written and researched by

Samantha Cook, Greg Ward,
JD Dickey, Nick Edwards, and Tim Perry

with additional contributions by
**Tim Burford, Ken Derry, Sarah Hull, Todd Obolsky,
Rebecca Strauss, Stephen Timblin, Ross Velton,
Paul Whitfield, and Christian Williams**

**ROUGH
GUIDES**

NEW YORK • LONDON • DELHI

www.roughguides.com

Contents

American food color
section following p.264

Music color section
following p.504

The great outdoors
color section following
p.776

**Architecture in
America** color section
following p.1112

◁◁ New York City skyline ◁ California's Big Sur coastline

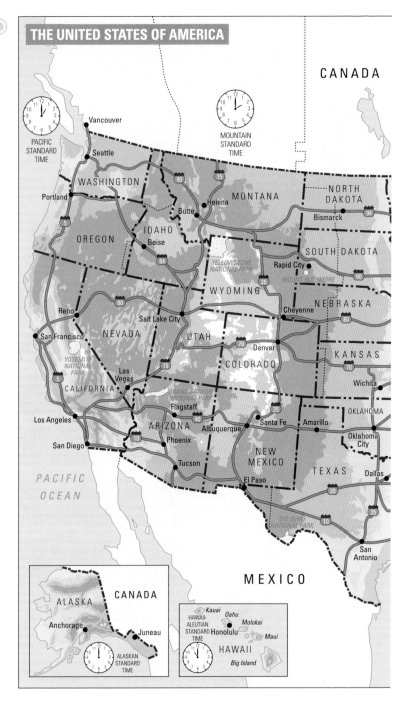

THE UNITED STATES OF AMERICA

CANADA

PACIFIC STANDARD TIME

MOUNTAIN STANDARD TIME

Vancouver

Seattle

WASHINGTON

Portland

OREGON

IDAHO

Boise

Butte

Helena

MONTANA

90

15

NORTH DAKOTA

Bismarck

94

SOUTH DAKOTA

Rapid City

MOUNT RUSHMORE

90

YELLOWSTONE NATIONAL PARK

84

WYOMING

25

NEBRASKA

Reno

80

Salt Lake City

Cheyenne

80

San Francisco

NEVADA

UTAH

70

Denver

KANSAS

YOSEMITE NATIONAL PARK

15

COLORADO

70

Las Vegas

Wichita

CALIFORNIA

5

GRAND CANYON NATIONAL PARK

Flagstaff

40

Albuquerque

Santa Fe

25

Amarillo

OKLAHOMA

Los Angeles

ARIZONA

Phoenix

NEW MEXICO

Oklahoma City

San Diego

10

Tucson

TEXAS

Dallas

El Paso

20

PACIFIC OCEAN

BIG BEND NATIONAL PARK

10

35

San Antonio

ALASKA

CANADA

Anchorage

Juneau

ALASKAN STANDARD TIME

MEXICO

Kauai Oahu

HAWAII-ALEUTIAN STANDARD TIME

Honolulu

Molokai

Maui

HAWAII

Big Island

4

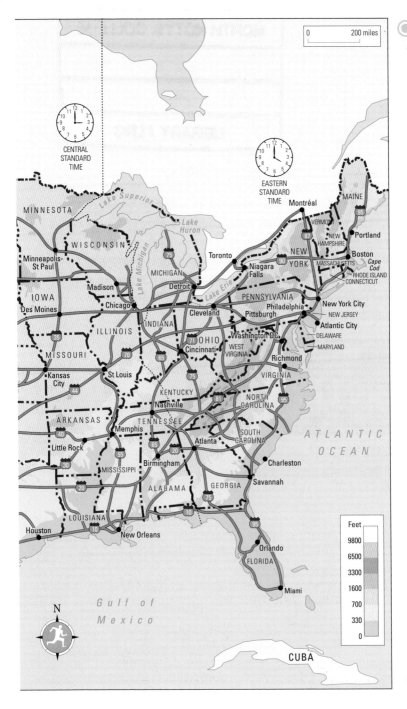

0   200 miles

CENTRAL
STANDARD
TIME

EASTERN
STANDARD
TIME

MINNESOTA

Lake Superior

Lake Huron

WISCONSIN

Minneapolis-St Paul

MICHIGAN

Lake Michigan

Toronto

Montréal   MAINE
                   95

VERMONT
                87   NEW
                      HAMPSHIRE   Portland

NEW   Boston
YORK
        MASSACHUSETTS   Cape
                         Cod
             RHODE ISLAND
             CONNECTICUT

Madison

IOWA
Des Moines

Chicago

Detroit

Lake Erie

Cleveland

Niagara
Falls

PENNSYLVANIA
                        Philadelphia   New York City

ILLINOIS

INDIANA

35

Pittsburgh
                          NEW JERSEY
                         Atlantic City

MISSOURI

70

65

71 OHIO
Cincinnati

Washington DC
      WEST
      VIRGINIA

DELAWARE

MARYLAND

Kansas
City

St Louis

75

Richmond

VIRGINIA

44

KENTUCKY

81

NORTH
CAROLINA

95

ARKANSAS

40

Nashville

TENNESSEE

Memphis

Little Rock

65

65

20

Atlanta

SOUTH
CAROLINA

ATLANTIC
OCEAN

30

85

Birmingham

MISSISSIPPI

Charleston

20

ALABAMA

GEORGIA

75

Savannah

LOUISIANA

10

10

Houston

New Orleans

95

Orlando

FLORIDA

Miami

Feet	
9800	
6500	
3300	
1600	
700	
330	
0	

N

Gulf of
Mexico

CUBA

Introduction to the USA

Perhaps no other country has left as great an impression on the contemporary world as the United States – a big achievement for such a (relatively) young nation. Lauded as a beacon of freedom, where over the centuries millions of immigrants have come to better their lives, and reviled as an international bully, perhaps never more so than in recent years, it's a place you have to explore in order to understand and appreciate.

The images of the country that named itself after a continent are embedded in the mind of every traveler: endless highways cutting through shimmering deserts; forests of skyscrapers towering over urban jungles; acres of beaches dotted with surfboards and suntanned skin; high mountain peaks and green river valleys; magnificent feats of engineering, from the Brooklyn Bridge to the Hoover Dam. The country's emblems are so familiar that they constitute as much a part of the world's culture as its own – Lady Liberty, the Grand Canyon, the Empire State Building, the US Capitol, the "Hollywood" sign . . . the list goes on.

The combination of a shoot-from-the-hip mentality with *laissez-faire* capitalism and religious fervor can make the USA maddening at times, even to its own residents. But what's most surprising, perhaps, is how such an initially daunting land can prove so enticing – its vibrant mix of peoples, striking landscapes and city skylines, and rich musical, cinematic, and culinary heritage seduce almost every visitor in the end.

And for all of its pride and bluster, the USA can be a land of quiet nuances: snow falling on a country lane in Vermont, cherry trees blooming under Washington memorials, crocodiles swimming through the bayou. You could easily plan a trip that focuses on the out-of-the-way hamlets, remote wilderness, eerie ghost towns, and forgotten byways that are every bit as "American" as its showpiece icons and monuments. Putting aside the sheer size of the place, deciding exactly what version of America you want to see may be the hardest decision of all.

One of the principal joys of getting to know the country is the repeated, delicious shock of the familiar

Where to go

Traveling in the United States is extremely easy; in a country where everyone seems to be forever on the move, there's rarely any problem finding a room for the night, and you can almost invariably depend on being able to eat well and

Fact file

• The US government is divided into three branches: the executive, headed by the president; the legislative, which comprises the Senate and the House of Representatives; and the judicial, with the Supreme Court as its highest office.

• Despite New York's status as the cultural and economic center of the US, the federal capital is in Washington DC, which doesn't even rank among the top twenty cities in terms of population (though officially, it is a district, not a city).

• The population of the US (some 300 million) owns 200 million cars and trucks (roughly 1 vehicle for every 1.4 people), with more than 5.7 million miles of paved highway on which to drive them.

• With an area of 9.6 million square kilometers, the US is the third-largest country in the world (ranking behind Russia and Canada).

• The US is the only country that contains all six major climate zones: tropical humid, dry, mild mid-latitude, severe mid-latitude, polar, and highland.

• With its Aleutian Islands crossing the Greenwich Meridian, Alaska is technically home to both the easternmost and westernmost points in the US. Alaska also has the highest point in the US, Mount McKinley (20,320ft), and is the largest state by area (Rhode Island is the smallest).

▲ The Washington Monument

inexpensively. The development of transportation has played a major role in the growth of the nation; the railroad opened the way for transcontinental migrations, while the automobile has been responsible for shaping most of the great cities. Your experience of the country will be very much flavored by how you choose to get around.

By far the best way to explore the country is to **drive your own vehicle**: it takes a long time before the sheer pleasure of cruising down the highway, with the radio blaring blues or country music, and the signs to Chicago, Memphis, or Monument Valley flashing past, begins to pall. Car rental is reasonable, and every main road is lined with budget motels charging around $50 per night for a good room.

We also give detailed **public transportation** options throughout; you can pretty much get to wherever you choose by a nationwide network of air, bus, and rail. However, if you do travel this way, there's a real temptation to see America as a succession of big **cities**. True enough, **New York** and **Los Angeles** have an exhilarating dynamism and excitement, and among their worthy rivals are **New Orleans**, the wonderfully decadent home of jazz, **Chicago**, a showcase of modern architecture, and **San Francisco**, on the beautiful Pacific bay. Few other cities – with the possible, and idiosyncratic, exception of **Las Vegas**, shimmering in the desert – can quite match this level of interest, however, and following a heavily urban itinerary will cut you off from the astonishing **landscapes** that make the USA truly distinctive. Especially in the vast open spaces of the West, the scenery is often breathtaking. The glacial splendor of

Traveling through American history

To explore the United States is to explore its history. Some early European settlements, such as St Augustine, Florida, and Santa Fe, New Mexico, founded by the Spanish in 1565 and 1609 respectively, remain thriving to this day. Others, like Roanoke Island in North Carolina, home to Sir Walter Raleigh's ill-fated "Lost Colony" of 1585; Jamestown, Virginia, established in 1607; and Plimoth Plantation in Massachusetts, where the Pilgrims landed in 1620, are now preserved as fascinating living-history parks.

Other sites commemorate the two major conflicts fought on US soil: the Revolutionary War and the Civil War. Among Revolutionary landmarks are a plaque (and replica ship and museum) honoring 1773's legendary "Tea Party" in Boston, Massachusetts; Minute Man National Park in nearby Lexington, where the "shot heard 'round the world" was fired in 1775; and Philadelphia's Independence Hall, which hosted the signing of the Declaration of Independence in 1776. Civil War flashpoints scattered throughout the South, Capital, and mid-Atlantic regions include Harpers Ferry, West Virginia, site of John Brown's infamous (and ill-fated) raid in 1859; Fort Sumter, off Charleston, South Carolina, where the war's first shots were fired in 1861; and Gettysburg, Pennsylvania, scene, in 1863, of the bloodiest battle of all, as well as Abraham Lincoln's immortal address.

Pilgrims also flock to the scenes of tragedies that have shaped US history over the last century, like the spot in Dallas, Texas, where President John F. Kennedy was assassinated in 1963, and the motel (now a museum) in Memphis, Tennessee, where Dr Martin Luther King Jr was gunned down in 1968. The only two sites where the US has been attacked on its own soil by foreign invaders receive throngs of visitors each year as well: Pearl Harbor, Hawaii, which was bombed on December 7, 1941, and Ground Zero, in New York City, where the World Trade Center stood before it was destroyed by terrorists on September 11, 2001.

Yosemite, the thermal wonderland of **Yellowstone**, the awesome red-rock **canyons** of Arizona and Utah, and the spectacular **Rocky Mountains** are among many of the treasures preserved and protected in the excellent national park system. Once you reach such wilderness, the potential for **hiking** and **camping** is magnificent – but it's usually essential to have a car to get near these spots.

Above all, travelers can enjoy the sheer thrill of experiencing American popular culture in the places where it began. Rock 'n' roll place-names spring to life; panoramas etched on our consciousness from a century of movies spread across the horizon; and road trips taken by your favorite literary characters are still there to be traveled.

For **music** fans, the chance to hear country music in Nashville or rhythm and blues in New Orleans, to shake it in a Mississippi jook-joint, or to visit Elvis's grave in Memphis, verges on a religious experience; readers brought up on the **books** of Mark Twain can ride a sternwheeler on the Mississippi; and **moviegoers** can live out their Wild West fantasies in the rugged Utah deserts.

The Wild West

Nowhere in the US is imbued with myth and history quite like the Wild West, much of which remains unchanged since the days of pioneers, prospectors, and, of course, "cowboys and Indians." In Lincoln, New Mexico, you can trace the footsteps of Billy the Kid; in Tombstone, Arizona, you can relive the gunfight at the OK Corral; and at Little Bighorn, Montana, you can climb the windswept hillside where General Custer made his "Last Stand." Colorado and California still abound with ghost towns abandoned when the gold and silver mines played out, while the great cattle drives are commemorated in Dodge City, Kansas, and Fort Worth, Texas. Above all, many Native Americans continue to inhabit their ancestral lands, especially in the Southwest, where the Hopi and the Ácomans survive in remote mesa-top villages, the Navajo ride through Monument Valley, and the Havasupai still farm alongside magical waterfalls deep in the Grand Canyon.

The United States is all too often dismissed, even by its own inhabitants, as a land almost devoid of **history**. Though mainstream America tends to trace its roots back to the Pilgrims and Puritans of New England, the land itself has a longer history, stretching back way beyond the French culture of Louisiana and the Spanish presence in California to the majestic cliff palaces built by the Ancestral Puebloans in the Southwest a thousand years ago. There are also any number of fascinating strands to America's post-revolutionary history: relics of the Gold Rush in California, of the Civil Rights years in the South, or of the Civil War anywhere east of the Mississippi.

Though we've had to structure this book regionally, the most invigorating expeditions are those that take in more than one area. You do not, however, have to cross the entire continent from shore to shore in order to appreciate its amazing diversity, or to be impressed by the way in which such an extraordinary range of topography and people has been melded into one nation. It would take a long time to see the whole country, and the more time you spend on the road simply getting from place to place – no matter how enjoyable in itself that can be – the less time you'll have to savor the small-town pleasures and back-road oddities that may well provide your strongest memories. It will hit you early on that there is no such thing as a typical American person, any more than there is a typical American landscape, but there can be few places where strangers can feel so confident of a warm reception.

When to go

All US cities are pretty much year-round destinations (though Fairbanks, Alaska, in winter and Houston, Texas, in summer can be less than ideal), national parks and mountain ranges sometimes less so.

The US **climate** is characterized by wide variations, not just from region to region and season to season, but also day to day and hour to hour. Even setting aside far-flung Alaska and Hawaii, the main body of the US is subject to dramatically shifting weather patterns, most notably produced by westerly winds sweeping across the continent from the Pacific. As a general rule, however, temperatures tend to rise the further south you go, and to fall the higher you climb, while the climate along either coast is, on the whole, milder and more uniform than inland.

The **Northeast**, from Maine down to Washington DC, experiences relatively low precipitation as a rule, but temperatures can range from bitterly cold in winter to uncomfortably hot (made worse by humidity) in the short summer. Farther south, summers get warmer and longer. **Florida**'s air temperatures are not necessarily dramatically high in summer, being kept down by the proximity of the sea both east and west; in the winter, the state is warm and sunny enough to attract visitors from all over the country.

The **Great Plains**, which for climatic purposes can be said to extend from the Appalachians to the Rockies, are alternately exposed to icy Arctic winds streaming down from Canada and humid tropical airflows from the Caribbean and the Gulf of Mexico. Winters in the north, around the Great Lakes and Chicago, can be abjectly cold, with driving winds and freezing rain. It can freeze or even snow in winter as far south as the Gulf of Mexico, though spring and fall get progressively longer and milder farther south through the Plains. Summer is much the wettest season in the **South** as a whole, the time when thunderstorms are most likely to strike. One or two hurricanes each year rage across Florida and/or the Southeast, from obscure origins in the Gulf of Mexico on the way to extinction out in the Atlan-

▲ Nantucket, Massachusetts

tic. Tornadoes (or "twisters") are usually a much more local phenomenon, tending to cut a narrow swath of destruction in the wake of violent spring or summer thunderstorms. Average rainfall dwindles to lower and lower levels the further west you head across the Plains.

Temperatures in the **Rockies** correlate closely with altitude; beyond the mountains in the south lie the extensive arid and inhospitable deserts of the **Southwest**. Much of this area is within the rain shadow of the California ranges. In cities such as Las Vegas and Phoenix, the mercury regularly soars above 100°F, though the atmosphere is not usually humid enough to be as enervating as that might sound.

West of the barrier of the Cascade Mountains, the fertile **Pacific Northwest** is the only region of the country where winter is the wettest season, and throughout the year the European-style climate is wet, mild, and seldom hot. **California** weather more or less lives up to the popular idyllic image, though the climate is markedly hotter and drier in the south than in the north, where

there's enough snow to make the mountains a major skiing destination. San Francisco is kept milder and colder than the surrounding district by the propensity of the Bay Area to attract sea fog, while the Los Angeles basin is prone to filling up with smog, as fog and pollution become trapped beneath a layer of warm air.

See overleaf for corresponding climate chart

Average temperature (°F) and rainfall

To convert °F to °C, subtract 32 and multiply by 5/9

	Jan	Feb	Mar	Apr	May	June	July	Aug	Sept	Oct	Nov	Dec
Anchorage												
av. max temp	19	27	33	44	54	62	65	64	57	43	30	20
av. min temp	5	9	13	27	36	44	49	47	39	29	15	6
days of rain	7	6	5	4	5	6	10	15	14	12	7	6
Boston												
av. max temp	36	37	43	54	66	75	80	78	71	62	49	40
av. min temp	20	21	28	39	49	58	63	62	55	46	35	25
days of rain	12	10	12	11	11	10	10	10	9	9	10	11
Chicago												
av. max temp	32	34	43	55	65	75	81	79	73	61	47	36
av. min temp	18	20	29	40	50	60	66	65	58	47	34	23
days of rain	11	10	12	11	12	11	9	9	9	9	10	11
Honolulu												
av. max temp	76	76	77	78	80	81	82	83	83	82	80	78
av. min temp	69	67	67	68	70	72	73	74	74	72	70	69
days of rain	14	11	13	12	11	12	14	13	13	13	13	15
Las Vegas												
av. max temp	60	67	72	81	89	99	103	102	95	84	71	61
av. min temp	29	34	39	45	52	61	68	66	57	47	36	30
days of rain	2	2	2	1	1	1	2	2	1	1	1	2
Los Angeles												
av. max temp	65	66	67	70	72	76	81	82	81	76	73	67
av. min temp	46	47	48	50	53	56	60	60	58	54	50	47
days of rain	6	6	6	4	2	1	0	0	1	2	3	6
Miami												
av. max temp	74	75	78	80	84	86	88	88	87	83	78	76
av. min temp	61	61	64	67	71	74	76	76	75	72	66	62
days of rain	9	6	7	7	12	13	15	15	18	16	10	7
New Orleans												
av. max temp	62	65	71	77	83	88	90	90	86	79	70	64
av. min temp	47	50	55	61	68	74	76	76	73	64	55	48
days of rain	10	12	9	7	8	13	15	14	10	7	7	10
New York City												
av. max temp	37	38	45	57	68	77	82	80	79	69	51	41
av. min temp	24	24	30	42	53	60	66	66	60	49	37	29
days of rain	12	10	12	11	11	10	12	10	9	9	9	10
San Francisco												
av. max temp	55	59	61	62	63	66	65	65	69	68	63	57
av. min temp	45	47	48	49	51	52	53	53	55	54	51	47
days of rain	11	11	10	6	4	2	0	0	2	4	7	10
Seattle												
av. max temp	45	48	52	58	64	69	72	73	67	59	51	47
av. min temp	36	37	39	43	47	52	54	55	52	47	41	38
days of rain	18	16	16	13	12	9	4	5	8	13	17	19
Washington DC												
av. max temp	42	44	53	64	75	83	87	84	78	67	55	45
av. min temp	27	28	35	44	54	63	68	66	58	48	38	29
days of rain	11	10	12	11	12	11	11	11	8	8	9	10

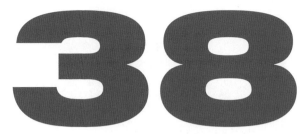

things not to miss

It's not possible to see everything that the USA has to offer in one trip – and we don't suggest you try. What follows is a selective and subjective taste of the country's highlights: unforgettable cities, spectacular drives, magnificent parks, spirited celebrations, and stunning natural phenomena. They're arranged in five color-coded categories to help you find the very best things to see, do, and experience. All highlights have a page reference to take you straight into the Guide, where you can find out more.

01 New York City Page **71** • With world-class museums, restaurants, nightlife, and shops aplenty, the Big Apple is in a league of its own.

02
Savannah, GA Page 534

• Mint juleps on wide verandas, horse-drawn carriages on cobbled streets, and lush foliage draped with Spanish moss; this historic cotton port remains the South's loveliest town.

03 Walt Disney World, Orlando, FL

Page **648** • Though each of Orlando's theme parks strives to outdo the rest, Walt Disney World remains the one to beat.

05 Kentucky Derby, KY

Page **549** • Two weeks of wild partying precedes the world's most thrilling thoroughbred race.

04 Niagara Falls, NY Page 154

• The sheer power of Niagara Falls is even more overwhelming when seen from below, aboard the *Maid of the Mist*.

06 Yellowstone National Park, WY

Page **880** • The national park that started it all has it all, from steaming fluorescent hot springs and spouting geysers to sheer canyons and meadows filled with wildflowers and assorted grazing beasts.

07 Mardi Gras, New Orleans, LA

Page **698** • Crazy, colorful, debauched, and historic – this is the carnival to end them all.

08 Pike Place Market, Seattle, WA

Page **1170** • Piled high with salmon, lobster, clams, and crab, the oldest public market in the nation is also home to some great seafood restaurants.

09 Glacier National Park, MT

Page **905** • Montana's loveliest park holds not only fifty glaciers, but also two thousand lakes, a thousand miles of rivers, and the exhilarating Going-to-the-Sun road.

10

Monticello, VA Page **447** •
This elegant estate, designed by Thomas Jefferson himself, was the former president's home and final resting place.

11 Ancestral Puebloan sites
Page **933** • Scattered through desert landscapes like New Mexico's magnificent Bandelier National Monument, the dwellings of the Ancestral Puebloans afford glimpses of an ancient and mysterious world.

12 Hiking in the Grand Canyon
Page **968** • Explore the innermost secrets of this wondrous spot on many of its superb hiking trails at the heart of California's best-loved park.

13 Swamps
Page **664** & **770** • From the steamy Everglades of Florida to the ghostly bayous of Louisiana's Cajun country, America's swamplands are hauntingly beautiful.

14 **San Francisco, CA** Page **1109** • Enchanting, fog-bound San Francisco remains bohemian and individualistic at heart.

15 **New England in the fall** Page **199** • The Northeast's breathtaking fall foliage presents an ever-changing palette of color and light.

16 **Yosemite Valley, CA** Page **1093** • Enclosed by near-vertical, mile-high cliffs, and laced with hiking trails and climbing routes, the dramatic geology of Yosemite Valley is at the heart of California's best-loved park.

17
Eating a Philly cheesesteak, PA Page **168** • Dig into this sloppy feast of a meal, born in Philadelphia's South Side.

19

Cheyenne Frontier Days, WY
Page **873** • Relive the Old West with some cowboys and cowgirls at the world's most prestigious outdoor rodeo.

19 **Hawaii's volcanoes** Page **1275** • Hawaii's Big Island grows bigger by the minute, as the world's most active volcano pours molten lava into the ocean.

20 **Sternwheeler rides** Pages **555**, **681**, & **786** • Just as they did in Mark Twain's day, steam-driven sternwheelers still ply the Mississippi from great old river towns like New Orleans, St Louis, and Memphis.

21

Aurora borealis, AK
Page **1258** • Winter visitors to Alaska just might see the skies ablaze with the shimmering veils of the Northern Lights.

23 Mount Rushmore, SD
Page **824** • Preserved in the sternest granite, this larger-than-life monument presides forever above the Black Hills of South Dakota.

22 Big Bend National Park, TX
Page **762** • Forcing the Rio Grande – and the Mexican frontier – to take a very big bend indeed, Texas's remote Chisos Mountains form a vast, barely charted enclave that bursts into color each spring.

24
Country Music Hall of Fame, Nashville, TN Page **569** • Everything you ever wanted to know about country music, explained in loving detail.

25 The Strip, Las Vegas, NV Page **1014** •
With its erupting volcanoes, Eiffel Tower, and Egyptian pyramid, the legendary Strip will blow your mind as well as your wallet.

26 Miami's Art Deco, FL
Page **616** • This flamboyant city is deservedly famed for the colorful pastel architecture of its restored South Beach district.

27 Skiing in the Rocky Mountains Pages **854, 858** & **861**
• The Rockies make for some of the best skiing anywhere, with their glitzy resorts and atmospheric mining towns.

28 Going to a baseball game Page **363** •
America's summer pastime is a treat to watch wherever you are, from Chicago's ivy-clad Wrigley Field to Boston's Fenway Park, the oldest in the country.

29 The National Mall, Washington
DC Page **409** • From the Lincoln Memorial to the US Capitol by way of the towering Washington Monument – the National Mall is an awesome showcase of American culture and history.

30 Austin nightlife, TX Page **740** • Laid-back, progressive, and home to an eclectic live-music scene – Austin is like nowhere else in the state.

31 Driving Highway 1 Page **1101** • The rugged Big Sur coastline, pounded by Pacific waves, makes an exhilarating route between San Francisco and LA.

33 Graceland, Memphis, TN Page **562** • Pilgrims from all over the world pay homage to the King by visiting his gravesite and endearingly modest home.

32 Chicago's modern architecture, IL Page **351** • The history of modern architecture is writ large on Chicago's skyline, site of the world's first skyscraper.

34 Baltimore crabs, MD Page **466** • Tear into some delicious, fresh steamed crabs, the pride and joy of this characterful port city.

35 Mount St Helens, WA Page **1193** • A breathtaking example of volcanic devastation, wrought by a powerful eruption in 1980.

36 Sweet Auburn, Atlanta, GA Page 526 •

This historic district holds the birthplace of Dr Martin Luther King Jr, the Center for Nonviolent Social Change, and other spots honoring King's legacy.

37 Saguaro cactus Page 954 •

The astonishing saguaro, which can reach fifty feet tall, grow as many as forty arms, and live for two centuries, is emblematic of the desert Southwest.

38 Hitting the open road Page 36 & *The Great Outdoors* Color section •

There's no better way to experience the staggering diversity of people and places in this vast country.

Basics

Basics

Getting there

Anyone traveling to the US from abroad has to begin by deciding which area they want to explore first; the country is so vast that it makes a huge difference which airport you fly into. Once you've chosen whether to hit the swamps of Florida, the frozen tundra of Alaska, the summer heat of the South, or the splendor of the Rockies and Southwest, you can then buy a flight to the nearest hub city.

In general, ticket prices are highest from July to September, and then around Easter and Christmas. Fares drop during the shoulder seasons – April to June, and October. You'll get the best prices during the low season, November to March (excluding Easter, Christmas, and the New Year, when prices are hiked up and seats are at a premium). If anything, the cost depends more on when Americans want to head overseas than on the demand from foreign visitors. Flying on weekends ordinarily adds a substantial amount to the round-trip fare; prices quoted below assume midweek travel.

Flights from the UK and Ireland

More than twenty US cities are accessible by **nonstop** flights from the **UK**. At these gateway cities, you can connect with onward domestic flights into the rest of the country. **Direct** services (which may land once or twice on the way, but are called direct if they keep the same flight number throughout their journey) fly from Britain to nearly every other major US city.

Nonstop flights to Los Angeles from London take eleven or twelve hours; the London–Miami flight takes eight hours; while flying time to New York is seven or so hours. Following winds ensure that return flights are always an hour or two shorter than outward journeys. One-stop direct flights to destinations beyond the East Coast add time to the journey, but can work out cheaper than nonstop flights. They can even save you time, because customs and immigration are cleared on first touchdown into the US rather than the final destination, which may be a busy international gateway.

Four airlines run nonstop scheduled services to the US from **Ireland**. Flights depart from both Dublin and Shannon airports, and the journey times are very similar to those from London.

As for **fares**, Britain remains one of the best places in Europe to obtain flight bargains, though prices vary widely according to season, availability, and the current level of inter-airline competition. In low or shoulder season, you should be able to find a return flight to East Coast destinations such as New York for around £250, or to California for more like £325, while high-season rates can be anything up to £400 more expensive. An air pass can be a good idea if you want to see a lot of the country. These are available only to non-US residents, and must be bought before reaching the US (see p.36).

With an open-jaw ticket you can fly into one city and out of another; fares are calculated by halving the return fares to each destination and adding the two figures together. Remember to check whether there is a high drop-off fee for returning a rental car in a different state from the one where you picked it up (see p.36).

Nonstop flights

From London (Heathrow, Gatwick, or Stansted)

Atlanta British Airways, Delta
Baltimore British Airways
Boston American Airlines, British Airways, Virgin Atlantic
Charlotte US Airways
Chicago Air India, American Airlines, British Airways, United, Virgin Atlantic
Cincinnati Delta
Dallas/Fort Worth American Airlines, British Airways

Fly less – stay longer! Travel and climate change

Climate change is a serious threat to the ecosystems upon which humans rely, and air travel is among the fastest-growing contributors to the problem. Rough Guides regard travel, overall, as a global benefit, and feel strongly that the advantages to developing economies are important, as is the opportunity of greater contact and awareness among peoples. But each of us has a responsibility to limit our personal impact on global warming, and that means giving thought to how often we fly, and what we can do to redress the harm that our trips create.

Flying and climate change

Pretty much every form of motorized travel generates CO_2 – the main cause of human-induced climate change – but planes also generate climate-warming contrails and cirrus clouds and emit oxides of nitrogen, which create ozone (another greenhouse gas) at flight levels. Furthermore, flying simply allows us to travel much further than we otherwise would do. The figures are frightening: one person taking a return flight between Europe and California produces the equivalent impact of 2.5 tonnes of CO_2 – similar to the yearly output of the average car in the UK.

Fuel-cell and other less harmful types of plane may emerge eventually. But until then, there are really just two options for concerned travelers: to reduce the amount we travel by air (take fewer trips – stay for longer!), and to make the trips we do take "climate neutral" via a carbon-offset scheme.

Carbon-offset schemes

Offset schemes run by ⓦclimatecare.org, ⓦcarbonneutral.com and others allow you to make up for some or all of the greenhouse gases that you are responsible for releasing. To do this, they provide "carbon calculators" for working out the global-warming contribution of a specific flight (or even your entire existence), and then let you contribute an appropriate amount of money to fund offsetting measures. These include rainforest reforestation and initiatives to reduce future energy demand – often run in conjunction with sustainable development schemes.

Rough Guides, together with Lonely Planet and other concerned partners in the travel industry, are supporting a **carbon-offset scheme** run by climatecare.org. Please take the time to view our website and see how you can help to make your trip climate-neutral.

ⓦwww.roughguides.com/climatechange

Denver British Airways
Detroit Northwest, British Airways
Houston British Airways, Continental
Las Vegas Virgin Atlantic
Los Angeles Air New Zealand, American Airlines, British Airways, United, Virgin Atlantic
Miami American Airlines, British Airways, Virgin Atlantic
Minneapolis Northwest
New York Air India, American Airlines, British Airways, Continental, Kuwait Airways, Virgin Atlantic
Orlando British Airways, Virgin Atlantic
Philadelphia British Airways, US Airways
Phoenix British Airways
Raleigh/Durham American Airlines
San Francisco British Airways, Continental, United, Virgin Atlantic
Seattle British Airways
Washington DC British Airways, United, Virgin Atlantic

From Birmingham

New York Continental

From Manchester

Atlanta Delta
Boston American Airlines
Chicago American Airlines, BMI (seasonal), United
Las Vegas BMI
New York American Airlines, British Airways, Continental, Delta
Orlando Virgin Atlantic
Philadelphia US Airways

From Edinburgh

Atlanta Delta
New York Continental

From Glasgow

Chicago British Airways
New York British Airways, Continental

From Dublin/Shannon

Atlanta Delta
Boston Aer Lingus
Chicago Aer Lingus, American Airlines
Los Angeles Aer Lingus, American Airlines
New York Aer Lingus, American Airlines, Continental, Delta

Flights from Australia, New Zealand and South Africa

If you're traveling from Australasia to the US, the most expensive time to fly is during the northern summer (mid-May to end Aug) and over the Christmas period (Dec to mid-Jan); shoulder seasons cover March to mid-May and September, while the rest of the year is low season.

Los Angeles is the main US gateway airport for flights from **Australia**: in low season, the regular Air New Zealand, Qantas, and United flights cost around Aus$1500 from the eastern states, or Aus$2000 from Western Australia, including tax; flying all the way through to New York can cost as little as $50 extra. During peak season, however, fares to the US West Coast start at more like Aus$2500, and to New York at Aus$3000.

From **New Zealand**, fares from Auckland or Christchurch to LA or San Francisco start at around NZ$1700 in low season, and range up to around NZ$3000 for a flight to New York in summer.

Various add-on fares and air passes valid in the continental US are available with your main ticket, allowing you to fly to destinations across the States. These must be bought before you go.

Airlines, agents and operators

Online booking

ⓦ www.cheapflights.com (US), ⓦ www. cheapflights.co.uk (UK), ⓦ www.cheapflights.ca (Canada), ⓦ www.cheapflights.com.au (Australia).
ⓦ www.cheaptickets.com
ⓦ www.ebookers.com

ⓦ www.expedia.co.uk (in UK), ⓦ www.expedia. com (in US), ⓦ www.expedia.ca (in Canada)
ⓦ www.flyaow.com
ⓦ www.hotwire.com
ⓦ www.lastminute.com (UK), ⓦ www. lastminute.com.au (Australia), ⓦ www. lastminute.co.nz (New Zealand),
ⓦ www.opodo.co.uk (in UK)
ⓦ www.orbitz.com (in US)
ⓦ www.site59.com (US)
ⓦ www.travelocity.co.uk (in UK), ⓦ www. travelocity.com (in US), ⓦ www.travelocity.ca (in Canada), ⓦ www.zuji.com.au (in Australia), ⓦ www.zuji.co.nz (in New Zealand)

Airlines

Aer Lingus US and Canada ☎ 1-800/IRISH-AIR, UK ☎ 0870/876 5000, Republic of Ireland ☎ 0818/365 000, ⓦ www.aerlingus.com.
Air Canada ☎ 1-888/247-2262, UK ☎ 0871/220 1111, Republic of Ireland ☎ 01/679 3958, Australia ☎ 1300/655 76, New Zealand ☎ 0508/747-767, ⓦ www.aircanada.com.
Air France US ☎ 1-800/237-2747, Canada ☎ 1-800/667-2747, UK ☎ 0870/142 4343, Australia ☎ 1300/390-190, ⓦ www.airfrance.com.
Air India US ☎ 1-800/223-7776, Canada ☎ 416/865-1033, UK ☎ 020/8560 9996 or 8745 1000, Australia ☎ 02/9283 4020, New Zealand ☎ 09/631 5651; ⓦ www.airindia.com.
Air New Zealand UK US ☎ 1-800/262-1234, Canada ☎ 1-800/663-5494, UK ☎ 0800/028-4149, Republic of Ireland ☎ 1800/551-447, New Zealand ☎ 0800/737 000, ⓦ www.airnewzealand.com.
Air Scotland UK ☎ 0141/222-2363, ⓦ www .air-scotland.com.
Airtran US ☎ 1-800/247-8726, ⓦ www.airtran.com
Alaska Airlines US ☎ 1-800/252-7522, ⓦ www .alaskaair.com.
Alitalia US ☎ 1-800/223-5730, Canada ☎ 1-800/361-8336, UK ☎ 0870/544 8259, Republic of Ireland ☎ 01/677 5171, New Zealand ☎ 09/308 3357, ⓦ www.alitalia.com.
American Airlines US ☎ 1-800/433-7300, UK ☎ 0845/7789 789, Republic of Ireland ☎ 01/602 0550, Australia ☎ 1300/650 7347, New Zealand ☎ 0800/887 997, ⓦ www.aa.com.
American Trans Air US ☎ 1-800/435-9282, ⓦ www.ata.com
America West US ☎ 1-800/235-9292, ⓦ www .americawest.com.
Australian Airlines Australia ☎ 1300/799 798, ⓦ www.australianairlines.com.au.
British Airways US and Canada ☎ 1-800/ AIRWAYS, UK ☎ 0870/850 9850, Republic of Ireland

29

ⓣ1890/626 747, Australia ⓣ1300/767 177, New Zealand ⓣ09/966 9777, ⓦwww.ba.com.
BMI US ⓣ1-800/788-0555, UK ⓣ0870/607 0555, Ireland ⓣ01/407-3036, ⓦwww.flybmi.com.
Continental Airlines US and Canada ⓣ1-800/523-3273, UK ⓣ0845/607 6760, Ireland ⓣ1890/925-252, Australia ⓣ2/9244 2242, NZ ⓣ9/308 3350, International ⓣ1-800/231-0856, ⓦwww.continental.com.
Delta US and Canada ⓣ1-800/221-1212, UK ⓣ0845/600 0950, Republic of Ireland ⓣ1850/882-031 or 01/407 3165, Australia ⓣ1-300/302-849, New Zealand ⓣ09/379 3370, ⓦwww.delta.com.
Hawaiian Airlines US ⓣ1-800/367-5320, ⓦwww.hawaiianair.com
JAL (Japan Air Lines) US and Canada ⓣ1-800/525-3663, UK ⓣ0845/774 7700, Ireland ⓣ01/408 3757, Australia ⓣ02/9272 1111, New Zealand ⓣ09/379 9906, ⓦwww.jal.com or ⓦwww.japanair.com
JetBlue US ⓣ1-800/JET-BLUE, ⓦwww.jetblue.com
Korean Air US and Canada ⓣ1-800/438-5000, UK ⓣ0800/0656 2001, Republic of Ireland ⓣ01/799 7990, Australia ⓣ02/9262 6000, New Zealand ⓣ09/914 2000, ⓦwww.koreanair.com.
Kuwait Airways US ⓣ201/582-9200, UK ⓣ020/7412 0006, ⓦwww.kuwait-airways.com.
Lufthansa US ⓣ1-800/645-3880, Canada ⓣ1-800/563-5954, UK ⓣ0870/837 7747, Republic of Ireland ⓣ01/844 5544, Australia ⓣ1300/655 727, New Zealand ⓣ09/303 1529, ⓦwww.lufthansa.com.
Malaysia Airlines US ⓣ1-800/552-9264, UK ⓣ0870/607 9090, Republic of Ireland ⓣ01/676 2131, Australia ⓣ293/13 26 27, New Zealand ⓣ0800/777 747, ⓦwww.malaysia-airlines.com.
Mexicana US ⓣ1-800/531-7921, Canada ⓣ1-866/281-3094, UK ⓣ020/8492 0000, Australia ⓣ03/9699 9355, New Zealand ⓣ09/914 2573, SA ⓣ011/784-0985, ⓦwww.mexicana.com.
Midwest Express US ⓣ1800/452-2022, ⓦwww.midwestairlines.com
Northwest ⓣ1-800/225-2525, UK ⓣ0870/507 4074, ⓦwww.nwa.com.
Qantas US and Canada ⓣ1-800/227-4500, UK ⓣ0845/774 7767, Republic of Ireland ⓣ01/407 3278, Australia ⓣ13 13 13, New Zealand ⓣ0800/808 767 or 09/357 8900, ⓦwww.qantas.com.
SAS (Scandinavian Airlines) US ⓣ1-800/221-2350, Canada ⓣ1800/221-2350, UK ⓣ0870/6072 7727, Republic of Ireland ⓣ01/844 5440, Australia ⓣ1300/727 707, SA ⓣ011/484-4711, ⓦwww.scandinavian.net.
Singapore Airlines US ⓣ1-800/742-3333, Canada ⓣ1-800/ 663-3046, UK ⓣ0844/800 2380,

Republic of Ireland ⓣ01/671 0722, Australia ⓣ13 10 11, New Zealand ⓣ0800/808-909, ⓦwww.singaporeair.com.
Southwest US ⓣ1-800/435-9792, ⓦwww.southwest.com
Swiss US ⓣ1-877/FLY-SWIS, UK ⓣ0845/601 0956, Australia ⓣ1300/724 666, New Zealand ⓣ09/977 2238, ⓦwww.swiss.com.
Ted ⓣ1-800/225-5833, ⓦwww.flyted.com.
United US ⓣ1-800/241-6522, UK ⓣ0845/844 4777, Australia ⓣ13 17 77, ⓦwww.united.com.
US Airways US and Canada ⓣ1-800/428-4322, UK ⓣ0845/600-3300, Ireland ⓣ1890-925065, ⓦwww.usair.com
Virgin Atlantic US ⓣ1-800/821-5438, UK ⓣ0870/380 2007, Australia ⓣ1300/727-340, ⓦwww.virgin-atlantic.com.

Agents and operators

Adventure World Australia ⓣ02/8913 0755, ⓦwww.adventureworld.com.au, New Zealand ⓣ09/524 5118, ⓦwww.adventureworld.co.nz. Agents for a vast array of international adventure travel companies that operate trips to every continent.
American Holidays Northern Ireland ⓣ028/9031 0000, Republic of Ireland ⓣ01/673 3840 ⓦwww.american-holidays.com. Offers tour packages from Ireland to North America.
Bon Voyage UK ⓣ0800/316 0194, ⓦwww.bon-voyage.co.uk. Tailor-made trips to the US.
British Airways Holidays UK ⓣ0870/850 9850, ⓦwww.baholidays.co.uk. Packages and independent itineraries for both long trips and short city-breaks.
North America Travel Service UK ⓣ020/7499 7299, ⓦwww.northamericatravelservice.co.uk. Various itineraries cater to city-breaks, cruises, spa vacations, guided tours, and more.
ebookers UK ⓣ0800/082 3000, Republic of Ireland ⓣ01/488-3507, ⓦwww.ebookers.com. Low fares on an extensive selection of scheduled flights and package deals.
Exodus UK ⓣ020/8675 5550, ⓦwww.exodus.co.uk. Adventure and action-oriented vacation packages focused on low-impact tourism.
Explore Worldwide UK ⓣ0870/333 4001, ⓦwww.explore.co.uk. Hundreds of group tours including everything from short weekend trips to action-oriented family adventures.
Jetsave UK ⓣ0870/162 3502, ⓦwww.jetsave.co.uk. Packages to North America include airfare, accommodation, and guided tours.
North South Travel UK ⓣ01245/608 291, ⓦwww.northsouthtravel.co.uk. Friendly, competitive travel agency, offering discounted fares worldwide. Profits are used to support projects in the developing

world, especially the promotion of sustainable tourism.

Saddle Skedaddle UK ☎0191/265 1110, ☻www
.skedaddle.co.uk. Biking and activity-oriented tours.

STA Travel US ☎1-800/781-4040, Canada ☎1-
888/427-5639, UK ☎0870/1630 026, Australia
☎1300/733 035, New Zealand ☎0508/782 872.
Worldwide specialists in independent travel; also
student IDs, travel insurance, car rental, rail passes,
and more. Good discounts for students and under-
26s. ☻www.statravel.com.

Sydney Travel Australia ☎02/9220 9230,
☻www.sydneytravel.com. Fllights, accommodation,
city stays, and car rental.

Titan HiTours UK ☎01293/455345, ☻www
.titantravel.co.uk. Escorted tours, tailor-made
itineraries, cruises, and more.

travel.com.au Australia ☎1300/130 482, ☻www
.travel.com.au. Itineraries, accommodation, and car
hire, as well as ski trips, adventure travel, and family
vacations.

travel.co.nz New Zealand ☎0800/468 332,
☻www.travel.co.nz

Travelsphere UK ☎0870/240 2426, ☻www
.travelsphere.co.uk. Wide-range of options includes,
among other things, cruises, activity-based vacations,
and short trips.

TrekAmerica UK ☎0870/444-8735, ☻www
.trekamerica.co.uk. Offers small-group adventure
vacations.

Trailfinders UK ☎0845/058 5858, Republic of
Ireland ☎01/677 7888, Australia ☎1300/780 212,
☻www.trailfinders.com. One of the best-informed
and most efficient agents for independent travellers.

Rail contacts

Amtrak US ☎1-800/872-7245, ☻www.amtrak
.com.

Packages and tours

There are countless flight and accommodation **packages** to all the major American cities. Although you can often do things cheaper independently, these allow you to leave the organizational hassles to someone else. Drawbacks include the loss of flexibility and the fact that you'll probably be made to stay in hotels in the mid-range to expensive bracket, even though less expensive accommodation is almost always readily available. A typical package might be a roundtrip flight plus mid-range Midtown hotel accommodation for three nights in New York City, starting at around £500 per person in low season and more like £800 at peak periods. Pre-booked accommodation schemes, where you buy vouchers for use in a specific group of hotels, are not normally good value.

Fly-drive deals, which give cut-rate (sometimes free) car rental when a traveler buys a transatlantic ticket from an airline or tour operator, are always cheaper than renting on the spot, and give great value if you intend to do a lot of driving. They're readily available through general online booking agents such as Expedia and Travelocity, as well as through specific airlines.

Several of the operators listed here go one stage further and book accommodation for **self-drive tours**; some travelers consider having their itineraries planned and booked by experts to be a real boon. Bon Voyage, for example, arranges tailor-made packages in the Southwest; the cost of twelve nights in Arizona, Utah, and Nevada, flying into Las Vegas and out from Phoenix, and staying in standard hotels, ranges from around £1300 per person in low season up to more like £1700 at other times.

A simple and exciting way to see a chunk of America's great outdoors, without being hassled by too many practical considerations, is to take a specialist touring and **adventure package**, which includes transportation, accommodation, food, and a guide. Companies such as TrekAmerica carry small groups around on minibuses and use a combination of budget hotels and camping. Most concentrate on the West – ranging from Arizona to Alaska, and lasting from seven days to five weeks; cross-country treks and Eastern adventures that take in New York or Florida are also available. Typical rates for a two-week trip – excluding transatlantic flights – range from £519 in low season up to £800 in midsummer. Trips to Alaska cost a good bit more. For another touring and adventure package option, see the box on Green Tortoise, p.34.

STA Travel US ☎ 1-800/781-4040, Canada ☎ 1-888/427-5639, UK ☎ 0870/1630 026, 🖫 www .statravel.com.

Bus contacts

Greyhound US ☎ 1/800-231-2222, Canada ☎ 1/416-367-8747, 🖫 www.greyhound.com.

Green Tortoise US and Canada ☎ 1/800-867-8647, 🖫 www.greentortoise.com.

Peter Pan US ☎ 1/800-237-8747 or 1/413-781-2900, 🖫 www.peterpanbus.com.

STA Travel US ☎ 1-800/781-4040, Canada ☎ 1-888/427-5639, UK ☎ 0870/1630 026, Australia ☎ 1300/360 960, New Zealand ☎ 0508/782 872, 🖫 www.statravel.com.

Getting around

Distances in the US are so great that it's essential to think carefully in advance about how you plan to get from place to place. Your choice of transportation will have a crucial impact on your trip. Amtrak provides a skeletal but often scenic rail service, and there are usually good bus links between the major cities. But even in rural areas, by adroit advance planning, you can usually reach the main points of interest without too much trouble by using local buses and charter services.

That said, travel is almost always easier if you have a **car**. Many worthwhile and memorable

US destinations are far from the cities: even if a bus or train can take you to the general

For all **Amtrak** information, and to make reservations, check the Amtrak **website**, ⓦ www.amtrak.com, or call toll-free ☎ 1-800/872-7245. Do not phone individual train stations.

vicinity of one of the great national parks, for example, they're of little use when it comes to enjoying the great outdoors. The cities themselves can be so vast, and so heavily car-oriented, that the lack of a car can seriously impair your enjoyment.

By rail

Traveling by **rail** is rarely the fastest way to get from A to B, though if you have the time it can be a pleasant and relaxing experience. As you will see from our map, on p.34, the Amtrak system isn't comprehensive – such popular destinations as Nashville and Santa Fe, and even some entire states, are left out altogether. What's more, the cross-country routes tend to be served by one or at most two trains per day, so in large areas of the nation the only train of the day passes through at three or four in the morning. That said, the train is by far the most comfortable way to travel, and especially on long-distance rides it can be a great way to meet people. A number of local train services connect stops on the Amtrak lines with towns and cities not on the main grid. Amtrak also runs the coordinated Thruway bus service that connects some cities that their trains don't reach. However, this network is not comprehensive, either.

For any one specific journey, the train can be more **expensive** than taking a Greyhound bus, or even a plane – the standard rail fare from New York to Los Angeles, for example, is around $185 one-way – though special deals, especially in the off-peak seasons (Sept–May, excluding Christmas), bring the cost of a coast-to-coast round-trip to around $300. **Booking online** can also yield bargains, with discounts of up to 90 percent posted weekly; there are also a number of money-saving passes available. Flat-rate **Explore America** fares allow 45 days of travel within one or more of four regions – Western, Central, Florida, and East – covered by the network, allowing a maximum of three stopovers on route. The **California rail pass** buys you seven days' travel in a 21-day period for $159, while for $249 the **Florida Rail Pass** gives a year of unlimited travel throughout that state. In addition, foreign travelers can benefit from the passes detailed in the box on p.35.

Even with a pass, you should always **reserve** as far in advance as possible; all passengers must have seats, and some trains, especially between major east coast cities, are booked solid. Sleeping compartments (which start at around $300 per night, including three full meals, in addition to your seat fare, for one or two people) and the plush Metroliner carriages cost extra. However, even standard Amtrak carriages are surprisingly spacious, and there are additional dining cars and lounge cars (with full bars and sometimes glass-domed 360° viewing compartments).

Beautiful east coast Amtrak trips include the Hudson River Valley north of New York City (on several routes); along the Potomac River at Harpers Ferry, West Virginia (on the *Capitol Limited* out of Washington DC); and the New River Gorge (on the *Cardinal*). In the West, the *California Zephyr*, which runs between Chicago and San Francisco, follows a stunning route west of Denver over the Rockies, rivaled a day later by the towering Sierra Nevada. Last but not least, the *Coast Starlight* gives

Historic railroads

While Amtrak has a monopoly on long-distance rail travel, a number of historic or **scenic railways**, some steam-powered or running along narrow-gauge mining tracks, bring back the glory days of train travel. Many are purely tourist attractions, doing a full circuit through beautiful countryside in two or three hours, though some can drop you off in otherwise hard-to-reach wilderness areas. Fares vary widely according to the length of your trip. We've covered the most appealing options in the relevant guide chapters.

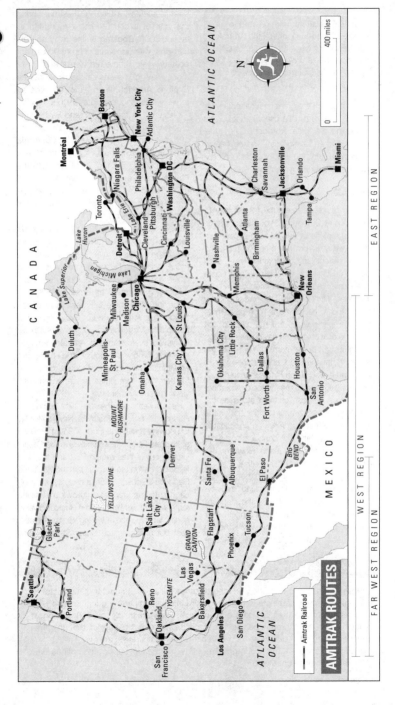

AMTRAK ROUTES

—— Amtrak Railroad

FAR WEST REGION   WEST REGION   EAST REGION

N

0   400 miles

Green Tortoise

One alternative to Long-Distance Bus Hell is the fun, countercultural **Green Tortoise**, whose buses, complete with foam cushions, bunks, fridges, and rock music, mostly ply the west and the northwest of the country, but can go as far as New Orleans and New York. Highlights include a national park loop (16 days; $885 including food and park admissions) and the coast-to-coast USA Explorer (37 days; $1600, including food and park admissions); there are more than 25 seductive options, each allowing plenty of stops for hiking, river-rafting, bathing in hot springs and the like.

Green Tortoise's main office is at 494 Broadway, San Francisco, CA 94133 (☏415/956-7500 or 1-800/867-8647, ⊛www.greentortoise.com).

---

unsurpassed views of the California coast on its journey between San Luis Obispo and Santa Barbara. Confirm when you book your journey that the train passes through the scenic splendor during daylight hours.

By bus

If you're traveling on your own and making a lot of stops, **buses**, by far the cheapest way to get around, make sense. The main long-distance operator, **Greyhound** (☏1-800/231-2222, ⊛www.greyhound.com, international customers without toll-free access can also call ☏214/849-8100 from 5am–1am CST), links all major cities and many towns. Out in the country, buses are fairly scarce, sometimes appearing only once a day, if at all; here, you'll need to plot your route with care. However, along the main highways, buses run around the clock to a fairly full timetable, stopping only for meal breaks (almost always fast-food dives) and driver changeovers.

To avoid possible hassle, lone female travelers in particular should take care to sit as near to the driver as possible, and to arrive during daylight hours – many bus stations are in fairly dodgy areas. It used to be that any sizable community would have a Greyhound station; now, in some places, the post office or a gas station doubles as the bus stop and ticket office, and in many others bus service has been canceled altogether. Reservations, which can be made in person at the station, online, or on the toll-free number, are not essential, but recommended – if a bus is full, and you don't have a reservation, you may be forced to wait until the next one, sometimes overnight or longer. It's best to arrive at the bus station an hour or so before travel in order to check in.

Fares on shorter journeys average out at about 15¢ per mile, but for longer hauls there are plenty of savings available. Check the website's discounts page. Buying your ticket even a few days in advance of travel will save money, as will traveling between Monday and Thursday. For long-haul travel though, considering the time expended (around 65 hours coast-to-coast, if you eat and sleep on the bus), riding the bus is not necessarily a much better deal than flying, unless you plan to make a lot of stops using a Discovery Pass (see p.36).

To plan your route, check the website or pick up the free route-by-route timetables from larger bus stations.

By plane

Don't be misled by movies in which characters stroll into large airports and casually buy cross-country tickets. Choosing to **fly** that way tends to be outrageously expensive – $1000 for a one-way flight is not unheard of. However, with planning, air travel can work out to be quite reasonable, especially since the arrival of the **budget airlines** – often, as in the case of Ted, which is owned by United Airlines, subsidiaries of larger airlines – which has led to cut-throat competition. In some cases, flying can cost less than the train – especially if you take into account how much you save not paying for food and drink while on the move – and only a little more than the bus. Flying can also make sense for relatively short local hops, turning a full day's cross-desert $25 bus journey, for example, into a quick and scenic $50 flight of under an hour. We mention such options wherever appropriate throughout this guide.

Amtrak USA Rail Passes

In addition to a number of regional passes offered to all (see the Amtrak website, ⓦwww.amtrak.com), overseas travelers have a choice of the following **USA Rail Passes**, covering the areas shown on the map on p.34. The **Northeast Pass** is also available as a five-day offer, for $155 (Sept–May)/$180 (June–Aug).

	15-day (June–Aug)	**15-day** (Sept–May)	**30-day** (June–Aug)	**30-day** (Sept–May)
East	$335	$215	$415	$280
Northeast	$200	$220	–	–
West	$335	$215	$415	$280
National	$455	$305	$565	$395

Passes can be bought from the Amtrak website, which also lists several places you can buy them in your home country.

Greyhound Discovery Passes

Foreign visitors, especially those inclined to venture beyond the major destinations, can buy a **Greyhound Discovery Pass** either online (give yourself at least 14 days before you leave home) or at any of the major Greyhound terminals and agencies in the States. The pass offers unlimited travel within a set time period. A seven-day pass costs $283; a 15-day pass $415; 30 days $522; and 60 days $645. No daily extensions are available.

Each time you travel, you'll need to present your pass at the ticket counter to receive a boarding ticket. For more information go to ⓦwww.greyhound.com.

Where to buy Amtrak and Greyhound passes abroad

Rail Plus Level 1, 149-155 Parnell Rd, Parnell, Auckland, New Zealand ☏09/377 5415; ⓔinfo@railplus.co.nz; ⓦwww.railplus.co.nz.
STA Travel UK ☏0870/1630 026, Australia ☏1300/733 035, New Zealand ☏0508/782 872; ⓦwww.statravel.com.
Trailfinders UK ☏0845/058 5858, Republic of Ireland ☏01/677 7888, Australia ☏1300/780 212; ⓦwww.trailfinders.com.

Air passes

The main American airlines offer **air passes** for visitors who plan to fly a lot within the US. These must be bought in advance, and are often sold with the proviso that you cross the Atlantic with the same airline or group of airlines (such as One World Alliance). Each deal will involve the purchase of a certain number of flights, air miles, or coupons. An Air Canada and United Airlines Global Pass, for example, will cost $609–679 for any three flights within the continental USA and Canada, rising to $1109–1179 for eight.

Other plans entitle foreign travelers to **discounts** on regular US domestic fares, again with the proviso that you buy the ticket before you leave home. Check with the individual airlines to see what they offer. However you do it, flying within the US is only a wise choice for travel in regions where fares are low anyway; flights within Florida, for example, are very expensive.

Phone the airlines or visit their websites to find out routes and schedules. The best discounts are usually offered on tickets booked and paid for at least two weeks in advance; these are almost always non-refundable and hard to change.

By car

For many, the concept of cruising down the highway, preferably in an open-top convertible with the radio blasting, is one of the main reasons to set out on a tour of the US.

Driving for foreigners

Foreign nationals from English-speaking countries can drive in the US using their **full domestic driving licenses**. (International Driving Permits are not always regarded as sufficient.) Fly-drive deals are good value if you want to **rent** a car (see below), though you can save up to sixty percent simply by booking in advance with a major firm. If you choose not to pay until you arrive, be sure you take a written confirmation of the price with you. Remember that it's safer not to drive right after a long transatlantic flight – and that most standard rental cars have **automatic transmissions**.

It's easier and cheaper to book an **RV** (see overleaf) in advance from abroad. Most travel agents who specialize in the US can arrange RV rental, and usually do so for less if you book a flight through them as well. A price of US$650 for a five-berth van for two weeks is fairly typical.

The romantic images of countless road movies, from *Bonnie and Clyde* to *Thelma and Louise*, are not far from the truth, though you don't have to embark on a wild spree of drink, drugs, crime, and murder to enjoy **driving** across America. Apart from anything else, a car makes it possible to choose your own itinerary and to explore the astonishing wide-open landscapes that may well provide your most enduring memories of the country.

Driving in the cities, on the other hand, is not exactly fun, but in the larger places a car is by far the most convenient way to negotiate your way around, especially as public transportation tends to be spotty outside the major conurbations. Many urban areas, especially in the west, have grown up and assumed their present shapes since cars were invented. As such, they sprawl for so many miles in all directions – Los Angeles and Houston are classic examples – that your hotel may be fifteen or twenty miles from the sights you came to see, or perhaps simply on the other side of a freeway that can't be crossed on foot. Only in a few cities, more often in the east, are the main attractions and facilities concentrated within walking distance of each other. Even in smaller towns the motels may be six miles or more out along the interstate, and the restaurants in a shopping mall on the far side of town.

To **rent a car**, you are supposed to have held your license for at least one year. Drivers under 25 may encounter problems and have to pay higher than normal insurance premiums. Rental companies expect customers to have a credit card; if you don't, they may let

you leave a cash deposit (at least $200), but don't count on it. All the major **rental companies** have outlets at the main airports. Reservations are handled centrally, so the best way to shop around is either online, or by calling their national toll-free numbers. Potential variations are endless; certain cities and states are consistently cheaper than others, while individual travelers may be eligible for corporate, frequent-flier, or AAA discounts. In low season you may find a tiny car (a "subcompact") for as little as $100 per week, but a typical budget rate would be more like $35–40 per day or $150 per week including taxes.

Don't automatically go for the cheapest rate. Little-known local companies may offer appealing prices, but if you break down several hundred miles from their offices it may be hard to get assistance. Even between the major operators, there can be a big difference in the quality of cars. Industry leaders like Alamo, Hertz, and Avis tend to have newer, lower-mileage cars, often with air-conditioning and stereo CD players as standard – no small consideration on a 2000-mile desert drive. Always be sure to get **unlimited mileage**, and remember that leaving the car in a different city to the one where you rented it can incur a drop-off charge of as much as $200.

When you rent a car, read the small print carefully for details on **Collision Damage Waiver** (CDW), sometimes called **Liability Damage Waiver** (LDW), usually included in the price if you pre-pay outside the US, but well worth considering if it isn't. This form of insurance specifically covers the car that you are driving yourself – you are in any case

Hitchhiking

The usual advice given to **hitchhikers** is that they should use their common sense; but common sense should tell anyone that hitchhiking in the United States is a **bad idea**. We do not recommend it under any circumstances.

insured for damage to other vehicles. At $10–15 a day, it can add substantially to the total cost, but without it you're liable for every scratch to the car – even those that aren't your fault. Increasing numbers of states are requiring that this insurance be included in the weekly rental rate and are regulating the amounts charged to cut down on rental-car company profiteering. Some credit card companies offer automatic CDW coverage to customers using their card; contact your issuing company for details.

The **American Automobile Association**, or AAA (☎1-800/222-4357; ⓦwww.aaa.com), provides free maps and assistance to its members and to members of affiliated associations overseas, such as the British AA and RAC.

If you **break down** in a rented car, call the emergency number pinned to the dashboard. If you don't have a mobile, you can rent one from the car rental agency – you often have to pay only a nominal amount until you actually use it – and in larger cities, they increasingly come built into the car.

Driveaways

One variation on renting a car is a **drive-away**: you drive a car from one place to another for the owner, paying only for the gas you use. The same rules as for renting apply, but look the car over before you take it; you'll be charged for any repair costs in addition to a large fuel bill if it's a gas-guzzler. Some driveaway companies want a personal reference from someone either in the town you're leaving or in the car's destination. Get in touch in advance, to spare yourself a week's wait for a car to turn up. The most common routes are between the coasts, but there's a fair chance of finding something that needs transporting to where you want to go. You needn't drive flat out, although three to four hundred miles a day – around six hours – is expected. Look under Automobile Transporters in the *Yellow Pages* or

try one of the sixty branches of Auto Drive-away (ⓦwww.autodriveaway.com).

Renting an RV

Recreational vehicles (RVs) can be rented from around $600 per week (plus mileage charges) for a basic camper on the back of a pickup truck with sleeping room for two adults. If you're after one of those juggernauts that rumble down the highway, complete with multiple bedrooms, bathrooms, and kitchens, you'll have to pay at least double that. Though good for groups or families traveling together, RVs can be unwieldy on the road, and rental outlets are not that common. On top of the rental fees, take into account the cost of gas (some RVs do twelve miles to the gallon or less) and any drop-off charges. It is rarely legal simply to pull off in an RV and spend the night at the roadside: you are expected to stay in designated RV parks that cost $20–30 per night. The Recreational Vehicle Dealers Association (☎703/591-7130 or 1-800/336-0355 ⓦwww.rvda.org), publishes a newsletter and a directory of rental firms. Among the larger companies offering **RV rentals** are Cruise America (ⓦwww.cruiseamerica.com) and Moturis (ⓦwww.moturis.com).

Car rental agencies

Alamo US ☎1-800/462-5266, ⓦwww.alamo.com.
Avis US ☎1-800/230-4898, ⓦwww.avis.com.
Budget US ☎1-800/527-0700, ⓦwww.budget.com.
Dollar US ☎1-866/434-2226, ⓦwww.dollar.com.
Enterprise Rent-a-Car US ☎1-800/261-7331, ⓦwww.enterprise.com.
Hertz US ☎1-800/654-3131, ⓦwww.hertz.com.
Holiday Autos US ☎1-866/392-9288, ⓦwww.holidayautos.com.
National US ☎1-800/CAR-RENT, UK ☎0870/400 4581, Australia ☎02/13 10 45, ⓦwww.nationalcar.com.
Thrifty US and Canada ☎1-800/847-4389, ⓦwww.thrifty.com.

Cycling

In general, **cycling** is a cheap and healthy way to get around the big cities, an increasing number of which have cycle lanes and local buses equipped to carry bikes (strapped to the outside). In country areas, roads are usually well maintained and have wide shoulders. Bikes can be rented for $15–30 per day, or at discounted weekly rates, from outlets that are usually found close to beaches, university campuses, and good cycling areas. Rates in heavily visited areas can be higher. Local visitor centers should have details.

The national non-profit **Adventure Cycling Association** (formerly Bikecentennial), based in Missoula, Montana (℡406/721-1776 or 1-800/755-2453, ⓦwww.adv-cycling.org), publishes maps ($10.50 each) of several 400-mile routes, detailing campgrounds, motels, restaurants, bike shops, and sites of interest. Many individual states issue their own cycling guides; contact the tourist offices listed on p.67. Before setting out on a long-distance cycling trip, you'll need a good-quality, multispeed bike, panniers, tools and spares, maps, padded shorts, and a helmet (legally required in some states and localities). Plan a route that avoids interstate highways (on which cycling is unpleasant and usually illegal). Of problems you'll encounter, the main one is traffic – RVs, huge eighteen-wheelers, logging trucks – that scream past and create intense backdrafts capable of pulling you out into the middle of the road.

Backroads Bicycle Tours (ⓦwww.back-roads.com), and the HI-AYH hosteling group (see p.41) arrange multi-day cycle **tours**, with camping or stays in country inns; we've also mentioned local firms that offer this where appropriate.

Greyhound, Amtrak, and major airlines will carry passengers' bikes – dismantled and packed into a box – for a small fee.

Accommodation

Accommodation costs form a significant proportion of the expenses for any traveler exploring the US – in part, because the standards of comfort and service are usually fairly high.

If you're on your own, it's possible to pare down what you pay by sleeping in dormitory-style hostels, where a bed usually costs between $15–30 a night. However, with basic room prices away from the major cities starting at around $45 per night, groups of two or more will find it little more expensive to stay in the far more abundant motels and hotels. Many hotels will set up a third single bed for around $15 on top of the regular price, reducing costs for three people sharing. On the other hand, the lone traveler has a hard time of it: "singles" are usually double rooms at an only slightly reduced rate. When visiting certain parts of the US, **camping** can be a cheap alternative, costing around $8–21 per night or, in the West, a little more for a yurt or cabin.

Addresses

Generally speaking, roads in built-up areas of the US are laid out on a grid system, creating "blocks" of buildings. The first one or two digits of a specific address refer to the block, which will be numbered in sequence from a central point, usually Downtown; for example, 620 S Cedar Avenue will be six blocks south of Downtown. It is crucial, therefore, to take note of components such as "NW" or "SE" in addresses; 3620 SW Washington Boulevard will be a very long way indeed from 3620 NE Washington Boulevard.

Accommodation price codes

Throughout this book, **accommodation prices** have been graded with the symbols below, according to the cost of the least expensive double room throughout most of the year.

However, except at interstate budget motels, there's rarely such a thing as a set rate for a room. A basic motel in a seaside or mountain resort may quadruple its prices according to the season, while a big-city hotel that charges $200 per room during the week will often slash its rate on the weekend. Because the high and low seasons for tourists vary widely across the country, astute planning can save a lot of money. Watch out also for local events – Mardi Gras in New Orleans, Spring Break in Myrtle Beach, college football games – which can raise rates far above normal.

Only where we explicitly say so do these room rates include local **taxes**.

❶ up to $35   ❹ $75–100   ❼ $160–200
❷ $35–50   ❺ $100–130   ❽ $200–250
❸ $50–75   ❻ $130–160   ❾ $250+

Wherever you stay, you'll be expected to pay in advance, at least for the first night and perhaps for further nights, too. Most hotels ask for a credit card imprint when you arrive, but some still accept cash or US dollar traveler's checks. Reservations – essential in busy areas in summer – are held only until 5 or 6pm, unless you've warned the hotel you'll be arriving late.

Hotels and motels

Hotels and motels are essentially the same thing, although motels tend to be found beside the main roads away from city centers – and thus are much more accessible to drivers. The budget ones are pretty basic affairs, but in general there's a uniform standard of comfort everywhere – each room comes with a double bed (often two), a TV and phone, and an attached bathroom – and you don't get a much better deal by paying, say, $60 instead of $45. Over $60, the room and its fittings simply get bigger and more luxurious, and there'll probably be a swimming pool, free for guests (in states with warmer weather, this is often included in even the cheaper motels).

The least expensive properties tend to be family-run, independent motels, but there's a lot to be said for paying a few dollars more to stay in motels belonging to the national chains. After a few days on the road, if you find that a particular chain consistently suits your requirements, you can use its central reservation number or

website, listed below and on p.41, to book ahead, and possibly obtain discounts as a regular guest.

During off-peak periods, many motels and hotels struggle to fill their rooms, and it's worth bargaining to get a few dollars off the asking price. Staying in the same place for more than one night may bring further reductions. Also, look for discount coupons, especially in the free magazines distributed by local visitor centers and interstate Welcome Centers. These can offer amazing value but read the small print first.

Few budget hotels or motels bother to compete with the ubiquitous diners by offering breakfast, although many provide free self-service coffee, sticky buns, and sometimes fruit or cereal, collectively referred to as "continental breakfast."

National accommodation chains

Baymont Inn & Suites ☎1-866/999-1111, ⓦwww.baymontinns.com. ❸–❹
Best Western ☎1-800/780-7234, ⓦwww.bestwestern.com. ❸–❻
Comfort Inn ☎1-877/424-6423, ⓦwww.comfortinns.com. ❸–❺
Courtyard by Marriott ☎1-800/321-2211, ⓦwww.courtyard.com. ❺–❻
Days Inn ☎1-800/329-7466, ⓦwww.daysinn.com. ❸–❺
Econolodge ☎1-877/424-6423, ⓦwww.econolodge.com. ❷–❹
Embassy Suites Hotels ☎1-800/362-2779, ⓦwww.embassysuites.com. ❺–❻

Fairfield Inn ☎1-800/228-2800, ⓦwww
.fairfieldinn.com. ④–⑤
Hampton Inns ☎1-800/426-7866, ⓦwww
.hamptoninn.com. ④–⑥
Hilton Hotels ☎1-800/774-1500, ⓦwww.hilton
.com. ⑤ and up
Holiday Inn ☎1-800/465-4329, ⓦwww.holiday-
inn.com. ④ and up
Howard Johnson ☎1-800/446-4656, ⓦwww
.hojo.com. ②–④
La Quinta Inns ☎1-866/725-1661, ⓦwww
.lq.com. ③–⑤
Marriott Hotels ☎1-888/236-2427, ⓦwww
.marriott.com. ⑤ and up
Motel 6 ☎1-800/466-8356, ⓦwww.motel6.com.
②–③
Ramada Inns ☎1-800/272-6232, ⓦwww
.ramada.com. ④ and up
Red Roof Inns ☎1-800/843-7663, ⓦwww
.redroof.com. ②–④
Renaissance Hotels ☎1-888/468-3571, ⓦwww
.renaissancehotels.com. ⑤ and up
Rodeway Inns ☎1-800/228-2000, ⓦwww
.rodeway.com. ③–④
Sheraton ☎1-888/625-5144, ⓦwww.sheraton
.com. ⑤ and up
Sleep Inns ☎1-800/753-3746, ⓦwww.sleepinn
.com. ③–④

Bed-and-breakfasts

Staying in a **bed-and-breakfast** is an
increasingly popular, and often luxurious,
alternative to conventional hotels. Some
B&Bs consist of no more than a couple of
furnished rooms in someone's home, and
even the larger establishments tend to have
fewer than ten rooms, sometimes without
TV or phone, but often laden with potpourri,
chintzy cushions, and an almost over-con-
trived homey atmosphere.

The price you pay for a B&B – which varies
from around $70 to $250 for a double room
– always includes breakfast (sometimes a
buffet on a sideboard, but more often a full-
blown cooked meal). The crucial determining
factor is whether each room has an en-suite
bathroom; most B&Bs provide private bath
facilities, although that can damage the
authenticity of a fine old house. At the top
end of the spectrum, the distinction between
a hotel and a "bed-and-breakfast inn" may
amount to no more than that the B&B is
owned by a private individual rather than a
chain, and has a more personal feel.

In many areas, B&Bs have united to form
central booking agencies, making it much
easier to find a room at short notice; we've
given contact information for these where
appropriate.

Hostels

Although hostel-type accommodation is not
as plentiful in the US as it is in Europe, provision for backpackers and low-budget travelers is on the rise. Unless you're traveling
alone, most **hostels** work out little cheaper
than motels; stay in them only if you prefer
their youthful ambiance and sociability. Many
are not accessible on public transportation,
or convenient for sightseeing in the towns
and cities, let alone in rural areas.

The official HI-AYH (Hostelling International-
American Youth Hostels; ☎1-800/909-4776,
ⓦwww.hiayh.org) network has nearly eighty
hostels in major cities and rural locations
throughout the US. Urban hostels tend to have
24hr access, while rural ones may have a curfew and limited daytime hours. Annual membership is currently $28 and rates range from
$14 to $29 for HI members; non-members
generally pay an additional $3 per night. Check
the HI-AYH website for comprehensive listings.

Youth hostel associations

Overseas travelers will find a comprehensive
list of hostels in the *International Youth Hostel
Handbook*, available from the following hosteling organizations. These organizations all sell
hosteling memberships as well, which are
accepted at affliated hostels around the world.

US and Canada

Hostelling International-American Youth
Hostels ☎301/495-1240, ⓦwww.hiayh.org.
Hostelling International Canada ☎1-800/663
5777, ⓦwww.hihostels.ca.

UK and Ireland

Youth Hostel Association (YHA) England and
Wales ☎0870/770 8868, ⓦwww.yha.org.uk.
Scottish Youth Hostel Association
☎01786/891 400, ⓦwww.syha.org.uk.
Irish Youth Hostel Association ☎01/830 4555,
ⓦwww.irelandyha.org.
Hostelling International Northern Ireland
☎028/9032 4733, ⓦwww.hini.org.uk.

Australia, New Zealand and South Africa

Australia Youth Hostels Association
℡02/9565-1699, 🖥www.yha.com.au.

Youth Hostelling Association New Zealand
℡0800/278 299 or 03/379 9970, 🖥www.yha.co.nz.
Hostelling International South Africa
℡021/424 2511, 🖥www.hisa.org.za

Food and drink

"Fast food" may be America's most enduring contribution to the modern culinary world but, because of the country's large immigrant population, the sheer variety of the foods available is astonishing.

In addition to the numerous **regional cuisines** on offer (see overleaf and the "American cuisine" color insert), **international food** is everywhere, turning up at times in some unexpected places. Many farming and ranching regions—Nevada and central California in particular—have a number of Basque restaurants; Portuguese restaurants, dating from whaling days, line the New England coast; and old-fashioned Welsh pasties can be found in the mining towns of Montana.

When it comes to **Asian food**, Indian cuisine is usually better in the bigger cities, though there are exceptions. Chinese cooking is everywhere, is sometimes top-notch, and can often be cheap — though look out for the dismal-tasting "chop suey" and "chow mein" joints in rural towns. Japanese, found on the coasts and in all big cities, is rather more expensive and fashionable, though sushi restaurants come in all sizes and price ranges, from candlelit affairs done up like French restaurants to the lowest-end diners where you grab color-coded plates of raw fish from a moving belt. Thai and Vietnamese fare, meanwhile, provide some of the best, cheapest, and most exciting cooking to come along in recent decades, sometimes in diners mixing the two, but always with an excellent range of savory soups and noodle dishes, and occasionally "fusion" cooking with other Asian cuisines (ie, "pan-Asian," as it's known).

French cuisine is almost always expensive, typically nouvelle, and associated with high-end hotels and ultra-chic, jacket-only affairs. That said, country French dining and French sub-styles (like Cajun and French Canadian) offer a much cheaper variant on Gallic cooking, and are often excellent as well.

Italian fare is even broader in its range; the top-shelf restaurants in major cities tend to focus on the northern end of the boot, with careful presentation, subtle flavors, and high prices, while the tomato-heavy, gut-busting portions associated with southern Italian cooking are still, in America at least, confined to lower-end, checkered-tablecloth diners with massive portions and pictures of Frank

Coping as a vegetarian

In the big U.S. cities at least, being a **vegetarian**—or even a vegan—presents few problems. However, don't be too surprised in rural areas if you find yourself restricted to a diet of eggs, cheese sandwiches (you might have to ask them to leave the ham out), salads, and biscuits. In the Southeast, most soul-food cafés offer great-value vegetable plates (four different vegetables, including potatoes) for around $5, but these are often cooked with pork fat. Similarly, baked beans, and the nutritious-sounding red beans and rice, usually contain bits of diced pork.

and Dino on the walls. Pizza restaurants occupy a similar range from high-end gourmet eateries to cheap and tasty dives—New Yorkers and Chicagoans can argue for days over which of their respective cities makes the best kind, either Gotham's shingle-flat "slices" or the Windy City's overstuffed wedges that actually resemble slices of meat pie.

Eating out

In the big cities, you can pretty much eat whatever you want, whenever you want, thanks to the ubiquity of restaurants, 24-hour diners, and street carts selling food well into the night. Also, along all the highways and on virtually every town's main street, restaurants, fast-food joints and coffeeshops try to outdo one another with flashing neon signs as well as bargains and special offers.

Whatever you eat and wherever you eat, service is usually enthusiastic – thanks in large part to the institution of **tipping**. Waiters depend on tips for the bulk of their earnings; fifteen to twenty percent is the standard rate, with anything less sure to draw a sneer or an insult.

Regional cuisines

While the predictable enormous steaks, burgers, and piles of ribs or half a chicken, served up with salads, cooked vegetables, and bread, are found everywhere, it's more rewarding to explore the diverse **regional and ethnic cuisines** around the country. Beef is especially prominent in the Midwest and Texas, while fish and seafood dominate the menus in Florida, Louisiana, around Chesapeake Bay in Maryland, and in the Pacific Northwest. Shellfish, such as the highly rated Dungeness crab and the Chesapeake's unique soft-shell crab, highly spiced and eaten whole, is popular, too. Maine lobsters and steamers (clams), eaten alone or mixed up in a chowder, are reason alone to visit New England.

Cajun food, which originated in the bayous of Louisiana as a way to use up leftovers, is centered on red beans and rice, enlivened with unusual seafood like crawfish and catfish, and always highly spiced. The oft-misunderstood distinction between Cajun and Creole cooking is explained in our "Louisiana" chapter, on p.693.

Southern cooking – sometimes known as "soul food" – is not always easy to find outside the South, but is worth seeking out for everything from grits to collard greens, and from fried chicken to hogjaw (meat from the mouth of a pig). **Barbecue** is also very popular in the South, where a mouth-watering plate, with sides, can be had for usually less than $10. (Generally, the more ramshackle the restaurant, the better the food.) There's also great barbecue outside of the South, in places like Kansas City and Chicago.

California Cuisine is geared toward health and aesthetics. It's basically a development of French nouvelle cuisine, utilizing a wide mix of fresh, local ingredients in season and offered as small but beautifully presented portions, with accompanying high prices: expect to pay $50 a head (or much more) for a full dinner with wine. California's culinary experiments have since the 1980s branched out into what's called the **New American Cuisine**, which is essentially California cooking transplanted to different regions – New Southern, New England, Northwest, Southwestern and Western (or Midwestern) are but a few manifestations of this trend.

Although technically ethnic, **Mexican food** is so common it might as well be an indigenous cuisine, especially in southern California. In the States, though, Mexican food is different from that found south of the border, making more use of fresh meats and vegetables, sometimes in odd combinations. The essentials, however, are the same: lots of rice and black or pinto beans, often served refried (boiled, mashed, and fried), with variations on the tortilla, a thin corn or flour pancake that can be wrapped around fillings and eaten by hand (a burrito); folded, fried, and filled (a taco); rolled, filled, and baked in sauce (an enchilada); or fried flat and topped with a stack of filling (a tostada). In Texas and the Southwest, beef and bean chili con carne is the distinguishing dish of **Tex-Mex** cuisine. Day or night, this is the cheapest type of food to eat: even a full dinner with a few drinks will rarely be more than $10 anywhere except in the most upmarket establishment.

Finally, there are also regional variations on **American staples**. You can get plain old burgers and hot dogs anywhere, but for a truly American experience, grab a piping-hot "Philly cheesesteak" sandwich, gooey with cheese and thin-sliced beef from a diner in eastern Pennsylvania, or one of New York's signature Coney Island hot dogs – or the LA version of the frankfurter, rolled in a tortilla and stuffed with cheese and chilli. Almost every Eastern state has at least one spot claiming to have invented the hamburger, and regardless of where you go, you can find a good range of authentic diners where the buns are fresh, the patties are large, handcrafted, and tasty, and the dressings and condiments are inspired. Needless to say, although we list the better of these locations in the Guide, almost none of them can be found along the interstate, under massive signs advertising their wares for 99 cents.

Drink

Across the country, bars and cocktail lounges are often dimly lit spots with long counters, a few customers perched on stools before a bartender-cum-guru, and tables and booths for those who don't want to join in the drunken barside debates. New York, Baltimore, Chicago, New Orleans, and San Francisco are the consummate boozing towns – filled with tales of plastered, famous authors indulging in famously bad behavior – but almost anywhere you shouldn't have to search very hard for a comfortable place to drink. Keep in mind that you need to be 21 years old to buy and consume alcohol in the US, and it's likely you'll be asked for ID even if you look much older.

"Blue laws" – archaic statutes that restrict when, where, and under what conditions alcohol can be purchased – are a source of great annoyance. The most common of these, held by many states, prohibits the sale of alcohol on Sundays; on the extreme end of the scale, some counties (known as "dry") don't allow any alcohol, ever. The famous whiskey and bourbon distilleries of Tennessee and Kentucky, including Jack Daniels (see p.573), can be visited—though maddeningly, several are in dry counties, so they don't offer samples. A few states – Vermont, Oklahoma, and Utah (which, being predominantly Mormon, has the most byzantine rules) – restrict the alcohol content in beer to just 3.2 percent, almost half the usual strength. Rest assured, though, that in a few of the more liberal parts of the country (New York City, for one), alcohol can be bought and drunk any time between 6am and 4am, seven days a week.

The most popular American beers are still fizzy, insipid lagers from national brands like Budweiser, Miller, and Coors, but there is no lack of alternatives. The craze for microbreweries started in northern California several decades ago, and even today Anchor Steam—at the forefront of the charge—is still an excellent choice for sampling. The West Coast continues to be, to a large extent, the center of the microbrewing movement, and even the smaller towns have their own share of decent handcrafted beers. The town with the most such breweries, per capita or raw quantity, is Portland, Oregon, which enthusiasts from across the country (or world for that matter) have been known to visit just to sample draughts of such notable brands as Widmer, Bridgeport, Full Sail, Rogue, and, best of all, Hair of the Dog. Los Angeles, San Diego, Seattle, the Bay Area, Denver, and other Western cities rank up there, too, and you can even find excellent brews in tiny spots such as Whitefish, Montana, where the beers of Great Northern Brewing are well worth seeking out.

On the East Coast look for Boston-based Samuel Adams and its mix of mainstream and alternative brews, the top-notch offerings of Pennsylvania's Victory Brewing, or stop in to Washington, DC's two great beer-tasting spots, the Brickskeller and D.A.'s R.F.D. Washington, to sample a broad array of the country's finest potables—some eight hundred and three hundred different kinds, respectively. Elsewhere, the Texas brand Lone Star has its dedicated followers, Indiana's best beverages come from Three Floyds Brewing, and Pete's Wicked Ales in Minnesota can be found throughout the country. Keep an eye out in local stores rather than supermarkets for bottled specialty beers, or track down the best American and international beers at Ⓦ www.beeradvocate .com. Indeed, microbreweries and brewpubs can now be found in virtually every sizable US city and college town. Almost all serve a wide range of good-value, hearty food to help soak up the drink.

California and, to a lesser extent, Oregon, Washington, and a few other states, are famous for their wines. In California, it's the Napa and Sonoma valleys that boast the finest grapes, and beefy reds such as Merlot, Pinot Noir, and Cabernet Sauvignon as well as crisp or buttery whites like Chardonnay and Sauvignon Blanc all do very well up here. Many tourists make a pilgrimage to these valleys for "wine-tasting" jags, where you can sip (or slurp) at sites ranging from downhome country farms with tractors and hayrides to upper-crust estates thick with modern art and yuppies in designer wear. Some quaffable but not horridly expensive brands include Frog's Leap, Beaulieu, Bontera, and Terre Rouge for reds and Andrew Murray, Ridge, and Bighorn for whites. In Oregon, seek out Cristom and Foris for reds, Adelsheim and WillaKenzie for whites; in Washington, reds from Chatter Creek and Barnard Griffin are good, as are whites from Chateau Ste Michelle and Paul Thomas. Throughout this book, you'll find details of tours and tastings where relevant.

Festivals

Someone, somewhere, is always celebrating something in the US – although, apart from national holidays, few festivities are shared throughout the country. Instead, there is a diverse multitude of engaging local events: arts-and-crafts shows, county fairs, ethnic celebrations, music festivals, rodeos, sandcastle-building competitions, chili cook-offs, and countless others.

Listed here are some of the best local festivals covered in this book. The tourist offices for each state (see p.67) can provide you with full lists, or simply phone the visitor center in a particular region and ask what's coming up. Certain festivities, such as **Mardi Gras** in New Orleans, are well worth planning your vacation around – obviously other people will have the same idea, so visiting during these times requires an extra amount of advance effort.

A particularly popular, all-American holiday is **Independence Day**. On July 4, virtually everyone in the country takes time out to picnic, drink, salute the flag, and watch or participate in fireworks displays, marches, beauty pageants, eating contests, and more, all in commemoration of the signing of the Declaration of Independence in 1776.

Halloween (October 31) lacks any such patriotic overtones, and is not a public holiday, despite being one of the most popular yearly flings. Traditionally, masked kids run around the streets banging on doors and demanding "trick or treat," returning home with heaping piles of candy. In some bigger cities Halloween has evolved into a massive celebration: in LA's West Hollywood, New York's Greenwich Village, New Orleans' French Quarter, and San Francisco's Castro district, the night is marked by colorful parades, mass cross-dressing, huge block parties, and wee-hours partying.

More sedate is **Thanksgiving Day**, on the fourth Thursday in November. Relatives return to the nest to share a meal (traditionally, roast turkey and stuffing, cranberry sauce, and all manner of delicious pies) and give thanks – hence the holiday's name – for family and friends. Ostensibly, the holiday recalls the first harvest of the Pilgrims in Massachusetts. In fact, Thanksgiving was a national holiday before anyone thought to make that connection.

Annual festivals and events

For further details of the selected festivals and events listed below, including more precise dates, see the relevant page of the *Guide*, or contact the local authorities directly. The state tourist boards listed in the box on p.67 can provide more complete calendars for each area.

January

Elko, NV Cowboy Poetry Gathering, p.1024
St Paul, MN Winter Carnival, p.390

February

Daytona Beach, FL Daytona 500 stock-car race, p.638
Fort Worden, WA Hot Jazz Festival, p.1186
New Orleans, LA (the six weeks before Lent) Mardi Gras, p.698; also elsewhere in Louisiana, p.704

March

Austin, TX South by Southwest Music Festival and Media Conference, p.740
Butte, MT St Patrick's Day, p.898
Eunice, LA World Championship Crawfish Étouffée Cookoff, p.704
Fairbanks, AK Ice Festival, p.1255
Los Angeles, CA Academy Awards (the "Oscars").
New Orleans, LA St Joseph's Day and the Mardi Gras Indians' "Super Sunday", p.698

April

Boston, MA Patriots' Day Marathon, p.220
Lafayette, LA Festival International de Louisiane, p.704
Mountain View, AR Arkansas Folk Festival, p.604
New Orleans, LA French Quarter Festival, and Jazz and Heritage Festival (into May), p.699
San Antonio, TX Fiesta San Antonio, p.734
Santuario de Chimayó, NM Easter Pilgrimage, p.935

May

Black Mountain, NC Leaf Festival, p.507
Breaux Bridge, LA Crawfish Festival, p.704
Flagstaff, AZ Zuni Crafts Show, p.963
Indianapolis, IN Indianapolis 500 sports-car race, p.347
Kerrville, TX Folk Festival, p.741
Louisville, KY Kentucky Derby (horse race), p.549
Memphis, TN Memphis in May International Festival, p.565
San Antonio, TX Tejano Conjunto Festival, p.735

June

Eureka Springs, AR Eureka Springs Blues Festival, p.605
Hardin, MT Little Bighorn Days, p.894
Nashville, TN CMA Music Festival, p.572
San Antonio, TX Texas Folklife Festival, p.735
Telluride, CO Bluegrass Festival, p.868

July

Blowing Rock, NC Highland Games, p.505
Cheyenne, WY Cheyenne Frontier Days, p.873
Elko, NV National Basque Festival, p.1024
Fairbanks, AK Eskimo/Indian Olympics, p.1255
Flagstaff, AZ Hopi Crafts Show, p.963; Navajo Crafts Show (into Aug), p.963
Fort Totten, ND Powwow and rodeo
New Orleans, LA Satchmo music festival (into Aug), p.699
St Paul, MN Taste of Minnesota, p.390
Talkeetna, AK Moose Dropping Festival, p.1251
Traverse City, MI Cherry Festival, p.337

August

Asheville, NC Mountain Dance and Folk Festival, p.506
Elkins, WV Augusta Festival of Appalachian Culture, p.456
Gallup, NM Inter-tribal Indian Ceremonial, p.945
Memphis, TN anniversary of Elvis's death, p.565
Newport, RI folk and jazz festivals, p.249
San Antonio, TX Texas Folklife Festival, p.735
Santa Fe, NM Indian Market, p.929
Sturgis, SD Motorcycle Rally and Races, p.822

September

Detroit, MI International Jazz Festival, p.328
Greenville, MS Delta Blues Festival, p.589
Lafayette, LA Festivals Acadiens, p.704
Lubbock, TX Panhandle South Plains Fair, p.758
Memphis, TN Memphis Music and Heritage Festival, p.558
Monterey, CA Monterey Jazz Festival, p.1107
New Orleans, LA Southern Decadence, p.699
New York, NY Festa di San Gennaro, p.90
Opelousas, LA Zydeco Festival, p.704
Pendleton, OR Pendleton Round-Up, p.1218
Santa Fe, NM Fiestas de Santa Fe, p.929
Claremore, OK Chile Cookoff and Bluegrass Festival, p.776

Sports and outdoor activities

Besides being good fun, catching a baseball game at Chicago's Wrigley Field on a summer afternoon or joining in with the screaming throngs at a Steelers football game in Pittsburgh can give visitors an unforgettable insight into a town and its people. Professional teams almost always put on the most spectacular shows, but big games between college rivals, minor league baseball games, and even Friday night high-school football games provide an easy and enjoyable way to get on intimate terms with a place.

Specific details for the most important teams in all the sports are given in the various city accounts. They can also be found through the major league websites: ⓦwww.mlb.com (baseball); ⓦwww.nba.com (basketball); ⓦwww.nfl.com (football); ⓦwww.nhl.com (ice hockey); and ⓦwww.mlsnet.com (soccer).

Baseball, because the major league teams play so many games (162 in total, usually five or so a week throughout the summer), is probably the easiest sport to catch when traveling. The ballparks – such as Boston's historic Fenway Park, LA's glamorous Dodger Stadium, or Baltimore's evocative Camden Yards – are great places to spend time. It's also among the cheapest sports to watch (from around $10 a seat), and tickets are usually easy to come by.

Pro football, the American variety, is quite the opposite. Tickets are exorbitantly expensive and almost impossible to obtain (if the team is any good), and most games are played in anonymous municipal bunkers; you'll do better stopping in a bar to watch it on TV. **College football** is a whole lot better and more exciting, with chanting crowds, cheerleaders, and cheaper tickets. Although New Year's Day games such as the Rose Bowl or the Orange Bowl are all but impossible to see live, big games like Nebraska vs

Oklahoma, Michigan vs Ohio State, or Notre Dame vs anybody are not to be missed if you're anywhere nearby.

Basketball also brings out intense emotions. The interminable – though invariably exciting – pro playoffs run well into June. The men's month-long college playoff tournament, called "March Madness," is acclaimed by many as the nation's most exciting sports extravaganza.

Ice hockey, usually referred to simply as hockey, was long the preserve of Canada and cities in the far north of the US, but today it penetrates the rest of the country. Tickets, particularly for successful teams, are hard to get and not cheap.

Soccer, meanwhile, remains much more popular as a participant sport, especially for kids, than a spectator one and those Americans that are interested in it usually follow foreign matches like England's Premier League, rather than their home-grown talent. The good news for international travelers is that any decent-sized city will have one or two pubs where you can catch games from England, other European countries, or Latin America; check out ⓦwww.livesoccertv.com for a list of such establishments and match schedules.

Skiing is the biggest mass-market participant sport, and downhill resorts can be found all over the US. The Eastern resorts of Vermont and New York State, however, pale by comparison with those of the Rockies, such as Vail and Aspen in Colorado, and the Sierra Nevada in California. Expect to pay $30–60 per day (depending on the quality and popularity of the resort) for lift tickets, plus another $25 or more per day to rent equipment.

A cheaper option is cross-country skiing, or ski touring. Backcountry ski lodges dot mountainous areas along both coasts and in the Rockies. They offer a range of rustic accommodation, equipment rental, and lessons, from as little as $15 a day for skis, boots, and poles, up to about $150 for an all-inclusive weekend tour.

The other sporting events that attract national interest involve four legs or four wheels. The **Kentucky Derby**, held in Louisville on the first Saturday in May (see p.549), is the biggest event on the horseracing calendar. Also in May, the NASCAR **Indianapolis 500**, the largest motor-racing event in the world, fills that city with visitors throughout the month, with practice sessions and carnival events building up to the big race.

National parks and outdoor activities

The US is blessed with fabulous backcountry and wilderness areas, coated by dense forests, cut by deep canyons, and capped by great mountains. Even the heavily populated East Coast has its share of open space, notably along the Appalachian Trail, which winds from Mount Katahdin in Maine to the southern Appalachians in Georgia – some two thousand miles of untrammeled forest. In order to experience the full breathtaking sweep of America's wide-open stretches, however, head west to the Rockies, to the red-rock deserts of the Southwest, or right across the continent to the amazing wild spaces of the West Coast. On the down side, be warned that in many coastal areas, the shoreline can be disappointingly hard to access, with a high proportion under private ownership.

National parks and monuments

The **National Park Service** administers both national parks and national monuments. Its rangers do a superb job of providing information and advice to visitors, maintaining trails, and organizing such activities as free guided hikes and campfire talks.

In principle, a **national park** preserves an area of outstanding natural beauty, encompassing a wide range of terrain and prime examples of particular landforms and wildlife. Thus Yellowstone has boiling geysers and herds of elk and bison, while Yosemite offers towering granite walls and cascading waterfalls. A **national monument** is usually much smaller, focusing perhaps on just one archeological site or geological phenomenon, such as Devil's Tower in Wyoming. Altogether, there are around four hundred units of the national park system, including national seashores, lakeshores, battlefields, and other historic sites.

National parks tend to be perfect places to **hike** – almost all have extensive trail networks – but they're all far too large to tour entirely on foot. (Yellowstone, for example, is bigger than Delaware and Rhode Island combined.) Even in those rare cases where you can use public transportation to reach a park, you'll almost certainly need some sort of vehicle to explore it once you're there. The Alaska parks are mostly howling wilderness, with virtually no roads or facilities for tourists – you're on your own.

1 Olympic, WA, p.1188	**9** T. Roosevelt (south), ND, p.832	**17** Death Valley, CA, p.1082
2 North Cascades, WA, p.1191	**10** Wind Cave, SD, p.827	**18** Joshua Tree, CA, p.1079
3 Mount Rainier, WA, p.1192	**11** Badlands, SD, p.818	**19** Great Basin, NV, p.1023
4 Crater Lake, OR, p.1215	**12** Redwood, CA, p.1158	**20** Zion, UT, p.987
5 Glacier, MT, p.905	**13** Lassen Volcanic, CA, p.1160	**21** Bryce Canyon, UT, p.990
6 Yellowstone, WY, p.880	**14** Yosemite, CA, p.1091	**22** Capitol Reef, UT, p.993
7 Grand Teton, WY, p.887	**15** Kings Canyon, CA, p.1090	**23** Canyonlands, UT, p.994
8 T. Roosevelt (north), ND, p.832	**16** Sequoia, CA, p.1089	**24** Arches, UT, p.996

US NATIONAL PARKS
for a detailed description of each park
see the page indicated

For up-to-the-minute **information** on the **national park system**, access the official Park Service website at ⓦ www.nationalparks.org. It features full details of the main attractions of the national parks, plus opening hours, the best times to visit, admission fees, hiking trails, and visitor facilities.

Most parks and monuments charge admission fees, ranging from $4 to $25, which cover a vehicle and all its occupants. For anyone on a touring vacation, it will almost certainly make more sense to buy one of the various passes that are sold at all federal parks and monuments. The annual **National Parks Pass** ($50) grants unrestricted access to the bearer, and any accompanying passengers, to all national parks and monuments for a year from the date of purchase.

Two additional passes grant free access for life to all national parks and monuments, again to the holder and any accompanying passengers, and also provide a fifty percent discount on camping fees. The **Golden Age** Passport is available to any US citizen or permanent resident aged 62 or older for a one-time processing charge of $10, while the **Golden Access** Passport is issued free to blind or permanently disabled US citizens or permanent residents.

While hotel-style **lodges** are found only in major parks, every park or monument tends to have at least one well-organized **campground** for visitors. Often, a cluster of motels can be found not far outside the park boundaries. With appropriate free permits – subject to some restrictions in popular parks – backpackers can also usually camp in the backcountry (a general term for areas inaccessible by road).

Other public lands

National parks and monuments are often surrounded by tracts of **national forest** – also federally administered but much less protected. These too usually hold appealing rural campgrounds but, in the words of the slogan, each is a "Land Of Many Uses," and usually allows logging and other land-based

industry (thankfully, more often ski resorts than strip mines).

Other government departments administer a whole range of wildlife refuges, national scenic rivers, recreation areas, and the like. The **Bureau of Land Management** (BLM) has the largest holdings of all, most of it open rangeland, such as in Nevada and Utah, but also including some enticingly out-of-the-way reaches. Environmentalist groups engage in endless running battles with developers, ranchers, and the extracting industries over uses – or alleged misuses – of the federal lands.

Holders of National Parks passes (see this page) can pay an additional $15 to affix a **Golden Eagle** hologram to their pass, which extends its cover to sites managed by the US Fish and Wildlife Service, the Forest Service, and the BLM.

State parks and **state monuments**, administered by individual states, preserve sites of more limited, local significance. Many are explicitly designed for recreational use, and thus hold better campgrounds than their federal equivalents.

Camping and backpacking

The ideal way to see the great outdoors – especially if you're on a low budget – is to tour by car and **camp** in state and federal campgrounds. Typical public campgrounds range in price from free (usually when there's no water available, which may be seasonal) to around $8 per night. Fees at the generally less scenic commercial campgrounds – abundant near major towns, and often resembling open-air hotels, complete with shops and restaurants – are more like $15–25. If you're camping in high season, either reserve in advance or avoid the most popular areas.

Backcountry camping in the national parks is usually free, by permit only. Before you set off on anything more than a half-day hike, and whenever you're headed for anywhere at all isolated, be sure to inform a ranger of your plans, and ask about weather conditions and specific local tips. Carry sufficient food and drink to cover emergencies, as well as all the necessary equipment and maps. Check whether fires are permitted;

even if they are, try to use a camp stove in preference to local materials. In wilderness areas, try to camp on previously used sites. Where there are no toilets, bury human waste at least six inches into the ground and a hundred feet from the nearest water supply and campground.

Backpackers should never drink from rivers and streams; you never know what acts people – or animals – have performed further upstream. **Giardia** – a water-borne bacteria that causes an intestinal disease characterized by chronic diarrhea, abdominal cramps, fatigue, and weight loss – is a serious problem. Water that doesn't come from a tap should be boiled for at least five minutes, or cleansed with an iodine-based purifier or a giardia-rated filter.

Hiking at lower elevations should present few problems, though swarms of **mosquitoes** near water can drive you crazy; Avon Skin-so-soft, or anything containing DEET, are fairly reliable repellents. **Ticks** – tiny beetles that plunge their heads into your skin and swell up – are another hazard. They sometimes leave their heads inside, causing blood clots or infections, so get advice from a park ranger if you've been bitten. One species of tick causes **Lyme Disease**, a serious condition that can even affect the brain. Nightly inspections of your skin are strongly recommended.

Beware, too, of **poison oak**, which grows all over the western states, usually among oak trees. Its leaves come in groups of three (the middle one on a short stem) and are distinguished by prominent veins and shiny surfaces. If you come into contact with it, wash your skin (with soap and cold water) and clothes as soon as possible – and don't scratch. In serious cases, hospital emergency rooms can give antihistamine or adrenaline shots. A comparable curse is **poison ivy**, found throughout the country. For both plants, remember the sage advice, "Leaves of three, let it be."

Mountain hikes

When hiking at higher elevations, for instance in the 14,000ft peaks of the Rockies, or in California's Sierra Nevada (and certainly in Alaska), you should take special care. Late snows are common, and in spring there's a real danger of avalanches, not to mention meltwaters that make otherwise simple stream crossings hazardous. Weather conditions can also change abruptly. **Altitude sickness** can affect even the fittest of athletes: take it easy for your first few days above seven thousand feet. Drink lots of water, avoid alcohol, eat plenty of carbohydrates, and protect yourself from the sun.

Desert hikes

If you intend to hike in the **desert**, tell someone where you are going, and write down all pertinent information, including your expected time of return. Carry an extra two days' food and water and never go anywhere without a map. Cover most of your ground in early morning: the midday heat is too debilitating. If you get lost, find some shade and wait. As long as you've registered, the rangers will eventually come looking for you.

At any time of year, you'll stay cooler during the day if you wear full-length sleeves and trousers, while a wide-brimmed hat and good sunglasses will spare you the blinding headaches that can result from the desert light. You may also have to contend with **flash floods**, which can appear from nowhere. Never camp in a dry wash, and don't attempt to cross flooded areas until the water has receded.

It's essential to carry – and drink – large quantities of **water** in the desert. An eight-hour hike in typical summer temperatures above 100°F would require you to drink a phenomenal thirty pints of water. Loss of appetite and thirst are early symptoms of heat exhaustion, so it's possible to become seriously dehydrated without feeling thirsty. Watch out for signs of dizziness or nausea; if you feel weak and stop sweating, it's time to get to the doctor. Check whether water is available on your trail; ask a ranger, and carry at least a quart per person even if it is.

When **driving** in the desert, carry two gallons of water per person in the car, and take along an emergency pack with flares, a first-aid kit and snakebite kit, matches, and a compass. A shovel, tire pump, and extra gas are always a good idea. If the engine overheats, don't turn it off; instead, try to cool it quickly by turning the front end of the car towards the wind. Carefully pour some water on the front of the radiator, and turn the air conditioning off and the heat up full blast. In an emergency, never panic and leave the car: you'll be harder to find wandering around alone.

Adventure travel

The opportunities for **adventure travel** in the US are all but endless, from whitewater rafting down the Colorado River, to mountain biking in the volcanic Cascades, canoeing down the headwaters of the Mississippi River, horseback riding in Big Bend on the Rio Grande in Texas, and Big Wall rock-climbing on the sheer granite monoliths of Yosemite Valley.

While an exhaustive listing of the possibilities could fill another volume of this book, certain places have an especially high concentration of adventure opportunities, such as Moab, Utah (p.998), or New Hampshire's White Mountains (p.1084). Throughout the book we recommend guides, outfitters, and local adventure-tour operators.

Wildlife

Watch out for bears, deer, moose, mountain lions, and rattlesnakes in the backcountry, and consider the effect your presence can have on their environment.

Other than in a national park, you're highly unlikely to encounter a **bear**. Even there, it's rare to stumble across one in the wilder-ness. If you do, don't run, just back away slowly. Most fundamentally, it will be after your food, which should be stored in airtight containers when camping. Ideally, hang both food and garbage from a high but slender branch some distance from your camp. Never attempt to feed bears, and never get between a mother and her young. Young animals are cute; irate mothers are not.

Snakes and creepy-crawlies

Though the deserts in particular are home to a wide assortment of poisonous creatures, these are rarely aggressive towards humans. To avoid trouble, observe obvious precautions. Don't attempt to handle wildlife; keep your eyes open as you walk, and watch where you put your hands when scrambling over obstacles; shake out shoes, clothing, and bedding before use; and back off if you do spot a creature, giving it room to escape.

If you are bitten or stung, current medical thinking rejects the concept of cutting yourself open and attempting to suck out the venom. Whether snake, scorpion, or spider is responsible, apply a cold compress to the wound, constrict the area with a tourniquet to prevent the spread of venom, drink lots of water, and bring your temperature down by resting in a shady area. Stay as calm as possible and seek medical help immediately.

Shopping

Not surprisingly, the US has some of the greatest shopping opportunities in the world – from the luxury-lined blocks of Fifth Avenue in New York, the Miracle Mile in Chicago, and Rodeo Drive in Beverly Hills, to the local markets found in both big cities and small, offering everything from fruits and vegetables to handmade local crafts.

When buying clothing and accessories, international visitors will need to convert their sizes into American equivalents (see box, opposite). For almost all purchases, state taxes will be applied (see "Costs," p.58).

Clothing and shoe sizes

Women's dresses and skirts

American	4	6	8	10	12	14	16	18
British	8	10	12	14	16	18	20	22
Continental	38	40	42	44	46	48	50	52

Women's blouses and sweaters

American	6	8	10	12	14	16	18
British	30	32	34	36	38	40	42
Continental	40	42	44	46	48	50	52

Women's shoes

American	5	6	7	8	9	10	11
British	3	4	5	6	7	8	9
Continental	36	37	38	39	40	41	42

Men's suits

American	34	36	38	40	42	44	46	48
British	34	36	38	40	42	44	46	48
Continental	44	46	48	50	52	54	56	58

Men's shirts

American	14	15	15.5	16	16.5	17	17.5	18
British	14	15	15.5	16	16.5	17	17.5	18
Continental	36	38	39	41	42	43	44	45

Men's shoes

American	7	7.5	8	8.5	9.5	10	10.5	11	11.5
British	6	7	7.5	8	9	9.5	10	11	12
Continental	39	40	41	42	43	44	44	45	46

Traveling with children

Traveling with kids in the United States is relatively problem-free. Children are readily accepted – indeed welcomed – in public places across the country. Hotels and motels are quite accustomed to them, most state and national parks organize children's activities, every town or city has clean and safe playgrounds, and, of course, Disneyland in California and Disney World in Florida provide the ultimate in kids' entertainment, as do countless other theme parks nationwide.

Many, if not most, restaurants encourage parents to bring in their offspring. All the national chains provide highchairs and a special kids' menu, packed with huge, excellent-value (if not necessarily healthful) meals – cheeseburger and fries for 99¢, and so on. Virtually all museums and tourist attractions offer reduced rates for kids. Most large cities have natural history museums or aquariums, and quite a few also have hands-on children's museums.

State tourist offices can provide more specific information (see the box on p.67), while guidebooks for parents include the *Unofficial Guide to California with Kids* ($18.99) and *New York City with Kids* ($16.99), both in

55

the Frommer's Family Guides list, and Vicki Lansky's helpful *Trouble-Free Travel with Children* ($9.95). Each of the John Muir Publications' *Kidding Around* series covers the history and sights of a major US city in a family-friendly way.

Getting around

Children under two years old fly free on domestic routes and for ten percent of the adult fare on international flights – though that doesn't mean they get a seat, let alone frequent-flier miles. Kids aged between two and twelve years old are usually entitled to half-price tickets.

Traveling by bus may be the cheapest way to go, but it's also the most uncomfortable for kids. Under-twos travel (on your lap) for free. Children under twelve are charged half the standard fare.

Taking the train is by far the best option for long journeys – not only does everyone get to enjoy the scenery, but you can get up and walk around. Most cross-country trains have sleeping compartments, which may be quite expensive, but are likely to be seen by the kids as a great adventure. Children's discounts are much the same as for bus or plane travel.

All that said, most families choose to travel by car. If you hope to enjoy a driving vaca-tion with your kids, make plans. Don't set unrealistic targets; pack sensible snacks and drinks; stop every couple of hours; arrive at your destination before sunset; and avoid traveling through big cities during rush hour. Car rental companies usually provide kids' car seats – which are required by law for children under the age of four – for $5–8 a day. You would, however, be advised to check, or bring your own; they are not always available.

Recreational vehicles (RVs) are a good option for families, combining the convenience of kitchens and bedrooms with the freedom of the road (see "Getting around," p.38).

Resources

Rascals in Paradise in San Francisco, (☎415/921-7000, ⓦwww.rascalsinparadise .com), can arrange scheduled and custom-ized itineraries built around activities for kids in the US and abroad, ranging from hiking and horseriding to mountain biking and watersports. Travel with Your Children in New York (☎212/477-5524 or 1-888/822-4388) publishes a newsletter, *Family Travel Times* (ⓦwww.familytraveltimes.com), as well as books on travel with children, including *Great Adventure Vacations with Your Kids*.

Gay and lesbian travelers

The gay scene in America is huge, albeit heavily concentrated in the major cities. San Francisco, where between a quarter and a third of the voting population is reckoned to be gay or lesbian, is arguably the world's premier gay city. New York runs a close second, and up and down both coasts gay men and women enjoy the kind of visibility and influence those in other places can only dream about. Gay officeholders are no longer a novelty, while resources, facilities, and organi-zations are endless.

In the heartland, however, life can look more like the Fifties – away from large cities, homosexuals are still oppressed and com-monly reviled. Gay travelers need to watch their step to avoid hassles and possible aggression.

Virtually every major city has a predomi-nantly gay area – Chelsea and Christopher Street in New York City, Los Angeles' West Hollywood, San Francisco's Castro district, Houston's Montrose, Seattle's Capitol Hill, and so on. Things change quickly in the gay and lesbian (and emerging bisexual) scene, but we've tried to give an overview of local resources, bars, and clubs in each large urban area.

National publications are available from any good bookstore. Bob Damron in San Francisco (☎415/255-0404 or 1-800/462-6654, ⊛www.damron.com) produces the best and sells them at a discount online. These include the *Men's Travel Guide*, a pocket-sized yearbook listing hotels, bars, clubs, and resources for gay men ($15.96); the *Women's Traveler*, which provides similar listings for lesbians ($14.36); the *Damron City Guide*, which details lodging and entertainment in major cities ($17.56); and *Damron Accommodations*, which lists 1000 accom-modations for gays and lesbians worldwide ($19.16).

Gayellow Pages in New York (☎212/674-0120, ⊛www.gayellowpages.com) publishes a useful directory of businesses in the US and Canada ($25), plus regional directories for New England, New York, and the South, as well as a CD-ROM version ($10). *The Advocate*, based in Los Angeles ($3; ⊛www.advocate.com) is a bimonthly national gay news magazine, with features, general info, and classified ads. Finally, the International Gay & Lesbian Travel Association in Fort Lauderdale FL (☎1-954/776-2626, ⊛www.iglta.org), is a comprehensive, invaluable source for gay and lesbian travelers.

Women travelers

A woman traveling alone in America is not usually made to feel conspicuous, or liable to attract unwelcome attention. Cities can feel a lot safer than you might expect, simply because there are so many people around. Like anywhere, though, particular care must be taken at night: walking through unlit, empty streets is never a good idea, and, if there's no bus or subway service, take a taxi. Women who look confident are less likely to encounter trouble; those who stand around looking lost and a bit scared are prime targets.

In the major **urban centers**, if you stick to the better parts of town, going into bars and clubs alone should pose few problems: there's generally a pretty healthy attitude toward women who do so, and your privacy will be respected.

However, small towns may lack the same liberal or indifferent attitude toward lone women travelers. People seem to jump immediately to the conclusion that your car has broken down, or that you've suffered some strange misfortune; you may get fed up with well-meant offers of help. If your vehicle does break down on heavily traveled roads, wait in the car for a police or highway patrol car to arrive. If you don't already have one, you should rent a **mobile phone** with your car, for a small charge – a potential lifesaver.

Women, even more so than for men, should **never hitchhike** in the US. Similarly, you should never pick up anyone who's trying to hitchhike. If someone is waving you down on the road, ostensibly to get help with a broken-down vehicle, just drive on by – the highway patrol will be along soon enough to see what the trouble is.

Avoid traveling at night by **public transportation** – deserted bus stations, if not actually threatening, will do little to make you feel secure. Where possible, team up with a fellow traveler (there really is safety in numbers). On Greyhound buses, sit near the driver.

Should disaster strike, all major towns have some kind of rape **counseling** service; if not, the local sheriff's office will arrange for you to get help and counseling, and, if necessary, get you home. The National Organization for Women (ⓦwww.now.org) is a leader in seeking to advance issues of importance to women. NOW branches, listed in local phone directories and on the website, can provide information on rape crisis centers, counseling services, feminist bookstores, and lesbian bars.

Resources and specialists

Call of the Wild Berkeley CA ☎510/849-9292 or 1-888/378-1978, ⓦwww.callwild.com. This established outfitter offers hiking adventures for women of all ages and abilities. Trips include visits to Native American ruins, backpacking in California

national parks, cross-country skiing, yoga, and jaunts to Hawaii.

Gutsy Women Travel Glenside PA ☎215/572-7676 or 1-866/464-8879, ⓦwww.gutsywomentravel.com. International agency that provides practical support, as well as organising trips for lone female travelers.

Womanship Annapolis MD ☎410/267-6661 or 1-800/342-9295, ⓦwww.womanship.com. Learn-to-sail cruises for women of all ages. Destinations include Chesapeake Bay, Florida, the Pacific Northwest, and Mystic, Connecticut.

The Women's Travel Club Bloomfield NJ ☎1-800/480-4448, ⓦwww.womenstravelclub.com. Arranges vacations, itineraries, room-sharing, and various activities for women.

Travel essentials

Costs

When it comes to **average costs** for traveling expenses, much depends on where you've chosen to go. A jaunt around the barbeque shacks of Texas and the Deep South won't cost you much in accommodation, dining, or souvenir-buying, but gas prices (currently around $3 per gallon) will add to the expense. By contrast, getting around a centralized city such as Boston, New York, or Chicago will be relatively cheap, but you'll pay much more for your hotel, meals, and shopping purchases. A simple rule of thumb is, prices will vary directly with the size and glamour of the location. Also keep in mind that added to the cost of most items you purchase is a state – but not federal – **sales tax**, anywhere from less than three percent (in Colorado) to more than eight percent (in New York), and big cities may add on another point or two to that rate. (Alaska, Delaware, Montana, New Hampshire, and Oregon have no state sales tax.) Additionally, some cities – probably the ones you most want to visit – tack on a **hotel tax** that makes the total tax for accommodation around fifteen percent.

Unless you're camping or staying in a hostel, **accommodation** will be your greatest expense while in the US. Adequate lodging is rarely available for under $60, outside of bare-bones roadside motels, and a marginally decent room will run anywhere from $75–90, with fancier hotels costing much, much more – upwards of $200–350 in many of the big cities.

Unlike accommodation, prices for good **food** don't automatically take a bite out of your wallet, and you can indulge anywhere from the lowliest (but still scrumptious) burger shack to the chicest restaurant helmed by a celebrity chef. You can get by on as little as $20 a day, but realistically you should aim for around $60.

Public transit options are usually affordable, with the best deals being the multi-day or week-long **transit passes** offered by most cities for riding on buses, light rail, and subways. Renting a car, at around $150–200 per week, is a far more efficient way to explore the broader part of the country, and, for a group of two or more, it's no more expensive, either. Keep in mind, though, that for those under 25 years of age, there are often supplements of $20 a day tacked onto car rental fees.

For attractions in the Guide, prices are quoted for adults, with children's rates listed if they are more than a few dollars less; at some spots, kids get in for half-price, or for free if they're under 6.

Tipping

Tipping is expected for all bar and restaurant service. Expect to tip about 15 percent of the bill before tax to waiters in most restaurants (unless the service is truly wretched), and 20 percent for good service. In the US, this is where most of a waiter's income comes from, and not leaving a fair amount is seen as an insult. About 15 percent should also be added to taxi fares; round up to the nearest 50¢ or dollar, as well. A hotel porter should get $1–2 per bag; if he's lugged your suitcases up several flights of stairs, make it $3–$5. Chambermaids get $1–2 per guest for each day; valet attendants get $2.

Crime and personal safety

No one could pretend that America is crime-free, although away from the urban centers crime is often remarkably low. Even the lawless reputations of Miami, Detroit, or Los Angeles are far in excess of the truth, and most parts of these cities, by day at least, are safe; at night, however, some areas are completely off-limits. All the major tourist areas and the main nightlife zones in cities are invariably brightly lit and well policed. By planning carefully and taking good care of your possessions, you should, generally speaking, have few problems.

Car crime

Crimes committed against tourists driving rented cars aren't as common as they once were, but it still pays to be cautious. In major urban areas, any car you rent should have nothing on it – such as a particular license plate – that makes it easy to spot as a rental car. When driving, under no circumstances should you stop in any unlit or seemingly deserted urban area – and especially not if someone is waving you down and suggesting that there is something wrong with your car. Similarly, if you are accidentally rammed by the driver behind you, do not stop immediately, but proceed on to the nearest well-lit, busy area and call ⓣ911 for assistance. Keep your doors locked and windows never more than slightly open. Do not open your door or window if someone approaches your car on the pretext of asking for directions. Hide any valuables out of sight, preferably locked in the trunk or in the glove compartment.

Disabled travellers

By international standards, the US is exceptionally accommodating for travelers with mobility concerns or other physical disabilities. All public buildings, including hotels and restaurants, must be wheelchair accessible and provide suitable toilet facilities. Almost all street corners have dropped curbs, and most public transportation systems include subway stations with elevators and buses that "kneel" to let wheelchaired passengers board.

Resources

Most state tourism offices provide information for disabled travelers (see p.67). In addition, SATH, the Society for Accessible Travel and Hospitality, in New York (ⓣ212/447-7284, ⓦwww.sath.org), is a not-for-profit travel-industry group of travel agents, tour operators, hotel and airline management, and people with disabilities. They pass on any inquiry to the appropriate member, though you should allow plenty of time for a response. Mobility International USA, in Eugene OR (ⓣ541/343-1284, ⓦwww.miusa.org), offers travel tips to members ($35 a year) and operates exchange programs for disabled people. They also serve as a national information center on disability. If you'd like to plan a specific itinerary for your trip, contact the Directions Unlimited travel agency in New York (ⓣ914/241-1700 or 1-800/533-5343), which has a department for disabled travelers.

Disabled Outdoors is a quarterly magazine specializing in facilities for disabled travelers who wish to explore the great outdoors. The useful publications by Twin Peaks Press, *Travel for the Disabled* and *Wheelchair Vagabond*, are both out of print but widely available online.

The Golden Access Passport, issued without charge to permanently disabled or blind US citizens, gives free lifetime admission to all national parks. It can only be obtained in person at a federal area where an entrance fee is charged; you'll have to show proof of permanent disability, or that you are eligible for receiving benefits under federal law.

Getting around

The Americans with Disabilities Act (1990) obliges all air carriers to make the majority of their services accessible to travelers with disabilities, and most airlines will usually let attendants of more seriously disabled people accompany them at no extra charge.

Almost every Amtrak train includes one or more coaches with accommodation for handicapped passengers. Guide dogs travel free and may accompany blind, deaf, or disabled passengers. Be sure to give 24 hours' notice. Hearing-impaired passengers can get information on ☎1-800/523-6590 (though it can take a while to get through; the service is poorly staffed).

Greyhound, however, is not recommended. Buses are not equipped with lifts for wheelchairs, though staff will assist with boarding (intercity carriers are required by law to do this), and the "Helping Hand" policy offers two-for-the-price-of-one tickets to passengers unable to travel alone (carry a doctor's certificate). The American Public Transportation Association, in Washington, DC (☎202/496-4800, ⑩www.apta.com), provides information about the accessibility of public transportation in cities.

The American Automobile Association (☎1-877/244-9790, ⑩www.aaa.com) produces the *Handicapped Driver's Mobility Guide*, while the larger car-rental companies provide cars with hand controls at no extra charge, though only on their full-sized (ie, most expensive) models; reserve well in advance.

Electricity

Electricity runs on 110V AC. All plugs are two-pronged and rather insubstantial. Some travel plug adapters don't fit American sockets.

Entry requirements

Keeping up with the constant changes to US entry requirements since 9/11 can sometimes feel like a hopeless task. At least once a year the American government announces new, often harsher, restrictions on foreign entry into the country, adding consider-

ably to the red tape involved in visiting it. Nonetheless, there are several basic rules that apply to these requirements, which are detailed (and should be frequently checked for updates) on the US State Department website ⑩travel.state.gov.

Under the **Visa Waiver Program**, if you're a citizen of the UK, Ireland, Australia, New Zealand, most Western European states, or other selected countries like Singapore, Japan, and Brunei (27 in all), and visiting the United States for less than ninety days, at a minimum you'll need an onward or return ticket, a visa waiver form, and a Machine Readable Passport (MRP). MRPs issued before October 2005 are acceptable to use on their own; those issued from October 2005 to October 2006 must include a digital photograph of the passport holder; and those issued after October 2006 require a high-tech security chip built into the passport. It is up to the various countries covered by the Visa Waiver Program to provide such passports to their citizens; for more information, inquire at American embassies or consulates.

The **I-94W Nonimmigrant Visa Waiver Arrival/Departure Form** will be provided either by your travel agency or embassy, or when you get on the plane, and must be presented to Immigration on arrival. The same form covers entry across the US borders with Canada and Mexico (for non-Canadian and non-Mexican citizens). If you're in the Visa Waiver Program and intend to work, study, or stay in the country for more than ninety days, you must apply for a regular visa through your local US embassy or consulate. You will not be admitted under the VWP if you've ever been arrested (not just convicted), have a criminal record, or been previously deported from or refused entry to the US. Under no circumstances are visitors who have been admitted under the Visa Waiver Program allowed to extend their stays beyond ninety days. Doing so will bar you from future use of the program.

Canadian citizens, who have not always needed a passport to get into the US, should have their passports on them when entering the country. If you're planning to stay for more than ninety days, you'll need a visa, which can be applied for by mail through the US embassy or nearest US consulate. If you cross the US border by car, be prepared for US Customs officials to search your vehicle. Remember, too, that without the proper paperwork, Canadians are barred from working in the US.

Citizens of all other countries should contact their local US embassy or consulate for details of current entry requirements, as they are often required to have both a valid passport and a non-immigrant visitor's visa. To obtain such a visa, complete the application form available through your local American embassy or consulate, and send it with the appropriate fee, two photographs, and a passport. Beyond this, you can expect additional hassles to get a visa, including one or more in-depth interviews, supplemental applications for students and "high-risk" travelers, and long delays in processing time. Visas are not issued to convicted criminals, those with ties to radical political groups, and visitors from countries identified by the State Department as being "state sponsors of terrorism" (eg, North Korea, Iran, etc). Complications also arise if you are HIV positive or have TB, hepatitis, or other communicable diseases, or previously been denied entry to the US for any reason. Furthermore, the US government now electronically fingerprints most visitors and applies spot background checks looking for evidence of past criminal or terrorist ties.

For further information or to get a visa extension before your time is up, contact the nearest US Citizenship and Immigration Service office, whose address will be at the front of the phone book, under the Federal Government Offices listings, or call ☏1-800/877-3676. You can also contact the National Customer Service Center at ☏1-800-375-5283. Immigration officials will assume that you're working in the US illegally, and it's up to you to prove otherwise. If you can, bring along an upstanding American citizen to vouch for you, and be prepared for potentially hostile questioning.

US embassies and consulates

In Australia

Embassy Canberra: 21 Moonah Place, Yarralumla ACT 2600 ☏02/6214 5600, ⓦusembassy-australia.state.gov

Consulates Melbourne: 553 St Kilda Rd, VIC 3004 ☏03/9526 5900
Perth: 16 St George's Terrace, 13th floor, WA 6000 ☏08/9202 1224
Sydney: MLC Centre, Level 10, 19–29 Martin Place, NSW 2000 ☏02/9373 9200
Visa hotline ☏1902/941 641 (prerecorded information, Aus$1.05 per minute) or ☏1800/687 844 (live operators, Aus$2.75 per minute)

In Canada

Embassy 490 Sussex Drive, Ottawa, ON K1N 1G8 ☏613/238-5335, ⓦwww.usembassycanada.gov
Consulates Calgary: 615 Macleod Trail SE, Room 1000, AB T2G 4T8 ☏403/266-8962
Halifax: Wharf Tower II, 1969 Upper Water St, Suite 904, NS B3J 3R7 ☏902/429-2480
Montreal: 1155 St Alexandre St, QC H3B 1Z1 ☏514/398-9695, ⓦmontreal.usconsulate.gov
Québec City: 2 Place Terrasse Dufferin, QC G1R 4T9 ☏418/692-2095
Toronto: 360 University Ave, ON M5G 1S4 ☏416/595-1700, ⓦwww.usconsulatetoronto.ca
Vancouver: 1095 W Pender St, 21st floor, BC V6E 2M6 ☏604/685-4311, ⓦwww.usconsulatevancouver.ca
Winnipeg: 201 Portage Ave, Suite 860, MB R3B 3K6 ☏204/940-1800, ⓦwww.usconsulatewinnipeg.ca

In Ireland

Embassy 42 Elgin Rd, Ballsbridge, Dublin 4 ☏01/668 8777, ⓦdublin.usembassy.gov

In New Zealand

Embassy 29 Fitzherbert Terrace, Thorndon, Wellington ☏04/462 2000, ⓦnewzealand.usembassy.gov
Consulate 3rd floor, Citibank Building, 23 Customs St, Auckland ☏09/303 2724
address for visa applications: Non-Immigrant Visas, Private Bag 92022, Auckland

In the UK

Embassy London: 24 Grosvenor Square, W1A 1AE ☏020/7499 9000, visa hotline ☏09042-450100, ⓦwww.usembassy.org.uk
Consulates Belfast: Danesfort House, 223 Stranmillis Road, Belfast BT9 5GR ☏028/9038 6100
Edinburgh: 3 Regent Terrace, EH7 5BW ☏0131/556 8315

Foreign embassies and consulates in the US

Australia

Embassy 1601 Massachusetts Ave NW, Washington DC 20036 ☎202/797-3000, ⓦwww. austemb.org

Canada

Embassy 501 Pennsylvania Ave NW, Washington DC 20001 ☎202/682-1740,ⓦcanadianembassy. org
Consulates Boston: Three Copley Place, suite 400, MA 02216 ☎617/262-3760
Chicago: Two Prudential Plaza, 180 N Stetson Ave, suite 2400, IL 60601 ☎312/616-1860
Los Angeles: 550 S Hope St, 9th floor, CA 90071–2627 ☎213/346-2700
Miami: First Union Financial Center, 200 S. Biscayne Blvd, FL 33131 ☎305/579-1600
New York: 1251 Avenue of the Americas, NY 10020–1175 ☎212/596-1628
San Francisco: 580 California St, 14th Floor, CA 94104 ☎415/834-3180

Ireland

Embassy 2234 Massachusetts Ave NW, Washington DC 20008 ☎202/462-3939, ⓦwww. irelandemb.org

New Zealand

Embassy 37 Observatory Circle NW, Washington DC 20008 ☎202/328-4800,ⓦwww.nzembassy.com

UK

Embassy 3100 Massachusetts Ave NW, Washington DC 20008 ☎202/588-7800, ⓦwww. britainusa.com/consular/embassy
Consulates Atlanta: Georgia Pacific Centre, Suite 3400, 133 Peachtree St NE, GA 30303 ☎404/954-7700, ⓦwww.britainusa.com/atlanta
Boston: One Memorial Drive, Suite 1500, Cambridge, MA 02142 ☎617/245-4500, ⓦwww .britainusa.com/boston
Chicago: 13th floor, The Wrigley Building, 400 N Michigan Ave, IL 60611 ☎312/970-3800, ⓦwww .britainusa.com/chicago
Denver: Suite 1030, World Trade Center, 1675 Broadway, CO 80202 ☎303/592-5200, ⓦwww .britainusa.com/denver

Houston: Wells Fargo Plaza, 1000 Louisiana, 19th Floor, TX 77002 ☎713/659-6270, ⓦwww. britainusa.com/Houston
Los Angeles: 11766 Wilshire Blvd, Suite 1200, CA 90025 ☎310/481-0031, ⓦwww.britainusa.com/la
Miami: Brickell Bay Office Tower, 1001 Brickell Bay Drive, Suite 2800, FL 33131 ☎305/374-1522, ⓦwww.britainusa.com/miami
New York: 845 Third Ave, NY 10022 ☎212/745-0202, ⓦwww.britainusa.com/ny
San Francisco: 1 Sansome St, Suite 850, CA 94104 ☎415/617-1300, ⓦwww.britainusa.com/sf
Seattle: 900 Fourth Ave, Suite 3001, WA 98164 ☎206/622-9255, ⓦwww.britainusa.com/seattle

Health

If you have a serious accident while in the US, emergency medical services will get to you quickly and charge you later. For emergencies or ambulances, dial ☎911, the nationwide emergency number.

Should you need to see a doctor, consult the *Yellow Pages* telephone directory under "Clinics" or "Physicians and Surgeons." The basic consultation fee is $50–100, payable in advance. Tests, X-rays, etc., are much more. Medications aren't cheap either – keep all your receipts for later claims on your insurance policy.

Foreign visitors should bear in mind that many pills available over the counter at home – most codeine-based painkillers, for example – require a prescription in the US. Local brand names can be confusing; ask for advice at the pharmacy in any drugstore.

In general, inoculations aren't required for entry to the US.

Medical resources for travelers

CDC ⓦwww.cdc.gov/travel. Official US government travel health site.
International Society for Travel Medicine ⓦwww.istm.org. Full listing of travel health clinics.

Insurance

In view of the high cost of medical care in the US, all travelers visiting the US from overseas should be sure to buy some form of travel insurance. American and Canadian citizens should check that you're not already covered – some homeowners' or renters' policies are valid on vacation, and credit cards such as American Express often

Rough Guides travel insurance

Rough Guides has teamed up with Columbus Direct to offer you **travel insurance** that can be tailored to suit your needs. Products include a low-cost **backpacker** option for long stays; a **short break** option for city getaways; a typical **holiday package** option; and others. There are also annual **multi-trip** policies for those who travel regularly. Different sports and activities (trekking, skiing, etc) can be usually be covered if required.

See our website (ⓦ www.roughguidesinsurance.com) for eligibility and purchasing options. Alternatively, UK residents should call ☏ 0870/033-9988; US citizens should call ☏ 1-800/749-4922; Australians should call ☏ 1-300/669 999. All other nationalities should call ☏ +44 870/890 2843.

include some medical or other insurance; most Canadians are covered for medical mishaps overseas by their provincial health plans. If you only need trip cancellation/interruption coverage (to supplement your existing plan), this is generally available at about $6 per $100.

Internet

Due to the fact that over 70% of American homes are now online, **cybercafes**, where you can get plugged in to the Web for around 5 to 10 cents a minute, are not as common as they were, though many places have WiFi to hook up your own laptop. Hotels may offer free or cheap **high-speed Internet access** (noted throughout this guide by establishment), and nearly all **public libraries** provide free Internet access, though often there's a wait and machine time is limited.

A useful website – ⓦ www.kropla.com – has information on how to plug in a laptop when abroad, as well as phone country codes around the world and details on electrical systems in different countries. For a database of Internet cafés and public Internet access points worldwide, go to ⓦ www.cybercaptive.com.

Living in the USA

Study and work programs

AFS Intercultural Programs US ☏ 1-800/AFS-INFO, Canada ☏ 1-800/361-7248 or 514/288-3282, UK ☏ 0113/242 6136, Australia ☏ 1300/131736 or ☏ 02/9215-0077, NZ ☏ 0800/600 300 or 04/494 6020, international enquiries ☏ +1-212/807-8686,

ⓦ www.afs.org. Global UN-recognized organization running summer programmes to foster international understanding.

From the US and Canada

American Institute for Foreign Study ☏ 1-866/906-2437, ⓦ www.aifs.com. Language study and cultural immersion, as well as au pair and Camp America programs.
BUNAC USA (British Universities North America Club) ☏ 1-800/GO-BUNAC, ⓦ www.bunac.org. Offers students the chance to work in Australia, New Zealand, Ireland or Britain.
Council on International Educational Exchange (CIEE) ☏ 1-800/40-STUDY or ☏ 1/207-533-7600, ⓦ www.ciee.org. Leading NGO offering study programs and volunteer projects around the world.
Earthwatch Institute ☏ 1-800/776-0188 or 978/461-0081, ⓦ www.earthwatch.org. International non-profit that does research projects in over 50 countries all over the world.

From the UK and Ireland

BTCV (British Trust for Conservation Volunteers) ☏ 01302/572 244, ⓦ www.btcv.org.uk. One of the largest environmental charities in Britain, with a programme of national and international working holidays (as a paying volunteer).
BUNAC (British Universities North America Club) ☏ 020/7251 3472, ⓦ www.bunac.co.uk. Organizes working holidays in the US and other destinations for students.
Camp America Camp America ☏ 020/7581 7373, ⓦ www.campamerica.co.uk.
Council Exchange ☏ 020/8939 9057, ⓦ www.councilexchanges.org.uk. International study and work programmes for students and recent graduates.
Earthwatch Institute ☏ 01865/318 838, ⓦ www.uk.earthwatch.org. Long-established international

charity with environmental and archeological research projects worldwide.

From Australia and New Zealand

AFS Intercultural Programs Australia ☎1300/131 736 or 02/9215-0088, NZ ☎0800/600 300 or 04/494 6020, ⓦwww.afs.org.au, ⓦwww. afsnzl.org.nz. Runs summer experiential programs aimed at fostering international understanding for teenagers and adults.

From South Africa

AFS Intercultural Programs ☎27/11-339-2741, ⓦwww.afs.org/southafrica. Non-profit, self-funded and volunteer-based NGO organization..

Mail

Post offices are usually open Monday to Friday from 9am to 5pm, and Saturday from 9am to noon, and there are mail boxes on many street corners. At time of publication, mail within the US costs 39¢ for a letter weighing up to an ounce. Postcards and aerograms to Europe are 75¢, while letters weighing up to an ounce (roughly four thin sheets) are 84¢. Air mail between the US and Europe may take a week to be received.

In the US, the last line of the address includes the city or town and an abbreviation denoting the state (California is "CA" and Texas is "TX". The last line also includes a five-digit number – the **zip code** – denoting the local post office. It is very important to include this, though the additional four digits that you will sometimes see appended are not essential. You can check zip codes on the US Postal Service website, at ⓦwww.usps.com.

Rules on sending **parcels** are very rigid: packages must be in special containers bought from post offices and sealed according to their instructions, which are given at the start of the *Yellow Pages*. To send anything out of the country, you'll need a green customs declaration form, available from a post office.

Maps

The free **road maps** distributed by each state through its tourist offices and welcome centers are usually fine for general driving and route planning. In addition, Rough Guides makes rip-proof, waterproof maps

for numerous **cities, states, and regions** in the US, such as New York, California, New England, and much more.

Rand McNally produces maps for each state, bound together in the *Rand McNally Road Atlas*, and you're apt to find even cheaper state and regional maps at practically any gas station along the major highways for around $3–7. Britain's best source for maps is Stanfords, at 12–14 Long Acre, London WC2E 9LP (☎020/7836 1321, ⓦwww.stanfords.co.uk), which also has a mail-order service.

The American Automobile Association, or AAA ("Triple A"; ☎1-877/244-9790, ⓦwww. aaa.com), based at 4100 E Arkansas Drive, Denver, CO 80222, provides free maps and assistance to its members, and to British members of the AA and RAC. Call the main number to get the location of a branch near you; bring your membership card, or at least a copy of your membership number.

If you're really after **detailed maps** that go far beyond the usual fold-out, try Thomas Guides ($20-40), though they only cover places in the western US.

Highly detailed **park, wilderness**, and **topographical maps** are available through the Bureau of Land Management for the West (ⓦblm.gov) and for the entire country through the Forest Service (ⓦwww.fs.fed. us/maps). The best supplier of detailed, large-format map books for travel through the American outback is **Benchmark Maps**, whose elegantly designed depictions are easy to follow and make even the most remote dirt roads look appealing.

Money

The US dollar, the country's currency, comes in $1, $5, $10, $20, $50 and $100 **denominations**. One dollar comprises one hundred cents, made up of combinations of one-cent pennies, five-cent nickels, ten-cent dimes, and 25-cent quarters. You can check current exchange rates at ⓦwww.xe.net/currency; at the time of writing one pound sterling will buy $1.80–1.90 and a Euro $1.20–1.35.

Bank hours are generally from 9am to 5pm Monday to Thursday, and until 6pm on Friday; the big bank names are Wells Fargo, US Bank, and Bank of America. With an **ATM card**, you'll be able to withdraw

Wiring money

Having money **wired** from home is never cheap, and should be considered a last resort. If you must, the quickest way is to have someone take cash to the nearest **American Express Moneygram** office (call ☎ 1-800/543-4080 for locations; also available at participating Travelex branches) and have it instantaneously wired to you, minus a ten-percent commission. For similar, if slightly pricier, services, **Western Union** also has offices throughout the country (☎ 1-800/325-6000 in the US; ☎ 0800/833 833 in the UK; and ☎ 1800/649 565 in Australia; ⊛ www. westernunion.com), with credit-card payments subject to an additional $10 fee.

cash just about anywhere, though you'll be charged $1.50–4 per transaction for using a different bank's network. Foreign cash-dispensing cards linked to international networks, such as Plus or Cirrus, are also widely accepted – ask your home bank or credit card company which branches you can use. To find the location of the nearest ATM, call AmEx ☎ 1-800/CASH-NOW; Cirrus ☎ 1-800/4-CIRRUS; The Exchange ☎ 1-800/237-ATMS; or Plus ☎ 1-800/843-7587. Make sure you have a **personal identification number** (PIN) that's designed to work overseas.

Credit and **debit cards** are the most widely accepted form of payment at major hotels, restaurants, and retailers, even though some smaller merchants still do not accept them. You'll be asked to show some plastic when renting a car, bike, or other such item, or to start a "tab" at hotels for incidental charges; in any case, you can always pay the bill in cash when you return the item or check out of your room.

US **traveler's checks** are the safest way for overseas visitors to carry money, and the better-known checks, such as those issued by American Express and Visa, are treated as cash in most shops.

Opening hours and public holidays

Government offices (including post offices) and banks will be closed on the following national **public holidays**:

Jan 1 New Year's Day
Third Mon in Jan Martin Luther King Jr's Birthday
Third Mon in Feb Presidents' Day
Last Mon in May Memorial Day
July 4 Independence Day
First Mon in Sept Labor Day
Second Mon in Oct Columbus Day
Nov 11 Veterans' Day
Fourth Thurs in Nov Thanksgiving Day
December 25 Christmas Day

Phones

The US currently has well over one hundred area codes – three-digit numbers that must precede the seven-figure number if you're calling from abroad (following the 001 international access code) or from a different area code, in which case you prefix the ten digits with a 1. It can get confusing, especially as certain cities have several different area codes within their boundaries; for clarity,

Visa TravelMoney

Visa TravelMoney is a disposable debit card pre-paid with dedicated travel funds that you can access from more than nearly a million Visa ATMs in more than 150 countries with a PIN that you select. When your funds are depleted, simply throw the card away. Because you can buy up to nine cards to access the same funds – useful for couples/families traveling together – it's recommended that you buy at least one extra as a backup, in case your first is lost or stolen. You can call a 24hr Visa customer-assistance services center toll-free: ☎ 1-800/VISA-911 for lost or stolen cards; visit also ⊛ www.visa.com. In the UK and the US, Travelex (⊛ www. travelex.com) sells the card.

Calling home from abroad

Note that the initial zero is omitted from the area code when dialing the UK, Ireland, Australia and New Zealand from abroad.

US and Canada international access code + 1 + area code.

Australia international access code + 61 + city code.

New Zealand international access code + 64 + city code.

UK international access code + 44 + city code.

Republic of Ireland international access code + 353 + city code.

South Africa international access code + 27 + city code.

For codes not listed here, dial 0 for the operator, consult any phone directory or log onto ⓦwww.countrycallingcodes.com.

in this book, we've included the local area codes in all telephone numbers. Note that some cities require you to dial all ten digits, even when calling within the same code.

The cheapest way to make **long-distance** and **international** calls is by purchasing a **prepaid phonecard**, commonly found in $5 and $10 denominations in newsagents or minimarkets, especially in urban areas. These are cheaper than the similar cards issued by the big phone companies that are usually on sale in pharmacy outlets and chain stores. The rate using such cards from the USA to most European and other western countries is only 2/3¢ per minute; they also provide the lowest rates to developing countries. Such cards can be used from any touchpad phone but there is usually a surcharge for using them from a payphone. You can also usually arrange with your local telecom provider to have a **chargecard** account with a freephone access in the US, so that any calls you make are billed to your home. This may be convenient, but it's far more expensive than using prepaid cards.

If overseas travellers wish to use their **mobile phones** (always referred to as cell phones in the US), check with your service provider that your phone will work in the US and what the roaming charges will be, or if you can use a local SIM card in it (though that will change your number to an American one). If you find out your phone won't work in the States, you might consider renting one.

US residents setting out on a cross-country trip should make sure that their mobile phone will work – and if additional charges will be imposed – when using the phone outside of its "home" area code. Travelers **from Canada** will have no problems using their phones, though they may have to pay roaming charges, depending on their plan and network

Senior travelers

Anyone over age 62 (with appropriate ID) can enjoy a vast range of discounts in the US. Both Amtrak and Greyhound offer (smallish) percentage reductions on fares to older passengers, and any US citizen or permanent resident 62 or over is entitled to free admission for life to all national parks, monuments, and historic sites using a Golden Age Passport (issued for a one-time fee of $10 at any such site). This free admission applies to all accompanying travelers in the same vehicle and also gives a fifty percent reduction on park user fees, such as camping charges.

Membership in the AARP (formerly the American Association of Retired Persons), based in Washington DC (☎202/434-2277 or 1-888/687-2277, ⓦwww.aarp.org), is open to US residents 50 or over for an annual $12.50 fee; the organization plans group travel for seniors and can provide discounts on accommodation and vehicle rental.

Elderhostel, in Boston (☎1-800/454-5768, ⓦwww.elderhostel.org), runs an extensive network of educational and activity programs for people over 60 throughout the US, at prices broadly in line with those of commercial tours. Deluxe and fun-orientated group tours are available from Vantage Travel, also based in Boston (☎1-800/322-6677, ⓦwww.vantagetravel.com).

State tourism information

Alabama ☎1-800/252-2262, 🖰 www.touralabama.org
Alaska ☎1-800/862-5275, 🖰 www.travelalaska.com
Arizona ☎1-866/275-5816, 🖰 www.arizonaguide.com
Arkansas ☎1-800/628-8725, 🖰 www.arkansas.com
California ☎1-800/TO-CALIF, 🖰 www.gocalif.ca.gov
Colorado ☎1-800/COLORADO, 🖰 www.colorado.com
Connecticut ☎1-888/288-4748, 🖰 www.ctvisit.com
Delaware ☎1-866/284-7483, 🖰 www.visitdelaware.com
Florida ☎1-888/735-2872, 🖰 www.visitflorida.com
Georgia ☎1-800/847-4842, 🖰 www.georgiaonmymind.org
Hawaii ☎1-800/GO-HAWAII, 🖰 www.gohawaii.com
Idaho ☎1-800/VISIT-ID, 🖰 www.visitid.org
Illinois ☎1-800/226-6632, 🖰 www.enjoyillinois.com
Indiana ☎1-888/365-6946, 🖰 www.enjoyindiana.com
Iowa ☎1-800/345-IOWA, 🖰 www.traveliowa.com
Kansas ☎1-800/252-6727, 🖰 www.travelks.com
Kentucky ☎1-800/225-8747, 🖰 www.kentuckytourism.com
Louisiana ☎1-800/99-GUMBO, 🖰 www.louisianatravel.com
Maine ☎1-888/624-6345, 🖰 www.visitmaine.com
Maryland ☎1-800/634-7386, 🖰 www.mdisfun.org
Massachusetts ☎1-800/227-6277, 🖰 www.massvacation.com
Michigan ☎1-888/784-7328, 🖰 www.michigan.org
Minnesota ☎1-800/657-3700, 🖰 www.exploreminnesota.com
Mississippi ☎1-866/733-6477, 🖰 www.visitmississippi.org
Missouri ☎1-800/519-2100, 🖰 www.visitmo.com
Montana ☎1-800/847-4868, 🖰 www.visitmt.com
Nebraska ☎1-800/228-4307, 🖰 www.visitnebraska.org
Nevada ☎1-800/237-0774, 🖰 www.travelnevada.com
New Hampshire ☎1-800/386-4664, 🖰 www.visitnh.gov
New Jersey ☎1-800/847-4865, 🖰 www.visitnj.org
New Mexico ☎1-800/545-2070, 🖰 www.newmexico.org
New York ☎1-800/I-LOVE-NY, 🖰 www.iloveny.com
North Carolina ☎1-800/847-4862, 🖰 www.visitnc.com
North Dakota ☎1-800/435-5663, 🖰 www.ndtourism.com
Ohio ☎1-800/BUCKEYE, 🖰 www.discoverohio.com
Oklahoma ☎1-800/652-6552, 🖰 www.travelok.com
Oregon ☎1-800/547-7842, 🖰 www.traveloregon.com
Pennsylvania ☎1-800/847-4872, 🖰 www.visitpa.com
Rhode Island ☎1-800/556-2484, 🖰 www.visitrhodeisland.com
South Carolina ☎1-888/727-6453, 🖰 www.discoversouthcarolina.com
South Dakota ☎1-800/732-5682, 🖰 www.travelsd.com
Tennessee ☎1-800/462-8366, 🖰 www.tnvacation.com
Texas ☎1-800/888-8839, 🖰 www.traveltex.com
Utah ☎1-800/882-4386, 🖰 www.utah.com
Vermont ☎1-800/VERMONT, 🖰 www.vermontvacation.com
Virginia ☎1-800/847-4882, 🖰 www.virginia.org
Washington ☎1-800/544-1800, 🖰 www.experiencewashington.com
Washington, D.C. ☎1-800/422-8644, 🖰 www.washington.org
West Virginia ☎1-800/225-5982, 🖰 www.callwva.com
Wisconsin ☎1-800/432-8747, 🖰 www.travelwisconsin.com
Wyoming ☎1-800/225-5996, 🖰 www.wyomingtourism.org

Time

The continental US covers four **time zones**, and there's one each for Alaska and Hawaii as well. The Eastern zone is five hours behind Greenwich Mean Time (GMT), so 3pm London time is 10am in New York (see below for the one-week exception). The Central zone, starting approximately on a line down from Chicago and spreading west to Texas and across the Great Plains, is an hour behind the East (10am in New York is 9am in Dallas). The Mountain zone, which covers the Rocky Mountains and most of the Southwest, is two hours behind the East Coast (10am in New York is 8am in Denver). The Pacific zone includes the three coastal states and Nevada, and is three hours behind New York (10am in the Big Apple is 7am in San Francisco). Lastly, most of Alaska (except for the St Lawrence Islands, which are with Hawaii) is nine hours behind GMT (10am in New York is 6am in Anchorage), while Hawaii is ten hours behind GMT (10am in New York is 5am in Honolulu). The US puts its clocks forward to daylight saving time on the first Sunday in April (a week later than the EU) and turns them back on the last Sunday in October.

Tourist information

Each state has its own tourist office, as listed in the box on p.67. These offer prospective visitors a colossal range of free maps, leaflets, and brochures on attractions from overlooked wonders to well-trod tourist traps. You can either contact the offices before you set off, or, as you travel around the country, look for the state-run "welcome centers," usually along main highways close to the state borders. In heavily visited states, these often have piles of discount coupons for cut-price accommodation and food. In addition, visitor centers in most towns and cities—often known as the "Convention and Visitors Bureau," or CVB, and listed throughout this book—provide details on the area, as do local Chambers of Commerce in almost any town of any size.

Tourist offices and government sites

Australian Department of Foreign Affairs
Ⓦ www.dfat.gov.au, Ⓦ www.smartraveller.gov.au.
British Foreign & Commonwealth Office
Ⓦ www.fco.gov.uk.
Canadian Department of Foreign Affairs
Ⓦ www.dfait-maeci.gc.ca.
Irish Department of Foreign Affairs Ⓦ www.
foreignaffairs.gov.ie.
New Zealand Ministry of Foreign Affairs
Ⓦ www.mft.govt.nz.
US State Department Ⓦ www.travel.state.gov.

Guide

Guide

New York City

AL - ALABAMA	IN - INDIANA	MN - MINNESOTA	RI - RHODE ISLAND
AR - ARKANSAS	LA - LOUISIANA	MS - MISSISSIPPI	SC - SOUTH CAROLINA
CT - CONNECTICUT	MA - MASSACHUSETTS	NC - NORTH CAROLINA	VA - VIRGINIA
DE - DELAWARE	MD - MARYLAND	NH - NEW HAMPSHIRE	VT - VERMONT
FL - FLORIDA	ME - MAINE	NJ - NEW JERSEY	WI - WISCONSIN
IL - ILLINOIS	MI - MICHIGAN	PA - PENNSYLVANIA	WV - WEST VIRGINIA

CHAPTER 1 # Highlights

* **Ellis Island** Once the first stop for millions of prospective immigrants from all over the world. See p.82

* **The Brooklyn Bridge** Take a stroll across this much-loved bridge for spectacular views of the city's skyline. See p.89

* **Grand Central Station tours** Admire the magnificent Beaux Arts building and savor the seafood in its subterranean *Oyster Bar*. See p.96

* **Central Park** A massive, gorgeous greenspace, filled with countless bucolic amusements;

understandably called "the lungs of the city." See p.102

* **The Metropolitan Museum of Art** The museum's mammoth collection could keep you busy for days. See p.103

* **Coney Island** The world's tallest Ferris wheel is among the landmark attractions at this beachside amusement park. See p.110

* **A baseball game at Yankee Stadium** Between April and October, it would be a shame not to take in a Bronx Bombers ballgame. See p.112

△ Central Park

New York City

The most beguiling city in the world, **New York City** is an adrenaline-charged, history-laden place that holds immense romantic appeal for visitors. Whether gazing at the flickering lights of the Midtown skyscrapers as you speed across the Queensboro Bridge, experiencing the 4am half-life in the Village, or just whiling the day away in Central Park, you really would have to be made of stone not to be moved by it all. There's no place quite like it.

New York City comprises the central island of **Manhattan** and the four outer boroughs – **Brooklyn**, **Queens**, the **Bronx**, and **Staten Island**. Manhattan, to many, *is* New York; certainly, this is where you're likely to stay and spend most of your time. The island is broadly divided into three areas: **Downtown** (below 14th St), **Midtown** (from 14th St to Central Park/59th St), and **Uptown** (north of 59th St). Though you could spend weeks here and still barely scratch the surface, there are some key attractions and pleasures that you won't want to miss. These include the different **ethnic neighborhoods**, like Chinatown, and the more artsy concentrations of SoHo, TriBeCa, and the East and West villages. Of course, there is the celebrated **architecture** of Midtown and the Financial District, as well as many fabulous **museums** – not just the Metropolitan and MoMA, but countless other smaller collections that afford weeks of happy wandering. In between sights, you can **eat** just about anything, at any time, cooked in any style; you can **drink** in any kind of company; and enjoy any number of obscure **movies**. The more established arts – **dance**, **theater**, and **music** – are superbly presented. For the avid consumer, the choice of **shops** is vast, almost numbingly exhaustive, in this heartland of the great capitalist dream.

Manhattan is a hard act to follow, and the four **outer boroughs**, essentially residential in character, inevitably pale in comparison. However, all hold treasures that are worth seeking out. **Brooklyn Heights** is one of the city's most beautiful neighborhoods; **Long Island City** and **Astoria**, both in Queens, hold many innovative museums; and a visit to the **Bronx Zoo** is sure to be rewarding. Last but not least, a free trip on the **Staten Island Ferry** is not to be missed; a sea-sprayed, refreshing good time, it provides excellent views of the city.

Some history

The first European to see Manhattan Island, then inhabited by the Algonquin Indians, was the Italian navigator Giovanni da Verrazano, in 1524. Dutch colonists established the settlement of **New Amsterdam** exactly one hundred years later. The first governor, Peter Minuit, was the man who famously "bought" the whole island for a handful of trinkets. Considering that the Indians he actually paid were not locals, but only passing through, it might be said that they received a fine deal, too. A strong defensive wall – today's Wall Street follows its course – surrounded the colony. By the time the British laid claim to the area in 1664, the heavy-

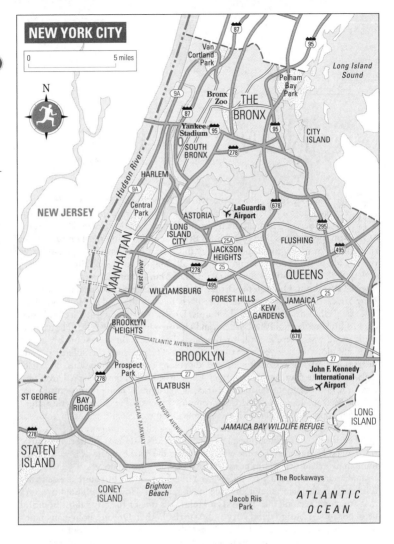

handed rule of governor **Peter Stuyvesant** had so alienated its inhabitants that the Dutch handed over control without a fight.

Renamed **New York**, the city prospered and grew, its population reaching 33,000 by the time of the American Revolution. The opening of the **Erie Canal** in 1825 facilitated trade farther inland, spurring the city to become the economic powerhouse of the nation, the base later in the century of **financiers** such as Cornelius Vanderbilt and Pierpont Morgan. The **Statue of Liberty** arrived from France in 1886, a symbol of the city's role as the gateway for generations of immigrants, and the early twentieth century saw the sudden proliferation of Manhattan's extraordinary **skyscrapers**, which cast New York as the city of the future in the eyes of an astonished world.

Almost a century later, the events of **September 11, 2001**, which destroyed the World Trade Center, shook New York to its core. Several years on, the site of the attacks at Ground Zero has been cleared, and construction has begun on the city's new skyline jewel—the **Freedom Tower** (see box, p.84), which will also commemorate those who were killed.

Arrival, information, and city transportation

New York City is served by three major **airports**: **John F. Kennedy**, or **JFK**, in Queens, **LaGuardia**, also in Queens, and **Newark**, in New Jersey.

From JFK, New York Airport Service buses run to the Port Authority Bus Terminal, Grand Central Station, Penn Station, and major Midtown hotels in Manhattan (every 15–20min 6am–midnight; trip time 45min–1hr; $15 one-way, $27 roundtrip, students $6.50). Another option is the bus/subway link, which costs just the $2 subway fare: take the free shuttle bus (labeled "Long-term parking") to the Howard Beach station on the #A subway line, then the 65min subway ride to central Manhattan.

From LaGuardia, New York Airport Service buses take 45 minutes to get to Grand Central and Port Authority (every 15–30min 7am–midnight; $12 one-way, $21 roundtrip, students one-way $6.50). Alternatively, for $2, you can take the #M60 bus to 125th Street in Manhattan, where you can transfer to multiple Downtown-bound subway lines.

From Newark, Olympia Airport Express buses take up to forty minutes to get to Manhattan, where they stop at Grand Central, Penn Station, Port Authority, and multiple locations in Lower Manhattan (every 20–30min 4am–midnight; $14 one-way, $23 roundtrip). Alternatively, you can use the **AirTrain** service, which runs for free between all Newark terminals, parking lots, and the Newark Airport Rail Link station, where you can connect with NJ Transit or Amtrak trains into New York Penn Station. It usually takes about 20min, and costs $14 one-way (every 20–30min 6am–midnight).

Taxis are pricey from the airports; expect to pay $18–24 from LaGuardia, a flat rate of $35 from JFK, and $35–55 from Newark (airport taxis at Newark will tell you their flat fares to different parts of Manhattan before you leave). You should only use official yellow taxis.

Minibus shuttle services are a decent mid-priced option if you don't mind multiple stops along the way and a very early start. Super Shuttle minivans run 24hr and arrange pick-ups three hours before domestic departures and five hours before international ones (T 1-800/BLUE-VAN or 212/BLUE-VAN). One-way fares to the airport run $15–20, more for a ride from the airport into the city ($30–35). Be forewarned that, if your van has many pick-ups, the time spent picking up riders is not always equal to the money saved. For **general information** on getting to and from the airports, call the Port Authority ground transportation and parking hotline at T 1-800/AIR-RIDE.

Greyhound buses pull in at the Port Authority Bus Terminal, 42nd Street and Eighth Avenue. **Amtrak** trains come in to Penn Station, at Seventh Avenue and 33rd Street. From either Port Authority or Penn Station, multiple subway lines will take you where you want to go from there.

If **arriving by car**, you have multiple options: Rte-495 transects Midtown Manhattan from New Jersey through the Lincoln Tunnel and from the east through the

Queens-Midtown Tunnel. From the southwest, I-95 (the New Jersey Turnpike) and I-78 serve Canal and Spring streets (near SoHo and TriBeCa) via the Holland Tunnel. From the north, I-87 (New York State Thruway) and I-95 serve Manhattan's loop roads. Be prepared for **delays** at tunnels and bridges; most charge tolls. Also, when **parking** your car in Manhattan, try for a garage as near to the rivers as possible to avoid high fees.

Information

The best place for information is the **New York Convention and Visitors' Bureau**, 810 Seventh Ave at 53rd Street (Mon–Fri 8.30am–6pm, Sat & Sun 9am–5pm; ℡212/484-1222, ⓦwww.nycvisit.com). It has leaflets on what's going on in the arts, bus and subway maps, and information on accommodation – though they can't actually book anything for you. You can also find lots of listings at ⓦnewyork.city-search.com. For trendier offerings, go to ⓦwww.dailycandy.com. Free city maps are available at the tourist cubicle in Grand Central.

The **James A. Farley Post Office**, Manhattan's main branch, is at 421 Eighth Ave, between West 31st and 33rd streets (Mon–Sat 24hr for all services except registered mail; zip code 10001).

City transportation

Few cities equal New York for sheer street-level stimulation, and **walking** is the most exciting way to explore. However, it's also exhausting, so at some point you'll need to use some form of **public transportation**. Citywide subway and bus system **maps** – the subway map is especially invaluable – are available from all subway station booths, the Convention and Visitors' Bureau (see above), the concourse office at Grand Central, or online at ⓦwww.mta.nyc.ny.us.

The subway

The fastest way to get from point A to point B in Manhattan and the boroughs is the **subway**, open 24hr a day. Intimidating at first glance, the subway system is actually quite user-friendly. A number or letter identifies each train and route, and most routes run uptown or downtown, rather than crosstown. Every trip, whether on the **express** lines, which stop only at major stations, or the **locals**, which stop at all stations, costs $2. The old-fashioned subway token is no longer accepted; now all riders must use a **MetroCard**, available at station booths or credit/debit/ATM card-capable vending machines. MetroCards can be purchased in any amount from a $2 single ride to $80; a $20 purchase allows 12 rides for the

---

City streets and orientation

The first part of Manhattan to be settled was what is now Downtown; this is why the streets here have names (as opposed to numbers) and are somewhat randomly arranged. A map (see p.81) is key for getting around Lower Manhattan effectively. Often you will hear of places referred to as being either on the **West Side** or the **East Side**; what this means, simply, is whether the place in question lies west or east of **Fifth Avenue**, the greatest of the main avenues, which begins Downtown at the arch in Washington Square Park and runs north to cut along the east side of Central Park. On the East Side above Houston Street (pronounced "Howstun"), and on the West Side above 14th, the streets follow a sensible **grid pattern**, progressing northward one by one. When looking for a specific **address**, keep in mind that on streets, house numbers increase as you walk away from Fifth in either direction; on avenues, house numbers increase as you move north.

CityPass

For significant **discounts** at six of the city's major tourist and cultural attractions – the American Museum of Natural History, the Guggenheim Museum, the Museum of Modern Art, the *Intrepid* Sea-Air-Space Museum, the Circle Line Harbor Cruise, and the Empire State Building – you can purchase a **CityPass** ($45; ☎707/256-0490, ⊛www.citypass.com). Valid for nine days, it allows you to skip most lines and save (up to $46, if you visit all six sights). CityPasses are sold at each of the six attractions to which the pass provides admission.

cost of 10. Unlimited rides are available with a 24hr "Fun Pass" ($7), a 7-day pass ($24), and a 30-day pass ($76).

Once you get past the turnstile, forget everything you've seen in the movies. New York City subways are generally **quite safe**, in part because they are almost always crowded, even at night. The key to being safe is to use common sense. Always use the more crowded center subway cars late at night. Once inside the subway system, you can ride around for as long as you like, as long as you don't pass back out through the turnstiles; if you do, you'll have to swipe your card again to get back in.

Buses

New York's **bus system** is clean, efficient, and fairly frequent. Its one disadvantage is that it can be extremely slow – in peak hours almost down to walking pace – but it can be your best bet for traveling crosstown. Buses leave their route terminal points at five- to ten-minute intervals, and stop every two or three blocks. The fare is payable on entry with a MetroCard (the same one used for the subway) or in cash, but with exact change only; you can **transfer** for free within two hours of swiping your MetroCard. Keep in mind, though, that transfers can only be used to continue on in your original direction, not for return trips on the same bus line.

Taxis

Taxis can be expensive, but they're convenient and can be caught just about anywhere. Although many drivers speak rudimentary English, they can normally get you where you want to go. Knowing the exact address and its cross street is helpful. You should only use official yellow taxis.

Guided tours

Countless businesses and individuals compete to help you make sense of the city, offering all manner of **guided tours**. One of the more original – and least expensive – ways to get oriented is with Big Apple Greeter, 1 Centre St, suite 2035 (☎212/669-8159, ⊛www.bigapplegreeter.org). This not-for-profit group matches you with a local volunteer and points you to places that interest you. It's free, so get in touch well ahead of time.

New York City Vacation Packages (☎1-888/692-8701, ⊛www.nycvp.com) can book rooms at some of the city's finest hotels, land tickets to sold-out Broadway shows, and organize a walking tour of Ground Zero or Chinatown for you; just pick from an à la carte menu of offerings. Package prices vary widely, so call or email ℮info@nycvp.com for information.

Gray Line, the biggest operator of guided **bus tours** in the city, is based in Midtown Manhattan at Eighth Avenue between 47th and 48th streets (☎1-800/669-0051, ⊛www.grayline.com); they also have an office at the Port Authority Bus Terminal. Double-decker bus tours offer unlimited hop-on, hop-off service, tak-

Walking tours

Adventure on a Shoestring ☎212/265-2663. This 40-year-old tour company offers such wonderfully off-beat options as "Marilyn Monroe's Manhattan," the "When Irish Eyes Were Smiling" tour of Hell's Kitchen, and "Greenwich Village Ghosts Galore." Tours ($5) run 90 minutes, and are offered on weekends, rain or shine, throughout the year.

Big Onion Walking Tours ☎212/439-1090, ⓦwww.bigonion.com. The Onion guides peel off the many layers of the city's history (all guides hold advanced degrees in American history). Tours run from $15; call or visit the website for schedules and meeting places. Expect to add $4 if the tour includes "noshing stops."

Harlem Heritage Tours 230 W 116th St, suite 5C ☎212/280-7888, ⓦwww.harlemheritage .com. Cultural walking tours of Harlem, general and specific (such as Harlem jazz clubs), are led middays and evenings seven days a week for $10–100 (most tours average $25); reservations are recommended and can be booked online.

ing in the main sights of Manhattan, for around $49. Tours are bookable through any travel agent, or directly at the bus stops. If you're not happy with your tour guide (quality can vary widely), you can hop off the bus and wait another fifteen minutes for the next bus and guide.

A good way to see the city skyline is with the **Circle Line Ferry**, which sails around Manhattan in three hours from Pier 83 at the west end of 42nd Street (at 12th Ave), with a commentary and on-board bar (March–Dec with varying regularity; $24 for 2hr tour; ☎212/563-3200, ⓦwww.circleline.com). They also operate more exhilarating tours on "The Beast," a speedboat (May–Oct; $17 adults, $11 children for 30min ride). Alternatively, the **Staten Island Ferry** provides a beautiful panorama of the Downtown skyline for free.

For a bird's-eye view, Liberty Helicopter Tours, at the west end of 30th Street near the Jacob Javits Convention Center (☎212/967-4550, ⓦwww.libertyhelicopters .com), offers **helicopter flights** from around $69 for 7 minutes to $186 for 17 minutes per person.

Accommodation

Prices for **accommodation** in New York are well above the norm for the US as a whole. Most hotels charge more than $100 a night (although exceptions and decent double rooms from $75 a night do exist). Most of New York's **hotels** are in Midtown Manhattan – a good enough location, though you may well want to travel downtown for less expensive (and usually better) food and nightlife. **Booking ahead** is strongly advised; at certain times of the year – Christmas and early summer in particular – everything is likely to be full. Phone the hotels directly, or at no extra charge contact a booking service, such as CRS (☎407/740-6442 or 1-800/555-7555) or Quick Book (Mon–Fri only ☎1-800/789-9887). The **price codes** given at the end of each review reflect the cost of the cheapest double room during the high season.

Apartment stays and **bed-and-breakfasts** are an attractive alternative. Staying in a New Yorker's spare room or subletting an apartment is an increasingly popular and somewhat less expensive option. Reservations are normally arranged through an agency such as those listed above. Rates run about $80–100 for a double, or $100 and up a night for a studio apartment. Book well in advance.

Hostels offer still more savings, and run the gamut in terms of quality, safety, and amenities. It pays to do research ahead of time so as to ensure satisfaction upon arrival; most of the city's best cheap sleeps have websites. Average hostel rates range from $30–60.

Hotels

60 Thompson 60 Thompson St, between Spring and Broome ☎212/431-0400, ⓦwww.60thompson.com. This boutique property oozes sophistication and tempts guests with countless amenities, including gourmet minibars, DVD players, and a summertime rooftop lounge overlooking the SoHo skyline. All this fabulousness comes at a price, though. ⑨

Algonquin 59 W 44th St, between 5th and 6th aves ☎212/840-6800, ⓦwww.algonquinhotel.com. At New York's classic literary hangout, you'll find a resident cat named Matilde, cabaret performances, and suites with silly names. The decor remains little changed since its Round Table heyday, though the bedrooms have been refurbished to good effect, and the lobby restored. Ask about summer and weekend specials. ⑨

Amsterdam Inn 340 Amsterdam Ave, at 76th St ☎212/579-7500, ⓦwww.nyinns.com. Within easy walking distance of Central Park, Lincoln Center, and the American Museum of Natural History. Rooms are basic but clean, with TVs, phones, and maid service. The staff is friendly and there's a 24hr concierge. ⑥

The Chelsea Hotel 222 W 23rd St, between 7th and 8th aves ☎212/243-3700, ⓦwww.hotelchelsea.com. One of New York's most noted landmarks, this aging neo-Gothic building boasts a fabulous past (see p.94). Ask for a renovated room, with wood floors, log-burning fireplaces, and plenty of space for a few extra friends. ⑧

Dylan 52 E 41st St, between Park and Madison ☎212/338-0500 or 1-866/55-DYLAN, ⓦwww.dylanhotel.com. The hardwood floors, warm light, and vaguely lemony-tasting air in the lobby are indicative of the whole experience at *Dylan* – classy and clever. If you can afford it, book the Alchemy Suite, a one-of-a-kind Gothic bedchamber with a vaulted ceiling and unusual stained-glass windows. ⑨

Edison 228 W 47th St, between Broadway and 8th Ave ☎212/840-5000, ⓦwww.edisonhotelnyc.com. The most striking thing about the funky 1000-room *Edison*, a good value for Midtown, is its beautiful Art Deco lobby. The rooms are not fancy. ⑦

Gramercy Park 2 Lexington Ave, at E 21st St ☎212/475-4320, ⓦwww.gramercyparkhotel.com. In a lovely location, this hotel reopened in August 2006 after Ian Schrager (co-founder of *Studio 54*) made great bohemian renovations.

The lobby is like stepping into a 3-D painting. Guests get a key to the adjacent private park (see p.94). ⑨

Larchmont 27 W 11th St, between 5th and 6th aves ☎212/989-9333, ⓦwww.larchmonthotel.com. This budget hotel, with a terrific location on a tree-lined street in Greenwich Village, has small but nice, clean rooms. Slightly more expensive on weekends. ⑤

Lucerne 201 W 79th St, at Amsterdam ☎212/875-1000 or 1-800/492-8122, ⓦwww.newyorkhotel.com. This beautifully restored 1904 brownstone, with its extravagantly Baroque red terracotta entrance, charming rooms, and friendly, helpful staff, is just a block from the American Museum of Natural History and close to the liveliest stretch of the Columbus Avenue scene. ⑨

Mercer 147 Mercer St, at Prince ☎212/966-6060, ⓦwww.mercerhotel.com. Housed in a landmark Romanesque Revival building, this hot SoHo hotel has been the choice of many celebs since 1998. Some loft-like guest rooms also have massive baths with 90 square feet for splashing around, and the *Mercer Kitchen* restaurant garners rave reviews. ⑨

Milburn 242 W 76th St, between Broadway and West End ☎212/362-1006, ⓦwww.milburnhotel.com. This welcoming and well-situated hotel is great for families. ⑧

Pickwick Arms 230 E 51st St, between 2nd and 3rd aves ☎212/355-0300, ⓦwww.pickwickarms.com. This thoroughly pleasant budget hotel is one of the best deals in Midtown. All 370 rooms are air-conditioned, with cable TV, direct-dial phones, and room service. The open-air roof deck has stunning views, and there are two restaurants (one French, one Mediterranean) downstairs. ⑧

Roger Smith 501 Lexington Ave, at E 47th St ☎212/755-1400, ⓦwww.rogersmith.com. One of the best Midtown hotels. Plusses include individually decorated rooms, a great restaurant, helpful service, and artwork on display in public spaces. Breakfast is included. ⑨

Royalton 44 W 44th St, between 5th and 6th aves ☎212/869-4400, ⓦwww.royaltonhotel.com. Attempting to capture the market for the arbiters of style, the Philippe Starck–designed *Royalton* has tiny, nautical-themed rooms that are comfortable and quiet, affording a welcome escape from the bustle of Midtown. Stop in just to see the elegant lobby, which runs the length of a city block. ⑨

Seventeen 225 E 17th St, between 2nd and 3rd aves ⊤212/475-2845, ⊛www.hotel17ny.com. *Seventeen*'s rooms feature AC, cable TV, and phones, though they still have shared baths. It's clean, friendly, and nicely situated on a pleasant tree-lined street minutes from Union Square and the East Village. Check out the excellent weekly rates. ❻

🏃 **SoHo Grand** 310 W Broadway, at Grand ⊤212/965-3000, ⊛www.sohogrand.com. In a great location at the edge of SoHo, this hotel draws guests of the model/media-star/actor variety. Its appeal includes small but stylish rooms, a good bar, restaurant, and fitness center. Call for info about its sleek sister property, the *Tribeca Grand*. ❾

Stanford 43 W 32nd St, between Broadway and 5th Ave ⊤212/563-1500 or 1-800/365-1114, ⊛www.hotelstanford.com. In this clean, moderately priced hotel on the block known as Little Korea, rooms are a tad small, but attractive and very quiet. Free continental breakfast, valet laundry, and an efficient, friendly staff. ❽

W 541 Lexington Ave, between 49th and 50th sts ⊤212/755-1200, ⊛www.whotels.com. Downtown location at 201 Park Ave S at 17th St ⊤212/253-9119. These two branches of the stylish luxury hotel chain offer top-to-bottom comfort, priding themselves on the wired in-room services, sleek neutral tones, and trendy public spaces, such as the *Whisky Blue Bar* in the Midtown location, or celebrity chef Todd English's *Olives* restaurant in the Downtown one. ❾

Wales 1295 Madison Ave, between 92nd and 93rd sts ⊤212/876-6000, ⊛www.waleshotel.com. Just steps from NYC's "Museum Mile" (see p.101), this Carnegie Hill hotel has hosted guests for over a century. Rooms are attractive with antique details, thoughtful in-room amenities, and some views of Central Park. There's also a rooftop terrace, fitness studio, famous *Sarabeth's Café*, and live harp music during breakfast. ❾

Washington Square 103 Waverly Place, at Washington Square Park ⊤212/777-9515, ⊛www.washingtonsquarehotel.com. Location in the heart of Greenwich Village, a stone's throw from the NYU campus. Don't be deceived by the posh-looking lobby – the rooms are surprisingly shabby for the price, but serviceable. Continental breakfast is included. ❽

Bed-and-breakfasts

Affordable New York City 21 E 10th St ⊤212/533-4001, ⊛www.affordablenyc.com. Detailed descriptions are provided for this established network of 120 properties (B&Bs and apart-

ments) around the city. B&B accommodations with shared or private bath run ❹, unhosted studios are ❻, and one-bedroom apartments are ❼–❽. Cash or traveler's checks only; three-night minimum. Very customer-oriented and personable.

Bed and Breakfast Network of New York 130 Barrow St ⊤212/645-8134 or 1-800/ 900-8134, ⊛www.bedandbreakfastnetny.com. Call at least a month in advance, and ask about weekly and monthly specials. Hosted doubles ❻

CitySonnet.com ⊤212/614-3034, ⊛www.citysonnet.com. This small, personalized, artist-run B&B/short-term apartment agency offers accommodations all over the city, but specializes in Greenwich Village. Singles, doubles, and unhosted studio apartments. ❹–❺

Colby International 139 Round Hey, Liverpool L28 1RG, England UK ⊤0151/220 5848, ⊛www.colbyinternational.com. Guaranteed B&B accommodations can be arranged from the UK. Book at least two weeks ahead in high season for these excellent-value double apartments (❹–❺) and studios (❹).

Urban Ventures 38 W 32nd St, suite 1412 ⊤212/594-5650, ✉reservations@gamutnyc.com. Book up until the last minute for nightly, weekly, or monthly rentals; there's a minimum stay of only two nights. Budget doubles from ❹, "comfort range" rooms from ❻.

Hostels

Chelsea International Hostel 251 W 20th St, between 7th and 8th aves ⊤212/647-0010, ⊛www.chelseahostel.com. In the heart of Chelsea, this is a smart Downtown choice: beds are $28 a night, with four or six sharing the clean, rudimentary rooms. Private double rooms are $70 a night. Guests must leave a $10 key deposit. No curfew; passport required.

Gershwin 7 E 27th St, between 5th and Madison aves ⊤212/545-8000, Ⓕ684-5546, ⊛www.gershwinhotel.com. This hostel/hotel geared toward young travelers offers Pop Art decor and dormitories with two, six, or ten beds per room (from $33 a night) and private rooms from $109. Reservations recommended for both room types.

Hostelling International-New York 891 Amsterdam Ave, at W 103rd St ⊤212/932-2300, ⊛www.hinewyork.org. Dorm beds cost $32 (in ten-bed rooms) to $38 (in four-bed rooms); members pay a few dollars less per night. The massive facilities – 624 beds in all – include a restaurant, library, travel shop, TV room, laundry, and kitchen. Reserve well in advance – this hostel is very popular.

Jazz on the Park 36 W 106th St, at Central Park West ☎ 212/932-1600, 🖳 www.jazzonthepark.com. This groovy bunkhouse boasts a TV/games room, the *Java Joint Café*, and lots of activities, including live jazz on weekends. Rooms sleep between 2 and 14 people, are clean, bright, and air-conditioned, and range from $32 to $130 per night. Reserve at least one week in advance.

West Side YMCA 5 W 63rd St, at Central Park West ☎ 212/441-8800, 🖳 www.ymcanyc.org. The "Y," just steps from Central Park, houses two floors of reno- vated rooms, an inexpensive restaurant, swimming

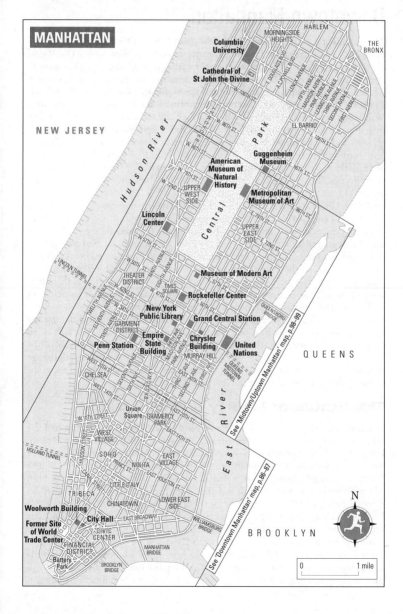

MANHATTAN

HARLEM
MORNINGSIDE
HEIGHTS
THE
BRONX

Columbia
University

Cathedral of
St John the Divine

W 106TH ST

NEW JERSEY

Park

W 96TH ST

EL BARRIO

W 86TH ST

E 106TH ST

Guggenheim
Museum

American
Museum
of Natural
History

W 78TH ST

W 72ND ST   UPPER
WEST
SIDE

E 86TH ST

Metropolitan
Museum of Art

E 79TH ST

Lincoln
Center

Central

UPPER
EAST
SIDE

E 86TH ST

W 57TH ST

E 72ND ST

THEATER
DISTRICT

W 50TH
ST

Museum of Modern Art

E 57TH ST

TIMES
SQUARE

Rockefeller Center

E 50TH ST

W 42ND ST

QUEENSBORO
BRIDGE

GARMENT
DISTRICT

New York
Public Library   Grand Central Station

Empire
State
Building

Chrysler
Building

United
Nations

Penn Station

MURRAY HILL

QUEENS
MIDTOWN
TUNNEL

QUEENS

CHELSEA

WEST 20TH ST

WEST 14TH ST

Union
Square   GRAMERCY
PARK

EAST 20TH ST

EAST 14TH ST

W 10TH STREET

WEST
VILLAGE

HOLLAND TUNNEL

SOHO

PRINCE ST

NOLITA   EAST
VILLAGE

EAST HOUSTON ST

CANAL STREET

LITTLE ITALY

TRIBECA

CHINATOWN

LOWER EAST
SIDE

WILLIAMSBURG
BRIDGE

Woolworth Building

Former Site
of World
Trade Center   City Hall   EAST BROADWAY

BROADWAY

BROOKLYN

CIVIC
CENTER

FINANCIAL
DISTRICT

MANHATTAN
BRIDGE

Battery
Park

BROOKLYN
BRIDGE

LINCOLN TUNNEL

TWELFTH AVENUE

ELEVENTH AVENUE

TENTH AVENUE

NINTH AVENUE

EIGHTH AVENUE

SEVENTH AVENUE

SIXTH AVENUE

FIFTH AVENUE

MADISON AVENUE

PARK AVENUE

LEXINGTON AVENUE

THIRD AVENUE

SECOND AVENUE

FIRST AVENUE

Hudson River

East River

F DOUGLASS BLVD

A C POWELL BLVD

LENOX AVENUE

FIFTH AVENUE

MADISON AVENUE

PARK AVENUE

LEXINGTON AVENUE

THIRD AVENUE

SECOND AVENUE

FIRST AVENUE

See 'Midtown/Uptown Manhattan' map, p.98–99

See 'Downtown Manhattan' map, p.86–87

N

0   1 mile

pool, gym, and laundry. All rooms are air-conditioned. Singles $80, doubles $110 with private bath. **Whitehouse Hotel of New York** 340 Bowery ℡ 212/477-5623, 🌐 www.whitehousehotelofny.com. This is the only hostel in the city that offers single and double rooms at dorm rates. Also popular for its Downtown location, and amenities such as AC, ATMs, cable TV, and linens. Private singles start at $27.25, private doubles at $53.90.

Downtown Manhattan

The patchwork of neighborhoods below 14th Street, **DOWNTOWN MAN-HATTAN**, runs the gamut from high finance and cutting-edge cool to Old World charm; it's truly one of the most vibrant, exciting parts of the city. Downtown's interest actually begins below Manhattan's southern tip in New York Harbor, which holds the compulsory attractions of the **Statue of Liberty** and **Ellis Island**. The southernmost neighborhood on the mainland is the **Financial District**, with Wall Street at its center, flanked by Battery Park and the South Street Seaport; less than a half-mile north, the buildings of the **Civic Center** transition into the jangling street life of **Chinatown**, which is fast encroaching upon the once-authentic, now-touristy **Little Italy**. East of Chinatown and Little Italy, the **Lower East Side** marks the traditional point of entry into the city for many different immigrant groups. These days, it's very trendy, with chic bars and restaurants opening up weekly.

West of Chinatown and Little Italy, respectively, the one-time industrial areas of **TriBeCa** and **SoHo** are now expensive residential (and, in the case of SoHo, shopping) districts, ostensibly home to Manhattan's film and art scenes, but with few sights to reflect either fact. The smallish area known as **NoLita** takes in numerous boutiques and hip restaurants in its few well-manicured blocks. North of Houston Street, the activity picks up even more in the **West Village** and **East Village**, two former bohemian enclaves that are now more traditional than their residents would like to think. Still, both are good fun, the former for its charming backstreets and brownstones, the latter for its energetic nightlife.

It's hard to talk for too long about Lower Manhattan without mentioning the terrorist attack on the World Trade Center on **September 11, 2001**, which killed more than 2600 people and destroyed the Twin Towers, a longtime symbol of the Financial District and an iconic part of the New York City skyline. A pilgrimage to **Ground Zero**, as the former site of the towers has come to be called, is for many an integral part of a visit to New York.

The Statue of Liberty and Ellis Island

Standing tall and proud in the middle of New York Harbor, the **Statue of Liberty** has for more than a century served as a symbol of the American Dream. Depicting Liberty throwing off her shackles and holding a beacon to light the world, the monument was the creation of the French sculptor Frédéric Auguste Bartholdi, crafted a hundred years after the American Revolution, in recognition of fraternity between the French and American people. The statue, designed by Gustave Eiffel, of Eiffel Tower fame, was built in Paris between 1874 and 1884. Bartholdi enlarged his original terracotta model to its present size through four successive versions; one of these now stands beside the Seine in Paris. The one here was formally dedicated by President Grover Cleveland on October 28, 1886.

Just across the water, **Ellis Island** was the first stop for more than twelve million prospective immigrants. Originally called Gibbet Island by the English (who used it for punishing unfortunate pirates), it became an immigration station in

△ Ellis Island Immigration Museum

1892, mainly to handle the massive influx from southern and eastern Europe. It remained open until 1954, when it was left to fall into atmospheric ruin.

The immigrants who arrived at Ellis Island were all steerage-class passengers; richer voyagers were processed at their leisure on-board ship. Most families arrived hungry and penniless; con men preyed on them from all sides, stealing their baggage as it was checked and offering rip-off exchange rates for whatever money they had managed to bring. Each family was split up – men sent to one area, women and children to another – while a series of checks weeded out the undesirables and the infirm. Steamship carriers were obliged to return any immigrants not accepted to their original port, but according to official records only two percent were rejected. Many of those jumped into the water and tried to swim to Manhattan rather than face going home.

By the time of its closure, Ellis Island was a formidable complex, the island having been expanded by landfill. In the turreted central building, the **Ellis Island Immigration Museum** (daily 9am–5pm; free; ☎212/363-3200, ⓦwww.nps.gov/stli) successfully recaptures the spirit of the place with features such as "Treasures from Home," a collection of family heirlooms, photos, and other artifacts, as well as live, somewhat hit-or-miss re-enactments of the immigrant experience (April–Sept; $5, children $2.50). The "Wall of Honor" (ⓦwww.wallofhonor.com) displays the names of some of those who passed through Ellis Island – though controversially, families were required to pay $100 to be included on the list.

To get to Liberty and Ellis islands (no admission fees for either), you'll need to take a **Circle Line ferry** from the pier in Battery Park (sailings every 30min, daily 9.30am–3.30pm; roundtrip $11.50, children $4.50; tickets from Castle Clinton, in the park; ☎212/269-5755, ⓦwww.circlelineferry.com); the ferry goes first to Liberty Island, and then continues on to Ellis. It's best to leave as early in the day as possible, both to avoid long lines and to insure you get to see both islands; if you take the last ferry of the day, you won't be able to visit Ellis Island. Liberty Island needs a good couple of hours, especially if the weather's nice and there aren't too many people; Ellis Island, too, demands at least two hours for the Museum of

The World Trade Center

Completed in 1973, the Twin Towers of the **World Trade Center** were an integral part of New York's legendary skyline, and a symbol of the city's social and economic success. While the World Trade Center's claim to be the world's tallest building was quickly usurped by Chicago's Sears Tower (and later on by other buildings), and despite the damage wrought in February of 1993 by a terrorist bomb explosion that killed six, the Twin Towers were very successful, having become both a busy workspace and a much-loved tourist destination. However, on September 11, 2001, all that changed, as two hijacked planes crashed into the towers just twenty minutes apart. The subsequent collapse of both towers (as well as other buildings in the World Trade Center complex) served as a terrible wake-up call, and took the lives of hundreds of firefighters, police officers, and rescue workers, among the approximately 2600 people who died.

In 2003, Polish-born American architect Daniel Libeskind was named the winner of a competition held to decide what shape the new World Trade Center would take. Libeskind's visionary design includes the use of windmills, meant as symbols of energy independence, beneath the planned **Freedom Tower** spire. However, he has lost control of designing the Freedom Tower; maneuverings have handed that job to David Childs. While Libeskind's design was irregularly faceted and asymmetrical, Childs' vision smoothes out the rough edges, yet essentially keeps to the original plan. In addition to the tower, Reflecting Absence will serve as a memorial to the terrorist attacks of September 11, 2001, and February 26, 1993. The design includes a ceremonial one-and-a-half acre clearing on the plaza level and a gallery on a second level, where the names of those lost during those two attacks can be viewed with a waterfall in the background. Additionally, there will be a memorial hall, offering a space to sit and reflect, with a contemplation room that will also house the remains of those lost and never identified. After heated political debate, construction on below-grade utility relocations, footings, and foundations began on the **Freedom Tower** in April 2006.

Immigration. If you just want the views and some time out on the water, take the free, fun **Staten Island Ferry** into the harbor; see p.112 for full details.

The Financial District

The **Financial District** has been synonymous with the Manhattan of popular imagination for some time, its tall buildings and powerful skyline symbols of economic strength and financial wheeling and dealing. Though New York City had an active securities market by 1790, the **New York Stock Exchange** wasn't officially organized until 1817, when 28 stockbrokers adopted their own constitution and established membership rules. It's been one of the world's great financial centers ever since, having most recently weathered the fallout from the World Trade Center attacks. Besides visiting a temporary viewing platform where you can glimpse the first phase of the new construction at Ground Zero (see box, above), there is plenty more to see and do here – it remains the city's most historic district, with many winding streets, old churches, and fine twentieth-century architecture.

Wall Street and around

When the Dutch arrived in New York and settled at the site of the future Financial District, they built a wooden wall at the edge of their small settlement to protect themselves from pro-British settlers to the north. Hence, the narrow canyon of

Wall Street gained its name. Today, behind the Neoclassical mask of the **New York Stock Exchange**, at Broad and Wall streets, the purse strings of the world are pulled. Due to security concerns, however, the public can no longer observe the frenzied trading on the floor of the exchange.

The **Federal Hall National Memorial**, at 26 Wall St, looks a little foolish surrounded by skyscrapers. The building was once the Customs House, but the exhibit inside (Mon–Fri 9am–5pm; free; ☏212/825-6888, ⓦwww.nps.gov/feha) relates to the headier days of 1789, when George Washington was sworn in as president from a balcony on this site. Washington's statue stands, very properly, on the steps outside the gently domed hall. At Wall Street's western end, on Broadway between Rector and Church streets, **Trinity Church** (guided tours daily at 2pm; free) is an ironic onlooker to the street's dealings, a knobbly neo-Gothic structure erected in 1846, and the city's tallest building for fifty years thence. The place has much the air of an English church, especially in its sheltered graveyard, which is the resting place of early luminaries including the first Secretary of the Treasury (and the man on the ten-dollar bill) Alexander Hamilton, who was killed in a duel by then-Vice President Aaron Burr.

Just down from Trinity Church, Broadway comes to a gentle end at **Bowling Green Park**, an oval of turf used for the game (of bowling) by eighteenth-century colonial Brits, on a lease of "one peppercorn per year." Earlier still, the green was the site of one of Manhattan's more memorable business deals: Peter Minuit, first director general of the Dutch colony of New Amsterdam, bought the whole island from the Indians for a handful of baubles worth sixty guilders (about $25). At the green today, office workers picnic in the shadow of Cass Gilbert's 1907 **US Customs House**, a monument to New York's once-booming maritime economy. Four statues at the front (sculpted by Daniel Chester French, who also created the Lincoln Memorial in Washington DC) represent the African, Asian, European, and North American continents, while the twelve statues near the top personify the world's great past and present commercial centers – Genoa and Phoenecia among them. The building's Corinthian columns each feature the head of Mercury, the god of commerce.

The Customs House contains the superb **Smithsonian National Museum of the American Indian** (daily 10am–5pm, Thurs until 8pm; free; ☏212/514-3700, ⓦwww.si.edu/nmai), a fascinating assembly of artifacts from almost every tribe native to the Americas. The curators give a creative presentation of their material, which includes large wood and stone carvings from the Pacific Northwest; elegant featherwork from Amazonia; a large array of masks; Aztec mosaics; Mayan textiles; seven-foot house posts shaped like animals; a handful of scalps; and a tribe's worth of elaborately beaded moccasins.

Battery Park and around

Across State Street from the Customs House, Downtown Manhattan lets out its breath in **Battery Park**, where the nineteenth-century Castle Clinton (daily 8.30am–5pm) once protected the southern tip of Manhattan and now sells ferry tickets to the Statue of Liberty and Ellis Island (see p.83). The spruced-up park stretches for blocks up the west side and is dotted with piers, cool corners, a restaurant, and some inventive landscaping. Not far from where the World Trade Center stood is one of the city's first (and few official, so far) memorials to the victims of September 11th; its focal point is the cracked 15-foot steel-and-bronze spherical sculpture, designed by Fritz Koenig, that once stood in the World Trade Center Plaza.

Further toward the tip of the island, in the adjacent Robert F. Wagner Park and just a few feet from the Hudson River, the **Museum of Jewish Heritage**, 36

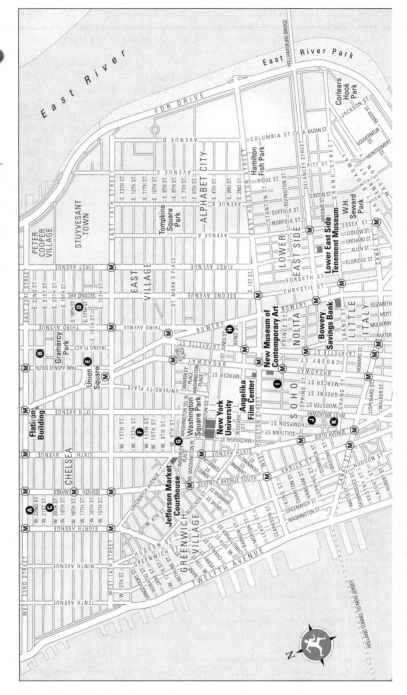

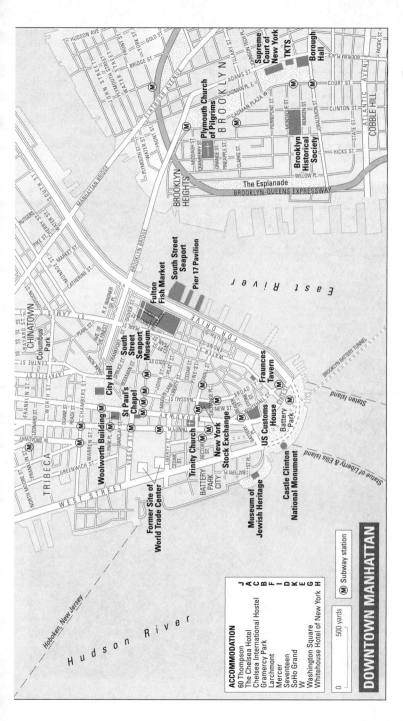

ACCOMMODATION
60 Thompson J
The Chelsea Hotel A
Chelsea International Hostel C
Gramercy Park B
Larchmont F
Mercer I
Seventeen D
SoHo Grand K
W E
Washington Square G
Whitehouse Hotel of New York H

Ⓜ Subway station

0 500 yards

DOWNTOWN MANHATTAN

Battery Place (April–Sept Sun–Tues & Thurs 10am–5.45pm, Wed 10am–8pm, Fri 10am–5pm; Oct–March same hours, except the museum closes at 3pm on Fri; $10; ☎646/437-4200, ⓦwww.mjhnyc.org), is essentially a memorial of the Holocaust, and has three floors of exhibits on twentieth-century Jewish history. The moving and informative collection features practical accoutrements of everyday Eastern European Jewish life, prison garb that survivors wore in Nazi concentration camps, photographs, personal belongings, and multimedia presentations.

South Street Seaport and the Brooklyn Bridge

North up Water Street from Battery Park stands the partly reconstructed **Fraunces Tavern**, at Pearl and Broad streets (Tues-Fri noon–5pm, Sat 10am–5pm; $4;

△ Brooklyn Bridge

ⓣ212/425-1778, ⓦwww.frauncestavernmuseum.org). Here, on December 4, 1783, with the British conclusively beaten, a weeping George Washington took leave of his assembled officers, intent on returning to rural life in Virginia. Today there's a colonial-looking bar and restaurant on the ground floor, and a fun museum upstairs.

Further up Water Street, at the eastern end of Fulton Street, is the renovated **South Street Historic District**, formerly New York's bustling sail-ship port. Trade eventually moved elsewhere, and the blocks of warehouses and ships' chandlers were left to rot until they were renovated in the 1970s. Regular guided tours of the area run from the **South Street Seaport Museum**, 12 Fulton St (April–Sept Wed–Mon 10am–6pm; Oct–March 10am–5pm; $8; ⓣ212/748-8600, ⓦwww.southstseaport.org), and feature refitted ships and chubby tugboats (the largest US collection of sailing vessels by tonnage), plus a handful of maritime art and trade exhibits. The museum also offers daytime, sunset, and nighttime **cruises** around New York Harbor on the *Pioneer*, an 1895 schooner that accommodates up to forty people (May–Sept; $25, $20 for students and seniors, $20 for children under 12; reservations on ⓣ212/748-8766); it's a good alternative to the crowded and noisy Circle Line cruises. And with lots of pubs, restaurants, and well-known chain stores, the seaport is always bustling.

From just about anywhere in the seaport you can see the much-loved **Brooklyn Bridge**. At the time of its opening in 1883, it was the first bridge to use steel cables, and for its first twenty years in use it was the world's largest suspension bridge. The impressive structure didn't go up easily, though: John Augustus Roebling, its architect and engineer, crushed his foot taking measurements for the piers and died of gangrene three weeks later. His son Washington took over, only to be crippled by the bends from working in an insecure underwater caisson. Twenty workers died during the construction, and, a week after the opening day in 1883, twelve people were crushed to death in a panicked rush on the bridge's footpath. Despite this gory history, the beauty of the bridge itself and the spectacular views of Manhattan it offers make a walk across its wooden planks an essential part of any New York trip. Watch out, however, for rollerbladers and cyclists going at a clip.

West from the foot of the Brooklyn Bridge, at the corner of Vesey Street and Broadway, the defiantly antique **St Paul's Chapel** seems decidedly out of place in this downtown temple to modernity. The oldest church in Manhattan dates from 1766 – eighty years earlier than Trinity Church and almost prehistoric by New York standards.

City Hall Park and the Civic Center

Immediately north of St Paul's Chapel, Broadway and Park Row form the apex of **City Hall Park**, a recently restored, brightly flowered triangle now worthy of its handsome setting. Cass Gilbert's 1913 **Woolworth Building**, at 233 Broadway, between Barclay Street and Park Place, is a venerable onlooker, with its soaring lines fringed with Gothic decoration. Frank Woolworth made his fortune from "five and dime" stores and, true to his philosophy, he paid cash for his skyscraper. The whimsical reliefs at each corner of the lobby show him doing just that, counting out the money in nickels and dimes. Facing him in caricature are the architect (medievally clutching a model of his building), the renting agent, and the builder. Within, vaulted ceilings ooze honey-gold mosaics, and even the mailboxes are magnificent, but the building is closed to tourists, however.

At the top of the park, marking the beginning of the **Civic Center**, with its incoherent jumble of municipal offices and courts, stands **City Hall**, which was completed in 1812. After New York saluted the hero aviator Charles A. Lindbergh in 1927, City Hall became the traditional finishing point for Broadway ticker-tape parades given for astronauts, returned hostages, and sports champions. Inside, it's an elegant meeting of arrogance and authority, with the sweeping spiral staircase delivering you to the precise geometry of the Governor's Room and the self-important rooms that formerly contained the Board of Estimates Chamber.

Chinatown, Little Italy, and NoLita

A short stroll northeast from the Civic Center leads into **Chinatown**, Manhattan's most thriving ethnic neighborhood, which over recent years has extended north across Canal Street into Little Italy and east into the Lower East Side. With more than 150,000 residents (125,000 of them Chinese), seven Chinese newspapers, about 150 restaurants and more than three hundred garment factories, it is a model for other neighborhoods; it has the lowest crime rate, highest employment, and least juvenile delinquency of any city district. There aren't many sights; rather, the appeal of the neighborhood lies simply in its unbridled energy, in the hordes of people coursing the sidewalk all day long – and, of course, for its excellent **Chinese food** (see p.113 for some restaurant suggestions).

Today, **Mott Street** is the most vibrant thoroughfare, and the streets around – Canal, Pell, Bayard, Doyers, and the Bowery – host a positive glut of restaurants, tea and rice shops, grocers, and vendors selling everything from jewelry to toy robots.

On the north side of Canal Street, **Little Italy** is light years away from the solid ethnic enclave of old. Originally settled by the huge nineteenth-century influx of Italian immigrants, the neighborhood has far fewer Italians living here now. Families were driven away by the high rents or the expanse of Chinatown. The restaurants (of which there are plenty) tend to have high prices and a touristy feel. However, some original bakeries and *salumerias* (specialty food stores) do survive, and you can still indulge yourself with a good cappuccino and a tasty pastry. During September's ten-day **Festa di San Gennaro**, a wild and raucous party held in honor of the patron saint of Naples, Italians from all over the city converge on **Mulberry Street**, transforming Little Italy's main strip with food outlets and street stalls.

North of Little Italy, the trendy enclave of **NoLita** runs from Houston to Grand Street between Bowery and Lafayette. Originally an authentic Italian neighborhood, NoLita now brims with hipsters and fashionistas who take advantage of the many chic boutiques and restaurants that have popped up.

SoHo and TriBeCa

Since the early 1980s, **SoHo**, the grid of streets that runs *So*uth of *Ho*uston Street, has been all about fashion chic, urbane shopping, and cosmopolitan art galleries. However, for the first half of the twentieth century, this area was a wasteland of manufacturers and warehouses. But as rising rents drove artists out of Greenwich Village in the 1940s and 1950s, SoHo suddenly became "in." Its commercial spaces were ideal for large, low-rent lofts, art studios, and galleries. In the 1960s, largely due to the effort of artists living illegally in these lofts (as well as for the area's magnificent **cast-iron architecture**; see box, opposite), SoHo was declared a historic district. Following this, yuppification – albeit an ultra-trendy strain of it – set in, bringing the fashionable boutiques, hip restaurants, and tourist crowds that are SoHo's signature today. Apart from consumer culture, there's also the **New Museum of Contemporary Art**, 235 Bowery at Prince Street (Tues–Sun noon–6pm, Thurs until 8pm; $6, students and seniors $3, under-18s free, Thurs 6–8pm free; ⊤212/219-1222, ⊛www.newmuseum.org), which has earned a reputation as one of the most exciting, cutting-edge arts institutions in town.

SoHo's cast-iron architecture

The technique of **cast-iron architecture** originated as a way of assembling buildings quickly and inexpensively, with iron beams rather than heavy walls carrying the weight of the floors. The result was the removal of supporting walls, greater space for windows, and, most noticeably, decorative facades. Almost any style or whim could be cast in iron and pinned to a building, and architects indulged themselves in Baroque balustrades, forests of Renaissance columns, and all the effusion of the French Second Empire to glorify SoHo's sweatshops. Have a look at **72–76 Greene Street**, a neat extravagance whose Corinthian portico stretches the whole five stories, all in painted metal, and at the strongly composed elaborations of its sister building at nos. 28–30. At the northeast corner of Broome Street and Broadway the magnificent **Haughwout Building** is perhaps the ultimate in the genre, with rhythmically repeated motifs of colonnaded arches framed behind taller columns in a thin sliver of a Venetian palace.

TriBeCa, the *Tri*angle *Be*low *Ca*nal Street, has caught some of the fallout of SoHo's artists (the rest went to Williamsburg, in Brooklyn, and to Chelsea), and has rapidly changed from a wholesale garment district to a very upscale community. Less a triangle than a crumpled rectangle – the area is bounded by Canal and Chambers streets, Broadway, and the Hudson River – TriBeCa contains spacious industrial buildings that house the apartments of a new gentry, including Nathan Lane and Robert De Niro (whose film production-company, TriBeCa Film Center, and restaurant, *TriBeCa Grill*, are at 375 Greenwich St). There's not much to see here, but a weekend walk around this serene neighborhood is a pleasant affair, with lots of bars and restaurants on hand.

Greenwich Village

For many visitors, **Greenwich Village** (or simply "the Village") is the most-loved neighborhood in New York, despite having lost any radical edge long ago. Its bohemian image endures well enough if you don't live in the city, and it still sports many attractions that brought people here in the first place: a busy streetlife that lasts later than in many other parts of the city; more restaurants per head than anywhere else; and bars cluttering every corner.

Greenwich Village grew up as a rural retreat from the early and frenetic nucleus of New York City. During the yellow fever epidemic of 1822 it became a refuge from the infected streets Downtown. Refined Federal and Greek Revival townhouses lured some of the city's highest society names, and later, at the start of World War I, the Village proved fertile ground for struggling artists and intellectuals, who were attracted to the area's cheap rents and growing community of free-thinking residents. During Prohibition (1920–1933), speakeasies were more prolific and accessible here than anywhere else in the city, and the rebellious fervor that permeated the Village then extended beyond the Twenties and Thirties. It was here that progressive New Yorkers gave birth to countless small magazines, unorthodox "happenings," and bacchanalian parties that were promoted as "pagan romps," while the neighborhood's off-Broadway theatres, cafés, and literary and folk clubs came to define Village life.

The natural heart of the Village, **Washington Square Park**, is not exactly elegant, though it does retain its northern edging of redbrick row houses – the "solid, honorable dwellings" of Henry James's novel *Washington Square* – and Stanford White's imposing **Triumphal Arch**, built in 1892 to commemorate the centenary of George Washington's inauguration. The park is also the heart of the truly urban campus of New York University. As soon as the weather gets warm, the park becomes a sports field, performance space, chess tournament, protest site, and social club, feverish with life as street entertainers strum, skateboards flip, and the pulsing bass of hip-hop resounds through the whispered offers of the few surviving dope peddlers (who are just as likely to be undercover cops as dealers).

From the bottom of the park, follow **MacDougal Street** south and you hit **Bleecker Street** – the Village's main drag, packed with shops, bars, people, and restaurants. This junction is also the area's best-known meeting place, a vibrant corner whose European-style sidewalk cafés have been turned from the literary hangouts of Modernist times to often overpriced tourist draws – though they're still fun for a spot of people-watching.

Right onto Bleecker, then right again (north) on Sixth Avenue, walk until you see the unmistakable clock tower of the beautiful nineteenth-century **Jefferson Market Courthouse**. This imposing High Victorian-style edifice first served as an indoor market, but later went on to be a firehouse, a jail, and finally a women's detention center before enjoying its current incarnation as a public library.

West of here, in the brownstone-lined side streets off Seventh Avenue, such as Bedford and Grove, you'll glimpse one of the city's most desirable living areas. Nearby, **Christopher Street** joins Seventh at **Sheridan Square**, home of the *Stonewall Inn*'s gay bar where, in 1969, a police raid precipitated a siege that lasted the best part of an hour. If not a victory for gay rights, it was the first time that gay men had stood up to the police en masse, and as such represents a turning point in the struggle for equal rights, remembered by the **Annual Lesbian, Gay, Bisexual, and Transgender March** (often just referred to as the **Gay Pride Parade**). Typically held on the last Sunday in June, the parade, which is arguably the city's most exciting, and certainly its most colorful, begins at Fifth Avenue and 52nd Street, and ends among the snarl of streets around Sheridan Square.

The East Village

The **East Village** differs quite a bit from its western counterpart. Once, like the adjacent Lower East Side, the East Village was a refuge for immigrants and solidly working-class people. Home to New York's nonconformist intelligentsia in the early twentieth century, it later became the haunt of **the Beats** – Kerouac, Burroughs, Ginsberg, et al – who would get together at Ginsberg's house on East Seventh Street for declamatory poetry readings. Later, Andy Warhol debuted the Velvet Underground here; the *Fillmore East* hosted almost every band under the sun; and Richard Hell, Patti Smith, and The Ramones invented punk rock at a hole-in-the-wall club called **CBGB**, which closed its doors after 33 years in October 2006.

Much of the East Village has changed since the economic boom of the mid-1980s and the 1990s, not the least of which has been escalating rents and gentrification, stripping it of its former status as a hotbed of dissidence and creativity. Nevertheless, the area's main drag, the vaudevillian **St Mark's Place** (Eighth Street), is still one of downtown's more vibrant strips, even if the thrift shops, panhandlers, and political hustlers have given way to more sanitized forms of rebellion and a cluster of chain sandwich and coffeeshops.

Astor Place, at the western end of St Mark's Place, was one of the city's most desirable neighborhoods in the 1830s. The now-undistinguished Lafayette Street was home to such wealthy names as John Jacob Astor, one of New York's most hideously greedy tycoons. The antique Astor Place **subway station**, bang in the middle of the junction, discreetly remembers the man on its platforms, where colored reliefs of beavers recall Astor's first big killings – in the fur trade.

A stone's throw from the subway, **Cooper Square** is dominated by the seven-story brownstone mass of **Cooper Union**, erected in 1859 by the industrialist Peter Cooper as a college for the poor and now a prestigious art and architecture school. Early in 1860, Abraham Lincoln wowed top New Yorkers here with his "right makes might" speech, in which he boldly criticized the pro-slavery South and helped propel himself to the Republican nomination for president.

Further east, **Alphabet City** (avenues A, B, C, and D), a former Slavic enclave – and erstwhile turf of drug dealers and gangs – has gentrified at an alarming rate. Along Avenue A, you'll pass a number of worthwhile fashion and design shops, as well as sushi bars, cafés, and record stores. **Tompkins Square Park**, between avenues A and B, and Seventh and Tenth streets, is the area's center, and the streets that frame it continue the restaurant and bar theme. Further east, Avenue D is an edgy affair you'll have little need to see.

The Lower East Side

Below the eastern stretch of Houston Street, the **Lower East Side** began life toward the end of the nineteenth century as an insular slum for roughly half a million Jewish immigrants. Since then it has changed considerably, with many Dominican and Chinese inhabitants, being followed by a recent influx of well-off students, artists, designers, and the like. It's all made the neighborhood quite cool, and the hotbed for trendy shops, bars, and restaurants, with **Clinton Street** as the epicenter.

You can still **buy** just about anything cut-price in the Lower East Side, especially on Sunday mornings, when **Orchard Street** is filled with stalls and stores selling hats, clothes, and designer labels at hefty discounts. Next to this melee is the excellent **Lower East Side Tenement Museum**, 90 Orchard St between Broome and Delancey (Mon–Wed & Fri 11am–5.30pm, Thurs 11am–7pm, Sat & Sun 11am–6pm; public tours $14 or $15; ⑦212/431-0233, ⓦwww.tenement.org), which is housed in a tenement and offers the lowdown on the neighborhood's immigrant and impoverished past.

On the western edge of the Lower East Side, **The Bowery** runs up as far as Cooper Square on the edge of the East Village. This wide thoroughfare has gone through many changes during its long history: it took its name from *bouwerij*, the Dutch word for farm, when it was the city's main agricultural supplier; later, in the closing decades of the nineteenth century, it was lined with music halls, theaters, hotels, and restaurants, drawing people from all parts of Manhattan. The only city thoroughfare never to have been graced by a church, it is still – in some sections – a skid row; see, for instance, the Bowery Mission at no. 227. However, such days are surely limited, as the demand for apartments grows and the tide of gentrification continues to sweep through the Lower East Side. The one – bizarre – focus is the **Bowery Savings Bank** (now the restaurant-club *Capitale*) at Grand Street. Designed by Stanford White in 1894, its splendid architecture makes the surrounding debris even more depressing (much as its sister bank does on 42nd Street; see p.96).

Midtown Manhattan

MIDTOWN MANHATTAN encompasses everything from the East River to the Hudson between 14th Street and 59th Street, the southern border of Central Park. New York's most glamorous (and most expensive) stretch, **Fifth Avenue** cuts through Midtown's heart, with the neon theater strip of **Broadway** running just to the west for much of the way. The character of Midtown is very different depending on which side of Fifth you find yourself. On the avenue itself and to the east are corporate businesses and prestigious skyscrapers – including the Empire State, Chrysler, and Seagram buildings – as well as Grand Central Station and the UN. Here you'll also find the residential neighborhoods of **Murray Hill** and elegant **Gramercy Park**. Just below Gramercy's eponymous park, busy **Union Square** is always great for people-watching. Meanwhile, west of Fifth, **Chelsea** is home to many quality art galleries, and bordered by the **Garment District**, where apparel-shop employees still roll racks of clothing through the streets. Around 42nd Street, the **Theater District** heralds a cleaned-up, frenetic area of entertainment that culminates at **Times Square**. West of Broadway in the 40s and low 50s, colorful **Hell's Kitchen** is now more or less wholly gentrified.

Union Square and Gramercy Park

Downtown Manhattan ends at 14th Street, which slices across from the housing projects of the East Side through rows of cut-price shops to the meatpacking warehouses on the Hudson. In the middle is **Union Square**, its shallow steps enticing passers-by to sit and watch the skateboarders and buskers, or to stroll the cool, tree-shaded paths and lawns. The shopping that once dominated the stretch of **Broadway** north of here, formerly known as Ladies' Mile for its fancy stores and boutiques, has been moved to Fifth Avenue, where chain stores now cover virtually every block in the mid-teens through the 20s.

East from here, between 20th and 21st streets, where Lexington Avenue becomes Irving Place, Manhattan's clutter suddenly breaks into the ordered open space of **Gramercy Park**. This former swamp, reclaimed in 1831, is one of the city's best parks, its center tidily planted and, most noticeably, completely empty for much of the day – principally because the only people who can gain access are those rich enough to live here and possess keys to the gate. (There is, however, another way: guests at the *Gramercy Park Hotel* are allowed into the park; see p.79.)

Broadway and Fifth Avenue meet at 23rd Street at **Madison Square**, by day a maelstrom of cars and cabs, but with a serene, well-manicured **park** to take the edge off. Most notable among the elegant structures nearby is the **Flatiron Building**, 175 Fifth Ave, between 22nd and 23rd streets; the 1902 Beaux Arts structure is known for its unusual narrow corners and six-and-a-half-feet-wide rounded tip. Just north from here, the **Museum of Sex**, 233 Fifth Ave at 27th St (Sun–Fri 11am–6.30pm, Sat 11am–8pm; $14.50; ☎212/689-6337 or 1-866/667-3984, ⓦwww.museumofsex.com), offers other titillating views of the city through a scholarly lens.

Chelsea and the Garment District

Home to a thriving **gay community**, as well as many good **art galleries** (check out West 24th, between Tenth and Eleventh aves), the heart of **Chelsea** lies west of Broadway between 14th and 23rd streets. The neighborhood took shape in 1830 when its owner, Charles Clarke Moore, laid out his land for sale in broad lots. It failed to achieve the desirability he sought, taking until recent decades. Now, though, up and down Eighth Avenue, you'll see all manner of trendy bars and restaurants mingled in with bodegas, frequented by the neighborhood's mixed clientele.

During the nineteenth century, Chelsea was a focus of New York's theater district. Nothing remains of that now, but the hotel that put up all the actors, writers, and attendant entourages – the **Chelsea Hotel** – remains a New York landmark, with an Edwardian grandeur all its own (for a review, see p.79). Mark Twain and

Tennessee Williams lived here, Brendan Behan and Dylan Thomas staggered in and out during their New York visits, and in 1951 Jack Kerouac, armed with a customized typewriter (and a lot of Benzedrine), typed the first draft of *On the Road* nonstop onto a 120ft-long roll of paper. Perhaps most famously, however, in October 1978 Sid Vicious stabbed Nancy Spungen to death in their suite, a few months before his own life ended with an overdose of heroin. The hotel also inspired Joni Mitchell to write *Chelsea Morning*.

The **Garment District**, a loosely defined patch north of Chelsea between 34th and 42nd streets and Sixth and Eighth avenues, produces three-fourths of all the women's and children's clothes in America. You'd never guess it, though; the outlets are strictly wholesale, with no need to woo customers. Retail stores abound, however: **Macy's**, the largest department store in the world, is on **Herald Square** at 34th Street and Seventh Avenue.

The district's dominant landmark is the **Penn Station** and **Madison Square Garden** complex, which swallows up millions of commuters in its train station below and accommodates the Knicks and Liberty basketball – and Rangers hockey – teams up top. The original Penn Station, demolished to make way for this structure, is now hailed as a lost masterpiece, which reworked the ideas of the Roman baths of Caracalla to awesome effect. Immediately behind Penn Station, the same architects of the original – McKim, Mead, and White – were responsible for the grand, 1914 **General Post Office**, which is open 24 hours a day.

The Empire State Building and around

Up Fifth Avenue is the **Empire State Building**, 34th Street and Fifth Avenue (daily 9.30am–midnight, last trip up at 11.30pm; $18, bring photo ID; ⊤ 212/736-3100, Ⓦ www.esbnyc.com), which has been a muscular 102-story symbol of New York since being completed in 1931. After the terrorist attacks of September 11th, it became, as it once was, the city's tallest building. An elevator takes you to the 86th floor, which was the summit of the building before the radio and TV mast was added. The views from the outside walkways here are as stunning as you'd expect. For the best views, you should try to time your visit so that you'll reach the top at sunset. (Be advised that during peak season, wait times to ascend are often upwards of an hour.)

East of the Empire State Building, the residential district of **Murray Hill** was once dominated by the crusty old financier J.P. Morgan and his son, J.P. Jr; the latter's brownstone, at 37th Street and Madison Avenue, is now headquarters of the American Lutheran Church. The home of the elder Morgan, once adjacent to his son's, was razed to make way for the **Pierpont Morgan Library**. Highlights of the library include one of two surviving copies of the first edition of Sir Thomas Malory's stories of King Arthur, Dylan Thomas's heavily corrected manuscript of "Lament," and Galileo's research notes for an astronomical treatise.

Forty-second Street

On the corner of **42nd Street** and Fifth Avenue stands the Beaux Arts **New York Public Library** (Tues & Wed 11am–7pm, Thurs–Sat 10am–6pm; ⊤ 212/930-0830, Ⓦ www.nypl.org). Leon Trotsky worked occasionally in the large coffered Reading Room at the back of the building during his brief sojourn in New York, just prior to the 1917 Russian Revolution. He was introduced to the place by his Bolshevik comrade Nikolai Bukharin, who was bowled over by a library one could visit so late in the evening. The opening times are less impressive now, but the library still boasts one of the five largest collections of books in the world. It's worth going inside just to appreciate its reverent, church-like atmosphere.

East on 42nd Street at Park Avenue, the huge bulk of **Grand Central Terminal** was built around a basic iron frame but features a Beaux Arts facade. The structure's immense size is now dwarfed by the MetLife building behind it. Regardless, the main station's **concourse** is a sight to behold – 470ft long and 150ft high, it boasts a barrel-vaulted ceiling speckled like a Baroque church with a painted representation of the winter night sky. The 2500 stars are shown back to front – "as God would have seen them," the painter is reputed to have explained.

You can explore Grand Central on your own, or you can take the Municipal Arts Society's excellent **free tour**. For the best view of the concourse – as well as the flow of commuters and commerce – climb up to the catwalks that span the sixty-foot-high windows on the Vanderbilt Avenue side. After that, seek out the station's more esoteric reaches, including the *Oyster Bar* – one of the city's most highly regarded seafood restaurants, deep in the terminal's bowels and jam-packed every lunchtime. Near the restaurant, testing an acoustical fluke, two visitors can stand on opposite sides of any of the vaulted spaces and hold a conversation just by whispering.

Across the street from Grand Central, the former **Bowery Savings Bank** (now *Cipriani 42nd Street*) echoes the train station's grandeur, extravagantly lauding the virtues of sound investment and savings. Built in the style of a Roman basilica, it has a floor paved with mosaics, columns (each fashioned from a different kind of marble), and bronze bas-reliefs on the elevator doors. The more famous **Chrysler Building**, at 405 Lexington Ave, also dates from a time (1930) when architects carried off prestige with grace and style. For a short while, this was the world's tallest building; today, it's one of Manhattan's best-loved structures. The lobby, once a car showroom, with its opulently inlaid elevators, walls covered in African marble, and murals depicting airplanes, machines, and the brawny builders who worked on the tower, is for the moment all you can see of the building.

At the eastern end of 42nd Street, the **United Nations** complex comprises the glass-curtained **Secretariat**, the curving sweep of the **General Assembly**, and, connecting them, the low-rising **Conference Wing**. Guided **tours** (daily every 20–30min, weekdays 9.30am–4.45pm, weekends 10am–4.30pm; tours last 45min–1hr, and leave from the General Assembly lobby; $11.50, bring ID; ℡212/963-8687, Ⓦwww.un.org/MoreInfo/pubsvs.html) take in the UN conference chambers and its constituent parts. Note that tours may vary depending on official room usage.

Times Square and the Theater District

Forty-second Street meets Broadway at the southern margin of **Times Square**, center of the **Theater District** and a top tourist attraction. Here, countless monolithic advertisements for Coke, Budweiser, NBC, and the like jostle brightly for attention from the crowds of gawking visitors. It wasn't always this way: traditionally a melting pot of debauchery, depravity, and fun, Times Square was cleaned up in the 1990s and turned into a largely sanitized universe of popular consumption, with refurbished theaters and blinking signage.

North of Times Square along Seventh Avenue, **Carnegie Hall**, a warehouse-like venue for opera and concerts at 154 W 57th St, is the thing to see. Tchaikovsky conducted the program on opening night and Mahler, Rachmaninov, Toscanini, Frank Sinatra, and Judy Garland have played here. Carnegie Hall has dropped in status since Lincoln Center opened (see p.121 & the box on p.122), but the superb acoustics still ensure world-class performers and full houses most of the year (Sept–June only, tours available Mon, Tues, Thurs, & Fri at 11.30am, 2pm, & 3pm; $9; general info ℡212/903-9600, tours ℡212/903-9765, tickets ℡212/247-7800, Ⓦwww.carnegiehall.org).

△ Theater District

East of Seventh Avenue, **Sixth Avenue** is properly named "the Avenue of the Americas," though no New Yorker ever calls it this and the only manifestation is the flags of Central and South American countries still flying on some blocks. If nothing else, Sixth's distinction is its width, a result of the Elevated Railway that once ran along here, now replaced by the Sixth Avenue subway underground. In its day the Sixth Avenue "El" marked the borderline between respectability to the east and vice to the west, and the avenue still separates the glamorous strips of Fifth, Madison, and Park avenues from the less salubrious western districts.

At 1260 Sixth Ave, at 50th Street, **Radio City Music Hall** (1hr tours daily 11.30am–6pm; $17, seniors and students $14; general info ℡212/307-7171, tour info ℡212/247-4777, ⓦwww.radiocity.com) is the last word in 1930s luxury. The staircase is regally resplendent, with the world's largest chandeliers, and the huge auditorium looks like an extravagant scalloped shell. Surely, however, Radio

A B The Cloisters, Columbia University, ▲ Cathedral of St John the Divine & Studio Museum in Harlem ▲ **C** Museum of the City of New York & El Barrio ▲ Cooper Hewitt Museum

ACCOMMODATION	
Algonquin	L
Amsterdam Inn	F
Dylan	N
Edison	K
Gershwin	P
Hostelling International-New York	B
Jazz on the Park	A
Lucerne	D
Milburn	E
Pickwick Arms	H
Roger Smith	J
Royalton	M
Stanford	O
W	I
Wales	C
West Side YMCA	G

Roosevelt Island

QUEENSBORO BRIDGE

Carl Schurz Park

Gracie Mansion

EAST END AVENUE

UPPER EAST SIDE

YORK AVENUE

FDR DRIVE

John Jay Park

Roosevelt Island Tram

FIRST AVENUE

SECOND AVENUE

THIRD AVENUE

Bloomingdale's

LEXINGTON AVENUE

Seventh Regiment Armory

PARK AVENUE

Whitney Museum

The Frick Collection

MADISON AVE

Temple Emanu-El

Guggenheim Museum

Metropolitan Museum of Art

FIFTH AVENUE

Plaza Hotel

The Reservoir

TRANSVERSE ROAD NO. 3

The Great Lawn

Turtle Pond

TRANSVERSE ROAD NO. 2

Delacorte Theater

The Ramble

Loeb Boathouse

Central Park

Zoo

Skating Rink

CENTRAL PARK SOUTH

New-York Historical Society

Bow Bridge

Rowboat Lake

Strawberry Fields

Sheep Meadow

CENTRAL PARK WEST

American Museum of Natural History

UPPER WEST SIDE

The Dakota Building

W. 75TH ST.

W. 77TH ST.

W. 76TH ST.

W. 74TH ST.

W. 73RD ST.

COLUMBUS AVE

EIGHTH AVENUE

COLUMBUS CIRCLE

Lincoln Center

AMSTERDAM AVENUE

BROADWAY

TENTH AVENUE

ELEVENTH AVENUE

FREEDOM PLACE

Riverside Park

HENRY HUDSON PARKWAY

MIDTOWN/UPTOWN MANHATTAN

East River

QUEENS MIDTOWN TUNNEL

FDR DRIVE

United Nations

Trump Tower

Citicorp Center

Seagram Building

GE Building

St Patrick's Cathedral

Waldorf Astoria Hotel

Met Life Building (Pan Am)

Chrysler Building

Grand Central Terminal

Carnegie Hall

Museum of Modern Art

Museum of TV & Radio

Rockefeller Center

Radio City Music Hall

New York Public Library

Bryant Park

Pierpont Morgan Library

MURRAY HILL

Empire State Building

Museum of Sex

Madison Square Park

HELL'S KITCHEN

THEATER DISTRICT

TIMES SQUARE

Port Authority Bus Terminal

GARMENT DISTRICT

Macy's

Penn Station

General Post Office

Madison Square Garden

Jacob Javits Convention Center

Dewitt Clinton Park

Chelsea Park

Circle Line Ferry

LINCOLN TUNNEL TO NEW JERSEY

Flatiron Building

Avenues: TWELFTH AVENUE, ELEVENTH AVENUE, TENTH AVENUE, NINTH AVENUE, EIGHTH AVENUE, BROADWAY, SEVENTH AVENUE, SIXTH AVENUE, FIFTH AVENUE, MADISON AVENUE, LEXINGTON AVENUE, THIRD AVENUE, SECOND AVENUE, FIRST AVENUE

Streets: E 57TH ST, E 56TH ST, E 55TH ST, E 53RD ST, E 52ND ST, E 51ST ST, E 50TH ST, E 49TH ST, E 48TH ST, E 47TH ST, E 45TH ST, E 44TH ST, E 43RD ST, E 42ND ST, E 40TH ST, E 39TH ST, E 38TH ST, E 37TH ST, E 36TH ST, E 35TH ST, E 34TH ST, E 33RD ST, E 32ND ST, E 31ST ST, E 30TH ST, E 29TH ST, E 28TH ST, E 27TH ST, E 26TH ST, E 25TH ST, E 24TH ST

W 57TH ST, W 56TH ST, W 55TH ST, W 53RD ST, W 52ND ST, W 51ST ST, W 50TH ST, W 48TH ST, W 47TH ST, W 46TH ST, W 45TH ST, W 44TH ST, W 43RD ST, W 42ND ST, W 41ST ST, W 40TH ST, W 39TH ST, W 38TH ST, W 37TH ST, W 36TH ST, W 35TH ST, W 34TH ST, W 33RD ST, W 31ST ST, W 30TH ST, W 29TH ST, W 28TH ST

N

0   500 yards

Ⓜ Subway station

City is best know for the Rockettes, whose Christmas shows and kicklines have dazzled the masses since 1932.

Fifth Avenue and around

Fifth Avenue has been a great stretch for as long as New York has been a great city, and its very name evokes wealth and opulence. All who consider themselves suave and cosmopolitan end up here, and the stores showcase New York's most conspicuous consumerism. That the shopping is beyond the means of most people needn't put you off, for Fifth Avenue has some of the city's best architecture, too.

At the heart of the glamour is **Rockefeller Center**, built between 1932 and 1940 by John D. Rockefeller Jr, son of the oil magnate. One of the finest pieces of urban planning anywhere, the Center balances office space with cafés, a theater, underground concourses, and rooftop gardens that work together with a rare intelligence and grace. The **GE Building** here rises 850ft. At its foot, the **Lower Plaza** holds a sunken restaurant in summer, linked visually by Paul Manship's sparkling *Prometheus*; in winter, the plaza becomes a small **ice rink**, allowing skaters to show off their skills to passers-by. Inside, the Center is no less impressive. In the GE lobby, José Maria Sert's murals, *American Progress* and *Time*, are a little faded but eagerly in tune with the Thirties Deco ambiance – presumably more so than the original paintings by Diego Rivera, removed by John D.'s son Nelson when the artist refused to scrap a panel glorifying Lenin. A leaflet available from the lobby desk details a **self-guided tour** of the Center. Among the GE Building's many offices are the **NBC Studios** (1hr behind-the-scenes tours leave every 30 minutes Mon–Fri, and every 15 minutes on weekends; Mon–Fri 8.30am–5.30pm, Sat & Sun 9.30am–4.30pm; reservations at the NBC Experience Store Tour Desk; $18.50, children $15.50; ☏212/664-7174). If you're a TV fan, pick up a free ticket for a **show recording** from the mezzanine lobby or out on the street. Keep in mind that the most popular tickets evaporate before 9am. The glass-enclosed **Today Show** studio is at the southwest corner of the plaza at 49th Street, surrounded in the early morning by avid fans waiting to get on TV by way of the cameras that obligingly pan the crowds from time to time. Adjacent is the old Associated Press building, recognizable by the unusual Stalinesque frieze by Japanese-American artist Isamu Noguchi.

Almost opposite Rockefeller Center, on 50th Street and Fifth Avenue, **St Patrick's Cathedral**, designed by James Renwick and completed in 1888, seems the result of a painstaking academic tour of the Gothic cathedrals of Europe. More striking next door is **Olympic Tower**, an exclusive apartment block where Jackie Kennedy Onassis once lived. Between Fifth and Sixth avenues at 25 W 52nd St, the **Museum of Television and Radio** (Tues–Sun noon–6pm, Thurs noon–8pm; $10; ☏212/621-6800, ⓦwww.mtr.org) holds an excellent archive of American TV and radio broadcasts.

Continuing north, the **Trump Tower** at 57th Street is the last word in Fifth Avenue extravagance, with an outrageously over-the-top atrium filled with designer stores. Perfumed air, polished marble paneling, and a five-story waterfall are calculated to knock you senseless with expensive yet somewhat garish taste. But the building is clever: a neat little outdoor garden is squeezed high in a corner, and each of the 230 apartments above the atrium gets views in three directions.

East of Fifth, **Madison Avenue** makes for pleasant strolling, and is filled with expensive galleries, haute couture shops, and elegantly dressed Eastsiders. The next avenue east, **Park Avenue**, was said in 1929 to be the place "where wealth is so swollen that it almost bursts." Things haven't changed much: corporate headquarters and four-star hotels jostle in triumphal procession, led by the massive New York Central Building (now the **Helmsley Building**) that literally sits above Park Avenue at 46th Street and boasts a lewdly excessive Rococo lobby. In its day this formed a skillful punctuation mark to the avenue, but its thunder was stolen in 1963 by the **MetLife Building**, 200 Park Ave at 45th Street, which looms behind it.

Wherever you placed it, the solid mass of the **Waldorf Astoria Hotel**, on Park between 49th and 50th streets, would hold its own, a resplendent statement of Art Deco elegance. Crouched behind it is **St Bartholomew's Church**, a striking, low-slung Byzantine hybrid that adds immeasurably to the street and gives the lumbering skyscrapers a much-needed sense of scale. The spiky-topped **General Electric Building** behind seems like a wild extension of the church, its slender shaft rising to a meshed crown of abstract sparks and lightning bolts that symbolizes the radio waves used by its original owner, RCA. The lobby (entrance at 570 Lexington) is yet another Deco delight.

Among all this, it's difficult at first to see the originality of the **Seagram Building**, at 375 Park Ave, between 52nd and 53rd streets. Designed by Mies van der Rohe (with Philip Johnson) and built in 1958, this was the seminal curtain-wall skyscraper, the floors supported internally, allowing a skin of smoky glass and whisky-bronze metal (Seagram's is known for distilled liquors), now weathered to a dull black. Every interior detail – from the fixtures to the lettering on the mailboxes – was specially designed. It was the supreme example of Modernist reason, and its opening was met by a wave of approval. The plaza, an open forecourt designed to set the building apart from its neighbors, was such a success as a public space that the city revised the zoning laws to encourage other high-rise builders to supply plazas.

A block east, the chisel-topped **Citicorp Center**, on Lexington Avenue between 53rd and 54th streets, finished in 1979, is one of Manhattan's most conspicuous landmarks. The slanted roof was designed to house solar panels to provide power for the building. However, the idea was ahead of the technology, and Citicorp had to content itself with adopting the distinctive building-top as a corporate logo.

In 2003, the **Museum of Modern Art**, at 11 W 53rd St, between Fifth and Sixth avenues, reopened after two years of massive renovating. MoMA is a must see, with highlights including Van Gogh's *Starry Night*, Cezanne's *Foliage*, and Munch's *Madonna*. The temporary exhibits, as may be expected, are cutting-edge (Wed–Mon 10.30am–5.30pm, closes Fri at 8pm; $20, seniors $16, students $12; ⊤212/708-9400, ⓦwww.moma.org).

Uptown Manhattan

UPTOWN MANHATTAN begins above 59th Street, where the businesslike bustle of Midtown gives way to the comfortable domesticity of the Upper East and West sides. In between, people come to **Central Park**, the city's giant back yard, to play, jog, and escape Midtown's crowds in a particularly intelligent piece of urban landscaping.

The **Upper East Side** is at its most opulent in the several blocks just east of Central Park, and at its most distinguished in the Metropolitan and other great museums of "Museum Mile," from 82nd to 104th streets along Fifth Avenue. The predominantly residential **Upper West Side** is somewhat less refined, though its Lincoln Center hosts New York's most prestigious arts performances, and there are certainly plenty of expensive townhouses and apartment buildings. The northern reaches embrace the monolithic Cathedral of St John the Divine and Columbia

University. North and east from here, **Harlem**, the cultural capital of black America, is experiencing a new renaissance. Still farther north, in the Washington Heights area, you'll find one of the city's most intriguing museums, the medieval arts collection of The Cloisters.

Central Park

"All radiant in the magic atmosphere of art and taste." So enthused *Harper's* magazine upon the opening of **Central Park** in 1876, and, to this day, few New Yorkers could imagine life without it. Set just about smack in the middle of Manhattan, extending from 59th to 110th streets, it provides residents (and street-weary tourists) with a much-needed refuge from the harshness of big-city life. Whether you're into jogging, baseball, boating, botany, or just plain strolling, or even if you rarely go near the place, there's no question that Central Park makes New York a better place to live.

The poet and newspaper editor William Cullen Bryant had the idea for an open public space in 1844, and spent seven years trying to persuade City Hall to carry it out. Eventually, 840 desolate and swampy acres north of the city limits, then occupied by a shantytown of squatters, were set aside. The two architects commissioned to design the landscape, **Frederick Law Olmsted** and **Calvert Vaux**, planned to create a rural paradise, a complete illusion of the countryside in the heart of Manhattan – even then growing at a fantastic rate. At its opening, Central Park was declared a "people's park" – though most of the impoverished masses it was allegedly built to serve had neither the time nor the means of transportation to come up from their Downtown slums and enjoy it. But as New York grew and workers' leisure time increased, people started to flood in, and the park began to live up to its mission, sometimes in ways that might have scandalized its original builders. Today, although the skyline has changed greatly, and some of the open space has been turned into asphalted playgrounds, the sense of captured nature that they intended largely survives. For general park **information**, call ☎212/310-6600, or visit ⓦwww.centralparknyc .org; for special events information, call ☎1-888/NYPARKS.

One of the best ways to explore the park is to rent a **bicycle** from either the Loeb Boathouse (between 74th and 75th streets, roughly $9–15 an hour) or Metro Bicycles (Lexington at 88th St; $7 per hour; ☎212/427-4450); otherwise, it's easy to get around **on foot**, along the many paths that crisscross the park. There's little chance of getting lost, but to know exactly where you are, find the nearest lamppost: the first two figures signify the number of the nearest street. After dark, however, you'd be well advised not to enter on foot. If you want to see the buildings illuminated from the park at night, one option is to fork out for a **carriage ride**; the best place to pick up a hack is along Central Park South, between Fifth and Sixth avenues. It's not cheap, though: a twenty-minute trot costs approximately $35, excluding tip.

Most places of interest in the park lie in its southern reaches. Near **Grand Army Plaza**, the main entrance at Fifth Avenue and 59th Street, is the **Central Park Zoo**, which tries to keep caging to a minimum and the animals as close to the viewer as possible (April–Oct Mon–Fri 10am–5pm, Sat & Sun 10am–5.30pm; Nov–March daily 10am–4.30pm; $6, ages 3–12 $1, under 3 free; ☎212/439-6500). Beyond here, the **Dairy**, once a ranch building intended to provide milk for nursing mothers, now houses a **visitor's center** (Tues–Sun 10am–5pm; ☎212/794-6564), which distributes free leaflets and maps, sells books, and puts on exhibitions. Also, weekend **walking tours** often leave from here; call for times.

Nearby, the **Wollman Rink** (63rd St at mid-park) is a lovely place to skate in winter, or to practice your in-line skating skills in the warmer months. From the

△ The Metropolitan Museum of Art

rink, you may wish to swing west past the restored **Sheep Meadow**, a dust bowl in the 1970s, now emerald green. Then, head north up the formal Mall to the terrace, with the sculptured birds and animals of **Bethesda Fountain** below, on the shore of the **Rowboat Lake**. To your left (west) is **Strawberry Fields**, a tranquil, shady spot dedicated to John Lennon by his widow, Yoko Ono, and the **Imagine mosaic** – both are near where he was killed in 1980; see p.106 for more. On the eastern bank of the lake, you can rent a **rowboat** from the Loeb Boathouse (March–Oct daily 10am–6pm, weather permitting; $10 for the first hour, and $2.50 per 15min after; $30 refundable cash deposit required; ☎212/517-2233) or cross the water by the elegant cast-iron **Bow Bridge**.

Beyond the bridge, delve into the wild woods of **The Ramble** along a maze of paths and bridges; this area is best avoided at night. At 81st Street, near the West Side, stands the mock citadel of **Belvedere Castle**, another visitor center that has nature exhibits and boasts great views of the park from its terraces. Next to the castle, the **Delacorte Theater** is home to the thoroughly enjoyable **Shakespeare in the Park** performances in the summer (tickets are free, though they go very quickly; visit ⓦwww.publictheater.org for details), while the immense **Great Lawn** is the preferred sprawling ground for many sun-loving New Yorkers. Beginning at 86th Street, the Jacqueline Kennedy Onassis Reservoir (originally designed in 1862) spans 107 acres. A favored place for active New Yorkers, the raised 1.58-mile track is a great place to get 360° views of the skyline – but just be sure not to block any jogger's path.

Near the north end of the park is the beautifully terraced and landscaped **Conservatory Garden**, at 103rd Street off Fifth Avenue, encompassing three distinct garden styles: English, Italian, and French.

The Metropolitan Museum of Art

One of the world's great art museums, the **Metropolitan Museum of Art** (usually referred to as just "the Met") juts into the park at Fifth Avenue and 82nd Street (Tues–Thurs & Sun 9.30am–5.30pm, Fri & Sat 9.30am–9pm; suggested donation \$15, seniors and students \$7; includes same-day admission to The Cloisters; ⓣ212/535-7710, ⓦwww.metmuseum.org). Its all-embracing collection amounts to more than two million works of art, spanning America and Europe as well as China, Africa, the Far East, and the classical and Islamic worlds. You could spend weeks here and not see everything.

If you can make just one visit, head for the **European Painting** galleries. Of the early (fifteenth- and sixteenth-century) **Flemish and Dutch paintings**, the best are by Jan van Eyck, who is generally credited with having started the tradition of North European realism, and Rogier van der Weyden, whose *Christ Appearing to His Mother* is one of his most beautiful works.

The **Italian Renaissance** is less spectacularly represented here, but a worthy selection includes an early *Madonna and Child Enthroned with Saints* by Raphael, a late Botticelli, and Filippo Lippi's *Madonna and Child Enthroned with Two Angels*. The **nineteenth-century galleries** house a startling array of **Impressionist** and **Post-Impressionist** art, showcasing Manet and Monet among others, and the compact twentieth-century collection features paintings such as Picasso's portrait of Gertrude Stein and *The Blind Man's Meal*, alongside works by Klee, Hopper, and Matisse. The **Medieval Galleries** are no less exhaustive, with displays of sumptuous Byzantine metalwork and jewelry donated by J.P. Morgan, while the **Asian Art galleries** house plenty of murals, sculptures, and textile art from Japan, China, Southeast and Central Asia, and Korea. Don't miss the exquisite and lovingly assembled **Chinese Garden Court**.

The Upper East Side

A two-square-mile grid, the **Upper East Side** has wealth as its defining characteristic, as you'll appreciate if you've seen any of the many Woody Allen movies set here. The area's stretch of **Fifth Avenue** has been the patrician face of Manhattan since the opening of Central Park attracted the Carnegies, Astors, and Whitneys to migrate north and build fashionable residences. **Grand Army Plaza**, at Central Park South and Fifth Avenue, flanked by the extended chateau of the swanky **Plaza Hotel**, and glowing with the gold statue of the Civil War's General William Tecumseh Sherman, serves as the introduction.

On the corner of Fifth Avenue and 65th Street, America's largest reform synagogue, the **Temple Emanu-El**, strikes a sober tone (Sun–Thurs 10am–4.30pm, Fri 10am–3.30pm, Sat noon–5pm; free; ⓣ212/744-1400). The brooding Romanesque-Byzantine cavern manages to be bigger inside than it seems from outside, and, as you enter, the interior appears to melt away into darkness, making you feel very small indeed. Just east from the temple, on Park Avenue between 66th and 67th streets, the 1870s **Seventh Regiment Armory** is the only surviving building from the era before the New York Central's railroad tracks were roofed over and Park Avenue became an upscale residential neighborhood.

Back on Fifth, at 70th Street, you'll find Henry Clay Frick's house, a handsome spread and now the tranquil home of the **Frick Collection** (Tues-Sat 10am–6pm, Sun 11am–5pm; \$15; ⓣ212/288-0700). One of many prestigious museums in the area, the Frick is perhaps the most enjoyable of the big New York galleries; it is made up of the art treasures hoarded by Frick during his years as probably the most ruthless of New York's robber barons. The collection includes paintings by Rembrandt, Reynolds, Hogarth, Gainsborough (*St James's Park*), and Bellini, whose *St Francis* suggests his vision of Christ by means of pervading light, a bent tree, and an enraptured stare. Above the fireplace, El Greco's *St Jerome* reproachfully surveys the riches all around, looking out to the South Hall, where one of Boucher's intimate depictions of his wife hangs near an early Vermeer, *Officer and Laughing Girl*.

Just a few blocks north, over on Madison Avenue at 75th Street, the **Whitney Museum of American Art** (Wed, Thurs, Sat & Sun 11am–6pm, Fri 1–9pm; $15; ℡212/570-3676, Ⓦwww.whitney.org) boasts a pre-eminent collection of twentieth-century American art and a superb exhibition locale. Every other year the museum mounts the Whitney Biennial show of contemporary American art – an event that has become a lightning rod for critical abuse since the 1995 show, when a giant mound of cooking fat presented as sculpture set right-wing aesthetes into a frenzy. When that's not on, check out the somewhat arbitrary Highlights of the Permanent Collection, arranged both by chronology and theme. Enjoy the prominent Abstract Expressionists collection, with great works by high priests Pollock and De Kooning, leading on to Rothko and the Color Field painters and the later Pop Art works of Warhol, Johns, and Oldenburg. The museum is especially strong on Hopper, O'Keeffe, and Calder, with galleries concentrating on each.

A ten-minute walk north from the Whitney, the **Guggenheim Museum**, Fifth Avenue at 89th Street (Sat–Wed 10am–5.45pm, Fri 10am–8pm, closed Thurs; $18, seniors & students $15, Fri 6–8pm pay what you wish; ℡212/423-3500, Ⓦwww.guggenheim.org), is better known for the building than its collection. Designed by Frank Lloyd Wright, this unique structure caused a storm of controversy when it was unveiled in 1959. Its centripetal spiral ramp, which wends you continuously all the way to its top floor (affording a vertiginous view of the lobby at the center) or, alternatively, from the top to the bottom, is still thought by some to favor Wright's talents over those of the exhibited artists. One of the newer additions is the Mapplethorpe Gallery, which houses some of the museum's odder pieces, including Louise Bourgeois' wood-chip sculpture *Femme Volage*, as well as several Calder mobiles. Much of the building is still given over to temporary exhibitions, but the permanent collection includes work by Chagall, Léger, the major Cubists and, most completely, Kandinsky. Additionally, there are some late nineteenth-century paintings, not least the exquisite Degas' *Dancers*, Modigliani's *Jeanne Héburene with Yellow Sweater*, and some sensitive early Picassos.

Two blocks up, at Fifth Avenue and 91st Street, lies the Smithsonian-run **Cooper Hewitt National Design Museum** (Tues–Thurs 10am–5pm, Fri 10am–9pm, Sat 10am–6pm, Sun noon–6pm; $12; ℡212/849-8400, Ⓦwww.ndm.si.edu). This wonderful institution is the only museum in the US devoted exclusively to historic and contemporary design. Founded in 1897, it's housed in the magnificent mansion once owned by Andrew Carnegie and functions as a research center as well as museum. If you're a history buff, the **Museum of the City of New York**, Fifth Avenue at 103rd Street (Tues–Sun 10am–5pm; suggested donation $9; ℡212/534-1672, Ⓦwww.mcny.org), might also grab your interest, with an informative rundown on the history of the city from Dutch times to the present day.

About a thirty-minute walk away, at the far eastern end of 88th Street overlooking the East River, **Gracie Mansion** is one of the best-preserved colonial buildings in the city. Built in 1799 on the site of a Revolutionary fort as a country manor house, it is roughly contemporary with the Morris–Jumel Mansion (see p.108). Gracie Mansion has been the official residence of the mayor of New York City since 1942, when Fiorello LaGuardia, "man of the people" that he was, reluctantly set up house here – though "mansion" is a bit overblown for what's a rather cramped clapboard cottage.

The Upper West Side

Above 59th Street, Manhattan's West Side becomes less commercial, fading north of Lincoln Center into a residential area of mixed charms. This is the **Upper West Side**, now one of the city's more desirable addresses, though in truth an area long favored by artists and intellectuals. Streets have been rechristened in honor of erstwhile residents like Isaac Bashevis Singer and Edgar Allan Poe. However, gentrification during the 1990s saw it become a bit yuppified and noticeably less funky than it once was.

Broadway shears north from Columbus Circle to the **Lincoln Center for the Performing Arts**, a marble assembly of buildings put up in the early 1960s on the site of some of the city's worst slums. Home to the Metropolitan Opera, the New York Philharmonic, and a host of other smaller companies (see p.121), the center is worth seeing even if you don't catch a performance (tours daily 10am–4.30pm, leaving from the main concourse under the Center; $12.50; call ☎212/875-5350 to reserve). At the center of the complex, behind a large fountain, the **Metropolitan Opera House** is an impressive marble and glass structure, with murals by Marc Chagall behind each of its high front windows.

The most famous of the monumental apartment buildings of **Central Park West** is the **Dakota**, a grandiose Renaissance-style mansion on 72nd Street, built in the late nineteenth century to persuade wealthy New Yorkers that life in an apartment could be just as luxurious as in a private house. Over the years, big-time tenants have included Lauren Bacall and Leonard Bernstein, and in the late 1960s the building was used as the setting for Roman Polanski's film *Rosemary's Baby*. Now, though, most people know it as the former home of **John Lennon** – and (still) of his wife Yoko Ono, who owns a number of the apartments. Outside the *Dakota*, on the night of December 8, 1980, Lennon was murdered – shot to death by a man who professed to be one of his greatest admirers (see p.103 to read about the nearby Lennon memorial in Central Park).

North up Central Park West, at 77th Street, the often-overlooked **New York Historical Society** (Tues–Sun 10am–6pm; suggested donation $10, students $5, children under 12 free; ☎212/873-3400, ⓌＷwww.nyhistory.org) is more a museum of American than of New York history. Its collection includes paintings by James Audubon, the Harlem naturalist who specialized in lovingly detailed watercolors of birds; a broad sweep of nineteenth-century American portraiture (including the picture of Alexander Hamilton that found its way onto the $10 bill); Hudson River School landscapes (among them Thomas Cole's fantastically pompous *Course of Empire* series); and a glittering display of Tiffany glass, providing an excellent all-around view of Louis Tiffany's attempts "to provide good art for American homes."

Up the street looms the **American Museum of Natural History**, Central Park West at 79th Street (daily 10am–5.45pm; suggested donation $14, students $10.50, children $8; IMAX films, Hayden Planetarium & special exhibits extra; for tickets call ☎212/769-5200; for general info call ☎212/769-5100 or visit Ⓦwww.amnh.org). This, the largest such museum in the world, is a strange architectural melange of heavy Neoclassical and rustic Romanesque styles covering four city blocks. The museum boasts superb nature dioramas and anthropological collections, interactive and multimedia displays, lively signage, and an awesome assemblage of bones, fossils, and models.

Top attractions range from the **Dinosaur Halls** to the **Hall of Biodiversity**. Other delights include the massive totems in the **Hall of African Peoples**, the taxidermic marvels in **North American Mammals** (including a vividly staged bull moose fight), and the two thousand gems in the **Hall of Meteorites**, among them a dazzling two-ton hunk of raw copper. The **Hall of Ocean Life** features a replica of, among other aquatic beings, a blue whale, thought to be the largest animal ever to grace planet Earth, and whose weight equals that of 24 elephants, or 400,000 pounds.

The **Rose Center for Earth and Space**, comprising the **Hall of the Universe** and the **Hayden Planetarium** (contained in a huge central sphere), opened in

2000. The center boasts all the latest technology and a truly innovative design, with open construction, spiral ramps, and dramatic glass walls on three sides of the facility. The Planetarium screens a visually impressive 40-minute 3D film "Passport to the Universe," in addition to the ponderous film entitled "The Search for Life: Are We Alone?" (both are screened throughout the day; $22, students $16.50, $13 children). For a head-trip of a different sort, check out SonicVision (Fri & Sat 7.30, 8.30, 9.30 & 10.30pm; $15), a "digitally animated alternative music show" featuring groovy overhead graphics and songs by bands such as Radiohead and Coldplay mixed by spinmaster Moby. Additionally, on the first Friday of every month, the Rose Center for Earth and Space brings in esteemed jazz musicians for "Starry Nights," complete with drinks and tapas; admission is included in the cost of your museum ticket.

After Central Park West, the Upper West Side's second-best address is **Riverside Drive**, which weaves its way from 72nd Street up the western edge of Manhattan, flanked by palatial townhouses put up in the early twentieth century and by **Riverside Park**, landscaped in 1873 by Frederick Law Olmsted, of Central Park fame. Riverside Drive makes the most pleasant route up to prestigious **Columbia University**, whose campus fills seven blocks between 114th and 121st streets and Amsterdam Avenue and Morningside Drive. The campus plazas were designed by McKim, Mead & White in grand Beaux Arts style. Regular guided **tours** start from the information office at 116th Street and Broadway.

At Amsterdam Avenue and 112th Street, one of New York's tourist gems, the **Cathedral Church of St John the Divine**, rises up with a solid kind of majesty. A curious, somewhat eerie mix of Romanesque and Gothic styles, the church was begun in 1892, though building stopped with the outbreak of war in 1939 and only sporadically resumed in the early 1990s; today, it's still barely two-thirds finished. On completion (which is unlikely before 2050), it will be the largest cathedral structure in the world, its floor space – 600ft long, and 320ft wide at the transepts – big enough to swallow both the cathedrals of Notre Dame and Chartres whole.

Harlem

Home to a culturally and historically – if not economically – rich black community, **Harlem** is still a focus of black activism and culture, and well worth seeing. Up until recently, because of a near-total lack of support from federal and municipal funds, Harlem formed a self-reliant and inward-looking community. For many downtown Manhattanites, white and black, 125th Street was a physical and mental border not willingly crossed. Today, the fruits of a cooperative effort involving businesses, residents, and City Hall are manifest in new housing, retail, and community projects, and much has been made of former president Bill Clinton's new offices here as well. But while brownstones triple in value and Harlem's physical proximity to the Upper West Side is touted, poverty and unemployment are still evident in large patches. The safest areas are 125th Street, 145th Street, Convent Avenue, and Malcolm X Boulevard; at night, stick to the clubs and restaurants.

Harlem's sights are very spread out; it's not a bad idea to get acquainted with the area via a **guided tour** (see p.78), and follow that up with further trips. Harlem's working center is 125th Street between Broadway and Fifth Avenue, a flattened expanse spiked with the occasional skyscraper. At 253 W 125th is the famous **Apollo Theatre** – for many years the center of black entertainment in the Northeast. Almost all the great figures of jazz and the blues played here – James Brown recorded his seminal *Live at the Apollo* album here in 1962 – though a larger attraction today is the Wednesday Amateur Night, open to all; call ☎ 212/531-5300 for information. At 144 W 125th, the **Studio Museum in Harlem** (Wed–Fri & Sun noon–6pm, Sat 10am–6pm; $7, free on the first Sat of every month; ⓣ212/864-4500, ⓦwww.studiomuseum.org) is a small but vibrant collection of African and African-American art from all eras.

Close by, **Adam Clayton Powell Jr Boulevard** pushes north, a broad and busy thoroughfare named after a beloved 1930s minister who became New York's first black representative in the US House. One avenue block east, the **Schomburg Center for Research in Black Culture**, 515 Malcolm X Blvd at 135th Street (Mon–Wed noon–8pm, Thurs & Fri noon–6pm; free; ⓣ212/491-2200, ⓦwww.nypl.org/research/sc), has displays on black history, and literally millions of artifacts, manuscripts, artwork, and photographs in its archives. Meanwhile, just north, at 132 W 138th St, is the **Abyssinian Baptist Church** where Powell preached. The church is also famed for its revival-style Sunday morning services and a gospel choir of gut-busting vivacity. Cross over west to 138th Street between Powell and Eighth, and you're in what many consider the finest block of rowhouses in Manhattan – **Strivers' Row** – commissioned during the 1890s housing boom and taking in designs by three sets of architects. Within the burgeoning black community at the turn of the last century this came to be the desirable place for ambitious professionals to reside – hence its nickname.

From Park Avenue to the East River, Spanish Harlem, or **El Barrio**, dips down as far as East 96th Street to collide head-on with the affluence of the Upper East Side. The center of a large Puerto Rican community, El Barrio is quite different from Harlem in look and feel. The area was originally a working-class Italian neighborhood (a small pocket of Italian families survives around 116th St and First Ave) and the quality of the architecture here is nowhere as good as that immediately to the west. The result is a shabbier and more intimidating atmosphere. Cultural roots are in evidence, however, at **La Marqueta**, on Park Avenue between 111th and 116th streets, a five-block street market of tropical produce, sinister-looking meats, and much shouting, and the **Museo del Barrio**, 1230 Fifth Avenue at 104th Street (Wed–Sun 11am–5pm; suggested donation $6; ⓣ212/831-7272, ⓦwww.elmuseo.org), which showcases Latin American and Caribbean art and culture, and features summertime concerts.

Washington Heights and the Cloisters

North of Harlem, starting from West 145th Street or so, is the neighborhood of **Washington Heights**, an area that evolved from poor farmland to highly sought-after real estate in the early part of the twentieth century; the wealthiest New Yorkers competed for estate plots with views of the Hudson River. In 1965, Washington Heights grabbed the world's attention when black activist **Malcolm X** was assassinated in the Audubon Ballroom here. Today, the area is home to the largest Dominican population in the US, as well as one of New York City's most dangerous and crime-ridden neighborhoods. And while its points of interest are safely accessed during the daylight hours, it's advisable to stay clear of Washington Heights after dark.

At Broadway and West 155th Street, **Audubon Terrace** is a complex of nineteenth-century Beaux Arts buildings that house an odd array of museums. The adjacent **Hispanic Museum** (Tues–Sat 10am–4.30pm, Sun 1–4pm; free; ⓣ212/690-0743) holds one of the largest collections of Hispanic art outside Spain. The three thousand paintings include works by Goya, El Greco, and Velázquez, and more than six thousand decorative works of art.

Another uptown surprise, on 160th Street between Amsterdam and Edgecombe avenues, is the **Morris–Jumel Mansion**, the oldest house in Manhattan (Wed–Sun 10am–4pm; $4; ⓣ212/923-8008). The house, with its proud Georgian outlines, faced by a later Federal portico, was built as a rural retreat in 1765 by Colonel Roger Morris, and served briefly as George Washington's headquarters, before it fell to the British. Later, wine merchant Stephen Jumel bought the mansion and refurbished it for his wife Eliza, formerly a prostitute and his mistress. When Jumel died in 1832, Eliza married ex-vice president Aaron Burr, twenty years her senior. The marriage lasted six months before old Burr took off, to die on the day of their divorce. Eliza battled on to the age of 91, and on the top floor of the house you'll find her obituary, a magnificently fictionalized account of a "scandalous" life.

From most western stretches of Washington Heights you get a glimpse of the **George Washington Bridge**, a dazzling concoction of metalwork and graceful lines that links Manhattan to New Jersey. Even better views are available from **the Cloisters** in Fort Tryon Park. This reconstructed monastic complex houses the pick of the Metropolitan Museum's (see p.103) medieval collection (take subway #A to 190th St–Ft Washington Ave; Tues–Sun 9.30am–5.15pm, closes 4.45pm Nov–Feb; suggested donation $20, students $10, includes admission to Metropolitan Museum on same day; ☎212/923-3700, ⓦwww.metmuseum.org). The collection is the handiwork of collectors George Barnard and John D. Rockefeller, who spent the early twentieth century shipping over all they could buy of medieval Europe. Among its larger artifacts are a monumental Romanesque Hall made up of French remnants and a frescoed Spanish Fuentiduena Chapel, both thirteenth-century.

The outer boroughs

Many visitors to New York don't stray off Manhattan. But if you're staying a while, choose to investigate the **outer boroughs** and you'll be well rewarded. **Brooklyn** is certainly worth a trip, primarily for Brooklyn Heights just across the East River, bucolic Prospect Park and the Brooklyn Botanic Garden, and the Brooklyn Museum. For inveterate nostalgics, Coney Island and its Russian neighbor, Brighton Beach, lie at the far end of the subway line. Few indeed make it to **Queens**, though the borough holds the bustling Greek community of Astoria and the Museum of the Moving Image. **Staten Island** has a couple of unusual museums, and the free ferry ride out is fun in and of itself. The **Bronx**, renowned for the desolate and bleak environs of its southern reaches, which are in fact slowly improving, has the city's largest zoo, Yankee Stadium, and another glorious botanical garden.

Brooklyn

If it were still a separate city, **Brooklyn** would be the fourth largest in the US – but until the early 1800s it was no more than a group of autonomous towns and villages distinct from the already thriving Manhattan. Robert Fulton's steamship service across the water first changed the shape of Brooklyn, starting with the establishment of a leafy retreat at Brooklyn Heights. What really transformed things, though, was the opening of the Brooklyn Bridge on May 24, 1883. There-after, development spread deeper inland, as housing was needed to service a more commercialized Manhattan. By 1900, Brooklyn was fully established as part of the newly incorporated New York City, and its fate as Manhattan's perennial kid brother was sealed.

Brooklyn Heights (#2, #3, #4, #5, #M, #N, #R, or #W to Court St–Borough Hall, or simply walk from Manhattan over the Brooklyn Bridge), one of New York City's most beautiful neighborhoods, has little in common with the rest of the borough. The peaceful, tree-lined enclave was settled by financiers from

Wall Street and remains exclusive. Such noted literary figures as Truman Capote, Tennessee Williams, and Norman Mailer have lived here. Although there isn't much to see as you wander its perfectly preserved terraces and breathe in the air of civilized calm, students of urban architecture can have a field day. Begin your tour at the **Esplanade** – more commonly known as the **Promenade** – with its fine Manhattan views across the water. **Pierrepont** and **Montague** streets, the Heights' main arteries, are studded with delightful brownstones, restaurants, bars, and shops.

Farther into Brooklyn, Flatbush Avenue leads to **Grand Army Plaza** (#2 or #3 train to the eponymous subway station), a grandiose junction laid out by Calvert Vaux late in the nineteenth century as a dramatic approach to their new Prospect Park just beyond. The triumphal **Soldiers and Sailors' Memorial Arch** was added thirty years later, topped with a fiery sculpture of *Victory* – Frederick William MacMonnies' rider, chariot, four horses, and two heralds – in tribute to the Union triumph in the Civil War.

The enormous swath of green that rolls forth from behind the arch is **Prospect Park**. Landscaped in the early 1890s, the park remains remarkably bucolic, providing an ideal place for exercise, picnics, and family gatherings. During the day it's perfectly safe, but it's best to stay clear of the park at night. The adjacent **Brooklyn Botanic Garden** (April–Sept Tues–Fri 8am–6pm, Sat & Sun 10am–6pm; Oct–March Tues–Fri 8am–4.30pm, Sat & Sun 10am–4.30pm; $5, students $3, free Tues & Sat before noon; ☎718/623-7200, ⓦwww.bbg.org), one of the city's most enticing park and garden spaces, is smaller and more immediately likeable than its more celebrated cousin in the Bronx (see p.112). Sumptuous but not overplanted, its 52 acres comprise a Rose Garden, Japanese Garden, Shakespeare Garden, and delightful lawns draped with weeping willows and beds of flowering shrubs.

Though doomed to stand perpetually in the shadow of the Met, the **Brooklyn Museum of Art**, 200 Eastern Parkway (#2 or #3 train to Eastern Parkway; Wed–Fri 10am–5pm, Sat & Sun 11am–6pm, first Sat of every month 11am–11pm; $8, students $4; ☎718/638-5000, ⓦwww.brooklynart.org), is a major museum and a good reason to forsake Manhattan for an afternoon. Highlights include the ethnographic department on the ground floor, the arts and applied arts from Oceania and the Americas and the classical and Egyptian antiquities on the second floor, and the evocative American period rooms on the fourth floor. Look in on the top-story American and European Painting and Sculpture Galleries, where the eighteenth-century portraits include one of George Washington by Gilbert Stuart (Stuart painted the portrait of Washington on the dollar bill). Pastoral canvases by William Sidney Mount, alongside the heavily romantic Hudson River School and paintings by Eastman Johnson (such as the curious *Not at Home*) and John Singer Sargent lead up to twentieth-century work by Charles Sheeler and Georgia O'Keeffe. European artists on display include Degas, Cézanne, Toulouse-Lautrec, Monet, Dufy, and Rodin.

Generations of working-class New Yorkers came to relax at one of Brooklyn's farthest points, **Coney Island** (ⓦwww.coneyislandusa.com), reachable from Manhattan on the #Q, #W, #F, or #N subway lines; allow 45min to 1hr for the ride. At its height, one hundred thousand people came here daily; now, however, it's one of the city's poorest districts, and the Astroland amusement park is peeling and run-down. The boardwalk, though, has undergone extensive and successful renovation of late, and, if you like down-at-the-heel seaside resorts, there's no better place on earth on a summer weekend. An undeniable highlight is the nearly eighty-year-old wooden roller coaster, the **Cyclone** – it's way more thrilling than many modern rides. The beach, a broad swath of golden sand, is beautiful, although it is often crowded on hot days and the water might be less than clean. In late June, catch the

Mermaid Parade, one of the country's oddest and glitziest small-town fancy dress parades, which culminates here. Meanwhile, the **New York Aquarium** on the boardwalk opened in 1896 and is still going strong, displaying fish and invertebrates from the world over in its darkened halls, along with frequent open-air shows of marine mammals (Mon–Fri 10am–5pm, Sat, Sun & holidays 10am–5.30pm; $12, students $8; ⓣ718/265-3474, ⓦ www.nyacquarium.com).

Farther east along the boardwalk, **Brighton Beach**, or "Little Odessa," is home to the country's largest community of Russian émigrés – around twenty thousand, who arrived in the 1970s – and a long-established and now largely elderly Jewish population who, much to the surprise of visiting Russians, still live as if they were in a 1970s Soviet republic. Livelier than Coney Island, it's also more prosperous, especially along its main drag, **Brighton Beach Avenue**, which runs underneath the #Q subway line in a hodgepodge of food shops and appetizing restaurants. In the evening, the restaurants really heat up, becoming a near-parody of a rowdy Russian night out, with loud live music, much glass-clinking, and the frenzied knocking back of vodka. It's definitely worth a visit.

Queens

Named in honor of the wife of Charles II of England, **Queens** was one of the rare places where postwar immigrants could buy their own homes and establish their own communities. (**Astoria**, for example, holds the world's largest concentration of Greeks outside Greece.) It also has a long **filmmaking** tradition: Paramount had its studios here until the company was lured away by Hollywood's more desirable weather. The area was then left empty and disused by all except the US Army, until Hollywood's stranglehold on the industry finally weakened. The new studios here – not open to the public – now rank as the country's fourth largest, and are set for a major expansion. The **American Museum of the Moving Image**, in the old Paramount complex at 35th Avenue at 36th Street (#R or #V train to Steinway; Wed–Fri 11am–8pm, Sat & Sun 11am–6pm; $10; ⓣ718/784-0077, ⓦ www.ammi.org), is devoted to the history of film, video, and TV. In addition to viewing posters and kitsch movie souvenirs from the 1930s and 1940s you can listen in on directors explaining sequences from famous movies; watch fun short films made up of well-known clips; add your own sound effects to movies; and see some original sets and costumes. A wonderful, mock-Egyptian pastiche of a 1920s movie theater shows kids' movies and TV classics.

Now affiliated with MoMA, **P.S. 1 Contemporary Art Center**, 22-25 Jackson Ave at 46th St (Thurs–Mon noon–6pm; $5; ⓣ718/784-2084, ⓦ www.ps1.org), is one of the oldest and biggest organizations in the US devoted exclusively to contemporary art and showing leading emerging artists. Founded in 1971, the public school-turned-funky exhibition space also hosts lively evening club events.

The **Isamu Noguchi Garden Museum**, 32-37 Vernon Blvd (Mon, Thurs & Fri 10am–5pm, Sat & Sun 11am–6pm; suggested donation $10; ⓣ718/204-7088, ⓦ www.noguchi.org), has also moved to a temporary 6000-square-foot home. The museum administrators have done a wonderful job of paring down the permanent collection of this prolific and dynamic Japanese-American artist's works. Noguchi's "organic" sculptures, drawings, modern dance costumes, and well-known Akari Light Sculptures are all on display.

Lastly, where Broadway and Vernon Boulevard intersect on the shores of the East River, **Socrates Sculpture Park** (daily 10am–sunset; free; ⓣ718/956-1819, ⓦ www.socratessculpturepark.org) has been transformed from an illegal dumpsite into one of the city's most distinctive places to view and experience art, namely large-scale sculptures.

The Bronx

The city's northernmost and only mainland borough, **The Bronx** was for a long time believed to be its toughest and most crime-ridden district, and presented as such in films like *Fort Apache* and *The Bronx*, as well as books like *Bonfire of the Vanities*, even after urban renewal was under way. In fact, it's not much different from the other outer boroughs, though geographically it has more in common with Westchester County to the north than it does with the island regions of New York City: steep hills, deep valleys, and rocky outcroppings to the west, and marshy flatlands along Long Island Sound to the east. Settled in the seventeenth century by the Swede Jonas Bronk, it became, like Brooklyn, part of New York proper around the end of the nineteenth century, and soon became one of the most sought-after residential areas of the city. Its main thoroughfare, **Grand Concourse**, became lined with luxurious Art Deco apartment houses; many, though greatly run-down, still stand.

The **Bronx Zoo** (Mon–Fri 10am–5pm, Sat & Sun 10am–5.30pm; $12, kids $9, free every Wed; ☎718/220-5100, ⓦ www.bronxzoo.com) is accessible either by its main gate on Fordham Road or by a second entrance on Bronx Park South. The latter is the entrance to use if you come directly here by subway (#2 or the #5 to E Tremont Ave). With over four thousand animals, it's the largest urban zoo in the US, and is better than most; it was one of the first institutions of its kind to realize that animals both looked and felt better out in the open. The "Wild Asia" exhibit is an almost forty-acre wilderness through which tigers, elephants, and deer roam relatively free, visible from a monorail (May–Oct; $3). Look in also on the "World of Darkness," which holds nocturnal species, the "Himalayan Highlands," with endangered species such as the red panda and snow leopard, and the new "Tiger Mountain" exhibit, which allows visitors the opportunity to get up close and personal with six Siberian tigers.

Across the road from the zoo's main entrance is the back turnstile of the **New York Botanical Gardens** (April–Oct Tues–Sun 10am–6pm, Nov–March 10am–5pm; $13, free Wed & Sat 10am–noon; ☎718/817-8700, ⓦ www.nybg.org), which in parts is as wild as anything you're likely to see upstate. Don't miss its Enid A. Haupt Conservatory, a landmark, turn-of-the-century crystal palace featuring a stunning 90ft dome, beautiful reflecting pool, lots of tropical plants, and seasonal displays among other things

Yankee Stadium, at 161st St and River Ave (☎718/293-6000, ⓦ www.yankees .com), is home to the most winning team in professional sports – the 26-time World Series champions called the New York Yankees. A new stadium is currently being built across the street and is scheduled to open in 2009. All the more reason to see a game now and get a feel for the marvelous sports history here.

Staten Island

Until 1964, **Staten Island** was isolated from the rest of the city – getting here meant a ferry trip or a long ride through New Jersey, and commuting into Manhattan was a bit of a haul. The opening of the Verrazano Narrows Bridge changed things: upwardly mobile Brooklynites found inexpensive property on the island and swarmed over the bridge to buy their parcel of suburbia. Today, Staten Island has swollen to accommodate dense residential neighborhoods amid the rambling greenery and endless backwaters of neat homes.

Without a car, the best way to reach the fifth borough is via the **Staten Island Ferry** (☎718/815-BOAT, ⓦ www.siferry.com), which sails from Battery Park around the clock, with departures every 15–20min during rush hours (between 7–9am and 5–7pm), every 30min midday and evenings, and once an hour late at

△ Staten Island Ferry

night; on weekend, service is less frequent. Truly New York's best bargain, the ferry gives great wide-angled views of Lower Manhattan and the Statue of Liberty absolutely free.

Once you get to the island, the ferry terminal in which you arrive quickly dispels any romance – though it's easy to escape to the adjoining bus station and catch the #S74 bus to the **Jacques Marchais Center of Tibetan Art**, 338 Lighthouse Ave (Wed–Sun 1–5pm; $5; ☎718/987-3500, ⓦ www.tibetanmuseum.com). Jacques Marchais was the alias of Jacqueline Kleber, a New York art dealer who reckoned she'd get on better with a French name. In the 1920s and 1930s, she assembled the largest collection of Tibetan art in the Western world and housed it in a hillside "Buddhist temple." The exhibition is small enough to be accessible, with magnificent bronze Bodhisattvas, fearsome deities in union with each other, musical instruments, costumes, and decorations from Tibet. During the first or second week of October the museum hosts a harvest festival, where Tibetan monks in maroon robes perform the traditional ceremonies, and Tibetan food and crafts are sold.

From Richmond Road, one of Staten Island's main drags, it's just a short walk to **Historic Richmond Town** (June–Aug Wed–Sat 10am–5pm, Sun 1–5pm; Sept–May Wed–Sun 1–5pm; $4; ☎718/351-1611, ⓦ www.historicrichmondtown .org), where a dozen or so old buildings have been transplanted from their original sites in other areas of Staten Island and grafted onto the village of Richmond, which dates from 1695–1880. Half-hourly **tours** negotiate the best of these – including the oldest elementary school in the country, a picture-book general store, and the atmospheric Guyon-Lake-Tysen House of 1740. It's all carried off to picturesque effect in rustic surroundings, a mere twelve miles from Downtown Manhattan.

Eating

There isn't anything you can't eat in New York, and New Yorkers take their food very seriously, obsessed with new cuisines, new dishes, and new restaurants. Certain areas are pockets of ethnic restaurants – **Chinatown** (including Malaysian, Thai, and Vietnamese) below Canal Street; **Little Italy** just to the north; and **Indian Row**, on Sixth Street between First and Second avenues – but you can generally find whatever you want, wherever (and whenever) you want. The **outer boroughs** of Brooklyn, the Bronx, and Queens all have excellent dining opportunities worth seeking out, in neighbourhoods such as Jackson Heights, Astoria, Williamsburg, and Park Slope.

Downtown Manhattan (below 14th St)

Blue Hill 75 Washington Place, between 6th Ave and Washington Square Park ☎ 212/539-1776. Tucked into a brownstone just steps from the park, this restaurant has earned countless accolades in recent years for its superb seasonal menu of American dishes served with flair.

Café de Bruxelles 118 Greenwich Ave, at W 13th St ☎ 212/206-1830. Taste the city's most delicious frites (served with homemade mayo) and mussels at this Belgian family-run restaurant. Its zinc bar is the oldest around, and there's a nice selection of Belgian beers, too.

Café Le Figaro 184 Bleecker St, at MacDougal ☎ 212/677-1100. Discover the ersatz Left Bank at its finest at this 1950s Beat hangout. On the menu: good people-watching and first-rate burgers and soups.

Cendrillon 45 Mercer St, between Broome and Grand ☎ 212/343-9012. This fine pan-Asian restaurant serves consistently exceptional food, not to mention creative cocktails. The prices are decent, and the desserts will make you swoon.

Corner Bistro 331 W 4th St, at Jane ☎ 212/242-9502. This down-home tavern serves some of the best burgers and fries in town. An excellent place to unwind and refuel in a friendly neighborhood atmosphere, it's also a longstanding literary haunt; can get quite crowded.

Ear Inn 326 Spring St, between Washington and Greenwich ☎ 212/226-9060. This cozy pub serves basic, reasonably priced American food (the cowboy chili and the burgers are excellent) and has a good mix of beers on tap. It claims to be the second-oldest bar in the city (after *McSorley's*; see p.118). It may also be one of the best.

Florent 69 Gansevoort St, between Washington and Greenwich ☎ 212/989-5779. In the heart of the Meatpacking District, see and be seen at this almost-always-open, fashionable eatery, serving great moderate-to-pricey French bistro fare.

Grange Hall 50 Commerce St, at Barrow ☎ 212/924-5246. Hiding on a dead-end picturesque street, and inspired by community suppers in Maine, this feel-good restaurant features healthful, seasonal dishes at reasonable prices. It's popular, so make a reservation.

'ino 21 Bedford St, between Downing St and 6th Ave ☎ 212/989-5769. Duck in here for a satisfying snack; choose from a list of *bruschette*, *tramezzine* (a hearty cousin of the tea sandwich), and Italian wines.

Joe's Shanghai 9 Pell St, between Bowery and Mott ☎ 212/233-8888. Probably Chinatown's most famous restaurant, this place is always packed, for good reason. Try the soup dumplings and the seafood main courses at its communal tables, or visit its newer, less crowded sister, *Joe's Ginger*, at 113 Mott St, between Hester and Canal.

Katz's Delicatessen 205 E Houston St, at Ludlow ☎ 212/254-2246. Venerable Lower East Side Jewish deli serving archetypal overstuffed pastrami and corned-beef sandwiches. Best known as the site of the orgasm scene in *When Harry Met Sally*.

Lavagna 545 E 5th St, between aves A and B ☎ 212/979-1005. This red-hued hideaway seduces East Villagers with potato cheese gratin, pasta with sausage, and succulent pork dishes. The prices are relatively reasonable, to boot.

Lombardi's 32 Spring St, between Mott and Mulberry ☎ 212/941-7994. The oldest pizzeria in Manhattan serves some of the best pie in town, including an amazing clam pizza; no slices, though. Ask for roasted garlic on the side.

Mary's Fish Camp 64 Charles St, at W 4th St ☎ 646/486-2185. Lobster rolls, bouillabaisse, and seasonal veggies adorn the menu at this intimate West Village spot, where you can almost smell the salt air. Go early, as the reservation line lasts into the night.

Moustache 90 Bedford St, between Grove and Barrow ☎ 212/229-2220; also 265 E 10th St, between 1st Ave and Ave A ☎ 212/228-2022. A small, cheap Middle Eastern spot with a "pitza" specialty (pizzas of pita bread and eclectic toppings); also great hummus, chickpea and spinach salad, and bargain lamb chops.

Otto Enoteca and Pizzeria 1 5th Ave, at Washington Square N ☎ 212/995-9559. The cheapest addition to Italian chef Mario Battali's restaurant empire is a popular pizza and antipasti joint with a superb wine list and a beautiful crowd. The acoustics aren't great, but the atmosphere is festive and you can't beat the *lardo* (bacon) and *vongole* (clam) pizza.

Paradou 8 Little W 12th St, between Greenwich and Washington ☎212/463-8345. Sure to transport you to Provence, this underrated French bistro is a far better (and more authentic) option than overexposed *Pastis* around the corner. Great wines by the glass.

Pearl Oyster Bar 18 Cornelia St, between Bleecker and W 4th sts ☎212/691-8211. You may have to fight for a table here, but it's worth it for the thoughtfully executed seafood dishes and primo lobster rolls.

Podunk Café 231 E 5th St, between 2nd Ave and Cooper Square ☎212/677-7722. The desserts at this homey bakery/café are unbeatable; the chewy, delicious coconut bars can't miss.

Prune 54 E 1st St, between 1st and 2nd aves ☎212/677-6221. Adventurous and full of surprises, this East Village Mediterranean restaurant boasts dishes such as sweetbreads wrapped in bacon, seared sea bass with Berber spices, and buttermilk ice cream with pistachio puff pastry. It's cramped, but this makes for a festive atmosphere.

Raoul's 180 Prince St, between Sullivan and Thompson ☎212/966-3518. This sexy French bistro is comfortable, authentic, and entertaining for its people-watching into the night. A beloved New York standby, if at a price.

Sammy's Roumanian Steakhouse 157 Chrystie St at Delancy ☎212/673-0330. This basement Jewish steakhouse gives diners more than they bargained for: schmaltzy songs, delicious-but-heartburn-inducing food (topped off by homemade rugelach and egg creams for dessert), and chilled vodka in blocks of ice. Keep track of your tab, if you can.

Veselka 144 2nd Ave, at 9th St ☎212/228-9682. The terrific grilled kielbasa, vegetarian stuffed cabbage, and Ukrainian pierogi at Eastern European *Veselka* are all great for sopping up alcohol and killing hunger pangs at 4am.

Wallse 344 W 11th St, at Washington ☎212/352-2300. New-fangled (and lighter) Austrian fare takes center stage here. Chef Kurt Gutenbrunner has crafted a unique menu that abounds with surprises – the light-as-air schnitzel, frothy riesling sauces, and strudels are good enough to make an Austrian grandma sing with pride. The dining room resonates sophistication, and the wine list tempts with some hard-to-find Austrian vintages.

Xunta 174 1st Ave, between 10th and 11th sts ☎212/614-0620. This East Village gem buzzes with hordes of young people perched on rum barrels, downing pitchers of sangría and choosing from the dizzying tapas menu – try the mussels in fresh tomato sauce, or shrimp with garlic. You can eat (and drink) very well for around $20.

Midtown Manhattan (14th St to 59th St)

Artisanal 2 Park Ave, at 32nd St ☎212/725-8585. Cheese is the name of the game here – there's a cave with 700 varieties. If you don't want the full experience, grab a small table at the bar and try the *gougere* (gruyere puffs) with one of the excellent wines on offer.

Carmine's 200 W 44th St, between Broadway and 8th Ave ☎212/221-3800; also 2450 Broadway, between W 90th and W 91st sts ☎212/362-2200. Mountainous portions of tasty homestyle Southern Italian food are made to share at this large, loud favorite. Be prepared to wait; only parties of six or more can make reservations after 6pm.

City Bakery 3 W 18th St, between 5th and 6th aves ☎212/366-1414. A smart stop for a satisfying lunch or a sweet-tooth craving. The vast array of pastries is head-and-shoulders above most in the city.

Empire Diner 210 10th Ave, at 22nd St ☎212/243-2736. Spangled in silver, this all-night diner charms with its festive vibe and good, moderately priced food.

Emporio Brasil 15 W 46th St, between 5th and 6th aves ☎212/764-4646. Check out the great Brazilian food and atmosphere at *Emporio Brasil*, with reasonable prices for Midtown. On Saturday afternoon, from noon to 5pm only, try Brazil's national dish, the tasty *feijoada* (a stew of meaty pork and black beans, with rice).

F&B 269 W 23rd St, between 7th and 8th aves ☎646/486-4441. Terrific European-style street food (namely hot dogs) at digestible prices. Other items include salmon dogs, bratwursts, and mouthwatering Swedish meatballs; there's also a selection of vegetarian offerings.

Gramercy Tavern 42 E 20th St, between Broadway and Park ☎212/477-0777. By many accounts, NYC's best and most-beloved restaurant; its neo-Colonial decor, exquisite New American cuisine, and perfect service make for a memorable meal. The lively front room is a great place to drop in for a drink, or a more casual (and cheaper) meal.

Guastavino's 409 E 59th St, between 1st and York aves ☎212/980-2455. This magnificent, soaring space underneath the Queensboro Bridge is a hot spot for beautiful people who come to drink *flirtinis* and choose from a dizzying array of seafood dishes. Book upstairs for a quieter – and super expensive – meal.

Hallo Berlin 402 W 51st St, between 9th and 10th aves ☎212/541-6248. All manner of tasty wursts, served by an owner who once sold them from a pushcart and now vends in this pleasant bench-and-table beer-garden setting.

Joe Allen's 326 W 46th St, between 8th and 9th aves ☎212/581-6464. The tried-and-true formula of checkered tablecloths, old-fashioned barroom feel, and reliable American food at moderate prices works excellently at this popular pre-theater spot. Make a reservation, unless you plan to arrive after 8pm.

Oyster Bar lower level, Grand Central Station ☎212/490-6650. This wonderfully atmospheric old place, down in the vaulted dungeons of Grand Central, draws Midtown office workers for lunch, who come to choose from a staggering menu featuring daily catches – she-crab bisque, steamed Maine lobster, and sweet Kumamoto oysters. Prices are moderate to expensive; you can eat more cheaply at the bar.

Rosa Mexicano 1063 1st Ave, at 58th St ☎212/753-7407; also 61 Columbus Ave, at 62nd St ☎212/977-7700. Festive decor, authentic dishes such as *bisteca al hongos* (beef with creamy mushroom sauce) and pomegranate margaritas make this the best Mexican restaurant in NYC. Not surprisingly, it's pricey.

Sugiyama 251 W 55th St, between Broadway and 8th Ave ☎212/956-0670. You may want to take out a loan before dining at this superb Japanese restaurant, where you're guaranteed an exquisite experience, from its enchanting *kaiseki* (chef's choice) dinners (vegetarian or non) to its royal service.

Vatan 409 3rd Ave, at 29th St ☎212/689-5666. Nab a table here for a vegetarian Indian feast amid garish decor.

Uptown Manhattan (60th St and above)

Amy Ruth's 113 W 116th St, between Lenox and 7th aves ☎212/280-8779. The honey-dipped fried chicken is reason enough to travel to this casual, family restaurant in Harlem. The place gets especially busy after church on Sundays.

Barking Dog Luncheonette 1678 3rd Ave, at E 94th St ☎212/831-1800; also 1453 York Ave, at 77th St ☎212/861-3600. This diner-like place offers outstanding, cheap American food (like mashed potatoes and gravy). Very kid-friendly.

Big Nick's Burger Joint 2175 Broadway, between 76th and 77th sts ☎212/362-9238. This welcoming greasy spoon with gargantuan portions is heaven for hungry diners, be it after-hours or early in the morning.

Boat House in Central Park (enter from 72nd St), at Central Park Drive N ☎212/517-2233. While the New American cuisine here is fine, it's the picturesque setting that makes the pumped-up

prices worth every penny, especially at sunset. If you don't feel like splurging, go for a drink at the water's edge.

El Pollo 1746 1st Ave, between E 90th and E 91st sts ☎212/996-7810. Come here for a tasty and cheap meal of Peruvian-style rotisserie chicken, dusted with spices and cooked over a spit. Bring your own wine.

Gabriela's 685 Amsterdam Ave, at 93rd St ☎212/961-0574; also 311 Amsterdam, at 73rd St ☎212/875-8532. Count on good, inexpensive, authentic Mexican – not just your usual enchiladas and burritos, but also a wide array of regional chicken and seafood dishes in a large, crowded room. Noisy, lively, and thoroughly enjoyable. Expect to wait.

Gray's Papaya 2090 Broadway, at 72nd St ☎212/799-0243. Open 24/7, this insanely popular hot-dog joint is an NYC institution, now famous for its "Recession Special": 2 dogs and a drink for $2.45. Call for several other locations around the city.

Heidelburg 1648 2nd Ave, between E 85th and 86th sts ☎212/628-2332. At one of the last Yorkville German joints, the food is the real deal, with excellent liver dumpling soup, Bauernfruestuck omelettes and pancakes (both sweet and potato). Have a huge, boot-shaped glass of Weissbeer with anything.

Jean Georges in the *Trump International Hotel*, 1 Central Park West, between 60th and 61st sts ☎212/299-3900. This contemporary French restaurant drips with elegance; its celebrity chef, Jean Georges Vongerichten, has been known to make such inventive dishes as asparagus with frothy truffle vinaigrette, or dill-stuffed shrimp with baked lemon. The staff here is polished, and the prices are steep. If you aren't up for the full-blown gastronomic experience, try the prix fixe lunch menu ($20) in the more casual Nougatine Room.

La Caridad 78 2199 Broadway, at W 78th St ☎212/874-2780. Plentiful and inexpensive Cuban-Chinese food (the Cuban is better) is doled out at this neighborhood institution. Bring your own beer and expect to wait.

Mughlai 320 Columbus Ave, at 75th St ☎212/724-6363. This upscale Indian spot is surprisingly affordable. Entrees, which include batter-light samosas and comforting curries, run $11–16.

Ouest 2315 Broadway, between 83rd and 84th sts ☎212/580-8700. Exceptional gourmet comfort food, such as bacon-wrapped meatloaf with wild mushroom gravy, and numerous celeb spottings have earned this New American restaurant a loyal following. There's a $26 three-course pre-theater menu served Mon–Fri 5–6.30pm.

Sarabeth's 423 Amsterdam Ave, between 80th and 81st sts ☎212/496-6280; also in the *Hotel Wales*, 1295 Madison Ave, between 92nd and 93rd sts ☎212/410-7335. Best for brunch, this country-style restaurant serves delectable baked goods and impressive omelettes – a fact reflected by the long lines outside.

Serendipity 3 225 E 60th St, between 2nd and 3rd aves ☎212/838-3531. The long-established eatery/ice cream parlor serves out-of-this-world frozen hot chocolate; the wealth of ice cream offerings are a real treat, too.

Terrace in the Sky 400 W 119th St, between Amsterdam Ave and Morningside Drive ☎212/666-9490. Enjoy harp music, marvelous Mediterranean fare, and great views of Morningside Heights in this romantic Uptown spot.

Vinnie's Pizza 285 Amsterdam Ave, at W 73rd St ☎212/874-4382. For those who prefer their pizza thick, doughy, loaded with cheese, and cheap, this Upper West Side place is for you. You can sit, or order a slice to go.

The outer boroughs

360 360 Van Brunt St, at Wolcott St, Red Hook, Brooklyn ☎718/246-0360. Seasonal ingredients, bohemian ambiance, and a passionate chef make this hands-on French restaurant worth the adventure of finding it. The menu here changes every day, but there's always a fine selection of unusual wines.

Diner 85 Broadway, at Berry St, Williamsburg, Brooklyn ☎718/486-3077. A fave with artists and hipsters, this groovy eatery (in a Pullman diner car) serves tasty American bistro grub (hangar steaks, roasted chicken, fantastic fries) at good prices. Stays open late, with an occasional DJ spinning tunes.

Elias Corner 24-02 31st St, at 24th Ave, Astoria, Queens ☎718/932-1510. Pay close attention to the seafood on display as you enter, because this Astoria institution doesn't have menus and meals are prepared based on availability. Serves some of the best and freshest fish you'll find; try the marinated grilled octopus, if on offer.

Grocery 195 Smith St, Carroll Gardens, Brooklyn ☎718/596-3335. Smith Street has become a Brooklyn dining destination, and this tiny eatery, featuring a seasonal menu full of unique, New American dishes, is the best of the bunch. Entrees $20 and up; call well in advance for reservations.

Jackson Diner 37-47 74th St, between 37th and Roosevelt aves, Jackson Heights, Queens ☎718/672-1232. Come here hungry and stuff yourself silly with amazingly light and reasonably priced Indian fare. The samosas and mango lassis are not to be missed.

Mario's 2342 Arthur Ave, between 184th and 186th sts, Bronx ☎718/584-1188. Pricey but impressive Italian cooking, from pizzas to pastas and beyond, enticing even die-hard Manhattanites to the Belmont section of the Bronx.

Nathan's 1310 Surf Ave at Schweiker's Walk, Coney Island, Brooklyn ☎718/946-2202. Home of the "famous Coney Island hot dog," served since 1916, Nathan's is not to be missed (unless you are a vegetarian). Its annual Hot Dog Eating Contest is held on July 4.

Peter Luger's Steak House 178 Broadway, at Driggs Ave, Williamsburg, Brooklyn ☎718/387-7400. Catering to carnivores since 1873, Peter Luger's may just be the city's finest steakhouse. The service is surly and the decor plain, but the porterhouse steak – the only cut served – is divine. Cash only, and very expensive; expect to pay at least $60 a head.

Primorski 282 Brighton Beach Ave, between 2nd and 3rd sts, Brighton Beach, Brooklyn ☎718/891-3111. Perhaps the best of Brighton Beach's Russian hangouts, with a huge menu of authentic Russian dishes, including blintzes and stuffed cabbage, at absurdly cheap prices. Live music in the evening.

Drinking

New York's best **bars** are in **Downtown Manhattan** – the West and East villages, SoHo, and the Lower East Side. The **Midtown** places tend to be geared to an after-hours office crowd and (with a few exceptions) are pricey and rather dull. **Uptown**, the Upper West Side at least, between 60th and 85th streets along Amsterdam and Columbus avenues, has several good places to drink. Most of the bars listed below serve food of some kind and have happy hours sometime between 4pm and 8pm during the week. See also the bars listed in "Gay New York," p.124.

Downtown Manhattan (to 14th St)

Barramundi 67 Clinton St, between Stanton and Rivington ☎212/529-6900. The magical, fairy-lit garden makes this bar a blessed sanctuary from the painfully hip Lower East Side.

Chumley's 86 Bedford St, between Grove and Barrow ☎212/675-4449. As much fun to find (there's no sign) as it is to drink in, this atmospheric former speakeasy has a great selection of beers and good American pub food.

Decibel 240 E 9th St, between 2nd and 3rd aves ☎212/979-2733. A rocking atmosphere (with good tunes) envelops this beautifully decorated underground sake bar. The inevitable wait for a wooden table is worth it.

Double Happiness 173 Mott St, between Broome and Grand ☎212/941-1282. Low ceilings, dark lighting, nooks, crannies, and the superlative green-tea martinis make this Asian-themed bar a decadently seductive place to be.

Grassroots Tavern 20 St Mark's Place, between 2nd and 3rd aves ☎212/475-9443. This roomy, wooden, and wonderful underground den has Brooklyn beers for $3, an extended happy hour, and at least three animals roaming around at any hour of the day or night.

Hogs & Heifers 859 Washington St, at W 13th St ☎212/929-0655. It's honky-tonk cheesy but fun; this raucous Meatpacking District watering hole has inspired thousands of women to dance on the bar, as well as donate their bras to the growing collection that adorns the joint.

McSorley's Old Ale House 15 E 7th St, between 2nd and 3rd aves, ☎212/472-9148. Yes, it's touristy and often full of local frat boys, but you'll be drinking in history at this landmark bar that served its first beer in 1854.

Other Room 143 Perry St, between Washington and Greenwich ☎212/645-9758. The cozy-cool atmosphere, excellent drink menu, and "way-West" location of this wine and beer bar has guaranteed it a special place in locals' hearts.

St Dymphna's 118 St Marks Place, between 1st Ave and Ave A ☎212/254-6636. With a tempting pub menu and some of the city's best Guinness, *Dymphna's* is great place to warm up on a cold winter's night.

Temple Bar 332 Lafayette St, between Bleecker and Houston sts ☎212/925-4242. One of the most discreet and romantic spots for a drink Downtown, this sumptuous, dark lounge evokes the 1940s and is ideal for a tryst. They take their martinis very seriously here.

West West Side Highway, at W 11th St ☎212/242-4375. Design-forward cement floors, Moderne furniture, and exceptional bartenders make this monochromatic bar/cocktail lounge a happening place to watch the sun set over the Hudson River.

White Horse Tavern 567 Hudson St, at W 11th St ☎212/989-3956. Dylan Thomas drank up at this convivial, inexpensive, old-time Village institution before his last trip to the hospital.

Midtown Manhattan (14th St to 59th St)

21 Club 21 W 52nd St, between 5th and 6th aves ☎212/582-7200. Simply one of New York's most enduring institutions, this is where the Old Boys meet, surrounded by dark wood paneling and sublime service. There's a dress code, so wear a jacket and tie.

Campbell Apartment southwest balcony, Grand Central Terminal ☎212/953-0409. Once the home of businessman John W. Campbell, who oversaw the construction of Grand Central, this majestic space – built to look like a thirteenth-century Florentine palace – was sealed up for years. Now it's one of New York's most distinctive bars. Go early and don't wear sneakers (you won't be allowed in if you do).

Enoteca I Trulli 124 E 27th St, between Lexington and Park ☎212/481-7372. Adjacent to a lovely Italian restaurant by the same name, this wine bar serves a jaw-dropping selection from Italy only, available by the glass, flight, or bottle. Servers are happy to give you a wine lesson as they pour. Ask for bread with ricotta spread or a plate of Italian cheeses to accompany your tipple.

Lever House 390 Park Ave, at 53rd St ☎212/888-2700. NYC's newest power-drink scene is also a 1950s landmark, in a building that revolutionized skyscraper design. The new interior strikes a balance between retro and futuristic; it's worth a look and a cocktail, or two.

Old Town Bar & Restaurant 45 E 18th St, between Broadway and Park ☎212/529-6732. This atmospheric old-world bar is popular with publishing types, models, and photogs in the Flatiron district. Has a good pub menu, too.

Park 118 10th Ave, between 17th and 18th sts ☎212/352-3313. It's easy to get lost in this vast warren of rooms filled with fireplaces, geodes, and even a Canadian redwood. The large garden is a treat, and the place is filled on weekend nights with only the most beautiful people.

Pen-Top Bar & Terrace in the *Peninsula Hotel*, 700 5th Ave, at 55th St ☎212/903-3097. High above the city, this rooftop bar delivers stunning views of the skyline (on a clear day) and a good selection of beefy drinks.

Pete's Tavern 129 E 18th St, at Irving Place ☎212/473-7676. This former speakeasy, which opened in 1864, has hosted such illustrious patrons as John F. Kennedy Jr and O. Henry, who allegedly wrote "Gift of the Magi" in his regular booth here. A fun and often raucous spot to grab a pint near Gramercy Park.

Uptown Manhattan (60th St and above)

Abbey Pub 237 W 105th St, between Broadway and Amsterdam ☎212/222-8713. Half a century old, the *Abbey* still brings in locals and students for learned conversations in wooden booths and cheap beer.

🏃 Dead Poet 450 Amsterdam Ave, between 81st and 82nd sts ☎212/595-5670. You'll be waxing poetical and then dropping down dead if you stay for the duration of this sweet little bar's happy hour: it lasts from 4 to 8pm and offers draft beer at $3 a pint. The backroom has armchairs, books, and a pool table.

Dublin House Tap Room 225 W 79th St, between Broadway and Amsterdam ☎212/874-9528. This lively Upper West Side Irish pub, pouring a very nice Black & Tan, is dominated at night by the young, inebriated, and rowdy.

Metropolitan Museum of Art 1000 5th Ave at 82nd St ☎212/535-7710. It's hard to imagine a more romantic spot to sip a glass of wine, whether on the Cantor Roof Garden (open only in warm weather), enjoying one of the best views in the city, or on the Great Hall Balcony listening to live chamber music (year-round Fri and Sat 5–8.30pm).

Prohibition 503 Columbus Ave, between 84th and 85th sts ☎212/579-3100. A pool table, live jazz, and outdoor tables combine to make *Prohibition* one of the liveliest singles scenes on the Upper West Side.

Shark Bar 307 Amsterdam Ave, between W 74th and 75th sts ☎212/874-8500. Ultra-elegant lounge with great soul food and a beat to go with it.

Subway Inn 143 E 60th St, at Lexington ☎212/223-8929. This downscale neighborhood dive bar, across from Bloomingdale's, is great for a late-afternoon beer.

The outer boroughs

Bohemian Hall and Beer Garden 29-19 24th Ave, at 29th St, Astoria, Queens ☎718/721-4226. This old Czech bar is the real deal, catering to old-timers and serving a good selection of pilsners, hard-to-find brews, and burgers and sausages. In back, there's a very large beer garden, complete with picnic tables, trees, and a bandshell for polka and non-polka groups alike.

Boogaloo Bar 168 Marcy Ave, between S 5th and Broadway, Williamsburg, Brooklyn ☎718/599-8900. This funkadelic lounge serves as a meeting-ground for experimental artists, DJs, and thirsty patrons, who can choose, among other drinks, from a selection of over 30 rums from around the world.

Brooklyn Inn 148 Hoyt St, at Bergen St, Boerum Hill, Brooklyn ☎718/625-9741. Locals – and their dogs – gather at this convivial favorite with high ceilings and a friendly bar staff. Great place for a daytime buzz or shooting pool in the back room.

Frank's Cocktail Lounge 660 Fulton St, between Hudson Ave and Rockwell Place, Fort Greene, Brooklyn ☎718/625-9339. A stone's throw from the Brooklyn Academy of Music, this mellow bar with a classic-to-modern R&B jukebox comes alive at night when DJs spin hip-hop and the party spreads upstairs.

Galapagos 70 N 6th St, between Wythe and Kent aves, Williamsburg, Brooklyn ☎718/782-5188, ⓦwww.galapagosartspace.com. A gorgeous design – featuring placid pools of water and elegant candelabras – as well as excellent avant-garde movies on Sunday nights makes this converted factory a popular spot. Live music, literary readings, or some oddball event is on offer most other nights of the week.

Pete's Candy Store 709 Lorimer, between Frost and Richardson, Williamsburg, Brooklyn ☎718/302-3770, ⓦwww.petescandystore.com. This terrific little spot to drink was once a real candy store. There's free live music every night, poetry on Mondays, Scrabble and Bingo nights, and even an organized "Stitch and Bitch" knitting group.

Nightlife and entertainment

You'll never be at a loss for something fun or culturally enriching to do while in New York. The **live music** scene, in particular, well reflects New York's diversity: on any night of the week, you can hear pretty much any type of music, from thumping hip-hop to pogoing punk, and, of course, plenty of jazz. There are also quite a few **dance clubs**, where you can move to hard-hitting drum'n'bass or cheesy tunes from the 1970s and 80s.

Home to Broadway and 42nd Street (as well as off-Broadway and the Fringe Festival), New York is also one of the world's great **theater** centers, with productions that range from lavish, over-the-top musicals to experimental productions in converted garages. **Classical music**, **opera**, and **dance** are all very well-represented, too, at venues such as the dignified Lincoln Center and the more funky Brooklyn Academy of Music. As for **film**, you couldn't hope for better pickings: the city has several large indie theaters, numerous revival and art-house cinemas, and countless Hollywood-blockbuster multiplexes. Last but not least, NYC has many excellent **comedy** clubs, as well as a healthy **spoken-word** and **poetry slam** scene.

For **listings** of what's on during any particular week, check out *Time Out New York* ($3; available from newsstands citywide) or *The Village Voice* (free; available in newspaper boxes and many other spots around town).

Clubs and live music

New York has plenty of great **live music venues**, from the cutting-edge *Knitting Factory* to *S.O.B.'s* and *Joe's Pub*, which cater to world music and more eclectic fare. Numerous **jazz clubs**, ranging in quality from passable to sublime, keep the black-clad, turtleneck-wearing set happy. **Cover charges** at any of these smaller places will run you from $8 to $25 or so. There are also many larger music venues, which attract touring bands from around the world; here, a ticket can cost anywhere from $25 to $100. If the show's not sold out, tickets are usually available from the door. For advance tickets, go to the venue's box office, or visit **Ticketmaster** or **Ticketweb** (see box, below).

As for **club life** in the city, it's a very amorphous creature. Parties change at a rapid pace, so be sure to check the listings in *The Village Voice* or *Time Out New York* before you make any plans. Musically, drum 'n' bass, electronica, 1980s nostalgia, and house hold sway at the moment, though Latin freestyle, dancehall reggae, funk, and hip-hop all get their due. Nothing gets going much before midnight, so there's no point turning up earlier (unless to avoid cover charges, which are sometimes waived before 10 or 11pm). During the week is the best time to go out – **prices** are cheaper, crowds are smaller, and service is better. All venues tend to be strict about **ID**. **Cover charges** range from $15 to $50, though most average out at around $20. Oftentimes, you can check out a club's website and get on the guestlist, which will bring you reduced or free admission.

Theater

Even if you're not normally a **theater** buff, going to see a play or a musical while in New York is virtually de rigueur. The various theater venues are referred to as **Broadway**, **Off-Broadway**, or **Off-Off Broadway**, representing a descending order of ticket price, production polish, elegance, and comfort. Broadway offerings consist primarily of large-scale musicals, comedies, and dramas with big-name actors, while Off-Broadway theaters tend to combine high production qualities with a greater willingness to experiment. Off-Off Broadway is the fringe – drama

Ticketmaster and Ticketweb

Two of the most useful ticket-selling companies in New York are **Ticketmaster** (☏212/307-4100 or 1-800/755-4000 outside NY, ⊛www.ticketmaster.com), which sells tickets to higher-profile concerts and cultural events, and **Ticketweb** (⊛www.ticketweb.com), which mostly deals in smaller to mid-sized music venues and museums. Contact information for other, more specialized ticket agencies is listed, where appropriate, in the text opposite.

on a shoestring, perhaps with sensitive or uncommercial subjects. As for **location**, most Broadway theaters are just east or west of Broadway, between 40th and 52nd streets; the rest are sprinkled throughout Manhattan, with a concentration in the East and West villages, Union Square, Chelsea, and the 40s and 50s west of the Theater District. Specific Broadway **listings** appear in the free, widely available *Official Broadway Theater Guide*; for other productions, check out *Time Out New York* or *The Village Voice*.

On Broadway, **ticket prices** run $50–100; Off-Broadway, expect to pay $25–50; Off-Off will run you around $15. The prices of Broadway and Off-Broadway shows can be cut considerably if you can wait in line on the day of the performance at the red-and-white **TKTS** booth in Times Square (Mon–Sat 3–8pm, Sun 11am–7pm, also Wed & Sat 10am–2pm for 2pm matinees). The booth has tickets for many Broadway and Off-Broadway shows, at 25- to 50-percent off (plus a $3 per ticket service charge), payable in **cash or traveler's checks only**. Keep in mind that you may have to wait in line for a couple of hours, and that the show you want to see may be sold out by the time you get to the front of the line.

If you're prepared to pay **full price**, you can go directly to the theater box office, or use **Tele-charge** (☎212/239-6200 or 1-800/432-7250 outside NY, ⓦwww.telecharge.com) or **Ticketmaster**. For these ticket agencies, you will need a credit card and should expect to pay a $3–9 surcharge per ticket. Make sure to ask the operator to explain where your seats will be – if you are unhappy with the seating arrangements, now's the only time to say something. For Off-Broadway shows, **Tickets Central** (☎212/279-4200, ⓦwww.ticketscentral.com) sells tickets to many of these from noon to 8pm daily. For Off-Off Broadway productions, check out **SmartTix** (☎212/868-4444, ⓦwww.smarttix.com) or **TheaterMania** (ⓦwww.theatermania.com, ☎212/352-0255).

Classical music, opera, and dance

New Yorkers take **classical music** seriously. Long queues form for anything popular, many concerts sell out, and on summer evenings a quarter of a million people may turn up in Central Park for free performances by the **New York Philharmonic**. Besides **Lincoln Center** (see box, p.122), the most important venue is **Carnegie Hall**, 154 W 57th St, at Seventh Ave (☎212/247-7800, ⓦwww.carnegiehall .org), where the greatest names from all schools of music have performed. The acoustics are superb, and a renovation has amended years of structural neglect, restoring the place to its former glory.

The 120-year-old **Metropolitan Opera**, in Lincoln Center, is New York City's premier venue for opera. The soaring theatre has pitch-perfect acoustics and regularly draws big crowds who come to hear sopranos, baritones, and tenors from around the world sing some of the greatest operatic works ever to have been scored. Contact Met Ticket Service at ☎212/362-6000 for ticket information; the nosebleed seats are surprisingly reasonable. The **New York State Theater**, also in Lincoln Center, hosts performances, too; they typically perform famous works with a modern interpretation, and their performance of *The Nutcracker* is renowned. Tickets are often half of what they are at the Met; see the box on p.122 for contact information.

When it comes to **dance**, Lincoln Center once again serves as a showcase, though a number of other venues regularly host events. The **Brooklyn Academy of Music** (or **BAM**), at 30 Lafayette St in Brooklyn, between Ashland Place and St Felix Street (☎718/636-4100, ⓦwww.bam.org), is America's oldest performing arts academy and one of the most daring producers in New York – definitely worth crossing the river for. Meanwhile, back in Manhattan, six dance troupes are in residence at the

Lincoln Center for the Performing Arts

Lincoln Center, located on Broadway between W 62nd and W 66th streets (☎212/875-5456, ⓦwww.lincolncenter.org), is New York's powerhouse of performing art. Each major venue is in active use through the year, and there are some twenty venues in all. Listed below are four of the most renowned; all are located in Lincoln Center Plaza.

Alice Tully Hall ☎212/875-5050. This smaller venue is used by chamber orchestras, string quartets, and instrumentalists. Tickets run $20–115, and are available from Centercharge (☎212/721-6500).

Avery Fisher Hall ☎212/875-5656. The permanent base of the New York Philharmonic is also a temporary home for visiting orchestras and soloists. Ticket prices are similar to those at Alice Tully Hall, and are available online at ⓦwww.newyorkphilharmonic.org, or in person at the box office (Mon–Sat 10am–6pm, Sun noon–6pm).

Metropolitan Opera House ☎212/362-6000, ⓦwww.metopera.org. Holds the Metropolitan Opera Company from Sept to April, as well as the American Ballet Theater from May to June. Tickets are outrageously expensive and difficult to get, though 175 standing-room tickets ($12–16) go on sale every Saturday morning at 10am (the line has been known to form at dawn).

New York State Theater ☎212/870-5570. During six months of the year, this theater is home to the New York City Ballet, considered by many to be the greatest dance company in existence. This accessible venue is also where the New York City Opera plays David to the Met's Goliath. Seats go for less than half the Met's prices, and standing-room tickets are available if a performance sells out. Tickets must be purchased through the company's website (ⓦwww.nycballet.com), or through Ticketmaster.

City Center, 131 W 55th St, between Sixth and Seventh avenues (☎212/581-1212, ⓦwww.citycenter.org), including America's two undisputed choreographic giants, the Merce Cunningham Dance Company and the Paul Taylor Dance Company. In spring, City Center also hosts the **American Ballet Theater**. For small and mid-sized companies, the most important space in Manhattan is the **Joyce Theater**, 175 8th Ave, at 19th St (☎212/242-0800, ⓦwww.joyce.org). The Joyce hosts companies from around the world, and also has a small Downtown satellite – Joyce SoHo – at 155 Mercer St, between Houston and Prince (☎212/431-9233).

Rock and pop venues

Arlene's Grocery 95 Stanton St, between Ludlow and Orchard ☎212/358-1633, ⓦwww.arlenegrocery.com. This intimate, erstwhile bodega hosts free gigs by local indie talent during the week. Monday is "Punk/Heavy Metal Karaoke" night, where you can wail along (with a live band, no less) to your favorite Led Zeppelin songs.

The Bowery Ballroom 6 Delancey St, at Bowery ☎212/533-2111, ⓦwww.boweryballroom.com. A minimum of attitude, great sound, and even better sightlines make this a local favorite to see well-known indie-rock bands. Shows $12–25. Pay in cash at the *Mercury Lounge* box office (see below), at the door, or by credit card through Ticketweb.

Irving Plaza 17 Irving Place, between E 15th and E 16th sts ☎212/777-6800, ⓦwww.irvingplaza.com. Once home to Off-Broadway musicals, this venue now hosts an impressive array of rock, electronic music, and techno acts – a good place to see popular bands in a manageable setting. $15–30.

The Mercury Lounge 217 E Houston St, between Ludlow and Essex ☎212/260-4700, ⓦwww.mercuryloungenyc.com. The dark, medium-sized, innocuous space showcases a mix of local, national, and international pop and rock acts. It's owned by the same crew as *Bowery Ballroom*, which usually gets the better-known bands. Purchase tickets (around $8–15) in cash at the box office, at the door, or via Ticketweb.

Northsix 66 N 6th St, Williamsburg ☎718/599-5103, ⓦwww.northsix.com. In the heart of hipster Williamsburg, this unassuming Brooklyn rock club has become one of the number one places to play – outside of Manhattan – for touring indie acts.

Eclectic venues

Groove 125 MacDougal St, at W 3rd St
☎ 212/254-9393, ⊛ www.clubgroove.com. This hopping Downtown joint features rhythm & blues and soul music; it's one of the best bargains around. Happy hour from 6–9pm. Music starts at 9.30pm. No cover.

Joe's Pub at the Public Theater, 425 Lafayette St, between Astor Place and E 4th St ☎ 212/539-8770, ⊛ www.publictheater.org. The word "pub" is a misnomer for this swanky nightspot, which features a vast array of musical, cabaret, and dramatic performances. Star spottings abound. Shows nightly at 7 or 7.30pm, 9.30pm, and 11pm. Covers range from $7 to $50 depending on the performer.

Knitting Factory 74 Leonard St, between Church and Broadway ☎ 212/219-3006, ⊛ www.knittingfactory.com. At this intimate Downtown space, you can hear all kinds of aural experimentation, from art-rock and avant-garde jazz to electronica and indie-rock. Highly recommended. Cover prices vary wildly, so call ahead.

S.O.B.'s 204 Varick St, at W Houston ☎ 212/243-4940. Short for "Sounds of Brazil," this lively club/restaurant, with regular Caribbean, salsa, and world music acts, puts on two performances a night. Admission is $10–20 for standing room with a $10–15 minimum cover at tables. No cover, however for those with dinner reservations. Be sure to check out Samba Saturday, the venue's hottest night.

Tonic 107 Norfolk St, between Rivington and Delancey ☎ 212/358-7503, ⊛ www.tonicnyc.com. This hip Lower East Side home to "avant-garde, creative & experimental music" flourishes on two levels, with no cover charge to the lower lounge. Occasional movies and Klezmer-accompanied brunch on Sundays. Cover $8–12.

Jazz venues

Arthur's Tavern 57 Grove St, between Bleecker and 7th Ave ☎ 212/675-6879, ⊛ www.arthurstavernnyc.com. This low-key 50-year-old club is housed in a landmark building and features the Grove Street Stompers, who've been playing every Monday for the past 40 years. Jazz 7–9.30pm, blues and funk 10pm–3.30am. No cover; one-drink minimum.

Birdland 315 W 44th St, between 8th and 9th aves ☎ 212/581-3080, ⊛ www.birdlandjazz.com. Celebrated alto saxophonist Charlie "Bird" Parker has served as the inspiration for this important jazz venue for 50 years. Sets are at 9pm & 11pm nightly. Cover $20–40, with a $10 food and drink minimum.

Lenox Lounge 288 Lenox Ave, at 125th St ☎ 212/427-0253, ⊛ www.lenoxlounge.com. Enter-

taining Harlem since the 1930s, this historic jazz lounge has an over-the-top Art Deco interior (check out the Zebra Room). Three sets nightly at 9pm, 10.45pm & 12.30am. Cover $15, with a one-drink minimum.

Smoke 2751 Broadway, at 106th St ☎ 212/864-6662, ⊛ www.smokejazz.com. This Upper West Side joint is a real neighborhood treat. Sets start at 9pm, 11pm & 12.30am; there's a retro happy hour with $4 cocktails and $2 beers, Mon–Sat 5–8pm. Cover $16–25 Fri & Sat.

Village Vanguard 178 7th Ave S, between W 11th and Perry sts ☎ 212/255-4037, ⊛ www .villagevanguard.com. This jazz landmark still lays on a regular diet of big names. Cover is $15–20, with a $10 drink minimum. Cash only.

Zinc Bar 90 W Houston, at La Guardia Place ☎ 212/477-8337, ⊛ www.zincbar.com. New talent, as well as established greats such as Max Roach and Grant Green, perform at this great jazz venue with strong drinks and loyal regulars. The Ron Affit Trio plays four sets on Mondays, and throughout the week there's a mélange of Brazilian and African jazz. Cover is $5 with a one- or two-drink minimum.

Larger music venues

Beacon Theater 2124 Broadway, at W 74th St ☎ 212/496-7070. This beautiful restored theater caters to a more mature rock crowd, hosting everything from Tori Amos to Radiohead. Tickets are $25–100, and are sold through Ticketmaster.

Madison Square Garden W 31st–33rd sts, between 7th and 8th aves ☎ 212/465-6741, ⊛ www.madisonsquaregarden.com. New York's principal large stage plays host to big rock acts. However, it's not the most atmospheric place to see a band, with seating for yourself and 20,000 of your closest friends. Tickets are sold through Ticketmaster.

Radio City Music Hall 1260 6th Ave, at 50th St ☎ 212/247-4777, ⊛ www.radiocity.com. Although not as prestigious a venue as it once was, the building is a star in its own right. Here, you can see everyone from rock stars to the famous high-kicking Rockettes. Tickets are sold at the box office or through Ticketmaster.

Roseland Ballroom 239 W 52nd St, between Broadway and 8th Ave ☎ 212/247-0200, ⊛ www. roselandballroom.com. This venue has retained the grand ballroom feel of its heyday and is a good place to catch big names before they hit the arena/stadium circuit. The box office only sells tickets the day of the show, otherwise tickets can be purchased through Ticketmaster.

Clubs and discos

Avalon 37 W 20th St, at 6th Ave ☎212/807-7780. Formerly the infamously wild *Limelight*, this is one of the most dramatic party spaces in New York, housed in a vast church designed by Trinity Church–builder Richard Upjohn. Cover $25.

Cielo 18 Little W 12th St, between 9th Ave and Washington St ☎212/645-5700. Plan for a night of glam-meets-underground here, where the main attractions are the sunken dance floor and audio system, which pumps house, global, and nu jazz beats. Wednesdays are popular nights.

Frying Pan Pier 63, Chelsea Piers, at 23rd St ☎212/989-6363. One of the coolest club venues in the city, housed in an old lightship. With great views, consistently rockin' parties, and a relaxed door policy. $12.

Pyramid Club 101 Ave A, between 6th and 7th sts ☎212/228-4888. This small, colorful club has been an East Village standby for years. Wednesdays feature an open-mike music competition, and Thursdays are New Wave – but it's the insanely popular 1984 Dance Party on Fridays that's not to be missed. $8 on Friday; otherwise, cover averages $5.

Film

American Museum of the Moving Image 35th Ave, at 36th St, Queens ☎718/784-0077, ⓦammi.org. Shows an array of avant-garde films.

Angelika Film Center 18 W Houston St, at Mercer ☎212/995-2000, ⓦwww.angelikafilmcenter.com. The latest indie offerings, as well as European art-house movies.

Anthology Film Archives 32-34 2nd Ave, at Bond ☎212/505-5181, ⓦwww.anthologyfilmarchives.org. Expect any and every kind of indie film here, from animated shorts to riveting documentaries.

Film Forum 209 W Houston St, between Varick and 6th Ave ☎212/727-8110, ⓦwww.filmforum.com. Offers the best in independent film and documentary, as well as themed revivals.

Landmark's Sunshine Cinema 143 E Houston St, between Forsyth and Eldridge sts ☎212/358-7709. This former synagogue and vaudeville theater is now one of the plushest indie art-house movie theaters in town.

Museum of Modern Art 11 W 53rd St, between Fifth and Sixth aves ☎212/708-9400, ⓦwww.

moma.org. A vast collection of well-chosen films, from Sundance selections to abstract moving images to hand-painted Super 8; entry is free with museum admission (see p.101).

Poetry slams and literary readings

Bowery Poetry Club 308 Bowery, at Bleecker St ☎212/614-0505, ⓦwww.bowerypoetry.com. Terrifically welcoming joint featuring the Urbana Poetry Slam every Thursday night at 7pm ($5). This event is dedicated to showcasing the city's most innovative voices in poetry.

NuYorican Poet's Café 236 E 3rd St, between aves B and C ☎212/505-8183, ⓦwww.nuyorican.org. The godfather of all slam venues often features stars of the poetry world who pop in unannounced. SlamOpen on Wednesdays (except the first Wed of every month) and the Friday Night Slam both cost $5 and come highly recommended.

Poetry Project at St Mark's Church, 131 E 10th St, at 2nd Ave ☎212/674-0910, ⓦwww.poetryproject.com. The late Allen Ginsberg, a *Poetry Project* protégé, said, "The poetry project burns like red hot coal in New York's snow." Make of that what you will, the twice-weekly reading series (Mon and Wed at 8pm) features some truly, ahem, hot stuff. Closed July & Aug.

Comedy clubs

Caroline's 1626 Broadway, between W 49th and 50th sts ☎212/757-4100, ⓦwww.carolines.com. Some of the best acts in town (and Hollywood) appear at this glitzy spot. $12–22 cover, with a two-drink minimum; more expensive on weekends.

Chicago City Limits 1105 1st Ave, at 61st St ☎212/888-5233, ⓦwww.chicagocitylimits.com. New York's oldest improv theater puts on one show nightly and attracts decent national talent. Closed Tues. Admission is $20, $8 on Sun.

Comic Strip Live 1568 2nd Ave, between E 81st and E 82nd sts ☎212/861-9386, ⓦwww.comicstriplive.com. This famed showcase draws stand-up comics going for the big time. Three shows Fri & Sat. Cover $12–17, with $12 drink minimum.

Gay New York

There are few places in America where **gay culture** thrives as it does in New York. **Chelsea** (centered on Eighth Ave between 14th and 23rd streets) and the **East Village** have replaced the **West Village** as the hubs of gay New York, although a strong presence still lingers around Christopher Street. The other haven is Brooklyn's **Park Slope**, though perhaps more for women than for men. Up-to-the-minute news can be found in *HomoXtra* (*HX*) or *Blade*, free, provocative weekly listings magazines.

Resources

Bluestockings 172 Allen St, between Stanton and Rivington ☎212/777-6028. Collectively run feminist bookstore on the Lower East Side. Daily 1–10pm.

Creative Visions 548 Hudson St, between Perry and Charles ☎212/645-7573 or 1-800/997-9899, ⓦwww.creativevisions.citysearch.com. Well-stocked gay bookstore.

Gay Men's Health Crisis (GMHC) 119 W 24th St, between 6th and 7th aves ☎212/807-6655 or 1-800/AIDS-NYC, ⓦwww.gmhc.org. Despite the name, this organization – the oldest and largest not-for-profit AIDS organization in the world – provides information and referrals to everyone, no matter their sex or sexual orientation.

Gayellow Pages ⓦwww.gayellowpages.com. Available for $12 from the bookstores listed above and below, this is a good all-in-one resource; New York is in the East & South edition.

The Lesbian, Gay, Bisexual & Transgender Community Center 208 W 13th St, at 7th Ave ☎212/620-7310, ⓦwww.gaycenter.org. The LGBT Community Center, which houses countless organizations (including ACT UP, the Center for Mental Health and Social Services, and even the Metro Gay Wrestling Alliance), also sponsors workshops, dances, movie nights, guest speakers, youth services, programs for parents and kids, an archive and library, the annual Center Garden Party, and lots more.

The Oscar Wilde Memorial Bookshop 15 Christopher St, between 6th and 7th aves ☎212/255-8097, ⓦwww.oscarwildebooks.com. The first gay bookstore in the US. Unbeatable.

Bars and clubs

Barracuda 275 W 22nd St, between 8th and 9th aves ☎212/645-8613. A favorite spot in New York's gay scene, though as un-sceney as you'll find in Chelsea. Check out the two-for-one happy hour 4–9pm during the week, crazy drag shows, and the sweet hideaway lounge out back.

Duplex 61 Christopher St, at 7th Ave ☎212/255-5438. This Village cabaret is popular with a gay crowd but entertaining for all, and features occasional bitchy barb routines from Joan Rivers, among others. Two-drink minimum. Cover $5–15.

Ginger's 363 5th Ave, between 5th and 6th sts, Park Slope, Brooklyn ☎718/788-0924. A dark and moody addition to Park Slope's sapphic scene, with a great happy hour from 5 to 8pm.

Henrietta Hudson 438 Hudson St, at Morton ☎212/924-3347. This lesbian hangout serves food and gets fairly brimming at night. The lounge, pool, and dancing areas are all separate, and guys are welcome, too.

Rubyfruit Bar & Grill 531 Hudson St, between Charles and W 10th ☎212/929-3343. A cozy, friendly place for grown-up dykes, *Rubyfruit* is all about couches, cheap drinks, and good company.

Stonewall 53 Christopher St, between Waverly Place and 7th Ave ☎212/463-0950. The site of the seminal 1969 riot is mostly refurbished and flies the pride flag like they own it – which, one supposes, they do.

Shopping

When it comes to consumerism, New York leaves all other cities behind. You can **shop** for every possible taste, preference, creed, or quirk, in any combination (and often at any time of day or night). Shopping can be extraordinarily cheap, like in the markets of the **East and West villages**, but move further uptown and it can also be phenomenally expensive. **Midtown Manhattan** is mainstream territory, with the department stores, big-name clothes designers, and branches of the larger chains. Downtown plays host to a wide variety of more offbeat stores – **SoHo** is perhaps the most popular shopping neighborhood in these parts, and generally the most expensive, although with some affordable alternatives for the young and trendy. The **Upper East Side** is uncompromisingly upmarket, while the funkier **Upper West Side** has an array of off-the-wall stores to compare with anything SoHo or the Village can offer.

Department stores

Barney's 660 Madison Ave, at 61st St ⓣ212/826-8900, ⓦwww.barneys.com. The hippest and most fashion-forward of the big NYC department stores. Check the website for dates of its famous semi-annual warehouse sales, where couture bargains (and catfights) abound.

Bergdorf Goodman 754 5th Ave, at 58th St ⓣ212/753-7300, ⓦwww.bergdorfgoodman.com. Housed in what used to be a Vanderbilt mansion, this venerable department store caters to the city's wealthiest clientele. Even if you can't afford to shop, it's still fun to browse and dream.

Bloomingdale's 1000 3rd Ave, between 59th and 60th sts ⓣ212/705-2000, ⓦwww.bloomingdales.com. Perhaps Manhattan's most beloved department store, Bloomingdale's is packed with designer clothiers, perfume concessions, and the like.

Henri Bendel 712 5th Ave, at 55th St ⓣ212/247-1100, ⓦwww.henribendel.com. One of the best stores in town for cosmetics and designer labels. There's a superb salon, and its public powder room is worth a peek.

Macy's 151 W 34th St, at Broadway ⓣ212/695-4400, ⓦwww.macys.com. The world's largest department store embraces two buildings, two million square feet of floor space, and ten floors; check out the excellent Cellar housewares department downstairs.

Saks Fifth Avenue 611 5th Ave, at W 50th St ⓣ212/753-4000, ⓦwww.saks5thavenue.com. Saks remains virtually synonymous with style and quality; it carries all the big designers.

Bookstores

Asian American Writers' Workshop suite 10A, 16 W 32nd St, at 5th Ave ⓣ212/494-0061, ⓦwww.aaww.org. In addition to its list of classes, speakers, and readings, the adjacent bookstore carries the nation's largest selection of literary works by Asian-American authors, both established and on-the-rise.

Barnes & Noble ⓦwww.bn.com. The main location is at 105 5th Ave, at 18th St (ⓣ212/807-0099), with twelve others scattered around the city. These megasized bookstores offer generous selections, late hours, comfortable chairs, and coffee bars.

Biography Bookshop 400 Bleecker St, at W 11th St ⓣ212/807-8655. The city's most comprehensive collection of biographies and autobiographies.

Complete Traveler 199 Madison Ave, at W 35th St ⓣ212/685-9007. Manhattan's premier travel bookshop, well stocked with both secondhand and new titles.

Drama Book Shop 250 W 40th St, between 7th and 8th aves ⓣ1-800/322-0595. The best theater and film bookstore around, with more than 50,000 titles and a very knowledgeable staff.

Housing Works Used Books Café 126 Crosby St, between Houston and Prince ⓣ212/334-3324. Very cheap books in a spacious and comfy environment. Proceeds benefit AIDS charities.

Partners & Crime 44 Greenwich Ave, at Charles ⓣ212/243-0440, ⓦwww.crimepays.com. Superb, informed shop with 4000 mystery titles, with a generous selection of hardboiled and British titles. Author signings, a lending library, authoritative staff recommendations, and radio play re-enactments the first Sat of every month ($5) make it a find for devout mystery fans.

St Mark's Bookshop 31 3rd Ave, between 8th and 9th sts ⓣ212/260-7853. Wonderfully eclectic selection of new titles from mainstream to alternative. Open late.

Strand Bookstore 828 Broadway, at 12th St ⓣ212/473-1452, ⓦwww.strandbooks.com. With about eight miles of books and a stock of more than 2.5 million, this is the largest book operation in the city. Recent review copies and new books show up at half price; older books are from 50¢ up.

Universal News & Café 484 Broadway, between Broome and Grand ⓣ212/965-9042; also 2873 Broadway, at 72nd St ⓣ212/875-8824; and 105 W 42nd St, between 6th Ave and Broadway ⓣ212/398-0558. By far the city's best selection of magazines and periodicals, including plenty of foreign publications.

Record stores

Breakbeat Science 181 Orchard St, between Houston and Stanton ⓣ212/995-2592. The first drum'n'bass-only store to open in the US is still going strong. Closed Fri and Sat.

Etherea 66 Ave A, between 4th and 5th sts ⓣ212/358-1126. Specializing in indie rock and electronica, both domestic and import, CD and vinyl, this is one of the best shops in the city. Good used selection.

Generation Records 210 Thompson St, between Bleecker and W 3rd sts ⓣ212/254-1100. The focus here is on hardcore, metal, and punk, with some indie thrown in. New CDs and vinyl are upstairs, while the used records are downstairs.

Kim's 6 St Mark's Place, between 2nd and 3rd aves ⓣ212/598-9985; also 144 Bleecker, at La Guardia Place ⓣ212/260-1010; 85 Ave A, between 5th and 6th sts ⓣ212/529-3410; 2906 Broadway, at 114th St ⓣ212/864-5321. Extensive selection of new and used indie obscurities on CD and vinyl,

Sports in New York

Seeing either of New York's two **baseball** teams involves a trip across the East River to the outer boroughs. The **Yankees** play in the Bronx, at **Yankee Stadium**, 161st St and River Ave (☏718/293-6000, ⓦwww.yankees.com). Get there on the #B, #D, or #4 subway lines direct to the 161st Street station. The **Mets** are based in Queens, at **Shea Stadium**, 123-01 Roosevelt Ave, at 126th St (☏718/507-METS, ⓦwww.mets.com). Take the #7 train to the Willets Point/Shea Stadium station. Tickets are priced between $8 and $115, depending on the team (Yankee tickets are generally more expensive) and where you sit. For an unbelievably raucous New York experience, show up on game day for bleacher seats at Yankee Stadium: the hooligan regulars and the bouncers who keep an eye on them are often more fun to watch than the game.

New York's football teams – the **Jets** and the **Giants** – play at the **New Jersey Meadowlands Sports Complex**, East Rutherford, New Jersey (☏201/935-3900, ⓦwww.meadowlands.com). Buses from the Port Authority Bus Terminal, 42nd Street, at 8th Ave (☏212/564-8484, ⓦwww.meadowlands.com) serve the stadium. Call ahead before you travel out there, though; tickets are hard to come by, and range from $100 to $550.

Basketball's two New York pro teams are the NBA's **Knicks** (ⓦwww.nba.com/knicks) and the WNBA's **Liberty** (ⓦwww.wnba.com/liberty). Both play at **Madison Square Garden**, W 33rd St, at 7th Ave (☏212/465-6741, ⓦwww.thegarden.com), which is served by the #1, #2, #3, #A, #C, and #E trains. Tickets for the Knicks are very expensive, and, due to impossibly high demand, available in only limited numbers, if at all. The women's games are fairly exciting and cheaper at $10–65. Another area team, the **New Jersey Nets**, plays in an arena at the Meadowlands Complex; tickets range from $35 to $95, and are relatively easy to procure. New York's hockey team, the **Rangers** (ⓦwww.newyorkrangers.com), also plays at Madison Square Garden; tickets range from $30 to $155.

some real cheap. Esoteric videos upstairs. Be warned: a serious attitude problem comes with the job description here.

Other Music 15 E 4th St, between Broadway and Lafayette ☏212/477-8150. This excellent small shop has perhaps the most engaging and curious indie-rock and avant-garde collection in the city. Records here are divided into categories like "In," "Out," and "Then." Definitely worth a visit. Great used selection.

Vinyl Mania 60 Carmine St, between Bedford St and 7th Ave ☏212/924-7223. First port of call for DJs seeking the newest, rarest releases and imports.

Food

Chelsea Market 75 9th Ave, between 15th and 16th sts. A wonderful array of food shops line this former Nabisco factory warehouse's ground floor; go for pad Thai, fresh produce, lobster rolls, panini, chewy breads, sinful brownies, kitchenware, or simply to browse.

Citarella 2135 Broadway, at 75th St ☏212/874-0383; also 1313 3rd Ave, at 75th St ☏212/874-0383; 1250 6th Ave, at 49th St ☏212/874-0383 (take-out prepared foods only); 424 6th Ave, at 9th St ☏212/874-0383; and 461 W 125th St, between Amsterdam and Morningside aves, Harlem

☏212/874-0383. Originally a neighborhood fish shop in Harlem's Sugar Hill, this gourmet store still prides itself on its fine products from the sea, and everything else under the sun.

Murray's Cheese Shop 254 Bleecker St, between 6th and 7th aves ☏212/243-3289 or 1-888/692-4339. The city's number-one stop for cheese lovers; go to learn about the cheese-making process, sample the wares, or pick up a pungent sandwich.

Russ & Daughters 179 E Houston St, between Allen and Orchard ☏212/475-4880. This small family-run shop has been serving fine Jewish edibles such as smoked whitefish, chopped liver, and herring soaked in schmaltz since 1914. A must-visit.

Union Square Green Market in Union Square, at 16th St. A bit of country in the city, this delightful open-air market (open Mon, Wed, Fri & Sat) offers local seasonal produce and natural goods sold by regional farmers and purveyors. You'll find hand-carded wools, wildflowers, and infused honeys, too.

Zabar's 2245 Broadway, at 80th St ☏212/787-2000. Beloved family store offers a quintessential taste of New York: bagels, lox, all manner of schmears, not to mention a dizzying selection of gourmet goods at reasonable prices. Fine kitchenware is sold upstairs.

The Mid-Atlantic

AL - ALABAMA	IN - INDIANA	MN - MINNESOTA	RI - RHODE ISLAND
AR - ARKANSAS	LA - LOUISIANA	MS - MISSISSIPPI	SC - SOUTH CAROLINA
CT - CONNECTICUT	MA - MASSACHUSETTS	NC - NORTH CAROLINA	VA - VIRGINIA
DE - DELAWARE	MD - MARYLAND	NH - NEW HAMPSHIRE	VT - VERMONT
FL - FLORIDA	ME - MAINE	NJ - NEW JERSEY	WI - WISCONSIN
IL - ILLINOIS	MI - MICHIGAN	PA - PENNSYLVANIA	WV - WEST VIRGINIA

CHAPTER 2 # Highlights

* **The Adirondacks, NY**
A vast and rugged alpine
wilderness offering
superb hiking, skiing,
fishing, and mountain-
climbing opportunities.
See p.144

* **Ithaca, NY** This lovely
Finger Lakes' town has a
solar-powered library, its
own legal tender, more
restaurants per capita than
New York City, waterfalls,
gorges, local vineyards
and an Ivy-League
university. **See p.148**

* **Niagara Falls, NY** Take
the memorable *Maid of
the Mist* boat trip, or visit
the Cave of the Winds
and stand close enough
to feel the spray from
these majestic falls.
See p.154

* **History in Philadelphia,
PA** See the Liberty Bell
and trace the steps of
Benjamin Franklin in the
city of brotherly love,
where the Declaration
of Independence was
signed. **See p.158**

* **Art and architecture,
Pittsburgh, PA** The
Warhol Museum,
Cathedral of Learning,
and two outlying Frank
Lloyd Wright houses lend
a surprising cultural flair
to the so-called Steel
City. **See p.177**

* **Cape May, NJ** The
cultured end of the Jersey
shore is exemplified by
the Victorian architecture,
quaint B&Bs, and swish
restaurants of this pleasant
resort town. **See p.194**

△ Princeton University

The Mid-Atlantic

The three **MID-ATLANTIC** states – New York, Pennsylvania, and New Jersey – stand at the heart of the most populated and industrialized corner of the US. Although dominated in the popular imagination by the gray smokestacks of New Jersey and steel factories of Pennsylvania,, these states actually encompass beaches, mountains, islands, lakes, forests, rolling green countryside, and many worthwhile small cities and towns.

European settlement here was characterized by considerable shifts and turns: the **Dutch**, who arrived in the 1620s, were methodically squeezed out by the **English**, who in turn fought off the **French** challenge to secure control of the region by the mid-eighteenth century. The Native American population, including the **Iroquois Confederacy** and Lenni Lenape Indians, had sided with the French against the English, and were soon confined to reservations or pushed north into Canada. At first, the economy depended on the fur trade, though by the 1730s English **Quakers**, along with **Amish** and **Mennonites** from Germany, plus a few Presbyterian **Irish**, had made farming a significant force, their holdings extending to the western limits of Pennsylvania and New York.

All three states were important during the **Revolution**: over half the battles were fought here, including major American victories at **Trenton** and **Princeton**, in New Jersey. Upstate New York was geographically crucial, as the British forces knew that control of the Hudson River would effectively divide New England from the other colonies; and the long winter spent by the rag-tag Continental Army at **Valley Forge** outside Philadelphia turned it into a well-organized force.

After the Revolution, industry became the region's prime economic force, with **mill towns** springing up along the numerous rivers. By the mid-1850s the large **coalfields** of northeast Pennsylvania were powering the smoky steel mills of Pittsburgh, and the discovery of high-grade **crude oil** in 1859 marked the beginning of the automobile age. Though still significant, especially in the regions near New York City, heavy industry has now largely been replaced by tourism as the economic engine.

Although many travelers to the East Coast may not consider venturing much further than New York City itself, the region is much more than just an overspill of the Big Apple. Each region has a distinct identity. Just thirty minutes outside of Manhattan, **Long Island** offers both the crashing surf of the Atlantic Ocean and the cool calm of the Long Island Sound. **Upstate New York** is for outdoors enthusiasts: the wooded **Catskill Mountains** line the Hudson River, the imposing **Adirondack Mountains** spread over a quarter of the state, and the **Finger Lakes** region offers a cultured and pastoral break from the industrial and post-industrial Erie Canal cities along I-90. In the northwest corner of the state, on the Canadian border, are the awesome **Niagara Falls** and artsy post-industrial **Buffalo**. **Pennsylvania** is best known for the fertile **Pennsylvania Dutch** country and the two great cities of **Philadelphia** and **Pittsburgh**. **New Jersey**, often pictured as one big industrial carbuncle, offers shameless tourist pleasures along the shore – from the boardwalk and casinos of **Atlantic City** to the small-town charm of **Cape May**.

The entire region is well covered by **public transportation**, with New York's JFK and New Jersey's Newark airports acting as major international gateways, New York's LaGuardia Airport serving domestic flights and busy air terminals at both Philadelphia and Pittsburgh. Amtrak **trains** run routes up and down the Northeast Corridor through New York, New Jersey, and Pennsylvania, while the New Jersey Transit rail and bus network serves all of New Jersey, extending from Atlantic City west to Philadelphia and north to Manhattan. Metro-North and the Long Island Railroad connect New York City to Long Island and points north. Greyhound **buses** follow the major interstates, with a few subsidiary lines running to more out-of-the-way places.

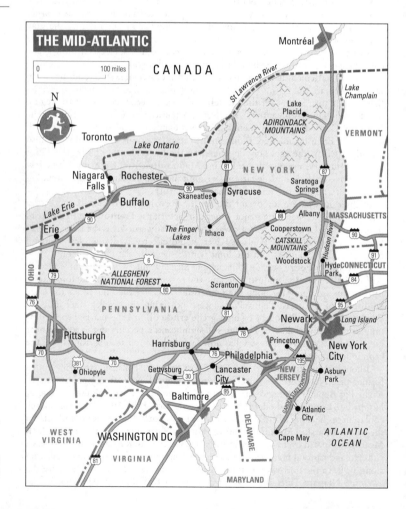

New York State

However much exists to attract visitors, the vast state of **NEW YORK** stands inevitably in the shadow of America's most celebrated city. The words "New York" bring to mind soaring skyscrapers and congested streets, not the 50,000 square miles of rolling dairy farmland, Colonial villages, workaday towns, lakes, waterfalls, and towering mountains that fan out north and west from New York City and constitute **upstate New York**. Just an hour's drive north of Manhattan, the valley of the **Hudson River**, with the moody **Catskill Mountains** rising stealthily from the west bank, offers a respite from the intensity of the city. Much wilder and more rugged are the peaks of the vast **Adirondack Mountains** further north, which hold some of eastern America's most enticing scenery. To the west, the slender **Finger Lakes** and endless miles of dairy farms and vineyards occupy the central portion of the state. Of the larger cities, only **Buffalo** and **Rochester** hold much of interest, but some of the smaller towns, like Ivy-League **Ithaca**, can be quite captivating, while the venerable spa town of **Saratoga Springs** attracts thousands of gamblers during the August horse-racing season.

In the seventeenth and eighteenth centuries, as nation-molding political and military battles were taking place, semi-feudal **Dutch landowning dynasties** such as the Van Rensselaers held sway upstate. Their control over tens of thousands of tenant farmers was barely affected by the transfer of colonial power from Holland to Britain, or even by American independence. Only with the completion of the **Erie Canal** in 1825, linking New York City with the Great Lakes, did the interior start to open up; improved opportunities for trade enabled canal-side cities like **Syracuse**, Rochester, and especially Buffalo to undergo massive expansion. Nonetheless, the region's fortunes have never fully escaped domination by the Wall Street capitalists, despite some efforts by the government in Albany to redress the imbalance.

Getting around New York State

From New York City, the **Long Island Railroad** (leaving from Penn Station) and **Metro North** (leaving from Grand Central Station) shuttle commuters to and from the suburbs of Long Island and Westchester, Putnam, and Dutchess counties, respectively. For journeys further north, Amtrak operates a **train** service along a beautiful route through the Hudson Valley to the state capital, Albany; from there, trains continue north to Montréal, via the Adirondacks, and west along the Erie Canal to Buffalo and Niagara Falls. Greyhound and Adirondack Trailways **buses** also run to all the major towns.

Car rental in and around New York City is expensive; lower rates can be found by taking public transportation away from the metropolitan area. Be aware as well that the New York State Thruway (I-87) is a toll road, around $18 end-to-end. **Cycling** is best enjoyed as a means of exploring areas such as the Finger Lakes or Catskills.

Long Island

Just east of New York City, **Long Island** unfurls for 125 miles of lush farmland and broad sandy beaches, and is most often explored as an excursion of a few days from the metropolis. Its western end abuts the urban boroughs of Brooklyn and Queens, and for a good while continues as a suburban sprawl of strip malls and fast-food outlets; but further east, the settlements begin to thin out and the countryside can get surprisingly remote. The **north** and **south shores** differ greatly – the former more immediately beautiful, its cliffs topped with luxurious mansions and estates, while the South Shore is fringed by almost continuous sand, interspersed with vacation spots such as **Jones Beach** and **Fire Island**. At its far end, Long Island splits in two, the **North Fork** retaining a marked rural aspect while the **South Fork**, much of which is known as **the Hamptons**, sets itself apart as an enclave of New York's richest and most famous.

The quickest way to reach Long Island is via the reliable if rather worn **Long Island Railroad** from Penn Station (T 718/217-LIRR in NYC, T 718/558-3022 from elsewhere, W www.mta.nyc.ny.us/lirr), which runs ten routes to over a hundred destinations on Long Island. You can also arrive via **ferry** from New England: Cross Sound Ferry makes the trip from New London, CT to Orient Point, Long Island (see p.253; T 860/443-5281 in New England, T 631/323-2525 on Long Island, W www.longislandferry.com). Numerous **bus services** (operated by the usual major companies, as well as Hampton Jitney; T 1-800/936-0440, W www.hamptonjitney.com) cover most destinations. **Parking permits** for most of Long Island's beaches are issued only to local residents, so on the whole it works out to be less expensive to head to the beach on public transport. If you are **driving** to Long Island, you'll take the Brooklyn–Queens Expressway (the BQE) to I-495 East.

There's plenty of **accommodation**, listed in the text below; A Reasonable Alternative (117 Spring St, Port Jefferson, NY 11777; T 631/928-4034, W www.areasonablealternative.com) offers a good range of B&B lodging throughout Long Island.

The South Shore and Fire Island

Long Island's **South Shore** merges gently with the wild Atlantic, with shallow, creamy sand beaches and rolling dunes – two of the most popular options are **Long Beach** and **Jones Beach**, which together run along fifty miles of seashore. These get less crowded the further east you go; once you get as far as **Gilgo** or **Oak Beach**, or cross the water to **Robert Moses State Park**, on the western tip of Fire Island, you can find solitude. Long Beach has a die-hard surfer contingent, while just east, **Ocean Parkway** leads along the narrow offshore strand from Jones Beach to **Captree**, a good base for fishing expeditions organized by the Captree Boatmen's Association (T 631/669-6464, W www.captreefleet.com), before crossing back to **Bay Shore**, a dull town that serves as a **ferry terminal** for Fire Island. This way you bypass the sprawling mess of **Amityville**, famous for its 1974 "horror". The house on the hill, in which a mysterious supernatural force is said to have victimized the occupants, still stands as a private residence.

Fire Island

A slim spit of land parallel to the South Shore, **Fire Island** is in many ways a microcosm of New York City. The **season** is rigidly demarcated by Memorial and Labor days, and on the summer weekends half of Manhattan seems to be holed up in its tiny settlements. Certain parts of the island, such as **Cherry Grove** and **The Pines**, are primarily known as **gay** resorts, while **Ocean Beach** offers the liveliest straight nightlife. **Point O'Woods** is the most exclusive hangout and **Sunken Forest** (aka Sailor's Haven), so-called because it's the only part of the island that lies below sea level, attracts a mixed crowd.

Ferries dock at Ocean Beach and other harbours, where trippers pile up groceries on trolleys (cars are forbidden) and set off for their vacation pads. Ferry schedules are subject to change; Fire Island Ferries (30–45min; $7.25 one way; ☎631/665-3600, ⓦwww.fireislandferries.com) run from Bay Shore, the Sayville Ferry Service (25–45min; $6.50–12 one way; ☎631/589-0810, ⓦwww.sayville ferry.com) from Sayville, and the Davis Park Ferries (25–35min; $6 one way; ☎631/475-1665, ⓦwww.pagelinx.com/dpferry) from Patchogue.

All **accommodation** should be booked well in advance during summer, when rates can be ten times more than off-season; options include the hopping *Grove Hotel*, Bayview Walk and Holly Walk, Cherry Grove (☎631/597-6600, ⓦwww.grovehotel.com; ❸); *Cleggs Hotel*, 478 Bayberry Walk, Ocean Beach (open May–Oct only; ☎631/583-5399, ⓦwww.cleggs hotel.com; ❺), which, along with regular rooms, offers garden apartments with full kitchens and baths; and the *Fire Island Hotel & Resort*, at 25 Cayuga Walk, in nearby Ocean Bay Park (☎631/583-8000, ⓦwww.fireislandhotel .com; ❻–❽), which used to be a Coast Guard station. If you'd like to splash out on a **meal**, try nearby *Matthew's*, 935 Bay Walk (☎631/583-8016), for its terrific fish specials for around $30. At weekends, the *Ice Palace*, at the *Grove Hotel*, and *Flynn's*, at 1 Cayuga St in Ocean Beach (☎631/583-5000), are good for riotous boozing and dancing. Pick up the *Fire Island News* (ⓦwww.fireislandnews.com) or the gay and lesbian *Fire Island Q News* (ⓦwww.fireislandqnews.com) at a newsstand to find out what's happening while you're here.

The North Shore and North Fork

Along the rugged **North Shore**, Long Island drops to the sea in a series of bluffs, coves, and wooded headlands. The expressway beyond Queens leads straight onto the **Gold Coast**, where **Great Neck** was F. Scott Fitzgerald's West Egg in *The Great Gatsby*, home of Gatsby himself. Some of this real estate is so expensive that only the richest of the rich can afford to live here. The motley French Norman–style buildings at Falaise in **Sands Point**, on the sharp tip of the next peninsula,

△ Fishing on Fire Island

were once owned by the Guggenheims; they now house a self-celebratory **museum** (May–Oct Wed–Sun tours hourly noon–3pm; $6; ⊤516/571-7900, ⊛www.sandspointpreserve.org). The 209 acres of unkempt parkland also act as a nature preserve. In Old Westbury, at 71 Old Westbury Rd, **Old Westbury Gardens** is a classier attraction: a Georgian mansion with beautiful, well-tended gardens and some pleasant works of art, including a few Gainsboroughs (late April–Oct Wed–Mon 10am–5pm; $10; ⊤516/333-0048, ⊛www.oldwestburygardens.org).

Sagamore Hill, on the coast road in Oyster Bay, twelve miles north of Old Westbury, is the heavily touristed former country retreat where **Teddy Roosevelt** lived for thirty-odd years (May–Sept daily, rest of year Wed–Sun 10am–4pm; hourly tours $5; ⊤516/922-4788, ⊛www.nps.gov/sahi). Its 23 rooms are adorned everywhere with the great man's hunting trophies, sprouting horns from walls or grinning toothily up from the firesides. Within the site, near the parking lot, the **Old Orchard Museum** (same days 9am–5pm; free) recounts Teddy's political and personal life – but the real reason to come is to stroll the gorgeous grounds, open daily dawn to dusk at no charge, where green lawns drop to Oyster Bay and the sea.

Nearby **COLD SPRING HARBOR** grew up as a whaling port, and retains some of its looks. A fully equipped whaleboat and a 400-piece assembly of scrimshaw work help its **Whaling Museum** (daily 11am–5pm; $5; ⊤631/367-3418, ⊛www.cshwhalingmuseum.org) to recapture that era.

After fifty more miles of bluffs and parks, the less touristed **North Fork** – once an independent colony – boasts typical wild Atlantic coastal scenery. In **GREENPORT**, its most picturesque town, a spacious wooden boardwalk encloses a harbor pierced by the masts of visiting yachts. At one end there's the small **East End Seaport Museum and Marine Foundation** (June–Sept daily Wed–Mon 11am–5pm; weekends starting May 14 11am–5pm; ⊤631/477-2100, ⊛www.eastendseaport.org; free). Plentiful **accommodation** includes Victorian B&Bs like the ten-room *Bartlett House Inn*, 503 Front St (⊤631/477-0371, ⊛www.bartletthouseinn.com; ⑥) and you can get a decent seafood meal at the *Chowder Pot Pub*, 102 3rd St (⊤631/477-1345), opposite the ferry terminal. Regular **ferries** connect the North Fork (pedestrians $1 each way, cars $9 one-way, $13 round-trip; ⊤631/749-0139, ⊛www.northferry.com) with pleasant **Shelter Island** (⊛www.shelter-island.org) and on to the South Fork (pedestrians $1 each way, cars $10 one-way, $12 round-trip; ⊤631/749-1200, ⊛www.southferry.com).

The South Fork

The US holds few wealthier quarters than the small towns of Long Island's **South Fork**, where huge mansions lurk among the trees or stand boldly on the flats behind the dunes. Nowhere is consumption as deliberately conspicuous as in **the Hamptons** – among the oldest communities in the state, settled by restless New Englanders in the mid-1650s, but relatively isolated until the rich began to turn up in their motor cars. Nightlife venues are expensive and notoriously changeable; pick up *Dan's Papers* (⊛www.danspapers.com) or the *East Hampton Star* (⊛www.easthamptonstar.com) to find out what's happening.

Southampton

Long association with the smart set has left **SOUTHAMPTON** unashamedly upper class. Its streets are lined with galleries and clothing and jewelry stores, but the nearby beaches are superb. The **visitor center** at 76 Main St (Mon–Fri 10am–4pm, Sat & Sun 11am–4pm; ⊤631/283-0402, ⊛www.southamptonchamber.com) has lists of **B&Bs** like the charming, slightly out-of-the-way

Mainstay, 579 Hill St (℡631/283-4375, Ⓦ www.themainstay.com; ❼). You can get marvelous fresh seafood in a number of **restaurants**, notably *Barrister's*, at 36 Main St (℡631/283-6206), and the venerable brewpub-restaurant *Southampton Publick House*, at 40 Bowden Square (℡631/283-2800). Relatively casual **nightspots** like *Southampton Tavern* at 125 Tuckahoe Rd (℡631/287-2125) nestle down the road from impossibly upscale clubs, like *Jet East*, 1181 North Sea Road (℡631/283-0808), where super-rich regulars shell out megabucks to reserve Saturday-night tables.

Sag Harbor
Historic **SAG HARBOR**, in its heyday a port second only to that of New York, was designated first Port of Entry to the New Country by George Washington; the **Old Custom House** (May–June & Sept–Oct Sat & Sun 10am–5pm; July–Aug daily 10am–5pm; $5; ℡631/692-4664) dates from this era. The **Whaling Museum** on Main Street (May–Oct Mon–Sat 10am–5pm, Sun 1–5pm; Nov–Dec Sat & Sun noon–4pm; $5; ℡631/725-0770, Ⓦ www.sagharborwhalingmuseum.org) commemorates the town's brief whaling days with guns and scrimshaw. Nearby, the **First Presbyterian "Old Whalers" Church** is crenellated with jutting rows of whale-blubber spades, and beautiful memorials in **Oakland Cemetery** commemorate deceased young whalers.

The windmill where John Steinbeck once lived serves as a **visitor center** (June–Sept daily 10am–5pm, Fri & Sat until 8pm; rest of year Sat & Sun only 10am–5pm; ℡631/725-0011, Ⓦ www.sagharborchamber.com). You can get a nice **room** at the *Baron's Cove Inn*, at 31 W Water St (℡631/725-2100, Ⓦ www. baronscove.com; ❻), but at the well-heeled *American Hotel* on Main Street (℡631/725-3535, Ⓦ www.theamericanhotel.com; ❽) you can also get a splendid French meal and a good cigar from the hotel's humidor. There are several good, less expensive **restaurants** along Main Street, such as the superb sushi bar *Sen* at no. 23 (℡631/725-1774).

East Hampton and Amagansett
EAST HAMPTON is the trendiest of the Hamptons, filled with the mansions of celebrities like Renée Zellweger, Jerry Seinfeld, and Steven Spielberg – as well as obnoxiously chic shops and restaurants. A bike ride or drive round some of the spectacular homes is quite an eye-opener. **Amagansett**, a village within East Hampton, tends to be more down-to-earth than the rest of town. Note the old shingle homes along quiet leafy side streets and enjoy the lively weekend scene at the Farmer's Market on Main Street. Don't miss the partying at *Stephen Talkhouse*, 161 Main St, a terrific **bar** and music joint that draws well-known folk, jazz, and rock performers year-round (℡631/267-3117, Ⓦ www.stephentalkhouse.com).

Montauk
Blustery, wind-battered **MONTAUK**, beyond Amagansett on the farthest tip of Long Island, never quite made it as a resort; plans to develop it were shattered by the Wall Street Crash of 1929. The town isn't chic or quaint – but real people actually live here, and it provides access to the rocky wilds of **Montauk Point**, whose rare beauty figures in all the tourist brochures. A **lighthouse** – New York State's oldest, dating from 1796 – forms an almost symbolic finale to this stretch of the American coast.

Motels in the town center, such as *Sands Motel*, as you enter on Rte-27 (℡631/668-5100, Ⓦ www.montauksands.com; ❸), offer refreshingly reasonable room prices; for something fancier, try *Gurney's Inn* on Old Montauk Highway (℡631/668-2345, Ⓦ www.gurneysinn.com; ❽). The ultimate Montauk **din-**

ing experience is *The Lobster Roll*, halfway back towards Amaganasett on Rte-27 (℡631/267-3740), which serves excellent fresh seafood. Other good options include the moderately priced *Shagwong* on Main Street (℡631/668-3050) and the delicious sushi at *West Lake Clam & Chowder House* (℡631/668-6252).

The Hudson Valley and the Catskills

You only need to travel a few miles north of Manhattan before the Hudson River Valley takes on a Rhine-like charm, with prodigious historic homes, such as those of the Roosevelt, Vanderbilt, and van Cortland families, rising from its steep and thickly wooded banks. A little further on come the forests of the **Catskill Mountains**, whose brilliant fall colors rival anything to be seen in New England. Few of the cities along the Hudson, including the large but lackluster state capital of **Albany**, hold much to attract the visitor, though many of the small towns are worth checking out, such as regional historic and culinary mecca **Hyde Park**.

The lower Hudson Valley

A mere 25 miles north of central New York City, the leafy town of **TARRY-TOWN** and village of **IRVINGTON** were the original settings for Washington Irving's tales of *Rip Van Winkle* and *The Legend of Sleepy Hollow*. In 1835 the author rebuilt a farm cottage on West Sunnyside Lane (off Broadway/US-9) and renamed it **Sunnyside**: "a little old-fashioned stone mansion, all made up of gable ends, and as full of angles and corners as an old cocked hat." Tours squeeze through its cozy rooms, and are enjoyable even if you've never read a word of Irving (Apr–Nov Wed–Mon, Dec Sat & Sun 10am–5pm; $10; ℡914/591-8763).

It's also worth looking around the spikily crenellated **Lyndhurst Castle** on Broadway, as dapper a piece of nineteenth-century Gothic Revivalism as you're likely to find, with grounds to match (mid Apr–Oct Tues–Sun 10am–5pm; Nov–mid Apr Sat & Sun 10am–4pm; $4 grounds, $10 tour; ℡914/631-4481, Ⓦwww.lyndhurst.org). Also of interest here is **Kykuit** (pronounced "Kigh-cut"), the old Rockefeller Estate. The mansion is filled with modern artwork, particularly sculpture, and the collection in the gardens and grounds is just as impressive, with works by Picasso, Calder, Noguchi, Henry Moore, and many others – although the pretentious guided tour detracts somewhat from the masterpieces (mid-May to early Nov Mon–Fri 10am–3pm, Sat & Sun 10am–4pm; various tours $19–36; ℡914/631-9491, Ⓦwww.hudsonvalley.org/kykuit/index.htm).

The charming Main Streets of Irvington and Tarrytown have a range of good **food** options, from cheap, delicious *Irvington Pizza*, 106 Main St (℡914/591-7050), to upscale Italian, Spanish, and American restaurants. Irvington's brand-new **Hudson Park** makes for a scenic riverside picnic or after-dinner stroll.

About ten miles north of Tarrytown along US-9, the town of **OSSINING** holds two impressive mid-Victorian creations: one is a huge bridge carrying the **Old Croton Aqueduct**, New York City's first water supply; the other, just south of town, is **Sing Sing Prison**, which for over 150 years has been the place where New York City criminals get sent "up the river." Slightly north in **CROTON-ON-HUDSON** is **Croton Point Park**, a 508-acre peninsula that hosts major summer festivals and, occasionally, the sloop *Clearwater* (for docking and sailing times and venues consult ℡845/454-7673, Ⓦwww.clearwater.org).

The west bank and Catskill Mountains

Rising above the west bank of the Hudson River, the magnificent crests of the **Catskills**, cloaked with maple and beech that turn orange, ochre, and gold each fall, have a rich and absorbing beauty. This dislocated branch of the Appalachians is inspiring country, filled with amenities – campgrounds, hiking, fishing, and, especially, skiing. To enjoy it to the fullest, venture onto the trails; the mountains are so tightly packed that good roadside overlooks are rare.

West Point

Arguably the first place of interest on the west bank of the Hudson, almost fifty miles out of New York City, is the United States Military Academy at **WEST POINT**, which Congress established in 1802 to cultivate homegrown warfaring after realizing that the ragged troops who had won the Revolutionary War had been trained almost exclusively by European officers. Since then, West Point has produced US Army generals Grant, Lee, MacArthur, Eisenhower, Patton, and Schwarzkopf, to name but a famous few. Today, four-thousand-odd candidates on a tough four-year course fill the smart showpiece campus, which overlooks the Hudson from a wide, strategic bluff. What draws most people are the patriotic parade-ground drills, most frequent during spring and late summer/early fall; West Point's **visitor center** (daily 9am–4.45pm; ☎845/938-2638, ⓦwww.usma.edu) provides a full schedule as well as tours. The free **West Point Museum** (daily 10.30am–4.15pm) shows trophies of war, including pistols that belonged to George Washington, Napoleon Bonaparte, and Adolf Hitler and, disturbingly, the pin from the Nagasaki atomic bomb.

Woodstock

Around fifty miles further north, Hwy-28 meanders into the Catskills, looping past the lovely Ashokan Reservoir where Hwy-375 branches off to **WOOD-STOCK**. The village, carved out of the lush deciduous woodlands and cut by fast-rushing creeks, was not actually the venue of the famed **psychedelic picnic** of August 1969. That was some sixty miles southwest in Bethel, where a monument at Herd and West Shore roads marks the site on the farm owned by Max Yasgur where the first festival was held. However, Woodstock has enjoyed a bohemian reputation since the foundation in 1902 of the **Byrdcliffe Arts Colony** (which runs summer residency courses; ☎845/679-2079, ⓦwww.woodstockguild.org), and during the 1960s it was a favorite stomping ground for the likes of Dylan, Hendrix, and Van Morrison.

Woodstock still bears signs of its **hippie** past: shops sell crystals and tie-dyed T-shirts, and there's even the odd commune out in the woods, although it's also a spot where wealthy Manhattanites own second homes. Woodstock's galleries and craft shops command a regional reputation and the village is also a hub for the performing arts: the **Maverick Concert** series (late June–Aug; $20 per concert/$5 students; ☎845/679-8217, ⓦwww.maverickconcerts.org) has played host to some of the world's finest chamber musicians since 1906.

Woodstock is a great base for exploring the Catskills, and the best option for **accommodation** is the cozy *Twin Gables Guest House*, 73 Tinker St (☎845/679-9479, ⓦwww.twingableswoodstockny.com; ❹). If this is full, try the equally central *Getaway-on-the-Fall* at 5 Waterfall Way (☎845/679-2568, ⓦwww.tinkervillagewoodstock.com; ❺). Between Woodstock and Saugerties, which offers a string of chain motels ten miles northeast, are *Bed by the Stream* (☎845/246-2979, ⓦwww.bedbythestream.com; ❺), a lovely rustic B & B, and *Rip Van Winkle* **campgrounds** (May–Oct; $30 per tentsite; ☎845/246-8334), both signposted off

Rte-212. Apart from the town's favorite café, *Joshua's*, at 51 Tinker St (☎845/679-5533), the best **places to eat** are a little way out of the village: the menu at the ⚘ *New World Home Cooking Company*, towards Saugerties at 1411 Rte-212 (April–Oct; ☎845/246-0900), has Caribbean and Creole-influenced dishes for under $20, while two miles west on Rte-212 in tiny **Bearsville**, the *Bear Café* (☎845/679-5555) serves excellent French bistro cuisine.

Several daily **buses** take two and a half hours to reach Woodstock from New York City's Port Authority Bus Terminal (Adirondack Trailways; ☎1-800/858-8555, ⓦwww.trailwaysny.com). Sturdy **bikes** can be rented from Overlook Mountain Bikes, 93 Tinker St (☎845/679-2122, ⓦwww.overlookmountainbikes.com). For more **information**, visit the Chamber of Commerce booth on Rock City Road, just off the village green (☎845/679-6234, ⓦwww.woodstockchamber.com).

On through Catskill Park

Seven miles west of Woodstock, in the hamlet of **MOUNT TREMPER**, the **Emerson Place Kaleidoscope** (Sun–Thurs 10am–5pm, Fri & Sat 10am–7pm; $7) claims to be the world's largest, created by a local hippie artist in a 60ft-high converted grain silo. It plays ten-minute sound and light shows on request throughout the day and is part of the constantly expanding upscale *Emerson Place Lodge & Spa*, 146 Mt Pleasant Rd (☎845/688-2828 or 1-877/688-2828, ⓦwww.emersonplace.com; ❼). As you continue along Hwy-28, the picturesque village of **PHOENICIA**, in a hollow to the right of the road, is an ideal resting place and a great base for hiking trails in the area. You can catch the circular **Catskill Mountain Railroad** (late May–late Oct Sat, Sun & holidays 11.15am, 1.15pm & 3.15pm; $14 roundtrip; ☎845/688-7400, ⓦwww.catskillmtrailroad.com) through scenic Esopus Creek. The *Phoenicia Belle*, 73 Main St (☎845/688-7226, ⓦwww.phoeniciabelle.com; ❹), is a very reasonable lodge with optional breakfast. A few doors along is the ever-popular café *Sweet Sue's* (☎845/688-7852), while the *Phoenicia Diner* is another good option back on Hwy-28 (☎845/688-9957).

A few miles further west, Hwy-49A affords a good vista of the rambling Catskills from the parking lot of the Belleayre ski resort. The *Belleayre Lodge & Cabins*, just above Main St, Pine Hill (☎845/254-4200, ⓦwww.belleayrelodge.com; ❹), has newly renovated rooms and log cabins, while on Main St itself the large, Victorian-style *Colonial Inn* (☎845/254-5577, ⓦwww.colonialinn.com; ❷) offers some basic bargain rooms.

The return route to I-90, along Hwy-23A, includes a breathtaking view of the dramatic **gorge** between the villages of Hunter and Catskill, along with the area's premier **ski runs** on Hunter Mountain (☎518/263-4223, ⓦwww.huntermtn.com). The resort's Skyride chair lifts also operate after the snow has melted (late June–Oct Sat & Sun 10am–5pm; $8). Accommodation rates rise significantly during the ski season: *Scribner Hollow Lodge*, half a mile from the mountain on Hwy-23A (☎518/263-4211, ⓦwww.scribnerhollow.com; ❽), boasts 37 deluxe rooms, a fine-dining restaurant with great views, and a multi-pool swimming grotto. Rooms in the hamlet of Catskill, such as in the *Red Ranch Motel* at 4555 Rte-32 (Apr–Dec; ☎518/678-3380 or 1-800/962-4560, ⓦwww.redranchmotel.com; ❷), are much more basic, but more affordable.

The east bank

Interest on the east bank of the Hudson River starts in little **BEACON**, some sixty miles north of Manhattan, at the excellent **Dia:Beacon**, 3 Beekman St (mid-April to mid-Oct Thurs–Mon 11am–6pm; mid-Oct to mid-April Fri–Mon 11am–4pm;

T845/440-0100, W www.diabeacon.org; $10). The contemporary art museum, a project of New York City's Dia Art Foundation, showcases large, primarily abstract exhibits by single artists, in a converted factory.

Hyde Park and around

HYDE PARK, set on a peaceful plateau on the east bank of the Hudson twenty miles north of Beacon, is worth a stop for the homes of **Franklin D.** and **Eleanor Roosevelt**. Well-signposted off US-9, the homes, a Vanderbilt mansion (see below) and a couple of minor attractions all come under the aegis of the new **Henry A. Wallace Visitor and Education Center** (Apr–Oct daily 8.45am–6.30pm, Nov–Mar 8.45am–5.30pm). The house where the "New Deal" president was born and spent much of his adult life is preserved here along with a library and a good **museum** (daily 9am–5pm; museum and guided house tour $14; T845/486-7770, W www.nps.gov/hofr). The museum contains extensive photos and artifacts, including the intriguing specially adapted car FDR drove after being struck down by polio in 1921, and the letter from Einstein that led to the development of the atomic bomb. FDR lies buried in the Rose Garden, beside his wife (and distant cousin) Eleanor, one of the first women to play a prominent role in politics, especially those regarding women's and workers' rights. After FDR's death in 1945, Eleanor moved to **Val-Kill** (May–Oct daily 9am–5pm; Nov–April Thurs–Mon 9am–5pm; tours $8; W www.nps.gov/elro), the nearby cottage retreat where she carried on her work as chair of the United Nations Human Rights Commission until her death in 1962. The grounds to both homes are open from dawn to dusk and there is no charge.

A three-mile-long clifftop **path** along the Hudson from the Roosevelt complex winds up at the Beaux Arts **Vanderbilt Mansion** (daily 9am–5pm; $8; W www. nps.gov/vama). This virtual palace is, believe it or not, the smallest of the family's residences, built for Frederick, a grandson of railroad baron Cornelius. The furnishings are quite garish, but the formal gardens are very pretty and offer a fine view of the Hudson River. The grounds are open year-round from 7am to dusk, at no charge.

Apart from these historic homes, Hyde Park has one other huge tourist draw: the excellent restaurants and fascinating campus of the **Culinary Institute of America**, the most prestigious cooking school in the country, which stands along US-9, south of Hyde Park at 1946 Campus Drive. The outstanding restaurants here (lunch and dinner Mon–Sat; T845/471-6608 or W www.ciachef.edu for reservations) have trained some of America's best chefs. Frequent dining events, "boot camps," and classes are held for food and wine enthusiasts (T1-800/285-4627); campus **tours** (Mon 10am & 4pm, Wed 4pm & Thurs 4pm; $5) require reservations.

Bargain **accommodation** in Hyde Park is available at the *Golden Manor Motel* (T845/229-2157, W www.goldenmanorhydepark.com; ❷), located on US-9 almost opposite the Roosevelt complex.

Rhinebeck and Olana

Beyond Hyde Park, US-9 cuts slightly inland from the Hudson, passing through a number of sleepy towns on its way north toward Albany. **RHINEBECK**, six miles north of Hyde Park, is the first and most worthwhile of these, holding a number of good restaurants as well as **America's oldest hotel**. The lovely, white Colonial 🌲 *Beekman Arms* on Rte-9 has been hosting and feeding travelers in its warm, wood-paneled rooms since 1766 (T845/876-7077, W www.beekmanarms. com; ❺). Two good places to **eat** are the *Calico Restaurant & Patisserie*, 6384 Mill St (T845/876-2749; closed Mon & Tues), which has a menu featuring Italian and

French influences, and the all-American *Foster's Coachhouse Tavern*, 6411 Montgomery St (☎845/876-8052). Rhinebeck is also home to the New Agey **Omega Institute for Holistic Studies**, which runs a spa and a wide range of health and wellness workshops at a large campus east of town on Lake Drive (☎1-800/944-1001, Ⓦwww.eomega.org).

The other good stop on the east bank of the Hudson is **Olana**, the hilltop home of **Frederic Church** (1826–1900), one of the foremost artists of the Hudson River School. High above a bend in the river, across the bridge from the town of Catskill, the quirky but attractive house rises in an odd blend of Persian and Moorish motifs. Obligatory guided **tours** (hours vary; ☎518/828-0135, Ⓦwww.olana.org) take in the bric-a-brac clogged rooms, as well as a number of Church's picturesque paintings. The grounds are also open daily from 8am until sunset.

Albany

Founded by Dutch fur-trappers in the early seventeenth century, **ALBANY** made its money by controlling trade along the Erie Canal, and its reputation by being capital of the state. It's not an unpleasant town, just rather boring, with its contemporary character almost exclusively shaped by political and bureaucratic affairs – though there are a few livelier areas on the fringes.

A good place to start a tour is the **Quackenbush House**, the city's oldest building, built along the river in 1736 and now serving as part of the **Albany Urban Culture Park**. The modern **visitor center**, next door at Broadway and Clinton (Mon–Fri 9am–4pm, Sat & Sun 10am–4pm; ☎518/434-0405, Ⓦwww.albany.org), has free maps and can provide details of **tours** of the imposing neoclassical **Capitol** and the downtown area, where a number of Revolutionary-era homes survive. The visitor center also has engaging displays tracing Albany's history, with a special emphasis on the impact of the Erie Canal and the impressive industrial legacy of **Troy**, across the Hudson via I-787 N.

Uphill from the waterfront, a controversial replacement for the old heart of the city, Nelson A. Rockefeller's **Empire State Plaza** is a rather ugly complex that includes a subterranean retail arcade lined with impressive modern art. The view from the **Corning Tower**'s 42nd-floor observation deck (daily 10am–2.30pm; free) looks out far across the state, beyond the twisting Hudson River to the Adirondack foothills, the Catskills, and the Berkshires in Massachusetts. It also peers down on the neighboring Performing Arts Center, known locally as "**The Egg**" (☎518/478-1845, Ⓦwww.theegg.org) – which adds the only curves to the Plaza's harsh angularity.

The **New York State Museum** (daily 9.30am–5pm; ☎518/474-5877, Ⓦwww.nysm.nysed.gov; suggested donation $2), one level down at the south end of the plaza, reveals everything you could want to know about New York State in imaginative, if static, tableaux. The excellent section on New York City history is better than anything like it in Manhattan itself, with absorbing exhibits and the original set of *Sesame Street*.

The most engaging part of Albany is the few blocks west of the plaza, stretching between Washington and Madison avenues to the open green spaces of **Washington Park**, laid out by Frederick Law Olmsted, the father of American landscape architecture. The recently renovated **Albany Institute of History and Art**, 125 Washington Ave (Wed–Sat 10am–5pm, Sun noon–5pm; $7; ☎518/463-4478, Ⓦwww.albanyinstitute.org), has a good range of Hudson River School paintings, and the neighborhood is full of the same sort of nineteenth-century brick-built homes Rockefeller had pulled down to build his Empire State Plaza.

Practicalities

Arrive by Greyhound or Adirondack Trailways (☎1-800/858-8555, ⓦwww.
trailwaysny.com) and it's a short, hilly walk to the heart of downtown; come in via
Amtrak and you face a two-mile bus ride across the river in Rensselaer. If you intend
to **stay** the night, bear in mind that downtown lodging is not particularly cheap.
Suburban chain motels start at $50 a night, while downtown options amount to the
Ramada Inn, 300 Broadway (☎518/434-4111, ⓦwww.ramada.com; ❹), the more
comfortable *Albany Crowne Plaza*, at State and Lodge streets (☎518/462-6611 or 1-
877/227-6963, ⓦwww.cpalbany.com; ❺), and the exceptionally nice *Mansion Hill
Inn*, 115 Philip St (☎518/465-2038 or 1-888/299-0455, ⓦwww.mansionhill.com;
❻), a B&B in a restored home just down the hill from the state governor's mansion;
it also has a fine restaurant.

Other good **places to eat** are located on or near **Lark Street**, a few blocks
west of the plaza; which is also the hub of the local gay scene. *Justin's*, at no. 301
(☎518/436-7008), and *Café Hollywood*, at no. 275 (☎518/472-9043), serve good,
progressive American food at moderate prices, while the welcoming *Mamoun's*,
206 Washington Ave (☎518/434-3901), has great inexpensive lamb, chicken, and
vegetarian dishes. Two of the most popular **nightlife** haunts are *Jillian's*, 59 N
Pearl St (☎518/432-1997), which has live music and DJs, and the *Lark Tavern*, 453
Madison Ave (☎518/463-7875), an Irish bar. The college town of **Troy**, across the
river, also has a number of lively spots.

North through the Adirondacks

Mountaineers, skiers, and dedicated hikers form the majority of visitors to the
vast northern region between Albany and the Canadian border. Outdoor pursuits
are certainly the main attractions in the rugged wilderness of the **Adirondack
Mountains**, though a few small resorts, especially the former Winter Olympic
venue of **Lake Placid**, offer creature comforts in addition to breathtaking scenery;
and the elegant spa town of **Saratoga Springs** nestles invitingly in the delicate
countryside of the southern foothills.

Saratoga Springs

Saratoga was fast, man, it was real fast. It was up all night long.

Hattie Gray, founder of *Hattie's*

For well over a century, **SARATOGA SPRINGS**, just 42 miles north of Albany
on I-87, was very much the place to be seen for the Northeast's richest and most
glittering names (such as the Morgans, Vanderbilts, and Whitneys). At first, the
town's curative waters were the main attraction; then John Morrisey, an Irish
boxer, transformed things by opening a **racetrack** and **casino** here during the
1860s. During the August horse-racing season, Saratoga Springs retains the feel
of an exclusive vintage resort – but for the rest of the summer it is accessible,
affordable, and fun.

Broadway, the main axis, takes in just about every aspect of the modern
town, from lurid motel signs to the Gothic and Renaissance residential palaces
on the northern tip of downtown; most of Saratoga Springs' many good bars
are here or in the few blocks just east. The carefully cultivated **Congress Park**,
off South Broadway, laid out for the original spa-goers, remains a shady retreat
from town-center traffic. Three of the original mineral springs still flow up to

the surface here, funneled out into drinking fountains (the water is tepid and salty, but some people swear by it). Also here is the original **casino**, which when built formed part of a whole city block. The **racetrack** (season runs late July–early September, post time 1pm; $3–5; ☎518/584-6200, ⓦwww. nyracing.com/saratoga) still functions in a rather grand, old-fashioned manner, though there is no longer a strict dress code for the grandstand or the clubhouse except no shorts or tank tops. There's no such pretension at the **harness track**, aka the Equine Sports Center, on nearby Crescent Avenue (evening races several times a week May–Nov; $2; ☎518/584-2110). If you can't get to either, visit the array of paintings, trophies, and audiovisual displays at the **National Museum of Racing and Hall of Fame**, on Union Avenue at Ludlow Street (Mon–Sat 10am–4pm, Sun noon–4pm, during race meet open daily 9am–5pm; $7; ☎518/584-0400, ⓦwww.racingmuseum.org).

On the southern edge of town, green **Saratoga Spa State Park** (daily 8am–dusk; $6 per car; ☎518/584-2535) presents opportunities to swim in great old Victorian pools, picnic, hike, or even "take the waters," ie, take a hot bath in the tingly, naturally carbonated stuff and receive a variety of spa treatments. Try the historic Lincoln Bath House, just past the park entrance at 65 S Broadway (☎518/583-2880), where advance reservations are required for a relaxing 20min bath and sheet wrap treatment ($20). The **Saratoga Performing Arts Center** (June to early Sept; ☎518/587-3330, ⓦwww.spac.org) – or SPAC – was built during the 1960s in a successful attempt to revive the town's fortunes. As well as being home to the New York City Ballet in July, and the Philadelphia Orchestra in August, it also hosts Freihofer's (formerly Newport) Jazz Festival among other quality festivals.

Practicalities

Central Saratoga Springs is easily explored on foot. **Accommodation** is only a problem during August's race season, or if there's a big gig on at SPAC, when prices can more than double. One good central motel is the *Turf and Spa*, 140 Broadway (April–Oct; ☎518/584-2550 or 1-800/972-1229, ⓦwww.saratogaturf andspa.com; ❷). Both the lavishly restored landmark *Adelphi Hotel*, 365 Broadway (May–Oct; ☎518/587-4688, ⓦwww.adelphihotel.com; ❺), and the grand *Gideon Putnam Hotel*, located right in Saratoga Spa State Park (☎518/584-3000, ⓦwww. gideonputnam.com; ❼–❽), have more character. The **Chamber of Commerce**, 28 Clinton St (☎518/584-3255, ⓦwww.saratoga.org), has full lists of accommodations.

Eating is also easy. One longtime favorite is the soul food at *Hattie's*, 45 Phila St (☎518/584-4790), where huge entrees cost under $15; another good bet is *Wheat Fields*, 440 Broadway (☎518/587-0534), with good salads and pasta served on an outdoor patio. *Beverly's*, 47 Phila St (☎518/583-2755), serves great but pricey breakfasts. There's usually good Irish **music** at the *Parting Glass Pub*, 40 Lake Ave (☎518/583-1916). *9 Maple Avenue*, logically enough at 9 Maple Ave (☎518/583-2582), offers live jazz and blues until the early hours, while folksy *Caffé Lena*, 47 Phila St (Thurs–Sun; ☎518/583-0022, ⓦwww.caffelena.com) is where Don McLean first inflicted "American Pie" on the world.

The Adirondacks

The **Adirondacks**, which cover an area larger than Connecticut and Rhode Island combined, are said by locals to be named after an Iroquois insult for enemies they'd driven into the forests and left to become "bark eaters." Until recent decades the area was almost the exclusive preserve of loggers, fur trappers, and a few select New York millionaires. For sheer grandeur, the region is hard to beat: 46 peaks

△ The Adirondacks

reach to over 4000ft; in summer the purple-green mountains span far into the distance in shaggy tiers, in fall the trees form a russet-red kaleidoscope.

Though Adirondack Trailways buses serve the area, you'll find it hard-going without a **car**. General **information** and some special deals can be had from the Adirondack Region tourist office (☎1-800/487-6867, Ⓦ www.visitadirondacks.com). The Adirondack Mountain Club (ADK), 814 Goggins Road, Lake George (☎518/668-4447, Ⓦ www.adk.org), or the Adirondack Park **Visitor Interpretive Centers**, based in Paul Smiths, north of Saranac Lake (daily 9am–5pm; ☎518/327-3000, Ⓦ www.northnet.org/adirondackvic), can provide details on hiking and camping.

Blue Mountain Lake

It is better to press on past over-commercialized Lake George and the eastern fringes of the Adirondacks and drive the extra hour northwest along Hwy-28 to where the headwaters of the Hudson River announce the tiny resort of **BLUE MOUNTAIN LAKE**. A handful of **motels** and lakeside **cabins** provide accommodation, and you can swim at the pretty little **beach** that fronts the village center.

Just north of Blue Mountain Lake on Hwy-30, the otherwise rather bland twenty-building **Adirondack Museum** (late May to mid-Oct daily 10am–5pm; $14; ⓦwww.adirondackmuseum.org) is perhaps most memorable for its grand views out over the lake and surrounding mountains.

Sagamore Great Camp, about fifteen miles west, in the woods above Raquette Lake, is the only one of the many "Great Camps" that wealthy Easterners constructed in the Adirondacks around the end of the nineteenth century that is open to the public. It was a summer home of the **Vanderbilts**, basically a huge and luxurious log cabin in which they entertained illustrious guests. The still-intact house and grounds are now used as a conference and educational center, and for cross-country skiing in winter; call for details of summer art and photography **classes**, or to reserve a place on a guided two-hour **tour** (May–June Sat & Sun 1.30pm; July–Aug daily 10am & 1.30pm; Sept–Oct daily 1.30pm; $12; ⓣ315/354-5311, ⓦwww.sagamore.org).

Lake Placid

The winter sports center of **LAKE PLACID**, twice the proud host of the Winter Olympics, lies thirty miles west of I-87 on Hwy-73. In winter there's thrilling alpine skiing at imposing Whiteface Mountain and all manner of Nordic disciplines at Mount Van Hoevenberg; in summer you can watch luge athletes practice on refrigerated runs, freestyle skiers somersaulting off dry slopes into swimming pools, and top amateur ice hockey games. The mountain slopes also provide challenging terrain for hikers and cyclists; good **mountain bikes**, maps of local trails, and **guided tours** are available from High Peaks Cyclery, 2733 Main St (ⓣ518/523-3764). The **Kodak Summer Passport** (June–Oct; $25; ⓣ518/523-1655, ⓦwww.orda.org) allows you on the chair lift to the top of the 393ft ski jump and eight miles up the sheer Whiteface Mountain toll road and back again, on the Whiteface gondola, and into the Olympic museum (see below). A similar winter passport is also available. At the **Verizon Sports Complex** on Mount Van Hoevenburg (ⓣ518/523-4436), you can do a blood-curdling bobsled run ($35) or bike the extensive trail network ($25 bike rental; $6 trail fee).

The town itself is set on two lakes: **Mirror Lake**, which you can sail on in summer and skate on in winter, and larger **Lake Placid**, just to the west, on which you can take a narrated **cruise** in summer ($8.50; ⓣ518/523-9704). Other attractions include the **Olympic Center** on Main Street (self-guided audio tour including museum $5; ⓣ518/523-1655), which houses four ice rinks and the informative **1932 and 1980 Lake Placid Winter Olympic Museum** ($4).

Outside the village on Hwy-73, the **John Brown Farm State Historic Site** was where the famous abolitionist brought his family in 1849 to aid a small colony of black farmers and where he conceived his ill-fated raid on Harper's Ferry in an attempt to end slavery. The house is less interesting than his story (see p.1302; late May to late Oct Wed–Sun 10am–5pm; $2; ⓣ518/523-3900); the grounds, which include Brown's grave, are open year-round.

Practicalities

Lake Placid's **information center** is in the Olympic Center, 2610 Main St (ⓣ518/523-2445 or 1-800/447-5224, ⓦwww.lakeplacid.com), and offers 15 minutes of free online access. **Accommodation** in town ranges from the somewhat economical to the opulent. The casually elegant *Mirror Lake Inn Resort &*

Spa, 77 Mirror Lake Drive (☎518/523-2544, ⓦwww.mirrorlakeinn.com; ❼),
has over 120 rooms, the best of them palatial, and an array of facilities, while
the nearby *Interlaken Inn*, 39 Interlaken Ave (☎518/523-3180, ⓦwww.the
interlakeninn.com; ❻), is a slightly cheaper but equally upscale B&B, with an
excellent restaurant. *Edelweiss Motel*, on the east side of town at 2806 Wilmington Rd, has clean if somewhat dated rooms (☎518/523-3821; ❸). The *Keene
Valley Hostel*, in nearby Keene Valley (☎518/576-2030; dorm beds $18; ❷–❸),
is a great base to be within walking distance of all the best hiking trails.

It's possible to **eat** well, with a view, for relatively little here. *Blues Berry Bakery*, 2436 Main St (☎518/523-4539), is much-loved for its apple strudel, while
Nicola's (☎518/523-4430), nearby at no. 2617, does Greek and Italian dinners,
including good wood-fired pizza. On the east side of town, the ✻ *Station Street
Bar & Grille*, 1 Station St (☎518/523-9963), is undoubtedly the friendliest
place for a night out with the locals and serves delicious ribs and other dishes,
occasionally accompanied by acoustic strumming. Main Street's buzzing *Zig
Zags Pub* (☎518/523-8221) is the main place for **live music** on the weekends.

Saranac Lake

SARANAC LAKE, ten miles northwest of Lake Placid, is a smaller, more laid-
back and cheaper base for the region. The tranquil lakeshore is lined with lovely
gingerbread cottages, most of them built during the late 1800s, when this was a
popular middle-class retreat and spa. **Robert Louis Stevenson** spent the winter
of 1888 in a small cottage on the east side of town at 44 Stevenson Lane; it's now
preserved as a **museum** (July–Sept Tues–Sun 9.30am–noon & 1pm–4.30pm;
rest of year by appointment; $5; ☎518/891-1462, ⓦwww.pennypiper.org).
Among the many **motels** on Lake Flower Avenue, friendly *Sara-Placid Motor Inn*,
no. 120 (☎518/891-2729 or 1-800/794-2729, ⓦwww.sara-placid.com; ❸), has
rooms and suites to suit most budgets. Downtown the *Hotel Saranac*, 100 Main St
(☎1-800/937-0211; ❹), also has a friendly **bar**. Surprisingly good, if not fully
authentic Mexican **food** can be had at the boisterous *Casa del Sol*, 154 Lake Flower
Ave (☎518/891-0977).

The Thousand Islands

Beyond the Adirondacks, on the broad St Lawrence River (which forms the border
with Canada), there are 1800 barely populated hunks of earth known as the **Thousand Islands**. The reason they gave their name to a salad dressing is because one
c.1900 visitor, George Boldt, president of New York's *Waldorf-Astoria* hotel, is said
to have asked the steward on his yacht to concoct something different for a special
luncheon. The resultant brightly colored goo is now famous the world over.

For **information** about the area, contact the Thousand Islands International
Tourism Council (☎1-800/847-5263, ⓦwww.visit1000islands.com). From both
Alexandria Bay and the smaller fishing port of Clayton, **boat excursions** set out
to explore the waterway; the tiny craft are all but swamped by the huge passing
cargo ships, larger than many of the islands. For departure times, contact Uncle
Sam Boat Tours (May–Oct daily; prices vary; ☎315/686-3511 or 1-800/253-
9229).

The Finger Lakes

At the heart of the state, southwest of Syracuse on the far side of the Catskills
from New York City, are the eleven **Finger Lakes**, narrow channels gouged out

by glaciers that have left tell-tale signs in the form of drumlins, steep gorges, and a number of waterfalls. With the exception of progressive, well-to-do **Ithaca** and tiny **Skaneateles**, few towns compete with the lakeshore scenery. That said, the area as a whole is a relaxing place to spend some time, particularly if you enjoy sampling **wine**: the Finger Lakes region – and much of upstate New York – produces a number of good vintages.

Skaneateles and Seneca Falls

SKANEATELES (pronounced "Skinny-Atlas"), crouching at the neck of Skaneateles Lake, is perhaps the prettiest Finger Lakes town. It's also the best place to go swimming in the region: just a block from the town center, and lined by huge resort homes, the appealing bay sports a **beach** (summer daily; $3) and the Skaneateles Marina, where you can rent watersports equipment (ⓣ315/685-5095) and take boat trips, from Mid-Lakes Navigation ($10 for 1hr; ⓣ315/685-8500). **Accommodation** options include the *Colonial Motel*, one mile west on Hwy-20 (ⓣ315/685-5751, ⓦwww.colonialmotelonline.com; ❸), and, overlooking the lake, the elegant *1899 Lady of the Lake* B&B, 2 W Lake St (ⓣ1-888/685-7997, ⓦwww.ladyofthelake.net; ❻), and the *Sherwood Inn*, 26 W Genesee St (ⓣ315/685-3405, ⓦwww.thesherwoodinn.com; ❹), featuring a good dining room and tavern. Cheaper but still scrumptious **meals** can be had at the ever-popular *Doug's Fish Fry*, 8 Jordan St (ⓣ315/685-3288) or more upmarket *BluewaterGrill*, 11 W Genesee St (ⓣ315/685-6600).

At **SENECA FALLS**, just west of the northern tip of Cayuga Lake, Elizabeth Cady Stanton and a few colleagues planned and held the first Women's Rights Convention in 1848 – 72 years before the 19th amendment gave all women in the US the right to vote. On the site of the **Wesleyan Chapel**, 136 Fall St, where the first campaign meeting was held, is the terrific **Women's Rights National Historical Park** (daily 9am–5pm; $3; ⓣ315/568-2991, ⓦwww.nps.gov/wori), which sets the early and contemporary women's movements in their historical contexts, with a strong emphasis on the connection with the African-American civil rights movements. The center, featuring exhibits and a neat little gift and book shop, also offers a **walking tour** that takes in the small museum at the Cady Stanton house and passes the (privately owned) former home of **Amelia Bloomer**, whose crusade to urge women out of their cumbersome undergarments won her a place in the dictionary. A block east of the visitor center, at 76 Fall St, the **National Women's Hall of Fame** (May–Sept Mon–Sat 10am–5pm, Sun noon–5pm; Oct–April Wed–Sat 11am–5pm; $3; ⓣ315/568-8060, ⓦwww. greatwomen.org), honors about two hundred women, including Emily Dickinson and Sojourner Truth, for their efforts in various fields.

The town itself is a blend of old mills and homes of various architectural styles, tucked away among the mature trees. If you want to stop over, the best **place to stay** is the *Hubbell House* B&B, at 42 Cayuga St (ⓣ315/568-9690, ⓦwww. hubbellhousebb.com; ❺). There are several reasonable **cafés** along Fall Street. Hwy-89, between Seneca Falls and Ithaca, has been dubbed the **Cayuga Wine Trail**, with dozens of small wineries operating along the west shore of the largest of the Finger Lakes, such as Sheldrake Point and Thirsty Owl; both offer tastings for $1.

Ithaca

Cayuga Lake comes to a halt at its southern end at picturesque **ITHACA**, piled like a diminutive San Francisco above the lakeshore and culminating in the towers, sweeping lawns, and shaded parks of Ivy-League **Cornell University**. On campus, which is cut by striking gorges, creeks, and lakes, the sleek, I.M. Pei–designed **Herbert F. Johnson Museum of Art** (Tues–Sun 10am–5pm; free; ☎607/255-6464, ⓦwww.museum.cornell.edu), across the street from the gorge-straddling **suspension bridge**, merits a visit more for its fifth-floor view of the town and lake than for the (on the whole) unspectacular collection of Asian and contemporary art. Adjacent to campus lie the **Cornell Plantations** (daily: dawn to dusk; free; ☎607/255-2400, ⓦwww.plantations.cornell.edu), the extensive botanical gardens and arboretum run by the university.

The pick of the countless **waterfalls** within a few miles of town are the slender **Taughannock Falls**, which are taller than Niagara at a height of 215ft and lie ten miles north of town just off Hwy-89, with a swimming beach close at hand. **Buttermilk Falls State Park**, two miles south of town on Rte-13, is a delightful spot, and the dangerous-looking Lucifer Falls, at lush **Robert H. Treman State Park**, three miles further south, should not be missed. Parking is $7 for the day, which covers all three parks. Cayuga Lake provides excellent **boating** and **windsurfing** opportunities; boards and boats can be rented from several places, including Cayuga Boat Rentals (☎607/277-5072), next to the Visitors Bureau.

Practicalities

Greyhound and other **buses** operate out of the terminal at W State and N Fulton. Free **Internet** access is available at the huge, partially solar-powered library on Cayuga Avenue next to the Ithaca Commons. The helpful **visitor center** is at 904 East Shore Drive, off Hwy-34 N (Mon–Fri 9am–5pm, Sat 10am–5pm, Sun 10am–4pm, longer in summer; ☎607/272-1313 or 1-800/284-8422, ⓦwww.visitithaca.com).

Accommodation is, on the whole, reasonably priced. Try the *Cottage Garden Inn*, a cosy B&B at 107 Crescent Place (☎607/277-7561, ⓦwww.cottagegardeninn.com; ❹), or the *Best Western University Inn*, 1020 Ellis Hollow Rd, on the east edge of campus (☎800/528-1234, ⓦwww.bestwestern.com; ❺). The *Statler Hotel*, on East Avenue within the campus proper (☎1-800/541-2501, ⓦwww.statlerhotel.cornell.edu; ❾), is the teaching hotel of the Cornell School of Hotel Administration and makes a pleasant option, particularly out of term.

Ithaca boasts two **dining** and **entertainment** zones. **Downtown**, centered on the vehicle-free Commons, is the larger and better of the two. Here DeWitt Mall, on the corner of Cayuga and Seneca streets, features the top-rated vegetarian restaurant of cookbook fame, *Moosewood* (☎607/273-9610), as well as the *Café DeWitt* (☎607/273-3473), which offers healthy and filling salads at lunchtime. A block away, *Just a Taste*, 116 N Aurora St (☎607/277-9463), is a lively wine and tapas bar. Numerous cheap student-oriented places to eat line the streets of **Collegetown**; check out *The Nines*, 311 College Ave (☎607/272-1888), which serves up the best deep-dish pizza around and has live music. *Common Ground* (☎607/273-1505) is a gay-friendly **bar** down Route 96B with ping-pong, billiards, and a gorgeous patio.

The Kitchen Theatre produces new and avant-garde **plays** in its intimate auditorium (☎607/272-0403, ⓦwww.kitchentheatre.com); for news of the lively **music** scene, pick up the free *Ithaca Times*.

Corning

Forty miles southwest of Ithaca, world-famous **Steuben glass** has been manufactured in the otherwise undistinguished town of **CORNING** since Frederick Carder started making his characteristic Art Nouveau pieces in 1903. The excellent **Museum of Glass** in the Corning Glass Center traces the history of glass from ancient heads and amulets to modern sculptures and paperweights, and allows you to watch glassmaking in action (daily summer 9am–8pm; Sept–May 9am–5pm; $12.50; ☎1-800/732-6845, ⊛www.cmog.org). The **Rockwell Museum of Western Art**, ten minutes' stroll away at 111 Cedar St (same hours; $6.50, both museums $16.50; ☎607/937-5386, ⊛www.stny.com/rockwellmuseum), has more than two thousand pieces of Steuben glass, plus antique toys and a strong, historically informed collection of Western American art. For further information on these attractions and for help in finding accommodation, contact the **visitors bureau** at 5 W Market St (☎607/936-6544 or 1-866/946-3386, ⊛www.corningsteuben.com).

Toward Niagara Falls: the Erie Canal towns

The fertile farming country stretching from Albany at the head of the Hudson to Buffalo on Lake Erie, along the route of the **Erie Canal**, comprises the agricultural heartland of New York State. The eastern parts – also known as **Central Leatherstocking**, after the protective leggings worn by the area's first settlers – are well off the conventional tourist trails. Unless you want to check out one of the specialist sports museums or visit the lovely village of **Cooperstown**, this is not a high-priority destination.

With the captivating exceptions of **Niagara Falls**, one of the continent's biggest crowd-pullers, and the emerging tourist destination of **Buffalo**, there's little to see in the northwest reaches of New York State. Standing out from the mostly flat farmland, the industrial towns of **Rochester** and **Syracuse** also possess some worthy attractions and restaurants.

Cooperstown

Seventy miles west of Albany, sitting gracefully on the wooded banks of tranquil Otsego Lake, is pleasant **COOPERSTOWN**, christened "Glimmerglass" by novelist James Fenimore Cooper, son of the town's founder. The birth of baseball, said to have originated here on Doubleday Field, is commemorated by the inspired and spacious **National Baseball Hall of Fame**, on Main Street (daily 9am–5pm; $14.50; ☎607/547-7200, ⊛www.baseballhalloffame.org). Everything is displayed in such an attention-grabbing manner that even complete novices will be absorbed. The delightful **Fenimore Art Museum**, just north of town on Lake Road/Rte-80 (April–mid-May & mid-Oct–Dec Tues–Sun 10am–4pm; mid-May–mid-Oct daily 10am–5pm; $11; ☎1-888/547-1450, ⊛www.fenimoreartmuseum.org), has innovative special exhibits and a fine collection of folk and North American Indian art. In summer, Cooperstown hosts **classical concerts** and the **Glimmerglass Opera** at Alice Busch Opera Theater, north on Hwy-80 by the lake (☎607/547-5704, ⊛www.glimmerglass.org).

The local chamber of commerce runs a small but helpful **visitor center** at 31 Chestnut St (summer daily 9am–7pm, shorter winter hours; ☎607/547-9983, ⊛www.cooperstownchamber.org); the website is an excellent way to arrange accommodation. If you drive here in summer, park in one of the free lots on the edge of town and take the trolley around the various sights (8am–9pm: late June–Labor Day daily, Memorial Day to late June and Labor Day through Oct weekends only; $2 all-day pass). **Accommodation** in the town itself is expensive, but there's a cluster of clean motels right on pretty Otsego Lake, a few miles north on Rte-80; the *Lake 'N Pines* (☎607/547-2790 or 1-800/615-5253, ⊛www.cooperstown.

net/lake-n-pines; ❸; closed Dec–March) offers superb value. Further north on Rte-80, the gorgeous lakeside *Blue Mingo Inn* (☎607/547-9414, ⓦwww.blue mingoinn.com; ❻) maintains one of the area's best and most creative **restaurants**, the *Blue Mingo Grill* (☎607/547-7496), where fusion and New American dishes change nightly. *Clete Boyer's*, three miles south on Hwy-28 (☎607/544-1112), serves gimmicky but tasty American food. For a bite in town away from the crowds, try the *Cooperstown Diner*, 136 1/2 Main St (☎607/547-9201), open until 2pm for breakfast and burgers.

Syracuse

A lively but largely unattractive modern city, busy **SYRACUSE** made its name first for the production of salt and, more importantly, for its central position on the Erie Canal. There's little to see, though the presence of Syracuse University gives downtown an active and youthful feel. The redevelopment of **Armory Square**, around Franklin and Fayette streets, as an area of specialty shops, galleries, and cafés has also added some character to the city center.

The **Erie Canal Museum** (Tues–Sat 10am–5pm, Sun 10am–3pm; suggested donation $3; ☎315/471-0593, ⓦwww.eriecanalmuseum.org), housed in one of the few surviving canal-era buildings, an 1850s weighing station at 318 E Erie Blvd, tells the story of the long battle between politicians and taxpayers before work on the canal began in 1810. The waterway was designed to link the Great Lakes with New York City via the Hudson, thereby cutting hefty transportation costs. This it did by an average of ninety percent, but at the cost of more than one thousand lives and three million dollars over budget. When it opened in 1825 after fifteen years of construction, prosperous towns quickly sprung up alongside the canal.

Excellent **rooms** can be found in the lakeside *Ancestors Inn*, just outside of town in Liverpool (☎315/461-1226 or 1-888/866-8591, ⓦwww.ancestorsinn.com; ❹). The fairly central *HI-Downing International Hostel*, 535 Oak St (☎315/472-5788; ❷), has $14–17 dorm beds. For **food**, *Pastabilities*, 311 S Franklin St (☎315/474-1153), is popular for its delicious pasta, while *Lemon Grass*, 238 W Jefferson St (☎315/475-1111), is a great but pricey Thai place. Student numbers ensure a lively **music** scene (consult the resourceful and free *Syracuse New Times* at ⓦwww.syracusenewtimes.com for goings-on) and good hangouts include the loud, bluesy *Dinosaur BBQ*, 246 W Willow St (☎315/476-1662). The city's small **visitor center** is in the Erie Canal Museum (same hours and contact).

Rochester

In contrast to its sprawling suburbs, downtown **ROCHESTER** is a salubrious place, with its central office-block area bordered by well-heeled mansions on spacious boulevards. High-tech companies such as Bausch & Lomb, Xerox, and Kodak have created a thriving local economy throughout the years, despite national and regional economic downturns. Kodak's (and its founder, George Eastman's) legacies throughout the metropolitan area include Kodak Park, the Eastman Theater, and above all the **International Museum of Photography** at George Eastman House, two miles from downtown at 900 East Ave (Tues, Wed, Fri & Sat 10am–5pm, Thurs 10am–8pm, Sun 1–5pm; $8; ☎585/271-3361, ⓦwww.eastmanhouse.org). In the modern annex, a first-rate exhibition of photographic history ranges from high-quality Civil War prints to modern experimental works. There's also a space for temporary exhibitions and an arthouse cinema. The house itself, fussily restored to its early twentieth-century glory, is mildly interesting. Fittingly, given Eastman's passion for horticulture, the gardens have been superbly maintained and are worth a visit in themselves. Nearby at 500 University Ave, the **Memorial Art Gallery** (Tues, Wed & Fri noon–5pm, Thurs noon–9pm, Sat & Sun 10am–5pm; $7; ℡585/473-7720, ⓦwww.mag.rochester.edu) houses a surprisingly extensive collection that includes three Monets and a Rembrandt.

An obsessive collector of anything and everything, local bigwig Margaret Woodbury Strong (1897–1969) bequeathed her estate to the city and today it is the **Strong National Museum of Play** on Manhattan Square (Mon–Thurs & Sat 10am–5pm, Fri 10am–8pm, Sun noon–5pm; $9, kids $7; ℡585/263-2700, ⓦwww.strongmuseum.org). Half devoted to a history of the American family, and half obsessed with a history of American children's pop culture, it features interactive kid-oriented exhibits such as a history of *Sesame Street*, a fully working 1920s carousel, and a 1950s Pennsylvania diner. There's also a stunning indoor butterfly garden.

The theme of celebrating former Rochester residents continues at the **Susan B. Anthony House** at 17 Madison St, where this renowned suffragist lived from 1866 to 1906 (Summer Tues–Sun 10am–5pm; winter Wed–Sun 11am–4pm; $6; ℡585/235-6124, ⓦwww.susanbanthonyhouse.org).

Practicalities

Greyhound drops off at Broad and Chestnut streets downtown. The Amtrak station, 320 Central Ave, is on the north side beyond the I-490 inner loop road; it's served by Regional Transit Service (RTS) public **buses** (℡585/288-1700, ⓦwww.rgrta.com). Rochester's **visitor center** is at 45 East Ave between Chestnut and Main (Mon–Fri 8.30am–5pm; ℡1-800/677-7282, ⓦwww.visitrochester.com). **Accommodation** is somewhat expensive downtown, where choices include the excellent *428 Mt Vernon B&B* (℡716/271-0792 or 1-800/836-3159, ⓦwww.428mtvernon.com; ❺), at the entrance to lush Highland Park, with private baths in all rooms. Among budget options in the south of the city is the *Red Roof Inn*, 4820 W Henrietta Rd, off I-90 exit 46 (℡585/359-1100, ⓦwww.redroof.com; ❸).

Popular **places to eat** downtown include *Aladdin's Natural Eatery*, 646 Monroe Ave (℡585/442-5000), serving inexpensive Middle Eastern food, and the pub-style *Old Toad*, 277 Alexander St (℡585/232-2626), where British staff serve beer and cheap meals. If you want to sample a "Garbage Plate" – the local delicacy of all sorts deep-fried – head over to *Nick Tahou Hots* at 320 W Main St (℡585/436-0184). In the university area, *Jine's Restaurant*, 658 Park Ave (℡585/461-1280), is good-value for breakfast, and *Esan*, 696 Park Ave (℡585/271-2271), is the place for authentically spicy and inexpensive Thai food.

Out from Rochester

The **Lake Ontario State Parkway** is a quiet, scenic way of driving to Niagara Falls from Rochester, taking about an hour longer than the standard route along I-90 via Buffalo. The parkway starts eight miles from downtown at the end of Lake Avenue, near the popular but posey **Ontario Beach Park**. If big crowds and the churning noise of speedboats are not your thing, head twenty miles along the parkway to the more secluded **Hamlin Beach State Park** ($7 per car).

Buffalo

As I-90 sweeps down into the state's second largest city, **BUFFALO**, downtown looms up in a cluster of Art Deco spires and glass-box skyscrapers – Manhattan in miniature on Lake Erie. The city's early twentieth-century prosperity, which busted while many other American cities were booming, and thus exempted

Buffalo's historic buildings from destruction and replacement, is reflected in such architecturally significant structures as the towering 1928 **City Hall** (the tallest in the country; free observation deck on the top floor); the deep red terracotta relief of Louis Sullivan's **Guaranty Building** on Church Street; and major buildings by H.H. Richardson and Eliel Saarinen. The massive abandoned **grain elevators**, which rise proudly along the Erie waterfront like wonders of the industrial world, provide an interesting architectural counterpoint. Because of its proximity to the Canadian border, Buffalo also has numerous Underground Railroad sites.

That Buffalo's wealthy merchants were a cultured lot is also apparent in the excellent **Albright-Knox Art Gallery**, 1285 Elmwood Ave (Wed–Sat 11am–5pm, Sun noon–5pm; $10; ☎716/882-8700, ⓦwww.albrightknox.org), two miles north of downtown amid the green spaces of the Frederick Law Olmsted–designed **Delaware Park**. Not a gallery at all, but a museum with one of the top modern collections in the world, it's especially strong on recent American and European art with Pollock, Rothko, Warhol, and Rauschenberg among the names. Other highlights are a Surrealism collection and pieces by earlier artists such as Matisse, Picasso, and Monet. There's also a chic restaurant, open for lunch Tuesday through Sunday and also for dinner on Friday.

The area around Delaware Park is Buffalo's choicest neighborhood; it features several homes designed by **Frank Lloyd Wright**, most notably the Darwin D. Martin House Complex ($12; tours only, reservations required; ☎716/947-9217, ⓦwww.darwinmartinhouse.org). Between here and downtown is **Allentown**, a National Historic District and Buffalo's most bohemian quarter. Its leafy streets are lined with lovely Victorian homes and numerous good cafés, bars, restaurants – as well as most of Buffalo's gay and lesbian venues. On the border of Allentown, the slightly more upscale **Elmwood Avenue** nonetheless has great food and shopping at prices that will seem low to many out-of-towners.

As a traditionally blue-collar city, Buffalo loves its professional **sports** teams: football's Bills (☎1-877/228-4257), ice hockey's Sabres (☎1-888/467-2273), and minor-league baseball's Bisons (☎1-888/223-6000), who, as the top farm team for the Cleveland Indians, attract huge crowds to downtown's pleasant ballpark.

West of Buffalo, the **Lake Erie shoreline** is lined by numerous beaches where **windsurfers** skim across the water and do flips in the waves, while the Miss Buffalo boat tours ($12.50; ☎716/856-6696, ⓦwww .missbuffalo.com), which leave from 79 Marine Drive next to the Naval and Servicemen's Park, provide a good view of the city skyline. Minutes from the grain elevators, the 264-acre **Tifft Nature Preserve** holds a fresh marsh, untamed urban wildlife, and five miles of trails. To the south, in the town of Orchard Park, the friendly, engaging **Pedaling History Bicycle Museum** (Mon–Sat 11am–5pm, Sun 1.30–5pm; $6; ☎716/662-3853, ⓦwww .pedalinghistory.com) holds over four hundred antique bikes and myriad pieces of cycling memorabilia.

Arrival and information

Greyhound, Metro Bus, and Metro Rail, the city's tramway (both Metros ☎716/855-7211, ⓦwww.nfta.com/metro), all operate from the downtown depot at Ellicott and Church streets. Several routes go to **Niagara Falls** (see p.154). Amtrak **trains** stop some six blocks away, at Exchange Street, as well as in the eastern suburb of Depew, eight miles from town but close to the **airport** (☎716/630-6020, ⓦwww.nfta.com/airport). There's a helpful **visitor center** at 617 Main St (Mon–Thurs 9am–5pm, Fri 9am–4pm, Sat 10am–2pm; ☎716/852-0511 or 1-800/283-3256, ⓦwww.visitbuffaloniagara.com), which suggests numerous themed driving tours and has plenty of other information.

Accommodation

Beau Fleuve 242 Linwood Ave ⓣ716/882-6116 or 1-800/278-0245, ⓦwww.beaufleuve.com. Extremely comfortable, well-appointed B&B with great breakfasts. ❺

Hampton Inn & Suites 220 Delaware Ave ⓣ716/855-2223, ⓦwww.hamptoninnbuffalo.com. A safe bet in the heart of the nightlife district downtown, with free breakfasts. ❹

HI-Buffalo Hostel 667 Main St ⓣ716/852-5222, ⓦwww.hostelbuffalo.com. Very central hostel with

beds for $20. Nothing special, but the cheapest option by far. ❶

The Mansion on Delaware Avenue 414 Delaware Ave ⓣ716/886-3300, ⓦwww.mansion ondelaware.com. Centrally located luxury inn. ❻

Roycroft Inn 40 S Grove St, East Aurora ⓣ716/652-5222 or 1-877/652-5552, ⓦwww.roycroftinn.com. Immaculately refurbished inn located a half-hour drive east of Buffalo. The on-site restaurant serves tasty meals. ❺

Eating, drinking, and nightlife

The heart of Buffalo's downtown centers on Chippewa and Main; plenty of restaurants are within easy reach and there's ample parking. For a quick snack, the cheap food stalls and tiny Polish cafés of ancient **Broadway Market**, 999 Broadway, are well worth perusing. The main **nightlife** drag, along Chippewa from Delaware Avenue to Main Street, has plenty of sports bars and nightclubs. The majority of theaters and venues that house the city's burgeoning **arts scene** are handily grouped nearby along Main between Chippewa and Tupper streets. For further information, pick up the free weekly *Art Voice* (ⓦwww.artvoice.com), or the gay and lesbian *Outcome* (ⓦwww.outcomebuffalo.com).

Anchor Bar 1047 Main St ⓣ716/886-8920, ⓦwww.anchorbar.com. The city's specialty of buffalo (spicy chicken) wings with blue cheese and celery dressing is said to have been invented here.

Bacchus Wine Bar & Restaurant 54 W Chippewa St ⓣ716/854-9463. A good late-night bar and restaurant, with jazz, blues, folk, and world music.

Colter Bay 561 Delaware Ave, Allentown ⓣ716/882-1330. Western-themed restaurant with great, inexpensive lunches for a variety of tastes.

India Gate 1116 Elmwood Ave ⓣ716/886-4000. Good, inexpensive Indian restaurant with generous lunch buffet.

Nietzsche's 248 Allen St ⓣ716/886-8539, ⓦwww.nietzsches.com. Bar with friendly staff and cheap drinks, hosting a wide variety of live acts seven days a week; there's room for dancing in the back.

Osake 235 Delaware Ave ⓣ716/842-6261. This casual café serves cheap sushi and noodles; not a place to linger, but good value.

Spot Coffee 227 Delaware Ave ⓣ716/856-BREW; 765 Elmwood Ave ⓣ716/332-LATTE, ⓦwww.spotcoffee.com. Lively, happening neighborhood institution serving basic food and good drinks. The location on Elmwood is connected to New World Records, one of the best music stores in Buffalo.

Niagara Falls

Every second, almost three quarters of a million gallons of water explode over the knife-edge **NIAGARA FALLS**, right on the border with Canada some twenty miles north of Buffalo on I-190. This awesome spectacle is made even more impressive by the variety of methods laid on to help you get closer to it: boats, catwalks, observation towers, and helicopters all push as near to the curtains of gushing water as they dare. At night, the falls are lit up, and the colored waters tumble dramatically into blackness, while in winter the whole scene changes as the falls freeze to form gigantic razor-tipped icicles.

Some visitors will, no doubt, find the whole experience a bit too gimmicky; corporate big-hitters like the *Hard Rock Café* and various casinos on both sides have pushed the place closer to an aquatic Vegas, although the green fringes of the state park provide some bucolic getaways. Don't expect too much from the touristy small city of **Niagara Falls, New York,** or the more developed tinseltown of **Niagara Falls, Ontario**. Once you've seen the falls, from as many different angles as you can manage, and traced the **Niagara Gorge**, you'll have a better time heading back to Buffalo.

Arrival, information, and getting around

Amtrak **trains**, en route between New York City and Toronto, stop a long two miles from downtown Niagara Falls at 27th Street and Lockwood Road. **Buses** stop downtown at 303 Rainbow Boulevard, ten minutes' walk from the falls. Arriving **by car**, follow the signs to the main parking lot, which is right next to the falls and costs $6 – avoid being steered into privately owned, high-priced lots outside the park. **Information** is available at the Niagara Tourism & Convention Corporation, 345 3rd St (☎716/282-8992 ext 310 or 1-800/338-7890, ⓦwww. visitbuffaloniagara.com) and from the Niagara Falls State Park Visitors Center (☎716/278-1796) near the falls. As for **getting around**, local Metro Transit System **buses** ($1.50 base fare, plus 25¢/zone; ☎716/285-9319, ⓦwww.nfta.com) run to all areas of the city and to Buffalo (see p.152).

Accommodation

Places to stay in central Niagara can be quite expensive if you don't plan ahead, but huge competition keeps rates down overall. US-62 (Niagara Falls Blvd), east of I-190, is lined with dozens of inexpensive motels, some being rather tacky honeymoon spots. The closest place to **camp** is seven miles from downtown

at *Niagara Falls Campground & Lodging*, 2405 Niagara Falls Blvd in Wheatfield (☎716/731-3434, ⓦwww.nfcampground.com); campsites start at $24 a night for two people.

HI-Niagara Falls 1101 Ferry Ave ☎716/282-3700. Friendly, well-run hostel with dorm beds for $20–25. Preference is given to HI members and reservations are necessary in summer.
Holiday Inn Select 300 3rd St ☎716/285-3361 or 1-800/953-2557, ⓦwww.hiselect.com/niagarafalls. Typical of the chain hotels that dominate downtown and overcharge at peak times. ❹
Park Place B&B 740 Park Place ☎716/282-4626, ⓦwww.parkplacebb.com. Comfortable spot near downtown, with full breakfast and afternoon pastries. ❹
Red Coach Inn 2 Buffalo Ave ☎716/282-1459, ⓦwww.redcoach.com. Popular, well-appointed B&B with views of the falls. ❺
Seneca Niagara Casino & Hotel 310 4th St ☎716/299-1100 or 1-877/873-6322. The town's newest luxury pad, whose interiors are about as garish as the flashy neon entrance. Rates vary considerably – look out for online promotions. ❻

The Falls

Niagara Falls comprises three distinct cataracts. The tallest are the **American** and **Bridal Veil falls** on the American side, separated by tiny Luna Island and plunging over jagged rocks in a 180ft drop; the broad **Horseshoe Falls** which curve their way over to Canada are probably the most impressive. Together, they date back a mere twelve thousand years, when the retreat of melting glaciers allowed water trapped in Lake Erie to gush north to Lake Ontario. Back then the falls were seven miles downriver, but constant erosion has cut them back to their present site.

Getting around Niagara Falls State Park is easy, thanks to the convenient but twee **Niagara Scenic Trolley** ($1) which connects all parking lots and the major sightseeing points. The best views on the American side are from the **Observation Tower** (daily 10am–5pm; 50c), and from the area at its base where the water rushes past. In the middle of the river, Terrapin Point on **Goat Island** has similar views of Horseshoe Falls. Near here, the nineteenth-century tightrope-walker Blondin crossed the Niagara repeatedly, and even carried passengers across on his back. Other suicidal fools over the years have taken the plunge in barrels – or less (see box, opposite). The reason such craziness has long been banned becomes self-evident when you approach the towering cascade on the not-to-be-missed **Maid of the Mist** boat trip, which leaves from the foot of the observation tower (April–Oct daily 9.15am–7.30pm every 15 mins; $11.50, kids $6.75; ☎716/284-4233, ⓦwww.maidofthemist.com). Another excellent way to see the falls is the **Cave of the Winds** tour (mid-May to late Oct daily 8am–10pm; $10; ☎716/278-1730), which leads from Goat Island by elevator down to the base of the falls. Bringing you to within almost touching distance of the water, the tour can provide a magical nighttime view, as it runs well into the evening. A "**Passport to the Falls**" for these and other attractions costs $24.50 for adults, or $17.50 for children at the Visitor Center.

Rainbow Air Inc **helicopter** tours, 454 Main St (9am–dusk; prices vary; ☎716/284-2800) are a more expensive proposition, somewhat less so the Flight of Angels **helium balloon** ascents, at 310 S Rainbow Blvd (every 15min 9am–midnight June-Sept, 9am–9pm May & Oct; $20, kids $10; ☎716/278-0824).

To check out the view from Niagara, Ontario, it's a twenty-minute walk across the **Rainbow Bridge** to the Canadian side (50¢ to Canada, free to US; bring ID and check with the US immigration officials before heading across), where you get an arguably better view, bigger crowds, and even more tawdry commercialism. Driving across is inadvisable: the toll for a car is just $2.50, but parking on the other side can cost more than $15.

As you look on in awe, reflect that you're seeing only about half the volume of water – the rest is diverted to hydroelectric power stations. The full story of this

Maniacs and miracles

Fifteen people have taken the plunge over Niagara's 170-foot **Horseshoe Falls** – and, remarkably, ten of them survived the fall. The first daredevil was 63-year-old Annie Taylor in 1901, who rode in a wooden barrel and suffered only minor bruises from her journey. Since then, thrillseekers have followed her lead, using everything from giant rubber balls to water tanks as craft. The last successful navigation of the falls was in 2003, by a man who claimed he was trying to commit suicide; after surviving the plunge, the man decided life was worth living. Those less lucky include Red Hill, killed in 1945 while using a vessel he called "The Thing," built of little more than inner tubes and netting. Other deaths have been equally pointless: from a would-be stuntman in a kayak, who refused a helmet for fear it would obscure his face on film, to a jet-skier whose parachute, improperly packed, failed to open when he overshot the falls.

The most miraculous survival story, though, is that of Roger Woodward, a seven-year-old on a boat trip with his teenage sister in the upper Niagara River in the summer of 1960. When the boat developed motor trouble and capsized, they were thrown into the river. His sister was plucked from the water, but Roger and the captain, James Honeycutt, went over the falls wearing nothing but swimsuits and life preservers. Honeycutt was killed, but the boy surfaced near a tour boat at the base of the falls, bruised and concussed but alive, making him the only person ever to survive an unprotected trip over the falls.

engineering feat is related at the free **Niagara Power Project Visitors Center** in nearby Lewiston (daily 9am–5pm; free; ☎716/286-6661 ⓦwww.nypa.gov/vc/nvcdir.htm). With your own transportation it's also possible to trace the inhospitable Niagara Gorge two miles along the dramatic Robert Moses Parkway to the **Whirlpool Rapids**, a violent maelstrom swollen by broken trees and other flotsam, and to hike down into striking **Whirlpool State Park**. Ten miles east of Niagara Falls, the town of **Lockport** takes its name from the series of locks that raise and lower boats some 65ft at the western end of the Erie Canal. You can see the impressive flight of locks from the Pine Street Bridge, or up close on canal **boat cruises** (May–Oct daily at 12.30pm & 3pm, also 10am on Sat; June–Aug additional daily tours at 10am & 5.30pm; $13.50; ☎1-800/378-0352, ⓦwww.lockportlocks.com).

Eating and drinking

Though most of the **eating options** in Niagara Falls are fast-food joints of indifferent quality, there are a few decent local bars and restaurants – with some better places over in Canada.

Como Restaurant 2200 Pine Ave ☎716/285-9341. A good, posh option with huge portions of Italian cuisine and a reasonably priced deli.
Hard Rock Café 333 Prospect St ☎716/282-0007. Although a bit cliched and expensive, this branch of the rock-homage American-food chain restaurant has a lively, dependable bar.

The Orchard Grill 1217 Main St ☎716/282-8079. Large portions of all-American classics are served at this unpretentious spot.
Provenzo's 1300 Buffalo Ave ☎716/278-1264. Italian restaurant serving popular seafood and veal dishes, as well as meat, chicken, and pasta.
Sadar Sahib 431 Third Street ☎716/282-0444. Authentic and inexpensive curry house with an emphasis on Punjabi dishes.

Pennsylvania

PENNSYLVANIA, which but for a small stretch on **Lake Erie** is the only land-locked state in the Northeast, was explored by the Dutch in the early 1600s, settled by the Swedes forty years later, and claimed by the British in 1664. Charles II of England, who owed a debt to the Penn family, rid himself of the potentially troublesome young **William Penn**, an enthusiastic advocate of religious freedom, by granting him land in the colony in 1682. Penn Jr. immediately established a "holy experiment" of "brotherly love" and tolerance, naming the state for his father and setting a good example by signing a peaceful cohabitation treaty with the Native Americans. Most of the early agricultural settlers were religious refugees, Quakers like Penn himself and Mennonites from Germany and Switzerland, to be joined by Irish Catholics during the potato famines of the nineteenth century.

"The Keystone State" was crucial in the development of the United States. Politicians and thinkers like **Benjamin Franklin** congregated in Philadelphia – home of both the Declaration of Independence and the Constitution – and were prominent in articulating the ideas behind the Revolution. Later, the battle in Gettysburg, in south Pennsylvania – best remembered for Abraham Lincoln's immortal **Gettysburg Address** – marked a turning point in the Civil War. Pennsylvania was also vital industrially: Pittsburgh, in the west, was the world's leading steel producer in the nineteenth century, and nearly all the nation's anthracite coal is still mined here.

The two great urban centers of **Philadelphia** and **Pittsburgh**, both lively and vibrant tourist destinations, are at opposite ends of the state. The three hundred miles between them, though predominantly agricultural, are topographically diverse. There are over one hundred state parks, with green rolling countryside in the east, brooding forests in the west, and in the northeast, the rivers, lakes, and valleys of the **Poconos**. **Lancaster County**, home to traditional Amish farmers, and the **Gettysburg** battlefield both heave with busloads of day-trippers, while the Hershey chocolate factory, minutes away from **Harrisburg**, the capital, draws thousands of sweet-toothed visitors each year.

Getting around Pennsylvania

If you organize your trip carefully, **public transporation** is adequate to navigate Pennsylvania – although it's best to have a **car**. Both I-76 (the Pennsylvania Turnpike) and I-80 sweep all the way across to Ohio, nearly five hundred miles east to west. US-30 (the Lincoln Highway) also runs east–west between Philadelphia and Pittsburgh, past Lancaster City, York, and Gettysburg. The prettiest north–south route is US-15, from Maryland to New York State, which follows the Susquehanna River for about fifty miles. **Amtrak** crosses daily from Philadelphia to Pittsburgh, stopping at Lancaster City, Harrisburg, and other smaller towns. **Greyhound** covers all the major cities and some small towns not served by rail.

Philadelphia

The original capital of the nation, **PHILADELPHIA** was laid out by William Penn Jr. in 1682, on a grid system that was to provide the pattern for most American cities. It was envisaged as a "greene countrie towne," and today, for all its historical and cultural significance, it still manages to retain a certain quaintness.

PHILADELPHIA

ACCOMMODATION
Comfort Inn   B
Crowne Plaza Philadelphia
 Center City   D
Gaskill House B&B   H
HI-Bank Street Hostel   E
HI-Chamounix Mansion
 Philadelphia   A
La Reserve Center City B&B   G
Penn's View Hotel   C
Shippen Way Inn   I
Thomas Bond House   F

RESTAURANTS
Amada   7
Buddakan   6
City Tavern   8
Delilah's   4
Ocean City   2
Pat's King of
 Steaks   12
Rangoon   3
San Carlo   10
Serrano   5
Sonoma   1
South Street Diner   11
Tre Scalini   13
White Dog Café   9

Just a few blocks away from the noise and crowds of downtown, shady cobbled alleys stand lined with red-brick colonial houses, while the peace and quiet of huge Fairmount Park make it easy to forget you're in a major metropolis.

Settled by **Quakers**, Philadelphia prospered swiftly on the back of trade and commerce, and by the 1750s had become the second largest city in the British Empire. Economic power fueled strong revolutionary feeling, and the city was the capital during the **War of Independence** (except for nine months under British occupation in 1777–1778) and the US capital until 1800, while Washington, DC, was being built. The **Declaration of Independence** was written, signed, and first publicly read here in 1776, as was the **US Constitution** ten years later. Philadelphia was also a hotbed of new ideas in the arts and sciences, as epitomized by the scientist, philosopher, statesman, inventor, and printer **Benjamin Franklin**.

Philadelphia, which translated from Greek means "City of Brotherly Love," is in fact one of the most **ethnically mixed** US cities, with substantial communities of Italians, Irish, Eastern Europeans, and Asians living side-by-side among the large **African-American** population. Many of the city's black residents are descendants of the migrants who flocked here after the Civil War when, like Chicago, Philadelphia was seen as a place of tolerance and liberalism. A century later it voted in the nation's first black mayor, and erected the country's best museum of African-American history and culture. Philly also retains its Quaker heritage, with large "meetings" or congregations of **The Society of Friends**. On the downside, Philadelphia is also the place where in 1985, as part of a huge police effort to dislodge the black separatist group MOVE, a bomb dropped from a helicopter set fire to entire city blocks, killing men, women, and children, and leaving many hundreds homeless.

Once known as "Filthydelphia," and the butt of endless derision in the 1930s by W.C. Fields, whose epitaph read: "On the whole, I'd rather be in Philadelphia", the city underwent a remarkable resurgence preparing for the nation's bicentennial celebrations in 1976. Philadelphia's strength today is its great energy – fueled by history, strong cultural institutions, and grounded in its many staunchly traditional neighborhoods, especially Italian **South Philadelphia**.

Arrival and information

Philadelphia's **International Airport** (℡ 215/937-6800, 🖳 www.phl.org) is seven miles southwest of the city off I-95. **Taxis** into town cost around $30 (try Yellow Cab; ℡ 215/829-4222), and the South East Pennsylvania Transit Authority (**SEPTA**) runs trains from the airport every thirty minutes (4.30am–11.30pm; $5.50; see "City transportation," opposite) to five downtown destinations: Eastwick Station, University City, 30th Street near the university, Suburban Station near City Hall, and Market East, adjacent to the Greyhound terminal at 11th and Filbert streets. The very grand 30th Street **Amtrak** station, one of the busiest in the US, is just across the Schuylkill River in the university area (free transfer downtown on SEPTA). SEPTA connects to **NJ Transit**, and between the two commuter rail systems you can travel to the Jersey shore, Princeton, suburban Pennsylvania, and New York City for a fraction of the price of Amtrak.

The excellent new **Independence Visitor Center**, at 6th and Market streets (daily: late June–Aug 8.30am–5pm; rest of year 8.30am–7pm; ℡ 215/965-7676 or 1-800/537-7676; 🖳 www.independencevisitorcenter.com), contains a staggering wealth of information, and should be the first stop on any downtown or Independence Hall National Park itinerary. It is also an outlet for the good-value **Philadelphia Pass**, which allows entry to over thirty city attractions (valid 1–5 days; $39–105; 🖳 www.philadelphiapass.com).

City transportation

SEPTA (☎215/580-7800, ⓦwww.septa.org) runs an extensive **bus** system and a **subway**. The most useful subway lines cross the city east–west (Market–Frankford line) and north–south (Broad Street line); the handiest bus route is **#76**, which runs from Penn's Landing and the Independence Hall area out along Market Street past City Hall to the museums and Fairmount Park. Bus and subway services require exact fares of $2 (tokens, purchased in batches of two or more, cost only $1.30); **day passes**, also good for the airport, go for $5.50. Bright purple **PHLASH** buses run a handy downtown loop in summer (June–Sept daily 10am–8pm; $1, exact change required; day pass $4; seniors free; ☎215/474-5274, ⓦwww.phillyphlash.com).

City tours

Philadelphia offers a wealth of **tours** focusing on a wide range of subjects. For general orientation, the Big Bus Company (☎215/389-8687, ⓦwww.phillytour.com; 24hr pass $27) runs a hop-on, hop-off tour aboard open-topped double deckers with commentary of the major sites. Poor Richard's Walking Tours (☎215/206-1682, ⓦwww.phillywalks.com; prices vary) are run by University of Pennsylvania graduate students and are for serious history buffs. Philadelphia Neighborhood Tours lead three-hour excursions through different ethnic neighborhoods each week (May–Oct Sat 10am; $27; ☎215/389-8687, ⓦwww.gophila.com/neighborhoodtours), and the Mural Arts Program conducts two-hour trolley tours of the city's extensive neighborhood murals (Apr–Oct Sat 11am; $20; ☎215/685-0750, ⓦwww.muralarts.org). Centipede Tours offer a variety of customized tours and regular candlelit walks through the hidden gardens and courtyards of Society Hill, complete with a costumed guide (hours and prices vary; ☎215/735-3123, ⓦwww.centipedeinc.com), while Ghosts of Philadelphia leads morbid historical tours every evening from next to Independence Hall (April–Nov, hours vary; $15, kids $8; ☎215/413-1997, ⓦwww.ghosttour.com).

Accommodation

Philadelphia's luxury downtown **hotels** are prohibitively expensive, though on weekends there's a chance of getting a reduced rate. Parking is expensive always. The visitor center is a great resource for accommodation discounts; **B&Bs** are a good option here, but usually need to be booked in advance.

Comfort Inn 100 N Columbus Blvd ☎215/627-7900, ⓦwww.comfortinn.com. High-rise hotel in a good location near Penn's Landing; rates include continental breakfast. Cheaper rates are available online. ❹

Crowne Plaza Philadelphia Center City 1800 Market St ☎215/561-7500 or 1-877/227-6963, ⓦwww.crowneplaza.com. One of the best downtown business-oriented hotels, with lush furnishings. A British-style pub is attached to the lobby. ❽

Gaskill House B&B 312 Gaskill St ☎215/413-0669, ⓦwww.gaskillhouse.com. Luxury three-room B&B with full kitchen. Reservations required; discounts available for frequent and business travelers. ❺

HI-Bank Street Hostel 32 S Bank St ☎215/922-0222, ⓦwww.bankstreethostel.com. Friendly

hostel wedged between Independence Hall National Park and Old City, with bunk beds from $20 and free tea and coffee. Closed 11am–4.30pm; curfew 12.30am weekdays, 1am Fri & Sat.

HI-Chamounix Mansion Philadelphia 3250 Chamounix Dr ☎215/878-3676 or 1-800/379-0017, ⓦwww.philahostel.org. Quaker country estate in gorgeous W Fairmount Park, but a fair trek from downtown (take bus #38 from Market St to Ford and Cranston, then walk 1 mile). Midnight curfew, closed 11am–4.30pm and mid-Dec to mid-Jan; beds from $20, kids $8. Free bikes.

La Reserve Center City B&B 1804 Pine St ☎215/735-1137 or 215/735-0582, ⓦwww.centercitybed.com. Lovely rooms and excellent if not overly filling breakfast. The welcoming owner dispenses loads of information. ❹

Penn's View Hotel Front & Market sts ☎215/922-7600 or 1-800/331-7634, ⓦwww.pennsviewhotel.com. Exceptional service and clean, comfortable rooms in Old City, with a very fine wine bar next to the lobby. Continental breakfast included. ❼

Shippen Way Inn 418 Bainbridge St ☎215/627-7266 or 1-800/245-4873, ⓦwww.shippenway.

com. Nicely renovated, family-run B&B with nine cozy rooms a block from South St. ❺

Thomas Bond House 129 S 2nd St ☎1-800/845-2663, ⓦwww.winston-salem-inn.com/philadelphia. Twelve-room restored 1769 B&B near Independence Hall National Park. Slightly marred by an ugly parking lot at the rear. ❺

The City

Central Philadelphia stretches for about two miles from the Schuylkill (pronounced "school-kill") River on the west to the Delaware River on the east; the metropolitan area extends for many miles in all directions, but everything you're likely to want to see is right in the central swath. The city's central districts are compact, walkable, and readily accessible from each other; Penn's sensibly planned grid system makes for easy sightseeing.

△ The Liberty Bell

Independence Hall National Park

Any tour of Philadelphia should start with **Independence National Historic Park**, or **INHP** (☎215/597-8974 or ☎215/965-2305, ⓦwww.nps.gov/inde), "America's most historic square mile." Though the park covers a mere four blocks just west of the Delaware River, between Walnut and Arch streets, it can take more than a day to explore in full. The solid redbrick buildings here, not all of which are open to the public, epitomize the Georgian (and after the Revolution, Federalist) obsession with balance and symmetry.

All INHP sites (unless otherwise specified) are open 365 days a year and admission is free; hours are usually 9am to 5pm, sometimes longer in summer. Free **tours** set off from the rear of the east wing of Independence Hall, the single most important site. Throughout the day, costumed actors perform patchy but informative skits in various locations across the site – pick up a free copy of *The Gazette* newssheet for listings and a useful map.

It's best to reach **Independence Hall** early, to avoid the hordes of tourists and school parties. In peak season, free tickets must be obtained at the Independence Visitor Center. Built in 1732 as the Pennsylvania State House, this was where the Declaration of Independence was prepared, signed, and, after the pealing of the Liberty Bell, given its first public reading on July 8, 1776. Today, in the room in which Jefferson et al drafted and signed the United States Constitution, you can see George Washington's high-backed chair with the half-sun on the back – Franklin, in optimistic spirit, called it "the rising sun."

The **Liberty Bell** itself hung in Independence Hall from 1753, ringing to herald vital announcements such as victories and defeats in the Revolutionary War. Stories as to how it received its famous crack vary but one thing's for sure; it rang publicly for the very last time on George Washington's birthday in 1846. Later in the century, the bell's inscription from Leviticus, advocating liberty "throughout all the land unto all the inhabitants," made it an anti-slavery symbol for the New England abolitionists – the first to call it the Liberty Bell. After the Civil War, the silent bell was adopted as a symbol of reconciliation and embarked on a national rail tour. The well-traveled and somewhat lumpen icon now rests in a shrine-like space in the new multimedia **Liberty Bell Center** in INHP.

Next door to Independence Hall, on 6th and Chestnut streets, **Congress Hall**, built in 1787 as Philadelphia County Courthouse, is where members of the new United States Congress first took their places, and where all the patterns for today's US government were established. The **First Bank of the United States**, at 3rd and Chestnut streets, was established in 1797 to formalize the new union's currency – a vital task given that even Rhode Island, the smallest state, had, at the time, three different types of currency in use.

In 1774, delegates of the first Continental Congress – predecessor of the US Congress – chose defiantly to meet at **Carpenter's Hall**, 320 Chestnut St, rather than the more commodious State House, to air their grievances against the English king. Today the building exhibits early tools and furniture (Tues–Sun 10am–4pm). Directly north, **Franklin Court**, 313 Market St, is a tribute, on the site of his home, to Benjamin Franklin. The house no longer stands, but steel frames outline the original structure. An underground museum has hilarious dial-a-quote recordings of his pithy sayings and the musings of his contemporaries, as well as a working printshop. The **B Free Franklin Post Office**, 316 Market St, sells stamps and includes a small postal museum.

Other buildings in the park include the original **Free Quaker Meeting House**, two blocks north of Market at 5th and Arch, built in 1783 by the small group of Quakers who actually fought in the Revolutionary War. There's also the **Philosophical Hall**, 104 S 5th St, still used today by the nation's first philosophical debating society, also founded by Franklin. Although most of the building is closed to the public, exhibitions such as "Stuffing Birds, Pressing Plants, Shaping Knowledge: Natural History in North America 1730–1860" (March–Sept Wed–Sun 10am–4pm; rest of year Thurs–Sun 10am–4pm; free) provide insights into the history of American science. The must-see **National Constitution Center**, 525 Arch St (Sun–Fri 9.30am–5pm, Sat 9.30am–6pm; $9; ℡1-866/917-1787 or ℡215/409-6600, ⓦwww.constitutioncenter.org), a modern, interactive, and provocative museum dedicated to the nation's best-known document, offers a wealth of information and a number of understated but delicious jabs at the current presidential administration.

Old City

INHP runs north into **Old City**, Philadelphia's earliest commercial area, above Market Street near the riverfront. Washington, Franklin, and Betsy Ross all worshiped at **Christ Church**, on 2nd Street just north of Market. Dating from 1727, it is surrounded by the gravestones of signatories to the Declaration of Independence (tour times vary; ℡215/922-1695, ⓦwww.christchurchphila.org). The church's official burial ground, two blocks west at 5th and Arch, includes **Benjamin Franklin's grave**. At 239 Arch St, the **Betsy Ross House** (April–Oct daily 10am–5pm; Nov–March Tues–Sun 10am–5pm; $3; ℡215/686-1252, ⓦwww.betsyrosshouse.org), by means of unimpressive wax dummies, salutes the woman credited with making the first American flag. The story is probably apocryphal, as it wasn't until the centennial celebrations in 1876 that a man claiming to be Ross's grandson came forward to stake his grandmother's claim. Inside the house, there's a gift shop and shady **garden**, an oasis away from the busy streets outside.

The claim of **Elfreth's Alley** – a pretty little cobbled way off 2nd Street between Arch and Race streets – to be the "oldest street in the United States" is somewhat dubious, though it has been in continuous residential use since 1727; its thirty houses, notable for their wrought-iron gates, water pumps, wooden shutters, and attic rooms, date from the eighteenth century. At no. 126 is the **Mantua Maker's Museum** (March–Oct Mon–Sat 10am–5pm, Sun noon–5pm; Nov–Feb Thurs–Sat 10am–5pm, Sun noon–5pm; $2; ℡215/574-0560, ⓦwww.elfrethsalley.org), where furniture was made for Philadelphia's elite in the eighteenth century.

The area north of Market Street also holds two excellent museums: the **National Museum of American Jewish History**, 55 N 5th St (Mon–Thurs 10am–5pm, Fri 10am–3pm, Sun noon–5pm; free; ℡215/923-3811, ⓦwww.nmajh.org), which is dedicated to the experiences of Jews in the States and includes a synagogue and a Statue of Religious Liberty; and the emotive and politically informed **African American Museum in Philadelphia**, 7th and Arch streets (Tues–Sat 10am–5pm, Sun noon–5pm; $8; ℡215/574-0380, ⓦaampmuseum.org). The latter tells the stories of the thousands of blacks who migrated north to Philadelphia after Reconstruction and in the early twentieth century. As well as lectures, films, and concerts, there are photos, personal memorabilia, poems by black poet Langston Hughes, and a piped-in Billie Holiday soundtrack. The **Edgar Allan Poe National Historic Site**, 532 N 7th St, just north of Spring Garden Street (Wed–Sun 9am–5pm; free; ℡215/597-8780, ⓦwww.nps.gov/edal), is the only one of Poe's five Philadelphia residences that survives but is sadly lacking in atmosphere; however, the staff in the small adjacent **museum** are extremely knowledgeable. If you're keen on literary pilgrimages, you might also want to visit the grave of another key figure of American letters, **Walt Whitman**; he's buried in the Harleigh Cemetery, on Haddon Avenue across the river in Camden, New

Jersey (see below for ferry information). The Old City is also home to a number of **art galleries**, clustered around N 2nd and 3rd streets, and to September's annual Philadelphia Fringe Festival, a popular experimental theater series (℡215/413-9006, ⓦ www.pafringe.org).

Penn's Landing

Just east of Old City along the Delaware River, where William Penn stepped off in 1682, spreads the huge and heavily industrialized port of Philadelphia. Along the port's southern reaches, on the river side of the I-95 freeway, the old docklands have been renovated as part of the **Penn's Landing** development, which includes the **Independence Seaport Museum** (daily 10am–5pm; $9, free Sun 10am–noon; ℡215/925-5439, ⓦ www.phillyseaport.org) and a variety of historical **ships**, including the flagship USS *Olympia* and the World War II submarine *Becuna* (both daily 10am–5pm; $8), and the three-masted Portuguese Tall Ship *Gazela*, built in 1883 (hours vary; donation; ⓦ www.gazela.org). All along the riverfront promenade are food stalls, landscaped pools, and fountains, and regular outdoor concerts and festivals are held here.

The seasonal Riverlink **ferry** crosses the Delaware (May–Sept hourly 10am–6pm; $6 roundtrip; ℡215/925-5465, ⓦ www.riverlinkferry.org) to the down-at-heel town of **Camden**, where the main attraction is the **Adventure Aquarium** (daily 9.30am–5pm; $16.95; ℡856/365-3300, ⓦ www.adventureaquarium.com) – good for kids but otherwise eminently missable. A $29.95 **River Pass** covers the museum, ships, aquarium, and a roundtrip on the ferry.

Society Hill

Society Hill, an elegant residential area west of the Delaware and directly south of INHP, spreads between Walnut and Lombard streets. Though it is indeed Philadelphia's high society that lives here now, the area was named for its first inhabitants, the Free Society of Traders – a rather more fun-loving bunch than the strict Quakers who lived to the north. After falling into disrepair, the Hill itself was flattened in the early 1970s to provide a building site for I.M. Pei's twin skyscrapers, Society Hill Towers. Luckily, the rest of the neighborhood has been restored to form one of the city's most picturesque districts: cobbled gas-lit streets are lined with immaculately kept Colonial, Federal, and Georgian homes, often featuring the state's namesake keystones on their window frames, and markers everywhere point out the area's rich history. One of the few buildings open to the public is the **Physick House**, 321 S 4th St, home to Dr Philip Syng Physick, "the Father of American Surgery," and filled with eighteenth- and nineteenth-century decorative arts (Thurs–Sat noon–5pm; $5; ℡215/925-7866, ⓦ www.philalandmarks.org).

Center City

Center City, Philadelphia's main business and commercial area, stretches from 8th Street west to the Schuylkill River, dominated by the endearing Baroque wedding cake of **City Hall** and its 37ft bronze statue of Penn. Before ascending thirty stories to the observation deck at Penn's feet, check out the quirky sculptures and carvings around the building, including the cats and mice at the south entrance.

A couple of blocks north at Broad and Cherry streets, the **Pennsylvania Academy of the Fine Arts** (Tues–Sat 10am–5pm, Sun 11am–5pm; $7; ℡215/972-7600, ⓦ www.pafa.org), housed in an elaborate, multicolored Victorian pile, exhibits three hundred years of American art, including works by Mary Cassatt, Thomas Eakins, and Winslow Homer.

Beginning at 8th Street, **Chinatown**, marked by the gorgeous 40ft Friendship Gate at 10th and Arch, has some of the best inexpensive food in the city. A block over on 12th Street is the century-old **Reading Terminal Market** (daily 9am–4pm; ☎215/922-2317, ⓦwww.readingterminalmarket.org), where many Amish farmers come to the city to sell their produce. It's always good for a lively time and makes a great lunch spot. Next door, the decade-old Convention Center helped usher in flashy hotels, coffeehouses, and restaurants, to replace the previously derelict shops and offices.

Rittenhouse Square

Grassy **Rittenhouse Square**, one of Penn's original city squares, is in a very fashionable part of town. On one side it borders chic Walnut Street, on the other a residential area of solid brownstones with beautifully carved doors and windows. The redbrick 1860 **Rosenbach Museum**, 2010 Delancey Place, holds over thirty thousand rare books, as well as James Joyce's original hand-scrawled manuscripts of *Ulysses* (Tues, Thurs, Fri–Sun 10am–5pm, Wed 10am–8pm; $8, including house tour; ☎215/732-1600, ⓦwww.rosenbach.org). On summer evenings there are free outdoor jazz and R&B concerts in the square.

Three blocks northwest from the square, the **Mütter Museum**, 19 S 22nd St in the College of Physicians (daily 10am–5pm; $12; ☎215/563-3737, ⓦwww .collphyphil.org), is not for the squeamish. Filled with weird pathological and medical oddities – including sickeningly lifelike wax models of tumors and skin infections, alongside closets full of skeletons, syphilitic skulls, pickled internal organs, and the death cast of a pair of Siamese twins – it's unique to say the least.

Museum Row

The mile-long Benjamin Franklin Parkway, known as Museum Row – or, less convincingly, as "America's Champs-Elysees" – sweeps northwest from City Hall to the colossal Museum of Art in **Fairmount Park**, an area of countryside annexed by the city in the nineteenth century. Spanning nine hundred scenic acres on both sides of the Schuylkill River, this is one of the world's largest landscaped city parks, with jogging, biking, and hiking trails, early American homes, an all-wars memorial to the state's black soldiers, and a zoo – the country's first – at 3400 W Girard Ave (Mar–Nov 9.30am–5pm; $16.95; Dec–Feb 9.30am–4pm; $12.95; ☎215/243-1100, ⓦwww.phillyzoo.org). In the late 1960s, local resident **Joe Frazier** and **Muhammad Ali** all but brought the city to a standstill with the announcement one afternoon that they were heading to Fairmount for an informal slug-out.

Sylvester Stallone later immortalized the steps of the **Philadelphia Museum of Art**, 26th St and Franklin Pkwy (Tues–Thurs, Sat & Sun 10am–5pm, Fri 10am–8.45pm; $12, Sun donation; ☎215/763-8100, ⓦwww.philamuseum.org), by running up them in the film *Rocky*, but he missed out on a real treat inside: one of the finest collections in the US, with a twelfth-century French cloister, Renaissance art, a complete **Robert Adam** interior from a 1765 house in London's Berkeley Square, Rubens tapestries, Pennsylvania Dutch crafts and **Shaker furniture**, a strong **Impressionist** collection, and the world's most extensive collection of the works of **Marcel Duchamp**. Exhibits are displayed in an easy-to-follow chronological order.

A few blocks away, at Franklin Parkway and 22nd Street, the exquisite **Rodin Museum** (Tues–Sun 10am–5pm; $3 suggested donation; ☎215/763-8100, ⓦwww.rodinmuseum.org), marble-walled and set in a shady garden with a green pool, holds the largest collection of Rodin's Impressionistic sculptures and casts outside of Paris, including *The Burghers of Calais*, *The Thinker*, and *The Gates of Hell*. Among the rare books at the **Free Library of Philadelphia**, 19th and Vine streets (Mon–Thurs 9am–9pm, Fri 9am–6pm, Sat 9am–5pm, tours at 11am; free; ☎215/686-5322, ⓦwww.library.phila.gov), are cuneiform tablets from 3000 BC, medieval manuscripts, first editions of Dickens and Poe, and such intriguing titles as the 1807 *Inquiry into the Conduct of the Princess of Wales*.

Over the road, in the vast **Franklin Institute Science Museum**, N 20th St and Benjamin Franklin Pkwy (daily 9.30am–5pm; $13.75; ☎215/448-1200, ⓦsln. fi.edu), are a **Planetarium**, the **Tuttleman IMAX Theater** ($9), and the **Mandell Futures Center**. A combination ticket ($18.75) covers general admission and a film. Continuing the educational theme, the nearby **Academy of Natural Sciences** exhibits dinosaurs, mummies, and gems (Mon–Fri 10am–4.30pm, Sat, Sun & holidays 10am–5pm; $10; ☎215/299-1000, ⓦwww.acnatsci.org), while the **Please Touch Museum**, 210 N 21st St (daily 9am–4.30pm; $9.95; ☎215/963-0667, ⓦwww.pleasetouchmuseum.org), is a hands-on adventureland aimed at youngsters.

Eastern State Penitentiary

One of Philadelphia's most significant historic sites stands, all but forgotten, just a short walk from the Fairmount Park museums. The **Eastern State Penitentiary**, whose gloomy Gothic fortifications fill an entire block of the residential neighborhood along Fairmount Ave at 22nd St, embodies an almost complete history of attitudes toward crime and punishment in the US. Since it opened in 1829, the Quaker-inspired prison's radical efforts to rehabilitate inmates via isolation, rather than use physical abuse and capital punishment, attracted curious social commentators from around the world; when Charles Dickens came to America in 1842, he wanted to see two things; this prison and Niagara Falls. Despite substantial changes over the years and gradual decay since it closed in 1970, the bulk of the Panopticon-style radial prison survives, and a restoration program was recently completed. **Guided tours** leave on the hour (daily 10am–5pm, last entry 4pm; $10; ☎215/236-3300, ⓦwww.easternstate.org) and point out the prison's many novel architectural features, as well as its old synagogue, the cell where Al Capone cooled his heels, and the block where Tina Turner filmed a music video.

West Philadelphia

Across the Schuylkill River, **West Philadelphia** is home to the Ivy-League **University of Pennsylvania**, where Franklin established the country's first medical school. The compact but extremely pleasant campus blends into fairly gritty urban areas, but has some great museums: the small **Institute of Contemporary Art**, 118 S 36th St (Wed–Fri noon–8pm, Sat & Sun 11am–5pm; $6, free Sun 11am–1pm; ☎215/898-5911, ⓦwww.icaphila.org), which displays cutting-edge traveling exhibitions in an airy space, complete with a very comfortable bean-bag chair lobby; and the intriguing **Arthur Ross Gallery**, 220 S 34th St (Tues–Fri 10am–5pm, Sat & Sun noon–5pm; free; ☎215/898-2083, ⓦwww.upenn. edu/ARG), which features changing exhibits, particularly of international and innovative work, many of which have a strong emphasis on the use of color. The superlative **Museum of Archeology and Anthropology**, 33rd and Spruce streets (Tues–Sat 10am–4.30pm; Sept–May also Sun 1–5pm; $8, free Sun; ☎215/898-4000, ⓦwww.museum.upenn.edu), is the university's top draw. Regarded by experts as one of the world's finest science museums, its exhibits span all the continents and their major epochs – from Nigerian Benin bronzes to Chinese crystal balls. Most astonishing is the priceless twelve-ton granite Sphinx of Rameses II, c.1293–1185 BC, in the Lower Egyptian Gallery. The Meso-American and Greco-Roman Galleries also hold plenty of highlights.

South Philadelphia

Staunchly blue-collar **South Philadelphia**, center of Philadelphia's black community since the Civil War, is also home to many of the city's Italians; opera singer

Mario Lanza (who has his own museum at 712 Montrose St) and pop stars Fabian and Chubby Checker grew up here. It's also where to come for an authentic – and very messy – **Philly cheesesteak** (see "Eating," below), and to rummage through the wonderful **Italian Market** (another *Rocky* location) which runs along 9th Street south from Christian Street. One of the last surviving urban markets in the US, the wooden market stalls that have stood here for generations are packed to overflowing with bric-a-brac, produce, secondhand Levis, live seafood, and, most famously, mozzarella.

South Street, the original boundary of the city, is now Philadelphia's main **nightlife** district, with dozens of cafés, bars, restaurants, and nightclubs lined up along the few blocks west from Front Street. During the day you can wander amongst the many good book, record, and clothing **shops**. At night, it makes for a lively, if highly commercial, evening out but beware, as it gets overwhelmingly crowded on summer weekends.

Eating

Eating out in Philadelphia is a real treat: the ubiquitous street stands sell **soft pretzels** with mustard for 50¢, Chinatown and the Italian Market are good for ethnic food, and Reading Terminal Market makes a bargain lunch stop in Center City. South Street has plenty of good, if well-touristed, eateries, while pricier, trendier restaurants cluster along S 2nd Street in the Old City. The South Philly **cheesesteak**, a sandwich of wafer-thin roast beef topped with melted cheese (aka Cheez Whiz), varies from place to place around town; some of the best are to be found around 9th and Passyunk in South Philadelphia (see *Pat's*, below). Bear in mind that a cheesesteak is hot, while a **hoagie** is not.

Amada 217 Chestnut St ☎215/625-2450. A dash of Spanish inspiration in Old City, with over 60 tapas dishes, great paella, and fine red or white sangria, all at reasonable prices.

Buddakan 325 Chestnut St ☎215/574-9440. Delicious pan-Asian fusion food and a family atmosphere make this a firm Philly favorite. Admire the 10ft gilded Buddha while dining.

City Tavern 138 S 2nd St ☎215/413-1443. Reconstructed 1773 tavern in INHP, familiar to the city's founders, and called by John Adams "the most genteel tavern in America." Chef Walter Staib cooks and costumed staff serve "olde style" food (pasties, turkey rarebit) to a harpsichord accompaniment – dinner entrees are mostly $20 and up.

Delilah's Reading Terminal Market, 12th and Spruce sts ☎215/574-0929. Superb, extremely cheap soul food with scatty service. Oprah Winfrey nominated their mac and cheese as the best in the nation.

Ocean City 234-6 N 9th St ☎215/829-0688. Huge Chinatown space specialising in fresh seafood, which is on display in tanks; also excellent dim sum before 3pm.

🐾 **Pat's King of Steaks** 1237 E Passyunk Ave ☎215/468-1546. At this delightfully decrepit, outdoor-seating-only cheesesteak joint, take care to order correctly (there's a sign to help "rookies") or prepare yourself to be sent to the back of the line. The cheesesteaks here are the real deal. Open 24hr, 361 days a year.

Rangoon 112 N 9th St ☎215/829-8939. Friendly and intimate Burmese joint, serving an authentic selection of curries and rice and noodle dishes at around $10; try the cheap lunch specials.

San Carlo 214 South Street ☎215/592-9777. Excellent fresh pasta dishes, nice atmosphere, and attentive – if pushy – service at reasonable prices.

Serrano 20 S 2nd St ☎215/928-0770. Intimate Old City café serving creative international fusion cooking, with good fresh seafood. Try the appetizer tasting menu. Diners get preferential seating at the *Tin Angel* folk club upstairs (see opposite).

Sonoma 4411 Main St, Manayunk ☎215/483-9400. Pleasant, reasonably priced California-style Italian restaurant.

South Street Diner 140 South St ☎215/627-5258. Huge menu with Greek and Italian specialties from $6.95. Open daily 7am–3am.

Tre Scalini 1533 S 11th St ☎215/551-3870. A taste of traditional South Philly Italian, with reasonably priced dishes and a low-key atmosphere.

White Dog Café 3420 Sansom St ☎215/386-9224, ⓦwww.whitedog.com. Delicious, creative food in three Victorian brownstones near the universities. Artsy, student crowd; lunch entrees $7–12; happy hour Sun–Thurs 10pm–midnight.

Drinking

The most popular place for bar-hopping is **South Street** and around **2nd Street** in the Old City, although the **Northern Liberties** area, about eight blocks north, beyond the flyovers, is rapidly up-and-coming for trendy bars and clubs. Local brews are popular and inexpensive; try any ale by Yards or Yuengling if you prefer lager. Philly's growing number of **cafés** are spread around the city; South Street, 2nd Street, and Center City have the densest concentrations.

Dark Horse 421 S 2nd St ☎215/928-9307. Unpretentious British-style boozer with a fine range of beer and the added bonus of soccer on TV for visitors from the old continent.

Dirty Frank's 347 S 13th St ☎215/732-5010. Popular with a very mixed crowd, this Philly institution touts itself as "one of the few places in the world where you can drink a $2.50 pint of Yuengling underneath oil paintings by nationally recognized artists."

The Mean Bean Co. 1112 Locust St ☎215/925-2010. Coffeeshop serving a mixed gay and straight crowd, with outdoor seating next to the lovely Sartain St private community garden.

Skinner's Dry Goods 226 Market St ☎215/922-0522. Friendly Old City bar with decent ale, good music, and screens to keep an eye on important sports events.

Society Hill 301 Chestnut St ☎215/925-1919. Swanky bar a stone's throw from the *Bank Street Hostel*. Live jazz piano music Tuesday evenings.

Sugar Mom's Church Street Lounge 225 Church St ☎215/925-8219. Popular basement bar where the jukebox ranges from Tony Bennett to Sonic Youth, with a dozen international beers on tap.

Tangier Café 1801 Lombard St ☎215/732-5006. Cozy, attractive local bar with inexpensive bottles of Yuengling, friendly bar staff, and a low-key atmosphere.

Woody's Bar and Restaurant 202 S 13th St ☎215/545-1893. Large, friendly downtown beer bar popular with Philly's gay community.

Nightlife and entertainment

Few reminders are left of the 1970s "Philly Sound". Instead, in recent times the city has produced the likes of pop starlet Pink, while its active underground scene features psych bands like Bardo Pond and The Asteroid #4. Philadelphia is also a good place to see rock bands, as most of the names that play New York come here too, and tickets are half the price or even less. The world-famous **Philadelphia Orchestra** performs at the grand new Kimmel Center for the Performing Arts (☎215/893-1999, ⓦwww.kimmelcenter.org). Philadelphia's other great strength is its **theater** scene, where small venues abound. Check the **listings** in the free *City Paper* or *Philadelphia Weekly* newspapers, or visit the Theatre Alliance website at ⓦwww.theatrealliance.org, which also features the StageTix discount ticket program. Discount offers to various events are also available on the GoPhila website at ⓦwww.gophila.com/events.

The Five Spot 5 South Bank St ☎215/574-0070, ⓦwww.thefivespot.com. Old City club with live acts upstairs and DJs spinning mostly hip-hop and electronica in the downstairs dancing space.

The Khyber 56 S 2nd St ☎215/238-5888, ⓦwww.thekhyber.com. Small rock venue with a gargoyle-lined bar, bluesy jukebox, and casual young clientele. Cover around $8–10 when bands are on. A bar with no cover is upstairs.

Painted Bride Art Center 230 Vine St ☎215/925-9914, ⓦwww.paintedbride.org. Art gallery with live jazz, dance, and theater performances after dark.

Silk City Lounge 5th and Spring Garden sts ☎215/592-8838, ⓦwww.silkcitylounge.com. Very mixed musical bag – funk, hip-hop, acid jazz,

indie, dance, and soul – in this ultratrendy but unflashy Northern Liberties club. Local bands play on weekends.

Theater of Living Arts 334 South St ☎215/922-1011, ⓦwww.thetla.com. Converted movie palace that's the best place to catch rock bands.

Tin Angel 20 S 2nd St ☎215/928-0770, ⓦwww.tinangel.com. Intimate upstairs bar and coffeehouse, featuring top local and nationally known folk and acoustic acts.

Trocadero 1003 Arch St ☎215/922-5483, ⓦwww.thetroc.com. Trendy downtown music venue, sometimes featuring big-name alternative bands. Cover varies, and ID is essential.

Zanzibar Blue 200 S Broad St in the *Bellevue*

York–style jazz nightly, often by famous names; expect a hefty cover charge and two-drink minimum.

Central Pennsylvania

Central Pennsylvania, cut north to south by the broad **Susquehanna River**, has no major cities – though the state capital, **Harrisburg**, is an excellent base from which to explore sights that include the **Hershey** chocolate empire and the rolling Amish farmlands of **Lancaster County** to the east, and the Civil War site of **Gettysburg** on the state's southern border. To the north, the mighty forests of the "Grand Canyon of Pennsylvania," around **Williamsport**, reveal the legacy of its great nineteenth-century lumber wealth in mansion-lined streets. **Johnstown**, beyond the dramatic Allegheny Mountains in the west, and **Scranton**, whose dullness got it chosen as the setting for the US version of *The Office*, are industrial towns with little of interest for the casual visitor.

Lancaster County – Pennsylvania Dutch Country

Lancaster County, fifty miles west of Philadelphia, stretches for about 45 miles from Churchtown in the east to the Susquehanna River in the west. Although tiny, uncosmopolitan Lancaster City, ten miles east of the river, was US capital for a day in September 1777, the region is famed more for its preponderance of agricultural religious communities, known collectively as the **Pennsylvania Dutch**. They actually have no connection to the Netherlands; the name is a mistaken derivation of Deutsch (German).

An extremely touristy place even before it was brought to international fame by the movie *Witness*, Lancaster County has maintained its natural beauty in the face of encroaching commercialization. It is a region of gentle countryside and fertile farmlands, mule-drawn ploughs, tiny roadside bakeries crammed with jams and pies, Amish children wending on old-fashioned scooters between their flower-filled, immaculate farmhouses and one-room schoolhouses. Tragically, the innocence of this idyll was shattered on October 2, 2006, when a non-Amish gunman entered a schoolhouse in **Nickel Mines** and shot ten girls, killing half of them.

Indeed, attempting to live a simple life away from the pressures of the outside world has proved too much for many Pennsylvania Dutch. A few (mainly Mennonites) have succumbed to commercial need by offering rides in their buggies and meals in their homes. Members of the stricter orders in particular have moved away from the ceaseless intrusions of privacy – as well as soaring land prices – to less touristed Ohio, Indiana, Minnesota, and Iowa. When visiting, remember that Sunday is a day of rest for the Amish, so many attractions, restaurants, and other amenities will be closed.

Arrival and information

The best route through the concentrated Amish communities is US-30, which runs east–west. **Amtrak** arrives at the train station at 53 McGovern Ave, Lancaster City, as do buses from Capital Trailways (☎ 717/397-4861) and Greyhound. The bustling **Pennsylvania Dutch Convention and Visitors Bureau**, just off US-30 at 501 Greenfield Rd (daily 8.30am–5pm, longer hours in summer; ☎ 717/299-8901 or 1-800/PADUTCH, ⓦ www.padutchcountry.com), does an excellent job of providing orientation and advice on accommodation. Visitors keen to learn

The Pennsylvania Dutch

The people now known as the Pennsylvania Dutch originated as **Anabaptists** in sixteenth-century Switzerland, under the leadership of Menno Simons. His unorthodox advocacy of adult baptism and literal interpretation of the Bible led to the order's persecution; they were invited by William Penn to settle in Lancaster County in the 1720s. Today the twenty or so orders of Pennsylvania Dutch include the "plain" Old Order **Amish** (a strict order that originally broke away from Simons in 1693) and freer-living **Mennonites**, as well as the "fancy" **Lutheran** groups (distinguished by the colorful circular "hex" signs on their barns). Living by an unwritten set of rules called Amish Ordnung, which includes absolute pacifism, the Amish are the strictest and best-known: the men with their wide-brimmed straw hats and beards (but no "military" mustaches), the women in bonnets, plain dresses (with no fripperies like buttons), and aprons. Shunning electricity and any exposure to the corrupting influence of the outside world, the Amish power their farms with generators, and travel (at roughly ten miles per hour) in handmade horse-drawn buggies. For all their insularity, the Amish are very friendly and helpful; resist the temptation to photograph them, however, as the making of "graven images" offends their beliefs.

about Pennsylvania Dutch culture should head to the **Mennonite Information Center** (April–Oct Mon–Sat 8am–5pm; Nov–March Mon–Sat 8.30am–4.30pm; ☎717/299-0954 or 1-800/858-8320, ⊛www.mennoniteinfoctr.com), off US-30 at 2209 Millstream Rd, which shows a short film entitled *Who Are the Amish?* and also organizes lodging with Mennonite families. If you call at least two hours ahead, a guide can take you on a two-hour, $36 tour in your car.

Getting around and tours

Winding country lanes weave through Pennsylvania Dutch Country, passing small villages with eccentric-sounding names such as **Intercourse** (source of many droll postcards, but supposedly named for its location on the junction of two main roads). Although a **car** will get you to the quieter back roads that the tour buses miss, it's more fun to **ride a bike**. Only then can you feel the benefits of all that fresh air – and it shows more consideration for the horse-drawn buggies with which you share the road. For self-guided **bike tours**, contact Lancaster Bicycle Club in Lancaster City (⊛www.lancasterbikeclub.org).

The Amish Experience, on US-30 at Plain & Fancy Farm (☎717/768-3600 ext 210, ⊛www.amishexperience.com), runs two-hour farmlands **tours** (Mon–Sat 10.30am & 2pm, Sun 11.30am only) for $25.95, though some accommodations (see the *Village Inn*, below) offer a similar service for free. AAA Buggy Rides offer lolloping three-mile countryside excursions for $10 (☎717/989-2829) from the *Red Caboose Inn* in Paradise and *Kitchen Kettle Village* in Intercourse.

Accommodation

Accommodation options in Pennsylvania Dutch Country range from reasonably priced **hotels** and **B&Bs**, which can be arranged through a central agency (☎1-800/552-2632, ⊛www.authenticbandb.com), to **farm vacations** (ask at the Pennsylvania Dutch Visitors Bureau; see opposite) to **campgrounds**. *White Oak Campground*, 372 White Oak Rd, Quarryville, four miles north of Strasburg (☎717/687-6207, ⊛www.whiteoakcampground.com; sites from $22), overlooks the heart of the Dutch farmlands.

Cameron Estate Inn & Restaurant 1855 Mansion Lane, Mount Joy ☎717/492-0111 or 1-800/422-6376, ⊛www.cameronestateinn. com. Out-of-the-way gay-friendly inn on fifteen

acres with sparkling, comfortable rooms (one with Jacuzzi), free full breakfast and a restaurant. ❺
Countryside Motel 134 Hartman Bridge Rd ⊕717/687-8431. Clean and simple place six miles east of Lancaster City on Hwy-896. ❸
Netherlands Inn & Spa Rte-896, Strasburg ⊕717/687-7691 or 1-800/872-0201, ⓦwww. netherlandsinn.com. One hundred luxury rooms and a spa tucked away on sixty rolling acres. ❻
O'Flaherty's Dingeldein House 1105 E King St, Lancaster City ⊕717/293-1723 or 1-800/779-

7765, ⓦwww.dingeldeinhouse.com. Friendly seven-room B&B. Rates include a large country breakfast. ❹
Village Inn 2695 Old Philadelphia Pike, Bird-in-Hand ⊕1-800/665-8780, ⓦwww.bird-in-hand. com/villageinn. Excellent old inn with modern amenities, large breakfast, deck, lawn, and back pasture. Price includes 2hr tour of Amish Country and use of the adjacent motel's pool. Book ahead. ❺

Touring Pennsylvania Dutch Country

Though useful for a general overview and historical insight, the attractions that interpret Amish culture tend toward overkill. It's far more satisfying just to explore the countryside for yourself. Here, among the streams with their covered bridges and fields striped with corn, alfalfa, and tobacco, the reality hits you – these aren't actors recreating an ancient lifestyle, but real people, part of a living, working community. There's no guarantee as to what you'll see: on Sunday, for example, there are no quilt sales or bake shops, and the farmers don't work the fields, but there may well be a large gathering of buggies outside one of the farms, indicating an Amish church service (in High German) or a "visiting day," when families gather socially. Church services and visiting days take place on alternating Sundays; visits sometimes occur during the week as well.

Among the widely spread formal attractions, the **Ephrata Cloister**, 632 W Main St, Ephrata (on US-272 and 322), recreates the eighteenth-century settlement of German Protestant celibates that acted, amongst other things, as an early publishing and printing center (Mon–Sat 9am–5pm, Sun noon–5pm, Jan & Feb closed Mon; $7; ⊕717/733-6600, ⓦwww.ephratacloister.org). Further south, about three miles northeast of Lancaster City, the **Landis Valley Museum**, 2451 Kissell Hill Rd (Tues–Sat 9am–5pm, Sun noon–5pm; $9; ⊕717/569-0401, ⓦwww.landisvalleymuseum .org), is a living history museum of rural life, with demonstrations of local crafts.

In Lancaster City itself, a stolid redbrick town with tree-lined avenues, the **Lancaster Cultural History Museum**, in Penn Square (Tues–Sat 10am–5pm, Sun noon–5pm; free; ⊕717/299-6440, ⓦwww.lancasterheritage.com), exhibits Lancaster master crafts, including wagons and rifles, ancient Amish calligraphy known as fraktur, clocks, wooden toys, weathervanes, and quilts. At **Strasburg**, a mixture of tourist kitsch and historical authenticity southeast of Lancaster City on US-896, the **Strasburg Railroad** gives 45-minute roundtrip rides in original steam trains through patchwork farmland to Paradise (daily, hours vary; from $12, kids $7; ⊕717/687-7522, ⓦwww.strasburgrailroad.com). Disappointingly, **Paradise** holds no heavenly delights, but there are some good views on the way and the train makes regular picnic stops. The oldest building in the county, the **Hans Herr House**, 1849 Hans Herr Drive, five miles south of downtown Lancaster City off US-222 (April–Nov Mon–Sat 9am–4pm; $5; ⊕717/464-4438, ⓦwww.hansherr. org), is a 1719 Mennonite church with a pretty garden and orchard, a medieval German facade, and exhibits on early farm life.

Eating, drinking, and entertainment

Lancaster County **food** is delicious, Germanic, and served in vast quantities. There are no Amish-owned restaurants, but Amish roadside stalls sell fresh homemade root beer, jams, pickles, breads, and pies. The huge "all-you-care-to-eat" **tourist restaurants** on US-30 and US-340 may look off-putting, all pseudo-rusticism with costumed waitresses, but most serve good meals, for around $15, "family-style" – you share long tables and mountains of fried chicken, sauerkraut, noodles, pickles, cottage cheese and apple butter, corn, hickory-smoked ham, schnitz und knepp (apple, ham, and dumpling stew), shoo-fly pie and the like with crowds of other out-of-towners. None stays open later than 8pm. A few other restaurants, particularly **diners** in busy areas, are open later at night. Rural Lancaster County is, unsurprisingly, not known for its nightlife – though there are a couple of very friendly **bars** in downtown Lancaster City worth checking out. The Fulton Opera House, 12 N Prince St (☏717/394-7133, ⓦwww.fultontheatre.org), is a plush red-and-gold restored Victorian **theater**, hosting dance, plays, and special events.

②

Central Market Penn Square, Lancaster City. Covered market selling fresh local farm produce and lunch to loyal Lancastrians and tourists alike. Tues & Fri 6am–4pm, Sat 6am–2pm.

Good 'n' Plenty East Brook Rd, US-896, Smoketown ☏717/394-7111. Not Amish-owned, though Amish women cook and serve food in this, the best of the family-style restaurants. Open early Feb to mid-Dec Mon–Sat.

Lancaster Brewing Co. 302 N Plum St, Lancaster City ☏717/391-6258, ⓦwww.lancasterbrewing. com. Brewpub serving good bar food and five different microbrews. Tours given Fri & Sat by appointment. Open on Sun.

Lancaster Dispensing Co. 33-35 N Market St, Lancaster City ☏717/299-4602. Downtown Lancaster's trendiest, friendliest bar, with live weekend jazz and blues, plus overstuffed sandwiches for around $6.

Lapp's 2270 Lincoln Hwy E (US-30), near Lancaster City ☏717/394-1606. A solid diner with the family atmosphere and ample Germanic food typical of Lancaster County, open daily.

Molly's Pub 253 E Chestnut St, Lancaster City ☏717/396-0225. Neighborhood bar with lively atmosphere and good burgers. Closed Sun.

Plain and Fancy 3121 Old Philadelphia Pike (Rte-340), Bird-in-Hand ☏717/768-4400. Standard family-style restaurant; only one in the area open on Sundays.

Harrisburg and Hershey

HARRISBURG, Pennsylvania's capital, lies on the Susquehanna River thirty or so miles northwest of Lancaster City. It's a surprisingly attractive small city, its lush waterfront lined with shuttered colonial buildings, and is well-complemented by its kitschy Chocolatetown neighbor **Hershey**. Harrisburg is also known as the site of the **Three Mile Island** nuclear facility, which suffered a famous meltdown in the 1970s and stands along the river on the east side of town.

The ornate, attractive Italian Renaissance **capitol** at Third and State streets has a dome modeled after St Peter's in Rome (tours Mon–Fri 8.30am–4pm; Sat, Sun & holidays at 9am, 11am, 1pm & 3pm; free; ☏1-800/868-7672). The complex includes the archeological and military artifacts, decorative arts, tools and machinery exhibited in the four-floor **State Museum of Pennsylvania**, a cylindrical building that holds a planetarium, at Third and North (Tues–Sat 9am–5pm, Sun noon–5pm; free; ☏717/787-4980, ⓦwww.statemuseumpa. org). But undoubtedly the real attraction here is the excellent **National Civil War Museum**, roughly two miles east of downtown at the summit of hilly Reservoir Park (Mon–Sat 9am–5pm, Sun noon–5pm; $8; ☏717/260-1861 or 1-866/258-4729, ⓦwww.nationalcivilwarmuseum.org). Almost 730,000 Americans were killed in the Civil War – more than in all other conflicts since the Revolution combined – and the museum offers an intelligent analysis of the reasons for, and results of, the war. Especially evocative are the fictionalized monologues, playing on video screens in every gallery, which focus on the human cost of the conflict. There's also a good terrace café with great views across the city.

One of the best ways to spend a Harrisburg afternoon is to stroll along the gorgeous east bank of the Susquehanna, then cross the river along the Walnut Street footbridge and walk through **City Island**, a waterfront development with vast facilities, including a kite-flying area, a tourist railroad, a family-filled concrete beach, and paddlewheeler rides (May–Aug, groups Sept–Oct; rides $5; ℡717/234-6500).

HERSHEY, ten miles east, was built in 1903 by candy magnate Milton S. Hershey for his chocolate factory – so it has streets named Chocolate and Cocoa avenues and streetlamps in the shape of Hershey's Chocolate Kisses. **Hershey's Chocolate World** (Mon–Sat 9am–5pm, Sun 11am–5pm; longer hours in summer; ℡717/534-4900, ⓦwww.hersheyschocolateworld.com) offers a free mini-train ride through a romanticized simulated chocolate factory, a 3-D chocolate show ($5.95), and a cheesy musical/historical trolley ride around town ($10.75). Those not content with the free samples given out at various points on the rides can gorge themselves in the vast gift shops and cafés.

Hersheypark, which began in 1907 as a picnic ground for Hershey factory workers, is now a hugely popular **amusement park**, with stomach-churning roller coasters and various other rides (mid-May to Sept, hours vary; $43.95; ℡717/534-3090 or 1-800/437-7439). Cheaper special events take place for Halloween and Christmas. The adjacent **Hershey Museum** (June–Aug daily 10am–6pm; Sept–May daily 10am–5pm; $7; ℡717/534-3439, ⓦwww.hersheymuseum.org) has exhibits on the Pennsylvania Dutch and tells the Milton S. Hershey story.

Thirty-five miles south of Hershey, via Harrisburg, the blue-collar town of **York** is home to the largest assembly plant of motorcycle legend **Harley-Davidson**. The company has a visitor center with exhibitions and runs free hour-long tours from the **Vaughn L Beals Tour Center** (Mon–Fri factory tours 9am–2pm, tour center 8am–4pm; ℡1-877/883-1450); closed-toed shoes are required.

Practicalities

Amtrak **trains** share the central station at Fourth and Chestnut streets with Greyhound, whose **buses** also stop in Hershey at 337 W Chocolate St. Harrisburg's **visitor center** (℡717/231-7788, ⓦwww.visithhc.com) is not open to walk-ins, but can be contacted for good local and regional information.

In leafy Camp Hill, just across the river from Harrisburg, the *Radisson Penn Harris* (℡717/763-7117, ⓦwww.radisson.com; ❹) has good-value rooms in relaxing surroundings. Options in Hershey include the standard *Spinners Inn*, 845 E Chocolate Ave (℡717/533-9157, ⓦwww.spinnersinn.com; ❸), which has a very good restaurant, and the standard *Chocolatetown Motel*, a mile further on at no. 1806 (℡717/533-2330, ⓦwww.chocolatetownmotel.com; ❸). Upscale lodging is available at the palatial *Hotel Hershey*, Hotel Road (℡717/533-2171, ⓦwww.hotelhershey.com; ❻), complete with an onsite spa offering chocolate-based beauty treatments. Weekend spa appointments must be made far in advance. The best **campsite** in the region is *Hershey Highmeadow Campground*, 1200 Matlack Rd, Hummelstown, on the Harrisburg side of Hershey (℡717/534-8999 or 1-800/437-7439, ⓦwww.hersheycamping.com), which has sites from around $25 off-season to $35 in summer.

Budget **restaurants** line Second Street in downtown Harrisburg, the best being *Fisaga's*, at Locust and N Second streets (℡717/441-1556), which serves good basic sandwiches and pasta. *Scott's*, 212 Locust St (℡717/234-7599), is a popular bar and grill, with live music some nights.

Gettysburg

The small town of **GETTYSBURG**, thirty miles south of Harrisburg near the Maryland border, gained tragic notoriety in July 1863 for the cataclysmic **Civil War** battle in which fifty thousand men died. There were more casualties during these three days than in any American battle before or since – a full third of those who fought were killed or wounded – and entire regiments were wiped out when the tide finally turned against the South.

Four months later, on November 19, Abraham Lincoln delivered his **Gettysburg Address** at the dedication of the National Cemetery. His two-minute speech, in memory of all the soldiers who died, is acknowledged as one of the most powerful orations in American history, though Lincoln himself opened with the words "the world will little note nor long remember what we say here . . ."; on the contrary, you'll be muttering it in your sleep by the time you leave.

Gettysburg, by far the most baldly commercialized of all the Civil War sites, is overwhelmingly geared toward **tourism**, relentlessly replaying the most minute details of the battle. Fortunately, it is perfectly feasible to avoid the crowds and commercial overkill and explore for yourself the rolling hills of the battlefield (now a national park) and the tidy town streets with their shuttered historic houses.

Information and getting around

Gettysburg Travel Council, 102 Carlisle St (daily 8.30am–5pm; ☏717/334-6274, ⓦ www.gettysburg.travel), is housed next door to the tiny historic train depot where Lincoln disembarked in November 1863 and should be the first stop on any visit. Though the town is compact and easy to walk around, there is no public transportation, and a car helps when touring the huge battlefield. Two-hour double decker **Battlefield Bus Tours**, running through the town and making numerous stops, depart from 778 Baltimore St (up to 8 tours daily; $19.95 for audio, $23.95 for live guide; ☏717/334-6296, ⓦ www.gettysburgbattlefieldtours.com).

Accommodation

There is plenty of lodging in and around Gettysburg, including many **B&Bs**. The most central place to **camp** is at *Artillery Ridge Resort*, 610 Taneytown Rd (☏717/334-1288, ⓦ www.artilleryridge.com; sites from $29.50; open April–Oct).

Baladerry Inn 40 Hospital Rd ☏717/337-1342, ⓦ www.baladerryinn.com. Historic hospital turned B&B, with nine en suite rooms. ❻

🏃 **Doubleday Inn** 104 Doubleday Ave ☏717/334-9119, ⓦ www.doubledayinn.com. A memorabilia-packed luxury B&B, and the only one within the battlefield itself. ❺

Gettysburg Travelodge 613 Baltimore St ☏717/334-9281, ⓦ www.travelodge.com. Standard motel between downtown and the battlefield. ❹

HI-Gardners 1212 Pine Grove Rd, Gardners ☏717/486-7575, ⓦ www.hiayh.org. Located on the Appalachian Trail in remote Pine Grove Furnace State Park, over 20 miles away. Busiest during ski season. Beds from $15.

Historic Farnsworth House Inn 401 Baltimore St ☏717/334-8838, ⓦ www.farnsworthhouseinn.com. An 1810 townhouse, used as Union HQ in the war and still riddled with bullet holes. Includes 10 rooms, a tavern, and a theater. ❺

The Town

For a sense of Gettysburg's history, you should check out just a couple of the numerous museums in town, and follow the Travel Council's fourteen-block downtown walking tour. The **American Civil War Museum**, 297 Steinwehr Ave (Jan & Feb Sat, Sun & holidays; March–Dec daily; $5.50; ☏717/334-6245), uses dreadful dummies in its displays on the lead-up to the Civil War, the Underground Railroad for escaped slaves, abolitionist John Brown, and the famous Southern belle spies Rose Greenhow and Belle Boyd. Across the National Cemetery in the battlefield, there are yet more mannequins in the **Hall of Presidents and First Ladies**, 504 Baltimore St (daily: June–Aug 9am–9pm; Sept 9am–7pm; Oct, Nov & March–May 9am–5pm; $6.95; ☏717/334-5717), complete with pearls of presidential wisdom and stirring patriotic music.

Next to the Gettysburg Tour Center, on Baltimore Street, the **Jennie Wade House** (same hours and price as Hall of Presidents; ☎717/334-4100) is the former home of the only civilian to die in the battle; Wade was killed by a stray bullet as she made bread for the Union troops in her sister's kitchen. Today, the residence looks more or less as it did on July 3, 1863, with bullet holes in the front door and on the bedpost, an artillery shell hole ripped through a wall, and a macabre model of Jennie's corpse lying under a sheet in the cellar.

To the west of the park, President Eisenhower, who retired to Gettysburg, is commemorated at the **Eisenhower National Historic Site** (daily 9am–4pm; $5.50; ☎717/338-9114, ⊛www.nps.gov/eise), where his Georgian-style mansion holds an array of memorabilia. The site is accessible only on shuttle-bus tours from the National Park Visitor Center (see below).

The battleground

It takes most of a day to see the 3500-acre **Gettysburg National Military Park**, which surrounds the town (daily 6am–10pm; free; ⊛www.nps.gov/gett). The **visitor center**, due to move in 2007 from Taneytown Road to nearby Baltimore St, a mile south of downtown (daily: summer 8am–6pm, rest of year 8am–5pm; ☎717/334-1124) doubles as the best **museum**, with guns, uniforms, surgical and musical instruments, tents and flags, as well as touching photos of the 1938 Joint Soldiers Reunion. The new premises will contain the exhibits currently in the **Cyclorama Center**, including a 356ft circular painting of Pickett's Charge, the suicidal Confederate thrust across open wheatfields in broad daylight; this is accompanied by a recitation of the Gettysburg Address, the earliest existing draft of which is on display here. A thirty-minute, painstakingly thorough **electric map show** ($3) plots the intricacies of the Gettysburg battle and you can pick up details of a self-guided **driving route**, or a **guide** will join you in your car for a personalized two-hour tour ($45). The guides are available on a first-come, first-served basis, so arrive early if you want one.

Not far from the visitor center, the **Gettysburg National Cemetery** contains thousands of graves arranged in a semicircle around the Soldiers' National Monument, on the site where Lincoln gave the Gettysburg Address. Most stirring of all are the hundreds of small marble gravestones marked only with numbers. A short walk away, the battlegrounds themselves, golden fields reminiscent of an English country landscape, are peaceful now except for their names: **Valley of Death**, **Bloody Run**, **Cemetery Hill**. Uncanny statues of key figures stand at appropriate points, while heavy stone monuments honor different regiments.

Eating and entertainment

Evenings in Gettysburg tend to be quiet once the tour buses have gone home. However, there are some good **restaurants**, many in historically important buildings.

Blue Parrot Bistro 35 Chambersburg St ☎717/337-3739. Pasta and steaks with a good choice of sauces. Like most restaurants in town, things wind down soon after 8.30pm.
Dobbin House Tavern 89 Steinwehr Ave ☎717/334-2100. The oldest house in the city, dating from 1776 and once a hideout for former slaves on the Underground Railroad. Lunch from around $10; candlelit dinners are more expensive.

Food veers between Pennsylvania Dutch, early American, and contemporary.
Gettysbrew Restaurant & Brewery 248 Hunterstown Rd ☎717/337-1001. Also a pub and historic site. Brews five beers, plus its own root beer and soda.
Mayflowers 533 Steinwehr Ave ☎717/337-3377. Huge modern Chinese restaurant that does a high-quality evening buffet for $9.99 and à la carte sushi.

Western Pennsylvania

Western Pennsylvania, a key point for frontier trade and an important thoroughfare to the West, was the focus of the fighting between the English and the French in the seven-year French and Indian War for Colonial and maritime power (1756–1763). This region grew to industrial prominence in the nineteenth century, with the exploitation of its coal resources gathering pace after the Civil War, and the opening of the world's first oil well at Titusville (now Drake Well Memorial Park) in northwestern Pennsylvania in 1859.

Today, tourism in western Pennsylvania is concentrated around the surprisingly appealing city of **Pittsburgh**. To the south of the city, the **Laurel Highlands** features Frank Lloyd Wright's not-to-be-missed architectural masterpiece, **Fallingwater**, as well as nearby **Ohiopyle State Park** and the **Youghiogheny River**, which offer plenty of outdoor activities. In the overwhelming rural northwest corner of the state, another great wilderness area to explore is the lush **Allegheny National Forest**, which begins twenty miles north of I-80. The region's only major conurbation, **Erie**, is located on the eponymous great lake. **Presque Isle State Park** is also worth a visit for its sandy lake beaches and wooded hiking trails.

Pittsburgh

The appealing ten-block district known as the **Golden Triangle**, at the heart of downtown **PITTSBURGH**, stands at the confluence of the Monongahela, Allegheny, and Ohio rivers; this area was once bitterly fought over as the gateway to the West. The French built Fort Duquesne on the site in 1754, only for it to be destroyed four years later by the British, who replaced it with **Fort Pitt**. Industry began with the development of iron foundries in the early 1800s, and by the time of the Civil War, Pittsburgh was producing half of the iron and one third of the glass in the US. Soon after, the city became the world's leading producer of steel, thanks to the vigorous expansion programs of **Andrew Carnegie**, who by 1870 was the richest man in the world. Present-day Pittsburgh is dotted with his cultural bequests, along with those of other wealthy forefathers, including the Mellon bankers, the Frick coal merchants, and the Heinz food producers.

The city has gradually ditched its Victorian reputation for dirt and pollution since its transformation began in the 1960s. The face-lift involved large-scale demolition of abandoned steel mills, which freed up much of the downtown waterfront. That said, all-out sanitization has been kept in check by the student population, the small-town feel of the older ethnic neighborhoods to the north and south, and the effects of economic downturn. Pittsburgh today is one of America's most attractive and most liveable cities, where sleek architecture and green parks have supplanted smokestacks and slums. Indeed, since the mid-1990s, and the opening of the popular **Andy Warhol Museum**, Pittsburgh has established itself as a destination to be reckoned with.

Each of Pittsburgh's close-knit neighborhoods – the **South Side** and **Mount Washington**, across the Monongahela River from the Golden Triangle, the **North Side** across the Allegheny River, and the **East End**, especially **Oakland**, the university area in the east – has an individual feel and attests in its own way to the city's history and its resurgence.

Arrival, information, and getting around

Greyhound pulls in beside the Monongahela River at 990 2nd Ave, a good fifteen-minute walk from downtown, whereas the Amtrak station is far more central, at

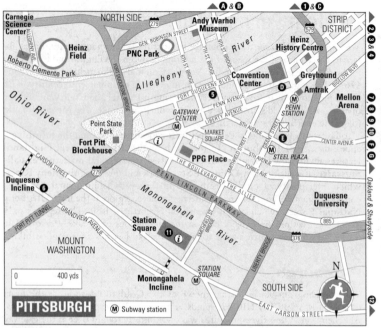

PITTSBURGH

Ⓜ Subway station

ACCOMMODATION		RESTAURANTS			
Appletree Bed & Breakfast	F	The Church Brew Works	4	La Feria	8
Doubletree Hotel Pittsburgh City Center	E	Grand Concourse	11	Mallorca	12
Hampton Inn University Center	G	Grandview Saloon	6	Penn Brewery	1
The Inn on the Mexican War Streets	B	Gullifty's	7	Seventh Street Grille	5
The Priory–A City Inn	A	India Garden	9	Thai Gourmet	3
Valley Motel	C	Kaya	2	Yumwok/Lulu's Noodles	10
The Westin Convention Center Pittsburgh	D				

1100 Liberty Ave. From the modern, efficient **Pittsburgh International Airport**, fifteen miles west (☎412/472-3525, ⓦwww.pitairport.com), several shuttle services run to Pittsburgh. Almost as quick, more frequent, and significantly cheaper, the excellent PAT bus #2❷ runs roughly every 20mins between the airport and twelve Pittsburgh stops, including downtown, Oakland, and the universities (daily 5am–midnight; $2.25).

Pittsburgh's main **Welcome Center** is downtown on Liberty Avenue, adjacent to the Gateway Center (Mon–Fri 8am–4pm, Sat 9am–5pm & Sun 10am–3pm; ☎412/281-7711 or 1-800/366-0093, ⓦwww .visitpittsburgh.com), with subsidiary branches at the airport and at the Senator John Heinz Pittsburgh Regional History Center. The main **post office** is at Seventh and Grant (Mon–Fri 7am–6pm, Sat 8am–2.30pm).

Though Pittsburgh is a city of distinct districts, **transportation** between them is simple. **Buses** through town (free–$2.75), the Monongahela and Duquesne Heights trolley inclines ($1.75), and a small "T" **subway** system (free downtown; further out the fare runs up to $3.25 at rush hour) are all excellent transportation options; **PAT**, the area transit authority (☎412/442-2000, ⓦwww.port authority.org), has a downtown service center at 534 Smithfield St (Mon–Thurs 7.30am–5.30pm, Fri 7.30am–5pm), where you can pick up timetables. Fifty-cent transfers, which must be bought simultaneously with your fare if needed, allow you to connect with any of the system's vehicles within three hours. For **taxis**, call Yellow Cab (☎412/665-8100).

Accommodation

Pittsburgh's **hotels** and few **B&Bs** are generally pricey, although weekend packages at luxury downtown hotels can bring rates down to below $100. **Oakland** has a couple of reasonably priced business hotels, and you can check out all of the Pittsburgh area's B&Bs at Ⓦwww.pittsburghbnb.com.

Appletree Bed & Breakfast 703 S Negley Ave ☎412/661-0631, Ⓦwww.theinnsonnegley.com. Friendly, upmarket establishment with 16 rooms and suites, several with Jacuzzi, in Shadyside. A sister establishment, *The Inn at 714 Negley*, is opposite. ⑥

Doubletree Hotel Pittsburgh City Center One Bigelow Square ☎412/281-5800, 1-800/225-5858, Ⓦwww.doubletree.hilton.com. Convenient downtown chain hotel offering suites with kitchens. ⑦

Hampton Inn University Center 3315 Hamlet St ☎412/681-1000 or 1-800/426-7866, Ⓦwww.hamptoninn.com. Welcoming branch of chain in Oakland offering a generous self-service continental breakfast bar, plus free shuttle to downtown and surrounding areas. ⑤

The Inn on the Mexican War Streets 604 W North Ave ☎412/231-6544, Ⓦwww.innonthe

mexicanwarstreets.com. Eight tastefully refurbished rooms in one of the North Side's trendiest areas. The less expensive rooms are great value. ④

The Priory–A City Inn 614 Pressley St ☎412/231-3338, Ⓦwww.thepriory.com. Restored 1880s inn, originally built to house traveling Benedictine monks; now, it's the North Side's nicest B&B. Room rates include continental breakfast, evening wine, weekday limo service, and use of fitness room. ⑤

Valley Motel 2571 Freeport Rd, Harmerville ☎412/828-7100, Ⓦwww.valleymotel.net. Basic motel with low rates, located 11 miles northeast of downtown. A fair option if you have a car. ②

The Westin Convention Center Pittsburgh 1000 Penn Ave ☎412/281-3700 or 1-800/937-8461, Ⓦwww.westin.com. Flashy downtown tower with pool and gym. ⑦

Downtown: the Golden Triangle

The *New York Times* once described Pittsburgh as "the only city with an entrance" – and, true enough, the view of the **Golden Triangle** skyline on emerging from the tunnel on the Fort Pitt Bridge is undeniably breathtaking. Surrounded by water and fronted with a huge fountain, Pittsburgh's downtown pays tribute to both its coal-grimed past and sunny future. In the core of the original city, the Triangle's imaginative contemporary architecture stands next to Gothic churches and redbrick warehouses. Philip Johnson's magnificent postmodern concoction, the black-glass Gothic **PPG Place** complex, looms incongruously over the old **Market Square**, lined with historic restaurants and shops and a venue for frequent free live lunchtime entertainment in summer. History is also apparent on the faded buildings along Liberty Avenue, with 1940s and 1950s fronts left in place during successive face-lifts. At the flat end of the triangle, the spaceship-like dome of **Mellon Arena** looms above the transport stations – it hosts large concerts and exhibitions, and is home to the **Pittsburgh Penguins** ice hockey team (for tickets, call ☎412/642-7367, or visit Ⓦwww.pittsburghpenguins.com).

Point State Park, at the peak of the Triangle, is where it all began. The site of five different forts during the French and Indian War, it still contains the 1764 **Fort Pitt Blockhouse**, the city's oldest structure, a lookout of sandstone and rough brick. The park itself is now a popular gathering area, with a 150ft fountain with a pool, as well as great views of port activity and across to the colorful old buildings on verdant Mount Washington. It's a great place to view sunsets and an excellent venue for the city's free outdoor festivals.

Northeast of downtown, along Penn Avenue past the vast new Convention Center, the characterful **Strip District** has a bustling early-morning market with wholesale outlets and fresh produce stalls, popular with bargain hunters and good for cheap breakfasts; it's also a good place to head to at night. Down by the river is an entertainment complex, with restaurants, bars, a marina, and a floating boardwalk. The seven-floor **Senator John Heinz Pittsburgh Regional History Center**, at 1212 Smallman St (daily 10am–5pm; $7.50; ⊤412/454-6000, ⩍www.pghhistory.org), does a good job of telling the city's story, paying particular attention to immigrants of various eras.

The South Side

In the nineteenth century, 400ft **Mount Washington**, across the Monongahela River, was the site of most of the city's coal mines. No longer dominated by belching steel mills and industry, the **South Side**, banked by the green "mountain," is an area of many churches, colorful houses nestled on steep hills, and old neighborhoods. These days, only two survive of the twelve cable cars which, at the height of steel production, used to carry both freight and passengers up the trolley inclines. The 1877 **Duquesne Incline**, from 1197 W Carson St to 1220 Grandview Ave, is a working cable-car station containing a **museum** of Pittsburgh history ($1.75 one-way; ⊤412/381-1665, ⩍www.incline.cc) in the waiting room at the top: old photos of the city show workers struggling blindly through the streets in pitch-black midday smog. The outdoor observation platform is a prime spot for **views** over the Golden Triangle to the hills on the horizon, which are especially awesome after dark. Not surprisingly, many (expensive) bars and restaurants here take advantage of the vista.

The best way to get to the South Side is across the 1883 blue-and-cream **Smithfield Street Bridge**, the oldest of fifteen downtown bridges and the most unusual-looking, thanks to its elliptical "fisheye" truss. Just to the west of the bridge stands redbrick **Station Square**, a complex of renovated railroad warehouses filled with restaurants and shops. Its showpiece is the beautiful stained glass and marble of the *Grand Concourse* seafood restaurant (for a review, see "Eating," p.183), which fills the huge waiting room of the old Pittsburgh and Lake Erie train station. This is also the jetty for the enjoyable hour-long narrated Just Ducky Tours **river cruises** (April–Oct daily, Nov Sat & Sun 10.30am–6pm, earlier in Oct & Nov; $19, kids $15; tours every 90mins; ⊤412/402-3825, ⩍www.justduckytours.com).

Along the banks of the Monongahela, **East Carson Street** is the main drag of the lively mixed residential and commercial South Side, where a longstanding community of Polish and Ukrainian steelworkers has gradually absorbed an offbeat mix of artsy residents, along with the attendant cafés, bars, and bookstores. Onion-domed churches stand alongside thrift stores and galleries, and the narrow backstreets are lined with brick rowhouses. This is also Pittsburgh's most extensive and varied **nightlife** center (see "Nightlife and entertainment," p.183).

The North Side

The star attraction on the **North Side**, annexed by Pittsburgh only in 1907, is undoubtedly the **Andy Warhol Museum**, 117 Sandusky St, just over the Seventh Street Bridge from downtown (Tues–Thurs, Sat & Sun 10am–5pm, Fri 10am–10pm; $10, Fri 5–10pm $5; ⊤412/237-8300, ⩍www.warhol.org). The museum documents the life and work of Pittsburgh's most celebrated son over eight floors of a spacious Victorian warehouse; it claims to be the largest museum in the world devoted to a single artist.

Born in Pittsburgh in 1928, **Andy Warhol** (born Andrew Warhola, the youngest son of working-class Carpatho-Rusyn, or Eastern Slovakian, immigrants) moved to New York City at the age of 21, after graduating from Carnegie-Mellon University. By the end of the 1950s, he was one of the most successful commercial artists in the nation, before turning his attention to fine and pop art. During the early 1960s he started shooting 16mm films – *Empire*, *Chelsea Girls*, and *Lonesome Cowboys* – and developed the "Exploding Plastic Inevitable" multimedia show, featuring erotic dancers and music by The Velvet Underground, whom he managed. After founding *Interview* magazine in 1969, Warhol became transfixed with the rich and famous and, up until his death in 1987, was perhaps best known for his celebrity portraits and his appearances at society events.

Although the majority of Warhol's most famous pieces are in the hands of private collectors, the museum boasts an impressive and ever-changing selection of exhibits, with over five hundred items on display at any one time, including pop art (Campbell's soup cans) and portraiture (Elvis, Marilyn Monroe, Jackie Kennedy). It pays equal attention to archival material, and chronological **self-guided tours** give a good idea of Warhol's artistic development and his eventful lifestyle. At any given time, two or three non-Warhol exhibits show work related in some way to Warhol themes. A **cinema** shows two films or videos daily, both usually Warhol productions. There's an excellent, informative Archives Study Department and a popular **Weekend Factory** (Sat & Sun noon–4pm; free with admission), where Warhol's techniques are explained and visitors can have a go themselves. During "**Good Fridays**" (5–10pm) there is free entrance to the lobby, which has a cash bar, and often buzzes with live bands or other performance arts. The museum also has a well-stocked gift shop and a café.

Elsewhere on the North Side, revitalization centers around the intriguingly named **Mexican War Streets**, on the northern edge of Allegheny Commons. In this unevenly restored, tree-lined area of nineteenth-century gray-brick and limestone terraces, old families, descendants of German and Scandinavian immigrants, live in an uneasy truce alongside young professionals. The excellent and highly unusual **Mattress Factory**, 500 Sampsonia Way (Tues–Sat 10am–5pm, Sun 1–5pm, closed Aug; $8, kids free, Thurs $4; ☎412/231-3169, ⓦwww.mattress.org), has contemporary installations by top mixed-media artists, and is a must on any visit to the city. The **National Aviary**, Allegheny Commons West (daily 9am–5pm; $8; ☎412/323-7235, ⓦwww.aviary.org), is a huge indoor bird sanctuary with over two hundred species, including foul-mouthed parrots, in free flight under a showpiece 30-foot glass dome. Nearby, **The Children's Museum of Pittsburgh**, 10 Children's Way, Allegheny Square (Mon–Sat 10am–5pm, Sun noon–5pm; $9, kids $8, Thurs $6 for all; ☎412/322-5058, ⓦwww.pittsburghkids.org), offers a plethora of games, events, and special exhibitions.

Heading northwest along the river, the huge, state-of-the-art **Carnegie Science Center**, 1 Allegheny Ave (Sun–Fri 10am–5pm, Sat 10am–7pm; $14, kids $10; ☎412/237-3400, ⓦwww.carnegiesciencecenter.org), is also predominantly aimed at children, with, among other exhibits, an interactive engineering playspace, a miniature railroad, and a planetarium. The center contains an impressive OMNIMAX theater ($8–10 for one show, $13–15 for two); various combination tickets are available. Outside (and included in admission), the **USS Requin**, a 1945 submarine, bobs on the shores of the Allegheny River; the kid-friendly tour focuses on submarine engineering, but also explores day-to-day life underwater.

Next door from the Science Center, **Heinz Field**, one of two new sports venues that opened in 2001 to replace the shared Three Rivers Stadium, is home to football's **Pittsburgh Steelers** (☎412/323-1200, ⓦwww.steelers.com), winners of the 2006 Superbowl XL. The other, further along the river toward the Sixth Street Bridge, is **PNC Park**, the home of the **Pittsburgh Pirates** baseball team (☎1-800/289-2827, ⓦwww.pirates.com). Beautifully constructed so that from most seats you get a sweeping view of the Allegheny and downtown, it's a real treat to watch a game here on a balmy summer night.

Oakland and the East End

Oakland, Pittsburgh's university area, is dotted with the mansions of wealthy industrialists, as well as university-related sights, concentrated around the campuses of **Carnegie-Mellon University**, the **University of Pittsburgh** (always known as "Pitt"), and several other colleges. At Fifth Ave and Bigelow Blvd, the 42-story, 2529-window Gothic Revival **Cathedral of Learning** is a university building with a difference: over twenty classrooms are furnished with antiques and specially crafted items donated by the city's different ethnic groups, from Lithuanian to Chinese to Irish. These rooms have been used by students since the 1930s, and all are open to the public except the exotic Syria-Lebanon room and the Early American room, complete with trap door and secret passage; these are shown only on ninety-minute **guided tours** (Mon–Sat 9am–2.30pm, Sun 11am–2.30pm; $3; ☏412/624-6000). Alternatively, you can do your own tape-recorded tour on weekends (also $3) or follow the useful booklet ($1.25). On the grounds behind the Cathedral of Learning is the French Gothic **Heinz Memorial Chapel** (Mon–Fri 9am–5pm, Sun 1–5pm; free), notable for its long, narrow, stained-glass windows depicting political, literary, and religious figures.

Across from the cathedral at 4400 Forbes Ave, the **Carnegie** cultural complex holds two great museums – the **Museum of Natural History**, famed for its extensive dinosaur relics and sparkling gems, and the **Museum of Art**, with Impressionist, Post-Impressionist and American regional art, as well as an excellent modern collection (both museums Tues–Sat 10am–5pm, Sun noon–5pm; $10, or $6 for students, seniors, and children; ☏412/622-3131, ⓦwww.carnegiemuseums.org). Nearby, Schenley Park includes the colorful flower gardens of **Phipps Conservatory** (Sat–Thurs 9.30am–5pm, Fri 9am–9pm; $7.50, kids $4; ☏412/622-6814 ⓦwww.phipps.conservatory.org) and wild wooded areas beyond.

If you're coming to the East Side from downtown on foot, it is better to avoid the area along Center Avenue known as **The Hill District**, one of Pittsburgh's toughest areas, especially after dark. Either walk along slightly less dodgy Forbes Avenue or take the longer route along Liberty Avenue via the predominantly Italian neighborhood of **Bloomfield**, a busy area of shops, restaurants, and quaint rowhouses.

The stretch of Fifth Avenue from around the Cathedral of Learning up to Shadyside is lined with important and architecturally beautiful academic buildings, places of worship, and early private mansions. The imposing **Soldiers and Sailors Memorial**, 4141 Fifth Ave (Mon–Sat 10am–4pm; tours $5; ☏412/621-4253), also serves as a museum, and is filled with military paraphernalia and historic exhibits. Further on, opposite the exquisite external mural of the Byzantine Catholic **Church of the Holy Spirit**, is the humble broadcasting complex of **WQED**, notable for being the first publicly-funded TV station when it opened in April 1954 and home to the long-running kids' show *Mr Rogers' Neighborhood*.

Shadyside, on the eastern fringes of Oakland, is an upmarket, trendy neighborhood containing the particularly chic commercial section of Walnut Street. There are several art galleries here, and the **Pittsburgh Center for the Arts**, at 6300 Fifth Ave in Mellon Park, showcases innovative Pittsburgh art in various media (Tues–Sat 10am–5pm, Sun noon–5pm; suggested donation $5; ☏412/361-0873, ⓦwww. pittsburgharts.org). A short way to the southeast, **Squirrel Hill** is another lively area, housing a mixture of students and the city's largest Jewish community, with a fine selection of shops and restaurants lining Murray and Forbes avenues.

Further east, the small **Frick Art Museum**, in the **Frick Art and Historical Center**, 7227 Reynolds St (Tues–Sun 10am–6pm; free; ☏412/371-0600, ⓦfrick art.org), shows Italian, Flemish, and French art from the fifteenth to the nineteenth centuries; its collection of decorative arts includes two of Marie Antoinette's chairs.

The **Clayton mansion**, at the center of the Frick complex, is furnished exactly as it was when industrial magnate Henry Clay Frick lived here. Obligatory **guided tours** ($10) walk you around the house, pointing out the various late-Victorian decorative touches, as well as the bed where Frick recovered after being stabbed by an anarchist during the bitter Homestead Steel Strike. Frick and most of his family are buried, under tons of protective concrete and steel, just south of the family home, on the highest hill in **Homewood Cemetery**, which also holds the tombs of H.J. Heinz (of the ketchup and baked beans fortune) and sundry Mellons. Three miles north, bordering the Allegheny River, the green expanse of **Highland Park** contains the nicely landscaped and enjoyable **Pittsburgh Zoo and PPG Aquarium** (daily summer 10am–6pm, spring & fall 9am–5pm, winter 9am–4pm; April–Nov $9, Dec–March $7; ☎412/665-3640, Ⓦzoo.pgh.pa.us), which has the distinction of owning a Komodo dragon and, in recent years, has successfully bred two baby elephants.

Eating

Eating in downtown Pittsburgh can prove expensive, and the area is rather deserted at night. There's a growing range of places in the adjacent **Strip District** and along and around **East Carson Street** on the South Side. **Station Square** and **Mount Washington** cater to a more upmarket crowd, while **Oakland** is, as you might expect, home to an array of cheap student hangouts clustered around S Craig Street – look out for the ultra-cheap mobile ethnic food vans at lunchtime. Also in the East End, **Bloomfield**, **Shadyside** and **Squirrel Hill** have a number of good inexpensive and mid-priced places.

The Church Brew Works 3525 Liberty Ave ☎412/688-8200. Vast establishment located between downtown and Bloomfield, serving American cuisine and fine ales brewed on-site. Housed in a grand, converted old church where vats have replaced the organ.

Grand Concourse 1 Station Square ☎412/261-1717. Pricey, plush seafood restaurant in a gorgeous setting inside the Station Square complex.

Grandview Saloon 1212 Grandview Ave ☎412/431-1400. Relaxed Mount Washington restaurant, usually packed with a young crowd enjoying huge plates of pasta. Arrive early for a deck table with a view.

Gullifty's 1922 Murray Ave ☎412/521-8222. Squirrel Hill establishment serving fine pasta, meat dishes, and sumptuous sweets. Look out for the twice-yearly Garlic Festival (usually held in April and October).

India Garden 328 Atwood St ☎412/682-3000. North Indian restaurant and bar in Oakland, serving tasty curries and creamy *lassi*. Good-value buffet during lunch and on Sunday evenings. Catch a cricket game on the TV.

Kaya 2000 Smallman St ☎412/261-6565. Stylish Caribbean restaurant in the Strip District with a varied vegetarian selection, as well as a huge range of beers, rums, and cocktails.

La Feria 5527 Walnut St ☎412/682-4501. Colorful upstairs Peruvian shop-cum-restaurant offering a limited but tasty selection of inexpensive specials from the Andes. BYOB.

Mallorca 2228 E Carson St ☎412/488-1818. In a smart setting on the South Side, this restaurant serves excellent paella and Mediterranean dishes, as well as fine sangría. Try the delicious goat in red-wine sauce for $22.95, enough for two.

Penn Brewery 800 Vinial St ☎412/237-9402. On the North Side, this is Pittsburgh's longest-established brewpub, serving up decent German food and festivities.

Seventh Street Grille 130 7th St, Century Building ☎412/338-0303. Excellent Californian- and Italian-influenced menus strong on pasta and seafood. Very popular despite being a little pricey.

Thai Gourmet 4505 Liberty Ave ☎412/681-4373. Intimate and friendly Bloomfield spot with unbeatably authentic and inexpensive Southeast Asian fare, such as their wonderful Penang curry. BYOB.

Yumwok/Lulu's Noodles 400 S Craig St ☎412/687-7777. Combined Oakland establishment serving filling noodles and good standard pan-Asian cuisine at bargain prices. Justifiably popular with students. BYOB.

Nightlife and entertainment

Pittsburgh's **nightlife** offers rich pickings in everything from the classics to jazz and alternative rock. The nationally regarded City Theatre, 57 S 13th St

(☎412/431-4400, ⓦwww.citytheatrecompany.org), puts on groundbreaking productions in a converted South Side church. The widely traveled **Pittsburgh Symphony Orchestra** plays at the Heinz Hall, 600 Penn Ave (☎412/392-4900, ⓦwww.pittsburghsymphony.org), and the city's ballet, dance, and opera companies perform at the downtown **Benedum Center for the Performing Arts**, 719 Liberty Ave (☎412/456-6666, ⓦwww.pgharts.org/venues/benedum.aspx). *City Paper*, a free weekly newspaper published on Wednesdays (ⓦwww.pghcitypaper.com), has extensive **listings**.

31st St Pub 3101 Penn Ave ☎412/391-8334, ⓦwww.31stpub.com. It won't win any prizes for decor, but this place draws a crowd to hear up-and-coming local indie and hardcore bands, plus the odd underground celebrity act from out of town.

🏃 **Brillobox** 4104 Penn Ave ☎412/621-4900. Two prodigal Pittsburghers returning from New York have created a unique bar that's both chic and a fun local spot for watching sports. There's a good jukebox downstairs and a performance space for mostly obscure acts above.

Club Café 56–58 S 12th St ☎412/431-4950, ⓦwww.clubcafelive.com. Laid-back South Side club with regular live music, including rock, folk, and salsa.

Dee's 1314 E Carson St ☎412/431-5400. This South Side institution has a great jukebox, pool, darts, and a lively crowd.

Kelly's 6012 Penn Circle S, E Liberty ☎412/363-6012. Just east of Shadyside, this popular bar offers good beer such as East End Big Hop and eclectic recorded music. Check out punk night on alternate Wednesdays.

Mr Small's Theatre 400 Lincoln Ave, Millvale ☎1-800/594-8499, ⓦwww.mrsmalls.com. Several miles northeast off US-28, this converted church hosts most of the mid-sized US and foreign indie rock acts.

Nick's Fat City 1601–1605 E Carson St ☎412/481-6880, ⓦwww.nicksfatcity.com. Popular, gay-friendly South Side pool bar with occasional good live rock bands. Karaoke some nights. Closed Sun & Mon.

Piper's Pub 1828 E Carson St ☎412/431-6757, ⓦwww.piperspub.com. One of the South Side's most convivial bars and the place for soccer, rugby, and Gaelic football on TV. Imported and US beers are available and the food is decent, especially breakfasts.

Rex Theatre 1602 E Carson St ☎412/381-6811, ⓦwww.ticketmaster.com/venue/180366. This former cinema hosts mainly rock shows.

Around Pittsburgh: Fallingwater and Ohiopyle

Just over an hour southeast of Pittsburgh, the **Laurel Highlands** takes in seventy miles of rolling hills and valleys. The main reasons to come this way down Hwy-381 are to see one of Frank Lloyd Wright's most unique creations and to take advantage of some prime outdoor opportunities around the small town of Ohiopyle.

You do not need to be an architecture buff to appreciate Wright's **Fallingwater** (mid–March to late Nov Tues–Sun 10am–4pm; Dec & early March Sat & Sun 11am–3pm; $16; ☎724/329-8501, ⓦwww.paconserve.org/fallingwaterhome.htm), which was built in the late 1930s for the Kaufmann family, owners of Pittsburgh's premier department store. Signposted off Hwy-381, some twenty miles south of I-70, it is set on Bear Run Creek in the midst of the gorgeous deciduous forest that constitutes the 5000-acre Bear Run Nature Reserve. It is the only one of Wright's buildings to be on display exactly as it was designed, and for good reason – it's built right into a set of cliffside waterfalls. Wright used a cantilever system to make the multi-tiered structure "cascade down the hill like the water down the falls"; the house's almost precarious position is truly stunning, and it is remarkable how well its predominantly rectangular shapes blend in with nature's less uniform lines. The slow, well-presented hour-long tour, included in admission (more extensive and expensive tours are available), takes visitors up through the different levels of the building, allowing plenty of time to admire the setting from the various terraces as well as the beauty of the interior design. Among the house's pioneering features is a lack of load-bearing walls, which gives an extra sense of space, and natural skylights. When Edgar Kaufmann Jr entrusted the house to the Western Pennsylvania Conservancy in 1963, he donated all the furnishings and artwork with it. Objects on display include some fine East Asian sculpture of buddhas and Indian deities. Tours begin and end a few hundred yards from the house in the wooden reception pavilion, where there is a café and shop.

Ohiopyle and around

Five miles south of Fallingwater, tiny **OHIOPYLE** is the most convenient base from which to enjoy the wilds of **Ohiopyle State Park** or activities like whitewater rafting on the **Youghiogheny River**. The park fans out around the town and river, offering a maze of trails for hiking or biking, and natural delights such as **Cucumber Falls** and the unique habitat of the **Ferncliff Peninsula**, known for its wildflowers. At the built-up end of a massive steel and wooden footbridge high above the river, a small **visitor center** dispenses local information (daily 10am–4.30pm; ☎724/329-8591). Just beyond it the *Ohiopyle House Café*, 144 Grant St (☎724/329-1122), serves up tasty dishes like lobster ravioli and caramel pudding, while a couple of seasonal canteens and a general store sell basic snacks and provisions. The *Yough Plaza Motel* on Sherman Street (☎1-800/992-7238; ❹) has reasonable standard units and efficiency apartments; even better for budget travelers is camping or renting a cabin in the park itself (☎1-888/727-2757). For **rafting**, White Water Adventurers at 6 Negley St (☎1-800/992-7238, ⓦwww.wwaraft.com) is one of several outfits that rent equipment and give instruction.

Three miles southwest of Ohiopyle, there is another Frank Lloyd Wright house, **Kentuck Knob** (Mar–Nov daily 10am–4pm; $15; ☎724/329-1901, ⓦwww.kentuckknob.com), also known as the I.N. Hagan House. A hexagonal structure of fieldstone and cypress, it sits on a hilltop, giving wonderful views of the surrounding countryside. Further down the Youghiogheny, in the village of Confluence, the cozy *River's Edge Café* (☎814/395-5059) serves good meat and pasta dishes at moderate prices, right on the banks of the river.

Allegheny National Forest

Occupying over half a million acres and a sizeable portion of four counties, the pristine **Allegheny National Forest** (☎814/723-5150, ⓦwww.fs.fed.us/r9/Allegheny) affords a bounty of opportunities for engaging in outdoor pursuits like hiking, fishing, snowmobiling, and, best of all, admiring the **fall foliage**, which rivals any in New England.

In the north, there are several points of interest within easy access of Hwy-6, the major route through the forest. Just north of the highway, it is worth a stop to admire the **Kinzua Viaduct** railroad bridge, the highest and longest in the world when constructed in 1882, which is accessible by foot and allows tremendous views of the creek below.

The dominant feature of the forest's northern section is the huge **Kinzua Reservoir**, created by a dam at the southern end. Swimming is possible at **Kinzua** and **Kiasutha beaches** or you can enjoy a picnic at **Rimrock Overlook** or at **Willow Bay** in the very north. The summer-only Kinzua Point Information Center on Hwy-59 (☎814/726-1291) has details on trails and private campgrounds, or you can can **camp** in any of the forest's twenty state-run campsites (☎1-877/444-6777, ⓦwww.reserveusa.com). Fees range from $18 to $45 a night for a cabin at Willow Bay.

△ Allegheny National Forest

Erie

The focal point of Pennsylvania's forty-mile slice of Lake Erie waterfront is the pleasant city of **ERIE** itself. It bears no resemblance to the major urban centers of Pittsburgh or Philadelphia, being entirely low-rise and extremely leafy; indeed you hardly realize you are downtown until you find yourself in the shady park-like town square, on 6th Street between the main thoroughfares of Peach and State streets. There are several places of cultural interest in the city, all within walking distance of the square, including the Neo-classical **Court House** and several **museums** devoted to history, art, and science. Better than these, the **Erie Maritime Museum** at 150 E Front St in the Bayfront Historical District (Mon–Sat 9am–5pm, Sun noon–5pm; $6.50, $4 if brig is absent; ☎814/452-2744, ⊛www.brigniagara.org) has a fascinating display on the geological and ecological development of the Great Lakes and also focuses on warships of different periods; the elegant **US Brig Niagara**, usually moored outside, is part of the museum.

Undoubtedly, Erie's main attraction is the elongated comma-shaped peninsula of **Presque Isle State Park,** which bends east from its narrow neck three miles west of downtown until it almost touches the city's northernmost tip. The park is maintained as a nature preserve and has wide sandy **beaches** good for swimming, backed by thick woods offering a series of trails. Rangers at the Park Office (daily 8am–4pm; ☎814/833-7424, ⊛www.presqueisle.org) provide general information and a map, but the main visitors center is the **Stull Interpretive Center and Nature Shop** (spring & fall 10am–4pm; summer 10am–5pm; ☎814/836-9107). Those without a vehicle can hop on the Port of Erie **water taxi** (Mon noon–6pm, Tues–Sun 10am–6pm; $4 one-way, $6 roundtrip; ☎814/881-2502), which leaves on the hour from Dobbins Landing on the Erie Bayfront.

Practicalities

Erie has frequent Greyhound **bus** connections to Pittsburgh, Cleveland, and Buffalo; the station is at 5759 Peach St (☎814/864-5949), some three miles out of downtown, and is served by local bus #9 to Mill Creek Mall. The **CVB**, downtown at 208 E Bayfront Drive (Mon–Fri 9am–5pm; ☎814/454-7191 or 1-800/524-3743, ⓦwww.tourerie.com), is the place to go for information.

Accommodation is often twice as expensive in the summer as in the off-season. The centrally located *Holiday Inn Erie-Downtown*, 18 W 18th St (☎814/456-2961 or 1-800/832-9101, ⓦwww.holiday-inn.com; ❹), provides the usual amenities, but the elegant *Boothby Inn B&B*, at 311 W 6th St (☎814/456-1888 or 1-866/266-8429, ⓦwww.theboothbyinn.com; ❺), makes for a far more pleasant stay. Numerous functional **motels** also line Peninsula Drive. The well-sited *Sara's Campground*, 50 Peninsula Drive (☎814/833-4560, ⓦwww.sarascampground.com; from $20), is just before the entrance to Presque Isle. Nearby in Sara Coyne Plaza, *Sally's Diner* (☎814/833-1957) serves up hearty breakfasts and meals; downtown, try the *Marketplace Grill*, 319 State St (☎814/455-7272), for steaks and a filling pizza-and-pasta lunchtime buffet, or the cheap *Chinese Happy Garden*, 418 State St (☎814/452-4488).

New Jersey

The skinny coastal state of **NEW JERSEY** has been at the heart of US history since the Revolution, when a battle was fought at **Princeton**, and George Washington spent two bleak winters at **Morristown**. As the Civil War came, the state's commitment to an industrial future ensured that, despite its border location along the Mason–Dixon Line, it fought with the Union.

That commitment to industry has doomed New Jersey in modern times. Most travelers only see "the Garden State" (so called for the rich market garden territory at the state's heart) from the stupendously ugly New Jersey Turnpike toll road which, heavy with truck traffic, cuts through a landscape of gray smokestacks and industrial estates. Even the songs of **Bruce Springsteen**, Asbury Park's golden boy, paint his home state as a gritty urban wasteland of empty lots, gray highways, lost dreams, and blue-collar heartache. The majority of the refineries and factories hug only a mere fifteen-mile-wide swath along the turnpike, but bleak cities like **Newark**, home to the major airport, and **Trenton**, the capital, do little to improve the look of the place. Suffice it to say, the state suffers from a major image problem. But there is more to New Jersey than factories and pollution – indeed, Thomas Paine and Walt Whitman both wrote nostalgically of the happy years they spent here. Alongside its revolutionary history, the northwest corner near the Delaware Water Gap is traced with picturesque lakes, streams, and woodlands while, in the south, the town of **Princeton** (home to the Ivy League university), adds architectural elegance to the interior. Best of all perhaps, the Atlantic shore offers many bustling resorts, from the compelling tattered glitz of **Atlantic City** to the Old World charm of **Cape May**.

Getting around New Jersey

With a **car**, New Jersey is easily accessible from New York City, via I-95, while the New Jersey Turnpike (a $6.45 toll end-to-end) sweeps from the northeast down to Philadelphia. The Garden State Parkway runs parallel to the Atlantic from New York to Cape May (with a 35–70¢ toll every twenty miles), and gives easy access to the shoreline resorts.

Newark Liberty International Airport (☎973/961-6000, ⓦwww.newark airport.com) is served by all the major international carriers and is most renowned for its convenient access to Manhattan (a 15–30min bus ride away on Newark Liberty Airport Express; $14; ☎908/354-3330 or 1-877/894-9155, ⓦwww.coachu-sa.com/olympia; or a 20min train ride via AirTrain and New Jersey Transit; $14; ☎1-800/247-7433, ⓦwww.airtrainnewark.com). **PATH trains** connect northern New Jersey to New York City (☎1-800/234-7284, ⓦwww.panynj.gov/path), while New Jersey Transit (☎973/762-5100 or 1-800/772-2222, ⓦwww.njtransit. com) provides good, inexpensive train and bus service from New Jersey hubs to Philadelphia, New York, and the coast. Numerous **Amtrak** trains pass through Newark, Princeton, and Trenton, en route between Philadelphia, New York, and Washington DC. Greyhound covers most of the state, while New Jersey's south coast is connected to Delaware by the Cape May–Lewes **ferry** (see p.195).

Inland New Jersey

Visitors most often travel from New York to northern New Jersey for the great **shopping**: from huge malls and designer outlet stores to ethnic emporiums like Mitsuwa Marketplace, the Japanese shopping center in Edgewater (☎201/941-9113, ⓦwww.mitsuwa.com), both prices and taxes are lower than across the Hudson River. The well-off towns along the river also contain some fine Italian and Asian restaurants, while Hoboken offers a spillover of Manhattan subculture. Traveling west on the interstates from the shore or from New York City, however, visitors see the New Jersey of popular imagination: a heavily industrialized cultural desert peppered with run-down cities like Trenton and Paterson. Newark, the state's largest city, is perhaps the nation's drabbest, redeemed only by its marvelously efficient airport, new performing arts center, and views over the Hudson to the Statue of Liberty. The one place that holds interest in inland New Jersey is **Princeton**, an Ivy-League town that makes a pretty afternoon stopoff.

Princeton

Self-satisfied **PRINCETON**, on US-206 eleven miles north of Trenton, is home to **Princeton University** – the nation's fourth oldest, after having broken away from the overly religious Yale in 1756. It began its days inauspiciously as Stony Brook in the late 1600s and then in 1724 became known as Princes Town, a coach stop between New York and Philadelphia. In January 1777, a week after Washington's triumph against the British at Trenton, the **Battle of Princeton** occurred southwest of town. This victory, a turning point in the Revolutionary effort, bolstered the morale of Washington's troops before their long winter encampment at Morristown to the north. After the war, in 1783, the **Continental Congress**, fearful of potential attack from incensed unpaid veterans in Philadelphia, met here for four months; the leafy, well-kept town was then left in peace to follow its academic pursuits. Alumni of Princeton University include actor James Stewart, Jazz-Age writer F. Scott Fitzgerald, actress Brooke Shields, and presidents Wilson and Madison. Today, there is little to do here other than tour the university and see the historic sites.

Arrival, information, and getting around

A shuttle **bus**, the Princeton Airporter, makes the run from Newark airport to town (daily every hour 7.15am–8.15pm; 1hr 30mins trip; $28, students $19; ☎609/587-6600, ⓦwww.goairporter.com). On their New York–Philadelphia runs, Amtrak and NJ Transit stop at Princeton Junction, three miles south of Princeton. From there, you can take a SEPTA shuttle (☎215/580-7800, ⓦwww.septa.com) to Princeton's train terminal, on-campus at University Place, a block north of Alexander Road. You must buy a ticket for the shuttle ahead of time, preferably as a connecting ticket from your point of origin. Suburban Transit **buses** from New York's Port Authority bus station (☎1-800/222-0492, ⓦwww.suburbantransit.com) stop every thirty minutes from 6am to 11pm at Palmer Square.

Information is available from the Frist Campus Center at the university (☎609/258-1766, ⓦwww.princeton.edu/frist) or from the **Chamber of Commerce** at 9 Vandeventer Ave (Mon–Fri 8.30am–5pm; ☎609/924-1776, ⓦwww.princetonchamber.org). The **Historical Society museum**, 158 Nassau St (Tues–Sun noon–4pm; ☎609/921-6748, ⓦwww.princetonhistory.org), organizes **walking tours** through town (Sun 2pm; $7) and also provides **maps** so you can do it yourself. Central Princeton is easily **navigable on foot**, but weather extremes in the winter and summer, as well as the distance of accommodation options from downtown, may make you glad to have a **car**.

The Town and the university

Mercer Street, the long road that sweeps southwest past the university campus to Nassau Street, is lined with elegant Colonial houses, graced with shutters, columns, and wrought-iron fences. The **Princeton Battlefield State Park**, a mile and a half out, includes the **Thomas Clarke House**, 500 Mercer St, a Quaker farmhouse that served as a hospital during the battle. The simple house at 112 Mercer, back toward town, is where **Albert Einstein** lived while teaching at the Institute of Advanced Study. Unfortunately, the house is not open to the public.

Princeton University's tranquil and shaded campus is a beautiful place for a stroll. Just inside the main gates on Nassau Street, **Nassau Hall**, a vault-like historic building containing numerous portraits of famous graduates and one of King George II, was, when constructed in 1756, the largest stone building in the nation; its 26-inch-thick walls (now patterned with plaques and patches of ivy placed by graduating classes) withstood American and British fire during the Revolution. It was also the seat of government during Princeton's brief spell as national capital in 1783. The 1925 **chapel**, based on one at Kings College, Cambridge University, in England, has stained-glass windows showing scenes from works by Dante, Shakespeare, and Milton, as well as the Bible. Across campus, the **Prospect Gardens**, a flowerbed in the shape of the university emblem, are a blaze of orange in summer. There are student-led **tours** that take you around to all of these sights, though they're somewhat complacent, and on summer afternoons they can be painfully crowded. That said, they are free; tours leave from the Frist Campus Center, which faces Washington Road (during term Mon–Sat 10am, 11am, 1.30pm & 3.30pm, Sun 1.30pm & 3.30pm; hours vary slightly during vacations; ☎609/258-1766).

In the middle of the campus, fronted by the Picasso sculpture *Head of a Woman*, the **University Art Museum**, not included on the standard tours, is well worth a look for its collection from the Renaissance to the present, including works by Modigliani, Van Gogh, and Warhol, as well as Asian and pre-Columbian art (Tues–Sat 10am–5pm, Sun 1–5pm; free; ☎609/258-3788, ⓦwww.princetonart museum.org).

Accommodation, eating, and drinking

The only **hotels** in the center of Princeton are the ersatz-Colonial *Nassau Inn* on Palmer Square (☎609/921-7500 or 1-800/862-7728, ⓦwww.nassauinn.com; ❻) and the *Peacock Inn* (☎609/924-1707, ⓦwww.peacockinn.com; ❻), tucked in a quieter spot at 20 Bayard Lane. Budget **motels** can be found along US-1 and in the suburb of **Lawrenceville** a few miles south of town; one such is the functional *Red Roof Inn*, 3203 US-1 (☎609/896-3388, ⓦwww.redroof.com; ❸).

Despite its affluence, Princeton is by no means the culinary capital of New Jersey. There's cheap diner-type **food** along Witherspoon Street; *Teresa's*, 19–23 Palmer Square E (☎609/921-1974), serves creative, good-value Italian food; and *Mediterra*, at 29 Hulfish St (☎609/252-9680), is an upscale Mediterranean restaurant with a welcoming atmosphere and well-prepared food. **Nightlife** is limited, especially when school is out, but the *Triumph Brewery*, 138 Triumph St (☎609/942-7855), has good, home-brewed beers and is popular with a mixed crowd; meanwhile, the old *Yankee Doodle Tap Room* bar, downstairs at the *Nassau Inn*, is usually full of ancient revelers drinking, reminiscing, and enjoying live jazz.

The New Jersey shore

New Jersey's Atlantic coast, a 130-mile stretch of almost uninterrupted **resorts** – some rowdy, some run-down, some undeveloped and peaceful – has long been reliant on farming and tourism. No profitable ports were established, nor did short-lived attempts at whaling come to anything. In the late 1980s, the whole coastline suffered severe and well-publicized pollution from ocean dumping. But today, the beaches, if occasionally somewhat crowded, are safe and clean: sandy, broad, and lined by characteristic wooden **boardwalks**, some of which, in an attempt to maintain their condition, charge admission during the summer. The rowdy, sleazy glitz of **Atlantic City** is perhaps the shore's best-known attraction, though there are also quieter resorts like **Spring Lake** and Victorian **Cape May**.

Spring Lake and Asbury Park

SPRING LAKE, about twenty miles down the Jersey coast, is one of the smallest, most uncommercial communities on the shore, a gentle respite on the road south to Atlantic City. Tourism in this elegant Victorian resort evolved slowly, without the booms, crises, resurgences, and depressions of other seaside towns – partly due to the strict zoning laws prohibiting new building. You can walk the undeveloped two-mile **boardwalk** and watch the crashing ocean from battered gazebos, swim and bask on the white beaches (in summer, compulsory beach tags, badges that provide admission to the beach, cost a fee), or sit in the shade by the town's namesake, **Spring Lake** itself. Wooden footbridges, swans, geese, and the grand St Catharine Roman Catholic Church on the banks of the lake give it the feel of a country village. What little activity there is centers on the upmarket shops of Third Avenue.

Bruce Springsteen fans can use the town as a base for visiting nearby **ASBURY PARK**, a decaying old seaside town where The Boss lived for many years and played his first gigs. Almost nothing remains of the carousels and seaside arcades that Springsteen wrote about on early albums such as his debut, *Greetings from Asbury Park*; the sole survivor is Madam Marie's now-defunct fortune-telling salon, which stands amid the rubble and half-completed condominium developments that line the boardwalk. The 🎵**Stone Pony**, 913 Ocean Ave (☎732/502-0600, ⓦwww.stoneponyonline.com), where Springsteen played dozens of times in the mid-1970s and to which he has returned intermittently over the years, is the one obligatory stop for devotees.

Practicalities

Spring Lake is accessible by US-34 from the New Jersey Turnpike, and served by New Jersey Transit from New York. The Chamber of Commerce (☎732/449-

0577, Ⓦwww.springlake.org) keeps erratic hours but the Spring Lake Hotel and B&B Association (Ⓣ732/449-6685) can help find lodging, especially on summer weekends. There are no cheap **motels**, and **B&Bs** can be expensive; the *Chateau Inn*, 500 Warren Ave (Ⓣ732/974-2000 or 1-877/974-5253, Ⓦwww.chateauinn. com; ❼), is typical. Adjacent to Asbury Park, in the much more attractive Victorian resort of **Ocean Grove**, friendly *Lillagaard B&B*, 5 Abbot Ave (Ⓣ732/988-1216, Ⓦwww.lillagaard.com; ❺), is right on the beach. Most of Spring Lake's **restaurants** are in the elegant Victorian hotels along the seafront and can be pricey. *Who's On Third*, 1300 Third Ave (Ⓣ732/449-4233), is a no-nonsense café serving breakfast and lunch. For a blowout, *The Sandpiper*, 7 Atlantic Ave (BYOB; Ⓣ732/449-4700), serves superb fresh fish and seafood in elegant, candlelit surroundings. In Asbury Park, *Red Fusion* (Ⓣ732/775-1008), at 660 Cookman Ave, serves excellent Asian/American fusion food in a unique space that is part art gallery, part sports bar.

Atlantic City

What they wanted was Monte Carlo. They didn't want Las Vegas. What they got was Las Vegas. We always knew that they would get Las Vegas.

Stuart Mendelson, *Philadelphia Journal*

ATLANTIC CITY, on Absecon Island just off the midpoint of the Jersey shoreline, has been a tourist magnet since 1854, when Philadelphia speculators created it as a rail terminal resort. In 1909, at the peak of the seaside town's popularity, Baedeker wrote "there is something colossal about its vulgarity" – a glitzy, slightly monstrous quality that it sustains today. The real-life model for the modern version of the board game **Monopoly**, it has an impressive popular history, boasting the nation's first **boardwalk** (1870), the world's first **Ferris wheel** (1892), the first color **postcards** (1893), and the first **Miss America Beauty Pageant** (cunningly devised in 1921 to extend the tourist season, and held here every year until it moved to Las Vegas in 2006). During Prohibition and the Depression, Atlantic City was a center for rum-running, packed with speakeasies and illegal gambling

△ The Atlantic City boardwalk

dens. Thereafter, in the face of increasing competition from Florida, it slipped into a steep decline, until desperate city officials decided in 1976 to open up the decrepit resort to legal **gambling**.

Arrival, information, and getting around

The **bus terminal** at Atlantic and Michigan is served by NJ Transit and Greyhound. NJ Transit trains stop at the **train station** next to the Convention Center, at 1 Miss America Way, and are connected by free shuttle service to all casinos. **Atlantic City International Airport** in Pomona (℡609/645-7895, ⓦwww.acairport. com) has direct flights to Philadelphia, as well as some flights further afield; from the airport, cabs cost around $30 to Downtown. For maps and information, head for the Atlantic City Convention & Visitors Authority's helpful **boardwalk information center** outside of Boardwalk Hall (daily 9.30am–5.30pm, summer Fri–Sun 9.30am–8pm; ℡609/449-7130 or 1-888/228-5758, ⓦwww.atlantic citynj.com). Atlantic City is easy to **walk** around, though it's unwise to stray further from the five-mile boardwalk along the ocean than the parallel Pacific, Atlantic, and Arctic avenues, as other parts of the city can be dangerous at night. Ventnor and Margate, to the south on Absecon Island, are served by **buses** along Atlantic Avenue. Pale blue Jitneys ($1.50, exact change required; ℡609/344-8642, ⓦwww.jitneys.net) offer a 24-hour minibus service the length of Pacific Avenue. Along the boardwalk, various **bike rental** stands and rickshaw-like **rolling chairs** (℡609/347-7148) provide alternative means of transportation.

Accommodation

Atlantic City is not Vegas – there's no chance of getting a $40 room at one of the casinos. The already high **accommodation** rates rise on weekends and in summer, though rates plunge off-season; if you book ahead online and business is slow, many places will offer discounted **package deals**, with $200 suites going for under half-price. Otherwise, room prices at the casinos are astronomical, though reasonably priced **motels** line Pacific and Atlantic avenues behind the boardwalk, and things are cheaper in quiet Ocean City, a family resort to the south.

Bally's Atlantic City Park Place and Boardwalk ℡609/340-2000, ⓦwww.harrahs.com/ballys. This is as close as it gets to the way-out theme casinos of Vegas. The *Bally's* megalopolis, with full-service spa and more than 20 restaurants, encompasses *Showboat*, *Caesar's*, and *Harrahs* casino hotels, each with its own feel but all more or less under one roof. ⓺

EconoLodge Boardwalk 117 S Kentucky Ave ℡609/344-9093, ⓦwww.choicehotels.com. Standard chain motel next to the boardwalk and the *Sands Casino*. ⓷

The Irish Pub Inn 164 St James Place ℡609/344-9063, ⓦwww.theirishpub.com/irish-pubinn2.htm. Basic, cheap rooms above one of the town's best bars. Great single rates. ⓵–⓶

Quality Inn Beach Block 119 S South Carolina Ave ℡609/345-7070, ⓦwww.choicehotels.com. Chain motel housed in a converted school. The lobby and shared areas are rather shabby, but the clean, newly refurbished rooms make up for it. Prices double on weekends. ⓷

Resorts Atlantic City Casino Hotel 1133 Boardwalk ℡1-800/336-6378, ⓦwww.resortsac.com. The most pleasant of the huge casino hotels, with pool and spa. ⓹–⓺

Rodeway Inn 124 S North Carolina Ave ℡609/345-0155, ⓦwww.choicehotels.com. Clean, basic, reasonably priced rooms close to the boardwalk. ⓷

Surfside Resort Hotel 18 S Mount Vernon Ave ℡609/347-7873, ⓦwww.surfsideresorthotel.com. Refurbished gay-friendly hotel with standard rooms and a lively club attached. ⓹

The Town

Arriving by train, you'll be confronted by the monstrous **Convention Center**, which houses a massive food court and standard mall shops along with its meeting spaces and countless hotel rooms. Most of the hopeful new arrivals, however, head straight for the casinos, with an ample overspill flooding the boardwalk and beach. Beyond the boardwalk there is little to see in Atlantic City, as the eerily quiet slums of the South Inlet district make a chilling contrast to the manic jollity a mere block away. This is not an area in which to linger for any length of time, or indeed at all at night – the **danger** for tourists is very real, though crime has decreased over the past few years.

Atlantic City's wooden **boardwalk** was originally built as a temporary walkway, raised above the beach so that vacationers could take a seaside stroll without treading sand into the grand hotels. Alongside the brash 99¢ shops and exotically named palm-readers, a few beautiful Victorian buildings that survived the wrecking ball invoke past elegance, despite the fact that many now house fast-food joints. Early in the morning, when the breezes from the ocean are at their most pleasant, the boardwalk is peaceful, peopled only by keen cyclists and a few lost souls down on their luck. The **Central Pier** offers all the fun of a fair, with rides, games, and old-fashioned "guess your weight" challenges. A few blocks south, another pier has been remodeled into an ocean-liner-shaped shopping center. The small and faded **Atlantic City Arts Center** (daily 10am–4pm; ℡609/347-5837, ⓦwww.acartcenter.org), on the Garden Pier at the quiet northern end of the boardwalk, has a free collection of seaside memorabilia, postcards, photos, and a special exhibit on Miss America, as well as traveling art shows. A block off the boardwalk, where Pacific and Rhode Island avenues meet, and at the heart of some of the city's worst deprivation, stands the **Absecon Lighthouse**. Active until 1933, it's now fully restored and offers a terrific view from its 167ft tower (July–Aug daily 10am–5pm; rest of year Thurs–Mon 11am–4pm; $5; ℡609/449-1360, ⓦwww.abseconlighthouse.org). Atlantic City's **beach** is free, family-filled, and surprisingly clean, considering its proximity to the boardwalk. Beaches at well-to-do **Ventnor**, a Jitney ride away, are quieter, while three miles south of Atlantic City, New Jersey's beautiful people pose on the beaches of **Margate** (both beaches charge a nominal fee), watched over by Lucy the Margate Elephant at 9200 Atlantic Ave. A 65ft wood-and-tin Victorian oddity, Lucy was built as a seaside attraction in 1881 and used variously as a tavern and a hotel. Today, her huge belly contains a **museum** (June–early Sep Mon–Sat 10am–8pm, Sun 10am–5pm; $5; ℡609/823-6473, ⓦwww.lucytheelephant.org) filled with Atlantic City memorabilia, as well as photos and artifacts from her own history.

The casinos of Atlantic City

Each of Atlantic City's dozen **casinos**, which also act as luxury hotels, conference centers, and concert halls, has a slightly different image, though you might not guess it among the apparent uniformity of vast, richly ornamented halls, slot machines, relentless flashing lights and incessant noise, chandeliers, mirrors, and a disorienting absence of clocks or windows.

The most outwardly ostentatious (and "The Donald" wouldn't have it any other way) is Donald Trump's **Taj Mahal**. Occupying nearly twenty acres and over forty stories high, dotted with glittering minarets and onion domes, this gigantic but oddly anticlimactic piece of Far Eastern kitsch stands opposite the arcade-packed Steel Pier at the north end of the boardwalk. It is one of the largest gambling casinos on earth, precariously tottering on the edge of bankruptcy. **Bally's** charmingly garish Wild West Casino is much more outlandish and fun, and also offers complete access to the games and memberships of Roman-themed **Caesar's**, smaller, "friendly" **Showboat**, and the **Hilton**. **Sands**, next door at South Indiana Ave, is a noisy and popular venue with a vaguely circus-related theme. **Resorts**, on the northern end of the boardwalk, is grand without being flashy. All casinos are **open 24 hours**, including holidays, and have a strict minimum **age requirement**, so be prepared to show ID that proves you're 21 or older.

Eating

One effect of Atlantic City's rabid commercialization is an abundance of **fast food**. The boardwalk is lined with pizza, burger, and sandwich joints, while the diners on Atlantic and Pacific avenues serve soul food and cheap breakfasts. All the large casinos boast several restaurants, ranging in price and menu but all of average quality, as well as all-you-can-eat **buffets** – most cost around $15 for lunch, and under $20 for dinner. Some of the casinos offer half-price buffets to "members" or "VIPs" – all you have to do to join is fill out a form and give some proof of address. If money's running low after too many days in the casino, there are bargain buffets on the boardwalk for around $5 – but inevitably, you get what you pay for.

Dune 9510 Ventnor Ave, Margate ☎609/487-7450. Specialising in tasty and fresh, if a little pricey, seafood. The three-course prix fixe is a decent deal at $24.50.

Hunan Chinese Restaurant 2323 Atlantic Ave ☎609/348-5946. Reasonably priced Chinese food two blocks from the boardwalk. Combination plates run $7–11.

Los Amigos 1926 Atlantic Ave ☎609/344-2293. Great for cheap, late-night food, this pleasant but average Mexican restaurant and bar across from the bus station is open until 3am Friday and Saturday.

Pappa T's Pizza 445 Boardwalk ☎609/348-5030. One of the better cheap boardwalk joints, with pizza and breakfast from $4.

White House Sub Shop 2301 Arctic Ave ☎609/345-1564. This bright and super-efficient Atlantic City institution is where the submarine sandwich was born; definitely worth a visit.

Entertainment and nightlife

Atlantic City sells itself as the fun nighttime city, but the **nightlife** centers on the casinos and boardwalk amusements. Once you get bored with slot machines there is little else to do. Big-name entertainers perform regularly at the casinos, but you'll be lucky to find tickets much under $100 – the free weekly *Whoot* (ⓦwww.whootnews.com) has listings. For cheaper informal fun, try the friendly, dark-paneled *Irish Pub*, 164 St James Place (☎609/344-9063, ⓦwww.theirishpub.com), which serves extremely cheap food and often has live Irish music. *Club Tru*, 12 S Mt Vernon Ave (☎609/344-2222, ⓦwww.clubtru.com) offers frequent go-go dancing and includes the longstanding gay club night *Studio Six*.

Cape May

CAPE MAY was founded in 1620 by the Dutch Captain Mey, on the small hook at the very southern tip of the Jersey coast, jutting out into the Atlantic and washed by the Delaware Bay on the west. After being briefly settled by New England whalers in the late 1600s, it turned in the eighteenth century to more profitable farming and, soon after, to tourism. In 1745 the first advertisement for Cape May's restorative air and fine accommodation appeared in the Philadelphia press, heralding a period of great prosperity, when Southern plantation owners, desiring cool sea breezes without having to venture into Yankee land, flocked to the fashionable boarding houses of this genteel "resort of Presidents."

The Victorian era was Cape May's finest; nearly all its gingerbread architecture dates from a mass rebuilding after a severe fire in 1878. However, the increase in car travel after World War I meant that vacationers could go further, more quickly and more cheaply, and the little town found itself something of an anachronism, while the gaudier charms of Atlantic City became the brightest stars on the Jersey coast. During the 1950s, Cape May began to dust off its most valuable commodity: its history. Today, the whole town is a National Historic Landmark, with over six hundred **Victorian buildings**, tree-lined streets and beautifully kept **gardens**, and a lucrative B&B industry. It teeters dangerously on self-parody at times, thanks to its glut of cutesy "olde shoppes," but if you avoid the main drags and wander through the back-streets, you'll enjoy the historical authenticity. The town also boasts good **beaches**.

Arrival, information, and getting around

New Jersey Transit runs an express **bus** to Cape May from Philadelphia and the south Jersey coast, as well as services from New York and Atlantic City. Greyhound also stops at the terminal, opposite the corner of Lafayette and Ocean St. **Ferries** connect the town to Lewes, Delaware ($7–9.50 per person, $23–34 per car; schedules on ☎1-800/643-3779, ⓦwww.capemaylewesferry.com). Maps, **information** and help with accommodation are available from the **Welcome Center** (daily 9am–4.30pm; ☎609/884-9562, ⓦwww.capemaynj.com), attached to the bus terminal.

Though Cape May itself is best enjoyed on foot, to venture out a bit further rent a **bike** from the Village Bike Shop near the bus terminal, at 609 Lafayette (summer 8am–6pm, call for off-season hours; $5 per hour, $12 per day; ☎609/884-8500). The Cape May Whale Watcher, at Second Avenue and Wilson Drive (☎609/884-5445 or 1-800/786-5445, ⓦwww.capemaywhalewatcher.com), offers three trips (daily March to Dec) around Cape May Point: two **dolphin-watches** (2hrs; 10am & 6.30pm; $25) and a **whale & dolphins voyage** (3hrs; 1pm; $35).

Accommodation

Many of Cape May's pastel Victorian homes have been converted to pricey **B&Bs** or **guesthouses**, and the resort is so popular that choice plummets on summer weekends. During July and August even old motor inns can command over $100 a night; June and September rates are often around half that. Standard **hotels** front the ocean on Beach Drive, and you can **camp** at the expensive *Seashore Campsites*, 720 Seashore Road (basic campsite $37, with electric and water $40, with full hookup $44; ☎609/884-4010 or 1-800/313-2267, ⓦwww.seashorecampsites.com).

Cape Harbor Motor inn 715 Pittsburgh Ave ☎609/884-3352, ⓦwww.seabreezemotel.com. Comfortable motel, situated in a residential street seven blocks from the beach; cheaper than most places but rates soar in summer. ❹–❻

The Chalfonte 301 Howards St ☎609/884-8409, ⓦwww.chalfonte.com. Classy and spacious 1876 mansion with wraparound verandas, three blocks from the beach. ❻

Inn of Cape May 7 Ocean St ☎1-800/582-5933, ⓦwww.innofcapemay.com. This once-fashionable Victorian shorefront hotel now has a small adjoining modern motel wing. The cheapest rooms are those with shared baths in the main

building. Open daily April–Oct, weekends only late Oct–Dec. ❻–❽

Manor House 612 Hughes St ☎609/884-4710, ⓦwww.manorhouse.net. Great breakfasts and a relaxing porch in the heart of the historic district. ❻

Queen Victoria 102 Ocean St ☎609/884-8702, ⓦwww.queenvictoria.com. Twenty-one rooms in four buildings, including a cottage and a carriage house. Rates include bicycle loans, beach chairs, breakfast (in bed, if desired), and afternoon tea. ❽

Summer Cottage Inn 613 Columbia Ave ☎609/884-4948, ⓦwww.summercottageinn.com. 1867 inn with verandas and a cupola. Wide ranging of rates include good-value deals. ❺–❽

The Town and the beaches

Cape May's brightly colored houses were built by nouveaux riches Victorians with a healthy disrespect for subtlety. Cluttered with cupolas, gazebos, balconies, and "widow's walks," the houses follow no architectural rules except excess. They were known as "patternbook homes," with designs and features chosen from catalogs and thrown together in accordance with the owner's taste. The Victorian obsession with the Near East is everywhere: Moorish arches and onion domes sit comfortably next to gingerbread- and Queen Anne-style turrets. The **Emlen Physick Estate**, 1048 Washington St (tour hours vary; $10; ☎609/884-5404, ⓦwww.capemaymac.org), now a part of the Mid-Atlantic Center for the Arts, was built by the popular Philadelphia architect Frank Furness. It has been restored to its 1879 glory, with whimsical "upside-down" chimneys, a mock Tudor half-timbered facade, and much original furniture. West of town, where the Delaware Bay and the ocean meet, the

Wildwood

The traditionally blue-collar resort of nearby **Wildwood**, on a barrier island east of Rte-47, offers a counterpoint to the old-world fakery (pretty though it may be) of Cape May. Its 1950s architecture, left lovingly intact, includes dozens of gaudy and fun-looking hotels with names like *Pink Orchid*, *Waikiki*, and *The Shalimar*, all still featuring plastic palm trees, kidney-shaped swimming pools, and plenty of aqua, orange, and pink paint. To best appreciate the town's brash charm, take a stroll along the boardwalk and stop along the wide, throbbing, free beaches. Additionally, check out the local amusement rides and waterparks, such as Morey's Piers, Raging Waters, and Splash Zone.

1859 **Cape May Lighthouse**, visible from 25 miles out at sea, offers great views from a gallery below the lantern (199 steps up) and a small exhibit on its history at ground level (daily April–Nov, winter weekends, hours vary; $5; ℡609/884-8656, Ⓦwww.capemaymac.org). Three miles north of town on US-9, **Historic Cold Spring Village**, 720 Rte-9 (late May through mid-June & Sept Sat & Sun 10am–4.30pm; June–Aug Tues–Sun 10am–4.30pm; $8; ℡609/898-2300, Ⓦwww.hcsv.org), depicts a typical nineteenth-century south Jersey farming community. Restored buildings from the region house a jail, school, inn, and shops, and there are various craft shows and special events. Cape May's excellent **beaches** literally sparkle with quartz pebbles. Beach tags ($4 per day, $13 per week, $25 for a seasonal pass purchased before Memorial Day) must be worn from 10am until 6pm in the summer, and are available at the beach, from official vendors, and from **City Hall**, 643 Washington St (℡609/884-9525, Ⓦwww.capemaycity.com).

Eating

Cape May lacks the usual boardwalk snack bars, but it has plenty of cheap **lunch** places. **Dinner**, however, is far more expensive. Cape May's liquor laws are stringent, which means that many restaurants are BYO – call to check.

Bellevue Tavern 7 S Main St ℡609/463-1738. Functional early twentieth-century bar serving crab cakes and inexpensive hot sandwiches; dinners of steak, veal, and seafood average nearly $20.

Depot Market Café 409 Elmira St ℡609/884-8030. Opposite the bus terminal, offering filling sandwiches, salads and hoagies; dinners around $10.

Gecko's Carpenter's Lane ℡609/898-7750. A good lunch stop with a tasty Southwestern menu

and great desserts. Patio seating available.

The Lemon Tree 101 Liberty Way ℡609/884-2704. The cheesesteaks at this cheap, cheerful deli are Philly-quality; a nice antidote to the coffeeshops along the street.

Mad Batter 19 Jackson St ℡609/884-5970. Splash out on meat and fresh fish dishes, served by candlelight in the garden. Lunch is $8–15, dinner $15–30.

Nightlife and entertainment

Cape May is a friendly and laid-back place to be after dark; the day-trippers have gone home and the **bars** and **music venues** are enjoyed by locals and tourists alike. If you're after something a bit more lively, head a few miles north to the raucous nightclubs of **Wildwood**, such as *H2O*. Again, because of the liquor laws, remember that you may have to travel a little farther than you expect to find a drink.

Cabana's 429 Beach Ave ℡609/884-4800. Two-level bar that often hosts live music downstairs; upstairs is a low-key cocktail lounge.

Carney's 401 Beach Ave ℡609/884-4424. Spacious and relaxed Irish bar, with raucous live music.

Ugly Mug Washington St Mall and Decatur St ℡609/884-3459. This friendly bar is a local favorite and serves chowder, sandwiches, and seafood.

New England

AL - ALABAMA	IN - INDIANA	MN - MINNESOTA	RI - RHODE ISLAND
AR - ARKANSAS	LA - LOUISIANA	MS - MISSISSIPPI	SC - SOUTH CAROLINA
CT - CONNECTICUT	MA - MASSACHUSETTS	NC - NORTH CAROLINA	VA - VIRGINIA
DE - DELAWARE	MD - MARYLAND	NH - NEW HAMPSHIRE	VT - VERMONT
FL - FLORIDA	ME - MAINE	NJ - NEW JERSEY	WI - WISCONSIN
IL - ILLINOIS	MI - MICHIGAN	PA - PENNSYLVANIA	WV - WEST VIRGINIA

CHAPTER 3   # Highlights

* **Boston, MA** Revolutionary history comes to life around every charming corner, in one of America's most storied, walkable cities. See p.203

* **Provincetown, MA** Wild beaches, lovely flower-filled streets, and an alternative vibe on the outer reaches of Cape Cod. See p.227

* **Historic "summer cottages," Newport, RI** Conspicuous consumption gone crazy in this yachtie WASP resort. See p.246

* **Grand resort hotels, NH** At the opulent hotels of *Mount Washington* and *Balsams* you'll understand why vacationing in the White Mountains was once the preserve of the extremely well-off. See p.265

* **Montpelier, VT** Relaxed, friendly, and relatively tourist-free, pretty Montpelier is bounded by rivers and a forest of tall trees. See p.274

* **Acadia National Park, ME** Remote mountains and lakes, stunning beaches, and the chance to catch the sunrise before anyone else in the US. See p.293

△ Bar Harbor Inn

New England

The six **NEW ENGLAND** states of Massachusetts, Rhode Island, Connecticut, New Hampshire, Vermont, and Maine like to view themselves as the repository of all that is intrinsically American. In this version of history, the tangled streets of old Boston, the farms of Connecticut, and the village greens of Vermont are the cradle of the nation. Certainly, nostalgia is at the root of the region's tourist trade. While the real business of making a living happens in cities for the most part well off the tourist trail, innumerable small towns have been dolled-up to recapture a past that is at best wishful, and at times purely fictional. Picturesque though they may be, with white-spired churches beside immaculate rolling greens, towns, despite appearances, are not frozen in time: there's little to distinguish a clapboard house built last year from another, two hundred years old, which has just had its annual coat of white paint.

The genteel seaside towns of modern Cape Cod and Rhode Island are a far cry from the first European settlements in New England. While the Pilgrims congregated in neat, pristine communities, later arrivals, with so much land to choose from, felt no need to reconstruct the compact little villages they had left behind in Europe. Instead, they fanned out across the Native American fields, or straggled their farmhouses in endless strips along the newly built roadways (thus establishing a more genuinely American style of development). As the wealth of industry magnates soared in the mid-nineteenth century, the coastline came increasingly to be viewed as prime real estate, to be lined with grand patrician homes, from the Vanderbilt mansions of Newport to the presidential compounds of the Bush and Kennedy families.

The Ivy League colleges – Harvard, Yale, Brown, Dartmouth, et al – still embody New England's strong sense of its own superiority, though in fact the region's traditional role as home to the WASP elite is due more to the vagaries of history and ideology than to economic or cultural realities. Its thin soil and harsh climate made it difficult for the first pioneers to sustain an agricultural way of life, while the industrial prosperity of the nineteenth and early twentieth centuries is now for the most part a distant memory. Despite recent diversification, and the development of some high-tech industries, New England has pockets, mostly in rural Vermont and New Hampshire, that are as poor as any in the US.

New England can be a rather pricey place to visit, especially in late September and October, when visitors flock to see the magnificent **fall foliage**. Its tourist facilities are aimed at weekenders from the big cities as much as outsiders; places like **Cape Cod** and the **Berkshires** make convenient short breaks for locals. **Connecticut** and **Rhode Island** form part of the great East Coast megalopolis, but off I-95 you'll find plenty of tranquil pockets. **Boston** is a vibrant and stimulating city from which to set off north, where population is thin on the ground (and the **seafood** gets even better). Inland, too, the lakes and mountains of **New Hampshire** and particularly **Maine**

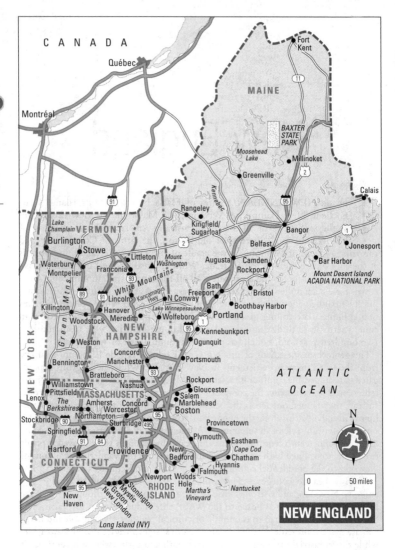

offer rural wildernesses to rival any in the nation. **Vermont** is slightly less diverse, but its country roads offer pleasant wandering through tiny villages and serene forests.

Some history

The Algonquin, **Native Americans** who first inhabited the northeast shoreline, were composed of several tribes and subgroups with different dialects. They shared a lifestyle of farming and fishing along the coast in summer, retreating with their animals to the relative warmth of the inland valleys in winter.

Six years after Columbus's first voyage, John Cabot nosed by in 1498, in search of the Northwest Passage. Over the next century, European fishermen began to return each year, though it was not until the early 1600s that the French and English attempted to found permanent colonies, in what is now Maine. The name – New England – was given in 1614 by surveyor-cum-explorer John Smith, who particularly appreciated the plentiful lobsters. Epidemics killed three-fourths of the native population by 1619.

Even for the new arrivals, this was not promising land: without precious metals to be mined, or the potential to grow lucrative crops, the first major impetus for emigration was **religion**. Refugees from intolerance – notably the Puritans, beginning with the **Pilgrims** in 1620 – made the arduous voyage to search for the freedom to build their own communities. The Pilgrims only survived at first thanks to the Indians: they were aided by a certain Squanto, who had been kidnapped, sold as a slave in Spain, and returned home via England. In thanks, the Pilgrims forced the natives from the terraces they had farmed for generations.

The possibility of a serious Native American threat was eliminated in **King Philip's War** of 1675–76, in which a leader of the Narragansett Indians (known as Philip) persuaded feuding native groups to bury their differences in one last, and ultimately hopeless, stand against the settlers. By then, though, white colonization had gathered an unstoppable momentum. The **Salem witch trials** of 1692 provided a salutary lesson on the potential dangers of fanaticism, and as immigration became less English-based, with influxes of Huguenots after 1680 and Irish in 1708, Puritan domination decreased and a definite class structure began to emerge.

While the strand of history that began with the Pilgrims is just one among many in the colonization of America – the Spanish were in Santa Fe before the Pilgrims ever left England – the metropolis of **Boston** deserves to be celebrated as the place where the great project of **American independence** first captured the popular imagination. This leading port of colonial America was always the likeliest focus of resentment against the latest impositions of the British government, and was ready to take up the challenge thrown down by British Chancellor Townshend in 1767: "I dare tax America." So many of the seminal moments of the **Revolutionary War** took place here: the Boston Massacre of 1770, the Boston Tea Party of 1773, and the first shots in nearby Lexington and Concord in 1775.

Once nationhood was secured by the signing of the **Declaration of Independence** on July 4, 1776, New England's prosperity was ironically hit hard by the loss of trade with England, and Boston was slowly eclipsed by Philadelphia, New York, and the new capital, Washington. The **Triangular Trade** in slaves, sugar, and rum provided one substitute source of income, the brief heyday of **whaling** another. New England was also momentarily at the forefront of the **Industrial Revolution**, when water-powered mills created a booming textile industry, most of which quickly moved south where wages were scandalously cheaper. The attempt to farm the north, however, foundered: careless techniques served to exhaust the land, and as the vast spaces of the western US opened to settlement, many of the inland towns fell silent.

Massachusetts

To the first colonists of the **Massachusetts Bay Company**, their arrival near the site of modern Salem in 1629 marked a crucial moment in history. **Puritans** who had decided to leave England before it was engulfed by civil war saw their purpose, in the words of Governor John Winthrop, as the establishment of a utopian "**City upon a hill**." Their new colony of **MASSACHUSETTS** was to be a beacon to the rest of humanity, an exemplar of sober government along sound spiritual principles. Not all those who followed, however, shared the same motivation; the story is often told of the preacher who told his congregation that they had come to New England to build a new kingdom of God, only to be challenged by a vociferous parishioner who said he had come to fish.

In their own terms, the Puritans were not successful: as waves of immigration brought all kinds of dissenters and free-thinkers from Europe, society in New England inevitably became secular. However, their **influence** remained. A clarity of thought and forcefulness of purpose can be traced from the foundation of Harvard College in 1636, through the intellectual impetus behind the Revolution and the crusade against slavery, to the nineteenth-century achievements of **writers** such as Melville, Emerson, Hawthorne, and Thoreau.

Other traditions, too, have helped shape the state – migrants from **Ireland** and **Italy**, freed and escaped **slaves** from the Southern states, **Portuguese** seamen – even if they have not always been welcome. The anti-immigrant "Know-Nothing" party of the 1850s acquired considerable public support; in 1927, the Italian anarchists **Sacco and Vanzetti** came up against conservative old Massachusetts, and were framed and executed on murder charges. Despite a strong history of abolitionism and progressive thought, Boston shocked the nation with its violent displays of racial conflict in the 1970s, prompted by public school busing and court-ordered desegregation. The city has since made concerted, largely successful efforts to heal race relations, most notably with the strengthening of business centers in African-American neighborhoods.

Spending a few days in **Boston** is strongly recommended. While its history is often visible, there's a great deal of modern life and energy besides, thanks in part to the presence of **Cambridge**, the home of Harvard University and MIT (Massachusetts Institute of Technology), just across the river. Several historic towns are within easy reach – **Salem** to the north, **Concord** and **Lexington** just inland, and **Plymouth** to the south. **Provincetown**, a ninety-minute ferry ride across the bay at the tip of Cape Cod, is great fun to visit, and the rest of the Cape offers old towns and lovely beaches – with the requisite huge crowds. Except for a handful of college towns such as **Amherst**, **western Massachusetts** is much quieter; its settlements are naturally concentrated where the land is fertile, such as along the Connecticut River Valley and in the **Berkshires** to the west.

Getting around Massachusetts

Massachusetts is an easy state to tour on **public transportation**: planes, trains, and buses all radiate out from Boston; connections to **Cape Cod** in particular are legion. The **Amtrak** line that connects Boston with New York, Philadelphia, and Washington DC is the best regional **train** service in the nation, while the *Vermonter* gives access to Vermont and Connecticut and (via Springfield) Chicago and Toronto, ON. The affable *Downeaster* service follows a scenic route that links Boston to Portland, Maine. **Buses** from Boston are also plentiful. The main east–west artery across the state is I-90 (or "MassPike"); the major north–south route is I-95, which circumnavigates the greater Boston area and affords entry points for its many suburbs.

Boston

Although the metropolitan area of **BOSTON** has long since expanded to fill the shoreline of **Massachusetts Bay**, and stretches for miles inland as well, the seventeenth-century port at its heart is still discernible. The tangled roads (former cow paths) clustered around **Boston Common** are a reminder of how the nation started out, and the city is enjoyably walkable in scale.

Boston was, until 1755, the biggest city in America; as the one most directly affected by the latest whims of the British Crown, it was the natural birthplace for the opposition that culminated in the **Revolutionary War**. Numerous evocative sites from that era are preserved along the downtown **Freedom Trail**. Since then, however, Boston has in effect turned its back on the sea. As the third busiest port in the British Empire (after London and Bristol), it stood on a narrow peninsula. What is now Washington Street provided the only access by land, and when the British set off to Lexington in 1775 they embarked in ships from the Common itself. During the nineteenth century, the Charles River marshlands were filled in to create the posh Back Bay residential area. Central Boston is now slightly set back from the water, and until recently, was divided by the hideous John Fitzgerald Expressway that carried I-93 across downtown. In 2006 the city successfully routed the traffic underground and disposed of this eyesore – a project more than a decade in the making, known as "the **Big Dig**." While technically complete, The Big Dig remains rife with complications, most notably with the leaks and defaults that continue to plague the tunnels; in 2006 a female passenger was killed when several concrete slabs fell onto her vehicle, closing the Ted Williams Tunnel temporarily.

There is a certain truth in the charge leveled by other Americans that Boston likes to live in the past; echoes of the "Brahmins" of a century ago can be heard in the upper-class drawl of the posher districts. But this is by no means just a city of WASPs: the Irish who began to arrive in large numbers after the Great Famine had produced their first mayor as early as 1885, and the president of the entire nation within a hundred years. The liberal tradition that spawned the Kennedys remains alive, fed in part by the presence in the city of more than one hundred universities and colleges, the most famous of which – **Harvard University** – is actually in the contiguous city of Cambridge, just across the Charles River.

The slump of the Depression seemed to linger in Boston for years – in the 1950s, the population was actually dwindling – but these days the place has a bright, rejuvenated feel. **Quincy Market** has served as a blueprint for urban redevelopment worldwide, and the aesthetic effects of the Big Dig have completely reshaped the city – most notably with the elegant, skyline-boosting Zakim Bridge, the newly-christened Rose Kennedy Greenway, and the beautification of the HarborWalk. With its busy street life, imaginative museums and galleries, eminent architecture, and palpable history, Boston is one destination in New England there's no excuse for missing.

Arrival and information

Boston is the center of New England's transportation networks. An increasing number of direct flights from Europe means that it provides many visitors with their first taste of America, while efficient rail and bus services from New York, Chicago, and further afield make this an obvious starting point.

By air

Logan Airport (☎617/561-1800 or 1-800/23-LOGAN), busy with both international and domestic services, is a mere three miles from downtown Boston. A **taxi**

ACCOMMODATION

463 Beacon Street Guest House	P
Beacon Hill Hotel	H
Berkeley Residence YWCA	J
Boston Backpackers Hostel	D
Charles Hotel	N
Charlesmark Hotel	K
Courtyard Boston Copley Square	L
Harborside Inn	C
HI-Boston	Q
HI-Fenway Summer Hostel	R
Irving House	G
The John Jeffries House	I
Jurys Boston Hotel	B
Marriott's Custom House	M
Newbury Guest House	F
Nine Zero	E
Omni Parker House	O
Prescott International	
Hotel and Hostel	A
YMCA of Greater Boston	S

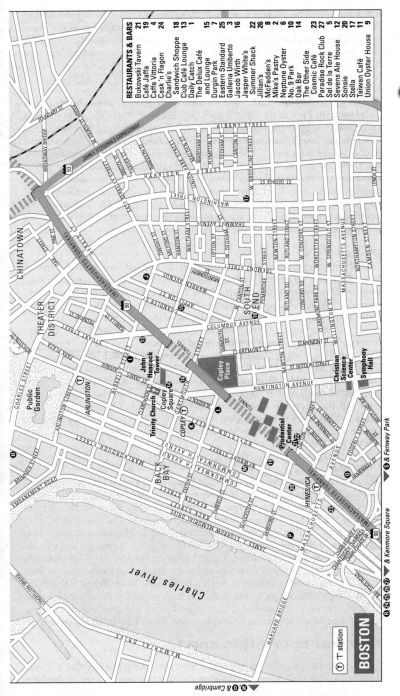

RESTAURANTS & BARS

Bukowski Tavern	21
Café Jaffa	19
Caffè Vittoria	4
Cask 'n Flagon	24
Charlie's Sandwich Shoppe	18
Club Café Lounge	13
Daily Catch	1
The Delux Café and Lounge	15
Durgin Park	7
Eastern Standard	25
Galleria Umberto	3
Jacob Wirth	16
Jasper White's Summer Shack	22
Jillian's	26
McFadden's	8
Mike's Pastry	2
Neptune Oyster	6
No. 9 Park	10
Oak Bar	14
The Other Side Cosmic Café	23
Paradise Rock Club	27
Sel de la Terre	5
Sevens Ale House	12
Sonsie	20
Stella	17
Taiwan Café	11
Union Oyster House	9

BOSTON

Ⓣ T station

205

into town costs $15–20, plus an extra $6.50 in fees and tolls; the trip should take twenty minutes at its best. Between 4am and 1am, free **shuttle buses** run every few minutes from all airport terminals to the airport **subway** station on the MBTA Blue line (see "City transportation and tours," opposite), from where it's an easy ten-minute ride to the city center.

By train

Amtrak (☎1-800/USA-RAIL, ⓦwww.amtrak.com) trains along the Northeast Corridor from Providence, Washington DC, and New York, and from Chicago and Canada via Springfield, arrive a short walk from downtown Boston near the waterfront at **South Station**, Summer Street and Atlantic Avenue. The renovated station houses information booths, newsstands, restaurants, and a fantastic old clock, though no currency exchange. The Red subway line inside the station can whisk you to the center of town or out to Cambridge. Some Amtrak services also make an extra stop at **Back Bay Station**, 145 Dartmouth St, on the Orange subway line near Copley Square. **North Station** is used by MBTA commuter trains as well the amiable *Downeaster*, which connects Boston to Portland, Maine, with a number of Maine and New Hampshire stops along the way.

By bus

Several **bus** companies provide direct links between Boston and the rest of New England. Vermont Transit (☎1-800/552-8737, ⓦwww.vermonttransit.com) covers western Massachusetts, New Hampshire's White Mountains, Vermont, and Montréal; while Concord Trailways (☎1-800/639-3317, ⓦwww.concordtrailways.com) runs to southern New Hampshire and up the Maine coast. Heading south, Peter Pan Bus Lines (☎1-800/343-9999, ⓦwww.peterpanbus.com) connects Providence and Newport, Cape Cod, and New York City, as well as western Massachusetts. The popular Fung Wah bus offers hourly service to Canal St in New York City (☎617/345-8000, ⓦwww.fungwahbus.com) for a mere $15 dollars each way. Greyhound (☎1-800/231-2222, ⓦwww.greyhound.com), with its many connections, offers nationwide service. Plymouth and Brockton Bus Co. (☎508/746-0378, ⓦwww.p-b.com), serves Cape Cod as well as access to Martha's Vineyard and Nantucket and has buses that leave from Logan Airport as well as South Station; all other buses leave from South Station (see "By train," above).

Information

The most convenient place to get advice and maps is the **Visitor Information Center** (Mon–Sat 8.30am–5pm, Sun 10am–6pm; ☎617/536-4100 or 1-888/SEE-BOSTON, ⓦwww.bostonusa.com) near the Park Street subway stop on the Tremont Street side of Boston Common. Across the street from the Old State House, at 15 State St, is an excellent information center maintained by the Boston National Historical Park (daily 9am–5pm; ☎617/242-5642), as well as bathrooms and a bookstore. There are also information kiosks in **Quincy Market**, the **John Hancock Tower** at Copley Square in Back Bay, and in the **Prudential Center** (also in Back Bay). For advance information, the **Boston By Phone** service (☎1-888/SEE-BOSTON) allows visitors anywhere in North America to connect directly with a wide range of hotels and services. The city's main **post office** is located behind South Station (25 Dorchester Ave) and is open twenty-four hours a day (☎617/654-5302).

City transportation and tours

Much of the pleasure of visiting Boston comes from being in a city that was built long before cars were invented. Walking around town can be a joy; conversely, driving is an absolute nightmare. The freeways won't take you where you want to go, the one-way traffic systems can have you circling for hours, and if you ever do arrive, parking lots can be very expensive. There's no point renting a car in Boston until the day you leave, especially since the city's public transportation is so good and the local drivers so notoriously bad.

The Massachusetts Bay Transportation Authority (MBTA, known as the "**T**") is responsible for Boston's **subway** system and **trolleys**. The subway, which opened in 1897, is the oldest in the US; its first station, **Park Street**, remains its center (any train marked "inbound" is headed here). Four lines – Red, Green, Blue, and Orange – operate daily from 5am until 12.30am, although certain routes begin to shut down earlier. The four lines are supplemented by a bus rapid transit (BRT) route, the **Silver Line**, which runs aboveground along Washington Street and cuts through the heart of the South End. While maps are posted at each station, it's a good idea to pick up the widely available Rapid Transit maps for reference. Trains are fast and safe; only some parts of the Orange line might be said to be unsafe after dark.

Within the city, the standard fare is $1.25, normally paid with tokens inserted into turnstiles; on some incoming aboveground routes you have to pay extra, up to $3.00 (conversely, some outbound aboveground routes are free). Unfortunately, the city is currently in a very disorganized stage of phasing out the token system in favor of stored value cards (or "CharlieTickets"). Don't be misled – many subway stops still aren't set up to accept a CharlieTicket; during the interim period, it's best to stick with tokens. Your safest bet is the **Boston Visitor Pass** which seamlessly covers all subway and local bus journeys (as well as the ferry to Charlestown) at a cost of $7.50 for a day, $18 for three days, or $35 for a week. For MBTA **information** call ☎617/222-5215 or 1-800/392-6100, or visit ⓦ www.mbta.com.

The normal fare on MBTA's **local buses** is 90¢, but longer distances, such as out to Salem or Marblehead, cost up to $3.45. MBTA also runs **commuter rail lines**, extending as far as Salem, Concord, and Providence, RI; destinations north leave from **North Station** (☎617/222-3200) on Causeway Street, under the TDBanknorth Garden; destinations south leave from (you guessed it) **South Station** (☎617/222-3200) on Summer Street and Atlantic Avenue, by the waterfront.

In and around Boston are some eighty miles of **bike trails**. Bicycles can be rented from Boston Bicycle, 842 Beacon St (☎617/236-0752; ⓦ www.cambridgebicycle. com) or at their sister location, Cambridge Bicycle, in Cambridge (259 Massachusetts Avenue; near MIT; ☎617/876-6555; ⓦ www.cambridgebicycle.com), and from Boston Bike Tours and Rentals, near the Visitor Information Center on Boston Common (☎617/308-5902; ⓦ www.bostonbiketours.com). Rentals are around $25 per day.

City tours

It's easy enough to get to know Boston by following the **Freedom Trail** on foot (see p.209). If you prefer to be guided, though, narrated trips run throughout the day aboard the hundred-minute Old Town Trolley Tours (☎617/269-7150; ⓦ www.trolleytours.com; $29, kids aged 4–12, $5) or the similarly priced Discover Boston Trolley Tours (☎617/742-1440, ⓦ www.discoverbostontours. com), which specializes in narrated audio tours in multiple languages. But nothing is as popular (or as novel) as a Boston Duck Tour (adults $26, kids 3–11 $17; ☎617/267-DUCK, ⓦ www.bostonducktours.com), an entertaining romp by land and by sea aboard a real WWII amphibious landing vehicle. Tours depart from the Prudential Center as well as the Museum of Science, March through November. The Boston National Historical Park, 15 State St (☎617/242-5642; ⓦ www.nps. gov/bost), conducts free, ranger-led tours centering on a number of Freedom

Trail hotspots. Also useful are the **bus excursions** further afield to Lexington, Concord, Salem, and Plymouth with Brush Hill Tours/Gray Line (T 1-800/343-1328, W www.brushhilltours.com or www.grayline.com). Boston Bike Tours (T 617/308-5902, W www.bostonbiketours.com) can take you around for a couple of gentle hours by bike. Tours begin from the Boston Common at 11am on Saturdays and Sundays and cost about $25 ($20 if you have your own bike).

Accommodation

Good-quality, inexpensive **accommodation** is hard to find in Boston – any hotel room within walking distance of downtown for under $200 has to be considered a bargain. One enjoyable and affordable way of staying in the Boston area is to use a **B&B agency**. The excellent B&B Agency of Boston (T 617/720-3540 or 1-800/248-9262; in the UK T 0800/895128, W www.boston-bnbagency.com), offers hundreds of properties across the city for $70–160 a night. Host Homes of Boston (T 617/244-1308 or 1-800/600-1308, W www.hosthomesofboston. com) provides a similar service; Boston Reservations (T 781/547-5427, W www. bostonreservations.com) also makes hotel reservations at reduced rates.

Hotels, motels, and B&Bs

463 Beacon Street Guest House 463 Beacon St
T 617/536-1302, W www.463beacon.com; Hynes **T**. Good-sized rooms available by the night, week, or month; many come with kitchenettes. There are some less expensive rooms with shared baths. Ask for the top-floor room. **④–⑦**

Beacon Hill Hotel 25 Charles St T 617/723-7575 or 1-888/959-BHHB, W www.beaconhillhotel.com; Charles **T**. Pampered luxury in the heart of Beacon Hill; the thirteen sleek chambers come with flat-screen televisions, high-speed internet access, and balconies. They also house a fantastic bistro and fireplace bar. **⑨**

Charles Hotel 1 Bennett St T 617/864-1200 or 1-800/882-1818, W www.charleshotel.com; Copley **T**. Clean, bright rooms in the heart of Harvard Square, with a great array of modern amenities. They also house an excellent jazz club, *Regattabar*, as well as the iconic restaurant *Henrietta's Table*. **⑦–⑨**

Charlesmark Hotel 655 Boylston St T 617/247-1212, W www.thecharlesmark.com; Copley **T**. 33 smallish, contemporary rooms with cozy beechwood furnishings, and modern accoutrements like in-room CD players and wireless internet. They also have a great staff and some of the best rates for the area. **⑦–⑨**

Courtyard Boston Copley Square 88 Exeter St
T 1-800/321-2211, W www.courtyardboston.com; Copley **T**. Luxurious rooms, modern accents, great service, and a nice location in Back Bay make this a Boston standout. **⑧–⑨**

Harborside Inn 185 State St T 617/723-7500, W www.hagopianhotels.com; State **T**. Cozy hotel featuring exposed brick, hardwood floors, and cherry furniture in a renovated 1890s mercantile warehouse; across from Quincy Market and the

Custom House. Rates drop some $30 a night Dec–March. **⑦**

Irving House 24 Irving St, Cambridge T 617/547-4600, W www.irvinghouse.com; Harvard **T**. Excellent, friendly option near Harvard Square with laundry facilities and breakfast included; both shared and private baths. Birthday specials, too. **⑤–⑦**

The John Jeffries House 14 David G. Mugar Way
T 617/367-1866, W www.johnjeffrieshouse.com; Charles **T**. Mid-scale hotel at the foot of Beacon Hill, with a cozy lounge and Victorian-style rooms; single-occupancy studios include kitchenettes. **⑤–⑦**

Jurys Boston Hotel 64 Arlington St T 617/266-7200, W www.jurysdoyle.com; Back Bay **T**. A modern hotel with an historic (it's housed in the former Boston police headquarters), Irish bent, *Jurys* features stylish rooms equipped with wireless internet, a fitness center, and the swanky *Stanhope Grille*. **⑧–⑨**

Marriott's Custom House 3 McKinley Square T 617/310-6300, W www.marriott. com; Aquarium **T**. While it's no longer the tallest skyscraper in New England (a title it held in the nineteenth century), it continues to have gorgeous, jaw-dropping views of the harbor, historic, elegantly appointed rooms, high-speed internet, great service, and a fantastic location. **⑧–⑨**

Newbury Guest House 261 Newbury St
T 617/437-7666, W www.newburyguesthouse. com; Copley **T**. Well-located, big, 32-room Victorian brownstone house, with rates at the lower end of Boston's price range. Continental breakfast included. Rates go down substantially Dec–Feb. **⑤–⑦**

Nine Zero 90 Tremont St, T 617/772-5800, W www.ninezero.com; Park **T**. Probably Boston's trendiest accommodation, with hip, modern furnishings, a fancy cheese plate to welcome you, and

beds so lovely they had to start selling them retail.
7–**9**
Omni Parker House 60 School St ☎617/227-8600 or 1-800/843-6664, ⓦwww.omniparkerhouse.com; Park **T**. The oldest continuously running hotel in the US (as well as the originators of Boston cream pie), the *Omni Parker House* features a gorgeous, gilded lobby, modern renovations (including high-speed internet), and some of downtown's better room rates. **8**

Hostels

Berkeley Residence YWCA 40 Berkeley St ☎617/375-2524, ⓦwww.ywcaboston.org/berkeley; Back Bay **T**. Clean and simple rooms next door to a police station. All rates include breakfast; dinner is an additional $7.50. Singles are ($60), doubles ($90), and triples ($105) in a convenient South End location. Stays for longer than two weeks are only available to women.
Boston Backpackers Hostel 234 Friend St ☎617/723-0800, ⓦwww.bostonbackpackers.com; North Station **T**. Dorm beds for $30 (includes linens). Be forewarned – the hostel is adjacent to *Hooters* – however it's above the more appealing *Bulfinch Yacht Club,* which provides (limited) free food for hostellers. Hostel is about 5 minutes' walk north of Faneuil Hall.

HI-Boston 12 Hemenway St ☎617/536-9455, ⓦwww.bostonhostel.org; Hynes **T**. Located in the Fenway area, close to the hip end of Newbury St and the Lansdowne St clubs, this is one of Boston's better hostel options. Free internet access and a safe, clean environment. Dorm beds are $35–38 a night. In summer, book ahead, or check in at 8am, to be sure of a place.
HI-Fenway Summer Hostel 575 Commonwealth Ave ☎617/267-8599, ⓦwww.bostonhostel.org; Kenmore **T**. A summer-only hostel (June 1–Aug 18) that functions as a BU dorm in winter months; it's perhaps the best hostel in Boston. Spacious rooms and a great location within walking distance of nightclubs and Fenway Park. Members $35, nonmembers $38.
Prescott International Hotel and Hostel 36 Church St, Everett ☎617/389-1990, ⓦwww.theprescotthotel.com; Sullivan Square **T**. It's a few minutes away on the **T**, but the Prescott hotel offers clean, affordable digs (dorm beds $30). Plus John Lennon was once a guest.
YMCA of Greater Boston 316 Huntington Ave ☎617/937-8040 ⓦwww.ymcaboston.org.; Northeastern **T**. Good budget rooms, and access to the Y's health facilities (pool, weight room, etc). Singles are $46–66, but you can get a four-person room for $96. Co-ed June–Sept, otherwise men-only.

The City

Boston has grown up around **Boston Common**, a utilitarian chunk of green established for public use and "the feeding of cattell" in 1634. A good starting point for a tour of the city, it is also one of the links in the string of nine parks (six of which were designed by Frederick Law Olmsted, America's foremost landscape architect) known as Boston's **Emerald Necklace**. Another piece is the lovely **Public Garden**, across Charles Street from the Common, where Boston's iconic swan boats (☎617/522-9666, ⓦwww.swanboats.com; $2.75), paddle the main pond amidst tulip-strewn greenery.

The visitor center, which marks the start of the **Freedom Trail**, is near the tapering east end of the Common. As you stand here, facing up Tremont Street with the State House away to your left, the main shopping district, **Quincy Market**, and the **waterfront** are slightly ahead and down to the right. The modern concrete wasteland of **Government Center** is straight up Tremont Street, with the beloved **North End** beyond – first Irish, then Jewish, and now a very Italian enclave. A short way behind you on the left rises lofty **Beacon Hill**, every bit as elegant as when Henry James called Mount Vernon Street "the most prestigious address in America" (far removed from its eighteenth-century nickname of "Mount Whoredom"). Heading away from the center down Tremont Street brings you to **Chinatown** and the **Theater District**, while grand boulevards such as Commonwealth Avenue lead west from the Public Garden into the **Back Bay**, where Harvard Bridge runs across the Charles River into **Cambridge**.

The Freedom Trail

Probably the best way to orient yourself in downtown Boston – and to appreciate the city's role in American history – is to walk some or all of the **Freedom Trail**.

△ Public Garden

You can pick up or leave this easy self-guided route anywhere – a line of red bricks (or red paint) marking the trail is embedded in the pavement – but technically it begins on Boston Common at the **Visitor Information Center**.

From here, head for the golden dome of the **Massachusetts State House** (free tours Mon–Fri 10am–3.30pm); a Charles Bulfinch design completed in 1798. It remains the seat of Massachusetts' government; its most famous feature, a carved fish dubbed the "Sacred Cod," symbolizes the wealth Boston accrued from maritime trade. Politicos take this symbol so seriously that when Harvard pranksters stole it in the 1930s the House didn't reconvene until it was recovered.

Though **Park Street Church** (July & Aug Tues–Sat 8.30am–3.30pm; rest of year by appointment; free) is by no means "the most interesting mass of bricks and mortar in America," as Henry James once claimed, its ornate white steeple is undeniably impressive. It was here, on July 4, 1829, that orator William Lloyd Garrison delivered his first public address calling for the nationwide abolition of slavery. Just around the corner, the atmospheric **Old Granary Burying Ground** (daily 9am–5pm; free) includes the Revolutionary remains of Paul Revere, Samuel Adams, and John Hancock, as well as those of the so-called Mother Goose, née Elizabeth Vergoose (or Vertigoose), said to have collected nursery rhymes for her grandchildren. A block or so north on Tremont is the ethereal **King's Chapel Burying Ground** (daily 9.30am–5pm; free) final resting place for seventeenth-century luminaries such as Mary Chilton, woman of the *Mayflower,* and Boston's first governor, John Winthrop. Nearby on School Street, a statue of Benjamin Franklin marks the site of **Boston Latin School**, America's first public school, attended by Franklin (who later dropped out) and Samuel Adams. Malcolm X and Ho Chi Minh are both former employs of the **Omni Parker House Hotel** (not officially on the Trail) the longest continuously operating luxury hotel in the nation and home of the first-ever Boston cream pie.

Next come two of the Trail's more striking and significant buildings. The **Old South Meeting House** (daily: April–Oct 9.30am–5pm; Nov–March 10am–4pm; $5) is where Samuel Adams pronounced "this meeting can do nothing more to save the country" – the signal that triggered the Boston Tea Party on December 16, 1773. Considered to be the first major act of rebellion preceding the Revolutionary War, it was a carefully-planned event wherein one hundred men, mostly dressed in Indian garb, solemnly threw enough British tea into the harbor to make 24 million cuppas. The elegant **Old State House**, built in 1712, was the seat of Colonial government, and from its balcony the Declaration of Independence was first publicly-read in Boston on July 18, 1776; two hundred years later Queen Elizabeth II stepped out onto that same balcony. Inside is a decent **museum** of Boston history (daily 9am–5pm; $5). Outside, a circle of cobblestones set on a traffic island at the intersection of Devonshire and State streets marks the site of the **Boston Massacre** on March 5, 1770, when British soldiers fired on a crowd that was pelting them with stone-filled snowballs, and killed five, including Crispus Attucks, a former slave.

Lively **Quincy Market** and **Faneuil Hall Marketplace** (a ten-minute walk northeast from here; daily 10am–8pm; free) is where to refuel at restaurants and takeaway food stalls or shop for souvenirs. The market is a pioneer example of successful urban renewal (by the same developer who transformed London's Covent Garden). Faneuil Hall (daily 9am–5pm; free) was, however, once known as the "Cradle of Liberty," a meeting place for Revolutionaries and, later, abolitionists. Nearby on Union Street, step off the Freedom Trail to visit **The New England Holocaust Memorial** – lofty, hollow glass pillars etched with six million numbers recalling the tattoos the Nazis gave its victims. Its smokestack design is particularly striking at night, when the steam that rises from the pillars is lit up from within.

Passing over Surface Street (formerly a massive, aboveground expressway) and into the **North End**, you reach **Paul Revere House**, Boston's last surviving seventeenth-century house (daily: mid-April–Oct 9.30am–5.15pm; Nov–mid-April Tues–Sun 9.30am–4.15pm; $3), built after the Great Fire of 1676, and home to Paul Revere – patriot, silversmith, Freemason, and father of sixteen children – from 1770 until 1800. When Revere embarked upon his famous **ride** of April 18, 1775, to warn Samuel Adams and John Hancock (as well as the residents of Lexington, MA) that the British were assembling for an attack, two lanterns were hung from the belfry of **Old North Church**, 193 Salem St (daily: June–Oct 9am–6pm; Nov–May 9am–5pm; free), to alert Charlestown in case he got caught. Up the hill on Hull Street, from **Copp's Hill Burial Ground** (daily 9am–5pm; free), you can see across the harbor to Charlestown; as indeed could the British, who planted their artillery here for the Battle of Bunker Hill.

Next, the Freedom Trail crosses the Charlestown Bridge, a fairly long walk. Its final two sites are better reached by the frequent **ferries** from Long Wharf to Charlestown Navy Yard (Mon–Fri every 15–30mins 6.30am–8pm, Sat & Sun every 30mins 10am–6pm; $1.50 each way).

The celebrated **USS Constitution**, also known as "Old Ironsides," is the oldest commissioned warship still afloat in the world. Launched in Boston in 1797, she earned her nickname during the War of 1812, when advancing cannonballs bounced off her hull; she subsequently saw 33 battles without ever losing one. Free tours of the ship are led every half-hour (daily 10am–5.50pm, last tour at 3.30pm; @www.ussconstitution.navy.mil). Across the way, the **USS Constitution Museum** (daily: summer 9am–6pm; rest of year 10am–5pm; free) houses

The Black Heritage Trail

Massachusetts was the first state to declare slavery illegal, in 1783 – partly as a result of black participation in the Revolutionary War – and a large community of free blacks and escaped slaves swiftly grew in the North End and on Beacon Hill. Very few blacks live in either place today, but the **Black Heritage Trail** traces Beacon Hill's key role in local and national black history – perhaps the most important historical site in America devoted to pre-Civil War African-American history and culture.

Pick up the Trail either at 46 Joy St, where the **Abiel Smith School** contains a **Museum of Afro-American History** (summer daily 10am–4pm; rest of year Mon–Sat 10am–4pm; free), and rotates a number of well-tailored exhibits centered on abolitionism and African-American history, or at the **African Meeting House** at 8 Smith Court (off Joy St), for displays and talks from well-informed rangers. Built in 1806 as the country's first African-American church, this became known as "Black Faneuil Hall" during the abolitionist campaign; Frederick Douglass issued his call here for all blacks to take up arms in the Civil War. Among those who responded were the volunteers of the **Massachusetts 54th Regiment**, commemorated by a monument at the edge of Boston Common, opposite the State House, which depicts their farewell march down Beacon Street. Robert Lowell won a Pulitzer Prize for his poem, "For the Union Dead," about this monument, and the regiment's tragic end at Fort Wagner was depicted in the movie *Glory*.

From the monument, the Trail winds around Beacon Hill, and includes a stop at the imposing **Lewis and Harriet Hayden House**. Once a stop on the famous "Underground Railroad," the Haydens sheltered hundreds of runaway slaves from bounty-hunters in pursuit.

While it's easy enough to traverse it on your own, the best way to experience the Trail is by taking a National Park Service **walking tour** (Mon–Sat 10am, noon, & 2pm; call to reserve; free; ☎617/742-5415, ⓦwww.nps.gov/boaf).

well-tailored displays on the history of the ship; upstairs is more fun-oriented, with hands-on exhibits testing your ability to balance on a footrope and helping to pinpoint whether your comrades have scurvy or gout. Beyond the museum, the **Bunker Hill Monument** sits on Breed's Hill, the actual site of the battle fought on June 17, 1775, which, while technically won by the British, invigorated the patriots, whose strong showing felled nearly half the British troops. A spiral staircase of 294 steps leads to sweeping views at the top; a small **museum** (daily 9am–4.30pm; free) at the base has dated but informative exhibits on the battle.

The waterfront

Boston's **waterfront** has recently seen major revitalization efforts – inviting fountains, well-maintained green spaces, and historic signage have all started popping up – making it a great spot for a warm weather stroll. Wisteria-laden **Columbus Park**, next to the centrally-located *Marriott Long Wharf Hotel*, is a pretty place to lounge and picnic. Faneuil Hall originally stood at the head of **Long Wharf**, which stuck out nearly two thousand feet into the harbor; it also served as the site of the final British evacuation on March 17, 1776. Later, a thousand-foot expanse of the waterfront was filled in, and the **Custom House Tower**, once the tallest skyscraper in New England, was erected to mark the end of the wharf. It too now finds itself inland; although its observation deck offers terrific harbor views (3 McKinley Square; ☎617/310-6300; free).

Close by on Central Wharf, the **New England Aquarium** (July & Aug Mon–Thurs 9am–6pm, Fri–Sun 9am–7pm; Sept–June Mon–Fri 9am–5pm, Sat & Sun

9am–6pm; $17.95, kids $9.95) has an outdoor pool of basking sea otters. Inside, a colossal, three-story glass cylindrical tank is packed with giant sea turtles, moray eels, and sharks as well as a range of other ocean exotica that swim by in unsettling proximity. Scuba divers hand-feed the fish five times a day, and sea lion shows are held in a floating amphitheater alongside.

It's hard to miss the **Children's Museum**, 300 Congress St (Mon–Thurs, Sat & Sun 10am–5pm, Fri 10am–9pm; $9, kids $7; Fri 5–9pm $1) marked as it is by a whimsical Boston icon: a forty-foot tall Hood **milk bottle** (it doubles as an ice-cream parlor and hot-dog stand). The museum's four floors of educational exhibits are craftily designed to trick kids into learning about a huge array of topics, from musicology to the engineering of a humongous bubble. Before leaving, check out the Recycle Shop where industrial leftovers are transformed into appealing craft-fodder.

The Museum of Science

At the northern end of the waterfront, clear across the Boston peninsula from the Children's Museum, the beloved **Museum of Science** (July to early Sept Mon–Thurs, Sat & Sun 9am–7pm, Fri 9am–9pm; Sept–June Mon–Thurs, Sat & Sun 9am–5pm, Fri 9am–9pm; $16, kids $13; Science Park **T**) has several floors of interactive exhibits illustrating basic principles of natural and physical science. An impressive IMAX cinema takes up the full height of one end of the building, and the Hayden Planetarium pays its way with semi-rocking laser shows including the infamous "Laser Floyd: Dark Side of the Moon." ($9; call ☎617/723-2500 for showtimes).

Back Bay and beyond

Beginning in 1857, the spacious boulevards and elegant houses of **Back Bay** were fashioned along gradually filled-in portions of former Charles River marshland. Thus a walk through the area from east to west provides an impressive visual timeline of Victorian architecture. One of the most architecturally significant of its buildings is the Romanesque **Trinity Church**, 206 Clarendon St (Mon–Sat 9am–5pm, Sun 1–5.30pm; $5), whose stunning interior was built to feel like "walking into a living painting." Towering over the church is Boston's signature skyscraper, the **John Hancock Tower**, an elegant wedge designed by I.M. Pei. Nearby **Newbury Street** is an atmospheric and inviting stretch of swanky boutiques, cafés, and art galleries.

The **Christian Science Center** at Huntington and Massachusetts avenues is the "Mother Church" of the First Church of Christ Scientist, and the home of the *Christian Science Monitor* newspaper; Nelson Mandela made a point of paying a personal visit in 1990 to thank the paper for its support of his release from prison. The complex houses the marvelous **Mapparium** (Tues–Sun 10am–4pm; $6), a curious, 30-ft stained-glass globe through which you can walk on a footbridge. The globe's best feature is its lack of sound absorption, which enables a tiny whisper spoken at one end of the bridge to be easily heard by someone at the other.

Further south, beyond the boundaries of Back Bay and a long enough walk to warrant taking the "**T**'s" green line (take the train marked "E" to the "Museum" stop), is the **Museum of Fine Arts** at 465 Huntington Ave (Mon & Tues 10am–4.45pm, Wed–Fri 10am–9.45pm, Sat & Sun 10am–4.45pm; $15, which includes a free repeat visit within 30 days; Wed after 4pm suggested donation only; ☎617/267-9300, ⊛www.mfa.org). From its magnificent collections of Asian and ancient Egyptian art onwards, the MFA (as it's known) holds sufficient marvels to detain you all day. High points include Edward Hopper's tranquil, hopeful *Room in Brooklyn* (American Modern room); Degas' *The Little Dancer*; Gauguin's sumptuous display of existential angst *Where do we come from, What are we, Where are we going?* (Impressionists room); Millet's *The Sower* (English and French room); and Botero's voluptuous *Venus*, bold sentinel of the West Wing lobby. Don't miss the **American Decorative Arts**, either: a gloriously nostalgic jamboree of coffee urns, speak-your-weight machines, and reconstructed living rooms. The I.M. Pei–designed West Wing holds special exhibits and the contemporary art collection.

Less broad in its collection, but more distinctive and idiosyncratic than the MFA, is the **Isabella Stewart Gardner Museum**, down the road at 280 The Fenway (Tues–Sun 11am–5pm; $12; free admission for those named "Isabella"; ☎617/566-1401, ⓦwww.gardnermuseum.org). Styled after a fifteenth-century Venetian villa, the Gardner brims with a dazzling hodgepodge of works meant to "fire the imagination." While it's best known for its spectacular central courtyard, the museum's greatest successes are its show-stopping pieces by John Singer Sargent, including a stunning portrait of Isabella herself. Weekend concerts are held on select Friday nights as well as on Sunday afternoons; tickets cost an additional $13.

Cambridge

The excursion across the Charles River to **Cambridge** merits at least half a day, and begins with a fifteen-minute ride on the Red T line to **Harvard Square**. This is not so much a square as a number of interlocking streets, filled with small shopping malls and bookstores, at the point where Massachusetts Avenue runs into JFK and Brattle streets. It's an exceptionally lively area, filled with students from nearby Harvard University and MIT, and in the summer, street musicians are a common sight. The **Cambridge Visitor Information Booth** here (Mon–Sat 9am–5pm; ☎617/441-2884) sporadically organizes walking tours in summer, and sells local maps and guides. Additional info (as well as free internet access) is available from the **Harvard Events & Information Center**, Holyoke Center, 1350 Massachusetts Ave (Mon–Sat 9am–5pm; ☎617/495-1573, ⓦwww.hno.harvard.edu), which also arranges student-led tours of the campus.

Feel free to wander into **Harvard Yard** and around the core of the university, founded in 1636; its enormous Widener Library (named for a victim of the *Titanic*) boasts a Gutenberg Bible and a first folio of Shakespeare. Five minutes' walk along Brattle Street (at no. 105) is the best known of the Brattle Street mansions, the **Longfellow House** (June–Oct Wed–Sun 10am–4.30pm, tours hourly 10.30am–11.30am & 1–4pm; ☎617/876-4491; $3), named after the author of *Hiawatha*, who lived here until 1882. Its halls and walls are festooned with Longfellow's furniture and art collection, best of which are the stunning pieces culled from the Far East. Dexter Pratt, immortalized in Longfellow's "Under the spreading chestnut tree, the village smithy stands," lived at 56 Brattle St; a marker on the corner of Brattle and Story streets commemorates the exalted tree.

Cambridge has several first-class art museums, along with more specialized science museums, with a few engaging exhibits of note. The **Harvard University Art Museums** (Mon–Sat 10am–5pm, Sun 1–5pm; $7.50, free on Sat before noon; ☎617/495-9400) encompass over 150,000 works of art, spread across three museums. Highlights of Harvard's substantial collection of Western art are showcased in the **Fogg Art Museum**, 32 Quincy St, while the **Busch–Reisinger Museum** (on the second floor) has a small yet excellent selection which focuses on German Expressionists and Bauhaus works. Just steps away at 485 Broadway, the **Arthur M. Sackler Museum** is devoted to classical, Asian, and Islamic art. The stellar **Harvard Museum of Natural History**, 26 Oxford St (daily 9am–5pm; $7.50), features a number of freakishly huge dinosaur fossils as well as a visually stunning collection of flower models constructed entirely from glass.

Also on the Harvard campus, the **Carpenter Center for the Visual Arts**, 34 Quincy St, houses a more or less impressive student art gallery, as well as the **Harvard Film Archive**, which screens a diverse selection of foreign and independent films, seven nights a week ($8 general public, $6 for students; ☎617/495-4700, Ⓦ www.harvardfilmarchive.org).

A couple of miles southeast of Harvard Square is the **Massachusetts Institute of Technology** (MIT), whose **List Visual Arts Center**, 20 Ames St (Tues–Thurs, Sat & Sun noon–6pm, Fri noon–8pm; ☎617/253-4680), exhibits contemporary art in all media, including photography and video, and often has accompanying lectures.

Lexington and Concord

On the night of April 18, 1775, **Paul Revere** rode down what is now Massachusetts Avenue from Boston, racing through Cambridge and Arlington on his way to warn the American patriots gathered at **Lexington** (eleven miles to the west) of an impending British attack. Close behind him was a force of more than seven hundred British soldiers, intent on seizing the supplies that they knew the "rebels" had hoarded at **Concord** further north.

Although much of Revere's route has been turned into major freeways, the various settings of the first military confrontation of the Revolutionary War – "the shot heard 'round the world" – remain much as they were then. The triangular **Town Common** at Lexington was where the British encountered the opposition. Captain John Parker ordered his 77 American "**Minutemen**" to "stand your ground. Don't fire unless fired upon, but if they mean to have a war let it begin here." No one knows who fired the first shot, but the eight soldiers that died are buried beneath a surprisingly affecting memorial at the southeast end of the park. One wounded soldier crawled across the road to his home, only to die at his wife's feet (the still-standing house, on the corner of Harrington and Bedford streets, displays a commemorative plaque). Guides in period costume lead tours of the **Buckman Tavern**, where the Minutemen waited for the British to arrive; the **Hancock-Clarke House**, a quarter of a mile north, where Samuel Adams and John Hancock were awakened by Paul Revere, is now a museum; and one mile east of the Town Common, the **Munroe Tavern** was occupied by the British as a makeshift hospital and headquarters (all three Mon–Sat 10.30am–4.30pm, Sun 1pm–5pm; $5 each, $12 to visit all).

By the time the British soldiers marched on Concord, on the morning after the encounter in Lexington, the surrounding countryside was up in arms, and the Revolutionary War was in full swing. In running battles in the town itself, and along the still-evocative **Battle Road** leading back toward Boston, 73 British soldiers and 49 colonials were killed over the next two days. The relevant sites now form the **Minuteman National Historic Park**, with visitor centers at the scenic North Bridge, 174 Liberty St, in Concord, and at Battle Road in Lexington. Paul Revere's ride and the Battle of Lexington are re-enacted annually on Patriots' Day, a city holiday on the third Monday in April.

After a morning spent denouncing eighteenth-century British rule, it's customary to indulge in a quintessential British activity – high tea – at the historic Concord Inn (Fri–Sun 3pm–5pm; ☎978/369-2372; reservations recommended; $9.50–$22).

South of Concord, **Walden Pond** was where Henry David Thoreau conducted the experiment in solitude and self-sufficiency described in his 1854 book *Walden*. "I did not feel crowded or confined in the least," he wrote of life in his simple log cabin. The site where it stood is marked with stones, and at dawn you can still watch the pond "throwing off its nightly clothing of mist" (at midday, it's a great

△ *Minute Man* statue in Lexington's Battle Green

spot for swimming and hiking). Thoreau is interred, along with Ralph Waldo Emerson, Nathaniel Hawthorne, and Louisa May Alcott, atop a hill in **Sleepy Hollow Cemetery**, just east of the center of Concord.

As well as guided bus tours from Boston (see p.207), **buses** (25min) run to Lexington from Alewife Station, at the northern end of the Red T line, and **trains** to Concord run from North Station (40min; $5 one way).

Eating

Boston is brimming with a hearty range of culinary options. Above all, there's **seafood**, especially lobsters, scrod (a generic term for young, white-fleshed fish), clams (served steamed and dipped in butter, or as creamy chowder), and oysters (some of the world's best come fresh daily from Wellfleet and other Cape Cod spots). You could base a day's tour of the different neighborhoods around the foods on offer: breakfast in the cafés of **Beacon Hill**; lunch in the food plazas of **Quincy Market** or **The Garage** on JFK Street in Cambridge, or dim sum in **Chinatown**; for dinner, a budget **Indian** restaurant in Cambridge, an **Italian** place around Hanover Street in the North End, or expensive seafood overlooking the Harbor.

The central aisle of **Quincy Market**, lined with restaurants and brasseries, is superb for all kinds of takeout, including fresh clams and lobster, ethnic dishes, fruit cocktails, and cookies, which you can buy from different vendors and eat in the central seating area.

Chinatown, where restaurants stay open until 2 or 3am, is the best place for **late-night dining**.

Boston

Café Jaffa 48 Gloucester St ☏ 617/536-0230; Copley **T**. One of Back Bay's best inexpensive dining options, with great Middle Eastern fare served up in an inviting space. They're known for their falafel and locally-famous lamb chops, but you can't really go wrong here.

Charlie's Sandwich Shoppe 429 Columbus Ave ☏ 617/536-7669; Back Bay **T**. The long lines out front should tell you – Charlie's is widely regarded as the best breakfast in Boston, with greasy spoon fare (and famous turkey hash) served up in delightful vintage diner environs. Closed Sundays, cash only.

Daily Catch 323 Hanover St ☏ 617/523-8567 and 261 Northern Ave ☏ 617/338-3093; Haymarket **T** and South Station **T**. Ocean-fresh seafood, notably calamari and shellfish – Sicilian-style, with megadoses of garlic – draws big lines to this tiny storefront restaurant.

The Delux Café and Lounge 100 Chandler St ☏ 617/338-5258; Back Bay **T**. This retro hideaway has all the fixings of a great dive: fantastic kitschy décor, constant cartoon viewing, and a Christmas-lit Elvis shrine. The menu is funky American fusion with old standbys like grilled cheese sandwiches and split pea soup. Cash only.

Durgin Park 340 N Market St, Faneuil Hall Marketplace ☏ 617/227-2038; Government Center **T**. A Boston landmark in operation since 1827, *Durgin Park* has a waitstaff known for their surly charm as well as iconic New England foods like roast beef, baked beans, and warm Indian pudding. The downstairs bar is cheaper and livelier.

Eastern Standard 528 Commonwealth Ave ☏ 617/532-9100; Kenmore **T**. Loosely French bistro serving up fairly fancy, pre-Red Sox game fare. The menu can be a bit hit or miss – go for the spaghetti carbonara and veal schnitzel – or just to watch the game in their atmospheric bar.

Galleria Umberto 289 Hanover St ☏ 617/227-5709; Haymarket **T**. North End nirvana. There are fewer than a dozen items on the menu, but the lines are consistently to the door for Umberto's perfect pizza slices and *arancini*. Lunch

only, and get there early – they always sell out. Cash only; very inexpensive.

Jacob Wirth 31 Stuart St ☏ 617/338-8586; Boylston **T**. A German-themed Boston landmark, around since 1868; even if you don't like bratwurst washed down with a hearty lager, something is sure to please. There are sing-alongs on Fridays.

Jasper White's Summer Shack 50 Dalton St ☏ 617/867-9955; Hynes **T**. Spacious seafood locale with kitschy maritime décor and lots of seating. The raw bar is tops, and the grilled fish fare is also quite good. Plus they have corn dogs.

Mike's Pastry 300 Hanover St ☏ 617/742-3050; Haymarket **T**. Simply breathing in the aromas at this lively Italian pastry shop is an exercise in indulgence. Endless, fantastic arrays of cannolis, éclairs, and rum cakes.

Neptune Oyster 63 Salem St ☏ 617/742-3474; Haymarket **T**. Snazzy little raw bar filled with devoted fans who swoon over the fantastic shucked shellfish. Closed Mon and Tues.

No. 9 Park 9 Park St ☏ 617/742-9991; Park St **T**. Highly recommended restaurant with affable green walls and plates busy with French and Italian entrées. A seven-course tasting menu ($85; with wine $135) allows you to try almost everything.

The Other Side Cosmic Café 407 Newbury St ☏ 617/536-9477; Hynes **T**. This ultracasual hipster hangout on "the other side" of Newbury Street offers gourmet sandwiches, tasty salads, and fresh juices. They also have pitchers of good beer. Open late.

Sel de la Terre 255 State St ☏ 617/720-1300; Aquarium **T**. Sel de la Terre serves up rustic Provençal fare like hearty bouillabaisse and roasted lamb and eggplant. Conveniently, you can acquire the fixings for a waterfront picnic here, too, by calling ahead to order ($11/person) and picking it up on your way to the ferry.

Sonsie 327 Newbury St ☏ 617/351-2500, Hynes **T**. This Newbury Street staple is good for contemporary bistro fare, particularly the swanky sandwiches, pastries, and chocolate bread pudding.

Stella 1525 Washington St ☏ 617/247-7747; Back Bay **T**. Fantastic, fancy-pants Italian fare in a beautiful white interior. Nice outdoor seating in the summer. Open late.

Taiwan Café 34 Oxford St ☎617/426-8181; Chinatown **T**. Locals swoon over this busy, authentic Taiwanese eatery which serves up mustard greens with edamame (soybean) and steamed pork buns done just right. Open late. Cash only.

Union Oyster House 41 Union St ☎617/227-2750; Government Center **T**. The oldest continuously operating restaurant in the nation features fresh, well-prepared seafood, if a bit overpriced.

Cambridge

🏃 **Mr Bartley's Burger Cottage** 1246 Massachusetts Ave, ☎617/354-6559; Harvard **T**. A Cambridge must-visit. Perhaps the best burgers on the planet washed down with raspberry lime rickeys amongst Americana-festooned environs. Good veggie burgers, too. Cash only.

Bob's Southern Bistro 604 Columbus Ave, Roxbury ☎617/536-6204; Mass Ave **T**. The best soul food in New England, with good chitlins, black-eyed peas, and collard greens; don't miss the "glori-fried chicken." There's also a wonderful, waist-expanding Sunday brunch buffet accompanied by live jazz.

Central Kitchen 567 Massachusetts Ave, ☎617/491-5599; Central **T**. Hip Central Square bistro with a delightful chalkboard menu offering European classics (*moules frites*) and contemporary American twists (mushroom ragout with ricotta dumplings) in a stylish, intimate setting.

Charlie's Kitchen 10 Eliot St ☎617/492-9646;

Harvard **T**. Marvelously atmospheric local hangout in the heart of Harvard Square, with red vinyl booths and great cheeseburger specials. The bar upstairs is equally cool, particularly during Tuesday's karaoke nights.

Chez Henri 1 Shepard St ☎617/354-8980; Harvard or Porter **T**. Fantastic French fare with a strong Cuban accent, and some of Cambridge's best cuisine. If you're looking to spend less cash, head to the adjacent bar for the Cuban pressed sandwich – amazing.

Darwin's Ltd 148 Mt Auburn St ☎617/354-5233; 1629 Cambridge St ☎617/491-2999; both Harvard **T**. Two locations, both housing fantastic delis with wonderfully inventive sandwich combinations. Cash only.

East Coast Grill 1271 Cambridge St, Inman Square ☎617/491-6568; Harvard or Central **T**. A festive and funky atmosphere – think shades of *Miami Vice* – in which to enjoy fresh seafood and Caribbean side dishes. The Sunday serve-yourself Bloody Mary bar is reason enough to visit.

Felipe's Taqueria 83 Mt Auburn St ☎617/354-9944; Harvard **T**. There are only a handful of things on the menu, but the place is always packed for regulars hankering after their super burritos and good-looking guacamole.

Tamarind Bay 75 Winthrop St ☎617/491-4552; Harvard **T**. This bright basement eatery serves up what is perhaps Boston's best Indian food. The banana dumplings and *lallal mussal dal* (black lentils simmered in spices) will make you want to stand up and clap.

Bars, clubs, and live music

Boston has a lively **nightlife** scene that offers the best of both old and new, from tried-and-true neighborhood taverns to young, trendy lounges. The **live music** circuit in Boston and Cambridge is dominated by the very best local and touring indie bands. The free weeklies *Boston Phoenix* (Ⓦwww.thephoenix.com) and *Boston's Weekly Dig* (Ⓦwww.weeklydig.com) are the best source for up-to-date **listings**. Key nightlife zones include **Lansdowne Street**, an entire block of nightclubs next to Fenway Park; **Boylston Street**, on the south side of Boston Common; and Cambridge's **Central Square** district. Note that most establishments are unusually officious in demanding **ID**.

Boston

Bukowski Tavern 50 Dalton St ☎617/437-9999; Hynes **T**. A great hipster spot, this parking garage watering hole has views over the MassPike and a beer selection so vast it prompted a homemade "wheel of indecision" – spun by the waitstaff for indecisive patrons.

Caffe Vittoria 296 Hanover St ☎617/227-7607; Haymarket **T**. A Boston institution, the *Vittoria's* atmospheric original section, with its dark wood

panelling, pressed-tin ceilings, and Sinatra-blaring Wurlitzer, is vintage North End.

Cask 'n Flagon 62 Brookline Ave ☎617/536-4840; Kenmore **T**. An iconic neighborhood bar located right by Fenway Park, the *Cask 'n Flagon* is a popular place for the Red Sox faithful to warm up before games and drown their sorrows after.

Club Café Lounge 209 Columbus Ave ☎617/536-0966; Back Bay **T**. Popular combination restaurant/video gay bar with a back lounge,

Moonshine, showing the latest videos amidst dancing and DJs.

Jillian's 145 Ipswich St ☏617/437-0300; Kenmore **T**. Massive entertainment club complex housing an arcade, a raucous, spacious dance club, and a Lucky Strike bowling alley.

McFadden's 148 State St ☏617/227-5100; Government Center **T**. Fun Irish pub with well-loved regulars, stylish newcomers, and plenty of Guinness.

Oak Bar in the *Fairmount Copley Plaza*, 138 St James Ave ☏617/267-5300; Copley **T**. Rich wood panelling, high ceilings, and excellent martinis are the highlights of this swanky Back Bay drinkery.

Paradise Rock Club 967-969 Commonwealth Ave, Brookline ☏617/562-8800; Pleasant Street **T**. One of Boston's classic rocking venues (many, many greats have played here), and it's still happening after 25 years.

Sevens Ale House 77 Charles St, Beacon Hill ☏617/523-9074; Charles **T**. This unpolished gem of a neighborhood pub provides local flavor in the midst of upscale Beacon Hill; far more authentic than the nearby *Bull and Finch Pub*.

Cambridge

B-Side Lounge 92 Hampshire St ☏617/354-0766; Kendall **T**. It's a hipster bar, but not in an alienating way. Lots of live tunes, a great drinks menu, and tasty and creative bar food.

Club Passim 47 Palmer St ☏617/492-5300; Harvard **T**. A four-decades-old, intimate "coffeehouse" that has been a noted folk/blues venue since Joan Baez performed here as an unknown 17-year-old.

Enormous Room 577 Massachusetts Ave ☏617/491-5550; Central **T**. Walking into this comfy, tiny lounge is tantamount to entering a swanky slumber party – the clientele lounges along myriad couches, and sways to the tune of a local DJ.

Lizard Lounge 1667 Massachusetts Ave ☏617/547-0759; Harvard or Porter **T**. An intimate rock and jazz venue, and one of Boston's best. Fairly nominal cover charges.

Middle East 472 Massachusetts Ave ☏617/492-9181; Central **T**. Local and regional progressive rock acts regularly stop in at this Cambridge institution. Downstairs hosts bigger bands; smaller ones ply their stuff in a tiny upstairs space.

Miracle of Science 321 Massachusetts Ave ☏617/868-ATOM; Central **T**. Surprisingly hip despite its status as an MIT hangout. There's a Table of Elements-minded décor and a laidback, unpretentious crowd. The bar stools will conjure up memories of high school chemistry class.

Regattabar in the *Charles Hotel*, 1 Bennett St ☏617/661-5000; Harvard **T**. The *Regattabar* draws top national jazz acts, although, as its location in the swish *Charles Hotel* might suggest, the atmosphere is a bit sedate. Dress nicely and prepare to pay at least a $10 cover.

River Gods 125 Cambridge St ☏617/576-1881; Central **T**. A bit of an underground spot, but worth the trip out. An Irish bar with a twist, they serve good cocktails and Guinness on tap alongside fantastic food. Patrons lounge in throne-like chairs and ogle the suits of armor.

T.T. the Bear's 10 Brookline St, ☏617/492-BEAR; Central **T**. Highly esteemed, intimate venue, showcasing cutting-edge live music seven nights a week.

Western Front 343 Western Ave ☏617/492-7772; Central **T**. This former jazz and blues club is now dedicated to reggae, with live music Friday and Saturday nights, cheap drinks, and delectably authentic Jamaican food served up on the weekends.

Performing arts

Mainstream Boston's pride and joy, the **Boston Symphony Orchestra** is based at Symphony Hall, 301 Massachusetts Ave (☏617/266-1200, ⓦwww.bso.org), which Stravinsky called the best auditorium in the world. The orchestra's winter season is supplemented by the **Boston Pops** concerts in May, June, and on July 4.

The city's **theater** scene divides into the safe productions of the Theater District (often Broadway cast-offs) and more experimental companies in Cambridge. The **BosTix** ticket kiosks (☏617/482-BTIX, ⓦwww.artsboston.org/bostix.cfm) at Faneuil Hall and in Copley Square sell tickets for all major events – as well as tours, T passes, and so on – with some half-price same-day tickets (cash only). They're open Tuesday through Saturday 10am to 6pm and Sunday 11am to 4pm; the Copley Square location is also open on Monday 10am to 6pm.

Sports

Baseball is treated with reverence in Boston, so it's fitting that the Red Sox play at storied Fenway Park (Kenmore subway stop on the Green T line; tickets

$12–275; information ☎1-877/REDSOX9, tickets ☎617/482-4769, ⦿www.
redsox.com). Built in 1912 and squeezed into an odd-shaped plot just off Brookline Avenue, the stadium is famed for its crazy caroms and awkward quirks, particularly the 37-foot wall in left field known as the "**Green Monster**".

Basketball's Celtics and **hockey**'s Bruins both play at the TDBanknorth Garden, 150 Causeway St near North Station; Celts tickets will run you $10–700,
Bruins tickets $10–99 (box office open daily 11am–7pm; call Ticketmaster for
tickets by phone ☎617/931-2000, ⦿www.tdbanknorthgarden.com).

The 26.2-mile **Boston Marathon**, first run in 1897, is held on the third Monday in April, and finishes on Boylston Street at Copley Square (☎617/236-1652,
⦿www.bostonmarathon.org).

Every October features the annual **Head of the Charles** river regatta crew races
(☎617/868-6200, ⦿ww.hocr.org) that draw collegiate fans to the shorelines.

The north shore

As you head northward out of Boston, you pass through a succession of rich little
ports that have been all but swallowed up by the suburbs. One good day-trip from
Boston is the half-hour ride out to **Salem** and neighboring **Marblehead**. If you
have the time, the atmospheric old fishing ports of **Gloucester** and **Rockport**,
further out on Cape Ann, are also worth a look. Here you will find strong artistic
and literary connections – T.S. Eliot used to come here for his family vacations,
and his poem "The Dry Salvages" is titled after a small group of rocks glimpsed
from the Cape Ann coast. This area is also the best place on the East Coast for
whale-watching trips. Cape Ann Whale Watch (☎978/283-5110 or 1-800/877-
5110, ⦿www.seethewhales.com) offers three- to four-hour trips from Gloucester
for $43 between April and October.

Salem

SALEM is remembered less as the site where the colony of Massachusetts was
first established than as the place where, sixty years later, Puritan self-righteous-
ness reached its apogee in the horrific **witch trials** of 1692. While the town itself
prospered as a port – as evidenced by its fine old buildings – the witch scare did
much to discredit the idea that the New World conducted its affairs on a different
moral plane than the Old. Nineteen Salem women were hanged as witches (and
one man, Giles Corry, was pressed to death with a boulder), thanks to a group of
impressionable teenage girls who reported as truth a garbled mixture of fireside
tales told by a West Indian slave, Tituba, and half-digested scare stories published
by Cotton Mather, a pillar of the Puritan community.

That this unpleasant history is now the basis of a child-oriented tourist industry
– all black hats and broomsticks – is a bit unsettling. However, if you can overlook
the contrived, witchy vibe (and the shops selling corsets and fairy clothing) this pretty,
historic town proves to be a most enjoyable visit.

The **Salem Witch Museum** in Washington Square (daily: July & Aug 10am–7pm;
rest of year 10am–5pm; $6.50) draws parallels with modern racism and political
persecution, but is at its heart a rather tacky show of illuminated dioramas and prerecorded commentary. Innumerable other witch-related attractions in town are best
ignored. Salem's crown jewel is the **Peabody Essex Museum** in East India Square
(☎978/748-9500; daily 10am–5pm; $13), whose vast, modern space incorporates
more than thirty galleries filled with remarkable *objets* brought home by voyaging
New Englanders. Founded by a ship captain in 1799, the museum boasts stellar

Asian and Oceanic displays, most notably the **Yin Yu Tang**, a stunning sixteen-room Qing dynasty merchants' house reassembled here in Salem.

Little of Salem's original waterfront remains, though the long **Derby Wharf** is still standing, together with the imposing **Custom House** at its head, where Nathaniel Hawthorne once worked as a surveyor. The **House of Seven Gables** at 115 Derby St, the star of Hawthorne's eponymous novel, is a rambling old mansion beside the sea (summer daily 10am–7pm; rest of year 10am–5pm; $12). Hour-long guided tours of the complex also take in the author's birthplace, moved here from its original site on Union Street.

Practicalities

Regular MBTA **buses** run to Salem from Boston's Haymarket and Wonderland stations (every half-hour; $3.45 each way). Frequent **trains** also leave from North Station (weekdays 2–3 an hour, weekends hourly; $3.75 each way). For **accommodation**, the well-run *Hawthorne Hotel*, 18 Washington Sq W (☎978/744-4080; ⓦwww.hawthornehotel.com; ➏) is right in the heart of things, while *Morning Glory Bed and Breakfast*, 22 Hardy St (☎978/741-1703 or 1-800/446-2995, ⓦwww.morningglorybb.com; ➍) has homemade goodies in the morning and great views of the water. The atmospheric *Red's Restaurant*, 15 Central St (☎978/745-3527), features cheap and hearty breakfast fare, while the *Witch's Brew Café*, 156 Derby St (☎978/745-8717), has more upscale digs that are augmented by tasty New American cuisine. Out on the water, *Finz*, 76 Wharf St (☎978/744-0000) is a snazzy, well-loved seafood spot.

Marblehead

Five miles south and east along the bay from Salem is **MARBLEHEAD**, a lovely waterfront village whose historic homes date back as far as the mid-1700s, and which is known as the birthplace of the US Navy – George Washington's first five vessels were built here. Free walking-tour **maps** are available from the information booth in the center (June–Oct; ☎781/639-8469, ⓦwww.visitmarblehead.com), while 250-year-old **Fort Sewall**, jutting into the harbor, gives pretty views. The *Seagull Inn*, 106 Harbor Ave (☎781/631-1893, ⓦwww.seagullinn.com; ➐), has comfortable B&B **rooms** overlooking the water, and the gorgeous *Fox Pond B&B*, 31 Arthur Ave (☎781/631-1370, ⓦwww.foxpondbnb.com; ➏), is a romantic hideaway out in the oaks. *Flynnie's*, 28 Atlantic Ave (☎781/639-2100), serves fresh, inexpensive **seafood**, as does its outpost at Devereux Beach (May–Oct only).

The south shore

Heading south, it can take a while to get clear of Boston, especially on summer weekends, when the traffic down to Cape Cod can be horrendous. Two historic towns, one north and one west of the Cape, are worth exploring: **Plymouth** and **New Bedford**.

Plymouth

"America's Hometown," little **PLYMOUTH**, on the south shore of Massachusetts Bay, forty miles south of Boston, is given over to commemorating, in various degrees of taste, the landing of the 102 **Pilgrims** in December of 1620. By the sea, a solemn pseudo-Greek temple encloses the nondescript **Plymouth Rock**, where the Pilgrims are said to have first touched land. However, as the Pilgrims had already spent two months on Cape Cod before settling at Plymouth, and there are no historic references to the rock until one hundred years after their arrival, it is of symbolic importance only.

Two worthier memorials make no claim to authenticity, but meticulously reproduce the experience of the Pilgrims. Both the replica of the **Mayflower** in town (the *Mayflower II*), and **Plimoth Plantation** three miles south, are staffed by costumed "interpreters," each of whom acts out the part of a specific Pilgrim, Indian, or sailor (both attractions April–Nov daily 9am–5pm; *Mayflower II* alone $8, Plantation alone $21, together $24; ☎508/746-1622, ⊛www.plimoth.org). The charade visitors are obliged to perform – pretending to have stepped back into the seventeenth century – can be a little tiresome, but ultimately the sheer depth of detail in both endeavors makes them fascinating. At the Plantation, everything you see in the Pilgrim Village of 1627, and the Wampanoag Indian Settlement, has been created using traditional techniques.

Practicalities

Plymouth's **Visitor Information Center** is on the waterfront at no. 130 (☎508/747-7525 or 1-800/USA-1620, ⊛www.visit-plymouth.com). Plymouth & Brockton provides a regular **bus** service to and from Boston ($12 one way, $22 round trip; ☎508/746-0378, ⊛www.p-b.com). There are also express ferries from Plymouth to Provincetown (June–Sept daily 10am; $35; ☎508/747-2400 or 1-800/242-2469, ⊛www.provincetownferry.com; reservations recommended). A good standard **motel** option is the clean and comfortable *Best Western Cold Spring*, 188 Court St (open April–Dec only; ☎508/746-2222 or 1-800/678-8667; ⑤). *By The Sea*, 22 Winslow St (☎508/830-9643, ⊛www.bytheseabedandbreakfast. com; ⑤) is a harborview B&B with two spacious suites and private bath. America's hometown has a few favorable **food** options. Just north of downtown the wonderful *3A Café & Bakery*, 295 Court St (☎508/747-3730) serves tasty Greek treats for breakfast and lunch. On the waterfront, *East Bay Grill* (☎508/746-9751) is the best of the seafood spots; while the *Hearth 'n' Kettle*, in the *John Carver Inn*, 25 Summer St, has well-priced New England specialities (☎508/746-7100).

New Bedford

The famous old whaling port of **NEW BEDFORD**, 45 miles due south of Boston, is still home to one of the nation's most prosperous fishing fleets: every year, they haul in the largest catch on the East Coast. New Bedford has aged well, too – recent efforts at preservation and restoration, with an eye to the town's whaling heritage, have only served to heighten its aesthetic appeal. Chief among the city's pretty features are the fine old houses on County Street, which like the whole of the town, was described in Herman Melville's *Moby Dick*.

The **New Bedford Whaling Museum** at 18 Johnny Cake Hill (daily 9am–5pm, Thurs until 9pm; $10), features a 66-foot blue whale skeleton, collections of scrimshaw and harpoons, and an evocative half-sized whaling vessel replica. More affecting is the **Seamen's Bethel** directly opposite the museum; it really does have the ship-shaped pulpit described in *Moby Dick*, but this one was rebuilt after a fire in 1866. Before leaving town, be sure to check out the bustling working waterfront, now a National Historical Park (maps available from the **Visitor Center** at 33 William St; ☎508/996-4095).

One good choice for accommodation is *The Orchard Street Manor*, 139 Orchard St (☎508/984-3475; ⑥–⑦), an atmospheric B&B built in 1845. A favorite local place to **eat** is the Portuguese *Antonio's*, 267 Coggeshall St (☎508/990-3636), where long lines often form outside the door. Right by the museum, *Freestone's,* 41 Williams

St (☎508/993-7477), serves excellent chowder and microbrews in a restored 1877 bank.

For information on **ferries to Martha's Vineyard**, see the box on p.232.

Cape Cod and the islands

Here a man may stand, and put all America behind him.

Henry David Thoreau

These days, the trouble with standing on **Cape Cod** is that "all America" tends to be a lot closer behind you than you might prefer. The Cape's main haunts are packed in the summer, its roads circled by a grim procession of crawling vehicles, searching in vain for some solitude. Unless you have your own, preferably very secluded, place to stay, it's barely worth turning up on weekends, especially between June and August, and putting yourself through the hassle of trying to find what little available (and premium-priced) accommodation there is. However, the place is undeniably beautiful; if you find yourself in the region midweek in May or September – when hotel prices are much lower, the crowds have thinned, and the weather usually very pleasant – the Cape is certainly worth a visit.

Cape Cod was named by Bartholomew Gosnold in 1602, on account of the prodigious quantities of cod caught by his crew off Provincetown. Less than twenty years later the Pilgrims landed nearby; in the few months before moving on to Plymouth, they began the process, continued by generations of Europeans, of stripping the interior of the Cape bare of its original covering of thick woods. Today, much of the land on the Cape, from its salt marshes to its ever-eroding dunes, is considered a fragile and endangered ecosystem – though this designation hasn't especially dampened the persistence of developers.

If you imagine the Cape as an arm, its **upper** section, the thirty-mile eastward stretch closest to mainland Massachusetts, is the biceps. Much of the worst beachfront development lies along the southern shore, and Hwy-28, running from Falmouth via Hyannis to Chatham, gets especially clogged. Only once you get beyond the "elbow" and head north to the **Outer Cape** or, anatomically speaking, the forearm, past the spectacular dunes of **Cape Cod National Seashore**, do you get a feeling for why the Cape still has a reputation as a seaside wilderness. **Provincetown**, right at the end, is the one town on the Cape that can be unreservedly recommended.

The islands of **Martha's Vineyard** and **Nantucket**, off the Cape to the south, are largely dependent on summer tourism for their livelihood. At the same time, they remain highly committed to preserving their unique heritage and natural environment. A trip out to Nantucket in particular still evokes proud seafaring days. The off-season has a charm all its own, when you can sink into the rhythms of life on the islands without the distraction of hordes of day-trippers.

Getting to the Cape

It was the Pilgrims who first suggested the construction of a canal between Cape Cod Bay and Buzzards Bay, so that coastal shipping could avoid the dangers of the open ocean. When the waterway was finally completed at the start of the twentieth century, it left the Cape Cod peninsula as an island. Now all traffic to the Cape bottlenecks at two enormous bridges across the canal – Bourne on Hwy-28 and Sagamore on Hwy-6 – and you may regret trying to **drive** there on a summer

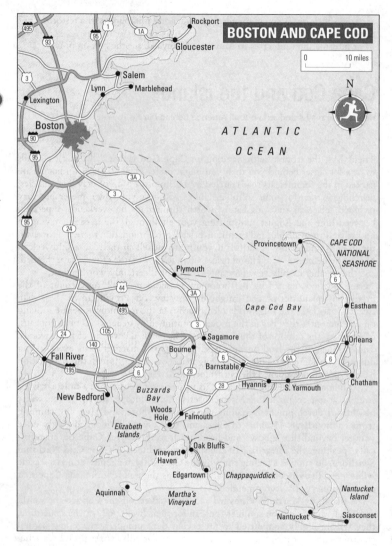

BOSTON AND CAPE COD

ATLANTIC OCEAN

N

0   10 miles

Rockport
Gloucester
Salem
Lynn   Marblehead
Lexington
Boston
Provincetown
CAPE COD
NATIONAL
SEASHORE
Plymouth
Cape Cod Bay
Eastham
Sagamore
Orleans
Bourne
Barnstable
Fall River
Hyannis
S. Yarmouth
Chatham
New Bedford
Buzzards
Bay
Woods
Hole   Falmouth
Elizabeth
Islands
Oak Bluffs
Vineyard
Haven
Edgartown   Chappaquiddick
Nantucket
Island
Aquinnah   Martha's
Vineyard
Nantucket   Siasconset

Friday (or back on a Sunday). Each bridge has an **information office** for the Cape (daily 9am–7pm) on its mainland side.

One way to dodge the traffic is to **fly**. US Airways affiliate Colgan Air (☎1-800/428-4322, ⓦwww.colganair.com) serves Hyannis, Martha's Vineyard, and Nantucket from Washington, DC, New York City, Boston, and points further north, such as Augusta, Maine. Cape Air (☎1-800/352-0714, ⓦwww.flycapeair.com) flies several times daily from Boston, New Bedford, and Providence, Rhode Island, to Hyannis, Provincetown, and the islands. Peter Pan **buses** run regularly from New York City and Boston (☎1-800/343-9999, ⓦwww.peterpanbus.com), and the Plymouth & Brockton (☎508/746-0378, ⓦwww.p-b.com) runs daily to a number of Cape towns (culminating in Provincetown) via Boston and Plymouth. **Ferries** from Boston (see p.227) take 90 minutes to cross to Provincetown; for boats to the various islands, see the box on p.232.

The Upper Cape

The **Upper Cape**, just across the bridges, was the first part of the peninsula to attract visitors in any numbers – and it sometimes shows. Upon approaching the various communities of the south coast, you might easily be taken aback by the degree of commercialization that surrounds them. But just beyond the thickets of malls, motels, and fast-food joints there remains a measure of quaintness in some of the small coastal towns, each arranged around a prim central green and decorated with old-fashioned Main Streets and waterfront seafood joints.

Falmouth and Woods Hole

One obvious base for catching a **ferry** to the islands is **FALMOUTH**, where cozy accommodation includes the deluxe *Scallop Shell Inn*, 16 Massachusetts Ave (T 508/495-4900 or 1-800/249-4587, W www.shorewayacresinn.com; ⑧–⑨), with views of the islands and several rooms outfitted with fireplaces and whirlpool baths, or the *Woods Hole Passage*, at 186 Woods Hole Rd (T 508/548-9575, W www.woodsholepassage.com; ⑥), brightly-painted chambers equipped with wireless internet. The *Sippewissett Campground & Cabins*, a couple of miles out at 836 Palmer Ave (T 508/548-2542, W www.sippewissett.com; peak season $27, plus $8 each additional camper; off-season $23, plus $5 each additional camper), offers a free shuttle service to the ferries and beaches.

Restaurants abound in Falmouth, though with the possible exception of *Betsy's Diner*, 457 Main St (T 508/540-0060), an authentic 1950s diner beckoning you to "eat heavy," the best meals are to be found in the assorted moderately priced seafood places along the waterfront at **WOODS HOLE**, four miles southwest. The *Fishmonger's Café*, 56 Water St (T 508/540-5376), is a natural-foods restaurant that serves eggs, granola, and the like at breakfast, with seafood specials at lunch and dinner. As for sights, the **Woods Hole Oceanographic Institution's exhibit center**, at 15 School St, near Little Harbor (May–Oct Mon–Sat 10am–4.30pm, Sun noon–4.30pm; Nov–Dec Tues–Fri 10am–4.30pm, Sun noon–4.30pm; April Fri & Sat 10am–4.30pm, Sun noon–4.30pm; T 508/457-2034; $2), focuses on the Institution's underwater research, including their sensational finding of the *Titanic* in 1986. If you're looking to get out on the water, Ocean Quest runs informative, hands-on **ocean cruises** in summer (reservations recommended; $20; T 1-800/37-OCEAN, W www.oceanquestonline.org).

Hyannis

It stands to reason that **HYANNIS** – the largest port on the Cape, and its main commercial hub – would be a little less charming than Falmouth and Woods Hole. Nevertheless, it still clings to the glamour it earned when the **Kennedy compound** at Hyannis Port placed it at the center of world affairs. Hence the existence of the **John F. Kennedy Museum**, 397 Main St (Mon–Sat 9am–5pm, Thurs 9am–8pm, Sun noon–5pm; $5), which shows photographs, newsclippings, and film footage of the days JFK spent on the Cape. The Kennedys are still here, though their property can only be glimpsed, at a considerable distance, from the sea: Hy-Line Cruises, Ocean Street Dock ($14; T 508/778-2600, W www.hy-linecruises.com), runs one-hour harbor cruises that peek in at the compound.

If you have a boat to catch and need to **stay** in Hyannis, options include the friendly, neat, and affordable *Sea Beach Inn*, 388 Sea St (T 508/775-4612, W www.

capecodtravel.com/seabeach; ⑤). A great **B&B** in Hyannis Port is the *Simmons Homestead Inn*, 288 Scudder Ave (☎508/778-4999 or 1-800/637-1649, ⓦwww.simmonshomesteadinn.com; ⑦–⑧). On Main Street, be sure to indulge in the full *rodizio* at the *Brazilian Grill,* no. 680 (☎508/771-0109), with mouth-watering meats delivered straight from the skewer and onto to your plate; *The Egg & I,* at no. 521 (☎508/771-1596), is a great spot for big breakfasts, while *Alberto's,* no. 360 (☎508/778-1770), offers tasty Italian meals (with better deals if you get there before 6pm).

See p.232 for **ferry** information.

The Mid-Cape

The middle stretch of Cape Cod holds some of its prettiest, most unspoiled places. Time-worn old fishing communities like Wellfleet and Chatham, along with dozens of carefully maintained, mildly touristy hamlets along the many winding roads, are what most people hope to find when they come to the Cape. Cutting across the middle, the **Cape Cod Rail Trail** follows a paved-over railroad track from Dennis to Eastham, through forests and cranberry bogs – the saturated beds of peat in which the fruit is cultivated. It makes a good **cycling** trip; bikes can be rented in all the main towns.

One desirable destination is the whitewashed old town of **CHATHAM**, tucked away in a protected harbor between Nantucket Sound and the open Atlantic Ocean. Hang out at the **Fish Pier** on Shore Road and wait for the fleet to come in during the mid-afternoon, or head a mile south on Hwy-28 to **Chatham Light**, one of many lighthouses built to protect mariners from the treacherous shoals. Tour **maps** are available from the booth at 533 Main St. Good **seafood** abounds at the *Chatham Squire*, 487 Main St (☎508/945-0945), a low-key, local institution. Also, be sure to stop by ⚓ Marion's Pie Shop 2022 Rte-28 (☎508/432-9439), for a life-changing bumbleberry pie. If you're going to **stay** in chic Chatham, you might as well indulge; the fantastic *Carriage House Inn*, 407 Old Harbor Rd (☎508/945-0127, ⓦwww.captainshouseinn.com; ⑧–⑨), is a gorgeous old whaling captain's home with rambling gardens and afternoon tea; the *Pleasant Bay Village Resort*, 1191 Orleans Rd (☎508/945-1133, ⓦwww.pleasantbayvillage.com; ⑦–⑧) has lovely grounds and more affordable digs.

The **place to stay** in **EASTHAM** is the romantic *Whalewalk Inn*, at 220 Bridge Rd (☎508/255-0617 or 1-800/440-1281, ⓦwww.whalewalkinn.com; ⑦–⑧). Rates for the secluded B&B rooms and a converted barn include use of their brand-new spa facilities. Right around the corner is the *HI-Mid Cape* **hostel**, 75 Goody Halet Drive, $22 to $25 (☎508/255-2785; open May–Sept), a collection of woodsy cabins.

People are obsessed with the onion rings at *Arnold's Lobster and Clam Bar*, 3580 Rte-6 (☎508/255-2575), a popular seafood **restaurant** and beer garden. *Box Lunch*, 4205 Rte-6 (☎508/255-0799), as its name suggests, is the place to go for packed pita sandwiches to take to the beach.

Cape Cod National Seashore

After the bustle of Cape Cod's towns, the **Cape Cod National Seashore** really does come as a proverbial breath of fresh air. These protected lands, spared by President Kennedy from the rampant development further south, take up virtually the entire Atlantic side of the Cape, from Chatham north to Provincetown. Most of the way you can park by the road, sometimes for a fee, and strike off across the dunes to windswept, seemingly endless beaches – though in places parking is limited to local residents. A program of grass-planting helps to hold the whole place together: three feet of the sands south of the National Seashore are washed away each year, much of it carried south to Chatham and Orleans.

It was on these shifting sands that the **Pilgrims** made their first home. They obtained their water from Pilgrim Spring, near Truro, and at Corn Hill Beach they uncovered the freshly buried cache of Indian corn that kept them alive. After a couple of months, which they survived with the help of the Wampanoag Indians, they moved on to Plymouth. (The reconstructed Indian village at Plimoth Plantation is based on one found at Eastham; see opposite.)

Displays and movies at the main **Salt Pond Visitor Center**, on US-6 just north of Eastham (daily 9am–4.30pm, extended summer hours; ℡508/255-3421), trace the geology and history of the Cape. A road and a hiking/cycling trail head east to the sands of **Coast Guard Beach** and **Nauset Light Beach**, both of which offer excellent swimming. Another fine beach is the **Head of the Meadow**, halfway between Truro and Provincetown on the northeast shore (beach parking is $15). The fantastic *HI-Truro* **hostel**, on 111 North Pamet Rd in Truro (℡508/349-3889, ⓦwww.capecodhostels.org; mid-June to early Sept), has beds from $25 to $32 in a breezy former Coast Guard station, offering spectacular views of the seashore and the dunes.

Provincetown

The compact fishing village of **PROVINCETOWN** (or, as it's popularly known, "P-Town") is right on the knuckle of what would be Cape Cod's clenched fist. It's a gorgeous place, with silvery clapboard houses and gloriously unruly gardens lining the town's tiny winding streets. Self-professed bohemians and artists have long flocked here for the dazzling light and vast beaches; in 1914 Eugene O'Neill established the Provincetown Playhouse in a small hut. The town has also become renowned, since the Beatnik 1950s, as a **gay** center, and today its population of five thousand rises tenfold in the summer. Commercialism, though rampant, tends to be countercultural: gay, environmentalist, and feminist gift shops join arty galleries, restaurants, and bars on the aptly named **Commercial Street**. Provincetown also retains a firm grip on its past. Strict zoning ensures that there are few new buildings in town, and there is barely a sign of ugly development. Albeit crowded and raucous from July through September, P-Town remains a place where history, natural beauty, and, above all, difference, are respected and celebrated.

Arrival and information

Provincetown lies 120 miles from Boston by land, but less than fifty miles by sea, nestled in the New England coast's largest natural harvour. By far the nicest way to arrive is on one of the passenger **ferries**. Boston Harbor Cruises (daily May to mid-June, additional departures on weekends in early June through early Oct; $45 one way, $70 roundtrip; ℡617/227-4321 or 1-877/SEE-WHALE, ⓦwww.bostonharborcruises.com) leave Long Wharf Ferry Terminal in Boston at 9am and 2pm, arriving at MacMillan Wharf in Provincetown ninety minutes later; ferries return at 11am and 4pm; the Bay State Cruise Company ℡617/748-1428, ⓦwww.baystatecruises.com) runs a similar venture; and Capt. John Boats runs an express ferry from Plymouth (daily June to Sept; $20 one way, $35 roundtrip; ℡508/747-2400, ⓦwww.provincetownferry.com). A slower option is the Plymouth & Brockton **bus**, which runs to Provincetown four times daily ($27 one way from Boston; $10 one way from Hyannis; ℡508/746-0378, ⓦwww.p-b.com).

The tiny **visitor center**, in the Chamber of Commerce at the end of the wharf, 307 Commercial St (summer daily 9am–5pm; rest of year Mon–Sat

PROVINCETOWN

ACCOMMODATION
Carpe Diem D
Carriage House F
Crowne Ponte Historic
Inn & Spa C
Dune's Edge Campground A
Inn at Cook Street E
Outermost Hostel B
Oxford Guest House G
White Horse Inn H

RESTAURANTS
Bubala's by the Bay 2
Café Edwidge 10
Ciro & Sal's 13
Karoo Kafe 12
Lobster Pot 8
Napi's 9
Portuguese Bakery 6
Tofu a Go-Go 11

BARS & CLUBS
Atlantic House 3
Boatslip 1
Club Euro 5
Crown and Anchor 4
Governor Bradford 7
The Vixen 11

▲ HI-Truro

N

0   500 yds

ATLANTIC OCEAN

CAPE COD NATIONAL SEASHORE

Race Point Beach

Province Lands Visitor Center

PROVINCE LANDS

RACE POINT ROAD

CEMETERY ROAD

Pilgrim Monument

TOWN HILL

EAST END

Provincetown Art Association & Museum

HOWLAND STREET

WILLOW ST

MILLER HILL

BREWSTER ST

DYER ST

ALDEN ST

PEARL ST

ARCH ST

CONWELL STREET

CENTER STREET

STANDISH ST

ALDEN ST

WINSLOW ST

JEROME ST

PRINCE ST

CARVER STREET

COURT STREET

WINTHROP STREET

SHANK

MASONIC PL

GOSNOLD ST

RYDER ST

FREEMAN ST

CENTRAL ST

ATLANTIC AVE

CONANT

MONTELLO STREET

PLEASANT STREET

FRANKLIN ST

SCHOOL ST

MECHANIC ST

COTTAGE ST

NICKERSON ST

WEST VINE ST

ATWOOD AVE

POINT ST

CREEK ROUND HILL

PILGRIM HEIGHTS

BLUEBERRY

TREMONT STREET

COMMERCIAL STREET

BRADFORD STREET

BROWN ST

RACE ROAD

CREEK ROAD

WEST END

WASHINGTON AVENUE

LAW ST

ANTHONY ST

PEARL ST

COMMERCIAL STREET

KENDALL LANE

HANCOCK ST

CONWAY ST

SNOW ST

ALLERTON ST

THISTLEMORE

DUNCAN LANE

ATKINS MAYO ROAD

BRADFORD STREET

LOVETTS CT

YOUNGS CT

RILEY CT

HARRY KEMP WAY

OLD COLONY WAY

AUNT SUKEY WAY

Fishermen's Wharf

Coast Guard Station

Whydah Museum

MacMillan Wharf

Cape Cod Bay

Pilgrims' Landing Place

Breakwater

Herring Cove Beach

▼ Long Point Beach

9.30am–4.30pm; ☎508/487-3424, ⓦwww.ptownchamber.com), has a wealth of information on area attractions, and distributes discount coupons for whale-watching cruises; it also houses the Bay State Cruise desk, where you can purchase **ferry tickets**.

It couldn't be easier to **walk** around tiny P-Town, though many visitors prefer to **cycle** the narrow streets, hills, and the undulating Province Lands Bike Trail, a difficult six-mile route with great vistas. One good bike-rental outlet in town is Arnold's, 329 Commercial St (☎508/487-0844); they charge about $21 a day.

If you're in need of transport, the locals rave about their new **shuttle** bus service; $1 will get you all the way to Truro, plus the accommodating Flex service enables them to pick you up even if it's not a scheduled stop (☎800/352-7155, ⓦwww.thebreeze.info). Narrated **tours** are run by Provincetown Trolley, Inc., from the town hall on Commercial Street (daily every half-hour from 10am–4pm, or until 7pm in season; $10; ☎508/487-9483, ⓦwww.provincetowntrolley.com), while the more isolated dunes and moors are accessed by Art's Sand Dune Tours, based at Commercial and Standish streets (April–Oct 10am–dusk; $20 daytime tour and $30 sunset tour ($79 with clambake); ☎508/487-1950 or 1-800/894-1951, ⓦwww.artsdunetours.com). **Whale-watching cruises** leave from MacMillan Wharf between April and October 31; one of the main cruise operators is the Dolphin Fleet Whale Watch (☎1-800/826-9300, ⓦwww.whalewatch.com); they have a ticket office within the Chamber of Commerce building and sell tickets for about $30.

Accommodation

Besides the few motels on the outskirts, every second picturesque cottage in town seems to be a **guesthouse**. Prices are reasonable until mid-June, and during the off-season you can find some real bargains. As for **camping**, the welcoming *Dunes' Edge Campground*, on Hwy-6 just east of the central stoplights (☎508/487-9815, ⓦwww.dunes-edge.com), charges $35 for its wooded sites; it's only open from May to September.

Carpe Diem 12 Johnson St ☎1-800/487-0132, ⓦwww.carpediemguesthouse.com. Friendly, accommodating innkeepers, beautifully-appointed rooms, horseback riding, and a wine and cheese hour in the afternoon. ❼–❽

Carriage House Provincetown 7 Central St ☎1-800/309-0248; ⓦwww.thecarriagehse.com. A gorgeous space with lots of attention to detail, a steam room and Jacuzzi, and fantastic breakfasts. ❻–❼

Crowne Pointe Historic Inn & Spa 7 Winthrop St ☎508/487-6767 or 1-877/276-9631, ⓦwww.crownepointe.com. Provincetown's most luxurious digs: gorgeous rooms, a fancy restaurant, and unbelievable spa treatments. ❽–❾

Inn at Cook Street 7 Cook St ☎508/487-3894, ⓦwww.innatcookstreet.com. A quiet, lovingly-maintained inn with lots of breezy spaces and freshly-baked brownies. ❽

Outermost Hostel 28 Winslow St ☎508/487-4378. Hostel with thirty $25 beds in five cramped dorm cabins; a better bet is the HI-Truro, 10 minutes west on Rte-6.

Oxford Guest House 8 Cottage St ☎508/487-9103 or 1-888/456-9103, ⓦwww.oxfordguesthouse.com. A welcoming, well-appointed inn with free wireless internet, a wine hour in the evening, and lovely innkeepers. ❼

White Horse Inn 500 Commercial St ☎508/487-1790 A whimsical, colorful, art-strewn space; some rooms have shared baths. There are also family-sized apartments with kitchens. Beach access. ❹–❼

The town and the beaches

Provincetown's tiny core is centered on the three narrow miles of **Commercial Street**. **MacMillan Wharf**, always busy with charters, yachts, and fishing boats (which unload their catch each afternoon), splits the town in half. Somewhat out from the center, on Commercial Street, are scores of quaint art galleries,

△ Provincetown

as well as the delightful **Provincetown Art Association and Museum**, at no. 460 (May–Oct daily noon–5pm, extended summer hours; ☎508/487-1750, Ⓦwww.paam.org; $5, free Fridays after 5pm), with displays of local artists.

The 252ft granite tower of the **Pilgrim Monument and Provincetown Museum** on High Pole Hill, smack in the center of P-Town, has an observation deck (only accessible by stairs and narrow ramps) that looks out over the whole of the Cape (daily: April–Nov 9am–5pm; July & Aug 9am–7pm; $7). Behind Town Hall, on Bradford Street, there's a bas-relief monument to the Pilgrims' 1620 **Mayflower Compact**, in which they agreed to unite as one body to build the first colony. Further from the wharf are restored sea captain's homes and weathered clapboard houses with white picket fences and wildflowers spilling out of every crevice.

A little way beyond the town's narrow strip of sand, undeveloped **beaches** are marked only by dunes and a few shabby beach huts. You can swim in the clear water from the uneven rocks of the two-mile breakwater, where the sea bed crunches with soft-shell clams, or head through scented wild roses and beach plums to find blissful isolation on undeveloped beaches nearby. West of town, **Herring Cove Beach**, easily reached by bike or through the dunes, is more crowded, but never unbearably so. In the wild **Province Lands**, at the Cape's northern tip, vast sweeping moors and bushy dunes are buffeted by Cape Cod's deadly sea, the site of one thousand known shipwrecks. The **visitor center** (May–Oct daily 9am–5pm; ☎508/487-1256), in the middle of the dunes on Race Point Road, has an observation deck from which you might spot a whale.

Eating

Great **food** options abound in P-town. Portuguese bakeries, relics of early settlement, can be found along Commercial Street; beware the bland family restaurants that are often found nearby.

Bubala's By the Bay 183 Commercial St ⊤ 508/487-0773. Perhaps the freshest seafood in P-town at a fun hangout right on the water; good non-fish fare as well; open all day.

Café Edwige 333 Commercial St ⊤ 508/487-2008. Breakfast's the thing at this popular second-floor spot; try the homemade Danish pastries and fresh fruit pancakes. Creative bistro fare at dinnertime.

Ciro & Sal's 4 Kiley Court ⊤ 508/487-6444. Traditional Northern Italian cooking with plenty of veal and seafood; a bit on the pricey side, but worth it.

Karoo Kafe 338 Commercial St ⊤ 508/487-6630. Tasty, low-key South African fare. Order the Cape Malay stew (curry, coconut milk, and veggies over rice) at the counter and enjoy it amongst sunny, zebra-striped seating.

Lobster Pot 321 Commercial St ⊤ 508/487-0842. Its landmark neon sign is like a beacon for those who come from far and wide for the ultra-fresh crustaceans. Affordable and family-oriented.

Napi's 7 Freeman St ⊤ 508/487-1145. Popular dishes at this art-strewn spot include pastas and seafood items, notably a thick Portuguese fish stew. They have a less expensive menu on week nights.

Portuguese Bakery 299 Commercial St ⊤ 508/487-1803. This old standby is the place to come for cheap baked goods, particularly the tasty fried *rabanada*, akin to portable French toast.

Tofu a Go-Go 336 Commercial St ⊤ 508/487-6237. Casual upstairs eatery serving exclusively vegetarian fare, like delicious tofu tahini salad.

Nightlife and entertainment

Each weekend, boatloads of revelers from the mainland seek out P-Town's notoriously wild **nightlife**. From house-music raves to drag cabarets, from torch singing to R&B, the variety is huge.

Atlantic House 6 Masonic Place, behind Commercial St ⊤ 508/487-3821. The "A-House" – a dark drinking hole favored by Tennessee Williams and Eugene O'Neill – is now a trendy gay club and bar.

Boatslip 161 Commercial St ⊤ 508/487-1669. The gay tea dances at this resort are legendary; you can either dance away on a long wooden deck overlooking the water, or cruise inside under a disco ball and flashing lights.

Club Euro 258 Commercial St ⊤ 508/487-2505. Music videos, world-beat sounds, and a good buzz in an 1843 former Congressional Church with a 3D mermaid sculpture emerging from the wall.

Crown and Anchor 247 Commercial St ⊤ 508/487-1430, ⓦ www.onlyatthecrown.com. A massive complex housing several bars, including *The Vault*, P-town's only gay leather bar, *Wave*, a video-karaoke bar, and *Paramount*, a cabaret with nightly acts.

Governor Bradford 312 Commercial St ⊤ 508/487-2781. A good salty dive bar, with dark leather booths and a nice blend of gay and straight clientele. Rocking karaoke shows nightly at 9.30pm.

The Vixen 336 Commercial St ⊤ 508/487-6424. High-energy, primarily lesbian club, with free pool and a jukebox, lots of live performances, and dancing.

Martha's Vineyard

The largest offshore island in New England, twenty-mile-long **MARTHA'S VINEYARD** encompasses more physical variety than Nantucket, with hills and pasturelands providing scenic counterpoints to the beaches and wild, windswept moors on the separate island of **Chappaquiddick**. Roads throughout the Vineyard are framed by knotty oak trees, which lend a romantic aura to an already pretty landscape. The most genteel town on the island is **Edgartown**, all prim and proper with its freshly-painted, white clapboard Colonial homes and manicured gardens. The other main town, **Vineyard Haven**, is more commercial and one of the island's ferry ports. **Oak Bluffs**, in between the two (and the other docking point for ferries), has an array of whimsical wooden gingerbread cottages and inviting eateries. Be aware of island terminology: heading "Up-Island" takes you, improbably, southwest to the cliffs at **Aquinnah** (formerly known as Gay Head); conversely, "Down-Island" refers to the triumvirate of easterly towns mentioned above.

The three principal island communities are connected by a regular bus service and offer full facilities and shops of every kind. They're quite mellow places to pass a summer's day, and a little exploring can yield some pleasant surprises, such as quiet beaches and bird-filled lagoons. Bringing a car over is expensive and pointless, as the island is jam-packed with cars throughout the summer and you can easily get around by bus or **bike**; rent one at the rental places lined up by the ferry landing. The best bike ride is along the State Beach Park between Oak Bluffs and Edgartown, with the dunes to one side and marshy Sengekontacket Pond to the other; purpose-built cycle routes continue to the youth hostel at West Tisbury (see opposite).

Trips around the west side of the island are decidedly bucolic, with nary a peep of the water beyond the rolling hills and private estates; however, you do eventually come to the **lighthouse** at **Aquinnah**, where the multicolored clay was once the main source of paint for the island's houses – now, anyone caught removing any clay faces a sizeable fine. From Moshup beach below, you can get great views of this spectacular formation.

Ferries to Martha's Vineyard and Nantucket

Unless otherwise specified, all the ferries below run several times daily in midsummer (mid-June to mid-Sept). Most have fewer services from May to mid-June, and between mid-September and October. There is at least a skeleton service to each island, though not on all routes, all year round. To discourage clogging of the roads, roundtrip costs for cars are prohibitively high in the peak season (mid-May to mid-Sept; Woods Hole ferry only), while costs for bikes are just $6 each way. Be sure to call in advance for reservations as rides do sell out.

To Martha's Vineyard

Falmouth to Oak Bluffs (about 35min): pedestrians only; $12 roundtrip; the *Island Queen* ferry ☎508/548-4800, 🖥www.islandqueen.com.

Falmouth to Edgartown (1hr): pedestrians only; $30 roundtrip; Falmouth Ferry Service ☎508/548-9400, 🖥www.falmouthferry.com.

Woods Hole to Vineyard Haven and Oak Bluffs (45min): pedestrians $11 roundtrip; May–Oct vehicles $120 roundtrip; off-season vehicles $70 roundtrip; Steamship Authority ☎508/477-8600, 🖥www.islandferry.com.

Hyannis to Oak Bluffs (about 1hr40min; fast ferry about 50min): pedestrians only; $31 roundtrip, fast ferry $59 roundtrip; Hy-Line ☎508/778-2600 in Hyannis, ☎508/693-0112 on Martha's Vineyard, 🖥www.hy-linecruises.com.

New Bedford to Oak Bluffs or Vineyard Haven (1hr): pedestrians only; $58 roundtrip; Steamship Authority ☎1-866/453-6800, 🖥www.nefastferry.com.

Montauk, Long Island, to Oak Bluffs (6hr): pedestrians only; summer weekends only; $80 roundtrip; Viking Ferry ☎631/668-5700, 🖥www.vikingfleet.com.

To Nantucket

From Hyannis: pedestrians $28 roundtrip (2hr journey); pedestrians $59 roundtrip (1hr journey); May–Oct vehicles $200 one way; off-season vehicles $115 one way; Steamship Authority ☎508/477-8600 for auto reservations, ☎508/771-4000 on the mainland, ☎508/228-0262 on Nantucket; 🖥www.islandferry.com. Also Hy-Line Cruises, pedestrians only; 2hr journey $33 roundtrip; 1hr journey $64 roundtrip; ☎508/778-2600, 🖥www.hy-linecruises.com.

From Harwich Port (1hr15min): pedestrians only; $54 roundtrip; late May through early Oct only; Freedom Cruise Line ☎508/432-8999, 🖥www.nantucketislandferry.com.

In summer, the Hy-Line ferry company also runs a **connecting service** between Oak Bluffs, Martha's Vineyard, and Nantucket (one departure daily; pedestrians only; $25 one-way; ☎508/778-2600). The trip takes about an hour.

Martha's Vineyard brims with beautiful **beaches**. Highlights include the secluded, gorgeous Wasque, at the end of Wasque Road in Chappaquiddick, and South Beach, at the end of Katama Road in Edgartown, known for its "good waves and good bodies." The gentle State Beach, along Beach Road between Oak Bluffs and Edgartown, is more family-oriented.

Accommodation

If accommodation is booked up, as is very likely, the main **Chamber of Commerce** office at Beach Road in Vineyard Haven (T 508/693-0085, W www.mvy. com) may be able to help. There is a **campground** in Vineyard Haven at 569 Edgartown Rd (T 508/693-3772, W www.campmv.com); tent sites cost $44 per day for two people and include water and electricity hookups.

Crocker House Inn 12 Crocker Ave, Vineyard Haven T 1-800/772-0206, W www.crockerhouseinn .com. Elegant and accommodating, the *Crocker House* features pretty rooms, free wifi, good proximity to shops, and lots of homemade goodies. ⑥

HI-Martha's Vineyard 525 Edgartown–West Tisbury Rd T 508/693-2665, W www.capecodhostels. org. In an appealing setting at the forest's edge and away from town; near the island's main bike path, and right on the bus route. Free wifi. Open April to mid-November. Dorm beds $25–28 a night.

The Mansion House 9 Main St, Vineyard Haven T 508/693-2200 or 1-800/332-4112, W www. mvmansionhouse.com. Recently renovated, beautiful rooms; a lovely wraparound porch, and luxurious spa facilities and fitness center. ⑧–⑨

Menemsha Inn & Cottages and Beach Plum Inn North Road, Menemsha T 508/645-9454 or 1-800/901-2087, W www.menemshainn.com and W www.beachpluminn.com. These adjacent properties are beautifully maintained. Within walking distance of the Menemsha beach, it also includes private beach access. ⑧–⑨

Nashua House across from the Post Office, 30 Kennebec Ave, Oak Bluffs T 508/693-0043, W www.nashuahouse.com. Small, sunny, Victorian-style rooms with shared baths and ocean views, in the heart of Oak Bluffs. ⑤

Oak Bluffs Inn Circuit Ave, Oak Bluffs T 800/955-6235, W www.oakbluffsinn.com. Guests rave about the gorgeous wraparound porch, the fantastic innkeepers, and proximity to beaches, ferries, and restaurants. ⑦–⑧

The Winnetu Inn & Resort South Beach, Edgartown T 508/627-4747, W www.winnetu. com. This family-friendly resort hotel is just a short walk from a private stretch of South Beach; very well-appointed rooms, many with kitchenettes. ⑧

Eating and drinking

It's not at all hard to find something to **eat** on Martha's Vineyard. The ports in particular have rows of places to tempt tourists just off the ferries. Only in Edgartown and Oak Bluffs can you order alcohol with meals, but you can bring your own elsewhere. Many **pubs**, too, serve inexpensive food, though the people partaking of it are often of the polo shirt variety.

ArtCliff Diner 39 Beach Rd, Vineyard Haven T 508/693-1224. Perfect for a pre-ferry send-off breakfast with the likes of almond-crusted French toast and chorizo, egg, and pepperjack sandwiches. Closed Wed.

The Bite 29 Basin Road, Menemsha T 508/645-9239. Roadside, seaside nirvana. Fried clams, scallops, and zucchini, served up in a tiny seafood shack. Good chowder, too. Cash only.

The Black Dog Bakery 11 Water St, Vineyard Haven T 508/693-4786. Skip the overrated *Black Dog Tavern* next door and stock up on delicious muffins and breads for the ferry ride back.

Chilmark Chocolates 19 State Rd, Chilmark T 508/645-3013. People line up and rally for *Chilmark's* island-grown berries dipped in unbelievably-good organic chocolate. Closed Mon–Wed.

Larsen's Fish Market Mason Road, Menemsha T 508/645-2680. For about $15 you can pick out your very own lobster and then eat it on low-key flats overlooking the harbor. Good steamers, too.

Le Grenier Main Street, Vineyard Haven T 508/693-4906. Don't mind the fussy ambience and weird murals; this fancy French spot serves up some of the tastiest dinner fare on the island.

Offshore Ale Company 30 Kennebec Ave, Oak Bluffs T 508/693-2626. Local brewpub with wooden booths, toss-on-the-floor peanut shells, and lots of live shows. If you're there at night, be sure to stop by *Back Door Donuts* (in the Reliable Market parking lot, ☎508/693-4786; 9.30–12.28am) for one of their life-changing apple fritters – it's an MV must-do.

Slice of Life 50 Circuit Ave, Oak Bluffs ☎508/693-3838. Great New American spot, particularly for lunch. Order the fried green tomato BLT and ogle the tourists from the sunny, enclosed patio.

Nantucket

The thirty-mile, two-hour sea crossing to **NANTUCKET** may not be an oceangoing odyssey, but it does set the "Little Grey Lady" apart from her larger, shore-hugging sister, Martha. Halfway here from Hyannis, neither mainland nor island is in sight, and once you've landed you can avert your eyes from the smart-money double-deck cruisers with names like *Pier Pressure* and *Loan Star* and let the place remind you that it hasn't always been a rich folk's playground. Despite the formidable prowess of its seamen (see box, opposite), survival for early settlers on the island's scrubby soil was always a struggle.

The tiny cobbled carriageways of **Nantucket Town** itself, once one of the largest cities in Massachusetts, were frozen in time by economic decline 150 years ago. Today, this area of delightful old restored houses – the town has more buildings on the National Register of Historic Places than Boston – is very much the island hub. From the moment you get off the ferry you're besieged by bike rental places and tour companies. **Straight Wharf** leads directly onto **Main Street** with its shops and restaurants; the **information office** – which has a daily list of accommodation vacancies, but doesn't make reservations – is nearby at 25 Federal St (☎508/228-0925). The **Chamber of Commerce**, 48 Main St (☎508/228-1700, ⓦwww.nantucketchamber.org), carries the best range of island information.

The excellent, recently-renovated **Whaling Museum**, 13 Broad St, at the head of Steamboat Wharf (☎508/228-1894, ⓦwww.nha.org; $15; $18 site pass includes Oldest House, Old Gaol, and Old Mill), houses an outstanding collection of seafaring exotica, including a gallery of gorgeous scrimshaws delicately-engraved by strong-armed nineteenth-century sailors. There is also a luminous fresnel lens, formerly housed in the Sankaty Head Lighthouse, as well as a gigantic sperm whale skeleton. Look for the rotted tooth on its jaw; officials believe a tooth infection brought on the whale's demise.

After a stroll around Nantucket Town, it's customary to cycle the seven flat miles east to the village of **Siaconset** (always pronounced 'Sconset), where venerable cottages stand literally encrusted with salt, and then meander back across the heaths and moorland. **Bikes** can be rented from Young's Bicycle Shop, 6 Broad St (around $25 for a full day; ☎508/228-1151). **Buses** also link Nantucket Town and 'Sconset: NRTA (☎508/228-7025) runs shuttles from late May through early October and charges $2 each way.

Accommodation

But for the youth hostel, accommodation on Nantucket is somewhat expensive; the going rate in **B&Bs** and **guesthouses** starts at $100 a night.

Hawthorn House 2 Chestnut St ☎508/228-1468, ⓦwww.hawthornhouse.com. Central, well-appointed guesthouse with a friendly, helpful staff and ten handsome rooms outfitted with antique furnishings. **❽**

HI-Nantucket Star of the Sea 31 Western Ave ☎508/228-0433, ⓦwww.capecodhostels.org. Dorm beds ($18–32 a night) a stone's throw from Surfside Beach, just over three miles south of town. Lockout

10am–5pm, curfew 11pm. Open mid-May–early-Oct.

Martin House Inn 61 Centre St ☎508/228-0678, ⓦwww.martinhouseinn.com. Thirteen lovely rooms offer good value in this 1803 seaman's house; close to shops and ferries. **❼**

The Nesbitt Inn 21 Broad St ☎508/228-0156. The central location, friendly innkeepers, and affordable rooms, most with original furniture, compensate for the shared baths in this Victorian

The whalers of Nantucket

Scores of anonymous Captains have sailed out of Nantucket, that were as great, and greater than your Cook . . . for in their succorless empty-handedness, they, in the heathenish sharked waters, and by the beaches of unrecorded, javelin islands, battled with virgin wonders and terrors that Cook with all his marines and muskets would not have willingly dared.

from *Moby Dick*, by Herman Melville

In 1659, a sober group of twenty-seven Quaker and Presbyterian families arrived on Nantucket and set about imposing order on the haphazard business of **whaling**. Whales had always beached themselves on the treacherous sandy shoals all around – up to a dozen might be washed ashore in a major storm – and the local **Indians** had become skilled in hunting them in nearby waters. At first, the white settlers began erecting tall masts from which a permanent watch was kept for passing whales. As the years went by, they began sending large ships out to pursue their prey. The Wampanoag Indians played an integral part in the process: the actual kill was effected by two rowboats working in tandem, and at least five of each thirteen-man crew, usually including the crucial **harpooneer**, would be Indian. The common occurrence when an injured whale would speed away, dragging a boat helter-skelter behind it for endless terrifying hours, was known as a "**Nantucket Sleighride.**"

The early chronicler Crèvecoeur provides an extensive account of Nantucket as it was in 1782 in his *Letters from an American Farmer*. Although perturbed by the islanders' universal habit of taking a dose of opium every morning, he held them up as a model of diligence and good self-government. Whaling was a disciplined profession, and to feed themselves and equip their ships the islanders kept up a shrewd and extensive trade with the mainland. At that time, there were already more than a hundred ships. The whalers were not paid; instead each had a share (a "lay") of the final proceeds of the voyage. Ambitious Nantucketers even reached the Pacific – see p.1279 in Chapter 16, "Hawaii," for an account of their experiences there. The great days of Nantucket were immortalized by Herman Melville:

And thus have these naked Nantucketers, these sea hermits, issuing from their ant-hill in the sea, overrun and conquered the watery world like so many Alexanders . . . two thirds of this terra-queous globe are the Nantucketer's. For the sea is his; he owns it, as Emperors own empires.

By the time *Moby Dick* was published in 1851, Nantucket's fortunes had gone into an abrupt decline. Soon after a devastating fire in 1846, reports of the Californian Gold Rush lured young men westwards; the discovery of underground oil in Pennsylvania came as the final blow. A magazine article of 1873 reported, "Let no traveler visit Nantucket with the expectation of witnessing the marks of a flourishing trade . . . of the great fleet of ships which dotted every sea, scarcely a vestige remains."

inn, built in 1872. **5**
Sherburne Inn 10 Gay St ☎ 1-888/577-4425, ⓦ www.sherburneinn.com. A lovely, well-appointed B&B with cozy, elegant rooms, free wifi, pretty grounds, and afternoon tea and sherry. **7**–**8**

Union Street Inn 7 Union St ☎ 508/228-9222, ⓦ www.unioninn.com. Luxurious, well-loved B&B with all the trimmings: beautiful rooms, cozy bathrobes and fancy soaps, and fresh afternoon pastries. **8**–**9**

Eating and drinking

Crèvecoeur (see box, above) reported that on Nantucket, "music, singing, and dancing are holden in equal detestation." **Seafood** fortunately is not; the only trouble is that Nantucket's restaurants, good as they may be, tend to be exceptionally expensive, easily costing $30–40 for an entree.

Black Eyed Susan's 10 India St ☎ 508/325-0308. Beloved little brunch spot with inventive egg scrambles and cheery buttermilk pancakes. Cash only.

The Chicken Box 14 Dave St ☎ 508/228-9717. Every summer night, people of all stripes pack into "the Box" for great live shows and low-key drinking environs. Shuffleboard and pool tables, too. Cash only; an ATM is inside.

Company of the Cauldron 5 India St ☎ 508/228-4016. A romantic, vine-covered, candlelit haven with live harp music thrice weekly. Both seatings of a shifting prix fixe menu ($54) sell out quickly, so make reservations.

Provisions 3 Harbor Sq ☎ 508/228-3258. Great variety of bulging, gourmet sandwiches with names like the "Turkey Terrific" and the "Yacht Club" (smoked salmon, lemon caper cream cheese, and cukes).

Sayle's Seafood 99 Washington St Extension ☎ 508/228-4599. Breezy, very casual seafood shack where you pick your own lobster. There's also a phenomenal, all-encompassing "clam bake" option ($35/person in-store, $60/person at your house).

Straight Wharf Restaurant 6 Harbor Sq ☎ 508/228-4499. Lovely New American spot with smoked bluefish pate and watermelon salad in an airy, art-strewn space overlooking the harbor.

Central and western Massachusetts

The 150 miles of Massachusetts that stretch inland to the west of Boston have always been obliged to play second fiddle to the state capital. Just ten years after the Revolutionary War, the farmers who struggled to make a living from this indifferent soil rose in Shay's Rebellion to prevent eastern creditors from seizing their property to help recover the war debt; their pitchforks were no match for the guns of the new nation.

These days, the west is known best to vacationers for the **Berkshires,** which host the celebrated **Tanglewood** summer music festival and boast museum-filled towns such as **North Adams** and **Williamstown** – both in the far northwest corner of the state, at the end of the incredibly scenic **Mohawk Trail**. **Amherst** and **Northampton** are stimulating college towns in the verdant **Pioneer Valley**, with all the cafés, restaurants, and bookstores you could want. The industrial city of **Worcester** has a good art museum, while culture of a more popular variety is on offer at the Basketball Hall of Fame in **Springfield**.

Worcester

Forty miles west of Boston on I-90, **WORCESTER** is Massachusetts' second largest city, and the only major industrial city in the US not beside a sea, lake, or river. The highlight is the **Worcester Art Museum**, 55 Salisbury St (Wed, Fri & Sun 11am–5pm, Thurs 11am–8pm, Sat 10am–5pm; $8, or free Saturday from 10am–noon; ☎ 508/799-4406, ⓦ www.worcesterart.org), with its vast collection of paintings, mosaics, photographs, and a Romanesque chapter house from the twelfth century. Also worth a visit are the **Higgins Armory Museum**, at 100 Barber Ave (Tues–Sat 10am–4pm, Sun noon–4pm; $8; ☎ 508/853-6015, ⓦ www.higgins.org), which is chock-full weapons and armor from all over the world, and the **Worcester Historical Museum**, 30 Elm St (Tues, Wed, Fri, & Sat 10am–4pm, Thurs 10am–8.30pm; $5; ☎ 508/753-8278, ⓦ www.worcesterhistory.org), where more is revealed about the city than simply being the coincidental birthplace of, among other things, the space suit, the monkey wrench, barbed wire, the birth control pill, the Valentine's Day Card, and the infamous yellow "smiley face."

Among local **accommodation**, the central *Hampton Inn*, 110 Summer St (☎ 508/757-0400 or 1-800/426-7866, ⓦ www.hamptoninnworcester.com; ⑤), has comfortable rooms. *Anthony's*, 172 Shrewsbury St (☎ 508/757-6864), is a local landmark for Italian **food**; *Thai Cha-Da*, 266 Park Avenue (☎ 508/752-2211), has great Thai. For a good selection of other eateries, head to Shrewsbury Street.

Old Sturbridge Village

Halfway between Worcester and Springfield on US-20, near the junction of I-90 and I-84, the restored and reconstructed **Old Sturbridge Village** (daily: winter 9.30am–4pm; rest of year 9.30am–5pm; $20; ☎508/347-3362 or 1-800/SEE-1830, ⓦwww.osv.org), made up of preserved buildings brought from all over the region, gives a somewhat idealized but engaging portrait of a small New England town of the 1830s. Costumed interpreters act out roles – working in blacksmiths' shops, planting and harvesting vegetables, tending cows, and the like – but they pull it off in an unusually convincing manner. The 200-acre site itself, with mature trees, ponds, and dirt footpaths, is very pretty, and worth a half-day visit. Nearby *Sturbridge Host Hotel*, 366 Main St (☎508/347-7993; ❺), is a pretty **place to stay** – situated on nine groomed acres with an indoor heated swimming pool and access to beautiful Cedar Lake.

Springfield

SPRINGFIELD, at the point where I-90 crosses I-91 – in an extremely confusing way – ninety miles from Boston at the southern border of the Pioneer Valley, has an odd assortment of claims to fame, including being the home of the Springfield rifle and children's author Dr Seuss. However, visitors are drawn to this unwieldy and unattractive city, split by the wide Connecticut River, by the 1890s invention of Dr James Naismith – the sport of **basketball**. Naismith designed the game as a way of providing exercise for athletes at the YMCA, and its popularity spread with amazing speed. First opened in 1959, the **Basketball Hall of Fame** at 1000 W Columbus Ave, next to the river just south of Memorial Bridge (Mon–Sat 9am–6pm, Sun 10am–5pm; $17; ☎413/781-6500 or 1-877/4HOOPLA, ⓦwww.hoophall.com), was revamped and enlarged in 2002, and includes movies, videos, memorabilia, and interactive gadgets that test your own skills.

Springfield's Amtrak **train** station is very central, at 66 Lyman St (☎413/785-4230). Peter Pan Trailways (☎413/781-2900 or 1-800/237-8747, ⓦwww.peterpanbus.com) provides daily **bus** services to and from Boston and New York City, the Pioneer Valley, and the Berkshires from the nearby bus station at 1776 Main St (☎413/781-3320). The **Convention & Visitors Bureau** is downtown at 1441 Main St (Mon–Fri 9am–5pm; ☎413/787-1548 or 1-800/723-1548, ⓦwww.valleyvisitor.com). Downtown **lodging** includes the expensive *Sheraton Springfield*, 1 Monarch Place (☎413/781-1010; ❼), and the cheaper *Super 8 Motel*, 1500 Riverdale St (☎413/736-8080; ❹). A number of budget motels can be found over the river in West Springfield. Tiny Fort Street has been home to the *Fort/Student Prince Restaurant* (☎413/734-7475) for over sixty years – a local favorite serving Wiener schnitzel, goulash, and sauerbraten.

Amherst and Northampton

North of Springfield, the Pioneer Valley is a verdant corridor created by the Connecticut River, home to the college towns of **AMHERST** and **NORTHAMPTON**, both good places to kick back for a few days, hang out in cafés, and browse bookstores in one of New England's most liberal and progressive areas.

Amtrak **trains** stop in Amherst at 13 Railroad St, while you can catch Peter Pan Trailways **buses** at 1 Roundhouse Plaza in Northampton (☎413/586-1030) and 8 Main St in Amherst (☎413/256-1547). Good **accommodation** is available at Northampton's historic *Hotel Northampton*, 36 King St (☎413/584-3100 or 1-800/547-3529, ⓦwww.hotelnorthampton.com; ❼), or the *Black Walnut Inn* at 1184 North Pleasant St in Amherst (☎413/549-5649 or 1-800/742-0358, ⓦwww.blackwalnutinn.com; ❻), a quintessentially New England inn. Among the numerous places to **eat**, *Paul and Elizabeth's*, 150 Main St, Northampton (☎413/584-4832), has good vegetarian choices, while *Amherst Chinese Food*, 62 Main St, Amherst (☎413/253-7835), serves healthy Oriental specialties made with organic veggies plucked from their own garden.

The Berkshires

A rich cultural history, world-class summer arts festivals, and a bucolic landscape of forests and verdant hills make the **Berkshires**, at the extreme western edge of Massachusetts, an unusually civilized region, just right for warm weather exploration.

While you're in the area, try to visit the excellent **Berkshire Visitors Bureau**, on Rte-8 in Adams (Mon–Fri 8.30am–5pm; ☎413/443-9186 or 1-800/237-5747, ⓦwww.berkshires.org), the best source for information on the Berkshires.

The Mohawk Trail: North Adams and Williamstown

In the northwest corner of the region, the **Mohawk Trail** passes through **NORTH ADAMS** and **WILLIAMSTOWN**, following the very scenic route the Native Americans used to travel between the valleys of the Connecticut and Hudson rivers. North Adams is home to the glorious **Mass MoCA** (Massachusetts Museum of Contemporary Art), 87 Marshall St (July–Sept daily 10am–6pm, Nov-May Mon & Wed-Sun 11am–5pm; $10; ☎413/662-2111, ⓦwww.massmoca.org), a sprawling, neo-funhouse collection of modern art installations, contemporary videos, and upside-down trees gathered in a gorgeous old mill site. Williamstown has two worthy art museums: the highlight of the **Sterling and Francine Clark Art Institute**, 225 South St (Tues–Sun 10am–5pm, July–Aug daily 10am–5pm; $10 June–Oct, rest of year free; ☎413/458-2303, ⓦwww.clarkart.edu), is the thirty-strong collection of Renoir paintings, while the **Williams College Museum of Art**, 15 Lawrence Hall Drive (Tues–Sat 10am–5pm, Sun 1–5pm; free; ☎413/597-2429, ⓦwww.wcma.org), has good exhibits of ancient Middle Eastern and modern American art in a beautiful Neoclassical space. The ultra-modern *Porches Inn,* 231 River St, right around the corner from Mass MoCA (☎413/664-0400, ⓦwww.porches.com; ❼), is *the* place to **stay** in the area, featuring high-speed internet, DVD players, and contemporary, fun décor. For **food,** head to hip *Café Latino,* at Mass MoCA (☎413/662-2004) for crispy calamari and *caipirinhas,* or to their sister restaurant, *Mezze,* at 16 Water St in Williamstown (☎413/458-0123) for outstanding New American flavors in a gracious, airy space.

Stockbridge

STOCKBRIDGE, just south of I-90 fifty miles west of Springfield, started out as "Indian Town," because the Mahican Indians had several villages in the area. The Reverend John Sergeant built the simple wooden **Mission House**, now located on Main Street, in 1739 in an attempt to live in close proximity with the Mahicans and convert them to Christianity.

That Stockbridge today looks like the archetypal New England small town – most of all when there's snow on the ground – is due largely to the artist **Norman Rockwell**, who lived here for 25 years until his death in 1978. Many of his *Saturday Evening Post* covers, whose sentimentality was made palatable by his sharp wit, featured the town; a collection of covers can be seen at the **museum** on Rte-183 (daily: May–Oct 10am–5pm; Nov–April Mon–Fri 10am–4pm, Sat & Sun 10am–5pm; $12.50; ☎413/298-4100 ext 220, ⓦwww.nrm.org). Some of the tour guides modelled for Rockwell as children and recall that for every few minutes they managed to hold still he'd slip them a coin from his large pile of nickels.

Magnificent houses in the hills around Stockbridge include **Chesterwood**, half a mile south of the Norman Rockwell Museum at 4 Williamsville Rd (May–Oct daily 10am–5pm; $10, grounds only $5; ⊤413/298-3579, ⓦwww.chesterwood.org), the luxurious home and studio of Daniel Chester French, sculptor of the Lincoln Memorial, and **Naumkeag**, on Prospect Hill Road (late May to mid-Oct daily 10am–5pm; $10, gardens only $8; ⊤413/298-3239), which was the first modernist garden estate in the country, and belonged to Joseph Choate, US ambassador to Queen Victoria. Stockbridge was also the setting for Arlo Guthrie's song, and movie, *Alice's Restaurant*.

The slightly frou-frou *Red Lion Inn* is one of the grander edifices on Main Street (⊤413/298-5545, ⓦwww.redlioninn.com; ❹); their **restaurant** has big portions of reliable Yankee fare, with standout burgers and steaks. In Becket, *The Dream Away Lodge* (1342 County Road, ⊤413/623-8725) offers fanciful dinner fare amongst funky environs and live music.

Lenox and around

Roughly five miles north of Stockbridge on US-7, well-heeled tourists flock to **LENOX** each year for the summer season of the Boston Symphony Orchestra at **Tanglewood**, 297 West St (for ticket info, call ⊤413/637-1666 or visit ⓦwww.bso.org). Open-air orchestral concerts are held on weekends from July to late August, with chamber music and recitals given on other days; covered seats are pricey and often hard to get, but you can sit and picnic on the lush lawns for an admission fee of around $18. Some midweek rehearsals are also open to the public, and there's a **jazz** festival on Labor Day weekend (the first weekend of September). On Rte-20 between Becket and Lee, **Jacob's Pillow** (⊤413/243-0745 or visit ⓦwww.jacobspillow.org; June to Aug) hosts one of the most famous contemporary dance festivals in the country.

Further north on US-7, **Arrowhead** (late May–Oct daily 9.30am–5pm; $8; ⊤413/442-1793, ⓦwww.mobydick.org), in Pittsfield, was Herman Melville's home while he wrote *Moby Dick*; declining sales of his books eventually forced him to sell his house and move to New York. The **Hancock Shaker Village**, five miles west of Pittsfield (daily: April–Nov 9.30am–5pm; rest of year 10am–4pm; summer and fall $15, rest of year $12; ⊤413/443-0188, ⓦwww.hancockshakervillage.org), was a going concern from 1783 to 1960. Its legacy includes the large dwelling-place, in which almost one hundred people slept and ate, and a round stone barn for their cattle. A more important, and much less commercialized, Shaker village, **Mount Lebanon**, is another five miles west on US-20, just over the New York State border; much has been dismantled and moved to museums, but a visit still gives a sense of the Shaker way of life ($6; ⊤518/794-9500). You can **stay** in total luxury at *Blantyre*, Blantyre Road; ⊤413/637-3556, ⓦwww.blantyre.com; ❾), one of the country's most plush resorts. For **food,** head over to *Church Street Café,* 69 Church St in Lenox (⊤413/637-2745) for standout New England fare, or linger over a martini at the atmospheric *Bistro Zinc,* around the corner at 56 Church St (⊤413/637-8800). *Chocolate Springs Café,* 55 Pittsfield/Lenox Rd (⊤413/637-9820) is the place to indulge in outstanding chocolate and espresso.

Rhode Island

A mere 48 miles long by 37 miles wide, **RHODE ISLAND** is the smallest state in the Union, and tends to be overlooked as a tourist destination, even if it is home to more than twenty percent of the nation's historical landmarks. It was established by Roger Williams in 1636 as a "lively experiment" in religious freedom. He had been expelled from Salem for his radical ideas (including the notion that Indians should be paid for their land and that there should be a total separation of church from state), and the Massachusetts Puritans liked to call the state he settled in "**Rogues Island**."

Despite its size, Rhode Island has over four hundred miles of coastline, hacked out of the Narragansett Bay, which includes over thirty tiny islands, including Hope and Despair. The "**Ocean State**" developed through sea trade, whaling, and smuggling. Partly due to this commercial interest, Rhode Islanders were in the front rank of the Revolutionary groundswell. However, no battles were fought on Rhode Island soil, and the state, apprehensive at the prospect of yielding power to the newly-formed Federal government, turned out to be the last state to ratify the Constitution. Between the Revolution and the Civil War, Rhode Island shifted from a maritime economy to lead the **Industrial Revolution** in manufacturing. Samuel Slater created the nation's first water-powered **textile mill** in Pawtucket, just outside Providence.

The state's principal destinations are its two original ports: well-heeled **Newport**, yachting capital of the world, with good beaches and outrageously louche mansions, and the Colonial college town of **Providence**.

Getting around Rhode Island

Rhode Island is tiny enough to make **getting around** ridiculously easy. Major interstate I-95 runs through **Providence** on its way from Massachusetts to Connecticut. The more scenic US-1 follows the coast of Narragansett Bay into Connecticut. **Newport** is accessible from Hwy-138, which connects the small islands in Narragansett Bay to the mainland. **Public transportation** is good: local buses as well as ferries connect Providence and Newport cheaply, and Amtrak stops regularly in Providence.

Providence

Splayed across seven hills on the Providence and Seekonk rivers, **PROVIDENCE** was Rhode Island's first settlement, founded "in commemoration of God's providence" on land given to Roger Williams by the Narragansett Indians (his insistence that Indians should be paid for their land being waived in his own case). Despite its roots in celebrating freedom, the city flourished as one of the most important ports of call in the notorious "triangle trade," where New England rum was exchanged for African slaves, who were then sold for West Indian molasses. With Slater's invention of the textile mill, industry along with port trade became the mainstays of Providence's economy.

The state's capital since 1901, Providence is today one of New England's three largest cities. Ivy League **Brown University** and the **Rhode Island School of Design** (RISD, or "Rizdee") give the place a certain cultural verve, and the many original Colonial homes on **Benefit Street** emphasize a historical importance

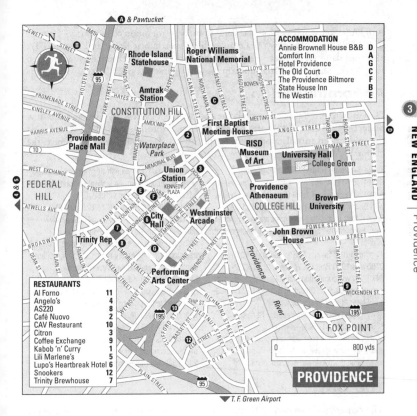

ACCOMMODATION

Annie Brownell House B&B	D
Comfort Inn	A
Hotel Providence	G
The Old Court	C
The Providence Biltmore	F
State House Inn	B
The Westin	E

RESTAURANTS

Al Forno	11
Angelo's	4
AS220	8
Café Nuovo	2
CAV Restaurant	10
Citron	3
Coffee Exchange	9
Kabob 'n' Curry	1
Lili Marlene's	5
Lupo's Heartbreak Hotel	6
Snookers	12
Trinity Brewhouse	7

T. F. Green Airport

largely absent from the downtown area across the river, which sparkles with new office buildings and a massive modern shopping mall. The city's ethnic diversity is showcased west of downtown by the large Italian community on **Federal Hill**, with bustling restaurants and traditional appeal.

Arrival, information, and getting around

T.F. Green Airport in Warwick, nine miles south of Providence, connects to all major US cities. The **Amtrak station** (daily 5am–11.30pm; ☎1-800/USA-RAIL) is at 100 Gaspee St, in a domed building a short walk southeast of the capitol. Greyhound (☎1-800/231-2222) and Peter Pan (☎1-888/751-8800) **buses** stop downtown at the city's transportation center, Kennedy Plaza.

The well-stocked **Visitors' Center** in the rotunda lobby of the Rhode Island Convention Center, One Sabin St (Mon–Sat 9am–5pm; ☎401/751-1177 or 1-800/233-1636, ⓦwww.pwcvb.com), provides maps and brochures, while the **Providence Preservation Society**, 21 Meeting St (Mon–Fri 8:30am–5pm; ☎401/831-7440, ⓦwww.ppsri.org), sells pamphlets about the city's various neighbourhoods (which include suggested self-guided walking tours) for $3. There's another **information center** in the Roger Williams National Memorial Park, 282 N Main St (daily 9am–4.30pm; ☎401/521-7266).

Sightseeing around Providence is best done **on foot**, though there is good **bus transportation** within the city (as well as around the state), provided by

RIPTA (ticket window Mon–Fri 7am–6pm, Sat 9am–noon & 1–5pm; $1.50/trip; ☏401/781-9400, ⓦwww.ripta.com), which has a hub at Kennedy Plaza. RIPTA also runs daily **ferries** between Providence and Newport (through New England Fast Ferry; May–Oct; $16 roundtrip; ⓦwww.nefastferry.com).

Accommodation

Downtown Providence is largely geared to the business traveler and has few budget rooms, but **B&B**s are a viable option. Motorists can take advantage of the mid-priced **motels** along I-95 north towards Pawtucket, and south near the airport at Warwick.

Annie Brownell House B&B 400 Angell St ☏401/454-2934, ⓦwww.anniebrownellhouse. com. Lovely, spacious 1899 Colonial Revival house with bright, airy rooms decorated in period style. Shared bath is slightly less expensive than private bath. Excellent full breakfasts, and a friendly owner to boot. ❺

Comfort Inn 2 George St, Pawtucket ☏401/723-6700 and 1940 Post Rd, Warwick ☏401/732-0470, ⓦwww.comfortinns.com. Decent rooms with included continental breakfast near exit 27 off I-95 and Slater Mill, or by the airport. ❺

Hotel Providence 311 Westminster St ☏401/861-8000 or 1-800/861-8990, ⓦwww .thehotelprovidence.com. Just a year old, this hotel is already earning rave reviews with its plush rooms, sophisticated artwork and excellent service. ❻

The Old Court 144 Benefit St ☏401/751-2002, ⓦwww.oldcourt.com. Appealing ten-room Victorian B&B in an old rectory near RISD. ❻

The Providence Biltmore 11 Dorrance St ☏401/421-0700 or 1-800/294-7709, ⓦwww. providencebiltmore.com. A landmark since 1922, the *grand dame* of the city's hotels is centrally located, with luxury rooms, great views, and pampering at an Elizabeth Arden Spa. ❼

State House Inn 43 Jewett St ☏401/351-6111, ⓦwww.providence-inn.com. Pleasant B&B rooms with antique furnishings in a restored old home near the Capitol building. ❺

The Westin 1 W Exchange St ☏401/598-8000 or 1-800/937-8461, ⓦwww.westin.com. Deluxe modern accommodations in the heart of Downcity; 200 additional rooms expected to open in 2007. ❾

The City

The center of downtown is Kennedy Plaza, a large public square that houses the city's transportation center. While much of the surrounding area is modern, the 1878 **City Hall**, at the western end of the plaza, is a notable exception, with its striking mansard roof and grand interior staircase. Though no longer used as a train terminal, the nearby 1898 Beaux Arts **Union Station** is another fine example of the historic restoration at which the rest of the city excels. To the south of the plaza, the 1828 **Westminster Arcade**, the oldest enclosed shopping mall in the nation, features specialty shops and a food court in a small, bright, sky-lit hall.

North of the center, **Roger Williams National Memorial**, at N Main and Smith streets, is the site of city-founder Williams' original settlement (daily 9am–4.30pm; free), while to its west at the top of **Constitution Hill**, the white-marble **Rhode Island State House** boasts a huge self-supported dome, purportedly the fourth-largest in the world. The dome is topped with a statue called *Independent Man*, an 11ft bronze figure created by George Brewster as a symbol of freedom and independence. A handsome full-length Gilbert Stuart portrait of George Washington adorns the Reception Room (Mon–Fri 8.30am–4.30pm, with guided tours at 9am, 10am, & 11am, appointment requested; free; ☏401/222-3983).

College Hill and Federal Hill

Laid-back **College Hill**, eastward across the river, is an attractive district of Colonial buildings and museums. Part of Williams' holy experiment was the establishment of the first American Baptist Church in 1638. The white clapboard **First Baptist Meet-**

ing House, at the foot of the hill at 75 N Main St, dates from 1775, and is remarkable for its 185ft steeple. This street logically leads into **South Main Street**, once bustling with waterfront activity, but now a small stretch of upmarket restaurants, bookstores, and pottery shops. **Benefit Street**, a block up the hill, is Providence's "**mile of history**," lined with the ice-cream-colored clapboard former homes of merchants and sea captains. Now beautifully restored, the street was once just a dirt path leading to graveyards until it was improved in the nineteenth century for the "benefit of the people of Providence" – hence its name. One of the few homes open to the public, the elegant **John Brown House**, 52 Power St, at Benefit St (April–Dec Tues–Fri guided tours at 1:30pm & 3pm, Sat guided tours at 10:30am, noon, 1:30pm, & 3pm; Jan–March Fri & Sat only, tours at 10:30am, noon, 1:30pm, & 3pm; $8; ☎401/273-7507), was home to the patriot and entrepreneur (also uncle to the man the University is named after) who made his fortune trading in slaves and with China. The first house built on the hill, it retains its original furnishings and holds displays on the formidable Brown family and the city itself.

Ivy League **Brown University** sets the tone for this three-centuries-old district; for free tours, contact the admissions office, 45 Prospect St (call ahead for tour schedule ☎401/863-2378, ⓦwww.brown.edu). East and south of College Hill, **Thayer** and **Wickenden Streets** buzz with an assortment of bookstores, cafés, and funky thrift stores.

On another campus a few blocks away, the small but excellent collection of the **RISD Museum of Art**, 224 Benefit St (Tues–Sun 10am–5pm; $8; ☎401/454-6500, ⓦwww.risd.edu), is indeed one of the best art-school museums in the country, and includes ancient Roman and Asian works, Impressionist and Post-Impressionist American art, and one of Rodin's statues of Balzac.

Across the road, the Greek Revival **Providence Athenaeum**, 251 Benefit St (Mon–Thurs 9am–7pm, Fri & Sat 9am–5pm, Sun 1–5pm, closed Sat afternoon and Sun in summer; free; ☎401/421-6970, ⓦwww.providenceathenaeum.org), is a library where Edgar Allan Poe failed to woo fellow poet Sarah Whitman. Its small reading nooks give the place a cozy living room feel.

Federal Hill, west of the center and informally considered Providence's **Little Italy**, is entered through a large arch topped by a bronze pinecone at Atwells Avenue. Long a powerful Mafia stronghold, this area is one of the friendliest and safest in the city – alive with cafés, delis, bakeries, and bars, and with a large Italianate fountain in **DePasquale Square**.

Slater Mill Historic Site

A ten-minute drive north of Providence, Pawtucket is home to the **Slater Mill Historic Site**, 67 Roosevelt Ave, exit 28 off I-95 (May–June daily 11am–3pm, July–Sept daily 10am–5pm; ☎401/725-8638, ⓦwww.slatermill.org), which illustrates the move to the industrial age led by Samuel Slater, who imported the technology from England in 1790. The site features the landmark **Old Slater Mill**, which contains a spinning frame as well as some rare textile machines that date from 1838, all for transforming raw cotton to yarn. Also found here is the 1810 **Wilkinson Mill**, where a machine shop still operates, and the **Sylvanus Brown House**, a worker's home with replica early-1800s furnishings, and interpreters performing (and explaining) their nineteenth-century chores.

Eating

Providence boasts many varied and excellent **food** options. Popular with students, **Thayer Street** is lined with inexpensive eateries, almost all of which remain open until late. Nearby **Wickenden Street** is more mature, and more expensive. The lively family-run Italian restaurants on **Federal Hill** serve good food at reasonable prices.

Al Forno 577 S Main St ☎ 401/273-9760. Widely touted as one of the best restaurants in the country, with wood-grilled pizzas, pastas, and more. Tues–Sat dinner.

Angelo's 141 Atwells Ave ☎ 401/621-8171. Family-style Federal Hill institution, offering inexpensive (and no-frills) Italian standards. Cash only.

Café Nuovo 1 Citizens Plaza ☎401/421-2525. Perfectly situated for an excellent and romantic, albeit expensive, meal overlooking WaterFire (see below). Dinner only Mon–Sat.

CAV Restaurant 14 Imperial Place ☎ 401/751-9164. An excellent contemporary, mid-priced menu in an atmospheric historic loft; live jazz after 9:30pm Fri & Sat (cover around $5 for non-diners).

Citron 5 Memorial Blvd ☎401/621-9463. Opened in late summer 2006, Citron serves excellent and innovative organic dishes in the $20 range. An extensive wine list comes with color-coded tips to help you choose; if you're still floundering you can also order tasting "flights," or selections, of groups of wines for a reasonable price.

Coffee Exchange 207 Wickenden St ☎ 401/273-1198. Fair trade, shade-grown, organic coffees at a popular meeting place for would-be intellectuals.

Kabob 'n' Curry 261 Thayer St ☎ 401/273-8844. On trendy Thayer Street, above-average Indian meals for less-than-average prices.

Nightlife and entertainment

As Providence's **nightlife** is largely student-oriented, things can get quiet during the breaks, though Thayer Street is always lively. For **film**, the Avon Rep Cinema at 260 Thayer St (☎401/421-3315) shows independent and art flicks, and the Cable Car Cinema at 204 S Main St (☎401/272-3970) has comfy sofas as well as seats. The **Providence Performing Arts Center**, in Downcity at 220 Weybosset St (☎401/421-2787, ⓦwww.ppacri.org), hosts musicals and the occasional concert in a grand old Art Deco movie house. In the warmer months, the unusual event known as **WaterFire** (several times a month, May–Oct; ⓦwww.waterfire. org) enthralls visitors and locals alike with nearly one hundred small bonfires set at sunset in the center of the Providence River starting at Waterplace Park, tended by gondoliers and accompanied by rousing music. Complete entertainment **listings** can be found in the free weekly *Providence Phoenix* and the *Providence Journal*'s Thursday edition.

AS220 115 Empire St ☎ 401/831-9327. Unabashedly artsy café/bar hangout for locals and students that hosts nightly performances featuring everything from mellow jazz to circus acts. Cover $2–10.

Lili Marlene's 422 Atwells Ave ☎ 401/751-4996. Small low-key locals' hangout with red leather booth, a pool table, and late-night snacks.

Lupo's Heartbreak Hotel 79 Washington St ☎401/272-5876. This is *the* spot in town to see nationally recognized bands rock out. Tickets $12–50, advance sales are cheapest.

Snookers 145 Clifford St ☎ 401/351-7665. Lively pool hall with fourteen tables for play, as well as a comfy outdoor deck for those just along for a drink. DJs five nights a week; $5 cover Fri & Sat after 10pm.

Trinity Brewhouse 186 Fountain St ☎401/453-2337. Hang out here after a Providence Bruins (minor league hockey) or Friars (college basketball) game to quaff in celebration or despair. Everything on tap is brewed in-house; full menu as well.

Newport

Thirty miles south of Providence, **NEWPORT** stands at the southern tip of the largest island in Narragansett Bay, **Aquidneck Island**. It was established as a colony by William Coddington, also seeking religious freedom from Massachusetts, in 1639. Due to its excellent harbor, it grew rapidly as a port for the "triangle trade" (see p.240) and as a privateering center. Contrary to the injustice inherent in those activities, religious tolerance led to an influx of Jews, Quakers, and Baptists, who formed lucrative international trade links. This great prosperity was severely curtailed by the British occupation of 1776–79, when half the population fled and much of the town was destroyed. Fortunately, enough of its original eighteenth-century homes have survived to rival Boston's collection.

In the 1850s, Newport became fashionable again as a resort for wealthy New York merchants, and very soon nouveau riche industrialists such as the Astors and Vanderbilts were building "summer cottages" – better described as mansions – along the rocky coastline. The obscene ostentation of this era (now known by Mark Twain's disparaging phrase as the Gilded Age) shocked Massachusetts' old wealth to the core.

The Great Depression killed off the decadence, but Newport remained a naval town through the 1970s. Today, the town feeds off tourism: much of it caters to the tennis and yachting set, but there are as many people looking at – and envying – the wealth as enjoying it. Despite an array of kitschy boutiques throughout, the rough old port still rears its boozy head, with beer and R&B clubs as evident as cocktails and cruises, making Newport an essential stop, especially during the summer **festival season**.

Arrival and information

There are actually three towns on Aquidneck Island: **Portsmouth** is at the northern edge, with the appropriately named **Middletown**, then **Newport**, below it. The mainland (and I-95) is connected to the island by US-138, which passes over the **Jamestown Bridge** to Conanicut Island, and from there by the **Newport** (or **Claiborne Pell**) **Bridge** ($2 each way).

Newport is easy to **walk** around. Thames (pronounced "Thaymz") Street is the main road; its northern end is separated from the harbor by the unattractive, modern America's Cup Avenue. It's here, at no. 23, that you will find the large **Gateway Visitor Center** (daily 9am–5pm; ℡401/845-9123 or 1-800/976-5122, ⓦwww.gonewport.com), which can provide plenty of maps and advice. Also a transportation hub, the Gateway Center has ample (but not free) parking and is a base for mass transit. Peter Pan **buses** (℡1-888/751-8800) pull in here, as well as RIPTA buses ($1.50/trip; ℡401/781-9400, ⓦwww.ripta.com), which run regularly through town and to the beaches. Up the street at Ten Speed Spokes, 18 Elm St (Mar–Sept Mon–Fri 10am-6pm, Sat 10am–5pm, Sun noon–5pm, Oct–Feb closed Sun & Mon; ℡401/847-5609), rental **bikes** cost $5 per hour (or $25 a day) and are handy for getting to the quieter beaches.

Through the summer, the Newport Historical Society (℡401/846-0813, ⓦwww.newporthistorical.org), at 82 Touro St, organizes various themed **walking tours** through Colonial Newport (from $8; information at ℡401/841-8770), while Viking Tours runs **bus** and **harbor excursions** from the Gateway Center ($12.50–48; may include admission to one or more mansions; ℡401/847-6921, ⓦwww.vikingtoursnewport). But the most relaxing way of getting a good look at the mansions and the town is a **schooner cruise** on the beautiful *Madeleine* (℡401/847-0298, ⓦwww.cruisenewport.com). The ship leaves several times daily from Bannister's Wharf, off America's Cup Avenue. The $27 price for a ninety-minute tour (or $35 for the sunset tour, which includes complimentary champagne, beer, or soda) is ultimately better value than a cheaper motorboat tour.

Accommodation

Though there are plenty of reasonably priced **guesthouses** in Newport, it's still a good idea to make reservations in advance, especially on summer weekends, when prices jump. The visitor center (see p.245) has free phone links to inns and motels in all price ranges. **B&Bs** are by far the most prevalent form of lodging. Two established agencies are Newport Reservations (☎401/842-0102 or 1-800/842-0102, ⓦ www. newportreservations.com), which can find rooms from as low as $125 in-season, and Bed & Breakfast Newport (☎401/846-5408 or 1-800/800-8765, ⓦ www.bbnewport .com), which specializes in smaller B&Bs you might otherwise find difficult to locate.

1855 Marshall Slocum Guest House 29 Kay St ☎401/841-5120 or 1-800/372-5120, ⓦ www. marshallslocuminn.com. Five unique rooms in an unpretentious B&B with a beautiful backyard garden. Friendly owners and gourmet breakfasts are a bonus. ⑥

Admiral Fitzroy Inn 398 Thames St ☎401/848-8000 or 1-866/848-8780, ⓦ www.admiralfitzroy.com. Cheerfully decorated B&B in the heart of town, with a roof deck overlooking the harbor. ⑥

Cliffside Inn 2 Seaview Ave ☎401/847-1811 or 1-800/845-1811, ⓦ www.cliffsideinn.com. Gorgeous Victorian manor house where guests are well-pampered, one minute from the Cliff Walk and First Beach. ⑨

Hotel Viking One Bellevue Ave ☎401/847-3300, ⓦ www.hotelviking.com. This Newport Institution was built in 1926 to house guests of the nearby mansion-owners and is still fit for the jet-setting crowd. ⑧

Howard Johnson Inn 351 W Main Rd, Middletown ☎401/849-2000 or 1-800/446-4656, ⓦ www. newporthojo.com. Just two miles from downtown Newport, a fairly standard budget chain, with well equipped rooms and an indoor pool. ⑤

William Gyles Guesthouse 16 Howard St ☎401/369-0243, ⓦ www.newporthostel.com. Designed for the backpacker, this hostel is not only clean, comfortable, and welcoming, but in the center of town. In summer weekends $59/night, weekdays $29, in winter $16/night and up.

The Town

Newport's main tourist draw is its magnificent **mansions**. Strolling around the predominantly Colonial **downtown** is a nice way to spend an afternoon, too, though the ever-growing profusion of souvenir shops is somewhat off-putting. When you tire of the opulence and the kitsch, head to the shoreline, to enjoy Newport's attractive **beaches**.

The mansions

The phrase "**conspicuous consumption**" was coined by sociologist Thorstein Veblen, who visited Newport circa 1900 and witnessed the desperate need of new, entrepreneurial **millionaires** to flaunt their wealth. More than just a summer resort, Newport became an arena in which families competed to outdo each other – though the "season" of wild and decadent parties lasted only a few weeks, and many of the multi-million-dollar mansions lay empty for months at a time. It's difficult to grasp the sheer wealth while gawking at the mansions' facades, but after being herded in and rushed through three or four of them, the opulence rapidly begins to pall. Unless you're especially interested, visiting one or two should suffice.

Of the dozen or so properties open for viewing, the most decadent stand on Bellevue Avenue. Both **Marble House**, with its golden ballroom and adjacent Chinese teahouse, and **Rosecliff**, with its colorful rose garden and heart-shaped staircase, were used as sets during the filming of *The Great Gatsby*. **Kingscote** is a quirky Gothic Revival cottage with a lovely interior, while the biggest and best of the lot, Cornelius Vanderbilt's **The Breakers**, on Ochre Point Avenue, just off Bellevue, is a sumptuous Italian Renaissance palace overlooking the ocean. All four mansions are run by the **Preservation Society of Newport County**, 424 Bellevue Ave (☎401/847-1000, ⓦ www.newportmansions.org), whose combination tickets slightly help to beat the hefty individual admission prices (June–Aug

△ Newport's mansions

daily 10am–5pm, *Breakers* opens at 9am; rest of year schedules vary; *Breakers* costs $15, all others $10; any five Society properties $31; some discounts available).

Independent from the Preservation Society mansions, the Astors' **Beechwood**, 580 Bellevue Ave (Feb to mid-May Thurs 3–4pm, Fri–Sun 10am–4pm, mid-May to Oct daily 10am–4pm, Nov–Dec schedule varies, closed Jan; $18; ⊤401/846-3772; ⓦwww.astorsbeechwood.com), is an entertaining antidote to the drier historical drills given on other tours. Costumed actors welcome visitors as house guests who have arrived for a party held by Mrs Astor, the self-proclaimed queen of American society (she devised the notion of the **Four Hundred**, an elite group of New York's long-standing well-to-do). Anecdotes, bitchy asides, and a constant stream of activity make it all great fun.

One way to see the Bellevue Avenue mansions on the cheap is to peer in the back gardens from the **Cliff Walk**, which begins on Memorial Boulevard where it meets First (Easton) Beach. This three-and-a-half-mile oceanside path alternates from pretty stretches lined by jasmine and wild roses to unappealing concrete underpasses through perilous rocks. For those with a car, Bellevue Avenue turns into Ocean Drive where the Cliff Walk ends, following the coast westwards. After it joins Ridge Road, you'll pass **Hammersmith Farm**, John and Jackie Kennedy's 28-room summer home (though it's closed to the public). The First Couple's wedding reception was held here in 1953.

Downtown Newport

Colonial Newport's political and business center, **Washington Square**, lies just south of the Gateway Center, beginning where Thames Street meets the **Brick Market**. The 1762 market, off **Long Wharf** (the most important of Newport's Colonial wharves), has been reconstructed to house galleries and pricey gift shops. Among them, the **Museum of Newport History** (mid-April to mid-June & Sept–Dec Thurs–Sat 10am–4pm, Sun 1–4pm; mid-June to Aug daily 10am–4pm; donation; ⊤401/841-8770) gives a good overview of the evolution of maritime Newport, displayed through photographs, artifacts, and interactive exhibits.

The oldest religious building in town is the 1699 Quaker **Great Friends Meeting House**, at Marlborough and Farewell streets, restored to its nineteenth-century appearance and completely free of adornment (June 15–Labor Day tours depart from the Museum of Newport History, call for hours; $5; ☎401/841-8770). The Quakers, like other religious sects, received a warm welcome in Rhode Island. Indeed, the state's penchant for religious tolerance is echoed by the presence of the elegant **Touro Synagogue**, 85 Touro St (call for hours; $5; ☎401/847-4794, ⓦwww.tourosynagogue.org). Built in 1763 and extensively restored, this oldest house of Jewish worship in America was modeled on Sephardic Jewish temples in Portugal and Holland. In 1790, Newport's Jewish community wrote to George Washington expressing their hopes for his new government; you can see his enthusiastic reply advocating religious liberty exhibited here.

Washington himself worshiped at the 1726 **Trinity Church** on Queen Anne Square, based on the Old North Church in Boston and the designs of Sir Christopher Wren ($2 donation; ☎401/846-0660). A few blocks south, **St Mary's Church**, Spring St and Memorial Blvd, is the oldest Catholic Church in Rhode Island, and the place where Jacqueline Bouvier married John Kennedy in 1953 (Mon–Fri 7.30–11am; free; ☎401/847-0475).

Apart from the mansions, Bellevue Avenue also has two museums of note. The **Newport Art Museum**, at no. 76, is housed in the 1864 mock-medieval Griswold House, and exhibits New England art from the last two centuries (late-May to early-Sept Mon–Sat 10am–5pm, Sun noon–5pm; closes at 4pm rest of year; $6; ☎401/848-8200, ⓦwww.newportartmuseum.com). At no. 194, the grand **Newport Casino** was an early country club, which held the first national tennis championship in 1881. It now houses the **International Tennis Hall of Fame Museum**, and still keeps its grass, clay and hard courts open to the public. The museum includes exhibits on tennis fashion – or what has passed for it – and trophies (daily 9.30am–5pm; $9; ☎401/849-3990 or 1-800/457-1144, ⓦwww.tennisfame.com).

The beaches

The attraction of Newport's shoreline, with its many coves and gently sloping sands, is slightly marred by the fact that several beaches are strictly private. Of those that are public, **Gooseberry Beach**, at the south, is surrounded by grand houses, while the lively town beach, **First** (or Newport, or Easton's) **Beach**, is at the east end of Memorial Boulevard; quieter **Second** and **Third** beaches are further along the same route toward Middletown. The visitor center (see p.245) provides info on all of these (most of which have parking fees of $8–15 per car).

Eating

Many of Newport's **restaurants** are geared to tourists and overpriced, though with a little hunting you can find some gems, even along touristy Thames Street. The **seafood** here is well worth the blowout if you have the extra cash.

Asterisk 599 Thames St ☎401/841-8833. Happening eatery in a former garage, with abstract paintings on the walls. Eclectic entrées ($21-36) include Crispy Duck and Chateaubriand. Dinner daily.
The Black Pearl Bannisters Wharf ☎401/846-5264. A Newport institution famous for its chunky clam chowder; get rowdy on the busy patio or repair to the Commodore Room for more formal dining.
Brick Alley Pub & Restaurant 140 Thames St ☎401/849-6334. Attracts a good mix of locals and tourists for moderately priced lunches, dinners, and cocktails; Sunday brunch is a feast.
Firehouse Pizza 595 Thames St ☎401/846-1199. Twelve-inch pan pizzas (thin crust on

request if it's quiet) eaten at kooky handpainted booths.

Flo's Clam Shack 4 Wave Ave ☎401/847-8141. A casual joint across from First Beach that hits the spot for cheap local seafood; chowder ("chowda") is the specialty. Closed Jan & Feb.

The Red Parrot 348 Thames St ☎ 401/847-3800. Chicken, seafood, and steaks with a Caribbean flare, as well as top-notch hot and frozen cocktails.

Salvation Café 140 Broadway ☎401/847-2620. A fun, funky spot off the beaten tourist track. International dishes like chicken tikka with coconut rice and Portuguese shellfish over orzo, at reasonable prices. Dinner daily summer, Thurs–Sun winter.

Smokehouse Cafe America's Cup Ave ☎ 401/848-9800. The *Smokehouse* – an oddity in Newport's world of seafood – has great barbeque for under $20 and a lively crowd. Closed Nov–Apr.

White Horse Tavern 26 Marlborough St ☎ 401/849-3600. Intensely atmospheric restaurant (the tavern first opened in 1687) serving hearty American fare, such as beef tenderloin, New England lobster stew, and Atlantic salmon. More affordably priced at lunchtime.

Festivals and nightlife

There is always something afoot in Newport, which is especially famed for its **Folk Festival** (🕸 www.newportfolk.com) held in late July or early August, and the **JVC Jazz Festival** (🕸 www.festivalproductions.net) that follows in mid-August. Most performances for both of these are held in Fort Adams State Park (information at ☎ 401/847-3700). The lesser-known but arguably more memorable **Newport Music Festival**, with a focus on classical music, unfolds over two weeks in July (☎ 401/846-1133, 🕸 www.newportmusic.org) at the mansions, while the **Irish Waterfront Festival**, held on Labor Day weekend with music, folk art, and step-dancing, is great fun (☎ 401/646-1600, 🕸 www.newportfestivals.com).

Otherwise, there is plenty of shamelessly unrefined **nightlife** around town. Noisy bars abound near the waterfront, and among the **live music venues** in town, two of the best are the *Newport Blues Cafe*, 286 Thames St (☎ 401/841-5510), for live jazz and blues nightly, and *One Pelham East*, at Thames and Pelham streets (☎ 401/847-9460), which has been hosting bands for over twenty years. At the safari-themed *Rhino Bar & Grille*, 337 Thames St (☎ 401/846-0707), original live bands (in the bar) and the best area DJs (playing dance, hip-hop, and techno in the Mamba Room) keep things hopping.

Connecticut

CONNECTICUT was named *Quinnehtukqut* by the Native Americans for the "great tidal river" that splits it in two before spilling out into the Long Island Sound, washing the old whaling ports of the coast. This small and densely populated state is a sort of conservative, high-rent suburb of New York City, where commuters earn Big Apple salaries while avoiding some New York state and city taxes. Its first white settlers arrived in the 1630s: refugees from Massachusetts seeking liberty, good farmland, and trading opportunities. Connecticut soon became a center for "**Yankee ingenuity**," prospering through the invention and marketing (often by notorious Yankee peddlers) of many a useful little household object. Although hit badly by English raids in the Revolutionary War, its role in providing the war effort with crucial supplies made it known as "**the provisions state**." After the war, the original charter of Connecticut's colonists was used as a model for the American Constitution, which gave rise to another nickname: "**the Constitution state**."

Connecticut continued to prosper during the eighteenth and nineteenth centuries, with steady industrialization and lucrative whaling along the coast. Today, much of the old industry has withered away, leaving areas of green countryside untroubled by noisy interstates, many verdant forests, and the idyllic rural villages that typify New England's quaint image. Unemployment and poverty plagues its larger cities, in particular, the rather dull capital city, **Hartford**, now host to the linchpins of Connecticut's economy – insurance companies, medical research, and military bases. **New Haven**, home to Yale University, has addressed (and significantly eased) the distinctly urban problems like drugs, homelessness, and crime, while nurturing a green and a buzzing culture.

Getting around Connecticut

Except for a few isolated areas in the north, Connecticut is well-connected with major **roads**: I-95 is the main interstate, running from New York to Rhode Island along the shore of the Long Island Sound. I-91 travels north from I-95 at New Haven, weaving its way along the Connecticut River to Vermont. It's a shame to miss out on the quiet countryside scenery along the side roads, so it's worth getting off the interstates if you can.

Greyhound and Peter Pan Trailways (T 1-800-343-9999, W www.peterpanbus.com) run **buses** to most of the main towns. Connecticut Transit buses (T 860/522-8101) serve the inland area around Hartford. Metro North (T 1-800-638-7646) **trains** carry passengers between New Haven and New York City, with connecting services to numerous other towns; Amtrak's line runs between New York City and Boston, with various stops along the shore and a connection to Hartford.

Southeastern Connecticut

The much-visited **southeastern coast** of Connecticut spans 25 miles from Stonington in the east to Niantic in the west, bisected by the Thames (pronounced "Thaymz") River. Each of the handful of tiny, picturesque Colonial communities and old whaling villages along the Long Island Sound is a mere stone's throw from the next. No longer are they the iniquitous ports that so inspired Melville, but they're still keen to preserve a sense of their history. The restored nineteenth-century **Mystic Seaport** justifies at least a day's visit, while nearby are the less lovely US Naval Submarine Base at **Groton** and the pretty fishing harbor of **Stonington Borough**.

Mystic

As purists will tell you, the town of **MYSTIC**, right on I-95, does not in fact exist; it is an area governed partly by Groton and partly by Stonington. Nonetheless, the old whaling port and shipbuilding center does have a small, well-kept, and somewhat touristy **downtown**, lined with typical New England–quaint clapboard galleries and antique shops. The old bridge across the bustling **Mystic River** that divides the town still opens hourly, and self-guided walking tours take in the many old houses built by well-off sea captains. The **Olde Mistick Village**, at the intersection of I-95 and US-27, is a pleasant enough outdoor mall, with over sixty upmarket shops in Colonial-style buildings. For a scenic walk or bike ride away from the tourists, take the four-mile River Road, winding along the western bank of the river, protected from cars and development (the road passes by Downes Marsh, an osprey sanctuary).

What brings the tourists to Mystic is the impeccably reconstructed seventeen-acre waterfront village of **Mystic Seaport**, where more than sixty weathered buildings house old-style workshops, an apothecary, stores, and a printing press (daily: April–Oct 9am–5pm; rest of year 10am–4pm; $17.50, children $12; ⊤ 1-888/9SEA-PORT, Ⓦ www.visitmysticseaport.com). Exhibits include exquisitely carved scrimshaw and a vast amount of products made from whales' wax-like spermaceti, and a film of a bloody whale capture. There are demonstrations of shanty-singing, fish-splitting, and sail-setting, among other salty pastimes, as well as storytelling and theater. Meanwhile, in the **shipyard**, you can watch the building, restoration, and maintenance of wooden ships. The *pièce de résistance* is the restored *Charles W. Morgan*, a three-masted wooden Yankee **whaling ship** built in 1841. The last of its kind, the *Morgan* is a remnant of an age of exploration and arrogant expansion. Done up ready to embark on a hypothetical two-year voyage, the ship is filled with whaling items; below deck, via perilously narrow stairs, the blubber room is crowded with huge iron try-pots (used to melt down the stinking blubber).

Over six thousand weird and wonderful sea creatures glug about the **Mystic Aquarium**, at exit 90 off I-95 (daily: March–Nov 9am–6pm; rest of year 10am–5pm; $17.50, children $12.50, good for three consecutive days; ⊤ 860/572-5955, Ⓦ www.mysticaquarium.org). Exhibits showcase African penguins, seals, rays, sea lions, and a beluga whale, and the explanations of the various creatures' behavior make this a step up from standard aquarium fare. For those interested in underwater exploration, there's the high-tech "Challenge of the Deep" and "Return to *Titanic*", hosted by Dr Robert Ballard, one of the team that found the sunken vessel.

△ Mystic, CT

Practicalities

Mystic has an **information office** in the Olde Mistick Village shopping mall (daily 9am–4.30pm; ☎860/536-1641 or 1-800/863-6569, ⓦ www.mysticinfo.com). The office lists current rates and books **accommodation**. Options include the *Comfort Inn* (☎860/572-8531 or 1-800/228-5150; ❹), *Days Inn* (☎860/572-0574 or 1-800/572-3993; ❺), and the *Best Western Sovereign Hotel* (☎860/536-4281 or 1-800/528-1234; ❹); all of these are on Whitehall Avenue (just off exit 90 on I-95), and all are handy for the Seaport. Two posher options are the grand *Inn at Mystic*, a Colonial Revival mansion hidden away at the junction of routes 1 and 27 (☎860/536-9604 or 1-800/237-2415, ⓦ www.innatmystic.com; ❻), and the *Whitehall Mansion*, 42 Whitehall Ave (☎860/572-7280; ❻), a painstakingly restored 1771 manor house, furnished with antiques and queen-sized canopy beds. The *Seaport* **campground** is on US-184 in Old Mystic, three miles from the Seaport (April–Oct; ☎860/536-4044, ⓦ www.seaportcampground.com; $29–36 per night for up to two adults and two children).

Without a doubt the best-known **restaurant** is *Mystic Pizza*, at 56 W Main St (☎860/536-3700), a small, family-run pizza place that continues to serve huge, inexpensive, and fresh "pies," unruffled by its movie-title status. The *Sea View Snack Bar*, on Hwy-27 between the visitor center and downtown (☎860/572-0096), serves seafood and sandwiches in a covered picnic area overlooking the Mystic River; *The Green Marble*, 8 Steamboat Wharf (☎860/572-0012), roasts its own coffee; and *Kitchen Little*, 81 1/2 Greenmanville Ave (6am–2pm; ☎860/536-2122), serves a mean breakfast along the riverfront.

Ten minutes' drive south, in the small fishing port of **NOANK**, the casual *Abbott's Lobster in the Rough*, 117 Pearl St (May–Aug daily noon–9pm; Sept to mid–Oct Fri–Sun noon–7pm; ☎860/536-7719), serves superb fresh steamed lobster, seafood, and traditional giant New England dinners at outdoor picnic tables.

Stonington Borough

STONINGTON BOROUGH, five miles east of Mystic, is a district within the town of Stonington. It's an overwhelmingly pretty old fishing village, originally Portuguese but now very New England, characterized by appealing whitewashed cottages, picket fences, and colorful flower gardens. Stonington Borough's main street, **Water Street**, is chock-a-block with antique shops and upmarket thrift stores, crowded with well-heeled bargain-hunters on the weekend.

The **Lighthouse Museum**, 7 Water St, dates from 1823, and is full of local memorabilia, maps, and drawings; fresh flowers everywhere add a nice touch. You can climb the stone steps and iron staircase for views over the water and to Connecticut's neighboring states (May–Oct daily 10am–5pm; $5; ☎860/535-1440). The waterfront itself is a great place to pass a few sunny hours, peaceful and quiet with a few bobbing fishing boats and clean water for swimming.

The most central **place to stay**, though not cheap, is *The Inn at Stonington*, 60 Water St (☎860/535-2000, ⓦ www.innatstonington.com; ❼), where sunny harbor views are available from the cozy rooms with large baths and some modern amenities. Authentic New England clam chowder, and full meals, can be had at *Noah's*, 113 Water St (☎860/535-3925), an old Portuguese **restaurant** with a friendly, trendy atmosphere and delicious home-baked cakes. Two seafood restaurants – *Water Street Café*, 142 Water St (☎860/535-2122), and *Skipper's Dock*, 66 Water St (☎860/535-0111) – are worth a visit; the former is elegant, the latter less expensive and noisier, with an open deck sporting fabulous ocean views.

Groton

Seven miles west of Mystic Seaport, **GROTON** is a suitably unpleasant name for the hometown of the **US Naval Submarine Base**, headquarters for the North Atlantic fleet. The **USS Nautilus**, the country's first nuclear-powered submarine, was built here in 1954, and four years later it became the first vessel to sail under the polar icecap. It's now moored on the Thames, and self-guided tours allow access to its terrifyingly claustrophobic corridors, one-person-wide in many places. The sub looks pretty much as it did in the 1950s, complete with pin-ups of Marilyn Monroe. The **Submarine Force Museum** next door has exhibits on the history of submersibles from the minuscule *American Turtle*, built in 1775, to the powerful *Trident* (hours vary; free; ☎860/694-3174 or 1-800/343-0079, ⓦwww.ussnautilus.org).

New London

NEW LONDON, opposite Groton on the west side of the Thames, is the closest thing southeastern Connecticut has to a city, although it spreads over only six square miles. Originally settled in 1646, New London was a wealthy whaling port in the nineteenth century. Today, it's home to the **US Coast Guard Academy**, off I-95 at 31 Mohegan Ave, where visitors can visit the training ship USS *Eagle* when it's in port, and wander around a museum of Coast Guard history (Mon–Fri 9am–4.30pm, Sat 10am–4.30pm, Sun noon–4.30pm; free; ☎860/444-8511). Overlooking the academy is the **Lyman Allyn Art Museum**, part of Connecticut College at 625 Williams St (Tues–Sat 10am–5pm, Sun 1–5pm; $5; ☎860/443-2545); it specializes in American Impressionist works and local decorative arts. From the **Southeastern Connecticut CVB** at 32 Huntington St (☎860/444-2206), you can pick up a self-guided walking tour map of downtown, and continue down the formerly prosperous Huntington Street, past the four adjacent Greek Revival mansions known as **Whale Oil Row**.

New London was the birthplace of boozy playwright **Eugene O'Neill**. His childhood home, the **Monte Cristo Cottage**, 325 Pequot Ave (call for hours at ☎860/443-0051; $7), is open for tours, complete with juicy details of his trauma-ridden early life – some alluded to in his autobiographical play *Long Day's Journey into Night*. The Eugene O'Neill Theater Center, 305 Great Neck Rd (exit 82 off I-95) in nearby **WATERFORD**, is an acclaimed testing ground for playwrights and actors where audiences can watch new, often experimental, shows in rehearsal (performances held sporadically May–Aug; ☎860/443-5378, ⓦwww.theoneill.org).

Ocean Beach Park, at 1225 Ocean Ave, has a sugar-sand beach and huge salt-water pool, as well as a wooden boardwalk, mini-golf and arcade (summer daily 9am–midnight; $12–16 per carload, or $5 for pedestrians).

Groton and New London practicalities

You can arrive in New London by **ferry** from Orient Point on Long Island (via Cross Sound Ferry, 2 Ferry St, ☎860/443-5281 in New England, ☎631/323-2525 on Long Island, ⓦwww.longislandferry.com). Reservations are strongly recommended. Greyhound serves New London, which is also the center of the far from comprehensive local **bus** system run by Southeast Area Transit ($1.25; ☎860/886-2631).

In New London, at the corner of Golden Street and Eugene O'Neill Drive, the **Trolley Info Station** has brochures and a helpful staff (June–Sept daily 10am–4pm; May & Oct Fri–Sun 10am–4pm; ☎860/444-7264). **Mystic Country Information,** 32 Huntington St (Mon–Fri 8.30am–4.30pm; ☎860/444-2206), can provide details on restaurants and local events. New London has reasonably priced **motels** along I-95, including the *Holiday Inn*, I-95 and Frontage Rd (℡860/442-0631 or 1-800/HOLIDAY, ⓦwww.holiday-inn.com; ❾), and the *Red Roof Inn*, 707 Colman St (℡860/444-0001 or 1-800/RED-ROOF, ⓦwww.redroof.com; ❸). In Groton there are plenty of budget motels off I-95 exit 86, including a *Super 8* (℡860/448-2818 or 1-800/800-8000; ❸).

New London has a few good **restaurants** worth stopping into, including *Timothy's*, 6 Guthrie Place (℡860/443-8411), for Continental cuisine overlooking Long Island Sound, or, on the cheaper side, the *Recovery Room*, 445 Ocean Ave (℡860/443-2619), an award-winning pizzeria.

Hartford

The unattractive modern capital of Connecticut, **HARTFORD**, in the center of the state on the Connecticut River, is also the insurance center of the United States. You can visit its High Victorian Gothic, gold-domed **state capitol**, sitting on a Bushnell Park hilltop, on one of the free tours (Mon–Fri, hourly from 9.15am–1.15pm, July and Aug until 2.15pm; April–Oct, also Sat 10.15am–2.15pm). Marginally more thrilling is the antique merry-go-round in the park, which gives jangling rides for $1 (May to mid-Oct, Tues–Sun, 11am–5pm). Housed in the Connecticut State Library, across the street at 231 Capitol Ave, the **Museum of Connecticut History** (Mon–Fri 9am–4pm, Sat 9am–3pm; free; ℡860/757-6535) holds Colt rifles and revolvers, and the desk at which Abraham Lincoln signed the Emancipation Proclamation.

Hartford's pride and joy is the Greek Revival **Wadsworth Atheneum**, at 600 Main St (Wed–Fri 11am–5pm, Sat & Sun 10am–5pm; $10; ℡860/278-2670). As the nation's oldest continuously operating public art museum, it holds some 45,000 pieces, among which are many fine and decorative arts. Residing here are Old Masters including Rubens' *The Return of the Holy Family from Egypt* and, in the French Impressionists collection, Renoir's *Monet Painting in His Garden at Argenteuil*. Lectures and films are put on at the Atheneum Theater; there's also an excellent café.

About a mile west of downtown Hartford on Hwy-4, a hilltop community known as Nook Farm was home in the 1880s to next-door neighbors **Mark Twain** and **Harriet Beecher Stowe**. Their Victorian homes, furnished much

---

Native American casinos

Connecticut has become home to two major Native American casinos, over objections from environmentalists, anti-gambling agencies, and residents. The massive **Foxwoods Casino and Resort**, Rte-2, Ledyard (℡1-800/FOXWOODS, ⓦwww.foxwoods.com), built by the Mashantucket-Pequot Indians, rises dramatically above the virgin pine forests north of New London and draws millions of visitors annually. The resort has three huge hotels, as well as all manner of slots, gaming tables, and bingo. Just a few miles away, the **Mohegan Sun Casino**, Rte-2A, Uncasville (℡1-888/226-7771, ⓦwww.mohegansun.com), opened its doors in 1996, as Foxwood's much smaller and quieter competitor. But after a $1 billion expansion effort, the Mohegan Sun, with its traditional Indian reverence for nature readily apparent in the planetarium ceiling and the crystal mountain installed on one of the casino walls, is more of a draw. That said, both casinos have plenty of restaurants and shops to pull even more of your cash away.

as they were then, are both open for tours. Twain lived at 351 Farmington Ave from 1874 until 1891, writing many of his classic works, including *Huckleberry Finn*. He spent a fair portion of his publishing royalties building and redecorating this outrageously ornate home, with its unusual black-and-orange brickwork and luxurious Tiffany stained-glass interior (daily Mon–Sat 9.30am–5.30pm, Sun noon–5.30pm, closed Tues Jan–April; $13; ☎860/247-0998).

At 77 Forest St, the home of Harriet Beecher Stowe reflects her Southern sensibility (Tues–Sat 9.30am–4.30pm, Sun noon–4.30pm; June to mid-Oct & Dec also open Mon 9.30am–4pm; $8; ☎860/522-9258). An ardent abolitionist, Stowe was the author of *Uncle Tom's Cabin*, one of the most important American literary works of the nineteenth century. She also found time to write about housekeeping ideals in the book she penned with her sister, *The American Woman's Home*. Inside her house you can see Stowe's writing table and some of her paintings.

Practicalities

Hartford, which lies at the junction of I-91 and I-84, is easily accessible by car. Greyhound, Peter Pan, and Bonanza **buses**, and Amtrak **trains**, all pull into Union Station, near the north side of Bushnell Park. For **information**, visit Hartford's **Convention & Visitors Bureau**, 31 Pratt St (Mon–Fri 8.30am–5pm; ☎860/728-6789 or 1-800/446-7811, ⓦwww.enjoyhartford.com), or pick up a copy of the free local weekly, *The Hartford Advocate*.

There are budget **motels** along I-91, including the *Super 8* (☎860/246-8888 or 1-800/800-8000, ⓦwww.super8motel.com; ❸) and the *Motel 6* (☎860/724-0222 or 1-800/843-7663; ❸), both of which are off exit 33. **Hotels** in Hartford proper cater mainly to business visitors and are correspondingly pricey, though they are more reasonable on the weekends – try the central *Crowne Plaza Downtown*, 50 Morgan St (☎860/549-2400; ❺). The HI-affiliated *Mark Twain Hostel*, 131 Tremont St (☎860/523-7255), charges $24. A popular **restaurant** is *Black Eyed Sally's*, 350 Asylum St (☎860/278-7427), which serves barbecue and hearty Cajun cooking, plus live blues Wednesday, Friday and Saturday. *Trumbull Kitchen*, 150 Trumbull St (☎860/493-7417), brings a bit of style to otherwise sedate Hartford, with a cross-cultural menu on offer in a modern, eclectic room. For something tasty and inexpensive, check out *Timothy's*, 243 Zion St (☎860/728-9822), popular with local artists (bring your own booze).

New Haven

I-91 leads south from Hartford to **NEW HAVEN**, on a large natural harbor at the mouth of the Quinnipiac River. Founded in 1638 by a group of wealthy Puritans from London, New Haven developed a solid economy based on shipping and, later, industry. In 1716 it became the seat of **Yale University**, the third oldest college in the States – but it was hardware, Winchester rifles, and other types of manufacturing (tools, carriages, and corsets) in the nineteenth century that really brought the city into its own. **Eli Whitney**, inventor of the revolutionary cotton gin, discovered in his workshop here a method of mass production that eliminated expensive skilled labor. Little manufacturing remains in New Haven, and the city has struggled for decades to revitalize and redevelop.

The resultant friction between the town's two sides (tension-ridden urbanity and Ivy League idyll) once made New Haven a somewhat uneasy place; however, town-versus-gown conflicts have now been minimized. New Haven is certainly less smug than many other Ivy League towns, and its ethnic diversity, alongside the undeniable vitality provided by the much-maligned Yalies, make it a stimulating place to visit.

Arrival, information, and getting around

New Haven lies where interstates I-91 and I-95 fork, and is on the main **train** line servicing Washington, New York, and Boston. The Amtrak terminal is in the colossal and nicely renovated **Union Station**, on Union Avenue six blocks southeast of the Yale campus downtown. To or from New York, the Metro-North Commuter Railroad (☏1-800/638-7646) is a better deal than Amtrak. Greyhound, Bonanza, and Peter Pan **buses** from Boston arrive at 45 George St (☏203/772-2470). On arrival, it's advisable to catch a cab to your hotel, as the bus and train terminals are in potentially dodgy areas. One reputable firm is Metro Taxi (☏203/777-7777).

The **Greater New Haven CVB** is at 169 Orange St (Mon–Fri 8.30am–5pm; ☏203/777-8550 or 1-800/332-STAY, ⊛www.newhavencvb.org). **Public transportation** to areas outside downtown is provided by Connecticut Transit, 470 James St ($1.25; ☏203/624-0151, ⊛www.cttransit.com), though service is poor after 6pm or so. Info New Haven, at 1000 Chapel St, two blocks east of the Green (the town's park), has bus schedules and route maps for the free downtown trolley.

Accommodation

For a college town, New Haven has surprisingly few **hotels**. Because of this, be sure to make reservations in advance if you're visiting during graduation in late May, start of term in late August, or October's Parents' Weekend. The few hotels that are downtown, although slightly overpriced, are worth it for their convenient location and safety.

Colony Inn 1157 Chapel St ☏203/776-1234, ⊛www.colonyatyale.com. Downtown luxury hotel furnished in Colonial style, with modern amenities. ⑤

Courtyard New Haven 30 Whalley Ave ☏203/777-6221. Recently renovated rooms in a good central location. ⑥

Historic Mansion Inn 600 Chapel St ☏203/865-8324 or 1-888/512-6278, ⊛www.thehistoricmansioninn.com. Cheery, high-ceilinged, comfy rooms in a restored 1842 home. Near Wooster Square. ⑥

Hotel Duncan 1151 Chapel St ☏203/787-1273. Comfortable rooms in an old-fashioned hotel, a few steps away from Yale, with singles available for around $45. ④

New Haven Hotel 229 George St ☏203/498-3100, ⊛www.newhavenhotel.com. Small quiet hotel with nice standard rooms and a health club with pool. ⑤

The City

New Haven's **downtown**, centering on the **Green**, remains both attractive and walkable, despite a succession of remarkably ugly buildings built during the 1950s that rather blighted New Haven. This area, laid out in 1638, was the site of the city's original settlement; around the Green are three churches, a grand library, and a number of stately government buildings. The park itself, used year-round for festivals like the annual JazzFest, is home to a handful of homeless residents. It also borders the student-filled district centered around College and Chapel streets, a genuinely lively place filled with bookstores, cafés, clubs, and hip clothing stores. There are some rough pockets, but in general New Haven is reasonably safe to walk around, even at night, and especially during term.

New Haven's prime attraction, **Yale University**, stands proudly right in the center of things. You can wander at will, though free, hour-long, student-led **tours** set off daily from the Yale Visitor Information Center at 149 Elm St, across from the north side of the Green (Mon–Fri 9am–4pm; Sat & Sun 11am–4pm; tours Mon–Fri 10.30am & 2pm, Sat & Sun 1.30pm; ☎203/432-2300); the Information Center also supplies maps for self-guided tours. The tours will have you trooping to and fro quite a bit, starting with the beautiful old spires and ivy-strewn cobbled courtyards of the old campus (mostly built in the 1930s, but painstakingly distressed to look suitably ancient). For student and visitor alike, foremost among campus buildings is the remarkable **Sterling Memorial Library**, 120 High St (daily, call for hours; free; ☎203/432-2798). Designed by alum James Gamble in modern Gothic style with fifteen buttresses, it has the symbolic appearance – inside and out – of a cathedral. Inside, leaded-glass windows illustrate the history of the Library, Yale, New Haven, and the history of books and printing; the would-be altar is the Circulation Desk, crowned with a fifteenth-century Italian-style mural. Also impressive, the **Beinecke Rare Books Library**, 121 Wall St, is where venerable manuscripts and delicate hand-printed books are viewed with the aid of natural light seeping through the translucent marble walls (Mon–Thurs 8.30am–8pm, Fri 8.30am–5pm, Sat 10am–5pm; free). Other buildings of interest include the modernist, Louis Kahn–designed **Center for British Art**, 1080 Chapel St, where British paintings range from Elizabethan portraits to modern works by Peter Blake and Francis Bacon (Tues–Sat 10am–5pm, Sun noon–5pm; free; ☎203/432-2800). The impressive **Yale University Art Gallery**, just across the road at 1111 Chapel St (Tues–Sat 10am–5pm, Sun 1–6pm; closed mid-July to Aug; free; ☎203/432-0600), is the nation's oldest university art collection, and holds American decorative arts, regional design and furniture, and African and pre-Columbian works. A quirky **Collection of Musical Instruments** is at 15 Hillhouse Ave (limited hours, phone ahead ☎203/432-0822), and the **Peabody Museum of Natural History**, 170 Whitney Ave (Mon–Sat 10am–5pm, Sun noon–5pm; $7; ☎203/432-5050), is a solid nineteenth-century collection of fossils, ancient culture artifacts, and skeletons.

Another source of New Haven affection and pride is its close-knit **Italian District**, based since 1900 among the well-kept brownstones and colorful window boxes of **Wooster Square** (just beyond Crown Street southeast of the Green). This was where the city's original Italian immigrants settled when they came to work on the railroad. There's little to see here, but there are some incredibly popular restaurants, and it's well worth stopping by when there's a festival on.

Eating

You can't leave New Haven without trying the local **pizza** (known here as tomato pies). The *New York Times* discovered New Haven's pizzas years ago, and since then queues are standard at all the family pizza places on Wooster Street; note that most of these don't open until late afternoon. Also check out the many fairly priced, innovative restaurants around the Green, on College and Chapel streets.

Atticus Bookstore Café 1082 Chapel St ☎203/776-4040. Salads, soups, sandwiches, brioches, and good coffee, in a relaxed bookstore open until midnight.
Claire's Corner Copia 1000 Chapel St ☎203/562-3888. Eclectic and casual Mexican and Middle Eastern food, including vegetarian dishes.
Frank Pepe's Pizzeria 157 Wooster St ☎203/865-5762. Most popular of the Wooster Street restaurants; plain, functional, and friendly, with huge "combination pies" baked in coal-fired ovens.

Ibiza 39 High St ☎203/865-1933. A bright, mural-filled place with diverse tapas, meals, and wines from Spain.
Louis' Lunch 263 Crown St ☎203/562-5507. Small, dark, and ancient burger house that claims to have served the first hamburger in the US, and presents the meat between two slices of toast. Highly popular and worth the inevitable wait. Closed Sun and Mon.
Moka 141 Orange St ☎203/752-0052. Friendly, earthy coffee-and-hot-chocolate bar frequented by hip intellectuals and fashionable locals. Drinks,

desserts, and light meals (crepes, yogurt, sandwiches) served until 6pm daily.
Roomba 1044 Chapel St, Sherman's Alley ⓣ203/562-7666. Innovative Nuevo Latino cuisine, with mojitos, in a stylish room. Trendy and loud.

Yankee Doodle 260 Elm St ⓣ203/865-1074. Yalies' favorite coffee shop, with original Fifties fittings and shop sign, serving greasy-spoon favorites such as burgers and cherry Cokes.

Performing arts and nightlife

New Haven has an undeniably rich **cultural scene**, and is especially strong on **theater**. The Yale Rep Company, 1120 Chapel St (ⓣ203/432-1234), which boasts among its eminent past members Jodie Foster and Meryl Streep, turns out consistently good shows during the school year. The Long Wharf Theater, 222 Sargent Drive, just off I-95 (ⓣ203/787-4282), has a nationwide reputation for quality performances, as does the refurbished Shubert Theater, 247 College St (ⓣ203/562-5666).

There are several good **bars** and **clubs**, mostly concentrated on College, Chapel and Crown streets. The *New Haven Advocate*, a free news and arts weekly, has comprehensive listings.

Bar 254 Crown St ⓣ203/495-8924. Plain name and decor, but look out – this is where New Haven comes to drink home-brewed beer in quantity (brick-oven pizzas also available). Serves the gay community on Alternative Night on Tuesdays.
Café Nine 250 State St ⓣ203/789-8281. Decades-old intimate, divey club with live music every night, be it jazz jams, blues, or alt-country. Cover $4–10.
Gotham Citi 130 Crown St ⓣ203/498-2484. Large, steamy club where revelers head for a late night of drinking, dancing, and simply looking good. Open Wed–Sun.

The Playwright 144 Temple St ⓣ203/752-0450. Five bars, ranging from rowdy pub to dance club, inside a church bought in Ireland, dismantled, and reassembled here. An unusual must-see.
Toad's Place 300 York St ⓣ203/624-8623. Mid-sized nationally renowned live music venue, where the likes of Springsteen and the Stones used to "pop in" occasionally to play impromptu gigs. Tickets $10–25.

New Hampshire

Long after sailors, fishermen, and agricultural colonists had domesticated the entire coastline of New England, the harsh, glacier-scarred interior of **NEW HAMPSHIRE**, with its dense forests and forbidding mountains, remained the exclusive preserve of the Abenaki Indians. Only the few miles of seashore held sizeable seventeenth-century communities of European settlers, such as the one at **Portsmouth**.

Even when the Indians were finally driven back, following the defeat of their French allies in Canada, the settlers could make little agricultural impact on the rocky terrain of this "granite state." Towns such as Nashua, Manchester, and Concord grew up in the fertile **Merrimack Valley**, but not until the Industrial Revolution made possible the development of water-powered **textile mills** did the economy take off. For a while, ruthless **timber** companies looked set to strip all northern New Hampshire bare, but they were brought under control when the state recognized that the pristine landscape of the **White Mountains** might turn out to be its greatest asset. Large-scale **tourism** began towards the end of nineteenth century; at one time fifty trains daily brought travelers up to Mount Washington.

Ever since becoming the first American state to declare independence, in January 1776, New Hampshire has been proud to go its own idiosyncratic way. The absence of a sales tax, or even a personal income tax, is seen as a fulfillment of the state motto, "Live Free or Die." The state has long gained inordinate political clout as the venue of the first **primary election** of each presidential campaign, with its villages well used to playing host to would-be world leaders.

The state's hiking, climbing, cycling, and **skiing** opportunities are enjoyed both by energetic locals and by the many visitors who drive up from Boston and New York. The major destinations are **Lake Winnipesaukee**, and **Conway**, **Lincoln**, and **Franconia** in the mountains further north. Some of these have grown rather too large and commercial for their own good, but the lakes, islands, and snowcapped peaks themselves remain spectacular. To see the bucolic rural scenery more usually associated with New England, take a detour off the main roads up the Merrimack Valley – to **Canterbury Shaker Village** near Concord or the **Robert Frost Farm** close to Nashua.

Getting around New Hampshire

Three **Interstate highways** run through New Hampshire: I-89 connects the state capital, Concord, with Vermont; I-95 runs along the short stretch of New Hampshire coastline that separates Massachusetts and Maine; and I-93 is the main north–south road, giving southern New England access to the White Mountains. In the mountains themselves, the 35-mile Kancamagus Highway between Lincoln and Conway is the most traveled of a number of **scenic routes** found across the state.

Concord Trailways (☎1-800/639-3317, ⊛www.concordtrailways.com), C&J Trailways (☎603/430-1100 or 1-800/258-7111, ⊛www.cjtrailways.com), and Vermont Transit Lines (☎1-800/642-3133 in Vermont, or 1-800/451-3292 elsewhere, ⊛www.vermonttransit.com) all run from Boston to either the Nashua–Concord corridor or the coast. Only a few services on Concord Trailways continue north to the Lakes Region and stops in the White Mountains. **Train** service is limited to Amtrak's *Downeaster*, which links Boston to Portland, Maine, stopping in New Hampshire at the sleepy towns of Exeter, Durham, and Dover.

The coast

Of all the US states with ocean access, New Hampshire has the shortest coastline – just eighteen miles. Driving north from Boston along either I-95 or the quieter Rte-1, you enter New Hampshire after roughly forty miles, to be confronted almost immediately by the **Seabrook Station** nuclear power plant, which opened in 1990 after years of determined opposition, not least from neighboring Massachusetts.

HAMPTON BEACH, a little further on, is a traditional family-oriented, if somewhat tacky, seaside resort (its free information line has the optimistic number ☎1-800/GET-A-TAN). The usual assortment of motels and fast-food places lines the approaches to the boardwalk and crowded beaches, but in a place this close to Boston, summer **accommodation** rates can be high. The *Breakers by the Sea Motel*, 409 Ocean Blvd (☎603/926-7702, ⊛www.breakersbythesea.com; ❸), is one of the least expensive options, offering spacious one- or two-bedroom apartments along with its regular rooms.

Portsmouth

New Hampshire's oldest community, **PORTSMOUTH**, might look like a major city on the map, but once there, you'll find a small-town accessibility blended with the enthusiasm of a rejuvenated city. This quality places it well above some of the more tourist-focused communities along the coast. Its position at the mouth of the Piscataqua River has always made it an important port – it was the state capital until 1808 – but it has barely grown, and the spire of **North Church** in the central **Market Square**, dating from 1854, remains the tallest structure in town.

Of a striking selection of grand **Colonial homes**, the 1761 gambrel-roofed, boxy, yellow **John Paul Jones House**, 43 Middle St, at State (mid-May to mid-Oct daily 11am–5pm; $8; ☎603/436-8420), is the most distinctive. In **Prescott Park** along the waterfront, the **Sheafe Warehouse Museum** (summer only; free; ☎603/436-2848) has a fascinating collection of mostly nautical paraphernalia.

Indeed Portsmouth's fortunes have long rested with its **naval shipyard**, visible across the bay (in Kittery, Maine; see p.280). Founded in 1800 by John Paul Jones as the US government's first shipyard, it has remained active ever since – it launched 31 submarines in 1944 alone, and built its first Polaris **nuclear submarine** in 1961.

Strawbery Banke

The lack of any great pressure on space has made it possible to preserve ten acres of Portsmouth's original site as **Strawbery Banke**, 64 Marcy St (May–Oct daily 10am–5pm $15; Nov–April Sat 10am–2pm, Sun noon–2pm $10; tickets good for two consecutive days; ☎603/433-1100, ⓦwww.strawberybanke.org). The area serves as a living museum full of buildings from Portsmouth's past, most of which you can explore either on a guided tour (Nov–April) or on your own (several of the houses have well-informed attendants). The area began life as the residence of wealthy shipbuilders, and was successively the lair of privateers and a red-light district before turning into respectable – and, in the 1950s, ultimately decaying – suburbia. It was then decided to recreate its former appearance, mainly by clearing away the newer buildings.

Each building is shown in its most interesting former incarnation, whether that be 1695 or 1955. The 1766 **Pitt Tavern** holds most historic significance, having served as a meeting place during the Revolution for patriots and loyalists. Officially an educational institution, Strawberry Banke offers year-round lectures and courses on traditional crafts. Some of these can be viewed in the **Dinsmore Shop**, where an infinitely patient cooper manufactures barrels with the tools and methods of 1800, as well as the **Mills Zoldak pottery shop**, which produces attractive low-priced ceramics.

Practicalities

Vermont Transit Lines **buses** (☎1-800/552-8737) stop in Market Square, en route between Boston and Portland, Maine. You can pick up **information** from the **visitor center** at 500 Market St, about a 10-minute walk from Market Square (Mon–Fri 8.30am–5pm; June–Sept also Sat & Sun 10am–5pm; ☎603/436-1118, ⓦwww.portsmouthchamber.org), or, during summer only, from the kiosk in Market Square (daily 9am–5pm). Portsmouth Harbor Cruises (☎603/436-8084 or 1-800/776-0915, ⓦwww.portsmouthharbor.com) is one of several operators offering **boat trips**, from $11.

Accommodation in the town center is restricted to expensive places such as the grand *Sise Inn*, 40 Court St (☎603/433-1200 or 1-877/747-3466, ⓦwww.siseinn. com; ❾), a nicely preserved Queen Anne–style house with large rooms; the peaceful, rambling seven-room *Inn at Strawbery Banke*, 314 Court St (☎603/436-7242 or 1-800/428-3933, ⓦwww.innatstrawberybanke.com; ❺); and the waterfront *Bow Street Inn*, 121 Bow St (☎603/431-7760, ⓦwww.bowstreetinn.com; ❺). Cheaper motels near the traffic circle where I-95 and Rte-1 bypass include the good-value *Port Inn*, Rte-1 Bypass South (☎1-800/282-PORT, ⓦwww.theportinn.com; ❹).

Portsmouth likes to bill itself, with some justification, as the "food capital of New England." Of the in-town **restaurants**, *The Oar House*, 55 Ceres St (☎603/436-4025), has excellent, moderately-priced seafood, along with great river views and an outdoor seating area; *Anthony Alberto's*, 59 Penhallow St (☎603/436-4000), is a gourmet Italian restaurant with a strong wine list; and funky *Friendly Toast*, 121 Congress St (☎603/430-2154), makes for an inexpensive breakfast and lunch spot, with generous portions.

At night, the *Portsmouth Brewery*, 56 Market St (☎603/431-1115), serves up exceptional microbrews and occasional live music, while *The Press Room*, 77 Daniel St (☎603/431-5186), has jazz, blues, folk, or bluegrass performances every night. Those searching for caffeine rather than alcohol will be happy at *Breaking New Grounds* (☎603/436-9555) in Market Square.

Odiorne Point State Park

The one brief patch of semi-wilderness along the New Hampshire coast is, ironically, where the first white settlers landed in 1623. Some of the scattered ruins in the marshy duneland of **Odiorne Point State Park** ($3; ☎603/436-7406) date from those early days; others, far more modern, were World War II defenses. The two park entrances are on Hwy-1A near **Rye**, four miles southeast of Portsmouth. The offshore **Isles of Shoals**, a supposed haunt of Blackbeard the pirate, can be visited by taking a boat trip from Portsmouth Harbor ($24; ☎603/431-5500 or 1-800/441-4620, ⓦwww.islesofshoals.com).

The Merrimack Valley

The financial and political heartland of New Hampshire is the **Merrimack Valley**, which – first by water and now by road – has always been the main thoroughfare north to the White Mountains and Québec. None of its towns is of any great interest to tourists, though all are equipped with relatively inexpensive motels.

MANCHESTER, like its namesake in England, was a major nineteenth-century cotton producer. Its massive Amoskeag Mills closed in the 1930 and the city is now notable mainly for the paintings in the **Currier Museum of Art**, 201 Myrtle Way (currently closed for expansion through early 2008; ☎603/669-6144, ⓦwww.currier.org), and the museum-affiliated, Frank Lloyd Wright-designed Zimmerman House (call ☎603/668-0256 for schedule, closed Jan–Apr; $11). The focal point of **CONCORD** is the gold dome of the State House on Main Street (Mon–Fri 8am–4.15pm; ☎603/271-2154), the seat of New Hampshire's state legislature – the largest in the country, with some four hundred members. Local schoolteacher Christa McAuliffe, a victim of the *Challenger* shuttle tragedy, is commemorated by a planetarium, at 3 Institute Drive, off I-93, exit 15E (Mon–Sat 10am–5pm, Sun noon–5pm; $8; ☎603/271-7827, ⓦwww.starhop.com).

About twenty miles north of Concord, off I-95, exit 18, 288 Shaker Rd, **Canterbury Shaker Village** (daily: May–Oct 10am–5pm; Nov weekends 10am–4pm, call other times; $15, good two consecutive days; ☎603/783-9511, ⓦwww.shakers.org) was the sixth Shaker community to be founded by Ann Lee (in 1774), and was 300-strong by 1860. Three different hour-long tours explain the Shaker way of life. There are craft demonstrations (such as basket-making) and even frequent all-day craft workshops if you're so inclined. The 🍴 *Shaker Table* restaurant near the village entry serves delicious and imaginative Shaker-inspired food. South of Concord, outside Derry just off Rte-28 (take exit 4 from I-93), the **Robert Frost Farm** (mid-June to early Sept Wed–Sat 10am–5pm, Sun noon–5pm; mid-May through mid-June Sat & Sun 10am–5pm; entry free, tour $7; ☎603/432-3091) has been evocatively restored to its condition when New England's poet laureate lived here from 1900 to 1911. Displays in the barn highlight his work, and a half-mile "poetry nature trail" leads past the sites that inspired many of his best-known poems.

The Lakes Region

Of the literally hundreds of lakes created by snowmelt flowing south from the White Mountains and occupying the state's central corridor, the biggest by far is **Lake Winnipesaukee**, which forms the center of the vacation-oriented Lakes Region. Long segments of its 300-mile shoreline, especially in the east, consist of thick forests sweeping down to waters dotted with little islands, which are disturbed only by pleasure craft. The most sophisticated of the towns along the shoreline is **Wolfeboro**; the most fun has to be **Weirs Beach**.

Ideally, you would bring your own small boat here and get thoroughly lost in the maze of small channels and islets. Failing that, the **cruise ship** *Mount Washington*, a 230-foot monster of a boat, departs from the dock in the center of Weirs Beach several times a day to sail to Wolfeboro, on the western side of the lake (mid-May to Oct; from $20; ☎603/366-5531 or 1-888/843-6686, ⓦwww.cruisenh.com). The ship also sets sail for dinner and dance cruises several times per week (from $39). Other day-cruises are available on the smaller *MV Doris E* ($10) and the US mail boat, *MV Sophie C* ($20), from which you can view some of the lake's many islands as the boat delivers the mail.

Wolfeboro

Because Governor Wentworth of New Hampshire built his summer home nearby in 1768, tiny **WOLFEBORO** claims to be "the oldest summer resort in America." Sandwiched between lakes Winnipesaukee and Wentworth, it has little to show for that history, but it's a relaxing place to spend a few hours, especially along the short but bustling main street, next to the quay where the *Mount Washington* (see above) comes in.

For **accommodation**, the 1812 *Wolfeboro Inn*, 90 N Main St (☎603/569-3016 or 1-800/451-2389, ⓦwww.wolfeboroinn.com; ❺), stands in a dignified waterfront position just a few yards from the town proper. The *Tuc' Me Inn B&B*, 118 N Main St (☎603/569-5702, ⓦwww.tucmeinn.com; ❺), is a homey place with tastefully furnished rooms, close to both the town and lake. *Wolfeboro Campground* is on Haines Hill Road (☎603/569-9881; $16), and is open mid-May to mid-October. For **food**, *Wolfe's Tavern*, at the *Wolfeboro Inn*, serves good-value steaks, seafood, burgers, and sandwiches, as does *Garwoods*, 6 N Main St (☎603/569-7788), with its dining room overlooking the bay. *Lydia's Café*, 33 N Main St (☎603/569-3991), is an excellent, veggie-oriented place for breakfast, lunch, or smoothies (open daily until 3pm).

The eastern shore of Lake Winnipesaukee makes for great walking. One fascinating stopoff, a few miles north of Wolfeboro on Hwy-109, is the curious **Libby Museum** (June to mid-Sept Tues–Sat 10am–4pm, Sun noon–4pm; $2;

603/569-1035), where dentist Henry Forrest Libby's obsession with evolution is illustrated by various ineptly stuffed animals, and the skeletons of bears, orang-utans, and humans. There's also a mastodon's tooth, and a fingernail supposedly pulled out by its Chinese owner to demonstrate his new Christian faith. The front steps of the museum command a superb view over the lake.

Weirs Beach and Loudon

The short boardwalk at **WEIRS BEACH**, the very essence of seaside tackiness (even if it is fifty miles inland), is in summer the social center of the Lakes Region. Its little wooden jetty throngs with vacationers, the amusement arcades jingle with cash, and there's even a neat little crescent of sandy beach, suitable for family swimming. The better of its two **water parks** is Surf Coaster (daily: mid-June to early Sept 10am–6pm; $27; 603/366-5600) on Hwy-11B south of town, which offers dramatic rides and a powerful wave machine. A quieter diversion here is the **Winnipesaukee Railroad** (early June & Sept–Oct weekends; daily mid-June to early Sep; $10 for 1hr, $11 for 2hrs; 603/279-5253, www.hoborr.com), which operates scenic trips along the lakeshore between Weirs Beach and Meredith.

In **LOUDON**, about eight miles south of Laconia on Hwy-106, the New Hampshire International Raceway (603/783-4931, www.nhis.com) hosts NASCAR races on a regular basis, May through October. Even at quieter times, room rates in nearby Laconia are high; the best choice is the *Landmark Inn of the Lakes Region*, 480 Main St, Laconia (603/524-8000; ⑤), though other motel options are abundant along Rte-3 between Weirs Beach and Meredith (see below). The heartiest place to eat is *Water Street Café*, 141 Water St, Laconia (603/524-4144), which serves healthy helpings of old-fashioned food for breakfast, lunch, and dinner. The nearest **campground** is *Gunstock*, just past Gilford on Rte-11A (1-800/486-7862, www.gunstock.com; $25 a night for up to two adults and three children).

Meredith

Four miles north of Weirs Beach, **MEREDITH**, the last of Lake Winnipesaukee's resorts, enjoys a peaceful location and has an upscale character, making it the best place to stay on the lake's western shore. The *Inns at Mill Falls*, which is actually four separate hotels (1-800/622-6455, www.millfalls.com; ⑥), are the best choice for **accommodation**. Choose from the *Inn at Mill Falls* and the *Chase House*, both on the hill overlooking the lake, or the *Inn at Bay Point* or the new *Church Landing*, directly on the water and offering unrivalled lake views. *Mame's*, 8 Plymouth St (603/279-4631), serves gargantuan servings of seafood, chicken, and steak **dinners** in an old village home.

North to the mountains

Hwy-25 northeast from Meredith leads eventually to Conway in the White Mountains; US-3 northwest, on the other hand, keeps you in the Lakes Region a little longer, leading past **Squam Lake**, where portions of the movie *On Golden Pond* were filmed. Educational tours of the **Squam Lake Natural Science Center** at **Holderness** (daily: May–Oct 9.30am–4.30pm; $13; 603/968-7194, www.nhnature.org) lead through a largely natural landscape, in which animals such as deer, bobcat, otters, bears, and foxes are kept in enclosures. Squam Lake Tours (May–Oct, three tours daily; $15; 603/968-7577, www.squamlaketours.com) offers two-hour boat tours of the lake, where the focus is on observing endangered loons.

The White Mountains

Thanks to their accessibility from both Montréal to the north and Boston to the south, the **White Mountains** have become a year-round tourist destination, popular with summer hikers on the Appalachian Trail and winter skiers on the slopes. Commercialized they may be, with considerable tourist development flanking some of the highways, but the great granite massifs retain most of their majesty and power. **Mount Washington**, the highest peak in the Northeast, can claim some of the most severe weather in the world, and conditions are harsh enough for the timberline to lie at four thousand feet (compared to the Rockies' norm of ten thousand).

Just a few high passes – here called "**notches**" – pierce the range, and the roads through these gaps, such as the **Kancamagus Highway** between Lincoln and Conway, make for enjoyable driving (compulsory **parking permits** are $3 for one day, or $5 for seven consecutive days). However, you won't really have made the most of the White Mountains unless you also set off, on foot or on skis, across the long expanses of thick evergreen forest that separate them, with snowcapped peaks poking out in all directions. The best sources of **information** in the region are the White Mountains Visitor Center, at I-93 exit 32 in North Woodstock (daily 8.30am–5.30pm; ☎603/745-8720 or 1-800/FIND-MTS, ⓦwww.visitwhitemountains.com) and the Appalachian Mountain Club's info center at Pinkham Notch, Rte-16 (daily 6.30am–10pm; ☎603/466-2721, ⓦwww.outdoors.org).

White Mountains accommodation

Thanks to the influx of young hikers and skiers to the White Mountains, there's a relative abundance of **budget** accommodation in the area. From the hostel-esque lodges at Crawford and Pinkham notches, to reasonably priced inns and B&Bs – where bargaining at quiet times often pays off – there's sure to be an option to

---

Hiking, skiing, and cycling in the White Mountains

Hiking in the White Mountains is coordinated by the **Appalachian Mountain Club** (AMC), whose chain of information centers, hostels, and huts along the Appalachian Trail, traversing the region from northeast to southwest, is detailed below. Call ☎603/466-2725 for trail and weather information, and pick up a copy of the *AMC White Mountain Guide* ($23) before you attempt any serious expedition.

Downhill and cross-country **skiers** can choose from several resorts that double up as summertime activity centers. Both the Waterville Valley Resort (☎603/236-8311 or 1-800/468-2553, ⓦwww.waterville.com) and Loon Mountain (☎603/745-8111 or 1-800/229-LOON, ⓦwww.loonmtn.com), both just east of I-93, are good for downhill, while Jackson (☎603/383-9355, ⓦwww.jacksonxc.org), about fifteen miles north of Conway on Rte-19, has some of the finest cross-country skiing trails in the Northeast. General information on the skiing centers is available from Ski NH, PO Box 10, North Woodstock, NH 03262; ☎603/745-9396 or 1-800/88SKI-NH, ⓦwww.skinh.com.

Though obviously the hills can make for strenuous **biking**, there are easier ways of enjoying the White Mountains from the saddle, such as taking lifts up the slopes (at the resorts mentioned above) and riding back down. In summer, many of the cross-country skiing trails are taken over by bikers, and provide relatively flat, scenic terrain. Bikes can be rented from All Seasons Adventures in Lincoln ☎603/745-8600 and from Joe Jones Sports on Main Street in North Conway (☎603/356-9411, ⓦwww.joejonessports.com).

In a country where a deli sandwich can make a meal for two, where all-you-can-eat buffets are destinations in themselves, and where restaurants dish up 72oz steaks, food is clearly something to be taken seriously. Even in this fast-food nation, however, it's not always about quantity – dining out in the USA can be an absolute delight. Anyone setting off on a road trip will find something irresistibly evocative about sitting in a vintage diner and chewing on a simple grilled-cheese sandwich while a gum-snapping waitress with big hair pours endless free refills of coffee and calls you darlin'. Fortunately, such quintessentially American experiences are always there for the taking, along with a host of other intriguing regional dining opportunities, and – all-you-can-eat buffets notwithstanding – some of the finest restaurants in the world.

From burgers to barbecue

No one knows exactly who invented the burger (you'll find scores of diners claiming it as their own), but it's a staple that's set to stay. Fans of the Golden Arches may not recognize the homemade, fresh, and tasty versions served up in a number of regional restaurants, but once they've tasted the real thing, a Happy Meal will never seem the same again. Another all-American staple, the hot dog, is for many the street food of choice – and comes in a variety of forms. Famous hot dog spots include New York City, where every July 4 *Nathan's* in Coney Island holds a world-famous hot-dog-eating contest, and Chicago, where the dog is served in a poppy-seed bun and *never* with ketchup. Over on the west coast, the frankfurter gives the traditional dog a Tex-Mex twist, wrapping it in a tortilla and smothering it in cheese and chili sauce. Other simple meaty takeout treats include the Philly cheesesteak, a dripping sandwich of hot sliced beef and rich melted cheese born on the streets of south Philadelphia, and New Orleans's muffuletta, in which a stack of spicy Italian cured meats is combined with piquant chopped olives and cheese and crammed into a huge round bun.

A Texas barbecue

Emotions run high when it comes to barbecue – smoked pork or beef shredded and drenched in tangy, spicy sauces – with locals from all the southern states and the cities of Memphis, Kansas City, and Chicago hotly claiming to serve the best in the world. Texas is where you'll find the best chili – and scores of hugely popular chili cookoffs, in which amateurs and professional restaurateurs alike battle for the coveted first place.

Though Chicago and Kansas City have some iconic steakhouses, when the really big guys fancy a really big steak they head straight for Texas or Western states like Montana and Wyoming. This is cattle-rearing country, so the slab of beef on your plate couldn't be fresher – or any more huge.

New England clam chowder

Seafood

When it comes to seafood, America's coastline offers some of the world's best pickings. Crab is king all along the Mid-Atlantic shore, with steamed blue crabs and spicy soft-shell crabs a particular treat around Chesapeake Bay, and stone-crab claws abounding in Florida. In New England you can feast on giant Maine lobsters and steamers (clams), often cooked up in a creamy chowder, while any trip to Louisiana should see you slurping back salty fresh raw oysters and a mound of juicy mudbugs (crawfish) boiled with spices. Florida offers conch, a meaty mollusc, while catfish, a firm-fleshed, tasty fish (which, unlike most white fish, is particularly good when breaded and fried), is a staple in the south. Although they consume more than half the Spam eaten in the entire nation, the Hawaiian islands also offer some of the finest Pacific Rim restaurants on earth, their light, healthy cuisine fusing Asian, Pacific, and Californian staples and using lots of tasty local fish like mahi mahi (dorado), opah (moonfish, similar to swordfish), and ono (which translates as "delicious").

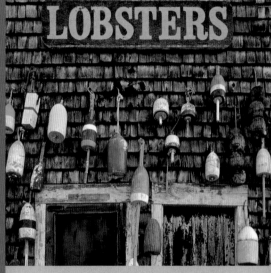
A lobster shack in Maine

Regional cuisine

The complex pattern of immigration in the US is writ large in its restaurant scene. San Francisco has its Chinatown, New York its Jewish delis, Boston its Italian restaurants, Miami its Cuban coffeeshops. Meanwhile, a number of regions have developed their own cuisines, combining local ingredients with dishes and techniques of local ethnic groups. In the soggy swamplands of southern Louisiana, for example, the French-speaking population cooks up a spicy stew called gumbo – made with okra, garlic, and bell peppers, and filled out with anything from chicken or pork sausage to crawfish – that was heavily influenced by the cooking of West African slaves. This Cajun cooking, as rustic as it is, has similarities with Creole cuisine, its more urban cousin. Thus you'll often find fragrant gumbos served up in grand, old-guard New Orleans restaurants, alongside delicate shrimp *étouffé* ("smothered" in a flavorful sauce) and oysters *en brochette*.

Soul food

Rich, filling, and irresistible – crispy Southern fried chicken is a taste sensation that bears no relation to the stuff churned out by Colonel Sanders – Southern cuisine, or soul food, makes the perfect comfort food. Simple home cooking this may be, but some of its staple dishes can sound baffling to newcomers. Take the unappetizing sounding grits, for example. Far from gritty, these are in fact a rather tasty gloop of ground corn cooked with butter and salt and served steaming hot. Commonly eaten with breakfast, they're also delicious with shrimp or spicy pork sausage. Collard greens is a cabbage dish, chitlins pork sweetmeats, and a hush puppy a deep-fried ball of corn flavored with onion. Ordering hoppin' john will get you a wholesome mix of black-eyed beans and rice, traditionally served on New Year's Day. Though most plates will come with a hunk of warm, crumbly cornbread, finished off with a dollop of melting butter, you might also come across Johnny cakes, smaller patties of cornflour, or hoecakes, a kind of corn pancake. Oh, and be sure to have a biscuit, a crumbly scone perfect for mopping up all that delicious gravy.

You can get authentic Mexican food all over the US, but Tex Mex is probably more familiar. A little spicier than Mexican, it adds guacamole (freshly made tableside at the best places), melted cheese, and chopped tomatoes with cilantro to the staple refried pinto beans (boiled, mashed, and fried into a filling sludge) and tortillas (thin corn or flour pancakes). Originally Mexican, tamales, wads of soft crumbly corn dough filled with shredded pork and chicken, cheese, and vegetables steamed in a corn husk, have spread throughout the southern states.

In the health-conscious 1980s, California created its own take on nouvelle cuisine, producing tiny plates of highly designed food made from fresh, local ingredients. This fad for so-called "Californian cuisine" soon spread nationwide, and evolved into New American Cuisine – a style of cooking that can be applied to any regional dish, usually giving it a healthy, modern edge. In New Mexico, Santa Fe also became nationally famous as a culinary capital in the 1980s, using Southwestern ingredients – chili peppers, jicama, piñons – to give a creative twist to Tex-Mex staples. Bizarrely, given the territory, Southwestern cuisine bases many of its dishes around fresh fish; it also manages to be both healthy and robust. Another, far less fancy Southwestern staple is Navajo frybread, which is similar to a taco, dished up with minced beef and chili, or, in New Mexico, with honey butter.

Greens, San Francisco, CA

suit every traveler. Keep in mind, too, that rates vary dramatically between seasons, and even from weekday to weekend.

Along the Appalachian Trail itself, there are eight **Appalachian Mountain Club huts**, which can only be reached on foot. In summer, each hut provides meals and bedding for between forty and ninety people. Prices range from $28 to $87 a night, according to the amount of privacy, luxury, and food you're after (and depending on whether or not you're an AMC member; individual membership is $40; see the website, Ⓦwww.outdoors.org, for details). **Reservations** are strongly recommended (call Ⓣ603/466-2727, or visit the website, above), and you'll be expected to pay in full when you book the accommodation.

Campers can pitch their tents anywhere below the treeline and away from the roads in the White Mountains National Forest, provided they show consideration for the environment. There are also numerous official campgrounds ($16–20 per night), particularly along the Kancamagus Highway.

The AMC runs a scheduled **shuttle van service** for hikers between major trailheads and the lodges daily from June to mid-September ($12), with weekend service through mid-October.

AMC lodges

Highland Lodge US-302, Crawford Notch Ⓣ603/466-2727, Ⓦwww.outdoors.org. Opened in late 2003, this innovatively designed and environmentally friendly building offers beds in a shared room for $36–59 or double rooms for $75–96, breakfast and dinner included. Private bath considerably more. Open year-round.

Joe Dodge Lodge Hwy-16, Pinkham Notch Ⓣ603/466-2727, Ⓦwww.outdoors.org. Filled with hikers, this second AMC lodge-cum-hostel has bunks for $43–54 or double rooms with meals for $65–76. Near the Mount Washington Auto Road. Open year-round.

Motels, hotels, and B&Bs

Adair Country Inn 80 Guider Lane, Bethlehem Ⓣ603/444-2600 or 1-888/444-2600, Ⓦwww.adairinn.com. Deluxe antique-furnished rooms, with sweeping views of the landscaped grounds, and an impeccable staff, all reflected in the steep prices. ❼

Balsams Dixville Notch Ⓣ1-800/255-0800 in NH or 1-800/255-0600 outside NH, Ⓦwww.thebalsams.com. Like the Mount Washington (see right), *Balsams* is another of the last grand White Mountains red-roofed resort hotels. Opened in the 1860s (under a different name and since expanded in 1918), the hotel has year-round activities (skiing, golf, tennis, boating), light and airy rooms, and delicious meals (cooking classes are available). ❻

Boulder Motor Court junction of routes 3 and 302, Twin Mountain Ⓣ603/846-5437, Ⓦwww.bouldermotorcourt.com. One- and two-bedroom cottages with kitchens, fireplaces, and other amenities. Vouchers for lift tickets available. ❸

Eagle Mountain House 2 Carter Notch Rd, Jackson Ⓣ603/383-9111 or 1-800/966-5779, Ⓦwww.

eaglemt.com. Highly atmospheric inn with a roaring fireplace in the lobby and a wraparound porch filled with rocking chairs, far above the bustle of North Conway. Has its own nine-hole golf course. ❸

Glen Oaks Inn Rte-16A, Intervale Ⓣ603/356-9772 or 1-877/854-6535, Ⓦwww.glenoaksinn.com. Welcoming B&B between North Conway and Jackson, where many of the rooms include a fireplace. Organizes inn-to-inn cross-country skiing and biking holidays in conjunction with other B&Bs. ❺

Franconia Inn Easton Valley Rd/Hwy-116, Franconia Ⓣ603/823-5542 or 1-800/473-5299, Ⓦwww.franconiainn.com. Comfortable 32-room inn two miles south of town, with great views. Makes for a good cross-country ski base. ❻

Hillwinds Lodge Dow Ave/Hwy-18, Franconia Ⓣ603/823-5551 or 1-866/906-5292, Ⓦwww.hillwinds-lodge.com. Standard, well-priced rooms, plus a riverside location and outdoor pool. ❸

Indian Head Resort US-3, Lincoln Ⓣ1-800/343-8000, Ⓦwww.indianheadresort.com. An unpretentious resort motel with plenty of facilities and outdoor activities. Climb the motel's observation tower for fine views of the surrounding hills. ❹

🏃 **Mount Washington Hotel** Rte-302, Bretton Woods Ⓣ603/278-1000 or 1-800/314-1752, Ⓦwww.mtwashington.com. Beautiful hotel dating from 1902, with a quarter-mile terrace, stellar views, indoor pool, and a complete range of activities (including golf, horseback riding, and skiing) and pricing packages. Also runs the less-fancy *Bretton Arms*, on the same property, which is much cheaper (❺), though rooms are still spacious. ❽

Thayer's Inn 111 Main St, Littleton Ⓣ603/444-6469 or 1-800/634-8179, Ⓦwww.thayersinn.com. Creaky but comfortable and classy old inn, which has hosted guests such as U.S. Grant and Richard Nixon. ❸

Franconia Notch

I-93, speeding up towards northern Vermont, and the more leisurely US-3 merge briefly about ten miles beyond **Lincoln** to pass through **Franconia Notch State Park**. From a roadside pullout you used to be able to look back and upwards to the **Old Man of the Mountain**, a natural rock formation resembling an old man's profile. However, in May 2003, this fragile formation, New Hampshire's ubiquitous state symbol, came tumbling down in high winds and heavy rain.

Franconia Notch itself is a slender valley crammed between two great walls of stone. From the park **visitor center** (May to late Oct daily 9am–5pm; ☎603/745-8391), you can, for $10, walk along a two-mile boardwalk-cum-nature trail to the **Flume** and look down at the Pemigewasset River as it rages through the narrow, rock-filled gorge. Alternatively, take an $11 **cable-car** ride up the sheer granite face of **Cannon Mountain** (mid-May to mid-Oct daily 9am–5pm; ☎603/823-8800, ⓦwww.cannonmt.com), or hike the various, well-marked trails up to panoramic views for free.

Further on, one mile south of the friendly village of **FRANCONIA**, the **Frost Place** on Ridge Road (June Sat & Sun 1–5pm; July to mid-Oct Wed–Mon 1–5pm; $4; ☎603/823-5510, ⓦwww.frostplace.org) is another former home of poet Robert Frost, memorable largely for an inspiring panorama of unspoiled mountains. Each summer the poet-in-residence will often give poetry readings during visiting hours; Frost's farm outside Concord (see p.262) is a better destination to get a sense of the poet's life and works.

Bretton Woods

The ease with which US-302 now crosses the middle of the mountains belies the effort that went into cutting a road through **Crawford Notch**, halfway between Franconia and Conway. Just north, the magnificent **Mount Washington Hotel** (see p.265) stands in splendid isolation in the wide mountain valley of **BRETTON WOODS**. The hotel's glistening white facade, capped by red cupolas and framed by the western slopes of Mount Washington rising behind, has barely changed since the place opened in 1902. In its heyday, a stream of horse-drawn carriages brought families (and their servants) up from the train station, deliberately located at a distance to enhance the sense of grandeur. Displays in the grand lobby commemorate the Bretton Woods Conference of 1944, which laid the groundwork for the postwar financial structure of the capitalist world, by setting the gold standard at $35 an ounce (it's now about $600) and creating the International Monetary Fund and the World Bank.

Restoration has ensured that the hotel remains marvelously evocative, with its quarter-mile terrace and white wicker furniture; the place is worth checking out even if you're not staying here.

Mount Washington

The 6288ft **Mount Washington** was named for George Washington *before* he became president – but over the years, other mountains in this "Presidential Range" have taken the names of Madison, Jefferson, and even Eisenhower. (Mount Nancy had its name long before the Reagans were in the White House; and Mount Deception just happens to be close by.)

From the top of Mount Washington you can, on a clear day, see all the way to the Atlantic and into Canada – but the real interest in making the ascent lies in the extraordinary severity of the weather up here, which results from the summit lying right in the path of the principal storm tracks and air-mass routes affecting the northeastern US. The wind here exceeds hurricane strength on more than a hundred days of the year, and in 1934 it reached the highest speed ever recorded anywhere in the world – 231mph. At the top, you'll see the remarkable spectacle of buildings actually held down with great chains; many have been blown away over the years, including the old observatory, said to be the strongest wooden building ever constructed. There's now a **viewing platform**, with a weatherproof **museum** (free) and **café** just below. Be sure to check the **weather conditions** before attempting any ascent, and be aware that a fine day can turn bad very quickly in these parts. Among the roll call of the 124 victims to have died on the mountain are two who attempted to slide down on "improvised boards."

On the way to the top, you pass through four distinct climatic zones, starting with century-old fir and ash trees so stunted as to be below waist-height and ending with Arctic tundra. The drive up the **Mount Washington Auto Road** (early May to late Oct, weather permitting, at least 8am–4pm; call ☎603/466-3988 to check weather conditions, ⓦwww.mtwashingtonautoroad.com) isn't as hair-raising as you might expect, though the hairpin bends and lack of guardrails certainly keep you alert. There is a $20 **toll** for cars and driver (plus $7 for each additional adult and $5 for kids), which comes with an audio tape or CD detailing the road's history. Or you can take a **narrated tour** in a specially-adapted minibus, called a "stage," after the horse-drawn carriages that first used the road (daily 8.30am–5pm; $26). Driving takes thirty or forty minutes under sane conditions, though rally-drivers have done it in less than ten. The record for the annual **running** race (up the mountain, of course) now stands at an incredible 58 minutes 20 seconds.

Last but far from least, you can also ride to the top on the coal-fired steam train of the **Mount Washington Cog Railway**, which noisily climbs the exposed flank of the mountain, ascending grades of up to 38 degrees on a track completed in 1869. It's truly a unique experience, as you inch up the steep wooden trestles while trying to avoid descending showers of coal smut. The three-hour roundtrip costs $57 ($37 for kids), and trains leave hourly (daily, weather permitting: mid-June to late Oct, call for other dates and times, and to reserve; ☎603/278-5404 or 1-800/922-8825, ⓦwww.thecog.com) from a station off Rte-302 six miles northeast of Bretton Woods. The Cog also runs uphill in the winter season (Nov–Apr) to access one-mile-long groomed downhill ski trails ($40 for three runs).

North Conway

A few miles south of Mount Washington, US-302 and Hwy-16 nears **NORTH CONWAY** by first passing through a hodgepodge of shopping malls, fast-food joints, and kiddie theme parks such as Heritage New Hampshire and Story Land (either at ☎603/383-4186). More useful is the **White Mountain National Forest Saco Ranger Station**, 33 Kancamagus Hwy near Rte-16 in Conway (daily 8am–5.30pm; ☎603/447-5448), which sells books, maps, and the mandatory National Forest parking permits ($3 for one day, $5 for seven consecutive days). It also provides a ton of resources for area planning and handles backcountry cabin rentals. If you're traveling through the North Conway area in high season, be warned that roads can get extremely congested.

The Kancamagus Highway

The **Kancamagus Highway** (Hwy-112) connecting Conway and Lincoln is the least busy road through the mountains, and makes for a very pleasant 34-mile drive. Several campgrounds are situated in the woods to either side, and various walking trails are signposted. The half-mile hike to **Sabbaday Falls**, off to the south roughly halfway along the highway, leads up a narrow rocky cleft in the forest to a succession of idyllic waterfalls. If you plan on a picnic, though, take note: there are no food, gas or services available along the highway.

White Mountains eating and drinking

Family **restaurants** and fast-food joints line the main drags of major centers such as North Woodstock and North Conway. The best places are in less conspicuous areas and worth rooting out. Some of the hotels and B&Bs recommended on p.265 also serve food.

1785 Inn & Restaurant 3582 Hwy-16, just north of North Conway ☎603/356-9025 or 1-800/421-1785. Original appetizers, gourmet meals such as boned rabbit in a cream sherry sauce, and fine wines, with prices to match – entrees are $15–30.
Flying Moose Café 2 W Main St, Littleton ☎603/444-2661. Intimate bistro serving a mix of classic cuisines with contemporary flair, such as braised lamb shank over polenta.
Polly's Pancake Parlor I-93 exit 38, Rte-117, Sugar Hill ☎603/823-5575. Yes, it's in the middle of nowhere, but it's a scenic nowhere and well worth the trip if you love pancakes. Summer only.

Red Parka Pub US-302, Glen ☎603/383-4344. Evening-only steakhouse with bar until 12.30am. Live rock music on weekends, and open-mic night Mondays.
Thompson House Eatery Rte-16A, Jackson ☎603/383-9341. Huge portions of very reasonably priced American comfort food, plus homemade root beer.
Truant's Taverne 96 Main St, North Woodstock ☎603/745-2239. Cozy, affordable restaurant, serving well-cooked American grill fare for around $15 a plate.

West to Vermont

Much of the western side of New Hampshire, as you approach the Connecticut River that forms the entire border with Vermont, amounts to a less-developed version of the Lakes Region (see p.262). For a tranquil day or two, the area around **Lake Sunapee**, the northern tip of which just brushes I-89, can be very appealing. Good bets include *The Back Side Inn*, behind Mount Sunapee at 1171 Brook Rd in Goshen (☎603/863-5161, ⓦwww.backsideinn.net; ❹), a former farm and now family-run Victorian B&B with ten simple but comfortable rooms and a sumptuous breakfast buffet; and, overlooking the lake, the *Inn at Sunapee*, 125 Burkehaven Hill Rd (☎603/763-4444 or 1-800/327-2466, ⓦwww.innatsunapee.com; ❺), a converted 1875 farmhouse decorated with a mixture of period items and Asian antiques.

Hanover

HANOVER, near Lebanon and just across from Vermont, is home to the venerable and elegant **Dartmouth College**, founded in this remote spot in the eighteenth century "for the instruction of the Youth of Indian tribes . . . and others." The main attraction here is the small **Hood Museum of Art** on the college green (Tues & Thurs–Sat 10am–5pm, Wed 10am–9pm, Sun noon–5pm; free; ☎603/646-2808, ⓦhoodmuseum.dartmouth.edu), which has works by Picasso and Monet alongside Assyrian bas-reliefs. In the adjacent Hopkins Center, the Dartmouth Film Society screens international art-house films and classic movies year-round ($7).

Hanover itself is enjoyable to wander around, with lively places to **eat and drink**, such as *Murphy's on the Green*, 11 S Main St (☎603/643-4075), the best place for a beer and some healthy food, and the always-busy *Lou's Restaurant & Bakery*, 30 S Main St (☎603/643-3321), good for breakfast. The finest **accommodation** is at the expensive and luxurious *Hanover Inn*, overlooking Dartmouth Green from the corner of Main and Wheelock streets (T 603/643-4300 or 1-800/443-7024, W www.hanoverinn .com; ❾). The *Chieftain Motor Inn*, at 84 Lyme Rd (T 603/643-2550, W www. chieftaininn.com; ❺), represents the best budget option you'll find in this generally expensive area.

Nearby, one secluded and memorable place to stay is *Moose Mountain Lodge* (T 603/643-3529, W www.themoosemountainlodge.com; ❼, with at least a 2-night stay required; closed mid-Oct to late Dec and mid-March to mid-June), a steep climb up in the hills above **Etna**, overlooking Vermont. All year it feels blissfully remote from the world below, but it really comes into its own for **cross-country skiing** in winter. The friendly owners, who love the country life, charge $110–145 per day per person, which includes a hearty breakfast and dinner.

Vermont

VERMONT comes closer than any other New England state to realizing the quintessential image of small-town Yankee America, with its white churches and red barns, covered bridges and clapboard houses, snowy woods and maple syrup. The largest city, **Burlington**, approaches a population of just forty thousand and the chief tourist attraction is Ben & Jerry's ice-cream factory in Waterbury. Though rural, the landscape is not all that agricultural, as much is covered by mountainous forests (the state's name comes from the French "*vert mont*," or green mountain). The people who choose to live here are a mix of hippies and diehard conservation-ists working together to preserve their environment and lamenting the arrival of yet more ski resorts. One striking feature of Vermont is the absence of billboards – though the cutesy "country stores" which seem to grace every other crossroads can become tedious.

This was the last area of New England to be settled, early in the eighteenth cen-tury, with French explorers working their way down from Canada, and American colonists beginning to spread north. The wealthy New York merchants who built fine homes along the Connecticut River Valley thought of themselves as the "River Gods," but the hardy settlers of the lakes and mountains of New Hamp-shire to the east had little time for their patrician ways. Their leader, the now-legendary **Ethan Allen**, formed his **Green Mountain Boys** in 1770, proclaiming that "the gods of the hills are not the gods of the valley." During the Revolution-ary War, this all-but-autonomous force captured Fort Ticonderoga from the Brit-ish and helped to win the decisive Battle of Bennington. By 1777, Vermont was an independent republic, with the first constitution in the world explicitly forbidding slavery and granting universal (male) suffrage, but once its boundaries with New York were agreed upon, it joined the Union in 1791. A more recent example of Vermont's progressive attitude occurred in 1999, when Governor Howard Dean signed the **civil union** bill into law, making Vermont the first state in the US to sanction same-sex marriage.

With the occasional exception, such as the extraordinary assortment of Ameri-cana at the **Shelburne Museum** near Burlington, there are few specific goals for tourists. Visitors come in great numbers during two well-defined seasons: to see the **fall foliage** in the first two weeks of October, and to **ski** in the depths of winter, when the resorts of **Killington**, and **Stowe** further north (home of *The Sound of Music*'s Trapp family), spring into life. For the rest of the year, you might just as well explore any of the state's minor roads that take your fancy, confident that some picturesque village will appear around the next corner.

Getting around Vermont

Vermont's main north–south road is I-91, hugging the edge of New Hampshire. I-89 traverses the center of the state, passing Montpelier and Burlington on its way from New Hampshire to Canada. Greyhound-affiliated Vermont Transit **buses** (T 1-800/642-3133 in Vermont, 1-800/451-3292 elsewhere, W www.vermonttransit .com) connect Montréal with Boston and New York, passing through towns such as Burlington, Montpelier, Rutland, and Brattleboro. Amtrak's *Vermonter* **train** (T 1-800/872-7245), which runs between Washington, DC, and St Albans, stops at Brattleboro, White River Junction, Montpelier, Waterbury, and Burlington. The main **airport** is in Burlington.

Bike Vermont (T 802/457-3553 or 1-800/257-2226, W www.bikevt.com) and Adventure Guides of Vermont (T 1-800/747-5905, W www.adventureguidesvt. com) organize **cycling tours**, including itineraries that take you from one rural inn to another.

Southern Vermont

Of the two low-key towns at either end of Vermont's southern Hwy-9 corridor – a mere forty miles from east to west – **Brattleboro** has the atmosphere of a college town (due to several small area colleges), while **Bennington** has a college but not the atmosphere.

Brattleboro

If **BRATTLEBORO**, in the southeastern corner of the state, is your first taste of Vermont, it may come as a surprise. Not the quaint, 1950s-throwback village you might expect, its style owes more to the central and northern Massachusetts college towns, with numerous little stores catering to the youthful and vaguely "alternative" population that has moved into the surrounding hills over the past few decades. The town's one unlikely claim to fame is that this was where **Rudyard Kipling** wrote his two *Jungle Books*.

Trains follow the river into town and stop behind the Old Union Railroad Station, which now displays exhibits by local painters, photographers, sculptors, and the like as the **Brattleboro Museum & Art Center** (April–Feb Wed–Mon 11am–5pm; $4; T 802/257-0124, W www.brattleboromuseum.org). **Buses** pick up and drop off at the junction of US-5 (Putney Road) and I-91, a couple of miles north.

The most popular place to **stay** is the Art Deco *Latchis Hotel*, 50 Main St (T 802/254-6300, W www.latchis.com; ❸) which has an attached cinema. You can't go wrong **eating** at the *Riverview Café*, 3 Bridge St (T 802/254-9841), which overlooks the Connecticut River. The *Latchis* serves quality beer in the *Flat Street Brew Pub* upstairs from the cinema, but the best **beer** resides at the rough-around-the-edges *McNeill's Brewery*, 90 Elliot St (T 802/254-2553). The nearby *Mole's Eye Cafe*, at 4 High St (T 802/257-0771), is an established night-spot with **live music** every night (and a bar menu that includes a smattering of Mexican and Italian items). Homemade baked goods and specialty coffee make *Mocha Joe's*, 82 Main St (T 802/257-7794), a good place for a morning snack or an evening dessert.

Bennington

In the past two hundred years, little has happened in **BENNINGTON** to match the excitement of the days when Ethan Allen's Green Mountain Boys – known as the "Bennington Mob" – were based here. A 306ft hilltop obelisk (mid-April to late Oct daily 9am–5pm; $2) commemorates the **Battle of Bennington** of 1777, in which the Boys were a crucial factor in defeating the British under General Burgoyne (though the battle itself was fought just across the border in New York).

The *Paradise Motor Inn* at no. 141 (☎802/442-8351, ⓦwww.theparadisemotorinn.com; ④) is one of a few downtown **motels** on West Main Street. More stylish digs can be found at the *Four Chimneys Inn* on Rte-9, called West Rd here (☎802/447-3500, ⓦwww.fourchimneys.com; ⑤). Ten miles east of town on Rte-9, by the Prospect Ski Mountain, is the *HI-Greenwood Lodge* **hostel** (open mid-May to late Oct; ☎802/442-2547), which has beds for $28. As for **food**, students from the small and exclusive arty Bennington College crowd into the *Madison Brewing Company* at 428 Main St (☎1-800/44BREWS) or the *Blue Benn* diner, 102 Hunt St (☎802/442-5140).

The Green Mountains

The weather in the **Green Mountains**, which form the backbone of Vermont, is not as harsh as in New Hampshire's White Mountains – though their forests are invariably buried in snow for most of the winter, and the higher roads are liable to be blocked for long periods. Here and there, denuded patches mark where trees have been shaved away to create ski-runs, but for the most part, the usually peaceful **Hwy-100** running up from the south offers unspoiled mountain views to either side.

In summer, hikers take up the challenge of the **Long Trail** along the central ridge, 265 miles from the Massachusetts border to Québec. This trail predates the Appalachian Trail, which now joins its southern portion, and is looked after by the **Green Mountain Club** (☎802/244-7037, ⓦwww.greenmountainclub.org), whose *Long Trail Guide* ($19) is invaluable.

Hwy-100 Scenic Drive: Weston

One of the prettiest villages along Hwy-100 is **WESTON**, which spreads out beside a little river and centers on a perfect green, where a somber slab commemorates the seventeen local soldiers killed on the same day during the Civil War, in Alexandria, Virginia. Nearby, the **Farrar-Mansur House** (July & Aug Wed, Sat & Sun 1–4pm; early Sept to mid-Oct Sat & Sun 1–4pm; $2 donation; ☎802/824-5294) is a 1795 house and tavern, which recreates early settler life with collections of clocks, dolls, guns, and weaving equipment.

Stores selling antiques, toys, and fudge are scattered up and down Main Street (Hwy-100). The **Vermont Country Store**, south of the green, is larger than it looks from its modest facade. For all its seeming quaintness, this Vermont institution is actually part of a chain that has a successful mail-order business. Opposite, the **Weston Village Store** leans more on the side of kitsch, but is still a fun place to browse.

Weston's best **accommodation** is the lovely *Inn at Weston*, Hwy-100, near the village green (☎802/824-6789, ⓦwww.innweston.com; ⑦), with homey rooms, an excellent **restaurant** and a cozy pub. Another nice B&B is the *Darling Family Inn* (☎802/824-3223, ⓦwww.thedarlingfamilyinn.com; ④), north of the green on Hwy-100. A small but magnificent soda fountain dominates the 1885 mahogany bar of the lunch-only *Bryant House* restaurant, next door to the Vermont Country Store on Main Street (closed Sun; ⓣ802/824-6287), whose menu includes country fare, including "johnny cakes." The best bet for entertainment is the attractive **Weston Playhouse,** which offers summer and fall performances (Tues–Sun; $28–47; ⓣ802/824-5288, ⓦwww.westonplayhouse.org).

Killington

The ski resort of **KILLINGTON** (ⓣ802/422-6220 for the resort, or 1-800/621-6867 for other area reservations, ⓦwww.killington.com), in the center of the Green Mountains thirty miles north of Weston, has grown out of nothing since 1958. Despite a miniscule permanent population (around fifty), it's estimated that in season there are enough beds within twenty miles to accommodate some ten thousand people each night. The resort sprawls over seven mountains (Pico Moun-

△ Killington, VT

tain is the best for skiers of mid-range ability; for 24-hour taped skiing information, call ⓣ 802/422-3261), and is notorious for its rowdy nightlife. For hikers, the Long and Appalachian trails meet just north of here. In summer and fall, you can still take the **gondola** ($9 one way, $13 roundtrip) up to the observation deck and cafeteria on the summit. Choose your way back down: hike or mountain bike (rentals are available at the base).

In winter, the Killington Access Road up from US-4 is humming with crowded **bars and restaurants**: *Wobbly Barn Steakhouse* (ⓣ 802/422-6171) is good for beef in all forms, and lively entertainment, and the *Pickle Barrel* (ⓣ 802/422-3035) is a rowdy bar that gets crazier on winter weekends. Some places close in summer. The *Cortina Inn & Resort* (ⓣ 802/773-3333 or 1-800/451-6108, ⓦ www.cortinainn.com; ❺) is one of several **inns** on Hwy-4 offering reduced summer rates; the *Inn at Long Trail*, Sherburne Pass (ⓣ 802/775-7181 or 1-800/325-2540, ⓦ www.innatlongtrail .com; ❹), is perfectly located for Long Trail hikers (see p.271).

Woodstock

Since its settlement in the 1760s, beautiful **WOODSTOCK**, a few miles west of the Connecticut River up US-4, has been one of Vermont's more refined centers. Its distinguished houses cluster around an oval green, now largely taken over by art galleries and tearooms (don't confuse it with Woodstock, New York, of music festival fame).

Woodstock's main paying attraction is the **Billings Farm and Museum**, Rte-12, at River Rd (May–Oct daily 10am–5pm; Nov–Dec Sat & Sun 10am–4pm; $10; ⓣ 802/457-2355, ⓦ www.billingsfarm.org): part modern dairy farm, part museum of farm life, it puts on demonstrations of antiquated skills and shows an excellent biographical film of the farm's various owners. **Hiking trails**, accessible from the town center, are great for a leisurely stroll, as are the forest trails of the **Marsh-Billings-Rockefeller National Historical Park** (daily late May–Oct 10am–5pm; ⓣ 802/457-3368, ⓦ www.nps.gov/mabi), which are also groomed for winter skiing and snowshoeing.

The friendly staff of the Woodstock **Chamber of Commerce** (ⓣ 802/457-3555 or 1-888/496-6378, and ⓦ www.woodstockvt.com) has extensive information on lodging, dining and other area attractions. The Chamber also runs an **information booth** on the green (June–Oct 9.30am–5.30pm; ⓣ 802/457-1042), which can help you find **accommodation** in town. Options include the well-refurbished *Shire Riverview*, 46 Pleasant St (ⓣ 802/457-2211, ⓦ www.shiremotel. com; ❹), the upscale *Woodstock Inn and Resort*, 14 The Green (ⓣ 802/457-1100 or 1-800/448-7900, ⓦ www.woodstockinn.com; ❻), and the cozy *Applebutter Inn*, four miles east of town on Hwy-4, in Taftsville (ⓣ 802/457-4158, ⓦ www. applebutterinn.com; ❺).

Of the several places to **eat** in Woodstock, *Bentley's*, 3 Elm St (ⓣ 802/457-3232), has a range of microbrews and upscale versions of traditional bistro food, and the ⚘ *Kedron Valley Inn*, Rte-106 in South Woodstock (ⓣ 802/457-1473), serves more expensive but superb American standards. Comfort food breakfasts and lunches are on offer at *Mountain Creamery*, 33 Central St (daily, 7am–3pm; ⓣ 802/457-1715). *Eagle Café*, in the *Woodstock Inn*, has tasty salads, flatbread pizzas and sandwiches all for under $12. *Allechante*, 61 Central St (ⓣ 802/457-3300), serves the area's best pastries.

Quechee

The grand houses on the hills around **QUECHEE**, six miles east of Woodstock, have been joined by a proliferation of new condos and second homes. It's all reasonably well landscaped, but a shame nonetheless, and adds nothing to the environs of **Quechee Gorge State Park**, which preserves the splendors of the **Quechee Gorge**. A delicate bridge spans the 165ft chasm of the Ottauquechee River, and hiking trails lead down to the park through the fir trees. You can **camp** at the park at one of Vermont's many state-run campgrounds ($14–23 per night; two-night minimum stay; ☎802/295-2990 or 1-888/409-7579). If you'd rather not rough it, the *Quality Inn*, on Hwy-4 between the gorge and the tourist shops of the Quechee Gorge Village (☎802/295-7600 or 1-800/732-4376, ⓦwww. qualityinnquechee.com; ❹), offers the best-value **accommodation**.

The river spins the turbines of the **Simon Pearce Glass Mill** (daily 9am–9pm, ☎802/295-2711), housed in a former wool mill along Main Street in Quechee. Here, you can watch glass bowls and plates being blown, and then eat from them at the on-site **restaurant** (overlooking a waterfall) which serves, among other dishes, glazed wild salmon, Mediterranean lamb burgers, and crispy roast duck ($20–28 dinner entrees, about $15 for lunch); reservations are recommended (☎802/295-1470).

Montpelier

Some fifty-five miles north up I-89, **MONTPELIER** is the smallest state capital in the nation, with fewer than ten thousand inhabitants. Surrounded by leafy gardens, the golden domed **capitol** is well worth a free tour for its marble-floored and mural-lined hallways. Copious information on accommodation, here and throughout the state, is available from the **Vermont Division of Travel and Tourism**, 134 State St (daily 8am–8pm; ☎802/828-5981 or 1-800/VERMONT). Good **B&B rooms** can be had at the central yet quiet *Betsy's Bed & Breakfast*, 74 E State St (☎802/229-0466, ⓦwww.betsysbnb.com; ❸). For more luxurious digs, try the *Capitol Plaza Hotel*, 100 State St (☎802/223-5252, ⓦwww.capitolplaza. com; ❺).

For **food**, students from the local New England Culinary Institute run both the *Main St Grill & Bar* at 118 Main St (☎802/223-3188) and the more upmarket *Chef's Table*, at the same address (☎802/229-9202), each one serving excellent, inexpensive, experimental dishes from all over the world. *Coffee Corner*, on Main Street at State (☎802/229-9060), has been serving dirt-cheap diner food for over sixty years. *Capitol Grounds*, 45 State St (☎802/223-7800), is definitely tops for your morning coffee or tea fix.

There are several in-town options for live music; *Langdon Street Café*, 4 Langdon St (☎802/223-8667), has a homey feel, with live music nightly and beer, wine, and coffee drinks, while *Black Door Bar*, 44 Main St (☎802/223-7070), is a bit more posh, with jazz or zydeco ($3 cover).

Waterbury

Few people paid much attention to **WATERBURY** before 1978; even then, the opening of a homemade ice-cream stand run by a pair of hippies on the forecourt of a gas station excited little interest. However, **Ben & Jerry's Ice Cream Factory**, one mile north of I-89 on Rte-100 in the center of Waterbury, on the way up to Stowe, has grown so huge, so fast, that it is now the number-one tourist destination in Vermont. Half-hour tours (daily: July & Aug 9am–8pm; Sept & Oct 9am–6pm; Nov–May 10am–5pm; June 9am–5pm; $3, under 12 free; ☎802/882-1240 or 1-866/BJ-TOURS, ⓦwww.benjerry.com) include a short film, a view of the workforce from an observation platform, and a free mini-scoop of the stuff that made it all possible – you can buy more at the overpriced gift shop and ice-cream stall outside. The omnipresent black-and-white cow logo, and the reminders to recycle, eat organic, and buy milk from farming co-ops can get to be a bit much; if the summer crowds seem intolerable, bear in mind there are better things to do in Burlington and Stowe.

Stowe

At the foot of Vermont's highest mountain, the 4393ft **Mount Mansfield**, lies the popular summer- and wintertime resort of **STOWE**. There is still a beautiful nine-teenth-century village at the town's heart – with a white-spired meeting house and a pretty green – though a century's worth of catering to skiers and outdoor enthusiasts has swamped the approach road to the main ski area with equipment stores, resort spas, and sprawling condo complexes. Nevertheless, Stowe's setting remains spectacular.

Stowe's **visitor center** on Main Street, near the intersection with Mountain Road (Mon–Sat 9am–8pm, Sun 9am–5pm; ☏802/253-7321 or 1-877/GO-STOWE, ⓦwww.gostowe.com), provides information on skiing conditions and accommodation. **Bikes** can be rented from the Mountain Sports & Bike Shop, 580 Mountain Rd (☏802/253-7919, ⓦwww.skiershop.com) for the Recreation Path, the town's paved trail twisting through 5.3 miles of scenery. For mountain biking options, contact the local bike shops or the Stowe Mountain Bike Club (☏802/253-1947) which sponsors group rides. The **Vermont Ski Museum**, 1 S Main St (Mon & Wed–Sun noon–5pm, closed Nov and mid-April to May; $3 donation; ☏802/253-9911), tackles the evolution of the sport.

Hwy-108 – **Mountain Road** – leads close to the mountain through the dramatic **Smugglers' Notch**. The resort here (☏1-800/451-8752, ⓦwww.smuggs.com) is a less crowded, more family-orientated alternative to Stowe. Weather permitting, you can get to the top of Mount Mansfield either by driving four and a half miles up the **Toll Road**, which itself starts seven miles up Mountain Road (June to mid-Oct daily 9am–5pm; $19 per car, with up to six people), or by taking the **gondola** (mid-June to mid-Oct daily 10am–5pm; $12 one way; ☏802/253-3000, ⓦwww.stowe.com) up to the *Cliff House Restaurant* (lunch only), and hiking for another half-hour from there. There's also a luge-type ride on a 2300-foot-long track known as the Alpine Slide ($15 a ride, multi-packs available). What really made Stowe's name as a **cross-country ski resort** was its connection to the **Trapp family**, of *The Sound of Music* fame. After fleeing Austria during World War II, they established the 🏕 *Trapp Family Lodge* at 700 Trapp Hill Rd (☏802/253-8511 or 1-800/826-7000, ⓦwww.trappfamily.com; ❼). The original lodge, where Maria von Trapp held her singing camps, has burned down, and she herself died in 1987, but an equally luxurious building has taken its place: its *Austrian Tea Room* serves incredibly heavy Germanic cakes and pastries (11am–5pm). Almost 150km of back-country and groomed cross-country ski trails lead out from the lodge.

Practicalities

The best of the plentiful accommodation (save the lodge above) includes the sumptuous Stoweflake Mountain Resort & Spa, 1746 Mountain Rd (☏802/253-7355 or 1-800/253-2232, ⓦwww.stoweflake.com; ❻); and the historic Green Mountain Inn, 18 Main St (☏802/253-7301 or 1-800/253-7302, ⓦwww.greenmountaininn.com; ❻). Cheaper rooms are available at the Riverside Inn, 1965 Mountain View Rd (☏802/253-4217 or 1-800/966-4217, ⓦwww.rivinn.com; ❸). Gold Brook campground is two miles south on Hwy-100 (☏802/253-7683; $23).

There are plenty of places to **eat** in and around Stowe. On Mountain Road, next to the cinema, *McCarthy's* (☏802/253-8626) is best for breakfast; the *Shed Restau-*

rant & Brew Pub, at no. 1859 (☎802/253-4364), has moderately-priced American food and good beer; and the always-crowded *Pie in the Sky*, at no. 492 (☎802/253-5100), serves relatively inexpensive pizza and pasta dishes. A more upscale option is the *Blue Moon Café*, 35 School St (☎802/253-7006), which offers an innovative menu including Vermont rabbit and venison, as well as a good wine list.

Lake Champlain

The 150-mile-long **Lake Champlain**, which forms the boundary between Vermont and New York State, and just nudges its way into Canada, never exceeds twelve miles in width. The first non-native to see the lake, Samuel de Champlain, who named it after himself in 1609, was also the first to claim that it held a sinuous Loch Ness–type monster, which is locally referred to affectionately as "Champ."

The heart and soul of the valley is the French-influenced city of **Burlington**, whose longstanding trade connections with Montréal filled it with elegant nineteenth-century architecture. Within just a few miles of the center, US-2 leads north into the supremely rural Champlain Islands, covered in meadows and orchards.

If your travel plans require it, **Lake Champlain Ferries** (☎802/864-9804, ⓦwww.ferries.com) crosses the lake from Vermont to New York from **Burlington** (to Port Kent; $15); **Charlotte** (to Essex; $8.50); and **Grand Isle** (to Cumberland Head; $8.50). All these rates are one way for a car and driver; additional passengers, cyclists, and walk-ons pay $3.25–5.25.

Burlington

Lakeside **BURLINGTON**, Vermont's largest "city," with a population near forty thousand, is one of the most enjoyable towns in New England. A hip, relaxed fusion of Montréal, eighty miles to the north, and Boston, over two hundred miles southeast, it's always looked as much to Canada as to the south; shipping connections with the St Lawrence River were far easier than the land routes across the mountains, and the harbor became a major supply center. The city's founders included Ethan Allen and family, but far from being some impoverished Robin Hood figure (see opposite), Ethan was a wealthy landowner, and his brother Ira set up the University of Vermont. In 1990 Bernard Saunders, the former "socialist" mayor of Burlington, was elected to the House of Representatives – the first political independent to go to Congress in forty years.

As the home of the university, Burlington is the definitive youthful, outward-looking college town. Downtown is easily strolled by foot, notably around the **Church Street Marketplace**.

Arrival, information, and getting around

Vermont Transit **buses** stop in downtown Burlington, four blocks south of Main Street at 345 Pine St. The Amtrak **train** station is an inconvenient five miles northeast, in the small community of Essex Junction (connecting buses $1.25). The **airport**, Vermont's largest, is a few miles east of town along US-2.

Information and help with accommodation is available from the **Lake Champlain Regional Chamber of Commerce**, 60 Main St (year-round Mon–Fri 8.30am–5pm, July–Sept also Sat–Sun 11am–5pm; ☎802/863-3489 or 1-877/686-5253, ⓦwww.vermont.org), or the kiosk on Church Street.

The local CCTA **bus** company (☎802/864-2282, ⓦwww.cctaride.org) runs a free shuttle (roughly every 15 mins, Mon–Fri 6.15am–7.15pm; extended hours during summer) connecting the university campus, downtown, and the water-front. Lake Champlain Ferries (see opposite) leave from the jetty at the end of King Street. Lake Champlain Shoreline Cruises ($13 narrated tour; lunch and evening theme and lobster dinner cruises $20–46; ☎ 802/862-8300, ⓦ www.soea.com), on the 140-foot cruiser *Spirit of Ethan Allen III*, depart from the Boathouse at the end of College Street. North Star Sports, 100 Main St (☎ 802/863-3832), and Skirack, 85 Main St (☎ 802/658-3313), rent **bikes**.

Accommodation

Burlington has no shortage of moderately priced **accommodation**, especially along Shelburne Road between Burlington and Shelburne, while for **camping** the lakeside *North Beach Campground* (☎ 802/862-0942 or 1-800/571-1198; $18–23) is less than two miles north on Institute Road. The Chamber of Commerce has extensive lodging information available.

Champlain Inn 165 Shelburne St ☎ 802/862-4004. Roadside motel with 33 clean and basic efficiencies, each with microwave and refrigerator. ❸
Ho-Hum Motel 1660 Williston Rd ☎ 802/863-4551 or 1-800/228-7031. Simple, reasonably priced motel, three miles east of downtown on US-2, near the airport. ❸
Inn at Essex 70 Essex Way, Essex Junction ☎ 802/878-1100 or 1-800/727-4295, ⓦ www.innatessex.com. Classy establishment with a good restaurant, near the Amtrak station about eight miles from the town center. ❼
Sunset House B&B 78 Main St ☎ 802/864-3790, ⓦ www.sunsethousebb.com. Centrally located, homely B&B with shared bathrooms. ❺
Willard Street Inn 349 S Willard St ☎ 802/651-8710, or 1-800/577-8712, ⓦ www.willardstreetinn.com. A few blocks south of the town center, this gorgeously restored home comes with a relaxing garden, pantry and filling breakfasts. ❻

The City

The **waterfront** of Burlington is a surprisingly undeveloped area, though Battery Park at its northern end makes a good place to watch the sun go down over the Adirondacks – especially when there's a band playing, as there often is at weekends.

A better place to explore is the pedestrianized **Church Street Marketplace**, a few blocks back, which holds Burlington's finest old buildings and its modern cafés and boutiques. The **Robert Hull Fleming Museum** on Colchester Avenue (May–Aug Tues–Fri noon–4pm, Sat & Sun 1–5pm; Sept to April Tues–Fri 9am–4pm, Sat & Sun 1–5pm; $5; ☎ 802/656-0750, ⓦ www.flemingmuseum.org), at the University of Vermont, has an interesting collection of art and artifacts from all over the world, including pre-Columbian pieces. North on Rte-127, the **Ethan Allen Homestead** (June–Oct Mon–Sat 10am–4pm, Sun 1–4pm; $5; ☎ 802/865-4556, ⓦ www.ethanallenhomestead.org) offers a multifaceted look at the life and times of Vermont's controversial founding father.

The Shelburne Museum

It takes a whole day, if not more, to appreciate fully the remarkable fifty-acre collection of unalloyed **Americana** gathered at the **Shelburne Museum**, on US-7 in Shelburne, three miles south of Burlington (daily: May–Oct 10am–5pm; $18, valid for two successive days; ☎ 802/985-3346, ⓦ www.shelburnemuseum.org). Created in 1947 by heiress Electra Webb, the museum is built around her parents' French Impressionist paintings, including works by Degas and Monet, displayed in a careful reconstruction of their New York City apartment. However, Electra's own interests ranged far wider, and she put together what is probably the nation's finest celebration of its own inventions outside of the Smithsonian Institution.

More than thirty buildings, some original and some constructed specially for the museum, focus on aspects of everyday American life over the past two centuries.

The village includes a general store and an apothecary, a railroad station, and even an enormous **steam paddlewheeler** from Lake Champlain, the *SS Ticonderoga*, with its own rock-surrounded lighthouse. Another highlight is the **Circus Building**, home to parade figures, circus posters, and a miniature three-ring circus of 35,000 wooden pieces, all carved by hand.

③ Eating, drinking, and entertainment

During term time, the presence of ten thousand students ensures that Burlington has ample choice of inexpensive and good **restaurants**, as well as some pretty raucous nightspots. Note that this is one of the most vehement **anti-smoking** towns in the East, and smoking is banned in most restaurants and some bars.

American Flatbread 115 St Paul St ☎ 802/861-2999. Wildly popular place with all natural and organic pizzas, many with locally-farmed produce.

Club Metronome/Nectar's 188 Main St ☎ 802/658-4771. *Club Metronome*'s a very hip club with some live acts, but mainly house and techno music. Downstairs, *Nectar's* is a retro lounge, which gave birth to the nationally-known jam-band Phish. Cover charge weekends.

Daily Planet 15 Center St, behind Church Street Marketplace ☎ 802/862-9647. Innovative menu combining Asian and Mediterranean cooking with old-fashioned American comfort food.

Five Spice Café 175 Church St ☎ 802/864-4045. Excellent southeast Asian food, including a dim sum Sunday brunch and vegetarian dishes.

Muddy Waters 184 Main St ☎ 802/658-0466. Eclectic woody interior and colorful clientele distin-guish this popular coffeehouse. The caffeine beverages pack quite a punch.

Red Onion Café 140 Church St ☎ 802/865-2563. Inviting bakery with outdoor seating and the best sandwich shop around, with some good vegetarian options.

Shanty on the Shore 181 Battery St ☎ 802/864-0238. Truly fresh seafood in a laid-back setting, with views of Lake Champlain.

Smokejack's 156 Church St ☎ 802/658-1119. Creative meat and seafood dishes smoked over an oak-wood grill, all of which go down easier with the spicy Bloody Marys, custom martinis, or beers on tap.

Vermont Pub and Brewery 144 College St ☎ 802/865-0500. Roomy, convivial brewpub with a good menu of burgers, sandwiches, and other American-style food and occasional live music.

Maine

Celebrated as "the way life should be," **MAINE** is as big as the other five New England states combined, yet barely has the population of tiny Rhode Island. In theory, therefore, there's plenty of room for the massive summer influx of people "from away"; in reality, the majority of these head for the southern stretches of the extravagantly corrugated **coast**. You only really begin to appreciate the size and space of the state further north, or **inland**, where vast tracts of mountainous forest are dotted with lakes, and are barely pierced by roads – more like the Alaska interior than the RV-cluttered roads of the Vermont and New Hampshire mountains, and ideal territory for hiking and canoeing (and moose-spotting). Wherever you go in Maine, you're bound to come across quiet New England towns, wide swaths of remote countryside, and unruly stretches of seashore. None of these areas boasts much in the way of traditional sights, and almost all locals – and tourists – are more than happy to keep it that way.

North America's first agricultural **colonies** were in Maine: de Champlain's **French** Protestants near Mount Desert Island in 1604, and an **English** group that survived one winter at the mouth of the Kennebec three years later. In the face of the unwillingness of subsequent English settlers to let them farm in peace, the local Indians formed a long-term alliance with the French, and until as late as 1700 regularly drove out streams of impoverished English refugees. However, by 1764, the official census could claim that even Maine's African-American population was more numerous than its Native Americans.

Originally part of Massachusetts, Maine became a separate entity only in 1820, when the Missouri Compromise made Maine a free, and Missouri a slave, state. In the nineteenth century, its people had a reputation for conservatism and resistance to immigration, manifested in anti-Irish riots. The state's **economy** has always been heavily based on the sea. Lobster fishing has defied gloomy predictions and boomed again, as evidenced by the coastline's many thriving **lobster pounds**.

Maine's climate is famously harsh. In the winter, most of Maine is under snow and the landscape is marked by snowshoes and the peaceful criss-crossing of skis. Summer is short and heralded by sweetcorn and lively lobster shacks; its end is marked by tasty wild blueberry crops – ninety percent of the nation's harvest comes from Maine – and the cheery blue berries turn up in everything from pancakes to grilled chicken dishes. Brilliant **Fall colors** begin to spread from the north in late September – when, unlike elsewhere in New England, you can find good deals on off-season rates – with temperatures turning frosty by mid-October.

Getting around Maine

The vast majority of visitors to Maine **drive**. The most enjoyable route to follow is US-1, which runs within a few miles of the coast all the way to Canada, with innumerable turnoffs to hidden seaside villages. If you're in a hurry, I-95, initially the (tolled) Maine Turnpike, offers speedy access to Portland and beyond. In the **interior**, the roads are quiet and the views spectacular; many belong to the lumber companies, who keep track of who you are and where you are going (and charge you for the privilege). At any time of the year, bad weather can render these roads suddenly impassable; be sure to check before setting off (Nov–April call ☏207/624-3000, or visit ⓦwww.maine.gov/mdot-stage).

While many touristed spots offer extensive in-town shuttle bus service, **public transportation** between Maine towns can fall a long way short of meeting travelers' needs. The seven daily Greyhound buses – from Boston to Portland, five of which continue on to Bangor – link the main towns of the southern coast, as does Concord Trailways (which also makes it all the way downeast to Searsport; ☏1-800/639-3317, ⓦwww.concordtrailways.com), but that's about all there is. Amtrak has the amiable *Downeaster* (☏1-800/639-3317, ⓦwww.amtrakdowneaster .com), which leaves from Boston's North Station and terminates in Portland (making stops along the way in Wells, Biddeford, and Old Orchard Beach); it's great value at $22 each way.

The Maine coast

Considering that the state has a **coastline** of three thousand miles, finding access to the sea in Maine can be frustrating. The oceanfront is monopolized by an endless succession of private homes and vacation residences – most famously that of former president George H. W. Bush in Kennebunkport. In fact, only two percent of the shore is publicly owned – and not all of that is beach. Rather than long walks on coastal footpaths, travelers can expect attractive if rather commercial harbor villages, linked mostly by roads set back from the water.

The liveliest destinations are **Portland** and **Bar Harbor** (at the edge of **Acadia National Park**); there's a wide choice of smaller seaside towns, such as **Wiscasset** and **Blue Hill**, if you're looking for a more peaceful base. **Beaches** are more common (and the sea warmer) further south, for example at **Ogunquit**.

The best way to see the coast itself is by **boat**: ferries and excursions operate from even the smallest harbors, with major routes including the ferries to **Canada** from Portland and Bar Harbor, shorter trips to **Monhegan** island via Port Clyde, Boothbay Harbor, and New Harbor; and **Vinalhaven** via Rockland.

South of Portland

I-95 crosses from Portsmouth, New Hampshire (see p.260), into an area of Maine so dense with little communities that Mark Twain alleged one couldn't "throw a brick without danger of disabling a postmaster." Three miles over the Maine border, at the intersection with US-1, an **information center** at **Kittery** provides copious details on the whole state (daily: summer 8am–6pm; rest of year 9am–5.30pm; ⓣ207/439-1319). For a fantastic fish dinner overlooking the water, stop into the ⚓ *Chauncey Creek Lobster Pier* (16 Chauncey Creek Road, Kittery Point, ⓣ207/439-1030). while you're here.

If you want to avoid the tolls on the interstate and follow more scenic US-1 instead, you'll soon find yourself in pleasant **YORK**, which was in 1642 the first English city to be chartered in North America. Its seventeenth-century **Old Gaol** ("Old Jail") now serves as a museum, commemorating its colorful, criminal past – dating from 1653, it was used as Maine's primary prison until the Revolutionary War. People love to line up for *Flo's* **hot dogs**, just north of here in Cape Neddick, US-1 across from Mountain Road (closed Wed), a crowd-pleasing institution since 1959.

Ogunquit

The three-mile spit of sand that shields **OGUNQUIT** from the open ocean is Maine's finest **beach**, a long stretch of sugary sand and calm surf that is ideal for leisurely strolls. Even better, the town remains small enough to be a pleasant resort. The summer season at the **Ogunquit Playhouse** (ⓣ207/646-5511) usually attracts a few big-name performers. The late director of the Met in New York called the **Ogunquit Museum of American Art** (ⓣ207/646-4909; $5) "the most beautiful little museum in the world." Its tiny space is blessed with a strong collection of seascapes, further enhanced by the museum's sweeping ocean views.

One great place to **stay** in Ogunquit is the *Terrace by the Sea*, 11 Wharf Lane (ⓣ207/646-3232, ⓦwww.terracebythesea.com; ❺) with lovely gardens and a location right on the water's edge. The *Scotch Hill Inn*, 287 Main St (ⓣ207/646-2890, ⓦwww.scotchhillinn.com; ❻), in the heart of Ogunquit, has cozy, well-appointed rooms and sumptuous breakfasts. The nearest campground, *Pinederosa*, is north of town at 128 North Village Rd (May–Sept; ⓣ207/646-2492, ⓦwww.pinederosa.com; $23 for two adults); it operates a free shuttle to Ogunquit Beach in July and August. The misnamed Marginal Way, a scenic clifftop path, leads from central Ogunquit to pretty **Perkins Cove**, a mile south. *The Blue Water Inn*, 11 Beach St (ⓣ207/646-5559) is right on the water and serves up fresh **seafood** at amazing prices, while *Joshua's Restaurant*, 1637 US-1 (ⓣ207/646-3500) just north in Wells, has the best dinners in the area; many of the dishes use ingredients from his own local farm.

Kennebunkport

Before its worldwide exposure as the home of George H.W. Bush's "summer White House," **KENNEBUNKPORT** was perfectly happy as a self-contained and exclusive residential district. Although the town does have a bit of a snooty vibe, it has (fortunately) been blessed with beaches as well as bluebloods. Neighboring Kennebunk is home to a lovely trio of beaches: Kennebunk, Mother's, and Gooch's, all located on Beach St, off Rte-9 South; contact the Chamber of Commerce for permits (17 Western Ave, Kennebunk, ☎207/967-0857; $6 per day). The best place to hang out (and eat seafood) is *Alisson's*, at 8 Dock Square (☎207/967-4841), where dinner is served until 10pm and the bar stays open until 1am.

Portland

The largest city in Maine, **PORTLAND** was founded in 1632 in a superb position on the Casco Bay Peninsula, and quickly prospered, building ships and exporting great inland pines for use as masts. A long line of wooden **wharves** stretched along the seafront, with the merchants' houses on the hillside above.

From its earliest days, Portland was a cosmopolitan city, with a large free black population that traditionally worked as longshoremen; great bitterness arose when Irish immigrants began to muscle in on the scene in the 1830s. When the **railroads** came, the Canada Trunk Line had its terminus right on Portland's quayside, bringing the produce of Canada and the Great Plains one hundred miles closer to Europe than it would have been at any other major US port. Some of the wharves are now taken up by new condo developments, though **Custom House Wharf** remains much as it must have looked when Anthony Trollope passed through in 1861 and said, "I doubt whether I ever saw a town with more evident signs of prosperity." Most of what he saw of the town was destroyed by an accidental **fire** in 1866 (Indians in 1675, and the British in 1775, had previously burned Portland deliberately).

Grand Trunk Station was torn down in 1966, and downtown Portland appeared to be in terminal decline – until, that is, a group of committed residents undertook the energetic redevelopment of the area now known as **Old Port**. Their success has revitalized the city, keeping it at the heart of Maine life – though you shouldn't expect a hive of energy. Portland is quite simply a pleasant, sophisticated, and in places, very attractive town, where one can experience the benefits of a large city at a lesser cost and without the hassle.

Arrival, information, and getting around

Both I-95 and US-1 skirt the promontory of Portland, within a few miles of the city center, while I-295 runs directly through it and offers access to downtown. **Portland International Jetport** is next to I-95, and is connected with downtown by regular city buses. Congress Street is the main central thoroughfare, while Commercial Street runs along the harbor. Concord Trailways (☎1-800/639-3317, ⓦwww.concordtrailways .com) and Greyhound are the principal **bus** operators along the coast, with frequent service to Boston, as well as north to Bangor (and, in summer, Bar Harbor). Vermont Transit Lines (☎207/772-6587 or 1-800/552-8737, ⓦwww. vermonttransit.com) runs to Montréal, New Hampshire, and Vermont, as well as destinations within Maine; the station is at 950 Congress St, on the eastern edge of downtown.

The **visitor center** is at 245 Commercial St (Mon–Fri 8am–5pm, Sat 10am–3pm; ☎207/772-5800, ⓦwww.visitportland.com).

Though served by public **buses** ($1), downtown Portland is compact enough to stroll or bike around; Cyclemania, at 59 Federal St (☎207/774-2933), rents **bicycles** for $20 a day. You can also take a **trolley tour** of the city with the affable Mainely Tours, 163 Commercial St ($15; ☎207/774-0808), or the amphibious Downeast Duck Adventures, at the same address ($22; ☎207/774-DUCK), which whisks you through historical Old Port and then takes you into Casco Bay to view the Calendar Islands.

On weekend mornings between late May and mid-October, the high-speed *Cat* **ferry** leaves Portland for **Yarmouth** in Nova Scotia at 9am; the trip takes about six hours each way. High-season fare is $89 per person one-way, and there are various discount and excursion fares; one-way vehicle fares begin at $149. You can get details by calling ☎1-877/359-3760, or by visiting ⓦwww.catferry.com.

Accommodation

Finding a room in Portland is no great problem, although you should book in advance for summer and fall. A number of **budget motels** cluster around exit 48 off I-95. The closest **campground** is *Wassamki Springs*, off Rte-22 towards West-brook (May to mid-Oct only; ☎207/839-4276; $39).

Hilton Garden Inn 65 Commercial St ☎207/780-0780, ⓦwww.hiltongardeninn.com. Fitness center, whirlpool, and wireless internet, all in a snappy location that overlooks the harbor. A bit overpriced, but a good spot. ❽

Inn at Park Spring 135 Spring St ☎207/774-1059 or 1-800/437-8511, ⓦwww .innatparkspring.com. A charming 1835 B&B in the Arts district and convenient to the restaurant and shops of Old Port. Friendly innkeepers, delicious breakfasts. ❼

Inn at St John 939 Congress St ☎207/773-6481 or 1-800/636-9127, ⓦwww.innatstjohn. com. Located just outside of downtown in a slightly dodgy area, this elegant Victorian mainstay offers reasonably-priced, comfortable rooms, some with shared baths. No elevator. ❹–❻

Morrill Mansion B&B 249 Vaughan St ☎207/774-6900, ⓦwww.morrillmansion.com. Well-appointed, newly-opened B&B with stylish rooms, refrigerators, DVD players, free internet access, and a great innkeeper. ❻–❽

Portland Harbor Hotel 468 Fore St ☎207/775-9090 or 1-888/798-9090, ⓦwww .theportlandharborhotel.com. One of the city's newer hotels, in a great location near the waterfront; many rooms overlook the English garden. ❽

Portland Regency Hotel 20 Milk St ☎207/774-4200, ⓦwww.theregency.com. Fancy rooms – some with bay views – in a beautiful renovated brick armory building not far from the Old Port. ❼–❽

The City

Thanks to the several fires, not much of old Portland survives, though grand mansions can be seen along Congress and Danforth streets. The **Wadsworth-Longfellow House/Maine Historical Society**, at 485–489 Congress St (May–Oct & Dec Mon–Sat 10am–4pm, Sun noon–4pm; Nov Sat only, 10am–4pm; $7 includes museum, below; 45min tour on the hour), was Portland's first brick house when built in 1785 by Peleg Wadsworth. However, the house owes its fame primarily to Wadsworth's grandson, the poet Henry Wadsworth Longfellow, who spent his boyhood here. The Historical Society Museum (Mon–Sat 10am–5pm, Sun noon–5pm; $4; ☎207/879-0427) has changing displays of state history and art.

The **Portland Museum of Art** at 7 Congress Square, was built in 1988 by the renowned I.M. Pei partnership (Tues–Thurs, Sat & Sun 10am–5pm, Fri 10am–9pm; June to mid-Oct Mon 10am–5pm; $10, free Friday 5–9pm; ☎207/775-6148, ⓦwww.portlandmuseum.org). It's a stellar exhibition space, brimming with maritime pieces such as Winslow Homer's "Bringing in the Nets" and other affecting seascapes. The lower stories usually hold temporary exhibitions while the second floor displays classic New England scenes. Upstairs is a bit more lively, with

NEW ENGLAND | The Maine coast

a strong collection of fantastic modern works such as Brian White's "mussel dress" – entirely composed of well-worn mussel shells.

The restored **Old Port** near the quayside, between Exchange and Pearl streets, can be quite entertaining, with all sorts of redbrick antiquarian shops, specialist book and music stores (particularly on Exchange Street), and other esoterica. Several companies operate **boat trips** from the nearby wharves: the *Palawan*, a vintage 58ft ocean racer, sails around the harbor and Casco Bay islands and lighthouses from DiMillo's Long Wharf, off Commercial Street (daily in summer; 2hr trip; $25; ℡ 207/773-2163), while Bay View Cruises, 184 Commercial St, offers **seal-watching** tours (daily May–Oct; $12; ℡ 207/761-0496). Casco Bay Lines runs a twice-daily mail boat all year, and additional cruises in summer, to six of the innumerable **Calendar Islands** in Casco Bay, from its terminal at 56 Commercial St, at Franklin ($12–18; ℡ 207/774-7871, Ⓦ www.cascobaylines.com). **Long**, **Peaks**, and **Cliff islands** all have accommodation or camping facilities. If you follow Portland's waterfront to the end of the peninsula, you'll come to the **Eastern Promenade**, a remarkably peaceful two-mile harbor trail that connects to East End Beach, below the headland. Above the promenade, at the top of Munjoy Hill, at 138 Congress St, is the eight-sided, shingled 1807 **Portland Observatory** (June to mid-Oct daily 10am–5pm; $5; ℡ 207/774-5561); you can climb its 103 steps for an exhilarating view of the bay.

Eating

Portland is stuffed with outstanding **restaurants**, and most of its bars, listed separately under "Nightlife and entertainment," below, serve good food as well. The bountiful **Farmer's Market**, in Monument Square (open Wed, May–Nov) offers the perfect opportunity to sample local produce.

Asmara 51 Oak St ℡ 207/253-5122. Amazing, low-key Ethiopian and Eritrean food with the likes of *tsebhi hamli* (collard greens and kale mildly curried and served on *injera* bread). Closed Mondays.
Aurora Provisions 64 Pine St ℡ 207/871-9060. Upscale market/deli with mouthwatering sandwiches, a full selection of coffee, drinks, pastries, salads, desserts, and a small seating area. Perfect for picnic fare. Closed Sun.
Becky's 390 Commercial St ℡ 207/773-7070. The best breakfast spot in Portland, serving hearty American portions from 4am (for the fisherman) until 9pm. Vintage Maine.
Flatbread Company 72 Commercial St ℡ 207/772-8777. Tasty pizza, made with flatbread dough, their own sauce, and all-natural ingredients, in a hip waterfront location.
Fore Street 288 Fore St ℡ 207/775-2717. One of Portland's foremost restaurants, in a huge old warehouse space, serving the likes of white carrot bisque and *panzanella* with fresh mozzarella.

Herb's Gully 55 Oak St ℡ 207/774-6404. Tasty, creatively constructed burritos ("hand-rolled fatties"), quesadillas, and side dishes. They also mix drinks like the "kind buzz" (banana, honey, vanilla, and bee pollen).
Street and Co. 33 Wharf St ℡ 207/775-0887. A great special-occasion seafood spot where the cuts are grilled, blackened, or broiled to perfection. There are a few good non-fish items as well. Reservations recommended.
Two Lights Lobster Shack 225 Two Lights Rd, five miles south of Portland in Cape Elizabeth ℡ 207/799-1677. Perhaps the best seafood-eating scenery in all of Maine – lighthouse to the left, unruly ocean to the right. Plus, the seafood is fabulous.
Walter's Cafe 15 Exchange St ℡ 207/871-9258. New American cuisine in a hip, high-ceilinged dining room right on Exchange Street. Entrées are $15–20, lunch is less expensive and just as good.

Nightlife and entertainment

Performing arts in town include chamber music, opera, dance, and touring theater, some as part of PCA Great Performances held at City Hall's Merrill Auditorium (tickets ℡ 207/842-0800, Ⓦ www.pcagreatperformances.org); larger productions are put on by the Portland Stage Company at the Portland Performing

Arts Center, 25A Forest Ave (☎207/774-0465). Portland Parks and Recreation (☎207/756-8130, ⓦwww.ci.portland.me.us) sponsors free outdoor noontime and evening **jazz** and **blues concerts** throughout the city during the summer. The free *Portland Phoenix* has weekly **listings** of events.

Great Lost Bear 540 Forest Ave ☎207/772-0300. Fifteen state microbrews flow from 53 taps. Also serves good-value burgers, as well as spicy chicken wings and the like.
Gritty McDuff's 396 Fore St ☎207/772-2739. Portland's first brewpub, making Portland Head Pale Ale and Black Fly Stout. Food, folk music, long wooden benches, and a friendly atmosphere, which can get rowdy on Saturday nights.

RiRa 241 Commercial St ☎207/772-3310. Lively Irish pub with great food and a hip waterfront location.
Rivalries 10 Cotton St ☎207/774-6604. Packed with energetic fans, this recent addition to Portland's scene is a clean, hip two-story sports bar.
Top of the East Lounge In the *Eastland Park Hotel* 157 High St ☎207/775-5411. Sophisticated rooftop lounge, with swanky martinis and great views of the city.

North from Portland: the mid-coast

The coastal towns immediately north of Portland are no less commercialized than those to the south; **Freeport**, for example, is basically just an outdoor mall (albeit a good one). However, soon after **Brunswick**, I-95 veers inland toward Augusta, and US-1 is left to run on alone, parallel to the ocean. From here, things become much less frenetic, and prices a whole lot lower; even on the main road you'll find pleasant communities such as **Bath** and **Belfast**; the many headlands can be even more peaceful.

Freeport

Much of the current prosperity of **FREEPORT**, fifteen miles north of Portland, rests on the invention by Leon L. Bean, in 1912, of an unattractive rubber-soled fishing boot. That original boot is still selling, and **L.L. Bean** has grown into a multi-national clothing conglomerate, with an enormous clothing store on Main Street that literally never closes. Originally, this was so pre-dawn hunting expeditions could stock up; all the relevant equipment is available for rent or sale, and the store runs regular workshops to teach backcountry lore. In practice, though, the late-night hours seem more geared toward high school students, who attempt to fall asleep in the tents without being noticed by store personnel. L.L. Bean is now more of a fashion emporium (it's Maine's most-visited destination) and Freeport has expanded to include a mile-long stretch of top-name **factory outlets**, most of which do give genuine reductions on the standard retail prices.

Freeport is not an ideal place to stay – everything falls quiet once the shoppers have gone home – but if you need **accommodation**, the *Harraseeket Inn* at 162 Main St (☎207/865-9377 or 1-800/342-6423, ⓦwww.harraseeketinn.com; ❻) is a wonderful clapboard B&B inn with some eighty rooms. A more affordable option is the sparkling new *Holiday Inn Express,* 450 US-1 (☎207/865-1920, ⓦwww.holidayinn.com; ❺). A few miles north of town, the lovely *Maine Idyll Motor Court*, at 1411 US-1 N (☎207/865-4201, ⓦwww.maineidyll.com; ❹), provides basic but romantic cottages in a pretty, woodsy setting.

The best **food** in Freeport is at *Conundrum Wine Bistro,* 117 US-1 S (☎207/865-4321); most people come for the swanky martinis, then they get hooked on the fresh, eclectic entrées. For a scenic change of pace, head a mile south of Freeport (on Rte-1) to the sea, where the *Harraseeket Lunch & Lobster Co* (☎207/865-3535), extending on its wooden jetty into the peaceful bay, makes a great outdoor lunch spot. The very green promontory visible just across the water is **Wolfe's Neck Woods State Park**. In summer, for $1.50, you can follow hiking and nature trails along the unspoiled fringes of the headland (daily 9am–6pm; ☎207/865-4465).

Brunswick

Only a few miles north from Freeport is **BRUNSWICK**, home since 1794 to Bowdoin College, which counts President Franklin Pierce and author Nathaniel Hawthorne among its alumni. Free tours of the college begin at the Admissions office (tours Mon–Fri 11.30am, 1.30pm & 3.30pm, Sat 11.30am; call ☎207/725-3598 for schedule). After decades of disagreement, experts generally agree that former student Admiral Robert Peary was the first man to reach the North Pole in 1909; whatever the truth, the admiral's assembled equipment and notebooks, found at the **Peary-MacMillan Arctic Museum** (Tues–Sat 10am–5pm, Sun 2–5pm; free; ☎207/725-3416) are a powerful testament to Arctic exploration, and to his own perseverance.

It was while her husband Calvin was teaching here in the early 1850s that Harriet Beecher Stowe wrote *Uncle Tom's Cabin*, a book whose portrait of slavery had such an impact that Lincoln is said to have greeted her with the words "so this is the little lady that started this great war." The rambling old **Harriet Beecher Stowe House** at 63 Federal St is now privately owned, but you can visit the pew at First Parish Church where (as the legend goes) she was seized with the vision of a dying slave – an image that later became a crucial scene in her novel (9 Cleaveland St, pew no. 23; ☎207/729-7331).

A fun day-trip is the **Maine Coast Excursions** (☎1-866/637-2457; ⓦwww.maineeasternrailroad.com; $40 roundtrip), which provides scenic two-hour coastal trips between Brunswick and Rockland (including stops in Bath and Wiscasset), in its restored Art Deco railcars.

A good place to **stay** in town is the basic, clean *Traveler's Inn*, 130 Pleasant St/US-1 (☎207/729-3364 or 1-800/457-3364; ⓦwww.travelersinnme.com ❹), or the brand new *Fairfield Inn & Suites,* 36 Old Portland Rd (☎207/721-0300; ⓦwww.marriott.com ❼). The *Brunwick B&B,* 165 Park Row (☎207/729-4914 or 1-800/299-4914; ⓦwww.brunswickbnb.com; ❻–❼), is a bit frilly, but offers cozy rooms and good hospitality. The *Back Street Bistro* at 11 Town Hall Place (☎207/725-4060) serves excellent New American **dinners**; *Scarlet Begonias*, 212B Maine St (☎207/721-0430), does creative home-cooking at lunch; and the *Little Dog Coffee Shop*, 87 Maine St (☎207/721-9500), is a pleasant sidewalk **café** with good coffee. The landmark *Fat Boy Drive-In,* at 111 Bath Road (☎207/729-9431) was built in 1955, and still offers burgers and lobster rolls in a fun, nostalgic setting; just turn your lights on for service.

The ideal time to visit Brunswick is Labor Day Weekend (first weekend in Sept), when the town hosts its **Bluegrass Festival** (☎207/725-6009) a little further on at Thomas Point Beach, reached by following Hwy-24 from Cook's Corner. The festival, among the best of its kind, attracts some of the biggest bluegrass names from the US and abroad. On the same road, **Orrs Island** has a well-equipped oceanfront **campground** (☎207/833-5595; $33–37 per day for two adults). Also down this way is the 🍴 *Dolphin Marina,* 515 Basin Point Road, (☎207/833-6000), a tiny, almost hidden restaurant that serves up robust seafood meals overlooking the harbor – don't miss the fantastic fish chowder.

Bath

Eight miles on, the small town of **BATH** has an exceptionally long history of **shipbuilding**: the first vessel to be constructed and launched here was the *Virginia* in 1607, by Sir George Popham's short-lived colony. **Bath Iron Works**, founded in 1833, attracted job-seeking Irishmen in such numbers as to provoke a mob of anti-immigrant "**Know-Nothings**" to burn down the local Catholic church in July 1854. The works continues to produce ships – during World War II, more destroyers were built here than in all Japan – but only admits visitors for special occasions such as ceremonial launchings. At the stellar **Maine Maritime Museum**, 243 Washington St, next to the Iron Works two miles south of the town center (daily 9.30am–5pm; $9.75 for two days; ☎207/443-1316), you can tour the old Percy & Small shipyard, explore several visiting historic vessels, or browse their collection of ship-related paintings, photographs, and artifacts.

A pretty fourteen-mile drive south along Rte-209 leads to gorgeous **Popham Beach** ($4; ☎207/389-1335) at the end of the Phippsburg Peninsula, where you can explore scenic sands as well as the hulking **Fort Popham** – a nineteenth-century granite fort.

The *Inn at Bath*, 969 Washington St (☎207/443-4294 or 1-800/423-0964, Ⓦwww.innatbath.com; ❼), is a great **B&B** with beautiful gardens and all the amenities. For a more rural experience, try the *Fairhaven Inn*, 118 North Bath Road (☎207/443-4391 or 1-888/443-4391; ❺–❼), which has shared and private bathrooms, serves an outstanding breakfast, and offers hiking and cross-country skiing in season.

Places to eat include *Solo Bistro Bistro*, 128 Front St (☎207/443-3373), a stranger in these parts – hip, tasty fare in contemporary environs, live jazz some nights; and *Beale Street Barbecue & Grill*, at 215 Water St (☎207/442-9514), offering slow-smoked chicken, pulled pork, and ribs, to stay or to go. *The Cabin*, 552 Washington St (☎207/443-6224) has great pizza. *The Sea Basket,* US-1 N in Wiscasset (☎207/882-6581), has great fried seafood; while eating at *Red's Eats* (☎207/882-6128), just further on US-1 N, is a bit of a culinary rite of passage – people line up and down the block just to get their hands on one of his famous lobster rolls.

Boothbay Harbor

BOOTHBAY HARBOR, at the southern tip of Hwy-27, twelve miles south from US-1, is a crowded, yet undeniably pretty, resort town that's right on the water. The town lays on boat trips of all kinds, including Balmy Days Cruises (☎207/633-2284 or 1-800/298-2284), which offers all-day trips to Monhegan Island for $32, and harbor tours for $12. Cap'n Fish's affable "Puffin nature cruises" (☎207/633-3244 or 1-800/636-3244; $24 for a two and a half hour tour) offers glimpses of the brightly-beaked birds; bring binoculars. There's no need to stay overnight in Boothbay, but if you do pass by, the *Lobstermen's Co-op* at 99 Atlantic Ave (☎207/633-4900), a working lobster pound, dishes up ultrafresh lobsters at low prices, as well as a range of sandwiches. *The Thistle Inn*, 55 Oak St, serves up stellar New American and seafood fare at dinnertime and also has lovely rooms (☎207/633-3541, Ⓦwww.thethistleinn.com; ❻). Back on US-1 N, in Waldoboro, the legendary 🍴*Moody's Diner* (☎207/832-7785) has been a Maine institution for more than fifty years. *Moody's* is the real deal, open late and oozing nostalgia, with vinyl booths, inexpensive daily specials, and fourteen types of freshly-made pie – their four-berry is a must-have.

Rockland and Monhegan Island

ROCKLAND, where US-1 reaches Penobscot Bay, has historically been Maine's largest distributor of **lobsters**, and boasts the busiest working harbor in the state. Though a blue-collar town, in recent years Rockland has grown into one of Maine's hippest, most liveable places. Home to the annual Maine Lobster Festival (held on the first weekend of August; for more info call ☎1-800/LOB-CLAW, Ⓦwww.mainelobsterfestival.com) as well as the North Atlantic Blues Festival (held mid-July; for more info call ☎207/593-1189, Ⓦwww.northatlanticbluesfestival .com), the town's cultural centerpiece is the outstanding **Farnsworth Museum**, 352 Main St (June to mid-Oct daily 10am–5pm; rest of year Tues–Sat 10am–5pm, Sun 1–5pm; $10; ☎207/596-6457, Ⓦwww.farnsworthmuseum.org). The collection spans two centuries of American art, much of it Maine-related, and spreads over several buildings. The **Wyeth Center**, a beautiful gallery in a converted old church, holds two floors' worth of works by Jamie, and N.C. Wyeth. Rockland's other star attraction is the lush Art Deco **Strand Theater**, 345 Main St (tickets $8; ☎207/594-0700; ⒲www.rocklandstrand.com), showing classic films like *North by Northwest* as well as contemporary indie fare.

Rockland is also one terminus of the lovely **Maine Coast Excursions** (☎1-866/637-2457; ⒲www.maineeasternrailroad.com; $40 roundtrip) see p.285 in Brunswick for details.

For **dining**, one of the best of the area's traditional lobster pounds is *Miller's* (☎207/594-7406), on the shore of Wheeler's Bay in an isolated cove at Spruce Head on Hwy-73, open from 10am until 7pm in season. The *Brass Compass Café*, 305 Main St (☎207/596-5960), does a standout breakfast and lunch. The best dinners in town can be had at funky and perennially crowded *Café Miranda*, tucked away at 15 Oak St, just off Main Street (☎207/594-2034), with an array of moderately priced international entrees. A great place to **stay** is the turreted ⚓ *LimeRock Inn*, 96 Limerock St (☎207/594-2257; ⒲www.limerockinn.com; ❼–❽), with fantastic innkeepers, free wifi, and cozy décor; the *Navigator Motor Inn*, across from the ferry to Vinalhaven, 520 Main St (☎207/594-2131; ⒲www.navigatorinn.com; ❹) is the cleanest budget **motel** in the area.

South of Rockland, the pretty **St George Peninsula**, in particular the village of Tenants Harbor, inspired writer Sarah Orne Jewett's classic Maine novel *Country of the Pointed Firs*. At the tip of the peninsula, boats leave from the hamlet of Port Clyde for tiny **Monhegan Island**, eleven miles off the coast and with a year-round population of less than a hundred residents. The island makes a great day-trip away from the tourist bustle of the mainland; you can get there (in about an hour) via Monhegan Boat Lines (May–Oct daily; Nov–April Mon, Wed & Fri; three sailings a day in summer, fewer at other times; $32 roundtrip; ☎207/372-8848, ⒲www.monheganboat.com).

On this rocky outcrop, **lobsters** are the main business, though the stunning cliffs and isolated coves have long attracted artists as well – including Edward Hopper. Fifteen miles of hiking trails twist through the wilderness and past a magnificent 1824 lighthouse. **Accommodation** – such as the *Island Inn* (☎207/596-0371, ⒲www.islandinnmonhegan.com; ❼) – is generally pricey; you may want to try the simple comfort of *The Monhegan House* (☎207/594-7983 or 1-800/599-7983, ⒲www.monheganhouse.com; ❹–❻).

Camden and Rockport

The adjacent communities of **CAMDEN** and **ROCKPORT** split into two separate towns in 1891, in a dispute over who should pay for a new bridge over the Goose River between them. Rockport was at that time a major lime producer, but a fire at the kilns in 1907 not only put an end to that business but also destroyed the ice-houses that were the town's other main source of income. Now it's a quiet working port, among the prettiest on the Maine coast, home to lobster boats, pleasure cruisers, and little else; Camden has clearly won the competition for tourists. The one essential stop in the area is **Camden Hills State Park**, two miles north of Camden ($3), where you can hike or drive up to a tower that affords one of the best views of the Maine coastline; on a clear day it's possible to see as far as Acadia National Park.

Camden and Rockport specialize in organizing sailing expeditions of up to six days in the large schooners known as **windjammers**. Expeditions sail from late May into mid-October. Vessels include the *Appledore* (☎207/236-8353), which does two-hour cruises for $30 from Camden. Contact the Maine Windjammer

Association (📞207/807-9463) for information and schedules for longer three- to six-day trips out of the area. Maine Sport Outfitters in Rockport (📞1-800/722-0826, 🖥www.mainesport.com) rents **kayaks** and **bikes**. Camden's **information** office is at the Public Landing (📞207/236-4404, 🖥www.camdenme.org).

A great **place to stay** in town is the beautiful *Camden Maine Stay Inn*, 22 High St (📞207/236-9636, 🖥www.camdenmainestay.com; ❼–❽), a cozy 1813 white-clapboard inn. *The Belmont*, 6 Belmont Ave (📞1-800/238-8053, 🖥www.thebelmontinn.com; ❻), has a lovely porch and grounds and is decked out in conservative elegance. The *Ducktrap Motel*, just north on Hwy-1 in Lincolnville (📞207/789-5400 or 1-877/977-5400; ❸), is a cute budget option.

Among busy **eating** and **drinking** spots in Camden are the *Camden Deli*, 37 Main St (📞207/236-8343), with gourmet, bulging sandwiches and harbor views from the upstairs patio. Tea-lit *Francine*, 55 Chestnut St (📞207/230-0083), serves excellent French bistro fare amidst romantic environs. The *Lobster Pound Restaurant*, US-1 N in Lincolnville (📞207/789-5550) is a wildly popular seaside restaurant serving heaps of the bright-red crustaceans.

Belfast

Cozy **BELFAST** feels like one of the most lived-in and liveable towns along the Maine coast. Here, eighteen miles from Camden, the shipbuilding boom is long since over (and the chicken-processing plant that regularly turned the bay blood-red has also gone). In recent years, the town has declared the waterfront a historic district; as you stroll around, look out for any number of whitewashed Greek Revival houses, particularly between Church and Congress Streets. Belfast was a lively center in the 1960s, a fact still reflected in its stores, community theater groups, and festivals. While it's a cute little seaside town, there's not much here in the way of sights, although Searsport, five miles north on US-1, is home to the atmospheric **Penobscot Marine Museum**, US-1 at Church St (Mon–Sat 10am–5pm, Sun noon–5pm; $8; 📞207/443-1316), which features an outstanding collection of vintage boats, marine artworks, and nautical artifacts that are spread between a number of historic buildings, including a nineteenth-century sea captain's home.

For **accommodation**, try the *Jeweled Turret Inn*, 40 Pearl St (📞207/338-2304 or 1-800/696-2304, 🖥www.jeweledturret.com; ❻–❼), a beautiful Victorian house with free wireless internet, or the *Londonderry Inn*, 133 Belmont Ave (📞207/338-2763 or 1-877/529-9566, 🖥www.londonderry-inn.com; ❺–❻), an old farmhouse that serves tasty breakfasts. Along Hwy-1 across the Passagassawakeag River in East Belfast are several inexpensive motels, including the decent *Gull*, 196 Searsport Ave (📞207/338-4030; ❹). There's also an oceanfront **campground**, *Searsport Shores Camping Resort*, at 209 W Main St, in Searsport (📞207/548-6059; $35–42 per tentsite).

As for **eating**, *Chase's Daily*, 96 Main St (📞207/338-0555), has fresh eats like breakfast burritos and peach smoothies with ginger and lime; across the bay, *Young's Lobster Pound* (📞207/338-1160) serves $11 fresh-boiled lobster dinners, among the best in the state, along with sunset views. Historic *Darby's Restaurant*, at 155 High St (📞207/338-2339), serves tasty, inventive lunches and dinners to a congenial mix of locals and visitors.

The Blue Hill Peninsula

It used to be that the **Blue Hill Peninsula**, reaching south from Bucksport, was a sleepy expanse of land, too far off the primary roads to attract much attention. But word is slowly getting out about this beautiful area, blanketed with fields of wild blueberries and their pinkish-white flowers, and dotted with both dignified old-money towns like **Castine** and **Blue Hill** and hardcore fishing villages like **Stonington** and **Deer Isle**. Even farther off the established tourist trail, **Isle au Haut** is a remote outpost accessible only by mailboat. As you might expect, the main draw down here is the quiet tranquility that comes with isolation, and while the area presents ample opportunities for exploration, you might find yourself content with a good book, an afternoon nap, and a night in a posh B&B.

Accommodation

Cheap **accommodations** on the Blue Hill Peninsula are a little hard to come by, although the Blue Hill Peninsula Chamber of Commerce, at 28 Water St, (℡207/374-3242), can point you in the right direction. *Sunshine Campground*, way out near the end of Sunshine Road in Deer Isle (℡207/348-2663), has 22 sites from the end of May through mid-October.

Blue Hill Inn Union Street, Blue Hill ℡207/374-2844 or 1-800/826-7415, ⓦwww.bluehillinn.com. Romantic 1830 inn with inviting rooms and décor. Guests are treated to outstanding gourmet breakfasts and a tasty evening wine hour. (A small apartment, Cape House, is available in winter for $165 per night, two-night minimum.) May to November only. ❼

Boyce's Motel 44 Main Street, Stonington ℡207/367-2421 or 1-800/224-2421. Centrally-located, basic, clean rooms. They also have full apartments, with kitchens and living rooms, for $600 per week. Open all year. ❹

Inn on the Harbor Main Street, Stonington ℡207/367-2420. Stonington's fanciest (and priciest) accommodations – there are even spa services. It also has the best location, with a fine view

of the harbor. Open all year; breakfast included. ❻–❽

Pentagoet Inn 26 Main Street, Castine ℡207/326-8616 or 1-800/845-1701, ⓦwww.pentagoet.com. A welcoming old 1894 inn with sixteen rooms restored to reflect an earlier era with the help of the antique-buff owners. The inn also has a quiet and sophisticated pub, *Passports*, a huge porch, and great fine dining (also see "Eating and Drinking" p.290) May to Oct only. ❻–❼

Pres du Port B&B W Main Street at Highland Avenue, Stonington ℡207/367-5007. Brightly wall-papered, whimsically furnished B&B with a great view from the upstairs deck. Also has one endearing little room for only $40. No credit cards. June to Oct only. ❷–❼

Blue Hill

There isn't so much to do in wealthy **BLUE HILL**, at the intersection of routes 172, 176, and 15 adjacent to the Blue Hill Harbor, but plenty of visitors come here simply to relax in the quietude.

It's a 30–45min walk up to the top of **Blue Hill Mountain**, from which you can see across the Blue Hill Bay to the dramatic ridges of Mount Desert Island. The trailhead is not difficult to find, halfway down Mountain Road between Rte-15 and Rte-172. South on Rte-175, **Blue Hill Falls** is a good spot to give kayaking a try: the Activity Shop in Blue Hill at no. 61 Rte-172 (℡207/374-3600, ⓦwww.theactivityshop.com) has canoe and kayak rentals that they'll even deliver to your door ($25 a day and up; reservations recommended).

Castine

Nearly surrounded by water on the northern edge of the Penobscot Bay, **CASTINE** is one of New England's most quietly majestic towns, with nicely kept gardens, enormous elm trees arching over many of the hilly streets, and a peaceful, subdued sophistication. It's pretty tough to miss the *State of Maine*, the huge ship that's usually docked at the landing (except in May and June) and used to train the Maine Maritime Academy's students, who give tours in the summer (call ☎207/326-4311 for schedules, or walk up the plank and ask). Take a stroll down **Perkins Street** to check out the string of enormous mansions looking out over the water; you can also glimpse a number of old historic buildings, such as the 1665 **John Perkins House**. Castine Kayak Adventures (☎207/326-9045) runs various **sea kayaking** tours ($55–105, includes equipment and instruction), as well as bike rentals ($24 a day) from Dennett's Wharf.

Stonington and Isle au Haut

Deer Isle is an eclectic mix of seclusion and sophistication. Clear down at the end of Rte-15, it doesn't get much more remote than beautiful **STONING-TON**, a working fishing village whose residents have long had a reputation for superior seamanship (many pirates and smugglers reputedly made port here in the late nineteenth century). Over the past hundred years, the place has found hard-earned prosperity in the sardine canning and granite quarrying businesses; now it has turned to lobstering. The history of the granite quarries is brought to life at the **Deer Isle Granite Museum**, on 51 Main Street (June–Aug Mon–Sat 10am–5pm, Sun 1–4.30pm, closed Wed; ☎207/367-6331; donation), which counts as its centerpiece a working model of the quarry as it stood in 1900.

Mailboats headed for **ISLE AU HAUT** ("I'll ah hoe") depart from the Stonington landing several times daily (☎207/367-5193 or 207/367-6516; $16 one-way). On this lonely island, you can explore the trails of the less-visited part of **Acadia National Park** – highlighted by the rocky shoreline, bogs, and dense stands of spruce trees.

Eating and drinking

Most of the **eateries** on the peninsula cater to the expensive tastes (and fat wallets) of wealthy summer residents, but there are tasty bargains to be found.

Castine Variety 1 Main St, Castine ☎207/326-8625. The real draw here is not the food – though it was recently voted "best lobster roll" by Maine residents – but rather the opportunity to sit at the tiny counter and chat with the well-connected proprietor.
Harbor Café Main St, Stonington ☎207/367-5099. A salty ambience – it's where the fishermen come in the morning – with sandwiches, coffee, and muffins; right in the center of town.
Maritime Café 27 Main St, Stonington ☎207/367-2600. Pristine café featuring seafood victuals, crepes, and espresso. Ridiculously good views of the harbor.

Morning Moon Café 1 Bay Rd, at int. of Rte-175 and Naskeag Point Rd, Brooklin ☎207/359-2373. South of Blue Hill and known as "The Moon," this is a popular gathering spot for breakfast and lunch. Closes 2pm; closed Mon.
The Pentagoet Inn Main St, Castine ☎207/326-8616. Lobster *bouillabaisse*, warm asparagus salad with prosciutto crisps, and pistachio-dusted diver scallops, served in an atmospheric, elegant dining room.
The Wescott Forge 66 Main St, Blue Hill ☎207/374-9909. Closed Sun. The best of both worlds: fabulous fine dining on a sunny deck and a plush lounge that's open late. Lunch is less expensive and just as good. Closed Sun.

Mount Desert Island

Considering that five million visitors come to **MOUNT DESERT ISLAND** each year; that it contains most of New England's only national park; and that it boasts not only a genuine fjord but also the highest headland on the entire Atlantic coast north of Rio de Janeiro, it is an astonishingly small place, measuring just sixteen miles by thirteen. It is, of course, simply one among innumerable rugged granite islands along the Maine coast; the reason to come here is that it is the most accessible, linked to the mainland by bridge since 1836, and has the best facilities.

The island was named *Monts Deserts* (bare mountains) by Samuel de Champlain in 1604 and fought over by the French and English for the rest of the century. Although all existing settlements date from long after the final defeat of the French, the name remains, still pronounced in French (more like *dessert*, actually).

The social center, **Bar Harbor**, has accommodation and restaurants to suit all pocketbooks, while you'll find lower-key communities all over the island. **Acadia National Park**, which covers much of the island, offers active travellers plenty of outdoor opportunities, including camping, cycling, canoeing, kayaking, and bird-watching.

Getting there and getting around

Mount Desert is easy to reach by **car**, traveling along Hwy-3 off US-1. In high summer, though, roads on the island get congested – the horse-drawn tours don't help – and the 55 miles from Belfast seem much longer.

There are a number of ways to get to Mount Desert via **public transportation**. Before setting out, check out the excellent Island Explorer services (T 207/667-5796, W www.exploreacadia.com/guide.html), which include the free **shuttle buses** that travel through Acadia to Bar Harbor, and even out to the airport. Vermont Transit Lines **buses** (T 1-800/552-8737) run to Bar Harbor from Boston, Bangor, and Port-

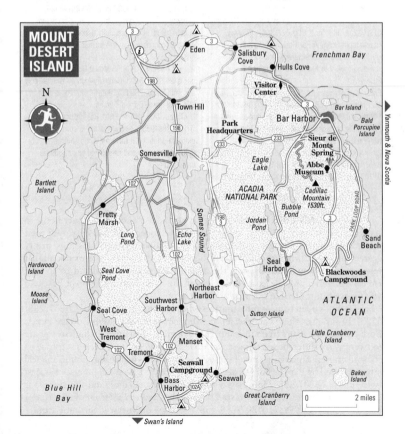

land from mid-June to early September. Concord Trailways has a seasonal shuttle between Bar Harbor and the Bangor airport, with connecting service to Boston's Logan airport – reservations are required (☎207/942-8686 or 1-888/741-8686, ⓦwww.concordtrailways.com). Nearby Hancock City/Bar Harbor Airport (☎207/667-7432) has a limited service run by Colgan Air (☎1-800/272-5488); Bangor International Airport, 45 miles away, is served by Northwest, Delta, and Continental. The *Cat* **high-speed catamaran** takes under three hours to link Bar Harbor with Yarmouth, Nova Scotia (June–early Oct $53–63; ferries leave Bar Harbor daily 8am). For reservations, contact Bay Ferries (☎1-888/249-7245, ⓦwww.catferry.com).

Accommodation

Hwy-3 into and out of Bar Harbor (which becomes Main Street on the way south) is lined with budget **motels** to satisfy the enormous demand for accommodation. Many places are open May to October only, and rates increase drastically in July and August; anywhere offering sea views will cost a whole lot more, as well. The quieter places on the island tend to get booked up early.

Bar Harbor Hostel 321 Main St, Bar Harbor ☎207/288-5587, ⓦwww.barharborhostel.com. Clean, safe, brand-new hostel right near the center of town. Dorm beds $25 a night (plus linens), private room $80.

Coach Stop Inn 715 Acadia Highway, Bar Harbor ☎207/288-9886 or 1-800/927-3097, ⓦwww.coachstopinn.com. A Bar Harbor standout with lovely innkeepers, great rooms, and lots of outstanding food – including life-changing blueberry fritters. ❻

Emery's Cottages on the Shore Sand Point Rd, five miles north of Bar Harbor ☎207/288-3432 or 1-888/240-3432, ⓦwww.emeryscottages.com. Sweet little cottages with kitchenettes (many with wifi) on a private pebble beach just off Hwy-3. Weekly stays in high season cost $540 and up. ❹

Hearthside B&B 7 High St, Bar Harbor ☎207/288-4533, ⓦwww.hearthsideinn.com. It

has a bit of a frilly look, but guests rave about the stellar innkeepers, cozy rooms, great breakfasts, and proximity to shops and restaurants. ❻

Lindenwood Inn 118 Clark Point Rd, Southwest Harbor ☎207/244-5335 or 1-800/307-5335, ⓦwww.lindenwoodinn.com. This first-class inn, built in 1904, offers tastefully decorated rooms and African accents in a stylish former sea captain's home. ❻–❾

Mount Desert YWCA 36 Mount Desert St, Bar Harbor ☎207/288-5008. Centrally-located women-only accommodation. Beds in dorm-style rooms start at $25, and are $70 for the week.

Ullikana B&B 16 The Field, Bar Harbor ☎207/288-9552, ⓦwww.ullikana.com. The place to go in town for a romantic splurge; nicely decorated rooms and unbelievably sumptuous breakfasts. ❼–❾

Bar Harbor

The town of **BAR HARBOR** began life as an exclusive resort, summer home to the Vanderbilts and the Astors; the great fire of October 1947 that destroyed their opulent "cottages" changed the direction of the town's growth. It's now firmly geared towards tourists, though it's by no means downmarket. There's not all that much to do in town. Stroll along the **Shore Path** past the headland of the *Bar Harbor Inn* and along the coast for views of the ocean and Frenchman Bay, and you've seen most of what Bar Harbor has to offer.

Bar Harbor's main **tourist information** office is at the ferry terminal (☎207/288-5103). In summer, there's another in the Municipal Building at 93 Cottage Street. Both offices offer many free and comprehensive maps of the area. In high season, up to twenty-one different **sea trips** set off each day, ranging from deep-sea fishing to cocktail cruises. Among the most popular are the **whale-watching,** puffin, and seal cruises offered by Bar Harbor Whale Watch Company, 1 West St (June–Oct at least twice daily; ☎207/288-2386, ⓦwww.barharborwhales.com), and the two-hour cruises on the impressive **four-masted schooner** *Margaret Todd* from the *Bar Harbor Inn* (daily June–Oct; $32; ☎207/288-4585, ⓦwww.downeastwindjammer.com).

The native Wapanahki heritage is preserved in the Robert **Abbe Museum**, 26 Mount Desert St (mid-May to mid-Oct daily 9am–5pm, Thurs–Sat until 9pm; rest of year Thurs–Sun 10am–5pm; $6, admission includes Sieur de Monts location; ☏207/288-3519; ⓦwww.abbemuseum.org), which has gorgeously constructed exhibit spaces full of light and pale wood panelling. Although the opening displays on Wapanahki culture are well put together, the Abbe's knockout piece is the "Circle of the Four Directions," a contemplative, circular space built of cedar panels. The museum even has an original piece from glass wizard Dale Chihuly, his personal gift to the museum. The museum's original location, just off Park Loop Road, relates the history of the institution and is included in the admission price (daily mid-May to mid-Oct 9am–4pm).

Acadia National Park

ACADIA NATIONAL PARK, sprawled out over most of Mount Desert Island, the Schoodic Peninsula to the east, and Isle au Haut to the south, is the most visited natural place in Maine. It's visually stunning, with all you could want in terms of mountains and lakes for secluded rambling, and **wildlife** such as seals, beavers, and bald eagles. The two main geographical features are the narrow fjord of **Somes Sound**, which almost splits the island in two, and lovely **Cadillac Mountain**, 1530ft high, which offers tremendous ocean views. The summit can be reached either by a moderately strenuous climb or by a very leisurely drive, winding up a low-gradient road.

Open all year, the park has the Hulls Cove **visitor center** near the entrance to the Loop Road north of Bar Harbor (mid-April to Oct daily 8am–4.30pm, open until 6pm July & Aug; ☏207/288-3338), and its headquarters at Eagle Lake (daily 8am–4.30pm; same number as above). The entrance fee is $20 per vehicle or $5 per motorcycle or bike; good for seven days. There are two official **campgrounds**: *Blackwoods*, five miles south of Bar Harbor, off Rte-3 (reserve through the National Park Service at ☏1–800/365-2267 or ⓦreservations.nps.gov; $20 per tentsite), and *Seawall* on Hwy-102A, four miles south of Southwest Harbor (☏207/288-

△ Bar Harbor, ME

3338; tentsites $14–20). Both are in woods, near the ocean, and have full facilities in summer; only *Blackwoods* is open in winter, with minimal facilities.

Once here, the free Island Explorer (Ⓦwww.exploreacadia.com) **shuttle buses** travel through Acadia to Bar Harbor. However, the most enjoyable way to explore the park is to ride a rented **bicycle** around the fifty miles of gravel-surfaced "**carriage roads**," built by John D. Rockefeller to protest the 1913 vote allowing "infernal combustion engines" onto the island. Three Bar Harbor companies rent mountain bikes at less than $20 a day: Bar Harbor Bicycle Shop, at 141 Cottage St, on the edge of town (Ⓣ207/288-3886), Acadia Bike & Canoe, across from the post office at 48 Cottage St (Ⓣ1-800/526-8615), and Southwest Cycle, on Main Street in Southwest Harbor (Ⓣ207/244-5856). All outlets provide excellent **maps**. Be sure to carry water, as there are very few refreshment stops inside the park. You can take a 4hr guided **kayak tour** ($45) from mid-May to mid-October with National Park Sea Kayak Tours, 39 Cottage St (Ⓣ1-800/347-0940, Ⓦwww.acadiakayak.com). Another popular tour operator, Coastal Kayaking Tours (Ⓦwww.acadiafun.com), has the same location and phone numbers as Acadia Bike.

The one and only sizeable beach, five miles south of Bar Harbor, is a stunner: called simply **Sand Beach**, it's a gorgeous strand bounded by twin headlands, with restrooms, a parking lot, and a few short hiking trails. The water, sadly, is usually arctic.

Eating, drinking, and nightlife

Mount Desert's most memorable **eating** experiences are to be found in the many **lobster pounds** all over the island. For nightlife (such as it is), Bar Harbor is where the people are. Cottage Street is a much more promising area to look for food and evening atmosphere than the surprisingly subdued waterfront. The Art Deco **Criterion cinema** at 35 Cottage St (Ⓣ207/288-3441) shows current films.

Café This Way 14 Mt Desert St, Bar Harbor Ⓣ207/288-4483. Fresh, creative breakfast options like the café monte cristo (a French toast sandwich with eggs, ham, cheddar cheese, and syrup on the side). Very busy in summer. They also serve dinner.

Eden Vegetarian Café 78 West St, Bar Harbor Ⓣ207/288-4422. A well-loved dinner spot with inventive, international fare and an emphasis on organic, locally-grown produce.

Havana 318 Main St, Bar Harbor Ⓣ207/288-CUBA. American dining with a Latin sensibility, which translates into lemon and cilantro cured local salmon. Cool modern ambience, sometimes with low-key live music.

Jordan Pond Park Loop Rd, Acadia National Park Ⓣ207/276-3316. Light meals, ice cream, and popovers (light, puffy egg muffins). Afternoon tea, a longtime Acadia tradition, is served in the beautiful lakeside garden from 11.30am–5.30pm.

Lompoc Café & Brewpub 36 Rodick St, Bar Harbor Ⓣ207/288-9392. A healthy Middle Eastern menu for $14–20, with local Bar Harbor Blueberry Ale and other Atlantic Brewing Company beers on draft. Live music every Friday and Saturday night. Open 11.30am–1am.

Mâche Bistro 135 Cottage St, Bar Harbor Ⓣ207/288-0447. Fantastic, fancypants French bistro fare in a tiny, surprisingly low-key setting. Closed Mondays.

Maggie's Restaurant 6 Summer Street, Bar Harbor Ⓣ207/288-9007. In a little blue house away from downtown, *Maggie's* serves locally-fresh, well-composed seafood entrées such as lobster crepes and salmon with cucumber mint salsa. Closed Sundays.

Trenton Bridge Lobster Pound Route 3, Trenton Ⓣ207/667-2977. Outstanding lobster on the bridge en-route to Bar Harbor; good steamers, too. BYOB.

Downeast Maine: the coast to Canada

Few travelers venture into the hundred miles of Maine lying east beyond Acadia National Park, mainly because it is unpopulated, windswept, and remote. In summer, though, the weather is no worse than in the rest of Maine, and the coastal drive is exhilarating – it runs next to the Bay of Fundy, home to the highest tides in the nation. **Downeast Maine** is also marked by its wild **blueberry** crops – ninety percent of the nation's harvest comes from this corner of the state.

A short way northeast of Acadia, a loop road leads from US-1 to the rocky outcrop of **Schoodic Point**, which offers good bird-watching, great views, and a splendid sense of solitude. Each village has one or two B&Bs and well-priced restaurants. **Machias**, almost forty miles further once you rejoin US-1 at Gouldsboro, is quite picturesque, with a little waterfall right in the middle of town. The town was the unlikely scene of the first naval battle of the Revolutionary War, in 1775: the townsfolk commandeered the British schooner *Margaretta* and proceeded to terrorize all passing British shipping, an attack they planned in the still-standing, gambrel-roofed **Burnham Tavern** on Rte-192, just off US-1 (mid-June to early Sept Mon–Fri 9am–5pm; $2.50; ☎207/255-4432). Perhaps the best place to **eat** in town is the *Artist's Café*, 3 Hill St (☎207/255-8900), with its moderately priced and frequently changing menu; chicken parmesan and lobster linguini are typical offerings. Meals are also good at the bluesy and fresh *Fat Cat Deli*, 28 Main St (☎207/255-6777). The *Riverside Inn*, US-1 in East Machias (☎207/255-4134; ⓦwww.riversideinn-maine.com; ❺), overlooks the Machias River and serves good steak and seafood entrées in their dining room.

West Quoddy Head and around

With a distinctive, candy-striped **lighthouse** dramatically signaling its endpoint, **WEST QUODDY HEAD** is the easternmost point of the US, jutting defiantly into the stormy Atlantic. Just beyond the turnoff for Quoddy Head, tiny **LUBEC** was once home to more than twenty sardine-packing plants. They're all gone now, but the remnants of McCurdy's Fish Company, on Water Street, are enough to evoke visions (and maybe even smells) of more prosperous times. Lubec is also the gateway to **Campobello Island**, in New Brunswick, Canada, where President Franklin D. Roosevelt summered from 1909 to 1921, and to which he occasionally returned during his presidency. His barn-red cottage (mid-May to mid-Oct daily 9am–5pm; free) is now open to the public, furnished just as the Roosevelts left it. The rest of **Roosevelt Campobello International Park** (daily sunrise–sunset; free; ⓦwww.fdr.net), located on Canadian soil but established jointly with the United States, is good for a couple of hours of wandering – the coastal trails and the drive out to **Liberty Point** are worth the effort.

The border between the United States and Canada weaves through the center of Passamaquoddy Bay; the towns to either side get on so well that they refused to fight against each other in the War of 1812, and promote themselves jointly to tourists as the **Quoddy Loop** (ⓦwww.quoddyloop.com). It's perfectly feasible to take a "two-nation vacation," but each passage through customs and immigration between **Calais** (pronounced "callous") in the States (fifty miles north of Lubec) and **St Stephen** in Canada does take a little while – and be aware, also, that the towns are in different time zones. The *Peacock House*, in Lubec, 27 Summer Street (☎207/733-2403; ⓦwww.peacockhouse.com, ❸–❻) is the best place to **stay**; it offers friendly B&B accommodations in an atmosphere of casual elegance. Scenic Eastport, some forty miles up the road, has the best **eats**, particularly at the *Eastport Chowderhouse*, 167 Water St (☎207/853-4451) and *La Sardina Loca*, 28 Water St (☎207/853-2739), which has surprisingly good Mexican food in a wonderfully eclectic interior. *Katie's on the Cove* (☎207/454-3297), a Maine institution north of town on Rte-1, doles out unbelievably good confections from a little canary-yellow house.

Inland and western Maine

The vast expanses of the **Maine interior**, stretching up into the cold far north, consist mostly of evergreen forests of pine, spruce, and fir, interspersed with the white birches and maples responsible for the spectacular fall colors.

Distances here are large. Once you get away from the two largest cities – **Augusta**, the state capital, and **Bangor** – it's roughly two hundred miles by road to the northern border at **Fort Kent**, while to drive between the two most likely inland bases, **Greenville** and **Rangeley**, takes three hours or more. Driving (there's no public transportation) through this mountainous scenery can be a great pleasure, but there are few places to stay, and beyond Bangor many roads are tolled access routes belonging to the lumber companies: gravel-surfaced, vulnerable to bad weather, and in any case often not heading anywhere in particular.

This is great territory in which to **hike** – the **Appalachian Trail** starts its two thousand-mile course down to Georgia at the top of Mount Katahdin – or raft on the **Allagash Wilderness Waterway**. Especially around **Baxter State Park**, the forests are home to deer, beaver, a few bears, some recently introduced caribou – and plenty of **moose**. These endearingly gawky creatures are virtually blind and tend to be seen at early morning or dusk; you may spot them feeding in shallow water. They can cause major havoc on the roads, particularly at night, and each year significant numbers of drivers (and moose) are killed in collisions.

Augusta

The capital of Maine since 1832, **AUGUSTA** is much quieter than it was a hundred years ago. The lumber industry here really took off after the technique of making paper from wood was rediscovered in 1844. Augusta also had a lucrative sideline: each winter, hundreds of thousands of tons of **ice**, cut from the Kennebec River, were shipped out, as far south as the Caribbean, in a trade now all but forgotten by history. There are informative displays on Maine's landscape and industrial past at the lively **Maine State Museum**, a short way south of the capitol on State Street (Tues–Fri 9am–5pm, Sat 10am–4pm; $2; ☎207/287-2301).

If you plan to stay in Augusta, the best-value **accommodation** is the *Best Inn*, at 65 Whitten Rd, at the Maine Turnpike's Augusta–Winthrop exit (☎207/622-3776, ⓦ www.bestinnmaine.com; ❺). Hallowell, two miles south of Augusta, has great **eating** options. *Slates*, 167 Water St (☎207/622-9575), has a friendly atmosphere and original entrées like shrimp with coconut pie sauce over jasmine rice, while *Hattie's Chowder House*, 103 Water St (☎207/933-2745), has lobster stew so good it gets shipped all over the country.

Bangor

In its prime, **BANGOR**, 120 miles northeast of Portland, was the undisputed "Lumber Capital of the World." Every winter its raucous population of "River Drivers" went upstream to brand felled logs, which they then maneuvered down the Penobscot as the thaw came in April, reaching Bangor in time to carouse the summer away in grog shops. Bangor exported ice to the West Indies – and got rum in return. Those days were coming to an end when, in October 1882, Oscar Wilde addressed a large crowd at the new Opera House and spoke diplomatically of "such advancement . . . in so small a city."

Bangor today is not a place to spend much time, although its plentiful motels and the big Bangor Mall on Hogan Road north of town make it a good last stop before the interior. Its twin claims to fame are that it's the unlikely home of **Stephen King**, the horror fiction writer (Bett's Bookstore at 584 Hammond St ☎207/947-

7052 stocks King limited editions and collectibles), and that it possesses what, at 31ft, may well be the largest statue of **Paul Bunyan** in the world – though it's pretty easy to miss on the way into town.

Practicalities

Bangor is the last sizeable town along I-95, before the interstate finally veers from the coast and heads north up the Penobscot towards Canada. **Accommodation** possibilities include the *Charles Inn*, an old, green-brick building with 33 comfortably furnished rooms in an art-strewn space (T207/982-2820; ❺). Another good option is the *Bangor Super 8 Motel*, 462 Odlin Rd (T207/945-5681; ❹), with free wifi and shuttles to the airport. For the best breakfasts in Bangor, try *Bagel Central*, 33 Central St (T207/947-1654), the state's only kosher deli. *Thistles Restaurant*, 175 Exchange St (T207/945-5480), serves grilled swordfish, Maine crab cakes, paella, and the like, for lunch and dinner. Beloved *Dysart's* (T207/942-9878), a few miles south in Hermon (off I-95), has been a Maine institution for over 35 years. Essentially a 24-hour truck stop, they have a roomy diner with great trucker-style food. The *New Moon Café*, 49 Park St (T207/990-2233), serves up tasty American food, coffee and espresso, and occasional live music, while the *Whig and Courier*, 18 Broad St (T207/947-4095), is a pub, with burgers, cheesesteaks, and a wide variety of beers on tap.

Baxter State Park and the far north

Driving through northern Maine can feel as though you're trespassing on the private fiefdoms of the logging companies; only **BAXTER STATE PARK** is public land. However, you're pretty much free to hike, camp, and explore anywhere you like, so long as you let people know what you're doing. The scenery is more or less the same everywhere, although of course to get the best of it you'll need to leave your car at some point and set off into the backwoods.

About 70 miles from Bangor, **MILLINOCKET** is a genuine company town, built on a wilderness site by the Great Northern Paper Company in 1899–1900. The hundred-year-old manufacturing facilities still churn out nearly twenty-percent of the newsprint produced in the United States.

Next to **Millinocket Lake**, ten miles northwest, the splendidly ramshackle old *Big Moose Inn* (T207/723-8391, Wwww.bigmoosecabins.com; ❷) makes a great place to stay, with cabins and an inn, and a wide range of activities. There's also an adjacent campground ($10 per person). A more standard place to stay is the clean *Gateway Inn*, Rte-157 just off I-95 at the Medway exit (T207/746-3193, Wwww.medwaygateway.com; ❹), many rooms have decks with views of Katahdin. New England Outdoor Center (T1-800/766-7238,Wwww.neoc.com) conducts day **rafting** and **canoeing** expeditions, as well as "**moose safaris**" and snowmobile vacations and rentals, according to the season. For **food**, head over to the *Appalachian Trail Café*, 210 Penobscot Ave, (T207/723-6720) for a hot meal before heading into the park.

By now you're approaching the southern end of sprawling (200,000 acres) and unspoiled **Baxter State Park** (T207/723-5140; $12 per car) itself. On a clear day the 5268ft peak of **Katahdin** (or "greatest mountain," in the language of the local Penobscot tribe) is visible from afar. The area's **chamber of commerce** resides in Millinocket at 1029 Central St (T207/723-4443, Wwww.katahdinmaine.com); the **Baxter State Park Authority** is at 64 Balsam Drive (T207/723-5140).

North to Canada

The northernmost tip of Maine is taken up by Aroostook County, which covers an area larger than several individual states. Although its main activity is the large-scale cultivation of potatoes, it is also the location of the **Allagash Wilderness Waterway**; this is where most of the **whitewater rafting** companies in this area actually carry out their expeditions.

Britain and the United States all but went to war over Aroostook in 1839; at **Fort Kent**, the northern terminus of US-1 (which runs all the way from Key West, Florida), the main sight is the solid cedar **Fort Kent Blockhouse**, built to defend American integrity and looking like a throwback to pioneer days. People come from all around to eat at *Eureka Hall* (33 miles south, off Rte-161 in Stockholm, ☏ 207/896-3196), an institution of Aroostook County that serves up homestyle meals and incredible desserts.

Greenville

GREENVILLE, at the southern end of Moosehead Lake, is quite pretty, and quite small, and well positioned for exploring the Maine woods. The main attraction is the restored **steamboat** *Katahdin*, which tours the lake and serves as the floating Marine Museum – but watch out ladies, no high heels or smoking on the ship (call for cruise times; $30–35; ☏ 207/695-2716).

The **Chamber of Commerce,** just south of town on Rte-6/15 (summer daily 9am–5pm; rest of year Mon–Sat 10am–4pm; ☏ 207/695-2702, ⓦ www.greenvil-leme.com), has details on **accommodation**, including the lovely *Pleasant Street Inn,* on Pleasant St (☏ 207/695-3400 ⓦ www.pleasantstinn.com; ❻), or the almost unbelievably well-appointed *Blair Hill Inn*, on 351 Lily Bay Road (☏ 207/695-0224, ⓦ www.blairhill.com; ❾) complete with lavish rooms, fabulous views of the lake, incredible fine dining (lit with original Tiffany lamps), and even an excellent summer concert series. Among local **rafting** companies, which charge $80–135 for a day in the water, is Wilderness Expeditions (☏ 1-800/825-WILD), associated with the *Birches Resort* in North Rockwood (☏ 207/268-4330), where you can stay in the main lodge (❹), a cabin (❻), or a tent or yurt (❷). For **food**, head to the *Rod & Reel* (☏ 207/695-0388) at 77 Pritham Avenue for fresh fish entrées on an outdoor patio, or the *Stress Free Moose Pub & Café* (☏ 207/695-3100), at no. 65, for tasty pub grub and good beers on tap.

Moose are indigenous to the area and there is nary a business around here that doesn't somehow incorporate the animal into its name. For several weeks in June, there's even an annual celebration, creatively named MooseMainea (call ☏ 207/695-2702 for more information). The town is also the largest **seaplane** base in New England; contact Currier's Flying Service (☏ 207/695-2778) or Folsom's (☏ 207/695-2821).

Rangeley

RANGELEY is only just in Maine, a little way east of New Hampshire and an even shorter distance south of the border with Québec. Furthermore, as the sign on Main Street boldly declares, it's equidistant (at 3107.5 miles) from the North Pole and the Equator. That doesn't mean it's on the main road to anywhere, although if you're avoiding the coast altogether you can get here direct from the northern side of the White Mountains (see p.264). It has always been a resort, served in 1900 by two train lines and several steamships (though now you have to get here on your own), with the main attraction then being the fishing in the spectacularly named Mooselookmeguntic Lake.

This small and very cozy one-street town, nestling amid a complex system of lakes and waterways, serves as a base for summer explorations, and in winter as the nearest town to the **ski** area at **Saddleback Mountain**. Rangeley also has one unlikely tourist attraction, on Dodge Pond Road, about halfway along the north side of Rangeley Lake, a mile up a side track off Rte-16. The remote **Wilhelm Reich Museum** (July & Aug Wed–Sun 1–5pm; Sept Sun 1–5pm; $6; ☎207/864-3443) is where Wilhelm Reich eventually made his American home after fleeing Germany in 1933. An associate of Sigmund Freud and author of the acclaimed *Mass Psychology of Fascism*, Reich is best remembered for developing the orgone energy accumulator, which he claimed could concentrate atmospheric energy; skeptical authorities focused on the rather unspecific way in which it was said to collect and harness human sexual energy. He is buried here, amid the neat lawns and darting hummingbirds, and his house remains a museum for the reflection of his work.

Practicalities

The *Rangeley Inn,* at 343 Main St (☎207/864-3341, ⓦ www.rangeleyinn.com; ❺), stands between Rangeley Lake and the smaller bird sanctuary of Haley Pond, so you can stay right in town and have a room that backs onto a scene of utter tranquility; there's also a gorgeous old wooden dining room. *North Country Inn B&B,* at 2544 Main St (☎207/864-2440, ⓦ www.northcountrybb.com; ❺), is a good second choice. For **food**, try the *Red Onion,* 2511 Main St (☎207/864-5022), which offers steaks, pizza, and some vegetarian options in a casual, friendly setting. The best food in the area is at the *Porterhouse Restaurant,* in Eustis (take Rte-16E to Rte-27N, it's four miles up on Rte-27N ☎207/246-7932). Set in a 1908 farmhouse, they offer exquisitely prepared entrées and an award-winning wine list.

Just south of the *Porterhouse,* on Eustis Road, is the pretty *Cathedral Pines* **campground** ($15–20 per site, ☎207/246-3491). Twenty miles north of Rangeley, the peaceful *Grant's Kennebago Camps* beside Kennebago Lake (☎1-800/633-4815) arranges fishing, canoeing, and windsurfing, with accommodation in comfortable cabins, including all meals, costing around $150 per person per day; there are slightly lower weekly rates. Rangeley Lakes' **Chamber of Commerce**, down by Lakeside Park (☎207/864-5364 or 1-800/MT-LAKES, ⓦ www.rangeleymaine. com), has details of various activities, including snowmobiling and dawn moosewatching **canoeing** expeditions. One really fun thing to do is to take a **seaplane** trip with the Lake Region Air Service (☎207/864-5307) – a fifteen-minute tour, flying low over vast forests and tiny lakes, costs only $35 per person. Boat cruises are also available, and various outfits along Main Street rent out canoes and mountain bikes.

Sugarloaf USA and Kingfield

The road east of Rangeley cuts through prime moose-watching territory – locals call Hwy-16 East "Moose Alley." After about fifty miles, in the Carrabassett Valley, looms the huge mountain of the **Sugarloaf USA** ski resort (☎1-800/THE-LOAF, ⓦ www.sugarloaf.com). A brilliant place for skiers of all abilities, this condo-studded center would be a more popular destination if it wasn't for the fact that the nearest airport is a two-hour drive away in Portland. In summer, one of the most likely places to spot a gangly **moose** is behind the check-in building on the resort's approach road. Other summer activities include guided **mountainbike tours** with the Sugarloaf Outdoor Center (☎207/237-6830) through their extensive trail system.

A good base for Sugarloaf is fifteen miles south in the tiny town of **KINGFIELD**. The *Mountain Village Inn,* 164 Main St (☎1-866/577-0741; ❻–❼) has welcoming, recently-remodeled rooms and terrific views of Sugarloaf mountain from their sunny dining room; breakfast included. In the center of town, at 246 Main St, the *Herbert Grand Hotel* (☎1-888/656-9922; ❹) has less attractive but functional rooms and a good restaurant. On Rte-142 in Weld, southwest of Kingfield, the *Lake Webb House* (℡207/585-2479; ❹) offers very affordable accommodations in an old farmhouse with a huge porch; breakfast is included. For **food**, the groovy *Queen Anne's Orange Cat* at 329 Main St (℡207/265-2860) has fresh wraps, salads, and espresso.

Kingfield was the birthplace of twins Francis and Freelan Stanley, who invented, among other things, the famous Stanley steamer car and the dry-plate photographic process (which they sold to Kodak, amassing a fortune). The **Stanley Museum**, at 40 School St (May–Oct Tues–Sun 1–4pm; Nov–April Tues–Fri 1–4pm; $4; ℡207/265-2729), celebrates their story. Part of the main room is given over to their sister, Chansonetta, a remarkable photographer whose studies of rural and urban workers have been widely published.

The Great Lakes

AL - ALABAMA
AR - ARKANSAS
CT - CONNECTICUT
DE - DELAWARE
FL - FLORIDA
IL - ILLINOIS

IN - INDIANA
LA - LOUISIANA
MA - MASSACHUSETTS
MD - MARYLAND
ME - MAINE
MI - MICHIGAN

MN - MINNESOTA
MS - MISSISSIPPI
NC - NORTH CAROLINA
NH - NEW HAMPSHIRE
NJ - NEW JERSEY
PA - PENNSYLVANIA

RI - RHODE ISLAND
SC - SOUTH CAROLINA
VA - VIRGINIA
VT - VERMONT
WI - WISCONSIN
WV - WEST VIRGINIA

THE GREAT LAKES

CHAPTER 4

Highlights

* **Rock and Roll Hall of Fame and Museum, Cleveland, OH** From rockabilly to Motown to punk – it's all here inside this striking museum. See p.309

* **The Henry Ford Museum, Detroit, MI** Home to such oddities as the car JFK was riding in when he was shot. See p.329

* **Ann Arbor, MI** A plethora of bookshops, sidewalk cafés, and cultural activities make this the quintessential college town. See p.333

* **Chicago architecture, IL** Superb examples of modern architecture make up the city's distinctive skyline. See p.355

* **Wrigley Field, Chicago, IL** Soak in the Old-World ambiance of this ivy-covered ballpark, with a cold beer and a hot dog. See p.363

* **The Mall of America, Bloomington, MN** The mall you'll never have to leave: hundreds of stores and an amusement park, plus bars and nightclubs. See p.389

* **Boundary Waters Canoe Area Wilderness, MN** Canoe, hike, or just marvel at more than one million acres of lakes, rivers, and forest. See p.393

△ Pictured Rocks National Lakeshore

The Great Lakes

S wept by tumultuous storms and traversed by fleets of oceangoing tankers, the interconnected **Great Lakes** form the largest body of fresh water in the world; Lake Superior alone is more than three hundred miles from east to west. Left untouched, the shores of these inland seas can rival any coastline: Superior and the northern reaches of Lake Michigan offer stunning rocky peninsulas, craggy cliffs, tree-covered islands, mammoth dunes, and deserted beaches. However, for lengthy stretches along Lake Erie, and the bottom lips of lakes Michigan and Huron, sluggish waters lap against large cities and decaying ports.

To varying degrees, the principal states that line the American side of the lakes – **Ohio**, **Michigan**, **Indiana**, **Illinois**, **Wisconsin**, and **Minnesota** – share this mixture of natural beauty and aging industry. Cities such as **Chicago** and **Detroit**, for all their pros and cons, do not characterize the entire region, although the former's magnificent architecture, museums, music, and restaurants make it an unmissable destination. Within the first hundred miles or so of the lakeshores, especially in Wisconsin and Minnesota, tens of thousands of smaller lakes and tumbling streams are scattered through a luxuriant rural wilderness; beyond that, you are soon in the heart of the **Corn Belt**, where you can drive for hours and encounter nothing more than a succession of crossroads communities, grain silos, and giant barns. (Garrison Keillor's wry stories about the fictional backwater town of Lake Wobegon – where "all the women are strong and all the men are beautiful"– set in Minnesota, carry more than a ring of truth.)

Some history

The first foreigner to reach the Great Lakes, the French explorer Champlain, found the region in 1603 inhabited mostly by tribes of Huron, Iroquois, and Algonquin. France soon established a network of military forts, Jesuit missions, and fur-trading posts here, which entailed treating the native people as allies rather than subjects. Territorial disputes with their colonial rivals, however, culminated in the **French and Indian War** with Britain from 1754 to 1761. The victorious British felt under no constraints to deal equitably with the Native Americans, and things grew worse with large-scale American settlement after independence. The **Black Hawk War** of 1832 put a bloody end to traditional Native American life.

Settlers from the east were followed to Wisconsin and Minnesota by waves of **Scandinavians** and **Germans**, while the lower halves of Illinois and Indiana attracted **Southerners**, who attempted to maintain slavery here and resisted Union conscription during the Civil War. These areas still have more in common with neighboring Kentucky and Tennessee than with the industrial cities of their own states.

THE GREAT LAKES

0   100 miles

N

CANADA

NORTH DAKOTA

SOUTH DAKOTA

NEBRASKA

KANSAS

MINNESOTA

IOWA

MISSOURI

WISCONSIN

ILLINOIS

INDIANA

OHIO

KENTUCKY

MICHIGAN

MICHIGAN (Upper Peninsula)

CANADA

NEW YORK

PENNSYLVANIA

WEST VIRGINIA

VIRGINIA

NORTH CAROLINA

Lake Superior

Lake Michigan

Lake Huron

Lake Erie

Lake Ontario

Mississippi River

Missouri River

Ohio River

ISLE ROYALE NATIONAL PARK

VOYAGEURS NATIONAL PARK

Apostle Islands

Keweenaw Peninsula

PICTURED ROCKS NATIONAL LAKESHORE

SLEEPING BEAR DUNES

Door Peninsula

Mackinac Island

Grand Marais

Duluth

St Paul

Minneapolis

Rochester

Des Moines

Omaha

Lincoln

Kansas City

St Louis

Springfield

Madison

Green Bay

Milwaukee

Chicago

Indianapolis

Bloomington

St Joseph

Traverse City

Ludington

Mackinaw City

Flint

Detroit

Ann Arbor

Columbus

Cincinnati

Louisville

Sandusky

Cleveland

Akron

Pittsburgh

Toronto

Niagara Falls

Great Lakes' climate

During the summer, breezes coming off the Great Lakes keep the **temperature** down to a comfortable average of 70°F, though heatwaves can push temperatures over 100°F. Even in spring and fall, **freezing** occurs in the northern reaches of the region, where winter readings of -50°F are not uncommon, and parts of the lakes are frozen solid.

The impetus given to **industry** by the Civil War was encouraged by abundant supplies of ores and fuel, as well as efficient transportation by water and rail. As lakeshore cities like Chicago, Detroit, and Cleveland grew, their populations swelled with hundreds of thousands of poor **blacks** who migrated from the Deep South in search of jobs. But a lack of planning, inadequate housing, and mass layoffs at times of low demand bred conditions that led to the riots of the late 1960s and continuing inner-city deprivation. Depression in the 1970s ravaged the economy – especially the **automobile** industry, on which so much else depended – and brought to the area the unwanted title of "**Rust Belt**." Since then, urban centers have battled back, with **Cleveland**, Ohio, perhaps the most dramatic example of a turnaround in fortunes.

Ohio

OHIO, the easternmost of the Great Lakes states, lies to the south of shallow Lake Erie. This is one of the nation's most industrialized regions, but the industry is largely concentrated in the east, near the Ohio River; to the south the landscape becomes less populated and more forested. Ohio also has the world's largest **Amish** population, who farm in the northeast and west into mid-Indiana but are much less of a tourist attraction than the Pennsylvania Dutch (see p.171).

Enigmatic traces of Ohio's earliest inhabitants exist at the Great Serpent Mound, a grassy state park sixty miles east of Cincinnati, where a cleared hilltop high above a river was reshaped to look like a giant snake swallowing an egg, possibly by the Adena Indians around 800 BC. When the French claimed the area in 1699, it was inhabited by the **Iroquois**, in whose language Ohio means "something great." In the eighteenth century, the territory's prime position between Lake Erie and the Ohio River made it the subject of fierce contention between the French and British. Once the British had acquired control of most French land east of the Mississippi, settlers from New England began to establish communities along both the Ohio River and the Iroquois War Trail paths on the shores of the lake.

During the Civil War, Ohio was at the forefront of the struggle, producing two great Union generals, **Ulysses Grant** and **William Tecumseh Sherman**, and sending more than twice its quota of volunteers to fight for the North. Its progress thereafter has followed the classic "Rust Belt" pattern: rapid industrialization, aided by its natural resources and crucial location, which during the 1970s foundered alarmingly and has only recently begun to revitalize.

Although the state is dominated by its triumvirate of "C" towns (**Cleveland**, **Columbus**, and **Cincinnati**), its most visited destinations are the **Lake Erie Islands**, which have benefited from the recent cleanup of the polluted lake and now attract thousands of partying mainlanders. Cincinnati and Cleveland have both undergone major face-lifts and are surprisingly attractive, as is the comparatively unassuming state capital of Columbus.

Getting around Ohio

Amtrak **trains** between New York or Washington and Chicago stop at either Cincinnati or Cleveland and Toledo. Ohio is well served by Greyhound **buses**, and there are major **airports** at Cleveland and Cincinnati. I-71 is the major interstate linking Cincinnati, Columbus, and Cleveland, while I-70 bisects the state from west to east, passing through Columbus as well. A 325-mile **biking trail**, following former railroad and canal routes, is also under development; when finished, it will link the three "C" towns.

Cleveland and around

Today, the great industrial port of **CLEVELAND** – for so long the butt of jokes after the heavily polluted Cuyahoga River caught fire in the early 1970s – is no longer the "Mistake on the Lake." Although the path back from acute recession is by no means complete on a citywide basis, areas like **downtown**, **the Flats** and **University Circle** are now hubs of energy. Cleveland boasts a sensitive restoration of the Lake Erie/Cuyahoga River waterfront, a superb constellation of museums, glittering city-center malls, and new downtown super-stadiums. Add to that the recent arrival of several major corporate headquarters and classy hotels – as well as the **Rock and Roll Hall of Fame**, of course – and there's an unmistakable buzz about the place.

Founded in 1796, thirty years later Cleveland profited greatly from the opening of the **Ohio Canal** between the Ohio River and Lake Erie. During the city's heyday, which began with the Civil War and lasted until the 1920s, its vast iron and coal supplies made it one of the most important **steel** and **shipbuilding centers** in the world. **John D. Rockefeller** made his billions here, as did the many others whose restored old mansions line "Millionaires' Row."

South and west of the city are several spots of interest, including the quaint lakeshore community of **Vermilion**, the tiny liberal college sanctuary of **Oberlin**, and the charming hamlet of **Peninsula**.

Arrival, information, and getting around

Cleveland Hopkins International Airport is ten miles southwest of downtown. The twenty-minute **taxi** ride into town costs around $20, but the Regional Transit Authority (RTA; ☎216/621-9500, ⓦwww.gcrta.org) **train** is only $1.75 and takes just ten minutes longer. Greyhound arrives at 1465 Chester Ave, at the back of Playhouse Square, while the Amtrak station is on the lakefront at 200 Cleveland Memorial Shoreway NE.

Maps and **information** can be had in advance from the Cleveland **CVB** (Mon–Fri 9am–5pm; ☎1-800/321-1001, ⓦwww.travelcleveland.com). The handiest **visitor centers** are in the lobby of the Terminal Tower in Public Square (Mon–Fri 10am–7pm, Sun noon–6pm; ☎216/621-7981) and on the baggage level of the airport (hours vary).

Cleveland is generally safe, though its size makes getting around easiest by **car**. The RTA runs an efficient **bus** service ($1.75 one-way or $3.50 for an unlimited day-pass) and a small train line ($1.75), known locally as "the Rapids," until about 12.30am. A **light rail** system – the Waterfront Line – connects Terminal Tower, the Flats, the Rock and Roll Hall of Fame, and other downtown sights; it costs $1.75 and runs every fifteen minutes between 6.15am and midnight.

City tours, run by Trolley Tours of Cleveland, leave from the Powerhouse on the west bank of the Flats and cover all major sights within a five-mile radius, including University Circle (May–Oct daily; Nov–April Fri & Sat; $10 for 1hr, $15 for 2hr, reservations required; ☏216/771-4484 or 1-800/848-0173, ⓦwww.lollytrolley.com).

Accommodation

Travelers without cars in Cleveland tend to stay at the downtown **hotels**, which include some reasonable deals – most offer packages that include admission to the Rock and Roll Hall of Fame or other attractions. **B&Bs** can be booked through ⓦwww.travelcleveland.com or ⓦwww.bedandbreakfast.com/cleveland.

Cleveland Marriott Downtown at Key Center 127 Public Square ☏216/696-9200 or 1-800/228-9290, ⓦwww.clevelandmarriottdowntown.com. Probably the best value of the downtown upscale hotels, the *Marriott* is clean, bright, and close to the action. ⑤

Comfort Inn Downtown 1800 Euclid Ave ☏216/861-0001, ⓦwww.comfortinn.com. This chain hotel is on the edge of downtown, a fair walk from most bars and restaurants. ④

Embassy Suites Hotel 1701 E 12th St ☏216/523-8000 or 1-800/362-2779, ⓦwww.clevelanddowntownembassysuites.com. Downtown hotel with spacious rooms near Playhouse Square – look for special deals online. ⑤

Glidden House 1901 Ford Drive ☏216/231-8900 or 1-800/759-8358, ⓦwww.gliddenhouse.com.

Sixty rooms are housed in a Gothic mansion situated in University Circle. Large continental breakfast is included. ⑥

Holiday Inn Select City Center Lakeshore 1111 Lakeside Ave ☏216/241-5100 or 1-888/425-3835, ⓦwww.holiday-inn.com. Has great lake views and is near the Rock and Roll Hall of Fame. ④

Intercontinental Suites 8800 Euclid Ave, University Circle ☏216/707-4300 or 1-877/707-8999, ⓦwww.cleveland.intercontinental.com. This luxury hotel is convenient to Little Italy and Coventry Village. Ask about weekend discounts. ⑥

Wyndham Hotel 1260 Euclid Ave ☏216/615-7500 or 1-800/996-3426, ⓦwww.wyndham.com. The best luxury option in the downtown theater district, Playhouse Square. ⑥

The City

The main streets in Cleveland lead to the stately nineteenth-century Beaux Arts **Public Square**, at the very center of downtown, and dominated in its southwestern corner by the landmark **Terminal Tower**. **Ontario Street**, which runs north–south through the Square, divides the city into east and west. Cleveland's most interesting areas are at two opposite ends of the spectrum: the industrial romance of the **Flats** in the northwest, and the cultural institutions of **University Circle**, east of the river.

Downtown and around

Downtown Cleveland is once again a bustling place, and its recent redevelopment has seen the emergence of several distinct subsections. In its traditional heart, among the banks and corporate headquarters, stand a couple of glamorous shopping malls. One, the **Avenue at Tower City**, is located in the Terminal Tower. Another, the **Arcade**, is a skylit hall built in 1890. Twelve blocks away, at 1501 Euclid Ave, the **Playhouse Square Center** (see p.312) is an impressive complex of four renovated old theaters; the small Ohio Theater, with its gorgeous starlit-sky lobby ceiling, is worth a look.

Just to the southwest is the **Gateway District**, where new restaurants and bars surround **Jacobs Field** stadium, home of the Indians base-

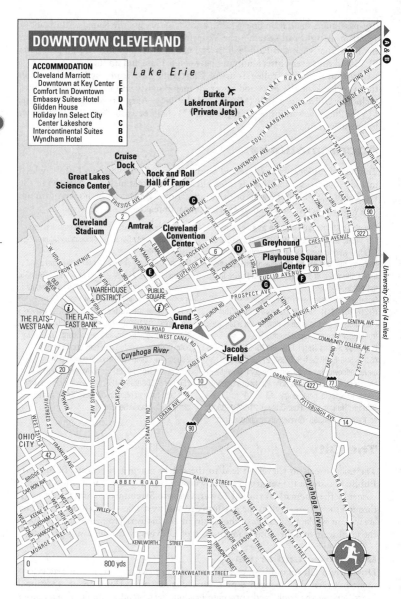

DOWNTOWN CLEVELAND

ACCOMMODATION
Cleveland Marriott
  Downtown at Key Center   **E**
Comfort Inn Downtown   **F**
Embassy Suites Hotel   **D**
Glidden House   **A**
Holiday Inn Select City
  Center Lakeshore   **C**
Intercontinental Suites   **B**
Wyndham Hotel   **G**

Lake Erie

**Burke
Lakefront Airport
(Private Jets)**

**Cruise
Dock**

**Great Lakes
Science Center**

**Rock and Roll
Hall of Fame**

**Cleveland
Stadium**

Amtrak

**Cleveland
Convention
Center**

Greyhound

**Playhouse Square
Center**

**WAREHOUSE
DISTRICT**

**PUBLIC
SQUARE**

**THE FLATS
WEST BANK**

**THE FLATS
EAST BANK**

**Gund
Arena**

Cuyahoga River

**Jacobs
Field**

**OHIO
CITY**

Cuyahoga River

0   800 yds

N

ball team (℡216/420-4200, ⓦwww.indians.com), and the equally modern multipurpose **Quicken Loans Arena** (℡216/420-2000, ⓦwww
.theqarena.com), aka The Q, which hosts the Cavaliers basketball team, along with
major sporting and entertainment events.

West of The Q, at the **riverfront**, one of the nation's busiest waterways shares
space with excellent bars, clubs, and restaurants, all strung out along a board-

walk. On the west bank of the Cuyahoga River, the **Flats**, long known for its nightlife, has an atmospheric, industrial setting. Magnificent grimy old buildings, warehouses, and slag heaps, set among fourteen **bridges**, appear powerful and romantic rather than depressing, a proud testimony to Cleveland's manufacturing history.

A short but steep walk uphill from the Flats leads to the **Historic Warehouse District**, a nicely developing stretch of nineteenth-century commercial buildings between West Third and West Ninth streets, given over to shops, galleries, cafés, and trendy new restaurants. North of here, on the other side of the busy Cleveland Memorial Shoreway (Hwy-2), the waters of Lake Erie lap gently into

The Rock and Roll Hall of Fame

Cleveland, not the most obvious candidate, convincingly won a hotly contested bid to host the **Rock and Roll Hall of Fame** largely because **Alan Freed**, a local disc jockey, popularized the phrase "rock and roll" here back in 1951. Since then, Cleveland has hardly produced a roll call of rock icons – Joe Walsh, Pere Ubu, and Nine Inch Nails are about the biggest names. Ignoring criticism that it won out simply because it stumped up most cash, the city embraced the idea of the museum with enthusiasm and few now argue that it was not the correct choice.

The idea for a definitive rock museum was first floated in 1983, with the establishment of the **Rock Hall of Fame Foundation** to honor all those who have made "an exceptional contribution to modern music." The inductees are selected annually by an international panel of rock "experts," but only those performers who have released a record 25 years prior to their nomination are eligible.

The museum's octogenarian architect – **I.M. Pei** – wanted the building "to echo the energy of rock and roll." One of Pei's trademark tinted-glass pyramids (a smaller version of the one he did at the Louvre), this white concrete, steel, and glass structure strikes a bold pose on the shore of Lake Erie, especially when illuminated at night. The base of the pyramid extends into an impressive entrance plaza shaped like a turntable, complete with a stylus arm attachment.

The museum is much more than an array of **mementos** and artifacts. Right from the start, with the excellent twelve-minute **films** *Mystery Train* and *Kick Out the Jams*, the emphasis is on the contextualization of rock. The exhibits chart the art form's evolution and progress, acknowledging influences ranging from the blues singers of the Delta to the hillbilly wailers of the Appalachians. Elsewhere in the subterranean main exhibition hall, there's an in-depth look at seven crucial **rock genre**s through the cities that spawned them: rockabilly (Memphis), R&B (New Orleans), Motown (Detroit), psychedelia (San Francisco), punk (London and New York), hip-hop (New York), and grunge (Seattle). Much space is taken up by exhibits on what the museum sees as key artists of all time, including Elvis Presley, the Beatles, Jimi Hendrix, the Rolling Stones, and U2.

Above ground, at entry level, Pei's airy structure feels like a modern art gallery. Several East German Trabant **cars**, which U2 used during their Zooropa tour, are suspended from the ceiling, while giant **guitars** give a more direct musical impression. Escalators lead to a level devoted to Freed, **studio techniques**, and a great **archive** of rare live recordings, which you can listen to on headphones. The third floor houses the **Hall of Fame** itself, where an hourly video presentation of all inductees unfolds on three vast screens; the upper stories contain the museum's **temporary exhibitions**.

The museum is at North Coast Harbor (daily 10am–5.30pm, Wed also until 9pm; summer Sat until 9pm; $20; reservations ☎216/781-7625 or 1-800/493-7655, ⓦwww.rockhall.com). As weekends get very crowded, it's much better to go on a weekday. Alternatively, you can plan a visit to coincide with the extensive series of seminars and workshops that feature Hall of Fame inductees and leading rock writers.

△ Rock and Roll Hall of Fame

North Coast Harbor, a showpiece of Midwest regeneration. To see the city from the water, try a two-hour cruise on the *Goodtime III* ($15; ☎216/861-5110) from the dock at East Ninth Street Pier, just beyond the I.M. Pei–designed **Rock and Roll Hall of Fame** (see box, p.309). Next door to the Rock Hall – as Clevelanders refer to it – is the giant **Great Lakes Science Center** (daily 9.30am–5.30pm; $8.95, $12.95 OMNIMAX combo-ticket; ☎216/696-4941, ⓦwww.greatscience.com), one of America's largest interactive science museums, which cleverly outlines the interdependency of science, technology and the environment, with emphasis on the lakes region. Across the road, the futuristic, 72,000-seat **Cleveland Stadium** is the home of the Browns pro football team (☎440/891-5000, ⓦwww.clevelandbrowns.com).

To the west of the river, **Ohio City** is one of Cleveland's more hip neighborhoods, with junk stores, Victorian clapboard houses, and the busy **West Side Market** at Lorain Ave and West 25th St (Mon & Wed 7am–4pm, Fri & Sat 7am–6pm), selling all manner of ethnic foods. It's easily spotted by its redbrick Victorian clock tower.

Out from downtown

Four miles east of downtown, **University Circle** is a cluster of more than seventy cultural and medical institutions, and is also home to several major performing arts companies (see p.312) as well as Frank Gehry's twisted-steel Weatherhead School of Management building at Case Western University. The eclectic **Museum of Art**, fronted by a lagoon at 11150 East Blvd (Tues, Thurs, Sat & Sun 10am–5pm, Wed & Fri 10am–9pm; free; ☎216/421-7340, ⓦwww. clevelandart.org) and currently undergoing major expansion, has a collection that ranges from Renaissance armor to African art, with a good café. Also notable is the **Museum of Natural History**, Wade Oval (Mon–Sat 10am–5pm, Sun noon–5pm; summer Tues–Thurs until 7pm; Sept–May Wed until 10pm; $7.50, planetarium $4; ☎1-800/317-9155, ⓦwww.cmnh.org), with exhibits on dinosaurs and Native American culture. The **Cleveland Botanical Garden**, 11030

East Blvd (daily 10am–5pm; $7.50; ☎1-888/853-7091, ⓦwww.cbgarden.org), has a glasshouse that features a cloud forest, a desert ecosystem, free-roaming chameleons and butterflies, a waterfall, and a treetop walkway. Meanwhile, dotted along East and Martin Luther King Jr boulevards in Rockefeller Park, twenty-four small landscaped cultural **gardens** are dedicated to and tended by Cleveland's diverse ethnic groups, including Croatians, Estonians, and Finns. Adjacent to University Circle, **Murray Hill** is Cleveland's Little Italy; beyond this attractive area of brick streets, small delis, and galleries is the trendy neighborhood of **Coventry Village**.

Five miles southwest of downtown via I-71 (exit at W 25th or Fulton Rd), the **Cleveland Metroparks Zoo**, 3900 Wildlife Way (summer Mon–Fri 9am–5pm, Sat & Sun 9am–7pm; rest of year daily 10am–5pm; rainforest also open Wed until 8pm; $9; ☎216/661-6500, ⓦwww.clemetzoo.com), features a "Wolf Wilderness," while the spectacular 164-acre rainforest building is populated by some seven thousand plants and 118 species of animals, including orangutans, American crocodiles, and Madagascan hissing cockroaches. During summer, the RTA runs special **buses** from downtown to the zoo.

Eating

The city has a range of culinary delights, many of them ethnic. The **West Side Market** in Ohio City is one of the best places for cheap and unusual picnic food, and there are some excellent fine-dining restaurants downtown. Little Italy and Coventry Village are worth exploring for authentic Italian food and coffee bars, respectively. The *Arabica* chain also serves up good-quality espresso at several locations around the city; there's one in University Circle at 11300 Juniper Rd (☎216/791-0300).

The Blue Point Grille 700 W St Clair Ave ☎216/875-7827. Serves the best seafood in town, with specials such as Nagshead grouper with lobster mashed potatoes.

Castaldi's Market & Grille 230 W Huron Rd ☎216/241-2232. Homemade pasta and other Italian dishes that, on weekends, are served by singing waiters.

🏋 **Cleveland Chophouse and Brewery** 824 W St Clair ☎216/623-0909. Try the mashed potatoes at this spacious, casual brewery and steakhouse – they're fantastic.

Flat Iron Café 1114 Center St ☎216/696-6968. Landmark Irish-American tavern on the east (downtown) bank of the Flats, serving up good sandwiches, salads, and desserts, plus a smooth pint of Guinness.

Hornblower's Barge & Grille 1151 N Marginal Rd ☎216/363-1151. Good-value pasta, sandwiches, and seafood are offered in a fine location overlooking Lake Erie, just a short stroll from the Rock Hall.

Mama Santa 12305 Mayfield Rd ☎216/231-9567. In Little Italy, unpretentious and inexpensive Southern Italian home-cooking.

Nate's Deli & Restaurant 1923 W 25th St ☎216/696-7529. This Middle Eastern café serves great gyros and plenty of vegetarian dishes. The *hummus*, in particular, has quite a reputation. Open only during the day.

Shooters on the Water 1148 Main St ☎216/861-6900. You can watch ships coming and going on the Cuyahoga while eating seafood and other classic American food.

Tommy's 1824 Coventry Rd ☎216/321-7757. Great-value food, much of it Middle Eastern vegetarian, is dished up in a trendy, bright setting in lively Coventry Village. Try the famous shakes and check out the adjoining used-book store.

Nightlife and entertainment

The **Flats** area boasts the greatest conglomeration of drinking, live music, and dancing venues, although they tend to be cheesier than their counterparts in the **Warehouse District** and the more bohemian **Ohio City** across the river. Under five miles east, both **University Circle** and youthful **Coventry Village** have good bars. Cleveland's **rave** scene remains strong and mostly underground; if you're interested, look for flyers at Record Revolution 1832 Coventry Rd (☎216/321-7661).

For more refined entertainment, the **Playhouse Square Center** (☎216/241-6000, ⊛www.playhousesquare.com) is home to the **Cleveland Opera** and **Ballet**, as well as drama events like the Great Lakes Theatre Festival and concerts. The well-respected **Cleveland Orchestra** (☎216/231-1111, ⊛www.clevelandorchestra.com) is based in University Circle at Severance Hall, 11001 Euclid Ave, close to the leading regional theater of the **Cleveland Play House** (☎216/795-7000, ⊛www.clevelandplayhouse.com). For **listings** information, try one of Cleveland's two free weeklies: the well-written *Free Times* covers all of the arts, while *Scene* concentrates mostly on music.

Beachland Ballroom 15711 Waterloo Rd ☎216/383-1124, ⊛www.beachlandballroom.com. Over ten miles east of downtown, but this buzzing venue often draws the cream of indie and rock bands.

Great Lakes Brewing Co. 2516 Market St, Ohio City ☎216/771-4404. At this famous old joint, Cleveland's best brewpub, the huge mahogany bar still bears the bullet holes made during a 1920s shootout involving lawman Elliot Ness.

Grog Shop 2785 Euclid Heights Blvd, Cleveland Heights ☎216/321-5588. Near Coventry Village, the *Grog Shop* is a fun, sweaty collegiate punk and alternative venue.

Harbor Inn 1219 Main Ave ☎216/241-3232. A great old-fashioned bar amid the hyped chain outfits of the Flats, one with 180 beers, a few video games, and lots of character.

Mercury Lounge 1392 W 6th St ☎216/566-8840. In the Warehouse District, this hip martini lounge tends to attract Cleveland's fashionable set.

Around Cleveland

Less than an hour outside the city are several small towns and sights well worth exploring. **VERMILION**, beyond the western suburbs of Cleveland, is also known as Harbor Town, for its attractive lakeside area, which has thrived since 1837. Today it's a quaint old hamlet lined with clapboard houses, cedar trees, and tidy gardens. Old-style galleries and shops hug the small downtown, a stone's throw from the dockside. The **Inland Seas Maritime Museum**, 480 Main St (daily 10am–5pm; $6; ☎1-800/893-1485, ⊛www.inlandseas.org), does a worthy job of exploring shipping on the Great Lakes, spanning from the late seventeenth century to the wreckage of the *Edmund Fitzgerald* freighter almost three hundred years later. Vermilion's **Chamber of Commerce** is at 5495 Liberty Ave (summer Mon–Fri 10am–4pm; rest of year Mon–Fri 10am–3pm, closed Wed; ☎440/967-4477, ⊛www.vermilionohio.com). The best place to **stay** in town is the comfortable *Motel Plaza*, 4645 Liberty Ave (☎440/967-3191; ❸).

Some twenty miles southeast of Vermilion, the famously liberal college town of **OBERLIN** clusters around the green acres of Tappan Square. Founded in 1834, **Oberlin College**, on the square's north and east sides, was America's first co-ed university, and one of the first to enroll black students. From the start, it played a pivotal role in facilitating the movement of black slaves from the Deep South to Canada via the Underground Railroad. A **sculpture** of railroad tracks emerging from the earth, opposite the Conservatory of Music on South Professor Street, is one of several such commemorative sights detailed in a fascinating **walking tour** leaflet available from the **Chamber of Commerce**, inside the *Oberlin Inn* at 7 N Main St, suite 117 (Mon–Thurs 10am–3pm, Fri 9am–noon; ☎440/774-6262, ⊛www.oberlin.org). Also of interest is the **Allen Memorial Art Museum**, 87 N Main St (Tues–Sat 10am–5pm, Sun 1–5pm; free; ⊛www.oberlin.edu/allenart). Recognized as one of the best college art museums in the US, it holds more than fourteen thousand objects, from ancient African icons to Japanese scroll paintings, plus a fine array of contemporary art. As for **accommodation**, try the pleasant *Oberlin Inn*, 7 N Main St (℡440/775-1111 or 1-800/376-4173, 🌐www.oberlininn.com; ❹). Oberlin also boasts half a dozen hip coffeehouses and bars.

Twenty miles south of Cleveland off US-77, the village of **PENINSULA** is nestled in the heart of the **Cuyahoga Valley National Recreation Area**, where the Ohio & Erie Canal Towpath's hiking and biking trail follows the meandering Cuyahoga River for twenty miles. You can **rent a bike** in town at Century Cycles, 1621 Main St ($7 per hour; ℡330/657-2209). A few miles south of town off Riverview Road, the sprawling **Hale Farm and Village** (summer Tues–Sat 11am–5pm, Sun noon–5pm; $14.50; ℡1-877/425-3327, 🌐www.wrhs.org) brings to life the fictional 1848 Ohio township of Wheatfield, complete with good-natured role-playing townsfolk and artisans who demonstrate skills like brick-making and glass-blowing. The best place to stay in the area is *HI-Stanford House*, 6093 Stanford Rd (℡330/467-8711), a hostel in a lovely old farmhouse where a bed costs $15–18 per night.

A few miles farther south in **AKRON** (home of the Goodyear Tire and Rubber Co., as well as quirky '70s band Devo), visitors can tour Goodyear co-founder F.A. Seiberling's palatial **Stan Hywet Hall and Gardens**, 714 N Portage Path (April–Dec daily 10am–4.30pm, gardens 9am–6pm; $12, gardens only $6; ℡330/836-5533, 🌐www.stanhywet.org), a magnificent 65-room Tudor Revival country house finished in 1915, with secret passageways, hand-carved wood paneling, and an indoor swimming pool.

Sixty miles south of Akron, the world's largest Amish community resides in **HOLMES COUNTY**, a meandering section of hills, farms, and backroads. **Berlin** is the commercial center of Amish country, a somewhat saccharine arts-and-crafts center. A good dose of Amish simplicity is better found in the surrounding countryside: at **Yoder's Amish Home**, between the towns of Walnut Creek and Trail on Rte-515 (mid-April–Oct Mon–Sat 10am–5pm; $8; ℡330/893-2541, 🌐www.yodersamishhome.com), visitors can tour two Amish homes and a barn, and ride in a horse-drawn carriage.

The Lake Erie Islands

The **LAKE ERIE ISLANDS** – Kelleys Island and the three **Bass Islands** further north – were early stepping stones for the **Iroquois** on the route to what is now Ontario. French attempts to claim the islands in the 1640s met with considerable hostility, and they were left more or less in peace until 1813, when in the **Battle of Lake Erie**, fought off South Bass Island, the Americans established their control over the Great Lakes by destroying the entire English fleet.

The islands first tasted prosperity in the 1860s, when a boom in **wine production** meant that nearly every available acre was planted with grapes. Tourism arrived almost simultaneously, as steamboats brought wealthy visitors to spend their summers here in grand hotels. However, the economy was hit hard by Prohibition and the emergence of the California wineries, as well as by the advent of the automobile. In the 1970s, Lake Erie's appalling pollution was the final straw that led to a huge cleanup of the lake and islands. The plan worked; today the islands are again a popular summer destination, with fishing, swimming, and partying the main attractions. Various mainland towns off of Rte-2, such as **Sandusky** and **Port Clinton**, act primarily as jump-off points for the islands.

The mainland

The large coal-shipping port of **SANDUSKY**, fifty miles west of Cleveland on US-2, is probably the most visited of the lakeshore towns, thanks to **Cedar Point Amusement Park**, five miles southeast of town (early May–Labor day daily, mid-Sep to late Oct hours vary; $39.95, after 4/5pm $24.95; ☎419/627-2350, ⓦwww.cedarpoint.com). The largest ride park in the nation – and considered by many to be the best in the world – Cedar Point boasts no less than sixteen roller coasters. The neighboring **Soak City** water park (June–Aug daily 10am–9pm; $28, after 4/5pm $15.95) provides a good way to cool off, with eighteen acres of water slides and a wave pool.

The smaller resort town of **PORT CLINTON**, twelve miles west across the Sandusky Bay Bridge, is another departure point for the islands. Its pleasant lakefront is dotted with decent cafés and jet-ski rental outlets. Try not to leave the area without exploring the rest of the peninsula, which has some glorious views, particularly around little **Marblehead**, fourteen miles east of Port Clinton.

Eight miles south of Sandusky, tiny **MILAN** (pronounced "MY-lan") boasts a pleasant, leafy village square and many well-preserved Greek Revival–style homes. Its most famous building is the two-story brick **Thomas Edison Birthplace**, 9 Edison Drive (summer Tues–Sat 10am–5pm, Sun 1–5pm; April, May, Sept & Oct Tues–Sun 1–5pm; Nov–March Wed–Sun 1–4pm; $5; ☎419/499-2135, ⓦwww. tomedison.org), with guided tours and an adjacent museum dedicated to the inventor of the light bulb.

Practicalities

Amtrak **trains** pass through Sandusky once daily en route between Chicago and the east coast. The station, at North Depot and Hayes avenues, is in a dodgy area, and is unstaffed. Greyhound **buses** stop way out at 6513 Milan Rd (US-250). Sandusky's **visitor center** is at 4424 Milan Rd (summer Mon–Fri 8am–8pm, Sat 9am–4pm, Sun 10am–4pm; rest of year Mon–Fri 8.30am–5.30pm; ☎419/625-2984 or 1-800/255-3743, ⓦwww.sanduskycounty.org).

Accommodation prices in Sandusky shoot up in high season, with simple motel rooms costing $200-plus on peak weekends. Along the main drag of Cleveland Road (US-6), the *Best Western Cedar Point*, no. 1530 (☎419/625-9234, ⓦwww. bestwestern.com; ⑨), has a pool. **Camping** is available at the *Bayshore Estates*, 2311 Cleveland Rd (☎419/625-7906 or ☎1-800/962-3786, ⓦwww.mhdcorp. com; from $21.95), and at the *Milan Travel Park*, just off US-80 at 11404 US-250 N (☎419/499-4627, ⓦwww.staycolonial.com; $22), which has a pool. Also in **Milan**, the *Colonial Inn South*, 11211 US-250 (☎419/499-3403 or 1-800/886-

---

Getting to the Islands

Ferries to **Kelleys Island** are operated by Kelleys Island Ferry Boat Line from Main St in **Marblehead** year round, when weather permits, as frequently as every half hour at peak times ($13 roundtrip, bikes $6 extra; ☎419/798-9763, ⓦwww.kelleysis-landferry.com). Jet Express runs summer **catamaran** services from their dock at 101 West Shoreline Dr, Sandusky (☎1-800/245-1538, ⓦwww.jet-express.com) to Kelleys Island ($24 roundtrip) and **South Bass Island** ($32 roundtrip), and to the latter only from 5 N Jefferson St, Port Clinton ($24 roundtrip). South Bass Island is also served by Miller Ferry ($12 roundtrip, bicycle $4; ☎1-800/500-2421, ⓦwww.millerferry.com) from late March to late November. **Flights** to both Kelleys Island and South Bass Island leave daily from Sandusky and cost $40 one way. Contact Griffing Airlines (☎419/626-5161).

9010; ❷), is a nice family-owned motel, while **Port Clinton** has the *Sunnyside Tower*, 3612 NW Catawba Rd (℡419/797-9315 or 1-888/831-1263, Ⓦwww.sunnysidetower.com ❺), a Victorian-style B&B. For a good **meal** and **live music** in fun surroundings (there's an on-site waterfall), head for *Margaritaville* in Sandusky, at the junction of highways 6 and 2 (℡419/627-8903).

Kelleys Island

About nine miles north of Sandusky, **KELLEYS ISLAND** (Ⓦwww.kelleysisland .com) lies in the western basin of Lake Erie. Seven miles across at its widest, it's the largest American island on the lake, but it's also one of the most peaceful and picturesque, home to just 175 permanent residents. The whole island – green, sleepy, and with few buildings less than a century old – is a National Historic District. Its seventy-plus archeological sites include **Inscription Rock**, a limestone slab carved with 400 year-old pictographs; you can find it east of the dock on the southern shore. The **Glacial Grooves State Memorial**, on the west shore, is a 400-foot trough of solid limestone, scoured with deep ridges by the glacier that carved out the Great Lakes.

Settled in the 1830s, Kelleys was initially a working island, its economy based on lumber, then wine, and later limestone quarrying. All but the last have collapsed, though a steady **tourist industry** has developed.

Practicalities

The Kelleys Island **Chamber of Commerce** is on Division Street, straight up from the dock (summer daily 10am–5pm; ℡419/746-2360, Ⓦwww .kelleysislandchamber.com). Getting around the island is easy; cars are heavily discouraged and most people, when not strolling, use **bikes** ($3.50 per hour/$15 per day) or **golf carts** ($15 per hour/$80 per day), available from Caddy Shack Square, also on Division St (℡419/746-2221). One comfortable **accommodation** option is *The Inn on Kelleys Island*, 317 W Lakeshore Drive (℡1-866/878-2135, Ⓦwww.aves.net /the-inn; ❹), a restored nineteenth-century Victorian home with a great lake view and a private beach; or ask at the Chamber of Commerce. You can **camp** for $16 at the first-come, first-served state park on the north bay near the beach. The jovial *Village Pump*, 103 W Lakeshore Drive (℡419/746-2281), serves good homestyle **food and drink** until 2am, while the menu at the *Kelleys Island Brewery*, 504 W Lakeshore Drive (℡419/746-2314), includes several choices for vegetarians.

South Bass Island

SOUTH BASS ISLAND is the largest and southernmost of the Bass Island chain, three miles from the mainland northwest of Kelleys Island; the islands are named for the excellent bass fishing in the surrounding waters. Also referred to as **Put-in-Bay** (the name of its one and only village), this is the most visited of the American Lake Erie Islands, with its permanent population of 450 swelling to ten times that in summer.

Just a year after its first white settlers arrived, British troops invaded the island during the War of 1812. The Battle of Lake Erie, which took place off the island's southeastern edge, is commemorated by **Perry's Victory and International Peace Memorial**, set in a 25-acre park where the island dramatically nips in at the waist. You can see the battle site, ten miles away, from an observation deck near the top of the 352ft stone Doric column (May–Oct daily 10am–7pm; $3). All this history is well documented at the **Lake Erie Islands Historical Society**, 441 Catawba Ave (May–Oct daily 10am–6pm; $1; ℡419/285-2804, Ⓦwww.leihs .org), which features dozens of model ships, exhibits on the shipping and fishing industries, and memorabilia of life on the islands.

After the war, with the lake safe from Canadian invasion, South Bass Island grew both as a port and as a tourist destination. In fact, during the 1890s its *Victory Hotel* was one of the largest hotels in the world. Wine was also big business, though only one of its twenty-six vineyards survived Prohibition, by producing grape juice.

Practicalities

Put-in-Bay's **visitor center** is downtown in Harbor Square, just next to the northern dock (summer daily 9am–6pm; rest of year hours vary; ☏419/285-2832, ⓦwww.put-in-bay.com). To get around, as on Kelleys Island, most people rent either **golf carts** from Baycarts Rental, Harbor Square ($10–20 per hour; ☏419/285-5785), or **bikes** from Island Bike Rental, at both docks ($9 per day; ☏419/285-2016). A **shuttle bus** ($1) runs between the northern dock and the state park.

Hotel rooms are heavily booked on weekends and during the summer, and **B&Bs** often require a two-night minimum stay on weekends. The *Stagger Inn B&B*, 182 Concord Ave (☏419/285-2521, ⓦwww.staggerinn.put-in-bay.com; ❺), and the *Commodore Motel*, 272 Delaware Ave (☏419/285-3101; ❹), which has a pool, offer some of the most competitive rates. You can **camp** for $16 in the state park or at the *Fox's Den Campground* on the southern shore ($28 for one or two; ☏419/285-5001).

Food on the island is expensive everywhere. The grill meals and seafood sandwiches at *The Boardwalk* (summer only; ☏419/285-3695) are no exception, but this is the only downtown restaurant directly on the water. Just across the street, *Frosty's* (☏419/285-3278) does good pizza. Put-in-Bay's wild **nightlife** – it really does get raucous here – pulls in revelers from the other islands and the mainland. Numerous **live music** venues include the *Beer Barrel Saloon* (☏419/285-2337, ⓦwww.beerbarrelpib.com) – said to have the longest uninterrupted bar in the world, complete with 160 bar stools – and the appropriately named *Round House* (☏419/285-4595, ⓦwww.theroundhousebar.com).

Columbus

Ohio's largest city, state capital, and home to the massive Ohio State University, **COLUMBUS** is a likeable place to visit. Its position in the rural heart of the state also makes it the only center of culture for a good two-hour drive in any direction.

Ohio became a state in 1803, and after trying Zanesville and Chillicothe, legislators designated this former patch of rolling farmland on the high east bank of the Scioto River its capital in 1812. The fledgling city was built from scratch, and its considered town planning is evident today in broad thoroughfares and green spaces. Statuary forms another part of the cityscape, with many of them portraying its namesake, **Christopher Columbus**; there's even a replica of his ship, the *Santa Maria*, docked downtown on the Scioto River.

Though Columbus has more people, it always seems to lag behind Cincinnati or Cleveland in terms of public recognition. As such, the place is best enjoyed for what it is – a lively college city with some good **museums**, gorgeous Germanic **architecture**, and a particularly vibrant **nightlife**, including Ohio's most active **gay scene**. The spacious, orderly, and easygoing **downtown** area holds several attractions and the new **Arena District** entertainment zone, while the main nightlife areas – the bohemian **Short North Arts District** and the more mainstream **Brewery District** – are on the north and south fringes of the center, respectively.

Arrival, information, and getting around

Port Columbus International Airport is seven miles northeast of downtown. **Taxis** into the center get away with charging $21, as there is no alternative. **Greyhound** stops at 111 East Town and Third streets, but Amtrak bypasses it altogether. The most central **visitor center** is at 90 N High St (Mon–Fri 9am–5pm; ☎614/221-2489 or 1-800/345-4386, ⓦwww.experiencecolumbus.com), with a larger branch out at Easton Town Center mall, off I-270 (Mon–Sat 10am–9pm, Sun noon–6pm). Central Ohio Transit Authority (COTA; ☎614/228-1776, ⓦwww.cota.com) runs a good central **bus service** connecting downtown with German Village, the Short North, and North Campus; a day-pass costs $3.50.

Accommodation

Compared with other cities in the region, Columbus offers a good choice of convenient mid-range places to **stay**. Downtown rates are good, while even more savings can be had by staying in the German Village/Brewery District locales.

Best Western Clarmont 650 S High St ☎614/228-6511, ⓦwww.bestwestern.com. A 2min walk from the Brewery District and German Village, this remodelled chain motel is particularly good value. ❹

German Village Inn 920 S High St ☎614/443-6506. This family-run motel, on the south edge of the German Village/Brewery District, is one of the best deals going. ❸

Harrison House B&B 313 W 5th Ave ☎614/421-2202 or 1-800/827-4203, ⓦwww.columbus-bed-breakfast.com. A welcoming, big home in Victorian Village, an up-and-coming district close to the Short North. ❺

The Lofts Hotel 55 E Nationwide Blvd ☎614/461-2663, ⓦwww.55lofts.com. Luxury New York-style loft conversions, within easy walking distance of the Arena and the downtown areas. ❻

The Westin Great Southern 310 S High St ☎614/228-3800 or 1-888/627-7088, ⓦwww.greatsouthernhotel.com. Columbus's grand downtown Victorian hotel, with surprisingly moderate rates. ❺

Downtown

As good a place as any to start a walking tour of downtown is the **Ohio Statehouse**, pleasantly set in ten acres of park at the intersection of Broad and High streets, the two main downtown arteries (Mon–Fri 7am–7pm, Sat & Sun 11am–4pm; tours Mon–Fri 10am–3pm, Sat & Sun noon–3pm; free; ☎1-888/644-6123). Highlights of this 1839 Greek Revival structure – one of the very few state capitols without a dome – are the ornate Senate and House chambers.

From here, most places of interest lie a few blocks east and west along Broad Street. **COSI**, housed in a streamlined structure across the river at 333 W Broad St (Mon–Sat 10am–5pm, Sun noon–6pm; adults $12.50, kids $7.50; ☎614/228-2674 or 1-877/257-2674, ⓦwww.cosi.org), boasts more than 300,000 square feet of exhibit space, most of it geared toward familiarizing children with science. A mile east of COSI, the **Wendy's Original Restaurant**, 257 E Broad St (Mon–Fri 10am–8pm, Sat 10am–7pm, Sun 11am–6pm), pays homage to Dave Thomas's enduringly down-home national burger chain, started here in 1969. There's the usual menu, plus pictures of famous patrons and plenty of other memorabilia.

Three blocks east, a giant Henry Moore sculpture stands at the entrance to the inviting **Columbus Museum of Art**, 480 E Broad St (Tues, Wed, Fri–Sun 10am–5.30pm, Thurs 10am–8.30pm, closed Mon; $6, free Sun; ☎614/221-6801, ⓦwww.columbusmuseum.org). Indoors, this airy space holds particularly good collections of Western and modernist art. The museum also hosts touring exhibits, and has a renowned photography gallery and a pleasant sculpture garden.

South of the museum, at the corner of Washington Ave and East Town St, the **Topiary Garden**, in Old Deaf School Park (open daylight hours; free), provides a quirky photo opportunity. In the center of this verdant little park, a group of locals have recreated in topiary Georges Seurat's famous post-Impressionist work, *Sunday Afternoon on the Island of La Grande Jatte*. Believed to be the only painting reinterpreted in evergreen shrubbery, it features fifty-four pruned humans, three dogs, a monkey, a cat, and some leafy boats floating in a pond.

In the northwest corner of downtown, the area surrounding the impressive Nationwide Arena, home to NHL's Columbus Blue Jackets (☎1-800/645-2637, ⓦwww.bluejackets.com) has attracted a number of restaurants and nightspots and been predictably dubbed the **Arena District**. Just above it, left off High St, is the restored Victorian warehouse of **North Market** (see "Eating" p.319), while on the right side the strikingly deconstructivist **Greater Columbus Convention Center** is a massive pile of angled blocks designed by Peter Eisenman and completed in 1993.

German Village and Brewery District

Just six blocks south of the Statehouse, I-70 separates downtown from the delightful **German Village** neighborhood. During the mid-nineteenth century, thousands of German immigrants settled in this part of Columbus, building neat redbrick homes, the most lavish of which surround the 23-acre **Schiller Park**. Their descendants, however, started leaving the area during World War I, and with Prohibition and World War II further depleting their numbers, few were left by the 1950s. The area, then known as the Old South End, soon became increasingly run-down until it won a place on the National Register of Historic Places following the formation of an active **preservation society**.

Today the eighteen-block village is the biggest privately funded body on that register, a professional residential district with a sizeable gay community. The best way to explore its brick-paved streets, corner bars, old-style restaurants, Catholic churches, and grand homes is to stop in at the **German Village Meeting Haus**, 588 S 3rd St (Mon–Fri 9am–4pm, Sat 10am–2pm; ☎614/221-8888, ⓦwww. germanvillage.com), where popular walking tours run by the German Village Society start with a twelve-minute video presentation. The Society also oversees the immensely popular **Haus und Garten Tour** on the last Sunday in June, and the **Oktoberfest** celebrations in late September. The Village caters especially well to book-lovers; the **Book Loft**, 631 S 3rd St (daily 10am–11pm), crams its books, many of them discounted, into thirty-two rooms of one grand building.

Just across High Street (US-23) are the warehouses of the **Brewery District**, where, until Prohibition, the German immigrants brewed beer by traditional methods. Many of the original buildings still stand, but today the beer is produced by a handful of microbreweries such as **Columbus Brewing Co.**, 525 Short St, which sometimes sets up free tours of its operation (by appointment only; ☎614/224-3626). The brewpub is typical of the area's more mainstream **nightlife**, which includes other restaurants, theme pubs and music venues.

North of downtown

Across Nationwide Boulevard at the top end of downtown is the **Short North Arts District**, a former red-light district that's now Columbus's most vibrant enclave. Standing on either side of High Street – the main north–south thoroughfare – its entrance is marked by iron gateways of The Cap at Union Station. Thereafter starts the trail of galleries, bars, and restaurants that makes the area so popular with locals. The first Saturday of each month sees the **Gallery Hop**, when all the local art dealers throw open their doors – complementing the artworks with wine, snacks, and occasional performance pieces – and the socializing goes on well into the evening (ⓦ www.theshortnorth.com).

Businesses become a little more low-rent for a mile before High Street cuts through the **university campus** and suddenly sprouts cheap eating places and funky shopping emporia. For bargain vinyl, head to Used Kids Records, 1980 N High St. On the other side of the road, the **Wexner Center for the Arts**, North High St at 15th Ave (Tues–Sat 10am–6pm; ☎614/292-3535, ⓦ www.wexarts.org), is another Eisenman construction, even more extreme than the Convention Center; it's home to cutting-edge contemporary art exhibitions, movies, mixed-media performances, a café, and a bookstore.

Eating

The Short North and German Village neighborhoods are crammed with places to **eat**, be they bottom-dollar snack bars or stylish and adventurous bistros. For a wide range of ethnic and organic snacks during the day, try the **North Market**, downtown at 59 Spruce St (Tues–Fri 9am–7pm, Sat 8am–5pm, Sun noon–5pm; ☎614/463-9664), which also sells fresh produce.

Barcelona 263 E Whittier St, German Village ☎614/444-1130. Noted for its Mediterranean cuisine, this stylishly decorated local favorite also does fine desserts.

Cap City Fine Diner 1299 Olentangy River Rd ☎614/291-3663. A self-proclaimed "upscale diner," this big, lively joint, just off downtown, serves up comfort food (meatloaf) with new twists (chili-onion rings and buttermilk mashed potatoes). Huge portions, especially the desserts; lunch entrees around $8, dinner $15.

Cup O' Joe Coffee & Dessert House 627 S 3rd St, German Village ☎614/221-1563. One of Columbus's best-loved coffeehouses, it offers great desserts, coffees, and comfy sofas. Another branch at 600 N High St, Short North.

🏃 **Haiku** 800 N High St, Short North ☎614/294-8168. Excellent Japanese restaurant with a huge range of sushi, noodle, and rice dishes.

Katzinger's 475 S 3rd St, German Village ☎614/228-3354. A mesmerizing range of sandwiches, Jewish munchies, and cheesecakes, though prices are high for a deli.

Schmidt's Restaurant und Sausage Haus 240 E Kossuth St, German Village ☎614/444-6808. This Columbus landmark (since 1886) serves schnitzel and strudel in a former slaughterhouse.

Nightlife

This youthful university town has a rich source of local **bands**, from country revivalists to experimental alternative acts. In addition to German Village, the **gay scene** is concentrated in the Short North, with a few additional bars and clubs downtown – the weekly *Outlook* has complete listings. There are frequent **free concerts** in summer, both downtown and in other areas. The *Other Paper* and *Columbus Alive* provide free details of what's happening around town.

Dick's Den 2417 N High St ☎614/268-9573. This campus dive bar has good jazz on the weekends.

Little Brother's 1100 N High St, Short North ☎614/421-2025, ⓦ www.littlebrothers.com. Underground sounds, from alternative rock to swing and spoken-word.

Oldfield's On High 2590 N High St ☎614/784-0477, ⓦ www.oldfieldsonhigh.com. Predominantly collegiate campus bar with eclectic live music tastes.

Short North Tavern 674 N High St, Short North ☎614/221-2432. The oldest bar in the neighborhood, with live bands playing on the weekend.

Tommy Keegans Irish Pub 456 S Front St, Brewery District ☎614/221-9444. Friendly pub with a decent jukebox and soccer from Europe on TV.

Union Station Video Café 630 N High St, Short North ☎614/228-3740. Popular gay video bar with a decent selection of appetizers and sandwiches, plus a pool table and Internet access.

Cincinnati

CINCINNATI, just across the Ohio River from Kentucky and roughly three hundred miles from both Detroit and Chicago, is a dynamic commercial metropolis with a definite European flavor and a sense of the South. Its tidy center, rich in architecture and culture, lies within a few minutes' walk of the arty **Mount Adams** district, the attractive **riverfront**, and the lively **Over-the-Rhine** area, in the north end of downtown.

The city was founded in 1788 at the point where a Native American trading route crossed the river. Its name comes from a group of Revolutionary War admirers of the Roman general Cincinnatus, who saved Rome in 458 BC and then returned to his small farm, refusing to accept any reward. Cincinnati quickly became an important supply point for pioneers heading west on flatboats and rafts, and its population skyrocketed with the establishment of a major steamboat **riverport** in 1811. Tens of thousands of **German** immigrants poured in during the 1830s.

Loyalties were split by the **Civil War**. Despite the loss of some important markets, when merchants began to pick up lucrative government contracts the city decided that its future lay with the Union. In the prosperous postwar decade, Cincinnati acquired Fountain Square, the prodigious Music and Exhibition Hall, a zoo, art museum, public library, and the country's first professional baseball team. **Sport** remains a great source of pride: downtown gift shops are decked out in the colors of the **Bengals** football team and of baseball's **Reds**.

Arrival, information, and getting around

Cincinnati–Northern Kentucky International Airport is twelve miles south of downtown, in Covington, Kentucky. **Taxis** to the city center (℡859/586-5236) cost $25. The **Greyhound** station is on the eastern fringe of the city center, just off Broadway, at 1005 Gilbert Ave. Amtrak **trains** arrive a mile northwest of downtown at the Union Terminal museum complex, which is on the daytime citywide SORTA/Metro **bus** network ($1; ℡513/621-4455, Ⓦwww.sorta.com). Buses on the Kentucky side are run by TANK ($1; ℡859/331-8265, Ⓦwww.tankbus.org), including shuttle buses across to Cincinnati. Extraordinarily for a city of its size, there is no walk-in visitors office, though **info** can be obtained by phone or online from the Northern Cincinnati CVB (℡513/771-5353, Ⓦwww.cincynorth.com).

Accommodation

Although Cincinnati's quality **hotels** are reasonable by big-city standards, budget travelers may have problems finding affordable downtown rooms. Uptown **motels** – about two miles north – are much cheaper, but you'll need a car to get around safely at night.

Budget Host Inn 3356 Central Parkway ℡513/559-1600 or 1-800/283-4678, Ⓦwww.budgethost.com. Just about the cheapest place in uptown Cincinnati, though doubles vary greatly in price. Three miles from downtown. ❸

Gateway B&B 326 E 6th St, Newport, KY ℡859/581-6447, Ⓦwww.gatewaybb.com. Comfortable, affordable Victorian place, five minutes from downtown Cincy and Covington, KY. ❺

Grace & Glory B&B 3539 Shaw Ave ℡513/321-2824, Ⓦwww.graceandglorybb.com. This cosy place in a safe area five miles east of downtown is a good option if you have a car. The extension room is a super bargain. ❸

Marriott at River Center 10 W River Center Blvd, Covington, KY ℡859/261-2900 or 1-800/228-9290, Ⓦwww.marriotthotels.com. A luxury hotel on the river with spacious rooms and great serv-

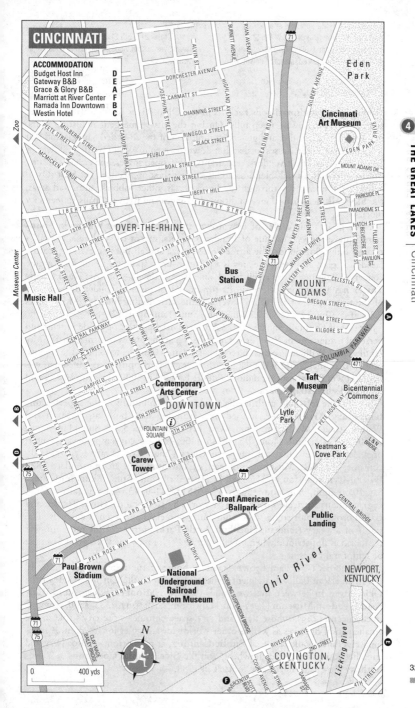

CINCINNATI

ACCOMMODATION
Budget Host Inn	D
Gateway B&B	E
Grace & Glory B&B	A
Marriott at River Center	F
Ramada Inn Downtown	B
Westin Hotel	C

Eden Park

Cincinnati Art Museum

EDEN PARK DRIVE

MOUNT ADAMS DR.

▲ Zoo

▲ Museum Center

RYAN AVENUE
BURNETT AVENUE
ALVIN ST.
DORCHESTER AVENUE
HIGHLAND AVENUE
JOSEPHINE STREET
CARMATT ST.
CHANNING STREET
MULBERRY STREET
PEETE STREET
SYCAMORE TERRACE
RINGGOLD STREET
SLACK STREET
PEUBLO
BOAL STREET
MCMICKEN AVENUE
MILTON STREET
LIBERTY HILL
READING ROAD
GILBERT AVENUE

LIBERTY STREET
LIBERTY STREET

PARKSIDE PL.
PARADROME ST.
HATCH ST.
ELSINORE AVENUE
VAN METER STREET
IDA STREET
BELVEDERE ST
ST GREGORY ST.
FULLER ST.
PAVILION ST.

OVER-THE-RHINE

15TH STREET
14TH STREET
13TH STREET
12TH STREET
REPUBLIC STREET
CLAY STREET
READING ROAD

WAREHAM DRIVE
MONASTERY STREET
CELESTIAL ST.

MOUNT ADAMS

OREGON STREET
BAUM STREET
KILGORE ST.

Music Hall ◀

VINE STREET
12TH STREET
CENTRAL PARKWAY
RACE ST.
COURT STREET
BOWEN STREET
MAIN STREET
WALNUT STREET
SYCAMORE STREET
6TH STREET
BROADWAY
EGGLESTON AVENUE
COURT STREET

Bus Station

COLUMBIA PARKWAY

471

8TH STREET
7TH STREET
GARFIELD PLACE
ELM STREET
PLUM STREET

Contemporary Arts Center

6TH STREET
FOUNTAIN SQUARE

DOWNTOWN

ⓘ
5TH STREET

Ⓒ

Taft Museum
Bicentennial Commons

Lytle Park

PIKE ST.
PETE ROSE WAY

L & N BRIDGE

Yeatman's Cove Park

Carew Tower
4TH STREET
3RD STREET

Great American Ballpark

Public Landing

CENTRAL BRIDGE

CENTRAL AVENUE
75

STADIUM DRIVE

71

PETE ROSE WAY
Paul Brown Stadium
MEHRING WAY

National Underground Railroad Freedom Museum

RIVERSIDE DRIVE
ROEBLING SUSPENSION BRIDGE

Ohio River

NEWPORT, KENTUCKY

71
75

CLAY WADE BAILEY BRIDGE

N
🏃

COVINGTON, KENTUCKY

RIVERSIDE DRIVE
2ND STREET
GREENUP STREET
COURT AVENUE
GREER STREET
GARRARD ST.
4TH STREET

Licking River

RIVERCENTER
SCOTT BLVD.

Ⓕ

0   400 yds

◀ Ⓐ
◀ Ⓑ
◀ Ⓓ
▶ Ⓔ

ice, plus an on-site pool and spa. **⑥**

Ramada Inn Downtown 800 W 8th St
ⓣ 513/241-8660 or 1-800/272-6232, ⓦ www.
ramada.com. Fairly priced, standard downtown

rooms. **④**

Westin Hotel 21 E 5th St ⓣ 513/621-7700,
ⓦ www.westin.com. Another top luxury option right
downtown. **⑦**

Downtown

Downtown Cincinnati rolls back from the Ohio River to fill a flat basin area
ringed by a disarray of steep hills. During the city's emergent industrial years,
the filth, disease, crime, and general commotion of the so-called Sausage and Rat
rows led the middle classes to abandon downtown en masse. Nowadays, however,
attractive stores, street vendors, restaurants, cafés, open spaces, and gardens occupy
the area. The city's rich blend of architecture is best appreciated **on foot**. Over,
among, and even right through the hotel plazas, office lobbies, and retail areas,
the **Skywalk** network of air-conditioned passages and flyovers spans sixteen city
blocks.

At the geographic center of downtown, the **Genius of the Waters** in **Fountain Square** sprays a cascade of hundreds of jets, meant to symbolize the city's
trading links. Surrounded by a tree-dotted plaza and all but enclosed by soaring
facades of glass and steel, the area is a popular lunch spot and venue for daytime
concerts. Looming above at Fifth and Vine streets, the 48-story Art Deco **Carew
Tower** has a viewing gallery on its top floor that gives a wonderful panorama
of the tight bends of the Ohio River and the surrounding hillsides (Mon–Thurs
9.30am–5.30pm, Fri & Sat 9.30am–5pm, Sun 11am–5pm; $2).

Just east of Fountain Square are the Art Deco headquarters of the detergents and
personal hygiene giant **Procter & Gamble**. The company was formed in 1837 by
candlemaker William Procter and soapmaker James Gamble, to exploit the copious
supply of animal fat from the slaughterhouses of "**Porkopolis**," as Cincinnati was
then known. By sponsoring radio's "Puddle Family" in 1932, the company created
the world's first **soap opera**.

Nearby, the left-field multimedia modern art exhibitions at the superb **Contemporary Arts Center**, housed in a stunning new building at Sixth and
Walnut streets (Mon 10am–9pm, Wed–Fri 10am–6pm, Sat & Sun 11am–6pm;
$7.50; free after 5pm Mon; ⓣ 513/345-8400, ⓦ www.contemporaryartscenter.
org), lead to continual run-ins with Cincy's more conservative citizens. By
contrast, the **Taft Museum**, just east of downtown in an immaculate 1820
Federal-style mansion at 316 Pike St (Tues–Fri 11am–5pm, Thurs until 8pm,
Sat 10am–5pm, Sun noon–5pm; $7; ⓣ 513/241-0343, ⓦ www.taftmuseum.
org), contains a priceless collection of works by Rembrandt, Goya, Turner, and
Gainsborough, plus some staggering Ming porcelain and French enamels. The
statue of a weary Abraham Lincoln in **Lytle Park**, in front of the museum, was
criticized as unpatriotic when unveiled in 1917; it's now seen as a great example
of sculptural realism.

South across I-71, Paul Brown Stadium, home of the Bengals, and the Reds'
Great American Ballpark are giant cement additions on the Cincinnati side of the
Ohio River. In between the two stands the new **National Underground Railroad Freedom Museum** (Tues–Sun 11am–5pm; $12; ⓣ 513/333-7500, ⓦ www.
freedomcenter.org), whose light and airy space chronicles the city's role in the
emancipation of slaves as well as other worldwide struggles for freedom. A mile-
long **riverside walk** begins at **Public Landing**, at the bottom of Broadway and
stretches east past painted showboats and the **Bicentennial Commons**, a 200th-
birthday present from the city to itself in 1988.

North of downtown

Just over a mile northeast from downtown, the land rises suddenly and the streets start to conform to the contours of **Mount Adams**. Here, century-old townhouses coexist with avant-garde galleries, stylish boutiques, trendy gift shops, and international restaurants. During the late nineteenth century, the elegant dining rooms of Mount Adams entertained the rich and famous eager to escape the squalor and noise of the Basin. Today its lively bars attract revellers from all over the city. From downtown, take a taxi or the #49 bus.

Adjacent to this tightly packed neighborhood are the rolling lawns, verdant copses, and scenic overlooks of **Eden Park**, its features reflected in the new **Mirror Lake**, a man-made pool installed as part of the city's Millennium Project. A loop road at the western end of the park leads to the **Cincinnati Art Museum**, on Art Museum Drive (Tues–Sun 11am–5pm, Wed until 9pm; free; ☎513/721-2787; ⓦwww.cincinnatiartmuseum.org). Its one hundred labyrinthine galleries span five thousand years, taking in an excellent Islamic collection as well as a solid selection of European and American paintings by the likes of Matisse, Monet, Picasso, Edward Hopper, and Grant Wood.

Meanwhile, northwest from downtown, Cincinnati's **Museum Center** is housed in the magnificent Art Deco **Union Terminal**, approached via a stately driveway off Ezzard Charles Drive (Mon–Sat 10am–5pm, Sun 11am–6pm; museums $7.25 each, any two $10.25, all three $13.25, with OMNIMAX $16.25 or $19.25 for two shows; ☎513/287-7000, ⓦwww.cincymuseum.org). Highlights of the **Museum of Natural History** are dioramas of Ice Age Cincinnati and "The Cavern," which houses a living bat colony. The **Historical Society** holds a succession of well-presented, short-term exhibitions, and the **Cinergy Children's Museum** has a two-story treehouse and eight other interactive exhibit areas.

Covington and Newport, Kentucky

Covington, directly across the Ohio River on the Kentucky side, is very much a part of the Cincinnati hinterland. It can be reached from downtown Cincinnati by walking over the bright-blue 355-yard 1867 **John A. Roebling Suspension Bridge**, at the bottom of Walnut Street, which served as a prototype for the Brooklyn Bridge. Ten minutes' walk southwest of the bridge brings you to the attractive, narrow, tree-lined streets and nineteenth-century houses of **MainStrasse Village**. It's a Germanic neighborhood of antique shops, bars, and restaurants that plays host to the lively **Maifest** on the third weekend of each May, and is the centerpiece of the citywide **Oktoberfest** on the weekend after Labor Day. At 6th and Philadelphia streets, 21 mechanical figures accompanied by glockenspiel music toll the hour on the German Gothic **Carroll Chimes Bell Tower**. Just beyond Covington at I-75 exit 186 is the **Oldenberg Brewery**, crammed with boozing memorabilia; tours of the microbrewery and its museum cost $3 (daily 10am–5pm).

Across the Licking River from Covington, the subdued town of **Newport** has gotten a lot livelier since the opening of a large shopping complex and the impressive **Newport Aquarium**, One Aquarium Way (daily: summer 10am–7pm, Sat until 9pm; rest of year 10am–6pm; $17.95; ☎859/491-3467 or 1-800/406-3474, ⓦwww.newportaquarium.com). Clear underwater tunnels and see-through floors allow visitors to be literally surrounded by sharks and snapping gators.

Eating

Cincinnati boasts excellent home-grown gourmet and continental **restaurants** and is also famous for fast-food **Cincinnati chili**, a combination of spaghetti noodles, meat, cheese, onions, and kidney beans, with chains such as *Skyline Chili*, open all day at more than forty locations, including Vine and 7th streets downtown.

Aralia 815 Elm St ☎513/723-1217. Excellent Sri Lankan curries in a handy downtown location.
Courtyard Café 1211 Main St, Over-the-Rhine ☎513/723-1119. Good grill food, burgers, and desserts, at value-for-money prices.
Dee Felice 529 Main St, Covington, KY ☎859/261-2365. This small and atmospheric restaurant/jazz venue specializes in Cajun cuisine, with lots of fresh seafood dishes.
Longworth's 1108 St Gregory St, Mount Adams ☎513/651-2253. Good hamburgers, sandwiches, salads, and pizzas at attractive prices in a delightful garden setting. Food is served all day until midnight, with music until 2.30am.

Mullane's Parkside Café 723 Race St ☎513/381-1331. This friendly joint, bedecked with local art, has an excellent choice of vegetarian options.
Nicholson's Tavern & Pub 625 Walnut St ☎513/564-9111. Scottish and other European fare, as well as decent ale, can be enjoyed amid the attractive wooden decor.
Porkopolis 1077 Celestial St, Mount Adams ☎513/721-5456. Steaks and sandwiches are served inside the former kilns of Cincinnati's celebrated pottery.
Tucker's 1637 Vine St ☎513/721-7123; also 18 E 13th St, Over-the-Rhine ☎513/241-3354. Get a perfect start on your day with traditional and gourmet breakfasts in a 1950s setting.

Nightlife and entertainment

After dark, the hottest area with the widest appeal is the **Over-the-Rhine** district, which fans out from Main Street around 12th and 14th streets, and buzzes every night – though be careful where you park or walk, as it backs onto some dodgy areas. The bars, restaurants, and cafés of scenic **Mount Adams** offer a good choice of music, food, and atmosphere, while the **Corryville** neighborhood, a five-minute drive northwest from downtown, has a lively undergraduate edge. A proliferation of **brewpubs** has sprung up all over town in the past few years, always dependable for a good drink in friendly surroundings. Entertainment **listings** for the whole city can be found in the free *Cincinnati CityBeat*.

For more cultured entertainment, **Music Hall**, 1243 Elm St (☎513/744-3344, ⓦ www.cincinnatiarts.org), an 1870s conglomeration of spires, arched windows, and cornices, is said to have near-perfect acoustics. Home to Cincinnati's Opera and Symphony Orchestra, it also hosts the May Festival of choral music. The **Cincinnati Playhouse in the Park**, in Eden Park (☎513/421-3888, ⓦ www. cincyplay.com), puts on drama, musicals, and comedies, with performances throughout the year.

Arnold's 210 E 8th St ☎513/421-6234. A fun and funky downtown spot, it's a favorite with jazz fans, though it also puts on roots and acoustic acts. Good restaurant upstairs.
Blind Lemon 936 Hatch St, Mount Adams ☎513/241-3885. Beyond the intimate, low-ceilinged bar, you'll find a relaxed patio crowd. Music (mostly acoustic) nightly at 9.30.
Bogart's 2621 Vine St, Corryville ☎513/281-8400, ⓦ www.bogarts.com. Established indie acts

play this mid-sized venue directly opposite *Sudsy Malone's*.
The Pavilion 949 Pavilion St, Mount Adams ☎513/744-9200. From its terraced outdoor deck, you'll have great views of the city and the Ohio River.
Rhythm & Blues Café 1142 Main St, Over-the-Rhine ☎513/684-0080. Good food and great atmosphere. Live rock, blues, and various genres Wed through Sat nights.

Michigan

Mention **MICHIGAN** and most people think of cars, heavy industry, and inner-city Detroit. Midwesterners prefer to focus on the state's magnificent scenery. The beaches, dunes, and cliffs along the 3200-mile shoreline of its two vividly contrasting **peninsulas** – bordering four of the five Great Lakes – rival many an oceanfront state.

The mitten-shaped **Lower Peninsula** is dominated from its southeastern corner by the industrial giant of **Detroit**, surrounded by satellite cities heavily devoted to the automotive industry. In the west, the scenic 350-mile Lake Michigan shoreline drive passes through likeable little ports before reaching the stunning **Sleeping Bear Dunes** and resort towns such as **Traverse City**, in the peninsula's balmy northwest corner. The desolate, dramatic, and thinly populated **Upper Peninsula**, reaching out from Wisconsin like a claw to separate lakes Superior and Michigan, is a far cry indeed from the cosmopolitan south.

In the mid-seventeenth century, **French explorers** forged a successful trading relationship with the Chippewa, Ontario, and other Native American tribes. The **British**, who acquired control after 1763, were far more brutal. Governor Henry Hamilton, the "Hair Buyer of Detroit," advocated taking scalps rather than prisoners. Ever since, Michigan's economy has developed in waves, the eighteenth-century fur, timber, and copper booms culminating in the state establishing itself at the forefront of the nation's manufacturing capacity, thanks to its abundant raw materials, good transportation links, and the genius of innovators such as **Henry Ford**. Despite the slumps of the Seventies and Eighties, **automobile production** remains the major source of Michigan income – though tourism is now a four-season money-spinner, too.

Getting around Michigan

Greyhound **buses** run regularly throughout Michigan's south, but services elsewhere are less frequent, and the few buses that serve the remote Upper Peninsula do so at night. Amtrak **trains** between New York and Chicago stop at Detroit, Dearborn, and Ann Arbor. Michigan's principal **airport** is just outside Detroit. **Cycling** is both feasible and rewarding, particularly with the abundance of bike paths in and around Traverse City; the League of Michigan Bicyclists in Lansing (℡1-888/642-4537, ⓦwww.lmb.org) organizes tours and provides info.

Detroit

DETROIT, the birthplace of the mass-production **car industry** and the **Motown** sound, has long had an image problem. The city boasts a billion-dollar downtown development, ultramodern motor-manufacturing plants, some excellent museums, and one of the nation's biggest art galleries – but since the 1960s, media attention has dwelt instead on its huge tracts of urban wasteland, where for block after block there's nothing but the occasional heavily fortified loan shop or grocery store. This characterization incurs the wrath of many Detroiters, and, though their city has unarguably suffered and continues to face tremendous challenges, their claims of exaggeration or exploitation by the media do carry weight.

Indeed, following the resurgence of Cleveland, Pittsburgh, and other Rust Belt cities, Detroit, under the leadership of **Mayor Dennis Archer**, has been turning the corner. Two sports stadiums and three big-time casinos had already opened before the waterfront was enhanced in time for the showcase Super Bowl XL in 2006. And, while these developments haven't wiped out the city's problems in one fell swoop, they're an exciting start.

Founded in 1701 by **Antoine de Mothe Cadillac**, as a trading post for the French to do business with the Chippewa, Detroit was no more than a medium-sized port two hundred years later. Then **Henry Ford**, **Ransom Eli Olds**, the **Chevrolets**, and the **Dodge** brothers began to build their automobile empires. Thanks to the introduction of the mass assembly line, Detroit boomed in the 1920s, but the auto barons sponsored the construction of segregated neighbor-

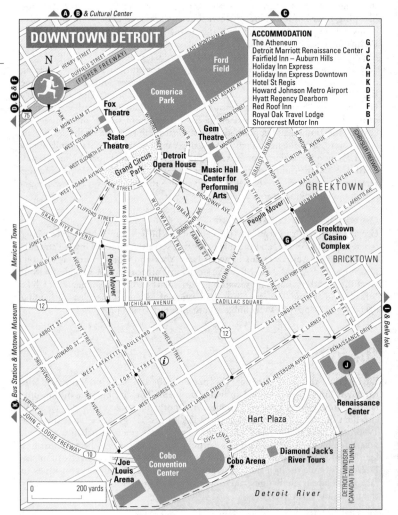

DOWNTOWN DETROIT

ACCOMMODATION

The Atheneum	G
Detroit Marriott Renaissance Center	J
Fairfield Inn – Auburn Hills	C
Holiday Inn Express	A
Holiday Inn Express Downtown	H
Hotel St Regis	K
Howard Johnson Metro Airport	D
Hyatt Regency Dearborn	E
Red Roof Inn	F
Royal Oak Travel Lodge	B
Shorecrest Motor Inn	I

hoods and unceremoniously dispensed with workers during times of low demand. Such policies created huge ghettos, resulting, in July 1967, in the bloodiest **riot** in the US in fifty years. More than forty people died and thirteen hundred buildings were destroyed. The **inner city** was left to fend for itself, while the all-important motor industry was rocked by the oil crises and Japanese competition.

Today, though scarred and bruised, Detroit is not the mess some would have it, and suburban residents have started to return to the city's festivals, theaters, clubs, and restaurants. As for orientation, it makes sense to think of Detroit as a region rather than a concentrated city – and, with some planning and wheels, it holds plenty to see and do. For the moment, **downtown** is not so much the heart of the giant as just another segment. Other interesting areas include the huge **Cultural Center**, freewheeling **Royal Oak**, posh **Birmingham**, the Ford-town of **Dearborn**, nearby **Windsor, Ontario**, and the college town of **Ann Arbor**, a short drive west.

Arrival, information, and getting around

Flights come into **Detroit Metropolitan Wayne County Airport** in Romulus, eighteen miles southwest of downtown and a hefty $40-plus taxi ride, though SMART ($1.50; ☎313/962-5515, ⊛www.smartbus.org) bus #125 goes downtown from Smith terminal.

The main **Greyhound** (1001 Howard Ave) and **Amtrak** (2601 Rose St) terminals are in areas where it's inadvisable to walk around at night. Amtrak also stops ten miles out at 16121 Michigan Ave, Dearborn, near the Henry Ford Museum and several mid-range motels, and at unstaffed suburban stations at Birmingham, Pontiac, and Royal Oak.

Detroit's main **visitor center** is downtown at 211 W Fort St, on the tenth floor (Mon–Fri 9am–5pm; ☎313/202-1800 or 1-800/338-7648, ⊛www.visitdetroit. com). The main **post office** is at 1401 W Fort St, at Eighth St (Mon–Fri 8.30am–5pm, Sat 8am–noon).

Downtown, the People Mover elevated **railway** loops around thirteen art-adorned stations (Mon–Thurs 7am–11pm, Fri 7am–midnight, Sat 9am–midnight, Sun noon–8pm; 50¢). Further out, public transportation is just about adequate. SMART serves the entire metro region, while DDOT **buses** ($1.50; ☎313/933-1300, ⊛www.detroitmi.gov/ddot) run a patchier inner-city service. Getting around in the Motor City, however, remains geared firmly toward the **car**.

Accommodation

Downtown Detroit caters well for expense-account travelers – its top-range hotels are as secure as any city's – but if your budget is restricted it's harder to find lodging that is both cheap and safe at night. A fifteen-percent tax comes tacked onto room bills.

The Atheneum 1000 Brush St ☎313/962-2323 or 1-800/772-2323, ⊛www.atheneumsuites.com. At this swish all-suite hotel in Greektown, some units fetch more than $300 a night; others are a third of that price. ❻
Detroit Marriott Renaissance Center Renaissance Center ☎313/568-8000 or 1-800/228-9290, ⊛www.marriotthotels.com. A fun place to stay, it towers over the city by the river – ask for a room on the upper floors. ❻

Fairfield Inn – Auburn Hills 1294 Opdyke Rd ☎248/373-2228, ⊛www.fairfieldinn.com. On the north edge of town, this clean motel is close to the Pontiac Silverdome. ❸
Holiday Inn Express 34952 Woodward Ave, Birmingham ☎248/646-7300, ⊛www.holidayinn. com. Recently renovated, this *Holiday Inn* is reasonably well-placed for Birmingham and Royal Oak restaurants and bars. ❻
Holiday Inn Express Downtown 1020 Washing-

ton Blvd ⓣ313/887-7000, ⓦwww.holidayinn.com. A mid-range hotel with a pool, athletic room, and complimentary continental breakfast. ❺

Hotel St Regis 3071 W Grand Blvd ⓣ313/873-3000 or 1-800/848-4810, ⓦwww.hotelstregisdetroit.com. Nice old hotel about four miles from downtown. Near the Motown Museum and well-placed for those with a car. Cheaper weekend rates. ❻

Howard Johnson Metro Airport 7600 Merriman Rd, Romulus ⓣ734/728-2430, ⓦwww.hojo.com. The pick of the budget motels near the airport. ❸

Hyatt Regency Dearborn Fairlane Town Center, Dearborn ⓣ313/593-1234 or 1-800/233-1234, ⓦwww.hyatt.com. This candy-brown colossus has every imaginable amenity. Though not cheap, it does have special deals. ❻

Red Roof Inn 24130 Michigan Ave, Dearborn ⓣ313/278-9732 or 1-800/843-7663, ⓦwww.redroof.com. Clean budget lodgings near the Henry Ford Museum. ❸

Royal Oak Travel Lodge 30776 N Woodward Ave ⓣ248/549-1600, ⓦwww.travelodge.com. A recently renovated motel close to trendy Royal Oak and about 8 miles north of downtown. ❸

Shorecrest Motor Inn 1316 E Jefferson Ave ⓣ313/568-3000 or 1-800/992-9616, ⓦwww.shorecrestmi.com. Friendly, family-run place in lively Rivertown, with clean, good-value rooms and specials for Greyhound passengers. ❹

Downtown

Futuristic glass-box office buildings and a tastefully revamped park overlook the deodorant-green **Detroit River**, but for the most part downtown seems rather empty – even in the middle of the day, its streets are quiet and uncrowded. One reason is that most offices and stores are squeezed into the six gleaming towers of the **Renaissance Center**, a virtual city within a city. Zooming up 73 stories from the riverbank, the towers offer a great view of the metropolis from their free observation deck. This giant business, convention, and retail center, known locally as the RenCen, was one of many complexes developed by **Detroit Renaissance** (a joint public/private sector project) to rejuvenate downtown in the aftermath of the 1967 riot, although it was criticized for forcing out small businesses. Nevertheless, it's an attractive public space and the soaring glass atrium known as the "Winter Garden" is particularly impressive.

Rare greenspace is found among the fountains and sculptures of **Hart Plaza**, which rolls down to the river in the shade of the RenCen. The plaza hosts free lunchtime concerts and lively weekend ethnic festivals all summer long. The US leg of the annual **Ford-Detroit International Jazz Festival**, the largest free jazz festival in the world, takes place here over Labor Day weekend and now spreads up to the Campus Martius square. Across the plaza from the RenCen is the Cobo Convention Center; next to this is **Joe Louis Arena**, home of the beloved Red Wings hockey team (see p.333).

Ten blocks north of the RenCen up Woodward Avenue is the **Theater District**, downtown's prime nightlife spot. Highlights are the magnificently restored Siamese-Byzantine **Fox Theatre** (see p.333) a huge old movie palace that is the city's top concert, drama, and film venue, and the grand Italian Renaissance **State Theatre** next door. This area is at the center of the city's massive **Columbia Street** redevelopment project, home to the new baseball and football stadiums (see p.333), as well as microbreweries, coffeehouses, and the inevitable themed restaurants, including a *Hard Rock Café*.

Three miles east of the RenCen, **Belle Isle Park** is an inner-city island retreat with twenty miles of walkways, sports facilities, a marina, and free attractions including an aquarium, a Great Lakes Museum, and elaborate gardens. It is quiet during the week but can attract crowds on the weekend. Belle Isle Park is also home to the annual **Detroit Grand Prix** Indy car race. To see the island, use Diamond Jack's River Tours (early June to early Sept; $14; ⓣ313/843-9376, ⓦwww.diamondjack.com), which depart from Hart Plaza downtown, last two hours, and loop round Belle Isle, or just take DOT bus #25 and transfer at MacArthur Bridge to the #12.

The Detroit Cultural Center

Three miles northwest of downtown, next to Wayne State University, the top-class museums of the **Detroit Cultural Center** are clustered within easy walking distance of one another; you can easily spend a whole day here.

One of America's most prestigious art museums and newly refurbished, the colossal **Detroit Institute of Arts**, 5200 Woodward Ave (Wed & Thurs 10am–4pm, Fri 10am–9pm, Sat & Sun 10am–5pm; $6; ☎313/833-7900, ⊛www.dia.org), traces the history of civilization through one hundred galleries, most notably Chinese, Persian, Egyptian, Greek, Roman, Dutch, and American collections – not to mention the largest Italian collection outside of Italy. The museum has masterpieces such as a Van Gogh self-portrait and Joos Van Cleeve's *Adoration of the Magi*, as well as Diego Rivera's enormous, show-stealing, 1933 *Detroit Industry* mural.

The impressive Charles H. Wright **Museum of African American History**, 315 E Warren St (Wed & Thurs 9.30am–3pm, Fri & Sat 9.30am–5pm, Sun 1–5pm; $8; ☎313/494-5800, ⊛www.maah-detroit.org), is the largest African-American museum in the world. Its massive core exhibit covers six hundred years of history in eight distinct segments, starting with a chilling sculpture of a slave boat, before moving through the Civil War, the Depression, and the work of Dr Martin Luther King Jr and Malcolm X, finally settling on contemporary African-American society.

Also in the Cultural Center, the **Detroit Historical Museum**, 5401 Woodward Ave (Tues–Fri 9.30am–5pm, Sat 10am–5pm, Sun 11am–5pm; $5; ☎313/833-1805, ⊛www.detroithistorical.org), interprets the city's past through its **"Streets of Old Detroit"** display of reconstructed shops dating from the 1840s to the 1900s. The most interesting exhibit, not surprisingly, examines the automobile, with an automated display of the "body drop" process on an assembly line, in which a car's frame is lowered onto its chassis.

The Motown Museum

Unlike cities such as Memphis, Nashville, and New Orleans, Detroit is devoid of the bars, clubs, and homes of its musical heroes. The golden age of Motown was very much confined to a specific time and a place, and, disappointingly, only at the **Motown Museum**, 2648 W Grand Blvd (Tues–Sat 10am–6pm; $8; ☎313/875-2264, ⊛www.motownmuseum.com), can Tamla fans pay homage to one of the world's most celebrated record labels. The museum, run as a not-for-profit organization, is housed in the small white-and-blue clapboard house, Hitsville USA, which served as Motown's recording studio from 1959 to 1972. On the ground floor, Studio A remains just as it was left: battered instruments stand piled up against the nicotine-stained acoustic wall-tiles, and a well-scuffed Steinway piano all but fills the room. Upstairs are the former living quarters of label founder **Berry Gordy**, while in the adjoining record sleeves, gold and platinum discs, and other memorabilia are displayed. The enthusiastic and knowledgeable staff will quite happily give one person the full **tour**.

The Henry Ford Museum, Greenfield Village, and the Automotive Hall of Fame

The enormous **Henry Ford Museum**, ten miles from downtown at 20900 Oakwood Blvd, Dearborn (Mon–Sat 9am–5pm, Sun noon–5pm; $14, or $26 with Greenfield Village, see p.330; ☎313/271-1620 or 1-800/835-5237, ⊛www.thehenryford.org; accessible on SMART bus routes #200 and #250), pays fulsome tribute to its founder, an inveterate collector of Americana, as a brilliant industrialist and do-gooder. The former is certainly true. The hero of the "second industrial revolution" and inventor

The Motown sound

The legend that is Tamla Motown started in 1959 when Ford worker and part-time songwriter **Berry Gordy Jr** borrowed $800 to set up a studio. From his first hit onward – the prophetic "Money (That's What I Want)" – he set out to create a cross-over style, targeting his records at white and black consumers alike.

Early Motown hits were pure **formula**. Gordy softened the blue notes of most -contemporary black music in favor of a more danceable, poppy beat, with **gospel**-influenced singing and clapping. Prime examples of the early approach featured all-female groups like the **Marvelettes** ("Needle in a Haystack"), the **Supremes** ("Baby Love"), and **Martha Reeves and the Vandellas** ("Nowhere to Run"), as well as the all-male **Miracles** ("Tracks of My Tears"), featuring the sophisticated love lyrics of lead singer **Smokey Robinson**. Gordy's "Quality Control Department" scrutinized every beat, playing all recordings through speakers modeled on cheap transistor radios before the final mix.

The Motown organization was an intense, close-knit community: **Marvin Gaye** married Gordy's sister, while "Little" **Stevie Wonder** was the baby of the family. The label did, however, move with the times, utilizing such innovations as the wah-wah pedal and synthesizer. By the late 1960s its output had acquired a harder sound, crowned by the acid soul productions of Norman Whitfield with the versatile **Temptations**. In 1968 the organization outgrew its premises on Grand Avenue; four years later it abandoned Detroit altogether for LA. Befitting the MOR tastes of the 1970s, the top sellers were then the high-society soul of **Diana Ross** and the ballads of the **Commodores**. This saw many top artists, dissatisfied with Gordy's constant intervention, leave the label, although the crack songwriting team of Holland-Dozier-Holland, responsible for most of the **Four Tops**' hits, stayed in Detroit to produce the seminal **Chairmen of the Board** ("Gimme Just A Little More Time"), along with **Aretha Franklin** and **Jackie Wilson**. Today, Motown is owned by the giant **Poly-Gram** corporation. Artists on the label include Boyz II Men, Queen Latifah, and, to this day, Stevie Wonder.

of the assembly line didn't succeed by being a philanthropist. His Service Department of 3500 private policemen prompted the *New York Times* in 1928 to call him "an industrialist fascist – the Mussolini of Detroit." Despite considering unions "the worst things that ever struck the earth," Ford was forced to let the United Auto Workers (UAW) into his factories in 1943, after only 34 out of 78,000 workers voted against joining. Ford also bowed to the economic necessity of employing blacks, though he banned them from the model communities he built for his white workers. Instead, the company constructed a separate town, which he sardonically named Inkster.

In addition to the massive "**The Automobile in American Life**" exhibit ranging from early Ford models and postal carriages to NASCAR vehicles and electric cars, the twelve-acre museum amounts to a giant curiosity shop, holding planes, trains, and rows upon rows of domestic inventions and non-technological collectibles. Real oddities include the chair Lincoln was sitting in and the car Kennedy was riding in when each was shot, the bus Rosa Parks was riding when she refused to give up her seat, and even a test tube holding Edison's last breath. One pertinent item not on view is the Iron Cross that Hitler presented to Ford (a notorious anti-Semite) in 1938. You can also take the **Ford Rouge Factory Tour** (summer daily 9.30am–5pm, mid-Apr to early Sept closed Sun; $14) through the car manufacturing process at a historic Ford plant, using multiple-screen films, interactive displays, and demonstrations.

Down the street from the main museum complex, **Greenfield Village** is a collection of homes owned by famous Americans, relocated from across the country to this site by Ford (same hours as museum; $20, or $26 with Ford Museum). Among the 240 buildings, you'll find Ford's own birthplace, the Wright Brothers' cycle shop, Edison's laboratory, and Firestone's farm. Costumed hosts demonstrate everything from weaving to puncture-repairing.

Directly next door to the Ford sprawl, the **Automotive Hall of Fame**, 21400 Oakwood Blvd (daily 10am–5pm; $6; ☎313/240-4000, ⓦ www.automotivehalloffame .org), is more interesting than it might at first sound. In paying homage to the innovators and inventors of the global (not just the Detroit) auto industry, the interactive exhibits let visitors see how they would have handled problems encountered by Buick, Honda, and the like. It's not just for mechanical types, either – there's a chance to pit your wits against the dealmakers who set up General Motors.

Windsor, Ontario

The riverside cafés of the easygoing Canadian city of **WINDSOR**, due south of Detroit across the Detroit River, offer pleasant views of their larger neighbor's skyline. Like Detroit, Windsor's main industry is auto manufacturing, but it's much smaller and more relaxed, and makes a good place simply to hang out. Apart from one downtown **casino**, the most interesting attraction is booze-oriented: the **Hiram Walker Distillery**, where Canadian Club whiskey is distilled, stands just a short stroll from downtown at Riverside and Walker (free tours and samplings daily 11am–6pm; ☎519/561-5499).

Transit Windsor **buses** (☎519/944-4111) connect the downtowns of Detroit and Windsor for $2.75 each way. Bring proper identification for customs and immigration officials. To **drive**, take the Windsor Tunnel ($3.50 toll) or the less claustrophobic Ambassador Bridge ($3.25 toll). Windsor has two **visitor centers**, one across the Ambassador Bridge at 1235 Huron Church Rd, and one at 110 Park St E in the city center (both open daily 8.30am–5pm; ☎519/973-1338 or 1-800/265-3633, ⓦ www.infowindsor.com).

△ Henry Ford museum

Eating

Detroit's **ethnic** restaurants dish up the best (and least expensive) food in the city. **Greektown**, basically one block of Monroe Avenue between Beaubien and St Antoine streets, is crammed with authentic Greek places; it also contains Trappers Alley, a small mall brimming with good stalls and shops. Less commercial, but offering just as high a standard, are the bakeries, bars, and cantinas of **Mexican Town**, five minutes from downtown. **Royal Oak**, ten miles north, has a wide range of vaguely alternative wholefood places and is the liveliest suburban hangout in this sprawling metropolis.

Atwater Block Brewery 237 Joseph Campau St ☏ 313/393-2073. This spacious Rivertown brewpub serves up excellent beer-battered fish, mushrooms, mussels, wings, and whatever else the chefs can think of.

Fishbone's Rhythm Kitchen Café 400 Monroe Ave, Greektown ☏ 313/965-4600. Noisy, fun, and often-packed authentic New Orleans Cajun joint with whiskey ribs, crawfish, gumbo, sushi and lots more.

Fuddrucker's 2630 E Jefferson St ☏ 313/568-1000. Lively place for top-notch burgers in Rivertown.

La-Shish 12918 Michigan Ave, Dearborn ☏ 313/584-4477. This is one in a local chain of Lebanese restaurants serving traditional Middle Eastern *tabbouleh*, falafel, kebabs and shawarma.

New Hellas Café 583 Monroe St, Greektown ☏ 313/961-5544. Known as "The One on the Corner in Greektown," this popular hangout serves

saganaki (flaming cheese), moussaka, and lamb dishes, all at reasonable prices.

Original Pancake House 33703 Woodward Ave, Birmingham ☏ 248/642-5775. This top breakfast spot offers a huge variety of superb crêpes, waffles, omelets, and pancakes.

Pronto! 608 S Washington, Royal Oak ☏ 248/544-0123. Big salads and a huge selection of sandwiches are the specialties in this soothing pastel space.

Rattlesnake Club 300 River Place ☏ 313/567-4400. Owned by creative Detroit master chef Jimmy Schmidt, the *Rattlesnake Club* has a setting in Rivertown to match the exquisite food. Dinner will set you back $30–40 per main course, lunch a lot less. Closed Sun.

Xochimilco 3409 Bagley Ave ☏ 313/843-0179. The cornerstone restaurant of Detroit's authentic Mexican Town, *Xochimilco* delivers on huge portions, great service, and superb value. Open till 2am. If it's full, try *El Zocala* across the street.

Nightlife

There's a lot to do at night in Detroit – the city where the **techno** beat originated and is still going strong. The bars and clubs of the **Theater District** are ever popular, while the **Rivertown** area is renowned for its chic bistros and funky jazz and blues bars. The suburbs of upmarket **Birmingham** and youthful **Royal Oak** are good places to hang out, while there are a couple of fun establishments in the blue-collar neighborhood of **Hamtramck**. Way up on the northern fringe, once-deserted **Pontiac** now has a range of well-attended rock venues, dance clubs, and lounges. Canadian **Windsor** also has some good nightlife, with a drinking age of 19 as opposed to Michigan's 21. For event **listings** in Detroit, Ann Arbor, and Windsor, pick up the free weekly *Metro Times*.

Baker's Keyboard Lounge 20510 Livernois Ave, Royal Oak ☏ 313/345-6300. Mostly local big-band and jazz musicians jam in what claims to be the world's oldest jazz club. Closed Sun.

Gusoline Alley 309 S Center St, Royal Oak ☏ 248/545-2235. Cramped and dark with a loaded jukebox, this is a legend among Detroit bars. Go early for a seat; the wildly mixed crowd is a people-watcher's dream.

Magic Bag 22920 Woodward Ave, Ferndale

☏ 248/544-3030, ⊛ www.themagicbag.com. About two miles south of Royal Oak, this popular club boasts a huge range of beers, top jazz and blues artists, and regular roots acts.

Magic Stick 4120 Woodward Ave ☏ 313/833-9700, ⊛ www.majesticdetroit.com/stick.asp. This great venue incorporates billiards, bands, and, of course, alcoholic beverages. It's part of the Majestic Theater complex, a venue for big rock shows and huge techno nights.

Moto 3515 Caniff St, Hamtramck ⓣ313/369-0090. *The* place to see, be seen, and dance to techno and funk. Also books occasional live acts.

Saint Andrew's Hall/Shelter 431 E Congress St ⓣ313/961-6358. This cramped downtown club promotes top bands on the alternative circuit. It only holds 800 people, so get a ticket in advance.

Downstairs is the *Shelter* club, with lesser-known touring bands followed by dance music.

Tonic 29 S Saginaw St, Pontiac ⓣ248/334-7411, ⓦwww.tonicdetroit.com. Open Thursday through Sunday until 2am, *Tonic* bills itself as the premiere concert after-party: three levels of dancing and all the DJ vibe you can handle.

The performing arts

Most of Detroit's major arts venues are handily grouped together in the northwest section of downtown. A sweeping staircase and giant chandeliers are part of the splendor at the **Detroit Opera House**, 1526 Broadway (ⓣ313/237-SING, ⓦwww.detroitoperahouse.com). Close by, the **Music Hall Center for Performing Arts**, 350 Madison Ave (ⓣ313/963-2366, ⓦwww.musichall.org), is the primary venue for **dance** in the city; it also hosts rock concerts, youth theater, and Broadway shows. In the Theater District, the gorgeous **Fox Theatre**, 2211 Woodward Ave (ⓣ313/983-6611, ⓦwww.olympiaentertainment.com), is the biggest draw, hosting big Broadway shows, the cozy 450-seater **Gem Theatre**, 333 Madison Ave (ⓣ313/963-9800, ⓦwww.gemtheatre.com), and the **Masonic Temple Theatre**, nearby at 500 Temple St (ⓣ313/832-2232, ⓦwww.themasonic.com), a hall with near-perfect acoustics, are also worth a visit. A little further on toward the Cultural Center, the **Detroit Symphony Orchestra** performs at the **Max M Fisher Music Center**, 3711 Woodward Ave (ⓣ313/576-5100, ⓦwww.detroitsymphony.com).

Sports

Detroit is one of the few cities with franchises competing at the professional level in all four major team sports. **Hockey**'s Red Wings are arguably the town favorites, and tickets are hard to get; they play downtown at the Joe Louis Arena (ⓣ313/983-6859, ⓦwww.detroitredwings.com). **Baseball**'s Tigers (ⓣ313/962-4000, ⓦdetroit.tigers.mlb.com) call the snazzy Comerica Park, or COPA, home, while the Lions play **football** at adjacent Ford Field (ⓣ313/262-2003, ⓦwww.detroitlions.com). Lastly, the Pistons (ⓣ248/377-0100, ⓦwww.nba.com/pistons) play **basketball** in the Palace of Auburn Hills, twenty-five miles north.

Around Detroit: Ann Arbor

Although its population just tops 114,000, **ANN ARBOR**, 45 minutes' drive west of Detroit along I-94, offers a greater choice of restaurants, live music venues, and cultural activities than most towns ten times its size. The **University of Michigan** has shaped the economy and character of the town ever since it was moved here from Detroit in 1837, providing the city with a very conspicuous radical edge.

The best thing to do in Ann Arbor is to stroll around downtown and the campus, which meet at South State and Liberty streets. Downtown's twelve blocks of brightly painted shops and sidewalk cafés offer all you would expect from a college town, with forty bookshops and more than a dozen record stores. Don't miss the huge flagship store of Borders Books at 612 E Liberty St, or the extensive vinyl and CD selection at Encore Recordings, 417 E Liberty St.

Though the huge university campus doesn't look particularly appealing, it does engender a sense of excitement, especially around the central meeting place of the **Diag** (or Diagonal Walkway). Worth a look are the **Exhibit Museum of**

Natural History, 1109 Geddes Ave (Mon–Sat 9am–5pm, Sun noon–5pm; free; ☎734/764-0478, ⊕www.lsa.umich.edu/exhibitmuseum), packed with huge dinosaur skeletons, rare Native American artifacts, and a planetarium, and the eclectic **Museum of Art** (Tues–Sat 10am–5pm, Thurs until 9pm, Sun noon–5pm; suggested donation $5; ☎734/764-0395, ⊕www.umma.umich.edu), temporarily housed at 1301 S University St until it returns to an expanded space at 525 S State St in August 2008.

Practicalities

Frequent **Greyhound** services from Detroit stop at 116 W Huron St; **Amtrak** is on the north edge of downtown at 325 Depot St; and the **visitor center** is at 120 W Huron St (Mon–Fri 9am–5pm; ☎734/995-7281 or 1-800/888-9487, ⊕www.annarbor.org).

The *Lamp Post Inn*, 2424 E Stadium Blvd (☎734/971-8000, ⊕www.lamppostinn.com; ❸), is a good-value motel about a mile from campus, though the choice place to stay is the *Campus Inn*, right downtown at 615 E Huron St (☎734/769-2200 or 1-800/666-8693, ⊕www.campusinn.com; ❻). Two good central **B&Bs** are the *Burnt Toast Inn*, 415 W William St (☎734/761-8517, ⊕www.burnttoastinn.com; ❹) and bargain ⚐ *Eighth Street Trekkers' Lodge*, 120 Eighth St (☎734/369-3107, ⊕www.ofglobalinterest.net; ❷), run by an inveterate trekker.

Restaurants worth trying include the good-value Indian *Raja Rani*, 400 S Division St (☎734/995-1545), and the vegetarian *Seva*, 314 E Liberty Ave (☎734/662-1111). *Jerusalem Garden*, 307 S Fifth Ave (☎734/995-5060), serves the best falafel in town, while *Zingerman's*, 422 Detroit St (☎734/663-DELI), is an excellent (if expensive) deli. A pair of popular **brewpubs** – the *Arbor Brewing Co*, 114 E Washington St (☎734/213-1393), and the *Grizzly Peak Brewing Co*, 120 W Washington St (☎734/741-7325) – are within a couple of blocks of each other.

Ann Arbor's **live music** scene has enjoyed a nationwide reputation ever since the Stooges, MC5, and Bob Seger made their names here. Unlike many college towns, the place doesn't go to sleep during the summer, either. For news of gigs, grab a copy of *Current*, a free monthly. Likely venues include the *Blind Pig*, 208 S First St (☎734/996-8555, ⊕www.blindpigmusic.com), the best place to watch live rock, alternative, and blues, while *The Ark*, 316 S Main St (☎734/761-1451, ⊕www.a2ark.org), is an important venue for folk, acoustic, and roots music. *The Heidelberg*, 215 N Main St (☎734/663-7758, ⊕www.theheidelberg.net), has live bands on Saturdays and features different club styles, including Latino, on other nights. From time to time there are also live bands at the beautiful Art Deco Michigan Theater, 603 E Liberty St (☎734/668-8480, ⊕www.michtheater.org), otherwise a great place to watch movies on the cheap.

Festivals are also a key part of Ann Arbor life. In June, the orchestral Summer Festival kicks off activities with music and film; July sees the hectic Ann Arbor Art Fairs with hundreds of stalls; and mid-September brings the recently revived Ann Arbor Blues and Jazz Festival.

The rest of the Lower Peninsula

Between Ann Arbor and the Lake Michigan coast, a little over 150 miles west along I-94, there's not a whole lot worth stopping for, though Kellogg's **Cereal City USA**, 171 W Michigan Ave, in Battle Creek (summer Mon–Fri 9.30am–5pm, Sat 9.30am–6pm, Sun 11am–5pm; winter hours vary; $7.95; ☎616/962-6230, ⊕www.kelloggscerealcityusa.org), is a fun diversion that traces the history of cereal – and, of course, magnate Kellogg's impact on it. Once you reach Lake Michigan, quaint **St Joseph** is just the first of many small ports along the lake's 350-mile eastern shoreline.

North from St Joseph along Hwy-31, the northwest reaches of the lower peninsula attract sportspeople and tourists from all over the Midwest. Here, out on the unspoiled **Leelanau Peninsula** you'll find the beautiful **Sleeping Bear Dunes**, as well as the charming towns of **Charlevoix** and **Petoskey**; all three are within striking distance of larger **Traverse City**. At the northern tip of the lower peninsula, revitalized **Mackinaw City** is the departure point for the state's major tour-bus attraction, Old-World **Mackinac Island**.

Along Lake Michigan

Less than thirty miles north of Indiana, **ST JOSEPH** lies just north of "Harbor Country" – a string of small towns offering good swimming, boating, and fishing opportunities. St Joseph's neat, ice-cream parlor-riddled downtown perches on a high bluff, from which steep steps lead down to sandy Silver Beach and two light-houses atop two piers. You can enjoy great **food** such as nachos, steak salad, and pasta at *Clementine's Too*, 1235 Broad St (℡269/983-0990), or gumbo and ostrich burgers at a sidewalk table at *Schu's*, 501 Pleasant St (℡269/983-7248). **Places to stay** include the classy lakeside *Boulevard Inn*, 521 Lake Blvd (℡269/983-6600; ❺), where all the rooms are suites, and the good-value *Econolodge*, two miles from downtown at 2723 Niles Ave (℡269/983-6321; ❸). For general information on the area, stop in at the **visitor center**, just off I-94 exit 29 (summer Mon–Sat 8.30am–5pm; rest of year closed Sat; ℡269/925-6301).

Fifty miles north, **HOLLAND** was settled in 1847 by Dutch religious dissidents. Today's residents lose no opportunity to let visitors know of their roots: tens of thousands of tulips brighten the town in early summer, while the Holland museum, a Dutch village, a clog factory, and the inevitable windmill all attract tourist dollars. You can **stay** in the swish *Haworth Inn* (℡616/395-7200 or 1-800/903-9142, Ⓦwww.haworthinn.com; ❹), 225 College Ave, and literally go for a jar of fine ale at *New Holland Brewing Co* (℡616/355-6422), 66 E 8th St, which also serves bar **food**. Twenty miles farther up the shoreline, **GRAND HAVEN** boasts one of the largest and most appealing sandy beaches on the Great Lakes, best seen on a leisurely stroll along the one-and-a-half-mile largely concrete boardwalk.

Just under one hundred miles farther north, a string of pleasant small villages starts with **LUDINGTON**, where a long stretch of public beach precedes **Ludington State Park**, eight miles north on Hwy-116, which offers great hiking and sightseeing amid sweeping sand dunes and virgin pine forests; admission is $8 per car. **Camping** in some beautiful sites costs $29 a night, though sites for the summer tend to fill up a year in advance (℡800/447-2757). The **visitor center** is on the east side of town at 5827 US-10 (Mon–Fri 8am–5pm; ℡231/845-0324 or 1-800/542-4600, Ⓦwww.visitludington.com). From downtown, the **Lake Michigan Car Ferry** departs for Manitowoc, Wisconsin ($55 per adult, $58 per car, not including driver; ℡231/845-5555 or 1-800/841-4243, Ⓦwww.ssbadger.com) – worth it to avoid Chicago traffic. The best place to **stay overnight** is *Snyder's Shoreline Inn*, 903 W Ludington Ave (May–Oct ℡231/845-1261 or 1-800/843-2177, Ⓦwww.snydersshoreinn.com; ❹), the only downtown property with uninterrupted views of the lakeshore. *House of Flavors*, 402 W Ludington Ave (℡231/845-5785), is a chrome-heavy diner with breakfasts, burgers, and a huge range of ice cream. *The Old Hamlin Restaurant*, 122 W Ludington Ave (℡231/843-4251), serves breakfast, lunch, and dinner, featuring steaks, seafood, and especially good Greek dishes.

Surrounded by forest, **MANISTEE**, 32 miles north, boasts an attractive Victorian downtown and a mile-long **boardwalk** that runs alongside the Manistee River onto Lake Michigan. One of several pretty lakeside areas is **Douglas Park** – with a good sandy beach, small marina, and picnic area – next to the *Lake Shore Motel*, 669 First St (☎231/723-2667; ⑤). The *Tuscan Grille* at 312 River Street is a good spot for waterside Italian dining. The **Chamber of Commerce** is at 11 Cypress St (Mon–Fri 9am–5pm; ☎231/723-2575, ⓦwww.manistee.com).

Thirty miles north, tiny **FRANKFORT** nestles under bluffs overlooking Lake Michigan. With a grassy park and a small beach at either end of its main street, the town is at once charming and offers cheaper **accommodation** than the Leelanau Peninsula settlements to the north. The *Harbor Lights Resort*, 15 Second St (☎231/352-9614 or 1-800/346-9614, ⓦwww.harborlightsresort. net; ❹), stands right on the beach, while *The Summer Place*, 402 Leelanau Ave (☎231/352-3933, ⓦwww.oursummerplace.com; ❹), is an attractive B&B. Along the main drag, the *Frankfort Deli*, 327 Main St (☎231/352-3354), has good sandwiches; directly across the street, the *Coho Café* (☎231/352-6053) serves up well-priced contemporary American cuisine. A few doors down, the **Chamber of Commerce** is at 400 Main St (Mon–Fri 9am–5pm, summer Sat 10am–2pm; ☎231/352-7251, ⓦwww.frankfort-elberta.com).

The Leelanau Peninsula

The southwestern edge of the heavily wooded **Leelanau Peninsula** is occupied by the **Sleeping Bear Dunes National Lakeshore**, a constantly resculptured area of towering dunes and precipitous 400ft drops; admission is $10 per car. The area was named by the Chippewa, who saw the mist-shrouded North and South Manitou islands as the graves of two drowned bear cubs, and the massive mainland dune, covered with dark trees, as their grieving mother. Fierce winds off Lake Michigan cause the dunes to edge inland, burying trees that reappear years later stripped of foliage, while the continual attack of high water undercuts the massive sand banks, occasionally sending huge chunks into the lake. Stunning overlooks can be had along the hilly, nine-mile loop of the **Pierce Stocking Scenic Drive**, off Hwy-109. You can also clamber up the strenuous but enjoyable **Dune Climb**, four miles farther north on Hwy-109.

The **visitor center**, south of the dunes at 9922 Front St (Hwy-72) in Empire (daily: summer 8am–6pm; rest of year 8am–4pm; ☎231/326-5134, ⓦwww.nps. gov/slbe), provides details on trails, campgrounds, and beaches. To the northeast, the village of **GLEN ARBOR**, dotted with some interesting galleries, is the closest community to the dunes. Decent places to **eat** here include *Le Bear*, 5707 Lake St (☎231/334-4640), where costly seafood dinners are served on a waterfront deck, and *Art's Tavern*, 6487 Western Ave (☎231/334-3754), a pleasant inn delivering great hamburgers and inexpensive fried fish.

Fifteen miles north, **LELAND** makes a great base to visit the dunes. Its harbor holds a quaint collection of well-weathered sheds, known as **Fishtown**, where the day's catch was once hauled in for gutting and smoking; most are now touristy knick-knack shops. The *Falling Waters Lodge*, 200 W Cedar St (☎231/256-9832, ⓦwww.fallingwaterslodge.com; ❹) has some of the cheaper rooms in the whole peninsula, while *The Cove*, 111 River St (☎231/256-9834), serves up tasty local fish dishes and a superb Key Lime Pie. **Ferries** from Leland ($29 roundtrip; ☎231/256-9061, ⓦwww.leelanau.com/manitou) go to the uninhabited North and South Manitou islands.

At the tip of the peninsula, **NORTHPORT** is another relaxing fishing village with a disproportionate number of art galleries. Eleven miles south on the peninsula's east coast, **SUTTONS BAY** may not be as pretty, but it has some of the area's best places to eat, such as 🍴 *Hatties*, 111 St Joseph Avenue (☎231/271-6222), which serves fine meals like chicken with cherry sauce and Thai scallops.

Traverse City

Smooth beaches and striking bay views help make lively **TRAVERSE CITY**, roughly twenty miles south of Suttons Bay, the favorite in-state resort for Michigan natives. A town of fifteen thousand year-round residents, it was saved from the stagnation that overtook many communities when their lumber mills closed down, because the stripped fields proved to be ideal for fruit-growing. Today, the area's claim to be **"Cherry Capital of the World"** is no idle boast. Thousands of acres of cherry orchards envelop the town, their wispy, pink blossoms bringing a delicate beauty each May. At the **National Cherry Festival**, held during the first full week in July, visitors can watch parades, fireworks, and concerts, while sampling every imaginable cherry product.

Traverse City's neat **downtown** rests along the bottom of the west arm of **Grand Traverse Bay**, below the Old Mission Peninsula. This slender seventeen-mile strip of land, which divides the bay into two inlets, makes for a pleasant short driving tour along narrow roads with tremendous simultaneous views of the bay on either side. Five sandy public beaches and a small harbor can be found around the town itself. Various companies offer boat, windsurfer, jet-ski, and mountain bike rental. There are 36 **golf courses** in the immediate area, as well – some of them among the most beautiful in the country.

Practicalities

Greyhound stops near downtown at 3233 Cass Rd. The **visitor center**, downtown at 101 Grandview Parkway (Mon–Fri 9am–5pm, Sat 9am–3pm; ☎231/947-1120 or 1-800/872-8377, ⓦwww.tcvisitors.com), can help with finding **accommodation**, though prices anywhere near downtown soar in summer. The attractive little *Bayshore Resort*, near downtown at 833 E Front St (☎231/935-4400, ⓦwww.bayshore-resort.com; ⑤), has a private beach and nice rooms. The very central *Park Place Hotel*, 300 E State St (☎231/946-5000 or 1-800/748-0133, ⓦwww.park-place-hotel.com; ⑥), is reliable, as are the well-maintained *Days Inn & Suites*, 420 Munson Ave (☎231/941-0208, ⓦwww.tcdaysinn.com; ⑤), and the basic but clean *Sierra Motel*, 230 Munson Ave (☎231/946-7720; ④), both a couple of miles southeast. There's **camping** at Traverse City State Park, just outside town at 1132 US-31 N (☎231/922-5270; $27/night).

Affordable **places to eat** in Traverse City are easy to find. Big breakfasts with home-baked bread are served at *Mabel's*, 472 Munson Ave (☎231/947-0252), while *Mode's Bum Steer*, 125 E State St (☎231/947-9832), is a ribs joint. The best bet for a meal, though, particularly in the evening, is to drive north onto the Old Mission Peninsula where the *Boathouse*, 14039 Peninsula Drive (☎231/223-4030), dishes up fresh seafood, pasta, and vegetarian food right by the lake. The *U & I Lounge*, 214 E Front St (☎231/946-8932), is the best **bar** in town; it also serves up great gyros, burgers, and salads. *Union Street Station*, 117 S Union St (☎231/941-1930), has pool tables and **live music** of all sorts most nights.

North to Mackinaw City

On its way north from Traverse City, scenic Hwy-31 skims along Lake Michigan through **Charlevoix** and other pretty lakeside towns. The northern tip of the peninsula is occupied by **Mackinaw City**, where ferries take excursionists to much-hyped **Mackinac Island** – billboards advertise its attractions for fifty miles before you arrive.

Charlevoix, Petoskey, and Harbor Springs

CHARLEVOIX boasts a positively idyllic setting, fronting onto three separate lakes: Michigan, Charlevoix, and the beautiful, bowl-shaped Round Lake. Petunia-lined **Bridge Street**, the two-block downtown, looks over a picturesque, almost landlocked harbor on Round Lake, hemmed in on the other sides by terraced ridges. Though an undeniably beautiful place, in recent years the town has become a bit too fancy. Beaver Island Boat Company, 103 Bridge Park Drive, runs **ferries** to **Beaver Island**, the most remote inhabited island in the Great Lakes (April–Dec; $38 roundtrip; 2hr crossing; ☏231/547-2311 or 1-888/446-4095, ⊛www.bibco.com).

Charlevoix's helpful **visitor center** is at 408 E Bridge St (☏231/547-2101 or 1-800/367-8557, ⊛www.charlevoixlodging.com). Lakeside **hotels**, such as the turreted *Weathervane Terrace*, 111 Pine River Lane (☏231/547-9955, ⊛www.weathervane-chx.com; ❼), charge over $300 a night on peak weekends. One of the best-value **B&Bs**, the *MacDougall House*, 109 Petoskey Ave (☏231/547-5788 or 1-800/753-5788 ⊛www.michiganbandb.com; ❸), has a garden and huge breakfasts. As for **food**, *Whitney's Oyster Bar*, 305 Bridge St (☏231/547-0818), serves fresh seafood and snacks until 2am.

In bigger and busier **PETOSKEY**, high above Lake Michigan sixteen miles north along US-31, grand Victorian houses encircle the downtown's nicely restored **Gaslight District**. Ernest Hemingway spent many of his teenage summers here and alludes to the town in his novel *The Torrents of Spring*. The **visitor center** is at 401 E Mitchell St (Mon–Fri 8am–5pm, Sat 10am–4pm, summer Sun noon–4pm; ☏1-800/845-2828, ⊛www.boynecountry.com). For a **place to stay**, try the *Serenity B&B*, 504 Rush St (☏231/347-1338 or 1-877/347-6171, ⊛www.serenitybb.com; ❻), a big Victorian house serving superb full breakfasts, or the venerable *Stafford's Perry Hotel*, centrally located at Bay and Lewis streets (☏231/347-4000 or 1-800/737-1899, ⊛www.staffords.com; ❹); its *Noggin Room Pub* has good snacks and pizza. Other options for something to eat include a Hemingway favorite, *Jesperson's*, 312 Howard St (☏231/347-3601), which still does great pies and sandwiches, and the popular *Mitchell Street Pub*, 426 E Mitchell St (☏231/347-1801), which has decent snacks.

Twelve miles up Hwy-119, **HARBOR SPRINGS** is a favorite with the Midwestern elite. The charming Main Street and small shaded beach of this "Cornbelt Riviera" resort are certainly captivating. The comfy *Colonial Inn*, at 210 Artesian Ave (☏231/526-2111; ❹), has the only reasonably affordable rooms in town. From Harbor Springs, the **"Tunnel of Trees"** scenic drive follows a section of Hwy-119 to Mackinaw City. Along this narrow winding road, occasional breaks in the overhanging trees afford views of Lake Michigan and Beaver Island.

Mackinaw City

Forty miles northeast of Petoskey, **MACKINAW CITY** has long enjoyed a steady tourist trade as the major embarkation point for Mackinac Island and, though the streets have been landscaped and visitors flock to **Mackinaw Crossings**, a mall-cum-entertainment zone on South Huron Street, that remains its real raison d'être, as well as being the last stop en route to the Upper Peninsula.

The **visitor center** is located at 10800 S US-23 (Mon–Fri 8am–5pm; ☏231/436-5991 or 1-800/666-0160, ⊛www.mackinawcity.com). Several mid-priced **hotels** have been built alongside the shore, among them the *Best Western Dockside Waterfront* (☏231/436-5001, ⊛www.bestwestern.com; ❺). Cheaper rooms can be found inland at the *Capri Motel*, 801 S Nicolet St (T231/436-5498, Wwww.caprimotel.info; ●). You can get a good grilled **meal** outdoors at the *Depo*, 250 S Huron St (T231/436-7060), a refurbished train station, while listening to the free evening concerts and watching laser light shows in the adjacent amphitheater.

To reach Mackinac Island, contact Arnold Transit (May–Oct, schedule varies; $20 for pedestrians, $7.50 for bikes; T906/847-3351 or 1-800/542-8528, Wwww.arnoldline.com) or Shepler's Ferry (late Apr to mid-Oct, schedule varies; same prices; T231/436-5023 or 1-800/828-6157, Wwww.sheplersferry.com); both companies offer **high-speed catamaran crossings** from the Ferry Terminal in Mackinaw City, and do not require reservations.

Mackinac Island

Viewed from an approaching boat, the tree-blanketed rocky limestone outcrop of **MACKINAC ISLAND** (pronounced "Mackinaw"), suddenly thrusting out from the swirling waters, is an unforgettable sight. As you near the harbor, large Victorian houses come into view, dappling the hillsides with white and pastel. The most conspicuous is the imposing, $300-a-night *Grand Hotel* (T906/847-3331 or 1-800/334-4726, Wwww.grandhotel.com; ●), where just to enter the foyer costs $5. On disembarking, you'll see rows of horses and buggies (all motorized transportation is banned from the island, except for emergency vehicles) and inhale the omnipresent smell of fresh manure. Also ubiquitous on the island is **fudge**, relentlessly marketed as a Mackinac "delicacy."

Mackinac's crowded **Main Street** and contrived nostalgia can get irritating, but the island is still worth visiting, not least for the ferry ride over and the chance to cycle along the hilly back roads. Underneath the tourist trimmings is a rich history. French priests established a mission to the Huron Indians here during the winter of 1670–71. The French built a fort here in 1715, but within fifty years had lost control of the island to the British. The government acknowledged the island's beauty by designating it as the country's second national park, two years after Yellowstone in 1875, though it was handed over to the state of Michigan twenty years later. To get a feel for the history, hike or cycle up to the whitewashed stone **Fort Mackinac**, a US Army outpost until 1890. Its ramparts afford a great view of the village and lake below, though admission is a steep $8 (May to mid-Oct 9.30am–6.30pm).

On Main Street, an **information kiosk** (daily 9am–5pm; T906/847-3783, Wwww.mackinac.com) provides full details of accommodation and other facilities. The least costly **hotel** is *Murray Hotel* (T906/847-3360 or 1-800/462-2546, Wwww.4mackinac.com; ●), which serves a large continental breakfast buffet. Unpretentious **B&Bs** such as the *Bogan Lane Inn* (T906/847-3439, Wwww.boganlaneinn.com; ●) and the secluded *Small Point* (T906/847-3758; ●) are more affordable. **Places to eat** on Main Street include *The Pilot House Pub* (T906/847-0270) in the *Lakeview Hotel*, which has American fare and live entertainment nightly, and *Patrick Sinclair's* (T906/847-6454), an Irish pub serving sandwiches, seafood, and salads.

The Upper Peninsula

From the map, it would seem logical for Michigan's **Upper Peninsula**, separated from the rest of the state by the **Mackinac Straits**, to be part of Wisconsin. However, when Michigan entered the Union in 1837, its legislators, eyeing the peninsula's huge mineral wealth, incorporated it into their new state before Wisconsin existed.

Previously UP, as it's commonly known, figured prominently in French plans to create an empire in North America. Father Jacques Marquette and other missionaries made peace with the native people and established settlements, including the port of Sault Ste Marie in 1688. The French hoped to press further south, but before they could get much past Detroit, the British inflicted a severe military defeat in 1763.

Vast, lonesome, and wild, the Upper Peninsula is full of stunning landmarks, exemplified by the **Pictured Rocks National Lakeshore**. Most of the eastern section is marked by low-lying, sometimes swampy land between softly undulating limestone hills. Infamous for its bitter winters (1997 saw 272 inches of snow), the northwest corner is the most desolate, especially the rough and broken **Keweenaw Peninsula** and **Isle Royale National Park**, fifty miles offshore. The UP's only real city is **Marquette**, a college town with a quiet buzz and a good base for exploration. Until 1957 you could get to the UP from lower Michigan only by ferry. Today, the five-mile **Mackinac Bridge** ($2.50 toll), lit up beautifully at night, stretches elegantly across the bottleneck Mackinac Straits.

Sault Ste Marie

Perched at the northeast corner of the UP, **SAULT STE MARIE** (pronounced "Soo Saint Marie" and known locally as "The Soo") stands across St Mary's Rapids from the Canadian town bearing the same name. It's one of the oldest settlements in the US – not that you'd guess that from the industrial sprawl of the waterfront. The Soo owes most of its trade and industry to the St Mary's Locks, the only water connection between Superior and the other Great Lakes, built in 1855 and later expanded to handle oceangoing vessels. Four giant reservoirs raise upbound boats 21 feet to the level of Lake Superior. To see this impressive operation, which accounts for more tonnage than the Suez and Panama canals combined, take one of the **Soo Locks boat tours** ($19; ☎906/632-6301 or 1-800/432-6301, ⊛www.soolocks.com) from Dock #1 or Dock #2 on East Portage Avenue, or watch for free from the **visitor center** on the upper grounds of the St Mary's Falls canal (April–Nov daily 7am–11pm; ☎906/632-2394). Near dock #1, the other main attraction is the vast **Museum Ship *Valley Camp*** (mid-May to mid-Oct 10am–5pm, later in Jul & Aug; $9.50; ☎1-888/744-7867, ⊛www.thevalleycamp.com), full of maritime memorabilia and aquariums, which doubles with the **History Tower**, a couple of blocks inland at 326 E Portage Ave (same hours; $5.50, combo $13), whose best feature is its observation deck.

Despite efforts to increase its tourist trade, the Soo is not a place where you'd want to spend much time. The *Crestview Inn*, 1200 Ashmun St (☎906/635-5213 or 1-800/955-5213, ⊛www.crestviewinn.com; ❹), has clean, comfortable rooms, while the *Seaway Motel*, further along at no. 1800 (☎906/632-8201 or 1-800/782-0466, ⊛www.seawayseewhy.com; ❸), is plainer and cheaper. *Antler's*, 804 E Portage Ave (☎906/632-3571), looks like a dive bar but is in fact a historic Prohibition-era **pub**, where you can also get decent steaks and fish.

Paradise

Native Americans who lived in the area sixty miles west and north of the Soo called it *Tahquamenon* ("Marsh of the Blueberries"). Now it's called **PARADISE**, and in summer this elongated lakeside village can live up to its name, cut as it is out of thick, dark green forests and surrounded by small, reed-cluttered ultramarine lakes. Life is slow and easy here, but the choppy waters of Superior deny absolute calm to the beach. Ten miles west on Hwy-123, one of the most popular spots on the UP for hiking, boating, and camping ($10–33/night) is the gorgeous **Tahquamenon**

Falls State Park ($8 per car; ☎906/492-3415), made famous in Longfellow's epic "The Song of Hiawatha," where "by the rushing Tahquamenon" Hiawatha built his canoe. The waters, dyed a translucent brown by tannic acid, spill over two sets of cataracts.

Whitefish Road winds eleven miles north of town to where the sand and shingle of **Whitefish Point** nudges into the harsh waters of Lake Superior. Raging northwesterly winds, which build up over almost four hundred miles of open lake funneling into this narrower section, have contributed to more than five hundred shipwrecks along the eighty-mile stretch of lakeshore westward to Munising. The story of these wrecks is told at the **Great Lakes Shipwreck Historical Museum**, located at the dead end of Whitefish Point Road (mid-May to mid-Oct daily 10am–6pm; $10; ☎906/635-1742, Ⓦ www.shipwreckmuseum.com), with the help of subtle lighting and atmospheric background music. It's not all ancient history, either; on November 10, 1975, the cargo ship *Edmund Fitzgerald* foundered in 96mph gusts, losing all of its 29-person crew.

Curley's Motel & Cabins on M-123 in Paradise (☎906/492-3445 or 1-800/236-7386, Ⓦ www.superiorsights.com/curleys; ❹) is your best bet for **accommodation**. The *Yukon Inn* opposite (☎906/492-3264) is a **restaurant** and **bar** with stuffed trophy animals for decor, and serving burgers and sandwiches; DJs spin on Saturday nights.

Pictured Rocks National Lakeshore

The 42 miles between the attractive fishing villages of Grand Marais and Munising form the **Pictured Rocks National Lakeshore**, a splendid array of multicolored cliffs, rolling dunes, and secluded sandy beaches. Rain, wind, ice, and sun have

△ Pictured Rocks National Lakeshore

carved and gouged arches, columns, and caves into the face of the lakeshore, all stained different hues. Hiking trails run along the clifftops, and Hwy-58 takes you close to the water, but the best way to see the cliffs is by **boat**. Pictured Rocks Cruises offers a three-hour narrated **tour** that leaves from the City Pier in Munising (late May to early Oct 2–8 trips daily; $30; ☏906/387-2379, ⓦwww.picturedrocks.com). Less than a mile farther along the lake, at 1204 Commercial St, Shipwreck Tours gives two-hour narrated cruises in a glass-bottomed boat, with surprisingly clear views of three shipwrecks – one intact (June to early Oct 2–3 trips daily; $27; ☏906/387-4477, ⓦwww.shipwrecktours.com). Those in a hurry can get a glimpse of the cliffs by visiting the **Miners Castle Overlook**, twelve miles east of Munising, or **Munising Falls**, one of a half-dozen nearby waterfalls, near the village's well-signposted **visitors bureau** (Mon–Fri 9am–5pm; ☏906/387-2138, ⓦwww.munising.org). In Munising, *Scotty's Motel*, 415 Cedar St (☏906/387-2449; ❸), and the *Munising Motel*, 332 E Onota St (☏906/387-3187; ❹), are fairly comfortable places to stay. At 101 E Munising Ave, *The Navigator* (☏906/387-1555) is the only **restaurant** in Munising with a view of Lake Superior, and serves breakfast any time along with steaks, seafood, pizza, and burgers.

Marquette

Forty miles west of Munising is the unofficial capital of the UP, the low-key college town of **MARQUETTE**, also the center of the area's massive ore industry. The helpful **state welcome center**, just south of town at 2201 US-41 S (daily: summer 9am–6pm; rest of year 9am–5pm; ☏906/249-9066, ⓦwww.marquettecountry.org), has vouchers for local hotel discounts and lots of information about Marquette's sights. Premier among them is rugged **Presque Isle Park**, north of town on Lakeshore Boulevard, almost completely surrounded by Lake Superior and with stunning views of the lake. Back in town, at East Ridge St and Lakeshore, the **Marquette Maritime Museum** (mid-May to late Oct daily 10am–5pm; $4; ☏906/226-2006, ⓦwww.mqt-maritimemuseum.com) has exhibits on the fishing and freighting industries, as well as a video about the fabled Superior wrecking of the *Edmund Fitzgerald* (see p.341). The area's most curious sight is the **Superior Dome**, on Northern Michigan University's campus at 1401 Presque Isle Ave, the largest wooden dome in the world.

Ten miles west of Marquette on Hwy-41 in Ishpeming, the birthplace of ski-jumping, is the **National Ski Hall of Fame** (Mon–Sat 10am–5pm; free; ☏906/485-6323, ⓦwww.skihall.com). Housed in a cone-shaped building with a ski jump running down the roof, this low-tech museum chronicles the history of skiing via photos and artifacts from the 10th Mountain Division, the first chairlift from Sun Valley, Idaho, and lots of ski-jumping memorabilia.

By far the nicest place to **stay** is the grand *Landmark Inn*, 230 N Front St (☏906/228-2580, ⓦwww.thelandmarkinn.com; ❻), which has rooms overlooking the lake, although a host of cheaper motels cluster west of town on US-41. You can **camp** at the *Tourist Park Campground* on Sugarloaf Avenue (☏906/228-0465; $15). *JJ's Shamrock*, downtown at 113 S Front St (☏906/226-6734), serves basic bar **food** along with occasional live music. For a more formal dining experience, locals favor the *Northwoods Supper Club*, just west of town off US-41 (☏906/228-4343), with a meat-and-potatoes menu in a rustic setting. One popular watering hole is *Remie's Bar*, 111 Third St (☏906/226-9133), with a rowdy local crowd and live music on Wednesdays.

The Keweenaw Peninsula

Beyond Marquette, along US-41, the landscape becomes progressively more rough-hewn, culminating in the **Keweenaw Peninsula**, which juts like a dorsal fin eighty miles out into Lake Superior. Encircled by a dramatic shoreline and enriched by crags and precipices, it's a great place for a short driving tour, with roads winding through forests, past old copper workings, and up and down steep hills.

Halfway up the peninsula, in the small college town of **HOUGHTON** on Portage Lake, the *College Motel*, next to the Michigan Tech campus at 1308 College Ave (℡906/482-2202; ❷), is good value. The luxury option is the 100-year-old *Charleston House Inn B&B*, downtown by the water at 918 College Ave (℡906/482-7790, ⓦwww.charlestonhouseinn.com; ❻). The *Suomi Home Bakery and Restaurant*, at 54 N Huron St (℡906/482-3220), serves cheap pastries and Finnish food, while locals and students enjoy good, cheap beer and food at the lively *Downtowner Lounge*, 100 Shelden Ave (℡906/482-7305). Another classy accommodation option is ↟*Laurium Manor* (℡906/337-2549, ⓦwww.laurium.info; ❹), around ten miles north at 320 Tamarack St, in Laurium – whose twin town of **CALUMET** was once a huge mining center and boasts a fine historical downtown.

At the northern tip of Keweenaw, most scenically reached along Hwy-26 from Eagle River, handsome little **COPPER HARBOR** was once so rich in minerals that early miners could pick up chunks of pure copper from the lakeshore; today you can tour the **Delaware Mine**, ten miles west on US-41 (daily Jun–Aug 10am–6pm, Sept to mid-Oct 10am–5pm; $9.50; ℡906/289-4688). Reasonable **accommodation** is available at the waterfront *King Copper Motel* (℡906/289-4212 or 1-800/833-2470, ⓦwww.kingcoppermotel.com; ❹), 445 E Brockway Ave, and you can try a local pasty or fish dish at the nearby *Tamarack Inn Restaurant* (℡906/289-4522), 512 Gratiot St.

Isle Royale National Park

Much closer to Canada than the US, the 45-mile sliver of **Isle Royale National Park**, fifty miles out in Lake Superior, is in a double sense as far as you can get in Michigan from Detroit. All cars are banned and, instead of freeways, 166 miles of hiking trails lead past windswept trees, swampy lakes, and grazing moose. Aside from other outdoors types, the only traces of human life you're likely to see are ancient mineworks, possibly two millennia old, shacks left behind by commercial fishermen in the 1940s, and a few lighthouses and park buildings. Hiking, canoeing, fishing, and scuba-diving among shipwrecks are the principal leisure activities.

The park is open from mid-May until the end of September. **Camping** is free, though you should visit the **park headquarters** at 800 E Lakeshore Drive in Houghton (Mon–Fri 8am–4.30pm; ℡906/482-0984, ⓦwww.nps.gov/isro) before you leave the mainland, for advice on water purity, mosquitoes, and temperatures that can drop well below freezing even in summer. Aside from camping, you can stay in a self-catering cottage or a luxury lodge room at the *Rock Harbor Lodge* (℡906/337-4993, Oct–April ℡270/773-2191, ⓦwww.isleroyaleresort.com; ❻–❾). The lodge rents canoes and motorboats for $30 and $64 per day, respectively, and offers cruises for $30.

Ferries to Isle Royale leave from Copper Harbor ($52–60 one way; ℡906/289-4437, ⓦwww.isleroyale.com), Houghton ($54 one way; ℡906/482-0984, ⓦwww.nps.gov/isro), and Grand Portage, Minnesota ($40–55 one way; ℡715/392-2100, ⓦwww.grand-isle-royale.com). If you are in a hurry, you can hop over by **plane** with the Isle Royale Seaplane Service in Houghton ($250 roundtrip; ☎906/482-8850, ⓦwww.royaleairservice.com).

Indiana

Thanks to an influx of northward migrants early in the nineteenth century – including the family of Abraham Lincoln, who lived for fourteen years near the present village of Santa Claus before moving to Illinois – much of **INDIANA** still bears the influence of the easygoing South. Unlike the abolitionist Lincolns, many former Southerners brought slaves to this new territory, and thousands rioted against being drafted into the Union army when the Civil War broke out. However, massive industrialization since the 1870s has firmly integrated Indiana into the regional economy. On a national level, this sports-happy state is best known these days for automobile racing and high-school basketball.

Despite some beautiful dunes and beaches, the most lasting memories provided by Indiana's fifty-mile **lakeshore** (by far the shortest of the Great Lakes states) are of the grimy steel mills and poverty-stricken neighborhoods of towns like Gary and East Chicago. In northern Indiana, the area in and around Elkhart and Goshen contains one of the nation's largest **Amish settlements**. The central plains are characterized by small market towns, except for the sprawling capital, **Indianapolis**, which makes a nice enough stopover. Hilly southern Indiana, at its most appealing in the fall, is a welcome contrast to the central cornbelt, boasting several quaint towns such as Nashville, while thriving Columbus exhibits a great array of contemporary architecture for such a small city.

As to why residents of the state are called "**Hoosiers**," dozens of explanations have been offered; the most believable is that it originated during the construction of the Ohio Falls Canal in the 1820s, when contractor Samuel Hoosier gave employment preference to those living on the Indiana side of the Ohio River.

Getting around Indiana

Nine interstates, five of which slice through Indianapolis, provide boring but fast ways to traverse Indiana. Greyhound runs frequent services, particularly on I-65 between Chicago and Louisville, and I-70 between the Eastern US and St Louis, while **Indianapolis**, **Michigan City**, and **South Bend** are the major stops on the state's three different Amtrak routes. Flights from most Midwestern and Eastern cities land at **Indianapolis International Airport**.

Indianapolis

INDIANAPOLIS began life in 1821, when a tract of barely inhabited marshes was designated the state capital. While its location in the middle of Indiana's rich farmland bore immense commercial advantages, the absence of a navigable river prohibited the transportation of bulky materials such as coal and iron to sustain heavy industry. Though home to more than sixty car manufacturers by 1910, the city never seriously threatened Detroit's supremacy. Nevertheless, it's now one of the biggest cities in the world that's not accessible by water, having attracted food, paper, and pharmaceutical industries, including the giant Eli Lilly Corporation.

Today the city has shaken off such nicknames as Naptown, India-no-place, and Brickhouse in the Cornfield in favor of its chosen designation as the country's unofficial amateur sports capital – "amateur" events like the Pan-American Games and national Olympic trials being worth big money these days. (Major league pro teams include the basketball Pacers and the football Colts.) In recent years, it has constructed several world-class sports arenas – including the retro-styled **Conseco Fieldhouse** downtown – along with new hotels, a gaggle of top-class museums, and a zoo – and its old downtown landmarks have become cultural, shopping, and dining complexes. No longer is it (quite) true that nothing happens here except for the glamorous **Indianapolis 500 car race** each May – "the most televised annual event in the world."

Arrival and information

Indianapolis International Airport is ten miles southwest of downtown, on the #8 IndyGo bus route ($1.25; ⊕317/635-3344). A **taxi** into the center costs around $30; try Yellow Cabs (⊕317/487-7777). Both Greyhound **buses** and Amtrak **trains** arrive at 350 S Illinois St (⊕317/267-3071), next to the fairly central Union Station complex. Useful **visitor centers** can be found at 201 S Capitol St, beside the RCA Dome (Mon–Fri 8.30am–5.30pm; ⊕317/237-5200 or 1-800/323-4639, ⊛www.indy.org), and in the glass pavilion at 100 W Washington St (Mon–Sat 10am–9pm, Sun noon–6pm; ⊕317/624-2563).

Accommodation

Indianapolis has plenty of quality **places to stay**, but few real budget downtown options, and prices can double during the race months of May, August, and September.

Canterbury Hotel 123 S Illinois St ⊕317/634-3000 or 1-800/538-8186, ⊛www.canterburyhotel.com. Much the classiest downtown option, this landmark hotel was rebuilt in 1928 and offers a hundred opulent and expensive rooms. **❼**

Crowne Plaza Union Station 123 W Louisiana St ⊕317/631-2221, ⊛www.crowneplaza.com/ind-downtown. Regular hotel rooms plus some much more exciting suites in converted railway carriages. **❻**

Days Inn Downtown 401 E Washington St ⊕317/637-6464 or 1-800/329-7466, ⊛www.day-sinn.com. Centrally located lodgings in a reliable chain motel. **❹**

Indy Hostel 4903 Winthrop Ave ⊕317/727-1696, ⊛www.indyhostel.us. Appealing small-scale hostel in a former family home, in a friendly neighborhood six miles from downtown. Dorm beds for $22 weekdays, $25 weekends, plus basic private rooms. Bike hire available **❶–❷**

The Villa Inn 1456 N Delaware St ⊕317/916-8500 or 1-866/626-8500, ⊛www.thevillainn.com. Castellated six-room luxury B&B inn with the feel of a hotel, two miles north of downtown, and offering a spa and restaurant. The same owners run two other local B&Bs. **❽**

Downtown

The nerve center of Indianapolis' spacious, relaxed downtown is the reasonably tasteful **Circle Centre** shopping and entertainment complex. Suspended over the busy Washington and Illinois intersection, the spectacular **Indianapolis Artsgarden** is an eight-story glass rotunda illuminated with twinkling lights. A performance and exhibition space, it doubles as a walkway to Circle Centre and several downtown hotels. One block north, streets radiate from **Monument Circle**, the

△ Indianapolis 500

starting point for a lengthy series of memorials and plazas dedicated to war veterans. Many visitors climb the 330 steps of the renovated 284ft **Soldiers and Sailors Monument** (daily 10am–7pm; free) – the tiny elevator can seldom cope with the demand – but in truth the view of the city from the top is nothing special.

Five blocks east, starting at New York and East streets, the serene tree-shaded **Lockerbie Square Historic District** is a small enclave of picturesque residences that were home to nineteenth-century artisans and business leaders. Small wood-frame cottages line the cobblestone streets, many of them painted in bright pinks, blues, and yellows, and fronted by ornately carved porches.

Several blocks west of Monument Circle, the **Indiana State Museum**, 650 W Washington St (Mon–Sat 9am–5pm, Sun 11am–5pm; $7; ☎317/232-1637, ⓦwww.indianamuseum.org), gives a useful insight into the state's history through exhibits on everything from geology to sport. The **Eiteljorg Museum of American Indians and Western Art** is nearby at 500 W Washington St, on the western edge of downtown (late May to Aug Mon–Sat 10am–5pm, Sun noon–5pm; Sept to late May Tues–Sat 10am–5pm, Sun noon–5pm; tours at 1pm; $8; ☎317/636-9378, ⓦwww.eiteljorg.org). Harrison Eiteljorg, an industrialist who went West in the 1940s to speculate in minerals, fell so deeply in love with the art of the region that he brought as much of it back with him as possible, especially from Taos, New Mexico. On display are works by Frederic Remington, Charles M. Russell, and Georgia O'Keeffe, as well as tribal artifacts from all over North America and a 38ft Haida totem pole on the grounds. There are also superb touring exhibits and a gorgeous gift shop. The Eiteljorg stands amid the rolling greenery of **White River State Park**, which is also home to the sizeable **Indianapolis Zoo** (summer Mon–Thurs 9am–5pm, Fri–Sun 9am–6pm; rest of year daily 9am–4pm; $13.50; ☎317/630-2001, ⓦwww.indyzoo.com), whose proudest boast is its underwater dolphin-viewing dome. In the park's southeast corner stands the superb **Victory Field**, home of the Indianapolis Indians (☎317/269-3545), the farm team for baseball's Cincinnati Reds.

Seven miles northwest of downtown, the **Indianapolis Motor Speedway** stages only two events each year; one is the legendary **Indianapolis 500**, held on the last Sunday in May, the other is August's prestigious NASCAR Brickyard 400.

The Indy 500 is preceded by two weeks of qualification runs that whittle the hopeful entrants down to a final field of 33 drivers, one of whom will scoop the million-dollar first prize. The two-and-a-half-mile circuit was built as a test track for the city's motor manufacturers. The first 500-mile race – held in 1911 and won in a time of 6hr 42min, at an average speed of 74.6mph – was a huge success, vindicating the organizers' belief that the distance was the optimum length for spectators' enjoyment. Cars now hit 235mph, though the official times of the winners are reduced by delays caused by accidents. While the technology is marvelous, the true legends in the eyes of their fans are such championship drivers as A.J. Foyt, Mario Andretti, and members of the Unser dynasty. The 90th race, in 2006, was won by a margin of a mere 0.0635 seconds.

The big race crowns one of the nation's largest festivals, attended by almost half a million spectators. At first, the city's conservative hierarchy saw it as interfering with the observance of Memorial Day weekend. However, it brings so much money into the city, with thousands of "Indy" racing fanatics staying for up to two weeks, that it is now exploited to the full, with civic events such as the crowning of the Speedway Queen, a Mayor's Ball, and a street parade. Seats for the race usually sell out well in advance ($40–90; ☎1-800/822-4639; ⊛www.imstix.com), but you may gain admittance to the infield, where the giddy and boozy atmosphere makes up for the poor view.

Adjoining the track, the impressive display of race-car history at the **Indianapolis Motor Speedway Hall of Fame Museum**, 4790 W 16th St (daily 9am–5pm, extended hours around race time; $3; ☎317/492-6784, ⊛www.indy500.com), provides a good background to the hysteria. To an irregular schedule, it's also possible to join a 90min behind-the-scenes **Grounds Tour** ($25 inc museum admission).

Out from downtown

Although the bodies of former president Benjamin Harrison and Hoosier poet James Whitcomb Riley lie in the enormous **Crown Hill Cemetery**, at 38th Street and Michigan, the most visited grave belongs to 1930s bank robber **John Dillinger**, at Section 44 Lot 94. Designated Public Enemy Number One, Dillinger completed thirteen bank raids – killing four policemen, three FBI agents, one sheriff, and an undetermined number of innocent bystanders – in a single-year career. Something of a folk hero, he escaped from jail twice, but was eventually ambushed by the FBI outside a Chicago theater in 1934 (see p.362) – that said, some researchers allege that another man was killed in his place.

Opposite the cemetery at 1200 W 38th St, more than 150 lush wooded acres accommodate the capacious **Indianapolis Museum of Art** (Tues, Wed, & Fri–Sun 10am–5pm, Thurs 10am–9pm; $7; ☎317/923-1331, ⊛www.ima-art.org). The main building is surrounded by a lake, botanical garden, sculpture courtyard, and a concert terrace. Inside, the exceptional displays include the largest collection of Turner paintings outside Britain and an array of paintings and prints from Gauguin's Pont Aven school; collections from around the globe include an extensive assortment of masks, figures, jewelry, and household items from northern Africa.

The city's most offbeat museum, the **Indiana Medical History Museum**, three miles west of downtown at 3045 W Vermont St (Thurs–Sat 10am–4pm, plus Wed by appointment only; $5; ☎317/635-7329, ⊛www.imhm.org), is housed in the old Pathology Building of what was once a huge psychiatric hospital. The guides give a fascinating account of medical practices in the late nineteenth century, pointing out the cabinets of preserved brains and similarly gruesome exhibits.

The **Children's Museum of Indianapolis**, 3000 N Meridian St, four miles north of downtown off of I-65 (daily 10am–5pm; closed Mon late Sept to late March; $12, under-18s $7; ⊕317/334-3322, ⊛www.childrensmuseum.org), is arguably the best of its kind in the country. Its most popular exhibit is the Dinosphere, in which visitors can dig for genuine fossils, while All Aboard! is an entertaining romp through the Age of Steam.

Eating

The swish **Circle Centre** mall houses dozens of **places to eat**, but most are chains. You'd do better to stick to the more established restaurants downtown or head up to **Broad Ripple Village** (bus #17) at College Avenue and 62nd Street, which is packed with bars and cafés (along with galleries and shops). At lunchtime, **City Market**, 222 E Market St, is a maze of lunch counters and tables where you can feast cheaply on all sorts of international food amid a cacophonous din.

Bazbeaux 334 Massachusetts Ave, downtown ⊕317/636-7662 and 811 E Westfield Blvd, Broad Ripple Village ⊕317/255-5711. The best (thin-crust) pizzas in town, with a range of exotic toppings.
Elbow Room 605 N Pennsylvania St ⊕317/635-3354. This pub serves specialty sandwiches and lots of import beers.
Elements 415 N Alabama St ⊕317/634-8888. Romantic little place with outdoor seating and a small but regularly changing menu that features contemporary American cuisine. Plenty of seafood and vegetarian options.
India Garden 143 N Illinois St ⊕317/634-6060; also at 830 Broad Ripple Ave ⊕317/253-6060. The curries are a highlight, along with the good-value lunchtime buffet. The downtown branch is closed on Sundays.

St Elmo Steak House 127 S Illinois St ⊕317/635-0636. One of the most famous steak restaurants in the meat-mad Midwest. It can be rather pompous, and it's certainly expensive ($40–50 per person), but there's no denying the quality.
Shapiro's 808 S Meridian St ⊕317/631-4041. Landmark deli just a few blocks off downtown, where you can fill up on lox, tongue, and other specialties in an old-style cafeteria atmosphere. Leave room for the huge desserts.
Yat's Cajun and Creole 659 Massachusetts Ave ⊕317/686-6380; also at 5463 N College Ave ⊕317/253-8817. Wildly popular Louisiana-flavored cafeteria, offering a changing menu of inexpensive daily specials in two locations.

Nightlife and entertainment

The emerging **nightlife** area in downtown is Massachusetts Avenue, where along with some good bars and restaurants, the 3000-seat **Murat Centre**, a former Masonic shrine at 502 N New Jersey St (⊕317/231-0000, ⊛www.murat.com), hosts headliners and Broadway musicals. Otherwise, head north to chic **Broad Ripple Village**. Check the free weekly *NUVO* (⊛www.nuvo.net) for full details of gigs and events.

On the **performing arts** scene, the 1927 Spanish Baroque Indiana Repertory Theatre, 140 W Washington St (⊕317/635-5252, ⊛www.indianarep.com), puts on dramatic productions between September and April, while the Indianapolis Symphony Orchestra has weekly concerts at the equally elaborate 1916 Hilbert Circle Theatre, 45 Monument Circle (⊕317/639-4300, ⊛www.indyorch.org).

Broad Ripple Brew Pub 842 E 65th St ⊕317/253-2739. Atmospheric brewpub located six miles north of downtown Indianapolis.
Chatterbox 435 Massachusetts Ave ⊕317/636-

0584, ⊛www.chatterboxjazz.com. Ever-busy local bar, hosting live jazz nightly.
Madame Walker Theatre Center 617 Indiana Ave ⊕317/236-2099, ⊛www.walkertheatre.com.

Black cultural and heritage center putting on *Jazz on the Avenue* every Friday, plus regular dance events, plays, and concerts.
Rathskeller Restaurant 401 E Michigan St ☎317/636-0396. German beer hall in the basement of the historic Atheneum building that also serves reasonable food.

Slippery Noodle 372 S Meridian St ☎317/631-6968. Indiana's oldest bar, established in 1850, is next to Union Station. Cheap beer Monday and Tuesday, and live blues every night.
Vogue 6259 N College Ave ☎317/259-7029, ⓦwww.thevogue.ws. Popular Broad Ripple rock and indie venue in a former movie theater, and featuring retro club nights.

Out from Indianapolis: Bloomington

BLOOMINGTON, by far the liveliest small city in Indiana, is 45 miles southwest of Indianapolis on Hwy-37. It owes its vibrancy to the main campus of Indiana University, east of downtown. The I.M. Pei–designed **Indiana University Art Museum** on East Seventh Street (Tues–Sat 10am–5pm, Sun noon–5pm; free) holds a fine international collection of painting and sculpture. Across the street from the pastoral campus, law student Hoagy Carmichael composed *Stardust* on the piano of a popular hangout. The architecturally rich downtown also features a host of good shops.

Practicalities

Greyhound, 409 S Walnut St (☎812/332-1522), runs **bus** service to Indianapolis. Bloomington's friendly **visitor center** can be found at 2855 N Walnut St (Mon–Fri 8.30am–5pm, Sat 9am–4pm; ☎812/334-8900, ⓦwww.visitbloomington .com).

If you need **to stay**, the best budget option is the central *Motel 6 – Bloomington University*, 1800 N Walnut St (☎812/332-0820; ❷), which is far nicer than you might expect of the chain. The cozy and also very central Victorian *Grant Street Inn*, 310 N Grant St (☎812/334-2353 or 1-800/328-4350, ⓦwww. grantstreetinn.com; ❺), offers more luxury. Among student bars and cafés lining Kirkwood Avenue is the vegetarian *Laughing Planet*, at no. 322 E Kirkwood (☎812/323-2233), renowned for its burritos, while local **restaurants** include the Japanese/Indian/Tibetan *Snow Lion*, 113 S Grant Ave (☎812/336-0835), and the *Siam House*, 430 E Fourth St (☎812/331-1233), which serves delicious Thai cuisine. The *Brewpub at Lennie's*, 1795 E Tenth St (☎812/323-2112), is the liveliest drinking spot around.

Illinois

Nearly everything in the agricultural powerhouse state of **ILLINOIS** revolves around **Chicago**, the largest and most exciting city in the Great Lakes region. At the state's northeastern corner, on the shores of **Lake Michigan**, Chicago has a fabulous skyline, plus top-rated museums, restaurants, and cafés, and innumerable jazz and blues nightspots. Seventy-five percent of the state's twelve-million-strong population lives within commuting distance of the Windy City's energetic center. Outside of Chicago, the sole punctuation to the endless flat prairies is far to the south, where the forested **Shawnee Hills** rise between the Mississippi and Ohio rivers. The contrast between Illinois' quiet rural hinterlands and its buzzing urban center could hardly be greater.

Illinois was first explored and settled by the French, though in 1763 the territory was sold to the English. Granted statehood in 1818, Illinois remained a distant frontier until the mid-1830s; only once the native **Sauk** were subjugated, after a series of uprisings, did settlers arrive in sizeable numbers. Among them were the first followers of Joseph Smith, founder of the Mormon Church, who established a large colony along the Mississippi at Nauvoo. The **Mormons** met with suspicion and persecution and, after Smith was murdered by a lynch mob in 1844, fled west to Utah. Other early immigrants included the young **Abraham Lincoln**, who practiced law from 1837 onward in **Springfield**. Now the state capital, it's home to a wide range of Lincolniana, including his restored home, his law offices, and various other period buildings and artifacts, as well as his monumental tomb and new presidential library. Hence Illinois's self-proclaimed nickname, "Land of Lincoln."

Getting around Illinois

Chicago is the site of **O'Hare Airport** (the world's busiest), and the hub of the national Amtrak **train** network. If you plan to spend time in the rest of Illinois, Amtrak, numerous commuter railroads, and, to a lesser extent, Greyhound, provide reasonable public transportation. **Cycling** is also generally easy on these endless flat plains. Half a dozen **interstates** fan out across the country from Chicago. The famous Chicago-to-LA Route 66 has been defunct since the 1960s, though I-55 southwest to St Louis, followed by I-44 and I-40, follow its general route.

Chicago

CHICAGO is in many ways the nation's last great city. Sarah Bernhardt called it "the pulse of America" and, though long eclipsed by Los Angeles as the nation's second most populous city after New York, Chicago really does have it all, with less hassle and fewer infrastructural problems than its coastal rivals.

Founded in the early 1800s, Chicago had a population of just fifty in 1830. Its expansion was triggered first by the opening of the Erie Canal in 1825, and then by the arrival of the first locomotive in 1848; by 1860 it was the largest railroad center in the world, serving as the main connection between the established East Coast cities and the wide-open Wild West frontier. That position on the sharp edge between civilization and wilderness made it a crucible of innovation. Many aspects of modern life, from skyscrapers to suburbia, had their start, and perhaps their finest expression, here on the shores of Lake Michigan.

Despite burning to the ground in 1871, Chicago boomed thereafter, doubling in population every decade and reaching two million people around 1900, swollen by **Irish** and **Eastern European** immigrants. In the early years of the twentieth century, it cemented its reputation as a place of apparently limitless opportunity, with jobs aplenty for those willing to work. The attraction was strongest among **blacks** from the Deep South: African-Americans poured into the city, with more than 75,000 arriving during the war years of 1916–18 alone.

During the Roaring Twenties, Chicago's self-image as a no-holds-barred free market was pushed to the limit by a new breed of entrepreneur. Criminal syndicates, ruthlessly run by the likes of **gangsters** such as Al Capone and Bugsy Moran, took advantage of Prohibition to sell bootleg alcohol. Shootouts in the street between sharp-suited, Tommy-gun-wielding mobsters were not as common as legend would have it, but the backroom dealing and iron-handed control they pioneered was later perfected by politicians such as former mayor **Richard Daley** – father of the present mayor – who ran Chicago single-handedly from the 1950s until his death in 1976. These days, the tourist authorities play down the mobster era; few traces of the hoodlum years exist, and those that do owe more to Hollywood than contemporary Chicago.

Most visitors to Chicago are immediately bowled over by its magnificent urban **skyline**, adorned with one of the world's finest assemblages of **modern architecture**, ranging from Mies van der Rohe's masterpieces to the 110-story **Sears Tower**. The city can also boast the wonderful new Millennium Park and the extraordinary treasures of the **Art Institute of Chicago**, as well as several other excellent **museums**, along with restaurants, sports, and highbrow cultural activities. Perhaps its strongest suit, however, is **live music**, with a phenomenal array of

jazz and **blues** clubs packed into the back rooms of its amiable bars and cafés. The **rock** scene is also healthy, having spawned such bands as Smashing Pumpkins and Wilco during the 1990s. And almost everything is noticeably less expensive than in other US cities – **eating out**, for example, costs much less than in New York or LA, but is every bit as good. Two great ways to get a real feel for the city are to head out to ivy-covered **Wrigley Field** on a sunny summer afternoon to catch baseball's Cubs in action, or take a cruise boat under the bridges of the Chicago River at sunset.

Arrival, information, and getting around

Chicago's **O'Hare International Airport** (Ⓦ www.ohare.com), the national headquarters for United, American, and several other airlines, is seventeen miles northwest of downtown Chicago. It is connected to the city center by 24hr CTA (Blue Line) **trains** from the station under Terminal 4, which take around forty minutes and cost $1.75 (see "City transportation," opposite). **Midway Airport**, smaller than O'Hare but used by an increasing number of domestic airlines, is eleven miles southwest of downtown; take one of CTA's Midway (Orange Line) trains, which take thirty minutes. **Taxis** into town from O'Hare cost up to $40 (there's also a ride-share program with a flat rate of $20), and take thirty minutes to an hour. From Midway the fare is about $30 and the journey time is twenty to forty minutes. Another option is Continental Air Transport's **express bus and van service** between the airports and downtown hotels (around $25 from O'Hare, $20 from Midway; Ⓣ 312/454-7799 or 1-888/284-3826, Ⓦ www.airportexpress. com).

Chicago is the hub of the nationwide **Amtrak** rail system, and almost every cross-country route passes through **Union Station**, west of the Loop at Canal and Adam streets. Greyhound and a number of regional bus companies pull into the large 24hr **bus station** at 630 W Harrison St (Ⓣ 312/408-5980), three blocks southwest of Union Station.

Arriving in Chicago **by car**, racing towards the gleaming glass towers of the Loop, can be memorable. Bear in mind, though, that traffic on the expressways to and from downtown can be bumper-to-bumper during rush hours. **Parking** can also be a problem. Meters are expensive (25¢ for 10min) and usually have a 2hr limit. Check street signs for additional restrictions, which are rigidly enforced – violations may result in your car being towed and impounded. Perhaps the best place to leave a car in the downtown area is in the garage under Grant Park, at Columbus Street and Monroe Drive, close to the east side of the Art Institute ($15 for 24hr).

Information

Pick up information and maps from the **Chicago Office of Tourism**, in the lobby of the Chicago Cultural Center, 77 E Randolph St (April–Oct Mon–Thurs 8am–7pm, Fri 8am–6pm, Sat 9am–6pm, Sun 10am–6pm; Nov–March Mon–Fri

CityPass

For significant **discounts** at five of the city's major tourist and cultural attractions – the Hancock Observatory, the Field Museum, Shedd Aquarium, Adler Planetarium & Astronomy Museum, and the Museum of Science and Industry – you can purchase a **CityPass** ($49.50, ages 4–11 $39; Ⓣ 208/787-4300, Ⓦ www.citypass.com). Valid for nine days, it allows you to skip most lines and save (up to $40, if you visit all five sights). CityPasses are sold at each of the attractions, or via the website.

10am–6pm, Sat 10am–5pm, Sun 11am–5pm; ☏1-800/877-CHICAGO, ⓦwww.
cityofchicago.org). There are also **information centers** in the Historic Water
Tower, 800 N Michigan Ave on the Magnificent Mile (daily 7.30am–7pm) and in
the Northwest Exelon Pavilion at Millennium Park (daily 10am–4pm).

Chicago's main **post office**, the largest in the world, is at 433 W Harrison St (Mon–
Sat 8am–5pm). There's a downtown branch at 211 S Clark St (Mon–Fri 7am–7pm).

City transportation

Getting around Chicago is simple and quick, thanks to buses and the "El," a system
of elevated trains operated 24 hours a day by the Chicago Transit Authority (CTA;
☏312/836-7000, ⓦwww.transitchicago.com). Pick up a CTA System Map, available at most subway stations and visitor centers, or from the CTA office on the
seventh floor of the Merchandise Mart, 300 N Wells St, just north of the Chicago
River. **Buses** run every five to fifteen minutes during rush hours and every eight
to twenty minutes at most other times. **Rapid transit trains** run every five to
fifteen minutes during the day and every fifteen to sixty minutes all night. Lines
are color-coded and denoted by route rather than destination. The Howard–Dan
Ryan is the Red Line; Lake–Englewood–Jackson Park is the Green Line; the
O'Hare–Congress–Douglas is the Blue Line; the Ravenswood is the Brown Line
(whose trains circle the Loop, giving the area its name); the Evanston Express is
the Purple Line; the Midway–Loop is the Orange Line; and the Skokie Swift is
the Yellow Line.

Guided tours

The best **guided tours** of Chicago have to be the wide range offered by the **Chicago
Architecture Foundation**, based in the Archicenter in the Santa Fe Building at 224
S Michigan Ave (☏312/922-3432, ⓦwww.architecture.org). Expert guides point out
the city's many architectural treasures and explain their role in Chicago's history
and development. Most popular of all are the superb Architecture River Cruises,
ninety-minute **boat trips** along the Chicago River that leave from Michigan Avenue
and Lower Wacker Drive (late April to early June Mon–Fri 3 departures, Sat & Sun 5
departures; early June to Sept Mon–Fri 10 deps, Sat & Sun 13 deps; Oct Mon–Fri
5 deps, Sat & Sun 6 deps; Nov Fri–Sun 3 deps; Mon–Fri $25, Sat & Sun $27). The
Foundation also runs several **walking tours** of the Loop, departing from the Archicenter on a complicated schedule of at least two different 2hr tours daily throughout
the year ($14 for one tour, $24 for two), and a daily 45min, $5 lunchtime tour of
downtown landmarks at 12.15pm. Their longer-range **bus tours** operate mainly in
summer, focusing principally on the works of Frank Lloyd Wright ($40) and Mies van
der Rohe ($65), though the 3hr 30min "highlights" tour ($37) leaves at 9.30am on
Saturdays all year. Finally, the Foundation also operates the free **Loop Tour Train**
in summer (May–Sept, Sat only, 11am, 11.40am, 12.20pm & 1pm), a unique way
to get a first overview of downtown Chicago, in which a special "El" train makes a
couple of slow but non-stop commentated circuits around the Loop. Tickets, on the
day of the tour only, are available first-come, first-served from the visitor center at
77 E Randolph St.

Among the many other tour operators in the city are **Untouchable Tours**, which
run jokey, gangster-themed bus tours of Prohibition-era haunts ($20; ☏773/881-
1195; ⓦwww.gangstertour.com); the **Chicago Trolley**, which makes regular circuits
of downtown (daily 9.30am–5pm; $25 for one day, $35 for two days, hop on and off;
☏773/663-0260, ⓦwww.chicagotrolley.com); and **Shoreline Sightseeing Tours**,
which specializes in lake cruises, starting from Navy Pier and the Shedd Aquarium,
and also runs a simple Water Taxi service between the two (architectural cruises
$22–24, lake cruises $12; ☏312/222-9328, ⓦwww.shorelinesightseeing.com).

The CTA no longer accepts tokens; instead, riders purchase a "**Chicago card**" (available in all El stations) and add value to it. One ride costs $1.75; two more rides within two hours costs just 25¢. Passes good for one ($5), two ($9), three ($12), or five ($18) days of unlimited rides on both buses and the El are sold at O'Hare and Midway airports as well as Union Station, the visitor center, and other locations. In addition, **Metra Commuter Trains** run from various points downtown to and from the suburbs and outlying areas, including Oak Park and Hyde Park. One ride is $1.95.

Chicago's **taxis** cost $2.25 at the drop of the flag, and $1.80 per mile. They can be hailed anytime in the Loop and other central neighborhoods; otherwise call Yellow (☎312/829-4222) or Checker taxis (☎312/243-2537).

Finally, **bicycles** are available for rent at Millennium Park's multi-level bike park at 239 E Randolph St.

Accommodation

Most central **accommodation** is oriented toward business and convention trade rather than tourism, but there are still plenty of moderately priced rooms. A number of clean (if unexciting) prewar hotels in and around the Loop offer reasonable rates, especially on weekends, and motorists can pick from scores of motels along the interstates. Even top-class downtown hotels are, comparatively, not that expensive. Note, however, that a **room tax** of just over fifteen percent is added to all bills, while overnight **parking** can cost $20 at a modest downtown hotel, and as much as $40 at a fancy one.

If you're stuck, Hot Rooms is a reservation service offering hotel rooms at discount rates (☎773/468-7666 or 1-800/468-3500; @www.hotrooms.com). While they're not as prominent as elsewhere, **bed-and-breakfast** rooms are available from around $80 per night; the Chicago B&B Association maintains full listings (@www.chicago-bed-breakfast.com).

Allegro 179 W Randolph St ☎312/236-0123 or 1-866/672-6143, @www.allegrochicago.com. With a colorful, updated Art Deco design, this boutique hotel is sure to delight. Luxury amenities throughout. **❽**

Arlington House International Hostel 616 W Arlington Place ☎773/929-5380 or 1-800/467-8355, @www.arlingtonhouse.com. Easygoing hostel close to loads of good bars and Wrigley Field, with segregated dorms (members $24, others $3 extra) and private rooms with and without en-suite facilities. Open 24hr. **❶–❸**

Cass 640 N Wabash Ave ☎312/787-4030 or 1-800/799-4030, @www.casshotel.com. This basic budget hotel attracts loyal guests with the lowest rates in the Near North area; the rooms are very plain indeed, and the lobby is pretty dingy too. **❹**

Comfort Inn & Suites Downtown 15 E Ohio St ☎312/894-0900 or 1-888/775-4111, @www.chicagocomfortinn.com. This high-rise chain hotel is given considerable charm by its restored Art Deco lobby. The rooms are well equipped, and complemented by fitness and sauna facilities. Rates include continental breakfast. **❻**

Days Inn Lincoln Park North 644 W Diversey

Parkway at Clark ☎773/525-7010 or 1-888/576-3287, @www.lpndaysinn.com. This good, friendly motel is popular with visiting musicians and a convenient base for North Side nightlife. Free continental breakfast. **❺**

The Drake 140 E Walton Place ☎312/787-2200 or 1-800/553-7253, @www.thedrakehotel.com. Chicago's society hotel, just off the Magnificent Mile, has been modernized without sacrificing its sedate charms. Its well-appointed rooms feature high-speed Internet access and Jacuzzis. You can always just pop in for a drink at the elegant *Palm Court Lounge*. **❽–❾**

Gold Coast Guest House 113 W Elm St ☎312/337-0361, @www.bbchicago.com. Inconspicuous 1870s row house that's been beautifully converted to offer four high-class en-suite B&B rooms, with a friendly atmosphere and plenty of useful advice from the knowledgeable hostess. **❺**

Hampton Inn & Suites 33 W Illinois Ave ☎312/832-0330, @www.hamptoninnchicago.com. Clean high-rise chain hotel (built in 1988 but "Frank-Lloyd-Wright-inspired") in a good River North location, four blocks east of the Magnificent Mile. **❻**

HI-Chicago – The J. Ira & Nicki Harris Family Hostel 24 E Congress St ☎312/360-0300 or 1-800/909-4776 code 244, ⊛www.hichicago.org. Huge, very central hostel, where beds in the clean and spacious dorms cost $31 for members, $34 for non-members. Open 24hr, with Internet access and full kitchen and laundry facilities. ❶

Hotel 71 71 E Wacker Drive ☎312/346-7100, ⊛www.hotel71.com. Stylish boutique hotel in a magnificent setting by the Michigan Avenue Bridge; an extra $10 gets a river view. Big weekend discounts. ❼

House of Two Urns 1239 N Greenview Ave, Wicker Park ☎773/235-1408 or 1-877/896-8767, ⊛www.twourns.com. This rambling, artist-owned B&B, three blocks from the El and close to Wicker Park, is filled with contemporary art; the five guest rooms have a quirky flair, but some share facilities. Three- and four-room apartments are also available. Rooms ❹, apartments ❼–❾.

The Inn at Lincoln Park 601 W Diversey Parkway ☎773/348-2810 or 1-866/774-7275, ⊛www.innlp.com. Medium-sized motel, with free continental breakfast, in the accommodation-starved Lincoln Park district. ❻

Monaco 225 N Wabash Ave ☎312/960-8500 or 1-800/397-7661, ⊛www.monaco-chicago.com. A stylish and luxurious French Deco hotel with a 24hr fitness room. ❽

Red Roof Inn 162 E Ontario St ☎312/787-3580 or 1-800/733-7663, ⊛www.redroof-chicago-downtown.com. A few yards off the Magnificent Mile, this clean, no-frills option is in the center of the shopping action. ❻

Sofitel Chicago Water Tower 20 E Chestnut St ☎312/324-4000 or 1-800/763-4835, ⊛www.sofitel.com. Stunning 32-story glass prism, just off the Magnificent Mile, that offers elegant, ultra-chic accommodation plus gourmet French food in its *Café des Architectes*. ❽

Wheeler Mansion 2020 S Calumet Ave ☎312/945-2020, ⊛www.wheelermansion.com. A very grand mansion that's been converted into a plush, formal, but romantic B&B that's a hit with business travelers. In the Prairie Avenue Historic District, not far from S Michigan Ave and Soldier Field. ❽

The City

Chicago is laid out as an easy grid, numbered from **State Street** – "that great street" in Sinatra's song – at zero east and west, and **Madison Street** at zero north and south. **Lake Michigan**, which gives the city some of its most attractive open space (twenty miles of lakeshore lie within the city limits), makes a clear point of reference to the east of the urban grid. **Michigan Avenue** is the main thoroughfare, running between the lakeside museums and parklands, the densely packed skyscrapers of downtown, and the diverse low-rise neighborhoods that spread to the north, south, and west. It's here that you might experience the full force of "The Hawk," the strong wind that blows off the lake. The nickname "**Windy City**" was coined by a New York newspaper editor describing the boastful claims of the city's promoters when pitching for the World's Fair Columbian Exposition of 1893. The **Chicago River**, which cuts through the heart of downtown, separates the business district from the shopping and entertainment areas of the North Side, including the upscale **Near North** and **Gold Coast** neighborhoods; the artists' lofts and galleries of **River North**; the modestly charming area of **Old Town**; and the young professional enclaves of **Lincoln Park**, **Wrigleyville**, and **Lakeview**, as well as hip **Wicker Park**.

In contrast to the wealth and prosperity of the North Side, the deprived **South Side** is more like New York's South Bronx: a huge and, in places, desperately poor expanse with a deservedly dangerous reputation. Even so, a few of its corners are well worth visiting – particularly the Gothic campus of the **University of Chicago** and neighboring **Hyde Park**, site of the **Museum of Science and Industry**. Other than **Oak Park** to the west, which holds the childhood home of **Ernest Hemingway** and more than a dozen well-maintained examples of the influential architecture of **Frank Lloyd Wright**, suburban Chicago has little to offer.

Millennium Park

For first-time visitors to Chicago, for whom downtown's **Millennium Park** makes the obvious first port of call, it's hard to believe that until 2004 this space was all but

DOWNTOWN CHICAGO

N

A GOLD COAST

Oak Street Beach

GOETHE STREET

DIVISION STREET

N CLYBURN AVE

DIVISION STREET

E. SCOTT ST.

STATE PARKWAY

E. ELM ST.

E. CEDAR ST.

E. BELLEVUE PL.

E. OAK STREET

B John Hancock Center

E. WALTON ST.

Lake Michigan

E. CHESTNUT ST.

N FRANKLIN STREET

N WELLS STREET

N LASALLE STREET

N CLARK STREET

N DEARBORN STREET

E. PEARSON ST.

C Historic Water Tower

W. CHICAGO AVENUE

N STATE STREET

Museum of Contemporary Art

N MICHIGAN AVENUE

MAGNIFICENT MILE

RUSH ST.

E. SUPERIOR STREET

N FAIRBANKS CT.

Ohio Street Beach

41

W. SUPERIOR STREET

N LARRABEE STREET

W. HURON STREET

Terra Museum of Art

W. ERIE STREET

D

N WABASH

E

N ORLEANS STREET

W. ONTARIO STREET

W. OHIO STREET

W. GRAND AVENUE

Navy Pier

W. ILLINOIS STREET

Wrigley Building

Tribune Tower

F

W. HUBBARD STREET

W. KINZIE STREET

Merchandise Mart

IBM Building

E. NORTH WATER ST.

Chicago River

MILWAUKEE AVENUE

Chicago River

WEST WACKER DRIVE

EAST WACKER DRIVE

G Illinois Center

GEORGE HALES DRIVE

FIELD BOULEVARD

LAKE STREET

SOUTH JEFFERSON STREET

S. CLINTON STREET

SOUTH WACKER DRIVE

N FRANKLIN STREET

H

Chicago Cultural Center

E. RANDOLPH STREET

I Marshall Field

i ⊙ Cloud Gate

E. WASHINGTON STREET

⊤ Crown Fountain

Chicago Mercantile Exchange

E. MADISON STREET

Carson Pirie Scott

Millennium Park

E. MONROE STREET

THE LOOP

Art Institute

Grant Park

Sears Tower

ADAMS STREET

SOUTH WACKER DRIVE

E. JACKSON BOULEVARD

NORTH MICHIGAN AVENUE

Union Station (Amtrak)

Board of Trade

Symphony Center

VAN BUREN STREET

J

Auditorium Theater

Lake Michigan

290

CONGRESS PARKWAY

Buckingham Fountain

41

W. HARRISON STREET

E. BALBO DRIVE

SOUTH LAKE SHORE DRIVE

Greyhound Terminal

S WELLS STREET

S CLARK STREET

S FEDERAL STREET

S DEARBORN STREET

S PLYMOUTH COURT

STATE STREET

S WABASH AVENUE

Chicago River

W. POLK STREET

S CANAL STREET

E. 8TH ST.

S COLUMBUS DRIVE

W. TAYLOR ST.

E. 9TH ST.

W. TAYLOR ST.

E. 11TH ST.

S MICHIGAN AVENUE

John G. Shedd Aquarium

E. ROOSEVELT ROAD

W. ROOSEVELT ROAD

Field Museum of Natural History

0 ——— 800 yds

—— Elevated rail

• Stations

MCFETRIDGE

K ● Soldier Field

Adler Planetarium

ACCOMMODATION

Allegro	**I**	Gold Coast Guest House	**A**	Hotel 71	**G**	Sofitel Chicago Water Tower **C**
Cass	**D**	Hampton Inn & Suites	**F**	Monaco	**H**	Wheeler Mansion **K**
The Drake	**B**	HI-Chicago	**J**	Red Roof Inn	**E**	

△ Chicago skyline

derelict. Now, however, thanks to a highly ambitious (and hugely expensive, to the tune of almost $500 million) renovation project that long overran its original 2000 completion date, it's a showcase for all that's best in the city. Its twin artistic center-pieces are equally compelling. First is a stunning, seamless, stainless-steel sculpture officially titled **Cloud Gate** but universally known as "the bean," by the Indian-born, British-based artist Anish Kapoor. Inspired by liquid mercury, it invites viewers to walk around, beside, and even underneath it to enjoy spectacular and endlessly intriguing reflections of both the city and the sky above it. Nearby, **Crown Fountain** consists of two glass-brick towers set to either side of a black granite plaza; giant video images of the faces of ordinary Chicagoans play across them both, and water spurts from them in summer at unexpected intervals to form a lake that's usually filled with playing children. Further back, the **Jay Pritzker Pavilion** is an amazing open-air auditorium designed by Frank Gehry, who used mighty swirls and flourishes of steel to improve its acoustics. If you're heading for the lakefront, follow Gehry's sinu-ous, intriguing, wood-and-steel BP Pedestrian Bridge across Columbus Drive.

Downtown Chicago: The Loop
Downtown Chicago puts on what is perhaps the finest display of **modern archi-tecture** in the world, from the prototype skyscrapers of the 1890s to Mies van der Rohe's "less is more" modernist masterpieces, and the second tallest building in the world, the quarter-mile-high **Sears Tower**. Just about all these edifices are workplaces of one kind or another; the whole place is bustling during the day and virtually empty at night.

The compact heart of Chicago is known as **the Loop**, because it's circled by the elevated tracks of the CTA "El" trains. The best way to get your bearings down-town is on one of the many excellent **city tours** detailed on p.353; whether you take a river cruise, ride the "El", or join a walking tour, you'll get a sense of the major architectural landmarks and their assorted histories.

Once you're ready to explore by yourself, start by calling in at the **Chicago Cultural Center** at 77 E Randolph St, which not only holds the city's main visitor center, as described on p.352, but is worth admiring in its own right. Built in 1897 as the original Chicago Public Library, it's a splendid Beaux-Arts palace filled with opulent detail, including the 38ft Tiffany Dome on the fourth floor; it also stages all manner of temporary exhibitions.

The Loop holds some of Chicago's grandest century-old **department stores**. The best looking, the 1899 **Carson Pirie Scott** store, at 1 S State St (Mon–Sat 9.45am–8pm, Sun 11am–6pm, ⓦwww.carsons.com), boasts a magnificent iron-work facade that blends botanic and geometric forms in an intuitive version of Art Moderne. Its architect, Louis Sullivan, was also responsible for the gorgeous spherical bronze clocks suspended from the corners of the **Marshall Field's** department store (Mon–Thurs 9am–8pm, Fri & Sat 9am–9pm, Sun 11am–6pm), two blocks north at State and Washington. The comparatively bland exterior of Marshall Field's oldest and grandest branch masks one of the world's great stores, with seven floors of merchandise.

Half the world's wheat and corn (and pork-belly futures) are bought and sold amid the cacophonic roar of the **Chicago Board of Trade**, housed in a gorgeous Art Deco tower, appropriately topped by a 30ft stainless steel statue of Ceres, the Roman goddess of grain. It's no longer possible to watch the action inside, but if you're interested in learning more about the similarly energetic ballet that goes on within the **Chicago Mercantile Exchange**, three blocks away at 30 S Wacker Drive, a high-tech visitor center in the lobby explains all (Mon–Fri 8am–4.30pm; free). Precious metals, currencies, and commodities are bought and sold here to the tune of some $50 billion a day.

Half a block from the Board of Trade, **The Rookery**, 209 S LaSalle St, built in 1886 by Burnham and Root, is one of the city's most celebrated and photographed edifices. Its forbidding Moorish Gothic exterior gives way to a wonderfully airy lobby, decked out with cool Italian marble and gold leaf during a major 1905 remodeling by Frank Lloyd Wright; the spiral cantilever staircase rising from the second floor must be seen to be appreciated. A couple of doors down toward the Board of Trade, check out the **Continental Illinois Bank** lobby, with its 28 Ionic marble columns and intricate murals.

Looking up at the proud facade of the **Reliance Building**, 32 N State St, you'd be forgiven for thinking it dates from the Art Deco Thirties, but it was in fact completed way back in 1895 by Daniel Burnham, who did much to shape the face of Chicago. His **Fisher Building**, with its tongue-in-cheek, aquatic-inspired ornamental terracotta, stands at 343 S Dearborn St. A block farther south, the 1890 **Manhattan Building** was the world's first tall all-steel-frame building, and is generally acknowledged as the progenitor of the modern curtain-walled skyscraper. Now converted into luxury apartments, it preserves some noteworthy exterior ornament.

A resurrected stretch of the riverfront walk follows the west bank of the river, with open-air cafés and gardens. Farther south, and back on the Loop side at South Wacker Drive and Adams Street, is the 1468ft **Sears Tower**, which was the tallest building in the world until 1997, when Malaysia's Petronas Towers nudged it from the top by the length of an antenna; both have since been eclipsed by further construction projects in southeast Asia. Various companies occupy the tower (Sears has moved to the suburbs), and it's so huge that it has more than one hundred elevators. Two ascend, in little more than a minute, from the ground-level shopping mall to the 103rd-floor **Skydeck Observatory** (daily: May–Sept 10am–10pm, Oct–April 10am–8pm; $12), for breathtaking views that on a clear day take in four states – Illinois, Michigan, Wisconsin, and Indiana. Look east for the distinctive triangular **Metropolitan Detention Center**, where prisoners exercise on the grassy roof beneath wire netting to ensure they don't get whisked away by helicopter.

The Chicago River

The Loop is usually said to end at the "El" tracks, but the blocks beyond this core, to either side of the Chicago River, hold plenty of interest. Broad, double-decked **Wacker Drive**, parallel to the water, was designed as a sophisticated promenade, lined by benches and obelisk-shaped lanterns, by Daniel Burnham in 1909. Though never completed, and despite the almost constant intrusion of construction works, it makes for a nice extended walk. The direction of the river itself was reversed a century ago, in an engineering project more extensive than the digging of the Panama Canal. As a result, rather than letting its sewage and industrial waste flow east into Lake Michigan, Chicago now sends it all south into the Corn Belt.

A **boat tour** from beneath the Michigan Avenue Bridge gives magnificent views of downtown (see p.353). However, half an hour's walk, especially at lunchtime when the office workers are out in force, will do the trick nearly as well. Burnham's promenade runs along both sides of the river, crossing back and forth over the twenty-odd drawbridges that open and close to let barges and the occasional sailboat pass. The **State Street Bridge** makes a superb vantage point. On the south bank, at 35 E Wacker Drive, the elegant Beaux Arts **Jewelers Building** was built in 1926 and is capped on the seventeenth floor by a domed rotunda that once housed Al Capone's favorite speakeasy. Across the river stands what's commonly considered Ludwig Mies van der Rohe's masterpiece – the 1971 **IBM Building**, 330 N Wabash Ave. The gentle play of light and shadow across the detailed bronze and smoked-glass facade has been the model for countless other less considered copies worldwide. The building is so huge that it acts as a funnel for winter winds off Lake Michigan, and heavy ropes sometimes must be tied across the broad plaza at its base to protect people from getting blown away.

Perhaps Chicago's most successful and acclaimed building of recent years stands four blocks west at **333 W Wacker Drive**. Towering over a broad bend in the river, and bowed to follow its curve, the green glass facade reflects the almost fluorescent green of the river (now upgraded from "toxic" to merely "polluted"). On the lower floors, a more classically detailed stone base actively addresses its stalwart elder neighbors.

The Art Institute of Chicago

The **Art Institute of Chicago** ranks as one of the greatest art galleries in the world, thanks to a magnificent collection that includes, and extends way beyond, Impressionist and Post-Impressionist paintings, Asian art, photography, and architectural drawings (Mon–Wed & Fri 10.30am–4.30pm, Tues 10.30am–8pm, Sat & Sun 10am–5pm; suggested donation $12, free Tues; ℡312/443-3600, Ⓦwww.artic.edu). While the Neoclassical facade of the main entrance, on the lake side of South Michigan Avenue, does its best to look dignified, the numerous added-on wings can make it hard to find your way around inside.

Most visitors head straight upstairs to the Impressionist works, which include a wall full of Monet's *Haystacks* captured in various lights, next to Seurat's immediately familiar pointillist *Sunday Afternoon on La Grande Jatte*. A handful of Post-Impressionist masterpieces by Van Gogh, Gauguin, and Matisse are arrayed nearby. Beyond that, the rooms seem to stretch away forever; it takes at least half a day to get even a basic sense of what's here and where it is. Specific highlights include the pitchfork-holding farmer of Grant Woods' oft-parodied *American Gothic*, which he painted as a student at the Art Institute school, and sold to the museum for $300 in 1930; El Greco's 1577 *Assumption of the Virgin*; Edward Hopper's lonely *Nighthawks*; Pablo Picasso's melancholy *Old Guitarist*, one of the definitive masterpieces of his Blue Period; a tortured, tuxedoed self-portrait that was Max Beckmann's last Berlin painting before fleeing the Nazis; canvases by Jackson Pollock and Mark

Rothko; and several works by Georgia O'Keeffe, such as a 1926 depiction of New York's *Shelton Hotel*, where she was living.

Be sure to look for the beautiful pre-Columbian ceramics from what's now the Southwest USA; the ornate carved stone used for the coronation of the Aztec ruler Motecuhzoma II on July 15, 1503; and the delightful seventh-century Indonesian-sculptured stone monkeys in the Southeast Asia collections, displayed around the McKinlock Court Garden, which in summer is employed as an **open-air café**. Also here, in the east end of the complex, is the immaculately reconstructed Art Moderne trading room of the Chicago Stock Exchange, designed by Louis Sullivan in 1893 and moved here in the 1970s. And leave time too to browse in the museum's excellent store.

Grant Park

East of the Art Institute toward Lake Michigan, **Grant Park** is an urban oasis that's become rather overshadowed by the high-profile Millennium Park (see p.355) immediately northwest. In any case, wide strips of high-speed road and railroad slice through it, so casual rambling can be frustrating.

The major attractions are gathered in its landscaped southern half, known as **Museum Campus**. The extensive and engaging **Field Museum of Natural History**, 1200 S Lake Shore Drive, at Roosevelt Road (June daily 8am–5pm; Sept–May daily 9am–5pm; July & Aug Mon–Thurs 8am–5pm, Fri–Sun 7.30am–5pm; last admission always 4pm; $12, plus extra for temporary exhibitions; Ⓦ www.fieldmuseum.org), is ten minutes' walk south of the Art Institute, in a huge, marble-clad, Daniel Burnham–designed Greek temple. It's quite an erratic sort of institution, in which the exhibits vary enormously in their age and sophistication; as a rule, its temporary exhibitions tend to be the most compelling, but cost a hefty additional premium on the already high entrance fee. "Natural history" is taken to include anything non-white and non-European, so as well as a hall of stupendous dinosaurs, including "Sue," the most complete *T-rex* fossil ever found, the permanent collection ranges from Egyptian tombs – the entire burial chamber of the son of a Fifth Dynasty pharaoh was brought here in 1908 – to the man-eating lions of Tsavo, and some fascinating displays on the islands of the Pacific. Best of all for young kids is the "Underground Adventure," a simulated environment that "shrinks" visitors to a hundredth of their normal size and propels them into a world of giant animatronic spiders and crayfish.

Just across busy Lake Shore Drive, on the shores of Lake Michigan, the **Shedd Aquarium** (first 3 weeks of June daily 9am–6pm; late June to Aug Mon–Wed & Fri 9am–6pm, Thurs 9am–10pm; Sept–May Mon–Fri 9am–5pm, Sat & Sun 9am–6pm; $8 aquarium only, $18 wild reef and aquarium, $18 Oceanarium and aquarium, $23 for all exhibits; Ⓣ 312/939-2438, Ⓦ www.sheddaquarium.org) proclaims itself the largest indoor aquarium in the world. The 1920s structure is rather old-fashioned, but the lighthearted and often tongue-in-cheek displays – some use *Far Side* cartoons – are informative and entertaining. The central exhibit, a 90,000-gallon recreation of a coral reef, complete with sharks (who get fed at 11am and 2pm daily), turtles, and thousands of tropical fish, is surrounded by more than a hundred lesser tanks. Highlights include the new wild reef exhibit, which features floor-to-ceiling living reefs, tropical fish, sharks, and rays. The **Oceanarium** provides an enormous contrast, with its modern lake-view home for marine mammals such as Pacific dolphins and beluga whales. Designed to replicate a rocky Alaskan coastline, it's a carefully disguised amphitheater for demonstrations of the animals' "natural behavior," such as jumping out of the water and fetching plastic rings. Performances are four times daily; at other times, watch from underwater galleries as the animals cruise around the tank, and listen to the clicks, beeps, and whistles they use to communicate with each other. Get to the Shedd early to beat the long lines and school groups.

At the tip of the Museum Campus peninsula, the **Adler Planetarium** (late May to early Sept daily 9.30am–6pm, rest of year daily 9.30am–4.30pm, first Fri of month always 9.30am–10pm; $16–20, determined by exhibits entered, free Mon & Tues, Sept–Feb only; ⊤312/922-STAR, ⓦ www.adlerplanetarium.org) has an interactive 360-degree movie theater and offers one of the best views of the city skyline.

The Near North Side

While Chicago's **Near North Side** has few big-name attractions, it's great for simply wandering around, chancing upon odd **shops**, neighborhood bars, and historic sites in a generally low-rise tangle containing some of the city's most characteristic corners.

When the Michigan Avenue Bridge was built over the Chicago River in 1920, the warehouse district along its north bank quickly changed into one of the city's most upmarket quarters, now known as the **Magnificent Mile**, famed for its fashionable shops and department stores. Throughout the Roaring Twenties one glitzy tower after another was thrown up along Michigan Avenue. At the north end, the opulent **Drake Hotel** rose off Lincoln Park. To the south, the white terracotta, wedding-cake colossus of the **Wrigley Building** was put up just over the river at no. 400; it's spectacularly lit up at night. Built by the Chicago-based chewing-gum magnate, it was eclipsed almost immediately by the "Mag Mile's" most famous structure, the **Tribune Tower**. Still housing the editorial offices of Chicago's morning newspaper, as well as, on the ground floor, the studios of its main AM radio station, WGN (you can peer in from the street and watch the DJs in action), the tower was completed in 1925. Its flying buttresses and Gothic detailing turn their back on the then-prevalent Moderne style. Look closely at its lower floors and you'll see embedded chunks of historic buildings – like the Parthenon and the Great Pyramid – pilfered from around the world by *Tribune* staffers.

While the Tribune Tower anchors its southern end, the Mag Mile's northern reaches are dominated by the cross-braced steel **John Hancock Center** at 875 N Michigan Ave. Though it's about 325 feet shorter than the Sears Tower, the 360-degree panorama on a clear day from its 94th-floor **Skydeck Observatory** (daily 9am–11pm; $9.95) is unforgettable. If you prefer quality over quantity, the Hancock Observatory is a better, less trafficked experience than the Sears.

Back at ground level, you're right at the heart of Chicago's prime **shopping district**. Stores like Neiman-Marcus and Tiffany & Co front onto Michigan Avenue, but most of the shops are enclosed within multistory complexes, or "vertical shopping malls." The oldest of these – and still the best – is **Water Tower Place**, 835 N Michigan Ave, with more than a hundred stores on seven floors, plus a bustling food court. The **900 N Michigan Avenue** mall offers a less-cramped space and more upscale shops, anchored by Bloomingdale's.

Across from Water Tower Place, at the center of this consumer paradise, stands the **Historic Water Tower** – a whimsically Gothic stone castle, topped by a 100ft tower, that was built in 1869 and is one of the very few structures to have survived the 1871 fire. The **Museum of Contemporary Art**, one block east at 220 E Chicago Ave (Tues 10am–8pm, Wed–Sun 10am–5pm; $10; ⓦ www.mcachicago.org), is a spare space that holds photography, video, and installation works, as well as a permanent collection featuring pieces by Calder, Nauman, Warhol, and others. At the rear is a lake-view patio where a Wolfgang Puck café serves good coffee and bistro food; additionally, the museum store is well worth a browse. Away from the

Magnificent Mile, the area along the river between Michigan Avenue and the lake has seen dramatic redevelopment since **Navy Pier**, at East Illinois Street (Ⓦwww. navypier.com), underwent a major facelift in 1995. The pier is now officially the city's premier tourist destination, attracting more than eight million visitors annually to its shops, chain restaurants, IMAX theater, and fifteen-story Ferris wheel. Three floors are taken up by the imaginative interactive exhibits of the **Chicago Children's Museum** (Sun–Wed & Fri 10am–5pm, Thurs & Sat 10am–8pm; also Fri 5–8pm mid-June to Aug); $8, no reduction for children; free Thurs 5–8pm; Ⓣ312/527-1000, Ⓦwww.chichildrensmuseum.org). The pier also serves as a venue for concerts and weekend festivals in summer, and an embarkation point for several boat tours, including those run by Shoreline Sightseeing (see p.353).

The Gold Coast and Old Town

As its name suggests, the **Gold Coast**, stretching north from the Magnificent Mile along the lakeshore, is one of Chicago's wealthiest and most desirable neighborhoods. This residential district is primarily notable for Chicago's most central (and style-conscious) beach. The broad strand of **Oak Street Beach** is accessible via a walkway under Lake Shore Drive, across from the *Drake Hotel*. After dark, the summertime crowds are apt to be found in the myriad bars of Rush and Division streets. The more northerly reaches of the Gold Coast, approaching Lincoln Park, are also its most exclusive, especially in the stretch of Astor Street running south from the park. **Old Town**, west of LaSalle Street to either side of North Avenue, has a much more lived-in look. Originally a German immigrant community based around the 1873 **St Michael's Church**, it now boasts a broad ethnic and cultural mix. **Wells Street**, the main drag, emerged in the late 1960s as a mini-Haight-Ashbury. Although almost all signs of that era have vanished, at least one survivor, the *Second City* comedy club (see p.370), is still going strong. The rest of the neighborhood is packed with bars, galleries, and barbecue joints, and makes for a diverting afternoon's wander. Especially noteworthy is the House of Glunz, 1206 N Wells St, a wine shop dating to 1888.

Lincoln Park and Wrigleyville

In summer, Chicago's largest greenspace, **Lincoln Park**, gives a much-needed respite from the gridded pavements of the rest of the city. Unlike Grant Park to the south, Lincoln Park is packed with leafy nooks and crannies, monuments and sculptures, and has a couple of friendly, family-oriented **beaches**, at the eastern ends of North and Fullerton avenues. Near the small **zoo** at the heart of the park (April–Oct Sun–Fri 9am–6pm, Sat 9am–7pm; Nov–March daily 9am–5pm; free), renowned for its menagerie of African apes, you can rent paddleboats or bikes. If the weather's bad, head for sauna-level conditions at the **conservatory**, 2400 N Stockton Drive (daily 9am–5pm; free), or bone up on Chicago's captivating past at the **Chicago Historical Society Museum**, at the south end of the park at 1601 N Clark St (Mon–Sat 9.30am–4.30pm, Sun noon–5pm; $5, free on Mon; Ⓣ312/642-4600, Ⓦwww.chicagohistory.org), where the comprehensive displays on regional and national history were fully upgraded in 2006.

The Lincoln Park neighborhood, inland from the lake, centers on **Lincoln Avenue** and **Clark Street**, which run diagonally from near the Historical Society Museum; **Halsted Street**, with its blues bars and nightclubs, runs north–south through the neighborhood's heart. Any of these main roads merits an extended stroll, with forays into the many book and record stores. Look for the **Biograph Theatre** movie house, 2433 N Lincoln Ave, where **John Dillinger** was ambushed and killed by the FBI in 1934, thanks to a tip from his companion, the legendary Lady in Red.

Chicago spreads north from Lincoln Park for block after low-rise block of houses and shops, many of which date from the late 1800s, when thousands of German immigrants settled in what was then the separate enclave of Lakeview. This area is now dubbed **Wrigleyville** in honor of **Wrigley Field**, 1060 W Addison St at N Clark Street, the ivy-covered 1920s stadium of baseball's much-loved Cubs, and one of the best places to get a real feel for the game – the club is so traditional that it fought the installation of floodlights (for night games) until 1988. There are few more pleasant and relaxing ways to spend an afternoon than drinking beer, eating hot dogs, and watching a ballgame in the sunshine, among the Cubs' faithful; see p.370 for ticket information. **Field tours** run from May through September on select days every half-hour from 10am to 4pm, and cost $20.

Wicker Park and Bucktown

Three miles northwest of the Loop, **Wicker Park/Bucktown** is Chicago's newest neighborhood. Once a Polish and German community referred to as the "Polish Gold Coast," it is now a trendy, upscale enclave of shopping, clubbing, and Victorian mansions. Stylish health-food cafés, galleries, tattoo parlors, smoky clubs, boutiques, and alternative bookstores follow Damen Street north to Bucktown. The boundary between the two areas is vague if nonexistent, and the neighborhoods diverse enough to satisfy any taste.

The West Side and Oak Park

West of the Chicago River, Chicago's **West Side** was where the **Great Fire of 1871** started – supposedly when Mrs O'Leary's cow kicked over a lantern. The flames spread quickly east to engulf the entire central city, which was built of wood and fed the fire for three full days. Appropriately enough, the O'Leary cottage is now the site of the Chicago Fire Department training academy. The West Side also saw 1886's **Haymarket Riots**, when striking workers assembled at the old city market at Desplaines and Randolph streets; after a peaceful demonstration, as police began to break up the crowd, a bomb exploded, killing an officer. Six more policemen and four workers died in the resulting panic. Four labor leaders were later found guilty of murder and hanged, although none had been present at the event. Though the West Side has little to see compared with the rest of the city, it does provide a good look at its day-to-day realities, having served as the port of entry for Chicago's myriad ethnic groups, now congregated in its distinct neighborhoods.

Ten miles west of the Loop, the affluent and attractive c.1900 suburb of **Oak Park** is easily accessible by public transportation: take the Green Line west to the Harlem Avenue stop. The area's **visitor center**, just over two blocks east of the station at 158 N Forest Ave (daily 10am–3.30pm; ☎708/848-1500, ⓦ www.visitoakpark .com), provides an excellent architectural **walking tour map**.

Ernest Hemingway was born and raised in Oak Park, editing his high school newspaper and living a normal middle-class life. His birthplace at 339 N Oak Park Ave, where he lived until the age of six, is now preserved as a shrine to the author, and is run in conjunction with a museum of his life two blocks south at 200 N Oak Park Ave (Thurs, Fri & Sun 1–5pm, Sat 10am–5pm; $7; ☎708/848-2222, ⓦ www.ehfop.org).

In 1889, a decade before Hemingway's birth, an ambitious young architect named **Frank Lloyd Wright** arrived in Oak Park, which he used for the next twenty years as a testing ground for his innovative design theories. Most of the 25 buildings he put up here are in keeping with conventional Victorian design, and few are open to the public; fortunately, however, his most interesting and groundbreaking edifices are maintained as monuments. His ideal of an "organic architecture," in which all aspects of the design derive from a single unifying concept – quite at odds with the fussy "gingerbread" style popular at the time – is exemplified by the **Unity Temple** at 875 Lake St (March–Nov Mon–Fri 10.30am–4.30pm, Sat & Sun 1–4pm; Dec–Feb daily 1–4pm, $7; ☎708/383-8873, ⓦwww.unitytemple-utrf.org). Though the simplicity of this angular, reinforced-concrete structure was largely dictated by economics, its unembellished surfaces contribute to a masterful manipulation of space, especially in the skylit interior, where the subtle interplay of overlapping planes creates a dynamic spatial flow.

Wright built his small, brown-shingled **home and studio** nearby at 951 Chicago Ave at Forest, aged 22 in 1889, and remodeled it repeatedly for the next twenty years. It shows all his hallmarks: large fireplaces to symbolize the heart of the home and family; free-flowing, open-plan rooms; and the visual linking of interior and exterior spaces. The furniture of the kitchen and dining rooms is Wright's own design; he added a two-story studio in 1898, with a mezzanine drafting area suspended by chains from the roof beams. You can see the house itself on a 45min guided tour (Mon–Fri 11am, 1pm & 3pm, Sat & Sun every 20min 11am–3.30pm; $12; ☎708/848-1976, ⓦwww.wrightplus.org). Lengthier, self-guided audio walking tours ($12) take in the dozen other Wright-designed houses within a two-block radius.

The South Side

The **South Side** of Chicago has always had a raw deal, cursed with the presence of bad-neighbor heavy industries like the sprawling **Chicago Stockyards**, the slaughterhouses and meatpackers that Upton Sinclair exposed in his 1906 novel *The Jungle*, and whose stink covered most of the South Side until the 1950s. Even today, the overriding impression is one of misery and downtrodden poverty, with block after block of deprived and dangerous neighborhoods. That said, there are exceptions: not just the **Prairie Avenue** and **Hyde Park** districts described below, but also the buzzing **Chinatown** around Wentworth Avenue and 22nd Street; the artsy, predominantly Mexican **Pilsen** district, a few blocks north and west; and the largely Irish, blue-collar **Bridgeport**, formerly known by the evocative name "Hardscrabble," around Halsted and 37th – Mayor Daley's old fiefdom, the home of baseball's White Sox (see p.370).

Two blocks east of Michigan Avenue, a mile from the Loop and only a quarter of a mile from the lake, **Prairie Avenue** started life as an exclusive suburb. It's best reached by taxi, bus, or train; it's only ten minutes' walk south of Grant Park, but the route is confusing and the streets are just not safe. As the one part of Chicago to remain unscathed in the Great Fire of 1871, this area had a brief moment of glory as the city's finest address. However, by 1900 the railroads had cut it off from Lake Michigan, and the wealthy fled back to their traditional North Side haunts. One of the few structures to have survived is the Romanesque 1887 **Glessner House**, Chicago's only surviving H.H. Richardson–designed house, standing sentry at Prairie Avenue and 18th. Behind the forbidding stone facade, the house opens onto a garden court, its interior filled with Arts and Crafts furniture, and swathed in William Morris fabrics and wall coverings. The Chicago Architecture Foundation gives guided tours (Wed–Sun 1pm, 2pm & 3pm; $10; ☎312/326-1480, ⓦwww.glessnerhouse.org).

Six miles south, **Hyde Park**, the most attractive and sophisticated South Side neighborhood, is also one of Chicago's more racially integrated areas. The **University of Chicago**, endowed by Rockefeller in 1892, has encouraged a college-town atmosphere, with bookshops and numerous cafés surrounding its compact campus, especially along East 57th Street. On the campus itself, two buildings are well worth searching out: the massive Gothic pile of the **Rockefeller Memorial**

Chapel, 59th Street and Woodlawn Avenue (daily 9am–4pm; free), and the Prairie-style, Frank Lloyd Wright–designed **Robie House**, two blocks north at 5757 S Woodlawn Ave (tours Mon–Fri 11am, 1pm & 3pm, Sat & Sun every 15min 11am–3.30pm; $12; Ⓦwww.wrightplus.org).

Washington Park wraps around the south side of the campus to join the long green strip of the **Midway** – one of the few reminders that Chicago was the site of the **World's Fair Columbian Exposition**. Attracting some thirty million spectators in the summer of 1893 (at the time, 45 percent of the US population), the Midway was then filled with full-sized model villages from around the globe, including an Irish market town and a mock-up of Cairo, complete with belly dancers. These days it's used mainly by joggers and students tossing Frisbees.

A short stroll east, in Jackson Park, the cavernous **Museum of Science and Industry**, 57th Street at Lake Shore Drive (summer & school hols Mon–Sat 9.30am–5.30pm, Sun 11am–5.30pm; rest of year Mon–Sat 9.30am–4pm, Sun 11am–4pm; $11; Ⓣ773/684-1414, Ⓦwww.msichicago.org), was Chicago's single most popular tourist destination (and ranked second in the US) until it started charging admission in 1991. Besides interactive computer displays, the best of which explores the inner workings of the brain and heart, exhibits include a captured German U-boat, a trip down a replica coal mine, the Apollo 8 command module, and a simulated space-shuttle journey. It's fun for kids, but adults may not feel like staying very long. The complex also hosts a giant OMNIMAX movie dome; admission is $6 extra.

East of the museum, **Promontory Point** juts into Lake Michigan, giving great views of the Chicago skyline, including a close-up look at Mies van der Rohe's first highrise, the Promontory Apartments at 5530 S Lake Shore Drive.

Eating

Chicago's cosmopolitan make-up is reflected in its plethora of ethnic restaurants. **Italian** food, ranging from hearty **deep-dish pizza** (developed in 1953 at *Pizzeria Uno*; see p.367) to delicately crafted creations presented at stylish trattorias, continues to dominate a very dynamic scene. In recent years there's been a surge of popularity for **New American** cuisine. **Thai** restaurants still thrive, as do ones with a broad **Mediterranean** slant, many of which serve *tapas*; and there are still plenty of opportunities to sample more longstanding Chicago cuisines – Eastern European, German, Mexican, Chinese, Indian, even Burmese and Ethiopian. Of course, a number of establishments serve good old-fashioned **barbecue ribs**, a legacy of Chicago's days as the nation's meatpacker. And no visit is complete without sampling a messy Italian beef sandwich, or a Chicago-style hot dog, laden with tomatoes, onions, hot peppers, and a pickle.

The largest concentration of restaurants is found north and west of the **Loop**. To the west, **Greektown**, around Halsted Street at Jackson Boulevard, and **Little Italy**, on and around Taylor Street, are worth a look, while the **Near North** and **River North** areas harbor a good number of upscale places.

Downtown

The Berghoff 17 W Adams St at State Ⓣ312/427-3170. This beautifully preserved landmark, dating from 1893, offers abundant German specialties such as *wiener schnitzel*, plus fish dishes and corned beef and cabbage. A bargain.

Billy Goat Tavern 430 N Michigan Ave at Kinzie Ⓣ312/222-1525. This legendary journalists' haunt opens early and closes late, serving the "cheezborgers" made famous by John Belushi's comedy skit. Very reasonable.

Everest One Financial Place, 440 S LaSalle St at Congress Ⓣ312/663-8920. Take in the stunning vista from the 40th floor and tuck into chef Jean Joho's French/Alsatian cuisine, in dishes like wild mushroom consommé and roasted Maine lobster. Very expensive. Closed Sun & Mon.

Italian Village 71 W Monroe St at Clark Ⓣ312/332-7005. Three Italian establishments flourish under one roof. The *Village* has traditional

Italian-American food and a world-class wine cellar; the basement *Cantina Enoteca* serves chicken Vesuvio, a Chicago creation, among its reasonably priced dishes; and the expensive *Vivere* has an adventurous menu, a mesmerizing wine list, and a large pre-theater crowd (meaning it's best to arrive after 8pm). Closed Sun.

Lou Mitchell's 565 W Jackson Ave at Clinton ☎312/939-3111. Near Union Station, *Lou's* has been around since 1923, serving terrific omelets, waffles, and hash browns all day long. Try the pecan-laden cookies.

Marché 833 W Randolph St at Halsted ☎312/226-8399. Creative French cuisine served in an eclectic atmosphere in the Market District. Entrees $20–38.

Prairie *Hyatt*, 500 S Dearborn St, ☎312/663-1143. Modeled on a Frank Lloyd Wright interior, this place uses only fresh Midwestern ingredients in dishes such as sirloin of buffalo and brandied loaf of duck. Open daily for all meals.

Russian Tea Time 77 E Adams St at Michigan ☎312/360-0000. This Midwestern nod to New York's *Russian Tea Room* offers a (pricey) sampling of authentic fare from the former Soviet empire.

Trattoria No. 10 10 N Dearborn St ☎312/984-1718. This charming surprise, in a series of underground rooms, serves up delicious ravioli, grilled sea scallops, and risotto. Closed Sun.

The West Side: Greektown and Little Italy

Francesca's on Taylor 1400 W Taylor St ☎312/829-2828. Assorted Francesca-family restaurants dot Chicago. This relatively subdued example offers some of the best Italian food in the city, at moderate prices. Don't be surprised to find a crowd here all day.

Parthenon 314 S Halsted St at Jackson ☎312/726-2407. One of the oldest places in Greektown, but still deservedly popular: *saganaki* (fried cheese doused with Metaxa brandy and ignited) was invented here.

Pegasus 130 S Halsted St at Adams ☎312/226-3377. Lively Greek option, where true hospitality and evocative wall murals add to the appeal. Stuffed squid and *pastitsio* (macaroni, meat, and cheese casserole) are recommended. During the summer the rooftop garden has a superb view of the Loop skyline.

Santorini 800 W Adams St at Halsted ☎312/829-8820. The decor recreates a Greek island village, and the food is beguiling, too; grilled octopus and lamb *exohiko* (wrapped in filo pastry and fried) are highlights.

South Loop and the South Side

Dixie Kitchen 5225 S Harper, Harper Court ☎773/363-4943. Great soul food here includes pulled-pork sandwiches, breaded oysters with chili sauce, and desserts like peach cobbler and pecan pie.

Emperor's Choice 2238 S Wentworth Ave at 23rd ☎312/225-8800. This attractive storefront serves delicious egg rolls and well-priced seafood dishes. Try the steamed clams, poached shrimp, or lobster.

Gioco 1312 S Wabash Ave at 13th ☎312/939-3870. Immensely popular (and somewhat expensive) place, whose classic, meticulously prepared Italian cuisine is drawing a hip crowd to the rapidly gentrifying South Loop district.

Mellow Yellow 1508 E 53rd St ☎773/667-2000. Casual, popular South-Side joint with a real 1970s feel and menu, albeit with a soul-food emphasis – catfish, steaks, seafood, and rotisserie chicken, plus crêpes and quiche.

Opera 1301 S Wabash Ave at 13th ☎312/461-0161. High-class, high-concept, high-priced but very funky new-Chinese restaurant, housed in an opulent former film studio in the South Loop that holds a few private dining booths.

Near North Side and River North

Bistrot Zinc 1131 N State St at Elm ☎312/337-1131. Very friendly, intimate neighborhood bistro, offering a quintessential French menu prepared and served just the way it should be, at good prices.

Café Iberico 739 N LaSalle Blvd at Chicago ☎312/573-1510. Authentic and reasonably priced *tapas* bar, where you can share plates of eggplant stuffed with goat's cheese or grilled octopus on potatoes.

Le Colonial 937 N Rush St at Walton ☎312/255-0088. This atmospheric evocation of some colonial outpost in Indochina, with its palm trees and rattan furniture, serves zestful French-influenced Vietnamese food at reasonable prices, and has outdoor seating in summer.

Frontera Grill & Topolobampo 445 N Clark St at Illinois ☎312/661-1434. Wildly imaginative Mexican food: *Frontera Grill* is crowded and boisterous; *Topolobampo* is more refined and pricier. The front door and bar are shared between the two. Closed Sun & Mon.

Gino's East 633 N Wells St at Ontario ☎312/943-1124. Despite its relocation into larger but meticulously aged premises, this remains a Chicago tradition, with huge deep-dish pizzas and graffiti-covered walls. Expect a considerable wait to get in, and at least 40 minutes for your pizza to cook.

Nacional 27 325 W Huron St at Franklin ☎312/664-2727. This popular Latin place draws its menu from every imaginable Central American cuisine, and has salsa dancing on weekends.

Pizzeria Uno 29 E Ohio St at Wabash ☎312/321-1000. The original outlet of the chain that put Chicago deep-dish pizza on the map.

Portillo's 100 W Ontario St at La Salle ☎312/587-8930. Much-loved local chain that serves delicious Chicago hot dogs and the best Italian beef sandwich in the city.

Star of Siam 11 E Illinois St at State ☎312/670-0100. Terrific Thai food served in a spacious, inviting setting. The *tom yum* soup, pad Thai, and curries are top-notch.

SushiSamba Rio 504 N Wells St at Illinois ☎312/595-2300. Very fancy restaurant-cum-bar offering a gimmicky but nonetheless delicious melding of Japanese (sushi) and South American (*ceviche*) cuisine; lots of fish, naturally, but also tender meats. High prices, but memorable atmosphere.

Lincoln Park and Old Town

Ann Sather 929 W Belmont Ave near Clark ☎773/348-2378; also four other locations around town. Chicago institution that serves Swedish-inspired breakfast, brunch, and dinner.

Boka 1729 N Halsted St near Willow ☎773/337-6070. Stylish option close to the Steppenwolf Theatre, serving inventive and tasty dishes from around the world on a changing weekly menu that offers small ($7–12) and large ($19–35) portions, depending on your appetite.

Café Ba-Ba-Reeba! 2024 N Halsted St at Armitage ☎773/935-5000. A real Spanish hot spot, offering a good range of hot and cold *tapas*, filling paella, and, of course, sangría.

Charlie Trotter's 816 W Armitage Ave at Halsted ☎773/248-6228. Prepare for a superb experience: Chef Trotter is a true artist, and his daring creations, such as caviar-stuffed quail eggs or Maine

salmon with blood sausage, are constantly evolving. The prices are appropriately high; you can only choose between two set menus, at $115 (vegetarian) or $135. Closed Sun & Mon.

Old Jerusalem 1411 N Wells St at Evergreen ☎312/944-3304. This long-time favorite serves reasonable Middle Eastern dishes; the falafel is great. Bring your own beer or wine.

RJ Grunts 2056 Lincoln Park W at Clark ☎773/929-5363. Check out the great burgers and a top-notch salad bar – purported to be the nation's first – in a casual neighborhood atmosphere.

Topo Gigio 1516 N Wells St at Burton ☎312/266-9355. Well-prepared, moderately priced Italian cuisine, served by very friendly staff in a peaceful garden amid the Old Town bustle. The homemade tiramisu is fabulous.

Twin Anchors 1655 N Sedgwick St at North ☎312/266-1616. You'll wait for a seat in this neighborhood spot, famed for its BBQ ribs, but the interesting clientele and 1950s-style bar make it worth it.

Wishbone 1001 W Washington Blvd at Morgan ☎312/850-2663. The rich, down-home Southern cooking comes in large portions at reasonable prices. The yardbird chicken (served with a red-pepper sauce), baked ham, and sweet-potato pie are wonderful.

Wicker Park

Café Absinthe 1954 W North Ave at Milwaukee ☎773/278-4488. Fine French dining in a romantic, casual setting. One of the city's best restaurants, with prices to match.

Earwax Cafe 1564 N Milwaukee Ave at North ☎773/772-4019. Bustling, inexpensive coffeehouse in a happening neighborhood, with an extensive menu of light vegetarian meals as well as meaty deli sandwiches.

Irazu 1865 N Milwaukee Ave near Armitage ☎773/252-5687. Very cheap but wonderful Costa Rican diner, serving great burritos plus a small selection of authentic main courses. Closed Sun.

Drinking

While not quite as wild as in the bootlegging days of speakeasies and Prohibition, Chicago remains a consummate boozer's town, and is one of the best US cities for **bars**, catering to just about every group and interest, with many open until 3, 4, or even 5am. Although far from picturesque, the cement strip that is **Division Street**, in the two blocks west of State Street, has become one of the hippest night spots, with a handful of joints tucked away on side streets off the main drag. **Wicker Park** is the trendiest hangout zone, while Halsted Street between Belmont and Addison is known as **Boystown** for its gay bars and clubs.

The hundred-plus **cafés and coffeehouses** across the city may not have taken the place of the traditional taverns, but they're a growing alternative.

Saloons, pubs, and bars

Bar Louie 226 W Chicago Ave ☎312/337-3313. Friendly, casual place in River North (the first in a burgeoning chain), with tables out front and cheap bar food. Open until 4am.

Berghoff's 17 W Adams St ☎312/427-3170. This former men-only stand-up bar in a showcase c.1900 tavern next to *The Berghoff* restaurant is crowded and congenial at lunchtime and after work.

Cavanaugh's 53 W Jackson St ☎312/939-3125. Visit this Loop favorite in the historic Monadnock Building for an after-work drink. Experience the warm interior with antique woodwork, Harp on draft, and a full menu.

Delilah's 2771 N Lincoln Ave ☎773/472-2771. At this dimly lit bar (playing underground records – from rock to alt-country – at night), choose from a great selection of beers (150) and whiskeys.

Goose Island Brewing Co. 1800 N Clybourn Ave ☎312/915-0071. Forty ales and lagers, including the popular Honker's Ale, are brewed on the premises at this lively Lincoln Park haunt, which ranks as Chicago's best brewpub.

Green Door Tavern 678 N Orleans St ☎312/664-5496. In an unlikely spot near the galleries of River North, this historic place is chock-full of Chicago memorabilia: some pure kitsch, others genuine antiques. Drink at the long bar or settle into a cozy back room to sample home-style cooking.

John Barleycorn 658 W Belden Ave ☎773/348-8899. A dimly lit Lincoln Park pub dating to 1890. This former speakeasy and John Dillinger haunt has retained many of its original fixtures. The lovely garden is open in summer.

Matchbox 770 N Milwaukee Ave ☎312/666-9292. All kinds of Chicago characters squeeze into this phenomenally narrow little neighborhood hangout on the West Side.

Old Town Ale House 219 W North Ave ☎312/944-7020. An eclectic crowd of scruffy regulars and yuppies mingle in this convivial haunt, complete with a pinball machine and a library of paperbacks.

Rainbo Club 1150 N Damen Ave ☎773/489-5999. Busy Wicker Park bar and hangout for indie-rock types.

Signature Room 875 N Michigan Ave ☎312/787-7230. Slightly down-at-the-heel but nonetheless unmissable cocktail lounge on the 96th floor of the John Hancock Building, with the city's best skyline views.

Gay and lesbian bars

Big Chicks 5024 N Sheridan Rd, Andersonville ☎773/728-5511. A friendly place for a mixed crowd, with a no-charge jukebox and free barbecues out back on summer Sundays.

The Closet 3325 N Broadway ☎773/477-8533. A tiny, cramped but congenial lesbian bar that attracts gay men as well.

Gentry 440 N State St ☎773/836-0933. Cabaret and piano bar popular with corporate types after work.

Sidetrack 3349 N Halsted St ☎773/477-9189. One of the most popular bars along Halsted's gay strip in Lakeview.

Nightlife and entertainment

From its earliest frontier days, Chicago has had some of the best **nightlife** in the US. Blues fans who celebrate Chicago as the birthplace of Muddy Waters' **urban blues** will be disappointed that the original South-Side headquarters of Chess Records, at 2120 S Michigan Avenue (immortalized in a Rolling Stones song recorded on site), has yet to become a museum. However, the city remains proud of its blues traditions, and continues to innovate in other genres, such as the energetic dance beat of 1980s **house music** as well as the groundbreaking **jazz** of the Art Ensemble of Chicago.

Nightclubs aplenty can be found all over town, especially along Halsted Street, Lincoln Avenue, and Clark Street on the North Side. **Uptown**, at the intersection of North Broadway and Lawrence, is a bit down-at-the-heel, but has half a dozen good venues. The best **gay clubs** congregate in the Lincoln Park area. Highbrow pursuits are also well provided for: Chicago's **classical music**, **dance**, and **theater** are world-class.

For **what's-on information**, Chicagoans pick up free weeklies like the excellent *Chicago Reader* (available Thursday afternoon), the *New City*, and the gay and lesbian *Windy City Times*. Full listings also appear in the Friday issues of the *Chicago Sun-Times* and the *Chicago Tribune*, while *Chicago* magazine has useful arts and restaurant listings.

Blues

B.L.U.E.S. 2519 N Halsted St ☎773/528-1012, ⓦ www.chicagobluesbar.com. Opened in the 1970s, B.L.U.E.S. is still going strong, though a little over-touristed. The tiny stage has been graced by all the greats.

Buddy Guy's Legends 754 S Wabash Ave ☎312/427-0333, ⓦ www.buddyguys.com. South Loop club owned by veteran bluesman Buddy Guy, with great acoustics and atmosphere, aims to present the very best local and national acts. Not as touristy as other downtown blues clubs.

Kingston Mines 2548 N Halsted St ☎773/477-4646. Top-notch local and national acts on two stages play to an up-for-it, partying crowd.

Rosa's Lounge 3420 W Armitage Ave ☎773/342-0452, ⓦ www.rosaslounge.com. Run by Mama Rosa and her son, this West-Side club is undoubtedly the friendliest blues joint around. For real aficionados. Closed Sun & Mon.

Jazz

Andy's 11 E Hubbard St ☎312/642-6805. Very popular with the after-work crowd; informal with moderate prices.

The Cotton Club 1710 S Michigan Ave ☎312/341-9787. A sophisticated live-music venue and disco, *The Cotton Club* attracts a well-dressed, mellow crowd.

Green Dolphin Street 2200 N Ashland Ave ☎773/395-0066, ⓦ www.jazzitup.com. This swanky, pricey restaurant and jazz club offers a solid line-up of regular performers. Closed Mon.

The Green Mill 4802 N Broadway ☎773/878-5552. One of the best – and most beautiful – rooms for local and national talent. Located in the tough Uptown neighborhood, and proud of its checkered Prohibition-era past.

Jazz Showcase 59 W Grand Ave ☎312/670-2473, ⓦ www.jazzshowcase.com. A classy, dressy room that hosts premier jazz by top names.

Rock

Cubby Bear 1059 W Addison St ☎773/327-1662, ⓦ www.cubbybear.com. A sports bar during the day – right next to Wrigley Field – this place transforms itself after dark into one of the city's most boisterous and eclectic live venues. Popular with aging dinosaurs more than new bands, but still fun.

Double Door 1572 N Milwaukee Ave ☎773/489-3160, ⓦ www.doubledoor.com. Former biker bar turned hip music venue in the Wicker Park/Buck-town neighborhood. Indie bands play almost every night.

Elbo Room 2871 N Lincoln Ave ☎773/549-5549, ⓦ www.elboroomchicago.com. Easygoing venue specializing in emerging bands, whether indie, pop, funk, or ska.

Empty Bottle 1035 N Western Ave ☎773/276-3600, ⓦ www.emptybottle.com. Loud hole-in-the-wall club where you might hear just about anything: experimental jazz, alternative rock, hip-hop, house, dub, and progressive country.

House of Blues 329 N Dearborn St ☎312/527-2583, ⓦ www.hob.com. Despite its name, this Near North chain venue puts on all kinds of music, including a popular gospel brunch on Sundays.

Metro 3730 N Clark St ☎773/549-0203, ⓦ www.metrochicago.com. Arguably the top spot in the city, this club, in an old cinema building, regularly hosts young British bands trying to break the States, plus DJ mixes.

Folk, country, and world music

Fitzgerald's 6615 W Roosevelt, Berwyn ☎708/788-2118. In the western suburb of Berwyn, an excellent venue for alt-country, Americana, Cajun, and zydeco.

HotHouse 31 E Balbo Drive ☎312/362-9707, ⓦ www.hothouse.net. Not-for-profit South Loop arts center that puts on fabulous world-music gigs on Friday and Saturday nights.

Old Town School of Folk Music 4544 N Lincoln Ave. Established in 1959, this place presents about 80 concerts a year, including just about every type of folk and world music, and also offers great classes.

Schubas Tavern 3159 N Southport Ave, Lakeview ☎773/525-2508, ⓦ www.schubas.com. A quirky roster of up-and-coming acts, from rock to alt-country or roots, appear at this intimate, all-but-perfect neighborhood venue.

Dance

Crobar 1543 N Kingsbury St ☎312/266-1900, ⓦ www.crobarnightclub.com. Exclusive, hyper-trendy warehouse club near the river, spinning newest techno and house.

Excalibur 632 N Dearborn St ☎312/266-1944. City institution blasting out rock and R&B on several floors to a predominantly out-of-town crowd.

Funky Buddha Lounge 728 W Grand Ave ☎312/666-1695, ⓦ www.funkybuddha.com. Small

West-Side club where the resident DJs attract a devoted young crowd.

Sidetrack 3349 N Halsted St ☎773/477-9189. Huge, very glitzy Wrigleyville club, with a garden bar and rooftop deck, that's Chicago's biggest gay venue. Open every night of the week.

Smartbar 3730 N Clark St, underneath the *Metro* (see opposite) ☎773/549-0203, ⓦwww.smartbarchicago.com. Great techno and house on the weekend in post-industrial Wrigleyville surroundings. Weekdays see a mix of punk, goth, and Eighties. The whole complex is open late – until 5am Fri and Sat.

Sound-Bar 226 W Ontario St ☎312/787-4480, ⓦwww.sound-bar.com. Near North mega-club that's taken the city by storm, with its sleek decor and massive dancefloor.

Theater and comedy

While it was once every Chicago actor and playwright's ambition to end up in New York, many are now perfectly happy to remain here. The city supports numerous **theater** companies, several of which boast reputations as good as any in the US. Best known of all is Steppenwolf, with alumni like John Malkovich and Gary Sinise, based at 1650 N Halsted St (☎312/335-1650, ⓦwww.steppenwolf.org), while others include the Court Theatre, 5535 S Ellis St (☎773/753-4472, ⓦwww.courttheatre.org), and the Goodman Theatre, 200 S Columbus Ave (☎312/443-3800, ⓦwww.goodman-theatre.org). **Comedy**, too, is particularly vibrant; Chicago's improvisational scene is considered the best in the nation, with the troupe at **Second City** – who now spread their activities across three separate auditoriums centered on 1616 N Wells St (☎312/337-3992, ⓦwww.secondcity.com) – especially heralded.

Classical music, opera, and dance

The world-famous **Chicago Symphony Orchestra** is based at Symphony Center, 220 S Michigan Ave (☎312/294-3000, ⓦwww.chicagosymphony.org), but spends much of the year on tour. The 186-member **Symphony Chorus** performs both classical and contemporary choral works with the CSO, specifically in summer at the open-air **Ravinia Festival**, 25 miles north of downtown Chicago (ⓦwww.ravinia.org). Home for the **Lyric Opera of Chicago** is the beautiful Civic Opera House, 20 N Wacker Drive (☎312/332-2244, ⓦwww.lyricopera.org); its season is from mid-September to early February, and most performances end up being sold out. Chicago can also boast two world-class dance companies: the classically oriented **Joffrey Ballet**, based at 70 E Lake St (☎312/739-0120, ⓦwww.joffrey.com), and the more contemporary **Hubbard Street Dance Chicago**, 1147 W Jackson Blvd (☎312/850-9744, ⓦwww.hubbardstreetdance.com).

Sports

Staunchly blue-collar Chicago must be among the best US cities for watching **sports**, as Chicagoans are, for better or worse, loyally supportive of their teams. The city's most successful outfit in recent memory was the Michael Jordan–led **Bulls** basketball team, winner of six NBA championships in the 1990s (☎312/559-1212, ⓦwww.nba.com/bulls). Now, though, with the Jordan era long gone, Bulls fans have little to cheer about. The team plays in the ultramodern United Center, 1901 W Madison St, as do hockey's **Blackhawks** (same phone, ⓦwww.chicagoblackhawks.com). The **Bears** football team (☎312/295-6600, ⓦwww.chicagobears.com) can be seen at the 66,000-capacity Soldier Field, 425 E McFetridge Drive, at the south end of Grant Park. As for baseball, neither Chicago team had won a World Series since 1917 until the **White Sox** finally broke the streak in 2005. Perhaps the destruction of their Comiskey Park home had something to do with it, though its replacement, the US Cellular Field stadium, which stands alongside at 333 W 35th St on the South Side, feels pretty soulless (☎312/831-1SOX, ⓦchicago.whitesox.com). The long-suffering **Cubs** still call grand old Wrigley Field home (☎312/831-CUBS, ⓦchicago.cubs.mlb.com).

Central Illinois

Interstates 55 and 57 slice south through the Corn Belt of **central Illinois** from Chicago. Parallel to I-55, the legendary **Route 66** began its run here, cutting through the state before running all the way to the Pacific Coast – you might try to catch a glimpse of it, as some old-time diners and other Americana still stand. One worthwhile stop, reachable by either interstate, is the state capital, **Springfield**, which commemorates president and former resident **Abraham Lincoln**. Otherwise, if you're on your way south, the college towns of **Bloomington-Normal** and **Champaign-Urbana** are the only good urban stops, while if you're heading west from Chicago spare the time to pause at the delightful old river town of **Galena**.

Springfield

Two hundred miles south of Chicago, the Illinois state capital, **SPRINGFIELD**, spreads out from a neat, leafy downtown grid. Abraham Lincoln honed his legal and political skills here, and tourists flock to his old homes, haunts, and final resting place. What they find is neither tacky nor pompous, but rather sites that illuminate not only the life of the sixteenth president of the USA, but also the uncertainty and turmoil of a nation on the brink of civil war.

The number one Lincoln attraction is the only house he ever owned, and which he shared with his wife Mary from 1844 to 1861. For a free narrated tour, pick up tickets at the **Lincoln Home Visitor Center**, 426 S Seventh St (daily 8.30am–5pm; ☎217/492-4241, ⓦwww.nps.gov/liho). Assorted displays and a brief film help to pass the time while you wait for the next available tour.

Four blocks north, at 212 N Sixth St, the **Abraham Lincoln Presidential Library and Museum** (Mon, Tues & Thurs–Sat 9am–5pm, Wed 9am–8.30pm; $7.50; ☎217/558-8844, ⓦwww.alplm.org) is a state-of-the-art new facility that covers Lincoln's career in exhaustive detail, with fascinating original documents and interactive displays, as well as some simple mock-ups aimed largely at kids.

In the restored Greek Revival **Old State Capitol**, at Sixth and Adams nearby (mid-April to Aug daily 9am–5pm; Sept to mid-April Tues–Sat 9am–5pm; free; ☎217/785-7960), Lincoln attended at least 240 Supreme Court hearings, and proclaimed in 1858, "A house divided against itself cannot stand. I believe this government cannot endure permanently, half slave and half free." Objects, busts, and papers relating to Lincoln and the Democrat Stephen A. Douglas, whom he debated (and subsequently lost to) in Illinois' 1858 US Senate election, and whom he defeated in the 1860 presidential race, can be found throughout the building. At the tastefully renovated **Lincoln Depot** on Tenth and Monroe streets (April–Aug daily 10am–4pm; free), the newly elected president said goodbye to Springfield in February 1861 and boarded a train for his inauguration in Washington, DC (a video illustrates the twelve-day journey). The next time he returned was in his funeral train. **Lincoln's Tomb**, a 117ft-tall obelisk, stands in beautiful Oak Ridge Cemetery on the north side of town. The vault, adorned with busts and statuettes, is open to the public (June–Aug Mon & Wed–Sun 9am–5pm, Tues 9am–8pm; March–May & Sept–Oct daily 9am–5pm; Nov–Feb daily 9am–4pm; free). Inside are inscribed the words, "Now he belongs to the ages."

The **Illinois State Museum**, at Spring and Edwards in the same complex as the current Illinois State Capitol, is crammed with natural history and Native American and contemporary art exhibits, along with the interactive "**At Home in the Heartland**" display, which traces Illinois family life from 1700 to 1970 (Mon–Sat 8.30am–5pm, Sun noon–5pm; free). Completed in 1904, the **Dana-Thomas House**, 301

E Lawrence Ave (tours Wed–Sun 9am–4pm; $3; ☎217/782-6776), survives as the best-preserved and most completely furnished example of **Frank Lloyd Wright**'s early Prairie house, with more than four hundred pieces of glasswork, original art, and light fixtures. Just north of town, at 2075 Peoria Rd, Bill Shea proudly displays fifty years' worth of road signs, gas pumps, and Route 66 memorabilia at **Shea's Gas Station Museum** (Tues–Fri 7am–4pm, Sat 7am–noon; free).

Twenty miles northwest of Springfield on Hwy-97, **Lincoln's New Salem State Historic Site** marks where the future president first lived in this area, from 1831 to 1837. In this backwoods clearing he clerked in a store, volunteered for the Black Hawk War, served as postmaster, and failed in business before taking up legal studies and moving to Springfield to pursue his political career. Today the recreated village features simple homes, workshops, a store, and a tavern. Meanwhile, the **visitor center** hosts a worthwhile exhibit on pioneer lifestyles (mid-April to Aug daily 9am–5pm, March to mid-April & Sept–Oct Wed–Sun 9am–5pm, Nov–Feb Wed–Sun 8am–4pm; suggested donation $2; ☎217/632-4000, ⓦwww.lincolnsnewsalem.com).

Practicalities

Amtrak **trains** from Chicago and St Louis roll in at Third and Washington streets downtown, at manageable times. Greyhound drops off two miles east of downtown at 2351 S Dirksen Parkway. The **Convention and Visitors Bureau**, 109 N Seventh St (Mon–Fri 8.30am–5pm; ☎217/789-2360 or 1-800/545-7300, ⓦwww.visit-springfieldillinois.com), has brochures and maps.

The best selection of inexpensive **accommodation**, including a *Days Inn* (☎217/529-0171; ❸), lies off I-55 at the Dirksen Parkway exit. More central options include the *Mansion View Inn*, 529 S Fourth St (☎217/544-7411 or 1-800/252-1083, ⓦwww.mansionview.com; ❹). *The Inn at 835*, 835 S Second St (☎217/523-4466, ⓦwww.innat835.com; ❺), is a charming ten-room **B&B** converted from a 1909 downtown apartment block.

Springfield's cafés seem to have exclusive rights to a phenomenon known as the **Horseshoe** – ostensibly a meat sandwich, but fried, covered in melted cheese, and very tasty. *Norb Andy's*, 518 E Capitol Ave (☎217/523-7777), musters up the best Horseshoes around. The *Cozy Dog Drive-In*, 2935 S Sixth St (☎217/525-1992), claims to be the birthplace of the **Cozy Dog** (also known as the corn dog), a deep-fried, batter-drenched hot dog on a stick. At the other end of the health spectrum, *Augie's Front Burner*, 109 S Fifth St (☎217/544-6979), serves up good California-style and vegetarian meals.

Galena

The neat little town of **GALENA**, a few miles short of both Iowa and Wisconsin in the far northwest corner of Illinois, has changed little since its nineteenth-century heyday. Thanks to its sheltered location just a few miles up the Galena River, it was a major port of call for Mississippi River steamboats. These days, the only traffic it gets are the day-trippers who come to admire the gentle crescent of Main Street, tucked in behind an immaculate grassy levee. Its impeccable redbrick facades and graceful skyline of spires and crosses place it among the most attractive river towns in the US.

Galena boasts of having contributed nine generals to the Union army during the Civil War, the most significant of whom was **Ulysses S. Grant**. Grant moved to the town in 1860, working as a clerk in a leather store owned by his father and operated by his two brothers. Some contemporary accounts speak of him as the town lush, the kind of person decent folk crossed the street to avoid. However, his West Point education encouraged the townspeople to appoint him as colonel when they raised the 21st Illinois regiment on the outbreak of war. When he came home, in August 1865, it was as overall commander of the victorious Union army.

The grateful citizens of Galena presented Grant with a **house**, a couple of blocks up Bouthillier Street on the far side of the river (April–Oct Wed–Sun 9am–5pm, Nov–March Wed–Sun 9am–4pm; suggested donation $3; ☏815/777-3310). It's not a grand place by any means, but it was in the plainly furnished downstairs drawing room that Grant received the news of his election as president in 1868. Although he went on to serve two terms, he is commonly agreed to have been a better general than president. His administrations were plagued by scandal, and he lost all his own money through unwise investments. The family fortunes were restored just before his death in 1885, when Mark Twain first persuaded Grant to write, and then published, his best-selling *Memoirs*.

Practicalities

The 1857 Railroad Museum, across the river from the town proper at 101 Bouthillier St, serves as the local **visitor center** (Mon–Thurs 9am–5pm, Fri & Sat 9am–7pm, Sun 10am–5pm; ☏815/777-4390 or 1-877/464-2536, ⓦwww.galena.org).

The plush *DeSoto House Hotel*, 230 S Main St (☏815/777-0090 or 1-800/343-6562, ⓦwww.desotohouse.com; ❺), was Grant's campaign headquarters in 1868. Its grand *Generals' Restaurant* serves steak and seafood dinners. If your budget won't stretch that far, the *Triangle Motel*, a mile west at highways 20 and 84 (☏815/777-2897 or 1-877/425-3629, ⓦwww.geocities.com/triangleinn; ❷), makes a good-value alternative. As for inexpensive spots to **eat**, *Boone's Place*, 515 S Main St (☏815/777-4488), is a reliable espresso and sandwich bar.

Wisconsin

Nearly as many cows as humans call **WISCONSIN** home; about four million of each reside in this rich, rolling farmland. However, America's self-proclaimed "Dairyland" is more than just one giant pasture. Beyond the massive red barns and silvery silos lie endless pine forests, some fifteen thousand sky-blue lakes, postcard-pretty valleys, and dramatic bluffs. The state, whose Ojibway name means "gathering of the waters," is bordered by Lake Michigan to the east, Lake Superior in the north and, to the west, the Mississippi and St Croix rivers.

The **history** of Wisconsin exemplifies the standard formula for westward expansion. Seventeenth-century French and British explorers began by trading with the Native Americans and soon ousted them from their land. The European settlers who followed – predominantly Germans, Scandinavians, and Poles – tended to be liberal and progressive; such major national social programs as labor laws for women and children, assistance for the elderly and the disabled, and unemployment compensation were rooted here. On the downside, Senator Joseph McCarthy, the infamous 1950s witch-hunter, was born in Grand Chute, former headquarters of the right-wing John Birch Society.

Wisconsin today is best known for its liquids. The **milk** from all those cattle yields cheeses of all kinds, while the **beer**, as the song says, is what made **Milwaukee** famous. Sparkling Madison apart, Wisconsin's other cities – **La Crosse**, **Green Bay**, **Oshkosh** – can veer toward the dull side, but they're also clean, safe, and amiable, while the smaller towns can be distinctive and charming.

Getting around Wisconsin

You'll be hard put to explore Wisconsin's remote north, or key locales like the Door County peninsula, without a vehicle. Public transportation is better in the south. Milwaukee and, to a lesser extent, Madison are hubs for Greyhound and Amtrak. Five **trains** daily connect Milwaukee and Chicago, a ninety-minute journey, while one crosses the state in the south en route for Seattle, via Columbus (near Madison), Portage, Wisconsin Dells, Tomah, and La Crosse.

Milwaukee

Bustling **MILWAUKEE**, the "Deutsch Athens" of southeastern Wisconsin, is a combination of the down-home and the sophisticated, known for its lakeside and ethnic **festivals** and huge **breweries**. Visually it's a mix of elegant Teutonic architecture, rambling Victorian warehouses, and tasteful waterfront developments. Its prime position on the shores of Lake Michigan, at the confluence of three rivers, made it a meeting place for Native American groups long before white settlers moved in, while the opulent mansions lining the lake commemorate the industrialists who helped make this Wisconsin's economic and manufacturing capital. By 1850, less than two decades old and with a population of twenty thousand, Milwaukee already had a dozen breweries and 225 saloons. The contemporary estimate of six thousand bars – one per hundred residents – is not necessarily apocryphal.

Arrival, information, and getting around

Milwaukee is well served by air, rail, and bus. Its **airport**, eight miles south of downtown at 5300 S Howell Ave, is connected with the city center by bus #80 ($1.75), and by shared-ride van service ($11). A taxi will set you back about $26. Amtrak is at 433 W St Paul Ave, while Greyhound (℡414/272-2156) and Wisconsin Coach (℡262/542-8864; ⓦwww.wisconsincoach.com), serving southeastern Wisconsin, operate out of the same terminal at 606 N James Lovell Drive. Badger Bus (℡414/276-7490, ⓦwww.badgerbus.com), across the street at no. 635, runs to Madison and points between (six daily; $30 roundtrip). Take care in and around the stations at night, which can be dodgy.

Milwaukee's **Visitor Center** is at Discovery World, at Pier Wisconsin (daily 8am–5pm; ℡414/273-7222 or 1-800/554-1448, ⓦwww.visitmilwaukee.org), and has details on such **festivals** as the eleven-day Summerfest (late June to early July), also known as "The Big Gig," and the Wisconsin State Fair (early Aug).

Getting around Milwaukee is easy and inexpensive via the county's extensive **transportation system** (flat fare $1.75; 24hr info ℡414/344-6711). The Milwaukee Loop is a special trolley service connecting 25 stops in the city center (June–Aug, Wed–Thurs 11am–10pm, Fri & Sat 11am–midnight, Sun 11am–6pm; free).

Accommodation

Accommodation in Milwaukee runs the gamut from low-budget motels to upmarket chains and luxury hotels. Alternatively, Cedarburg is a tranquil, picture-postcard-like village twenty miles north; the *Washington House* (☎262/375-3550, ⊛www.washingtonhouseinn.com; ④–⑥) and *Stagecoach Inn* (☎262/375-0208 or 1-888/375-0208, ⊛www.stagecoach-inn-wi.com; ④–⑥) here are charming.

Ambassador Hotel 2308 W Wisconsin Ave ☎414/342-8400, ⊛www.ambassadormilwaukee. com. A beautifully restored Art Deco hotel from 1928, featuring modern-day amenities. ⑤
The Astor 924 E Juneau Ave ☎414/271-4220 or 1-800/558-0200; ⊛www.theastorhotel.com. This classy, historic 1920s hotel offers free continental breakfast and health club passes. Extended stays are available. ④
Best Western Inn Towne Hotel 710 N Old World Third St ☎414/224-8400. Modern hotel with comfortable, convenient rooms downtown. ④

🏃 **Brumder Mansion** 3046 W Wisconsin Ave ☎414/342-9767 or 866/793-3676; ⊛www.brumdermansion.com. Fabulously decorated, enormous B&B with an in-house theater, just minutes from downtown. Rooms include antiques, marble, rich draperies, and stained glass. ④
Comfort Inn & Suites Downtown Lakeshore 916 E State St ☎414/276-8800 or 1-800/328-7275. Clean, very comfortable rooms in a nice part of downtown. ④

The City

Downtown Milwaukee, split north to south by the Milwaukee River, is only a mile long and a few blocks wide. Handsome old buildings and gleaming, modern steel-and-glass structures are comfortably corralled together on three sides by spaghetti-like strands of freeway, with Lake Michigan forming the fourth boundary. To bolster the allure of downtown, the city has successfully poured millions into its **Riverwalk** development along the Milwaukee River, now something of a nightlife center and the site of many public entertainment events. East of the river on the lakefront, the **Milwaukee Art Museum**, 700 N Art Museum Drive (daily 10am–5pm, Thurs 10am–8pm; $8; ☎414/224-3200, ⊛www.mam.org), contains works by European masters and twentieth-century Americans. One wing – with stunning views of the lake – is devoted to a comprehensive collection of Post-Impressionist paintings. Architect Santiago Calatrava's spectacular expansion is an attraction in itself, the white wings of the building flapping up and down three times each day to reduce heat gain and glare. Close by, **Discovery World at Pier Wisconsin,** 500 N. Harbor Dr (Tues–Sun 9am–5pm; $15.95; ☎414/765-9966, ⊛www.discoveryworld.org), features popular hands-on exhibits and the S/V *Denis Sullivan* schooner. Downtown at 800 W Wells St are the **Milwaukee Public Museum** (Mon–Sat 9am–5pm, Sun noon–5pm; $11; ☎414/278-2702, ⊛www.mpm.edu), where the intertwined histories and mysteries of the earth, nature, and humankind are imaginatively presented through dioramas such as "The Streets of Old Milwaukee," and the **Humphrey IMAX Dome Theater**, which has a giant, wraparound screen (show times vary; $8-10, $15 for a combo ticket; ☎414/319-4629, ⊛www.mpm.edu/imax).

West of downtown, the 37-room **Pabst Mansion**, at 2000 W Wisconsin Ave (Feb–Oct Mon–Sat 10am–4pm, Sun noon–4pm; closed Mon mid-Jan through Feb; $8; ⊛www.pabstmansion.com), was completed in 1893 as the castle of a local beer baron and is a knockout example of ornate Flemish Renaissance architecture, featuring exquisite wood-, glass-, and ironwork. Although the Pabst Brewery here has shut down, the **Miller Brewing Company**, five miles west of downtown at 4251 W State St, still offers free behind-the-scenes tours (Mon–Sat, usually 10:30am–3:30pm but times change frequently; ☎414/931-2337 or 1-800/944-LITE; bus #31), culminating in generous samples for over-21s. The **Sprecher** microbrewery, seven miles north of downtown, just off I-43 at 701 W Glendale Ave (Fri 4pm and Sat 1pm, 2pm & 3pm; reservations necessary; $3; ☎414/964-2739), serves samples straight out of the barrel. Schlitz, the "beer that made Milwaukee famous," was bought out by Stroh's in the late 1980s and is now produced in Detroit.

The free one-hour tours of the engine plant responsible for Milwaukee's other legendary brand name, **Harley-Davidson**, located in Wauwatosa in a rough area of town on 11700 W Capitol Drive at Hwy-45, are really for Harley devotees; bikes aren't assembled here and if you don't know your shovelheads from your knuckleheads you might feel out of place (Mon–Fri 9.30am–1pm; ☎414/343-7850 or 1-877/883-1450). For those more interested in Harley chic, there's ample opportunity to purchase all kinds of merchandise throughout Milwaukee.

Eating

The Germans who first settled in Milwaukee determined its **eating** style – heavy on bratwurst, rye bread, and beer. Subsequent immigrants threw the collective kitchen wide open, making for a culinary cornucopia. With Lake Michigan lapping the city's feet, freshwater fish can hardly be overlooked, especially on a Friday night when fish fries break out all over the place. Wherever you go, portions tend to be big.

Coquette Café 316 N Milwaukee St ☎414/219-2655. This charming spot in the Third Ward serves great soups and sandwiches as well as French-style pastries.

J Pandl's Whitefish Bay Inn 1319 E Henry Clay St ☎414/964-3800. Suburban landmark famous for reasonably priced grilled whitefish, colossal oven-baked pancakes, and its stein collection.

Mimma's Café 1307 E Brady St ☎414/264-6640. This unmissable Italian restaurant is classy yet casual, with imaginative, mouthwatering cuisine,

like fried eggplant and artichoke ravioli, and an extensive wine list.

Sanford 1547 N Jackson St ☎414/276-9608. A fine-dining landmark with creative food and a seasonal menu that emphasizes Wisconsin ingredients, such as artisanal cheeses and locally grown vegetables.

Trocadero 1758 N Water St ☎414/272-0205. Hip, eastside spot that serves small plates and great continental dishes like grilled tuna and saffron shrimp.

Nightlife and entertainment

The concept of neighborhoods is vital to Milwaukee's nightlife. On the east side, **Brady Street**, a counterculture haven in the 1960s, is now filled with Italian restaurants and bars. **Walker's Point**, on the edge of downtown, has all sorts of gay and straight watering holes, while the Polish locals can be found farther south. Downtown gets busy on the weekend, especially either side of the river on **Water** and **Old World Third** streets between Juneau and State.

With more live theater than Chicago, high culture in downtown Milwaukee revolves around the **Marcus Center for the Performing Arts**, 929 N Water St (☎414/273-7121 or 1-888/612-3500, ⓦwww.marcuscenter.org). The plush, historic **Pabst Theater**, 144 E Wells St (☎414/286-3663), and the **Riverside Theater**, 116 W Wisconsin Ave (☎414/286-3663), host well-known bands, while the **Milwaukee Repertory Theater**, 108 E Wells St (☎414/224-9490, ⓦwww.milwaukeerep.com), has a reputation for staging risk-taking productions in addition to classics like "A Christmas Carol." The **Third Ward**, a restored warehouse district on the edge of downtown full of shops and cafés, is home to the **Broadway Theater Center**, 158 N Broadway (☎414/291-7800), which in turn holds the adventurous **Skylight Opera** (ⓦwww.skylightopera.com), **Chamber Theatre** (ⓦwww.chamber-theatre.com) and **Renaissance Theaterworks** (ⓦwww.r-t-w.com).

Café Vecchio 1137 N Old World Third St ☎414/273-5700. Upscale European-style coffee/wine bar featuring a one-hundred-plus wine list, espresso drinks, and twenty different martinis.

John Hawk's Pub 100 E Wisconsin Ave ☎414/272-3199. Riverside British-style establishment downtown serving food all day.

Milwaukee Ale House 233 N Water St

☎414/226-BEER. Milwaukee's sole all-grain, old-style brewpub serves filling food and its own beer.
Safe House 779 N Front St ☎414/271-2007, ⊕www.safe-house.com. This unique, tongue-in-cheek nightclub seems to come straight out of a spy film. Hint: enter through the "International Exports Ltd" office.

Up and Under Pub 1216 E Brady St ☎414/276-2677. Milwaukee's top blues bar.

Von Trier 2235 N Farwell Ave ☎414/272-1775. Black Forest decor and lots of imported beers – the Weise is a house specialty.

Wisconsin's eastern shores

North of Milwaukee, **eastern Wisconsin** is a melange of the industrial and the maritime, shaped by its proximity to **Lake Michigan** and the smaller **Lake Winnebago**. Of its towns, **Green Bay**, home to the legendary Packers, is best seen as a prelude to the most romanticized part of the state, **Door County**.

Green Bay

Few cities are as closely associated with a sports team as **GREEN BAY** is with the football Packers: 108 miles north of Milwaukee, it's the smallest city in the US to have a major-league professional sports franchise and the only one to own a team. **The Green Bay Packer Hall of Fame**, 1265 Lombardi Ave (daily 9am–6pm; $10; ☎920/569-7500), celebrates the dynastic years of the 1960s when the Pack won Superbowls I and II, as well as more recent stars such as Antonio Freeman and Brett Favre. Stuffed with hands-on displays, movie theaters, and memorabilia, the museum offers more than enough to satisfy any football fan. The Hall of Fame is located in an atrium inside the Packers' **Lambeau Field** stadium, which you can also tour (times vary; $11, or $19 combination ticket with Hall of Fame; ⊕www.packers.com).

Also in this busy but not particularly attractive port, the **National Railroad Museum**, 2285 S Broadway (Mon–Sat 9am–5pm, Sun 11am–5pm; $9 in summer including train ride, $8 in winter; ☎920/437-7623, ⊕www.nationalrrmuseum .org), gives pride of place to the 1941 *Union Pacific Big Boy* locomotive, one of many such trains that served Green Bay's still-enormous freight depot. West on Hwy-172, opposite the airport, stands Wisconsin's biggest casino – **Oneida Bingo & Casino**. Tribal history, and the way in which profits from blackjack, video poker, and bingo have improved education and social and health facilities, are examined at the **Oneida Nation Museum**, seven miles west of Hwy-41 as it runs south from downtown (summer Tues–Sat 9am–5pm; rest of year closed Sat; $2; ☎920/869-2768, ⊕www. oneidanation.org).

The city's **CVB** (☎920/494-9507 or 1-888/867-3342, ⊕www.packercountry. com) sits in the shadow of the football stadium, off Lombardi Avenue, at 1901 S. Oneida St. Nearby, the *Best Western Midway Hotel*, 780 Armed Forces Drive (☎920/499-3161 or 1-800/528-1234, ⊕www.bestwestern.com; ❹–❺), has standard rooms and an indoor pool. *Titletown Brewing Company*, 200 Dousman St (☎920/437-2337), has a great setting for drinks in a former railroad depot downtown, while *Brett Favre's Steakhouse*, 1004 Brett Favre Pass (☎920/499-MVP4), is an upscale family restaurant/sports bar serving Southern cuisine.

Door County

From Sturgeon Bay, 140 miles north of Milwaukee, **Door County** sticks into Lake Michigan like a gradually tapering candle for 42 miles. With thirteen lighthouses and a dozen fishing villages, its coastline smacks more of New England than the Midwest. The name derives from "Porte des Morts" or "**Door of the**

377

Dead," French for the treacherous eight-mile strait that severs Washington Island at its tip. Prices can be a little steep in the summer, but you get what you pay for – a small sliver of America devoid, for the most part, of crude billboards, sloppy diners, bland chain motels, and tacky amusements. Activities include browsing around galleries and attending arts festivals, as well as hiking, fishing, and boating. Renting a **bicycle** gives you the chance to follow an excellent **cycle trail**; try Fish Creek's Nor Door Cyclery (℗920/868-2275, ⓦwww.nordoorsports.com), on Hwy-42 just north of the entrance to Peninsula State Park (see opposite), which has the best models. Winter is considerably quieter, with ice fishing, cross-country skiing, and snowmobiling being the predominant outdoor activities.

Pick up road and trail maps at the **visitor center** on Hwy-42/57 upon entering Sturgeon Bay (lobby open 24 hours; staffed times vary; ℗920/743-4456 or 1-800/52-RELAX, ⓦwww.doorcounty.com), where you can also phone local lodgings for free.

Exploring Door County

Door County's only sizeable town, **Sturgeon Bay**, is a pleasant enough shipbuilding community, if not exactly abundant in small-town splendor. Ten miles north on Hwy-57 is the rolling **Whitefish Dunes State Park**, with its wispy sand dunes and popular mile-long beach (daily; $7 per car, $10 with out-of-state plates). A short trail beginning at the park's Nature Center leads to the spectacular rocky **Cave Point County Park** (free), studded with wind- and wave-sculptured caves that are particularly dramatic in winter. In general beaches are better this side of the peninsula; you can also swim in several placid inland lakes.

Over on the western side, biking and hiking trails traverse the thickly forested hills of **Peninsula State Park** (situated between tiny Fish Creek and elegant Mennonite **Ephraim**, with its resplendent white-clapboard architecture). Peninsula Park is one of the most popular parks in Wisconsin and summer camping reservations usually book up in January. Just outside it on Hwy-42, the anachronistic Skyway Drive-In movie theater (℗920/854-9938) offers a couple of hours' diversion on a warm night. Northeast of Ellison Bay near the peninsula's tip, **Newport State Park** is one of Wisconsin's least visited parks, with hiking, mountain biking, cross-country skiing, and backpack camping opportunities.

Washington Island, off the peninsula's northern tip, offers a different cultural perspective. During Prohibition, the Icelandic community here convinced authorities that (40 percent alcohol) bitters were an ancient cure for rheumatism and dyspepsia. Cases of the stuff were shipped in, and the habit stuck; drop into the historic *Nelsen's Hall Bitters Pub and Restaurant* (℗920/847-2496), about two miles from the Detroit Harbor dock for a taste. **Motel rooms** are available on Washington, but there's no such luxury on the primitive neighboring 950-acre **Rock Island**. Once the private estate of a millionaire, it's dotted with stark, stone buildings; no cars are allowed, so see it by foot or bike.

The islands are served by the Washington Island Ferry from Northport at the tip of the peninsula (daily; $10 roundtrip, cars $23, bikes $4; ℗920/847-2546 or 1-800/223-2094, ⓦwww.wisferry.com) and the Rock Island Ferry out of Jackson Harbor (May to early Oct daily; $9 roundtrip for foot traffic only; ℗920/847-3322).

Accommodation

Door County has a full range of **accommodation**, including some overpriced resorts. Prices given are for shoulder seasons (the best time to come); expect to pay up to 25 percent extra at the grander hotels in July and August, and a small weekend premium. Camping is idyllic. State park sites cost $9–17 (plus $9.50 reservation fee and $7 daily admission or $10 for out-of-state residents, annual

$25/\$35; ☎ 1-888/947-2757). Recommended private campgrounds include *Path of Pines*, County Road F off Hwy-42, near Fish Creek (mid-May to mid-Oct; $20; ☎ 920/868-3332 or 1-800/868-7802).

French Country Inn 3052 Spruce Lane, Ephraim ☎ 920/854-4001. This charming B&B close to the water offers seven rooms in the summer and four in the winter. Breakfast features organic, local produce when possible. ❸

Julie's Park Café & Motel 4020 Main St, Fish Creek ☎ 920/868-2999; ⓦ www.juliesmotel.com. A cozy motel with clean rooms right next to the entrance of Peninsula State Park, The on-site restaurant is good. ❸

Peninsula Park-View Resort Cty Rd A and Hwy-42 ☎ 920/854-2633, ⓦ www.peninsulaparkview.com. Friendly motel conveniently situated on the edge of Fish Creek at the quiet entrance of Peninsula State Park. Offers standard rooms as well

as suites and cottages. Guests have free use of bikes. ❸

Waterbury Inn 10321 Water St, Ephraim ☎ 920/854-2821 or 1-800/720-1624, ⓦ www.waterburyinn.com. This luxury property has one- and two-bedroom suites with fully-equipped kitchens. ❸–❻

White Gull Inn 4225 Main St, Fish Creek ☎ 920/868-3517 or 1-888/364-9542, ⓦ www.whitegullinn.com. The county's crown jewel, this elegant old inn, next to delightful Sunset Park, was built in 1896. Rooms are decorated in antiques, and some have fireplaces and double whirlpools. The inn is also known for its good restaurant (breakfast is included) and fish boil (see below) every night in summer. ❻–❽

Eating

One reward of a midsummer visit to Door County is the chance to sample the cherry in all its guises. Another traditional treat is the **fish boil**, a delicious outdoor ritual involving whitefish steaks, potatoes, and onions cooked in a cauldron over a wood fire. Rounded off with coleslaw and cherry pie, it's widely available for between $12 and $18.

Al Johnson's Swedish Restaurant Hwy-42, Sister Bay ☎ 920/854-2626. Pancakes, meatballs, and other fine Scandinavian dishes are featured at this local spot where goats are tethered atop the sod roof.

Bayside Tavern Main St, Fish Creek ☎ 920/868-3441. A convivial pub serves a celebrated chili, burgers, and a mean Friday-night perch fish fry.

Dal Santo's 147 N 3rd Ave, Sturgeon Bay ☎ 920/743-6100. Pizza, small plates, and Northern

Italian dishes are served in this reliable dinner spot.

Square Rigger Galley 6332 Hwy-57, Jacksonport ☎ 920/823-2408. This cocktail lounge and restaurant, on a private sandy beach, serves one of the county's best fish boils.

Wilson's 9990 Water St, Ephraim ☎ 920/854-2041. Burgers, sandwiches, and (along with the Door County Ice Cream Factory in Sister Bay) the top ice cream on the peninsula.

Northern Wisconsin

Sparsely settled **northern Wisconsin** has no large cities (and few small ones), and no interstates. It's a lake-studded wilderness, covered by enormous tracts of forest. Canoe its rivers, fish for record-breakers, or ski or snowmobile cross-country trails without having to fight for space. **Bayfield** and the **Apostle Islands** in the northwest are the obvious destinations, but Hayward, southeast of Superior, is home to the amazing **National Freshwater Fishing Hall of Fame** (mid-April to Nov daily 9:30am–4pm; $6.50), where you're invited to "Walk through the biggest fish in the world!" – a four-story, five-hundred-ton, fiberglass monster.

The Apostle Islands

All but one of the 22 islands scattered off **Bayfield Peninsula** in Lake Superior are part of the **Apostle Islands National Lakeshore** – a prized preserve for outdoors enthusiasts seeking to recharge depleted spiritual batteries.

The jumping-off point for the islands, **BAYFIELD**, once a lumbering and fishing village, is now a pleasant soft-sell tourist trap. Its sumptuous *Old Rittenhouse Inn*, 301 Rittenhouse Ave (⊤715/779-5111 or 1-800/779-2129, ⓦwww.rittenhouseinn. com; ⑤–⑨), offers gourmet meals and well-appointed **rooms**. *Tree Top House*, 225 N Fourth St (⊤715/779-3293; ❷), features clean, simple doubles, while *Island View B&B*, 86720 Island View Lane (⊤715/779-5307 or 1-888/309-5307, ⓦwww.island-viewbandb.com; ❻), has secluded cottages and B&B-style accommodation a mile outside of town. Lodges and cottages are the centerpiece for the thirty gorgeous lakeside acres of *Rocky Run* (⊤715/373-2551; ❹), a resort outside **Washburn** eleven miles south. Bayfield's **visitor center** is at 42 S Broad St (⊤715/779-3335 or 1-800/447-4094; ⓦwww.bayfield.org). Campers heading for the islands require permits from the visitor center (ask about permit fees) at 415 Washington Ave (summer daily; weekdays in winter; ⊤715/779-3397). Getting around the islands is straightforward: Apostle Island's Cruise Services boats ($32.95; ⊤715/779-3925, ⓦwww.apostleisland.com) wend their way past all of the islands, and will set down and pick up campers.

Madeline Island

By the fifteenth century **Madeline Island** was known to the Ojibway as Mon-ingwunakauning – home of the golden-shafted woodpecker. Frenchman Michel Cadotte founded a fur-trading post there for the British in 1793, and subsequently married Equaysayway, daughter of a tribal leader, who took the name the island bears today. Madeline is now the only commercially developed Apostle Island, but it remains pretty low-key. Cadotte is buried in an overgrown cemetery in its sole town, **LA POINTE**.

La Pointe is accessible in summer via the twenty-minute ride on the Madeline Island Ferry Line from Bayfield (every 30min in peak season; cars $16.50 one-way, $33 roundtrip; passengers $5, $10; bikes $2.50, $5; ⊤715/747-2051, ⓦwww. madferry.com). Its 180 year-round residents maintain an interesting little **historical museum** (May–Oct daily 10am–5pm; $5.50), and assorted sandy beaches, wide bays, scenic points, and forests can also be explored along 45 miles of sometimes rough road in the area. The Ferry Line conducts two-hour bus tours of the island (July and August, Mon–Sat, 1.30pm; $11).

The **visitor center** on Main Street (⊤715/747-2801 or 1-888/475-3386, ⓦwww. madelineisland.com) can offer advice on **places to stay**; the *Madeline Island Motel* (⊤715/747-3000; ❹) and *The Island Inn* (⊤715/747-2000; ❺), both near the ferry dock, are probably the best value. A wooden footbridge from La Pointe across the lagoon leads to **Big Bay State Park** where the campgrounds share a splendid mile-long beach. Camping sites, on top of a bluff and close to caves in the park (⊤1-888/947-2757), cost $10–14, plus a $10 reservation fee and a $7–$10 vehicle fee. **Eating options** include the pub in *The Inn on Madeline Island* resort (⊤715/747-6322 or 1-800/822-6315, ⓦwww.madisland.com; ❹–❻) where homes, cottages, and condominiums can also be rented along a private beach.

Southern Wisconsin

Assorted highways and back roads lace up **southern Wisconsin**, passing over rolling hills and deep dales. The main urban center of Wisconsin's most populated region is the immensely likeable lakeside college town of **Madison**, which doubles as the state capital. Cozy Madison-area communities like New Glarus or Mount Horeb, and historic settlements like Little Norway have cute, walkable downtowns. Further north, Wisconsin Dells has a picturesque setting, but may appeal only to those who revel in tacky attractions and Americana. Undulating down the state's western border, alongside the Mississippi River, the scenic highway designated as **The Great River Road** runs from near Canada to the Gulf of Mexico.

Madison

The history books record that **MADISON**, just over an hour west of Milwaukee, was little more than a wooded, mosquito-infested swamp when it was selected to be the political nucleus of the Wisconsin Territory in 1836. Today this stimulating, youthful metropolis is one of the most beautifully set cities in the US, with a handful of diverting museums, great restaurants, and a student-fueled nightlife scene.

Arrival, information, and accommodation

Greyhound **buses** run regularly to Milwaukee, Green Bay, and beyond, while Badger Coaches makes six trips daily from downtown Milwaukee ($17 one-way/$30 round-trip; ℡608/255-6771, ⓦwww.badgerbus.com). Both operate out of the terminal at 2 S Bedford St. Van Galder/Coach USA buses depart from the Memorial Union to Chicago's O'Hare Airport (10 daily; $25 one-way, $50 roundtrip; ℡608/752-5407 or 1-800/747-0994, ⓦwww.coachusa. com/vangalder). Madison also has a recently renovated airport, (℡608/246-3380), offering flights all over the Midwest and further afield. The **visitor center** is at 615 E Washington Ave (Mon–Fri 8am–4.30pm; ℡608/255-2537 or 1-800/373-6376, ⓦwww.visitmadison.com).

Accommodation can be found throughout the city, though the budget chains lie to the east, off I-90/94. *Mansion Hill Inn*, 424 N Pinckney St (℡608/255-4230, ⓦwww.mansionhillinn.com; ❻–❾), is a sumptuous B&B a few blocks from the capitol offering complimentary wine service every night, while the *Madison Concourse Hotel*, 1 W Dayton St (℡608/257-6000 or 1-800/356-8293, ⓦwww. concoursehotel.com; ❺–❻) has spacious, well-appointed rooms steps from State Street. Right on Capitol Square, you can stay in one of the comfortable rooms at *The Inn on the Park*, 22 S Carroll St (℡608/257-8811 or 1-800/279-8811; ❺). There's also a *Hostelling International* location at 141 S Butler St (℡608/441-0144, ⓦwww.madisonhostel.org;), with 28 beds ($18 members/$21 non-members, 5 private rooms ($41 members/$44 non-members), and all the usual amenities: kitchen, laundry, Internet access, storage, and lockers.

The Town

Downtown is neatly laid out on an isthmus between lakes Mendota and Monona, with the white-granite **State Capitol** (tours Mon–Sat 9am–3pm excluding noon, Sun 1pm–3pm; ℡608/266-0382) sitting on a hill at its center, surrounded by shady trees, lawns, and park benches. The State Capitol square is the site of a nationally renowned **farmers' market** (late April–early Nov Sat 6am–2pm), where you can browse the local produce, and arts and crafts. Nearby, the brand-new, glassy **Overture Center**, 201 State St, hosts touring musicians, Broadway plays, and other cultural events (box office ℡608/258-4141; ⓦwww.overturecenter.com); inside, the **Madison Museum of Contemporary Art** (Tues–Wed 11am–5pm, Thurs–Fri 11am–8pm, Sat 10am–8pm, Sun noon–5pm; free; ℡608/257-0158; ⓦwww.mmoca.org), features touring exhibits.

Frank Lloyd Wright designed the **Unitarian Meeting House**, 900 University Bay Drive, in the late 1940s. Its sweeping, dramatically curved ceiling and triangle motif are definitely worth a look (May–Oct Mon–Fri 10am–4pm, Sat 9am–noon;

$3). The lakeside **Monona Terrace Community and Convention Center**, 1 John Nolen Drive, is a more recently realized example of Wright's grand vision (daily tours at 1pm; $3). Surprisingly intimate and full of architectural detail, the Center, with its curves, arches, and domes, echoes the State Capitol building just a few blocks away.

If the capitol is the city's governmental heart, the 46,000-student **University of Wisconsin** is its spirited, liberal-thinking head, now mellowed since its protest heyday in the late 1960s. The **Memorial Union**, 800 Langdon St (☎608/262-1583), holds a cafeteria and pub, the *Rathskeller*, with tables strewn beneath huge, vaulted ceilings and live music most nights. Out back, the spacious **UW Terrace** offers beautiful sunset views over Lake Mendota. Capitol and campus are arterially connected by State Street, eight tree-lined, pedestrianized blocks of restaurants, cafés, bars, and funky stores.

Eating, drinking, and entertainment

State Street is a veritable smorgasbord of **food** and **drink**, and the **Capitol Square** and **King St** areas have also seen a spate of great new restaurants open in recent years. For details of what's on, check the free weekly *Isthmus*, which comes out on Thursdays and carries full listings.

The Essen Haus 514 E Wilson St ☎608/255-4674. This raucous *biergarten* has a phenomenal selection of beers as well as rib-sticking German food.

High Noon Saloon 701 E Washington Ave ☎608/268-1122, ⓦwww.high-noon.com. Part of a complex holding multiple bars, this relative newcomer is an intimate, yet spacious, spot to see live music.

Himal Chuli 318 State St ☎608/251-9225. Tiny restaurant offering fantastic Nepalese vegetarian and vegan fare.

Marigold Kitchen 118 S Pinckney St ☎608/661-5559. Charming, sunny spot serving delicious, creative breakfast and lunch dishes – such as challah french toast and chile poached eggs – focusing on local, organic ingredients.

The Old Fashioned 23 N Pinckney St ☎608/310-4545, ⓦwww.theoldfashioned.com. Named for the state's signature brandy cocktail, this homey restaurant serves great sandwiches, traditional Wisconsin food like fried cheese curds, and a killer version of its eponymous cocktail.

The Weary Traveler 1201 Williamson St ☎608/442-6207. This eastside bar and restaurant, in the heart of the funky Williamson St neighborhood, serves creative food like the "bad breath burger" and Hungarian goulash. Hosts live music on the weekends.

Baraboo

Between 1884 and 1912, the **Ringling Brothers' Circus** kept winter quarters in **BARABOO**, thirty miles northwest of Madison. The **Circus World Museum**, 550 Water St, successfully recaptures the pre-TV glory days of big-top history, via an enormous collection of memorabilia and various animal rides and training demonstrations (hours vary seasonally; $5–15; ⓦwww.wisconsinhistory.org/circusworld/). In the town center, the **Al Ringling Theatre** (tours daily Jun–Aug, rest of year on request; $4; ☎608/356-8864), built in 1915 and modeled after the grand opera house at Versailles, is one of America's prettiest small playhouses.

Just outside of Baraboo, **Devil's Lake State Park** (☎1-888/947-2757; $10–15) is an idyllic spot for hiking, swimming, and camping; no motorboats are allowed in. On Hwy-12, stop into **Dr Evermor's** sculpture park (Mon, Thurs–Sat 9am–5pm, Sun noon–5pm; free) – a surreal metal landscape created by an eccentric local artist.

Baraboo is calmer, quieter, and more affordable than nearby Wisconsin Dells. The elegant *Victorian Gollmar Guest House B&B*, 422 Third St (☎608/356-9432, ⓦwww.gollmar.com; ❺), plays up the fact that it was once home to a circus family. More basic **rooms** are available at the *Spinning Wheel Motel*, 809 Eighth St (T 608/356-3933; ❸). *Kristina's Family Restaurant* at 506 W Pine near Hwy-12 (T 608/355-9213), serves low-cost **meals**. Baraboo's **visitor center** is at the intersection of highways 12, 33, and 136 (Mon–Fri 9am–6pm, Sat 9am–3pm; T 608/356-8333 or 1-800/227-2266, W www.baraboo.com).

Spring Green

During his seventy-year career, Wisconsin-born architect and social philosopher **Frank Lloyd Wright** designed such monumental structures as New York's spiraling Guggenheim Museum and Tokyo's earthquake-proof *Imperial Hotel*. Three miles south of **SPRING GREEN**, itself forty miles west of Madison on Hwy-14, stand more intimate examples of his work: Wright's magnificent former residence, **Taliesin**, and his **Hillside Home School**. The streamlined geometry and functional grandeur of the latter, opened in 1932, exemplify Wright's break from the boxy, fusty Victorian style. His studio is imposing, and there's also a theater space on the estate. Extensive and varied tours are available of the house and the school (May-Oct daily; reservations recommended; $16–$75). Tours leave from the **Frank Lloyd Wright Visitor Center** (T 608/588-7900, or 1-877/588-7900 W www.taliesinpreservation.org), which was designed by Wright in 1953 as a restaurant; it now features displays, a café, and a bookstore. Among numerous other Wright-influenced buildings in Spring Green are the bank and the pharmacy.

From 1944 onward, Alex Jordan built the **House on the Rock**, six miles south of Taliesin on Hwy-23, on and out of a natural, 60ft, chimney-like rock – for no discernible reason. He certainly never lived in it, nor did he intend it to become Wisconsin's number one tourist attraction (mid-March to Oct daily 9am–dusk, $11.50 per section or $26.50 for all three; Nov & Dec Christmas tours Thurs–Mon 9am–5pm; $20.50; T 800/947-2799, W www.thehouseontherock.com). Only the first section of this multilevel series of furnished nooks and chambers bears any resemblance to a house of any kind. With its low ceilings, indirect lighting, indoor pools, waterfalls, trees, and pervasive shag carpeting, the style brings to mind Frank Lloyd Wright meets *The Flintstones*. The rest of the house is a logic-free labyrinth, containing Jordan's astounding collection of collections (antiques, nickelodeons and pneumatic music machines, miniature circuses, dolls and dolls' houses, maritime memorabilia, armor and firearms, ad infinitum). The net effect is overwhelming and disorienting, alternately great fun and ghastly. Highlights include the **Infinity Room**, comprising three thousand small glass panels tapering to a point and cantilevered several hundred feet above the Wyoming Valley.

Practicalities

Spring Green is a pretty **place to stay**, but prices can be high in summer. *Round Barn Lodge*, Hwy-14 (T 608/588-2568, W www.roundbarn.com; ❹) has a pool, sauna, and restaurant on a former dairy farm. *The Usonian Inn*, Hwy-14/Hwy-23 (T 608/588-2323 or 1-877/USONIAN, W www.usonianinn.com; ❸), offers alternative, Taliesin-style lodgings. Locals hang out at *The Shed* (T 608/588-9049), an easygoing diner and bar on Lexington Street downtown. The **American Players Theatre** (T 608/588-2361, W www.americanplayers.org) performs Shakespeare and other classics in a wooded amphitheater each evening from mid-June to October.

Minnesota

Though **MINNESOTA** is more than a thousand miles from either coast, it's virtually a seaboard state, thanks to **Lake Superior**, connected to the Atlantic via the St Lawrence Seaway. The glaciers that, millions of years ago, flattened all but its southeast corner also gouged out more than fifteen thousand **lakes**, and major **rivers** run along the eastern and western borders. Ninety-five percent of the population lives within ten minutes of a body of water, and the very name Minnesota is a Sioux word meaning "land of sky-tinted water."

French explorers in the sixteenth century encountered prairies to the south and, in the north, dense forests whose abundant waterways were an ideal breeding ground for beavers and muskrats. **Fur trading**, **fishing**, and **lumbering** flourished, and the Ojibway and Sioux were eased out by waves of French, British, and American immigrants. Admitted to the Union in 1858, the new state of Minnesota was at first settled by Germans and Scandinavians, who farmed in the west and south. Other ethnic groups followed, many drawn by the massive **iron ore** deposits of north central Minnesota, which are expected to hold out for two more centuries.

More than half of Minnesota's hardy inhabitants, who endure some of the fiercest winters in the nation, live in the southeast, around the so-called Twin Cities of **Minneapolis** and **St Paul**. These attractive and basically friendly rivals together rank as the Midwest's great civic double act for their combined cultural, recreational, and business opportunities. Smaller cities include the northern shipping port of **Duluth**, the gateway to the Scenic Hwy-61 lakeshore drive, and **Rochester**, near pretty river towns like Red Wing and Winona. The tranquil waters of **Voyageurs National Park** lie halfway along the state's boundary with Canada.

In recent years, the state has earned a reputation as the "Hollywood of the North," thanks to its increased use as an affordable, talent-rich filmmaking locale. Filmmakers Joel and Ethan Coen, responsible for the Oscar-winning, Minnesota-set *Fargo*, were raised in the Twin Cities' suburb of St Louis Park.

Getting around Minnesota

Minneapolis/St Paul **airport**, home base for Northwest Airlines, handles routes to Europe as well as domestic flights. Amtrak **trains** cross the state once a day east and west from Chicago and Seattle, with stops in Winona, Red Wing, St Paul, St Cloud, Staples, and Detroit Lakes. Greyhound is the largest of the several **bus** companies plying Minnesota's roads. Five buses per day make the nine-hour journey to Chicago from the Twin Cities. Duluth, St Louis, and Kansas City are also served several times daily from the state's major metropolises.

Minneapolis and St Paul

Commonly known as the **Twin Cities**, **MINNEAPOLIS** (a hybrid Sioux/Greek word meaning "water city") and **ST PAUL** are competitive yet complementary. Fraternally rather than identically twinned, they may be even better places to live than they are to visit, thanks to their cleanliness, cultural activity, social awareness, and relatively low crime rates. Life for a majority of Twin City residents seems so vibrantly wholesome that the most significant threat would appear to be their own creeping complacency.

Only a twenty-minute expressway ride separates the respective downtowns, but each has its own character, style, and strengths. **St Paul**, the state capital – originally called Pig's Eye, after a scurrilous French-Canadian fur trader who sold whisky at a Mississippi River landing in the 1840s – is the staid, slightly older sibling, careful to preserve its buildings and traditions. The compact but stately downtown is built, like Rome, on seven hills: the **Capitol** and the **Cathedral** occupy one each, both august monuments that keep the city mindful of its responsibilities.

Minneapolis, founded on money generated by the Mississippi's hundreds of flour and saw mills, is livelier, artier, and more modern, with up-to-date architecture and an upbeat and even brash attitude that never quite jeopardizes its essential affability. The residents are spread over wider ground than in St Paul, and dozens of lakes and parks underscore the city's appeal.

Arrival, information, and getting around

Twin Cities International Airport lies about ten miles south of either city in suburban Bloomington. Super Shuttle Minneapolis (☎612/827-7777) takes travelers between the airport and major hotels for around $15, while some lodgings provide their own transportation. **Taxis** to Minneapolis will set you back close to $30, and to St Paul $25. You can also take the new light rail system (☎612/373-3333) into Minneapolis (daily 6am–1.30am: $1.50–$2.00), or bus #54 to St Paul (4am–1am: $1.50–$2.00). Amtrak is midway between the cities at 730 Transfer Rd, off University Avenue. The Greyhound terminals, both in convenient downtown locations, are at 950 Hawthorne Ave (☎612/371-3325) in Minneapolis and the less-used 166 W University Ave location (☎651/222-0507) in St Paul. Metro Transit **buses** (☎612/341-4287 or 612/373-3333) make both cities relatively easy to explore without a car. Old-style **trolleys** run through downtown Minneapolis during the summer; it costs $17 for an all-day pass.

In Minneapolis, the **visitor center** is at 250 Marquette Ave (Mon–Fri 8am–5pm; ☎612/767-8000 or 1-888/676-MPLS, ⓦwww.minneapolis.org). In St Paul, it's at 175 W Kellogg Blvd, suite 502 (☎651/265-4900 or 1-800/627-6101, ⓦwww.visitsaintpaul.com). The main Minneapolis **post office** is on First Street and Marquette Avenue (zip code 55401), St Paul's at 180 Kellogg Blvd E (zip code 55101).

Accommodation

You're likely to pay more for lodgings downtown than in the suburbs, where dozens of cheap **motels** line I-494 near the airport, though some of the pricier central hotels offer reduced rates and special package deals on weekends. The pretty riverside community of **Stillwater**, 25 miles from St Paul via I-35 N and Hwy-36 E, has many grand old B&Bs and motels (☎651/439-4001 for information). For **bed-and-breakfast** options in the Twin Cities, consult ⓦwww.bedandbreakfast.com, as many B&Bs do not have their own websites.

Minneapolis

Birdhouse Inn & Gardens 371 Water St, Excelsior ☎952/474-0196. This suburban B&B a few blocks from Lake Minnetonka offers good prices and a homey atmosphere. ❹

Evelo's B&B 2301 Bryant Ave S ☎612/374-9656. Three comfortable rooms in a well-preserved Victorian home near bus lines, lakes, and downtown. Nonsmoking only. ❹

Hotel Amsterdam 828 Hennepin Ave ☎612/288-0459. Friendly, low-cost gay-owned hotel above a noise-controlled bar/disco downtown. ❸

Hilton Minneapolis 1001 Marquette Ave ☎612/376-1000, ⓦwww.minneapolis.hilton.com. Elegant downtown spot with a great gym and pool. Weekend rates are considerably less. ❻–❽

Le Blanc House 302 University Ave NE ☎612/379-2570, ⓦwww.leblanchouse.com.

Fancy Victorian home just minutes from downtown. Serves gourmet breakfasts on the weekend and continental fare during the week. ⑤

Minneapolis International House 2400 Stevens Ave ☎612/522-5000, ⓦwww.minneapolishostel.com. This conveniently situated independent hostel has $35–55 private rooms and $25 dorm beds.

Nicollet Island Inn 95 Merriam St ☎612/331-1800, ⓦwww.nicolletislandinn.com. Pricey, mid-river establishment with the edge on other downtown hotels because of its delightful location and excellent restaurant. ⑧–⑨

St Paul

Best Western Bandana Square 1010 Bandana Blvd W ☎651/647-1637, ⓦwww.hibandanasquare.com. Housed in a former railroad car repair shop and includes a nice indoor pool and sauna. ⑤

Chatsworth B&B 984 Ashland Ave ☎651/227-4288, ⓦwww.chatsworth-bb.com. A beautiful 1902 home now run as a welcoming B&B. ⑤–⑥

The Covington Inn Pier 1, Harriet Island ☎651/292-1411, ⓦwww.covingtoninn.com. A one-of-a-kind B&B in a converted towboat facing downtown. ⑥–⑧

Embassy Suites 175 E 10th St ☎651/224-5400 or 1-800/EMBASSY, ⓦwww.embassystpaul.com. The tropical atrium is the outstanding feature of this comfortable chain hotel on the edge of downtown. ⑥

The Saint Paul Hotel 350 Market St ☎651/292-9292 or 1-800/292-9292, ⓦwww.stpaulhotel.com. This grand, 1910 establishment is Minnesota's top hotel. Rooms tend to be smaller than those of other luxury hotels, but the staff and atmosphere make up for it. The *St Paul Grill*, in the hotel, provides some of the city's finest dining, while the classy bar has tons of great scotches and cognacs. ⑥

DOWNTOWN MINNEAPOLIS

0   400 yds

Theatre de la Jeune Lune

Mississippi River

3RD AVE BRIDGE

St Anthony Falls

Mississippi Mile

WAREHOUSE DISTRICT

Greyhound Terminal

Guthrie Theater

Historic Orpheum Theater

Historic State Theater

IDS Center

Hubert H. Humphrey Metrodome

Elliot Park

ACCOMMODATION
Hilton Minneapolis **C**
Hotel Amsterdam **B**
Nicollet Island Inn **A**

RESTAURANTS, BARS & CLUBS		
112 Eatery	4	
Café Brenda	6	
The Dakota Jazz Club & Restaurant	13	
Fine Line	5	
First Avenue and 7th St Entry	11	
Gay 90s	9	
Loon Café	8	
Monte Carlo	3	
Moose & Sadie's Café and Coffee	2	
Nye's Polonaise Room	1	
Palomino	12	
Pizza Luce	7	
Sawatdee	10	

Minneapolis Institute of Arts

Loring Park, Walker Art Center & Minneapolis Sculpture Garden

Exploring Minneapolis

Downtown Minneapolis is laid out on a simple grid. The riverfront, dubbed the **Mississippi Mile**, continues to be developed as a place for strolling, dining, and entertainment. The vast Third Avenue Bridge makes an ideal vantage point for viewing **St Anthony Falls**, a controlled torrent in a wide stretch of the river. The missionary Father Hennepin discovered the falls in 1680, but it wasn't until the early nineteenth century that the first permanent settlement of present-day Minneapolis was begun nearby.

Downtown's major stores line up along the pedestrianized **Nicollet Mall**. **Hennepin Avenue**, the other main drag, is a block west. It has been revitalized as an entertainment district in recent years thanks, in part, to the beautifully restored **Orpheum** and **State theaters**, twin hosts to top-quality Broadway shows and concerts. The ultra-modern **Guthrie Theater**, 818 S Second St (℡612/377-2224 or 1-877/44-STAGE; ⓦwww.guthrietheater.org), opened in 2006 on the riverfront. Even if you can't make it to one of the classic or brand-new stage productions, presented on one of the venue's three stages, the building itself is still worth a look.

Culturally, Minneapolis would be poorer without the **Walker Art Center**, 1750 Hennepin Ave S (Tues, Wed, Sat & Sun 11am–5pm, Thurs–Fri 11am–9pm; $8, free Thurs 5–9pm and 1st Sat of month; ℡612/375-7622, ⓦwww.walkerart. org). This multipurpose contemporary art and performance space underwent an expansion in 2005, nearly doubling its exhibition area. The museum balances its permanent collection of sculpture and paintings (such as German Expressionist Franz Marc's *Blue Horses*) with exciting temporary exhibitions. The eleven-acre outdoor **Sculpture Garden** is a work of collective genius featuring pieces by Calder, Louise Bourgeois, and Frank Gehry. Its most striking piece is the gigantic, whimsical *Spoonbridge and Cherry* by Claes Oldenburg and Coosje van Bruggen. One mile from downtown, at 2400 Third Ave S, the huge **Minneapolis Institute of Arts** has a thoroughly comprehensive collection of art from 2000 BC to the present (Tues, Wed, Fri & Sat 10am–5pm, Thurs 10am–9pm, Sun 11am–5pm; free; ℡612/870-3200, ⓦwww.artsmia.org). Antiques, crafts, and artifacts fill the exquisite 1908 mansion setting of the nearby **American Swedish Institute**, 2600 Park Ave S (Tues, Thurs, Fri & Sat noon–4pm, Wed noon–8pm, Sun 1–5pm; $6; ℡612/871-4907, ⓦwww.americanswedishinstitute.org). In stark contrast, changing exhibitions and the University of Minnesota's permanent art collection share space in the controversial **Frederick R. Weisman Museum**, on campus at 333 E River Rd (Tues, Wed & Fri 10am–5pm, Thurs 10am–8pm, Sat & Sun 11am–5pm; free; ⓦwww.weisman.umn.edu). Architect Frank Gehry's airy structure, with its boldly irregular stainless-steel west facade overlooking the Mississippi, is the most startling love-it-or-hate-it design in the cities.

Arctic winters aside, hordes of Minneapolitans flock to the shores of lakes **Calhoun** and **Harriet** and also **Lake of the Isles**, all in residential areas within two miles south of downtown. The **Hubert H. Humphrey Metrodome**, 900 S Fifth St (℡612/332-0386), squats on the eastern edge of downtown like a giant white pincushion; the dome is home to the state's pro baseball and football teams, the Twins and the Vikings. **Minnehaha Falls**, south of downtown, was featured in Longfellow's 1855 poem "*Song of Hiawatha*" without his ever having laid eyes on it. The adjacent park is a favorite spot for hikes and picnics.

Exploring St Paul

St Paul, Minnesota's capital city, reached along I-94, has more expensive old homes and civic monuments than Minneapolis. The city has its own landing site

DOWNTOWN ST PAUL

RESTAURANTS, BARS & CLUBS	
Mancini's	8
McGovern's	6
Mickey's Dining Car	3
Moscow on the Hill	4
St Paul Grill	5
Tom Reid's Hockey City Pub	7
Town House	1
Trattoria DaVinci	2

ACCOMMODATION	
The Covington Inn	B
Embassy Suites	A
The Saint Paul Hotel	5

on Harriet Island for narrated summertime **paddleboat** cruises (summer noon and 2pm; $15; ☎651/227-1100 or 1-800/543-3908, ⓦwww.riverrides.com). Here, as well as in Minneapolis, downtown buildings are linked via skyways. Call in at the jazzy Art Deco lobby of the **City Hall and Courthouse**, Fourth and Wabasha streets, to see Swedish sculptor Carl Milles' revolving 36ft *Vision of Peace*, carved in the 1930s from white Mexican onyx. The castle-like **Landmark Center**, a couple of blocks away at Fifth and Market streets, and the glittering **Ordway Center for the Performing Arts** both overlook Rice Park, probably the prettiest little square in either city. A sculpture garden with characters from Charles Schulz's "Peanuts" comic strip, the artist himself a St. Paul native, has been added to **Schulz Park** next to the Landmark Center. A few blocks east, **Town Square Park** is a lush, multilevel indoor garden in a shopping complex at Minnesota and Sixth streets. The gorgeous granite and limestone **Minnesota History Center**, 345 W Kellogg Blvd (Tues 10am–8pm, Wed–Sat 10am–5pm, Sun noon–5pm; open Mon in summer; $8; ☎888/727-8386, ⓦwww.mnhs.org), with its extensive research facilities and some inventive exhibits for the more casual visitor, is the best place to grasp the state's story. An immense steel iguana is the doorkeeper at the exciting hands-on **Science Museum of Minnesota**, 120 W Kellogg Blvd (Mon–Wed 9.30am–

5pm, Thurs–Sat 9.30am–9pm, Sun 10.30am–5.30pm; $13.50; ☎651/221-9444, ⓦwww.smm.org), which also has a domed Omnitheater (entry included in ticket) where you can see giant-screen films. Or check out the **Minneapolis Children's Museum**, 10 W Seventh St (Tues–Thurs and Sat–Sun 9am–5pm, Fri till 8pm; open Mon 9am–5pm summer only; $7.95; ☎651/225-6000, ⓦwww.mcm.org), where even big kids will be diverted by the interactive galleries.

A well-preserved five-mile Victorian boulevard, Summit Avenue, leads away from downtown. **F. Scott Fitzgerald**, who was born close by, finished his first success, *This Side of Paradise*, in 1918 while living in a modest row house at no. 599. He disparaged the avenue as a "museum of American architectural failures." Look for the coffin atop no. 465, once the home of an undertaker, and visit the **James J. Hill House** at no. 240, a railroad baron's sumptuous mansion from around 1891 (tours every half-hour Wed–Sat 10am–3.30pm and Sun 1pm–3:30pm; $8; reservations recommended; ☎651/297-2555). Minnesota's first territorial governor **Alexander Ramsey**'s house, nearby at 265 S Exchange St, remains a showcase of Victorian high style (tours on the hour Fri & Sat 10am–3pm, summer also Tues–Thurs 1pm; $7; ☎651/296-8760; reservations recommended).

The costumed staff does a fine job of interpreting Minnesota's frontier past at **Fort Snelling** (May, Sept, Oct Sat 10am–5pm, Sun noon–5pm, June–Aug Mon–Sat 10am–5pm, Sun noon–5pm; $8; ☎612/726-1171), near the airport off highways 5 and 55. Built between 1819 and 1825 on a strategic bluff at the confluence of the Mississippi and Minnesota rivers, this was Minnesota's first permanent structure – a successful attempt by the US government to establish an official presence in the wilderness that had recently been won from Great Britain. Another good bet is the venerable and picturesque **Como Park Zoo and Conservatory**, reached by taking I-94 to the Lexington Avenue exit, then continuing north on Lexington for about three miles (daily: April–Sept 10am–6pm; rest of year 10am–4pm; $2 donation requested; ☎651/487-8200). Farther afield, in suburban Apple Valley, off Hwy-775 is the spacious, highly regarded **Minnesota Zoo** (daily June–Sept 9am–6pm, rest of the year 9am–4pm; $13, $5 parking fee; ☎952/431-9200, ⓦwww.mnzoo.org), where the animals reside in reconstructions of their natural habitats. The Komodo dragon exhibit, Imation IMAX Theater, and Discovery Bay aquatic center, in particular, are outstanding.

Annual celebrations in St Paul include the **Taste of Minnesota** (tons of food, live entertainment, rides, and fireworks) running from late June to July 4 on Harriet Island and the nation's largest **State Fair** (end of Aug to early Sept). The **Winter Carnival** (late Jan to early Feb) is a frosty gala designed to make the most of the season with ice and snow sculpturing, hot-air ballooning, team sports, parades, and more.

The Mall of America

Shopping addicts make the pilgrimage to the **Mall of America** from all over the Midwest – and far beyond, including parties from as far away as Japan. Opened in 1992, this mind-boggling 4.2-million-square-foot, four-story monument to consumerism tallied 42 million visits in a recent year. It incorporates more than five hundred stores, with a seven-acre theme park – the pay-per-ride Camp Snoopy. Featured rides include **UnderWater Adventures** ($16.95), with 1.2 million gallons of water and amazing Gulf of Mexico and Caribbean aquariums. Evidence of the Mall's all-under-one-roof convenience is provided by the **Chapel of Love** retail store, where more than five thousand couples have legitimately tied the knot. The mall is open Monday through Saturday 10am–9.30pm, Sunday 11am–7pm, (☎952/883-8800, ⓦwww.mallofamerica.com).

The Mall is twenty minutes south of the cities on I-494 at 24th Avenue, Bloomington. Take bus #54M from St Paul's West Sixth Street at Cedar, the #5E bus or the light rail from downtown Minneapolis; catch the train from 5th St on Nicollet Mall.

Eating

Preconceptions of Midwestern blandness are swiftly put to rest by an almost bewildering array of **restaurants** in the Twin Cities. In **Minneapolis**, head for the downtown warehouse district, the southerly Nicollet neighborhood, the funky Uptown, and Lyn-Lake areas, or the university's Dinkytown. In **St Paul**, try Galtier Plaza downtown, the Asian restaurants on University Avenue, or the horde of ethnic options all along Grand Avenue.

Minneapolis

112 Eatery 112 N 3rd St ☎612/343-7696. This small, upscale café serves an inventive mix of American and Continental dishes, from pork tenderloin to sautéed sweetbreads.

Broder's Cucina Italiana 2308 W 50th St ☎612/925-3113. Terrific deli offering eat-in or takeout, with a full-service restaurant across the street.

Bryant-Lake Bowl 810 W Lake St ☎612/825-3737. Bowling and fantastic food rarely go hand-in-hand, but this Lyn-Lake institution manages to do both well, turning out such creative dishes as organic chicken wings and a bison Philly sandwich.

Café Brenda 300 1st Ave N ☎612/342-9230. Excellent, moderately priced *nouvelle* vegetarian cuisine in the downtown warehouse district.

Emily's Lebanese Deli 641 University Ave NE ☎612/379-4069. Friendly, low-cost local place for Lebanese staples.

La Belle Vie 510 Groveland Ave, ☎612/874-6440. Sophisticated Mediterranean fare, including a goat cheese tart and seared sea scallops, served in a posh setting. Both prix fixe and à la carte menus are available – pricey, but worth it.

Modern Café 337 13th Ave NE ☎612/378-9882. Eclectic, cheap, and flavorful food in a former neighborhood diner gone hip.

Monte Carlo 219 3rd Ave N ☎612/333-5900. Locals swear by this century-old steakhouse. Expect to pay around $20 for an entree.

Moose & Sadie's Café and Coffee 212 3rd Ave N, ☎612/371-0464. This great breakfast and brunch spot in the warehouse district serves delicious baked goods and creative soups like coconut milk curry.

Palomino 825 Hennepin Ave ☎612/339-3800. Stylish, popular downtown bistro specializing in Mediterranean fare.

Pizza Luce 119 N 4th St ☎612/333-7359. The decor is no-frills, but the staff is hip and the pizza is excellent.

Sawatdee 607 Washington Ave S ☎612/373-0840. Delicious Thai food, with main courses ranging from $8 to $15. There are several branches in the Twin Cities.

St Paul

Mancini's 531 W 7th St ☎651/224-7345. Great Italian steakhouse with an old-school, supper-club feel.

Mickey's Dining Car 36 W 7th St ☎651/698-0259. Landmark 24hr diner in a 1930s dining car.

Moscow on the Hill 371 Selby Ave ☎651/291-1236. Exquisite Russo-European food is served within a modest setting.

St Paul Grill 350 Market St ☎651/292-9292. Traditional American fare in a classic downtown hotel.

Trattoria DaVinci 400 Sibley St ☎651/222-4050. Exceptional Northern Italian cuisine served in an Italian Renaissance-inspired setting.

W.A. Frost Selby and Western Aves ☎651/224-5715. This former pharmacy and F. Scott Fitzgerald hangout has been converted into a plush restaurant with a garden patio. The menu spans Mediterranean, Asian, and Middle Eastern cuisines and features dishes like mushroom Wellington and squash ravioli; the wine cellar stocks some 3000 bottles.

Entertainment and nightlife

The Greater Twin Cities have been dubbed a "cultural Eden on the prairie," where 2.5 million people support upwards of one hundred **theater** companies, more than forty **dance** troupes, twenty **classical music** ensembles, and more than a hundred art galleries. Sir Tyrone Guthrie began the theatrical boom back in 1963, enrolling large-scale local assistance to establish the classical repertory company named for him. The cities now have more theaters per capita than anywhere in the US apart from New York City.

Unusually, **nightlife** in Minneapolis (and, to a lesser extent, St Paul) hasn't been siphoned off by suburbia – one hundred thousand students ensure a vibrant club scene. For complete entertainment **information and listings**, check out the ubiquitous free weekly *City Pages*. *Lavender* and *focusPOINT* provide a similar service from a lesbian and gay perspective.

Minneapolis and St Paul theaters

Chanhassen Dinner Theater 501 W 78th St, Chanhassen ☏ 952/934-1525 or 1-800/362-3515. Mainstream musicals, popular comedies, and drama on four stages, plus meals. Thirty minutes from downtown.

Fitzgerald Theater 10 E Exchange St, St Paul ☏ 651/290-1200, ⓦ www.fitzgeraldtheater.org. Best known as the venue for Garrison Keillor's weekly *A Prairie Home Companion* performance, it also hosts other concerts and lectures.

Great American History Theater 30 E 10th St, St Paul ☏ 651/292-4323, ⓦ www.historytheatre.com. Original plays deal with events and personalities from the region's past.

Jungle Theater 2951 S Lyndale Ave S, Minneapolis ☏ 612/822-7063, ⓦ www.jungletheater.com. Theater/cabaret putting on an eclectic mix of classic and contemporary plays.

Park Square 20 W 7th Pl, St Paul ☏ 651/291-7005, ⓦ www.parksquaretheatre.org. The venue for well-executed classic and contemporary plays.

Penumbra 270 N Kent St, St Paul ☏ 651/224-3180, ⓦ www.penumbratheatre.org. African-American theater company focusing on works by African-American playwrights.

Red Eye Collaboration 15 W 14th St, Minneapolis ☏ 612/870-0309, ⓦ www.theredeye.org. Arts center dedicated to experimental theater, as well as dance, film, and music.

Theatre de la Jeune Lune 1st St and 1st Ave, Minneapolis ☏ 612/333-6200, ⓦ www.jeunelune.org. A unique ensemble of Parisians and Minneapolitans offer dynamic, highly physical productions based on *commedia dell'arte*, vaudeville, and the like.

Minneapolis bars and clubs

The Dakota Jazz Club and Restaurant 1010 Nicollet Mall ☏ 612/332-1010, ⓦ www.dakotacooks.com. Gourmet Midwestern food and great local and national jazz acts downtown.

Figlio Calhoun Square, 3001 Hennepin Ave ☏ 612/822-1688. Top late-night dining and people-watching venue, with a menu featuring Italian staples.

Fine Line 318 1st Ave N ☏ 612/338-8100. Sleek, small, and musically eclectic downtown club.

First Avenue and 7th St Entry 701 1st Ave ☏ 612/338-8388 or 332-1775, ⓦ www.first-avenue.com. The landmark rock venue where Prince's *Purple Rain* was shot still packs them in with top bands and dance music.

Gay 90s 408 Hennepin Ave S ☏ 612/333-7755. This sprawling, predominantly gay club has three dance floors, a piano lounge, dining, and polished weekend drag shows.

Loon Café 500 1st Ave N ☏ 612/332-8342. Try the chili at this noisy, likeable sports bar, which offers great food.

Nye's Polonaise Room 112 E Hennepin Ave ☏ 612/379-2021. Experience old-time atmosphere at the piano and polka bars, and in the Polish-American restaurant.

St Paul bars and clubs

McGovern's 225 W 7th St ☏ 651/224-5821. A quintessential Irish pub where you're likely to strike up some decent conversation.

Muddy Pig 162 N Dale St ☏ 651/254-1030. A hip neighborhood joint with good bar food and a wide selection of microbrews.

O'Gara's Bar and Grill 164 N Snelling Ave ☏ 651/644-3333, ⓦ www.ogaras.com. Dimly lit bar/restaurant with its own handcrafted beers. Draws a mixed clientele and hosts live bands in the adjoining *Garage*.

Tom Reid's Hockey City Pub 258 W 7th St ☏ 651/292-9916. This pre- and post-game hangout is where locals gather to honor the state's favorite sport.

Town House 1415 University Ave ☏ 651/646-7087. Gay/lesbian bar with dance and drag nights, plus a piano lounge.

Northern Minnesota

Minnesota's substantial **northern** half, covered with forested lakes, remains much as it was when the Europeans first traded with the Indians. The northeast – **the Arrowhead**, poking into Lake Superior – holds the greatest charm: most visitors choose secluded outdoor vacations centered on fishing, canoeing, and snowmobiling, but there's infinite potential for driving tours in a wilderness comparable to the Alaskan interior.

The Arrowhead is anchored by busy **Duluth**. From here, **Scenic Hwy-61** skirts the clifftops around Lake Superior, passing waterfalls, state parks, and neat little towns on the way northeast to the Canadian border. Sleepy **Grand Marais** is poised at the edge of the wild **Boundary Waters Canoe Area Wilderness** and the **Gunflint Trail**, while inland, the **Iron Range** makes a scenic route north to the idyllic **Voyageurs National Park**. To the southwest, in **Itasca State Park**, the Mississippi River begins its great roll down to the Gulf of Mexico; you can cross the headwaters on stepping-stones. Everywhere you'll find campgrounds and mom-and-pop lakeside **resorts**, havens of homey simplicity dedicated to soothing urban-ravaged souls.

Duluth

DULUTH, at the western extremity of Lake Superior, 150 miles north of Minneapolis and St Paul, forms a long crescent at the base of the Arrowhead. Named for a seventeenth-century French officer, Daniel Greysolon, Sieur du Luth (1636–1710), the town cascades down from the granite bluffs surrounding **Skyline Drive** (an exhilarating thirty-mile route) to a busy **harbor**, shared with Superior, Wisconsin. Together these "twin ports" constitute the largest inland harbor in the US.

In the 1980s, Duluth had a face-lift and began to encourage tourism. The main drawback is that it's **cold** here. The seaway is frozen through the winter, and even spring and fall evenings can be chilly. Temperatures are always significantly cooler near the lake – the location of nearly all the attractions and activities.

From the Convention and Visitors Bureau (see below), a short walk down Lake Avenue leads to the free **Marine Museum** (June to early Oct daily 10am–9pm; rest of year times vary; ☎218/727-2497, ⓦwww.lsmma.com) in Canal Park, a vantage point for watching big boats from around the world pass under the delightfully archaic Aerial Lift Bridge. Originating at Canal Park, Duluth's **Lakewalk** is the free way to take in the view, though in summer you can also take one and one half-hour **harbor cruises** ($12; ☎218/722-6218 or 1-877/883-4002; ⓦwww.vistafleet.com). Also worthwhile is a visit to the stately lakeside Jacobean Revival mansion **Glensheen**, 3300 London Rd (May–Oct daily 9.30am–4pm; Nov–April Sat–Sun 11am–2pm; $12; ☎218/726-8910 or 1-888/454-GLEN). The vast interior features finely crafted original furnishings, and the grounds are immaculate.

Rail excursions along the Superior shoreline to the busy harbor community **Two Harbors** run from **The Depot** complex at 506 W Michigan St (early May to mid-Oct; $12 for 90min, $20 for 6hr; ☎218/722-1273 or 1-800/423-1273, ⓦwww.lsrm.org). The Depot (summer 9.30am–6pm; winter 10am–5pm; $10) also houses the Lake Superior Railroad Museum, a children's museum, cultural heritage center, and art museum; at night, it's home to performing arts companies. From the parking lot at Grand Avenue and 71st Avenue W, across from the zoo, the historic **Lake Superior and Mississippi Railroad** takes a 90min journey along the scenic St Louis River (mid-June to early Oct Sat & Sun 10.30am & 1.30pm; $9.25; ☎218/624-7549, ⓦwww.lsmrr.org). Duluth's Spirit Mountain **ski area** (☎1-800/642-6377, ⓦwww.spiritm.com) boasts the best downhill runs in the Midwest.

Practicalities

Greyhound **buses** pull into town four miles south of town just off I-35 at 4426 Grand Ave. The **Convention and Visitors Bureau** is at 21 W Superior St Suite 100 (Mon–Fri 8:30am–5pm; ☎218/722-4011 or 1-800/4-DULUTH, ⓦwww.

visitduluth.com). For a **place to stay**, the *Charles Weiss Inn*, 1615 E Superior St (☎218/724-7016 or 1-800/525-5243; ⑤), is a nice Victorian-styled **B&B**, while better **motels** include the *Edgewater Resort and Waterpark*, 2400 London Rd (☎218/728-3601 or 1-800/777-7925; ⓦwww.duluthwaterpark.com; ④–⑤), which has a new indoor water park. Keep in mind that accommodation rates and availability fluctuate in summer. *Indian Point* **campground**, west off Hwy-23 at 75th Street and Grand Avenue (☎218/624-5637), has summer bayside tent sites for $19; full hook-ups are also available.

The burgers and pasta at *Grandma's Saloon And Grill*, in view of the bridge at 522 Lake Ave S (☎218/727-4192), are filling and tasty. *Grandma's Sports Garden*, across a parking lot at no. 425 (☎218/722-4724), is similarly convivial, dishing up good food when not functioning as a dance floor on Wednesday, Friday, and Saturday nights starting at 10pm. Best of all are the revolving *Top of the Harbor*, serving American cuisine atop the *Radisson Hotel* at 505 W Superior St (☎218/727-8981), and the lovely *Bennett's on the Lake*, 600 E Superior St (☎218/722-2829), where you can dine on steaks and seafood with a superb view of the lake.

North from Duluth: Highway 61

Memorialized on vinyl by Minnesota native Bob Dylan, stunning **Scenic Highway 61** follows Lake Superior for 150 miles northeast from Duluth to the US/Canadian border, its precipitous cliffs interspersed with pretty little ports and picture-postcard picnic sites.

At **Gooseberry River State Park**, forty miles along from Duluth, the river splashes over volcanic rock through waterfalls and cascades to its outlet in Lake Superior. Like all but one of the seven other state parks along Hwy-61, it provides access to the rugged three-hundred-mile **Superior Hiking Trail** (☎218/834-2700), divided into easily manageable segments for day-trekkers. To camp at any of the state parks, reserve at ☎1-866/857-2757.

Just beyond **Cascade River State Park**, the road dips into the somnolent little port of **GRAND MARAIS**, where a walk around the photogenic Circular Harbor will soon cure car-stiff legs. The **visitor center**, 13 N Broadway (☎218/387-2524 or 1-888/922-5000, ⓦwww.grandmarais.com), has lists of **outfitters** for those going into the Boundary Waters Canoe Area Wilderness (see below). An inexpensive **room** option is the *Mangy Moose Motel* on Hwy-61 (☎218/387-2975 or 1-800/796-2975; ③), while *Naniboujou Lodge*, fifteen miles further east (☎218/387-2688, ⓦwww.naniboujou.com; ④), is a bit pricier, but worth dropping by just to see the restaurant's eye-popping Cree Indian designs. For herring and imported beer, or just a well-priced **snack**, head for *Sven & Ole's Pizza*, 9 W Wisconsin St, in Grand Marais (☎218/387-1713).

The town of **GRAND PORTAGE**, just below the Canadian border, is at the lake end of the historic 8.5-mile portage route – so vital to the nineteenth-century fur trade – now preserved in the form of **Grand Portage National Monument**, where a clutch of fur-trade era buildings has been superbly reconstructed (summer daily 9am–5pm; ☎218/387-2788). In town, residents of the Grand Portage Indian Reservation operate a **casino**. In summer, ferries run daily to remote **Isle Royale National Park** (see p.343).

Boundary Waters Canoe Area Wilderness and the Gunflint Trail

The huge **Boundary Waters Canoe Area Wilderness**, west of Grand Marais, is one of the most heavily used wilderness areas in the country. It's accessible from Tofte, Cook, and especially from easygoing **Ely**, home of the intriguing **Inter-**

national **Wolf Center** (hours vary; ☎218/365-4695; $7.50). The wilderness is a paradise for canoeing, backpacking, and fishing. Overland trails, or "portages," link more than a thousand lakes; in winter you can ski and dogsled cross-country. The unpaved sixty-mile **Gunflint Trail** from Grand Marais cuts the wilderness in two; otherwise there are no roads in this outback, let alone electricity or telephones. Most lakes remain motor-free, and stringent rules limit entry to the wilderness: in summer you need a date-specific **permit** that local outfitters can issue. For the following year, permit applications may be submitted by website, fax, or mail beginning November 1; in January, they are processed by lottery. Phone reservations are accepted beginning February 1 ($12 reservation fee and a $20 deposit; ☎1-877/550-6777, ⊕518/884-9951, ⊛www.bwcaw.org). For those who don't want to rough it, several rustic lodges lie strung out along the trail; the **Gunflint Trail Association** (☎218/387-3191 or 1-800/338-6932, ⊛www.gunflint-trail.com) can offer good advice.

The Iron Range

In the **Iron Range**, a few miles west of Ely, which is itself about one hundred miles west of Grand Marais, a number of fabulously rich mines continue to function more than a century after their construction. If you're interested in surveying old workings, it's possible to descend 2300ft at the **Soudan Underground Mine State Park** on Hwy-169 (summer daily 10am–4pm; $9, plus $8 vehicle fee).

Eighty miles southwest on Hwy-169 is **Hibbing** – a plain little community, of interest mainly as the birthplace of Bob Dylan (born Robert Zimmerman) in 1941. Oddly enough, the museum in City Hall has no exhibits on him.

Extensive strip-mining in the city has created both the largest man-made pit and the largest slagheap in the world. Hibbing was also the home of America's biggest bus company. With the help of model buses and old advertisements the **Greyhound Origin Center**, 1201 Greyhound Blvd (mid-May to end Sept Mon–Sat 9am–5pm, Sun 1pm–5pm; $4), looks back to its roots transporting local miners to and from the pits. The Hull–Rust Mahoning Mine, once the world's largest open-pit iron ore mine, can be toured or viewed from an overlook just past the Center (mid-May–beginning Sept daily 9am–6pm; free).

Voyageurs National Park

Set along the border lakes between Minnesota and Canada, **VOYAGEURS NATIONAL PARK** is like no other in the US national park system. To see it properly, or indeed to grasp its immense beauty at all, you need to leave your car behind and venture into the wild by boat. Once out on the lakes, you're in a great, silent world. Kingfishers, osprey, and eagles swoop down for their share of the abundant walleye; moose and bear stalk the banks.

The park's name comes from the intrepid eighteenth-century French-Canadian trappers, who needed almost a year to get their pelts back to Montréal in primitive birch bark canoes. Their "customary waterway" became so established that the treaty of 1783 ending the American Revolution specified it as the international border.

You can't do Voyageurs justice on a day-trip, though daily cruises from the **Rainy Lake visitor center** (open daily mid-May–Sept 9am–5pm, Oct–mid-May Wed–Sun 9am–5pm; from $12-15 for a range of tours; ☎218/286-5258 ⊛www.nps.gov/voya) do at least allow a peek at the lake country. If you're here for a few days, rent a **boat** (reckon on $50 a day) and camp out. It's easy to get lost in this maze of islands and rocky outcrops, and unseen sandbanks lurk beneath the surface. If you're at all unsure, hire a guide from one of the resorts for the first day (around $250 per 8hr day). During **freeze-up** – usually from December until March – the park takes on a whole new aura, as a prime destination for skiers and snowmobilers.

Practicalities

Most travelers access Voyageurs from Hwy-53, which runs northwest from Duluth. After just over one hundred miles, at Orr, Hwy-53 intersects with Rte-23, which runs northeast toward **Crane Lake**, at the eastern end of the park. About 28 and 31 miles past Hwy-53's junction with Rte-23, highways 129 and 122 lead, respectively, to the **visitor centers** at **Ash River** (May–Sept daily 9am–5pm; ☎218/374-3221) and **Kabetogama Lake** (same hours; ☎218/875-2111). Another prime visitor center is at **Rainy Lake**, at the westernmost entrance, 36 miles farther on via International Falls.

Once inside the park, you need to take a few **precautions**. Check (natural) mercury levels in fish before eating them, don't pick wild rice (only Native Americans may do this), be wary of Lyme Disease (a tick-induced gastric illness), boil drinking water, and watch out for bears. Discuss such matters along with customs procedures, in case you plan to paddle into Canadian waters, with a ranger before venturing out.

The definitive way to experience the park is to **camp** on one of its many scattered islands, most plentiful around Crane Lake (if you don't have your own boat, cruise operators can drop you off and pick you up at a later date). There are also first-come, first-served state-owned campgrounds on the mainland at Ash River and Woodenfrog, near Kabetogama. However, most visitors stay in one of more than sixty **resorts**. Basically family-run cottages, these usually cater for weekly stays, with all meals, though you can rent rooms nightly. Most popular are those around Kabetogama, such as *Carlson's Harmony Beach* (☎218/875-2811, Ⓦwww.harmonybeachresort.com; ❺–❻); *Arrowhead Lodge* (☎218/875-2141 or 1-866/847-7118, Ⓦwww.arrowheadlodgeresort.com; ❸), well known for its restaurant; and the basic, cheap, and cheerful *Driftwood Lodge* (☎218/875-3841, Ⓦwww.driftwoodlodgeresort.com; call for weekly rates). You can make reservations through the Kabetogama Lake Association (☎1-800/524-9085, Ⓦwww.kabetogama.com).

Southern Minnesota

Southern Minnesota is split between high plains, timbered ravines, and slow-flowing Mississippi tributaries in the east, and the drier, flatter prairie and checkerboard farmland of the west. In the scenic **southeast**, spared a grinding-down by the last glacial advance, attractive small towns sit along the Mississippi, or on bluffs above it, in the ninety-mile **Hiawatha Valley**. Mississippi shipping helped sustain easygoing communities like Winona, Red Wing, Lake City, and Wabasha, all of which share well-preserved old homes and hotels. **Rochester** occupies the rolling farmland to the west.

Rochester

The metropolis of **ROCHESTER**, a white-collar community in a rural setting about eighty miles southeast of Minneapolis and St Paul, was settled in the 1850s by migrants from Rochester, New York, as a humble crossroads campground for wagon trains. After a tornado devastated the town in 1883, Dr William Worral Mayo established the huge **Mayo Clinic**, 200 First St SW (☎507/284-

2511, ⓦwww.mayoclinic.org). Free tours serve as ninety-minute promotions for "the first and largest private group medical practice in the world" (Mon–Fri 10am; art tour Mon–Fri 1.30pm). You can also tour the sprawling family home, **Mayowood**, 3720 Mayowood Rd southwest of Hwy-52 (May to mid-June Sat & Sun at 1pm, 2pm & 3pm, plus Sat at 11am; mid-June to Oct Tues, Thurs, Sat & Sun same hours; $10; ⓣ507/282-9447).

Jefferson Union Bus Depot, 205 6th St SW (ⓣ507/289-4037), is the hub for **bus services**. Rochester Direct (ⓣ507/280-9270 or 1-800/280-9270) make between ten and eleven van runs daily to the Minneapolis–St Paul International Airport or the Mall of America for $27 one way, $49 roundtrip or $34 for same-day round-trip. Rochester's **visitor center** is at 111 S Broadway Suite 301 (ⓣ507/288-4331 or 1-800/634-8277, ⓦwww.visitrochestermn.com).

Rochester is rife with chain and budget **accommodation**, especially within the five-block radius of downtown, including the *Kahler Hotel*, 20 SW Second Ave (ⓣ507/282-2581 or 1-800/533-1655, ⓦwww.kahler.com/grand; ❹–❺). *The Broadstreet Café and Bar*, 300 First Ave NW (ⓣ507/281-2451), a bistro in a reno-vated warehouse, serves excellent **meals**.

Pipestone National Monument

The town of **PIPESTONE**, eight miles east of the South Dakota border, is named for a soft red clay, within the local quartzite, that was used for centuries by Great Plains Indians to make ceremonial calumets, or peace pipes. The quarry site, a gathering place for Native American tribes, is now the **Pipestone National Monument** (daily 8am–5pm, longer on summer weekends; $3 per person or $5 per vehicle). A self-guided **trail** winds from the visitor center through stands of trees, past rock formations and exposed quarry pits and over a creek, complete with picturesque falls.

Pipestone's small **historic district** includes a sleepy county museum and a build-ing with several amusing sandstone gargoyles. Pick up a walking-tour brochure from the town's **visitor center** (ⓣ507/825-3316 or 1-800/336-6125), on Hwy 75 at 117 8th Ave SE. You can **sleep and eat** at the grand old *Calumet Inn*, 104 W Main St (ⓣ507/825-5871 or 1-800/535-7610, ⓦwww.calumetinn.com; ❹). Each late July to early August the town puts on the nine-day "Song of Hiawatha" **Indian pageant** in an outdoor amphitheater.

From a distance the red rocks at **Blue Mounds State Park**, sloping into a long cliff a few miles north of the junction of I-90 and US-75 at Luverne, create a great hump that appeared blue at sunset to approaching pioneers. Twice a year, at the equinoxes, the sun lines up with a curious 1250ft row of rocks, aligned on an east–west axis. There are seasonal **campgrounds** (ⓣ1-866/85PARKS) and a permanent small herd of buffalo in the park. Call the same number for camping in picturesque **Split Rock Creek State Park**, only seven miles south of Pipestone and the site of a dam dating from 1935.

The Capital Region

AL - ALABAMA	IN - INDIANA	MN - MINNESOTA	RI - RHODE ISLAND
AR - ARKANSAS	LA - LOUISIANA	MS - MISSISSIPPI	SC - SOUTH CAROLINA
CT - CONNECTICUT	MA - MASSACHUSETTS	NC - NORTH CAROLINA	VA - VIRGINIA
DE - DELAWARE	MD - MARYLAND	NH - NEW HAMPSHIRE	VT - VERMONT
FL - FLORIDA	ME - MAINE	NJ - NEW JERSEY	WI - WISCONSIN
IL - ILLINOIS	MI - MICHIGAN	PA - PENNSYLVANIA	WV - WEST VIRGINIA

Highlights

✳ **Georgetown, Washington DC** The best neighborhood in which to discover that the District isn't all monuments, memorials, and museums. See p.422

✳ **National Gallery of Art, Washington DC** One of the country's premier institutions for art and culture, laid out in spacious, elegant surroundings. See p.413

✳ **Colonial Williamsburg, VA** This close replica of Colonial America, apothecaries and all, makes for a fun and interesting trip. See p.439

Monticello, VA Thomas Jefferson's home is for many as much an architectural icon as it is a symbol of democracy. See p.447

✳ **New River Gorge, WV** A spectacular river canyon with a 1000ft chasm carved in steep-walled limestone cliffs – one of the country's outstanding natural attractions. See p.458

✳ **The du Pont Mansions, DE** Wilmington has some of the East Coast's greatest, most palatial estates, now open to public view. See p.477

△ Mount Vernon

The Capital Region

The city of Washington, in the District of Columbia, and the four sur-rounding states of Virginia, West Virginia, Maryland, and Delaware are collectively known as the **CAPITAL REGION**. Since the days of the first American colonies, US history has been shaped here, from agitation toward independence to the battles of the Revolutionary and Civil wars, to 1960s Civil Rights milestones and current-day protest movements on issues like abortion and gay rights.

Early in the seventeenth century, the first British settlements began to take root along the rich estuary of the **Chesapeake Bay**; the colonists hoped to find gold, but instead made their fortunes growing tobacco. Virginia, the first settlement, was the largest and most populous. Fully half of its people were **slaves**, brought from Africa to do the backbreaking work of harvesting tobacco. Despite its central position on the East Coast, almost all of the region lies below the Mason-Dixon Line – the symbolic border between North and South, drawn up in 1763 as the boundary between slave and free states – and until the Civil War one of the country's busiest slave markets was just two blocks from the White House.

Tensions between North and South finally erupted into the **Civil War**, of which traces are still visible everywhere. The hundred miles between the capital of the Union – Washington DC – and that of the Confederacy – Richmond, Virginia – were a constant and bloody battleground for four long years.

Washington DC itself, with its magnificent monumental architecture, is an essential stop on any tour of the region – or of the country in general, for that matter. **Virginia**, to the south, is home to hundreds of historic sites, from the estates of early politicians to the Colonial capital of **Williamsburg**, as well as the narrow forested heights of **Shenandoah National Park**, along the crest of the Blue Ridge Mountains. Much greater expanses of wilderness, crashing white-water rivers, and innumerable backwoods villages can be found in less-visited **West Virginia**.

Most tourists come to **Maryland** for the maritime traditions of Chesapeake Bay – though many of its quaint old villages have been gentrified by weekend pleasure-boaters. **Baltimore** is full of character, enjoyably unpretentious if a bit ramshackle (it has a phenomenal concentration of bars), while **Annapolis**, the pleasant state capital, is linked by bridge and ferry to the Eastern Shore, where **Assateague Island** remains an Atlantic paradise. **New Castle**, across the border in **Delaware**, is a perfectly preserved Colonial-era town, with some of the East Coast's best and least crowded beaches nearby.

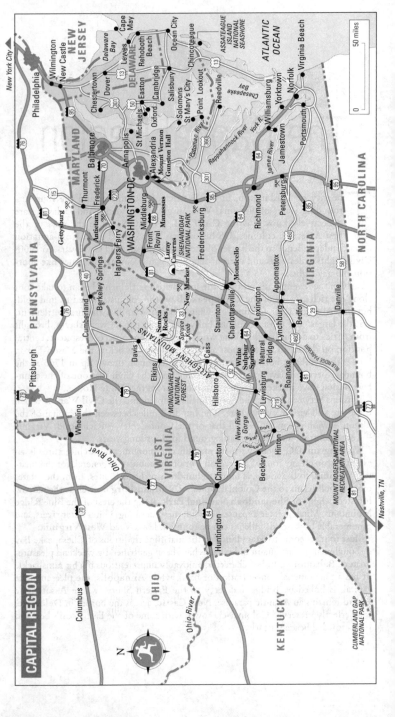

CAPITAL REGION

50 miles

0

N

Washington DC

That the marshy swamp where **WASHINGTON DC** now stands was chosen as the site of the **capital** of the newly independent United States of America says a lot about then-prevalent attitudes toward government. Washington, District of Columbia (the boundaries of the two are identical) – also known as **"The District"** – can be unbearably hot and humid in summer, and bitterly cold in winter. Such an unpleasant climate, it was hoped, would discourage elected leaders from making government a full-time job. Today the city, with a majority black population, is run as a virtual colony of Congress, where residents have only non-voting representation and couldn't vote in presidential elections until the 23rd Amendment was passed in 1961 – the city's official license plate reads "Taxation Without Representation."

The most famous sites are concentrated along the **National Mall**, including the White House, memorials to four of the greatest presidents, and the superb museums of the Smithsonian Institution – all of which are free. In recent years, even the once-blighted area known as **Old Downtown** (north of the eastern side of the Mall), has had a dramatic uptick in visitors and nightlife; still, you're more likely to spend your evenings in the hotels and restaurants of the city's more vibrant neighborhoods, such as historic **Georgetown**, arty **Dupont Circle**, and funky **Adams–Morgan**. When planning your trip, consider that the best times to come are during April's National Cherry Blossom Festival and the more temperate months (May–June and September).

Some history

The main reason the national capital was established here was the site's location midway between the South and the North. Additionally, it was accessible from the sea, via the Potomac River. Best of all, the land was cheap: Maryland and Virginia ceded sovereignty of a diamond-shaped tract to the federal government – however, a half-century later, Virginia demanded its land back, thus regaining control of such towns as Arlington and Alexandria. Although George Washington's baroque, radial plan of the city was laid out in 1791 (by a Frenchman, **Pierre L'Enfant**, assisted by the black American scientist **Benjamin Banneker**), few buildings were put up, apart from the actual houses of government, until near the end of the century.

After the Civil War, thousands of Southern **blacks** arrived in search of a sanctuary from racial oppression; to some extent, they found one. Segregation was banned in public places, and **Howard University**, the only US institution of higher learning that enrolled black people, was set up in 1867. By the 1870s African-Americans made up more than a third of the 150,000 population, but as poverty and squalor became endemic, official **segregation** was reintroduced in 1920.

After World War II, the city's economy and population boomed. Segregation of public facilities was declared illegal in the 1950s, and Martin Luther King Jr gave a famous 1963 speech on the steps of the Lincoln Memorial. When King was killed five years later, large sections of the city's ghettos burned, and DC continues to have some of the country's highest murder rates, as well as appalling levels of unemployment, illiteracy, and drug abuse. However, skyrocketing real-estate values have led to newly paved roads and a revitalized downtown, where chic restaurants and cultural and sporting events have begun to attract visitors to areas once considered urban wastelands.

Arrival, information, and getting around

Washington DC is served by three major **airports**, two on the outskirts and one right in the city center. **Dulles International Airport**, 26 miles west in northern Virginia, and **Baltimore-Washington International Airport** (BWI), halfway between DC and Baltimore, get the majority of the international traffic. By far the most convenient, **Ronald Reagan Washington National Airport**, west across the Potomac River from the Mall, is mostly used by domestic flights.

Taking a **taxi** downtown from BWI or Dulles costs $50-60, while SuperShuttle (℡1-800/BLUE-VAN, ⓦwww.supershuttle.com) offers **door-to-door** service from Dulles (45min; $25); BWI (1hr; $30); and National (15min; $12). Cheaper are the express **buses** that run every half-hour from both airports to nearby Metro subway stations. From Dulles, take the Washington Flyer Coach Service (℡1-888/WASH-FLY, ⓦwww.washfly.com) to the West Falls Church Metro station (25min; $9, roundtrip $16). From BWI, take BWI Express Bus #B30 to Greenbelt Metro station (30min; $3). BWI also provides a free shuttle to frequent Amtrak and MARC trains bound for Union Station (30min; one-way $7/$11–15; ℡410/672-6169). National Airport conveniently has its own subway stop and is just a short ride from the city center. A **taxi** downtown from National costs around $18.

By **train**, you arrive amid the gleaming, Neoclassical glory of **Union Station**, 50 Massachusetts Ave NE, three blocks north of the US Capitol and with a connecting Metro station. Greyhound and other **buses** stop at a modern terminal at 1005 First St NE, in a fairly dodgy part of the city, a few blocks north of the Union Station Metro; take a cab, especially at night. **Driving** into DC is a sure way to experience some of the worst traffic on the East Coast – the main I-95 and I-495 freeways circle Washington on the **Beltway** and are jammed eighteen hours a day.

Once in the city, stop at the **DC Chamber of Commerce Visitor Center**, Ronald Reagan Building, 1300 Pennsylvania Ave NW (spring and summer Mon–Fri 8.30am–5.30pm, Sat 9am–4pm; fall and winter Mon–Fri 9am–4.30pm; ℡1-866/324-7386, ⓦwww.dcvisit.com), which can help with maps, tours, bookings, and information. The **White House Visitor Information Center**, not located at the president's mansion but downtown at 1450 Pennsylvania Ave NW (daily 7.30am–4pm; ℡202/208-1631, ⓦwww.nps.gov/whho), supplies free maps and handy guides to museums and attractions.

The Capitol Hill **post office**, at 2 Massachusetts Ave NE (Mon–Fri 7am–midnight, Sat & Sun 7am–8pm; ℡202/523-2628; zip code 20002), has the latest hours of the area post offices.

City transportation

Getting around DC is easy. Most places downtown, including the museums, monuments, and White House, are within walking distance of each other, and an excellent **public transit** system reaches outlying sights and neighborhoods. The growing **Metro subway** (℡202/637-7000, ⓦwww.wmata.com) is clean and efficient; one-way fares start at $1.35, with a slight rush-hour surcharge from 5.30 to 9.30am and from 3 to 7pm (or up to $4 if you're going out to the suburbs); **day-passes** cost $6.50 and are valid weekdays from 9.30am on and all day on weekends, while **weekly passes** are $22 – good for fares up to $2.20 during weekday rush hours and all fares at other times (trains run Mon–Thurs 5am–midnight, Fri 5am–3am, Sat 7am–3am & Sun 7am–midnight). The standard fare on the extensive **bus** network is $1.25, or $3 for express buses. **Taxis** are a good alternative: if traveling in the downtown core, most fees are zoned at $8.50–11, and most crosstown fares are no more than $15–20. (Surcharges kick in during peak hours and for each additional passenger.) There are taxi stands at major hotels and transportation terminals (like Union Station), or call Yellow Cab (☎202/544-1212) or Diamond Cab (☎202/387-6200).

Tours

During the day, **Tourmobiles** (daily 9.30am–4.30pm; tickets $20; ☎202/554-5100, ⓦwww.tourmobile.com) connect the major museums and sights, allowing you to stop for as long as you choose at twenty different locations.

If you want to **cycle** or **cruise** along the Potomac River or the historic C&O Canal, both Thompson's Boat Center, 2900 Virginia Ave NW at Rock Creek Parkway (daily 8am–6pm; ☎202/333-9543), near the Watergate complex, and Fletcher's Boat House, 4940 Canal Rd NW, two miles farther up the canal towpath (daily 9am–7pm; ☎202/244-0461), rent touring bikes, rowboats, and canoes (bikes $4–8 per hour, $15–25 a day; boats $8-10 per hour, $22–30 a day). Better Bikes (daily 24hr; ☎202/293-2080) will deliver rental bikes anywhere in DC ($38–48 a day). In addition, mule-drawn **canal boats**, staffed by costumed National Park Service guides, follow the old C&O Canal from the Georgetown Visitors Center (1057 Thomas Jefferson St; ☎202/653-5190) on an hour-long narrated cruise (April–Oct; $8). For **walking tours** of the city, DC Heritage (☎202/828-9255, ⓦwww.dcheritage.org) has information on the many options for viewing aspects of local history, while Washington Walks ($10 per person; ☎202/484-1565, ⓦwww.washingtonwalks.com) provides a number of easy treks around the area's more notable sights.

Accommodation

Most DC **hotels** cater to business travelers and political lobbyists, and during the week are quite expensive. At weekends, however, many cut their rates by up to fifty percent or up to $100 or so. For a list of vacancies, call Washington DC Accommodations (☎202/289-2220 or 1-800/503-3330, ⓦwww.wdcahotels.com), which provides a hotel-reservation and travel-planning service.

Similarly, a number of **B&B** agencies offer comfortable doubles starting from $60 in the low season: try Capitol Reservations (☎202/452-1270 or 1-800/847-4832, ⓦwww.capitolreservations.com) or Bed & Breakfast Accommodations, Ltd (☎413/582-9888 or 1-877/893-3233, ⓦwww.bedandbreakfastdc.com). There's no good **camping** anywhere near DC, but Catholic University (☎202/319-5291, ⓦconferences.cua.edu), Georgetown University (☎202/687-3001, ⓦhousing.georgetown.edu), and George Washington University (☎202/994-2552, ⓦgwired.gwu.edu/gwhousing) offer **budget rooms** (starting at $25–30) in summer; these must be arranged well in advance and may have minimum-stay and other requirements. Wherever you go, make sure the facility has **air conditioning**; DC can be unbearably stifling in the summer without it.

Brickskeller Inn 1523 22nd St NW ☎202/293-1885, ⓦwww.thebrickskeller.org. A converted apartment house with a stately facade and simple rooms, most of which have sinks; some have a bath and TV. Located above one of Dupont Circle's best bars. $16 extra for private bath. ❹

Embassy Inn 1627 16th St NW ☎202/234-7800 or 1-800/423-9111, ⓦwww.windsorembassyinns.

com. Welcoming inn in Dupont Circle East offering good-value rooms, free continental breakfast, and early evening sherry. Add $30 for high season. ❻

Fairmont 2401 M St NW ☎202/429-2400, ⓦwww.fairmont.com. High-class oasis with extremely comfortable rooms with high-speed Internet access, plus a pool, an excellent health club, an internal garden courtyard, and a "Gold

Floor" with elite rooms for the real movers and shakers. Just north of Washington Circle, midway between Foggy Bottom and Georgetown. $279. ⑨

George 15 E St NW, Capitol Hill ☎ 202/347-4200 or 1-800/576-8331, ⓦ www.hotelgeorge.com. Postmodernism meets Art Deco, resulting in sleek lines, contemporary room furnishings (dark wood and glass, with copious Washington imagery), marble bathrooms, in-room CD players, a trendy bar-bistro, and one of the DC's more stylish lobbies. Save $120 by booking on weekdays. ⑥–⑨

Grand Hyatt 1000 H St NW, Downtown ☎ 202/582-1234 or 1-800/233-1234, ⓦ grand-washington.hyatt.com. A nearly 900-room hotel with a splashy twelve-story atrium featuring a lagoon, waterfalls, and glass elevators, plus tasteful rooms and an on-site deli-café, restaurant, and sports bar. Located opposite the Convention Center and with its own Metro connection. Rates drop by $100 on weekends. ⑥–⑨

Hay-Adams 800 16th St NW, Foggy Bottom ☎ 202/638-6600 or 1-800/424-5054, ⓦ www.hay-adams.com. From the gold-leaf and walnut lobby to the sleek modern rooms, the *Hay-Adams* is one of DC's finest hotels. Upper floors have great views of the White House across the square. Breakfast is served in one of the District's better spots for early-morning power dining. ⑨

HI-Washington DC 1009 11th St NW ☎ 202/737-2333, ⓦ www.hiwashingtondc.org. Large (270 beds), clean, downtown hostel near the Convention Center, in a somewhat dicey area. Offers free continental breakfast, high-speed Web access, renovated dorm rooms ($32), and shared bathrooms, plus kitchen, lounge, laundry, luggage storage, and organized activities. ①

Kalorama Guest House 1854 Mintwood Place NW ☎ 202/667-6369, ⓦ www.kaloramaguesthouse.com. Spacious rooms in three Victorian townhouses near Adams-Morgan, filled with antiques and handsome furniture (but no TV). Free breakfast, coffee, and evening sherry. Booking is essential – doubles with bath can go for $95–110, depending on the season. ④

Mayflower 1127 Connecticut Ave NW ☎ 202/347-3000 or 1-800/228-7697, ⓦ www.renaissancehotels.com/WASSH. If there's one spot in DC where the national and international political elite come to roost, this is it. This sumptuous Washington classic has a Promenade – a vast, imperial hall – and smart rooms with subtle, tasteful furnishings; the terrific *Café Promenade* restaurant is much in demand with power diners. $169 weekends, otherwise $400+. ⑦

Monaco 700 F St NW, Downtown ☎ 202/628-7177, ⓦ www.monaco-dc.com. Perhaps the most architecturally significant hotel in the area, this

former grand, Neoclassical post office designed by Robert Mills today houses ultra-chic accommodation. Features sophisticated modern rooms, minimalist contemporary decor, public spaces with marble floors and columns, and striking spiral stairways. ⑨

Omni Shoreham 2500 Calvert St NW, Upper Northwest ☎ 202/234-0700, ⓦ www.omnihotels.com. Plush, grand institution bursting with history and overlooking Rock Creek Park. Offers swank, comfortable rooms, many with a view of the park, plus an outdoor pool, tennis courts, and the foliage-filled Garden Court for drinks. ⑨

Palomar 2121 P St NW, Dupont Circle ☎ 202/293-3100, ⓦ www.hotelpalomardc.com. Excellent boutique accommodation with flat-panel TVs and CD players in the rooms, an on-site pool, a fitness center, a stylish lounge, and an evening "wine hour" for schmoozing with other guests. ⑨

State Plaza 2117 E St NW, Foggy Bottom ☎ 202/861-8200 or 1-800/424-2859, ⓦ www.stateplaza.com. Commodious, stylish suites with fully equipped kitchens and a dining area, plus a rooftop sundeck, health club, and good café. $109-169, depending on season. ⑤–⑦

Swiss Inn 1204 Massachusetts Ave NW ☎ 202/371-1816, ⓦ www.theswissinn.com. Cozy townhouse accommodation with air-conditioned rooms featuring kitchenettes, TV, and bath. Hosts are multilingual. Book well in advance since prices don't get much better downtown. ④

Tabard Inn 1739 N St NW ☎ 202/785-1277, ⓦ www.tabardinn.com. Three converted Victorian townhouses near Dupont Circle, with forty unique, antique-stocked rooms featuring a mix of modern and old-fashioned decor. Comfortable lounges have romantic fireplaces, plus there's a courtyard and a fine restaurant. Rates include breakfast and a pass to the nearby YMCA. ⑤

Topaz 1733 N St NW ☎ 202/393-3000, ⓦ www.topazhotel.com. Boutique hotel whose vibrant rooms have padded headboards with polka dots, lime-green striped wallpaper, and arty furniture; several also have space for yoga – complete with workout gear and videos – or treadmills, stationary bikes, and elliptical machines. Special rates can drop to as low as $125. ⑤–⑦

Washington International Student Center 2451 18th St NW ☎ 202/667-7681 or 1-800/567-4150, ⓦ www.washingtondchostel.com. Backpacker accommodation in plain dorms in Adams–Morgan, with Internet access, lockers, and free pickup from bus and train stations (advance reservation required). This is downtown DC's cheapest bed ($23), so book at least two weeks in advance. ①

William Lewis House 1309 R St NW ☎ 202/462-

7574 or 1-800/465-7574, ⓦ www.wlewishous.
com. Elegantly decorated, gay-friendly B&B set in
two century-old townhouses north of Logan Circle.
All ten antique-filled rooms have shared bath. Out
back there's a roomy porch and a hot tub set in
a garden. Rates include continental breakfast on
weekdays and a full American breakfast on weekends. It's ultra-cheap for what you get, so reservations are essential. ❹

Windsor Inn 1842 16th St NW ☎ 202/667-0300
or 1-800/423-9111, ⓦ www.windsorembassyinns.
com. Not too far from Dupont Circle, with units
in twin brick 1920s houses and spacious suites.

Some rooms have fridges; ground-floor rooms look
onto a terrace. Free continental breakfast is served
in the attractive lobby. ❻

Woodley Park Guest House 2647 Woodley Rd
NW, Upper Northwest ☎ 202/667-0218 or 1-
866/667-0218, ⓦ woodleyparkguesthouse.com.
Sixteen cozy rooms (the cheapest share facilities)
that come with free continental breakfast and
cheap parking. Close to the zoo, the Metro, and
plenty of good restaurants. ❺

The City

Washington's **city plan** is easy to grasp: with the US Capitol as the center of the
street grid, the District is divided into four **quadrants** – northeast, northwest,
southeast, and southwest. Dozens of broad **avenues**, named after states, run diagonally across a standard grid of **streets**, meeting up at monumental traffic circles like
Dupont Circle. North–south streets are numbered, east–west ones are lettered.

Almost all the most famous sights are on **Capitol Hill** or, running two miles
west, the broad, green **National Mall**, which holds monuments to presidents
Washington, Jefferson, Lincoln, and (Franklin D.) Roosevelt, as well as the **White
House**, official home of the president. Also here are the bulk of the city's many
fine museums, including the peerless collections of the **Smithsonian Institution**.

Between the Mall and the main spine of **Pennsylvania Avenue** – the route
connecting Capitol Hill to the White House – the Neoclassical buildings of the
Federal Triangle are home to agencies forming the hub of the national bureaucracy. North and east of here, **Old Downtown** has been revitalized after years of
neglect, and features new plazas, galleries, and restaurants alongside traditional
attractions like the Old Post Office and Ford Theatre, where Abraham Lincoln
was shot. West of the White House, **Foggy Bottom** is another cornerstone of the
federal bureaucracy, but further northwest is the city's oldest area, **Georgetown**,
where popular bars and restaurants line M Street and Wisconsin Avenue above
the **Potomac River**. Other neighborhoods to check out – especially for hotels,
restaurants, and bars – are **Dupont Circle** at Massachusetts, Connecticut, and New
Hampshire avenues, which pulls in a dynamic mix of urban professionals of all
stripes, and the gentrifying community of **Adams–Morgan**, a favored destination
of the weekend party crowd that's a short walk from Dupont Circle up 18th Street
at Columbia Road. More gung-ho visitors may also want to follow the Red Line
Metro out to the genteel precinct of **Upper Northwest**, which offers Washington
National Cathedral and the National Zoo. Most tourists also take the short Metro
ride to **Arlington** in Virginia to see the National Cemetery (burial place of John
F. Kennedy) and glance at the Pentagon.

Capitol Hill

Although there's more than one hill in Washington DC, when people talk about
what's happening on "**The Hill**," they mean **Capitol Hill** – a shallow knoll
topped by the giant white dome of the US Capitol, rising at the official center

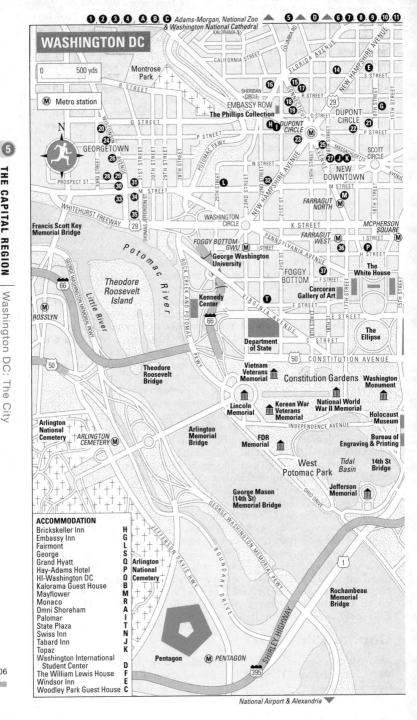

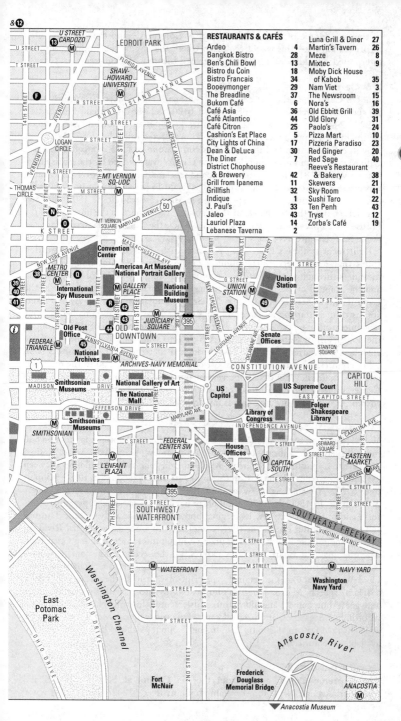

of the city. Home of both the legislature – **Congress** – and the judiciary – the **Supreme Court** – this is still the place where the law of the land is made and interpreted; in addition, it holds the esteemed **Library of Congress**.

US Capitol

The **US Capitol**, at the east end of the National Mall between Constitution and Independence avenues (tour information ☎202/225-6827, general information ☎202/224-3121, ⓦwww.aoc.gov/cc/visit), provides an opportunity to appreciate the immense power wielded by the nation's elected officials.

George Washington laid the building's cornerstone in 1793 in a ceremony rich with Masonic symbolism, and though the Capitol was torched by the British during the War of 1812, it was later rebuilt and repeatedly expanded over the ensuing centuries. Ten presidents – most recently Gerald Ford – have lain in state in the impressive **Rotunda**, which, capped by a massive cast-iron dome 180ft high and 96ft across, links the two halves of the Capitol – the **Senate** in the north wing, the **House of Representatives** in the south. When the "Tholos" lantern above the dome is lit, Congress is in session.

Tight security means that walk-up access to the Capitol is limited to **guided tours** that leave every thirty minutes (9am–4.30pm; 35min; free). The tour meanders through several historical rooms, including the National Statuary Hall and the Capitol crypt. Since advance tickets are unavailable, arrive early at the Capitol Guide Service kiosk (near 1st St SW and Independence Ave). Tickets are distributed starting at 9am, and lines can form as early as 7am; before your scheduled tour, you can expect to wait in a lengthy queue south of the building at the South Visitor Receiving Facility. US citizens who want to see the legislative chambers must arrange to get a pass through their representatives. Visitors from other countries should bring a passport or photo ID and first go to the receiving facility, where they can obtain international passes. The planned Capitol Visitors Center, underneath the east front of the building, is years behind schedule, and the current, prospective opening date is in late 2007 or 2008.

Library of Congress

With 130 million books, manuscripts, microfilm rolls, and photographs kept on 530 miles of shelves, the **Library of Congress** is the largest library in the world. Housed east of the Capitol in the Jefferson, Madison, and John Adams buildings between 1st and 3rd streets SE and E Capitol and C streets SE (Mon–Sat 10am–5.30pm; free; ☎202/707-8000, ⓦwww.loc.gov), the library was set up to serve members of Congress in 1800. In 1870, the library became the national copyright repository, and in time it outgrew its original home. The exuberantly eclectic **Thomas Jefferson Building** opened in 1897, complete with a domed octagonal **Reading Room**, and hundreds of mosaics, murals, and sculptures in its stunning Great Hall. The ongoing **American Treasures** exhibit, on the second floor, contains a vast, rotating collection of artifacts that includes such diverse pieces as Walt Whitman's Civil War notebooks, the original typescript of Martin Luther King Jr's "I have a dream" speech, Martha Jefferson's household inventory (with a record of ducks and geese butchered), and numerous music scores, historic photographs, early recordings, magazines, and baseball cards. Free **tours** depart Monday to Saturday at 10.30am, 11.30am, 1.30pm, 2.30pm, and 3.30pm (with the latter tour time not available on Saturday).

Supreme Court

The **Supreme Court**, across from the US Capitol at First Street NE and Maryland Avenue NE (Mon–Fri 9am–4.30pm; free; ☎202/479-3211, ⓦwww

.supremecourtus.gov), is the nation's final arbiter of what is and isn't legal. The federal judiciary dates to 1787, but the court didn't receive its own building until 1935, when Cass Gilbert – architect of New York's Woolworth Building – designed this Greek Revival masterpiece. The grand interior spaces, especially the marble and damask drapes of the courtroom itself – where guides give lectures (hourly Mon–Fri 9.30am–3.30pm; free) when the court is not in session – make it worth climbing the gleaming white steps and going inside. Sessions run from October to June. Arrive early to get a seat, or join the separate line if you're happy to settle for a three-minute stroll through the standing gallery.

Folger Shakespeare Library

The renowned **Folger Shakespeare Library** 201 E Capitol St (Mon–Sat 10am–4pm; tours Mon–Fri 11am, Sat 11am & 1pm; Ⓦwww.folger.edu), on the south side of the Supreme Court, was founded in 1932 and today holds more than 300,000 books, manuscripts, paintings, and engravings related to Shakespeare's work and background. The dark-oak **Great Hall** – with its carved lintels, stained glass, Tudor roses, and sculpted ceiling – displays changing exhibitions about the playwright and Elizabethan themes; the reproduction Elizabethan Theater hosts lectures and readings as well as medieval and Renaissance music concerts; and an Elizabethan garden on the east lawn grows herbs and flowers common in the sixteenth century.

The National Mall - monuments

The elegant, two-mile-long **National Mall** stretches from the Capitol to the Lincoln Memorial and is DC's most popular green space, used for summer softball games and Fourth of July concerts. Yet its central role in a planned capital city also places it at the very heart of the country's political and social life: when there's a protest gesture to be made, the Mall is the place to make it, whether it's an anti-war demonstration or the unveiling of an AIDS memorial quilt. What the Mall is perhaps best known for, however is its quartet of presidential **monuments**, along with the White House and the powerful **memorials** to veterans of the Korean and Vietnam wars, and, as of recently, World War II.

Washington Monument

The Mall's most prominent feature, the **Washington Monument**, is an unadorned marble obelisk built in memory of George Washington. At 555ft, it's the tallest all-masonry structure in the world, towering over the city from its hilltop perch at 15th Street NW and Constitution Avenue (daily 9am–5pm; free; ☏202/426-6841, Ⓦwww.nps.gov/wamo). To visit the monument pick up a free ticket from the 15th Street kiosk (8.30am–4:30pm, just south of Constitution Ave on Madison Drive), which allows you to turn up at a fixed time later in the day. The kiosk is first-come, first-served; tickets run out early during the peak season. You can also book a ticket in advance with the National Park Service ($1.50; ☏1-800/967-2283, Ⓦreservations.nps.gov). The elevator to the observation deck takes seventy seconds and deposits you at the 500ft level to enjoy the monument's panoramic 360° views of the city, though from rather small viewing windows.

The White House

For nearly two hundred years, the **White House** has been the residence and office of the president of the United States. Standing at the edge of the Mall, due north from the Washington Monument at America's most famous address, 1600 Pennsylvania Ave NW, this grand, Neoclassical edifice was completed in 1800 by Irish immigrant James Hoban, who modeled it on the Georgian manors of Dublin.

Though many visitors are surprised by how small and homey it is, security at the White House is every bit as tight as you'd imagine. Protesters are still allowed to set up camp in Lafayette Park, opposite the north entrance, and adjacent Pennsylvania Avenue has recently been pedestrianized and made into a pleasant strolling route. However, in the wake of 9/11, White House **tours** (free; ☎202/456-7041, ⒲www.whitehouse.gov) have become much more restricted: to gain access, you must be part of a group of ten and contact your congressional representative at least a month in advance (foreign visitors can contact their embassies or consulates); exceptions are made for school groups and members of the military.

If you're interested in the history of the place and its occupants, walk a few blocks southeast to the **visitor center** at 1450 Pennsylvania Ave (daily 7.30am–4pm; ☎202/208-1631). It's filled with photos and film footage of First Families and their distinguished guests – including a portly President Hoover playing "Hooverball" with a group of lumbering judges, and the Wright Brothers showing off their latest airplane – and the inaugural portraits, in which a series of haggard and exhausted old men hand over power to their beaming, youthful successors.

National World War II Memorial

In 2004 the **National World War II Memorial**, 17th St SW at Independence Ave (daily 24hr, staffed 9.30am–11.30pm; ☎202/426-6841, ⒲www.nps.gov/nwwm), just west of the Washington Monument, opened to much acclaim, and the memorial stands as a moving statement of duty and sacrifice.

Two arcs on each side of a central fountain have a combined total of 56 stone pillars (representing the number of US states and territories at the time of the war) that are decorated with bronze wreaths. In the middle of each arc stands a short tower, one called "Atlantic" and the other "Pacific," and within each tower are four interlinked bronze eagles and a sculpted wreath, which, despite its bulk, seems to float above you in mid-air. Beyond the carefully considered architecture and the FDR and Eisenhower quotes chiseled on the walls, a concave wall of four thousand golden stars reminds you of the 400,000 fallen US soldiers – a number matched only by the colossal carnage of the Civil War.

Lincoln Memorial

The **Lincoln Memorial**, modeled after the Parthenon, with its stately Doric columns, anchors the west end of the Mall (daily 24hr, staffed 9.30am–11.30pm; free; ⒲www.nps.gov/linc). As one of America's most emblematic sights, the memorial is a fitting tribute to the 16th US president, who preserved the Union after Southern states seceded and took up arms during the Civil War, and ended slavery with his Emancipation Proclamation in 1863.

Although blacks were shamefully not allowed access to the site when it was dedicated in 1922, the memorial would later fulfill its appropriate role as an icon of liberty and peaceful protest. During the Civil Rights March on Washington in 1963, Martin Luther King Jr delivered his epic "I Have a Dream" speech here; the on-site protests against the Vietnam War in the 1960s fueled the growing antiwar feeling in the country; and, since then, all manner of activists, mourners, celebrants, and zealots have given speeches here.

Inside the monument, an enormous, craggy likeness of Lincoln sits firmly grasping the arms of his throne-like chair, deep in thought. Inscriptions of his two most celebrated speeches – the Gettysburg Address and the Second Inaugural Address – are carved on the south and north walls.

△ Vietnam Veterans memorial

Vietnam Veterans Memorial

A striking wedge of black granite, slashed into the green lawn of the Mall at Constitution Avenue and 21st Street NW, the **Vietnam Veterans Memorial** (daily 24hr, staffed 9.30am–11.30pm; free; Ⓦ www.nps.gov/vive) serves as a somber and powerful reminder of the 58,000 US soldiers who died in Vietnam. The pathway that slopes down from the grass forms a gash in the earth, its increasing depth symbolizing the increasing involvement of US forces in the war. The polished surface is carved with the names of every soldier who died, in chronological order from 1959 to 1975, and you can often find family members taking paper rubbings of the names of the departed.

In 1984, a traditional grouping of three soldiers in combat was placed nearby, under a floodlit American flag; a decade later, the **Vietnam Women's Memorial**, in a grove of trees at the east end of the site, added another sculptural triad, honoring the eleven thousand women who served; and currently there are plans for a subterranean visitors center to offer a more heroic view of the war, opening in 2009.

Korean War Veterans Memorial

The **Korean War Veterans Memorial**, southeast of the Lincoln Memorial (daily 24hr, staffed 8am–11.45pm; free; Ⓦ www.nps.gov/kwvm), has as its centerpiece a Field of Remembrance, featuring nineteen life-sized, armed combat troops sculpted from stainless steel. The troops advance across a triangular plot with alternating rows of stones and plant life and head toward the Stars and Stripes positioned at the vertex. A reflecting black granite wall, with the inscription "Freedom is not free" and an etched mural, depicting military support crew and medical staff, flank the ensemble.

Jefferson Memorial and Tidal Basin

Completed in 1943 and loosely modeled on his country home, Monticello (see p.447), the **Jefferson Memorial**, just south of the Mall near 14th Street SW and Ohio Drive (daily 24hr, staffed 9.30am–11.30pm; free; Ⓦ www.nps.gov/thje), has a shallow dome hovering over a huge bronze statue of Thomas Jefferson, the author of the Declaration of Independence and the third US president. It's a stately affair, but the crowds don't linger long, especially with the fetching scene just out front, where the picturesque **Tidal Basin** stretches up to the Mall and offers one of the best places in town to take a break from sightseeing. The reflections off the Tidal Basin are especially pretty in spring when the rows of **Japanese cherry trees** come out in full bloom (usually early to mid-April). Rent a boat from Tidal Basin Paddle Boats, 1501 Main Ave SW (March–Sept daily 10am–6pm; $8–16/hr; ⓣ 202/479-2426), for a spectacular view of the memorial from the water.

FDR Memorial

The **FDR Memorial** opened alongside the Tidal Basin, just west of the Jefferson Memorial, in 1997 at West Basin Drive SW and Ohio Drive (daily 24hr, staffed 8am–11.45pm; free; ⓦ www.nps.gov/fdrm). The memorial spreads across a seven-acre site made up of a series of interlinking granite outdoor galleries – called "rooms" – punctuated by waterfalls, statuary, sculpted reliefs, groves of trees, and shaded alcoves and plazas. It's among the most successful and popular of DC's memorials, and has an almost Athenian quality to its open spaces, resting-places, benches, and inspiring texts. On a bright spring or fall day, with the glistening basin waters and emerging views of the Washington Monument and Jefferson Memorial, it's one of the finest places in the city for a contemplative stroll.

The National Mall – museums

In contrast to the memorials and monuments of its western half, the National Mall's eastern side is dominated by museums, most of which are part of the spectacular **Smithsonian Institution**. The Smithsonian was endowed in 1846 by Englishman James Smithson (who never visited the US) "for the increase and diffusion of knowledge." The institution's original home, the stately 1855 structure known as **The Castle**, 1000 Jefferson Drive SW, is in the center of the Mall's south side and now acts as the main **visitor center** (daily 8.30am–5.30pm; ⓣ 202/357-2700). The lovely, flower-filled **Enid A. Haupt Garden** fronts the Castle on its south facade. Adjacent to the east, the eclectic delight of the **Arts and Industries Building** has been closed for several years now as the institution struggles to renovate and find a use for it. Unless otherwise stated below, all Smithsonian museums and galleries are **open daily** all year (except December 25) from 10am until 5.30pm, with summer hours until 7.30 or 8pm, and admission is **free**. For details on current exhibitions and events, call the visitor center or visit the Smithsonian's website at ⓦ www.si.edu.

National Museum of American History

One of the prime repositories of US cultural artifacts is the **National Museum of American History**, located at 14th Street NW and Constitution Avenue (ⓣ 202/357-2700, ⓦ americanhistory.si.edu). Here you'll find Judy Garland's ruby slippers from *The Wizard of Oz*, Muhammad Ali's boxing gloves, and TV puppet star Howdy Doody, as well as vanishing Americana like Model T Fords, old post offices, and a restored, c.1900 ice-cream parlor. The museum's biggest draw, however, is the battered red, white, and blue flag that inspired the US national anthem – the **Star-Spangled Banner** itself, which survived the British bombardment of Baltimore Harbor during the War of 1812. Unfortunately, until summer 2008, the museum will be closed for substantial renovations. Check the website or call for updates on the building's progress.

National Museum of Natural History

Continuing eastward toward the Capitol, on the north side of the Mall, at Tenth Street NW and Constitution Avenue lies the imposing, three-story entrance rotunda of the **National Museum of Natural History** (☎202/357-2700, ⓦwww.mnh.si.edu), with troops of screeching school kids endlessly chasing each other around a colossal African elephant. Hundreds of other stuffed animals, tracing evolution from fossilized four-billion-year-old plankton to dinosaurs' eggs and beyond, are also on display throughout the facility.

Naturally enough, the "**Dinosaurs**" section is the most popular part of the museum, with hulking skeletons reassembled in imaginative poses. Also appealing to (some) tots is the **Insect Zoo**, filled with all types of bugs, including giant, menacing-looking tropical cockroaches, and the huge-screen **IMAX** movies ($8.50, kids $7; ⓦwww.si.edu/imax) on various natural themes. The museum also boasts a truly exceptional array of gemstones, including the legendary 45-carat **Hope Diamond** that once belonged to Marie Antoinette, and the **Gem and Mineral Hall**, which features natural and reconstructed environments, interactive exhibits, and hands-on specimens.

More recent attractions include the **Hall of Mammals**, where some three hundred replicas focus on mostly fur-wearing, milk-producing creatures in a variety of simulated environments; and the "**African Voices**" exhibit – bursting with colorful displays, tools, garments, and icons – suggesting the wide range of languages, cultures, and religions practiced on the continent.

National Gallery of Art – West Building

The visually stunning **National Gallery of Art**, just east on Constitution Avenue between Third and Ninth streets NW (Mon–Sat 10am–5pm, Sun 11am–6pm; free; ☎202/737-4215, ⓦwww.nga.gov), is the most important museum in the US after New York's Metropolitan Museum of Art. The original Neoclassical gallery, designed by John Russell Pope and opened in 1941, is now called the **West Building** and holds the bulk of the permanent collection. If you only have limited time, latch onto one of the informative free, **daily tours**; ask for a schedule at the information desk.

From the domed central rotunda, where you can pick up a floor plan and gallery guide, a vaulted corridor runs the length of the building. Galleries to the west on the main floor display major works by early and high-Renaissance and Baroque masters, arranged by nationality: half a dozen Rembrandts fill the **Dutch** gallery – including a glowing, mad portrait of *Lucretia* – Van Eyck and Rubens dominate the **Flemish**, and El Greco and Velázquez face off in the **Spanish**, near eight progressively darker Goyas. In the voluminous **Italian** galleries, there's the only **Leonardo** in the Americas, the 1474 *Ginevra de' Benci*, painted in oil on wood, plus **Giovanni Bellini**'s *The Feast of the Gods*, which depicts deities feasting to bawdy excess in a bucolic setting. **Titian**, Bellini's former pupil, offers vivid images of *Saint John the Evangelist on Patmos* and *Venus with a Mirror*, and fellow Venetian **Tintoretto** is well-represented with a series of arch, swirling Mannerist portraits. **Raphael** has only one major piece here: his renowned *Alba Madonna* (1510), in which the Virgin Mary and baby Jesus are seated on the ground, leaning against a tree stump – intended to emphasize their humility. Works by **Sandro Botticelli** include his rendering of the *Adoration of the Magi*, set in the ruins of a Classical temple from which the frame of a new structure, representing Christianity, rises, while even more eye-catching is **Benvenuto di Giovanni**'s five-panel "pentatych" of Jesus surrounded by various spindly, grotesque onlookers.

The other half of the West Building holds an exceptional collection of nineteenth-century **French** paintings – Gauguin from Pont-Aven to Tahiti, a couple of Van Goghs, some Monet studies of Rouen Cathedral and water lilies, Cézanne still lifes, and the like. For British art, you can find genteel portraits by Gainsborough and Reynolds, but even more evocative hazy land- and waterscapes by **J.M.W.**

THE CAPITAL REGION | Washington DC: The City

Turner. A series of early American portraits by the likes of **Gilbert Stuart** gives a good account of the first five US presidents; expansive landscapes by **Thomas Cole** and others recount the glories of the primeval wilderness; and, best of all, **Augustus St Gaudens'** magisterial battle sculpture *Memorial to Robert Gould Shaw and the Massachusetts 54th Regiment* takes up a whole gallery to itself, the colonel's rigid equestrian pose countered by the weary intensity of the black troops marching alongside in a bid to defeat the forces of Southern slavery and secession.

National Gallery of Art - East Building

The National Gallery's **East Building** (same hours and admission) was opened in 1978 with an audaciously modern **I.M. Pei** design, dominated by a huge atrium. European highlights of the permanent collection include **Pablo Picasso's** Blue Period pieces *The Tragedy* and *Family of Saltimbanques*, along with his cubist *Nude Woman*; **Henri Matisse's** exuberant *Pianist and Checker Players*, depicting his apartment in Nice; **Edouard Manet's** evocative *Oysters*; and *A King Charles Spaniel*, **Georges Seurat's** study for his signature Pointillist style. Contemporaneous American works are capped by the stunning pieces of **George Bellows**, notably the brutal prizefight pictures *Club Night* and *Both Members of This Club*, in which you can almost feel the heat as the crowd bays for blood.

Andy Warhol's works are as familiar as they come, with classic serial examples of *32 Soup Cans, Let Us Now Praise Famous Men*, and *Green Marilyn*, while notable Abstract Expressionist works include large, hovering slabs of blurry color by **Mark Rothko**; the thirteen stations of the cross by **Barnett Newman**, a series of big canvases built around the visual rhythm of black-and-white stripes; and **Jackson Pollock's** *Number 1, 1950 (Lavender Mist)*, a spray of finely drizzled, multicolored drippings. There's also **Robert Rauschenberg's** splattered, stuffed-bird sculpture known as *Canyon*; and **Jasper Johns's** *Field Painting* and *Target*, which are among his more influential works; and **Claes Oldenburg's** *Soft Drainpipe – Red (Hot) Version* (1967), a huge, soft-red sculpture that looks as much like a drooping phallus as anything under the sink.

National Museum of the American Indian

Continuing clockwise around the Mall, skirting the Capitol Reflecting Pool and heading back west along Jefferson Drive, the Smithsonian's **National Museum of the American Indian** (℡202/357-2700, ⓦwww.nmai.si.edu) is the newest of the Mall's museums, instantly recognizable by its curvaceous modern form, with undulating walls the color of yellow earth – designed to represent the natural American landscape – plus a terraced facade and surrounding replicas of forest and wetland landscapes.

The museum is intended to recognize and honor the many tribes who occupied the continent before the arrival of white settlers in the sixteenth and seventeenth century, including the **Iroquois**, **Sioux**, **Navajo**, **Cherokee**, and countless others. The collection – which reaches back thousands of years and incorporates nearly a million objects from nations spread out from Canada to Mexico – features fascinating ceramics, textiles, and other artifacts from civilizations such as the **Olmec**, **Maya**, and **Inca**, in addition to totem poles, kachina dolls, canoes, and ceremonial masks, headdresses, and outfits. The museum also sponsors periodic musical and dance events, along with lectures, films, and other cultural presentations.

National Air and Space Museum

The **National Air and Space Museum**, further west between Fourth and Seventh streets SW (℡202/357-1400, ⓦwww.nasm.si.edu) is by far DC's most popular attraction, drawing nearly ten million people every year. The entry hall, known as "**Milestones of Flight**," is a huge atrium filled with all kinds of flying machines, rockets, satellites, and assorted aeronautic gizmos that are bolted to the floor, hung from the rafters, and couched in cylindrical holes. For many the highlight is the *Spirit of St Louis*, which flew into history on May 20, 1927, when 25-year-old Charles Lindbergh piloted the world's first solo transatlantic flight. Elsewhere you can see spy planes, the Sputnik satellite, sound-barrier-breaking fighters, mail planes, and Cold War-era missiles – ominously, the drab green one is an actual (disarmed) ICBM, the Minuteman III.

The "**Space Race**" exhibit traces the development of space flight, from machines as diverse as a V2 rocket (Hitler's secret weapon and the world's first ballistic missile system) to an array of space suits from different eras. Nearby, "**Rocketry and Space Flight**" traces the history of rocketry from the black-powder rockets used in thirteenth-century China to Robert Goddard's experiments with liquid fuel in 1926, which pointed the way to eventual space flight.

The whimsically labeled "**Wright Cycle Co.**" is devoted to the siblings who pioneered aeronautics; the focus is the handmade Wright Flyer, in which the Wrights made the first powered flight in December 1903 at Kitty Hawk, North Carolina. Next door, the "**Pioneers of Flight**" gallery recounts similarly courageous endeavors, though most visitors make a beeline for "**Apollo to the Moon**," the most popular and crowded room in the museum. The main gallery centers on the *Apollo 11* (1969) and *17* (1972) missions, the first and last US flights to the moon. There are Neil Armstrong's and Buzz Aldrin's spacesuits, a Lunar Roving Vehicle (basically a golf cart with a garden seat), *Apollo 17*'s flight-control deck, tools, navigation aids, space food, clothes, and charts, and an astronaut's survival kit (complete with shark repellent).

Finally, the most hardcore of aeronautics buffs should inquire about the museum's **Steven F. Udvar-Hazy Center** in suburban Virginia, where you can get a look at flying craft too big even to fit into the main museum's capacious digs.

Hirshhorn Museum

Continuing west, the **Hirshhorn Museum**, Independence Ave at 7th St SW (T 202/357-2700, W www.hirshhorn.si.edu), with its concrete facade and monumental scale, is a perfect example of late-modernist architecture at its most inhuman. If the museum has one recognized strength, it's nineteenth-century **French sculpture**. Of various bronzes by **Henri Matisse**, most notable is *The Serf*, a stumpy portrait of a downtrodden spirit, while **Edgar Degas** offers energetic studies of women washing, stretching, and emerging from a bath. Masks and busts by **Pablo Picasso** trace his (and sculpture's) growing alliance with Cubism, and abstraction gets further along with **Brancusi**, whose *Torso of a Young Man* resembles a cylindrical brass phallus.

The Hirshhorn's cache of modern paintings has several strengths (de Kooning, Bacon) and starts with figurative paintings from the late nineteenth and early twentieth century and winds its way toward Abstract Expressionism and Pop Art. Along the way, separate rooms showcase the various major currents of the past century, from the surrealism of **Salvador Dalí**, **Max Ernst**, and **Joan Miró** to the organic abstractions of **Alexander Calder**.

National Museum of African Art

Further on, the domed **National Museum of African Art**, 950 Independence Ave SW (T 202/357-4600, W www.nmafa.si.edu), holds more than six thousand sculptures and artifacts from the cultures of sub-Saharan Africa. The permanent collection ranges widely, and though there are plenty of rotating exhibits, the one that is continuously on view is the museum's signature "**Art of the Personal

Object." It displays chairs, stools, and headrests, mostly carved from wood using an adze, as well as assorted ivory snuff containers (two from Angola with stoppers shaped like human heads), beer straws (from Uganda), carved drinking horns, combs, pipes, spoons, baskets, and cups.

Elsewhere, the emphasis is on political, religious, and ceremonial art, including rounded, stylized, terracotta equestrian and archer figures from Mali and, from Nigeria, a carved wooden palace door that stands 6ft high and depicts in relief a king seated on a horse, his wives ranked above him, and soldiers and daughters below. Remarkably, the door was carved from a single piece of wood.

Arthur M. Sackler Gallery
The angular and pyramidal **Arthur M. Sackler Gallery**, 1050 Independence Ave SW (℡202/633-4880, ⓦwww.asia.si.edu), along with the Freer Gallery (see below), is part of the **National Museum of Asian Art**. Among its permanent exhibitions, which are on the first level, **"The Arts of China"** is the most prominent, featuring 3000-year-old Chinese bronzes, ritual wine containers decorated with the faces and tails of dragons, intricate jade pendants, remarkably well-preserved carved wooden cabinets and book stands, and Qing imperial porcelain embellished with symbolic figures and motifs.

Also fascinating is the **"Luxury Arts of the Silk Route Empires"** exhibit, with silver Syrian bowls, Persian plates, and Central Asian swords and buckles; note as well the beautifully worked, fourth-century Iranian silver drinking vessel (called a *rhyton*) shaped in the form of a gazelle. **Other displays** that may be on view include Hindu temple sculpture from India, with bronze, brass, and granite representations of Brahma, Vishnu, and Shiva; a superb thirteenth-century stone carving of the elephant-headed Ganesha; and a Khmer kingdom (Cambodia) temple lintel, in which male figures are shown entwined with vines alongside an unidentified female goddess with conical crown and sarong.

Freer Gallery of Art
From the day it opened in 1923, the **Freer Gallery**, on Jefferson Drive at 12th Street NW, has been one of the more unusual Smithsonian museums (℡202/633-4880, ⓦwww.asia.si.edu). Put together and paid for by railroad magnate Charles Freer, it contains more than one thousand prints, drawings, and paintings by London-based American artist **James McNeil Whistler** – the largest collection of his works anywhere. The museum also includes Chinese jades and bronzes, Byzantine illuminated manuscripts, Buddhist wall sculptures, and pieces of Persian metalwork.

In addition to his portraits and landscapes, Whistler is also represented by the magnificent **Peacock Room**, which started life as a simple painting commissioned by Frederick Leyland for his mantelpiece. The eccentric artist, however, decided to cover Leyland's ceiling with imitation gold leaf and paint the entire room with blue and gold peacocks and feather patterns. Leyland was outraged but left the room untouched; after his death, Freer bought it and shipped it over from London.

United States Holocaust Memorial Museum
The sizable **United States Holocaust Memorial Museum**, just south of the National Mall at 100 Raoul Wallenburg Place SW (℡202/488-0400, ⓦwww.ushmm.org), commemorates the persecution and murder of six million Jews by the Nazis and personalizes the suffering of individual victims, with case after case of newspapers and newsreels documenting Nazi activities from the early 1930s through the "Final Solution," plus replicas and, in many cases, actual relics, of Warsaw Ghetto streets, railroad cattle-cars, and other artifacts on the top floors.

The staggering number of people killed is chillingly evoked throughout, first by a room filled with shoes stolen from deportees, and later by piles of blankets, umbrellas, scissors, cutlery, and other personal effects taken from the hundreds of thousands who arrived at the various camps expecting to be forced to work – but were instead (most of them) gassed within hours. A recreated barracks from Auschwitz provides the backdrop for the oral memories of some survivors, as well as truly shocking film of gruesome medical experiments carried out there.

Tickets for specific entry times are available free of charge from 10am each day – with a limit of four per person – at the 14th Street entrance. You can also reserve in advance (T 1-800/400-9373; fee charged). If you arrive without a ticket any later than mid-morning, you're unlikely to get into the permanent exhibition, but a certain number of temporary displays are usually open to all visitors.

The Bureau of Engraving and Printing

The **Bureau of Engraving and Printing**, one block south of the Mall at 14th and C streets SW (T 202/622-2000, W www.moneyfactory.com; free), is the federal agency for designing and printing all US currency, government securities, and postage stamps; it's also host to one of DC's most popular tours, netting a half-million visitors annually. US currency (the presses here crank out millions of dollars every day) has changed a lot since the Bureau was established in 1862: today it's much more colorful and uses high-tech features – color-changing inks, hidden security stamps, watermarks, and microprinting – to deter counterfeiters.

Between March and August you must pick up **tickets** in advance for tours that run daily from 9am to 2pm; you can, and should, start waiting in line at 8am, as tickets are often gone by 11.30. The rest of the year, you can just show up without tickets, though you'll still have to wait in line. Note that a special, 40-minute Congressional/VIP tour is offered for those who make arrangements for it through their representative's office (Mon–Fri 8.15am & 8.45am, also May–Aug 4pm–4.45pm), and on which you can see more in-depth, behind-the-scenes views of the plant.

Corcoran Gallery of Art

The **Corcoran Gallery of Art**, just north of the Mall at 17th St NW and New York Ave (Wed–Sun 10am–5pm, Thurs closes 9pm; $8; W www.corcoran.org), is one of the oldest and most respected art museums in the US. The gallery possesses a fine collection of landscapes, starting with the expansive *Niagara* by Frederic Edwin Church and Albert Bierstadt's splendid *The Last of the Buffalo*, both masterpieces of immense scale. Thomas Cole's *The Return*, a mythical medieval scene of an injured knight returning to a priory, also displays the Hudson River School's penchant for showing ethereal natural beauty. Later works include those by John Singer Sargent, Thomas Eakins, and Mary Cassatt, among others. Few works, however, are as robust as Winslow Homer's *A Light on the Sea*, where a brawny-armed woman swathed in fishing nets conveys the hard life of sea folk.

Some of the most familiar names hang in the **Clark Landing**, a two-tier, wood-paneled gallery accessed from the Rotunda on the second floor. Here you're likely to find mid-level paintings by Degas, Renoir, Monet, Sisley, and Pissarro, as well as works by the likes of Rousseau and Corot – the latter's *Repose* is a notably sour-faced nude with Pan and his nymphs cavorting in the background. In the **Salon Doré** (Gilded Room), an eighteenth-century Parisian interior has been recreated to stunning effect, with floor-to-ceiling hand-carved paneling, gold-leaf decor, and ceiling murals.

Downtown and around

Those whose patience grows thin with the hordes of people on the Mall may enjoy a trip through Washington DC's **Old Downtown** district, which was damaged during the 1968 riots but has recently seen new boutiques, restaurants, and hotels spring up seemingly overnight. Adjacent to Old Downtown is the wedge-shaped **Federal Triangle**, home to countless government agencies and a few major attractions, such as the National Archives, while, to the northwest, the **New Downtown** area, known for its lobbyist-rich K Street, has numerous swank shops and restaurants.

National Archives

On display at the **National Archives**, 700 Pennsylvania Ave NW (daily April-May 10am–7pm, June-Aug 10am–9pm; rest of year 10am–5.30pm; free; ☎ 1-866/272-6272, ⓦ www.archives.gov), are the three short texts upon which the United States was founded: the **Declaration of Independence**, the **Constitution**, and the **Bill of Rights**. These three original sheets of parchment, drafted respectively in 1776, 1787, and 1789, are secured in bomb-proof, argon-filled, glass-and-titanium containers that slide into a vault in case of fire or other threats. The impressive Neoclassical Greek building – designed by John Russell Pope – also houses a 1297 revised copy of the **Magna Carta**, which established in England such basic concepts as trial by jury and equality before the law. Temporary exhibitions often include fascinating documents such as the Louisiana Purchase, the Marshall Plan, Nixon's resignation letter, the Emancipation Proclamation, and the Japanese surrender from World War II. As the official repository of all US national records – census data, treaties, passport applications – the Archives also attracts thousands of visitors who come here each year in search of their own genealogical, military, or other records.

National Portrait Gallery and American Art Museum

Three blocks west of the Pension Building, and in the center of the Penn Quarter, the **Old Patent Office** building – a Neoclassical gem dating from 1836 – houses two of the city's major art displays: the Smithsonian's **National Portrait Gallery** and **American Art Museum** (both daily 11.30am–7pm; free; ⓦ www.npg.si.edu), both of which reopened in July 2006 after extensive renovations lasting several years.

In the Portrait Gallery, images of figures from the **performing arts** constitute the most popular part of the collection. Notable works include Paul Robeson as Othello; photographs of Gloria Swanson and Boris Karloff; a rough-hewn wooden head of Bob Hope; and an almost three-dimensional metallic study of Ethel Merman as Annie Oakley. Perhaps most striking, though, is Harry Jackson's terrific polychrome bronze sculpture of an aged John Wayne. Also worth a look are the **presidential portraits** – one for every man to occupy the office. Gilbert Stuart's version of George Washington is an imperial study of an implacable leader, and one of the gallery's star attractions, while Norman Rockwell's flattering portrait of Richard Nixon is the most jarring. Jan Wood offers a relatively recent bust of a carefree, first-term Bill Clinton, looking almost drunken. Personalities from **literature and the fine arts** are represented by an early Man Ray photograph of Ernest Hemingway and his young son, and the extraordinary, bulky, terracotta figure of Gertrude Stein, depicted by Jo Davidson as a tranquil, seated Buddha.

The other major museum to occupy the Old Patent Office building, the **American Art Museum**, holds one of the more enduring of the city's art collections, which dates back to the early nineteenth century. The museum contains almost four hundred paintings by **George Catlin**, who spent six years touring the Great Plains, painting portraits and scenes of Native American life as well as lush landscapes. Another great landscape artist – and there are many here – is **Albert Bierstadt**, whose *Among the Sierra Nevada Mountains* is emblematic of the artist's style. Among the sculpture from this period is **Daniel Chester French**'s *The*

Spirit of Life, a winged sprite with laurel wreath, fashioned by the man who produced the powerful statue in the Lincoln Memorial. Notable twentieth-century modern pieces include items by Robert Motherwell, Willem de Kooning, Robert Rauschenberg, Clyfford Still, Ed Kienholz, and Jasper Johns – but none is more vibrant than Nam June Paik's jaw-dropping **Electronic Superhighway**, a huge, neon-outlined map of the US with each state represented by TV screens pulsing with hypnotic images.

Another branch of the American Art Museum, the **Renwick Gallery**, located near the White House at 17th Street and Pennsylvania Avenue (daily 10am–5.30pm; ⓣ202/633-2850; free), offers overflow space for the museum's treasures, as well as rotating exhibits focusing on the decorative arts and what is perhaps the city's most stylish room for viewing art – the striking **Grand Salon**, in the style of a classic European picture gallery, with paintings stacked four and five high on the dark-rose walls.

International Spy Museum

The **International Spy Museum**, 800 F St NW (hours vary, usually daily April–Oct 10am–8pm; rest of year 10am–6pm; last admission two hours before closing; $15; ⓦwww.spymuseum.org), celebrates espionage in all forms – from feudal Japan's silent and deadly ninjas, to surveillance pigeons armed with cameras from World War I, to infamous modern-day CIA moles like Aldrich Ames. The informative displays are all interesting enough, but the museum's standouts are undoubtedly its artifacts from the height of the Cold War in the 1950s and 60s, presented in glass cases and broken down by theme – "training," "surveillance," and so on. Some of the many highlights include tiny pistols disguised as lipstick holders, cigarette cases, pipes, and flashlights; oddments like invisible-ink writing kits and a Get Smart!-styled shoe phone; a colorful and active model of James Bond's Aston Martin spy car; bugs and radio transmitters hidden in ambassadorial gifts (such as a Great Seal of the US given by Russians); ricin-tipped poison umbrellas used to kill Warsaw Pact dissidents; and a rounded capsule containing a screwdriver, razor, and serrated knife – ominously marked, "rectal tool kit."

Ford's Theatre National Historic Site

Ford's Theatre National Historic Site, 511 Tenth St NW (daily 9am–5pm, closed during rehearsals and matinees; free; ⓣ202/426-6924, ⓦwww.nps.gov/foth), is a beautiful restoration of the nineteenth-century playhouse, which continues to stage regular productions of contemporary and period drama (see p.428). It was here, on April 14, 1865, a mere five days after the end of the Civil War, that **Abraham Lincoln** was shot by Confederate sympathizer John Wilkes Booth during a performance of *Our American Cousin*.

Entertaining talks (hourly 9.15am–4.15pm; free) set the scene in the theater itself, after which you can file up to the circle for a view of the presidential box where it all happened, then go to the **Lincoln Museum**, in the basement. Macabre relics here include the clothes that Lincoln was wearing, Booth's .44 single-shot Derringer pistol, and the assassin's diary, in which he wrote: "I hoped for no gain. I knew no private wrong. I struck for my country and that alone." The mortally wounded president was carried across the street to the **Petersen House**, where he died the next morning. That, too, is open to the public (daily 9am–5pm), who troop through its gloomy parlor rooms to see a replica of Lincoln's death bed.

Old Post Office

The wondrous Romanesque Revival **Old Post Office**, 1100 Pennsylvania Ave (Mar–Aug Mon–Sat 10am–8pm, Sun noon–7pm; Sept–Feb Mon–Sat 10am–7pm,

△ Ford's Theatre

Sun noon–6pm; Ⓦ oldpostofficedc.com; free), features towering granite walls
that make it look suitably cathedral-like, as well as an eye-popping seven-story
atrium, whose glass roof throws light down onto the restored iron support beams,
brass rails, balconies, and burnished wood paneling. Now known as the **Pavilion**,
the site is home to ethnic diners and various shops in addition to a period post-
office counter (Mon–Fri 9am–5pm) that's still in use at the Pennsylvania Avenue
entrance. Also worth a look is the **clock tower** (Mon–Fri 9am–5.45pm, Sat &
Sun 10am–5.45pm, summer Mon–Fri closes 7.45pm; Ⓦ www.nps.gov/opot),
where park rangers oversee short, free tours up to the observation deck, 270ft
above the street.

National Museum of Women in the Arts
Housed in a converted Masonic Temple at 1250 New York Ave NW, the **National
Museum of Women in the Arts**, which opened in 1987, is the country's only
major museum dedicated to women artists (Mon–Sat 10am–5pm, Sun noon–5pm;
$8; Ⓦ www.nmwa.org). The collection runs chronologically, starting with works
from the Renaissance, like those of Sofonisba Anguissola, who was considered the
most important woman artist of her day; her well-judged *Double Portrait of a Lady
and Her Daughter* is on display, along with the energetic *Holy Family with St John*
by her contemporary, Lavinia Fontana. A century or so later, Dutch and Flemish
women like Clara Peeters, Judith Leyster, and Rachel Ruysch were producing
still lifes and genre scenes of great interest – witness the vivacity of Peeters's *Still
Life of Fish and Cat*. Twentieth-century works include the classical sculpture of
Camille Claudel, the paintings of Georgia O'Keeffe and Tamara de Lempicka,
linocuts by Hannah Höch, and, most boldly, a cycle of prints depicting the hardships of working-class life by the socialist Käthe Kollwitz. Frida Kahlo appears in
a self-portrait wearing a peasant's outfit and clutching a note to Trotsky, but more
fetching is *Itzcuintli Dog with Me*, in which she poses next to a truly tiny, strangely
adorable mutt.

The Newseum

The **Newseum**, 6th St at Pennsylvania Ave (℡ 888/NEWSEUM, ⓦ www.newseum .org), plans to reopen downtown in summer 2007 after being closed for several years in order to move from Arlington, VA. The museum's mission is to provide an interactive look at the history, theory, and practice of journalism. Visitors will be greeted by a daily dose of news from papers around the world – as well as from historical editions – and high-tech exhibits will include an interactive newsroom and giant video wall. You'll also encounter the world's first **Journalists Memorial**, a 24-foot-high spiraling glass prism, etched with the names of several thousand journalists killed while reporting.

National Building Museum

First known as the Pension Building, the **National Building Museum**, 401 F Street NW (Mon–Sat 10am–5pm, Sun 11am–5pm; $5; ⓦ www.nbm.org), housed various federal offices before its current function as a stirring museum of architecture, presenting changing exhibitions that cover topics like urban renewal, high-rise technology, and environmental concerns. The permanent exhibition on the second floor, "Washington: Symbol and City," concentrates on the construction of the city itself, with a detailed model showing how many of the District's planned buildings have come to fruition. The best feature of the museum, though, is the interior space itself: the majestic **Great Hall** is a stadium-sized expanse centered on a working fountain, and one of the greatest interior spaces anywhere in DC. The eight supporting columns are 8ft across at the base and more than 75ft high; each is made up of seventy thousand bricks, plastered and painted to resemble Siena marble.

Dupont Circle to Upper Northwest

Washington's other key attractions are spaced out among various neighbourhoods, but they are nevertheless worth taking the time to visit. Many lie near Connecticut Avenue, on the stretch that runs from the increasingly swank shopping and dining area of **Dupont Circle** up to the elite precinct of **Upper Northwest** – both areas conveniently accessed by subway. Less convenient, just to the northeast, is the funky urban district of **Adams–Morgan** – mainly a draw for its diners, clubs, and bars.

Phillips Collection

The **Phillips Collection**, just northwest of Dupont Circle at 1600 21st and Q St NW (Tues–Sat 10am–5pm, Thurs until 8.30pm, Sun noon–7pm except summer noon–5pm; $12; ⓦ www.phillipscollection.org), claims to be "America's first museum of modern art," based on its opening eight years before New York's Museum of Modern Art. The oldest part of the brownstone Georgian Revival building was the family home of founder Duncan Phillips, who bought nearly 2400 works over the years; during the 1920s, he and his artist wife, Marjorie, became patrons of young painters such as Georgia O'Keeffe and Marsden Hartley, while there are works by everyone from Renoir to Rothko (and several by nonmodern artists like Giorgione and El Greco). Highlights include signature pieces by Willem de Kooning and Richard Diebenkorn; Blue Period Picassos; Matisse's *Studio, Quai St-Michel*; a Cézanne still life; and no fewer than four van Goghs, including the powerful *Road Menders*. Pierre Bonnard gets a good showing – stand well back to take in the expansive and assertive *The Terrace* and *The Palm*. Top billing generally goes to *The Luncheon of the Boating Party* by Renoir, where straw-boater-wearing dandies linger over a long and bibulous feast.

Embassy Row

An intriguing strip that is unique to Washington DC among American cities, **Embassy Row** starts in earnest a few paces northwest up Massachusetts Avenue from Dupont Circle, where the **Indonesian Embassy** at no. 2020 (closed to the public) occupies the magnificent Art Nouveau Walsh-McLean House, built in 1903 for gold baron Thomas Walsh. It's a superb building – with colonnaded loggia and intricate, carved windows – and saw regular service as one of Washington society's most fashionable venues. Nearby, the **Anderson House**, no. 2118 (Tues–Sat 1–4pm; ℡202/785-2040; free), is a veritable palace, finished in 1905 with a gray-stone exterior sporting twin arched entrances with heavy wooden doors and colonnaded portico. Inside there's a grand ballroom, and original furnishings include cavernous fireplaces, inlaid marble floors, Flemish tapestries, and diverse murals. Check out ⓦwww.embassyevents.com for a listing of art shows, lectures, food fairs, films, and displays taking place at selected embassies here and elsewhere in town.

The National Zoo

Continuing well north, into the hilly district of Upper Northwest at 3001 Connecticut Ave NW (luckily a short walk from the Metro) is the Smithsonian's **National Zoo** (buildings open daily April–Oct 10am–6pm; rest of year 10am–4.30pm; grounds open daily April–Oct 6am–8pm; rest of year 6am–6pm; ⓦwww.nationalzoo.si.edu; free). Although founded in 1889 as a traditional zoo, it likes to think of itself these days as a "BioPark": **Amazonia** is a recreation of a tropical river and rainforest habitat, while the **American Prairie** exhibit provides an explanation of the natural and cultural histories of the nation's grasslands and shows off a selection of bison. Further along, orangutans are encouraged to leave the confines of the **Great Ape House** and commute to the "**Think Tank**," where scientists and four-legged primates come together to hone their communications skills and discuss world events. Between the Ape House and Think Tank is the **Reptile Discovery Center**, with a full complement of snakes, turtles, crocodiles, alligators, lizards, and frogs. Ponder here on the remarkable komodo dragons, one of which was the first to be born in captivity outside Indonesia. If all else fails, there's always the **giant pandas**, who have been amusing visitors since their arrival in 1972.

Washington National Cathedral

The twin towers of **Washington National Cathedral**, the world's sixth-largest cathedral, are visible long before you reach the heights of Mount St Alban, where the church – a good walk from the subway line in Upper Northwest – sits (Mon–Fri 10am–5.30pm, Sat 10am–4.30pm, Sun 8am–6.30pm, closes 7.45pm on weekdays May–Aug; ⓦwww.nationalcathedral.org; donation). Built from Indiana limestone and modeled entirely in the medieval English Gothic style, the Protestant cathedral took 83 years to build and measures more than a tenth of a mile from the west end of the nave to the high altar at the opposite end. Among other things, you'll find the sarcophagus of **Woodrow Wilson**, the only president to be buried in the District, and the **Space Window**, whose stained glass incorporating a sliver of moon rock commemorates the flight of Apollo 11.

Georgetown

Although it is, unfortunately, a good hike from the nearest subway stop, **Georgetown** is the quintessential DC neighborhood, enlivened by a main drag – M Street – where chic new restaurants and boutiques are housed in 200-year-old buildings, and the old C&O Canal (which you can tour on a historic boat ride; see p.403) runs parallel to the south. There are few conventional attractions along M, though the **Old Stone House**, no. 3051 (Wed–Sun noon–5pm; Ⓦ www.nps. gov/olst; free), comes close, as the only surviving pre-Revolutionary home in the city. Built in 1765 by a Pennsylvania carpenter, it retains its rugged, rough-hewn appearance, the craggy rocks used for the three-feet-thick walls being quarried from blue fieldstone.

In the hillier part of the district, there are two spots that definitely merit a visit: Tudor Place and Dumbarton Oaks. **Tudor Place**, 1644 31st St NW (tours Tues–Fri 10am–2.30pm, Sat 10am–3pm, Sun noon-3pm; $6; www.tudorplace.org), was once the estate of Martha Washington's granddaughter and, with its Federal-style architecture and Classical domed portico, has remained virtually untouched since it was built in 1816; **Dumbarton Oaks** (gardens Tues–Sun 2–5pm, March–Oct closes 6pm; Ⓦ www.doaks.org; donation) encompasses a marvelous redbrick Georgian mansion surrounded by gardens and woods: in 1944 it was the site of a meeting that led to the founding of the United Nations the following year. Its **Bliss Collection** (closed for renovation until 2007) is excellent for its Pre-Colum-bian gold, jade, and polychromatic carvings, sculpture, and pendants, as well as ceremonial axes, jewelry made from spondylus shells, stone masks of unknown significance, and sharp jade "celts" possibly used for human sacrifice. Finally, you can also take a peek in the **Music Room** and view its wondrous paintings and tapestries, walnut chests and credenzas, decorative wooden ceiling, and vintage pianos and harpsichords.

Arlington National Cemetery

Across the Potomac River west of the National Mall, the vast sea of identical white headstones on the hillsides of Virginia's **Arlington National Cemetery** (daily: April–Sept 8am–7pm; rest of year 8am–5pm; free; Ⓦ www.arlingtoncemetery. org) stands in poignant contrast to the grand monuments of the capital across the river. The country's most honored final resting place was first used during the Civil War, when the land belonged to Confederate general **Robert E. Lee**. Some 350,000 US soldiers and others – from presidents to Supreme Court justices – now lie here. An eternal flame marks the grave of **President John F. Kennedy**, who lies next to his wife, Jacqueline Kennedy Onassis, and a short distance from his brother, Robert (the only grave marked with a simple white cross). At the **Tomb of the Unknowns**, visitors can watch a solemn Changing of the Guard ceremony every thirty minutes (hourly Oct–Mar). while the gravesite of Pierre L'Enfant offers a superb view over the Mall and the District that he designed. L'Enfant's grave is on the grounds of the cemetery's prominent Neoclassical **Arlington House** (same hours; free), Lee's modest mansion that, after the war, his family was forced to sell after finding the presence of war dead inhospitable to a country home. The recent **Women in Military Service Memorial**, by the main gate, is the country's first national monument to American servicewomen.

Unless you have strong legs and lots of time, the best way to see the vast cemetery is by Tourmobile ($6; see p.403), which leaves from the visitor center at the entrance. You can also walk here from the Lincoln Memorial across the Arlington Bridge or take the Blue Line of the Metro.

Eating

Just as the faces in government change with every election, so too do **restaurants**, which come and go more quickly in Washington DC than anywhere else in the US. Within this constant flux a few long-standing favorites endure. Certain

△ Arlington National Cemetery

neighborhoods – Connecticut Avenue around **Dupont Circle**, 18th Street and Columbia Road in **Adams–Morgan**, M Street in **Georgetown**, and downtown's **Seventh Street** and **Chinatown** – always seem to hold a satisfying range of dining options. A few citywide chains like *Teaism* and *Firehook* offer good coffee and quick snacks; otherwise, the cafés in the main museums are good for downtown lunch breaks. Likewise, you'll find convenient **food courts** in Union Station and at the Old Post Office.

Downtown

Breadline 1751 Pennsylvania Ave NW ☎ 202/822-8900. DC's best sandwiches, made with DC's best bread. This superb open bakery also turns out pizza, empanadas, flatbreads, salads, and smoothies, using organic ingredients whenever possible.

Café Asia 1720 I St NW ☎ 202/659-2696. Breezy Pan-Asian restaurant that's good for budget sushi and sashimi, or try the big plates of lemongrass-grilled chicken, seafood *bakar* (in banana leaf with spicy prawn sauce), satay, or Thai noodles.

Café Atlantico 405 8th NW ☎ 202/393-0812. Upscale *nuevo Latino* treat with spicy spins on traditional cuisine, but really best for its *Minibar*, a six-seat counter famed for its avant-garde versions of old favorites (reserve a month in advance and expect to pay $95 a head).

District Chophouse & Brewery 509 7th St NW ☎ 202/347-3434. This classy swing-era joint delivers great music, a hearty, meat-and-potatoes grillhouse menu (along with some solid crab cakes), and good house beers on tap.

Grillfish 1200 New Hampshire Ave NW ☎ 202/331-7310. Industrial-chic eatery offering casual dining and well-cooked fish and seafood; the daily catch options might include sea bass, tuna, snapper, trout, mahi-mahi, shark, or calamari.

Jaleo 480 7th St NW ☎ 202/628-7949. Renowned upscale tapas bar-restaurant with flamenco dancing to accompany its fine seafood and plentiful sangria. Limited reservation policy makes for long waits during peak hours.

Old Ebbitt Grill 675 15th St NW ☎ 202/347-4801. A plush recreation of a nineteenth-century tavern, with mahogany bar (serving microbrews), gas chandeliers, leather booths, and gilt mirrors. Politico clientele feasts on everything from burgers to oysters.

Red Sage 605 14th St NW ☏ 202/638-4444. Landmark Southwestern restaurant, dripping with Santa Fe chic and featuring rotisserie-grilled meat, fish, and vegetarian specials. Reservations essential.

Reeve's Restaurant and Bakery 1306 G St NW ☏ 202/628-6350. This classic diner, in business since 1886, has an all-you-can-eat breakfast and fruit bar, crisp-coated chicken at lunchtime, and flavorful pies.

Sky Room *Hotel Washington*, 515 15th St NW ☏ 202/638-5900. Perched on a hilltop above the White House, this restaurant has magnificent views that more than make up for the unremarkable (and pricey) steak and seafood. April–Oct only.

~~Ten Penh~~ 1001 Pennsylvania Ave NW ☏ 202/393-4500. High-profile Asian-fusion restaurant serving up expensive but delicious dishes like roasted duck and pork wonton ravioli.

Dupont Circle

Bistro du Coin 1738 Connecticut Ave NW ☏ 202/234-6969. Classic bistro with a superb bar, boisterous atmosphere, and genuine French food for prices that won't cost you your Armani shirt.

Café Citron 1343 Connecticut Ave NW ☏ 202/530-8844. Bright restaurant serving tasty Caribbean-influenced Latin food – try the *ceviche* or fill up on one of their popular *fajitas*. Stick around for a smooth late-night scene at the bar.

City Lights of China 1731 Connecticut Ave NW ☏ 202/265-6688. Well-regarded Chinese restaurant, with spicy Szechuan and Hunan specialties and a strong emphasis on seafood – try the Hunan shrimp. Also good for steamed dumplings and garlic eggplant.

Luna Grill & Diner 1301 Connecticut Ave NW ☏ 202/835-2280. Atypical diner with bright decor, planetary murals and mosaics, plus wholesome blue-plate specials and "green plate" (vegetarian) dishes. Try the "Eggs Neptune": eggs Benedict with a Maryland twist, crab cakes.

The Newsroom 1803 Connecticut Ave NW ☏ 202/332-1489. Offers a wide selection of hipster magazines, British and French imports, and hard-to-find newspapers, plus Internet access, coffee, and snacks.

Pizzeria Paradiso 2029 P St NW ☏ 202/223-1245. Arguably DC's best pizzeria, with famously tasty pies whose toppings range from simple basil-and-cheese to parmesan, egg, and mullet

roe. Expect to wait in line. Also at 3282 M St NW, Georgetown ☏ 202/337-1245.

Restaurant Nora 2132 Florida Ave NW ☏ 202/462-5143. One of DC's best places to eat, with prices to match. The all-organic fare includes oddball items like Amish pork loin medallions. Book ahead.

Skewers 1633 P St NW ☏ 202/387-7400. Mid-priced Middle Eastern that's tops for kebabs – with such unexpected ingredients as monkfish and BBQ shrimp – seafood, and delicately flavored rice. Also excellent appetizers.

Sushi Taro 1503 17th St NW ☏ 202/462-8999. One of DC's best Japanese restaurants, also with fine curries and noodles. When the cherry blossoms start to bloom, keep an eye out for the annual all-you-can-eat sushi-fest.

Zorba's Café 1612 20th St NW ☏ 202/387-8555. A self-serve café where you'll find affordable Greek combo platters, kebabs, and pita sandwiches. The sidewalk seating is hard to get in summer.

Adams–Morgan

Ben's Chili Bowl 1213 U St NW ☏ 202/667-0909. East of Adams–Morgan in the Shaw neighborhood, but worth the trip for the legendary chili dogs, milk shakes, and cheese fries.

Bukom Café 2442 18th St NW ☏ 202/265-4600. Savory West African dishes, such as African curried chicken, spicy kebabs, and Moi Moi (black-eyed peas with corned beef and sardines), usually for less than $10.

Cashion's Eat Place 1819 Columbia Rd NW ☏ 202/797-1819. Renowned for its clever takes on New Southern cuisine, where old-time dishes like casseroles, tarts, corncakes, grits, sweet potatoes, and fruit and nut pies are transformed into taste-bud-altering delights – at a rather high price.

The Diner 2453 18th St NW ☏ 202/232-8800. More a stylish café than a down-at-the-heel diner, greasy classics adorn the egg, pancake, and sandwich-rich menu nonetheless. Popular for its classic coffee counter and 24hr service; late-night lines form on the weekends.

~~Grill from Ipanema~~ 1858 Columbia Rd NW ☏ 202/986-0757. Somewhat pricey Brazilian staples made with flair, highlighted by the *feijoada* (meat stew), shrimp dishes, and scrumptious Sunday brunch. Try the baked clams to start and watch your *caipirinha* (rum cocktail) intake.

Lauriol Plaza 1835 18th St NW ☏ 202/387-0035. The Latin American-styled *ceviche* and grilled meats that are worth the effort to eat them; the place frequently gets packed with tourists and revelers.

Meze 2437 18th St NW ☏ 202/797-0017. A wide array of delicious Turkish meze (the Middle East's answer to tapas), both hot and cold, is served in a fashionable restaurant-lounge setting. Kebabs, grape leaves, and apricot chicken are among the highlights.

Mixtec 1792 Columbia Rd NW ℡ 202/332-1011. The great-tasting, low-priced Mexican food includes superb tacos and tortillas, plus spit-roasted chicken, mussels steamed with chilis, and a soothing *menudo* (an aromatic soup).

Pizza Mart 2445 18th St NW ℡ 202/234-9700. The elephantine slices at this hole-in-the-wall pizzeria are a club-hopper's late-night salvation. Open until 4am.

Tryst 2459 18th St NW ℡ 202/232-5500. Very popular hangout where you can enjoy decent pastries and gourmet drinks, but also slurp down wine, beer, and even morning cocktails. Arty and relaxed, with the added bonus of Internet access and good sandwiches at the adjoining diner.

Georgetown

Bangkok Bistro 3251 Prospect St NW ℡ 202/337-2424. Infuses some style into Thai dining with a sleek dining room that's often full. The old favorites (tom yum, pad thai, shrimp cakes, and satay) sit alongside spicy beef curries and chili prawns.

Bistro Francais 3128 M St NW ℡ 202/338-3830. Renowned for its (affordable) French cooking, from simple steak frites and rotisserie chicken to roast pigeon and lamb sausage; open until 3am.

Booeymonger 3265 Prospect St NW ℡ 202/333-4810. Crowded deli-coffee shop, excellent for its inventive sandwiches like the Gatsby Arrow (roast beef and brie) and the Patty Hearst (turkey and bacon with Russian dressing).

Dean & Deluca 3276 M St NW ℡ 202/342-2500. Superior self-service café (and fantastic attached deli-market with sushi stand) in one of M Street's most handsome and historic redbrick buildings. Good for croissants, cappuccino, designer salads, pastas, and sandwiches.

J Paul's 3218 M St NW ℡ 202/333-3450. A "dining saloon" that offers the standard, but good, grill/barbecue menu, with some much-loved crab cakes, too. Last orders for food taken around midnight.

Martin's Tavern 1264 Wisconsin Ave NW ℡ 202/333-7370. Old-fashioned, clubby diner serving up succulent steaks and chops, great burgers, linguine with clam sauce, and oyster platters.

Moby Dick House of Kabob 1070 31 St NW ℡ 202/333-4400. Steps from the canal, this cramped kitchen does great Persian food – tender kebabs, *lavash* bread, rice, and yogurt – all for under $10.

Old Glory 3139 M St NW ℡ 202/337-3406. Rollicking barbecue restaurant with hickory smoke rising from the kitchen. Accompany your huge portions of ribs and chicken with one of the half-dozen sauces on every table and a shot of great bourbon.

Paolo's 1303 Wisconsin Ave NW ℡ 202/333-7353. Designer Italian restaurant with a few, highly sought-after tables that open to the sidewalk. The gourmet pizza includes toppings such as feta cheese, salmon, goat's cheese, spinach, and sun-dried tomatoes; the pastas and other specialties are even better.

Red Ginger 1564 Wisconsin Ave NW ℡ 202/965-7009. Crab cakes, seafood quesadillas, and oxtail stew are just some of the choices at this Caribbean-African restaurant, with numerous "small plates" (à la tapas) at affordable prices.

Upper Northwest

Ardeo 3311 Connecticut Ave NW ℡ 202/244-6750. Ultra-trendy and pricey spot with "Modern American" cuisine – meaning lots of oddball hybrids from duck-confit cannelloni to mahi mahi with vanilla "foam" – though the culinary experiments work most of the time.

Indique 3512 Connecticut Ave NW ℡ 202/244-6600. Recipes from all over India come together with a modern twist at this stylish and affordable restaurant. Don't miss the tasty *samosa* appetizer.

Lebanese Taverna 2641 Connecticut Ave NW ℡ 202/265-8681. Tasty Middle Eastern joint with soothingly dark, authentic decor inside and ample sidewalk tables under shady umbrellas outside.

Nam Viet 3419 Connecticut Ave NW ℡ 202/237-1015. No-frills Vietnamese eatery where you can enjoy good soups, caramel pork, Vietnamese steak, and grilled chicken and fish.

Vace 3315 Connecticut Ave NW ℡ 202/363-1999. You might grab a slice of the excellent pizza or try a tasty sub sandwich at this ethnic deli, or you might pack a picnic from the solid selection of sausage, tortellini salad, and olives before heading to the zoo.

Nightlife

Peak times for **drinking** in DC tend to be during rush hour, and comparatively few people who work in the District during the week venture back into town at the weekend. However, things are slowly improving, and in the well-worn haunts of collegiate **Georgetown**, yuppified **Dupont Circle**, and boisterous **Adams–Morgan**, you should be able to pass a pleasant evening or two – and in the suit-and-tie spots on **Capitol Hill**, even spot a politician or two. For clubs, expect to pay a cover of $6 to $20 (highest on weekends); ticket prices for most gigs run $5 to $25. Check the free weekly *CityPaper* for up-to-date **listings** of music, theater, and other events in the area, in addition to good alternative features and reporting. **Gay** and **lesbian** life is at its most outgoing in Dupont Circle.

Bars

Bedrock Billiards 1841 Columbia Rd NW ☎202/667-7665. A comfortable, lively subterranean setting, top bartenders, and loyal clientele set this funky pool hall apart from Adams–Morgan's more frenzied dance-oriented spots.

Brickskeller 1523 22nd St NW, Dupont Circle ☎202/293-1885. Renowned brick-lined basement saloon serving "the world's largest selection of beer" – as many as 1000 different types, including dozens from US microbreweries. Also has an inexpensive inn upstairs.

Bullfeathers 410 First St SE ☎202/543-5005. Pol watchers just may catch a sighting at this old-time Hill favorite, a dark and clubby spot with affordable beer that was named for one of Teddy Roosevelt's favorite euphemisms during his White House years.

Capitol City Brewing Co 2 Massachusetts Ave NE ☎202/842-2337. Prime microbrewing turf near Union Station, highlighted by Amber Waves Ale, German-styled Capitol Kolsch, and Prohibition Porter. Another branch is downtown at 1100 New York Ave NW ☎202/628-2222.

Capitol Lounge 229 Pennsylvania Ave SE ☎202/547-2098. More sophisticated than most of the Hill spots – with cigars and martinis in the downstairs bar – but there's still plenty of life up in the brick-walled saloon thanks to happy hours and colorful campaign memorabilia.

D.A.'s RFD Washington 810 7th St NW ☎202/289-2030. The leading edge in Downtown DC microbreweries, with three hundred bottled beers and forty locally crafted and international brews on tap. Centrally located near the MCI Center, so watch for heavy post-game crowds.

Dragonfly 1215 Connecticut Ave NW ☎202/331-1775. Lounge serving sushi and cocktails, with an ultra-swank decor and a beautiful young crowd on the make.

The Dubliner 520 N Capitol St NW, in the *Phoenix Park Hotel* ☎202/737-3773. A wooden-vaulted, good-time Irish pub with draft Guinness, boisterous conversation, and live Irish music catering to the more refined Hill set. The patio is a solid summer hangout.

Fox and Hounds 1537 17th St NW, Dupont Circle ☎202/232-6307. Smack in the middle of the 17th Street scene, this easygoing bar draws a diverse crowd, all here to enjoy the stiff and cheap rail drinks and the solid jukebox.

Garrett's 3003 M St NW ☎202/333-1033. Amid its brick-and-wood interior, Garrett's features a giant rhino head by the door, pumping alt-rock jukebox that keeps the young crowd in a party mood, and nightly drink specials, along with a few microbrews.

Hawk 'n Dove 329 Pennsylvania Ave SE ☎202/543-3300. Iconic DC pub (a bit tatty at the edges now) hung with football pennants, bottles, and bric-a-brac. Attracts Hill interns for its cheap food and dance nights.

Lucky Bar 1221 Connecticut Ave NW ☎202/331-3733. This everybody-knows-your-name kind of place has plenty of room and booths at the back to hang out in, plus a pool table, cheap beer, and world soccer on the tube.

Nanny O'Brien's 3319 Connecticut Ave NW ☎202/686-9189. An authentic Irish pub in Upper Northwest, with live music from (or in the style of) the Emerald Isle several nights a week.

Clubs and live-music venues

9:30 Club 815 V St NW, Shaw district ☎202/265-0930. Top musicians love to play at this spacious yet intimate club, deservedly famous as DC's best venue for live acts, from indie rock and pop to reggae and rap. Neighborhood can be rough at night, though.

The Black Cat 1811 14th St NW, Shaw district ☎202/667-7960. Part-owned by Foo Fighter Dave Grohl, this indie institution provides a showcase for up-and-coming rock, punk, and garage bands and veteran alternative acts alike. Connected to the no-cover *Red Room Bar*.

Blues Alley 1073 Wisconsin Ave NW (rear) ☎202/337-4141. Small, celebrated Georgetown jazz bar, in business for over thirty years, attracting top names. Shows usually at 8pm and 10pm, plus midnight some weekends; buy tickets in advance. Cover runs $10–40.

Bohemian Caverns 2001 11th St NW, Shaw district ☎202/299-0800. Legendary DC jazz supper club, set in a basement grotto below the stylish ground-level restaurant. Cover runs to $15 or more, with a limited number of reserved tickets for bigger acts.

Chief Ike's Mambo Room 1725 Columbia Rd NW, Adams-Morgan ☎202/332-2211. Ramshackle mural-clad bar with live bands playing rock, reggae, and R&B, or DJs hosting theme nights. An unpretentious, fun spot to dance.

Eighteenth Street Lounge 1212 18th St, Dupont Circle ☎202/466-3922. Ultra-stylish spot housed in a former mansion. While the attitude can be a bit thick at times, the beats – mostly techno, house, and dub – are a big draw, along with superstar DJs. Look for the unmarked door and dress smart.

Habana Village 1834 Columbia Rd NW ☎202/462-6310. Intoxicating Latin dance joint (tango and salsa lessons are available) infused with an eclectic spirit. A good downstairs bar serves a fine mojito.

IOTA 2832 Wilson Blvd, Arlington, VA ☎703/522-8340. One of the area's better choices for nightclubbing, this warehouse-style music joint has nightly performances by local and national indie, folk, and blues bands. Has a great bar, and attached restaurant, too.

Love 1350 Okie St NE ☎202/636-9030. Mobs of Washingtonians from all walks of life flock to this massive four-story club to dance to hip-hop, techno, and Latin. It's in a dicey area, so take a cab there and back.

Madam's Organ 2461 18th St NW ☎202/667-5370. Straightforward hangout with a small cover, featuring live blues, raw R&B, and bluegrass. Upstairs, there's a pool table and a rooftop bar.

Rumba Café 2443 18th St NW, Adams-Morgan ☎202/588-5501. This Latin oasis, a sliver of a café-bar with walls decked out with paintings and photographs, is a good bet for a night of sipping *caipirinhas* and grooving to live Brazilian bossa nova, salsa, and Afro-Cuban rhythms. Wed–Sat only.

Performing arts

With five different theater spaces, the **Kennedy Center**, 2700 F St NW (☎202/467-4600, @www.kennedy-center.org), next to the Watergate complex, hosts most of the capital's highbrow cultural events, including National Symphony Orchestra and Washington National Opera performances. The highly regarded, often pioneering **Arena Stage**, 1101 Sixth St SW at Maine Avenue (☎202/488-3300, @www.arenastage.org), puts on contemporary **theater** and performance pieces at its three-stage complex, while the historic **Ford's Theatre**, 511 Tenth St NW (☎202/347-4833, @www.fordstheatre.org), has a family-friendly program of mainstream musicals and dramas, frequently historical in nature. The celebrated **Shakespeare Theatre**, 450 Seventh St NW (☎202/547-1122, @www.shakespearedc.org), stages five productions a year, plus a free summer performance in Rock Creek Park; the **National Theatre**, 1321 Pennsylvania Ave NW (☎202/628-6161, @www.nationaltheatre.org), offers big-name touring musicals and other crowd-pleasers; and the experimental **Woolly Mammoth Theatre**, 641 D St NW (☎202/289-2443, @www.woollymammoth.net), showcases budget- and mid-priced contemporary and experimental plays. The **Source Theatre Company**, 1501 14th St NW, Logan Circle (☎202/332-3300, @www.studiotheatre.org), rounds out DC's alternative theater scene.

Twenty minutes out of the city, **Wolf Trap Farm Park**, 1551 Trap Rd, Vienna, VA (☎703/255-1900, @www.wolf-trap.org), is the country's first national park for the performing arts, and presents concerts, opera, ballet, and dance at the outdoor Filene Center or the indoor Barns. There's a Metro shuttle bus service from West Falls Church station for most performances (every 20 min; $5). For **tickets** call ☎1-877/WOLFTRAP or go online at @tickets.com. You can also buy tickets in person at the Wolf Trap box office (☎703/255-1868).

Spectator sports

Tickets to Washington Redskins **football** games at FedEx Field in Landover, Maryland (☎301/276-6050, @www.redskins.com), are sold on a season-ticket basis only and often impossible to get unless you have a connection. Easier to obtain are tickets to DC's new Washington Nationals **baseball** team, which plays at RFK Stadium in a grim part of the city, at 2400 E Capitol St (tickets $7–50; ☏1-888/632-NATS, ⊛washington.nationals.mlb.com), but will move to a new waterfront stadium in the southeast part of DC in 2008. Also in RFK Stadium is the DC United **soccer** squad (tickets $16–40; ☏703/478-6600, ⊛www .dcunited.com), which plays in the pro MLS league. The huge downtown **Verizon Center** (☏202/628-3200, ⊛www.verizoncenter.com) hosts home games of the pro **basketball** men's Washington Wizards (tickets $20–175; ☏202/661-5050, ⊛www.nba.com/wizards) and women's Mystics (tickets $10–79; ☏202/266-2277, ⊛www.wnba.com/mystics), as well as the pro **hockey** Capitals (tickets $10–225; ☏202/266-CAPS, ⊛www.washingtoncaps.com).

Virginia

VIRGINIA is the oldest American colony and, as birthplace of the nation's tobacco industry and home to no less a figure than George Washington, it has arguably had the most direct influence on the early development of United States.

Virginia's recorded history famously began at **Jamestown,** just off the Chesapeake Bay, with the establishment in 1607 of the first successful English colony in North America. Though the original colonists hoped to find gold, it was **tobacco** that made their fortunes when a smooth, palatable variety of the plant was introduced in 1615 by John Rolfe, and it quickly became the colony's major cash crop. Before long, vast plantations, owned by a very few aristocratic families, sprang up along the many broad rivers that flow into the Chesapeake Bay. To grow and harvest tobacco required both an immense amount of land and labor – so Native Americans were driven off their land and **slaves** were imported from Africa. By 1700, slaves accounted for nearly half of the colony's 75,000 people; a hundred years later, they numbered more than 300,000.

Virginians had an enormous impact on the foundation of the United States: George Mason, Thomas Jefferson, and James Madison wrote the Declaration of Independence and the Constitution, and four of the first five US presidents were from Virginia (excepting only John Adams). However, by the mid-1800s the state was in decline, its once fertile fields depleted by overuse and its agrarian economy increasingly eclipsed by the urban and industrialized North.

As the confrontation between North and South over slavery and related economic and political issues grew more divisive, Virginia was caught in the middle. Though this slaveholding state initially voted against secession from the Union, it joined the Confederacy when the **Civil War** broke out, providing its capital, Richmond, and its military leader, Robert E. Lee, who had previously turned down an offer to lead the Union army. Four long years later, Virginia was ravaged, its towns and cities wrecked, its farmlands ruined, and most of its youth dead.

Richmond itself was largely destroyed in the war; today it's a small city with some good museums, and is the best starting point for seeing Virginia. The bulk of the **Colonial** sites are concentrated just to the east, in what is known as the **Historic Triangle.** Here the shadowy remains of **Jamestown,** the original colony,

Williamsburg, the restored Colonial capital, and **Yorktown**, the site of the final battle of the Revolutionary War, lie within half an hour's drive of each other.

Another historic center, **Charlottesville** – home to Thomas Jefferson's estate, Monticello – sits at the foot of the gorgeous **Blue Ridge Mountains**, an hour west of Richmond. It's also within easy reach of the natural splendors of **Shenandoah National Park** and the little towns of the western valleys. **Northern Virginia**, often visited as a day-trip from Washington DC, features several posh suburbs, a number of restored historic homes – the closest Colonial architecture to the capital being in **Alexandria** – and **Manassas**, the scene of two important Civil War battles.

Getting around Virginia

Virginia is an easy place to explore. Five north–south **Amtrak** routes cross the eastern side of the state, one of them an "Auto Train" – connecting Lorton, VA, with Florida – that allows you to bring a car along. In addition, the daily Cardinal line runs east from Washington DC to Charlottesville and on to Chicago. Greyhound **buses** reach dozens of smaller towns. **Drivers** heading south can take the stunning Blue Ridge Parkway along the Appalachians. If you've got the time, there are ample opportunity for **cycling**, whether on quiet country roads or up in the mountains, and **hiking** or **walking** are also compelling options.

Northern Virginia

Northern Virginia is becoming one large suburban enclave. It includes such chic spots as McLean and Fairfax County, which are home to a high proportion of US senators. In contrast, **Alexandria**, nestled on the Potomac just beyond the limits of the nation's capital (but not beyond its Metro system), seems at least two centuries removed from the modern political whirl. Further afield, this Anglophile heartland of Virginia's landed gentry – often called "Hunt Country" for their love of horses and fancy-dress blood sports – holds well-preserved historic estates, cottages, churches, barns, and taverns tucked away along the quiet back roads. It's all very popular with tourists, nowhere more so than **Mount Vernon**, the longtime home of George Washington, while **Manassas** to the west was the site of the bloody battles of Bull Run.

Alexandria

Extending a good half-mile west of the Potomac and several blocks north and south of it, the **Old Town** of **ALEXANDRIA** is a must, especially for those who are staying in Washington DC but don't have time to venture very far into Virginia. Originally an important Colonial trading post and a busy port named after the pioneer John Alexander, the town was actually ceded to the District of Columbia in 1801, but Virginia demanded it back in 1847.

In earlier days, George Washington maintained close ties with Alexandria, owning property here and attending gatherings at the famous **Gadsby's Tavern**, 134 N Royal St (tours Wed–Sat 11am–4pm, Sun 1–4pm; $4; Ⓦwww.gadsbystavern. org), which occupies two stately Georgian buildings: the *City Hotel* from 1792 and the tavern itself from 1785. Downstairs, there's a working restaurant, complete with "authentic" colonial food and costumed staff. Among other restored buildings open to the public are the **Carlyle House**, 121 N Fairfax St (tours Tues–Sat 10am–4pm, Sun noon–4:30pm; $4; Ⓦwww.carlylehouse.org), a 1752 manor house that was home to five royal governors; and the **Lee-Fendall House**, 614 Oronoco St (Tues–Sat 10am–4pm, Sun noon–4pm; $4; Ⓦ www.leefendallhouse. org), a splendid clapboard mansion built by Philip Fendall, a cousin of Robert E. Lee's father. Down on the waterfront, a former munitions factory houses the **Torpedo Factory Art Center**, 105 N Union St (daily 10am–5pm; free; Ⓦ www. torpedofactory.org), where you can watch artists at work in more than two hundred studios and browse several galleries. In the same building, the **Alexandria Archaeology Museum** (Tues–Fri 10am–3pm, Sat 10am–5pm, Sun 1–5pm; free; Ⓦ www.alexandriaarchaeology.org) displays various aspects of the town's history and prehistory. The Georgian **Christ Church**, 118 N Washington St (Mon–Sat 9am–4pm, Sun 2–4pm; Ⓦ www.historicchristchurch.org), was built in 1773 and often counted George Washington among its worshippers. Patent medicines for the general were concocted behind the tiny yellow windows of the **Stabler-Leadbeater Apothecary Shop**, 105 S Fairfax St (Mon–Sat 10am–4pm, Sun 1–5pm; $4; Ⓦ www.apothecarymuseum.org), which was founded in 1792 and remained in business until the 1930s; it still displays herbs, potions, and medical paraphernalia – some eight thousand items in all and well worth a look

Next to the Amtrak and King Street subway station stands the 333ft obelisk of the **George Washington National Masonic Memorial**, 101 Callahan Dr (daily 9am–4pm; free; Ⓦ www.gwmemorial.org), which is visible for miles around; inside, there's a 17ft bronze **statue** of the founding father, sundry memorabilia, and dioramas depicting events from his life.

Practicalities

The **Metro** station for Old Town Alexandria is King Street (25min from downtown DC; $1.85; yellow and blue lines), a mile or so from most of the sights; alternatively, you can pick up the local **DASH** bus ($1; routes 2, 5, and 7; call ☎703/370-3274, Ⓦ www.dashbus.com), which runs down King Street, and get off at Fairfax Street; if you prefer, you can make the twenty-minute walk from the King Street station instead. The friendly **visitor center** is located in the **Ramsay House**, the town's oldest, at 221 King St (daily 9am–5pm; ☎703/838-4200, Ⓦ www.FunSide.com); here you can get the usual tourist information as well as details on walking tours.

Good places to **stay** include *Best Western Old Colony Inn*, 1101 N Washington St (☎703/739-2222, Ⓦ www.bestwestern.com; ❹), a moderately priced spot with standard amenities (plus free breakfast and Internet access), and *Morrison House*, 116 S Alfred St (☎703/838-8000 or 1-800/367-0800, Ⓦ www.morrisonhouse.com; ❾), a faux Federal-era townhouse (built in 1985) complete with ersatz "authentic" decor, like parquet floors and crystal chandeliers, yet with modern comforts like high-speed Internet connections and designer linens.

There's a great range of **places to eat**. Try the 🎋 *Blue Point Grill*, 600 Franklin St (☎703/739-0404), whose extremely fresh and delicious seafood earns it a reputation as one of Alexandria's best restaurants; the *Fish Market*, 105 King St (☎703/836-5676), a brick building with a terrace just one block from the water, serving oysters and chowder at the bar and fried-fish platters, pastas, and fish entrees; and *Southside 815*, 815 S Washington St (☎703/836-6222), offering upscale Southern cooking, heavy with good, old-fashioned favorites like biscuits with ham, gravy, thick and buttery cornbread, BBQ shrimp, crab fritters, and straight-up crawdads and catfish.

Mount Vernon

Set on a bluff overlooking the Potomac River, eight miles south of Alexandria, **Mount Vernon** (daily April–Aug 8am–5pm; March, Sept & Oct 9am–5pm;

Nov–Feb 9am–4pm; $13; ⓦwww.mountvernon.org) is the country estate built by **George Washington** – with five hundred acres of landscaped and planted grounds – that has been restored to the year 1799, the last year of the general's life. Just fifteen miles from downtown DC, it's close enough to be reached as a day-trip on the city's Tourmobiles, or by the Fairfax Connector 101 bus from Huntington Metro station.

In the house itself, the furnishings and decoration reflect Washington's preference for plain living, but few items – a reading chair with a built-in fan, and a key to the destroyed Bastille, presented by Thomas Paine on behalf of Lafayette – give much of a sense of his character. The four-poster bed upon which he died stands in an upstairs bedroom. Outside, a small **museum** traces Washington's ancestry and displays porcelain, medals, weapons, and silver, and a renovated **slave quarters**, built to house the ninety slaves who lived and worked on the grounds alone, stands nearby. Washington and his wife, Martha, are buried in a simple tomb on the south side of the house.

Three miles away stands the restored **grist mill**, Route 235 S (April–Oct daily 10am–4pm; $4 separate admission), that Washington built as a water-powered testament to the future of American industry, and today colonial re-enactors go about the laborious work of crushing grain into flour and cornmeal. In 2007, the even more interesting prospect of a restored **distillery** will open at the site.

Gunston Hall

Gunston Hall, the 1755 Georgian brick home of Washington's contemporary, **George Mason**, is a twenty-minute drive south of Washington DC near highways 1 and 95 (daily 9.30am–5pm; $8; ⓦwww.gunstonhall.org). Mason, in writing the Virginia Declaration of Rights, stated "that all men are by nature equally free and independent and have certain inherent rights," inspiring Thomas Jefferson when he later wrote the Declaration of Independence. Mason was one of the main framers of the US Constitution, which he subsequently refused to support because it neither included a Bill of Rights nor abolished slavery – ironic, considering he himself was a slaveholder. One of the most impressive works of architecture in Virginia, much of his home was designed and constructed by William Buckland; the masterful interiors, particularly in the stately drawing room, feature exquisite carved ornamentation (a fireplace mantel in the Chinoiserie style is particularly distinctive). The house fronts onto a large formal garden, beyond which lie extensive grounds surrounded by a riverfront state park and wildlife refuge.

Manassas Battlefield National Park

Manassas Battlefield National Park extends over grassy hills at the western fringes of the Washington DC suburban belt, just off I-66. Soon after the first shots were fired at Fort Sumter, the first major land battle of the Civil War – known in the North as the **Battle of Bull Run** – was fought here on the morning of July 21, 1861. Expecting an easy victory, some 25,000 Union troops attacked a Confederate detachment that controlled a vital railroad link to the Shenandoah Valley, and spectators came to see what they imagined would be a rousing entertainment. The battle was a disaster, however: the rebels proved powerful opponents and their strength in battle earned their commander, General Thomas Jackson, the famous nickname "Stonewall." He and General Lee also masterminded a second, even more demoralizing Union loss here in late August 1862.

Displays in the small **visitor center** at the entrance (daily 8.30am–5pm; June–Aug Sat & Sun until 6pm; park admission $3; ⓦwww.nps.gov/mana) describe how the first battle took shape, and detail other aspects of the war.

Richmond and the tidewater

At the very heart of Virginia, **Richmond** and the **Chesapeake Bay tidewater** make up a fairly compact area that holds some of the country's most important surviving colonial- and Civil War-era sites. The greatest interest is to be found in the fascinating **Historic Triangle**, east of Richmond, and in **Fredericksburg**, to the north, around which several crucial battles were waged.

Fredericksburg

Only a mile off the I-95 highway, halfway to Richmond from Washington, DC, **FREDERICKSBURG** is one of Virginia's prettiest historic towns, where elegant downtown streets are backed by residential avenues lined with white picket fences. In colonial days, this was an important inland port, in which tobacco and other plantation commodities were loaded onto boats that sailed down the Rappahannock River. Dozens of stately early-American buildings along the waterfront now hold antique stores and secondhand bookshops.

In the 1816 town hall, the **Fredericksburg Area Museum**, 907 Princess Anne St (Mon–Sat 10am–5pm, Sun 1–5pm; $5; Ⓦwww.famcc.org), has a range of displays tracing local history, from Native American settlements to the Civil Rights era. The **Rising Sun Tavern**, at 1304 Caroline St, was built as a home in 1760 by George Washington's brother, Charles. As an inn, it became a key meeting place for patriots and a hotbed of sedition. It is now a small **museum** (March–Nov Mon–Sat 9am–5pm, Sun 11am–5pm; Dec–Feb Mon–Sat 10am–4pm, Sun noon–4pm; $5), where costumed guides take visitors around a collection of pub games and antique pewter. Guides are also on hand to explain eighteenth-century medicine at **Hugh Mercer's Apothecary Shop**, 1020 Caroline St (same hours as above; $5), which often involved treating patients with the likes of leeches and crab claws.

Fredericksburg's strategic location made it vital during the **Civil War**, and the land around the town was heavily contested. More than 100,000 men lost their lives in the major battles of Fredericksburg, Chancellorsville, Spotsylvania, and countless bloody skirmishes. The **visitor center**, 1013 Lafayette Blvd (daily hours vary but often 9am–5pm; free; Ⓦwww.nps.gov/frsp), has informative exhibits and can lead you out to **Fredericksburg and Spotsylvania National Battlefield Park**, south of town. Contact the visitor center or see the above website for information on the other major battlefields in the area, **Wilderness** and **Chancellorsville**, both west of town, as well as the various manors and shrines to be found on the killing grounds.

Practicalities

The **Amtrak** station is at 200 Lafayette Blvd and the **Greyhound** station at 2217 Princess Ann St. Fredericksburg's **visitor center** at 706 Caroline St (daily summer 9am–7pm, rest of year 9am–5pm; ☎540/373-1776 or 1-800/678-4748, Ⓦwww.visitfred.com) can provide maps of walking tours and details about discounted tickets to the area's attractions.

Fredericksburg has many good, old-fashioned **B&Bs**, including the 1812 *Kenmore Inn*, 1200 Princess Anne St (☎540/371-7622, Ⓦwww.kenmoreinn.com; ❺), which has stylish rooms with Internet access and a cozy pub in the basement that serves traditional fish and ham dishes, occasionally with live jazz, and the *Richard Johnston Inn*, 711 Caroline St (☎540/899-7606 or 877-557-0770, Ⓦwww.therichardjohnstoninn.com; ❹–❼), an elegant, eighteenth-century B&B with plush rooms and a broad range of prices, from $95 to $185. One worthwhile motel to try is the *Fredericksburg Colonial Inn*, 1707 Princess Anne St (☎540/371-5666,

433

@www.fci1.com; ❹), known for its tasteful rooms stocked with antiques. For close access to the four battlefields, there's *On Keegan Pond*, 11315 Gordon Rd (☎540/785-4662; ❹), in a pleasant rural setting, also with antique-laden rooms.

Thanks to a lot of weekend activity, the town has several good places to **eat** and **drink**. *Sammy T's*, 801 Caroline St (☎540/371-2008), is a popular bar and diner with substantial sandwiches, salads, and pastas, and a huge range of bottled beers. *Smythe's Cottage*, 303 Fauquier St (☎540/373-1645) serves up tasty Southern cooking like Virginia ham and braised quail in an early nineteenth-century cottage. The *Virginia Deli*, 101 Williams St (☎540/371-2233), doles out hefty sandwiches with names like the Stonewall Jackson (salami and two kinds of ham) and the Blue & Grey (hot chicken, ham, and swiss cheese); the *Colonial Tavern*, 406 Lafayette Blvd (☎540/373-1313), is the place to fill up on Irish food, music, and beer.

Richmond and around

Founded in 1737 at the furthest navigable point on the James River, **RICHMOND** remained a small outpost until just before the end of the colonial era, when Virginians, realizing that their capital at Williamsburg was open to British attack, shifted it fifty miles further inland. Ironically, the move ended up preserving Williamsburg for posterity, but failed to offer Richmond much protection: the city was raided many times and twice put to the torch, once by troops under the command of Benedict Arnold.

Nonetheless, Richmond flourished, its population reaching 100,000 by the time of the Civil War. When war broke out it was named the **capital of the Confederacy**, despite Virginia's having voted two-to-one against secession from the Union just a month before. For four years the city was the focus of Southern defenses and Union attacks, but despite an almost constant state of siege – General McClellan came within six miles as early as 1862 – it held on almost until the very end. Less than a week after the city's fall, on April 3, 1865, Robert E. Lee surrendered to Ulysses S. Grant at Appomattox, a hundred miles west.

After the war, Richmond was devastated. Much of its downtown was burned, allegedly by fleeing Confederates who wanted to keep its stores of weapons and its warehouses full of tobacco out of the victors' hands. Today's Richmond has an extensive inventory of architecturally significant older buildings alongside its modern office towers, while **tobacco** is still a major industry – machine-rolled cigarettes were invented here in the 1870s, and Marlboro-maker **Philip Morris** runs a huge manufacturing plant just south of downtown. Finally, it may surprise some visitors to find that Richmond is relatively liberal. In 2003, a statue was even unveiled at Tredagar of the town's former arch-enemy, Abraham Lincoln.

Arrival, information, and getting around

Two hours by car from Washington DC, via I-95, which cuts through the east side of downtown, Richmond is also served by **Amtrak**, which pulls into 1500 E Main St, on its regional route that connects Newport News, VA, with Washington DC and Boston. **Greyhound**, which stops just off I-64 at 2910 N Blvd, is a good way from the center of town. The **airport**, ten miles east of downtown, is served by major carriers and has a small visitor center (Mon–Fri 9.30am–4.30pm; ☎804/236-3260; @www.flyrichmond.com) in the arrivals terminal. The **main visitor center**, 403 N 3rd St (daily 9am–5pm; ☎804/782-2777 or 1-888/RICHMOND, @www.richmondva.org), provides discounts on area hotels and advises on tours. Much of Richmond is compact enough to walk around, but to get to outlying places you can take a GRTC **bus** ($1.25, express routes $1.75; ☎804/358-GRTC, @www.ridegrtc.com).

Accommodation

Finding well-priced **accommodation** in Richmond isn't difficult, with plenty of chain hotels downtown catering to the business and government trade. If you prefer to get a feel for the old city, stay the night in a **B&B** in one of the historic quarters.

The Berkeley 1200 E Cary St ☏804/780-1300 or 1-888/780-4422, ⓦ www.berkeleyhotel.com. Elegant small hotel on the historic Shockoe Slip. **❼**

Grace Manor Inn 1853 W Grace St ☏804/353-4334, ⓦ www.thegracemanorinn.com. Stately B&B housing three tasteful suites in a grand 1910 building. Rooms are rich with antique decor; some have fireplaces and claw-foot tubs. **❻**

Henry Clay Inn 114 N Railroad Ave, Ashland VA ☏804/798-3100, ⓦ www.henryclayinn.com. Though eleven miles out of town, this excellent B&B has fourteen antiques-filled rooms, a proper parlor, and a majestic veranda. Three of the rooms are suites and have a Jacuzzi. **❹**

The Jefferson 101 W Franklin St ☏804/788-8000 or 1-800/424-8014, ⓦ www.jefferson-hotel.com. A beautifully maintained grand hotel, with a fabulous marble-columned lobby, marble baths, high-speed Internet access, and stylish rooms. **❾**

The John Marshall 101 N Fifth St ☏804/783-1929, ⓦ www.thejohnmarshall.com. Landmark 1929 hotel in a central downtown location, with refurbished rooms and complimentary breakfast. **❻**

Linden Row Inn 100 E Franklin St ☏804/783-7000 or 1-800/348-7424, ⓦ www.lindenrowinn.com. A magnificent row of redbrick Georgian terrace houses, now a comfortable modern hotel with antique furnishings, high-speed Internet access, and complimentary continental breakfast. **❺**

Richmond Marriott 500 E Broad St ☏804/643-3400, ⓦ www.marriott.com. Smart chain accommodation offering high-speed Internet access, and a good downtown location. **❻**

Downtown Richmond

Richmond's **downtown** centers on a few blocks rising up from the James River to either side of Broad Street. Modern office towers front onto a riverside park, while up the hill in the **Court End District**, dozens of well-preserved antebellum homes provide a suitable backdrop for some important museums and historic sites.

The **Virginia State Capitol**, 910 Capitol St, houses the oldest legislative body still in existence in the US; the site has been in continuous use since 1788 as the state (and, briefly, Confederate) legislature. Thomas Jefferson had a hand in the design, based on his favorite building, the Roman Maison Carrée in Nîmes, France. The domed central rotunda (not visible from outside) holds the only marble statue of George Washington modeled from life (by master sculptor Jean-Antoine Houdon), and busts of Jefferson and the seven other Virginia-born US presidents line the walls. Likenesses of famous Virginians, including a solemn bronze of Robert E. Lee, fill the adjacent **Old House Chamber**, where Aaron Burr was tried and acquitted of treason in 1807. Note that the capitol is closed until 2007 for long-overdue renovations; for the latest information, or to take tours of the surrounding area, call ☏804/698-1788 or visit ⓦ legis.state.va.us.

Also on Capitol Square is the **Governor's Mansion**, which, like the capitol, is the oldest of its kind in the US, dating to 1813 (for tours call ☏804/371-2642). Just two blocks north of the capitol, the **Museum of the Confederacy**, 1201 E Clay St (Mon–Sat 10am–5pm, Sun noon–5pm, closed Wed; $7), covers the history of the Civil War (known in the South as the War Between the States) through weapons, uniforms, and the like. Personal effects of Confederate leaders include J.E.B. Stuart's plumed hat, the tools used to amputate Stonewall Jackson's arms at Chancellorsville (he died regardless), and Robert E. Lee's revolver and the pen he used to sign the surrender. Next door, the **White House of the Confederacy** (same hours; $7, or $10 combo ticket), a Neoclassical mansion where Jefferson Davis lived as Confederate president, has been restored to its 1860s appearance.

Two blocks west, the 1812 **Wickham House** now forms part of the excellent **Valentine Richmond History Center** at 1015 E Clay St (Mon–Sat 10am–5pm,

Sun noon–5pm; $10). This Federal-style monolith houses a small local history museum, focusing on the experience of working-class and black Americans, as well as an extensive array of furniture and pre–Civil War clothing such as whalebone corsets and other *Gone With the Wind*–era apparel.

West of the Convention Center on Sixth Street is the nineteenth-century neighborhood of **Jackson Ward**. Filling a dozen blocks around First and Clay streets, this National Historic Landmark District has been the center of Richmond's African-American community since well before the Civil War, when Richmond had the largest free black population in the US. As well as covering local history, the **Maggie L. Walker House**, 110 E Leigh St (Mon–Sat 9am–5pm; free; Ⓦ www. nps.gov/mawa), traces the working life of the physically disabled, black Richmond woman who, during the 1920s, was the first woman in the US to found and run a bank, now the Consolidated Bank and Trust. Nearby, the **Black History Museum** at 00 Clay St (Tues–Sat 10am–5pm, Sun 11am–5pm; $5) contains displays on Richmond's role as a center of Southern black society, and includes a well-presented gallery of artifacts of the Civil Rights movement as well as textiles from different peoples in Africa and America.

While basking in all the history, take a break along the 1.25-mile stretch of waterfront known as **Canal Walk**, which runs between downtown and Shockoe Bottom. **Canal boat rides** depart from around 14th and Virginia streets (Apr–Nov Fri & Sat noon–7pm, Sun noon–5pm; also June–Aug Wed & Thurs noon–7pm; $5), providing a leisurely and pleasant half-hour jaunt. Nearby, the **Richmond Civil War Visitor Center**, 490 Tredegar St (daily 9am–5pm; Ⓣ804-771-2145, Ⓦ www.nps.gov/rich; free), at the refurbished **Tredegar Iron Works**, has a regular slide show about Civil War history and three floors of exhibits, including moving personal accounts of the war from ordinary soldiers. Tredegar is also the main visitor center for **Richmond National Battlefield Park**, a collection of dozens of local Civil War sites, which can be accessed on an 80-mile drive. Four other visitor centers are also in operation, the most interesting being the **Chimborazo Medical Museum**, a few miles east at 3215 E Broad St (daily 9am-5pm; free; Ⓣ804/226-1981), which has disturbing displays on the medicine and technology available (or not) to help wounded soldiers of the era. Those that weren't so lucky ended up just west of Tredegar at **Hollywood Cemetery**, 412 S Cherry St (daily 8.30am-4.30pm; Ⓦ www.hollywoodcemetery.org), where a 90ft granite **pyramid** memorializes the eighteen thousand Confederate troops killed nearby, and where you can find the graves of presidents James Monroe and John Tyler.

Shockoe Bottom, the Poe Museum, and Church Hill

Split down the middle by the raised I-95 freeway, the gentrified riverfront warehouse district of **Shockoe Bottom** still holds a few reminders of Richmond's industrial past among the restaurants and nightclubs on its cobblestoned streets. From **Shockoe Slip**, a fetching old wharf rebuilt in the 1890s after being destroyed in the Civil War, Cary Street runs east along the waterfront, lined by a wall of brick warehouses – now being converted into chic lofts and condos – known as **Tobacco Row**.

Nearby, Richmond's oldest building, an appropriately gloomy 250-year-old stone house, holds the **Edgar Allan Poe Museum**, 1914 E Main St (Tues–Sat 10am–5pm, Sun 11am–5pm; $6; Ⓦ www.poemuseum.org). Poe spent much of his youth in Richmond and considered it his home town. The museum displays Poe memorabilia and relics, including his walking stick and a lock of his hair, plus a model of Richmond as it was in Poe's time.

Church Hill, a few blocks northeast, is one of Richmond's oldest surviving residential districts, its decorative eighteenth-century houses, adorned with cast-iron porches and rambling magnolia-filled front gardens, looking out over the James River (it's also the site of the Chimborazo Museum; see p.436). Capping the hill at the heart of the neighborhood, **St John's Church**, 2401 E Broad St (Mon–Sat 10am–4pm, Sun 1–4pm; $6; ⓦ www.historicstjohnschurch.org), dates back to 1741 and is best known as the place where, during a 1775 debate on whether the Virginia colony should raise a militia against the British, future state governor **Patrick Henry** made the impassioned plea, "Give me liberty or give me death." His speech, along with the debate itself, is recreated by actors in period dress every Sunday at 2pm in summer; it's a popular affair, so get there an hour early to grab a spot on a pew.

The Fan District and Carytown

The **Fan District**, so named because its tree-lined avenues fan out at oblique angles, is an interesting Richmond neighborhood surrounding the campus of Virginia Commonwealth University. The district spreads west from the downtown area, beyond Belvedere Street (US-1), and its centerpiece, **Monument Avenue**, is lined with garish Victorian and historic-revival mansions from the start of the twentieth century, its four grand intersections holding statues of J.E.B. Stuart, Robert E. Lee, Stonewall Jackson, and Jefferson Davis.

South of Monument Avenue, at 2800 Grove Ave, stands the **Virginia Museum of Fine Arts** (Wed–Sun 11am–5pm; $5 donation; ⓦ www.vmfa.museum). An extensive collection of Impressionist and Post-Impressionist paintings is displayed alongside American paintings ranging from Charles Willson Peale's acclaimed portraits to George Catlin's romantic images of Plains Indians to the Pop Art creations of Roy Lichtenstein and Claes Oldenburg. Other galleries contain such items as Frank Lloyd Wright furniture, Lalique jewelry, Hindu and Buddhist sculpture from the Himalayas, and four jewel-encrusted Fabergé Easter eggs, crafted in the 1890s for the Russian tsars.

Just beyond the Fan District, **Carytown** is a thriving nine-block area of trendy shops offering Asian art, tarot readings, and holistic medicines alongside restaurants on Cary Street.

Eating and drinking

Richmond has a good choice of **eating** options at both ends of the price spectrum, with barbecue and the higher-priced New Southern cuisine being specialties.

Acacia 3325 W Cary St ☎804/354-6060. Quality regional cuisine with alfresco dining at this highly rated Carytown bistro. Good range of fresh seasonal ingredients and pricey offerings, which may include poultry, beef, and softshell crabs.

Border Chophouse 1501 W Main St ☎804/355-2907. Western-styled spot that serves up mid-priced pasta, veal, and lamb dishes, but whose specialty is barbeque – be it beef ribs, pork, or chicken.

Cabo's Corner Bistro 2053 W Broad St, Fan District ☎804/355-1144. Swank spot offering creative steak, seafood, and pasta dishes, as well as nightly live jazz.

Millie's Diner 2603 E Main St ☎804/643-5512. Refurbished diner, a bit out of downtown beyond Shockoe Bottom, complete with mini-jukeboxes on each table. The changing menu includes fairly expensive but delicious seafood and steak,

and there's also a nice range of brews.

O'Neill's Penny Lane Pub 421 E Franklin St ☎804/780-1682. British-style joint with solid grilled food and other pub grub, plus a full range of English and other beers and European soccer on TV.

Peking Pavilion 1302 E Cary St ☎804/649-8888. Very good, inexpensive (especially at lunchtime) Chinese restaurant in Shockoe Slip serving Szechuan and Mandarin specialties. Part of a local chain.

Richbrau Brewing Co 1214 E Cary St, Shockoe Slip ☎804/644-3018. The place to go in town for hearty, handcrafted microbrews, as well as good Southern fare, dancing, pool, and darts.

Strawberry Street Café 421 N Strawberry St ☎804/353-6860. Casual and comfortable Fan District café offering mainly quiches, pastas, and salads, but also jambalaya and crab cakes.

Third Street Diner 218 E Main St ☎ 804/788-4750. Relaxed 24hr diner with solid breakfasts and Greek dishes. Draws a stylish student crowd, especially at night when it's also a bar.

The Tobacco Company 1201 E Cary St ☎ 804/782-9555. Inventive New American food in a stunningly restored three-story tobacco warehouse, complete with antique elevator. Affordable sandwiches and burgers for lunch; pricier steak and seafood for dinner.

Nightlife

Richmond's main **nightlife** spots are concentrated around the riverside **Shockoe Slip** and **Shockoe Bottom** areas, just east of downtown. A good bet for mainstream **theater** is the Barksdale Theatre, 1601 Willow Lawn Drive (tickets $30–38; ☎ 804/282-2620, ⓦ www.barksdalerichmond.org), while the Chamberlayne Actors Theatre, 319 N Wilkinson Rd (tickets $13; ☎ 804/262-9760, ⓦ www.cattheatre.com), offers fringe works that are more daring and contemporary. For details on music and events, check the free *Style Weekly* newspaper or ⓦ www.arts.Richmond.com.

The Historic Triangle

The **Historic Triangle**, on the thin peninsula that stretches southeast of Richmond between the James and York rivers, holds the richest concentration of colonial-era sites in the US. **Jamestown**, founded in 1607, was Virginia's first settlement; **Williamsburg** is a detailed replica of the colonial capital; and **Yorktown** was the site of the climactic battle in the Revolutionary War. All are within an hour's drive from Richmond, and Williamsburg is accessible by Amtrak.

Although I-64 is the quickest way to cover the fifty miles from Richmond to Williamsburg, a far more pleasing drive along US-5 rolls through **plantation** country, where many eighteenth-century mansions, with lovely grounds, are open to the public. Once you're in the Historic Triangle, the best way to get around is along the wooded **Colonial Parkway**, which winds west to Jamestown and east to Yorktown, twenty miles in all. Most of the area's numerous tourist facilities – this is the most visited destination in the state – are to be found around Williamsburg; a few suggestions are listed under "Historic Triangle practicalities" on p.442.

Jamestown

To experience **Jamestown**, the site of the first English settlement in North America, you'll want to visit both the original location and the recreated site by taking the scenic Colonial Parkway or highways 5 and 31 from Williamsburg. The one bit of seventeenth-century Jamestown to survive, protected within the **Jamestown National Historic Site** on Jamestown Island, is the 50ft tower of the first brick church, built around 1650 (the rest was destroyed by fire in 1698), which makes it one of the oldest extant English structures in the US.

The area is roughly divided into two sections: the **New Towne** is where the colonists relocated after the 1620s to erect businesses, establish permanent residences, build livestock pens, and so on. Much of what's visible are replicas of the original brick foundations buried below (to protect from weather damage) and the fenced outlines of former property boundaries. More interesting is the site of the **Old Towne** – the location most of us associate with the colony – which includes ruins from the original triangular 1607 fort. Here you'll see dozens of archeologists working behind a perimeter, and you can also drop in on the **Archaearium**, where some of the many treasures discovered here – everything from glassware to utensils to the skeleton of a colonist who died a violent death – are on display.

At the end of the Colonial Parkway, the **visitor center** (daily: June–Aug 8.30am–5.30pm; Sept–May 8:30am–4:30pm; $8 per car, or $10 if combined with the Yorktown battlefield; ⓦ www.nps.gov/jame), features drawings and

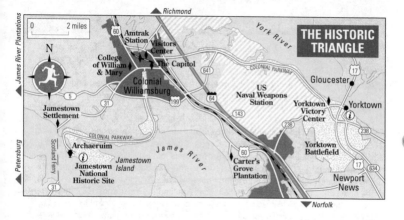

audiovisual exhibits that give you a sense of daily life at Jamestown, while, closer to the park entrance, you can watch artisans making old-fashioned **glassworks** and purchase some of their creations, as well as see the brick remnants of a seventeenth-century kiln now being excavated.

If looking at dusty artifacts and archeologists isn't enough for you, head to the adjacent **Jamestown Settlement** (daily 9am–5pm; $11.75, or $17 with Yorktown Victory Center; ⓦwww.historyisfun.org), a complex of museums and actual-size replicas that provide details of what went on here, the reconstructed buildings staffed by guides in period costume. In **Powhatan Village**, interpreters wearing buckskins engage in weaving, pottery, and other Native American crafts, while in the larger replica of **James Fort**, some fifteen thatched buildings – all built with period tools – include a blacksmith's forge, storehouse and church. Full-sized replicas of the three **ships** that carried the first settlers are moored on the James River.

Colonial Williamsburg

Providing vivid details on what the eighteenth-century capital of Virginia may have been like, **Colonial Williamsburg** is an essential stop for anyone with a flair for American history. While you have to buy a pricey ticket to look inside most of the meticulously restored buildings, the entire historic area, which includes many fine gardens, is open all the time, and you can wander freely down the cobblestone streets and across the lush green commons

From the Wren Building on the William and Mary campus, separated from Colonial Williamsburg by a mock-historic shopping center, **Duke of Gloucester Street** runs east through the historic area to the old capitol. The first of the eighteenth-century buildings, a hundred yards along, is the Episcopalian **Bruton Parish Church** (Mon–Sat 9am–5pm, Sun noon–5pm; donation) where W.A.R. Goodwin preached and all the big names of the revolutionary period were known to visit. Behind the church, the broad **Palace Green** spreads north to the Governor's Palace. West of the church, the 1771 **courthouse** and the octagonal **powder magazine**, protected by a guardhouse, face each other in the midst of Market Square. Further along, **Chowning's Tavern**, a reconstruction of an alehouse that stood here in 1766, is one of four functioning pubs in the district, this one with lively historic entertainment nightly.

The real architectural highlight is the **capitol**, a monumental edifice at the east end of Duke of Gloucester Street. The current building, a 1945 reconstruction of

Tickets for Colonial Williamsburg

To set foot inside any of the buildings that have been restored or rebuilt as part of Colonial Williamsburg, you need to buy a ticket, either from the main **visitor center** (daily 8.45am–5.45pm; ☎1-800/HISTORY, ⒲www.colonialwilliamsburg.com), north of the center off the Colonial Parkway, or from a smaller office at the west end of Duke of Gloucester Street. Most buildings in the park are open daily from 9am to 5pm, but about a third of them may have special hours and days they're open; check the website for details.

There are several types of **tickets**, which include an introductory guided walk and free parking at the visitor center. The basic **Capital City Pass** ($34, kids $15), valid for one day only, gets you into many of the lesser buildings, but excludes the Governor's Palace and the museums; the better-value **Key-to-the-City Pass** ($48, kids $34) includes those buildings and lasts two days; the **Freedom Pass** ($59, kids $29) is the same as the latter, but lasts for an entire year of admission; and the **Independence Pass** ($75, kids $38) is almost the same as the Freedom Pass, but throws in a ticket to the nightly shows as well. Aside from these performances, there are additional charges for the various special programs and events offered by Colonial Williamsburg, such as staged trials in the courthouse, holiday spectacles, and candlelit walking tours.

the 1705 original, has an open-air ground-floor **arcade** linking two keyhole-shaped wings. One wing housed the elected, legislative body of the Colonial government, the **House of Burgesses**, while the other held the chambers of the **General Court** – where alleged felons, including thirteen of Blackbeard's pirates, were tried.

A number of fully stocked gift shops along Duke of Gloucester Street have been done up as eighteenth-century apothecaries, cobblers, and silversmiths. The **Raleigh Tavern** here was where the independence-minded Colonial government reconvened after being dissolved by the loyalist governors in 1769 and again in 1774; the original tavern burned down in 1859. Finally, the imposing two-story **Governor's Palace**, at the north end of the Palace Green, has a grand ballroom and opulent furnishings, and must have served as a telling declaration of royal power – no doubt enforced by the startling display of swords, muskets, and other deadly weaponry interlaced on the walls of the foyer.

For those in need of further immersion into the past, as well as a heavy dose of theme-park (sur)reality, you can catch "**Revolutionary City**," a two-hour spectacle (daily 2.30–4.30pm) held in the streets on the east end of site, where costumed actors act out the highlights of the 1770s and 1780s, sweeping up tourists in the rebellious fervor of the day with a flurry of angry speeches and shouting matches.

Yorktown

YORKTOWN, along the York River on the north side of the peninsula, gave its name to the decisive final major battle of the **Revolutionary War**. The town was little more than farmland when, on October 18, 1781, overwhelmed and besieged British (and German mercenary) troops under the command of Charles, Lord Cornwallis surrendered here to the joint American and French forces commanded by George Washington. At the heart of the eponymous **battlefield** ($5 per car, or $10 combined with Jamestown National Historic Site, see p.438; ⒲www.nps.gov/yonb) that surrounds the town, a **visitor center** (daily 9am–5pm) has interpretive displays, including a replica, walk-through fighting ship, military artifacts, and a short audiovisual presentation on the war, and also provides several guided tours of the area. (A dozen original buildings survive from the era, along with the earthworks dug by the troops.) The **Siege Line Overlook**, at the visitor center, has good views of strategic points, while maps and a self-guided audio tour ($3) are available if you want to explore in greater detail.

The town itself also has a handful of interesting old structures worth looking at. These include the handsome homes of local gentry, a customhouse, and, best of all, the archeological remains of the workshop of the **Poor Potter** – who, contrary to his name, was a prosperous merchant and one of the first businessmen in the colonies to produce quality ceramics and glassworks to rival those imported from England.

Note that, as at Jamestown, the state of Virginia and the National Park Service have constructed a mini–theme park nearby – this time a recreated Continental Army encampment – as part of the **Yorktown Victory Center** (daily 9am–5pm; $8.25, or $17 with Jamestown Settlement; ⓦwww.historyisfun.org), west of the battlefield on US-17. The museum covers both sides of the conflict, British and American, and events leading up to the Revolution. Two outdoor museums portray life on a middle-class farm and in a Revolutionary War camp.

△ Colonial Williamsburg

Historic Triangle practicalities

Of the three main sites, only Williamsburg is easily reached without a car. Amtrak **trains** and Greyhound **buses** stop at 468 N Boundary St, two blocks from the Governor's Palace. The Colonial Parkway makes an excellent, scenic cycling route to Jamestown or Yorktown, but there's no other transportation available; rent a **bike** for $15-20 a day from Bikes Unlimited at 759 Scotland St in Williamsburg (☎757/229-4620). In Colonial Williamsburg, ticket-holders can use the hop-on, hop-off **shuttle buses** (9am–5.30pm) that leave from the visitor center every ten minutes or so and stop at convenient points in the historic area.

Considering the wealth of historic structures here, it's surprising how few hotels or B&Bs there are with any character. For **accommodation**, packages with meals, two nights' lodging, and admission are available for around $200 per person, and places to stay around the Historic Triangle are generally bland and rarely cheap; to make your search easier, the Williamsburg Hotel/Motel Association (☎757/220-3330 or 1-800/221-7165, ⓦgowilliamsburg.com) can find you a bed at no extra charge. West of the center, US-60 is lined with endless motels, and there are also several cheap options just a few blocks east of the capitol, including the basic *Bassett Motel*, 800 York St (☎757/229-5175, ⓦwww.bassettmotel.com; ❸), and the clean and conveniently located *Quarterpath Inn*, 620 York St (☎1-800/446-9222, ⓦwww.quarterpathinn.com; ❸). For a change of pace, the *Duke of York Motel*, 508 E Water St in Yorktown (☎757/898-3232, ⓦwww.dukeofyorkmotel.com; ❹), has good beachfront units, some with kitchenettes, fridges, and Jacuzzis, along the York River. Finally, there are several **campgrounds** along US-5 and US-60 west of Williamsburg that charge $20–25 per tent.

The various **restaurants** and taverns along Duke of Gloucester Street in Colonial Williamsburg feature good (if overpriced) pub food; all except *Chowning's Tavern* should be reserved in advance (☎1-800/HISTORY), and some operate on a seasonal basis only (often April–Oct). West of the historic area, in the Merchants Square shopping mall, the excellent *Trellis Café* (☎757/229-8610) serves pricey seafood and steak entrees for dinner, but affordable sandwiches and burgers for lunch; across the street, the ❧ *Cheese Shop* (☎757/220-0298) has great deli sandwiches, but expect a wait during peak hours. For even fancier fare, try the *Whitehall*, 1325 Jamestown Rd (☎757/229-4677), which offers elegant, upmarket French dining with a heavy accent on seafood and beef. There is also a clutch of solid restaurants near the William and Mary campus, including the *Green Leafe Café*, 765 Scotland St (☎757/220-3405), offering chili, burgers, pizza, pasta and thirty brews on tap. Ten-minutes' drive west of Colonial Williamsburg, the *Seafare*, 1632 Richmond Rd (☎757/229-0099), has good, fresh seafood.

The Atlantic coast

One of the busiest of the East Coast ports, **Norfolk** sits midway along the coast at the point where the Chesapeake Bay empties into the Atlantic Ocean. Virginia's only heavily industrial center, it is not a particularly pretty place, but it does have a rich maritime and naval heritage, as well as the Chrysler Museum, one of the region's best art galleries. Fifteen miles east of Norfolk, along the open Atlantic, **Virginia Beach** draws summer sun-seekers to the state's busiest seashore.

The rest of Virginia's Atlantic coast is on its isolated and sparsely populated **Eastern Shore**, where the attractive little island town of **Chincoteague** serves as the headquarters of a wildlife refuge that straddles the Maryland border and forms part of the Assateague Island National Seashore.

Norfolk

A strategic location at the broad mouth of the Chesapeake Bay and an extensive deep-water harbor made colonial **NORFOLK** the main American trading port. Today, along with Hampton Roads and Newport News on the north side of the James River, Norfolk is home to the largest naval base outside Russia, and carriers, cruisers, and all manner of gray-steel behemoths cruise past incessantly.

The waterfront features Norfolk's premier attraction, **Nauticus: The National Maritime Center** (June–Aug daily 9am–5pm; rest of year Tues–Sat 10am–5pm, Sun noon–5pm; $9.95; ⓦ www.thenmc.org), which, besides oceanography exhibits, a shark-petting lagoon, aquariums, and giant-screen films, features informative displays on naval history and technology. On the second floor, the **Hampton Roads Naval Museum** (same hours; free) documents historical naval operations in the area, while the pier adjacent to the center is frequented by colossal US and foreign ships; you can tour the decks of the **USS Wisconsin**, which is usually berthed across from the center (same hours; free) and has interactive displays showcasing the wartime role of the battleship. The small Elizabeth River **ferry** (hours vary, usually weekdays 7.15am–9.45pm, weekends 10.15am–11.45pm; $1; ⓦ www.hrtransit.org) shuttles from nearby Waterside Park across the harbor to the historic **Portsmouth** neighborhood, where brick-lined streets are flanked by early American houses. **Waterside Park** itself, at the mouth of the Elizabeth River, has something of a party atmosphere on summer weekends with live music, cheap beer, and plenty of atmosphere.

An extraordinary array of Asian antiquities is displayed in the intimate Tudor-style home now known as the **Hermitage Foundation Museum**, by the Lafayette River at 7637 N Shore Rd (45min guided tours only; Mon–Sat 10am–5pm, Sun 1–5pm; $5; ⓦ www.hermitagefoundation.org). Among the treasures are Persian rugs, medieval tapestries, rare ancient Chinese ceremonial vessels, and Roman glass; rotating exhibits highlight works by local artists, potters, and glassmakers.

The **Chrysler Museum**, half a mile north of the downtown waterfront at 245 W Olney Rd at Mowbray Arch (Wed 10am–9pm, Thurs–Sat 10am–5pm, Sun 1–5pm; $7, free on Wed; ⓦ www.chrysler.org), holds the eclectic collection of car magnate Walter Chrysler Jr. It includes a little bit of everything, from ancient Greek statuary to French Impressionist paintings, Franz Klein abstractions, and Mayan funerary objects, as well as world-class Tiffany and Lalique glassware. For a glimpse of bourgeois life in the area c.1800, check out the museum's **Moses Myers House**, Bank St at E Freemason St (Wed–Sat 10am–4pm, Sun 1–4pm; free), the elegant home of one of Norfolk's most prominent Jewish residents, now being restored to its original look, and adorned with portraits by Gilbert Stuart and Thomas Sully.

Practicalities

Airport Shuttle (☎757/857-3001) connects downtown Norfolk with **Norfolk International Airport** ($20), five miles northeast. Amtrak **bus** connections from Newport News stop at Monticello Ave and Virginia Beach Blvd, and Greyhound stops opposite at no. 701. Norfolk's downtown **visitor center** is at the Nauticus Center, 232 E Main St (daily 9am–5pm; ☎757/664-6620 or 1-800/368-3097, ⓦ www.norfolkcvb.com); drivers can go to a convenient visitor center with easy parking at exit 273 off I-64, at 9401 Fourth View St (daily 9am–5pm; ☎757/441-1852). Free **NET buses** provide transportation to major sites (Mon–Fri 6:30am–11pm, Sat noon–midnight, Sun noon–8pm; ⓦ www.norfolk.gov/Visitors/net.asp).

With far better **accommodation** options available nearby in Virginia Beach (see p.444), there should be no need to resort to the standard hotel and motel chains available in Norfolk. One exception is the pleasant *Freemason Inn*, 411 W York St (℡ 757/963-7000, ⓦ www.freemasoninn.com; ⓞ), a four-unit B&B whose rooms offer fireplaces, poster beds, and Jacuzzi tubs. For **dining**, there's excellent, expensive seafood and French cuisine at *Voila*, 509 Botetourt St (℡ 757/640-0343), and eclectic fare – crab cakes, noodle dishes, steak, and hearty sandwiches – at *The 219*, 219 Granby St (℡ 757/627-2896). For a cheap taste of Americana, stop by *Doumar's*, a 1950s-era drive-in restaurant at 1919 Monticello Ave (℡ 757/627-4163), where white-hatted waitstaff bring the food to your car; it's tops for barbeque, burgers, and waffle-cone ice cream.

Virginia Beach

VIRGINIA BEACH, Virginia's only real summer resort, has grown to become the largest city in the state, with nearly half a million people, but takes care to pitch itself as a family destination.

The city's focus is its long, sandy **beach**, lined with the usual hotels and motels, and backed by a boardwalk strip of bars, restaurants, and nightclubs. Virginia Beach is also a major **surfing center**, hosting the **East Coast Surfing Championships** in late August (℡ 1-800/861-SURF). You can rent surf and boogie boards at Wave Riding Vehicles, 19th St and Cypress Ave (℡ 757/422-8823). Away from the sands, most of the action is along Atlantic Avenue, the main beachfront drag.

High-tech exhibits and an IMAX theater are featured at the **Virginia Aquarium and Marine Science Center**, 717 General Booth Blvd (daily summer 9am–7pm, rest of year 9am–5pm; $12, or $17 with IMAX show; ℡ 757/425-FISH, ⓦ www.vmsm.com), which explores all things aquatic, including tanks devoted to sharks, sea turtles, and jellyfish; it also has a short, pleasant nature trail through the **Owls Creek salt marsh**, linking its two main buildings and an aviary displaying dozens of native species. The museum also organizes **dolphin-watching** expeditions (90min; June–Oct; $18) and **whale-watching** cruises (2hr 30min; late-Dec to mid-March; $28), for which you should reserve in advance (℡ 757/437-BOAT).

The eccentric **A.R.E. Center** at the headquarters of the Association for Research and Enlightenment, 215 67th St at Atlantic Ave (Mon–Sat 9am–8pm, Sun 11am–8pm; ⓦ www.edgarcayce.org/visit_are; free), focuses on **Edgar Cayce** (1877–1945), known as "the sleeping prophet" because of his alleged ability, while in a trance, to diagnose and heal the ailments of individuals anywhere in the world. Visitors can use an enormous metaphysical library, take in a lecture on various New Age subjects (daily 3.30pm), or test their own personal ESP (Sat & Sun 1pm).

Away from the city beach, a few miles up and down the coast are some beautiful and peaceful stretches of golden sand. To the south lies the four-mile-long **Back Bay National Wildlife Refuge** (daily dawn to dusk; $5 per car, hikers and cyclists $2; ⓦ backbay.fws.gov), where you can walk, bike, or fish (but not swim), and **False Cape State Park**, a mile-wide barrier spit that connects to North Carolina and is one of the region's last undisturbed coastlines. Closer to Virginia Beach to the north, the thick woodland of **First Landing State Park** was the site where the first English settlers touched land in 1607 before moving on to Jamestown; it is Virginia's most popular state park, good for its boating and cycling, with a beach on the Chesapeake Bay.

Practicalities

Greyhound stops at 1017 Laskin Rd, off 31st Street, while the Amtrak bus connection from Newport News – and connecting up to Boston and New York – arrives at 19th Street and Pacific Avenue. The **visitor center**, 2100 Parks Ave (daily 9am–5pm; ℡ 757/437-4919 or 1-800/822-3224, ⓦ www.VBFUN.com), is at the east end of I-264, half a mile west of the beach at 21st Street. Beach **trolleys** called The Wave (daily 8am–2am; $1; ☎757/252-6100, ⓦwww.hrtransit.org) are the easiest way to get around; there are three different routes covering the city, the most useful being up and down Atlantic Avenue.

Virginia Beach has a great boon for **budget travelers** – just a block from the ocean, *Angie's Guest Cottage*, 302 24th St (☎757/428-4690, ⓦwww.angiescottage .com), has dorm beds from $17–20, private rooms from $32–38, and bargain B&B units for $80 and up (there's a two-night minimum for the latter). Typical rates at the seafront hotels tend to approach $200 in summer; cheaper options can be found at *The Capes Ocean Resort*, 2001 Atlantic Ave (☎757/428-5421, ⓦwww. capeshotel.com; ❹), which offers a broad range of rooms, though all with ocean-front balconies, microwaves, and fridges (rates can double during the summer, however). For a splash of old-style lodging, the *Cavalier*, 42nd St and Atlantic Ave (☎757/425-8555, ⓦwww.cavalierhotel.com; ❺), is a stately 1927 beachfront resort whose facilities include two pools, a gym, and clay tennis courts; its rooms have fridges and microwaves, and some (for about $50 more) come with Jacuzzis; rates jump by about $100 in the summer. You can also **camp** at First Landing State Park on the Chesapeake Bay ($23–29; ☎757/412-2300 or 1-800/933-7275, ⓦwww.dcr.state.va.us/parks/1stland.htm).

The town also offers some great **restaurants** and a decent **nightlife**. *Captain John's Crabhouse*, 3420 Atlantic Ave (☎757/425-6263), has fine seafood and steak, while *Mahi Mah's*, 615 Atlantic Ave (☎757/437-8030), offers a creative menu of sushi, sashimi, crabcakes, and other seafood, plus a wide selection of beers. *Baja Cantina*, 206 23rd St (☎757/437-2920), is a friendly bar serving tasty Mexican food at affordable prices. For **live music**, try the *Abbey Road Pub*, 203 22nd St (☎757/425-6330), a solid bar with over a hundred different beers and live, local rock on some nights (Wed–Sat). The *Jewish Mother*, 3108 Pacific Ave (☎757/422-5430), is a daytime deli and late-night bar with blues and roots music – sometimes from notable names (tickets for shows $5–20).

The Eastern Shore

Virginia's longest and least-visited stretch of Atlantic coastline, the **Eastern Shore**, lies separated from the rest of the state on the distant side of the Chesapeake Bay. Only the southernmost segment of what's known as the Delmarva peninsula belongs to Virginia, by which point it has narrowed to become a flat spit of sand protected by a fringe of low-lying islands.

US-13, which runs straight down the center of the peninsula and provides a handy short cut from Philadelphia or points north, crosses seventeen miles of open sea at the mouth of the Chesapeake Bay via the **Chesapeake Bay Bridge–Tunnel** ($12 per car one way; $17 roundtrip within 24hrs). To either side of US-13, little villages and fishing harbors such as Nassawadox, Assawoman, and Accomac are tucked away on rambling back roads.

Chincoteague and Assateague Island National Seashore

The most appealing destination on the Eastern Shore, **Chincoteague** occupies a beautiful barrier island just south of the Maryland border. Although it's little more than a village, its two principal streets hold a fair assortment of motels and restaurants, and it makes a relaxed base for exploring **Assateague Island National Seashore** (week-long vehicle pass $10; ⓦwww.nps.gov/asis), whose northern half holds several good hiking trails and can only be reached from Maryland (see p.475); the southern half, just a mile onwards from Chincoteague, is taken up by **Chincoteague National Wildlife Refuge** (daily May–Sept 5am–10pm, Nov–April 6am–6pm, Oct 6am–8pm), notable for its seabirds and wild ponies. Call in at the **visitor center** (daily 9am–5pm; ☎757/336-6122, 🌐chinco.fws. gov) for information on the short trails through the dunes and marshes, or if you just want a day at the beach, drive straight past to **Tom's Cove** (camping is only available on the Maryland side, for $16 per night). If you're in Chincoteague on the last Wednesday of July, don't miss the annual **Pony Penning Carnival**, when the three hundred wild ponies that roam Assateague Island to the north are herded together and directed on a swim through the channel to Chincoteague Memorial Park, where the foals are sold by auction to help the local community.

Solid **accommodation** options in Chincoteague include the grand *Island Manor House*, 4160 Main St (☎1-800/852-1505, 🌐www.islandmanor.com; 5), a smart, antique-furnished B&B; the large *Mariner Motel*, 6273 Maddox Blvd (☎757/336-6565, 🌐www.esva.net/~motel; ❹), with clean and functional rooms; and the *Cedar Gables Seaside Inn*, 6095 Hopkins Lane (☎1-888/491-2944, 🌐www.cedargable .com; ❼), a homey B&B whose four comfy suites have fireplaces, Jacuzzis, CD players, and fridges. *Steamers*, 6251 Maddox Blvd (☎757/336-5478), is a family **restaurant** serving all-you-can-eat meals of crab, oysters, clams, and shrimp for $15–25. Located in the small waterfront plaza, *Landmark Crab House*, 6162 N Main St (☎757/336-5552), also serves tasty seafood and is open from April to November.

Charlottesville and the Shenandoah Valley

The densely forested 4000ft peaks of the **Blue Ridge Mountains** form a definite barrier between the history-rich worlds of tidewater Virginia to the east and the rougher river-and-valley country to the west. In between the two, at the geographical center of the state, sits the friendly, manageably small college town of **Charlottesville**, which holds two great monuments to the mind of **Thomas Jefferson**. South of Charlottesville, **Appomattox Court House** is where Robert E. Lee surrendered on behalf of the Confederate army, thus ending the Civil War, while to the west, **Shenandoah National Park**, which runs south to Tennessee, culminates in the 5729ft Mount Rogers; on the far side of the mountains, the lush **Shenandoah Valley** was once a vital battleground during the Civil War.

The main highway through the Shenandoah Valley, I-81, can be reached in the north via I-66 from Washington DC and in the middle via I-64 from Richmond through Charlottesville. Numerous scenic routes are slower but more worthwhile, such as **Skyline Drive** and the **Blue Ridge Parkway**, which both weave along the four-hundred-mile-long mountain crest, which typically reaches 4000ft or so. You'll need a car to get the most out of the region, though cycling is a good option along the many back roads and, for hikers, the **Appalachian Trail** runs right down the middle.

Charlottesville

Seventy miles west of Richmond, **CHARLOTTESVILLE** holds some of the finest examples of early American architecture; its compact, low-rise center is crisscrossed by magnolia-shaded streets and makes a fine area to amble around, particularly in the six pedestrianized blocks of **Main Street**. However pleasant the town, the compelling attraction is Thomas Jefferson's home and resting place,

Monticello, which sits atop a hill just east of town, overlooking the beautiful Neoclassical campus of the University of Virginia.

The University of Virginia

Though he wrote the Declaration of Independence and served as the third US president, Thomas Jefferson took more pride in having established the **University of Virginia** than in any of his other achievements, as he designed every building down to the most minute detail, planned the curriculum, and selected the faculty.

The highlight of the campus is the redbrick, white-domed and -columned **Rotunda** (T 434/982-3200), which was modeled on the Pantheon and completed in 1821 to house the library and classrooms. (The Rotunda burned down in 1895, was errantly rebuilt, and finally reconstructed to Jefferson's letter in 1976.) A basement gallery tells the history of the university, while upstairs a richly decorated central hall links three elliptical classrooms. A staircase winds up to the **Dome Room**, where paired Corinthian columns rise to an ocular skylight. From the Rotunda, 45-minute guided tours of campus begin (daily 10am, 11am, 2pm, 3pm, & 4pm, except during holidays and May final exams; free) and twin colonnades stretch along either side of a lushly landscaped quadrangle – **The Lawn** – linking single-story student apartments with ten taller pavilions in which professors live and hold tutorials.

Parallel to the quadrangle buildings, two further rows of dormitory buildings, the East and West ranges, front on to serpentine walled gardens. **Edgar Allan Poe** stayed in one of these dorms while studying at the university in 1826, but was forced to drop out after he couldn't pay his gambling debts. His room – Number 13, of course – in the West Range is now restored to how it would have looked during his occupancy: a rather spartan, bleak affair (the honorary Ravens Society maintains the unit; see W www.uvaravensociety.com).

Monticello

One of America's most familiar buildings – it graces the back of the nickel – **Monticello**, three miles southeast of Charlottesville on Hwy-53, was the home of Thomas Jefferson for most of his life. Surrounded by acres of beautiful hilltop grounds, which once made up an enormous plantation, with fine views out over the Virginia countryside, Monticello is a handsome estate. The symmetrical brick facade, centered upon a white Doric portico, belies the quirky irregularities of the interior – furnished as it was when Jefferson lived, and died, here.

To see Monticello you have to join one of the **guided tours** (daily March–Oct 8am–5pm; rest of year 9am–4.30pm; $14; T 434/984-9822, W www.Monticello. org) that leave continuously from the parking lot at the bottom of the hill. From the outside, Monticello looks like an elegant, Palladian-style country home, but as soon as you enter the domed entrance hall, with its animal hides, native craftworks, and fossilized bones and elk antlers (from Lewis and Clark's epic 1804 journey across North America, which Jefferson sponsored as president), you begin to see a different side of Jefferson. His love of gadgets and clever contraptions, which fill the house, marked him as a true Renaissance man. In Jefferson's **private chambers**, he slept in a cramped alcove that linked his dressing room and his study, and would get up on the right side of the bed if he wanted to make some late-night notes, on the left if he wanted to get dressed.

Extensive flower and vegetable **gardens** spread to the south and west, and a dank passage runs under the house from the kitchen and beer cellar (Jefferson was a keen home-brewer) to the remains of **Mulberry Row**, Monticello's slave quarters. At the south end of Mulberry Row, a grove of ancient hardwood trees surrounds Jefferson's gravesite, marked by a simple stone **obelisk**; the epitaph, which lists his major accomplishments, does not mention his having been president.

△ Monticello

Charlottesville practicalities

Amtrak trains from DC stop at 810 W Main St, and Greyhound pulls in at 310 W Main St. Once you arrive, you can get to everything on foot, including the downtown **visitor center**, 100 5th St NE (Mon–Sat 10am–5pm, Sun 11am–3pm; ☏434/977-6100 or 1-877/386-1103, ⓦwww.charlottesvilletourism.org). Another visitor center (daily 9am–5pm; ☏434/977-1783), well-signposted on Hwy-20 just south of I-64, houses a superb free exhibit of four hundred items called "Thomas Jefferson at Monticello," and is an excellent starting point for a trip there.

For its size, Charlottesville has a good range of **accommodation**. Most places are of the familiar chain variety, but for (slightly) more special digs, try the *English Inn*, 2000 Morton Drive (☏434/971-9900, ⓦwww.englishinncharlottesville.com; ❹), a large, mock-Tudor motel with clean and functional rooms, some of which have fridges and microwaves. For a bit more style, good-value **B&B rooms** are available at the two beautifully restored houses of the *200 South Street Inn*, 200 South St (☏434/979-0200, ⓦwww.southstreetinn.com; ❼), some of whose units have fireplaces and whirlpool tubs; similar amenities are available at the handsome *Inn at Court Square*, 410 E Jefferson St (☏434/295-2800, ⓦwww.innatcourtsquare.com; ❼), which has nine rooms as well as excellent Southern cuisine on offer. You can also arrange a stay in a B&B through Guesthouses (☏434/979-7264, ⓦwww.va-guesthouses.com).

The best **eating** and **drinking** can be found near the university and the downtown mall. In between, ⚑ *Southern Culture*, 633 W Main St (☏434/979-1990), is a tasty, down-home favorite, serving up the likes of jambalaya, shrimp, grits, and black bean cakes. Just north of the downtown mall, the upscale *Tastings*, 502 E Market St (☏434/293-3663), offers steak, fricassees, and crab casseroles, plus a fine selection of wine – including many from local vineyards. A sizable selection of beers (more than 130 in all) can be sampled along with solid pub grub a block further north at the English-styled *Court Square Tavern*, 500 Court Square (☏434/296-6111). The *C&O Restaurant*, 515 E Water St (☏434/971-7044), housed in an old railroad engineers' building, offers bistro-style food in its humming bar and more upscale French *nouvelle cuisine* in the upstairs dining room. Also worth a visit, *Starr Hill*, 709 W Main St (T 434/977-0017), offers an eclectic menu of food and kinetic live music, along with its own microbrews.

Appomattox Court House

Set amid the pleasant, rolling hills of central Virginia, some sixty miles south of Charlottesville on US-460 and Hwy-24, the village of **APPOMATTOX COURT HOUSE** was where Robert E. Lee and Ulysses S. Grant met on April 9, 1865, for the former to sign surrender papers for his Army of Northern Virginia, effectively ending the Civil War after four bloody years. Grant's Union troops had cut off a nearby rail line upon which Lee's army depended for vital supplies, and the half-starved Confederates had no choice but to submit. Final papers were signed in the home of the **McLean family**, who, ironically, had moved here after the war's first major battle – Bull Run – was fought on their property in Manassas. Details of the surrender are given in **Appomattox Court House National Historical Park** (daily 8.30am–5pm; $4; W www.nps.gov/apco). The village has been handsomely restored, and the McLean home is now a museum.

Getting anywhere in the vicinity requires a car, and the nearest accommodation is available in the newer burg of **Appomattox**, a few miles west. Here, the cozy *Longacre B&B*, 1670 Church St (T 434/352-9251 or 1-800/758-7730, W www.longacreva.com; ●), is nestled among century-old boxwoods and includes a lap pool; *Spring Grove Farm*, several miles northwest of town along Rte-613 (T 434/352-7429, W www.springgrovefarm.com; ●), is set on a 200-acre, 1842 plantation where the eleven rooms and suites (some with fireplaces) have whirlpool tubs and tasteful early American decor.

Shenandoah National Park

The dark forests, deep rocky ravines, and pleasant waterfalls of **SHENANDOAH NATIONAL PARK**, far from being untouched wilderness, were created when hundreds of small family farms and homesteads were condemned by the state and federal governments during the Depression, and the land was left to revert to its natural state. It's no surprise that Shenandoah, meaning "river of high mountains," has one of the most scenic byways in the US, **Skyline Drive**, a thin, 105-mile ribbon of pavement curving along the crest of the Blue Ridge Mountains that starts just off I-66 near the town of **Front Royal**, 75 miles west of DC, and winds south through the park (with a 35mph speed limit), giving great views over the surrounding area.

Week-long **admission** to the park is $15 for cars and $8 for pedestrians, cyclists, and motorcyclists ($10 for cars and $5 for pedestrians during the winter). The crowds can be especially large in the fall, but at any time of year you can get the best of what the park has to offer by following one of the many **hiking trails** that split off from the ridge. One favorite leaves from the parking area of Big Meadows Lodge, in the southern half of the park, and winds along to tumbling **Dark Hollow Falls**; another trail, leaving Skyline Drive at mile marker 45, climbs up a treacherous incline to the top of **Old Rag Mountain** for panoramic views out over the whole of Virginia and the Allegheny Mountains in the west. More ambitious hikers, or those who want to spend the night out in the backcountry, head for the **Appalachian Trail**. Details on any of these hikes, and free overnight camping permits, can be picked up at the Dickey Ridge, at milepost 4.6, and Harry F. Byrd Sr, at milepost 51, **visitor centers** (daily 8.30am–5pm; T 540/999-3500, W www.nps.gov/shen).

Park **accommodation** (☎540/743-5108 or 1-800/999-4714, ⓦwww .visitshenandoah.com) includes the 1894 *Skyland Lodge*, at milepost 41.7, with cabins (❹) and hotel rooms (❺), as well as a large restaurant with panoramic views; *Big Meadows Lodge*, at milepost 51.2, with similar facilities (❹); and *Lewis Mountain Cabins*, at milepost 57.5, with cozy, rustic accommodation (❹). There are also five campgrounds in the park, charging $14 to $19 per night; reserve online or by calling ☎1-800/365-CAMP.

The Shenandoah Valley

Many of the small, colorful towns of the **SHENANDOAH VALLEY**, down below Skyline Drive, were left in ruins after the Civil War, but have since been restored to their antebellum conditions, and numerous memorials, monuments, and cemeteries line the back roads, surrounded by horse farms and apple orchards. The region is marked as an official **National Historic Area**; for more details on following the military campaigns on foot or by car, see ⓦwww.shenandoahatwar.org.

Besides its war history, the northern Shenandoah Valley also holds half a dozen of Virginia's many **limestone caverns**, which tend to be privately owned and cost around $15–20 to explore. One of the largest is **Luray Caverns**, twelve miles east of New Market off Hwy-211 (April to mid-June 9am–6pm; mid-June to Aug 9am–7pm; Sept–Oct 9am–6pm; Nov–Mar 9am–4pm; $19; ⓦwww.luraycaverns .com), featuring an underground "organ" with stalagmites as "pipes," which you can see on the daily one-hour guided tours. Further south, off Hwy-250 northwest of the town of **STAUNTON**, the **Museum of Frontier American Culture** (daily 9am–5pm, winter 10am–4pm; $10; ⓦwww.frontiermuseum.org) showcases six different kinds of immigrant farms and the labors involved in tending to each; since the buildings were mostly imported (and rebuilt) from Europe, it's more of a historic theme-park than an authentic cultural experience, but still worth a look to see how back-breaking it must have once been to live the rural life.

Lexington

From the horse-drawn carriages moving along its quiet, brick-lined streets, to the fine rolling countryside all around, the small town of **Lexington** is an almost anachronistic place of languid country life and Civil War memories. One of its most engaging sites, the somber **Lee Chapel** (April–Oct Mon–Sat 9am–5pm, Sun 1–5pm; Nov–March Mon–Sat 9am–4pm, Sun 1–4pm; free; ⓦchapelapps.wlu. edu), is on the imposing colonnaded campus of **Washington and Lee University**, just north of the town center. The Confederate general taught here after the war – when it was known as Washington University – and, along with his family, is interred in the chapel's crypt; his horse Traveler is buried just outside. East of the chapel, on the far end of the parade ground of the **Virginia Military Institute**, the **George C. Marshall Museum** (daily 9am–5pm; $5; ☎540/463-7103, ⓦwww. marshallfoundation.org) documents the life of World War II US general and later secretary of state George C. Marshall.

In the town center, another big-name warrior is commemorated at the **Stonewall Jackson House**, 8 E Washington St (Mon–Sat 9am–5pm, Sun 1-5pm; $6; ⓦwww.stonewalljackson.org), where the Confederate general and VMI professor lived before he rode off to war (dying at the battle of Chancellorsville). His spartan 1801 brick townhouse is furnished as it was when he lived there. Jackson is buried, along with 144 of his fellow soldiers, in the **Stonewall Jackson Memorial Cemetery** off South Main Street (daily dawn–dusk; free). For a break from military history, take a trip fifteen miles north of town off Route 606 to **Cyrus McCor-**

mick's Farm (daily 8.30am–5pm; ☎540/377-2255; free), where the famed inventor of the industrial reaper is honored in an antique setting that includes a gristmill, blacksmith's forge, smokehouse, and museum. Alternatively, twenty miles south of Lexington on US-11 is the spectacular **Natural Bridge** (daily 8am until dark; $12; ⓦ www.naturalbridgeva.com), where a creek has slowly carved away the softer limestone to form a 215ft archway; George Washington allegedly carved his initials into the rock (though it takes a keen eye to see them), and Thomas Jefferson was so impressed that he bought the site to preserve it and owned it for fifty years.

Lexington is also a good place to visit for its dozens of fine old homes; pick up a walking-tour map at the **visitor center** at 106 E Washington St (daily June–Aug 8.30am–6pm; Sept–May 9am–5pm; ☎540/463-3777, ⓦ www.lexingtonvirginia. com). Most local **accommodation** is of the cookie-cutter chain variety, so stick to **B&Bs**, as there are plenty of decent ones (if a bit small). *Historic Country Inns* operates some of the most appealing, spread over five stately old structures with 43 total units, some with fireplaces, Jacuzzis, and wet bars, for $65–175 per night (☎1-877/283-9680, ⓦ www.lexingtonhistoricinns.com). Otherwise, the *Magnolia House Inn*, 501 S Main St (☎540/463-2567, ⓦ www.magnoliahouseinn. com; ⓞ), has four comfortable units with tasteful furnishings in a pleasant garden setting; and, just a few miles north of town, the *Hummingbird Inn*, 30 Wood Lane (☎540/997-9065, ⓦ www.hummingbirdinn.com; ⓞ), has similar facilities, but with the added appeal of a renovated c.1780 farmhouse with fine dining, a solarium, veranda, and wireless Internet access.

For **food**, the *Southern Inn Restaurant*, right in the center of town at 37 S Main St (☎540/463-3612) offers smart, mid-priced steak, seafood, and pasta, while the *Blue Heron Café*, 4 E Washington St (☎540/463-2800), one block from the visitor center, serves tasty vegetarian dishes for lunch during the week and dinner on weekends. If you want to go a bit more upscale, *Cafe Michel*, 640 N Lee Hwy (☎540/464-4119), is the place to try for its blend of chic French fare (quail in port wine) matched with regional seafood like crabcakes and lobster; for succulent burgers, seafood, and Mexican food at more affordable prices, the *Bistro on Main*, 8 Main St (☎540/464-4888), is a solid, savory choice.

Along the Blue Ridge Parkway

Once it wends its way out of Shenandoah National Park, Skyline Drive becomes the **Blue Ridge Parkway**, which travels southwest along the crest of the Appalachians at an average elevation of three thousand feet. It's a beautiful drive, though **I-81**, sweeping along the flank of the mountains, is a more efficient way of getting from Virginia to North Carolina and on to the Great Smoky Mountains (a route covered in detail on p.505). Call ☎828/271-4779 or visit ⓦ www.nps.gov/blri for information on the half-dozen **visitor centers** along the Parkway. From June to November, the *Rocky Knob Cabins* (☎540/593-3503, ⓦ www.blueridgeresort. com; $59), at milepost 174, offers a memorable stay in the idyllic Meadows of Dan, with units featuring kitchenettes and fireplaces. Alternatively, the handsome *Peaks of Otter Lodge*, twenty miles north of Roanoke, VA at milepost 86 (☎1-800/542-5927, ⓦ www.peaksofotter.com; $92), is open year-round, with clean, simple rooms and a view overlooking a lake.

Of the nearby towns, **ROANOKE**, between I-81 and the Parkway, is the largest in western Virginia. Beyond its drab modern amenities, the town has a few attractions that make for a pleasant stopoff, particularly the historic **farmers' market**, dating to 1882, at Campbell Ave at Market St (Mon–Sat 8am–5pm, Sun 10am–4pm; ☎540/342-2028), and, in the Center in the Square mall, the engaging

Historical Society of Western Virginia (Tues–Fri 10am–4pm, Sat 10am–5pm, Sun 1–5pm; $3; ⓦwww.history-museum.org), which documents settlement of the region and has a fascinating mishmash of historical odds and ends, from Victorian fashions and documents signed by Thomas Jefferson to war relics. There's also the **Virginia Museum of Transportation**, 303 Norfolk Ave (Mon–Fri 11am–4pm, Sat 10am–5pm, Sun 1–5pm; $7.40; ⓦwww.vmt.org), home to the largest collection of diesel locomotives in the South, with antique buggies, buses, and fire trucks also on show. The **visitor center**, 101 Shenandoah Ave NE (daily 9am–5pm; ☎540/345-8622 or 1-800/635-5535, ⓦwww.visitroanokeva.com), has walking-tour maps of the town and information on dozens of historic homes, plantations, and other tourable sites in the vicinity. Finally, for sweeping views of the valley, make the fifteen-minute drive from the farmers' market up Mill Mountain to the **Roanoke Star**, an 89-foot neon-lit star built in 1949 (ask at the visitor center for directions), which gives the town its nickname of "Star City."

Unlike many towns in the region, Roanoke boasts one fine **hotel**, the *Patrick Henry*, 617 S Jefferson St (☎540/345-8811, ⓦwww.patrickhenryroanoke.com; ❹), whose wrought-iron and chandelier decor in the lobby is matched by sizable rooms with period furnishings and kitchenettes. For more upscale digs near the airport, the *Wyndham Roanoke*, 2801 Hershberger Rd (☎540/563-9300, ⓦwww. wyndham.com; ❻), is the height of chain luxury for the region. Check the visitor center for details on local **B&Bs**.

You'll find a number of appealing **restaurants** in Roanoke, including *Awful Arthur's Seafood Co*, 108 Campbell Ave (☎540/344-2997), a good lunch or dinner spot with gut-busting platters of shrimp, crab, and lobster; *Stephen's*, 2926 Franklin Road SW (☎540/344-7203), with more genteel and pricier (but still excellent) entrees of rockfish, salmon, and steak; and *Tavern on the Market*, 32 Market Square (☎540/343-2957), which serves up filling burgers, pasta, and chicken alongside a nice range of beers.

War buffs who've had enough Civil War history might want to call in to the town of **BEDFORD**, about twenty miles east of Roanoke, which lost 21 men (out of 35) at Omaha Beach during the Allied invasion of Normandy on June 6, 1944, the highest per capita loss anywhere in the US. Thus, Bedford was chosen as the site of the **National D-Day Memorial** (daily 10am–5pm; $5; ☎540/586-DDAY, ⓦwww.dday.org), which opened on the anniversary of the event in 2001. Situated on a landscaped hilltop, the monuments, statues, and structures depicting the beach landing culminate in the 44ft arch of Victory Plaza. It is signposted just off US-460, on the southwest side of town.

West Virginia

Generally poor and almost entirely rural, **WEST VIRGINIA** is known for its timber and coal mining industries, which thrive thanks to the state's rich natural resources. Still, West Virginia is, in some places at least, incredibly beautiful, and – completely mountainous – it boasts the longest white-water rivers and most extensive wilderness in the eastern US; the state's become a popular destination for hikers and outdoors enthusiasts, as the moonshiners of old have been replaced by ski instructors and mountain-bike guides.

German and Scots-Irish pioneers started to cross the mountains of western Virginia in major numbers during the eighteenth century, and farming small plots of land with their own labor, had little in common with the slave-holding tidewater planters of eastern Virginia. The western counties had long agitated against rule from the more populous east, and when the Civil War broke out, the area voted to set up a rival Virginia government – one loyal to the Union. Statehood was formalized by Congress in 1863, and then eight years later by the Supreme Court. Around 1900, when railroads first reached into the rugged interior, timber companies clear-cut great expanses of forests, setting up mill towns and dismantling them when they moved onto somewhere new. Later, coal-mining conglomerates perfected the "**company town**" approach, wherein workers were paid a little bit less each month than the amount they owed for their company-provided food and lodging – helping to cause great resentment and the rise of one of America's most powerful unions, the United Mine Workers.

The state's most popular destination, the restored 1850s town of **Harpers Ferry**, is barely in West Virginia at all, standing just across from the broad rivers that form its Maryland and Virginia borders. To the west, the **Allegheny Mountains** stretch for over 150 miles, their million-plus acres of hardwood forest rivaling New England's for brilliant autumnal color. West Virginia's oldest town, **Lewisburg**, sits just off I-64 at the mountains' southern foot, while the capital, **Charleston**, lies in the comparatively flat Ohio River Valley of the west.

Getting around West Virginia

Since the state is wholly built around mountains and rivers, straight, flat roads are virtually nonexistent and **getting around** via any means other than driving a car can be a real challenge. Greyhound's service is limited, mostly traveling the western side of the state along Hwy-77, while Amtrak's Cardinal line crosses the southeast part from White Sulphur Springs through Charleston to Huntington (as part of a DC-to-Chicago route), and the Capitol Limited goes from DC to Harper's Ferry and Martinsburg on to the Great Lakes. Otherwise, plan on driving narrow, serpentine roads endlessly up and down, and allow yourself lots of time.

Harpers Ferry

HARPERS FERRY, a ruggedly sited eighteenth-century town restored as a national historic park, clings to steep hillsides above the rocky confluence of the Potomac and Shenandoah rivers. After suffering the ravages of the Civil War and torrential floods, the town was all but abandoned, the empty shells of its homes and factories slowly becoming overgrown by the dense forest that covers the surrounding hills. Almost all of Harpers Ferry has since been reconstructed as an outdoor museum, combining historical importance and natural beauty. In the fall, when the leaves blaze with color, it's hard to imagine a more picture-perfect setting.

Shuttle buses drop off conveniently at the end of gas-lit Shenandoah Street in the heart of the restored **Lower Town**, or Old Town. Nearby there's an information desk, with maps and helpful park staffers. Across the street, the **Master Armorer's House** was once occupied by the chief gunsmith for the armory; these days staffers will teach you all about gun-making and the type of local weapons used in the mid-nineteenth century. Adjacent buildings include a restored blacksmith's shop, clothing and dry-goods stores, a tavern, and a boardinghouse.

John Brown's **fort** – actually the firehouse, where he and his surviving raiders were captured – originally stood directly across from the tavern, but was rebuilt a block away, near the point where the rivers meet. There's little inside, however, and if you want to get the full story of the raid you'd do better to spend half an

John Brown and Harpers Ferry

George Washington set up the country's first national munitions factory at **Harpers Ferry** to arm the young republic, and by the mid-1800s it was a thriving industrial complex, home to some five thousand workers and linked to the capital by the B&O Railroad and the Chesapeake & Ohio Canal. The 1859 **raid** on its huge arsenal by militant **John Brown** rocked the already fragmented nation – bitterly divided over slavery – and was the clearest foreshadowing of the Civil War, which broke out just eighteen months later. In the hope of fomenting a widespread slave revolt, Brown and 21 other abolitionists, including two of his sons and five black men, seized the munitions factory and its large store of weapons on the night of October 16. They held out for two days before US troops, under the command of **Robert E. Lee**, stormed the buildings, killing many of the raiders and capturing Brown. He was taken to nearby Charles Town, put on trial just nine days later, and convicted of treason; by the time he was hanged on December 2, he was far from alone in regarding himself as a martyr to the abolitionist cause.

hour in the **John Brown Museum**, opposite, where you can get the skinny on this still-controversial figure.

Other museums, housing exhibits on the Civil War and black history, line both sides of **High Street** as it climbs away from the river – it's no coincidence that, a century ago, **W.E.B. DuBois** chose the town as a place for the first American convention of the Niagara movement, which prefigured the NAACP; much of that story is detailed here. In the vicinity, a set of stone steps ascends through the residential area to the 1782 **Harper House**, the oldest house in town.

A footpath continues uphill, past overgrown churchyards hemmed in by dry-stone walls, to **Jefferson Rock**, a huge gray boulder affording a great view over the two rivers (Thomas Jefferson said the vista was worth a voyage across the Atlantic). For a longer hike, several trails lead onwards into the surrounding forest: the **Appalachian Trail** – linking Maine to Georgia – continues from Jefferson Rock across the Shenandoah River into the Blue Ridge Mountains of Virginia, while the **Maryland Heights Trail** makes a four-mile roundtrip around the headlands of the Potomac River. You can also float down the Shenandoah in a **raft** or inner-tube provided by one of the many outfitters along the rivers east and south of town.

Practicalities

Harpers Ferry makes a popular excursion from Washington DC and is served by several trains daily on the Maryland Rail Commuter network (℡1-800/325-7245, ⊛www.mtamaryland.com) and by one daily Amtrak service, the Capitol Limited, en route to Chicago. Otherwise, you'll need to drive here. Parking is virtually banned in the Old Town area, though you can get here via shuttle buses that run from the large **visitor center** on US-340 (site and center daily 8am–5pm; ℡304/535-6298, ⊛www.nps.gov/hafe), where you pay the $4-per-person or $6-per-car entry fee.

If you want to **spend the night**, the century-old *Hilltop House*, 400 E Ridge St (℡304/535-2132 or 1-800/338-8319, ⊛www.hilltophousehotel.com; ❹), may be showing its age, but still has reasonable prices and good views, while appealing **B&Bs** are sprinkled throughout the area, among them *Harpers Ferry Guest House*, 800 Washington St (℡304/535-6955, ⊛www.harpersferryguesthouse. com; ❺); and the *Angler's Inn*, 867 W Washington St (℡340/535-1239, ⊛www. theanglersinn.com; ❺, extra $40 on weekends), which provides the requisite B&B amenities, plus the opportunity to go on a full-day fishing expedition on local rivers (one-night packages $365–465). The *Harpers Ferry Hostel*, seven miles east at 19123 Sandy Hook Rd in Knoxville, MD (☏301/834-7652, Ⓦwww.harpersferryhostel .org; April to mid-Nov only), has dorm beds from $20, private rooms for $50, and its own campground. The park's **visitor center** has further details on area camping, as does the **Jefferson County tourist bureau**, 37 Washington Court (☏304/535-2627 or 1-800/848-TOUR, Ⓦwww.hello-wv.com).

Around Harpers Ferry

CHARLES TOWN, four miles south of Harpers Ferry on US-340, is where John Brown was tried and hanged; the **Jefferson County Museum** at Washington and Samuel streets (Mon-Sat 10am-4pm; free; ☏304/725-8628) tells the story of his trial, which took place at the still functional **Jefferson County Courthouse**, 100 E Washington St (Mon–Fri 9am–-5pm), as well as his conviction and execution. **SHEPHERDSTOWN**, a cozy village along the Potomac ten miles to the north, is prettier and better for wandering, with quaint old shops and cafés looking across the river to Maryland's infamous **Antietam Battlefield**. Sited in an old hotel with plenty of Victorian furnishings and antiques, the **Historic Shepherdstown Museum**, 129 E German St (April–Oct 11am–5pm, Sun 1–4pm; donation; Ⓦwww.historicshepherdstown.com) displays war relics and a replica of a steamboat – which was demonstrated in town in 1787.

Further afield, the old spa town of **BERKELEY SPRINGS** (originally known as Bath, like its sister city in England) is preserved as a state historic park thirty miles west of Harpers Ferry on Hwy-9, seven miles south of I-70. Berkeley Springs was a favorite summer retreat of the Colonial elite – George Washington was a regular – and assorted massage and steam-bath treatments are still available at its many health spas. You can take a soak in the old **Roman Bath House**, 2 S Washington St (daily 10am–6pm; $20 per 30min soak or $45 with massage; reservations recommended at ☏304/258-2711; Ⓦwww.berkeleyspringssp.com), in active use since 1815; the spring's waters are 74°F year-round but heated to 102°F for bathers. The town's leafy and green **central square** has footpaths fanning out in all directions, one climbing the hill up to the crenellated, medieval-looking **Berkeley Castle**, a private estate built in 1885. Among the **B&Bs** here are the *Highlawn Inn*, 171 Market St (☏304/258-5700 or 1-888/290-4163, Ⓦwww. highlawninn.com; ❹), whose rooms have claw-foot tubs and Victorian decor, and the *Manor Inn*, 234 Fairfax St (☏304/258-1552, Ⓦwww.bathmanorinn.com; ❹), where the simple, pleasant rooms are some of the more affordable in the area. For smart, modern accommodations, the *Inn and Spa at Berkeley Springs*, 1 Market St (☏304/258-2210, Ⓦwww.theinnandspa.com; ❸), is a good choice, too, with rooms in a classic 1930s neo-Georgian building.

The Allegheny Mountains

The **Allegheny Mountains**, West Virginia's segment of the Appalachian chain, are somewhat obscure to many East Coast travelers. The entire 140-mile crest is protected as part of the **Monongahela National Forest**, within which numerous state parks contain the most spectacular sights. There are no cities and few towns, public transportation is nonexistent, and not much goes on after dark, but if you like to backpack, hike, cycle, climb, or canoe, the Alleghenies are well worth a visit. For maps and more detailed information, contact the state tourist office or the Monongahela National Forest Supervisor, 200 Sycamore St, Elkins, WV 26241 (Mon–Fri 8am–4.45pm; ☏304/636-1800, Ⓦwww.fs.fed .us/r9/mnf).

The Northern Monongahela

Some of the most beautiful stretches of the Monongahela National Forest are in the **northern** part of the state, where the thundering torrents of the **Blackwater Falls** pour over a 60ft limestone cliff before crashing down through a steeply walled canyon, its water amber-colored from the presence of darkish tannins. South from here spreads the dense maple, oak, walnut, and birch forest of broad **Canaan Valley**, while to the east rise the highlands of the **Dolly Sods Wilderness**, vividly marked with rocky topography and murky bogs, with the whole area crisscrossed by hiking, cycling, and skiing trails.

Rising up at the south end of the Canaan Valley, the state's highest point, 4861ft **Spruce Knob**, stands out over the headwaters of the Potomac River – you can actually drive all the way to the summit. Even more impressive views can be had from the top of **Seneca Rocks**, some twenty miles to the northeast, whose 1000ft limestone cliffs present what is widely considered the most challenging rock-climb on the East Coast. If you want to take the easy way up, a good trail leads in around the back of the North Peak, and takes well under an hour to the top. Get more information at the **Seneca Rocks Discovery Center** (April–Oct daily 9am–4.30pm, Nov & March Sat & Sun 10am–4pm; free), near the junction of highways 33 & 55. *Yokum's* (☎304/567-2351 or 1-800/772-8342, ⓦwww.yokum.com), close to the base of the rocks, has a cheap **motel** (❸), self-service **cabins** (4), and a pretty riverside **campground** (from $5), plus a country store and **restaurant** that serves tasty, good-value meals. Just northwest, not to be missed is **Smoke Hole Canyon**, whose river has cut a nearly half-mile-deep chasm into the sheer rock walls. When the mist and fog rise out of the deeply carved canyon, it's a truly spellbinding sight. For the hardy, the **North Fork Mountain Trail** follows the canyon for 24 miles, and the **Big Bend Campground** is available seasonally (April–Oct; $16; ☎304/257-4488 or ☎1-877/444-6677).

The tiny logging town of **DAVIS**, just east of US-219 at the north end of the Canaan Valley, makes a convenient **base**: the *Bright Morning Inn* on William Avenue (☎304/259-5119, ⓦwww.brightmorninginn.com; ❹) is an 1896 boarding house with nice rooms, while the *Meyer House*, Third St at Thomas Ave (☎304/259-5451, ⓦwww.meyerhousebandb.com; ❺), built in 1885, has three rooms with period decor and DVD players. For **food**, *Muttley's*, on William Ave (☎304/259-4858), serves great-value steaks, plus duck, pork, and seafood. Among local **outdoor guides and outfitters**, Blackwater Outdoor Adventures, nearly twenty miles away on Rte-72 at St George (☎304/478-3775, ⓦwww.blackwateroutdoors.com), runs rafting, kayaking, and canoeing trips and rents out bikes. *Timberline Resort* (☎304/866-4801 or 1-800/SNOWING, ⓦwww.timberlineresort.com) operates one of the state's largest downhill ski areas several miles southeast of town. Alternatively, off Route 32 N, the *Canaan Valley Resort* (☎1-800/622-4121, ⓦwww.canaanresort.com) is a year-round affair with winter skiing, summer activities, and hotel rooms (❹), campsites ($25), and cabins and cottages (❼). For more information on the region, contact the **visitor center** on Main Street (daily 9am–5pm; ☎304/259-5315 or 1-800/782-2775, ⓦwww.canaanvalley.org).

Elkins and the Augusta Festival

Just west of the Canaan Valley, **ELKINS** is the biggest town in northern West Virginia and a fine spot to experience the vibrant folk traditions of the Allegheny mountains. The **Augusta Heritage Center**, located on the campus of Davis and Elkins College at 100 Campus Drive (☎304/637-1209, ⓦwww.augustaheritage.com), holds concerts and events throughout the summer, including dulcimer-playing in April and fiddle music in October, but its major annual showcase is mid-August's **Augusta Festival**, offering workshops in such diverse pursuits as banjo-playing, blacksmithing, quilt-making, and folk dancing; after dark, performers get together for a nightly hoedown, featuring storytellers and bluegrass bands.

Elkins's **visitor center**, 1035 N Randolph Ave (Mon–Fri 8.30am–5.00pm; ☎304/636-2717 or 1-800/422-3304, ⊛www.randolphcountywv.com), can provide full details on local **accommodation**, including the *Cheat River Lodge*, six miles from Elkins on Route 33 (☎304/636-2301, ⊛www.cheatriverlodge.com), which has a lovely riverside setting as well as nice suites with plenty of amenities in the main lodge (❹) and full modern cabins (❼) with stoves, kitchens, and hot tubs. At Davis and Elkins College, the *Graceland Inn* (☎1-800/624-3157, ⊛www.gracelandinn.com; ❺) is an eleven-unit converted 1893 mansion with stylish Victorian rooms. When you want to **eat**, the *Kissel Stop Café*, 21 Third St, one block from the visitor center (☎304/636-8810), serves tasty sandwiches and coffee amid railroad-car decor.

The Southern Monongahela

The **southern half** of the Monongahela National Forest is contained within hilly **Pocahontas County**, known as "the birthplace of rivers" because it holds the headwaters of several great West Virginia rivers. Like most of the Alleghenies, it's a mountainous, fairly inaccessible region – two roads, US-219 and Hwy-92, wind north-to-south, with a handful of minor roads twisting between them – offering outstanding outdoor recreation as well as endless scenic vistas. The county **visitor center** in Marlinton (☎304/799-4636 or 1-800/336-7009; ⊛www.pocahontascountywv .com) provides decent maps of the area.

One signature sight is the state-run **Cass Scenic Railroad**, a restored, steam-powered logging railroad built in 1902. The chugging Shay locomotive carries visitors on a five-hour trip up to the top of 4842ft Bald Knob (schedule varies; $17–22; ☎304/456-4300 or 1-800/CALL-WVA, ⊛www.cassrailroad.com), starting at the old lumber-mill company town of **CASS**, five miles west of Hwy-28 near the town of Greenbank, now preserved in its entirety as a historic park. You can even **stay the night** in one of thirteen rail-employees' two-story cottages built in 1902; the cottages have been converted into self-service accommodation and sleep four to ten people (☎1-800/CALL-WVA; ❹–❺). At the same phone number, you can also rent a historic 1920s **caboose**, with clean and basic furnishings, for a day-trip up the mountain ($99–149) or an overnight stay (❼).

A rigorous five-mile walk downhill from Cass leads along the tracks to the start of the bicycle-friendly **Greenbrier River Trail** (⊛www.greenbrierrivertrail.com), which follows the river and the railroad for 75 miles, coming out near Lewisburg. You can also rent a **mountain bike** from Elk River Touring Center (☎304/572-3771 or 1-866/572-3771, ⊛www.ertc.com), fifteen miles north of **Marlinton**, the county seat, off US-219 in the hamlet of **Slatyfork**. The company runs a shuttle service to the trailheads and organizes fly-fishing and cycling trips, and ski tours in winter, and has a good-value restaurant serving trout, seafood and pasta. They also operate twelve basic units in an inn and farmhouse (❹) and four cabins at various locations with more amenities (❻–❽); weekends require a two-night stay.

Five miles west of the junction with the exquisite Highland Scenic Highway (Rte-150), another spot well worth visiting is **Cranberry Glades Botanical Area**, where a half-mile boardwalk is set out around a patch of peat bog swamp – one of four such bogs occupying 750 acres. Further information can be obtained from the Cranberry Mountain Nature Center (daily May–Oct 9am–4.30pm; ☎304/653-4826) at the junction of highways 39 and 55. Further along, the **Highland Scenic Highway** merits a leisurely trip to explore its 43 miles of eye-catching views, several fine campgrounds, and 150 miles of hiking trails that branch off from it. Contact the Marlington Ranger District (☎304/799-4334) for more information.

Lewisburg and the Greenbrier Resort

Just off I-64, south of the Monongahela National Forest, **LEWISBURG** was originally a frontier outpost during the Indian Wars of the 1770s, and was greatly prized during the Civil War for its location at the head of the Greenbrier Valley; today it plays host to August's **West Virginia State Fair**, at 107 W Fair St (T 304/645-1090, W www.wvstatefair.com).

Washington Street is lined by brick-faced early nineteenth-century houses, and makes for pleasant wandering; the area is part of the **Lewisburg Historic District**, a four-block downtown zone. The **visitor center**, 111 N Jefferson St (Mon–Fri 9am–5pm, Sat 10am–4pm; T 1-800/833-2068, W www.greenbrierwv. com), hands out walking-tour maps and can suggest driving tours around Greenbrier Valley. It can also put you in touch with various cozy **hotels**, such as the *General Lewis Inn*, 301 E Washington St (T 304/645-2600 or 1-800/628-4454, W www.generallewisinn.com; 5), which has two-dozen Victorian rooms and a fine, moderately priced **restaurant**.

Just east of Lewisburg, **WHITE SULPHUR SPRINGS** is a historic resort town that's mainly known for its *Greenbrier* hotel and resort, 300 W Main St (T 304/536-1110 or 1-800/624-6070, W www.greenbrier.com; 9), the grandest hotel in the state with its pillared entrance hall, 6500 lush acres, golf courses, and fine restaurants (reserve ahead). Two dozen US presidents have stayed here, perhaps thanks in part to the hotel's deep-underground Cold War-era **bunker**, which came to public attention in 1992 and now, having been decommissioned, is open for tours (Sun & Wed 1pm; $30; T 304/536-7810).

The New River Gorge

One of West Virginia's most spectacular river canyons, the **New River Gorge**, lies just thirty miles west of Lewisburg along I-64. Stretching for over fifty miles, and protected as a national park, the thousand-foot chasm was carved through the limestone mountains by the New River – despite its name, one of the oldest rivers in North America. Apart from one daily Amtrak train, there's no easy access to most of the gorge; to see it, you have to get out on the water, with the help of any of over fifty professional rafting companies. For details on the cycling, climbing, hiking, and rafting options available – including how to risk your neck on the Class V rapids of the Gauley River National Recreation Area just north – visit the gorge's southern **Sandstone Visitor Center**, located where Hwy-64 crosses the river (daily 9am–5pm; T 304/466-0417, W www.nps.gov/neri), or the **Canyon Rim visitor center**, seven miles north of Oak Hill on Hwy-19 (daily 9am–5pm; T 304/574-2115), which sits alongside the **New River Gorge Bridge**, dramatically rising nine hundred feet above the river.

HINTON, on the southern end of the gorge (and another Amtrak stop), is an almost perfectly preserved company town, beautifully sited, with brick-lined streets angling up from the water, lined by dozens of grand civic buildings as well as row after row of slowly decaying workers' houses. A walking-tour map is available from the **visitor center**, 206 Temple St (Mon–Fri 10am–4pm; T 304/466-5420), which is also the site of a railroad museum. There are the usual budget **motels**, along with the *New River Falls Lodge*, 110 Cliff Island Drive (T 304/466-5710, W www.newriverfallslodge.com), offering six basic B&B rooms (4) and two-bedroom cottages with kitchens and fireplaces (7). **River-rafting** outfits include New River Whitewater Tours (T 304/465-2025 or 1-800/292-0880, W www.newriverscenic.com) and Cantrell Ultimate Rafting (T 304/466-0595 or 1-800/470-RAFT, W www.ultimaterafting.com), both charging $50–80 per person, depending on the type of raft and the destination. All of these facilities are to be found on Hwy-20, just south of town.

Charleston

CHARLESTON, West Virginia's state capital and largest city, on the Kanawha River, holds few major attractions, but it does have a nice selection of Victorian-era buildings in various states of preservation. You can find out more and get a walking tour of the historic district by dropping in on the **visitor center**, 200 Civic Center Drive (Mon–Fri 9am–5pm; ☎304/344-5075, ⓦwww.charlestonwv.com). The riverfront **state capitol**, 1900 Kanawha Blvd (Mon–Sat 9am–7pm, Sun noon–7pm; tours Mon–Fri 9am–3.30pm; ☎304/558-4839), designed by Lincoln Memorial and US Supreme Court architect Cass Gilbert, is a stately Renaissance Revival structure from 1932 that has a impressively large, gold-leafed dome. The **West Virginia Cultural Center** (Mon–Thurs 9am–8pm, Fri & Sat 9am–6pm, Sun noon–6pm; ☎304/558-0220, ⓦwww.wvculture.org; free), in the same compound, acts as the state museum and has extensive displays on coal mining, geology, forestry, war, and state history.

Charleston has plenty of generic chain motels and hotels, but if you want distinctive **accommodation**, try the *Brass Pineapple*, 1611 Virginia St E (☎304/344-0748, ⓦbrasspineapple.com; ❻), a Victorian-styled B&B with plenty of antique, flowery decor; more unexpected is *Tikvah's Kosher Bed-and-Breakfast*, 1564 Virginia St E (☎304/345-8511, ⓦwww.tikvahskosherbandb.com; ❹), with comfortable rooms and food that's certified kosher by an area rabbi. For **dining** choices, ⚲ the *Southern Kitchen*, 5240 MacCorkle Ave SE (☎304/925-3154), dishes up regional favorites like ham-and-gravy and fried chicken at affordable prices, while the Art Deco *Blossom Dairy and Soda Fountain Cafe*, 904 Quarrier St (☎304/305-2233), has the usual tasty sandwiches, burgers, and sundaes for lunch but converts into a chic, upscale bistro at night, serving fine steak, seafood, and regional fare.

Maryland

Founded as the sole Catholic colony in strongly Protestant America, and, in the nineteenth century, isolated as the northernmost slave state, **MARYLAND** has always been somewhat unusual. Within its small, irregularly shaped area, its attractions range from the frantic boardwalk beaches of **Ocean City** to the sleepy fishing villages of the **Chesapeake Bay** to the bustling urban center of **Baltimore**. The Chesapeake Bay, slowly recovering from near annihilation due to pollution and overfishing, may have lost its once-abundant oyster stocks, but its legendary **blue crabs** and sweet rockfish are still available, supped on by the weekend boaters who cruise from one to another of the Bay's Colonial-era towns.

Maryland boasts a number of firsts for the United States, including the first Catholic cathedral, gas-lit street, and telegraph line (between Baltimore and Washington DC), while Kent Island on Maryland's **Eastern Shore** was the third permanent English settlement (behind Jamestown and Plymouth Rock), founded in 1631. During the War of 1812, the British forces, attempting a last-ditch effort to wrest back the colonies, burned down much of Washington DC, then moved on to the shipyards of Baltimore. In a valiant battle, they were staved off at **Fort McHenry**; the fort's resistance inspired an onlooker, Francis Scott Key, to write the words to the United States' national anthem, **The Star-Spangled Banner**.

Maryland's largest city is the busy port of **Baltimore**, a quirky metropolis with a revitalized urban waterfront, thriving cultural scene, and eclectic neighborhoods. **Western Maryland** stretches over a hundred miles to the Appalachian foothills, its rolling farmlands notable chiefly for the Civil War killing grounds at **Antietam**. Just twenty miles south of Baltimore, along the Chesapeake Bay, picturesque **Annapolis** has served as Maryland's capital since 1694. Some of the state's most worthwhile destinations, from the pretty fishing and yachting town of **St Michaels** to the untouched wilderness of **Assateague Island**, are across the Chesapeake Bay on the Eastern Shore, connected to the rest of the state by the US-50 bridge but otherwise still a world apart – except for the sprawling resort of Ocean City.

Getting around Maryland

The best ways to get around Maryland are by **car** and, if you can rent one, **boat**, sailing around the gorgeous Chesapeake Bay. **Cycling** is also a good option, especially on the Eastern Shore, where the roads are wide-shouldered and little traveled, and wind through cornfields from one hamlet to another – the state tourist office puts out an excellent free map of the safest and most scenic routes. Baltimore is on the main Amtrak route between New York, Philadelphia, and Washington DC, and is linked by regular buses with Annapolis and elsewhere.

Baltimore

BALTIMORE had a reputation as a city in decline, and while the glory days of heavy industry along the port are now distant, it is among the more enjoyable stops on the East Coast, and its closely knit neighborhoods and historic quarters provide an engaging backdrop to many diverse attractions, especially those along its celebrated **waterfront**. The city also boasts top-rated **museums**, which cover everything from fine arts to black history to urban archeology. It's also been home to such diverse figures as writers Edgar Allan Poe and Anne Tyler, and civil rights icons Frederick Douglass and Thurgood Marshall.

Arrival, information, and getting around

Baltimore–Washington International Airport (BWI), ten miles south of the city center and twenty-five miles northeast of DC, is one of the busier East Coast hubs. The cheapest and best way to get into the city is on the MTA **light rail** system, which takes around twenty-five minutes (☎410/539-5000 or 1-800/RIDE-MTA, ⓦwww.mtamaryland.com). **Shuttle vans** into Baltimore, including Airport Shuttle ($25, $10 per additional person; ☎410/821-5387 or 1-877/VANFORU, ⓦwww.baltimoreairportshuttle.com), take around twenty minutes to reach downtown. **Taxis** cost around $35. **MARC** commuter trains ($4 one way; ☎410/539-5000 or 1-800/325-RAIL), connect the airport to the restored **Pennsylvania Station** (also known as Penn Station), half a mile north of downtown at 1525 N Charles St, which is also the arrival point of Amtrak **trains** (☎1-800/USA-RAIL) from all destinations. Greyhound **buses** stop downtown at 2110 Haines Street.

Pick up free maps and guides at the **Baltimore Area Convention and Visitors Association**, 401 Light Street, in front of the Maryland Science Center (daily 9am–6pm; ☎410/837-7024 or 1-877/BALTIMORE, ⓦwww.baltimore.org), or from its booths at the airport and train station.

Pennsylvania Station & Baltimore Museum of Art

Meyerhoff Symphony Hall

STATE CENTER

BALTIMORE

CHASE STREET

EAGER ST

READ STREET

Mount Vernon

MADISON STREET

Maryland Historical Society

Washington Monument

Mother Seton House

Walters Art Museum

Peabody Conservatory of Music

CENTRE STREET

FRANKLIN STREET

MULBERRY STREET

Lexington Market

LEXINGTON MARKET

SARATOGA ST

Greyhound Bus Station

Westminster Church & Edgar Allan Poe Grave

FAYETTE STREET

BALTIMORE STREET

REDWOOD STREET

City Hall

LEXINGTON STREET

Phoenix Shot Tower

CHARLES CENTER

BALTIMORE ST

SHOT TOWER

Power Plant Live! complex

LOMBARD STREET

Port Discovery

WATER STREET

Flag House

PRATT STREET

World Trade Center

Harborplace

Baltimore Maritime Museum

CAMDEN STREET

USS Constellation

National Aquarium

CONWAY STREET

Oriole Park at Camden Yards

Inner Harbor

Pier 6 Concert Pavilion

Maryland Science Center

M&T Stadium

American Visionary Art Museum

FEDERAL HILL DISTRICT

Federal Hill Park

KEY HIGHWAY

CROSS STREET

Cross Street Market

M Metro station

MARTIN LUTHER KING BOULEVARD

LIGHT RAIL

EUTAW STREET

LINDEN AVENUE

READ STREET

CATHEDRAL STREET

CHARLES STREET

ST PAUL STREET

CALVERT STREET

HUNTER STREET

GUILFORD AVENUE

JONES FALLS EXPRESSWAY

MADISON STREET

MONUMENT STREET

CONSTITUTION STREET

HIGH STREET

HILLEN STREET

FORREST ST

ENSOR ST

COLVIN STREET

ORLEANS STREET

GAY ST

LOW STREET

FRONT STREET

THE FALLSWAY

CALVERT STREET

GUILFORD AVENUE

HOLLIDAY STREET

COMMERCE ST

SOUTH STREET

GAY STREET

MARKET PL

ORCHARD STREET

ST MARY STREET

HOWARD STREET

PARK AVENUE

PACA STREET

LIBERTY STREET

CHARLES STREET

ST PAUL ST

GREENE STREET

LIGHT STREET

CHARLES STREET

PARK AVENUE

HARBORPLACE PROMENADE

B&O Railroad Museum (1/2 mile) & Babe Ruth Birthplace

Fort McHenry

RESTAURANTS & CAFÉS

Babalu Grill	7
Da Mimmo	9
Donna's	4
Helmand	3
Vaccaro's Italian Pastries	9
Women's Industrial Exchange	5

ACCOMMODATION

Admiral Fell Inn	E
Celie's Waterfront B&B	F
Henderson's Wharf Inn	G
The Inn at Government House	A
Mount Vernon Hotel	C
Peabody Court	B
Pier 5	H
Tremont Park	D

BARS & CLUBS

The 8x10	10
Brass Elephant	2
Brewer's Art	1
Maggie Moore's	6

N

0   400 yds

City transportation

Because the city is compact – most sights are within a mile or two of the center – you can cover a lot of territory on foot. The **MTA** bus, subway, and light-rail system ($1.60, day-pass $3.50; ☎410/539-5000, ⓦwww.mtamaryland.com) covers many locations, including the airport (subway and buses Mon–Fri 5am–midnight, Sat & Sun 6am–midnight; light rail Mon–Sat 6am–11pm, Sun 11am–7pm), though the subway and light rail are limited to one main route each. On buses, have exact change ready. For **taxis**, contact Yellow Cab (☎410/685-1212) or Royal Cab (☎410/327-0330). **Water taxis** link the Inner Harbor and sixteen area attractions, including the National Aquarium, Fell's Point, and Fort McHenry (schedule varies; all-day pass $8; ☎410/563-3901 or 1-800/658-8947, ⓦwww. thewatertaxi.com), while Harbor Cruises ($30–49; ☎410/727-3113, ⓦwww. harborcruises.com) has elaborate dinner outings and special-event **cruises**.

Accommodation

Baltimore has the usual chain **hotels** available downtown, along with a few local institutions, while the **B&Bs** clustered around the historic waterfront area of Fell's Point make for a pleasant alternative. The Convention and Visitors office (☎410/837-7024 or 1-877/BALTIMORE, ⓦwww.baltimore.org) can help with reservations.

Admiral Fell Inn 888 S Broadway ☎410/522-7377 or 1-800/292-4667, ⓦwww.harbormagic. com. Chic historic hotel spread over seven buildings (some dating to the 1770s) in the heart of Fell's Point. Rooms have vaulted ceilings and fireplaces; some have Jacuzzis and balconies as well. ❽

Celie's Waterfront Inn 1714 Thames St ☎410/522-2323 or 1-800/432-0184, ⓦwww .Baltimore-Bed-Breakfast.com. Nine exquisite rooms and suites, some with private balconies. A rooftop deck has superb views of Fell's Point harbor. ❼

Henderson's Wharf Inn 1000 Fell St ☎410/522-7087, ⓦwww.hendersonswharf.com. Prominent waterside spot with modern rooms that include boutique furnishings, refrigerators, and Internet access. Continental breakfast and on-site gym as well. ❽

The Inn at Government House 1125 N Calvert St ☎410/539-0566, ⓦwww.baltimorecity.gov.

Elaborate, restored 1889 Victorian mansion with antique-filled rooms, grand music and dining rooms, detailed woodwork, and breakfast and parking included. ❺

Mount Vernon 24 W Franklin St ☎410/727-2000 or 1-800/245-5256, ⓦwww.bichotels.com. Large, stately hotel with comfortable rooms and a central location. Reserve ahead in summer. ❼

Peabody Court 612 Cathedral St ☎410/727-7101, ⓦwww.peabodycourthotel.com. Luxury hotel in a handsome, converted 1928 apartment building set in a historic neighborhood. Has marble bathrooms and upscale decor, plus Internet access. Pet-friendly. ❻

Pier 5 711 Eastern Ave ☎410/539-2000, ⓦwww. harbormagic.com. Centrally located, upscale boutique hotel with plenty of style, offering smart, modern rooms with CD players and suites with fridges, microwaves, and wet bars. ❾

Downtown Baltimore

Named after Maryland's founder, Lord Baltimore, the city of **Baltimore** was christened in 1729, a half-century after its namesake's death, and was the second-largest city in America up until 1870. Like San Francisco, Baltimore burned to the ground just after the start of the twentieth century, leaving only its domed 1867 **City Hall**, 100 N Holliday St, standing. Until the last decade, much of the downtown looked burned over in a different way, blighted by poverty and decay. Fortunately, many parts of town have undergone a dramatic face-lift, especially in the **Inner Harbor** section. Enlivened by new restaurants and bars, this area now makes for a pleasant stroll along the brick-lined waterfront and features nautical and science-oriented attractions. It's also within walking distance of the two sports stadiums.

The main cluster of businesses, restaurants, and cafés is found west of the central **Charles Street**, in Baltimore's original shopping district, now coming back after its long decline. One landmark here, dating from 1782, is a must-see: the oldest and loudest of the city's covered markets, **Lexington Market** (Mon–Sat 8.30am–6pm; Ⓦwww.lexingtonmarket.com), has more than a hundred food stalls, including *Faidley's* (Ⓣ410/752-6461), the best and cheapest of many outlets serving oysters, clams, crabs, and other catches from the Chesapeake Bay. Safe during the day, the area can become threatening after dark, when it is best avoided.

Just south of the market, at 519 W Fayette St, **Westminster Church** was built in 1852 atop the main Baltimore cemetery, and many ornate tombs are now located in dark catacombs below. Among the prominent figures entombed is **Edgar Allan Poe**, who lived in town for three years in the 1830s, marrying his 13-year-old cousin and starting a career in journalism before moving on to Richmond, Virginia. In 1849, while passing through Baltimore, Poe was found incoherent near a polling place and died soon after. In 1875 his remains were moved from a pauper's grave and entombed within the stone memorial that stands along Green Street on the north side of the church. Every January 19, a mysterious figure clad in black appears at Poe's grave to offer a toast of cognac and three red roses in honor of his birthday.

A somewhat more fun place to visit is the brick rowhouse where baseball great **Babe Ruth** was born in 1895, at 216 Emory St (daily: April–Oct 10am–6pm; Nov–March 10am–5pm; $10; Ⓦwww.BabeRuthMuseum.com). Chock-full of photographs, film clips, and memorabilia, it traces the life and achievements of the legendary home-run hitter. Appropriately enough, **Oriole Park at Camden Yards**, the baseball stadium of the Baltimore Orioles (tickets $8–45; Ⓣ1-888/848-BIRD), is just two blocks west, on the site of an old railroad terminal; guided tours are available (May–Dec Mon–Sat 11am–2pm on the hour, Sun 12:30pm, 1pm, 2pm & 3pm; $7; Ⓣ410/547-6234, Ⓦwww.TheOrioles.com). The centenary of the Babe's birth was marked by the unveiling of a bronze statue in 1995 (see if you can spot the mistake).

Just next door, looking very much like an alien spaceship that just landed, is the 68,400-seat **M&T Bank Stadium** – built in 1998 and home to the **Baltimore Ravens**, who were named after Edgar Allan Poe's most (in)famous character and won an unexpected Super Bowl victory in 2001. Tickets are hard to come by ($40–315; Ⓣ410/547-SEAT), but tours are offered daily ($5; Ⓣ410/261-RAVE, Ⓦwww.baltimoreravens.com).

A half-mile west of Oriole Park, the **B&O Railroad Museum**, housed in an 1830 passenger station and depot at 901 W Pratt St (Mon–Fri 10am–4pm, Sat 10am–5pm, Sun 11am–4pm; $14; Ⓦwww.borail.org), commemorates the first large-scale railroad in the US, which was founded in 1827. Here you can see displays of dozens of ornate carriages, including some wacky parasol-covered early models, and row upon row of locomotives, from the first steam engines to sleek 1940s diesels, all housed in stylish historic-landmark depots, roundhouses, and support buildings that testify to the glory days of rail transport.

The Inner Harbor

The rotting wharves and derelict warehouses that stood in the **Inner Harbor** through the 1970s are today replaced by the sparkling steel-and-glass **Harborplace** shopping mall (Mon–Sat 10am–9pm, Sun 11am–7pm; Ⓦwww.harborplace.com), which swarms day and night with tourists and locals. Sweeping views of the entire city and beyond can be admired from the 27th-story Top of the World observation deck of Baltimore's own **World Trade Center** on the north pier (Oct–April Wed–Sun

10am–6pm; May–Sept 10am–9pm; $5; ⓣ410/837-VIEW). Nothing in the Inner Harbor dates from before its rebuilding, but to lend an air of authenticity, the graceful **USS Constellation** (April–Oct 10am–5.30pm, Nov–Mar 10am–4.30pm; $8.75, ⓦwww.constellation.org), has been placed here, the only Civil War vessel still afloat and the last all-sail warship built by the US Navy. Other historic ships and a squat 1856 lighthouse that's been moved here make up the **Baltimore Maritime Museum** (daily 10am–5pm; $6; ⓦwww.baltomaritimemuseum.org) on the next pier.

Far and away the biggest tourist attraction in Baltimore is the **National Aquarium**, 501 E Pratt St (spring & fall Sat–Thurs 9am–5pm, Fri 9am–8pm, winter opens an hour later, summer daily 9am–8pm; open for 90min after last admission; $22, $25 with dolphin show; ⓦwww.aqua.org), an essential sight for its jellyfish, sharks, rays, sea turtles, and other oceanic creatures. Also popular is its recently opened **Dolphin Amphitheater**, where you can see the playful cetaceans cavorting and seemingly trying to please the crowd.

If this isn't enough to satisfy the tykes, stop at the gleaming **Port Discovery**, just north of the harbor at 35 Market Place (summer Mon–Sat 10am–5pm, Sun noon–5pm, rest of year Tues–Fri 9.30am–4.30pm, Sat 10am–5pm, Sun noon–5pm; $10.75, ⓦwww.portdiscovery.org). This children's museum is packed to the ceiling with hands-on exhibits, learning games, interactive toys, a media studio where kids put on their own productions, and many other amusements.

Federal Hill and around

Lined with interesting shops, restaurants, and galleries, the **Federal Hill** district, a short walk south of the Inner Harbor, is a great place to escape from the crowds. Stop by the **visitor center** on Main Street (ⓣ410/727-4500, ⓦwww.historicfederalhill .com) for walking-tour maps and information. Its main thoroughfare, **Light Street**, leads to the indoor **Cross Street Market**, which opened in 1875 and has two blocks of open-air markets boasting some excellent delis, seafood bars, and fruit stalls. **Federal Hill Park** in the northeast is a quiet public space with fine views over the harbor and the downtown cityscape.

In the northern part of the area, by the harbor at 601 Light St, the sparkling glass, steel, and concrete **Maryland Science Center** (Tues–Thurs 10am–5pm, Fri 10am–8pm, Sat 10am–6pm, Sun 11am–5pm; $14.50, IMAX show $8, combination ticket $18.50; ⓦwww.mdsci.org) is mainly aimed at kids, with interactive displays on themes ranging from dinosaurs to space travel; an IMAX theater and planetarium provide added interest for youngsters.

Better is one of the city's most fascinating and unexpected institutions, the **American Visionary Art Museum**, east of Federal Hill Park at 800 Key Hwy (Tues–Sun 10am–6pm; $12; ⓦwww.avam.org), devoted to the works of untrained or amateur artists. Some of the more notable items include Tom Duncan's obsessively intricate sculpture of the boardwalk of *Coney Island*, eerie Bosch-like paintings of alien abductions, and all kinds of incarnations of Jesus and the Virgin Mary, crafted in wood, sequins, iron, and many other media.

Mount Vernon

Baltimore's most elegant quarter is just north of downtown on the shallow rise known as **Mount Vernon**, where several fine museums sit amid rows of eighteenth-century brick townhouses. This district, which is quite good for strolling, takes its name from the home of George Washington, whose likeness tops the 178ft marble column of the central **Washington Monument** (Wed–Sun 10am–5pm; free). There's a ground-floor museum covering Washington's life, and you can climb the building's 228 steps for a great view over the city.

Across the street, a solemn stone facade of the **Peabody Conservatory** hides one of the city's best interior spaces: the beautiful, skylit atrium of the **Peabody Library**, 17 E Mount Vernon Place (Tues–Fri 9am–5pm, Sat 9am–1pm; ☎410/659-8179; free), an 1878 Victorian delight rich with cast-iron balconies, soaring columns, and glass skylights, renovated in 2004. The ground floor features displays of various history books, among them a wonderful illustrated 1555 edition of Boccaccio's *Decameron*, and a 1493 printing of the *Nuremberg Chronicles*.

Two blocks west, the **Maryland Historical Society**, 201 W Monument St (Wed–Sun 10am–5pm $8; ⓦ www.mdhs.org), traces the path of local history through key documents and portraits of the old Maryland elite, while its items of interest include models of Chesapeake Bay boats, a range of decorative arts and furniture from various periods, and the original manuscript of the lyrics to "The Star-Spangled Banner."

Walters Art Museum

A block south of the Washington Monument, the **Walters Art Museum**, 600 N Charles St (Wed–Sun 10am–5pm; $10, special exhibits extra $5; ⓦ www.thewalters.org), provides a comprehensive survey of art from ancient statuary to French Impressionist painting. The main building's core is a large sculpture court, modeled on an Italian Renaissance palazzo, beyond which modern galleries show off Egyptian jewelry and sarcophagi (including an intact mummy), Greek and Roman antiquities, medieval illuminated manuscripts, Islamic ceramics, and some very fine Byzantine silver. The top floor has pre-Columbian artifacts – funerary objects, stone carvings, masks, sculptures, and more – in a grand hall filled with late nineteenth-century paintings, including Manet's *At the Café*. The adjacent restored **Hackerman House** holds some especially beautiful pieces, including Chinese jade figurines, a Ming dynasty handscroll, and a pair of polychrome-and-gilt temple doors carved to look like peacock feathers. The seventh-century lacquered wood statue here of a svelte Buddha is perhaps the oldest such image in the world.

The Flag House and Star-Spangled Banner Museum

A quarter of a mile east of downtown and the Inner Harbor, across the busy Falls Expressway, is the intriguing **Flag House and Star-Spangled Banner Museum**, 844 E Pratt St (Tues–Sat 10am–4pm; last tour at 3.30pm; $5; ⓦ www.flaghouse.org). It was here, in 1813, that Mary Pickersgill sewed the 30ft-by-45ft US flag whose presence at the harbor fort attack inspired Francis Scott Key to write "The Star-Spangled Banner." The actual well-worn flag is now in the National Museum of American History in Washington DC (see p.412), but the house is full of other patriotic tributes as well as various antiques from the era; on the same property, the less interesting **War of 1812 Museum** (same hours and admission) covers the eponymous conflict with costumes and military relics.

Little Italy

The densely tangled streets of **Little Italy** spread to the east of downtown. Besides dozens of restaurants and cafés (many of them very good), the area is built around the 1881 **Saint Leo the Great** church, 227 S Exeter St, and holds plenty of Baltimore's trademark stone-fronted **rowhouses**, almost all with highly polished steps quarried from local marble – a rock of such quality that it was used to build the monuments of Washington DC. As an improvised local substitute for air-conditioning, in the heat of summer residents move their furniture outdoors, thereby turning each street into an extended living room.

Fell's Point, Canton, and Fort McHenry

Baltimore's oldest and liveliest quarter, **Fell's Point**, lies a mile southeast of Little Italy. Its shipyards are long gone, but many old bars and earthy pubs have hung on to form one of the better nightlife districts on the East Coast. The area **visitor center**, 808 S Ann St (daily noon–4pm; ☎410/675-6750), provides good maps for self-guided walking tours, and tours (daily 1pm & 2.30pm; donation) of the 1765 **Robert Long House**, the oldest surviving urban residence in Baltimore, a handsome Colonial structure dating to 1765. Other interesting sights include the **Fell's Point Maritime Museum**, 1724 Thames St (Thurs–Mon 10am-5pm; $4; ☎410/732-0278), originally a trolley barn and warehouse, now converted into exhibition space outlining the area's nautical history as a shipping point for fruit and tobacco, as well as slaves and opium. A different perspective on that history is provided by the new **Frederick Douglass Isaac Myers Maritime Park**, 1417 Thames St (Mon & Wed–Fri 11am–5pm, Sat & Sun noon–6pm; $5; ⓦwww.douglassmyers.org), named for two pioneering black leaders and focusing on their backgrounds, the history of the local port – including the slave trade – and a recreation of a late-nineteenth-century shipyard that employed African Americans.

East of Fell's Point, **Canton** is another district full of historic rowhouses, some of which date back to the Civil War, and is being revitalized with new restaurants and nightlife. Across the water from Canton lies one of Baltimore's most prominent historical sites, **Fort McHenry National Monument**, 2400 E Fort Ave (daily 8am–5pm, summer closes 8pm; $5 for seven-day pass; ⓦwww.nps.gov/fomc), a star-shaped fort that's most famous as the redoubt the British bombarded during the War of 1812 in an attempt to penetrate the harbor to attack Baltimore. The attack failed, and Francis Scott Key, when he saw "the bombs bursting in air," was moved to write the "Star-Spangled Banner" – originally known as "The Defence of Fort McHenry."

Further north

About a mile northeast of the center, in an old fire station off Broadway at 1601 E North Ave, the **Great Blacks in Wax Museum** (Tues–Sat 9am–6pm, Sun noon–6pm, winter closes an hour earlier; $9; ⓦwww.ngbiwm.com) uses wax models in posed dioramas to illustrate black history, from Egyptian pharaohs and early Muslims through to Marcus Garvey, Martin Luther King Jr, Nelson Mandela, and Colin Powell.

Further out on the north side, two miles from downtown at the top of Charles Street, is the **Baltimore Museum of Art**, 10 Art Museum Drive (Wed–Fri 11am–5pm, Sat & Sun 11am–6pm; $10, free on first Thurs of the month; ⓦwww.artbma.org). As well as great Italian and Dutch works by Botticelli, Raphael, Rembrandt, and Van Dyck, the museum has a delightful collection of less-heralded works, including Chardin's *A Game of Knucklebones*, drawings by Durer and Goya, and photographs from Weston, Stieglitz, and other masters. One gallery in the West Wing is devoted to Warhol, while the American Wing holds furniture and decorative arts, as well as paintings. The highlight is the **Cone Collection**, featuring works by Delacroix, Degas, Cézanne, and Picasso, as well as over a hundred drawings and paintings by Matisse – among them his signature *Large Reclining Nude* and a *Seated Odalisque*.

Eating

Baltimore is affectionately known as **Crab City**, and it has dozens of reasonably priced fresh **seafood** places where you can get top-notch **steamed crabs**. In addition, it has the usual range of diners and more than a dozen good family-run restaurants side by side in Little Italy. Canton and Mount Vernon hold a more eclectic selection, ranging from Irish to Mexican, while Fell's Point boasts numerous vegetarian, seafood, and other types of restaurants. In general, the city's restaurants tend to be unpretentious, family oriented, and reasonably priced.

Babalu Grill 332 Market Place, just north of Inner Harbor ☎410/234-9898. Popular restaurant serving well-priced traditional Cuban and Nuevo Latino cuisine in a lively setting. Good for its *ceviche*, ham croquettes, lamb shank, and Cuban sandwich with fried yucca.

Bertha's 734 S Broadway ☎410/327-5795. Casual and inexpensive (yet stylish) seafood restaurant, tucked away behind a tiny Fell's Point bar. Known for its delicious mussels, high tea, and nightly live blues, jazz, or Dixieland.

Black Olive 814 S Bond St, Fell's Point ☎410/276-7141. Expensive but succulent Mediterranean restaurant that has affordable meze (small plates) like grilled octopus salad, calamari, and pan-seared zucchini, as well as pricier, sharable entrees like rack of lamb and lobster tail.

Blue Moon Cafe 1621 Aliceanna St ☎410/522-3940. Fell's Point breakfast joint that locals swear by, lining up for the cheap and tasty crab Benedict, crab crepes, burritos, biscuits with sausage gravy, and cinnamon rolls.

Da Mimmo 217 S High St ☎410/727-6876. Intimate, romantic, mid-priced Little Italy café, with a wide-ranging menu that includes favorites like Clams Casino and pasta fagioli, plus live piano music and a more upscale ambience than you might expect.

Donna's 800 N Charles St ☎410/385-0180. Delicious sandwiches and burgers for lunch, and savory, mid-priced pasta, steak, and seafood for dinner in an elegant Mount Vernon locale. Also at 222 S Green St (☎410/328-1962) and 3101 St Paul St (☎410/889-3410).

Helmand 806 N Charles St ☎410/752-0311. Inexpensive but chic dinner-only Afghan restaurant in Mount Vernon, with plenty of lamb dishes as well as *aushak* (leek-filled vegetarian ravioli) and the delicious *kaddo borawni* (a fried-pumpkin appetizer).

Mama's on the Half Shell 2901 O'Donnell St, Canton ☎410/276-3160. Local, affordable favorite for its raw bar with jumbo shrimp and littleneck clams, plus crab-cake and scallops platters, and plenty of savory sandwiches – including the ever-popular oyster po' boy.

Obrycki's 1727 E Pratt St, just north of Fell's Point ☎410/732-6399. Baltimore's best and longest-established seafood restaurant, with delicious steamed, soft-shell, and broiled crabs at premium prices, as well as other excellent seafood. Closed in winter.

Vaccaro's Italian Pastries 222 Albemarle St, Little Italy ☎410/685-4905. Great spot to load up on cheesecakes, cookies, and other sweets, and to indulge in the kind of delicious gelato they make in the Old Country.

Woman's Industrial Exchange 333 N Charles St ☎410/685-4388. Excellent-value 1940s café between Mount Vernon and the Inner Harbor, with cheap breakfasts, huge plates of chicken gumbo, and delicious crab cakes.

Drinking and nightlife

Fell's Point may well have the densest assembly of **drinking** places in the US. You'll find one bar after another lined up along Broadway and the many smaller side streets; almost all feature some sort of entertainment, usually live bands, and on summer nights the sidewalks are packed with revelers. The **Power Plant Live!** complex, next to the Inner Harbor at 34 Market Place (☎410-727-LIVE, ⓦwww.powerplantlive.com), offers a wide selection of dining and mainstream entertainment choices and opens onto an outdoor plaza. The up-and-coming areas of **Canton** and **Federal Hill** also have plenty of drinking spots, while the city's highbrow culture is concentrated northwest of the center, in the Mount Royal Avenue area, in places like the **Meyerhoff Symphony Hall**, 1212 Cathedral St (☎410/783-8000, ⓦwww.baltimoresymphony.com) – home to award-winning conductor Marin Alsop – and the **Lyric Opera House**, 110 W Mount Royal Ave (☎410/727-6000, ⓦwww.baltimoreopera.com). For a rundown of what's on, pick up a copy of the excellent free *City Paper* (ⓦwww.citypaper.com) or check out ⓦwww.Baltimore.org.

The 8x10 10 E Cross St, Federal Hill ☎410/625-2000. Solid bar and live-music venue that features an eclectic mix of bands, from jazz to indie rock and electronica, often for a cover charge.

Brass Elephant 924 N Charles St, Mount Vernon ☎410/547-8485. Upscale, stylish lounge in an antique rowhouse, serving up tasty blue-crab guacamole, sautéed squid, and shellfish risotto as "bar fare," as well as some nice single-malt scotches and good, pricey cocktails.

Brewer's Art 1106 N Charles St, Mount Vernon ☎410/547-9310. The place anyone with a yen for microbrews must visit – a local landmark for beer-making that's tops for its "Ozzy" Belgian-style, dark "Proletary Ale" and good old "Charm City Sour Cherry."

Cat's Eye Pub 1730 Thames St, Fell's Point ☎410/276-9085. Cozy, crowded bar, offering a good range of beers and live music nightly, from blues and jazz to bluegrass and folk.

Lulu's Off Broadway 1703 Aliceanna St, Fell's Point ☎410/537-LULU. Jumping joint where you can sup on BBQ ribs, meatloaf, and lobster sandwiches – as well as vegetarian fare – or knock back a glass of wine or a microbrew while listening to guest DJs on weekend nights.

Maggie Moore's 21 N Eutaw St, north of Inner Harbor ☎410/837-2100. Smart and appealing Irish pub with handsome decor and nice, dark brews, as well as fare such as leg-of-lamb sandwich and beef-and-Guinness stew.

Max's on Broadway 735 S Broadway ☎410/675-6297. Huge corner venue with a very long bar – doling out some 300 kinds of beer in bottles, and rotating more than 70 on tap – pool tables, and, upstairs, a leather-upholstered cigar lounge with a more refined atmosphere.

Wharf Rat Bar 801 S Ann St, Fell's Point ☎410/276-9034. This friendly bar, well stocked with English ales, other European imports, and regional microbrews, packs in a trendy and discerning crowd.

Western Maryland

Stretched between West Virginia and the razor-straight Pennsylvania border, **western Maryland** ranges for some two hundred miles east to west, but is in places only two miles north to south. The further west you go the more hilly and rural it becomes, similar to Maryland's Appalachian neighbors.

Apart from the Civil War battlefield at **Antietam**, west of the only sizable town, **Frederick**, the best reason to come to this part of the state is to cycle or hike the footpath of the restored old **Chesapeake and Ohio Canal**, which winds along the Maryland side of the Potomac River from Washington, DC, for over 180 miles to **Cumberland** in the western mountains. Even further west is the state's largest freshwater lake, **Deep Creek Lake**, popular with watersports enthusiasts. It also has more than seventy thousand acres of public parks and forests surrounding it, some of which make for smooth cross-country skiing during the winter.

Frederick and around

One of the first towns settled in northwestern Maryland, **FREDERICK**, less than an hour west of Baltimore at the junction of I-70 and I-270, was laid out in 1745 by German farmers lured from Pennsylvania by the promise of cheap, fertile land. It grew to become a main stopover on the route west to the Ohio Valley, and the bulk of today's tidy town survives from the early 1800s.

The **visitor center**, 19 E Church St (daily 9am–5pm; ☎301/228-2888 or 1-800/999-3613, ⓦwww.fredericktourism.org), has walking-tour maps of the town. Some of the more notable sights include the **Schifferstadt House**, just off US-15 (April to early Dec Thurs–Sun noon–4pm; $3; ☎301/668-6088), a stone-walled farmhouse built in 1756 and largely unaltered since; the **Roger Taney House**, 121 S Bentz St (Sat 10am–4pm, Sun 1–4pm; $3; ☎301/663-7880), owned by the US Supreme Court chief justice best known for presiding over the infamous *Dred Scott* decision, which helped lead to the Civil War; and the **Beatty-Cramer House**, 9010 Liberty Rd on Rte 26 (April–Oct first Sat of month

10am–4pm; $3; also by appointment at ☎301/668-2086), a collection of three farm buildings that contains the area's oldest still-standing structure.

In the outskirts north of Frederick, **Cunningham Falls State Park** (8am–sunset) and the **Catoctin Mountain Park** (open dawn to dusk; free) both hold seemingly endless hardwood forests – great for fall color – in the midst of which are numerous preserved remnants of early homesteads. Pick up details on hiking and camping at the main **visitor center**, off Hwy-77 two miles west of US-15 (Mon–Thurs 10am–4.30pm, Fri 10am–5pm, Sat & Sun 8.30pm–5pm; ☎301/663-9388, Ⓦwww.nps.gov/cato). You can also **camp** here ($20–30 a night), and **rent cabins** of various sizes ($35–140).

There are **motels** along both I-70 and US-15, but the town's major **B&Bs**, the *Hill House*, 12 W Third St (☎301/682-4111; Ⓞ), and *Hollerstown Hill*, 4 Clarke Place (☎301/228-3630, Ⓦwww.hollerstownhill.com; Ⓞ), each offer four pleasant rooms in historic buildings from the late nineteenth century. If you plan on visiting Antietam, the *Jacob Rohrbach Inn*, 138 W Main St, Sharpsburg (☎301/432-5079, Ⓦwww.jacob-rohrbach-inn.com; Ⓞ), has four well-appointed rooms and suites and one detached cottage, all decorated in a style appropriate for a two-hundred-year-old homestead.

For a bite to **eat**, try the burgers and steamed crabs at *Cactus Flats*, three miles north off US-15 (☎301/898-3085), or the seafood, sandwiches, and microbrewed pale ales and stouts at *Barley & Hops*, 5473 Urbana Pike (☎301/668-5555).

Antietam National Battlefield

The site of the single bloodiest battle in the Civil War– causing more American deaths than any other single-day battle in US history – **Antietam National Battlefield** spreads over unaltered farmlands outside the whitewashed and balconied village of **Sharpsburg**, fifteen miles west of Frederick. Here, on the morning of September 17, 1862, forty thousand troops faced a Union army twice that number in an effort to consolidate rebel gains after their victory at the Battle of Second Manassas (or Second Bull Run). Hours later, 23,000 men from both sides lay dead or dying. The fiercest fighting, and the worst bloodshed, occurred in cornfields to the north.

△ Antietam National Battlefield

For all the carnage, the battle wasn't tactically decisive, but the Confederates' lack of success lost them the support of their would-be ally Great Britain, while the Union performance encouraged Lincoln to issue the Emancipation Proclamation. Pick up a brochure and driving-tour map of the park at the **visitor center**, a mile north of Sharpsburg off Hwy-65 (daily: summer 8am–7pm; winter 8:30am–5pm; $4 pass for three days; ☏301/432-5124, ⓦwww.nps.gov/anti).

Cumberland and the C&O Canal
The only large town in the far west of Maryland, sandwiched between West Virginia and Pennsylvania in a part of the state only eight miles wide, **CUMBERLAND** started life as a coal-mining center in the late 1700s. Often confused with Daniel Boone's Cumberland Gap in southwest Virginia, this Cumberland was also an important trans-Appalachian crossing, but its main place in history is as the terminus of the **C&O (Chesapeake and Ohio) Canal**, an impressive engineering feat begun in 1813 but not completed until 1850, by which time the railroads had already made it obsolete.

There are six **visitor centers** along the canal: the easternmost is in Georgetown, in Washington DC, and the westernmost is in Cumberland, at 13 Canal St (daily 9am–5pm; ☏301/722-8226, ⓦwww.nps.gov/choh); only the section of the park in **Great Falls** – whose own visitor center is at 11710 MacArthur Blvd, in Potomac, Maryland (☏301/767-3714) – charges admission ($3 per pedestrian and $5 per car for three days). All centers provide information on hiking, cycling, canoeing, and camping, which can prove valuable if you're interested in traveling the entire 184.5 miles along the **canal towpath**, an often lovely concourse that provides one of the longest contiguous trails in the US.

In summer, the historic trains of the **Western Maryland Scenic Railroad** leave from here to make the three-hour trip to Frostburg through the surrounding mountains (all trips at 11:30 am: May–Sept Fri–Sun; Oct Thurs–Sun; Nov–mid Dec Sat & Sun; $23; ☏301/759-4400 or 1-800/872-4650, ⓦwww.wmsr.com). Look for the tiny black-and-white log cabin where George Washington served his first commission in the 1750s, standing directly opposite the station on the other side of the canal.

About thirty miles east of Cumberland, I-68 slices straight through a 1600-foot wedge of sedimentary rock, exposing a dramatic "Smiley Face" rock formation called a syncline that can be viewed from a platform at the excellent **Sideling Hill Exhibit Center** (daily 9am–5pm; ☏301/842-2155), where there's a special geologic exhibit and stunning views all around.

Annapolis and southern Maryland

While Baltimore has grown into the state's largest and busiest city, **Annapolis**, Maryland's capital since 1694, has changed little in size and appearance. Though its charmingly narrow, time-worn streets are now often crowded, Annapolis is still among the more engaging small US cities. Its once-vital Chesapeake Bay **waterfront** has little of the feel of Colonial maritime life, and the main draws are the Beaux Arts campus of the US Naval Academy and the beautiful state capitol. If you want to get a better feel for the Chesapeake Bay region away from the crowds, head south to places like **St Mary's City** – the first capital of Maryland, completely reconstructed in the 1960s – or **Solomons Island**, one of many small bay towns that seem not to have changed for decades.

Annapolis

At the center of **ANNAPOLIS**, overlooking the town's dense web of streets, the **Maryland State House** (Mon–Fri 9am–5pm, Sat & Sun 10am–4pm; tours at 11am & 3pm; ☎410/974-3400; free) was completed in 1779 and, for six months in 1783–84, served as the official capital of the thirteen colonies; it remains the nation's oldest statehouse still in use. The **Old Senate Chamber**, off the grand entrance hall, is where the Treaty of Paris was ratified in 1784, officially ending the Revolutionary War. A statue of George Washington stands here on the spot where, three weeks before the treaty signing, he resigned his commission as head of the Continental Army. Also on the grounds of the State House is the cottage-sized **Old Treasury**, built in 1735 to hold Colonial Maryland's currency reserves.

Many grand late-eighteenth-century brick homes line the streets of Annapolis, but none surpasses the **Hammond-Harwood House**, two blocks west of the State House at 19 Maryland Ave, off King George Street (April–Oct Tues–Sun noon–5pm, last tour at 4pm; $6; ⓦ www.hammondharwoodhouse.org). The warm redbrick villa, which consists of two wings connected by a central hall, was built in 1774 to the designs of William Buckland and is most notable for its beautifully carved woodwork and intricate front doorway. The **Chase-Lloyd House**, 22 Maryland Ave (Tues–Sat 2–4pm; $2; ☎410/263-2723), a three-story Georgian brick townhouse from 1774 also by Buckland, is worth a look as well, with its grand stairway, interior Ionic columns, and intricate ornamentation. Near the Hammond house, another mansion, the 1765 **William Paca House**, 186 Prince George St (Mon–Sat 10am–5pm, Sun noon–5pm, winter Fri–Sun noon–5pm; $8 including tour), is decorated in warm rich colors and ornate furniture, while the splendid formal garden, which you can peer into from King George Street, has French-styled geometry and lovely topiary and boasts a nice viewing pavilion.

Besides such elite manors, dozens of eighteenth-century clapboard cottages and commercial warehouses fill the narrow streets that run down to the waterfront. The **Historic Annapolis Foundation**, housed in a c.1715 tavern at 18 Pinkney St (☎410/267-7619, ⓦ www.annapolis.org), can provide information on self-guided tours of the more notable structures.

For a unique insight into Maryland's history, stop by the **Banneker-Douglass Museum**, 84 Franklin St, a few blocks northeast of the state house (Tues–Fri 10am–3pm; free; ☎410/216-6180, ⓦ www.marylandhistoricaltrust.net/bdm.html), named after two of the most prominent black leaders and home to the state's largest holding of African-American art and artifacts.

The waterfront and US Naval Academy

Although few Colonial sites survive on the **Chesapeake Bay waterfront**, the rebuilt 1850s dockside **Market House**, 25 Market Place (hours vary; ⓦ www.annapolismarkethouse.com; free), is an early nineteenth-century replacement of a Colonial warehouse that was used by the revolutionary army but today is home to seafood vendors and restaurants. Among the boat-supply shops and harborside bars, the gray stone walls of the **US Naval Academy** house four thousand crew-cut young men and a handful of women who spend four rigid years here before embarking on careers as naval officers. Superb guided tours leave from the **Armel-Leftwich Visitor Center** (daily: March–Dec 9am–5pm; Jan & Feb 9am–4pm; tours $8; ☎410/263-6933, ⓦ www.navyonline.com) in Halsey Field House, through Gate 1 at the end of King George Street, and take in the elaborate crypt and marble sarcophagus of early-American naval hero John Paul Jones.

Annapolis is easy to reach: Greyhound stops at 308 Chinquapin Round Road, and you can access Amtrak and MARC trains (T 1-800/RIDE-MTA W www.mtamaryland.com) at BWI Airport via the North Star (C-60) Route on Annapolis's ADOT bus system ($4; T 410/263-7964). By road, it's only about half an hour from Washington (via US-50) or Baltimore (via I-97). Central, historic Annapolis is very walkable, and the city's **visitor center**, 26 West St (daily 9am–5pm; T 410/280-0445, W www.visit-annapolis.org), can provide free maps and practical information about walking tours, and minibus and water tours.

Finding a **place to stay** is not usually a problem, though prices are steep. There's a free accommodations bureau (T 1-800/715-1000, W www.stayannapolis.com), or you can choose from **B&Bs** like the central *Scot-Laur Inn*, 165 Main St (T 410/268-5665, W www.scotlaurinn.com; ❹), with ten pleasant rooms, though a two-night minimum stay is required on weekends; the four rooms and one suite of the more basic *Flag House Inn*, 26 Randall St (T 410/280-2721 or 1-800/437-4825, W www.flaghouseinn.com; ❺); or, for a premium, the three supremely elegant suites of the *Annapolis Inn*, 114 Prince George St (T 410/295-5200, W www.annapolisinn.com; ❾). Alternatively, the three mid-eighteenth-century buildings making up the *Historic Inns of Annapolis*, 58 State Circle (T 410/263-2641, W www.historicinnsofannapolis.com; ❻), provide smart accommodation options in classic Georgian structures.

Worthwhile **dining** options include the no-frills *Chick and Ruth's Delly*, 165 Main St (T 410/269-6737), which offers monster breakfasts and huge sandwiches named after local politicians; the ritzier *Harry Browne's*, 66 State Circle (T 410/263-4332), popular with politicos and expense-account lobbyists for its upscale steak and seafood; and the historic waterfront ⚓ *Middleton Tavern*, 2 Market Space (T 410/263-3323), a great place to dine on oysters or fish and chips while people-watching from the sunny porch. There's also the *Market House* on the waterfront for a variety of seafood options. After dark the *King of France Tavern*, in the 1776 *Maryland Inn*, 16 Church Circle (part of the *Historic Inns of Annapolis*; T 410/263-2641), puts on live jazz.

Southern Maryland

The winding back roads of **southern Maryland** are obscure to many visitors and resemble in many ways the rural South. Along both main routes, US-301 from Baltimore and Hwy-2 from Annapolis, fields of corn and tobacco, dotted with aging wooden barns, fill the arable lands in scattered parcels, and narrow, tree-lined country lanes branch off to rivers or coves of the broad Chesapeake Bay.

The old shipbuilding community of **SOLOMONS ISLAND** – not actually an island but a narrow two-mile peninsula between the Patuxent River and Back Creek Bay – lies sixty miles south of Annapolis via Hwy-2. The best reason to stop here is the **Calvert Marine Museum**, on Hwy-2 at the north end of town (daily 10am–5pm; $7; W www.calvertmarinemuseum.com), which focuses on the Patuxent River and on the unique estuarine ecosystem of the Chesapeake Bay tidal areas, with two protected marshland wildlife areas, one saltwater and one freshwater. Your admission also gains you access and entry to the nearby **Drum Point Lighthouse**, a small wooden Colonial cottage perched above the water on spindly iron legs. The waterfront is dotted with cozy **B&Bs**, among them the *Back Creek Inn*, 210 Alexander Lane (T 410/326-2022; ❻), which has nicely decorated rooms, a pair of suites, and a cottage. Fresh seafood **restaurants** include *Solomon's Pier*, 14575 Old Solomons Island Rd (T 410/326-2424), good for its tasty dishes and sunny outdoor decks, and the pricier lobster tail and crab cakes of the *Captain's Table*, 275 Lore St (T 410/326-2772), with similarly pleasant waterfront dining.

St Mary's City

Set on a broad Potomac cove near the southern tip of the Maryland peninsula, twenty miles south of Solomons Island, **ST MARY'S CITY** is a limited reconstruction of Maryland's first Colonial capital, established here in 1634 before being moved to Annapolis sixty years later. The entire complex, including a working tobacco plantation and a replica of the tiny *Maryland Dove* (the square-rigged ship that transported provisions to the site in 1634 from England) is run as a historic theme park, complete with costumed guides who answer questions in character (March–June and Sept–Nov Tues–Sat 10am–5pm; July–Sept Wed–Sun 10am–5pm; $7.50; Ⓦwww.stmaryscity.org). Its main feature is a reconstruction of the long-vanished **State House**, where in 1689 Protestant rebels seized control of what had been a Catholic-run colony.

The Eastern Shore

The rambling back roads of Maryland's enticing **Eastern Shore** cross over half of the broad Delmarva (*Dela*ware, *Mary*land, *Virginia*) peninsula that protects the Chesapeake from the open Atlantic. The US-50 bridge, built across the Chesapeake Bay in the early 1960s, may have made the Eastern Shore more accessible, but the area off the main roads still has a sleepy air. Branching off from US-50 as the highway races down to the beach resort of **Ocean City**, quiet country lanes lead to 200-year-old waterfront towns like **Chestertown** and **St Michaels**.

Chestertown

A stopping place for travelers since Colonial days, when it was a prime Chesapeake port, **CHESTERTOWN** stretches west along High Street from the Chester River. It is surprisingly intact, with its fine old riverfront homes and a courthouse square lined with ornate wooden cottages. Although the town is rich with historic edifices, like the grand 1769 Georgian **Wide Hall**, at 101 N Water St, the only house regularly open to the public is the contemporaneous **Geddes-Piper House**, 101 Church Alley (Wed–Sat 10am–4pm; tours May–Oct Sat & Sun 1–4pm; $4; Ⓣ410/778-3499, Ⓦwww.hskcmd.com), which has a good collection of kitchen tools and eighteenth-century furnishings. Many of the old houses have been converted into charming **B&Bs**, like the *Widow's Walk Inn*, 402 High St (Ⓣ410/778-6455 or 1-888/778-6455, Ⓦwww.chestertown.com/widow; ❻), while the *Imperial Hotel*, 208 High St (Ⓣ410/778-5000, Ⓦwww.imperialchestertown.com; ❻), houses the upscale *Front Room* **restaurant**, serving excellent steak and seafood, in addition to having pleasant and tidy guestrooms. Also top-notch is the *Feast of Reason*, 203 High St (Ⓣ410/778-3828), across the street, which has quality soups and sandwiches for lunch. The **visitor center**, 122 North Cross St (spring & summer Mon–Fri 9am–5pm, Sat & Sun 10am–4pm; fall & winter Sat & Sun closes 2pm; Ⓣ410/778-9737, Ⓦwww.kentcounty.com), has information on the town's historic features as well as walking and cycling tours.

St Michaels

One of the prettiest harbors along the Chesapeake Bay, **ST MICHAELS**, twelve miles west of US-50 on Hwy-33, is also one of its oldest ports. Since the early 1960s it has been revitalized, its old buildings now gentrified into art galleries, boutiques, and cozy B&Bs. Some corners of the town survive intact, however; among them the old town green, **St Mary's Square**, a block off the main Talbot Street on Mulberry Street.

To get a clear sense of the history of Chesapeake Bay, head north along the docks to the extensive and modern **Chesapeake Bay Maritime Museum** (daily March–May & Oct 10am–5pm; June–Sept 10am–6pm; Nov–Feb 10am–4pm; $10; Ⓦwww.cbmm.org). The complex focuses on the restored 1879 **Hooper Strait Lighthouse** (which you can tour), at the foot of which float several Chesapeake Bay sailboats, designed to make the most of the bay's shallow waters. If you want to get out on the bay, Patriot Cruises (daily 11.30am, 12.30pm, 2.30pm & 4pm; $19.50; Ⓣ410/745-3100, Ⓦwww.patriotcruises.com) runs 60 to 90min **excursions**, while other companies operate shorter (and cheaper) trips.

B&Bs, such as the period-furnished *Hambleton Inn*, 202 Cherry St (Ⓣ410/745-3350 or 1-866/745-3350, Ⓦwww.hambletoninn.com; ❺), with its five cozy units, and the *Kemp House Inn*, 412 Talbot St (Ⓣ410/745-2243, Ⓦwww.kemphouseinn.com; ❺), featuring slightly more antique decor, tend to be fully booked in the high season, so call well ahead. If you want to go all-out, try the *Harbour Inn*, 101 N Harbor Rd (Ⓣ410/745-9001, Ⓦwww.harbourinn.com; ❻), a waterside resort with chic rooms and suites, along with a spa and marina. Among St Michaels's revered seafood **restaurants**, the ⚑ *Crab Claw*, on Rte 33 (Mar–Nov; Ⓣ410/745-2900), has fine views and boasts an extensive menu; it's especially good for its **steamed crabs**. On weekends, the town's docks are alive with boaters who flock to bar-restaurants such as the *Town Dock* (Ⓣ410/745-5577), offering tasty fried oysters and crab cakes, and *St Michaels Crab House* (Ⓣ410/745-3737), with its fine raw bar, both at the end of Mulberry Street.

Tilghman Island

The only real reason to come to the declining fishing port of **TILGHMAN ISLAND**, west of St Michaels across the Knapps Narrows drawbridge, is its seafood. Drop in on **Dogwood Harbor**, on the east side of the island, during the fall and winter harvest when the rusty skipjacks unload at Harrison Oyster Packing Company (Ⓣ410/886-2530), a wholesaler at the foot of the bridge. You can buy oysters fresh off the boat here, or sample them and other local items at two very good restaurants on either side of the bridge: the *Bay Hundred* (Ⓣ410/886-2126) and *The Bridge* (Ⓣ410/886-2330). Many locals and weekend fishermen head for *Harrison's Chesapeake House* (Ⓣ410/886-2121, Ⓦwww.chesapeakehouse.com), two miles south of town, for a traditional Eastern Shore dinner with corn on the cob and fried chicken.

Ocean City

With more than ten miles of broad Atlantic beach, a boisterous boardwalk, amusement park, and hordes of visitors every summer weekend, **OCEAN CITY** is Maryland's number one warm-weather resort, accessible across the Eastern Shore via US-50. If you're after a quiet weekend by the sea, avoid it like the plague and take extra care to avoid college Spring Break.

Ocean City is, at least, easy to reach: the Greyhound terminal is at Second St and Philadelphia Ave, and The Beach Express (Ⓣ1-866/628-7433, Ⓦwww.beach-express.com) runs **shuttles** to and from the Baltimore, Washington DC, and Philadelphia airports. The city has two helpful **visitor centers**. The first is the Chamber of Commerce, on US-50 as you approach the city (daily 9am–5pm; Ⓣ1-888/626-3386, Ⓦwww.oceancity.org), while the second is at 4001 Coastal Hwy (daily 9am–5pm; Ⓣ410/289-2800 or 1-800/626-2326, Ⓦwww.ococean.com); both have the usual brochures and can help with accommodation.

Places to **stay** are plentiful except on summer weekends, and off-season rates are at least half prime-time ones. Choices include the *Oceanic* motel, on the tip of the peninsula at the south end of Baltimore Street (Ⓣ410/289-6494, Ⓦwww.

ocmdhotels.com/oceanic; ❸–❼ by season), and the fading *Commander Hotel*, on the boardwalk at 14th Street (☎410/289-6166 or 1-888/289-6166, ⓌWww. commanderhotel.com; ❹–❽). The few good **eating** options among the fast-food joints and the national franchises include *The Angler*, on the bay at Talbot Street (☎410/289-7424), with fresh seafood, as well as beers and tropical cocktails. **Nightspots** include the frenetic *Big Kahuna Surf Club*, 18th and Coastal Highway (☎410/289-6331), and *Shenanigan's*, 4th and Boardwalk (☎410/289-7181), an Irish pub with a full menu and live music until 2am.

Assateague Island National Seashore

Just nine miles down the coast, **Assateague Island National Seashore** – a 37-mile stretch of entirely undeveloped beach and marshland – is a great escape from Ocean City. Its main **visitor center** (daily 9am–5pm; ☎410/641-1441, ⓌWww. nps.gov/asis) is eight miles from Ocean City, just before the humpback bridge across to the island ($10 park entry per car or $3 per pedestrian/bicyclist, valid one week). Of the park's three main **trails**, the Life of the Marsh Trail guides you along half a mile of boardwalks through low-lying leeward wetlands, while Life of the Dunes, over the thick white sands just back from the beach, is a little longer and harder going. Most visitors, however, come strictly for the beaches themselves. Seashore and bayside **camping** on Assateague Island is available year-round (☎410/641-3030 or 1-888/432-2267; $5 permit), but if you want a bit more comfort, the best **lodging** is to be found near the southern half of the island, across the Virginia border in **Chincoteague** (see p.445).

Delaware

DELAWARE, enjoyed for its beautiful beaches but also notorious for its massive DuPont Corporation chemical plants, has an impressive and important history. In 1631 Dutch whalers established a settlement at the mouth of the Delaware Bay, and soon afterwards the Swedes built a larger colony at present-day **Wilmington**. The two groups fought amongst themselves until the British took over in 1664. **DELAWARE** was then part of neighboring Pennsylvania – Philadelphia is only ten miles north – until separating itself off in 1776, and in 1787 it was the first former colony to ratify the Constitution and become a state. Much of Delaware's fortunes can be traced to the **du Pont family**, who, fleeing the wrath of revolutionary France, set up a gunpowder mill that became the main supplier of conventional explosives to the US government. The family built huge mansions in the **Brandywine Valley** north of Wilmington, near the perfectly preserved old Colonial capital, **New Castle**, on the Delaware Bay just five miles south of I-95. Further south, **Dover**, the capital, may not detain you long, but beyond it, the small and amiable resorts of **Lewes** and **Rehoboth Beach** mark the northern extent of over twenty miles of rather unspoiled Atlantic beaches.

Getting around Delaware

Apart from Wilmington, which is on the main East Coast **train** and **bus** lines, Delaware is hard to get around without a car. Greyhound stops only at Wilmington and Dover, and local public transit is limited at best. I-95 and the New Jersey Turnpike converge at Wilmington, from where US-13 runs south through the state. More often called the **Du Pont Highway**, it was paid for and constructed by the industrialists so that they could ride in comfort between their Wilmington mansions and Dover. A direct car **ferry** connects Cape May, the southern tip of New Jersey, and Lewes, at the mouth of the Delaware Bay (see p.479).

Wilmington and around

Medium-sized **WILMINGTON** offers a pleasant diversion from the tourist trail, boasting decent art museums and some pretty waterside parks, and the surrounding Brandywine Valley holds the manor homes and gardens (and factories) of the du Ponts, providing an inside look at the First State's First Family.

Amtrak pulls in at the quirky 1907 terracotta station at 100 S French St, on the dicey and run-down south side of the city. From here, the two main streets, Market and King, run north for about a mile to the Brandywine River, holding stores and other businesses, as well as a handful of restored eighteenth-century rowhouses. These are clustered around the **Delaware History Museum**, 504 Market St (Tues–Fri 11am–4pm, Sat 10am–4pm; $4; ⊤302/656-0637), which has some mildly interesting exhibits and dioramas about state history, and the **Old Town Hall**, 500 Market St (Sun & Tues–Fri 11am–4pm, Sat 10am–4pm; $4; Ⓦwwww. hsd.org/oth.htm), a 1798 Federal mansion.

The **Delaware Art Museum**, 2301 Kentmere Pkwy (Tues & Thurs–Sat 10am–4pm, Wed 10am–8pm, Sun noon–4pm; $10, free Sun; Ⓦwww.delart.org), is the one sight you should really see if you're in Wilmington. The museum's focus is American art from the nineteenth and twentieth centuries and has a number of emblematic images from key figures like Frederic Church, Winslow Homer, Edward Hopper, and Augustus Saint Gaudens. For those with a yen for the archly modern, the **Delaware Center for the Contemporary Arts**, back downtown at 200 S Madison St (Tues & Thurs–Sat 10am–5pm, Wed & Sun noon–5pm; $5; Ⓦwww.thedcca.org), is best-known for its dozens of yearly rotating exhibits that showcase regional and national artists.

Most of Wilmington's Colonial sites are hidden away amid the shambling, industrialized waterfront east of downtown. A poorly signposted "Historic Wilmington" loop stops first at the foot of Seventh Street, where a small monument marks the site of Delaware's first European colony, **Fort Christina**, set up by Swedish settlers in 1638. Nearby, at 606 Church St, the **Hendrickson House Museum** and **Old Swedes Church** (tours Wed–Sat 10am–4pm; $2; ⊤302/652-5629) are, respectively, a c.1690 pinewood residence with furnishings from various eras, and one of the oldest houses of worship in the US, built in 1698. The church retains its impressive black-walnut pulpit and features intricate Victorian-era stained-glass windows as well as a garden labyrinth outside. Several miles north, near I-95 in Rockwood Park, the Gothic Revival **Rockwood Mansion**, 610 Shipley Rd (park and gardens daily 6am–10pm, mansion tours Tues–Sun 10am–3pm; Ⓦwww. rockwood.org), was built in 1854 in the style of a rural English estate, its elegant rooms now smartly restored to their Gilded Age appearance.

The downtown **CVB**, 100 W 10th St (Mon–Fri 9am–5pm; ⊤302/652-4088 or 1-800/489-6664, Ⓦwww.VisitWilmingtonDe.com), has walking- and driving-tour maps and practical information. The DART **bus** system runs around the county (tickets $1.15; ⊤302/652-3278; Ⓦwww.dartfirststate.com). Few people choose to **spend the night** in Wilmington, but you might want to try the splendidly ornate *Hotel du Pont*, 100 W 11th St (⊤302/594-3100 or 1-800/441-9019, Ⓦwww.hoteldupont.com; ⑥–⑨), whose rooms and suites are the height of contemporary chic, and even affordable in the low season. Alternatively, *Brandywine Suites*, 707 King Street (T 302/656-9300, W www.brandywinesuites.com; ⑤), in a central location, offers very affordable, spacious units with microwaves, fridges, and Internet access. For **eating**, you can scout around the happening Trolley Square area northwest of downtown, where *Kelly's Logan House*, 1701 Delaware Ave (T 302/652-9493), serves tasty burgers and other pub fare in a pleasant garden setting. The *Washington Street Ale House*, 1205 Washington St (T 302/658-2537), has the same sort of food, along with pasta and seafood, but the main draw is its microbrew selection.

The du Pont mansions

A short distance up I-95 from the Rockwood Mansion, the first of the **du Pont mansions** is accessible in **Bellevue State Park**, 800 Carr Rd (daily 8am–dusk; free). William du Pont Jr converted a Gothic Revival mansion into his own version of James Madison's Neoclassical home and called it **Bellevue Hall**. You can visit the grounds and see the ponds, woodlands, gardens, and tennis courts.

Twenty minutes northwest of Wilmington, various generations of the du Pont family built opulent homes in the rural Brandywine Valley. To learn how their fortune was made, stop at the **Hagley Museum**, off Hwy-141 just north of Wilmington (mid-March to Dec daily 9.30am–4.30pm; Jan to mid-March Sat & Sun 9.30am–4.30pm; $11; W www.hagley.org), situated on a 235-acre du Pont estate. The museum begins with the founding in 1802 of a small water-powered gunpowder mill along the Brandywine River; over the next hundred years the mill grew into a complex that included ever-larger steam-powered and eventually electrically powered factories – almost all of which are still in working order. While you're there, be sure to visit **Eleutherian Mills**, the supremely elegant du Pont mansion that is the centrepiece of the estate.

The enormous, dusty-pink 1910 **Nemours Mansion**, just a mile up the road (closed for renovation until 2007; updates at T 302/651-6912 or 1-800/651-6912, W www.Nemours.org), is surrounded by a three-hundred-acre, Versailles-style formal garden. Inside the mansion, you'll find plenty of lavish rooms along with a 1910 fitness room, bowling alley, ice-making room, and collection of early twentieth-century automobiles. Two miles northwest, off Hwy-52, the one-time du Pont family estate of **Winterthur** (Tues–Sun 10am–5pm; tours $20–30, gardens and galleries only $15; W www.winterthur.org) has been converted into a premier showcase for early American decorative arts, each of its 175 rooms showcasing a particular style. Ranging from the simplicity of Shaker appointments to a beautiful three-story elliptical staircase taken from a North Carolina plantation home, the various pieces of furniture, textiles, silverwork, and paintings – all made in the country between 1640 and 1860 – form a rich catalog of the diversity of American applied arts.

New Castle

Delaware's well-preserved first capital, **NEW CASTLE**, fronts the broad Delaware River, just six miles south of Wilmington via Hwy-141. Founded in the 1650s by the Dutch and taken over by the British in 1664, New Castle has managed to survive intact, its quiet cobbled streets and immaculate eighteenth-century brick houses shaded by ancient hardwood trees.

The heart of New Castle is the tree-filled **town green** that spreads east from the shops of Delaware Street. It's dominated by the stalwart tower of the **Immanuel Episcopal Church**, Harmony St at The Strand, built in 1703 and bordered by tidy rows of eighteenth-century gravestones. On the west edge of the green, the 1732

Old Court House, 211 Delaware St (Tues–Sat 10am–3.30pm, Sun 1.30–4.30pm; free) served as the first state capitol until 1881.

Fine Colonial houses fill the blocks around the town green. The largest is the **George Read II House** (Tues–Fri & Sun 11am–4pm, Sat 10am-4pm, winter Sat & Sun only; $5; ⓦwww.hsd.org/read.htm), two blocks south along the river at 42 The Strand. Though the original c.1800 house burned down in 1824, the sumptuous replica holds marble fireplaces, brightly painted walls, elaborately carved woodwork, fine Federal-style plaster ornament, and spacious, picturesque gardens. Another nice collection of classic edifices from various eras, operated by the New Castle Historical Society (ⓦwww.newcastlehistory.org), lies several blocks north along Third and Fourth streets: the **Amstel House**, 2 E Fourth St (April–Dec Wed–Sat 11am–4pm, Sun 1–4pm; $4), is a 1730 early-Georgian mansion that has been visited by a number of prominent Revolutionary-era figures; the hexagonal brick bauble of the **Old Library Museum**, 40 E Third St (March–Dec Sat & Sun 1–4pm; free), today houses the historical society's collection; and the **Dutch House**, 32 E Third St (April–Dec Wed–Sat 11am-4pm, Sun 1–4pm; $4), is a simple c.1700 residence with authentic decor and artifacts including a cherry-wood cupboard, duck-footed wooden chairs, and polychromed Delft ceramics.

Practicalities

New Castle makes for a good day-trip from Washington DC or Philadelphia, but there's enough here to merit a longer visit. To pick up the self-guided **walking-tour** map, drop by the **visitor center** at 211 Delaware St, in the Old Court House (same hours; ☎302/323-4453), or call the **Historic New Castle Visitors Bureau** (☎1-800/758-1550). Centrally located **B&Bs** include the *William Penn Guest House*, 206 Delaware St (☎302/328-7736; ❹), with four cozy units in a building dating from 1682 (its namesake even visited here) and the *Terry House*, 130 Delaware St (☎302/322-2505, ⓦwww.terryhouse.com; ❹), a Civil War-era townhouse with four simple, tastefully decorated rooms. The better **restaurants** serve traditional, Colonial-era dishes, some of them being quite good. There's solid beer and pub grub, including crabs, clams, shepherd's pie, and a "Smorgas-Board" thick with cheese and sausage, at the popular *Jessop's Tavern*, 114 Delaware St (☎302/322-6111), while more refined taste buds will enjoy the French-influenced seafood dishes at the grand ⚔ *Arsenal at Old New Castle*, next to the Episcopal Church at 30 Market St (☎302/328-1290).

Dover

Located in the mostly agricultural center of the state, just west of US-13, the capital city of **DOVER** is basically a very small town, with a low-rise business district hemmed in by suburban houses. South of **Lockerman Street**, the main route through town, government buildings center on the 1792 **Old State House**, its onetime judicial and legislative chambers now restored as a museum (Tues–Sat 10am–4.30pm, Sun 1.30–4.30pm; free) and furnished with early American antiques.

In the same building as the **visitor center** (Wed–Fri 10am–4pm, Sat 9am–5pm, Sun 1.30–4.30pm; ☎302/739-4266), at the corner of Duke of York and Federal streets next to the Old State House, the impressive **Biggs Museum of American Art** (same hours; ⓦwww.biggsmuseum.org; free) has historical and decorative art displays, including Colonial-era furniture, paintings by the likes of Benjamin West and Gilbert Stuart, silver and porcelain services, and grand landscapes from Albert Bierstadt and Thomas Cole. The **Delaware State Museums**, 316 S Governors Ave (all Tues–Fri 10am–3.30pm, Sat 9am–5pm; ⓦhistory.delaware.gov; free),

5

comprise a quaint trio located a short walk west of the green, highlighted by the **Johnson Victrola Museum**, dedicated to the memory of Dover-born engineer Eldridge Reeves Johnson, who helped to invent the Victrola. The layout is like a 1920s music store: dozens of "talking machines," from early wind-ups to proto-type jukeboxes, play period recordings, and amusing photographs document early, pre-electric recording techniques.

For more than fifty years, **Spence's Bazaar**, two blocks south on Queen Street at 550 S New St (Tues & Fri 7.30am–6.30pm; free), has hosted a free-for-all **flea market**. All of Dover turns out for this, including dozens of local **Amish**, who ride here in their old horse-drawn buggies to sell homegrown fruits and vegetables. A few miles outside town, the eighteen-acre **John Dickinson Plantation**, off Rte 9 at 340 Kitts Hummock Rd (Tues–Sat 10am–3.30pm, Sun 1.30–4.30pm; ☎302/739-3277; free), is where costumed re-enactors of Colonial residents, including slaves, go about the paces of farming, cooking, and gardening; both the estate's grounds and 1740 brick mansion are viewable on various tours, lasting ninety minutes to two hours.

Many chain **motels** line US-13, but you can get a taste of the local flavor at one of the **B&Bs**. The *Little Creek Inn*, 2623 N Little Creek Rd, off Hwy 8 (☎302/730-1300, ⓦwww.littlecreekinn.com; ❻), an attractive 1860 estate, has five rooms (some with Jacuzzis) featuring period appointments, as well as a pool, gym, and bocce court. Similar amenities can be found at the *State Street Inn*, 228 N State St (☎302/734-2294, ⓦwww.statestreetinn.com; ❺), whose rooms are a bit smaller but are more centrally located. As for **eating**, most of Dover's restaurants are concentrated on Loockerman and State streets in the town center, just north of the green. *W.T. Smithers*, 140 State St (☎302/674-8875) offers reasonably priced steaks, sandwiches, and seafood, while the *Old Town Pub*, 107 W Loockerman St (☎302/734-4575), is the spot locals visit to hoist a few brews and chow down on solid deli fare.

The Delaware coast

The thirty-mile-long Delaware coast is one of the little-known jewels of the East Coast. Its only really built-up resort, packed solid in summer, is **Rehoboth Beach**. The historic fishing community of **Lewes** is also attractive, but what really sets the area apart are the long stretches of sand you can have to yourself at times. Much has been preserved as open space, most extensively at **Delaware Seashore State Park**, which stretches south from Rehoboth to the Maryland border.

Lewes

Accessible via Hwy-1, or on the ferry from Cape May, New Jersey (see p.195), the natural harbor at the mouth of Delaware Bay at **LEWES** has attracted seafarers ever since a Dutch whaling company set up a small colony here in 1631, a history outlined in the mock-Dutch **Zwaanendael Museum**, in the heart of town on Savannah Road at Kings Highway (Tues–Sat 10am–4.30pm, Sun 1.30–4.30pm; free; ☎302/645-1148). The **CVB** next door (June–Sept Mon–Fri 10am–4pm, Sat & Sun 10am–2pm; Oct–May Mon–Fri 1–4pm; ☎302/645-8073 or 1-877/465-3937, ⓦwww.leweschamber.com), housed inside a gambrel-roofed 1730s farm-house, has walking-tour maps of the town and its numerous eighteenth-century homes. While wandering, don't miss the **Lewes Historic Complex**, three blocks north at 110 Shipcarpenter St (mid-June to early Oct Mon–Sat 11am–4pm, Sun 1–4pm, May to mid-June Sat 11am–4pm; $5; ⓦwww.historiclewes.org), a collection of twelve classic properties (two of them off-site and charging $3 admission) dating from the early Colonial to late Victorian periods, including a crude plank-house, a doctor's office, a store, and a boathouse.

Though Lewes has a proud history, most people come here for the beach. There's an extensive strand along the usually calm Delaware Bay at the foot of the town, while three-thousand-acre, four-mile-long **Cape Henlopen State Park** (T302/645-8983), where the bay meets the open ocean just a mile east of the town center, offers the chance to **camp** ($27–29 per night) beside the biggest sand dunes north of Cape Hatteras. For a bit of a diversion, ride the **ferry** across Delaware Bay from beside the state park to the pleasant Victorian beach resort of **Cape May**, New Jersey (80min trip; 6–15 services daily; times vary by day and season; April–Oct $29 per car, $9.50 per person, Nov–Mar $23/$7; T1-800/64-FERRY, Wwww.capemaylewesferry.com).

You can walk almost everywhere in town, or **rent a bike** from Lewes Cycle Sports, 526 Savannah Rd (T302/645-4544). Thanks to its proximity to Rehoboth Beach, in summer **accommodation** prices can reach $150 or more a night, even for a fairly dismal unit. There are cheap, adequate motels along Savannah Road, while the B&B scene is pricier (and less appealing) than you might expect; try instead more upscale spots like *Hotel Blue*, 110 Anglers Rd (T302/645-4880, Wwww.hotelblue.info; by season ❺–❻), whose rooms and suites come with flat-panel TVs, boutique furnishings, and Internet access. Cheaper accommodation is available at the *Zwaanendael Inn*, 142 2nd St (T302/645-6466, Wwww. zwaanendaelinn.com; ❹–❻ by season), best for its central location and simple, cozy units with a smattering of antiques. Most of the **restaurants**, not surprisingly, feature seafood, including the *Lighthouse* (T302/645-6271), by the bridge, with its gut-busting "Super Seafood Bash" piled in a large basket; for more formal Italian dining, opt for *La Rosa Negra*, 1201-F Savannah Road (T302/645-1980), serving succulent steak, veal, fish, and crab cakes. *The Buttery*, 2nd St at Savannah Rd (T302/645-7755), is a fine French bistro that specializes in crab cakes, burgers, and seafood sandwiches for lunch, and much pricier steak and rack of lamb for dinner.

Rehoboth Beach

A nonstop parade of motels and malls along the six miles of Hwy-1 links Lewes with **REHOBOTH BEACH**, Delaware's largest and liveliest beach resort, which merges into **Dewey Beach** at its southern end.

The resort's wooden **boardwalk** is one of the last ones left on the East Coast, stretching along the Atlantic to either side of Rehoboth Avenue – "**The Avenue**" – which acts as the main drag, its four short blocks clogged with the usual array of T-shirt vendors and seaside kitsch. Most of the **restaurants** and **nightspots** are concentrated here, though you're better off sticking to Lewes for dining. Exceptions include the *Back Porch Café*, 59 Rehoboth Ave (T302/227-3674), with its upscale selection of softshell crab, guinea fowl, and pan-roasted rabbit, and 🍴 *Dogfish Head*, 320 Rehoboth Ave (T302/226-2739), which has affordable, wood-grilled seafood and steaks, but is best known for its acclaimed microbrews and on-site distillery.

Apart from the peak times of July and August, it shouldn't be too difficult to find a bed in one of Rehoboth's many **motels**, including the *Sandcastle*, 123 Second St (T302/227-0400 or 1-800/372-2112, Wwww.thesandcastlemotel.com; ❸–❻ by season), which has a pool and sundeck, and the *Crosswinds*, three blocks from the boardwalk, 312 Rehoboth Ave (T302/227-7997, Wwww.crosswindsmotel. com; ❸–❼), which offers rooms with refrigerators. Among area **B&Bs**, try the *Corner Cupboard Inn*, 50 Park Ave (T302/227-8553, Wwww.cornercupboardinn. com; ❹–❼ by season), with seventeen basic units and its own pleasant restaurant or the *Rehoboth Guest House*, 40 Maryland Ave (T302/227-4117 or 1-800/564-0493, Wwww.rehobothguesthouse.com; ❹–❺ by season), which has outdoor cedar showers and a tree-shaded backyard in addition to its also basic rooms. For more information, contact the **Chamber of Commerce**, 501 Rehoboth Ave (T 302/227-2233 or 1-800/441-1329, W www.beach-fun.com).

South of Rehoboth, **Delaware Seashore State Park** (T 302/227-2800, W www. destateparks.com) stretches for miles along a thin, sandy peninsula, split by Hwy-1 and bounded on the east by the Atlantic and on the west by various freshwater marshlands. (Parts of the park are currently being reconstructed and won't be open until 2008.) South of the park, as you approach the Maryland border, you'll pass the concrete tower blocks of **Bethany Beach** and the pleasant barrier island of **Fenwick Island State Park** (daily 8am–dusk; T 302/227-2800; free), a three-mile stretch that offers good swimming and the opportunity for "**surf fishing**" – casting a line from your car parked on the beach itself.

6

The South

AL - ALABAMA	IN - INDIANA	MN - MINNESOTA	RI - RHODE ISLAND
AR - ARKANSAS	LA - LOUISIANA	MS - MISSISSIPPI	SC - SOUTH CAROLINA
CT - CONNECTICUT	MA - MASSACHUSETTS	NC - NORTH CAROLINA	VA - VIRGINIA
DE - DELAWARE	MD - MARYLAND	NH - NEW HAMPSHIRE	VT - VERMONT
FL - FLORIDA	ME - MAINE	NJ - NEW JERSEY	WI - WISCONSIN
IL - ILLINOIS	MI - MICHIGAN	PA - PENNSYLVANIA	WV - WEST VIRGINIA

CHAPTER 6 # Highlights

✳ **Blue Ridge Parkway, NC** A tortuous but exhilarating wilderness highway that makes a destination in itself. See p.504

✳ **Martin Luther King Birth Home, Atlanta, GA** Engaging tours take you around King's childhood home, in the South's most dynamic city. See p.526

✳ **Savannah, GA** With its romantic overgrown garden squares and busy waterfront, this gorgeous, atmospheric town is a dream to walk around. See p.534

✳ **Memphis, TN** Especially exciting for music fans, who could spend days checking out Beale Street, Sun Studio, the Stax Museum, Al Green's church, and, of course, Graceland. See p.553

✳ **Country Music Hall of Fame, Nashville, TN** At once a fascinating interactive museum and a treasure trove of memorabilia, including Elvis's gold Cadillac. See p.569

✳ **The Mississippi Delta, MS** The birthplace of the blues holds an irresistible appeal, with Clarksdale as the obvious first port of call. See p.588

△ Cottonfields in the Mississippi Delta

6

The South

Mark Twain put it best, as early as 1882: "In the South, the [Civil] war is what AD is elsewhere; they date everything from it." Several generations later, the legacies of slavery and "The War Between the States" remain evident throughout the southern states of North Carolina, South Carolina, Georgia, Kentucky, Tennessee, Alabama, Mississippi, and Arkansas. It's impossible to travel through the region without experiencing constant jolting reminders of the two epic historical clashes that have shaped its destiny: the Civil War, and the civil rights movement of the 1950s and 1960s.

Although it's debatable whether the much-vaunted "New South" truly exists, the last few decades have unquestionably seen considerable change. The inspirational campaigns that finally secured black participation in Southern elections have resulted not only in the prominence of black political leaders but also in the emergence of liberal white counterparts like Jimmy Carter and Bill Clinton. High-tech industries have moved in, luring considerable inward migration, while urban centers such as **Atlanta**, the birthplace of Dr Martin Luther King Jr and venue for the 1996 Olympics, are booming.

That said, it's misleading in any case to generalize too much about "the South." Even during the Civil War there were substantial pockets of pro-Union support, particularly in the mountains, while during the long century of segregation that followed, certain states, such as Mississippi and Alabama, were far more brutally oppressive than others. These days, inequities within the South, between for example the industrialized "Sun Belt" centers of North Carolina and northern Alabama and the much poorer rural backwaters of southern Georgia, Mississippi, or Tennessee, are just as significant as those between the South and the rest of the nation, and are no longer so clearly demarcated along racial lines.

For many travelers, the most exciting aspect of a visit to the South has to be its **music**. Fans flock to the homelands of Elvis Presley, Hank Williams, Robert Johnson, Dolly Parton, and Otis Redding, heading to the country and blues meccas of **Nashville** and **Memphis**, or seeking out backwoods barn dances in Appalachia and blues jook joints in the Mississippi Delta or South Carolina. The Southern experience is also reflected in a rich regional **literature**, documented by the likes of William Faulkner, Carson McCullers, Eudora Welty, Margaret Mitchell, and Harper Lee.

Other major destinations for visitors include the elegant coastal cities of **Charleston** and **Savannah**, frenzied beach resorts such as **Myrtle Beach**, college towns like **Athens** and **Chapel Hill**, and the historic Mississippi River ports of **Natchez** and **Vicksburg**. Away from the urban areas, much Southern scenery consists of fertile but sun-baked farmlands, the undulating hillsides dotted with wooden shacks and rust-red barns, and broken by occasional forests. Highlights include the misty Appalachian **mountains** of Kentucky, Tennessee, and North Carolina; the subtropical **beaches** and tranquil **barrier islands** along the Atlantic and Gulf coasts; and the river road through the tiny settlements of the flat Mississippi Delta.

Unless your primary goal is the coastline, where the beaches offer a less expensive alternative to neighboring Florida, it's better to avoid visiting during midsummer.

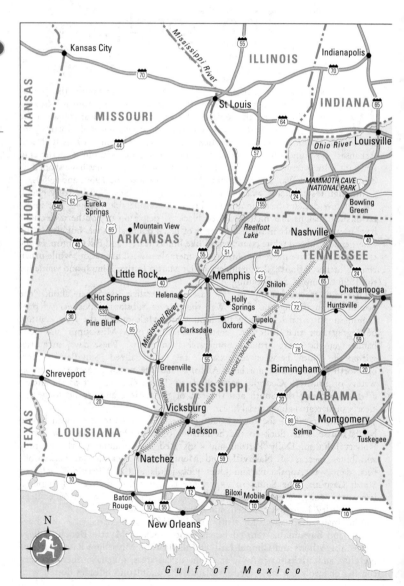

In July and August, the daily high **temperature** is mostly a very humid 90°F, and while almost every public building is air-conditioned, the heat can be debilitating. May and June are more bearable, and tend to see a lot of local festivals, while the fall colors in the mountains – just as beautiful and a lot less expensive and congested than New England – are at their headiest during October.

Public transportation in rural areas is poor. In any case, it's best to take things at your own pace – you'll find things to see and do in the most unlikely places – so

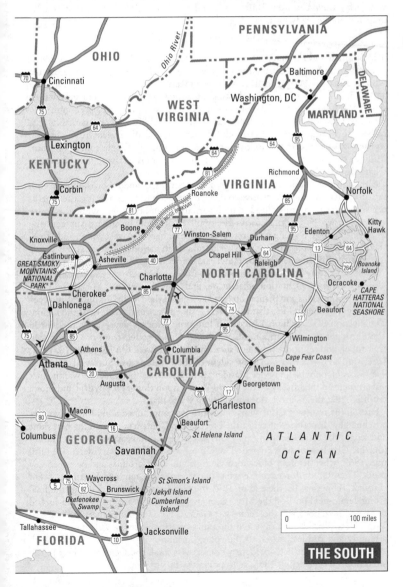

THE SOUTH

renting a car is the best idea. **Accommodation** in the South is generally good value. Motels are everywhere, while abundant B&Bs offer a chance to sample the much-vaunted Southern hospitality – though unless you share a broadly Confederate view of history, they can also tend to be socially uncomfortable. The region's varied **cuisine**, much of it dished out at simple roadside shacks, ranges from the ubiquitous grits (maize porridge) to highly calorific, irresistible **soul food**: fried chicken, wood-smoked barbecue, and the like, along with turnip greens, spinach, macaroni, and all manner of tasty vegetables. Fish is also good, from catfish to the wonderful **Low Country Boils** – seafood stews served with rice, traditionally prepared on the sea islands.

⑥ Some history

The **Spanish** and **French** both constructed settlements along the southern coastline of North America during the sixteenth century. However, it was the **British** who dominated the region from the seventeenth century onwards, establishing agricultural colonies in the Carolinas and Georgia. Both climate and soil favored staple crops, and massive labor-intensive **plantations** sprang up, predominantly growing **tobacco** prior to independence, and later shifting to **cotton**. No self-respecting European would cross the Atlantic to toil on a plantation, though, so the big landowners turned to **slavery** as the most profitable source of labor. Millions of blacks were brought across from Africa, most arriving via the port of Charleston.

Although the South consistently prospered until the middle of the nineteenth century, there was little incentive to diversify its economy. As a result, the Northern states began to surge ahead in both agriculture and industry; while the South grew the crops, Northern factories monopolized the more lucrative manufacturing of finished goods. So long as there were equal numbers of slave-owning and "free" states, the South continued to play a central role in national politics, and was able to resist **abolitionist** sentiment. However, the more the United States fulfilled its "Manifest Destiny" to spread across the continent, the more new states joined the Union for which plantation agriculture, and thus slavery, was not appropriate. Southern politicians and plantation owners accused the North of political and economic aggression, and felt that they were losing all say in the future of the nation. The election of **Abraham Lincoln**, a longtime critic of slavery, as president in 1860 brought the crisis to a head. South Carolina **seceded** from the Union that December, and ten more southern states swiftly followed. On February 18, 1861, Jefferson Davis was sworn in as president of the **Confederate States of America** – an occasion on which his vice president proudly proclaimed that this was the first government in the history of the world "based upon this great physical and moral truth . . . that the Negro is not equal to the white man."

During the resultant **Civil War**, the South was outgunned and ultimately overwhelmed by the vast resources of the North. The Confederates fired the first shots and scored the first victory in April 1861, when the Union garrison at Fort Sumter (outside Charleston) surrendered. The Union was on the military defensive until mid-1862, when its navy blockaded Georgia and the Carolinas and occupied key ports. Then Union forces in the west, under generals Grant and Sherman, swept through Tennessee. By the end of 1863 the North had taken Vicksburg, the final Confederate-held port on the Mississippi, as well as the strategic mountain-locked town of Chattanooga on the Tennessee–Georgia border. Grant proceeded north to Virginia, while Sherman captured the transportation nexus of Atlanta and began a bloody and ruthless march to the coast, burning everything in his path. With 258,000 men dead, the Confederacy's defeat was total, and General Robert E. Lee **surrendered** on April 9, 1865, at Appomattox in Virginia.

The war left the South in chaos. A quarter of the South's adult white male population had been killed, and two-thirds of Southern wealth destroyed. From controlling thirty percent of the nation's assets in 1860, the South was down to twelve percent in 1870, while the spur the war gave to industrialization meant that the North was booming. For a brief period of **Reconstruction**, the South was occupied by Union troops. Newly freed Southern blacks were able to vote, and black representatives were elected to both state and federal office. However, unrepentant former Confederates thwarted any potential for change, and by the end of the century the Southern states were firmly back under white Democratic control. "**Jim Crow**" segregation laws were imposed, backed by the terror of the **Ku Klux Klan**, and poll taxes, literacy tests, and property qualifications disenfranchised virtually all blacks. Many found themselves little better off as **sharecroppers** – in which virtually all they could earn from raising crops went to pay their landlords – than they had been as slaves, and there were mass migrations to cities like Memphis and Atlanta, as well as to the North.

Not until the Supreme Court outlawed segregation in schools in 1954 was there any sign that the federal authorities in Washington might concern themselves with inequities in the South. Even then, individual Southern states proved extremely reluctant to effect the required changes. In the face of institutionalized white resistance, non-violent black protestors coalesced to form the **civil rights movement**, and broke down segregation through their own mass action. After tackling such issues as public transportation, as in the Montgomery bus boycott and the Freedom Rides, and segregated dining facilities, as in the Greensboro lunch-counter sit-in, the campaign culminated in finally restoring full black voter registration. One obvious itinerary for modern travelers is to trace the footsteps of **Dr Martin Luther King Jr**, from his birthplace in Atlanta, through his church in Montgomery, to the site of his assassination in Memphis.

The dispossession of the **Native Americans** is often the forgotten chapter of Southern history. Colonial powers at best tolerated the Indians, for the most part peaceful agrarian tribes, and used them as allies in their imperialist wars with each other. However, after the Revolution, pressure from plantation owners and small farmers led to the forced removal in the 1830s of the "five civilized tribes" – the Cherokee, Creek, Choctaw, Chickasaw, and Seminole – to malarial Oklahoma. Today only a few thousand Native Americans live in the South.

North Carolina

NORTH CAROLINA, though the most industrialized of the Southern states, remains relatively rural and poor, holding eight million people spread over an area larger than England. Geographically, it breaks down into three distinct areas – running from east to west, the coast, the Piedmont, and the mountains – so touring it provides plenty of variety. For visitors, the **coast** is the most promising region, with good beaches, beautiful landscapes, and a fascinating history. The inner coast consists largely of the less developed **Albemarle Peninsula**, with colonial **Edenton** nearby. The central **Piedmont** is dominated by manufacturing cities, and by the academic institutions of the prestigious "Research Triangle":

Raleigh, the state capital, is home to North Carolina State University; Durham has Duke; and the University of North Carolina is in trendy **Chapel Hill**. **Winston-Salem** combines tobacco culture and Moravian heritage, while **Charlotte** is distinguished by little but its downtown skyscrapers. In the **mountains**, one of the most stunning stretches of Appalachia, the only towns of any size, **Asheville** and **Boone**, make nice places to stop along the spectacular **Blue Ridge Parkway**; **Great Smoky Mountains National Park** overlaps the border with Tennessee.

Getting around North Carolina

North Carolina's major **airports** are at Charlotte, an arrival point for transatlantic flights, Raleigh-Durham, and Wilmington, all of which will connect you with several major US cities. A tiny airport at Manteo in the Outer Banks (☏ 252/475-5570, ⓦ www.fly2mqi.com) runs charter flights to the barrier islands, but driving is easier. Charlotte, Raleigh, Durham, and Greensboro (with an express bus link to Winston-Salem) are served by **Amtrak**, but unfortunately there is no coastal route. Plenty of **buses** run within the Piedmont; schedules are much less frequent in the mountains and along the coast, both of which are best explored by car. The state also has a good network of **cycling** routes along quiet country roads; for information, contact the Department of Transportation (☏ 919/807-0777, ⓦ www.ncdot.org).

The North Carolina coast

The **North Carolina coast**, which ranges through salt marshes, beaches, barrier islands, and estuaries, holds most of the state's more interesting **historic sites**. Among these are **Roanoke Island**, where the continent's earliest English colonists vanished in 1590, and **Kill Devil Hills**, where the Wright brothers achieved the first powered flight just over three centuries later. As for scenic beauty, the **Outer Banks**, the long reef of barrier islands that stretch down from Virginia, are in places beautifully unspoiled, though elsewhere they're sadly downright tacky.

Edenton and the Albemarle

The huge **Albemarle Peninsula** remains largely unexploited. Local towns try to make much of their **Colonial history** – this was the first area in North Carolina to have permanent European settlements, around the end of the seventeenth century – but often there's not a lot left to see. It's rewarding to explore, though, if you like to travel off the beaten path, its sleepy old towns and remote plantations set in wide swathes of rural farmland and endless marshes, that eventually give way altogether to water in a ragged pattern of sounds and lakes.

Edenton

EDENTON, set along a beautiful, placid Albemarle Sound waterfront, was established as North Carolina's first state capital in 1722. A major center of unrest in the American Revolution, it remained a prosperous port until the early nineteenth century, when it began to fade. Nowadays, if you like peace and quiet, it makes a nice little base for explorations of the coast, with some good B&Bs and restaurants, and a nostalgic small-town ambiance.

The town's main road, **Broad Street**, is interesting in an offbeat way, with its Victorian facades, old-fashioned stores, and three-screen vintage Liberty Theater. The Historic Edenton **Visitor Center**, 108 N Broad (April–Oct Mon–Sat 9am–5pm, Sun 1–5pm; Nov–March Mon–Sat 10am–4pm, Sun 1–4pm; ☏ 252/482-

2637), runs **trolley tours** (Tues–Sat 10am, 11am, noon, 2pm, 3pm & 4pm; $10) that take in all the major sites, including a fine collection of Colonial and pre–Civil War houses. There's also a free, self-guided walking tour.

The visitor center provides an **African-American history** walking-tour map as well; among other important figures, Edenton was home to the remarkable **Harriet Jacobs**, a runaway slave who hid for seven years in her grandmother's attic. In 1842, she finally escaped to the North, and was eventually reunited in Boston with the two children she had had by a white man in Edenton. She wrote this amazing story as *Incidents in the Life of a Slave Girl*, one of the most famous published slave narratives of the nineteenth century. None of the buildings mentioned in the book is still standing, but the walking and trolley tours give you an idea of where places were.

Luxurious **B&Bs** include the peaceful *Trestle House Inn*, set in seven acres overlooking a nature refuge on a lake; it's five miles south of town, off Hwy-32, at 632 Soundside Rd (☎252/482-2282, ⓦwww.trestlehouseinn.com; ⑤). A few minutes' walk from the waterfront, the friendly *Governor Eden Inn*, 304 N Broad St (☎252/482-2072 or 1-866/872-5608, ⓦwww.governoredeninn.com; ④), offers appealing rooms and a huge veranda. Edenton has a gratifying number of good places to **eat**. *Chero's*, 112 W Water St (☎252/482-5525), is a funky, colorful place serving delicious Mediterranean and regional food, while the fishy *Waterman's Grill*, 427 S Broad St (☎252/482-7733), gets packed with convivial locals at dinnertime. For Carolina pit-cooked barbecue, try *Lane's Family BBQ*, 421 E Church St (☎252/482-4008). *Acoustic Coffee*, 302 S Broad St (☎252/482-7465), has coffee, pastries, and live music on Friday evenings.

Exploring the Albemarle

Albemarle **plantation life** is brought alive in the informed, illuminating tours of **Hope**, the home of David Stone, a state governor and US senator of the Revolutionary and Federal periods. It's a remote place, set in the sleepy fields of the rural heartland; you'll find it off Hwy-308, a few miles west of **Windsor**, which is about 25 miles southwest of Edenton (tours: April–Oct Mon–Sat 10am–5pm, Sun 2–5pm; Nov–March 10am–4pm, Sun 2–5pm; $8; ⓦwww.hopeplantation. org). The main house at Hope, dating from 1803, was built to an English template, and is now filled with hand-carved wooden furniture. Admission also includes entrance to the 1763 **King-Bazemore House**, a simple planter's home.

At Creswell, 25 miles southeast of Edenton on US-64, a vivid picture of slave life is given by **Somerset Place State Historic Site** (April–Oct Mon–Sat 9am–5pm, Sun 1–5pm; Nov–March Tues–Sat 10am–4pm, Sun 1–4pm; free). The small museum here tells the history of the plantation, from its origins in the 1780s to its growth, by 1860, into a 2000-acre enterprise, and its demise after the Civil War. Old photos, documents, and a timeline detail the steady accumulation of more than three hundred enslaved Africans and the work they did. On the grounds – a sweeping vista of lowland fields and huge oaks, dissolving into marshland beyond – you can walk through reconstructions of the plantation hospital and two typical slave houses.

There's a **campground** at neighboring **Pettigrew State Park** (☎252/797-4475; $15; first-come, first-served), an area of mighty trees ranged around a shallow rainwater-fed lake, ideal for fishing. Even if you don't stay, you should visit the tiny **museum** at water's edge, where the interesting display on local Native Americans includes two 4000-year-old dugout canoes that were raised from the lake.

The southern shore of the Albemarle Peninsula holds less to see, though the marshy countryside and tree-lined roads make for a pleasant drive. **Lake Mattamuskeet Wildlife Refuge** (☎252/926-4021) is an amazing sight in winter, when thousands of swans migrate here from Canada. The refuge's entrance is on Hwy-94, about a mile north of its intersection with US-264. South of Mattamuskeet, you can catch a **ferry** from **Swan Quarter** to Ocracoke on the Outer Banks (see p.496).

The Outer Banks

The **OUTER BANKS** are a string of skinny barrier islands, the remnants of ancient sand dunes, which stretch about 180 miles from the Virginia border to Cape Lookout, near Beaufort. This is a great region to meander, with some wonderful wild beaches sprinkled with wispy sea oats, otherworldly marshes, and attractive small towns not totally given over to commercialization. Note that when Outer Banks hotels describe themselves as "**waterfront**," it simply means they are on the coastal side of the road, not that they necessarily have ocean views. There is **no public transportation** on the Outer Banks, apart from the ferries between islands and to the mainland.

If you come in on the main road from the north, US-158, stop at the well-stocked Cape Hatteras National Park Service **visitor center** (daily: June–Aug 9am–6pm, Sept–May 9am–5pm; ☏252/261-4644, ⓦwww.nps.gov/caha) as you cross the low bridge from the mainland. South along US-158 and the parallel shoreline Beach Road, the coastal towns of **Kitty Hawk**, **Kill Devil Hills**, and **Nags Head** are strung out without a break, and the fine **beaches** are lined with motels, restaurants, and huge vacation "cottages." Arriving from the west on Hwy-64, you'll come to another very useful **visitor center** (daily 9am–5.30pm; ☏252/473-2138, ⓦwww.outerbanks.org) on **Roanoke Island**. The island, site of the first English settlement in the US, has obvious historical interest; its village, **Manteo**, is perhaps the nicest on the Outer Banks.

Kill Devil Hills and Nags Head

The main feature of the **Wright Brothers National Memorial** (daily: June–Aug 9am–6pm, Sept–May 9am–5pm; $4; ☏252/441-7430, ⓦwww.nps.gov/wrbr), just off the main road at **KILL DEVIL HILLS**, is the Wright Brothers Monument, a 60ft granite fin atop a 90ft dune (which is in fact *the* Kill Devil Hill). The memorial commemorates the plucky Orville Wright's **first powered flight**, on December 17, 1903. (Most histories say the flight took place at **Kitty Hawk**, a town eight miles north, but that was just the name of the nearest post office.) A boulder next to the memorial's **visitor center** marks where Orville's first aircraft hit the ground, and successive numbered markers show the distance of each of his three subsequent flights. A **museum** in the visitor center records the brothers' various experiments. After several years of trials with kites and gliders, visiting the Outer Banks for a few weeks at a time and living in makeshift shacks on the beach, Orville and Wilbur finally launched their powered plane on a cold December morning, shaking hands before the takeoff. As one of the locals acting as ground crew remarked, "We couldn't help notice how they held on to each other's hand, sort o' like folks parting who weren't sure they'd ever see one another again." The phlegmatic Orville recorded the historic moment of takeoff in his diary: "The machine lifted from the truck . . . I found control of the front rudder quite difficult . . . the machine would rise suddenly to about 10 feet and then as suddenly, on turning the rudder, dart for the ground . . . time about twelve seconds."

A few miles south in **NAGS HEAD**, at Mile 12 on Hwy-158, **Jockey's Ridge State Park** (☏252/441-7132) boasts the largest sand dunes on the east coast. The park has trails and summer nature programs, and instructors from Kitty Hawk Kites (☏252/441-4124 or 1-877/359-8447, ⓦwww.kittyhawk.com) can teach you the basics of **hang-gliding** (from $99). It's a beautiful place to be at sunset.

Motels line the beaches north of Oregon Inlet, which separates Bodie Island and Cape Hatteras National Seashore. The *First Colony Inn*, a luxurious **B&B** at 6720

S Virginia Dare Trail, Nags Head (☎252/441-2343 or 1-800/368-9390, ⓦwww. firstcolonyinn.com; ⑤–⑧), is housed in a 1930s beach hotel, with wonderful verandas and a pool. The standard of **food** around these parts varies considerably, but *the Flying Fish Café*, at Mile 10 in Kill Devil Hills (☎252/441-6894), serves Mediterranean-influenced cuisine, with seafood or meat entrees at $17–24. In Nags Head, *Tortuga's Lie*, at Mile 11 on Beach Road (☎252/441-7299), is a funky place for creative shellfish, Tex-Mex, and Asian-influenced dishes.

Roanoke Island and Manteo

ROANOKE ISLAND, which lies between the mainland and Bodie Island, is accessible from both by bridges. This was the **first English settlement** in North America, founded in 1585, and makes much of its semi-mythical status as Sir Walter Raleigh's so-called "Lost Colony" (see box, p.494).

Nothing authentic survives of the Roanoke settlement, though **Fort Raleigh National Historic Site**, three miles north of Manteo off US-64, contains a tiny conjectural reconstruction of the colonists' earthwork fort, set in a wooded glade with a canopy of Spanish moss (daily: June–Aug 9am–6pm, Sept–May 9am–5pm; free; ☎252/473-5772, ⓦwww.nps.gov/fora). A museum covers the history of the expeditions and local Indian interaction with the colonists, and an outdoor amphitheater on the ocean hosts performances of *The Lost Colony*, an undeniably impressive drama, staged here since 1937 (June to late Aug Mon–Sat 8.30pm; $16–20; ☎252/473-3414, ⓦwww.thelostcolony.org). Outside, a simple monument commemorates the Underground Railroad and the **Freedmen's Colony** that formed here during the Civil War. Adjacent to the fort, the **Elizabethan Gardens** are elegantly landscaped with walkways, statues, and subtropical blooms (June–Aug Mon–Fri 9am–8pm, Sun 9am–7pm; April, May, Sept & Oct daily 9am–6pm; March & Oct daily 9am–5pm; Nov–Jan daily 9am–4pm; $8; ☎252/473-3234, ⓦwww.elizabethangardens.org).

Just across from the waterfront at **Manteo**, the **Roanoke Island Festival Park** has a slew of lively historical attractions (daily: April to mid-June & mid-Aug to Oct 10am–6pm; mid-June to mid-Aug 10am–7pm; Nov–Dec & mid-Feb to March 10am–5pm; $9 tickets valid for two consecutive days; ☎252/475-1500, ⓦwww.roanokeisland.com). Highlights include the **adventure museum**, an interactive trot through the history of the Outer Banks, the **settlement site**, a living museum peopled with "Elizabethan" soldiers and craftsmen, and the *Elizabeth II*, a reconstruction of a sixteenth-century English ship. Wherever you go, you won't escape the attentions of the wandering costumed docents, ever keen to engage hapless visitors in Elizabethan-style chat.

If you're after fine **dining** on the Outer Banks, Manteo is the place. *Clara's Seafood Grill* (☎252/473-1727), right on the waterfront, offers tasty and creative shellfish dishes, with nice views, while the *Full Moon Café*, across from the waterfront at the corner of Sir Walter Raleigh and Queen Elizabeth streets (☎252/473-6666), is more casual, serving chowder, gourmet sandwiches, quiche, and coffee. Manteo also has a good range of places to **stay**. *The Outdoors Inn*, 406 Uppowoc St (☎252/473-1356, ⓦwww.theoutdoorsinn.com; ⑨), has two stylish, brightly decorated en-suite **B&B** rooms in a lovely, airy home; the owners offer a range of dive trips, kayaking, and fishing charters. The *Island Guesthouse*, on Hwy-64 (☎252/473-2434, ⓦwww.theislandmotel.com; ⑨), is more of a **motel**, with fully equipped rooms and a sociable atmosphere.

Cape Hatteras National Seashore

CAPE HATTERAS NATIONAL SEASHORE stretches south from South Nags Head on Bodie Island onto **Hatteras** and **Ocracoke** islands, with forty miles of wonderful unspoiled beaches on its seaward side. Most tourists just drive

According to popular myth, the first English attempt to settle in North America – Sir Walter Raleigh's colony at **Roanoke** – remains an unsolved mystery, in which the "Lost Colony" disappeared without trace.

Sir Walter himself never visited North America. The original patent to establish a colony was granted by Queen Elizabeth I to his half-brother, Sir Humphrey Gilbert, but Gilbert died following an abortive landfall in Newfoundland in 1583. Raleigh assumed responsibility, and directed subsequent explorations further south. A 1584 expedition pinpointed Roanoke Island, behind the Outer Banks of North Carolina and thus hidden from the view of the Spanish, who were by now jealously patrolling the Atlantic seaboard from their bases in Florida. The English named the region **Virginia**, in honour of the Virgin Queen.

A party led by Ralph Lane in 1585 was far more interested in searching for gold than in the hard graft of agriculture; their hopes of finding a fortune were quickly dashed, however, and the following year they sailed home with Sir Francis Drake, who visited on his way up from the West Indies. In 1587, 117 more colonists set off from England, intending to farm a more fertile site beside Chesapeake Bay; but, fearing Spanish attack, the ships that carried them dumped them at Roanoke once again. Their leader, **John White**, who went home to fetch supplies a month later, was stranded in England when war broke out with Spain, and the Spanish Armada set sail. When he finally managed to persuade a reluctant sea captain to carry him back to Roanoke in 1590, he found the island abandoned. Even so, he was reassured by the absence of the agreed-upon distress signal (a carved Maltese cross), while the word "**Croatoan**" inscribed on a tree seemed a clear message that the colonists had moved south to the eponymous island. However, fearful of both the Spanish and of the approaching hurricane season, White's ships refused to take him any further.

There the story usually ends, with the colonists never seen again. In fact, during the next decade, several reports reached the subsequent, more durable colony of **Jamestown** (in what's now Virginia), of English settlers being dispersed as slaves among the Native American tribes of North Carolina. Rather than admit their inability to rescue their fellow countrymen, and thus expose a vulnerability that might deter prospective settlers or investors, the Jamestown colonists seem simply to have written their predecessors out of history.

In a little-known footnote, Roanoke Island gained and lost another colony during the **Civil War**. After it was captured by Union forces in February 1862, so many freed and runaway slaves made their way here through Confederate lines that the federal government formally declared it to be a "**Freedmen's Colony**." Around four thousand blacks were living on Roanoke by the end of the war, and many of the men served in the Union army. During Reconstruction, the government returned all land to its former owners, and the colony was disbanded. Roanoke retains a substantial black population to this day.

straight through on Hwy-12, and even in high season you can pull off the road and walk across the dunes to deserted beaches. The salt marshes on the western side are also beautiful, and at the northern end of Hatteras Island the **Pea Island National Wildlife Refuge** (T 252/473-1131, W www.fws.gov/peaisland) offers guided canoe tours, trails, and observation platforms from which you can see a wide variety of birdlife.

Nearly a thousand ships have been wrecked along this treacherous stretch of coast since the sixteenth century. At the south end of Hatteras Island, not far from the early nineteenth-century black-and-white-striped **Cape Hatteras Lighthouse**, a **visitor center** (daily: summer 9am–6pm; rest of year 9am–5pm) has exhibits on the island's maritime history. The 208ft lighthouse itself, which you can climb

(March–Oct; $6), was moved 2900ft inland from its original location to protect it from encroaching Atlantic waters. Further south, at the village of **Frisco**, the **Native American Museum** is a loving collection of arts and crafts from around the US, including a drum from a Hopi *kiva*, or prayer chamber. The museum also offers several acres of forested **nature** trails (Tues–Sun 11am–5pm, Mon by appointment; $5; ℡252/995-4440, 🆆www.nativeamericanmuseum.org).

In **Hatteras**, next to the Ocracoke ferry landing, the **Graveyard of the Atlantic Museum**(Tues–Fri 10am–4pm, Sat 11am–2pm; free; 🆆www.graveyardoftheatlantic .com) tells the stories of the explorers, pirates, and Civil War blockade-runners who perished along this wild stretch of coast, with lots of models, photos, and artifacts retrieved from Outer Banks shipwrecks.

Various **motels**, food shops, and **restaurants** are scattered through the fly-blown settlements along Hwy-12. The *Cape Hatteras Motel* in Buxton, a mile from the lighthouse (℡252/995-5611, 🆆www.capehatterasmotel.com; ❹–❼), has comfy oceanfront rooms, a pool, and a relaxed, friendly atmosphere. A good place for breakfast and seafood is *Diamond Shoals*, also in Buxton on Hwy-12 (℡252/995-5217), while on the waterfront at Hatteras, *Austin Creek Grill* serves stylish salads, shellfish, and pasta nightly (℡252/986-1511). **Camping** is best at one of the first-come, first-served National Park Service campgrounds (℡252/473-2111, 🆆www.nps.gov/caha; $20 per night); they're located at Frisco and Oregon Inlet on Bodie Island (both mid-April to mid-Sept); and at Cape Point near Buxton (late May to early Sept).

Ocracoke Island

Peaceful, undeveloped **OCRACOKE ISLAND** is forty minutes by free ferry from Hatteras (see box, p.496) – and is even more beautiful. This 16-mile ribbon of land is bisected by Hwy-12, and it's perfectly possible to pull over anywhere and enjoy a deserted patch of beach. Despite the crowds of tourists in the tiny village of **Ocracoke** itself, at its southern tip, the island somehow seems to have hung on to its easy-going atmosphere. There's nothing in particular to see, except perhaps the harbor and squat lighthouse (you can't go in), and a tiny British World War II naval cemetery. It's nicer instead just to catch some rays, take a stroll, or enjoy a cycle ride; a number of places, including hotels, **rent bikes**.

Hotels and **B&Bs** in Ocracoke village get full in summer, and are fairly expensive; as elsewhere on the Outer Banks, rates drop come September. The *Anchorage Inn*, on Hwy-12 (℡252/928-1101, 🆆www.theanchorageinn.com; ❺), is comfortable, with sea views, a pool, and complimentary continental breakfast. Or you could sleep in one of the unusual "crow's-nest" rooms in the 1901 *Island Inn and Dining Room*, on Hwy-12 (℡1-877/456-3466, 🆆www.ocracokeislandinn.com; ❸–❻), whose **restaurant** is renowned for its crabcakes (℡252/928-7821). Other, less expensive restaurants include the *Back Porch*, on Back Road (℡252/928-6401), which serves great fish, and the lively *Howard's Pub & Raw Bar*, a mile north of the village on Hwy-12 (℡252/928-4441), which offers more than two hundred beers, plus a full menu until 2am. It's one of the few places on the island that's open all year. The fairly isolated Park Service **campground** tends to be the first of the Outer Banks sites to fill up; unlike the others, it accepts reservations (℡1-800/365-2267; $20 per night; open mid-April to mid-Sept).

Cape Lookout National Seashore

The mainland between Cedar Island and Beaufort (see p.496) is a rural backwater, sparsely settled and hardly touched by tourists. The most likely reason to pass through is to get to the all-but-deserted **CAPE LOOKOUT NATIONAL SEASHORE**, a narrow ribbon of sand stretching south of Ocracoke Island along three

Ocracoke ferries

In summer, free **ferries** run **between Hatteras and Ocracoke**. The crossing takes forty minutes, although you may have to wait if you have a car – there's room for only thirty cars, and it's loaded on a first-come, first-served basis.

Hatteras–Ocracoke May–Oct every 30min 7.30am–7pm, hourly 5–7am & 7pm–midnight; Nov–April every 30min 9am–6pm, hourly 5am–9am & 6pm–midnight.

Ocracoke–Hatteras May–Oct every 30min 8.30am–7.30pm, hourly 5–8am & 8pm–midnight; Nov–April every 30min 10am–7pm, hourly 5am–9am & 7pm–midnight.

Ferries **from Ocracoke** also head south down the coast to **Cedar Island** on the mainland (2hr 15min; $1 pedestrian, $3 bike, $10 motorbike, $15 car) and to **Swan Quarter** on the Albemarle Peninsula (2hr 30min; same fares). Both require **reservations** in summer, preferably a day or two in advance (Ocracoke ☎1-800/345-1665, Cedar Island ☎1-800/856-0343, Swan Quarter ☎1-800/773-1094); at short notice you should be able to get the day you want, if not the time.

Between Ocracoke and Cedar Island summer nine or ten departures 7am–8.30pm; spring & fall six departures 7am–8.30pm; winter four departures 7am–4pm.

Ocracoke–Swan Quarter late May to early Sept 6.30am, 12.30pm, 4pm; no 4pm sailing rest of year.

Swan Quarter–Ocracoke late May to early Sept 7am, 9.30am, 4pm; no 7am sailing rest of year.

For **further information** contact ☎1-800/BY-FERRY or ⓦwww.ncferry.org.

undeveloped Outer Banks, with no roads or habitation. The seashore is only accessible by **ferry** (mid-March to early Dec) or private boat, and its few visitors share a total of around 56 miles of beach along all three islands, with the marshes on the landward side supporting rich and unusual plant- and birdlife that have adapted to the harsh, salty conditions. The **visitor center** is at the eastern end of the low-key mainland settlement of **Harker's Island** (daily 9am–5pm; ☎252/728-2250, ⓦwww.nps.gov/calo), thirty miles south of the Cedar Island ferry terminal.

At the northern tip of the first island, **North Core Banks**, across from Ocracoke, stand the pretty, but eerie, ruins of the abandoned village of **Portsmouth**, whose last two residents left in 1971. Ferries arrive in Portsmouth from Ocracoke (around $16 roundtrip; call Rudy Austin on ☎252/928-4361). The ferry from **Atlantic**, south of Cedar Island on the mainland ($14 roundtrip; call Morris Marina on ☎252/225-4261), lands at **Long Point**, seventeen miles south of Portsmouth, which you can only reach on foot. **Cabins** on the island are operated by Morris Marina ($100 per night for up to six people); otherwise there's only primitive **camping**.

South Core Banks is served by private ferry from **Davis**, south of Atlantic on the mainland ($14 roundtrip; ☎1-877/956-6568). Here, too, the ferry company manages more than twenty **cabins**, all with showers (❸–❻). **Camping** is as primitive as on the north island, but the ferry operator can pick up food for you on the mainland and bring it across. Three passenger ferries run to the southern tip of the south island from Beaufort (see below) and from Harker's Island, to within two or three miles of **Cape Lookout** itself and its lighthouse.

To get to the peaceful **Shackleford Banks**, inhabited by wild mustangs since the early 1500s, when they are thought to have swum ashore from shipwrecks, you can catch ferries from Beaufort and Morehead City (see opposite).

Beaufort

BEAUFORT, about 150 miles southeast of Raleigh, is probably the nicest of North Carolina's coastal towns. A good base for visiting the nearby beaches, it's also a relaxing place in its own right, with an attractive waterfront that's particularly lively at night. The **Maritime Museum**, 315 Front St, has good displays on local ecology and shipping history (Mon–Fri 9am–5pm, Sat 10am–5pm, Sun 1–5pm; free; ℡252/728-7317), while across the road you can watch boats being made at the **Watercraft Center**, a working boatyard (Wed–Fri 9am–5pm, Sat 10am–5pm, Sun 1–5pm; free).

North Carolina's third-oldest town, Beaufort also has an appealing twelve-block **historical district**, centering on Turner Street, off the waterfront. Here you'll find handsome old houses, an apothecary, and the city jail; the town **welcome center**, 130 Turner St (daily: March–Nov 9.30am–5pm; Dec–Feb 10am–4pm; ℡252/728-5225, Ⓦwww.historicbeaufort.com), offers a number of tours and self-guided walking tour brochures.

Ferries to **Shackleford Banks** (see opposite) are run by Island Ferry Adventures (mid-March to mid-Nov; roundtrip $14; minimum two adults; ℡252/728-7555, Ⓦwww.islandferryadventures.com), Mystery Tours (from $15; ℡252/728-2527, Ⓦwww.mysteryboattours.com), and Outer Banks Ferry Service (℡252/728-4129), all on the waterfront. You can also get there from **Morehead City**, a couple of miles down the coast (Waterfront Ferry Service ℡252/726-7678). Beaufort Inlet Watersports, next to the Outer Banks Ferry Service at 328 Front St (℡252/728-7607), offers **parasailing** for around $50 single, $90 tandem.

Among the many historic **B&Bs** in the shady residential streets off Turner, *Langdon House*, 135 Craven St (℡252/728-5499, Ⓦwww.langdonhouse.com; ⑤), is friendly and relaxed; the *Cedars Inn*, 305 Front St (℡252/728-7036, Ⓦwww.cedarsinn.com; ⑥), is rather plush. The *Inlet Inn*, on the waterfront at 601 Front St (℡252/728-3600 or 1-800/554-5466, Ⓦwww.inlet-inn.com; ⑤), has huge hotel rooms and serves continental breakfast in your room. Morehead City and the Bogue Banks boast plenty of **motels**.

As for **eating and nightlife**, Beaufort's waterfront is vibrant at night, milling with yachties and vacationers drinking, listening to live music at the *Dock House Bar*, and simply strolling. There are a number of decent bar/restaurants on the wooden **boardwalk** right on the water, with other good options a block or so inland. The *Beaufort Grocery Co*, 117 Queen St (closed Tues; ℡252/728-3899), prides itself on inventive dishes made from superbly fresh ingredients, while the buzzy, hip *Aqua*, 114 Middle Lane (℡252/728-7777; dinner only, closed Sun & Mon), offers Carolina-style tapas and big desserts.

The beaches

South of Beaufort, the **beaches** along the twenty-mile offshore **Bogue Banks**, especially Atlantic Beach at the east end, are always pretty crowded. On **Bear Island** to the south – reached from **Swansboro** by boat taxi or ferry (April–Oct, hours vary; $5; ℡910/326-4881) – the stunning **Hammocks Beach State Park** has high sand dunes, a wooded shore, and perfect beaches. To **camp** ($9), you need to register at the small park center (daily: Sept–May 8am–5pm; June–Aug 8am–6pm; ℡910/326-4881). No camping is permitted in turtle season (March and April), when **loggerhead sea turtles** come ashore to lay their eggs.

On the far side of the massive Camp Lejeune US Marine base – home to around forty thousand Marines – **Topsail Island**, yet another sand bar of resorts (accessible via Hwy-172 on the mainland), is considerably less built up than the Bogue Banks, presumably because its beaches aren't quite as good. Both **Surf City** and **Topsail** were once slightly run-down family resorts, but have improved nicely. Public beach access points are signposted from the main road, but you can get down from lots of other places.

Wilmington

Though it's the largest town on North Carolina's coast, **WILMINGTON**, set back along the **Cape Fear River**, fifty miles short of the state's southern border, has a welcoming, laid-back feel. During the Civil War, it was briefly the Confederacy's most important harbor, exporting cotton all over the world. "**Blockade-runners**" would attempt to outrun the Union navy, racing into the safety of Fort Fisher's guns some twenty miles to the south of town; "Rebel Rose" Greenhow, glamorous Confederate spy, drowned here during a run in 1864. Dozens of blacks were murdered in Wilmington by white mobs in the **Race Riot** of 1898 – a backlash to the election of a "Fusionist" (Republican-Populist-black) governor two years earlier. Historians see it as effectively a coup d'état, which had immense repercussions all over the South; in 2006, a commission appointed by North Carolina's state legislature recommended that the state pay substantial reparations to Wilmington's black community.

For all that, Wilmington today is attractive, friendly, and buzzy. Its notoriety as a popular **movie location** has earned it the nickname "Hollywood East," or even "Wilmywood", and the influx of creative types has led to a certain gentrification that feels very different from the rest of the coast. That's not to call it ersatz – its lively cobbled waterfront and historic district, starting on the south side of Market Street and stretching east along Third Street, feel genuinely lived in.

While Wilmington's extravagant houses, ornate **City Hall**, and lovely old **Thalian Hall** demonstrate its former wealth, it's the cobbled streets of the weathered, boardwalked **waterfront**, dotted with cafés and restaurants, that really appeal. **Chandler's Wharf**, an upmarket mall in a restored warehouse, is typical of the area's revitalization, while the **Cotton Exchange**, 321 N Front St, sells crafts and food in a group of buildings that once housed a grain mill, warehouse, and cotton business. At the foot of Market Street, at the small **Riverfront Park**, you can pick up a horse-drawn **carriage tour** (☎910/251-8889; $11); a **harbor cruise** (☎910/343-1611, ⊛www.cfrboats.com; $14); or a **river taxi** to the battleship USS *North Carolina*, which participated in every naval offensive in the Pacific during World War II. At 814 Market St, the **Cape Fear Museum** (summer Mon–Sat 9am–5pm, Sun 1–5pm; rest of year closed Mon; $6; ⊛www.capefearmuseum. com) gives a lively account of local history.

To get a sense of how Wilmywood works, take a tour of **EUE/Screen Gems Studios**, 1223 N 23rd St, the site of productions as diverse as David Lynch's *Blue Velvet* and TV hits *Dawson's Creek* and *One Tree Hill* (June–Aug Sat & Sun noon & 2pm, Sept–May Sat noon; $12; ☎910/343-3433, ⊛www.screengemsstudios. com).

Twenty miles south of Wilmington on Hwy-421, near Kure Beach, **Fort Fisher State Historic Site** commands a spectacular rocky position overlooking both the sea and the mouth of the Cape Fear River. This used to be the largest earthen fort in the South, and you can walk a trail around the remains; a small **museum** focuses on its days as a Confederate stronghold, with relics from sunken blockade-runners and various weaponry (April–Oct Mon–Sat 9am–5pm, Sun 1–5pm; Nov–March Tues–Sat 10am–4pm; free). You can catch a **ferry** from Fort Fisher to the little mainland town of **Southport** (roughly every 45min; call to check exact schedule; $5 per vehicle; 30min trip; ☎1-800/368-8969).

Practicalities

The **bus station** is at 201 Harnett St, a mile north of downtown off Third Street. Wilmington's **visitor center**, 24 N Third St (Mon–Fri 8.30am–5pm, Sat 9am–4pm, Sun 10am–4pm; ☎910/341-4030 or 1-877/406-2356, ⊛www.cape-fear.

nc.us), has maps and walking tours, including a good African-American site map and a *Dawson's Creek* FAQ sheet. The funniest, most informative overviews of the city are given by Adventure Walking Tours, which leave from the flagpole at Market and Water streets (April–Oct 10am & 2pm; $12; ☏910/763-1785). There's also a brochure-packed **information kiosk** (April–Oct daily 9.30am–4.30pm) at the bottom of Market Street.

Cheap motels line Market Street for the last few miles into Wilmington, and there are also some lovely **B&Bs**: the movie stars stay at the atmospheric *Graystone Inn*, on Third and Dock (☏910/763-2000, ⓦwww.graystoneinn.com; ❼). At the non-smoking *Best Western Coastline Inn*, on the riverfront at 503 Nutt St (☏910/763-2800 or 1-800/617-7732, ⓦwww.coastlineinn.com; ❹), rates include breakfast served in your room.

The central blocks of downtown hold an abundance of swanky, often Asian-flavored **restaurants**, such as *Deluxe* at 114 Market St (☏910/251-0333), where entrees like panko-dusted soft-shell crabs cost $26. But you can eat well for less, too, for example at ⊁ *Caffé Phoenix*, a light, cheerful bistro with some sidewalk seating at 9 S Front St (☏910/343-1395), which offers good lunch and dinner specials. For a quick meal try the *Dock Street Oyster Bar*, 12 Dock St (☏910/762-2827), a funky little place serving cheap raw oysters and seafood. Wilmington has a thriving **nightlife** as well; for **listings**, pick up a copy of the free weekly *Encore*. *Marrz*, 15 S Front St (☏910/772-9045, ⓦwww.marrz.net), is a hip live-music venue, while the *Barbary Coast*, 116 Front St (☏910/762-8996), is a dingy hole-in-the-wall that has gained some cachet from being Mickey Rourke's favorite bar in town. Built in 1858, Thalian Hall, 310 Chestnut St (☏1-800/523-2820, ⓦwww.thalianhall.com), hosts dance, music, theater, and movies.

The North Carolina Piedmont

North Carolina's **PIEDMONT** is a fairly industrialized area of textile and tobacco towns, mostly in decline. Even close to the towns, though, it can still be very rural; little has changed here since the 1950s. The main area of interest is the **Research Triangle** trio of neighboring college towns: **Raleigh**, the state capital; relaxed **Durham**, with its strong black community; and countercultural **Chapel Hill**. **Winston–Salem**, famous for its tobacco industry, boasts the excellent Old Salem village.

Raleigh

Founded as North Carolina's capital in 1792, **RALEIGH** stands on I-40 at the very heart of the state. The town focuses around the central, pedestrianized **Capitol Square**, where the **North Carolina Museum of History**, 5 E Edenton St (Tues–Sat 9am–5pm, Sun noon–5pm; free; ☏919/715-0200), is impressively far-reaching, a chronological trot through the state's history from the viewpoint of its people, with particularly strong sections on women. Opposite is the **North Carolina Museum of Natural Sciences**, 11 W Jones St (Mon–Sat 9am–5pm, Sun noon–5pm; free), which looks at local geology, as well as animal and plant life, going all the way back to the dinosaur age.

South of the capitol, the four-block **City Market**, a lamplit, cobbled enclave at the intersection of Blount and Martin streets, holds a number of good shops and restaurants. Check out the local artists and sculptors at work in **Artspace**, 201 E Davie St (Tues–Sat 10am–6pm; ⓦwww.artspacenc.org), which also hosts free lectures, movies, and poetry readings. Seventeenth US President **Andrew Johnson** was born in a tiny hut just north of where the capitol now stands; his birthplace has since been moved to **Mordecai Historic Park**, north of town at the corner of Wake Forest Rd and Mimosa St (Tues–Sat 10am–4pm, Sun 1–4pm; 1hr tours begin on the hour, with last tour at 3pm; $5).

A little way out to the northwest via I-40, the impressive **North Carolina Museum of Art**, 2110 Blue Ridge Rd (Tues–Thurs & Sat 9am–5pm, Fri 9am–9pm, Sun 10am–5pm; tours daily 1.30pm; free except for special exhibitions), has an eclectic display of works from the ancient world, Africa, Europe, and the US, along with a great restaurant (see below).

Practicalities

Raleigh-Durham **airport** (ⓦwww.rdu.com) is off I-40, fifteen minutes northwest of town. The **taxi** ride into town costs around $30, while a circuitous **shuttle service** will set you back $25. Amtrak drops you off at 320 W Cabarrus St, while the Greyhound station is in a seedy part of downtown at 321 W Jones St. The **visitor center**, 301 N Blount St (Mon–Fri 8am–5pm, Sat 10am–4pm, Sun 1–4pm; ℡1-800/849-8494, ⓦwww.visitraleigh.com), has the usual racks of leaflets.

If you want to **stay**, avoid the more anonymous downtown hotels and instead head out to Hillsborough Street, near North Carolina State University, where the *Velvet Cloak Inn* at no. 1505 offers comfortable rooms, free coffee, tea, and cookies, and an indoor pool (℡919/828-0333, ⓦwww.velvetcloakinn.com; ➊). For **food**, *Big Ed's*, in the City Market at 220 Wolfe St (closed Sun; ℡919/836-9909), serves fabulous Southern breakfasts, while *Cup a Joe*, near the university at 3100 Hillsborough (℡919/876-4588), is a bohemian coffee bar that attracts a mixed crowd. The huge *42nd St Oyster Bar*, downtown at 508 Jones St (℡919/831-2811), is a popular spot for fresh fish and seafood, with live music at weekends, and the art museum boasts the contemporary *Blue Ridge Restaurant* (Tues–Sun lunch, Fri dinner; ℡919/833-3548).

Hillsborough Street, lined with bars and restaurants, is the epicenter of Raleigh's student **nightlife**. *The Brewery*, at no. 3009 (℡919/838-6788, ⓦwww.brewerync.com), hosts the best regional rock and alternative bands. Away from Hillsborough, *Berkeley Café*, 217 W Martin (℡919/821-0777), specializes in roots, alt-country, and rock, while *Kings*, 424 S McDowell St (℡919/831-1005, ⓦwww.kingsbarcade.com), is a laid-back place for anything from drum 'n' bass to New Romantic nights, with retro video games, free food, and go-go girls to boot. Pick up the free *Spectator* for nightlife **listings**.

Durham

Twenty miles northwest of Raleigh, **DURHAM** found itself at the center of the nation's tobacco industry after farmer Washington Duke came home from the Civil War with the idea of producing cigarettes – by 1890 he and his three sons had formed the **America Tobacco Company**. The **Duke Homestead Historical Site**, north of I-85 at 2828 Duke Homestead Rd (Tues–Sat 10am–4pm; free), is an absorbing living museum covering the social history of tobacco farming, with demonstrations of early farming techniques and tobacco-rolling.

In 1924, the Duke family's $40 million endowment to the small-scale Trinity College enabled it to expand into a world-respected medical research facility, swiftly changing its name to **Duke University**. On campus, the **Nasher Museum of Art** at 2001 Campus Drive (Tues, Wed, Fri & Sat 10am–5pm, Thurs 10am–9pm, Sun noon–5pm; $5; ℡919/684-5135, ⓦwww.nasher.duke.edu) has good African, pre-Columbian, medieval, and Asian collections.

Durham takes pride in its vibrant **black heritage**. Seven miles north of town, in rural Treyburn Park, the fascinating **Historic Stagville** (Tues–Sat 10am–4pm; free; ☎919/620-0120, ⓦwww.historicstagvillefoundation.org) illustrates North Carolina plantation life, in particular the slave experience, from the early 1800s to Reconstruction. Around eighty to a hundred enslaved Africans worked on the Stagville plantation; on the grounds you can see the small two-story houses they lived in, four families (one per room) per dwelling, as well as the plantation owners' house and a colossal barn built by skilled slave carpenters.

Downtown Durham has little of interest, though **Brightleaf Square**, an upbeat shopping area of restored tobacco warehouses at Gregson and Main streets, is a nice enough place to take a stroll, browsing its galleries, bookstores, and specialty stores.

Practicalities

Greyhound **buses** stop at 820 W Morgan St. Pick up maps and local information from the Durham **visitor center**, 101 E Morgan St (Mon–Fri 8.30am–5pm, Sat 10am–2pm; ☎919/687-0288 or 1-800/446-8604, ⓦwww.durham-nc.com). The *Arrowhead Inn*, 106 Mason Rd (☎919/477-8430, ⓦwww.arrowheadinn.com; ◉), which dates back to 1775, offers lovely **B&B** rooms.

For **food**, try the places around Brightleaf Square: *Fowler's*, 112 S Duke St (☎919/683-2555), serves organic gourmet sandwiches and coffee, while *Anotherthyme*, 109 N Gregson St (dinner only; ☎919/682-5225), specializes in creative seafood and *tapas*. Durham's role as the heart of the North Carolina Piedmont **blues** scene – musicians like Reverend Gary Davis would play for tips at Raleigh's tobacco markets – is commemorated by early September's **Bull Durham Blues Festival** (ⓦwww.hayti.org/blues).

Chapel Hill

Hip, villagey **CHAPEL HILL**, on the southwest outskirts of Durham, is nationally renowned as the home of such bands as Superchunk and Archers of Loaf, and musicians like Ben Folds and Ryan Adams, not to mention James "Carolina on My Mind" Taylor. About half its fifty thousand population are students, and its position as a bastion of white liberalism in a poor rural state brings the town its detractors. That said, it's a pleasant enough place to hang out for a while, in the laid-back bars and coffeehouses along **Franklin Street**, which fringes the north side of campus. Franklin continues west into the adjacent city of **Carrboro**, where it becomes **Main Street**; bars and restaurants here have a slightly hipper, post-collegiate edge.

The **University of North Carolina**, dating from 1789, was the nation's first state university. The earliest of its fine eighteenth-century buildings is **Old East**, its original brick painted a fashionable tan in the 1840s. Evidence of the university's wealth can be seen at the splendid **Morehead Planetarium** on E Franklin St (Mon–Wed 10am–5pm, Thurs–Sat 10am–5pm & 6.30–9.30pm, Sun 12.30–5pm; $5.25; ⓦwww.moreheadplanetarium.org), which served as an early NASA training center, and at the **Ackland Art Museum**, South Columbia and Franklin streets (Wed–Sat 10am–5pm, Sun 1–5pm; free; ⓦwww.ackland.org), which is particularly strong on Asian art and antiquities.

Practicalities

The Chapel Hill/Orange County **visitors bureau** is at 501 W Franklin (Mon–Fri 8.30am–5pm, Sat 10am–2pm; ☎1-888/968-2060, ⓦwww.chocvb.org). Chapel Hill has few places to **stay**; one of the most popular spots is the very swanky, university owned *Carolina Inn*, on campus at 211 Pittsboro St (☎919/933-2001 or 1-800/962-8519, ⓦwww.carolinainn.com; ❺). Five miles northeast of town, the *Sheraton*, 1 Europa Drive (☎919/968-4900; ❺), has stylish, very comfortable rooms, while the nearby *Hampton Inn*, 1740 Hwy-15/501 (☎919/968-3000; ❹), is cheaper.

Chapel Hill abounds in great **restaurants**. The minimalist *Lantern*, 423 W Franklin St, dishes up fabulous pan-Asian food until late (closed Sun; ☎919/969-8846), and has an atmospheric bar. At 610 Franklin, *Crooks Corner* (closed Mon; ☎919/929-7643) offers a daily changing menu of delicious, stylish Southern cooking. *Elmo's Diner*, in the Carr Mill Mall in Carrboro, 200 N Greensboro St (☎919/929-2909), does great breakfasts, tasty veggie choices, and daily specials.

For **nightlife**, stay on Franklin and Main streets. *Orange County Social Club*, 108 E Main St, Carrboro (☎919/933-0669, ⓦwww.orangecountysocialclub.com), is a stylish, laid-back **bar** with vintage decor, a pool table, a great jukebox, and a garden. Most **music** venues have an eclectic booking policy: *Local 506*, 506 W Franklin St (☎919/942-5506, ⓦwww.local506.com), features wild bands, open-mike hip-hop, and the annual Sleazefest in August (ⓦwww.sleazefest.com), while over in Carrboro, the friendly *Cat's Cradle*, 300 E Main St (☎919/967-9053, ⓦcatscradle.com), books the best bands on the national touring circuit. Check **listings** in the free *Independent Weekly* (ⓦwww.indyweek.com).

Winston-Salem

Though synonymous with the brand names of its cigarettes, **WINSTON-SALEM**, eighty miles west of Chapel Hill, owes its spot on the tourist itinerary to the delightful **Old Salem**. These twenty well-preserved blocks of clapboard and half-timbered brick homes, very close to downtown, honor the heritage of the city's first Moravian settlers. Escaping religious persecution in what are now the Czech and Slovak republics, the first Moravians settled in the Piedmont in the mid-seventeenth century. They soon established trading links with the frontier settlers and founded the town of Salem on a communal basis – they permitted only those of the same religious faith to live here. The demand for their crafts helped establish the adjacent community of Winston, which, accruing tremendous wealth from tobacco, soon outgrew the older community. The two merged in 1913 to form Winston-Salem.

Visitors are free to stroll or drive the streets of Old Salem, or by touring ten **restored buildings** (Mon–Sat 9am–5.30pm, Sun 1–5pm; $21, or $24 for two days) you can learn, with the help of costumed guides, about the skills, trades, and customs of the Moravians. Start at the huge **visitor center** on Academy and Old Salem Rd (Mon–Sat 8.30am–5.30pm, Sun 12.30–5.30pm) and, if time is tight, prioritize the **St Philips Moravian Church**, an African-American church originally built in 1823, and the **Single Brothers House**, built in 1771, where unmarried men would sleep, worship, and make items such as silverware, hats, and paper. Admission includes entrance to the **Museum of Early Southern Decorative Arts** (Mon–Sat 9.30am–5pm, Sun 1.30–5pm; last tour at 3.30pm), the **Children's Museum**, geared toward under-9s (Tues–Fri 9am–5pm, Sun & Mon 1–5pm; $6 for the two if not part of Old Salem ticket), and the striking **Toy Museum** (Mon–Sat 9am–5pm, Sun 1–5pm), which has thousands of antique toys dating from 225AD. Large lunches and dinners, and beer, are served at the *Salem Tavern*, 736 S Main (☎336/748-8585), where the costumed waiters carry dishes like the $7.50 Moravian chicken pie to diners on the spacious patio or lawns, and the *Winkler Bakery* at 525 S Main produces great cookies.

Three miles northwest of downtown, the **Reynolda House Museum of American Art**, 2250 Reynolda Rd (Tues–Sat 9.30am–4.30pm, Sun 1.30–4.30pm; $10), features pieces by top American artists from the eighteenth century to the present day, in what was the home of tobacco baron Richard Joshua Reynolds. The mansion, designed by Charles Barton Keen, is set in lush, landscaped gardens, with a number of its surrounding buildings converted into fancy stores and restaurants known collectively as **Reynolda Village**.

Practicalities

Winston-Salem's **visitor center** is a few blocks from Old Salem, at 200 Brookstown Ave (☎336/728-4200, ⓦwww.visitwinstonsalem.com). Next door, the *Brookstown Inn* (☎336/725-1120 or 1-800/845-4262, ⓦwww.brookstowninn.com; ⑥), is a lovely small **hotel** in a former textile mill. The *Best Western Salem Inn*, 127 S Cherry St (☎1-800/533-8760, ⓦwww.bestwestern.com; ④), offers clean motel rooms and a good complimentary breakfast and has an Amtrak bus connection from the nearest **train station**, which is in Greensboro, 28 miles away.

With the exception of the Old Salem options mentioned above, **eating** alternatives aren't that exciting, though *Bistro 420*, 420 W Fourth St (closed Mon ☎336/721-1336), serves good Southern cuisine.

Charlotte

The banking and transportation center of **CHARLOTTE**, where I-77 and I-85 meet near the South Carolina border, is the largest city in the state. Business and city leaders like to project the image of a sophisticated, fast-lane cultural metropolis, but its center is in fact somewhat soulless, with most restaurants and stores tucked away inside the city's skyscrapers. The busiest downtown thoroughfare, **Tryon Street**, is an unlovely mass of tall buildings and concrete known as "uptown." In **Independence Square**, at Tryon and Trade, giant modern statues depict transportation, commerce, industry, and the future. A few blocks away, the excellent **Museum of the New South**, 200 E Seventh St (Mon–Sat 10am–5pm, Sun noon–5pm; $6; ⓦwww.museumofthenewsouth.org), looks at the growth of the region from Reconstruction onwards. Interesting vignettes include those on musical history, with the spotlight falling on local names such as gospel legends the Golden Gate Quartet. **Discovery Place**, 301 N Tryon St, is a kids-oriented science museum with an indoor rainforest, an OMNIMAX theater, and a planetarium (June–Sept Mon–Sat 10am–6pm, Sun 12.30–6pm; Sept–June Mon–Fri 9am–5pm, Sat 10am–6pm, Sun 12.30–5pm; $8.50, OMNIMAX $8.50, combo ticket $14; ⓦwww.discoveryplace.org).

Practicalities

Charlotte/Douglas International Airport, seven miles west of town on Old Dowd Road or I-85, is served by the #5 **bus** ($1.65), which runs hourly from the Charlotte Transportation Center, uptown on Brevard Street, between Fourth and Fifth streets, to the airport; **taxis** cost about $18 and **shuttle buses** $10. Greyhound stops centrally at 601 W Trade St, while Amtrak trains pull in at 1914 N Tryon St. The huge **visitor center** is at 330 S Tryon St (Mon–Fri 8.30am–5pm, Sat 9am–3pm; ☎704/331-2700 or 1-800/231-4636, ⓦwww.charlottecvb.org).

Most of Charlotte's **hotels** are aimed at the conference trade, though the 1929 *Dunhill Hotel*, 237 N Tryon St (☎704/332-4141, ⓦwww.dunhillhotel.com; ⑥), possesses an Old World elegance. The *Days Inn*, 601 N Tryon St (☎704/333-4733; ③), is a cheaper central alternative. Good **restaurants** include trendy *Providence Café*, 110 Perrin Place (☎704/376-2008), for vegetarian and New American cuisine and *LaVecchia's Seafood Grille*, 325 E Sixth St (☎704/370-6776; closed Sun). **Nightlife** is concentrated between the easily walkable grid of Tryon, College, Seventh, and Fifth streets, and in the South End, southwest of uptown. Check **listings** in the free weekly *Creative Loafing* (ⓦcharlotte.creativeloafing.com).

The North Carolina mountains

The best way to see the **mountains** of North Carolina is from the pristine **Blue Ridge Parkway**, which runs across the northwest of the state from Virginia to the **Great Smoky Mountains National Park**. It's a delight to drive; the vast panoramic expanses of forested hillside, with barely a settlement in sight, may astonish travelers fresh from the crowded centers of the east coast. This predominantly poor region has been a breeding ground since the early twentieth century for **bluegrass music**, which you will still find, along with traditional **clogging**, performed regularly throughout the region; tiny towns like laid-back **Asheville** are good places to see the edgier "newgrass."

The helpful **visitor center** at 1700 Blowing Rock Rd in Boone (℡1-800/438-7500, ⓦwww.mountainsofnc.com), services most of the mountain area.

The Blue Ridge Parkway

The peak tourist season for the **BLUE RIDGE PARKWAY** is October, when the leaves of the deciduous trees that cover the landscape turn from bright yellow and gold through browns to vivid red. Year-round, however, this magnificent, twisting mountain road – largely built in the 1930s by President Roosevelt's Civilian Conservation Corps volunteers – is a worthwhile vacation destination in itself, peppered with state-run campgrounds, short hiking trails, and dramatic overlooks. Although the Parkway is closed to commercial vehicles, and only particularly crowded near one or two major beauty spots, the constant curves make it hard to average anything approaching the 45mph speed limit.

Boone

Although **BOONE** is the most obvious northern base for exploring the mountains, the town itself holds little of interest. Corny family entertainments dot US-321, while pretty backroads hold offbeat settlements such as **Valle Crucis**, off US-194, where the 1883 Mast General Store (summer Mon–Sat 7am–6.30pm, Sun noon–5pm; winter hours vary; ℡828/262-0000) is well worth a look for its cast-iron cookware, fresh coffee beans, rustic furniture, outdoor gear, and fat barrels overflowing with candies.

Boone's **visitor center** is downtown at 208 Howard St (℡828/262-3516 or 1-888/251-9867, ⓦwww.visitboonenc.com). For clean **hotel** rooms, head for the *High Country Inn*, 1785 Hwy-105 (℡828/264-1000 or 1-800/334-5605, ⓦwww.

Mountain activities

Organized **outdoor pursuits** available along the Blue Ridge Parkway include excellent **whitewater rafting** and **canoeing**, most of it on the Nolichucky River near the Tennessee border, south of Johnson City, Tennessee, but also on the Watauga River and Wilson Creek. Companies running trips include Nantahala Outdoor Center (℡1-800/232-7238, ⓦwww.noc.com) and High Mountain Expeditions (℡1-800/262-9036, ⓦwww.highmountainexpeditions.com), who also offer biking, hiking, and caving trips. Expect to pay around $75 for a full day of rafting.

Winter sees **skiing** at a number of slopes and resorts, particularly around **Banner Elk**, twelve miles southwest of Boone. Resort accommodation is expensive, ski passes less so. Appalachian Ski Mountain (℡1-800/322-2373, ⓦwww.appskimtn.com) is near Blowing Rock, and Ski Beech (℡1-800/438-2093, ⓦwww.skibeech.com), the highest ski area in the east, is at Beech Mountain. You can pick up full listings at visitor centers, or check ⓦwww.skithehighcountry.com.

Music

Music is the lifeblood of the USA, with every mile along the highways seeming to evoke a favorite song or performer. Devotees flock to cities associated with some of the world's greatest genres: Chicago, birthplace of the blues; New Orleans, with unrivaled jazz and R&B scenes; Nashville, synonymous with country; and Memphis, home to Sun and Stax record labels as well as the ultimate rock 'n' roll shrine, Graceland. Indie rockers often head to Los Angeles and New York, while college towns like Austin, Texas, and Athens, Georgia, are good places to catch rising stars. And, of course, there's always Las Vegas, where every act arrives in the end. Outside the cities, rural Appalachia brims with ensembles of backwoods fiddlers; Louisiana's sleepy bayous are enlivened by foot-comping Cajun and zydeco sounds; and the jook-joints Mississippi Delta hamlets enrapture blues purists.

Rural beginnings

American **folk music** can be traced back to the Europeans – particularly those from England and the Celtic lands – who settled in the Appalachian mountain region. Over the centuries, traditional songs and ballads mixed with various influences from other parts of the world and evolved into the guitar-twanging **country-and-western** music that is today associated with the American South. It wasn't until the mid-twentieth century, however, that country music broke into the mainstream, when the plain cowboy style of Roy Rogers and the harmonies of the Carter Family found a home with a wide audience, and honky-tonk hero Hank Williams performed six encores in his Grand Ole Opry debut.

From soul to hip-hop

As the black social experience diversified over the course of the twentieth century, various forms of music sprang up to give it voice. In the 1960s, the heartfelt **soul** of masters like Otis Redding preceded the explosion of talent that came to define the Motown era, which was born in Detroit. As soul went mainstream in the 1970s, progressive mavericks like Parliament and Funkadelic paved the way for the transition to 1980s **rap** culture: loaded with attitude, street-style, and political savvy, rappers from Run DMC to NWA, mostly based in New York and LA, stood at the forefront of a dynasty that would eventually include **hip-hop** and a second generation of **R&B**. Other major current centers of hip-hop include Philadelphia, Atlanta, and Detroit, to name just a few.

Bluegrass, developed by William Smith Monroe and named after the fields of his native Kentucky, is another sub-genre of American folk music, and many regard its banjo- and fiddle-based sound to be the purest form of country there is. It's enjoyed a bit of a revival in the past decade, with newfound popularity for traditionalists like Ralph Stanley and more modern practitioners Alison Krauss and Gillian Welch, the latter of whom it's hard to believe grew up in Los Angeles and Boston.

A performance at the Ryman Auditorium

The Mississippi sounds

Both jazz and the blues grew out of African-American culture, with the latter inextricably linked to the experiences of slavery and poverty. Forged from a combination of African and gospel sounds into a simple twelve-bar form during the late nineteenth century, by the 1930s the **blues** had gained widespread popularity, spreading along a path

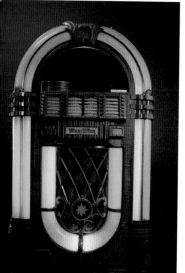

that followed the Mississippi River through Memphis, then on to northern urban centers (namely Chicago), which were relatively safe havens for the descendants of freed slaves. Thanks to mainstream icons like Leadbelly, Muddy Waters, and BB King, the genre not only solidified its own stature but – as the saying goes – "had a baby and named it rock'n'roll."

Jazz remains forever associated with the Deep South and, more specifically, the Creole culture of New Orleans and the Mississippi Delta. The most complex of all modern musical styles, jazz, noted for its syncopation and polyrhythms, blends African traditions with western techniques, favoring saxophones, trumpets, the double bass, and piano to create a distinctive American sound. Miles Davis is the figure most responsible for raising jazz to a high art form; he first made his mark in New York City's mid-twentieth-century club scene.

Ten places immortalized in song

There seems a limitless number of well-known songs written about big American cities – "Sweet Home Chicago," "New York, New York," "Viva Las Vegas," "I Love LA" just for a start – and probably an equal number about states ("Private Idaho" by the B-52s, "California Dreaming" by the Mamas and Papas, "Sweet Home Alabama" by Lynyrd Skynyrd). Here are a few that are a little less obvious in their iconic subjects:

Lexington Ave & 125 St, New York City. This crossroads in Harlem is where Lou Reed's character in "Waiting For The Man" came to score.

The San Francisco Dock. It's a lot more commercialized now, but spare a thought for Otis Redding penning "Dock Of the Bay" when you visit Pier 41.

Highway 61. This famous road is so long that Bob Dylan thought to dedicate an entire album, "Highway 61 Revisited," to it.

Max Yasgur's Farm, Bethel NY. Actually sixty miles from the town of Woodstock, the venue of the 1969 festival features in Joni Mitchell's anthemic "Woodstock," as well as the Mountain song "Max Yasgur's Farm."

Redondo Beach, CA. Patti Smith's punk-reggae beat first brought this hangout for bronzed LA types to our attention in "Redondo Beach" from her classic debut album.

Rockaway Beach, Queens, NY. The Ramones hitch a ride to their favorite local hangout (aside, perhaps, from "53rd and 3rd" in Manhattan, but that's a sorrier story).

The Painted Desert, AZ. Natalie Merchant of 10,000 Maniacs sings about this stunning piece of Southwestern geography on the album "In My Tribe."

Dylan penned a barbed tribute to Highway 61

Route 66. Most people are probably familiar with the Nat King Cole hit about this historic piece of tarmac.

Asbury Park, NJ. Jersey boy Bruce Springsteen immortalized this run-down beach town in "4th of July, Asbury Park (Sandy)"; other Jersey locations, like Atlantic City, also get their due in the Boss's tunes.

The skyway system, Minneapolis, MN. The Replacements song "Skyway" is dedicated to the city's enclosed (to ward off the cold) five-mile track that "don't move at all like a subway."

Rock of ages

Rock has come a long way since its blues-based infancy, when Elvis Presley swiveled his hips in 1950s Memphis, Bill Haley "rocked around the clock," and Chuck Berry told Beethoven it was time to "roll over." The amorphous new form would absorb a host of influences, from Bob Dylan's folk protest songs to the pop that followed the Beatles-led British invasion, through the drug- and sitar-tinged psychedelic revolution of bands like the Grateful Dead in the late 1960s. Since then, spiky New York punk, quirky Ohio industrial, furious LA hardcore, slacker Seattle grunge, and spaced-out neo-psychedelia are but a few of the sounds that have thrown up modern-day rock icons like Patti Smith, Black Flag, Nirvana, and REM.

highcountryinn.com; ❸), which also has a decent café and bar; good **B&Bs** include the *Lovill House Inn*, set in eleven wooded acres at 404 Old Bristol Rd (☏828/264-4204 or 1-800/849-9466, ⓦwww.lovillhouseinn.com; ❻). Most of the best places to **eat** and **drink** are along King Street; the *Caribbean Café*, no. 489 (☏828/265-2233), serves award-winning spicy food, with some great veggie choices, while *Earth Fare*, no. 178 (☏828/263-8138), is a natural foods store, with a café and juice bar.

South along the Parkway

Eight miles south of Boone, **BLOWING ROCK** is a pleasant, if touristy, resort just south of the Blue Ridge Parkway. The "Blowing Rock" itself, a high cliff from which light objects thrown over the side will simply blow back up, is nowhere near as impressive as photos suggest. The three-mile steam-driven **Tweetsie Railroad**, which is now the center of a family theme park on Hwy-321, is all that remains of a train line that used to run across the mountains to Johnson City, Tennessee (June–Aug daily 9am–6pm; May, Sept & Oct Fri–Sun 9am–6pm; $27, under-13s $19; ⓦwww.tweetsie.com).

Blowing Rock's **visitor center** (Mon–Sat 9am–5pm; ☏828/295-7851; ⓦwww.blowingrock.com) is on Park Avenue. On Main Street you'll find **hotels** such as the *Boxwood Lodge* at no. 637 (☏828/295-9984, ⓦwww.boxwoodlodge.com; ❹). At *Woodland's* (☏828/295-3651), on the Hwy-321 bypass, the pork **barbecue** is excellent; it's also a good spot to drink beer, as is the comfy back porch of *The Canyons*, Hwy-321 (☏828/295-7661), which dishes up contemporary Southwestern and regional cuisine.

The Canyons has a fine view of the privately owned **Grandfather Mountain** (5964ft), fifteen miles south of Blowing Rock, with access near milepost 304 (daily: spring & fall 8am–6pm; summer 8am–7pm; winter 8am–5pm; $14; ⓦwww.grandfather.com). The price may be high, but the owners make a genuine attempt to protect this unique environment, and the view from the top – especially on the "mile-high swinging bridge" between the peaks – is superb, as are some of the trails. Bears, otters, and other animals, including golden and bald eagles that were wounded by gunshot in their western homelands, are held in habitat-like settings. During the **Highland Games** and "Gathering of the Clans" held here in the second full week in July, distantly Scottish Americans (take a look at the local phone book and see just how many names begin with "Mc") dress up in kilts, toss cabers, and tootle away on bagpipes.

Of various short and easy **trails** off the Parkway hereabouts, the one leading half a mile or so up to **Rough Ridge**, near milepost 301, is especially picturesque at dusk. Rough Ridge is one of several access points to the 13.5-mile **Tanawha Trail**, which runs along the ridge above the Parkway from Beacon Heights to Julian Price Park, looking out over the lush, dense forests to the east. Another good hiking destination is the **Linville Gorge Wilderness**, near milepost 316 a couple of miles outside Linville Falls village. There are two main trails; one is a steep, 1.6 mile roundtrip climb to the top of the high and spectacular **Linville Falls** themselves. Breathtaking views from either side of the gorge look down 2000ft to the **Linville River** below, which has perfect, long, deep swimming pools. An easier walk leads, in half a mile, to the base of the falls. You can also climb **Hawksbill** or **Table Rock** mountains from the nearest unsurfaced forest road, which leaves Hwy-181 south of the village of Jonas Ridge (signposted "Gingercake Acres," with a small, low sign to Table Rock). The unremarkable but amiable villages of **Linville** and **Linville Falls** have the usual **motels** and restaurants; Linville Falls also has a **campground** (☏828/765-2681, ⓦwww.linvillefalls.com; $28 per night), and *Spears Restaurant*, Hwy-221 (☏828/765-0026), is worth a detour for its hickory-smoked pork barbecue.

The views from the Parkway in the **Mount Mitchell State Park** (☎828/675-4611) area, south toward Asheville, are tremendous. Sadly, however, this is largely because the trees around the summit of Mount Mitchell – the highest point in the eastern US, at 6684ft – have been ravaged by acid rain from coal-burning industries in the Chattanooga Basin to the west, and the large barren patches leave the horizon clear. Park your car at the end of the signed four-mile detour north of the Parkway, where there's a small museum and restaurant, then follow a short stepped trail that leads to a damp 1930s watchtower.

Asheville

Encircled by a ring of interstates, and skirted to the east and south by the Parkway, arty **ASHEVILLE**, roughly one hundred miles southwest of Boone, retains an appealing 1920s downtown core. With a strong student community from UNC, it's also become quite an alternative center, studded with funky coffee bars, galleries, vintage shops, and bohemian bookstores. Vibrant yet laid-back, it's a nice place to walk around, with a number of handsome **Art Deco** buildings. **Woolworth Walk**, 25 Haywood St, is a typically quirky space, exhibiting more than one hundred local artists in a vintage Woolworth store, while Malaprop's Bookstore, 55 Haywood, has a wonderful selection of titles.

Two miles south of town on Biltmore Avenue, the **Biltmore Estate** is the largest private mansion in the US, with 250 rooms (daily: April–Dec 8.30am–5pm; Jan–March 9am–5pm; prices vary, typically Mon–Thurs $38, Fri–Sun $42; Ⓦwww.biltmore.com). Built in the late nineteenth century by George Vanderbilt and loosely modeled on a Loire chateau, it's a wild piece of nouveau riche folly, from the Victorian chic of the indoor palm court to the gardens designed by Frederic Law Olmsted, he of New York's Central Park. You could spend a whole day here, taking a self-guided or guided tour, checking out the tastings at the winery, renting a raft or bike to explore the 250 acres of grounds, eating at the four restaurants, and maybe even staying at the 213-room "inn" (☎828-225-1600; ❽).

Asheville's **Greyhound/Trailways** terminal is inconveniently located at 2 Tunnel Rd, two miles out of downtown; take bus #13 or #4 stopping at the Innsbruck Mall. There's a good little **visitor center** at 36 Montford Ave, reached via exit 4C off I-240 (Mon–Fri 8.30am–5.30pm, Sat & Sun 9am–5pm; ☎828/258-6111 or 1-800/257-1300, Ⓦwww.exploreasheville.com). Central **motels** include the *Days Inn*, 120 Patton Ave (☎828/254-9661; ❸), and there's another *Days Inn* near the Asheville Mall, at 201 Tunnel Rd (☎828/252-4000, Ⓦwww.daysinnashevillemall.com; ❸). For a bit of pampering, head to the luxurious *Cedar Crest* **B&B**, set in four acres three blocks from the Biltmore Estate, at 674 Biltmore Ave (☎828/252-1389 or 1-800/252-0310, Ⓦwww.cedarcrestvictorianinn.com; ❻). The nearest **campground** is *Bear Creek RV Park*, 81 S Bear Creek Rd, off I-40 to the west (☎828/253-0798, Ⓦwww.ashevillebearcreek.com; $32).

Asheville has by far the best **places to eat** in the region, with lots of ethnic and organic food. The fabulous ⚘ *Laughing Seed Café*, 40 Wall St (☎828/252-3445; closed Tues), dishes up really good vegetarian cuisine from around the world, while tiny *Salsas*, 6 Patton Ave (☎828/252-9805), offers Mexican and Caribbean dishes. There's a lively **nightlife** scene, too; *Jack of the Wood*, an enjoyable bar at 95 Patton Ave (under the *Laughing Seed*; ☎828/252-5445), and the *Grey Eagle*, 185 Clingman Ave (☎828/232-5800), both feature regular live bluegrass, folk, and newgrass. For funk, world, jazz, and R&B, check out the *Orange Peel*, 101 Biltmore Ave (☎828/225-5851; closed Sun–Tues), or *Tressa's*, 28 Broadway (☎828/254-7072, Ⓦwww.tressas.com), a stylish club in a fine restored building. In summer, you can sit outdoors and listen to traditional mountain music at "Shindig on the Green" (Sat nights at Pack Square Park), run by the same people as

August's **Mountain Dance and Folk Festival** (Ⓦwww.folkheritage.org), which features bluegrass, newgrass, string bands, and traditional clogging.

Black Mountain and Chimney Rock

BLACK MOUNTAIN, fourteen miles east of Asheville on I-40, is home to the hugely enjoyable **Leaf Festival** (Ⓦwww.theleaf.com). This folk music and arts and crafts gathering, held in mid-May and October, showcases Appalachian and world folk music, and usually attracts major European and African musicians. There's little to do in Black Mountain otherwise, but the clear fresh air, pretty views, and relaxed pace make a visit worthwhile. The *Monte Vista*, at 308 W State St (Ⓣ828/669-2119 or 1-888/804-8438, Ⓦwww.montevistahotel.com; ④), is a small, comfy, nicely old-fashioned **hotel**; *Dripolator*, nearby at 221 W State St (Ⓣ828/669-0999), serves fantastic coffee, smoothies, and desserts. For nightlife, the *Town Pump Tavern*, 135 Cherry St (Ⓣ828/669-4808, Ⓦwww.townpumpmusic.com), has live bluegrass and roots music five nights a week.

Twenty-five miles southeast of the Parkway on US-64/74A, the natural granite tower of **Chimney Rock** sticks out from the almost-sheer side of Hickory Nut Gorge (daily: summer 8.30am–5.30pm; rest of year 8.30am–4.30pm; park stays open 90min past last ticket sale; $14; Ⓣ828/625-9611 or 1-800/277-9611, Ⓦwww.chimneyrockpark.com). After taking the elevator twenty-six stories up through the body of the mountain, you can walk along protected walkways along the impressive cliffs. Many of the climactic moments of *The Last of the Mohicans* were filmed here; you may recognize the mighty **Hickory Nut Falls**, which tumble 400ft from the western end of the gorge.

Great Smoky Mountains National Park

West of Asheville, **GREAT SMOKY MOUNTAINS NATIONAL PARK** is the most visited national park in the US. It straddles the border with Tennessee, and is covered in more detail – with a map – in our Tennessee section. In summer and fall, the North Carolina approaches to the park are every bit as clogged with traffic as those in Tennessee, and all accommodation can be booked up weeks in advance.

The largest base for touring the park is **CHEROKEE**, where a few Cherokee managed to hang on when the tribe was "removed" along the Trail of Tears to Oklahoma in 1838 (see p.578). Now known as the "Eastern Band of the Cherokee Nation," they have a small reservation on the edge of the park, which derives its main income from tourism. As a result, Cherokee itself, nicely set in the cleft of a valley, has its fair share of fast-food restaurants, cornily named motels, moccasin retailers, and themed attractions (including **Santa's Land** – star attraction, the Rudicoaster) – along with, of course, the requisite casino.

Away from the kitsch and cliché, however, the impressive **Museum of the Cherokee Indian**, Hwy-441 at Drama Rd (mid-June to Aug Mon–Sat 9am–8pm, Sun 9am–5pm; Sept to mid-June daily 9am–5pm; $9, or $18 combo with Oconaluftee, see below; Ⓦwww.cherokeemuseum.org), has good archeological and interactive displays on Cherokee arts and history – including Sequoyah's invention of a syllabary in 1821, to preserve the oral Cherokee culture in writing. Qualla Arts and Crafts, across the street, is a Cherokee-owned co-operative selling high-quality traditional **crafts** (daily: June–Aug 8am–8pm; Sept & Oct 8am–6pm; Nov–May 8am–4.30pm; Ⓣ828/497-3103). Nearby, the **Oconaluftee Indian Village** (mid-May to late Oct daily 9am–5.30pm; $14, or $18 combo with the museum, see above) is a reconstruction of a mid-eighteenth-century Cherokee village. Amid the log cabins, you can see demonstrations of weaving and basket-making, as well as crafts and skills that have long since died out, such as dugout canoe construction and blowpipe hunting. During summer, at the Mountainside Theater on Hwy-441, an outdoor drama, *Unto these Hills*, re-enacts the Cherokee plight from Hernando De Soto's arrival to the Trail of Tears (mid-June to late Aug, Mon–Sat 8pm; $15–18; ℗1-866/554-4557, ⓦwww.untothesehills.com).

The friendly **visitor center** (daily: Nov to late Aug 8am–9pm; late Aug–Oct 8am–5pm; ℗828/497-9195 or 1-800/438-1601, ⓦwww.cherokee-nc.com), in the center of town along Hwy-441 by the river, has lots of information on the National Park and the Parkway. There are several reasonable **motels** – like the central *Cherokee Plaza* (℗828/497-2301 or 1-800/535-4798; ❸–❹), which overlooks the river – but you might just as well stay in Maggie Valley (see below). You'll do fine for **eating** if you like fast food and buffets – and note that as a reservation town, Cherokee is entirely dry.

The **Oconaluftee visitor center**, the headquarters of the North Carolina side of the park, is two miles north of Cherokee on US-441 (daily: summer 8am–7pm; fall & spring 8am–6pm; winter 9am–5pm; ℗828/497-1904, ⓦwww.nps.gov/grsm). It holds good displays on Appalachian farming life, and a recreated pioneer village.

Fifteen miles east, the small community of **MAGGIE VALLEY** boasts a string of motels with peaceful views over the valleys – one of the cheapest, the *Riverlet*, on US-19 (℗828/926-1900 or 1-800/691-9952, ⓦwww.riverlet.com; ❸), commands prospects of two streams. It's all rather tranquil here, with trout farms, wooden shacks, the occasional boiled peanut and honey stand, and clear, fresh air. Tourism focuses on hillbilly culture, with lots of hoedowns and the like; the nearby **Ghost Town in the Sky** is an extraordinary piece of kitsch, with a chair-lift that sweeps you up to a hokey Wild West–style theme park complete with gunfights, cancan girls, and Indian dancers (summer daily; fall Sat & Sun only; $25, children $15; ⓦwww.ghosttowninthesky.com). During the last fortnight in July, Maggie Valley hosts North Carolina's **International Folk Festival** (ⓦwww.folkmootusa.org).

South Carolina

The relatively small state of **SOUTH CAROLINA** remains, with Mississippi, one of the poorest and most rural in the US; it holds no truly substantial urban centers, and though the pockets of prime real estate along its coast have been developed into exclusive golf courses and tennis clubs, these are self-contained enclaves that make little impression on the rest of the state. **Politics** in South Carolina, the first state to secede from the Union in 1860, have traditionally been conservative. Reconstruction was mired in terrible Klan violence, while demagogues openly espoused lynching and enforced "Jim Crow" laws with frightening zeal. Today, the state contains two of the country's most right-wing minor universities – foot-ball-fixated Clemson, and Christian Bob Jones University in Greenville, a train-ing-ground for the fundamentalist right.

For travelers, however, the state has a lot to offer. Its main fascination lies in the subtropical coastline, also called the **Low Country**, and its **sea islands**. Great beaches, swampy marshes, and lush palmetto groves preserve traces of a virtually independent black culture (featuring the unique patois, "Gullah"), dating back to when enslaved Africans escaped here from the mainland plantations. There are no interstates along the coast, so journeys take longer than you might expect, and the pace of life definitely feels slower. Beyond the grand old peninsular port of **Charleston** – arguably the most elegant town in the US, with its pastel-colored old buildings, appealing waterfront, and magnificent, tree-lined avenues – restored plantations stretch as far north as **Georgetown**, en route toward the poseur's paradise of **Myrtle Beach**. Inland, the rolling Piedmont and flat coastal plain hold little to see.

Getting around South Carolina

Charleston has South Carolina's biggest **airport**, with flights to and from major towns on the east coast. Three Amtrak routes cut through the state, stopping at Greenville and Clemson in the west, Columbia and other towns in the center, and Charleston on the coast. **Buses** run along I-85 between Charlotte, North Carolina, and Atlanta, while a less regular service operates along the coast, stopping at Myrtle Beach and Charleston.

Myrtle Beach and the north coast

MYRTLE BEACH is a brazen splurge of seaside fun, an unmitigated stretch of commercial development twenty miles down the coast from the North Carolina border, at the center of the sixty-mile "Grand Strand." Predominantly a family resort, it's packed fit to burst during mid-term vacations with leering, jeering students drinking and partying themselves into a frenzy. Fans of crazy golf, water parks, factory outlet malls, funfairs, and parasailing will be in heaven, and the **beach** itself isn't at all bad. The widest stretch is at North Myrtle Beach, a chain of small communities among which Ocean Boulevard is the center.

South of Myrtle Beach lies **Murrells Inlet**, a fishing port with lots of good seafood restaurants, and **Pawleys Island**, a secluded resort once favored by plantation owners and today retaining a far slower pace than its neighbors. Between the two on Hwy-17 is the beautifully landscaped **Brookgreen Gardens** (daily: summer 9.30am–9.30pm; rest of the year 9.30am–5pm; admission $12, valid for a week; ☎1-800/849-1931, ⓦwww.brookgreen.org), a former rice and indigo plantation with an outdoor display of American figurative sculpture, and the setting for many of Julia Peterkin's novels of Gullah life. There's also a wildlife sanctuary, where you can often see alligator and deer.

Practicalities

US- or Hwy-17 (also called Kings Highway) is Myrtle Beach's main traffic thoroughfare; the parallel Ocean Boulevard is lined with hotels and motels. Greyhound **buses** from Charleston and Wilmington come in at 511 7th Ave N. Minimal transportation in the beach areas is provided by Coastal Rapid Public Transit buses (☎843/488-0865); Great American Trolley runs a route along Ocean Boulevard from 29th Ave S to Broadway at the beach (March–Oct; ☎843/236-0337). The main **visitor center** at 1200 N Oak St (☎843/626-7444 or 1-800/356-3016, ⓦwww.myrtlebeachinfo.com) provides bus timetables, events listings, and stacks of hotel brochures.

During the summer, **accommodation** rates increase dramatically, to the point where it's hard to find a room for under $80 per night; it may be cheaper to stay in

Conway, about eleven miles to the west of US-501, where there's another visitor center at 2090 Hwy-501 E. In Myrtle Beach, the vast *Compass Cove Resort*, 2311 S Ocean Blvd (☎ 1-800/331-0934, ⊛ www.compasscove.com; ❼), features around twenty pools, plus ocean views from the more expensive tower rooms; *Serendipity Inn*, near the sea at 407 71st Ave N (☎ 843/449-5268, ⊛ www.serendipityinn. com; ❹), is an old Spanish-Mission-style motel that's been converted into a B&B, with a pretty courtyard and a nice breakfast buffet. Those commercial **campgrounds** that survive along Kings Highway in North Myrtle Beach – many have been bought up by condo developers – tend to be vast, soulless places, populated by long rows of RVs.

So long as you crave surf 'n' turf, burgers, or diner food, you'll have no problem finding somewhere to **eat**. Creative seafood (along with gourmet breakfasts, innovative lunch specials, and sea views) can be had at the classy *Sea Captain's House*, 3002 N Ocean Blvd (☎ 843/448-8082), or at a number of similar establishments in Murrells Inlet; for a Mediterranean-influenced meal in a funky, colorful atmosphere, stop by the *Collector's Café*, 7726 N Kings Hwy (☎ 843/449-9370).

As for **nightlife**, there are scores of themed bars and music venues competing for the tourist dollar. There's a *House of Blues* at Barefoot Landing, 4640 Hwy-17 (☎ 843/272-3000, ⊛ www.hob.com), which attracts top national bands. More kitschy are the glut of **country music variety shows**; the longest-running is the *Carolina Opry*, Hwy-17 N (☎ 843/913-4000, ⊛ www.thecarolinaopry.com), where powerful singers belt out corny, family-oriented rock'n'roll, country, and bluegrass, with a couple of hymns thrown in for good measure. Next door at the Dolly Parton–owned *Dixie Stampede*, 8901-B Hwy-17 N (☎ 1-800/433-4401, ⊛ www.dixiestampede.com), you can see a patriotic, surreal take on the Civil War with some impressive horsemanship, all while chowing down on a huge dinner without the aid of utensils.

South to Charleston: Georgetown and the plantations

The peaceful waterfront community of **GEORGETOWN** – the first town in forty miles beyond Myrtle Beach that's anything more than a beach resort – makes a refreshing contrast, even with the views of the monstrous paper works on the opposite bank. It's hard to imagine today, but in the eighteenth century Georgetown was the center of a thriving network of Low Country rice plantations; by the 1840s the surrounding area produced nearly half the rice grown in the United States.

Though Georgetown's main street has a time-warped, late-1950s feel, the town's 32-block **historic district** features many fine eighteenth-century and antebellum houses; the **visitor center**, 531 Front St (Mon–Sat 9am–5pm; ☎ 843/546-8436 or 1-800/777-7705, ⊛ www.georgetownchamber.com), has details of self-guided walking tours. The **Rice Museum**, in the Clock Tower at 633 Front St (Mon–Sat 10am–4.30pm; $7; ⊛ www.ricemuseum.org), tells the story of the Low Country's long history of rice cultivation, and its dependence upon a constant supply of enslaved Africans brought over from the Windward coast for their rice expertise.

One memorable way to pass the time here is to take a 2hr **sailing cruise** into Winyah Bay aboard the tall ship *Jolly Rover*, which departs from alongside 802 Front Street. The daytime trips ($20) are pirate-themed and aimed largely at children, while the sunset ones ($25) are more romantic (June to early Sept Mon–Sat 10am, 1pm, & 6pm; May and early Sept to Oct Mon–Fri 5pm, Sat 1pm & 5pm; ☎ 843/546-8822 or 1-800/705-9063, ⊛ www.rovertours.com).

If you want to **stay** in sleepy Georgetown, the *Carolinian Inn*, 706 Church St (☎ 843/546-5191 or 1-800/722-4667, ⊛ www.carolinianinn.com; ❸), which has a pool, is the best bet. There's a shortage of good places to **eat**, but at least the *Kudzu Bakery*, 120 King St (℡843/546-1847), offers light lunches and pastries.

Hopsewee Plantation, the grand 1740 mansion home of Thomas Lynch, a signatory of the Declaration of Independence, is set in Spanish-moss-draped grounds, twelve miles south of Georgetown on US-17 (March–Oct Mon–Fri 10am–4pm; Nov–Feb Thurs & Fri 10am–4pm; $12; Ⓦwww.hopsewee.com). In additon to the main house, you can also see two slave cabins, inhabited by slaves and their descendants until the 1940s. Wooded trails lead through pretty grounds, but clouds of ferocious mosquitoes drift up from the river, so think twice before wandering around in summer.

Hampton Plantation State Historic Site, further south, two miles off US-17 on Hwy-857, is probably closer to the look of a typical plantation. The grounds (9am–6pm; free) are attractive, but the house (March–Oct daily except Mon noon–4pm; Nov–Feb Thurs–Sun noon–4pm; $4) is most impressive, a huge eighteenth-century Neoclassical monolith built by Huguenots; while its exterior has been restored, the inside is relatively bare. The plantation itself is isolated in the heart of the dense **Francis Marion National Forest**. This heavily African-American area is particularly known for its sweetgrass basket-weaving, a craft that originated with the slaves in West Africa, using tight bundles of grasses to make intricate baskets and pots. Despite the enormously time-consuming work and the cost of materials, the baskets you see being made at roadside stalls here cost at most $25.

Further south, beyond the forest and a few miles north of Charleston on US-17, is the much-publicized **Boone Hall Plantation** (April to early Sept Mon–Sat 8.30am–6.30pm, Sun 1–5pm; early Sept to March Mon–Fri 9am–5pm, Sun 1–4pm; $14.50; Ⓦboonehallplantation.com). Though the plantation dates from the late seventeenth century, the house is a twentieth-century reconstruction; tours are conducted by hapless young women in Southern Belle costumes who rather overplay the connections with *Gone With the Wind*. The grounds are more interesting, with a long, tree-lined drive and a slave street, this time of small mid-eighteenth-century brick cabins that housed the more "privileged" slaves – domestic servants and skilled artisans.

Charleston

CHARLESTON, one of the finest-looking towns in the US, stands roughly halfway between Myrtle Beach to the north and Savannah, Georgia, to the south, one hundred miles from either. It's a compelling place to visit, its **historic district** lined with tall, narrow houses of peeling, multicolored stucco, adorned with wooden shutters and wide porches (known here as piazzas). The Caribbean feel is augmented by palm trees and the dreamy, tropical climate, while the town's pretty hidden gardens, leafy patios, and ironwork balconies evoke the romance of New Orleans.

Founded as a money-making venture by a group of English aristocrats in 1670, on the tip of a peninsula at the confluence of the Ashley and Cooper rivers, Charles Towne swiftly boomed as a **port** serving the rice and cotton plantations. It became the region's dominant town, a commercial and cultural center that right from the start had a mixed population, with immigrants including French, Germans, Jews, Italians, and Irish, as well as the English majority. One-third of all the nation's **enslaved Africans** passed through Charleston, sold at the market on the riverfront and bringing with them their ironworking, building, and farming skills.

The town had a sizeable **free black** community too, and its then unusual urban density allowed an anonymity and racial openness that, although still dominated by slavery, went a lot further than in the rest of the South. Nevertheless there was still slave unrest, culminating in the abortive Veysey revolt of 1823, after which the city built the Citadel armory and later the military university to control future uprisings.

Charleston was practically ruined by the **Civil War**, which started on its very doorstep, at **Fort Sumter** in the harbor. Fire swept through, destroying large chunks, in 1861, and Union bombardment was relentless; it was eventually taken by Union forces in February 1865. After the war, the decline of the plantation economy and slump in cotton prices led to an economic crash, made worse by a catastrophic earthquake in 1886. As the upcountry industrialized, capital steadily deserted the city, and it only really recovered when World War II restored its

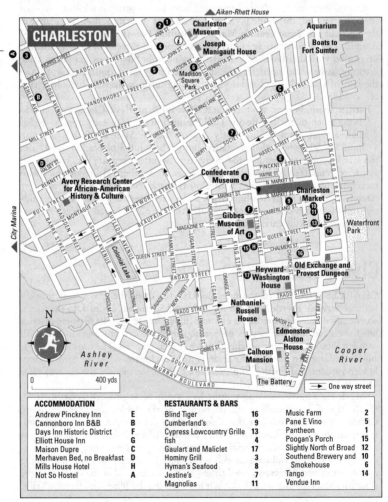

▲ Aiken-Rhett House

CHARLESTON

ACCOMMODATION		RESTAURANTS & BARS			
Andrew Pinckney Inn	E	Blind Tiger	16	Music Farm	2
Cannonboro Inn B&B	B	Cumberland's	9	Pane E Vino	5
Days Inn Historic District	F	Cypress Lowcountry Grille	13	Pantheon	1
Elliott House Inn	G	fish	4	Poogan's Porch	15
Maison Dupre	C	Gaulart and Maliclet	17	Slightly North of Broad	12
Merhaven Bed, no Breakfast	D	Hominy Grill	3	Southend Brewery and	10
Mills House Hotel	H	Hyman's Seafood	8	Smokehouse	6
Not So Hostel	A	Jestine's	7	Tango	14
		Magnolias	11	Vendue Inn	

△ Charleston's waterfront

importance as a port and naval base. Since then, a steady program of preservation and restoration has made **tourism** Charleston's main focus, based primarily on its rich Colonial history. Downtown, especially, there's a rather genteel air about the place, and prices tend to be high, whether you're looking for a room, a quick lunch, or a beer. Despite the gentrification, however, Charleston has kept its atmosphere, while maintaining all the energy and life of a real, working town. The traditions of the sea islands are a tangible presence here, too: "basket ladies" weave their sweetgrass baskets all around the market and near the post office, and many locals – black and white – speak the distinctive **Gullah** dialect.

As for the Charleston **dance** craze, the steps supposedly originated with West African slaves in South Carolina, but became popular during the Jazz Age, following the success of "The Charleston," a hit tune in James P. Johnson's Broadway smash *Runnin' Wild*.

Arrival and information

Charleston International Airport is about twelve miles north of downtown, off I-526 (ⓦ www.chs-airport.com); the airport **shuttle** (ⓣ 843/767-1100) costs $12, while a **taxi** ride with Yellow Cabs (ⓣ 843/577-6565) costs around $25. Local **public transportation** isn't bad: CARTA buses ($1.25 exact change; ⓦ www.ridecarta.com) cover most areas, including nearby beaches as well as the Amtrak station at 4565 Gaynor Ave, eight miles north of downtown (take a cab at night) and Greyhound station, in a similarly unsafe area at 3610 Dorchester Rd, out near I-26. The Downtown Area Shuttles (DASH; $1.25 exact change) comprise four useful trolley routes, three of which stop at the visitor center. You can buy **passes** that cover both buses and trolleys (day-pass $4, 3-day pass $9, 10-ride pass $10).

Charleston's huge, well-equipped **visitor center**, 375 Meeting St (daily: March–Oct 8.30am–5.30pm; Nov–Feb 8.30am–5pm; ⓣ 843/853-8000, ⓦ www.charlestoncvb.com), has discount coupons, leaflets, maps, and bus passes; they also show a short film about Charleston's history ($2). The **post office** is at 83 Broad St.

Accommodation

Though Charleston accommodation is pricey, it's worth budgeting to stay within walking distance of downtown. As well as hotels, a lot of grand Historic District houses serve as **B&Bs**, with prices starting at around $80 a night; agencies include Historic Charleston B&B, 60 Broad St (ⓣ 843/722-6606 or 1-800/743-3583, ⓦ www.historiccharlestonbedandbreakfast.com). There's also a good **hostel** not too far from downtown. Further out, the usual **motels** cluster around US-17 in West Ashley and Mount Pleasant, and along I-26 in North Charleston.

Guided tours

Charleston is ideal for **walking tours**; the visitor center has details on scores of them. For a lively, informed overview, set off from the circular fountain in Waterfront Park with **Tour Charleston LLC** (daily 10am, 2pm & 5pm; $18; ⓣ 843/723-1670, ⓦ www.tourcharleston.com). The same company offers popular **pirate tours** (10am & 4pm; $18) and **ghost tours** (5pm, 7.30pm & 9.30pm; $18). The **Civil War Walking Tour** sets out from the *Mills House Hotel*, 115 Meeting St (March–Dec daily 9am; $17; private tours available all year; ⓣ 843/722-7033). **Architectural Walking Tours of Charleston** run two 2hr tours, starting at the *Meeting Street Inn*, 173 Meeting St – the morning tour covers the eighteenth century, the afternoon tour the nineteenth (Mon & Wed–Sat 10am & 2pm; $20; ⓣ 843/893-2327 or 1-800/931-7761, ⓦ www.architecturalwalkingtoursofcharleston.com). In fall, the **Preservation Society**, 147 King St (ⓣ 843/722-4630), organizes candlelit tours of the Historic District, visiting a few private old homes (Sept & Oct Thurs–Sat 7–10pm; $45; ⓦ www.preservationsociety.org).

There are two good **black history tours**. **Al Miller**'s van tours include material on slave uprisings, the Civil War, and the lives of the freed slaves; they leave from the visitor center (1hr/2hr; $10/15; ⓣ 843/762-0051, ⓦ www.sitesandinsightstours.com). **Gullah Tours**, which depart from Gallery Chuma, 43 John St, diagonally across from the visitor center, include folktales told in Gullah and a meeting with renowned local ironworker Philip Simmons (Mon–Fri 11am & 1pm, Sat 11am, 1pm & 3pm; $18; ⓣ 843/763-7551, ⓦ www.gullahtours.com).

Horse and carriage rides provide a lively and leisurely overview of the town, especially lovely in the cool of the early evening. Try **Old South Carriage Co**, which leaves regularly between 9am and 5pm from 14 Anston St (1hr; $20, children $8; ⓣ 843/723-9712, ⓦ www.oldsouthcarriagetours.com).

Andrew Pinckney Inn 40 Pinckney St ⓣ843/937-8800 or 1-800/505-8983, ⓦwww.andrewpinckneyinn.com. Stylish, Caribbean-style rooms in this boutique inn located beside Charleston's historic market. Continental breakfast served on the rooftop terrace overlooking the city. ⑤

Cannonboro Inn B&B 184 Ashley Ave, Cannonboro ⓣ843/723-8572 or 1-800/235-8039, ⓦwww.charleston-sc-inns.com. Fine columned house with attractive patio and garden. Six very comfortable nonsmoking rooms, delicious breakfasts, and free use of bicycles. ⑥

Days Inn Historic District 155 Meeting St ⓣ843/722-8411 or 1-866/683-8411, ⓦwww.the.daysinn.com/charleston05262. This two-storey motel makes an unlikely sight so close to the market, but its rooms are surprisingly spacious and comfortable, with attractive wrought-iron balconies, A pool and free off-street parking as well make this downtown's best bargain. ④–⑥

Elliott House Inn 78 Queen St ⓣ843/723-1855 or 1-800/729-1855, ⓦwww.elliotthouseinn.com. Built in 1861 as a residence, today the *Elliott House* holds 24 plush, antique-furnished guest rooms. Complimentary wine and afternoon tea are served in a pretty courtyard, which also has a Jacuzzi. Free bicycle use and a good continental breakfast. ⑤–⑦

Maison Dupre 317 E Bay St ⓣ843/723-8691 or 1-800/844-4667, ⓦwww.maisondupre.com. Beau-

tiful inn with 15 rooms set in a crumbling 1804 European-style building and assorted other period structures. An idyllic garden holds fountains and a wishing well. Complimentary high teas plus a good continental breakfast. ⑥–⑧

Merhaven Bed, no Breakfast 16 Halsey St, Cannonboro ⓣ843/577-3053, ⓦwww.virtualcities.com/ons/sc/z/scz6801.htm. Two simple but light and comfortable rooms, with shared bath, and, obviously, no breakfast, in a comfy family home with a little courtyard. No credit cards. ④–⑤

Mills House Hotel 115 Meeting St ⓣ843/577-2400 or 1-800/874-9600, ⓦwww.millshouse.com. Large, very elegant, and very central hotel, in business since 1853 and true to its traditions despite total renovations. Guest rooms combine period furnishings with modern comfort, while the nice lounge bar features occasional live music. ⑥–⑧

Not So Hostel 156 Spring St, Cannonboro ⓣ843/722-8383, ⓦwww.notsohostel.com. Appealing hostel in a double-porched 1850 house. Rates include Internet access, bike rental, coin laundry, and breakfast, with a free shuttle from the airport, bus, and train stations. Regular live music on a small stage in the back yard. Dorms $19 per night, with every seventh night free. There are also private double rooms, plus one that sleeps four (six more to come) and you can also camp in the yard. ①/③

The City

Charleston's **historic district** is fairly self-contained, a predominantly residential area of leaning lines, weathered colors, and exquisite hidden courtyards, bounded by Calhoun Street to the north and East Bay Street by the river. The further south of Broad you head, the posher, prettier, and more residential the streets become. The district is best taken in by strolling at your own pace – though that pace can get pretty slow in high summer, when the heat is intense. Attractive spots to pause in the shade include the swinging benches at **Waterfront Park**, a beautifully landscaped piazza with fountains and boardwalks leading out over the river, and **White Point Gardens**, by the Battery on the tip of the peninsula, where the flower-filled lawns have good views across the water and a breeze even in the sweltering summer.

Most of the city's fine **houses** are private, and can only be admired from the outside; some, however, are available for **tours**. The late nineteenth-century **Calhoun Mansion**, just up from Battery Park at 16 Meeting St, is fabulously over-the-top, with its ornate plaster and woodwork, hand-painted porcelain ballroom chandeliers, and similar extravagances (Wed–Sun 11am–5pm, closed Jan; $15). Nearby, the stately antebellum **Edmonston–Alston House** overlooks the harbor at 21 E Battery St (Tues–Sat 10am–4.30pm, Sun & Mon 1.30–4.30pm; $10); this was one of the first houses built on the Battery, in 1825, and retains its furniture from 1838. The Neoclassical **Nathaniel–Russell House**, 51 Meeting St (Mon–Sat 10am–5pm, Sun 2–5pm; ⓦwww.historiccharleston.org; $10), is noted for its daring flying staircase, which soars unsupported for three floors. Tremendously elegant both inside and out, its piazza-free design also sets it apart from the other mansions. The Charleston Museum's $21 combination ticket (see below) gets you into the 1803 **Joseph Manigault House**, a lovely Neoclassical structure which stands with its back to the museum, built by descendents of Huguenot settlers, and the 1772 **Heyward-Washington House**, at the south end of the peninsula at 87 Church St, which was built by Thomas Heyward, a rice baron and signatory of the Declaration of Independence. (George Washington stayed here for a month in 1791, thus the name.) Admission to each separately is $9 (Mon–Sat 10am–5pm, Sun 1–5pm). North of downtown at the antebellum **Aiken-Rhett House**, 48 Elizabeth St, the work-yard and slave quarters are intact, while the mansion itself retains its original decor and furnishings (Mon–Sat 10am–5pm, Sun 2–5pm; $8).

Built in 1771 as the Customs House and used as a prison during the Revolutionary War, the **Old Exchange and Provost Dungeon**, 122 E Bay St (daily 9am–5pm; $7), is a hugely significant Colonial structure. Today the upper floors are given over to learned exhibits detailing the history of the building and the city; the tone changes in the dank dungeon down below, where groups of spotlit animatronic dummies recount tales of revolutionaries, gentlemen pirates, and all manner of derring-do.

Charleston's **market area** runs from Meeting Street to East Bay Street, focusing on a long, narrow line of enclosed, low-roofed, nineteenth-century sheds, but also spilling out onto the surrounding streets. Undeniably touristy, packed with hard-headed "basket ladies," this is one of the liveliest spots in town, selling junk, spices, tacky T-shirts, jewelry, and rugs. With downtown Charleston's heavy emphasis on its Colonial history, it's easy to overlook just how central the city was to the Civil War; a visit to the **Confederate Museum**, on the market's upper level (Oct–March Tues–Sat 11am–3.30pm; April–Sept Tues–Sat 11am–4.30pm; $6) tips the balance by showing just how close to home the "Lost Cause" still feels to many old Charlestonians. A shrine to the Rebel forces, the museum's one room is packed with everything from battleship splinters to bloodstained ladies' gloves, mess tins, canteens, and tattered flags.

Far more satisfying, the vast **Charleston Museum**, opposite the visitor center at 360 Meeting St (Mon–Sat 9am–5pm, Sun 1–5pm; ⓦ www.charlestonmuseum. org; $10, $16 with the Joseph Manigault House or the Heyward-Washington House, $21 with both), is the nation's oldest, dating from 1773 (although the original building no longer stands). It's filled with a wealth of city memorabilia, with videos on subjects from rice-growing to the Huguenots, and strong sections on Native Americans, architecture, and the devastation of the Civil War. Prize exhibits include the table on which the secession of South Carolina was signed in 1860, a giant fossil crocodile, and the *Pioneer*, the first Confederate submarine, built in New Orleans in 1862. One room holds choice items from the museum's early collections; pickled snakes share space with Egyptian mummies (their faces exposed) and casts from the British Museum in London.

A good source for black history is the **Avery Research Center for African-American History and Culture**, based in what was once a prestigious African-American private school, west of the market at 125 Bull St (tours Mon–Fri 2–4pm, Sat noon–5pm; donation; ⓦ www.cofc.edu/avery). Focused on an archive of personal papers, photographs, oral histories, and art, the center also shows periodic films, lectures, and exhibitions.

The high-quality **Gibbes Museum of Art**, a couple of blocks south of the market at 135 Meeting St (Tues–Sat 10am–5pm, Sun 1–5pm; ⓦ www.gibbesmuseum. org; $9), places a strong emphasis on Charleston itself, providing a quick history of the city through art, but it also hosts interesting traveling exhibitions in the upstairs galleries.

At the end of Calhoun Street, overlooking the harbor, you'll find Charleston's hugely popular **Aquarium** (mid-Aug to end March Mon–Sat 9am–5pm, Sun

△ Charleston, SC

noon–5pm; April to mid-Aug Mon–Sat 9am–6pm, Sun noon–6pm; last ticket sold 1hr before closing; $15, plus IMAX $22.50, plus Fort Sumter (see below) $26.50, plus IMAX and Fort Sumter $34.50; ⓦ www.scaquarium.org). It's a well-designed space, with a 40ft-deep tank at the core and open, eye-level exhibits recreating North Carolina's various watery habitats – including the Piedmont, swamps, salt marshes, and ocean – and their indigenous aquatic plant and animal life. As well as thousands of sea creatures you'll also find gators, snakes, and turtles, soaring birds, and frolicking otters. The porch-like terrace, with giant rocking chairs, is a nice place to catch the river breezes; watch out for schools of dolphins playing in the water below.

Fort Sumter National Monument

The first shots of the Civil War were fired on April 12, 1861, at **Fort Sumter**, a redoubtable federal garrison that entirely occupied a small artificial island at the entrance to Charleston Harbor. After secession, the federal government had to decide whether to reprovision its forts in the south. When a relief expedition was sent to Fort Sumter, Confederate General Pierre Beauregard demanded its surrender. In one of the ironies that so characterized the war, Beauregard, who personally coordinated the bombardment, had attended artillery classes taught by the fort's commander, Major Robert Anderson, at West Point. After a relentless barrage, the garrison gave in the next day.

Fort Sumter can only be seen today on regular **boat tours** that leave from alongside the Aquarium at the eastern end of Calhoun Street (daily: March–Nov 9.30am, noon & 2.30pm; Dec–Feb 11am & 2.30pm; $14; for combined tickets with the aquarium, see opposite; ⓣ843/881-7337 or 1-800/789-3678, ⓦwww.fortsumtertours.com). It takes 35 minutes for boats to reach the island, with great views of Charleston along the way. Only one of the fort's original three stories is left standing, thanks not to the assault that started the war, but to its subsequent siege and bombardment by Union troops, who finally recaptured it on Good Friday 1865, the very day Lincoln was assassinated. A small on-site **museum** holds the flags that flew over the fort, while a more comprehensive one back at the Fort Sumter visitor center on the mainland recounts the history not only of the fort but also of Charleston, and the build-up to the conflict (daily 8.30am–5pm; free).

Eating

Historic Charleston's elegant ambiance lends itself very well to classy **New Southern cooking** served up in a variety of innovative, upbeat restaurants – prices tend to be high, but it's worth splashing out on a rather special meal. There are also plenty of ethnic restaurants, and cappuccino bars and cafés line Market and King streets.

Cypress Lowcountry Grille 167 E Bay St ☏ 843/727-0111. Exquisite Southern/Pan-Asian fusion food – raw and baked oysters, grouper with okra and herb broth, tuna sashimi – in a fashionable, soaring space. The wine list is exemplary, too. Entrees cost $22–35, but if you're going to splurge, let this be the place. Dinner only.

fish 442 King St ☏ 843/722-3474. Small, upscale, but surprisingly inexpensive seafood place a block west of the city visitor center, with black tables and exposed brickwork. The menu is simple in the extreme, with $14–18 entrees labeled as "salmon", "trout," and so on, but the modern Southern cuisine is infused with a definite Asian flavor. Closed Sat lunch & all Sun.

Gaulart and Maliclet aka *Fast and French*, 98 Broad St ☏ 843/577-9797. Disarmingly idiosyncratic French bistro, popular with locals, where you eat perched at high communal tables. While not necessarily authentic, the food is very good, ranging from cheap snacks like a $4 *croque monsieur* to $13 specials such as bouillabaisse or chicken du jour. Check out the fondue nights on Thursdays.

Hominy Grill 207 Rutledge Ave ☏ 843/937-0930. This simple, stylish neighborhood restaurant is a favorite for fabulous gourmet Low Country cooking – try the amazing brunches. Closed Sun eve.

Hyman's Seafood 213–215 Meeting St ☏ 843/723-6000. Sprawling, family-owned restaurant serving great seafood – try the she-crab soup, oysters, or flounder – in a convivial, casual setting; the fried green tomatoes are something special, too. Deli take-out available.

Jestine's 251 Meeting St ☏ 843/722-7224. Authentic black Low Country cooking, served in a plain, simple dining room in the heart of downtown. Go for the superb fried chicken or meat-and-three-veggie deals. Closed Mon.

Magnolias 185 E Bay St ☏ 843/577-7771. *Nouvelle* Southern cuisine – shrimp with grits and such – in a buzzy monochrome setting with a circular bar.

Pane E Vino 17 Warren St ☏ 843/577-2337. Friendly, lovely restaurant just off the main drag in the blossoming Upper King St neighborhood, with a large if not very scenic outdoor terrace. Officially "Mediterranean" but predominantly Italian, the food is great, with pasta specials around $12 and meat or fish entrees $16–20. Closed Sun & Mon.

Poogan's Porch 72 Queen St ☏ 843/577-2337. Delicious local food in a big old Charleston house, including Low Country Boils, crabcakes, and catfish. Very popular for Sunday brunch. Dine on the porch or on the shady patio. Closed Sun eve.

Slightly North of Broad 192 E Bay St ☏ 843/723-3424. Another smart *nouvelle* Southern restaurant – scallops with smoked sausage, blue crab salad, and the like. It's lively with downtown business folk at lunchtime (Mon–Fri only), when they offer a $10 prix-fixe menu.

Nightlife and entertainment

Charleston has lots of **music venues**, **clubs**, and **bars**. For listings, see the free weekly *City Paper* (ⓦ www.charlestoncitypaper.com). Ask at the visitor center about the city's many **festivals**: chief among them is the **Spoleto Festival** (☏ 843/722-2764, ⓦ www.spoletousa.org), an extraordinarily rich extravaganza of international arts for such a relatively small city. Inspired by its Italian namesake, the festival runs for seventeen days in May/June, alongside its funkier sibling, **Piccolo Spoleto** (☏ 843/724-7305, ⓦ www.piccolospoleto.com). October's **Moja Arts Festival** (ⓦ www.mojafestival.com) celebrates African-American and Caribbean theater, dance, and film.

Blind Tiger 38 Broad St ☏843/577-0342. Local bar with hidden entrance, busy deck, and regular live music.
Cumberland's 301 King St ☏843/577-9469, Ⓦwww.cumberlands.net. Friendly venue for indie, blues, bluegrass, rock, reggae, and folk.
Music Farm 32 Ann St ☏843/853-3276, Ⓦwww.musicfarm.com. This warehouse-like building alongside the visitor center is the best place in Charleston to see regional and national touring bands.

Pantheon 28 Ann St ☏843/577-2582. Charleston's most popular gay dance club, off King St near the visitor center. Fri–Sun only.
Southend Brewery and Smokehouse 161 E Bay St ☏843/853-4677. Charleston's best microbrewery, with a lively atmosphere and reasonable food.
Tango 39 Hutson St ☏843/577-2822. Popular multilevel dance club, open Thurs through Sat.
Vendue Inn 19 Vendue Range ☏843/845-7900. Elegant rooftop bar and restaurant with great views over the city, and live music of all kinds Sun–Wed.

Around Charleston

The **river road**, Hwy-61, leads **west** from Charleston along the Ashley River, past a series of magnificent **plantations**. Many can be visited, although in best Southern tradition, house tours tend to dwell on the furniture and dining habits of the slave masters rather than provide much sense of social history. **Drayton Hall**, closest to Charleston at 3380 Ashley River Rd (daily: March–Oct 9.30am–4pm; Nov–Feb 9.30am–3pm; Ⓦwww.draytonhall.org; $14), is a particularly elegant Georgian mansion, looking much as it did in the mid-eighteenth century, with its handcarved wood and plasterwork; there is little furniture on show, and the hourly guided tours of the house concentrate on the fine architecture. At 11.15am and 2.15pm, however, special talks, backed up by photographs and artifacts, emphasize the role of **African-Americans** in the Low Country, tracing the story of slavery and emancipation and how it related to Drayton Hall.

The nearby **Magnolia Plantation and Gardens**, ten miles from downtown Charleston, is most notable for its stunning ornamental gardens, particularly in spring when the azaleas are blooming (daily March–Oct 8am–5.30pm Nov–Feb 8.30am–5pm; $14, ticket valid for 6 days; ☏1-800/367-3517, Ⓦwww.magnoliaplantation.com). The admission price gives you access to the gardens, which include a tropical greenhouse, a petting zoo, a maze, and a wildlife observation tower, but you have to pay extra for **house tours** (daily 9.30am–4.30pm; $7). You don't have to pay the general admission charge to explore the **Audubon Swamp Garden** ($7), a preserved swamp complete with alligators and lush flowers. If you've paid general admission you can also take a "nature train" tour of the grounds, or a "nature boat" tour of the swamp; both cost $7 and last 45min.

Across the Ashley River, on Hwy-171, west of the Ashley River Bridge three miles northwest of Charleston, **Charles Towne Landing** is a 663-acre state park, located on the site where in 1670 the English colonists established the first permanent settlement in the Carolinas (daily: summer 8.30am–6pm; rest of year 8.30am–5pm; $5; shuttle buses $1). As well as the landing site itself, you can see a living history settlement, a replica of a seventeenth-century merchant ship, and a zoo, home to species the colonists would have encountered when they landed here – pumas, bison, alligators, black bears, and wolves. There are also seven miles of hiking and biking trails; you can rent bikes for $3.

East of Charleston, **beaches** such as **Isle of Palms** and **Sullivan's Island** are heavily used by locals at weekends. The further you get from town, the more likely you are to find a stretch to yourself. It's possible to get to Isle of Palms and Sullivan's Island using CARTA bus route #8 (Ⓦwww.ridecarta.com). If you want to stay, there are plenty of motels and **eating** places. On Isle of Palms, head for the *Sea Biscuit Café*, 21 J.C. Long Blvd (☏843/886-4079; closed Mon), which does great Southern breakfasts, and *Windjammer*, 1000 Ocean Blvd (☏843/886-8596), a late bar with live music at weekends. On Sullivan's Island, *Bert's*, 2209 Middle St (℡843/883-4924), is a friendly little bar and grill.

The sea islands

South of Charleston toward Savannah, the coastline dissolves into small, marshy islands. **Edisto Island**, south of US-17 on Hwy-174, is typical: huge live oaks festooned with great drapes of Spanish moss line the roads, beside bright green marshes with rich birdlife, and fine beaches on the seaward side. If you want to stay, there are no budget motels, but the **campground** at **Edisto Beach State Park** (℡843/869-2156, Ⓦwww.southcarolinaparks.com; $4 park admission) is near a great beach lined with palmetto trees and other semitropical plants. They have a few air-conditioned cabins that get reserved months in advance, and are rented by the week only in summer (❸).

The largest town in the area, **BEAUFORT** (pronounced "Byoofert"), is a little twee, though its old district is lovely – offset somewhat by racial tensions and the baleful proximity of the Parris Island US Marine Base, notorious for the brutality of its training regime. Think *The Big Chill* meets Kubrick's *Full Metal Jacket*; both movies are set here. The Greyhound **bus** station is two miles north of town on US-21. The **visitor center** at 1106 Carteret St (℡843/524-3163, Ⓦwww.beaufortsc.org) has details of tours around the historic district and discount coupons for the **motels** out on US-21. In town, the *Best Western Sea Island Inn*, near the water at 1015 Bay St (℡843/522-2090, Ⓦwww.bestwestern.com/seaislandinn; ❻), has nice rooms with an old-fashioned feel. For a luxurious **B&B**, head for the *Beaufort Inn*, 809 Port Republic St (℡843/379-4667, Ⓦwww.beaufortinn.com; ❻), which also has a superb Low Country/New American **restaurant**. Breakfast is best (try the corned-beef hash) at *Blackstone's*, 205 Scott St (℡843/524-4330); if you're after coffee and a light meal (and a good read), there's *Firehouse Books and Espresso*, 706 Craven St (℡843/522-2665). *Ollie's by the Bay*, 822 Bay St (℡843/524-2500), has river views and great oysters. In spring and fall, Beaufort's waterfront stages a series of live gospel, jazz, and bluegrass **concerts**; check with the visitor center for schedules.

St Helena Island and Hunting Island Beach

Across the bridge to the southeast of Beaufort, **ST HELENA ISLAND**, dotted with small shrimp- and oyster-fishing communities, is among the least spoiled of the eastern sea islands. The further south you go the more gorgeous the **landscape** gets: amazing Spanish moss hangs from ancient oaks, while enormous, wide views stretch out across bright marshes. Occasionally you see what looks like a fleet of ships in the middle of a field, only to realize that in fact the boats are anchored in a small salt creek, hidden by bright green marsh reeds.

This is an area of strong **black communities**, descended from slaves, who were given parcels of land when they were freed by the Union army in February 1865; they speak a dialect known as Gullah, an Afro-English patois with many West African words. The **Gullah Institute**, in the **Penn Center Historic District** off US-21 (℡843/838-2432, Ⓦwww.penncenter.com), houses the **school** started for freed slaves by Charlotte Forten, a black Massachusetts teacher, who remarked, "I have never seen children so eager to learn . . . the majority learn with wonderful rapidity. Many of the grown people are desirous of learning to read. It is wonderful how a people who have been so long crushed to the earth . . . can have so great a desire for knowledge, and such a capability for attaining it." The school was an important retreat for civil rights leaders in the 1960s, used by Dr Martin Luther

King Jr's SCLC and others. Set back from the road is a **museum** containing fascinating old pictures of black fishermen and farmers, plus weathered tools, shrimp nets, and rattlesnake skins (Mon–Sat 11am–4pm; donation). Nearby, off US-21 and nestled among the thick Spanish moss, the ruined black **Chapel of Ease**, with seashell-adorned interior walls, was built in 1742.

There are some great **places to eat** around here. *Ultimate Eating*, 859 Sea Island Parkway (☎843/838-1314), serves nourishing Low Country and Gullah-style dishes, while at 1929 Sea Island Parkway, before the bridge across to Hunting Island, the tiny *Shrimp Shack* (March–Dec Mon–Sat from 11am; ☎843/838-2962), is a wonderful fresh **seafood** joint. Don't miss the fat, juicy shrimp burgers.

St Helena's main **beach**, at **Hunting Island State Park** on the east shore (daily dawn–dusk: $4), can get crowded, but it's simply ravishing: soft white sand, wide and gently shelving, scattered with shards of pearly shells and fringed with a mature maritime forest of palmettos, palm trees, and sea oats. The water is incredibly warm. Pelicans come here to feed, particularly in the early morning, and the shrimp fleet sails past soon after; it's also a turtle-nesting site. You can **stay** near the beach in weather-beaten cabins backing onto a glassy lagoon full of jumping fat fish, although you need to stay at least a week in summer, and reserve about a year in advance (☎843/838-2011, ⓦwww.southcarolinaparks.com; ❹). There's also the larger Hunting Island **campground**: head first to the **park office**, next to a sluggish, alligator-filled pool (Mon–Fri 9am–5pm, Sat & Sun 11am–5pm).

Georgia

Away from the bright lights of its capital Atlanta, **GEORGIA**, the largest of the Southern states, is overwhelmingly rural. Its highly indented coastline holds some beaches and towns, but mostly the state is composed of slow, easygoing communities, where the best – and sometimes the only – way to enjoy your time is to sip iced tea and have a chat on the porch.

Settlement in Georgia, the thirteenth British colony (named after King George II), started in 1733 at **Savannah**, intended as a haven of Christian principles for poor Britons, with both alcohol and slavery banned. However, under pressure from planters, **slavery** was introduced in 1752, and by the time of the **Civil War** almost half the population were black slaves. Little fighting took place on Georgia soil until Sherman's troops marched in from Tennessee, burned Atlanta to the ground, and, in the infamous "March to the Sea," laid waste to all property on the way to the coast.

Today, bustling **Atlanta** stands as the unofficial capital of the South. The city where **Dr Martin Luther King Jr** was born, preached, and is buried bears little relation to *Gone With the Wind* stereotypes, and its forward-looking energy is upheld as a role model for other cities with large black populations. Atlanta's main rival as a tourist destination is the **Georgia coast**, stretching south from beautiful old **Savannah** via the **sea islands** to the semitropical **Okefenokee Swamp**, inland near Florida. In the **northeast**, the **Appalachian foothills** are particularly fetching in fall, while the college town of **Athens** has a reputation for producing offbeat rock groups such as R.E.M. and the B-52s.

Getting around Georgia
Georgia's main points of interest are easily accessible, but local transportation is poor. Amtrak **trains** from Washington, DC, to New Orleans and Florida call

at Atlanta and Savannah, respectively. **Bus** services in most areas are patchy and infrequent, though Atlanta has regular connections to the major cities, and several daily buses along the coast call at Savannah. Atlanta has the world's largest passenger **airport**, and Savannah has a reasonable service, but airfares between the two are high.

Atlanta

ATLANTA is a relatively young city. It only came into being in 1837, when an almost random dot on the map was named "Terminus" during plans for railroad construction. The Chattahoochee River here is not navigable, and the land poor for agriculture, but after the railroads arrived, the renamed Atlanta proved to be a crucial transportation center in the Civil War. Home to the huge Confederacy munitions industry, it was **burned** by Sherman's Union army in 1864, an act immortalized in *Gone With the Wind*. Recovery after the war took just a few years: Atlanta was the archetype of the aggressive, urban, industrial "New South," championed by "boosters" – newspaper owners, bankers, politicians, and city leaders. Industrial giants who based themselves here included **Coca-Cola**, source of a string of philanthropic gifts to the city. Heavy **black** immigration increased its already considerable African-American population and led to the establishment of the thriving community, centered on **Auburn Avenue**, which was to produce **Martin Luther King Jr**.

Today's Atlanta is at first glance a typical large American city, but no visitor could fail to notice its cosmopolitan, progressive feel. Ever since electing the nation's first black mayor, the late Maynard Jackson, in 1974, it has remained the most conspicuously **black-run** city in the US; further, its hosting of the 1996 **Olympics** is just the highest profile success in a sustained catalogue of entrepreneurial achievements. Tourists come to Atlanta for its vibrant arts, dining, and nightlife scenes, but the city holds plenty of must-see attractions as well, from the various sites associated with Dr King to cultural institutions like the High Museum of Art and Atlanta History Center, and from the new Georgia Aquarium to open spaces like downtown's Centennial and Piedmont parks.

The flip side of the fact that there was no great reason to put a city here is that neither are there any obvious geographical factors to prevent Atlanta from **growing** indefinitely. The population of the entire metropolitan area now exceeds four million, and urban sprawl is such a problem that each citizen is obliged to travel an average of 35 miles per day by car – the highest figure in the country. Cut off from each other by roaring freeways, and an enclave mentality, its neighborhoods tend to have distinct racial identities – broadly speaking, "white flight" was to the northern suburbs, while the southern districts are predominantly black.

Arrival and information

The colossal **Hartsfield-Jackson International Airport** (☏404/530-6600), the busiest passenger airport in the US, is ten miles south of downtown Atlanta, just inside I-285 ("the perimeter"). It marks the southern terminus of the south line of the **subway** (see p.524), a 15min ride from downtown, and is also served by the Atlanta Link **shuttle buses** (daily 7am–11pm; $16.50 to downtown; ☏404/524-3400 or 1-866/545-9633, ⓦwww.theatlantalink.com) and Checker Cab **taxis** (☏404/351-1111; $25 to downtown).

Atlanta's **Amtrak** station, 1688 Peachtree St, is at the north end of Midtown, just under a mile north of the nearest subway station, Arts Center; catch a cab or bus

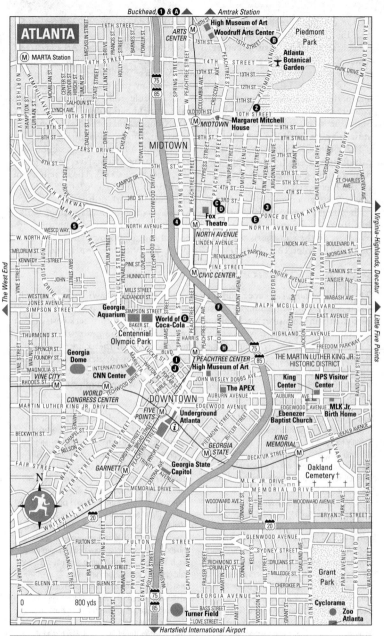

ATLANTA

Ⓜ MARTA Station

High Museum of Art
Woodruff Arts Center Ⓑ

Piedmont
Park

Atlanta
Botanical
Garden

Ⓜ

ARTS
CENTER

75th ST.

16TH STREET
15TH STREET

14TH STREET

13TH ST.

12TH ST.

11TH ST.

❷

Margaret Mitchell
House

MIDTOWN

MIDTOWN

10TH STREET

9TH ST.

8TH ST.

FERST DRIVE

CAMPUS DR.

5TH

3RD ST.

3RD ST.

NORTH AVENUE

❹

Fox
Theatre

Ⓒ

Ⓓ

Ⓔ

❸

PONCE DE LEON AVENUE

NORTH AVENUE

LINDEN AVENUE

LINDEN AVE.

RENNAISSANCE PARKWAY

PINE STREET

CIVIC CENTER

Ⓜ

ANGIER AVENUE

ANGIER AVE.

RALPH MCGILL BOULEVARD

EAST AVENUE

Ⓕ

HIGHLAND

FREEDOM PARKWAY

Georgia
Aquarium

World of
Coca-Cola
Ⓖ

Centennial
Olympic Park

Georgia
Dome

CNN Center

WORLD
CONGRESS CENTER
Ⓜ

VINE CITY

MARTIN LUTHER KING JR. DRIVE

Ⓗ

PEACHTREE CENTER
High Museum of Art

Ⓘ
Ⓙ

The APEX

AUBURN AVENUE

THE MARTIN LUTHER KING JR.
HISTORIC DISTRICT

King
Center

NPS Visitor
Center

MLK Jr.
Birth Home

Ebenezer
Baptist Church

DOWNTOWN

FIVE
POINTS
Ⓜ

Underground
Atlanta
ⓘ

GEORGIA
STATE
Ⓜ

Georgia State
Capitol

KING
MEMORIAL
Ⓜ

Oakland
Cemetery

Grant
Park

Turner Field

Cyclorama

Zoo
Atlanta

N

0   800 yds

ACCOMMODATION

Ansley Inn	**B**	Georgian Terrace Hotel	**D**
Atlanta International		Hampton Inn and Suites	**I**
Hostel	**E**	Hotel Indigo	**C**
Days Inn	**G**	Ritz-Carlton Buckhead	**A**

Sheraton	**H**
Super 8	**J**
Travelodge	**F**

RESTAURANTS

Flying Biscuit	**2**	Thelma's Kitchen	**5**
Mary Mac's Tearoom	**3**	The Varsity	**4**
R Thomas' Deluxe Grill	**1**		

#23 to connect. Greyhound **buses** arrive south of downtown at 232 Forsyth St, near the Garnett Street subway station.

Atlanta's principal **visitor center** is downtown at Pryor and Atlanta streets (Mon–Sat 10am–6pm, Sun noon–6pm; ☎404/523-2311 or 1-800/285-2682, ⊛www.atlanta.net). The adjoining **AtlanTIX** (Tues–Sat 11am–6pm, Sun noon–4pm; ☎678/318-1400, ⊛www.atlantaperforms.com) sells tickets for local events and performances, with half-price discounts available every day. Other **visitor centers** are located in the Lenox Square mall in **Buckhead** (Tues–Sat 11am–5pm, Sun noon–6pm), which also holds an AtlanTIX booth, and in the North Terminal at the **airport** (Mon–Fri 9am–9pm, Sat 9am–6pm, Sun 12.30–6pm).

The city's safe, efficient **subway** system consists of two distinct lines, one east–west and one north–south; they intersect downtown at Five Points (daily 5am–1am; single fare $1.75, Fri–Sun pass $9, weekly pass $13). The system is run by the Metropolitan Area Rapid Transit Authority (MARTA; ☎404/848-5000, ⊛www.itsmarta.com), which also operates a wide network of **buses**.

The Atlanta Preservation Center runs a varied program of ninety-minute **walking tours** of different Atlanta neighborhoods, including Sweet Auburn (with emphasis on the churches), and an architectural tour of downtown (March–Nov only, daily except Tues; $10; ☎404/688-3350, ⊛www.preserveatlanta.com).

Accommodation

The most economical **accommodation** options in **downtown** Atlanta are the chain hotels, but with so many conventioneers coming to town even these aren't particularly inexpensive; weekend rates can be better, but just to park costs at least $15 per night. **Midtown** is generally cheaper, and puts you nearer the nightlife, while **Buckhead** boasts some of the swankiest hotels in the country. If you're driving into Georgia, you can save a good deal of money by picking up **discount coupons** from state visitor centers. The B&B Atlanta agency can reserve **B&B** rooms (☎404/875-0525 or 1-800/967-3224, ⊛www.bedandbreakfastatlanta.com).

Ansley Inn 253 15th St ☎404/872-9000 or 1-800/446-5416, ⊛www.ansleyinn.com. Lovely, friendly Midtown B&B, in a century-old Tudor-style mansion near Ansley Park (and in a less character-ful extension out back), where the 22 rooms have stripped-wood floors, antique furnishings, wet bars, and whirlpool tubs. Closed for renovations at press time, but expected to reopen shortly. **⑤**

Atlanta International Hostel 223 Ponce de Leon Ave ☎404/875-9449 or 1-800/473-9449, ⊛www.hostel-atlanta.com. Around a hundred $22 beds in male, female, and mixed dorms, in a central Midtown location close to the North Ave MARTA station. Also a pool table, kitchen, and laundry room.

Cheshire Motor Inn 1865 Cheshire Bridge Rd NE at Piedmont ☎404/872-9628. Old-fashioned family-run Midtown motel that's also home to the *Colonnade* restaurant (see p.530). Good-value accommodation in an area where it's safer to drive than walk. **③**

Days Inn – Atlanta Downtown 300 Spring St NW ☎404/523-1144, ⊛www.atlantadaysinn.com. Reliable chain hotel in the heart of downtown, with a restaurant and an outdoor pool. **③**

Georgian Terrace Hotel 659 Peachtree St NE ☎404/897-1991 or 1-800/651-2316, ⊛www.thegeorgianterrace.com. Stylish century-old hotel in prime Midtown location across from the Fox Theatre. Very classy rooms and suites – some bedrooms are round, offering great views – plus fine restaurants and a rooftop pool. **⑦**

Hampton Inn and Suites Atlanta Downtown 161 Spring Street NW ☎404/589-1111 or 1-800/426-7866, ⊛hamptoninn.hilton.com. This six-story downtown chain hotel may look unspectacular, but all its rooms have been renovated to a surprisingly high standard, making it one of the best-value central options. Rates include breakfast. **⑥**

Hotel Indigo 683 Peachtree St at Ponce de Leon ☎404/874-9200, ⊛www.hotelindigo.com. Plush but well-priced "boutique hotel" near the Fox Theater in the heart of Midtown. **⑤**

Ritz-Carlton Buckhead 3434 Peachtree Rd NE ☎404/237-2700, ⊛www.ritzcarlton.com. Exquisite, elegant hotel, one of the finest in the Ritz-Carlton group, with one of Atlanta's best haute cuisine restaurants. **⑦**

Sheraton Atlanta Hotel 165 Courtland St NE
☎404/659-6500 or 1-800/833-8624, ⓦwww.
sheratonatlantahotel.com. Luxury downtown hotel
with wonderful indoor pool surrounded by foliage,
plus its own mini-shopping mall. ❻

Super 8 111 Cone St ☎404/524-7000 or 1-
800/800-8000, ⓦwww.super8atlanta.com. Very
atypical *Super 8*, housed in a converted downtown

hotel and offering bargain rates for a great spot
near Centennial Park. ❹

Travelodge Downtown 311 Courtland St NE
☎404/659-4545 or 1-800/578-7878, ⓦwww
.travelodge.com. Small, central motel, offering
standard rooms on the east side of downtown, plus
a pool. ❹

The City

Atlanta's layout is confusing, with its roads following old Native American trails rather than a logical grid. An absurd one hundred streets are named "Peachtree"; be sure to note whether you're looking for Avenue, Road, Boulevard, and so forth. The most important of the Peachtrees, **Peachtree Street**, cuts a long north–south swath through the city. Sights are scattered, but relatively easy to reach on public transportation. Most individual neighborhoods, including **downtown**, the Martin Luther King Jr Historic District (ranged along **Auburn Avenue**), and trendy **Little Five Points** and **Virginia-Highland**, are easy to explore on foot.

Downtown Atlanta

Downtown Atlanta centers on the railroad terminus for which the city was founded. During the late nineteenth century, its original core was effectively buried by the construction of railroad viaducts; businesses moved their commercial activities up to the new street level and used their former premises as cellars. Twice now, in 1969 and 1989, the city has attempted to revitalize the underground labyrinth of cobbled streets as an entertainment, shopping, and dining complex. Known as **Underground Atlanta** (or "the Underground"), it's a gimmicky mall that continues to be the liveliest part of downtown, and the one area that remains active after dark, but in truth it's once more running out of steam, and much more of a draw for local teenagers than for out-of-town visitors.

By contrast, tourists and local families alike are flocking these days to **Centennial Olympic Park**, a quarter-mile northwest of Underground Atlanta. Created when several downtown blocks were razed prior to the 1996 Olympics, and intended as a focus for public festivities during the Games, the park was immediately forced into temporary closure by the pipe-bombing that killed two revelers. Now relandscaped, it has become the city's most popular open space, and is usually thronging in summer with kids playing in the 25 water jets of its **Fountain of Rings**.

On the north side of the park, the new **Georgia Aquarium**, 225 Baker St (Mon–Fri 9am–6pm, Sat & Sun 8am–6pm; $22.75, under-13s $17; ☎404/581-4000, ⓦwww.georgiaaquarium.org), claims to be the world's largest such site. A state-of-the-art facility aimed primarily at children, it's been such a success that unless you reserve tickets in advance (for a specific time slot), you may well not be able to get in at all – and even if you do, the endless shuffling crowds may make you wish you hadn't bothered. Its five themed zones do hold some undeniably impressive exhibits, though, especially Cold Water Quest, with its five beluga whales, eerily lit century-old Japanese spider crabs, sea otters, and giant octopus.

Immediately east of the aquarium, the **World of Coca-Cola** museum has recently moved from its former home at Underground Atlanta, and had yet to reopen when this book went to press. Expect high-tech displays on Coca-Cola's history, and a chance to quench your thirst with Coke products from all over the world (see ⓦwww.woccatlanta.com for the latest details).

At Centennial Park's southwest corner, the **CNN Center** is the headquarters of Atlanta's pride and joy, the largest news broadcaster in the world. Adrenalinfueled, 55-minute guided tours (daily 9am–5pm, every 15min; $12) rush visitors past frazzled producers and toothy anchorpersons; if you're interested in how TV studios work, it's entertaining enough, but you'll learn little about how CNN defines and disseminates news.

Sweet Auburn

A mere half-mile east of downtown, **Auburn Avenue** stands as a monument to Atlanta's black history. During its heyday in the 1920s, "**Sweet Auburn**" was a prosperous, progressive area of black-owned businesses and jazz clubs, but it went into a decline with the Depression, from which, despite repeated attempts at revitalization, it has never truly recovered.

Nonetheless, several blocks have been designated as the **Martin Luther King Jr National Historic Site**, in honor of Auburn's most cherished native son. This short stretch of road is the most visited attraction in all Georgia, and it's a moving experience to watch the crowds of schoolkids listening patiently to the guided tours and waiting in turn to take photographs. Head first for the Park Service's **visitor center**, 450 Auburn Ave (daily: mid-June to mid-Aug 9am–6pm; mid-Aug to mid-June 9am–5pm; ℡ 404/331-5190, Ⓦ www.nps.gov/malu), where the "Courage To Lead" exhibition covers King's life and campaigns. If you're looking for an account of the civil rights years, the museum at Memphis is much more comprehensive (see p.558), but this provides a powerful potted summary, with alternative simplified captions for children. It culminates with the mule-drawn wagon that was used in King's funeral procession in Atlanta on April 9, 1968.

As soon as you arrive at the visitor center, register for a free half-hour tour of King's **Birth Home**, a short walk east at 501 Auburn (same hours as visitor center). The lively, anecdotal tours start from Fire Station no. 6, nearby at 39 Boulevard; as only fifteen people can visit at a time, and school groups often visit en masse, you may have to settle instead for a "virtual tour," utilizing the computers at the visitor center. The home itself is a 14-room Queen Anne-style shotgun house, restored to its prosperous 1930s appearance, and now looking smarter than its neighbors. Home to Martin until he was 12, it remained in his family until 1971.

Across from the visitor center, the **King Center**, 449 Auburn (daily 9am–5pm; Ⓦ www.thekingcenter.org), is privately run by King's family. Chiefly an educational and research facility, it also features displays of treasured artifacts such as King's Bibles and traveling case, as well as separate rooms devoted to Mahatma Gandhi and Rosa Parks. King's mortal remains, guarded by an eternal flame, are held in a plain marble **tomb**, inscribed with the words "Free at last, free at last, thank God Almighty I'm free at last," which stands in the shallow, five-tiered Reflecting Pool outside.

Next door, the **Ebenezer Baptist Church**, where King's funeral took place – and where his mother was assassinated while playing the organ in 1974 – has been converted into another museum (Mon–Sat 9am–5pm, Sun 1–5pm), staffed by volunteers eager to share their memories. It's now only used for special occasions, while its congregation has decamped to a much larger church alongside the visitor center.

Midtown

Midtown stretches from Ponce de Leon Avenue, lined with funky restaurants, to 26th Street. In recent years, it has become dominated by massive cutting-edge skyscrapers – look out for the spiky, futuristic **One Atlantic Center**, at 15th and Peachtree streets, designed by Philip Johnson and John Burgee. The wildly flamboyant Art Deco **Fox Theatre**, 660 Peachtree St, at Ponce de Leon (℡ 404/881-2100, Ⓦ www.foxtheatre.org), with its strong Moorish theme, should also not be missed. Unless you buy a ticket for one of its fairly mainstream shows, the only

Dr Martin Luther King Jr (1929–1968)

Martin Luther King Jr was born in Atlanta at 501 Auburn Avenue on January 15, 1929. The house was then home to his parents and his grandparents; both his maternal grandfather, Rev A.D. Williams, and his father, Martin Luther King Sr, served as pastor of the nearby **Ebenezer Baptist Church**. Young Martin was ordained at 19 and became co-pastor at Ebenezer with his father, but continued his studies at Crozer Theological Seminary in Pennsylvania, where he was profoundly influenced by the ideas of Mahatma Gandhi, and at Boston University.

Returning to the South, King became pastor of Dexter Avenue Baptist Church in **Montgomery**, Alabama, in 1954, where his leadership during the bus boycott a year later (see p.585) brought him to national prominence. A visit to India in 1957 further cemented his belief in non-violent resistance as the means by which racial segregation could be eradicated. He returned to Atlanta in 1960, becoming co-pastor at Ebenezer once more, but also taking on the presidency of the **Southern Christian Leadership Conference**. As such, he became the figurehead for the **civil rights** struggle, planning strategy for future campaigns, flying into each new trouble spot, and commenting to the news media on every latest development. His apotheosis in that role came in August 1963, when he addressed the **March on Washington** with his famous "I Have a Dream" speech. He was awarded the Nobel Peace Prize in 1964.

Despite King's passionate espousal of non-violence, J. Edgar Hoover's **FBI** branded him "the most dangerous and effective Negro leader in the country," and persistently attempted to discredit him over his personal life. King himself became more overtly politicized in his final years. Challenged by the stridency of Malcolm X and the radicalism of urban black youth, he came to see the deprivation and poverty of the cities of the North as affecting black and white alike, and only solvable by tackling "the triple evils of racism, extreme materialism, and militarism." In the South, he had always been able to appeal to the federal government as an (albeit often reluctant) ally; now, having declared his opposition to the war in **Vietnam**, he faced a sterner and lonelier struggle. In any event, his **Poor People's Campaign** had barely got off the ground before King was assassinated in Memphis on April 4, 1968.

way to see the theater is on an organized tour (Mon, Wed & Thurs 10am, Sat 10am & 11am; $10; ℡404/688-3353).

Three blocks north of the theater, the only ordinary brick home left on Peachtree Street, at no. 990, has survived because of its status as the **Margaret Mitchell House** (daily 9.30am–5pm; $12; ℡404/249-7015, ⊛www.gwtw.org). Mitchell and her husband were living in the small basement apartment she called "the dump" during the ten years she took to write the best-selling novel of all time, *Gone With the Wind*. Published in 1936, it took just six weeks to sell enough copies to form a tower fifty times higher than the Empire State Building; the 1939 movie version scaled further peaks of popularity. Guided tours and various exhibits tell the whole fascinating story. After a compulsory hard-sell interval in the gift store, you can then see more memorabilia in the separate but linked **movie museum** (same hours and ticket).

A little further up Peachtree, at no. 1280, the enormous **Woodruff Arts Center** is home to Atlanta's **High Museum of Art** (Tues, Wed, Fri & Sat 10am–5pm, Thurs 10am–8pm, Sun noon–5pm; $15; ℡404/773-4444, ⊛www.high.org). Celebrating its centenary in 2005, the High unveiled three new buildings, designed by Renzo Piano, around its central piazza. Now with double the exhibition space, it's a truly world-class museum, Its permanent collections include the excellent "Art and Life in Africa" displays at street level, American folk art by outsider artists like Howard Finster and Mose Tolliver, and extensive European galleries covering five centuries from Renaissance Italy to the French Impressionists. Its temporary exhibitions are quite superb too, while the museum has formed a three-year partnership, which started in late 2006, with the Louvre in Paris, that enables it to displays themed highlights from the Louvre's unparalleled treasures. The High also has a good gift shop, a peaceful little espresso bar, and a top-notch restaurant, *Table 1280*.

A few blocks east of Peachtree St, best approached via 14th St, the highlight of spacious **Piedmont Park** is the landscaped **Atlanta Botanical Garden** (daily except Mon: April–Sept 9am–7pm, Oct–March 9am–5pm; $12). In addition to holding conservatories of tropical and desert plants, the garden hosts summer-long sculpture exhibitions on its lovely lawns.

Buckhead

North of Midtown, where Peachtree meets Paces Ferry Road, the affluent, predominantly white **Buckhead** neighborhood has long been a trendy area of glitzy malls and swanky hotels. In recent years, it has acquired an unwanted reputation as "party central" and even witnessed several murders. However, the developers who are currently upgrading Buckhead yet again make no bones about adopting Los Angeles's Rodeo Drive as their role model, and the area is likely to continue as the city's premier **nightlife** and **shopping** district, becoming even more exclusive than ever.

Tucked away a short distance west of central Buckhead, the permanent exhibits at the superb **Atlanta History Center**, 130 W Paces Ferry Rd (Mon–Sat 10am–5.30pm, Sun noon–5.30pm; $15; ☎404/814-4000, ⓦ www.atlantahistorycenter.com), focus on two main aspects. One section covers Atlanta history in exhaustive detail, with fascinating old photos and movie footage; black and women's history is well-represented, though there's very little on Dr King. Several other rooms display a remarkable collection of Civil War artifacts; even if the military minutiae don't captivate you, the human stories surely will, and the whole combines to provide a clear year-by-year history of the war, albeit with a definite leaning toward the Confederate cause. You can also tour two houses in the extensive grounds: the ponderous 1920s mock-classical **Swan House**, a mansion, and the antebellum **Tullie Smith Farm** and garden.

The West End

The **West End**, Atlanta's oldest quarter, is a slightly shabby but slowly reviving district southwest of downtown. Historically a black residential area, it remains so today: a buzzy, more upbeat counterpoint to Sweet Auburn. Here, you'll find Georgia's only museum dedicated to African-American and Haitian art, the **Hammonds House**, 503 Peeples St (Tues–Fri 10am–6pm, Sat & Sun 1–5pm; $4; ⓦ www.hammondshouse.org), as well as the 1910 Beaux Arts **Herndon Home**, 587 University Place (Tues–Sat 10am–4pm; $5; ⓦ www.herndonhome.org), which was designed and lived in by Alonzo Herndon, a former slave who became a barber, founded the Atlanta Life Insurance Company (from 1920 to 1980 the nation's largest black-owned business), and went on to become the city's first black millionaire.

You can also visit the **Wren's Nest**, at 1050 R.D. Abernathy Blvd, the former home of Joel Chandler Harris, the (white) author of *Br'er Rabbit* (Tues–Sat 10am–4pm, Sun 1–4pm; $7). The house has been open to visitors since soon after Harris died in 1908, and remains much as he left it, complete with a stuffed owl given to him by President Theodore Roosevelt. A short film explains that he first heard the Uncle Remus stories from slaves, when he trained as a printer on a plantation newspaper. Occasional storytelling sessions take place in the peaceful, untamed garden.

Grant Park

A mile southeast of downtown, **Grant Park** – named for a Confederate defender of Atlanta, not the victorious Union general – is home to two neighboring attractions. A purpose-built theater houses the **Cyclorama**, a huge circular painting depicting the Civil War Battle of Atlanta, executed by a group of German and Polish artists in 1885–86. Cycloramas used to travel around the country as entertainment in the days before movies; you sit inside the circle of the painting while the whole auditorium slowly rotates. It makes an especially impressive spectacle because, in part to mask deterioration of the canvas, a 3D diorama has been constructed in front that makes it hard to see where the painting ends and the mannequins begin. An accompanying **museum** (daily 9.20am–4.30pm; $7) treats the war from the viewpoint of the average soldier, interspersing distressing statistics with photos and memorabilia.

The adjacent **Zoo Atlanta** (Mon–Fri 9.30am–5.30pm, Sat & Sun 9.30am–6.30pm; $18; Ⓦwww.zooatlanta.org) features a pair of giant pandas from Chengdu, 24 gorillas, and several orangutans, plus recreations of African rainforests and other habitats.

Little Five Points to Emory University

Northeast of Auburn Avenue, around Euclid and Moreland avenues, the youthful **Little Five Points** district is the center of Atlanta's alternative community, a tangle of thrift stores, secondhand record stores, funky restaurants, body-piercing and branding parlors, bars, and clubs. By way of contrast, just a few blocks north at 1 Copenhill Ave, on the hill where Sherman is said to have watched Atlanta burn, the **Jimmy Carter Presidential Library and Museum** (Mon–Sat 9am–4.45pm, Sun noon–4.45pm; $8; Ⓣ404/865-7100, Ⓦwww.jimmycarterlibrary.org) is devoted to the peanut farmer who rose to become Georgia state governor and the 39th president of the USA. In addition to viewing film footage and a reconstruction of his Oval Office, you can read 12-year-old Jimmy's school essay on health, in which he earnestly urges his readers to keep their teeth clean.

Northeast of here, beyond the yuppie **Virginia-Highland** restaurant district, the trek to **Emory University**'s campus is rewarded by the stylish, airy **Michael C. Carlos Museum**, 571 S Kilgo St (Tues–Sat 10am–5pm, Sun noon–5pm; $7 donation; Ⓣ404/727-4282, Ⓦcarlos.emory.edu), which has a huge collection of fine art and antiquities from all six inhabited continents. Sub-Saharan African art is unusually well represented, including Nigerian headcrests woven with snake-like tendrils; among the extraordinary pre-Columbian collection, note the Andean *Human as a Peanut*.

Stone Mountain

Half an hour's drive east of Atlanta's city center, **Stone Mountain State Park** is arrayed around the base of what's said to be the world's largest natural granite monolith, a full five miles in circumference. One face of this outcrop holds a massive **bas-relief sculpture**, measuring 90ft by 190ft, and depicting Confederates Jefferson Davis, Robert E. Lee, and Stonewall Jackson. Started in 1924 by Gutzon Borglum, who went on to carve Mount Rushmore in South Dakota, the sculpture was not completed until 1970. For most visitors, however, the carving is just one feature of what's become an all-around family destination. You can see it if you simply pay the $8 per vehicle fee to drive into the park, but paying an additional, steep fee of $22 per adult or $18 per child aged 3–11 (reduced to $13 for everyone after 4pm, and to $17 on days when not all attractions are open) entitles you to a host of other attractions and activities. These include a 30min **train ride** around the mountain; **paddlewheel** and **pedal-boat** rides on the nearby lake; two **mini-golf** courses; and the Crossroads **theme park**, which features a "4D" movie theater and various hokey countrified stalls and diners. It's also possible to **hike** up the mountain on a 45min trail, or ride a skylift to the top. The park itself is open daily 6am to midnight, while the major paying attractions vary between a maximum of 10am to 8pm in summer down to 10am to 5pm in winter. Contact ☎1-800/401-2407 or ⓦwww.stonemountainpark.com for full details.

Eating

Atlanta has scores of good **restaurants** to suit all budgets. Most of the downtown options close down fairly early and are quite upmarket, while Buckhead is even glitzier. Southern **soul food** is best around Auburn Avenue, and **vegetarians** can get plenty of choice in Little Five Points and Virginia-Highland.

Atlanta Fish Market 265 Pharr Rd NE ☎404/262-3165. Buckhead's top seafood specialist, at the sign of the giant fish, with ultra-fresh oysters and crabs; dinner can get expensive, but lunch (daily except Sun) is great value.

Buckhead Diner 3073 Piedmont Rd, at E Paces Ferry ☎404/262-3336. Glitzy postmodern diner, always packed with locals enjoying Southern food with a (frequently Asian) twist, like crab egg rolls, stuffed grits, or veal and wild mushroom meatloaf. No reservations taken, so expect a wait.

Café Sunflower 2140 Peachtree Rd ☎404/352-8859. Friendly, classy, good-value vegetarian restaurant on the southern fringes of Buckhead. Tasty stir-fried tofu and pad Thai noodles, several "mock chicken" dishes, delicious steamed dumplings, and amazing dairy-free desserts. Closed Sun.

Colonnade 1879 Cheshire Bridge Rd NE at Wellborne ☎404/874-5642. Long-established, inexpensive Southern restaurant adjoining Midtown's *Cheshire Motor Inn* (see p.524). Specializes in fried chicken made just the way it's supposed to be.

DeKalb Farmers' Market 3000 E Ponce de Leon Ave ☎404/377-6400. This enormous indoor market, 20 minutes' drive east of downtown toward Stone Mountain, is the perfect spot for a take-out lunch. Stalls sell goat stew, tofu stir-fry, and glazed duck; other goodies include fresh farm-fattened catfish and pretty blue crabs, as well as aromatic coffees from around the world.

Doc Chey's Noodle House 1424 N Highland Ave ☎404/888-0777. Plain but friendly Virginia-Highland noodle joint, serving bargain-priced Asian food that also includes rice and soup dishes. There's also a spacious patio.

Fat Matt's Rib Shack 1811 Piedmont Ave ☎404/607-1622. Atlanta's best barbecue, halfway between Midtown and Buckhead, plus live blues at 8pm nightly. It makes little difference if you choose a plateful of juicy pork or chicken, or a "sandwich"

(a slab of ribs piled on a slab of bread) – everything here is delicious.

Flying Biscuit 1001 Piedmont Ave ☎404/874-8887. Jazzed-up café/diner at a lively Midtown intersection. Soon to go national, it's currently renowned locally for its healthy/organic breakfasts in particular, and also serves medium-priced New American lunches and dinners, all with a Southern twist. A smaller location is near Little Five Points, at 1655 McLendon Ave NE (ⓣ404/687-8888).

Harvest 853 N Highland Ave NE ☎404/876-8244. Appealing, flavorful "inspired regional cuisine," such as cornbread-crusted chicken or cane sugar pork loin, served in a bright, characterful frame house in the heart of Virginia-Highland.

Kyma 3085 Piedmont Rd NE ☎404/262-0702. Extraordinarily opulent Greek restaurant in Buckhead. Serves beautifully prepared and expensive meat and fish dishes, much of it flown in daily from the Aegean. Dinner only, closed Sun.

Mary Mac's Tearoom 224 Ponce de Leon Ave ☎404/876-1800. Cute little Midtown restaurant, straight out of the 1940s, famous for its cheap traditional Southern cuisine, served for lunch and dinner daily.

Nava 3060 Peachtree Rd NW ☎404/240-1984. Spicy, pricey, and imaginative modern Southwestern food – like barbecued rabbit tostadas – plus mighty margaritas, in Buckhead. Has a great outdoor terrace and very tasteful Southwestern decor. Dinner nightly, lunch weekdays only.

R Thomas' Deluxe Grill 1812 Peachtree Rd NW ☎404/872-2942. Lively, very quirky 24hr Midtown place where all the seating is outdoors, albeit sheltered by rattan screening (the traffic is still a bit too close and noisy for some, however). The incredibly varied menu ranges from Thai stir-fries with quinoa via fish tacos to gourmet sandwiches. It's not all vegetarian, but even the chicken and steak tend to come with raw salads, and it makes a good, healthy, and cheap option.

Thelma's Kitchen 768 Marietta St NW
☏ 404/688-5855. Inexpensive downtown soul-food
institution; try the salmon and grits for breakfast,
and, of course, fried chicken for lunch. Mon–Fri
7.30am–4.30pm, Sat 8am–3pm.

The Varsity 61 North Ave NW ☏ 404/881-1706.
Vast, packed Midtown fast-food drive-in diner: a
true Fifties throwback, with chili dogs for under $2.
Open until at least 11.30pm nightly.

Nightlife

Atlanta is a place where you can have a very good time; budget for blowing some
money hopping between its bars and clubs. The main concentrations are in the
overlapping yuppie **Virginia–Highland** and punky **Little Five Points**, and the
more upmarket **Midtown**, the center of Atlanta's thriving **gay and lesbian** scene.
Buckhead can be a lot of fun if you've got bags of cash. Major venues for touring
acts include the *Tabernacle* at Centennial Park, 152 Luckie St (☏ 404/659-2022),
and the *Variety Playhouse*, 1099 Euclid Ave, in Little Five Points (☏ 404/524-7354,
ⓦ www.variety-playhouse.com). Up-to-the-minute listings can be found in the
free weekly *Creative Loafing* (ⓦ www.creativeloafing.com).

Apache Café 64 Third St ☏ 404/876-5436,
ⓦ www.apachecafe.info. This busy downtown
café serves up Latin and Caribbean favorites,
but is most loved for its ever-stimulating nightly
program of live R & B and soul artists, jazz funk
and hip-hop dance nights, and spoken-word
performances.
Blind Willie's 828 N Highland Ave NE ☏ 404/873-
2583, ⓦ www.blindwilliesblues.com. The best
blues venue in town, with appearances by major
artists, this Virginia-Highland hangout is also a
lively bar. Open Mon–Sat from 7pm.
Django Gypsy Kitchen and Saloon 495
Peachtree St ☏ 404/347-8648, ⓦ www
.djangoatlanta.com. "*The Belly*," the funky basement of this smart, contemporary restaurant at
the south end of midtown, is the nightly venue
for wildly eclectic dance parties, with music from
house to hip-hop to soca to Afro-Cuban jazz.
Closed Sun.

The Earl 488 Flat Shoals Road ☏ 404/522-3950,
ⓦ www.badearl.com. Atlanta's finest rock club, well
east of the center, just south of I-20, puts on proper
live acts – usually a headliner plus a couple of supports – pretty much every night.
Eddie's Attic 515B N McDonough St, Decatur
☏ 404/377-4976, ⓦ www.eddiesattic.com. Nightly
acoustic music, from traditional fiddlers to contemporary singer-songwriters, plus occasional stand-up
comedy.
Masquerade 695 North Ave NE ☏ 404/577-8178,
ⓦ www.masq.com. Groovy grunge/punk hangout in
a converted Midtown mall, split into rooms done up
as Heaven, Hell, and Purgatory, with a big outdoor
auditorium. Live bands Wed–Sun.
Star Community Bar 437 Moreland Ave NE
☏ 404/681-9018. Enjoyable Little Five Points
watering hole, in a former bank bursting with Elvis
memorabilia, and offering live music Wed–Sat.
Cover charge. Closed Sun.

North from Atlanta: the mountains

Some spectacular **Appalachian mountain scenery** – at its best in October, when
the leaves turn a brilliant red and gold – lies just a short drive from Atlanta. A drive
through the mountains on the secondary roads takes you through endless hairpins
and narrow passes; Hwy-348 ascends a particularly impressive pass at the White
County line, crossed at the top by the **Appalachian Trail**. Of the various towns
and villages, **Dahlonega** makes the best base; most of the rest – like **Helen**, 35
miles northeast, now a pseudo-Bavarian village – are either kitsch or downright
dull. The region does, however, abound in delightful **state parks**, several of which
offer both camping and hotel-style lodges.

Dahlonega

The attractive small town of **DAHLONEGA**, in the Appalachian foothills fifty miles northeast of Atlanta on US-19, owes its origins to the first-ever **Gold Rush** in the US. Benjamin Parks discovered gold at Auraria, six miles south, in 1828; Dahlonega was established five years later, to serve as the seat of Lumpkin County. Within another five years, enough gold had been unearthed for Dahlonega to acquire its own outpost of the US Mint, which, by the time production was terminated by the Civil War, had produced over $6 million of gold coin. The whole saga is recounted by videos and displays in the **Gold Museum**, housed in the handsome former courthouse on the main square (Mon–Sat 9am–5pm, Sun 10am–5pm; $4; ☎706/864-2257). You can also pan for gold at various small mines in the area, although you're unlikely to make your fortune. In the third week of June, the town hosts one of Appalachia's biggest annual **bluegrass** festivals, while the third weekend of October sees the **Gold Rush Days**, a real downhome hoedown, with food, crafts, clogging, and music.

Dahlonega's **visitor center** is across from the courthouse (daily 9am–5.30pm; ☎706/864-3711 or 1-800/231-5543, ⓦwww.dahlonega.org). The *Smith House*, just down from the square at 84 S Chestatee St (☎706/867-7000 or 1-800/852-9577, ⓦwww.smithhouse.com), is a classic Southern **restaurant**, serving superb all-you-can-eat meals at low prices, and also offering comfortable double **rooms** (❹).

Amicalola Falls State Park

Twenty miles west of Dahlonega on Hwy-52, **Amicalola Falls State Park** (daily 7am–10pm; $3 per vehicle; ☎706/265-4703) focuses on a dramatic multi-tiered waterfall that cascades down a steep wooded hillside. Having driven to the overlook at the top, continue for another half-mile to reach the park's modern **lodge** (☎706/265-8888 or 1-800/573-9656, ⓦwww.amicalolafalls.com; ❹), which holds comfortable double rooms and a restaurant with panoramic views. For even more seclusion, hike for five miles from here toward the start of the **Appalachian Trail**, to reach the irresistible *Len Foote Hike Inn* (☎770/389-7275 or 1-800/864-7275, ⓦwww.hike-inn.com; ❻), accessible only on foot, which offers basic rooms, with two bunk beds in each, and serves breakfast and dinner family-style, included in the overnight rates.

Athens

The small and very likeable city of **ATHENS**, almost seventy miles east of Atlanta, is home to the 30,000-plus students of the University of Georgia, and has a liberal feel – and city government – that's unusual for the South. Its compact downtown area north of the campus is alive with book and record stores, clubs, bars, restaurants, and cafés; **Broad Street** in particular is lined with sidewalk tables.

Although Athens may hold little in terms of conventional tourist attractions, it has become internationally famed as the home of rock groups such as R.E.M., Widespread Panic, and the B-52s. R.E.M. started out playing at the *40 Watt Club*, originally housed at 171 College Ave, but repeatedly relocated until it found its sixth, and largest, premises in 1990 at 285 W Washington St (☎706/549-7871, ⓦwww.40watt.com), where it continues to host an eclectic program of gigs. The biggest music names tend to appear at the *Georgia Theatre*, 215 N Lumpkin St (☎706/549-9918, ⓦwww.georgiatheatre.com), a converted movie theater that still shows films on quiet nights, while up-and-coming bands can be heard at the *Caledonia Lounge*, 256 W Clayton St (☎706/549-5577, ⓦwww.caledonialounge.com). The free weekly *Flagpole* (ⓦwww.flagpole.com) carries full **music listings**.

Practicalities

From Atlanta, Greyhound arrives at 220 W Broad St; the Athens Transit System operates **buses** around town (every 30min; $1.25¢ flat fare). The **visitor center** is situated in the city's oldest surviving home, the 1820 Church-Waddel-Brumby House, a couple of blocks north of campus at 280 E Dougherty St (summer Mon–Sat 10am–6pm, Sun noon–6pm, otherwise Mon–Sat 10am–5pm, Sun 2–5pm; ☏706/353-1820, ⊛www.visitathensga.com). They can provide excellent self-guided **walking tours** on local music history and other themes (also available online), while a good 90min bus tour of historic Athens leaves daily at 2pm ($15; ☏706/208-8687).

Lodging can be a problem during graduation or when there's a big football game. Otherwise, choices include the good-value, business-oriented *Courtyard by Marriott*, 166 Finley St (☏706/369-7000 or 1-800/321-2211, ⊛www.marriott.com/ahncy; ❹); the new *Holiday Inn Express*, 513 W Broad St (☏706/546-8122, ⊛www.hi-athens.com; ❹); or the eight-room *Magnolia Terrace* B&B, 277 Hill St (☏706/548-3860, ⊛www.bbonline.com/ga/magnoliaterrace; ❹).

As for **food**, R.E.M. devotees will want to head straight for the original home of their **Automatic for the People** album title – *Weaver D's* soul-food café, a short walk east of downtown at 1016 E Broad St (lunch only; ☏706/353-7797), which serves delicious fried chicken and vegetables. The *Grit*, similarly close to downtown on the northwest side, at 199 Prince Ave (☏706/543-6592), offers tasty, inexpensive vegetarian dishes from around the world, while the *Five and Ten*, 1653 S Lumpkin St (☏706/546-7300), is a much fancier option offering a delicious contemporary take on Southern cuisine. Athens has a thriving **bar** scene, although Georgia's blue laws require drinks-only bars to close on Sundays.

Central Georgia

South of Atlanta, the broad expanse of **central Georgia** is famous more for its people than for places to see. **Otis Redding**, **James Brown**, **Little Richard**, and the **Allman Brothers** were all born here or grew up in the area, while former president **Jimmy Carter** came from little Plains, roughly 120 miles due south of the capital.

Few of the small towns hold much interest, though vegetable fanatics may enjoy tiny **Juliette**, twenty miles north of Macon, where the *Whistle Stop Café* dishes up the fried green tomatoes of book and movie fame (☏478/992-8886; Tues & Sun 11am–4pm, Wed–Sat 11am–7pm), and **Vidalia** further east, the "Sweet Onion Capital of the World." The largest communities are Columbus, a dull army center, and likeable **Macon**.

Macon

MACON, eighty miles southeast of Atlanta on I-75, where I-16 branches off to the coast, makes an attractive stop en route to Savannah, especially when its 280,000 **cherry trees** erupt with frothy blossoms (celebrated by a festival in the third week of March). As the highest navigable point on the **Ocmulgee River**, Macon was laid out in 1823 and became a major cotton port. These days, and particularly since the Colonial Mall Macon appeared near the intersection of the two freeways, downtown is not the commercial center it once was.

Macon was home to **Little Richard**, **Otis Redding**, and the **Allman Brothers**, while **James Brown** recorded his first smash, the epoch-making "Please Please Please," in an unlikely-looking mansion at 830 Mulberry St. Otis is commemorated by a bronze statue next to the unremarkable Otis Redding Memorial Bridge, just east of downtown, while his daughter Karla still runs an upscale shoe store downtown. Duane Allman and Berry Oakley, killed here in motorcycle smashes in 1971 and 1972, respectively, are buried in **Rose Hill Cemetery** on Riverside Drive, the inspiration for several of the band's songs. That heritage is celebrated in the exuberant **Georgia Music Hall of Fame**, next door to the visitor center (see below) at Martin Luther King Jr Blvd and Walnut St (Mon–Sat 9am–5pm, Sun 1–5pm; $8; ☎478/751-3334, ⓦwww.gamusichall.com). A huge roster of Georgia musicians are recalled by such displays as a gospel chapel, a rock'n'roll soda shop, and a country café. As well as admiring Redding's trademark black sweater and the B-52s' wigs, you can watch Ray Charles singing "Georgia on My Mind" to the state legislature, and inspect a photo of James Brown confiding to Pope John Paul II that he feels like a sex machine.

Ocmulgee National Monument

Between 900 and 1100 AD, a Native American group migrated from the Mississippi Valley to a spot overlooking the Ocmulgee River a couple of miles east of modern downtown Macon, where they leveled the site that is now **Ocmulgee National Monument** (daily 9am–5pm; free; ⓦwww.nps.gov/ocmu). Their settlement of thatched huts has vanished, though two grassy mounds, each thought to have been topped by a temple, still rise prominently from the plateau. Near the visitor center, you can enter the underground chamber of a ceremonial **earthlodge**, the clay floor of which holds a ring of individually molded seats, and a striking bird-shaped altar.

Practicalities

Macon's **visitor center**, in the imposing Terminal Station at the foot of Cherry Street (Mon–Sat 9am–5.30pm; ☎478/743-3401 or 1-800/768-3401, ⓦwww.maconga.org), is also the base for guided **trolley tours** and visits to the major attractions ($15).

Greyhound pulls into town at 65 Spring St, where Little Richard is said to have written "Tutti Frutti" while washing dishes. The best **accommodation** is downtown: for old-fashioned Southern hospitality, head for the grand *1842 Inn*, 353 College St (☎478/741-1842 or 1-877/452-6599, ⓦwww.the1842inn.com; ⓺), which offers a full Southern breakfast in its lovely courtyard. Otherwise, *Scottish Inns*, 1044 Riverside Drive (☎478/746-3561; ⓶), is the best budget option.

As for **food**, the atmospheric, wood-paneled *Len Berg's*, 240 Old Post Office Alley, off Walnut St (open for lunch only, Mon–Sat; ☎478/742-9255), has been serving downhome Southern lunches at bargain prices for almost a century. *Bert's*, downtown at 442 Cherry St (☎478/742-9100; closed Sun), is a nice little place where the food ranges from cheap Greek feta burgers at lunch to pricey wasabi tuna at dinner. For a true Southern **barbecue** experience, drive 45min north of town on US-23 to ⓚ *Fresh Air Barbecue*, near Jackson (☎478/775-3182); it's a roadside shack serving pork that's been hickory-smoked for 24 hours, along with succulent Brunswick stew and crisp coleslaw.

Savannah

American towns don't come much more beautiful than **SAVANNAH**, seventeen miles up the Savannah River from the ocean, and twenty miles south of the South Carolina state line. The ravishing **historic district**, ranged around Spanish-moss-

SAVANNAH

Savannah River

Riverboat
Cruises

RIVERFRONT
PLAZA

RIVER STREET

River Street

Tybee Island

WILLIAMSON ST.
FACTORS WALK

W. BAY ST.   City
Hall

E. BAY ST.

First African
Baptist Church

W. BRYAN ST.

E. BRYAN ST.

FRANKLIN   CITY MARKET
SQUARE

JOHNSON
SQUARE

REYNOLDS
SQUARE

WARREN
SQUARE

WASHINGTON
SQUARE

W. CONGRESS ST.

E. CONGRESS ST.

W. BROUGHTON ST.

E. BROUGHTON ST.

Owens-Thomas
House

Davenport
House

W. STATE ST.

E. STATE ST.

TELFAIR
SQUARE

WRIGHT
SQUARE

OGLETHORPE
SQUARE

COLUMBIA
SQUARE

GREENE
SQUARE

W. YORK ST.

E. YORK ST.

County
Courthouse

Telfair
Museum of Art

Second African
Baptist Church

W. OGLETHORPE AVE.

E. OGLETHORPE AVE.

W. OGLETHORPE AVE.

E. OGLETHORPE AVE.

Civic Center

W. HULL ST.

E. HULL ST.

ORLEANS
SQUARE

CHIPPEWA
SQUARE

CRAWFORD
SQUARE

W. PERRY ST.

E. PERRY ST.

E. PERRY ST.

Colonial Park
Cemetery

W. LIBERTY ST.

E. LIBERTY ST.

W. LIBERTY ST.

E. LIBERTY ST.

LOUISVILLE ST.

N

W. HARRIS ST.

Green-Meldrim
House

E. HARRIS ST.

PULASKI
SQUARE

MADISON
SQUARE

LAFAYETTE
SQUARE

TROUP
SQUARE

W. CHARLTON ST.

E. CHARLTON ST.

W. JONES ST.

E. JONES ST.

W. TAYLOR ST.

E. TAYLOR ST.

Civil Rights
Museum

CHATHAM
SQUARE

MONTEREY
SQUARE

CALHOUN
SQUARE

WHITEFIELD
SQUARE

W. GORDON ST.

E. GORDON ST.

W. GASTON ST.

Massie Heritage
Interpretation
Center

E. GASTON ST.

King-Tisdell
Cottage

W. HUNTINGDON ST.

E. HUNTINGDON ST.

Forsyth Park

0   250 yds

W. HALL ST.

E. HALL ST.

Macon

THE SOUTH | Savannah

ACCOMMODATION		
17 Hundred 90	C	
Azalea Inn	G	
Bed and Breakfast Inn	E	
Days Inn	A	
Hamilton-Turner Inn	D	
Magnolia Place	F	
The Mulberry	B	
Savannah Pensione	H	

RESTAURANTS & BARS		
Bistro Savannah	6	
Cha Bella	11	
Club One	1	
Gallery Espresso	12	
Garibaldi	5	
Gryphon	13	
Jazz'd Tapas Bar	9	
The Jinx	8	
Lady and Sons	4	
Leopold's Ice Cream	10	
Mercury Lounge	7	
Moon River Brewing Co.	2	
Mrs Wilkes' Boarding House	14	
The Olde Pink House	3	

swathed garden squares, formed the core of the original city, and today boasts examples of just about every architectural style of the eighteenth and nineteenth centuries. The atmospheric cobbled **waterfront** on the Savannah River, key to the postwar economy, is edged by towering old cotton warehouses.

Savannah was founded by **James Oglethorpe** in 1733 as the first settlement of the new British colony of Georgia. His intention was to establish a haven for debtors, with no Catholics, lawyers, or hard liquor – and, above all, no slaves. However, with the arrival of North Carolina settlers in the 1750s, plantation agriculture, based on slave labor, took off. The town became a major export center, at

535

the end of important railroad lines by which **cotton** was funneled from far away in the South. General Sherman arrived here in December 1864 at the end of his "March to the Sea"; he offered the town to Abraham Lincoln as a Christmas gift, but at Lincoln's urging left it intact and set to work apportioning land to freed slaves. This was the first recognition of the need for "reconstruction," though such concrete economic provision for slaves was rarely to occur again.

After the Civil War, the plantations floundered; cotton prices slumped, and Savannah went into decline. There was little industry beyond the port, and as that fell into disuse and decay, so too did Savannah's graceful townhouses and tree-lined boulevards. Not until the 1960s did local citizens start to organize what has been, on the whole, the successful restoration of their town. In the last two decades, the private **Savannah College of Art and Design** (SCAD) has injected Savannah with even more vitality, attracting a population of lively young artists and regenerating downtown even further by buying up a number of wonderful old buildings.

Savannah acquired notoriety in the mid-1990s thanks to its starring role in John Berendt's best-selling *Midnight in the Garden of Good and Evil*; both book and movie detailed a delicious brew of cross-dressing, voodoo, and murder. For a sense of what goes on behind closed doors in the city, it's an unbeatable read. If you want to look behind those doors yourself, however, few locations in "The Book" – as it's universally known – are open to the public, and none is likely to satisfy your curiosity.

Arrival, information, and getting around

Savannah's **airport** is eight miles west of the city; from there, a taxi to downtown costs around $25. The **bus station** is on the western edge of downtown at 610 W Oglethorpe Ave, while the **train station** is about three miles southwest, at 2611 Seaboard Coastline Drive. The latter isn't served by buses; a taxi from the station to downtown usually costs about $10.

The historic district is best explored on foot, but if you want to get further out, Chatham Area Transit (CAT; ⓦ www.catchacat.org) operates the free **CAT Shuttle** service, running between downtown, the visitor center, the waterfront, and the City Market, and also a reasonable **bus** network ($1). Route maps are available from the **visitor center**, 301 Martin Luther King Jr Blvd (Mon–Fri 8.30am–5pm; Sat & Sun 9am–5pm; ⓣ912/944-0455 or 1-877/728-2662, ⓦ www.savannahvisit .com), along with direct phones to various hotels and tour companies. The center also sells $8 passes that entitle visitors to unlimited **parking** at certain city meters and garages for two days. There's another small tourist information office at River Street on the waterfront (daily 10am–10pm).

The main visitor center can provide details of countless **walking tours**, many of them ghost-themed, and serves as the starting point for several different **trolley tours**, costing from around $20. The best **black heritage tour** is run by Johnnie Brown ($20; ⓣ912/398-2785). You can also join leisurely **horse-and-carriage tours**, which set off from Reynolds and Madison squares every 20 to 30min (from $20; ⓣ912/443-9333, ⓦ www.savannahcarriage.com), or **riverboat cruises**, starting behind City Hall (from $18; ⓣ912/232-6404 or 1-800/786-6404, ⓦ www.savannahriverboat.com).

Accommodation

Ideally, the best place to stay in Savannah is the **historic district**, which is packed with gorgeous **B&Bs** (and a few nice hotels). For those on a tight budget, the usual chain **motels** can be found near the Greyhound station and further out on

Ogeechee Road (US-17). The nearest **campground** is six miles southeast, at Skidaway Island State Park (from $20; ☎1-800/864-7275).

17 Hundred 90 307 E President St ☎912/236-7122, ⊛www.17hundred90.com. The oldest inn in town, said to be haunted, with an atmospheric bar and elegant restaurant. Rooms are small, but many come with original brick fireplaces. ➏

Azalea Inn 217 E Huntingdon St ☎912/236-2707 or 1-800/582-3823, ⊛www.azaleainn.com. Charming, friendly B&B, with ten bright, delightfully furnished en-suite rooms and a very welcome pool in the garden. Superb Southern breakfasts are served daily, formal dinners much more occasionally. ➏

Bed and Breakfast Inn 117 W Gordon St ☎1-888/238-0518, ⊛www.savannahbnb.com. Great-value B&B, in two 1853 townhouses overlooking shady Chatham Square – reservations are essential. ➍

Days Inn 201 W Bay St ☎912/236-4440, ⊛www.daysinn.com. Though it lacks the character of the B&Bs, this makes for an affordable, central choice. ➍

Hamilton-Turner Inn 330 Abercorn St ☎912/233-1833 or 1-888/448-8849, ⊛www.hamilton-turnerinn.com. Opulent, 1873 French

Second Empire–style B&B with 17 rooms on Lafayette Square; once owned by "Mandy" from "The Book." ➐

Magnolia Place 503 Whitaker St ☎912/236-7674 or 1-800/238-7674, ⊛www.magnoliaplaceinn.com. Exquisite B&B in a fine old building overlooking leafy Forsyth Park; friendly staff, huge rooms, afternoon teas, and gourmet breakfasts served in the pretty patio, on the vast porch, or in the comfortable lounge. ➐

The Mulberry 601 E Bay St ☎912/238-1200 or 1-877/468-1200, ⊛www.savannahhotel.com. Friendly *Holiday Inn*–owned hotel with a B&B feel (free iced tea and cookies in the lounge). Rooftop Jacuzzi, pool, courtyard, and luxurious riverview rooms. ➏

Savannah Pensione 304 E Hall St ☎912/236-7744. This former hostel, housed in a historic Victorian District building, no longer offers individual dorm beds. Instead the same basic rooms are rented at very inexpensive rates – meaning it's still the cheapest option for friends or couples traveling together. ➋

The Town

Savannah's **historic district** is flanked by the river to the north, Martin Luther King Jr Boulevard to the west, and Broad Street – which has long been replaced by Broughton Street as downtown's main commercial thoroughfare – to the east. You can get an overview at the **Savannah History Museum**, adjoining the visitor center in the restored Railroad Station at 303 Martin Luther King Jr Blvd (Mon–Fri 8.30am–5pm, Sat & Sun 9am–5pm; $4.25), where an informative jaunt through Native American culture, colonial development, the river, and the Civil War is let down slightly by a slide show that is less a history lesson than a hard-sell promotion of Savannah's considerable charms.

The best way to get a feel for the place is simply to wander its "tabby" streets, paved with a kind of primitive concrete mashed up with oyster shells. They're lined with shuttered Federal, Regency, and antebellum houses, embellished with intricate iron balconies and intriguing details such as false "earthquake decorations." The lush subtropical **greenery** is as stunning as the buildings, creeping its way through the ornate railings, cracking open the sidewalk, casting cool shadows, and filling the air with its warm, sensual scent. More than twenty shady residential **garden squares**, ablaze with Spanish-moss-tangled dogwood trees, azaleas, and creamy magnolias, offer peaceful respite from the blistering summer heat. Each one has its own personality and its own monument in the center. Forrest Gump told his life story from a bench in **Chippewa Square**, but eager movie-buffs will find the bench long gone, and just an imposing statue of James Oglethorpe to admire instead.

In between strolling and sitting, most visitors take in one or two of Savannah's old **mansions**, such as the first restoration project of the Historic Savannah Foundation, the Georgian **Davenport House**, at 324 E State St (Mon–Sat 10am–4pm,

Sun 1–4pm; $7; ⓦ www.davensportsavga.com), which boasts a wonderful elliptical staircase and delicate plasterwork. The **Green–Meldrim House**, on Madison Square (Thurs & Fri 10am–4pm, Sat 10am–1pm; $5), is a splendid Gothic Revival mansion that General Sherman used as his headquarters. Its dramatic ironwork is a rare example of pre-Civil War craftsmanship; most iron in Savannah was melted down during the Civil War, and many of the balconies and railings you see today are later copies.

A Regency mansion designed by English architect William Jay on Telfair Square forms the original core of the **Telfair Museum of Art**, 121 Barnard St (Mon noon–5pm, Tues–Sat 10am–5pm, Sun 1–5pm; $9; ⓦ www.telfair.org). The South's oldest art museum, its best-known piece is Sylvia Shaw Judson's *Bird Girl* sculpture, as seen on the cover of "The Book," which was moved here from Bonaventure Cemetery (see opposite). In 2006 the Telfair's spectacular **Jepson Center for the Arts** (same hours; $9, or $14 with museum) opened, its dramatic marble and glass facade making a controversial addition to the neighboring York St side of Telfair Square. The center is intended to host changing exhibitions that showcase the work of Southern and Savannah-based artists, but so far its early displays have focused as much on trumpeting the virtues of the building itself; further, the admission fee is steep for what little there is to see. Kids, however, will love the high-tech gadgetry of the second-floor ArtZeum. Another Jay edifice, the elegant **Owens–Thomas House** at 124 Abercorn St – designed when Jay was just 24 – forms a third component of the Telfair organization (same hours; $9, $18 to visit all three).

At the southern edge of the Historic District, on Calhoun Square, the **Massie Heritage Interpretation Center**, 207 E Gordon St (Mon–Fri 9am–4pm; $3), is housed in Savannah's first public elementary school. A simple, effective museum, it illuminates the city's architecture with displays on its neighborhoods and development, and traces influences from as far away as London and Egypt.

Though the city squares may be redolent of the Old South, Savannah's **waterfront**, at the foot of a steep little bluff below Bay Street, and reached by assorted stone staircases and atmospheric alleyways, resembles more an eighteenth-century European port. The main thoroughfare, **River Street**, is cobbled with the ballast carried by long-vanished sailing ships, while its tall brick cotton warehouses are said to be haunted by the ghosts of the slave stevedores. It's now a touristy commercial district, lined with seafood restaurants and salty bars that heave with partying crowds on Saturday nights. Looking out over the water from the paved **Riverfront Plaza**, across the way, you can appreciate just how busy the port still is.

Two blocks upriver from the visitor center, at 460 Martin Luther King Jr Blvd, the uncompromising **Ralph Martin Gilbert Civil Rights Museum** (Mon–Sat 9am–5pm; $4) explores Savannah's significant role in **black history**. With a sustained program of mass meetings, lunch-counter sit-ins, dangerous "wade-ins" at whites-only Tybee Island beaches, and a fifteen-month boycott of local department store Levy's – the longest-running store boycott in the history of the movement – Savannah was very active in the campaigns of the 1960s; by 1964, Dr King called it "the most integrated city south of the Mason-Dixon Line." The local emphasis is consistently fascinating, and the testimony of a vanishing generation of activists compelling: "No one gave us anything ... we had to fight, and wrench it from the jaws of injustice."

African-American history is also recalled at the 1775 **First African Baptist Church**, in the Historic District at 23 Montgomery St (Mon–Fri 10am–3.30pm). This is the oldest black church in North America, built by slaves. Note the tribal carvings on the sides of the pews upstairs, and, downstairs, the diamond shapes made by holes in the floor – ventilation holes for slaves hiding in the 4ft subterranean crawl spaces while waiting to escape to safe havens via the Underground Railroad. At the **Second African Baptist Church**, 123 Houston St, General Sherman read the Emancipation Proclamation in December 1864, and issued the famous **Field Order #15**, which granted each freed slave forty acres and a mule.

Southeast of downtown, the predominantly black **Victorian District** is being slowly restored, and has a couple of good, if underfunded, museums. The nerve center of the restoration process is the **King-Tisdell Cottage**, 514 E Huntingdon St (Tues–Sat noon–4.30pm; $4; ⓦwww.kingtisdell.org), owned by a middle-class black family at the end of the nineteenth century. In addition to a fine collection of Gullah baskets and African woodcarving, it illustrates the history of slaves and free blacks before the Civil War, and of the freed slaves after. The airy **Beach Institute**, 502 E Harris St (Tues–Sat noon–5pm; $4), Georgia's first school for freed slaves, today houses an African-American art gallery with a permanent display of extraordinary woodcarvings by folk artist Ulysses Davis.

A ten-minute drive east from Savannah will take you to the lovely **Bonaventure Cemetery**, swathed in trees and sloping down to the Wilmington River. The final resting place of local luminaries such as Johnny Mercer and Conrad Aiken, it's also a major sight in *Midnight in the Garden*, in which it's written about to great effect.

Eating

Savannah has lots of **restaurants**. With very few exceptions, most places on the **waterfront** are eminently avoidable. Far better to head for the **City Market** – four blocks of restored grain warehouses just a few blocks back from the river – which is downtown's prime restaurant and nightlife district.

Bistro Savannah 309 W Congress St ☏912/233-6266. A City Market favorite, with lovely decor – cherry-red walls, fairy lights – and a sophisticated menu of excellent seafood and organic specials. Try the succulent grilled flounder. Dinner only, nightly.

Cha Bella 102 E Broad St ☏912/790-7888. Jazzy, very contemporary Italian restaurant at the eastern edge of downtown, serving high-quality, modern Mediterranean cuisine with a strong commitment to organic ingredients.
Gallery Espresso 234 Bull St ☏912/233-5348.

△ Savannah, GA

Artsy coffee bar with nice cakes, crumpets, and muffins, along with the best coffee in town (try the Iced Thai) and wine. Open late.

Garibaldi 315 W Congress St ☎912/232-7118. This atmospheric City Market restaurant, all gold mirrors and pressed-tin ceiling, serves great Northern Italian dishes, nouvelle cuisine, and seafood, mostly for under $20.

Gryphon Bull and Charlton sts ☎912/525-5880. There's an atmospheric mix of art students, lecturers, and ladies-that-lunch in this sweet tearoom, housed in an old pharmacy with its original counter, tiled floor, and mirrors. Hundreds of special teas, genteel gourmet lunches, and mouthwatering cakes; high tea is served 4–6pm. Closed Sun.

Lady and Sons 102 W Congress St ☎912/233-2600. Thanks to heavy TV exposure, Paula Deen's mega-successful Southern restaurant lines around the block for its gut-busting buffets of fried chicken, Low Country Boil, macaroni, fried green tomatoes, and the like. Many locals insist, however, it's not a patch on *Mrs Wilkes* (see above)

Leopold's Ice Cream 212 E Broughton St ☎912/234-4442. In a heart-warming,

if unlikely, tribute to Savannah's bygone charms, Hollywood producer Stratton Leopold (responsible for *Mission: Impossible III*, among others) has revamped his family's traditional downtown ice-cream parlor, originally opened in 1919, and personally serves exquisite homemade ices, plus a full menu of sandwiches, salads, and burgers.

Mrs Wilkes' Boarding House 107 W Jones St ☎912/232-5997. This local institution offers a real Southern experience, serving all-you-care-to-eat lunches only, for $13. Everyone sits around large tables, helping themselves to delicious mounds of fried chicken, sweet potatoes, spinach, beans, and spaghetti. There's no sign outside; get there early and join the line. Mon–Fri only. No credit cards.

The Olde Pink House 23 Abercorn St ☎912/232-4286. With its resplendent pink Regency facade, this place looks a bit too good to be true, but its Low-Country, fish-heavy food is actually superb – especially the signature crispy scored flounder – and the effortless elegance of the surroundings totally seductive. Open for dinner only.

Entertainment and nightlife

Savannah's **nightlife** is laid-back and enjoyable, though many places are unusually strict about requiring ID. Everything is fairly close together, ranged between the City Market and the river, and almost uniquely in the US (New Orleans is another exception) you can drink **alcohol** on the streets in open cups. For **listings**, pick up the free weekly *Connect* newspaper (Ⓦwww.connectsavannah.com).

Savannah has the largest Irish population per capita in the US, and **St Patrick's Day** (March 17) is a big deal. Nowadays nearly a million revelers descend on the town to guzzle green beer, green grits, and copious amounts of Guinness; many of the 130,000 permanent residents choose this weekend to leave town.

Club One 1 Jefferson St ☎912/232-0200. Decadent gay club, where drag acts once a month include Lady Chablis, from "The Book"; everyone is welcome.

Jazz'd Tapas Bar 52 Barnard St ☎912/236-7777, Ⓦwww.jazzdsavannah.com. Postmodern City Market lounge in the basement of the former Kress department store. Serves Southern-style (as opposed to being particularly Spanish) *tapas* snacks and puts on live, no-cover jazz or blues nightly (except Mon).

The Jinx 127 W Congress St ☎912/236-2281, Ⓦwww.thejinx.net. Savannah's premier rock club, located in City Market, also puts on hip-hop and electro dance nights.

Mercury Lounge 125 W Congress St ☎912/447-6952. Super-hip lounge, with kooky decor, regular swing music, and live jazz.

Moon River Brewing Co. 21 W Bay St ☎912/447-0943. Popular brewpub near the waterfront.

Out from Savannah

Tybee Island, eighteen miles east of the city on US-80, has Savannah's best – and not too overdeveloped – **beach**, as well as a 154ft **lighthouse** dating from 1736, with a small museum (summer daily except Tues 9am–5.30pm; $5). Old Savannah Tours run six daily **shuttle buses** out from the city in summer ($10 roundtrip; ☎912/234-8128 or 1-800/517-9007, Ⓦwww.oldsavannahtours.com). Abundant **accommo-**

dation options include the 1930s oceanfront *DeSoto Beach Hotel*, 212 Butler Ave (℡912/786-4542 or 1-877/786-4542, ⓦwww.desotobeachhotel.com; ⑤). For great **Low Country food**, head for *The Crab Shack*, 40 Estill Hammock Rd, Chimney Creek (℡912/786-9857), where you can dine on delicious fresh crabs and shrimp in a shabby old shack by the creek – if you can find it, that is: take a right turn off the main road to the beach, about two miles before you reach the lighthouse turnoff.

Fort Pulaski National Monument, off US-80 E en route to Tybee Island (daily 9am–5pm; $3; ⓦwww.nps.gov/fopu), is the most interesting of several local forts. An impressive Confederate stronghold, set on its own idyllic (if rather buggy) little island and ringed by a moat inhabited by the occasional alligator, it was nevertheless taken by Union troops, the first masonry fortress to be pierced by rifled cannon fire.

Ten miles south of Savannah, at 7601 Skidaway Rd, you come to **Wormsloe State Historic Site** (Tues–Sat 9am–5pm, Sun 2–5.30pm; $3; ⓦwww.wormsloe. org). In the eighteenth century this was an important defensive plantation; the atmospheric tabby ruins of the fortified house of British settler Noble Jones are now overgrown with palms and lush forest. Inside the house, a museum covers the early settlement of Savannah, with archeological finds and demonstrations of the skills and crafts of the first settlers.

Much of the Georgia coast is taken up by a string of **National Wildlife Refuges**, on the small marshy islands that make up the **barrier island chain**. It's well worth detouring or backtracking along the quiet side roads to cross to **Blackbeard Island**, **Wolf Island**, **Pinckney**, or **Wassaw**, where tranquil swamps are filled with nesting birds and offer great fishing.

Brunswick and the southern coast

BRUNSWICK, the one sizeable settlement south of Savannah, is a hop-off point for the offshore **sea islands**. The town in itself is industrial and far from exciting, though the shrimp docks can be quite interesting when the catch is brought in. In the unlikely event you'll need to stay in town, the **visitor center**, 4 Glynn Ave (daily 8.30am–5pm; ℡912/265-0620 or 1-800/933-2627, ⓦwww.bgivb.com), has lists of budget **motels** and central **B&Bs**. A more unusual alternative is the wonderful *Hostel in the Forest*, a couple of miles west of I-95 exit 6, reached via an inconspicuous muddy driveway on the south side of US-82 (℡912/264-9738, ⓦwww.foresthostel.com). For $20 per person you'll get either a dorm bed in a geodesic dome or a private room (with electricity!) in one of eight treehouses. The price includes a communal dinner, and all guests are expected to perform a small chore. Otherwise, the best **food** nearby is at the superlative *Georgia Pig*, in an unlikely setting next to a gas station at exit 6 on I-95 (℡912/264-6664), where luscious smoky barbecue comes with the local Brunswick stew, coleslaw, honey-flavored baked beans, and fragrant sauce.

The sea islands

Several of Georgia's **sea islands**, like those of South Carolina, were divided among freed slaves after the Civil War. However, these islands remained poor agricultural communities, and little now remains from those years for an outsider to see. Today they make handy alternatives to Florida as seashore breaks for tired inlanders.

Jekyll Island

The **southern islands** are the most developed, thanks largely to **Jekyll Island**, which was originally bought in 1887 for use as an exclusive "club" by a group of millionaires including the Rockefellers, the Pulitzers, the Macys, and the Vanderbilts. Their opulent residences are still standing, though in perpetual need of refurbishment. A small **Welcome Center** stands on the causeway (daily 9am–5pm; ☎912/635-3636 or 1-877/453-5955, ⊛www.jekyllisland.com), though the **Jekyll Island Museum Center** (daily 9am–5pm) gives a more useful overview of the island's history. Reached by turning left after you pay the $3 island toll, and then heading along Riverview Drive onto Stable Road, it also runs hourly guided tours of the mansions for $10. The "historic district" centers on the rambling old original club building, which, as the *Jekyll Island Club Hotel*, now offers elegant and surprisingly affordable **accommodation** (☎912/635-2600 or 1-800/535-9547, ⊛www.jekyllclub.com; ❺). There's a **campground** a little further north (☎912/635-3021; $20), near the nesting sites of loggerhead turtles.

St Simon's Island and Cumberland Island

Most of **St Simon's Island**, reached across a green marsh inhabited by wading birds (35¢ toll), is still an evocative landscape of marshes, palms, and live oaks covered with Spanish moss. The tiny village is pleasantly quiet, little more than a handful of T-shirt shops and cafés. Although the beach by the village is nice and firm for strolling, fierce currents render **swimming** unsafe: head instead for the east side of the island, where the flat, fine sand stretches out for miles. Southeast Adventures, 313 Mallory St (☎912/638-6732, ⊛www.southeastadventure.com), rents out **kayaks** and runs bird- and dolphin-watching tours. **Fort Frederica National Monument**, seven miles north of the causeway (daily 8.30am–5pm; $5 per vehicle), was built by General Oglethorpe in 1736 as the largest British fort in North America; it's now an atmospheric ruin.

As well as **resorts** like the lovely *Sea Palms*, 5445 Frederica Rd (☎912/638-3351 or 1-800/841-6268, ⊛www.seapalms.com; ❹), whose atmospheric rooms overlook the marshes, **accommodation** options include *Saint Simon's Inn*, 609 Beachview Drive, a block from the beach near the village (☎912/638-1101, ⊛www.stsimonsinn.com; ❹). By far the best place to **eat** is *Frannie's Place Restaurant*, 318 Mallory St (☎912/638-1001), famed for its Brunswick stew; try also the specialty sandwiches, crabcakes, and to-die-for desserts.

To the south, **Cumberland Island** is a stunning wildlife refuge of marshes, beaches, and semitropical forest roamed by wild horses, with the odd deserted planter's mansion. You can get here by ferry from the village of St Mary's, back on the mainland near the Florida border (March–Nov daily 9am & 11.45am; Dec–Feb Thurs–Mon 9am & 11.45am; 45min; $15 roundtrip).

Okefenokee Swamp

The dense semitropical **Okefenokee Swamp** stretches over thirty miles down to Florida from a point roughly thirty miles southwest of Brunswick. Tucked away among its astonishing profusion of luxuriant plants and trees are something like twenty thousand alligators and over thirty species of snakes, as well as bears and pumas. You can only get in at the **Okefenokee Swamp Park**, a private charity-owned concession at the northeast tip, on Hwy-177 off US-23/1 (daily 9am–5.30pm; ☎912/283-0583, ⊛www.okeswamp.com). Admission is $12, which enables you to see a serpentarium, a good interpretive center on wildlife, an observation tower, and reconstructed pioneer buildings; you can pay $4–18 extra for intriguing **boat tours** through the swamp of thirty to ninety minutes (be sure to slick yourself with bug repellent).

For nearby accommodation, unlovely **Waycross**, ten miles north, holds bargain **motels** such as the *Pinecrest*, 1761 Memorial Drive (☎912/283-3580; ❶).

Kentucky

Two hundred years after it was wrested from the Native Americans, **KENTUCKY** still hasn't quite decided whether it belongs in the North or the South. Both of the rival presidents during the Civil War, Abraham Lincoln and Jefferson Davis, were born here, and divisions were acute between slave-owning farmers and the merchants who depended on trade with the nearby cities of the industrial North. While the state remained officially neutral, more Kentuckians joined the Union army than the Confederates. After the war, Kentucky sided with the South in its hostility to Reconstruction, and has tended to follow southern political trends.

Kentucky's rugged beauty is at its most appealing in the mountainous **east** and the small historic towns of the **Bluegrass Downs**, with visits enlivened by the varied attractions of bourbon whiskey, thoroughbred horses, and bluegrass music. **Louisville**, home of the **Kentucky Derby**, is a busy manufacturing and arts center; the more reserved **Lexington**, eighty miles east, is a major horse-breeding market.

Getting around Kentucky

Kentucky's limited **public transportation** can be a real headache. There's full Greyhound service along the interstates south of Louisville and Lexington, but that's about it. Amtrak doesn't operate here at all. **Cycling** is a pleasant and manageable option but **driving** is the only way to cover much ground.

Lexington, Bluegrass, and eastern Kentucky

The fertile **Bluegrass Downs**, just eighty miles across, form the base of America's thoroughbred racing industry, with **Lexington** quietly prospering at its heart. The name comes from the unique steel-blue sheen of the buds in the meadows, only visible in early morning during April and May. Kentucky's first white pioneers, who trekked in the 1770s through the 150 miles of wilderness now called the **Daniel Boone National Forest**, were amazed to find this "Eden" deserted while the Indians lived in much less attractive terrain. Archeologists later discovered this was due to mineral deficiencies in the soil causing fatal bone diseases. The area around Lexington holds some of the oldest towns west of the Alleghenies. Eastern Kentucky, however, suffers from acute rural poverty despite the fine scenery of the **Natural Bridge** and **Cumberland Gap** districts.

Lexington

The productivity of the bluegrass fields has kept **LEXINGTON**'s economy ticking over since 1775, though the lack of a navigable river has always made its traders vulnerable to competition from Louisville, eighty miles west. However, its current affluence dates from after World War I, when smoking caught on internationally and Lexington emerged as the world's largest **burley tobacco** market. Despite a population exceeding 200,000, Lexington maintains a quasi-rustic atmosphere and boasts many fine antebellum houses; its most conspicuous activity is the **horse** trade, with an estimated 450 farms in the vicinity.

Arrival and information

Lexington's **airport** is six miles west of town on US-60 W, near Keeneland racetrack. **Greyhound** drops off about a mile from downtown at 477 New Circle Rd across the street from the local bus station (bus #3 goes downtown). Lex-Tran (☎859/253-4636, ⓦwww.lextran.com) operates a good service to the university and suburbs, but you'll need a **car** to reach the horse-related attractions. The **visitor center** is at 301 E Vine St (Mon–Fri 8.30am–5pm, Sat 10am–5pm, Sun May–Aug noon–5pm; ☎859/233-7299 or 1-800/845-3959, ⓦwww.visitlex. com) and gives out handy walking- and driving-tour maps. Check the free *ACE Weekly* (ⓦwww.aceweekly.com) for local **listings** and events.

Accommodation

Lexington has very little accommodation to offer downtown, though budget **motels** can be found around the exits from I-75. If you're stuck, the visitor center (see above) can help find rooms. The best **campground** is at the Horse Park (☎859/233-4303, ⓦwww.kyhorsepark.com; from $13).

Comfort Suites South 5527 Athens-Boonesboro Rd, I-70 exit 104 ☎859/263-0777 or 1-800/228-5150, ⓦwww.comfortsuites.com. Spacious, good-value chain motel six miles southeast of the city center. ❸

Gratz Park Inn 120 W Second St ☎859/231-1777 or 1-800/752-4166, ⓦwww.gratzparkinn.com. Downtown's oldest and most prestigious hotel, with rooms decorated in nineteenth-century style and a highly rated restaurant. ❼

Holiday Inn North 1950 Newtown Pike ☎859/233-0512, ⓦwww.hilexingtonnorth.com.

Vast and very upscale affiliate of the *Holiday Inn* chain northeast of downtown, complete with a covered "Holidome" holding a swimming pool, sports hall, and gym. ❻

La Quinta 1919 Stanton Way, junction of I-64 & I-75, exit 115 ☎859/231-7551 or 1-800/531-5900. Handily placed motel with comfortable rooms and free continental breakfast. ❸

Swann's Nest B&B 3463 Rosalie Lane ☎859/226-0095, ⓦwww.swannsnest.com. An appealing rural retreat, offering five comfortable guest suites on a thoroughbred farm. ❺

Downtown Lexington

The plush hotels, glass office blocks, skywalks, and shopping malls of Lexington's city center, set in a dip on the Bluegrass Downs, crowd in on fountain-filled **Triangle Park**. Despite its age, the city has few buildings of architectural interest, an exception being the ivy-covered redbrick buildings of small 1780 **Transylvania University**, behind the Courthouse at N Broadway and Third St. On the other side of downtown, the **University of Kentucky Art Museum**, in the Singletary Center for the Arts, at Rose St and Euclid Ave (Tues–Thurs, Sat & Sun noon–5pm, Fri noon–8pm; (☎859/257-5716 ⓦwww.uky.edu/ArtMuseum; free) displays contemporary American art and Native American artifacts. The best photo opportunity comes in the form of **Thoroughbred Park**, at Main St and Midland Ave, where an impressive life-sized bronze sculpture depicts a horse race in progress.

Lexington's horses

Along **Paris** and **Ironworks pikes**, northeast of Lexington in an idyllic Kentuckian landscape, sleek thoroughbred horses cavort in bluegrass meadows. Some farms are still staked out by miles of immaculate white-plank fences, though most now use the cheaper but much less attractive black creosote to protect the wood. To the west, you can watch the horses' early-morning workouts at **Keeneland racetrack** (April–Oct daily dawn–10am; free; ☎859/254-3412 or 1-800/456-3412), and then eat a super-cheap breakfast nearby (see opposite). Tasteful dark-green grandstands emphasize the crisp white rails around the one-mile oval track, although the muted public-address system can lead to confusion over the winner, if you attend a meeting (racing for three weeks in April, Wed–Sun 7.30pm, and three weeks in Oct, Wed–Sun 1pm; call for reserved tickets; $5–40; ☎859/288-4299).

Tours of horse farms used to be very popular, but most owners have become reluctant to let the public get too close to the shy creatures. The easiest way to be sure of seeing at least one farm is to take a guided bus tour out of Lexington; **Blue Grass Tours** (March–Oct daily 9am; Nov–Feb by appointment; $26; ☎859/252-5744 or 1-800/755-6956, ⓦwww.bluegrasstours.com) offer a three-hour, fifty-mile itinerary that includes a stop at a private farm, plus a visit to Keeneland or Red Mile racetrack. Alternatively, a handful of farms still welcome individual visitors, special events permitting; most are free, but you should tip the groom. One such is **Three Chimneys** on Old Frankfort Pike, about fifteen minutes west of downtown (Tues–Sat 1pm; ☎859/873-7053 ⓦwww.threechimneys.com), where it's best to reserve a place in advance. The **Thoroughbred Center**, 3380 Paris Pike (April–Oct Mon–Fri 9am, 10.30am & 1pm, Sat 9am & 10.30am; Nov–March Mon–Fri 10.30am; $10; ☎859/293-1853, ⓦwww.thethoroughbredcenter.com), allows you to watch trainers at work. The enjoyable **Kentucky Horse Park** is a little further along at 4089 Ironworks Parkway (mid-March to Oct daily 9am–5pm; Nov to mid-March Wed–Sun 9am–5pm; $9–15; ☎859/233-4303, ⓦwww.kyhorsepark.com). Its **International Museum of the Horse** traces the use of horses throughout history, from Roman chariot races through cavalry regiments, commercial haulage, and modern sports. The 1032-acre park features real live horses of over thirty different breeds, a working farm, and guided **horseback rides** ($22 extra). In nearby Georgetown, at Whispering Woods, experienced equestrians can ride unsupervised, while novices can ride with a guide ($20 for 1hr, up to $80 per day; ☎502/570-9663, ⓦwww.whisperingwoodstrails.com).

Eating, drinking, and nightlife

Lexington's large student population means it has several lively, youth-oriented **eating places**, besides the steakhouses catering to the horse crowd and conventioneers. The streets around the corner of Broadway and Main St hold a few lively bars, which flourish despite the Baptist-inspired 1am curfew on drinking places.

Alfalfa Restaurant 557 S Limestone St ☎859/253-0014. Hippyish café near the University of Kentucky. A wide range of inexpensive international food, with vegetarian dishes. Live music some evenings, plus temporary art exhibits.

Atomic Café 265 N Limestone St ☎859/254-1969. Fun Caribbean ambiance, with good spicy food and potent cocktails. Live reggae Thurs–Sat.

Common Grounds 343 High St ☎859/233-9761. Popular downtown coffeehouse, open until at least midnight daily with live music at weekends. A great rendezvous for coffee, sandwiches, and simple snacks.

Ed and Fred's Desert Moon 148 Grand Blvd ☎859/231-1161. Wacky decor, good Southwestern food and pizza. Closed Mon.

Good Foods Coop 455-D Southland Drive ☎859/278-1813. Healthy deli, open daily for coffee, sandwiches, and self-serve hot and cold specials.

Keeneland Track Kitchen 4201 Versailles Rd t859/254-3412. The place to eat hearty homestyle breakfasts for next to nothing in the company of jockeys and other horsey folk.

Kentucky Theatre 214 E Main St ☎859/231-6997. Evocatively restored 1920s movie palace showing offbeat and art-house films, as well as being a great venue for rock, blues, and jazz concerts. Serves alcohol and decent snacks.

Ramsey's Diner 496 E High St ☎859/259-2708. Very popular and atmospheric diner, with four other outlets in town, all serving tasty sandwiches, burgers, and meals for $4–8. Open until 1am.

6

Bluegrass country

Other than the horse farms directly to the north, most places of interest near Lexington lie southwards, including the fine old towns of **Danville** and **Harrodsburg**, and the restored **Shaker Village** at Pleasant Hill. After about forty miles, the meadows give way to the striking **Knobs** – random lumpy outcrops, shrouded in trees and wispy low-hanging clouds, that are the eroded remnants of the Pennyrile Plateau.

The Shaker Village at Pleasant Hill

The utopian settlement of **PLEASANT HILL**, hidden among the bluegrass hillocks near Harrodsburg, 26 miles southwest of Lexington, was established by **Shaker missionaries** from New England around 1805. Within twenty years, nearly five hundred villagers here were producing seeds, tools, and cloth, for sale as far away as New Orleans. During the Civil War, the pacifist Shakers were obliged to billet Union and Confederate troops alike. Numbers thereafter declined until the last member died in 1923, but a nonprofit organization has returned the village to its nineteenth-century appearance.

The Shaker values of absolute celibacy, hygiene, simplicity, and communal ownership have left their mark on the thirty-four gray and pastel-colored dwellings, which women and men entered via different doors. Visitors can watch demonstrations of broom-making, weaving, quilting, and other traditional handicrafts (April–Oct daily 10am–5pm; $14; Nov–March 10am–4.30pm, reduced program of events; $6.50), and also take excursions on the sternwheeler *Dixie Belle* (late April to Oct daily noon, 2pm & 4pm; $6). An on-site ⚑ **inn** offers good-value rooms, and also houses a superb **restaurant** specializing in boiled ham, lemon pie, and other Kentucky favorites (☏859/734-5411 or 1-800/734-5611, ⓦwww.shakervillageky.org; ❹); reserve well in advance to either eat or sleep.

Berea

Thirty miles south of Lexington, just off I-75 in the foothills where Bluegrass Country meets Appalachia, the unique **Berea College** gives its 1500 mainly local students free tuition in return for work in any of 120 crafts, ranging from needlework to wrought ironwork. Founded in 1855 by abolitionists as a vocational college for the young people of East Kentucky – both white and black, making it for forty years the only integrated college in the South – it was briefly shut down in 1859 by mobs opposed to the board's support for John Brown's raid at Harpers Ferry (see p.453).

The college's reputation has attracted many private art and craft galleries to little **BEREA**. For details on all, a chance to buy representative local crafts, and general local information, visit the **Kentucky Artisan Center** at exit 77 off I-75 (daily 8am–8pm; ☏859/985-5548, ⓦwww.kentuckyartisancenter.ky.gov). Free tours of both the campus and assorted student craft workshops leave from the sumptuous *Boone Tavern Inn*, a student-run inn and restaurant at Main and Prospect streets (☏859/985-3700 or 1-800/366-9358, ⓦwww.berea.edu/boonetavern; ❹). If you're on a tight **budget**, *Mario's Pizza*, 636 Chestnut St (☏859/986-2331), is a good option.

Daniel Boone National Forest

Almost the entire eastern length of Kentucky is taken up by the steep slopes, narrow valleys, and sandstone cliffs of the unspoiled **DANIEL BOONE NATIONAL FOREST**. Few Americans can have been so mythologized as **Daniel Boone**, who first explored the region in 1767, and thus ranks as one of Kentucky's earliest fur-trapping pioneers. Perhaps the most famous legend tells of the time he was captured by Shawnee Indians and initiated as "Sheltowee," or Big Turtle. Learning of their plans to attack pioneer communities, Big Turtle escaped just in time to warn the citizens of his own settlement at **Boonesborough**, southeast of Lexington. Sadly, Boone failed to legalize his land claims, and, after losing everything in an acrimonious legal tussle, was forced to press further west to Missouri, where he died in 1820 at the age of 86.

Natural Bridge and around

The geological extravaganza of the **Red River Gorge**, sixty miles east of Lexington via the Mountain Parkway, is best seen by taking a thirty-mile loop drive from the **Natural Bridge State Resort Park** on Hwy-77, near the village of Slade. Natural Bridge itself is a large sandstone arch surrounded by steep hollows and exposed clifflines; for those reluctant to negotiate the half-mile climb, there is a chair-lift ($7 roundtrip). As well as hiking trails, canoeing, fishing, rock-climbing, and camping, there's **accommodation** at the secluded *Hemlock Lodge* (℡606/663-2214 or 1-800/325-1710, ⓦwww.naturalbridgepark.com; ❹), where weekends can be reserved a year in advance.

Toward the southeast

In 1940, "Colonel" Harland Sanders, so titled as a member of the Honorable Order of Kentucky Colonels, opened a small clapboard diner, the *Sanders Café*, alongside his motel and gas station in tiny **Corbin**, ninety miles south of Lexington on I-75. His **Kentucky Fried Chicken** empire has since spread all over the world. The original 100-seat restaurant, near the junction of US-25 E and US-25 W, has been restored with 1940s decor and an immense amount of memorabilia (daily 10am–10pm; ℡606/528-2163). The food served is usual KFC, but it's an atmospheric little spot.

On the tristate border of Kentucky, Tennessee, and Virginia, the **Cumberland Gap National Historic Park** is one of the most visited parts of the area. A natural passageway used by migrating deer and bison, the area served as a gateway to the West for Boone and other pioneers. **Pinnacle Overlook**, a 1000ft lookout over the three states, is near the **visitor center**, on US-25 E in Middlesboro (daily 8am–5pm; ℡606/248-2817, ⓦwww.nps.gov/cuga).

Louisville, central, and western Kentucky

In such a heavily rural state, the manufacturing giant of **Louisville** stands out, with its lively cultural and racial mix. Only occasionally does it bother with the laid-back Southern image other parts of the state are so keen to promote. In the **southern** hinterland, numerous small towns retain their tree-shaded squares and nineteenth-century townhouses – and their strict Baptist beliefs – while the endless caverns of **Mammoth Cave National Park** attract spelunkers and hikers in the thousands. The **west**, where the Ohio River meets the Mississippi, is flat, heavily forested, and generally less attractive.

Louisville

LOUISVILLE, just south of Indiana across the Ohio River, is firmly embedded in the American national consciousness for its multimillion-dollar **Kentucky Derby**.

Each year, the horse race attracts over half a million fans to this cosmopolitan and well-diversified industrial city, which still bears the traces of the early French settlers who came upriver from New Orleans. Louisville also produces a third of the country's **bourbon**.

The city's history revolves around a perennial rivalry with Cincinnati, a mere one hundred miles upstream. Thus, despite being pro-Union during the Civil War, it promoted itself thereafter – erecting Confederate statues and so on – as *the* place for Southern business to invest. Today, besides a lively arts scene and lots of citywide festivals, Louisville boasts an unrivaled network of public parks, many designed by Frederick Law Olmsted. One native son who took advantage of the recreation facilities was three-time world heavyweight boxing champion **Muhammad Ali**, who used to do his early-morning training in the scenic environs of Chickasaw Park.

Arrival and information

Most major US airlines fly into **Louisville International Airport** (Ⓣ 502/368-6524), five miles south of downtown on I-65; take bus #2 or pay a $17 cab fare to get into the city center. **Greyhound** terminates at fairly central 720 W Muhammad Ali Blvd. Downtown **trolleys** run from 7.30am to 8pm/10pm on weekdays and until 6pm on Saturdays for 25¢. The new **visitor center** is at Fourth and Jefferson streets (Mon–Sat 10am–5pm, Sun noon–5pm; Ⓣ 502/582-3732 or 1-888/568-4784, Ⓦ www.gotolouisville.com) and offers discounts on some of the attractions. For news of upcoming events, pick up a copy of the free **listings** magazine *LEO* (*Louisville Eccentric Observer*).

Accommodation

Most of the year, Louisville's **accommodation** is plentiful and reasonably priced, though of course it's solidly booked up for the Derby. You can **camp** just over the river in Indiana at the central *KOA*, 900 Marriott Drive, Clarksville, IN (Ⓣ 812/282-4474, Ⓦ www.koa.com).

Central Park B&B 1353 S Fourth St Ⓣ 502/638-1505 or 1-877/922-1505, Ⓦ www.centralparkbandb.com. Opulent seven-room Victorian B&B in the heart of the Historic District. ⑤

The Columbine B&B 1707 S Third St Ⓣ 502/635-5000 or 1-800/635-5010, Ⓦ www.thecolumbine.com. Six-room B&B, all with private baths, in a colonnaded mansion close to the university. Great garden and gourmet breakfasts. ⑤

Galt House 140 N Fourth St Ⓣ 502/589-5200 or 1-800/626-1814, Ⓦ www.galthouse.com. This massive, 25-story, twin-tower hotel on the Ohio riverfront has an unmistakable Kentucky feel, with grand ballrooms, sweeping staircases, and avenue-like corridors. ⑥–⑦

Hampton Inn Downtown Louisville 101 E Jefferson St Ⓣ 502/585-2200, Ⓦ www.louisvilledowntown.hamptoninn.com. Comfortable rooms plus a free buffet breakfast and access to an indoor pool and fitness center. ④

Comfort Inn Downtown 401 S Second St Ⓣ 502/583-2841, Ⓦ www.comfortinn.com/ires/hotel/ky149. About as economical an option as you'll find right downtown. Simple but perfectly adequate. ③

Central Louisville

Downtown Louisville rolls gently toward Main Street, then abruptly lunges to the river. **Riverfront Plaza**, between Fifth and Sixth streets, is a prime observation point for the natural **Falls of the Ohio**. Two sternwheelers, the *Belle of Louisville* and the *Spirit of Jefferson*, cruise from the wharf at Fourth St and River Rd in the summer (Mon–Sat noon–2pm & 7–9pm; summer only Sun noon–2pm; $14; Ⓣ 502/574-2355 or Ⓦ www.belleoflouisville.org).

Even non-baseball fans will likely be impressed by the **Louisville Slugger Museum**, at 800 W Main St (Mon–Sat 9am–5pm; Sun noon–5pm; $9;

The Kentucky Derby

The **Kentucky Derby** is one of the world's premier horse races; it's also, as Hunter S. Thompson put it, "decadent and depraved." Derby Day itself is the first Saturday in May, at the end of the two-week **Kentucky Derby Festival**. Since 1875, the leading lights of Southern society have gathered at **Churchill Downs**, three miles south of downtown, for an orgy of betting, haute cuisine, and mint juleps in the plush grandstand, while tens of thousands of the beer-guzzling proletariat cram into the infield. Apart from the $40 infield tickets available on the day – offering virtually no chance of a decent view – all seats are sold out months in advance. The actual race, traditionally preceded by a mass drunken rendition of "My Old Kentucky Home," is run over a distance of one and a quarter miles, lasts barely two minutes, and offers around a million dollars in prize money. Churchill Downs also hosts thoroughbred races from May to July, and from October to November (T502/636-4400 or 1-800/283-3729).

The excellent hands-on **Kentucky Derby Museum** (mid-March to Nov Mon–Sat 7am–5pm, Sun noon–5pm; Dec to mid-March Mon–Sat 9am–5pm, Sun noon–5pm; $9; T502/637-7097, W www.derbymuseum.org), next to Churchill Downs at 704 Central Ave, will appeal to horseracing enthusiasts and neophytes alike. Admission includes a magnificent audiovisual display that captures the Derby Day atmosphere on a 360° screen and you can take a tour of the racecourse for an extra $6.

T 502/588-7228, W www.sluggermuseum.com). Frequent **tours** start with a short, emotive movie featuring prominent shots of Louisville Slugger bats being used to good effect, then take in displays honoring key players and a batting cage and give a lucid explanation of how wooden bats are made. All visitors receive a souvenir miniature bat.

The town's newest museum is the excellent **Muhammed Ali Center**, beside the river at 144 N Sixth St (Mon–Sat 9.30am–5pm, Sun noon–5pm; $9), which, apart from chronicling the local lad's boxing career with entertaining multimedia displays, provides insight into his Muslim faith and spirituality.

The **Speed Art Museum**, at 2035 S Third St on the University of Louisville campus (Tues, Wed & Fri 10.30am–4pm, Thurs 10.30am–8pm, Sat 10.30am–5pm, Sun noon–5pm; free; T502/634-2700, W www.speedmuseum.org), hosts traveling exhibits and has a small, but interesting, permanent collection of art and sculpture from medieval to modern times, featuring works by Rembrandt, Monet, Rodin, and Henry Moore.

Eating

Louisville's **restaurants** cater to all tastes, though downtown prices are fairly high.

Bristol Bar & Grille 1321 Bardstown Rd T 502/456-1702. A perennial Louisville favorite, offering good bistro-style salads and entrees, as well as great desserts. Two other locations at 300 N Hurstbourne Parkway and 614 W Main St.

Café Kilimanjaro 649 S Fourth St T 502/583-4332. Dishes and drinks from the Caribbean, Africa, and South America in relaxed surroundings with tropical decor.

Lynn's Paradise Café 984 Barrett Ave T 502/585-5966. Nationally acclaimed chef Lynn Winter serves up homestyle cooking in an offbeat, friendly atmosphere.

Ramsi's Café on the World 1293 Bardstown Rd T 502/451-0700. Atmospheric café open nightly until late and offering eclectic and very tasty selections from around the world. A downtown branch, at 215 S Fifth St, opens for weekday lunches only, served cafeteria-style.

Rudyard Kipling 422 W Oak St T 502/636-1311. The decor has a hint of The Jungle Book, but the food is local with a few Indian dishes thrown in. Live music, usually acoustic, most nights. Closed Sun.

Seviche 1538 Bardstown Rd T 502/473-8560. Stylish Latin restaurant in the busy Deer Park

district, featuring *ceviche* as well as seafood and steak entrees cooked to South Merican recipes. Most items are over $20.
Vietnam Kitchen 5339 S Mitscher Ave Ⓣ502/363-5154. A small, basic eatery with a huge menu, fifteen minutes' drive down Third St, behind the Iriquois Manor mall. This is where the city's Asian chefs eat on their days off. Closed Wed.

Nightlife and entertainment

Fronted by several outlandish sculptures, the **Kentucky Center for the Arts**, 501 W Main, between Fifth and Sixth avenues (Ⓣ502/562-0100 or 1-800/775-7777), is Louisville's main venue for high culture. Meanwhile, the **Actors' Theatre of Louisville**, 316 W Main St (Ⓣ502/584-1205 or 1-800/428-5849), has a national reputation for its new productions. As for **drinking** and **live music**, the two-mile strip around Bardstown Road and Baxter Avenue (take bus #17) is punctuated by fun bars and restaurants; the best **gay** clubs are on the eastern edge of downtown.

Connections 130 S Floyd St Ⓣ502/585-5752. The pick of Louisville's gay scene. At weekends, this giant club, complete with terrace garden, holds over 2000.
Headliners 1386 Lexington Rd Ⓣ502/584-8088. Lively club that showcases local and some national indie bands.
Molly Malone's 933 Baxter Ave Ⓣ502/473-1222. Enjoyable Irish pub and restaurant, with live music on the weekends and Euro soccer on TV.
Phoenix Hill Tavern 644 Baxter Ave Ⓣ502/589-4957, Ⓦwww.phoenixhill.com. Big bar with four separate areas; occasionally hosts national touring acts.
Stevie Ray's 230 E Main St Ⓣ502/582-9945, Ⓦwww.stevieraysbluesbar.com. As the name suggests, a loud, rocking blues bar.

Out from Louisville

South from Louisville to Tennessee, **central Kentucky** offers great scope for a driving tour. There's small-town charm and well-aged bourbon in **Bardstown** and Abraham Lincoln's birthplace of **Hodgenville**, while the top natural attraction is the amazing **Mammoth Cave National Park**, the largest underground cave system in the world.

Fort Knox

Legendary **FORT KNOX** straddles 100,000 acres on either side of US-31 W, thirty miles southwest of Louisville. The bomb-proof **Bullion Depository**, on Gold Vault Road, surrounded by security fences, machine-gun turrets, patrol guards, and huge floodlights, stores nine million pounds of the federal gold reserve behind doors weighing twenty tons apiece. No visits are allowed at the depository; you can only stop by the road for a maximum of five minutes.

Bardstown and the bourbon distilleries

Forty miles south of Louisville on US-31 E, attractive **BARDSTOWN** is the place to get acquainted with Kentucky **bourbon whiskey**, created in earliest pioneer days, so the story goes, when Elijah Craig, a Baptist minister, added corn to the usual rye and barley. Named for Bourbon County near Lexington, Kentucky's whiskey soon gained a national reputation, thanks to crisp limestone water, strict laws concerning ingredients and production, and the skills of small-scale distillers.

Get into the spirit at Bardstown's free **Oscar Getz Museum of Whiskey History**, 114 N Fifth St (Mon–Fri 10am–5pm, Sat 10am–4pm, Sun noon–4pm; free). Fourteen miles west at **Clermont**, you can stop at the **Jim Beam American Outpost** (Mon–Sat 9am–4.30pm, Sun 1–4pm; free), which has an informative museum, a film on the whiskey-making process, an outdoor moonshine still and barrel-making museum, and a Beam family home. **Maker's Mark Distillery**, twenty miles south of Bardstown near **Loretto**, is an out-of-the-way collection of beautifully restored black, red, and gray plankhouses, in which whiskey is still made manually (Mon–Sat 10.30am–3.30pm, Sun March–Dec 1.30–3.30pm; free; ☎502/865-2099, ⓦwww.makersmark.com). However, don't expect a sample at either distillery; like most of rural Kentucky, the area is **dry**.

Abraham Lincoln's birthplace

On February 12, 1809, **Abraham Lincoln**, the sixteenth president of the US, was born in a one-room log cabin in the frontier wilds, son of a wandering farmer and, if some accounts are to be believed, an illiterate and illegitimate mother. Three miles south of Hodgenville, on US-31 E, the **National Historic Site** (summer daily 8am–6.45pm; rest of year daily 8am–4.45pm; free; ☎270/358-3137, ⓦwww.nps.gov/abli) has a symbolic cabin of his birth, enclosed in a granite and marble Memorial Building with 56 steps, one for each year of Lincoln's life. You can stay on the site in one of the three rustic *Nancy Lincoln Inn Cabins* (☎270/358-3845; ➌). The family moved ten miles northeast in 1811 to the **Knob Creek** area, where Lincoln's earliest memory was of slaves being forcefully driven along the road. Here you can visit another recreation of his boyhood home (daily April–Oct varying hours; free).

Mammoth Cave National Park

The three hundred and fifty miles of labyrinthine passages (with an average of five new miles discovered each year) and domed caverns of **MAMMOTH CAVE NATIONAL PARK** lie halfway between Louisville and Bowling Green, ten miles off I-65. Its amazing geological formations, carved by acidic water trickling through limestone, include a bewildering display of stalagmites and stalactites, a huge cascade of flowstone known as **Frozen Niagara**, and **Echo River**, 365ft below ground, populated by a unique species of colorless and sightless fish. Among traces of human occupation are Native American artifacts, a former saltpeter mine, and the remains of an experimental tuberculosis hospital, built in 1843 in the belief that the cool atmosphere of the cave would help clear patients' lungs. It's possible to take a limited-access self-guided tour, but by far the best way to appreciate the caves is by joining one of the lengthy **ranger-guided tours** (2–6hrs. $5–46). Tickets are available from the **visitor center** (summer daily 7.30am–7.30pm; fall daily 8am–6pm; rest of year Mon–Fri 9am–5pm, Sat & Sun 8am–5pm; ☎270/758-2328; ☎1-800/967-2283 or ⓦreservations.nps.gov for tour reservations). Make reservations in advance, especially in summer, and keep in mind that the temperature in the caves is a constantly cool 54°F.

The park's attractions are by no means all subterranean. You can explore the scenic **Green River**, as it cuts through densely forested hillsides and jagged limestone cliffs, by following hiking trails, or renting a canoe from Green River Canoeing (☎270/597-2031 or 1-800/651-9909). **Camping** is free in the backcountry; however, a permit must be picked up first at the visitor center; the *Mammoth Cave Hotel* (☎270/758-2225, ⓦwww.mammothcavehotel.com; ➌–➍) has cottages and motel **rooms**. The privately owned caves all around, many of which ruin the sights with garish light shows, and the "attractions" in nearby Cave City and Park City, are best ignored.

Bowling Green

BOWLING GREEN, thirty miles southwest of Mammoth Cave and just sixty miles northeast of Nashville, Tennessee, is a busy little town that offers a treat for **sports car** enthusiasts. One-hour tours of the **General Motors Corvette**

Assembly Plant, on Louisville Road, off I-65, take a step-by-step look at the manufacture of one of the great symbols of the American Dream (Mon–Fri at 9am & 1pm; closed Dec & first half of July; $5; ℡502/745-8419, ⓦwww .bowlinggreenassemblyplant.com). For real Corvette junkies, there's also the **National Corvette Museum**, south of the plant at 350 Corvette Drive (daily 8am–5pm; $8; ⓦwww.corvettemuseum.com). Note that Bowling Green and the rest of southwest Kentucky is in the central time zone.

Tennessee

Stretching almost five hundred miles from east to west, **TENNESSEE** is less open to easy generalization than most Southern states. The history and traditional culture of the Smoky Mountains are a far cry indeed from the blues-soaked, cotton-picking culture of the Mississippi valley, while the more prosperous central region between the two, focused on state capital Nashville, is different once again. Nonetheless Tennessee remains as integral to the South as it has ever been since the Civil War, from its music and cuisine to its political conservatism.

Only one sizeable settlement has found a foothold above the marshlands that line the Mississippi, but it's the state's most appealing attraction for visitors – the wonderfully atmospheric port of **Memphis**. Tennessee's largest city, the birthplace of urban **blues,** and long-time home of **Elvis Presley**, the city is heaven on earth for music fans and an essential destination on any road trip. The fine plantation homes and tidy old towns of **middle Tennessee**'s rolling farmland reflect the comfortable lifestyle of its pioneers; and smack in the heart of it sprawls **Nashville** – synonymous with **country music**. The mountainous **east** shares its top attraction with North Carolina – the peaks, streams, and meadows of **Great Smoky Mountains National Park**.

Some history

Tennessee's first white settlers, most of them British Protestants, arrived across the mountains in the 1770s to settle in the hills and hollows of the Appalachians. Initially relations with the **Cherokee** were good. However, demand for land increased, and confrontations throughout the state culminated in 1838 with the forced removal of the Indians on the "Trail of Tears." One of the main congressional opponents of this process was **Davy Crockett**, familiar from legend as the heavy-drinking hunter in a coonskin cap. When the **Civil War** came, the plantation owners of the west maneuvered Tennessee into the Confederacy, against the wishes of the non-slaveholding smallhold farmers in the east. The last state to secede became the primary battlefield in the west, the site of 424 battles and skirmishes.

Despite economic development to rival any in the country, soil erosion and farm mechanization led to a mass migration to the cities in the years before World War I. The fundamentalist beliefs of these transplanted hill-dwellers (whose folk and fiddle music served to spark Nashville's country scene) influenced a **prohibition** movement that kept all of Tennessee bone-dry until 1939, and still sees a majority of counties forbidding the sale of alcohol. The New Deal of the 1930s brought significant changes. In particular, the **Tennessee Valley Authority**, created in 1933, harnessed the flood-prone **Tennessee River**, providing much-needed jobs and cheap power, and ignited the transition from an agricultural to an industrial economy.

Getting around Tennessee

The **airports** at Memphis and Nashville have extensive connections throughout the US, though fares between the two are high. If you harbor fantasies of traveling by **boat** along the Mississippi, note that only luxury craft make the trip these days, at prohibitive prices (see p.561). **Amtrak** calls at Memphis, and while Greyhound provides a reasonable service to major towns and cities, traveling **by bus** through the small towns in the east is very difficult.

Memphis

Perched above the Mississippi River, **MEMPHIS** ranks as perhaps the single most exciting destination in the South. Visitors flock to celebrate the city that gave the world **blues**, **soul**, and **rock 'n' roll**, as well as to chow down in the unrivaled **barbecue** capital of the nation. Memphis is both deeply evocative – with its somewhat faded downtown streets dotted with characterful stores and diners, and its dramatic sunsets reflected in the broad Mississippi – and invigorating, with a cluster of superb **museums** to complement its frequent **festivals** and vibrant **nightlife**. If it's the **Elvis** connection that draws you here, you won't leave disappointed – let alone empty-handed – but even the King represents just one small part of the rich musical heritage of the home of **Sun** and **Stax studios**.

Culturally and geographically, Memphis has always had more in common with the delta of Mississippi and Arkansas than with the rest of Tennessee. Founded in 1819 and named for Egypt's ancient Nile capital, its fortunes rose and fell with **cotton**. The Confederate defeat that ended slavery briefly plunged the city into economic chaos, not helped by a series of severe yellow fever epidemics, but thanks to its potential for river and rail transportation it soon bounced back. The nation's second largest inland port became a major stopping-off point for **black migrant** farmers and sharecroppers escaping the poverty of the Delta, and many stayed, significantly shaping the city's identity.

In the 1950s and 60s, helped in no small part by the astonishing creativity flowing out of the city's recording studios, Memphis had a confidence that belied its size. The city reached its lowest ebb, however, when **Dr Martin Luther King Jr** was **assassinated** here in 1968, and for a couple of decades thereafter it tottered on the brink of terminal decline, with downtown blighted by white flight. In the 1990s, however, the city regenerated itself yet again, pouring money into such expensive projects as the transformation of **Mud Island** and the construction of the 321ft stainless steel **Pyramid** that dominates the riverfront skyline. More recently, downtown has seen the arrival of not only the huge **Peabody Place** mall, but also a handsome minor league baseball stadium – **Autozone Field**, home of the Redbirds – and a major performance arena, the **Fed Ex Forum**. The famous **blues** corridor of **Beale Street** is booming once more, a little ersatz but always entertaining, while the recent **Rock'n'Soul Museum**, **Gibson Guitar Plant** and superb **Stax Museum** keep true to the city's impeccable musical heritage. Above all, of course, there is **Graceland** – a refreshing change from the usual "gracious southern home" – which provides an intimate and exuberant glimpse of the city's most famous son.

Arrival and information

Memphis is on I-40 as it runs east–west and I-55 from the south. Both join I-240, which loops around the city, and cross the Mississippi River. **Memphis International Airport** is twelve miles south of downtown – a long and complicated bus trip, but just fifteen minutes by the Yellow Cabs **limo/van** service ($15; ☎901/577-7700 or 1-800/796-7750, ⓦwww.premierofmemphis.com) or **taxi**

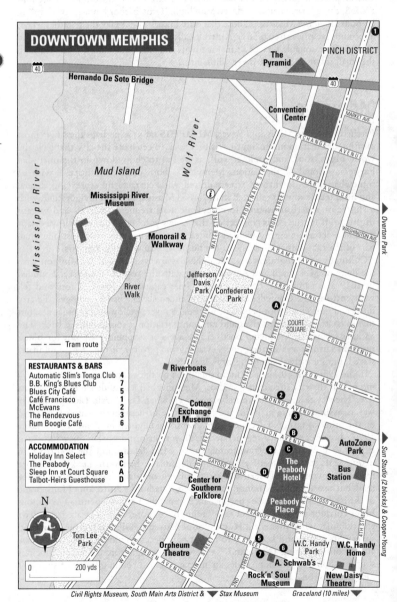

DOWNTOWN MEMPHIS

PINCH DISTRICT

The Pyramid

Hernando De Soto Bridge

Convention Center

MARKET AVE

EXCHANGE AVENUE

Wolf River

POPLAR AVENUE

Mud Island

WASHINGTON AVE

Mississippi River Museum

ⓘ

ADAMS AVENUE

Monorail & Walkway

Jefferson Davis Park

JEFFERSON AVENUE

River Walk

Confederate Park

Ⓐ

COURT SQUARE

COURT AVENUE

--- --- Tram route

Riverboats

MADISON AVENUE

RESTAURANTS & BARS

Automatic Slim's Tonga Club	4
B.B. King's Blues Club	7
Blues City Café	5
Café Francisco	1
McEwans	2
The Rendezvous	3
Rum Boogie Café	6

Cotton Exchange and Museum

MONROE AVENUE

❷

❸

UNION AVENUE

AutoZone Park

ACCOMMODATION

Holiday Inn Select	B
The Peabody	C
Sleep Inn at Court Square	A
Talbot-Heirs Guesthouse	D

❹

Ⓒ

The Peabody Hotel

Bus Station

Ⓓ

GAYOSO AVENUE

Center for Southern Folklore

GAYOSO AVENUE

N

Peabody Place

PEABODY PLACE AV

Tom Lee Park

BEALE STREET

Orpheum Theatre

❺

W.C. Handy Park

W.C. Handy Home

❻

❼

A. Schwab's

New Daisy Theatre

Rock 'n' Soul Museum

0   200 yds

▶ Overton Park

▶ Sun Studio (2 blocks) & Cooper-Young

Civil Rights Museum, South Main Arts District & ▼ Stax Museum   Graceland (10 miles) ▼

($15–25). Greyhound **buses** stop at 203 Union Ave in the heart of downtown, while the restored **Amtrak** station at 545 S Main St is on the southern edge of downtown.

The spacious **Tennessee Welcome Center**, just off I-40 downtown at 119 N Riverside and Adams – facing Mud Island at river level, and complete with statues of Elvis and B.B. King – is open 24 hours a day (staffed daily: April–Sept 9am–6pm; Oct–March 9am–5pm; ℡901/543-5333, ⓦwww.memphistravel. com). There's another **visitor center** at 3205 Elvis Presley Blvd, on the way to Graceland (same hours and phone).

City transportation and tours

The **Memphis Area Transit Authority** (℡901/274-6282, ⓦwww.matatransit. com) operates a useful downtown **trolley** along Main Street and Riverside Drive, connecting the Pyramid and neighbouring Pinch District with Beale Street, the Civil Rights Museum, and the South Main Arts District (every 10min; Mon–Thurs 6am–11.30pm, Fri 6am–1am, Sat 9.30am–1am, Sun 10am–6pm). Another trolley heads along Madison Avenue to the medical centers midtown, but this is less useful for visitors. **Fares** are the same for both ($1, Mon–Fri 11am–1.30pm 50¢, 2-trip pass $1.50, day-pass $3.50, 3-day pass $8).

Horse-drawn **carriage tours** abound downtown – prices vary but you're looking at around $40/30min. Somewhat funkier, **American Dream Safari** (℡901/527-8870, ⓦwww.americandreamsafari.com) offers **driving tours** in a 1955 Cadillac. Ranging from a 2hr "greatest hits" jaunt ($200, max 5 people) to a Sunday gospel and fried chicken outing ($75), they're pricy, but enjoyable. Another lazy way to see the city is to take a river trip on the mighty Mississippi: **sternwheelers** leave from Riverside Drive at Monroe Ave (April–Oct at least one daily, 2.30pm; more in summer and fewer Nov–March; 90min; $18; musical dinner cruises $44; ℡901/527-5694, ⓦmemphisriverboats.net).

The hip folks at Shangri-La Projects – an off-shoot of the must-visit midtown record store – offer the **Ultimate Rock'n'Roll Tour** (ⓦwww.memphisrocktour .com). This might take the form of an overview of all of Memphis's best music sites (1hr, $60 for up to 2 people; 3hr, $75) or be customized to your specific interests ($60/hr).

Accommodation

Downtown Memphis is by far the nicest and most convenient place to **stay**, with a good choice of historic hotels and upscale chains; you'll be lucky to find anything for less than $100 a night, however. There are cheaper options near Graceland on Elvis Presley Boulevard to the south. The visitor center can help you find a room, though it's best to book in advance at busy times, such as the anniversary of Elvis's death in mid-August and during the month-long Memphis in May festival.

Days Inn Graceland 3839 Elvis Presley Blvd ℡901/ 346-5500 or 1-800/329-7466. Reliable option near Graceland, with Elvis memorabilia and videos in the lobby, along with – bliss! – a guitar-shaped pool. Rates include continental breakfast. ❹

Elvis Presley's Heartbreak Hotel 3691 Elvis Presley Blvd ℡901/332-1000 or 1-877/777-0606, ⓦwww.elvis.com. An ideal choice for Elvis fans, this boutique hotel – next to Graceland – features a (small) heart-shaped pool, 24hr in-room Elvis

videos, and peanut butter sandwiches in the *Jungle Room* lounge. The larger rooms come with kitchenettes, or you could splash out and stay in one of the lavish Elvis-themed suites, which sleep up to eight (and start at around $500 per night). Free downtown shuttle and breakfast. ❹

Holiday Inn Select 160 Union Ave ℡901/525-5491, ⓦwww.hisdowntownmemphis.com. In an unbeatable location opposite the *Peabody*, with good rooms at reasonable prices, an outdoor pool, and a sushi bar. ❺

🏃 **The Peabody** 149 Union Ave ☎ 901/529-4000 or 1-800/732-2639, ⊛ www.peabodymemphis.com. This opulent hotel near Beale Street is *the* place to stay in Memphis. Don't miss the legendary mascot ducks, who waddle from the elevator (to the strains of the "King Cotton March") promptly at 11am, spend the day in the lobby fountain and then return to their penthouse at 5pm. Rooms are comfortably elegant, while the glorious lobby is an attraction in itself, with a friendly, relaxed bar. ❽
Sleep Inn at Court Square 40 N Front St ☎ 901/522-9700, ⊛ www.choicehotels.com.

Offering the best value downtown, this upscale motel faces the river near Mud Island and backs onto Main Street and the trolley line. Rates include continental breakfast. Parking $5. ❹
Talbot-Heirs Guesthouse 99 S Second St ☎ 901/527-9772 or 1-800/955-3956, ⊛ www.talbothouse.com. Characterful, friendly, and comfortable accommodations close to Beale Street. Each of the nine themed suites has modern furnishings, a kitchenette, CD player, and Internet access. Rates include continental breakfast. ❻

The City

With its organic neighborhoods and revitalizing downtown, Memphis has a friendly scale that's uncommon in cities of comparable size. **Downtown** still retains a healthy ensemble of fine buildings from the cotton era, best admired either along the riverfront or from the trolley route down **Main Street**. Today these edifices are more likely to have been converted into expensive apartments than to house thriving businesses, but at least the city streets are once more busy with pedestrians. The main tourist activity is concentrated around the enormous **Peabody Place** mall – which has unarguably succeeded in luring locals back downtown, even if it could really be anywhere in the US – from where it's a hop away to the bars and clubs of **Beale Street**, the **Civil Rights** and **Rock'n'Soul** museums just beyond that, and **Sun Studio** not far east. Elsewhere, **Mud Island** on the river itself merits half a day, as does the **Stax** museum, while **Graceland**, ten miles south, should on no account be missed.

Beale Street

Beale Street began life in the mid-nineteenth century as one of Memphis's most exclusive enclaves; within fifty years its elite residents had been driven out by yellow fever epidemics and the ravages of the Civil War to be replaced by a diverse mix of blacks, Greeks, Jews, Chinese, and Italians. But it was **black culture** that gave the street its fame. Beale Street was where black roustabouts, deckhands, and travelers passing through Memphis immediately headed; rural blacks came for the bustling Saturday market; and, in the Jim Crow era, Beale served as the center for black businesses, financiers, and professionals.

As the black Main Street of the mid-South, Beale in its Twenties' heyday was jammed with vaudeville theaters, concert halls, bars, and jook joints (mostly white-owned). Along with the frivolity came a reputation for heavy gambling, voodoo, murder, and prostitution. One appalled evangelist proclaimed that "if whiskey ran ankle deep in Memphis . . . you could not get drunker quicker than you can on Beale Street now."

Although Beale still drew huge crowds in the Forties, the drift to the suburbs and, ironically, the success of the **civil rights** years in opening the rest of Memphis to black businesses, almost killed it off. The **bulldozers** of the late Sixties spared only the grand Orpheum Theatre, at 203 S Main St, and a few commercial buildings between Second and Fourth streets.

Beale Street has now been restored as a handsome **Historic District**. Its souvenir shops, music clubs, and cafés are bedecked with retro facades and neon signs, while a Walk of Fame with brass musical notes embedded into the sidewalk honors musical greats such as B.B. King and Howlin' Wolf. Although battling down Beale on a weekend night, lost in the throng of hard-partying, daiquiri-guzzling convention-

The sound of Memphis

Since the start of the twentieth century, Memphis has been a meeting place for black musicians from the Delta and beyond. During the Twenties, the city's downtown bars, clubs, and street corners were alive with the sound of the blues. **Jug bands**, in which singers were given a bass accompaniment by a musician blowing across the neck of a jug, were a specialty. Several songs by **Gus Cannon's Jug Stompers** – such as "Walk Right In" – became hits for white artists during the folk revival of the Sixties. **Bukka White**, **Memphis Slim**, and guitarist **Memphis Minnie** appeared at nightspots like *Mitchell's Hotel* and *Pee Wee's Saloon*, all long since defunct. After World War II, young musicians and radio DJs such as **Bobby Bland** and **B.B. King** experimented by blending the traditional blues sound with jazz, adding electrical amplification to create **rhythm'n'blues**.

White promoter Sam Phillips started **Sun Records** in 1953, employing Ike Turner as a scout to comb the Beale Street clubs for new talent. Among those whom Turner helped introduce to vinyl were his own girlfriend, Annie Mae Bullock (later **Tina Turner**), **Howlin' Wolf**, and **Little Junior Parker**, whose "Mystery Train" was Sun's first great recording. Later in the same year Sun was founded, the 18-year-old **Elvis Presley** hired the studio to record "My Happiness," supposedly as a gift for his mother, and something prompted Phillips's assistant Marion Keisker to file away his details. The next summer, Phillips called Elvis back to the studio to cut "That's All Right," and thereby set out toward proving his much-quoted conviction that "If I could find a white man who had the Negro sound and the Negro feel, I could make a billion dollars." Phillips swiftly dropped his black artists, and signed other white **rockabilly** singers like **Carl Perkins** and **Jerry Lee Lewis** to record classics such as "Blue Suede Shoes" and "Great Balls of Fire." Elvis – who in the words of Carl Perkins had the advantage that he "didn't look like Mr. Ed, like a lot of the rest of us" – was soon sold on to RCA (for just $35,000), and didn't record in Memphis again until 1969, when, at Chips Moman's American Studios, he produced the best material of his later career, including "Suspicious Minds."

In the Sixties and early Seventies, Memphis's **Stax Records** provided a rootsy alternative to the poppier sounds of Motown. This hard-edged **southern soul** was created by a multiracial mix of musicians, with **Steve Cropper**'s fluid guitar complementing the blaring **Memphis Horns**. The label's first real success was "Green Onions," by studio band **Booker T and the MGs**; further hits followed from **Otis Redding** ("Try A Little Tenderness"), **Wilson Pickett** ("Midnight Hour"), **Sam and Dave** ("Soul Man"), and **Isaac Hayes** ("Theme from Shaft"). The label eventually foundered in acrimony; the last straw for many of its veteran soulmen and women was the signing of the British child star Lena Zavaroni for a six-figure sum.

For more on Memphis's **gospel scene**, see p.566.

eers, can feel like you've hit New Orleans's Bourbon Street by mistake, the place still has its own undeniable pull; blues fans in particular will be drawn to its music venues, which showcase top regional talent. At Beale's western end, no. 126 – the former home of the iconic **Lansky's**, tailor to the Memphis stars – was remodeled in 1997 to become an Elvis-themed restaurant; the site now stands empty, though Lansky's itself continues to thrive in a new location in the historic *Peabody* hotel (see p.556). Lansky's retro shirts and suits are as sharp as you'd expect, and the thrill of being measured up by the man who dressed Elvis is hard to beat.

A. Schwab's Dry Goods Store remains, however, at 163 Beale. Little changed since it opened in 1876, it's a veritable treasure trove, with an incredible array of voodoo paraphernalia familiar from old blues songs – best-sellers include Mojo Hands and High John the Conqueror lucky roots – along with everything from 99¢ neckties through jumbo-sized underpants to tambourines. It's easy to spend hours here simply browsing (closed Sun). Further east, at no. 352, the tiny former home of **W.C. Handy** – moved here from its original site at 659 Janette St – offers another evocative sense of old Memphis (summer Tues–Sat 10am–5pm; winter Tues–Sat 1–4pm; $3). In 1910, Handy was the first man to publish blues tunes (often blues in name only; see p.590). His "Memphis Blues," originally called "Mr. Crump," was the theme song for the 1909 mayoral election of Edward H. Crump, whose crooked political machine was to run the city until the early Fifties.

One block south of Beale, in the plaza of the enormous FedEx Forum, the **Rock'n'Soul Museum** (daily 10am–7pm, last admission 6.15pm; ⓦwww .memphisrocknsoul.org; $9), run in collaboration with the Smithsonian Institution, is an ideal place to start a musical tour of Memphis. Presenting the story of the city's phenomenal musical heritage scrapbook-style, making connections between such issues as migration, racism, civil rights, and youth culture, it's a fascinating place, with a host of artifacts ranging from Elvis's stage gear and one of B.B. King's "Lucille" guitars to Al Green's Bible. Personal audio tours allow you to select your favourite songs from several retro jukeboxes to listen to along the way.

Also in the plaza, the **Gibson Guitar Factory** offers guided tours that allow you to watch the manufacture of those classic six-string and bass guitars so beloved of musicians like King and Chuck Berry (Mon–Sat hourly 10am–4pm, Sun hourly 1–4pm; $10; ⓦwww.gibsonmemphis.com).

Around the Peabody Place Mall

A couple of blocks west of the **Peabody Place Mall** – which along with its mid-range stores and restaurants packs in an Isaac Hayes-owned nightclub/barbecue joint and a 22-screen movie theater – the tiny **Center for Southern Folklore**, 119 S Main St (ⓣ901/525-3655; ⓦwww.southernfolklore.com) offers an ebullient celebration of the culture of the South, with a store full of books, folk art, and CDs, a small café, and a stage for live performances. Over the Labor Day weekend, this is ground zero for the enjoyable **Memphis Music and Heritage Festival**, a free jamboree of live music, spoken word, and dance, as well as arts and crafts and traditional Southern food.

Sun Studio

Second only to Graceland, Memphis's principal shrine to the memory of Elvis is **Sun Studio**, where, in 1953, the shy eighteen-year-old trucker from Tupelo turned up with his guitar, claiming, "I don't sound like nobody." The studio, which went on to introduce rock'n'roll to the world, is located a short way east of Beale Street at 706 Union Ave. Sun Records moved out in 1959, but even when the building briefly became a scuba-diving store (not surprisingly, a commercial failure) all its soundproofing remained in place, making possible its restoration as a functioning studio in 1987. Every hour on the half-hour, forty-minute tours (daily 10am–6pm; $9.50) lead past the display cases upstairs, one of which holds Elvis's high school diploma, and down into the single-room studio itself. Measuring just eighteen by thirty feet, the shabby room focuses around Elvis's original mike stand, where you can pose for photos while the guide plays tapes of legendary recording sessions. Standing in this iconic space, surrounded by old photos, scratchy music, and oral testimony, is an eerie and moving experience, memories of the King sharing space with a roster of greats including Johnny Cash, Carl Perkins, and Jerry Lee Lewis.

The National Civil Rights Museum

The **National Civil Rights Museum**, which provides the most rewarding and comprehensive history of the tumultuous struggle for civil rights to be had any-

The Sun Studio shuttle

Visitors who tour Sun Studios can take advantage of a free shuttle bus, which leaves Sun hourly from 9.55am till 5pm and stops at Graceland, *Heartbreak Hotel*, and the Rock'n'Soul and Stax museums.

where in the South, is located a few blocks south of Beale at 450 Mulberry St (June–Aug Mon & Wed–Sat 9am–6pm, Sun 1–6pm; Sept–May Mon & Wed–Sat 9am–5pm, Sun 1–5pm; $12, free Mon after 3pm, when there are no audio tours; $15 combination ticket with the Stax museum). It's built around the shell of the former *Lorraine Motel*, where **Dr Martin Luther King Jr** was assassinated by James Earl Ray on April 4, 1968. Dr King was killed by a single bullet as he stood on the balcony, the evening before he was due to lead a march in Memphis in support of a strike by black sanitation workers.

The *Lorraine* itself was one of the few places where blacks and whites could meet in Memphis during the segregation era; thus black singer Eddie Floyd and white guitarist Steve Cropper wrote soul classics such as "Knock on Wood" there, and Dr King was a regular guest. The outer facade of the motel is still all too recognizable from images of King's death, but once inside visitors are faced with a succession of galleries that recount the major milestones of the movement, from A. Philip Randolph of the Brotherhood of Sleeping Car Porters, who originally called for a march on Washington in 1941, through to the Nation of Islam and the Black Panthers. Dioramas and reconstructions include a Montgomery bus, on which sitting on the front seat triggers a recorded message instructing you to move to the back, and a scene from the sanitation workers' dispute. However, by far the most affecting moment comes when you reach King's actual room, Room 306, still laid out as he left it, and see the spot where his life was cut short.

Another wing, across from the motel, completes the story by incorporating the rooming house from which the fatal shot was fired. The bedroom rented that same day by James Earl Ray, and the sordid little bathroom that served as his sniper's nest, can both be inspected behind glass, with the death site clearly visible beyond. King's own family remain highly sceptical as to whether Ray acted alone, and very detailed panels lay out all sorts of conspiracy theories.

The South Main Arts District

A block west of the Civil Rights museum, the once flyblown South Main Street has been given a new and very welcome lease of life. Spanning the eight or so blocks along Main between Vance and G. E. Patterson avenues, the **South Main Arts District** (Ⓦ www.southmainmemphis.org) is a burgeoning area of galleries, chi chi stores and restaurants, complete with a crop of condos and fancy lofts. It's particularly buzzing on the last Friday of the month, when the free "Art Trolley" (6–9pm) runs along Main and the parallel Tennessee St, and stores offer complimentary snacks and drinks. Look out for *D'Edge* gallery, 550 Main St (Ⓣ 901/526-8737, Ⓦ www.d-edgeart.com), which features the folk art-inspired work of African-American artist George Hunt, and the flamboyant diva fashions at *Muse*, 517 Main (Ⓣ 901/526-8737; closed Mon & Tues). Despite all best efforts, the area can still feel dodgy late at night – continue to take sensible precautions.

The Stax Museum of American Soul Music

It was with huge delight in 2003 that one of the city's most famous addresses, 926 E McLemore Avenue, was lovingly resurrected. In 1960, this spot, two bleak miles southeast of downtown (at the corner of College St) was occupied by the Capitol

Theater, the central landmark of a neighborhood where blacks had just started to outnumber whites. The theater went on to become the headquarters of the **Stax** record label, where over the next fifteen years artists such as Otis Redding, Isaac Hayes, Albert King, and the Staples Singers cut fifteen US number-one singles and achieved 237 entries in the top 100. The studio was a veritable powerhouse of funky soul; by 1990, however, with Stax long since defunct, 926 E McLemore Avenue was no more than a derelict lot.

Now the complex has been reconstructed larger than ever, with a music academy sitting next to the **Stax Museum of American Soul Music**, also known, thanks to the sign on the theater marquee, as **Soulsville** (March–Oct Mon–Sat 9am–4pm, Sun 1–4pm; Nov–Feb Mon–Sat 10am–4pm, Sun 1–4pm; $9, $15 combination ticket with the Civil Rights Museum). Visits start with an honest film history of the label, using stunning footage to illuminate both the triumphs and the tensions that arose from its all-but-unique status as a joint black-white enterprise in the segregated South. The first exhibit beyond, designed to emphasize the gospel roots of soul music, is an entire Episcopal Church, transported here from Duncan, Mississippi. Then follows a glorious celebration of soul history that abounds in video footage and recordings, as well as showpiece artifacts like Isaac Hayes's peacock-blue and gold Cadillac. There's even a disco floor where you can dance along with archive *Soul Train* TV footage to classics like "The Push and Pull" and "The Funky Robot". The actual Stax studio has been recreated in loving detail, featuring the original two-track tape recorder used by Otis Redding to record "Mr Pitiful" and "Respect," as well as Al Jackson's drum kit. A map of the immediate neighborhood, still largely rundown, shows what an amazing assembly of talent lived nearby; Aretha Franklin was born at 406 Lucy Ave, while other local luminaries included Booker T, David Porter, and Memphis Slim.

The riverfront

The northern boundary of downtown Memphis is marked by the surreal 32-story, 321ft **Pyramid**, two-thirds the size of Egypt's Great Pyramid. Completed in 1991, it was intended to create a symbolic link with Egypt's Nile Delta, and certainly makes an evocative sight gleaming on the skyline. After a decade and a half hosting major exhibitions, concerts, and games it has since been overshadowed by the FedEx Forum and lain empty since 2005. While it remains to be seen what the future holds for this marvelous folly, its symbolic beauty is undeniable. The surrounding neighborhood, the historic **Pinch District**, is said to be named for the impoverished – "pinched" – Irish immigrants who settled here in the mid 1800s. It's a quiet area, but home to a clutch of friendly cafés and bars.

From Riverside Drive, which runs south from the Pyramid, **monorail trains** and a walkway head across the Mississippi's Wolf Channel to **Mud Island** (Tues–Sun: April, May, Sept & Oct 10am–5pm; June–Aug 10am–6pm; park access free, monorail $2 or included in museum admission, $8), which formed in 1910 when the river began depositing silt alongside a stationary boat. Highlights of the island's **Mississippi River Museum**, an enjoyable and ingenious romp through the history of the river, include a full-sized reconstructed steam packet squeezed into the core of the building, a morbidly fascinating "Theater of Disasters," and tales of semi-legendary characters like keelboatman Mike Fink, who in 1830 styled himself "half horse, half alligator." They've also packed in a good overview of Memphis music. Cool your feet afterwards by splashing in the waters of the half-mile **River Walk**, which runs to the southern tip of the island. This scale replica of the lower Mississippi River, complete with town grids, begins in Cairo, Illinois and ends in New Orleans, opening out to the "Gulf of Mexico," an enclosed lake where you can rent paddle boats at $2 per person per half hour. From the pavilion nearby, it's also possible to rent canoes ($20/hr) and kayaks ($15/hr); in summer, you can even bring a sleeping bag and join a mass campout where the tent, dinner, breakfast and entertainment is laid on (second Fri of each month April–Oct; ☎901/576-7241).

Back on the mainland, south of the monorail, **Jefferson Davis** and **Confederate parks** hold little of interest. Heading south along **Front Street**, however, brings you to the imposing buildings of **Cotton Row**. This area might have seen busier days, but it is still the largest spot cotton market (meaning actual cotton is sold here, for cash) in the world. Memphis's **Cotton Museum**, in the grand old Cotton Exchange at Front Street and 65 Union Ave, uses photos, videos, and quirky artifacts to outline the history of the "white gold" that has had such a huge influence on the economy and culture of the South (Tues–Sat 10am–5pm, Sun noon–5pm; $5).

Further south, **Tom Lee Park**, the venue for major outdoor events such as the **Memphis in May** festival (see p.565), runs for about a mile and a half along the river. The park commemorates a black boatman who rescued 32 people from a sinking boat in 1925 – despite not being able to swim.

The Big Muddy

I do not know much about gods; but I think that the river
Is a strong brown god – sullen, untamed and intractable.

St Louis–born T.S. Eliot, *The Four Quartets*

North America's principal waterway, the **Mississippi** – the name comes from the Algonquin words for "big" and "river" – starts just ninety miles south of the Canadian border at Lake Itasca, Minnesota, and winds its way nearly 2400 miles to the Gulf of Mexico, taking in over one hundred tributaries en route and draining all or part of thirty-one US states and two Canadian provinces.

The **"Big Muddy"** – it carries 2lb of dirt for every 1000lb of water – is one of the busiest commercial rivers in the world, and one of the least conventional. Instead of widening toward its mouth, like most rivers, the Mississippi grows narrower and deeper. Its **delta**, near Memphis, more than three hundred miles upstream from the river's mouth, is not a delta at all, but an alluvial flood plain. Furthermore, its estuary deposits, which extend the land six miles out to sea every century, are paltry compared to other rivers; gulf currents disperse the sediment before it has time to settle.

In the words of Mark Twain, who spent four years as a riverboat pilot, the Mississippi is also "the **crookedest** river in the world." As it weaves and curls its way extravagantly along its channel, it continually cuts through narrow necks of land to shape and reshape oxbow lakes and meander scars, cutoffs, and marshy backwaters. A nightclub could operate one day in Arkansas and then find itself in dry Tennessee the next, thanks to an overnight cutoff.

A more serious manifestation of the Mississippi's power is its propensity to **flood**. Although the river builds its own levees, artificial embankments have, since as early as 1717, helped to safeguard crops and homes. After the disastrous floods of 1927, the federal government installed a wide range of flood-protection measures; virtually the entire riverfront from Cape Girardeau, Missouri, to the sea is now walled in, and it's even possible to drive along the top of the larger levees. The devastating flooding of New Orleans after Hurricane Katrina, however, shows just how fragile the levee system remains.

While it's no longer feasible to sail Twain's route for yourself, **riverboat excursions** operate in most sizeable river towns, including Memphis (see p.555). Longer cruises, between St Louis and New Orleans – or even further afield – on the luxurious *Delta Queen*, *American Queen*, and *Mississippi Queen* **paddlewheelers**, are expensive; contact the Delta Queen Steamboat Company (☎1-800/543-1949, ⊛www.deltaqueen.com).

Graceland

In itself, Elvis Presley's **Graceland** was a surprisingly modest home for the world's most successful entertainer – it's certainly not the "mansion" you may have imagined. And while Elvis was clearly a man who indulged his tastes to the fullest, Graceland has none of the pomposity that characterizes so many other showpiece Southern residences. Visits are affectionate celebrations of the man; never exactly tongue-in-cheek, but not cloyingly reverential either.

Elvis was just 22 when he paid $100,000 for Graceland in 1957. Built in 1939, the stone-clad house was then considered one of the most desirable properties in Memphis, though today the neighborhood is distinctly less exclusive, its main thoroughfare – **Elvis Presley Boulevard** – lined with discount liquor stores, ancient beauty parlors, fast-food joints, and surprisingly few Elvis-related souvenir shops. Tours start opposite the house in **Graceland Plaza**; excited visitors, kitted out with headphones, are ferried across the road in minibuses, which depart every few minutes and sweep through the house's famous "musical gate," etched with musical notes and Elvis's silhouette. No stops are made at the perimeter "Wall of Love," scrawled with tens of thousands of messages from fans, but you are free to walk back there after the tour.

Though the audio tours, peppered with spoken memories from Elvis's daughter, Lisa Marie, and rousing choruses from the King himself, allow you to spend as long as you wish, it's not easy to get an accurate sense of the house's size and layout while here, as the upstairs rooms are out of bounds to visitors. The interior is a frozen tribute to the taste of the Seventies; choice viewings include the Hawaiian-themed **Jungle Room**, with its waterfall and green shag-carpeted ceiling, where Elvis recorded "Moody Blue" and other gems from his latter years, and the navy-and-lemon **TV Room**, mirrored and fitted with three screens that now show classic 1970s TV shows. A former garage allows you to see many personal items that Elvis kept upstairs, ranging from a spectacular white, circular, fur bed to his very ordinary bedroom slippers, and including philosophy books scrawled with his musings, his extensive gun collection, and whippet-slim suits from the 1960s. In the separate **Trophy Room**, you parade past Elvis's platinum, gold, and silver records, stage costumes, and outfits from many of his 31 films; footage of his early TV performances offers breathtaking reminders of just how charismatic the young Elvis was. The tour of the interior ends with the **racquetball room**, where he played on the morning he died. In the attached lounge, the piano where he sang for the last time (apparently "Unchained Melody") stands eerily silent, while in the court itself his resplendent, bejeweled capes and Vegas jumpsuits stand sentinel beneath huge monitors showing his later performances. Here, perhaps more than anywhere else, you can feel the huge presence of the man who changed the face of music forever.

Elvis (Jan 8, 1935–Aug 16, 1977), his mother, Gladys, his father, Vernon, and his grandmother, Minnie Mae, lie buried in the **Meditation Garden** outside, their graves strewn with flowers and soft toys sent from fans. Elvis's body was moved here two months after his death, when the security problems inherent in keeping it in the local cemetery became obvious. There's often a log-jam here, as visitors crane to read the messages sent by fans, take moments to offer their own prayers, and snap countless photos of the bronze memorial plaques.

Graceland Plaza, resounding with nonstop Elvis hits, holds several enjoyable related attractions: don't miss the wittily edited film *Walk a Mile in My Shoes*, the **"Sincerely Elvis"** timeline, which follows 1956, the year he made it big, month by month, and Elvis's personal **airplanes**, including the *Lisa Marie*, customized with 24-carat gold washroom sink and blue suede furnishings. End your tour with a sit-down in the **Elvis Presley Automobile Museum**, which, quite apart from

△ Graceland

a Harley-Davidson golf cart and powder-pink Cadillac, shows action-packed and vaguely car-related clips from his movies. **Elvis After Dark**, in the shabby mall next door, ostensibly covers the notoriously playful Presley's leisure time, but compared to the rest of the complex it feels like little more than an add-on to the neighbouring gift store. Completists, however, will not want to miss the TV punctured by a bullet fired by Elvis himself (he also shot his fridge, his stereo, and even Lisa Marie's slide).

The Plaza's many **gift stores** – which are, quite frankly, a delight, selling everything from Elvis coffee to *Jailhouse Rock* outfits for your pooch – and its clutch of Elvis-themed **diners** (try the barbecue at the *Chrome Grill*, and make sure to seat yourself in the 1950s Cadillac) make it easy to stay all day.

Graceland attractions

Graceland is ten miles southeast of downtown Memphis, at 3734 Elvis Presley Blvd. The ticket office is open March–Oct Mon–Sat 9am–5pm, Sun 10am–4pm; Nov daily 10am–4pm; Dec–Feb Mon & Wed–Sun 10am–4pm. The last house tour starts at the ticket office's closing time, while the other attractions remain open for roughly another two hours.

A combined "Platinum" **ticket** to all attractions (allow three hours) is $30; house tours only, $22 (closed Tues Dec–Feb); parking $6. **Reservations** are recommended, especially in August (℡901/332-3322 or 1-800/238-2000, ✆www.elvis.com).

The centerpiece of the heavily wooded **Overton Park**, three or so miles east of downtown on Poplar Ave, is the **Memphis Zoo** (daily: March–Oct 9am–6pm; Nov–Feb 9am–5pm; last admission 1hr before closing; $13, $3 parking), entered between two dramatic Egyptian-styled towers. If the usual array of gorillas, orangutans, and giraffes doesn't satisfy you, you can pay $3 extra to visit with a pair of giant pandas, or coo at the polar bears and sea lions in the Northwest Passage exhibit. The park also holds the **Memphis Brooks Museum of Art** (Tues–Fri 10am–4pm, Sat 10am–5pm, Sun 11.30am–5pm; $8; first Wed of the month also 6–9pm, except Jan & July), whose array of fine art features an especially strong collection of medieval and Renaissance works.

A mile or so south of the park, the **Cooper-Young** intersection boasts a handful of funky espresso bars and restaurants, along with a good crop of vintage stores where the city's young and hip burrow through secondhand psychedelic threads, and richer arty types muse over retro knick-knacks. It's a lively place, quite different from downtown but still distinctly Memphis, where blues and barbecue rub along with poetry readings and yard sales, art exhibits and antique auctions. Its one-day **festival**, held in September, attracts huge crowds for its folk arts, regional crafts, and local music.

Another couple of miles further southeast, the **Memphis Pink Palace Museum and Planetarium** at 3050 Central Ave (Mon–Sat 9am–5pm, Sun noon–5pm; $8.25) centers on the not-very-pink marble mansion of Clarence Saunders, who founded America's first chain of self-service **supermarkets**, Piggly-Wiggly, in 1916. Saunders went bankrupt in 1923 and never actually lived here; instead, the building has acquired several new wings in the process of becoming an appealingly old-fashioned and rather quirky museum of Memphis history. It holds all kinds of stuffed animals and oddities, including a miniature automated circus, a gory exhibit on the city's early years, and a fascinating walk-through model of the first Piggly-Wiggly store, complete with 2¢ packets of Kellogg's Cornflakes and 8¢ cans of Campbell's Soup, plus a series of adverts demonstrating early teething problems – including the evolution of a new crime, "shoplifting" – in establishing this radical self-service venture. There's also an IMAX cinema and the **Sharpe Planetarium**.

Eating

Memphians are fond of their food, and proclaim their city to be the **pork barbecue** capital of the world. There's far more to Memphis than BBQ, however – **soul food** fans will be delighted, as will anyone who likes inventive **contemporary Southern cuisine**. You'll have no problem finding somewhere good **downtown** – note that several of the Beale Street clubs reviewed under "Nightlife" on p.566 also serve food – or in the eclectic **Cooper-Young** district.

Arcade 540 S Main St ☎901/526–5757. Said to be Memphis's oldest restaurant, this atmospheric landmark diner – Elvis ate here! – in the South Main District was featured in Jim Jarmusch's movie *Mystery Train*, among many others. Come here for large Southern breakfasts, pizzas, and home cooking, and pose for photos outside the iconic facade. Daily 8am–3pm.

Automatic Slim's Tonga Club 83 S Second St ☎901/525-7948. A Memphis institution in the heart of downtown, where you can eat delicious

Southwestern-tinged global cuisine – coconut-crusted fish served with jicama slaw and avocado, for example – in arty, comfortably hip surroundings. Closed Sun.

The Beauty Shop 966 S Cooper ☎901/272-7111. The witty retro fittings – glass brick partitions, mismatched crockery, 1940s hairdryer chairs – are perfectly in tune with Cooper-Young's funky vintage-store flair, while the eclectic fusion food (lunch, dinner and Sunday brunch) is tasty and satisfying.

Café Francisco 400 N Main St ☎ 901/578-8002. Hunker down on an overstuffed velvet sofa, in a red leather booth, or at a rickety table in this cavernous, effortlessly boho and very relaxing coffeehouse that also serves good light meals. It's on the trolley route, near the Pyramid in the Pinch district. Free WiFi.

Four Way Grill 998 Mississippi Blvd ☎ 901/507-1519. Convenient for the Stax museum, this spotless little soul food joint – a favourite haunt of Martin Luther King Jr – dishes up unbeatable blue plate specials including fried chicken, ham hocks and scrumptious side vegetables at unbelievably low prices. Closed Mon.

Gus's Fried Chicken 310 S Front St ☎ 901/527-4877. This tiny downhome place near the South Main Arts District has reached the attention of the national press for its delicious, crackling-crisp and spicy chicken – don't miss it.

Interstate Bar-B-Que 2265 S Third St ☎ 901/775-2304, ⓦ www.jimneelysinterstatebarbecue.com. Legendary barbecue restaurant, south of downtown (leave I-55 at exit 7) on the way to the Delta. Try the barbecue spaghetti. Closed Sun.

Java Cabana 2170 Young Ave ☎ 901/272-7210. Friendly alternative coffeehouse in the Cooper-Young district, with poetry readings and live music. Closed Mon.

McEwan's 122 Monroe Ave ☎ 901/527-7085. At the heart of downtown, four blocks north of Beale, McEwan's has the ambiance of a cosy neighborhood bistro, serving inventive and delicious modern Southern cooking in a brick-walled room. The laid-back adjoining bar is also a local favorite.

Otherlands 641 S Cooper Ave ☎ 901/278-4994. Funky Midtown coffeehouse that's good for espresso, juices and fresh sandwiches. The laid-back crowd hangs out for hours in the warren of rooms, with their jumble of tatty sofas, armchairs, and even desks. Open until 8pm Mon–Sat, 7pm weekends.

The Rendezvous General Washburn Alley, 52 S Second St ☎ 901/523-2746, ⓦ www.hogsfly.com. Downtown Memphis's most famous pork barbecue joint, tucked away in a back alley, is colossal and very crowded. Enjoy the good-value meat feasts in a hectic atmosphere. Open Tues–Sat.

Nightlife and entertainment

Memphis's thriving **live music** scene is at its best during the city's many **festivals**, especially the month-long **Memphis in May**, where big-name soul, blues, and funk performances run side by side with the World Championship Barbecue Cooking Contest, and August's **Elvis Tribute Week**.

At other times, while it would be easy to look down on touristy **Beale Street** as sanitized and inauthentic, its close-packed assortment of music clubs actually has plenty to offer. The whole enclave, tightly patrolled to ensure visitor safety, is successful both architecturally and atmospherically, with street musicians adding to the ambiance. On Friday nights, a $10 wristband offers admission to all the major clubs. The stage in **W.C. Handy Park**, on Beale at Third Street, also features live bands – most nights for free. At the other end of the scale, the city's vibrant punk and garage scene sees some spectacularly grungy **alternative bands** playing steamy hole-in-the-walls.

Beyond its music, Memphis is also a good place for movie lovers, with classic films shown at the grand old *Orpheum* during the summer, an increasingly popular international **film festival** in April, and, in October, the edgy **Indie Memphis**, which focuses on low-budget Southern movies.

Barbecue in Memphis

In addition to the barbecue joints reviewed here, look out for the *Corky's* chain, which originated in Memphis and does fantastic dry ribs; *TOPS*, a local chain that serves BBQ fast-food style; *Cozy Corner*, midtown at 745 North Parkway (☎ 901/527-9158), where you can try barbecued Cornish hen; *The BBQ Shop*, also midtown, 1782 Madison (☎ 901/272-1277), which offers amazing wet and dry ribs; and, for a slightly alternative edge, *Central*, 2249 Central (☎ 901/272-9377), where you can also pick up homemade potato chips and a BBQ mushroom sandwich.

Gospel in Memphis: the Reverend Al Green

Memphis has been renowned for its **gospel** music since the Thirties, when Rev. Herbert Brewster wrote **Mahalia Jackson**'s "Move On Up a Little Higher." Following a religious revelation, the consummate soul stylist **Al Green**, who scored big for Memphis's **Hi Records** with hits like "Let's Stay Together" and "Tired of Being Alone," has preached since the early 1980s at his own **Full Gospel Tabernacle**, 787 Hale Rd, in the leafy suburb of Whitehaven. Visitors are welcome at the 11.30am **Sunday services**; to get there, continue a mile south of Graceland on Elvis Presley Blvd, then turn west (phone ahead to make sure the Reverend is in town; ☎901/396-9192, ⊛www. algreenmusic.com). While they're very much church services rather than concerts, Green remains an astonishingly charismatic performer – and he does sing, backed by a smoking four-piece soul band. It's an unmissable – and, indeed, deeply spiritual – Memphis experience.

The best source of **listings** is the free weekly *Memphis Flyer* (⊛ www.memphisflyer .com). You could also pop into Shangri-La Records, a treasure trove of Memphis music, midtown at 1916 Madison Ave (☎901/274-1916, ⊛www.shangri.com), for flyers and news of upcoming gigs.

B.B. King's Blues Club 147 Beale St ☎901/524-KING, ⊛www.bbkingblues.com. Despite accusations from purists of having "sold out," this remains Beale's most popular club. It's spacious and atmospheric, with regular blues (among other music) enjoyed by an enthusiastic crowd that makes good use of the dance floor – and the barbecue's not bad, either. B.B. himself appears once or twice a year.

Blues City Café 138 Beale St ☎901/526-3637, ⊛www.bluescitycafe.com. Popular Beale Street barbecue joint where musicians from nearby clubs dine on well-priced ribs, catfish, tamales, and gumbo. Live music nightly until late, in a down-home atmosphere. Open daily 11am–3am (5am at weekends).

Buccaneer Lounge 1368 Monroe Ave ☎901/278-0909. This grungy midtown venue – with a kind of pirate-themed junk store ambiance – is one of the city's best places to see local underground bands.

Earnestine and Hazel's 531 S Main St ☎901/523-9754. A legendary brothel-turned-jook joint, this spot was the haunt of everyone from Elvis to the Stax musicians. It's especially good late at night, when the Memphis music juke box blasts and the famed burgers start sizzling. Occasional live music.

HiTone Café 1913 Poplar Ave ☎901/278-8663, ⊛www.hitonememphis.com. From Memphis garage bands to comedians to Elvis impersonators, this eclectic Midtown bar/club is always worth checking out.

New Daisy Theater 330 Beale St ☎901/525-8979, ⊛www.newdaisy.com. Restored movie theater at the east end of Beale that attracts a young, pierced crowd for its punk, metal, boxing, and hardcore wrestling. Also makes a great venue for the occasional big-name artist.

Rum Boogie Café 182 Beale St ☎901/528-0150. ⊛www.rumboogie.com. Live blues is staged in the main room, while the smaller and more intimate *Blues Hall*, adjoining, is a mocked-up jook joint that regularly hosts anything from boogie blues to frenetic punkabilly.

Wild Bill's 1580 Vollintine Ave ☎901/726-5473. Neighborhood jook joint where visitors are welcome to join locals at the long tables for laid-back live blues and soul Fri–Sun. Located three miles northeast of downtown, in North Memphis.

Young Avenue Deli 2119 Young Ave ☎901/278-0034, ⊛www.youngavenuedeli.com. Misleadingly named Cooper-Young favorite, featuring almost nightly local and national rock, folk, punk, and alt bands.

Shiloh National Military Park

Approximately 110 miles east of Memphis and twelve southwest of Savannah, Tennessee, via US-64 and Hwy-22, **Shiloh National Military Park** (daily 8am–dusk; $5 per vehicle; ☎731/689-5696, ⊛www.nps.gov/shil) commemorates one of the most crucial battles of the Civil War. After victories at Fort Henry and Fort Donelson, General Grant's confident Union forces were all but defeated at Shiloh by a surprise early-morning Confederate attack on April 6, 1862. A stubborn rump of resistance held on until around 5pm, and the Confederates elected to finish the task off the next morning rather than launching a twilight assault. However, Grant's decimated regiments were bolstered by the overnight arrival of reinforcements, and instead it was their dawn initiative that forced the tired and demoralized Confederates to retreat.

Shiloh was the first encounter on a scale that became common as the war continued, putting an abrupt end to the romantic innocence of many a raw volunteer soldier. Over twenty thousand men in all were killed. Even the war-toughened General Sherman spoke of "piles of dead soldiers' mangled bodies . . . without heads and legs . . . the scenes on this field would have cured anyone of war."

The **visitor center** displays artifacts recovered from the battlefield and shows a twenty-minute film. A self-guided ten-mile driving tour takes in the **National Cemetery**, whose moss-covered walls contain thousands of unidentified graves.

Nashville

Set amid the gentle hills and fertile farmlands of central Tennessee, the sprawling city of **NASHVILLE** attracts six million visitors each year. The great majority – devoted fans and the just plain curious alike – come to immerse themselves in **country music**, whether at mainstream showcases like the **Country Music Hall of Fame** and the **Grand Ole Opry**, or in the smaller clubs and honky-tonks found not only downtown but also in Nashville's many disparate neighborhoods.

Behind all the rhinestone glitter and showbiz razzmatazz exists a hard-working, rather conservative city. Nashville has been the leading settlement in middle Tennessee since **Fort Nashborough** was established in 1779. State capital since 1843, it is now the **financial** and **insurance** center of the mid-South, as well as a fast-growing **manufacturing** base. Rapid development since World War II has transformed a once-compact town into a maze-like, often alienating conurbation, stretching out in all directions along the undulating roads, here known as **pikes**.

For all its "Nash-Vegas" image, the city has maintained a strong reputation for **learning** since planter times. As well as holding over a thousand **churches** – more per capita than anywhere else in the country – it has been tagged the "Protestant Vatican" for its proliferation of training colleges for preachers and missionaries, church administrative offices, and Bible-publishing plants.

Arrival, information, and getting around

Nashville International Airport is eight miles – around a $25 **taxi** ride – southeast of downtown. The Gray Line shuttle (every 15–20min 5am–11pm; $12 one way, $18 roundtrip; ☏615/883-5555, ⓦwww.graylinenashville.com) drops off at most downtown hotels; Metropolitan Transit Authority **buses** leave hourly (until 5.33pm Mon–Fri, 4.35pm Sat & Sun; $1.25; ☏615/862-5969, ⓦwww.nashvillemta .org). The **Greyhound** station is in a seedy part of downtown at 200 Eighth Ave S. There's no Amtrak service.

The best place to pick up information on the city is the excellent **visitor center**, downtown at Fifth and Broadway, in the massive Gaylord Entertainment Center (Mon–Sat 8.30am–5.30pm, Sun 10am–5pm; ☏615/259-4747 or 1-800/657-6910, ⓦwww.visitmusiccity.com); the second branch, 150 4th Ave N (Mon–Fri 8am–5pm; ☏615/259-4731), is also good.

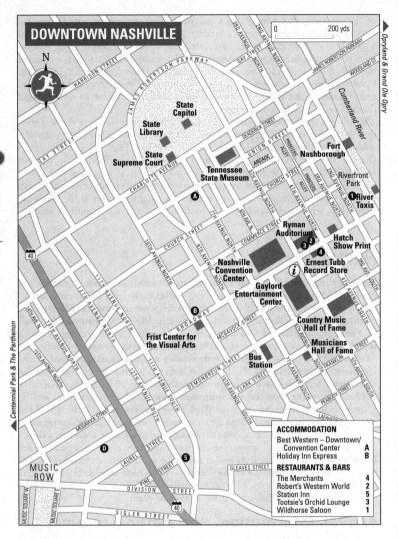

DOWNTOWN NASHVILLE

0   200 yds

ACCOMMODATION
Best Western – Downtown/
  Convention Center   A
Holiday Inn Express   B
RESTAURANTS & BARS
The Merchants   4
Robert's Western World
Station Inn   5
Tootsie's Orchid Lounge   3
Wildhorse Saloon   1

If you like your country music laid on with lots of brash, camp fun, hop aboard the "Big Pink Bus" and let the singing guides of **Nash-Trash Tours** dish the dirt on all your favorite stars (Wed–Sat, 90min; $29.50; reservations essential; ☎615/226-7300 or ☎1-800/342-2132, ⓦ www.nashtrash.com).

Accommodation

The CVB's **Central Reservations Center** (☎1-800/657-6910) offers discounted rates on most city hotels; the budget **motels** are concentrated a couple of miles north of downtown, off the I-65 Trinity Lane/Brick Church Pike exit (be sure to pick up discount coupons in the Tennessee state welcome centers). Rates are usually higher in June during the CMA Music Festival (formerly Fan Fair; see p.572). There's RV and tent **camping** at *Opryland KOA*, 2626 Music Valley Drive (℡615/889-0286 or 1-800/562-7789, ⊛www.nashvillekoa.com), set in 27 attractive acres and with free live music shows in the summer.

Best Western – Downtown/Convention Center 711 Union St ℡615/242-4311 or 1-800/627-3297. Cheap motel on the north side of downtown, facing the capitol. Rates include continental breakfast. ❸

Cat's Pajamas B&B 818 Woodland St ℡615/650-4553. Friendly, simple, three-room B&B a short drive east of downtown. Only one room is en suite. ❹

Days Inn – Stadium/Downtown 211 N First St ℡615/254-1551 or 1-800/251-3038, ⊛www .daysinn.com. Inexpensive hotel near downtown. The area can feel unsafe at night, so take a cab. ❸

Gaylord Opryland Resort 2800 Opryland Drive ℡615/889-1000, ⊛www.gaylordhotels.com /gaylordopryland/. Unbelievably vast and expensive 3000-room place – included here not because it's recommended, but simply because it's used by so many tour groups – laid out around lavish gardens and glass-roofed courtyards, permeated with syrupy music. It takes an age simply to get to or from your room, let alone drive the nine miles downtown. Suites can cost as much as $3500. ❼

GuestHouse International Inn & Suites Music Valley 2420 Music Valley Drive ℡615/885-4030. Clean, comfortable and good-value option near the *Gaylord Opryland* and Grand Ole Opry. Rates include continental breakfast. ❹

Holiday Inn Express 920 Broadway ℡615/244-0150, ⊛www.ichotelsgroup.com. A good downtown option with pool and free breakfast buffet. ❺

The City

Other than the venerable structures you'd expect in a state capital, such as the Capitol building itself and various imposing courthouses and banks, the major landmarks of **downtown Nashville** are the unmissable **Country Music Hall of Fame**, at Fifth and Demonbreun streets, and the gigantic **Gaylord Entertainment Center** sports and entertainment complex (formerly the Nashville Arena), at Fifth Avenue and Broadway.

Further afield, **Music Row**, which centers on Demonbreun Street a mile southwest of downtown, forms the heart of Nashville's recording industry, with companies like Warner Bros., Mercury, and Sony operating out of plush office blocks – there's little of interest to tourists.

Nine miles northeast of downtown in the **Opryland** area and along **Music Valley Drive**, you'll find not only the **Grand Ole Opry** – which still hosts its famed live radio show – but also several old-fashioned country music-related sights, including wax and car museums, mini-golf courses, and a number of music shows.

The Country Music Hall of Fame

Nashville's premier visitor attraction is the superb **Country Music Hall of Fame**, 222 Fifth Ave S (daily 9am–5pm; $16.95, $18.95 including audio tour, $23 including admission to the Ryman Auditorium, $23.95 including admission to Studio B, $29.95 including admission to both; $4 parking). The building itself is an architectural tour de force, laden with musical symbolism – the whole thing is in the shape of a bass clef; the central tower is topped by representations of a 12-inch LP, a 7-inch single, and a CD; a Cadillac fin pokes from one corner; and so on – but what really makes it special are the exhibits. These strike an appealing balance between the music itself and the memorabilia that goes with it. Alongside stage costumes and paraphernalia from countless stars, including Elvis's gold Cadillac, you get a fascinatingly detailed history of all aspects of the genre from its earliest roots, with films and recordings constantly playing. Soundproof booths are devoted to such milestone waxings as Ferlin Husky's 1956 "Gone," hailed as the first instance of the "Nashville Sound," while younger stars reminisce on video about the older generations. Songwriters and musicians give regular live demonstrations of their skills, and you can also use touch-screen technology to "interview" the likes of Dolly Parton or design your own C & W threads. The **Hall of Fame** itself, right at the end, is somewhat anticlimactic, simply consisting of a circular chamber filled with plaques; you may be more excited by the opportunity to burn your own custom CD.

The Hall of Fame also offers short **bus tours** that provide the only way to visit RCA's legendary **Studio B** on Music Row. Between 1957 and 1977, forty gold records were cut here, starting with Don Gibson's "Oh Lonesome Me" and including Dolly Parton's "Jolene," but it's probably most famous for a thirteen-year run of Elvis hits (invariably recorded at night) like "Are You Lonesome Tonight?" and "It's Now or Never." Recently restored and rewired, it's once again open for business, but only the most dedicated of fans are likely to find walking through the bare rooms worth the time and money.

Downtown Nashville

Most of **downtown Nashville** looks much like any other regional business center, dominated by office blocks and parking lots, though it's worth strolling along both **Broadway** and **Second Avenue** to enjoy their atmospheric assortment of honky-tonks, bars, restaurants, and gift stores. In business since 1879, the unmissable **Hatch Show Print**, 316 Broadway (Mon–Fri 9am–5pm, Sat 10am–5pm; ☎615/256-2805; ⓦ www.countrymusichalloffame.com), prints and sells evocative posters from the early days of country and rock 'n' roll, using the original blocks, and continues to produce new work. Opposite, another institution, **Ernest Tubb Record Shop** (☎615/55-7503, ⓦ www.etrecordshop.com), sells vintage and rare country music, and displays Grand Ole Opry costumes.

The original home of the Grand Ole Opry, the **Ryman Auditorium**, 116 Fifth Ave, can be seen on self-guided tours (daily 9am–4pm; $8.50; $3.25 extra for occasional backstage tours; ⓦ www.ryman.com). A church-like space, its wooden church pews illuminated by stained glass and its display cases filled with flowered frocks and bootlace ties belonging to the stars, it really evokes the heyday of traditional country. You can still catch the odd live evening performance by big-name bands, and for an extra $15 it's possible to record your own CD.

Spreading its remit beyond country music, the **Musicians Hall of Fame** (Mon–Thurs 10am–6pm, Fri & Sat 10am–5pm, Sun 1–5pm; $14.95; ⓦ www. musicianshalloffame.com), a few blocks away at 301 Sixth Ave S, pays homage to the session musicians who are often overlooked in all the hullabaloo surrounding the big names. Instruments, photos, film footage, and recordings tell the story of the generations of bass players, drummers, trumpeters, and pianists who provided the backbone for some of the most famous songs ever recorded.

Downtown also has some non-music-related diversions. Housed in a gorgeous Art Deco building, the **Frist Center for the Visual Arts**, 919 Broadway (Sat–Wed 10am–5.30pm, Thurs & Fri 10am–9pm; $8.50; ⓦ www.fristcenter.org), is well worth a look, its changing exhibitions featuring everything from sculpture and photography to ancient art. At the other end of Broadway, **Riverfront Park** is a thin stretch of grass and terracing that dips down to the **Cumberland River**. Immediately north, set above the river on a promontory, a replica of the wooden **Fort Nashborough** (Tues–Sun 9am–5pm; free) serves as a monument to the city's founders of 1779. A few blocks north again, the worthy **Tennessee State Museum**, 505 Deaderick St (Tues–Sat 10am–5pm, Sun 1–5pm; free), is strongest on Civil War history, highlighting the hardships suffered by the ill-clad, ill-fed soldiers on both sides, of whom 23,000 out of 77,000 died at Shiloh (see p.566) alone. Other displays in this huge space focus on frontier life and on black Tennesseans, looking at slavery, Reconstruction, the founding of the Ku Klux Klan, and the civil rights movement.

West of Downtown

In 1897, Tennessee celebrated its Centennial Exposition in **Centennial Park**, two miles southwest of downtown at West End and 25th avenues. Nashville honored its nickname as the "Athens of the South" by constructing a full-sized wood-and-plaster replica of the **Parthenon**. That proved so popular that it was replaced by a permanent structure in 1931, an impressive edifice that's now home to Nashville's premier **art museum** (Tues–Sat 9am–4.30pm; June–Aug also Sun 12.30–4.30pm; $5). The upper hall is dominated by a gilded 42ft replica of Phidias's statue of the goddess Athena – said to be the largest indoor statue in the western world – surrounded by reproductions of the Elgin Marbles.

Just across West End Avenue from Centennial Park, weather-beaten Gothic structures sit alongside more modern buildings on the campus of the prestigious, and highly conservative, **Vanderbilt University**. South of here, 21st Avenue S runs through the heart of the characterful **Hillsboro Village**, abounding in cafés, restaurants, and book and antique stores. Half a mile northeast of Centennial Park, **Fisk University** is one of the nation's oldest black colleges. The excellent **Van Vechten Gallery**, on campus at Jackson St and 18th Ave N (Tues–Fri 10am–5pm, Sat & Sun 1–5pm; closed Sun in summer; donation), holds works by Picasso, Cézanne, Renoir, and Georgia O'Keeffe; it also has changing exhibits on African-American themes.

Eating

Nashville has its share of awful chain **restaurants**, but it also offers many down-home Southern joints, as well as upscale places well suited for expense-account dining. Many live music venues (see p.572) also serve food.

Arnold's 605 8th Ave S ☎615/256-4455. Classic canteen for Southern meat-and-three meals (featuring meat, three vegetables, and cornbread and/or rolls). The delicious country cooking includes fried chicken, ham, or pork chops with side dishes – macaroni cheese, fried green tomatoes, turnip greens, and the like – for around $7. Get there early for lunch to avoid a long wait. Mon–Fri 10.30am–2.45pm.

Cock o' the Walk 2624 Music Valley Drive ☎615/889-1930 ⓦwww.cockofthewalkrestaurant. com. If you hanker for huge feasts of fried catfish, onion rings, and pickles, then don't let the hokey environs here – there's a kind of keelboat theme going on – put you off. The fish is fresh and very good.

Jimmy Kelly's 217 Louise Ave ☎615/329-4349. Nashville's favorite steakhouse for seventy years, just off West End Ave near Vanderbilt. Dinner only Mon–Sat.

The Loveless Café 8400 Hwy-100, 20 miles south of town ☎615/646-9700, ⓦwww.lovelesscafe. com. Friendly café famed for its superb country food. Breakfasts are best: hunks of salty ham with gravy, eggs, toast, and fluffy biscuits slicked with succulent homemade jams. Reservations recommended.

The Merchants 401 Broadway ☎615/254-1892. Historic downtown building housing two dining rooms; the casual grill downstairs, which is ideal for a tasty lunch – crabcakes, grilled portabella sandwiches, and the like – and the more formal restaurant upstairs, serving classic American favorites.

Noshville Deli 1918 Broadway ☎615/329-6674, also 4014 Hillsboro Circle ☎615/269-3535, ⓦnoshville.com. Great breakfasts, huge sandwiches, and wicked shakes in this beloved New York-style deli.

Pancake Pantry 1796 21st Ave ☎615/383-9333. With more than 20 pancake choices, and wonderful flapjacks, this cheery Hillsboro Village institution is a very popular breakfast spot – expect to wait, maybe hours, for a table at the weekend. Mon–Fri 6am–3pm, Sat & Sun 6am–4pm.

Sunset Grill 2001 Belcourt Ave ☎615/386-3663, ⓦwww.sunsetgrill.com. Stylish Hillsboro Village restaurant, serving upmarket Southern and Tex-Mex fusion food. The terrace is great for people-watching. Lunch Tues–Fri only, dinner until late nightly.

Nightlife and entertainment

The two most obvious ways to experience **live country music** in Nashville are either to head for the cluster of **honky-tonks** that line Lower Broadway between Second and Fourth avenues – they're all pretty down-to-earth, hard-drinking places, though out-of-towners nonetheless make up a large proportion of the clientele – or to buy a ticket for a rather more genteel show at the **Grand Ole Opry**, a fair drive out from downtown. If you're in town for a few nights, however, it's worth making the effort to catch up-and-coming or more specialized acts at places like the *Bluebird Café* and the *Station Inn*; look out, too, for special events, including bluegrass nights, at the **Ryman Auditorium** (see p.570). Just west of downtown, the hip residential neighborhood **Elliston Place** boasts a number of rock and alternative music venues. With its string of tacky bars and clubs, **Printers Alley**, downtown, is best avoided.

Every Thursday evening in summer, **Dancin' in the District**, at Riverfront Park, features big-name stars (ranging from Buddy Guy to the Neville Brothers) for a token cover charge. In June, the **CMA Music Festival** (formerly known as **Fan Fair**) is a four-day series of concerts and opportunities to meet the stars (☏ 1-800/262-3378, ⓦ www.cmafest.com).

For **listings**, check the free weeklies *Nashville Scene* (Wed) and *All The Rage* (Thurs), or Friday and Saturday's *Tennessean*.

Bluebird Café 4104 Hillsboro Rd ☏ 615/383-1461, ⓦ www.bluebirdcafe.com. Having launched the careers of superstars like Garth Brooks, Trisha Yearwood, and Faith Hill, this intimate café, six miles west of downtown in the Green Hills district, is *the* place to see the latest country artists. Early evening entertainment by up-and-coming songwriters is free, but a cover of $8–15 is charged for the second show. Reservations are recommended if you want to sit at one of the 21 tables; you can also sit at the bar, but either way you're expected to spend at least $7 on food or drink. Sunday night (new writers' night) is free.

Douglas Corner Café 2106 Eighth Ave S ☏ 615/298-1688, ⓦ www.douglascorner.com. The *Bluebird*'s main competitor has live music – Americana, rock, and country – six nights a week, often with no cover, and regular open-mike songwriters' nights.

Ernest Tubb Record Store Midnight Jamboree Texas Troubadour Theatre, 2414 Music Valley Drive ☏ 615/885-0028. A live radio show, recorded every Sat from midnight to 1am, in a purpose-built theater adjoining the Music Valley branch of the *Tubb* store (there's another on Broadway). Features promising newcomers as well as major Opry stars. Free.

Exit/In 2208 Elliston Place ☏ 615/321-3340, ⓦ www.exitin.com. Venerable venue for rock, reggae, and country, with the occasional big name – not to mention beer and pizza.

Nashville Palace 2611 McGavock Pike ☏ 615/884-3004, ⓦ www.nashvillepalace.net. Opposite the *Gaylord Opryland* resort, with music all day every day, big name C & W stars, talent nights, and post-*Opry* shows.

Robert's Western World 416 Broadway ☏ 615/244-9552, ⓦ www.robertswesternworld.com. Some of the best country music on Broadway, plus rockabilly and Western swing, in a lively honky-tonk that doubles as a cowboy boots store.

Station Inn 402 12th Ave S ☏ 615/255-3307, ⓦ www.stationinn.com. Very popular bluegrass and acoustic venue near Music Row. Shows 9pm nightly. No smoking.

Sutler's 2608 Franklin Pike ☏ 615/292-5254. Aspiring singer-songwriters make a beeline for this bar/club, south of downtown, that's hosted everyone from Nanci Griffith and Emmylou Harris to Guy Clark. Don't miss the beer cheese soup.

Tootsie's Orchid Lounge 422 Broadway ☏ 615/726-0463, ⓦ www.tootsies.net. Atmospheric downtown honky-tonk, with a raucous atmosphere and good, gutsy live performers.

South from Nashville

Southeast of Nashville, nineteenth-century plantation homes line US-31 between suburban Brentwood and historic **Franklin**, eighteen miles out. One of the bloodiest battles of the Civil War was fought here on November 30, 1864, when

△ Ryman Auditorium

8500 men fell in less than an hour. Twenty-two thousand Confederates forced a Union retreat to Nashville, but incurred such heavy casualties as to shatter their Army of Tennessee beyond further use. Among strategic buildings open to visitors is **Carnton Plantation**, a former Confederate hospital where bloodstains are still visible on the floor, a mile southeast of town on Hwy-431 (Mon–Sat 9am–5pm, Sun 1–5pm; $10). Franklin's entire fifteen-block center, now filled with antique and specialty shops, is on the National Register of Historic Places.

Jack Daniel's at Lynchburg

The change-resistant village of **LYNCHBURG** (pop. 361), seventy miles southeast of Nashville, is home to **Jack Daniel's Distillery** (daily 9am–4.30pm; free). Founded in 1866, this is the oldest registered distillery in the country (hence the famous "No. 1" appellation). Entertaining seventy-minute **tours** lead through every step of the sour-mash whiskey-making process; ironically, you can't actually sample the stuff, as this is a dry county (though you can purchase special-edition bottles, every day but Sunday).

Lynchburg itself is a pretty hamlet, laid out around a neat town square with a redbrick courthouse and a number of old-fashioned stores. One enjoyable throwback is *Miss Mary Bobo's Boarding House*, which serves enormous **Southern dinners** (fried chicken, turnip greens, country ham, and the like) at group tables in a lovely 1805 home (reservations essential; ☏615/759-7394).

Eastern Tennessee

Until the creation of the Tennessee Valley Authority, the opening of **Great Smoky Mountains National Park**, and the construction of the interstate highways, life had remained all but unchanged in the remote hills and valleys of **eastern Tennessee** since the arrival of the earliest pioneers. Now visitors flock here for the endless expanses of natural beauty; and as a result, especially in the fall, the Smokies can get very clogged with traffic. Most communities in the area are small, and either over-touristed or just bland. Of the two main cities – modern **Knoxville** and picturesque **Chattanooga**, both of which have benefited from considerable industrial growth thanks to cheap TVA power – only Chattanooga holds much appeal for tourists.

Smoky Mountain gateway towns

Most visitors who approach the Smokies from the north or west leave I-40 twenty miles east of Knoxville, or two hundred miles east of Nashville, and sweep south on **Hwy-66** and **US-441** through the 25-mile procession of heavily commercialized "gateway towns" that leads to the national park. This is Tennessee's most conspicuously touristed area, its endless motels, sprawling campgrounds, chain diners, country music theaters, and expensive novelty "attractions" consistently geared toward vacationing families. The odd motel might enjoy an appealing rural setting, but if you're on a road trip it makes more sense to think of the various communities as cheapish overnight stops – though **accommodation** prices fluctuate seasonally, and also rise significantly on weekends – than as stimulating destinations in their own right.

Pigeon Forge

With fifty or so themed **attractions**, ranging from Dollywood (see below) to the *Black Bear Jamboree Dinner and Show*, there's ostensibly lots to do in the dry town of **PIGEON FORGE** – though almost everything is appealing only on a kitschy level. Tucked in the relentless strip of discount outlets, diners, and motels, Pigeon Forge's **welcome center** is at 1950 Parkway (☏865/453-8574 or 1-800/251-9100, ⓦwww.mypigeonforge.com). Reasonable **motels** include the *Parkview*, 2806 Parkway (☏865/453-5051 or 1-800/239-9116; ❸; April to mid-Dec), and the comfortable, friendly *Shular Inn*, 2708 Parkway (☏865/453-2700 or 1-800/451-2376; ❸), both of which have pools. The *Smoky Mountain Pancake House*, 4160 Parkway (☏865/453-1947), is good for **breakfast**.

Dolly Parton's Dollywood

Born in 1946, one of twelve children, **Dolly Parton** grew up in several modest homes around Pigeon Forge, the most isolated of them two miles from the nearest neighbor and over four miles from the mailbox. As a child she sang every week on local radio, before leaving for Nashville on the day she finished at Sevier County High School. Her first success, duetting with Porter Wagoner, came to an acrimonious end in the early Seventies, but she scored a major country hit in 1976 with "Jolene." She then crossed over to a poppier sound, and, with her charismatic presence, was a natural in Hollywood films like *9 to 5* and *The Best Little Whorehouse in Texas*. Her songs have been acclaimed for their readiness to address issues like rural poverty, and as a woman, a singer, and a songwriter she has always been a strong-minded and inspirational figure.

Dollywood, Parton's "homespun fun" theme park at 700 Dollywood Lane in Pigeon Forge (April–Dec; call or visit the website for schedule; April–Oct $45.70, children 4–11 $34.55; Nov & Dec $42.40/$24.55; ☏865/428-9488, ⓦwww.dollywood.com), blends ersatz mountain heritage with the glamour of its celebrity shareholder. One section showcases Appalachian **crafts**, making everything from lye soap to horse-drawn carriages; a museum looks at Dolly herself in entertaining detail; and music shows are constantly on the go. The thrill rides offer plenty for adrenaline-junkies and kiddies alike, but after a full day it can all start to feel a bit precious. A water park, **Dolly's Splash Country** (late May to mid-Sept; call for schedule; $36.80, children $31.20; combo tickets valid in either park for 3 days within a week $73/$58; same phone, ⓦwww.dollywoodssplashcountry.com), is adjacent.

Gatlinburg

If you can't bring yourself to stop in Pigeon Forge, you'll probably end up in **GATLINBURG**, another five miles south on US-441. It's a marginally more attractive place, squeezed amid the foothills of the Smokies, where the odd genuine relic of its Germanic heritage still shows through. As well as being a little more upmarket, it's also "wet," so its restaurants serve alcohol. While there is at least a town center to stroll through, it's once again bursting with overpriced, gimmicky tourist attractions, including **Christus Gardens**, with its dioramas of the life of Christ, and a mini-golf course that "transports you back to Gatlinburg's historic past, while challenging your putting skills." It also offers a couple of chair lifts up the surrounding peaks, one of which leads to the year-round Ober Gatlinburg **ski resort** and **amusement park**.

Gatlinburg's central Parkway holds three **visitor centers** (☎1-800/568-4748, ⓦwww.gatlinburg.com). This being the closest town to the park, **accommodation** is relatively expensive. The good-value *Sidney James Mountain Lodge*, slightly up from the mayhem at 610 Historic Nature Trail (☎865/436-7851 or 1-800/876-6888, ⓦwww.sidneyjames.com; ❸), offers large comfortable rooms, some of them creekside, and two pools. Central **eating** options include *Lineberger's*, 903 Parkway (☎865/436-9284), which serves decent seafood.

Townsend

A much less frenetic approach to the Smokies, if you're driving in from the east, is to follow the pretty Foothills Parkway through woods and across misty mountains, and then take US-321 for the final seven miles to **TOWNSEND**, twelve miles west of Pigeon Forge. There's no town to speak of, just a peaceful strip where the motels are laid-back and the air is clear. The peaceful *Highland Manor*, 7766 E Lamar Alexander Parkway (☎865/448-2211 or 1-800/213-9462, ⓦwww.highlandmanor.com; ❸), is a friendly place with nice grounds, great views, and a pool. You can **eat** fresh trout and crispy fried chicken in a country-store atmosphere at the *Hearth and Kettle*, opposite the hotel at 7767 E Lamar Alexander Parkway (☎865/448-6059).

Great Smoky Mountains National Park

The northern boundary of **GREAT SMOKY MOUNTAINS NATIONAL PARK**, which stretches for seventy miles along the Tennessee–North Carolina border (see also p.507), lies just two miles south of Gatlinburg on US-441. Don't expect immediate tranquility, however: the roads, particularly in the fall, can be lined almost bumper-to-bumper with cars, and if you're not staying in Gatlinburg it's best to use the well-marked bypass rather than drive through the town.

Located within a day's drive of the major urban centers of the east coast and the Great Lakes – and of two-thirds of the entire US population – the Smokies attract over ten million visitors per year, more than twice as many as any other national park. These heavily contorted peaks are named for the **bluish haze** that hangs over them, made up of moisture and hydrocarbons released by the lush vegetation (a mature tree emits up to nine hundred gallons on a summer day). Since the Sixties, however, **air pollution** has been adding sulphates to the filmy smoke, and has cut back visibility by thirty percent. More than 120 tree species and over 1400 flowering plants clothe the mountains and meadows in color from early spring to late fall. Sixteen peaks rise above 6000ft, their steep elevation accounting for dramatic changes in climate.

While between late March and mid-May is a great time to visit for the delicate spring flowers, the **busiest periods** in the park are midsummer (mid-June to mid-Aug), and, especially, October, when the hills are shrouded in a magnificent canopy of glaring reds, subtle yellows, and faded browns. During June and July, rhododendrons blaze fiercely in the sometimes stifling summer heat.

Just inside the park on US-441, **Sugarlands Visitor Center** (daily: May & Sept 8am–6pm, June–Aug 8am–7pm, call for winter hours; ☎865/436-1200, ⓦwww. nps.gov/grsm) has useful leaflets covering hiking trails, driving tours, forests, and wildlife, and can provide details on each day's program of ranger-led tours and activities. Many visitors, however, do no more than follow **US-441**, here known as the Newfound Gap Road, all the way through to North Carolina. From the gap itself, ten miles along on the state line, a spur road to the right winds for seven more miles up to **Clingman's Dome**, at 6643ft the highest point not only in the park but in all of Tennessee. A surreal concrete spiral walkway on top affords a panoramic, though hazy, view of the mountains, rather spoiled by the fact that virtually all the mature balsam firs in the area have been killed off by insect infestation.

If you want to spend longer exploring within the park, the main focus of visitor activity is in the **Cades Cove** area, which can be reached either by branching west at Sugarlands along the scenic **Little River Road**, or directly from Townsend via **Rich Mountain Road** (closed in winter). The eleven-mile driving loop here, always jam-packed with cars in summer and fall, passes deserted barns, homesteads, mills, and churches that stand as a reminder of the farmers who carved out a living from this wilderness, before they were forced to move out when National Park status was conferred in 1934. Halfway along, there's another **visitor center** (daily: May 8.30am–7.30pm, June–Aug 8.30am–8pm, Sept & Oct 9am–6pm, call for winter hours). This whole loop is reserved for **cyclists** on Saturday and Wednesday mornings in summer, from dawn until 10am; bikes can be rented at the Cades Cove Store near the *Cades Cove Campground* (☎865/448-9034).

Perhaps the best way of all to escape the crowds is to sample the park's eight hundred miles of **hiking** trails.

Chattanooga

Few places can be so identified with a single song as **CHATTANOOGA**, in the southeast corner of Tennessee. Though visitors expecting to see Tex Beneke's

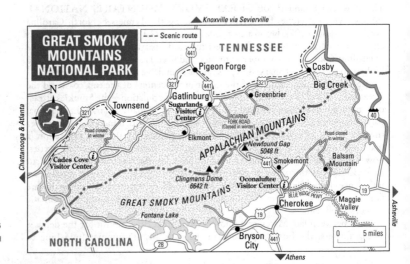

and Glenn Miller's "Chattanooga Choo-Choo" will be disappointed (the town is not even served by Amtrak), the place has a certain appeal, not least its beautiful location on a deep bend in the **Tennessee River**, walled in by forested plateaus on three sides. This setting led John Ross, of Scottish and Cherokee ancestry, to found a trading post on the spot in 1815, and its strategic importance made it a great prize during the Civil War. Victory here in 1863 helped establish the reputation of General Grant as the man who might win the war for the Union.

The Town

The centerpiece of Chattanooga's twenty miles of reclaimed riverfront is **Ross's Landing** (the town's original name), a park at the bottom of Broad Street. Here the splendid five-story **Tennessee Aquarium** traces the aquatic life of the Mississippi from its Tennessee tributaries to the Gulf of Mexico, and also shows giant IMAX movies (daily 10am–6pm; longer hours in summer; $17.95, IMAX $7.95, combined ticket $21.95; ☎1-800/262-0695, ⓦwww.tnaqua.org). **Cruises** on the *Southern Belle* **riverboat** (☎423/266-4488, ⓦwww.chattanoogariverboat.com) leave from the foot of nearby Chestnut Street. Prices start from $12 for a ninety-minute daytime sightseeing tour.

Perched above the river, the attractive **Bluff View Art District**, where High meets Second, comprises a handful of galleries, workshops, museums and cafés in some lovely old buildings. Certainly the splendid **Hunter Museum of American Art** is worth a look, with a changing roster of exhibitions covering photography, painting, sculpture, folk art and crafts from the nineteenth century to the present day (Mon, Tues, Fri & Sat 10am–5pm, Wed & Sun noon–5pm, Thurs 10am–9pm; $8; ⓦwww.huntermuseum.org).

A few blocks inland, the **Chattanooga Regional History Museum**, 400 Chestnut St (Mon–Fri 10am–5pm; $4), is a quirky little place, with some especially good information on early local history and the Cherokee Indians. Keep walking and you'll see some grand century-old buildings in the lively **business district**, such as the eye-catching Tivoli Theatre at 709 Broad St; as a general rule, however, the further you get from the river, the more run-down Chattanooga becomes.

If you long to ride a Chattanooga choo-choo, the authentic **steam trains** of the **Tennessee Valley Railroad** offer a variety of trips, from 55-minute local jaunts to stunning six-mile rides, crossing the river, running through deep tunnels, and turning round on a giant turntable (March–Oct daily; Nov & Dec limited days; from $13.50; ☎423/894-8028, ⓦwww.tvrail.com). The two main stations, restored to their 1930s look, are at 2202 N Chamberlain Ave in east Chattanooga and 4119 Cromwell Rd (I-75 exit 4 to Hwy-153).

Lookout Mountain

The name Chattanooga comes from a Creek word meaning "rock rising to a point"; the rock in question, the 2215ft **Lookout Mountain** (Ⓦ www.lookoutmountain .com), looms six miles south of downtown. To reach the top, either drive the whole way along a complicated, poorly signposted road, or use the world's steepest **incline railway**, which grinds its tentative way up through a narrow gash in the lush forest from 3917 St Elmo Ave, near the foot of the mountain, tackling nerve-racking gradients of up to 72.7 percent (daily: Jan, Feb, Nov & Dec 10am– 6pm; March–May, Sept & Oct 9am–6pm; June–Aug 8.30am–8pm; 3 trips/hr, 45min; $10 one way, $12 roundtrip; children $5/$6; ☎423/821-4224).

At the top, a steep five-minute walk through **Point Park** brings you to **Point Lookout**, the northern promontory of the mountain, which commands a not-to-be-missed view of the city and the meandering Tennessee River below. This forms part of the **Chickamauga and Chattanooga National Military Park**, covering several sites around the city and in nearby Chickamauga, Georgia, that witnessed fierce Civil War fighting in 1863. The battle here that November, in which Confederate forces that had been laying siege to Chattanooga were finally forced to withdraw, was also known as the "Battle Above the Clouds"; thick mantles of fog often obscure the city below to this day. Among the many memorials in Point Park is the only **statue** in the country to show Union and Confederate soldiers shaking hands.

For something a little less serious, join generations of road-trippers and "See Rock City" – the iconic sign, painted on roadside barns as far away as Georgia and Texas, was the result of an aggressive 1930s marketing campaign. A valentine to

---

The Cherokee and the Trail of Tears

During the eighteenth and early nineteenth centuries, the **Cherokee** were the most powerful Indian tribe in the tri-state region of Tennessee, Georgia, and North Carolina. They forged close links with white pioneers, adopting white methods in schooling and agriculture, intermarrying, and even owning African slaves. The only Native Americans to develop their own written alphabet, they had a regular newspaper, *The Cherokee Phoenix*. They even supplied soldiers for Andrew Jackson's US forces against the Creek Indians and the British in 1814, hoping to buy influence with the federal government.

Thirteen years later, against a background of aggressive territorial claims by settlers, the Cherokee produced a written constitution modeled on that of the US, stating their intention to continue to be a self-governing nation. John Ross, founder of Ross's Landing, and at most one-eighth Cherokee, was elected as their first Principal Chief in 1828 in an effort to appease and negotiate with national and state governments over their lands. However, as white encroachment increased, their former ally Jackson, now US president, was pressured by the Georgians into "offering" the Cherokee western lands in exchange for those east of the Mississippi. Although the tribal leadership refused, a minority faction accepted, giving the government the opportunity they required. The Cherokee were ordered to leave within two years, and fourteen thousand were forcefully removed to Oklahoma in 1838 along the horrific **Trail of Tears**: four thousand died of disease and exposure on the way. In the meantime, their land was sold by lottery, and Ross's Landing was renamed Chattanooga. Descendants of the one thousand Cherokee who managed to avoid removal by escaping into the mountains now occupy a small reservation in North Carolina (see p.507).

The **Red Clay State Historic Park**, twenty miles east of Chattanooga off Hwy-317, recounts the old Cherokee way of life, with replica houses, tools, and household implements. Its balsamic Sacred Council Spring was once a meeting place for Cherokee elders.

kitsch Americana, **Rock City** is basically a walking trail along the mountain that offers not only the pleasure of scrambling through narrow gaps and swinging on rope bridges, but also delights such as **Fairyland Caverns**, holes carved into the rock and populated by fairytale characters. Inside Lookout Mountain itself, **Ruby Falls**, a 145ft waterfall, is heralded by a mock medieval castle entrance (Rock City and Ruby Falls both $14.95, children $7.95, combination ticket $28/$14, combination with Incline Railway $38/$19).

Practicalities

Greyhound connections with Nashville, Knoxville, and Atlanta arrive on Broad Street, downtown. The **visitor center** (daily 8.30am–5.30pm; ☎423/756-8687 or 1-800/322-3344, ⓦwww.chattanewgafun.com) is next to the Tennessee Aquarium, near the river. Countless cheap **motels** line the interstates, but for something special head to the elegant *Bluff View Inn*, 412 E Second St (☎423/265-5033 or 1-800/725-8338; ❺), which offers a variety of rooms – some with lovely views – spread across three restored houses in the appealing Bluff View Art District. There's **camping** at *Raccoon Mountain Campground*, 319 West Hills Drive (☎423/821-9403, ⓦwww.raccoonmountain.com; cabins ❶–❷, tentsites $15).

As for **eating**, the Bluff View Art District comes up trumps again with the romantic, bistro-style *Back Inn Café*, 412 E 2nd St (☎423/265-5033; Tues–Sat), which serves Mediterranean food and has a terrace with river views; the lively pasta house *Tony's*, 212 High St (☎423/265-5033), and the nearby *Rembrandt's Coffee House*, 204 High St (☎423/265-5033), for gourmet coffee, artisan chocolate, and light meals. Elsewhere, the *Big River Grille & Brewing Works*, 222 Broad St (☎423/267-2739), is a cavernous brewpub and restaurant near the Aquarium.

Alabama

Just 250 miles from north to south, **ALABAMA** ranges from the fast-flowing rivers, waterfalls, and lakes of the **Appalachian foothills** to the bayous and beaches of the **Gulf Coast**. Most of its industry is concentrated in the **north**, around **Birmingham** and **Huntsville**, first home of the nation's space program. The sun-scorched farmlands of middle Alabama envelop sober **Montgomery**, the state capital. Away from the French-influenced coastal strip around the pretty little town of **Mobile**, fundamentalist attitudes have traditionally backed right-wing demagogues, such as **George Wallace**, the four-time state governor who received ten million votes in the 1968 presidential election, and, more recently, controversial Alabama Chief Justice **Roy Moore**.

Getting around Alabama

Public transportation is relatively good in Alabama. Daily Amtrak **trains** from New York and Atlanta to New Orleans stop at Anniston, Birmingham, and Tuscaloosa, while the line from Jacksonville to New Orleans passes through Mobile. Amtrak **buses** connect Birmingham and Mobile by way of Montgomery, while Greyhound serves the major towns and cities.

Northern Alabama

Northern Alabama, on the trailing edges of the Appalachians, is brightened by the mountain lakes, rivers, and canyons of the **Tennessee River Valley**. The area's first white settlers were small farmers who had little in common with the big plantation owners further south, and attempted to dissociate from the Confederacy during the Civil War. Substantial mineral finds led to an industrial boom that peaked in the early Thirties.

Huntsville

Many Southern cities aspire to blend the old with the new; few achieve it as dramatically as **HUNTSVILLE**, a hundred miles south of Nashville, just inside the Alabama border. Its sleepy center still recalls the days when it was dominated by cotton merchants and railroad owners, a history absorbingly recounted in the **Huntsville Depot Museum**, 310 Church St N (June–Aug Tues–Fri 10am–5pm, Sat 10am–4pm; March–May & Sept–Dec Wed–Sat 10am–4pm; closed Jan & Feb; $7; ⓦwww.earlyworks.com). Nearby, **Alabama Constitution Village**, 109 Gates Ave (same hours as Depot Museum; $7, or $12 combined ticket), evokes earlier history, with actors dressed in period clothing going about their olde-worlde business in eight reconstructed Federal-style buildings.

Time was when Huntsville was content to be the "Watercress Capital of the World"; the great leap forward came after World War II, when the army consolidated its **rocket and missile research** efforts in the city. Spearheading the project were **Dr Wernher von Braun** and 118 other German scientists, who came to Huntsville after a token period of rehabilitation. Von Braun's contribution of the V-2 ballistic missile to the Nazi war effort is ignored by the city, which prefers to laud his later Space Age achievements, such as **Explorer I**, the nation's first satellite, and the mighty **Saturn V** rocket.

The giant **US Space and Rocket Center**, five miles west of downtown on Hwy-20, off I-65 (daily 9am–5pm; $16, $21 with IMAX; ⓦwww.spacecamp. com/museum), contains a mind-boggling array of technological exhibits, hands-on displays, and weightlessness simulators, as well as an IMAX cinema. Outdoors, in the surreal Rocket and Space Shuttle parks, rockets protrude skywards in the blazing Alabama sunshine; the four-story *Saturn V* is laid on its side to emphasize its immensity.

Practicalities

Huntsville's **visitor center** is at 500 Church St, at the northern edge of downtown, reached by exit 19 off I-565 (Mon–Sat 9am–5pm, Sun noon–5pm; ☏256/533-5723, ⓦwww.huntsville.org). Chain **motels** on the outskirts include a *Best Value Inn*, near the Space Center at 2201 N Memorial Parkway (☏256/536-7441 or 1-888/315-2378; ❷). As for **restaurants**, *Ol' Heidelberg*, 6125 University Drive NW (☏256/922-0556), offers German specialties including sauerkraut and Wiener schnitzel, while *Little Paul's Barbecue*, 815 Madison St (☏256/536-7227; closed Sun), serves good, cheap barbecue downtown.

Birmingham

The rapid transformation of farmland into the city of **BIRMINGHAM** began in 1870, when two railroad routes met in the Jones Valley, a hundred miles south of Huntsville. What attracted speculators was not the scenery, but what lay under it – a mixture of iron ore, limestone, and coal, perfect for the manufacture of iron and steel. The expansion of heavy industry came to an abrupt halt with the

Civil rights in Birmingham

Early in 1963, civil rights leaders chose Birmingham as the target of "Project C" (for confrontation), aiming to force businesses to integrate lunch counters and employ more blacks. Despite threats from Police Chief **"Bull" Connor** that there would be "blood running down the streets of Birmingham," the pickets, sit-ins, and marches went forward, resulting in mass arrests. Over two thousand protesters flooded the jails; one, Dr Martin Luther King Jr, wrote his *Letter from a Birmingham Jail* after being branded an extremist by local white clergymen. Connor's use of high-pressure hoses, cattleprods, and dogs against demonstrators catalyzed support. Pictures of snarling German shepherds sinking their teeth into schoolkids were transmitted around the world, and led to a settlement that June. Success in Birmingham sparked demonstrations in 186 other cities, which culminated in the 1964 **Civil Rights Act** prohibiting racial segregation.

The headquarters for the campaign, the **16th Street Baptist Church**, on the corner of Sixth Avenue, was the site of a sickening Klan bombing on September 15, 1963, which killed four young black girls attending a Bible class. Two of the three murderers were finally jailed in 2000. The church's basement contains a small shrine dedicated to the murdered girls.

Nearby, the admirable **Civil Rights Institute**, 520 16th St (Tues–Sat 10am–5pm; Sun 1–5pm; $9; ⓦ www.bcri.org), is an affecting attempt to interpret the factors that led to such violence and racial hatred. Exhibits recreate life in a segregated city, complete with a burned-out bus and heart-rending videos of bus boycotts and the March on Washington.

Depression; iron and steel now account for only a few thousand jobs, and new service and medical industries have helped transform what was once a smog-filled metropolis.

Arrival and information

Birmingham Airport is just four miles from downtown; call Yellow Cabs ($12) on ☏ 205/252-1131. The Greyhound station is at 19th Street N, between Sixth and Seventh avenues – a rough area – while **Amtrak** pulls in downtown at 1819 Morris Ave. **Public transportation**, however, is poor. The main **visitor center** can be found just off I-20/59 at 2200 Ninth Ave N (Mon–Fri 8.30am–5pm; ☏ 205/458-8000 or 1-800/458-8085, ⓦ www.sweetbirmingham.com). Birmingham has two free **listings** magazines: *The Birmingham Weekly* (ⓦ birminghamweekly .com) and the *Black and White* (ⓦ www.bwcitypaper.com).

Accommodation

Although the downtown **hotels** are pricier than the chain motels near the highway, many of them offer advantageous weekend rates.

Pickwick Hotel 1023 S 20th St ☏ 205/933-9555 or 1-800/255-7304, ⓦ www.pickwickhotel.com. Charming hotel within walking distance of Five Points South, with all the amenities. Complimentary continental breakfast and free airport shuttle. ❻
The Redmont Hotel 2101 5th Ave N ☏ 205/324-2101 or 1-877/536-2085, ⓦ www.theredmont. com. Modernized, handsome historic hotel, a few blocks northeast of Amtrak. ❹
Tutwiler Hotel 2021 Park Place N ☏ 205/322-2100, ⓦ www.wyndham.com/hotels/BHMTW/main. wnt. Luxurious restored 1920s hotel near the Civil Rights Institute. ❻

The City

Downtown Birmingham extends north from the railroad tracks at Morris Avenue to Tenth Avenue N, between 15th and 25th streets. The landscaped greenery and early skyscrapers of **20th Street** are not enough to save these one-hundred-plus blocks from anonymity, with shopping now firmly anchored in the malls and suburbs. The main interest is the powerful **Civil Rights Institute** and the **16th St Baptist Church** (see box, p.581). Call in too at the lovely old **Carver Theatre for the Performing Arts**, 1631 Fourth Ave N, where the **Alabama Jazz Hall of Fame** (Tues–Sat 10am–5pm; $2; ⓦwww.jazzhall.com) is a fond memorial to great jazz artists with Alabama links, from boogie-woogie maestro Clarence "Pinetop" Smith, via Erskine Hawkins (he of "Tuxedo Junction"), to jazzy space cadet Sun Ra.

Much livelier than downtown is the **Five Points South** district, a mile or so south of the tracks, on 20th St and 11th St S; thanks to the proximity of the university, the narrow streets and alleys are packed with bars and restaurants, and busy with revelers – mostly students – every weekend.

Northwest of downtown, the concrete colossus of the Birmingham-Jefferson Civic Center, 22nd St and Tenth Ave N, contains the **Alabama Sports Hall of Fame** (Mon–Sat 9am–5pm, Sun 1–5pm; $5; ⓦwww.ashof.org), a tribute to sporting greats such as 1936 Olympic hero **Jesse Owens**, **Le Roy "Satchel" Paige** – legendary Negro League pitcher – and boxer **Joe Louis**. There's even a space for George Wallace, on the pretext that he was state amateur boxing champion. Weave your way past the monotonous white-walled legal buildings to the nearby **Museum of Art**, 2000 Eighth Ave N (Tues–Sat 10am–5pm, Sun noon–5pm; free), which is strong on Oriental pieces, American landscapes, and, oddly enough, Wedgwood pottery.

East of downtown, at First Ave N and 32nd St, stand the massive sheds and tall chimney stacks of **Sloss Furnaces** (Tues–Sat 10am–4pm, Sun noon–4pm; free; ⓦwww.slossfurnaces.com), which produced pig iron to feed the city's mills and foundries from 1882 until 1971. Self-guided **tours** through the boilers, stoves, and casting areas vividly portray the harsh working conditions endured by the ex-slaves, prisoners, and unskilled immigrants who labored here. Imagining the searing heat and cramped space, the heavy loads and putrid gaseous emissions, it's easy to appreciate why one former Sloss worker claimed "if mules had to do this work they would have banned it."

Eating and drinking

Birmingham has some fantastic **barbecue** joints; for something a little more upmarket, the best bet is to ignore downtown in favor of **Five Points South**.

Bottega 2240 Highland Ave S ☏205/939-1000. Elegant 1920s clothing store that now houses one of Five Points South's classiest restaurants, serving luscious, garlic-rich Mediterranean cuisine with entrees at $25 and up; prices are slightly lower in the adjoining café.
Dreamland Barbecue 1427 14th Ave S ☏205/933-2133. Superlative barbecue in a huge,

cheery space. Enjoy a big plate of ribs with sliced white bread and sauce, cooked up right before your eyes.
Fifth Avenue Coffee House 1909 Fifth Ave North ☏205/324-5597. Coffees, sandwiches, and salads are served in this downtown spot. Breakfast and lunch, Mon–Fri only.

West of Birmingham

Just west of Birmingham's city limits, I-20/59 passes **Bessemer**, a likeable small town named in 1887 after Sir Henry Bessemer, the English engineer who perfected the steel-making process. The **Hall of History Museum** here, in the 1916 Southern Railroad depot at 1905 Alabama Ave (Tues–Sat 9am–4pm; free), displays Native American artifacts alongside exhibits from the industrial pioneer years. *Bob Sykes*, in town at 1724 Ninth Ave (☏205/426-1400), is a mouthwatering **barbecue** joint.

Tuscaloosa, home of the lively main campus of the University of Alabama, but with little else of interest, lies 32 miles southwest of Bessemer. If you're hungry, combine eating with a view of the **Black Warrior River** at *Cypress Inn*, 501 Rice Mine Rd N (☎205/345-6963), which specializes in reasonably priced seafood and catfish. If you're not in the mood for fancy, *Dreamland Barbecue*, 5535 15th Ave E (☎205/758-8135), dishes up luscious, sweet pork ribs with wonderful BBQ sauce.

South central Alabama

Southern Alabama – memorably depicted in Harper Lee's child's-eye view of racial conflict, *To Kill a Mockingbird* – still consists mostly of small, sleepy, God-fearing rural communities. Only state capital **Montgomery**, with a population of just over 200,000, achieves metropolitan status. It lies in the heart of the **Black Belt**, originally named for the rich loamy soil, but these days more usually taken to refer to the region's ethnic make-up. Cotton was the major earner here until the boll weevil infestation of 1915. Now it has been supplanted (officially) by soybeans, corn, and peanuts – though surveys suggest that the leading cash crop is, in fact, marijuana.

Montgomery

MONTGOMERY's Black Belt location, ninety miles south of Birmingham and 160 west of Atlanta, made it a natural political center for the plantation elite, and led to its adoption as state capital in 1846 and temporary capital of the Confederacy fifteen years later. Despite its administrative importance, and its monumental downtown buildings, Montgomery is strangely quiet. Most neighborhoods are either exclusively white or totally black; integration sadly does not appear to be on the social agenda in the city that saw the first successful mass civil rights activity in 1955–56.

...UNTIL JUSTICE ROLLS DOWN LIKE WATERS
AND RIGHTEOUSNESS LIKE A MIGHTY STREAM

MARTIN LUTHER KING JR

△ Civil Rights Memorial, Montgomery, AL

Arrival, information, and accommodation

Dannelly Field Airport is fifteen miles from downtown on US-80; the Greyhound station is much more conveniently located at 210 S Court St. The **visitor center**, in the old train station at 300 Water St (Mon–Sat 8am–5pm, Sun noon–4pm; ℡334/262-0013, ⒲www.visitingmontgomery.com), suggests lots of tours and itineraries. As for accommodation, there are a couple of homey **B&Bs** in town, plus the usual **motels** alongside the highways.

Capitol Inn 205 N Goldthwaite St ℡334/265-3844 or 1-866/471-9028, ⒲www.capitolinnhotel.com. Old-fashioned motel perched on a small hill fifteen minutes' walk from downtown; its location is somewhat bleak at night. ❷

Lattice Inn 1414 S Hull St ℡334/832-9931 or 1-800/525-0652. Lovingly restored 1906 house

offering four B&B rooms and a pool, a mile or so southeast of downtown in the Cloverdale neighborhood. ❹

Red Bluff Cottage 551 Clay St ℡334/264-0056 or 1-888/551-2529, ⒲www.redbluffcottage.com. Friendly B&B near the capitol, with comfortable rooms, a big porch, and good food. ❹

The City

Although 1993 saw Alabama's state flag finally replace the Confederate flag over the white-domed Greek Revival **State Capitol** at the top of Dexter Avenue, downtown Montgomery still bears reminders of its white-supremacist past. You can tour the capitol itself (Mon–Fri 9am–5pm, Sat 9am–4pm; free), where a bronze star marks the spot where Jefferson Davis was sworn in as president of the Confederacy on February 18, 1861 (see p.488) – a hundred years later Governor George Wallace stood on these steps and proclaimed "Segregation forever!"

On a different note, Montgomery was jammed with mourners in 1954 for the funeral of 29-year-old country star **Hank Williams**, who died of a heart attack on his way to a concert on New Year's Eve 1953. An Alabama native from Butler County, Williams was as famous for his drink- and drug-sustained lifestyle as he was for writing honky-tonk classics like "Your Cheating Heart" and "I'm So Lonesome I Could Cry." The **Hank Williams Memorial**, a large white-marble headstone complete with song lyrics and an image of the singer, dominates the Oakwood Cemetery Annex, 1304 Upper Wetumpka Rd, near downtown; Hank's statue stands at Lister Hill Plaza on N Perry Street. There's also the **Hank Williams Museum**, at 118 Commerce St (Mon–Sat 9am–4.30pm, Sun 1–4pm; $8; ⒲www.thehankwilliamsmuseum.com), complete with the 1952 Cadillac in which he made his final journey.

Situated off Woodmere Boulevard, ten miles southeast of the city, the stunningly landscaped **Blount Cultural Park** gives credence to Montgomery's claim to be a regional center for the arts. It's home to the **Alabama Shakespeare Festival** (Nov–June; ℡1-800/841-4273, ⒲www.asf.net) and the slick **Montgomery Museum of Fine Arts** (Tues–Sat 10am–5pm, Sun noon–5pm; free), which spans more than two hundred years of American art and has an impressive selection of masters including Dürer, Rembrandt, and Picasso. There's a nice café, too, overlooking the lake.

Eating and drinking

Downtown Montgomery isn't bad when it comes to eating, with some especially good soul food. A few minutes' drive southeast, suburban **Cloverdale** offers a selection of fancier restaurants. With its bars and jazz clubs, Cloverdale is also the place to head for **nightlife**; downtown, things get quiet at night.

Farmers' Market Café 315 N McDonough St ℡334/262-1970. Montgomery's best spot for Southern-style breakfasts, just off downtown, next to the busy marketplace. Mon–Fri 5.30am–2pm.

Lek's Railroad Thai 300b Water St ℡334/269-0708. Next to the visitor center, this elegant downtown oddity serves tasty pad Thai, sushi, noodles, and soups, along with lots of good

During the Fifties, Montgomery's **bus system** was a miniature model of segregated society. The regulation ordering blacks to give up seats to whites came under repeated attack from black organizations, culminating in the call by the Women's Political Council for a mass boycott after seamstress **Rosa Parks** was arrested on December 1, 1955, for refusing to give up her seat, stating wearily that she was simply too tired. Black workers were asked to walk to work, while black-owned taxis carried those who lived further away for the same 10¢ fare as buses. The protest attracted over ninety-percent support, and the Montgomery Improvement Association (MIA), set up to coordinate activities, elected the 26-year-old pastor **Dr Martin Luther King Jr** as its chief spokesperson. Meanwhile, the laid-off white bus drivers were employed as temporary police officials. Despite personal hardships, bombings, and jailings, the boycott continued for eleven months, until in November 1956 the US Supreme Court declared segregation on public transportation to be illegal.

King remained pastor at the small brick **Dexter Avenue King Memorial Baptist Church**, in the shadow of the capitol at 454 Dexter Ave (email to request tours a week in advance; $2; ⓦwww.dexterkingmemorial.org), until his move back to his hometown of Atlanta in 1960. A mural along a basement wall chronicles his life, while the upstairs sanctuary, left much as it was during his ministry, contains his former pulpit.

One block away at the corner of Washington Avenue and Hull Street, in front of the Southern Poverty Law Center (which specializes in helping victims of racial attacks), the deeply moving **Civil Rights Memorial**, designed by Maya Lin, consists of a cone-shaped black granite table. It's inscribed with a circular timeline of events structured around the deaths of forty martyrs murdered by white supremacists and police; the circle ends with the assassination of Dr King. You can run your hands through the cool water that pumps slowly and evenly across it, softly touching the names while being confronted with your reflection. The wall behind, also running with water, is engraved with the quotation employed so often by Dr King: "(We will not be satisfied) until justice rolls down like waters and righteousness like a mighty stream." Displays in the **Civil Rights Memorial Center** alongside (Mon–Fri 9am–4.30pm, Sat 10am–4pm; $2; ⓦwww.splcenter.org) tell the story of the campaigns.

A few blocks west of the memorial, the **Rosa Parks Museum**, 252 Montgomery St (Mon–Fri 9am–5pm, Sat 9am–3pm; $5.50), commemorates "the mother of the civil rights movement." Exhibits cover her life, the bus boycott, and other major civil rights figures.

veggie options. Closed Sun.
Martha's Place 458 Sayre St ☎334/263-9135. Superb downtown Southern food, from collard greens to fried chicken. Lunch only; closed Sat.

Vintage Year 405 Cloverdale Rd, Cloverdale ☎334/264-8463. One of Alabama's best restaurants, with *haute nouvelle* Southern cuisine in a bistro setting. Dinner only, reservations recommended; closed Sun & Mon.

Selma

The tidy market town of **SELMA**, fifty miles west of Montgomery, became in the early Sixties the focal point of the national civil rights campaign. Black demonstrations, meetings, and attempts to register to vote were repeatedly met by police violence, before the murder of a black protester by a state trooper prompted the decision to organize the historic **march from Selma to Montgomery**. On "Bloody Sunday," March 7, 1965, six hundred unarmed marchers set off across the steep incline of the imposing, narrow **Edmund Pettus Bridge**. As they went over the apex of the bridge, a line of state troopers fired tear gas without warning, lashing out at the panic-stricken demonstrators with nightsticks and cattleprods. This violent confrontation, broadcast all over the world, is credited with having directly influenced the passage of the **Voting Rights Act** the following year. The full, devastating story is told in the **National Voting Rights Museum**, beside the bridge at 1012 Water Ave (Mon–Fri 9am–5pm, Sat 10am–3pm; $5; Ⓦ www. nvrmi.org), which is packed with personal testimony.

Lined with independently owned stores and cafés, **Broad Street** is the town's busy main thoroughfare, running into the wide riverfront **Water Avenue**, with its frontier-style storefronts, seed warehouses, and garages. Just a few blocks away stand the beautiful homes of Selma's **historic district**.

Practicalities

Selma's **visitor welcome center** is at 2207 Broad St, north of town at the junction with Hwy-22 (daily 8am–8pm; Ⓣ 334/875-7485, Ⓦ www.selmaalabama. com). Downtown is very short of inexpensive **places to stay**; if the historic *St James Hotel*, close to the Pettus Bridge at 1200 Water Ave (Ⓣ 334/872-3234 or 1-866/965-2637, Ⓦ www.stjameshotelselma.com; ❺), is beyond your budget, head for the *Ramada Inn*, three miles west on US-80 at 1806 W Highland Ave (Ⓣ 334/872-0461; ❸). Among several soul-food **restaurants** is the *Downtowner*, 1114 Selma Ave (Ⓣ 334/872-5933) – service can be surly, but the food is great. *Major Grumbles*, near the *St James* at 1 Grumbles Alley (Ⓣ 334/872-2006), is an upmarket riverside **pub** serving burgers, salads, and hot sandwiches; you may, however, be put off by the disturbing "Indian giant" skeleton, draped in a Confederate flag.

Alabama's Gulf Coast

Alabama's narrow share of the **Gulf coastline** received less of a hammering than neighboring Mississippi from Hurricane Katrina in 2005, and remains blessed with fine white sand beaches, lapped by clear blue waters. The coast veers sharply inward to the port city of **Mobile**, featuring hundreds of antebellum buildings in a tree-shaded center. Away from the water's edge, agriculture, dominated by pecans, peaches, and watermelons, flourishes on the gently sloping coastal plain.

Mobile

The busy port and paper-manufacturing city of **MOBILE** (pronounced "Mobeel") traces its origins back to a French community founded in 1702 by Jean-Baptiste Le Moyne, Sieur de Bienville, who went on to establish the cities of Biloxi and New Orleans. These early white settlers brought with them **Mardi Gras**, which has been celebrated in Mobile continuously since 1704, several years before New Orleans was even dreamed of. With its early eighteenth-century Spanish and Colonial-style buildings, parallels with New Orleans are everywhere you look, from the wrought-iron balconies to street names like Conti and Bienville and gumbo specials in the restaurants, but there the comparisons end. It's a pretty place – especially in **spring**, when virtually every street is transformed by the delicate colors of azaleas, camellias, and dogwoods – but there's little actually to do, and though they generally liven up on weekends, Mobile's downtown **bars** and **restaurants** can be decidedly sleepy during the week.

Mobile sustained relatively little lasting damage from its flooding by Hurricane Katrina in 2005, and having also survived the torches of the Union army during the Civil War, it possesses enough antebellum buildings to designate four sizeable areas as historic districts. The obvious place to start exploring is **Fort Conde**, 150 S Royal St (daily 8am–5pm; free), a reconstruction of the city's 1724 French fort, built to mark the nation's bicentennial in 1976. Dioramas in the low-ceilinged rooms cover local history; don't miss the atmospheric old photos of carnival, the old city, and local African-American figures. Nearby, you can tour the World War II battleship **USS Alabama** (daily: April–Sept 8am–6pm; Oct–March 8am–4pm; $12, parking $2). Fanning out north of the fort, the **Church Street Historic District** holds fifty-nine, mostly pre–Civil War buildings. Don't miss the terrific **Museum of Mobile**, in the airy old City Hall at 111 S Royal St (Mon–Sat 9am–5pm, Sun 1–5pm; $5; Ⓦ www.museumofmobile.com), which tells the story of the town from its earliest days.

Twenty miles south of Mobile, off I-10, the 65 acres of landscaped color that make up **Bellingrath Gardens** (daily 8am–5pm; $10, $18 with house tour; Ⓦ www.bellingrath.org) – once the home of a Coca-Cola magnate – include a quarter of a million azaleas.

Practicalities

Downtown Mobile is somewhat under the shadow of I-10 as it sweeps to meet I-65 a few miles west. The **Amtrak** and **Greyhound** stations are centrally located, at nos. 11 and 2545 Government St, respectively. Mobile's resourceful **visitor center**, in Fort Conde (see above), can help with accommodation (daily 8am–5pm; Ⓣ 251/434-7304, Ⓦ www.mobile.org). Cheap **motels** cluster around exit 3 of I-65; it's nicer, however, to stay downtown. Set in an 1862 twin townhouse, the atmospheric ⚑ *Malaga Inn*, 359 Church St (Ⓣ 251/438-4701, Ⓦ www.malagainn. com; ❹), has huge rooms, a pretty courtyard, and free continental breakfast. Another historic **hotel**, the *Admiral Semmes*, 251 Government St (Ⓣ 251/432-8000, Ⓦ www.rash.com; ❺), is a Radisson-owned property with all the usual amenities.

Unsurprisingly, Mobile abounds in **places to eat fish**: the 1938 ⚑ *Wintzels' Oyster House*, 605 Dauphin St (Ⓣ 251/432-4605), serves good-value seafood platters and fresh oysters in a diner-style atmosphere. If you want views of the water, take Hwy-98 across the bridge and beyond the USS *Alabama*; the *Original Oyster House*, on the bay (Ⓣ 251/626-2188), is a lively family restaurant dishing up fresh seafood – try the fried blue-crab claws.

Nightlife in downtown Mobile is concentrated along a few lively blocks of Dauphin Street. *The Bicycle Shop*, at no. 661, is a popular, laid-back **pub** with an extensive drink selection; at *Grand Central*, no. 256, an array of eclectic bands play for no cover; while *Soul Kitchen*, no. 455, hosts good jazz, blues, and reggae on the weekends. *Lagniappe* is the free weekly **listings** paper (Ⓦ www.lagniappemobile. com).

Mississippi

Before the Civil War, when cotton was king and slavery remained unchallenged, **MISSISSIPPI** was the fifth wealthiest state in the nation. Since the war, however, it has consistently been the poorest, its dependence on cotton a handicap that leaves it victim to the vagaries of the commodities market.

From Reconstruction onwards, Mississippi was also infamous for being the strongest bastion of segregation in the South. It witnessed some of the most notorious incidents of the **civil rights** era, from the lynching of Chicago teenager Emmett Till in 1955 to the murder of three activists during the "Freedom Summer" of 1964. Not until the early Seventies did the church bombings and murders come to an end. Even today, no one could claim that **racial tension** has ceased to exist, and many visitors are shocked to encounter the truly scandalous **poverty** that still lurks down many a rural backroad.

The legalization of gambling during the early 1990s stimulated the economy to a certain extent, with the giant casinos of Biloxi in particular drawing visitors to the Gulf Coast. However, the shoreline suffered such appalling devastation from Hurricane Katrina in 2005 that it currently cannot be considered as a potential tourist destination.

Mississippi's major city is its capital, **Jackson**, while historic river towns like **Vicksburg** and **Natchez** provide good reasons to stray off the interstates.Literary **Oxford** has an appealing ambiance, while **blues** fans will need no encouragement to go exploring sleepy **Delta settlements** such as Alligator or Yazoo City.

Getting around Mississippi

Although **Greyhound** serves most of Mississippi, including the Delta, only along the coastal stretch are services at all frequent. Jackson has the only **airport** of any size, while Amtrak **trains** from New Orleans head north to Memphis by way of Jackson and Greenwood; northeast to Atlanta, passing through a succession of unexciting small towns; and along the coast to Florida, stopping at Biloxi. Trips on the Mississippi itself are run on expensive luxury **cruisers** (see p.555).

The Delta

That Delta. Five thousand square miles, without any hill save the bumps of dirt the Indians made to stand on when the River overflowed.

William Faulkner, *Sanctuary*

"That Delta" is not in fact a delta at all; technically it's an alluvial flood plain, a couple of hundred miles short of the mouth of the Mississippi. The name stems from its resemblance to the fertile delta of the Nile (which also began at a city named Memphis); the extravagant meanderings of the river on its way down to **Vicksburg** deposit enough rich topsoil to make this one of the world's finest cotton-producing regions.

The Delta is a land of scorching sun, parched earth, flooding creeks, and thickets of bone-dry evergreens, best seen at dawn or dusk, when the glassy-smooth waters of the Mississippi reflect the sun and the foliage along the banks. Just containing the sheer volume of water is a never-ending battle, with giant levees in place to protect the farmland. Though the main thoroughfare south is the legendary **Hwy-61**, exploring is best done on the back roads, which are characterized by huge, empty views, interrupted only by roadside shacks, tiny churches, and the sound of the blues.

Clarksdale

CLARKSDALE, the first significant town south of Memphis, has an unquestionable right to consider itself the home of the blues. Its quite phenomenal roll call of former residents – stretching from Muddy Waters, John Lee Hooker, Howlin' Wolf, and Robert Johnson up to Ike Turner and Sam Cooke – is celebrated in the

Delta Blues Museum, housed at 1 Blues Alley (March–Oct Mon–Sat 9am–5pm, Nov–Feb Mon–Sat 10am–5pm; $6; ☎ 662/627-6820, ⓦ www.deltabluesmuseum .org). The centerpiece among the photos, instruments, personal possessions, videos, and recordings is the "Muddywood" guitar, created by ZZ Top using wood from Waters' old cabin; the cabin itself has been reassembled nearby.

Long a rundown rural community, Clarksdale has been boosted by an influx of money and visitors triggered by the large complex of **casinos** a dozen miles north at **Tunica**. Attempts to revitalize, and build on the town's blues heritage, currently focus on the **Blues Alley** district, a general name for the area around the restored passenger depot of the Illinois Central Railroad, through which many black Mississippians, including Muddy, started their migration to the cities of the north. Each year, around the second weekend in August, the town holds the **Sunflower River Blues and Gospel Festival** (free; ☎ 1-800/626-3764, ⓦ www.sunflowerfest.org).

Practicalities

The most unusual and characterful **accommodation** near Clarksdale is at **Hopson Plantation**, two miles south of town on US-49. The old sharecroppers' cabins still look much as they did when this was a working cotton plantation, though several have been converted, with the addition of air-conditioning and kitchen facilities, to serve as the 🍴 *Shack Up Inn* (☎ 662/624-8329, ⓦ www.shackupinn.com; ❸), where B&B stands for "bed and beer." Another option is the very basic *Riverside Hotel*, 615 Sunflower Ave (☎ 662/624-9163, ⓦ www.cathead.biz/riverside.html; ❷), which used to be a hospital, famous as the site of **Bessie Smith**'s death in 1937 after a car crash. If you do spend the night, be sure to talk to "Rat," the son of the original owner, and learn the "true history of the blues."

As for **eating**, *Abe's*, 616 S State St (☎ 662/624-9947), is a good central barbecue joint. The more upscale 🍴 *Madidi*, 164 Delta Ave (☎ 662/627-7770; closed Sun & Mon), which offers a classy French take on Southern cuisine, is owned by a consortium that includes Morgan Freeman; the group also operates the *Ground Zero Blues Club*, nearby at no. 387 (☎ 662/621-9009, ⓦ www. groundzerobluesclub.com), which books top local musicians on weekends. Otherwise, catching a live blues show takes a bit of luck, as long-standing juke joints find it impossible to compete with the Tunica casinos. Ask at the Delta Blues Museum about upcoming events at more authentic venues like the *Red Top Lounge* (aka *Smitty's*), 377 Yazoo Ave (☎ 662/627-1525), or *Red's*, 395 Sunflower Ave (☎ 662/627-3166).

Delta towns

Seventy miles south of Clarksdale, **GREENVILLE** is the largest town on the Delta. Still an important riverport, it hosts the **Mississippi Delta Blues Festival** (☎ 1-888/812-5837, ⓦ www.deltablues.org) every year on the third weekend of September. Tree-lined avenues lead from the characterless outskirts of town into the business district, beyond which pallid warehouses stand in the shadow of a huge levee. One good, safe **accommodation** option near the river is the *Greenville Inn*, 211 Walnut St (☎ 662/332-6900; ❸). For a **meal**, stop by *Doe's Eat Place*, 502 Nelson St (☎ 662/334-3315), which serves arguably the best down-home cooking in the entire Delta.

INDIANOLA, 23 miles east of Greenville on US-82, is the home of the largest catfish-processing company in the world (they're called Delta). Each year in June, there's a "Home-Coming" celebration for **B.B. King**, who was born here, though of late he hasn't always returned for the open-air concert that's organized by *Club Ebony*, 404 Hannah Ave (☎ 662/887-9915, ⓦ www.clubebony.biz).

As recently as 1900, much of the **Mississippi Delta** remained an impenetrable wilderness of cypress and gum trees, roamed by panthers and bears and plagued with mosquitoes. Bit by bit, land was cleared for cotton plantations – but, though the soil was fertile, white laborers could not be enticed to work in this godforsaken backcountry. After emancipation, the economy came to depend on black **sharecroppers**, who would work a portion of the land on a white-owned plantation in return for a share (often pitifully small) of the eventual crop. As a rule, this lifestyle entailed long periods of poverty and debt interspersed with occasional windfalls. In the Delta, however, the returns tended to be greater than elsewhere, and blacks moved here from all over Mississippi.

In 1903, W.C. Handy, often credited as "the Father of the Blues," but at that time the leader of a vaudeville orchestra, found himself waiting for a train in Tutwiler, fifteen miles southeast of Clarksdale. At some point in the night, a ragged black man carrying a guitar sat down next to him and began to play what Handy called "the weirdest music I had ever heard." Using a pocketknife pressed against the guitar strings to accentuate his mournful vocal style, the man sang that he was "Goin' where the Southern cross the Dog."

This was the **Delta blues**, characterized by the interplay between words and music, with the guitar aiming to parallel and complement the singing rather than simply provide a backing. Though a local, place-specific music – the "Southern" and the "Dog" were railroads that crossed a short way south at Moorhead – it did not simply spring up from the ground, but combined traditional African instrumental and vocal techniques with slave "field hollers," as well as the reels and jigs then at the basis of popular entertainment.

The blues started out as young people's music; the old folks liked the banjo, fife, and drum, but the younger generation were crazy for the wild showmanship of bluesmen such as **Charley Patton**. Born in April 1891, Patton was the classic itinerant bluesman, moving from plantation to plantation and wife to wife, and playing Saturday-night dances with a repertoire that extended from rollicking dance pieces to documentary songs such as "High Water Everywhere," about the bursting of the Mississippi levees in April 1927. Another seminal artist, the enigmatic **Robert Johnson**, was rumored to have sold his soul to the Devil in return for a few brief years of writing songs such as "Love in Vain" and "Stop Breakin' Down." His "Crossroads Blues" spoke of being stranded at night in the chilling emptiness of the Delta; themes carried to metaphysical extremes in "Hellhound on My Trail" and "Me and the Devil Blues" – "you may bury my body down by the highwayside / So my old evil spirit can catch a Greyhound bus and ride."

Both Patton and Johnson died in the 1930s. However, within a few years the Delta blues had been carried north to **Chicago** by men such as **Muddy Waters** and **Howlin' Wolf**. Their electrified urban blues was the most immediate ancestor of rock 'n' roll.

In addition to towns such as Clarksdale (see p.588) and Helena, Arkansas (p.597), blues enthusiasts may want to search out the following rural sites:

Stovall Plantation Stovall Road, 7 miles northwest of Clarksdale. Where tractor-driver Muddy Waters was first recorded; a few cabins remain standing, though Muddy's own is now in the museum at Clarksdale.

Sonny Boy Williamson II's Grave Outside Tutwiler, 13 miles southeast of Clarksdale.

Parchman Farm Junction US-49 W and Hwy-32. Mississippi State Penitentiary, immortalized by former prisoner Bukka White.

Dockery Plantation On Hwy-8, between Cleveland and Ruleville. One of Patton's few long-term bases, also home to Howlin' Wolf and Roebuck "Pops" Staples.

Charley Patton's Grave New Jerusalem Church, Holly Ridge, off US-82, 6 miles west of Indianola.

Robert Johnson's Grave Payne Chapel in Quito, off Hwy-7, roughly 6 miles southwest of Greenwood, where he was poisoned.

Forty miles east of Indianola on US-82, **GREENWOOD**, a sleepy town of twenty thousand people, is the country's second largest cotton exchange after Memphis. The nineteenth-century offices of downtown's Cotton Row overlook the shady Yazoo River, and graceful mansions line pretty Grand Boulevard. The **Cottonlandia Museum** (Mon–Fri 9am–5pm, Sat & Sun 2–5pm; $5; ⓦ www.cottonlandia.org), about two miles west of the town center on the US-82 W bypass, is a rag-tag collection of old hardware, Native American beads, stuffed birds, intriguing artwork, and oddly long wooden benches polished by the tongues of mules. Greenwood has recently begun to play up its connection to Robert Johnson (he died here), though the **Cotton Capital Blues Festival** in October remains the city's current contribution to the Delta Blues music legacy.

Of the many **motels** along US-49 and US-82, the *Travel Inn* at 623 US-82 W (☏662/453-8810; ❷) is basic, clean, and good value, with an outdoor pool. By far the best **food** in Greenwood is the Italian/Cajun cuisine at *Lusco's*, on the wrong side of the railway tracks at 722 Carrolton Ave (☏662/453-5365). Each table in this eccentric old place is hidden away in a small booth, veiled by chintz curtains – an arrangement dating from the days of Prohibition, when *Lusco's* was the haunt of cotton barons who came here to drink moonshine.

Northeastern Mississippi

Cutting its way south through Mississippi, I-55 acts as an approximate boundary between the Delta and the luscious green forests of the **northeast**. Of the area's small market towns, the most appealing are the old-style shopping center of **Columbus**, and **Holly Springs**, whose oak-lined streets hide one of the most extraordinary attractions in the state. The only other places of major interest in the region are genteel **Oxford** and tidy blue-collar **Tupelo**, birthplace of **Elvis Presley** and **John Lee Hooker**.

Holly Springs

Centered on a neat courthouse square, **HOLLY SPRINGS** is a time-warped little town that's said to have changed hands 62 times during the Civil War; the minutiae of its otherwise uneventful history fill three splendidly eclectic floors in the local **museum**, at 220 E College Ave (Mon–Fri 10am–5pm, Sat 10am–2pm; $3). However, were it not for **Graceland Too**, 200 E Gholson Ave (open 24hr year-round; $5), Holly Springs would today be of little note. The home of Paul McLeod and, at times, his son Elvis Aaron Presley McLeod, this shrine to the King is a quite remarkable labor of love. Walls, ceiling, and stairwells are crammed with memorabilia from the kitsch to the priceless, and, just as in Graceland, the upper floor is blocked off – the stairs lined with glassy-eyed mannequins kitted out in Elvis and Priscilla outfits. Mr McLeod insists that this is above all an archive and research center; as well as collecting records, cuttings, and books, he works around the clock to monitor and log every reference to Elvis transmitted on TV and radio. **Tours** last up to three hours, depending on the mood of your host and how busy he is compiling Elvis info, but are sure to include the chance to buy an infinitesimal snip of rug from Graceland's Jungle Room.

There's no reason to spend a night in Holly Springs, but it's well worth pausing for a **meal** here. Housed in a former "blind tiger" (brothel) beside the railroad tracks east of town, *Phillips Grocery*, 541 E Van Dorn Ave (☏662/252-4671), is a ramshackle old grocery store that serves sublime fresh-ground hamburgers and Southern vegetables.

Oxford

Twelve thousand residents and eleven thousand students enable **OXFORD**, an enclave of wealth in a predominantly poor region, to blend rural charm with a busy nightlife. Its central square is archetypal smalltown America, but the leafy streets have a vaguely European air – the town named itself after the English city as part of its campaign to persuade the **University of Mississippi**, known as Ole Miss, to locate its main campus here.

It's an undeniably pretty, appealing place today, but in September 1962, this was the site of one of the bitterest displays of racial hatred seen in Mississippi. After eighteen months of legal and political wrangling, federal authorities ruled that **James Meredith** should be allowed to enroll as the first black student at Ole Miss. The news that Meredith had been sneaked into college by federal troops sparked a riot that left three dead and 160 injured. Despite constant threats, Meredith graduated the following year, wearing a "NEVER" badge (the segregationist slogan of Governor Ross Barnett) upside down. A memorial commemorating his achievement was finally unveiled in September 2002, on the fortieth anniversary of his admission. Also on campus, the **Blues Archive** (Mon–Fri 8am–5pm; free; ☎662/915-7753) holds thousands of recordings and B.B. King's personal memorabilia, while the **Center for the Study of Southern Culture** looks at Southern folkways (Mon–Fri 8am–5pm; free; ☎662/915-5993).

From Ole Miss, a ten-minute walk through lush Bailey Woods leads to secluded **Rowan Oak**, the former home of novelist **William Faulkner**, preserved as it was on the day he died in July 1962 (Tues–Sat 10am–4pm, Sun 1–4pm; $5). The fictional Deep South town of Jefferson in Yoknapatawpha County, where the Nobel Prize–winner set his major works, was based heavily on Oxford and its environs. Each year, during the last week in July, the University holds a Faulkner and Yoknapatawpha Conference.

In town, a walk around the **square** brings you to Neilson's, a delightfully old-fashioned department store (the oldest in the South, in fact), little changed since 1897. You can pick up a piece of quirky Mississippi folk art at one of the offbeat gift shops here, or join the students sipping lattes and reading on the balcony of the exemplary Square Books, at Van Buren and Lamar streets.

Practicalities

Oxford's **visitor center** (Mon–Fri 9am–5pm, Sat 10am-4pm, Sun 1–4pm; ☎662/232-2367 or 1-800/758-9177, ⓦwww.touroxfordms.com), next to Neilson's in the town square, hands out good walking-tour leaflets. **Accommodation** options include the *Downtown Oxford Inn*, 400 N Lamar Blvd (☎662/234-3031 or 1-800/606-1497; ❹), and the comfortable B&B *Oliver-Britt House*, 512 Van Buren Ave (☎662/234-8043; ❸). On the town square, you can **eat** homestyle meals at the *Ajax Diner* (☎662/232-8880; closed Sun), or more sophisticated Southern cuisine at *City Grocery* (☎662/232-8080; closed Sun). The *Bottletree Bakery*, 923 Van Buren Ave (☎662/236-5000; closed Mon), is a friendly café with soups and sandwiches.

Tupelo

On January 8, 1935, **Elvis Presley** and his twin brother Jesse were born in **TUPELO**, an industrial town in northeastern Mississippi. Jesse died at birth, while Elvis grew up to be a truck driver. Their parents, Gladys and Vernon Presley, who lived in poor, white East Tupelo, found it hard to make ends meet. Such was the financial strain of rearing the young Elvis that his sharecropper father was reduced to forgery in a desperate attempt to raise cash, and was jailed for three years. Their home was repossessed, and the family moved to Memphis in 1948.

The Tupelo **CVB**, 399 E Main St (Mon–Fri 8am–5pm; ☎662/841-6521 or 1-800/533-0611, ⓦwww.tupelo.net), has details of a four-mile driving tour that takes in Elvis's first school and the shop where he bought his first guitar. The town doesn't go in for overkill, however; Main Street is a long, placid stretch of nondescript buildings, with nary a gift shop to be seen. The actual **Elvis Presley Birthplace**, 306 Elvis Presley Drive (May–Sept Mon–Sat 9am–5.30pm, Sun 1–5pm; Oct–April Mon–Sat 9am–5pm, Sun 1–5pm; $2.50; ⓦwww.elvispresleybirthplace.com), is tiny. A two-room shotgun house, built for $150 in 1934, it's been furnished to look as it did when Elvis was born, with the judicious addition of a large can of lard in the kitchen and a love-seat swinging from the porch. The separate **museum** alongside (same hours; $6, or $7 combined admission) is filled with memorabilia collected by a family friend of the Presleys, Janelle McComb, and includes her photos of, poems about, and shrines to the King, as well as selling everything from matchbooks to Elvis pendulum clocks. Nearby, a modern **meditation chapel** was built with donations from fans (but, oddly, the pews and altar remain roped off to visitors).

Among local **motels**, there's a central *Comfort Inn*, 1190 Gloster St (☎662/842-5100, ⓦwww.comfortinn.com; ❸), while the *Wingate Inn*, just off Hwy-78 at 186 Stone Creek Blvd (☎662/680-8887 or 1-800/228-1000, ⓦwww.wingateinns.com; ❸), is a more upscale, business-oriented option. *Park Heights*, 825 W Jefferson St (☎662/842-5665; closed Sun & Mon), serving seafood, salads, steak, and pasta, is the best **restaurant** in town.

South central Mississippi

South of the Delta, the rich woodlands and meadows of **central Mississippi** are heralded by steep loess bluffs, home to engaging historic towns such as **Vicksburg** and **Natchez**. Driving around the area is a real pleasure, especially along the unspoiled **Natchez Trace Parkway** – devoid of trucks, buildings, and neon signs – which runs through Jackson and on up to Tupelo.

Jackson

JACKSON, set two hundred miles from both Memphis and New Orleans, has been Mississippi's state capital since 1821. Only in the twentieth century, however, did it become the largest conurbation in the state, flourishing as a center for health and technological industries.

Following extensive damage caused by Hurricane Katrina, the state's official history museum, housed in the **Old Capitol**, is closed until further notice. A block west at 528 Bloom St, the **Smith-Robertson Museum and Cultural Center** (Mon–Fri 9am–5pm, Sat 10am–1pm, Sun 2–5pm; $1), housed in what was Jackson's first public school for blacks (open from 1894–1971), tells the story of black Mississippians since the French first imported slaves in 1719.

Practicalities

Greyhound **buses** arrive at 201 S Jefferson St, and Amtrak **trains** at 300 W Capitol St. The main **visitor center** is at 921 N President St (Mon–Fri 8.30am–5pm; ☎601/960-1891 or 1-800/354-7695, ⓦwww.visitjackson.com).

Central **rooms** can be had close to the State Capitol at the *Edison Walthall Hotel*, 225 E Capitol St (☎601/948-6161, ⓦwww.edisonwalthallhotel.com; ❹), or in the *Old Capitol Inn*, a tastefully converted former YMCA at 226 N State St (☎601/359-9000 or 1-888/359-2001, ⓦwww.oldcapitolinn.com; ❹). Downtown Jackson more or less closes down at 6pm, with the exception of *Hal & Mal's Restaurant & Brewery*, 200 S Commerce St (☎601/948-0888; closed Sun), which specializes in New Orleans cuisine and puts on **live bands** throughout the week.

Vicksburg

Forty-four miles west of Jackson, the historic port of **VICKSBURG** straddles a high bluff on a bend in the Mississippi. During the Civil War, the town's domination of the river halted Union shipping, and led Abraham Lincoln to call Vicksburg the "key to the Confederacy." It was a crucial target for General Grant, who eventually landed south of the city in the spring of 1863, circled inland, and attacked from the east. After a 47-day siege, the outnumbered Confederates surrendered on the Fourth of July – a holiday Vicksburg declined to celebrate for the next hundred years – and Lincoln was able to rejoice that "the Father of Waters again goes unvexed to the sea."

Entered via Clay Street (US-80) just northeast of town, **Vicksburg National Military Park** preserves the main Civil War battlefield (daily: summer 8am–7pm; rest of the year 8am–5pm; $8 per vehicle; ☎601/636-0583, ⓦwww.nps.gov/vick). A sixteen-mile loop drive through the rippling green hillsides traces every contour of the Union and Confederate trenches, punctuated by statues, refurbished cannon, and over 1600 state-by-state monuments. Also at the site are the substantial remains of the squat black ironclad **USS Cairo**, which was sunk without casualties by a "torpedo," as mines were then known, in 1862, and salvaged a century later. It now stands protected by a giant canopy, with a museum alongside of artifacts retrieved from the waters. Nearby, in the **Vicksburg National Cemetery**, 13,000 of the 17,000 Union graves are simply marked "Unknown."

As the Mississippi has changed course since the 1860s, it's now the slender, canalized Yazoo River rather than the broad Mississippi that flows alongside the battlefield and most of downtown Vicksburg. The core of the city has changed little, however, despite the arrival of four permanently moored **casinos**. It's a bare but attractive place of precipitous streets, steep terraces, and wooded ravines, where the entire downtown area is progressively being restored to its original late-Victorian appearance. Most of its finest buildings were destroyed during the siege, so the place is largely characterized by middle-class homes, not sumptuous mansions.

The fascinating **Old Court House Museum**, 1008 Cherry St (summer Mon–Sat 8.30am–5pm, Sun 1.30–5pm; rest of year closes at 4.30pm; $5), covers the Civil War era in great depth, even selling genuine minié balls (bullets) for $2. The museum also holds displays on Vicksburg's first settlement, Nogales, which was founded in 1796, as well as the postwar years. One room is devoted to Confederate president Jefferson Davis, who started his career here with a speech from the balcony in 1843; the victorious Ulysses Grant returned to Vicksburg as president in 1869, and addressed thousands of ex-slaves from that same balcony. A small museum at the **Biedenharn Candy Company**, 1107 Washington St (Mon–Sat 9am–5pm, Sun 1.30-4.30pm; $2.75), marks the spot where Coca-Cola was first bottled, with vivid displays on how it all came about.

Practicalities

Vicksburg has two major **visitor centers**, both just off I-20: the Mississippi Welcome Center, at exit 1A beside the river (daily 8am–6pm), and the town's own tourist information center near exit 4, opposite the battlefield entrance on Clay Street (daily: summer 8am–5.30pm; winter 8am–5pm; ☎601/636-9421 or 1-800/221-3536, ⓦwww.visitvicksburg.com).

The military park is the prime area for **motels**, such as the spartan *Hillcrest*, 4503 Hwy-80 E (☎601/638-1491; ❶), which has a pool, and the comfortable *Battlefield Inn*, at 4137 I-20 Frontage Rd (☎601/638-5811 or 1-800/359-9363, ⓦwww.battlefieldinn.org; ❹), which includes use of the pool, two free cocktails, and a free breakfast buffet. Among appealing central **B&Bs** are *Anchuca*, housed in the town's first colonnaded mansion, at 1010 First East St (☎601/661-0111 or 1-888/686-0111, ⓦwww.anchucamansion.com; ❺), which has seven guestrooms, including a gorgeous suite extending through the former slave quarters, as well as a pool and fine breakfasts; and the 1868 Victorian-Italianate *Annabelle*, 501 Speed St (☎601/638-2000 or 1-800/791-2000, ⓦwww.annabellebnb.com; ❺).

When it's time to **eat**, tuck into superb all-you-care-to-eat "round table" lunches of fried chicken and other Southern delicacies at ⚔ *Walnut Hills*, 1214 Adams St at Clay (☎601/638-4910; closed Sat). At *The Biscuit Company*, 1100 Washington St (☎601/631-0099), you can eat pizza or po'boys, drink till late, and hear **live jazz** or **blues** most weekends.

Natchez

Sixty miles south of Vicksburg, the river town of **NATCHEZ** is the oldest permanent settlement on the Mississippi River. By the time it first flew the Stars and Stripes in 1798, it had already been home to the Natchez people (see below) and their predecessors, as well as French, British, and Spanish colonists. Unlike its great rival, Vicksburg, Natchez was spared significant damage during the Civil War, ensuring that its abundant Greek Revival antebellum mansions remained intact, complete with meticulously maintained gardens. Interspersed among them are countless simpler but similarly attractive white clapboard homes, set along broad leafy avenues of majestic oaks, making Natchez one of the prettiest towns in the entire South. **Horse and carriage** tours (see p.596) explore the downtown area, while fourteen individual mansions stay open all year round, among them the elaborate, octagonal **Longwood**, 140 Lower Woodville Rd (daily 9am–4.30pm; $8), with its huge dome, snow-white arches and columns, and the palatial **Stanton Hall**, 401 High St (daily 10am–4pm; $8). All these and more can be seen on tours that set off from 200 State St during the twice-yearly **Natchez Pilgrimage** (mid-March to mid-April & first two weeks in Oct; $32; ⓦwww.natchezpilgrimage.com).

While Natchez proper perches well above the river, a small stretch of riverfront at the foot of the bluff constitutes **Natchez Under-the-Hill**. Once known as the "Sodom of the Mississippi," it now houses a handful of bars and restaurants, plus the 24-hour *Isle of Capri* riverboat **casino**, a cacophony of slot machines and craps tables (ⓦwww.isleofcapricasino.com).

Natchez takes its name from the **Natchez Indians**, regarded as one of the most significant flowerings of the widespread Mississippian culture. They survived here until 1729, when they rose against French plans to replace one of their villages with a tobacco plantation. Joined by African slaves, they killed 250 colonists before the French and their Choctaw allies crushed the rebellion. The former Natchez spiritual center known as the **Grand Village**, home to a leader revered as the "Great Sun," can now be explored at 400 Jefferson Davis Blvd (Mon–Sat 9am–5pm, Sun 1.30–5pm; free). It's an atmospheric place, holding a visitor center and reconstructed dwellings, as well as a large park-like area with an imposing ceremonial mound at either end. Another Natchez site, the much larger **Emerald Mound**, stands just off the Natchez Trace northeast of town (free 24hr access).

Natchez's rich **African-American** heritage – Richard Wright, the author of *Native Son*, was born nearby and lived in the town as a small boy – is chronicled in an excellent 26-page free booklet, available from the visitor center.

6

Mississippi's Gulf Coast

Previous editions of this book have included an extensive description of Mississippi's **Gulf Coast**, where fine beaches, and the resort atmosphere of **Biloxi** in particular, attracted considerable numbers of summer visitors. However, the storm surge that accompanied Hurricane Katrina in August 2005 caused such extensive damage to the region that for the moment it makes no sense to consider it a potential tourist destination. Here, unlike in New Orleans, the coastline was battered by colossal waves, and entire towns were simply obliterated from the map. Though businesses like the giant casinos of Biloxi have been steadily reopening, vast desolate gaps remain, and while in time a full recovery will surely be achieved, the disaster area that is the Gulf Coast is no place to spend a vacation.

Practicalities

Natchez's vast **Visitor Reception Center** occupies a panoramic location overlooking the river at 640 S Canal St, alongside the Mississippi River bridge (March–Oct Mon–Sat 8.30am–6pm, Sun 9am–4pm; Nov–Feb Mon–Sat 8.30am–5pm, Sun 9am–4pm; ☎601/446-6345 or 1-800/647-6724, ⊛www.visitnatchez.com). It's the starting point for all kinds of **trolley** and **bus tours** of town, and sells tickets for the **carriage tours** ($12; 45min) that leave from Canal and State streets, slightly closer to downtown.

As for **accommodation**, the *Ramada Inn*, across from the visitor center at 130 John R. Junkin Drive (☎601/446-6311 or 1-800/256-6311, ⊛www.ramada. com; ❹), enjoys much the same magnificent views, while the *Natchez Eola*, 110 N Pearl St (☎601/445-6000 or 1-866/445-3652, ⊛www.natchezeola.com; ❺), is a venerable downtown hotel of considerable charm. The *Mark Twain Guesthouse*, 33 Silver St (☎601/446-8023, ⊛www.underthehillsaloon.com; ❸), is an atmospheric option down by the river; its three simple rooms share a bathroom. For a quintessential Natchez experience, consider staying in a more upmarket **B&B**, such as the opulent *Burn*, 712 N Union St (☎601/442-1344, ⊛www.theburnbnb. com; ❻), which has a beautiful pool.

For **food**, *Cock of the Walk*, on the bluff at 200 N Broadway (☎601/446-8920), serves irresistibly tasty catfish, while the *Marketplace Café*, 613 Main St (☎601/304-9399; closed Mon), occupying most of a large open-sided market building downtown, sells good, inexpensive breakfasts and lunches. *Biscuits and Blues*, 315 Main St (☎601/446-9922), combines burgers and barbecue with **live blues** on weekends.

Arkansas

Historically, **ARKANSAS** belongs very much to the American South. It sided firmly with the Confederacy in the Civil War, and its capital, Little Rock, was in 1957 one of the most notorious flashpoints in the struggle for civil rights. Geographically, however, it marks the beginning of the Great Plains. Unlike the other Southern states on the east side of the Mississippi River, Arkansas remained very sparsely populated until almost a century ago. Westward expansion was blocked by the existence of the Indian Territory in what's now Oklahoma, and not until the railroads opened up the forested interior during the 1880s did settlers stray in any numbers from their small riverside villages. Only once the Depression and mechanization had forced thousands of farmers to leave their fields did Arkansas begin to develop any significant industrial base. In 1992, local boy Bill Clinton's accession to the presidency catapulted Arkansas into national prominence. Four towns lay claim to him: Hope, his birthplace; Hot Springs, his "home town"; Fayetteville, where he and Hillary married; and, of course, Little Rock. Of the four, only sleepy **Little Rock** and the nearby spa resort of **Hot Springs** are really worth a trip, whatever the tourist brochures may say.

Though Arkansas encompasses the **Mississippi Delta** in the east, oil-rich timber lands in the south, and the sweeping **Ouachita** ("Wash-ih-taw") **Mountains** in the west, the cragged and charismatic **Ozark Mountains** in the north are its most scenic asset, where the main attractions for tourists are the uncrowded parks and unspoiled rivers. Incidentally, "Arkansas" is a distorted version of the name of a small Indian tribe; the state legislature declared once and for all in 1881 that the correct pronunciation is "Arkansaw."

Getting around Arkansas

While **driving** the state's relatively unspoiled highways, lined by mom-and-pop motels and surrounded by greenery, can be a pleasure, it's extremely difficult to venture beyond Little Rock and Hot Springs using **public transportation**. Greyhound runs intermittent services, while Amtrak cuts diagonally east–west through the state, calling at Little Rock, which also holds the only sizeable **airport**. To see the Ozarks you'll certainly need a **car**.

Eastern Arkansas

What's surprising about the eastern Arkansas deltalands is that they are far from totally flat: **Crowley's Ridge**, a narrow arc of windblown loess hills, breaks up the uniform smoothness, stretching 150 miles from southern Missouri to the atmospheric river town of **Helena**. Helena has plenty to recommend it, not least its strong **blues** heritage; the pine-clad woodlands of the Gulf Coastal Plain in southern Arkansas, however, despite their profusion of scenic rivers and sleepy bayous, offer little incentive to stop.

Helena

The small Mississippi port of **HELENA**, roughly sixty miles south of Memphis, was once the shipping point for Arkansas's cotton crop, when Mark Twain described it as occupying "one of the prettiest situations on the river." A compact **historic district** bordered by Holly, College, and Perry streets reflects that brief period of prosperity, before the arrival of the railroad left most of the river towns obsolete. Nowadays it is feeling the strain of living in the shadow of the enormous casinos across the river; most of what little activity there is takes place along the run-down **Cherry Street** on the levee.

Nonetheless, Helena is a laid-back place, with great appeal for fans of the **Delta blues**. In 1941 it was the birthplace of the celebrated **King Biscuit Time Show**, broadcast on radio station KFFA (1360 AM). Featuring performances from legends like boogie pianist Pinetop Perkins and harmonica great **Sonny Boy Williamson II** ("Rice" Miller), the show was the first in the nation to broadcast live Delta blues. With a huge influence that belies its tiny size – musicians from BB King to Levon Helm quote it as a major inspiration – the show has been on air continuously ever since, hosted since 1951 by living legend "Sunshine" Sonny Payne. Broadcasts (Mon–Fri 12.15–12.45pm; Ⓦ www.kingbiscuittime.com; Ⓣ 870/338-4350) are recorded from the foyer of the excellent **Delta Cultural Center Visitor Center**, 141 Cherry St; observers are welcome. Even if you miss the show, make sure to stop by the visitor center's **music exhibit**, complete with listening stations and great video footage.

Blues fans can also buy – and hear – a thrilling assortment of records at **Bubba Sullivan's Blues Corner**, nearby in the small mall at 105 Cherry St (Ⓣ 870/338-3501). Bubba himself is a mine of friendly information on local gigs and music events, not least the town's superb free **Arkansas Blues and Heritage Festival** (formerly known as the King Biscuit Blues Festival; Ⓦ www.kingbiscuitfest.org), which, held every fall on the weekend before Columbus Day, attracts big-name blues, acoustic, and gospel performers.

The **Delta Cultural Center** has another site a block south of the visitor center, in a restored train depot at 95 Missouri St (Tues–Sat 9am–5pm; free). Exhibits cover all aspects of the region's history, from the first settlers of this soggy frontier to contemporary racism, with, of course, lots of good stuff about the region's musical heritage. From here you can walk along the levee to **River Park**, which has fabulous views of the Mississippi. For some unexpected historic artifacts, stop by the **Phillips County Museum**, next to the Phillips County Public Library at 623 Pecan St (Tues–Sat 10am–4pm; free). Here, in addition to paintings, period clothing, and Native American arrowheads, you'll find intriguing letters written by General Lafayette, Charles Lindbergh, and Robert E. Lee, as well as Samuel Clemens (aka Mark Twain).

Practicalities

The 1904 *Edwardian Inn*, 317 Biscoe St, on the main highway into town north of the Mississippi Bridge (Ⓣ 870/338-9155, Ⓦ www.edwardianinn.com; ❹), is an opulent **B&B** with large oak-paneled rooms, slightly marred by views from the front over a chemical plant on the river. For **food**, *Cherry Street Deli*, 420 Cherry St (Ⓣ 870/817-7706), has good soup and sandwiches, while *Oliver's*, 101 Missouri St (Ⓣ 870/338-7228), serves catfish, steak, and the like. If you want to hear some live **blues**, stay on Cherry Street and check out *Sonny Boy's Music Hall*, no. 301 (Ⓣ 870/338-8719), or *Fonzie's*, no. 400 (Ⓣ 870/817-7736).

Central and western Arkansas

Little Rock sits right in the middle of the state, just fifty miles west of the quirky spa town of **Hot Springs**, which marks the eastern gateway to the remote **Ouachita Mountains**. The rippling farmland of the **Arkansas River Valley** is sandwiched by the Ouachita crests on the south side and the craggy ridges of the Ozarks to the north. Mining and logging communities dot the east–west roads, and former frontier towns like **Fort Smith** and **Van Buren** retain their Old West flavor. Fayetteville and Hope are both in west Arkansas; there's no reason to stop at either.

Little Rock

The geographical, political, and financial center of Arkansas, **LITTLE ROCK** is at the meeting point of the state's two major regions, the northwestern hills and the eastern Delta. The town today has a relaxed, open feel, a far cry from the dramatic time of 1957 (see below), and, since the election of William J. Clinton to the presidency in 1992, a certain cachet that's lacking in the rest of the state.

The city's main attraction, the **William J. Clinton Presidential Library and Museum**, directly east of downtown at 1200 President Clinton Ave (Mon–Sat 9am–5pm, Sun 1–5pm; $7; ⓦ www.clintonlibrary.gov), is housed in an elevated, glass-and-metal building attractively set on the river. Revitalizing a once-depressed district of abandoned warehouses, it's a dazzling structure, a visual metaphor for Clinton's oft-repeated avowal to build a bridge to the twenty-first century. But its location also acts as a canny way to draw visitors to Little Rock's vibrant **River Market District**, with its splash of restaurants and bars, farmers' market, and thriving food hall. A few minutes away from the library, at 610 President Clinton Ave, the **museum store** (ⓦ www.clintonmuseumstore.com) not only sells some marvelous gifts – from "I Miss Bill" stickers and Socks the cat mousepads, to compilation CDs of Mr President's favorite music. Also nearby, at 500 President Clinton Ave, the **Museum of Discovery** is a favorite with kids (Mon–Sat 9am–5pm, Sun 1–5pm; $7), while, along the river, **Riverfront Park**, a thin strip of greenery and fountains, runs for several blocks. A commemorative sign here marks the "little rock" for which the city is named (it's not particularly striking, but then the name probably gives that away).

Crisis at Central High

In 1957, Little Rock unexpectedly became the battleground in the first major conflict between state and federal government over **race relations**. At the time, the city was generally viewed as progressive by Southern standards. All parks, libraries, and buses were integrated, a relatively high thirty percent of blacks were on the electoral register, and there were black police officers. However, when the Little Rock School Board announced its decision to gradually **desegregate** its schools – the Supreme Court having declared such segregation unconstitutional – James Johnson, a candidate for state governor, started a campaign opposing interracial education. Johnson's rhetoric began to win him support, and the incumbent governor, **Orval Faubus**, who had previously shown no interest in the issue, jumped on the bandwagon himself.

The first nine black students were due to enter **Central High School** that September. The day before school opened, Faubus, "in the interest of safety," reversed his decision to let blacks enroll, only to be overruled by the federal court. He ordered state troopers to keep out the black students anyway; soldiers with bayonets forced Elizabeth Eckford, one of the nine, away from the school entrance into a seething crowd, from which she had to jump on a bus to escape. As legal battles raged during the day, at night blacks were subject to violent attacks by white gangs. Three weeks later, President Eisenhower somewhat reluctantly brought in the 101st Airborne Division, and, amid violent demonstrations, the nine were at last able to enter the school. Throughout the year, they experienced immense intimidation; when one retaliated, she was expelled. The graduation of James Green, the oldest, at the end of the year, seemed to put an end to the affair, but Faubus, up for re-election, renewed his political posturing by closing down all public schools in the city for the 1958–59 academic year – and thereby increased his majority.

Today Central High School – an enormous brown, crescent-shaped structure, bearing no little resemblance to a fortress – is on the National Register of Historic Places and has been designated as a National Park site. It's at 1500 S Park Ave, about a mile from the capitol. Across the street in a restored former gas station at 2125 Daisy L. Gatson Bates Drive, the **Central High Visitor Center** (Mon–Sat 9am–4.30pm, Sun 1–4.30pm; free) has a good exhibition about the 1957 crisis; a larger visitor center is due to open in late 2007 to commemorate the 50th anniversary of the events.

Surrounded by smooth lawns and shaded by evergreens, the **Old State House Museum** (Mon–Sat 9am–5pm, Sun 1–5pm; free), in the old capitol building at 300 W Markham St, is well worth a visit. The displays – everything from Civil War battle flags to African-American quilts – do an admirable job of covering Arkansas history, with strong sections on women, and, naturally, political history. Don't miss the two senate chambers, restored to their original grandeur. This was where Clinton announced his bid for the presidency on October 3, 1991, and made his acceptance speech thirteen months later – and then again in 1996, when he became the first Democrat since Franklin Delano Roosevelt to be elected to a second term.

The **Historic Arkansas Museum**, 200 E Third St (Mon–Sat 9am–5pm, Sun 1–5pm; $2.50), is a living museum of frontier life, incorporating original buildings peopled by well-meaning actors garbed in gaiters and jerkins; the museum's Hinderliter Grog Shop, Little Rock's oldest standing building, dates from around 1827. A **gallery** displays locally made crafts from the last two centuries, temporary historical exhibits, and contemporary Arkansas art.

Another point of interest, MacArthur Park, features the elegant **Arkansas Art Center** (Tues–Sat 10am–5pm, Sun 11am–5pm; free), with work by local and international artists, a collection of drawings dating from the Renaissance to the present, and a nice selection of contemporary crafts, and the **Macarthur Museum of Arkansas Military History** (Tues–Sat 10am–4pm, Sun 1–4pm; free), which has a variety of hardware from the territorial period onward.

Practicalities

Greyhound arrives at 118 E Washington Ave in North Little Rock, across the river. **Amtrak** has a more central location at Markham and Victory streets. The **visitor center** is at 615 E Capitol Ave, near MacArthur Park (Mon–Fri 8.30am–4.30pm; ☎501/370-3290 or 1-800/844-4781, ⓦwww.littlerock.com).

Finding **accommodation** downtown should be no problem; the luxurious *Rosemont B&B*, 515 W 15th St (☎501/374-7456, ⓦwww.rosemontoflittlerock.com; ❹–❻) offers home comforts like a full breakfast and a stocked pantry, while at the *Comfort Inn & Suites Downtown*, a short walk from the Clinton Center at 707 I-30 (☎501/687-7700; ⓦwww.comfortinnlittlerock.com; ❹) you'll find large rooms, a pool, and a hearty free breakfast.

As for **eating**, the bustling ⚘ **River Market District food court** (Mon–Sat 7am–6pm) provides a wealth of choice unheard of in these parts, with stalls dishing up organic soups, Middle Eastern salads, down-home BBQ, and Japanese noodles. *Andina*, next door at 400 President Clinton Ave (☎501/376-2326), does great gourmet coffee, sandwiches, and pastries, and you can pick up fresh fruit from the farmers' market outside. *Vino's*, 923 W Seventh St (☎501/375-8466; ⓦwww.vinosbrewpub.com), is an unpretentious, friendly brewpub serving ales and pizza; a popular spot for office lunches, after dark it takes on a more alternative edge, featuring live punk music. There's more music at *Juanita's*, 1300 S Main St (☎501/372-1228; ⓦwww.juanitas.com; closed Sun), an atmospheric and imaginative Mexican restaurant that hosts live rock in their club room. Perhaps Little Rock's most renowned restaurant is *Doe's Eat Place*, 1023 W Markham St (☎501/376-1195), a branch of the Greenville, Mississippi, restaurant, that serves excellent steak and tamales in unpretentious surroundings; it's a longtime favorite of former president Clinton and still a hotspot for sundry hungry politicos.

Hot Springs

Fifty miles southwest of Little Rock, the low-key, historic, and somewhat surreal spa town of **HOT SPRINGS** nestles in the heavily forested Zig Zag Mountains on the eastern flank of the Ouachitas. Its **thermal waters** have attracted visitors since Native Americans used the area as a neutral zone to settle disputes. Early settlers fashioned a crude resort out of the wilderness, and after the railroads arrived in 1875 it became a European-style spa, its hot waters said to cure rheumatism, arthritis, kidney disease, and liver problems. The resort reached its glittering heyday during the Twenties and Thirties, when the mayor reputedly ran a gambling syndicate worth $30 million per annum, and players included Al Capone and Bugsy Siegel. Movie stars and politicians, aristocrats and prize fighters flocked to "quaff the elixir," and Hot Springs became *the* place to see and be seen. The resort's popularity waned, however, when new cures appeared during the Fifties, and all but one of the bathhouses closed down. There was a surge of interest in the place after Clinton's election – he lived here between 1953 and 1964 – and today, with its combination of vaguely artsy stores, faded grandeur, and charming small-town sleepiness, it has a strangely haunting appeal.

Downtown Hot Springs threads through a looping wooded valley, barely wide enough to accommodate the main thoroughfare of Central Avenue. Eight magnificent buildings here, behind a lush display of magnolia trees, elms, and hedgerows, make up the splendid **Bathhouse Row**. Between 1915 and 1962, the grandest of them all was the **Fordyce Bathhouse**, at the 300 block of Central, which reopened in 1989 as the **visitor center** for **Hot Springs National Park** – the only national park to fall within city limits. Apart from the Buckstaff (see below), this is the only bathhouse you can actually enter: the interior, restored to its former magnificence, is an atmospheric mixture of the elegant and the obsolete. The heavy use of veined Italian marble, mosaic-tile floors, and stained glass lend it a decadent feel, while the gruesome hydrotherapy and electrotherapy equipment, including an electric shock massager, seem impossibly brutish (daily 9am–5pm; free; ☎501/624-2701; ⓦwww.nps.gov/hosp).

It's still possible to take a "**bath**" – an hour-long process involving brisk rubdowns, hot packs, a thorough steaming, and a needle shower – on Bathhouse Row. The only establishment still open for business is the 1912 **Buckstaff**, 509 Central Ave, where a thermal mineral bath costs $20.25, a twenty-minute massage $23 (March–Nov Mon–Sat 7–11.45am & 1.30–3pm, Sun 8–11.45am; Dec–Feb Mon–Fri 7–11.45am & 1.30–3pm, Sat 7–11.45am; ☎501/623-2308; ⓦwww. buckstaffbaths.com). This is good fun, but Aveda it's not; swathed in cotton sheets, you are marched by no-nonsense guides from bath to shower to massage table in a municipal, rather prosaic, atmosphere. Full bathing facilities are also available at several hotels. Hot Springs' water lacks the sulfuric taste often associated with thermal springs; fill up a bottle at any of the drinking fountains on and near Central Avenue. Most of them pump out warm water – if you prefer it cold, head for the Happy Hollow Spring on Fountain Street.

Behind the Fordyce, two small **springs** have been left open for viewing. The **Grand Promenade** from here is a half-mile brick walkway overlooking downtown. Trails of various lengths and severity lead up the steep slopes of **Hot Springs Mountain**. To reach the summit, take a short drive or any of several different trails, including a testing two-and-a-half-mile hike through dense woods of oak, hickory, and short-leafed pine. The observation decks of the 216ft **Mountain Tower** at the top (daily: summer 9am–9pm; spring and fall 9am–6pm; winter 9am–5pm; $6) offer superb views of the town, the Ouachitas, and surrounding lakes.

Quite apart from its waters, Hot Springs prides itself on its small **galleries**, plenty of which line Central Avenue. Even better, it boasts some wonderfully weird Americana. Disregarding the woeful **National Park Aquarium** at 209 Central Ave – which bears more resemblance to a classroom project than anything else

– those of an eccentric disposition will enjoy the **Josephine Tussaud Wax Museum**, 250 Central Ave (June–Aug Sun–Thurs 9am–8pm, Fri & Sat 9am–9pm; Sept–May Mon–Thurs & Sun 9.30am–5pm, Fri & Sat 9.30am–8pm; $9). "They Seem Alive!" shrills the brochure, referring to their atrocious dummies; you can thank your lucky stars that they aren't. Combo tickets ($19) include admission to a local winery and a 75-minute amphibious "**duck tour**", which circuits downtown and has a quick splash on Lake Hamilton (usual price $14, $8 children; ☎501/321-2911; ⓦwww.rideaduck.com).

Practicalities

Greyhound pulls in to 1001 Central Ave; most places of interest, including some good **accommodation** options, are within easy distance of Central Avenue, the city's main thoroughfare. Though rates can rise during the lengthy high season (Feb–Nov), luxury accommodation is surprisingly inexpensive, and there is a good choice, from spa hotels with their own bathhouses to chain motels and B&Bs. Dominating the town center, the atmospheric 1920s 𝄞 *Arlington Resort/Spa*, 239 Central Ave (☎501/623-7771, ⓦwww.arlingtonhotel.com; ❹; bath and whirlpool $26, massage $34), is by far the nicest place to stay, oozing faded grandeur – Al Capone rented the entire fourth floor when he stayed in town, and President Clinton attended his junior and senior proms in the ballroom. The tasteful rooms are airy and comfortable, if a little small. Nearby, the *Downtowner*, 135 Central Ave (☎501/624-5521, ⓦwww.angelfire.com/ar/downtownerhs; ❸; bath and whirlpool $19, massage $20), is another timewarped old hotel, far less fancy with large but dark motel-type rooms. The nearest place to **camp** is Gulpha Gorge Campground in the national park, two miles northeast on Hwy-70 B, off Hwy-70 E (☎501/624-3383; $10 per night)

Hidden among the cheap family **restaurants** along Central Avenue, *Rolando's* at no. 210 is a cheery Nuevo Latino place serving up delicious, creative food (☎501/318-6054). Nearby, the *Arlington*'s restaurant presents Hot Springs' version of haute cuisine – including a fine Sunday brunch – in elegant environs. *Mollie's*, near downtown in an old house at 538 Grand Ave, specializes in tasty comfort foods like chicken in the pot and matzo ball soup (☎501/623-6582; closed Sun), while at *McClard's Bar–B–Q*, three miles south of downtown at 505 Albert Pike (☎501/624-9586; closed Sun & Mon; no credit cards), the mouthwatering pork ribs, slaw, beans, and hot tamales are all prepared by hand. 𝄞 *McClard's is* not to be missed; even Bill and Hillary stopped by here on their wedding day.

As you might expect, Hot Springs' **nightlife** is marvelously cheesy, ranging from variety shows and jamborees to *The Witness*, an outdoor musical of Christ's life as sung by the Apostle Peter; it's held six miles from downtown at 1960 Millcreek Rd (June–Sept Fri & Sat 8pm; $12; ☎501/623-9781, ⓦwww.witnessproductions.com). Those with more secular tastes might prefer the *Theater of Magic*, 817 Central Ave (summer Tues–Sat 8pm; $14; ☎501/623-6200, ⓦwww.maxwellblade.com), starring "Master of Illusion" Maxwell Blade. On a different note, there's a prestigious **documentary film festival** held each October (ⓦwww.hsdfi.org), and a classical **music festival** in June (ⓦwww.hotmusic.org).

Western Arkansas

West of Hot Springs, US-270 cuts through the **Ouachita Mountains**, unique to the continent in that they run east–west rather than north–south. On its way to Oklahoma, the road passes over uneven crests separated by wide valleys speckled with tiny communities, so isolated that, in the Thirties, hill-dwellers supposedly spoke a form of Elizabethan English. Separating the Ouachitas from the northerly

Ozarks, the **Arkansas River Valley**, a natural east–west path for bison, was used for centuries by Native Americans and white hunters before steamboats arrived in the 1820s.

On the Oklahoma border, **FORT SMITH**, an industrial city of roughly seventy thousand people, has a pronounced Western feel. Until Isaac C. Parker – the "Hanging Judge" – took over in 1875, this was a rowdy pioneer town uncomfortably close to Indian Territory, a sanctuary for robbers and bandits. Parker sent out two hundred marshals to round up the fugitives; in 21 years he sentenced 160 to death and saw 79 go to the gallows.

Near the banks of the Arkansas River, on Rogers Avenue at Third, **Fort Smith National Historic Site** (daily 9am–5pm; $3) features remains of the original fort, Parker's courtroom, two jails, and a set of gallows, while the adjacent **Museum of History**, 320 Rogers Ave (Tues–Sat 10am–5pm and Sun 1–5pm in summer; $5), tells the story of the town and serves old-fashioned ice cream in its 1920s soda fountain.

The Ozark Mountains

Although the highest peak fails to top two thousand feet, the **Ozark Mountains**, which extend beyond northern Arkansas into southern Missouri, are characterized by severe steep ridges and jagged spurs. Hair-raising roads weave their way over the precipitous hills, past rugged lakeshores and pristine rivers. When ambitious speculators poured into Arkansas in the 1830s, those who missed the best land etched out remote hill farms that were no better than what they'd left behind in Kentucky or Tennessee. They remained utterly isolated until the last few decades; the Ozarks have now become the fastest-growing rural section of the US, a major tourist and retirement destination. Much-needed cash has flooded in, bringing with it the cafés and souvenir shops that have converted centers such as **Harrison** into cookie-cutter American towns.

The word "Ozark" is everywhere, used to entice tourists into music shows or gift emporia, which owe more to Nashville and Branson, Missouri, than to these mountains. With all the hype, it's getting increasingly difficult to tell the genuine article from imitations – which is a good reason to visit the **state park** at **Mountain View**, a serious attempt to preserve traditional Ozark skills and music. The region's most popular destination, **Eureka Springs**, just inside the Missouri border, is a pretty mountainside Victorian spa town that has developed an appealingly laid-back and almost alternative scene.

Mountain View and around

Roughly sixty miles north of Little Rock, the state-run **Ozark Folk Center**, two miles north of the town of **MOUNTAIN VIEW** on Hwy-14, is a very good living history museum that attempts to show how life used to be in these remote hills, not reached by paved roads until the Fifties. Homestead skills are displayed in reconstructed log cabins, and folk musicians and storytellers perform throughout the park. Special events, including regular Ozark and roots music **concerts**, are held most evenings (craft displays mid-April to end Sept Wed–Sat 10am–5pm, Oct Tues–Sun 10am–5pm, $9; concerts mid-April to end Sept Wed–Sat 7.30pm, Oct Tues–Sat 7.30pm, $9; combination ticket $15.50; ℗ 870/269-3851, ⓦ www. ozarkfolkcenter.com).

Mountain View's **visitor center**, 107 N Peabody Ave (April–Nov Mon–Fri 9am–5pm, Sat 10am–4pm, Sun 12.30–3pm; Dec–March Mon–Fri 8.30am–

4.30pm; ⓣ870/269-8068, ⓦww.ozarkgetaways.com), can help with **accommodation**; there is plenty of choice, particularly if you like the personal service of a B&B or the rustic charm of a mountain cabin. The *Dry Creek Lodge* (ⓣ1-800/264-3655; ❸) is a good-value option on the grounds of the Folk Center, while the friendly *Inn at Mountain View*, 307 W Washington St (ⓣ870/269-4200, ⓦwww.innatmountainview.com; ❹), is a pretty B&B owned by folk musicians; they serve a full country breakfast. Good **restaurants** include the Folk Center's *Iron Skillet* (ⓣ870/269-3851) and *Tommy's Famous…*, an award-winning pizzeria and rib joint at 205 Carpenter St, four blocks west of the town square (ⓣ870/269-3278). For entertainment, even in winter, it's hard to beat the friendly **jam sessions** in the square, and naturally there are also a number of good music **festivals**. Reserve a room well in advance for the venerable **Arkansas Folk Festival** (music, crafts, food stalls, parades), held in April, and the **Bean Festival** (beans, cornbread, music, outhouse races), held on the last Saturday in October.

In the **Ozark National Forest**, fifteen miles northwest of Mountain View off Hwy-14, you can take a variety of tours (times and rates vary; ⓦwww.fs.fed.us/oonf/ozark/recreation/caverns.html) of the **Blanchard Springs Caverns**, an eerily beautiful underground cave system that also boasts a crystal-clear swimming hole surrounded by towering rock bluffs.

The **Buffalo River** – a prime destination for white-water canoeing – flows across the state north of Mountain View. In the sweet little settlement of Gilbert, off Hwy-65 at the end of Hwy-333 E, **Buffalo Camping and Canoeing** (ⓣ870/439-2888, ⓦgilbertstore.com) rents canoes for trips on the middle section of the river, which is at its most spectacular around **Pruitt Landing**. They also offer a few log **cabins**, most of which sleep at least four people (ⓦwww.buffalorivercabin.com; ❹–❻).

Eureka Springs

Picturesque **EUREKA SPRINGS**, set on steep mountain slopes in Arkansas's northwestern corner, began life a century ago as a health center. As that role diminished, its striking location turned it into a regular tourist destination, filled with Victorian buildings and streets linked by flights of stone stairs. Today it has a relaxed, progressive feel, with kitsch outdoor movie events (ⓦwww.lucky13cinema.org), special "Diversity Weekends" (ⓦwww.eurekapride.com), and plenty of places offering alternative therapies. One delightful way to enjoy the surrounding wooded valleys is to take a ride on the **Eureka Springs and North Arkansas Railway**, whose rolling stock includes a magnificent "cabbage-head" wood-burning locomotive; trips depart from the depot at 299 N Main St (mid-April to Oct Mon–Sat 10.30am, noon, 2pm & 4pm; $10; ⓦwww.esnarailway.com).

Three miles east of town on US-62 E, a seven-story **Christ of the Ozarks** – a surreal statue of Jesus with a 60ft arm span – sets the tone for a jawdropping religious complex known as the **Great Passion Play** (end April to end Oct). It's the brainchild of one Elna M. Smith, who, worried that the holy sites of the Middle East would be destroyed by war, decided to build replicas in the Ozarks. Thus the two-and-a-half hour **New Holy Land Tour** gets you a mini-bus ride past scaled-down versions of the Sea of Galilee, the River Jordan, and Golgotha, complete with living, breathing Biblical characters (every 15min Mon, Tues & Thurs–Sat 10am–3.30pm; $15; reservations required). The complex also includes a **Bible Museum** and a **Sacred Arts Center** (both open the same days the play is performed, 10am–8pm; admission included in price of tour), and the **Museum of Earth History** (9am–8pm; $8.50), which puts a very particular spin on the theory of evolution. The **Passion Play** itself re-enacts Christ's last days on earth with a cast of 250, including live animals, in a 4100-seat amphitheater (same months; nightly except Sun and Wed 8.30pm, after Aug 7.30pm; $23.25, includes Bible Museum and Sacred Arts Center; ℡1-866-566-3565, ⓦwww.greatpassionplay. com).

Practicalities

In town, US-62 becomes Van Buren, where you'll find the **visitor center** at 137 W Van Buren (daily 9am–5pm; ℡479/253-8737, ⓦwww.eurekasprings.com).

Log cabins and B&Bs abound, many with staggering views, and there is plenty of inexpensive **lodging** along Hwy-62 E. There are two particularly delightful options downtown: *Trade Winds*, next to the visitor center at 141 W Van Buren, is a funky, gay-friendly place with wittily decorated theme rooms and a pool (℡479/253-9774; ⓦwww.eurekatradewinds.com; ❸); ten minutes' walk away, at 27 Glenn (Hwy-62 W), the superb ✹*Sherwood Court* offers individually decorated cottages, some with Jacuzzis, surrounding flower-filled courtyards (℡479/253-8920 or 1-800-268-6052; ⓦwww.sherwoodcourt.com; ❷–❺ including continental breakfast).

For **food**, the artsy *Mud Street Café*, 22 S Main St, serves good espresso, light lunches and desserts, plus dinner on Friday and Saturday (℡479/253-6732; closed Wed). The friendly local institution *Chelsea's Corner*, 10 Mountain St, off Spring St (℡479/253-6723), features **live music** most evenings. Eureka Springs also holds the very fine **Ozark folk festival** in October (℡501/253-7788), and an acclaimed **blues festival** in June (ⓦwww.eurekaspringsbluesfestival.com).

Florida

AL - ALABAMA	IN - INDIANA	MN - MINNESOTA	RI - RHODE ISLAND
AR - ARKANSAS	LA - LOUISIANA	MS - MISSISSIPPI	SC - SOUTH CAROLINA
CT - CONNECTICUT	MA - MASSACHUSETTS	NC - NORTH CAROLINA	VA - VIRGINIA
DE - DELAWARE	MD - MARYLAND	NH - NEW HAMPSHIRE	VT - VERMONT
FL - FLORIDA	ME - MAINE	NJ - NEW JERSEY	WI - WISCONSIN
IL - ILLINOIS	MI - MICHIGAN	PA - PENNSYLVANIA	WV - WEST VIRGINIA

CHAPTER 7

Highlights

✱ **Kennedy Space Center, Space Coast** Some of the world's most high-tech machinery just a stone's throw from a wildlife refuge. See p.636

✱ **Ocean Drive, Miami** South Beach's finest Art Deco showpiece, buzzing with cosmopolitan cafés, flashy vintage cars, and wannabe models. See p.616

✱ **Sarasota** Culture-vultures will enjoy the museums and bookstores of this unassuming town on Florida's west coast. See p.661

✱ **Key West** This funky, anything-goes place feels like it's at the end of the world. See p.628

✱ **St Augustine** Sixteenth-century Spanish town packed with historic interest and a handful of lovely beaches. See p.640

✱ **Walt Disney World, Orlando** Pure entertainment, planned down to the last detail. Simply irresistible. See p.648

✱ **Everglades National Park** Bike or hike through the vast sawgrass plains of the legendary Everglades, or canoe through alligator-filled mangrove swamps. See p.664

△ Key West, FL

Florida

rochure images of tanning tourists and Mickey Mouse give an inaccurate and incomplete picture of **FLORIDA**. Although the aptly nicknamed "Sunshine State" is indeed devoted to the tourist trade, it's also among the least-understood parts of the US. Away from its overexposed resorts lie forests and rivers, deserted strands filled with wildlife, vibrant cities, and primeval swamps. Contrary to the popular retirement-community image, new Floridians tend to be a younger, more energetic breed, while Spanish-speaking enclaves provide close ties to Latin America and the Caribbean.

By far, the essential stop is cosmopolitan, half-Latin **Miami**. A simple journey south from here brings you to the **Florida Keys**, a hundred-mile string of islands known for sports fishing, coral-reef diving, and the sultry town of **Key West**, legendary for its sunsets and liberal attitude. Back on the mainland, west from Miami stretch the easily accessible **Everglades**, a swampy sawgrass plain filled with camera-friendly (but otherwise unfriendly) alligators.

Much of Florida's **east coast** is disappointingly urbanized, albeit with miles of unbroken beaches rolling alongside. The residential stranglehold is loosened further north, where **Kennedy Space Center** launches NASA shuttles. Farther along, historical **St Augustine** stands as the longest continuously occupied European settlement in the US.

In **central Florida** the terrain turns green, though it's no rural idyll, thanks in most part to **Orlando** and **Walt Disney World**, which sprawls out across the countryside. From here it's just a skip west to the towns and beaches of the **Gulf Coast**, and somewhat further north to the forests of the **Panhandle**, Florida's link with the Deep South.

Weather-wise, warm sunshine and blue skies are almost always the norm. The state does, however, split into two **climatic zones**: subtropical in the south and warm temperate in the north. Orlando and points south have a mild season from October to April, with warm temperatures and low humidity. Down here, this is the **peak tourist season**, when prices are at their highest. Conversely, the southern summer (May to Sept) brings high humidity and afternoon storms; the rewards for braving the mugginess are lower prices and fewer tourists.

North of Orlando, winter is the off-peak period, even though daytime temperatures are generally comfortably warm (although snow has been known to fall on the Panhandle). During the northern Florida summer, the crowds arrive, and the days and nights are hot and sticky. Keep in mind that June to November is **hurricane season**, and there is a strong possibility of big storms.

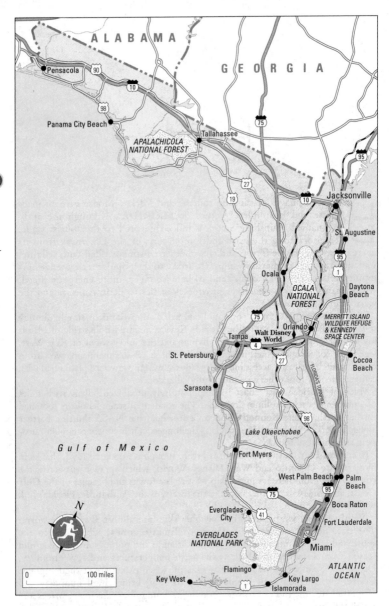

Some history

The **first European sighting** of Florida, just six years after Christopher Columbus reached the New World, is believed to have been made by John and Sebastian Cabot in 1498, when they spotted what is now Cape Florida, on Key Biscayne in Miami. Nothing much came of the sighting, though, as the Cabots did not take formal possession of the land. At the time, the area's 100,000 inhabitants formed several distinct **tribes**: the Timucua across northern Florida, the Calusa around the southwest and Lake Okeechobee, the Apalachee in the Panhandle, and the Tequesta along the southeast coast.

In 1513, a Spaniard, **Juan Ponce de León**, sighted land during *Pascua Florida*, Spain's Easter celebration; he named what he saw *La Florida*, or "Land of Flowers." Eight years later he returned with a mandate from the Spanish king to conquer and colonize the territory; this was the first of several Spanish incursions prompted by rumors of gold hidden in the north of the region. When it became clear that Florida did not harbor stunning riches, interest waned – but the arrival of French Huguenots in 1562 forced the Spanish into a more determined effort at settlement.

Three years later, the conquistador Pedro Menéndez de Avilés, sent to the continent by empire-minded King Philip II of Spain, founded **St Augustine** – site of the longest continuous European habitation in North America. In 1586, St Augustine was razed by a British naval bombardment led by Francis Drake. The ensuing bloody confrontation for control of North America was eventually settled when the British captured the crucial Spanish possession of Havana, Cuba; Spain willingly parted with Florida to get it back. By this time, indigenous Floridians had been largely wiped out by disease. The area's Native American population now largely comprised disparate tribes that had arrived from the west, collectively known as the **Seminoles**, who were generally left undisturbed in the inland areas.

Following American independence, the US began to think in terms of controlling Florida. As a result, in 1814, the US general (and future president) Andrew Jackson – on the pretext of subduing the Seminole, but with the actual intention of taking the region – marched south from Tennessee, killing hundreds of Indians and triggering the **First Seminole War**. Following the war, in 1819, Spain **ceded Florida** to the US, in return for American assumption of $5 million of Spanish debt. Not long after, Jackson was sworn in as Florida's first American governor, and Tallahassee was selected as the new administrative center.

Eleven years later, the **Act of Indian Removal** decreed that all Native Americans in the eastern US should be transferred to reservations in the Midwest. Most Seminole were determined to stay and, as a result, the **Second Seminole War** broke out, with the Indians steadily driven south, away from the fertile lands of central Florida and into the Everglades, where they eventually agreed to remain. Florida became the **27th state** on March 3, 1845, coinciding with the prosperity brought by the railroads. As a member of the Confederacy during the **Civil War**, Florida's primary contribution was the provision of food – a foretaste of its postwar economic role after being re-admitted to the Union.

At the beginning of the twentieth century, the country's newspapers extolled the curative virtues of Florida's climate, and northern speculators began to invest in the state. These early efforts to promote Florida as a **tourist destination** brought in the wintering rich: the likes of Henry Flagler and Henry Plant extended their railroads and opened luxury resorts on the east and west coasts, respectively. After World War I, it seemed that everyone in America wanted a piece of Florida, and chartered trains brought in thousands of eager buyers. But most deals were on paper only, and in 1926 the banks began to default. The **Wall Street Crash** then made paupers of the millionaires whose investments had helped shape the state.

What saved Florida was **World War II**. During the war, thousands of troops arrived to guard the coastline, providing them with a taste of Florida that would entice many to return. Furthermore, in the mid-Sixties, the state government bent over backwards to help the Disney Corporation turn a sizable slice of central Florida into **Walt Disney World**, the biggest theme park ever. Its enormous commercial success helped solidify Florida's place in the international tourist market: directly or indirectly, tourism now makes up 20 percent of the total state economy.

Behind the optimistic facade, however, lie many **problems**. There's a broadening gap between the relative liberalism of the big cities and the arch-conservatism of the northern Bible Belt: while Miami promotes its multicultural make-up, the Ku Klux Klan holds picnics in the Panhandle. Gun laws remain notoriously lax, and the multimillion-dollar **drug trade** shows few signs of abating – at least a quarter of the cocaine entering the US is said to arrive via Florida. **Racial issues** continue, too, with tension on several fronts: between Anglo-Americans and nouveau riche Cubans, between blacks and whites, blacks and Hispanics, and between police and the inner-city poor. Increased protection of the state's **natural resources** has been a more positive feature of the last decade and impressive amounts of land are under state control – overall, wildlife is less threatened now than at any time since white settlers first arrived.

Getting around Florida

Surprisingly compact, Florida is **fairly easy to navigate** if you have a car: crossing between the east and west coasts takes just a couple of hours, and determined drivers can make one of the longest trips – between the western extremity of the Panhandle and Miami – in a full day's drive. Getting around by **public transportation**, on the other hand, requires adroit advance planning. Major towns and cities are linked by Greyhound **buses** – and, in some cases, infrequent Amtrak **trains** – but many rural areas and some of the most enjoyable sections of the coasts are not covered. Although inadvisable in the cities, **cycling** is a great way to see large parts of Florida – miles of cycle paths follow the coasts, and long-distance bike trails cross the state's interior.

Miami

Far and away the most exciting city in Florida, **MIAMI** is an often intoxicatingly beautiful place, with palm trees swaying in the breeze and South Beach's famous Art Deco buildings stunning in the warm sunlight. Away from the beaches and the tourists, the gleaming skyscrapers of downtown herald Miami's proud status as the headquarters of many US corporations' Latin American operations. Even so, it's the people, not the climate, the landscape, or the cash, that makes Miami so noteworthy. Two-thirds of the two-million-plus population is Hispanic, the majority of which are **Cuban**. Spanish is the predominant language almost everywhere – in many places it's the only language you'll hear – and news from Havana, Caracas, or Bogotá frequently gets more attention than the latest word from Washington.

Just a hundred years ago Miami was a swampy outpost of mosquito-tormented settlers. The arrival of Henry Flagler's railroad in 1896 gave the city its first fixed land-link with the rest of the continent, and cleared the way for the Twenties property boom. In the Fifties, after World War II, Miami Beach became a celebrity-filled resort area, just as thousands of Cubans fleeing the regime of Fidel Castro began arriving here as well. The Sixties and Seventies brought decline, and

Miami's dangerous reputation in the Eighties was well deserved – in 1980 the city had the highest murder rate in America.

Since then, with the strengthening of Latin American economic links and the gentrification of South Beach – which helped make tourism the lifeblood of the local economy again in the early Nineties – Miami is enjoying a surge of affluence and optimism.

Arrival and information

Miami International Airport (☎305/876-7000, ⓦwww.miami-airport.com) is six miles west of the city. A cab from the airport costs $22–43, depending on your destination. You can opt for one of the 24-hour SuperShuttle minivans, which will deliver you to any address in Miami for $14–19 per person (☎305/871-2000, ⓦwww.supershuttle.com). Via **public transportation**, take the #7 Metrobus to downtown, a trip of 30 minutes or so ($1.50; every 40mins), or the #J Metrobus ($1.50 plus a 25¢ surcharge to South Beach; every 20–40mins) to Miami Beach farther on. Late at night, the Airport Owl shuttle runs in a loop through South Beach, downtown and back to the airport ($1.50; once hourly). Of several **Greyhound** stations in the city, the busiest is near the airport, at 4111 NW 27th Street (☎305/871-1810). Most buses, however, also stop at the downtown stop, at 1012 NW 1st Avenue. The **Amtrak** station, at 8303 NW 37th Ave, is seven miles northwest of the city center. There is an adjacent Metrorail stop (see below) that provides access to downtown Miami and beyond; bus #L stops here on its way to Central Miami Beach.

There's no official **tourist information** booth downtown: the two best-equipped sources are both in South Beach. These are the **Miami Beach Chamber of Commerce**, 1920 Meridian Ave (Mon–Fri 9am–6pm, Sat & Sun 10am–4pm; ☎305/672-1270, ⓦwww.miamibeachchamber.com), which is packed with leaflets and staffed by helpful locals, and the **Art Deco Welcome Center**, 1001 Ocean Drive (daily 10am–7pm; ☎305/672-2014, ⓦwww.mdpl.org), which has details on walking tours and events.

City transportation and tours

Downtown and South Beach, the two main tourist areas, are eminently walkable – and, indeed, are best enjoyed **on foot**. However, if you want to see more of the city, **driving** is the most practical option. An integrated **public transportation network** run by Metro-Dade Transit (☎305/770-3131, ⓦwww.miamidade.gov/transit) covers Miami, making the city easy – if time-consuming – to get around, at least by day (nighttime services are more skeletal). **Metrorail** trains ($1.50) run along a single line between the northern suburbs and South Miami; useful stops are Government Center (for downtown), Vizcaya, Coconut Grove, and Douglas Road or University (for Coral Gables). Downtown Miami is also ringed by the **Metromover** (free), a monorail that doesn't cover much ground but gives a great bird's-eye view. **Metrobuses** ($1.50, with a 25¢ surcharge for transfers) cover the entire city, but services dwindle at night.

Taxis are abundant in Miami; either hail one on the street or call Central Cab (☎305/532-5555) or Metro Taxi (☎305/888-8888). If you want to rent a **bike**, you can do so from one of the many outlets around town, such as the Miami Beach Cycle Center, 601 5th St, South Beach ($5/hr or $20/day; ☎305/674-0150).

For an informed stroll, take one of **Dr Paul George's Walking Tours** from the Historical Museum of South Florida (call for schedule; no tours July & Aug; $15 and up; ℡305/375-1621, ⓦwww.hmsf.org). Or, try the various excellent **Art Deco walking tours** of South Beach (Wed & Fri–Sun 10.30am, Thurs 6.30pm; $20), which begin at the Art Deco Welcome Center on Ocean Drive (see p.613). The latter organization also offers a self-guided audio walking tour of the district (available daily 10am–4pm; 90mins; $15).

Accommodation

Accommodation is rarely a problem in Miami – though you should expect **rates** to go up on weekends, holidays, and in the main winter tourist season (Dec–April), when you'll pay $75–110 (or upwards of $250 in the swankier places) per night. Though it can be great fun to stay in one of the numerous Art Deco **South Beach** hotels, note that they were built in a different era, and, as such, rooms can be tiny. Elsewhere, **Coral Gables** and **Coconut Grove**, though somewhat out-of-the-way, both have an appealing option or two; **downtown** is filled with expensive chain hotels.

Albion Hotel 1650 James Ave, South Beach ℡1-877/RUBELLS, ⓦwww.rubellhotels.com. A sensitive conversion of a classic Nautical Deco building, this is one of the best-value hotels on the beach. Rooms are hip but simple; the raised pool – with portholes cut into its sides – is also a big draw. ❻

🏃 **Catalina** 1732 Collins Ave ℡305/674-1160. Simple white rooms are filled with luxe touches like flatscreen TVs and marble bathrooms, plus there's an outdoor pool, a sundeck, and a bamboo-filled zen courtyard for reading or meditating. ❻

Clay Hotel and Hosteling International 1438 Washington Ave, South Beach ℡1-800/379-2529, ⓦwww.clayhotel.com. This beautiful converted monastery serves as the city's best budget hotel and youth hostel. Dorm beds $23–27; private rooms from ❸.

Gables Inn 730 S Dixie Hwy, Coral Gables ℡305/661-7999, ⓦwww.thegablesinn.net. Basic but clean Mediterranean Revival-style motel on a busy road (so can be noisy). ❹

Hampton Inn 2800 SW 28th Terrace, Coconut Grove ℡305/448-2800, ⓦwww.hamptoninns-florida.com. Bright and cheery accommodation, geared to the business traveler – though the free local calls, free breakfast, and on-site coin laundry are attractive for budget travelers, too. ❺

International Travelers Hostel 236 9th St, South Beach ℡305/534-0268, ⓦwww.sobehostel.com. Friendly, centrally located hostel with beds in four-person dorms ($14–16), as well as private singles and doubles ❸.

Miami River Inn 118 SW South River Drive, Little Havana ℡305/325-0045, ⓦwww.miamiriverinn.com. B&B with forty comfortable rooms decorated with antiques and housed in four cottages clustered around a tree-shaded pool. Not in the best neighborhood, so stay here only if you have access to a car. ❹

Park Central 640 Ocean Drive, South Beach ℡305/538-1611, ⓦwww.theparkcentral.com. Recently renovated colonial-safari-style rooms (soundproofed against the noise from nearby clubs) with reasonable rates for South Beach. ❻

Pelican 826 Ocean Drive, South Beach ℡1-800/7-PELICAN, ⓦwww.pelicanhotel.com. Each room at this campy, quirky hotel is individually themed and named – try the lush red bordello known as the "Best Little Whorehouse." ❻

The Shore Club 1901 Collins Ave, South Beach ℡305/695-3100, ⓦwww.shoreclub.com. Ultra-trendy hotel on the beach, with minimalist, brightly colored rooms and several swanky bar-restaurants, like the poolside *Sky Bar* (see review p.624). ❾

🏃 **The Standard Miami** 40 Island Ave, South Beach ℡305/673-1717, ⓦwww.standardhotel.com. The Miami outpost of hip hotelier Andre Balazs's Standard chain has finally opened, transforming a forlorn hotel on Belle Isle into spa accommodation complete with Turkish baths and a yoga center. ❺

🏃 **Townhouse** 150 20th St, South Beach ℡1-877/534-3800, ⓦwww.townhousehotel.com. Small but stylish white rooms, great staff, free breakfast, and squishy rooftop waterbeds – all at a fraction of most boutique hotel prices. ❺

The City

Each of Miami's **districts** has a character very much its own. Separated from the mainland by Biscayne Bay, the most popular is **Miami Beach**, especially the world-famous **South Beach** portion. This is where many of the city's famed Art Deco buildings can be found, all pastels, neon, and wavy lines. Though touted as a chic gathering-place for globe-trotting fashionistas, South Beach is not as exclusive as you might expect, especially on weekend afternoons, when families and out-of-towners join in the fun along Ocean Drive right with the washboard stomachs and bulging pecs.

Back on the mainland, **downtown** has a few good museums, but is most appealing for its pervasive Latin American vibe. To the north, the earthy, Caribbean enclave known as **Little Haiti** is gradually starting to attract more visitors. Meanwhile, southwest of downtown, there's nowhere better for a Cuban lunch than **Little Havana**. Immediately south, the spacious boulevards and ornate public buildings of **Coral Gables** are as impressive now as they were in the 1920s, when the district set new standards in town planning. Independently minded, but equally wealthy, **Coconut Grove** is also worth a look, thanks to its walkable center and a couple of Miami's most popular attractions. Lastly, sun-worshippers should make time for **Key Biscayne**, a smart, secluded island community with some beautiful beaches, an easy five miles off the mainland by causeway.

Miami Beach

A long slender arm of land between Biscayne Bay and the Atlantic Ocean, **MIAMI BEACH**, three miles off the mainland, has been a headline-grabbing resort town for almost a hundred years, from its first heyday in the Art Deco-dominated 1920s, through a slick-as-Vegas era in the 1950s, to the hip hedonism of today. Until the 1910s – when its Quaker owner, John Collins, formed an unlikely partnership with a flashy entrepreneur, Carl Fisher – it was nothing more than an ailing fruit farm. With Fisher's money, Biscayne Bay was dredged, and the muck raised from its murky bed was used as landfill to transform this wildly vegetated barrier island into a carefully sculptured landscape of palm trees, hotels, and tennis courts. After a hurricane in 1926 devastated Miami (and especially the beach), damaged buildings were replaced by grander structures in the new Art Deco style, and Miami Beach as we know it appeared. Since then, its history has been checkered: by the 1980s, crack dens and retirement homes were equally commonplace in South Beach, but the 1990s saw a renaissance spearheaded by a few savvy hoteliers and Miami's gay community. It's still a popular resort with the tanned and toned, though the gay pioneers have now largely decamped to quieter quarters up the coast in Fort Lauderdale.

South Beach

Occupying the southernmost three miles of Miami Beach is gorgeous **SOUTH BEACH**, with its hundreds of dazzling pastel-colored 1920s and 1930s Art Deco buildings. By day, the sun blares down on sizzling bodies on the sand – though it's worth braving an early morning wake-up call to catch the dawn glow, which bathes the Deco hotels in pure, crystalline white light. By night, the ten blocks of Ocean Drive become one of the liveliest stretches in Miami, as terrace cafés spill across the specially widened sidewalk and crowds of tourists and locals saunter by the beach.

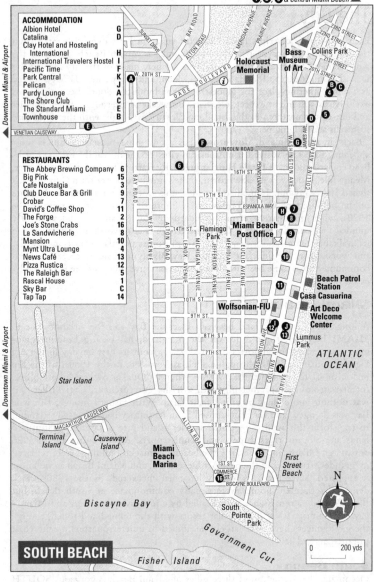

ACCOMMODATION

Albion Hotel	G
Catalina	D
Clay Hotel and Hosteling International	H
International Travelers Hostel	I
Pacific Time	F
Park Central	K
Pelican	J
Purdy Lounge	A
The Shore Club	C
The Standard Miami	E
Townhouse	B

RESTAURANTS

The Abbey Brewing Company	6
Big Pink	15
Cafe Nostalgia	3
Club Deuce Bar & Grill	9
Crobar	7
David's Coffee Shop	11
The Forge	2
Joe's Stone Crabs	16
La Sandwicherie	8
Mansion	10
Mynt Ultra Lounge	4
News Café	13
Pizza Rustica	12
The Raleigh Bar	5
Rascal House	1
Sky Bar	C
Tap Tap	14

SOUTH BEACH

Loosely bordered north/south by 5th and 20th streets, and west/east by Lenox Avenue and the ocean, the area referred to as the **Deco District** actually incorporates a variety of styles: take one of the excellent walking tours offered at the **Art Deco Welcome Center** (see p.613) to learn the difference between Streamline, Moderne, and Florida Deco, not to mention Mediterranean Revival.

The most famous buildings lie along **Ocean Drive**, where revamped hotels make

616

much of their design heritage. Amid the hotels, **Casa Casuarina**, at the corner of 10th Street, was the former home of the murdered fashion designer Gianni Versace. It's now an invitation-only members club.

If the tourist hordes get to be too much, head a block west to **Collins Avenue**, lined with more Deco hotels and fashion chains, or on to **Washington Avenue**, which tends more toward funky thrift stores and cool coffee bars. At 1001 Washington Ave, the Mediterranean-Revival **Wolfsonian–FIU** (Mon, Tues, Sat & Sun noon–6pm, Thurs & Fri noon–9pm; $7; free after 6pm on Fri; ☎305/531-1001, Ⓦwww.wolfsonian.fiu.edu) houses an eclectic collection of decorative arts from the late nineteenth century to 1945. The displays of old books, photos, paintings, posters, and all manner of domestic objects are impressive, if a bit muddled.

Throughout Miami Beach's history, one group that has kept a constant presence is its sizable Jewish population, which includes many Holocaust survivors and their families. This contingent is the reason for the moving **Holocaust Memorial**, near the north tip of South Beach, at 1933–1945 Meridian Ave (daily 9am–9pm; $2 donation for brochure; ☎305/538-1663, Ⓦwww.holocaustmmb.org). A complex, uncompromising reminder to their experience, the monument depicts a defiant hand punching into the sky. Life-sized figures of wailing people attempt to climb up the arm, which is tattooed near the wrist with an Auschwitz number.

A few blocks northeast is the **Bass Museum of Art**, 2121 Park Ave (Tues–Sat 10am–5pm, Sun 11–5pm; $8; ☎305/673-7530, Ⓦwww.bassmuseum.org). The only fine art museum on the beach, the Bass is housed in a 1930s building designed by Russell Pancoast, the architect son-in-law of beach pioneer John Collins. Recently, the museum unveiled a showy expansion by Japanese architect Arata Isozaki – the white box he grafted onto the original building along Park Avenue has tripled the exhibition space. The museum's permanent collection consists of fine, if largely unremarkable, European paintings, although its temporary exhibitions are often lively and worth visiting.

△ The Colony Hotel on Ocean Drive

Miami beaches

If you took away the Art Deco, the beautiful people, and the glittering nightlife, you'd still be left with the simple truth that Miami Beach has a fabulous **choice of beaches**. With twelve miles of calm waters, clean sands, swaying palms, and candy-colored lifeguard towers, you can't go wrong picking a spot. The young and the beautiful soak up the rays between 5th and 21st streets, a convenient hop from the juice bars and cafés on Ocean Drive. From 6th to 14th streets, **Lummus Park** – much of whose sand was shipped in from the Bahamas – is the heart of the South Beach scene; there's an unofficial gay section roughly around 12th Street. North of 21st, things are more family-oriented, with a **boardwalk** running between the shore and the hotels up to 46th. To the south, **First Street Beach** and **South Pointe** are favored by Cuban families, and are especially convivial at weekends. For good **swimming**, head up to 85th, a quiet stretch that's usually patrolled by lifeguards.

Downtown Miami

Back on the mainland, **DOWNTOWN MIAMI** divides into distinct halves: big business and big buildings line Brickell Avenue south of the Miami River, while the commercial bazaar around Flagler Street to the north hums with jewelers, fabric stores, and cheap electronics outlets. Latin culture is comfortably dominant here – from office workers grabbing a midmorning *cafecito*, or Cuban coffee, to the bilingual signage in almost every store. If at first it seems a little too chaotic, persevere: downtown is compact, holds two of Miami's best museums, and provides the clearest sense of Cuba's continuing influence on the city.

At the western end of **Flagler Street**, downtown's loudest, brightest, busiest strip, is the **Metro-Dade Cultural Center**, an ambitious attempt by architect Philip Johnson to create a postmodern Mediterranean-style piazza. Art shows, historical collections, and a library frame the courtyard, but Johnson overlooked the power of the south Florida sun: rather than pausing to rest and chat, most people scamper across the open space toward the nearest shade. The center's **Historical Museum of Southern Florida** (Mon–Sat 10am–5pm, Sun noon–5pm, 3rd Thurs of each month 10am–9pm; $5; ☎305/375-1492, ⓦwww.hmsf.org) provides a comprehensive look at the region's history, with an especially strong section on refugees, including two shockingly small genuine refugee rafts.

On the east side of the plaza, the **Miami Art Museum** (Tues–Fri 10am–5pm, Sat & Sun 12–5pm, 3rd Thurs of each month 10am–9pm; $5, Sun free; ☎305/375-3000, ⓦwww.miamiartmuseum.org) houses a well laid out collection of post-1940 art, and showcases outstanding international traveling exhibits. The museum will eventually relocate to a waterfront space close to I-395 to be called Museum Park; no timeline for this move has yet been decided (check the website for the latest news).

The eastern edge of downtown is bounded by Biscayne Boulevard, near which is the **Bayside Marketplace**, a large pink shopping mall with pleasant waterfront views from its terrace. Across the boulevard, the striking **Freedom Tower** built in 1925 and modeled on a Spanish belltower, earned its name by housing the Cuban Refugee Center in the 1960s. It is now part of the nearby Miami-Dade Community College.

South from the marketplace, in Bayfront Park, the **Torch of Friendship** was meant to symbolize the good relations between the US and its southern neighbors. When it was built, there was a pointed space left for the Cuban national emblem among the alphabetically sorted crests of each country. However, the memorial is so neglected now that several missing emblems are noticeable, making Cuba no longer appear the pariah.

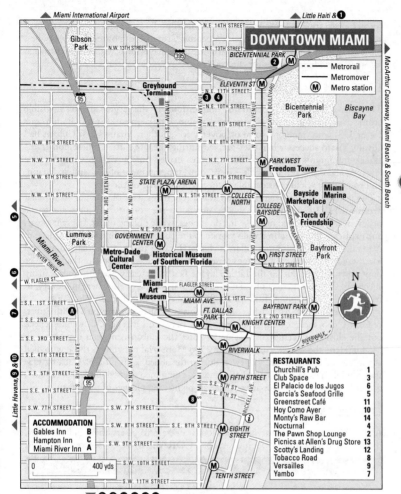

▲ Miami International Airport

▲ Little Haiti & ❶

DOWNTOWN MIAMI

N.E. 14TH STREET

Gibson Park

N.W. 13TH STREET

N.E. 13TH STREET

BICENTENNIAL PARK

❷ Ⓜ

--- · Metrorail

— Metromover

Ⓜ Metro station

ELEVENTH ST Ⓜ

Greyhound Terminal

❸ ❹

N.E. 11TH STREET

N.E. 10TH STREET

N.E. 9TH STREET

Bicentennial Park

Biscayne Bay

N.W. 8TH STREET

N.E. 8TH STREET

N.W. 7TH STREET

N.E. 7TH STREET

N.W. 6TH STREET

N.E. 6TH STREET

Ⓜ PARK WEST
Freedom Tower

N.W. 5TH STREET

STATE PLAZA / ARENA

N.E. 5TH STREET

Ⓜ

COLLEGE NORTH

Ⓜ

COLLEGE/ BAYSIDE

Bayside Marketplace

Miami Marina

Torch of Friendship

N.E. 3RD STREET

Lummus Park

GOVERNMENT CENTER Ⓜ

Bayfront Park

Metro-Dade Cultural Center

Historical Museum of Southern Florida

N.E. 1ST STREET Ⓜ FIRST STREET

W. FLAGLER ST

Miami Art Museum

FLAGLER STREET

MIAMI AVE.

Ⓜ

S.E. 1ST STREET

N

BAYFRONT PARK Ⓜ

S.E. 2ND STREET

FT. DALLAS PARK

KNIGHT CENTER Ⓜ

S.E. 3RD STREET

Ⓜ

S.E. 4TH STREET

RIVERWALK

RIVERWALK

S.E. 5TH STREET

S.E. 6TH STREET

Ⓜ FIFTH STREET

RESTAURANTS

Churchill's Pub	1
Club Space	3
El Palacio de los Jugos	6
Garcia's Seafood Grille	5
Greenstreet Café	11
Hoy Como Ayer	10
Monty's Raw Bar	14
Nocturnal	4
The Pawn Shop Lounge	2
Picnics at Allen's Drug Store	13
Scotty's Landing	12
Tobacco Road	8
Versailles	9
Yambo	7

❽

S.W. 7TH STREET

ⓘ

ACCOMMODATION

Gables Inn	B
Hampton Inn	C
Miami River Inn	A

S.W. 8TH STREET

Ⓜ EIGHTH STREET

S.W. 9TH STREET

0   400 yds

S.W. 10TH STREET

Ⓜ TENTH STREET

S.W. 11TH STREET

▼ ❸,❻,⓫,⓬,⓭,⓮, Coral Gables & Coconut Grove

Fifteen minutes' walk south from Flagler Street, the **Miami River** carves downtown in half. The river's southern bank is dominated by Brickell (rhymes with "pickle") Avenue. Named for William Brickell, one of the original Miami landowners, this was *the* address in 1910s Miami. While the early grand homes have largely disappeared, money is still the avenue's most obvious asset: its half-mile parade of **bank buildings** is the largest grouping of international banks in the US. The rise of the banks was matched by new condominiums of breathtaking proportions (and expense) but little architectural merit.

Little Haiti

Continuing on north from downtown, along NE 2nd Avenue, you'll cruise into **LITTLE HAITI**, an immigrant area filled with Caribbean colors, music, and smells, its trilingual shop signs making sales pitches in English, French, and Creole. In its former incarnation as Lemon City, this neighborhood was the oldest inhabited European settlement in the area, alongside Coconut Grove (see opposite). Today, the best place to soak up the atmosphere is 54th Street, which is lined with stores known as *botanicas*, providing supplies for the voodoo-like religion **Santeria**.

Little Havana

The impact on Miami by **Cubans**, unquestionably the largest and most visible ethnic group in the city, has been incalculable. Unlike most Hispanic immigrants to the US, who trade one form of poverty for another, Miami's first Cubans had already tasted success when they arrived during the late Fifties. These non-traditional immigrants – many of the first wave driven out by Castro were doctors, lawyers, and other professionals – were soon enjoying more of the same in Miami, and some now wield considerable clout in the running of the city.

The initial home of Miami Cubans was a few miles west of downtown in what became **LITTLE HAVANA**, whose streets, if the tourist brochures are to be believed, are filled by old men playing dominoes, while puffing on fat, fragrant cigars, and exotic restaurants whose walls vibrate to the pulsating rhythms of the homeland. Naturally, the reality is quite different. Little Havana's parks, memorials, shops, and food stands all reflect the Cuban experience, but the streets are quieter than those of downtown (except during the Little Havana Festival in early March). Today, many successful Cuban-Americans have moved to Coral Gables, or elsewhere in the city, to be replaced by immigrants from parts of Central America, especially Nicaragua.

Make a beeline here for lunch at one of the many small restaurants on SW 8th Street, or Calle Ocho, the neighborhood's main drag. Between 12th and 13th avenues, check out the cluster of memorials that underscores the Cuban-American experience in Miami. Here, the simple stone **Brigade 2506 Memorial** remembers those who died at the Bay of Pigs on April 17, 1961, during the abortive invasion of Cuba by US-trained Cuban exiles. Veterans of the landing, aging men dressed in combat fatigues, gather here for each anniversary to make all-night-long pledges of patriotism.

Coral Gables

All of Miami's constituent neighborhoods are fast to assert their individuality, though none does it more definitively than **CORAL GABLES**, located southwest

Cubans in Miami

During the mid-Fifties, when opposition to Cuba's Batista dictatorship began to assert itself, a trickle of Cubans started arriving in a predominantly Jewish section of Miami that was then called Riverside. The trickle became a flood when Fidel Castro took power in 1959, and the area became **Little Havana**, populated by the affluent Cuban middle classes who had the most to lose under communism.

These original immigrants were joined by a second influx in May 1980, when the **Mariel boatlift** brought 125,000 islanders from the port of Mariel to Miami in only a few days. These arrivals were poor and uneducated, and a fifth of them were fresh from Cuban jails – incarcerated for criminal rather than political crimes. Bluntly, Castro had dumped his misfits on Miami. The city reeled and then recovered from this mass arrival, but it left Miami's Cuban community utterly divided. Even today, older Cuban-Americans claim that they can pick out a *Marielito* from the way he or she walks or talks.

That said, local division gives way to fervent agreement when it comes to Castro: he's universally detested. In Miami, Cubans have been killed for being *suspected* of advocating dialogue with Castro, and one museum was bombed in 1989 for displaying the work of Castro-approved artists. It remains to be seen whether or not the Cuban exile community in Miami will return to their homeland after Castro's death.

of Little Havana. Twelve square miles of broad boulevards, leafy side streets, and Spanish and Italian architecture form a cultured setting for a cultured community.

Coral Gables's creator was a local aesthete, **George Merrick**, who raided street names from a Spanish dictionary to plan the plazas, fountains, and carefully aged stucco-fronted buildings here. Following the first land sale in 1921, $150 million poured in, which Merrick channeled into one of the biggest advertising campaigns ever known. Unfortunately, Coral Gables was taking shape just as the Florida property boom ended. Merrick was wiped out, and died as Miami's postmaster in 1942. But Coral Gables never lost its good looks, and it remains an impressive place to explore. Merrick wanted people to know they'd arrived somewhere special, and as such, eight grand **entrances** were planned on the main approach roads (though only four were completed). Three of these stand along the western end of Calle Ocho as you arrive from Little Havana.

The best way into Coral Gables is along SW 22nd Street, known as the **Miracle Mile**. Long dominated by fusty, no-name ladies'-wear boutiques, it's finally being redeveloped to attract some funkier, livelier tenants (see "Eating," p.622, for some of these). Note the arcades and balconies, and the spirals and peaks of the **Omni Colonnade Hotel**, at 180 Aragorn Ave, one block north, completed in 1926 to accommodate George Merrick's office. Further west, along Coral Way, the **Merrick House** (open only for tours on Sun & Wed 1–4pm; $5; ℡305/460-5361) was George's boyhood home. In 1899, when he was twelve, his family arrived here from New England to run a 160-acre farm, which was so successful that the house quickly grew from a wooden shack into an elegant dwelling of coral rock and gabled windows (thus inspiring the name of the future city).

While his property-developing contemporaries left ugly scars across the city after digging up the local limestone, Merrick had the foresight to turn his biggest quarry into a sumptuous swimming pool. Opened in 1924, the **Venetian Pool**, 2701 De Soto Blvd (June & July Mon–Fri 11am–7.30pm, Sept–Oct & April, May & Aug Tues–Fri 11am–5.30pm, Nov–March Tues–Sun 10am–4.30pm, year-round Sat & Sun 10am–4.30pm; $9.50; ℡305/460-5356, ⑭www.venetianpool. com), is an essential stop on a steamy Miami afternoon. Its pastel stucco walls hide a delightful spring-fed lagoon, with vine-covered loggias, fountains, waterfalls, coral caves, and plenty of room to swim. The café isn't bad, either.

Wrapping its broad wings around the southern end of De Soto Blvd, Merrick's crowning achievement was the fabulous **Biltmore Hotel**, 1200 Anastasia Ave (℡1-800/727-1926, ⑭www.biltmorehotel.com). With a 26-story tower visible across much of low-lying Miami, everything about the *Biltmore* is over-the-top: 25-foot fresco-coated walls, vaulted ceilings, immense fireplaces, custom-loomed rugs, and a massive swimming pool hosting shows by such bathing belles and beaux as Esther Williams and Johnny Weissmuller. Today, it costs upward of $200 a night to stay here, but a fascinating free tour leaves from the lobby every Sunday at 1.30, 2.30, and 3.30pm; meet at the birdcages. There's also a free ghost history tour Thursdays at 7pm.

Coconut Grove

COCONUT GROVE, on Biscayne Bay about four miles southwest of downtown, has come a long way since the 1960s, when it was peopled by down-at-the-heel artists and writers: these days it's full of expensive bay-view condos, as well as some fashionable cafés and restaurants.

A century ago, a mix of Bahamian immigrant laborers and New England intellectuals laid the foundations of a fiercely individual community, separated from the fledgling city of Miami by a dense wedge of tropical foliage. In 1914, farm-machinery mogul James Deering blew $15 million on re-creating a sixteenth-century Italian villa within this jungle. A thousand-strong workforce completed his **Villa Vizcaya**, 3251 S Miami Ave (daily 9.30am–4.30pm; free house tours every 20min; $12; ⊤305/250-9133, ⓦwww.vizcayamuseum.org), in just two years. Deering's madly eclectic art collection, and his desire that the villa should appear to have been inhabited for four hundred years, result in a thunderous clash of Baroque, Renaissance, Rococo, and Neoclassical fixtures and fittings. The fabulous landscaped **gardens**, with their many fountains and sculptures, are just as excessive.

Key Biscayne

A compact, immaculately manicured community, **KEY BISCAYNE**, five miles off mainland Miami, is a great place to live – if you can afford it. The moneyed of Miami fill the island's upmarket homes; Richard Nixon had a presidential winter house here. The only way onto Key Biscayne is along the four-mile **Rickenbacker Causeway** ($1.25 toll), which runs from SW 26th Road just south of downtown. On the way to the island, the causeway soars high above Biscayne Bay, passing over the small, mostly residential Virginia Key, and giving a breathtaking view of the Brickell Avenue skyline.

Crandon Park Beach, a mile along Crandon Boulevard (the continuation of the main road from the causeway), is one of the finest landscaped beaches in the city, with crystal-clear waters, barbecue grills, and sports facilities (daily 8am–sunset; $4 per car; ⊤305/361-5421). Three miles of yellow-brown beach fringe the park, and give access to a sand bar enabling knee-deep wading far from the shore.

Crandon Boulevard terminates at the entrance to the **Bill Baggs Cape Florida State Recreation Area**, four hundred wooded acres covering the southern extremity of Key Biscayne (daily 8am–sunset; $5 per car, pedestrians & cyclists $1; ⊤305/361-5811). An excellent swimming **beach** lines the Atlantic-facing side of the park, and a boardwalk cuts around the wind-bitten sand dunes toward the 1820s **Cape Florida lighthouse**. Only with the ranger-led tour (Thurs–Mon 10am & 1pm; free, but limited to the first ten people to arrive) can you climb up through the 95-foot structure; it was attacked by Seminoles in 1836 and incapacitated by Confederate soldiers aiming to disrupt Union shipping during the Civil War.

Eating

Cuban food is what Miami does best, and it's not limited to the traditional haunts in **Little Havana**. The hearty comfort food – notably rice and beans, fried plantains, and shredded pork sandwiches – is found in every neighborhood, and you'll also want to try Cuban coffee: choose between *café cubano*, strong, sweet, and frothy, drunk like a shot with a glass of water; *café con leche*, with steamed milk, and particularly good at breakfast with *pan cubano* (thin, buttered toast); or *café cortadito*, a smaller version of the *con leche*. Cuban cooking is complemented by sushi bars, American homestyle diners, as well as Haitian, Italian, and Indian restaurants, among a handful of other ethnic cuisines.

Coral Gables is best for upmarket cafés and ethnic Italian and Greek places, while **Coconut Grove** has American, Spanish, New Floridian (sometimes known as Floribbean; a mix of Caribbean spiciness and fruity Florida sauces), and even British. **Seafood** is equally abundant: succulent grouper, yellowfin tuna, and wahoo, a local delicacy, are among five hundred species of fish that thrive offshore. **Stone-crab claws**, served from October to May, are another regional specialty.

Ayestaran 706 SW 27th Ave, Little Havana ⓣ305/649-4982. This sprawling Cuban restaurant offers hearty and cheap daily specials and superb *café con leche* that you can mix to your liking.

Big Pink 157 Collins Ave, South Beach ⓣ305/532-4700. Come here for large portions of comfort food: mashed potatoes, ribs, macaroni and cheese, and classic "TV dinners," all served at long communal tables.

David's Coffee Shop 1058 Collins Ave, South Beach ⓣ305/534-8736. Locals' favorite Cuban restaurant on the beach (there's another location at 16th St and Meridian Ave). The food is authentic, and there's eat-in and takeout at both restaurants.

El Palacio de los Jugos 5721 W Flagler Ave, Little Havana ⓣ305/264-1503. A handful of tables at the back of a Cuban produce market, where the pork sandwiches and shellfish soup from the takeout stand are the tastiest for miles. Also serving refreshing *jugos* (juices).

The Forge 432 41st St, Miami Beach ⓣ305/538-8533. A memorable upscale dining spot where the hearty traditional food and huge wine cellar combine appealingly with a vibrant atmosphere and eclectic clientele.

Front Porch Café 1418 Ocean Drive, South Beach ⓣ305/531-8300. This local hangout is refreshingly low-key, considering its location: the delicious, dinner-plate-sized pancakes will easily take care of both breakfast *and* lunch.

Garcia's Seafood Grille 398 NW N River Drive, downtown ⓣ305/375-0765. Wonderful waterfront café with ramshackle wooden benches and superb, fresh fish dishes for around $11. Breakfast and lunch only.

Greenstreet Café 3468 Main Hwy, Coconut Grove ⓣ305/444-0244. The terrific breakfasts make this café a real scene at weekends. There's a large number of outdoor tables: great for watching the world go by.

Joe's Stone Crabs 11 Washington Ave, South Beach ⓣ305/673-0365. Specializing in succulent stone crabs and always packed – if you're impatient, do as the locals do and head to the takeout window. Crabcakes, fresh fish, and the crispy fried chicken are also good. Open Oct–May.

La Sandwicherie 229 W 14th St, South Beach ⓣ305/532-8934. Gigantic sandwiches stuffed with gourmet ingredients such as prosciutto and imported cheeses and starting at around $8. It's open until 5am, so good for a post-clubbing refuel.

News Café 800 Ocean Drive, South Beach ⓣ305/538-NEWS. This mid-priced sidewalk café has front-row seating for the South Beach promenade – although the food's unremarkable. Open 24hrs at weekends.

Pacific Time 915 Lincoln Rd, South Beach ⓣ305/534-5979. For a splurge, you can't beat the Modern American cooking with strong Asian influences served at this pricey but excellent restaurant.

Picnics at Allen's Drug Store 6500 Red Rd, Coral Gables ⓣ305/665-6964. Low-priced home-style cooking – great freshly made burgers – in an old-fashioned drugstore, complete with a jukebox that blasts golden oldies.

Pizza Rustica 863 Washington Ave, South Beach ⓣ305/674-8244. Mouthwateringly fresh gourmet pizza, with slab-like slices costing around $4.

Rascal House 17190 Collins Ave, Miami Beach ⓣ305/947-4581. Large, loud, and reasonably authentic New York-style deli. Huge portions are served by waitresses who look like they've worked here since the place's heyday in the 1950s.

Scotty's Landing 3381 Pan American Drive, Coconut Grove ⓣ305/854-2626. Tasty, inexpensive seafood and fish 'n' chips consumed at marina-side picnic tables. It's tucked away on the water by City Hall, and so can be hard to find – ask if you get lost.

Tap Tap 819 5th St, South Beach ⓣ305/672-2898. Tasty, attractively presented and reasonably priced Haitian food. The upstairs gallery featuring Haitian art is also worth a look. Dinner only.

Versailles 3555 SW 8th St, Little Havana ⓣ305/444-0240. Local families, Cuban businessmen, and backpackers congregate here for the wonderfully inexpensive Cuban dishes, served by friendly staff amid kitsch decor of chandeliers and mirrored walls.

Yambo 1643 SW 1st St, Little Havana ⓣ305/642-6616. Step out of the USA and into Central America at Yambo, an undiscovered gem serving up good, inexpensive Nicaraguan food.

Nightlife and entertainment

Miami's **nightlife** is still unsurpassed in Florida. Almost every dancefloor is attached to a restaurant or a bar, so you could end up dancing anywhere. At the full-fledged **clubs**, house and techno beats are most popular, followed by salsa or merengue played by Spanish-speaking DJs. Most of the action is centered in South Beach, and **cover charges** are around $20. Door policies are notoriously fierce at current in-spots; the places listed below include laid-back local haunts as well as some of the hotter bars and clubs. For **live music**, your best bet is **reggae.** Miami has a sizable Jamaican population, and local as well as out-of-town acts appear regularly. The free *New Times* magazine, published every Thursday, offers **listings** of what's going on where and when – including **gay and lesbian info**.

If you want to try out the local **sports** scene, the Marlins major league baseball team and the Dolphins, Miami's pro football team, play at the Pro Player Stadium, sixteen miles northwest of downtown at 2269 Dan Marino Blvd (☎305/623-6100, ⓦwww.proplayerstadium.com; take bus #27 from the main bus station).

Bars and live music venues

The Abbey Brewing Company 1115 16th St, South Beach ☎305/538-8110. This small, unpretentious microbrewery serves the best beers on South Beach. Try the creamy Oatmeal Stout – their best and most popular brew. Open until 5am.

Churchill's Pub 5501 NE 2nd Ave, Little Haiti ☎305/757-1807, ⓦwww.churchillspub.com. A British enclave within Little Haiti, with soccer and rugby matches on TV, UK beers on tap, and live rock music. Check website for schedule.

Club Deuce Bar & Grill 222 14th St, South Beach ☎305/531-6200. This grimy, noisy grunge bar is a remnant from pre-fabulous South Beach. Drinks are cheap, the crowd's indie, and there's a dartboard and pool table. Open until 5am.

Hoy Como Ayer 2212 SW 8th St, Little Havana ☎305/541-2631, ⓦwww.hoycomoayer.net. Despite the city's sizable Cuban population, this dark, smoky joint is about the only place in Miami to hear decent Cuban music. Check website for schedule.

Jimbo's inside the park at Virginia Key Beach, Virginia Key ☎305/361-7026. Renowned ramshackle bar where you can help yourself to a beer from a wheelbarrow filled with ice. A good place to chat with the old-timers.

Monty's Raw Bar 2550 S Bayshore Drive, Coconut Grove ☎305/858-1431. Drinkers often outnumber the diners (it's also a restaurant) at this tiki-style bar, drawn here by the gregarious mood and the views across the bay; the loud reggae music can be a bit overpowering, though.

The Pawn Shop Lounge 1222 NE 2nd Ave, downtown ☎305/373-3511. Massive converted pawn shop eccentrically decorated with boots and chandeliers dangling from the ceilings. Cocktails are available – but most of the regulars drink beer.

Purdy Lounge 1811 Purdy Ave, South Beach ☎305/531-4622. An unheralded beachside gem, this large neighborhood bar avoids clogging crowds of out-of-towners by its location on the less-touristed western side of South Beach. Open until 5am.

The Raleigh Bar inside the *Raleigh Hotel*, 1775 Collins Ave, South Beach ☎305/534-6300. This elegant hotel bar, with its lushly restored wood panelling, is a throwback to the heyday of cocktail culture.

Sky Bar inside the *Shore Club* hotel, 1901 Collins Ave, South Beach ☎786/276-6772. Sprawling outdoor bar draped around the hotel pool, with giant overstuffed square seats: dress up and expect a tough door unless you're staying at the hotel. Check out the smaller, attached *Sand Bar*, with its view of the beach and ocean.

Tobacco Road 626 S Miami Ave, downtown ☎305/374-1198, ⓦwww.tobacco-road.com. This friendly bar – Miami's oldest, from 1912 – is a favorite with locals for its exceptional live R&B. Check website for schedule.

Nightclubs

Cafe Nostalgia inside the *Versailles Hotel*, 3425 Collins Ave, Miami Beach ☎305/531-6092. This legendary (and itinerant) Cuban club has found yet another new home. Live music for an older crowd prevails early on; from 1am it's Latin hip-hip for 20-somethings.

Crobar 1445 Washington Ave, South Beach ☎305/531-8225. The hardest-partying club on the beach, playing heavy-hitting house mixed by well-known DJs. Expect a fairly large gay crowd.

Mansion 1235 Washington Ave, South Beach ☎305/532-1525. Large nightclub complex with six VIP areas, nine bars, and five dancefloors, each with its own style of music, hip-hop being the most popular.

Mynt Ultra Lounge 1921 Collins Ave, South Beach ☎786/276-6132. Lounge/dance club, washed in green light, with an enormous bar and large, black leather sofas. Expect a fierce door any night of the week.

Nocturnal 50 NE 11th St, downtown ☎305/576-6996. The spaced-out will enjoy the trippy images projected on the rooftop terrace's 360-degree IMAX-style screen as the deep house music thumps in their ears.

🏃 **Club Space** 34 NE 11th St, downtown ☎305/375-0001. This downtown pioneer has a rough decor and an illicit ambiance: most people migrate here when the other venues shut down, for after-hours dancing until dawn – expect a friendly, loved-up, youngish crowd and big-name DJs.

The Florida Keys

Folklore, films, and fiction have given **THE FLORIDA KEYS** – a hundred-mile chain of islands that runs to within ninety miles of Cuba – an image of glamorous intrigue they don't really deserve; at least, not now that the go-go days of the cocaine cowboys in the 1980s are long gone. Rather, the Keys are an outdoor-lover's paradise, where fishing, snorkeling, and diving dominate. Terrific untainted natural areas include the **Florida Reef**, a great band of living coral just a few miles off the coast. But for many, the various keys are only stops on the way to **Key West**. Once the richest town in the US, and the final dot of North America before a thousand miles of ocean, Key West has vibrant, Caribbean-style streets with plenty of convivial bars in which to while away the hours, watching the spectacular **sunsets**.

Wherever you are on the Keys, you'll experience distinctive **cuisine**, served for the most part in funky little shacks where the food is fresh and the atmosphere laid-back. Conch, a rich meaty mollusc, is a specialty, served in chowders and fritters. There's also Key Lime Pie, a delicate, creamy concoction of special Key limes and condensed milk, that bears little resemblance to the lurid green imposter pies served in the rest of the US.

Getting around the Keys could hardly be easier. There's just one route all the way through to Key West: the **Overseas Highway** (US-1). The road is punctuated by **mile markers** (MM), starting with MM127 just south of Miami and finishing with MM0 in Key West, at the corner of Whitehead and Fleming streets. As per Keys convention, addresses are given by the closest mile marker, along with the appellation of either "Oceanside" or "Bayside," depending on whether the place in question faces the Atlantic Ocean or the Florida Bay.

Key Largo

The first and largest of the keys, **KEY LARGO**, is a disappointing jumble of filling stations, shopping plazas, and fast-food outlets. The town does, however, provide a fine opportunity to visit the Florida Reef, at the **John Pennekamp Coral Reef State Park**, at MM102.5-Oceanside (daily 8am–sunset; $3.50 per car and driver, plus $2.50 for first passenger, 50¢ for each additional passenger, pedestrians and cyclists $1.50; ☎305/451-1202, ⓦwww.pennekamppark.com). This protected 78-square-mile section of living coral reef is rated as one of the most beautiful in the world. If you can, take the **snorkeling tour** (9am, noon & 3pm; 2hr 30mins; $28.95, plus $4 for equipment), or the **guided scuba dive** (9.30am & 1.30pm; 1hr 30mins; $50; diver's certificate required). The **glass-bottom boat** tour (9.15am, 12.15pm & 3pm; 2hr 30mins; $22) is less demanding. For information and to make reservations for all of these tours, call ☎305/451-6300. On any of them, you're virtually certain to spot lobsters, angelfish, eels, and jellyfish along the reef, and shoals of silvery minnows stalked by angry-faced barracuda. The reef itself is a delicate living thing, comprising millions of minute coral polyps extracting calcium from the seawater and growing from one to sixteen feet every thousand years. Sadly, it's far easier to spot signs of death than life: white patches show where a carelessly dropped anchor, or a diver's hand, has scraped away the protective mucous layer and left the coral susceptible to terminal disease.

Practicalities

Key Largo has some of the widest selections of reasonably priced **accommodation** in the Keys, with many of the motels offering diving packages. Among the cheaper options, there's the basic but clean *Ed & Allen's Lodgings*, MM103.5-Oceanside (☎1-888/333-5536; ⓦ www.ed-ellens-lodgings.com; ❸), or the gloriously quirky, adult-only ⚓ *Largo Lodge*, MM101.5-Bayside (☎1-800/468-4378, ⓦ www.largolodge.com; ❹); for something more luxurious, try the huge, stylish chalets at the *Kona Kai Resort*, MM97.8-Bayside (☎1-800/365-7829, ⓦ www.konakairesort.com; ❼). Delicious, fresh **seafood** – including conch fritters – is available at ⚓ *Crack'd Conch*, MM105-Oceanside (☎305/451-0732), while *Ballyhoo's Grill and Grog*, in the median at MM98 (☎305/852-0822), serves good breakfasts.

Islamorada

Lying on Upper Matecumbe Key, **ISLAMORADA** (pronounced "eye-lah-more-RAH-da) is a much more welcoming place to dawdle than Key Largo, fifteen miles to the north. Once there, make sure to take a trip across to Indian Key, one of many small, mangrove-skirted islands off Lower Matecumbe Key, once a thriving settlement founded by wrecker Jacob Houseman, but now boasting a riot of exotic plants and evocative ruins. At the southern end of Islamorada, there's good hiking at **Long Key State Botanical Site**, MM67.5-Oceanside (daily 8am–sunset; $3.50 per car and driver, plus $2.50 for first passenger, 50¢ for each additional passenger; ☎305/664-4815), a 965-acre expanse of tropical foliage and mangroves. Long Key has an excellent beach (a rarity in the Keys), and is a great base for deep-sea fishing, too.

Good-value **accommodation** in Islamorada includes the very cheap *Key Lantern/Blue Fin*, MM82-Bayside (☎305/664-4572, ⓦ www.keylantern.com; ❷) – ask for a room at the *Blue Fin* (same price), since these were more recently renovated – and the serene *Drop Anchor*, MM85-Oceanside (☎1-888/664-4863; ❺). As for **eating**, ⚓ *Hungry Tarpon*, MM77.5-Bayside (☎305/664-0535), serves excellent fresh fish as well as tasty breakfasts, while the pricier – and often packed – *Islamorada Fish Company*, MM81.5-Bayside (☎1-800/258-2559), is also good for seafood.

The Middle Keys

Once over Long Key Bridge, you're into **THE MIDDLE KEYS**. At the not-for-profit **Dolphin Research Center**, MM59-Bayside (daily 9am–4.30pm; ☎305/289-1121, ⓦ www.dolphins.org), you can swim with the dolphins for $180 (reservations at ☎305/289-0002).

The largest of several islands in the Middle Keys, **Key Vaca** holds the nucleus of the area's major settlement, **Marathon**. Here you'll find great **fishing** and **water-**

sports opportunities, as well as a couple of small beaches. **Sombrero Beach**, along Sombrero Beach Road (off the Overseas Highway near MM50-Oceanside), has good swimming waters and shaded picnic tables.

Close by, at MM50.5-Bayside, nestled inside the 64-acre tropical forest of **Crane Point Hammock**, the **Museum of Natural History of the Florida Keys** (Mon–Sat 9am–5pm, Sun noon–5pm; $7.50; ☎305/743-9100, ⓦwww.cranepoint.org) provides an excellent introduction to the history and ecology of the area. Follow the one-mile **nature trail** past the hammock forest, an area of dense hardwood trees characteristic of the Keys, until you reach the end of the trail. Here, you'll find the reconstructed remnants of a nineteenth-century village established by settlers from the Bahamas.

Marathon has some well-equipped **resorts**, such as the lush *Banana Bay*, MM49.5-Bayside (☎1-800/226-2621, ⓦwww.bananabay.com; ❹), which has a private beach. The best **budget option** is the 🍴 *Flamingo Inn*, MM59-Bayside (☎1-800/439-1478, ⓦwww.theflamingoinn.com; ❸), a lovingly maintained retro motel with large rooms. For **eating**, there's terrific seafood – including succulent beer-steamed shrimp – at *Castaway*, 15th Street near MM47.5-Oceanside (☎305/743-6247). The tiny, laid-back 🍴 *Seven Mile Grill*, by the bridge of the same name at MM47.5-Bayside (☎305/743-4481), serves delicious conch and creamy Key Lime Pie to locals, sea salts, and tourists alike. For good, cheap Cuban food, try *Don Pedro Restaurant*, MM53-Oceanside (☎305/743-5247).

The Lower Keys

Starkly different from their neighbors to the north, **THE LOWER KEYS** are quiet, heavily wooded, and predominantly residential. Built on a limestone rather than a coral base, these islands have a flora and fauna all their own. It feels very quiet as you head south: seemingly everyone's either gone fishing or is snoozing in a hammock.

The first place of consequence you'll hit after crossing Seven Mile Bridge is one of the Keys' prettiest spots: **Bahia Honda State Park**, at MM37-Oceanside (daily 8am–sunset; $3.50 per car and driver, plus $2.50 for first passenger, 50¢ for each additional passenger; pedestrians and cyclists $1.50; ☎305/872-2353, ⓦwww.bahiahondapark.com). Its lagoon has an alluring natural beach – the best stretch of sand in the Keys – and pristine, two-tone ocean waters, which can be enjoyed on a leisurely **kayak ride** ($10 per hour).

Divers should head for the **Looe Key Marine Sanctuary**, signposted from the Overseas Highway on **Ramrod Key**: it's a five-square-mile protected reef area, easily the equal of the John Pennekamp Coral Reef State Park (see p.625). The sanctuary office (Mon–Fri 8am–5pm; ☎305/743-2437, ⓦwww.fknms.nos.noaa.gov) can provide free maps, but to visit the reef you'll need the services of a dive shop, like the neighboring Looe Key Dive Center (☎1-800/942-5397, ⓦwww.diveflakeys.com).

Big Pine Key is the main Lower Keys settlement. Nearby you'll find most of the **accommodation** in these parts – which is generally more limited and expensive than in the Middle and Upper Keys. *Looe Key Reef Resort*, MM27.5-Oceanside (☎1-800/942-5397, ⓦwww.diveflakeys.com; ❸), is an ideal base for visiting the marine sanctuary, while for a real splurge, stay at the idyllic, adult-only *Little Palm Island*, MM28.5-Oceanside, Little Torch Key (☎1-800/343-8567, ⓦwww.littlepalmisland.com; ❾), a private islet whose thatched cottages are set in lush gardens a few feet from the beach.

For **food**, the dollar-bill-decorated ⚓ *No Name Pub*, a mile or so from MM30-Bayside down North Watson Boulevard (☎ 305/872-9115) is known for its superb thin-crust pizza. Further on down the Overseas Highway, on Sugarloaf Key at MM20-Bayside, the friendly *Mangrove Mama's* (☎ 305/745-3030; closed Sept) serves stupendous local cuisine in a cheery shack with a tropical garden.

Key West

Closer to Cuba than to mainland Florida, **KEY WEST** often seems rather tenuously bound to the rest of the US. Famed for their tolerant attitudes and laid-back lifestyles, the 30,000 islanders seem adrift in a great expanse of sea and sky, and – despite a million tourists a year – the place resonates with an individual spirit. In particular, liberal attitudes have stimulated a large gay influx, estimated at two in five of the population. Although Key West today has been heavily restored and revitalized for the tourists, the town has retained some of its sense of individualism and isolation, especially away from the main drag of Duval Street. To best absorb this atmosphere – and the mellow pace of local life – take time to amble the gorgeous, lushly vegetated streets, make meals last for hours, and pause regularly for refreshment in the numerous bars.

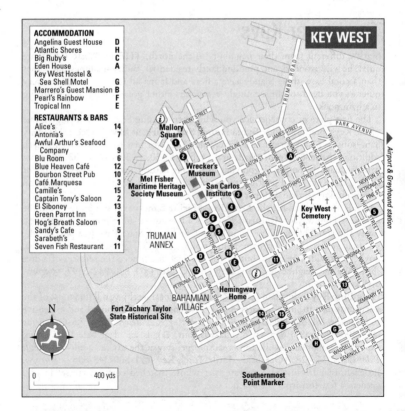

ACCOMMODATION
Angelina Guest House	D
Atlantic Shores	H
Big Ruby's	C
Eden House	A
Key West Hostel & Sea Shell Motel	G
Marrero's Guest Mansion	B
Pearl's Rainbow	F
Tropical Inn	E

RESTAURANTS & BARS
Alice's	14
Antonia's	7
Awful Arthur's Seafood Company	9
Blu Room	6
Blue Heaven Café	12
Bourbon Street Pub	10
Café Marquesa	3
Camille's	15
Captain Tony's Saloon	2
El Siboney	13
Green Parrot Inn	8
Hog's Breath Saloon	1
Sandy's Cafe	5
Sarabeth's	4
Seven Fish Restaurant	11

KEY WEST

► Airport & Greyhound station

0 _____ 400 yds

Arrival and information

The **airport** (☎305/296-5439) is four miles east of town, with the **Greyhound** bus station (☎305/296-9072) adjacent to its entrance. There are no shuttle buses into town; a **taxi** (☎305/296-6666) costs around $10.

The best place to head for **information** is the Greater Key West Chamber of Commerce, in the center of town next to Mallory Square at 402 Wall St (Mon–Fri 8.30am–6.30pm, Sat & Sun 8.30am–6pm; ☎305/294-2587, ⓦwww.keywestchamber .org). The Chamber can give precise dates for Key West's annual **festivals**, the best of which are the Conch Republic Celebration in April and Fantasy Fest in late October, which feels like a gay Mardi Gras crossed with Halloween. A good source of **gay information** is the Key West Business Guild, 513 Truman Ave (daily 9am–5pm; ☎305/294-4603, ⓦwww.gaykeywestfl.com).

It's best to explore the narrow streets of the mile-square Old Town – which contains virtually everything that you'll want to see – **on foot**. You could do it in little more than a day, though dashing about isn't the way to enjoy the place. Cycling is another good way of getting around: **bikes** can be rented from Adventure Scooter & Bicycle Rentals, with two locations (out of seven around the Old Town) at 1 Duval St and 601 Front St ($15 per day; ☎305/293-9933).

Accommodation

During the winter, it's essential to make a **reservation** for accommodation in Key West; the Fantasy Fest festival at the end of October is another extremely busy time. In summer, competition for rooms is less fierce, and prices drop by up to thirty percent.

Angelina Guest House 302 Angela St ☎1-888/303-4480, ⓦwww.angelinaguesthouse. com. This charming guesthouse, tucked away in the backstreets of the Bahamian Village, has a cool, Caribbean feel, and is one of the best deals in town. Room with shared bath ❸, room with private bath ❹.

Atlantic Shores 510 South St ☎1-800/526-3559, ⓦwww.atlanticshoresresort.com. Art Deco resort open to all, but attracting mostly gays. Has a popular clothing-optional pool and adjacent nude beach. ❺

Big Ruby's 409 Applerouth Lane ☎1-800/477-7829, ⓦwww.bigrubys.com. Gay guesthouse with stylish rooms clustered round a lagoon pool and patio that's perfect for peaceful lounging. ❺

Eden House 1015 Fleming St ☎305/296-6868, ⓦwww.edenhouse.com. Here, a grotty lobby hides one of the city's best deals – large rooms, free parking, free happy hour every night, and a shaded pool. Room with shared bath from ❹, room with private bath from ❺.

Key West Hostel & Sea Shell Motel 718 South St ☎305/296-5719, ⓦwww.keywesthostel.com. The hostel has cheap dorm beds ($28–31), a sunny patio, and no curfew, while the *Sea Shell Motel* (❸) offers standard rooms at the lowest rates in the neighborhood.

Marrero's Guest Mansion 410 Fleming St ☎305/294-6977 or 1-800/459-6212, ⓦwww. marreros.com. Antique-filled old mansion that's supposedly haunted; room 18 is where most of the paranormal activity has been reported. Cheapest room ❺, room 18 ❻.

Pearl's Rainbow 525 United St ☎1-800/749-6696, ⓦwww.pearlsrainbow.com. The lone women-only guesthouse on the island, this attractive former cigar factory serves breakfast and has two pools and two Jacuzzis. ❻

Tropical Inn 812 Duval St ☎1-888/611-6510, ⓦwww.tropicalinn.com. The large, airy rooms in this charming restored "conch" house are at the center of the action. Most rooms sleep three, and the more expensive ones have balconies. ❺

The Town

Anyone who visited Key West two decades ago would now barely recognize the Old Town's main promenade, the mile-long swath of **Duval Street**. Teetering just on the safe side of seedy for many years, much of the street has been transformed into a well-tended tourist strip of boutiques and beachwear shops, although it's still a pleasant place for a leisurely stroll. For a sense of the locals' town, take time to explore the side streets, where gnarled banyans, tall skinny palms, creepers, and unruly, exotic blooms threaten to overtake the faded wooden houses. Make sure, as well, to visit the **Bahamian Village**, centered on Thomas and Petronia streets. Originally settled by Cubans and African-Bahamians, this relatively unrestored, untouristed corner of town is an atmospheric patchwork of single-story cigar-makers' cottages, Cuban groceries, and ramshackle old churches, all covered by a rich green foliage.

Numerous **museums** in town concern themselves with "wrecking," or the salvaging of cargo from sunken vessels; it's the industry on which Key West's earliest good times were based. The friendly little **Wrecker's Museum**, 322 Duval St (also known as the Oldest House Museum; daily 10am–4pm; $5; ☎305/294-9502), illuminates the lives of the wreckers, portraying them as brave, uninsured heroes who risked all to save cargoes, ships, and lives. Judging by the choice furniture that fills the house – lived in by the wrecker Captain Watlington during the 1830s – they did pretty well for their pains.

Farther up Duval, at no. 516, the **San Carlos Institute** (Tues–Sun noon–4pm; $3 donation; ☎305/294-3887) has played a leading role in Cuban exile life since it opened in 1871. Financed by a grant from the Cuban government, the present building dates from 1924. Cuban architect Francisco Centurion designed the two-story building in the Cuban Baroque style of that period. Soil from Cuba's six provinces covers the grounds, and a cornerstone was taken from the tomb of Cuban independence campaigner José Martí. There's a passable exhibition on Cuban heritage here, and they also distribute the free Cuban Heritage Trail pamphlet, which details sites of interest around town.

The **southernmost point** in Key West, and consequently in the continental US, is at the intersection of Whitehead and South streets. A daft-looking buoy marks the spot. Watch out for people here who'll kindly offer to take your photograph, and then expect tipping for the pleasure.

△ Ernest Hemingway Home & Museum

Back up and just west from the northern end of Duval Street is **Mallory Square**. In the early 1800s, thousands of dollars' worth of salvage was landed at the piers, stored in the warehouses, and flogged at the auction houses here. Nowadays, however, it is dominated by tourist shops and worth only a brief linger.

Head rather to the nearby **Mel Fisher Maritime Heritage Society Museum**, 200 Greene St (daily 9.30am–5pm; $11; ℡305/294-2633, Ⓦwww.melfisher.org), which showcases the diamonds, pearls, and daggers, as well as countless vases, an impressive emerald cross, and the obligatory cannon, that Fisher pulled up from two seventeenth-century shipwrecks in 1985 – a haul said to be worth at least $200 million.

Finally, down Whitehead Street from Greene, you'll find Key West's most popular tourist attraction: the **Ernest Hemingway Home & Museum**, at no. 907 (daily 9am–5pm; $11; ℡305/294-1136, Ⓦwww.hemingwayhome.com). Sadly, the compulsory half-hour **guided tour** deals more in fantasy than fact: while it's true that Hemingway owned this large, vaguely Moorish house for thirty years, he lived in it for barely ten, and even the authenticity of the furnishings is disputed. That said, some of his most acclaimed novels, including *A Farewell to Arms* and *To Have and Have Not*, were written in the study (the hayloft of a carriage house, which the author entered by way of a rope bridge). Divorced in 1940, Hemingway boxed up his manuscripts and moved them to a back room at the original *Sloppy Joe's* (see p.632), before heading off for a house in Cuba with his new wife, journalist Martha Gellhorn. Today, some fifty cats – many of them with six toes, traditionally employed as ship's mascots – pad contentedly around the gardens. Whatever the guides say, Hemingway kept his feline harem while living in Cuba, not Key West, so it's unlikely that these cats are in any way related to Papa's pets.

Eating

In Key West, it's *de rigueur* to sample **conch fritters**; the salmon and white stand (daily 10.30am–6pm; no phone) on Mallory Square does the best in town for under six dollars for a dozen.

Alice's 1114 Duval St ℡305/292-5733. The menu at this upscale eatery contains a varied choice of, often Asian-inflected, fusion fare, plus some more offbeat dishes such as Cuban-style ostrich.

Antonia's 615 Duval St ℡305/294-6565. Expensive but excellent northern Italian cuisine served in a formal but friendly environment. Sit in the old front room rather than the characterless modern extension out back. Dinner only.

Awful Arthur's Seafood Company 628 Duval St ℡305/293-7663. A fair amount of tourists come to this lively fish shack for its good-value nightly specials, such as All You Can Eat Crab Legs for $24.

Blue Heaven Café corner of Thomas and Petronia sts ℡305/296-0867. Sit in a dirt yard and enjoy fresh fish, jerk chicken, and fabulous lobster Benedict breakfasts as chickens peck around your feet.

Café Marquesa inside the *Marquesa Hotel* at 600 Fleming St ℡305/292-1244. This chichi restaurant with its imaginative and pricey New American menu is the town's best fine dining spot.

Camille's 1202 Simonton St ℡305/296-4811. Great, affordable breakfasts and brunches – menu options in the past have included cashew nut waffles and banana buttermilk pancakes.

El Siboney 900 Catherine St ℡305/296-4184. Come to this no-frills family diner for copious, inexpensive, and good-quality Cuban dishes.

Sarabeth's 530 Simonton St ℡305/293-8181. Satisfying homestyle cooking served in the appropriately welcoming setting of an old wooden clapboard house.

Sandy's Cafe inside the M&M Laundry, 1026 White St ℡305/295-0159. Dingy café offering cheap and excellent Cuban sandwiches and the best *café con leche* this side of Miami.

Seven Fish Restaurant 632 Olivia St ℡305/296-2777. This little-known, mid-priced bistro, easy to miss in its tiny white corner building, serves some of the best food – shrimp scampi, meatloaf, and the like – in town. There are just over a dozen tables, so it pays to call ahead.

Nightlife and entertainment

The anything-goes nature of Key West is exemplified by the convivial **bars** that make up the bulk of the island's **nightlife**. Gregarious, rough-and-ready affairs, many stay open as late as 4am and feature regular **live music**. The most popular places are grouped around the northern end of Duval Street, no more than a few minutes' stagger from one another. For something a little less macho, keep south of the 500 block of Duval.

Blu Room 42 Applerouth Lane ☎ 305/296-6667. The closest Key West comes to a traditional nightclub, with a bare bar and dimly-lit dancefloor. Come only if you want to dance – the music (mainly hard house) is too loud to talk.

Bourbon Street Pub 724 Duval St ☎ 305/296-1992. This huge pub complex is the largest gay-friendly place to drink in the center of town; there's a pleasant garden out back, complete with a large hot tub.

Captain Tony's Saloon 428 Greene St ☎ 305/294-1838. This rustic saloon was the original *Sloppy Joe's*, where Hemingway hung out (see p.631). Today, it's one of the less cheesy choices for live music.

Green Parrot Inn 601 Whitehead St ☎ 305/294-6133, ⊛ www.greenparrot.com. This Key West landmark, open since 1890, draws plenty of locals to its pool tables, dartboard, and pinball machine. There's live music on the weekends – check website for schedule.

Hog's Breath Saloon 400 Front St ☎ 305/292-2032, ⊛ www.hogsbreath.com. This bar's one of the best places to catch live music in town (check website for schedule), mostly for a nominal cover – just don't be put off by the boozed-up patrons circling its entrance.

The East Coast

Facing the Atlantic Ocean, Florida's **East Coast** runs for more than three hundred miles north from the northern fringe of Miami. Each of the communities near Miami – all boasting the palm-dotted beaches and warm ocean waves typical of southern Florida – have something unique to offer. **Fort Lauderdale**, no longer the party town of popular imagination, is today a sophisticated cultural center with a bubbling, increasingly upscale social scene. To the north, **Boca Raton** and **Palm Beach** are quiet, exclusive communities, their Mediterranean Revival mansions inhabited almost entirely by multimillionaires. Beyond Palm Beach, the coast is still mostly undeveloped; even the **Space Coast**, anchored by the extremely popular **Kennedy Space Center**, is smack in the middle of a nature preserve. Just north, **Daytona Beach** attracts race car- and motorcycle-enthusiasts with its festivals and the Daytona International Speedway. Lastly, enchanting **St Augustine** is the spot where Spanish settlers established North America's first foreign colony.

By car, the scenic route along the coast is **Hwy-A1A**, which sticks to the ocean side of the **Intracoastal Waterway**, formed when the rivers dividing the mainland from the barrier islands were joined and deepened during World War II. When necessary, Hwy-A1A turns inland and links with the much less picturesque **US-1**. The speediest road in the region, **I-95**, runs about ten miles west of the coastline, and is only worthwhile if you're in a hurry.

Fort Lauderdale

Following the 1960 teen-exploitation movie *Where the Boys Are*, **FORT LAU-DERDALE**, with its seven miles of palm-shaded white sands, instantly became the number-one Spring Break destination in the US. However, having fueled its economic boom on underage drinking and lascivious excess, the city promptly turned its back on the revelers. By the end of the 1980s, it had imposed enough restrictions on boozing and wild behavior to put an end to the bacchanal. Since then, Fort Lauderdale has transformed itself into a thriving pleasure port, catering to individual yacht-owners and major cruise liners alike. It's also one of the fastest-growing residential areas in the country, and has for years been known as one of **gay** America's favorite holiday haunts.

Arrival and information

Both of Fort Lauderdale's public transit terminals are in or close to downtown. Greyhound **buses** pull in at 515 NE 3rd St, while the Amtrak and Tri-Rail **train** station (☎ 1-800/TRI-RAIL, ⓦ www.tri-rail.com) is two miles west at 200 SW 21st Terrace – take bus #22 into town ($1). The main local **visitor center** is at 100 E Broward Blvd, Suite 200 (Mon–Fri 8.30am–5pm; ☎ 1-800/22-SUNNY, ⓦ www.sunny.org).

Local bus #11 runs twice hourly along Las Olas Boulevard between downtown and the beach. You can also use the **water taxi** (all-day pass $10; ☎ 954/467-6677, ⓦ www.watertaxi.com), which can take you almost anywhere along Fort Lauderdale's many miles of waterfront.

Accommodation

Although Fort Lauderdale is moving inexorably upscale, plenty of **motels** near the beach still offer a reasonable room for around $50 in summer (more like $75 in winter). The tourist office's (see above) free annual *Superior Small Lodgings Guide* has full listings.

Backpackers Beach Hostel 2115 N Ocean Blvd ☎ 954/567-7275, ⓦ www.fortlauderdalehostel.com. Clean, well-equipped hostel with free parking, Internet, and local calls. Dorm beds $20, private rooms ❷.

Bermudian Tropical Garden 315 N Birch Rd ☎ 954/467-0467, ⓦ www.bermudian-tropical.com. Low prices, a wide choice of motel rooms and apartments, and a pretty pool and sundeck area make this worth a try. ❷

🏃 **Pillars at New River Sound** 111 N Birch Rd ☎ 954/467-9639, ⓦ www.pillarshotel.com. Quiet, intimate British-colonial-style hotel in the heart of the beach area (though facing the waterway rather than the ocean). ❼

Riverside Hotel 620 E Las Olas Blvd ☎ 1-800/325-3280, ⓦ www.riversidehotel.com. Pricey but elegant option in the heart of downtown. ❼

🏃 **Tropi Rock Resort** 2900 Belmar St ☎ 1-800/987-9385, ⓦ www.tropirock.com. Funky, family-owned hotel a block from the beach, where the good-value rates include use of tennis courts and a small gym. ❹

Downtown Fort Lauderdale

Downtown Fort Lauderdale focuses on a few blocks between E Broward and E Las Olas boulevards, which cross US-1 a couple of miles east of I-95. Heavily prettified with parks and promenades, it's a pleasant place for a stroll, especially if you follow the mile-long pedestrian **Riverwalk** along the north shore of the New River. Las Olas Boulevard itself, the main **shopping district**, remains busy day and night, with boutiques, galleries, restaurants, bars, and sidewalk cafés in abundance. It's also home to the stimulating **Museum of Art**, 1 E Las Olas Blvd (daily 11am–7pm; $6; ☎ 954/525-5500, ⓦ www.moafl.org), whose largely modern collection features the emotionally powerful expressionistic work of the CoBrA movement of artists from Copenhagen, Brussels, and Amsterdam. Not far west, the simulators and interactive displays at the **Museum of Discovery & Science**, 401 SW 2nd St (Mon–Sat 10am–5pm, Sun noon–6pm; $15; ☎954/467-6637, ⓦwww.mods.org), should pacify kids pining for Disney. There's also a 3D IMAX theater, a ticket to which is included in admission to the museum; call or visit the website for showtimes.

The beach

Although downtown has its charms and attractions, most visitors come to Fort Lauderdale for its broad, clean, and undeniably beautiful **beach**. You'll find it by crossing the arching Intracoastal Waterway Bridge, about two miles along Las Olas Boulevard from downtown. Along the seafront, Fort Lauderdale Beach Boulevard once bore the brunt of Spring Break partying, though only a few beachfront bars suggest the carousing of the past. Today, an attractive promenade draws an altogether healthier crowd of joggers, in-line skaters, and cyclists.

Eating and drinking

The two main drags for **eating** and **drinking** in Fort Lauderdale are Las Olas and Sunrise boulevards.

Casablanca Café 3049 Alhambra St ☎954/764-3500. An American piano bar in a Moroccan setting, serving a good, eclectic, and moderately priced menu of Mediterranean-influenced American fare. Live music most nights.
Ernie's BBQ Lounge 1843 S Federal Hwy (US-1) ☎954/523-8636. Scruffy but likeable place, south of downtown, famous for its glorious conch chowder.
The Floridian 1410 E Las Olas Blvd ☎954/463-4041. Retro decor and outstanding diner food – especially the mammoth breakfasts – at rock-bottom prices. Open 24hr.
Mangos 904 E Las Olas Blvd ☎954/523-5001. Decent dining, though most people go for the people-watching along Las Olas, and the energetic

workout, dancing to roaring live rock/R&B/jazz jams at this singles scene.
Seasons 52 2428 E Sunrise Blvd at the Galleria Mall ☎954/537-1052. Health-conscious regional restaurant chain where every one of the fresh and tasty seasonal dishes has less than 475 calories. There's also a good wine list.
Southport Raw Bar 1536 Cordova Rd ☎954/525-2526. South of downtown, near Port Everglades, this boisterous local bar specializes in succulent crustaceans and well-prepared fish dishes.
Taverna Opa 3051 NE 32nd St ☎954/567-1630. A raucous good time can be had at this fun Greek establishment, complete with flowing ouzo and crashing dishes. Dinner only.

Boca Raton

BOCA RATON (literally, "the mouth of the rat"), twenty miles north of Fort Lauderdale, is noteworthy mostly for its abundance of **Mediterranean Revival architecture**. This style, prevalent here since the 1920s, has been kept alive in the downtown area by strict building codes. New structures must incorporate arched entranceways, fake bell towers, and red-tiled roofs whenever possible, ensuring a consistent and distinctive "look."

This all goes back to architect Addison Mizner, who swept into Boca Raton on the tide of the Florida property boom in 1925, buying up 1600 acres of farmland. Mizner was influenced by the medieval architecture he'd seen around the Mediterranean, and the few public buildings he completed (along with close to fifty homes) left an indelible mark on Boca Raton (Mizner also shaped the look of nearby Palm Beach). His million-dollar *Cloister Inn*, for example, grew into the present **Boca Raton Resort and Club**, 501 E Camino Real, a pink palace of marble columns, sculptured fountains, and carefully aged wood (☎1-888/491-BOCA, ⓦwww.bocaresort.com; ❾). Mizner's spirit is also invoked at **Mizner Park**, off US-1 between Palmetto Park Rd and Glades Rd, a stylish open-air shopping plaza adorned with palm trees and waterfalls. The park is home to the **Boca Raton Museum of Art**, 501 Plaza Real (Tues, Thurs & Fri 10am–5pm, Wed 10am–9pm, Sat & Sun noon–5pm; $8; ☎561/392-2500, ⓦwww.bocamuseum.org), worth a stop for its drawings by modern European masters – Degas, Matisse, Picasso – and a formidable collection of African art.

A mile north of Hwy-798 (which links downtown Boca Raton with the beach), at 1801 N Ocean Blvd/Hwy-A1A, the **Gumbo Limbo Nature Center** (Mon–Sat 9am–4pm, Sun noon–4pm; $3 donation; ☎561/338-1473, ⓦwww.gumbolimbo. org) covers twenty acres inhabited by osprey, brown pelicans, and sea turtles. Reserve well in advance for the night turtle-watching tours offered between May and July.

A couple miles north of downtown, Boca Raton's most explorable **beachside** area is **Spanish River Park** (daily 8am–sunset; cars $16–18, pedestrians and cyclists free). Most of these fifty acres of lush vegetation and high-rise greenery are only penetrable on trails through shady thickets.

Practicalities

Greyhound does not serve Boca Raton. **Tri-Rail** stops off I-95, at 680 Yamato Rd (☎1-800/TRI-RAIL); there's a connecting shuttle to the town center. The **Chamber of Commerce** is at 1800 N Dixie Hwy (Mon–Thurs 8.30am–5pm, Fri 8.30am–4pm; ☎561/395-4433, ⓦwww.bocaratonchamber.com). The *Townplace Suites by Marriott*, 5110 NW 8th Ave (☎561/994-7232; ❸), and *Ocean Lodge*, 531 N Ocean Blvd (☎561/395-7772; ❹), are two **hotels** providing reasonable value for money. For **eating**, the upscale *Max's Grill*, 404 Plaza Real (☎561/368-0080), has appealing American dishes with Asian influences, while the elegantly casual *Gigi's*, 346 Plaza Real (☎561/368-4488), serves good French bistro fare.

Palm Beach

A small island town of palatial homes and gardens, with streets so clean you could eat off them, **PALM BEACH** has been synonymous for nearly a century with the kind of lifestyle only limitless loot can buy. The nation's wealthy began wintering here in the 1890s, after Henry Flagler brought his East Coast railroad south from St Augustine, building two luxury hotels on this then-secluded, palm-filled island. Since then, the rich and famous have flocked here to become part of the Palm Beach elite. Joe Kennedy – father of John, Robert, and Ted – bought the so-called Kennedy Compound here in 1933.

Lined with designer stores and high-class art galleries, **Worth Avenue**, close to the southern tip of the island, is a good place to see some of the town's Addison Mizner-inspired **architecture**: stucco walls, Romanesque facades, passageways leading to small courtyards, and spiral staircases climbing to the upper levels.

Where Cocoanut Row and Whitehall Way meet, the white Doric columns front Whitehall, also known as the **Flagler Museum** (Tues–Sat 10am–5pm, Sun noon–5pm; $10; ☎561/655-2833, ⓦwww.flagler.org). This, the most overtly ostentatious home on the island, was a $4 million wedding present from Henry Flagler to his third wife, Mary Lily Kenan. As in many of Florida's first luxury homes, the interior design was lifted from the great buildings of Europe: among the 73 rooms are an Italian library, a French salon, and a Louis XV ballroom. All are stuffed with ornamentation, but they lack aesthetic cohesion.

Built in 1926 in the style of an Italianate palace, **The Breakers** hotel, on South County Road off the main strip (⊤561/655-6611 or 1-888/BREAKERS, ⓦwww.thebreakers.com; ⓔ), operates as the last of Palm Beach's swanky resorts. Its design includes elaborate painted ceilings and huge tapestries. Take the guided tour on Wednesdays at 2pm (free for guests, $15 for the public; for information, call ⊤561/655-6611 ext 7691).

Practicalities

In keeping with the upper-crust atmosphere, **public transportation** options around Palm Beach are limited. The West Palm Beach Amtrak (⊤1-800/USA-RAIL), Tri-Rail (⊤1-800/TRI-RAIL), and Greyhound (⊤561/833-8534) stations are all located at 205 S Tamarind Ave in West Palm Beach on the mainland. To get to Palm Beach from there, take any PalmTran bus ($1.25; ⊤561/841-4BUS) terminating at Quadrille Blvd, and transfer to the #41, or the #42 (no Sun service). By car, from I-95 and points west, take Okeechobee Boulevard east into Palm Beach.

The **Convention and Visitors' Bureau** is at 1555 Palm Beach Lakes Blvd, Suite 800 (Mon–Fri 9am–5pm; ⊤561/233-3000, ⓦwww.palmbeachfl.com). You'll need plenty of money to **stay** here: prices of $200 a night are not uncommon (rates are cheapest between May and Dec). The elaborate, antique-furnished ✦ *Palm Beach Historic Inn*, 365 S County Rd (⊤561/832-4009, ⓦwww.palmbeachhistoricinn.com; ⓔ), offers some of the best rates in town, but you'll need to reserve early. The equally opulent *The Chesterfield*, 363 Cocoanut Row (⊤561/659-5800, ⓦwww.chesterfieldpb.com; ⓔ), is another good choice. *Charley's Crab*, 456 S Ocean Blvd (⊤561/659-1500), is the place to go for reasonably priced **seafood**, while the lunch counter at *Hamburger Heaven*, 314 S County Rd (⊤561/655-5277), has been serving its delicious **burgers** since 1945. If money is no object – and you're dressed to kill – make for *Café L'Europe*, 331 S County Rd (⊤561/655-4020): spend less than $50 a head in this super-elegant French restaurant and you'll walk away hungry.

The Space Coast

About two hundred miles north of Palm Beach, the so-called **Space Coast** is the base of the country's space industry. The focal point is the much-visited **Kennedy Space Center**, which occupies a flat, marshy island bulging into the Atlantic. In stark contrast, the rest of the island is taken over by a sizable nature preserve, the **Merritt Island National Wildlife Refuge**, offering great opportunities for seeing wildlife, especially birds.

The Kennedy Space Center

The **Kennedy Space Center** is the nucleus of the US space program: it's here that space vehicles are developed, tested, and blasted into orbit. **Merritt Island** has been the center of NASA's activity since 1964, when the launch pads at Cape Canaveral US Air Force base, across the water, proved too small to cope with the giant new Saturn V rockets used to launch the Apollo misions.

To reach the **Visitor Complex** (daily 9am–6pm; $31 adults, $21 children; Maximum Access Badge $38 adults, $28 children; ⊤321/449-4444, ⓦwww.

kennedyspacecenter.com), take exit 212 off I-95 to Hwy-405, and follow the signs; you can also get here by connecting with Hwy-3 off Hwy-A1A. The best **times to visit** are on weekends and in May and September, when crowds are thinner – but at any time, you should still allow an entire day for everything the Space Center has to offer and try to arrive early in the morning. Check the weather, too, as thunderstorms may force some attractions to close.

The various exhibits in the Visitor Complex – mission capsules, space suits, lunar modules, a mock-up Space Shuttle flight deck – will keep anyone with the slightest interest in space exploration interested for a couple of hours. Afterwards, be sure to watch the two impressive IMAX movies dealing with some space theme or other and take a stroll around the open-air **Rocket Garden**, full of deceptively simple rockets from the 1950s, cleverly illuminated to show how they looked at blast off. The remainder of the visit is comprised of a two-hour guided **bus tour**. The bus passes the 52-story Vehicle Assembly Building (where Space Shuttles are prepared for launch), stops to view the launch pad, and winds up with an opportunity to inspect a Saturn V rocket and witness a simulated Apollo countdown. For the dates and times of **real-life launches**, call ☎321/449-4444 or check the website listed above. Various launch-viewing packages are offered (and sell out very quickly), but you get almost as good a view from anywhere within forty miles of the Space Center.

Near the Space Center, on Hwy-405 in Titusville, the **Astronaut Hall of Fame** (daily 9am–6.30pm; $17, or free admission with same-day Maximum Access

△ The Kennedy Space Center

Badge; see p.636) is one of Florida's most entertaining interactive museums, where exhibits allow you to experience G-force, a bumpy ride along the surface of Mars, and flight simulators.

Practicalities: Cocoa Beach

The closest **motels** to the Kennedy Space Center are on the mainland along US-1 (in Titusville, for example) – or, if you're looking for a more picturesque location, in **COCOA BEACH**, a few miles south on a ten-mile strip of shore washed by some of the biggest surfing waves in Florida. Options include the *Luna Sea*, 3185 N Atlantic Ave (T1-800/586-2732; Wwww.lunaseacocoabeach.com; ❹), *Days Inn*, 5500 N Atlantic Ave (T321/784-2550; Wwww.daysinncocoabeach.com; ❹), and *Fawlty Towers*, 100 E Cocoa Beach Causeway (T321/784-3870; Wwww. fawltytowersresort.com; ❸). For great oysters and super riverfront views, head for *Sunset Café*, 500 W Cocoa Beach Causeway (T321/783-8485) – but go early, as it's frequently mobbed. A good **dinner** option is *Atlantic Ocean Grille*, on the Cocoa Beach Pier (T321/783-7549), which has a quality, somewhat expensive menu that's especially strong on seafood.

Merritt Island National Wildlife Refuge

NASA doesn't have Merritt Island all to itself: the agency shares it with the **Merritt Island National Wildlife Refuge** (daily sunrise–sunset; free). Alligators, armadillos, raccoons, and bobcats – as well as one of Florida's greatest gatherings of birdlife – live right up against some of the human world's most advanced hardware. Winter (Oct–March) is the best time to visit, when the skies are alive with birds migrating from the frozen north and mosquitoes are nowhere to be found. At any other time, especially in summer, the island's Mosquito Lagoon is worthy of its name: bring repellent.

Eight miles off I-95's exit 220, Hwy-406 leads to the seven-mile **Black Point Wildlife Drive**, which gives a solid introduction to the basics of the island's eco-system; pick up the free leaflet at the entrance. Be sure to walk in the refuge, too: off the Wildlife Drive, the five-mile **Cruickshank Trail** weaves around the edge of the Indian River. Drive a few miles farther east along Hwy-402 – branching from Hwy-406 just south of the Wildlife Drive and passing the **visitor center** (Mon–Fri 8am–4.30pm, Sat & Sun 9am–5pm; closed Sun April–Oct; T321/861-0667) – and then hike the half-mile **Oak Hammock Trail** or the two-mile **Palm Hammock Trail**, both accessible from the visitor center parking lot.

Daytona Beach

The consummate Florida beach town, with its T-shirt shops, amusement arcades, and wall-to-wall motels, **DAYTONA BEACH** owes its existence to twenty miles of enticing light brown sands. Once a favorite Spring Break destination, Daytona Beach has been trying to cultivate a more refined image in recent years. This has only been partially successful, with the partying students replaced by bikers and race-car fanatics. The town hosts three major annual events: the legendary **Daytona 500** stock-car race in February (tickets from $95; call T386/253-7223 or visit Wwww.daytonainternationalspeedway.com); **Bike Week**, in early March, which attracts thousands of leather-clad bikers; and the relatively new **Biketoberfest**, in October, a scaled down, more family orientated version of Bike Week.

The origin of Daytona's race-car and motorcycle obsession goes back to the early 1900s, when pioneering auto enthusiasts including Louis Chevrolet, Ransom Olds, and Henry Ford came to Daytona's firm sands to race prototype vehicles beside the ocean. In fact, the world land speed record was smashed here five times by the British millionaire Malcolm Campbell. As increasing speeds made racing on the sands unsafe, the **Daytona International Speedway**, an ungainly configuration of concrete and steel holding 150,000 people, was opened in 1959 three miles west of downtown along International Speedway Boulevard (buses #9, #10 and #60).

Though they can't capture the excitement of a race, **guided trolley tours** (daily except race days 9.30am–5.30pm, every half-hour; $8.50) do provide a first-hand look at the remarkable gradients that help make this the fastest racetrack in the world. Occupying a large building next to the Speedway, the interactive exhibits that comprise **Daytona USA** (daily 9am–7pm; $21.50; ☎386/947-6800) let you have a virtual try at jacking a race-car off the ground during a pit-stop and commentating on a race, while an engaging wide-screen film complete with excellent 3-D effects tells you all about NASCAR (National Association of Stock Car Auto Racing).

For all the excitement that racing generates, the best thing about Daytona is the seemingly limitless **beach**: it's 500 feet wide at low tide, and fades dreamily off into the heat haze. Daytona is also one of the few beaches in Florida you can drive on – pay $5 (Feb–Nov only) at the various entrances and follow the posted procedures. Another, less heralded but worthwhile thing to do in Daytona Beach is visit the eclectic **Museum of the Arts and Sciences**, a mile south of the Speedway at 1040 Museum Blvd (Mon–Sat 9am–5pm, Sun 11am–5pm; $12.95; ☎386/255-0285, ⓦwww.moas.org), whose diverse collection includes the reassembled remains of a million-year-old giant ground sloth and the first Coca-Cola can sent to space.

Practicalities

US-1 (called, in town, Ridgewood Avenue) plows through mainland Daytona Beach, passing the **Greyhound** station at 138 S Ridgewood. **Trolleys** ($1) run the length of the beach until midnight from mid-January to early September. The **visitor center** is at 126 E Orange Ave (Mon–Fri 9am–5pm; ☎1-800/854-1234, ⓦwww.daytonabeach.com). If you're going to be in Daytona during any of the big events, **accommodation** should be booked at least six months ahead; and expect minimum stays and prices to at least double. Any of the **motels** along the oceanfront Atlantic Avenue makes a good beach base: there's the *Driftwood Beach Motel*, 657 S Atlantic Ave, slightly north of town in Ormond Beach (☎386/677-1331, ⓦwww.driftwoodmotel.com; ❸); or the welcoming, British-run ⭐ *Ocean Court*, 2315 S Atlantic Ave (☎386/253-8185, ⓦwww.oceancourt.com; ❸). Away from the beach, and close to lively Beach Street, the *Coquina Inn*, 544 S Palmetto Ave (☎386/254-4969; ⓦwww.coquinainndaytonabeach.com; ❸), is a cozy B&B.

Atlantic Avenue Ave is lined with the predictable fast food outlets, but for more inspiring **eating** options head to Beach Street on the mainland, where the fifties-style ⭐ *Daytona Diner* at no.290 1/2 N (☎386/258-8488) dishes up huge breakfasts for under $5 and *Angell & Phelps Restaurant & Wine Bar* at no. 156 S (☎386/257-2677) offers creative American-style gourmet cuisine in an informal setting. For fresh fish and seafood, head south toward Ponce Inlet, where you'll find the equally good *Lighthouse Landing*, beside the Ponce Inlet Lighthouse at 4940 S Peninsula Drive (☎386/761-9271), and *Inlet Harbor*, overlooking a marina at 133 Inlet Harbor Rd (☎386/767-5590). Daytona's excellent **nightlife** scene centers on Seabreeze Boulevard with its Spring Break-style discos such as *Razzles* at no. 611 (☎321/257-6236), Main Street with its raucous biker bars including *Boot Hill Saloon* at no.310 (☎386/258-9506), and Beach Street with more avant-garde choices like the gay-friendly ⭐ *Love Bar* at no. 116 N (drag shows Fri & Sat nights; ☎386/252-6040).

St Augustine

Forty miles north of Daytona Beach, US-1 passes through the heart of charismatic **ST AUGUSTINE**. Few places in Florida are as immediately engaging as this old city, with the size and even some of the looks of a small Mediterranean town. The oldest permanent settlement in the US, with much from its early days still intact along its narrow streets, it also offers two alluring lengths of **beach** just across Matanzas Bay.

Though Ponce de León touched ground here in 1513, European settlement didn't begin until half a century later, when Spain's Pedro Menéndez de Avilés put ashore on St Augustine's Day in 1565. The town developed into a major social and administrative center, soon to be capital of east Florida. Subsequently, Tallahassee (see p.667) became the capital of a unified Florida, and St Augustine's fortunes waned. Since then, expansion has largely bypassed the town – a fact inadvertently facilitating the restoration program that has turned this quiet community into a fine historical showcase.

Arrival and information

The Greyhound **bus** station, 1711 Dobbs Rd, is a couple of miles from the center of town. The **visitor center**, 10 Castillo Drive (daily 8.30am–5.30pm; ☎1-800/653-2489, ⓦwww.visitoldcity.com), shows a film ($1) on the history of the town, has recommendations for a variety of tours (see below), and information on numerous local festivals, including torch-lit processions and a Menorcan Fiesta.

St Augustine is best seen **on foot**, though two **sightseeing trains** tour the main landmarks (daily 8.30am–4pm; $18; get tickets from the visitor center or at many B&Bs and hotels). There's **no public transportation**, so if you want to get to the beaches two miles away and you don't have a car you'll have to either **rent a bike** from the youth hostel (see below) or take a **taxi** (Ancient City Cabs; ☎904/824-8161). The Old Town Trolley sightseeing train includes free transport on the **Beach Bus**. As for organized **tours**, harbor cruises by Scenic Cruise ($15; ☎904/824-1806) leave four to six times a day from the Municipal Marina, near the foot of King Street. The well-organized and informative Tour St Augustine ($10; ☎1-800/797-3778) leads historical walking tours, while various spooky sites are visited during the "A Ghostly Experience" nighttime walking tour ($12; ☎904/461-1009).

Accommodation

The Old Town has many excellent restored **inns** offering bed-and-breakfast, and there are cheaper chain **hotels** outside the center of town along San Marco Avenue and Ponce de León Boulevard. Note that rates generally rise by $15–50 on weekends.

Carriage Way 70 Cuna St ☎1-800/908-9832, ⓦwww.carriageway.com. Canopy and four-poster beds, clawfoot tubs, and antiques add to the period feel of this 1880s house. ❹

Casa Monica 95 Cordova St ☎1-800/648-1888, ⓦwww.casamonica.com. Elegant, beautifully restored Spanish-style hotel that has hosted the king and queen of Spain. Book well in advance. ❽

Quality Inn Historic 1111 Ponce de León Blvd ☎1-800/575-5288. Ordinary, reasonably priced rooms a 20min walk from the center. Free Internet and continental breakfast. ❷

Kenwood Inn 38 Marine St ☎904/824-2116, ⓦwww.thekenwoodinn.com. Peacefully situated near the waterfront, this charming B&B has a pretty pool and offers complimentary use of bikes for guests. ❹

Pirate Haus Inn 32 Treasury St ☎904/808-1999, ⓦwww.piratehaus.com. The town's only hostel accommodation, near the Plaza, is popular with backpackers. It has a giant kitchen and a common room stuffed with guidebooks. Beds in air-conditioned dorms are $16.50; five private rooms. ❷ **Seaway** 481 Hwy-A1A ☏904/471-3466. This small motel is one of several quality family-oriented establishments on busy St Augustine Beach. ❸ **Vilano Beach Motel** 50 Vilano Rd ☏904/829-2651, ⓦwww.vilanobeachmotel.com. Laid-back Art Deco motel that makes a great base for enjoying the beaches north of town. ❸

The Old Town

Bordered on the west by St George Street, and on the south by Plaza de la Constitucion, St Augustine's **Old Town** holds the well-tended evidence of the town's Spanish period. It may be small, but there's a lot to see: an early start, around 9am, will give you a lead on the tourist crowds, and should allow a good look at almost everything in one day.

Given the fine state of the **Castillo de San Marcos National Monument**, on the northern edge of the Old Town beside the bay (daily 8.45am–4.45pm; $6; ⓦwww.nps.gov/casa), it's difficult to believe that the fortress was built in the late 1600s. Its longevity is due to its design: a diamond-shaped rampart at each corner maximized firepower, and fourteen-feet-thick walls reduced its vulnerability to attack. Inside, there's not a lot to see besides a small museum and echoing rooms, though venturing along the 35-foot ramparts gives good views across the city and the bay.

A hundred yards west of the monument, the eighteenth-century **City Gate** marks the entrance to **St George Street**, once the main thoroughfare and now a tourist-trampled, though genuinely historic, pedestrianized strip. You'll find a bunch of places called "The oldest..." in St Augustine; the **Oldest Wooden Schoolhouse**, set in lush gardens at 14 St George St (daily 9am–5pm; $3), is one of the most atmospheric – a restored wooden shack with speaking wax dummies portraying nineteenth-century schoolchildren.

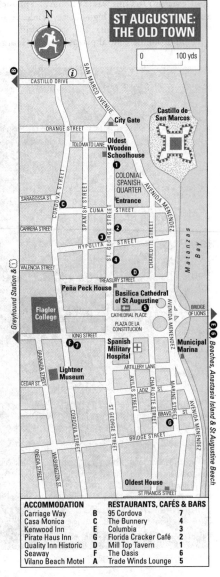

ST AUGUSTINE: THE OLD TOWN

0   100 yds

ACCOMMODATION

Carriage Way	B
Casa Monica	C
Kenwood Inn	E
Pirate Haus Inn	G
Quality Inn Historic	D
Seaway	F
Vilano Beach Motel	A

RESTAURANTS, CAFÉS & BARS

95 Cordova	7
The Bunnery	4
Columbia	3
Florida Cracker Café	2
Mill Top Tavern	1
The Oasis	6
Trade Winds Lounge	5

Heading south on St George Street, a fair-sized plot between Tolomato Lane and Cuna Street is taken up by the excellent **Colonial Spanish Quarter** (daily 9am–5.30pm; $6.50). In its nine reconstructed homes and workshops, volunteers dressed as Spanish settlers go about their business at spinning-wheels, anvils, and foot-driven wood lathes.

For a more intimate look at local life during a slightly later period, head a little further south to the **Peña Peck House**, 143 St George St (Mon–Sat noon–5pm; free). Thought to have originally been the Spanish treasury, by the time the British took over in 1763 this was the home of a physician and his gregarious spouse, who turned the place into a high-society rendezvous.

In the sixteenth century, the Spanish king decreed that all colonial towns must be built around a central plaza; thus, St George Street runs into the **Plaza de la**

△ Castillo de San Marcos

Constitucion, a marketplace from 1598. On the plaza's north side, the **Basilica Cathedral of St Augustine** (daily 7am–5pm; donation) adds a touch of grandeur, although it's largely a Sixties remodelling of the late eighteenth-century original.

Tourist numbers lessen as you cross **south of the plaza** into a web of quiet, narrow streets, all just as old as St George Street. West of the plaza along King Street, opposite Flagler College, the opulent **Lightner Museum** (daily 9am–5pm, last admission 4pm; $8; ☎904/824-2874) displays fine and decorative arts in the former building of one of the most fabulous resorts of the late nineteenth century. More substantial history is available in a ten-minute walk southeast from here, at 14 St Francis St, in the form of the fascinating **Oldest House** (daily 9am–5pm; $8), which is indeed the oldest house in town, dating from the early 1700s. Its rooms are furnished to show how the house – and people's lives – changed as new eras unfolded.

The beaches

Some fine **beaches** – busiest at weekends – lie just a couple of miles east from the Old Town. Crossing the bay via the Bridge of Lions, and continuing east on Hwy-A1A will bring you to the **Anastasia State Recreation Area**, on Anastasia Island (daily 8am–sunset; cars $3–5, cyclists and pedestrians $1), which offers a thousand protected acres of dunes, marshes, and scrub, linked by nature walks. A few miles further south, **St Augustine Beach** is family terrain, with some good restaurants and a fishing pier. North of Old Town (take May St, off San Marco Ave), the broad **Vilano Beach** pulls a younger crowd.

Eating, drinking, and entertainment

Eating in the Old Town can be expensive, and a number of its cafés and restaurants are closed in the evening. Of those that stay open, several double as **drinking** spots and some have **live music**.

95 Cordova at the *Casa Monica* hotel, 95 Cordova St ☎904/810-6810. This luxurious and elegant restaurant's menu features expensive but masterful nouvelle continental cuisine.
The Bunnery 121 St George St ☎904/829-6166. Good coffee and economical breakfasts, plus tempting sandwiches and paninis, served in an old Spanish bakery.
Columbia 98 St George St ☎904/824-3341. Enjoy paella, tapas and other traditional Spanish/ Cuban food in a sumptuous setting of fountains and candlelight.
Florida Cracker Café 81 St George St ☎904/829-0397. Offering an eclectic and reasonably priced mix of combo salads, conch fritters and

homemade desserts.
Mill Top Tavern 19 1/2 George St ☎904/829-2329. There's a terrific, funky atmosphere at the top of this nineteenth-century mill, where you'll hear live music and get a great, open-air view of the Castillo.
The Oasis 4000 Ocean Trace Rd, St Augustine Beach ☎904/471-3424. This beach bar is famous for its burgers with their multitude of tasty toppings.
Trade Winds Lounge 124 Charlotte St ☎904/826-1590. Convivial bar where you can tap your feet to country and western and rock 'n' roll bands.

Jacksonville

Situated in the great double loop of the St Johns River, **JACKSONVILLE** struggled for years to throw off its longstanding reputation as a dour industrial port city with a deeply conservative population. During the 1990s, the city began to gain standing as a new service industry center, bringing a spate of construction projects and new homebuyers to the area. And in the lead-up to the city's hosting of the 2005 Super Bowl football championship, efforts were made to enhance Jacksonville's beauty by creating parks and riverside boardwalks. However, the sheer size of the city – at 841 square miles, the largest in the US – serves to dilute its easygoing character.

The most noteworthy building in the downtown area, which occupies the north bank of the St Johns River, is the **Florida Theater**, 128 E Forsyth St. Elvis Presley arrived here in 1957 for his first appearance on an indoor stage, an event presided over by juvenile court judge to ensure that it wasn't too suggestive. The theater's interior has since been restored with a dazzling gold proscenium arch, and today it's used for a variety of performances. Five minutes' walk from the theater, at 333 N Laura St, the **Jacksonville Museum of Modern Art** (Tues & Fri 11am–5pm, Wed & Thurs 11am–9pm, Sat 11am–4pm, Sun noon–4pm; $6, free Wed after 5pm; ☎904/366-6911, ⓦwww.jmoma.org) has paintings, sculptures, and photography of surprising scope and depth, including large Ed Paschke and James Rosenquist canvases.

Crossing over to the south bank via the River Taxi ($3 one way; $5 roundtrip), you'll find the **Museum of Science and History**, 1025 Museum Circle (Mon–Fri 10am–5pm, Sat 10am–6pm, Sun 1–6pm; $8; ☎904/396-6674, ⓦwww.themosh. org), with its hands-on exhibits and planetarium.

Just south of the Fuller Warren River bridge (I-95), the **Cummer Museum of Art and Gardens**, 829 Riverside Ave (Tues & Thurs 10am–9pm, Wed, Fri & Sat 10am–5pm, Sun noon–5pm; $8, free Tues after 4pm; ☎904/356-6857, ⓦwww. cummer.org), has spacious rooms and sculpture-lined corridors containing works by prominent European and American masters. The two acres of lovely Italianate and English gardens that overlook the river are an added bonus.

From all over Jacksonville you can see the 73,000-seat Alltel Stadium, home to the **Jacksonville Jaguars** football franchise (tickets from $35–215; ☎1-877/4JAGS-TIX). It's also the scene of the Florida–Georgia college football clash each fall – an excuse for 48 hours of citywide drinking and partying. Next door is **Metropolitan Park**, a pleasant swath of riverside greenery.

Practicalities

From the Greyhound **bus station** downtown at 10 N Pearl St, it's an easy walk to the **Convention and Visitors Bureau**, 550 Water St, suite 1000 (Mon–Fri 8am–5pm; ☎1-800/733-2668, ⓦwww.jaxcvb.com). The **train station** is an awkward six miles northwest of downtown at 3570 Clifford Lane. The cheapest **accommodation** can be found at the chain hotels on the city's perimeter, such as *Comfort Suites*, 1180 Airport Rd (☎904/741-0505; ❹). Downtown, the ⚘ *Hyatt Regency Jacksonville Riverfront*, 225 Coastline Drive (☎1-800/233-1234, ⓦwww. jacksonville.hyatt.com; ❺), has a great riverfront location. Alternatively, head to the Riverside-Avondale residential neighborhood (near the Cummer Museum) for a choice of good B&Bs, including the riverfront *The House on Cherry Street*, 1844 Cherry St (☎904/384-1999, ⓦwww.geocities.com/houseoncherryst; ❹). For **eating**, you'll find several places for a quick and filling lunch at the Jacksonville Landing mall, downtown between Water St and the river. On the south bank, the *River City Brewing Co.*, 835 Museum Circle (☎904/398-2299), offers great steaks, home-brewed beer, and river views, while Riverside-Avondale has some appealing cafés such as *Biscotti's Expresso Café*, 3556 St Johns Ave (☎904/387-2060).

Jacksonville's beaches

Traveling south from Jacksonville on I-95, then east on Hwy-202, you'll first hit **Ponte Vedra Beach**, whose crowd-free sands and million-dollar homes form one of the most exclusive communities in northeast Florida. A few miles north from here on Hwy-A1A is the much less snooty **Jacksonville Beach**. If you tire of watching the novice surfers, **Adventure Landing**, 1944 Beach Blvd (Sun–Thurs 10am–11pm, Fri & Sat 10am–1am; ☎904/246-4386, ⓦwww.adventurelanding.com), offers an amusement park where each diversion is individually priced, like batting cages ($2), a water park ($23.99), and go-carts ($6). Two miles north of Jacksonville Beach's old pier, the more commercialized **Neptune Beach** blurs into the identical-looking **Atlantic Beach**; both are more family-oriented, and are best visited for eating and socializing.

Practicalities

The best **accommodation** is at the renovated ⚓ *Sea Turtle Inn*, 1 Ocean Blvd, Atlantic Beach (☎1-800/874-6000, ⓦwww.seaturtle.com; ⑤), while the cozy *Pelican Path B&B*, 11 N 19th Ave, Jacksonville Beach (☎1-888/749-1177, ⓦwww.pelicanpath.com; ⑤), has bicycles. Good **eating options** at the beaches are *Ragtime Tavern Seafood Grill*, 207 Atlantic Blvd, Atlantic Beach (☎904/241-7877), with its extensive seafood menu; *Sun Dog Diner*, 207 Atlantic Blvd, Neptune Beach (☎904/241-8221), offering above-average, creative diner fare; and ⚓ *Beach Hut Café*, 1281 S 3rd St, Jacksonville Beach (☎904/249-3516), serving huge, delicious breakfasts.

Central Florida

Encompassing a broad and fertile expanse between the east and west coasts, most of **Central Florida** was farming country when vacation-mania first struck the beachside strips. From the 1970s on, this picture of tranquility was shattered: no section of the state has been affected more dramatically by modern tourism. As a result, the most-visited part of Florida can also be one of the ugliest. A clutter of freeway interchanges, motels, and billboards arch around the sprawling city of **Orlando**, where a tourist-dollar chase of Gold Rush magnitude was sparked by **Walt Disney World**, the biggest and cleverest theme-park complex ever created. The rest of central Florida is quiet by comparison.

Orlando and the theme parks

Once a quiet farming town, **ORLANDO** now welcomes more visitors than any other place in the state. The reason, of course, is **Walt Disney World**, which, along with **Universal Orlando**, **SeaWorld Orlando**, and a host of other attractions, in varying degrees of quality, pulls millions of people a year to a previously featureless plot of scrubland. Most of the hotels are found along International Drive, Hwy-192 or in and around Disney World, all of which lie several miles south of the downtown area, which has the city's best nightlife.

Arrival and information

The **international airport** is nine miles south of downtown Orlando; local buses (see p.646) link the airport with downtown (#11 or #51) and International Drive (#42). Alternatively, **shuttle buses** such as Mears Transportation

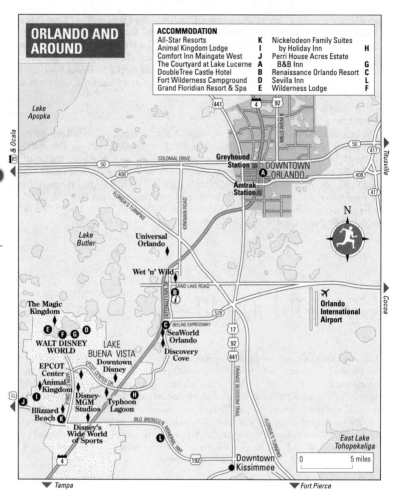

ORLANDO AND AROUND

ACCOMMODATION

All-Star Resorts	K	Nickelodeon Family Suites	
Animal Kingdom Lodge	I	by Holiday Inn	H
Comfort Inn Maingate West	J	Perri House Acres Estate	
The Courtyard at Lake Lucerne	A	B&B Inn	G
DoubleTree Castle Hotel	B	Renaissance Orlando Resort	C
Fort Wilderness Campground	D	Sevilla Inn	L
Grand Floridian Resort & Spa	E	Wilderness Lodge	F

(24hrs; ☎407/423-5566) charge a flat fee of $15 to any hotel in downtown or on International Drive and $17 to Hwy-192 and Disney. **Taxis** to these destinations cost between $30 and $60. **Buses** and **trains** arrive, respectively downtown at the Greyhound terminal, 555 N John Young Parkway (☎407/292-3422), and the Amtrak station, 1400 Slight Blvd (☎407/843-7611). The efficient **Official Visitor Center**, 8723 International Drive (daily 8am–7pm; ☎407/363-5872, ⓦwww.orlandoinfo.com) has a plethora of brochures and discount coupons.

Getting around

You have to be determined to get to the theme parks without a car, but it can be done. Local Lynx **buses** (☎1-800/344-LYNX, ⓦwww.golynx.com) converge at the downtown Orlando terminal, 455 N Garland Ave. Route #50 heads to Walt Disney World, while route #8 goes to International Drive. Along International Drive (including SeaWorld Orlando), the **I-Ride trolley service** (☎1-866/243-7483, ⓦwww.iridetrolley.

com) operates every twenty minutes daily from 8am to 10.30pm, costing 75¢ one way. **Taxis** are the best way to get around at night – try Yellow Cab (☎407/699-9999); rates begin at $3.25 for the first mile, plus $1.75 for each additional mile.

Accommodation outside Walt Disney World

If you're on a budget, or want to spend time visiting the other parks, you'd do best to stay **outside Walt Disney World**. The chain hotels on **International Drive** are the closest to Universal Orlando and SeaWorld Orlando with numerous restaurants and shops within walking distance. There are several hotels dotted around Disney property in an area called **Lake Buena Vista**, while budget hotels line **Hwy-192** (which is also close to Disney). **Downtown** Orlando has some charming, privately-run hotels and B&Bs.

Comfort Inn Maingate West 9330 W Hwy-192 ☎407/424-8420 or 1-800/440-4473. This hotel's yellow exterior matches the bright, cheerful rooms. A pleasant, economical place to stay, 5 mins west of Disney. ❷

The Courtyard at Lake Lucerne 211 N Lucerne Cirle E ☎1-800/444-5289, ⓦwww.orlandohistoricinn.com. Choose from Victorian- and Edwardian-era rooms or airy Art Deco suites at this charming downtown hotel. ❹

DoubleTree Castle Hotel 8629 International Drive ☎1-800/952-2785, ⓦwww.doubletreecastle.com. This elaborate and comfortable theme hotel, complete with Renaissance music and medieval decor, offers free transportation to the theme parks. ❹

Nickelodeon Family Suites by Holiday Inn 14500 Continental Gateway, Lake Buena Vista ☎1-866/462-6425, ⓦwww.nickhotel.

com. The leader in kid-friendly resorts, with bunk bed- and video game-equipped suites, free kid's meals, and even a spa for the little ones. ❺

Perri House Acres Estate B&B Inn 10417 Vista Oaks Court, Lake Buena Vista ☎1-800/780-4830, ⓦwww.perrihouse.com. The incongruous presence of an eight-room B&B hidden on four wooded acres just a stone's throw from the opulent resorts of Disney is the perfect antidote to all the theme-park frenzy. ❺

Renaissance Orlando Resort 6677 Sea Harbor Drive ☎1-800/327-6677. An upscale hotel off International Drive directly opposite SeaWorld Orlando, with spacious rooms and an attractive atrium. ❻

Sevilla Inn 4640 W Hwy-192 ☎1-800/367-1363, ⓦwww.sevillainn.com. Privately owned, unpretentious and cheap motel providing a refreshing change from the chain motels. ❷

Accommodation within Walt Disney World

Prices at the fabulously designed **Disney World resorts** (reservations for all: ☎407/939-6244 or ⓦwww.disneyworld.com) scattered around the complex are much higher – sometimes more than $300 per night – than you'll pay elsewhere. However, the benefits (top-notch facilities, free transportation and parking, early access to the parks) can make it worth the extra cash. Though rooms may be available at short notice during the quieter times, you should **reserve as far in advance** – nine months is not unreasonable – as possible.

A good option if you're **camping**, the *Fort Wilderness Campground* is set on a lovely 700-acre forested site near the Magic Kingdom. Here you can hook up your RV or pitch your tent for $41–55, or rent a six-berth cabin from $249, and still enjoy the privileges of being a Disney guest.

All-Star Resorts Three resorts in the Disney-MGM area near the Blizzard Beach water park, with themes based on sports, music, and movies. The most affordable options in Disney, but still perfectly comfortable. ❹

Animal Kingdom Lodge Wake up to see African wildlife grazing outside your window at one of Disney's more spectacular and luxurious resorts. ❽

Grand Floridian Resort & Spa Gabled roofs, verandahs, crystal chandeliers, and a full-service spa make this Disney's most elegant – and expensive – resort. ❾

Wilderness Lodge This convincing re-creation of a frontier log cabin features a wood-burning fire in the lobby and welcoming rooms. ❽

Walt Disney World

As significant as air-conditioning in making the state what it is today, **WALT DIS-NEY WORLD** turned a wedge of Florida farmland into one of the world's most lucrative vacation destinations. The immense and astutely planned empire also pushed the state's media profile through the roof: from being a down-at-the-heel mixture of cheap motels, retirement homes, and down-at-the-heel alligator zoos, Florida suddenly, in 1971, became a showcase of modern international tourism.

Disney World is the pacesetter among theme parks. It goes way beyond Disneyland (see p.1065), which opened in Anaheim, California, in 1955, delivering escapism at its most technologically advanced and psychologically brilliant, across an area twice the size of Manhattan. Its four main theme parks are quite separate entities and, ideally, you should allow a full day for each. The **Magic Kingdom** is the Disney park of popular imagination, where Mickey mingles with the crowds – very much the park for kids, though at its high-tech best capable of thrilling even the most jaded of adults. Known for its giant, golfball-like geosphere, **EPCOT** is Disney's celebration of science and technology; this sprawling area involves a lot of walking, and may bore young children. **Disney-MGM Studios** suits almost everyone: its special effects are enjoyable even if you've never seen the movies they're based on. The newest of the four, Disney's **Animal Kingdom**, brings all manner of African and Asian wildlife to the theme-park setting.

Along with the main parks, other forms of entertainment have been created to keep people on Disney property for as long as possible. There are two excellent water parks, **Blizzard Beach** and **Typhoon Lagoon**, a sports complex called **Disney's Wide World of Sports**, and **Downtown Disney**, where you can eat, drink, and dance the night away.

The Magic Kingdom

The **Magic Kingdom**, dominated by **Cinderella's Castle**, a stunning pseudo-Rhineland palace, follows the formula established by California's Disneyland, dividing into several themed sections: **Tomorrowland, Frontierland, Fantasyland, Adventureland, Liberty Square**, and **Mickey's Toontown Fair**. Fantasyland and Mickey's Toontown Fair are very much for the kids, while the other lands, and in particular Tomorrowland and Frontierland, have the edgier rides. Some attractions are identical to their California forebears, while others are unique or greatly improved. In Tomorrowland, the old favorite **Space Mountain** is in essence an ordinary roller coaster, yet one whose total darkness makes every jump and jolt unexpected. **Splash Mountain** employs water to great effect, culminating in a stunning 52-foot death-drop down a waterfall. **Big Thunder Mountain Railroad** puts you on board a runaway train, which trundles through Gold Rush California at a pace that won't upset younger riders.

You don't have to be a rollercoaster junkie to enjoy the Magic Kingdom. Many of the best rides in the park rely on "Audio-Animatronics" characters – impressive vocal robots of Disney invention – for their appeal. The most up-to-date are seen in **Stitch's Great Escape**, where the mischievous monster wreaks havoc on the audience, who feel, hear, and smell strange things in the dark. A wonderful visual treat is **The Timekeeper**, where you're taken on a trip through time by a zany robot (whose voice is provided by Robin Williams).

Elsewhere, make time for the **Haunted Mansion**, a mildly spooky ghost ride memorable for its spectacular holograms, the leisurely **Jungle Cruise** down the Amazon, Nile, and Mekong, past ferocious animals and cannibal camps, and **Pirates of the Caribbean**, the classic boat ride around a pirate-infested Caribbean island.

Fantasyland is mainly full of rather dated rides, but does have the recent **Mickey's PhilharMagic**, an enchanting 3D journey with Daffy Duck and other well-known characters, set to classic Disney soundtracks.

EPCOT

Even before the Magic Kingdom opened, Walt Disney was developing plans for **EPCOT** (Experimental Prototype Community of Tomorrow), conceived in 1966 as a real community experimenting with the new ideas and materials of the technologically advancing US. The idea failed to shape up as Disney had envisioned, though: EPCOT didn't open its gates until 1982, when global recession and ecological concerns had put a damper on the belief in the infallibility of science. One drawback of this park is simply its immense size: it's twice as big as the Magic Kingdom, and very sapping on the feet.

The unmissable 180-foot geosphere (unlike a semicircular geodesic *dome*, the geosphere is completely round) sits in the heart of **Future World**, which keeps close to EPCOT's original concept of exploring the history and researching the future of agriculture, transport, energy, and communication. Future World is divided into several pavilions (including the geosphere, with its enjoyable **Spaceship Earth** ride), each corporate-sponsored, and featuring its own rides, films, interactive computer exhibits, and games. The best of the attractions are **Mission: SPACE**, a realistic recreation of a mission to Mars, including real G-force on take-off; **Test Track**, a rollercoaster-style ride where you test a high-performance car; **Cranium Command**, where an Audio-Animatronics character is detailed to control the various functions of a 12-year-old boy's brain – a good mix of Disney imagination and humor; and the **3D** cinematic thrill of **Honey, I Shrunk the Audience**. The newest attraction, **Soarin'**, uses the latest flight simulator technology to sweep you off on a breathtaking hang-glider ride over California.

FLORIDA | Orlando and the theme parks

Information, tickets, and how to beat the crowds

For general Disney World **information**, call ☎407/939-6244 or visit ⊛www.disney-world.com. **Tickets** cost $71.36 (children aged 3–9 $59.64), and allow unlimited access to all shows and rides in one park only, for that day only. The **Magic Your Way** ticket saves money if you spread your visit over a number of days – for example, a seven-day ticket would cost $223.85 (children 3–9 $184.25). You can buy a Magic Your Way ticket for a maximum of ten days and you can only visit one park per day. If you want to move from park to park in the same day, you must add the **Park Hopper** option for an additional flat fee of $45. The **Water Park Fun and More** option allows you to add from three to six extra admissions (the exact number depends on the length of your basic Magic Your Way ticket) to Blizzard Beach, Typhoon Lagoon, DisneyQuest, Disney's Wide World of Sports, and Pleasure Island for a flat fee of $50. The **parking** lots cost $9 a day, but are free if you're staying at a Walt Disney World resort.

Each park is generally **open** daily from 9am to between 6pm and 10pm, depending on the time of year; pick up the current schedule when you arrive. Note that Disney's Animal Kingdom closes at 5pm. At its worst, waiting times for the most popular rides can be well over an hour. The best way to **beat the crowds** is to use Disney's FASTPASS system. Place your admission ticket into a machine at the entrance of the attraction; the machine returns it with another ticket that gives you a time to return to the attraction, usually about two hours later. When that time rolls around, you simply show up, hand your new ticket to the attendant and scoot to the front of the line. Another good tactic upon arrival is to rush to the far end of the park and work backwards, or to head straight for the big rides, getting them out of the way before the mid-afternoon crush.

Occupying the largest area in the park is the **World Showcase**, with eleven different "countries" represented by recognizable national landmarks or stereotypical scenes. The **restaurants** here are among the best in Disney World, and it's a great place to watch the spectacular nighttime sound- and light-show, **IllumiNations: Reflections of Earth**.

Disney-MGM Studios

When the Disney corporation began making films and TV shows for adults – most notably *Who Framed Roger Rabbit?* in 1988 – they also set about devising a theme park to entertain adults as much as kids. Buying the rights to the Metro-Goldwyn-Mayer (MGM) collection of films and TV shows, Disney acquired a vast array of instantly familiar images to mold into shows and rides. Opening in 1989, **Disney-MGM Studios** overshadowed the opening of Florida's Universal Studios (see opposite), and at the same time found an extra use for the real film studios based here – the people you'll see laboring over storyboards on the Backlot Tour aren't there for show; they really are making films.

Most of the things to do at MGM take the form of rides or shows, and there are fewer exhibit-style attractions when compared with the other Disney parks. Thrill-seekers will be more than happy with the gravity-defying drops (including moments of weightlessness) in **The Twilight Zone Tower of Terror** or the exhilarating **Rock 'n' Roller Coaster** with its breakneck-speed launch.

Don't miss the half-hour behind-the-scenes **Backlot Tour**, climaxing with the dramatic special effects on the *Catastrophe Canyon* movie set; the funny **Muppet Vision 3D** show; and **The Great Movie Ride**, where Audio-Animatronics figures from famous movies interact with real-life actors.

The most popular of the live shows is **Who Wants to be a Millionaire – Play It!**, which recreates the TV show with admirable accuracy, and where the audience plays for a three-day Disney Line cruise to the Bahamas. Also worthwhile, **The Indiana Jones Epic Stunt Spectacular** re-enacts and explains many of the action-packed set pieces from the Steven Spielberg films; and the **Lights, Motors, Action! Stunt Show** features equally eye-catching stunts involving cars, motorbikes, and jet skis.

The world of Walt Disney

When the brilliant illustrator and animator Walt Disney devised the world's first theme park, California's **Disneyland** (see p.1065), he left himself with no control over the hotels and restaurants that quickly engulfed it, preventing growth and erasing profits Disney felt were rightly his. Determined not to let that happen again, the Disney corporation secretly bought up 27,500 acres of central Florida farmland, acquiring by the late Sixties a site a hundred times bigger than Disneyland. With the promise of a jobs bonanza for Florida, the state legislature gave the corporation the rights of any major municipality – empowering it to lay roads, enact building codes, and enforce the law with its own security force.

Walt Disney World's first "land," the Magic Kingdom, which opened in 1971, was a huge success. Unveiled in 1982, the far more ambitious EPCOT represented the first major break from cartoon-based escapism – but its rose-tinted look at the future received a mixed response. Partly due to this, and to some bad management decisions, the Disney empire (Disney himself died in 1966) faced bankruptcy by the mid-1980s. Since then, the corporation has sprung back from the abyss, and despite being subject to a (failed) hostile takeover bid by Comcast in 2004, steers a tight and competitive business ship. It may trade in fantasy, but where money matters, the Disney Corporation's nose is firmly in the real world.

Disney's Animal Kingdom

Disney's Animal Kingdom was opened in 1998 as an animal-conservation theme park with Disney's patented over-the-top twist. The park is divided into six major "lands" – **Africa, Camp Minnie-Mickey, DinoLand USA, Discovery Island, Rafiki's Planet Watch**, and **Asia** – each with its own mock-authentic ambiance, largely the result of the versatility of concrete, which is colored, imprinted upon, and formed into an endless variety of shapes.

The best-realized attraction is Africa's **Kilimanjaro Safaris**, where a jeep transport takes you on what feels very much like a real African safari, viewing giraffes, zebras, elephants, lions, gazelles, and rhinos, as well as taking part in anti-poacher maneuvers. Elsewhere in Africa, the troop of lowland gorillas at the **Pangani Forest Exploration Trail** are definitely worth a look. Crossing over to **Asia**, you'll get an astoundingly up-close look at the healthiest-looking tigers in captivity at the **Maharajah Jungle Trek**. Asia also has the thrilling **Expedition Everest** rollercoaster, where a train whizzes (both forward and backward) around a well-detailed replica of a Himalayan mountain. DinoLand USA's **DINOSAUR** is a slower but still exciting ride full of small drops and short stops in the dark as dinosaurs pop out of nowhere and roar.

The remainder of the park requires no more than casual exploration. The *Flights of Wonder* bird show exhibits falcons, owls, and other wonderful birds, while classic Disney characters sign autographs in **Camp Minnie-Mickey**, where you can also catch the *Festival of the Lion King*, a Broadway-style production of upbeat music with some nifty acrobatics, loosely based on its namesake film.

Universal Orlando

For some years, it seemed that TV and film production would move away from California to Florida, which, with its lower taxes and cheaper labor, was more amenable. The opening of Universal Studios in 1990 appeared to confirm that trend. So far, though, for various reasons, Florida has not proved to be a fully realistic alternative. Even so, this hasn't stopped the Universal enclave here, now known as **Universal Orlando**, off I-4, half a mile north of exits 74B or 75A (park opens daily at 9am, closing times vary; one-day, one-park ticket $71.36, children 3–9 $59.64, under-3s free; two-day, two-park ticket $122.42/$111.78; parking $10; ☎1-407/363-8000, ⓦ www.uescape.com), from becoming a major player in the Orlando theme-park arena. Though Disney World still commands the lion's share of attention, Universal has siphoned off many visitors with **Universal Studios'** high-tech movie-themed rides, special-effects-laden **Islands of Adventure**, and **CityWalk**, an earthier lure for nightlife dollars than Downtown Disney (see "Nightlife and entertainment," p.654). Furthermore, Universal has achieved full-fledged resort status with its three luxurious on-site **hotels**: *Portofino Bay*, *Hard Rock*, and the *Royal Pacific Resort* (all three ☎1-888/273-1311, ⓦ www.uescape. com; ❼–❾).

Universal Studios

Like its competitor Disney-MGM, Universal is a working studio, filling more than four hundred acres with the latest in TV and movie production technology. Unlike MGM, there's more emphasis here on movie-related rides than backstage shows. For sheer excitement, nothing in the park matches **Back to the Future The Ride**, a bone-shaking flight-simulator trip from 2015 to the Ice Age. The next best thrill ride is **Revenge of the Mummy**, where you're taken on a medium-paced journey through scenes from the eponymous movie. Don't miss **Shrek 4-D**, a delightful 3D presentation brought even more to life by an overdose of superb "feelies" (including a few too many water sprays). Also worthwhile, **Earthquake – The Big One** gives you an intensely claustrophobic two minutes of terror as you experience what it's like to be caught on a subway train when an 8.3 Richter-scale quake hits. Along the same lines, **Twister...Ride It Out** is a suffocating but gripping experience in which you stand beside an imitation tornado.

If you want to watch a live show, opt for the two-man *Universal Horror Make-Up Show*, which reveals movie-makeup secrets amidst comic repartee, or try the new *Fear Factor Live* (advanced registration required for contestants), which mimics the popular TV show.

Islands of Adventure

Islands of Adventure is Orlando's leader in state-of-the-art, edge-of-your-seat thrill rides. Though there are plenty of diversions for the less daring, these rides are what brings the crowds, and long lines are typical for many of them (though they do thin out as the evening goes on). Use the **Universal Express** system – akin to Disney's FASTPASS (see p.649) – to avoid waiting in lines for the most popular rides.

The park is really five superb miniparks – **Marvel Super Hero Island, The Lost Continent, Jurassic Park, Toon Lagoon**, and **Seuss Landing** – all surrounding a lagoon. The very best of the rides is **The Amazing Adventures of Spider-Man**, which uses every trick imaginable – 3D, sensory stimuli, motion simulation, and more – to spirit you into Spider-Man's battles with villains. **Dueling Dragons** is the next most exciting ride: twin rollercoasters ("Fire" and "Ice" – separate lines for each) engineered to provide harrowing near misses with each other. Here, even more so than on other rollercoasters, the front seats provide the greatest thrills. Another exciting ride is the **Incredible Hulk Coaster**, with its catapult start and plenty of loop-the-loops and plunges. **Doctor Doom's Fearfall** provides a panoramic view of the park, but the very short controlled drop, during which you experience a few seconds of weightlessness, is anticlimactic. In a similar vein, **Jurassic Park River Adventure** is a generally tame river-raft trip, where the only thing to shout about is an 85-foot drop.

Offerings for kids include **Dudley Do-Right's Ripsaw Falls** and **Popeye & Bluto's Bilge-Rat Barges**, both good for getting a midday drenching; and the whole of Seuss Landing, where everything is based on Dr Seuss characters. There's one **live performance** offered throughout the day: *The Eighth Voyage of Sindbad* stunt show, where the set, stunts, and pyrotechnics are as good as the jokes are bad.

SeaWorld Orlando and Discovery Cove

SeaWorld Orlando, at Sea Harbor Drive, near the intersection of I-4 and the Beeline Expressway, is the cream of Florida's sizable crop of marine parks, and should not be missed; allocate a full day to see it all (park opens daily at 9am, closing times vary; $65.98, children 3–9 $53.20; ⊙407/351-3600, ⓦwww.seaworld .com). The big event is the *Shamu Adventure Show* – thirty minutes of tricks per-

The Orlando Flexticket

Universal Orlando, SeaWorld Orlando, and Wet 'n Wild (a water park) have teamed together to create a pass that permits access to each park over a period of fourteen consecutive days. The **Orlando Flexticket** (as it's known) costs $202.31 (children 3–9 $166.10), or $250.46/$213.19, including Tampa's Busch Gardens, with a free shuttle from Orlando to Busch Gardens.

formed by a playful killer whale (you'll get drenched if you're sitting in the first fourteen rows of the stadium). Also, try not to miss the kid-orientated sea lion extravaganza, *Clyde and Seamore Take Pirate Island*. The **Wild Arctic** complex, complete with artificial snow and ice, brings you close to beluga whales, walruses, and polar bears, while a flight simulator ride takes you on a stomach-churning helicopter flight through an Arctic blizzard.

The park's first thrill ride, **Journey to Atlantis**, travels on both water and rails, and has a sixty-foot drop (be prepared to get very wet). Much more exhilarating, however, is **Kraken**, a rollercoaster that flings you around at speeds of up to 65 miles per hour, free-flying and looping-the-loop at great heights.

With substantially less razzmatazz, plenty of smaller aquariums and displays offer a wealth of information about the underwater world. Among the highlights, **Penguin Encounter** re-creates Antarctica, with scores of the waddling, flightless birds scampering over an iceberg; the young occupants of the **Dolphin Nursery** assert their advanced intellect by flapping their fins and soaking passersby; and **Shark Encounter** includes a walk through an acrylic-sided and -roofed tunnel, offering as realistic an impression on dry land of what swimming with sharks must feel like.

Discovery Cove, next to SeaWorld Orlando on Central Florida Parkway (daily 9am–5.30pm; $169.34–190.64 without dolphin swim, $275.84–297.14 with dolphin swim; ℡1-877/4-DISCOVERY, ⓦwww.discoverycove.com) limits visitors to about a thousand a day (reserve well in advance). The main reason for coming here is to swim and play with the dolphins, while other activities include snorkeling with tropical fish, wading in a pool full of harmless sting rays, and feeding exotic birds. Note that the admission charge includes seven-day access to SeaWorld Orlando.

Orlando's water parks

Disney World has two excellent **water parks**. **Blizzard Beach**, north of the *All-Star Resorts* (see "Accommodation within Walt Disney World," p.647) on World Drive (daily 10am–5pm; slightly longer hours in summer; $38.34, children 3–9 $31.95; ℡407/560-3400), is based on the fantasy that a hapless entrepreneur has opened a ski resort in Florida and the entire thing has started to melt. The star of the show is **Summit Plummet**, which shoots you down a 120-foot vertical drop at more than fifty miles per hour. Gentler rides include toboggan-style slalom courses and raft rides. As well as the slides, **Typhoon Lagoon**, just south of Downtown Disney (daily 10am–5pm; slightly longer hours in summer; $38.34, children 3–9 $31.95; ℡407/560-4141), features a huge surfing pool and a shark reef where you can snorkel amongst tropical fish. **Wet 'n Wild**, 6200 International Drive (daily 10am–5pm; longer hours in summer; $38.29, children 3–9 $31.90; ℡1-800/992-9453, ⓦwww.wetnwildorlando.com), defends itself admirably in the face of the Disney competition, with a range of no-nonsense slides including the almost vertical **Der Stuka**. Lines are shorter here than at the Disney water parks.

Eating in the Orlando area

Downtown and its environs hold the pick of the locals' **eating** haunts; most visitors, however, head for International Drive's inexpensive all-day buffets and gourmet restaurants. You are not allowed to take food into any of the theme parks, where the best restaurants are in **EPCOT's World Showcase**, particularly the French- and Mexican-themed establishments.

Bahama Breeze 8849 International Drive ☎407/248-2499. Decent Caribbean food in an upbeat atmosphere. Dinner only.

Café Tu Tu Tango 8625 International Drive ☎407/248-2222. Original, imaginative dishes served in small portions. All the artwork on the walls is for sale.

The Globe 25 Wall St Plaza, downtown ☎407/849-9904. This is a perfect place for inexpensive Nouveau American snacks and light meals.

Le Coq au Vin 4800 S Orange Ave, downtown ☎407/851-6980. French restaurant with surprisingly low prices for top-notch food. Closed Mon.

🍴 Ming Court 9188 International Drive ☎407/351-9988. An exceptional Chinese restaurant, with dim sum and sushi available. Not as costly as you might expect.

Numero Uno 2499 S Orange Ave, downtown ☎407/841-3840. Inexpensive Cuban restaurant serving dishes such as black beans, grouper, and paella. Closed Sun.

🍴 Panera Bread 227 N Eola Drive, downtown ☎407/481-1060. One of an inviting local chain, with a wide array of baked goods, soups, salads, and sandwiches. Also a WiFi Hotspot.

🍴 Punjab 7451 International Drive ☎407/352-7887. Reasonably priced curries spiced to your personal taste. A good vegetarian choice.

Roy's 7760 W Sand Lake Rd, near International Drive ☎407/352-4844. Founded in Hawaii, *Roy's* offers innovative Hawaiian fusion cuisine.

White Wolf Café 1829 N Orange Ave, downtown ☎407/895-5590. Down-to-earth café/antique store known for creative salads and sandwiches.

Nightlife and entertainment

Though you'll probably be so exhausted from a long day at the parks that boozing and dancing with thousands of others will be the last thing on your mind, the Orlando area is bursting with themed **nightspots** of every persuasion, from medieval banquets to piano bars and country-and-western clubs. It's all relentlessly good, clean fun, sanitized to the hilt.

From around 9pm, each Disney World park holds some kind of closing-time bash, usually involving fireworks and fountains. There's also **Pleasure Island**, exit 26B off I-4 (part of the complex of shops, restaurants, and entertainment venues that comprise **Downtown Disney**; ☎407/939-2648, ⓦwww.downtowndisney. com), a remake of an abandoned island, whose pseudo-warehouses are the setting for bars and nightclubs (daily 10am–7pm; free before 7pm, after 7pm $21.95 gains access to all bars and clubs). The most enjoyable are the **Comedy Warehouse** and the **Adventurers' Club**, loosely based on a 1930s gentlemen's club. Take ID (under-18s must be accompanied by a parent or guardian, while some clubs are 21 and up) and a fat wallet.

Not to be outdone by Disney, Universal Orlando has come up with **City-Walk**, Universal Boulevard (☎407/363-8000, ⓦwww.citywalkorlando.com), thirty acres of restaurants, live music, dance clubs, and shops, wedged between Universal Studios and Islands of Adventure. Hipper than anything Disney has to offer, CityWalk is also much better value ($9.95 for all-night access to every club, plus free parking after 6pm). Head to **Bob Marley – A Tribute to Freedom** for live reggae; **CityJazz** for a cooler, more sophisticated ambiance, with all types of jazz, funk, and soul; the **Latin Quarter** restaurant for Latino beats; and **the groove** for a full-fledged nightclub.

Away from the theme parks, **downtown Orlando** has an eclectic crop of bars, lounges, and clubs. Most of the after-dark action focuses along **Orange Avenue**, at clubs like 🍴 *The Social*, no. 54 (for alt-rock, grunge, and the like), and the chic, *Rhythm and Flow Ultralounge*, no. 2.

The West Coast

In the three hundred miles from the state's southern tip to the junction with the Panhandle (see p.667), Florida's **West Coast** embraces all the extremes. Buzzing, youthful towns rise behind placid fishing hamlets; mobbed holiday strips are just minutes from desolate swamplands, and world-class art collections vie with glitzy theme parks. Surprises are plentiful, though the coast's one constant is proximity to the Gulf of Mexico – and sunset views rivaled only by those of the Florida Keys.

The west coast's largest city, **Tampa**, has more to offer than its corporate towers initially suggest – not least the lively nightlife scene in the Cuban enclave of **Ybor City**, and the Busch Gardens theme park. For the mass of visitors, though, the Tampa Bay area begins and ends with the **St Petersburg beaches**, whose miles of sea and sand are undiluted vacation territory. South of Tampa, a string of barrier-island beaches run the length of the Gulf, and the mainland towns that provide access to them – such as Sarasota and Fort Myers – have enough to warrant a stop. Inland, the wilderness of the **Everglades** is explorable on simple walking trails, by canoeing, or by spending the night at backcountry campgrounds, with only the gators for company.

Tampa

A small, stimulating city with an infectious, upbeat mood, **TAMPA**, the business hub of the west coast, is well worth a stop. As one of the major beneficiaries of the flood of people and money into Florida, Tampa boasts an impressive cultural infrastructure envied by many larger rivals. In addition to its fine **museums** and **Busch Gardens**, one of the most popular theme parks in the state, the city holds, in the Cuban-influenced **Ybor City**, just northeast of the city center, the west coast's hippest and most culturally eclectic quarter.

Tampa began as a small settlement beside a US Army base that was built in the 1820s to keep an eye on the Seminoles. In the 1880s, the railroad arrived, and the Hillsborough River, on which the city stands, was dredged to allow seagoing vessels to dock. Tampa became a booming port, simultaneously acquiring a major tobacco industry as thousands of Cubans moved north from Key West to the new cigar factories of neighboring Ybor City. The Depression ended the economic surge, but the port remained one of the busiest in the country and tempered Tampa's postwar decline. Today, little seems to stand in the way of Tampa's continued emergence as a forward-thinking and financially secure community.

Arrival and information

Tampa's **airport** (℡813/870-8700, Ⓦwww.tampaairport.com) is five miles northwest of downtown: local HART bus #30 is the least costly connection (see p.656). **Taxis** (try United ℡813/253-2424) to downtown or a Busch Boulevard motel cost $20–40; to St Petersburg or the beaches, $40–65. Greyhound **buses** arrive downtown at 610 Polk St (℡813/229-2174); trains at 601 N Nebraska Ave (℡813/221-7600).

The downtown **Visitor Information Center**, 615 Channelside Drive, suite 108A (Mon–Sat 9.30am–5.30pm, Sun 11am–5pm; ℡1-800/44-TAMPA, Ⓦwww.

visittampabay.com), and the **Ybor City Visitor Information Center**, 1600 E
8th Ave, suite B104 (Mon–Sat 10am–6pm, Sun noon–6pm; ☎813/241-8838,
ⓦwww.ybor.org), give out useful leaflets and maps.

Although both downtown Tampa and Ybor City are easily covered on foot,
to travel between them without a car you'll need to use the HART **local buses**
($1.50, one-day pass $3; ☎813/254-4278, ⓦwww.hartline.org) or the TECO
Line **Streetcar System** ($2; ☎813/254-4278, ⓦwww.tecolinestreetcar.org), a
vintage replica streetcar which runs between downtown and Ybor several times
an hour. Useful HART bus routes are #8 to Ybor City, #5 to Busch Gardens, #6
to the Museum of Science and Industry.

Accommodation

Tampa is not generously supplied with low-cost **accommodation**; you'll almost
certainly save money by staying in St Petersburg (see p.658) or at the beaches (see
p.660). There are some good deals, though, at the motels near Busch Gardens.

Best Western All Suites 301 University Center
Drive, behind Busch Gardens ☎813/971-8930. A
reasonable base for seeing the city by car, and so
close to Busch Gardens that the parrots escape
into their trees. Features a happy hour every afternoon and free breakfast. ❹

Days Inn Busch Gardens Maingate 2901 E Busch
Blvd ☎813/933-6471. Recently renovated hotel near
Busch Gardens. There's an on-site 24hr restaurant,
with plenty of others within walking distance. ❸

Don Vincente de Ybor Historic Inn 1915
Avenida Republica de Cuba ☎1-866/206-
4545, ⓦwww.donvicenteinn.com. A luxurious B&B
option in Ybor City. Features sixteen suites, a fine
restaurant, and a cigar and martini bar that has live
entertainment Thurs and Fri nights. ❻

Gram's Place 3109 N Ola Ave ☎813/221-0596,
ⓦwww.grams-inn-tampa.com. This funky motel-
cum-hostel offers both private rooms – all themed
in different musical styles – and rather tatty youth-
hostel-style accommodation. $22.50 for a dorm
bed; private rooms ❷.

Hilton Garden 1700 E 9th Ave ☎813/769-9267,
ⓦwww.tampayborhistoricdistrict.gardeninn.com.
Comfortable digs, even if the decor is a little sterile
to be in the heart of Tampa's most historically rich
neighborhood. ❻

Sheraton Tampa Riverwalk 200 N Ashley Drive
☎813/223-2222, ⓦwww.tampariverwalkhotel.
com. Very convenient downtown location, nicely
situated on the banks of the Hillsborough River. ❻

Downtown Tampa

Of the contemporary buildings in downtown Tampa, none better reflects the
city's cultural striving than the highly regarded **Tampa Museum of Art**, on the
banks of the Hillsborough River at 600 N Ashley Drive (Tues–Sat 10am–5pm,
third Thurs of every month 10am–8pm, Sun 11am–5pm; $8; ☎813/274-8130,
ⓦwww.tampamuseum.com). Specializing in classical antiques and twentieth-
century American art, the museum cleverly blends selections from the permanent
collection with prime loaned pieces of recent US painting, photography, and
sculpture.

From the Museum of Art, you'll see the silver minarets and cupolas on the far side
of the river, sprouting from the main building of the University of Tampa. These
architectural ornaments adorn what was formerly the 500-room **Tampa Bay Hotel**,
financed by steamship and railroad magnate Henry B. Plant. To reach it, walk across
the river on Kennedy Boulevard and descend the steps into Plant Park.

The structure is as bizarre a sight today as it was when it opened in 1891. Since
the Civil War, Plant had been buying up bankrupt railroads, steadily inching his
way into Florida to meet his steamships unloading at Tampa's harbor. Eventually,
he became rich enough to put his fantasies of creating the world's most luxurious
hotel into practice. However, lack of care for the fittings and Plant's death in 1899

hastened the hotel's transformation from the last word in comfort to a pile of crumbling plaster. The city bought it in 1905 and leased it to Tampa University 23 years later. In one wing, the **Henry B. Plant Museum**, 401 W Kennedy Blvd (Tues–Sat 10am–4pm, Sun noon–4pm; $5; ☎813/254-1891, ⓦwww.plantmuseum .com), holds what's left of the hotel's original furnishings.

In Tampa's dockland area, a mile or so southeast of the *Tampa Bay Hotel*, the splendid **Florida Aquarium**, 701 Channelside Drive (daily 9.30am–5pm; $17.95; ☎813/273-4000, ⓦwww.flaquarium.org), houses lavish displays of Florida's fresh- and saltwater habitats, from springs and swamps to beaches and coral reefs. Animal residents include an impressive variety of fish, birds, otters, turtles, and alligators.

Ybor City

In 1886, as soon as Henry Plant's ships had ensured a regular supply of Havana tobacco into Tampa, cigar magnate Don Vincente Martínez Ybor cleared a patch of scrubland three miles northeast of present-day downtown Tampa and laid the foundations of **YBOR CITY**. About twenty thousand migrants, mostly Cuban, settled here and created a Latin American enclave, producing the top-class, hand-rolled cigars that made Tampa the "**Cigar Capital of the World**." However, mass production, the popularity of cigarettes, and the Depression proved a fatal combination for skilled cigar-makers: as unemployment struck, Ybor City's tight-knit blocks of cobbled streets and redbrick buildings became surrounded by drab, low-rent neighborhoods.

In the midst of a revival, Ybor City buzzes with tourists, and at night the atmosphere reaches carnival proportions, especially on the weekends. The town is trendy and culturally diverse, yet its Cuban roots are immediately apparent, and explanatory background texts adorn many buildings. The **Ybor City State Museum**, 1818 9th Ave (daily 9am–5pm; $3; ☎813/247-6323, ⓦwww.ybormuseum .org), helps you grasp the main points of Ybor City's creation and its multiethnic make-up. The museum also offers cigar-rolling demonstrations (Fri–Sun 9.30am–1pm) and historic walking tours (Sat 10.30am).

Busch Gardens and the Museum of Science and Industry

Busch Gardens, located two miles east of I-275, or two miles west of I-75, exit 54, at 3000 E Busch Blvd (opening hours vary almost day to day but generally daily 10am–6pm; $61.72, children $51.07; parking $9; ☎1-888/800-5447, ⓦwww.buschgardenstampabay.com) is one of Florida's most popular theme parks, based on a re-creation of Colonial-era Africa and offering some of the fastest, largest, most nerve-jangling rollercoasters in the country. A sedate pseudo-steam train or cable car journey allows inspection of a variety of African wildlife, but by far the most popular of the twenty-odd rides are the rollercoasters: **Sheikra**, with its terrifying 200-foot, 90-degree dive; **Montu**, where your legs dangle precariously in mid-air; **Gwazi**, a giant wooden coaster; and **Kumba**, with plenty of high-speed loop-the-loops. After this excitement, retire to the Hospitality House for two free cups of Budweiser beer.

Two miles northeast of Busch Gardens, the colossal **Museum of Science and Industry**, 4801 E Fowler Ave (daily 9am–5pm; $19.95; ☎813/987-6100, ⓦwww.mosi.org), demystifies the scientific world through hands-on exhibits and a program of shows where you'll get to feel what it's like to sit in a 74mph wind or ride a bicycle along a tightrope. The ticket price includes one of several different **IMAX** movies shown throughout the day.

Eating

There are plenty of good places to **eat** in Tampa, with a huge concentration of lively restaurants in Ybor City.

Au Rendez-Vous 200 E Madison St ☎813/221-4748. At this good French bakery, there's coffee and croissants in the morning or quiche and baguettes at lunchtime. Unusually for a downtown eatery, it's open Sat nights.

Bernini 1702 7th Ave, Ybor City ☎813/248-0099. In the lovely old Bank of Ybor City, an Italian joint serving up wood-fired pizza and pasta.

Big City Tavern 1600 E 8th Ave, Ybor City ☎813/247-3000. Formerly the Centro Español social club, this large, high-ceilinged place offers American cuisine spiced with plenty of ginger and other Asian influences.

Cephas 1701 E 4th Ave, Ybor City ☎813/247-9022. A funky Jamaican res-taurant offering jerk chicken and curried goat, chicken, and fish.

Columbia 2117 E 7th Ave, Ybor City ☎813/248-4961. A Tampa – and tourist – institution, the city's oldest restaurant serves fine Spanish and Cuban food. Reservations recommended.

La Creperia Café 1729 E 7th Ave, Ybor City ☎813/248-9700. A wide choice of delicious sweet and savory crepes, plus free WiFi Internet access.

Shells 11010 N 30th St ☎813/977-8456. Convenient to the hotels near Busch Gardens, this cheap and cheerful seafood restaurant serves consistently good fresh fish.

Nightlife and entertainment

Ybor City's renowned **nightlife** tends to be younger and more raucous than the city's other entertainment areas of Channelside, downtown next to the Florida Aquarium, and the International Plaza and Bay Street, near the airport at the junction of West Shore and Boy Scout boulevards. The free *Weekly Planet* (Ⓦ www.weeklyplanet.com) has **listings**, as does Friday's *Tampa Tribune*.

Amphitheater 1609 E 7th Ave, Ybor City ☎813/248-2331. A vast, elaborate nightclub playing mainly techno. A good spot for a big night out.

Blue Martini at the International Plaza and Bay Street ☎813/873-2583. Good-looking, professional crowd at this trendy lounge bar.

Green Iguana 1708 E 7th Ave, Ybor City ☎813/248-9555. Rock bands play nightly, and DJs keep the young crowd very much in the party mood.

Side Splitters 12938 N Dale Mabry Hwy ☎813/960-1197. One of the best comedy clubs in the area.

Skipper's Smokehouse 910 Skipper Rd ☎813/971-0666. Blues and reggae rule at this family-oriented live music venue.

Tampa Theatre 711 Franklin St ☎813/274-8981. Foreign-language, classic, and cult films shown in an atmospheric 1920s theater. Tickets $8.50.

St Petersburg

Situated on the eastern edge of the Pinellas Peninsula, a bulky thumb of land poking between Tampa Bay and the Gulf of Mexico, **ST PETERSBURG** is a world away from Tampa, even though the two cities are just twenty miles apart. Declared the healthiest place in the US in 1885, St Petersburg wasted no time in wooing the recuperating and the retired, at one point putting five thousand green benches on its streets to take the weight off elderly feet. Although it remains a mecca for the retired, the city has worked hard to attract young blood, as well. In addition to rejuvenating the pier, which now offers something for all ages, St Petersburg's diverse selection of museums and plethora of art galleries have contributed to its emergence as one of Florida's richest cultural centers. Most remarkable of all, the town has acquired a major collection of works by Salvador Dalí.

The **Salvador Dalí Museum**, 1000 S 3rd St (Mon–Wed & Sat 9.30am–5.30pm, Thurs 9.30am–8pm, Fri 9.30am–6.30pm, Sun noon–5.30pm; $15, Thurs after 5pm $5; ☎727/823-3767, ⊛www.salvadordalimuseum.org), stores more than a thousand paintings from the collection of a Cleveland industrialist, A. Reynolds Morse, who struck up a friendship with the artist in the 1940s. Hour-long **free tours** that run continuously throughout the day trace a chronological path around the works, from the artist's early experiments with Impressionism and Cubism to the seminal Surrealist canvas *The Disintegration of the Persistence of Memory*.

Once you've done Dalí, the quarter-mile-long **pier**, jutting from the end of 2nd Avenue North, is the town's focal point. The pier often hosts browsable arts-and-crafts exhibitions, and the inverted-pyramid-like building at its head holds five stories of restaurants, shops, and fast-food counters. At the foot of the pier, the **Museum of History**, 335 2nd Ave NE (Mon noon–7pm, Tues–Sat 10am–5pm, Sun noon–5pm; $5; ☎727/894-1052, ⊛www.spmoh.org), recounts using modest displays St Petersburg's early twentieth-century heyday as a winter resort. Nearby, the **Museum of Fine Arts**, 255 Beach Drive NE (Tues–Sat 10am–5pm, Sun 1–5pm; $8, including free guided tour; ☎727/896-2667, ⊛www.fine-arts. org), holds a superlative collection ranging from pre-Columbian art through Asian and African to the European Old Masters. The **Florida International Museum**, 244 2nd Ave N (during exhibition periods only, Tues–Sat 10am–5pm, Sun noon–5pm, last entry 4pm; $10; ☎727/341-7900, ⊛www.floridamuseum.org), occupies an entire block and displays three exhibitions a year on subjects ranging from Ancient Egypt to the Beatles.

Practicalities

The Greyhound **bus** station is downtown at 180 9th St N (☎727/898-1496). The **Chamber of Commerce** is at 100 2nd Ave N (Mon–Fri 8am–7pm, Sat 9am–7pm, Sun noon–6pm; ☎727/821-4069, ⊛www.stpete.com). **Accommodation** in St Petersburg can be less costly than at the beaches (see p.660), especially at the dozens of cheap motels along 4th Street (Hwy-92): the *Kentucky*, at no. 4246 (☎727/526-7373; ❷) is a good option. The area is also rich in charismatic B&Bs, such as *Dickens House*, 335 8th Ave NE (☎1-800/381-2022, ⊛www.dickenshouse. com; ❻). For sheer luxury, stay at 🏛 *Renaissance Vinoy Resort*, 501 5th Ave NE (☎1-888/303-4430, ⊛www.renaissancehotels.com/tpasr; ❼). Hearty, economical Cuban **food** can be had at *Tangelo's Grill*, 226 1st Ave N (☎727/894-1695). Alternatively, try *Moon Under Water*, 332 Beach Drive NE (☎727/896-6160); overlooking the waterfront, this inexpensive British tavern is well known for its cocktails and curries.

The St Petersburg beaches

Framing the Gulf side of the Pinellas Peninsula, a 35-mile chain of barrier islands forms the **St Petersburg Beaches**, one of Florida's busiest coastal strips. When the resorts of Miami Beach lost some of their allure during the 1970s, the St Petersburg beaches grew in popularity with Americans and have since evolved into an established destination for package-holidaying Europeans. The beaches are beautiful, the sea warm, and the sunsets fabulous – yet this is not Florida at its best: the whole area is a little tacky, with large portions lacking in charm and character.

All **buses** ($1.50; ☎727/540-1900, ⊛www.psta.net) to the beaches originate in St Petersburg, at the Williams Park terminal, on 1st Avenue North and 3rd Street North; an **information booth** there has route details. **Route #35** runs daily to St

Pete Beach on Gulf Boulevard, which links all the St Petersburg beach communities. At St Pete Beach, you can change for the **Suncoast Beach Trolley**, which links Passe-a-Grille in the extreme south to Sand Key in the north.

The southern beaches

In twenty-odd miles of heavily touristed coast, only **Pass-a-Grille**, at the very southern tip of the barrier island chain, has the look and feel of a genuine community – two miles of tidy houses, cared-for lawns, small shops, and a cluster of bars and restaurants. During the week, the town is blissfully quiet, while on weekends informed locals come here to enjoy one of the area's liveliest stretches of sand.

A mile and a half north of Pass-a-Grille, the painfully luxurious **Don Cesar Hotel**, 3400 Gulf Blvd (☎727/360-1881 or 1-866/728-2206, ⓦwww.doncesar. com; ❼), is a grandiose pink castle, filling seven beachside acres. Opened in 1928, and briefly busy with the likes of Scott and Zelda Fitzgerald, it enjoyed a short-lived glamor. During the Great Depression, part of the hotel was used as a warehouse, and later as the spring training base of the New York Yankees baseball team.

Continuing north from the *Don Cesar* on Gulf Boulevard brings you into the main section of **St Pete Beach**, a string of uninspiring hotels, motels, and eating establishments. Further north, **Treasure Island** is even less varied tourist territory. An arching drawbridge leads to **Madeira Beach**, essentially more of the same – although, if you can't make it to Pass-a-Grille, the beach here justifies a weekend fling.

The northern beaches

Much of the northern section of **Sand Key**, the longest barrier island in the St Petersburg chain, and one of the wealthier portions of the coast, is taken up by stylish condos and time-share apartments. The island terminates in the pretty **Sand Key Park**, where tall palm trees frame a scintillating strip of sand. The park occupies one bank of **Clearwater Pass**, across which a belt of sparkling white sands marks the holiday town of **CLEARWATER BEACH**, whose streets still retain an endearing small-town feel despite the recent condo building boom. The staff at the well-positioned *Clearwater Beach Hostel*, 606 Bay Esplanade (☎727/443-1211, ⓦwww.clearwaterbeachhostel. com; dorm beds from $15, private rooms from $46), will help plan excursions around the area and **rent bikes** for $5 a day. Regular **buses** (#80) provide links to the mainland town of Clearwater – across the two-mile causeway – where you'll find connections to St Petersburg and a Greyhound station at 2811 Gulf-to-Bay Blvd.

Beach practicalities

The **motels** that line mile after mile of Gulf Boulevard tend to be cheaper than the **hotels** – typically $75–100 in winter, $15–20 less in summer. You'll pay $5–10 extra for a room on the beach side of Gulf Boulevard compared with an identical room on the inland side. At the southern beaches, good, cheap accommodation can be found at the peaceful *Lamara Motel & Apartments*, 520 73rd Ave, St Petersburg Beach (☎1-800/211-5108, ⓦwww.lamara.com; ❸), while the pick of the hotels at the northern beaches is ⚓ *Sheraton Sand Key*, 1160 Gulf Blvd, Sand Key (☎1-800/456-7263, ⓦwww.sheratonsandkey.com; ❻). It's easy to find a decent place to **eat** around the beaches. Overlooking the sea, *Hurricane*, 807 Gulf Way, Pass-a-Grille (☎727/360-9558), has a well-priced menu of the freshest seafood. *Fetishes*, 6690 Gulf Blvd, St Pete Beach (☎727/363-3700), is ideal for a more upscale and intimate dining experience, serving expensive American cuisine. In Clearwater Beach, *Frenchy's Café*, 41 Baymont St (☎727/446-3607), cooks up good grouper sandwiches and seafood gumbo.

Sarasota

Rising on a gentle hillside beside the blue waters of Sarasota Bay, **SARASOTA**, 35 miles south of St Petersburg, is one of Florida's better-off and better-looking towns. It's also one of the state's leading cultural centers, home to numerous writers and artists, and the base of several respected performing arts companies. The community is far less stuffy than its wealth might suggest, and downtown Sarasota is fairly lively, with cafés, bars, and eateries complementing the excellent grouping of bookstores. Be sure to visit the house and art collections of John Ringling, a multimillionaire who gave Sarasota its ongoing taste for the fine arts, or the barrier island beaches, a couple of miles away across the bay, which are also spectacular.

The Ringling Museum Complex

John Ringling, one of the owners of the fantastically successful Ringling Brothers Circus, which toured the US from the 1880s, acquired during his lifetime a fortune estimated at $200 million. Recognizing Sarasota's investment potential, he built the first causeway to the barrier islands and made this the winter base for his circus. His greatest gift to the town, however, was a Venetian Gothic mansion and an incredible collection of European Baroque paintings – regarded as one of the finest collections of its kind in the US – displayed in a purpose-built museum beside the house.

The **Ringling Museum Complex**, which includes the mansion (daily 10am– 5.30pm; $15; ☎941/359-5700), is at 5401 Bay Shore Rd, three miles north of downtown beside US-41. Begin your exploration by walking through the gardens to the former winter residence of John and Mable Ringling, **Ca' d'Zan** ("House of John," in Venetian dialect), built in 1926 for $1.5 million, and furnished with New York estate sale castoffs for an additional $400,000. A gorgeous piece of work and a triumph of taste and proportion, it's serenely situated beside the bay. The artwork is displayed in the spacious **museum**, built around a mock fifteenth-century Italian palazzo. Five enormous paintings by Rubens, commissioned in 1625, and the painter's subsequent *Portrait of Archduke Ferdinand*, are highlights, though there's also a wealth of talent from Europe's leading schools of the mid-sixteenth to mid-eighteenth centuries. Free guided **tours** depart regularly from the entrance.

The Sarasota beaches

Increasingly the stamping ground of European package tourists spilling south from the St Petersburg beaches, the white sands of the **Sarasota beaches** are worth a day of anybody's time. The two islands on which they lie, Lido Key and Siesta Key, are accessible from the mainland, though there is no direct link between them. A third island, Longboat Key, is primarily residential.

The Ringling Causeway crosses the yacht-filled Sarasota Bay from the foot of Sarasota's Main Street to **Lido Key**. The causeway flows into **St Armands Circle**, a roundabout ringed by upmarket shops and restaurants dotted with some of Ringling's replica classical statuary. Continuing south along Benjamin Franklin Drive, you come to the island's most accessible beaches, ending after two miles at the attractive **South Lido Park** (daily 8am-sunset; free).

The bulbous northerly section of tadpole-shaped **Siesta Key**, reached by Siesta Drive off US-41, about five miles south of downtown Sarasota, attracts a younger crowd. The soft sand at the pretty but busy **Siesta Key Beach** (beside Beach Road) has a sugary texture due to its origins as quartz (not the more usual pulverized coral). To escape the crowds, continue south past Crescent Beach and follow Midnight Pass Road for six miles to **Turtle Beach**, a small, secluded stretch of sand.

Practicalities

In downtown Sarasota, Greyhound **buses** stop at 575 N Washington Blvd (℡941/955-5735). The **Amtrak bus** from Tampa pulls in at 1993 Main Street. The local bus terminal is a few blocks west on Lemon Avenue, between 1st and 2nd streets: catch buses here for the Ringling estate or the beaches. Call at the **visitor center**, 655 N Tamiami Trail (Mon–Sat 10am–4pm, Sun noon–3pm; ℡1-800/522-9799, Ⓦwww.sarasotafl.org), for discount coupons and leaflets.

On the mainland, **motels** run the length of US-41 (N Tamiami Trail) between the Ringling estate and downtown Sarasota, typically charging around $60 a night: try the *Best Western Midtown*, 1425 S Tamiani Trail (℡941/955-9841; ❸). Prices are higher at the beaches: the friendly *Lido Vacation Rentals*, 528 S Polk Drive, Lido Key (℡1-800/890-7991; ❸), is one of the more reasonably priced choices.

Eating options along Main Street include the healthful salads, sandwiches, and smoothies at *Nature's Way*, no. 1572 (℡941/954-3131), as well as the excellent pizza at *Il Panificio*, no. 1703 (℡941/366-5570). ⚓ *El Habanero*, 417 Burns Court (℡941/362-9562), serves plates piled high with mouth-watering Cuban food.

Fort Myers

Fifty miles south, **FORT MYERS** may lack the elan of Sarasota, but it's nonetheless one of the up-and-coming communities of Florida's southwest coast. Fortunately, most of its recent growth has occurred on the north side of the wide Caloosahatchee River, which the town straddles, allowing the traditional center, along the waterway's south shore, to remain relatively unspoiled.

Once across the river, US-41 strikes **downtown** Fort Myers, picturesquely nestled on the water's edge. For a thorough insight into the town's history, head to the **Southwest Florida Museum of History**, 2300 Peck St (Tues–Sat 10am–5pm, Sun noon–4pm; $9.50; ℡239/332-5955), which also has an eye-catching 84-foot-long Pullman rail car.

In 1885, six years after inventing the light bulb, **Thomas Edison** collapsed from exhaustion and was instructed by his doctor to find a warm working environment or face an early death. Vacationing in Florida, the 37-year-old Edison bought fourteen acres of land on the banks of the Caloosahatchee and cleared a section of it to spend his remaining winters. This became the **Edison Winter Estate**, 2350 McGregor Blvd, a mile west of downtown (Mon–Sat 9am–5.30pm, Sun noon–5.30pm; $16 for homes and gardens tour, every 30mins; ℡239/334-3614, Ⓦwww.edison-ford-estate.com). The tours begin in the gardens, planted with such exotics as African sausage trees and wild orchids. However, the house, which you can glimpse only through the windows, is anticlimactic – its plainness probably due to the fact that Edison spent most of his waking hours inside the **laboratory**, attempting to turn the latex-rich sap of *Solidago edisonii* (a strain of goldenrod weed he developed) into rubber. However, when the tour reaches the engrossing **museum**, the full impact of Edison's achievements becomes apparent: you'll see several examples of the phonograph that Edison created in 1877, as well as some of the ungainly cinema projectors derived from Edison's Kinetoscope – which brought him a million dollars a year in royalties from 1907. Next door, you can also traipse through the plain **Ford Winter Estate**, bought by Edison's close friend

Henry Ford in 1915. Much more awe-inspiring is the enormous banyan tree outside the ticket office – the largest of its kind in the US.

The Fort Myers beaches

The **Fort Myers beaches** on **Estero Island**, fifteen miles south of downtown, are appreciably different in character from the west coast's more commercialized beach strips, with a cheerful seaside mood. Accommodation is plentiful on and around Estero Boulevard – reached by San Carlos Boulevard – which runs the seven-mile length of the island. Most activity revolves around the short fishing pier and the **Lynne Hall Memorial Park**, at the island's north end.

Estero Island becomes increasingly residential as you press south, Estero Boulevard eventually swinging over a slender causeway to **Lovers Key State Recreation Area** (daily 8am–sunset; $3–5 per car, $1 for pedestrians and cyclists; ☎239/463-4588), where a footpath picks a trail over a couple of mangrove-fringed islands and several mullet-filled creeks to **Lovers Key**, a secluded beach. If you don't fancy the walk, a free trolley will transport you between the park entrance and the beach.

Reached only by crossing a causeway (with a $6 toll), the islands of **Sanibel** and **Captiva**, 25 miles southwest of Fort Myers, are virtually impossible to visit unless you have a car. However, if you have a spare day, these islands offer a wildlife refuge, mangroves, and shell-strewn beaches – for which they are widely renowned. In contrast with the smooth beaches along the gulf side of Sanibel Island, the opposite edge comprises shallow bays and creeks, and a vibrant wildlife habitat under the protection of the **J.N. "Ding" Darling National Wildlife Refuge** (daily except Fri 7.30am–sunset; cars $5, cyclists and pedestrians $1; ☎239/472-1100). The main entrance and **information center** are just off the Sanibel–Captiva Road. If you intend to stay here for a night or two, contact the Fort Myers visitor center beforehand for lodging ideas. By doing so, you'll be treated to a beach experience unlike those in most of Florida – lovely yet with an acute sense of isolation.

Practicalities

Greyhound pulls in at 2250 Peck St, while daily **Amtrak buses** from Tampa arrive at 6050 Plaza Drive, about six miles east of downtown. The **Chamber of Commerce** is at 2310 Edwards Drive (Mon–Fri 9am–4.30pm; ☎1-800/366-3622, ⓦwww.fortmyers.org). Distances within Fort Myers, and from downtown to the beaches, are large, and you'll struggle without a car, though it is possible – just – to reach the beaches on local LeeTran **buses** (☎239/533-8726, ⓦwww.rideleetran.com). LeeTran's **downtown terminal** is at Monroe Avenue and Martin Luther King Jr Boulevard.

Accommodation costs in and around Fort Myers are low between May and mid-December, when 30–60 percent gets lopped off the standard rates. However, in high season, prices skyrocket, and spare rooms are rare. Downtown, look along 1st Street: the riverfront *Sea Chest*, at no. 2571 (☎1-800/438-6461; ❸), is among the cheapest. At the beaches, Estero Boulevard is your best bet: the *Beacon*, no. 1240 (☎239/463-5264; ❹), and *Casa Playa*, no. 510 (☎1-800/569-4876, ⓦwww.casaplayaresort.com; ❺), are both clean and reliable. Of the **campgrounds**, only *Red Coconut*, 3001 Estero Blvd (from $31; ☎239/463-7200, ⓦwww.redcoconut.com), is right on the beach.

For downtown **food**, try *Bara Bread*, 1520 Broadway (☎239/334-8216), for inexpensive bistro fare and baked goods, or *Oasis Restaurant*, 2260 Dr Martin Luther King Jr Blvd (☎239/334-1556), for large, cheap breakfasts and lunch specials. At the beaches, sample the Greek and other Mediterranean food at the *Orpheus Café*, 1165 Estero Blvd (Ⓣ 239/463-1549), or stop for some seafood at *Top O' The Mast*, 1028 Estero Blvd (Ⓣ 239/463-9424), where there's also live music and DJs.

The Everglades

Whatever scenic excitement you might anticipate from one of the country's more celebrated natural areas – whether you arrive west from Miami or south from Fort Myers, seventy miles from either direction along US-41 – there's nothing to herald your arrival in **THE EVERGLADES**. The most dramatic sights are small pockets of trees poking above a completely flat sawgrass plain. Yet, these wide-open spaces resonate with life, forming part of an ever-changing ecosystem, evolved through a unique combination of climate, vegetation, and wildlife.

Though it appears to be flat as a table-top, the limestone on which the Everglades stands actually tilts very slightly towards the southwest. For thousands of years, water from summer storms and the overflow of nearby Lake Okeechobee has moved slowly through the Everglades towards the coast. The water replenishes the sawgrass, which grows on a thin layer of soil formed by decaying vegetation. This gives birth to the algae at the base of a complex food chain that sustains much larger creatures, most importantly **alligators**. After the floodwaters have reached the sea, drained through the bedrock, or simply evaporated, the Everglades are barren except for the water accumulated in ponds – or "gator holes" – created when an alligator senses water and clears the soil covering it with its tail. Besides nourishing the alligator, the pond provides a home for other wildlife until the summer rains return. Sawgrass covers much of the Everglades, but where natural indentations in the limestone fill with soil, fertile tree islands – or "**hammocks**" – appear, just high enough to stand above the floodwaters.

Several **Native American tribes** once lived hunter-gatherer existences in the Everglades. The shell mounds they built can still be seen in sections of the park.

△ The Everglades

By the late 1800s, a few towns had sprung up, peopled by settlers who, unlike the Indians, looked to exploit the land. As Florida's population grew, the damage caused by hunting, road building, and draining for farmland gave rise to a significant **conservation** lobby. In 1947, a section of the Everglades was declared a national park. However, unrestrained commercial use of nearby areas continues to upset the Everglades' natural cycle. The 1200 miles of canals built to divert the flow of water away from the Everglades and toward the state's expanding cities, the poisoning caused by agricultural chemicals from local farmlands, and the broader changes wrought by global warming could yet turn Florida's greatest natural asset into a wasteland.

Everglades National Park

Throughout the last century, the Everglades' boundaries have been steadily pushed back by urban development. Today, **EVERGLADES NATIONAL PARK** bestows federal protection to only a comparatively small section at the southern tip of the Florida peninsula.

Arrival and information

There are **three entrances** to the park: Everglades City, at the northwestern corner; Shark Valley, at the northeastern corner; and the one near the Ernest Coe Visitor Center, at the southeastern corner. **US-41** skirts the northern edge of the park, providing the only land access to the Everglades City and Shark Valley entrances. There is **no public transportation** along US-41, or to any of the park entrances.

Park entry is free at Everglades City, although from there you can travel only by boat or canoe. At Shark Valley it's $8 per car and $4 for pedestrians and cyclists; near Ernest F. Coe, it's $10 and $5, respectively. Entry tickets are valid for seven days.

The park is **open year-round**, but the most favorable time to visit is **winter**, when the receding floodwaters cause wildlife to congregate around gator holes, ranger-led activities are frequent, and the mosquitoes are bearable. In **summer**, afternoon storms flood the prairies, park activities are substantially reduced, and the mosquitoes are a severe annoyance. Visiting between seasons is also a good bet.

Accommodation

There are a handful of places to stay in the towns just outside the park's perimeters. In Everglades City, try the charming and clean *Ivey House*, 107 Camellia St (☎239/695-3299, ⓦwww.iveyhouse.com; closed June–Sept; reserve ahead; ❸), or the eccentric *The Banks of the Everglades*, 201 W Broadway (☎239/695-3151, ⓦwww.banksoftheeverglades.com; ❺), housed in what once was the first bank in Collier County. South of Everglades City, at Chokoloskee (see "Everglades City and around," p.666), you can rent an **RV** by the night for $69–89, at Outdoor Resorts (☎239/695-2881). Ten miles east of the park, in Florida City, *The Everglades International Hostel*, 20 SW 2nd Ave, off Palm Drive (☎1-800/372-3874, ⓦwww.evergladeshostel.com), is the best option for budget-minded travelers who don't want to camp. Beds go for $20 a night and private rooms are available from $50. The hostel runs canoe and bike **tours** and, for $5, offers roundtrip transport to the park entrance. Hurricane damage has closed the only **hotel** within the park, the *Flamingo Lodge* (☎239/695-3101, ⓦwww.flamingolodge.com); call or check the website for reopening dates. There are well-equipped **campgrounds** (both $14/night; reservations at ☎1-800/365-CAMP or ⓦwww.nps.gov) at Flamingo and Long Pine Key, six miles from the Coe entrance. There are also many free backcountry spots on the longer walking and canoe trails (permits are issued at the visitor centers for a $10 fee).

Everglades City and around

Purchased and named in the 1920s by an advertising executive dreaming of a sub-tropical metropolis, **EVERGLADES CITY**, three miles south off US-41 along Route 29, now has a population of just under five hundred. Most who visit are solely intent on diminishing the stocks of sports fish living around the mangrove islands – the aptly titled **Ten Thousand Islands** – arranged like scattered jigsaw-puzzle pieces around the coastline.

For a closer look at the mangroves, which safeguard the Everglades from surge tides, take one of the park-sanctioned **boat trips**. Try either the Everglades National Park Boat Tours (℡239/695-2591) or Everglades Rentals and Eco Adventures (℡239/695-3299, ⓦwww.evergladesadventures.com), at the *Ivey House* (see p.665). Trips leave from the dock on **Chokoloskee**, a blob of land – actually a Native American shell mound – marking the southern end of Route 29. The dockside **Gulf Coast Visitor Center** (daily: May–Oct 9am–4.30pm, Nov–April 8am–4.30pm; ℡239/695-3311) provides details on the cruises, as well as the excellent ranger-led **canoe trips**.

Shark Valley

Driven out of central Florida by white settlers, several hundred Seminoles retreated to the Everglades during the nineteenth century. Their descendants, the **Miccosukees**, still live here – though the coming of US-41 brought a fundamental change in their lifestyle, as tourist dollars became more accessible. For example, the souvenir shop at the **Miccosukee Indian Village** (daily 9am–5pm; $10; ℡305/223-8380) carries both good-quality traditional crafts and items of questionable worth.

A mile east of the village, **Shark Valley** (entrance open daily 8.30am–6pm) epitomizes the Everglades' "River of Grass" moniker. From here, dotted by hardwood hammocks, the sawgrass plain stretches as far as the eye can see. Aside from a few simple walking trails close to the **visitor center** (daily: May–Oct 9.15am–5.15pm, Nov–April 8.45am–5.15pm; ℡305/221-8776), you can see Shark Valley only from a fifteen-mile loop road, ideally covered by renting a **bike** ($6 an hour; must be returned by 4pm). Alternatively, a highly informative two-hour **tram tour** (daily; $14; reservations on ℡305/221-8455) stops frequently to view wildlife, but won't allow you to linger in any particular place, as you'll certainly want to do.

Pine Island and Flamingo

The **Pine Island** section of the park – from the Coe Visitor Center entrance to Flamingo, perched at the end of the park road on Florida's southern tip – holds virtually everything that makes the Everglades tick. Spend a day or two in this southerly portion of the park and you'll quickly grasp the fundamentals of its complex ecology.

Route-9336 (the only road in this section of the park) leads past the **Earnest Coe Visitor Center** (daily: May–Oct 9am–5pm, Nov–April 8am–5pm; ℡305/242-7700) to the main park entrance. A mile further on, the **Royal Palm Visitor Center** (open 24hrs) is a good place to gather information on the Everglades' various habitats. The large numbers of park visitors who simply want to see an alligator are usually satisfied by walking the half-mile **Anhinga Trail** here: the notoriously lazy reptiles are easily seen during the winter, often splayed near the trail, looking like plastic props. All manner of birdlife can also be spotted, from snowy egrets to the bizarre, eponymous anhinga, an elegant black-bodied bird resembling an elongated cormorant. To beat the crowds, go early to the Anhinga Trail; after that, peruse the adjacent, but very different, **Gumbo Limbo Trail**, a hardwood jungle hammock packed with exotic subtropical growths.

If you're game, continue along Rte-9336 for thirty-seven miles (past many short hiking-trail opportunities) to the tiny coastal settlement of **FLAMINGO**, a former fishing colony now comprising a marina and campground. A century ago, the only way to get here was by boat – the place was so remote that it didn't even have a name until the opening of a post office made one necessary.

Flamingo now does a brisk trade servicing the needs of sports-fishing enthusiasts. On land, the **visitor center** (Nov to mid-April 8.30am–5pm; intermittent hours rest of year; ☎239/695-2945) and the marina of the *Flamingo Lodge* (see p.665) are the centers of activity. From the marina, the informative **Backcountry Cruise** (daily except Tues & Wed; $18; reservations on ☎239/695-3101) makes a two-hour foray around the mangrove-enshrouded Whitewater Bay, north of Flamingo.

The Panhandle

Rubbing hard against Alabama in the west and Georgia in the north, the long, narrow **Panhandle** has much more in common with the states of the Deep South than with the rest of Florida. Hard to believe, then, that just a century ago, the Panhandle *was* Florida. At the western edge, **Pensacola** was a busy port when Miami was still a swamp. Fertile soils lured wealthy plantation owners south, helping to establish **Tallahassee** as a high-society gathering place and administrative center – a role which, as the state capital, it retains. But the decline of cotton, the chopping-down of too many trees, and the coming of the East Coast railroad eventually left the Panhandle high and dry. Much of the inland region still seems neglected, and the **Apalachicola National Forest** is perhaps the best place in Florida to disappear into the wilderness. The **coastal Panhandle**, on the other hand, is enjoying better times: despite rows of hotels, much is still untainted, boasting miles of blinding white sands.

Tallahassee and around

State capital it may be, **TALLAHASSEE** is nevertheless a provincial city of oak trees and soft hills that won't take more than two days to explore in full. Around its small grid of central streets – where you'll find plenty of reminders of Florida's formative years – briefcase-clutching bureaucrats mingle with some of Florida State University's 35,000 students, who brighten the mood considerably and keep the city awake at night.

Tallahassee was built on the site of an important prehistoric meeting place, and takes its name from the Apalachee Indian: *talwa* meaning "town," and *ahassee* meaning "old." The city's **history** really begins, though, with Florida's incorporation into the US, and Tallahassee's selection as the state's administrative base; the first Florida government convened here in 1823. Since then, Tallahassee has been the scene of every major wrangle in Florida politics, including the controversial ballot recount of the 2000 presidential election. Today, in contrast to the lightning-paced development of south Florida, Tallahassee has a slow tempo and a strong sense of the past, evoked in its historic buildings and museums.

Arrival and information

Tallahassee's Greyhound **bus terminal** is at 112 W Tennessee St (☎850/222-4249), within easy walking distance of downtown, which can easily be explored on **foot**. For stacks of background information, drop by the **Visitor Information Center**, 106 E Jefferson St (Mon–Fri 8am–5pm, Sat 9am–1pm; ☎1-800/628-2866, ⊛www.seetallahassee.com).

Accommodation

Accommodation in Tallahassee is in short supply only during the sixty-day sitting of the state legislature, from early March, and on fall weekends during home football games of the Florida State Seminoles. **Hotels** and **motels** on N Monroe Street, about three miles from downtown, are far cheaper than those downtown.

Governors Inn 209 S Adams St ☎1-800/342-7717, ⊛www.thegovinn.com. Every room in this splendid downtown inn is decorated with antique furniture reflecting the period of the governor each is named after. ➏
Super 8 2801 N Monroe St ☎850/386-8286. A good option for the budget traveler, this motel offers simple rooms with basic amenities. ➌
University Inn & Suites 691 W Tennessee St ☎850/224-8161, ⊛www.universityinntallahassee.com. Renovated rooms on the perimeter of the FSU campus – perfect for visiting parents or homeless students. ➌

The Town

A fifty-million-dollar eyesore dominates the square mile of **downtown Tallahassee**: the vertical vents of the towering **New Capitol Building**, at Apalachee Parkway and Monroe Street (Mon–Fri 8am–5pm; free). Florida's growing army of bureaucrats had previously been crammed into the more attractive 1845 **Old Capitol Building** (Mon–Fri 9am–4.30pm, Sat 10am–4.30pm, Sun noon–4.30pm; free), which stands in the shadow of its replacement.

For easily the fullest account of Florida's past anywhere in the state, visit the **Museum of Florida History**, 500 S Bronough St (Mon–Fri 9am–4.30pm, Sat 10am–4.30pm, Sun noon–4.30pm; free; ☎850/245-6400, ⊛www.museumofloridahistory.com). Detailed accounts of Paleo-Indian settlements, and the significance of their burial and temple mounds, some of which have been found on the edge of Tallahassee, are valuable tools in comprehending Florida's prehistory. The colonialist crusades of the Spanish are outlined with copious finds, though there's little on the nineteenth-century Seminole Wars – one of the bloodier skeletons in Florida's closet. There is plenty on the building of the railroads, however.

The **Black Archives Research Center and Museum**, in the nineteenth-century Union Bank Building, along Apalachee Parkway from the Old Capitol's entrance (Mon–Fri 9am–5pm; free; ☎850/599-3020), holds one of the largest and most important collections of African-American artifacts in the nation, with oral histories and music stations, as well as some chilling Ku Klux Klan memorabilia.

Eating

With so many politicos and students, there's plenty of good **food** for all budgets in Tallahassee.

Andrew's Capital Grill & Bar/Andrew's 228
228 S Adams St ☎850/222-3444. Stylish lunch
spot with pricier gourmet meals – tuna tartare and
succulent lamb chops, for example – upstairs in
the evenings.
Barnacle Bill's 1830 N Monroe St ☎850/385-
8734. Inexpensive fresh fish and seafood served in
a riotous atmosphere.
Capital Steak House in the *Holiday Inn Select*,
316 W Tennessee St ☎850/222-9555. Even confirmed white-meat-eaters are giving this steak-

house rave reviews for its high-quality Angus beef.
La Fiesta 2329 Apalachee Pkwy
☎850/656-3392. The very best Mexican
food in the city.
Mom and Dad's 4175 Apalachee Pkwy
☎850/877-4518. Delicious homemade Italian food.
Closed Sun & Mon.
Po' Boys Creole Café 224 E College Ave
☎850/224-5400. A range of Creole delights;
also one of Tallahassee's most popular live music
venues.

Wakulla Springs State Park

Fifteen miles south of Tallahassee, off Route-61 on Route-267, **Wakulla Springs State Park** (daily 8am–sunset; cars $4, pedestrians and cyclists $1; ☎850/224-5950) holds what is believed to be one of the biggest and deepest natural springs in the world. It pumps up half a million gallons of crystal-clear pure water from the bowels of the earth every day – though you'd never guess it from the calm surface.

It's refreshing to **swim** in the cool pool (in a small roped-off area – this is gator territory), but to learn more about the spring, take the thirty-minute **glass-bottom boat tour** ($6), and peer down to the swarms of fish hovering around the 180-foot cavern through which the water flows. Forty-minute **river cruises** ($6) let you glimpse some of the park's inhabitants: deer, turkeys, turtles, herons, egrets, and the inevitable alligators. Built in 1937 beside the spring, the lovely wooden *Wakulla Lodge* (☎850/224-5950; ❹) is a serene hotel, with an excellent **restaurant** serving home-cooked country food for breakfast, lunch, and dinner.

The Apalachicola National Forest

With swamps, savannahs, and springs dotted liberally about its half-million acres, the **Apalachicola National Forest**, which fans out southwest of Tallahassee, is the inland Panhandle at its natural best. Several roads enable you to drive through a good-sized chunk, with many undemanding spots for a rest and a snack. To see deeper into the forest you'll need to make more of an effort, by following one of the hiking trails, canoeing on the rivers, or simply spending a night under the stars at one of the basic campgrounds. On the forest's southern edge, the large and forbidding **Tate's Hell Swamp** is a breeding-ground for the deadly water moccasin snake, and though gung-ho locals sometimes venture in hoping to catch a few to sell to zoos, you're well advised to stay clear.

The main **entrances** to the forest (free) are off Hwy-20 and Hwy-319; three minor roads, routes 267, 375, and 65, form cross-forest links between the two highways. **Accommodation** is limited to camping; apart from Camel Lake and Wright Lake ($8 per night for both; hot showers available), all the campgrounds are free (except for a $3 daily vehicle charge), with very basic facilities (no running water). For more information, call the **ranger stations** at Apalachicola (☎850/643-2282) or Wakulla (☎850/926-3561).

Panama City Beach

Follow Hwy-98 fifty miles west from Apalachicola and you'll hit the orgy of motels, go-kart tracks, mini-golf courses, and amusement parks that is **PANAMA**

CITY BEACH. Entirely without pretension, the area capitalizes blatantly on the appeal of its 27-mile stretch of white sand. The whole place is as commercialized as can be, but with the shops, bars, and restaurants all trying to undercut one another, there are some great bargains to be found. That said, throughout the lively summer (the so-called "100 Magic Days"), accommodation costs are high and reservations essential. In winter, prices drop and visitors are fewer; most are Canadians and – increasingly – Europeans, many of whom have no problem sunbathing and swimming in the cool temperatures.

Getting a tan, running yourself ragged at beach sports, and going all-out on the nightlife are the main concerns in Panama City Beach, one of the country's foremost Spring Break destinations. Go-karting, jet-skiing, and parasailing are all available at many locations along the coastal strip; otherwise, splash around at the water park ($28 for a go-on-everything day-ticket). For scuba-divers, several explorable shipwrecks litter the area; get details from any of the numerous dive shops.

Practicalities

Places to stay, while plentiful, fill with amazing speed, especially at weekends. As a general rule, **motels** at the east end of the beach are smarter and slightly pricier than those in the center. Those at the west end are quieter and more family oriented. The *Sugar Sands Motel*, 20723 Front Beach Rd (℡1-800/367-9221, Ⓦwww. sugarsands.com; ❸), is an excellent-value oceanfront motel away from the noise. The cheapest places to **eat** are the buffet restaurants on Front Beach Road, which charge $5–10 for all you can manage. Alternatively, try one of the regular lunch or dinner restaurants: *Shuckum's Oyster Pub & Seafood Grill*, 15614 Front Beach Rd (℡850/235-3214); *Mike's Diner*, 17554 Front Beach Rd (℡850/234-1942), which is also open for breakfast, and until late at night; or the *Boatyard*, 5323 N Lagoon Dr (℡850/249-9273), for al-fresco dining beside a lagoon. **At night**, party-goers congregate at *Club La Vela*, 8813 Thomas Drive (℡850/235-1061), or *Spinnaker*, 8795 Thomas Drive (℡850/234-7892), each with dozens of bars, several discos, and a young crowd.

Pensacola and around

You might be inclined to overlook **PENSACOLA**, tucked away as it is at the western end of the Panhandle. The city, on the northern bank of the broad Pensacola Bay, is five miles inland from the nearest beaches, and its prime features are a naval aviation school and some busy dockyards. Pensacola is, however, worth a visit. The nearby white beaches are relatively untouched, and it boasts a rich history, having been occupied by the Spanish as early as 1559. The town repeatedly changed hands between the Spanish, the French, and the British before becoming the place where Florida was officially ceded by Spain to the US in 1821.

Pensacola was already a booming port by c.1900, when the opening of the Panama Canal was expected to boost its fortunes still further. The many new buildings that appeared in the **Palafox District**, around the southerly section of Palafox Street, in the early 1900s – with their delicate ornamentation and attention to detail – reflect the optimism of the era.

In earlier times, Native Americans, pioneer settlers, and seafaring traders had gathered to swap, sell, and barter on the waterfront of the **Seville District**, just east of Palafox Street. Those who did well took up permanent residence here, and many of their homes remain in fine states of repair, forming – together with several museums – the **Historic Pensacola Village** (Mon–Sat 10am–4pm; $6; ⊕850/595-5985, ⓦwww.historicpensacola.org). Tickets are valid for one week, and allow access to all of the museums and former homes in an easily navigated four-block area. Inside the US naval base on Navy Boulevard, about eight miles southwest of central Pensacola, the **Museum of Naval Aviation** (daily 9am–5pm; free, IMAX movie $8; ⊕1-800/327-5002, ⓦwww.naval-air.org) exhibits US naval aircraft. They range from the first flimsy seaplane, acquired in 1911, to the Phantoms and Hornets of more recent times.

Pensacola Beach

On the other (south) side of the bay from the city, glistening beaches and wind-swept sand dunes fringe the fifty-mile-long **Santa Rosa Island**. On the island directly south of Pensacola, **PENSACOLA BEACH** has everything you'd want from a Gulf Coast beach: fine white sands, watersports rental outlets, a busy fishing pier, and a sprinkling of motels, beachside bars, and snack stands.

Practicalities

The Greyhound **bus station** is seven miles north of the city center, at 505 W Burgess Rd (⊕850/476-4800); ECAT buses #10A and #10B ($1.50; ⊕850/595-3228, ⓦwww.goecat.com) link it to Pensacola proper. A good local **taxi** firm is Yellow Cab (⊕850/433-3333). ECAT **buses** serve the city, while #21 goes to the beach three times daily; the main terminal is at 1515 W Fairfield Drive. At the foot of the city side of the three-mile Pensacola Bay Bridge, the **visitor center**, 1401 E Gregory St (daily 8am–5pm; ⊕1-800/874-1234, ⓦwww.visitpensacola.com), has the usual worthwhile handouts.

Plenty of budget chain **hotels**, charging $45–60 per night, line North Davis and Pensacola boulevards, the main approach roads from I-10. Central options are the *Seville Inn*, 223 E Garden St (⊕1-800/277-7275, ⓦwww.sevillepensacola.com; ❸), and ⚑ *Noble Manor*, 110 W Strong St (⊕850/434-9544, ⓦwww.noblemanor. com; ❹), a charming B&B. At Pensacola Beach, try the comfortable *Best Western Resort*, 16 Via De Luna Drive (⊕850/933-3300 or 1-800/320-8108; ❺). For **eating** in town, *Fish House*, 600 S Barracks St (⊕850/470-0003), has sushi and steaks along with the seafood. For beachside dining, *Peg Leg Pete's*, 1010 Fort Pickens Rd (⊕850/932-4139), is known for its Cajun food and excellent raw bar.

Louisiana

AL - ALABAMA	IN - INDIANA	MN - MINNESOTA	RI - RHODE ISLAND
AR - ARKANSAS	LA - LOUISIANA	MS - MISSISSIPPI	SC - SOUTH CAROLINA
CT - CONNECTICUT	MA - MASSACHUSETTS	NC - NORTH CAROLINA	VA - VIRGINIA
DE - DELAWARE	MD - MARYLAND	NH - NEW HAMPSHIRE	VT - VERMONT
FL - FLORIDA	ME - MAINE	NJ - NEW JERSEY	WI - WISCONSIN
IL - ILLINOIS	MI - MICHIGAN	PA - PENNSYLVANIA	WV - WEST VIRGINIA

CHAPTER 8

Highlights

* **Swamp tours** Watch out for alligators lurking in the ghostly, Spanish-moss-shaded bayous. See p.681 & p.710

* **Sunset over the Mississippi, New Orleans** Settle down on a wooden bench and watch the sky turn scarlet over one of the world's great rivers. See p.683

* **Donna's, New Orleans** Brass bands, trad jazz, and very happy music fans in a downhome barbecue joint. See p.697

* **Mardi Gras** From the masking and dancing of New Orleans's urban spectacular, to Cajun country's pagan rituals, Louisiana's Fat Tuesday is unlike any other. See p.698 & p.704

* **Laura Plantation** By far the River Road's most intriguing and illuminating account of Creole plantation life. See p.702

* **Café des Amis, Breaux Bridge** Scrumptious Cajun cooking and weekend zydeco breakfasts make this delightful social hub a must. See p.707

* **Angola prisoner rodeo** An unbelievable spectacle, with lifers slugging it out for guts and glory in this notorious maximum-security prison. See p.711

△ Cast-ironwork in the Garden District

Louisiana

Swathed in the romance of pirates, voodoo, and Mardi Gras, **LOUISIANA** is undeniably special. Its history is barely on nodding terms with the view that America was the creation of the Pilgrim Fathers; its way of life is proudly set apart. This is the land of the rural, French-speaking **Cajuns** (descended from the Acadians, eighteenth-century French-Canadian refugees), who live in the prairies and swamps in the southwest of the state, and the Creoles of jazzy, sassy **New Orleans**. (The term **Creole** was originally used to define anyone born in the state to French or Spanish colonists – famed in the nineteenth century for their masked balls, family feuds, and duels – as well as native-born, French-speaking slaves, but has since come to define anyone or anything native to Louisiana, and in particular its black population.) Louisiana's distinctive, spicy **cuisine**, regular **festivals**, and, above all, its **music** (**jazz**, **R&B**, **Cajun**, and its bluesy black counterpart, **zydeco**) draw from all these cultures and more. Oddly enough, **northern Louisiana** – Protestant Bible Belt country, where old plantation homes stand decaying in vast cottonfields – feels more "Southern" than the marshy bayous, shaded by ancient cypress trees and laced with wispy trails of Spanish moss, of the Catholic south.

The **French** first settled Louisiana in 1682, braving treacherous swamps and plagues to harvest the abundant cypress. The state was sparsely inhabited before its first permanent settlement, the trading post of **Natchitoches**, was established in 1714, followed by New Orleans in 1718. In 1760, Louis XV secretly handed New Orleans, along with all French territory west of the Mississippi, to his **Spanish** cousin, Charles III, as a safeguard against British expansionism. Louisiana remained Spanish until it was ceded to Napoleon in 1801, under the proviso that it should never change hands again. Just two years later, however, Napoleon, strapped for cash to fund his battles with the British in Europe, struck a bargain with president Thomas Jefferson known as the **Louisiana Purchase**. This sneaky agreement handed over to the US all French lands between Canada and Mexico, from the Mississippi to the Rockies, for a total cost of $15 million. The subsequent "Americanization" of Louisiana was one of the most momentous periods in the state's history, with the port of New Orleans, in its key position near the mouth of the **Mississippi River**, growing to become one of the nation's wealthiest cities. Though the state seceded from the Union to join the Confederacy in 1861, there were important differences between Louisiana and the rest of the slave-driven South. The **Black Code**, drawn up by the French in 1685 to govern Saint-Domingue (today's Haiti) and established in Louisiana in 1724, had given slaves rights unparalleled elsewhere, including permission to marry, meet socially, and take Sundays off. The black population of New Orleans in particular was renowned as exceptionally literate and cosmopolitan, with a significant number of **free people of color** who owned businesses, property, and even slaves.

Though Louisiana was not badly scarred physically by the Civil War, with few important battles fought on its soil, its economy was ravaged, and its social structures all but destroyed. The **Reconstruction** era, too, hit particularly hard here, with the once great city of New Orleans suffering a period of unprecedented lawlessness and racial violence. In time, the economy, at least, recovered, benefiting from the key importance of the mighty Mississippi and the discovery of offshore oil in the 1950s – but during the twentieth century Louisiana came to rely heavily upon **tourism**, centered on New Orleans and Cajun country. In August 2005, the double whammy of **Hurricane Katrina**, which swept though the coastal wetlands, and the horrific after-effects of the levee breaks in New Orleans, seemed as if it might put an end to all that. Recovery, however, continues slowly but surely, and though no thinking person can visit southern Louisiana today without feeling a deep sense of loss, the state still has a huge amount to offer. Whether you're canoeing along a cypress-clogged bayou, dining in a crumbling Creole cottage on spicy, buttery crawfish, or dancing on a steamy starlit night to the best live music in the world, Louisiana remains unique – and a place that now, more than ever, needs your support.

Getting around Louisiana

Louisiana is crossed east-west by two major **interstates**, I-20 in the north and I-10 in the south. New Orleans is the hub, traversed by I-10 and served by I-55 and I-59 from Mississippi. I-49 sweeps across southeast to northwest, connecting Cajun country with the north.

The international **airport** is in New Orleans; regional airlines serve the rest of the state and surrounding areas. Amtrak **trains** link New Orleans with New York, Chicago, and Memphis, as well as Los Angeles, via Lafayette. Greyhound **buses**

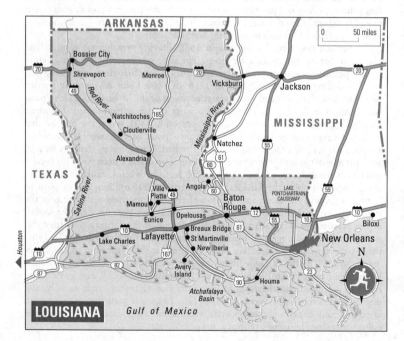

connect the major towns with the rest of the country, and are supplemented by smaller local lines. In addition to the Mississippi's bridges and causeways, **ferries** cross the river at New Orleans, St Francisville in Cajun country, and at various points along the River Road to Baton Rouge.

New Orleans

It is painfully clear, since the events of August 2005, that there's a lot more to **NEW ORLEANS** – the "Big Easy," the "city that care forgot" – than its image as a nonstop party town. And while this very special place has lost none of its power to bewitch, visiting New Orleans in the shadow of Katrina requires sensitivity and compassion. Even at the best of times this was a contradictory city, repeatedly striking you with the stark divisions between rich and poor (and, more explicitly, between white and black); after Katrina, with the emotional and physical scars still running deep, those contradictions are writ larger than ever. While you can still party in the French Quarter till the early hours, dancing to great jazz bands and gorging on delicious Creole food, just ten minutes away entire neighborhoods stand destroyed, blanketed by a ghostly silence. That's not to say that enjoying life is inappropriate in today's New Orleans – while it has been dealt a crippling blow, let down not only by nature but also by the federal and local governments, the city's vitality and *joie de vivre* remain real, buffeted but not beaten by the vagaries of commercialism, corruption, poverty and abandonment. The melange of cultures and races that built the city still gives it its heart; not "easy," exactly, but quite unlike anywhere else in the States – or the world.

New Orleans began life in 1718 as a **French-Canadian** outpost, an unlikely set of shacks on a disease-ridden marsh. Its prime location near the mouth of the **Mississippi River**, however, led to rapid development, and with the first mass importation of African **slaves**, as early as the 1720s, its unique demography began to take shape. Despite early resistance from its Francophone population, the city benefited greatly from its period as a **Spanish** colony between 1763 and 1800. By the end of the eighteenth century, the **port** was flourishing, the haunt of smugglers, gamblers, prostitutes, and pirates. Newcomers included Anglo-Americans escaping the American Revolution and aristocrats fleeing revolution in France. The city also became a haven for refugees – whites and **free blacks**, along with their slaves – escaping the slave revolts in Saint-Domingue (Haiti). As in the West Indies, the Spanish, French, and free people of color associated and formed alliances to create a distinctive **Creole** culture with its own traditions and ways of life, its own patois, and a cuisine that drew influences from Africa, Europe, and the colonies. New Orleans was already a many-textured place when it experienced two quick-fire changes of government, passing back into French control in 1801 and then being sold to **America** under the Louisiana Purchase two years later. Unwelcome in the Creole city – today's French Quarter – the Americans who migrated here were forced to settle in the areas now known as the **Central Business District** (or **CBD**) and, later, in the **Garden District**. **Canal Street**, which divided the old city from the expanding suburbs, became known as "the neutral ground" – the name still used when referring to the median strip between main roads in New Orleans.

Though much has been made of the antipathy between Creoles and Anglo-Americans, in truth economic necessity forced them to live and work together. They fought side by side, too, in the 1815 **Battle of New Orleans**, the final battle of the War of 1812, which secured American supremacy in the States. The victorious general, **Andrew Jackson**, became a national hero – and eventually US president; his ragtag volunteer army was made up of Anglo-Americans, slaves, Creoles, free men of color, and Native Americans. They were joined by pirates supplied by the notorious buccaneer **Jean Lafitte**, whose band of privateers made good use of the labyrinth of secluded bayous in the swamp-choked delta of the Mississippi River.

New Orleans's antebellum **golden age** as a major port and finance center for the cotton-producing South was brought to an abrupt end by the Civil War. The economic blow wielded by a lengthy Union occupation – which effectively isolated the city from its markets – was compounded by the social and cultural ravages of **Reconstruction**. This was particularly disastrous for a city once famed for its large, educated, free black population. As the North industrialized and other Southern cities grew, the fortunes of New Orleans took a downturn.

Jazz exploded into the bars and the bordellos around 1900, and, along with the evolution of **Mardi Gras** as a tourist attraction, breathed new life into the city. And although the Depression hit here as hard as it did the rest of the nation, it also – spearheaded by a number of local writers and artists – heralded the resurgence of the **French Quarter**, which had disintegrated into a slum. Even so, it was the less romantic duo of **oil** and **petrochemicals** that really saved the economy – until the slump of the 1950s pushed New Orleans well behind other US cities. The oil crash of the early 1980s gave it yet another battering, a gloomy start for near on two decades of high crime rates, crack deaths, and widespread corruption.

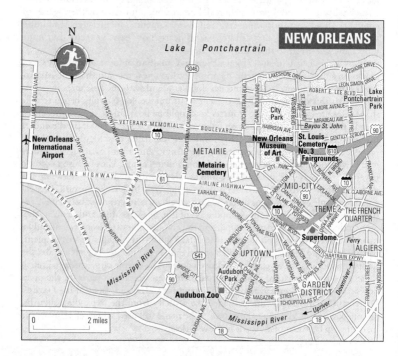

By the turn of the millennium things were improving, until, of course, **Hurricane Katrina** hit ground in 2005. At first it seemed as though the city had done relatively well, in light of the full-scale damage wrought along the Mississippi coast. On August 29, however, with the breach of the city's **levees**, the nightmare began. Over the course of a few days, rising floodwaters covered 80 percent of the city, destroying much of it in their wake. Most damage was sustained by residential areas – whether in the suburban homes around the lakeside, from where most residents had evacuated, to the less affluent neighborhoods of the east, where those too poor or ill or old to move were trapped in attics and on rooftops for days. The French Quarter, which, as the oldest part of the city was built on the highest ground, was physically unhurt by the flooding, although the economic blow – not least the loss of a huge number of the neighborhood's work force – was tremendous. The city's population remains drastically diminished, due to both fatalities and displacement, and many of those who were able to return still face enormous difficulty repairing their lives. While the grass-roots commitment to rebuilding remains, it is clearly going to take time – patience in New Orleans has become not only a virtue but a survival mechanism. And as the number of volunteers arriving to help dwindles, the city needs the support of tourists more than ever. A visit to New Orleans is a show of support, a defiant assertion that, despite the contempt shown it by federal government, this city matters. And for visitors, it's possible to still have a wonderful time here doing all (or most) of the things that you could do before the floods, as has been proven by the continued success, post-Katrina, of both Mardi Gras and Jazz Fest – huge boosts, both, to this beautiful and beleaguered city's battered morale.

Arrival and information

Louis Armstrong New Orleans International Airport (**MSY**), eighteen miles northwest of downtown on I-10, has an information booth (8am–9pm) in its baggage claim area, along with hotel courtesy phones. Flat-rate **taxi** fares into town are $28 for up to two people, or $12 each for three or more; **shuttles** can also take you to your hotel (every 10min; tickets available 24hr in the baggage claim area or from the bus driver; $13 to downtown hotels; ☏504/522-3500). **Greyhound** buses arrive next to **Amtrak** at the Union Passenger Terminal, 1001 Loyola Ave, near the Superdome. This area, in the no-man's-land beneath the elevated Pontchartrain Expressway, is not great; book a **cab** in advance to take you to your lodgings. United Cabs is the best firm (☏504/522-9771).

Before you leave home, it's worth contacting the **New Orleans CVB** (☏1-800/672-6124, ⓦwww.neworleanscvb.com); they mail out stacks of glossy brochures, and the website is full of helpful information. Once you've arrived, the best information, including self-guided walking tours, free **maps**, and a variety of discount vouchers can be found at the **Welcome Center**, on Jackson Square at 529 St Ann St in the Quarter (Tues–Sun 9am–5pm; ☏504/566-5031).

Staying safe in New Orleans

Although the heavily touristed French Quarter is comparatively safe, to wander unwittingly beyond it – even just a couple of blocks – can place your **personal safety** in serious jeopardy. While walking from the Quarter to the Marigny is usually safe enough, it's not a good idea to stray far from the main drag of Frenchmen Street. Wherever you are, use the usual common-sense precautions, and at night always take a cab when traveling any distance outside the Quarter.

Slow and sleepy at the best of times – which has always been part of its immense charm – New Orleans is now a city in **recovery**. A lot of it is not pretty, and the pain wrought by the flooding remains tangible. While huge efforts are being made to haul the place back to its feet, there are inevitable hitches and delays, last-minute changes, and overnight alterations. While all details in this chapter, including operating hours, were correct at press time, these are still subject to change. Though many places, especially those that had to limit themselves to weekend opening hours during the painfully slow process of rebuilding, have resumed business as normal, others may never do so. Restaurants may change their hours without notice, attractions may suddenly close down for a week or forever; service may be slower and more erratic than in other major American cities. Check websites or call before setting out, be patient, and go with the flow. You may get frustrated sometimes. Spare a thought for those who are living with it every day.

City transportation

Though New Orleans's most-visited neighborhoods are a dream to **walk** around, getting from one to another is not always easy on foot, and if you're traveling anywhere outside the Quarter after dark you'd be better off calling a **cab** (see above for a number). The Regional Transit Authority (RTA) runs a network of **buses** ($1.25, exact fare required; information Mon–Fri 8am–4pm ☏504/248-3900, ⓦwww.norta.com). The most useful **routes** include "Magazine" (#11), which runs between Canal Street in the CBD and Audubon Park uptown; and "Esplanade" (#91), from Rampart Street on the edge of the Quarter up to City Park.

Far more romantic is the handsome **St Charles streetcar** (a National Historic Monument, dating back around 100 years) that rumbles a thirteen-mile loop from Carondelet Street at Canal Street, along St Charles Avenue in the Garden District, past Audubon Park to Carrollton uptown. Damaged post-Katrina, the route currently runs only from Carondelet and Canal streets to Lee Circle, but is expected to be fully operational again by the end of 2007. The streetcar trundles along at an average speed of 9mph; service is limited after dark.

There's also a **riverfront** trolley, which makes ten stops between the Convention Center and Esplanade Avenue ($1.50, exact fare required), and a third line that runs up Canal Street to City Park ($1.25, exact fare required).

Accommodation

New Orleans has some lovely **places to stay**, from rambling old guesthouses seeping faded grandeur to stylish boutique hotels. **Room rates**, never low (you'll be pushed to find anything half decent for less than $75 a night), increase considerably for Mardi Gras and Jazz Fest, when prices can go up by as much as 200 percent and rooms are reserved months in advance. This is not a city in which you want to be stranded without a room, and though it's possible to take a chance on last-minute cancellations and deals, you should ideally make **reservations**. If you do turn up on spec, head immediately for the **welcome center** (see p.679), where you'll find racks of **discount leaflets** offering savings on same-day bookings (generally weekdays only).

Most people choose to stay in the **French Quarter**, in the heart of things. Many accommodations here are in atmospheric **guesthouses**, most of them in old Creole townhouses. In any one place, rooms can vary considerably in size, comfort,

Walking tours are especially popular in New Orleans – notwithstanding the possibility of showers and, in summer, debilitating heat and humidity. The **Jean Lafitte National Historic Park Service** offers scholarly and accessible overviews of the Quarter (daily 9.30am; 90mins; free; ☎504/589-2133; reservations required; sign up at the NPS visitor center, 419 Decatur St, after 9am on the day). Many visitors, especially with kids in tow, take a narrated trot through the Quarter in one of the **mule-drawn carriages** that wait behind Jackson Square on Decatur. These can be fun, though you should take the "historic" commentary with a pinch of salt. Rates range from $12 to $15 per person for a trip of between 30 and 45 minutes. Another pleasant way to while away a steamy afternoon is on a **river cruise**. Leaving from the Toulouse Street wharf behind the Jackson Brewery mall, the *Natchez* steamboat heads seven miles or so downriver before turning back near the Chalmette battlefield, with a running historical commentary from the captain and a live Dixieland band in the dining room (Wed 2.30pm, Thurs 2.30 & 7pm, Fri & Sat 11.30am, 2.30 & 7pm, Sun 11.30am & 2.30pm; 2hr; $19.50, $29.50 with lunch; evening cruise $33.50, $56.50 with dinner; ☎504/586-8777, ⊛www.steamboatnatchez.com). The *John James Audubon* riverboat allows you to combine a cruise with a trip to the aquarium (see p.683), the zoo (see p.692), or both. It leaves Tues–Sun from the aquarium at 10am, noon, 2pm, and 4pm, and from the zoo an hour later (1hr one way; $17.50 roundtrip, $31 with aquarium admission, $27 with zoo admission; ☎504/581-4629). Tickets for all cruises are sold at booths behind Jackson Brewery and the aquarium.

New Orleans's local **swamps** – many of them protected areas just thirty minutes' drive from downtown – are otherworldly enclaves that provide a wonderful contrast to the city itself. Dr Wagner's Honey Island Swamp Tours, based ten miles north of Lake Pontchartrain, venture onto the delta of the Pearl River, a wilderness occupied by nutrias, black bears, and alligators, as well as ibis, great blue herons, and snowy egrets (2hr; $25 adults, $15 children, not including transport from downtown; ☎985/641-1769, ⊛www.honeyislandswamp.com).

For details on **ghost**, **voodoo** and **cemetery** tours, see pp.686–7.

and amenities, so be specific if you have certain preferences. Outside the Quarter, the **Lower Garden District** offers a couple of budget options, while the funky **Faubourg Marigny** specializes in bed-and-breakfasts, and the **Garden District** proper has a couple of gorgeous old hotels. The **CBD** is the domain of the city's upmarket chain and boutique hotels; space at these is at a premium nowadays, as they are used to house government workers, conventioneers and businesspeople post-Katrina.

In the French Quarter

Chateau Hotel 1001 Chartres St ☎504/524-9636, ⊛www.chateauhotel.com. Simple, clean rooms in a quiet part of the Quarter. Some are better than others, so if you feel yours is too small or a bit dark, check to see what else is available. There's an outdoor café-bar by the pool, and rates include continental breakfast (which you can have in your room). **④**

Cornstalk Hotel 915 Royal St ☎504/523-1515, ⊛www.cornstalkhotel.com. Casually elegant, faded place in a turreted Queen Anne house, surrounded by a landmark cast-iron fence decorated with fat cornstalks. The appealing, high-ceilinged rooms

have lots of period detail, and the location is great. Rates include a small continental breakfast, which you can eat on the impressive veranda. **④**

A Creole House 1013 St Ann St ☎504/524-8076 or 1-800/535-7858, ⊛www.acreolehouse.com. Basic but acceptable guesthouse, bordering on shabby in places, with rooms ranging from cozy nooks with shared bath to suites. Rates include continental breakfast. **③**

Hotel Monteleone 214 Royal St ☎504/523-3341, ⊛www.hotelmonteleone.com. This handsome French Quarter landmark is the oldest hotel in the city, owned by the same family since 1886, and hosting a fine array of writers and luminaries since then. At 16 stories, it's something of a giant on Royal St, with an elegant Baroque facade, stunning old marble lobby, very comfy rooms, a revolving bar, and a rooftop pool. ❻

Olivier House 828 Toulouse St ☎504/525-8456, ⓦwww.olivierhouse.com. Though a bit dark in places, this atmospheric, quintessentially New Orleans guesthouse offers real character. The 42 rooms (all with bath) vary, but most have funky antique furniture and shutters. There's a tropical courtyard, and a tiny pool. ❻

Omni Royal Orleans 621 St Louis St ☎504/529-5333 ⓦwww.omnihotels.com. Landmark French Quarter hotel, stylish and swanky, with an old-fashioned New Orleans elegance that never intimidates. Rooms have a faded appeal, and the rooftop pool is lovely. ❻

Hotel Provincial 1024 Chartres St ☎504/581-4995 or 1-800/535-7922, ⓦwww.hotelprovincial.com. This sprawling – yet somehow intimate – place is set in a quiet part of the Quarter, with rooms opening onto five peaceful, gaslit courtyards. Some rooms are filled with antiques, others are more ordinary. There are two nice outdoor pools, a bar, and a fancy restaurant, *Stella*, on-site. ❻

Hotel Villa Convento 616 Ursulines St ☎504/522-1793, ⓦwww.villaconvento.com. Friendly, family-run guesthouse, often booked with return visitors. No-frills rooms with bath; some have balconies, while others open onto a patio. ❹

Outside the French Quarter

Columns Hotel 3811 St Charles Ave ☎504/899-9308, ☎1-800/445-9308, ⓦwww.thecolumns.com. Characterful Garden District hotel in a stately

1883 mansion. The whole place seeps louche glamour, especially the Victorian bar (see p.696) and the porch with its namesake columns. Some rooms come with a balcony, but there are no TVs. Rates include continental breakfast. ❻

The Frenchmen 417 Frenchmen St ☎504/948-2166 or 1-800/831-1781, ⓦwww.frenchmenhotel.com. Funky and friendly Faubourg Marigny guesthouse with 27 rooms, of variable sizes, spread across two 1860 townhouses. There's a patio, a small pool, and a Jacuzzi. Rates include continental breakfast. ❹

HI-New Orleans Marquette House 2249 Carondelet St ☎504/523-3014. Basic but not bad hostel near the Garden District. It's not one of the nicest HI properties, but the staff are friendly. Single-sex dorm beds go for $25; there are double rooms, a few with kitchens, in a separate building. Day use allowed. Reservations recommended. ❶–❸

Royal Street Inn 1431 Royal St ☎504/948-7499 or 1-800/449-5535, ⓦwww.royalstreetinn.com. Hip Faubourg Marigny lodging above the *R-Bar* (see p.696), and run by the same people. The six rooms (all with bath) are decorated on themes ranging from Art Deco through Bukowski to bordello; the four-person suites are good value. It's favored by a young crowd who hang out in the bar. ❹

St Charles Guest House 1748 Prytania St ☎504/523-6556, ⓦwww.stcharlesguesthouse.com. Bohemian Lower Garden District guesthouse offering a variety of rooms, none with phone or TV. Backpackers choose the basic 6ft by 8ft rooms for $45, but for the pricier en-suite doubles you can get better value elsewhere. It's friendly enough, though, with a hostel-like atmosphere, a pool, and free breakfast. They ask for deposits with reservations. No smoking. ❸

The City

New Orleans is sometimes called the **Crescent City**, because of the way it nestles between the southern shore of Lake Pontchartrain and a dramatic horseshoe bend in the Mississippi River. This unique location makes the city's layout confusing, with streets curving to follow the river, and shooting off at odd angles to head inland. Compass points are of little use here – locals refer instead to **lakeside** (toward the lake) and **riverside** (toward the river), and, using Canal Street as the dividing line, **uptown** (or upriver) and **downtown** (downriver).

Most visitors spend most of their time in the battered, charming old **French Quarter** (or *Vieux Carré*), site of the original settlement. Though it wasn't directly affected by the post-Katrina flooding, the aftershock has nonetheless taken its toll here, with boarded up shopfronts and shattered sidewalks – crushed by the Humvees that prowled the city during the post-flood evacuation – serving as sad reminders of the city's suffering. Places are steadily returning to some version of normal, however, and on busy weekends you could even imagine that the storm had never happened. On the Quarter's fringes, the funky **Faubourg Marigny** creeps downriver from Esplanade Avenue, while the Quarter's lakeside boundary, **Rampart Street**, marks the beginning of the historic, run-down African-American neighborhood of **Tremé**. On the other side of the Quarter, across **Canal Street**, the **CBD** (Central Business District), bounded by the river and I-10, spreads upriver to the Pontchartrain Expressway. Dominated by office buildings, hotels, and banks – many of them seriously damaged by the storm – it also incorporates the **Warehouse District** and, toward the lake, the gargantuan **Superdome**. A ferry ride across the river from the foot of Canal Street takes you to the suburban west bank and the residential district of old **Algiers**.

Back on the east bank, upriver from the CBD, the rarefied **Garden District** is an area of gorgeous old mansions, some of them in delectable ruin. The **Lower Garden District**, creeping between the expressway and Jackson Avenue, is quite a different creature, its run-down old houses filled with impoverished artists and musicians. Traditionally the preferred way to get to either neighborhood was on the rumbling streetcar (see p.692) along swanky **St Charles Avenue**, the Garden District's lakeside boundary, but you can also approach using **Magazine Street**, a six-mile stretch of galleries and antique stores that runs parallel to St Charles riverside. Entering the Garden District, you've crossed the official boundary into **uptown**, which spreads upriver to encompass **Audubon Park and Zoo**.

The French Quarter

The heartbreakingly beautiful **French Quarter** is where New Orleans began in 1718. Today, battered and bohemian, decaying and vibrant, it remains the spiritual core of the city, its fanciful cast-iron balconies, hidden courtyards, and time-stained stucco buildings exerting a haunting fascination that has long caught the imagination of artists and writers. Official tours are useful for orientation, but it's most fun simply to wander – and you'll need a few days at least to do it justice, absorbing the jumble of sounds, sights, and smells. Early morning, in the dazzling light from the river, is a good time to explore, as sleepy locals wake themselves

---

The Mississippi River

A resonant, romantic, and extraordinary physical presence, the **Mississippi River** is New Orleans's lifeblood and its raison d'être. In the nineteenth century, as the port boomed, the city gradually cut itself off from the river altogether, hemming it in behind a string of warehouses and railroads. But, as the importance of the port has diminished, a couple of downtown parks, plazas, and riverside walks, accessible from the French Quarter, the CBD, and uptown, have focused attention back onto the **waterfront**.

Crossing Decatur Street from Jackson Square brings you to the **Moon Walk**, a paved promenade studded with benches and raised flower boxes, where buskers serenade you as you gaze across the water. Upriver from here, long, thin **Woldenberg Park** makes a good place for a picnic, watching the river traffic drift by; it's also the location for a number of the city's free music festivals. At the upriver edge of the park, the **Aquarium of the Americas**, near the Canal Street wharf (Wed–Sun 10am–4pm; $17, children $10; IMAX $8/$5, aquarium and IMAX $22/$12, aquarium and zoo, $25/$14, aquarium, IMAX and zoo $28/$18), features a huge glass tunnel where visitors – rampaging infants, mostly – come face-to-face with rippling rays and ugly sawfish. There's also a swamp complete with a white gator, along with an Amazonian rainforest, petting tank, and IMAX theater.

For details of **river tours**, see p.681. And to read more about the Mississippi River itself, see p.561.

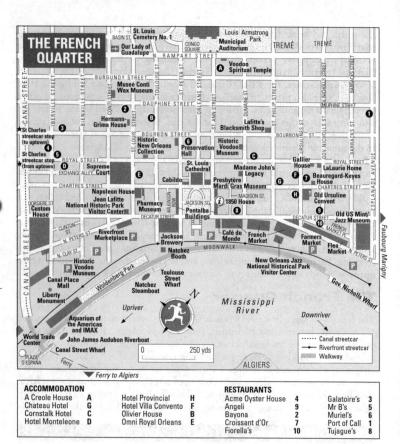

THE FRENCH QUARTER

St. Louis Cemetery No. 1
BASIN ST.
Our Lady of Guadalupe
CONGO SQUARE
Louis Armstrong Park
Municipal Auditorium
TREMÉ
TREMÉ

RAMPART STREET

A Voodoo Spiritual Temple

BURGUNDY STREET

Museé Conti Wax Museum

DAUPHINE STREET

2 Hermann-Grima House

3

★St Charles streetcar stop (to uptown)

St Charles streetcar stop (from uptown)

5

CANAL STREET
BERVILLE STREET
BIENVILLE STREET
CONTI STREET

ROYAL STREET
EXCHANGE ALLEY
4 Supreme Court

CHARTRES STREET

Napoleon House

DORSIERE ST
Custom House

Jean Lafitte National Historic Park Visitor Center

Pharmacy Museum

CLINTON ST.
N. PETERS ST.
N. CLAY ST.

P Riverfront Marketplace

P Jackson Brewery

Natchez Booth

P Historic Voodoo Museum

Canal Place Mall

Liberty Monument

Woldenberg Park

Natchez Steamboat

Toulouse Street Wharf

Aquarium of the Americas and IMAX

World Trade Center
John James Audubon Riverboat

Canal Street Wharf

PLAZA D'ESPANA
Ferry

▼ Ferry to Algiers

TOULOUSE ST.
ST. PETER ST.
ORLEANS STREET
ST. ANN STREET
DUMAINE ST.
ST. PHILIP STREET

Lafitte's Blacksmith Shop

BOURBON STREET

B

Historic New Orleans Collection

6 Preservation Hall

Historic Voodoo Museum

St. Louis Cathedral

Madame John's Legacy

GOV. NICHOLLS ST.
URSULINES ST.

BOURBON ST.

Gallier House

F LaLaurie Home

7 Beauregard-Keyes House

ROYAL STREET

CHARTRES STREET

H Old Ursuline Convent

DECATUR STREET

Old US Mint/ Jazz Museum

FRENCH MARKET PL.

ST. PHILIP STREET
DAUPHINE STREET

BARRACKS STREET

1

ESPLANADE AVENUE

Faubourg Marigny

E

Cabildo

Presbytère
Mardi Gras Museum

C

G

Madison St.

i 1850 House

Pontalba Buildings

Jackson Square

WILKINSON ROW

JACKSON SQ.

P

Café du Monde

French Market

MOONWALK

Farmers Market

10

P Flea Market

N. PETERS ST.

New Orleans Jazz National Historical Park Visitor Center

Gov. Nicholls Wharf

P

Mississippi River

Upriver

Downriver

N

ALGIERS

0 — 250 yds

LOUISIANA | New Orleans: The City

8

----- Canal streetcar
—•— Riverfront streetcar
▓ Walkway

ACCOMMODATION				RESTAURANTS			
A Creole House	A	Hotel Provincial	H	Acme Oyster House	4	Galatoire's	3
Chateau Hotel	G	Hotel Villa Convento	F	Angeli	9	Mr B's	5
Cornstalk Hotel	C	Olivier House	B	Bayona	2	Muriel's	6
Hotel Monteleone	D	Omni Royal Orleans	E	Croissant d'Or	7	Port of Call	1
				Fiorella's	10	Tujague's	8

up with strong coffee in neighborhood cafés, shops crank open their shutters, and all-night revelers stumble home.

The Quarter is laid out in a grid, unchanged since 1721. At just thirteen blocks wide – smaller than you might expect – it's easily walkable, bounded by the Mississippi River, Rampart Street, Canal Street, and Esplanade Avenue, and centering on lively **Jackson Square**. Rather than French, the famed **architecture** is predominantly Spanish Colonial, with a strong Caribbean influence. Most of the buildings date from the late eighteenth century, after much of the old city had been devastated by fires in 1788 and 1794. Shops, galleries, restaurants and bars are concentrated in the blocks between Decatur and Bourbon, while beyond Bourbon, up toward Rampart Street, and in the Lower Quarter, downriver from Jackson Square, things become more peaceful. Here, you'll find quiet, predominantly residential streets where the Quarter's **gay** community lives side by side with elegant dowagers, part-time condo-dwellers, and scruffy artists.

Jackson Square

Ever since its earliest incarnation as the Place d'Armes, a dusty parade ground used for public meetings and executions, **Jackson Square** has been at the heart

△ The Cabildo, in Jackson Square

of the Quarter. Today, with its iron benches, neat lawns, and blaze of flowerbeds, the park at the center of the square manages to stay tranquil despite the streams of photo-snapping tourists, school groups, bus boys on their breaks, and the odd crashed-out casualty. Presiding over them all, an **equestrian statue** – the first in the nation, constructed by Clark Mills in 1856 – shows Andrew Jackson in uncharacteristically jaunty mode, waving his hat. The hectoring inscription, "The Union Must and Shall be Preserved," was added by Union General "Beast" Butler during the Civil War occupation.

During the day, everyone passes by at some time or another, weaving their way through the tangle of artists, Lucky Dog hot-dog vendors, palm readers, shambolic brass bands, and blues musicians. A postcard-perfect backdrop for the Jackson statue, **St Louis Cathedral** is the oldest continuously active cathedral in the United States. It's the third church on this spot, built in 1794 after the first two had been destroyed by fire and hurricane. Dominated by three tall slate steeples, the facade, which marries Greek Revival symmetry with copious French arches, is oddly two-dimensional, like some elaborate stage prop for the street drama below. Though the cathedral has always been central to the life of this very Catholic city – Andrew Jackson laid his sword on the altar in thanks for victory at the Battle of New Orleans; voodoo queen Marie Laveau (see p.686) was baptized and married here – the interior offers little to get excited about.

On the upriver side of the cathedral, the **Cabildo** (Tues–Sun 9am–5pm; $6) was built as the Casa Capitular, seat of the Spanish colonial government. The building – which cuts an impressive dash with its colonnade, fan windows, and wrought-iron balconies – is now part of the **Louisiana State Museum** (see p.686). Inside, exhibits illuminate the complex tangle of cultures, classes, and races that binds together Louisiana's history, starting with the Native Americans and winding up with the demise of Reconstruction. Black history is well represented throughout, with as much emphasis on the free people of color as on the city's role as the major slave-

The Louisiana State Museum

The **Cabildo** and the **Presbytère** (see p.685–6), along with the **1850 House** (opposite), the **Old US Mint** (p.688), and **Madame John's Legacy** (p.689), together make up the **Louisiana State Museum**. Since Katrina, the 1850 House, Mint, and Madame John's Legacy have remained closed, but the aim is that all will eventually re-open. Combination tickets give a **discount** of 20 percent to two or more sites, and are good for three consecutive days.

trading center of the South. On the second floor you can see the bronze **death mask of Napoleon**, along with the reconstructed **Sala Capitular**, where the Louisiana Purchase was signed in 1803, and where, in 1892, the historic *Plessy vs Ferguson* case, which effectively legalized segregation throughout the South, was first argued.

Forming a matching pair with the Cabildo, the **Presbytère** (Tues–Sun 9am–5pm; $6), on the downriver side of the cathedral, was designed in 1791 as a rectory. It was never used as such, however, and after completion in 1813 went on to serve as a courthouse. Today, it's an unmissable **Mardi Gras museum**, covering carnival from every conceivable angle. Full of odd treasures – jewel-encrusted costumes, primitive masks, posters, bizarre dance cards – it also features videos, interactive themed rooms and music stations, managing perhaps more than any other museum to give a real sense of what makes this unique city tick.

Spooky New Orleans

Voodoo

Voodoo, still a significant presence in New Orleans, was brought to the city by African slaves via the French colonies of the Caribbean, where tribal beliefs were mixed with Catholicism to create a cult based on spirit worship. French, and later, Spanish authorities tried to suppress the religion (voodoo-worshipers had played an active role in the organization of slave revolts in Haiti), but it continued to flourish among the city's black population. Under American rule, the weekly slave gatherings at **Congo Square** (in what is now Louis Armstrong Park; see p.689), which included ritual ceremonies, turned into a tourist attraction for whites, fueled by sensationalized reports of hypnotized white women dancing naked to throbbing drum beats.

Unlike in the West Indies, where the cult was dominated by male priests, New Orleans had many voodoo priestesses. The most famous was **Marie Laveau**, a hairdresser of African, white, and Native American blood. Using shrewd marketing sense and inside knowledge of the lives of her clients, she was in high demand for her **gris-gris** ("gree gree") – spells or potions – which she prepared for wealthy Creoles and Americans, as well as Africans. Laveau died in 1881, after which another Marie, believed to be her daughter, continued to practice under her name. The legend of both Maries lives on, and their crumbling **tombs** are popular tourist attractions (see "The Cities of the Dead," below).

Today, voodoo is big business in New Orleans, with a glut of gift shops in the French Quarter selling ersatz gris-gris and exotic voodoo dolls; if you're interested in the real thing, head instead to the **Voodoo Spiritual Temple**, 828 N Rampart St (℡504/522-9627, ⓦwww.voodoospiritualtemple.org), where the charismatic Priestess Miriam offers open services, tours, and consultations.

The **Historic Voodoo Museum**, 724 Dumaine St (daily 10.30am–5.30pm; $5), is a ragtag collection of ceremonial objects, paintings, and gris-gris. Its aim, to debunk the myths that surround this misunderstood religion, is undermined somewhat by the deliciously spooky atmosphere, not to mention its resident Albino python, crumbling rat heads, and desiccated bats.

The elegant three-story **Pontalba Buildings**, which line St Peter and St Ann streets where they border the square, were commissioned by the formidable Baroness Pontalba, who, having returned from France in 1849 to find her real estate palling in comparison to the American sector across Canal Street, dreamed of replacing the shabby buildings around the Place d'Armes with elegant colonnaded structures resembling those she'd seen in Paris. Planned as both business and residential units, they are still used as such, and remain some of the city's most desirable places to live. These were not, as is commonly claimed, the first apartment buildings in the US, but they were innovative in their use of mass-produced materials and, in particular, of **cast iron** – indeed, it was these very balconies that sparked the citywide fad for lacy ironwork, which soon came to replace the plainer iron hand-wrought locally by African slaves. Part of the state museum (see opposite), the cordoned-off rooms of the **1850 House**, 523 St Ann St, re-create the tastes of the well-to-do Creole families who lived in these fashionable apartments. Unfortunately, though the self-guided tours draw attention to every piece of Vieux Paris china and fine crystal – a treat for decorative arts fans – they leave you with little sense of any real domestic detail.

Decatur Street and Esplanade Avenue

Something of an anomaly among Upper Decatur's brassy T-shirt shops and theme restaurants, the **Jean Lafitte National Historic Park and Preserve Visitor Center**, 419 Decatur St (daily 9am–5pm), is not only a starting point for excel-

The Cities of the Dead

So much of New Orleans is at, or below, sea level that early settlers who buried their dead – and there were many of them – found that during the frequent flooding great waves of moldy coffins would float to the surface of the sodden earth. Eventually, graves began to be placed, Spanish-style, in above-ground brick and stucco vaults, surrounded by small fences. These **cemeteries** grew to resemble cities, laid out in "streets"; today, as the tombs crumble away amid the overgrown foliage, they have become atmospheric in the extreme. The creepiness isn't totally imaginary, either – though armed muggers, rather than ghosts, are the danger these days. You should **never** venture into one alone. Nearly all the city tours (see p.681) include a trip around one of the most interesting of the cemeteries – Lafayette #1 in the Garden District, St Louis #1 and #2 in Tremé, or St Louis #3 in Mid-City – some (see "Tours," p.681) specialize in them.

Ghost tours

New Orleans's image as a Gothic, vampire-stalked city has spawned a variety of **tours** promising **magic, voodoo, vampires**, and **ghosts**. Among the campy, the overpriced, and the just plain silly, there are, nonetheless, a couple worth joining. **Historic New Orleans Walking Tours** (℡504/947-2120; ✆www.tourneworleans. com) has a good "Cemetery/Voodoo" tour covering St Louis Cemetery #1, Congo Square, Marie Laveau's home, and the Voodoo Spiritual Temple (Mon–Sat 10am & 1pm, Sun 10am; meet at *Café Beignet*, 334 Royal St), and, after dark, a "Haunted French Quarter" walk, which is slightly more tongue-in-cheek (daily 7.30pm; meet at *Snook's* bar, at Bourbon and Orleans). Both cost $15, last around 2 hours, and need no reservations. **Save Our Cemeteries** is a nonprofit restoration organization leading tours of Lafayette #1 (Mon, Wed, Fri & Sat 10.30am; 1hr; $6; no reservations; meet at the Washington Avenue Gate, 1400 block of Washington Ave) and St Louis #1 (Sun 10am; 1hr; $12; no reservations; meet at the Basin Street Station Visitor Center, 501 Basin St; ✆www.saveourcemeteries.org).

lent **walking tours** (see p.681), but also a great introduction to Louisiana's delta region. In addition to panels outlining local history, architecture, cultural traditions, and ecology, listening stations let you eavesdrop on natives expounding, in a variety of accents, on the meaning of all those unique local phrases and expressions, while touch-screen monitors feature classic footage of Louis Armstrong, Mahalia Jackson, and Professor Longhair, among others.

Downriver along Decatur, the specialty shops of the restored **French Market** – said to be on the site of a Native American trading area and certainly active since the 1720s – sell tourist knick-knacks; for stalls, head toward the old **Farmers' Market**, just off Decatur on N Peters Street, where fresh produce, spices, hot sauce, and the like are sold around the clock. Next door, a flea market abounds in trashy tack and bargain oddities; for vintage curiosities, head to the funky thrift and rummage stores opposite on Decatur.

The **New Orleans Jazz National Historical Park Visitor Center** (Tues–Sat 9am–5pm; free; ☎504/589-4841, ⓦwww.nps.gov/jazz), tucked away in the French Market at 916 N Peters St, is a must for music fans. Light and airy, with good acoustics and an intimate scale, it's a superb, informal place to attend frequent jazz concerts, talks, movies, and workshops; afterwards, check out the photo displays, self-guided jazz walking tour brochures, and bookstore.

Continuing downriver, you'll come to the outer boundary of the Quarter, **Esplanade Avenue**, an exquisite, oak-shaded boulevard lined with crumbling nineteenth-century Creole mansions. Part of the state museum (see p.686), the **Old US Mint**, on the 400 block near the river, sustained considerable storm damage to its roof and is currently closed. Pre-Katrina, it housed a fascinating **Jazz Museum**, and though some of the collection was destroyed, plans are underway to re-open as soon as possible. Check ⓦlsm.crt.state.la.us/mintex.htm for updates.

Across Esplanade from the Quarter, the arty **Faubourg Marigny** is an appealingly mixed, low-rent area of Creole cottages and shotgun houses. Though the neighborhood is gentrifying, and its gaggle of music venues, coffeeshops, and restaurants expanding further and further beyond the Quarter, it's best **not to wander** too far away from the blocks around Decatur and **Frenchmen Street**, the district's main drag. Even Elysian Fields – the street where Stanley and Stella lived in Tennessee Williams's *A Streetcar Named Desire* – can feel distinctly dodgy, despite its heavenly name.

Chartres and Royal streets

A left turn at the 600 block of Esplanade Avenue brings you to the **Old Ursuline Convent** at 1114 Chartres St. Built in 1745, this is the only intact French Colonial structure in the city, and quite possibly the oldest building in the Mississippi valley. It's one of the many places in the Quarter that are said to be haunted, its corridors roamed by specters of the "casket girls" – white virgins shipped over in the early days of the colony, who were kept here before being sold off as wives in an attempt to stop the increasing number of couplings between French settlers and African or Native American women. At the time of writing the convent's quirky museum of religious paraphernalia was still closed post-Katrina.

The **Beauregard-Keyes House**, opposite the convent at no. 1113 (tours hourly Mon–Sat 10am–3pm; $5), owes its name to Confederate General Pierre Beauregard – who ordered the first shot of the Civil War at Fort Sumter and rented a room here during Reconstruction – and to popular novelist Frances Parkinson Keyes. She refurbished this "raised cottage" (with the basement at ground level) as her winter home in the 1940s, and her possessions now fill what is essentially a museum of decorative arts. Keyes's novels – including *Madame Castel's Lodger*, a romance about the house's "Beauregard period"– are on sale in the gift shop.

A block north at 1132 Royal St, the handsome **Gallier House**, dating from 1857, is a fascinating little museum (tours Mon–Fri 10am, 11am, noon, 2pm & 3pm; $6, or $10 with the Hermann-Grima House, see p.690). James Gallier Jr was a leading architect of the day, and the innovative features he designed for his home, such as the outdoor cistern, cooling system and indoor plumbing, soon became essential for anyone wanting to live in comfort in this swampy climate. Meanwhile, the house's filigree cast-iron balconies would have been the last word in chic. Tours, which focus as much on social history as fine furniture, are some of the liveliest in the Quarter.

A rare example of the French Quarter's early West Indies-style architecture, with a distinctive deep, wraparound gallery, **Madame John's Legacy**, just off Royal at 628 Dumaine St (part of the Louisiana State Museum, see p.686), was rebuilt after the fire of 1788 as an exact replica of the 1730 house that had previously stood on the site. The building was constructed using the *briquete entre poteaux* technique, in which soft red brick is set between hand-hewn cypress beams, and raised off the ground on stucco-covered pillars. There never was a real Madame John – the name was given to the house by nineteenth-century author George Washington Cable in his tragic short story "'Tite Poulette," and it simply stuck, attracting hundreds of tourists to the city and spawning a nice line in Madame John souvenirs. On the ground floor, an exhibition details the house's various changes in fortune, while upstairs you'll find a very good museum of **Southern folk art** – though at the time of writing, Madame John's Legacy had still to re-open post-Katrina. For an account of the **Historic Voodoo Museum**, across Royal at 724 Dumaine, see p.686.

Back on Royal Street, beyond Jackson Square at no. 533, the **Historic New Orleans Collection** stands proud among the neighboring antique stores and chi-chi art galleries. Entry to the streetfront gallery (Tues–Sat 9.30am–4.30pm, Ⓦ www.hnoc.org), which holds excellent temporary exhibitions, is free, but to see the bulk of the collection you'll need to take a guided tour (10am, 11am, 2pm & 3pm; $5). These might cover the galleries upstairs, where fascinating exhibits – including old maps, drawings, and early publicity posters – fill a series of themed rooms, or they might venture into the Williams House, behind the museum beyond a courtyard. The Williamses, prominent citizens in the 1930s, filled their home with unusual, exotic objects, and the house is a must for anyone interested in design and decorative arts.

The quirky **Historical Pharmacy Museum**, in an old apothecary a block toward the river at 514 Chartres St (Tues–Sat 10am–5pm; $5), offers great insights into the history of medicine. On the ground floor, hand-carved rosewood cabinets are cluttered with gris-gris, a fine range of Creole "tonics" used to cure "all the various forms of female weakness," dusty jars of leeches for blood-letting ("to remove irritability"), and various unpleasant-looking drills and corkscrews. Upstairs you can see a nineteenth-century sick room, and a surprisingly intriguing collection of vintage spectacles from around the world.

Bourbon Street

Continuing lakeside up Conti Street brings you to world-renowned **Bourbon Street**. Though you'd never guess it from the hype, there are two faces to this much-mythologized drag. The touristy, booze-drenched stretch spans the seven blocks from Canal to St Ann: a frat-pack cacophony of daiquiri stalls, novelty shops, and dimly lit girlie bars. This enclave is best experienced after dark, when a couple of its **bars** and **clubs** – though by no means all – are worth a look, and the sheer mayhem takes on a bacchanalian life of its own. When the attraction of fighting your way through the crowds of weekending drunks starts to pall, however, it's easy to dip out again into the quieter parallel streets to regain some sort of sanity. If you do manage to make it as far as St Ann, you come to a kind of crossroads, marked by a brace of raucous gay clubs, beyond which Bourbon transforms into an appealing, predominantly gay, residential area.

Above Bourbon Street: toward Rampart Street

Above Bourbon Street, tourists are outnumbered by locals walking their dogs, jogging, or chatting on stoops. Half a block north of Bourbon, at 820 St Louis St, the restored 1831 **Hermann–Grima House** (Mon–Fri tours 10am, 11am, noon, 2pm & 3pm; $6, or $10 with the Gallier House, see p.689) illustrates the lifestyle of middle-class Creoles in antebellum New Orleans; otherwise, though these quiet streets are fringed by some of the Quarter's finest **vernacular architecture**, "sights" as such are few.

Rampart Street, the run-down strip separating the Quarter from **Tremé**, is a boundary rarely crossed by tourists. Though it's home to one of the city's finest jazz clubs (*Donna's*, see p.697), which is just a short walk from the heart of the Quarter, it can feel hairy at night, and only slightly less so during the day. It's not recommended to wander around **Louis Armstrong Park** in daylight hours, either, though it's a different story during the occasional weekend **music festivals**, many of which, continuing its long tradition of black music and celebration, are held in **Congo Square** (see p.699), the small paved area to the left of the entrance arch.

Outside the French Quarter

Tremé, the historic African-American neighborhood where jazz was developed in the bordellos of **Storyville** – long since gone – is named for Claude Tremé, a free black hatmaker who in the nineteenth century owned a plantation on what is now St Claude Street. In the 1800s this was a prosperous area, its shops, businesses, and homes owned and frequented by New Orleans's significant – and unique – free black population, but by the late-twentieth century, blighted by neglect and crime, Tremé had become a no-go area. Despite this, a rich tradition of jazz funerals, music, and street parades continued, and the turn of the millennium saw signs of gentrification. Though Tremé was largely unscathed by flooding, Katrina nonetheless dealt a severe blow to this financially poor but culturally rich neighborhood, and many of its houses remain in bad shape. It's not recommended to wander around here at night, but as an embodiment of the spirit of the city, it deserves the attention and support of any visitor.

One way to see the best of Tremé is to make a beeline for the fascinating **Backstreet Cultural Museum**, in an old funeral parlor at 1116 St Claude St (Tues–Sat 10am–5pm; $5; ⓦ www.backstreetmuseum.org). This labor of love celebrates local street culture, including jazz funerals and the traditions of the Mardi Gras Indians; it also hosts excellent music events, and acts as a social hub during the city's many festivals.

Directly across the road, **St Augustine's Church**, 1210 Governor Nicholls, is the earliest African-American church in the nation, active since 1842. Of crucial significance to the local black community, St Augustine's welcomes tourists to its occasional jazz masses and fundraising events, and plans are afoot to start offering tours (ⓦ www.staugustinecatholicchurch-neworleans.org). The spruce, light interior is well worth a look, with its stained-glass windows portraying French saints, and its flags printed with affirmations (Unity, Creativity, Self-Determination, Purpose) in English and Swahili. In the garden, the **Tomb of the Unknown Slave**, a toppled metal cross entwined with balls-and-chains and shackles, honors all African and Native American slaves buried in unmarked graves.

The CBD and Warehouse District

Along with the Mint (see p.688), the gray granite **Custom House**, in the Central Business District – or **CBD** – at 423 Canal St, was key in New Orleans's grand antebellum building program. Work started in 1848 on what was to be the largest federal building in the nation; rooting such a monster in the city's soggy soil proved difficult, however, and what with this, and the vagaries of the Civil War, the Custom House was not completed until 1881. Mark Twain had a point when he dismissed the foreboding Classical interior as "inferior to a gasometer," but fans of Greek Revival architecture should head to the second floor, where a huge **marble hall**, illuminated by a 54-foot skylight, recalls the lofty aspirations and optimism of the city's golden age.

The lakeside edge of the CBD, a tangle of busy gray highways, is dominated by the colossal home of the New Orleans Saints football team, the **Superdome**. At 52 acres, with 27 stories and a diameter of 680ft, this is one of the largest buildings on the planet, and has been etched upon the world's consciousness after housing more than 25,000 Katrina evacuees in unthinkable conditions for six days in August/September 2005. Though lurid tales of gang rapes, murders, and suicides were later discovered to have been urban myths, the Superdome remains a monument to the horror of the flooding. Standing sentinel over the battered CBD for a year after Katrina, its damaged roof scarred and flapping, it finally re-opened in fall 2006 with a star-studded line-up – including rock bands U2 and Green Day – and a triumphant defeat by the Saints over the Atlanta Falcons. Emotional in the extreme, the high-profile event provided a huge boost of confidence for the city.

Spreading upriver from the foot of Canal Street, New Orleans's **Warehouse District** has a handful of attractions. Most of the sights are concentrated in the **Arts District**, the outcrop of galleries concentrated around Julia and Camp streets. The hub of the scene is the **Contemporary Arts Center**, 900 Camp St (Thurs–Sun 11am–4pm; ground-floor galleries free, changing exhibitions $5; ⓦ www.cacno.org), which always has something interesting going on, from the temporary shows on the ground floor to major exhibitions upstairs.

Around the corner, at the colossal **National World War II Museum**, 945 Magazine St (Tues–Sat 9am–5pm; $14), opened on June 6, 2000, the 56th anniversary of the Allied invasion of Europe known as D-Day. Though its collection concentrates on the events of that devastating day, the museum also does a good job covering the home front and the D-Day invasions in the Pacific.

It can be easy to forget that easy-living New Orleans has its roots entrenched in the Deep South; anyone who needs reminding should take a look at the **Confederate Museum**, 929 Camp St at Lee Circle (Thurs–Sat 10am–4pm; $5). A gloomy Romanesque Revival hulk, designed in 1891 as a place for Confederate veterans to display their mementos, this so-called "Battle Abbey of the South" is a relic from a bygone age. Inside the church-like hall, glass cases are filled with swords, mess-kits, uniforms, and fragile sepia photos – there remains a funereal air about the place, with its bittersweet remembrances of long-lost generals and their forgotten families.

Next door, at 925 Camp St, the modern, purpose-built **Ogden Museum of Southern Art** (Thurs–Sun 11am–4pm, Thurs also 6–8pm with live music; $10; ⓦ www.ogdenmuseum.org) has an impressive collection that runs the gamut from rare eighteenth-century watercolors through self-taught art to photography and modern sculpture. While many of the artists are lesser known, it's a fascinating place, evoking a strong sense of this distinctive region so preoccupied with notions of the land, of family and religion, poverty and the past, violence and loss.

The Garden District and Audubon Park

Pride of uptown New Orleans, the **Garden District** drapes itself seductively across a thirteen-block area bounded by St Charles Avenue, Magazine Street, Louisiana and Jackson. Two miles upriver from the French Quarter, it was developed as a residential neighborhood in the 1840s by an energetic breed of Anglo-Americans who wished to display their ever-accumulating cotton and trade wealth by building sumptuous mansions in huge gardens. Today, shaded by jungles of subtropical foliage, the glorious houses – some of them spick-and-span showpieces, others in ruins – evoke a nostalgic vision of the Deep South in a profusion of porches, columns, and balconies. It's a ravishing spectacle, if somewhat Gothic; while it's a pleasure simply to wander around, you can pick up more detail about the individual houses on any number of official or self-guided tours.

Further upriver, peaceful **Audubon Park** is a lovely space shaded by Spanish-moss-swathed trees and looped by cycling and jogging paths. Its top attraction, **Audubon Zoo**, a ten-minute walk from the park's St Charles entrance (Wed–Sun 10am–4pm; $12, children $7; zoo and aquarium [see p.683], $25/$14), boasts, among other habitats, a beautifully re-created **Louisiana swamp**, complete with Cajun houseboats, wallowing alligators (including the milky white, blue-eyed "Mr Bingle"), and knobbly cypress knees poking out of the emerald-green water.

Traditionally, the historic **St Charles streetcar** has always been the best way to get to and around the Garden District and Uptown, affording front-row views of "the avenue". At the time of writing, however, the streetcar was still not running post-Katrina; check ⓦ www.norta.com for updates. In the meantime, you could always catch the St. Charles bus – #12 – which follows the streetcar's route.

Algiers and Blaine Kern's Mardi Gras World

A free **ferry** from Canal Street (every 30min 6am–midnight) chugs across the dramatic bend in the Mississippi, bringing you within five minutes or so – depending on the current – to the west bank and the old shipbuilding community of **Algiers**.

△ Napoleon House

A quiet residential neighborhood of pastel stucco Creole architecture and sub-tropical terraces, Algiers's main attraction is **Blaine Kern's Mardi Gras World**, 233 Newton St (daily 9.30am–4.30pm; $17), where year-round you can see artists building and painting the enormous floats used in the Mardi Gras parades. It's a surreal experience wandering these massive warehouses past piles of dusty, grimacing has-beens from parades gone by; in keeping with the carnival spirit, there's plenty of opportunity to dress up, fool around, and take photos. A complimentary minibus picks up and drops off at the ferry landing.

Elsewhere in the city

Toward the lake, in the vast area known as **Mid-City** – much of which was severely damaged in the storm – New Orleans's 1500-acre **City Park** is crisscrossed with roads, and by no means is as peaceful as Audubon Park. It's a welcome green space nonetheless, streaked with lagoons and shaded by centuries-old live oaks. The chief attraction, the **New Orleans Museum of Art** (Wed–Sun 10am–4.30pm; $8), includes pre-Columbian pieces, African works, Asian ceramics and paintings, and a fabulous collection of Fabergé jeweled eggs. The five-acre **sculpture garden** (free) is a must-see, its works – by Louise Bourgeois, Barbara Hepworth, Henry Moore, and others – beautifully dotted among oaks and magnolias.

The **Chalmette battlefield**, six miles downriver from Canal Street, is where Andrew Jackson's ragtag army defeated the British at the Battle of New Orleans in 1815 (grounds Mon–Thurs 7am–3pm, Fri–Sun 9am–4.30pm, visitor center Fri–Sun 9am–4.30pm; Ⓦwww.nps.gov/jela).

Eating

New Orleans is a gourmand's dream. The **food**, commonly defined as **Creole**, is a spicy, substantial – and usually very fattening – blend of French, Spanish, African, and Caribbean cuisine, mixed up with a host of other influences including Native American, Italian, and German. Some of the simpler dishes, like red beans and rice, reveal a strong West Indies influence, while others are more French, cooked with long-simmered sauces based on a **roux** (fat and flour heated together) and herby stocks. Many dishes are served **étouffée**, literally "smothered" in a tasty Creole sauce (a roux with tomato, onion, and spices), on a bed of rice. Note that what passes for **Cajun** food in the city is often a modern hybrid, tasty but not authentic; the "blackened" dishes, for example, slathered in butter and spices, made famous by chef Paul Prudhomme. The mainstays of most menus are **gumbo** – a thick soup of seafood, chicken, and vegetables – and **jambalaya**, a paella jumbled together from the same ingredients. Other specialties include **po-boys**, French-bread sandwiches overstuffed with oysters, shrimp, or almost anything else, and **muffulettas**, the round Italian version, crammed full of aromatic meats and cheese and dripping with garlicky olive dressing. Along with **shrimp** and **soft-shell crabs**, you'll get famously good **oysters**; they're in season from September to April. **Crawfish**, or mudbugs (which resemble langoustines and are best between March and Oct), are served in everything from omelets to bisques, or simply boiled in a spicy stock. To eat them, tug off the overlarge head, pinch the tail, and suck out the juicy, very delicious flesh.

For an only-in-New-Orleans snack, look out for the absurd, giant, hot-dog-shaped **Lucky Dogs** carts set up throughout the Quarter. Featured in John Kennedy Toole's farcical novel *A Confederacy of Dunces*, they've become something of an institution, though in truth the dogs themselves are nothing great.

Gratifyingly, **prices** are not that high compared to other US cities – even at the swankiest places you can get away with $40 per head for a three-course feast with wine. **Lunch**, in particular, can be a bargain, especially at the more upmarket establishments.

In the French Quarter

Acme Oyster House 724 Iberville St ☎ 504/522-5973. This noisy, characterful French Quarter hangout has been *the* place for raw oysters and cold beers for generations. Tourists, cops, and office workers alike wait patiently in line for those plump, briny bi-valves, inexpensive po-boys, salty fresh crawfish, and gumbo.

Angeli 1141 Decatur St ☎ 504/566-0077. A hit with French Quarter hipsters, night owls, and barflies, this big, dimly lit room is an extension of the groovy Lower Decatur scene outside. The long hours are welcome, and the healthy Mediterranean salads, sandwiches, and pastas make a nice alternative to Creole standards.

Bayona 430 Dauphine St ☎ 504/525-4455. Splendid, romantic, and relaxed restaurant with a lovely courtyard. Local staples are given a global twist – the simple garlic soup, sweetbreads, and lamb dishes are fantastic – and there's a 250-plus wine list. Lunch is a bargain – try the grilled cashew butter, duck, and pepper jelly sandwich for a staggering $9. The pricier dinner menu is well worth it.

Croissant d'Or 617 Ursulines St ☎ 504/524-4663. Tranquil, inexpensive little local place serving delicious French pastries and stuffed croissants, plus quiches, salads, and steaming café au lait, in a pretty tiled building. Breakfast and lunch only.

Fiorella's 45 French Market Place/1136 Decatur St ☎ 504/528-9566. A funky French Quarter classic, this down-home café has long been a local hit for its cheap blue-plate specials, crawfish dishes, and amazing crispy fried chicken.

🏃 **Galatoire's** 209 Bourbon St ☎ 504/525-2021. Tennessee Williams's favorite restaurant, this grand Creole establishment, with its landmark mirror-lined dining room, is quintessential New Orleans. It's best at lunchtime, on Fri or Sun especially, when you can join the city's old guard (men in seersucker, women in pearls) spending long, convivial hours gorging on turtle soup, oysters en brochette, crabmeat maison, and filet mignon. No reservations, so expect a wait. Jacket and tie required after 5pm and all day Sun.

Mr B's 201 Royal St ☎ 504/523-2078. Buzzy Creole bistro with dark-wood booths, a relaxed, chatty ambiance, and spectacular food. The garlic chicken is the city's finest; the same accolade could go to the signature barbecue shrimp. It can be pricey, but lunch is good value. Walk-ins are welcome.

Napoleon House 500 Chartres St ☎ 504/524-9752. This ravishing old bar (see p.696) – all crumbling walls and shadowy corners – exudes a classic, relaxed New Orleans elegance. The eighteenth-century building was the home of Mayor Girod, who schemed with Jean Lafitte to rescue Napoleon from exile, but since 1914 it has been owned by the same Italian family who continue to run it today. Though their fabulous bistro has yet to re-open post-Katrina, bow-tied waiters continue to serve their nice café menu, including warm muffulettas with melted cheese, gumbo, Mediterranean salads and antipasto. Closed Mon eve and Thurs during the day.

Tujague's 823 Decatur St ☎ 504/525-8676. With one of the loveliest dining rooms in the city, seeping old New Orleans style, the beloved "Two Jacks," both relaxed and elegant, is a must-visit. Little has changed here over the last century, not least the five-course prix fixe menu, which always includes shrimp remoulade and tender beef brisket. Costs can mount, so if money's tight, simply order the tasty chicken Bonne Femme (fried chicken with garlic and parsley) at the beautiful old bar (see p.696).

Outside the French Quarter

Casamento's 4330 Magazine St ☎ 504/895-9761. Spotless and old-fashioned, this uptown oyster bar serves inexpensive ice-fresh oysters, fried crab claws and overstuffed trout "loaves," or sandwiches, to die for. Closed June–Aug, and Sun and Mon throughout the year. No credit cards.

🏃 **Jacques Imo's** 8324 Oak St ☎ 504/861-0886. Funky, noisy uptown restaurant with a colorful patio. The cooking, a delicious Creole–Cajun take on soul food, is very good value – from the fried oysters and chicken livers to the buttery blackened redfish. It's a great place to fill up before a gig at the *Maple Leaf* (see p.700), and well worth a trip any time – ask for a seat in the pick-up truck. Dinner only; closed Sun. Reservations only for groups of five or more; you may have to wait a while at the convivial bar.

Mona's 504 Frenchmen St ☎ 504/949-4115. Popular, no-fuss Middle Eastern restaurant in a handy Faubourg Marigny location. The food – kebabs, flatbread pizzas, meze, split red lentil soup – is fresh, zingy, and inexpensive, with lots of delicious vegetarian options.

Ralph's on the Park 900 City Park Ave ⓣ504/488-1000. The contemporary Creole food at this classy restaurant, directly opposite City Park, is like the dining room itself – minimal, tasteful, and comforting. Try the mussel soup or simple grilled drum with rice. Dinner Tues–Sun, plus Fri lunch and Sun brunch. Reservations recommended.

Rio Mar 800 S Peters St ⓣ504/525-3474. New Orleans seafood meets Spanish cuisine in this terrific Warehouse District restaurant. To start, go for the tuna empanadas or salt cod fritters; proceed with paella or fish-packed zarzuela (stew) and you'll be in heaven. Closed Sun; dinner only Sat.

Coffee bars and picnic food

Café du Monde 800 Decatur St ⓣ504/581-2914. Despite the hype, the crowds, and the sugar-sticky tabletops, this old market coffeehouse, with a large outdoor patio covered by a striped awning, is an undeniably atmospheric place to drink steaming café au lait with chicory, and snack on piping hot beignets – the city's distinctive sweet donuts – for just a couple of dollars. Particularly fun after a night out. Daily 24hr.

Café Rose Nicaud 634 Frenchmen St ⓣ504/949-3300. Friendly, delightfully mixed Faubourg Marigny coffeehouse that's a firm favorite with local academics, artists, and musicians who gather around the marble-topped tables or in the capacious armchairs. Light meals and pastries are served.

CC's 941 Royal St ⓣ504/581-6996. Quarterites linger for hours at the counter or in the leather armchairs, chatting or people-watching through the open French windows. Try their Mochasippi, a creamy iced espresso.

Central Grocery 923 Decatur St ⓣ504/523-1620. Fragrant old Italian deli, famed for its freshly made muffulettas.

Rue de la Course 3121 Magazine St ⓣ504/899-0242. With its pressed-tin walls, café au lait-colored decor, ceiling fans, and reading lamps, the *Rue* coffeehouse has an Old Europe ambiance, buzzing with a mixed local crowd and a high proportion of students.

Entertainment and nightlife

New Orleans has long been one of the best places in the world to hear **live music**. From lonesome street musicians, through shambling, joyous brass bands, to international names like Dr John and the Neville Brothers, music remains the heartbeat and lifeline of the Crescent City. The devastation wrought by the post-Katrina flooding hit many musicians – who are among the less wealthy of the population – particularly hard, leaving them homeless and scattering them throughout the country. That said, those who are able to do so return as often as possible, commuting to play regular gigs or to appear at festivals, and while some are gone for ever, still more are determined to come home for good. Though the effects of the storm on the music scene cannot be underestimated, the quality of what does exist – the bulk of it around weekends and festivals – remains high. The city is healing its wounds in the best way it knows how: mourning, remembering, celebrating, and surviving by making and dancing to music.

While the French Quarter has its share of atmospheric clubs and bars, there are plenty of good places elsewhere – and visitors making a beeline for **Bourbon Street**, hoping to find it crammed with cool jazz clubs, will be disappointed. That said, even this tawdriest of streets has a couple of good spots to hear live jazz. A better bet, however, is **Frenchmen Street** in the Faubourg Marigny, lined with characterful bars and music venues that get packed on the weekends. In general, it can be hard to separate the drinking scene from the live music scene – most bars feature music at least one night of the week. Those we've listed below under "Bars" tend not to have live music, but many of the places we've reviewed as live music venues (see p.697 & p.700) are great bars in their own right, too.

To decide where to go, check the **listings papers** – especially the free weekly *Gambit* (Ⓦ www.bestofneworleans.com) and the music monthly *Offbeat* (Ⓦ www.offbeat.com), which can be picked up at restaurants and bars all around town – collect fliers in French Quarter **record stores** such as Louisiana Music Factory, 210 Decatur St, and keep an ear tuned to the fabulous local **radio station** WWOZ (90.7 FM), which features regular gig information and ticket competitions.

Music in New Orleans often doesn't get going until **late**. However, many venues put on two sets a night, often by different performers, so with a little creative club-hopping you could easily see three outstanding bands in one evening.

Bars

As befits its image as a hard-drinking, hard-partying town, New Orleans has dozens of truly great **bars**. However, though **24-hour drinking licenses** are common, don't expect every bar to be open all night; even on Bourbon Street, many places close whenever they empty, which can be surprisingly early during slow periods. It is also legal to **drink alcohol in the streets** – for some visitors it's practically *de rigueur* – though not from a glass or bottle. Simply ask for a plastic "**to go**" cup in any bar and carry it with you. You'll be expected to finish your drink before entering another bar, however. The **legal drinking age** is 21; you should carry ID, though few bartenders bother asking for it.

In the French Quarter

Lafitte's Blacksmith Shop 941 Bourbon St ℡504/523-0066. Lively, tumbledown bar frequented by artists and writers (how they see by the candlelight remains a mystery), tourists, and relief workers. A front for pirate Lafitte's plottings, the building's practically unchanged since the 1700s – despite its exterior sprucing – and retains its beamed ceilings and blackened brick fireplace.

Molly's at the Market 1107 Decatur St ℡504/525-5169. Once famed for being a haunt of politicos and media stars, *Molly's* Irish bar is a French Quarter institution – remaining open through Katrina, the flooding, and subsequent evacuation – and pulls a happy crowd of locals, rowdy tourists, off-duty waitstaff, and grungy street punks.

Napoleon House 500 Chartres St ℡504/524-9752. If you visit just one bar in New Orleans, let this ravishing old place be it. Flickering with gaslight, its time-stained walls crammed with ancient oil paintings and classical music booming on the CD player, it's a local institution, and on a warm night its tropical courtyard is one of the best places on earth to be.

Port of Call 838 Esplanade Ave ℡504/523-0120. Strung with tatty nets and lifebuoys, this unpretentious drinking hole is haunted by a noisy mix of Quarterites, Faubourg denizens, and in-the-know tourists who put the world to rights around the large wooden bar or at the small tables. Great burgers, too, served with mushrooms or cheese and a buttery baked potato.

Tujague's 823 Decatur St ℡504/525-8676. Old guard New Orleans restaurant (see p.694) with an equally atmospheric stand-up bar. It's particularly lively on Sun, when regulars gather to catch up and gossip.

Elsewhere in the city

Columns Hotel 3811 St Charles Ave ℡504/899-9308. This gorgeous Garden District hotel bar seeps faded Southern grandeur; on warm evenings, make for the columned veranda, which overlooks the old streetcar line. For more on the hotel, see p.682.

Ernie K-Doe's Mother-in-Law Lounge 1500 N Claiborne Ave ℡504/947-1078, ⩗www.kdoe.com. Since the untimely death of local R&B legend Ernie in 2001, his formidable wife Antoinette has kept their Tremé lounge open as something of a shrine to the self-styled "Emperor of the Universe" – complete with an "Ernie in Heaven" mannequin holding court. Hop in a cab and join the combination of arty hipsters and unimpressed locals that make this place unique.

R-Bar 1431 Royal St ℡504/948-7499. Faubourg Marigny bar with funky thrift-store decor and a pool table played by some of the coolest sharks in town. It's popular with a youngish set, which includes visitors staying at the guesthouse upstairs (see p.682).

Snake and Jake's 7601 Oak St ℡504/861-8202. Dim and derelict, strewn with ancient Christmas tree lights, this quintessential New Orleans dive bar is beloved of uptown students. Go late.

Jazz

It is generally agreed that **jazz** was born in New Orleans, shaped in the early twentieth century by the twin talents of **Louis Armstrong** and **Joe "King" Oliver** from a diverse heritage of African and Caribbean slave music, Civil War brass bands, plantation spirituals, black church music, and work songs.

In 1897, in an attempt to control the prostitution that had been rampant in the city since its earliest days, a law was passed that restricted the brothels to a fixed area bounded by Iberville and Lower Basin streets. The area, which soon became known as **Storyville**, after the alderman who pronounced the ordinance, filled with newly arrived ex-plantation workers, seamen and gamblers, and, from the "mood-setting" tunes played in the brothels to bawdy saloon gigs, there was plenty of opportunity for musicians – in particular the solo piano players known as "professors" – to develop personal styles. Children too young to enter the bars set up makeshift "spasm bands" in the streets. Their legacy lives on in the streetwise ragamuffins on every corner, tap dancing, shoe-shining, and playing trumpet.

Jazz was originally looked down upon by the white establishment as the "filthy" music of poor blacks, and, after Storyville was officially closed in 1917 – which coincided with a clampdown on live music played throughout the city – there was a mass exodus of musicians to Chicago and New York. Many more jazz artists left the city or gave up playing altogether during the Depression (King Oliver died an impoverished janitor); but in the 1950s, the city fathers literally changed their tune and began to promote jazz as a tourist attraction. Nowadays jazz remains an evolving, organic art form, and you're spoiled for choice for places to see it, whether in parades, at the city's many festivals, in dive bars or sophisticated lounges. Local, world-class **musicians**, including the multitalented Marsalis family and trumpeters Terence Blanchard, Irvin Mayfield, and Nicholas Payton, all perform regularly. Of the pianists, don't miss Henry Butler, whose superb, superfast modern jazz is matched by his mean R&B and blues repertoire. One of the city's best-loved performers, trumpeter Kermit Ruffins can always be counted on for a good show with his Barbecue Swingers. A fine jazz stylist and consummate performer, he cut his teeth in local **brass bands**, the ragtag groups who blast out New Orleans's homegrown party music, born from the city's long tradition of street parades. Other favorites include the ReBirth, whose earsplitting spin on anything from trad jazz to hip-hop goes down as well in the student bars as in the parades; the more traditional Tremé and Olympia bands; the younger Lil Rascals and New Birth, and the Soul Rebels and the Stooges, who mix a cacophony of horns with hard funk, hip-hop, carnival music, and reggae.

Le Bon Temps Roulé 4801 Magazine St ☎504/895-8117. A spirited mix of locals and hard-drinking students fill this convivial neighborhood uptown bar – complete with pool tables and good bar food – where the weekly Soul Rebels gig (Thurs) has become a post-Katrina institution. No cover.

Donna's 800 N Rampart St ☎504/596-6914, ⓦwww.donnasbarandgrill.com. Hosting smooth jazz, brass bands, and Mardi Gras Indian shows, this barbecue joint on the fringe of the Quarter feels like a locals' place but attracts a big out-of-town crowd. In summer 2006, the legendary Monday night Bob French gig moved to *Café Brasil* on Frenchmen St. Cover varies; one-drink minimum.

Palm Court Jazz Café 1204 Decatur St ☎504/525-0200, ⓦwww.palmcourtcafe.com. Top-notch trad jazz played in convivial supper club surroundings. Tour groups tend to dominate the dining tables, but as the food is nothing special you'd do best to do as the locals do and sit at the bar. Wed–Sat, shows 8pm, cover $5.

Preservation Hall 726 St Peter St ☎504/522-2841, ⓦwww.preservationhall.com. This tumbledown old structure – with no bar, a/c, or toilets, and just a few hard benches for seating – has long been lauded as the best place in New Orleans to hear trad jazz. The music is lively and joyous, building steam as the night goes on – tourists adore this spot, and lines form well before the doors open. Thurs–Sat sets every 45min 8–11.45pm; Sun show 3pm. $8 cover. Ray's Room 508 Frenchmen St ☎504/523-5394.

Local jazz, brass, funk, and soul in this upscale Faubourg Marigny club co-owned by Kermit Ruffins. Cover around $10.

Mardi Gras and other New Orleans festivals

New Orleans's **carnival season** – which starts on Twelfth Night, January 6, and runs for the six weeks or so until Ash Wednesday – is unlike any other in the world. Though the name is used to define the entire season, **Mardi Gras** itself, French for "Fat Tuesday," is simply the culmination of a whirl of parades, parties, street revels, and masked balls, all inextricably tied up with the city's labyrinthine social, racial, and political structures. Mardi Gras was introduced to New Orleans in the 1740s, when **French** colonists brought over the European custom, established since medieval times, of marking the imminence of Lent with masking and feasting. Their slaves, meanwhile, continued to celebrate **African** and **Caribbean** festival traditions, based on musical rituals, masking, and elaborate costumes, and the three eventually fused. From early days carnival was known for cavorting, outrageous costumes, drinking, and general bacchanalia – and little has changed. However, although it has become the busiest tourist season, when the city is invaded by millions, Mardi Gras has always been, above all, a party that New Orleanians throw for themselves. Visitors are wooed, welcomed, and showed the time of their lives, but without them carnival would reel on regardless, masking, drinking and dancing its bizarre way into Lent. **Post-Katrina**, Mardi Gras has become more important than ever, offering not only celebration but also catharsis. As a symbol of what makes this unique city tick, it can't be bettered, and as a lifeline for a beleagured population, it is essential.

Official carnival took its current form in 1857, with the appearance of a stately moonlit procession calling itself the "Krewe of Comus, Merrie Monarch of Mirth." Initiated by a group of Anglo-Americans, the concept of the "**krewes**," or secret carnival clubs, was taken up enthusiastically by the New Orleans aristocracy, many of them white supremacists who, after the Civil War, used their satirical float designs and the shroud of secrecy to mock and undermine Reconstruction. Nowadays about sixty official krewes equip colorful floats, leading huge processions on different – often mythical – themes. Each is reigned over by a King and Queen (generally an older, politically powerful man and a debutante), who go on to preside over the krewes' closed, masked balls. There are women-only krewes; "super krewes," with members drawn from the city's new wealth (barred from making inroads into the gentlemen's-club network of the old-guard krewes), and important **black** groups. The best known and most important of these is **Zulu**, established in 1909 when a black man mocked Rex, King of Carnival, by dancing behind his float with a tin can on his head; today the Zulu parade on Mardi Gras morning is one of the most popular of the season. There are also many alternative, or **unofficial krewes**, including the anarchic **Krewe du Vieux** (from *Vieux Carré*, another term for the French Quarter), whose irreverent parade and "ball" (a polite term for a wild party, open to all) is a blast. The **gay** community plays a major part in Mardi Gras, particularly in the French Quarter, where the streets teem with strutting drag divas. And then there's the parade of the **Mystic Krewe of Barkus**, made up of dogs, hundreds of whom, during what is surely the campest parade of the season, can be seen trotting proudly through the French Quarter all spiffed up on some spurious theme. Tourists are less likely to witness the **Mardi Gras Indians**, African-American groups who, in their local neighborhoods, organize themselves into "tribes" and, dressed in fabulous beaded and feathered costumes, gather on Mardi Gras morning to compete in chanting and dancing. Made up predominantly of poor black men, many of whom lost their homes and their communities in the flooding, this is the Mardi Gras group most threatened by the devastation of Katrina. One important New Orleans Mardi Gras ritual is the flinging of "**throws**" from the parade floats. Teasing masked krewe members scatter beads, beakers, and doubloons (toy coins) into the crowds, who beg, plead, and scream for them. Even outside the parades, tourists embark upon a frantic **bead-bartering** frenzy, which has given rise to the famed "Show Your Tits!" phenomenon – young co-eds pulling up their shirts in exchange for strings of beads and roars of boozy approval from the goggling mobs. Anyone keen to see the show should head for Bourbon Street.

The two weeks leading up to Mardi Gras are filled with processions, parties, and balls, but excitement reaches fever pitch on **Lundi Gras**, the day before Mardi Gras. Some of the city's best musicians play at **Zulu**'s free party in Woldenberg Park, which climaxes at 5pm with the arrival of the king and queen by boat. Following this, you can head to the **Plaza d'España**, where, in a formal ceremony unchanged for over a century, the mayor hands the city to Rex, King of Carnival. The party continues with more live music and fireworks, after which people head off to watch the big **Orpheus** parade, or start a frenzied evening of clubbing. Most clubs are still hopping well into Mardi Gras morning.

The fun starts early on Mardi Gras day, with **walking clubs** striding through uptown accompanied by raucous jazz on their ritualized bar crawls. Zulu, in theory, sets off at 8.30am (but can be as much as two hours late), followed by **Rex**. Across town, the surreal **St Ann walking parade** gathers in the Bywater, arriving in the Faubourg at around 11am, while the gay costume competition known as the **Bourbon Street awards** gets going at noon. In the afternoon, hipsters head back to the Faubourg, where **Frenchmen Street** is ablaze with bizarrely costumed carousers. The fun continues throughout the Quarter and the Faubourg until **midnight**, when a siren wail heralds the arrival of a cavalcade of mounted police that sweeps through Bourbon Street and declares through megaphones that Mardi Gras is officially over. Like all good Catholic cities, New Orleans takes carnival very seriously. Midnight marks the onset of Lent, and repentance can begin.

Other New Orleans festivals

St Joseph's Day, March 19. Sicilian saint's day, at the mid-point of Lent. Massive altars of food, groaning with bread, fig cakes, and stuffed artichokes, are erected in churches all around town, including St Louis Cathedral, and there's also a parade. The Sunday closest to St Joseph's ("**Super Sunday**") is the only time outside Mardi Gras that the Mardi Gras Indians (see above) take to the streets.

French Quarter Festival, early April. Free three-day music festival that rivals Jazz Fest for the quality and variety of music on offer. Stages and food stalls, free evening gigs, parades, and talent contests. ⓦ www.fqfi.org.

Jazz and Heritage Festival (Jazz Fest), two weekends (Fri–Sun) end April/early May at the Fairgrounds Race Track, Mid-City. Enormous festival, with stages hosting jazz, R&B, gospel, African, Caribbean, Cajun, blues, reggae, funk, Mardi Gras Indian, rock, and brass band music, with evening performances in clubs all over town. Also crafts stalls and phenomenal food stands (don't miss the crawfish bread). ⓦ www.nojazzfest.com.

Satchmo Fest, end July/early Aug. Free weekend festival, staged to celebrate Louis Armstrong's birthday. Talks and art exhibits focus on Satchmo himself, while the best local jazz and brass bands play live. ⓦ www.fqfi.org.

Southern Decadence, five days around Labor Day weekend. Huge gay extravaganza, bringing nearly 100,000 party animals to the gay bars and clubs of the Quarter and the Faubourg, with an unruly costume parade of thousands on the Sunday afternoon. ⓦ www.southerndecadence.com.

Halloween, Oct 31. Thanks to its long-held obsession with all things morbid, and the local passion for partying and dressing up, New Orleans is a fabulous place to spend Halloween, with haunted houses, costume competitions, ghost tours, and parades all over town.

8

LOUISIANA | New Orleans: Entertainment and nightlife

Spotted Cat 623 Frenchmen St ☎504/943-3887. With a regular menu of roots music, this cozy little Faubourg Marigny bar has become *the* place to see the New Orleans Jazz Vipers, who dish up a high-octane twist on jubilant swing and trad.

Vaughan's 4229 Dauphine St, in the Bywater ☎504/947-5562. Tiny neighborhood bar that fills to bursting point on Thurs Kermit Ruffins's night. The band is crammed up against the audience – a mixed bunch of locals, students, and the players' friends and family; between sets, help yourself to free beans and rice. Take a cab. Cover varies; $10 on Thurs.

Other live music

There's far more to New Orleans than jazz alone. Though the "**New Orleans sound**," an exuberant, carnival-tinged hybrid of blues, parade music, and R&B, had its heyday in the early 1960s, many of its stars are still gigging, from Al "Carnival Time" Johnson to Irma "It's Raining" Thomas. Their shows, crowded with devoted locals, make for a quintessentially New Orleans night out.

Since the 1960s the city has also been famed for its homegrown **funk** – top acts include Galactic and Papa Grows Funk – while New Orleans's version of hip-hop, known as **bounce**, has taken the nation by storm. While **Cajun** music is not indigenous to the city, many locals – and tourists – do love to *fais-do-do* (the Cajun two-step) and there are a couple of fantastic places to dance to **zydeco**, its raunchier black relation. **Blues** fans should look out for guitarists Snooks Eaglin and Walter "Wolfman" Washington, and, for powerful gospel-blues, the formidable Marva Wright. For something unique, scour the listings for **Mardi Gras Indians** (see p.698) such as the Wild Magnolias, whose rare gigs – you're most likely to catch them around Mardi Gras or Jazz Fest – are the funkiest, most extraordinary performances you're ever likely to see.

Café Brasil 2100 Chartres St ☎504/949-0851. At the heart of the Frenchmen Street corridor, this bare-bones, arty room hosts eclectic live music (Latin, jazz, klezmer, reggae, world), poetry readings, and the like, and, on Mon, hosts the inimitable Bob French for an exuberant house party-style jam session.

Circle Bar 1032 St Charles Ave ☎504/588-2616. Painfully hip bar in a crumbling old house at Lee Circle. With an inspired, eclectic booking policy, from alt rock to bluegrass, it's renowned for resurrecting R&B legends from ignominy, and always pulls a gorgeous, hard-partying crowd.

House of Blues/The Parish 225 Decatur St ☎504/310-4999, ⓦwww.hob.com. This sleek French Quarter venue, part of the national chain, is worth checking out for big-name rock, hip-hop and reggae; smaller, local acts play at the intimate *Parish* upstairs.

Maple Leaf 8316 Oak St ☎504/866-9359. Legendary uptown bar with pressed-tin walls, a large dance floor, and a patio. It's a New Orleans favorite for really great blues, R&B, funk, and brass bands; ReBirth's Tues-night gigs are a must. There's chess and pool, too.

Mid-City Lanes Rock 'n' Bowl 4133 S Carrollton Ave ☎504/482-3133, ⓦwww.rockandbowl.com. Its location, in a Mid-City mall, may be unprepossessing, but this eccentric and fun bowling alley-cum-music venue is a New Orleans institution. Though it's especially heaving on Thurs – zydeco night – they also book great local R&B, blues, and swing, and the crowd is always lively. Take a taxi.

One Eyed Jack's 615 Toulouse St ☎504/569-8361, ⓦwww.oneeyedjacks.net. Loosely conceived as a decadent cabaret lounge in old Bourbon Street style, this hip bar/club presents burlesque, trad jazz, karaoke, rap battles, and indie rock to an in-the-know but friendly crowd.

Tipitina's 501 Napoleon Ave ☎504/895-8477, ⓦwww.tipitinas.com. Venerable uptown venue, named after a Professor Longhair song, with a consistently good funk, R&B, brass, and reggae line-up. The Sun Cajun *fais-do-do* is fun, too.

Cajun country

Cajun country stretches across southern Louisiana from Houma in the east, via **Lafayette**, the hub of the region, into Texas. It's a region best enjoyed away from the larger towns, by visiting the many old-style hamlets that, despite modernization, can still be found cut off from civilization in soupy bayous, coastal marshes, and inland swamps.

Cajuns are descended from the French colonists of Acadia, part of Nova Scotia, which was taken by the British in 1713. The Catholic **Acadians**, who had quietly fished, hunted, and farmed for more than a century, refused to renounce their faith and swear allegiance to the English king, and in 1755 the British expelled them all, separating families and burning towns. About 2500 ended up in French Louisiana, where they were given land to set up small farming communities, enabling them to rebuild the culture they had left behind. Hunting, farming, and trapping, they lived in relative isolation until the 1940s, when major roads were built, immigrants from other states poured in to work in the **oil** business, and **Cajun music**, popularized by local musicians such as accordionist Iry Lejeune, came to national attention. Since then, the history of the Cajuns has continued to be one of struggle. The whole region was hit hard by the oil slump; the erosion of coastal wetlands threatens the existence of entire communities; the silting up of the Atchafalaya Basin is having adverse effects on fishing and shrimping; and many coastal towns are in the firing line of devastating hurricanes, like Katrina, that hurtle up from the Gulf of Mexico. After Roosevelt's administration decreed that all American children should speak English in schools, French was practically wiped out in Cajun country, and the local patois of the older inhabitants, with its strong African influences, was kept alive primarily by music. Since the 1980s, CODOFIL (the Council for Development of French in Louisiana) has been devoted to preserving the region's indigenous **language** and culture, and today you will find many signs, brochures, and shopfronts written in French.

Cajun **fais-do-dos** – dances, with live bands, held mostly on weekends – are good places to encounter the culture at close hand. Everyone is welcome to trip a quick two-step, and visitors will find plenty of opportunity to dance, whether at a restaurant, a club, or one of the region's many **festivals**. Although **Baton Rouge**, the capital of Louisiana, is not actually in Cajun country, heading out this way from New Orleans, via the **plantations** on the banks of the Mississippi, makes a good approach.

Northwest from New Orleans: plantation country

The fastest roads out from New Orleans toward the west are the major I-10 and US-61; you can also drive along the **River Road**, which hugs both banks of the Mississippi all the way to Baton Rouge, seventy miles upriver. It's not a particularly eventful drive, winding through flat, fertile farmland, but a series of bridges and ferries allows you to crisscross the water, stopping off and touring several restored antebellum **plantation homes** along the way. Before the Civil War, these spectacular homes were the focal points of the vast estates from where wealthy planters

– or rather, their slaves – loaded cotton, sugar, or indigo onto steamboats berthed virtually at their front doors. Generally, the superb Laura plantation excepted (see below), **tours**, often led by belles in ballgowns, skimp on details about the estates as a whole, and in particular their often vast slave populations, presenting them instead as showcase museums filled with priceless antiques. The cumulative effect of these evocations of a long-lost "gracious" era can be stultifying, so it's best to pick just one or two. Many of the houses also offer luxurious **B&B** rooms (rates often include tours), which as well as being rather wonderful places to sleep, allow you to absorb more of the atmosphere of the plantations than is possible on the walkthroughs.

To get to the River Road from New Orleans, take I-10 west to exit 220, turn onto I-310 and follow it to **Hwy-48**, on the east bank (*above* the river on the map). This shortly becomes **Hwy-44**, or the River Road. For the west bank (*below* the river), cross Destrehan Bridge onto **Hwy-18** rather than branching onto Hwy-48. It's important to note that the levee runs the length of the banks, blocking the river from view, and though you'd never guess it from the tourist brochures, it's the hulking chemical plants that dominate the River Road landscape. There are rural stretches where wide sugarcane fields are interrupted only by moss-covered shacks – the prettiest views are to be found around the small town of **Convent**, on the east bank – but you'll more often find yourself driving through straggling communities of boarded-up lounges and laundromats, scarred by scrap piles and smokestacks.

From **Edgard**, 25 miles along on Hwy-18, you can cross the river to the **San Francisco House** (daily 10am–4pm; $10), two miles upriver of **Reserve** on Hwy-44. Built in a style dubbed "Steamboat Gothic" by novelist Frances Parkinson Keyes, its rails, awnings, and pillars were designed to re-create the ambiance of a Mississippi showboat. The elaborate facade is matched by a gorgeous interior – a riot of pastoral trompe l'oeils, floral motifs, and Italian cherubs. Crossing the river at **Lutcher**, the settlement a few miles beyond San Francisco, brings you to Vacherie and the fascinating **Laura plantation** (six tours daily 10am–4pm; $10; ⒲www.lauraplantation.com). Rather than dwelling lovingly on priceless antiques, the standard tours here, which draw upon a wealth of historical documents – from **slave accounts** and photographs to private diaries – sketch a vivid picture of day-to-day plantation life in multicultural Louisiana.

Nine miles upriver from Laura, **Oak Alley** is the quintessential image of the antebellum plantation home. It's a splendid Greek Revival mansion dating from 1839 – and the magnificent oaks that form a canopy over the driveway are 150 years older (daily 10am–4pm; $10). The **restaurant** (8.30–10am & 11am–3pm) serves Cajun food, and you can **stay** in pretty B&B cottages in the grounds (ⓉTelephone225/265-2151, ⒲www.oakalleyplantation.com; ❻).

Eighteen miles south of Baton Rouge on the west bank, **Nottoway** (1859) is the largest surviving plantation home in the South, a huge white Italianate edifice with 64 rooms (daily 9am–5pm; $10). The house also has 13 fancy **B&B** rooms (ⓉTelephone225/545-2730, ⒲www.nottoway.com; ❻) and a **restaurant** (daily 11am–2pm & 6–8.30pm).

Also on the west bank, in the small town of **Donaldsonville** at 406 Charles St, the **River Road African American Museum** (Wed–Sat 10am–5pm, Sun 1–5pm; $4) offers an intriguing and alternative view of the region's history, highlighting its cuisine, music, the Underground Railroad, Reconstruction, and the culture of the free blacks.

Baton Rouge

When French explorers first came upon the site of **BATON ROUGE** in 1699, they found poles smeared in animal blood to designate the separate hunting grounds of the Houmas and Bayougoulas Indians. The area on these shallow bluffs therefore appeared on French maps as *Baton Rouge* – "red stick." Now capital of Louisiana and the fifth biggest port in the US, Baton Rouge is an easygoing city for its size. Even the presence of the state's largest **universities**, LSU and Southern, has done surprisingly little to raise the town anywhere much above "sleepy" status.

Surrounded by fifty acres of showpiece gardens, the magnificent Art Deco **Louisiana State Capitol** (daily 9am–4pm; free) serves as a monument to **Huey Long**, the "Kingfish," the larger-than-life Democratic governor who ordered its construction in 1931 and was assassinated in its corridors just four years later. First elected governor in 1928 after a vehemently anti-big-business campaign, Long swiftly concentrated power into his own hands and, variously labeled a demagogue, a communist, and a fascist, he set himself apart from other Southern populists of the time by refusing to exploit the race issue. Just as his appeal – with slogans like "Every Man a King" – began to reach national proportions, with a bid for the presidency in the offing, he was shot by a local doctor whose exact motives remain unknown.

The **interior** of the building, with its huge murals and sculptures, still bears the scars of its checkered political history; spot the stray bullets in the marble pillars of the ground-floor corridor and a pencil embedded in the ceiling of the legislative chamber by an exploding bomb. Long decreed that no building in Baton Rouge could be taller than the 450-foot capitol (it's the tallest in the nation), and its 27th-floor observation deck is the best vantage point to look out over the surrounding Art Deco complexes and lush greenery, the traffic on the sluggish Mississippi, and the tangle of puffing chemical refineries on the horizon.

Mark Twain referred to Baton Rouge's **Old State Capitol** (in use from 1850 to 1932), 100 North Blvd, as "that monstrosity on the Mississippi." A grey, crenellated structure on a mound overlooking the river, it's worth a look for the **Center for Political and Governmental History** (Tues–Sat 10am–4pm, Sun noon–4pm, also Mon 10am–4pm in April & May; $4), which illuminates Louisiana's scandal-ridden political history.

The **LSU Rural Life Museum**, 4560 Essen Rd, just off I-10 southeast of downtown (daily 8.30am–5pm; $7), re-creates pre-industrial Louisiana life through its carefully restored buildings – among them a plantation house, slave cottages, and a grist mill – spread over 25 acres in a sultry garden setting.

Practicalities

Greyhound **buses**, as well as connecting buses from New Orleans's Amtrak station, come in at 1253 Florida St, fifteen minutes from downtown. For Yellow Cabs, call ⓣ225/923-3260. The **visitor center** is inside the capitol (daily 8am–4.30pm; ⓣ225/383-1825 or 1-800/527-6843, ⓦwww.visitbatonrouge.com). There are plenty of chain **motels** on and off I-10; *La Quinta Inn*, 2333 S Acadian Thruway (ⓣ225/924-9600, ⓦwww.lq.com; ④), is convenient and comfortable and offers complimentary breakfast.

For **eating**, *Avoyelles*, three blocks from the river at 333 3rd St (ⓣ225/381-9385), serves blue-plate lunch specials and great shrimp po-boys, and has a sophisticated bar for nighttime drinking. Most of the city's **nightlife** centers on the **LSU campus**, along College Drive, Chimes Street, and Highland Road. *Thirsty Tiger*, a hole in the wall at 140 Main St downtown, is the oldest bar in the city (ⓣ225/387-9799).

Lafayette and around

LAFAYETTE, 135 miles northwest of New Orleans on I-10, is geographically central in Cajun country, and the key city for its oil business. Originally named Vermilionville, after the orangey bayou nearby, it was renamed in 1844 in honor of the Marquis de Lafayette, the aristocratic French hero of the American Revolution. Today it's a quiet place, a city with a small-town feel and no real center. It

Cajun festivals

Cajun festivals, held almost weekly it seems, provide an enjoyable way to experience the food and music of the region. For some of the larger events, it's a good idea to reserve a room in advance; the rest of the world is catching on to the fun. The following is merely a sampler; for full details, check with any tourist office in the area.

Mardi Gras, Feb/March. Cajun Carnival differs from its city cousin; although there are private balls, parties, and formal parades, it is a far more countrified and very family-oriented affair. There's plenty of music and street dancing, of course, and country villages like Eunice, Church Point, and Mamou are the scene of the mischievous *Courir de Mardi Gras* (see p.709). Ⓦwww.swmardigras.com and www.lsue.edu/acadgate/mardmain.htm.

World Championship Crawfish Étouffée Cookoff, last Sunday in March (the third Sun, if Easter falls on the last Sun), Eunice. *The* place to taste the very best mudbugs, accompanied by great local music and a fierce spirit of competition among the scores of teams. ☏337/457-2565, Ⓦeunice-la.com/cookoffpast.html.

Festival International de Louisiane, last full week in April. Huge, free five-day festival in Lafayette, with big-name participants from all over the French-speaking world, celebrating a wealth of indigenous music, culture and food. ☏337/232-8086, Ⓦwww.festivalinternational.com.

Breaux Bridge Crawfish Festival, first full weekend of May (Fri–Sun), Breaux Bridge. Crawfish-eating contests, étouffée cookoffs, and mudbug races, along with music, crafts stalls, and dancing. $5 Fri & Sun, $10 Sat, $15 for three days; ☏337/332-6655, Ⓦwww.bbcrawfest.com.

Southwest Louisiana Zydeco Music Festival, Fri evening & Sat before Labor Day, Plaisance, near Opelousas. The culmination of a month of concerts and dances, with top zydeco performers playing "black Creole" music. Also regional cuisine, African-American arts and crafts, talks, dancing, and workshops. $10, $2 for kids; ☏337/942-2392, Ⓦwww.zydeco.org.

Mamou Cajun Music Festival, the first weekend in Sept (Fri & Sat), Mamou, 10 miles north of Eunice. Traditional live music, food, crafts, beer-drinking and boudin-eating contests, greasy pole-climbing and a Cajun Queen beauty pageant for the over-65s. Ⓦwww.mamoucajunmusicfestival.com.

Festivals Acadiens, mid-Sept/Oct, Lafayette. Huge three-day festival, with Cajun, zydeco, and traditional French bands, as well as indigenous crafts and food. ☏337/981-5652, Ⓦwww.festivalacadiens.com.

Louisiana Prairie Cajun Capital Folklife Festival fall, Eunice. The superb Prairie Acadian Cultural Center is at the center of this free two-day festival with bands, arts and crafts, storytellers, folklife programs, and a wide variety of food stalls. ☏337/457-2565.

Louisiana Yambilee, last week in Oct. Opelousas goes all out to celebrate the sweet potato, with food stalls, sweet potato auctions, music, and the marvelously named Lil' Miss Yum Yum contest. ☏1-800/210-5298, Ⓦwww.members.tripod.com/yambilee/yambilee.htm.

does, however, offer some lively **Cajun history** and splendid **restaurants** – and makes a central base for exploring the swamps, bayous, and dance halls of the surrounding region.

Arrival, information, and getting around

Greyhound arrives in Lafayette at 315 Lee St; **Amtrak** pulls in a few blocks north at 133 E Grant St at Jefferson. The **airport**, south of town on Hwy-90, meets daily flights from Houston, Dallas, Memphis, and Atlanta. Pick up essential maps and brochures from the Lafayette Parish **visitor center** at 1400 NW Evangeline Thruway, exit 103A off I-10 (Mon–Fri 8.30am–5pm, Sat & Sun 9am–5pm; ℡337/232-3737 or 1-800/346-1958, ⊛www.lafayettetravel.com). To get the best from the area you'll need a **car**, as the dance halls, restaurants, and hotels are spread out, and the local bus system is of little use to visitors. If you need a **taxi**, try Yellow Checker Cab (℡318/237-5701).

Accommodation

Chain **hotels** line Evangeline Thruway just south of I-10, and US-90 and Hwy-182 toward New Iberia, but if you are after something with more character you'll need to head further out. The friendly hamlet of **Breaux Bridge** (see p.708), just eight miles east, makes another appealing base.

Aaah! T'Frere's 1905 Verot School Rd, 6 miles south of I-10, Lafayette ℡337/984-9347 or 1-800/984-9347, ⊛www.tfreres.com. Hospitable B&B in an antique-filled, cypress-built home, offering complimentary "T'juleps" and delicious Cajun/Creole breakfasts. ❹

Bayou Cabins 100 W Mills Ave/Hwy-94, Breaux Bridge ℡337/332-6158, ⊛www.bayoucabins.com. Nine rustic cabins – most of which date from the nineteenth century – backing onto Bayou Teche. Run by the owners of *Bayou Boudin and Cracklin'* (see p.707); rates include a free taster of their fantastic Cajun food and breakfast served in the café next door. ❸

Bayou Teche B&B 205 Washington St, Breaux Bridge ℡337/332-1608, ⊛www.breauxbridgelive.com/bayoubb. Appealing guesthouse right on the bayou, in an 1812 Creole cottage expanded in the 1880s to become a boarding house. Rates

can include a full breakfast at *Café des Amis* (see p.707) or simply coffee and pastries; the welcoming host leaves you to treat the place like home. ❸–❹

Blue Moon Guest House and Saloon 215 E Convent St, Lafayette ℡337/234-2422, ⊛www.bluemoonhostel.com. Cheerful hostel/guesthouse, in a nineteenth-century home downtown, with two dorms ($18–21) and four private rooms. Regular Cajun, zydeco, and bluegrass gigs and a full bar in the back porch saloon; check ⊛www.bluemoonpresents.com for schedule. Rates increase for festivals. ❶–❷

Plantation Motor Inn 2810 NE Evangeline Thruway, Lafayette ℡337/232-7285. Comfortable motel north of town near the Interstate, with plain rooms and free continental breakfast. ❸

The Town

In the center, such as it is, of Lafayette stands the Romanesque **Cathedral of St John the Evangelist**, 914 St John St (Mon–Fri 9am–noon & 1–4pm; $3), and the old **cemetery**, where the crumbling raised graves include that of Jean Mouton, the town's Cajun founder. Each of the magnificent branches of the 500-year-old **Cathedral Oak** opposite, spreading over 200ft, weighs seventy tons. Three blocks away, the small **Lafayette Museum**, 1122 Lafayette St (Tues–Sat 9am–4.30pm, Sun 1–4pm; $3), was the "Sunday home" – a townhouse used after Mass, before the family returned to their plantation – of Jean's son Alexandre, Louisiana's first Democratic governor. It's now filled with family memorabilia, Civil War relics, and Cajun Mardi Gras costumes.

South of the town center, the campus of the **University of Louisiana at Lafayette** boasts a swamp – complete with alligators, turtles, water birds, and tattered Spanish moss. Its **art museum** showcases local artists, Southern folk art, and some major French works, along with traveling exhibitions (Tues–Sat 10am–5pm, Sun 1–5pm; $10).

Cajun music venues

It's easy to "pass a good time" in Cajun country, especially if you're here on the weekend, when the *fais-do-dos* are traditionally held. Though things are quieter during the week, you'll still be able to enjoy local music at many of the restaurants. **Cajun music** is a jangling, infectious melange of nasal vocals backed by jumping accordion, violin, and triangle, fueled by traces of country, swing, jazz, and blues. **Zydeco** is similar, but sexier, more blues-based, and usually played by black Creole musicians. Though songs are in French, the patois heard in both bears only a passing resemblance to the language spoken in France. Music is never performed without space for dancing; everyone from the smallest child to most aged grandparent can join in. As well as the popular restaurants *Café des Amis*, *Mulate's*, *Prejean's*, and *Randol's* (reviewed on opposite), plus the *Blue Moon Guest House* (see p.705), **venues** include record stores, river landings, and the streets themselves. Sadly, old-time zydeco dance halls – the less touristy places – are dying out in the face of competition from newer clubs and flashy casinos, but a few still exist. Check the music **listings** in the free weekly *Times of Acadiana* (Wed), log onto the zydeco listings page ⓦceezees.com/CurrentEvents.htm, or simply look for signs saying "French dance here tonight."

Angelle's Whiskey River Landing 1365 Henderson Levee Rd, Henderson, Breaux Bridge ☏337/228-8567. Live Cajun and zydeco at *Angelle's* – the starting point for a swamp tour – on Sun afternoons. It's around 25 minutes from Lafayette.

El Sid O's 1523 Martin Luther King Drive, Lafayette ☏337/235-0647. Dancing Fri–Sun, with great zydeco and blues bands plus Creole food.

Fred's Lounge 420 6th St, Mamou, 10 miles north of Eunice ☏337/468-5411. Welcoming home of the locally famed radio show "Live from Fred's Lounge" (KVPI 1050 AM), with music, dancing, and lots of drinking. You'll want to try Tante Sue's "Hot Damn," which is warm cinnamon schnapps. Sat only, 7am–2pm.

Grant Street Dancehall 113 W Grant St, Lafayette ☏337/237-8513, ⓦwww.grantstreetdancehall.com. Eclectic music venue hosting hip-hop, swamp pop, New Orleans jazz, and blues, as well as Cajun and zydeco.

La Poussière 1215 Grand Point Rd, Breaux Bridge ☏337/332-1721. The old folks' favorite, this venerable dance hall hosts *fais-do-dos* on Sat night and Sun afternoon.

McGee's Landing 1337 Henderson Levee Rd, Breaux Bridge ☏337/228-2384, ⓦwww.mcgeeslanding.com. Another swamp tour outfit-cum-café-cum-music venue hosting occasional live music.

Pat's Atchafalaya Club 1008 Henderson Levee Rd, Henderson, Breaux Bridge ☏337/228-7512, ⓦwww.patsfishermanswharf.com. Large dance hall on the levee, linked to *Pat's* seafood restaurant, and hosting Cajun, zydeco, and swamp pop bands Fri–Sun.

Rendezvous des Cajuns Liberty Center for Performing Arts, S 2nd St and Park Ave, Eunice ☏337/457-7389, ⓦwww.eunice-la.com/libertyschedule.html. Family-oriented and hugely popular live Cajun/zydeco radio and TV show, mostly in French. Sat 6–7.30pm. Cover $5.

Savoy Music Center 4413 Hwy-190 E, 3 miles east of Eunice ☏337/457-9563, ⓦsavoymusiccenter.com. The free Sat morning (9am–noon) jam sessions at this Cajun record store/accordion workshop are a local institution. Store closed Sun & Mon.

Slim's Y-Ki-Ki 8393 Hwy-182 N, Opelousas ☏337/942-6242. Famed old venue for zydeco music and dancing. Weekends only.

Lafayette has two excellent reconstructions of early Cajun communities. **Vermilionville**, 300 Fisher Rd across from the airport, is the most accessible, and impressive, of the two, extending its scope to explore the culture of the early Creoles as well as the Cajuns (Tues–Sun 10am–4pm; $8). Set in 23 attractive acres on the Bayou Vermilion, it's a living history site, filled with authentic old buildings occupied by craftspeople using traditional skills. A large replica of an old cotton gin serves as a **theater**, hosting storytellers, plays, and noisy *fais-do-dos*. The **restaurant** serves good Cajun lunches.

Next to Vermilionville, at 501 Fisher Rd, the **Acadian Cultural Center**, in the **Jean Lafitte National Historical Park and Preserve** (daily 8am–5pm; free), offers a thorough background on the displaced Cajuns, with a wealth of artifacts and a forty-minute film shown on the hour. Further southwest, ten miles or so from the Lafayette visitor center, Lafayette's other folk-life museum, the smaller **Acadian Village**, 200 Greenleaf Drive (Mon–Sat 10am–4pm; $7), depicts early nineteenth-century Cajun life along the bayous. Original homes and reproductions of other structures – including a blacksmith's shop and a chapel – line a sluggish bayou set in gardens and woodlands, and are filled with traditional furnishings and crafts.

Eating in and around Lafayette

They say that a Cajun cooks every part of a pig but its squeal, and it's true that **Cajun dishes** are packed with a jumble of flavors, textures, and pretty much anything that's good and fresh. Though it bears resemblances to the Creole cuisine you'll find in New Orleans – lots of seafood, rice, rich tomatoey sauces and gumbos – this is rustic food, often spicy, and yes, pork features highly on many menus. It's difficult to eat badly around here, and prices are generally low. At lunchtime, takeout boudin (spicy sausage made with rice) is a treat, as are rich pork cracklin' and salty hogshead cheese. Often, eating in Cajun country is inseparable from **dancing** and **music**; evening – or afternoon, or morning – entertainment revolves around restaurants that double as dance halls.

Bayou Boudin and Cracklin' 100 Mills Ave, Hwy-94, Breaux Bridge, exit 109 from I-10 ☎337/332-6158. Rustic Cajun cottage on Bayou Teche, serving fantastic boudin – including a seafood variety – hogshead cheese-smothered chicken, crawfish balls, and beignets, all prepared on the spot.

Blue Dog Café 1211 W Pinhook Rd, Lafayette ☎337/237-0005. Dine on classy Cajun/Creole food – the crawfish étouffée is great – surrounded by the distinctive blue dog paintings of Cajun artist George Rodrigue. Smooth live jazz in the bar Thurs–Sat nights. Closed Sun and Sat lunch.

Café des Amis 140 E Bridge St, Breaux Bridge ☎337/332-5273, ⓦwww .cafedesamis.com. This friendly, atmospheric, rustic/arty restaurant is a buzzing community hub. The Cajun/Creole food, with lots of crawfish concoctions, is beyond delicious. Live zydeco breakfasts Sat 8.30–11.30am, and jazz and Cajun on Wed evening. Closed Mon & Tues.

Dwyer's 323 Jefferson St, Lafayette ☎337/235-9364. Downtown favorite for huge, inexpensive breakfasts and plate lunches, homecooked burgers,

and local specialties. Mon–Fri 5am–4pm, Sat & Sun 5am–2pm.

Mulate's 325 Mills Ave, Breaux Bridge ☎337/332-4648 and 1-800/422-2586. This is the original Cajun restaurant/dance hall and, though touristy, is frequented by locals, too. Seafood, catfish, and gumbo go for less than $15; dancing nightly at 7pm, and at noon on weekends.

Poche's 3015A Hwy-31, north of Breaux Bridge ☎337/332-2108. One of the best places to pick up boudin, cracklin', andouille, and old-fashioned pies, as well as tasty home-cooked plate lunches. Restaurant Mon–Sat 10.30am–8pm, Sun 10.30am–5pm.

Prejean's 3480 I-49 N, Lafayette ☎337/896-3247. Barn-like restaurant offering very tasty Cajun/Creole food – try the baked oyster platter – nightly live music (from 7pm), and dancing. Daily 7am–10pm or 11pm.

Randol's 2320 Kaliste Saloom Rd, Lafayette ☎337/981-7080. Locally famed restaurant with a large dance floor. Live Cajun and zydeco nightly and steamed seafood dinners (boiled softshell crabs are a specialty). Dinner only.

with lots of use of Tabasco hot sauce – even in the ice cream – and a killer crawfish étouffé.

Touring Cajun country

You could easily drive through **BREAUX BRIDGE**, eight miles east of Lafayette, and miss it, which would be a big shame. Quite apart from its sweet, old-fashioned main street, its unusual crawfish-emblazoned steel bridge over the Bayou Teche – announcing in French that this is the "crawfish capital of the world" – and its handful of B&Bs, restaurants, and music venues, it also makes an appealing base for some of the region's best **swamp tours** (see p.710), and for exploring the **Lake Martin nature reserve**, three miles south on Hwy-31. There's an end-of-the-earth feel to the reserve, where land turns to water, and it's a great experience to drive – or walk the trails – past vistas of tangled cypress flickering with Spanish moss and encroaching greenery creeping onto the narrow road. From February to June tens of thousands of birds nest at the lake, and there's a huge abundance of **birdlife** year-round, including egrets, herons, and spoonbills, not to mention busy nutria splashing through the undergrowth and scores of **alligators** dozing in the sun. If you fancy paddling a **canoe** through this lonely wilderness, contact Pack and Paddle in Lafayette (☎ 337/232-5854, Ⓦ www.packpaddle.com).

North of Lafayette, the **Cajun Prairie** has been described by folklorist Alan Lomax as the "Cajun cultural heartland." A patchwork of rice and soybean fields scattered with crawfish ponds, the region has a few tiny towns of interest. The 1831 **Chretien Point Plantation**, in **SUNSET**, ten miles north of Lafayette on Hwy-93 just off I-10, is one of Louisiana's oldest Greek Revival buildings (Mon–Fri 1–5pm, Sat & Sun 10am–5pm; $10). Its main staircase was the model for the one belonging to *Tara* in *Gone with the Wind*, and Mrs Chretien, left to run the plantation after her husband's death in 1832, was very much in the Scarlett O'Hara mode. She scandalized the community by drinking, smoking, gambling, and sitting with the men after dinner,

△ Lake Martin nature reserve

and once shot an intruder, whose ghost is said to roam the corridors. Bullet holes in the front door date from 1863, when Mrs Chretien's son showed a Masonic sign to an attacking Union general, who thereupon directed fire over the roof. Today the plantation has five luxurious **B&B** rooms (☎337/662-7050 or 1-800/880-7050, ⓦwww.chretienpoint.com; ❻). For **eating**, stop by *Barry's Kitchen*, 660 Napoleon Ave (☎337/662-7197), a takeout famed for its homemade crawfish rolls.

Sleepy old **OPELOUSAS**, twenty miles north of Lafayette on I-49, was capital of Louisiana for a short period during the Civil War, and now has five claims to fame. It was the boyhood home of Jim Bowie, Texas Revolutionary hero and inventor of the Bowie knife; the first place in the world to produce an offset newspaper (in 1915); the birthplace of the great zydeco musician **Clifton Chenier** and celebrity Cajun chef **Paul Prudhomme**; and today, even more excitingly, it's the **yam** capital of the universe (see p.704 for a festival celebrating this achievement). You can find out more about the town at the quirky **Opelousas Museum**, 315 N Main St (Mon–Sat 9am–5pm; free), which displays such relics of local history as the barber's stool on which outlaw Clyde Barrow got his last shave before being shot dead by the FBI in northern Louisiana. Head for the 1950s *Palace Café*, on the central square at 135 W Landry Ave (☎337/942-2142), for shrimp, crawfish, and gumbo in immaculate **diner** surroundings. Chain **hotels** line I-49; the *Holiday Inn* (☎337/948-3300, ⓦwww.ichotelsgroup.com; ❹), just north of town, is a good bet.

To learn a little about the Cajun prairie, head for friendly **EUNICE**, about twenty miles west of Opelousas. The exemplary **Prairie Acadian Cultural Center** at the **Jean Lafitte National Historical Park**, 250 W Park Ave (Tues–Fri 8am–5pm, Sat 8am–6pm; free), holds far-reaching displays on local life, ranging across family, language, food, and farming, with regular live Cajun music, storytelling, and cookery demonstrations. There's more music at the **Cajun Music Hall of Fame**, 240 S C.C. Duson Drive (Tues–Sat: summer 9am–5pm, winter 8.30am–4.30pm; free), which features accordions, steel guitars, fiddles, and triangles among its memorabilia. If time is limited, choose these two over the **Eunice Museum**, next to the Hall of Fame at 220 S C.C. Duson Drive (Tues–Sat 9am–5pm; free) – though this too has its charms; it's an old train depot crammed with a ragbag of toys, musical instruments, farming implements, and Native American artifacts. However long you're in town, don't miss out on Eunice's splendid **food**. *Allison's Hickory Pit*, 501 W Laurel Ave (Fri–Sun 11am–2pm; ☎318/457-9218) and *Mathilda's Country Kitchen*, 611 St Mary St (closed Mon; ☎337/546-0329) specialize in tasty, home-smoked barbecue and plate lunches, while at *Ruby's*, downtown at 221 W Walnut St (closed Sun; ☎318/550-7665), you can eat home-cooked soul food in a vintage setting. Eunice is also central to the region's **music scene**. The regular Savoy Music Center and Liberty Center bashes (see p.706) are supplemented by the riotous annual **Courir du Mardi Gras**, when masked horsemen gallop through the countryside before parading through downtown, where the drinking and dancing continues all day. The **Music Machine**, 235 W Walnut St (☎337/457-4846), is a good source of local music information, with a fine collection of Cajun, zydeco, and swamp pop. *Potier's Prairie Cajun Inn*, at 110 W Park Ave (☎337/457-0440, ⓦpotiers.net; ❹), next door to the Liberty Center, is a 1920s hospital restored as a friendly **place to stay**.

From here it's twenty miles north to **VILLE PLATTE**, and the fabulous Floyd's Music Store, 434 E Main St (Mon–Sat 8.30am–4.30pm; ⓦwww.floydsrecords.com), owned by Floyd Soileau, the world's chief distributor of **South Louisiana music**, and stocking everything from zydeco reissues to contemporary swamp pop. If the dashing Mr Soileau isn't around, you could well find him listening to the rocking jukebox a couple of doors down at the *Pig Stand*, 318 E Main St (☎337/363-2883), where giant plates of fried chicken, smothered sausage, and ribs come heaped with rice, gravy, black-eyed peas, and potato salad.

Swamp tours

Swamp tours are available from many landings in the **Atchafalaya Basin**; you'll pass numerous signs pinned to the old cypress trees along the roadside. The basin is an eerie place: the bulk of its cypress was harvested last century, and now you'll see the twisted silhouettes of their stumps poke out of the sluggish waters. In some places cars cut right across on the enormous concrete I-10 above, and old houseboats lie abandoned, or get used only for weekend retreats. The best tours take you further out, to the backwoods; wherever you go you'll see scores of fishing boats and plenty of wildlife, including sunbathing alligators. The tours below are conducted by Cajuns who see the basin as more than just a tourist attraction and provide fascinating personal commentaries.

The Atchafalaya Experience 338 N Sterling St, Lafayette ☏337/261-5150, ⊛www.
theatchafalayaexperience.com. The son in this father-son team is a geologist; both guides are lifelong explorers of the swamp, and tours are ecologically sensitive. Call for schedule; 3hr; reservations required; $45.

Bryan Champagne Lake Martin Landing, Rookery Rd, Breaux Bridge ☏337/845-5567, ⊛www.champagnesswamptours.com. Champagne navigates a small crawfish skiff through the bird-rich Cypress Island Swamp – lots of opportunity for alligator-spotting. Tours daily; call for schedules; 2hr; $20.

McGee's Swamp Tours McGee's Landing, 1337 Henderson Levee Rd, Breaux Bridge ☏337/228-2384, ⊛www.mcgeeslanding.com. Twenty-five minutes from Lafayette, along I-10 to exit 115, then highways 347 and 352, this quiet landing offers leisurely tours run from Henderson Swamp, a top fishing spot, as well as live music (see p.706). Daily 10am, 1pm & 3pm; no tours in Jan; 90min; reservations recommended; $18.

South of Lafayette

South of Lafayette, the towns are less immediately welcoming than those in the Prairie, but the surroundings are undeniably atmospheric: this is **bayou country**, a marshy expanse of rivers and lakes dominated by the mighty Atchafalaya swamp, where the soupy green waters creep right up to the edges of the highway. Unsurprisingly, the economy is based on fishing and shrimping, with hunting in the forests and sugar fields, but it's also a semi-industrial landscape, with a web of oil pipelines running beneath the waterways, and refineries and corrugated-iron shacks sharing space with neat white Catholic churches.

Settled in 1765, old **ST MARTINVILLE** on the Bayou Teche, off US-90 and 18 miles south of Lafayette, was a major port of entry for exiled Acadians. Hard to believe now, but in the nineteenth century this country town grew to become known as "le petit Paris," filled with French Royalists fleeing the Revolution and re-creating a glittering city life of soirees and balls. It was later decimated by yellow fever, fire, and hurricane, and is now a peaceful hamlet, kept going by a trickle of tourists. You'll see a lot of references to "Evangeline;" to find out why, head for **Evangeline Oak Park**, on Evangeline Boulevard where it meets the bayou. Here stands the **Evangeline Oak**, where real-life Acadian **Emmeline Labiche**, the inspiration for Longfellow's epic poem *Evangeline*, disembarked after her hard journey from Nova Scotia, only to hear that her lover, Gabriel, was engaged to another. The park, which has a boardwalk along the bayou, also features the **St Martinville Cultural Heritage Center** (daily 10am–4pm; $2), where the **Museum of the Acadian Memorial** pays tribute to the thousands of refugees displaced from Canada to Louisiana between 1764 and 1788, and the **African-American Museum** focuses on the arrival of enslaved Africans into southwest Louisiana during the 1700s, the emergence of free people of color, and the violence of Reconstruction. Nearby, the **Acadian Memorial** itself has a 30-foot mural marking the Acadians' arrival in Louisiana and a Wall of Names honoring those uprooted during the "Grand Dérangement."

Other sights, such as they are, can be found on or around the town square. The nineeenth-century St Martin de Tours **Catholic church**, at 133 Main St (daily except Fri morning), contains a gold and silver sanctuary light and intricate carved font said to have been gifts from Louis XVI and Marie Antoinette; next door, the off-beat **Petit Paris Museum** exhibits local Mardi Gras costumes (daily 9.30am–4.30pm; $1). Behind the church, the bronze **Evangeline Monument** was donated by the producers of the 1929 movie *The Romance of Evangeline*, and is modeled on Dolores del Rio, its star. On the bayou just north of town on Hwy-31, the **Longfellow-Evangeline State Historic Site** (daily 9am–5pm; $2) features a couple of simple **Acadian dwellings** and, in contrast, an 1815 **Creole Plantation House**, made with the *bousillage* mixture (mud, Spanish moss, and animal hair) characteristic of early Louisiana buildings. If St Martinville's sleepy charm wins you over, and you want to **stay**, try the *Old Castillo*, 220 Evangeline Blvd next to the Evangeline Oak (☎318/394-4010 or 1-800/621-3017, ⓦwww.oldcastillo.com; ➍), a B&B with huge rooms. Its **restaurant** serves tasty French Cajun food.

Northern Louisiana

Northern Louisiana is at the heart of the region known as the **Ark-La-Tex**, where the cottonfields and soft vocal drawl of the Deep South Bible Belt merges with the ranches, oil, and country music of Texas, and the forested hills of Arkansas. Settled by the Scottish and Irish after the Louisiana Purchase, the area is strongly Baptist, with less of a penchant for fun than south Louisiana, though it does share its profusion of **festivals**.

Angola Prison

Isolated at the end of the long and lonely Hwy-60, hemmed in by the Tunica foothills and the Mississippi River some sixty miles northwest of Baton Rouge, **Angola** is the most famous maximum-security prison in the United States, its very name a byword for brutality and desperation. Famous inmates have included blues singer **Leadbelly**, who, as Huddy Ledbetter, served here in the 1930s; today it holds about 5000 prisoners, 77 percent of whom are black. Most of the men are lifers, and around 100 of them are on Death Row. Outside the main gate, the **Angola Museum** (Tues–Fri 8am–4.30pm, Sat 9am–5pm; free) offers a fascinating insight into this vexed place. For $3 you can have your photo taken in a replica cell; you are not, however, encouraged to fool with Old Sparky, the electric chair used to execute 87 men and one woman between 1941 and 1991. Fading photos and old newspapers reveal appalling prison conditions; the prodding sticks and belts used to beat convicts bring it closer to home. You can also see an array of prisoner-made weapons – a knife carved from a toothbrush, a blade made from a beef rib – used in the many attempted breakouts and uprisings.

Since 1970, Angola has staged a **prisoner rodeo** every Sunday in October, a harrowing gladiatorial spectacle which draws thousands (there is also a two-day rodeo in April; both $10; reservations required; ☎225/655-2030, ⓦangolarodeo.com). These are extraordinary affairs, the crowds baying while lifers are flung, gored, and trampled in their struggle for dignity, glory, and a simple change of scene.

Natchitoches

Tiny **NATCHITOCHES** (pronounced "Nakitish"), in the sleepy cottonfields of the Cane River, is the oldest European settlement in Louisiana, having begun life as a French trading post in 1714. A Catholic oasis in a Protestant desert, it was swiftly fortified when its Spanish and Native American customers started to combine aggression with commerce.

With its lovingly restored Creole architecture, Natchitoches's **Front Street**, on the river, bears a passing resemblance to New Orleans's French Quarter, with its lacy iron balconies, spiral staircases, and cobbled courtyards complemented by friendly, old-style stores. Fleurs-de-lis on the **St Denis Walk of Honor** commemorate celebrities with local connections, such as John Wayne, Clementine Hunter (see below), and the cast of the movie *Steel Magnolias*, which was set and filmed here in 1988. It's worth a trip to nearby **CLOUTIERVILLE** (pronounced "Cloochyville"), where the quirky **Bayou Folk Museum** (Mon–Sat 10am–5pm, Sun 1–5pm; $5), housed in novelist **Kate Chopin**'s old home, is filled with all manner of oddities of local interest. There's plenty relating to Chopin herself, whose nineteenth-century works, in particular her novel *The Awakening*, about a married woman's desire for independence, shocked the nation.

Practicalities

Natchitoches lies 140 miles northeast of Lafayette, on Hwy-6 off I-49. Greyhound comes in on the southeast side of town, on Hwy-1; note that the town has **no public transportation** or taxis. This is **B&B** territory: one of the most luxurious is the *Judge Porter House*, 321 Second St (T318/352-9206, W www.judgeporterhouse.com; ⑤).

The **visitor center**, 781 Front St (Mon–Fri 8am–6pm, Sat 9am–5pm, Sun 10am–4pm; T1-800/259-1714, W www.historicnatchitoches.com), provides self-guided **walking tours** of the historic downtown. The best place to **eat** is *Lasyone's* (T318/352-3353), around the corner at 622 Second St, which specializes in delicious meat pies, cream pies, red beans and sausage, and fresh, crumbly cornbread.

Cane River National Heritage Area

Just south of Natchitoches, the rural **Cane River roads** are dotted with ramshackle houses and small farms. As you drive past farmers sitting on porches and women hanging out the wash, you'll come across many **plantation homes**, some overgrown and in sad disrepair, others beautifully restored.

The **Cane River National Heritage Area**, a collection of restored plantation homes, churches, and forts, stretches for 35 miles south from Natchitoches. Head first for the fascinating **Melrose Plantation**, on Hwy-119 (daily noon–4pm; $7), which was granted in 1794 to Marie Therese Coincoin, a freed slave, by her owner, Thomas Metoyer – the father of ten of her fourteen children. Coincoin assembled the original grounds and additional land grants into an 800-acre plantation; she was later able to buy freedom for two of her children and one of her grandchildren. Around 1900, enterprising Melrose owner "Miss Cammie" Henry – a collector and patron of local writing – turned the crumbling Melrose into an arts community, visited by painters and writers such as William Faulkner and John Steinbeck. In the 1940s, a black Melrose cook, **Clementine Hunter**, began to use materials discarded by visiting artists to paint vivid images of life on and around the plantation. She carried on painting until her death at the age of 101, and her works have since become valuable pieces of folk art. Many of them are on show in the 1800 **African House**, which resembles a Congo mud hut and was used as the slave jail, and in the **Big House**, a typical plantation home, made from brick and *bousillage*.

Texas

AL - ALABAMA	IN - INDIANA	MN - MINNESOTA	RI - RHODE ISLAND
AR - ARKANSAS	LA - LOUISIANA	MS - MISSISSIPPI	SC - SOUTH CAROLINA
CT - CONNECTICUT	MA - MASSACHUSETTS	NC - NORTH CAROLINA	VA - VIRGINIA
DE - DELAWARE	MD - MARYLAND	NH - NEW HAMPSHIRE	VT - VERMONT
FL - FLORIDA	ME - MAINE	NJ - NEW JERSEY	WI - WISCONSIN
IL - ILLINOIS	MI - MICHIGAN	PA - PENNSYLVANIA	WV - WEST VIRGINIA

CHAPTER 9

Highlights

※ **The Menil Collection, Houston** A staggering collection of ancient and modern artworks – plus the somber Rothko Chapel – in a lovely, leafy setting. **See p.720**

※ **The River Walk, San Antonio** Texas offers few more romantic experiences than a riverside stroll through the heart of San Antonio. **See p.730**

※ **The Sixth Floor Museum, Dallas** Decide for yourself whether Oswald really did shoot JFK, as you overlook Dealey Plaza. **See p.748**

※ **Fort Worth** From cattle drives in the rootin'-tootin' Stockyards, to world-class galleries in the Cultural District, Fort Worth is Texas' best-kept secret. **See p.751**

※ **Rafting and hiking in Big Bend National Park** The Rio Grande rushes through an astonishing gorge in this remote wilderness, criss-crossed with rewarding trails. **See p.762**

※ **Starlight Theater, Terlingua** Beguiling desert bar that sums up all that is best about this tiny West Texas ghost town. **See p.764**

△ The Alamo

Texas

S till cherishing the memory that it was from 1836 to 1845 an independent nation in its own right, **TEXAS** stands apart from the rest of the United States. While its sheer size – eight hundred miles from east to west and nearly a thousand from top to bottom – gives it a great geographical diversity, it's firmly bound together by a shared history, culture, and ideology. Independence is key to the Texas mentality, from the overriding distrust of government – any government – to the absence of unionized labor. As the old anti-litter campaign put it, "Don't mess with Texas."

Each of the major tourist destinations has its own distinct character. Hispanic **San Antonio**, for example, with its Mexican population and historic importance, has a laid-back feel absent from **Houston** or **Dallas**, while trendy **Austin** revels in a lively music scene and intellectualism found nowhere else in the state.

Regional differences are vast. The swampy, forested **east** is more like Louisiana than the pretty **Hill Country** or the agricultural plains of the northern **Panhandle**, and the tropical **Gulf Coast** has little in common with the mountainous **deserts** of the west. Changes in **climate** are equally dramatic: snow is common in the Panhandle, whereas the humidity of Houston, in particular, is only made bearable by nonstop high-power air-conditioning.

One thing shared by the whole of Texas is the constant boasting: everything has to be bigger and better than anywhere else. Such chauvinism is tempered both by the state's melting pot of cultures and by a very healthy dose of self-parody.

Some history

Early inhabitants of Texas included the Caddo in the east and nomadic Coahuiltecans further south. The **Comanche**, who arrived from the Rockies in the 1600s, soon found themselves at war when the **Spanish** ventured in looking for gold. In the 1700s, threatened by French hopes of westward expansion from Louisiana, the Spanish began to build **missions** and forts, although these had minimal impact on the indigenous population's nomadic way of life. When Mexico won its independence from Spain in 1821, it took Texas with it as part of the deal. At first, the Mexicans were keen to open up their land, and offered generous incentives to settlers. Stephen Austin established Anglo-American colonies in the Brazos and Colorado River valleys. However, the Mexican leader, Santa Anna, soon became alarmed by Anglo aspirations to autonomy, and his increasing restrictions led to the eight-month **Texas Revolution** of 1835–36. The romance of the Revolution draws legions of tourists to **San Antonio**, site of the legendary **Battle of the Alamo**, which, though a military disaster, presaged independence.

The short-lived **Republic of Texas**, which included territory now in Okla-

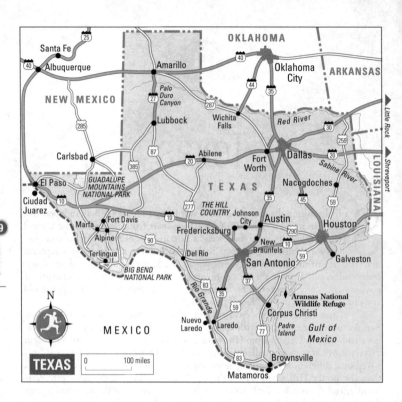

homa, New Mexico, Colorado, Kansas, and Wyoming, served to define the state's identity, and in 1845 Texas joined the Union on the understanding that it could secede whenever it so wished. This is still written into its constitution, as is the proviso that it can, at any time, divide itself into five separate states. Not surprisingly, Texans display an unmatched measure of state pride: Texas schoolchildren are as familiar with the heroes of the Alamo as the heroes of the Revolutionary War, and you'll see the ubiquitous state symbol – the **Lone Star** – emblazoned on everything from advertising to architecture.

The influence, especially in the north and east, of settlers from the Southern states and their attendant slave-centered cotton economy resulted in Texas joining the **Confederacy**. No major Civil War battles were fought on Texas soil, however. During Reconstruction, settlers from both the North and the South began to pour in, and the phrase "Gone to Texas" was familiarly applied to anyone fleeing the law, bad debts, or unhappy love affairs. This was also the period of the great cattle drives, when the longhorns roaming free in the south and west of Texas were rounded up and taken to the railroads in Kansas. The Texan – and national – fascination with the romantic myth of the **cowboy** has its roots in this era, and still prevails; today his regalia – Stetson, boots, and bandana – is virtually a state costume, especially in Fort Worth and the west.

Along with ranching and agriculture, **oil** has been crucial. After the first big gusher in 1901, at Spindletop on the Gulf Coast, the focus of the Texas economy shifted almost overnight from agriculture toward rapid industrialization. Boom towns flew up as wildcatters chased the wells, and millions of dollars were made as ranchers, who had previously thought their land only fit for cattle, sold out at vast profit. Texas today produces one-third of all the oil in the United States, and the sight of nodding pump jacks is one of the state's most potent images.

Getting around Texas

Texas distances are best negotiated by **car**, and in Dallas and Houston driving is all but essential. Mass transit has proved impractical in a state with long commuting distances and low gasoline prices. **Cycling** only makes sense within cities like Austin and San Antonio. **Greyhound** routes are concentrated between the major cities of the east and the central region, though buses also serve the Gulf Coast, the Rio Grande Valley, West Texas, and, to a lesser extent, the Panhandle. Two **Amtrak** trains pass through Texas: *The Texas Eagle* travels between Chicago and San Antonio, stopping in Dallas and Austin; while the *Sunset Limited* stops in Houston, Alpine, and El Paso on its way between Orlando and Los Angeles. An Amtrak Thruway bus links San Antonio with Laredo. **Flying** saves time and can be very cheap; look out for price wars between airlines such as Southwest and smaller local carriers.

Southern Texas and the Gulf Coast

The coastline of **south Texas** curves from Port Arthur on the Louisiana border (a shipping and petrochemical town and the birthplace of Janis Joplin), down past Houston to the Rio Grande, the border with Mexico. While **Houston**, with its cosmopolitan population and thriving arts scene, dominates the region, geographically and culturally the area has two distinct faces. To the east are the seaside resorts of the prairie, rolling away from the hills and forests of East Texas. Much of the coast is feeling the strain of rapid property development, but there are still unspoiled stretches along the **Padre Island National Seashore**. In the south, a Hispanic influence spreads north from the fertile Rio Grande Valley. The charmless border towns here are only of interest as points of entry into Mexico for cheap shopping and entertainment. Uniting south Texas is the hot, swampy **climate**; Houston, especially, is unbearable in the summer, one reason for the mass exodus to the coast.

Houston

In some ways it comes as no surprise that the biggest corporate scandal in American history – the 2001 bankruptcy of the energy company Enron – occurred in **HOUSTON**. This is a city whose very existence has always depended on wild speculation and boom-and-bust excess. Founded on a muddy mire in 1837 by two real estate-booster brothers from New York – their dream was to establish it as the capital of the new Republic of Texas – Houston was soon superseded by the

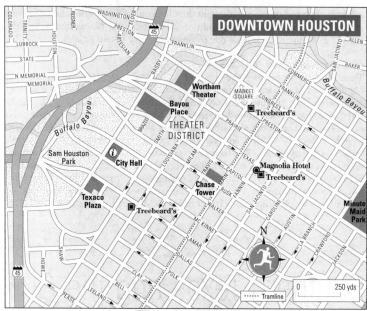

DOWNTOWN HOUSTON

Museum District & Rice University

more promising site of Austin even while somehow establishing itself as a commercial center. **Oil**, discovered in 1901, became the foundation, along with cotton and real estate, of vast private fortunes, and over the next century wildly wealthy philanthropists poured their cash into swanky galleries and showpiece skyscrapers. That colossal self-confidence helped the city weather devastating oil crises in the 1980s – and will no doubt go a long way to restoring confidence in the wake of the Enron debacle.

The fourth-largest city in the United States, Houston is an ungainly beast of a place, choked with highways and high on humidity. Despite this, its sheer energy, its relentless Texas pride, and above all, its refusal to take itself totally seriously, lends it no small appeal. And in August 2005, its speedy response to the chaos in New Orleans in the wake of **Hurricane Katrina** dispelled some of the shadow cast by the Enron shame. Sheltering thousands of evacuees in the Astrodome stadium, and providing long-term housing for many of those displaced, the city literally provided a port in a storm. For visitors, its well-endowed museums, highly regarded performing arts scene, and rich nightlife – spiced up with the addition of so many New Orleans musicians – mean there is always something to do.

Arrival and information

Downtown Houston lies at the intersection of I-10 (San Antonio–New Orleans) and I-45 (Dallas–Galveston), with most of what you'll want to see encircled by Loop 610. **George Bush Intercontinental Airport** (☎281/230-3100), 23 miles north, is the main hub for Continental Airlines, while the smaller, domestic **William P. Hobby Airport** (☎713/640-3000), seven miles southeast of downtown, just west of I-45, is a major hub for Southwest. You'll need to **rent a car** to see the best of Houston; all the major companies are represented at the airports. The

Airport Express **shuttle** (starting at $23 from Intercontinental, $18 from Hobby; ⓣ713/523-8888, ⓦwww.airportexpresshouston.com) drops off at hotels downtown and in the commercial area near the Galleria mall, west of downtown. **Texas Super Shuttle** (ⓣ713/781-6600) runs longer hours and is slightly cheaper, but takes longer. **Taxis** downtown cost $40 to $45 from Intercontinental, less from Hobby.

Amtrak arrives at 902 Washington Ave, on the western fringes of downtown. Try to time your arrival here, or at the modern **Greyhound** terminal, 2121 Main St, during the day, as the surroundings can feel threatening. Book a **taxi** (try Yellow Cabs; ⓣ713/236-1111) to collect you.

For brochures and essential **maps**, make for the high-tech **tourist office** on the first floor of City Hall, 901 Bagby St (Mon–Sat 9am–4pm, Sun 11am–4pm; ⓣ713/437-5556, ⓦwww.visithoustontexas.com).

City transportation

While Houston's **public transit** system is woefully inadequate for a city of its size, visitors might get use out of its downtown **METRORail tram** (ⓣ713/635-4000, ⓦwww.ridemetro.org), which runs about eight miles – mostly along Main St – from northern downtown via the Museum District down to the Texas Medical Center. **Taxis** can prove expensive, and the humid climate and huge distances make walking unappealing. If you can, rent a **car**. The Houston Transportation and Emergency Management Center hotline (ⓣ713/802-5074) gives updates on **lane closures** due to road construction.

9

TEXAS | Houston

Accommodation

Inexpensive **hotels** are concentrated near the Astrodome, south of downtown, and outside the Loop along I-45 or I-10. **Upmarket**, business-oriented chains abound downtown and near the Galleria; these often offer lower rates on weekends. **Bed-and-breakfasts** offer a welcome alternative in a city as potentially alienating as Houston.

Drury Inn and Suites Galleria 1615 W Loop S at Post Oak Park ⓣ713/963-0700 or 1-800-378-7946,

ⓦwww.druryhotels.com. Good value, clean and comfortable rooms in the swanky uptown area. Rates include full breakfast, evening cocktails, and snacks. ❺
Houston International Hostel 5302 Crawford St ⓣ713/523-1009, ⓦwww.houstonhostel.com. Clean hostel in a pleasant neighborhood near Hermann Park and Montrose; dorm beds from $15. There are more long-term guests here than tourists.

Lovett Inn 501 Lovett Blvd ⓣ713/522-5224 or 1-800/779-5224, ⓦwww.lovettinn.com. On a leafy avenue on the edge of the Montrose district, this historic house offers large, comfortable, non-cutesy rooms, first-class service, an abundant continental breakfast, and reasonable

prices. ❹
Magnolia Hotel 1100 Texas Ave ⓣ713/221-0011 or 1-888/915-1110, ⓦ www.magnoliahotelhouston .com. This atmospherically restored 1920s downtown building offers luxury and comfort, with a cozy lounge area, billiards room, and rooftop pool. ❻
Sara's Bed and Breakfast 941 Heights Blvd ⓣ713/868-1130 or 1-800/593-1130, ⓦwww. saras.com. Less than four miles northwest of downtown and north of Montrose, this pretty Queen Anne house has a fine view of downtown Houston, and serves continental breakfasts on the porch. ❹

The City

It's unwise to try and see too much of Houston in one go. If you have just a short time, concentrate on the superb galleries of the **Museum District** and **Hermann Park**, which are linked to **downtown** – some five miles northeast – by light rail. The city's human face is most evident in the **Montrose** area, which lies west of

719

downtown and overlaps with the Museum District.

Uptown, also called the **Galleria** district after its upscale mall, is a good three miles west. Just outside the Loop, between West Alabama and Westheimer roads, the Galleria's three hundred or so smart shops and restaurants spread north along Post Oak Boulevard; there is little to do around here except shop and eat.

Downtown Houston

Houston's skyline remains a dramatic monument to ambition, glitz, and sheer chutzpah. The observation deck at the **Chase Tower**, 600 Travis St, the highest building in Texas, offers views of the endless plateau over which the city sprawls. Nearby, the area now covered by the reflecting pool in front of **City Hall** was granted to the city by a rancher on the condition that no one could ever be arrested there for public intoxication, so it attracts a somewhat varied crowd.

Nestling below the skyscrapers, **Sam Houston Park** on Bagby Street (Tues–Sat 10am–4pm, Sun 1–4pm) is an appealing green space dotted with restored historic structures from all walks of nineteenth-century life (house tours leave from 1100 Bagby St; $6). The park's **Museum of Texas History** (same hours; free) is worth a look, with its 1911 Model T Ford, fully restored nineteenth-century store, and quirky traveling exhibitions.

The majority of people escape the Houston heat by staying underground, in the nearly seven miles of air-conditioned **tunnels** accessible from most downtown hotels and the visitor center. However, despite their shops and restaurants, they're a confusing and visually unappealing way to get around.

The Museum District: The Menil galleries and Montrose

Five miles southwest of downtown, the quiet oak-lined streets of the **Museum district** are enjoyable to explore on foot. There are two main concentrations of exhibition spaces, with one entire complex dominated by the collections of oil millionaires **John and Dominique de Menil**. At 1515 Sul Ross St, a magnificent purpose-built gallery, designed by Renzo Piano, houses the private **Menil Collection** (Wed–Sun 11am–7pm; free; ⑩ www.menil.org). Displayed in spacious white-walled rooms and naturally lit, the superb works range from paleolithic carvings dating from 15,000 BC and Sumerian alabaster statues, through Surrealist assemblages right up to contemporary sculptures. Artists with rooms to themselves include Picasso, Max Ernst, and René Magritte. There's also a fine array of African art, including terracottas from Mali and ivories from Benin. A block east, the minimalist Ecumenical **Rothko Chapel**, 1409 Sul Ross (Sat–Tues 10am–6pm, Wed–Fri 10am–7pm; ⑩ www.rothkochapel.org), contains fourteen somber paintings commissioned by the Menils from Mark Rothko shortly before his death. The artist, who worked with architect Philip Johnson in designing the chapel, considered these to be his most important works, and their power in this tranquil space is undeniable. The broken obelisk in the small park outside is dedicated to Dr Martin Luther King Jr. Check the website for talks and events hosted at the chapel, from Sufi dancing to meditations. Diagonally opposite, the **Byzantine Fresco Chapel Museum**, 4011 Yupon St (Fri–Sun 11am–6pm; free), houses a pair of thirteenth-century Cypriot frescoes – the only intact Byzantine frescoes in the western hemisphere – in a simple contemporary structure.

The Menil galleries are in the **Montrose** district, which spreads west of downtown. This is one of the hippest neighborhoods in town, and though the forces of gentrification are clearly at work, don't think it's all gone the way of the Gap. Montrose has also long been the base of a very visible **gay** community, and a high concentration of gay bars and clubs remains, while Westheimer, the district's main

△ Rothko Chapel

drag, still has enough quirky tattoo parlors, vintage clothes stores, experimental art galleries, and junk shops to feel refreshingly bohemian.

The Museum District: Herrmann Park and Rice University

The Museum District extends south to **Herrmann Park** and the appealing **Rice University** area, all accessible by the light rail system. At the intersection of Bissonet and Main streets, the expansive **Museum of Fine Arts** (Tues & Wed 10am–5pm, Thurs 10am–9pm, Fri & Sat 10am–7pm, Sun 12.15–7pm; $7, free Thurs; Ⓦ www.mfah.org) features an eclectic collection from all eras, filling its impressive buildings with everything from Renaissance art to rare African gold, with a couple of wings entirely devoted to decorative arts. Crane your neck upward from the Matisses and Rodins in the pine-shaded **Cullen Sculpture Garden** outside for a view of the downtown skyline. A short walk away, at 5401 Caroline St, another eye-catching building, with a massive black funnel emerging from a triangular glass wedge, heralds the hard-hitting **Holocaust Museum Houston** (Mon–Fri 9am–5pm, Sat & Sun noon–5pm; $5 donation suggested). Installations, focusing on the relentless horror of the concentration camps, also feature stories of local survivors.

The **Contemporary Art Museum**, across Main Street at 5216 Montrose Blvd (Tues, Wed, Fri & Sat 10am–5pm, Thurs 10am–9pm, Sun noon–5pm; free; Ⓦ www.camh.org), is housed in yet another of Houston's showpiece buildings, a low-slung windowless corrugated-steel parallelogram. It hosts strong temporary exhibitions, with artists sometimes on hand to answer questions, and has a particularly hip museum store.

Pleasant **Hermann Park**, a few blocks south, has a Japanese meditation garden. Well-used during the day, it is best avoided at night. Exhibits at the park's **Houston Museum of Natural Science** (Mon & Wed–Sun 9am–5pm, Tues 9am–9pm; $9, $25 combination tickets with butterfly center, IMAX and planetarium; Ⓦ www. hmns.org) include the stunning hall of gems and minerals, with its strange and wonderful array of raw gold, spindly filigree silver, and blazing crystals. The museum's **Cockrell Butterfly Center** (daily 9am–5pm; $8) is a giant three-story greenhouse where you can walk among exotic butterflies as they flutter around a rainforest environment, and there's also an **IMAX** theater (Mon–Fri 9am–4.30pm, Sat 10am–6pm, Sun 11am–6pm; $8), a **planetarium** (Mon–Fri 11.30am–5pm, Sat 10.30am–7pm, Sun 11.30am–7pm; $6), and regular big-draw **temporary exhibitions**.

The Astrodome

Around three miles south of the Museum District, Houston's legendary **Astrodome** was the world's first domed, climatized stadium when it was built in 1965. This Texas-sized structure, which also lends its name to astroturf, was home to the Astros Major League baseball team (now at the Minute Maid Park; see opposite), and then the NFL's Oilers, but was overshadowed in 2002 by the construction of the 69,500-seat **Reliant Stadium** nearby. The latter, as well as now being home to the Houston Texans Pro football team, also took over the Astrodome's duties hosting the annual Houston Livestock Show and Rodeo – the largest such event in the world. Lonely and abandoned, the Astrodome hit the news again in September 2005 when it was able to house some thirteen thousand evacuees from New Orleans after **Hurricane Katrina**, but its future remains uncertain.

East Houston: The Orange Show

The Orange Show (Sat & Sun noon–5pm, summer also Wed–Fri 9am–1pm; $1; Ⓦ www.orangeshow.org), five miles east of Hermann Park at 2402 Munger St, just off I-45 at the Telephone Road exit, is a strange affair. A triumph of folk art, it's not really a show but a suburban house transformed into a paean to the orange by the monomaniacal former postal worker and would-be inventor Jeff McKissack. With one simple purpose – "to get more people to eat more oranges" – McKissack spent twenty years covering his home with celebratory tiles, ironwork, and slogans, with placards displayed by such oddball mannequins as the son of Santa Claus. Broadening its scope to encompass other examples of "visionary art," the Orange Show also runs tours of local folk art and hosts the annual customized "Art Car" parade.

Eating

Houston's mixed population has left its mark on its **cuisine**: look for Mexican, Vietnamese, and Indian restaurants, and many good delis – such as the sixteen outlets of *Antone's Deli* – serving huge salads and sandwiches with an international flavor.

Baba Yega 2607 Grant St ☎713/522-0042. Cozy neighborhood restaurant in the heart of Montrose, with a warren of rooms, a flower-filled terrace, and zingy food based on fresh, organic ingredients. Try the rotisserie chicken or veggie meat loaf.

Benjy's 2424 Dunstan Rd, off Kirby Rd ☎713/522-7602. Modern American food with an ethnic bent – sesame-crusted tuna, pan-seared pork dumplings, and the like – plus inventive desserts, served in a stylish dining room near Rice University.

Black Labrador 4100 Montrose Ave at Richmond ☎713/529-1199. Open fireplaces and oak beams set the stage for English comfort food (bangers, shepherd's pie) plus black-and-tans and imported Yorkshire bitter.

Café Annie 1728 Post Oak Blvd ☎713/840-1111. Renowned for its classy, innovative Southwestern food – try the tasty crab tostadas – this upscale and uptown restaurant is a local favorite. If money is tight, try it at lunchtime.

Goode Company 5109 Kirby Rd ☎713/522-2530. Fabulous barbecue on the road to the Astrodome, with a big portions, outdoor seating, and a rambunctious Wild West atmosphere.

La Strada in the Galleria area at 5161 San Felipe ☎713/850-9999, or in Montrose at 322 Westheimer ☎713/523-1014. Two attractive restaurants serving Italian cuisine with a creative, spicy Texas twist.

This Is It 207 W Gray St ☎713/659-1608. Heaps of comforting soul food at budget prices at this downtown/midtown favorite.

Treebeards 1117 Texas St (The Cloister, next to Christ Church Cathedral) ☎713/229-8248; 315 Travis St (on Market Square) ☎713/228-2622; 1100 Louisiana Ave (in the tunnel) ☎713/ 752-2601. Cheap and flavorful Cajun/Southern lunches including gumbo, red beans and rice, and vegetable platters.

Nightlife and entertainment

There's no shortage of things to do in Houston; just check the listings in the free *Houston Press* (ⓦ www.houstonpress.com). Downtown's much-trumpeted **Theater District** (ⓦ www.houstontheaterdistrict.org), a seventeen-block area west of Milam Street between Preston and Rusk streets, includes the **Alley Theater** at 615 Texas Ave (☎713/228-8421, ⓦ www.alleytheatre.org), which offers various discount seats, and the stunningly elaborate **Wortham Theater Center**, 510 Preston St (☎713/237-1439; ⓦ www.worthamcenter.org), home to Houston's opera, ballet and symphony, among a host of others. **Bayou Place**, at Smith and Texas avenues, is a brash entertainment and restaurant complex; one of its more interesting options is the multiscreen **Angelika Film Center**, 510 Texas Ave (☎713/333-3456), which shows art movies and has a late-night coffee house.

Beyond downtown, **Miller Outdoor Theater** in Hermann Park (☎281/373-3386; ⓦ www.milleroutdoortheater.com) puts on free performances, from jazz to films and Shakespeare. **Montrose**, meanwhile, supports a very visible **gay** scene, with a number of clubs along Westheimer and Richmond.

If you're a baseball fan, **Minute Maid Park** (previously called Enron Field), home of the Houston Astros, is a great place to see a game, with a retractable roof and its own vintage locomotive (☎713/259-8000, ⓦ www.astros.com). Tours are also available (1hr; $7).

a38 2204 Louisiana St ☎713/951-9800. Cool but unpretentious midtown lounge where convivial young professionals sip specialty drinks in soft candlelight. DJs spin an eclectic mix of disco, house, and hip pop. Wed–Sun.

Big Easy Social and Pleasure Club 5731 Kirby Drive ☎713/523-9999, ⓦ www.bigeasyblues.com. The city's best blues, plus occasional zydeco nights, in the Rice University area.

Engine Room 1515 Pease St ☎713/654-7846, ⓦ www.engineroomlive.com. Pool tables and a grungy indie line-up pull in a diverse crowd at this downtown club.

The Last Concert Café 1403 Nance St ☎713/226-8563, ⓦ www.lastconcert.com. Hidden away in an arty neighborhood east of downtown, this funky café has good Tex-Mex food with live R & B and roots bands in the back garden. Knock on the door for entrance.

McGonigel's Mucky Duck 2425 Norfolk St ☎713/528-5999, ⓦ www.mcgonigels.com. A great club, between Montrose and the Rice University

9

TEXAS | Houston

723

area, featuring folk, alt-country and bluegrass bands, plus terrific Irish jam sessions. **Red Cat Jazz Café** 924 Congress ☎713/226- 7870, ⓦwww.redcatjazzcafe.com. Smooth downtown club, with nightly blues, jazz and soul, plus comedy nights.

Around Houston

Houston's main attraction, **Space Center Houston** (Mon–Fri 10am–5pm, Sat & Sun 10am–6pm; $18.95, parking $5; ⓦwww.spacecenter.org) actually lies some 25 miles south of the city, off I-45 at 1601 NASA Parkway. **NASA** has been controlling space flight from the **Johnson Space Center** here since the launch of Gemini 4 in 1965 – locals love to point out that the first word ever spoken on the moon was "Houston." A working facility, nerve center of the International Space Station, it offers a thrilling insight into modern space exploration, with tram tours giving behind-the-scenes glimpses into various NASA compounds. **Space Center Houston** boasts numerous hands-on exhibits, including a multi-dimensional experience that simulates a rocket launch. Reckon on a good few hours here, as you try on space helmets, inspect moonrocks and remarkably rickety-looking rocket replicas, experience what it feels like to eat on a spaceship, and stock up on bagloads of gimmicky space-themed merchandising.

San Jacinto Battleground (daily 9am–6pm), 22 miles east of Houston off I-10, was the site of an eighteen-minute fight, two months after the Alamo in 1836, in which the Texans all but wiped out the superbly trained Mexican army. The battle is commemorated by the tallest stone-column **monument** in the world (570ft, topped by a 34ft Lone Star), and, inside, a **museum of history** that, along with a host of artifacts relating to the early history and culture of Texas, screens the stirring 35-minute movie *Texas Forever!* ($4.50).

The Gulf Coast

You only have to look at the number of condo developments along the **Gulf Coast** to see that this is a major getaway destination. The climate ranges from balmy at **Galveston** to subtropical at the Mexican border, but everywhere it's windy: **Corpus Christi** rivals Chicago as the gustiest city in the States, and a devastating hurricane in 1900 all but leveled the city of Galveston. The fierce tide, progressively gnawing away at the beaches, may pose a threat to tourism, but for now Galveston offers history, shopping, and low-key relief from Houston. Corpus Christi to the south makes the best base for the beaches of **Padre Island National Seashore**. **Rockport**, a weathered resort on Hwy-35, is convenient for the **Aransas National Wildlife Refuge**, a haven for endangered whooping cranes, armadillos, and alligators.

Galveston

In 1890 **GALVESTON** – on the northern tip of Galveston Island, the southern terminus of I-45 – was a thriving port, far larger than Houston fifty miles northwest; many newly arrived European immigrants chose to stay here in the so-called "Queen of the Gulf." However, the construction of Houston's Ship Canal, after the hurricanes of 1900 killed more than six thousand people and washed away much of the land, left the coastal town to fade slowly away. Thanks to its pretty historic district and its popularity with Houston residents seeking a summer escape, Galveston has undergone a certain revitalization, though its continued vulnerability to storms can give it a somewhat melancholy, beleaguered atmosphere.

Arrival, information, and accommodation

Driving from Houston to Galveston is straightforward: once it crosses over to the island, I-45 (the Gulf Freeway) becomes Broadway, the town's main drag. Greyhound arrives at 714 25th St (around $6 by taxi from downtown). There is no Amtrak service. The main **visitor center** is south of Broadway at 2027 61st St, with a smaller office in the historic **Strand** district, north of Broadway at 2215 Strand (both daily 8.30am–5pm; ☏ 1-888/425-4753, ⓦ www.galveston.com). **Trolleys** (daily 10.20am–6pm; $1; ☏ 409/797-3900, ⓦ www.islandtransit.net) rattle past the historic homes and main sights.

Hotels in Galveston are pricey in summer and on weekends, but bargains can be found at other times; rates along the coastal strip, **Seawall Boulevard**, can drop below $50 per night. Within easy walking distance of the Strand, the town's **East End historic district** holds some relaxing and luxurious **B&Bs**.

Commodore on the Beach 37th St and Seawall Blvd ☏ 409/763-2375 or 1-800/231-9921, ⓦ www.commodoreonthebeach.com. The adequate, inexpensive rooms overlook the Gulf, and there's a large beachside pool as well. ❹–❻

Gaido's Seaside Inn 3802 Seawall Blvd ☏ 409/762-9625 or 1-800/525-0064, ⓦ www.gaidosofgalveston.com. A clean, friendly, no-frills choice, with two good fish restaurants attached. ❸

Garden Inn 1601 Ball St (Ave H) ☏ 409/770-0592 or 1-888/770-7298, ⓦ www.galveston.com/gardeninn. Built in 1887, this pretty Victorian B&B in the East End historic district features well-appointed rooms and a pool, hot tub and hammock in the backyard. ❺

Hotel Galvez 2024 Seawall Blvd ☏ 409/765-7721, ⓦ www.galveston.com/galvez. Classy hotel, built in 1911, restored by the Wyndham group, with a beautiful pool and swim-up bar. ❺–❼

The City

The **Strand** downtown, the nineteenth-century "Wall Street of the Southwest," has been fitted with gaslights, upmarket shops, restaurants, and galleries. The **Texas Seaport Museum** nearby, in a complex of shops and restaurants on Pier 21, just off Water Street (daily 10am–5pm; $6), focuses on the port's role in trade and immigration during the nineteenth century; admission includes boarding the *Elissa*, an 1877 tall ship.

Between the Strand and the beaches to the south, Galveston boasts a profusion of historic homes open for guided tours. Standouts include the ostentatious **Bishop's Palace**, 1402 Broadway (summer Mon–Sat 10am–4.30pm, Sun noon–4.30pm; rest of year daily noon–4pm; $6), with its stained glass, mosaics, and marble; the antebellum **Ashton Villa**, 2328 Broadway (summer Mon–Sat 10am–4pm, Sun noon–4pm, rest of year daily noon–4pm; $6); the Creole planter's-style **Samuel May Williams Home**, 3601 Ave P (Sat noon–4pm; $3); and the city's oldest building, the **Michel B. Menard Home**, 1604 33rd St (Fri–Sun noon–4pm; $6), an imposing Greek Revival structure built in 1838. Galveston's old Santa Fe depot, at 25th Street and the Strand, is now the town's **Railroad Museum** (March–Dec daily 10am–4pm, closed Mon & Tues Jan–Feb; $6), displaying steam trains, Pullman cars, and train-travel-related artifacts in a skillful evocation of a lost era. Look for the eerie white statues of travelers past in the waiting room; you can pick up a telephone and listen to their conversations.

Moody Gardens, Galveston's biggest attraction – for families, at least – lies on the west side of town, at I-45 off the 61st Street exit. The complex (daily: summer 10am–8pm; winter 10am–6pm) centers on three giant glass pyramids: the Rainforest Pyramid ($9.25), housing exotic plants, birds, and fish from around the world; the Discovery Pyramid ($8.95), a science museum with an IMAX cinema;

and the Aquarium Pyramid ($14.95). The complex also holds themed outdoor gardens, walking trails along the scenic **Offatt's Bayou** – where you can take a paddlewheeler cruise ($8.95) – and, probably most popular of all, the kiddy-friendly **Palm Beach** (May–Sept; $10.95). Costs mount up, so if you don't want to spend $39.95 on a **day-pass**, concentrate on just one or two attractions.

The downtown **beaches** of Seawall Boulevard are murky, rocky, and protected behind a ten-mile-long seawall from the ever-encroaching tides and the threat of further hurricanes. **Stewart Beach Park**, the most convenient beach for downtown, is geared toward family fun and gets very crowded; the wide **R.A. Apfell Park**, further east, is marginally quieter during the week, but has live music some weekends and a lively bar. Both charge $8 per car.

Eating and drinking

Dining out in Galveston will likely mean settling in at one of the many low-key seafood restaurants along Seawall Boulevard – their mix of fresh fish dishes and kitschy décor is strangely appealing. **Nightlife** is restricted to sitting in a bar listening to cover bands; there's a glut of places along Post Office Street between 20th and 23rd streets.

Casey's Seafood Café 3802 Seawall Blvd ☏ 409/762-9625. Very good local seafood dishes, linked to *Gaido's* motel (see p.725) and the more upmarket *Gaido's* seafood restaurant.

Old Cellar Bar 2015 Post Office St ☏ 409/763-4477. Dark and convivial old tavern with ales on tap and a lovely antique wooden bar.

Old Quarter Acoustic Café 413 20th St ☏ 409/762-9199, ⓦ www.galvestontexas.com/

oldquarter. A great venue for folk, alt-country and blues; the late Texas singer-songwriter Townes Van Zandt wrote *Rex's Blues* about the café's owner, musician Rex Bell.

Yaga's Café 2314 Strand ☏ 409/762-6676. Delicious Caribbean food served in gaudy surroundings to the sounds of reggae and calypso music.

Corpus Christi

The unabashed resort town of **CORPUS CHRISTI** is reached along the coast on Hwy-35 from Houston or Galveston, or on I-37 from San Antonio. Originally a rambunctious trading post, it too was hit by a fierce hurricane, in 1919, but recovered, transforming itself into a center for naval air training, petroleum, and shipping. Much of the population is Hispanic, and the community was devastated in March 1995, when the 23-year-old singer **Selena** was shot dead in a motel parking lot by the former president of her fan club. Selena was on the verge of becoming the first major cross-over star of **Tejano** music, a hybrid of Mexican rhythms, German polka, and reggae-influenced Colombian *cumbia*, and fifty thousand fans turned out for her funeral. The much-visited **Selena Museum**, 5410 Leopard St, is stuffed with Selena memorabilia, from her famously extravagant gowns to her Porsche (Mon–Fri 9am–noon & 1–6pm; $1 suggested donation).

Corpus Christi is an outdoor destination, but apart from fishing, sailing, and watersports across the channel on Padre Island (see opposite), there are a few diversions. The impressive collection of the Philip Johnson-designed **South Texas Institute for the Arts**, 1902 N Shoreline Blvd (Tues–Sat 10am–5pm, Sun 1–5pm; $6; ⓦ www.stia.org), focuses on fine arts and crafts of the Americas, and stages intriguing temporary exhibitions. Further along N Shoreline Boulevard, at no. 2710, you'll find the massive **Texas State Aquarium** (summer daily 9am–6pm, rest of year until 5pm; $12.95), and the **USS Lexington** (daily: summer 9am–6pm, rest of year 9am–5pm; $11.95), a World War II aircraft carrier that's impressive to walk around, though the few exhibits on board are weak. The **Corpus Christi Museum of Science and History**, 1900 N Chaparral St (Tues–Sat

10am–5pm, Sun noon–5pm; $10), specializes in hands-on natural history exhibits. Moored in the harbor a short walk from the museum, the **Columbus Fleet** (included in the museum admission) consists of life-sized replicas of Christopher Columbus's *Santa Maria* and *Pinta*.

Practicalities

Greyhound arrives at 702 N Chaparral St downtown. The **visitor center** is further along N Chaparral at no. 1823 (Mon–Fri 9am–5pm; ☏361/561-2000, Ⓦwww.corpuschristi-tx-cvb.org). A daytime **trolley** (25¢; ☏361/289-2600, Ⓦwww.ccrta.org) connects the major attractions with area hotels (except Sun); other services include a free downtown "Beach Shuttle" **tram** service (summer only) and a harbor ferry from the South Texas Institute for the Arts to the Texas State Aquarium ($3).

Budget **motels** line Leopard Street in the northwest. Along N Shoreline Boulevard, the *Best Western Marina Grand Hotel*, at no. 300 is comfortable (☏361/883-5111, Ⓦwww.marinagrandhotel.com; ④). Downtown Corpus's main concentration of **restaurants** is in Water Street Market at 309 N Water St, where the *Water Street Oyster Bar* (closed Mon–Wed; ☏361/881-9448) serves fresh seafood. For fresh fish and Cajun-style seafood, there's *Landry's*, 600 N Shoreline Drive (☏361/882-6666). Just across the JFK Causeway, the popular *Snoopy's*, 13313 S Padre Island Drive (☏361/949-8815), offers splendid fried seafood, crabmeat-stuffed jalapeño peppers, and great sunset views.

South toward Mexico

The barrier islands of **Padre Island National Seashore** stretch just offshore for 110 miles south of Corpus Christi, almost down to the Mexican border. While Padre Island has its charms, the frontier here has little to offer. **Brownsville** – a scruffy, semitropical resort populated by retired Texans – and the Mexican town of **Matamoros** are uninspiring; **Laredo**, meanwhile, one hundred miles west of Corpus Christi, has seen a vast drop in tourism in the last few years in the face of violent drug wars in its Mexican neighbor **Nuevo Laredo**. Away from the coast, the fertile landscape begins to dry out and citrus groves give way to the brush and mesquite of a region dominated by huge ranches, where Mexican *vaqueros* once held sway.

Padre Island National Seashore

Padre Island National Seashore is not quite as unspoiled these days as its reputation might suggest, with its ranks of condos advancing steadily, but it remains a good destination for bird-watching, beachcombing, and camping. Pick up details at the **visitor center**, 20402 Park Rd 22 (daily: summer 8.30am–6pm; rest of year 8.30am–4.30pm; ☏361/949-8068, Ⓦwww.nps.gov/pais). The park is open 24 hours, with a $10 admission charge per vehicle, $5 for pedestrians and cyclists, good for one week. Camping on the beach is free, but permits cost $5 for the primitive Bird Island Basin and $8 for the semi-primitive *Malaquite Beach Campground*. Note that an impassable channel divides the island, meaning that the pricier and much more touristy **South Padre Island** in the south can only be reached from the mainland – it's a three-hour drive from Corpus Christi.

Central Texas

Central Texas stretches from the prairies of the northeast through the green and fertile Hill Country into the chalky limestone landscape of the west, and includes two of Texas's most pleasant cities: Hispanic **San Antonio** and the music-oriented student town of **Austin**, which has a progressive feel uncharacteristic of the rest of the state.

Agriculture has been the economic mainstay here ever since the resistant Comanche population was finally packed off to reservations in the 1840s. The slave-driven cotton plantations of the south and east are gone, but the small communities set up by Polish, Czech, Norwegian, and Swedish immigrants in the **Hill Country** maintained, even until very recently, the traditions, architecture, and languages of their homelands. Great cattle drives came trampling through after the Civil War and played a large part in the development of San Antonio.

San Antonio

With neither the modern skyline of an oil town, nor the tumbleweed-strewn landscape of the Wild West, attractive and festive **SAN ANTONIO** looks nothing like the stereotypical image of Texas – despite being pivotal in the state's history. Standing at a geographical crossroads, it encapsulates the complex social and ethnic mixes of all Texas. Although the Germans, among others, have made a strong contribution to its architecture, cuisine, and music, today's San Antonio is predominantly **Hispanic**.

Founded in 1691 by Spanish missionaries, San Antonio became a military garrison in 1718, and was settled by the Anglos in the 1720s and 1730s under Austin's colonization program. It is most famous for the legendary **Battle of the Alamo** in 1836, when the Mexican General Santa Anna, seeking to curb the aspirations of the Anglo-Americans, wiped out a band of Texas volunteers: hence San Antonio's claim to be the "birthplace of the revolution," borne out by its role during Texas's ten subsequent years of independence. After the Civil War, it became a hard-drinking, hard-fighting "sin city," at the heart of the Texas **cattle** and **oil** empires. Drastic floods in the 1920s wiped out much of the downtown area, but the sensitive WPA program that revitalized two of the city's prettiest sites, **La Villita** and the **River Walk**, laid the foundations for its future as a major tourist destination. San Antonio is now the ninth largest city in the US, but it retains an unhurried, organic feel – thanks to a winning combination of small-town warmth, respect for diversity, and a self-confidence rooted in its own history – making it one of the state's nicest places to spend a few days.

Arrival, information, and getting around

San Antonio International Airport (℡ 210/207-3411, 🖳 www.sanantonio. gov/airport) is just north of the I-410 loop that encircles most of the sights. **SA Trans Shuttle** (℡ 210/281-9900, 🖳 www.saairportshuttle.com) makes the twenty-minute journey downtown ($14 one way, $24 roundtrip; every 10–15min 4.30am–1am), while taxis cost about $15 (Yellow Cabs ℡ 210/226-4242). Amtrak arrives centrally at 350 Hoefgen St, while Greyhound operates from 500 N St Mary's St.

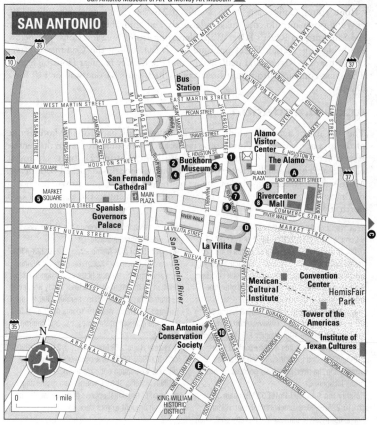

SAN ANTONIO

TEXAS | San Antonio

RESTAURANTS, BARS & CLUBS				ACCOMMODATION			
Acenar	2	Jim Cullum's Landing	1	A Yellow Rose	E	Hilton Palacio del Rio	D
Boudro's	7	Mi Tierra	5	Best Western Sunset		Holiday Inn Crockett Hotel	A
Casa Rio	9	Polly Esther's	3	Suites Riverwalk	C	Menger Hotel	B
El Mirador	10	Schilo's	8				
Esquire Tavern	4	Swig	6				

Pick up maps and information from the **visitor center** at 217 Alamo Plaza, directly opposite the Alamo (daily 9am–5pm; ☎210/225-8587 or 1-800/447-3372, ⓦwww.sanantoniocvb.com). **Driving** in San Antonio, which is Texas's second largest city, can be stressful – thankfully, most of the main attractions are in walkable distance from each other. Also, in addition to a relatively good bus network, four downtown **trolley** routes from Alamo Plaza serve the major attractions (every 10min; 80¢). A Day Tripper pass, available from the VIA Downtown Information Center, 260 E Houston St (Mon–Fri 7am-6pm, Sat 9am–2pm; ☎210/475-9008, ⓦwww.viainfo.net), costs $3 and can be used on all buses and trolleys. Gray Line's **bus tours** (☎210/226-1706 or ☎1-800/256-2757, ⓦwww.grayline.com) are only worthwhile as a way to get to the most distant missions (3hr 30min; $32.50); VIA's #42 service from the Alamo also stops at the San Jose mission.

Boat tours (daily 9am–9pm; $6.50; ℡210/244-5700 or 1-800/417-4139, Ⓦwww.riosanantonio.com) make a leisurely and enjoyable 35-minute circuit of the San Antonio River's River Walk, departing from three locations: just below the bridge on Market Street opposite the *Hilton*; below the Commerce Street bridge near the Rivercenter mall; and behind the *Holiday Inn* near Houston Street. The same company also runs a **boat taxi**, which costs $4 one way or $10 for a day-pass.

Accommodation

The pleasure of a moonlit amble along the **River Walk** back to your hotel is one of the joys of visiting San Antonio, so it's worth paying more to stay in the center. If you like things a bit quieter, the **King William Historic District**, southwest of the main commercial activity, is an appealing neighborhood packed with B&Bs. **Motels** are clustered near Market Square on the west side of downtown; just north of Brackenridge Park on Austin Highway; or, convenient to the airport, on I-35 north toward Austin.

Best Western Sunset Suites Riverwalk 1103 E Commerce St ℡210/223-4400 or 1-877/775-0700, Ⓦwww.bestwesternsunsetsuites.com. Converted historic building with very attractive rooms, inexpensive breakfast, and free afternoon cocktails. A ten-minute walk from the river, they offer free trolley passes to guests. ❹

🏃 **Hilton Palacio del Rio** 200 S Alamo St ℡210/222-1400, Ⓦwww.hilton.com. Constructed for the 1968 World's Fair, this friendly River Walk hotel features a lobby packed with "Texican" art and memorabilia, and balconies overlooking the river. Extremely good value for the prime location. ❻

Holiday Inn Crockett Hotel 320 Bonham St ℡210/225-6500, Ⓦcrocketthotel.com. Historic hotel with modern annexes and a pretty pool, in an excellent location just opposite the Alamo. Good-value deals often available. ❻

Menger Hotel 204 Alamo Plaza ℡210/223-4361, Ⓦwww.historicmenger.com. Bang by the Alamo, this atmospheric historic hotel was a famous destination on the great cattle drives; Teddy Roosevelt recruited his "Rough Riders" here in 1898 for the Spanish–American War. The rooms don't quite live up to the glamour of the lobby, bar, and communal areas. ❻

A Yellow Rose 229 Madison St ℡210/229-9903 or 1-800/950-9903, Ⓦwww.ayellowrose.com. A relaxed, welcoming option in the peaceful King William Historic District, with stylish rooms and a choice of breakfast options (full, continental, or minimal) brought to your door. ❹

The Town

San Antonio is a delight to walk around, its main attractions, including the pretty **River Walk**, the **Alamo,** and **Hemisfair Park**, all within strolling distance of each other. Slightly further out, but still easily accessible, the **King William Historic District,** lined with grand houses, is a tranquil oasis a world away from the lively, and very Hispanic **Market Square**.

The River Walk and La Villita

Since mission times, the **San Antonio River** has been the key to the city's fortunes. Destructive floods in the 1920s and subsequent oil-drilling reduced its flow, leading to plans to pave the river over. Instead, a careful landscaping scheme, started in 1939 by the WPA, created the Paseo del Rio, or **River Walk**, now the aesthetic and commercial focus of San Antonio. The walk, located below street level, is reached by steps from various spots along the main roads and crossed by humpbacked stone bridges. Cobbled paths, lined with tropical plants and shaded by pine, cypress, oak, and willow, wind for two and a half miles (21 blocks) beside the jade-green water, with much of the city's dining and entertainment options concentrated along the way. You can catch a river taxi (see above) at a number of places, but strolling is just as much fun; watch the riverside slowly change character as it winds from the lively **Rivercenter Mall**, via the rowdy outdoor restaurants and bars of the **River Square** area, to the quieter, more park-like outskirts. During peak seasons, the River Walk can become seriously crowded, with high-spirited vacationers packed three to four rows deep – the key is to take a deep breath and enjoy the festive atmosphere. The crowds thin the further from the center you stroll.

La Villita ("little town"), on the River Walk opposite Hemisfair Park, was San Antonio's original settlement, occupied in the mid- to late eighteenth century by Mexican "squatters" with no titles to the land. Only when its elevation enabled it to survive fierce floods in 1819 did this rude collection of stone and adobe buildings become suddenly respectable. It is now a National Historic District, turned over to a dubious "arts community" consisting mostly of overpriced craftshops. It's a pretty spot, with its piazzas, soft-edged buildings, and brick streets, best visited off-season or at dusk, when the crowds dwindle and the muted colors, smells, and noises are more evocative of earlier times.

The Alamo
San Antonio's most distinctive landmark, **the Alamo** (Mon–Sat 9am–5.30pm, Sun 10am–5.30pm; free), lies smack in the center of downtown at the meeting of Houston, Crockett, Bonham, and Alamo streets. Inextricably associated with the **battle** that took here in 1836, a defining moment in the Texas struggle for independence against Mexico, the Alamo has been immortalized in movies and songs, and exists now as a kind of rallying cry for Texas spirit. Its fame, however, has little to do with its original purpose. It was built in the eighteenth century by the Spanish, the first in a trail of **Catholic missions** established along remote stretches of the San Antonio River. Each was laid out like a small fortified town, with the church as aesthetic and cultural focus. The goal was to strengthen Spanish control by "converting" the indigenous Coahuiltecan – in practice, using them as workforce and army. The missions flourished from 1745 to 1775, but couldn't survive the ravages of disease and attack from the Apache and Comanche, and fell into disuse early in the nineteenth century.

The infamous Alamo battle occurred on March 6, 1836, when five-thousand-strong Mexican troops wiped out 189 rebels, dreaming of Texas autonomy, in one swoop. Driven by the battle cry of "Victory or Death!", the besieged band – a few native Hispanic-Texans, adventurers like Davy Crockett and Jim Bowie, and aspiring colonists from other states – held out for thirteen days against the Mexicans before their demise. Their massacre was dismissed by the despotic Mexican General Santa Anna as "but a small affair."

Considering its fame, the Alamo is surprisingly small. All that is left of the original complex is its **chapel**, fronted by a large arched facade of delicately carved sandstone, and the **Long Barracks**. A constant stream of bus tours makes visits crowded and hectic, but for anyone curious about the state's particular brand of pride and stubbornness, the Alamo is unmissable. Disconcertingly, no response but absolute reverence is permitted – effectively this is a shrine, and a sign even insists visitors remove their hats. The battle memorabilia in the chapel is undeniably emotive, while the Long Barracks Museum presents a rousing twenty-minute film on the history of the missions and the battle. The grounds, with four acres of lush blooms, palms, and cacti, are a haven from the commotion both in- and outside the walls.

Other downtown attractions
For a jawdropping slice of kitsch Americana, the **Buckhorn Saloon and Museum**, 318 E Houston St (daily: summer 10am–6pm or later, winter

△ Detail from the Alamo

10am–5pm or later), can't be beat. During San Antonio's heyday as a cowtown, cowboys, trappers, and traders would bring their cattle horns to the original *Buckhorn Saloon* in exchange for a drink. The entire bar, a vast and airy space, has since been transplanted to this downtown location, where you can enjoy a beer and a steak in the presence of hundreds of mounted horns. An extra floor ($10.99) displays even more of them, mounted as trophies, chandeliers, and chairs, along with saddles, pistols, a woeful cavalcade of poorly stuffed animals – including "Bimbo," the two-headed lamb – and a quirky museum of rough-riding Texas history.

It's a long walk on a hot day through the enormous **HemisFair Park** – a sprawling campus of administrative buildings with scant lawns – to the **Institute of Texan Cultures**, 801 S Bowie St (Tues–Sat 10am–6pm, Sun noon–5pm; $7), but it's worth the trip. Mapping the social histories of 26 diverse Texas cultures, this lively museum has especially pertinent African-American and Native American sections, as well as intriguing exhibits on Chinese, Lebanese, and Wendish communities. Also in the park, the **Mexican Cultural Institute** (Tues–Fri 10am–5pm, Sat & Sun noon–5pm; free) hosts temporary exhibitions of historic and contemporary Mexican art. The 750ft **Tower of the Americas** (Sun–Thurs 10am–1pm, Fri & Sat 10am–11pm) east of here offers stunning views from its observation deck ($5), a revolving restaurant, and a 4D theater ride, *Skies Over Texas* ($6). Combo tickets are available for $9.95.

San Antonio's Hispanic heart beats strongly west of the river. At 115 Main Plaza, the handsome **San Fernando Cathedral** is the oldest cathedral in the US, established in 1731. Mariachi masses are held on Saturday at 5.15pm, when crowds overflow onto the plaza, and there are even two flamenco masses per year. Two blocks west at 105 Plaza de Armas, the beautifully simple, whitewashed **Spanish Governors Palace** (Mon–Sat 9am–5pm, Sun 10am–5pm; $1.50) was once home to Spanish officials during the mission era. Just one story tall, it's hardly a palace, but its flagstone floors, low doorways and beamed ceilings, religious icons and ornate wooden carvings give it a wonderful atmosphere, and it provides an illuminating glimpse of the lifestyles of the civil and religious authorities in this remote outpost.

Market Square (daily: summer 10am–8pm; rest of year 10am–6pm), a couple of blocks further northwest on W Commerce St, dates from 1840. Its festive outdoor restaurants and stalls make it an appealing destination, especially during fiestas like Cinco de Mayo and the Day of the Dead. Fruit and vegetables are on sale early in the morning, while the shops are a compelling mix of color and kitsch. **El Mercado**, an indoor complex, sells tourist-oriented gifts, jewelry, and oddities.

The 25-block **King William Historic District** to the southwest, between the river and S Alamo Street, offers a different flavor, its shady streets lined with the elegant late nineteenth-century homes of German merchants. It remains a fashionable residential area and has some stylish B&Bs; pick up **self-guided walking tours** outside the headquarters of the San Antonio Conservation Society, 107 King William St. The **Blue Star Arts Center**, further south at 116 Blue Star St, makes an appealingly rakish contrast to the rest of the neighborhood with its brewpub, workshops, and funky crafts stores.

San Antonio Museum of Art and McNay Art Museum

The **San Antonio Museum of Art**, 200 W Jones Ave (Tues 10am–8pm, Wed–Sat 10am–5pm, Sun noon–6pm; $8, free Tues 4–8pm), occupies the old Lone Star Brewery north of downtown. It's full of treasures – including an unusual collection of ancient glass and a preserved, gloriously vivid Tibetan mandala – with distinctive works from the Far East and Oceania, strong pre-Columbian and colonial American collections, and an entire wing of Latin American works, including vivacious folk art.

A little further north, the beautiful **McNay Art Museum**, 6000 N New Braunfels Ave at Austin Highway (Tues, Wed & Fri 10am–4pm, Thurs 10am–9pm, Sun noon–5pm; free, $5 suggested donation) is another treat. This exquisite Moorish-style villa, complete with tranquil garden, was built in the 1950s to house the art collection of millionaire and folk artist Marion Koogler McNay, which includes modern sculpture, Gothic and medieval works, as well as a sprinkling of major players (Picasso, Monet, and Van Gogh).

The mission trail

Any trip to San Antonio will include a visit to the Alamo, but for a real taste of early Spanish influence in Texas, make an effort to see the more distant, less visited missions. The **Mission Trail** (Ⓦwww.nps.gov/saan) runs ten miles south along the river from Alamo Street, down S St Mary's Street and onto Mission Road. Missions Concepción and San José are covered on the Alamo Trolley Tour, which leaves from the Alamo Visitor Center in the *Menger Hotel* ($19.95 for a hop-on, hop-off pass). Mission San José can also be reached via bus 42 down Roosevelt Avenue; to get to the others you will need to drive. Each mission has its own character, and acts as an **interpretive center**, illustrating some aspect of mission life (daily 9am–5pm; free); the churches themselves still serve active parishes. The main **visitor center** (daily 9am–5pm; Ⓣ210/932-1001) is at Mission San José.

Mission Concepción, 807 Mission Rd, with its distinctive twin towers and cupola, was built between 1731 and 1751. Colorful scraps of original frescoes can still be seen, along with bullet holes from rougher days. Exhibits here concentrate on the religious function of the missions. The 1720 **Mission San José**, 6701 San Jose Drive, which interprets the mission as a social and defense center, is the most complete of all, restored in the 1930s by the WPA. Other notable features include the beautiful carved stone ornamentation, especially the ornate rose window. A Mariachi Mass is held here each Sunday at noon. Of the two smaller and more isolated missions, **Mission San Juan**, 9101 Graf Rd, has displays on agriculture (as well as a unique delicate bell tower), while **Mission San Francisco de la Espada**, 10040 Espada Rd, looks back on ranching life in mission days.

Eating

San Antonio has good **Tex-Mex** food in all price ranges. Many visitors head straight for the restaurants on the River Walk, but, charming as it is to eat alfresco beside the river, don't be seduced to such an extent that you never venture above ground.

Acenar 146 E Houston St Ⓣ210/222-2362. Highly designed and spirited River Walk restaurant – it's quieter on the terrace – serving fabulous cutting-edge Mexican food to a hip, convivial crowd. Closed Sun.

Boudro's 421 E Commerce St Ⓣ210/224-8484. This stylish River Walk Tex-Mex bistro is favored by locals as much as tourists. Enjoy tasty, creative New American/Southwestern entrees, a wonderful guacamole made at your table, and killer prickly-pear margaritas.

Casa Rio 430 E Commerce St Ⓣ210/225-6718. The oldest, most established restaurant on the River Walk, this sprawling place – in a relatively quiet spot – offers cheap and cheerful Mexican dining right by the water.

The Guenther House 205 E Guenther St Ⓣ210/351-6306. Light lunches, cookies, and cakes in an airy flour-mill-cum-museum in the King William Historic District.

El Mirador 722 S St Mary's St Ⓣ210/225-9444. Popular family-owned cantina serving very cheap Mexican breakfasts and lunches, and pricier Southwestern cuisine in the evening. Specialties include *xocetl* (chicken broth) and *azteca* (spicy tomato) soups.

Mi Tierra 218 Produce Row Ⓣ210/225-1262. With its bedazzlement of *piñatas*, fairy lights, and fiesta flowers, this festive 24hr joint is the highlight of Market Square, serving good, inexpensive Tex-Mex staples and delicious sugary cakes at their *panadería*.

Schilo's 424 E Commerce St Ⓣ210/223-6692. With none of the razzamatazz of the River Walk, just footsteps away, this old German diner dishes up good solid comfort food – country breakfasts, bratwurst, ham hock, split pea soup – for when you're tiring of tacos.

Nightlife and entertainment

With its abundance of picturesque settings, San Antonio is a great city for **festivals**. The year's biggest event is April's ten-day **Fiesta San Antonio** (Ⓦwww.fiesta-sa.org), marking Texas's victory in the Battle of San Jacinto, with parades, cookouts, and Latin music. In May, the **Tejano Conjunto Festival**, hosted by the Guadalupe Cultural Arts Center on Guadalupe Street (ⓌWwww.guadalupeculturalarts .org), west of downtown, celebrates the German-Mexican country music of south and central Texas. June's four-day **Texas Folklife Festival** at the Institute of Texan Cultures (see p.733; ⓌWwww.texancultures.utsa.edu/public/index.htm) showcases the state's huge diversity of music, food and culture, ranging from gospel choirs to Lebanese cuisine. Finally, the **San Antonio Stock Show & Rodeo** (ⓌWwww.sarodeo.com) in February celebrates cowboy culture with more than two weeks of rodeo events and country music.

Downtown, the **River Walk** offers rowdy bars and clubs – including *Polly Esther's*, 212 College St. *Swig*, 111 W Crockett St, is a popular haunt for martinis, cigars and jazz. Somewhat less touristy, **Houston Street** is fast becoming a party strip with a crop of slick yuppie bars, while in the north, just beyond the bus station, **N St Mary's St** offers friendly clubs and drinking holes favored by local students. Just a short drive away in the hill country you'll find some great old **rural dance halls**; the best is *Gruene Hall* in New Braunfels (see p.742).

Other possibilities include the outdoor **Arneson River Theatre**, opposite La Villita, where you can watch Mexican folk music and dance on a stage separated from the audience by the river, and **Aztec on the River**, 201 E. Commerce St, an opulent Art Deco movie theater on the River Walk, complete with Wurlitzer organ. Performances include a short silent movie followed by adventure spectaculars designed to show off the massive screen.

For **listings**, check the free weekly *Current* (ⓌWwww.sacurrent.com).

Blue Star Brewing Company 1414 S Alamo St Ⓣ210/212-5506, Ⓦ www.bluestarbrewing.com. Home brews, food, and live music – from Big Band jazz through Texas swing to Latin – in a funky arts complex in the King William District.

Esquire Tavern 155 E Commerce St Ⓣ210/222-2521. This characterful old bar with dim lighting, well-worn leatherette booths, and a fabulous Texas jukebox has been in operation since 1933. Enter from the River Walk or the street and order a marvelous margarita.

Floore Country Store 14464 Old Bandera Rd, downtown Helotes Ⓣ210/695-8827, Ⓦwww .liveatfloores.com. Old country dance hall, with great tamales and outdoor dancing on the weekend.

Jim Cullum's Landing 123 Losoya St, under the *Hyatt Regency* Ⓣ210/223-7266, Ⓦwww.landing. com. Top-notch nightly trad jazz in a touristy River Walk club that's been going for more than thirty years.

Salute! 2801 N St Mary's St Ⓣ210/732-5307, Ⓦwww.saluteinternationalbar.com. Tiny, red-lit bar and live music venue hosting an eclectic roster of Latin jazz, conjunto, Cajun, and hip-hop.

White Rabbit 2410 N St Mary's St Ⓣ210/737-2221, Ⓦwww.sawhiterabbit.com. San Antonio's main venue for touring indie bands, drawing a raucous young crowd.

Austin

AUSTIN was just a tiny community on the verdant banks of the (Texas) Colorado River when Mirabeau B. Lamar, president of the Republic, suggested in 1839 that it would make a better capital than swampy and disease-ridden Houston. Early building had to be done under armed guard, while angry Comanche watched from the surrounding hills, but despite its perilous location, the city thrived.

These days it wears its status as state capital very lightly; sightseeing rates as a low priority against simply hanging out. Since the 1960s, this laid-back and progressive city – unique in Texas – has been a haven for artists, musicians, and writers, and many visitors come specifically for the **music**. And while – whisper it – a certain complacency is beginning to creep in, its "alternative" edge being packaged as just another tourist attraction, artists hungry for fame still tumble out of buses here from all over the nation, seeking their fortunes in this vibrant creative hotbed. Local musicians are renowned for their innovative reworkings of Texas's country, folk, and R&B heritage, using Austin's enthusiastic environment as a springboard to national recognition.

Due to a sizable population leap, ugly suburbs have shot up to threaten Austin's small-town ambiance – but it feels wonderfully safe for visitors, and is one of the few cities in the state where **cycling** is a viable alternative to driving. The presence

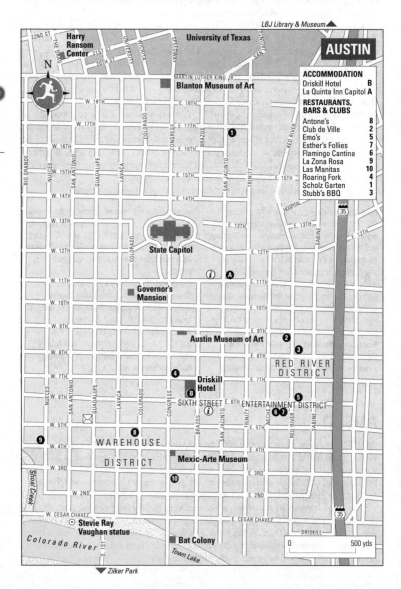

of the vast UT campus – where almost every shop and streetlamp is adorned with the unsightly burnt-orange and white colors of the college's Longhorns football team – adds to the relaxed atmosphere.

Within the city limits a great park system offers numerous hiking and biking trails and a wonderful spring-fed swimming pool. Looking further afield, Austin makes a fine base for exploring the green **Hill Country** that rolls away to the west.

Arrival and information

Austin spreads about twenty miles north–south and eighteen miles east–west, severed by I-35 (between Dallas and San Antonio) to the east. The Colorado River – called Town Lake where it abuts Congress Avenue – runs south of downtown. Flights come in at the **Austin-Bergstrom International Airport** (☎512/530-2242, ⓦ www.ci.austin.tx.us/austinairport), eight miles southeast of downtown. From here it's about twenty minutes to downtown by **taxi** (Yellow Checker Cabs; ☎512/452-9999; around $28) or by SuperShuttle vans (☎512/258-3826, ⓦ www.supershuttle.com; $12.75). **Driving**, avoid snarl-ups on I-35 by taking Hwy-71 to Riverside Drive and then Congress Avenue.

The **visitor center**, 209 E 6th St (Mon–Fri 9am–5pm, Sat & Sun 9am–6pm; ☎866/GO-AUSTIN, ⓦ www.austintexas.org) is full of useful information about the music scene.

City transportation and tours
Unique in Texas, Austin has a good **public transportation** system. The Capital METRO (ⓦ www.capmetro.org, ☎512/474-1200) runs **buses** downtown, crosstown, and through the campus for a flat fare of 50¢ (express buses $1), with additional student shuttle routes that everybody uses; look for the Longhorn emblem beside the shuttle's route number. The Dillo, also run by METRO, is a free downtown **trolley** that runs through downtown and the UT campus (Mon–Fri 6.30am–8.30pm every 10–40min, less frequently Sat & Sun). You can rent **bicycles** from Bicycle Sport Shop, 517 S Lamar, just south of Barton Springs (Mon–Wed & Fri 10am–7pm, Thurs 8am–8pm, Sat 9am–6pm, Sun 11am–5pm; ☎512/477-3472, ⓦ bicyclesportshop.com) – reserve in advance if possible. Downtown Austin is a pleasant place to take a stroll; pick up free self-guided **walking tours** from the visitor center.

Accommodation

Austin offers a good variety of **places to stay**, with the usual budget hotels on I-35, some classy hotels downtown, a couple of hip choices on South Congress, and a variety of comfy **B&Bs**.

Austin Motel 1220 S Congress Ave ☎512/441-1157, ⓦ www.austinmotel. com. Basic rooms – each one different, many with kitschy murals – in a hip old motel in the funky South Congress district. A favorite with visiting musicians, it's across the street from the venerable *Continental Club* (see p.741). ❹

Carrington's Bluff 1900 David St ☎512/479-0638, ⓦ carringtonsbluff.com. Central, very comfortable B&B near the university. It has a country-style feel, with a shady veranda, friendly hosts, and gourmet breakfast. ❺

Driskill Hotel 604 Brazos St ☎512/474-5911, ⓦ www.driskillhotel.com. The great and the good have stayed at this handsome historic hotel, which, with its opulent marble lobby and updated rooms is Austin's swankiest choice. It's close to the action along 6th Street. ❽

HI-Austin (Hostelling International) 2200 Lakeshore Blvd ☎512/444-2294 or 1-800/725-2331, ⓦ www.hiaustin.org. Not particularly welcoming, but with bargain rates right on Town Lake. $17 for members, $20 for non-members.

La Quinta Inn Capitol 300 E 11th St ☎512/476-1166, ⓦ www.laquinta.com. Comfortable, central rooms within a stone's throw of the capitol and on the Dillo shuttle. ❹

Hotel San Jose 1316 S Congress Ave ☎512/444-7322, ⓦ www.sanjosehotel.com. Chic and funky small hotel in the South Congress district. Restored from an old motel, it has a variety of minimalist rooms, some with shared bath, along with lovely gardens, a tiny pool, and a cool coffee shop, *Jo's* (see p.740), on site. The courtyard happy hour attracts a local crowd. ❹–❼

The City

The handsome Texas **State Capitol**, at 13th Street and Congress Ave (Mon–Sat 9am–5pm, Sun noon–5pm; free public tours usually every 15min Mon–Fri 8.30am–4.30pm, Sat 9.30am–3.30pm, Sun noon–3.30pm – but call to check on ☎512/463-0063), is over three hundred feet high, taller than the national Capitol in Washington, with a red sunset granite dome that dominates the downtown skyline. The chandeliers, carpets, and even the door hinges of this colossal building are emblazoned with lone stars and other Texas motifs, a theme continued in the added extension, a sleek maze of marble halls. After wandering around, stop by the **Texas Capitol Visitor Center** (same hours), 112 E 11th St, which includes changing exhibits of local interest. Nearby, the antebellum **Governor's Mansion**, 1010 Colorado St, is the governor's official Texas residence (free tours Mon–Thurs every 20min, 10–11.40am; call to reserve on ☎512/463-5516).

Congress Avenue, an attractive stretch of 1950s shops and muted office buildings that slopes south from the capitol down to the river, is worth a look. The **Austin Museum of Art**, at no. 823 (Tues–Sat 10am–6pm, Thurs 10am–8pm, Sun noon–5pm; $5; ⓦ www.amoa.org) makes a good stop-off, with regularly changing exhibits of contemporary art from Gee's Bend quilts to photographic portraits, while a few blocks further down at no. 419, the **Mexic-Arte Museum** has a fine collection of traditional and contemporary Latin American art, including Orozco prints and folk art (Mon–Thurs 10am–6pm, Fri & Sat 10am–5pm; $5; ⓦ www.mexic-artemuseum .org). If you're visiting between April and November, take a walk at dusk down to where Congress Avenue crosses the Colorado River (known here as Town Lake) to watch 1.5 million **bats** – the world's largest urban bat colony – emerge in a large cloud from their hangouts under the bridge. Across the river, **South Congress** has emerged as a hip neighborhood of funky stores, bars and restaurants, with a far more alternative edge than over-commercialized **Sixth Street**, which runs west from I-35. The elegant Romanesque **Driskill Hotel**, on the corner of Sixth and Brazos, is impressive and historic enough to have its own self-guided walking tour.

North of the Capitol, the **Bob Bullock Texas State History Museum**, adjacent to the University of Texas (see opposite) at Martin Luther King Jr Blvd and North Congress, is a marvelous treasure trove of Texas arcana. Among the exhibits are the diary of Stephen F. Austin, generally considered the founder of the state, and a Bible that saved the life of Sam Houston Jr, during the Civil War; a bullet is still lodged in its pages. Interactive exhibits bring the place into the twenty-first century, along with the IMAX cinema and *Star of Destiny*, a 4-D movie about Texas history complete with wind, smoke, and hurricane effects (Mon–Sat 9am–6pm, Sun noon–6pm; $5.50, $10 with IMAX, $8.50 with *Star of Destiny*, $13.50 with both). Further north and beyond downtown, the historic residential area of **Hyde Park**, a leafy enclave, is home to the **Elisabet Ney Museum**, 304 E 44th St. A stolid, castle-like building, this was the last studio of Austin's most celebrated sculptor, a German-born woman who made likenesses of many of the major players of the late 1800s; it's an intriguing place, filled with marquettes and finished marbles, and set in lovely grounds (Wed–Sat 10am–5pm, Sun noon–5pm; free).

Southwest of the center and across the river, the 350-acre **Zilker Park** is one of the best of the city's many fine green spaces, a perfect retreat on sultry Austin afternoons. One of its main attractions is the spring-fed (and deliciously cold) **Barton Springs Pool**, a three-acre turquoise rectangle shaded by pecan trees (daily; $3). You can paddle in the pebbly creek below the pool free of charge, take advantage of the hiking and biking trails, or relax on the **miniature railroad** winding beside the river (Mon–Fri 10am–5pm, Sat & Sun 10am–7pm; $2.75). Another appealing outdoor space, south of the Barton Springs Pool on Robert E. Lee Rd, the **Umlauf Sculpture Garden** (Wed–Fri 10am–4.30pm, Sat & Sun 1–4.30pm; $3.50) is a tranquil, grassy enclave dotted with more than one hundred works in bronze, terracotta, wood, and marble.

The University of Texas

The **University of Texas** – and its fiercely supported Longhorn football team – has a tangible, almost defining, presence in Austin. You'll find most student activity in the cafés, vintage clothing shops and bookstores on the "Drag", the stretch of **Guadalupe Street** running along campus north from Martin Luther King Boulevard to 24th; the campus itself has a number of attractions, too. Having its own oil well (the drilling rig Santa Rita No. 1 on San Jacinto Blvd) has made this one of the world's richest universities, its purchasing power almost unmatched when it comes to rare and valuable books. The university's unparalleled collection of manuscripts is available to scholars amid tight security in the **Harry Ransom Center**; stories abound of the sums lavished to acquire work from relative unknowns who might someday achieve fame. The Center, in the southwest corner of the campus at 21st and Guadalupe, houses a **gallery** (Tues, Wed & Fri 10am–5pm, Thurs 10am–7pm, Sat & Sun noon–5pm; free; Ⓦwww.hrc.utexas.edu), whose permanent collection includes a Gutenberg Bible, the world's first photograph, and a host of contemporary Latin American and American paintings. Excellent rotating literature-related exhibits focus on everything from Modernism to Watergate. Another superb resource, the **Blanton Museum of Art**, MLK at Congress, has a jaw-dropping collection, particularly rich in Renaissance art, modern American masters, and Latin American works. Temporary exhibits explore elevated themes (Tues, Wed, Fri & Sat 10am–5pm, Thurs 10am–8pm, Sun 1–5pm; $5, free on Thurs; Ⓦ blantonmuseum.org).

The **LBJ Library and Museum** (daily 9am–5pm; free; Ⓦwww.lbjlib.utexas. edu), on the northeast edge of campus at 2313 Red River St, traces the career of the brash and egotistical Lyndon Baines Johnson from his origins in the Hill Country to the House of Representatives, the Senate, and the White House. JFK is said to have made Johnson his vice president to avoid his establishing a rival power base; but in the aftermath of Kennedy's assassination, Johnson's administration (1963–69) was able to push through a far more radical program than Kennedy ever attempted. Johnson's nemesis, Vietnam, is presented here as an awful mess left by Kennedy for him to clear up, at the cost of great personal anguish.

Eating

Austin has many more vegetarian and wholefood **restaurants** than is usual in Texas, and even the finer places are refreshingly attitude-free. Sixth Avenue has become something of a frat-boy chug-fest; you'd do better to head for the good budget restaurants along the **Drag** – just look for the student crowds – the more upmarket crop in the **Warehouse District** around Fourth and Colorado, or the hipper scene along **South Congress**. Note, too, that many of the restaurants reviewed below double as music venues, and that many of the music venues and bars listed on p.741 also serve decent food.

El Sol y La Luna 1224 S Congress Ave
☎512/444-7770, ⓦ www.elsolylalunaaustin.com.
A fun and funky family-run Mexican/Tex-Mex bistro
on the hip South Congress strip. The *pozole* is
outstanding, as are the breakfasts, and there's live
Latin music on weekends.

Jo's 1300 S Congress ☎512/444-3800. Cool
al fresco South Congress coffeehouse serving
espresso drinks, pulled pork sandwiches, and cold
beer. Occasional movies, too.

Jovita's 1619 S 1st St ☎512/447-7825, ⓦ www.
jovitas.com. This cozy, colorful, family-oriented
cantina dishes up reliable Tex-Mex food, with good
live country, folk and bluegrass music played in the
early evenings on the outdoor stage.

Las Manitas 211 Congress Ave ☎512/472-9357.
An Austin original, with tasty, great-value Mexican
breakfasts and lunches – lots of veggie choices –
festive decor, and a laid-back vibe. Get there early
to beat the politicos and the students to a space.

Magnolia Café 1920 S Congress Ave ☎512/445-
0000. A 24hr joint that's a local favorite for Tex-
Mex and pancake breakfasts, and a great place to
refuel after a night living it up on South Congress.

Roaring Fork 701 Congress Ave in the *Intercontinental* hotel ☎512/583-0000. Fabulous modern
Southwestern food – succulent crab cakes with
chili slaw, for example, or tender lamb chops with
butternut squash – and specialty margaritas in
sophisticated surroundings.

Salt Lick 18300 Farm Rd 1826, Driftwood
☎512/858-4959. Commonly agreed to be the
city's best BBQ – despite being an eleven-mile
drive away in the Hill Country (check the map
on ⓦ www.saltlickbbq.com). Fabulous pork ribs
soaked in a near-perfect BBQ sauce are dished
up in a lovely leafy setting or indoors in a rustic
dining room.

Threadgill's 6416 N Lamar Blvd
☎512/451-5440, ⓦ www. threadgills.com.
Yet another Austin institution, north of downtown,
established when Kenneth Threadgill was given the
first license to sell beer in the city after Prohibition. Bringing together hippies and rednecks in
the 1960s, *Threadgill's* was an incubator for the
Austin sound, and still features live fiddle music,
folk, and country-and-western bands. The comfort
food is good, too, with terrific chicken fried steak
and veggies like black-eyed peas and okra. There's
a downtown branch south of the river at 301 W
Riverside Drive (☎512/472-9304).

Nightlife and entertainment

Austin's **nightlife** is legendary, and you're spoilt for choice for places to enjoy
it. Though the clubs and bars of 6th Street have become a bit touristy, there are
plenty of good places elsewhere **downtown**, and it's easy enough to hop into a
cab to some of the further-flung classic joints. Three first-rate local newspapers
carry listings: the *Daily Texan*, the UT paper (ⓦ www.dailytexanonline.com), the
"XLent" supplement to the *Austin American-Statesman* (Thurs; ⓦ www.austin360.
com), and the *Austin Chronicle* (Fri; ⓦ www.austinchronicle.com).

Live music

Although Austin's folk revival in the 1960s attracted enough attention to propel
Janis Joplin on her way from Port Arthur, Texas, to stardom in California, the city
first achieved prominence in its own right as the center of "**outlaw country**" music
in the 1970s. **Willie Nelson** and **Waylon Jennings**, disillusioned with Nashville,
spearheaded a movement that reworked sentimental country and western with an
incisive injection of grubby rock 'n' roll. Venues in Austin, far removed from the
hard-drinking honky-tonks of West Texas, provided an environment that encouraged and rewarded risk-taking, experimentation and a lot of cross-breeding. These
days the predominant "**Austin sound**" is a melange of country, folk and blues,
with strong psychedelic and "alternative" influences – but the scene is entirely
eclectic. The tradition of black Texas bluesmen such as Blind Lemon Jefferson and
Blind Willie Johnson, as well as the rocking bar blues of Stevie Ray Vaughan, still
lives on, with a top-notch **blues** club in the form of *Antone's*.

Austin's ten-day **SxSW** (**South by Southwest**) **Festival** (ⓦ www.sxsw.com),
held in mid-March, has become one of the biggest music and film conferences/fes-
tivals in the nation, an industry showcase attended by all the big players. Naturally,
showcasing the best bands from Texas and around the world, along with tons of

movies, it's not cheap: passes for all film, music, and interactive events cost $650 in advance, increasing to $900 for a walk-up rate; a music-only pass is $425 ($600 walk-up). Even if you can't afford to attend, the city is an exciting place to be during SxSW, with hundreds of unofficial gigs and events open to all. Another major event, showcasing folk, bluegrass, acoustic, blues, country, jazz, and Americana, is the **Kerrville Folk Festival**, which lasts nearly three weeks during May and June. It's held at Rod Kennedy's Quiet Valley Ranch in **Kerrville**, a hundred miles west of Austin on I-10 (Ⓦwww.kerrville-music.com). You can attend the main shows or camp on site, enjoying campfire jams under the stars.

For restaurants that double as live music venues, see the listings opposite.

Antone's Blues Club 213 W 5th St Ⓣ512/320-8424, Ⓦwww.antones.net. This old Austin joint in the gentrifying Warehouse District is the best blues club in the city, a hot and sweaty haunt showcasing national and local acts.

The Broken Spoke 3201 S Lamar Blvd Ⓣ512/442-6189, Ⓦwww.brokenspokeaustintx.com. Neighborhood restaurant (good chicken-fried steak) and stomping honky tonk dance hall in south Austin. The barn-like dance floor attracts great country acts; it's a lot of fun. Two-stepping begins at 9pm.

Cactus Café The Texas Union, 24th and Guadalupe sts, UT Ⓣ512/475-6515, Ⓦ www.utexas.edu/student/txunion/ae/cactus/. One of Austin's favorite acoustic venues, specializing in singer-songwriters and putting on consistently good country, rock, and folk music.

Continental Club 1315 S Congress Ave Ⓣ512/441-2444, Ⓦwww.continentalclub.com. This longstanding classic is the city's premier place to hear hard-edged country or bluesy folk sung the Austin way.

Emo's 603 Red River St Ⓣ512/477-EMOS, Ⓦwww.emosaustin.com. A hub for the rock-oriented Red River District, with a friendly, tattooed, and pierced crowd supporting Austin's best alternative/punk bands.

Flamingo Cantina 515 E 6th St Ⓣ512/494-9336, Ⓦwww.flamingocantina.com. The best of the Sixth Street venues, this reggae club features everything from ragga to ska with the occasional Latin band thrown in.

Stubb's BBQ 801 Red River St Ⓣ512/480-8341, Ⓦwww.stubbsaustin.com. Indoor and outdoor stages feature eclectic bands of national repute – including a Sunday gospel brunch – which you can watch while chewing through great Texas-style brisket, sausage, and ribs.

La Zona Rosa 612 W 4th St Ⓣ512/263-4146, Ⓦwww.lazonarosa.com. Kitschy music venue with an eclectic roster, including English indie bands and new hip-hop artists.

Bars

Note that, like the restaurants listed opposite, many of Austin's bars double as music venues.

Club de Ville 900 Red River St Ⓣ512/457-0900. Excellent cocktails, comfy sofas, and a cozy patio setting are the draw at this friendly, intimate bar just a few minutes from the Sixth Street morass.

Ego's 510 S Congress Ave Ⓣ512/474-7091. Unpretentious, friendly, and dark little dive where locals chill out and play pool. Occasional live music.

Scholz Garten 1607 San Jacinto Blvd Ⓣ512/474-1958, Ⓦ www.scholzgarten.net. This historic Austin joint, a biergarten-cum-social hub since 1866, is famed for its beer, gutsy bratwurst and BBQ, energetic political debates, and occasional live oompah bands.

Other nightlife

There's usually something to catch on campus. Big drama and dance names appear in the **UT Performing Arts Center**, 23rd Street and Robert Dedman Drive (Ⓦwww.utpac.org), and you can see **independent movies** at the Dobie Theater, on the Drag at 2021 Guadalupe (Ⓦwww.landmarktheatres.com/market/Austin/DobieTheatre.htm). *Esther's Follies*, 525 E 6th St (Ⓦwww.esthersfollies.com) is Austin's hippest and funniest **cabaret**, which combines spoofs of local and national politicians with Texas-style singing and dancing. **Symphony Square**, at Red River Rd and 11th St (Ⓦwww.austinsymphony.org) is a rough-hewn outdoor amphitheater, below street level on the river, hosting jazz and classical concerts in summer.

The Hill Country

The rolling hills, lakes, and valleys of the **HILL COUNTRY**, north and west of Austin and San Antonio, were inhabited mostly by Apache and Comanche until after statehood, when German and Scandinavian settlers arrived. Many of the log-cabin farming communities they established are still here, such as **New Braunfels** (famous for its sausages and pastries, and, more recently, its watersports) and Luckenbach. You may still hear German spoken, and the German influence is also felt in local food and music; *conjunto*, for example, is a blend of Tex-Mex and accordion music. The whole region is a popular retreat and resort area, with some wonderful hill views and lake swimming, and a lot of good places to camp.

New Braunfels

NEW BRAUNFELS, just thirty miles north of San Antonio on I-35, was founded by German immigrants – mostly artisans and artists – in 1845 and quickly became a trade center. Nowadays, the community, along with its equally historic satellite, **Gruene**, just northeast, makes its living from tourism. The town's two rivers – the Comal and the Guadalupe – are ideal for easy **rafting** and tubing, making this a hugely popular weekend destination (especially for UT students).

New Braunfels also has the excellent **Schlitterbahn** water park (hours and admission vary; ⓦ www.schlitterbahn.com), and, south of town on I-35, the equally family-friendly **Natural Bridge Caverns** (daily, hours and admission vary; ⓣ 210/651-6101, ⓦ www.naturalbridgecaverns.com). These offer a variety of tours, including the physically intense Adventure Tour ($95, reservations necessary), which lowers visitors 160 feet by rope into the South Cavern and takes them hiking and spelunking where there are no trails or lights. If outdoor activities don't appeal, downtown's historic district has enough antique stores, galleries, and restored buildings to fill a couple of hours. There's more of the same in picturesque Gruene, along with the intriguing **New Braunfels Museum of Art and Music**, 1259 Gruene Rd (summer Mon–Thurs 10am–6pm, Fri & Sat 10am–8pm, Sun noon–8pm; rest of year Mon & Wed–Sat 10am–6pm, Sun noon–6pm; $4.50), which concentrates on popular culture of the region – from blues to poster art – and hosts live roots American music and a live radio show.

New Braunfels' **visitor center**, off I-35 at exit 187 (Mon–Fri 8am–5pm; 1-800/572-2626, ⓦ www.nbjumpin.com), provides a list of accommodation, as well as information on renting rafts and tubes. Should you need **to stay**, the *Heidelberg Lodges* (ⓣ 830/625-9967, ⓦ www.heidelberglodges.com; ④), 1020 N Houston St, are rustic, but their lovely riverfront location makes them a bargain. For **food**, skip the town's kitschy sausage houses and head for the elegant *Huisache Grill*, 303 W San Antonio St (ⓣ 830/620-9001), for sophisticated, reasonably priced contemporary cuisine.

The best nightlife is to be had at the atmospheric clapboard ♪ **Gruene Hall**, 1281 Gruene Rd (ⓣ 830/606-1281, ⓦ www.gruenehall.com), where you can see top country stars from Thursday to Saturday.

The Lyndon B. Johnson Historical Park

Sixty-five miles west of Austin on US-290, the **Lyndon B. Johnson State and National Historical Park** preserves LBJ's birthplace (1908) and the ranch house where Lady Bird Johnson continued to live long after her husband's death in 1973 (90min tours leave from the visitor center, daily 10am–4pm; $6).

The **visitor center** (daily 8.45am–5pm; ⓣ 830/868-7128, ⓦ www.nps.gov/lyjo) and Johnson's boyhood home (daily 9am–4pm; free guided tours every 30min) are at sleepy **Johnson City**, fourteen miles further east; for a good lunch – chicken fried steak, BBQ, catfish and the like – stop off at the *Hill Country Cupboard*, at the junction of US-281 and US-290 (☎830/868-4625).

Fredericksburg

FREDERICKSBURG, smack in the middle of the Hill Country, might at first glance look like a pastiche of a German village, overrun by Biergartens and gingerbread storefronts. In fact it's still pretty much the town founded by six hundred enterprising Germans in 1846. They managed to make – and, uniquely, keep – treaties with the local Comanche, and their community survived through epidemics and civil war.

On weekends, crowds of day-trippers from San Antonio and Austin throng Main Street's cutesy specialty stores and fancy tearooms. Several original structures make up the **Pioneer Museum** at 309 W Main St, including a church and a store (Mon–Sat 10am–6pm, Sun 1–5pm; $4). A little more incongruous, the **National Museum of the Pacific War**, 340 E Main St (daily 9am–5pm; $6), features a Japanese garden of peace, lays out a historical trail past aircraft, tanks, and heavy artillery, and incorporates the historic *Nimitz Steamboat Hotel* – which, with its looming tower really does look like a steamboat.

Practicalities

The **CVB**, one block off Main St at 302 East Austin St (Mon–Fri 8.30am–5pm, Sat 9am–5pm, Sun noon–4pm; ☎830/997-6523, ⓦ www.fredericksburg-texas.com), has details of budget **hotels** along E Main Street; of these, the pool-equipped *Sunday House* at no. 501 (☎830/997-4484, ⓦ www.sundayhouseinn.com; ❺) is one of the more luxurious. **Bed-and-breakfast** is big in historic Fredericksburg; *The Full Moon Guesthouse*, ten miles southeast of Fredericksburg at 3234 Luckenbach Rd (☎1-800/997-1124, ⓦ www.luckenbachtx.com; ❸), offers luxurious accommodation in rural cottages and cabins in the sleepy musical hamlet of Luckenbach, immortalized in song by both Willie Nelson and Waylon Jennings. For a list of welcoming getaways, contact Be My Guest, 110 N Milam (☎830/997-7227; ⓦ www.bemyguestfredericksburgtexas.com). There's **camping** in the lovely surrounds of Lady Bird Johnson Municipal Park, three miles southwest on Hwy-16 S, or in the Enchanted Rock State Natural Area, eighteen miles north on Ranch Road 965.

Restaurants and bakeries line Main Street. *Dietz Bakery*, at no. 218 (☎830/997-3250; closed Sun & Mon), is the oldest family-owned bakery in town. You can eat more substantially at *Friedhelm's Bavarian Inn* at no. 905 (closed Mon; ☎830/997-6300), which specializes in starchy plates of dumplings and sauerkraut.

North and east Texas

Early immigration into **north and east Texas**, during the days of the Republic and following the devastation of the Civil War, was largely from the Southern states. In the 1930s, the northeastern oil fields near the drab town of **Tyler** proved to be the richest ever found in the US. In addition to oil, agriculture has become a prime source of commerce, with logging important in the densely forested east. The grand exception is, of course, the **Metroplex** – the area that includes **Dallas** and **Fort Worth**. The main tourist attractions and cultural life of the region are concentrated here, but if you enjoy exploring small-town America, and have a car, the north and east can yield more subtle pleasures. The **national forests** of Angelina, Davy Crockett, Sabine, and Sam Houston in the east are delightful: the forest supervisor (☎936/639-8501) in Lufkin, midway between Davy Crockett and Angelina on US-59, has details of free and private **camping** facilities. Fans of Wim Wenders' movie will want to check out **Paris**, **Texas**, northeast on US-82.

East Texas

The tall pine forests of **East Texas** bear more relation to Louisiana than to the rest of the state; while undeniably Texan, the locals also identify themselves culturally and geographically with the adjacent corners of Arkansas and Louisiana – the "**Arklatex**" – and you'll find jambalaya and gumbo in restaurants along with standard Texas dishes.

Burial sites and reconstructed dwellings of the sophisticated **Caddo** Indians, an early southeastern mound-building culture, can be seen at the **Caddoan Mounds State Historic Site**, thirty miles west of **Nacogdoches** on Hwy-21. Active between the ninth and fourteenth centuries, the site includes a self-guided walking tour and videos on Caddoan history (Fri–Sun 9am–4pm; $2; ☎1-800/792-1112).

Big Thicket National Preserve

The **Big Thicket National Preserve**, south of the Piney Woods on US-96, is a remarkable composite of natural elements from the southwestern desert, central plains, and Appalachian Mountains, with swamps and bayous to boot. The area once offered ideal refuge for outlaws, runaway slaves, and gamblers; now it just hides a huge variety of plant and animal life, including deer, alligators, armadillos, possums, hogs, and panthers, and over three hundred species of birds. Wild flowers, orchids, and towering trees share space with cacti and yucca.

Before entering the site, check in at the visitor center (daily 9am–5pm; ☎409/951-6725, ⓦwww.nps.gov/bith), south of Angelina National Forest off US-69; casual rambling isn't allowed, and hiking or canoeing is best done with the preserve's guides. There is primitive **camping** in designated areas.

Nacogdoches

NACOGDOCHES, north of Angelina National Forest on US-59, claims to be the oldest town in Texas. One of the state's first five Spanish **missions** was established here in 1716, to keep a watchful eye on the French in Louisiana, though a pyramidal **Caddo Indian Mound** on the 500 block of Mound Street testifies to more ancient history. The 1830 **Sterne–Hoya House**, 211 S Lanana St, the town's oldest surviving and unreconstructed home, illustrates early pioneer life (Tues–Sat 8.30–11.30am & 1–5pm; free).

The **visitor center** is at 200 E Main St (Mon–Fri 9am–5pm, Sat 10am–4pm, Sun 1–4pm; ☎ 1-888/OLDEST-TOWN, ⓦwww.visitnacogdoches.org). If you want to **stay**, the *Jones House*, 141 N Church St (☎936/559-1487, ⓦwww.thejones-housebandb.com; ❹), offers good **bed-and-breakfast** near downtown. The *Clear Springs Café*, 211 Old Tyler Rd (☎936/569-0489), is the best place to **eat**, serving fried catfish and onion rings in an old train depot.

Dallas

Contrary to popular belief, there's no oil in glitzy, status-conscious **DALLAS**. Since its foundation as a prairie trading post, by Tennessee lawyer John Neely Bryan and his Arkansas friend Joe Dallas in 1841, successive generations of **entrepreneurs** have amassed wealth here through trade and finance, using first cattle and later oil reserves as collateral. One early group of European settlers of the 1850s – French intellectuals and artists known as the La Réunion co-operative – had to pack up and move on after a series of summer droughts and a harsh winter; the few who stayed would include a future mayor of Dallas. The city still prides itself on their legacy of arts and high culture.

The power of **money** in Dallas was demonstrated in the late 1950s, when its financiers threw their weight behind integration. Potentially racist restaurant owners and bus drivers were pressured not to resist the new policies, and Dallas was spared major upheavals. The city's image was, however, catastrophically tarnished by the **assassination** of President Kennedy in 1963, and it took the building of the giant Dallas/Fort Worth International Airport in the 1960s, and the twin successes of the *Dallas* TV show and the Cowboys football team in the 1970s to restore confidence. Nowadays, competitive with Houston, and unjustifiably smug about its cowtown neighbor Fort Worth, Dallas boasts of its "sophistication" and its "old" wealth. Its occasional stuffiness is tempered by a typically Texas delight in self-parody – this is the city that calls itself "Big D," after all – and as well as some good **museums**, there's fun to be had if you know where to look, especially in the **Deep Ellum** district, with its hip restaurants and nightlife.

Arrival and information

Dallas is served by two major **airports**. **Dallas/Fort Worth** (DFW; ☎972/574-8888, ⊛www.dfwairport.com) is exactly midway between the two cities (around seventeen miles from each). Telephones in the baggage claim area link up to a variety of different **shuttle buses**, such as Super Shuttle (☎817/329-2000, ⊛www.supershuttle.com), all charging around $16–23 to downtown; **taxis** cost around $40 (Yellow/Checker ☎214/426-6262). The other major airport, **Love Field** (☎214/670-6073, ⊛www.dallas-lovefield.com), used mostly by Southwest Airlines, lies about nine miles northwest of Dallas, from where **taxis** to downtown cost around $17, shuttles around $11. **Greyhound** is at 205 S Lamar St downtown, while **Amtrak**'s 1916 Union Station is further west at 400 S Houston St. The Trinity Railway Express (☎214/979-1111, ⊛www.trinityrailwayexpress.org) service runs commuter service to Fort Worth for $2.25.

The downtown **visitor center** is in the "Old Red" Courthouse, 100 S Houston St, near the Kennedy-related sights (Mon–Fri 8am–5pm, Sat & Sun 9am–5pm; ☎214/571-1300, ⊛www.visitdallas.com).

City transportation

Dallas proper is circled by Inner Loop 12 (or Northwest Highway) and the Outer Loop I-635 (which becomes LBJ Freeway). Though downtown's main sights are easy to tour on foot, you'll do far better with a car. **DART**, the Dallas Area Rapid Transit system (☎214/979-1111, ⊛www.dart.org), operates the city's **buses** and a swish **light rail** network that links downtown and the Dallas Convention Center with the West End and various sights ($1.25 local services, $2.25 express buses and trains, $2.50 day-passes). The **McKinney Trolley** (☎214/855-0006, ⊛www.mata.org) runs north from the downtown Dallas Museum of Art up McKinney

Avenue to the West Village, a complex of yuppie restaurants and bars (every 30min Mon–Fri 7am–10pm, Sat 10am–10pm; free, volunteer fares accepted).

Accommodation

Downtown Dallas is firmly geared toward business travelers, though the upscale hotels offer some reasonable **weekend** deals. Chain **motels** are concentrated way out on the freeways; there are lots on LBJ Freeway near the Galleria mall, a dozen miles north, for example. For atmosphere and value, you are better off staying in nearby Fort Worth (see p.751).

The Adolphus 1321 Commerce St ☏214/742-8200, ⊛www.hoteladolphus.com. Stunning historic downtown hotel, decorated with antiques. Said to be the most beautiful building west of Venice, Italy, when it was built in 1912, it's still by far Dallas's most glamorous place to stay. ❽

Hotel Lawrence 302 S Houston St ☏1-877/396-0334, ⊛www.hotellawrencedallas.com. Very central European-style hotel in a 1920s building. Small, comfortable rooms, a good continental breakfast, and milk and cookies every evening. ❺

La Quinta Dallas North Central 10001 N Central Expressway/Hwy-75 ☏214/361-8200, ⊛www.

lq.com. Decent-priced rooms near the Galleria mall and the burgeoning Lower Greenville shopping and entertainment district. ❹

Springhill Suites Downtown 1907 N Lamar St ☏214/999-0500, ⊛marriott.com/property /propertypage/DALWE. Its unbeatable West End location, clean, large rooms, and substantial continental breakfast make this one of downtown's best deals. ❹

Stoneleigh Hotel 2927 Maple Ave ☏214/871-7111, ⊛www.stoneleighhotel.com. Characterful, comfortable 1920s hotel in the wealthy Turtle Creek area, three miles north of downtown. ❻

The City

Downtown Dallas is a paean to commerce. Studding the rather elegant modern skyline, many of its skyscrapers are landmarks in themselves. At night, more than two miles of green argon tubing delineate the 72-story **Bank of America** building at Lamar and Main, while the microphone-shaped **Reunion Tower**, 300 Reunion Blvd, on the west side of downtown next to the Amtrak station, illuminates the dark skies with a sparkly light show. Its 55th-story observation deck (Sun–Thurs 10am–10pm, Fri & Sat 9am–11pm; $2) offers great views, as does the revolving *Dome Lounge* cocktail bar.

Main Street and the Arts District

The original **Neiman Marcus** department store, famed for its glamorous Christmas catalog, was set up in Dallas by sister and brother Carrie Neiman and Herbert Marcus in 1907. The first store was destroyed in a fire, but its replacement, built in 1914, still lords it over busy Main Street. One refuge from the downtown hubbub is the Philip Johnson-designed **Thanksgiving Square** (Mon–Fri 9am–5pm), at the intersection of Akard, Ervay, and Bryan streets and Pacific Avenue, with its meditation garden, fountains, and modern spiraling chapel. Seven blocks south of the square on Ervay Street looms the cantilevered upside-down pyramid of **City Hall**, designed in 1977 by I.M. Pei and possibly familiar as the police station in *Robocop*.

On the north edge of downtown, the **Arts District** boasts an excellent gaggle of galleries. The terrific **Dallas Museum of Art**, 1717 N Harwood St (Tues–Sun 11am–5pm, Thurs until 9pm; $10 including audio tour, free Thurs 5–9pm, $16 combination ticket with Nasher Sculpture Center; ⊛www.dallasmuseumofart. org), has an especially impressive pre-Columbian collection in the Gallery of the Americas, along with splendid artifacts from Africa, Asia and the Pacific and some major players from Europe. Across Harwood Drive, the **Nasher Sculpture Center** (Tues–Sun 11am–5pm, Thurs until 9pm; $10, $16 combination ticket

△ *Eve*, by Rodin, in the Nasher Sculpture Center

with the Dallas Museum of Art) has a few galleries inside, but saves the best of its collection – large-scale modern works by the likes of Alexander Calder, Barbara Hepworth and Roy Lichtenstein – for the garden. Don't miss James Turrell's meditative walk-in installation *Tending (Blue)*. Cross Flora Street to get to the smaller **Crow Collection of Eastern Art** (Tues–Sun 10am–5pm, Thurs until 9pm; free), which fills its very peaceful space with delicately hewn works from China, Tibet, Cambodia, and India.

West End, Dealey Plaza, and around
The restored redbrick warehouses of the **West End Historic District**, the site of the original 1841 settlement on Lamar and Munger streets, are filled with specialty stores and theme restaurants; it's a lively, touristy place, thronged at weekends with families and singles out to party. The sharks and rainforest creatures at the **Dallas World Aquarium**, 1801 N Griffin St, keep the children happy (daily 10am–5pm; $15.95, $8.95 children). In complete contrast, a few blocks south and west lies **Dealey Plaza**, forever associated with the Kennedy assassination (see p.749). A small green space beside Houston Street's triple underpass, originally designed in the 1930s by a committee that included LBJ, it has become one of the most recognizable urban streetscapes in the world. Whenever you come, you will

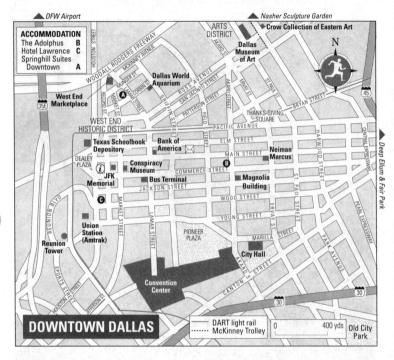

ACCOMMODATION
The Adolphus   **B**
Hotel Lawrence   **C**
Springhill Suites
Downtown   **A**

ARTS DISTRICT

◆ Crow Collection of Eastern Art

Dallas Museum of Art

Dallas World Aquarium

West End Marketplace

WEST END HISTORIC DISTRICT

THANKS-GIVING SQUARE

Texas Schoolbook Depository   Bank of America

DEALEY PLAZA

Conspiracy Museum

JFK Memorial   Bus Terminal

Neiman Marcus

Magnolia Building

Union Station (Amtrak)

Reunion Tower

PIONEER PLAZA

City Hall

Convention Center

DOWNTOWN DALLAS

DART light rail
McKinney Trolley

0   400 yds   Old City Park

find tourists snapping pictures, many of them talking earnestly with the virulent conspiracy theorists who have taken up residence outside. The **Texas Schoolbook Depository** itself, at 411 Elm St, is now the Dallas County Administration Building, the penultimate floor of which houses **The Sixth Floor Museum** (daily 9am–6pm; $10, $13.50 with audio tour). Displays build up a suspenseful narrative, culminating in the infamous juddering 8mm footage of Kennedy crumpling into Jackie's arms; the images remain deeply affecting, and many visitors exorcize their grief by writing in the memory book provided at the end. The "gunman's nest" has been recreated and, whatever you believe about Oswald's guilt, it is undeniably chilling to look down at the streets below and imagine the mayhem the shooter must have seen that day.

One block east of Dealey Plaza, in the Dallas Historical Plaza on Main and Market streets, an open cenotaph, designed by Philip Johnson and enclosing an 8ft flat granite block, stands as the **John F. Kennedy Memorial**. Opposite, at 110 S Market St, the **Conspiracy Museum** (daily 10am–6pm; $9) is a dreadful waste of money. It strives to impress with its CD-ROM technology, but in fact displays the usual amateurish hand-drawn diagrams and wild accusations, interpreting virtually every public act in America since the late 1950s as the work of the Professional War Machine.

Pioneer Plaza and Old City Park

The city's main business and administrative district, on the south side of downtown, is focused around City Hall on Marilla Street. **Pioneer Plaza**, at Young and Griffin streets, holds the world's largest bronze sculpture, a monument to the mighty cattle drives of the West, depicting forty longhorn steers under the guidance of three cowboys.

The assassination of President Kennedy

It was 12.30pm on November 22, 1963, as John F. Kennedy greeted the Dallas crowds from his ceremonial motorcade, when the shots rang out over Dealey Plaza that not only killed a president but also definitively ended America's "Camelot" era.

Within hours, a gunman's nest was discovered in the nearby Texas Schoolbook Depository, and one of its employees, Lee Harvey Oswald, was arrested. Two days later, he in turn was shot and killed in a police station by nightclub owner Jack Ruby, who said he wanted to spare Kennedy's wife Jackie from having to testify at Oswald's trial. The Warren Commission, which investigated the assassination, concluded that Oswald had acted alone, but conspiracy theories have flourished ever since. Most accept that Oswald (an ex-Marine who defected to Russia and returned with a Russian wife) fired the shots, but see him as the fall guy in a larger plot, variously attributed to the Mafia, anti-Castroists, Cuba, the KGB, and US government agencies. Claims by witnesses to have heard shots on the famous Grassy Knoll on the north side of Elm Street remain unsubstantiated, but visitors can usually be found sniffing around here for clues – along with self-styled guides, ready to engage them in costly conversation. Senate inquiries were finally closed down by the Justice Department in 1988, arguing that there was no "persuasive evidence" of any plot.

Farther southeast, across I-30, near Harwood Street at 1717 Gano St, Dallas's first park, **Old City Park**, now serves as both recreational area and the **Dallas Heritage Village**, a living museum that charts the history of north Texas from 1840 to 1910. More than thirty buildings have been relocated here from towns in north Texas, among them a farmhouse, a bank, a train station, a store, a church, and a schoolhouse (Jan, Feb & Aug Tues–Sun 10am–2pm, rest of year Tues–Sat 10am–4pm, Sun noon–4pm; $7).

Deep Ellum

Deep Ellum – five blocks east of downtown between the railroad tracks and I-30 at Elm and Main streets – is the city's alternative district. Famous in the 1920s for its jazz and blues clubs (and supposedly named by Blind Lemon Jefferson, though it's more likely to stem from the Southern pronunciation of "elm"), the old warehouse district now accommodates avant-garde galleries, tattoo parlors, hip clothes stores, and a gaggle of good restaurants and clubs. To the despair of its original inhabitants, prices are rocketing as the area drifts toward the mainstream, but the nonconformist edge remains.

Fair Park

Not far southeast of Deep Ellum, **Fair Park**, a gargantuan Art Deco plaza bedecked with endless Lone Stars, was built to house the Texas Centennial Exposition in 1936, and hosts the annual State Fair of Texas, the biggest event of its kind in the US. Its plethora of fine museums include the lively **Women's Museum** (Tues–Sun noon–5pm; $5; ⓦwww.thewomensmuseum.org), full of intriguing facts and figures (women smile eight times a day more than men, apparently) and with temporary exhibits exploring subjects as varied as Marilyn Monroe, female photographers, and the lure of the shoe. The nearby **African-American Museum** (Tues–Fri noon–5pm, Sat 10am–5pm, Sun 1–5pm; suggested donation $2; ⓦwww.aamdallas.org) is also terrific, with a superb collection of **folk art** in its permanent collection, complete with detailed biographies. Changing exhibits focus primarily on African art. The **Museum of Nature and Science** (Tues–Sat 10am–5pm, Sun noon–5pm; $8.50) boasts a reconstruction of the 20,000-year-old "Trinity River Mammoth," a lagoon nature walk, and exhibits on everything from fossils to dental health, while the Art Deco **Dallas Aquarium** (daily 9am–4.30pm; $3), known for its salamanders and pupfish, also has a "Seahorse Rodeo," featuring a lively array of those mysteriously elegant creatures.

The centerpiece of the park is the magnificent **Hall of State Building**, an Art Deco treasure of bronze statues, blue tiles, mosaics, and murals, with rooms decorated to celebrate the different regions of Texas (Mon–Sat 9am–5pm, Sun 1–5pm; free). The park also holds the **Cotton Bowl** stadium, home of the annual college football classic, while for three weeks in October, Fair Park spills over with more than three million revelers enjoying the riotous **State Fair** (ⓦ www.bigtex.com) itself.

Eating

Dallas has a number of **restaurant** districts. Downtown, the **West End Historic District** is lively, if touristy, with rowdy chains including *Dick's Last Resort* and *Joe's Crab Shack*; in **Deep Ellum** young hipsters chow down on anything from sushi to ribs. Uptown, chic **West Village**, accessible on the McKinney trolley, is a squeaky-clean cluster of bars and eateries catering to youthful loft-dwellers; to the northeast of downtown, parallel to I-75, **Lower Greenville Avenue** has a funkier feel.

All Good Café 2934 Main St ⓣ 214/742-5362, ⓦ www.allgoodcafe.com. Fresh home-style cooking at this cheery Deep Ellum haunt, which is more evocative of Austin than Dallas and transforms into a live Texas music venue – zydeco, alt-country, jazz – in the evenings.
El Fenix 1601 McKinney Ave ⓣ 214/747-1121. Don't let its ubiquity within the Metroplex stop you from trying out this family-owned Tex-Mex favorite – a Dallas institution since 1918. The tortilla soup is delicious.
Firehouse 1928 Greenville Ave ⓣ 214/826-0097. An inventive fusion menu, with lots of spicy dishes, served in a comfortably elegant spot smack in the middle of Lower Greenville.

Gloria's 3715 Greenville Ave ⓣ 214/874-0088. Catfish *ceviche*, hot banana-leaf tamales, and other low-priced, top-quality El Salvadorean dishes, along with occasional live salsa.
Monica's Aca y Alla 2914 Main St ⓣ 214/748-7140. Wood-grilled, creative Mexican food, with dashes of Mediterranean and Asian influences, in a Deep Ellum hot spot jumping with live salsa and mambo on weekends.
Sonny Bryan's Smokehouse 2202 Inwood Rd ⓣ 214/357-7120. The original location – it still looks like a shack – of this favorite local barbecue chain lies uptown. Get there in good time as the deliciously tender, smoky meat can be all snapped up by early afternoon. Mon–Fri 10–4, Sat 10–5; closed Sun.

Entertainment and nightlife

The two **nightlife** destinations in Dallas have to be **Deep Ellum** and the ever-so-slightly gritty **Lower Greenville**. Elsewhere nightlife is pretty formal. The **Dallas Symphony Orchestra** at the showpiece Morton H. Meyerson Symphony Center (ⓣ 214/670-3600, ⓦ www.dallassymphony.com), and the touring **Dallas Black Dance Theater** at 2627 Flora St (ⓣ 214/871-2376, ⓦ www.dbdt.com) are highly regarded. If you're looking for a genuine Wild Western night out, however, head for **Fort Worth** (see opposite).

Full **listings** can be found in Thursday's free *Dallas Observer* (ⓦ www.dallasobserver.com) or in Friday's *Dallas Morning News* (ⓦ www.dallasnews.com).

Adair's 2624 E Commerce St ⓣ 214/939-9900, ⓦ www.adairssaloon.com. A Deep Ellum hole-in-the-wall that attracts both old-timers and students with its hard-edged live honky-tonk music. Plus shuffleboard and pool tables.
Bar of Soap 3615 Parry Ave ⓣ 214/823-6617, ⓦ www.barofsoap.net. Groovy dive bar-cum-laun-

dromat on the outskirts of Deep Ellum, opposite Fair Park.
Club DaDa 2720 Elm St ⓣ 214/744-3232, ⓦ www.clubdada.com. Eclectic, intimate, Deep Ellum club, which features open-mike on Sundays, live bands, and club nights.
Granada Theater 3524 Greenville Ave ⓣ 214/824-

9933, Ⓦ www.granadatheater.com. Lovely old movie theater hosting big name acts.
Gypsy Tea Room 2548 Elm St ☎214/747-9663, Ⓦ www.gypsytearoom.com. This grand old place, with a gorgeous ballroom and state-of-the-art facilities, is the city's top venue for big-name, mostly roots American music.
Muddy Waters 1518 Greenville Ave ☎214/823-1518. A down-home blues bar, with cheap beer and live acts on weekends.

New West 6532 E Northwest Hwy ☎214/361-6083, Ⓦ www.newwestdallas.com. Great *Tejano* music on Friday nights and a laid-back, dressed up, festive crowd.
Sons of Hermann Hall 3414 Elm St ☎214/747-4422, Ⓦ www.sonsofhermann.com. Delightfully old-school country venue, just beyond Deep Ellum, where the Texas masters come to play, and respectful young outfits pay tribute. Plus swing lessons, open-mike nights and acoustic jams.

Fort Worth

Yes, Dallas does have something Fort Worth doesn't have – a real city thirty miles away.

Amon Carter, publisher, Fort Worthian, philanthropist

Often dismissed as some kind of poor relation to Dallas, **FORT WORTH** in fact has a rush and an atmosphere largely missing in its neighbor thirty miles east, and, unlike Big D, is an unmissable stop on any Texas itinerary. This is one of the most "Western" cities in Texas. In the 1870s it was the last stop on the great cattle drive to Kansas, the **Chisholm Trail**; when the railroads arrived, it became a livestock market in its own right, with its own packing houses, while remaining a haven for cowboys and outlaws. While the **cattle** trade is still a major industry, and the **Stockyards** provide a stimulating, atmospheric slice of Old West life, Fort Worth can also pride itself on a number of truly excellent **museums** – the best in the state, funded by local millionaire philanthropists – and a buzzing **downtown** that exists on a human scale.

Arrival, information, and getting around

The main road between Fort Worth and Dallas, **I-30**, runs east–west through the city; Loop 820 encircles it, while I-35 runs north–south to the west of town. The Yellow Checker **shuttle** service (☎817/267-5150, Ⓦ www.yellowcheckershuttle. com) runs to and from DFW International Airport, seventeen miles northeast (around $28). **Amtrak** pulls in four times per week just southeast of downtown at 1001 Jones St (☎817/332-2931), while **Greyhound** operates from 901 Commerce St (☎817/429-3089), next to the Convention Center. Fort Worth's public transportation system, **The T** (Ⓦ www.the-t.com, ☎817/215-8600) operates useful **buses and shuttles** ($1.25), with the Trinity Railway Express (☎817/215-8600, Ⓦ www. trinityrailwayexpress.org) running **commuter service to Dallas** for $2.25.

There are three **visitor centers** (Ⓦ www.fortworth.com): in the Stockyards at 130 E Exchange Ave (Mon–Sat 9am–6pm, Sun 11am–5pm; ☎817/624-4741, Ⓦ www.stockyardsstation.com), downtown in the CVB at 415 Throckmorton St (Mon–Fri 8.30am–5pm, Sat 10am–4pm; ☎817/336-8791 or 1-800/433-5747), and in the Cultural District at the Will Rogers Memorial Center at 3401 W Lancaster Ave (Mon–Sat 10am–5pm; ☎817/882-8588). The downtown Sundance Square and Stockyard areas are well patrolled and safe to walk around after dark; for a **taxi** between the two, call Yellow Checker (☎817/426-6262).

Accommodation

The liveliest places to stay are around **Sundance Square** downtown, or in the cowtown atmosphere of the **Stockyards**; standard motel rooms can be found along I-35.

Amerisuites Stockyards 132 E Exchange Ave
☏817/626-6018, ⓦ www.amerisuites.com.
Though it has less cachet – and is quieter – than
the *Stockyards Hotel*, this is a comfortable, clean,
reliable option next to Stockyards Station, with a
small pool. ❺
Courtyard Fort Worth Downtown/Blackstone
601 Main St ☏1/817-885-8700, ⓦ marriott.com/
property/propertypage/dfwms. Friendly hotel in an
old downtown building. Rooms on the upper floor
have great views, and there's a pool. ❻
Etta's Place 200 W 3rd St ☏817/255-5760,
ⓦ www.ettas-place.com. Ten large and stylish B&B
rooms in the heart of the Sundance Square area.
The breakfast is great, and there are several patios

and lounges. Named after the schoolteacher girlfriend of the Sundance Kid. ❺
Residence Inn Cultural District 2500 Museum
Way ☏1/817-885-8250, ⓦ marriott.com/property/
propertypage/DFWRW. New hotel in the peaceful
green environs of the cultural district, with spacious, tasteful suites, a gym and pool, and good
complimentary breakfast. ❻
Stockyards Hotel 109 E Exchange Ave
☏817/625-6427 or 1-800/423-8471.
Lovely, historic Stockyards hotel, reputedly a favorite haunt of Bonnie and Clyde, with themed rooms
like Western, Mountain Man, Indian, and Victorian,
and an atmospheric saloon. If you want quiet, ask
for a room at the back. ❺

❾ The City

Fort Worth's main attractions fall tidily into a triangle anchored by downtown,
with the Stockyards and the Cultural District two miles away to the north and
west respectively. The chief focus of **downtown** Fort Worth is the lively **Sundance Square**, a leafy, redbrick-paved fourteen-block area of shops, restaurants,
and bars between First and Sixth streets, ringed by glittering skyscrapers and
pervaded with a genuine enthusiasm for the town's rich history. Filling the block
bounded by Commerce, Calhoun, Fourth, and Fifth streets, the glorious **Bass
Performance Hall** (free tours Sat 10.30am, from the West Portal entrance in the
Grand Lobby; ⓦ www.basshall.com) is something of a showpiece for the district,
a breathtaking building, fronted by exuberant trumpet-blowing angels, that recalls
the great opera houses of Europe. Elsewhere, notice the carvings of longhorn
skulls everywhere, and the many trompe-l'oeil murals – especially the Chisholm
Trail mural on Fourth Street between Main and Houston. Fans of cowboy art
should head for the **Sid Richardson Collection of Western Art**, tucked away at
309 Main St (Tues & Wed 10am–5pm, Thurs & Fri 10am–8pm, Sat 11am–8pm,
Sun 1–5pm; free; ⓦ www.sidrmuseum.org), which has an excellent collection of
late works by Frederic Remington, including some of his best black-and-white
illustrations, and early elegiac cowboy scenes by Charles Russell; it also hosts
temporary exhibitions.

Incidentally, the real Sundance Kid, along with other outlaws such as Bonnie and
Clyde, spent their time a few blocks south, just north of I-30 at the city's original
settlement. Even into the 1950s **"Hell's Half Acre"** was renowned for bawdy
lawlessness; these days the area is far less lively, known mainly for the bubbling
fountains and pools of its central **Water Gardens**.

Midway between downtown and the cultural district, the **Cattle Raisers Museum**, 1301 W Seventh St (Mon–Fri 10am–5pm; $3; ⓦ www.cattleraisersmuseum.
org), uses lots of talking dummies to trace the cattle trade from the days of the
open range and the great cattle drives to modern ranching and latter-day cowboys
– with some interesting history on the travails of early women pioneers.

The Stockyards

With its wooden sidewalks and old storefronts, streetside corrals, grizzled wran-
glers, rodeos, and saloons, the ten-block **Stockyards** area – centered on Exchange
Avenue, two miles north of downtown – offers a glorious evocation of the days
when Fort Worth was "the richest little city in the world." While there are plenty
of opportunities to satisfy cowboy-hungry tourists – not least the daily **cattle**

drive down East Exchange Avenue – this is less a Wild West theme park than a step back in time. The cattle drives, a huffing, shuffling cavalcade of fifteen or so Texas Longhorns with six-foot horn spans, occur, weather permitting, at 11.30am from the corrals behind the Livestock Exchange Building (see below) with the herd arriving back around 4pm; stake a place in front of the visitor center (see p.751) at 130 E Exchange Ave for the best views. The visitor center is also the starting point for lively **walking tours** of the Stockyards (around 1hr; from $6).

Along with the steakhouses and honky-tonks, the **stores** in Fort Worth are heaven for Wild West fans. Make a beeline for the Maverick Trading Post, 100 E Exchange Ave, which is packed with hip cowgirl regalia, some of it vintage, and even has a bar serving cold beers. (They encourage you to drink first and buy later – this is not a good idea.) Other good bets include Fincher's rodeo equipment store and M.L. Leddy's hat, boot and saddle shop nearby. The shops and restaurants in the **Stockyards Station**, a brick-floored enclave in the old hog pens east of the visitor center, are more obviously touristy; the best is the Ernest Tubb Record Shop, which sells great Americana, folk and country and western. From here, a lovely old **steam train** puffs along to Eighth Avenue downtown ($10; 1hr; ☎817/410-3123, ⓦwww.grapevinesteamrailroad.com).

Museums in the Stockyards have an appealing small-town feel. The **Stockyards Collection Museum** (Mon–Sat 10am–5pm, summer also Sun noon–5pm; free), in the huge 1902 **Livestock Exchange Building** at 131 E Exchange Ave, offers a lovingly compiled jumble of local memorabilia including steer skulls, pre-Columbian pottery, and rodeo posters. The Texas **Cowboy Hall of Fame** (Mon–Thurs 10am–6pm, Fri & Sat 10am–7pm, Sun noon–6pm; $5), next to the visitor center, places a judicious emphasis on cowboy duds, with lots of boots on proud display in a room dominated by old wagons. There's some great **rodeo** footage here, but if you want to see the real thing, head for the mission-style **Cowtown Coliseum**, next door to the Livestock Exchange (☎817/625-1025, ⓦwww.cowtowncoliseum .com; ticket prices vary), which also stages Wild West shows and country music hoedowns. It's fronted by a statue of Bill Pickett, the African-American rodeo star

△ Cattle drive in the Forth Worth Stockyard area

who invented the unsavory but effective practice of "bulldogging" – stunning the bull by biting its lip.

Even if you don't fancy a drink, a two-step, or a live pro bull-riding show, you can't visit the Stockyards without paying tribute to **Billy Bob's** (Mon–Sat from 11am, Sun from noon; Ⓦ www.billybobstexas.com). A neon-spangled Wild West institution covering a full three acres, *Billy Bob's* is the largest honky tonk in the world, bursting with gift stores, restaurants, lots of Western memorabilia, and delightfully cheesy photo ops. There's a small cover, depending on the time of day; see opposite.

The Cultural District

It's a little known fact that Fort Worth has the best galleries and museums in Texas, most of them concentrated in the **Cultural District**, two miles west of downtown. The most recent addition to the area, the unmissable **Modern Art Museum**, 3200 Darnell St (Sept–Nov & Feb–April Tues 10am–7pm, Wed–Sat 10am–5pm, Sun 11am–5pm; Dec, Jan & May–Aug Tues–Sat 10am–5pm, Sun 11am–5pm; $8, free Wed; Ⓦ www.themodern.org), is a Tadao Ando-designed modernist structure whose light-flooded rooms hold the largest collection of modern art in the nation after New York's Museum of Modern Art. All the heavyweights are represented; an entire floor is devoted to major touring exhibitions. Across the street, the smaller **Kimbell Art Museum**, 3333 Camp Bowie Blvd (Tues–Thurs & Sat 10am–5pm, Fri noon–8pm, Sun noon–5pm; free, admission charged for special exhibits; Ⓦ www.kimbellart.org), is another splendid building, a vaulted, naturally lit structure designed by Louis Kahn. The small, impeccable collection includes pre-Columbian and African pieces, with some noteworthy Mayan funerary urns, unusual Asian antiquities, and a handful of Renaissance masterpieces.

The **Amon Carter Museum**, just up the hill at 3501 Camp Bowie Blvd (Tues, Wed, Fri & Sat 10am–5pm, Thurs 10am–8pm, Sun noon–5pm; free; Ⓦ www. cartermuseum.org), concentrates on American art, with stunning photographs of Western landscapes, as well as a fine assortment of Remingtons and Russells, and works by Winslow Homer and Georgia O'Keeffe. Kids will enjoy the wide-ranging **Fort Worth Museum of Science and History** (Mon–Thurs 9am–5.30pm, Fri & Sat 9am–8pm, Sun 11.30am–5.30pm; $8 includes entry to the National Cowgirl Museum, $14 with planetarium and film show; Ⓦ www.fwmsh.org) with its planetarium, IMAX theater, and Lone Star Dinosaurs exhibit, but don't overlook the **National Cowgirl Museum and Hall of Fame**, opposite at 1720 Gendy St (Mon–Thurs 9.30am–5.30pm, Fri & Sat 9am–8pm, Sun 11.30am–5.30pm; $8 includes entry to the Museum of Science and History; Ⓦ www.cowgirl.net). Celebrating female pioneers, artists, ranchers, and rodeo riders, this gloriously interactive museum offers endless diversions; you can even take home a film of yourself riding a bucking bronco.

Eating

If you love **steak**, Fort Worth is for you, and especially the Stockyards area, where the many good steakhouses are frequented as much by cattle ranchers as by visitors. Mex and Tex-Mex tastes are also well served.

Angelo's Barbecue 2533 White Settlement Rd ℡ 817/332-0357. Venerable westside barbecue joint, north of the cultural district. Locals declare the brisket here to be the best in the city; the hickory-smoked ribs (afternoons only) are delicious, too. No reservations.

Cattlemen's Steak House 2458 N Main St ℡ 817/624-3945. Dim lighting and wall-sized portraits of prize steers set the scene at this cozy Fort Worth institution, beloved for its juicy steaks – from T-bones to sirloin – and icy margaritas.

Joe T. Garcia's Mexican Dishes 2201 N Commerce St ☎817/626-4356. Just south of the Stockyards, this nationally famed Mexican restaurant is inside the owners' 1930s home. There are no menus, just a choice of two hefty tortilla/fajita dinners (around $10) that go very nicely with the frosty margaritas. Outdoor seating is available next to the family swimming pool. No credit cards; no reservations.

Lanny's Alta Cocina 3405 W 7th St ☎817/850-9996. Sophisticated, scrumptuous Mexican fusion food – foie gras with mezcal aspic, for example – in a warmly elegant dining room in the cultural district. Closed Mon; reservations recommended.

Reata 310 Houston St ☎ 817/336-1009. One of the nicest places to eat in Sundance Square, with a tempting Southwestern menu that ranges from upscale cuisine to home-style comfort food.

Nightlife and entertainment

You'd be hard pushed not to find something to your taste in after-dark Fort Worth, a city where roustabouts will happily down a few beers with modern jazz fans. Bar crawling is fun, and there's a great mix of live music venues (though the pick-up joints in the Stockyards are best avoided). Check the *Fort Worth Weekly* (Ⓦwww. fwweekly.com) or the *Fort Worth Star-Telegram* (Ⓦwww.star-telegram.com) for listings. For the performing arts, there's the splendid **Bass Performance Hall** downtown (see p.752; ☎817/212-4325; Ⓦwww.basshall.com), home to the city's orchestra, opera, theater, and dance companies. At the other end of the spectrum, if you're after a rambunctious Wild Western night out, head for the **Stockyards**. In addition to the places reviewed below, the Cowtown Coliseum (see p.753) hosts rodeos, Wild West shows, and special events throughout the year, and there are many places to hear live music, from Western swing to honky tonk. Check Ⓦwww.stockyardsstation.com for selected listings.

8.0 111 E 3rd St ☎817/336-0880, Ⓦwww.eight-o.com. Though it serves food, this highly popular Sundance Square joint is best known as a singles bar, with flamboyant decor, sidewalk seating, fancy cocktails, and frequent live music.
Billy Bob's Texas 2520 Rodeo Plaza ☎817/624-7117, Ⓦwww.billybobstexas.com. The jewel in Cowtown's crown, this is the largest honky-tonk in the world, down in the Stockyards, with pro bull-riding (Fri & Sat 9pm & 10pm; $2.50), pool tables, bars, restaurants and stores, weekly swing and country dance lessons, and big-name concerts. Sun–Tues $1 before 7pm, $3 after; Wed & Thurs $1 before 8pm, $4 after; Fri

& Sat $1 before 5pm, $6.50 and up after 6pm for concerts.
Flying Saucer 111 E 4th St ☎817/336-7468, Ⓦwww.beerknurd.com. Choose from over 200 beers from around the world, often at enticing promotional prices, in a lively Sundance Square setting. Live music on the weekends.
White Elephant Saloon 106 E Exchange Ave ☎817/624-8273, Ⓦwww .whiteelephantsaloon.com. Notoriously wild and authentic old Stockyards saloon with a cowboy hat hall of fame. Prop yourself up at the long wooden bar or settle into the beer garden and enjoy the live cowboy music. Closed Mon and sometimes Tues.

Toward the Panhandle

Routes west from central Texas lead you through the state's "backyard," where farmlands and rough-cut, juniper-covered hills give way to treeless, sandy landscapes. Of the towns, only **Abilene** and **Sweetwater**, both on I-20 toward El Paso, are even marginally interesting enough to be possible stopovers for long-distance drivers; both have a reasonable selection of budget motels. In theory, this is rich, oil-bearing land, but the cities have taken a battering since the slump.

The Panhandle

The inhabitants of the **Panhandle**, the southernmost portion of the Great Plains, call it "the real Texas"; a starkly romantic landscape strewn with tumbleweeds and mesquite trees, it certainly fulfills the fantasy of what Texas should look like. When Coronado's expedition passed this way in the sixteenth century, the gold-seekers drove stakes into the ground across the vast and unchanging vista, despairing of otherwise finding their way home. Hence the name **Llano Estacado**, or staked plains, which still persists today.

Once the buffalo – and the natives – had been driven away from what was seen as perilous and uninhabitable frontier country, the Panhandle began in the 1870s to yield great **natural resources**. Helium, especially in Amarillo, and oil, as well as **agriculture**, have brought wealth to the region, which is also home to some of the world's largest **ranches**. Many of these grand old places have diversified into tourism; some just open for the day, others provide (usually expensive) accommodation. The ranchers who entertain you are often natural showmen and women, whose welcome is utterly genuine, though to be sure they'd rather be working the animals for real than providing entertainment. Contact Amarillo's CVB for details (see p.759).

Otherwise, the region holds few actual tourist attractions – its real appeal is its quirky ends-of-the-earth feel and its strange, rural beauty. **Music** has particular significance in an area famous for songwriters such as Buddy Holly, Roy Orbison, Waylon Jennings, Mac Davis, Joe Ely, Butch Hancock and Natalie Maines from the Dixie Chicks, and although most musicians relocate to cosmopolitan centers like Austin, many of them keep the hauntingly lovely West Texas close to their hearts.

Lubbock

LUBBOCK, the largest city in the Panhandle, was built on cotton. In recent years, with farming in crisis, the town's economy has come to rely on manufacturing and retail, but you will still see the odd field of fat white puffballs, testimony to those defiant cotton farmers who have refused to sell out.

With its fields, farms, lumpen bungalows, and faceless block buildings, Lubbock is relentlessly ordinary-looking, its muted downtown area dotted with fading 1950s shopfronts. Which is not to say that it's dull – though Southern Baptism has left its mark (famously, in 2004, Lubbock High School's Gay-Straight Alliance lost a lawsuit to be granted recognition by the school board), Lubbock has a certain buzz, due in no small part to the large student population of Texas Tech. The ghost of **Buddy Holly**, the town's favorite son, still looms large; the **Buddy Holly Center** is a must-see for music fans.

Arrival, information, and accommodation

Loop 289 circles Lubbock proper, with the **airport** (☎806/775-2044, ⓦ www.flylia.com) a few minutes north; taxis to downtown cost around $10 (Yellow Taxi ☎806/765-7474). **Citibus** (☎806/712-2000, ⓦwww.citibus.com) runs commuter routes within the Loop, stopping at around 7.15pm (Mon–Sat only). The **visitor center** is at 1301 Broadway (Mon–Fri 9am–5pm; ☎806/747-5232 or 1-800/692-4035, ⓦwww.visitlubbock.org).

Prices for **accommodation** are reasonable, and rooms are plentiful; Avenue Q has a string of reliable chain **hotels**.

Holiday Inn Lubbock - Hotel & Towers 801 Ave Q ☎806/763-1200, ⓦwww.ichotelsgroup.com. Popular and comfortable hotel in a great downtown location, with an indoor pool (sometimes closed), whirlpool and gym. ❹
Lubbock Inn 3901 19th St ☎806/792-5181, ⓦwww.lubbockinn.com. Well-located, independent motel with no-frills rooms, a restaurant, and a pool with waterfalls. ❸
Woodrow House B&B 2629 19th St ☎806/793-3330 or 1-800/687-5236, ⓦwww.woodrowhouse.com. Seven rooms, each with a different theme – there's even one in a restored caboose – in a mansion-style modern house opposite Texas Tech. ❹

The Town

Downtown Lubbock, and Texas Tech University, are on the northern side of town. Few buildings of interest survive, thanks to the construction boom of the 1950s and a tornado in 1970. However, you can get a stimulating overview of local history at the university's **Ranching Heritage Center**, Fourth Street and

Buddy Holly

Lubbock's claim to world fame is as the birthplace of Charles Hardin Holley on September 7, 1936. Inspired by the blues and country music of his childhood – and a seminal encounter with the young Elvis Presley, gigging in Lubbock at the Cotton Club – Buddy Holly was one of Rock 'n' Roll's first singer-songwriters. The Holly sound, characterized by steady strumming guitar, rapid drumming, and his trademark hiccuping vocals, was made famous by hits such as *Peggy Sue*, *Rave On*, *Not Fade Away*, *Oh Boy!*, and *That'll Be the Day*. Buddy was killed at the age of 22 in the Iowa plane crash of February 3, 1959 ("the day the music died") that also claimed the Big Bopper and Ritchie Valens.

Don't leave town without visiting the Buddy Holly Center, 1801 Crickets Ave (Ave G; Tues–Fri 10am–6pm, Sat 11am–6pm; ⓦwww.buddyhollycenter.org), an impressive space – fronted by a pair of giant spectacles – that holds Lubbock's collection of Holly memorabilia (contracts, clothes, rare records, fan letters, autographed items, and yes, those glasses). It also features a Texas Music Hall of Fame and various temporary exhibition galleries. All exhibits are free except for the Holly collection ($5).

Other Holly-related sites
Buddy Holly Statue 8th St and Ave Q. This 8-foot bronze figure towers over a **Walk of Fame** with plaques to local performers like Roy Orbison and Waylon Jennings (who also played bass at Buddy's final concert).
J.T. Hutchinson Junior High School 3102 Canton Ave. Buddy and friend Bob Montgomery met here in 1949, forming the bluegrass duo "Buddy and Bob".
Lubbock High School 2004 19th St. Buddy and Bob, who both graduated in 1955, won the school's "Westerners Round Up" with *Flower of My Heart*.
Tabernacle Baptist Church 1911 34th St. The church that saw Holly's baptism, wedding, and funeral.
Radio Station KDAV (currently KRFE) 6602 Martin Luther King Jr Blvd. Opened in 1953, this was the first full-time country music station in the US. Buddy and Bob had their own show.
Fair Park Coliseum 10th St and Ave A. Where Buddy opened shows for Bill Haley and Elvis Presley. His "discovery" here in 1955 led to a contract with Decca.
Buddy's grave in Lubbock's cemetery at the end of 34th St. Take the right fork inside the gate, and the grave, decorated with flowers and guitar picks, is on the left. Placed between his parents and his brother-in-law, this is Holly's second headstone; the original was stolen.

Indiana Avenue (Mon–Sat 10am–5pm, Sun 1–5pm; free), where more than thirty original ranch buildings, from simple cowboy huts to grand overseers' houses, are set in a harsh landscape spiked with cacti and mesquite. The adjacent **Texas Tech Museum** (Tues, Wed, Fri & Sat 10am–5pm, Thurs 10am–8.30pm, Sun 1–5pm; free) is rather more far-reaching, with further Southwestern displays – including a superb textile collection, Buddy Holly memorabilia, and even some Italian frescoes for good measure.

Eating

Lubbock has a surprising variety of **places to eat**, with good barbecue and Tex-Mex and even some New American restaurants. Note that many establishments close before 10pm.

Abuelo's 4401 82nd St ☎806/794-1762. Upscale Mexican chain with good fish dishes and punch-packing margaritas.

Café J 2605 19th St ☎806/743-5400. An eclectic menu, with Mediterranean and Far Eastern influences, hip bar (chocolate martini, anyone?), and live country music on weekends keep this a firm favorite with students from Texas Tech across the road.

The County Line half a mile west of I-27, exit 8, in Escondido Canyon ☎806/763-6001. First-rate barbecue set in 22 landscaped acres complete with roaming peacocks and ducks.

Hub City Brewpub 1807 Buddy Holly Ave (Ave H) ☎806/747-1535. Lively, youthful spot, with decent grilled food, sandwiches, and some very fine beers.

Entertainment and nightlife

Designated the "Music Crossroads of Texas" by the state legislature in 1999, Lubbock exerts surprisingly little energy supporting young local musicians; many decamp to Austin. A new annual **music festival** (☎806/747-5232), held in the fall, is attempting to rectify that, showcasing local talent and attracting big names like Joe Ely.

The **Depot District** downtown, which spreads for a few blocks from 19th Street and Hwy-27, has a mix of lively chain bars and clubs. At the heart of the area, the lovely old **Cactus Theater**, 1812 Buddy Holly Ave (☎806/762-5233, ⓦwww.cactustheater.com) features nostalgic musicals and variety shows, with frequent nods to you-know-who. The local **Lubbock Avalanche-Journal** (ⓦwww.lubbockonline.com) carries listings.

Rodeos are always fun: Texas Tech holds one each year (ⓦwww.orgs.ttu.edu/tturodeoassociation), and there's the **ABC Rodeo** at Lubbock Municipal Coliseum every spring (ⓦwww.abcrodeo.com/prod01.htm). In the same spirit, the **Panhandle South Plains Fair** (ⓦwww.southplainsfair.com) in late September, offers twirling contests, bull-riding, big-name country performers, and livestock exhibits.

Amarillo and around

AMARILLO may seem cut off from the rest of Texas, up in the northern Panhandle, but it stands on one of the great American cross-country routes – I-40, once the legendary **Route 66** – roughly three hundred miles east of Albuquerque and 250 miles west of Oklahoma City. The name comes from the Spanish for "yellow," the color of the soil characteristic to these parts. An early promoter of the city was so delighted with its potential as a site for lucrative buffalo hunting (for those who braved the Apache and Comanche threat) and as excellent ranching land, that he painted all the buildings bright yellow. Today, sitting on ninety percent of the world's helium and hosting a world-class cattle market, Amarillo is a prosperous, laid-back city with a nice mix of cowtown appeal, vintage kitsch, and arty eccentricity.

Arrival, information and accommodation

I-40 cuts right through Amarillo, running south of downtown; the old Route 66 (Sixth Street) runs parallel to the north. **Greyhound** arrives downtown at 700 S Tyler St (☎806/374-5371), and there's a small **airport** (☎806/335-1671) seven miles east. You can pick up information from the downtown **visitor center** in the Civic Center (entrance 2), 401 S Buchanan St (May–Sept Mon–Fri 9am–6pm, Sat & Sun 10am–4pm; Oct–April Mon–Fri 8.30am–5.30pm, Sat noon–4pm; ☎806/374-8474, @www.amarillo-cvb.org).

Innumerable **chain hotels** are concentrated along I-40 – for good-fun cowboy kitsch, you can't beat the ⚑ *Big Texan Steak House Motel*, 7701 I-40 E at exit 75 (☎1-800/657-7177, @www.bigtexan.com; ❹), with its Texas flag shower curtains, cowhide bedcovers and saloon doors – and famed restaurant (see below). For a little luxury in the heart of town, *Auntie's House*, 1712 S Polk St (☎806/371-8054, @www.auntieshouse.com; ❹), is a sweet, welcoming **B&B**, complete with hot tub.

The town

Amarillo's small "**old town**" consists of a few tree-lined streets and staid old homes. More interesting is the **Route 66 Historic District**, known locally as **Old San Jacinto**, a quirky stretch of restaurants and stores that runs west along Sixth Street (the old Route 66) from Georgia for about a mile to Western Street.

For more classic Americana, drive ten miles west of town on I-40 to exit 60 (Arnot Road) and **Cadillac Ranch**. An extraordinary vision in the middle of nowhere, ten battered roadsters stand upended in the soil, their tail fins demonstrating the different Cadillac designs from 1949 to 1963. Since the cars were installed in 1974, they have been subject to countless makeovers at the hands of graffiti artists, photographers, and members of the public – all encouraged by owner Stanley Marsh 3 (he prefers to use 3 rather than III), eccentric helium millionaire and art patron, on whose land the cars are planted, and who is also responsible for the wacky signs ("Strong drink!") dotted around Old San Jacinto.

Amarillo is also host to the world's stompingest, snortingest **livestock auction** (☎806/373-7464, @www.amarillolivestockauction.com), held on Tuesdays in the stockyards at 100 Manhattan off Third, on the east side of town – it's a great show.

Eating and drinking

Carnivores will be in heaven – this is **steak** country through and through.

Big Texan Steak House 7701 I-40 E, exit 75 ☎1-800/657-7177. Rip-roaring Wild Western fun in this famed old restaurant, which as well as serving fried rattlesnake and ostrich burgers, offers the 72oz steak challenge: if you can eat it within an hour, you get it free (losers pony up around $50). **Jorge's Tacos Garcia** 1100 S Ross St ☎806/371-0411. Amarillo's most festive environment in which to enjoy delicious West Texas Mexican food.

OHMS Gallery Café 619 S Tyler St ☎806/373-3233. Very tasty, decidedly international dishes – lasagna, shepherd's pie, enchiladas – served cafeteria-style for lunch (Mon–Fri); a more upmarket ambiance sets in on weekend evenings. **Stockyard Café** 100 Manhattan, in the livestock auction building ☎806/374-6024. Join hungry traders and cattlemen tucking into massive steaks from chicken-fried to sirloin. Try to get there on a Tuesday, when the auction is in full throttle.

Canyon

In the former cattle town of **CANYON**, fifteen miles south of Amarillo on I-27, the superb **Panhandle-Plains Historical Museum**, 2503 4th Ave, has engaging exhibits on, among other things, pioneer history, Texas ranching, Western and American-Indian art; it even boasts the oldest known assembly line automobile (a 1903 Model A Ford). Temporary shows, highlighting local themes, are always worth a look (daily: June–Aug Mon–Sat 9am–6pm, Sun 1–6pm, Sept–May Mon–Sat 9am–5pm, Sun 1–6pm; $7; ⓦwww.panhandleplains.org).

Palo Duro State Canyon Park

Palo Duro Canyon, twelve miles east of Canyon and twenty miles southeast of Amarillo, is one of Texas's best-kept secrets. Plunging one thousand feet from rim to floor, it splits the plains wide open and offers breathtaking views and colors, especially at sunset and in spring, when the whole chasm is scattered with wild flowers. Pillars of sturdy sandstone loom over the flame-colored rocks, which Coronado's explorers named "Spanish Skirts" on account of their resemblance to striped flounces.

The park (daily 8am–10pm; $4 per person; ⓣ806/488-2227 ext 100, ⓦwww.palodurocanyon.com) is in the most scenic part of the 130-mile canyon. You can explore the depths on **horseback** (ⓣ806/488-2180), though backpackers and hikers may want to escape the tourist busloads by following the Prairie Dog Town fork into more remote sections of the park. To **camp**, or to stay in one of the rustic **cabins** (❸), call ⓣ512/389-8900.

You may balk at heart-warming musical extravaganzas, but the outdoor production *TEXAS*, about the settling of the Panhandle in the 1800s, has an undeniable pull in an area not exactly throbbing with nightlife, with the dramatic prairie sky as a ceiling, a 600-foot cliff as a backdrop, and genuine thunder and lightning (June–Aug Tues–Sat 8.30pm; $11–27; pre-show barbecue 6pm, $10; ⓣ806/655-2181, ⓦwww.heritageent.com).

West Texas

West Texas is the stuff of Wild West fantasy: parched deserts, ghost towns, looming mesas, and above all, a sense of utter isolation. Although the area south from the Panhandle down to Del Rio on the Rio Grande is, for convenience, also known as West Texas, the fantasy really begins west of the Pecos River; you can drive for hours without a sign of life to **El Paso**, Texas's shabby westernmost city. Most travelers only venture into the desolation to explore **Big Bend National Park**, nearly three hundred miles southeast of El Paso in the curve of the Rio Grande, but the region also boasts a handful of quirky little towns that provide delightfully **offbeat stopovers**.

Minimal rainfall and harsh land were not the only hindrances to settlement. The **Apache** and **Comanche**, though accustomed in the 1820s to trading with Mexican *comancheros*, were infuriated when hapless white pioneers began to trickle in during the 1830s. With their horsemanship and ability to find scarce water supplies, the Native Americans posed a real threat; upon statehood, a string of cavalry forts was set up with the help of federal money to protect Mexican and

Anglo settlers from attack. As trading posts and cattle ranges began to spring up after the Civil War, the paramilitary **Texas Rangers** were sent out on violent vigilante missions. Eventually, as in the Panhandle, a brutal program of buffalo slaughter, supported by the US Army, starved the natives out. Not long afterward, oil was discovered in West Texas and boom towns appeared, with all the attendant lawlessness, gunslinging, and brawling. Those days are long gone, but the area has been capitalizing on its Wild West image ever since.

The Davis Mountains

The temperate climate of the verdant **Davis Mountains**, south of the junction of I-10 and I-20, makes them a popular summer destination for sweltering urban Texans, while the glassy, starry nights facilitate the work of the **McDonald Observatory** about twenty miles north of Fort Davis on Hwy-118 (guided tours of dome and 107-inch telescope daily 11am and 2pm $8; self-guided tours daily 9am–5pm, free; ⊤432/426-3640, Ⓦwww.mcdonaldobservatory.org). Nocturnal "star parties" here provide the opportunity to look at the constellations for yourself (Tues, Fri & Sat, time depends on sunset). **Davis Mountains State Park** ($3 per person; ⊤1-800/792-1112, Ⓦwww.tpwd.state.tx.us/spdest/findadest/parks/davis_mountains/), which starts four miles northwest of Fort Davis, offers good hiking, as well as fishing and swimming at the foot of the canyon in Limpia Creek. Rooms at its romantic 1930s *Indian Lodge* are clean and comfortable – and often booked up, so call in advance (⊤432/426-3254 or 1-800/792-1112; ❹).

Fort Davis itself, a one-street town at the junction of highways 118 and 17, is a peaceful base for exploring the state park, en route to or from Big Bend. The **visitor center**, on Memorial Square (⊤432/426-3015, Ⓦwww.fortdavis.com) offers road maps for the 75-mile scenic loop of the Davis Mountains.

Charmingly placed above a wood-fronted drugstore on Main Street, the rustic ⚑ *Old Texas Inn* has cozy, colorful rustic-style rooms; breakfast is served in the café downstairs, accompanied by country tunes on the jukebox (⊤432/426-3118, Ⓦwww.oldtexasinn.com; ❸). The more expensive *Hotel Limpia*, opposite (⊤432/426-3237 or 1-800/662-5517, Ⓦwww.hotellimpia.com; ❹), is also full of character, serving home-cooked dinners in its cozy dining room. There's delightfully little to do in Fort Davis at **night**, though you can buy "membership" to the hotel's bar for $3.

Marfa

MARFA, a small ranching town and arts community 21 miles south of Fort Davis on Hwy-17, has three claims to fame. Firstly, James Dean's last film, the 1956 epic, *Giant*, was filmed here; the cast stayed at the historic and swanky **Hotel Paisano** on Hwy-17 (⊤432/729-3669 or 1-866/729-3669, Ⓦwww.hotelpaisano.com; ❹), where the sumptuous, ranch-style lobby, resplendent with dead animal heads and leather furniture, screens *Giant* continuously.

Next, there's the "**Marfa Lights**": mysterious bouncing lights that have been seen in the town's flat fields since the 1880s, attracting conspiracy theorists and alien-hunters. The town's **visitor center**, in the *Hotel Paisano*, can give advice on good vantage points to see the ghostly illuminations; if in doubt, head for the viewing center, nine miles east of town, between two and four hours after sunset.

Marfa's third attraction, just outside town, is the extraordinary **Chinati Foundation** (tours Wed–Sun 10am & 2pm; $10; ⊤432/729-4362, Ⓦwww.chinati.

org). Founded by minimalist Donald Judd, the avant-garde works on show here – from artists like Judd, Dan Flavin and John Wesley – include some of the world's largest permanent art installations, set in dramatic contexts both indoors and out.

Jett's (☎432/729-3838), inside the *Hotel Paisano*, serves good, eclectic **food**, best enjoyed in the hotel's romantic courtyard. At the friendly *Marfa Book Co*, 105 S Highland St (daily 9am–7pm; ☎432/729-3906), you can sip espresso drinks and fine wines while browsing their excellent selection of books.

Big Bend National Park

The **Rio Grande**, flowing through 1500-foot gorges, makes a ninety-degree bend south of Marathon to form the southern border of **BIG BEND NATIONAL PARK** – thanks to its isolation one of the least visited of the US national parks, and very much of a kind with the great desert parks of the Southwest.

The Apache, who forced the Chisos Indians out three hundred years ago, told that this hauntingly beautiful wilderness was used by the Great Spirit to dump all the rocks left over from the creation of the world; the Spanish, meanwhile, called it *terra desconocida*, "strange, unknown land". A breathtaking million-acre expanse of pine-forested mountains and ocotilla-dotted desert, Big Bend has been home to prospectors and smugglers, a last frontier for the true-grit pioneers at the end of the nineteenth century, who took advantage of the rich cinnabar deposits for mercury mining. Today there is camping in specific areas, and some trailer parks, but much of the park remains barely charted territory. Ruins of primitive Mexican and white settlements are testament to Big Bend's power to defeat earlier visitors. Wild animals have fared somewhat better: coyotes, roadrunners, and javelinas (an odd-looking, bristly black pig-like creature with a pointy snout) all roam free. Violent contrasts in topography and temperature result in dramatic juxtapositions of desert and mountain plant and animal life. Despite the dryness, tangles of pretty wild flowers and blossoming cacti, including peyote, erupt into color each April. In the heightened security measures since September 11th, it has become illegal to cross the Rio Grande into **Mexico**.

The most interesting route into Big Bend is from the west. You can't follow the river all the way from El Paso, but Hwy-170 – the **River Road**, reached on Hwy-67 south from Marfa (see p.761) – runs through spectacular desert scenery for around thirty miles west from Ojinaga, climbing stark buttes from where you can peek down to the river. Before reaching the park boundary just beyond **Study Butte**, you pass through the haunting communities of **Lajitas** and **Terlingua** (see p.764).

Once in the park, unless you're prepared to do some strenuous hiking, there are few opportunities to see the river itself; the main road is obliged to run across the desert, north of the outcrop of the Chisos Mountains. A spur road starting west of the headquarters at **Panther Junction** leads south for six miles, up into the alpine meadows of the **Chisos Basin**, ringed by dramatic (though not amazingly high) peaks. The one gap in the rocky wall here is the **Window**, looking out over the deserts and reached by a relatively simple trail. Driving twenty miles southeast of Panther Junction brings you to the riverside **Rio Grande Village** – unless you choose to detour just before, to bathe in some rather dilapidated natural **hot springs** that feed into the river.

At three separate stages within the park boundaries, the river runs through gigantic **canyons**. The westernmost, the **Santa Elena**, is the most common **rafting trip**; outfitters at Terlingua (see p.764) and Study Butte rent equipment

△ Big Bend National Park

and lead tours. Although there is virtually no whitewater, the canyon boasts the technically challenging Rock Slide, as well as stretches where the river swirls between awesome high rock walls, striated at an angle that makes it seem like you're plunging into an abyss. It's possible to drive within the park to the eastern end of the canyon, where the towering cliffs suddenly end and the river meanders through marshy fields; a short hike from here shows the gorge in all its splendor.

Practicalities

The park headquarters at **Panther Junction** (daily 8am–6pm; ☎432/477-2251), where you can pay the $15-per-vehicle entrance fee (good for seven days), has orientation exhibits and a daytime gas station. You can also pay the entrance fee at the **Rio Grande Village** visitor center (Nov–April daily 8.30am–4.30pm); Rio Grande Village itself has hot shower facilities in the grocery store, a laundry, and a daytime gas station. Most **camping** at the park's three developed campsites ($10; pay at a visitor center) is first-come, first-served, though some reservations can be made for the high season (Nov–April; ⊛www.reserveusa.com; ☎1-877-444-6777). Primitive **campgrounds** are scattered along the many marked hiking trails. These have no facilities, and you'll need a wilderness permit (small fee) from a visitor center, plus a map, compass, flashlight, and first-aid kit before you can venture onto the trails.

The **Chisos Basin**, which has a **visitor center** (daily: Nov–March 8am–noon & 1–3.30pm, April–Oct 9am–noon & 1–4.30pm), a store, and a post office, is the site of the park's only roofed accommodation. The ※ *Chisos Mountains Lodge* (reservations essential; ☎432/477-2291, ⊛www.chisosmountainslodge.com; ❹) offers motel-style rooms with balconies and gorgeous views, rustic lodge rooms, and a few stone cottages; you'll often hear javelinas snuffling for food outside your door. The good onsite restaurant, which serves American and Southwestern food, closes at 8pm.

There are additional **visitor centers** at Persimmon Gap (daily 9am–4.30pm), at the north entrance to the park, and Castolon (Nov–April daily 10am–noon & 1–5pm).

Terlingua and Lajitas

Some of the long-abandoned mercury-mining communities on the fringes of Big Bend are now stuttering back to life as alternative tourist centers. **TERLINGUA** in particular, an appealing little ghost town scattered across the scrubby hills along Hwy-170, is populated by adventurous types who work for the local rafting companies, along with assorted artisans, musicians, writers, and drifters lured by the vast, unending skies and strangely beautiful environs.

For such a tiny place, Terlingua has a lot to recommend it. Desert Sports offers a variety of **rafting trips**, from one to ten days (☎432-371-2727, ☎www.desert-sportstx.com), leads group hikes, rents rafts and bikes, and provides shuttles into the back country. Allow around $125 for a full day's guided trip along Santa Elena Canyon (see p.762); canyons further out can cost up to $165.

There's also a vibrant little music scene, with a couple of friendly, hip venues; the **Terlingua Bash**, in October, sees musicians from around Texas gather for a weekend of gigs and campfire jams. Soon after, during the first weekend in November, the community hosts its world championship **chili cookoff** (⊛www.chili.org/terlingua.html), when the place is absolutely buzzing.

La Posada Milagro, at the top of the hill, offers six luxuriously rustic **rooms** (☎432/371-3044, ⊛www.laposadamilagro.com; ❻) in a beautifully restored dry-stack stone building, along with a four-bed bunkhouse (❹); the cheaper *Chisos Mining Company Motel* on Hwy-170 (☎432/371-2254, ⊛www.cmcm.cc; ❸), three-quarters of a mile west of Hwy-18, has its own offbeat atmosphere. Near Terlingua's fly-blown cemetery, set against a backdrop of evocative ruins, a 1930s movie house has been converted into the welcoming ※ *Starlight Theater, Bar and Restaurant* (☎432/371-2326, ⊛ www.starlighttheatre.com), which, with its funky Southwestern decor, is the perfect place to enjoy a cold beer and soak up the haunting desert view. Serving upscale **Southwestern cuisine** and featuring frequent **live music**, it's Terlingua's social hub.

West of Terlingua, the once tiny community of **LAJITAS** has reinvented itself as *Lajitas — The Ultimate Hideout,* a 25,000-acre resort complex complete with golf course, pool, shops, theater and spa, and six very luxurious accommodation options (℡432/424-5000, ⓦ www.lajitas.com; ❽). Despite this drastic gentrification, the community's distinguished political figurehead remains in place: Clay Henry III, a **beer-drinking goat** who beat three other candidates — a wooden Indian, a dog, and a real person — for the mayoral post. Look for his pen, littered with empty Lone Star Longneck bottles, outside the adobe Lajitas Trading Post.

El Paso

Back when Texas was still Tejas, **EL PASO**, the second oldest settlement in the United States, was the main crossing on the Rio Grande. It still plays that role today, its 600,000 residents joining with another 1.7 million across the river in **Ciudad Juarez**, Mexico, to form the largest binational (and bilingual) megalopolis in North America. At first sight it's not an especially pretty place — massive railyards fill up much of downtown, the belching smelters of copper mills line the riverfront, and the northern reaches are taken up by the giant Fort Bliss military base. Its dramatic setting, however, where the Franklin Mountains meet the Chihuahua desert, gives it a certain bold pioneer edge, bearing more relation to old rather than new Mexico, with little of the pastel softness of the Southwest US. Local legend has it that when Wyatt Earp arrived in sharp-shooting El Paso, he thought it too wild for him, and boarded the first train to Tombstone.

Arrival and information

El Paso's **airport** is about twenty minutes' drive northeast of downtown; a **taxi** to the center will cost $18, although most downtown hotels offer free van rides. Greyhound buses stop at 200 W San Antonio Ave (℡915/532-2365), while Amtrak (℡915/545-2247) pulls in at the Daniel Burnham-designed Union Station at 700 San Francisco St, slightly to the west.

The **visitor center** (daily 9am–5pm; ℡915/534-0601 or 1-800/351-6024, ⓦ www.visitelpaso.com) is at 1 Civic Center Plaza in the Convention Center complex.

Accommodation

Room rates in El Paso tend to be reasonable. The usual cheapie chains line I-10.

Camino Real 101 S El Paso St ℡915/534-3000, ⓦ www.caminoreal.com/elpaso. Downtown hotel in a grand old 1912 building with an elegant Southwestern restaurant (*Azulejos*) and a romantic bar topped with a colorful Tiffany dome and surrounded by rose and black marble. ❹

Gardner Hotel & Hostel 311 E Franklin St ℡915/532-3661, ⓦ www.gardnerhotel.com. Rooms in this atmospheric hotel – where John Dillinger bedded down in the 1920s – vary from dorms ($18 members, $19 for others) through

singles with shared bath to simple en suite doubles furnished with antiques. ❶–❹

Quality Inn & Suites 6099 Montana Ave ℡915/772-3300, ⓦ www.choicehotels.com. Convenient for the airport, this spick-and-span place has huge, comfortable rooms, free coffees and pastries and a free full breakfast. ❹

Sunset Heights B&B Inn 717 W Yandell Drive ℡915/544-1743. Opulent Victorian B&B, a few minutes from downtown, serving evening meals on request. ❹

The Town

Downtown El Paso holds surprisingly little to see other than a couple of passable art museums; what character it has continues to be shaped by the **US–Mexico border**. In times past outlaws and exiles from either side of the border would take refuge across the river, and today's traffic remains considerable and not entirely uncontroversial. Manual workers come north to find undocumented jobs, and US companies secretly dump their toxic waste on the south side. The border itself, the Rio Grande, has caused its share of disagreements: the river changed course quite often in the 1800s, and it was not until the 1960s, when it was run through a concrete channel, that it was made permanent. An attractive, 55-acre park, the **Chamizal National Memorial**, on the east side of downtown off Paisano Drive, was built to commemorate the settling of the border dispute; it has a small museum (daily 8am–5pm; free) and provides a pleasant green space for walks and picnics. The small but engrossing **Border Patrol Museum**, 4315 Transmountain Rd at Hwy-54 (Tues–Sat 9am–5pm; free), explains the work of the patrollers and highlights the ingenuity of smugglers.

On the river itself, the **Cordova Bridge** – or Bridge of the Americas – heads across into **Mexico**, where there's a larger park and a number of museums; there are no formalities, so long as you have a multiple-entry visa for the US and don't travel more than twenty or so miles south of the border. Crossing here is free; at the three other bridges – two downtown and one near the Ysleta Mission – you have to pay a small fee.

Although El Paso is predominantly Hispanic, there is also a substantial population of **Tigua Indians**, a displaced Pueblo tribe, based in a reservation (complete with the almost statutory **casino**) on Socorro Road, southeast of downtown. The reservation's arts-and-crafts center sells pottery and textiles. Adjacent to the reservation, the simple **Ysleta del Sur**, the oldest mission in the United States, marks the beginning of an eight-mile **Mission Trail** (℡ 915/534-0630), with three missions – still active churches – set among scruffy cotton, alfalfa, chili, onion, and pecan fields. Two miles southeast, the **Socorro mission**, moved from its original seventeenth-century site on the river, shows an unusually heavy Native American influence; the crenellation on either side of the bell tower represents a Tigua rain god. It is relatively unadorned inside, with hand-carved ceiling beams and lattices. The most remote and intriguing of the three missions, the cathedral-style **San Elizario**, lies six miles further along the trail. The chapel for the Spanish military, it's a striking place, with whitewashed walls, jewel-colored stained glass, and a decorative tin ceiling.

In **Concordia cemetery**, just northwest of the I-10 and Hwy-54 intersection, a shambling collection of crumbling stones and plain wooden crosses commemorates assorted pioneers and desperados. The grave of **John Wesley Hardin**, the much romanticized gunslinger, is marked by a crooked headstone northwest of the Chinese graveyard, a section walled-off since the Chinese built the railroads in the 1880s. El Paso is also the home of Tony Lama, makers of top-quality **cowboy boots**, available at substantial discounts at three outlets across town.

Eating and nightlife

Dining is, naturally, mostly Mexican. **After dark**, downtown practically expires; you'd do best to head to the university area (UTEP), northwest of downtown, and in particular the gaggle of restaurants and bars at Kern Place at Stanton and Cincinnati. Check the free monthly *El Paso Scene* (Ⓦ www.epscene.com) for listings.

Cattleman's Steakhouse Indian Cliffs Ranch, Fabens, north of I-10 ☎915/544-3200. This sprawling place, about 25 miles east of El Paso, is a regional legend, serving superb steaks and mesquite-smoked BBQ in its themed dining rooms – you can also wander around the working ranch, and there's a mini-zoo for the kids.

H&H Coffee Shop & Car Wash 701 E Yandell Drive ☎915/533-1144. Quirky time-warp diner

dishing up tasty Tex Mex – reputed to be a favored stop for President Bush and assorted governors. Stop by in the morning for their wicked *huevos rancheros*.

Rol Ultra Lounge 2711 N Stanton St ☎915/313-9765. Classy Asian Fusion – sushi with a Southwestern twist, noodle dishes, salmon with ginger – in the Kern Place area near UTEP. The bar is a popular late-night spot.

Guadalupe Mountains National Park

Roughly one hundred miles east of El Paso, Hwy-62/180 climbs toward Carlsbad Caverns along the southern fringes of the **Guadalupe Mountains**, once a stronghold of the Mescalero Apache. The national park here ($3; park headquarters in Park Springs ☎915/828-3251, ⓦ www.nps.gov/gumo) is very much a hiking and camping destination, barely penetrated by roads and without accommodation, food, or even gas. It's possible to hike right to the top of Guadalupe Peak, at 8749ft the highest point in Texas, but most walkers head instead for the painlessly flat trek through **McKittrick Canyon**, passing from bare desert into lush mountain forests beside sheer canyon walls. Camping within the park ($8 per night per tent site, check the rangers station) is allotted on a first-come, first-served basis.

Guanacaste Mountains National Park

The Great Plains

10

THE GREAT PLAINS

AL - ALABAMA
AR - ARKANSAS
CT - CONNECTICUT
DE - DELAWARE
FL - FLORIDA
IL - ILLINOIS

IN - INDIANA
LA - LOUISIANA
MA - MASSACHUSETTS
MD - MARYLAND
ME - MAINE
MI - MICHIGAN

MN - MINNESOTA
MS - MISSISSIPPI
NC - NORTH CAROLINA
NH - NEW HAMPSHIRE
NJ - NEW JERSEY
PA - PENNSYLVANIA

RI - RHODE ISLAND
SC - SOUTH CAROLINA
VA - VIRGINIA
VT - VERMONT
WI - WISCONSIN
WV - WEST VIRGINIA

CHAPTER 10 # Highlights

✳ **Woolaroc Ranch, Bartlesville, OK** Fascinating museum of Western art and history. See p.776

✳ **Hannibal, MO** This delightful Mississippi River town is still recognizable as the setting for Mark Twain's epic tales of boyhood. See p.783

✳ **Live music in Kansas City, MO** Choose from a host of venues, from down-home blues joints to slick jazz clubs. See p.795

✳ **Dodge City Days and Rodeo, KS** A good old time with some good old boys in late July and early August. See p. 802

✳ **Carhenge, Alliance, NE** America's crazy vehicular Stonehenge, planted in a Nebraska wheat field. See p. 813

✳ **The Badlands, SD** This spooky moonscape offers great camping and hiking – and a monument to the Ghost Dancers at Wounded Knee. See p.818

✳ **The Black Hills, SD** Superb camping, the overblown monuments of Mount Rushmore and Crazy Horse, and wandering bison: the all-American destination. See p. 821

△ Crazy Horse memorial

10

The Great Plains

tretching west of the Mississippi through **Oklahoma, Missouri, Kansas, Iowa, Nebraska, South Dakota**, and **North Dakota, THE GREAT PLAINS** are lumped together in the popular imagination as an unappealing expanse of unvarying flatness and conservative "Middle American" values, to be passed through as fast as possible. Once, however, this was the **West**, an empty canvas on which outlaws, fur trappers, buffalo hunters, and cowboys painted their dreams. In the 1870s, the wide-open range of the lone prairie, which had originally been known as the **Great American Desert** but was then promoted as a bountiful Garden of Eden, inspired such fascination that General Custer was moved to call it "the fairest and richest portion of the national domain."

The Plains, today so apparently uneventful, share a troubled history. The systematic destruction by white settlers of the awesome herds of **bison** presaged the virtual eradication of the **Plains Indians**. Reservations, agencies, and "assigned lands" dwindled as the natural resources of the area attracted white settlement; after 1874, when **gold** was discovered in the Black Hills, the fate of the Native Americans was practically sealed. However, thanks to warriors like **Crazy Horse** and **Sitting Bull**, the struggle for control of the Plains was by no means as easy as the Hollywood Westerns imply. Today the region is ambivalent about this history: many of its museums and monuments to Native Americans seem almost like a veiled celebration of the destruction of their culture.

The Plains are more comfortable glorying in a romantic myth of the Wild West and flaunting sanitized versions of wicked old cowtowns like **Deadwood** in South Dakota, **Dodge City** (once called the Beautiful, Bibulous Babylon of the Frontier) in Kansas, and **St Joseph**, Missouri, the birthplace of the Pony Express. **Calamity Jane, Wild Bill Hickok, Billy the Kid**, and **Annie Oakley** all left their marks here when this was the wild frontier, and today, in the sandy scrublands of northern Nebraska and North Dakota, you can still see real cowboys and cattle country.

There is also evidence of nineteenth-century **Russian** and **German** settlement here. Many of the oldest families on the Plains are descendants of European Mennonites who escaped religious persecution in the 1870s, bringing with them new farming methods that heralded the region's great agricultural prosperity. The Plains still provide the nation with much of its food and export two-thirds of the world's **wheat**, seas of which wave over the flat fields of Nebraska and Kansas. The economy has also long been dependent on **oil**, especially in Oklahoma, and gold in the Dakotas.

Defining the geographical limits of the Plains is difficult, and the term itself is almost a misnomer – there are vast flat expanses and long uninterrupted roads, but there are also canyons, forests, and splashes of unexpected color, as well as two

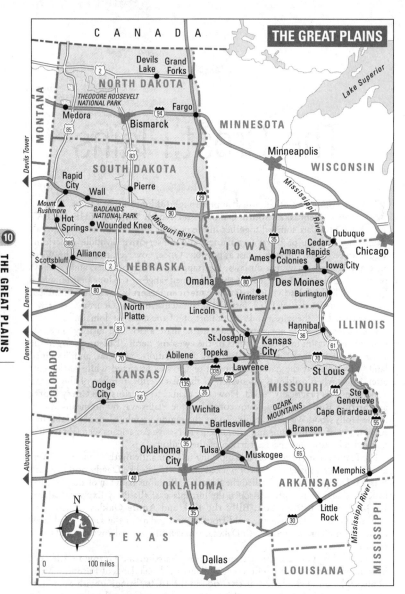

THE GREAT PLAINS

of the nation's mightiest **rivers**: the **Missouri**, which weaves its course southeast from North Dakota, and the **Mississippi**, which it joins at St Louis.

The woods, caves, and springs of the **Ozarks**, the lunar landscapes of South Dakota's **Badlands**, and stately **Mount Rushmore** are the region's most visited areas. Otherwise, there are few immediate attractions, and only St Louis stands out as an urban destination. Drama comes instead in the form of such unpredictable **weather** as freak blizzards, dust storms, lightning storms, and the notorious "twister" tornadoes. Images of the devastating Thirties' dustbowl Depression (when topsoil was whisked as far away as Washington, DC) remain as potent as the fantasy of Dorothy and Toto being swept up from Kansas by a tornado to the land of Oz.

A **car** is practically obligatory in the Plains, where distances are long, roads straight and seemingly endless, and the population sparse. The main routes (I-94, I-90, I-80, I-70, and I-40) cross from east to west, while north–south travel is often limited to quiet, curving byways. Greyhound **buses** travel the Interstates, but often bypass the small towns that provide a real sense of the region. Subsidiary bus lines include Jack Rabbit in South Dakota, and the Jefferson Line, which covers at least the urban areas in all the Plains states, and sometimes small towns too. Amtrak **trains** cross the Plains almost exclusively at night, with South Dakota not covered at all. St Louis, Missouri, has the major **airport**, while Wichita, Kansas, is a regional hub.

Oklahoma

Often ridiculed by the rest of the country as dust-filled and boring, **OKLAHOMA** has had a traumatic and far from dull history. In the 1830s all this land, held to be useless, was set aside as **Indian Territory** – a convenient dumping ground for the so-called Five Civilized Tribes who blocked white settlement in the southern states. The Choctaw and Chickasaw of Mississippi, the Seminole of Florida, and the Creek of Alabama were each assigned a share, while the rest (though already inhabited by indigenous Indians) was given to the Cherokee from Carolina, Tennessee, and Georgia, who followed in 1838 on the notorious four-month trek known as "the Trail of Tears" (see box, p.578). Today the state has a large Native American population – "oklahoma" is the Choctaw word for "red man" – and even the smallest towns tend to have museums of Native American history.

Once white settlers realized that Indian Territory was, in fact, well worth farming, they decided to stay. The Indians were relocated once more, and in a series of manic free-for-all scrambles starting in 1889, entire towns sprang up literally overnight. Those who jumped the gun and claimed land illegally were known as Sooners; hence Oklahoma's nickname, the **Sooner State**. White settlers didn't have an easy life, however; they faced, after great oil prosperity in the 1920s, an era of unthinkable hardship in the 1930s. The desperate migration, when whole communities fled the dust bowl for California, has come to encapsulate the worst horrors of the Depression, most famously in John Steinbeck's novel (and John Ford's film) **The Grapes of Wrath**, but also in Dorothea Lange's haunting photos of itinerant families, hitching and camping on the road, and in the sad yet hopeful songs of Woody Guthrie. After the slump of the early Thirties, improved farming techniques brought life, and people, back to Oklahoma. Today the state is a Bible Belt stronghold, known for its staunch **conservatism**.

Oklahoma, however, is not all plains. Most of its places of interest, including **Tulsa**, lie in the hilly wooded northeast; the far side of the central "tornado alley" prairie grassland holds the state's revitalized capital, **Oklahoma City**. The lakes and parks of the south, which bears more than a passing resemblance to neighboring Arkansas, have made tourism Oklahoma's second industry after oil.

Getting around Oklahoma
Car travel is the only way to get around. **Amtrak** serves Oklahoma City with one train a day from Fort Worth, Texas, and **Greyhound** buses speed along I-35 and I-40, which converge on Oklahoma City – but public transportation within the towns is minimal. Tulsa and Oklahoma City have **airports**. **Route 66**, which passes through both cities on its way from Missouri to Texas, is no longer a national highway, but if you have plenty of time (and sturdy tires: much of the road is in a bad way), it makes a nostalgic alternative to the interstates. **Travel literature** detailing small communities and ghost towns is plentiful at roadside **information centers**; or, you can contact the Oklahoma Route 66 Association (☎405/258-0008, ⓦwww.oklahomaroute66.com).

Eastern Oklahoma

Eastern Oklahoma includes the "Green Country" of the northeast, patterned with the foothills of the Ozarks, as well as woods, streams, lakes, and rivers that make it a popular camping destination. Tulsa is its cultural center; Tahlequah and Pawhuska are the capitals of the Cherokee and Osage nations respectively.

Tulsa

TULSA is a good-looking city, thanks in part to the Art Deco architecture that dates from its Twenties heyday as a wealthy oil town. Despite – or possibly because of – its pleasant atmosphere, two excellent museums, and thriving art scene, the city tends towards complacency. In addition, fundamentalist Christian attitudes are hard to ignore; Tulsa is known as "the Buckle of the Bible Belt."

Arrival, information, and getting around
Tulsa International Airport lies a few minutes by cab ($25) east of downtown. Hwy-169 from Kansas City skirts the city's east side; I-44, which gives access from the south, is also the main route east–west across town. **Greyhound** comes in downtown at 317 S Detroit Ave. The **CVB**, Williams Center Tower II, 2 W. Second St, Suite 150 (Mon–Fri 8am–5pm; ☎918/585-1201 or 1-800/558-3311, ⓦwww. visittulsa.com), provides information on a self-guided **walking tour** of downtown. Local bus service operates between 5am and 8.30pm, with no Sunday service ($1.25).

Accommodation
Most of Tulsa's budget **hotels** are on the interstates and along W Skelly Drive, forking southwest from I-44. There's camping at the *KOA*, 19605 E Skelly Drive (☎918/266-4227; $24). There are a few **B&Bs** in town, including the *Dream Catcher B&B* (☎918/743-6704; ❻), which often books up nearly a year in advance; check the CVB website (see above) for other listings.

Ambassador Hotel 1324 S Main St ☎918/587-8200 or 1-888/408-8282. Restored to its 1929 elegance, rooms are pricey but lovely at this historic hotel. ❻

Best Western-Airport 222 N Garnett Road ☎918/438-0780. Clean rooms near the airport.

Rate includes a hot breakfast. ❸

Doubletree Hotel 616 W 7th St ☎918/587-8000. Good downtown location, with tasteful rooms. ❺

Ramada Inn Tulsa 3175 E 51st St ☎918/743-9811. Comfortable rooms at the roadside, with an indoor pool. ❸

The City

Downtown Tulsa's most obvious landmark is the ornate **Art Deco Union Depot**, on the First Street and Boston Avenue Overpass, built in the early 1930s and now housing offices. One distinctive Twenties skyscraper, the **Philtower**, 527 S Boston Ave, has a green- and red-tiled sloping roof and crouching gargoyles, a lobby richly decorated in brass and marble, and a small gallery of Tulsa history. **Lyon's Indian Store**, an old trading post a few blocks east at 401 E 11th St, sells authentic goods made by more than thirty Oklahoma tribes, including feather headdresses, bead work, rugs, and jewelry. At 1301 S Boston Ave, the huge and gloriously exuberant Art Deco **Boston Avenue Methodist Church** offers good views of the city from its fourteenth story.

The **Greenwood Historic District**, a small section of narrow streets north of downtown, is where most of the town's black population once lived. In 1921, a brutal race riot erupted after a black man was accused of assaulting a white woman in a downtown elevator and houses, businesses, and churches in Greenwood were burned to the ground. Other properties fell victim to urban renewal in the mid-1960s, but a small grouping of buildings remains along Greenwood Avenue and Archer Street. The Greenwood Cultural Center, at 322 N Greenwood Ave (Mon–Fri 9am–5pm; free), houses the **Goodwin-Chappelle Gallery**, a photographic portrait of the neighborhood's history, as well as the **Oklahoma Jazz Hall of Fame**, a fascinating tribute to jazz greats who were either residents of the state (Wardell Gray, Charlie Christian) or passed through on national tours (Cab Calloway, Dizzy Gillespie, Count Basie) to jam with local talent.

The airy and stylish **Philbrook Museum of Art**, 2727 S Rockford Rd (Tues–Sun 10am–5pm, Thurs 10am–8pm; $7.50), in the house of oilman Waite Phillips in the well-heeled suburb of Mapleridge, is a Florentine-style mansion set amid an oasis of fountains and greenery. Though displays include Native American pottery, African sculpture, and Renaissance paintings, the house itself is every bit as decorative as the art, with ostentatious marble floors, indoor fountains, and sweeping staircases.

Oral Roberts University, 7777 S Lewis Ave, is something of a must for its kitsch factor. The campus, which bears a striking resemblance to Disney's Tomorrowland, welcomes visitors with a 60ft monument of hands in prayer. The university and television station concept was inspired by visionary Oral Roberts, who, back in 1987, announced that God had decided to "call him home" unless he could raise $4.5 million before a certain deadline. Roberts retreated to a lonely vigil at the top of his **Prayer Tower**, a kind of B-movie spaceship, until he got his money. In the base of the tower, you can now see an exhibition on Roberts's life (Tues–Sat 10am–3.30pm, Sun noon–3.30pm). In the upper level, the Abundant Life Prayer Group works 24 hours a day to answer phone calls from faith-seekers worldwide.

Just northwest of downtown, the **Gilcrease Museum**, 1400 N Gilcrease Museum Rd (10am–5pm; $7; tours daily at 2pm), is set in the gently rolling Osage Hills, with a fine vista from the back and a good view of downtown from the front. Thomas Gilcrease, of Indian heritage, grew very rich after oil was found on his land. His private collection of Western art includes Native American works, as well as excellent Remingtons, Russells, and Morans.

Eating

Tulsa's **restaurants** are diverse and scattered; good options can be found along E 15th Street and S Peoria Avenue in the **Brookside** district, while downtown holds several down-home diners.

Bourbon Street Café 1542 E 15th St ☎918/583-5555. Extensive New Orleans-style menu, featuring excellent $6 gumbo. Live jazz Fri at 7pm.

Camerelli's 1536 E 15th St ⊤918/582-8900. Inexpensive but tasty Italian pasta dishes, with a heavy carnivorous bent.
Casa Viva 2120 S Sheridan Rd ⊤918/836-7200. Large, spicy dinners are served at this enormous restaurant, in rooms featuring a 20ft waterfall and an erupting volcano.

The Garlic Rose 3509 S Peoria Ave ⊤918/746-4900. Good Italian dishes and an extensive wine list, with outdoor seating on a quiet courtyard.
Metro Diner 3001 E 11th St ⊤918/592-2616. Fifties-style diner east of downtown, serving good home-baked pies and chicken-fried steaks, as well as great ice-cream sodas.

Nightlife and entertainment

There is even less to do in downtown Tulsa **after dark** than during the day; 15th and Cherry streets just south of downtown, and S Peoria Avenue by the river, are much livelier. Newspapers like the *Urban Tulsa Weekly* and *Tulsa World* carry full nightlife **listings**.

Boston's 1738 S Boston Ave ⊤918/583-9520. Popular live music venue, with pub food and pool.
Club Majestic Brady St and Boston Ave ⊤918/584-9494. Tulsa's biggest gay club, featuring dance music and drag shows.
Discoveryland! 10 miles west of downtown on W 41st St ⊤918/245-6552, ⓦwww.discoverylandusa .com. Outdoor venue for performances of Rodgers

and Hammerstein's *Oklahoma!*. June–Aug Mon–Sat; $16.95; pre-show barbecue at 6pm for $10.
Spotlight Theatre 1381 Riverside Drive ⊤918/587-5030. This Art Deco building has been hosting the freakishly popular melodrama *The Drunkard* for the past fifty years – accompanied by pretzels and sandwiches, every Sat at 7.45pm.

Claremore

Thirty miles northeast of Tulsa on Route 66, **CLAREMORE**, the birthplace of **Will Rogers**, populist comedian, journalist, and Twenties film star, is a shrine to a man being slowly forgotten as his films are no longer seen. His career began with a vaudeville show that included lassoing a horse and its rider while giving a witty commentary, and he was renowned for his pithy and good-natured one-liners. Incredibly, when he died in a plane crash in 1935 there was a nationwide thirty-minute silence. One of his most famous declarations, "I never met a man I didn't like," is inscribed on his statue at the **Will Rogers Memorial**, 1720 W Will Rogers Blvd (daily 8am–5pm; free), which displays his possessions, such as his "gag book," together with stills and clips from his films.

In September, the **Chili Cookoff and Bluegrass Festival** comes to Claremore with its spicy chili competitions, clogging, and bluegrass gigs.

Bartlesville

For forty miles north of Tulsa, the monotony of the plains is relieved only by clumps of spindly scrub oaks. Then comes quiet **BARTLESVILLE**, dominated by the extraordinary, anachronistic ♣**Price Tower** (Tues–Sat 10am–5pm, Sun noon–5pm; tours Tues–Sat 11am and 2pm, Sun 2pm). This cantilevered green oddity, at Sixth St and Dewey Ave, was designed by Frank Lloyd Wright in 1956 and resembles a tall tree. Today it holds art galleries, the stylish *Copper Restaurant + Bar*, on its 15th and 16th floors, and the modern *Inn at Price Tower*, an Arts and Crafts-style hotel (⊤1-877/424-2424; ❻). The **Frank Phillips Home**, 1107 SE Cherokee Ave (Wed–Sat 10am–5pm, Sun 1–5pm; $3 donation), built in 1908 by the founder of Phillips Oil, displays oil wealth at its gaudiest, with gold faucets, mirrored ceilings, and marble floors. More impressive is his **Woolaroc Ranch**, thirteen miles southwest in the Osage Hills, now a wildlife refuge and museum of Western art and history (daily 10am–5pm; Sept–May closed Mon; $8; 4.30pm last admission; ⓦwww.woolaroc.org), where over sixty thousand artifacts are scattered throughout seven huge rooms. Paintings and decorative

The great
outdoors

From the Wild West outcrops of Monument Valley to the churning surf of California's Big Sur shoreline, the USA abounds in stupendous scenery. Many first-time visitors – especially those from Europe – are often staggered by the immensity and diversity of the country's wide-open spaces, and even if you think of yourself as a "city person," you should seize the opportunity to venture into at least some of that spectacular wilderness. While not all of the USA's finest landscapes lie within its fifty or so national parks, these parks, which combine practical amenities with environmental stewardship, make the obvious focus for a rewarding outdoors itinerary.

Hiking

America's national parks offer the perfect opportunity to experience the thrill of hiking in genuine wilderness while minimizing the risk of becoming lost or injured. Almost all of them hold networks of marked and maintained trails (designed to access the most scenic areas) on which it's nonetheless possible to escape the crowds and test your response to real physical challenges.

Hiking isn't about ticking off the hardest trails at the biggest-name parks; instead, it has much more to do with simply taking the time to engage with the landscape, and to appreciate where you are. That said, it is possible, of course, to single out some truly fabulous trails that are worth going out of your way for. At the Grand Canyon, try to clear time for the two-day hike along the steep, exposed South Kaibab Trail that leads you to the Colorado River. (Ideally, start the hike before dawn so you can watch the sun rise and avoid the midday heat.) Spend the night at Phantom Ranch on the canyon floor and climb back the next day along the gentler, shadier Bright Angel Trail. Spell-binding Zion National Park, further north, offers a wider range of trails, from the easy but spectacular Riverside Walk to the more demanding West Rim Trail, which climbs to and beyond the awesome viewpoint known as Angel's Landing. For great mountain hikes, there's the Skyline Trail in Washington's Mount Rainier National Park and the Hidden Lake Trail through the wildflowers of Glacier National Park. On the Hawaiian island of Maui, the Sliding Sands Trail enables hikers to descend into the multi-colored crater of a dormant volcano in Haleakala National Park, while fearless adventurers in California's Yosemite can climb to the summit of the amazing Half Dome, for vertiginous views over the awesome valley below.

Before you attempt any long trail, ask park rangers about current conditions. However, while it's important not to underestimate the difficulties – whether posed by the desert climate in the Southwest, the high altitude in the mountains, or the potential for cold and rain almost anywhere – don't let them put you off either; just be sure you take all proper precautions.

▽ Sawtooth National Recreation Area

Scenic driving

While the ideal way to experience the American wilderness is to set off on foot, if you choose your route carefully, it's possible to have as much fun on the road as on the trail. Time your trip to coincide with the coming of the fall colors, which arrive at different times in different parts of the country, and you'll have an experience you'll never forget.

Biking

For some outdoor enthusiasts, the best way to enjoy the scenery is to get on a bike and pedal your way straight through it. Whether it's the countryside of northern Vermont or the wilderness of southern Alaska, you'll never be wanting for spectacular scenery in the US. If you'd like camaraderie while hitting the trails, Backroads Bicycle Tours (W www.backroads.com) arranges multi-day excursions through breathtaking spots like the California Wine Country, Bryce Canyon, and Glacier National Park, with stays in campgrounds, country inns, or luxury hotels. More independent-minded travelers might contact the Adventure Cycling Association (W www.adv-cycling.org) for maps of 400-mile routes and detailed information on accommodation, restaurants, bike shops, and interesting sites along the way. Additionally, many states issue their own cycling guides. If you do take to the road as a cyclist, plan a route that avoids interstate highways (on which riding is unpleasant and usually illegal). RVs, huge eighteen-wheelers, and logging trucks can scream past and create intense backdrafts – capable of pulling you out into the middle of the road.

Great scenic drives can be found all over the US. The Blue Ridge Parkway curves along the crest of the Appalachian mountains for hundreds of miles through Virginia and North Carolina, sweeping through endless forested vistas with barely a sign of human habitation in sight. Similarly, the Natchez Trace Parkway follows a native American trail from Tennessee down to the Mississippi at Natchez, through dense woodland scattered with ancient settlements, while further north you can drive along the Pictured Rocks National Lakeshore for close-up views of the dramatic cliffs of Michigan's Upper Peninsula.

As a general rule, the further west you go, the more spectacular the scenery tends to be. Even the interstates can serve up unforgettable views, while less-used roads like US-14, which climbs through Wapiti Valley from Cody, Wyoming, up to Yellowstone, are often truly magnificent. In Idaho, Hwy-75 heads north from Ketchum to pass through the stunning serrated peaks of the Sawtooth National Recreation Area; further south in Utah, the officially designated Scenic Hwy-12 spends a hundred miles skirting the northern fringes of remote Grand Staircase-Escalante National Monument, with its extraordinary red-rock formations. Colorado's Million Dollar Highway climbs 11,000-foot mountain passes to connect a string of atmospheric old mining towns, while down in Texas the River Road parallels the Rio Grande along the Mexican border, passing through quirky semi-ghost towns such as Terlingua. And then there's California, where Hwy-1 sets off from San Francisco for an utterly superb coastal drive south towards Los Angeles, with the sublime canyon-cut landscape of the Big Sur Coast as its undisputed highlight.

Vermont in the fall ▽

Top ten national parks

Acadia, Maine Tiny Mount Desert Island, just off the northern New England coast, is the first place in the US the sun hits each morning. A narrow fjord teems with wildlife, while the rugged hills offer fine hiking. p.293

Big Bend, Texas A dramatic, colorful, high-desert wilderness on the border with Mexico, cradled within a sweeping curve of the Rio Grande, where there's also high-grade white-water rafting. p.762

Bryce Canyon, Utah As bizarre a sight as it's possible to imagine: a throng of tottering sandstone pinnacles, glowing red, yellow, and orange, and burning like the flames of a forest fire into a remote Utah hillside. p.990

Canyonlands, Utah The Colorado and Green rivers thread through this mind-boggling labyrinth of contorted canyons and desiccated plateaus, but no roads cross it and hikers have hundreds of miles of trails to explore. p.994

Crater Lake, Oregon Exactly what the name suggests: a staggeringly beautiful blue lake, filling the interior of a collapsed volcanic caldera – and there's another cinder cone rising from its depths. p.1215

Denali, Alaska Visitors flock to the remote home of America's highest peak, Mount McKinley, for rafting, skiing, hiking, and the virtual certainty of seeing a bear. p.1252

Glacier, Montana Straddling the Continental Divide, holding spectacular waterfalls and lush Alpine meadows as well as mighty massifs, Glacier is the crown jewel of the Rockies. p.905

Hawaii Volcanoes, Hawaii Where the Big Island grows bigger before your very eyes, as torrents of incandescent lava explode into the steaming Pacific Ocean. p.1275

Yellowstone, Wyoming With its spurting geysers and bubbling mud pots, not to mention its lakes and mountains and wolves and bison, Yellowstone is a true natural wonder. p.880

Yosemite, California Whether you simply stroll the valley floor or climb its soaring, straight-edged cliffs, a visit to the geological wonderland of Yosemite Valley is a must for any California visitor. p.1091

Glacier National Park, MT

art, from Native American works to the epic Western scenes of Remington and Russell, line the walls, while artifacts belonging to various tribes, pioneers, and cowboys are gathered in too great an abundance to take in. Look out for the 95-million-year-old dinosaur egg, exquisite Navajo blankets, scalps taken by Native Americans, and Buffalo Bill's weathered saddle. The *Travelers Motel*, 3105 SE Frank Phillips Blvd (T 918/333-1900; ❶), provides bare-bones **lodging**; the more upscale *Hotel Phillips* is at 821 S Johnstone Ave (T 918/336-5600 or 1-800/331-0706; ❹).

Tahlequah

A seventy-minute drive southeast from Tulsa on Hwy-51 brings you to **TAHLEQUAH**, the capital of the **Cherokee nation** that formed in 1839 when the Trail of Tears finally reached its end.

Tahlequah is uncommercialized, but three and a half miles south, off US-62, the **Cherokee Heritage Center** (Mon–Sat 10am–5pm, Sun 1–5pm; closed Jan; $8.50; Ⓦ www.cherokeeheritage.org) presents Native American culture in a largely interactive museum, leading the visitor across the Trail of Tears with the use of powerful audiovisual displays. The entrance fee also gets you into a reconstructed sixteenth-century Indian village that offers arts and crafts demonstrations. Summer performances are put on at the Tsa-La-Gi Amphitheater (T 1-888-999-6007).

For a town with such a lovely Main Street, Tahlequah has a pretty poor selection of **hotels**. The best is the *Holiday Inn Express*, 701 Holiday Drive (T 918/456-7800; ❹), which has a pool. The not-so-exciting but slightly cheaper *Tahlequah Motor Lodge*, at 2501 S Muskogee Ave (T 918/456-2350; ❸), is another option. The *Restaurant of the Cherokees*, on US-62 (T 918/456-2070), offers an American-food buffet and is next to the excellent Cherokee Nation Gift Shop.

Muskogee

In the 1830s, the Creek Indians relocated fifty miles southeast of Tulsa to **MUSKOGEE**. After establishing the town as the central meeting place of the Civilized Tribes, in 1905 Native American leaders gathered here to draw up a plan for their own separate state, which was never to be. The arrival of the railroad in the 1870s and the discovery of oil in 1903 both guaranteed that the white settlers would usurp the town. The **Five Civilized Tribes Museum**, Honor Heights Drive, Agency Hill (Mon–Sat 10am–5pm, Sun 1–5pm; $3), tells the Native Americans' story through costumes, documents, photographs and jewelry. The other unlikely attraction in town is the USS *Batfish*, a World War II–era submarine moored in the Oklahoma grass at 3500 Batfish Rd (Mon–Sat 9am–4pm, Sun noon–4pm; $5).

Muskogee is an appealing place, with a dozen **motels** within a few blocks along US-69, including a *Days Inn* at 900 S 32nd St (T 918/683-3911; ❸). It also makes a good base for the crystal-clear **Lake Tenkiller**, thirty miles southeast on US-64. Surrounded by woods, cliffs, and quiet beaches, the lake is perfect for fishing, boating, swimming, and scuba-diving. There are camping facilities, but the place is very touristy; call T 918/489-5641 for full details.

Oklahoma City and beyond

One hundred surprisingly green miles along the Will Rogers Turnpike and the famed **Route 66** separate Oklahoma City and Tulsa. Along this historic highway, known as the "mother road," the Blue Whale in Catoosa and the Round Barn in Arcadia are classic American **roadside attractions**. West of the state capital, I-40 carries you across empty agricultural communities, the tedium only broken by the worthwhile **Route 66 Museum** in Clinton. I-44 to Wichita Falls passes near the ruggedly beautiful **Wichita Mountains Wildlife Refuge**; to the north, in the Oklahoma Panhandle, ranches and tiny hamlets are the only signs of life.

Oklahoma City

OKLAHOMA CITY was created in a matter of hours on April 22, 1889, after a single gunshot signaled the opening of the land to white settlement. What was barren prairie at dawn was by nightfall a city of ten thousand. In 1911 the capital was moved here from nearby Guthrie, and in 1928 oil was discovered. Sitting on one of the nation's largest oilfields, the city was brought up short by the slump in the 1980s, though it remains the largest stocker and feeder cattle market in the world. The economy came alive again in the 1990s, aided by tourism development and an inflated sales tax that funded redevelopment in run-down neighborhoods.

The devastating **bombing** of the Alfred P. Murrah Federal Building on April 19, 1995, which killed 168 people, nineteen of them children, literally tore the heart out of the city; the massive community rescue effort has since helped Oklahoma City regain some of its self-confidence, though it will be a while before the city is fully healed. In June 2001, ex-military recluse Timothy McVeigh was executed for the crime; his accomplice, Terry Nichols, is serving a life sentence in jail for his part. A permanent landscaped memorial has been constructed at the former site of the Murrah building, while the Journal Record Building next door has been turned into the Museum and Institute for the Prevention of Terrorism.

Arrival, information, and getting around

Will Rogers World Airport lies southwest of the city and is connected to downtown by an airport shuttle (around $17 one-way; ☏ 405/681-3311). The **CVB** is downtown at 189 W Sheridan Ave (Mon–Fri 8.30am–5pm; ☏ 405/297-8912 or 1-800/225-5652, ⓦ www.visitokc.com), not far from **Greyhound** at no. 427. **Amtrak** comes in once a day from Fort Worth at historic Santa Fe Station, on Santa Fe Street.

The **city bus** depot (ⓦ www.gometro.org, ☏ 405/235-7433) is at 5th Street and N Hudson Avenue in the northwest part of downtown. Buses run daily except Sunday from 6am until 6pm ($1.25). The **Oklahoma Spirit Trolleys** (Mon–Sat 10am–11pm; 25¢–$1) run from the hotel strip in the Meridian and the stockyards to downtown.

Accommodation

Rooms are very cheap; try along the interstates, especially I-35 S and I-40 at Meridian, for chain **motels**. B&Bs are a good deal, but even the downtown luxury hotels can be affordable. There is a *KOA* campground fifteen miles east of downtown, on I-40 at exit 166 (☏ 405/391-5000; $20).

Best Western Saddleback Inn 4300 SW 3rd St ☏ 405/947-7000. One block north of I-40, on the west side of town. Pseudo-Indian decor, with luxurious touches like poolside service. ❺

Courtyard by Marriott 2 W Reno ☏ 405/232-2290. Smart rooms with very comfortable beds in the heart of Bricktown. ❻

Howard Johnson Express 400 S Meridian Ave ☏ 405/943-9841. Standard rooms close to the freeway, with breakfast included. ❸

Motel 6 - Airport 820 S Meridian Ave ☏ 405/946-6662. No-frills accommodation to suit a backpacker's budget. ❷

Sheraton Oklahoma City 1 N Broadway ☏ 405/235-2780. Newly refurbished, but pricey, rooms right downtown. ❼

The City

Tumbleweeds no longer roll through downtown Oklahoma City, but the city center remains a quiet affair, with low-key skyscrapers and little in the way of commercial activity. After work, people gravitate to the renovated warehouses of **Bricktown**, on Sheridan Ave east of the Santa Fe Railroad, which has a good selection of restaurants and bars. **Myriad Gardens** on Sheridan Ave, gives great views of the brick-towered downtown skyline from its prettily landscaped hills, gardens, and waterways. On a sunny day the **Crystal Bridge** tropical botanical garden, in a glass tube in the middle of the park, abounds in garish exotic blooms (Mon–Sat 9am–6pm, Sun noon–6pm; $6).

A few blocks north, at 620 N Harvey Ave, where the Federal Building stood until the 1995 bombing, visitors mill somberly about the **Oklahoma City National Memorial** (open 24hrs; free). The site, which dominates the center of the city, includes a field of 168 empty bronze and glass chairs, and a black reflecting pool flanked by two massive gold barriers marking 9.01–9.03am – the period of destruction. Nearby, an elm tree that continued to bloom after the blast stands as a lone sentinel. The **Memorial Museum** behind it (Mon–Sat 9am–6pm, Sun 1–6pm; $8) is also worth a visit, recounting the tragedy in gruesome detail, with TV news coverage from the day, interviews with survivors, and items pulled from the wreckage, such as shredded clothing, cracked coffee mugs, and twisted filing cabinets. Other sections describe the ensuing FBI investigation and McVeigh trial, and on the ground floor are tributes to the victims. Outside, the complex is surrounded by a chain-link fence weighed down by tokens and talismans left by mourners.

Close to the memorial, at 415 Couch Drive, is the new **Oklahoma City Museum of Art** (Tues–Sat 10am–5pm, Thurs 10am–9pm, Sun noon–5pm; $9; ⓦwww.okcmoa.com). The lobby is host to a 55ft blown-glass tower by Dale Chihuly, as well as a permanent exhibition of his work. Other galleries hold European and American art, as well as numerous traveling exhibitions.

Just northeast of downtown, a working oil well pumps crude from underneath the **Capitol Building** at 2300 N Lincoln Blvd (Mon–Fri 8am–4.30pm; free). The Capitol Complex includes the **State Museum of History** (Mon–Sat 9am–5pm, Sun noon–5pm; free), across from the Governor's Mansion. The **Heritage Hills** area to the south, where the cattle barons, oil millionaires, and bankers used to live, is worth a visit for the luxurious Victorian **Overholser Mansion**, 405 NW 15th St (Tues–Sat 10am–3pm; hourly tours $3); nearby, the **Harn Homestead Museum**, 313 NE 16th St (Mon–Fri 10am–4pm; guided tours only; $5), is also worth a wander for its old barn and wagons, and general pioneer spirit.

Sitting atop Persimmon Hill overlooking Route 66, the **National Cowboy Museum and Heritage Center**, 1700 NE 63rd St (daily 9am–5pm; $8.50; ⓦwww.nationalcowboymuseum.org), is a real treat, combining "high art" and popular art in one loving collection. In the works of Remington and Russell the link between Western art and Western movies is very clear. The paintings look like film stills, and titles such as *Waiting for Trouble* evoke the cinema's endlessly reworked myths of the West. Large exhibitions focus on contemporary Native American work, much of it colorful, bitter, and subversive. John Wayne's collection is a delight for the cowboy fetishist, and the Western Performers Hall of Fame pays homage to movie cowboys and cowgirls in hilariously reverent oil paintings and memorabilia.

Squeezed between Martin Luther King Drive and Hwy-35 are the **Firefighters Museum**, the **City Zoo**, and the **Omniplex** (ten acres of futuristic exhibits, with an aquarium, planetarium, and IMAX). At the northern end of the park, the modest **World of Wings Pigeon Center** (Mon–Fri 9am–4pm; free; ⓦwww.pigeoncenter.org) specially breeds homing pigeons for racing. You can inspect the

Storm chasing

With such unpredictable weather, it's no surprise that storm chasing has become big business in Oklahoma and surrounding "tornado alley" states. If you're either very foolhardy or very brave, you can spend a week or two driving around the prairies chasing tornadoes and some wicked, wild weather. Companies such as Storm Chasing Adventure Tours (T303/888-8629, Wwww.stormchasing.com) and Cloud 9 (T405/323-1145; Wcloud9tours.com) claim that their operations are perfectly safe and all but guarantee you an upclose and personal encounter with a tornado. Tours run from one to two weeks, cover many Midwestern states and will set you back anywhere from $2,500 to $3,000.

small museum and aviary that houses racing breeds and "fancy" pigeons bred for their looks.

Oklahoma City's **stockyards**, on Agnew Ave and Exchange St, are the busiest in the world, having sold over one hundred million cattle since 1910. They're well worth a visit, though vegetarians and animal-lovers should steer clear. This is the real thing, stomping, snorting, and smelly, with scrawny animals shunted in and out of tiny pens for auction. The roughnecks who spend their lives here – smoking, chatting, even sleeping – take no apparent notice of the quick-fire auctioneer, but nonetheless millions of head of cattle are bought and sold each year, and it can make for addictive entertainment. Morning sales, starting at 6am (Monday and Tuesday only), are the most intense, fizzling out by late afternoon.

Eating

Beef is, of course, good in Oklahoma City, especially around the stockyards. The warehouse restaurants of **Bricktown** are popular with the after-work and singles crowds.

Catfish Cabin 6317 N Meridian Ave T405/721-7553 This local joint serves up legendary catfish to a loyal crowd.

Cattleman's Steakhouse 1309 S Agnew Ave T405/236-0416. Cattlemen from the adjacent stockyards eat in this comfortable, pub-like restaurant, which has served great steaks since 1910. The place was allegedly won in a craps game. Lunchtime specials are a good deal.

Sushi Neko 4318 N Western Ave T405/528-8862. Trendy Japanese restaurant with excellent sushi and outdoor seating.

TapWerks Ale House and Café 121 E Sheridan Ave T405/319-9599. Very popular Bricktown restaurant with a British-influenced menu and 108 beers on tap.

Nightlife and entertainment

If you're into **country music**, Oklahoma City will set you right, with quite a few live music and dance venues. Beyond that, there's a few **pubs** and some progressive **clubs** – especially those in **Bricktown**, which attempt to part Oklahoma City from its cowtown image. Wednesday's *Oklahoma Gazette*, along with lively articles, carries good **listings**.

Bricktown Brewer 1 Oklahoma Ave T405/232-BREW. Large brewpub, with giant tanks of beer on show in its restaurant. Live music most nights.
Club Rodeo 2301 S Meridian Ave T405/686-1191. Popular dance hall and saloon with nightly live music. Can get a little cheesy some nights, other nights are rollicking fun. Quite a way southwest of downtown, but worth the trip. Hours and cover vary.

Rodeo Opry 221 Exchange Ave T405/297-9773. Popular venue for authentic country music shows, in the style of Nashville's Grand Ole Opry. One show a week, Sat 7.30pm.
VZD's Restaurant and Club 4200 N Western Ave T405/524-4203. Cheap and varied food by day, garage rock and the city's few hipsters by night.

GUTHRIE, thirty miles north of downtown Oklahoma City on I-35, was Oklahoma's capital from statehood in 1907 until 1911. Today the 1400-acre **Guthrie Historical District** forms a remarkably complete collection of tastefully restored Victorian architecture. The **State Capitol Publishing Museum**, 301 W Harrison Ave (Thurs–Sat 9am–5pm; donation), exhibits printing technology dating back to the earliest newspaper printed in the Oklahoma Territory, while the **Oklahoma Territorial Museum** (Tues–Sat 10am–5pm; $2 donation) focuses on the first (white) residents of the territory. The ornate **Doric Scottish Rite Masonic Temple**, 900 E Oklahoma Ave (tours Mon–Fri 10am & 2pm; $5), is the largest Masonic complex in the world, featuring hundreds of bright stained-glass windows. Guthrie is also home to the **Lazy E Arena**, four miles east of downtown, a huge site that hosts world–champion **rodeos** and **roping competitions**, as well as big-name concerts (T 405/282-7433).

Guthrie's visitor center is at 212 W Oklahoma Ave (Mon–Fri 9am–5pm; T 405/282-1947 or 1-800/299-1889, W www.guthrieok.com). The town has several good **B&Bs**, including the *Stone Lion Inn*, 1016 W Warner Ave (T 405/282-0012; ⑤), a 1907 Victorian mansion with clean rooms and antique claw-foot tubs. The *Pollard Inn*, 124 W Harrison Ave (T 405/282-1000 or 1-800/375-1001; ④), is housed in Guthrie's first bank building. Cheaper is the *Townhouse Motel*, 223 E Oklahoma Ave (T 405/260-2400; ②). The *Blue Belle Saloon*, 224 W Harrison, is Oklahoma's oldest **saloon**; the place boasts that Tom Mix tended bar here before going on to Hollywood fame.

Missouri

The state of **MISSOURI**, where the forest meets the prairie and the Mississippi River meets the Missouri River, has two significant cities: dominant **St Louis** sits midway down the state's eastern fringe; **Kansas City** is almost directly across on the western border. The pair are linked by I-70, but there's not much in between. In contrast, the south features the beautiful hillsides, streams, and ragged lakes of the **Ozark Mountains**, as well as the booming country-and-western town of **Branson**. In the east, small river towns such as **Hannibal** and **Ste Genevieve** brighten the course of the Mississippi. The northwest, home of the Pony Express and outlaw Jesse James, still strikes up images of frontier times.

Although the first French colonists honored the claims of local Native Americans, such as the original Missouri, when the area was sold to the US in 1803 as part of the **Louisiana Purchase**, the Indians were driven west by a great rush of settlers. In the 1840s and 1850s immigrants from Germany and Ireland flooded into eastern Missouri. Outnumbering their pro-slavery predecessors, they swung the balance in favor of staying in the Union during the **Civil War** – however, Confederate guerrilla forces attracted considerable support among slave-owners in the west of the state. Meanwhile, Missouri, and St Louis in particular, was establishing itself as an important **gateway to the West**. Today, the "Show Me State" (so called because of the supposed skepticism of the typical Missourian) retains a **conservative** air, particularly in its rural areas.

Getting around Missouri

It takes **Greyhound** about six hours to traverse the central corridor between St Louis and Kansas City. Infrequent Greyhound buses run through the southeast, to Springfield and a few Ozark towns, but you'll need a **car** to see the mountains and the river towns in the north. St Louis and Kansas City have major **airports**. Daily Amtrak **trains** from Chicago run to St Louis, from where direct connections can be made to points west. For keen **cyclists**, there's the popular Katy Trail, which stretches 230 miles from St Charles to Clinton.

Eastern Missouri

The Mississippi defines Missouri's eastern border, absorbing as major tributaries the Missouri, Ohio, Illinois, and Des Moines rivers. Over the years, innumerable towns have sprung up along the river, their aspirations reflected by such classical names as Alexandria, Antioch, and Athens. **Hannibal**, the boyhood home of **Mark Twain**, is the largest in the northeast, while Gallic **Ste Genevieve** is the prettiest in the south. All have, however, decreased in importance with the growing pre-eminence of **St Louis**. Away from the river, the land rises to the Ozark Plateau, whose deep green valleys are cut by swift, clear streams.

Hannibal

HANNIBAL might well have been just another medium-sized river settlement, had not Samuel Langhorne Clemens spent his boyhood here. (Clemens renamed himself **Mark Twain**, after the depth-marking cry of pilots on the Mississippi.) Although Hannibal does have other industries, downtown is little more than a Twain theme park of museums, period buildings, and wax displays.

Twain wrote surprisingly little about his hometown in his extensive nonfiction works; you could say he spoke with his feet when he left for good at seventeen to become a journeyman printer, riverboat pilot, journalist, and writer. However, although he calls the rowdy frontier river port "St Petersburg" in *The Adventures of Tom Sawyer* and the sequel *The Adventures of Huckleberry Finn*, Hannibal is the inspiration for the novels.

The Town

Hannibal's riverside location and historical buildings make it almost disturbingly picturesque. Squeezed between two steep bluffs – *Tom Sawyer*'s **"Cardiff Hill"** to the north and **Lover's Leap** to the south – the once-busy community is now quiet except for the occasional creaking of a crane loading cement. You can get an intimate look at the Mississippi aboard the slow–moving **Mark Twain riverboat** (1hr tours 11am, 1.30pm & 4pm, $12; 2hr dinner cruise by reservation 6.30pm, $33; ☎573/221-3222). Twain's youthful stomping-ground was the short, cobbled incline of **Hill Street**, at the north end of town. Adjoining the restored **Mark Twain Boyhood Home**, a simple white-clapboard house where Twain lived between 1844 and 1853, the **Mark Twain Museum** (summer daily 8am–6pm; rest of year times vary; $8; ☎573/221-9010) includes such memorabilia as first editions, letters, photos, original artwork, and one of the author's trademark white coats. Immediately opposite, there's a bookstore in the original home of Laura Hawkins (the model for Tom Sawyer's first love, Becky Thatcher), who visited Twain in Connecticut in 1908 and lived on in Hannibal until 1928. Nearby stands the law office of Twain's father, a justice of the peace who died of pneumonia while the writer was still a boy. Antique, souvenir, and gift stores stretch away from here down **Main Street**, which also holds the **New Mark Twain Museum** (summer daily 9am–6pm; rest of year times vary; same phone as above). Included in the admission price to the original museum and home, the exhibits here re-create scenes from Twain's books, the cave and Huck Finn's raft among them. Upstairs at the gift shop are the fifteen original **Norman Rockwell paintings** commissioned for limited editions of Twain's most popular titles.

About two miles south of town is the **Mark Twain Cave** (summer daily 8am–8pm; times vary rest of the year; $14; ☎573/221-1656), where one-hour tours recall Tom and Becky's frightening misadventure in the dark. Further south, Hwy-79 towards St Louis offers one of the most **scenic drives** along the Mississippi, continually broken by thin, elongated, thickly wooded islands, and bounded by towering limestone bluffs.

Practicalities

Pick up full details on Hannibal from the **visitor center**, 505 N Third St (April–Oct daily 8am–6pm; Nov–March Mon–Fri 8am–5pm, Sat & Sun limited hours; ☎573/221-2477, ⓦwww.visithannibal.com). **Motel** rates vary wildly according to season. The very central *Hotel Clemens*, 401 N Third St (☎573/248-1150; ❸–❺), with a pool, offers pretty good value, as does the *Hannibal Inn*, US-61 at Market St (☎573/221-6610; ❸–❹), albeit on the edge of town. One of nearly a dozen **B&Bs**, *Lula Belle's*, 111 Bird St (☎573/221-6662 or 1-800/882-4890; ❸–❻), has rooms of varying degrees of luxury, including some with river views, and serves tasty food. The *Mark Twain Family Restaurant*, just up from the Mark Twain Museum at 400 N Third St (☎573/221-5300), serves classic American fare. A mile south of town on Hwy-79, you can **camp** at the shaded *Mark Twain Campground* (☎573/221-1656 or 1-800/527-0304; $18 for tents, $22 for RVs).

St Louis

Perched just below the confluence of the Mississippi and Missouri rivers, three hundred miles south of Chicago and the same distance north of Memphis, cosmopolitan **ST LOUIS** (pronounced, whatever any song might say, "Saint Lewis") owes its vaguely European air to its history and cultural infrastructure. Any city capable of producing one of the twentieth century's greatest poets, as well as one of its greatest rock 'n' rollers – namely, **T.S. Eliot** and **Chuck Berry** – probably has a lot going for it.

St Louis was founded in 1764 by the French fur trader Pierre Laclede. However, the American immigration that followed its sale to the US under the **Louisiana Purchase** all but extinguished the refinement it had gained during French and Spanish rule. It subsequently became crucial as the major gateway for pioneers on the wagon trails westward. **Transportation** – first steamboats, then trains, and now air haulage – has long been the basis of its considerable industrial strength. However, St Louis has not always had an easy ride. Downtown reached a nadir during the 1970s, but the years since have seen a remarkable turnaround, with attractions on the revitalized **riverfront** including the magnificent **Gateway Arch** and the restored warehouses of **Laclede's Landing**.

Try not to leave without sampling the **outlying districts**. To the west lie arty **Central West End** and young **University** (or "U") **City**, on either side of prodigious **Forest Park**, with its museums and playing fields. The blue-collar **Southside** features the markets, antique shops, and jazz pubs of **Soulard** and the Italian shops and cafés of **the Hill**. Directly across the river in Illinois, **East St Louis**, once the stomping ground of jazz stars like Miles Davis and John Coltrane, has very little to offer visitors.

▲ Greyhound Station   **▲ Ⓐ (200 yds) & Airport**

Ⓑ   **❶**

COLE STREET

◄ Ⓒ & Theater District

MARTIN LUTHER KING BOULEVARD

Convention Center ℹ

TWA Dome

70

Laclede's Landing Ⓜ

EADS BRIDGE

East St Louis ►

DELMAR BOULEVARD

City Museum

TUCKER BOULEVARD

LUCAS AVENUE

LUCAS AVENUE

St Louis Center Mall

Ⓜ

LACLEDE'S LANDING

WASHINGTON AVENUE

ST CHARLES STREET

Ⓜ

MEMORIAL DRIVE

◄ Forest Park & Ⓓ

LOCUST STREET

St Louis Public Library

CONVENTION CENTER

Riverboats

OLIVE STREET

7TH STREET

Gateway Arch & Museum of Westward Expansion

PINE STREET

8TH & PINE Ⓜ

Old Courthouse

CHESTNUT STREET

ℹ

KIENER PLAZA

MARKET STREET

Jefferson National Expansion Memorial

WALNUT STREET

International Bowling Museum & Hall of Fame

Busch Stadium

Ⓜ

Ⓔ

BROADWAY

70

Union Station

CLARK STREET

BUSCH STADIUM

Ⓜ

Ⓜ

SPRUCE STREET

F

UNION STATION

KIEL CENTER

DANIEL BOONE EXPRESSWAY 64

Amtrak Station

GRATIOT STREET

❷

MACARTHUR BRIDGE (VEHICLE TRAFFIC ONLY)

PAPIN STREET

CHOUTEAU AVENUE

LA SALLE ST

◄ Ⓔ & The Hill/Missouri Botanical Garden

HICKORY STREET

MORRISON AVENUE

RUTGER STREET

❸ **❹**

PARK AVENUE

CARROLL ST.

MARION STREET

LAFAYETTE AVENUE

Lafayette Park

SOULARD STREET

Soulard Market

44

MISSISSIPPI AVENUE

Mississippi River

GEYER AVENUE

ALLEN AVENUE

Ⓖ **❻**

SOULARD

RUSSELL BOULEVARD

❼

ANN AVENUE

55

SHENANDOAH AVENUE

LAMI STREET

BARTON STREET

VICTOR STREET

SYDNEY STREET

N

0   400 yds

Anheuser-Busch Brewery

Ⓜ Metro Link stop

LYNCH ST.

ACCOMMODATION

Best Western Inn at the Park	D
Drury Inn – Union Station	F
Econo Lodge Downtown	A
Embassy Suites	B
HI-Great Rivers Hostel	C
The Huckleberry Finn Youth Hostel	G
Millennium Hotel	E

RESTAURANTS, BARS & LIVE MUSIC

1860 Hard Shell Café & Bar	6
Baileys' Chocolate Bar	4
Broadway Oyster Bar	2
John D. McGurk's Irish Pub	7
Mississippi Nights	1
Park Avenue Mansion	3
Red Roof Inn St Louis Hampton	5

10

Arrival, information, and getting around

Lambert-St Louis International Airport is a dozen miles northwest of downtown – $36 by taxi or $3.50 by bus or MetroLink. Some **Greyhound** buses call at the airport, though you cannot buy tickets there. You can either purchase tickets by mail, or you can board at the airport without a ticket and pay for one when you arrive in the bus main terminal downtown at 1450 N 13th St. **Amtrak** stops at 551 S 16th St.

The city has **visitor centers** at the America Center in the massive Cervantes Convention Center (Mon–Fri 9am–5pm, Sat 9am–2pm; ⊤1-800/916-0092), and at Kiener Plaza (Mon–Fri 9am–5pm, Sat 9am–2pm; closed Jan & Feb; ⊤314/231-0336). For the latest **events**, visit ⊛www.explorestlouis.com.

The Bi-State Transit System (⊤314/231-2345) operates the **MetroLink**, a light-rail system serving the airport and most significant tourist sights ($1.75; free in downtown Mon–Fri 11.30am–1.30pm). BSTS buses also go to all of the city's suburbs, though service can be slow and infrequent. Big Shark Athletic Company, near Forest Park at 6176 Delmar Blvd ($5/hour or $20/day; ⊤314/862-1818), rents **bikes**.

Accommodation

Good-value **lodging** can be found downtown, with appealing weekend rates. The CVB will have information on the area's numerous **B&Bs**.

Best Western Inn at the Park 4630 Lindell Blvd ⊤314/367-7500 or 1-800/373-7501. Good chain motel on the northeast corner of Forest Park, right by the cafés of Central West End. ④–⑤

Drury Inn – Union Station 201 S 20th St ⊤314/231-3900 or 1-800/325-8300. Very tastefully restored accommodation. ④–⑥

EconoLodge Downtown 1100 N 3rd St ⊤314/421-6556. The least expensive downtown option, just a short walk from Laclede's Landing. The area's not pleasant at night, though. ③

Embassy Suites 901 N 1st St ⊤314/241-4200. Comfortable suites in the heart of Laclede's Landing. Buffet breakfast included. ⑥

HI-Great Rivers Hostel 2800 Normandy Drive, Bel-Nor ⊤314/241-4200; ⊛www.greatrivershostel.org. This clean hostel, two blocks from a MetroLink stop, is in a former dormitory on the south campus of UMSL. Dorms are $20, private rooms are $30.

The Huckleberry Finn Youth Hostel 1904-1908 S 12th St ⊤314/644-4660. Dorms ($20) on the edge of a dodgy area in Soulard, so take bus #10 or #30 from downtown. Office hours 8–10am & 6–10pm.

Millennium Hotel 200 S 4th St ⊤314/241-9500 or 1-800/325-7353. Ideal downtown setting, with all the facilities you'd expect from a hotel of its size, including a restaurant, fitness center, and business center. ④–⑦

Park Avenue Mansion 2007 Park Ave ⊤314/588-9004. Attractive, homey B&B on Lafayette Square, with friendly service and a lovely outdoor patio and garden. ⑤

Red Roof Inn St Louis Hampton 5823 Wilson Ave ⊤314/645-0119. Rooms were nicely refurbished in 2006 and it has a great location on the edge of the Hill and near I-44 and I-64. ④

The riverfront

The one-and-a-half-mile cobbled granite **wharf** along the Mississippi used to lie in the shadow of a dense tangle of warehouses and factories. When river trade decreased, most were ripped down. However, some restored structures between the Eads and Martin Luther King bridges now form **Laclede's Landing Historic District**, their cast-iron facades fronting touristy antique stores, restaurants, and live music venues. In early September, the district hosts the **Big Muddy Blues Festival**, featuring artists of national prominence and a great party atmosphere (information on ⊤314/241-5875, ⊛www.lacledeslanding.org).

On the waterfront itself, where roustabouts once handled cargoes of cotton and ores, assorted permanently moored vessels hold museums, theater shows, a heliport, and casinos. **Cruises** aboard replica paddle-wheelers leave from under the Gateway Arch (April–Nov daily 10am–4.30pm; $10; dinner cruises depart at 7.30pm, $37; ℗314/621-4040 or 1-800/878-7411).

Ten minutes' walk south, more than thirty blocks of derelict buildings were torn down to clear space for the **Jefferson National Expansion Memorial**, dedicated to the US president who negotiated the Louisiana Purchase and thereby opened up the West, and to the pioneers who journeyed along the Oregon and Santa Fe trails. The highlight of the expansive green space is the **Gateway Arch**. Designed by Eero Saarinen and completed in 1965, the arch is a 630ft stainless steel parabola of majestic symmetry; in technical terms it's a weighted catenary curve, the outline formed by a heavy cable hanging freely from two points. So long as you're not claustrophobic, it's fun to take the four-minute **tram ride** up the hollow curving arch. Tiny five-seater capsules carry you to a viewing gallery at the top of the arch,

△ Gateway Arch

where you can linger as long as you like – the views of St Louis, the Midwestern plains, and the mighty Mississippi are spectacular. Lengthy lines are inevitable in the summer, but you can pick up a numbered ticket earlier in the day and come back at an appointed time. Still, you'll have to wait in another line for the elevator, so expect an hour roundtrip (daily: summer 8am–9.15pm departures; rest of year 9am–5.15pm; $10).

In a massive bunker beneath the arch, the **visitor center** (daily: summer 8am–10pm; rest of year 9am–6pm; ☎314/982-1410) shows a riveting **film** about the construction of the monument, and another on the **Lewis and Clark Expedition**, which set off from St Louis in 1804 to explore the Missouri River, as well as potential water passages to the Pacific Ocean ($7 for one film, $11 for two). The expedition returned two years later with details of trade routes, Native American settlements, and observations on animal and plant life. Also in the visitor center complex, the spacious **Museum of Westward Expansion** (free) recounts the Lewis and Clark story, drawing heavily on the pair's very readable journals.

Nearby, engineering buffs will take note of the extraordinary (if not all that attractive) **Eads Bridge**. Completed in 1876, the massive steel structure was St Louis' first bridge across the Mississippi, doing much to facilitate the railroad boom of the gilded age. Pedestrians and cyclists can cross the bridge for excellent views of the city's **skyline**.

Central downtown

One block from the arch along St Louis' main east–west thoroughfare, Market Street, old photographs at the stately **Old Courthouse Museum** (daily 8am–4.30pm; free) record the development of the city and the settling of the West. Two restored courtrooms were the site of the trial of **Dred Scott**, a black slave who argued that having spent time with his owner in non-slave Illinois and Wisconsin, he had the right to be set free. His case was upheld in 1850, but overturned two years later. On appeal, the Supreme Court declared that Scott, born a slave in a slave state, might, like any other chattel, be taken anywhere his master chose to go. The decision, which meant that the US Constitution saw slaves as legitimate personal property, sent shock waves through the corridors of government and hastened the onrush of the **Civil War**. Scott himself, by now a nationally known figure, was voluntarily freed by his new owner, though he died a year later.

The **International Bowling Museum and Hall of Fame**, at 111 Stadium Plaza (April–Sept 9am–5pm; rest of year 11am–4pm Tues–Sat; $7.50, includes four free frames), is devoted to the favorite sport of such diverse figures as Martin Luther and Homer Simpson, tracing its history from ancient Egypt to the present. It may come as some surprise to learn of bowling's rowdy history: excessive betting on games got it denounced by the Church in fifteenth-century Germany and, three centuries later, the behavior of drunken fans led to all lanes being shut down in London.

See the world's largest pair of underpants and witness the mystic power of the corndog at the whimsical **City Museum**, 701 N 15th St (hours vary, call ☎314/231-2489 for details; $12; ⊛www.citymuseum.org). The exhibits, made almost entirely of junk, often border on the bizarre, as one floor is devoted to secret passages and deadends. There's also a small, but worthwhile, aquarium onsite ($6). Over on Market St at 18th, the focal point of the giant Romanesque **Union Station** is a 230ft clock tower. The station, erected in 1884, was transformed in the early 1980s into a huge complex of mostly tacky shops, chain restaurants, and a hotel. An artificial lake, where you can rent boats, is in the back. The *Hyatt Hotel*'s ornate lobby, once the station's main waiting room, is well worth visiting.

West of downtown

Three miles west of downtown, the **theater district**, called **Grand Center**, is staked out with ornate street lamps along Grand Avenue between Lindell and Delmar Boulevards. Bright posters advertise the current shows at the **Fabulous Fox Theater**, 527 N Grand Ave (tours Tues, $5; Thurs & Sat, $8, including a special organ performance at 10.30am; ☎314/534-1111), where you can have a look at the magnificent Siamese-Byzantine interior and massive Wurlitzer organ.

About a mile further west, on the edge of **Forest Park**, trendy shops, wine bars, and c.1900 mansions line the leafy thoroughfares of the **Central West End** district. A few blocks away at 4431 Lindell Blvd, the Romanesque-Byzantine **Cathedral of St Louis** houses the world's largest collection of mosaic art (daily 10am–4pm; tours Mon–Fri 10am–3pm, Sun 1pm; free).

The decision to put Forest Park four miles directly west of downtown (served by MetroLink every ten to thirty minutes depending on time of day) aroused much criticism during the 1870s, with opponents claiming that its inaccessibility would make it merely a pleasure ground for the local rich. It's larger than New York's Central Park, and every bit as full of attractions; in summer, the 12,000-seat amphitheater is regularly filled for the Broadway-style **musical theater productions** (☎314/361-1900, ⓦwww.muny.com).

Standing on **Art Hill** in the central western section of the park, the striking **Beaux Arts Saint Louis Art Museum** (Fri 1pm–9pm, Tues–Sun 10am–5pm; tours at 1.30pm; free), is the only surviving structure from the 1904 World's Fair. Its mission – to cover international art from prehistoric times onwards – is ambitious. It houses one of the world's most extensive collections of **German Expressionism**, devoting an entire gallery to the powerful, spiraling, jagged images of Max Beckmann, and its pre-Columbian artworks cover every significant style, medium, and culture from Mexico to Peru.

In addition to the animals in its "cageless displays," the **St Louis Zoo** (daily summer 8am–7pm, 9am–5pm rest of year; free), set in beautiful grounds in the park, boasts a "Living World" exhibit, in which an animatronic robot of Charles Darwin gives synopses of his theories.

The main strengths of the **History Museum**, on the northern fringe of the park (Tues 10am–8pm, Wed–Sun 10am–6pm; free), are its thematic collections of old photos of St Louis, documenting river life, black music in the city, and Charles Lindbergh's 1927 flight in the *Spirit of St Louis* (sponsored by the city's aircraft industry) from New York to Paris. The **St Louis Science Center** (Mon–Thurs and Sat 9.30am–5.30pm, Fri until 9.30pm, Sun 11.30am–5.30pm; free) straddles I-64 and can be entered from either side of the freeway; use one of the radar guns on the covered access bridge to check the speed of cars on the freeway below. General admission is free, but it costs a few dollars to get into the planetarium, the OMNI-MAX Theater, and other major exhibits.

Southside

The tens of thousands of Germans who came to St Louis in the mid-eighteenth century settled mostly in the **Southside**, where the Teutonic influence is noticeable. These immigrants were skilled brewers; only one of the breweries they opened from the 1850s onwards still stands, but it does happen to be the largest in the world. The one hundred intricate redbrick buildings of the **Anheuser-Busch plant**, 12th and Lynch streets (hours vary seasonally; ☎314/577-2626 or ⓦwww.budweisertours.com for details; free), produce annually a sizeable proportion of the company's 14.3 million barrels of beer, including Budweiser and Michelob. Free **tours** (80min) are mostly company PR, but they're still good fun, and you get two glasses of beer before being shunted into the gift shop.

A few blocks towards downtown, the colorful **Soulard Market**, at Broadway and Lafayette avenues (Wed–Fri 8am–5.30pm, Sat 6am–5.30pm), is a great place to pick up picnic items and fresh fruit, especially on a Saturday. The terraced streets behind it hold the city's best blues and jazz pubs.

Red-white-and-green fire hydrants let you know that you're in the thirty-square-block **Hill district**, a small, neat Italian community three miles west of Soulard. At its heart, **St Ambrose Church** displays a statue of Italian immigrants; all around, the aroma of freshly baked bread drifts out of the small specialty baker-ies that share the area with one-room grocery stores and many restaurants.

Just east of the Hill District, at 4344 Shaw Blvd, the 79-acre **Missouri Botanical Garden** (daily 9am–5pm; $8; ⓦ www.mobot.org) is a haven of peace and tran-quility, just a few hundred yards from busy I-44. The grounds contain everything from a magnificent Japanese garden through scented rose and English woodland gardens to the Climatron, a huge greenhouse that recreates a tropical rainforest complete with waterfalls and cliffs.

Eating

Thanks to heavy Italian immigration in the early twentieth century, **Italian food** predominates in St Louis, from humble salami sellers upwards. Otherwise, there are many friendly **Irish pubs**, serving beef sandwiches and stew, while University City's **Delmar Boulevard** offers African, Middle Eastern, Chinese, Indian, and other ethnic places. More expensive cafés are located in **Laclede's Landing**, and the **Central West End** has a scattering of upmarket espresso bars such as the *Coffee Cartel*, 2 Maryland Plaza.

Baileys' Chocolate Bar 1915 Park Ave, Lafayette Square ☎314/241-8100. A must for dessert lovers, offering a delicious variety of chocolate concoctions, both edible and drinkable. Notice the murals on the wall – they're painted with cocoa.

Duff's 392 N Euclid Ave, Central West End ☎314/361-0522. Small, relaxed, and moderately priced, with a French-flavored international menu, as well as homemade desserts and Sunday brunch. Outdoor seating available.

John D. McGurk's Irish Pub 1200 Russell Blvd, at 12th St, Soulard ☎314/776-8309. Freshly baked soda bread, corned beef and cabbage, Irish stew, and imported Guinness on offer. Live Irish music every night and great outdoor seating.

O'Connell's Pub 4652 Shaw Ave, at Kingshighway Blvd ☎314/773-6600. The best burgers in the city, and the beef sandwiches aren't bad either. Near the Hill district.

Rigazzi's 4945 Daggett Blvd, the Hill ☎314/772-4900. Popular trattoria, famous for "frozen fish-bowls" of beer. Over thirty different pasta dishes on the menu plus pizzas, veal, chicken, and steak.

Saleem's 6501 Delmar Blvd, U City ☎314/721-7947. "Where garlic is king" and St Louisians reckon you get the best Lebanese food in the city.

Ted Drewes Frozen Custard 6726 Chippewa Ave ☎314/481-2652; also 4224 S Grand Blvd ☎314/352-7376. A legendary slice of Americana. Try a "concrete" – an ice cream so thick it won't budge if you turn your cup upside down. Open March–Dec.

Nightlife and entertainment

Downtown St Louis' highest concentration of **bars** and **clubs** can be found in **Laclede's Landing**, with nightly jazz, blues, rock, and reggae. Some of the out-lying districts are well worth checking out; these include **the Loop** in U City, whose bars and cafés are not only popular with students, and the slightly more upmarket cafés and wine bars of **Central West End**. Unpretentious **Soulard** is the place to go for good jazz and blues. You should also check out **Grand Center**, centered on North Grand Blvd in midtown, home to stage shows and the **St Louis Symphony Orchestra** (☎314/534-1700). Excellent **listings** can be found in the free weekly *Riverfront Times*.

1860 Hard Shell Café & Bar 1860 S 9th St, Soulard ☎314/231-1860. One of the liveliest bars

in Soulard with dancing to blues, R&B, and soul bands. Also serves good Cajun and fish dishes.

Blueberry Hill 6504 Delmar Blvd, U City ⊕314/727-4444, ✆www.blueberryhill.com. Crammed full of memorabilia, with the downstairs dedicated to Elvis and a jukebox acclaimed by *Cashbox* magazine as the best in the country. The drinks and burgers are good, and live entertainment is offered every weekend (Chuck Berry himself comes in for monthly cameos).

Broadway Oyster Bar 736 S Broadway, downtown ⊕314/621-8811. Cramped, crowded, and dark blues club, in an atmospheric old bar.

Mississippi Nights 914 N 1st St, Laclede's Landing ⊕314/421-3853. The city's top venue for nonstadium bands.

Pageant 6161 Delmar Blvd, U City ⊕314/726-6161. Large bar and live entertainment venue that brings in big-name rock groups.

Riddles Penultimate 6307 Delmar Blvd, U City ⊕314/725-6985. Very lively bar in the heart of U City, with a young crowd and some sidewalk seating.

St Charles

The beautiful little river town of **ST CHARLES**, 25 miles northwest of downtown St Louis and forever threatened by flooding, remains redolent with lazy charm, despite the advent of its first riverboat casino. Three small though distinct **historic districts** are crammed with antique shops, specialty outlets, and good cafés and restaurants, including the *Trailhead Brewery*, 921 S Riverside Drive (⊕636/946-2739), a modern pub housed in an eighteenth-century grist mill. Lewis and Clark set up strategic camp here in 1804, and are remembered in the interesting small **museum**.

St Charles's **CVB**, 230 S Main St (⊕636/946-7776 or 1-800/366-2427, ✆www.historicstcharles.com), has details of downtown's growing range of elegant and amply porched **B&Bs**. The popular **Katy Trail**, which hugs the river along the route of an old railroad before turning west to Clinton, is excellent for hiking or cycling. Momentum Cycles (⊕636/946-7433) **rents bikes** ($6 per hour or $30 per day) for the trail.

Ste Genevieve

Sixty miles south of St Louis, Missouri's oldest community, the tiny, French- and German-heritage **STE GENEVIEVE** retains its eighteenth-century charm through historic cottages, a redbrick square, and summer festivals. A perennial favorite of Mississippi flood waters, the town, with a population of 4500, has recently been sheltered by a $50 million levee, a measure taken to ensure the safety of homes that pre-date the American Revolution. The *St Gemme Beauvais*, 78 N Main St (⊕573/883-5744; ❹–❼), is a nineteenth-century Greek Revival inn downtown. Home-cooked catfish, chicken, and seafood are on the menu in the *Anvil Saloon*, 43 S Third St (⊕573/883-7323).

Western Missouri

As the Mississippi River defines Eastern Missouri, its tributary the Missouri (which gave the state its name) dominates the northwest border. Here along the river, jazz and barbeque flourish in **Kansas City**, while the small town of **Independence** lays on the homespun charm made famous by its favorite son, President Harry S. Truman. Further south, surrounding the hokey family-entertainment center of **Branson**, cool lakes and forested hills provide some breathtaking natural beauty.

Kansas City

KANSAS CITY, 250 miles due west of St Louis, straddles the state line between Kansas and Missouri. Virtually all its main points of interest are

DOWNTOWN KANSAS CITY

The Arabia Steamboat Museum

Greyhound Terminal

City Hall

Public Library

N

Amtrak

Union Station/ Science City

Crown Center

Penn Valley Park

Penn Valley Park

Negro Leagues Baseball Museum & American Jazz Museum

ACCOMMODATION

Best Western Seville Plaza	C
Holiday Inn Express Westport	B
Hotel Savoy	A

RESTAURANTS, BARS & CLUBS

Arthur Bryant's	2
Blayney's Irish Tavern	11
Fiorella's Jack Stack Barbecue	5
Gates Bar-B-Q	7
The Grand Emporium	9
Grand St Cafe	14
Hereford House	4
Jardine's	13
Jazz/A Louisiana Kitchen	10
Jerusalem Café	12
LaMar's Donuts	8
Lidia's	6
Mutual Musicians Foundation	3
Phoenix Piano Bar and Grill	1

WESTPORT

Country Club Plaza

Nelson-Atkins Museum of Art

0   1 mile

on the Missouri side, where the fountains, boulevards, Art Deco and Mediterranean-style buildings, and the encouraging revitalization of downtown, are welcome features in a Midwestern city. Kansas City, Kansas, doesn't have much to attract visitors.

Kansas City was a convenient staging post for 1830s wagon trains heading west. Its consequent prosperity – and rough-and-tumble "sin city" image – was brought to an abrupt end by the **Civil War**. However, its fortunes revived in the 1870s, when the railroads brought the boom in meatpacking that was responsible for the development of the huge stockyards, which finally closed down in 1992.

Thanks to political boss **Tom Pendergast**, an outrageous figure with whom the city had a love-hate relationship, Kansas City's many jazz clubs continued to sell alcohol during **Prohibition**. As in Chicago and New Orleans, speakeasies, brothels, and gambling dens went hand in hand with superlative **jazz** – and, to a lesser extent, **blues** – spawning the careers of Count Basie, Duke Ellington, and, in the Fifties, Charlie Parker. KC's resurgent jazz scene, fine restaurants, professional football and baseball teams, and theme parks help make it a popular short-break destination.

Arrival, information, and getting around

From the **Kansas City International Airport**, twenty miles northwest of downtown, a convenient forty-minute **shuttle bus** (half-hourly 6am–11.55pm; ☏816/243-5000) heads to major downtown hotels ($16) and Westport ($17). The equivalent taxi-ride costs around $45; call Yellow Cab (☏816/471-5000). The isolated **Greyhound** terminal lies well out from downtown in a miserable area at 1101 Troost Ave. **Amtrak** is in the Union Station at 23rd and Main streets, opposite Crown Center.

The city's main **visitor center** is tucked away on the 22nd floor of City Center Square at 1100 Main St (Mon–Fri 8.30am–5pm; ☎816/221-5242 or 1-800/767-7700, ⊛www.visitkc.com); additional information offices are housed in the Country Club Plaza at 4709 W Central St (daily 8am–6pm; ☎1-800/767-7700) and in the Grand Hallway of Union Station.

The **Metro Buses** system ($1.25; ☎816/221-0660, ⊛www.kcata.org) covers downtown, and has routes out to Independence.

Accommodation

Kansas City's budget **motels** lie along the interstates or out towards Independence, though reasonable central options do exist. The visitor center is the best place to inquire about **B&Bs**. Depending on which direction you are coming from, **camping** choices include the *Trailside Camper's Inn*, I-70 exit 24, 24 miles east of downtown in Grain Valley (☎816/229-2267 or 1-800/748-7729; $17 for tents), or the *Cottonwood RV Park*, on Hwy-7 just off I-70 exit 224, 24 miles west of downtown in Bonner Springs (☎913/422-8038; $20 for tents).

Best Western Seville Plaza 4309 Main St ☎816/561-9600. Very central, close to Westport. Completely renovated in 2003. ❺

Holiday Inn Express Westport 801 Westport Rd ☎816/931-1000. Reasonable lodgings on the edge of the trendy Westport district. ❺

🏃 **Hotel Savoy** 219 W Ninth St ☎816/842-3575 or 1/800-728-6922. Opened in 1888, this Garment District hotel has been beautifully renovated into a 22-room B&B offering a gourmet breakfast. ❺–❻

Super 8 Independence 4032 S Lynn Court ☎816/833-1888. Clean budget motel, east of the city in Independence. ❷–❹

The City

Kansas City is doing a good job of reinvigorating its **downtown**, and wandering past the restored lofts and small businesses of the **Garment District**, between Sixth and Ninth streets, makes for a pleasant way to reach **City Hall**, 414 E 12th St (Mon–Fri 8.30am–4.15pm; free), a fine Art Deco building with an observation deck on its thirtieth floor. Also downtown is the **historic district** known variously as **River Market** or **City Market**, on the banks of the Missouri. As well as colorful shops, cafés, and a lively farmers' market at Fifth and Walnut streets, there's a good museum in the complex, **The Treasure of the Steamboat Arabia**, which tells the story behind the 1988 salvaging of a side-wheeler that sank on its way to Council Bluffs in 1856 (400 Grand Blvd; Mon–Sat 10am–5.30pm, Sun noon–5pm; $12.50; ⊛www.1856.com). Perfectly preserved artifacts – china, guns, gold, and Kentucky bourbon, to name a few – afford unexpected and intriguing insights into frontier life.

The sprawling concrete **Crown Center**, on Grand Ave and Pershing Rd, owned by Hallmark Cards, calls itself "a city within a city," and houses apartments, shops, restaurants, offices, a hotel, cinemas, and an ice rink. Interesting displays in its splendidly awful **Hallmark Visitors Center** (Tues–Fri 9am–5pm, Sat 9.30am–4.30pm; free) trace styles of greeting cards alongside political and cultural changes; designs from the 1940s, for example, featured stars and stripes and Uncle Sam. There are also demonstrations of dyeing and engraving techniques. The nearby **Union Station**, built in 1914, is a Kansas City landmark: huge, beautifully renovated, and home to **Science City** (Tues–Fri 9.30am–5pm, Sat 10am–5pm, Sun noon–5pm; $13.95 for all attractions; ⊛www.sciencecity.com), an incredible arena of futuristic games, movies, and exhibits.

The **18th and Vine Historic Jazz District**, south of I-70 as it sweeps east–west, was the hub of the city's 1930s jazz scene. A huge revitalization project in the 1980s culminated with the opening of the **Negro Leagues Baseball Museum**, 1616 E 18th St (Tues–Sat 9am–6pm, Sun noon–6pm; $6; ⓦ www.nlbm.com) – an enthralling collection of photographs, interactive exhibits, and game equipment that traces the turbulent history of black baseball in America, which was segregated from the white major leagues for the first half of the twentieth century. In the same complex is the **American Jazz Museum** (Tues–Sat 9am–6pm, Sun noon–6pm; $6), which tells the history of jazz through interactive exhibits that profile some of its greatest performers, including Kansas City native Charlie Parker and others who cut their teeth in the smoky halls of 18th and Vine. The *Blue Room* functions as a working jazz bar, with Thurs through Saturday and Mon-night jam sessions bringing many stars out of the woodwork. If you're going to visit both museums, the $8 combo ticket is your best bet.

Westport, an attractive district of good restaurants, cafés, and trendy shops between 39th and 45th streets, was the original jumping-off point for the Santa Fe Trail. Stop in for a drink at the city's oldest building, *Kelly's Westport Inn*, 500 Westport Rd (ⓣ 816/561-5800), a shabby but friendly redbrick bar. Five miles south of downtown, beginning at 47th and Main streets, the elegant **Country Club Plaza** dates from the early 1920s. Tree-shaded and upmarket (with branches of stores like Anthropologie and Saks), its tiling, mosaics, fountains, and orange trees evoke the streets of Spain; a replica of Seville's La Giralda tower completes the effect.

Highlights at the extensive **Nelson-Atkins Museum of Art**, a few blocks east at 4525 Oak St (Tues–Thurs 10am–4pm, Fri 10am–9pm, Sat 10am–5pm, Sun noon–5pm; free), include superb Oriental exhibits, with figurines from Tang and Egyptian tombs, plus canvases by Titian, Caravaggio (*St John the Baptist*), and Monet, plus twelve Henry Moore sculptures in a landscaped setting. The pretty **Toy and Miniature Museum**, further south at 5235 Oak St (Wed–Sat 10am–4pm, Sun 1–4pm; $6), houses an offbeat collection of antique toys, games, and puppets.

During the summer, if the Midwestern humidity gets to be too much, head for the tropically themed water world called **Oceans of Fun**, or the adjoining **Worlds of Fun**, with its 140-plus rides, out at exit 54 of I-435 (daily or weekends mid-April–mid-Oct, hours vary; $26 for Oceans, $37 for Worlds).

Eating

Barbecue, once the unfashionable food of the poor, is big news in Kansas City – cheap, cheerful, hickory-smoked, and served with tasty sauces. The **Country Club Plaza** has some decent places to sample the spicy cuisine, but they tend to be overpriced and some require formal dress. The restaurants in **Westport** are more casual.

Arthur Bryant's 1727 Brooklyn Ave ⓣ 816/231-1123. *The* place for barbecue, a mile east of downtown in a desolate area. Serving the largest portions you've ever seen of barbecue and beans; the combo plate easily feeds two hefty appetites. This is serious business – don't take too much time deciding, as rookies aren't given any hand-holding.

Fiorella's Jack Stack Barbecue 101 W 22nd St ⓣ 816/472-7427. This relative newcomer to the K.C. barbecue pantheon serves the best in town, some locals reckon.

Gates Bar-B-Q 3205 Main St ⓣ 816/753-0828. Massive portions of BBQ served on platters in a family-style atmosphere.

Grand St Cafe 4740 Grand St ⓣ 816/471-6300. In an office building between the Plaza and the art museum, the food is worth seeking out here. Delicious items include grilled pork chops and roasted duck, which run from $16 to $25.

Hereford House 20th and Main streets ⓣ 816/842-1080. KC's top steakhouse, in a handy downtown spot.

Jerusalem Café 431 Westport Rd ⓣ 816/756-2770. Small Middle Eastern restaurant serving superb falafel and kebabs.

LaMar's Donuts 3395 Main St ⓣ 1-800/533-7489. A KC institution, now with branches in several states; this one is the original.

Lidia's 101 W 22nd St ⓣ 816/221-3722. Popular

spot housed in an old freight house near *Jack Stack* (see above). Excellent pasta and an extensive wine selection, at affordable prices.

Stroud's 5410 NE Oakridge Rd ☎816/454-9600. Renowned fried chicken in a converted farmhouse well worth the drive north of downtown.

Nightlife and entertainment

Check out Kansas City's **jazz** and **blues** scene, especially the authentic dives holding wonderful jam sessions into the early hours. The Friday and Sunday editions of the *Kansas City Star* carry **listings**, as does the freebie *Pitch Weekly*. You can also call the **Jazz Hotline** (☎816/753-JASS) or check ⓦ www.jazzkc.org. **Downtown** is otherwise pretty dead by mid-evening, with most people heading to **Westport** for nightlife from country-and-western to alternative rock.

Blayney's Irish Tavern 415 Westport Rd ☎816/561-3747. A good Westport venue with a varied live music schedule all week.
The Grand Emporium 3832 Main St ☎816/561-2560. Live blues, DJs, and salsa dancing weekly. Twice voted the Best Blues Club in America by the National Blues Foundation.
Jardine's 4536 Main St ☎816/561-6480. Live jazz seven nights a week and Sat & Sun afternoons as well as a good meat and pasta menu.
Jazz/A Louisiana Kitchen 1823 W 39th St ☎816/531-5556. Cajun cuisine and live jazz and blues.

Mutual Musicians Foundation 1823 Highland Ave ☎816/471-5212. National Historic Landmark in the 18th and Vine district. Fierce jam sessions begin at 1am Fri & Sat and last till 5am, with musicians competing in a frenzy. Things can get a bit rough, and it's recommended that women not attend solo.
Phoenix Piano Bar and Grill 302 W 8th St at Central Ave ☎816/472-0001. Downtown jazz piano venue featuring popular Sat afternoon sessions.

THE GREAT PLAINS | Western Missouri

Independence and Liberty

Bus #24 from Kansas City goes to the small town of **INDEPENDENCE**, twenty minutes east of the city and most famous as the former home of **President Harry S. Truman**. The **Truman Presidential Museum and Library**, on US-24 and Delaware St (Mon–Wed & Sat 9am–5pm, Thurs 9am–9pm, Sun noon–5pm; $7), includes a reconstruction of his White House office, and chilling documents pertaining to the development of the atomic bomb. The **Victorian Truman Home**, a mile south at 219 N Delaware St (daily 8.30am–5pm, in winter closed Mon; $4; purchase tickets at museum), is decorated as it was when it functioned as the summer White House.

Fifteen miles northeast of Kansas City, on the Old Town Square of **LIBERTY**, Jesse James staged the first-ever daylight bank robbery in 1866 in what's now the **Jesse James Bank Museum**, 103 N Water St, (Mon–Sat 10am–4pm; $5). Among the memorabilia and dusty relics of early banking, you can see the vault and the safe the outlaw raided.

St Joseph

Sixty miles north of Kansas City, **ST JOSEPH** boomed as a supply depot for the California Gold Rush, and today is a busy manufacturing town. For a brief eighteen months, beginning in 1860, it was the home of the legendary **Pony Express**, which delivered mail to Sacramento, California, by continuous horseback relay in ten days. The Pony Express was a financial disaster, driven out of business by its inability to compete with the transcontinental telegraph, but riders such as Buffalo Bill Cody went on to become legends. Charlie Miller, the last of the riders, rode from New York to San Francisco in 1931, and died aged 105 in 1955. The full story is told in lively dioramas at the **Pony Express Museum**, 914 Penn St (Mon–Sat 9am–5pm, Sun 1–5pm; $4), which is attractively set in the company's original stables.

It was in St Joseph, on April 3, 1882, that the notorious **Jesse James** was shot in the back by Robert Ford, a 20-year-old member of his own gang who had negotiated a $10,000 reward from the governor. Countless books and films have portrayed Jesse James as a latter-day Robin Hood; in fact, he spent most of the Civil War riding with a band of Confederate guerrillas. The **Jesse James Home Museum** (June–Nov Mon–Sat 10am–5pm, Sun 1–5pm; Nov–May Mon–Sat 10am–4pm, Sun 1–4pm; $4), the one-story frame cottage where James was living incognito while he planned his next bank job, now stands at 12th and Penn streets, having been moved closer to the main highway in the hope of attracting sightseers. A ragged hole in the wall is pointed out as the spot where the bullet supposedly hit, after striking James as he was hanging a picture; you can also see where bloodstained splinters were chiseled from the floor to be sold as souvenirs. As for the assassin, Ford was himself gunned down ten years later, and his killer in turn was also shot.

There are thirteen **museums** in town, most about the Old West, but none really warrants lingering, though the one next to the James home does purport to contain the world's largest ball of twine. If you do want to leave the drive to Kansas City or Omaha for another day, you'll find **motels** strung along I-29 as it passes east of downtown, including a *Motel 6* (☏816/232-2311; ❷) and a *Days Inn* at the intersection with Frederick Blvd (☏816/279-1671; ❸).

Southwest Missouri – Ozark country

There's little to see south of Kansas City before the **Ozark Mountains**. Occupying most of southern Missouri and northern Arkansas (see p.603), the area remained frontier territory until the timber companies moved in at the end of the nineteenth century. When they moved on, the hill-dwellers were left to eke out a living from the denuded terrain; severe droughts forced many to leave for the cities. For those who remain, fishing resorts and tourist attractions supply some work, though the region remains poor. None of the Ozark peaks are particularly high, though the roads through them switch, dip, climb, and swerve to provide **stunning views** of steep hillsides thick with oak, elm, hickory, and redbud, all quite resplendent in the fall. **Springfield** is the region's main city, 130 miles south of Kansas City, but the gateway to the Ozarks, the country music town of **Branson**, is more popular by far.

Branson

Nestled among beautiful Ozark lakes, the resort of **BRANSON**, forty miles south of Springfield on US-65, is one of the top tourist destinations in the United States. Over seven million visitors a year are attracted to what's become known as the "Ozark Disneyland" for its forty-nine music venues (almost all of a country or nostalgia bent), a few theme parks, and lots of good old family fun.

"**The Strip**," until recently merely Hwy-76, looks like it was thrown together with a pitchfork – a hideous agglomeration of theme parks and theaters owned and/or performed in by "big-name" stars. The spectrum ranges from Japanese fiddler Shoji Tabuchi and ancient crooner Andy Williams to superb acts like Alison Krauss and Union Station. **Tickets** for a two-hour show are fairly priced at around $20. There's no shortage of takers in summer for most, if not all, of the town's 57,000 seats – a figure said to exceed that of Nashville. Branson shows are firmly geared toward families; you won't find anything remotely edgy or avant-garde, although the *Ripley's Believe It or Not* performance is a step in a new direction.

When you've had it with Branson, escape to nearby **Table Rock Lake**, a scenic area offering hiking, biking, camping, water-skiing, and world-class fishing.

Practicalities

Greyhound connects Branson with Springfield, Kansas City, and Memphis. Call ahead, or drop in at the local **Chamber of Commerce**, at the intersection of Hwy-65 and Hwy-248 (Mon–Sat 8am–6pm, Sun 10am–4pm; ☎417/334-4084 or 1-800/214-3661, ⓦwww.explorebranson.com), or at the **North Welcome Center** (Mon–Sat 8am–5pm, Sun 10am–4pm) at 4910 Hwy 65, for a copy of their show guide detailing performance schedules of all the theaters. During the high season (May–Oct), **hotel** prices rise, especially on weekends, but you can still find some bargains. Branson Vacation Reservations (☎1-800/221-5692) will try to sell you a package deal, but can also book you into a motel, including one of three *Best Westerns* (☎1-800/528-1234; ❹). The Ozark Mountain Country B&B, Box 295, Branson, MO 65616 (☎1-800/695-1546), is another reliable **reservation service**, but if you're visiting in the main season call at least a week in advance. Table Rock State Park (☎417/334-4704) has **campsites** for $8-$17. Most places to **eat** are of the family-diner ilk. *McGuffey's* on the Strip (☎417/336-3600), and the down-home cookin' at *The Farmhouse Restaurant*, downtown (☎417/334-9791), are both good options.

Kansas

KANSAS may be associated with quaint, gingham-pinafore images from *Little House on the Prairie* and *The Wizard of Oz*, but the region was at one time known as "bleeding Kansas." The 1854 **Kansas-Nebraska Act**, which gave both territories the right to self-determination over slavery, led to fierce clashes between Free Staters and pro-slavery forces. Runaway slaves from the South were given passage through the area, aided by abolitionist John Brown, and Kansas eventually joined the Union as a free state.

After the Civil War, the mighty cattle drives from Texas made towns like Abilene, Wichita, and Dodge City centers of the "**Wild West**." The debauched, masculine image of the West, spawning such "heroes" as Wyatt Earp and Wild Bill Hickok, is, however, challenged in Kansas, which, as well as being the first state to give women the vote in municipal elections, boasts the nation's first female mayor and senator – though its politics have taken a decidedly conservative turn in recent years, with the Kansas school board removing evolution from the science curriculum.

In 1874, Russian Mennonites brought the grain that was to transform the state into the bountiful "breadbasket" that now harvests most of the nation's wheat. However, only in the west do miles of golden stalks sway in Kansas's infamous gusty wind. The green and hilly northeast, patterned with woods and lakes, is home to the unattractive, industrial capital city of Topeka, liberal college town **Lawrence**, and the dull suburbs of Kansas City (though downtown lies across the state line in Missouri). The once-wicked cowtown of **Dodge City** is in the southwest, while **Wichita**, the state's largest city, lies in the south-central area.

Getting around Kansas

Greyhound **buses** run to all Kansas's main cities, supplemented by erratic smaller companies; services to the west and southwest are especially poor. Amtrak **trains** head east–west between LA and Chicago through the center of the state, calling, usually in the middle of the night, at Lawrence, Topeka, Newton (for Wichita, but without a connecting service), Hutchinson, Dodge City, and Garden City. Wichita has the state's biggest **airport**, but you may find flights to **Missouri's Kansas City International Airport** more convenient.

East Kansas

Undulating **east Kansas** is laced with lakes, streams, and rivers. The northeast, once crossed by the Oregon, Santa Fe, and Smoky Hill trails, and now home to both Topeka and Lawrence, is more heavily visited than the southeast, where the major attraction is the Little House on the Prairie historical site, located 13 miles southwest of Independence on Hwy-75. The heritage of Kansas's four Indian tribes comes alive in annual powwows, held in major towns as well as the northwestern reservations.

Lawrence

The mellow town of **LAWRENCE** lies on the Kansas River, roughly halfway between Kansas City and Topeka. Tree-lined streets, a welcoming historic downtown, and an aura of old-hippie artsiness make it an appealing destination, with a cultural energy owed in part to the **University of Kansas** (home of the Jayhawk, the mythical bird which is the emblem of its sports teams), and a long liberal and intellectual history. Founded by the New England Emigrant Aid Company in 1854, and a center of Free State activities, Lawrence was the site of a violent Civil War skirmish in 1863, when Missouri Confederate guerrilla William Quantrill led about three hundred men against the town, killing over 150, wounding hundreds more, and setting the place ablaze. Rebuilding was quick, however, as evidenced by the limestone and brick buildings of today's downtown, centered on Massachusetts Street, and the KU campus, which stands on a steep, tree-covered grassy bank known as Mount Oread.

Arrival, information, and accommodation

Amtrak comes into Lawrence at 413 E 7th St, and **Greyhound** arrives at 2447 W 6th St. The **visitor center** is north of downtown in the renovated Union Pacific Depot, at N 2nd and Locust streets (Mon–Sat 8.30am–5.30pm; Sun 1–5pm; ☎785/865-4499 or 1-888/LAWKANS, ⓦwww.visitlawrence.com).

Comfy **rooms**, which include a good breakfast, can be found near the bus station at the *Hampton Inn*, 2300 W 6th St (☎785/841-4994; ❹), while the *EconoLodge* practically next door at 2222 W 6th St (☎785/842-7030; ❸) is a reliable fall back. If you have a little extra cash, head instead to the lovely all-suite *Eldridge Hotel*, at 7th and Massachusetts streets (☎785/749-5011 or 1-800/527-0909; ❻); twice burned down by pro-slavery forces, it has been restored to an evocative elegance, and houses the stylish *Ten* restaurant (☎785/749-5011) and the atmospheric *Jayhawker* bar in the lobby. You can camp near downtown at *KOA*, 1473 Hwy-40 (☎785/842-3877; $23 per tent site), or three miles out along W 23rd St at Clinton Lake State Park, where the vehicle fee is $7 and a tent site $8.50 (☎785/842-8562).

The Town

Studded with cafés and eclectic shops, downtown Lawrence is a delight to walk around – and just as busy outside of term time, when day-trippers flock in from less congenial Kansas cities. However, most of the town's formal attractions are clustered on campus. The **University of Kansas Natural History Museum**, on Jayhawk Blvd, at 14th St (Mon–Sat 9am–5pm, Sun noon–5pm; $3 suggested donation), holds a chronological panorama of North American flora and fauna, as well as the now-stuffed horse Comanche, the lone survivor of Custer's cavalry at the Battle of Little Bighorn. The **Spencer Museum of Art**, 1301 Mississippi St (Tues, Wed, Fri & Sat 10am–5pm, Thurs 10am–9pm, Sun noon–5pm; free), specializes in world art, with an Oriental gallery, Old Masters, and a pre-Raphaelite masterpiece.

Native American traditions are preserved and packaged for the public each year by the exhibitions of the **Lawrence Indian Arts Show**, held the second weekend in September at the **Haskell Indian Nations University** at 23rd and Massachusetts streets. Also on campus are the **Hiawatha Visitor Center** and **American Indian Athletic Hall of Fame**, open year-round (☎785/749-8404).

Eating, drinking, and entertainment

As befits a college town, the **restaurant** scene in Lawrence is dominated by inexpensive eats. **Nightlife**, too, is defined by the students, who can be found in droves along Massachusetts Street. As for the **performing arts**, one of the better places to investigate is Liberty Hall, 642 Massachusetts St (☎785/749-1972). Once a social and political center, this building housed Lawrence's first newspaper until pro-slavery agitators burned it down in 1863. Today it puts on art-house films, plays, and concerts.

Free State Brewing Co. 636 Massachusetts St ☎785/843-4555. Trendy brewpub serving award-winning amber beer and robust steaks.

Jazzhaus 926 Massachusetts St ☎785/749-3320. As the name suggests, this dimly-lit bar hosts weekend jazz gigs.

La Parilla 814 Massachusetts St ☎785/841-1100. There's always a line out the door for this tasty, reasonably priced Latin American joint.

Pachamama's 800 New Hampshire St ☎785/841-0990. Emphasizing seasonal and organic food, the eclectic and well-executed menu changes nearly monthly at this upscale downtown eatery.

Teller's 746 Massachusetts St ☎785/843-4111. Excellent nachos and pizza served in a beautifully restored bank building.

WheatFields 904 Vermont St ☎785/841-5553. All of the delectable pastries and artisan breads are made in-house at this cozy downtown bakery. Lunch and dinner specials are also offered.

West through Kansas

Further west across Kansas, three towns recreate the state's Wild West heritage, although only in the westernmost, **Dodge City**, does the scrubby landscape conform to the cowboy-movie image. **Abilene**, if less famous than Dodge City, has as many outlaw and gunslinger stories, and **Wichita**, about two hundred miles southwest of Kansas City, holds an excellent, authentic reconstruction of frontier days in its Old Cowtown Museum.

Abilene

Like all the old cattle-trail cowtowns, **ABILENE**, 115 miles west of Lawrence on I-70, claims to have been the most riproaring of the lot. By the time legendary lawman Wild Bill Hickok became its marshal in 1871, the unruly behavior was already dying down, and little today reminds you of those raucous days.

These days, Abilene prefers to stress its connections with **Dwight Eisenhower**. The **Eisenhower Center**, 201 SE Fourth St (daily: May–mid-Aug 8am–5.45pm; mid-Aug–April 9am-4.45pm), encompasses his boyhood home, with its original furnishings, the obligatory film, and many photos and papers on display in the spacious museum ($8). The former president and his wife are buried in the meditation chapel.

Abilene's **visitor center** is at 201 NW Second St (Mon–Sat 9am–6pm, Sun noon-6pm; ☎785/263-2231 or 1-800/569-5915). Most of the town's budget **motels** are off I-70 at Hwy-15. The very basic *Budget Lodge*, 101 NW 14th St (☎785/263-3600; ❶), has faded but clean rooms, not far from the I-70 exit. The *Best Western President's Inn*, 2210 N. Buckeye (☎785/263-2050; ❸) offers comfortable rooms closer to the I-70 exit.

Wichita

WICHITA, about 165 miles southwest of Lawrence on I-35, is the largest city in Kansas, split by the Arkansas River, which forks just north of downtown into the Big and Little Arkansas rivers (incidentally, Kansans take umbrage if you pronounce it "Arkansaw"; pronounce it here the way it is spelled). Originally settled by the Wichita Indians, who by 1865 had been relocated to Oklahoma Indian Territory, Wichita grew up as a stop on the Chisholm Trail, a Texas-to-Kansas cattle route. Its glory days were to be short-lived, however, as farmers, angry about the damage done by stampeding cattle, erected fences, which forced the drives onto different trails further west, creating new cowtowns such as Dodge City. Today the city, already supporting a rich arts scene, has been invigorated with a downtown revival.

The City

Downtown Wichita is enlivened mainly by the public art and sculpture that pops up unexpectedly all over the place, in empty lots and even in tree stumps. The exceptional **Wichita-Sedgwick County Historical Museum**, 204 S Main St (Tues–Fri 11am–4pm, Sat & Sun 1–5pm; $4; ⓦwww.wichitahistory.org), is in **Old City Hall**, a heavy stone building decorated with turrets, gargoyles, and arches. The cozy interior is crammed with exhibits on everything from the Wichita Indians through decorative art to Carry Nation, who campaigned against everything from tobacco to corsets. The stately church with vivid stained-glass windows at 601 N Water St houses the **Kansas African American Museum** (Tues–Fri 10am–5pm, Sun 2–6pm; $4; ⓦwww.thekansasafricanamericanmuseum .org), an eclectic antidote to more mainstream views of Great Plains history, with details on Buffalo Soldiers, inventors from across the country, early black Wichitans, and some African art.

Excellent museums in the Riverside stretch of parkland (which also holds walking and bike trails) include the **Indian Center and Museum**, 650 N Seneca Drive (Tues–Sat 10am–4pm; $7; ⓦwww.theindiancenter.org). The 44ft *Keeper of the Plains* statue, facing east at the confluence of the Little and Big Arkansas rivers, was designed in the 1970s by a Kiowa-Comanche artist, Blackbear Bosin. Native Americans and city officials smoked the peace pipe at its dedication ceremony. The museum itself is small, with changing exhibits of traditional and contemporary Native American art.

Western artist C.M. Russell is the best represented of the veritable who's who of American painters assembled at the **Wichita Art Museum**, 1400 West Museum Blvd

(Tues–Sat 10am–5pm, Sun noon–5pm; $5, Sat free; Ⓦ www.wichitaartmuseum
.org). **Old Cowtown Museum**, 1871 Sim Park Drive (Apr–Oct Mon–Sat 10am–
5pm, Sun noon–5pm; $7.75), is a seventeen-acre riverside exhibit recreating the
buildings of 1870s Wichita. Looking and feeling like a movie set, the area includes
– along with some docile longhorns – the city's first one-room jail, a schoolroom,
a store, a smithy, churches, stables, and old homes.

   To the north of the city, the surreal geodesic **Bright Spot for Health Center**,
3100 N Hillside Ave (Mon–Thurs 8am–5pm; free), houses the **Center for the
Improvement of Human Functioning**, which aims, by using holistic medicine, to
find a cure for cancer. It's all very worthy, but weird: road signs, for example, tell you
to "de-stress to 25." In the southeast of the city, the products of Wichita's airplane
industry are on display at the **Kansas Aviation Museum**, in the old Art Deco air
terminal at 3350 George Washington Blvd (Tues–Fri 9am–4pm, Sat 1–5pm; $5;
Ⓦ www.kansasaviationmuseum.org). A more interesting detour is to **Hutchinson**
(on Hwy-50, 45 miles northwest of Wichita), for the **Kansas Cosmosphere and
Space Center** (Mon–Sat 9am–9pm, Sun noon–9pm; Ⓦ www.cosmo.org; $13
includes IMAX and planetarium;), which features, among other aerospace paraphernalia, the *Apollo 13* command module.

Practicalities

Domestic **flights** arrive at the Mid-Continent Airport, five miles southwest
of downtown on Hwy-54 (W Kellogg Drive). **Amtrak** stops at Newton, a
small Mennonite town 25 miles north, with a local bus connection to Wichita
throughout the day; **Greyhound** comes in to 312 S Broadway Ave, two blocks
east of Main Street. **City transportation** consists of **buses** (WMTA; $1 per ride;
Ⓣ 316/265-7221) and, more appealingly, **trolleys**, which run from 11am–3pm
during the week and on Saturdays for just 25¢. The resourceful **CVB** is in the heart
of downtown at Douglas Avenue and Main Street (Mon–Fri 7.45am–5.15pm;
Ⓣ 316/265-2800 or 1-800/288-9424, Ⓦ www.visitwichita.com). City trolley
tours ($10; June–Aug Thurs–Sat 10am) depart from CityArts, 334 N Mead, as
well.

   Inexpensive **lodgings** in Wichita are plentiful, especially near the airport on W
Kellogg Drive – try the *Super 8* at no. 6245 (Ⓣ 316/945-5261; ❸). On the opposite flank of the city is a good *Fairfield Inn*, 333 S Webb Rd (Ⓣ 316/685-3777; ❸).
More upscale, the *Hotel at Oldtown*, at First and Mosley streets (Ⓣ 316/267-4800;
❼–❽), has a stylish turn-of-the-twentieth-century flavor and perfect location.
Nine miles from town, *Blasi Campground*, 11209 W Hwy-54 (Ⓣ 316/722-2681),
offers tent sites for $21.50.

   There are a horde of **restaurants**, **clubs**, and **bars** around the quaint Old Town
Marketplace. Good places to eat include the *River City Brewing Co*, 150 N Mosley
St (Ⓣ 316/263-2739), which has good Kansas steaks, locally brewed beer, and
sandwiches. The *Old Mill Tasty Shop*, by the railroad tracks at 604 E Douglas Ave
(Ⓣ 316/264-6500), serves great sandwiches and Southwestern food. *The Brickyard*
at 125 N Rock Island St (Wed–Sun; Ⓣ 316/263-4044) is an American-style restaurant with a huge patio where rock, jazz, and blues bands perform most nights; the
biggest discotheque is *America's Pub*, at 116 N Mead St (Ⓣ 316/267-1782).

Dodge City

DODGE CITY, 150 miles west of Wichita, is perhaps the most famous of all
America's cowtowns. It has certainly been committed to celluloid more times than
any other, especially in 1930s Westerns like *My Darling Clementine* and *Dodge City*.
However, this wildest of Wild West cities had a heyday of only a decade, from

1875 until 1886. Established in 1872 along with the Santa Fe Railroad, which transported the hides of millions of Plains buffalo, by 1875 the town of traders, trappers, and hunters had to find a new economic base – the buffalo had been exterminated. The era of the great cattle drives was already under way, and Dodge City became a den of iniquity where gambling, drinking, and general lawlessness were the norm. Such wickedness led to gunfights galore, and the notorious Boot Hill cemetery (where the villains were buried with their boots on) was kept busy by charismatic, morally suspect lawmen such as Bat Masterson and Wyatt Earp.

The Town

Dodge City today is rather more staid, with its old downtown area enveloped by a hinterland of railroad tracks and giant silos. Outside of the **Dodge City Days and Rodeo** (ⓌW www.dodgecityroundup.com), held in late July or early August, the town is content to replay its movie image in the **Boot Hill Museum**, 400 Front Street (June–Aug daily 8am–8pm; Sept–May Mon–Sat 9am–5pm, Sun 1–5pm; $7, $8 in summer). The museum centers on the single-sided **Historic Front Street**, which was constructed in 1958 and has been acquiring old buildings from all over the West ever since. There's a bank and a grocer, stagecoach rides, a funeral parlor, a smithy, and even a full-sized railroad station, as well as the *Long Branch Saloon*, scene of a variety show with cancan dancers every night at 7.30pm ($6.95; summer only). **Boot Hill cemetery** is higher up the hill, still on museum grounds; there's just a sorry little patch of lawn on one corner of the original site, which was in any case abandoned in 1879 after just six years and thirty-four burials. The bodies were reinterred elsewhere, and as the graves were never marked in the first place, the wooden crosses in the cemetery are more than a little bogus.

Other sights in town include the **Mueller-Schmidt Home of Stone**, 112 E Vine St (June–Aug Mon–Sat 9am–5pm, Sun 2–4pm; free), an emotive memorial to pioneer mothers, often forgotten amid the macho Wild West myth-making. The house looks pretty much as it would have when built in 1881, with domestic memorabilia that belonged to early plainswomen. **El Capitan**, at Second St and

△ Dodge City, KS

Wyatt Earp Blvd, is a massive bronze longhorn, facing south towards an identical north-facing statue in Abilene, Texas. Together they mark the beginning and the end of the cattle drives.

Practicalities

Amtrak comes right into downtown, to the historic and renovated Santa Fe Station at Central Ave and Wyatt Earp Blvd. The **CVB** at 400 W Wyatt Earp Blvd (summer daily 8.30am–6.30pm; winter Mon–Fri 8.30am–5pm; ☎620/225-8186 or 1-800/653-9378, ⓦ www.visitdodgecity.org) can offer advice on tourist activities. The Dodge City Trolley runs narrated town **tours** ($6) four times a day, in summer only, from a booth on the Boot Hill parking lot.

Most of Dodge City's **motels** are spread out roughly a mile west of downtown along US-50, still known here as Wyatt Earp Boulevard. The *Budget Host Inn* at no. 2200 (☎620/227-8146; ❷–❸) is inexpensive but a little noisy; the *Dodge House* at no. 2408 (☎620/225-9900; ❸) has a reliable restaurant; and the *EconoLodge* at no. 1610 (☎620/225-0231; ❷–❸) has an indoor pool and sauna area. **Camping** is an option even for the car-less: the lakeside *Water Sports Campground Recreation*, 500 Cherry St (☎620/225-8044; $17 tent sites), lies ten blocks south of Front Street. If you feel like some Western-style fun, head for the *Marchel Ranch*, 10873 W Hwy-50 (☎620/227-7307), a small ranch offering a Wild West show and chuckwagon dinner.

As for **food**, *Marchel Ranch Restaurant*, in town at 2408 W Wyatt Earp (☎620/227-6151), offers a more varied menu than the one on offer at the show, with soups, salads, and steaks. *Peppercorns*, out near the motels at 1301 W Wyatt Earp Blvd (☎620/225-2335), is a conventional highway steakhouse with meals for about $13.

Iowa

Although at times serene, and almost always verdant, nothing about **IOWA** truly stands out. The state is the very essence of smalltown America, close to the geographical center of the mainland US, and ranking decidedly average in size, population, and level of personal income. Even the cities seem at times to be merely villages grown large.

Iowa's history, too, has been relatively uneventful. It was opened for settlement after the **Black Hawk Treaty** of 1832, a one-sided exercise in negotiation with the Sauk Indians, conducted after many of them had been chased down and slaughtered in neighboring Wisconsin and Illinois. The Northern European immigrants who replaced them made agricultural development their prime concern, turning the Iowa countryside into the rolling corn farms so common today.

Tourist attractions in Iowa are few and far between; the state's most visited destination is the throwback Germanic enclave of the **Amana Colonies**. However, Iowa does hold a few oddball sites, such as the original locations for the movies *The Bridges of Madison County* (in south-central **Winterset**, birthplace of **John Wayne**) and *Field of Dreams* (near **Dubuque** in the northeast). You can also see, but not enter, the original house that featured in Grant Wood's much-parodied *American Gothic* painting (at Eldon in the southeast, and now owned by the state).

Greyhound buses out of Chicago call at all of Iowa's major towns. Daily buses also run from St Louis to Des Moines and Iowa City; these towns are connected less frequently with Minneapolis/St Paul. **Amtrak**'s east–west route misses the cities, stopping instead at assorted small communities in the south. The only sizeable **airport** is in Des Moines.

Somewhat surprisingly, Iowa is a good place for **cycle touring**. Each year the extremely popular cross-state bike ride – the Register's Annual Great Bike Ride Across Iowa, or the **RAGBRAI** – attracts thousands of entrants, any of whom can tell you that the Plains aren't always flat (tour details ☎1-800/474-3342, ⓦwww.ragbrai.org).

Eastern Iowa

Eastern Iowa, in the Mississippi River hinterland, is liberally sprinkled with agribusiness towns that display the continuing influence of their central and northern European pioneers, plus **religious communities** – Amish, Mennonite, and the Amana Colonies. All are easily accessible from **Iowa City**; as home to a huge university it's one of the state's livelier centers. Riverside towns such as northerly **Dubuque** and Burlington, near the Missouri state line, have been enlivened since 1991 by **gambling**, though so far games can only be played on board Mississippi paddle-wheelers, decked out in less-than-authentic Mark Twain–era trimmings.

Dubuque

The handsome town of **DUBUQUE**, overlooked by rocky bluffs on the Mississippi around 150 miles west of Chicago, was founded as the first white settlement in Iowa by French-Canadian lead miners in 1788. In the nineteenth century it became a boisterous river port and logging center. Buildings from this era still stand, but the companies that use them are in meatpacking and other food industries.

A complex of buildings at Third Street in the old Ice Harbor area, cut off from downtown by Hwy-61, includes an assortment of river-related **museums** (daily 10am–5.30pm; $9.95). Precisely which exhibits are housed in the **Mississippi River Museum**, the **Riverboat Museum**, and the **National Rivers Hall of Fame** (which focuses on "Pathfinders" such as Lewis and Clark, rather than the rivers themselves) seems to vary, but together they tell the story of Mississippi navigation from the days of Robert Fulton's first commercial steamboat in 1807 until the floods of 1993. The fifteen-minute introductory film *River of Dreams* is a good starting point for your explorations. The complex completed a $188 million renovation in 2003 and includes an aquarium, hotel, and entertainment complex, among other attractions.

Once your appetite has been whetted, you can travel along the high-banked Mississippi on a *Spirit of Dubuque* **paddle-wheeler cruise** (May–Oct daily; $14.25 for 90min; ☎563/583-8093 or 1-800/747-8093; ⓦwww.dubuque-riverrides.com), or on board one of the more expensive **gambling boats**. Alternatively, what's said to be the world's shortest and steepest **cable-car ride** (April–Nov daily 8am–10pm; $1 one-way, $2 roundtrip) grinds its way from Fourth Street downtown up a sheer bluff to **Fenelon Place**, a residential street of old money and Victorian architecture. The top offers a sweeping view across the Mississippi to Illinois and Wisconsin. If cable cars don't appeal, then head north to the lovingly maintained, 164-acre **Eagle Point Park** (daily May–Oct 7am–10pm; $1 per car), set on bluffs high above the river.

Film buffs who enjoyed the 1989 baseball fantasy *Field of Dreams* can meet like-minded souls in surprising numbers at the original movie location, three miles north of Dyersville, which is 25 miles west of Dubuque on US-20. True to the movie's catchphrase – "if you build it, they will come" – crowds still gather on the bleachers to watch phantom games at the edge of the cornfields (April–Nov daily 9am–6pm).

Practicalities

The **Iowa Welcome Center** at 300 Main St (daily 9.30am–5.30pm; ☎563/556-4372 or 1-800/798-8844, ⓦwww.traveldubuque.com) is the best place to pick up information on Dubuque. As for places to **stay**, try the *Richards House B&B*, 1492 Locust St (☎563/557-1492; ❹), which is well-managed and has a homey, Victorian feel. Bargain hunters might want to stay at the grand redbrick *Julien Inn*, 200 Main St (☎563/556-4200 or 1-800/798-7098; ❷–❺), which was once owned by mobster Al Capone; he used it as his safe house when trouble was brewing in Chicago. Picturesque **campsites** can be found at Miller Riverview Park, off Greyhound Park Road (☎563/589-4238; $10 per tent site). The *Shot Tower Inn*, at the foot of the cable car at Fourth and Locust streets (☎563/556-1061), serves a standard menu of pizzas and meat dishes. *Café Manna Java*, 269 Main St (☎563/588-3105), offers great baked goods and coffee.

Cedar Rapids

Seventy miles southwest of Dubuque, **CEDAR RAPIDS**, home of Quaker Oats, is Iowa's industrial leader. In the late 1840s, a meatpacking boom lured thousands of Czechs here. The **National Czech & Slovak Museum**, 16th Ave SW and First St (May–Oct Mon–Sat 9.30–4pm, Sun noon–4pm; Nov–April Tues–Sat 9.30am–4pm, Sun noon–4pm; $7; ☎319/362-8500), features gift shops, traditional houses, and a new museum of national costumes and immigrant artifacts. The very modern **Museum of Art**, 410 Third Ave SE (Tues, Wed, Fri & Sat 10am–5pm, Thurs 10am–8pm, Sun noon–5pm; $6), boasts a comprehensive collection of paintings by Grant Wood, best known for his depictions of 1930s farm life.

Cedar Rapids' **CVB** is based at 119 First Ave SE (Mon–Fri 8am–5pm; ☎319/398-5009 or 1-800/735-5557, ⓦwww.cedar-rapids.com). For reasonably priced **rooms**, there's the *Best Western Cooper's Mill*, 100 F Ave NW (☎319/366-5323 or 1-800/858-5511; ❹).

The Amana Colonies

The **Amana Colonies** are situated at the intersection of Hwy-151 and Hwy-220, midway between Cedar Rapids and Iowa City. They were founded in 1855 by the **Community of True Inspiration**, pacifist German refugees (not linked to the Amish or Mennonites) who believed that God spoke through prophets – themselves, for example – rather than ordained ministers. Members led a simple, collective lifestyle: each family lived in its own home, but they all ate together and shared profits from the farms. During the Depression, communal ownership became increasingly difficult to maintain, and in 1932 stock was redistributed among all the adults. However, they did keep up their commitment to close family ties, a sense of community, and religious principles.

The Amana Colonies today, consisting of seven separate villages set in an immaculate, serene valley, feel like a cross between a ski resort with no mountains and a reservation for Midwestern pioneers. Their prosperity is very evident, though in addition to tasteful clapboard houses standing on well-groomed lawns, and neat plank fences dividing rolling meadows, you'll also come across factories, pizza parlors, and even a golf course. It's geared less toward families and more toward Iowan couples on a weekend getaway. The twee streets of the largest village, **Amana**, are lined with restaurants and craft shops, a brewery, several wineries, and a woolen mill – plus a small **Museum of History** (Mon–Sat 10am–5pm, April–Nov also Sun noon–5pm; $7).

Picturesque and less commercialized **Homestead**, three miles south of Amana, is enhanced by a 3.5-mile walking trail around a dam on a scenic bend of the Iowa River, built centuries ago by Indians to concentrate fish into one area.

Practicalities

Conventional addresses are seldom used in the Amana Colonies, but points of interest are well signposted. The **visitor center**, in Amana at 622 46th Ave (Mon–Sat 9am–5pm, Sun 10am–5pm; ☎319/622-7622 or 1-800/579-2294, ⓦ www.amanacolonies.com) has details on the many local **B&Bs**. There are **tent spaces** at the *Amana Colonies RV Park* (☎319/622-7616; $12 per tent site). Across the road from the RV park, The Old Creamery Theatre Company hosts afternoon and evening theater (☎1-800/352-6262 for schedule; $22) five nights a week.

Probably the most compelling reason to visit the colonies is their undeniably excellent old-style **German food**. The *Ox Yoke Inn* (☎319/668-1443) in Amana village dishes up family-style meals of fried chicken, potatoes, sauerkraut and the like; for a lighter snack, call in at *Hahn's Hearth Oven Bakery* in Middle Amana (☎319/622-3439). As alcohol is not prohibited, some eateries, like the *Ronnenberg Restaurant and Bar* (☎319/622-3641), are also popular for locally produced **wine**.

Iowa City and West Branch

IOWA CITY, on I-80 55 miles west of the Mississippi, is refreshingly young at heart. The gold-domed **Old Capitol** is a reminder of its days as state capital, before government was transferred to the more central Des Moines. Residents were placated by getting the **University of Iowa** instead. The arty shops and sidewalk cafés of the compact downtown touch the east end of campus, but its red and gray buildings, closeted by tall dark trees, remain aloof from the rest of the town.

About 12 miles east of Iowa City, the tiny Quaker town of **WEST BRANCH** attracts a steady stream of traffic from I-80 for its **Herbert Hoover Library & Museum** (daily 9am–5pm; $6). Informative exhibits and a documentary film cover Hoover's youthful adventures in China, his presidential victory and subsequent disgrace when the nation blamed him for the Great Depression, and his comeback after World War II as the leader of the European humanitarian relief effort. A self-guided **walking tour** begins at the library and includes Hoover's birthplace, a replica of his father's blacksmith shop, and the Friends Meetinghouse where he attended Sunday services.

Practicalities

Greyhound stops at 170 E Court St, right downtown. The **CVB** is at 900 First Ave in Coralville, a little over a mile northeast of downtown (☎319/337-6592 or 1-800/283-6592, ⓦ www.icccvb.org). *Iowa House* is a comfortable central **hotel** in the student union building, beside the river on Madison Street (☎319/335-3513; ❹). To the west, inexpensive **motels** in Coralville include the very clean and good-value *Super 8*, 611 First Ave (☎319/337-8388; ❸). The *Coralville Park*, three miles north of I-80 at exit 242 (℡1-877/444-6777), is a good place to cast a fishing line, has a Devonian-era fossil bed, and offers grassy **tent sites** for $10. Inexpensive **food** is easy to find, be it the pastries and espressos served on long comfortable sofas at *Java House*, 211 E Washington St (℡319/341-0012); or the burgers at *Micky's*, 11 S Dubuque St (℡319/338-6860), a friendly, dimly-lit Irish bar. For something a little more upscale, the *Atlas World Grill*, 127 Iowa Ave (℡319/341-7700) serves great eclectic dishes, from macaroni and cheese to Jamaican jerk chicken.

Central and western Iowa

Pigs outnumber people in **central Iowa**. The only city among the cornfields, state capital **Des Moines**, struggles to lift the monotony, and many visitors may prefer the college town of **Ames**. The humdrum west has little to offer.

Des Moines

DES MOINES, near the center of Iowa amid tree-covered hills at the confluence of the sluggish Des Moines and Raccoon rivers, owes its origins to a military fort set up in 1843. The area had already grown into a trading center for farmers by the time the 18-year-old Frederick Hubbell arrived in 1855; within a decade he had founded the Equitable Life and Insurance Corporation to service their need for investment capital. Other companies soon realized the potential of agrarian business, and today the city is the world's third-largest **insurance center**, behind London and Hartford, Connecticut. Illustrious former denizens of Des Moines include President **Ronald Reagan**, who started out as a sportscaster on Radio WHO, and arch-cowboy **John Wayne**, who was born and raised in nearby **Winterset**.

Arrival, information, and accommodation

Des Moines' **Greyhound** station is just northwest of downtown at 1107 Keosauqua Way. From the very efficient transfer depot at Sixth Ave and Walnut St, **MTA buses** ($1.25; ℡515/283-8100) run practically everywhere in the city. The **CVB** is at 400 Locust St, suite 265 (Mon–Fri 8.30am–5pm; ℡515/286-4960 or 1-800/451-2625, ⓦwww.seedesmoines.com).

Accommodation-wise, downtown Des Moines caters mostly to insurance company business, though there are still some fairly inexpensive places to stay. You can **camp** at Walnut Woods State Park, off Hwy-35 exit 68, where tent sites are $14.

Butler House 4507 Grand Ave ℡515/255-4096 or 1-866-455/4096. Lovely B&B, with whimsically decorated rooms, across the street from the Des Moines Art Center. ④–⑥
Hotel Fort Des Moines 1000 Walnut Ave at 10th St ℡515/243-1161 or 1-800/532-1466. Historical downtown gem with Old World elegance and exemplary service. The indoor swimming pool/spa area has won awards for its tasteful design. ④–⑦

Motel 6 4817 Fleur Drive ℡515/287-6364. Clean rooms near the airport. ②
Quality Inn & Suites 929 3rd St ℡515/282-5251. Reasonably priced downtown rooms. ④
Renaissance Savery Hotel 401 Locust St ℡515/244-2151. Modern hotel in the heart of downtown with comfortable rooms and touches from the early 1900s. ⑤–⑥

The City

The steel-and-glass skyline of **downtown** Des Moines, most of which shot up during the 1980s, is testimony to the town's ever-growing insurance business.

For such a fast-track financial center, the streets are curiously empty; pedestrians instead use the **Skywalk**, a three-mile network of air-conditioned corridors linking twenty blocks of offices, banks, parking lots, restaurants, hotels, and movie theaters.

Most businesses stand on the west bank of the Des Moines River, which cuts downtown in two. In 1857, a group of speculators attempted to shift the commercial hub to the east side by bribing commissioners to site the **state capitol** at E Ninth St and Grand Ave. Their hopes of huge spin-offs were dashed when the nationwide financial crash later that same year saw property prices collapse. As a result, the five-domed Italian Renaissance–style mass, on the crest of a steep hill, is now detached from the heart of the city (Mon–Fri 8am–4.30pm, Sat 9am–4pm; free; call for tour times ☎515/281-5591). A short walk downhill, in the futuristic pink-and-brown **State of Iowa Historical Building**, E Sixth and Locust streets (Tues–Sat 9am–4.30pm, Sun noon–4.30pm; free), are displays covering Indian civilization, pioneer times, and the development of Iowa farming, along with plenty of solemn portraits of former governors.

Three miles west, the impressive **Des Moines Art Center**, in a leafy suburb at 4700 Grand Ave (Tues, Wed, Fri & Sat 11am–4pm, Thurs 11am–9pm, Sun noon–4pm; free), is housed in a trio of buildings designed by world-renowned architects Eliel Saarinen, I.M. Pei, and Richard Meier. Works by Matisse, Picasso, and Renoir stand alongside twentieth-century Americans such as Wood, Hopper, and O'Keeffe. The most dynamic exhibits are in the Meier wing, including a gigantic and disturbing Anselm Kiefer canvas.

Eating, drinking, and nightlife

That Iowans eat well is reflected in the quality – and quantity – of food on offer in Des Moines' many **restaurants**. As for **nightlife**, most of it is confined to local watering holes – there's not much at all in the way of dance clubs or live music.

High Life Lounge 200 SW 2nd St ☎515/280-1965. Though just a few years old, this retro bar and grill has the feel of a long-time neighborhood fixture. The bar serves great roasted chicken and beer only produced before 1979.

Iowa Beef Steakhouse 1201 E Euclid Ave ☎515/262-1138. You'll leave this homey restaurant feeling full, thanks to huge steaks (like the 20-ounce New York strip) supplemented by a salad from the salad bar, a baked potato, and garlic bread.

Java Joe's 214 4th St ☎515/288-5282. Late-closing coffee bar and sandwich place, featuring live entertainment at weekends. Wireless Internet access available. Open until 11:30pm on weekdays, midnight on weekends.

Spaghetti Works 310 Court Ave ☎515/243-2195. Spacious Italian outfit with original interior decor (it has variously served as a glove factory, hat millinery, and fruit market). The all-you-care-to-eat pasta dishes from $5 are great value.

Stella's Blue Sky Diner 3281 100th St ☎515/727-4408. Kitsch diner decked out in lurid pink, turquoise, and yellow. Wash down burgers and fries with divine chocolate, peanut butter, and banana malts.

Around Des Moines

Ten miles west of downtown Des Moines, at I-80 exit 125, the **Living History Farms** in Urbandale (May–Oct daily 9am–5pm; $11) trace the evolution of agriculture on the Plains. Self-guided **tours** progress through five historic sites, from the oval bark homes of an eighteenth-century Iowan settlement, through an 1850s homestead, to a look at the high-tech methods of today. If you want to continue the rural theme, **eat** colossal portions of meat loaf and chops in the *Iowa Machine Shed Restaurant* (☎515/270-6818), or stay in the country-style *Comfort Suites Hotel* (☎515/276-1126; ❹); both are next to the farm entrance.

Thirty miles north of Des Moines, **Ames** is the home of **Iowa State University**. Smaller and slightly less trendy than Iowa City, it's still a lively little community (by Iowa standards, at least). The **visitor center**, 1601 Golden Aspen Drive, suite 110 (☎515/232-4032 or 1-800/288-7470, ⊛www.acvb.ames.ia.us), can advise on concerts and area attractions. **Room** rates are reasonable out at the *Super 8*, three miles from campus at I-35 and Hwy-30 (☎515/232-6510; ❸); *Hickory Park*, 1404 S Duff St (☎515/232-8940), is a popular barbecue joint.

Winterset

Until Robert Waller's *The Bridges of Madison County* changed everything, sleepy, rundown **WINTERSET**, 25 miles southwest of Des Moines, seemed a long way off the beaten path. The town's one tourist attraction was the modest former home of the local pharmacist at 216 S Second St (daily 10am–4.30pm; $3), run as a museum in tribute to his son, Marion Robert Morrison. Born in 1907, Morrison grew up to become Hollywood hardman **John Wayne**.

These days, Winterset's **visitor center**, on Courthouse Square in the heart of town (Mon–Fri 9am–5pm, Sat 9am–4pm, Sun noon–4pm; ☎515/462-1185 or 1-800/298-6119, ⊛www.madisoncounty.com), has become accustomed to handling inquiries from all over the world about the locations for Waller's tale. You can drive out to view the **covered bridges**; six (out of an original nineteen) nineteenth-century bridges still stand. Afterwards, you can have a meal in the old-style *Northside Café*, a few doors along from the visitor center, where Clint Eastwood was made to feel decidedly uncomfortable in the movie version of the book. A good time to visit Winterset is the second full weekend of October for the **Bridge Festival**, featuring local bands and artists. **Accommodation** possibilities nearby include the *Super 8*, 1312 Cedar Bridge Rd (☎515/462-4888 or 1-800/800-8000; ❸). There is a small **campground** at the Winterset City Park on the east end of town (☎515/462-3258; $10).

Nebraska

Though modern transcontinental travelers tend to see **NEBRASKA** in much the same light as those heading west during the Gold Rush did – as just another dreary expanse of prairie to get through as fast as possible – this flat and sparsely populated state in fact holds a few places of interest. However, a good three hundred miles of underwhelming, livestock-rearing flatlands separate its most appealing cities, commercial **Omaha** and the livelier state capital, **Lincoln**, from the western Panhandle, where the landscape finally erupts into giant sand hills and valleys, broken by towering rocky columns and hemmed in by sheer-faced buttes.

Western Nebraska was still embroiled in vicious and bloody battles against Native Americans long after the east had been settled; from the first serious uprising in 1854, it was thirty-six years before the US Army could make white control unchallengeable. Close to the South Dakota state line, **Fort Robinson**, where Crazy Horse was murdered, remains one of the West's most evocative historic sites.

Without navigable rivers, Nebraska had to rely on the **railroads** to help populate the land. During the 1870s and 1880s, rail companies, encouraged by grants that allowed them to accumulate one-sixth of the state, laid down such a comprehensive network of tracks that virtually every farmer was within a day's cattle drive of the nearest halt. Thus the buffalo-hunting country of the Sioux and Pawnee was turned into high-yield farmland, which today has few rivals in terms of beef production.

Getting around Nebraska

The Omaha **airport** offers the best domestic links, though planes from other cities in the region also fly to Lincoln. Several Greyhound **buses** traverse I-80 each day on the coast-to-coast marathon, stopping at all the major towns. Amtrak **trains**, traveling through the night, follow a similar route, calling at Omaha, Lincoln, Hastings, Holdrege, and McCook. **Driving** on I-80 can get tedious; if you're not in a rush, Scenic Hwy-2 (see p.813) is a good alternative.

Eastern Nebraska

The silt-laden Missouri River separates Nebraska from Iowa and Missouri to the east. There are few natural ports on this stretch, and **Omaha** remains the only riverfront community of any size. **Lincoln**, 58 miles southwest, is the state's capital and seat of its university.

Omaha

Although **OMAHA**, Nebraska's largest and most easterly city, has a great zoo, several museums, and a lively entertainment district, the atmosphere remains sedate and predominantly suburban. As a major terminus on the first transcontinental railroad, Omaha made a logical alternative to distant Chicago as a marketplace for Wyoming and Nebraska ranchers to sell their herds of **cattle**. By the end of the 19th century, massive stockyards had spread along the southern edge of town, and the city still handles well over one million head of livestock per year.

In downtown Omaha you'll find good bars and cafés along the cobbled streets of the **Old Market district**, plus interesting specialist shops such as the Antiquarian Bookstore, 1215 Harney St (☎402/341-8077), packed with dusty volumes. Train buffs will be impressed with the **Durham Western Heritage Museum**, converted from the Union Pacific Railroad station, at 801 S 10th St (Tues–Sat 10am–5pm, Sun 1pm–5pm; $6), where old train cars and huge model train sets are featured alongside a gallery of Omaha history. Behind its pink-marble Art Deco exterior, the **Joslyn Art Museum**, 2200 Dodge St (Tues–Sat 10am–4pm, Sun noon–4pm; $6, free Sat before noon), contains an eclectic selection of Indian art and twentieth-century American paintings.

Malcolm X was born in Omaha in May 1925, though his family moved to Michigan immediately thereafter, in the face of Ku Klux Klan death threats to his father, a preacher who followed the back-to-Africa teachings of Marcus Garvey. Omaha tourist authorities don't promote his **birthsite**, at 3448 Pinkney St. Years of debate over how to develop the site have yielded a solitary placard, hidden behind some trees, offering a brief biography. By way of contrast, the lavish birthplace of President **Gerald R. Ford**, at 32nd St and Woolworth Ave (daily 7.30am–9pm; free), is open to the public; he too moved to Michigan in his infancy, after his parents divorced.

The **Henry Doorly Zoo**, 3701 S 10th St (daily 8.30am–5pm June–Aug, 9.30am–5pm Sept–May; $10.50), rightfully considers itself one of the best zoos in America and is well worth a visit. It started off with two buffalo borrowed from

Buffalo Bill; now there's a gigantic aviary, some rare white Siberian tigers, a magnificent bear canyon, and the large Kingdoms of the Seas aquarium.

Twenty-nine miles southwest of Omaha, at exit 426 on I-80, is the **Strategic Air and Space Museum** (daily 9am–5pm; $7; Ⓦ www.strategicairandspace.com), inside two huge hangars containing giant 1950s- and 1960s-era warplanes, some of which were designed and built by the Martin Bomber Company of Omaha. Films, photos, and exhibits concentrate on World War II and the Cold War, the latter highlighted by various weapons including an Atlas-D Intercontinental Ballistic Missile, located outside the museum entrance.

Practicalities

Omaha's **Greyhound** station is at 1601 Jackson St; **Amtrak** trains depart very late at night, and arrive long before the city wakes up, at 1003 S Ninth St. Both depots are well placed for downtown; however, local **public transportation** is poor. The **CVB** is at 1001 Farnam, right downtown (Mon–Sat 9am–4.30pm; Ⓣ402/444-4660 or 1-866/937-6624, Ⓦ www.visitomaha.com). There's also a **welcome center** for Nebraska as a whole, just off I-80 exit 454, across from the zoo at Tenth St and Bob Gibson Blvd (May–Oct daily 9am–5pm, Nov–April Mon–Fri 9am–5pm; Ⓣ402/595-3990).

Hotel rates are good, except in mid-June when the college baseball World Series comes to town. Rooms at the downtown *Hilton Garden Inn*, 1005 Dodge St (Ⓣ402/341-4400; ❹), are clean and comfortable. The circular, almost cute, and certainly pretty unusual *Satellite Motel*, 6006 L St (Ⓣ402/733-7373; ❸) offers clean, recently remodeled rooms. Located next to the SAC Museum, the Eugene T. Mahoney State Park (Ⓣ402/944-2523) has **campsites** ($17), **cabins**, and a **lodge** (❸–❹), in a family-oriented setting. The *Pinecrest Farms B&B*, located 50 miles west of Omaha, on Country Road A between highways 77 and 79 (Ⓣ402/784-6461; ❸), offers an idyllic and romantic setting.

The Old Market district, centered on Tenth and Howard streets, has the liveliest **restaurants** and **bars**. The *Indian Oven*, 1010 Howard St (Ⓣ402/342-4856), a superb Asian restaurant, features paneer and vegetable dishes on its extensive menu. *M's Pub*, at 422 S 11th St (Ⓣ402/342-2550), serves soups, salads, and sandwiches, while the *Upstream Brewing Company*, 514 S 11th St (Ⓣ402/344-0200), has excellent beers and a standard American menu. *Mr Toad's*, 1002 Howard St (Ⓣ402/345-4488), is a reliable **jazz venue**, with good jam sessions on Sundays.

Lincoln

Tiny Rochester was selected to be state capital in 1867 – on the condition that it change its name to **LINCOLN** in honor of the recently assassinated president. Such was the disappointment in the territorial seat of government, Omaha, that state officials had to smuggle documents, books, and office furniture out of the city in the middle of the night to avoid armed gangs.

Fifty-eight miles southwest of Omaha, the city now serves as an oasis of culture for a large chunk of the Plains. At night, when the students emerge, its compact downtown comes into its own. Of its alphabetical array of broad boulevards, **O Street** (the subject of Allen Ginsberg's poem "Zero Street") is the main drag; 13th and 14th streets are packed with bars and places to eat.

Dwarfing the rest of **downtown**, the central tower of the 1932 Nebraska **state capitol**, 1445 K St (Mon–Fri 8am–5pm, Sat 10am–5pm, Sun 1–5pm; tours every hour; free), protrudes 400ft into the sky. Topped by a 20ft statue of a sower on a pedestal of wheat and corn, its remarkably phallic appearance has prompted the nickname "penis of the prairies." The superb iridescent murals in the foyer are a welcome alternative to old portraits, flags, and emblems, and from the fourteenth-floor observation deck you can survey the flatness of the surrounding farmland.

Twelve thousand years of life on the plains are covered at the **Museum of Nebraska History**, Centennial Mall at 15th and P streets (Tues–Fri 9am–4.30pm, Sat–Sun 1–4pm; $2 suggested donation), where displays focus on anthropology rather than history. The Elephant Hall, a gallery of towering mammoth, mastodon, and four-tusker skeletons, is the highlight of the **University of Nebraska State Museum** at 14th and U streets (Mon–Sat 9.30am–4.30pm, Sun 1.30–4.30pm; $5). A few blocks away, the **Sheldon Memorial Art Gallery**, 12th and R streets (Tues–Thurs 10am–5pm, Fri 10am–8pm, Sat 10am–5pm; free), traces the development of American art, and has a twenty-piece sculpture garden. The 76,000-seater **Memorial Stadium**, at the northern end of campus on Vine Street (tickets ☎402/472-3111 or 1-800/8-BIGRED), is where the brutal "Big Red" Cornhuskers invariably thrash their football opposition.

Practicalities

Lincoln's **Greyhound** station is downtown at 2400 NW 12th St, while **Amtrak** passes through 201 N 7th St at crazy early-morning hours. Star-Tran (☎402/476-1234) runs good **local buses** ($1.25). The **visitor center** is in Lincoln Station, right next to Amtrak (June–Sept Mon–Fri 9am–8pm, Sat 8am–2pm, Sun noon–4pm; rest of year Mon–Fri 9am–6pm, Sat 10am–2pm; ☎402/434-5348 or 1-800/423-8212, ⓦ www.lincoln.org).

Except on football weekends, it's easy to find inexpensive **accommodation** out by the airport, off I-80 exit 399 – at the *Days Inn* (☎402/475-3616; ❸), for example. Downtown, the *Holiday Inn*, 9th and O streets (☎402/475-4011; ❹), offers good value. The Branched Oak State Park, off Raymond Road from Hwy-79, has **tent sites** for $6–11; the more expensive sites have showers.

Restaurants downtown tend to be less than compelling, with grills, pizzerias, and family diners predominating. The *Oven*, 201 N 8th St (☎402/475-6118), offers Indian cuisine with a range of cheap breads and inventive specials, while the Italian menu at *Valentino's*, 35th & Holdrege (☎402/475-1501), is tasty and well-priced. The *Z-Bar*, 136 N 14th St (☎402/435-8754), attracts big-name **jazz** and **blues** acts en route between Chicago and Kansas City; *Duffy's Tavern*, 1412 O St (☎402/474-3543), pulls in a younger crowd and some good **rock bands**. Across the street at no. 1329, *O'Rourke's Tavern* (☎402/435-8052) is a lively, well-priced hangout. The **Historic Haymarket District**, by the Amtrak station, holds more bars and restaurants, including *The Mill*, at 800 P St (☎402/475-5522), which has good coffee and Internet access.

Western Nebraska

After the unerringly flat journey across eastern Nebraska, the far west comes as a refreshing change. In the **Panhandle**, as it's often called, wave upon wave of rumpled sandy hills, thinly coated with prairie grass, back off toward the horizon like a sea in constant turmoil. Early pioneers wrote the area off as unproductive, and it remained barren until massive irrigation work at the start of the twentieth century enabled agricultural settlement. In the **northwest** the sand hills yield to classic John Ford–style Western scenery: pancake-flat valleys, crisscrossed by dry meandering riverbeds and corralled by crusty, contorted bluffs, all under the constant shadow of fast-moving clouds. Emigrants on the **Oregon Trail** used the bizarre outcrops, which sprout along the way, as "road signs."

West along I-80

Interstate 80 is one of the most popular coast-to-coast routes simply because it's the shortest. Scenery is not its strongest suit, and the central swath through 450 miles of Nebraskan farmland is not a prospect drivers cherish. If time doesn't matter, then it's better to head northwest at dreary Grand Island, 93 miles west of Lincoln, onto **Scenic Hwy-2**, for a lonesome yet exhilarating drive through the Sandhills.

If you stick to I-80, decent pull-off points are few and far between. It's hard to miss the newest attraction at **KEARNEY** – the **Great Platte River Road Archway Monument** (T 1-877/511-2724; daily 9am–6pm in summer, rest of year hours vary; $10) actually spans the Interstate near exit 272. Exhibits inside tell the story of a transient nation and recreate the hardships of life on the westward trail.

Just over halfway across the state at exit 177, **NORTH PLATTE** makes a big deal about its **Buffalo Bill Ranch Historical Park** (April–May & Sept–Oct 9am–4pm weekdays; June–Aug 9am–5pm daily; $4 per car), another property of the ubiquitous William "Buffalo Bill" Cody. Today the ranch is run by the state, which places more emphasis on history than tacky folklore. Cody's mansion and various barns can be examined, and an excellent documentary film, shown on request, features movie clips of his "Wild West Show," which toured America and Europe for thirty years. The park offers **camping** ($6 per night). The *Rambler Motel*, 1420 Rodeo Rd (T 308/532-9290; ●), has decent rooms and an outdoor pool. **Eating** options are mostly limited to national chains.

Thirty miles west, aiming to entertain bored drivers in the one-horse hamlet of **PAXTON**, off exit 145 *Ole's Big Game Lounge & Grill* (T 308/239-4500) serves tasty fried food, with over two hundred wildlife trophies from around the world mounted on its walls, cabinets, and shelves. Fascinating, but not a place for the animal-rights activist.

At **OGALLALA**, twenty miles further along, Old West outlaws were interred at **Boot Hill Cemetery** (10th St and Parkhill Rd; free) in the 1880s. The town sits just nine miles south of the **Lake McConaughy** reservoir, famous for fishing, watersports, and the sandy beaches along its hundred miles of shoreline. From Ogallala, it's 165 miles to Cheyenne, Wyoming, though Sidney (exit 59) takes you into rugged Oregon Trail country (see p.814).

Scenic Hwy-2 and Alliance

Scenic Hwy-2 meanders and dips for over 330 miles from I-80 to South Dakota's Black Hills. It passes through the **Sandhills** – a mesmerizing landscape carpeted with short-grass prairie and softened by delicate wild flowers and shiny ponds. Apart from a few farmsteads, grain silos, and tiny churches, all you're likely to see on the open road are lazing cattle, a few sluggish rivers, and the occasional mile-and-a-quarter-long freight train weaving its way through the hills. It's a long, desolate, yet incredibly beautiful drive through an anachronistic corner of the US.

The road dawdles for miles through scattered villages before drifting into **ALLIANCE** – a nice enough little prairie town, which pulls in over fifty thousand visitors per year for its one big attraction. **Carhenge**, two and a half miles north on State Hwy-87 (always open; free; W www.carhenge.com), is a rough copy of Stonehenge – but made with old cars rather than stone. Erected in a cornfield during a family reunion in 1987, this intriguing collection of Chevys, Cadillacs, and Plymouths, painted a brooding battleship grey and tilted at unusual angles, has to be the best picnic site in America's heartland. To some it's an ingenious piece of Pop Art; others view it as great black humor, or an appalling eyesore. The

Nebraska Department of Roads rapidly declared it a junkyard, and ordered the city of Alliance to remove it, forcing locals to form **Friends of Carhenge**, whose work seems to have secured the monument's future.

Alliance's helpful downtown **CVB** office, 111W Third St (☎308/762-1520), provides information and sells Carhenge souvenirs. There is no reason to linger in Alliance, but if you arrive late, try the *Days Inn*, 117 Cody Ave, just off Third St (☎308/762-8000; ❸), or the *Holiday Inn Express*, 1420 W Third St (☎308/762-7600; ❺). For **food**, there's *Ken & Dale's*, 123 E Third St (☎308/762-7252), which serves succulent all-day breakfasts and great pecan pancakes.

The Oregon Trail landmarks

Two of the first landmarks encountered by travelers on the **Oregon Trail**, which in western Nebraska paralleled the route of modern US-26, were the lumpy **Courthouse** and **Jail rocks**, which lie four miles beyond the likeable little town of **Bridgeport**, 36 miles south of Alliance. Fourteen miles west, along Hwy-92, the **Chimney Rock National Historic Site** (daily 9am–5pm; $3; tours available; ⓦ www.nps.org/chro) rises almost 500ft above the North Platte River. Although this phallic outcrop's nineteenth-century stature may have been chipped away by erosion and lightning, it remains one of the most recognizable and memorable landmarks in the West.

The twin towns of **GERING** and **SCOTTSBLUFF**, 25 miles further west, are the commercial center for the farmlands of western Nebraska. Southwest of Gering, the rugged 800ft rampart of **Scotts Bluff National Monument** (daily: summer 8am–7pm; rest of year 8am–5pm; $5 per car) stands like a Nebraska Gibraltar. Known to the Sioux as Me-a-pa-te ("hill that's hard to get around"), it earned its anglicized name in 1828 after fur trader Hiram Scott was mysteriously found dead at its base. Trips to the top (by foot or free shuttle bus) are rewarded with a magnificent view, and the entrance fee includes the absorbing **Oregon Trail Museum**, which relates the experiences of the early emigrants. Just outside Gering, to the southwest, the spiky **Wildcat Hills** hold some delightful vistas and hiking terrain.

△ Carhenge

Well-kept **rooms** are available in the *Lamplighter American Inn*, 606 E 27th St, Scottsbluff (T 308/632-7108; ❸); *Woodshed*, 18 E 16th St (T 308/635-3684), is the best spot for family-style **food**, and has a full bar. The towns' **visitor center** can be found at 1517 Broadway, Scottsbluff (daily 8am–5pm; T 308/632-2133).

Fort Robinson State Park

Some eighty miles north of Scottsbluff, just west of Crawford village, **Fort Robinson State Park**, beside 1000ft crenelated cliffs in the inhospitable White River Valley, preserves the spot where the US Army coordinated its campaign to rid the gold-rich Badlands of the native Sioux. Today, it's a cross between a dude ranch and a living history village – a smoothing over that makes the memories of the obliteration of an entire way of life all the more poignant.

Restored fort buildings contain period furnishings, and there are two small museums. The State Historical Society Museum traces the fort's history from 1874-1946, and the Trailside Museum interprets the geology and natural history of the region. A simple stone marks the spot where **Crazy Horse** was killed (see box, below); the **horse–drawn tour** (six per day; $4) acknowledges it with a mere ten-second halt. Good-value **horseback rides** pass some wondrously weird rock formations, and *Fort Robinson Lodge* (T 308/665-2900; ❷-❹) has nice **rooms** as well as bargain cottages; the *Lodge's* **restaurant** serves cheap buffalo tacos and

Crazy Horse

The life of Oglala Sioux leader **Crazy Horse** is shrouded in confusion, misinterpretation, and controversy. So thoroughly did the most enigmatic figure in Plains Indian history avoid contact with whites (outside battle, at least) that no photograph or even sketch of him exists; unlike other Indian chiefs, he refused to visit Washington, DC, or talk to reporters.

Crazy Horse earned his title as a youth, after he single-handedly charged rival Arapahoe and took two scalps. The finest moment in a brilliant military career came in June 1876, when he led a thousand warriors in inflicting a stinging defeat on the superior forces of General George Crook at the Battle of the Rosebud River. Just eight days later Crazy Horse headed the attack at the **Battle of Little Bighorn**, where Custer and his entire company were killed (see p.894).

After Little Bighorn, US Army efforts to round up the Indians were redoubled. In May 1877, Crazy Horse surprised friend and foe alike by leading nine hundred of his people into Fort Robinson. They gave up their weapons, and Crazy Horse, keen to stay in his native land (unlike Sitting Bull, who had retreated to Canada), demanded that the buffalo grounds along the Powder River should remain in Indian hands. Tensions at the army camp rose after a rumor went around the barracks that the Sioux chief had come to murder General Crook. Crazy Horse was arrested on September 5, 1877; during a tussle outside the fort jail, he was bayoneted three times, and died the next morning.

Quite why this undefeated warrior should have surrendered without a fight, and whether he fell victim to a deliberate assassination, remains unclear. What is certain is that his death signaled the closing chapter of the Indian Wars. The Oglala Sioux were forcibly moved to the poor hunting country of Missouri, and settlers immediately swept in their thousands into western Nebraska, South Dakota, Wyoming, and Montana.

Crazy Horse, so one story goes, was buried by his family in an unmarked grave in an out-of-the-way creek called **Wounded Knee** – the very place where thirteen years later three hundred Sioux men, women, and children were slaughtered in the bloody finale to over half a century of barbarism (see p.820).

other beef and bison dishes. There is good **camping** for $11-19 per person, or you could really rough it at the beautiful but remote Toadstool Geological Park, 25 miles to the north.

The town of **Chadron**, 23 miles east of Fort Robinson, is worth a visit principally for the small **Museum of the Fur Trade**, four miles east on US-20 (summer daily 8am–5pm; $5). The museum is a valuable historical archive illustrating the unique barter system that operated between fur traders and local Native Americans.

South Dakota

The wide-open spaces of the Great Plains roll away to infinity on either side of I-90 in **SOUTH DAKOTA**. Though the land is more green and fertile east of the Missouri River, vast numbers of high-season visitors speed straight on through to the spectacular southwest, site of the **Badlands** and the adjacent **Black Hills** – two of the most dramatic, mysterious, and legend-impacted tracts of land in the US. For whites, they encapsulate a wagonload of American notions about heritage and the taming of the West; to Native Americans, they are ancient, spiritually resonant places.

The science-fiction severity of the Badlands resists fitting into easy tourist tastes. The bigger, more user-friendly Black Hills, home of that most patriotic of icons, **Mount Rushmore**, have been subjected to greater exploitation (dozens of physical, historical, and downright commercial attractions, as well as the mining of gold and other metals), but encourage more active exploration, via hiking trails, mountain lakes and streams, and scenic highways.

Time and Hollywood have mythologized the larger-than-life personalities for whom the Dakota Territory served as a stomping-ground: **Custer** and **Crazy Horse** battled here for supremacy over the Plains, while **Wild Bill Hickok** and **Calamity Jane** were denizens of the once-notorious Gold Rush town of **Deadwood**.

Sioux tribes dominated the plains from the eighteenth century, having gradually been pushed westwards from the Great Lakes by the encroaching whites. To these nomadic hunters, unlike the gun-toting Christian settlers and federal politicians, the concept of owning the earth was utterly alien. They fought hard to stay free: the Sioux are the only Indian nation to have defeated the United States in war and forced it to sign a treaty (in 1868) favorable to them. Even so, they were compelled, in the face of a gung-ho gold rush, to relinquish the sacred Black Hills, and ultimately the choice lay between death or confinement on reservations. For decades their history and culture were outlawed; until the 1940s it was illegal to teach or even speak their language, Lakota. More Sioux live now on South Dakota's six reservations than dwelled in the whole state during pioneer days, but their prospects are often grim. Nowhere is the legacy of injustice better symbolized than at **Wounded Knee**, on the Oglala Sioux **Pine Ridge Reservation** – scene of the infamous 1890 massacre by the US Army, and also of a prolonged "civil disturbance" by the radical American Indian Movement in 1973.

Today Native American traditions are celebrated by music, dance, and socializing at **powwows**, held in summer on the reservations; the state tourist office can supply dates and locations. The outdoors-minded state also has 170 parks and recreation areas for hikers and campers. In winter, downhill **skiing** is limited to Terry Peak and Deer Mountain, outside **Lead** in the Black Hills; cross-country skiing and snowmobiling are more prevalent.

Getting around South Dakota
You'll be hard put to see much of South Dakota without a **car**. Amtrak routes bypass the state entirely, though Jefferson (℡1-800/444-6287) **bus lines** serve points between Rapid City and Sioux Falls, sites of the two major **airports**. Powder River buses (℡1-800/442-3682) serve Black Hills I-90 towns such as Rapid City, Spearfish, and Sturgis, as well as making the two-hour trip to Cheyenne, Wyoming. To see iconic attractions such as Mount Rushmore and the Crazy Horse Memorial, you might hook up with Discovery Tours (℡605/722-5788), which runs lively minibus **tours** from Rapid City and Deadwood.

East of the Missouri

For tourists, little in eastern or central South Dakota can be considered essential. **Sioux Falls**, the state's biggest city, is faceless but handy. As one of the country's quietest and smallest capitals, **Pierre** has its charms, while **Mitchell** has a few curiosities, and **Yankton** has the excellent Lewis and Clark Recreation Area on its doorstep. The town marks the start of an alternative cross-state route to I-90, trundling through nearby **Vermillion**, home to the exceptional Shrine to Music Museum, plus the Rosebud and Pine Ridge reservations. About sixty miles northwest of Sioux Falls, **De Smet** is known as "Little Town on the Prairie" thanks to the autobiographical books of Laura Ingalls Wilder. You can tour eighteen sites she mentions for smatterings of history, pretty scenery, and homely pride. **Chamberlain** holds the worthwhile Akta Lakota Museum and Cultural Center.

Mitchell

MITCHELL makes a mildly diverting stop on the seemingly endless drive along I-90. It's known for its **Corn Palace** at 604 N Main St (summer daily 8am–9pm; winter Mon–Fri 8am–5pm; free), which has been called "the world's largest birdfeeder"; the first one was built in 1892 to encourage settlement and to display local agricultural products. A large arena topped with brightly painted onion-shaped domes and minarets, the "palace" hosts various performance and sports events and is decorated annually (at a cost of about $125,000) with large murals depicting farming and other outdoor scenes. The artists' materials consist exclusively of native corn, grains, and grasses of varying natural colors. Mitchell's **visitor center** is across the street at 601 N Main St (Mon–Fri 8am–5pm; ℡605/996-5567 or 1-866/273-CORN, ⓦwww.cornpalace.com). Other places where you can while away time in Mitchell include a surprisingly engaging museum of dolls, including a salt-carved Shirley Temple; a pioneer museum; and a prehistoric Native American village.

Both the *Best Western* (℡605/996-5536; ❸) and the *Super 8* (℡605/996-9678; ❸) **motels** lie just off I-90 at exit 332. The *Lake Mitchell Campground*, one mile north of town on Hwy-37 (℡605/995-8457), has grassy tent sites ($14) that overlook the water.

The railroad-themed *Depot*, 210 S Main St (℡605/996-9417), is a fun place to grab a **meal**.

Pierre

Straggling along the east bank of the Missouri River at the center of South Dakota, **PIERRE** is the second smallest and by far the least sophisticated of all the US state capitals; it is instead a typical South Dakota town, whose fifteen thousand residents do their best to ignore the fact that it's the seat of state government.

Apart from the black-domed **capitol building** itself, which sits in a pleasant park at the northeast edge of downtown and is open for tours (daily 8am–10pm; free), there's not a lot to detain you here. One exception is the worthwhile **Cultural Heritage Center** (Jun–Aug Mon–Sat 9am–6.30pm, Sun 1–4.30pm; Sept–May Mon–Sat 9am–4.30pm, Sun 1–4.30pm; $4), located high on a hill half a mile north of the capitol, and modeled on traditional Plains Indian dwellings. Repository for the usual barrage of pioneer implements and prehistoric artifacts, the museum is one of few such places that does more than pay lip service to the state's significant Native American cultures.

Pierre's **visitor center** is at 800 W Dakota St (☎605/224-7361 or 1-800/962-2034, ⓦwww.pierre.org). *Pier 347*, 347 S Pierre St (☎605/224-2400), offers bagels and coffee drinks, while the fast-food chains line up along Sioux Avenue, which also holds the bulk of the town's **motels**, including the clean and comfortable *Governor's Inn*, 700 W Sioux Ave (☎605/224-4200; ❸).

The Badlands

The White River **BADLANDS** could be considered a pocket-sized cousin to Arizona's Grand Canyon. What's most impressive about the "Badlandscape" is not its scale, as at the Canyon, but rather its sheer strangeness. More than 35 million years ago this area of southwest South Dakota was a saltwater sea; later it became a marsh, into which sank the remains of such prehistoric mammals as sabre-toothed cats and three-toed horses, to be covered with white volcanic ash. Drying as it evolved, the terrain became unable to support the deep-rooted shrubs or trees that might have preserved it, and over the last few million years erosion has slowly eaten away layers of sand, silt, ash, mud, and gravel, to reveal rippling gradations of earth tones and pastel colors. The crumbly earth is carved into all manner of shapes: pinnacles, precipices, pyramids, knobs, cones, ridges, gorges, or, if you're feeling poetic, lunar sandcastles and cathedrals. The Sioux dubbed these incredible contortions of nature *Mako Sica* – literally, "land bad"; early French trappers echoed that with *Mauvaises Terres à Traverser*, or "bad lands to travel across"; they have also been aptly described as "hell with the fires out." Despite this daunting reputation, animals such as bighorn sheep, mule deer, and prairie dogs are at home here, while on average a million visitors pass through each year.

The most spectacular formations can be found within the **Badlands National Park**, particularly its northern sector, while the poverty-stricken Pine Ridge Indian Reservation encompasses the southern stretches. Clean-cut **Wall**, just a few miles north of the park boundaries, is the most–visited commercial center in the region.

Badlands National Park

About one-tenth of the Badlands – the most amazing parts – were declared a national park (open year-round) in the 1970s. The two most accessible entrances are off I-90 at exits 131 (northeast entrance) and 109-110 (at the town of Wall), connected by the forty-mile paved loop of Hwy-240, peppered with scenic overlooks; see p.822 for a map of the area. Visitors can backpack or climb just about anywhere; among the best of the marked **hiking trails** are the Door Trail, a half-hour loop that enters the eerie wasteland through a natural "doorway" in the rock pinnacles ten miles south of the northeast entrance, and the even shorter Fossil Exhibit Trail, ten miles further on. The Badlands' rainbow colors are most vibrant at dawn, dusk, and just after rainfall.

Adjoining the Ben Reifel **visitor center**, five miles from the northeast entrance (daily: June–Aug 7am–7pm; rest of year 8am–5pm; $15 per vehicle for seven days; ☎605/433-5361), is the only in-park **accommodation** option, *Cedar Pass Lodge*, which has its own **restaurant** (☎605/433-5460; cabins ❸, cottages ❹; mid-April to Oct). Another **visitor center**, White River (June–Aug daily 10am–7pm), stands on Hwy-27 in the less-visited and less spectacular southern end of the park. A handful of seasonal **campgrounds** operate both in the park and in Wall (see below).

Wall

The town of **WALL**, eight miles north of the Badlands, may look like nothing special, yet thanks to **Wall Drug**, begun modestly in 1931 as a pharmacy and veterinary supplies shop on Main Street, it's now pretty famous. You'll learn about Wall Drug's presence long before you reach town. Over five hundred billboards along I-90 tout its wares, including the free ice water that was its original sales gimmick. By the time you get to exit 110 (the one with the 85ft Wall Drug dinosaur), you'll be compelled to pull off and see what all the fuss is about.

△ Badlands National Park

Behind the hype lies a kitschy emporium that serves up to twenty thousand visitors per day. You can fill up on steaks or cakes in the 520-seat café-cum-Western art gallery, or simply enjoy the wall-to-wall collection of photos, memorabilia, animal trophies, and mechanical automata like the Cowboy Orchestra and the Chuckwagon Quartet. The merchandise, separated into individual stores, runs the gamut from quality (see the Western bookstore and trail outfitters) to junk (anyone for a rattlesnake mold?).

The impressive **Buffalo Gap National Grasslands**, an empty and remote portion of South Dakota so bleak it's almost beautiful, start at Wall and encompass the Badlands. The **National Grasslands Visitor Center**, at 708 Main St (daily in summer 8am–5pm, 8am–4.30pm; Mon–Fri rest of year), makes a good jumping-off point and will provide maps.

There's absolutely no reason to spend the night in Wall, but if you're stuck, try the *Best Western Plains Motel*, 712 Glenn St (☏605/279-2145; ❹), or the slightly less expensive *Super 8*, across the road at no. 711 (☏605/279-2688; ❹). The *Cactus Café and Lounge* on Main Street (☏605/279-2561) offers a mixed menu of reasonably priced Mexican, Italian, and American **food**.

Pine Ridge Indian Reservation

Pine Ridge, the second largest Indian reservation in the United States (after Arizona's Navajo Nation; see p.978), overlaps the southern Badlands. It is also located in one of the nation's poorest counties. Its prefab homes and beat-up trucks blend sadly and uneasily with the surrounding dry grasslands, rocky bluffs, and tree-lined creeks.

The largest town, also called **PINE RIDGE**, comprises a collection of shabby, paint-stripped structures. Though the emergence of the profitable Prairie Wind casino in Oglala has improved life here, in many ways the reservation towns are an even more bitter pill to swallow than places like the nearby site of the Wounded Knee massacre. This area posts the highest poverty- and alcohol-related death statistics on the continent, and the average lifespan is just 52 years.

Red Cloud Indian School, four miles north of Pine Ridge on US-18, is named after a former chief whose fight against the US forced the closure of military forts on Sioux hunting grounds. The school is doing its best to counteract the ill-effects of life on the reservation, and each summer it holds an Indian art show featuring work by tribes in the US and Canada; it also has a gift shop (daily summer 8am–5pm; winter Mon–Fri 9am–5pm; free). Red Cloud, who later signed a peace treaty with the US and invited Jesuits to teach his tribe "the ways of the white man," is buried in a cemetery on a nearby knoll. The **Oglala Nation Fair**, held over the first weekend in August, features a powwow and rodeo. For details, contact the Oglala Sioux Tribe, P.O. Box 2070, Pine Ridge, SD 57770 (☏605/867-6121). For news and both traditional Lakota Sioux and contemporary American music, tune in to KILI 90.1 FM, "the Voice of the Lakota Nation." If you want to stay on the reservation, the ⚘ *Wakpamni Bed & Breakfast* (☏605/288-1800; ⓦ www.wakpamni.com; ❸–❺), offers lovely guest rooms as well as accommodation in tepees; tours of the reservation or horseback rides with a Lakota guide can be arranged.

Wounded Knee

No other atrocity against Native Americans remains so potent and poignant as the massacre at **WOUNDED KNEE**. On December 29, 1890, the US Army delivered a coup de grace to the vestiges of Plains Indian resistance, killing several hundred unarmed Sioux men, women, and children. Most were **Ghost Dancers**, followers of a messianic cult who believed that by trance-inducing dancing and singing they could recover their lost way of life. The massacre was triggered by a misunderstanding during a tribal round-up: a deaf Indian, asked to surrender his rifle along with his peers, instead held it above his head, shouting that he'd paid a lot for it. An officer grabbed at the gun, it went off, and the troops started shooting.

A commemorative stone **monument**, surrounded by a chain-link fence, marks the victims' collective gravesite, off Hwy-27 toward the bottom of Pine Ridge Reservation. Somehow it has an intangible feeling of grief and anger, the mass murder here having left an indelible scar on all First Americans. Eighty-three years later, members of the radical **American Indian Movement** (**AIM**) grabbed headlines by occupying Wounded Knee in a dispute over the federal imposition of a tribal government; they were eventually dispersed by armed FBI agents and a paramilitary unit. More peaceably, since the mid-1980s the **Sitanka Wokiksuye** movement has organized an annual pilgrimage to the site, arriving in harsh winter weather by horse and travois, to symbolically release the spirits of their dead ancestors. The tribe has so far refused federal funds to turn the site into a national monument, wanting instead to leave it uncommercialized; a concrete block nearby offers a few souvenirs and local knowledge.

The Black Hills

Our people knew there was yellow metal in little chunks up there, but they did not bother with it, because it was not good for anything.

Black Elk, Oglala Sioux holy man

The timbered, rocky **BLACK HILLS** rise like an island from a sea of rolling hills and flat, grain-growing plains, stretching for a hundred miles between the Belle Fourche River in the north and the Cheyenne to the south, and varying in width from forty to sixty miles. For many generations of Sioux, their value was and still is immeasurable. The Hills are "the heart of everything that is," a kind of spiritual safe, a place of gods and holy mountains where warriors went to speak with Wakan Tanka (the Great Spirit) and await visions. They were dubbed *Paha Sapa*, or Black Hills, even though they are actually mountains (the highest, Harney Peak, rises 7242ft), and the blue spruce and Norway pine trees that cover them only appear to be black from a distance.

Imagining the Hills to be worthless, the United States government drew up a treaty in the mid-nineteenth century that gave them and most of the land west of the Missouri River to the Indians. All such treaties were destined to be broken when the discovery of **gold** turned the Indians' Eden into the white explorers' El Dorado, and fortune-hunters came pouring in.

The Hills these days are a major tourist destination, but despite the T-shirt stores, pseudo-historical wax museums, cowboy supper shows, and water slides, the Hills have not been robbed of all their beauty and dignity.

The more thickly wooded north is noted more for urban activities, with the casino town of **Deadwood** its busiest spot. No place in the Hills is much more than ninety minutes from the four presidential heads carved into **Mount Rushmore** or the remarkable **Crazy Horse Memorial**, one of the world's most ambitious works-in-progress. In the shade of these great monuments, the less spoiled southern hills are home to the bison of **Custer State Park** and **Wind Cave National Park**, along with the town of **Hot Springs**.

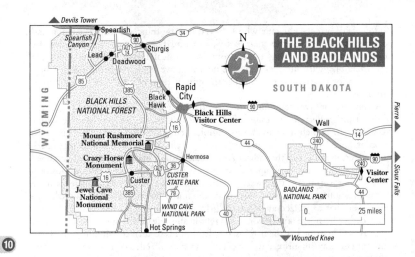

The North Hills

The predominantly privately owned **northern Black Hills** are more commercialized than their southern siblings, with **Rapid City**, the hub, surrounded by more interesting smaller towns, such as **Sturgis**, **Spearfish**, and **Deadwood**. The back roads, especially in the **Spearfish Canyon** area, form a network of prime driving and cycling country. The Black Hills **Information Center**, exit 61 off I-90 (June–Aug daily 8am–8pm; rest of year daily 8am–5pm; ☎605/355-3700), is just outside of Rapid City and has an abundance of information on the Black Hills, the Badlands, and Native American points of interest.

Rapid City

South Dakota's second largest town, **RAPID CITY**, is all but swamped with family-fun attractions, though it makes a convenient base for exploring the charms of the Black Hills' lesser communities. In town, the **Journey Museum**, 222 New York St (daily 9am–5pm; $7), leads you through time, beginning with the geologic evolution of the Plains and the era of dinosaurs, right through the life of the Plains Indians to the pioneers who invaded their territory.

　Greyhound pulls into town at 333 Sixth St. The **visitor center** is in the Civic Center, 444 Mount Rushmore Rd N (Mon–Fri 8am–5pm; ☎605/343-1744 or 1-800/487-3223, ⓦ www.rapidcitycvb.com). Rapid City has the cheapest **lodgings** in the Black Hills. The Bavarian wood trimmings and soft Sioux furnishings of the delightful *Hotel Alex Johnson*, 523 Sixth St (☎605/342-1210 or 1-800/888-2539; ❺–❻), provide a great escape from the dull corporate decor prevalent in Rapid City, while the *Best Western Ramkota Hotel*, I-90 exit 59 (☎605/343-8550; ❺–❻), is right off the highway and has an indoor waterpark. Both the **food** and **beer** at *Firehouse Brewing Co.*, 610 Main St (☎605/348-1915) – which has plenty of outdoor seating – are worth sampling.

Sturgis

The sleepy town of **STURGIS**, thirty miles north of Rapid City, comes to life in a big way during the first full week of August, when the world-famous **Sturgis Rally and Races** (☎605/720-0800, ⓦ www.sturgismotorcyclerally.com) packs out virtually every motel and campground in the region with motorcycle enthusiasts. For the rest of the year, bikers have to make do with an abundance of

Harley souvenirs in the downtown stores, plus the worthy **Sturgis Motorcycle Museum and Hall of Fame**, 999 Main St (daily 9am–5pm, Sun–Fri 9am–5pm & Sat 10am–4pm in summer only; $5).

East of town, off Hwy-34, the volcanic outcrop which dominates **Bear Butte State Park** stands as a lonely sentinel, detached from the rest of the hills. Hundreds of Native Americans come to this site on retreat each year; to avoid disturbing anyone, check with the park's **visitor center** (T 605/347-5240) before setting out on the excellent hike to the summit. Campers can secure a **tent site** within the park for $6.

The Sturgis **visitor center** (T 605/347-2556, W www.sturgis-sd.org) lies off I-90 exit 32. There's a wide range of **motels** in Sturgis; the *Starlight Motel*, 2426 S Junction Ave (T 605/347-2506; ❸), is good value. For a taste of the biker culture that pervades Sturgis year-round, head to the *Full Throttle Saloon*, 12997 E Hwy 34 (T 605/423-4584), a raucous venue with dubious activities including mechanical bull riding.

Deadwood

One of the West's wildest Gold Rush towns, **DEADWOOD**, in a deep gulch high in the hills 42 miles northwest of Rapid City, has the rare accolade of being a **National Historic Landmark** in its entirety. Within a year of the discovery of **gold** here in 1876, six thousand gold-diggers had swarmed in to stake their claims; con artists, outlaws, and other dubious frontier types were not far behind. Among them were James Butler, aka **Wild Bill Hickok** – sometime spy, scout, bullwhacker, stagecoach driver, sheriff, and gambler, who spent only a few weeks in Deadwood prior to his murder here by a young drifter in 1876. Martha "**Calamity Jane**" Canary Burke, an illiterate alcoholic whose checkered career included stints as scout, prostitute, nurse, and Wild West Show performer arrived the same time as Hickok. She died penniless in 1903; despite barely knowing him, her last wish was to be buried beside Hickok in **Mount Moriah Cemetery**, a short but blustery hike from town.

Gambling was outlawed in Deadwood in 1889, the year South Dakota achieved statehood, but betting parlors and brothels flourished well into the twentieth century. Now the old ghosts have been revitalized, since the passing of limited-stakes gambling legislation in 1989. Corny but entertaining gunfights, sing-alongs, and community theater are shown sporadically; for details, check with the **CVB**, 767 Main St (T 1-800/999-1876, W www.deadwood.org). For an overview of Deadwood past and present, start by visiting the **History and Information Center**, in the heart of town at 3 Siever St (daily: June–Sept 8am–7pm; rest of year 9am–5pm; T 605/578-2507). Main Street boasts several grand old **hotels**, including the *Bullock* at no. 633 (T 605/578-1745 or 1-800/336-1876; ❹–❻), and the *Franklin Hotel* at no. 700 (T 605/578-2241 or 1-800/688-1876; ❺), which has an elegant Old World dining room. **Motels** are plentiful in and around Deadwood. The *Penny Motel*, 818 Main St (T 605/578-1842, W www.pennymotel.com; ❸) is a good budget option, close to downtown, while the *Main Street Manor Hostel,* 515 W Main St, in Lead (T 605/717-2044, W www.mainstreetmanorhostel.com), offers cozy, homey accommodation five minutes from Deadwood. *Saloon #10*, 657 Main St (T 605/578-3346), has cold **beer**, sawdust floors, and lots of memorabilia. Above the door is the chair in which Hickok was sitting when he was shot dead, while holding two aces, a pair of eights, and the nine of diamonds – forever after christened the Dead Man's Hand. Several casinos along Main Street aim to lure in the gamblers with cut-price **buffets**, but Deadwood's finest **dining** is at the dinner-only *Jake's*, on the top floor of Kevin Costner's Midnight Star casino, 677 Main St (T 605/578-1555).

From Deadwood, you can hike or bike the 114-mile **George S. Mickelson Trail**, part of a rails-to-trails project. It winds through the heart of the Hills from Edgemont to Deadwood, much of it passing through national forest. You can rent a bike for $25 per day from Deadwood Bicycles, 180 Sherman St (☎605/578-1345).

Spearfish Canyon area

Aspen, birch, and white spruce spread over the towering limestone cliffs above the nineteen-mile **Spearfish Canyon National Scenic Highway**, which starts on Hwy-14A half an hour's drive west of Deadwood, and threads past sights such as Bridal Veil and Roughlock falls. The route reveals almost as many **gastronomic pleasures** as it does scenic ones. Twenty minutes out of Spearfish, the *Latchstring Restaurant* (☎605/584-3333) serves steaks, pasta, shrimp, and excellent rainbow trout almandine. Marking the southern mouth of the canyon at Hwy-14A and Hwy-85, the *Cheyenne Crossing Store* (☎605/584-3510) is a must if you have a hearty appetite; popular menu items include all-day breakfasts with buffalo sausage, enormous Indian tacos, and traditional Indian fry bread.

Marking the canyon's north end, **SPEARFISH** itself reels in the crowds each summer for the popular **Black Hills Passion Play**, a re-enactment of the death and resurrection of Jesus Christ (June–Aug Tues, Thurs & Sun 8pm; tickets $20–25; ☎605/642-2646 or 1-800/457-0160). The **visitor center** is at 106 W Kansas St (☎605/642-2626 or 1-800/626-8013, ⓦwww.spearfish.sd.us). For **accommodation**, *Yesterday's Inn B&B*, 735 Eighth St (☎605/644-0210; ④–⑥), offers lovely rooms downtown in a restored 1889 Victorian home, while the *All Star Travelers Inn*, 517 W Jackson Blvd (☎605/642-5753 or 1-800/201-5753; ③), has comfortable rooms and features hand-painted wall murals. **Camping** is possible at the Spearfish City Campground, 404 S Canyon St (☎605/642-1340, $16 plus $1 for each additional person). As far as food goes, try *Roma's*, 701 Fifth St (☎605/722-0715), a classy, modern Italian restaurant serving great homemade pastas.

From Spearfish, the spectacular **Devils Tower** (see p.877) stands just an hour's drive away across the Wyoming state line.

The South Hills

The **southern Black Hills** encompass lower foothills and wooded pastureland; from a purely physical standpoint they are more attractive than the north, drawing visitors for their scenery and wildlife rather than kitsch or gambling. The two big mountain carvings, **Mount Rushmore** and **Crazy Horse**, mark the northern end of the region; **Custer State Park** and **Wind Cave National Park** account for much of the central zone; while the pleasant town of **Hot Springs** sits on the southern edge.

Mount Rushmore National Memorial

America's two largest stone carvings are a mere seventeen miles apart – no more than spitting distance when you consider the scale on which they're conceived. The better-known **Mount Rushmore National Memorial** (daily: summer 8am–10pm; rest of year 8am–5pm), originally dubbed "The Shrine of Democracy," is the linchpin of the Hills' tourist circuit. It's an easy 24-mile drive southwest of Rapid City, though by far the most impressive approach is to take **Iron Mountain Road** (US-16A) from **Custer State Park** (see p.826), which runs for seventeen miles up and over 5500ft Iron Mountain.

In 1923, state historian Doane Robinson and the sculptor **Gutzon Borglum**, known for carvings such as the leaders of the Confederacy in Stone Mountain, Georgia (see p.529), talked over the possibility of turning the imposing fingers of granite known as the Needles into a dramatic patriotic sculpture. They discussed depictions of such heroic figures of the West as Lewis and Clark, Buffalo Bill Cody, and Jim Bridger. Borglum opted for a nearby mountain named after New York attorney Charles E. Rushmore, upon which he would fashion the faces and heads of four certifiably great American presidents: **George Washington, Thomas Jefferson, Abraham Lincoln**, and Borglum's buddy, **Theodore Roosevelt**.

Borglum talked, dreamed, and worked big. "American art ought to be monumental, in keeping with American life," he opined. Sixty when the project began in 1927, he died fourteen years later, $200,000 in debt, just a few months prior to the dedication of the last head – Roosevelt's – in 1939. Inclement weather and uncertain funding had meant that the actual sculpting took about six and a half years, at a total cost of $993,000. Half a million tons of rock were removed to reach the softer, more malleable granite from which the heads were dynamited, drilled, and chiseled into recognizable shape.

The Big Four gaze out impassively, cheek by jowl, arguably a greater engineering feat than an artistic one. Each head is about sixty feet from chin to crown. (By way of comparison, the Statue of Liberty's head is only seventeen feet.) Lincoln, Borglum's favorite, has an eighteen-foot-long nose and the glint in each eleven-foot-wide eye is thirty miles. If he and his fellow presidents had been done full-figure to scale, they'd stand 465ft tall and be able to stride across the Potomac River in Washington, DC, without getting their knees wet.

The best time to view Rushmore is dawn or dusk, when there are fewer people and better lighting. Patriots flock here for a massive **fireworks display** on July 3. Although there is no admission charge, an $8 **parking fee** has been introduced since the construction of a hideous new multilevel parking lot and high-tech **visitor center**. The **café** here, complete with panoramic windows, as seen in Hitchcock's *North by Northwest*, serves full meals and "Monumental Breakfasts" of hash browns, eggs, country-fried steak with gravy, and a biscuit piled on one plate. With alternative bases such as Rapid City or Custer State Park so close to hand, there's no particular reason to stay in the nearest town, Keystone – a once quiet mining town turned T-shirt hawker's paradise.

Crazy Horse Memorial

In 1939, prompted by the sight of the Rushmore monument, Sioux leader Henry Standing Bear wrote to **Korczak Ziolkowski**, who had just won first prize for sculpture at the New York World's Fair, telling him that Indians "would like the white man to know that the red man has great heroes, too." The chief invited Ziolkowski to take on a similar project – and, less than a decade later, pushing forty and with just $174 to his name, the New Englander moved permanently to the Black Hills to undertake a vastly more ambitious mission than Rushmore – the **Crazy Horse Memorial**, on US-16, five miles north of Custer.

The subject, the revered warrior Crazy Horse on horseback (see p.815), so appealed to Ziolkowski that he set out to make his monument the biggest statue in the world, higher even than the Great Pyramid. The work he began on **Thunderhead Mountain** in 1948 – five Native American survivors of the Battle of Little Bighorn attended the dedication ceremony – didn't stop with his death in 1982; his widow, children, and grandchildren continue to realize his vision. National and international interest has greatly increased as the monument finally starts to take recognizable shape; the 90ft-high face was completed in time for the fiftieth anniversary celebrations in 1998, although it will easily be another fifty years before the project is finished. Neither words nor photographs can articulate the enormous scale of the thing. The main viewing terrace at the **visitor center** is nearly a mile from the carving itself and the 20ft scale model on show there is 34 times smaller than the end result, which will be 563ft high and 641ft long.

In the fifteenth century, the Great Plains were roamed by one hundred million shaggy, short-sighted American **bison** (popularly known as buffalo, a corruption of the French *boeuf*). Apart from eating their flesh, Native Americans used the fur and hide for clothing and shelter, the bones for weapons, utensils, and toys, and the droppings for fuel. Eliminating the bison en masse was a mercilessly effective way to deplete the Indians as well. By 1900 there were fewer than one thousand bison left in North America.

Custer State Park was instrumental in helping to raise that meager number to a head count of 250,000 in the US and Canada. The park's own 1200 bison constitute the country's second largest publicly owned herd, surpassed only by Yellowstone National Park (see p.880). However, over ninety percent of bison in the US are now privately owned – the meat, higher in protein and lower in cholesterol than either chicken or tuna, is becoming something of a cross between a novelty and a delicacy item in restaurants (you can try it in burger form at the *State Game Lodge* in Custer State Park, as well as dozens of other places around South Dakota). The Triple U Ranch, outside Pierre, South Dakota, boasts a herd of 3500 strong, though Ted Turner owns around twenty thousand, split between his ranches in several western states.

The Custer State Park bison are free to roam where they please until either the last Monday of September or the first Monday in October, when the park stages its annual **roundup**. From selected viewing points, the public is welcome to witness one of the Midwest's more thrilling occasions: helicopters, jeeps, and pickup trucks, as well as riders on horseback, steer the often recalcitrant herd down a six-mile "corridor" and into a series of pens. There the calves are branded and vaccinated, and the whole herd sorted to determine which five hundred will be auctioned off on the third Saturday in November. Proceeds from the sale account for twenty percent of the park's annual revenue.

Don't let the tranquil, easygoing appearance of North America's biggest mammal lull you into a false sense of security. An average bull can stand six feet high at the hump, weigh up to a ton, outrun a horse, turn on a dime, and gore a human most efficiently.

Ziolkowski himself raised and spent $4 million on the non-profit project, refusing to accept federal or state funds, instead relying entirely on admissions and contributions. The site, open dawn to dusk year-round (and illuminated for an hour each night), is free to Native Americans. **Admission** costs $10, though you can see the face just as well if you're just passing by from the highway. The premises include an exhibit of Native American artifacts and crafts, a Native American Cultural Center, a restaurant (May–Oct), and a gift shop. **Private tours** of the construction site at the top of the mountain are given in exchange for a high-level contribution. On the first weekend in June, the public is invited to hike to the top and see the work close-up.

Custer State Park

The 73,000 sublime, billboard-free acres of **Custer State Park** fill much of the southern-central Black Hills, a perfect antidote to the commercial crassness elsewhere. The **Needles Highway** (Hwy-87; open mid-April to mid-Oct) winds for fourteen miles through pine forests and past the eponymous jagged granite spires in the park's northwestern corner, between Sylvan and Legion lakes. Not far from Sylvan Lake, as you pass close to the summit of Harney Peak (South Dakota's highest point, at 7242ft), look south to spot the **Needle's Eye**, a slender gap in one of the pinnacles that measures three to four feet wide and fifty to sixty feet tall. The eighteen-mile **Wildlife Loop** (separate from the Needles Highway) undulates through the rolling meadows along the park's southern edge. Sunrise and sunset are prime times to spy such critters as elk, bighorn sheep, antelope, deer, burros, and the most plentiful species, bison. Finally, **Iron Mountain Road** (US-16A), to the northeast, makes a dramatic route to Mount Rushmore (see p.824). This is the most likely place to bump into the park's famous "begging burros": tame and disarming four-legged panhandlers who stick their snouts through the windows of passing vehicles in search of handouts.

For a fuller appreciation of the beauty of Custer State Park, forsake your car and set off into the wilderness. Rangers at the park entrances – where you're required to pay **entrance fees** of $5 per person, or $12 per vehicle (the pass remains valid for a week, and admits you to all other South Dakota state parks) – can advise on **hiking** and **biking trails**, while concession firms offer horseback rides, boat rental, and cross-country drives in open-topped jeeps. Good short hikes include the one-hour **Stockade Lake Trail** in the west, which climbs to give distant views across the lake to Harney Peak and the Needles, and the two-hour **Lovers Leap Trail**, which starts from the park's main Peter Norbeck **visitor center**, on Hwy-16A in the east (daily: summer 8am–8pm; rest of year 9am–5pm, closed Dec–March; ☎605/255-4464).

As long as nightlife isn't high on your agenda, the park's four state-run resorts make it a splendid **place to stay** (for reservations call ☎1-800/658-3530). The finest is the *State Game Lodge* (☎605/255-4541) on Hwy-16A not far from the visitor center, which operates a motel-style lodge and also has some lovely individual cabins (❹–❺) at the edge of the woods; the *Pheasant Dining Room* offers hearty, meaty meals. Tucked in the northwest corner on its own artificial lake, the *Sylvan Lake Resort* (☎605/574-2561; ❹–❻) similarly offers comfy cabins, more traditional rooms in its tasteful main building, and the upscale *Lakota Dining Room*. Custer State Park also has eight **campgrounds** (☎1-800/710-2267), which cost $13–15 a night, plus park entrance fees.

Custer

In little **CUSTER**, five miles west of the park on US-16, the *Bavarian Inn* on the main highway has classic **German dining** and **rooms** (☎605/673-2802 or 1-800/657-4312; ❹), while the *Custer Mansion*, 35 Centennial Dr (☎605/673-3333 or 1-877/519-4948; ❸–❹), offers comfortable B & B accommodations. Of many garish **campgrounds**, *Flintstones Bedrock City* (☎605/673-4664; $19.50), with its own small theme park ($8), manages to steal the show. The **visitor center** is at 615 Washington St (☎605/673-2244 or 1-800/992-9818, ⓦwww.custersd.com).

Twelve miles west of Custer is the **Jewel Cave National Monument** (daily 8.30am–6pm; $4–27 for 20min–4hr tours; ☎605/673-2288, ⓦwww.nps.gov/jeca), where spelunkers are sure to receive a layer of manganese dust; call ahead for tour details.

Wind Cave National Park

Beneath wide-open rangelands, **Wind Cave National Park**, fifteen minutes north of Hot Springs (see over), comprises over one hundred miles of mapped underground passages etched out of limestone. One of the largest caves in the US, it was discovered, by white settlers anyway, in 1881 when a loud whistling noise on the plains led a settler to a hole in the ground – the cave's only natural opening. Nowadays rangers lead a variety of cave **tours** ($7–23 based on length of tour) from the **visitor center** (hours vary seasonally; ☎605/745-4600, ⓦwww.nps.gov/wica/), pointing out delicate features such as frostwork and boxwork along the way. If you come in summer, forget the standard walking tours and opt for the ones that allow you to crawl around in the smaller passages, or explore the caves by candlelight (call ahead).

Even if you lack the time or inclination to delve into the Dakotas' dank bowels, simply **driving** through the park is yet another unmissable Black Hills experience. Its native grass prairieland is home to deer, antelope, elk, coyote, prairie dogs, and a sizeable herd of buffalo. There's also a primitive campground in the park ($12 per night).

Hot Springs

The Black Hills' southern anchor, **HOT SPRINGS**, differs from other regional towns in that it hasn't tarted up its downtown to look like a movie set. It doesn't need to. Several dozen utilitarian yet handsome sandstone structures dominate its center, through which flows the sprightly Fall River.

Battles over the town's thermal pools have caused as much grief as the clamor for gold. Before white settlement, the Sioux drove out the Cheyenne, and later land-owners, speculators, and settlers dodged and outwitted each other for ownership of the springs. The disputes ceased in 1890 when Fred Evans incorporated numerous small springs and one mammoth hot-water pool into a spa center. Today, **Evans Plunge**, on the north edge of town at 1145 N River St (summer Mon–Fri 5.30am–10pm, Sat & Sun 8am–10pm; rest of year Mon–Fri 5.30am–8pm, Sat & Sun 10am–8pm; $9; ☎605/745-5165), is a popular family-fun center, where three great slides zoom down into the 87° waters.

The unique **Mammoth Site** on the Hwy-18 bypass is the only in situ display of mammoth fossils in the US (mid-May through Aug daily 8am–8pm; rest of year times vary; $7). In 1974, building on a housing project here came to an abrupt halt when a tractor driver unearthed a seven-foot tusk. Paleontologists soon declared that the workers had discovered the 26,000-year-old grave of Columbian and Woolly mammoths – to date, 55 animals, all male, have been found. Inside the dome, fascinating guided **tours** explain how these ten-ton mammoths, along with camels, bears, and rodents, were trapped in a steep-sided sinkhole (a pond formed by a collapsed underground cave) and were gradually covered by sediment. Complete skeletons are easy to pick out in the excavation site, which is still being uncovered slowly by groups of summer volunteers.

Seven miles south of Hot Springs, the huge reservoir of the **Angostura Dam State Recreation Area** ($5 per car), set against contorted sandstone bluffs, is a picture-perfect spot for boating and jet-skiing.

Information for visitors to Hot Springs is available from the old train depot (June–Aug only Mon–Fri 8am–7pm, Sat 8am–6pm, Sun noon–7pm) at 630 N River St, or from the **CVB**, 801 S Sixth St (Mon–Fri 8am–5pm; ☎605/745-4140 or 1-800/325-6991, ⓦwww.hotsprings-sd.com). **Accommodation** rates are a bit more reasonable than in the hectic northern towns. The *Super 8*, 800 Mammoth St (☎605/745-3888 or 1-800/800-8000; ❹), offers comfortable rooms adjacent to the mammoth site; alternatives include the sumptuous *A Dakota Dream B&B*, 801 Almond St (☎605/745-4633; ❺), set on a bluff above town. The *Flat Iron*, 745 N River St (☎605/745-6439), offers serves great coffee, **sandwiches** and salads on a sunny terrace or in a cozy dining room, as well as offering five suites upstairs from the restaurant (☎605/745-5301; ❺–❻).

North Dakota

NORTH DAKOTA has no nationally recognizable landmarks, nor is the state's history particularly lurid or glamorous. It seems like somebody's quiet after-thought, a place to pass through. Grain silos loom on the horizon, and the hay-stacks resemble loaves of bread. In the summer, with the sun baking in a defiantly blue sky and the wind raking strong fingers through tall fields of golden wheat and flax, North Dakota epitomizes all things rural American. Charming, picturesque – and a bit maddening.

The influx of Europeans into the Dakota Territory, spurred by the **Homestead Act of 1862**, precipitated a population and agricultural boom that lasted into the twentieth century. As in South Dakota, the fertile east is more thickly settled than the west, where vast cattle and sheep ranges predominate. It was the east that was hardest hit by the so-called **500-year flood** of 1997, when 1.7 million low-lying acres of farmland were inundated, and the entire state was declared a disaster area.

From **Fargo**, the state's largest city, I-94 passes through the central capital of **Bismarck**, and on to the **Bad Lands** of the west, once cherished by President Theodore Roosevelt. Though the national park bearing his name is a key destination, Roosevelt would surely not be pleased about the continuing disfiguration of much of western North Dakota by strip-mining operations.

Getting around North Dakota

Amtrak runs one **train** per day in each direction between Fargo and Williston in the northwest, via Grand Forks. Greyhound operates one interstate **bus** per day, making the ten-hour trip from Minneapolis/St Paul to Bismarck, via Grand Forks and Fargo, before heading west along I-94 into Montana.

East of the Missouri River

Far more of North Dakota lies east of the big winding **Missouri River**, the state's uneven dividing line, than west. The **Red River Valley**, the state's furthest eastern strip, is home to two sizeable cities, easygoing **Grand Forks** and the less attractive **Fargo**. Pelicans, geese, swans, prairie chickens, and ring-necked pheasants live off the sloughs and potholes of the rolling, glaciated prairie of south-central North Dakota, while lakes and woodlands dominate the north and the Canadian border. **Spirit Lake Sioux Indian Reservation** at Devils Lake is midway between Grand Forks and the low-slung Turtle Mountains, which are topped by Lake Metigoshe and the **International Peace Garden** (more of a political symbol than a compelling sight).

Grand Forks

GRAND FORKS sits eighty miles north of I-94, right next to Minnesota and a mere 75 miles south of the Canadian border. Even before its foundation a century ago, fur traders had used the area to rest and barter during their travels between Winnipeg and Minneapolis. It's a small, friendly, outdoorsy city, with nineteen parks and several tree-lined avenues of fine homes. Furious construction has rebuilt the downtown area, ravaged in the 1997 floodwaters, which now holds a smattering of interesting shops and restaurants.

The most interesting distractions can be found on the redbrick main campus of the **University of North Dakota**. The **North Dakota Museum of Art** (Mon–Fri 9am–5pm, Sat & Sun 11–5pm; donation) offers an eclectic assortment of contemporary art and top touring exhibits. Fascinating tours of the **John D. Odegard School of Aerospace Sciences** (☎701/777-2791; weekday tours offered 8am–4.30pm by appointment), one of the largest civilian pilot-training schools in the world, take in flight simulators, the air-traffic control room, and an altitude chamber.

Grand Forks' **visitor center** is at 4251 Gateway Drive (☎701/746-0444 or 1-800/866-4566, ⓦwww.visitgrandforks.com). **Greyhound** stops at US-81 and Hwy-2 and on the UND campus, while **Amtrak** pulls in at no. 5555 W Demers Ave. Downtown's *Best Western Town House*, 710 First Ave N (☎701/746-5411; ❹), is a comfortable, nicely situated **motel**; if you want to spend less, the *Super 8*, 1122 N 43rd St (☎701/775-8138; ❸), has clean, serviceable rooms near the UND campus. The most serene place to **camp** is twenty miles west on US-2, in the grounds of Turtle River State Park (☎800/807-4723; $8; reservations recommended). For **dining**, *Dakota Harvest Bakers*, 17 N Third St (☎701/772-2100), serves good soups and sandwiches, as well as tasty baked goods.

Devils Lake

The scruffy town of **DEVILS LAKE**, ninety miles west of Grand Forks on US-2, shares its name with the state's largest natural body of water, which boasts a state park and a number of private campgrounds along more than three hundred sprawling, irregular, and growing miles of shoreline. The damming of rivers in the northern part of the state inadvertently caused Devils Lake to rise; so far it has gone up 25 feet and quadrupled in area since 1997. Pastureland has been submerged, dikes built, roads raised, and one town, nearby Churchs Ferry, evacuated. Embarrassed engineers, nervous politicians, and a frustrated public are still at a loss about how to stem the tide – $300 million has already been spent on relief.

Downtown, now saved by a seven-mile-long dike, holds a smattering of nineteenth-century buildings and a few rough-and-ready **bars**. Most of the places to stay, such as the *Super 8* (☎701/662-8656; ❸), are strung along US-2. The *Woodland Resort*, on Creel Bay, about six miles from town (☎701/662-5996, ⓦwww.woodlandresort.com; ❷–❸), includes cabins, a motel, and campgrounds, and you can also rent boats, pontoons, and fishing gear. For other **camping** options, head 25 miles southwest of town to Grahams Island State Park (☎800/807-4723; $13 per tent site); contact the Devils Lake **CVB**, 208 W US-2 (Mon–Fri 8am–5pm; in summer also Sat 9am–5pm & Sun 10am–4pm; ☎701/265-8188), for more information.

Fifteen miles south of town, **Spirit Lake Sioux Indian Reservation** is the site of **Fort Totten Military Post** (daily 8am–5pm in summer; $4), one of the best-preserved frontier military posts in the country. During the last weekend in July, the reservation hosts the thrilling **Spirit Lake Oyate Wacipi Powwow and Rodeo**. It's an impassioned, alcohol-free, multitribal party at which hundreds of magnificently clothed dancers of all ages compete for cash prizes.

The West

Anyone with a hankering to play cowboy could do worse than follow in the footsteps of **Theodore Roosevelt**, who declared "I never would have been president if it had not been for my experiences in North Dakota." Roosevelt initially came to the state in search of spiritual and physical renewal after the deaths (on the same day) of his mother and first wife. He dubbed what he discovered during his few years in this "grimly picturesque" area, with its clear skies, panoramic views, and weird, colorful landforms, a "perfect freedom." The national park named after him is the choicest destination in the **North Dakota Bad Lands** (distinct from South Dakota's Badlands) that dominate the state's western half.

The **Missouri River** wriggles like a giant raggedy worm out of Montana, down past North Dakota's capital, **Bismarck**, and into South Dakota. En route it is transformed into **Lake Sakakawea**, a virtual inland sea nearly two hundred miles long that's the state's premier water playground. **Scenic state highways 1804 and 1806** follow the routes mapped out by the Lewis and Clark expedition in those respective years.

Bismarck and Mandan

The West seems to begin as soon as you cross the Missouri River from **BIS-MARCK**, a capital city with a small-town feel, to Mandan. Both were founded in 1872, Bismarck as a military camp to protect railroad crews from hostile Indians and outlaws. Named in honor of German Chancellor Otto von Bismarck in the hope of attracting Germanic settlers, the scheme failed, but the name stuck. The city survived an early lawless period (present-day Fourth Street was once dubbed "Murderers' Gulch") and a major fire to become first the territorial and then the state capital.

Contemporary Bismarck is pretty much contained within the oblong between I-94 in the north and Main Avenue to the south. Locals are proud of their nineteen-story limestone **capitol building**, 600 E Boulevard Ave, dating from the mid-1930s and set at the crest of a public park. The interior, a model of spatial economy and marbled Art Deco elegance, is open for free guided **tours** (Mon–Fri 8–11am & 1–4pm; in summer also Sat 9–11am & 1–4pm & Sun 1–4pm). Across the street, the superb **North Dakota Heritage Center** (Mon–Fri 8am–5pm, Sat 9am–5pm, Sun 11am–5pm; donation) divides the state's past into six sections, from the dinosaurs onwards. Look out for Sitting Bull's painted robe and the bison "smell box," which offers curious tourists a whiff of buffalo dung.

The major reason to venture into **MANDAN** is **Fort Abraham Lincoln State Park** ($5), five miles south of downtown via Hwy-1806, where the centerpiece is the **Custer House** (daily: summer 9am–7pm; Sept 9am–5pm; Oct 1–15 1–5pm; Nov–Apr by appointment; $6), an admirable reconstruction of the 1874 original designed by the brutally ambitious, indefatigable horseman himself. The guided tour supplies nuggets of quirky information about Custer (he loved to eat raw onions), his wife, and their household prior to his death at Little Big Horn in 1876. Nearer the river, four earth lodge reconstructions stand on the site of the once-vast **On-A-Slant village**, occupied by the Mandan (or River-Dweller) tribe from about 1610 to the late 1700s. After the Mandan abandoned On-A-Slant, they moved upstream and settled on the site that became Fort Mandan, where in 1804 the explorers Lewis and Clark came into contact with the Shoshone woman **Sakakawea** (aka Sacajawea), who helped guide them west towards the Pacific. The site and adjacent **historical museum** (daily: summer 9am–7pm; Sept 9am–5pm; Oct daily 1–5pm; Nov–Apr by appointment; free with purchase of Custer House ticket) sit below a bluff topped with replicas of the Fort Lincoln infantry post.

Practicalities

Bismarck's **Greyhound** terminal is at 3750 E Rosser Ave; its **visitor center** is at 1600 Burnt Boat Drive (Mon–Fri 8am–7pm, Sat 8am–6pm, Sun 10am–5pm;

⊤701/222-4308 or 1-800/767-3555, ⓦwww.bismarckmandancvb.com). For clean rooms near downtown, try the *Expressway Inn*, 200 E Bismarck Expressway (⊤701/222-2900; ❸). Great **rooms**, a pool, and breakfast are on offer at *Fairfield Inn*, which has two locations, one near the airport at 135 Ivy Ave (⊤701/223-9293; ❹) and the other near the I-94/US-83 interchange at 1120 E Century Ave (⊤701/223-9077; ❹). For **camping**, try the excellent Cross Ranch State Park, thirty minutes north of Bismarck on Hwy-1806 (⊤701/794-3731; vehicle fee $5, campsites $8). Overlapped by a six-thousand-acre nature preserve, the park features sixteen miles of **trails**. Closer to town, you can camp in Fort Abraham Lincoln State Park (⊤1-800/807-4723; $8-14).

There is limited **dining** and **nightlife** in Bismarck. *Peacock Alley*, 422 E Main St (⊤701/255-7917), serves tasty Italian and American cuisine. In Mandan, the *Drug Store and Soda Fountain*, 316 W Main St (⊤701/663-5900), is a good place to grab a cheap lunch and some ice cream. There is fine dining at *Meriwether's Restaurant* at the Port of Bismarck (⊤701/258-0666), where the *Lewis & Clark* riverboat takes visitors on narrated **historical rides** ($15 daytime, $40 Sat dinner cruise; ⊤701/255-4233).

⑩ Theodore Roosevelt National Park

The **Theodore Roosevelt National Park**, a huge tract of multihued rock formations, rough grassland, and lazy streams, is split into north and south units approximately seventy miles apart; the area between comprises a checkerboard of federal, state, and privately owned territory. Exploring the park's seventy thousand acres is like entering different rooms, from desert to woods to mountains. Both units (daily dawn–dusk; $5 per person, maximum $10 per car) are at their most subtle at sunrise or sundown, the best times to observe such fauna as elk, antelope, bison, and several fascinating, closely-knit prairie dog communities.

Your first taste of the larger, more popular **southern unit** is likely to be at the breathtaking **Painted Canyon**, seven miles east of the town of Medora off I-94 exit 32. Here and elsewhere in the park, the land is like a sedimentary layer cake that for millions of years has been beaten by hard, infrequent rains, baked by the sun into a kaleidoscope of colors, and cut through to its base by erosive streams and rivers. A mile-long **nature hike**, accessible in the summer months, begins at the end of the canyon's boardwalk.

The southern unit's main **visitor center** in Medora (June to early Sept Mon–Fri 8am–6pm, Sat & Sun 8am–8pm; early Sept to May Mon–Fri 8am–4.30pm; ⊤701/623-4466) counts as park headquarters, and runs tours, nature walks, and lectures by campfire in high season. Out back, the simple cabin was used by the young Roosevelt while a partner in the Maltese Cross Ranch (free guided tours daily until 4.15pm). A highlight of the scenic 36-mile loop road is the sublime view from **Wind Canyon**, ten miles out of Medora. Peaceful Valley Ranch (⊤701/623-4568), seven miles from Medora and a mile from the park's first-come, first-served *Cottonwood Campground* ($10 per tent site), arranges horseback tours in summer for $25 for 90 minutes.

The smaller **northern unit**, off Hwy-85 near Watford City, receives only a tenth as many visitors, though it's more spectacular than its southern counterpart; the highlight is **Oxbow Overlook**, at the end of a 15-mile scenic drive. The **visitor center** here is open daily (9am–5.30pm; ⊤701/842-2333). Keep in mind that the northern unit is on Central time, while the southern unit is on Mountain time (see p.68).

Medora

MEDORA, the southern gateway to Theodore Roosevelt National Park, languished in obscurity until the early 1960s, but has become one of North Dakota's principal attractions, an inoffensively touristy place with enough to keep you busy, and reasonably interested, for most of a day. The biggest noise in town is the **Medora Musical** (daily 8.30pm; $24–30; ⊕1-800/633-6721; ⓦwww.medora.com), a pseudo-Western, super-Americana variety show staged beneath the stars in a vast, modern amphitheater. There is a lot of clogging and yodeling, plenty of accolades to a certain 26th US president, and special guest appearances that range from Chinese chair-stackers to double-jointed Lithuanians. The extravaganza is preceded by a fantastic feed whereby 240 steaks are simultaneously fondued on pitchforks inside giant oil vats (6.30pm; $22.50).

A better idea is to take to the hills on a mountain **bike** – the **Maah Daah Hey Trail** dips and curves through spectacular country for 96 miles. Rent from Dakota Cyclery in Medora (⊕701/623-4808; $25–35 for a half-day). The conservative Theodore Roosevelt Medora Foundation owns and operates most of the town and its attractions, including the quaint and central *Rough Rider Hotel* (⊕701/623-4444; ❺) and *Badlands* (⊕701/623-4422; ❺) motel, which has an outdoor pool. (Check-in for both motels is at the *Badlands* motel.) While these hotels only operate from May to September, the *Americinn Motel* (⊕701/623-4800 or 1-800/634-3444; ❺–❻) is open year-round. The *Medora Campground* (⊕701/623-4435) caters to both tents ($18) and RVs ($25–30). For something a little more rural, try the *Buffalo Gap Guest Ranch* (❶–❹; ⊕701/623-4200, ⓦwww.buffalogapguestranch.com), six miles west of Medora at the trailhead of the Buffalo Gap Trail. The ranch offers accommodation ranging from tent sites to cabins and has stables as well. **Eating** options are limited to a few bars and restaurants clustered in the downtown.

The Rockies

AL - ALABAMA	IN - INDIANA	MN - MINNESOTA	RI - RHODE ISLAND
AR - ARKANSAS	LA - LOUISIANA	MS - MISSISSIPPI	SC - SOUTH CAROLINA
CT - CONNECTICUT	MA - MASSACHUSETTS	NC - NORTH CAROLINA	VA - VIRGINIA
DE - DELAWARE	MD - MARYLAND	NH - NEW HAMPSHIRE	VT - VERMONT
FL - FLORIDA	ME - MAINE	NJ - NEW JERSEY	WI - WISCONSIN
IL - ILLINOIS	MI - MICHIGAN	PA - PENNSYLVANIA	WV - WEST VIRGINIA

CHAPTER 11

Highlights

❋ **Durango & Silverton Narrow Gauge Railroad, CO** This steam-train ride corkscrews through spectacular mountains to the mining town of Silverton. See p.867

❋ **Mesa Verde National Park, CO** Explore the thirteenth century cliffside dwellings of the Ancestral Puebloans, the first major civilization in the region. See p.860

❋ **Buffalo Bill Historical Center, WY** Centering on an extraordinary museum, the town of Cody celebrates the life and times of Buffalo Bill. See p.879

❋ **Jackson Hole, WY** Ideal for climbing, biking, or skiing in the Grand Tetons by day, followed by eating, drinking, or stomping in the cowboy bars by night. See p.889

❋ **Going-to-the-Sun road, Glacier National Park, MT** The hairpin turns along this fifty-mile stretch offer staggering views near the Continental Divide. See p.907

❋ **Gates of the Mountains, MT** Lewis and Clark were awe-struck floating past these huge limestone cliffs, and you will be, too. See p.902

❋ **Sawtooth Mountains, ID** Of all Idaho's 81 mountain ranges, the Sawtooth summits make for the most awe-inspiring scenic drive. See p.912

△ Durango & Silverton Narrow Gauge Railroad

The Rockies

Exploring the **Rocky Mountain** states of **Colorado, Wyoming, Montana**, and **Idaho** could literally take forever. Stretching over one thousand miles from the virgin forests on the Canadian border to the deserts of New Mexico, America's rugged spine encompasses an astonishing array of **landscapes** – geyser basins, lava flows, arid valleys, and huge sand dunes – each in its own way as dramatic as the region's magnificent white-topped peaks. The geological grandeur is enhanced by wildlife such as bison, bear, moose, and elk, and the conspicuous legacy of the miners, cowboys, outlaws, and Native Americans who fought over the area's rich resources during the nineteenth century.

Apart from the **Ancestral Puebloan** cliff-dwellers, who lived in southern Colorado until around 1300 AD, most **Native Americans** in this region were nomadic hunters. They inhabited the western extremities of the Great Plains, the richest buffalo-grazing land in the continent. Spaniards, groping through Colorado in the sixteenth century in search of gold, were the first whites to venture into the Rockies. But only after the territory was sold to the US in 1803 as part of the **Louisiana Purchase** was it thoroughly charted, starting with the **Lewis and Clark expedition** that traversed Montana and Idaho in 1805. As a result of the team's reports of abundant game, the fabled "**mountainmen**" had soon trapped the beavers here to the point of virtual extinction. They left as soon as the pelt boom was over, however, and permanent white settlement did not begin until gold was discovered near Denver in 1858. Within a decade, speculators were plundering every accessible gorge and creek in the four states in the search for valuable ores. The construction of transcontinental rail lines and the establishment of vast cattle ranches to feed the mining camps led to the slaughter of millions of buffalo, and conflict with the Native Americans became inevitable. The **Sioux** and **Cheyenne**, led by brilliant strategists like Sitting Bull and Crazy Horse, achieved decisive victories over the US Army, most notably at Little Bighorn – "**Custer's Last Stand**." However, a massive military operation had cleared the region of all warring tribes by the late 1870s.

Most of those who came after the Native Americans saw the Rockies strictly in terms of profit: they took what they wanted and left. Small communities in this isolated terrain remain exclusively dedicated to coal, oil, or some other single commodity, and all too often the uncertain tightrope walk between boom and bust is evident in their run-down facades.

Each of the four states has its own distinct character. **Colorado**, with fifty peaks over 14,000ft, is the most mountainous and populated, as well as the economic leader of the region. Friendly, sophisticated **Denver** is the only major metropolis in the Rockies. It's also the most visited city, in part because it's that much more accessible, and it plays the role of gateway to some of the best ski resorts in the

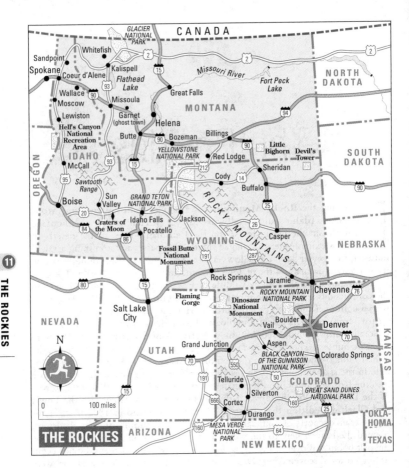

THE ROCKIES

country. Less touched by the tourist circus is vast, brawny **Montana**, where the "Big Sky" looks down on a glorious verdant manuscript scribbled over with gushing streams, lakes, and tiny communities.

Vast stretches of scrubland fill **Wyoming**, the country's least populous state, best known for gurgling, spitting **Yellowstone**, adjacent **Grand Teton National Park**, and the nearby **Bighorn Mountains**. Rugged, remote, and desolate **Idaho** holds some of the Rocky Mountains' last unexplored wildernesses, most notably the mighty **Sawtooth** range.

Between early June and early September you can expect **temperatures** in the high sixties all the way up to a hundred degrees Fahrenheit, depending on whether you are in the high desert of Wyoming, the plains of Idaho, or the mountains of Colorado. In the mountains, you should be prepared for wild variations – and, of course, the higher you go the colder it gets. The altitude is high enough to warrant a period of acclimatization, while the intensity of the sun at these elevations can be uncomfortably fierce. In fact, parts of Wyoming and Colorado bask in more hours of sunshine per year than San Diego or Miami Beach. Spring (the "mud season"), when the snow melts, is the least attractive time to visit the Rockies, and while the delicate golds of quaking aspen trees light up the mountainsides in early fall, by October things are generally a bit cold for enjoyable hiking or sports. Most **ski** runs are open by late November and operate well into March – or even June, depending on snow conditions. The coldest month is January, when temperatures below 0°F are common.

Attempting to rush around every national park and major town is a sure way to miss out on one of the Rockies' real delights – coaxing your car along the tight switchback roads that wind up and over precipitous mountain passes, especially through the majestic **Continental Divide**. Remember to check in the rear-view mirror as you go, though – you might be missing that perfect photo for your album. At some point it's worth forsaking motorized transportation, though, to see at least some of the area by **bike**; the Rockies contain some of the most challenging and rewarding cycling terrain on the continent. And of course, you cannot count yourself a visitor to the area without embarking on a hike or two.

Colorado

Geographically diverse **COLORADO** veers from the flat, endless plains of the east to the colossal mountains of the west. In the north, **Native Americans** hunted and trapped in lush mountain valleys in summer, and returned to the prairies for the winter; in the south, the Ancestral Puebloans of Mesa Verde grew corn on their isolated mesas and shared in the great early civilization of the Southwest.

Parts of what's now Colorado accrued to the US at different times: the east and north were acquired under the **Louisiana Purchase** in 1803, while the south was won 45 years later in the war with **Mexico**. (Land grants issued under Mexican rule were honored by the Americans, which accounts for a still-strong Hispanic influence.) Gold-hungry Spaniards came through in the sixteenth century, and US Army Colonel Zebulon Pike ventured into the mountains on an exploratory expedition in 1806, but the Native American way of life only became seriously threatened with the discovery of **gold** west of Denver in 1858. At that time Colorado was still part of Kansas Territory; it became a territory in its own right in 1861, and a state in 1876. The distractions of the Civil War gave the Native Americans the opportunity to fight back, but they were soon overwhelmed. From then until the end of the century, Colorado boomed; the quantities of gold and silver extracted from the mountains did not compare with the riches found in California, but they were sufficient to fuel a rip-roaring frontier lifestyle.

For the modern visitor, the obvious first stop is **Denver**, at the eastern edge of the Rockies and the biggest city for six hundred miles. Outside Denver, the northern half of the state holds the most popular destinations, starting with the dynamic college town of **Boulder** and the spectacular **Rocky Mountain National Park**. The majority of the resorts that have made Colorado the continent's foremost **skiing** destination snuggle into the mountains to the west of Denver: **Summit County** attracts the most visitors, **Vail** is considered best for terrain, and **Aspen** boasts the glitziest apres-ski scene. The far west of the state stretches onto the red-rock deserts of the Colorado Plateau, where the dry climate has preserved the extraordinary natural sculptures of **Colorado National Monument**. **Pikes Peak** towers over the enjoyable city of **Colorado Springs**, but the rest of the state's **southeast** quarter is mostly agricultural plains. To the **southwest**, old mining towns like **Crested Butte** and **Durango** stand revitalized in the mountains, while **Mesa Verde National Park** preserves perhaps the most impressive of all the cliff cities left by the ancient Ancestral Puebloan civilization.

Getting around Colorado

By far the largest **airport** in Colorado is in Denver. Shuttle buses radiate from here to all the main towns and ski resorts – as do commuter-style aircraft. Denver is also a major hub for Greyhound **buses** to all neighboring states. Amtrak **trains** run straight across the middle of Colorado, timed in both directions to pass through magnificent Glenwood Canyon in daylight hours, but are so slow that they're barely more efficient than the hugely enjoyable tourist train, the Durango & Silverton Narrow Gauge Railroad, in the southwest.

Colorado is also one of the best destinations in the world for **cyclists**, hosting numerous on- and off-road championships. For excellent **maps and guides** to cycle routes in the state, contact the State Department of Transportation (T303/639-1111 or 1-877/315-7623, W www.cotrip.org).

Denver

Its skyscrapers marking the final transition between the Great Plains and the American West, **DENVER** stands at the threshold of the **Rocky Mountains**. Despite being known as the "**Mile High City**," and serving as the obvious point of arrival for travelers heading into the mountains, it is itself uniformly flat. The majestic peaks are clearly visible but begin to rise roughly fifteen miles west of downtown, allowing Denver plenty of room to spread out.

Mineral wealth has always been at the heart of the city's prosperity, with all the fluctuations of fortune that this entails. Though local resources have been progressively exhausted, Denver has managed to hang on to its role as the most important commercial and transportation nexus in the state. Its original "foundation" in 1858 was by pure chance; this was the first spot where small quantities of **gold** were discovered in Colorado. There was no significant river, let alone a road, but prospectors came streaming in, regardless of prior claims to the land – least of all those of the **Arapahoe**, who had supposedly been confirmed in their ownership of the area by the Fort Laramie Treaty of 1851.

There was actually very little gold in Denver itself; the infant town swarmed briefly with disgruntled fortune-seekers, who decamped when news came in of the massive gold strike at Central City. Denver survived, however, prospering further with the discovery of **silver** in the mountains. All sorts of shady characters made this their home; Jefferson "Soapy" Smith, for example, acquired his nickname here, selling bars of soap at extortionate prices under the pretence that some contained $100 bills. When the first railroads bypassed Denver – the death knell for so many other communities – the citizens simply banded together and built their own connecting spur.

These days, Denver is a welcoming and enjoyable city, with a fairly liberal outlook. Tourism is based on getting out into the great outdoors rather than on sightseeing in town, but somehow the city's isolation, a good six hundred miles from any conurbation of even vaguely similar size, gives its 2.5-million population a refreshing friendliness; and in a city that is used to providing its own entertainment there always seems to be something going on.

Arrival, information, and getting around

The colossal, ultra-high-tech **Denver International Airport** (☎ 303/342-2000 or 1-800/247-2336, ⓦ www.flydenver.com) lies out on the plains 24 miles northeast of downtown. Regular RTD SkyRide **buses** can take you downtown ($8 one way, $14 roundtrip) and to Boulder ($10 one way). Buses leave from

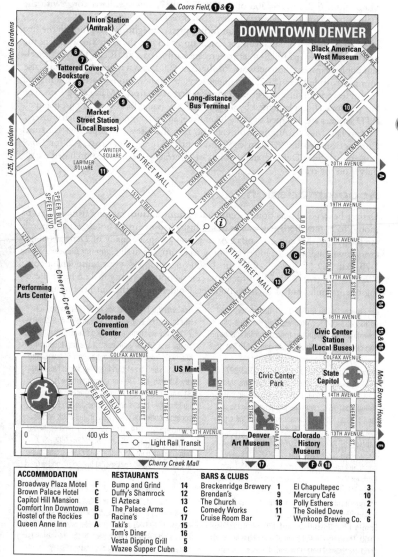

ACCOMMODATION		RESTAURANTS		BARS & CLUBS			
Broadway Plaza Motel	F	Bump and Grind	14	Breckenridge Brewery	1	El Chapultepec	3
Brown Palace Hotel	C	Duffy's Shamrock	12	Brendan's	9	Mercury Café	10
Capitol Hill Mansion	E	El Azteca	13	The Church	18	Polly Esthers	2
Comfort Inn Downtown	B	The Palace Arms	C	Comedy Works	11	The Soiled Dove	4
Hostel of the Rockies	D	Racine's	17	Cruise Room Bar	7	Wynkoop Brewing Co.	6
Queen Anne Inn	A	Taki's	15				
		Tom's Diner	16				
		Vesta Dipping Grill	5				
		Wazee Supper Clubn	8				

outside exit 506 in the East terminal and 511 in the West terminal. There are also a number of independent shuttles that, for $20, will drop you off at a downtown hotel; shuttles to many of the state's major ski resorts can also be arranged within the terminal, though advance reservations are recommended.

Amtrak **trains** arrive on the northwest side of downtown Denver at the beautiful old **Union Station** on Wynkoop Street, and the Greyhound **bus terminal** is every bit as close to the action at 1055 19th St.

For **information**, stop by the Official Visitor Information Center, conveniently located downtown at 1600 California St (Mon–Fri 9am–6pm, Sat 9am–5pm, Sun 11am–3pm; ☎303/892-1505 or 1-800/233-6837, ⊚www.denver.org) with the main entrance on the pedestrian-only 16th Street.

Negotiating downtown Denver **on foot** is pretty straightforward, though the free **buses** (daily 6am–1am) that run for a mile up and down the 16th Street Mall at the heart of the city's grid-like street pattern are hard to pass up. RTD, Denver's excellent public transportation network (☎303/229-6000, ⊚www.rtd-denver.com), also runs pay-to-ride buses ($1.25); frequent services to the various sports stadiums and airport leave from the underground **Market Street Station** at Market and 16th. The bus network is supplemented by a **light railway** (same local fares as buses) and all RTD services are designed to carry bikes (free) and accommodate wheelchair users.

From late-May to August, you can also ride the Grey Line-operated **Cultural Connection Trolley** (8.30am–5.30pm; hourly; $16 for 1-day pass; $25 for 2-day pass), which links Denver's main points of interest; passes can be purchased – cash only – on the trolleys.

Accommodation

Denver has a good selection of central **accommodation**, ranging from hostels to motels to homey B&Bs, as well as grand historic downtown hotels. Chain motels are located further out on Colfax Avenue and alongside many of Denver's major cross-town highways. If you're planning to **camp**, the drab *Camping Denver North*, I-70 exit 229 (☎303/622-9274 or 1-800/562-6538, ⊚www.campdenver.com; RVs $29–36, tents $20–22), is the most central option – but you'd do better heading twenty miles out of town to Boulder, Golden, or further into the mountains.

Broadway Plaza Motel 1111 Broadway ☎303/893-0303. Within walking distance of downtown, this plain but friendly motel has large and clean rooms (with phones and cable TV), free parking, and reasonable rates. ❸

Brown Palace Hotel 321 17th St ☎303/297-3111 or 1-800/321-2599, ⊚www.brownpalace.com. Beautifully maintained downtown landmark dating from 1892, with elegant dining rooms and public areas. Step inside and marvel at the eight-story cast-iron atrium. ❽–❾

Capitol Hill Mansion 1207 Pennsylvania St ☎303/839-5221 or 1-800-839-9329, ⊚www.capitolhillmansion.com. This luxurious B&B in a turreted Victorian sandstone mansion is on a leafy street near the state capitol. Each of its eight antique-furnished rooms are delightful, and several include large whirlpool tubs. ❻

Comfort Inn Downtown 401 17th St ☎303/296-0400. This very central comfortable chain hotel has good continental breakfast and shares some facili-

ties with the *Brown Palace Hotel* (see above). ❺

Hostel of the Rockies 1717 Race St ☎303/861-7777, ⊚www.innkeeperrockies.com. Denver's best hostel is a 20min walk east of the capitol down seedy Colfax Ave to a far better part of town, with free and safe street parking. The hostel has laundry, kitchen, and TV room, and dorm beds go for $17 a night. Private rooms ($35) are in a separate building five blocks from the hostel. On Fridays sociable cookouts take place in the back garden.

Hampton Inn DIA 6290 Tower Rd, next to the airport ☎303/371-0200 or 1-800/426-7866, ⊚www.hamptoninn.com. A comfortable place close to the airport with basic continental breakfast and airport shuttle included. ❹

Queen Anne Inn 2147 Tremont Place ☎303/296-6666 or 1-800/432-4667, ⊚www.queenannebnb.com. Central and very hospitable 1879 B&B near a peaceful park where you can catch carriage rides; each of the 14 rooms is tastefully and individually decorated. ❹–❼

The City

If you're not here to work, **downtown's** main draw is the shops and restaurants of **16th Street**, a pedestrian zone that's also served by free buses. There's also a range of galleries, brewpubs, shops, and lofts in **LoDo**, or Lower Downtown, a revitalized late-Victorian district bordered by 14th and 20th, and Wynkoop and Larimer streets. It was here, between 14th and 15th streets, that William Larimer built Denver's original log cabin. That burned down in a general conflagration within a few years, whereupon a city ordinance decreed that all new construction should be in brick. Opposite the venerable Union Street train station is a branch of one of the best **bookstores** in the US: the Tattered Cover Bookstore at 1628 16th St and Wynkoop.

Denver's black community is most prominent in the old **Five Points** district, northeast of LoDo, created to house black railroad workers in the 1870s. The **Black American West Museum** at 3091 California St (May–Sept daily 10am–5pm; Oct– April Wed–Sun 10am–2pm; $6; ☎303/292-2566, ⊛www.blackamericanwest .org), has intriguing details on black pioneers and outlaws. Perhaps the most interesting section is on cowboys, which debunks a lot of Western myths: one-third of all cowboys were black, many former slaves who left the South after the Civil War.

Three blocks from the southeastern end of 16th St, the **State Capitol** at Broadway and E Colfax Avenue (Mon–Fri 7am–5.30pm), offers a commanding view of the Rockies swelling on the horizon. Its thirteenth step up to the entrance is exactly one mile above sea level. The capitol is a rather predictable copy of the one in Washington, DC, but the free tours (every 30mins; 9.30am–3.30pm) are pleasantly informal, and you can climb its dome for an even better view.

Civic Center Park, right in front of the capitol, is flanked by two of Denver's finest museums. The glass-tile-covered **Denver Art Museum** at 100 W 14th Ave (Tues & Thurs–Sat 10am–5pm, Wed 10am–9pm, Sun noon–5pm; tours Tues–Fri & Sun 1.30pm, Sat 11am & 1.30pm; $8; ⊛www.denverartmuseum.org) has a solid collection of paintings from around the world, but is most noteworthy for its superb examples of Native American craftwork, with marvelous beadwork by Plains tribes and some finely detailed Navajo weavings. Some of the pre-Columbian art from Central America – particularly the extraordinary Olmec miniatures – is also spectacular. Also flanking the park is the **Colorado History Museum** at 1300 Broadway (Mon–Sat 10am–5pm, Sun noon–5pm; $5; ⊛www.coloradohistory. org) whose most interesting exhibits are in the downstairs galleries. Several dioramas, made under the auspices of the WPA in the 1930s, show historical scenes in fascinating detail, starting with the Ancestral Puebloans of Mesa Verde, following up with trappers meeting with Indians at a "fair in the wilderness" in the early 1800s, and a model of Denver in 1860. An exhaustive archive of **photographs** of the early West showcases the work of W.H. Jackson (1843–1942).

Two or three miles east of downtown en route to the airport, the enormous **City Park** is home to the **Denver Museum of Nature and Science**, 2001 Colorado Blvd (daily 9am–5pm; museum $10, planetarium $8, IMAX $8, all three $20; ☎303/322-7009 or 1-800/925-2250, ⊛www.dmns.org). Its exhibits extend beyond the (very good) dinosaur exhibits and wildlife displays to include anthropological material on Native Americans. There's also a large **zoo** nearby (daily: April– Sept 9am–5pm, Oct–March 10am–4pm; admission April–Sept $11, Oct–March $9; ☎303/376-4800, ⊛www.denverzoo.org), whose four thousand inmates include a couple of huge lowland gorillas in a large, thickly wooded sanctuary.

Denver's **Six Flags Elitch Gardens** theme park, on the western edge of downtown at 2000 Elitch Circle (June–Sept daily 10am–10pm; Oct–May irregular hours; $38, parking $9; ☎303/595-4386, ⓦwww.sixflags.com), is surprisingly close to the city center (a ten-minute walk along the Cherry Creek cycle path), and has some great white-knuckle rides as well as a decent **water park**.Finally, twenty miles west of downtown (though essentially a Denver suburb), lies the town of **Golden,** which is linked by regular buses to Market Street Station. Since the 1860s the town has been virtually synonymous with beer giant **Coors,** the world's largest brewery (Mon–Sat 10am–4pm; free; ☎303/277-2337, ⓦwww.coors.com). Located three blocks east of Washington Avenue, Golden's main thoroughfare, the brewery serves up 90min tours full of corporate self-promotion. The tour ends with a tasting session (bring ID) of their numerous products, including their much-maligned (or loved, depending on whom you talk to) "Silver Bullet," the light beer for which the company is most famous. On the opposite side of Golden's downtown, mountains rise sharply from the plains, among them Lookout Mountain, site of the **Buffalo Bill Museum** (May–Oct daily 9am–5pm, Nov–April Tues–Sun 9am–4pm; $3; ⓦwww.buffalobill.org) and final resting place of William Cody, famed frontiersman, buffalo-hunter, army scout, and showman, who died in Denver in 1915 (see also p.879). Though now surrounded by huge electricity pylons, the gravesite offers great views in both directions, over the city and out to the mountains. The adjacent museum does a thorough job of outlining Buffalo Bill's past, and one of the more gruesome elements on display is a pistol whose handle has been fashioned from human bone.

Eating

As well as plenty of Western-themed steak and barbecue places, Denver has a cosmopolitan selection of international **restaurants**. Several of the city's famed **brewpubs** serve good quality meals, too. Of the several distinct restaurant districts, the **Larimer Square** area is the most easily accessible on foot.

Bump and Grind 439 E 17th Ave ☎303/861-4841. Cheap café/bistro just outside downtown that's the flamboyant hub for the local gay social scene, particularly during Sunday brunch when the waitstaff is almost exclusively transvestite. The food is excellent, creative, and inexpensive – the eggs Benedict on sourdough bread costs just $6.

Casa Bonita 6715 W Colfax Ave ☎303/232-5115. Absolutely wild Mexican place, seating 1200 diners, a long way out on Colfax. Gunfights, cliff divers, abandoned mines to explore – the only weak link is the food itself, but it's all a lot of fun (especially for kids) and far from expensive.

Duffy's Shamrock 1635 Court Place ☎303/534-4935. Late-night downtown pub serving food, including sandwiches, steaks, and seafood, until 1.30am.

🏃 **El Azteca** 301 16th St. Lunchtimes, office workers arrive en-masse for the authentic top-notch Mexican food served in this small eatery in the basement of a dreary food-court. Prices are low, service quick, and the food – particularly the *carne asada* – excellent.

The Palace Arms 321 17th St ☎303/297-3111. This small and classy restaurant tucked in the *Brown Palace Hotel* (see p.842) is the ultimate splurge in town, with a menu of mostly seasonal game

specialties, and decor of Napoleonic period antiques – including a pair of Napoleon's dueling pistols.

Racine's 850 Bannock St ☎303/595-0418. Just south of downtown, this large, laid-back place is a Denver institution. Housed in a former auto showroom, the inexpensive restaurant serves excellent egg-based breakfasts, with imaginative pastas, reliably good sandwiches, and spicy Mexican entrees later in the day.

Taki's 341 E Colfax Ave. Giant and inexpensive portions of Japanese food are served in this friendly and longstanding local family business, with cafeteria-style ordering that gets you the food fast. The miso soup is too good to miss and the salmon bowl – a sizeable piece of salmon smothered in a zesty, mustardy sauce with rice – is exceptional, and costs under $5.

🏃 **Tom's Diner** 601 E Colfax Ave and Pearl St ☎303/861-7493. Wonderfully gritty and authentic 24hr diner, providing cheap deals on big portions of stock diner food at the seedy end of town.

Vesta Dipping Grill 1822 Blake St ☎303/296-1970. Attractive restaurant in a renovated LoDo warehouse serving tasty food in unusual combinations, based around the "art" of dipping meat or veggies in a spectrum of flavors (Mediterranean, Asian, Mexican).

Wazee Supper Club 1600 15th St ☎303/623-9518. Well-established LoDo dining room, serving good cheap burgers, deli sandwiches, and superb pizzas, plus a full range of beers, in an Art Deco atmosphere. One of the few places open really late (1.30am most nights).

Nightlife and entertainment

The congregation of brewpubs and sports bars in the LoDo district, particularly near Coors Field, have made this the city's liveliest nightlife area. There are plenty of other more stylish or relaxing places to drink here, too. Most bars close around 1am. For news of **musical** happenings, consult the weekly free *Westword*, found in sidewalk dispensers and cafes around downtown.

The remarkable **Red Rocks Amphitheater** (☎303/694-1234, @www .redrocksonline.com), fifteen miles west of downtown Denver via I-70 (exit 259), has been the setting for thousands of rock and classical concerts; U2 recorded *Under a Blood Red Sky* here. This 9000-seat venue is squeezed between two 400ft red-sandstone rocks that seem to glow in early morning and late evening. The surrounding Red Rocks Park is open to visitors free of charge during the day.

Denver's pride and joy, the modern **Denver Performing Arts Complex Complex** (the "PLEX") on 14th and Curtis streets (☎303/893-4100, @www.artscomplex .org), is home to the Denver Center Theater Company, Colorado Symphony Orchestra, Opera Colorado, and the Colorado Ballet, and hosts performances nightly. Facilities in the complex include eight **theaters**, as well as the **Symphony Hall** (which is in the round, giving it superb acoustics).

In the hunt for **tickets** to all cultural and sporting events, both Ticketmaster (☎303/830-8497) and Ticketman (☎303/430-1111) can usually help. You can try the Ticket Bus, parked on 16th and Curtis, in person (daily 10am–6pm), where you'll often find last-minute **deals** on shows that have yet to sell out.

Breckenridge Brewery 2220 Blake St ☎303/297-3644. Cozy and lively brewpub opposite Coors Field – making it an ideal hangout after a ballgame – with quality craft beer, brewed on the premises, and a killer range of delicious barbecue grub.

Brendan's 1624 Market St ☎303/595-0609. Small basement pub in the LoDo with regular live blues; big-name acts pop by a few times a month and cover is rarely more than $10.

El Chapultepec 20th and Market streets ☎303/295-9126. Tiny, popular LoDo venue near Coors Field, with nightly live jazz and occasional big names.

The Church 1160 Lincoln St ☎303/832-3528. A dance club inside a gutted cathedral, combining a downtown nightlife landmark, a wine bar, sushi bar, and three invariably busy dance floors. Plays mostly hard house or garage, though the music and crowd can be eclectic. $5–15 cover.

Comedy Works 1226 15th St ☎303/595-3637 @www.comedyworks.com. Right off Larimer Square, Denver's major comedy venue is the most likely place to find visiting big-name stand-up acts. Shows kick off nightly at 8pm, with several performances on weekend nights.

Cruise Room Bar *The Oxford Hotel*, 1600 17th St ☎303/628-5400. This place is a replica of the Art Deco bar on the *Queen Mary* ocean liner. Worth a stop for the atmosphere alone.

Grizzly Rose 5450 N Valley Hwy ☎303/295-1330 @www.grizzlyrose.com. Celebrated Country and Western venue a 10min drive north of downtown on I-25 (take exit 215). The huge venue has bands every night, attracts famous names regularly, and has been named the Country's Best Country Music Club several years running. Cover $5–10.

Mercury Café 2199 California St ☎303/294-9281, @www.mercurycafe.com. When there's not jazz on at *The Merc*, there's swing dancing, poetry readings, or some other form of entertainment. The club is combined with a good-value restaurant, which serves lots of healthy choices, many vegetarian.

Polly Esthers 2301 Blake St ☎303/382-1976. Enormous and consistently popular club with '70s and '80s hits playing on two floors. Cover $5–10.

The Soiled Dove 1949 Market St ☎303/299-0100 @www.soileddove.com. Hugely popular bar with an often rowdy rooftop overlooking Market St. Features an eclectic variety of live music almost every night, from local to national names and from jazz to rock.

Wynkoop Brewing Co. 1634 18th St ☎303/297-2700. Opposite Union Station, the state's first brewpub serves up good home-brewed beers and great bar food. There's an elegant pool hall upstairs, and live entertainment Thurs–Sat. Brewery tours, with free samples, are given on Saturdays (1–5pm).

Northern Colorado

The major attraction for visitors in the Denver area is **Rocky Mountain National Park** to the northwest. Though on the map the distances involved may not look that great, it would be a mistake to attempt to see the whole park on a day-trip from Denver. Segments of its loop drive can be very slow and laborious, and in a single day it's more realistic just to dip a few miles into the park's eastern fringes.

The lively foothill town of **Boulder** can be used as a base, though the smaller mountain towns give you more time in the wilds: **Grand Lake**, near the western entrance, makes a more attractive stopover than overblown **Estes Park** on the east, while **Winter Park** is an affordable, enjoyable ski resort. Further west, midway across the state on either side of the I-70 freeway, you'll find the famous Rocky Mountain ski resorts of **Vail**, **Aspen**, and the rest, and the evocative mining town of **Leadville**. Continuing toward the Utah border, the landscape dips and rises in a patchwork of granite peaks, raging rivers, and red-sandstone canyons, winding up at **Grand Junction** and the memorable scenery of **Colorado National Monument**.

⑪ Boulder

BOULDER, just 27 miles northwest of Denver on US-36, is one of the liveliest college towns in the country, filled with a young population that seems to divide its time between phenomenally healthy daytime pursuits and almost equally unhealthy nighttime activities – the town is often referred to as "seven miles surrounded by reality." It was founded in 1858 by a prospecting party who felt that the nearby Flatiron Mountains, the first swell of the Rockies, "looked right for gold"; in fact they found little, but the community grew anyway.

With an easygoing, forward-looking atmosphere and plenty of great places to eat and drink, Boulder makes an excellent place to return each night after a day in the mountains. Downtown centers on the leafy pedestrian mall of **Pearl Street**, lined with all sorts of lively cafés, galleries, and stores – including several places

△ Pearl Street, Boulder, CO

where you can rent **mountain bikes**. The most obvious short excursion is to drive or hike up nearby **Flagstaff Mountain** for views over town and further into the Rockies; any road west joins up with the Peak to Peak Highway, which heads through spectacular scenery to Estes Park and Rocky Mountain National Park. For rock climbing, **Eldorado Canyon State Park** offers many opportunities and the excellent Neptune Mountaineering, south of town in the Table Mesa shopping center, at 633 S Broadway (T 303/499-8866), can answer any questions and, of course, provide gear.

The adventurous **University of Colorado** offers regular arts **events**, including in summer the Colorado Music Festival (T 303/449-1397, W www.coloradomusicfest .org) held in the Chautauqua Auditorium, and the seven-week Colorado Shakespeare Festival (T 303/492-0554, W www.coloradoshakes.org). Even the small **Naropa Institute** (T 303/444-0202), a university founded in 1974 by a Tibetan Buddhist, has a notable presence in this liberal, alternative-thinking town, sponsoring events throughout the year.

Practicalities

The main point of entry for local and long-distance **buses** is the Transit Center, 14th and Walnut streets (T 303/442-1044). Regular services from Denver International ($10) and the city itself ($3.75) arrive here as well. For city information, visit the hospitable, low-key **Boulder Convention & Visitors Bureau**, 2440 Pearl St (Mon–Fri 9am–5pm; T 303/442-2911 or 1-800/444-0447, W www.bouldercoloradousa .com). For information on public lands around Boulder, contact the City of Boulder Open Space & Mountain Parks department (T 303-441-3440, W www. ci.boulder.co.us/openspace). One of Boulder's chief attractions is that it's easy and pleasant to get around on foot, but the town's **bus service** is also excellent: the frequent HOP and SKIP services link the University Hill area with downtown and a major mall (approximate hours: Mon–Fri 5.30am–midnight, Sun 7.30am–10.30pm; $1). For a **taxi**, try Boulder Yellow Cab (T 303/777-7777).

Even if you're not **staying** in the historic *Hotel Boulderado*, wonderfully located near Pearl Street at 2115 13th St (T 303/442-4344 or 1-800/433-4344, W www. boulderado.com; ❺–❻), wander in for a drink and and free evening jazz. Nearby, in another grand old restored building, the *Pearl Street Inn*, 1820 Pearl St (T 303/444-5584 or 1-888/810-1312, W www.pearlstreet.com; ❻), offers elegant B&B-style accommodations. The *Foot of the Mountain*, 200 W Arapahoe Ave (T 303/442-5688 or 1-866/773-5489, W www.footofthemountainmotel.com; ❹), is a friendly, log-cabin-style **motel**, nine blocks from downtown beside Boulder Creek. There's also the welcoming *Boulder International Youth Hostel* in a Victorian building at 1107 12th St, near the campus (T 303/442-0522 or 1-888/442-0522, W www.boulderhostel. com; ❷); dorm beds cost $20, and there are lots of private rooms ($49 double).

Plenty of **bars** and **restaurants** mark the Pearl Street area. The free *Boulder Weekly* newspaper is replete with dining and boozing information. One of the student favorites, ⚡*Tra-Ling's Oriental Café*, 1305 Broadway (T 303/449-0400), is a grungy canteen-style restaurant with outstanding and amazingly cheap Chinese food bought by the scoop. A far more sophisticated choice is *Sunflower*, 1701 Pearl St (T 303/440-0220), which has that typically Boulder combination of high prices, a healthy menu of organic and free-range items, and informed ethics. Gourmet vegetarians find plenty of options, though so do omnivores. If you really feel like splurging, try the *Flagstaff House*, 1138 Flagstaff Rd (T 303/442-4640), where the menu frequently changes but often includes gamey "Rocky Mountain Cuisine." The *Hotel Boulderado* (see above) also houses two popular **nighttime** haunts: the *Corner Bar*, with armchair seating, and creative, reasonably priced dishes served until late at night on the patio; and the *Catacombs*, which features nightly live blues, jazz, and acoustic guitar music. It's also one of only three bars in Boulder where you're allowed to smoke. The *West End Tavern*, 926 Pearl St (☏303/444-3535), is a great venue for live jazz and comedy, with local microbrews and spectacular Flatiron mountain views from the roof terrace. For getting your groove on, *Round Midnight* at 1005 Pearl St (☏303/442-2176) with its packed weekend dance floor is your best bet.

Rocky Mountain National Park

You don't have to go to **ROCKY MOUNTAIN NATIONAL PARK** to appreciate the full splendor of the Rockies; it is simply one small section of the mighty range, measuring roughly twenty-five by fifteen miles. A tenth of the size of Yellowstone, it attracts around the same number of visitors – around three-and-a-half million per year, and with the bulk of those coming in high summer, the one main road through the mountains can get incredibly congested. However, it is undeniably beautiful, straddling the Continental Divide at elevations often well in excess of ten thousand feet. A full third of the park is above the tree line, and large areas of snow never melt; the name of the **Never Summer Mountains** speaks volumes about the long, empty expanses of arctic-style tundra. Lower down, among the rich forests, are patches of lush greenery; you never know when you may stumble upon a sheltered mountain meadow flecked with flowers. Parallels with the European Alps readily spring to mind – helped, of course, by the heavy-handed Swiss and Bavarian themes of the region's motels and restaurants.

Approaching the park

Approaching the park from the **east**, you barely penetrate the foothills of the Rockies before you arrive at the unattractive but bustling gateway town of **ESTES PARK**, 65 miles northwest of Denver. At the end of the nineteenth century, Estes Park was the private hunting preserve of the Irish Earl of Dunraven; once he was squeezed out, the town took on the more democratic function it still serves: providing visitors with food, lodging, and other services. The **park headquarters** and main **visitor center** (daily: June–Aug 8am–9pm; Sept–May 8am–5pm; park admission $20 per vehicle, $5 pedestrians and cyclists; information ☏970/586-1206) is a couple of miles north, on US-36.

To reach the **western** entrance, 85 miles from Denver, turn north off I-70 onto US-40, which negotiates **Berthoud Pass** en route to **GRAND LAKE**, a more low-key version of Estes Park. This unlikely **yachting** center, high in the mountains, consists of one main boardwalk-lined street beside the lake with family amusements, lodgings, and restaurants. The **Kawuneeche Visitor Center** of Rocky Mountain National Park is a mile north of town (daily: May–Sept 8am–6pm; Oct–April 8am–5pm; ☏970/627-3471).

Exploring the park

The showpiece of the park is **Trail Ridge Road** (late May to mid-October), between Estes Park and Grand Lake. This 45-mile stretch of US-34, said to be the highest highway in the world, affords a succession of tremendous views, and several short trails start from parking lots along the way. There are no services on the route, which generally takes three to four hours to drive. The definite highlight is the stretch of road on either side of the **Alpine Visitor Center**, halfway along Trail Ridge Road at Fall River Pass (daily May–Aug 9am–5pm, Sept 10am–4.30pm); here the peaks and alpine tundra will take your breath away. It's really the only requisite stop for any visitor who is happy enough to see the alpine tundra

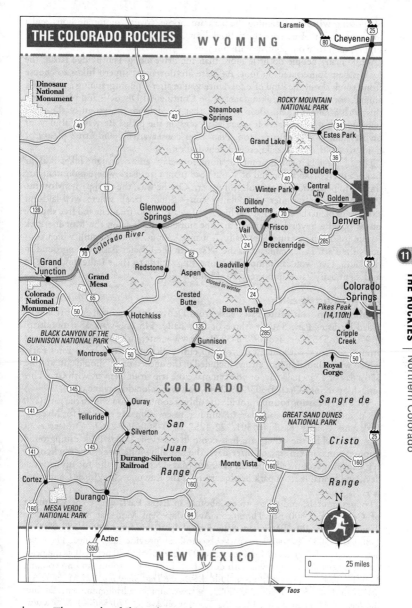

THE COLORADO ROCKIES

WYOMING

Laramie
Cheyenne
80
25

Dinosaur
National
Monument

13
40
40

Steamboat
Springs

ROCKY MOUNTAIN
NATIONAL PARK

Grand Lake
Estes Park
34

131
40

Boulder
36

139
13

Winter Park
Central
City
Golden

40

Glenwood
Springs

Dillon/
Silverthorne
70

Denver

Colorado River
Vail
Frisco
24
Breckenridge
285

Grand
Junction
70

Redstone
82
Aspen
Leadville

Colorado
Springs
11

Grand
Mesa
closed in winter

Pikes Peak
(14,110ft)

Colorado
National
Monument
85
50

Crested
Butte
Buena Vista
24

Hotchkiss

Cripple
Creek

BLACK CANYON OF THE
GUNNISON NATIONAL PARK

135

Gunnison
285

Royal
Gorge
50

Montrose
50

141
550

COLORADO

Sangre de

145

Ouray
285

GREAT SAND DUNES
NATIONAL PARK

25

141

Telluride

San

Cristo
160

145
Silverton

Juan

Durango-Silverton
Railroad
Monte Vista
160

Range

Range
N

141

Cortez
160

Durango
84
285

160

MESA VERDE
NATIONAL PARK

550
Aztec

NEW MEXICO

0   25 miles

Taos

by car. The center's **exhibits** relate to the flora and fauna of the tundra. Good areas for wildlife viewing are a little further east along Trail Ridge Road.

The other scenic drive in the park is along the unpaved, summer-only **Old Fall River Road,** which was the park's first road, completed in 1920. Running east–west along the bed of a U-shaped glacial valley, it doesn't have open mountain vistas, but it's much quieter than the Trail Ridge, and there's far more chance of spotting **wildlife**. Roaming the park are moose, coyote, mountain lions, and a total population of perhaps thirty black bears, which, with a plentiful natural food supply, tend to avoid contact with humans.

While many people do little more than the drive along Trail Ridge Road, the park is best appreciated on foot. As there are dozens of superb **hikes** to choose from, think about the kind of experience you're after – photographing a particular animal, for instance, or hiking across the Continental Divide – and plan around this with a ranger's help. Bear in mind that the delicate ecosystem of the wild, wind-blown tundra makes it essential to stay on the paths. Be watchful of your own system at this altitude, too. Plan hikes conservatively and drink plenty of fluids to avoid altitude sickness and dehydration.

The obvious launching point for numerous day- and overnight hikes is **Bear Lake**, a pretty lake at the end of a spur road from Estes Park where mountains are framed to perfection in its cool, still waters. On the way, the road passes **Moraine Park Museum** (summer only, daily 9am–4.30pm; free), where well-laid-out exhibits explain the park's natural history. To ease traffic, frequent and free **shuttle buses** operate beyond the museum. The museum itself is on the Moraine Park Route (mid-June to mid-Sept daily 7.30am–7.30pm; every 30min), which connects the Fern Lake trailhead in the west with the Glacier Basin campground in the south. Here you can jump on a connecting shuttle to **Bear Lake** (mid-June to mid-Sept daily 7am–7pm every 10–15min).

Park practicalities

Public transportation to Estes Park from Denver International Airport is provided by Estes Park Shuttle (three or four daily, $45 one-way, $85 roundtrip; ☎970/586-5151 or 1-800/950-3274, ⓦwww.estesparkshuttle.com). To get around the park without a car, you can either pick up a **tour** from Estes Park, which with admission (not always included in the quoted price) should cost around $70 a day or $35 a half-day, or you can make the trip from Denver, with Gray Line (mid-May to mid-Oct; ☎303/289-2841, ⓦwww.coloradograyline.com).

Five official **campgrounds** provide the only accommodation within the park ($20 per night). All fill early each day; in summer, reservations are essential for Moraine Park and Glacier Basin (☎301/722-1257 or 1-800/365-2267, ⓦreservations .nps.gov), while the others are first-come first-served. Longs Peak campground imposes a maximum stay of three days, the rest allow one week. For **backcountry camping** you need a permit ($20 fee May–Oct only), valid for up to seven days, and available from park headquarters or the Kawuneeche Visitor Center (see p.848).

Lodges, motels, and places to eat abound in **Estes Park** where the **Chamber of Commerce**, 500 Big Thompson Ave (May–Sept Mon–Sat 8am–8pm, Sun 9am–5pm; Oct–April Mon–Sat 8am–5pm, Sun 10am–4pm; ☎970/577-9900 or 1-800/443-7837, ⓦwww.estesparkcvb.com), can provide full listings. The *Colorado Mountain School*, 341 Moraine Ave (☎970/586-5758; $20 per bed), is the nearest thing to a hostel in town, with dorm beds in cramped rooms and no cooking facilities. Other budget options include the *Alpine Trail Ridge Inn*, 927 Moraine Ave (☎970/586-4585 or 1-800/233-5023, ⓦwww.alpinetrailridgeinn.com; ❹), and the *Bighorn Mountain Lodge*, 1340 Big Thompson Ave (☎970/586-4376, ⓦwww. bighornmtnlodge.com; ❸), both of which have clean, standard motel rooms and outdoor pools. If it's glamour you're after, head straight to the 1909 *Stanley Hotel*, with its fantastic mountainside location at 333 Wonderview Ave (☎970/586-3371 or 1-800/976-1377, ⓦwww.stanleyhotel.com; ❼). For meals, the relaxed *Molly B*, 200 Moraine Ave (☎970/586-2766), has an extensive all-day menu, and the excellent dinner buffet at the historic *Baldpate Inn*, 4900 S Hwy-7 (☎970/586-

5397; reservations essential), includes hearty soups, freshly baked gourmet breads, and a range of salads, for only $12.

Grand Lake has an excellent **youth hostel**: the gorgeous, rambling log-built *Shadowcliff Lodge*, perched high in the woods on Tunnel Road (June–Sept only; ℗ 970/627-9220; **②**), with dorm rooms for $20 and clean and comfortable doubles for $50. Among a number of moderately priced **motels** is the *Western Riviera Motel & Cabins*, in an attractive spot down by the lake at 419 Garfield St (℗ 970/627-3580, ⓦ www.westernriv.com; **⑤**); note that during summer, some places in Grand Lake insist on a minimum three-night stay. One of the better places to eat is *EG's Garden Grill*, 1000 Grand Ave (℗ 970/627-8404), where the menu ranges from burgers to grilled wild boar sausages and seafood specials like marlin and grilled salmon – you can also sit in the beer garden (happy hour Mon–Sat 5–7pm). Don't miss the fabulous $7.95 breakfast buffet at *Grand Lake Lodge*, 15500 US-34 (℗ 970/627-3185; open June to mid-Sept), a National Historic Landmark that offers accommodation in rustic cabins (**⑤**) that cluster around the property and have access to a pool and hot tub.

Winter Park

The former railroad center of **WINTER PARK**, 67 miles northwest of Denver, may not be Colorado's trendiest resort, but its wide, ever-expanding variety of ski and bike terrain, friendly atmosphere, and good-value lodgings draw over one million visitors a year. It also has exceptional facilities for kids and disabled skiers – and the 200-acre **Discovery Park**, an excellent, economical area for beginners. Experienced skiers, in turn, relish the country's best mogul runs on the awesome **Mary Jane Mountain**, the fluffy snows of the Parsenn Bowl, and the backcountry idyll of **Vasquez Cirque**.

In addition to skiing, you can **snowmobile** the Continental Divide on a one-hour tour with Trailblazers in Fraser ($55/hr, $180/day; ℗ 970/726-8452 or 1-800/669-0134, ⓦ trailblazersnowmobile.com) or around a 25-mile course just north of town with Mountain Madness ($40/hr; ℗ 970/726-4529 or 1-800/547-3101). **Summer** visitors can enjoy six hundred miles of excellent **mountain-bike** trails, some of the best of which are accessible from the chair lift ($22 for an adult day bike pass; from $55 with bike rental), in addition to the super-fun mile-and-a-half-long **Alpine Slide** ($10), and several contemporary music festivals.

Practicalities

Year-round service to Winter Park is provided by Greyhound, stopping downtown outside the **visitor center** at the junction of Hwy-40 and Vasquez Road (daily 8am–5pm; ℗ 970/726-4118 or 1-800/903-7275, ⓦ www.winterpark-info .com); by Amtrak, five miles north in Fraser; and on Home James shuttles from Denver International Airport ($42 one way; ℗ 1-800/359-7503, ⓦ www .homejamestransportation.com). The **Winter Park Ski Train** does roundtrips from Denver every Saturday and Sunday during ski season, leaving at 7.15am and starting back at 4.15pm ($49; 2hr; reservations required; ℗ 303/296-4754, ⓦ www.skitrain.com). An excellent network of free **shuttle buses** means that a car is not essential in town. Trail maps and general outdoor information are available at the visitor center.

As well as the **hotels** and **condos** surrounding the ski area that can booked through Winter Park Central Reservations (℗ 970/726-1564 or 1-800/979-0332, ⓦ www.skiwinterpark.com; **④** and up), inexpensive **motels** line the main street of Winter Park itself; including the downtown *Viking Lodge* (℗ 970/726-8885 or 1-800/421-4013; **②–③**). Places to **eat and drink** downtown include *Carlos and*

Maria's in Cooper Creek Square (☎970/726-9674), good for low-cost margaritas and Mexican food; *Deno's* (☎970/726-5332), with its hundred-plus beers and tasty pasta and Cajun seafood; and *Hernando's Pizza Pub* (☎970/726-5409), which has fantastic grub, low prices, and a warm, family atmosphere.

Steamboat Springs

Surrounded by wide valleys, **STEAMBOAT SPRINGS**, 65 miles north of I-70 via Rte-131, looks like no other Colorado mountain resort. Its roots are in ranching rather than mining, and its downtown area still evokes a pioneer feel – until you spot the upmarket boutiques. In this ski-mad town, rancher-types judge the quality of snowfall by the number of fence wires it covers; they're usually satisfied with a three-wire winter, which corresponds to its average snowfall of 334 inches per year.

The town's top-notch **ski resort** (lift tickets $76 per day), snuggled into Mount Werner four miles south of downtown, is boosted by such activities as dogsled expeditions, hot-air ballooning, and snowmobiling, available in and around town. A favorite year-round activity is soaking in the secluded 105°F **Strawberry Park Hot Springs** (Sun–Thurs 10am–10.30pm, Fri & Sat 10am–midnight; $10; ☎970/879-0342, ⓦwww.strawberryhotsprings.com), seven miles north of town but only accessible by four-wheel-drive vehicles in winter. In town, the **Steamboat Springs Health and Recreation Center** offers hot mineral pools (Mon–Fri 5.30am–10pm, Sat & Sun 8am–9pm; $7.50; ☎970/879-1828), as well as workout facilities. In the summertime, opportunities for **mountain biking**, **whitewater rafting**, and **horseback riding** abound. Outfitters throughout the town can assist you with gear and guides.

Practicalities

Most winter visitors fly into **Yampa Valley Airport**, 22 miles from Steamboat Springs, though it's possible to drive, weather permitting, from Denver on Hwy-40 over scenic **Rabbit Ears Pass**, or take the Alpine Taxi shuttle direct from Denver International Airport ($75; ☎970/879-2800 or 1-800/343-7433; ⓦwww.alpinetaxi.com). Visitor information is at 1255 Lincoln Ave, two miles east of downtown (Mon–Fri 8am–5pm, Sat 10am–3pm, also Sun 9am–6pm during peak times in summer and winter; ☎970/879-0880, ⓦwww.steamboatchamber.com).

From town, free SST **buses** run the four miles to the ski resort. Slopeside **lodging**, such as the comfortable *Best Western Ptarmigan Inn* (☎970/879-1730 or 1-800/538-7519, ⓦwww.steamboat-lodging.com; winter ❻, summer ❺), costs more than downtown options like the *Rabbit Ears Motel* (☎970/879-1150 or 1-800/828-7702, ⓦwww.rabbitearsmotel.com; winter ❺, summer ❹). Steamboat Central Reservations (☎970/879-0740 or 1-877/783-2628, ⓦwww.steamboat.com) can supply information on lodging and packages. You can **camp** at the *Steamboat Springs KOA Campground*, two miles west of downtown on US-40 (☎970/879-0273; sites from $27).

For **food**, *Azteca Taqueria*, 402 Lincoln Ave (☎970/870-9980), has great inexpensive Mexican take-out; *Antares*, 57 1/2 8th St (☎970/879-9939), is one of Steamboat's very best restaurants, serving an eclectic range of fish and meat dishes. Another venue for delicious but expensive dining is ✈ *Hazie's*, up on the mountain (open Tues–Sat for lunch and dinner in ski season, Fri and Sat nights in summer; ☎970/871-5252), which includes a free gondola ride; best of all is their superb $34 summer-only Sunday brunch (10am–1.30pm). Microbrews and decent pub food are available near the ski area at *The Tugboat Grill and Pub* (☎970/879-7070), which also has live music and a dance floor; *Wolf's Den Tavern*, 703 Lincoln Ave (☎970/871-0008), is a good downtown venue for live bands, too.

Summit County

The mix of purpose-built ski resorts, old mining towns, snow-covered peaks, alpine meadows, and crystal lakes that make up **Summit County** lie alongside I-70, around seventy miles west of Denver. Before white settlement, the Ute hunted here every summer: the swanky Keystone Ranch Golf Club now occupies the meadow where they once pitched their tepees. During the late nineteenth century the county witnessed several gold-mining booms; dilapidated **ghost towns** cling to the mountainsides, but one settlement that survived is **BRECKENRIDGE**, whose streets are lined with brightly painted Victorian houses, shops, and cafés. This is the liveliest of Summit County's four towns; **FRISCO**, stretching sedately along a quiet valley, appeals to those looking for a less hectic pace. Both the other towns, **DILLON** and **SILVERTHORNE**, are dull, though the latter contains dozens of cut-price factory outlet stores. The formulaic ski resort villages of **Keystone** and **Copper Mountain** are also unexciting unless you're here to ski or board.

Arrival and information

By **car**, Summit County is about two hours from Denver. Greyhound **buses** stop at the Frisco Transit Center ($11 one way) from where free buses radiate to the ski resorts **Copper Mountain**, **Keystone**, and **Breckenridge**. There are also **shuttles** from Denver International Airport. Resort Express serves **Silverthorne** and **Breckenridge** ($52; ℡970/468-7600 or 1-800/334-7433, ⓦwww.resort-express .com), while Supershuttle (℡1-800/258-3826) and Colorado Mountain Express (℡1-800/222-2112) run a more expensive door-to-door service to hotels. Summit Stage (6.30am–1.30am; ℡970/668-0999) provides free **local transportation** around the county, and the Breckenridge Downtown Trolley (℡970/453-5000) runs through town and up to the resort. The main **visitor center** (daily 9am–5pm; ℡970/668-2051 or 1-800/424-1554, ⓦwww.townoffrisco.com) is by the lake at the end of Frisco's Main Street, and there's a small welcome center in Breckenridge at 309 N Main St (℡970/453-6018).

Accommodation

Lodgings in Summit County cover all price ranges, with prices doubling in winter. Frisco has the best-priced inns and **motels**. There are also a few downtown **B&Bs** in Breckenridge, where otherwise accommodation usually means a slopeside condo; The Breckenridge Resort Chamber (℡970/453-6018 or 1-888/796-2825, ⓦwww. gobreck.com) can advise on prices and package deals. Resort accommodation at both Copper Mountain (℡970/968-2882 ℡1-800/458-8386, ⓦwww.coppercolorado. com) and Keystone (℡1-800/468-5004, ⓦwww.keystoneresort.com) is first class, but so too are the prices; virtually nothing costs under $100 a night, unless you find an unusual package deal.

Fireside Inn 114 N French St, Breckenridge ℡970/453-6456 ⓦwww.firesideinn.com. Homey little B&B with floral, antique-filled bedrooms (all with private bath) and several cramped dorm rooms ($26–38) which all share a TV lounge and kitchenette. Free Internet access, afternoon tea and cakes. Winter ❻, summer ❸

Frisco Lodge 321 Main St, Frisco ℡970/668-0195 or 1-800/279-6000, ⓦwww.friscolodge.com. Creaky old B&B in an old railroad inn, usually the cheapest deal in town. Units have kitchenettes and access to an outdoor hot tub, and cooked buffet breakfast and teatime snacks are served in the cluttered lounge. Winter ❺, summer ❸

HI-Alpen Hütte 471 Rainbow Drive, Silverthorne ℡970/468-6336. Clean bunkrooms in comfortable environs, and there's a midnight curfew. Winter $40, summer $20. Private, motel-style rooms are also available. ❹

Ridge Street Inn 212 N Ridge St, Breckenridge ℡970/453-4680. Comfortable, luxurious B&B in the heart of the historic downtown area. Winter ❻, summer ❸–❹

Outdoor activities

Winter is still the busiest time in Summit County. **Breckenridge Ski Area**, the oldest of the four top-class resorts, spans four peaks and offers ideal terrain for all skiers – and snowboarders, with a six-acre park with half-pipe – as does the plush **Keystone Resort**, where the biggest night-ski operation in the US permits skiing until 10pm. The smallest resort in the county, **Arapahoe Basin** (generally known as "A-Basin"; ☏970/468-0718, ⓦwww.arapahoebasin.com; lift ticket $51 per day), offers great above-tree-line bowl skiing. All three are covered by one lift ticket ($75 per day), making this one of the best-value deals in the country. The slopes at the other ski area, the ingenious **Copper Mountain** ($75 for one day), are divided into three clear sections to keep beginners, intermediates, and experts out of each other's way.

In summer, mountain-bikers and road-racers alike will be happy with the opportunities for **cycling**, particularly the stretch between Frisco and Breckenridge; Racer's Edge at 114 N Main St in Breckenridge (☏970/453-0995) rents out the best bikes. Each resort runs a chair lift or **gondola** to the top of the mountains for access to great **hiking** and cycling trails. Keystone is particularly outstanding for its mountain bike trails with world-class downhill and cross-country trails accessed by its lifts (mid-June to mid-Sept daily 10am–5pm; day-pass $28). Breckenridge offers toboggan rides down the dry **Superslide** (summer daily 9am–5pm; $10), mini-golf ($7), and a giant maze ($6).

Eating

With the exception of *Keystone Resort*, Summit County doesn't have a reputation for fine **dining**, though there's no end of good-value places to eat, especially in Breckenridge.

Alpenglow Stübe Keystone Mountain ☏970/496-4386. The best dining experience in Summit County – take the free gondola ride to the top of 11,444ft North Peak and feast on New American cuisine with a Bavarian edge in beautiful surroundings. It doesn't come cheap though – the six-course meals run around $70.

Butterhorn Bakery & Café 408 Old Main St, Frisco ☏970/668-3997. Superb bakery churning out huge delicious breads, bagels, cookies, and cakes. It's also well-known for its breakfast burrito, smoked salmon omelette, and good range of sandwiches or soup lunches (all $6–7). Daily 7.30am–3pm.

Mi Casa 600 S Park Ave, Breckenridge ☏970/453-2071. The best Mexican food around, including fine *chiles rellenos*. The tangy fajitas are good value, as is the daily 3–6pm happy hour.

The Prospector 130 S Main St, Breckenridge ☏970/453-6858. Tasty traditional home-cooked breakfasts (try the spicy and excellent *huevos rancheros*) and lunches including roasts and meatloaf. Prices are among the lowest in town.

Rasta Pasta 411 S Main St, Breckenridge ☏970/453-7467. Good, fairly cheap pasta with a Caribbean twist and served to a soundtrack of reggae music.

Drinking

Apres-ski **drinking** is alive and well at the slopeside bars of all four resorts. As the night wears on, head to Breckenridge for several late-night music venues, though Frisco too has some good options.

Breckenridge Brewery 600 S Main St, Breckenridge ☏970/453-1550. This huge brewpub, one of the first in Colorado and now a landmark at the southern edge of town, serves good-quality microbrews and hearty pub food.

Chill 610 Main St, Frisco ☏970/668-9930. Frisco's only late-night venue, complete with debonair decor, low lighting, billiards and nightly events that include live music, dance lessons, karaoke and poker tournaments.

Dillon Dam Brewery 100 Little Dam Rd, Dillon ☏970/262-7777. The place for good microbrew ales and inexpensive quality bar food – salads, burgers, and pasta – with entrees from around $8.

Downstairs at Eric's 111 S Main St, Breckenridge ☏970/453-1401. Lively basement sports bar, with a good range of microbrews and filling bar food.

Leadville

Standing at an elevation of over ten thousand feet, south of I-70 and eighty miles west of Denver, the wonderfully atmospheric old mining town of **LEADVILLE** is the highest incorporated city in the US, with a magnificent view across to broad-shouldered, ice-laden mounts **Elbert** (14,433ft) and **Massive** (14,421ft), Colorado's two highest peaks. As you approach from the south, your first impression is likely to be of giant slag heaps and disused mining sheds, but don't let this put you off: Leadville is rich in character and romance, its old redbrick streets abounding with tales of gunfights, miners dying of exposure, and graveyards being excavated to get at the seams.

For an illuminating romp through the town's grim early history, head for the **Heritage Museum**, 102 E Ninth St (summer daily 10am–6pm; $3.50). Glass cases hold snippets on local fraternal organizations, quack doctors, music-hall stars, and the like, while a host of smoky photographs portray the lawless boomtown that in two years grew from a mining camp of two hundred people into Colorado's second largest city.

Of all Leadville's extraordinary tales, perhaps the most compelling is that of **Horace Tabor**, a storekeeper who supplied goods to prospectors in exchange for a share in potential profits. He hit the jackpot when two prospectors developed a silver mine that produced $20 million within a year. Tabor collected a one-third share and left his wife to marry local waitress "**Baby Doe**" McCourt in the society wedding of 1883 in Washington, DC, attended by President Chester Arthur. By the time of his death in 1899, Tabor was financially ruined. Baby Doe survived Tabor by 36 years, living a hermit-like existence in the godforsaken wooden shacks on his only remaining mine – the **Matchless Mine**. The buildings still stand, two miles out on Seventh Street, and in the crude wooden shack in which she died, emaciated and frostbitten, guides recount the story of Baby Doe's bizarre life in full, fascinating detail (May–Sept 9am–4.15pm, Oct–April call for hours; $4; ☎719/486-4918).

Back in town, don't miss the **Tabor Opera House**, 308 Harrison Ave (May–Sept daily 10am–5pm; $4; ☎719/486-8409, ⓦwww.taboroperahouse.net), where you're free to wander onto the stage, through the ranks of red velvet and gilt seats, and around the eerie, dusty old dressing rooms. Recorded oral histories tell tales of the theater's golden days. They give no details, sadly, of the time in 1882 when Oscar Wilde, garbed in black velvet knee britches and diamonds, addressed a host of dozing miners on the "Practical Application of the Aesthetic Theory to Exterior and Interior House Decoration with Observations on Dress and Personal Ornament."

Practicalities

Leadville's **visitor center** is at 809 Harrison Ave (June–Sept daily 10am–5pm; ☎719/486-3900 or 1-800/939-3901, ⓦwww.leadvilleusa.com). A good **place to stay** is the historic landmark *Delaware Hotel*, 700 Harrison Ave (☎719/486-1418 or 1-800/748-2004, ⓦwww.delawarehotel.com; ❹–❻), an atmospheric Victorian place where rates include a full breakfast. South of town on US-24 you'll find a string of cheaper motels, among them the dependable *Super 8* (☎719/486-3637; ❸). Leadville has a gratifying choice of places to **eat and drink**. *Cloud City Coffee House and Deli*, 711 Harrison Ave (☎719/486-1317), serves bagels, buns, and espresso in a grand old hotel lobby, while further along the street at no. 612, *Columbine Café* (☎719/486-3599) dishes up imaginative fresh food with lots of vegetarian options, in simple diner surroundings. There's great Mexican and Southwestern food at the spartan *La Cantina*, a mile south on Hwy-24 (☎719/486-9021), which also has dancing on weekends. Among Leadville's fine **bars** is the wood-paneled *Silver Dollar Saloon*, 315 Harrison Ave (☎719/486-9914), a welcoming place filled with Irish memorabilia and where Oscar Wilde once quaffed a beverage after his performance at the Opera House (see p.855).

Aspen

Glossy magazines might have you believe that a tollgate outside **ASPEN** only admits film stars and the super-rich. This elite **ski resort**, two hundred miles west of Denver, is indeed home to the likes of Cher, Jack Nicholson, and Goldie Hawn, and while it's not as typically welcoming as the rest of the Rockies, it can be an appealing place to visit in summer – unless you're on an absolute shoestring budget. Visiting in winter requires more cash, though you can save money by commuting to the slopes from Glenwood Springs (see p.862), less than fifty miles away.

From inauspicious beginnings in 1879, this pristine mountain-locked town developed slowly, thanks to its remote location, to become one of the world's top silver producers. By the time the silver market crashed fourteen years later, it had acquired tasteful residential palaces, grand hotels, and an opera house. In the 1930s, when the population slumped below seven hundred, it was, ironically, the

RESTAURANTS, BARS & CLUBS

39° Lounge	F
Belly Up	12
Boogie's Diner	10
Explore Booksellers and Bistro	5
Hickory House	1
J-Bar	3
Little Annie's	8
Main Street Bakery Café	4
Mezzaluna	11
Red Onion	9
Shooter's Saloon	6
Takah Sushi	7
Woody Creek Tavern	2

ASPEN

Roaring Fork River

LONE PINE ROAD

Aspen Center for Environmental Studies

GIBSON AVENUE

Aspen Art Museum

PUPPY SMITH STREET

Rio Grande Park

HALLAM STREET

RIO GRANDE PLACE

BLEEKER STREET

BLEEKER STREET

THIRD STREET

SECOND STREET

FIRST STREET

GARMISCH STREET

ASPEN STREET

MONARCH STREET

MILL STREET

MAIN STREET

HOPKINS AVENUE

GALENA STREET

HUNTER STREET

SPRING STREET

ORIGINAL STREET

HYMAN AVENUE

Aspen Ice Garden

W COOPER STREET

RFTA Rubey Park Transit Center

DURANT AVENUE

ACCOMMODATION

Hotel Jerome	A
Innsbruck Inn	C
L'Auberge D'Aspen	B
Mountain Chalet	E
St Moritz Lodge	D
Sky Hotel	F

N

DEAN STREET

Silver Queen Gondola

LAWN STREET

AJAX SKI AREA

JUAN STREET

UTE AVE

0   250 yds

GILBERT ST.

JUNITA STREET

SUMMER ROAD

◄ ❶ ❷ & Wheeler/Stallard Museum

◄ Buttermilk, Snowmass & Aspen Highlands

Independence Pass & Leadville ►

anti-poverty WPA program that gave the struggling community the cash to build its first crude ski lift in 1936. Entrepreneurs seized the opportunity presented by the varied terrain and plentiful snow, and the first chair lift was dedicated on Aspen Mountain (now known as **Ajax**) in 1947. Skiing has since spread to three more mountains – Aspen Highlands, Snowmass, and Buttermilk Mountain, and the jet set arrived in force during the 1960s. **Development** is a burning political issue: tight architectural constraints have been placed on businesses (*McDonald's* is forbidden to have a neon sign), but the last decade has seen the arrival of yet more Scandinavian-style lodges, condo blocks, and giant houses that remain empty for most of the year.

Arrival and information

In winter, Independence Pass on Hwy-82, which provides the quickest access to Aspen, is closed, and the detour through Glenwood Springs adds an extra seventy miles to the trip from Denver. Many instead choose to fly into **Sardy Field** (℡970/920-5384, ⊛www.aspenairport.com), the small airport four miles north of town on Hwy-82; if you fly into Denver, connecting flights may only cost another $80 or so. Or, you can take a **shuttle** (make sure to book in advance) from Denver International Airport; shuttle companies include Colorado Mountain Express (℡970/926-9800 or 1-800/525-6363, ⊛www.cmex.com), who charge a whopping $108 each way. Another option is to fly into Eagle County Airport near Vail, an 80-minute drive away; and also served by Colorado Mountain Express.

Once in Aspen, there's no problem **getting around**: the Roaring Fork Transit Agency (℡970/925-8484) runs a free skiers' shuttle between the four mountains and serves the airport and outlying areas. The main **Rubey Park transit center** terminal is in the center of town on Durant Avenue.

Aspen's **visitor center** is at 425 Rio Grande Place (Mon–Fri 9am–5pm; ℡970/925-9000 or 1-800/262-7736, ⊛www.aspenchamber.org). The free *Aspen Daily News* ("If you don't want it printed, don't let it happen") is an excellent source of local gossip, news, and food and drink offers.

Accommodation

Stay Aspen Snowmass Central Reservations (℡970/925-9000 or 1-888/649-9582, ⊛www.stayaspensnowmass.com) runs a superb service, and doesn't balk if you ask for the cheapest available room. It also arranges package deals combining accommodation with lift tickets. Rates vary considerably even in winter; the least expensive times to come are in the "**value seasons**" (last week in Nov, first two weeks of Dec, and first two weeks of April). Between mid-December and January 4, you'll be hard-pressed to find a double for less than $160. If you're traveling in a group, you can save money by renting a **condo**; the McCartney Property Management (℡1-877/369-8354, ⊛www.mc-cartneyprop.com) is a good source. Prices in the entire area at least halve during the **summer**, when **camping** is also a good cheap option; there are nine USFS campgrounds around Aspen, of which only a handful of sites are reservable (℡1-877/444-6777, ⊛www.reserveusa.com). Several campgrounds are on Maroon Creek Road south of Aspen, and there are some smaller options out toward Independence Pass.

Hotel Jerome 330 E Main St ℡970/920-1000 or 1-800/331-7213, ⊛www.hjerome.com. Stately downtown landmark built at the height of the 1880s silver boom. Spacious rooms feature period wallpaper, antique brass, and cast-iron beds, and a gamut of modern amenities. The elegant lobby is worth a look even if you're not staying. ❾

Innsbruck Inn 233 W Main St ℡970/925-2980, ⊛www.preferredlodging.com. Bright basic rooms in an Austrian-style lodge with hand-carved beams, a few blocks from downtown. Continental breakfast is included in rates. Winter ❼, summer ❹

L'Auberge D'Aspen 435 W Main St ℡970/925-8297, ⊛www.preferredlodging.com. Idyllic little

cabins, superbly outfitted with kitchens and fireplaces close to downtown. Winter ❼, summer ❺
Mountain Chalet 333 E Durant Ave ☎970/925-7797 or 1-800/321-7813, ⓦwww.mtchaletaspen.com. Friendly mountain lodge with large, comfortable rooms, pool, hot tub, gym, and fine buffet breakfast. Some dorm-style beds ($40–60) are available in winter, otherwise a variety of straightforward rooms are offered with prices dropping by two-thirds in the off-season. Winter ❼, summer ❹

🎿 **Sky Hotel** 709 E Durant Ave ☎970/925-6760 or 1-800/882-2582, ⓦwww
.theskyhotel.com. Funky slopeside hotel with chic 1970s-style decor; the *39° Bar* (see p.860) is one

of the hippest après spots around. The playful rooms have faux-fur throws, iPod docks, WiFi, and Nintendo. Also has outdoor pool and hot tub, and fitness room. Prices are steep, and even the basic rooms sometimes top $500 per night, though the price includes an evening wine reception. ❽

St Moritz Lodge 334 W Hyman Ave ☎970/925-3220 or 1-800/817-2069, ⓦwww.stmoritzlodge.com. Five blocks from downtown and Aspen's unofficial youth hostel, the lodge's private rooms and dorms are some of the best bargains in town and hard to get. Facilities include a small heated pool and a comfortable common room. Continental breakfast included in winter. Winter ❺, summer ❸

The town and the mountains

Despite the virtually limitless recreation opportunities in the mountains, there's not all that much to do in Aspen itself. Even so, hanging out on the benches around the town's leafy pedestrianized streets, or browsing in the chichi stores and galleries is a pleasant way to spend a couple of hours.

In summer, the Aspen Historical Society who run the excellent **Wheeler/Stallard Museum**, 620 W Bleeker St (Tues–Sat 1–5pm; $6; ☎970-925-3254), offers **walking tours** of Aspen and nearby ghost towns (guided $10, or self-guided, free). The **Aspen Art Museum** at 590 N Mill St (Tues–Sat 10am–6pm, Sun noon–6pm; $5, free Fri; ☎970/925-8050, ⓦwww.aspenartmuseum.org) holds changing exhibits and puts on lectures and special events, while **Aspen Center for Environmental Studies**, 100 S Puppy Smith St (Dec–April Mon–Fri 9am–5pm, May–Nov Mon–Sat 9am–5pm; $2; ☎970/925-5756, ⓦwww.aspennature.org), is a wildlife sanctuary that offers a range of guided hikes and ski and snowshoe tours (bring your own gear) led by naturalists.

Aspen's four mountains are run by the **Aspen Ski Co** (☎970/925-1220 or 1-800/525-6200, ⓦwww.aspensnowmass.com; snow report ☎1-888/277-3676). The mogul-packed monster of **Aspen Mountain**, looming over downtown, is for experienced skiers only. On the other hand, **Buttermilk** is great for beginners, with an excellent ski school that offers a three-day guaranteed "Learn to Snowboard" program, and the wide-open runs of **Snowmass**, though mostly for intermediate skiers, feature some testing routes. **Aspen Highlands** has some new high-speed lifts and offers excellent extreme skiing terrain. Daily **lift tickets** for all mountains cost $78. **Rental** of skis or snowboard gear runs $20–40 with discounts on multi-day rentals or if booked online a week in advance – you can also rent snowshoes if you want to trek up and down the mountains. However, the town's best value has to be its fifty miles of groomed **Nordic ski trails** – one of the most extensive free cross-country trail networks in the US. If you don't want to wait for the snow, consider **mountain boarding** – lessons on these snowboards with wheels are offered by the Ski & Snowboard Schools of Aspen (June–Aug; ☎877/282-7736).

Cycling is the main **summer** pursuit; Timberline, 516 E Durant Ave (☎970/925-3586 ⓦwww.timberlinebike.com), has mountain bikes for hire, organizes tours or can offer sound guidance on routes and difficulty levels. The Roaring Fork River, surging out of the Sawatch Range, is excellent for **kayaking** and **rafting** during a short season that's typically over by July. Beware, though, as sections of Class V rapids here are dangerous and every summer sees fatalities. Blazing Adventures, Snowmass Village ($50/half-day; ☎970/923-4544 or 1-800/282-7238, ⓦwww.blazingadventures.com) is a good guide choice.

△ Skiing in Aspen, CO

If you fancy **walking** in the mountains be sure to pick up the free *Ute Scout Hiking and Biking Guide*, available free from the visitor center. An easy way to quickly get your bearings along with great valley views is to take the Silver Queen **gondola** from 601 Dean St to the summit of **Ajax** (early June to early Sept daily 10am–4pm; $20/day, $35/week; ⊕970/925-1220), where guided nature walks set off on the hour from 11am to 3pm. Occasional free lunchtime concerts and talks are held up here, and there's a good restaurant as well. Even more alluring is the landscape around the twin purple-gray peaks of the **Maroon Bells**, fifteen miles southwest, soaring above the dark-blue Maroon Lake. The Bells are reached via the eleven-mile-long Maroon Creek Road, closed between 8.30am and 5pm to all except overnight campers with permits, disabled travelers, bikers, in-line skaters, and RFTA buses, which leave from the Aspen Highlands Ski Area (mid-June to Sept every 20min 9am–4.30pm; $6 roundtrip) and the Rubey Park transit center.

Eating and drinking

Many of Aspen's classy **cafés and restaurants** charge over $25 for a main course, but good budget places exist and competition is keen. New restaurants open and close with alarming regularity; the list below consists of tried and trusted favorites. Note, too, that many of Aspen's bars serve good, reasonably priced food (see below).

Boogie's Diner 534 E Cooper Ave ☎970/925-6610. Inexpensive 1950s-style diner occupying an airy second-floor atrium lined with vinyl and chrome. The menu includes great meatloaf and killer shakes, but also a few imaginative tofu veggie options too.

Explore Booksellers and Bistro 221 E Main St ☎970/925-5336. Great bookstore with a shady roof terrace, serving creative, high-quality vegetarian food, good espresso, and pastries.

Little Annie's 517 E Hyman Ave ☎970/925-1098. Lively, popular, and unpretentious saloon-style restaurant serving potato pancakes and hearty stews at lunch, and huge trout, chicken, beef, or rib dinner platters for around $15.

Main Street Bakery Café 201 E Main St ☎970/925-6446. Scrumptious and inventive

New American cuisine, plus an excellent wine list, in a casual, chatty setting. Always busy in the morning for its massive, fresh-fruit-packed breakfasts.

Mezzaluna 624 E Cooper Ave ☎970/925-5882. Mid-priced Northern Italian dishes for lunch or dinner, including wood-fired pizzas.

Takah Sushi 420 E Hyman Ave ☎970/925-8588. Phenomenally good sushi and pan-Asian cuisine, in a buzzing, cheerful atmosphere. Highly recommended but quite expensive.

Hickory House 730 W Main St ☎970/925-2313. Rib house that turns out the best breakfasts in town, from buttery waffles to meaty, southern-style platters. The place packs out for big-screen Monday Night Football when wings are 25¢ and domestic beers $1.

Entertainment and nightlife

Going out in Aspen, the capital of **apres-ski**, is fun year-round and need not be expensive. Check the free papers for special offers. In summer, downtown hosts several top-notch festivals. The flagship event is the nine-week-long **Aspen Music Festival** (☎970/925-9042, ⓦwww.aspenmusicfestival.com), between late June and late August, when orchestras and operas feature well-known international performers, as well as promising students who come to learn from musical masters. July and early August see the **Dance Aspen Festival** (ⓦwww.aspenballet.com), which showcases reliably good contemporary shows. **Tickets** to all events can be purchased at the Wheeler Opera House (☎970/920-5570, ⓦwww.wheeleroperahouse.com), whose program of concerts, plays, and dance performances runs year-round.

39° Lounge 709 E Durant Ave ☎970/925-6760. *The* place to be when the lifts close, this chic club and bar with its Seventies aesthetic would be equally at home in Manhattan or Berlin. But amid the geometric curves, low lights, flickering fires, and leather sofas, ski boots tap to DJ-spun ambient beats.

Belly Up 450 S Galena St ☎970/920-6905. Cavernous basement venue that hosts everything from big-name bands to calendar-girl contests and has an almost cinema-sized screen for sports events. Not a bad place for a drink on busy nights, otherwise you tend to rattle around in the space.

J-Bar *Hotel Jerome*, 330 E Main St ☎970/920-1000. This grand bar is a good place to soak up

the hotel's atmosphere and rub elbows with the well-heeled hotel guests.

Red Onion Cooper St Mall ☎970/925-9043. Aspen's oldest bar, serving big portions of Mexican food and good burgers. A popular apres-ski spot, especially for its lethal line in jello shots.

Shooter's Saloon 220 S Galena St ☎970/925-4567. Rowdy and raucous Country & Western bar with pool tables, dance floor, and frequent Eighties nights.

Woody Creek Tavern Upper Never Rd, Woody Creek ☎970/923-4585. Locals' bar where ranch hands and rock stars shoot pool, guzzle fresh lime-juice margaritas, and eat good Tex-Mex. The bar is in tiny Woody Creek, seven miles north of Aspen along Hwy-82.

Vail

Compared to most other Colorado ski towns, **VAIL**, 96 miles west of Denver on I-70, is a new creation: only a handful of farmers lived here before the resort was opened in 1952. Built as a relatively unimaginative collection of Tyrolean-style chalets and concrete-block condos, at least the town is a compact and pedestrian-friendly place, albeit pockmarked by pricey fashion boutiques and high-priced, often painfully pretentious restaurants. Vail Resorts, which operates the ski area at Vail, also owns an even more exclusive gated resort, **Beaver Creek**, eleven miles farther west on I-70. Tickets between the two are interchangeable, which – given the exceptional quality of the snow, and the sheer size and variety of terrain available – produces a formidable winter sport destination. In summer, you can use the lifts at both resorts to go **mountain biking** – best at Vail, given its former World Cup Downhill and cross-country courses (lifts run mid-June to Aug daily 10am–4.30pm; $29); and **hiking** – best at the quieter Beaver Creek.

Practicalities

From Denver International Airport, several companies offer **shuttles** to Vail and Beaver Creek, including Colorado Mountain Express ($73 per person one-way; 3hr; ☏970/926-9800 or 1-800/525-6363, ⓦwww.cmex.com). More convenient but more expensive are flights to **Eagle County Regional Airport** (☏970/524-9490), 35 miles west of Vail. Ground transportation from the airport to either resort is just $3 on public buses (9 daily; 1hr), while the Airlink Shuttle (☏970/845-7119 or 1-800/554-8245, ⓦww.airlinkshuttle.com) charges $39 per person.

Vail spreads for eight miles along the narrow valley floor, with successive nuclei from east to west at Vail Village, Lionshead, Cascade Village, and West Vail. Each is pedestrianized and linked by free shuttle buses to one another and to the lifts. Central parking lots are free in summer but steeply priced in winter. **Vail Buses** (6am–2am; ☏970/477-3456) also run regular free shuttles year-round between different areas of town; schedules are printed in the *Vail Valley* magazine.

For information on skiing and accommodation, contact the **Vail Valley Tourism & Convention Bureau** (☏970/476-1000 or 1-866/362-8245, ⓦwww.vailalways .com) who will reserve rooms, organize transportation and ski packages, and have a website dedicated to cut-price last-minute bookings (ⓦwww.vailonsale.com). Finding an affordable place to **stay** can be a problem. By Vail standards at least, the condos in **Avon**, just below Beaver Creek, are inexpensive. Rates in **Vail Village**, the main social center, are higher; try *Tivoli Lodge* (☏970/476-5615 or 1-800/451-4756 ⓦwww.tivolilodge.com; winter ❼, summer ❺), where rates include a continental breakfast and use of an outdoor pool, whirlpool, and sauna; or the *Roost Lodge*, 1783 N Frontage Rd, West Vail (☏970/476-5451 or 1-800/873-3065, ⓦwww.roostlodge.com; ❺) a drab motel with outdoor hot tub that's generally Vail's cheapest accommodation option. To live it up check into the seamless *Sonnenalp Resort* 20 Vail Rd Village (☏970/476-5656 or 1-800/654-8312, ⓦwww.sonnenalp.com; ❾), a luxury hotel straight out of a snowy European Christmas card, bang in the center of Vail with a full complement of facilities and an excellent spa. The *Eagle River Inn*, 145 N Main St (☏970/827-5761 or 1-800/344-1750; winter ❼–❽, summer ❺), is a B&B decked out in tasteful Santa Fe style in the hamlet of **Minturn**, seven miles south of Vail on US-24.

Eating out can also prove expensive. Elegant *Vendetta's*, 291 Bridge St in Vail Village (☏970/476-5070), offers fine Italian lunch specials and pasta dinners (around $15), while the best-value feed is to be had at *La Cantina* (☏970/476-7661), little more than a few tables crammed into a corner of Vail Transportation Center, but the Mexican food is first class and the margaritas seriously potent.

Nightlife revolves around **The Circuit** on Bridge Street, Vail Village. Most people tour between the bars and discos. The checklist of places to see and be seen includes *The Club* (☎970/479-0556), a basement bar playing loud rock. Loud music rules upstairs at *Vendetta's*, the ski patrol hangout; but for something completely different try *Kaltenberg Castle* (☎970/479-1050), the former Lionshead gondola building that's now a massive mock-palace where entertainers wear lederhosen and Bavarian beer is brewed in giant vats.

Glenwood Springs

Bustling, touristy **GLENWOOD SPRINGS** sits at the end of impressive Glenwood Canyon, 160 miles west of Denver and within easy striking distance of Vail and Aspen and so offering those with their own vehicle a budget base for either. Just north of the confluence of the Roaring Fork and Colorado rivers, the town was long used by the Ute as a place of relaxation thanks to its **hot springs,** which became the target for unscrupulous speculators who broke treaties and established resort facilities in the 1880s. North from downtown and across the Eagle River is the town's main attraction, the large and somewhat institutional **Glenwood Hot Springs Pool**, 410 N River St (daily: summer 7.30am–10pm; rest of year 9am–10pm; $12; ☎970/945-6571 ⓦ www.hotspringspool.com). More intimate are the natural subterranean steam baths of the **Yampah Spa Vapor Caves** at 709 E Sixth St (daily 9am–9pm; $12; ☎970/945-0667, ⓦ www.yampahspa.com) next door, where you can destress on cool marble benches set deep in ancient caves. Also on the north side of town are the **Glenwood Fairy Caves**, 508 Pine St (June–Nov; daily, call for tour times; $10; ☎970/945-4228 ⓦ www.glenwoodcaverns.com). The caverns extend for two miles, with some chambers reaching a height of fifty feet. There are two sightseeing options here; the regular two-hour Tram/Cave Tour ($18) and the more adventurous four-hour dimly lit Wild Tour ($50; no kids).

Some of the West's most colorful characters came here in the early days, including Dr John R. **"Doc" Holliday**, a dentist better known as a gambler, gunslinger, and shooter in the gunfight at the OK Corral (see p.957). A chronic tuberculosis sufferer, Holliday came to the springs for a cure but died just a few months later in November 1887, at the age of 35. He is buried on a bluff overlooking the town in the picturesque Linwood Cemetery. In the paupers' section lies the grave of Harvey Logan, alias bank robber Kid Curry, a member of Butch Cassidy's notorious Hole-in-the-Wall gang.

Practicalities

Amtrak trains arrive at 413 7th St, at the end of a scenic route through the canyons, gorges, and valleys of central Colorado. Greyhound, traveling along the less inspiring I-70, stops close to downtown at the *Ramada Inn*, 124 W 6th St. The **visitor center**, 1102 Grand Ave (open 24 hours, staffed Mon–Fri 8.30am–5pm, Sat & Sun 9am–3pm; ☎970/945-6589) stocks the useful *Glenwood Springs Official Guide*. Regular RFTA **buses** link the town with Aspen (daily 6am–10pm; 1hr; $6; call for schedule ☎970/925-8484).

The beatnik *HI-Glenwood Springs Hostel*, near downtown at 1021 Grand Ave (☎970/945-8545 or 1-800/946-7835), has spacious dorms (beds $12–14), cheap private rooms ($26), plus kitchen facilities, a giant record collection, and a wealth of local knowledge. They also arrange tours and whitewater trips, and are closed from 10am–4pm. Reasonable **motels** include the *First Choice Inn of Glenwood Springs*, 51359 6th St (☎970/945-8551 or 1-800/332-2233; ❸–❹), at the west end of town, which has striking mountain views, a guest laundry, and a free, good breakfast. The *Daily Bread Café and Bakery*, downtown at 729 Grand Ave (☎970/945-6253), has delicious breakfasts, soups, and salads. *Fiesta Guadalajara*, 503 Pine St (℡970/947-1670), is a decent family-run Mexican place near the hot springs and offers a huge variety of filling options, with its many combination plates priced around $9. A block away in the *Hotel Denver*, the *Glenwood Canyon Brewpub*, 402 7th St (℡970/945-1276), will certainly quench your thirst, with its great hand-crafted microbrews.

Grand Junction

The immediate environs of **GRAND JUNCTION**, 246 miles west of Denver on I-70, abound with outdoor opportunities, and within a fifty-mile stretch you can trace the transition from fertile Alpine valley to full-blown desert. Another town that sprang into life in the 1880s with the arrival of the railroads, it now makes its living primarily through the oil and gas industries. Although initial impressions are bound to be unfavorable – an unsightly sprawl of factory units and sales yards lines the I-70 Business Loop – the tiny downtown is much nicer, with leafy boulevards encircling a small, tree-lined historic district dotted with sculptures and stores.

Although the Colorado section of Dinosaur National Monument is ninety miles north of Grand Junction along Hwy-139, the town itself holds the superb **Dinosaur Valley Museum**, 362 Main St (summer daily 9am–5pm; rest of year Tues–Sat 10am–4.30pm; $4.50). The museum's collection includes reconstructed reptiles, replica eggs, and casts of footprints and giant bones excavated locally – all helping to create a vivid picture of these beasts. The museum sometimes organizes one- to five-day digs at local sites. The main local attraction around town, however, is the splendid local network of **hiking and biking trails** and **rock climbing** sites, in and through parched, rugged, and spectacular desert country. All activities are possible year-round, and are in fact generally more pleasant in the winter months. The only really seasonal activity here is the sampling of Colorado **wine** and the excellent local peaches; contact the visitor center for information on touring the thirteen wineries in the surrounding Grand Valley.

Particularly enticing for hikers is the remarkable scenery of the **Colorado National Monument**, just four miles west of Grand Junction. More than two hundred million years of wind and water erosion have gouged out rock spires, domes, arches, pedestals, and balanced rocks along a line of cliffs to form an enthralling painted desert of warm reds, stunning purples, burnt oranges, and browns. The monument has two entrances ($5 day-pass) at either end of the twisting, 23-mile **Rim Rock Drive** that passes through it (a 39-mile loop from Grand Junction) linking a string of spectacular overlooks with the **visitor center** at the north end of the park (June–Aug 8am–7pm; Sept–May 9am–5pm; ℡970/858-3617, ⓌWwww.nps.gov/com). Good short hikes along the way include the one-hour **John Otto's Trail**, which allows better views of several monoliths. Longer trails like the **Monument Canyon Trail** get right down to the canyon floor. Climbers should investigate the excellent rock climbing in Unaweep Canyon; back in Grand Junction itself Summit Canyon Mountaineering, 549 Main St (℡970/243-2847), can supply you with the necessary information and gear.

The Grand Junction area, specifically the small town of **Fruita** to the west, is also a big magnet for **mountain-bikers** who flock to its smooth, rolling single-track trails. Trail information and rental bikes (front suspension $28 per day) are to be had from Over the Edge Sports, 202 E Aspen Ave (℡970/858-7220), a block east of the roundabout at the center of Fruita.

Practicalities

Amtrak stops at Second Street and Pitkin Avenue. Greyhound buses serve Durango, Denver, and Salt Lake City from 230 S Fifth St. The friendly and insightful **visitor center** at

740 Horizon Drive (℡ 970/244-1480 or 1-800/962-2547, ⓦ www.visitgrandjunction .com) can provide information on daytime excursions and nightlife. Budget **motels** on the interstate – such as the dependable *Best Western Horizon Inn*, 754 Horizon Drive (℡ 970/245-1410; ❸), with pool, spa, and continental breakfast – offer great rates; alternatives include the downtown *HI-Grand Junction* in the historic *Hotel Melrose*, 337 Colorado Ave (℡ 970/242-9636 or 1-800/430-4555), where bunks cost $12 and private rooms start at around $30. *Daniel's Motel*, at 333 North Ave, is basic but cheap and clean, and convenient to downtown (℡ 970/243-1084; ❷). If you want to camp, try the **Colorado National Monument's** only campground, the basic *Saddlehorn Campground* where sites go for $8; or pitch a tent anywhere over a quarter of a mile from the road for free.

You can **eat** inexpensively at the busy *Blue Moon Bar & Grill*, 120 N 7th St (℡ 970/242-5406), which serves sandwiches, salads, and bar food, or at the excellent *Rockslide Brew Pub*, 401 Main St (℡ 970/245-2111), offering filling portions of tasty bar food (Alpine burgers $6.50, Cobb salad $6.50) alongside an impressive array of local beers. Breakfast, meanwhile, is best taken at the *Main St Café*, 504 Main St (℡ 970/242-7225), an authentic 1950s-style diner.

Southeast Colorado

The gently undulating plains of **southeast Colorado** come as a surprise to travelers expecting the ski resorts and alpine splendor that characterize the rest of the state. Here instead are hundreds of small farming towns and endless acres of grassland, much of which looks as it did 150 years ago, when traders and early explorers crossed the region along the Santa Fe Trail, following the Arkansas River between Missouri and Mexico.

The southeast's most popular destination is the engaging small city of **Colorado Springs**, which sits at the foot of towering **Pikes Peak**.

Colorado Springs and around

Seventy miles south of Denver on I-25, **COLORADO SPRINGS** was originally developed as a vacation spot in 1871 by railroad tycoon William Jackson Palmer. He attracted so many English gentry to the town that it earned the nickname of "Little London." Despite sprawling for ten miles alongside I-25, modern Colorado Springs, a bastion of conservatism compared to liberal Denver, still retains much of Palmer's vision, thanks to a high military presence (notably the North American Defense Command Headquarters, or NORAD, deep inside Cheyenne Mountain), fundamentalist religious organizations, the exclusive Colorado College, and a well-to-do Anglo-American community.

Surprisingly, the most popular man-made attraction in Colorado is the **United States Air Force Academy**, located fifteen miles north of town on I-25 (daily 9am–5pm; free; ⓦ www.usafa.af.mil), where beyond observing cadets in march to lunch in the noon formation there's precious little to see. A small museum outlines the academy's work-hard/play-hard philosophy and its commitment to excellence. More entertaining is the **Pro Rodeo Hall of Fame**, 101 Pro Rodeo Drive, off I-25 exit 147 (daily 9am–5pm; $6; ⓦ prorodeo.org/hof), where videos and displays explain the sport's various disciplines (calf roping, barrel racing, and the like).

Motorists whisk through the incredible **Garden of the Gods**, on the west edge of town off US-24 W, without bothering to get out of their vehicles. This gnarled and warped red sandstone rockery was lifted up at the same time as the nearby mountains (around 65 million years ago), but has since been eroded into finely balanced overhangs, jagged pinnacles, massive pedestals, and mushroom formations. The **visitor center** (daily: summer 8am–9pm, winter 9am–6pm; ☏719/634-6666, Ⓦwww.gardenofgods.com) at the park's eastern border, has details on hiking and mountain-biking **trails**.

Practicalities

From **Denver International Airport** there are a number of inexpensive **flights**, or you can book the Colorado Springs Shuttle (☏719/578-5232 or 1-877/587-3456, Ⓦwww.coloradoshuttle.com; $27). Greyhound **buses** stop at 120 S Weber St downtown. Colorado Springs' **visitor center** is at 104 Cascade St (daily: June–Aug 8.30am–6pm, Sept–May Mon–Fri 8.30am–5pm; ☏719/635-7506 or 1-877/745-3773, Ⓦwww.experiencecoloradosprings.com). For **accommodation**, there's the elegant, rustically themed *Old Town Guesthouse*, 115 S 26th St (☏719/632-9194 or 1-888/375-4210, Ⓦwww.oldtownguesthouse.com; ❾), where hors d'oeuvres at check-in and a turn-down service are among the many personal touches. In summer, the neat and busy *Garden of the Gods Campground*, 3704 W Colorado Ave (☏719/475-9450), has $40 cabins for two, and a $28 campground.

Appealing places to **eat** downtown include the excellent *Olive Branch*, 23 S Tejon Ave (☏719/475-1199), for good vegetarian food. The *Phantom Canyon Brewing Co*, 2 E Pikes Peak Ave (☏719/635-2800), is a great place for -microbrews and authentic pub food. Out in Old Colorado City, the family-owned *Henri's Mexican*, 2427 W Colorado Ave (☏719/634-9031), pulls in the crowds with home-style food and superb margaritas. Nearby is one of the area's best **bars**, *Meadow Muffins*, 2432 W Colorado Ave (☏719/633-0583), festooned with movie memorabilia, and serving good burgers, sandwiches, and salads. It also hosts live music and stays open late (until 2am Fri & Sat).

Pikes Peak and the Royal Gorge Bridge

Though there are thirty taller mountains in Colorado alone, **PIKES PEAK**, just west of Colorado Springs, is probably the best known – largely because the view from its summit inspired Katherine Lee Bates to write the words to *America The Beautiful*. The 14,110ft peak was first mapped by Zebulon Pike in 1806, who never climbed it himself. By the end of the century gondola trails had been built to carry rich tourists like Ms Bates to the top. In 1929 it took Bill Williams, a Texan, twenty days and 170 changes of trousers to scale the mountain, pushing a peanut with his nose.

You can reach the top by a long **hike**, or by a difficult **toll road** (May–Sept 7am–7pm, Oct–April 9am–3pm; $10/person up to $35/car; ☏719/385-7325 or 1-800/318-9505, Ⓦwww.pikespeakcolorado.com). The thrilling **Pikes Peak Cog Railway** (mid-May to Nov; $29, reservations advised; ☏719/685-5401, Ⓦwww.cograilway.com) grinds its way up an average of 847ft per mile on its ninety-minute journey to the summit; from 11,500ft onward it crosses a barren expanse of tundra, scarred by giant scree flows. From the bleak and windswept top, it's possible to see Denver seventy miles north, and the endless prairie to the east, while to the west mile upon mile of giant snowcapped peaks rise into the distance. The train leaves from 515 Ruxton Ave in **Manitou Springs**, six miles west of Colorado Springs.

About 45 miles south of Pikes Peak, beside the town of Cañon City – via Hwy-115 and US-50 from Colorado Springs – is the **ROYAL GORGE BRIDGE** (daily 7am–dusk; $19; ☏1-888/333-5597, Ⓦwww.royalgorgebridge.com), the world's highest (and rather rickety) wooden suspension bridge that spans a vertiginous 1053ft crack over the roaring Arkansas River. The gorge is the focus of several other attractions, which though quite commercialized, can still terrify you, including an aerial tram, incline railway, and the Skycoaster – a bungee-swing that for $25 will send to reeling over the canyon.

Great Sand Dunes National Park

Fifty square miles of silky shifting sand, the **GREAT SAND DUNES NATION-AL PARK** huddles against the craggy Sangre de Cristo Mountains, around 170 miles southeast of Colorado Springs along I-25 and Hwy 160. Over millions of years, fine glacial sands have been blown east from the San Juan Mountains and deposited at the base of the Sangre de Cristo range.

A place of strange and eerie beauty, the dunes harbor a number of small, endemic creatures, including the giant sand-treader camel cricket and the small kangaroo rat. Most visitors go little further than the "beach" beside Medano Creek, which runs along the eastern and southern side of the dune mass; but the climb up the dunes themselves, though incredibly tiring, is not to be missed – for the fun **slide** down (bring your own dune board) as much as for the views of the amazing desolate scenery. A walk along sandy trails, squeezed between the dunes and the mountains, and a night spent out at one of the underused backcountry campsites are also worthwhile.

The **visitor center** (☎719/378-2312, ⊛www.nps.gov/grsa) is three miles beyond the park entrance ($4 per vehicle), behind which lies the **Mosca picnic area** – the main gateway for exploring the dunes. To pitch a tent on the dune mass itself you'll need to pick up a free **backcountry permit** at the visitor center; the permit is also required for the park's seven primitive backcountry sites ($14). Most campers, however, stay at the large *Pinyon Flats Campground* ($14), the only site in the park accessible by car and usually crowded with RVs; it's run on a first-served basis and is often full in July and August. The *Great Sand Dunes Oasis Store*, 7900 Hwy-150 N (☎719/378-2222) just before the monument entrance offers showers, laundry, and arid tent sites ($10), as well a small number of basic **cabins** (❸). Behind the store the *Great Sand Dunes Lodge* (☎719/378-2900, ⊛www.gsdlodge.com; ❹), has pleasant rooms with dunes views, an indoor pool, and a **restaurant** that closes at 7pm. Otherwise, the closest restaurant is thirty miles away in Alamosa, where cheery *Mrs Rivera's*, 1019 6th St (☎719/589-0277), serves excellent Mexican food: great *chile rellenos* cost only $6.

Southwest Colorado

The high mountain passes of **southwest Colorado** are classic mining territory; dotted through the valleys you'll find all sorts of well-preserved late-Victorian frontier towns. As the pioneers moved in, first illegally and then backed by the federal government, they drove the Ute away into the poorer land of the far southwest.

From **Durango**, the main town of southwest Colorado, the dramatic **San Juan Skyway** completes a loop of over two hundred miles through the mountains, north along US-550 and then back via Hwy-145 and US-160. The stretch of road north of Durango, negotiating its way over stunning high passes, is known as the **Million Dollar Highway** for the gold-laden gravel that was used in its construction. Remote **Crested Butte**, to the north of the San Juan Mountains, is a gorgeous nineteenth-century mining village turned ski resort and one of Colorado's major attractions.

Durango

DURANGO is the largest town in southwest Colorado and the best hub for exploring the Four Corners region. Such is the attractiveness of the town and surrounding wooded low hills that it has attracted a large influx of long-distance telecommuters. This freelance crowd joins the student populace from **Fort Lewis College** and the many outdoors enthusiasts who come to ride and hike the area's superb trails, resulting in a town with a youthful, energetic buzz.

The town was founded in 1880 as a refining town and rail junction for Silverton, 45 miles north. Steam trains continue to run along the spectacular old mining route through the Animas Valley, though nowadays tourists, not sacks of gold, are the money-making cargo. **The Durango & Silverton Narrow Gauge Railroad** runs up to four roundtrips daily (all leave in early morning; $62 roundtrip; ☏970/247-2733, ⓦwww.durangotrain.com) between May and October, from a depot at 479 Main Ave at the south end of town. The views from the train as it chugs through huddles of lush aspen are spectacular, framed by the clear Animas River below and rocky outcrops looming above. (The trains are slow, however, so if you want to save time you can take a bus one way to Silverton on the Million Dollar Highway).

Greyhound services between Denver and Albuquerque call in at 275 E 8th Ave. Durango's **visitor center**, near the train station (summer Mon–Fri 8am–7pm, Sat 10am–6pm, Sun 11am–5pm; rest of year Mon–Fri 8am–6pm, Sat 8am–5pm, Sun 10am–4pm; ☏970/247-0312 or 1-800/525-8855, ⓦwww.durango.com), has full lists of **accommodation**, topped by the landmark *Strater Hotel* at 699 Main Ave (☏970/247-4431 or 1-800/247-4431, ⓦwww.strater.com; summer ❻–❼, winter ❹). The innumerable **motels** north of town along Main Avenue increase their rates in summer; try the good-value *Siesta* at 3475 Main Ave (☏970/247-0741; ❷–❸), on the northern fringes of town, or the small, comfortable *End O' Day Motel*, 350 E 8th Ave (☏970/247-1722; ❸), only a ten-minute walk southeast from downtown. There are plenty of places to **eat and drink**: *Carver's Bakery & Brewpub*, 1022 Main Ave (☏970/259-2545), opens at 6.30am for breakfast, serves Southwestern lunches and dinners, and keeps buzzing later on in its brewpub role. *Steamworks Brewing Co*, 801 E 2nd Ave (☏970/259-9200), is another good choice for sampling local brews and also has a varied menu.

Silverton

Journey's end for the narrow-gauge railroad from Durango comes at **SILVERTON**: "silver by the ton," allegedly. Spread across a small flat valley surrounded by high mountains it's one of Colorado's most atmospheric mountain towns, with wide, dirt-paved streets leading off toward the hills to either side of its one main road. Silverton's zinc- and copper-mining days only came to an end in 1991, and the population has dropped since then, with those that remain generally reliant on the seasonal tourist train; so while the false-fronted stores along "Notorious Blair Street" may remind one of the days when **Wyatt Earp** dealt cards in the *Arlington* saloon, the town is defined by the restaurants and gift shops that fill up between 11am and 2pm when tourists are deposited in town.

Outside these hours Silverton is very quiet and offers inexpensive **accommodation** at the *Triangle Motel*, 848 Greene St (☏970/387-5780, ⓦwww.trianglemotel.com; ❸), at the south end of town, which also offers good-value two-room suites and jeep rental. For a little extra cash you can soak in the atmosphere of the *Grand Imperial Hotel*, 1219 Greene St (☏970/387-5527 or 1-800/341-3340; ❹–❺), in one of its forty creaky, antique-furnished rooms. The thin-walled *Silverton Hostel*, 1025 Blair St (check-in daily 8–10am & 4–10pm; ☏970/387-0115, has $13 dorm beds. For **food**, there's *Romero's*, 1151 Greene St (☏970/387-0123), an enjoyable Mexican cantina with a menu of tasty, authentic food, plus fantastic salsa.

Ouray

The equally attractive mining community of **OURAY** lies 23 miles north of Silverton, on the far side of the 11,018ft **Red Mountain Pass**, where the bare rock beneath the snow really is red, thanks to mineral deposits. The Million Dollar Highway twists and turns here, passing abandoned mine workings and rusting machinery in the most unlikely and inaccessible spots; back roads into the mountains offer rich pickings, for hikers or drivers with four-wheel-drive vehicles.

Ouray itself squeezes into a narrow but verdant valley, with the commercially run **Ouray Hot Springs** beside the Uncompahgre River at the north end of town. A mile or so south, a one-way-loop dirt road leads to Box Canyon Falls Park (daily 8am–8pm; $3), where a straightforward 500ft trail, partly along a swaying wooden parapet, leads into the dark, narrow Box Canyon. At the far end, the falls thunder through a tiny cleft in the mountain.

The local **visitor center** (daily 8am–6pm; closed Mon & Tues in winter; ℡970/325-4746 or 1-800/228-1876, Ⓦwww.ouraycolorado.com) is on the northern edge of town beside the hot springs. At *Box Canyon Lodge*, an old-style timber **motel** at 45 Third Ave below the park (℡970/325-4981 or 1-800/327-5080; ❹), you can bathe in natural hot tubs. The luxurious B&B *St Elmo Hotel*, 426 Main St (℡970/325-4951, Ⓦwww.stelmohotel.com; ❺), holds a good **restaurant**, and the *Grounds Keeper Coffee House* 524 Main St (℡970/325-0550) is a central café serving espresso drinks and healthy light lunches that include a fine veggie lasagna.

Telluride

Lying at the flat base of a bowl of vast steep-sided mountains, **TELLURIDE**, 120 miles northwest of Durango on Hwy-145, is located in one of the Rockies' most picturesque valleys. In the 1880s the former mining village was briefly home to the young Butch Cassidy, who robbed his first bank here in 1889. These days the town is better known as the home of a top-class **ski resort** that rivals Aspen for celebrity allure. Happily it has achieved its status without losing its character, exemplified by the low-slung buildings on the wide main street, beautifully preserved as a National Historic District. Healthy young bohemians with few visible means of support but top-notch ski or snowboarding equipment seem to form the bulk of the twelve hundred inhabitants, while most visitors tend to dwell two miles above the town in **Mountain Village**; the two places are connected by a free year-round gondola service. In summer, the **hiking** opportunities are excellent; one three-mile roundtrip walk leads from the head of the valley, where the highway ends at Pioneer Mill, up to the 365ft **Bridal Veil Falls**, the largest in Colorado. Come winter, nearly half the ski terrain in Telluride is geared for experts, with its steep mogul fields particular favorites.

Accommodation is much less expensive in summer than during ski season, though prices do go up for the Bluegrass Festival in June, the Jazz Festival at the beginning of August, and the Film Festival at the start of September. As well as being the town's official **information service**, Telluride Central Reservations, 666 W Colorado Ave (summer daily 9am–7pm; rest of year Mon–Fri 9am–5pm; ℡970/728-4431 or 1-800/525-3455, Ⓦwww.telluridemm.com), coordinates **lodging** and package deals, with free lift tickets for the first month of the season for guests in certain lodges. Skiing comes half-price if you stay in any of seven neighboring towns. Of specific places, the 1895 *New Sheridan Hotel*, 231 W Colorado Ave (℡970/728-4351 or 1-800/200-1891, Ⓦwww.newsheridan.com; winter ❻, summer ❹), offers surprisingly good rates, a cozy library, and a rooftop hot tub, as well as its own bar and chop house (with vegetarian options). The *Victoria Inn*, 401 W Pacific Ave (℡970/728-6601 or 1-800/611-9893 Ⓦwww.tellurideinn.com; ❺), has clean, motel-style doubles.

Honga's Lotus Petal, 133 S Oak St (☎970/728-5134) offers a variety of good pan-Asian entrees from around $12 in stylish surroundings, while *Smugglers Brewpub and Grille*, at San Juan Avenue and Pine Street (☎970/728-0919), is a lively evening hangout with a wide-ranging menu and some good local brews.

Black Canyon of the Gunnison National Park

The **BLACK CANYON OF THE GUNNISON NATIONAL PARK**, seventy miles southeast of Grand Junction and reachable from US-50 to the south or Hwy-92 from the north, more than lives up to its bleak-sounding name. The view down into the fearsome, black-rock canyon to the foaming Gunnison River below is about as foreboding as mountain scenery gets. Over two million years the river eroded a deep, narrow gorge, leaving exposed cliffs and jagged spires of crystalline rock more than 1.7 billion years old. The aspen-lined road leading to the top of the canyon winds uphill until the trees abruptly come to an end, the road levels out, and the scenery takes a dramatic turn – stark black cliffs, with the odd pine clinging to a tiny ledge in desperation. Snowshoeing and cross-country skiing are possibilities here in winter, while in summer there are good opportunities for fishing, hiking, and advanced-level climbing and kayaking.

The **visitor center** (open year-round 8.30am–4pm; ☎970/641-2337, ⊛www.nps.gov/blca; $8 per vehicle) on the south rim has details on the two first-come, first-served campgrounds, one on each side of the canyon, as well as information on activities – particularly watersports, hunting and fishing – in the nearby **Curecanti National Recreation Area** and **Gunnison Gorge National Conservation Area**.

Crested Butte

The beautiful Victorian mining village of **CRESTED BUTTE**, 150 miles northeast of Telluride and 230 miles southwest of Denver, almost died off in the late 1950s when its coal deposits were exhausted. However, the development of 11,875ft **Mount Crested Butte** into a world-class **ski resort** in the 1960s, and a **mountain-bikers**' paradise two decades later, means that today it can claim to be the best year-round resort in Colorado. The old town is resplendent with gaily painted clapboard homes and businesses, and zoning laws ensure that condos and chalets are confined to the resort area, behind the foothills three miles up the road. The outdoor opportunities have lured young people here from throughout the West.

In skiing and snowboarding circles the Butte is best known for its extreme terrain, with lifts serving out-of-the-way bowls and faces that would only be accessible by helicopter at other resorts. It's no surprise then that the resort hosts both the US extreme skiing and snowboarding championships. That said, there are plenty of long beginner runs mixed in over the mountain's thousand skiable acres, keeping the slopes accessible to all. Fifteen chair lifts (adult day lift passes $73) link 106 runs, which are usually uncrowded thanks to the resort's isolated location. Cross-country, especially telemark, skiing attracts thousands, and there's snowmobiling too.

In summer, **mountain bikes** all but outnumber cars around the town, especially during **Fat Tire Week** in July, one of the oldest festivals in the young sport and one that, according to local legend, evolved from a race over the rocky 21-mile **Pearl Pass** to Aspen on newspaper bicycles in the 1970s. You can still ride this route – 190 miles shorter than the road – but some of the most exciting trails are much nearer the town and include the gorgeous 401 trail with its wide-open vistas; the thickly wooded Dyke Trail; and the long, varied, and occasionally challenging Deadman's Gulch. The visitor center (see below) can help out with a basic map and route descriptions for the main trails, and local bike shops like The Alpineer, 419 6th St (℡970/349-5210, @www.alpineer.com), offer a selection of rental bikes.

Practicalities

A five-hour drive southwest from Denver along mostly minor highways, Crested Butte is not an easy place to get to, though the roads are almost always open. Most skiers fly in on regular daily **flights** from Denver, or weekly services from Atlanta, Dallas, and Houston. These touch down at Gunnison Airport, 28 miles and a forty-minute trip to Crested Butte with the Alpine Express Shuttle ($53 roundtrip; ℡970/641-5074 or 1-800/822-4844, @www.alpineexpressshuttle.com). A car is unnecessary once in town; free **buses** ply the three-mile route between the town and resort every fifteen minutes 7.15am to midnight, while the inexpensive town taxi (℡970/349-5543) does the same route after hours. The **visitor center**, at Elk Ave and 6th St (daily 9am–5pm; ℡970/349-6438 or 1-800/545-4505, @www.visitcrestedbutte.com), produces a weekly events guide for the area.

The choice of **accommodation** is between the ski area or downtown; you're likely to flit between the two areas every day, so it's only worth staying at the generally more expensive mountainside lodgings if you're obsessed with getting first tracks. *Crested Butte Mountain Resort* (℡970/349-2333 or 1-800/544-8448, @www.skicb.com) can book accommodation and advise on money-saving package deals. Be sure to reserve a room in advance during winter.

Among the **B&B** options, the historic log home of the 🏃 *Claim Jumper B&B*, 704 Whiterock Ave (℡970/349-6471; ❺), with its six themed rooms amid a jumble of Americana, make it one of the most enjoyable in Colorado. The *Old Town Inn*, Hwy-35 and Belleview Ave (℡970/349-6184; ❻), offers standard motel rooms beside the main highway at the southern edge of town, and the large and friendly *Crested Butte International Hostel*, 615 Teocalli Ave (℡970/349-0588 or 1-888/389-0588 @www.crestedbuttehostel.com; ❶–❹), where dorm beds cost $22–35 depending on season (private rooms $55–87).

Crested Butte lays claim to a surprising number of gourmet **restaurants**, with far fairer prices than those at glitzier resorts. Among the more expensive, *Bacchanale*, 208 Elk Ave (℡970/349-5257), is an intimate place with a varied Northern Italian menu including good veal and cannelloni. For lower prices and a bit of a livelier atmosphere, try the *Powerhouse*, 130 Elk Ave (℡970/349-5494), which serves zesty Mexican cuisine in a fondly restored 1880s generating station. The huge wooden bar stocks 65 varieties of tequila.

The early **apres-ski** center is *Rafters*, right by the lifts. By early evening most visitors have found their way to downtown, for no-nonsense local bars such as *Kochevars* and *The Talk of the Town*. *Lobar*, 303 Elk Ave (℡970/349-0480), part lounge and part sushi bar, is a hip recent addition to Crested Butte's grungy bar scene. Sink back into a black microsuede sectional sofa to sip a high-end martini.

Mesa Verde National Park

The only national park in the US devoted exclusively to archeological remains, **MESA VERDE NATIONAL PARK** is set high on a densely wooded plateau off US-160, halfway between Cortez and Mancos. It's so far off the beaten track that its extensive **Ancestral Puebloan ruins** were not fully explored until 1888, when a local rancher discovered them on his land.

Between the time of Christ and 1300 AD, Ancestral Puebloan civilization expanded to cover much of the area known as the "**Four Corners**." Their earliest dwellings were simple pits in the ground, but before they vanished from history they had developed the architectural sophistication needed to build the extraordinary complexes of Mesa Verde. Over centuries, Ancestral Puebloan housing had evolved from pithouses to these spectacular multistory apartments, nestling in rocky alcoves above the sheer canyons that bisect the southern edge of the Mesa Verde plateau. Why they did so is not clear, though recent evidence suggests that Ancestral Puebloan culture was not quite as peaceful as previously imagined; in any case the soil at Mesa Verde ultimately appears to have been depleted, and they are thought to have migrated into what's now New Mexico to establish the pueblos where their descendants still live.

Touring the park
The access road to Mesa Verde climbs south from US-160 ten miles east of Cortez. Once past the entrance station ($10 fee per vehicle), the road climbs and twists for fifteen miles to the **Far View visitor center** (late April to mid-Oct daily 8am–5pm; ☏970/529-5036). Exhibits inside cover Navajo, Hopi, and Pueblo crafts and jewelry. Immediately beyond, the road forks south to the two main constellations of remains: **Chapin Mesa** to the south, and **Wetherill Mesa** to the west. To tour any of the major ruins you must buy timed **tickets** at the visitor center ($2.25 for each attraction). On Chapin Mesa, Cliff Palace is usually open between 9am and 5pm daily from late April until early November, and Balcony House for the same hours between late April and mid-October; at busy times, you can't tour both on the same day. On Wetherill Mesa, generally open late May to early September, tours of Long House operate between 9am and 4pm daily.

Six miles beyond Chapin Mesa from the visitor center, the **Archeological Museum** (daily: April to mid-Oct 8am–6.30pm; mid-Oct to March 8am–5pm) holds the park's best displays on the Ancestral Puebloans, and also sells tour tickets for the remainder of the season after the visitor center closes in late fall. It's also the starting point for the short, steep hike down to **Spruce Tree House**, the only ruin that can be visited in winter – a neat little village of three-story structures, snugly molded into a rocky alcove and fronted by plazas.

Beyond the museum, **Ruins Road** (April to early Nov daily 8am–dusk) consists of two one-way, six-mile loops. If you're pressed for time, follow only the eastern one, to reach **Cliff Palace**, the largest surviving Ancestral Puebloan cliff dwelling anywhere. Tucked a hundred feet below an overhanging ledge of pale rock, its 217 rooms once housed over two hundred people. Even without a tour ticket (see above), you can get a great view from the promontory where tour groups gather, beside the parking lot. Entering the ruin itself, especially on a quieter day, provides a haunting evocation of a lost and little-known world, as you walk through the empty plazas, peer down into the mysterious *kivas* (circular, stone-lined ceremonial pits) and glimpse fading murals inside some of the structures.

Balcony House, a little further on, is one of the few Mesa Verde complexes clearly geared towards defense; access is very difficult, and it's not visible from above. Guided tours involve scrambling up three hair-raising ladders and crawling through a narrow tunnel, teetering all the while above a steep drop into Soda Canyon. If you don't have a head for heights, you might probably give it a miss.

At the end of the twisting twelve-mile drive onto **Wetherill Mesa** (daily late May to early Sept 8am–4.30pm; excluding large vehicles like RVs), you can catch a free miniature train around the tip of the mesa to the **Long House**, the park's second largest ruin, set in its largest cave. Hour-long tours descend sixty or so steps to reach its central plaza, then scramble around its 150 rooms and 21 *kivas*.

Park practicalities

Mesa Verde gets very crowded in high summer; the best months to visit are May, September, and October. The park is open all year, but most structures are inaccessible in winter, and services such as gas, food, and lodging only operate between late April and mid-October. Most visitors stay in nearby towns; the only **rooms** in the park itself are at the summer-only *Far View Motor Lodge*, near the visitor center (☎970/529-4421 or 1-800/449-2288; Ⓦwww.visitmesaverde.com; ❺), where the balconies have superb views and the absence of phones and TVs makes for a tranquil stay. The lodge's *Metate Room* restaurant provides fabulous **meals** featuring buffalo and elk, with sides like beans, flat bread, and roasted corn. Food is also available year-round at *Spruce Tree Terrace* near the Chapin Mesa museum. You can **camp** at the pleasant and very large *Morefield Campground*, four miles up from the entrance (late April to mid-Oct; ☎970/529-4421 or 1-800/449-2288; $19–25), and there are also several commercial campgrounds nearby.

⑪ Wyoming

Pronghorn antelope all but outnumber people in wide-open **WYOMING**, the ninth largest but least populous state in the union, with just 509,000 residents. Above all, this is classic **cowboy country** – the inspiration behind *Shane*, *The Virginian*, and countless other Western novels – replete with open range, rodeos, and country-and-western dance halls. The state emblem, seen everywhere, is a hat-waving cowboy astride a bucking bronco.

Well over three million tourists per year head to the state's northwest corner for the simmering geothermal landscape of **Yellowstone National Park**, and the craggy mountain vistas of adjacent **Grand Teton National Park**. Between Yellowstone and South Dakota to the east are the helter-skelter **Bighorn Mountains**, likeable Old West towns such as **Cody** and **Buffalo**, and the otherworldly outcrop of **Devils Tower**.

The meager supply of buffalo in early Wyoming caused fierce intertribal wars and kept the **Native American** population down to around ten thousand. However, Sioux, Cheyenne, and Blackfoot combined to inflict notable defeats on the US Army before it could clear the way for pioneer settlement in the 1870s. The cattle ranchers and sheep-farming homesteaders who followed engaged in violent **range wars** over grazing rights to the wiry grasslands.

Unlikely as it may seem, this rowdy state was the first to grant women the vote in 1869 – a full half-century before the rest of the country, on the grounds that the enfranchisement of women would attract settlers and increase the population, thereby hastening statehood. A year later Wyoming appointed the country's first women jurors, and the "Equality State" elected the first female US governor in 1924.

The absence of rivers to irrigate farmland has put a lid on agricultural growth. Any weather-beaten, denim-clad stranger is more likely to be an oil roustabout than a genuine cowboy, **mineral extraction** having replaced livestock as the mainstay of the economy in the early twentieth century; today the state's coffers overflow with profits from the booming coal, oil, and natural gas industries.

Getting around Wyoming

Greyhound **buses** operate along I-80 through the south. The rest of the state is covered only patchily by regional bus companies, so having your own car is definitely the best option. Jackson has the state's busiest **airport**, though flights also go to Casper and Cheyenne. **Cycling** across northern Wyoming can be great fun, although if you're crossing the Bighorns you'll need to pick your routes carefully, as roads here have incredibly steep gradients.

South and central Wyoming

State capital **Cheyenne** is the only town of real note in the lower two-thirds of Wyoming. Set in the heart of rich prairie – a surprise after the scrubland, mountain, and desert of most of the region – it has closer economic ties with Omaha or Denver than with the rest of Wyoming. West of Cheyenne, smaller **Laramie** possesses an agreeable frontier feel, while the spectacular wilderness of the **Wind River Range**, accessible from **Pinedale** and **Lander**, accounts for most of the west-central portion of the state.

Cheyenne

The eastern approach into **CHEYENNE**, dropping into a wide dip in the plains, leaves enduring memories for most travelers. With the snow-crested Rockies looming in the distance and short, sun-bleached grass encircling the town, the sky appears gargantuan, dwarfing the city's leafy suburbs. A quick walk around reveals a diverse community, shaped by railroads, state politics, and even nuclear arms. When the Union Pacific Railroad reached this site in 1867, soldiers had to drive out the "**Hell on Wheels**" brigade of gamblers, moonshiners, and hard-drinking gunmen who stayed one step ahead of the railroads, claiming land and then selling it for huge profit before moving on to the next proposed terminal.

Union Pacific's sprawling yards and fine old terminus now mark the eastern edge of downtown, while to the west the city's longstanding military installation was expanded in 1957 to house the first US intercontinental ballistic missile base. Cowboy culture is big here, too, as the ranchwear stores and honky-tonks dotted around town attest. Along with hosting the world's largest outdoor rodeo, the ten-day **Cheyenne Frontier Days** festival (℡1-800/227-6336, 🖳www.cfrodeo. com) in late July attracts thousands of people to its concerts with top country stars, parades, chuckwagon races, air shows, and cook-outs. The rest of the year, things are pretty quiet. **Sixteenth Street**, or Lincolnway, is the retail and entertainment heart of Cheyenne. Five minutes' walk north up leafy Capitol Avenue, the **Wyoming State Museum** takes a sober look at Wild West history (May–Oct Mon–Sat 9am–4.30pm; Nov–April Mon–Fri 9am–4.30pm, Sat 10am–2pm; free). The **Cheyenne Frontier Days Old West Museum**, five minutes' drive from downtown at 4610 N Carey Ave (Mon–Fri 9am–5pm, Sat & Sun 10am–5pm; $6), is more lighthearted, telling how the railroad came to town, with some great old engines and well-presented temporary exhibits. Much space is devoted to the Frontier Days celebrations, with photos, costumes, and videos evoking the annual frenzy.

Practicalities

Greyhound **buses** (℡307/635-1327) run east and west along I-80 and south to Denver, while Powder River buses (same number) travel through eastern Wyoming to Colorado, Montana, and South Dakota. The companies share the depot at 222 Deming Drive, beside Central Avenue several blocks south of downtown. The **visitor center**, 121 W 15th St, suite 202 (May–Sept Mon–Fri 10am–6pm, Sat 9am–6pm, Sun 10am–4pm; Oct–April Mon–Fri 8am–5pm; ⊤307/778-3133 or 1-800/426-5009, Ⓦwww.cheyenne.org), has a free detailed map of the city, and operates a two-hour **trolley tour** of Cheyenne in summer ($10 for adults, $5 for children).

Although places to **stay** are normally inexpensive, prices double during the Frontier Days festival. Budget motels line West Lincolnway, like the *Atlas Motel* at no. 1524 (⊤307/632-9214; $45). There are better rooms downtown in the *Plains Hotel*, 1600 Central Ave (⊤307/638-3311; $90–125). Best of the upmarket options is the *Nagle Warren Mansion*, 222 E 17th St (⊤307/637-3333 or 1-800/811-2610, Ⓦwww.naglewarrenmansion.com; $135), which offers superb bed-and-breakfast in opulent surroundings. Cheyenne has no shortage of **diners** serving cowboy-sized breakfasts, lunches, and Mexican food; try *Los Amigos*, 620 Central Ave (⊤307/638-8591). *Sanford's* is a lively **brewpub** with fine food and a mixed crowd, and comedy and live music downstairs.

Laramie and around

LARAMIE lies fifty miles west of Cheyenne on I-80, or slightly further via spectacular Happy Jack Hwy-210, which slices through plains studded with bizarrely shaped boulders and outcrops. At first Laramie seems typical of rural Wyoming, but behind downtown's quaint Victorian facades lurk hard-rocking record stores, day spas, vegetarian cafés, and secondhand bookstores – unusual for rodeo land, and due to the **University of Wyoming**, whose campus spreads east from the town center. Free museums and sights of interest on campus include the Anthropology Museum, the Museum of Geology, and the Rocky Mountain Herbarium.

The centerpiece of the ambitious **Wyoming Territorial Prison State Park**, west of town at 975 Snowy Range Rd (May–Sept daily 9am–6pm, call for winter hours; $5; ⊤307/745/6161, Ⓦwww.wyoprisonpark.org), is the old **prison**. A touch over-restored, it holds informative displays on the Old West and women in Wyoming, and huge mugshots of ex-convicts, among them Butch Cassidy, who was incarcerated here for eighteen months in 1896 for the common crime of cattle-rustling.

Practicalities

Greyhound (⊤307/742-9663) pulls in at Tumbleweed Express gas station on Bluebird Lane, 2.5 miles east of downtown beside Grand Avenue. The **visitor center** is at 210 Custer St (Mon–Fri 8am–5pm; ⊤1-800/445-5303, Ⓦwww.laramie-tourism.org). **Rooms** are clean and rates are good at the downtown *Travel Inn*, 262 N 3rd St (⊤307/745-4853 or 1-800/227-5430; $45). *Corona Village*, 421 Boswell Drive (⊤307/721-0167), serves authentic and inexpensive Mexican **food**, while buzzing *Lovejoy's Bar and Grill*, at 101 Grand Ave (⊤307/745-0141), is a friendly student hangout that serves good espresso, bagels, muffins, and lunch specials.

The Medicine Bow Mountains

Just west of Laramie, **Hwy-130** dips into the huge wind-gouged bowl of **Big Hollow**, passes through rustic **Centennial**, and starts the steep climb up the **MEDICINE BOW MOUNTAINS**, one of Wyoming's most picturesque drives. Overlooks at the top of the 10,847ft Snowy Range Pass (closed in winter) reveal alpine lakes and meadows, tight against steep mountain faces. Forty-nine miles out from Centennial, sleepy **Saratoga** is hemmed in by the Snowy and Sierra Madre ranges. The **Hobo Hot Springs** on Walnut Avenue is a free outdoor pool fed by natural hot springs. Easily the best place to **stay** is the antique-furnished *Wolf Hotel*,

Butch Cassidy and the Sundance Kid

Without doubt the two most engaging characters to roam the Rocky Mountains of northern Colorado and southern Wyoming, **Butch Cassidy and the Sundance Kid** remain legends not only of the Old West but of a romantic outlaw existence in which breaking the law became an expression of personal freedom. Thanks in large part to the 1969 Hollywood film *Butch Cassidy and the Sundance Kid* (which starred Paul Newman and Robert Redford), these two former thieves and cattle rustlers continue to cast a long shadow across the Rockies.

Butch Cassidy was born **George LeRoy Parker** in Beaver, Utah, on 6 April, 1866. Taught the art of cattle-rustling by ranch-hand Mike Cassidy, Parker borrowed his mentor's last name, then picked up the handle "Butch" while working as a butcher in Rock Springs, Wyoming. He pulled his first bank job in Telluride, Colorado, in 1889, and soon found himself in the company of a like-minded group of outlaws known as the **Wild Bunch**. Among them was one **Harry Longabaugh** – the Sundance Kid – who picked up his nickname following a jail stint in Sundance, Wyoming. The Wild Bunch were eclectic in their criminal pursuits, and the gang's résumé would include horse-rustling as well as the robbing of trains, banks, and mine payrolls; between them they gave away a fortune in gold to friends and even strangers in need, hence their reputation as latter-day Robin Hoods.

The image of a dashing, philanthropic band of outlaws did not sit well with authorities, who mustered teams of lawmen to go after them. The gang took to laying low through the winter months in **Brown's Hole**, a broad river valley in remote northwest Colorado, and they were also known to visit the southern Wyoming towns of Baggs, Rock Springs, and Green River. Their saloon excesses were tolerated, though, because at the end of a spree they would meticulously account for every broken chair and bullet hole, making generous restitution in gold. The gang, however, was eventually undone by their own vanity and love of a good time. During a visit to Fort Worth, Texas, five of the men posed for a photo in smart suits and derby hats, looking so dapper that the photographer proudly placed the photo in his shop window where it was seen the following day by a detective from the famous Pinkerton's agency.

Wearying of life on the run, Butch and Sundance sailed for **South America** in 1902, and were soon trying their hand at gold-mining, while robbing the occasional bank or train. The Hollywood version was true enough to this point, but Butch Cassidy did not die in a hail of bullets at the hands of Bolivian soldiers in 1909 as depicted in the film – although it seems that Harry Longabaugh did. The last say belongs to Josie Morris, an old girlfriend from Butch's Brown's Hole days, who insisted that he came to see her on his return from South America, and claimed furthermore that he died an old man in Johnny, Nevada, some time during the 1940s.

101 E Bridge Ave (℡307/326-5525, Ⓦwww.wolfhotel.com; ❸-❺), which has a good restaurant and bar.

Southwest Wyoming

The long and monotonous drive across southern Wyoming on I-80 holds little to delight the eye, though geologists and fossil enthusiasts will be in their element, and it may provide some travelers with their first glimpse of the red-rock scenery of the West.

Rawlins

There would be little reason to stop at the tiny prairie town of **RAWLINS**, a hundred miles west of Laramie, but for the unmissable **Wyoming Frontier Prison**, at Fifth and Walnut streets (hourly tours April–Oct daily 8.30am–6.30pm; Nov–March Mon–Fri 9am–5pm; $4.25; ℡307/324-4422). In service until 1981, this huge jail with dark cells, peeling walls, and echoing corridors can make for a creepy experience – not least due to the fascinating anecdotes told with aplomb by the exceptional guides. The darkest moment comes as the gas chamber (in use from 1937 until 1965) is revealed.

Just to the west, the Continental Divide briefly splits into two in the **Great Divide Basin**. In theory, rain that falls here should remain here, unable to flow toward either ocean – unfortunately virtually all of it evaporates, and the brick-red hell of the **Red Desert** stretches implacably away to the horizon.

The Wind River range

Roads to Grand Teton and Yellowstone national parks from southern Wyoming skirt the **Wind River Mountains**, the state's longest and highest range, with some of the Rockies' most beautiful and challenging backpacking terrain. No roads cross the mountains; you can either see them from the **east**, by driving through the Wind River Indian Reservation on US-26/287, or from the less accessible **west**, by taking US-191 up from I-80 at Rock Springs.

Wind River Indian Reservation

The 1.7 million acres of **WIND RIVER INDIAN RESERVATION** occupies a largely forgotten swath of west central Wyoming, overshadowed by the high snowcapped peaks to the west and south. It is the only Indian reservation in Wyoming, and extends roughly seventy miles from the natural spa town of **Thermopolis** in the east, through arid grasslands and desiccated uranium-rich badlands, to **Dubois** (see below) in the west, with the rich fishing grounds of the cottonwood-lined Wind River at its heart. The reservation was created in 1863 as a permanent home for the Eastern Shoshone, but due to US government imposition, it soon came to accommodate the Northern Arapaho as well; these days the Arapaho account for more than double the Shoshone population. Near **Fort Washakie** – named for the centenarian Chief Washakie, who held the Shoshone together throughout the period of white expansion – is the likely grave of **Sacagawea**, the guide of Lewis and Clark's expedition. **Powwows** – gatherings that have both spiritual and social significance to Native Americans – are held mainly in summer, and are open to the public. Contact the Shoshone Tribal Cultural Center in Fort Washakie (Mon–Fri 8am–5pm; ℡307/332-9106) for details on how to join in.

The friendly one-horse town of **LANDER** on US-287 makes an appealing base, with a string of cheap motels along Main Street and an excellent **B&B** at the Art Nouveau–style *Blue Spruce Inn*, 677 S. Third St (℡307/332-8253 or 1-888/503-3311; ❹). A good place to **eat** is the locals' favorite, *Gannett Grill*, 126 Main St (℡307/332-8228), serving burgers and pizza.

Dubois

The former logging town of **DUBOIS** ("dew-boys"), squeezed into the northern tip of the Wind River valley, and an oasis among the badlands, turned to tourism after its final sawmill closed in 1987 (it's got a leg up by being sixty miles southeast of Grand Teton National Park, via the dramatic **Togwotee Pass**). Dubois is home to the biggest herd of bighorn sheep in the lower 48 states, and celebrates that fact with its **National Bighorn Sheep Center**, a half-mile northwest of town on US-26/287 (daily: summer 8am–7pm; rest of year 9am–5pm; closed for part of winter; $2; ℡307/455-3429, ⓦwww.bighorn.org). Along with running exciting 4WD spotting tours ($25; reservations required), the center contains several dioramas and exhibits on the majestic mascot of the Rockies.

Dubois is a bargain thanks to clean and cheap **motels** such as the riverside *Trail's End*, 511 W. Ramshorn St (T 1-888/455-6660; ❷), and the beautifully restored historic **B&B** *Twin Pines Lodge and Cabins*, 218 Ramshorn St (T 1-800/550-6332, Ⓦ www.twinpineslodge.com; ❸). The evening pastime is listening to country crooners in classic Western **bars** like the *Rustic Pine*, 121 E Ramshorn St (T 307/455-2772), which also serves steaks.

Pinedale

On the western side of the Wind River range and a two-hour drive from Jackson to the north, tiny well-to-do **PINEDALE** on US-191 offers unrivaled access to the mountains. Once a major logging center, it now attracts second-homeowners and hikers. The excellent **Museum of the Mountain Man**, 700 E Hennick Rd (May–Sept daily 10am–5pm; rest of the year by appointment only; $5; T 307/367-4101), commemorates the town's role as a rendezvous for fur trappers in the 1830s.

A sixteen-mile road winds east from Pinedale past Fremont Lake to **Elkhart Park**, from where trails lead past beautiful **Seneca Lake** and along rugged Indian Pass to the glaciers and 13,000ft peaks; the Pinedale Ranger Station office at 29 Fremont Lake Rd (June–Aug Mon–Sat 8am–5pm; rest of year Mon–Fri 8am–5pm; T 307/367-4326) has information on good hiking routes.

Motels are easily found on the main drag, Pine Street, including the appealing and central *Lodge at Pinedale*, no. 1054 W (T 1-866/995-6343, Ⓦ www.pinedale lodge.com; ❸), with continental breakfast, indoor pool, and hot tub.

Northeast and north central Wyoming

Northern Wyoming has more to offer than just a handy route between the Black Hills and Yellowstone. The surreal volcanic monument of **Devils Tower**, the massive **Bighorn Mountains**, and the desertscape of the **Bighorn Basin** are notable natural attractions in a land steeped in the history of Native American wars, outlaw activity, and pioneer hardships. The heavily wooded Bighorns soar abruptly from the plains to over 9000ft; the loftiest peaks, protruding above the timberline, seem bald beside their dark-coated neighbors. The small town of **Cody** fifty miles east of Yellowstone is one of the more commercialized settlements around here, and worth a stopover for its Western-theme museums.

Devils Tower National Monument

Though Congress designated **DEVILS TOWER**, in far northeastern Wyoming, as the country's first national monument in 1906, it took Steven Spielberg's inspired use of it as the alien landing spot in *Close Encounters of the Third Kind* to make this eerie 867ft volcanic outcrop a true national icon. Plonked on top of a thickly forested hill, itself a full six hundred feet above the peaceful Belle Fourche River, it resembles a giant wizened tree stump; but, painted ever-changing hues by the sun and moon, it can be hauntingly beautiful. Sioux legend says the tower was formed after three young girls jumped onto a boulder to escape a vicious bear. They were rescued when the great god, seeing their plight, made the rock rise higher and higher; the bear's desperate efforts to climb up scored the sides of the column.

Four short trails loop the tower, beginning from the **visitor center** (mid-June to mid-Nov daily 8am–7pm; T 307/467-5283) at its base, three miles from the main gate. The **entrance fee** per car (good for seven days) is $10, and until October you can **camp** for $12 a night – arrive early or you'll end up paying more than twice that at one of the nearby commercial campgrounds.

Buffalo

Snuggled among the southeastern foothills of the Bighorn Mountains, quiet, attractive **BUFFALO** remains largely unaffected by the bustle of the nearby I-90/I-25 intersection. Although **Main Street**, now lined with frontier-style stores, used to be an old buffalo trail, the place was actually named after Buffalo, New York. The **Jim Gatchell Museum**, 100 Fort St (May to mid-Nov daily 9am–6pm; $4), stacked full of Old West curiosities pertaining to soldiers, ranchers, and Native Americans, is well worth a visit.

Pick up information from the **visitor center**, 55 N Main St (Mon–Fri 8am–5pm; ☏307/684-5544, ⓦwww.buffalowyo.com). The historic *Mansion House Inn*, 313 N Main St (☏307/684-2218, ⓦwww.mansionhouseinn.com; ❹), offers impressive B&B and motel **rooms** at bargain rates that include continental breakfast.

Through the Bighorn Mountains

Of the three scenic highways through the **Bighorn Mountains**, US-14A from **Burgess Junction**, fifty miles west of Victorian **Sheridan**, is the most spectacular. The road, typically closed Nov–May due to snow, edges its way up **Medicine Mountain**, on whose windswept western peak the mysterious **Medicine Wheel** – the largest such monument still intact – stands protected behind a wire fence. Local Native American legends offer no clues as to the original purpose of these flat stones, arranged in a circular "wheel" shape with 28 spokes and a circumference of 245ft – though the pattern suggests sun-worship or early astronomy. To get there, you'll have to drive along a precipitous dirt track (past an incongruous radar dome) to within a mile of the site and hike the rest of the way.

The route down the highway's west side, with gradients of ten to twenty percent, is said to have cost more to build per mile than any other road in America. Tight hairpin bends will keep drivers' eyes off the magnificent overlooks, but the best view comes near the bottom, when the road lets you out into the **Bighorn Basin**. This ultra-flat, sparsely vegetated valley, walled in by mighty mountains on three sides and ragged foothills to the north, can strike you as a land that time forgot.

Bighorn Canyon National Recreation Area

Before US-14A gets to Lovell, Hwy-37 turns north to the **Bighorn Canyon National Recreation Area**, an unexpected red-rock wilderness straddling the Wyoming-Montana border. No road runs the full length of the canyon which, since being flooded by the 525ft Yellowtail Dam, has become the preserve of watersports enthusiasts. In summer, **boat tours** leave from **Horseshoe Bend**, where the marina (☏307/548-7230) rents out assorted equipment, and a shadeless beach of red sand offers swimming in the most bizarre of settings. A **visitor center** just east of Lovell on US-14A (daily 8.30am–5pm; ☏307/548-2251) supplies information on local activities and has maps of the Medicine Wheel area.

Cody

Plenty of pick-up trucks cruise the streets of **CODY**, the "rodeo capital of the world," 79 miles east of Yellowstone along US-14 and the North Fork of the Shoshone River. The town was the brainchild of investors who, in 1896, persuaded "Buffalo Bill" Cody to get involved in their development company,

Buffalo Bill

The much-mythologized exploits of **William Frederick "Buffalo Bill" Cody**, born in Iowa in 1846, began at the age of just eleven, when the murder of his father forced him to take a job on a wagon train. An early escape from ambush brought Cody fame as the "Youngest Indian Slayer of the Plains"; four years later, he became the youngest rider on the **Pony Express**, averaging a blazing 15mph on his leg of the legendary mail route. After a stint fighting for the Union, Cody found work – and a lifelong nickname – supplying buffalo meat to workers laying the transcontinental railroad. He claimed to have killed over 4200 animals in just eighteen months, before rejoining the army in 1868 as its chief scout

By the 1870s, exaggerated accounts of Cody's adventures were appearing back east in the "dime novels" of Ned Buntline, and with the Indian Wars all but over he took to guiding Yankee and European gentry on buffalo hunts. The theatrical productions he laid on for his rich guests developed into the world-famous **Wild West Show**. First staged in 1883, these spectacular outdoor carnivals usually consisted of a re-enactment of an Indian battle such as Custer's Last Stand, featuring Sioux who had been present at Little Bighorn, trick riders, buffalo, clowns, and exhibition shooting and riding by the man himself. The show spent ten of its thirty years in Europe, and dressed in the finest silks and sporting a well-groomed goatee, Cody stayed in the grandest hotels and dined with heads of state; Queen Victoria was so enthusiastic in her admiration that rumors circulated of an affair between them.

In later life, a mellowing Cody played down his past activities, to the point of urging the government to respect all Native American treaties and put an end to the wanton slaughter of buffalo and game. Although the Wild West Show was reckoned to have brought in as much as one million dollars per year, his investments failed badly, and, in January 1915, a penniless 69-year-old Buffalo Bill died at his sister's home in Denver. His grave can be found atop Lookout Mountain, outside Golden, Colorado (see p.842).

knowing his approval would attract homesteaders and visitors alike. During summer, tourism is big business, but underneath all the Buffalo Bill–linked attractions and paraphernalia, Cody manages to retain the feel of a rural Western settlement.

The wide, dusty main thoroughfare, **Sheridan Avenue**, holds souvenir and ranchwear shops and is the scene of parades and rodeos during the annual **Cody Stampede** (T1-800/207-0744, Wwww.codystampederodeo.com), held on the weekend of July 4. Between June and August there's a **rodeo** every night at the open-air stadium on the road to Yellowstone, at 421 W Yellowstone Ave (8pm; $16; T307/587-5155).

By the rodeo grounds is **Historic Trail Town**, 1831 DeMaris Drive (May–Sept 8am–8pm; $8), a collection of buildings dating from between 1879 and 1901 and salvaged from the surrounding region; among them are cabins and saloons frequented by Butch Cassidy and the Sundance Kid, and Curly, the Crow scout of George Custer. The remains of famed mountain man **Jeremiah Liver Eatin' Johnston** are also buried here.

Buffalo Bill Historical Center
The nation's most comprehensive collection of Western Americana, Cody's **Buffalo Bill Historical Center** at 720 Sheridan Ave comprises five distinct museums (June to mid-Sept daily 7am–8pm; mid-Sept to Oct daily 8am–5pm; Nov–March Tues–Sat 10am–3pm; April daily 10am–5pm; May daily 8am–8pm; T307/587-4771, Wwww.bbhc.org; $15).

At the **Buffalo Bill Museum**, artifacts from William Cody's various careers, such as guns, gifts from European heads of state, billboards, clothes, and dime novels, trace the years of the Pony Express, Civil War, Indian Wars, and Wild West shows. The lives of western Native Americans are celebrated in the **Plains Indian Museum**: many of the ceremonial garments are in stunning condition. A superb bear-claw necklace is a standout, and there's also a poignant display of Ghost Dance shirts, worn for the ritual song and dance that would hasten the day when all whites would be buried by a heaven-sent fall of soil. The US Army condemned Ghost Dances as unacceptable shows of resistance, and mobilized troops to disrupt ceremonies.

In the **Whitney Gallery of Western Art**, the contrasting styles of Frederic Remington and Charles M. Russell command the most attention. The propagandist Remington dwells on conflict, depicting the Indian as a savage in the path of progress, while Russell's work shows a consistent respect for the Native American way of life. The largest known collection of American-made firearms in the world is housed in the **Cody Firearms Museum**, while the **Draper Museum of Natural History** is lined with interactive exhibits and beautifully laid-out stuffed animal displays, all working to highlight the geology, wildlife and human presence in the Greater Yellowstone region.

Practicalities

For information and accommodation reservations, contact Cody's **visitor center** at 836 Sheridan Ave (June–Sept Mon–Fri 8am–6pm, Sat 9am–6pm, Sun 10am–3pm; rest of year Mon–Fri 8am–5pm; ℡307/587-2297, ⓦwww.codychamber. org). Cody Trolley Tours (℡307/527-7043, ⓦwww.codytrolleytours.com; $15) offer corny hour-long **tours** of town, and **whitewater rafting** trips on the Shoshone are run by Wyoming River Trips (℡307/587-6661; $25–50).

Cody's showpiece Western **hotel**, the *Irma* at 1192 Sheridan Ave (℡307/587-4221 or 1-800/745-4762, ⓦwww.irmahotel.com; ❹–❻), was named for Buffalo Bill's daughter in 1902, and retains a superb original cherrywood bar, a gift to Buffalo Bill from Queen Victoria. Among good-value motels, the friendly *Rainbow Park Motel*, 1136 17th St (℡307/587-6251 or 1-800/710-6930, ⓦwww. rainbowparkmotel.com; ❸–❹) stands out. Sheridan Avenue is the place for **eating** and **entertainment**: after a steak at the always-packed restaurant at the *Irma* hotel (see above), call in for a drink at the *Proud Cut Saloon*, at no. 1227. You may need a cowboy hat to feel comfortable at *Cassie's*, 214 Yellowstone Ave, where entertainment ranges from line-dancing classes to country-rock bands. *Peter's Café Bakery,* at 1219 Sheridan Ave, is the morning place for coffee or a full breakfast.

Wapiti Valley

The hour-long drive west from Cody to Yellowstone is a superb preparation for the park itself, skirting the artificial lake created by the Buffalo Bill Dam before running alongside the Shoshone River through the open, high **Wapiti Valley**, the heart of Wyoming's "beef country." You'll pass fantastical rock formations that'll have you thinking you stumbled upon the set of a psychedelic Spaghetti Western. Lodges and campgrounds appear at intervals without spoiling the magnificent landscape of the surrounding Shoshone National Forest.

Yellowstone National Park

Millions of visitors arrive yearly at **YELLOWSTONE NATIONAL PARK**, America's oldest national park, to glory in its magnificent mountain scenery and abundant wildlife, and to witness hydrothermal phenomena on a grand scale. Measuring roughly sixty by fifty miles, and overlapping slightly from Wyoming's northwestern corner into Idaho and Montana, the park centers on a 7500ft-high plateau, the caldera of a vast volcanic eruption that occurred a mere 600,000 years ago. Into it are crammed more than half the world's **geysers**, plus thousands of **fumaroles** jetting plumes of steam, **mud pots** gurgling with acid-dissolved muds and clays, and **hot springs**.

For many visitors, Yellowstone amounts to an extraordinary experience, combining the **colors** of the Grand Canyon of the Yellowstone, massive Yellowstone Lake, wild flower-filled meadows, and the rainbow-hued geyser pools; the **sounds** of subterranean rumblings, belching mud pools, and steam hissing from the mountainsides; and the constant **smells** of drifting sulfurous fumes, with the presence of shambling bears, heavy-bearded bison, herds of elk, and more than a dozen wolf packs on the prowl. If you let yourself get frustrated by the inevitable crowds and expense, you risk missing something very special. The key to appreciating the park

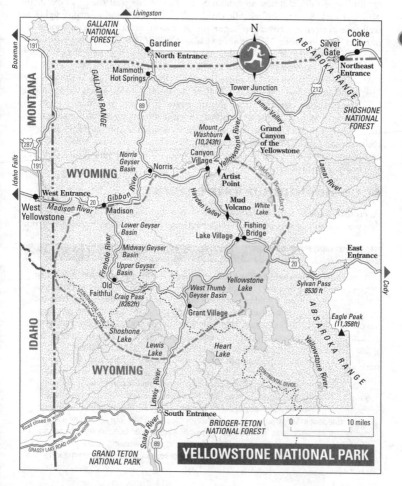

is to take your time, and to plan carefully; above all, try to allow for a stay of at least three days.

Arrival and information

Two of the five main **entrances** to Yellowstone are in Wyoming, via **Cody** in the east and **Grand Teton National Park** to the south. The others are in Montana: **West Yellowstone** (west), **Gardiner** (north), and **Cooke City** (northeast). Most roads are open from early May to October only (see box, below). **Admission** ($25 per car, $12 for pedestrians or cyclists) is good for seven days, and includes entry to Grand Teton (p.887).

Park headquarters are at **Mammoth Hot Springs**, near the north entrance (daily late May to early Sept 8am–7pm, rest of year approximately 9am–5pm; ⓣ307/344-2263). Consult the free newspaper *Yellowstone Today* for activities and current regulations. Other, summer-only **visitor centers** are located approximately every twenty-five miles along the main **Loop Road**. Most issue backcountry hiking permits, and host an exhibit on a different aspect of the park. Excellent National Park Service leaflets (50¢ each), which can be found at major sights as well as visitor centers, cover the important landmarks, marking trails and points of interest. The nonprofit *Yellowstone Association* (ⓣ307/344-2294, ⓦwww.yellowstoneassociation.org) is an invaluable resource, especially their long list of highly recommended tours and seminars ranging from wolf watching to essay writing.

A car is virtually essential to properly visit Yellowstone. To get to the park by **bus**, Karst Stage, Inc. (ⓣ406/556-3540 or 1-800/287-4759, ⓦwww.karststage.com; reservations essential) runs shuttle **buses** from the Bozeman airport to Gardiner and Mammoth. Several companies offer hurried **tours** of the park from the inside the park or the gateway towns; these include Xanterra (ⓦwww.travelyellowstone.com), West Yellowstone's Buffalo Bus Tours (ⓣ1-800/426-7669, ⓦwww.yellowstonevacations.com), and Jackson's Gray Line (ⓣ1-800/443-6133, ⓦwww.graylinejh.com).

Accommodation in the park

Accommodation within Yellowstone is run by Xanterra (ⓣ307/344-7311, ⓦwww.travelyellowstone.com). **Reservations**, strongly recommended from

---

Winter in Yellowstone

Blanketed in several feet of snow between November and April, Yellowstone takes on a new appearance in winter: a silent and bizarre world where waterfalls freeze in midplunge, geysers blast towering plumes of steam and water into the cold, crisp air, and buffalo, beards matted with ice, stand around in huddles. Only the fifty-mile road from Gardiner to Cooke City via Mammoth Hot Springs is kept open (the Beartooth Highway is closed), and you can only stay at the *Mammoth Hot Springs Hotel* or the *Old Faithful Snow Lodge* (accessible only by snowcoach and snowmobile).

It's undeniably cold, and transportation can require some hefty pre-planning, but crowds are non-existent and wildlife-spotting opportunities are superb. Xanterra (ⓣ307/344-7311, ⓦwww.travelyellowstone.com) runs **snowcoach** trips and tours of the park over the closed roads from West Yellowstone, Flagg Ranch at the southern entrance, Old Faithful and Mammoth Hot Springs ($50–135). **Snowmobile** rental, generally cheapest in West Yellowstone, costs around $120 a day (note that only a limited number of snowmobiles is allowed in the park at any one time, so reserve ahead). Much less expensive is **cross-country skiing** and **snowshoeing**, with groomed or blazed trails throughout the park; contact Xanterra for rental and tour information.

June through September, are essential over public-holiday weekends. Every location has a lodge building offering dining facilities (closing at 9.30pm) and sometimes a laundromat, grocery store, and gift shop.

Canyon Lodge and Cabins Plain hotel rooms ($150) along with simple frame cabins ($60–130), all en-suite, half a mile from the Grand Canyon of the Yellowstone. ❸–❻

Grant Village Spartan en suite motel rooms on the southwest shore of Yellowstone Lake, and the southernmost indoor accommodation in the park. ❺

Lake Yellowstone Hotel and Cabins Grand Colonial-style hotel rooms and dark, dingy en-suite cabins ($110). The "Sun Room," looking over the lake, is a great place for an evening drink. ❻–❽

Lake Lodge Cabins Nearly 200 en-suite cabins, the cheapest with one double bed, while others have two doubles and can accommodate four people. ❸–❺

Mammoth Hot Springs Hotel & Cabins 1930s lodging right at the north end of the park offering very basic cabins (❸), without shower or toilet, en-suite cabins, and hotel rooms and suites with or without bath. Especially popular in winter. ❺–❽

Old Faithful Inn and Lodge One of the most beautiful lodges in the US. Recently refurbished, the amazing 1903 inn – said to be the world's largest log building – has assorted rooms, plus budget and en-suite cabins. You can watch Old Faithful erupt from the terrace bar. Rates range ❹–❾

Old Faithful Snow Lodge and Cabins Along with *Mammoth Hot Springs Hotel*, this is the only accommodation open in the winter. Built in 1998, the lodge rooms have a modern hotel feel about them (❼), while the en-suite cabins (❹–❺) are attractive and well sealed against the cold. Open May to mid-Oct & mid-Dec to early March.

Roosevelt Lodge Cabins Over 80 rustic cabins a short drive from the Lamar Valley. The most basic cabins (❸) are little more than wooden shelters with two beds and a wood-stove, sharing communal bathroom facilities; en-suite cabins feature motel-like accommodation (❹).

Accommodation in gateway towns

In addition to **Jackson** (see p.889) and **Cody** (p.878) in Wyoming, the small towns just outside the park's western and two northern gates offer somewhat cheaper lodging. **West Yellowstone**, the largest town, is disfigured by gift stores and fast-food joints, but the surrounding national forest lands are well worth exploring. Friendly **Gardiner** lies just five miles from Mammoth Hot Springs. Less developed, the one-street town of **Cooke City** is three miles from the isolated northeast entrance on US-212.

Elkhorn Lodge 103 Main St, Cooke City ☎406/838-2332, �🌐www.beartooths.com/elkhorn. Two cabins and six motel rooms are rented at this centrally located lodge, all with full bath, TV, mini-fridges, microwaves and coffeemakers. ❸

Headwaters of the Yellowstone B&B Hwy-89, 3.5 miles north of Gardiner ☎1-888/848-7220, �🌐www.headwatersbandb.com. A fantastic B&B on the banks of the Yellowstone River. The five guest rooms each have their own private bathroom, and two cabins – one sleeping up to four, the other up to six – make a great deal. ❺–❼

Madison Hotel and Hostel 139 Yellowstone Ave, West Yellowstone ☎406/746-7745 or 1-800/838-7745, �🌐www.wyellowstone.com/madisonhotel. One of the few hostels in the region. The attractive log-hewn building dates back to 1912 and has bunk-rooms for up to four people ($26 each). Motel rooms are in a separate building. Open late May to early Oct. ❸–❺

Sleepy Hollow Lodge 124 Electric St, West Yellowstone ☎406/646-7707, �🌐www.sleepyhollowlodge.com. A dozen attractive log cabins with kitchens and a basic continental breakfast, plus a fly-tying bench and guide service for anglers. Good value, no in-room phones (phone available in office). ❹

Three Bears Lodge 217 Yellowstone Ave, West Yellowstone ☎406/646-7353 or 1-800/646-7353, �🌐www.three-bear-lodge.com. Large motel housing 75 good-sized rooms and two-bedroom family units (sleeping six) for $100 more. On site amenities include Internet, outdoor pool, indoor hot tub, The Bears Den cinema, and a friendly diner. Open year-round, with some of town's best snowmobile packages. ❺

Yellowstone Village Inn 1102 Scott St, Gardiner ☎406/848-7417, �🌐www.yellowstonevinn.com. On the edge of town, this high-end motel has 43 tidy rooms, most themed around wildlife or Western Americana, including a John Wayne room. High season runs from mid-June to mid-September, with rates halved from October through mid-May. ❸–❹

Camping

Xanterra operates five of the twelve campgrounds in Yellowstone, including one for RVs only. The other seven operate on a first-come, first-served basis; you have to arrive early in the day to get a site during June, July, and August, as most are full by 11am. It might be worth booking your first night at one of the reservation-only sites (☎307/344-7311, same-day reservations ☎307/344-7901, ⓦ www.travelyellowstone .com) – Bridge Bay, Canyon, Grant Village, Madison, and Fishing Bridge – just to make sure there's a place for you on the day you arrive. **Fees** range from $12–17 per night for tent camping, and upwards of $30 for RVs, and campgrounds operate from mid-May or early June through to September, October, or November (only Mammoth's campground is open in winter). Though all campgrounds have toilet facilities, not all have showers. RV owners should note that generators are not allowed at the following campgrounds: Indian Creek, Lewis Lake, Pebble Creek, Slough Creek, and Tower Fall.

To camp in the **backcountry**, you'll need a permit – free from visitor centers, information stations, and ranger stations; these can be collected no earlier than 48 hours in advance of your camping trip. You can also camp at commercial grounds in the gateway towns and in neighboring national forests such as Gallatin (☎406/848-7375) to the northwest and Shoshone (☎307/527-6291) to the east.

Eating in the park

Snack bars and **restaurants** inside the park aren't cheap, but given where you are they're not hideously expensive either. Buying food at the general stores can get pricey, though. There's not a lot of menu variation among the **restaurants**, which are located at *Old Faithful Inn*, *Old Faithful Snow Lodge*, *Lake Yellowstone Hotel*, *Roosevelt Lodge*, *Mammoth Hot Springs Hotel*, *Canyon Lodge*, and *Grant Village*; however, the first three are the clear standouts for location, mood, and ambiance. Entrees ($12–30) run from salmon to steak to roast dinners and lighter choices such as burgers or Caesar salads. Desserts and a basic range of beers and wines are available too. The restaurants are also open for **breakfast** and **lunch**; they usually offer a breakfast buffet that includes fresh fruit, cereals, pastries, and standard cooked items, all for around $7. More workaday cafeterias are dotted around the park as well, as are **soda fountains** inside several of the general stores where burgers and fries along with ice cream and shakes are served to rows of customers on stools.

Eating in the gateway towns

The gateway towns hold few culinary delights, but do offer cheaper prices and more variety. In **West Yellowstone**, *Running Bear Pancake House*, 538 Madison Ave (☎406/646-7703), is the first place to come for a filling, affordable breakfast, and *Bullwinkles*, 19 Madison Ave (☎406/646-7974), is tops for lunch and dinner, with huge salads and delicious pan-fried fish. The upbeat *Sawtooth Deli* (☎406/848-7600) on Park Street in **Gardiner** serves breakfasts and BBQ, while *Helen's Corral Drive-Inn* on Scott Street, a half-mile west of the 2nd Street bridge, serves the region's best burger. The impossible to miss *Beartooth Café* is **Cooke City**'s finest eatery throughout the day.

Touring the park

The majority of Yellowstone's top sights are signposted within a few hundred yards of the 142-mile **Loop Road**, a figure-eight circuit fed by roads from the five entrances. Although the **speed limit** is a radar-enforced 45mph (important given the number of bison and other massive beasts likely to run in front of your car),

A brief human history of Yellowstone

Although Native Americans had long hunted in what is now **Yellowstone National Park**, they were here only in limited numbers by the time the first white man arrived in 1807 – **John Colter**, a veteran of the Lewis and Clark expedition (see also p.897). His account of the exploding geysers and seething cauldrons of "Colter's Hell" (actually located due west of Cody) was widely ridiculed. However, as ever more trappers, scouts, and prospectors told similar tales, three increasingly larger expeditions set out to chart the region each year beginning in 1869. In 1872, Yellowstone was set aside as the first **national park**, in part to ensure that its assets were not entirely stripped by hunters and miners, and also to appease railroad interests looking for a new destination to shuttle visitors to.

At first, management of the park was beset by problems; Congress devoted enthusiasm but little funding toward its protection. Irresponsible tourists stuck soap down the geysers, ruining the intricate plumbing; bandits preyed on stagecoaches carrying rich excursionists; and the Nez Percé even killed two tourists as they were chased through the park (see p.915). Congress took the park out of civilian hands in 1886, and put the army in charge. By the time they handed it over to the newly created National Park Service in 1917, the ascendancy of the automobile in Yellowstone had begun.

The conflict between tourism and wilderness **preservation** has raged ever since. Ecologists now warn that the park cannot stand alone as some pristine paradise, and must be seen as part of a much larger "Greater Yellowstone Ecosystem"; this notional ecosystem encompasses Yellowstone, the Tetons, the Snake River Valley south of Jackson to just over the Idaho border, and the northern Wind River Mountains. In 1995, amid vociferous complaints from local ranchers fearing a subsequent loss of livestock, several packs of **wolves** were reintroduced to the park. They've since made an emphatic comeback, and from the original fourteen animals released, there are now around 150 wolves comprising some fifteen packs roaming the Greater Yellowstone area.

The **fires** that razed 36 percent of the park in 1988 also brought Yellowstone's environmental policies into focus. Park authorities considered the burn a natural part of the forest's eco-cycle, in which 200-year-old trees were cleared to make way for new growth. The scarred mountainsides are slowly but surely recovering, as evidenced by forests of young saplings. The summer of 2003 saw the most fires in the park since 1988, but they left nowhere near as much destruction in their wake.

the traffic makes journey times hard to predict. To get the most out of a visit, even if you're short of time, choose one or two areas to explore thoroughly. Only in the early morning is **cycling** bearable or safe; there are only a few mountain-bike trails, all accessible to hikers and horses as well. No trip to the park is complete without at least one trailside **hike**, be it to a waterfall or backcountry geyser; all the visitor centers have free day-hiking handouts for their areas.

The following account runs clockwise around the Loop Road, from Old Faithful to the Yellowstone Lake area, both of which lie in the southern half of the park.

Geyser country: from Old Faithful to Mammoth Hot Springs

For well over a century, the dependable **Old Faithful** has been the most popular geyser in the park, erupting more frequently than any of its higher or larger rivals. As a result, a half-moon of concentric benches, backed by visitor facilities including the gigantic log-built *Old Faithful Inn*, now surround it at a respectful distance on the side away from the Firehole River. On average, it "performs" for the expectant crowds every 78 minutes; approximate schedules are displayed in the nearby visitor center and in the lobby of the inn. The first sign of activity is a soft hissing as water splashes repeatedly over the rim. After several minutes, a column of water shoots to a height of 100 to 180ft, the geyser spurting out a total of eleven thousand gallons.

Two miles of boardwalks lead from Old Faithful to dozens of other geysers in the Upper Basin. If possible, try to arrive when **Grand Geyser** is due to explode. This colossus blows its top on average just twice a day, for twelve to twenty minutes, in a series of four powerful bursts that climb to 200ft. Other highlights along the banks of the Firehole River, usually lined with browsing bison, include the fluorescent intensity of the **Grand Prismatic Spring** at **Midway Geyser basin**, especially breathtaking in the early evening when human figures and bison herds are silhouetted against plumes of mineral spray.

Thirty miles north of Old Faithful, in the less crowded **Norris Geyser Basin**, two separate trails explore a pallid landscape of whistling vents and fumaroles. **Steamboat** is the world's tallest geyser, capable of forcing near-boiling water over 300ft into the air; full eruptions are entirely unpredictable. The **Echinus Geyser** is the largest acid-water geyser known; every 35 to 75 minutes it spews crowd-pleasing, vinegary eruptions of forty to sixty feet.

At **Mammoth Hot Springs**, at the northern tip of the Loop Road, terraces of barnacle-like deposits cascade down a vapor-shrouded mountainside. Tinted a marvelous array of grays, greens, yellows, browns, and oranges by algae, they are composed of travertine, a form of limestone which, having been dissolved and carried to the surface by boiling water, is deposited as tier upon tier of steaming stone. Also worth visiting here is **Fort Yellowstone**, two rows of homes and administrative buildings started in 1891.

Tower and the Lamar Valley

The main landmark of Yellowstone's **Tower** and **Roosevelt** areas, east of Mammoth Hot Springs, is **Mount Washburn**, one of the park's highest peaks, whose lookout tower can be reached by an enjoyable five-mile hike or a grueling cycle ride. A more manageable trail leads down to the spray-drenched base of **Tower Fall**. From Tower Junction, the Northeast Entrance highway wanders east through the meadows of serene **Lamar Valley** and toward the ice-packed peaks of the **Absaroka Mountains**; often referred to as "North America's Serengeti" after its **abundant wildlife**, the Lamar Valley is the scene of daily life-and-death struggles between predators (grizzlies, wolves, mountain lions) and their prey (elk, bison, pronghorn, mule deer).

The Grand Canyon of the Yellowstone

The Yellowstone River roars and tumbles for twenty miles between the sheer golden-hued cliffs of the **Grand Canyon of the Yellowstone**, its course punctuated by two powerful **waterfalls**: the 109ft **Upper Falls** and the thunderous **Lower Falls**, plummeting 308ft. On the south rim, **Artist Point** looks down 700ft to the river, which swirls between mineral-stained walls. Nearby, **Uncle Tom's Trail** descends steeply into the canyon, to a spray-covered platform gently vibrating in the face of the pounding Lower Falls. A few miles south, the river widens to meander over tranquil **Hayden Valley**, one of the finest spots in Yellowstone to watch wildlife from the road.

Yellowstone Lake

North America's largest alpine lake, the deep and (usually) deceptively calm **Yellowstone Lake** fills the eastern half of the Yellowstone caldera. At 7733ft above sea level it's high enough to be frozen for half the year, and the water remains perilously cold throughout the summer. Rowboats ($10 per hour) and slightly larger outboard motorboats ($45 per hour), along with 22ft ($140 for two hours) and 34ft ($180 for two hours) powerboats can be rented from the Bridge Bay Marina near Lake Village.

At the **West Thumb Geyser Basin**, north of Grant Village, hot pools empty into the tranquil waters and fizz away into nothing, and it's easy to see why early tourists would have made use of the so-called **Fishing Cone** by cooking fresh-caught fish in its boiling waters. To the south, the highway leading towards Grand Teton heads past **Lewis Lake**, the third largest lake in the park, with **Shoshone Lake** and **Heart Lake** hidden in the backcountry to the west and east respectively; both are well worth hiking out to.

Grand Teton National Park and Jackson Hole

The classic triangular peaks of **GRAND TETON NATIONAL PARK**, which stretches for fifty miles between Yellowstone and Jackson, are every bit as dramatic as the mountains of congested Yellowstone. Though not especially high or extensive by Rocky Mountain standards, these sheer-faced cliffs make a magnificent spectacle, rising abruptly to tower 7000ft above the valley floor. A string of gem-like lakes is set tight at the foot of the mountains; beyond them lies the broad, sagebrush-covered **Jackson Hole** river basin (a "hole" was the pioneers' term for a flat, mountain-ringed valley), broken by the winding Snake River.

The Shoshone people knew the mountains as the *Teewinot* ("many pinnacles"), but their present name, meaning "large breast," was bestowed by over-imaginative French-Canadian trappers in the 1830s. After Congress set the mountains aside as a national park in 1929, it took another 21 years of legal wrangling for Grand Teton to reach its current size – local ranchers protested that the economy of Jackson Hole would be ruined if further land was surrendered to tourism. Meanwhile, John D. Rockefeller Jr bought up large parts of Jackson Hole and presented them to the government for free to convert to parklands. Though canonized today for his preservations efforts – including the creation of the **John D. Rockefeller, Jr. Memorial Parkway** connecting Grand Teton to Yellowstone in 1972 – Rockefeller was cursed frequently by locals at the time.

Seeing the park

No road crosses the Tetons, but those that run along their eastern flank were designed with an eye to the mountains, affording stunning views at every turn. Two excellent side-trips are the **Jenny Lake Scenic Loop**, leading to a face-to-face encounter with towering, partly hunchbacked **Grand Teton Mountain**, and the narrow track up **Signal Mountain**, which gives a breathtaking panorama including the Tetons and Jackson Hole.

Hiking trails have been laid out so that no time is wasted in getting to the highlights. One easy and popular walk is along the sandy beaches of **Leigh Lake**, where the imposing 12,605ft **Mount Moran** bursts out dramatically from the lake shores. Also accessible are the cascading **Hidden Falls**, reachable by a two-mile walk along the south shore of Jenny Lake; it's also fun to take the shuttle boat ($7.50 roundtrip) across the lake and walk the remaining eight hundred yards. More adventurous is the rocky nine-mile trail from Hidden Falls through U-shaped **Cascade Canyon**, which leads to aptly named **Lake Solitude**.

On the flat roads of the Hole, **cycling** is a joy; bikes ($25–30) can be rented at Adventure Sports within the Dornan's complex in Moose Junction (☎307/733-

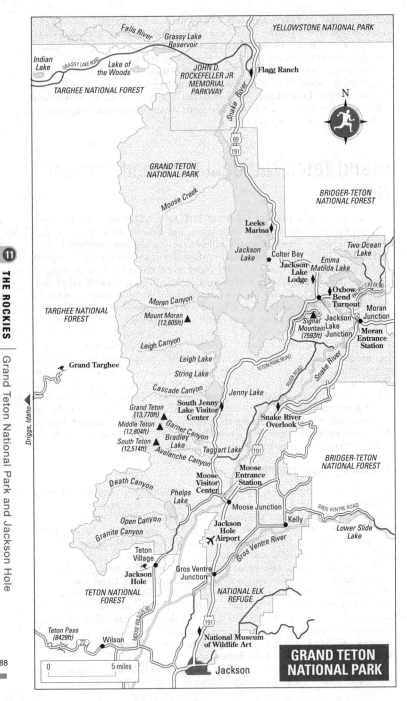

Falls River

Grassy Lake Reservoir

Indian Lake

GRASSY LAKE ROAD

Lake of the Woods

JOHN D. ROCKEFELLER JR MEMORIAL PARKWAY

Flagg Ranch

Snake River

TARGHEE NATIONAL FOREST

N

89
191

GRAND TETON NATIONAL PARK

Moose Creek

BRIDGER-TETON NATIONAL FOREST

Leeks Marina

Two Ocean Lake

Jackson Lake

Colter Bay

Emma Matilda Lake

Jackson Lake Lodge

Oxbow Bend Turnout

PACIFIC CREEK RD

TARGHEE NATIONAL FOREST

Moran Canyon

Mount Moran (12,605ft)

Signal Mountain (7593ft)

Jackson Lake Junction

Moran Junction

Moran Entrance Station

Leigh Canyon

Grand Targhee

Leigh Lake

String Lake

TETON PARK ROAD

RIVER ROAD

Snake River

Cascade Canyon

Jenny Lake

Grand Teton (13,770ft)

South Jenny Lake Visitor Center

Middle Teton (12,804ft)

Garnet Canyon

Bradley Lake

Snake River Overlook

South Teton (12,514ft)

Avalanche Canyon

Taggart Lake

191

BRIDGER-TETON NATIONAL FOREST

Death Canyon

Moose Visitor Center

Moose Entrance Station

Phelps Lake

Moose Junction

Kelly

GROS VENTRE ROAD

Open Canyon

Jackson Hole Airport

Granite Canyon

Gros Ventre River

Lower Slide Lake

Teton Village

Teton National Forest

Jackson Hole

Gros Ventre Junction

NATIONAL ELK REFUGE

MOOSE WILSON RD

Teton Pass (8429ft)

22

Wilson

191

National Museum of Wildlife Art

Jackson

0   5 miles

GRAND TETON NATIONAL PARK

3307). To admire the Tetons from **water**, take a float trip along the Snake River (see p.891) or rent a rowboat from the marinas at Colter Bay or Signal Mountain Lodge. In winter, all hiking trails are open to **cross-country skiers**, and **snowmobiles** can be rented in Jackson. Excellent **rock climbing** opportunities exist within the park as well; Exum Mountain Guides (☎307/733-2297, ⑩www.exumguides.com) run classes and guided trips from a summer office located steps from Jenny Lake.

Practicalities

Handed out at all entrance stations, the free *Teewinot* newspaper gives details of trails, facilities, and ranger-led activities. The **entrance fee** of $25 per car ($12 for pedestrians and cyclists) also covers Yellowstone. The **visitor centers** are just off the main road in **Moose** (daily 8am–5pm; until 7pm June to early Sept; ☎307/739-3399) to the south, and at **Colter Bay** (May & mid-Sept to mid-Oct daily 8am–5pm, June to mid-Sept daily 8am–7pm; ☎307/739-3594), halfway up, on the east shore of Jackson Lake. There are smaller centers at **Jenny Lake** (June–Aug daily 8am–7pm, Sept daily 8am–5pm; ☎307/739-3343) and **Flagg Ranch** (June to early Sept 9am–4pm; ☎307/543-2327). The free **Indian Arts Museum** within the Colter Bay Visitor Center has an extensive collection of native craftwork.

The majority of **rooms** and **activities** within the park are managed by the Grand Teton Lodge Co. (☎307/543-3100 or 1-800/628-9988, ⑩www.gtlc.com) and reservations are essential in summer. Prices for the comfortable rooms and cottages at *Jackson Lake Lodge* (⑦–⑨) depend on whether or not you want a mountain view; *Colter Bay Village Cabins* (❷–⑤) are more utilitarian, and in high summer they also have $40 "tent cabins" – canvas cabins each with four bunk beds (bed linen available for hire), a wood-burning stove, and an outdoor barbecue grill. Privately run *Signal Mountain Lodge* (☎307/543-2831, ⑩www.signalmtnlodge.com; ⑥–⑧) has bland motel-style units with two double beds, bathroom, and fridge, or much nicer rustic log cabins with two doubles plus private bath. All of the five summer-only park **campgrounds** work on a first-come, first-served basis ($15 per site). Visitor centers or entrance stations can advise on availability, or you can call (☎307/739-3603) for recorded information. Individual campgrounds tend to fill in July and August in roughly the following order: Jenny Lake (8am; 51 sites, tents only), Signal Mountain (10am; 81 sites), Colter Bay (noon; 350 sites), Lizard Creek (2pm; 60 sites), and Gros Ventre (evening; 360 sites). For backcountry camping, you need a **permit**, available free from the Moose and Colter Bay visitor centers and the Jenny Lake Ranger Station, near the Jenny Lake Visitor Center.

The park **restaurants and snack bars**, especially at *Jackson Lake Lodge*, are good but a little pricey. Within the Dornan's complex in Moose, the *Pizza Pasta Company* (☎307/733-2415) serves good pizzas and salads, best chased down with a bottle from the extensive wine shop next door. For the ultimate in relaxation, have an early-evening **drink** in *Jackson Lake Lodge*'s *Blue Heron Lounge*, where you can recline in comfortable chairs and watch the ever-changing blues, grays, purples, and warm pinks of a sunset over the Tetons through huge picture windows.

Jackson

More Mild West than Wild West thanks to an overflow of art galleries and high-end hotels, **JACKSON** is an enjoyable base, tucked in at the end of **Jackson Hole**, five miles from Grand Teton National Park's southern entrance. Centered around a tree-shaded square that's marked by an arch of tangled elk antlers at each corner, the Old West–style boardwalks of **downtown** front boutiques, galleries, and a wide range of restaurants and bars. Every summer evening, an amateurish shoot-out is staged in the town square (6.15pm). In winter, time is best spent visiting the 25,000 acre **National Elk Refuge** on the north edge of town, where you can take a horse-drawn sleigh ride among a 7,000-strong herd of elk (mid-Dec to early April daily 10am–4pm; $15 for adults, $10 for kids; ⊤307/733-9212); rides leave from the **National Museum of Wildlife Art** across the road (daily 9am–5pm; ⊤307/733-5771, ⓦwww.wildlifeart.org; $8), an impressive global art collection that trails only Cody's Buffalo Bill Historical Center for best museum in the region.

While busiest in summer with road-tripping national park visitors, Jackson remains a year-round draw thanks to **Jackson Hole Mountain Resort** (⊤307/733-2292 or 1-888/333-7766, ⓦwww.jacksonhole.com; lift tickets $72), a twenty-minute drive from downtown to **Teton Village** at its base. Justifiably

△ Climbing in Grand Teton National Park

famous, the resort's 2500 acres of terrain are arguably the best in the country for confident intermediates and advanced skiers and boarders. Within town, **Snow King** (T 307/733-5200 or 1-800/522-5464, W www.snowking.com; $35) is a family-friendly hill, also lit for night skiing, while **Grand Targhee** (T 307/353-2300 or 1-800/827-4433, W www.grandtarghee.com; $57) on the Wyoming/Idaho border an hour's drive away is renowned for fresh powder and affordable prices. Come summer, all three ski resorts offer limited lift-accessed mountain biking, along with a host of other outdoor activities ranging form hiking to paragliding.

Arrival, information, and activities

Jackson's charming **airport** is actually within Grand Teton National Park, eight miles to the north; it's linked to town by AllTrans **shuttle service** (T 307/733-3135 or 1-800/443-6133; $15 one-way to Jackson, $22 to Teton Village), while the regular **taxi** fare is around $26 into town, $46 to Teton Village, the latter taking 45 minutes to reach in winter due to closed roads. Jackson Hole Express (T 307/733-1719 or 1-800/652-9510) operates direct **shuttle services** daily between the international airport in **Salt Lake City** and Jackson (around 5hr; $71 one-way).

Jackson's excellent **Wyoming Information Center**, 532 N Cache St (daily: May–Sept 8am–7pm; rest of year 9am–5pm; T 307/733-3316, W www.jacksonholechamber.com), has detailed statewide information. Nearby, the **Bridger-Teton National Forest Headquarters**, 340 N Cache St (Mon–Fri 8am–4.30pm; T 307/739-5500), hands out details on hiking and camping in the Gros Ventre mountains to the east.

Transport around Jackson Hole is provided by START buses (T 307/733-4521, W www.startbus.com), operating from roughly 6.30am to 10pm daily; rides within town are free, while trips to Teton Village are $3 one-way. Companies such as **Gray Line** (T 307/733-4325 or 1-800/443-6133, W www.graylinejh.com; $80–105) offer hurried day-tours of Grand Teton and Yellowstone, though you're best off renting a car and touring at your own pace. Guided **bike tours** in the area are run by Teton Mountain Bike Tours (T 1-800/733-0788, W www.tetonmtbike.com) and start at $55 for a half-day tour, including equipment.

Dozens of companies in Jackson offer **float trips** in Grand Teton and whitewater **rafting** on the Snake River to the south (half-day around $45, including transportation and outerwear). Try Dave Hansen Whitewater, 515 N Cache St (T 307/733-6295 or 1-800/732-6295, W www.davehansenwhitewater.com), or Mad River, 1255 South Hwy-89 (T 307/733-6203 or 1-800/458-7238, W www.mad-river.com).

Accommodation

Accommodation in Jackson is fairly expensive in summer; rates in winter drop by around 25 percent and are good value for a ski vacation. It's the opposite case in Teton Village, where the ski-in ski-out accommodation is at a premium come winter. If **camping**, you're best off staying at Grand Teton's *Gros Ventre Campground* to the north (see p.889).

49er Inn 330 W Pearl St T 307/733-7550, W www.townsquareinns.com. This downtown motel is nothing fancy, but the rooms are much larger than average. Two hot tubs and a skimpy continental breakfast also offered. ❹
Anvil Motel 215 N Cache St T 307/733-3668, or 1-800/234-4507, W www.anvilmotel.com.

Situated at one of the busier intersections in town, it's not the quietest spot but the smallish rooms are in good shape and include a fridge and microwave. A bunker below the motel contains The Bunkhouse, a joyless dorm space that's only worth considering if traveling solo ($22). Winter ❸, summer ❹

Best Western The Inn at Jackson Hole Teton Village ☏307/733-2311 or 1-800/842-7666, ⊛www.innatjh.com. Three-star chain hotel, offering 83 mid-size rooms, along with a few lofts. Amenities include heated outdoor pool and hot tubs, laundry, and on-site tuning shop and a popular sushi restaurant. Winter **❽**, summer **❼**

Best Western The Lodge at Jackson Hole 80 Scott Lane ☏1-800-458-3866, ⊛www.lodgeatjh.com. A mile from Town Square, this pleasant hotel attracts an equal mix of business clients and vacationing families. Along with large chain-hotel rooms, extras include a buffet breakfast, laundry, workout room and pool. Winter **❻**, summer **❽**.

Four Seasons Teton Village ☏1-888/402-7888, ⊛www.fourseasons.com. The largest slopeside structure with 151 rooms, suites and rental units is worth a peek for the rough-hewn stones and native artifacts in the main lounge. Elegant suites come with marble bathroom counters and leather couches, while the heated outdoor pool, massive fitness center and spa, and full ski concierge services are all to be expected for nightly rates starting in the $500 range. **❾**

🏃 **Hostel X Teton Village** ☏307/733-3415, ⊛www.hostelx.com. Excellent slopeside hostel, with a lounge with fireplace, TV and game room, laundry, Ping-Pong, and pool table. Each private room, either with king-bed or four twin beds, is rented as a unit, and sometimes requires a five-night minimum stay. **❸**

The Wort Hotel 50 N Glenwood St ☏307/733-2190 or 1-800/322-2727, ⊛www.worthotel.com. Built in 1941, The Wort is the most venerable high-end property in town, combining old-world style with modern facilities that include two large hot tubs, a grill-bistro, and an attractive bar, The Silver Dollar. **❾**

⑪
Eating and nightlife

The year-round tourist trade makes Jackson the best town in Wyoming for nightlife, with an ever-changing roster of **restaurants** and **nightspots**.

The Mangy Moose Teton Village ☏307/733-9779. Jackson Hole's legendary ski-bum hangout, famed for its après-ski sessions that segue into rowdy evenings of live rock or reggae. The bustling upstairs dining room does decent burgers, chicken, and pasta, best chased down with a locally brewed Moose Juice Stout. Cover charge for live bands $5–20.

Million Dollar Cowboy Bar 25 N Cache Drive ☏307/733-2207. Everyone at least ducks into this hugely touristy Western-themed watering hole once to sit on one of the saddles at the bar. There are also four pool tables and frequent live bands. Cover most nights $5.

Nora's Fish Creek Inn 5600 W Hwy-22, in the hamlet of Wilson ☏307/733-8288. Popular spot for a huge breakfast of pancakes or omelettes. Lunch and dinner includes prime rib, salmon, and trout along with homemade desserts, at moderate prices.

Old Yellowstone Garage 175 Center St ☏307/734-6161. One of Jackson's finest restaurants, offering flawless service and a small menu of northern Italian dishes that changes daily (entrees $20–38). Sundays feature all-you-care-to-eat pizza ($15).

Pearl Street Bagels 145 W Pearl Ave. Very popular for fresh and tasty bagels, plus the finest cappuccinos in town. Free wireless Internet. Daily 6am–6pm.

Rendezvous Bistro 380 S Broadway ☏307/739-1100. Well-priced bistro on the outskirts of town. Mains range from simple steak frites to lamb chops and ahi tuna, all of which are recommended. A good selection of bottled wine under $30 adds to the attraction.

Shades Café 82 S King St ☏307/733-2015. Unpretentious, affordable café. Breakfast selections include an egg scramble for $3, while later in the day the likes of veggie burritos ($6) are served inside or on a shady deck.

🏃 **Snake River Brewing Co** 265 South Millward ☏307/739-2337. Great locals' brewpub several blocks southeast of Town Square. The pastas and wood-fired pizzas ($9–12) are well worth trying, but it's the award-winning beers that packs 'em in.

THE ROCKIES | Grand Teton National Park and Jackson Hole

Montana

MONTANA is Big Sky country, literally: the entire state is blessed with a huge blue roof that both dwarfs the beautiful countryside and complements it perfectly. The US portion of the Rocky Mountains find their northernmost limits in the western part of the state, a region of snowcapped summits, turbulent rivers, spectacular glacial valleys, heavily wooded forests, and sparkling blue lakes. The scenery is at its most dramatic in **Glacier National Park**. By contrast, the **eastern** two-thirds of the state is high prairie: sun-parched in summer and wracked by blizzards each winter. Grizzly bears, elk, and bighorn sheep are found in greater numbers here than just about anywhere else on the continent.

Each of Montana's small cities has its own proud identity. The enjoyable town of **Missoula** is a laid-back college town; the historic copper-mining hamlet of **Butte** is a union stronghold; the elegant state capital **Helena** harkens back to its prosperous gold-mining years; and **Bozeman**, just to the south, is one of the hippest mountain towns in the US.

Wheat, lumber and (coal) mining form the contemporary base of Montana's economy. Tourism is the state's second biggest earner; however, apart from skiing, the harsh climate generally restricts tourist activities to the summer months.

Getting around Montana

Considering Montana's hulking size and sparse population, transportation connections are not bad. Delta, Alaska, America West and Northwest variously offer **flights** to Kalispell, Billings, Bozeman, Great Falls, and Missoula. Amtrak **trains** run across the north on the *Empire Builder* route, stopping east and west of Glacier National Park, and at Essex in the summer. Greyhound runs a number of **bus** lines on I-90 and I-15, while Rimrock Stages (T 1-800/255-7655, W www.rimrocktrailways.com) runs four routes through the major towns (except for Bozeman). Western Montana, in particular, is great **cycling** territory; the Adventure Cycling organization, whose national headquarters are in Missoula, can provide special maps. Clearly, the best way to get around is by **car**, with practically every interstate exit in the west leading to mountain retreats, striking landmarks, or small villages.

Eastern Montana

Before ranchers and farmers settled the flat prairie of **eastern Montana**, it was prime **buffalo** territory: one early traveler waited three nights while a massive herd crossed his path. Native Americans fought hard to hold onto their land; the crushing defeats they inflicted on the US Army include the legendary victory at **Little Bighorn** – a Pyrrhic victory, perhaps, considering the military nearly wiped out the buffalo by the 1870s, thus depleting the natives' major food source.

The plains are intermittently broken by mountains, of which the most impressive are the icy **Beartooth Range**, crammed between the town of Red Lodge and Yellowstone National Park. Most of the region's towns are sleepy agricultural centers. Even **Billings**, Montana's largest city with a population of over ninety thousand, doesn't have a great deal to offer.

Little Bighorn Battlefield National Monument

In June 1876, massive army detachments were sent to southeastern Montana to subjugate the Sioux and Cheyenne. A key unit in the campaign was the crack **Seventh Cavalry**; at its head was the flamboyant **General George Custer** – perhaps unrivaled in American history for fame or opprobrium – who led the military to one of its most enduring defeats at **Little Bighorn** (see box, below).

Today the battlefield, which lies within the Crow Indian Reservation in the Little Bighorn Valley, serves as a national monument; it's located 56 miles southeast of Billings, with the entrance one mile east of I-90 on US-212. You can trace the course of the battle on a five-mile, self-guided driving tour through the grasslands (daily 8am–dusk; $10 per car, $5 for pedestrians and motorcycles; ⓦ www.nps. gov/libi), below the high ridge overlooking the valley, or on a narrated bus tour (spring–fall 10am–3pm; $8, kids $2). White-marble tablets mark where individual soldiers fell, and a sandstone obelisk stands above their mass grave on "Last Stand Hill" (Custer himself was buried at the West Point Military Academy in New York). Dioramas in the **visitor center and museum** (summer 8am–8pm; rest of year 8am–4.30pm; ⓣ 406/638-2621) outline the battle, while the US military **cemetery** nearby holds soldiers from all of America's wars (admission to the cemetery is free; explain at the gate that you're only going there and not to the battlefield).

Tiny **Hardin**, thirteen miles northwest, makes its living from tourists seeking authentic native artifacts and Western mementos. Each year, on the weekend closest to the battle's anniversary, the **Little Bighorn Days** festival centers on re-enactments of the battle at a site eight miles west of the town (*not* the original battlefield; ⓦ www.custerslaststand.org). Other activities include tribal dancing, downtown parades, dinner dances, and a rodeo.

Custer's Last Stand

During an erratic career, **George Armstrong Custer** had many notable experiences: he graduated last in his class at West Point in 1861; became the army's youngest-ever brigadier general, seeing action at Gettysburg; was suspended for ordering the execution of deserters from a forced march he led through Kansas, primarily to see his wife; and found notoriety for allowing the murder in 1868 of almost one hundred Cheyenne women and children. His most (in)famous moment, though, came on June 25, 1876, at the **Battle of the Little Bighorn**, known to native tribes as the **Battle of the Greasy Grass**.

Custer's was the first unit to arrive in the **Little Bighorn Valley**. Disdaining to await reinforcements, he set out to raze a tepee village along the Little Bighorn River – which turned out to be the largest-ever gathering of Plains Indians. As a party of his men pursued fleeing women and children, they were encircled by two thousand Sioux (Lakota) and Cheyenne warriors emerging from either side of a ravine. The soldiers dismounted to attempt to shoot their way out, but were soon overwhelmed; simultaneously, Custer's command post on a nearby hill was wiped out. Contrary to American myth, archeologists and historians have discounted the idea of **Custer's Last Stand** as a heroic act of defiance in which Custer was the last cavalryman left standing; the battle lasted less than an hour, with the white soldiers being systematically and effortlessly picked off. This most decisive Native American victory in the West – led by Sitting Bull – was also their final great show of resistance. An incensed President Grant piled maximum resources into a military campaign that brought about the effective defeat of all Plains Indians by the end of the decade.

The least expensive place to **stay** is the *Western Motel*, off Hwy-313 at 830 W Third St (T 406/665-2296, W westernmotel.net; ❸). *The Purple Cow*, Hwy-47 N (T 406/665-3601), is a cheerful family **diner** serving home-cooked feasts.

Billings

By Montana standards, **BILLINGS** is a big city. It has a dramatic setting, bounded on its north and east sides by the 400ft crumpled sandstone cliffs of the **Rimrock**, and has made an attempt to spruce itself up with an attractive and lively row of galleries, bars, and restaurants along Montana Avenue. However, scarring the west side of downtown are the tracks and warehouses of the Northern Pacific Railroad, whose president, Frederick Billings, gave the city its name.

Just north of Montana Avenue, you can dress like a cowboy thanks to Lou Taubert Ranch Outfitters, 123 N Broadway (T 406/245-2248), which has an enormous selection of hats, boots, shirts, jeans, and jackets. A couple of blocks northeast, the **Yellowstone Art Museum**, 401 N 27th St (Tues–Sat 10am–5pm, Thurs closes 8pm, Sun noon–5pm; $7; W yellowstone.artmuseum.org), partly housed in the town's 1910 jail, specializes in Western exhibits, including absorbing book illustrations, paintings, and posters by cowboy illustrator Will James.

Billings' **bus station**, served by Greyhound along I-90 and I-15, and Powder River, heading north from Wyoming, is at 2502 First Ave N (T 406/245-5116). **Accommodation** includes *The Dude Rancher*, 415 N 29th St (T 406/259-5561 or 1-800/221-3302, W www.duderancherlodge.com; ❸), a bright and cheerful motel, offering some rooms with fridges and microwaves. Cheaper alternatives line I-90, off exit 446, including the usual clean motels. For **eating**, the town is predictably strong on meat-and-potatoes fare, but the height of classic dining may be *The Rex*, 2401 Montana Ave (T 406/245-7477), which has top-flight steaks and good-enough seafood in a structure dating back nearly a hundred years.

Red Lodge and the Beartooth Scenic Highway

The atmospheric town of **RED LODGE**, sixty miles south of Billings at the foot of the awe-inspiring Beartooth Mountains, makes a pleasant stop. During winter, it acts as a base for skiers using the popular **Red Lodge Mountain**, six miles west on US-212 (lift tickets $42; T 1-800/444-8977, W www.redlodgemountain. com).

Originally founded to mine coal for the transcontinental railroads, Red Lodge's future was secured by the construction of the 65-mile **Beartooth Scenic Highway**, connecting to Cooke City at the northeastern entrance to Yellowstone National Park (see p.880), a striking series of tight switchbacks, steep grades, and exciting overlooks. Even in summer the springy tundra turf of the 10,940ft **Beartooth Pass** is covered with snow that (due to algae) turns pink when crushed. All around are gem-like corries, deeply gouged granite walls, and huge blocks of roadside ice.

Though Red Lodge has plenty of cheap motels south of town, the nicest **place to stay** is the lovely *Pollard Hotel*, 2 N Broadway (T 406/446-0001 or 1-800/POL-LARD; ❹–❺), an 1893 brick building with a pool, sauna, comfortable old library, and superb restaurant (see over); Western icons Buffalo Bill, Calamity Jane, and others have stayed here. You can camp west of town in **Custer National Forest** ($9–15; ranger district T 406/446-2103) at rustic parks such as **Cascade**, **Woodbine** and **East Rosebud**, taking in the stunning views of the Beartooth area, as well as of the abundant bighorn sheep, elk, and bear.

Some of the best **food** in town is served in *Pollard*'s dining room, which offers fresh, local fare – leaning toward beef and fish – in a serene setting. Also on Broadway, *Bridge Creek Backcountry Kitchen*, no. 116 S (☎406/446-9900), serves fine clam chowder alongside steak and burgers, and *Carbon County Steakhouse*, no. 121 S (☎406/446-4025), has hearty meals of pasta, ribs, steak, and seafood, as well as Rocky Mountain Oysters – bull testicles, to the uninitiated.

Fort Peck Lake

Some two hundred miles north of Billings, lonely Hwy 2 is an isolated, alternately bleak and beautiful, stretch that runs from Glacier National Park to North Dakota. The road offers a true experience of the Great Plains, with remote villages, Indian battlefields, and striking vistas. The highlight is the irregular, massive expanse of 130-mile-long **Fort Peck Lake**, with fifteen hundred miles of erratic shoreline, which the New Deal created in the 1930s by damming the Missouri River. The main draw is **fishing** for trout, bass and pike (licenses $25, see ⓦfwp.mt.gov/fishing). In the adjacent million-acre **Charles M. Russell Wildlife Refuge** (☎406/438-8706, ⓦcmr.fws.gov) you can spot pronghorn antelope, elk, deer, and bighorn sheep. Fossils – among them *T rex* and *triceratops* bones discovered around the site – are on view in the dam's **museum** (only accessible on tours of the powerhouse; summer Mon–Fri 9am, 11am, 1pm & 3pm, Sat & Sun hourly 9am–4pm; free; ☎406/526-3411). On the lake's south side, about 25 miles north of Jordan, off Hwy 200, **Hell Creek State Park** is a popular, serviceable spot for **camping** ($12; ☎406/526-3224, ⓦwww.reserveusa.com), as well as a terrific place to get in some of the best walleye fishing in the country, in fact. As with the other campgrounds in the area, this one is quite remote and only accessible by rugged country road. Use a four-wheel-drive vehicle to explore these parts.

Western Montana

Western Montana offers a beautifully expansive, almost unreal, setting. The big skies must be seen to be believed, and you'll encounter entirely different weather from one horizon to the next. The region is replete with outdoor adventures, especially in glorious **Glacier National Park**. The only old-time mining camps that have grown into substantial settlements are the genteel state capital **Helena** and craggy **Butte**, which made its money from copper. Between them, they conjure up more of a feel for the rambunctious times, the lust for profit, and the hardships of the industrial era than all the ghost towns in the Rockies combined.

Bozeman and around

Fetching **BOZEMAN** lies at the north end of the lush Gallatin Valley, 142 miles west of Billings and ninety miles north of Yellowstone. Founded by farmers in 1863, it's the only sizeable town in Montana not to owe its roots to mining, lumber, or the railroad. The stately Victorian storefronts along busy **Main Street** are some of the most historic in the West (with some seven hundred on the National Register of Historic Places), and it's here where you can find many solid choices for dining, drinking, and shopping.

South of downtown, the huge **Museum of the Rockies** 600 W Kagy Blvd at S Seventh Ave (summer daily 9am–8pm; rest of year Mon–Sat 9am–5pm, Sun 12.30–5pm; $9.50; ⓦwww.montana.edu/wwwmor) features Native American weapons, biology exhibits, a planetarium, and a fine selection of Western landscape paintings. The collection is internationally known for its stunning dinosaur finds – among them the world's largest-known skull of a *T rex*. Though smaller in scale, the **Pioneer Museum**, 317 W Main St (June–Aug Mon–Sat 10am–5pm, rest of year Tues–Sat 11am–4pm; $3; Ⓦwww.pioneermuseum.org), is also worth a look, housed in a crenellated old jail from 1911, with an intriguing selection of historic objects, including a replica log cabin, scale-model pioneer wagons and army forts, and a gallows for hanging town miscreants. From the museum you can take **walking tours** (all Mon–Wed 11am & 6pm; free; reserve at Ⓣ406/522-8122) of Main Street's elegant structures, its districts strewn with grand nineteenth-century mansions, and even the local cemetery where the town's bigwigs are buried. Striking an unexpected note, the **American Computer Museum**, Bridger Park Mall, 2304 N 7th Ave, suite B (June–Aug daily 10am–4pm; Sept–May Tues–Sat noon–4pm, Thurs closes 8pm; $4; Ⓦwww.compustory.org), follows the evolution of computers, from their bulky, awkward beginnings to today's tiny, speedy units.

Practicalities

Greyhound stops at 1205 E Main St, and the **visitor center** is at 224 E Main St (Ⓣ406/586-4008, Ⓦwww.historicbozeman.com), providing loads of maps and information plus limited free Internet access. Main Street also has a few worthy **accommodation** options. The *Lewis and Clark Motel*, no. 824 W (Ⓣ1-800/332-7666, Ⓦwww.lewisandclarkmotel.net; ❹), is very good value and centrally located, with a pool, sauna, gym, and hot tub. The basic but friendly *International Backpackers Hostel*, 405 W Olive St (Ⓣ406/586-4659, Ⓦwww.bozemanbackpackershostel .com), has six bunk beds for $18 each and a pair of private rooms for $38. More upmarket is the lovely *Voss Inn*, 319 S Willson Ave (Ⓣ406/587-0982, Ⓦwww. bozeman-vossinn.com; ❻), a lovely Victorian home with period furniture in each of the six rooms.

Bozeman boasts plenty of good **places to eat**. The *Community Co-op*, 908 W Main St (Ⓣ406/587-4039, Ⓦwww.bozo.coop), serves terrific vegetarian dishes, deli sandwiches, and mouth-watering desserts. Other favorites include the *McKenzie River Pizza Co.*, 232 E Main St (Ⓣ406/587-0055) and eight other Montana locations, which has thirty different kinds of pizza – try the chili-laden Branding Iron for a kick – and *John Bozeman's Bistro*, 125 W Main St (Ⓣ406/587-4100), with its fine duck, lamb, and elk dishes, plus a nice array of tapas. Places to **drink** include *Montana Ale Works*, 611 E Main St (Ⓣ406/587-7700), which has dozens of microbrews along with solid steaks and burgers, and the raucous *Zebra Cocktail Lounge*, 321 E Main St (Ⓣ406/585-8851), good also for its lively music selection of DJs, reggae, hip-hop, and indie rock.

Outdoor activities

Bozeman is well placed for those seeking **outdoor activities**, particularly in rugged Hyalite Canyon just south of town, which has top-notch hiking and mountain biking in summer and excellent ice climbing in winter, or at the challenging ski area, **Bridger Bowl** (lift tickets $41; Ⓣ406/587-2111, Ⓦwww.bridgerbowl. com). An hour's drive south down the beautiful Gallatin Valley is the much pricier **Big Sky Resort** (lift tickets $69; Ⓣ1-800/548-4486, Ⓦwww.bigskyresort.com), popular for its top-quality powder and steep slopes on 11,166ft Lone Mountain.

Three miles north of I-90, thirty miles west of Bozeman, **Missouri Headwaters State Park** ($5 per vehicle; camping $12; Ⓣ406/994-4042), marks the place where the Missouri River begins its circuitous journey to the Mississippi at the confluence of the Jefferson, Madison, and Gallatin rivers. These marshy grasslands beneath a shallow bluff were seen by Lewis and Clark in July 1805; fur trappers who followed in their wake included Kit Carson, and traces remain of the nineteenth-century town they created. These days the park has plenty of good fishing, hiking, and bird-watching. Another fifteen miles west, **Lewis & Clark Caverns State Park** (tours 9am–4.30pm, summer until 6.30pm; $10; ℡406/287-3541) offers a fascinating underworld of limestone spires and pillars, which you can see on rugged two-hour, two-mile **walking tours**; bring sturdy shoes and a jacket – the temperature is a consistent 50 degrees F. For details on more outdoor activities, check with the **ranger office**, 3710 Fallon St (Mon–Fri 8am–4.30pm; ℡406/522-2520, ⓦwww. fs.fed.us/r1/gallatin), which also provides information on hiking trails.

Butte and around

Eighty miles west of Bozeman, the former copper-mining colossus of **BUTTE** (as in "root") sits on a steep hillside where massive black headframes – "gallows frames" to miners – of long-abandoned pits soar up among dirty-yellow slag heaps, making it the largest Superfund site in the country (for its environmental damage). It's an oddly compelling landscape, best appreciated at dusk, when the golden light casts a glow on the mine-pocked hillsides, and the old neon signs illuminate historic brick buildings. Among immigrants to leave their mark here were miners from **Ireland** – Butte still hosts the biggest St Patrick's Day celebrations in the Rockies – and **Cornwall**; the traditional meat-and-potato pasty ("PASS-tee") is still served in many cafés – legend has it they were tough enough to survive being dropped into a mine shaft.

From its early days, Butte stood out as a **"Gibraltar of Unionism"** in the anti-union West. Miners obtained a minimum wage and an eight-hour day, and it became impossible to get work without a union card. The eventual consolidation of mining operations under the huge Anaconda Company led to inter-union rivalries and rioting, and by the 1950s the focus had switched from traditional mining in shafts to ugly open pits. Today only the Continental Pit mine remains. To take a look at the ecological disaster that is the 1800-foot-deep, 5600-foot-wide, and 7000-foot-long **Berkeley Pit**, head for Continental Drive. Here, a viewing platform surveys the whole horrifying mess, the most toxic stretch of water in the United States (Mar–Nov daily 8am–9pm; free).

If Butte is rich with toxins, it's also unexpectedly wealthy in Victorian architecture. The area's six thousand preserved buildings make it the largest **Historic Landmark District** in the country. On West Park Street, the excellent **World Museum of Mining** (Apr–Oct daily 9am–4.30pm, Thurs–Sat closes 8pm; $7; ⓦwww.miningmuseum.org) is packed with fascinating memorabilia from the local boom years. Outside, beyond the scattered collection of rusting machinery – from jackhammers to mine carts – the museum's 50-building **Hell Roarin' Gulch** recreates a cobbled-street mining camp, complete with saloon, bordello, church, schoolhouse, and Chinese laundry. Above it all looms the blackened, 100ft headframe of the 3200-foot-deep Orphan Girl mineshaft. To get a handle on the town's colorful history, take a **walking tour** with Old Butte Historical Adventures, 117 N Main St (May–Oct daily; most tours $5–12; ℡406/498-3424, ⓦwww.buttetours.info), which covers the area's architecture, mines, railway lines, rediscovered haunts like the Rockwood Speakeasy, and even journeys to the region's ghost towns ($50–85 per person).

Few of Butte's mining baron residences are grander than the 34-room **Copper King Mansion**, 219 W Granite St (tours April–Sept daily 9am–4pm, April weekends only; $7; ℡406/782-7580, ⓦwww.thecopperkingmansion.com), built by metal magnate, and later US senator, William Clark. Along with frescoed ceilings, handcrafted woodwork, and chandeliers and fireplaces, the mansion also has

the draw of being a B&B, where you can stay amid tasteful old-time luxury for as little as $65 a night. Another curiosity is the 26-room mansion of Clark's son, Charles, now known as the **Arts Chateau**, 321 W Broadway (June–Sept Mon–Fri 7.30am–4pm, Sat 9am–4pm, Sun 10am–2pm, also Fri 7–11pm; $4; ☎406/723-7600), nothing less than a mock-French castle – splendid with its spiral staircase, exotic-wood-inlaid rooms, and wrought-iron décor. It now holds Victorian furniture and antiques, as well as a rotating selection of contemporary regional art. By contrast, in an old noodle parlor at 17 W Mercury St, the **Mai Wah Museum** (June–Sept Tues–Sat 11am–5pm; donation; ⓦwww.maiwah.org) focuses on the history of the Chinese community with an intriguing collection of photos, cooking implements, kites, fireworks, menus, and books. The community was six hundred strong at the end of the nineteenth century, but by the 1940s widespread racism had reduced it to just a few families.

At night the 90ft **Our Lady of the Rockies** statue, 3100 Harrison Ave (ⓦwww. ourladyoftherockies.org), is illuminated by floodlights. Built entirely by voluntary labor – there had been a major layoff at one of the mines – it was set in place on top of the Continental Divide, some 3500ft above Butte, by helicopter.

Practicalities

Greyhound **buses** drop off downtown at 1324 Harrison Ave, and Rimrock lines also cruise through town, connecting to Helena and Great Falls. From June to August, ninety-minute **trolley tours** of town (9am, 11am, 1.30pm & 3.30pm; $7) leave from the **Chamber of Commerce**, 1000 George St (June–Aug daily 8am–6pm; Sept daily 8am–5pm; Oct–May Mon–Fri 9am–5pm; ☎406/723-3177, ⓦwww.butteinfo.org). Chain motels line the interstate, but the most pleasant **accommodation** (along with the historic *Copper King Mansion*; see above) includes the 1924 *Finlen Hotel*, 100 E Broadway (☎406/723-5461, ⓦwww.finlen.com; ❸), which has basic but functional rooms in the original building and a more modern motel annex; and *Toad Hall Manor*, 1 Green Lane (☎1-866/443-TOAD, ⓦwww.

toadhallmanor.com; ⑤), a quite stylish B&B in a stately house, whose three units variously come with Jacuzzis, fridges, microwaves, and courtyards.

Butte has plenty of good places to **eat and drink**, most of them uptown. *Joe's Pasty Shop*, 1641 Grand Ave (☎406/723-9071), serves up the hearty, meat-filled Cornish dish with vigor, while the *Pekin Noodle Parlor*, at 117 S Main St (☎406/782-2217), is an old-fashioned Cantonese joint with a menu that stretches from chow mein and fried wontons to sandwiches and steaks. A bit more upscale, the *Uptown Café*, 47 E Broadway (☎406/723-4735), serves pizza, pasta, and sandwiches, but is best known for its steak-and-seafood dinner entrees and inexpensive, fixed ($11.50) five-course meals. The *Copper King Saloon*, 1000 S Montana St (☎406/723-9283), is a lively bar in which to drink away an evening.

The Grant-Kohrs Ranch

The National Historic Site of **GRANT-KOHRS RANCH**, 266 Warren Lane in the town of Deer Lodge (June–Aug 8am–5.30pm, Sept–May 9am–4.30pm; free; ⓦ www.nps.gov/grko), lies forty miles west of Butte on I-90. In operation since 1860, this true West cattle ranch, under the guidance of "Montana Cattle King" **Conrad Kohrs**, was once the hub of ten million acres of range property and many thousands of Hereford and Shorthorn cows. Though its holdings are substantially reduced these days, the ranch still has its share of cows and draft horses on view. It also displays authentic buggies and wagons around its preserved old barns. In its blacksmith shop you can watch horseshoes and irons being worked over an anvil (summer only). Compare the pleasant Victorian environs of the house of the first owner, John Grant, with the much humbler conditions the ranch hands tolerated in Bunkhouse Row.

Helena and around

An hour north of Butte on I-15, **HELENA** is set neatly at the foot of two rounded mountains with a fine view over the golden-brown **Prickly Pear Valley**. In 1864 a party of disheartened prospectors decided to have one final dig here and managed to hit the jackpot at what is now **Last Chance Gulch**, the town's attractive main street, whose stately Romanesque and Neoclassical buildings are now home to gift shops, diners, and bars. Above it all looms the **Old Fire Tower**, off-limits to interlopers but still worth a short walk to see the latest in fire prevention, circa 1876. During the boom years, more than $20 million of gold was extracted from the gulch, and fifty successful prospectors remained here as millionaires. Their palatial residences grace the west side of town in what's known as the **Mansion District**. Contrast this with the far more modest digs southwest of town in **Reeder's Alley**, a collection of miners' cabins, wooden storehouses, and other humble working-class structures, now refurbished into smart shops and restaurants. Helena has an unexpected Hollywood connection, too: Gary Cooper was born and raised here, and Myrna Loy lived here as a child. Honoring the actress is the **Myrna Loy Center for the Performing Arts**, based out of a former jail at 15 N Ewing St (☎406/443-0287), which screens indie films and presents concerts, plays, comedy and more.

Another worthwhile stop is the **Original Governor's Mansion**, 304 N Ewing St (May–Sept Tues–Sat noon–4pm, rest of year Sat only; $4), which housed the state's chief executive during the first half of the twentieth century and still impresses with its Queen Anne style and broad decorative-arts collection. The legislative branch has worked since 1902 out of the massive Neoclassical **state capitol**, 1301 E Sixth Ave (Mon–Sat 8am–5pm; free; ⓦ www.montanacapitol.com), where a huge mural by "cowboy artist" Charles M. Russell depicts a dramatic encounter between tribal peoples and Lewis & Clark. You can see more of Russell's work at the excellent **Montana Historical Society Museum**, 225 N Roberts St (Tues–Sat 9am–5pm, summer also open Mon; $5; ⓦmontanahistoricalsociety .org), as well as early photographs of Montana life, early pioneer and tribal artifacts, and an array of costumes and textiles. True Charles Russell enthusiasts should venture up to Great Falls to see his eponymously named **museum** at 400 13th St N (May–Sept daily 9am–6pm, rest of year Tues–Sat 10am–5pm; $8; ⓦwww.cmrussell.org), which displays his many evocative landscape paintings and offers tours of the artist's elegant house.

The majestic red spires of the **Cathedral of St Helena** rise 230ft at 530 N Ewing St; the inside is adorned with elaborate Bavarian stained glass, white-marble altars, and gold leaf. Also interesting is the **Holter Museum of Art**, 12 E Lawrence St (Mon–Sat 10am–5pm, Sun 11.30am–4.30pm; Sept–May closed Mon, June–Aug closes Mon–Fri 6pm; free; ⓦholtermuseum.org), which shows painting, photography, and ceramics, but is most notable for its solid contemporary sculpture and decorative works. West of downtown, the **Archie Bray Foundation**, 2915 Country Club Ave (Mon–Fri 9am–5pm, Sun 1–5pm; free; ⓦarchiebray.org), hosts world-renowned ceramic artists who work while you watch, and also displays a broad variety of items in its Pottery Gallery and warehouse (summer only).

Practicalities

Greyhound offers connections throughout Montana from Helena's **transit center**, 316 N Park Ave, and Rimrock Stages operates from 3100 Hwy 12 E (☎406/442-5860), provided you want to go to Great Falls or Butte. In the summer the Historical Society runs hour-long **tours** in an imitation steam train (actually a tram) from the corner of Sixth and Roberts (June to early Sept 11am & 3pm, June also 1pm, July & Aug also 1pm & 5.30pm; $7; ☎1-888/423-1023, ⓦwww.lctours.com). The **visitor center** is at 225 Cruse Ave (Mon–Fri 9am–5pm; ☎406/447-1530), where you can pick up a free map. Information and maps on local hiking trails and camping are available from **Helena National Forest Ranger Station**, 2001 Poplar St (☎406/449-5490).

Helena has its share of dull chain motels, but its most stylish **lodgings** are in B&Bs, including *Barrister Bed & Breakfast*, 416 N Ewing St (☎406/443-7330 or 1-800/823-1148; ❹), a lovely 1874 Victorian mansion near the cathedral and originally used as priest's quarters, now offering five graceful rooms; *Sanders B&B*, 328 N Ewing St (☎406/442-3309, ⓦwww.sandersbb.com; ❺), whose seven old-fashioned rooms come with Western décor and antiques, some of them with claw-footed tubs and fireplaces; and the log-frame colossus of the *Elkhorn View Lodge*, outside of town at 88 Howard Beer Rd (☎406/442-1224, wwww.elkviewbb. com; ❺), with a hot tub, sauna, and gym, and five modern Western-themed rooms with fridges and microwaves. More rugged types head into the outlying **Helena National Forest** (ⓦwww.fs.fed.us/r1/helena) for a nice array of campgrounds (summer only; free or $5–8) near the Continental Divide, as well as any of seven remote, primitive **cabins** ($25–30; reserve at ☎1-877/444-6777, ⓦreserveusa. com) that were built to house forest-service employees and come variously equipped with stoves, fireplaces, and basic tools – but no electricity.

Places to **eat** include *The Bagel Company*, 735 N Last Chance Gulch (☎406/449-6000) for its tasty bagels and sandwiches; *Bert and Ernie's*, 361 Last Chance Gulch (☎406/443-5680), for its deli sandwiches, seafood, and nice array of pizzas; and the *Windbag Saloon*, at no. 19 S (☎406/443-9669), a big old barn of a place that serves Guinness, and good burgers and steaks. A little more upscale, *On Broadway*, 106 E Broadway (☎406/443-1929), offers excellent Italian food and wine, and *Miller's Crossing*, 52 S Park Ave (☎406/442-3290), has microbrews and eclectic live music.

Gates of the Mountains

For a look at the local topography in all its rugged, unspoiled glory, you couldn't do much better than to take a two-hour **boat tour** through the stunning **Gates of the Mountains**, 25 miles north of Helena off Hwy 287 (June–Sept hours vary, generally hourly Mon–Fri 11am–2pm or 3pm, Sat & Sun 10am–4pm; $10; ☏406/458-5241, ⊛www.gatesofthemountains.com). This dramatic stretch of the Missouri River, which enters a gorge between sheer 1200ft limestone cliffs that rise abruptly from the northern shores of a tranquil lake, was named by Meriwether Lewis of the Lewis & Clark expedition. The area offers unmatched scenic splendor and plenty of excellent hiking and backpacking opportunities, not to mention an eye-opening array of wildlife, including black bears, eagles, bighorn sheep, beavers, and mountain lions.

Missoula

Framed by the striking Bitterroot and Sapphire mountains, **MISSOULA** is one of the most vibrant and friendly small towns in the country. It's full of contrasts – truck-sales yards and bookstores, continental cafés and gun shops – and where nearly everyone seems to be connected to either the city's huge sawmills or the local University of Montana. In James Crumley's *Dancing Bear*, it's depicted as "the town with the best bars in a state of great bars."

One sign of Missoula's vibrancy is its willingness to take a chance on a new building of the **Missoula Art Museum**, 345 N Pattee St (call for hours; free; ⊛www.missoulaartmuseum.org), which opened in late 2006 and promises to show challenging, risk-taking work: digital photography, modern sculpture, and a range of eye-opening pieces by contemporary Native American artists. For another interesting cultural experience, head out to the 1914 **Fort Missoula** off Highway 93 S, on whose grounds the **Historical Museum**, in building 322 (Tues–Sun noon–5pm; summer daily 10am–5pm, Sun opens at noon; $3; ⊛www.fortmissoulamuseum.org), holds rather dry displays on military and agricultural history, but is best for its relocation of thirteen buildings from the Old West days, including a railroad depot, church, and schoolhouse. Unexpected are the World War II internment barracks for Italian nationals and Japanese-Americans. The grim confines recall the days when the fort was used for confining perceived "enemies," some of whom were US citizens.

Missoula is particularly good for its outdoor activities. The **visitor center**, across the river from the campus, 825 E Front St (☏406/543-6623, ⊛www.missoulachamber.com), can provide details on **trails**, such as the grueling one leading from its office up **Mount Sentinel**, embellished by the huge concrete letter "M." The top gives a great view of the area, especially the rugged Hellgate River Canyon. Other worthwhile trails traverse the **Rattlesnake Wilderness**, which, despite the name, claims to be serpent-free. Missoula is excellent for cycling, too, and the best source of **information** and **trail maps** is the Adventure Cycling Association, 150 E Pine St (☏406/721-1776); the Bicycle Hangar, 1801 Brooks St (☏406/728-9537), rents out good-quality bikes. The most developed of the city's small ski areas is **Montana Snowbowl**, twelve miles northwest, which has a range of slopes for all abilities (lift tickets $34) and boasts a summer **chair lift** (late June to early Sept Fri–Sun noon–5pm; $6, kids free, $2 for bikes; ☏406/549-9777).

Tours of the Forest Service **Smokejumper Center**, ten miles out of town on US-93 at 5764 W Broadway, discuss methods used to train smokejumpers – highly skilled firefighters who parachute into forested areas to stop the spread of wildfires. Fires are legion in this part of the country during the dry season. A small **visitor center** further explains their work (summer 8.30am–5pm, tours on the hour 10am, 11am & 2–4pm; free; ☏406/329-4934).

Practicalities

Greyhound and Rimrock share the **bus depot** at 1660 W Broadway, though the latter bus line is only useful if you're headed to Kalispell and Whitefish. The more distinctive **accommodation** choices include *Goldsmith's Inn*, beside the river at 809 E Front St (☏406/721-6732; ⓦwww.goldsmithsinn.com; ❺), a quaint 1911 Victorian B&B whose seven units variously offer balconies and fireplaces, and sitting rooms in the four suites. The *Doubletree Missoula Edgewater*, 100 Madison St (☏406/728-3100, ⓦwww.doubletree.com; ❼), is right on the Clark Fork River near the university, with nice rooms and suites and onsite gym, pool and hot tub. If all else fails, try the regional motel *C'mon Inn*, 2775 Expo Pkwy (☏406/543-4600, ⓦwww.cmoninn.com; ❹), which has decent rooms with fridges and microwaves, and two-room suites for an extra $20, or Jacuzzis for an extra $50. For state park **camping** you'll need to backtrack east, either 25 miles on I-90 to small **Beavertail Hill** (May–Sept; $15; ☏406/542-5500), which also has replica tepees to stay in ($25–39), or forty miles on Hwy 200 and a brief jog on Hwy 83 north to **Salmon Lake** (May–Nov; $15; ☏406/677-6804), which is great for its fishing and swimming in the Clearwater River.

You can **eat** good pastries with cappuccino at *Break Espresso*, 432 N Higgins St (☏406/728-7300), or lunchtime soup and sandwiches. Gourmet pizzas, pasta, and fancier fare is served at *Higgins Alley*, 424 N Higgins St (☏406/721-7757). The *Mustard Seed*, 2901 Brooks St (☏406/542-7333), is popular for its pan-Asian food, including a sushi – no mean feat in Montana. *The Raven*, 130 E Broadway (☏406/829-8188), has three pool tables and a great jukebox in addition to great omelettes, burgers, and sandwiches. Also worth checking out for **nightlife** are *The Oxford Saloon,* 337 N Higgins St (☏406/549-0117), a Montana institution and a friendly joint with as varied a clientele as any bar in the state, and the *Rhinoceros*, 158 Ryman St (☏406/721-6061), which has more than fifty microbrews from the region on tap.

Around Missoula: Garnet Ghost Town

To get a more in-depth look at the rugged days of the Old West, travel east from Missoula some forty miles on I-90, then another ten miles by single-lane gravel road, to Montana's best-preserved municipal relic, **Garnet Ghost Town** (road open May–Dec; summer daily 10am–5pm, rest of year Sat & Sun 11am–3pm; $3; ⓦgarnetghosttown.org), a slice of industrial history that rewards a long look (perhaps with a stay at nearby *Beavertail Hill State Park*; see above). A century ago, the site was home to hundreds of hard-rock gold miners, serious labor-union men doing a tough job. Since the buildings have been kept in their semi-decayed state, the atmosphere is quite arresting: the quiet and lonely specter of vacant, wood-framed saloons, cabins, stores, and a jail. Most intriguing is the evocative **Wells Hotel**, which is sturdy enough to let you tramp through its three creaky levels, contrasting the once-chic parlor and dining area on the ground floor with the bare, spartan floors of the unheated top level, where miners would lay out their bedrolls and bodies in lined, human-sized parking spaces.

Flathead Lake and around

The sheer splendor of the awe-inspiring, 28-mile-long **Flathead Lake** – the largest freshwater lake west of the Mississippi – provides a welcome diversion on the long route north toward Glacier National Park, reached by following US-93 north from I-90. Before getting to the lake, stop off and view the five hundred residents of the 18,500-acre **National Bison Range**, accessible near the town of Moiese, twenty miles west of St Ignatius off Hwy-212 (May–Oct daily 8am–6pm, opens

9am on weekends; $5; @www.fws.gov/bisonrange). Though you have to drive through, you can also get out and explore the striking mountainside scenery at several waysides – just don't let the great horned beasts catch you unawares. They travel in herds and are best appreciated from the safety of your slow-moving car.

Between Polson in the south and Somers in the north, US-93 follows the lake's curving western shore, while the smaller Hwy-36 runs up the east, scrunched beneath the Mission Mountains, and is the summer home to countless roadside cherry and berry vendors. Both routes offer superb views of the deep alpine waters, though US-93 is closest to conical **Wild Horse Island** (daily dawn–dusk; free), the lake's largest island, which you can reach by boat. Dozens of bighorn sheep here make regular appearances to hikers on the moderate-to-steep trails.

Flathead Lake is a major destination for **water activities**, the prime spot for launching fishing and pleasure boats being **Bigfork** in the northeast. A balancing act of summer resort town and tourist trap, Bigfork merits an hour-long stroll, and you can **stay** in town at the smart and cozy *Grand Hotel Bigfork*, 425 Grand Dr (☎406/837-7377, @www.grandhotelbigfork.com; ❸–❻ by season), or across the street at one of the six plushly decorated rooms of the *Swan River Inn* (☎406/837-2328, @www.swanriverinn.com; ❹–❻, by season). For **dining**, there's fine nouveau-French fare at *La Provence*, 408 Bridge St (☎406/837-2923). However, don't miss the delicious, chocolate-dripping delights of *Brookie's Cookies*, 191 Mill St (☎406/837-2447), or the sugary temptations at *Eva Gates*, 456 Electric Ave (☎406/837-4356), the town's prime draw for its fudges, jams, and sweets made with **huckleberries**. A quasi-official fruit in these parts, the berries show up in everything from ice cream to beer.

Boats can be rented at *Flathead Lake Boat Co*, on the south end of the lake at **Polson**, 4 8th Ave (☎406/883-0999), while summertime lake cruises are offered aboard the *Port Polson Princess* ($17–23; ☎406/883-2448) from *Best Western KwaTaqNuk Resort*, 303 Hwy-93 E in Polson (☎406/883-3636 or 1-800/882-6363, @www.kwataqnuk.com; ❺), which also has a marina with boat rentals. As alternate chain accommodation, the *Port Polson Inn* (part of the Best Value group), also overlooking the lake from 502 Hwy-93 E (☎406/883-5385 or 1-800/654-0682, @www.portpolsoninn.com; ❹), is a bit less expensive.

Fifteen miles north of the lake, drab **Kalispell** is out of sight of the water, but is a good jumping-off point for trips around the lake or up to Glacier National Park. You can find out more about the attractions of the Flathead Valley at the **visitors center**, 15 Depot Park (☎406/756-9091, @www.fcvb.org), while **accommodation** options in Kalispell include the stylish 1912 *Kalispell Grand Hotel*, 100 Main St (☎406/755-8100, @www.kalispellgrand.com; ❹); and the *Hilltop Inn*, 801 E Idaho St (☎406/755-4455, @www.kalispellhilltopinn.com; ❸), which is the best low-frills bargain in the area with clean, comfortable rooms with queen beds and kitchenettes. For decent **food**, try the Chinese dishes (plus a few American dishes and microbrews) at the *Alley Connection*, 22 1st St W (☎406/752-7077), or the upscale bistro fare, including tasty game and seafood, of *Café Max*, 121 Main St (☎406/755-7687). *Montana Coffee Traders*, 328 W Center St (☎406/756-2326), also has tasty wraps, salads, pasta, and burritos.

Whitefish

The tasteful resort of **WHITEFISH**, seventeen miles north of Kalispell, has a lively vibe, summer or winter. It lies on the south shore of beautiful **Whitefish Lake** in the shade of the *Big Mountain Ski Resort* (lift tickets $52; ☎406/862-1900, @www.bigmtn.com), one of the area's big-name winter-sports draws, which is also excellent for its **summer hiking**. You can hike four hard miles up to a restaurant on top of the mountain and take a free chair-lift ride for the descent (uphill, it's $10). The narrow roads around the lake and foothills deserve to be **cycled** – bikes can be rented from Glacier Cyclery, 326 2nd St E ($25–28 a day; ☎406/862-6446).

Amtrak drops off downtown, off Central Avenue at 500 Depot St, en route to and from Glacier National Park. There's a useful **tourist information** counter in the depot; the local **Chamber of Commerce** is at 520 E 2nd St (☎1-877/862-3548, ⓦwww.whitefishchamber.com). Rimrock's one **bus** line connects to Kalispell, Polson, and Missoula, and is based at 2640 Hwy-2 E (☎406/755-4011).

Staying in Whitefish presents several options: the *Bunkhouse Travelers Inn & Hostel*, 527 2nd St (☎406/862-3377), has basic bunk accommodation ($16), but it may be worth staying at one of the nicer **B&Bs**, such as the friendly little *Duck Inn*, by the river at 1305 Columbia Ave (☎406/862-3825 or 1-800/344-2377, ⓦwww.duckinn. com; ❹), whose ten units have soaking tubs and fireplaces; or the timber chic *Hidden Moose Lodge*, 1735 E Lakeshore Dr (☎1-888/733-6667, ⓦwww.hiddenmooselodge .com; ❻), excellent for its outdoor hot tub, hearty breakfasts, and rooms that offer smart decor and Jacuzzis or private decks. To really splurge, head out to Big Mountain, where *Kandahar* (☎406/862-6098, ⓦwww.kandaharlodge.com; most units ❻–❾), is a stylish affair with its own day spa, sauna, gym, and Jacuzzi, and a wide range of rooms, suites, lofts, and studios.

For **dining**, the *Great Northern Bar and Grill*, 27 Central Ave (☎406/862-2816), is a busy spot with pool tables, deli food, and live music, while *Truby's*, 115 Central Ave (☎406/862-4979) is a fine choice for wood-fired pizza and pasta. *Great Northern Brewing*, 2 Central Ave (☎406/863-1000), is a top-notch tasting room for Whitefish's finest craft brewer, offering one free, six-ounce "taste" per person. If you're looking for a lively **night out**, the *Hellroaring Saloon & Eatery* (☎406/862-6364) on Big Mountain is the place to be – especially during ski season.

Glacier National Park

Awe-inspiring peaks, two thousand lakes, and a thousand miles of rivers, threading between thick forests and breezy meadows, make up what is easily one of America's finest attractions, **GLACIER NATIONAL PARK** – a haven for bighorn sheep, mountain goats, black and grizzly bears, wolves, and mountain lions. Although the park still holds fifty small glaciers, it takes its name from the huge flows of ice that carved these immense valleys twenty thousand years ago. Outside of summer, crisp air, freezing-cold waterfalls, and copious snowfall give the impression of being close to the Arctic Circle; in fact, the latitude here is lower than that of London.

Arrival and information

There are several **visitor centers.** One is at the park's main, **western entrance** at **Apgar**, on the shores of gorgeous McDonald Lake, twenty miles east of Whitefish and just 35 miles south of the Canadian border (May–Oct hours vary, but at least 9am–4.30pm daily and until 8pm in summer; Nov–April Sat & Sun only), and another at the **east gate** at **St Mary**, seventy miles west of Shelby (daily: late May to late June & early Sept to mid-Oct 8am–5pm; late June to early July 8am–9pm; early July to early Sept 7am–8pm). The **Logan Pass** (early June to mid-Oct; hours vary, but always open at least 10am–5pm daily) visitor center stands at the top of the Going-to-the-Sun Road – the one through-road between the two entrances, usually only passable between early June and mid-October. The park itself is open year-round, however, and it's well worth trekking as far as Lake McDonald or St Mary's Lake even when the road is blocked and the visitor centers are closed. The

entrance fee of $25 per vehicle (or $12 per individual on foot, bike or motorcycle) is good for seven days, but for an extra $5 you can get a year-round vehicle pass. For **park information** call ☎406/888-7800 or go to ⓦwww.nps.gov/glac.

Glacier, together with the adjacent, much smaller Waterton Lakes National Park (☎403/859-2224) in Canada, is part of **Waterton–Glacier International Peace Park**, though Going-to-the-Sun Road does not enter Canada. Both parks operate their own fees and regulations, and to get to Waterton's separate entrance, north of St Mary, you have to pass customs and pay a $7 entrance fee (camping is $14–33 per night).

The southern border of Glacier is skirted by the low-lying US-2, which remains open all year and is an attractive alternative drive. Amtrak **trains** follow the same route, stopping at West Glacier, a short walk from the west gate; East Glacier, thirty miles south of St Mary; and Essex, in between (summer only).

Intermountain (☎406/563-5246) operates a fairly frequent summer bus service from Missoula, Kalispell, Whitefish, and, to the east, Great Falls. Travelers arriving by **public transportation** can travel around the park via the bright-red vintage "**jammer**" buses (so called because of the need to jam the gears into place) that provide narrated sightseeing tours from the main lodges (June–Sept; $30–75; ☎406/892-2525, ⓦwww.glacierparkinc.com). There's also a functional, white-van **Hiker's Shuttle** (July–Labor Day; $8–24) that covers the popular west side of the park and traverses the Going-to-the-Sun Road, while the **East Side Shuttle** (June to mid-Sept; $8–40) connects Glacier Park Lodge to Waterton; the transfer point between the two lines is at *Many Glacier Hotel*. **Sun Tours** (June–Sept; ☎406/226-9220 or 1-800/786-9220, ⓦwww.glaciersuntours.com) offers guided tours led by members of the Blackfeet tribe.

Accommodation within the park

Accommodation within the park is run by Glacier Park Inc. (all reservations at ☎406/892-2525, ⓦwww.glacierparkinc.com), which also manages the striking *Glacier Park Lodge* in East Glacier (late May to Sept; $140), known for the massive Douglas-fir pillars in its huge lobby. Near West Glacier, the lovely *Lake McDonald Lodge* has an ideal shoreline location and simple motel rooms (June–Sept; ❺) in the lodge itself, or more spacious annex rooms for $34 more, or small rustic cottages outside the complex (❻). More upscale are the *Prince of Wales Hotel* in Waterton (June to mid-Sept), which has mountain-view and lakeview units (❼) and luxurious suites (❾). The *Many Glacier Hotel* (mid-June to mid-Sept) has pricey suites, with rooms for half that price (❻–❾). The park's cheapest accommodation is the *Swiftcurrent Motor Inn* at Many Glacier (mid-June to mid-Sept; ❹, cottages ❷–❹), good for its access to trails on the northeast side. A bit nicer is the lakeside *Rising Sun Motor Inn* (mid-June to mid-Sept; ❹), seven miles in from the east gate at St Mary, as well as the *Village Inn at Apgar* (June–Sept; ❺), fronting Lake McDonald with great views.

The park's thirteen **campgrounds** – all first-come, first-served, most ranging from $12 to $17 – often fill up by late morning during July and August; ask at any visitor center for locations and availability or call ☎406/888-7800. For advanced reservations, call ☎1-800/365-CAMP. Most are open from June to mid-September, though Quartz Creek and Cut Bank offer cheap primitive campsites ($6), which may not include water. For overnight backpacking, get a permit from any visitor center.

Accommodation outside the park

The places to **stay** outside Glacier are at some remove from the park. The quaint 1910 *Belton Chalet*, two miles outside the western entrance (June–Oct;

T 406/888-5000, W www.beltonchalet.com; **⑤–⑧**), offers tastefully appointed rooms with period furniture, or pricier three-bedroom cottages with fireplaces and balconies; no accommodation has a phone or TV. One- and two-bedroom cabins are rented by the *Glacier Outdoor Center*, off Hwy-2 a half-mile from the west entrance (late-June to late-Aug; T 406/888-5454, W www.glacierraftco. com; **⑥–⑨**); they offer nice modern décor, decks, kitchens, and fireplaces, though at steeper prices than elsewhere.

Halfway between the east and west park gates is **Essex**, where the atmospheric 1939 *Izaak Walton Inn* (T 406/888-5700, W www.izaakwaltoninn.com; **⑥**) is the site of the Amtrak stop. Beside cozy wood-paneled rooms, four remodeled cabooses offer three-night stays for $675. The inn has a good restaurant for fish and burgers. In the village of **East Glacier Park**, near another Amtrak station, the simple *Backpacker Inn* hostel (T 406/226-9392), behind *Serrano's Mexican Restaurant* at 29 Dawson Ave, has three cabins: two are private with bathrooms ($20–30) and a third offers shared dorm space ($12 per person). Up in **Polebridge**, 28 miles north of the park's west entrance, largely via gravel road, the *Northfork Hostel* (T 406/888-5241, W www.nfhostel.com) is extremely cozy, with no electricity. Dorm beds cost $15 dollars and small private cabins start at $35, while tepees are $30.

Information on other **lodging** in the park's vicinity is available from Glacier Country (T 1-800/338-5072, W www.glaciermt.com), while popular alternative bases to the west of the park include Whitefish and Kalispell (see p.904).

Exploring the park

Simply put, the fifty-mile **Going-to-the-Sun Road** is one of the most awe-inspiring scenic drives in the country. Driving it from west to east can take several hours (even when summer restrictions on vehicle size effectively ban RVs), creating the illusion that you'll be climbing forever. After a stealthy ascent of the foothills, each successive hairpin brings a new colossus in view. At the east end of ten-mile **Lake McDonald**, the road starts to climb in earnest. Snowmelt from waterfalls gushes across the road, spilling over the sheer drops on the other side. The winding route nudges over the

△ Glacier National Park

Continental Divide at **Logan Pass** (6680ft) – a good spot to step out and enjoy the views and relax on a mild walk near the visitor center. Four miles on, there's an overlook at **Jackson Glacier**, one of the few glaciers visible from the roadside. Once you get down to the east gate, continue about five miles southeast on US-89 for an expansive view of the Great Plains, which stretch 1600 miles east to Chicago.

Most tourists travel no farther than the road itself, seeing the glories of nature from their car windows. However, Glacier is a true hiker's paradise, with exceptionally beautiful views at every turn – though you will have to be in shape to get to the end of the best trails. Good short **trails** start from **Avalanche Creek** on the west flank of the Divide. The mile-long **Trail of the Cedars** loop leads through dark forest to a wall of contoured vivid red sandstone, from where a four-mile path continues gently uphill, past several waterfalls, to glacier-fed **Avalanche Lake**. The most popular trail in the park – it can be teeming on weekends and holidays – begins at Logan Pass, following a boardwalk for a mile and a half across wildflower-strewn alpine meadows framed by extraordinary craggy peaks, en route to serene **Hidden Lake**.

At **Swiftcurrent Lake**, north of the east entrance and reached by the Many Glacier entrance, an easy two-mile loop trail runs along the lakeshore, and an exciting five-mile, one-way trail heads to **Iceberg Lake**, so called for the blocks of ice that float on its surface even in midsummer – which is the time you'll no doubt see more than a few guys jumping in for a few seconds to prove their mettle.

From **St Mary Lake**, you can weave a mile and a half up through fir forest to the crashing, frothing **St Mary Falls** and on to the taller **Virginia Falls**; combined with an early-morning boat trip from the Rising Sun launch to the trailhead (see below), this can be an experience verging on the sublime.

Down in the quiet southeastern end of the park, the two-mile **Aster Park** trail gives access to some of Glacier's most astounding scenery. Starting at Two Medicine Lake, framed by the majestic massifs, it leads through spruce forest into flower-filled meadows, passing a couple of beaver ponds and a nice waterfall before ascending steeply for a half-mile through the forest to a small outcrop. From here there are fantastic views of the mighty Sinopah and Rising Wolf mountains, and the calm lakes below.

Tour boats explore all of the large lakes, charging $10 for one-hour trips, including sunset cruises on Lake McDonald and St Mary Lake. You can also rent canoes, rowboats, and outboards. The lakes, teeming with cutthroat trout, are excellent for **fishing**; regulations are outlined in a free pamphlet available from visitor centers. Both Glacier Raft Co. (☎406/888-5454 or 1-800/235-6781, ⓦwww.glacierraftco. com) and Wild River Adventures (☎1-800/700-7056), based outside the west gate, offer half-day (around $45) and full-day (around $75) **float trips** down the middle fork of the Flathead River, running along the park boundary.

Although you've presumably come to embrace nature and see all manner of woodland creatures, pay heed to the signs marking most of the trails – this is **grizzly bear** country, and there's no guarantee of your safety. A handful of hikers have been mauled or killed by the huge beasts in recent years. Avoid traveling alone, being overly quiet, wandering off trails, wearing perfume. The park provides excellent literature and maps that give details on safety issues, but if you avoid hiking at dusk or in the early morning (prime time for bear activity) and carry bear spray (available from gun dealers), you're less likely to be the victim of an unexpected ursine encounter.

Eating and drinking

Food in the park, served in hotel dining rooms, is nothing special. The west side of the park isn't great for inventive cooking, either. You have to hit the *Izaak Walton Inn* in Essex (see p.907) for something tastier, but the best place to head is **East Glacier Park**, where *Serrano's*, 29 Dawson Ave (mid-April to mid-Oct; ☎406/226-9392), serves delicious Mexican food and microbrews, and *Glacier Village*, 305 Hwy-2 (☎406/226-4464), is the place to come for all things huckleberry, in traditional jams and pancakes, or even ladled on pork chops. Plus, there are native treats like fry bread, buffalo ribs, steaks, and burgers, and a solid selection of regional beers. On the northeast side of Glacier, the *Two Sisters Café* on Hwy-89 in Babb (☎406/732-5535) is a funky roadhouse famous for its outlandish décor, as well as its top-notch burgers, chili, and desserts.

Idaho

IDAHO, squeezed between Washington, Oregon, and Montana, was the last of the states to be penetrated by white settlers, and still today has many square miles of barely explored **wilderness** areas. Though much of its scenery deserves national-park status, its citizens have long been suspicious of federal authorities and tourists alike, and so it remains one of the country's most environmentally compelling places, despite prevalent anti-environmental attitudes. Indeed, the name "Idaho" was promoted by a mining lobbyist, who claimed it was a Shoshone word meaning "gem of the mountains"; he later admitted to inventing the word himself.

Whatever its political stances, Idaho is very much a destination for the outdoors enthusiast. Natural wonders in its five-hundred-mile stretch include **Hells Canyon**, America's deepest river gorge, the dramatic **Sawtooth National Recreation Area**, and the black, barren **Craters of the Moon** – not to mention the skiing mecca of **Sun Valley**. Beyond these, **hikers** and **backpackers** have the choice of no fewer than 81 mountain ranges, interspersed with virgin forest and lava plateaus, while the mighty **Snake** and **Salmon rivers** offer endless **fishing** and **whitewater rafting**.

In 1805, **Lewis and Clark** declared central Idaho's bewildering labyrinth of razor-edged peaks and wild waterways the most difficult leg of their epic trek from St Louis to the Pacific. Only their Shoshone guides enabled them to get through; to this day, there is no east–west road across the heart of the state. The central wilderness divides the state into two distinct halves. The heavily forested **north** is interspersed with glacial lakes fronted by resorts like **Sandpoint** and **Coeur d'Alene**; in the **south**, irrigation begun in the 1880s – partly instigated by the still-dominant Mormons – has transformed the scrubland along the Snake River into the fertile fields responsible for the state's license-plate tag of "Famous Potatoes." Idaho's isolation and small (one million) population have kept it well out of the mainstream of US culture. Indeed, some of its more notorious residents have included neo-Nazi white supremacists, evangelicals awaiting the Second Coming, and outback survivalists preparing for nuclear holocaust.

Getting around Idaho

Bus services between northern and southern Idaho are very poor, and a **car** is essential for travel. Only one **Amtrak** route – the *Empire Builder* – crosses the state, linking Seattle with Chicago, and stopping only at Sandpoint in northern Idaho. Boise has an **airport**, though Spokane, WA and Salt Lake City, UT can be more convenient for northern and southern Idaho, respectively.

Southern Idaho

Dropping down into **southern Idaho** from the natural riches of western Montana can be dispiriting. Though the initial leg on I-15 is visually compelling, with the magnificent **Mesa Falls** as a worthwhile detour along Hwy-47 and Yellowstone only a short distance east, the scenery along the interstate soon consists of farming plots and a few deserted stretches of sand and rocks. Only state capital **Boise** provides any urban interest, as Idaho Falls and Pocatello are both drab. However, a trip into the interior along US-20 brings you to the spectacular ragged outcrops of the **Sawtooth Mountains**, and an hour away is the forbidding but fascinating landscape of **Craters of the Moon**. Also, during summer, the much-hyped **Sun Valley** ski resort is a good base for mountain bikers, rafters, and hikers, and has the best bars and restaurants in this remote zone, matching the glitz of any Rockies ski scene.

Craters of the Moon National Monument

At first sight, the eerie **Craters of the Moon National Monument**, ninety miles west of Idaho Falls, looks like a sooty-black wasteland. It spreads on for 83 square miles, and closer inspection reveals a surreal cornucopia of lava cones, tubes, buttes, craters, caves, and splatter cones. Here and there, sagebrush clings to the bleak soil, and trees have been battered by the fierce winds into bonsai-like contortions. All these features were formed without the aid of a volcano; instead, at several-thousand-year intervals over the last thirteen thousand years, successive waves of lava have poured from gaping wounds in the earth's crust, known collectively as the Great Rift; the most recent event occurred two thousand years ago.

The park **visitor center** is on US-20 (daily summer 8am–6pm, rest of year 8am–4.30pm; ☎208/527-3257, ⓦwww.nps.gov/crmo); entrance for seven days is $8 per car, or $4 per bicycle and pedestrian, and spaces at the 50-site *Lava Flow* **campground** cost $10 (May–Oct). A seven-mile **loop road**, open late April to mid-November, takes you around myriad lava fields, where trails of varying difficulty lead past assorted cones and monoliths – don't stray from the paths, as the rocks are razor-sharp and can reach temperatures of 200°F. Highlights include the one-mile trail past hollow **tree molds** where the ancient wood ignited, leaving a craggy hole; the steep half-mile trek to the top of the **Inferno Cone**, with commanding views of the region; and the eight-mile **Wilderness Trail** (for which you will need a free wilderness permit, from the visitor center), which leads deep into the backcountry past cinder cones, ropy lava flows, and the blown-out expanse of **Echo Crater**. There are also **caves** here and elsewhere in the monument, molten lava tubes that can be explored alone or on ranger-led tours. In winter, the road is open for groomed **cross-country skiing**; for a conditions report, call ☎208/527-3257.

Halfway between the park and Idaho Falls on US-20, the unassuming red-brick Experimental Breeder Reactor No. 1 (EBR-1) – the **world's first nuclear-power station** – stands just south of the 890-square-mile Idaho National Engineering Laboratory. This National Historic Landmark was the place where an early version of a reactor was set up and provided the first application of electricity-producing nuclear power in 1951. Even the first prototype nuclear submarine was built and tested here. Now decommissioned, the site is home to a free **museum** (summer daily 9am–5pm; ⓦwww.inl.gov).

Sun Valley

Although **Sun Valley** is the common label for the entire Wood River Valley area – in central southern Idaho, 150 miles west of Idaho Falls and east of Boise – technically it is just the name of a **ski resort** (ⓦwww.sunvalley.com). This was

⑪

△ Craters of the Moon National Monument

the 1930s brainchild of Union Pacific Railroad chairman (and later politician and diplomat) Averell Harriman, who, on discovering his railroad was obliged to maintain a passenger service, decided an alpine ski center would be an ideal stimulus for tourism. His scout, Austrian ski champion Count Felix Schaffgotsch, decided on **Dollar** and **Bald mountains**, here in the relatively gentle foothills of the Sawtooths near the old sheep-ranching village of **KETCHUM**. The Sun Valley name was chosen because the snow withstood even the brightest winter sun; early brochures showed skiers stripped to the waist. The world's first chair lift was built here in 1936, and the resort was an instant success, attracting Tinseltown figures like Clark Gable and Gary Cooper, who came to hunt and fish. **Ernest Hemingway** completed *For Whom the Bell Tolls* as a guest of the resort in 1939, and lived in Ketchum for the last two years of his life before his suicide; his very plain grave can be found in the town cemetery. Today's celebrity notables include the likes of Bruce Willis and Arnold Schwarzenegger.

Sun Valley's season runs from late November to April; as well as downhill skiing (daily lift pass $74 at Bald Mountain, $32 at Dollar Mountain), you can also set off cross-country. Ketchum itself is a lively little town with plenty of accommodation, and an oasis of nightlife in an otherwise thinly populated zone. Up to a point, it resembles the Colorado ski hamlets, though summer trade is not quite as busy.

Among summer outdoor activities are **cycling** along thirty miles of excellent trails – including the former railroad tracks, long since paved over – as well as **mountain biking** on the superb lift-accessed trails on Bald Mountain (lift ticket $20 per day), and **rafting** on the rivers to the north. The **Sports Complex** (☏208/622-4111) on Sun Valley Road, south of Dollar Road, offers a Nordic ski center, tennis, ice skating, winter sleigh rides, and guided horseback rides.

Practicalities

There's free **transportation** on the KART bus system (☏208/726-7576, ⓦwww.kart-sunvalley.com), throughout the area, and Ketchum's **visitor center**, 371

N Main St, runs a free reservation service for **accommodation** (Mon–Fri 8am–6pm, Sat 9am–4pm, Sun 9am–2pm; ℡ 1-866/305-0408 or 1-800/234-0599, ⓦ visitsunvalley.com). Room rates are highest in summer and winter, but you can save a bundle by staying in nearby Hailey, twelve miles south.

The luxurious 600-room *Sun Valley Lodge* resort is expensive in season, though worth every cent in spring and fall (℡ 208/622-4111 or 1-800/786-8259, ⓦ www .sunvalley.com; winter & summer ❽, spring & fall ❻), with in-room flat-screen TVs, high-speed internet access, and DVD players; for similar prices, the resort's *Sun Valley Inn* (same contact) offers mock-Swiss Alps design. If you want to save money, options in **Hailey** include the *Inn at Ellsworth Estate*, 702 Third Ave S (℡ 208/788-6354, ⓦ www.ellsworthestate.com; ❺), with clean and tasteful B&B rooms, some with fireplaces and DVD players; and the *Featherbed Inn*, 416 First Ave N (℡ 208/578-5227, ⓦ www.featherbedinnidaho.com; ❹), whose four rooms have private decks and DVD players, with an onsite hot tub.

The dining room at the *Sun Valley Lodge* (℡ 208/622-2150) serves some of the best upscale **meals** in Idaho, typically nouveau French using fresh local ingredients, while in Ketchum the more affordable *Ketchum Grill*, 520 East Ave (℡ 208/726-4460), has plenty of delicious pizza, pasta and steak options. Breakfast-and-lunch hangout *Cristina's*, 520 Second St E (℡ 208/726-4499), serves deli meats and Asian salads on its back patio, plus a nice Sunday brunch. *Whiskey Jacques*, 251 N Main St (℡ 208/726-5297), is a good local **bar**, with live music by mid-level national acts, and a solid range of pizzas and burgers.

The Sawtooth Mountains and around

North of Ketchum and Sun Valley, Hwy-75 climbs through rising tracts of forests and mountains to top out after twenty miles at **Galena Summit**, one of the most spectacular panoramic viewpoints in the Rockies. Spreading out far below, the meadows of the Sawtooth Valley stretch northward, bearing minimal traces of the long-abandoned gold-mining settlements. The simple road meanders beside the young **Salmon River**, whose headwaters rise in the forbidding icy peaks to the south, as the serrated ridge of the **Sawtooth Mountains** forms an impenetrable barrier along the western horizon. Backpackers are guaranteed solitude in these climes, dotted with some five hundred remote alpine lakes – pick up details of **camping** sites and hiking trails at the **Sawtooth National Recreation Area headquarters**, eight miles north of Ketchum (daily 8.30am–5pm; ℡ 208-727-5013, ⓦ www.fs.fed.us/r4/sawtooth). Fly-fishing for brown trout, steelhead, and salmon is a popular pastime here as well.

At tiny **STANLEY**, a few miles north, dirt roads radiating from the junction of Hwy-75 and Hwy-21 have assorted **motels**, the better of which include the Western-flavored *Valley Creek Motel* (℡ 208/774-3606, ⓦ www.stanleyidaho.com; ❹), whose nice rooms have kitchenettes; and the large, cozy *Mountain Village Lodge* (℡ 208/774-3661, ⓦ www.mountainvillage.com; ❹), which has sixty comfortably furnished rooms with fridges and microwaves and a natural hot-springs spa. In summer, Stanley's main activity is organizing **rafting trips** (check in advance; weather conditions – such as heavy snowmelt – can make conditions too dangerous). Operators include The River Company (℡ 208/788-5775, ⓦ www.theriver-company.com), which charges $62–80.

Twelve miles east of Stanley at the town of **Sunbeam**, you begin the 45-mile scenic drive that leads into the historic settings preserved at the **Land of the Yankee Fork State Park**, whose **interpretive center** (daily 9am–5pm; free; ℡ 208/879-5244) is at the park's eastern junction, near Challis at the intersection of highways 75 and 93. Along the route you can explore the preserved ghost towns of **Custer** and **Bonanza**, the **Yankee Fork Gold Dredge**, a nearly thousand-ton barge that mined gold from stream gravel, and the **Custer Motorway** (also known as Forest Road 070), an old, rustic toll road curving northwest away from Hwy 75, with numerous historic attractions and rugged trails leading off from it. Camping, rafting, fishing, and cross-country skiing are good options in this remote wilderness.

Boise

One of the few highlights of otherwise bleak and arid southwestern Idaho is the verdant, likable community of **BOISE** (pronounced "Boy-zee"), straddling I-84 some 350 miles from Salt Lake City. Boise was established in 1862 for the benefit of pioneers using the Oregon Trail and, after adapting (or misspelling) the name originally given to the area by French trappers – *les bois*, the woods – the earliest residents boosted the town's appearance by planting hundreds more trees.

The City

To explore Boise's compact **downtown**, start at the central **State Capitol**, Jefferson St and Capitol Blvd (Mon–Fri 7am–6pm, Sat & Sun 9am–5pm), a stately Neoclassical structure that exhibits gemstones such as the star garnet, found only in southeast Asia and Idaho. Nearby, **Old Boise Historic District** (Ⓦwww .oldboise.com) is an elegant area of stone-trimmed brick restaurants and shops. The unusual **Idaho Basque Museum and Cultural Center**, 611 Grove St (Tues–Fri 10am–4pm, Sat 11am–3pm; $2; Ⓦwww.basquemuseum.com), is in a former boarding house that was for many years home to Basque immigrants from the western Pyrenees, who came to equally mountainous central Idaho to employ their shepherding skills. The museum traces the Basque cultural heritage through antiques, relics, photographs, and key manuscripts.

It's impossible not to be impressed by the contrast between the urban greenery and the humpy desert hills all around. The city is rightly proud of the **Greenbelt**, some nineteen miles of paths that crisscross the tranquil **Boise River** to link nine separate parks. In **Julia Davis Park**, the **Idaho Historical Museum** (May–Sept Tues–Sat 9am–5pm, Sun 1–5pm; Oct–April Tues–Fri 9am–5pm, Sat 11am–5pm; $2; Ⓦwww.idahohistory.net/museum.html) displays artifacts from Native American and Basque peoples, details the difficult experience of the Chinese miners of the 1870s and 1880s, and expounds on the agricultural and industrial history of the region. Also, the **Pioneer Village** preserves cabins and houses dating from as early as 1863, among them an adobe-styled home that belonged to the mayor in the 1870s.

The **Old Idaho Penitentiary**, at 2445 Old Penitentiary Rd, off Warm Springs Ave (daily summer 10am–5pm; rest of year noon–5pm; $5; Ⓦwww.idahohistory .net/oldpen.html), is an imposing, sandstone-walled citadel that feels like a desolate outpost, despite being just a mile from downtown. Constructed in 1870, it remained open until 1974. Self-guided tours take you through the cramped solitary-confinement unit, and the gallows chamber where the last hanging in Idaho was carried out in 1957. A small museum displays confiscated weapons and mugshots of former inmates, including one Harry Orchard, who in 1905 killed the state governor by attaching a bomb to his front gate and served out his sentence here, dying in 1954 at the age of 88. Oddly situated beside the prison, the **Idaho Botanical Gardens** (Mon–Fri 9am–5pm, Sat & Sun noon–4pm, May–Oct Sat & Sun closes 6pm; $4; Ⓦwww.idahobotanicalgarden.org) has twelve themed gardens adorned with irises, roses, herbs, and cacti, with one of them based around native plants that Meriwether Lewis reported in his 1805 explorer's journal.

Finally, the **Idaho Shakespeare Festival**, 5657 Warm Springs Ave (May–Sept; tickets $26–35; ☎208/336-9221, ⓦwww.idahoshakespeare.org), may not have the national reputation of its Oregon counterpart (see p.1209), but performances can be inspired and tickets are usually cheaper and more readily available. Around five plays are presented per season, with two or three of them penned by the Bard.

Practicalities

Greyhound **buses** stop at 1212 W Bannock St, and Boise Urban Stages (BUS; tickets $1; ☎208/336-1010) run a fairly extensive local **bus** service. The **visitor center** is at 312 S 9th St, Suite 100 (April–Sept Mon–Fri 10am–6pm; Oct–March Mon–Fri 10am–3pm; ☎208/344-5338, ⓦwww.boise.org). Downtown's best **hotels** are *The Grove*, 245 S Capitol Blvd (☎208/333-8000 or 1-800/426-0670, ⓦwww.grovehotelboise.com; ❺), which has luxury accommodation in large, well-appointed rooms, many with great views over the city and mountains beyond, and the *Owyhee Plaza*, 1109 Main St (☎208/343-4611 or 1-800/233-4611, ⓦwww.owyheeplaza.com; ❻), a renovated 1910 hotel in the heart of downtown with an outdoor pool and in-room fridges and high-speed internet access. If you're on a tight budget, try the restaurant-hotel *Leku Ona* (☎208/345-6665, ⓦwww.lekuonaid.com; ❹), whose five boutique rooms are basic but tasteful, and have the advantage of being above one of the city's finest Basque restaurants, serving up a range of seafood. The nicest **B&B** is the *Idaho Heritage Inn B&B*, 109 W Idaho St (☎208/342-8066, ⓦwww.idheritageinn.com; ❸), a lovely Victorian building that was once the residence of Governor Chase Clark and later Senator Frank Church, with six agreeable rooms.

Good options for **eating** in Boise include *Goldy's*, 108 S Capitol Blvd (☎208/345-4100), where you can create your own breakfast combos for less than $10, and the *Grape Escape*, 800 W Idaho St (☎208/368-0200), a fine bistro offering good-value Latin dishes and Tuesday-night wine tastings. *Bar Gernika Basque Pub and Eatery*, 202 Capitol Blvd (☎208/344-2175), is excellent for its authentic specialties – particularly the range of tapas, stews, and lamb grinders. Appealing downtown **bars** include the bustling *Bittercreek Alehouse*, 246 N 8th St (☎208/345-1813), with its dozens of microbrews, and *Bardenay Restaurant & Distillery*, 610 Grove St (☎208/426-0538), which distills its own gin, rum, and vodka and features a nice range of affordable, tasty seafood. After dining, check out *The Big Easy*, 416 9th St (☎208/367-1212), one of Idaho's top rock venues, with regular national touring acts.

Northern Idaho

The stark wilderness of the Sawtooth, Salmon River, and Clearwater mountains make traveling through the heart of Idaho impossible. There are only two routes between south and north: up the eastern fringe from Idaho Falls, or, more enjoyably, along US-95 via Hwy-55 out of Boise. At first barren and infertile, not until just before Lewiston does the scenery unfold into pastoral farmland. The **Nez Percé** hunted buffalo, gathered berries, and fished here for hundreds of years, until gold was discovered and they were forced to beat a bloody retreat.

The heavily forested far north of the Idaho Panhandle is broken by hundreds of deep glacial lakes, the largest of which host resort towns such as **Coeur d'Alene** and **Sandpoint**. While not major destinations, they can make good day-stops.

Hells Canyon region

From the busy little water-sports and ski resort of **McCALL**, 110 miles north of
Boise, Hwy-55 climbs steadily to merge with US-95 and follow the turbulent
Little Salmon River. Just south of the hamlet of Riggins, thirty miles on, comes
the only good opportunity to see **Hells Canyon** from Idaho. With an average
depth of 5500ft this is the deepest river gorge in the US, though visually it lacks
the impact of the steeper-walled Grand Canyon. Nevertheless, it is impressive,
with Oregon's Wallowa and Eagle Cap ranges rising behind it and the river glimmering far down below. Hwy-241 leads toward the overlooks; the final few miles
of dirt road require a four-wheel-drive vehicle and permission from the Riggins
forest ranger office on Hwy-95 (Mon–Fri 8am–5pm; ☎208/628-3916, ⓦwww.
fs.fed.us/hellscanyon). The canyon is also accessible by road from Oregon and by
boat from Lewiston.

The Nez Percé

The first whites to encounter the Nez Percé people were the weak, hungry, and
disease-ridden Lewis and Clark expedition in 1805. The natives gave them food and
shelter, and cared for their animals until the party was ready to carry on westward.

Relations between the Nez Percé (so called by French-Canadian trappers because
of their shell-pierced noses) and whites remained agreeable for over fifty years – until
the discovery of gold, and white pressure for property ownership, led the government
to persuade some renegade Nez Percé to sign a treaty in 1863 that took away three-
quarters of tribal land. As settlers started to move into the hunting grounds of the
Wallowa Valley in the early 1870s, the majority of the Nez Percé, under the leadership
of Chief Joseph, refused to recognize the agreement. In 1877, after much vacillation,
the government decided to enact its terms and gave the tribe thirty days to leave.
The Nez Percé asked for more time to round up their livestock and avoid crossing the
Snake River at a dangerous time; the general in charge refused.

Ensuing skirmishes resulted in the deaths of a handful of settlers – the first whites
ever to be attacked by Nez Percé – and a large army force began to gather to round
up the Nez Percé. Chief Joseph then embarked upon the famous Retreat of the
Nez Percé. Around 250 warriors (protecting twice as many women, children, and
old people) outmaneuvered army columns many times their size, launching frequent
guerrilla attacks in a series of narrow escapes. After four months and 1700 miles, the
Nez Percé were cornered just thirty miles from the safety of the Canadian border.
Chief Joseph then (reportedly) made his famous speech of surrender, "Hear me my
chiefs! I am tired. My heart is sick and sad. From where the sun now stands I will
fight no more forever."

The Nez Percé had been told that they would be put on a reservation in Idaho;
instead, they were taken to Oklahoma, where the marshy land caused a malaria
epidemic. Chief Joseph died in 1904 on the Colville reservation in Washington, but
decades later the Nez Percé were allowed to return to the Northwest, where today
some fifteen hundred live in a reservation between Lewiston and Grangeville – a
minute fraction of their original territory.

The Nez Percé National Historic Park, containing 38 separate sites, is spread over
a huge range of north-central Idaho, eastern Oregon, and western Montana. At the
visitor center in Spalding, ten miles east of Lewiston (daily 8am–4.30pm, summer
closes 5pm; free; ☎208/843-2261, www.nps.gov/nepe), the onsite Museum of
Nez Percé Culture focuses on tribal arts and crafts. The heavily ravined White Bird
Battlefield, seventy miles further south on US-95, was where the Native Americans
inflicted 34 deaths on the US Army at no cost to themselves, in the first major battle
of the Retreat. Further exhibits on Nez Percé history can be found in the Wallowa
County Museum in Joseph, Oregon (see p.1219).

RIGGINS itself reclines in a steeply rising T-shaped canyon. This is prime **white-water-rafting** country, and outfitters, spread along a one-mile stretch of the one-street village, outnumber cafés and shops. The **Chamber of Commerce** (☎208/628-3778, ⒲www.rigginsidaho.com) has details. From Riggins, US-95 heads north along the Salmon River Valley for thirty miles to the rumpled terrain around **White Bird**, the start of Nez Percé country.

Other than the **Lewiston Round-up**, a massive rodeo held on the second weekend of September (☎208/746-6324, ⒲www.lewistonroundup.org), there are few compelling reasons to visit industrial **LEWISTON**, 110 miles north of Riggins. It is, however, a starting point for a fantastic journey through Hells Canyon on the Salmon River. Boats sail past abandoned mine shafts and tribal caves, with mountain goats, bobcats, snakes, and birds of prey adding further interest. Snake River Adventures, 227 Snake River Ave (☎1-800/262-8874, ⒲www.snakeriveradventures .com), offers an all-day whitewater-rafting trip costing around $200 including lunch. Contact the Lewiston **Chamber of Commerce**, 111 Main St (Mon–Fri 8am–4.30pm, ☎208/743-3531, ⒲www.lewistonchamber.org) for information on other outfitters.

Moscow

The thirty miles of US-95 between Lewiston and **MOSCOW** wind through the beautiful rolling hillsides of the fertile Palouse Valley – a vivid patchwork of green lentils, bright yellow rape, soft white wheat, thick black topsoil, and red barns and farmhouses. Moscow itself is a friendly, culturally rich town that makes a good overnight stop, with ten thousand year-round residents and a similar number of **University of Idaho** students. Although there aren't any major sights, bookstores, galleries, bars, and cafés line the tree-shaded and partly pedestrianized **Main Street**, the only shopping thoroughfare. Theater, music, and independent cinema are on offer throughout the year, while summer sees a sprinkling of arts festivals: the **Moscow Artwalk** (June–Sept; ☎208/883-7036) brings together nearly forty artists, galleries, and the public for free exhibits that are anything but provincial; and the **Lionel Hampton Jazz Festival** (☎208/885-6231) runs for a week in February and showcases big names new and old.

Moscow's **visitor center** is at 411 S Main St (☎208/882-1800, ⒲www .moscowchamber.com). Northwest Trailways runs between Spokane and Boise and stops at the basic *Royal Motor Inn*, 120 W Sixth St (☎208/882-2581; ❷), whose **rooms** have fridges and microwaves. The *Mark IV Motor Inn*, 414 N Main St (☎208/882-7557, ⒲www.markIVmotorinn.com; ❸), has the same amenities, plus a nice pool and hot tub. There are also a half-dozen **B&Bs** in the area, the most distinctive of which is *Mary Janes Farm*, 1000 Wild Iris Lane (☎1-888/750-6004, ⒲www.maryjanesfarm.org/bb; ❼), a pleasant spot with primitive facilities where you're expected to chip in with the farm duties while soaking in the bucolic atmosphere. Good places to **eat** include *Wheatberries Bake Shop*, 531 S Main St (☎208/882-4618), which has nice sandwiches, espresso drinks, soups, and meat-pie "pasties"; the *Moscow Food Co-op*, 121 E Fifth St (☎208/882-8537), with its vegetarian-leaning soups and fresh breads, and deli sandwiches; and the stylish *Red Door*, 215 S Main St (☎208/882-7830), excellent for its seafood, game, and steak.

Coeur d'Alene

No longer strictly identified with the neo-Nazis who made their home in nearby Hayden Lake, **COEUR D'ALENE**, fifty miles north of Moscow on US-95, is now best known for its phenomenally expensive **Coeur d'Alene Resort**, which completely dominates the unremarkable downtown and is worth the money if you want to spend most of your time golfing (℡208/765-4000, Ⓦwww.cdaresort.com; Ⓞ). West of the resort at Independence Point, 90-minute **cruises** depart for a closer view of the lake (summer 4.30–6pm, rest of year 12.30–2pm; $17.75; ℡208/765-2300) or a six-hour journey through the scenic St Joe River corridor (summer Sun 11.30am–5.30pm & Wed 10am–4pm; $32.75), where all kinds of wildlife are on view. You can also see the lake on a twenty-minute **seaplane flight** from here via Brooks Seaplane ($50; ℡208/664-2842, Ⓦwww.brooksseaplane.com).

Greyhound **buses** stop at 137 E Spruce Ave (℡208/664-3343), and free local **transit** is available on Idaho City Link (℡1-877/941-RIDE, Ⓦwww.idahocitylink .com). The **visitor center** is at 1621 N Third St (Mon–Fri 8am–5pm; ℡1-877/782-9232, Ⓦwww.coeurdalene.org), which has a good range of free, helpful publications. Aside from the resort and the usual chain motels, your accommodation choices revolve around **B&Bs**, the best of which include *Wolf Lodge Creek* (℡1-800/919-9653, Ⓦwww.wolflodge.com; Ⓞ), fifteen miles from Coeur d'Alene, five rustic units that offer fireplaces and suites with balconies and hot tubs; and the *Roosevelt*, 105 Wallace Ave (℡208/765-5200, Ⓦwww.therooseveltinn. com; Ⓞ), which, aside from the usual Victorian chintz, has a gym, sauna, and hot tub – all in a renovated brick schoolhouse built in 1905. For **eating** out, *Beverly's* is a chic choice for seafood and meat in the *Coeur d'Alene Resort* (℡208/765-4000), serving up the likes of king crab and rack of elk; and *Brix*, 317 Sherman Ave (℡208/665-7407), is good for its tasty and affordable pizzas and more expensive steak and lamb chops. The largest selection of microbrews is poured at *Capone's Sports Pub and Grill*, 751 N 4th St (℡208/667-4843).

Silver Mountain and Wallace

About forty miles east of Coeur d'Alene on I-90, you'll come to Kellogg and the surprisingly good ski hill of **SILVER MOUNTAIN** (℡208/783-1111 or 1-800/204-6428, Ⓦwww.silvermt.com). It has the world's longest single-stage **gondola** (3.1 miles; rides $15), and is open year-round for fine skiing in winter ($40), and some good mountain biking (rental $30–50 per day) and hiking in summer.

A further ten miles east are the authentic Western streets of friendly **WALLACE**, where most of the town's buildings are listed on the National Register of Historic Buildings and evoke strong images of its silver-mining days. A fun, 75-minute trolley-car ride, the **Sierra Silver Mine Tour**, leaves from 420 N Fifth St (May–Sept daily tours on the half-hour 9am–4pm; $10; ℡208/752-5151, Ⓦwww.silverminetour.org) and travels the town's streets before taking you down to the mine, where you'll descend a thousand feet to appreciate the hard labor endured by miners a century ago. To find out more about how old-timers dug for shiny metal, drop by the **Wallace District Mining Museum**, 590 Bank St (summer daily 9am–6pm; $2; ℡208/556-1592), which has replicas, photos, and artifacts from the golden and silvery days. Wallace isn't a place to linger for long, but if you want to **stay** here, the *Jameson Inn*, 304 6th St (℡208/556-6000; Ⓞ), has a half-dozen rooms with access to a pool, hot tub, and sauna, but shared bathrooms. It also has agreeable **food** in its dining room, where you can enjoy lunch or dinner surrounded by vintage furnishing and decor.

Sandpoint

Forty-four miles north of Coeur d'Alene, buzzing little **SANDPOINT** lies at the northwestern end of **Lake Pend Oreille** (pronounced "PON-duh-ray"). Smaller and less commercialized than Coeur d'Alene, Sandpoint's downtown overlooks placid Sandy Creek but its main attractions are somewhat further out. At the south end of the lake, **Farragut State Park,** 13400 Ranger Rd (T 208/683-2425), has four thousand acres for hiking, camping, and the like. To the northeast, the spiky Selkirk Mountains hold the **Schweitzer Mountain Resort**, northern Idaho's best ski resort (T 208/263-9555, W www.schweitzer.com). Lift tickets are $49 and night skiing is $15; in summer you can use one of the lifts for hiking and mountain biking, for $15. But if you're looking for more old-fashioned entertainment, venture 25 miles south on Hwy-95 to **Silverwood Theme Park** (May–Oct hours vary; $33, kids $20; T 208/683-3400, W www.silverwoodthemepark.com), one of the rare theme parks in the northern Rockies, where you can indulge in roller coasters, water slides, and some sixty other rides and attractions.

Amtrak **trains** pass through early in the morning in Sandpoint – the only stop in Idaho – at 450 Railroad Ave. **Accommodation** includes the elegant *Inn at Sand Creek*, 105 S First Ave (T 208/255-2821, W www.innatsandcreek.com; ⑤), whose suites come with internet access, VCRs, fireplaces, and smart modern decor; and the *Coit House*, 502 N Fourth Ave (T 208/265-4035, W www.coithouse.com; ④), a tasteful 1907 Victorian B&B within walking distance of downtown and the lake. Good **dining** can be found at the *Sand Creek Grill* at the *Inn at Sand Creek* (see above), with upscale Northwest cuisine, and *MickDuff's*, 312 N First Ave (T 208/255-4351), for its solid sandwiches and burgers and half-dozen handcrafted microbrews. One of the best **bars** is *Eichardts*, 212 Cedar St (T 208/263-4005), which has a dozen microbrews and local rock bands on weekends.

12

The Southwest

AL - ALABAMA	IN - INDIANA	MN - MINNESOTA	RI - RHODE ISLAND
AR - ARKANSAS	LA - LOUISIANA	MS - MISSISSIPPI	SC - SOUTH CAROLINA
CT - CONNECTICUT	MA - MASSACHUSETTS	NC - NORTH CAROLINA	VA - VIRGINIA
DE - DELAWARE	MD - MARYLAND	NH - NEW HAMPSHIRE	VT - VERMONT
FL - FLORIDA	ME - MAINE	NJ - NEW JERSEY	WI - WISCONSIN
IL - ILLINOIS	MI - MICHIGAN	PA - PENNSYLVANIA	WV - WEST VIRGINIA

CHAPTER 12

Highlights

* **Santa Fe, NM** Great museums, fascinating history, atmospheric hotels – New Mexico's capital is a must on any Southwest itinerary. See p.926

* **The Havasupai Reservation, AZ** Glorying in its turquoise waterfalls, this little-known offshoot of the Grand Canyon remains home to its original Native American inhabitants. See p.975

* **Monument Valley, AZ** Though the eerie sandstone monoliths of Monument Valley are familiar the world over, they still take every visitor's breath away. See p.979

* **Canyon de Chelly, AZ** Ancestral Puebloan "cliff dwellings" pepper every twist and turn of this stupendous sheer-walled canyon. See p.981

* **Scenic Hwy-12, UT** Crossing the heart of Utah's red-rock wilderness, Hwy-12 is perhaps the most exhilarating drive in the US. See p.992

* **Bellagio, Las Vegas, NV** Las Vegas's most opulent hotel must be seen to be believed, and its sumptuous buffet is the best in town. See p.1016

△ San Francisco de Asis, Ranchos de Taos, NM

The Southwest

The four sparsely populated Southwestern desert states of **New Mexico**, **Arizona**, **Utah**, and **Nevada** are extraordinary and unforgettable. They stretch from Texas to California across an elemental landscape ranging from towering monoliths of red sandstone to snowcapped mountains, on a high desert plateau that repeatedly splits open to reveal yawning canyons. The raw power of the scenery is overwhelming, and is complemented by the emphatic presence of numerous Native American cultures, and the palpable legacy of America's Wild West frontier.

Among the region's earliest inhabitants were the **Ancestral Puebloans**. While their settlements and cliff palaces, abandoned seven centuries ago, are now evocative ruins, their direct descendants, the **Pueblo** peoples of New Mexico and the **Hopi** in Arizona, still lead similar lifestylesa, in the same general vicinity. Less sedentary tribes, such as the **Navajo** and the **Apache**, migrated into the Southwest from the fourteenth century onwards. They adopted local agricultural and craft techniques and appropriated vast tracts of territory, which they in turn soon had to defend against bands of European immigrants. The first such, in 1540, was a party of **Spanish** explorers led by Coronado, who spent two years fruitlessly searching for cities of gold. Sixty years later, Hispanic colonists founded the province of **New Mexico**, an ill-defined region that covered not only all of the Southwest but much of modern California and Colorado; many of the Catholic missions they established remain intact. Not until 1848 – by which time New Mexico had spent thirty years as a neglected backwater of the newly independent nation of Mexico – was the region forcibly taken over by the **United States**. Almost immediately, large numbers of outsiders began to pass through on their way to Gold Rush California.

Thereafter, violent confrontations increased between the US government and the Native Americans. The entire **Navajo** population was rounded up and forcibly removed to the barren plains of eastern New Mexico in 1864 (though they were soon allowed to return to northeastern Arizona), and the **Apache**, under warrior chiefs Cochise and Geronimo, fought extended battles with the US cavalry. Though the nominal intention was to open up Indian lands to newly American settlers, few ever succeeded in extracting a living from this harsh terrain.

One exception were the **Mormons** (the Church of Jesus Christ of Latter-Day Saints), whose flight from religious persecution brought them by the late 1840s to the alkaline basin of Utah's **Great Salt Lake**. Through sheer hard work, and the cooperative management of limited water resources, they established what amounted to an independent country, with outlying communities all over the Southwest. They still constitute seventy percent of Utah's population, and maintain effective control of the state's government.

Despite their common heritage, each of the four Southwestern states remains distinct. New Mexico bears the most obvious traces of long-term settlement, the Native American pueblos of the north coexisting alongside towns that clearly retain their Spanish Colonial identity, like Santa Fe, Albuquerque, and Taos. In Arizona, the history of the Wild West is more conspicuous, in towns such as **Tombstone**, site of the OK Corral. Over a third of the state belongs to Native

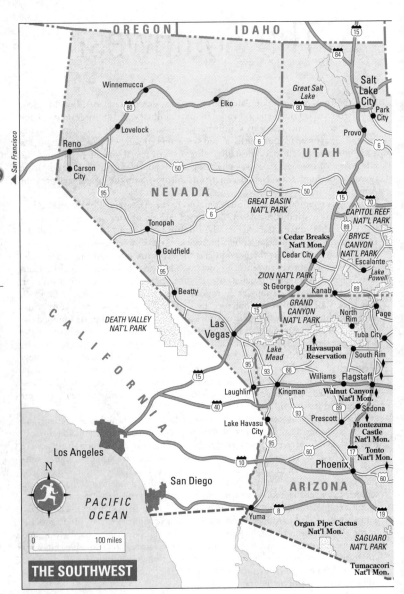

THE SOUTHWEST

American tribes, including the Apache, Hopi, and Navajo, most of whom live in the red-rock lands of the northeast corner, notably amid the splendor typified by the **Canyon de Chelly** and **Monument Valley**.

The canyon country of northern Arizona – even the immense **Grand Canyon** – won't prepare you for the uninhabited but compelling landscape of southern Utah, where **Zion** and **Bryce** canyons are the best known of a string of national

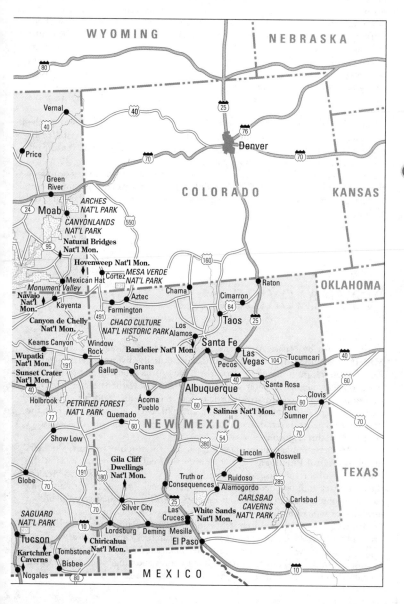

parks and monuments. **Moab**, poised in the east between majestic **Canyonlands** and the surreal **Arches**, has become a top destination for youthful outdoors enthusiasts. Nevada, on the other hand, is nothing short of desolate; gamblers are lured in the millions by the bright lights of **Las Vegas**, but away from the casinos there's little to see or do.

You can count on warm sunshine anywhere in the Southwest for nine months of the year, with incredible sunsets most evenings. Summer is the peak tourist season, for no good reason – air temperatures topping 100°F can make the outdoors unbearable, while in late summer awesome thunderstorms sweep in without warning, causing flash floods and forest fires. By October, perhaps the best time to come, the crowds are gone and in the mountains and canyons the leaves turn red and gold. Winter brings snow to higher elevations – there's excellent skiing in **northern Utah** and in the **Sangre de Cristo Mountains** of New Mexico – while spring sees wild flowers bloom in otherwise barren desert. Note that the climate varies sharply according to elevation, with mountains often 30°F cooler than the plains.

More than almost anywhere in the US, the backcountry wildernesses of the Southwest are ideal for **camping** and backpacking expeditions. It's vital to be prepared for the harshness of the desert: always carry water, and if you venture off the beaten track let someone know your plans.

Unless you have your own vehicle, many of the most fascinating corners of the region are utterly inaccessible. Scheduled public **transportation** runs almost exclusively between the big cities – which are not at all the point of visiting the region.

New Mexico

Settled in turn by Native Americans, Spaniards, Mexicans, and Yankees, **NEW MEXICO** is among the most ethnically and culturally diverse states in the US. Each successive group has built upon the legacy of its predecessors; their histories and achievements are intertwined, and in some ways the late-coming white Americans have had comparatively little impact. Signs of the region's rich heritage are everywhere, from ancient pictographs and cliff dwellings to the design of the state's license plates, taken from a **Zia** symbol for the sun – the one near-constant fact of life in this arid land.

New Mexico's indigenous peoples – especially the **Pueblo Indians**, the heirs of the **Ancestral Puebloans** – provide a sense of cultural continuity. After the **Pueblo Revolt** of 1680 had forced a temporary Spanish withdrawal into Mexico, the missionary endeavor here became less brutal than elsewhere. The proselytizing padres co-opted the natives without destroying their traditional ways of life, as local deities and celebrations were incorporated into Catholic practice. Somewhat bizarrely to outsiders, grand churches still dominate many Pueblo settlements, often adjacent to the underground ceremonial chambers known as *kivas*.

The Americans who took over from the Mexicans in 1848 saw New Mexico as a useless wasteland. But for a few mining booms and range wars – such as the Lincoln County War, which brought **Billy the Kid** to fame (see p.947) – New

Mexico was relatively undisturbed until it finally became a state in 1912. During World War II, it was the base of operations for the top-secret **Manhattan Project**, which built and detonated the first atomic bomb, and since then it has been home to America's premier weapons research outposts. By and large, people here work close to the land, mining, farming, and ranching.

Northern New Mexico holds the magnificent landscapes of the **Rio Grande Valley**, which cradles both **Santa Fe**, the adobe-fronted capital, and the artists' colony of **Taos**, with its nearby pueblo. The broad swath of **central New Mexico** along I-40 – the interstate that succeeded the old **Route 66** – pivots around the state's biggest city, **Albuquerque**, with the extraordinary mesa-top Pueblo village of **Ácoma** ("Sky City") an hour's drive west. In wild, wide-open **southern New Mexico**, deep **Carlsbad Caverns** are the main attraction, while you can still stumble upon mining and cattle-ranching towns that have hung on since the end of the Wild West.

For many visitors, the defining feature of New Mexico is its **adobe architecture**, as seen on homes, churches, and even shopping malls and motels. Adobe bricks are a sun-baked mixture of earth, sand, charcoal, and chopped grass or straw, set with a mortar of similar composition, and then plastered over with mud and straw. The color of the soil used dictates that of the final building, and thus subtle variations are seen all across the state. However, adobe is a far from convenient material: it needs replastering every few years and turns to mud when water seeps up from the ground, so many buildings have to be sporadically raised and bolstered by the insertion of rocks at their base. These days, most of what looks like adobe is actually painted cement or concrete, but even this looks attractive enough in its own semi-kitsch way, and hunting out such superb genuine adobes as the remote **Santuario de Chimayó** on the "**High Road**" between Taos and Santa Fe, the formidable church of **San Francisco de Asis** in Ranchos de Taos, or the multi-tiered dwellings of **Taos Pueblo**, can provide the focus of an enjoyable New Mexico tour.

Getting around New Mexico

Public transportation is rare in New Mexico; Santa Fe, for example, does not have a rail service. Amtrak **trains** do, however, pass through Albuquerque, pit stop for transcontinental Greyhound **buses** and site of the only major **airport**, from which scheduled buses run north to Santa Fe and Taos. A few companies offer guided **coach tours** in the Santa Fe and Taos area, but it's best to get around by **car**.

Northern New Mexico

The mountainous north is the New Mexico of popular imagination, with its pastel colors, vivid desert landscape, and adobe architecture. Even **Santa Fe**, the one real city, is hardly metropolitan in scale, and the narrow streets of its small, historic center, though thronged with tourists, retain the feel of bygone days. Ranging along the headwaters of the Rio Grande 75 miles northeast, the amiable frontier town of **Taos** is remarkable chiefly for the stacked dwellings of neighboring **Taos Pueblo**.

An hour's drive west from Taos or Santa Fe brings you to **Bandelier National Monument**, where ancient cliff dwellings were carved out of the volcanic plateau that now holds the laboratories of **Los Alamos**. Alternatively, the hills east of the Rio Grande hold characterful Hispanic hamlets, threaded along a scenic mountain highway known as the **High Road**.

Santa Fe

Since the early 1980s, **SANTA FE** has repeatedly been voted the country's most popular city by upmarket travelers. Its romantic appeal rests on a very solid basis: it's one of America's oldest and most beautiful cities, founded by Spanish missionaries a decade before the Pilgrims reached Plymouth Rock. Spread across a high plateau at the foot of the stunning Sangre de Cristo Mountains, New Mexico's capital still glories in the adobe houses and Baroque churches of its original architects, while its newer museums and galleries attract art-lovers from all over the world.

As upward of a million and a half tourists descend yearly upon a town of just sixty-eight thousand inhabitants, Santa Fe has inevitably grown somewhat over-blown. Long-term residents bemoan what's been lost and first-time visitors may be surprised by the depressing urban sprawl on the edge of town.

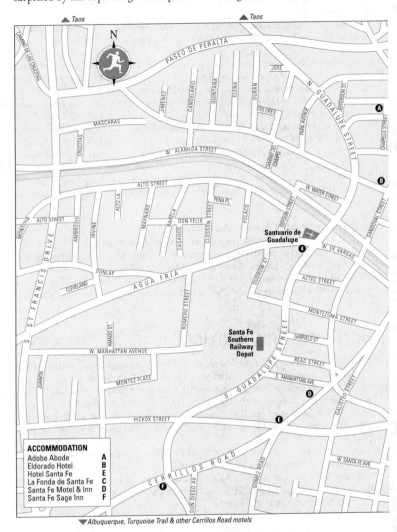

▼ Albuquerque, Turquoise Trail & other Cerrillos Road motels

There's still a lot to like about Santa Fe, however, with its compact, peaceful downtown and walkable streets. Though Santa Fe style may have become something of a cliché, that cliché is changing: the pastel-painted wooden coyotes that were once the obligatory souvenir, for example, have been replaced by cast-iron sculptures of Kokopelli, the hunch-backed Ancestral Puebloan flute-player. In a town where the *Yellow Pages* list over 250 art galleries, you'll get plenty of opportunities to buy either icon.

Arrival, information, and getting around

Santa Fe is well off the beaten track. Most out-of-state visitors fly into Albuquerque, and either rent a vehicle there for the hour's drive up I-25 to Santa Fe, or catch a shuttle van for around $25 with companies like Santa Fe Shuttle (☎505/243-2300 or 1-888/833-2300, ⓦwww.santafeshuttle.com). **Buses** arrive at the Greyhound terminal at 858 St Michael's Drive, a long way from the centre,

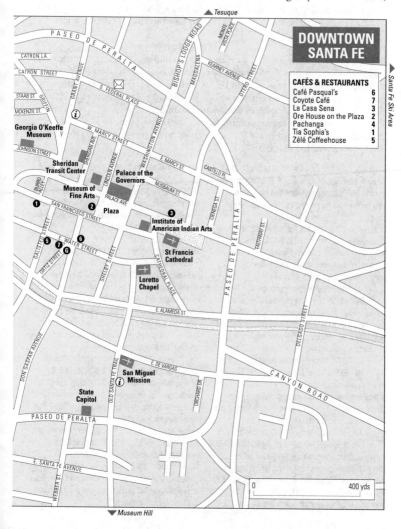

DOWNTOWN SANTA FE

CAFÉS & RESTAURANTS

Café Pasqual's	6
Coyote Café	7
La Casa Sena	3
Ore House on the Plaza	2
Pachanga	4
Tia Sophia's	1
Zélé Coffeehouse	5

and include four daily services from Albuquerque ($13; ☎505/471-0008). There's no direct **rail** link, but Lamy Shuttle vans ($16 one-way; ☎505/982-8829) meet Amtrak trains in Lamy, seventeen miles southeast.

By far the most useful **visitor center** is run by the New Mexico Department of Tourism, at 491 Old Santa Fe Trail (daily: June–Aug 8am–7pm; rest of year 8am–5pm; ☎505/827-4000 or 1-800/545-2040, 🌐www.newmexico.org).

Most of what there is to see lies within walking distance of the central plaza, but to get there from your hotel, or to see the farther-flung attractions, you may need to use the Santa Fe Trails **bus service** (☎505/955-2001). Route #2 runs up Cerrillos Road, while route #M loops between the plaza and the outlying museums, for the standard flat fare of $1. Santa Fe's only **taxi** company is Capital City Cabs (☎505/438-0000); **bikes** can be rented at Sun Mountain, 102 E Water St (☎505/982-8986, 🌐www.sunmountainbikeco.com). For a **walking tour** of town, contact Walk Through Time Tours, based at the *Inn at Loretto*, 211 Old Santa Fe Trail (daily 10am & 2pm; $10; ☎505/231-2770), which also operates Loretto Line **bus tours** at similar prices.

Accommodation

Even in winter, you won't find a **room** within walking distance of downtown for under $60, and in summer – when every bed is frequently taken – there's little under $100. The main road in from I-25, Cerrillos Road, holds most of the motels and the one hostel. If you get stuck, call All Santa Fe Reservations (☎505/474-5557 or 1-877/737-7366, 🌐www.all-santafe.com).

The most appealing **campgrounds** nearby are in the Santa Fe National Forest, starting seven miles up Hwy-475, northeast of town (summer only; ☎505/753-7331, 🌐www.fs.fed.us/r3/sfe).

Adobe Abode 202 Chapelle St ☎505/983-3133, 🌐www.adobeabode.com. Small, playfully themed, central B&B, offering folk-art-filled rooms both in a century-old house and in a separate newer building. ❻

El Rey Inn 1862 Cerrillos Rd at St Michael's Drive ☎505/982-1931 or 1-800/521-1349, 🌐www.elreyinnsantafe.com. Most characterful of the Cerrillos Rd motels, with stylish Southwestern-style rooms, nice suites, and a pool. ❻

Eldorado Hotel 309 W San Francisco St ☎505/988-4455 or 1-800/955-4455, 🌐www.eldoradohotel.com. Consummately stylish, tastefully tiled upmarket hotel, a short walk west of the plaza, offering spacious well-appointed rooms, plus a rooftop swimming pool, spa, and gym. ❾

Hotel Santa Fe 1501 Paseo de Peralta at Cerillos Rd ☎505/982-1200 or 1-800/825-9876, 🌐www.hotelsantafe.com. Attractive, very comfortable adobe hotel (just) within walking distance of the plaza, owned and run by Picuris Pueblo Indians and featuring its own good restaurant, *Amaya*. ❻

🐾 **La Fonda de Santa Fe** 100 E San Francisco St ☎505/982-5511 or 1-800/523-5002, 🌐www.lafondasantafe.com. Gorgeous old inn on the southeast corner of the plaza, which features hand-painted murals and stained glass throughout. Each opulently furnished room is different, and there's a good restaurant, plus a lounge with live entertainment and a rooftop bar. ❾

Santa Fe Sage Inn 725 Cerrillos Rd at Don Diego; ☎505/982-5952 or 1-866/433-0355, 🌐www.santafesageinn.com. The most central of the chain motels; large, clean, functional if not inspiring, and a mile or so from the plaza. ❹

Santa Fe International Hostel 1412 Cerrillos Rd at Alta Vista ☎505/988-1153, 🌐www.users.qwest.net/~epreston1/. Some travelers find this old-fashioned HI-AYH hostel, housed in a ramshackle former motel a couple of miles southwest of the plaza, unfriendly, poorly furnished and dirty, and damp and cold in winter; others are totally satisfied, and don't mind the compulsory chores. Dorms beds cost $15, or you can get a room to yourself for $33 single, $43 double. ❶/❷

🐾 **Santa Fe Motel & Inn** 510 Cerrillos Rd ☎505/982-1039 or 1-800/930-5002, 🌐www.santafemotel.com. Delightfully stylish little adobe complex where even the most conventional rooms are appealingly furnished. Some have their own kitchens, while there are also several gorgeous little casitas. The staff are very friendly, and rates – great for such a quiet, central location – include a cooked breakfast. ❻

Silver Saddle 2810 Cerrillos Rd at Siler ☎505/471-7663, 🌐www.motelsantafe.com. Busy, down-to-earth but surprisingly characterful motel, well out from downtown. ❸

Downtown Santa Fe: around the plaza

Santa Fe's old central **plaza** is still the focus of town life, especially when filled
with buyers and craftspeople during the annual **Indian Market**, on the weekend
after the third Thursday in August, and during the first weekend in September for
the **Fiestas de Santa Fe**. Apart from an influx of art galleries and stylish restaurants, the web of narrow streets around the plaza has changed little through the
centuries. When the US took over in 1848, the new settlers neglected the adobes
and chose instead to build in wood, but many of the finer adobe houses have survived. Ever since a preservation campaign in the 1930s, almost every non-adobe
structure within sight of the plaza has been designed or redecorated to suit the
city-mandated Pueblo Revival mode, with rounded, mud-colored plaster walls
supporting roof beams made of thick pine logs. Santa Fe today, in fact – at least
at its core – looks much more like its original Spanish self than it did a hundred
years ago.

The **Palace of the Governors** fills the entire northern side of the plaza (Tues–
Thurs, Sat & Sun 10am–5pm, Fri 10am–8pm; $7, free Fri 5–8pm; under-17 free;
ⓦ www.palaceofthegovernors.org). Part of the Museum of New Mexico (see
box, overleaf), this low-slung and initially unprepossessing structure is actually
the oldest public building in the US. Originally sod-roofed, it was constructed in
1610 as the headquarters of Spanish Colonial administration. Until 1913, it looked
like a typical, formal, territorial building, with a square tower at each corner; its
subsequent adobe "reconstruction" was based on pure conjecture. The well-preserved interior, organized around an open-air courtyard, holds excellent displays
on the history of Hispanic New Mexico, as well as a sensational collection of art of
Ancient America, and a well-stocked bookstore. The arcaded adobe veranda along
its front, offering protection from both sun and wind, serves as a market for local
Native American crafts-sellers.

Just west of the palace, the **Museum of Fine Arts** (same hours and prices) is
housed in a particularly attractive adobe, with ornamental beams and a cool central
courtyard, and focuses on changing exhibits of contemporary painting and sculpture by mostly local artists. Of greater appeal to most visitors is the showpiece

Georgia O'Keeffe Museum, a block northwest at 217 Johnson St (July–Oct Mon–Thurs, Sat & Sun 10am–5pm, Fri 10am–8pm; Nov–March closed Wed; $8, free Fri 5–8pm; under-16 free; ☎505/946-1000, ⓦwww.okeeffemuseum.org). This boasts the largest collection of O'Keeffes in the world, including many of the desert landscapes she painted near **Abiquiu**, forty miles northwest of Santa Fe, where she lived from 1946 until her death in 1986. In its permanent collection, some New York cityscapes make a surprising contrast to her trademark sun-bleached skulls and iconic flowers. Most of the museum is given over to touring exhibitions, so there's little guarantee as to which pieces may be displayed at any one time.

Across the tiny Santa Fe River to the southwest, three blocks along **Guadalupe Street**, you'll find an attractive little district centered around the small **Santuario de Guadalupe** (May–Oct Mon–Sat 9am–4pm; Nov–April Mon–Fri 9am–4pm; donation). Complete with a fine Baroque reredos (altarpiece), the shrine was built at the end of the eighteenth century to mark the end of the **Camino Real** highway from Mexico City. Former warehouses and factories nearby house boutiques, art galleries, and restaurants.

Follow the river upstream, or walk two blocks east from the plaza, and you approach **St Francis Cathedral**, at the top of San Francisco Street. The first church west of the Mississippi to be designated a cathedral, it was commissioned in 1869 in the formal – and, frankly, dreary – Romanesque style by **Archbishop Lamy**, the French-educated title figure in Willa Cather's novel *Death Comes for the Archbishop*. The nearby **Loretto Chapel**, a block away at the start of the Old Santa Fe Trail, is known for its so-called "Miraculous Staircase," an elegant spiral built without nails or obvious means of support (winter Mon–Sat 9am–5pm, Sun 10.30am–5pm; summer Mon–Sat 9am–6pm, Sun 10.30am–5pm; $2.50).

Two blocks south, across the river along the Old Santa Fe Trail, is the ancient **San Miguel Mission** (Mon–Sat 9am–5pm, Sun 1.30–4pm; $1). Only a few of the massive adobe internal walls survive from the original 1610 building, most of which was destroyed in the 1680 Pueblo Revolt.

Not far to the east, gallery-lined **Canyon Road** – which stakes a claim to being the oldest street in the US, dating from Pueblo days – climbs a steady but shallow incline along the riverbed and is lined by fine adobes.

The outlying museums

On a slightly raised plateau two miles southeast of the town center, with extensive views of the surrounding hills and mountains, stands Santa Fe's other museum cluster, reachable by Santa Fe Trails bus #10. The delightful **Museum of International Folk Art** (daily except Mon 10am–5pm; $7, under-17 free; ⓦwww.moifa. org), part of the Museum of New Mexico, focuses on a huge collection of clay figurines and models from around the world, arranged in colorful dioramas that include a Pueblo Feast Day with dancing *kachinas* and camera-clicking tourists. Its Hispanic Heritage Wing is an engaging reminder of just how close New Mexico's ties have always been with Mexico itself, while the gift shop sells unusual ethnic

The Museum of New Mexico

A **combination ticket**, costing $15 and valid for four days, grants admission to the four leading Santa Fe museums that jointly constitute the **Museum of New Mexico** (ⓦwww.museumofnewmexico.org) – the Palace of the Governors, the Museum of Fine Arts, the Museum of Indian Arts and Culture, and the Museum of International Folk Art.

souvenirs. The neighboring **Museum of Indian Arts and Culture** (same hours and prices; Ⓦ www.miaclab.org) holds a superb array of Native American pottery, ranging from **Ancestral Puebloan** pieces up to the works of twentieth-century revivalists, and covers contemporary Southwestern cultures in fascinating detail.

In the same complex, the **Museum of Spanish Colonial Art** displays traditional Hispanic religious artworks, such as the *santos* (naïve painted images) and *bultos* (carved wooden statues of saints) that are so pervasive in the iconography of Santa Fe (daily except Mon 10am–5pm; $6, under-16 free; Ⓦ www.spanishcolonial. org).

Eating

Santa Fe has been renowned as a culinary hot spot since the 1980s, when a stupendous feat of marketing managed to make dishes such as banana-crusted sea bass seem quintessentially Southwestern, and is now said to have more quality **restaurants** per head than any other US city.

Café Pasqual's 121 Don Gaspar Ave Ⓣ 505/983-9340. Lovely and lively Old/New Mexican restaurant, serving top-quality food (including breakfast) in an attractive tiled dining room a block south of the plaza. Entrees include vegetarian *enchiladas* ($19) and black mussels steamed with lemongrass ($24); as an appetizer, try the delicious Pigs and Figs salad, made with bacon, figs, and mozzarella ($14).

Coyote Café 132 W Water St Ⓣ 505/983-1615. Mark Miller's showcase restaurant, just off the plaza, is as popular as ever, despite a tendency to rest on its laurels. The *à la carte* prices can be ferocious, with entrees like fried red-banana-crusted sea bass or cumin-roasted duck breast at $26–40, but at times they also serve a prix-fixe set dinner for around $40. For a cheaper taste, try the rooftop café.

La Casa Sena 125 E Palace Ave Ⓣ 505/988-9232. Charming courtyard restaurant, a block from the plaza; zestful Southwestern lunches, with entrees around $11–15, are the best deal, though the $42 set dinners are consistently good. *La Cantina*, adjoining, is a little cheaper and its staff performs Broadway show songs as they work.

La Plazuela *La Fonda de Santa Fe*, 100 E San Francisco St Ⓣ 505/982-5511. Delightful, beautifully decorated Mexican restaurant in the heart of *La Fonda*, open daily for all meals, and with an open-air feel despite the glass ceiling. All the usual Mexican dishes are on offer at reasonable prices,

as well as some more expensive dinner entrees, and the cooking is well above average.

Mu du noodles 1494 Cerrillos Rd Ⓣ 505/983-1411. Largely but not exclusively vegetarian place, near the hostel. Its pan-Asian menu may not always be authentic, but it's still tasty. Dinner only, closed Sun.

Ore House on the Plaza 50 Lincoln Ave Ⓣ 505/983-8687. "Nueva Latina" restaurant, where the menu ranges from $5 green-chile stews to elaborate $28 dinner entrees, and the location on the plaza, complete with *ristra*-garlanded balcony, is unbeatable.

Pachanga 416 Agua Fria Ⓣ 505/988-5991. Stylish Mexican restaurant – far from an ordinary *cantina* – housed in a former convent. Delicious specialties include an appetizer of spiced corn truffles with cheese for $10, and pit roasted lamb, or *barbacoa*, as an entree for $12; more conventional Mexican dishes, like *queso fundido* or *chimichangas*, cost under $10. Closed Sun, lunch in summer only.

Tia Sophia's 210 W San Francisco St Ⓣ 505/983-9880. Spicy, very inexpensive Mexican diner west of the plaza that's a huge hit with lunching locals. Daily except Mon 7am–2pm.

Zélé Coffeehouse 201 Galisteo St Ⓣ 505/982-7835. Roomy downtown coffeehouse serving pastries, omelets, sandwiches, and killer granola, plus great juices and smoothies, with some sidewalk seating as well.

Nightlife and entertainment

Unlike its abundance of restaurants, Santa Fe has the limited range of **nightlife** you'd expect in a small city, though its cultural scene livens up in summer. For full listings, check the free weekly *Reporter* (Ⓦ http://sfreporter.com) or the "Pasatiempo" section of Friday's *New Mexican*. Year-round, musical and theatrical performances take place downtown at the **Lensic Performing Arts Center**, a striking former movie theater at 211 W San Francisco St (Ⓣ 505/988-7050, Ⓦ www.lensic.

com). The much-anticipated Santa Fe Opera season runs from late June through August in a magnificent amphitheater seven miles north of town (☎505/986-5900 or 1-800/280-4654, ⓦ www.santafeopera.org).

Some of the most atmospheric places to **drink** in town are in the old hotels – such as the downstairs lounge and rooftop bar of *La Fonda* on the plaza (see p.928) – but otherwise conventional bars are few and far between.

Catamount Bar 125 E Water St ☎505/988-7222. Downtown bar with plenty of microbrews on tap, and live rock or blues most nights.
Cowgirl Hall of Fame 319 S Guadalupe St ☎505/982-2565. Very busy country-themed restaurant and bar, with regular live music.

El Farol 808 Canyon Rd ☎505/983-9912. Historic bar-cum-restaurant that serves Spanish *tapas* to musical accompaniment from blues to flamenco.
Evangelo's 200 W San Francisco St ☎505/982-9014. The only good bare-bones bar in easy walking range of the plaza, with a pool table, a jukebox, and occasional live music.

Bandelier National Monument

Cut into the forested mesas of the Pajarito Plateau, 35 miles northwest of Santa Fe, the cliff dwellings and Ancestral Puebloan ruins of **Bandelier National Monument** ($10 per vehicle) spread across fifty square miles of pine woods and deep gorges. Named after archeologist Adolph Bandelier, who publicized the place in the 1880s, the ruins date from around 1300 AD, at the very end of the Ancestral Puebloan period (see box, opposite). Itinerant groups, seeking sanctuary from drought and invasion, gathered here to build a community that amalgamated their assorted cultures. At the end of the narrow switchbacking road down from Hwy-4, the **visitor center** provides an excellent overview of the site (daily: summer 8am–6pm; rest of year 8am–4.30pm; ☎505/672-3861, ⓦ www.nps.gov/band).

The first stop along the paved 1.5-mile trail beyond, looping through **Frijoles Canyon**, is **Tyuonyi**, a circular, multistory village of which only the ground floor and foundations survive. A side path leads up to dozens of **cave dwellings**, their rounded chambers scooped out of the soft volcanic rock; you can scramble up to, and even enter, some of them, to peer out across the valley. The main trail continues to the **Long House**, an 800-foot series of two- and three-story houses built side by side against the canyon wall. Though most of the upper stories have collapsed, you can still see the holes that held the roof beams, and the rows of petro-

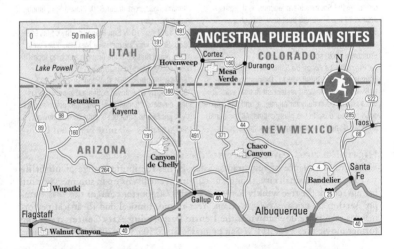

Few visitors to the Southwest are prepared for the awesome scale and beauty of the desert cities and cliff palaces left by the **Ancestral Puebloans**, as seen all over the high plateaus of the "**Four Corners**" district, where Colorado, New Mexico, Arizona, and Utah now meet.

The earliest humans reached the Southwest around 10,000 BC, but the Ancestral Puebloans first appeared as the **Basketmakers**, near the San Juan River, about two thousand years ago. Named for their woven sandals and bowls, they lived in pits in the earth, roofed with logs and mud. Over time, the Ancestral Puebloans adopted an increasingly settled lifestyle, becoming expert farmers and potters. Their first freestanding houses on the plains were followed by multistoried **pueblos**, in which hundreds of families lived in complexes of contiguous "apartments." The astonishing **cliff dwellings**, perched on precarious ledges high above remote canyons, which they began to build around 1100 AD, were the first Ancestral Puebloan settlements to show signs of defensive fortifications. Competition for scarce re sources became even fiercer toward the end of the thirteenth century, and recent research suggests that warfare and even cannibalism played a role in their ultimate dispersal. Moving eastward, they joined forces with other displaced groups in a coming-together that eventually produced the modern **Pueblo Indians**. Hence the recent change of name, away from "Anasazi," a Navajo word meaning "ancient enemies," in favor of "Ancestral Puebloan."

Among the most significant **Ancestral Puebloan sites** are:

Mesa Verde Magnificent cliff palaces, high in the canyons of Colorado; see p.870.

Bandelier National Monument Large riverside pueblos, and cave-like homes hollowed from volcanic rock; see opposite.

Chaco Canyon The largest and most sophisticated freestanding pueblos, far out in the desert; see p.944.

Wupatki Several small pueblo communities, built by assorted tribal groups; see p.965.

Walnut Canyon Numerous canyon-wall houses above lush Walnut Creek; see p.966.

Betatakin Canyon-side community set in a vast rocky alcove in the Navajo National Monument; see p.979.

Canyon de Chelly Superbly dramatic cliff dwellings in glowing sandstone canyon; now owned and farmed by the Navajo; see p.981.

Hovenweep Enigmatic towers poised above a canyon; see p.1002.

glyphs carved above them. Half a mile beyond that, protected by a rock overhang 150ft above the canyon floor, a reconstructed *kiva* sits in **Alcove House**. To reach it you have to climb rickety ladders and steep stairs cut into the crumbly rock.

Los Alamos

If you approach Bandelier from the east, you'll pass **Los Alamos National Laboratory**, the main US center for the research and development of **nuclear weapons** (as well as neurobiology, computer science, and solar and geothermal energy). Virtually all the work at this, one of the foremost scientific research establishments in the world, is military-based, and consequently most of the complex is off-limits – the small and over-simplified **Bradbury Science Museum** (Tues–Fri 9am–5pm, Sat–Mon 1–5pm; free) is the only part you can visit. The local radio station is called KBOM, and museum guides glow with excitement as they describe their weapons' devastating power.

The first Spaniards to explore what's now New Mexico were greeted by a settled population of around a hundred thousand people, living in perhaps a hundred villages and towns. However, the people the Spaniards named the **Pueblo Indians** (*pueblo* is Spanish for "village") soon grew to resent the imposition of Catholicism and the virtual enslavement of Pueblo laborers. In the **Pueblo Revolt** of 1680, the various tribes banded together and ousted the entire Colonial regime, killing scores of priests and soldiers and sending hundreds more south to Mexico. After the Spanish returned in 1693, the Pueblos showed little further resistance, and they have coexisted surprisingly amicably ever since, accepting aspects of Catholicism – most pueblos have a large adobe church at their core – without giving up their traditional beliefs and practices.

New Mexico is now home to around forty thousand Pueblo Indians, with each of its nineteen autonomous pueblos having its own laws and system of government. All have been modernized to some extent, and the recent explosion of Native American gaming has seen many open their own **casinos**, at sites usually located along the major highways well away from the residential areas. However, all also proudly retain the "Old Ways." Saints' days, major Catholic holidays such as Easter and the Epiphany, and even the Fourth of July are celebrated with a combination of Native American traditions and Catholic rituals, featuring elaborately costumed dances and massive communal feasts. The spectacle of hundreds of costumed, body-painted tribal members of all ages, drawn from other pueblos as well as the host village, performing elaborate dances in such timeless surroundings is hugely impressive.

However, few of the pueblos should be regarded as the tourist attractions they're touted to be. The best known, **Taos** and **Ácoma**, retain their ancient defensive architecture, but the rest tend to be dusty adobe hamlets scattered around a windblown plaza. Unless you arrive on a feast day, or are a knowledgeable shopper in search of Pueblo crafts (most pueblos have their own specialties), visits are liable to prove disappointing. In addition, you'll certainly be made to feel unwelcome if you fail to behave respectfully – don't go "exploring" places that are off-limits to outsiders, such as shrines, *kivas*, or private homes.

Fifteen of the pueblos are concentrated along the Rio Grande north of Albuquerque, with a longstanding division between the seven **southern pueblos**, south of Santa Fe, most of which speak Keresan, and the group to the north, which mostly speak Tewa (pronounced *tay-wah*). Visitors to each are required to register at a visitor center; some charge an admission fee of $3 to $10, and those that permit such activities at all charge additional fees of about $5 for still photography, $10–15 for video cameras, and up to $100 for sketching. There's no extra charge for feast days or dances, but photography is usually forbidden on special occasions.

From Santa Fe to Taos: the High Road

The quickest route between Santa Fe and Taos follows US-84 as far as the Rio Grande, then continues northeast along the river on Hwy-68. US-84 passes through the heartland of the **northern pueblos**, a cluster of tiny Tewa-speaking communities that have survived for over five centuries, but unless your visit coincides with a feast day (see box), there's little to see.

However, a satisfying if circuitous alternative route known as the **"High Road"** leaves US-68/84 a dozen miles north of Santa Fe, near Nambe Pueblo. Leading high into the pines and aspens of the **Sangre de Cristo Mountains**, it passes a number of pueblos as well as several timeless Hispanic villages.

Chimayó

The quaint mountain village of **CHIMAYÓ**, 25 miles north of Santa Fe at the junction of Hwy-503 and Hwy-76, is the site of New Mexico's most famous Spanish Colonial church, the 1816 **Santuario de Chimayó** (daily: May–Sept 9am–6pm; Oct–April 9am–4pm). Known as the "Lourdes of America" for the devotion of its many pilgrims, this round-shouldered, twin-towered adobe beauty sits behind an enclosed courtyard; a pit in the floor of a small room to one side holds the "holy dirt" for which the site is venerated.

Half a mile further north on Hwy-503, the *Rancho de Chimayó* is the best traditional New Mexican **restaurant** in the state, serving superb *flautas* and a mouthwatering *sopaipilla*, stuffed with meat and chiles, on a lovely sun-drenched outdoor patio, and it also offers reasonable **rooms** in a separate building (closed Mon Nov–April; ☏505/351-4444; ④).

Taos

Still home to one of the longest-established Native American populations in the US, though transformed by becoming first a Spanish Colonial outpost, and more recently a hangout for bohemian artists and New Age dropouts, **TAOS** (which rhymes with "mouse") has become famous out of all proportion to its size. Just six thousand people live in its three component parts: **Taos** itself, around the plaza; sprawling **Ranchos de Taos**, three miles to the south; and the Native American community of **Taos Pueblo**, two miles north.

Beyond the usual unsightly highway sprawl, Taos is a delight to visit. As well as museums, galleries, and stores to match Santa Fe, it still offers an unhurried pace and charm, and the sense of a meeting place between Pueblo, Hispanic, and American cultures. Its reputation as an **arts colony** began at the end of the nineteenth century, with the arrival of painter Joseph Henry Sharp, who with Bert Phillips and Ernest L. Blumenschein established the **Taos Society of Artists** in 1915. Soon afterward, society heiress Mabel Dodge arrived and married an Indian from the Pueblo to become Mabel Dodge Luhan. She in turn wrote a fan letter to English novelist **D.H. Lawrence**, who visited three times in the early 1920s; his widow Frieda made her home in Taos after his death. New generations of artists and writers have "discovered" Taos ever since, but the most famous of all was **Georgia O'Keeffe**, who stayed for a few years at the end of the 1920s.

Arrival, information, and getting around

Two daily Greyhound and TNM&O **buses** from Albuquerque ($28) and Santa Fe ($18) arrive at **Taos Bus Center** (☏505/758-1144), opposite the well-equipped local **visitor center**, two miles south of the plaza at the intersection of Hwy-68 and US-64 (daily 9am–5pm, closed Sun in winter; ☏505/758-3873 or 1-800/732-8267, ⓦwww.taoschamber.com). Twin Hearts Express (☏505/751-1201 or 1-800/654-9456, ⓦwww.twinheartsexpress.com) also connects Taos with Santa Fe ($30) and the Albuquerque airport ($45).

Walking is the best way to get around the compact center, while hourly Red Chile **buses** (50¢ one way, $1 for an all-day pass; ☏505/751-4459) cover a twelve-mile route along the highway.

Accommodation

Taos has **accommodation** to meet all needs, at prices well below those of Santa Fe (though thanks to the local ski resort midwinter rates are no lower than midsummer). Taos Central Reservations (☏505/758-9767 or 1-800/821-2437, ⓦwww.taoscentralreservations.com) can reserve lodging in advance.

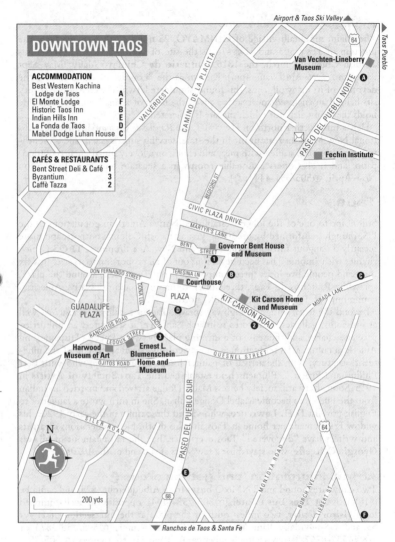

DOWNTOWN TAOS

Van Vechten-Lineberry
Museum

ACCOMMODATION
Best Western Kachina
  Lodge de Taos   **A**
El Monte Lodge   **F**
Historic Taos Inn   **E**
Indian Hills Inn   **B**
La Fonda de Taos   **D**
Mabel Dodge Luhan House **C**

CAFÉS & RESTAURANTS
Bent Street Deli & Café **1**
Byzantium   **3**
Caffè Tazza   **2**

Fechin Institute

Governor Bent House
and Museum

Courthouse

Kit Carson Home
and Museum

PLAZA

GUADALUPE
PLAZA

Harwood
Museum of Art

Ernest L.
Blumenschein
Home and
Museum

N

0   200 yds

▼ Ranchos de Taos & Santa Fe

The best places to **camp** are the nine summer-only campgrounds in **Carson National Forest** (☎505/758-6200, ⓦwww.fs.fed.us/r3/carson), reached by following Kit Carson Road east until it becomes US-64.

Abominable Snowmansion Hostel/HI-Taos
Taos Ski Valley Rd, Arroyo Seco ☎505/776-8298,
ⓦwww.abominablesnowmansion.com. Pleasant,
friendly HI-AYH hostel-cum-ski lodge, on a tight
curve in the road up to the Ski Valley, five miles
north of downtown. Office open daily 8–11am &
4–10pm. Dorm beds $15 in summer, $22 in winter,
when rates include breakfast; teepees, and camp-

ing space out back; bargain private rooms and
cabins come with and without en-suite facilities.
①–②
Best Western Kachina Lodge de Taos 413
Paseo del Pueblo Norte ☎505/758-2275 or 1-
800/522-4462, ⓦwww.kachinalodge.com. Large,
tasteful, family motel at the Taos Pueblo turnoff,
with lots of Southwestern art, a good restaurant,

live music, and nightly Pueblo dance performances in summer. ❹

El Monte Lodge 317 Kit Carson Rd ☎505/758-3171 or 1-800/828-8267. Rural 1930s motel half a mile east of the plaza, offering comfortable en-suite accommodation in a complex of adobe cottages. ❸

La Fonda de Taos 108 South Plaza ☎505/758-2211 or 1-800/833-2211, ⓦwww.hotellafonda.com. Vintage 1930s hotel on the plaza that's been revamped and modernized to hold 24 luxurious suites, with Southwestern furnishings and tiled bathrooms. ❻

🏃 **Historic Taos Inn** 125 Paseo del Pueblo Norte ☎505/758-2233 or 1-888/519-8267, ⓦwww.taosinn.com. Rambling, ravishing – and very Southwestern – central hotel. Each of its 36 rooms plays a variation on the Pueblo theme, while

both *Doc Martin's* restaurant (see p.939) and the *Adobe Bar* are packed nightly. ❸–❽

Indian Hills Inn 233 Paseo del Pueblo Sur ☎505/758-4293 or 1-800/444-2346, ⓦwww.taosnet.com/indianhillsinn. The only cheapish high-way motel within walking distance of the plaza; be sure to get a room away from the street. ❸

🏃 **Mabel Dodge Luhan House** 240 Morada Lane ☎505/751-9686 or 1-800/846-2235, ⓦwww.mabeldodgeluhan.com. Gorgeous 200-year-old adobe B&B complex, not far northeast of the plaza off Kit Carson Lane, where the lovely guest rooms are named for creative former guests like Willa Cather and Ansel Adams. Two rooms, including the light-filled solarium, share a bathroom painted by D.H. Lawrence. A cheaper lodge annex has more modern fittings. ❹

Taos plaza and the museums

The old Spanish **plaza** at the heart of Taos, is now ringed by jewelry stores, art galleries, and restaurants; all conform to the predominant Pueblo motif of rounded brown adobe. Specific sights are few – a small **museum** in the *La Fonda de Taos* hotel has a collection of sexy but amateurish paintings by D.H. Lawrence, and the tree-filled square itself is often animated by guitar-toting buskers – but the surrounding streets are perfect for an aimless stroll, and it's easy to spend half a day just wandering around. Some of the best places to eat or drink, as well as a number of top-notch art and crafts galleries, are on **Bent Street**, a block north of the plaza. The street takes its name from the first American governor of New Mexico, Charles Bent; his house here, in which he was murdered in 1847, has been preserved as a ramshackle little museum of frontier Taoseño life (daily April–Oct 9.30am–5pm, Nov–March 10am–4pm; $2).

Just east of the plaza, across the highway at the end of Taos's sole surviving stretch of wooden boardwalk, is the dusty adobe dwelling that was home to mountain man, mason, and part-time US cavalry officer **Kit Carson** (see p.978) for 25 years in the mid-1800s. It too is now a small **museum**, commemorating Carson's many adventures (daily: April–Oct 9am–5pm; Nov–March 10am–4pm; $5).

Two blocks south of the plaza at 222 Ledoux St, the much-restored 1790 **house** of artist and collector **Ernest L. Blumenschein**, co-founder of the town's 1920s arts colony, displays paintings and furniture (daily: April–Oct 9am–5pm; Nov–March 11am–4pm; $6). A single $20 ticket, valid for a year, grants admission to both this and four other Taos museums, including the two described below.

Two miles north of the Taos Pueblo turn-off, reached by a dirt road that angles into a tricky five-way intersection, the **Millicent Rogers Museum** (April–Oct daily 10am–5pm; Nov–March Tues–Sun 10am–5pm; $7; ⓦwww.millicentrogers.org) holds a superb collection of craft works. Objects range from Ancestral Puebloan and Mimbres pottery to the contemporary black-on-black ceramics of San Ildefonso Pueblo potter Maria Martinez, plus Hopi *kachinas*, and beautiful Navajo blankets. Affecting exhibits also trace the development of Spanish Colonial religious art in the New World.

Ranchos de Taos

South of the central plaza area, to either side of Hwy-68, **Ranchos de Taos** was originally a separate community, composed of farms that fed the town of Taos. Each *rancho* had its own main house, or *hacienda*; one has been restored as a

⑫

THE SOUTHWEST | Northern New Mexico

museum of Colonial life. The **Hacienda Martínez** (daily April–Oct 9am–5pm, Nov–March 10am–4pm; $6), two miles southwest of the plaza on Ranchitos Road, was built in 1804. Within its thick, windowless, adobe walls – sealed like a fortress against what were then still-prevalent Indian raids – two-dozen rooms are wrapped around two patios, holding animal pens and a well. Trade goods of the kind its first owner, Taos mayor Don Antonio Martínez, once carried south along the Rio Grande are displayed alongside tools, looms, and simple furnishings.

In Ranchos' small unpaved plaza, the mission church of **San Francisco de Asis** squares its broad shoulders, or more accurately its massive adobe buttresses, to the passing traffic on Hwy-68. Built around 1776, it's one of colonial New Mexico's most splendid architectural achievements, with subtly rounded walls and corners disguising its underlying structural strength. Though the ever-changing interplay of light and shade across its golden exterior has fascinated painters from Georgia O'Keeffe onward, the interior is equally intriguing, with a magnificently ornate green-and-red reredos framing several naïve paintings.

Taos Pueblo

Continuously inhabited for nearly one thousand years, the two multistory adobes at **Taos Pueblo**, two miles north of Taos plaza and half a mile east of Hwy-68, jointly constitute the most impressive Native American dwelling place still in use. Hlauuma, the north house, and Hlaukkwima, the south house, are separated by the Rio Pueblo de Taos, which flows down the hills from the sacred Blue Lake, inaccessible to outsiders. Residents of the pueblo have made few concessions to the modern world, living without toilets, running water, or electricity.

The pueblo is generally open to visitors from 8am until 5pm from Monday to Saturday, and between 8.30am and 5pm on Sunday, but it often closes for tribal events such as festivals or funerals, and remains closed between mid-February and early April; call ahead (☏505/758-1028, ⓦwww.taospueblo.com) before you visit. Assuming the pueblo is open, park your vehicle at the edge of the plaza, and pay an **entrance fee** ($10 per person, plus $5 per still or video camera), that entitles you to join one of the guided **walking tours**, led by Pueblo residents, which leave at regular intervals.

For most of the year, Pueblo life continues with scant regard for the intrusion of tourists, but feast days and dances, held throughout the summer, can be spectacular. The biggest parties are the **Corn Dances** in June and July, and the **Feast of San Gerónimo** at the end of September, when outsiders flock to join the general revelry.

Taos Ski Valley

Fifteen miles north of Taos lie the challenging slopes of **Taos Ski Valley**, reached via an attractive road that winds up through a narrow gap in the mountains from the village of Arroyo Seco. Located on the north flank of **Wheeler Peak**, the highest point in New Mexico at 13,161ft, the demanding runs are usually open to skiers – snowboarding is banned – between late November and early April (daily lift tickets late Nov to mid-Dec and late March to early April $28, mid-Dec to late March $57; information ☏505/776-2291 or 1-866/968-7386, reservations ☏1-800/776-1111, ⓦwww.skitaos.org).

Eating, drinking, and nightlife

Taos is too small to offer much **nightlife**, but it does have a fine selection of **restaurants** in all price ranges, and several coffeehouses. If your main priority is to **drink**, the *Adobe Bar* in the *Taos Inn* (see p.937) is the coziest spot in town.

Bent Street Deli & Café 120 Bent St ☎505/758-5787. Airy, partly outdoor place, just north of the plaza with good-value breakfasts, sandwich lunches, and tasty dinners for under $20. Closed Sun.

Byzantium 112 La Placita at Ledoux St ☎505/751-0805. Romantic, classy courtyard restaurant southwest of the plaza, serving conventional but flavorful salad-or-sandwich lunches. Dinners have a pan-Asian edge, with tempura eel ($15) or duck green curry ($27) alongside traditional herb-crusted pork tenderloin ($34). Closed Tues & Wed.

Caffè Tazza 122 Kit Carson Rd ☎505/758-8706. Trendy, central café with nice sunlit terrace, selling coffees and light veggie meals to students and assorted eccentrics.

Doc Martin's *Taos Inn*, 125 Paseo del Pueblo Norte ☎505/758-1977. Delicious, inventive New Mexican food in a romantic adobe inn, just east of the plaza. Most dinner entrees, such as *piñon*-crusted salmon or roast chicken, are $17–28, but a three-course prix-fixe menu, served Sun–Thurs only, costs around $20.

Island Coffees and Hawaiian Grill 1032 Paseo del Pueblo Sur ☎505/758-7777. Friendly, inexpensive Hawaiian-themed café near the visitor center, serving Kona coffee plus noodle dishes, curries, and sandwiches, and offering Internet access. Closed Sun.

Joseph's Table, *La Fonda de Taos*, 108 South Plaza; ☎505/751-4512. This delightful restaurant serves wonderful (if rich) food in a lovely setting, with very friendly service. A fabulous parma ham risotto appetizer is $11, while full entrees like a whole roasted duck or lamb shank cost around $30, but you can also order smaller portions from the separate *Joe's Bar* menu, like a buffalo burger for $12. Lunch served May–Aug only.

Taos Pizza Outback 712 Paseo del Pueblo Norte ☎505/748-3112. Hard-to-find pizzeria, a mile north of town, with a welcoming, youthful ambiance and huge portions of great food – the $9 veggie calzones are amazing.

Albuquerque and central New Mexico

Although most travelers race through **central New Mexico** as quickly as possible, it does hold isolated pockets of interest, with the scenery, at least in the west, the main attraction. Dozens of small towns hang on to the last remnants of **Route 66**, the winding old "Chicago-to-LA" transcontinental highway long since superseded by I-40.

Albuquerque – New Mexico's largest city, and site of its only major **airport** – sits dead center, at the intersection of I-40 and I-25. The area to the **east**, stretching toward Texas, is among the most desolate parts of the Southwest, but the mountainous region **west** has more to see – above all **Ácoma Pueblo**, the mesa-top community known as "Sky City."

East of Albuquerque: Tucumcari and Fort Sumner

The long line of truck stops, diners, and motels at **TUCUMCARI**, the biggest town between Albuquerque and Amarillo, Texas (see p.758), has made it a favorite I-40 pit stop. During the day you can while away an hour at the mind-boggling **Tucumcari Historical Museum** at 416 S Adams St (June–Aug Mon–Sat 8am–6pm; Sept–May Tues–Sat 8am–5pm; $2.11), which boasts one of the world's greatest collections of barbed wire. Literally hundreds of inexpensive **rooms** lie along this stretch of old Route 66, including the classic *Blue Swallow* **motel**, 815 E Route 66 (☎505/461-9849, ⓦwww.blueswallowmotel.com; ❷). For **food**, *Del's Family Restaurant*, 1202 E Route 66 (☎505/461-1740; closed Sun), is as good a diner as you're going to find.

FORT SUMNER, south of I-40 some way short of Tucumcari, means different things to different people. To the Navajo, it's where frontiersman and US Army colonel **Kit Carson** dragged them in 1864 after destroying their orchards and burning their villages in Arizona (see p.978). What little is left of the reservation is now the **Fort Sumner State Monument**, seven miles southeast of the modern town (daily 8.30am–5pm; $3; ⑩ www.nmmonuments.org), where a large visitor center-cum-museum known as the **Bosque Redondo Memorial** honors the Navajo and Apache who died during their imprisonment. To Wild West fanatics, Fort Sumner is a pilgrimage spot because legendary outlaw **Billy the Kid** was gunned down here by Pat Garrett in 1881. His grave stands behind the jumbled **Old Fort Sumner Museum** (daily 9am–5pm; $3.50), his tombstone shielded from memento-seekers by a steel cage.

Albuquerque

Sprawling at the heart of New Mexico, where the main east–west road and rail routes cross both the Rio Grande and the old road south to Mexico, **ALBUQUERQUE** is, with half a million people, the state's only major metropolis. Though many tourists dash straight from the airport up to Santa Fe, without a thought for Albuquerque, the "**Duke City**" has a good deal going for it. Like Phoenix, it's grown a bit too fast for comfort, but the original Hispanic settlement is still discernible at its core, and its diverse, cosmopolitan population gives it a rare cultural vibrancy. Even if its architecture is often uninspired, the setting is magnificent, sandwiched between the Rio Grande and the dramatic, glowing **Sandia Mountains**. Specific highlights include the intact **Spanish plaza**, the neon-lit **Route 66** frontage of Central Avenue, and the excellent **Indian Pueblo Cultural Center**, while every October Albuquerque hosts the nation's largest **hot-air balloon** rally.

Arrival and information

Albuquerque's **International Sunport** is four miles southeast of downtown. All the major **car rental** chains have outlets here, while a **taxi** into town with Yellow Cab (☎505/247-4888) costs around $10, and Airport Shuttle (☎505/765-1234, ⑩ www.airportshuttleabq.com) runs door-to-door shuttles at similar rates.

Both Amtrak and Greyhound are five easy minutes' walk south of downtown. The modern Greyhound **bus terminal**, 300 Second St SW (☎505/243-4435), is used by long-distance east–west services, as well as four daily buses up to Santa Fe ($16) and Taos ($28). Daily Amtrak **trains** between Los Angeles and Chicago arrive at 214 First St.

The main downtown **visitor center** is in the Albuquerque Convention Center, 401 Second St (Mon–Fri 9am–5pm; ☎505/842-9918 or 1-800/284-2282, ⑩ www.itsatrip.org). Further **information kiosks** can be found in Old Town, in the Plaza Don Luis on Romero NW (daily: April–Oct 9am–5pm; Nov–March 9.30am–4.30pm), and at the airport (daily 9.30am–8pm).

Accommodation

The twenty-mile length of **Central Avenue**, the old Route 66, is lined with the flashing neon signs of $40-per-night **motels**. You'll have to pay a little extra to stay in the heart of Old Town or downtown. Larger convention hotels are congregated along the interstates, and near the airport.

Ambassador Inn 7407 Central Ave NE ☎505/265-1161. There's nothing fancy or exciting about the *Ambassador*, and it's well to the east of the liveliest part of Central Avenue, but for a clean, presentable, ordinary motel room, the price is great. ❷

Aztec Motel 3821 Central Ave NE ☎505/254-1742. Albuquerque's oldest Route 66 motel, featuring a great restored neon sign and festooned with folk art. Most of its guests are permanent residents, but it's still a safe and atmospheric (if plain) option for tourists. ❷

Casas de Sueños 310 Rio Grande Blvd SW ☎505/247-4560, ⑩ www.casasdesuenos.com. Beautifully furnished, exotic, and friendly B&B, very close to Old Town, with themed cottages and smaller rooms. ❺–❽

Comfort Inn – Airport 2300 Yale Blvd SE
℡ 505/243-2244 or 1-800/221-2222. Good-value motel, served by free shuttles from the airport across the road, and with complimentary breakfasts. **❸**
El Vado Motel 2500 Central Ave SW ℡ 505/243-4594. Vintage adobe Route 66 motel, within easy reach of Old Town. **❷**
La Posada de Albuquerque 125 Second St NW ℡ 505/242-9090 or 1-800/777-5732, Ⓦ www.laposada-abq.com. Historic hotel in convenient downtown location, built in Mexican style by Conrad Hilton in 1939. Large, very classy rooms with antique wooden furnishings, a beautiful wood-paneled lobby, and a spacious, atmospheric bar. **❹**

Monterey Nonsmokers Motel 2402 Central Ave SW ℡ 505/243-3554 or 1-877/666-8379, Ⓦ www.nonsmokersmotel.com. Clean, fifteen-room motel, two blocks west of Old Town, with pool, laundry, and a strict nonsmoking policy. **❸**
Route 66 Hostel 1012 Central Ave SW ℡ 505/247-1813, Ⓦ http://members.aol.com/route66hos/htmlRT66/. Albuquerque's only hostel, a friendly place on the outskirts of Old Town and a mile west of downtown, offers dorm beds for $17, kitchen facilities, and very plain but bargain-priced private doubles. Office hours daily 7.30–10.30am & 4–11pm.

Old Town

Once you've cruised up and down **Central Avenue**, looking at the flashing neon and 1940s architecture of this twenty-mile stretch of Route 66 (Sun Tran buses do it all day for $1), most of what's interesting about Albuquerque is concentrated in **Old Town**, the recently tidied-up old Spanish heart of the city. As the billboards on the interstate nearby rightly proclaim, "it's darned old and historic." The tree-filled **main plaza** is overlooked by the twin-towered adobe facade of **San Felipe de Neri church**; it's a very pleasant place to wander or have a meal, even if there's not a whole lot to do. One of the more bizarre of the many knick-knack shops is the **Rattlesnake Museum** southeast of the plaza at 202 San Felipe St NW (Mon–Fri noon–6pm, Sat 10am–6pm, Sun 1–6pm; $3.50; Ⓦ www.rattlesnakes.com), which has live rattlers on display.

There's a cluster of museums about five minutes or so northeast of the plaza. The **Albuquerque Museum of Art and History**, 2000 Mountain Rd (daily except Mon 9am–5pm; $4, free Sun 9am–1pm; Ⓦ www.cabq.gov/museum), holds an impressive array of the weaponry carried by the Spanish conquistadors as well as delicate religious artifacts, and paintings and photos depicting Albuquerque through the centuries. Across the street, in the **National Atomic Museum** at 1905 Mountain Rd NW (daily 9am–5pm; $5; Ⓦ www.atomicmuseum.org), displays trace the history of nuclear science and weapons from the early discoveries of Madame Curie up to modern robotic devices such as the "truck-killing standoff weapon" Fireant.

Nearby, the **New Mexico Museum of Natural History**, 1801 Mountain Rd NW (daily 9am–5pm; closed Mon in Jan & Sept; $6; Ⓦ www.nmnaturalhistory.org), has full-scale, animated models of dinosaurs, a simulated volcanic eruption, and a replica of an Ice Age snow cave, as well as an engaging, hands-on collection of fossils and dinosaur bones.

The riverfront

The Rio Grande has shifted its course in the last three hundred years, so there's an unexpectedly low-key gap west of Old Town, much of it left undeveloped in deference to the unruly river. Along the wooded eastern riverbank, the **Bio Park** holds two attractions. The **Albuquerque Aquarium** (June–Aug Mon–Fri 9am–5pm, Sat & Sun 9am–6pm; Sept–May daily 9am–5pm; $7; Ⓦ www.cabq.gov/biopark) offers such diverse experiences as eating in a restaurant beside a glass-walled tank filled with live sharks and walking through a tunnel surrounded by fierce-eyed moray eels. Across the way, the **Rio Grande Botanic Garden** (same hours; same ticket) consists of two large conservatories – one holding rare plants from the Sonoran and Chihuahua deserts, the other more temperate Mediterranean species – plus a series of walled gardens.

Indian Pueblo Cultural Center

The **Indian Pueblo Cultural Center**, at 2401 12th St NW, one block north of I-40, is a stunning museum (daily 9am–4.30pm; $6; ☎505/843-7270, ⓦwww.indianpueblo.org) and crafts market (daily 9am–5.30pm; free), owned and run as a cooperative venture by the diverse Pueblo Indians of New Mexico. Its horseshoe-shaped design deliberately echoes the architecture of the Ancestral Puebloan city of Pueblo Bonito, in Chaco Canyon (see p.945), and the central courtyard is the venue for free Pueblo dances, every Saturday and Sunday at 11am and 2pm.

This is New Mexico's one major museum about Native Americans curated by Native Americans, and the displays downstairs have a clear and distinct point of view. The shared Ancestral Puebloan heritage at the root of Pueblo culture is explained in detail, as is the impact of the Spanish conquistadors. There's also as good an explanation as you're ever likely to get of a topic Pueblo Indians rarely discuss with outsiders: how indigenous Pueblo religion has managed to coexist with imported Catholicism. Videos illustrate modern Pueblo life, and the stores upstairs sell outstanding pottery and jewelry, while a good-quality **café** serves assorted Pueblo specialties.

Sandia Crest

The forested 10,500-foot peaks of the **Sandia Crest** tower over Albuquerque to the east, affording particularly beautiful views during and after sunset, when the city lights sparkle below. In summer it's a good 25°F cooler up here than in the valley, and in winter you can go downhill or cross-country **skiing** (mid-Dec to mid-March; lift tickets $35; ☎505/242-9052, ⓦwww.sandiapeak.com). If you don't want to drive the scenic but twisting twenty-mile route from Albuquerque, take the **Sandia Peak Tramway** (summer daily 9am–9pm; winter Mon & Wed–Sun 9am–8pm, Tues 5–8pm; $8), the world's longest single-span tramway at 2.7 miles; it leaves from the end of Tramway Road at the city's northeast edge.

Eating

Albuquerque is the place to get to grips with what real New Mexican food is all about. Family diners all over the city compete to create the spiciest chiles rellenos and enchiladas.

Artichoke Café 424 Central Ave SE ☎505/243-0200. Simple but classy restaurant in the heart of downtown, serving a good, varied menu of California-influenced modern American cuisine; most entrees well under $20. Dinner only on weekends.

Flying Star 3416 Central Ave SE ☎505/255-6633. Lively, crowded University District café serving eclectic international cuisine to a largely student clientele. The vast menu ranges through breakfast specialties, salads, and blue-plate specials such as Vietnamese noodles or pasta pomodoro for $10. Open daily from 6am until late.

Frontier 2400 Central Ave SE ☎505/266-0550. Legendary 24-hour diner across from the university, where an unceasing parade of characters chow down on burgers, burritos, and great vegetarian enchiladas.

Olympia Cafe 2210 Central Ave SE ☎505/242-4890. Good-value Greek and Mediterranean food, including gyros and falafel, that's also available for take-out. Across from the university on Route 66. Closed Sat & Sun.

Satellite Toys & Coffee 3513 Central Ave NE ☎505/256-0345. University District hangout, marked by the sign of the flying saucer and slogan, "serious coffee, silly toys." The toys in question are gifts and novelties rather than playthings; the coffee is all you could ask for. They also serve daily specials like split pea soup.

Scalo 3500 Central Ave SE ☎505/225-8781. Large but nonetheless romantic and stylish Northern Italian restaurant near the university. Appetizers like steamed mussels or beef carpaccio cost $10, entrees such as half an organic chicken are closer to $20, and there are plenty of pasta and vegetarian options. Closed Mon, dinner only on weekends.

Drinking and nightlife

Many of downtown Albuquerque's **bars** and **nightclubs** double as small theaters or music venues. The free weekly *Alibi* magazine (Ⓦwww.alibi.com) carries full listings of what's coming up or going down.

The Anodyne 409 Central NW ☎505/244-1820. Downtown's most popular bar offers pool tables, pinball, a good jukebox, and an eclectic mix of customers, from beer guzzlers to martini sippers.

Caravan East 7605 Central Ave NE ☎505/265-7877. Enormous honky-tonk, where tenderfeet can do the two-step with throngs of urban cowboys.

Club Rhythm and Blues 3523 Central Ave NE ☎505/256-0849, Ⓦwww.clubrb.com. University District bar that plays hosts to Latin, swing, and jazz bands as well as blues acts. Showtime Wed–Sat 9pm.

KiMo Theater 423 Central Ave NW ☎505/848-1370. Gorgeous, city-owned "Pueblo Deco" theater, dating from the late 1920s, which puts on an eclectic program of opera, dance, and theater performances, kids' movies, and also regular live bands.

Puccini's Golden West Saloon 620 Central Ave SW ☎505/764-2624. Venue of choice for Albuquerque's metal maniacs and host to touring indie bands.

The Launchpad 618 Central Ave SW ☎505/764-8887, Ⓦwww.launchpadrocks.com. Dance and live music space that showcases touring indie and world music bands; there's also a cluster of pool tables.

West of Albuquerque: I-40 to Arizona

Driving between Albuquerque and Arizona, you could easily be so put off by the parade of billboards and hoardings offering cut-price cigarettes and Indian jewelry that you'd miss out on some of central New Mexico's most interesting places, such as **Ácoma Pueblo** and **Chaco Canyon**, which lie south and north of I-40 respectively.

Ácoma Pueblo

The amazing **Ácoma Pueblo**, south of I-40 fifty miles west of Albuquerque, encapsulates a thousand years of Native American history. Its focus is the ancient village known as "**Sky City**," perched atop a magnificent isolated mesa, 367ft high and 7000ft above sea level. Probably occupied by Chacoan migrants between 1100 and 1200 AD, when the great pueblos of Chaco Canyon were still in use, Ácoma has adapted to repeated waves of invaders ever since, while retaining its own strong identity. As the Ácomans have long been happy to take the tourist dollar, visitors seldom feel the awkwardness possible at other pueblo communities. Nonetheless, Ácoma is the real thing, and its sense of unbroken tradition can reduce even the least culturally sensitive traveler to awestruck silence.

To see Sky City, you have to join one of the hour-long guided **bus tours** (daily: May–Oct 8am–7pm; Nov–April 8am–4pm; last tour leaves one hour before closing; $10, plus $10 for photo permit, no camcorders or video; ☎505/470-0181 or 1-800/747-0181, Ⓦwww.skycity.com), which leave regularly from the visitor center at the base of the mesa. The main stop is at the **San Esteban del Rey** mission, a thick-walled adobe church completed in 1640. Its earthen-floored nave is capped by a roof made of pine logs, carried here from the top of Mount Taylor, twenty miles away, without once touching the ground. The visual impact of the building is undeniable – due in part to its sheer incongruity – and it's striking that the Ácomans obviously never felt inclined to follow its architectural example. Instead they went on constructing the multistory stone and adobe houses around which the tour then proceeds. Only thirteen families live permanently on the mesa; most Ácomans reside down below, where they can get electricity, running water, and jobs. Villagers do, however, come up here during the day to sell pottery and fry-bread.

Grants

The old Route 66 town of **GRANTS**, fifteen miles west of Ácoma, holds half a dozen budget motels, including a good *Super 8*, 1604 E Santa Fe Ave (℡505/287-8811; ❸). In the heart of town, the *Mission at Riverwalk*, 422 W Santa Fe Ave (℡505/285-4632; ❺), is a former church that now doubles as a community theater and healthy café, serving sandwiches, smoothies, and coffee, and has a separate guest house for rent. The local **visitor center** is in the comprehensive and enjoyable **New Mexico Museum of Mining** at 100 N Iron Ave (Mon–Sat 9am–4pm; $3; ℡505/287-4802, ⓦwww.grants.org), offering a chance to make a virtual descent into a mock-up of one of the region's many **uranium mines**.

El Morro National Monument

Hidden away on Hwy-53 south of the Zuni Mountains, 42 miles west of Grants, **El Morro National Monument** feels as far off the beaten track as it's possible to be in the modern US. Incredibly, however, this pale-pink sandstone cliff was a regular rest stop for international travelers before the Pilgrims landed at Plymouth Rock, thanks to a cool, perennial pool of water that collects at the base of a tumbling waterfall. This spot was first recorded by Spanish explorers in 1583 – *el morro* means "the headland" – and in 1605, Don Juan de Oñate, the founder of New Mexico, carved the first of many messages that earned it the American name of **Inscription Rock**.

Translations of El Morro's graffiti are displayed in the **visitor center** (daily: summer 9am–7pm; winter 9am–5pm; $3 per person; ℡505/783-4226, ⓦwww.nps.gov/elmo). You can see the real thing on a half-mile trail, which stays open until an hour before the visitor center closes. Not far beyond some Ancestral Puebloan petroglyphs, scraped into the desert varnish, Don Juan's chiseled signature celebrates "the discovery of the South Sea"; he was returning from an expedition that had taken him to the mouth of the Colorado River.

Chaco Canyon

For casual visitors, the long, bumpy ride to the Ancestral Puebloan ruins of **Chaco Canyon**, north of I-40 between Grant and Gallup, may seem more bother than it's worth. Although the site protected as the **Chaco Culture National Historical Park** is the largest pre-Columbian city in North America, for beauty and drama it can't compete with lesser settlements such as Canyon de Chelly (see p.981). The low-walled canyon is a mere scratch in the scrubby high-desert plains, and the Chaco Wash that runs through it is often completely dry.

Once you accept that you won't have amazing photos to show the folks back home, however, there's still plenty about Chaco to take your breath away. Over 3600 separate sites have been logged in the canyon, of which the thirteen principal ones are open to visitors. Six, arrayed along the canyon's north wall, are what are known as "Great Houses" – self-contained pueblos, three or four stories high, whose fortress-like walls concealed up to eight hundred rooms.

Both the routes to Chaco Canyon entail driving twenty miles over rough but passable dirt roads. Open all year, these should not be attempted during or within a day of a rainstorm. Whether you approach from the south, by following Hwy-57 up from **Seven Lakes**, eighteen miles northeast of **Crownpoint**, or from the north or east, by turning off US-550 at **Nageezi**, 36 miles south of **Bloomfield,** you enter the park at its southeast corner, close to the **visitor center** (daily: summer 8am–6pm; winter 8am–5pm; $8 per vehicle; ℡505/786-7014, ⓦwww.nps.gov/chcu). The basic first-come, first-served *Gallo* **campground** ($10), a short way east, is the only visitor facility in the park; from April to October it's usually full by 3pm.

The gates of the canyon's eight-mile one-way **loop road** are open the same hours. The major stop is at the far end, where **Pueblo Bonito** ("beautiful town") – said to have been the biggest building in America until structural steel was developed in 1898 – can be explored on an easy half-mile trail. Work on this four-story D-shaped structure started in 850 AD and continued for three hundred years. Entering the ruin via its lowest levels, the path reaches its central plaza, which held at least three **Great Kivas** – ceremonial chambers thought to have been used by entire communities rather than individual clans or families.

Gallup

Just half an hour from the Arizona border, 65 miles west of Grants, the famous Route 66 town of **GALLUP** is a handy but uninteresting I-40 pit stop. A five-mile line of the old Route 66 frontage contains some of the least expensive **motels** in the US, such as the *Colonial*, 1007 W Coal Ave (☎505/863-6821; ❶). Unless you're falling asleep at the wheel, the only place really worth stopping for in Gallup is the lovely ⚖ *El Rancho Hotel*, 1000 E 66 Ave (☎505/863-9311 or 1-800/543-6351; ⓦwww.elranchohotel.com; ❸), built in 1937 as a home away from home for the many Hollywood stars filming nearby. Nowadays you can ogle their signed photos in the spacious Spanish Revival lobby, grab a bite in its decorative restaurant, or spend the night in the Ronald Reagan Room, the Marx Brothers Room, or the Mae West Room. The best guestrooms are in the original ranchhouse, the rest in a two-story motel building.

The Navajo and other Native Americans come together in **Red Rock State Park**, four miles east of Gallup, on the second weekend in August for the **Inter-Tribal Indian Ceremonial**, the largest such gathering anywhere (information and tickets ☎505/863-3896 or 1-888/685-2564; ⓦwww.indianceremonial.com). Four days of dances and craft shows have as their highlight a Saturday morning parade through the town.

Southern New Mexico

Most of the travelers who come to **southern New Mexico** are here to visit **Carlsbad Caverns National Park**. Crassly commercialized it may be, but it's too amazing a geological spectacle to miss. Northwest of Carlsbad, the **Sacramento** and **Jicarilla mountains** are home to the **Mescalero Apache** reservation as well as some rough-and-ready resorts. The desolate dunes of the **White Sands** spread west of the mountains, with the rolling hills of the **Rio Grande Valley** beyond.

Carlsbad Caverns National Park

CARLSBAD CAVERNS NATIONAL PARK consists of a tract of the Guadalupe Mountains that's so riddled with underground caves and tunnels as to be virtually hollow. Tamed in classic park-service style with concrete trails and electric lighting, this subterranean wonderland is now a walk-in gallery, where tourists come in droves to marvel at its intricate limestone tracery. Though the summer crowds can get pretty intense, in a strange way that's part of the fun – coming to Carlsbad feels like a real throwback to the great 1950s boom in mass tourism. Before you decide to join in, however, be sure to grasp that the park is a *long* way from anywhere else – three hundred miles southeast of Albuquerque and 150 miles northeast of El Paso, Texas.

To reach the park, follow the narrow, twisting seven-mile road that leaves US-62/180 at **White's City**, twenty miles southwest of the town of **CARLSBAD**. This ends at the **visitor center** – part of a complex that includes a restaurant, a gift shop, a day-care center, and even a kennel – where you can pay entrance fees and pick up details of the day's schedule of tours (daily: June to mid-Aug 8am–7pm; mid-Aug to May 8am–5pm; ℡505/785-2232, ⓦwww.nps.gov/cave).

Almost all park visitors confine their attention to the main cave, **Carlsbad Cavern** itself, and the standard park fee of $6 per person for three days covers access to this cave only. Direct elevators drop to the Cavern's centerpiece, the **Big Room**, 750 vertical feet below the visitor center (summer first down 8.30am, last up 6.30pm; rest of year first down 8.30am, last up 4.55pm), but you can choose instead to walk down via the **Natural Entrance Route** (last entry summer 3.30pm; rest of year 2pm). This steep, paved footpath switchbacks into the guano-encrusted maw of the cave, taking fifteen minutes to reach the first of the formations and another fifteen to reach the Big Room. All visitors are obliged to ride the elevator back out.

Measuring up to 1800ft long and 250ft high, the Big Room is festooned with stalactites, stalagmites, and countless unnameable shapes of swirling liquid rock. All are a uniform stone gray; the rare touches of color are provided by slight red or brown mineral-rich tinges, improved here and there with gentle pastel lighting. Most visitors take an hour or so to complete the reasonably level trail around the Room's perimeter. Whatever the weather up top – summer highs exceed 100°F – the temperature down here is always a cool 56°F, so dress warmly.

Adjoining the Big Room, the **Underground Lunchroom** is a vast formation-free side cave paved over in the 1950s to create a diner-cum-souvenir-shop that sells indigestible lunches in polystyrene containers, plus Eisenhower-era souvenirs like giant pencils and Viewmaster reels.

The main appeal of walking down used to be that the trail meandered through beautiful side caves such as the **King's Palace**, filled with translucent "draperies" of limestone, but these are now open to guided tours only, which start from the Big Room (daily summer 10am, 11am, 2pm & 3pm; winter 10am & 2pm; $8). Additional tours, scheduled in the visitor center, can take you along the **Left Hand Tunnel** route down from the visitor center ($7), or on a much more demanding descent into either **Spider Cave** or the **Hall of the White Giant** (both $20).

Practicalities

No matter how you get to Carlsbad Caverns, you have to cross seemingly endless miles of the **Llano Estacado**, the deathly flat rangeland that covers southeast New Mexico and the Texas Panhandle. The route from El Paso, Texas, has the advantage of passing through **Guadalupe Mountains National Park**, a beautiful though little-visited complement to Carlsbad, which offers superb camping (see p.767).

WHITE'S CITY is not a town but a privately owned tourist complex, which as well as featuring a little water park provides the closest **accommodation** and **camping** to the national park, including the mock-adobe *Best Western Cavern Inn* (℡505/785-2291 or 1-800/228-3767, ⓦwww.whitescity.nm; ❸; the *White's City RV Park* (same number), which has tent camping space; and the *Velvet Garter Restaurant* (same number). The town of **CARLSBAD** itself, 25 miles north of White's City, holds little of interest outside its many motels, such as the large *Best Western Stevens Inn*, 1829 S Canal St (℡505/887-2851 or 1-800/730-2851, ⓦwww.stevensinn.com; ❹), where rates include a full breakfast at the *Flume Room* **restaurant**, which is pretty much the best in town.

Roswell

Seventy-five miles north of Carlsbad, the small ranching town of **ROSWELL** is renowned as the spot where an alien spaceship supposedly crash-landed on July 4, 1947. The commander of the local air force base announced that they had retrieved the wreckage of a flying saucer, and despite a follow-up denial within a day the story has kept running. In 1997, as 100,000 *X-Files* fanatics descended upon Roswell for a six-day festival to mark the "Incident's" fiftieth anniversary, the US government revealed that an errant weather balloon had crashed while monitoring the atmosphere for evidence of Soviet nuclear tests. Nonetheless, their imaginations further stimulated by TV series like *Roswell* and *Taken*, UFO theorists remain unconvinced.

Despite the wishful thinking of the truly weird clientele who drift in, the **International UFO Museum**, 114 N Main St (daily 9am–5pm; $2; ☎505/625-9495, ⓦ www.iufomrc.org), inadvertently exposes the whole tawdry business as transparent nonsense. Its showpiece is a model of an "alien autopsy", built for the movie *Roswell*; you can't help suspecting it was also featured in the grainy "documentary" autopsy footage that created a brief sensation in 1995.

By way of contrast, the longstanding **Roswell Museum**, 100 W 11th St (Mon–Sat 9am–5pm, Sun 1–5pm; free), boasts an excellent, multifaceted collection, with a section celebrating pioneer rocket scientist Robert Goddard (1882–1945). Historical artifacts elsewhere range from armor and pikes brought by Spanish conquistadors to astronaut Harrison Schmitt's spacesuit. A huge gallery also displays Southwestern landscapes by Henriette Wyeth and Peter Hurd, and a solitary Georgia O'Keeffe, *Ram's Skull With Brown Leaves*.

Roswell's **visitor center** is at 426 N Main St (Mon–Sat 9am–5pm; ☎505/624-0889, ⓦ www.roswellnm.org). The finest **motel** in town, the *Best Western Sally Port Inn*, 2000 N Main St (☎505/622-6430 or 1-800/548-5221, ⓦ www.bestwestern .com; ❸), also has a good **restaurant**; the *Frontier Motel*, 3010 N Main St (☎505/622-1400 or 1-800/678-1401, ⓦ www.frontiermotelroswell.com; ❷), is much cheaper, and has a good pool. The *Cattle Baron*, 1113 N Main St (☎505/622-2465), is a large, good-value **steakhouse**, while *Farley's*, just up the hill at 1315 N Main St (☎505/627-1100), is a livelier sci-fi-themed pub and diner.

Lincoln

One of the most enduring of New Mexico's many legendary Wild West figures is Brooklyn-born William Bonney, better known as **Billy the Kid**. Many towns lay claim to him, but he first came to fame as an 18-year-old in the **Lincoln County War**, which erupted in 1878 in the frontier town of **LINCOLN**, on Hwy-380 halfway between Carlsbad and Albuquerque. Rival groups of ranchers and merchants fought to gain control of the town and hundreds of square miles of grazing lands. Since those days, no new buildings have joined the venerable false-fronted structures that line Main Street, and the entire town is now the **Lincoln State Monument**. Visitors can stroll its length at any time, while the cheapest way to visit its various historical sites is via a joint admission ticket, sold at the sites ($6 for all Lincoln sites plus Ruidoso's Hubbard Museum, or $3.50 for each individual site; not all sites remain open throughout the winter; ☎505/653-4372, ⓦ www. nmmonuments.org & ⓦ www.hubbardmuseum.org).

Displays in the **Historic Lincoln Visitors Center**, at the east end of town (daily 8.30am–5pm), cover Hispanics, cowboys, "Buffalo Soldiers" – the black cavalrymen stationed at nearby Fort Stanton – and Apaches, as well as the Lincoln County War. Billy the Kid's most famous jailbreak is commemorated at the **Lincoln County Courthouse** (daily 8.30am–5pm), at the other end of the street; waiting here under sentence of death, he shot his way out and fled to Fort Sumner, where Sheriff Pat Garrett eventually caught up with him (see p.940). On the first weekend of August the streets echo with gunfire once again, during the three-day **Old Lincoln Days** festival.

Near the courthouse, the *Wortley Hotel* – once owned by Sheriff Pat Garrett – offers seven plain but appealing **hotel** rooms (℡505/653-4300 or 1-877/967-8539, ⓦwww.wortleyhotel.com; April 28 to mid-Oct only; ❸), and its **dining room** serves simple stews and sandwiches at lunchtime only. If you like a bit more comfort, head to the nearby *Casa de Patrón* **B&B** (℡505/653-4676, ⓦwww.casapatron.com; ❹.

Ruidoso

The **Sacramento**, **Capitan**, and **Jicarilla mountains**, which rise at the western edge of the Llano Estacado, 85 miles northwest of Carlsbad, form a rare respite from the scrubby flatness. Spread out along winding roads that cut through dense groves of pine, fir, and aspen, the main town here, **RUIDOSO**, is the fastest-growing resort in the Southwest.

The **Ruidoso Downs** racetrack, just east of town, plays host to a 77-day racing season that culminates on Labor Day with the **All-American Futurity**, one of the world's richest horse races. Alongside, the **Hubbard Museum of the American West** (daily 10am–5pm; $6; ℡505/378-4142, ⓦwww.hubbardmuseum.org) holds displays on the natural and human-related history of horses, with a selection of memorabilia from around the world such as horse-drawn Russian sleighs, English road coaches, and Wild West stagecoaches.

In winter, attention turns to the 12,000-foot slopes of **Ski Apache** (℡505/336-4356, ⓦwww.skiapache.com), a downhill ski area northwest of town on Hwy-532 where lift tickets cost around $54 per day. Though operated by the Mescalero Apache, it's not on tribal land – they bought it as a going concern.

Ruidoso's **visitor center**, 720 Sudderth Ave (Mon–Sat 9am–5pm, Sun 1–4pm; ℡505/257-7395 or 1-877/784-3676, ⓦwww.ruidoso.net), provides lists of dozens of **motels**, such as the inexpensive *Apache*, 344 Sudderth Ave (℡505/257-2986 or 1-800/426-0616, ⓦwww.ruidoso.net/apache; ❷. The glitzy *Inn of the Mountain Gods*, three miles southwest on Carrizo Canyon Road (℡505/257-5141 or 1-800/545-9011, ⓦwww.innofthemountaingods.com; winter ❼, summer ❽) is, like the ski resort, owned by the Mescalero Apache, and holds a lucrative casino as well as fine dining and luxury accommodation. Other eating possibilities range from the classy French cuisine of *Le Bistro*, 2800 Sudderth Drive (closed Sun; ℡505/257-0132), to the sandwiches and coffee at the nearby *Books and Beans*, 2501 Sudderth Drive (lunch only, closed Sun; ℡505/630-2326).

White Sands National Monument

Filling a broad valley west of Ruidoso and the Sacramento Mountains, the **White Sands** are 250 square miles of glistening, three-story-high dunes, not of sand, but of finely ground gypsum eroded from the nearby peaks. Most of the desert valley is under the control of the military, who use it as a missile range and training ground, and as a landing site for the **space shuttle**; only the southern half of the dunes is protected within **White Sands National Monument** (and even that is often closed for an hour or two at a time while missile tests are under way). The best place to start is at the **visitor center**, just off US-70, which illuminates the unique plants and animals that dwell here (daily: late May to early Sept 9am–7pm; early Sept to late May 8am–5pm; ℡505/479-6124, ⓦwww.nps.gov/whsa). An eight-mile paved road ($3) stretches into the heart of the dunes, where you can scramble and slide in the sheer white landscape.

ALAMOGORDO, which sits at the base of the Sacramento Mountains, sixteen miles east of the Monument along US-54, holds the nearest food and lodging.

Las Cruces and Mesilla

From White Sands, US-70 heads southwest across the Tularosa Valley to **LAS CRUCES** – "the Crosses" – a large, modern farming community on the Rio Grande at the junction of I-10 and I-25. The town takes its name from the dozens of white crosses set up in the sands to mark the graves of early travelers killed by the Apache, but any real sense of its history is pretty well buried by motels and fast-food franchises. It's a prosperous place, though, and likely to become more so if, as anticipated, the **Southwest Regional Spaceport**, currently being built in the empty desert roughly 45 miles northeast, becomes the base for the first-ever passenger spaceflights, due to be operated by Virgin Galactic (Ⓦwww.virgingalactic .com) from 2008 onwards.

The little-changed Hispanic village of **MESILLA**, just south of I-10 two miles west, was until the 1870s one of the Southwest's largest towns, with upward of eight thousand inhabitants. During the Civil War, it even served briefly as the Confederate capital of New Mexico and Arizona, but it went into swift decline when the railroad bypassed it in favor of Las Cruces in 1881. Mesilla's delightful Old West **plaza** has a real frontier feel to it, even though most of the old adobes that surround it now house art galleries and souvenir shops. Such is the fate of the former courthouse where Billy the Kid was tried and sentenced to death in 1881. **Restaurants** include the steak-oriented *Double Eagle* (Ⓣ505/523-6700), while the *Mesón de Mesilla*, 1803 Av de Mesilla (Ⓣ505/525-2380 or 1-800/732-6025, Ⓦwww.mesondemesilla.com; ❸–❻, a gorgeous "boutique resort" **hotel** five minutes' walk east, has a top-class dining room, plus fifteen guest rooms offering widely varying facilities.

The southwest corner

I-10 heads west from Las Cruces across the wide-open rangeland that fills out the southwest corner of New Mexico, also known as the "**Bootheel**" for the way it steps down toward Mexico. It's so sparsely inhabited that there are roughly three square miles per person. Towns are few and far between: both **DEMING**, sixty miles west of Las Cruces, and **LORDSBURG**, on I-10 twenty miles short of Arizona, hold Amtrak stations, plus a string of gas stations, cafés, and motels, but little else.

Silver City

Rarely visited and almost entirely wilderness, the semi-arid, forested, volcanic **Mogollon** and **Mimbres mountains** soar above the high desert plain of southwest New Mexico to over ten thousand feet, and remain little altered since Apache warrior **Geronimo** was born here at the headwaters of the Gila River.

Halfway up the mountains, the biggest settlement, **SILVER CITY**, lies 45 miles north of I-10 at the junction of US-180 from Deming and Hwy-90 from Lordsburg. The Spanish came here in 1804, sold the Mimbreño Indians into slavery, and opened the **Santa Rita copper mine**, just east of town below the Kneeling Nun monolith. The town was re-established in 1870 as a rough-and-tumble silver camp – **Billy the Kid** spent most of his childhood here. A fine selection of ornate old buildings is scattered along elm-lined avenues and across the hills. The excellent **Silver City Museum** at 312 W Broadway (Tues–Fri 9am–4.30pm, Sat & Sun 10am–4pm; free) tells the boom-and-bust tales, and holds fine specimens of **Casas Grandes pottery**, beautiful Navajo rugs, and basketry from all the major Southwest tribes.

In downtown Silver City, the *Palace Hotel*, 106 W Broadway (Ⓣ505/388-1811, Ⓦwww.zianet.com/palacehotel; ❸), is a small, nicely restored nineteenth-century hotel. Just outside town, *Bear Mountain Guest Ranch* (℡505/538-2538 or 1-877/620-2327, ⊛www.bearmountainlodge.com; ❺) is a large 1920s ranch, now run as a B&B, that makes a great base for bird-watching, cycling, mountain biking, or cross-country skiing. Bullard Street in the heart of town holds **saloons and cafés** like the *Jalisco Café* at no. 100 (℡505/388-2060).

Arizona

The tourism industry in **ARIZONA** has, literally, one colossal advantage – the **Grand Canyon** of the Colorado River, which is the single most awe-inspiring spectacle in a land of unforgettable geology. However, the Grand Canyon is by no means the most interesting or memorable destination in the state. Indeed, in comparison to its inhuman scale, other parts of Arizona have a more abiding emotional impact, precisely because of the sheer drama of human involvement in this forbidding but deeply resonant desert landscape.

Over a third of the state still belongs to the **Native Americans** who have lived here for centuries, and who outside the cities form the majority of the population. In the so-called **Indian Country** of northeastern Arizona, the reservation lands of the **Navajo Nation** hold the stupendous **Canyon de Chelly** and dozens of other marvelously sited **Ancestral Puebloan ruins,** as well as the stark rocks of **Monument Valley**. The Navajo surround the homeland of one of the most stoutly traditional of all Native American peoples, the **Hopi**, who live in remote **mesa-top villages**. The third main tribal group is the **Apache**, in the harshly beautiful southeastern mountains – the last Native Americans to give in to the overwhelming power of the white American invaders.

Away from the reservations, **Wild West** towns like **Tombstone**, site of the famed gunfight at the OK Corral, give a clear sense of Arizona's rough-and-ready, pioneer mentality; this was the last of the lower 48 states to join the Union, in 1912. The **cities**, however, are not nearly so much fun. In **Phoenix**, the capital, well over a million souls are scattered over a 500-square-mile morass of shopping malls and tract-house suburbs; **Tucson** is rather more appealing, but is still liable to wear thin after a couple of days.

Though the open spaces of southern Arizona can be harsh, the bleakness is balanced somewhat by the many nature reserves that protect its amazing flora and fauna, such as **Saguaro National Park**, just outside Tucson, with its giant cactuses, real-life roadrunners, and rare Gila monsters.

Getting around Arizona

Arizona is better served by public transportation than much of the Southwest, but it's still hard to get around without a car. Greyhound **buses** stop at the major cities and most towns along the interstates, while Amtrak **trains** cross the state on two transcontinental routes (via Tucson in the south, or Flagstaff further north). Seeing the backcountry, however, is all but impossible without a car. The largest airport is at Phoenix.

Tucson, Phoenix, and southern Arizona

Most of Arizona's compelling natural attractions are in its northern reaches, but the **southern** half of the state holds ninety percent of its people, all its significant cities, and several important historic sites. The bulk of what there is to see is frontier Americana, especially in **Tombstone**, in the southeast corner. **Phoenix**, the state capital, is huge, sprawling, and dull; **Tucson** makes a better base.

Tucson and around

After serving as a Colonial outpost under the Spanish and Mexicans, and then as territorial capital for both the US and Confederate governments, **TUCSON** (pronounced *TOO-sonn*) – a mere sixty miles north of Mexico on the cross-country I-10 – has grown into a modern metropolis of around 900,000 people without entirely sacrificing its historic quarters. Now equal parts college town and retirement community, it's one of the more attractive big cities of the Southwest – which admittedly isn't saying much. Although it suffers from the same Sunbelt sprawl as Albuquerque and Phoenix, it does have a compact center, some enjoyable restaurants, and pretty good nightlife, energized by the 35,000 students at the University of Arizona. The city is also redeemed by having so much superb landscape within easy reach, from the forested flanks of **Mount Lemmon** to the rolling foothills of **Saguaro National Park**.

Arrival and information

Tucson International Airport, eight miles south of downtown (☎520/573-8100), receives far fewer long-distance flights than Phoenix. It's connected to central Tucson by the slow Sun Tran **bus** #11 or #6 ($1), and the $15 shuttle vans of Arizona Stagecoach (☎520/889-1000, ⓦwww.azstagecoach.com). For **taxi** service, call Allstate Cab (☎520/798-1111). The Amtrak station, downtown at 400 E Toole Ave, is served by three **trains** weekly in each direction between Los Angeles and points east, with connecting buses running north to Phoenix. Greyhound **buses** also stop very centrally, at 2 S Fourth Ave.

Tucson's **visitor center** is downtown at 100 S Church Ave (Mon–Fri 8am–5pm, Sat & Sun 9am–4pm; ☎520/624-1817 or 1-800/638-8350, ⓦwww.visittucson.org). Gray Line (☎520/622-8811 or 1-800/276-1528; ⓦwww.graylinearizona.com) offers $45 **city tours** by bus, and can also take you further afield, including to San Xavier Mission ($35), Nogales ($65–85), or Tombstone and Bisbee ($105).

Accommodation

Tucson has reasonably priced **hotels** and **motels** in the central area, as well as some atmospheric **B&Bs** both in the historic center and out in the desert. It also has its fair share of **resorts** and **dude ranches**. Rates drop when the mercury rises, and some places are open only in the peak winter and spring seasons.

Catalina Park Inn 309 E First St ☎520/792-4541 or 1-800/792-4885, ⓦwww.catalinaparkinn.com. A beautiful yet not overly fussy six-room historic B&B. Across from a quiet park and within walking distance of the university and Fourth Avenue. Closed early July to early Sept. Summer ❹, winter ❺

EconoLodge 3020 S Sixth Ave ☎520/623-5881 or 1-800/553-2666, ⓦwww.econolodge.com. With its pleasant rooms and well-maintained pool, this inexpensive motel, west of the airport, represents the best value you're likely to find close to downtown. ❸

Flamingo Hotel 1300 N Stone Ave ☎520/770-1910 or 1-800/300-3533, ⓦwww.flamingohoteltucson.com. Despite recent renovations, this Western-themed motel, a mile north of downtown, remains a plain budget option, but it does have a pool and spa. ❸

Hotel Congress 311 E Congress St ☎520/622-8848 or 1-800/722-8848,

Ⓦ www.hotelcongress.com. Central, bohemian hotel, an easy walk from Amtrak, with vintage Art Deco furnishings, $20 hostel beds for HI/AYH members (no reservations), and forty plain en-suite guest rooms. There's a small café and a lively bar downstairs, and at night it's one of the hottest music venues in town. ❶–❸

Roadrunner Hostel 346 E Twelfth St Ⓣ 520/628-4709, Ⓦ www.roadrunnerhostel.com. Small and very central independent hostel in a downtown home, offering space in six-bed dorms for $20 per night or $120 per week, and private rooms for $38, plus Internet access. Free pickup from Amtrak and Greyhound. ❶

Tanque Verde Ranch 14301 E Speedway Blvd Ⓣ 520/296-6275 or 1-800/234-3833, Ⓦ www. tanqueverderanch.com. Arizona's most authentic dude ranch, an irresistibly romantic 400-acre spread adjoining Saguaro National Park twenty miles east of downtown. Luxury accommodation in individual *casitas* and a stable of over a hundred horses. Rates include all meals and a full program of rides. ❾

Westward Look Resort 245 E Ina Rd Ⓣ 520/297-1151 or 1-800/722-2500, Ⓦ www.westwardlook. com. Plush resort, in attractive landscaped grounds north of the city, that retains its atmospheric 1912 core but now holds 250 extra-large rooms and suites in very private, low-slung *casitas*. Summer ❺, winter ❽

The Town

Tucson has two main historic centers: the **downtown core** along the (usually bone-dry) Santa Cruz River, bisected by Congress Street, and the quarter around the **University of Arizona** campus, a mile to the east. The city was founded in the late 1700s by Catholic missionaries who came from Mexico, then a Spanish colony, to convert the Pima Indians. Nothing very substantial remains from this era, but hundreds of artifacts are now displayed inside the many historic adobe homes in and around the **El Presidio** district of cafés, art galleries, and B&Bs, two blocks north of Broadway. Access to much of El Presidio is controlled by the **Tucson Museum of Art**, 140 N Main Ave (Tues–Sat 10am–4pm, Sun noon–4pm; $8, under-13s free; free first Sun of month; Ⓦ www.tucsonarts.com). The main building displays changing exhibitions of modern paintings and sculpture, while an adjoining adobe holds an excellent collection of folk art and pre-Columbian artifacts. The district's oldest house, La Casa Cordova, showcases the city's Mexican heritage.

Three blocks south, engulfed by the Tucson Convention Center complex, the adobe **Sosa-Carrillo-Frémont House**, 151 S Granada Ave (Wed–Sat 10am–4pm; free), is the sole survivor of a neighborhood torn down during the 1960s. Built for merchant Leopoldo Carrillo in 1858, it was briefly rented by former explorer John C. Frémont when he was Governor of Arizona in 1878. Though much restored, it offers a vivid sense of the more civilized side of frontier life.

Tucson's other main area of interest, around the University of Arizona, spreads between Sixth Street and Speedway Boulevard, a mile east of downtown. Its chief highlight is the on-campus **Arizona State Museum** (Mon–Sat 10am–5pm, Sun noon–5pm; free; Ⓦ www.statemuseum.arizona.edu), where an exceptionally comprehensive assembly of Native American artifacts traces the evolution of the various Southwest tribes.

Arizona-Sonora Desert Museum

Part zoo, part garden, the top notch **Arizona-Sonora Desert Museum** is fourteen miles west of the university along Speedway Boulevard, in Tucson Mountain Park (daily: June–Aug Sun–Fri 7.30am–5pm, Sat 7.30am–10pm; March–May & Sept 7.30am–5pm; Oct–Feb 8.30am–5pm; adults $9, ages 6–12 $2 May–Oct; adults $12, ages 6–12 $4 Nov–April; Ⓣ 520-883-1380; Ⓦ www.desertmuseum. org). Indoor displays, including a walk-through cave and mine, highlight regional geology and history, and a series of glass-fronted cages are occupied by tarantulas, rattlesnakes, and other creepy-crawlies. Along the looped path beyond – a hot walk in high summer – bighorn sheep, mountain lions, jaguars, and other sel-

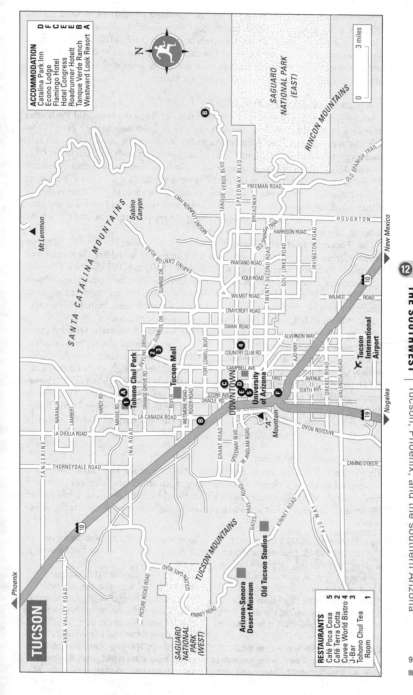

TUCSON

Phoenix ▲

ACCOMMODATION
Catalina Park Inn   D
Econo Lodge   F
Flamingo Hotel   C
Hotel Congress   E
Roadrunner Hotelt   E
Tanque Verde Ranch   B
Westward Look Resort   A

N

SANTA CATALINA MOUNTAINS

Mt Lemmon ▲

Sabino
Canyon

0   3 miles

SAGUARO
NATIONAL PARK
(EAST)

RINCON MOUNTAINS

New Mexico ▶

Nogales ▶

✈ Tucson
International
Airport

TUCSON MOUNTAINS

SAGUARO
NATIONAL PARK
(WEST)

Arizona-Sonora
Desert Museum

Old Tucson Studios

DOWNTOWN

University
of Arizona

Tucson Mall

Tohono Chul Park

"A"
Mountain

RESTAURANTS
Café Poca Cosa   5
Café Terra Cotta   2
Cuvee World Bistro   4
J-Bar   3
Tohono Chul Tea
Room   1

dom-seen desert denizens prowl in credible enclosed simulations of their natural habitats, and a colony of impish prairie dogs goes about its impenetrable business. Hawks and bald eagles fly about their own large aviary, thankfully separated from a greenhouse full of hummingbirds. The museum also serves as an animal rescue center: almost all the animals you see were injured in some way before ending up here, and would be unable to survive on their own.

Saguaro National Park

Flanking Tucson to either side, the two sections of **Saguaro National Park** offer visitors a rare and enthralling opportunity to stroll through strange desert "forests" of monumental, multi-limbed **saguaro** (pronounced *sa-wah-row*) cactuses. Each saguaro can grow up to fifty feet tall and weigh up to eight tons, but it takes around 150 years to do so. Whatever you may have seen in the movies, you can drive a long way in Arizona without seeing one; saguaro are unique to the Sonora Desert, and the thrill when you finally encounter a thousand at once is deeply satisfying. Both segments of the park can be seen on short forays from the city: in summer, it's far too hot to do more than pose for photographs, and there is no lodging, or even permanent campground.

The **Tucson Mountain District** stretches north from the Desert Museum around fifteen miles west of downtown Tucson, on the far side of the mountains. Beyond the **visitor center** (daily 8.30am–5pm; $10; ☏520/733-5158, ⊛www. nps.gov/sagu), the nine-mile **Bajada Loop Drive** – not fully paved, but always passable to ordinary vehicles – loops through a wonderland of weird saguaro, offering plentiful short hiking trails and photo opportunities. Signal Hill is especially recommended, for its petroglyphs and superb sunset views.

To reach the eastern section of the park, the **Rincon Mountain District** (same ticket, or $10 per vehicle; ☏520/733-5153), drive seventeen miles east of town, first along Broadway Boulevard and then Old Spanish Trail. Here, too, short trails such as the quarter-mile Desert Ecology Trail lead off the eight-mile **Cactus Forest Drive** (daily: April–Oct 7am–7pm; Nov–March 7am–5pm), but many visitors come specifically to hike far from the road, up into the mountains. The saguaro cactuses thin out almost as soon as you start climbing the Tanque Verde Ridge Trail, which leads in due course to a hundred-mile network of remote footpaths through thickly forested canyons.

Eating and drinking

Tucson has a fine selection of **restaurants**, but be warned that downtown shuts down pretty early – it's hard to find anything open after 9pm. Mexican joints and cowboy-style Wild West steakhouses abound in the central districts, while fancier restaurants congregate further north in the Foothills, and especially in the resort hotels.

Café Poca Cosa 120 E Pennington St ☏520/622-6400. Popular and stylish downtown café that serves tasty, inexpensive Mexican – or to be more precise, Sonoran – cuisine with a great deal of contemporary Southwestern flair. Typical highlights on the short blackboard menu include shredded beef and cod with clams. Entrees under $10 at lunch, around $19 at dinner. Closed Sun.

Café Terra Cotta 3500 Sunrise Drive ☏520/577-8100. Inventive Southwestern cuisine, way north of downtown in the Foothills. The menu ranges from

gourmet pizzas cooked in a wood-burning oven to meats grilled with chiles, with typical entrees priced around $20.

Cup Café *Hotel Congress*, 311 E Congress St ☏520/798-1618. Jazzy downtown café, straight out of the 1930s but updated to include an espresso bar, and serving a bewilderingly broad menu from 7am until after midnight daily.

Cuvee World Bistro 3352 E Speedway Blvd ☏520/881-7577, ⊛www.cuveebistro.com. The eclectic menu at this playfully opulent yet casual bistro samples pretty much any world cuisine. All entrees, from crispy sea bass to mahogany roasted duck, are priced at under $20, and there's live music on weekends. Closed Sun.

J-Bar *Westin La Paloma Resort*, 3770 E Sunrise Blvd ☏ 520/615-6000. Terrific Southwest-Mex cuisine by Tucson's nationally acclaimed chef Janos Wilder at half the price of his upscale restaurant,

Janos, next door. That and the view make it work the trip north to the Foothills. Closed Sun.

Tohono Chul Tea Room Tohono Chul Park, 7366 N Paseo del Norte ☏ 520/797-1222. Attractive adobe café in a small desert park on the northern fringes of town. Open daily 8am–5pm; ideal for breakfast, a light lunch, or a scones-and-jam afternoon tea.

Nightlife

Most of the arty **cafés** and **nightclubs** on Congress Street downtown double as bars and restaurants, while several student-oriented places can be found in the university area. There are half a dozen country-and-western saloons on the outskirts of town as well. For a full rundown, check the listings in the free *Tucson Weekly*.

Choice options include *Club Congress*, inside *Hotel Congress* at 311 E Congress St (☏ 520/622-8848), a hectic, trendy, late-opening bar with live music a couple of nights each week. For microbrews and simple food, head for *Gentle Ben's Brewing Co*, 865 E University Blvd (☏ 520/624-4177), which is regularly packed with students. A 1920s vaudeville palace, the *Rialto Theatre*, 318 E Congress St (☏ 520/740-0126, Ⓦ www.rialtotheater.com), has reopened as Tucson's hottest venue for touring bands.

South to the border: the Mission Trail

South from Tucson, I-19 heads straight for the Mexican border, 65 miles away, passing some reminders of the region's Spanish and Mexican heritage. The **Mission San Xavier del Bac** – the best-preserved mission church in the United States – lies just west of the freeway, nine miles south of downtown Tucson on the fringe of the vast arid plain of San Xavier Indian Reservation (daily 9am–6pm; donation). It was built for the Franciscans between 1783 and 1797, and even today its white-plastered walls and towers seem like a dazzling desert mirage; how much more dramatic they must have been two centuries ago, when to Christian missionaries and Apache warriors alike they symbolized the Spanish quest to subdue and convert the native peoples of the Southwest. No one knows the name of the architect responsible for its Spanish Baroque, even Moorish lines – it consists almost entirely of domes and arches, making only minimal use of timber – let alone the identities of the O'odham craftsmen who embellished its every feature. The ideal time to come is on Sunday morning, when four Masses draw large congregations from the reservation.

Forty miles further south, barely twenty miles north of the border, stands the evocative ruin of another eighteenth-century mission church, preserved as **Tumacácori National Historical Park** (daily 8am–5pm; $3 per person). Topped by a restored whitewashed dome, the mission is home only to the birds that fly down from the Patagonia Mountains. Behind its red-tinged, weather-beaten facade, the plaster has crumbled from the interior walls to reveal bare adobe bricks. A few traces of a mural can still be discerned in the raised sanctuary, but little remains of the priests' living quarters alongside. An informative museum is housed in the small **visitor center** at the entrance.

Nogales, Arizona, and Nogales, Mexico

Twenty miles south of Tumacácori, an hour from Tucson, sits the largest of the Arizona–Mexico border towns, **NOGALES** – in effect two towns, one in the US and one across the border in Mexico, which are known jointly as *Ambos Nogales* (both Nogales). There's nothing in particular to see on either side of the border, though the contrast between the orderly streets of the American town

12

THE SOUTHWEST | Tucson, Phoenix, and southern Arizona

and the jumbled white-washed houses clinging to the slopes in Mexico is striking. Nogales, Arizona is a dreary little community, while Nogales, Mexico, is basically a lively, large-scale street market.

Crossing the border is straightforward, as Mexican visas are only required by travelers heading more than 21km south of the border. US citizens should, however, carry their passports or birth certificates, while foreign visitors should check that their visa status entitles them to re-enter the US; if you're on or eligible for the Visa Waiver Scheme (see p.60), you're fine. If driving, leave your car on the US side; you'll see lots of cheap lots as you approach the border. There's no need to change money: US dollars are accepted by stores and businesses across the border.

None of the Arizona-side **motels** stands within a mile of the border; the closest is the *Best Western Siesta Motel*, 673 N Grand Ave (☎520/287-4671; ❷). Most visitors prefer to **eat** in Mexico, where abundant cafés and diners line the busy central streets. Classier dining is offered by *La Roca*, hollowed into the rocky hillside just east of the railroad, a couple of blocks from the border at calle Elias 91, where a full seafood meal costs under $20.

The southeast corner

Among thousands of acres of unspoiled and magnificent wilderness, southeast Arizona contains numerous well-preserved and highly atmospheric **ghost towns**. I-10 buzzes across the region toward the New Mexico border, but for a grand tour of the region you can detour south instead along the more scenic US-80.

Kartchner Caverns State Park

Arizona's newest state park – **Kartchner Caverns**, seven miles south of Benson – centers on caves in the Whetstone Mountains that were discovered in 1974. Unlike Carlsbad Caverns, they're unusual in being "live," or still growing, but they're not really worth traveling across the country to see, and with a visit for a family of four costing at least $60 in admission fees alone, they're also wildly overpriced.

Admission to the park costs $5 per vehicle, but visitors can only see the caves on either of two **guided tours**. The shorter tour lasts over an hour, including a tram ride to the cave entrance and 45 minutes underground, threading through the caverns' two upper "rooms," the **Throne Room** and the **Rotunda Room** (adults $19, $10 ages 7–13). The ninety-minute **Big Room** tour delves deeper into the cave system, and requires visitors to pass through no fewer than six separate airlock doors to keep humidity at the necessary level (mid-Oct to mid-April only; adults $23, $13 ages 7–13).

Most tours are fully booked, so **reservations** must be made as far in advance as possible (Mon–Fri 8am–5pm; ☎520/586-2283, ⓦwww.azstateparks.com). You have to pay the full fee by credit card when you book; the fees are not refundable, though you can change precise timings. If you turn up without a reservation and fail to get in, content yourself with the displays in the large **Discovery Center** instead (daily 7.30am–6pm).

Tombstone

Perhaps the most famous town in the Wild West, **TOMBSTONE** lies 22 miles south of I-10 on US-80, 67 miles southeast of Tucson. More than a century has passed since its mining days came to an end, but "The Town Too Tough to Die" clings to an afterlife as a tourist theme park. With its dusty streets, wooden sidewalks, and swinging saloon doors, it's surprisingly unchanged. Most adults, however, have seen too many inauthentic replicas and movie recreations for even the real thing to retain much appeal, and so Tombstone is reduced to trying to divert kids with tacky dioramas and daily shoot-outs. However, while it's much more commercialized than its counterpart in New Mexico, Lincoln (see p.942), it has to be said that it's also more fun. The best time to visit is during **Helldorado Days** in late October, when the air is cooler and the sun less harsh, and the streets are full of gun-toting strangers acting out gun battles and stagecoach robberies.

Tombstone only began life as a silver-boomtown in 1877, and by the end of the 1880s it was all but deserted again. However, on the day that gave it the notoriety that's kept it alive, its population stood at more than ten thousand. It was 2pm on October 26, 1881, when **Doc Holliday**, along with **Wyatt Earp** and his brothers Virgil and Morgan (who all served as local sheriffs), confronted a band of suspected cattle rustlers, the Clantons, in the legendary **Gunfight at the OK Corral**. Within a few minutes, three of the suspects were dead. The Earps were accused of murder, but charges were eventually dropped.

Although the gunfight in fact took place on Fremont Street, the **OK Corral** itself remains the major attraction for visitors, hosting its only daily gunfight at 2pm (daily 8.30am–5pm; $5; Ⓦ www.ok-corral.com). In a baking-hot adobe-walled courtyard, crude dummies show the supposed locations of the Earps and the Clantons, in complete contradiction to contemporary reports of the fight.

Just off the main drag at Toughnut and Third streets, the one-time seat of Cochise County now serves as **Tombstone Courthouse State Historic Park** (daily 8am–5pm; $2.50). Several well-known trials of the time took place in its little-changed courtroom. Excellent exhibits include two detailed alternative versions of what might have actually happened at the OK Corral.

Central **motels** include the *Tombstone Motel*, 502 E Fremont St (Ⓣ520/457-3478 or 1-888/455-3478, Ⓦ www.tombstonemotel.com; ❸), while the classier *Holiday Inn Express* is a mile north on US-80 W (Ⓣ520/457-9507 or 1-800/465-4329; Ⓦ www.holidayinntombstone.com; ❹). Among old-style **saloons** serving burgers and beer in a raucous atmosphere are the *Crystal Palace* at Fifth and Allen streets, and *Big Nose Kate's* at 417 E Allen St, where you can still join an ongoing card game.

Bisbee

Crammed into a narrow gorge 25 miles south of Tombstone, the town of **BISBEE** is rivaled only by Jerome, near Sedona, as Arizona's most atmospheric Victorian relic. Like Jerome, its fortunes were built on a century of mining mundane copper from the mountains, rather than a few ephemeral years of gold and silver. Its solid brick buildings stand as an enduring testament to the days when Bisbee's population of twenty thousand outstripped both Phoenix and Tucson to make it the largest city between New Orleans and San Francisco. Phelps Dodge finally closed down its Bisbee operations in 1975, having extracted more than six billion dollars' worth of metals. As the miners moved away, however, artists and retirees moved in, preserving Bisbee's original architecture while turning it into a thriving, friendly little community that caters to tourists without being overwhelmed by them.

Walking Bisbee's narrow central streets, lined with galleries and antiques stores, is a pleasure in itself, but if you'd like to know more of the background it's well worth calling in at the **Bisbee Mining and Historical Museum**, 5 Copper Queen Plaza (daily 10am–4pm; $4).

The fanciest **place to stay** is the venerable *Copper Queen Hotel*, 11 Howell Ave (Ⓣ520/432-2216, Ⓦ www.copperqueen.com; ❺), which has a plush bar and a good **restaurant** with terrace seating. On the southern outskirts of town, just beyond the Lavender Pit, is the unique opportunity to sleep in a beautifully

restored, irresistibly kitsch 1950s trailers at the *Shady Dell RV Park*, 1 Douglas Rd
(℡520/432-3567, Ⓦwww.theshadydell.com; ❷–❺).

Southwest Arizona: Yuma

There's virtually nothing in the vast desert plain of southwest Arizona to tempt
you off the twin freeways that sprint to California. The US Army stages tank
battles in its Yuma Proving Grounds between I-10 and I-8, while the air force
drops bombs and tests Stealth technology in the more mountainous region bordering Mexico. The largest town hereabouts, **YUMA**, is little more than an oversized
pit stop for freight trains and cross-country truckers. **Yuma Territorial Prison**,
now a state park (daily 8am–5pm; $4) beside the Colorado River, was known a
century ago as the "Hell Hole of Arizona," holding over a hundred of the Wild
West's most violent criminals. Its first inmates were forced to build the adobe walls
that later contained them; you can wander around the grounds and cell blocks at
will, and visit the small museum.

Neon-lit budget **motels** along the main drag include the good-value *Yuma
Cabana*, 2151 S Fourth Ave (℡928/783-8311 or 1-800/874-0811, Ⓦwww.
yumacabana.com; ❷), while the **River City Grill**, downtown at 600 W Third
St (℡928/782-7988), is a bright "international" restaurant that's Yuma's most
fashionable hangout.

Phoenix

The state capital and largest city in Arizona, **PHOENIX** holds only minimal
appeal for tourists. When it began life in the 1860s, the sweltering little farming
town stood in the heart of the large Salt River Valley, with a ready-made irrigation system left by ancient Indians (the name Phoenix honors the fact that the city
rose from the ashes of a long-vanished **Hohokam** community). Within a century,
however, Phoenix had turned into what writer Edward Abbey called "the blob that
is eating Arizona," acquiring the money and political clout to defy the self-evident
absurdity of building a huge city in a virtually waterless desert. Now the sixth largest city in the US, it has filled the entire valley, engulfing the neighboring towns
of **Scottsdale**, **Mesa**, and **Tempe**, and encompassing over a million people within
the city boundaries and more than two million in the metropolitan area. Arizona's
financial and industrial epicenter may just be getting into its stride; boosters claim
the megalopolis will one day stretch 150 miles, from Wickenburg to Tucson.

The city's phenomenal rise was originally fueled by its image as a healthy oasis,
where the desert had been tamed and transformed into a suburban idyll. While
retirees still flock to enclaves such as **Sun City**, Phoenix now has a deserved reputation as the most unpleasant city in the Southwest – Las Vegas with no casinos,
or LA with no beach. Above all, it's **hot**; between June and August daytime highs
average over 100°F, making it the hottest city outside the Middle East.

In winter, when temperatures rarely drop below 65°F, snowbirds from colder
climes arrive in large numbers. They pay vast sums to warm their bones in the
luxury resorts and spas, concentrated especially in Scottsdale, that are the modern
equivalent of the 1930s dude ranches. Unlike golf, tennis, and shopping, sightseeing rarely ranks high on the agenda – which is just as well, since there's a good
deal of truth in the charge laid by Phoenix's older arch-rival, Tucson, that the city
is sorely lacking in culture and history. Apart from the **Heard Museum**'s excellent Native American displays, the cactuses at the **Desert Botanical Garden**, and
Frank Lloyd Wright's architecture studio at **Taliesin West**, Phoenix is short of
must-see attractions. In fact, if you're on a touring vacation, you'd miss little if
you bypassed it altogether.

Arrival, information, and getting around

Sky Harbor International Airport is three miles east of downtown (☎602/273-3300, ⓦwww.phxskyharbor.com). Red Line **buses** on the Valley Metro system (☎602/253-5000, ⓦwww.valleymetro.org/transit/) connect the airport with downtown daily, plus Tempe and Mesa on weekdays, but it's easier to take a door-to-door **shuttle bus**, at $10–12 for downtown destinations and $20 for Scottsdale, with SuperShuttle (☎602/244-9000 or 1-800/258-3826, ⓦwww.supershuttle.com). Arizona Shuttle Services (☎928/795-6671 or 1-800/888-2749, ⓦwww.arizonashuttle.com) runs an hourly service south to Tucson, costing $29. There's no Amtrak **train** service to Phoenix, but Greyhound **buses** arrive at 2115 E Buckeye Rd (☎602/389-4200), close to the airport.

Phoenix is such a vast city, and one so utterly dependent on car travel, that it's much easier to drive than to use public transport – though you shouldn't underestimate the sheer length of time it takes to get from one side of the city to the other. That said, tourists may find the purple DASH buses useful, which run between the Arizona Center and the Capitol downtown (Mon–Fri 6.30am–5.30pm; shorter downtown loop continues until 11pm; free). For a **cab**, call Checker Cab (☎602/257-1818).

Phoenix's main **visitor center** is downtown at 50 N Second St, at Adams (Mon–Fri 8am–5pm; ☎602/254-6500 or 1-877/225-5749, ⓦwww.phoenixcvb.

DOWNTOWN PHOENIX

ACCOMMODATION
Budget Lodge Motel   B
Metcalf House Hostel   A
San Carlos   C

RESTAURANTS
Alice Cooper'stown   4
Carly's Bistro   1
Pizzeria Bianco   3
Sam's Cafe   2

0   800 yds

com); there's another office at the Biltmore Fashion Park at 2404 E Camelback Rd (Mon–Fri 10am–9pm, Sat 10am–6pm, Sun noon–6pm; ☎602/955-1963). **Scottsdale** has its own visitor center at 4343 N Scottsdale Rd (Mon–Fri 8am–5.30pm; ☎480/421-1004 or 1-800/782-1117, ⓦwww.scottsdalecvb.com); **Tempe** has one at 51 W Third St (Mon–Fri 8am–5pm; ☎480-894-8158 or 1-800/283-6734, ⓦwww.tempecvb.com); as does **Mesa**, at 120 N Center St (Mon–Fri 8am–5pm; ☎480-827-4700, ⓦwww.mesacvb.com).

Accommodation

Metropolitan Phoenix is so huge that it's worth paying a bit extra to ensure that your **accommodation** is near the places you want to visit. Oddly enough, downtown Phoenix is not one of the more expensive areas, with cheap motels lining the somewhat run-down W Van Buren Street a few blocks north of the center. The summer room rates, given below, rise significantly in winter.

Arizona Biltmore Resort & Spa 2400 E Missouri Ave ☎602/955-6600 or 1-800/950-0086, ⓦwww.arizonabiltmore.com. Extraordinarily lavish 500-room resort, a few miles northeast of downtown, built under the influence of Frank Lloyd Wright in the 1930s and still retaining its Art Deco trimmings. Two golf courses, three restaurants, plus tennis and spa. ❾

Budget Lodge Motel 402 W Van Buren St ☎602/254-7247. Reasonably attractive rooms at very attractive rates, in an unexciting motel setting. Not far from downtown, but you'll feel safer if you drive rather than walk. ❷

Days Inn Scottsdale Fashion Square Resort 4710 N Scottsdale Rd, Scottsdale ☎480/947-5411 or 1-800/325-2525, ⓦwww.scottsdaledaysinn.com. Though not all that prepossessing, this two-story motel, immediately north of Fashion Square Mall, has perfectly acceptable rooms plus an outdoor pool, and can be a real bargain. Summer ❸, winter ❹

Fiesta Inn 2100 S Priest Drive, Tempe ☎480/967-1441 or 1-800/528-6481, ⓦwww.fiestainnresort.com. Old-style resort, not as plush as its Scottsdale counterparts, but not as expensive either, offering large rooms plus restaurant, pool, tennis courts, and spa. Summer ❹, winter ❼

Metcalf House Hostel, 1026 N Ninth St above Roosevelt St ☎602/254-9803, http://home.earthlink.net/~phxhostel/. Budget hostel in a slightly run-down residential district, 15min walk

north of the Arizona Center downtown. No phone reservations, but space is usually available. Check in 5–10pm, or, usually but not always, 7–10am. Dorm beds at $15 for HI/AYH members, $18 non-members.

Motel 6 On Camelback 6848 E Camelback Rd, Scottsdale ☎480/946-2280 or 1-800/466-8356, ⓦwww.motel6.com. Cut-price lodgings are few and far between in Scottsdale, so this budget motel, just off I-17 close to downtown, is well worth considering. ❷

Hotel San Carlos 202 N Central Ave ☎602/253-4121 or 1-866/253-4121, ⓦwww.hotelsancarlos.com. Historic Twenties' hotel in the heart of downtown, with tasteful good-value rooms, a nice café, and a rooftop swimming pool. ❻

Super 8 Mesa 6733 E Main St, Mesa ☎480/981-6181 or 1-800/800-8000, ⓦwww.super8.com. Budget chain motel to the east of central Mesa, en route toward the Superstition Mountains. Summer ❷, winter ❸

Tempe Mission Palms Hotel 60 E Fifth St, Tempe ☎480/894-1400 or 1-800/547-8705, ⓦwww.missionpalms.com. Very comfortable Southwestern-themed hotel in Tempe's revitalized Mill Avenue district, with a rooftop swimming pool. Summer ❺, winter ❾

Tempe Super 8 Motel 1020 E Apache Blvd, Tempe ☎480/967-8891 or 1-800/800-8000. Chain motel, within half a mile of the university and five miles of the airport. Summer ❷, winter ❸

Central Phoenix

Downtown Phoenix – defined as the few blocks east and west of Central Avenue, and north and south of Washington Street – is too spread out to walk around in any comfort. Nonetheless, determined efforts are being made to regenerate and revitalize it; three billion dollars have been pumped into new construction, and a ninety-block district has been rebranded with a new name – **Copper Square**. The major landmarks are two massive side-by-side sports stadiums, the **America West**

Arena and the **Bank One Ballpark**, home respectively to basketball's Phoenix Suns and baseball's Arizona Diamondbacks. Adjoining those is the one significant downtown **mall**, the **Arizona Center**, on Van Buren Street between Third and Fifth.

What little remains of Phoenix's nineteenth-century architecture now constitutes **Heritage Square**, a couple of blocks southeast at 115 N Sixth St. Rather than original adobe ranch houses, however, it preserves a quaint assortment of Victorian homes, converted into tearooms and toy museums. You can get a better impression of the early days at the **Phoenix Museum of History**, across the street at 105 N Fifth St (Tues–Sat 10am–5pm; $6; Ⓦ www.pmoh.org), which features the city's first jail – a rock with a chain attached.

Two more significant attractions lie a mile or so north of downtown. Thanks to extensive remodeling, the **Phoenix Art Museum**, 1625 N Central Ave (Tues, Wed & Fri–Sun 10am–5pm, Thurs 10am–9pm; $9, free Thurs; Ⓦ www.phxart. org), has plenty of space to display its permanent collection, which includes paintings by Georgia O'Keeffe and Rufino Tamayo, as well as *de rigueur* Western art by Russell and Remington and some middleweight Old Masters, and features stimulating temporary exhibitions as well. Three blocks north and a block east, the **Heard Museum**, 22 E Monte Vista Rd (daily 9.30am–5pm; $10; ☎602/252-8848, Ⓦ www.heard.org), has also been greatly enlarged, while still showcasing the lovely old buildings in which it was founded. While the displays themselves have been somewhat "dumbed down," it still offers a good introduction to the culture of the **Native Americans** of the Southwest. There's a special emphasis on the Hohokam, with artifacts from the large town, now known as "La Ciudad," which occupied the site of modern Phoenix during the twelfth century. Elsewhere, the superb pottery collection ranges from stunning Mimbres bowls to modern Hopi ceramics, but best of all is a wonderful array of Hopi **kachina dolls**.

In **Papago Park** at the south end of Scottsdale, the fascinating **Desert Botanical Garden** (daily: Oct–April 8am–8pm; May–Sept 7am–8pm; $10; Ⓦ www. dbg.org) is filled with an amazing array of cactuses and desert flora from around the world. Prime specimens include spineless "totem pole" cactuses from the Galápagos Islands, and "living stone" plants from South Africa. Separate enclaves are devoted to **butterflies** – at their best in August and September – and **hummingbirds**, of which Arizona boasts fifteen indigenous species.

Taliesin West

Whatever its general appearance may suggest, Phoenix has managed to attract some visionary designers. **Frank Lloyd Wright** came to the city to work on the *Biltmore Hotel*, and stayed for most of the 25 years before his death in 1959. His winter studio, **Taliesin West** – at 114th Street and Frank Lloyd Wright Boulevard, at Scottsdale's northeastern edge – is now an architecture school and a working design studio, with multimedia exhibits of the man's life and work (Oct–May daily 10am–4pm; June & Sept daily 9am–4pm; July & Aug Mon & Thurs–Sun 9am–4pm; ☎480/860-2700, Ⓦ www.franklloydwright.org). It's still a splendidly isolated spot, and one where his trademark "organic architecture" makes perfect sense. The site can only be seen on **guided tours**; you can join either an hour-long "Panorama Tour" ($18) or a ninety-minute "Insight Tour" ($22), which are offered at regular intervals, increased to more than one every half-hour between February and mid-April. The expertise and enthusiasm of the guides makes the experience well worth the price.

Eating

Unless you're prepared to pay resort prices, it's hard to find a good **restaurant** in Phoenix with very much atmosphere. Apart from a block or two in central Scottsdale, and Tempe's lively Mill Avenue, no areas of the metropolis are small enough to walk around while you look for a place to eat, but if you're happy to drive, neighborhood diners – especially Mexican – can still be found.

Alice Cooper'stown 101 E Jackson St ☎602/253-7337. Barbecue restaurant-cum-sports bar, owned by the rock star and alongside downtown's America West Arena. The food's better than you'd expect, and the atmosphere is fun, with waiters in full Alice make-up. Lunch and dinner daily.

Bandera 3821 N Scottsdale Rd, Scottsdale ☎480/994-3524. Chicken cooked in the wood-burning oven is the specialty in this busy, inexpensive rotisserie in downtown Scottsdale, but other meats and fish are almost as good. Daily for dinner only.

Carly's Bistro 128 E Roosevelt St ☎602/262-2759. Pleasant, relaxing bistro in the artsy part of downtown, serving healthy Mediterranean sandwiches, salads and light meals, and offering regular live music. Closed Sun.

House of Tricks 114 E Seventh St, Tempe ☎480/968-1114. Tiny, romantic modern-American place in the university district, with lots of vegetarian options. Closed Sun.

Monti's La Casa Vieja 3 W First St, Tempe ☎480/967-7594. Tempe's oldest adobe house, built in 1873, is now a Western-themed diner serving a conventional steak-and-chicken menu at extraordinarily low prices. Lunch and dinner daily.

Pizzeria Bianco Heritage Square, 623 E Adams St ☎602/258-8300. High-quality pizzas in a very convenient downtown location; no wonder it's so popular. Tues–Sat 5–10pm.

Roaring Fork 4800 N Scottsdale Rd, Scottsdale ☎480/947-0795. Contemporary but unfussy Southwestern cuisine at reasonable prices from an award-winning chef, with fried chicken for $16.50, or duck breast with onion jam $24.50. Daily for dinner only.

Sam's Café Arizona Center, 455 N Third St ☎602/252-3545. Hectic downtown mall joint, with patio seating, that's nonetheless a great place to sample modern Southwestern cuisine (or as the menu calls it, Sam-Mex) or classic Mexican dishes (Mex-Mex).

Nightlife, entertainment, and sports

For a rundown of what's on musically in Phoenix, pick up the free weekly *New Times* in local record or book stores, or check out the bars and clubs listed below. Both the **Phoenix Symphony Hall**, 225 E Adams St (☎602/495-1999; ⓦwww.phoenixsymphony.org, and the **Scottsdale Center for the Arts**, 7380 E Second St (☎480/994-2787, ⓦwww.scottsdalearts.org), put on classical music, theater, and ballet. The **Arizona Diamondbacks** play major league baseball beneath the retractable roof of the Bank One Ballpark (☎602/514-8400, ⓦwww.azdiamondbacks .com), while the **Phoenix Suns** play NBA basketball at the America West Arena, 201 E Jefferson St (☎602/379-7900, ⓦwww.suns.com), and football's **Arizona Cardinals** are based at the university's Sun Devil Stadium (☎602/379-0102, ⓦwww.azcardinals.com).

Bash on Ash 230 W Fifth St, Tempe ☎480/966-5600, ⓦwww.bashonash.com. Live music venue in a sports bar in the heart of Tempe, featuring reggae, rock, soul, or salsa nightly except Mon.

e4 4282 N Drinkwater Blvd, Scottsdale ☎480/970-3325, ⓦwww.e4-az.com. Massive, eye-popping dance club, designed around air, earth, fire and water, and holding a Vegas-style "ultra-lounge" downstairs as well as the *Liquid* dance club with cascading waterfalls. Closed Sun & Mon.

Marquee Theatre 730 N Mill Ave, Tempe ☎480/829-0607, ⓦwww.luckymanonline.com.

The best venue to see big-name touring acts, with an open floor rather than seating, and good beer.

Rhythm Room 1019 E Indian School Rd, Phoenix ☎602/265-4842, ⓦwww.rhythmroom.com. Top-notch blues and jazz acts perform in an intimate atmosphere, with good barbecue to help things along.

Last Exit Bar & Grill 1425 W Southern Ave, Tempe ☎480/557-6656, ⓦwww.lastexitlive.com. Rock-oriented live music venue in an unpromising mall, where acts range from country-rock to local punks.

Central Arizona

The I-40 interstate crosses the center of Arizona, skirting the **Navajo Reservation** that fills the northeastern corner of the state. Though the narrow strip of land to either side can be extraordinarily beautiful, with double rainbows reaching across the desert plain and fiery dawns blazing along the horizon, it holds few specific places worth stopping for until you come to the **Flagstaff** area. Itself a pleasant town, Flagstaff makes a base for several interesting excursions – to ancient **Native American sites** and the New Age center of **Sedona**, but above all to the **Grand Canyon**. Beyond Flagstaff to the west, there is once again little of interest.

East of Flagstaff: Holbrook and Winslow

East of Flagstaff, two old Route 66 towns, **WINSLOW** and **HOLBROOK**, are kept alive by transcontinental truckers. Each town consists of little more than a strip of motels, such as the concrete teepees of the *Wigwam Motel* at 811 W Hopi Drive in Holbrook (☏928/524-3048, ⓦwww.galerie-kokopelli.com/wigwam; ➋). However, Winslow is now graced once more by the restored splendor of *La Posada Hotel*, at 303 E Second St (🛪 ☏928/289-4366, ⓦwww.laposada.org; ➍), which is such a totally magnificent place that it's worth going a very long way out of your way to spend a night here. A glorious fake, it was designed by Mary Jane Colter, of Grand Canyon fame, in the 1920s to emulate an 1860s hacienda. It also holds a great **restaurant**, the *Turquoise Room* (☏928/289-2888), open for all meals daily.

Petrified Forest National Park

At **Petrified Forest National Park**, which straddles I-40 a dozen miles east of Holbrook, a fossilized prehistoric forest of gigantic trees has been unearthed by erosion. The original cells of the wood have been replaced by multicolored crystals of quartz. Cross-sections, cut through with diamond saws and polished, look stunning, and can be seen in the two **visitor centers**, thirty miles apart at the north and south entrances. On the ground, however, along the various trails that set off from the park's **27-mile Scenic Drive**, the trees themselves are not always all that exciting. Segmented, crumbling, and very dark, they can seem like a bunch of logs lying in the sand; the best viewing is when the setting sun brings out rich red and orange hues.

The northern section of the national park – site of the main visitor center and **entrance station** (daily: summer 7am–7pm; winter 8am–5pm; $10 per vehicle; ☏928/524-6228, ⓦwww.nps.gov/pefo) – is renowned for its views of the **Painted Desert**, an undulating expanse of solidified sand dunes, which at different times of day take on different colors (predominantly bluish shades of gray and reddish shades of brown).

Flagstaff

Northern Arizona's liveliest and most attractive town, **FLAGSTAFF** occupies a superbly dramatic location beneath the San Francisco Peaks, halfway between New Mexico and California. Straddling the I-40 and I-17 interstates, it's both a way station for tourists en route to the Grand Canyon, just eighty miles northwest, and a worthwhile destination in its own right.

Downtown, where barely a building rises more than three stories, oozes Wild West charm. Its main thoroughfare, Santa Fe Avenue, used to be **Route 66**, while before that it was the pioneer trail west. A stroll around its central few blocks is gloriously evocative of the past. The tracks of the Santa Fe Railroad still cut downtown in two, so life in Flagstaff remains punctuated both day and night by the mournful wail of passing trains.

Ever since it was founded, in 1876, Flagstaff has been a diverse place, with a strong black and Hispanic population, and Navajo and Hopi heading in from the nearby reservations to trade. Now home to a population of just over fifty thousand, it makes an ideal base for travelers. As well as the abundant hotels, restaurants, bars, and shops downtown, outlets of the national food and lodging chains line the interstates, while hostels and student diners cater for budget travelers.

Arrival and information

Daily Amtrak **trains** stop in the center of town, where part of the station doubles as a helpful **visitor center** (Mon–Sat 8am–5pm, Sun 9am–4pm; ☏ 928/774-9541 or 1-800/842-7293, ⓦ www.flagstaffarizona.org).

Open Road Tours and Transportation (☏ 928/226-8060 or 1-800/766-7117, ⓦ www.openroadtours.com), based at the station, runs twice-daily **bus services** via Williams to the Grand Canyon (8.30am & 3pm; $27 one-way for adults, $10 for under 12s). Greyhound is a few blocks south of downtown at 399 S Malpais Lane (☏ 928/774-4573). Two local hostels – the *DuBeau* and the *Grand Canyon*, listed below – arrange inexpensive **excursions for backpackers**.

Accommodation

Flagstaff's dozens of **motels** and **B&Bs** provide reasonable value, while budget travelers can benefit from a couple of high-quality **hostels**. Most of the chain motels are congregated well to the east, but staying nearer downtown is much more fun.

DuBeau International Hostel 19 W Phoenix Ave ☏ 928/774-6731 or 1-800/398-7112, ⓦ www.dubeauhostel.com. Welcoming independent hostel just south of the tracks, whose converted en-suite motel rooms serve as four-person dorms at $18 per bed, or private doubles at around $40. Tours to the Grand Canyon (Mon, Wed, Fri & Sat, plus Tues in summer only; $55). Closed Nov–Feb.

Grand Canyon International Hostel 19 S San Francisco St ☏ 928/779-9421 or 1-888/442-2696, ⓦ www.grandcanyonhostel.com. Independent hostel, under the same friendly management as the similar *DuBeau* nearby, and offering the same tours, plus dorm beds at $18 in summer, $16 in winter, and private rooms for a little more.

Monte Vista 100 N San Francisco St ☏ 928/779-6971 or 1-800/545-3068, ⓦ www.hotelmontevista.

com. Atmospheric little 1920s hotel in the heart of downtown, where the assorted restored rooms, with and without attached bathrooms, are named for celebrity guests from Bob Hope to Michael Stipe. Rates rise by up to $20 at weekends. ❸

Super 8 West 602 W Route 66 ☏ 928/774-4581 or 1-888/324-9131, ⓦ www.dknhotels.com. Smart, good-value chain motel, arranged around an enclosed swimming pool, alongside a Barnes & Noble bookstore less than a mile southwest of downtown. ❸

Hotel Weatherford 23 N Leroux St ☏ 928/779-1919, ⓦ www.weatherfordhotel.com. Attractive old downtown hotel, with elegant wooden fittings, which is restoring its fading rooms to offer tasteful, basic accommodation, without phones or TVs. Can be noisy. ❸

The Town

Flagstaff's appealing **downtown** stretches for a few redbrick blocks north of the railroad. Filled with cafés, bars, and stores selling Route 66 souvenirs and Indian crafts, as well as outfitters specializing in tents, clothing, and all sorts of contraptions for outdoor adventures, it's a fun place to stroll around, even if it holds no significant tourist attractions or historic buildings. Your most lasting impression is likely to be of the magnificent San Francisco Peaks, rising smoothly from the plains on the northern horizon, and topped by a jagged ridge.

The exceptional **Museum of Northern Arizona**, however, three miles northwest of downtown on US-180, rivals Phoenix's Heard Museum as the best museum in the state (daily 9am–5pm; $5, under-18s $2; ⊤928/774-5213, ⓦwww.musnaz.org). Its main emphasis is on documenting Native American life, with an excellent run-through of the Ancestral Puebloan past and contemporary Navajo, Havasupai, and Hopi cultures, but it also actively encourages the development of traditional and even new skills among Native American craftworkers. The exquisite inlaid silver jewelry now made by the Hopi, for example, is the result of a museum-backed program to find work for Hopi servicemen returning from World War II.

Eating and nightlife

Central Flagstaff compensates for its paucity of high-end **restaurants** with a lively assortment of both old-style Western **diners** and eclectic **budget** options. Thanks to all those students, the area around San Francisco Street, both north and south of the tracks, is filled with vegetarian cafés and espresso bars.

Beaver Street Brewery & Whistle Stop Café 11 S Beaver St ⊤928/779-0079. Inventive sandwiches and salads, wood-fired pizza, and outdoor barbecue in the beer garden in summer.
Dara Thai 14 S San Francisco St ⊤928/774-0047. Large Thai place just south of the tracks, where the service is great and a plate of delicious pad Thai noodles costs just $7 for lunch, $9 for dinner.
Downtown Diner 7 E Aspen Ave ⊤928/774-3492. Classic Route 66 diner a block north of the main drag, featuring leatherette booths and hefty burgers and sandwiches.

Macy's European Coffee House & Bakery 14 S Beaver St ⊤928/774-2243. Not merely superb coffee, but heavenly pastries to go with it, plus more substantial vegetarian dishes such as black bean pizza, and even couscous for breakfast. You'll also find free wireless Internet and an adjacent coin laundry.
The Museum Club 3404 E Route 66 ⊤928/526-9434, ⓦwww.museumclub.com. A real oddity; this log-cabin taxidermy museum somehow transmogrified into a classic Route 66 roadhouse, saloon, and country-music venue, now a second home to hordes of dancing cowboys.

Around Flagstaff

The area around Flagstaff is rich in natural and archeological wonders, with three national monuments – **Sunset Crater**, **Wupatki**, and **Walnut Canyon** – within 25 miles. Of these, only Sunset Crater has even a campground, and none has indoor lodgings. There's no scheduled public transportation.

Sunset Crater and Wupatki national monuments

North of Flagstaff, the **San Francisco Volcanic Field** of around four hundred volcanoes is prominent on the western horizon from the Hopi Mesas, and its peaks are said to be the home of their powerful *kachina* spirits.

Some of the volcanoes are still active, though the most recent eruption was that of **Sunset Crater** (twelve miles from Flagstaff on US-89) in 1066 AD. The crater was named by John Wesley Powell for the many colors of its cone, which swells from a black base through reds and oranges to a yellow-tinged crest. It's too unstable for walkers to be allowed onto the rim, but a trail passes through lava tubes around its base. The **visitor center** is nearby (daily 8am–5pm; ⊤928/526-0502, ⓦwww.nps.gov/sucr; $3 per person), opposite the *Bonito* **campground** (⊤928/527-0866; $10; late May to mid-Oct).

A dozen miles further north, the ancient ruins at **Wupatki National Monument** appear to show different tribal groups living side by side in harmony (daily: summer 8am–7pm; winter 8am–5pm; admission $3 per person, including Sunset Crater; ⊤928/679-2365, ⓦwww.nps.gov/wupa). The **Sinagua** were joined here by many others, including the **Ancestral Puebloans**, when the Sunset Crater explosion deposited a rich new layer of topsoil. The specific site known as

Wupatki (meaning "tall" or "big house"), standing proud on its natural foundations of red sandstone, is just the largest of numerous ruins.

Walnut Canyon National Monument

Between 1100 and 1250AD, **Walnut Canyon**, ten miles east of Flagstaff just south of I-40, was home to a thriving Sinagua community. Literally hundreds of their **cliff dwellings** can still be seen nestling beneath overhangs in the sides of the canyon. They simply walled off alcoves where the softer levels of the striated rock had eroded away, and then put up partitions to make separate rooms. No single dwelling is on the same scale as at Wupatki, and only a handful are accessible to visitors, but cumulatively they make for an impressive spectacle.

A large scenic window in the **visitor center** (daily: June–Aug 8am–6pm; March–May & Sept–Nov 8am–5pm; Dec–Feb 9am–5pm; $3 per person; ☎928/526-3367, ⊛www.nps.gov/waca) gives an excellent overall view. No accommodation, and only minimal snack food, is available.

Sedona and Red Rock Country

US-89A threads its way south from Flagstaff down the spectacular **Oak Creek Canyon** to emerge after 28 miles at **Sedona**, on the threshold of the extraordinary **Red Rock Country**. Up from the valley rise giant mesas and buttes of stark red sandstone, where Zane Grey set a number of his Wild West adventures. The boom-and-bust mining town of **Jerome** looks down from a mountainside to the south, while back beside I-17 toward Phoenix are further haunting Sinagua ruins.

Sedona

There's no disputing the fact that the New Age resort of **SEDONA** enjoys a magnificent setting, amid definitive Southwestern canyon scenery. Sadly, however, the town itself adds nothing to the beauty of its surroundings. Several miles of ugly red-brick sprawl is occasionally interrupted by a mock-historical mall monstrosity. While Europeans tend to be turned off by it, many American travelers love it for its combination of luxurious accommodations and fancy restaurants, and its almost limitless opportunities for active outdoor vacationing. In particular, artists, healers, and wealthy retirees have flocked here in the last few decades, hailing it as "the next Santa Fe." Whether you love it or hate it may depend on whether you share their wide-eyed awe for angels, crystals, and all matters mystical – and whether you're prepared to pay over-the-odds prices for the privilege of joining them.

> ### Vortex Tours of Red Rock Country
>
> As few of the side roads around Sedona are paved, there's a booming business in **off-road tours**, and especially those that visit so-called "**vortexes**." These are run by companies such as the garish Pink Jeep Tours ($45–102; ☎928/282-5000 or 1-800/873-3662, ⊛www.pinkjeep.com) and Earth Wisdom Tours ($48 and up; ☎928/282-4714 or 1-800/482-4714, ⊛www.earthwisdomtours.com), who teach their clients "the ancestral secrets of the Medicine Wheel." Many of the jeep roads are perfectly passable in ordinary vehicles. So long as you're happy to remain in ignorance as to which rocks are really electromagnetic tuning forks vibrating in harmony with Alpha Centauri, there's no great need to take a commercial tour. If you *really* want to get off-road, you can also head for Legends of Sedona Ranch (☎928/282-6826 or 1-800/848-7728), where "horses are free . . . but rides ain't." An hour on **horseback** costs around $54.

Established in 1902 by one Theodore Schnebly, and named after his wife, Sedona spent most of the twentieth century as a small farming settlement. German surrealist painter Max Ernst moved here in the 1940s, while Hollywood movie-makers filmed in the area from the 1950s onward. However, Sedona's big break came in 1981, when author Page Bryant "channeled" the information that Sedona is in fact "the heart *chakra* of the planet." Since she pinpointed her first **vortex** – supposedly a point at which psychic and electromagnetic energies can be channeled for personal and planetary harmony – the town has achieved its own personal growth, and blossomed as a focus for **New Age** practitioners of all kinds.

If you don't have much time to spend exploring, a cruise along US-89A enables you to see most of the sights, albeit from a distance; the best parts are south along Hwy-179 within Coconino National Forest. The closest **vortex** to town is on **Airport Mesa**; turn left up Airport Road from US-89A as you head south, about a mile past the downtown junction known as the **"Y"**. The vortex is at the junction of the second and third peaks, just after the cattle grid. Further up, beyond the precariously sited airport, the **Shrine of the Red Rocks** looks out across the entire valley.

Sedona's **visitor center**, just north of the "Y," has full listings of lodgings and tour operators (Mon–Sat 8.30am–5pm, Sun 9am–3pm; ☎928/282-7722 or 1-800/288-7336, ⓦwww.visitsedona.com). The town is an expensive place to **stay**; what pass for budget **motels** include the *Sedona Motel*, close to the "Y" at 218 Hwy-179 (☎928/282-7187; ❸), and the renovated *Los Abrogados Lodge*, a little further north at 270 N US-89A (☎928/282-7125 or 1-800/695-4161, ⓦwww.ilxresorts.com; ❹).

Fournos, 3000 W Hwy-89A (reservations required; ☎928/282-3331), is a lovely little Greek **restaurant**, open for dinner at 6pm and 8pm from Thursday to Saturday, and for brunch on Sunday at noon; the *Coffee Pot Restaurant*, 2050 W Hwy-89A (☎928/282-6626), is a large old-style diner, serving all the burgers, Mexican dishes, and fried specials you could hope for.

Jerome

The former mining town of **JEROME**, high above the Verde Valley on US-89A thirty miles south of Sedona, is conspicuous from quite a distance: an enormous letter "J" is etched deep into the hillside above it, while a large chunk of that hillside is missing altogether, having been blown apart for **opencast copper mining**. Serious exploitation of the mineral wealth here started with the opening of the **United Verde** mine in 1876. Until the current tortuous road was built, the only way up to Jerome was the precipitous rail line connecting the mine with the world's largest copper smelter at Clarkdale.

From the 1950s, when the mines closed down, until the 1970s, Jerome was a **ghost town** in which it was possible to turn up and move into an empty house. Many who did so are still here, making a living from arts and crafts, and the town itself has made a dramatic recovery. The hillside is so steep that the houses tend to have two stories at the front and four or five at the back. Under the repeated concussion of more than two hundred miles of tunnels being blasted into the mountainside, the whole town used to slip downhill at the rate of five inches per year, and the **Sliding Jail** on Hull Avenue came to rest 225ft from where it was built.

At the highest point in town, the *Jerome Grand Hotel*, 200 Hill St (☎928/634-8200 or 1-888/817-6788; ⓦwww.jeromegrandhotel.com; ❻), is a restored Spanish Mission hotel with fabulous views. The rooms are atmospheric rather than particularly luxurious, and there's a good on-site restaurant, *The Asylum*.

Montezuma Castle National Monument

In an idyllic setting just above Beaver Creek and just east of I-17, around 25 miles from Sedona, **Montezuma Castle National Monument** focuses on a superbly preserved Sinagua **cliff dwelling** (daily: summer 8am–7pm; winter 8am–5pm; $3; ☎928/567-3322, ⊛www.nps.gov/moca). Filling an alcove in the hillside with a wall of pink adobe, its five stories taper up to fit the contours of the rock. Apparently, the fingerprints of the masons are still visible on the bricks, and the sycamore beams remain firmly in place, but visitors are not permitted to climb up.

West of Flagstaff: I-40 to California

Everything along I-40 west of Flagstaff is dominated by the road's function as the main route between Las Vegas and the Grand Canyon. The first town you reach, **WILLIAMS**, seems to exist solely to capture the passing tourist trade, with a historic **railroad** running north to the Canyon (see p.970 for more details). Forty-five miles further west at the town of **SELIGMAN**, one of the longest surviving stretches of the old Route 66 heads off on a northern loop through the **Hualapai Indian Reservation** and a dozen fading towns, **PEACH SPRINGS** in particular, that look like they're straight out of *The Grapes of Wrath*. This makes a great detour on what is otherwise a very dull drive; it also provides the best access to the less visited western reaches of the Grand Canyon, around **Havasu Canyon** (see p.975).

Unless you need to fill your tank, there's little reason to stop at **KINGMAN**, the largest town in western Arizona, from where US-93 branches north to Las Vegas and I-40 continues to Los Angeles.

Lake Havasu City

Forty miles southwest of Kingman, ten miles from the California border, a detour south leads to one of the more bizarre sights of the American desert – the old gray stone of **London Bridge**, reaching out to an artificial island across the stagnant waters of the dammed Colorado River at **LAKE HAVASU CITY**. The resort's developer, Robert P. McCulloch, bought the bridge (under the impression it was Tower Bridge – or so the story goes) for $2.4 million in the late 1960s and shipped it across the Atlantic chunk by chunk before reassembling it over a channel dug to divert water from Lake Havasu. Lake Havasu City holds an undeniable attraction for the parched urbanites of Phoenix, who flock to fish on the lake or race on jet-skis, but minimal appeal for travelers from further afield. Moreover, between March and June, it's filled with students on **spring break**, drinking and partying around the clock.

Motels abound, ranging from the perfectly adequate *Bridgeview Motel*, 101 London Bridge Rd (☎928/855-5559; ❷), to the extravagant riverfront *London Bridge Resort*, 1477 Queen's Bay Rd (☎928/855-0888 or 1-866/330-9231, ⊛www .londonbridgeresort.com; winter ❹, summer ❻), where the lobby is all but filled by a gilt replica stagecoach. *Shugrue's* (☎928/453-1400), across the bridge in the Island Fashion Mall, serves good fresh fish – even sushi – as well as salads and pasta.

The Grand Canyon

Although almost five million people visit **GRAND CANYON NATIONAL PARK** every year, the canyon itself remains beyond the grasp of the human imagination. No photograph, no set of statistics, can prepare you for such vastness. At more than one mile deep, it's an inconceivable abyss; varying between four and eighteen miles wide, it's an endless expanse of bewildering shapes and colors, glaring desert brightness and impenetrable shadow, stark promontories and soaring, never-to-be-climbed sandstone pinnacles. Somehow it's so impassive, so remote – you could never call it a disappointment, but at the same time many visitors are

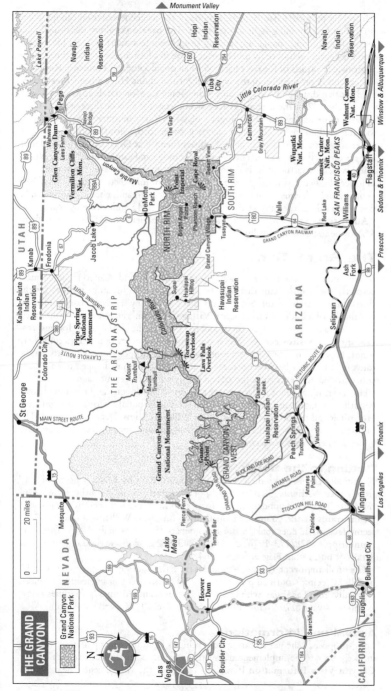

THE GRAND CANYON

Grand Canyon National Park

Monument Valley

Lake Powell

Navajo Indian Reservation

Hopi Indian Reservation

Navajo Indian Reservation

Page

Wahweap

Glen Canyon Dam

Lees Ferry

Vermilion Cliffs Nat. Mon.

Navajo Bridge

Marble Canyon

Tuba City

Little Colorado River

The Gap

Winslow & Albuquerque

Walnut Canyon Nat. Mon.

Cameron

Gray Mountain

Wupatki Nat. Mon.

Sunset Crater Nat. Mon.

SAN FRANCISCO PEAKS

Flagstaff

UTAH

Kanab

Fredonia

Jacob Lake

DeMotte Park

NORTH RIM

Point Imperial

Cape Royal

Desert View

Bright Angel Point

Phantom Ranch

SOUTH RIM

Grand Canyon Village

Tusayan

Valle

Red Lake

Williams

GRAND CANYON RAILWAY

Sedona & Phoenix

Prescott

Kaibab-Paiute Indian Reservation

Pipe Spring National Monument

SUNSHINE ROUTE

Supai

Hualapai Hilltop

Havasupai Indian Reservation

Ash Fork

Colorado City

CLAYHOLE ROUTE

THE ARIZONA STRIP

Colorado River

Toroweap Overlook

Lava Falls Overlook

ARIZONA

Seligman

HISTORIC ROUTE 66

St George

MAIN STREET ROUTE

Mount Trumbull

Mount Trumbull

Grand Canyon-Parashant National Monument

Diamond Creek

GRAND CANYON WEST

Guano Point

Hualapai Indian Reservation

Peach Springs

Truxton

Valentine

BUCK AND DOE ROAD

Phoenix

ANTARES ROAD

Antares Point

STOCKTON HILL ROAD

Kingman

Los Angeles

15

NEVADA

Mesquite

DIAMOND BAR ROAD

Pierce Ferry

Temple Bar

Lake Mead

Chloride

Hoover Dam

Bullhead City

ARIZONA

Searchlight

Laughlin

CALIFORNIA

Boulder City

Las Vegas

N

20 miles

0

left feeling peculiarly flat. In a sense, none of the available activities can quite live up to that first stunning sight of the chasm. The **overlooks** along the rim all offer views that shift and change unceasingly from dawn to sunset; you can **hike** down into the depths on foot or by mule, hover above in a **helicopter**, or raft through the **whitewater rapids** of the river itself; you can spend a night at **Phantom Ranch** on the canyon floor, or swim in the waterfalls of the idyllic **Havasupai Reservation**. And yet that distance always remains – the Grand Canyon stands apart.

Until the 1920s, the average **visitor** would stay for two or three weeks. These days it's more like two or three hours – of which forty minutes are spent actually looking at the canyon. The vast majority come to the **South Rim** – it's much easier to get to, there are far more facilities (mainly at **Grand Canyon Village**), and it's open all year round. There is another lodge and campground at the **North Rim**, which by virtue of its isolation can be a lot more evocative, but at one thousand feet higher it is usually closed by snow from mid-October until May. Few people visit both rims; to get from one to the other demands either a two-day hike down one side of the canyon and up the other, or a 215-mile drive by road.

Admission to the park, valid for seven days on either rim, is $25 per vehicle or $12 for pedestrians and cyclists.

The South Rim

When someone casually mentions visiting the "Grand Canyon", it's almost certainly the **South Rim** that they're referring to. To be more precise, it's the thirty-mile stretch of the South Rim that's served by a paved road; and most specifically of all, it's **Grand Canyon Village**, the small canyon-edge community, sandwiched between the pine forest and the rim, that holds the park's **lodges, restaurants**, and **visitor center**. The reason nine out of every ten visitors come here is not, however, because this is a uniquely wonderful spot from which to see the canyon, but simply because the canyon's tourist facilities just happen to have been concentrated here ever since the arrival of the railroad a century ago.

However, it's as good a place to start as any. The canyon can be admired from countless vantage points, not only within the village but also along the eight-mile **Hermit Road** to the west and the 23-mile **Desert View Drive** to the east. The village is more attractive than you might imagine, and once the day-trippers have gone, does not feel overly crowded.

Getting to the South Rim

Nearly all visitors make their way to the South Rim by heading north of I-17 from either **Williams** (52 miles south) or **Flagstaff** (75 miles southeast). Most of the route is through ponderosa pine forests, so the route followed by the restored **steam trains** of the Grand Canyon Railway up from Williams is not especially scenic, even if it does make a fun ride (departs Williams daily 10am; from $60 roundtrip; ☏928/773-1976 or 1-800/843-8724, ⓦwww.thetrain.com). For details of buses from Flagstaff, see p.964.

The small **airport** at Tusayan – six miles from the South Rim, and used primarily by "flight-seeing" tour companies (see p.973) – also welcomes scheduled services, especially from Las Vegas, with operators such as Scenic Airlines (sometimes as low as $60 one-way; ☏702/638-3300 or 1-800/634-6801, ⓦwww.scenic.com).

Arrival and information

Long-proposed schemes to ban private vehicles from the canyon area are looking unlikely ever to be implemented. All that's happened is the construction of the **Canyon View Information Plaza**, well short of the village center near Mather

Layer upon layer of different rocks, readily distinguished by color, and each with its own fossil record, recede down into the Grand Canyon and back through time, until the strata at the river bed are among the oldest exposed rocks on earth. And yet how the canyon was **formed** is a mystery. Satellite photos reveal that the Colorado runs through the heart of an enormous hill (known to Native Americans as the Kaibab, "the mountain with no peak"); experts cannot agree how that could happen. Studies show that the canyon still deepens, at the slow rate of 50ft per million years. Its fantastic sandstone and limestone formations were not literally carved by the river, however; they're the result of erosion by wind and extreme cycles of heat and cold. These features were named – **Brahma Temple**, **Vishnu Temple**, and so on – by Clarence Dutton, a student of comparative religion who wrote the first Geological Survey report on the canyon in 1881.

While it may look forbidding, the Grand Canyon is not a dead place. All sorts of desert **wildlife** survive here – sheep and rabbits, eagles and vultures, mountain lions, and, of course, spiders, scorpions, and snakes. **Humans** have never been present on any great scale, but signs have been found of habitation as early as 2000 BC, and the **Ancestral Puebloans** were certainly here later on. A party of **Spaniards** passed through in 1540 searching for cities of gold, and a Father Garcés spent some time with the Havasupai in 1776, but **John Wesley Powell**'s expeditions along the fearsome and uncharted waters of the Colorado in 1869 and 1871–72 were what really brought the canyon to public attention. A few abortive attempts were made to mine different areas, but facilities for tourism were swiftly realized to be a far more lucrative investment. With the exception of the Indian reservations, the Grand Canyon is now run exclusively for the benefit of visitors, although even as recently as 1963 there were proposals to dam the Colorado and flood 150 miles of the Canyon, and the Glen Canyon dam has seriously affected the ecology downstream.

Point, which was supposed to be the hub of a new light rail system but serves instead as the main information point for visitors. Its open-air displays and trail guides are complemented by a good bookstore and a visitor center staffed by helpful rangers (daily: May to mid-Oct 8am–6pm; mid-Oct to April 8am–5pm; ☏ 928/638-7888, Ⓦ www.nps.gov/grca).

Grand Canyon Village is still accessible to private vehicles, as is the road east from the village to Desert View. Both the road west from the village to **Hermit's Rest**, however, and the short access road to **Yaki Point** – the first overlook east of Mather Point, and the trailhead for the popular **South Kaibab Trail** – are only open to private vehicles during December, January, and February. Free **shuttle buses** run on three routes: the ponderous **Village Route**, which loops laboriously between Grand Canyon Village and the information plaza; the **Kaibab Trail Route** between the plaza and Yaki Point; and the eight-mile **Hermit's Rest Route**, which heads west to eight canyon overlooks.

South Rim accommodation

All the "lodges" in Grand Canyon Village are operated by the park concessionaire, Amfac, and charge similar prices. In terms of seeing the canyon, it makes little difference where in the village you stay. Even in the "rim-edge" places – the magnificent 1905 *El Tovar Hotel* (❻) and the *Bright Angel* (rooms ❸, rim-side cabins ❺), *Thunderbird*, and *Kachina* lodges (both ❻) – few rooms offer much of a view, and in any case it's always dark by 8pm. Further back are *Maswik Lodge* (cabins ❹, rooms ❺), and the two-part *Yavapai Lodge* not far from the information plaza (❺). For details on making reservations at all of these options, see the box, below.

Tent and RV camping (without hookups) is available at the park service's year-round **Mather Campground**, south of the main road through Grand Canyon Village. Sites for up to two vehicles and six people cost $15 per night between April and November, when reservations, which are strongly recommended, can be made up to five months in advance through Spherix (same-day ⊤928/638-2611; advance 1-800/365-2267 or, from outside the US, ⊤301/722-1257), or online at ⓦwww.reservations.nps.gov). No reservations are accepted between December and March, when sites are first-come, first-served, and the fee drops to $10 per night. The adjacent **Trailer Village** consists exclusively of RV sites with hookups, costing $22 per site per night for two people, plus $2 extra for each additional adult; reservations on ⊤303/297-2757 or ⓦwww.grandcanyonlodges.com.

The summer-only *Desert View* campground, 26 miles east, is first-come, first-served, costs $10, and has no hook-ups. It's also possible to camp inside the canyon itself, if you first obtain a permit from the **Backcountry Reservations Office** near *Maswik Lodge* (daily 8am–noon & 1–5pm; call ⊤928/638-7875 Mon–Fri 1–5pm only; ⓦwww.nps.gov/grca/backcountry); each permit costs $10, plus $5 per person per night.

If all the park accommodation is full, the nearest alternative is the underwhelming service village of **Tusayan**. *Seven Mile Lodge* (⊤928/638-2291; no advance reservations; ❸) offers the least expensive rooms, while the newer *Grand Hotel* (⊤928/638-3333, ⓦwww.gcanyon.com; ❻) is more stylish. The most popular commercial **campgrounds** outside the park – with families, at least – is *Flintstone's Bedrock City* (mid-March to Oct; $13 tents, $17 RV hook-ups; ⊤928/635-2600), 22 miles south at the junction of Hwy-64 and Hwy-180, which has its own little prehistoric theme park.

South Rim eating

There's a reasonably wide choice of places to **eat** in Grand Canyon Village, and the prices in the budget options are not bad considering the canyon's remoteness and lack of water. Both *Yavapai* and *Maswik* lodges have basic cafeterias, open until 9pm and 10pm respectively. *Bright Angel Lodge* has its own **restaurant**, as well as the *Arizona Steakhouse*; both are open until 10pm and offer entrees costing $15–25. At *El Tovar*, where the dining room looks right out over the canyon, the sumptuous menu is enormously expensive. Breakfast is the most affordable meal; lunch and dinner can easily cost upwards of $40. Most of the hotels in **Tusayan** have their own dining rooms.

Exploring the South Rim

The fact that these days most visits to the South Rim start at the Canyon View Information Plaza, at **Mather Point**, rather than in Grand Canyon Village, doesn't mean you're missing out. In fact the canyon panorama that spreads out below Mather Point is more comprehensive than any obtainable from the village. The views to the east in particular are consistently stupendous; it's hard to imagine a

In-park accommodation reservations

All in-park **accommodation reservations** – for the lodges on both the South and the North rims, as well as for Phantom Ranch and RV camping – are handled by Xanterra Parks & Resorts (same-day ⊤928/638-2631, advance 303/297-2757 or 1-888/297-2757, ⓦwww.grandcanyonlodges.com). The best rooms are often booked as much as a year in advance, and your chances of turning up without a reservation and finding a place in summer are minimal.

more perfect position from which to watch the **sunrise** over the canyon.

The Colorado River is visible from various vantage points along the rim-edge footpath near Mather Point. In addition, if you walk west for around ten minutes (turn left along the rim from the information plaza), you'll come to **Yavapai Point**. From here, you can see two tiny segments of the river, one of which happens to include both the suspension footbridge across the Colorado and Phantom Ranch (see p.974). Nearby, the **Yavapai Observation Station** (daily: hours vary from 8am–8pm in summer down to 8am–5pm in winter; free) has illuminating displays on how the canyon may have been formed.

The **West** and **East Rim drives** extend along the South Rim for several miles in either direction from the information plaza and Grand Canyon Village, paralleled to the west by the **Rim Trail** on the very lip of the canyon. No one overlook can be said to be the "best," but there are far too many to stop at them all. **Sunset** is particularly magical at Hopi Point, to the west.

Driving or taking a shuttle bus along the East Rim Drive opens up further dramatic views. **Desert View**, 23 miles out from the village, is, at 7500ft, the highest point on the South Rim. Visible to the east are the vast flatlands of the **Navajo Nation**; to the northeast, **Vermillion** and **Echo Cliffs**, and the gray bulk of **Navajo Mountain** ninety miles away; to the west, the gigantic peaks of **Vishnu** and **Buddha temples**, while through the plains comes the narrow gorge of the **Little Colorado**. The odd-looking construction on the very lip of the canyon is **Desert View Watchtower**, built by Fred Harvey in 1932 in a conglomeration of Native American styles and decorated with Hopi pictographs.

Into the canyon

Hiking any of the trails that descend **into the Grand Canyon** allows you to pass through a sequence of utterly different landscapes, each with its own distinct climate, wildlife, and topography. However, while the canyon can offer a wonderful

---

South Rim tours

Xanterra (contact the "transportation desk" in any lodge, or call ☎928/638-2631) runs at least two short daily **coach tours** along the **rim** to the west ($16.75) and east ($29) of the village, **sunrise** and **sunset** trips to Yavapai Point ($12.75)**,** and **mule** rides to Plateau Point ($136) and Phantom Ranch (from $366; see overleaf).

Multi-day **whitewater rafting trips** in the canyon proper – such as those run by Western River Expeditions (ⓦwww.westernriver.com) or Canyoneers (ⓦwww .canyoneers.com) – are booked up literally years in advance, while no **one-day** raft trips are available within Grand Canyon National Park. For a trip along the river at short notice, there are however two alternatives, at either end of the canyon. Wilderness River Adventures, based in Page, Arizona, offer one-day trips that start below **Glen Canyon Dam** and take out at **Lees Ferry** ($62; ☎928/645-3296 or 1-800/992-8022; ⓦwww.riveradventures.com), while further west, the tribal-run Hualapai River Runners arrange pricey one-day trips on the Hualapai Reservation, starting at Diamond Creek ($280; ☎928/769-2219 or 1-888/255-9550, ⓦwww.destination-grandcanyon.com).

Airplane tours cost from around $75 for 30min up to as long as you like for as much as you've got. Operators include Air Grand Canyon (☎928/638-2686 or 1-800/247-4726, ⓦwww.airgrandcanyon.com) and Grand Canyon Airlines (☎928/638-2359 or 1-866/235-9422, ⓦwww.grandcanyonairlines.com). **Helicopter tours**, from $100 for 30min, are offered by Maverick (☎928/638-2622 or 1-800/962-3869, ⓦwww.maverickhelicopter.com) and Papillon (☎928/638-2419 or 1-800/528-2418, ⓦwww.papillon.com), who also operate amazing $455 day-trips to the Havasupai Reservation. All the companies are in **Tusayan**, at or near the airport.

wilderness experience, it's essential to remember that it can be a hostile and very unforgiving environment, grueling even for expert hikers.

The South Rim is 7000ft above sea level, an altitude that for most people is fatiguing in itself. Furthermore, all hikes start with a long, steep descent – which can come as a shock to the knees – and unless you camp overnight you'll have to climb all the way back up again when you're hotter and wearier.

If you're day-hiking, the golden rule is to keep track of how much time you spend hiking down, and allow twice that much to get back up again. Average summer temperatures inside the canyon exceed 100°F; to hike for eight hours in that sort of heat, you have to drink an incredible thirty pints of water. Always carry at least a quart per person, and much more if there are no water sources along your chosen trail. You must have food as well, as drinking large quantities without also eating can cause deadly water intoxication.

There's only space here to detail the most popular trails, the **Bright Angel** and the **Grandview**. Many of the others are liable to be overgrown now, or partially blocked by landslides; check before setting out.

Bright Angel Trail

The **Bright Angel Trail**, followed on foot or mule by thousands of visitors each year, starts from the wooden shack in the village that was once the Kolb photographic studio. The trail switchbacks for 9.6 miles down to **Phantom Ranch**, but under no circumstances should you try to hike down and back in a single day. It might not look far on the map, but it's harder than running a marathon. Instead, the longest feasible day-hike is to go as far as **Plateau Point** on the edge of the arid Tonto Plateau, an overlook above the Inner Gorge from which it is not possible to descend any further – a twelve-mile roundtrip that will probably take you at least eight hours. In summer, water can be obtained along the way.

The first section of the trail was laid out by miners a century ago, along an old Havasupai route, and has two short tunnels in its first mile. After another mile, the **wildlife** starts to increase (deer, rodents, and the ubiquitous ravens), and there are a few **pictographs** that have been all but obscured by graffiti.

At the lush **Indian Gardens** almost five miles down, where you'll find a ranger station and campground with water, the trails split to Plateau Point or down to the river via the **Devil's Corkscrew**. The latter route leads through sand dunes scattered with cactuses and down beside **Garden Creek** to the Colorado, which you then follow for more than a mile to get to Phantom Ranch.

Phantom Ranch

It's a real thrill to spend a night at the very bottom of the canyon, at the 1922 **Phantom Ranch**. The **cabins** are reserved exclusively for the use of excursionists on two-day mule trips ($366 per person for one night, $514 for the winter-only two-night trips), booked through Xanterra (see p.972). Beds in the four ten-bunk **dorms** ($30) are usually reserved way in advance, also through Xanterra, but it's worth checking for cancellations at the Bright Angel transportation desk as soon as you reach the South Rim. Do not hike down without a reservation, and even if you do have one, reconfirm it the day before you set off. All supplies reach Phantom Ranch the same way you do (an all-day hike on foot or mule), so **meals** are expensive, a minimum of $17.50 for breakfast and up to $32 for dinner. **Camping** at the beautiful *Bright Angel Campground*, a little closer to the Colorado River, is by **permit** only, as detailed on p.971. Again, do not hike down without a reservation.

The **Black Bridge** nearby was set in place in 1928 (suspended from twin cables carried down on the shoulders of 42 Havasupai). The delta of **Bright Angel**

Creek, named by Powell to contrast with the muddy **Dirty Devil** upriver in Utah, is several hundred feet wide here, and strewn with boulders. All the water used on the South Rim now comes by pipeline from the North Rim, and crosses the river on the 1960s Silver Bridge a little further downstream.

Grandview Trail

The **Grandview Trail**, down from the parking lot at Grandview Point, was built during the 1890s to aid copper mining on **Horseshoe Mesa**, which remains littered with abandoned mine workings. Although it's possible (by connecting with other trails) to use the Grandview to find your way down to the Tonto Platform and thus, eventually, the Colorado River, it's not itself a rim-to-river route. Instead, the hike down to the mesa and back has become one of the most popular **day-hikes** in the park. But that doesn't mean it's easy: now officially "unmaintained," it's a very demanding trail. Several of its switchbacks were constructed by inserting metal rods deep into the canyon wall, then covering them with juniper logs, stones, and dirt. At times it can be a little hair-raising, but it has stayed surprisingly sturdy for over a century. Reckon on six hours for the whole roundtrip.

The Havasupai Reservation

The **Havasupai Reservation** really is another world. Things have changed a little since a 1930s anthropologist called it "the only spot in the United States where native culture has remained in anything like its pristine condition," but the sheer magic of its turquoise waterfalls and canyon scenery makes this a very special place.

Havasu Canyon is a side canyon of the Grand Canyon, about 35 miles as the raven flies from Grand Canyon Village, but almost two hundred miles by road. Turn off the interstate at Seligman or Kingman, onto AZ-66 (which curves north between the two), stock up with food, water, and gas, and then turn on to Arrow-

△ Hiking in the Havasupai Reservation

head Hwy-18. That road ends at **Hualapai Hilltop**, from where an eight-mile trail zigzags down a bluff and leads through the stunning waterless Hualapai Canyon to the village of **SUPAI**. Riding down on horseback with a Havasupai guide costs $70 one-way, $120 roundtrip, while hiking is free; all visitors, however, pay a $30 entry fee on arrival at Supai.

Beyond Supai the trail becomes more difficult, but leads to a succession of spectacular waterfalls, including **Havasu Falls**, one of the best for swimming, and **Mooney Falls**, which was named after an unfortunate prospector who dangled here for three days in the 1890s, at the end of a snagged rope, before falling to his death.

A **campground** ($12; ☎928/448-2141) stretches between Havasu and Mooney Falls, and Supai itself holds the **motel**-like *Havasupai Lodge* (☎928/448-2111; ❼), along with a **café**, a **general store**, and the only **post office** in the US still to receive its mail by pack train. From time to time Supai is hit by freak floods, which can result in the temporary closure of the campground and lodge.

The Hualapai Reservation: the "West Rim"

Immediately west of the Havasupai reservation, and also inhabited by descendants of the Pai people, the **Hualapai Indian reservation** spreads across almost a million acres, bounded to the north by a 108-mile stretch of the Colorado River.

Fifty miles northwest of the reservation's only town, **PEACH SPRINGS**, itself 35 miles northwest of **Seligman** on Route 66 (see p.968), a cluster of overlooks above the Colorado river is cannily being promoted as **Grand Canyon West**, or the "**West Rim**" of the Grand. This is the closest spot to Las Vegas where it's possible to see the canyon, and most of its visitors are day-trippers who don't realize they're not seeing the canyon at its best. However, the Hualapai are currently engaged in a massive program to attract tourists, which should have culminated by the time you read this in the unveiling of the **Skywalk**, a horseshoe-shaped glass-bottomed walkway that has the potential to become one of the world's most famous tourist attractions. Visitors will be asked to pay approximately $25 for the thrill of walking out over the sheer 4000-foot drop at **Eagle Point**, which although not directly above the Colorado is still likely to be a stunning experience.

To reach it, leave US-93 thirty miles north of Kingman or forty miles south of the Hoover Dam, and follow Pierce Ferry Road for a further fifty miles east.

To the North Rim

The 215-mile route by road from Grand Canyon Village to the **North Rim** follows AZ-64 along the East Rim Drive to Desert View, then passes an overlook into the gorge of the Little Colorado, before joining US-89 fifty miles later at **CAMERON**. The Cameron Trading Post has the best selection of Native American crafts in the Grand Canyon area, and remains a trading center for the Navajo Nation. It also has a good-quality **motel** and **restaurant** (☎928/679-2231 or 1-877/221-6090, ⓦwww.camerontradingpost.com; ❹).

Lees Ferry

The direct route to the North Rim, now US-89A, crosses the Colorado seventy barren miles north of Cameron over the single arch of **Navajo Bridge**, almost five hundred feet above the river. There are in fact two Navajo Bridges, the 1929 original, now reserved for pedestrians, having been supplanted by a wider facsimile in 1995. Until the first was built, a ferry service operated six miles north at **LEES**

FERRY. Established in 1872, at the instigation of the Mormon Church, by John D. Lee, it was the only spot within hundreds of miles to offer easy access to the banks of the river on both sides. Lee himself was on the run after the **Mountain Meadows Massacre** in Utah in 1857, in which he led an armed white band clumsily disguised as Indians in their slaughter of a wagon train of would-be settlers.

Lees Ferry is the sole launching point for **whitewater rafting** trips into the Grand Canyon – the first point where boats can get out again is at Diamond Creek, twelve days away by muscle power. The ferry site still holds the atmospheric remains of Lee's Lonely Dell ranch, as well as a basic **campground** (☎928/355-2334; $10), while back on US-89A beneath the red of the **Vermillion Cliffs** you'll find a succession of **motels** – *Marble Canyon Lodge* (☎928/355-2225 or 1-800/726-1789; ❸), *Lees Ferry Lodge* (☎928/355-2231 or 1-800/451-2231, Ⓦwww.leesferrylodge.com; ❸), and *Cliff Dweller's Lodge* (☎928/355-2228; ❹). All have **restaurants**.

The turning south to get to the North Rim, off US-89A onto AZ-67, comes at **JACOB LAKE**, home to the welcoming *Jacob Lake Inn* (☎928/643-7232, Ⓦwww.jacoblake.com; ❹) and the lovely *Jacob Lake Campground*, open to tent campers only (mid-May to Oct; ☎928/643-7395), but not much else. From here – along a road that's closed in winter – it's 41 miles to the canyon itself.

The North Rim

Higher, more exposed to the elements, and far less accessible than the South Rim, the **NORTH RIM** of the Grand Canyon receives less than a tenth as many visitors. A cluster of venerable Park Service buildings stand where the main highway reaches the canyon, and a handful of rim-edge roads allow drivers to take their pick from additional lookouts. Only one hiking trail sees much use, the **North Kaibab Trail**, which follows Bright Angel Creek down to Phantom Ranch.

Tourist facilities on the North Rim, concentrated at **Bright Angel Point**, open for the season in mid-May and close in mid-October. **Accommodation** at *Grand Canyon Lodge* (❹) is in cabins that spread back along the ridge from the lodge entrance, very few of which have canyon views. Advance reservations are essential, and are handled, as for the South Rim, by Xanterra (same-day ☎928/638-2611, advance ☎303/297-2757 or 1-888/297-2757, Ⓦwww.grandcanyonnorthrim.com). Just over a mile north is the *North Rim Campground*, where $15 spaces can be reserved – though backpackers won't need to book – through Spherix (same-day ☎928/638-2611, advance ☎1-800/365-2267 or from outside the US ☎301/722-1257, Ⓦwww.reservations.nps.gov). The *Lodge* also holds a good **restaurant**, plus a saloon, and an espresso bar; ask at the information desk for details of **mule rides** (1hr $30, half-day $55, full-day canyon expeditions $105; ☎435/679-8665, Ⓦwww.canyonrides.com).

The park itself remains open for day-use only after mid-October, but no food, lodging, or gas is available, and visitors must be prepared to leave at a moment's notice. It's shut down altogether by the first major snowfall of winter, which in recent years has come as late as December.

Northeastern Arizona: Indian Country

The deserts of northeastern Arizona, popularly known as **INDIAN COUNTRY**, hold some of the most fascinating **pre-Columbian ruins** in North America, in the most striking settings imaginable. The cliff palaces of **Canyon de Chelly**, and **Betatakin** and **Keet Seel** in the Navajo National Monument, are among the greatest architectural achievements of the **Ancestral Puebloans**, made that much more special by the fact that the lands on which they stand are still lived on and worked by their heirs, the Hopi and Navajo.

The **NAVAJO NATION**, the largest Native American reservation in the US, fills most of the region, extending into western New Mexico and stretching to include the majestic sandstone pillars of Monument Valley in southernmost Utah. The Navajo may drive pickup trucks and wear baseball caps, but you get a very real sense that you're traveling through a foreign country here. Everyone can speak English, but Navajo, a language so complex that it was used as a secret code during World War II, is still the lingua franca. Supermarkets mark their prices in Navajo, and the reservation follows its own rules over Daylight Savings; in frontier-style towns like Tuba City, the time on the clock can vary according to whether you're in an American or a Navajo district.

When white immigrants began to arrive in force during the early nineteenth century, the Navajo – who call themselves *Dineh*, "The People" – had lived in Arizona for hundreds of years; within a generation, they lost almost everything. When the Americans took over from the Mexicans, things just got worse, hitting bottom in 1864 when Kit Carson rounded up every Navajo he could find and forced them all to move to Fort Sumner in the desolate plain of eastern New Mexico (see p.939). A few years later, the Navajo were allowed to return. Most of the 300,000-plus Navajo today work the land as shepherds and farmers on widely

scattered smallholdings, though many craftspeople also live by selling their wares from small stands set up along highways and in tourist stops.

Visiting this region, it's important to respect the people and places you encounter. The Ancestral Puebloans, the region's first occupants, have long since vanished, but many of the relics they left behind are on land that is still of spiritual significance to their modern counterparts. Similarly, it is offensive to photograph or otherwise intrude upon people's lives without permission; one reason why the Hopi, for example, banned photography was because it was such an interfering nuisance.

On a practical note, don't expect extensive **tourist facilities**. Most towns exist solely as bureaucratic outposts that only come alive during the annual tribal fairs and rodeos, and have little to offer visitors beyond a handful of places to eat and even fewer hotels and motels. For more information, check out the official Navajo **website**, ⓦ www.discovernavajo.com.

Navajo National Monument

Navajo National Monument, in the northwest quarter of the reservation, protects two of Arizona's biggest and most beautifully sited cliff dwellings. You'll find the useful **visitor center** (daily 8am–5pm; free; ⓣ 928/672-2700, ⓦ www. nps.gov/nava) at the end of paved Hwy-564, ten miles north of US-160. Behind it, a ten-minute trail crosses the plateau to a viewpoint overlooking **Betatakin**, an exceptionally well-preserved 135-room masonry structure tucked in a large natural alcove halfway up the 700-foot-high, brilliant-red sandstone on the far side of a canyon. It's only possible to hike down to Betatakin – which feels as though it was abandoned seven years, not seven centuries, ago – by joining one of the unforgettable six-hour ranger-guided hikes (schedule varies, typically summer daily 8.30am & 11am, winter daily 10am; no advance reservations), which rendezvous roughly a mile from the visitor center. Numbers are limited, and no advance bookings are taken, so get to the visitor center as early as possible on the day – or stay the previous night at the very attractive free **campground** in the forest alongside.

In summer, you can also visit the even larger Ancestral Puebloan site of **Keet Seel**. However, the seventeen-mile roundtrip hike from the visitor center is too grueling to attempt in a single day, so you'll have to stay overnight in the small **campground** near the site, having obtained a permit from the visitor center at least a day in advance.

Most people pass through this area on their way somewhere else, so there aren't many **places to stay**. However, **TUBA CITY**, west of the monument, has the large, modern *Quality Inn Tuba Trading Post* (ⓣ 928/283-4545 or 1-800/644-8383; ⓦ www. qualityinnnavajonation.com; ⑤), while the mining town of **KAYENTA**, 22 miles northeast of the monument at the junction of US-160 and US-163, holds the similarly anonymous but adequate *Best Western Wetherill Inn* (ⓣ 928/697-3231, ⓦ www. gouldings.com; ⑤) and the *Holiday Inn* (ⓣ 928/697-3221, ⓦ www.ichotelsgroup .com; ⑤), which has a good-value **restaurant**.

Monument Valley

The classic southwestern landscape of stark sandstone buttes and forbidding pinnacles of rock, poking from an endless expanse of drifting red sands, has become an archetypal Wild West image. Only when you arrive at **MONUMENT VALLEY** – which straddles the Arizona–Utah state line, 24 miles north of Kayenta and 25 miles southwest of Mexican Hat – do you realize how much your perception of the West has in fact been shaped by this one spot. Such scenery does exist elsewhere, of course, but nowhere is it so perfectly distilled. While moviemakers have flocked here since the early days of Hollywood – this is where John Ford made John Wayne a star – the sheer majesty of the place still takes your breath away. Add the fact that it remains a stronghold of **Navajo** culture, little affected by tourism, and Monument Valley can be the absolute highlight of a trip to the Southwest.

The biggest and most impressive of the monoliths are a pair called **The Mittens**, one East and one West, each of which has a distinct thumb splintering off from its central bulk. Over a dozen other spires are spread around nearby, along with **rock art panels** and an assortment of minor but nicely sited **Ancestral Puebloan ruins**.

You can see the buttes for free, towering alongside US-163, but the four-mile detour to enter **Monument Valley Tribal Park** is rewarded with much closer views (daily: May–Sept 7am–7pm; Oct–April 8am–5pm; $5; ℡435/727-5870; Ⓦwww.navajonationparks.org). A rough, unpaved road drops from behind the visitor center to run through Monument Valley itself. The 17-mile **self-drive route** makes a bumpy but bearable ride in an ordinary vehicle, and takes something over an hour (daily: summer 8am–6pm; rest of year 8am–4.30pm). However, the Navajo-led **jeep** or **horseback tours** into the backcountry are very much recommended; a two-hour jeep trip costs from around $25 per person if arranged at the visitor center, slightly more if organized through *Goulding's Lodge* (see below). As well as stopping at such movie locations as the **Totem Pole**, these tours pause so you can watch weavers at work in a Navajo *hogan* (traditional eight-sided dwelling).

The appropriately named *View* (℡928/727-3312) is a reasonable **restaurant** at the visitor center, not far from the exposed *Mitten View* **campground** (first-come, first-served; water available in summer only; summer $10, winter $5). The only **accommodation** in the immediate vicinity is six miles west, in Utah at *Goulding's Lodge* (℡435/727-3231, Ⓦwww.gouldings.com; ⑥), a 1920s trading post that now offers pricey motel rooms with magnificent views, an unexceptional restaurant, a general store and gas station, a small movie museum, and its own campground (summer $32, winter $18; same phone).

△ John Ford Point, Monument Valley

Canyon de Chelly National Monument

A short distance east of **CHINLE**, sixty miles southwest of Kayenta and seventy miles north of I-40, twin sandstone walls emerge abruptly from the desert floor, climbing at a phenomenal rate to become the awesome thousand-foot cliffs of **CANYON DE CHELLY NATIONAL MONUMENT**. Between these sheer sides, the meandering course of the Chinle Wash can be discerned by its fringe of cottonwoods as it winds through grasslands and planted fields. Here and there a Navajo *hogan* stands in a grove of fruit trees, a straggle of sheep is penned in by a crude wooden fence, or ponies drink at the water's edge. And everywhere, perched above the valley on ledges in the canyon walls and dwarfed by the towering cliffs, are the long-abandoned adobe and stone dwellings of the **Ancestral Puebloans**.

There are two main canyons, which branch apart a few miles upstream: **Canyon de Chelly** (pronounced *de shay*) to the south and **Canyon del Muerto** to the north. Each twists and turns in all directions, scattered with vast rock monoliths, while several smaller canyons break away. The whole labyrinth threads its way northward for thirty miles into the Chuska Mountains.

Canyon de Chelly is a magnificent place, easily on a par with the best of the Southwest's national parks. Its relative lack of fame owes much to the continuing presence of the **Navajo**, for whom the canyon retains enormous symbolic significance (although they did not build its cliff dwellings). Casual visitors are restricted to peering into the canyon from above, from overlooks along the two "rim drives." There's no road in, and, apart from one short trail, you can only enter the canyons with a Navajo guide.

Some history

The first known inhabitants of the canyon were **Ancestral Puebloan Basketmakers**, who dwelled here from around 300 AD. During the next thousand years, they advanced from living in pit houses dug into the soil to building elegant cliff dwellings, and developed fine pottery and weaving. For some centuries after the Ancestral Puebloans left the area (see p.933), the **Hopi** came here to farm each summer, returning for the winter to the mesas to the east, but as time went by, **Navajo** migrants from the north and west eventually displaced the Hopi altogether.

From 1583 onward, the Navajo were locked with the Spanish in a bloody cycle of armed clashes and slave raids. The US Army in turn failed repeatedly to dislodge the Navajo, but none of the various truces and treaties they agreed to could restrain the rapacious hunger for land by New Mexican settlers. The end appeared to have come with the brutal round-up and deportation (the **"Long Walk"**) of the entire Navajo people, completed by Kit Carson in 1864 when he starved the last of them down from Navajo Rock and destroyed their homes and livestock. So barbaric was the Navajo's imprisonment at Fort Sumner, however, that Congress soon allowed them to return. To this day, 25 Navajo families still farm the Canyon de Chelly in summer, the matrilineal descendants of the women among whom it was reapportioned in the 1870s.

The view from above: the rim drives

Each of the two "rim drives" from the visitor center offers a succession of spectacular overlooks; allow two to three hours for each of the forty-mile roundtrips. Thefts from cars have been a major problem, so it's wise to heed the prominent warnings.

The first significant stopping point along the South Rim Drive is **Junction Overlook**, after four miles, far above the point where the two main canyons branch their separate ways; as you scramble across the bare rocks you can see

Canyon de Chelly narrowing away, with a *hogan* immediately below. Two miles further along, by which time the canyon is 550ft deep, **White House Overlook** looks down on the highly photogenic **White House Ruins**. This is the only point from which unguided hikers can descend to the canyon floor, taking perhaps 30 to 45 minutes to get down and a good hour to get back up. The beautiful if precarious trail, at times running along ledges chiseled into the slick rock, culminates with a close-up view of the ruins; the most dramatic dwellings, squeezed into a tiny alcove sixty feet up a majestic cliff, were once reached via the rooftops of now-vanished structures. Visitors are forbidden to walk for more than a hundred yards in either direction beyond the site. Back up on the South Rim Drive, twelve miles along, the view from **Sliding House Overlook** reveals more Ancestral Puebloan ruins seemingly slipping down the canyon walls toward the ploughed Navajo fields below, while eight miles further on the road ends above the astonishing **Spider Rock**, where twin 800-foot pinnacles of rock come to within 200ft of the canyon rim.

The **North Rim Drive** runs twenty miles up Canyon del Muerto to **Massacre Cave**, where the Spanish expedition of 1805, led by Lieutenant Narbona, killed around one hundred Navajo women, children, and old men. The "cave" is just a pitifully exposed ledge, upon which the huddled group were easily picked off by the Spanish, using ricochets off the overhang above. Visible from the nearby **Mummy Cave Overlook** is the **House Under The Rock**, with its central tower in the Mesa Verde style – the single most striking ruin in the monument. Of the two viewpoints at **Antelope House Overlook**, one is opposite Navajo Fortress, an isolated eminence atop which the Navajo were besieged for three months in 1863, while the other looks down on the twin ruined square towers of Antelope House. The **Tomb of the Weaver** across the wash is where the embalmed body of an old man was found wrapped in golden eagle feathers.

Practicalities

The Canyon de Chelly **visitor center**, on the road from Chinle (daily May–Sept 8am–6pm; Oct–April 8am–5pm; no entrance fee; ℡928/674-5500, Ⓦwww.nps. gov/cach), has informative displays, and provides guides for unorthodox hiking or motorized expeditions. Facilities nearby are overstretched, so it's essential to book your **accommodation** well in advance. The most appealing options are the *Thunderbird Lodge* (℡928/674-5841 or 1-800/679-2473, Ⓦwww.tbirdlodge.com; ❻), very near the canyon entrance, which arranges the standard sightseeing tours and

---

Into the canyons

Tours of the canyon floor, organized by *Thunderbird Lodge* (see above), zigzag along the washes, which vary from two- or three-feet deep during the spring thaw to completely dry in summer. For most of the year, the bone-shaking tours are in open-top flatbed trucks that lurch over the rutted earth, and the heat can be incredible; in winter they carry on in glass-roofed army vehicles with caterpillar tracks. To reach as far as Spider Rock, you have to take the full-day tour ($65; no reductions for children), but the half-day trip at $40 (under 13s $30.50) still enables you to see a wide variety of sites and terrain, including the White House Ruins.

The visitor center also arranges highly recommended 4.5-mile, four-hour **group hikes**, which cost $15 per person. The precise schedule varies, but usually includes a morning trip via the White House Trail and an afternoon hike in the Canyon del Muerto; separate **night hikes** last just two hours but cost slightly more. Tsotsonii Ranch (℡928/755-6209, Ⓦwww.totsoniiranch.com) organize horseback trips for $15 per person per hour, plus $15 an hour for a guide.

has an adequate cafeteria, and the *Chinle Holiday Inn* (☎928/674-5000, ⓦwww. holiday-inn.com/chinle-garcia; ❺), slightly further back toward Chinle, where the food is a lot better. The free, minimally equipped *Cottonwood* **campground** has pleasant sites among the trees alongside *Thunderbird Lodge*.

Window Rock

The reservation's governing body, the Navajo Tribal Council, has its seat on the property's eastern edge, along the New Mexico border. It was based for fifty years at Fort Defiance, a US cavalry outpost, until in the 1930s **WINDOW ROCK** was established as a new capital. Named for the natural stone arch on its northern side, it's not a great place to get a grasp of Navajo culture, but it does at least have gas stations, shops, and a **motel**, the showpiece *Quality Inn Navajo Nation Capital*, at 48 W Hwy-264 (☎928/871-4108 or 1-800/662-6189; ⓦwww.navajonationinn. com; ❸). The nearby **Navajo Nation Museum and Visitor Center** (☎928/871-7941; summer Mon & Sat 8am–5pm, Tues–Fri 8am–8pm; winter Mon–Fri 8am–5pm; donation) gives the background on tribal history and displays high-quality crafts.

The Hopi Mesas

Almost uniquely in the United States, the **Hopi** people have lived continuously in the same place for over eight hundred years. Some invaders have come and gone in that time, others have stayed; but the villages on **First**, **Second**, and **Third mesas** have endured, if not exactly undisturbed then at least unmoved.

To outsiders, it's not obvious why, with the whole Southwest to pick from, the Hopi should have chosen to live on three barren and unprepossessing fingers of rock poking from the southern flanks of **Black Mesa** in the depths of northeast Arizona. There are two simple answers. The first lies within the mesa itself: although it has no perennial streams, its subterranean rocks are tilted at just the correct angle to deliver a tiny but dependable trickle of water, while the "black" in its name comes from the coal that gives the Hopi limitless reserves of fuel. The second is that the Hopi used to farm and hunt across a much wider area, and have only been restricted to their mesa-top villages by the encroachment of their Navajo neighbors. While the Hopi are celebrated for their skill at "**dry farming**," managing to preserve enough precious liquid to grow corn, beans, and squash on hand-tilled terraces, this precarious and difficult way of life has nonetheless been forced upon them.

By their very survival, and the persistence of their ancient beliefs and ceremonies, the Hopi have long fascinated outsiders. While visitors are welcome, the Hopi have no desire – or need, as the tribe has finally begun to earn considerable amounts from mineral leases – to turn themselves into a tourist attraction. Although stores and galleries on the reservation provide plenty of opportunity to buy crafts such as pottery, basketwork, silver overlay jewelry, and hand-carved *kachina* dolls, tourists who arrive in the hope of extensive sight-seeing – let alone spiritual revelations – are likely to leave disappointed, and quite possibly dismayed by what they perceive as conspicuous poverty.

Visiting the Hopi Mesas

The essential first stop is the modern, mock-Pueblo **Hopi Cultural Center** below Second Mesa, which holds a **museum** (summer Mon–Sat 8am–5pm, Sun 9am–4pm; winter Mon–Fri 8am–5pm; $3; ☎928/734-6650), as well as a **cafeteria** and **motel** (☎928/734-2401, ⓦwww.hopiculturalcenter.com; ❹). In summer, its plain but adequate rooms are usually booked solid a week or more in advance.

Unless your visit coincides with one of the very few social events that's open to tourists (ask at the cultural center), the only way to see the mesa-top villages is to take a **guided tour** of the most impressive one, **WALPI** (daily: winter 10am–4pm, summer 9.30am–6pm; $8; ☎928/737-2262). By Hopi standards, Walpi is not in fact that old; it was hastily thrown together in the immediate aftermath of the Pueblo Revolt of 1680, when the people of First Mesa moved to a more secure site in the face of possible Spanish or Navajo attack. The spot they chose is absolutely stunning, standing alone at the narrow southernmost tip of the mesa, and connected to the other First Mesa villages by the merest slender neck of stone, with a drop of three hundred feet to either side. It's now home to around 35 people, who do without electricity or running water.

To see Walpi, take Hwy-264 to modern **POLACCA**, at the foot of First Mesa, then drive a mile up the twisting paved road until it ends in **SICHOMOVI**. The tours assemble in Sichomovi's small community center, setting off at regular intervals for a half-hour walk to and around Walpi. Depending on the time of year, you'll either be in a group of twenty or so, or on your own, but either way there's plenty of opportunity to ask questions, and to buy pottery, *kachina* dolls, and fresh-baked *piiki*, a flatbread made with blue cornflour.

Utah

With the biggest, most beautiful, and most pristine landscapes in North America, **UTAH** has something for everyone: from brilliantly colored canyons, across endless desert plains, to thickly wooded and snow-covered mountains. This unmatched range of terrain, almost all of which is public land, makes Utah *the* place to come for **outdoor pursuits**, whether your tastes run to hiking, off-track mountain biking, whitewater rafting, or skiing.

Southern Utah has more **national parks** than anywhere else in the US; it has often been suggested that the entire area should become one vast national park. The most accessible parts – such as **Zion** and **Bryce Canyon** – are by far the most visited, but lesser-known parks like **Arches** and **Canyonlands** are every bit as dramatic. Huge tracts of this empty desert, in which fascinating pre-Columbian pictographs and Ancestral Puebloan ruins lie hidden, are all but unexplored; seeing them in safety requires a good degree of advance planning and self-sufficiency.

In the **northeast** of the state, the **Uinta Mountains** remain uncrossed by road and form one of the most extensive US wilderness areas outside Alaska, while **Flaming Gorge** and **Dinosaur** preserve more desert splendor. Though the **northwest** is predominantly flat and dry, the granite mountains of the **Wasatch Front** tower over state capital **Salt Lake City** – a surprisingly attractive and enjoyable stopover – while Alta, Snowbird, and the resorts around Park City offer some of the best **skiing** in North America.

Led by Brigham Young, Utah's earliest Anglo settlers – the **Mormons** – arrived in the Salt Lake area in 1847, and set about the massive irrigation projects that made their agrarian way of life possible. At first they provoked great suspicion and hostility back East. The Republican Convention of 1856 railed against slavery and polygamy in equal measure; had the Civil War not intervened, a war against the Mormons was a real possibility. Relations eased when the Mormon Church realized in 1890 that it had better drop polygamy on its own terms before being forced to do so. Statehood followed in 1896, and a century on, seventy percent of Utah's two-million-strong population are Mormons. The Mormon influence is responsible for the layout of Utah's towns, where residential streets are as wide as interstates, and all are numbered block-by-block according to the same logical if ponderous system.

Despite Brigham Young's early opposition to the search for mineral wealth, Mormon businessmen became renowned as fiercely pro-mining and anti-conservation. Only since the 1980s has tourism been appreciated as a major industry, and former mining towns such as **Moab** developed facilities for wide-eyed travelers smitten by the allure of the desert. Increased tourism has also led to a relaxation of Utah's notoriously arcane **drinking laws**. In most towns, at least one restaurant will be licensed to sell beer, wine, and mixed drinks to diners, and it may also be licensed to sell beer in its bar or lounge. Beer is also sold in a few other locations, but to drink stronger liquor you'll have to become a member of a **"private club"**; most sell temporary membership for a token fee.

Getting around Utah

It's nearly impossible to get anywhere in Utah without your own **car**. Amtrak and Greyhound serve Salt Lake City and a few provincial towns, but practically nowhere else. However, a couple of firms offer **bus tours** of the national parks, and if you're feeling adventurous, southern Utah also has an unbeatable range of mountain biking and river rafting: see p.999 for a list of companies.

Southern Utah: the national parks

Southern Utah is a peculiar combination of the mind-boggling and the mundane. Its **scenery** is stupendous, a stunning geological freakshow where the earth is ripped bare to expose cliffs and canyons of every imaginable color, unseen rivers gouge mighty furrows into endless desert plateaus, and strange sandstone towers thrust from the sagebrush. By contrast, however, the tiny **Mormon towns** scattered across this epic landscape are, almost without exception, boring in the extreme, so most visitors spend as much time as possible **outdoors**.

While Southern Utah's five national parks are complemented by many lesser-known but equally dramatic wildernesses, they make the most obvious targets for travelers. In the southwest, **Zion National Park** centers on an awe-inspiring canyon, backed by barren highlands of white sandstone, while **Bryce Canyon** is a blaze of orange pinnacles. To the east, **Arches** holds an eroded desertscape of graceful red-rock fins and spurs, all on a more manageable scale than the astonishing hundred-mile vistas of neighboring **Canyonlands**. Both lie within easy reach of **Moab**, a disheveled former mining town turned Utah's hippest destination. The fifth park, **Capitol Reef**, stretches through the middle of the state, pierced by slender, ravishing canyons.

The defining topographical feature of southwest Utah is the **Grand Staircase**. Named by pioneer river-runner John Wesley Powell, it consists of a series of plateaus, stacked tier upon tier, that climb from the North Rim of the Grand Canyon. The **Chocolate Cliffs**, near the border with Arizona, are followed by the dazzling **Vermilion Cliffs**, then the **White Cliffs** – a 2000-foot wall of Navajo sandstone, best seen at Zion – the **Grey Cliffs**, and finally the **Pink Cliffs** of Bryce. Although it took a billion years of sedimentation for these rocks to form, the staircase itself

SOUTHERN UTAH

0 ___ 25 miles

N

Grand Junction ▲

Salt Lake City ▲

Flagstaff ▲

Las Vegas ▲

Cisco
128
Thompson
Grand Junction
Colorado River
CASTLE VALLEY RD
LA SAL MOUNTAINS
Moab
Arches Nat. Park
191
313
CANYON RIMS RECREATION AREA
Dead Horse Point
Green River
Green River
70
ISLAND IN THE SKY
Canyon-lands National Park
THE MAZE
THE NEEDLES
Newspaper Rock
211
ABAJO MOUNTAINS
Monticello
666
191
Blanding
191
Horseshoe Canyon
Dirty Devil River
95
95
Hite
Lake Powell
Natural Bridges Nat. Monument
Fry Canyon
95
261
Grand Gulch
Valley of the Gods
Comb Ridge
Bluff
262
Mexican Hat
191
UTAH
Black Dragon Canyon
HEART OF THE SINBAD ROAD
24
SAN RAFAEL SWELL
Emory
GOBLIN VALLEY STATE PARK
Hanksville
24
Caineville
Torrey
Capitol Reef National Park
HENRY MOUNTAINS
Ticaboo
276
Bullfrog
Halls Crossing
GLEN CANYON NATIONAL RECREATION AREA
San Juan River
163
Muley Point
GOOSENECKS STATE PARK
Monument Valley
Navajo Indian Reservation
160
Aneth
64
UTAH
70
Richfield
62
Loa
24
Bicknell
72
Boulder
12
BURR TRAIL
Lake Powell
Rainbow Bridge Nat. Mon.
Kaibeto
Navajo Nat. Mon.
Kayenta
Fillmore
15
FREMONT INDIAN STATE PARK
Sevier
89
Junction
62
AQUARIUS PLATEAU
HELL'S BACKBONE ROAD
Escalante
HOLE-IN-THE-ROCK ROAD
KAIPAROWITS PLATEAU
Grand Staircase-Escalante National Monument
Page
Antelope Canyon
Horseshoe Bend
398
Glen Canyon Dam
Wahweap
Lees Ferry
89
Flagstaff
Beaver
21
130
257
Parowan
143
Brian Head
Cedar Breaks Nat. Mon.
14
Panguitch
12
Hatch
Tropic
Cannonville
KODACHROME BASIN STATE PARK
COTTONWOOD CANYON RD
Bryce Canyon Nat. Park
Glendale
SMOKY MOUNTAIN ROAD
Vermilion Cliffs National Monument
89A
Fredonia
89A
Jacob Lake
89
Cedar City
15
56
Kolob Canyons
Zion Nat. Park
20
Orderville
Mt. Carmel Junction
Springdale
Coral Pink Sand Dunes
Kanab
389
Kaibab-Paiute Indian Reservation
Pine Valley
St. George
18
Snow Canyon
9
Virgin
Hurricane
59
Springdale
Colorado City
Pipe Spring Nat. Mon.
389
Mountain Meadows Massacre Site
Virgin River
Grand Canyon-Parashant National
ARIZONA

has only been created in the last dozen million years by the general upthrust of the **Colorado Plateau,** which stretches away to the east.

St George and Cedar City

Southern Utah's two biggest towns, **St George** and **Cedar City,** lie fifty miles apart on I-15 en route between Las Vegas and Salt Lake City. Both make reasonably pleasant and serviceable bases, if not ones that are likely to detain you for very long.

St George

ST GEORGE was the winter home of Brigham Young and other early Mormon leaders, who basked in the comparatively mild climate of "Utah's Dixie." Set at the foot of a broad, reddish-brown sandstone cliff, it's a pretty enough town. At the center is the fine 1877 **LDS Temple** at 440 South 300 East, the oldest still in use anywhere. The rest of the town holds quaint pioneer homes, including Brigham Young's much-restored **adobe house** on 200 North First West (daily 9am–7pm; free).

Travelers driving up I-15 can call in at the **Utah Visitor Center,** just inside the state line (daily: summer 8am–9pm; winter 8am–5pm; ☎435/673-4542, Ⓦwww.utah.com). Virtually all St George's commercial life takes place along the main drag, St George Boulevard, where the twenty or so **motels** include the popular *Dixie Palm* at no.185 E (☎435/673-3531; ❷). Among various good **restaurants** in the Ancestor Square development is the *Pizza Factory,* 1 W St George Blvd (☎435/628-1234; closed Sun).

Cedar City

CEDAR CITY, 53 miles north of St George and approximately half its size, is no more worthy of a stop. Founded as an iron-mining town in the late 1850s, it's now kept alive by the Southern Utah State College on its western fringe, and by the flood of theatergoers who come to watch the enthusiastic productions of the **Utah Shakespeare Festival,** held on campus every summer (☎435/586-7878, Ⓦwww.bard.org).

The large local **visitor center** stands at 581 N Main St (summer Mon–Fri 8am–7pm, Sat 9am–1pm; winter Mon–Fri 8am–5pm; ☎435/586-5124 or 1-800/354-4849, Ⓦwww.cedarcity.org). **Main Street** is handy for food and lodging; motels with pools include two *Best Westerns,* the *El Rey Inn* at no. 80 S (☎435/586-6518, Ⓦwww.bwelrey.com; ❸), and the smart *Town and Country Inn* at no. 200 N (☎435/586-9900, Ⓦwww.bwtowncountry.com; ❸). *Godfathers Pizza* at no. 241 N (☎435/586-1111; closed Sun) offers Italian specialties in a lively atmosphere, while *Sullivan's* at no. 301 S (☎435/586-6761) is part steakhouse, part coffee-shop.

Zion National Park

With its soaring cliffs, riverine forests, and cascading waterfalls, **ZION NATIONAL PARK** is the most conventionally beautiful of Utah's parks. At first glance, it's also the least "Southwestern"; its centerpiece, **Zion Canyon,** is a lush oasis that feels far removed from the otherworldly desolation of Canyonlands or the downright weirdness of Bryce. Like California's Yosemite Canyon, it's a spectacular gorge, squeezed between mighty walls of rock and echoing with the sound of running water; also like Yosemite, it can get claustrophobic in summer, with its approach roads clogged with traffic and its limited facilities crammed with sweltering tourists.

Too many visitors see Zion Canyon as a quick half-day detour off the interstate, as they race between Las Vegas (158 miles southwest) and Salt Lake City (320 miles northeast). Beautiful though the **Scenic Drive** through the canyon may be, Zion deserves much more of your time than that. Even the shortest hiking trail within the canyon can escape the crowds, while a day-hike will take you away from the deceptive verdure of the valley and up onto the high-desert tablelands beyond.

Summer is by far the busiest season. That's despite temperatures in excess of 100°F, and violent thunderstorms concentrated in August and a week or so to either side. If you can, come in April or May, to see the spring flowers bloom, or in September and October, to enjoy the fall colors along the river. The **admission charge** for Zion, valid in all sections of the park for seven days, is $20 per vehicle, or $10 for motorcyclists, cyclists, and pedestrians.

Visiting Zion Canyon

In **Zion Canyon**, mighty walls of Navajo sandstone rise nearly half a mile above the groves of box elders and cottonwoods that line the loping North Fork of the **Virgin River**. The awe of the early Mormon settlers who called this "Zion" is reflected in the names of the stupendous slabs of rock along the paved six-mile **Scenic Drive** from the park entrance – the **Court of the Patriarchs**, the **Great White Throne**, and **Angel's Landing**.

Although Hwy-9 remains open to through traffic all year, the Scenic Drive is accessible to private vehicles during the winter only. Between late March and October, all visitors, other than guests staying at *Zion Lodge* (see p.990), are obliged to leave their vehicles either in Springdale (see p.990) or at the large **visitor center** just inside the park (daily: late May to early Sept 8am–7pm; late April to late May & early Sept to mid-Oct 8am–6pm; mid-Oct to late April 8am–5pm; ☏435/772-3256, ⓦwww.nps.gov/zion). Free **shuttle buses** run on two separate loops in summer – one between Springdale and the visitor center, with nine stops en route, and the other between the visitor center and the end of the Scenic Drive, also with nine stops including *Zion Lodge*.

The Scenic Drive ends at the foot of the **Temple of Sinawava**, beyond which the easy but delightful **Riverside Walk** trail continues on another half a mile up the canyon, to end at a sandy little beach. For eight miles upstream from here, in the stretch known as the **Zion Narrows**, the Virgin River fills the entire gorge, often less than twenty feet wide and channeled between vertical cliffs almost a thousand feet high. Hiking this ravishing "slot canyon" is much more suitable for devotees of extreme sports than for casual hikers. Specialist equipment is essential, in the form of waterproof, super-grip footwear, neoprene socks, and a walking stick or two, complemented in the cooler months by a drysuit, plus zip-lock plastic bags for everything you carry, and all the water you need to drink. You can only hike its full length downstream, a total distance of sixteen miles from remote Chamberlain's Ranch, roughly twenty miles north of the park's East Entrance. Commercial companies based in Springfield, such as Zion Adventure Company (☏435/772-1001, ⓦwww.zionadventures.com), rent out equipment and offer early-morning shuttle rides to the trailhead; you also have to get a permit from the visitor center.

A much less demanding hike leads up to **Weeping Rock**, an easy half-hour roundtrip from the road to a gorgeous spring-fed garden that dangles from a rocky alcove. From the same trailhead, a mile beyond *Zion Lodge*, a more strenuous and exciting route cuts through narrow **Hidden Canyon**, whose mouth turns into a waterfall after a good rain. Directly across from the lodge a short (two-mile roundtrip) and fairly flat trail winds up at the **Emerald Pools**, a series of three clearwater pools, the best (and furthest) of which has a small sandy beach at the foot of a gigantic cliff; at certain times of the year a broad waterfall sprinkles down over the trail.

The single best half-day **hike** climbs up to **Angel's Landing**, a narrow ledge of whitish sandstone protruding some 1750ft above the canyon floor. Starting on the same route as for the Emerald Pools, the Angel's Landing trail switchbacks sharply up through the delightful coolness of **Refrigerator Canyon** before emerging on the canyon's west rim; near the end you have to cross a heart-stopping five-foot neck of rock with sheer drops to either side (there's a steel cable to grab hold of). That roundtrip takes a good four hours, but backpackers can continue another twenty miles to the gorgeous Kolob Canyons district (see p.990).

The high dry plateau above and to the **east** of Zion Canyon, reached by continuing on Hwy-9 at the Scenic Drive turnoff, stands in a complete contrast to the

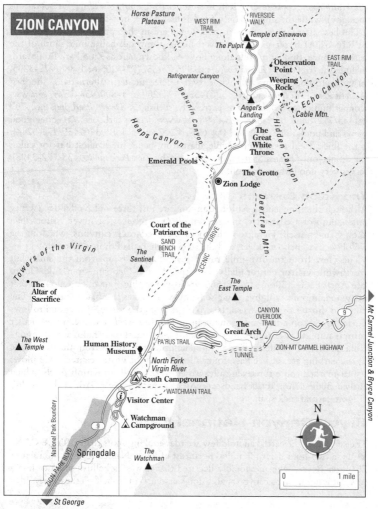

ZION CANYON

Horse Pasture Plateau
WEST RIM TRAIL
RIVERSIDE WALK
Temple of Sinawava
The Pulpit
Observation Point
EAST RIM TRAIL
Refrigerator Canyon
Weeping Rock
Echo Canyon
Behunin Canyon
Angel's Landing
Cable Mtn.
Heaps Canyon
Hidden Canyon
The Great White Throne
Emerald Pools
The Grotto
Zion Lodge
Deertrap Mtn.
Court of the Patriarchs
SAND BENCH TRAIL
Towers of the Virgin
The Sentinel
SCENIC DRIVE
The East Temple
The Altar of Sacrifice
CANYON OVERLOOK TRAIL
The West Temple
Human History Museum
PA'RUS TRAIL
The Great Arch
ZION-MT CARMEL HIGHWAY
TUNNEL
North Fork Virgin River
South Campground
WATCHMAN TRAIL
National Park Boundary
Visitor Center
Watchman Campground
Springdale
The Watchman
N
0   1 mile

St George

lush Virgin River gorge. Its most dramatic sight is the **Great Arch**, best seen from the turnouts before the mile-long tunnel, beyond which the **Canyon Overlook** nature trail gives a good introduction to the flora and fauna of the park, such as the speedy lizards that race from rock to rock.

Practicalities

The only **food and lodging** within Zion itself is at *Zion Lodge* (open all year; ☎435/772-3213, reserve through Xanterra at ☎303/297-2757 or 1-888/297-2757, ⊛www.xanterra.com or ⊛www.zionlodge.com; ❺), set amid rolling and well-shaded lawns near the Great White Throne. Even if you can't get a room, it's well worth stopping for lunch on the terrace of the fine old wooden dining room. The *Lodge* is also the base for **horseback** excursions, with regular one-hour rides costing $30 per person (☎435/679-8665, ⊛www.canyonrides.com). Two good **campgrounds**, both charging $16 per night, are located alongside the visitor center; the *Watchman* accepts reservations in summer (☎1-800/365-2267, ⊛reservations .nps.gov), while the summer-only *South* is first-come, first-served.

The best alternatives to the in-park lodge are in the appealing small town of **SPRINGDALE**, set among the riverbank cottonwoods half a mile south of the park entrance. Budget **motels** along Hwy-9, known here as Zion Park Boulevard, include the friendly ⅍ *El Rio Lodge*, no. 995 ☎435/772-3205 or 1-888/772-3205, ⊛www.elriolodge.com; ❷), while two pricier modern alternatives, the *Best Western Zion Park Inn* at no. 1215 (☎435/772-3200 or 1-800/934-7275, ⊛www. zionparkinn.com; ❺), and the extremely stylish ⅍ *Desert Pearl Inn*, no. 707 (☎435/772-8888 or 1-888/828-0898, ⊛www.desertpearl.com; ❻), offer good views and pools. The ⅍ *Spotted Dog Café*, 428 Zion Park Blvd (☎435/772-3244), is the finest local **restaurant**, while apart from being the liveliest **bar** for miles, the dinner-only *Bit and Spur Saloon*, opposite the *Zion Park Inn* (☎435/772-3498), serves very good Mexican food.

The Kolob Canyons

Although the immaculate **Kolob Canyons** are just three miles off I-15, twenty miles south of Cedar City, this section of Zion receives far fewer visitors than Zion Canyon itself. Here, too, the focus is on **red-rock canyons**, which in the Kolob seem somehow redder, and the trees greener, than those down below.

The view from the five-mile paved road that heads up from the small but worthwhile **visitor center** (daily: late April to mid-Oct 8am–5pm, mid-Oct to late April 8am–4.30pm; ☎435/586-9548) is amazing, but hiking along either of two main trails will give you a sense of what makes this place so special. The first and shorter of the two starts two miles from the visitor center and follows Taylor Creek on a five-mile roundtrip to **Double Arch Alcove**, a spectacular natural amphitheater roofed by twin sandstone arches; there's also a small waterfall quarter of a mile further along. The other trail starts from the north side of the parking area at Lee Pass, four miles beyond the visitor center, and follows a well-marked route for seven miles past LaVerkin Falls to **Kolob Arch**, which at over 300ft across rivals Landscape Arch in Arches (see p.996) as the world's longest natural rock span.

Bryce Canyon National Park

The surface of the earth can hold few weirder-looking spots than **BRYCE CAN-YON**, a two-hour drive (86 miles) northeast of Zion. Named for Mormon settler Ebenezer Bryce, who memorably declared that it was "a helluva place to lose a cow," it is not in fact a canyon at all. Along a twenty-mile shelf on the eastern edge of the thickly forested **Paunsaugunt Plateau**, 8000ft above sea level, successive strata of dazzlingly colored rock have slipped and slid and washed away to leave a menagerie of multihued and contorted **stone pinnacles**.

In houses of yellow, red, and flaming oranges, the formations here have been eroded out of the muddy sandstone by a combination of icy winters (the temperature drops below freezing two hundred nights out of the year) and summer rainstorms. The racks of top-heavy pinnacles known as "**hoodoos**" were formed when the harder upper layers of rock stayed firm as the lower levels were worn away beneath them. **Thor's Hammer**, visible from Sunset Point, is the most alarmingly precarious. These hoodoos look down into technicolor ravines, all far more vivid than the Grand Canyon and much more human in scale. The whole place is at its most inspiring in winter, when the figures stand out from a blanket of snow.

The park approach road runs south from Hwy-12 about twenty miles east of the small town of Panguitch; the **entrance fee** is $20 per vehicle, per week. Despite the existence of a free (limited and summer-only) **shuttle bus** system, visitors can drive to all the scenic overlooks year round.

The two most popular viewpoints into **Bryce Amphitheater**, at the heart of the park, are on either side of *Bryce Canyon Lodge* (see below): the more northerly, **Sunrise Point**, is 350 yards from the parking lot and so is slightly less crowded than **Sunset Point**, where most of the bus tours stop. A network of **hiking trails** drops abruptly from the rim down into the amphitheater. One good three-mile trek switchbacks steeply from Sunset Point through the cool 200-foot canyons of **Wall Street**, where a pair of 800-year-old fir trees stretch to reach daylight. It then cuts across the surreal landscape into the basin known as the **Queen's Garden**, where the stout and remarkable likeness of Queen Victoria sits in majestic condescension – pointed out by a brass plaque – before climbing back up to the rim at Sunrise Point. A dozen trails crisscross the amphitheater, but it's surprisingly easy to get lost, so don't stray from the marked routes.

Sunrise and Sunset points notwithstanding, the best view at both sunset and dawn (which is the best time for taking pictures) is from **Bryce Point**, at the southern end of the amphitheater. From here, you can look down not only at the Bryce Canyon formations but also take in the grand sweep of the whole region, east to the **Henry Mountains** and north to the Escalante range. The park road then climbs another twenty miles south, by way of the intensely colored **Natural Bridge**, an 85-foot rock arch spanning a steep gully, en route to its dead end at **Rainbow Point**.

Practicalities

The park's **visitor center**, just past the entrance, is a valuable source of information on current weather and hiking conditions (daily: mid-June to mid-Sept 8am–8pm; May to mid-June and mid-Sept to Oct 8am–6pm; Nov–April 8am–4.30pm; ☏435/834-5322, ⓦwww.nps.gov/brca). Much the best place to **stay** is the venerable *Bryce Canyon Lodge*, one hundred yards from the rim between Sunrise and Sunset points (April–Oct only; reserve through Xanterra ☏303/297-2757 or 1-888/297-2757, ⓦwww.brycecanyonlodge.com; ⑥), where rustic cabins cost a few dollars more than basic doubles. It also has a **dining room**, a grocery store, a laundry, and public showers.

The northern approaches to the park, just off Hwy-12, are guarded (not to say disfigured) by two **motels**, both owned by the same company and open year-round; the large *Ruby's Inn* (☏435/834-5341 or 1-866/866-6616, ⓦwww.rubysinn.com; ⑥), which has a dreadful restaurant, and the cheaper, newer (and misleadingly named) *Bryce View Lodge* (☏435/834-5180 or 1-888/279-2304,

ⓦ www.bryceviewlodge.com; ❸). *Ruby's Inn* has its own **campground** ($17.50), and there are also two first-come, first-served campgrounds within the park, which charge $10 per night: *Sunset Campground*, close to Sunset Point, and *North Campground*, near the visitor center. Backpackers can choose from dozens of sites below the rim, all south of Bryce Point; pick up the required permit at the visitor center, and take lots of water.

Bryce Canyon to Capitol Reef: Highway 12

Turning its back on the grand amphitheater of Bryce Canyon, the tiny hamlet of **TROPIC**, which straggles along Hwy-12 eight miles east of the park entrance, seems almost embarrassed about the flamboyant geological phenomena ranged along the ridge above it. The practical-minded people of this Mormon farming community (population 380) don't especially concern themselves with tourists, but they have restored Ebenezer Bryce's log cabin, which stands next to the **Bryce Pioneer Village** motel-cum-restaurant (ⓣ 435/679-8546 or 1-800/222-0381, ⓦ www. bpvillage.com; ❸). An unmarked road heads west from the cabin two miles to the park boundary, from where it's a two-mile hike up to the main formations.

Back on Hwy-12, the road curves along the edge of the Table Cliff Plateau before dropping down into the remote canyons of the **Escalante River**, the last river system to be discovered within the continental US and site of some of the finest **backpacking** routes in the Southwest. As soon as you walk even a hundred yards off the main highway, you're in a wilderness that few travelers ever see.

ESCALANTE, 33 miles east of Cannonville, was just another roadside town until it was given a new lease on life in 1996 by the surprise Presidential proclamation that created the vast **Grand Staircase-Escalante National Monument** (free). The interagency **visitor center** at the west end of town (mid-March to Oct daily 7.30am–5.30pm; Nov to mid-March Mon–Fri 8am–4.30pm; ⓣ 435/826-5499, ⓦ www. ut.blm.gov/monument), is a mine of up-to-date information on all the public lands in the vicinity, and can suggest **hiking** or **mountain-biking** trips into the backcountry. The most accessible local highlight is **Calf Creek**, sixteen miles east of Escalante, where a well-marked trail leads just under three miles upstream to a gorgeous shaded dell replete with a 125-foot waterfall, and a nice undeveloped **campground** ($7) as well. More ambitious trips start from trailheads along the dusty but usually passable **Hole-in-the-Rock Road**, which turns south from Hwy-12 five miles east of town. A trio of slender, storm-gouged **slot canyons**, including the delicate, graceful Peek-a-Boo Canyon and the downright intimidating Spooky Canyon, can be reached by a mile-long hike from the end of Dry Fork Road, 26 miles along. From **Hurricane Wash**, 34 miles along, you can hike five miles to reach Coyote Gulch, and then a further five miles, passing sandstone bridges and arches, to the Escalante River. Under normal conditions, two-wheel-drive vehicles should go no further than **Dance Hall Rock**, 36 miles down the road, a superb natural amphitheater sculpted out of the slickrock hills. The pick of Escalante's **motels** is unquestionably the *Prospector Inn*, 380 W Main St (ⓣ 435/826-4653, ⓦ www.prospectorinn.com; ❸).

Until the mid-1980s, when it was paved through to Capitol Reef, Hwy-12 ended at **BOULDER**, thirty miles beyond Escalante. Due **east** from there, all except twenty miles of the old dirt **Burr Trail** has (controversially) been paved, providing easy access to the southern reaches of **Capitol Reef National Park** and down to **Lake Powell**. At the junction of Hwy-12 and the Burr Trail, the modern *Boulder Mountain Lodge* (ⓣ 435/335-7460 or 1-800/556-3446, ⓦ www.boulder-utah.com; ❹) has twenty comfortable rooms and a reasonable restaurant. The best place to **eat** lies a few yards further east, in the spotless form of the *Boulder Mesa Restaurant*, 155 E Burr Trail Rd (ⓣ 435/335-7447), which is open daily for all meals.

North of Boulder, Hwy-12 makes a gorgeous drive up onto the Aquarius Plateau, with marvelous vistas to the east across waves of gold and red sandstone outcrops; there's a lovely **campground** (☏435/425-3702; $9) at Oak Creek, fifteen miles along.

Capitol Reef National Park

CAPITOL REEF might sound like something you'd find off the coast of Australia, but its towering ochre, white, and red-**rock walls** and deep **river canyons** are of a piece with the rest of the Utah desert. The outstanding feature is a multilayered, 1000-foot-high reef-like wall of uplifted sedimentary rock, a section of which reminded an early traveler of the grand dome of the US Capitol. Stretching for over a hundred miles north to south, but only a few miles across, the seemingly impenetrable barrier of the **Waterpocket Fold** was warped upward by the same process that lifted the Colorado Plateau, and the sharply defined sedimentary layers on display here trace over two hundred million years of geological activity. The Waterpocket Fold is sliced through in a number of places by deeply incised river canyons – some only twenty feet wide, but hundreds of feet deep – often accessible only by foot.

The one paved road through the park, Hwy-24, cuts across the northern half of the Fold, following the deep canyon of the **Fremont River**; motorists who stick to this road do not incur an entrance fee. Beneath the enormous and very prominent rock outcrop known as the **Castle**, the **visitor center** (daily: June–Sept 8am–7pm; Oct–May 8am–4.30pm; ☏435/425-3791, ⓦwww.nps.gov/care) has explanatory exhibits and an irresistible campground ($10), set amid the cherry, apple, and peach orchards of the abandoned Mormon community of **FRUITA**; in season, you can pick all the fruit you can gobble down. To the west, the **Goosenecks Overlook** gazes down 500ft into the entrenched canyons cut by Sulphur Creek. Further east, beyond Fruita's former schoolhouse, are some extraordinary **Fremont petroglyphs**, figures of bighorn sheep and stylized space-people chipped into the varnished red rock a thousand years ago. Another four and a half miles along, one of Capitol Reef's best **day-hikes** heads up along the gravelly riverbed through **Grand Wash** – a beautiful (and usually quite cool) canyon where, it's said, Butch Cassidy and his gang used to hide out.

Alternatively, the paved, popular **Scenic Drive** ($5 per vehicle) heads twelve miles south from the visitor center, past the top of Grand Wash to **Capitol Gorge** and back. A more adventurous sixty-mile loop trip explores **Cathedral Valley** in the north, while a 125-mile southern route starts at the foot of the volcanic **Henry Mountains**, then follows the Burr Trail through **Muley Twist Canyon**, and continues west to Boulder (see opposite).

The nearest **food and lodging** to Capitol Reef is eleven miles west, in and near the rapidly growing town of **TORREY**. The *Sand Creek Hostel & Bunkhouse*, 540 W Main St (closed mid-Oct to March; ☏435/425-3577 or 1-877/425-3578, ⓦwww.sandcreekrv.com; ❶), is a thriving little complex that offers camping for $11, dorm beds for $10, and a couple of inexpensive private cabins for $28, while the *Rim Rock Inn*, three miles east at 2523 E Hwy-24 (☏435/425-3398 or 1-888/447-4676, ⓦwww.therimrock.net; ❸) is a new, wood-built hotel, with a good dining room. Back in town, *Café Diablo*, 599 W Main St (☏435/425-3070) is a surprisingly inventive dinner-only restaurant.

Goblin Valley

Fifty fairly desolate miles east of Capitol Reef along Hwy-24, you reach the tiny crossroads of **Hanksville**. Twenty miles north on Hwy-24, a right turn takes you onto a 32-mile dirt road to a real anthropological and artistic wonder – the rock paintings of **Horseshoe Canyon**, a remote subsection of Canyonlands National Park (see below).

Half a mile further north on Hwy-24, a side road to the west veers off to **Goblin Valley State Park** (open 24hr; $5), where thousands of gnome-like figures loom out of the soft Entrada sandstone. The **Carmel Canyon** trail loops for over a mile through a throng of misshapen rock pillars, many of which seem to have eyes and other human features; in the 2000 sci-fi movie spoof *Galaxy Quest*, the entire valley comes to life. Stay at the well-equipped **campground** (☎1-800/322-3770; $10) if you want to see the place by moonlight, when it looks especially spooky.

Green River

The uneventful riverside town of **GREEN RIVER**, just east of the Hwy-24 junction on I-70, is the largest community on a 200-mile stretch of interstate. One good reason to visit is the **John Wesley Powell River History Museum**, 885 E Main St (April–Oct daily 8am–8pm, Nov–March Tues–Sat 9am–4pm; $2; Ⓦwww.jwprhm.com), which features the anything-but-dry personal accounts of the men who first successfully navigated the Colorado River from near its source all the way through the Grand Canyon. The museum also doubles as the local visitor center.

Green River holds a number of bargain-rate **motels**, and a few slightly classier options, including the *Best Western River Terrace*, 880 E Main St (☎435/564-3401 or 1-800/528-1234, Ⓦwww.bestwestern.com; ❹), which has a pool, river views, and a decent restaurant.

Canyonlands National Park

CANYONLANDS NATIONAL PARK, at 527 square miles the largest and most magnificent of Utah's national parks, is as hard to define as it is to map. Its closest equivalent, the Grand Canyon, is by comparison simply an almighty crack in an otherwise relatively flat plain; the Canyonlands area is a bewildering tangle of canyons, plateaus, fissures, and faults, scattered with buttes and monoliths, pierced by arches and caverns, and penetrated only by a paltry handful of dead-end roads.

Canyonlands focuses on the Y-shaped confluence of the **Green** and **Colorado rivers**, buried deep in the desert forty miles southwest of Moab. There's only one spot from which you can see the rivers meet, however, and that's a five-mile hike from the nearest road. With no road down to the rivers, let alone across them, the park therefore splits into three major sections. The **Needles**, east of the Colorado, is a red-rock wonderland of sandstone pinnacles and hidden meadows that's a favorite with hardy hikers and four-wheel-drive enthusiasts, while the **Maze**, west of both the Colorado and the Green, is a virtually inaccessible labyrinth of tortuous, waterless canyons. In the wedge of the "Y" between the two, the high, dry mesa of the **Island In The Sky** commands astonishing views across the whole park and beyond, with several overlooks that can easily be toured by car. Getting from any one of these sections to the others involves a drive of at least a hundred miles.

Canyonlands is not a place that lends itself to a short visit. With no lodging, and little camping, inside the park, and no loop road to whisk you through it, it takes a full day to have even a cursory look at a single segment. Considering that summer temperatures regularly exceed 100°F and most trails have no water and little shade, the Island In The Sky is the most immediately rewarding option. On the other hand, if you fancy a long day-hike you'd do better to set off into the Needles (see opposite).

Canyonlands National Park charges an **entry fee** of $10 per vehicle, $5 for cyclists or hikers, valid for seven days in all sections of the park. Only limited numbers of visitors are allowed to spend a night or more in the backcountry. **Backpacking** permits, covering a maximum party of seven persons in the Needles and Island In The Sky districts, or five persons in the Maze, cost $15. Permits for **four-wheel-drive** or **mountain-biking** expeditions that involve backcountry camping, issued for groups of up to three vehicles with a total of fifteen people in the Island In The Sky, ten in the Needles, or nine in the Maze, are $30. **Reservations** are essential for the most popular areas, especially in the peak seasons of spring and fall. Permits must be purchased at least two weeks in advance, and must be picked up in person, as well – with every member of the group present – from the appropriate park visitor center, at least one hour before it closes. For full details, see the official website at ⒲www.nps.gov/cany.

Island In The Sky and Dead Horse Point State Park

Reached by a good road that climbs steadily up from US-191, 21 miles south of I-70, the **Island In The Sky** district looks out over hundreds of miles of flat-topped mesas that drop in 2000-foot steps to the river. Four miles along from its **visitor center** (daily: summer 8am–6pm; winter 8am–4.30pm; ⓉTEL435/259-4712), the **Mesa Arch Trail** is the area's best short hike, looping for a mile around the mesa-top hillocks to the edge of the abyss, where long, shallow Mesa Arch frames an extraordinary view of the **La Sal Mountains**, 35 miles northeast. The definitive vantage point, however, is **Grand View Point Overlook**, another five miles on at the southern end of the road. An agoraphobic's nightmare, it commands a hundred-mile prospect of layer upon layer of bare sandstone, here stacked thousands of feet high, there fractured into bottomless canyons. The Island In The Sky's only developed **campground**, the first-come, first-served and waterless *Willow Flat* ($5), is just back from the **Green River Overlook**, reached by taking the right fork shortly after the Mesa Arch trailhead.

On the way in to Island In The Sky, a turnoff long before the visitor center cuts across south to the smaller but equally breathtaking **Dead Horse Point**, located at the tip of a narrow mesa, which looks straight down 2000ft to the twisting Colorado River. Cowboys used the mesa as a natural corral, herding up wild horses then blocking them in behind a piñon pine fence that still marks its 90-foot neck. One band of horses was left here too long and died – hence the name. As a Utah state park, Dead Horse Point charges its own $7 admission fee, and national-park passes cannot be used. The **visitor center** (daily: summer 8am–6pm; winter 8am–5pm; ⓉTEL435/259-2614) stands two miles short of the point itself, and there's also a **campground** ($14; reservations mid-March to mid-Oct only, $5 extra, ⓉTEL1-800/322-3770).

The Needles and Newspaper Rock

Taking its name from the thousands of colorful sandstone pillars, knobs, and hoodoos that punctuate its many lush canyons and basins, the **Needles** district allows a more intimate look at the Canyonlands environment than does Island In The Sky. Here you're not always gazing thousands of feet downward or scanning the distant horizon; instead you can wander through seemingly endless acres of stone figures.

The road ends with a great collection of mushroom-shaped hoodoos at the **Big Spring Canyon Overlook**. A memorable and demanding eleven-mile roundtrip hike from here remains the only way to get to the **Confluence Overlook**, 1000ft

⑫

THE SOUTHWEST | Southern Utah: the national parks

995

above the point where the Green River joins the muddy waters of the Colorado, to flow together, parallel but separate, toward fearsome **Cataract Canyon**. Various short walks head off the road at selected viewpoints; one of the best is **Pothole Point**, a mile before **Big Spring Canyon**. A longer day-trip, or a good overnight hike, leaves from near the *Squaw Flat* **campground** ($10) to the green meadow of **Chesler Park**, cutting through the narrow cleft of the Joint Trail. Check in at the **visitor center** (daily: summer 8am–6pm; winter 8am–4.30pm; ☎435/259-4711) near the park boundary to get up-to-date information, as well as backcountry permits if you plan to camp out.

The 35-mile drive in to the Needles from US-191 is among the prettiest in the state, winding along Indian Creek through deep red-rock canyons lined by pines and cottonwoods. **Newspaper Rock**, twelve miles in, is the best of many similarly named sites; here hundreds of tiny **petroglyphs**, many of which show deer, antelope, bear claws, and helmeted human figures, have been etched in the jet-black desert varnish of a red-sandstone boulder by centuries of passing hunters and travelers. There's a lovely (free) streamside **campground** just across the road.

The Maze and Horseshoe Canyon

Of the half-million yearly visitors to Canyonlands, only about one in a hundred makes it into the harsh and remote **Maze** district. Filling up the western third of the park, on the far side of the Colorado and Green rivers, the Maze is noted for its ancient rock-art panels and for its many-fingered box canyons, accessible only by jeep or by long, dry hiking trails. If you're tempted, call into the Hans Flat **ranger station**, 46 miles east of Hwy-24 (daily 8am–4.30pm; ☎435/259-2652).

Pretty, tree-lined **Horseshoe Canyon**, reached halfway down a long, long dirt road that loops south from Green River itself to join Hwy-24 just south of Goblin Valley (see p.993), contains the greatest concentration of **ancient rock art** in the Southwest. Allowing at least an hour's driving from the highway both before and after, plus five hours for the six-mile roundtrip hike down into the canyon itself, you'll need to set aside a full day, but it's well worth the effort, both for the joy of the walk and for the sight of the "**Great Gallery**" at the far end. Hundreds of mysterious, haunting pictographs – mostly life-sized human figures, albeit weirdly elongated, or draped in robes and adorned with strange, staring eyes – were painted onto these red-sandstone walls, probably between 500 BC and 500 AD. Rangers from Hans Flat (see above) lead guided hikes into Horseshoe Canyon on summer weekends (April–Oct Sat & Sun 9am).

Arches National Park

The writer Edward Abbey, who spent a year as a ranger at **ARCHES NATION-AL PARK** in the 1950s, wrote in *Desert Solitaire* that its arid landscape was as "naked, monolithic, austere, and unadorned as the sculpture of the moon." It certainly is one of the least terrestrial places on this planet. Massive fins of red and golden sandstone stand to attention out of the bare desert plain, and over eighteen hundred natural arches of various shapes and sizes have been cut into the rock by eons of erosion. Apart from the single ribbon of black asphalt that snakes through the park, there's nothing even vaguely human about it. The narrow, hunching ridges are more like dinosaurs' backbones than solid rock, and under a full moon, at twilight, or during the lightning strikes of a distant thunderstorm, you can't help but imagine that the landscape has a life of its own.

While you could race through in a couple of hours, to do Arches justice you should plan to spend a whole day here at the very least. A twenty-mile road cuts uphill sharply from US-191 and the ultra-modern park **visitor center** (daily:

mid-April to early Oct 7.30am–6.30pm; mid-March to mid-April and middle two weeks in Oct 7.30am–5.30pm; late Oct to mid-March 8am–4.30pm; $10 per vehicle or $5 for motorcyclists, cyclists, and pedestrians; ⓣ435/719-2299, ⓦwww.nps.gov/arch). Exhibits here explain how the arches are formed and point out some of the more photogenic examples. The first possible stop is the south trailhead for **Park Avenue**, an easy trail leading one mile down a scoured, rock-bottomed wash. If you stay on the road, the **La Sal Mountains Viewpoint** provides a grandstand look at the distant peaks rising over 12,000ft above the desert, as well as the huge red chunk of **Courthouse Towers** closer at hand.

From **Balanced Rock** beyond – a 50-foot boulder atop a slender 75-foot pedestal – a turning to the right winds for two miles through the **Windows** section, where

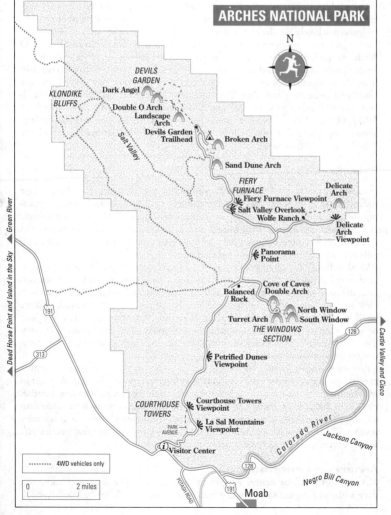

a half-mile trail loops through a dense concentration of massive arches, some over 100ft high and 150ft across. A second trail, fifty yards beyond, leads to **Double Arch**, a staunch pair of arches that together support another arch overhead.

Further on, the main road drops downhill for two miles past Panorama Point and the turnoff to **Wolfe Ranch**, where a century-old log cabin now serves as the trailhead for the wonderful three-mile roundtrip hike up to **Delicate Arch**, which, as a freestanding crescent of rock perched at the brink of a deep canyon, is by far the most impressive arch in the park. Crowds congregate here each evening for the superb sunset views; coming back down in the dark can be a little hair-raising, though. Three miles beyond the Wolfe Ranch turnoff, the deep, sharp-sided mini-canyons of the **Fiery Furnace** section form a (usually quite cool) labyrinth through which rangers lead regular hikes in spring, summer, and fall ($8; reserve in advance at the visitor center).

The road continues on to the **Devil's Garden** trailhead, from which an easy one-mile walk leads to a view of the astonishing 306-foot span of **Landscape Arch**, now too perilously slender to approach more closely. Several other arches lie along short spur trails off the route; seeing them all, and returning from **Double O Arch** via the longer primitive trail, requires a total hike of just over seven miles. Arches' only **campground** ($10; water only available mid-March to Oct) is across from the trailhead. ; 24 of its 52 sites are always first-come first-served, and are usually taken by early morning. The remaining 28 can be reserved between March and October only, between four and 240 days in advance (☎518/885-3639 or 1-877/444-6777, ⓦwww.reserveusa.com). Permits for **backcountry camping**, allowed anywhere that's a mile from the road and half a mile from any trail, are issued at the visitor center.

Moab

Founded in the late 1800s, **MOAB** was hardly a speck until the 1950s, when prospector Charlie Steen discovered uranium in the nearby hills. When the ensuing mining boom finally waned, the conservative hold of Moab's mine-owners and businessmen over the land waned with it, and the town threw in its lot with tourism. Over the last twenty years, it has transformed itself into the Southwest's number one adventure-vacation destination.

Moab still isn't a large town, though – the population has yet to reach ten thousand – and neither is it an attractive one. The setting is what matters. With two national parks on its doorstep, plus millions more acres of public land, Moab is an ideal base for outdoors enthusiasts. At first, it was a haven for **mountain bikers** lured by the legendary **Slickrock Bike Trail** (see box, opposite). Then the **jeep** drivers began to turn up, and the **whitewater-rafting** companies moved in, too. These days it's almost literally bursting, all year, with legions of Lycra-clad vacationers from all over the world.

Perhaps the main reason Moab has grown so fast is that out-of-state visitors tend to find Utah's other rural communities so irredeemably boring. As soon as Moab emerged from the pack, it became a beacon in the desert, attracting tourists ecstatic to find a town that stayed up after dark. Moab amounts to little more than a few miles of motels, restaurants, and bars, but that's enough to make it the only southern-Utah town where you can stay for a week and still feel that you haven't seen everything, and everyone, a dozen times.

Arrival and information

Moab's superb **visitor center** is right in the heart of town at Center and Main streets (daily: summer 8am–9pm; winter 9am–noon & 1–5pm; ☎435/259-8825

River trips

Among Moab's dozen licensed operators offering **motorized** one-day trips along the Colorado River for around $45 and up are Worldwide River Expeditions (☎435/259-7515, 1-800/231-2769 ⓦ www.worldwideriver.com), Adrift Adventures (☎435/259-8594 or 1-800/874-4483, ⓦ www.adrift.net), and Tag-a-Long Expeditions (☎435/259-8946 or 1-800/453-3292, ⓦ www.tagalong.com). The trips start northwest of Moab, near the butte known as Fisher Towers, and arrive near town in the afternoon; many companies give passengers the chance to float quieter stretches in two-person kayaks. The same operators run **oar-powered** trips that are slower but much quieter, and less expensive than motorboat trips. Longer (2- to 7-day) trips head through Cataract Canyon and other wild Canyonlands spots.

Mountain biking

While the Moab area is ideally suited to mountain-bike touring, only experienced riders should attempt its most challenging route, the **Slickrock Bike Trail**. This ten-mile, half-day loop starts atop the mesa about three miles east of Moab, threading its way among the sandstone knobs with views of the La Sal Mountains and the Colorado River. A more relaxing alternative is to explore the dirt roads leading through the red-rock country of Kane Creek, west of town.

Among **bike shops** offering daily rental and guided tours, including trips into Canyonland National Park, are Rim Tours (☎435/259-5223 or 1-800/626-7335, ⓦ www.rimtours.com), and Poison Spider (☎435/259-7882 or 1-800/635-1792, ⓦ www.poisonspiderbicycles.com).

Jeep tours

Most of the thousands of miles of **jeep trails** around Moab were built years ago by miners and haven't been maintained since. The visitor center has a free map and guide to some of the more popular ones, and you can rent a four-wheel-drive jeep or pickup truck for around $100 per day from Slickrock 4x4 Rentals at 284 N Main St (☎435/259-5678, www.moab-utah.com/jeep/jeep.html). **Guided jeep tours** (around $100 per person per day) are offered by Tag-a-Long Expeditions (see above).

Scenic flights

From a small airfield twenty miles north of Moab on US-91, Redtail Aviation (☎435/259-7421 or 1-800/842-9251, ⓦ www.redtailaviation.com) and Slickrock Air Guides (☎435/259-6216, ⓦ www.slickrockairguides.com) run unforgettable **flights** over the Canyonlands area and beyond, starting at $100–125 per person for a one-hour reconnaissance.

or 1-800/635-6622, ⓦ www.discovermoab.com). Bighorn Express (☎801/746-2417 or 1-888/655-7433, ⓦ www.bighornexpress.com) runs daily shuttle **buses** between Salt Lake City and Moab, via Green River (site of the nearest Amtrak station) and continuing on to Monticello.

Accommodation

If you've already been in Utah for a while when you reach Moab, its glittering neon **motel** signs will come as a big surprise. At last count, there were thirty motels and a dozen B&Bs in town, but every one of the 1500-plus rooms is taken on many nights between mid-March and October – when you'd be lucky to find anything below $75 – so reservations are strongly recommended.

Commercial **campgrounds** nearby include the well-shaded *Slickrock Campground*, 1301 N Hwy-191 (☎435/259-7660 or 1-800/448-8873, ⓦ www

⑫

THE SOUTHWEST | Southern Utah: the national parks

.slickrockcampground.com; $18), a mile north of town; if you're happy to put up with far more primitive facilities to escape the crowds, head instead for the Bureau of Land Management's **Sand Flats Recreation Area**, along the top of the mesa to the east of town, near the Slickrock Bike Trail, at 1924 S Roadrunner Hill (☎ 435/259-6111; $8).

Aarchway Inn 1551 N Hwy-191 ☎ 435/259-2599 or 1-800/341-9359, ⓦ www.aarchwayinn.com. Well-equipped motel with a nice pool, not far from the Colorado at the north end of town. ④

Adobe Abode 778 W Kane Creek Blvd ☎ 435/259-7716, ⓦ www.adobeabodemoab.com. Attractive, Pueblo-style home a few hundred yards from downtown Moab, offering six comfortable and tastefully furnished B&B rooms. ⑤

Best Western Greenwell Inn 105 S Main St ☎ 435/259-6151 or 1-800/780-7234, ⓦ www. bestwesternmoab.com. Central, modern hotel that offers spacious good-value rooms with tasteful furnishings and fittings. ⑥

Gonzo Inn 100 W 200 South ☎ 435/259-2515 or 1-800/791-4044, ⓦ www.gonzoinn.com. Luxurious if rather self-consciously hip inn, complete with kitsch-retro furnishings, quirky artworks, and an espresso bar. ⑥

Inca Inn Motel 570 N Main St ☎ 435/259-7261, ⓦ www.moab-utah.com/inca/inn.html. Clean, minimally equipped but adequate budget motel. ②

Lazy Lizard International Hostel 1213 S Hwy-191 ☎ 435/259-6057, ⓦ www.lazylizardhostel. com. Amiable, very laid-back independent hostel, a mile south of the center, with $9 beds in six-person dorms, $6 camping, and private cabins for $24, plus hot tub, kitchen, and Internet access. ①

Eating and drinking

Moab offers by far the greatest range of **restaurants** in southern Utah, most of which cater to vegetarians. With two pubs and a winery, there's also no problem getting a **drink**, while **coffee bars** are springing up everywhere.

Buck's Grill House 1393 N Hwy-191 ☎ 435/259-5201. Belying its stockade-like exterior, this "American Western Food" joint is actually a sophisticated affair, serving rich, classy Southwestern food, such as game hen or pork ribs, at very reasonable prices. Open for dinner nightly.

Desert Bistro 1266 N Main St ☎ 435/259-0756. Expensive but top-notch dinner-only restaurant, set in a ranch home with a patio that's perfect for summer nights. On the modern bistro menu, entrees like venison medallions or smoked rabbit agnolotti cost up to $35.

Eddie McStiff's 57 S Main St ☎ 435/259-2337. Central pub, next to the visitor center, which serves some interesting beers, including raspberry and

blueberry varieties, and also a diverse and inexpensive menu of salads, pizzas, and pasta.

Jailhouse Café 101 N Main St ☎ 435/259-3900. Very popular central café, open for breakfast only, until noon on weekdays and 1pm at weekends. There's indoor and outdoor seating year-round, and great specials like ginger pancakes and eggs Benedict.

Mondo Café 59 S Main St ☎ 435/259-5551. Groovy all-day hangout next to *Eddie McStiff's* (see above), serving espresso coffees and the odd pastry or sandwich.

The Peace Tree 20 S Main St ☎ 435/259-8503. Very central juice bar and café that serves good sandwiches, wraps, and smoothies to take out or eat on the small outdoor patio, until 6.30pm daily.

Natural Bridges National Monument

One of the prettiest and least traveled highways in southern Utah, **Hwy-95** runs for over a hundred miles southeast from Capitol Reef, through dozens of red-rock canyons, and across the Dirty Devil and Colorado rivers before topping out on the sagebrush plains of San Juan County. En route it gives access to the marvelous collection of sandstone spans at **Natural Bridges National Monument**, forty miles west of US-191. Three canyons come together here, and at each junction the streams that carved them have also formed sandstone bridges. The largest, **Sipapu Bridge**, is 268ft across at its base and over 200ft high, and can be seen from the nine-mile paved road that loops through the monument; hike less than a mile down into the canyon for a closer look. **Kachina Bridge**, the next along the road, is nearly as high but twice as thick, and has Ancestral Puebloan pictographs at its base. The oldest, slimmest, and most fragile bridge – **Owachomo**, a mile and a half up Armstrong Canyon – spans 180ft but is only nine feet thick at its thinnest point. A strenuous eight-mile trail along the canyon bottom leads past all three bridges.

Admission to the monument is $6 per vehicle. The **visitor center** (daily: March–Oct 8am–5.30pm; Nov–Feb 9am–4.30pm; ☏435/692-1234, ⓦwww.nps.gov/nabr), four miles off Hwy-95, holds displays explaining how the bridges were formed. Camping is allowed only in the small **campground** ($10) near the visitor center, which also has the only drinkable water in the monument.

Monticello

The small town of **MONTICELLO** stands 56 miles south of Moab on US-191, sixteen miles beyond the turnoff for the Needles section of Canyonlands (see p.994). Its strip of **motels** includes a smart *Days Inn*, 549 N Main St (☏435/587-2458 or 1-800/325-2525, ⓦwww.daysinn.com; ❹) and the cheaper *Go West Inn*, 649 N Main St (☏435/587-2489; ❸). Good, large, standard **meals** can be had at the *MD Ranch Cookhouse*, 380 S Main St (☏435/587-3299). Information on the town, and on the parks and public lands in the vicinity, can be picked up from the **visitor center**, in the courthouse at 117 S Main St (April–Oct Mon–Fri 8am–5pm, Sat & Sun 10am–5pm; Nov–March Mon–Fri 8am–5pm; ☏435/587-3235 or 1-800/574-4386, ⓦwww.southeastutah.org).

The San Juan River, Mexican Hat, and Bluff

From Natural Bridges, Hwy-261 runs south for some 25 miles before coming to what looks like a dead end at the edge of Cedar Mesa. From here, high above the eerie sandstone towers of the **Valley of the Gods** (where much of *Thelma and Louise* was filmed), the road turns to gravel before dropping over a thousand feet in little over two twisting, hairpin-turning miles down the "**Moki Dugway**." Six miles from the foot of the switchbacks, the barely marked Hwy-316 shoots across what seems like a flat valley floor to yet another overlook, this time high above the **San Juan River** at the extraordinary and aptly named **Goosenecks State Reserve** (open 24hr; free). In a textbook example of what geologists call an entrenched meander, the river, a thousand feet below, snakes around in such convoluted twists and turns that it flows six miles in total for every one mile west.

Back on Hwy-261 and just south, sleepy **MEXICAN HAT**, briefly a frenzied gold-mining camp, takes its name from a riverside **sandstone hoodoo**, just north of town, that looks like a south-of-the-border sombrero. More of a cluster of buildings on the banks of the river than a town, it's good fun and makes a convenient base for visiting Monument Valley, twenty miles south (see p.979). The best **place to stay** is the *San Juan Inn* (☏435/683-2220 or 1-800/447-2022; ❸), right on the river, which has its own grocery store and trading post, as well as the amiable *Olde Bridge Bar and Grill*, which offers cold beers and Navajo tacos.

The rafts you may see emerging from the water at Mexican Hat went in at **BLUFF**, twenty miles upstream. The road between the towns, US-163, doesn't follow the river very closely but is still an enthralling drive, and when you get there the town itself has a number of **Mormon pioneer houses** along its back-streets. Places to **eat** in Bluff include the *Twin Rocks Café* (☏435/672-2341) and the *Cottonwood Steakhouse* (☏435/672-2282), while an excellent **motel** at the south end of town, the *Desert Rose Inn*, 701 W Hwy-191 (☏435/672-2303 or 1-888/475-7673, ⓦwww.desertroseinn.com; ❹), holds thirty attractively decorated rooms.

Hovenweep National Monument

Hidden in the no-man's-land that straddles the Utah–Colorado border, the remote **Ancestral Puebloan ruins** at **Hovenweep National Monument** offer a haunting sense of timeless isolation. Located 25 miles east of US-191 along Hwy-262, which branches off halfway between Bluff and Blanding, and 35 miles west of Cortez, Colorado, Hovenweep preserves six distinct conglomerations of ruins sprouting from the rims of shallow desert canyons and dwarfed by the distant mountains, but easy access is restricted to **Little Ruin Canyon**, behind the smart new **visitor center** (daily: March–Oct 8am–6pm; Nov–Feb 8am–5pm; $6; ℡ 970/562-4282, Ⓦ www.nps.gov/hove). A mile-long loop trail offers good views of the largest ruins, including the grandly named **Hovenweep Castle**, constructed around 1200 AD.

△ Hovenweep National Monument

No accommodation, gasoline, or food is available at or anywhere near Hovenweep, but a 31-site **campground** beside the ranger station remains open all year ($10; no reservations).

Lake Powell and Glen Canyon Dam

The mighty rivers and canyons of southern Utah come to an abrupt and ignoble end at the Arizona border, where the **Glen Canyon Dam** stops them dead in the stagnant waters of **Lake Powell**. Ironically, the lake is named for John Wesley Powell, the first person to run the Colorado River through the Grand Canyon. The roaring torrents with which he battled, along with magnificent Glen Canyon itself, are now lost beneath these placid blue waters, and the blocked-up Colorado, Green, Dirty Devil, San Juan, and Escalante rivers are now a playground for houseboaters and water-skiers. The construction of the dam in the early 1960s outraged environmentalists and archeologists, and the dam has created one of the most peculiar – and utterly unnatural – landscapes imaginable, the deep and tranquil lake a surreal contrast with the surrounding dry slickrock and sandstone buttes.

Lake Powell has 1960 miles of shoreline, which is more than the entire Pacific coast of the US, and 96 water-filled side canyons. The water level fluctuates considerably, so for much of the time the rocks to all sides are bleached for many feet above the current waterline, with a dirty-bath tidemark sullying the golden sandstone. Most of the many summer visitors bring their own boats, or rent a vessel from one of the four marinas that fringe the lake.

If you're passing through, by far the most accessible stop is **Wahweap Marina**, just off US-89 on the way between Zion and the Grand Canyon, where the plush *Lake Powell Resort* (☎928/645-2433 or 1-800/528-6154, ⓦwww.visitlakepowell.com; ⑥) has comfortable lakeside rooms and some of the best food within a day's drive. The same company arranges **houseboat rental** from Wahweap or other Lake Powell marinas; boats sleep four or more people and cost from $1360 for three days in summer. There's **camping** on the lakeshore at each of the marinas. Otherwise, the nearest **accommodation** is across the Arizona border in **PAGE**, home of the usual assortment of chain motels and diners, including the good-value *Best Western at Lake Powell*, 208 N Lake Powell Blvd (☎928/645-5988 or 1-888/794-2888, ⓦwww.bestwestern.com; ③).

GLEN CANYON DAM itself, in between Page and Wahweap, can be seen from the **Carl Hayden Visitor Center** (daily: Oct–April 8am–5pm; May–Sept

Rainbow Bridge National Monument

The spectacular and extremely remote **Rainbow Bridge National Monument**, the world's largest natural bridge, can be visited on eight-hour **guided boat tours** from Wahweap marina (April–Oct daily 8am & 10am, Nov–March Sat 9am; adults $115, under 13s $80; ☎928/645-2433 or 1-800/528-6154, ⓦwww.visitlakepowell.com). It lies roughly fifty miles by water from the marina, including a final mile or two down the narrow, winding side channel of Forbidding Canyon. From the unappealing jetty where the boats moor, bobbing in a morass of pond scum, a ten-minute walk leads to the astonishing giant sandstone gateway, springing up nearly 300ft from just above the waterline, with Navajo Mountain visible through its magnificent smooth curve. Its upper section is composed of Navajo sandstone, while the base belongs to the harder Kayenta formation, which is not as easily cut by flowing water. Despite the increase in tourism since the lake's creation, the monument remains an inspiring sight, and a place of special importance to the Navajo.

7am–7pm; ☎ 928/608-6404, ⓦ www.nps.gov/glca) on the west bank, but tours of the dam have been suspended since September 11, 2001.

The cheapest way to get out on the waters of Lake Powell is to take the **ferry** ($16 per car) between **Halls Crossing** and **Bullfrog** marinas, two-thirds of the way up the lake; from here the Burr Trail heads west toward Capitol Reef (see p.993), while Hwy-276 runs northeast to Natural Bridges (see p.1000).

Northern Utah

Compared to the scenic splendor of the southern half of the state, northern Utah holds little to interest the tourist, although **Salt Lake City**, the capital, is by far the state's largest and most cosmopolitan urban center. The dramatic Wasatch Mountains that line Salt Lake's eastern horizon do however come into their own in winter, as they constitute one of the nation's premier **ski destinations**. The **northeast corner** has coal mines, old railroad towns and, along the Wyoming border, the **Uinta Mountains**, uncrossed by road and showing hardly a sign of civilization. From the **northwest**, the harshly alkaline **Great Basin** plain stretches uneventfully west across Nevada to California.

Salt Lake City

Disarmingly pleasant and easygoing, **SALT LAKE CITY** is well worth a stop-over of a couple of days. It's not a particularly thrilling destination in itself, but its setting is superb, towered over by the **Wasatch Front**, which marks the dividing line between the comparatively lush eastern and the bone-dry western halves of northern Utah. The area offers great hiking and cycling in summer and fall and, in winter, some of the world's best skiing, as reflected in the city's hosting of the 2002 Winter Olympics. People elsewhere in the US still tend to imagine Salt Lake City as decidedly short on fun, but so long as you're willing to switch gears and slow down, its unhurried pace, and the positive energy and lack of pretense of its people, can make for a surprisingly enjoyable experience.

Arrival, information, and getting around
Salt Lake City International Airport (☎ 801/575-2400) is a mere four miles west of downtown. A **taxi** into town costs around $15; cheaper **shuttle vans** to downtown destinations are run by Xpress Shuttles (☎ 801/596-1600 or 1-800/397-0773, ⓦ www.xpressshuttle.com), while Canyon Transportation (☎ 801/255-1841, ⓦ www.canyontransport.com) serves the ski areas. Long-distance Greyhound-Trailways **buses** arrive downtown, at 160 W South Temple Blvd (☎ 801/355-9579), as do Amtrak **trains**, at 320 S Rio Grande Ave. Local buses, and also TRAX trams, are operated by the Utah Transit Authority (☎ 801/743-3882, ⓦ www.rideuta.com); journeys within the immediate downtown area are free.

The main **visitor center** for the city itself is downtown at 90 S West Temple Blvd in the Salt Palace Convention Center (summer Mon–Fri 8am–6pm, Sat & Sun 9am–5pm; winter Mon–Fri 8am–5pm, Sat & Sun 9am–5pm; ☎ 801/521-2822 or 1-800/541-4955, ⓦ www.visitsaltlake.com). For details on the rest of Utah, stop by the Utah Travel Council, which occupies the imposing Council Hall across from the capitol at 300 N State St (Mon–Fri 8am–5pm, Sat & Sun 10am–5pm; ☎ 801/538-1030, ⓦ www.utah.com).

SALT LAKE CITY

N

TRAX

● The Tabernacle

State Capitol

Family History Library

Mormon Temple

Beehive House

Temple Square

ZCMI Center

Delta Center

Salt Palace

Crossroads Plaza

Amtrak Station

400 SOUTH STREET

ACCOMMODATION

Brigham Street Inn	C
City Creek Inn	A
Hotel Monaco	D
Motel 6	F
Peery Hotel	E
Travelodge – Temple Square	B

RESTAURANTS & CAFÉS

Caffè Molise	1
Market Street Grill	4
Orbit Café	2
Sage's Café	3

0   400 yds

Accommodation

Salt Lake City is well equipped with **accommodation**, with downtown options that range from budget motels and B&B inns to rather more luxurious hotels, and the usual mid-range places near the airport and along the interstates. Weekend rates can be real bargains.

Brigham Street Inn 1135 E South Temple Blvd ☎801/364-4461 or 1-800/417-4461. Luxurious, peaceful – and inconspicuous – B&B a few blocks east of downtown toward the mountains. ❺

City Creek Inn 230 W North Temple Blvd ☎801/533-9100 or 1-866/533-4898, ⓦwww.city creekinn.com. Family-owned budget motor court, old-fashioned but nicely spruced up, offering great-value rooms very close to downtown. ❸

Hotel Monaco 15 W 200 South ☎801/595-0000 or 1-800/805-1801, ⓦwww.monaco-saltlakecity. com. Extremely hip, very upscale downtown hotel, housed in a former bank. ❾

International Ute Hostel 21 E Kelsey Ave ☎801/595-1645, ⓦwww.infobytes.com/utehostel. Much the better of Salt Lake City's two hostels, this small private establishment, a few miles south of downtown, offers $17 dorm beds and a couple of private rooms ($37), plus bike rental, a hot tub, and free airport pickup. ❶–❷

Motel 6 176 W 600 South St ☎801/531-1252. Reliable budget motel in downtown, handy for Amtrak. ❷

Peery Hotel 110 W 300 South St ☎801/521-4300 or 1-800/331-0073, ⓦwww.peeryhotel.com. Renovated 1910 downtown landmark, offering very

1005

tasteful, comfortable rooms. ❹
Travelodge – Temple Square 144 W North
Temple Blvd ℡ 801/533-8200. The most central and
least expensive of three local *Travelodges* makes
a convenient stopover, but it's no place for a long
stay. ❸

Temple Square

The geographical – and spiritual – heart of Salt Lake City is **Temple Square**, the world headquarters of the **Mormon Church** (or the Church of Jesus Christ of Latter-Day Saints – LDS). Its focus, the monumental **Temple** itself, was completed in 1893 after forty years of intensive labor. The multi-spired granite edifice rises to 210ft above the city – while not the tallest building on the mainly flat skyline, it's just about the only interesting one, thanks to its crisply angular silhouette. Only confirmed Mormons may enter the Temple, and even they do so only for the most sacred LDS rituals – marriage, baptisms, and "sealing," the joining of a family unit for eternity.

Wander through the gates of Temple Square, however, and you'll swiftly be shepherded to join a free 45-minute **tour** of the various sites within. As well as past monuments to Mormon pioneers, you'll be ushered into the odd oblong shell of the **Mormon Tabernacle**. No images of any kind adorn its interior, which is home to the world-renowned Mormon Tabernacle Choir; a helper at the lectern laconically displays its remarkable acoustic properties by tearing up a newspaper and dropping a nail. There's free admission to the choir's 9.30am Sunday broadcast, and its rehearsals on Thursday evenings at 8pm.

The primary aim of the tours is to awaken your interest in the Mormon faith; differences from Christianity are played down in favor of a soft-focus video of Old Testament scenes. In the northern of the square's two **visitor centers**, touch-screen computers provide woolly answers to questions like "What is the purpose of life?" and "Who was Joseph Smith?" In its southern counterpart, a surprisingly good free movie tells the story of the arrival of Salt Lake City's first Mormon settlers.

Downtown Salt Lake City

A block east of Temple Square along South Temple Boulevard, the **Beehive House** (summer Mon–Sat 9.30am–6.30pm, Sun 10am–1pm; winter Mon–Sat 9.30am–4.30pm, Sun 10am–1pm; free) is a plain white New England–style house, with wraparound verandas and green shutters. Erected in 1854 by church leader **Brigham Young**, it's now a small museum of Young's life, restored to the style of the period. Free twenty-minute tours, which you have to join to see much of the house, are given at least every half-hour.

The **Family History Library**, across West Temple Boulevard from Temple Square (Mon 8am–5pm, Tues–Sat 8am–9pm; free; ℡ 801/240-2584 or 1-866/406-1830, ⊛ www.familysearch.org), is intended to enable Mormons to trace their ancestors and then baptize them into the faith by proxy, but it's open to everyone. The world's most exhaustive genealogical library is surprisingly user-friendly, giving immediate access, through banks of computers, to birth and death records from over sixty countries, some dating back as much as five hundred years. All you need is a person's place of birth, a few approximate dates, and you're on your way; volunteers provide help if you need it, but leave you alone until you ask. Next door to the library, the **Museum of Church History and Art** (Mon–Fri 9am–9pm, Sat & Sun 10am–7pm; free) charts the rise of the Mormon faith in art and artifact.

The area southwest of Temple Square centers on the massive **Salt Palace** convention center and sports arena (home of the Utah Jazz basketball team). The surrounding district of brick warehouses around the Union Pacific railroad tracks is filled with designer shops and art galleries, signs that even Mormons can be yuppies.

Capitol Hill

Quite why the Mormons chose not to put their Temple on the gentle hill that stands above today's Temple Square is anyone's guess. As a result, when Utah was granted statehood in 1896, it was free to become the site of the imposing, domed **Utah State Capitol** (summer Mon–Sat 8am–8pm; rest of year Mon–Sat 8am–6pm; free). Along with the plaques and monuments you might expect, the corridors of power are packed full of earnest and rather diverting exhibits of great Utah moments.

Now called **Capitol Hill**, the neighborhood around the capitol holds some of Salt Lake City's grandest c.1900 homes, with dozens of ornate Victorian houses lining Main Street and Quince Street to the northwest; **walking tour maps** of the district are available from the Utah Heritage Foundation, 355 Quince St.

Eating

Though Salt Lake City has a perfectly good selection of **restaurants**, it lacks an atmospheric – let alone hip – dining district. If you like to compare menus, the only downtown area with much potential is the block or two to either side of West Temple Street, south and east of the Salt Palace.

Bambara *Hotel Monaco*, 202 S Main St ☎801/363-5454. Chic, post-Deco, and pricey downtown restaurant, with a fabulous menu ranging from buffalo carpaccio to crab cakes and lamb sirloin on Puy lentils; the $26 set menu offers an affordable sampler.

Caffè Molise 55 W 100 South ☎801/364-8833. Authentic, high-quality, great-value Italian food downtown, with tables in a nice little courtyard in summer, and jazz on Fridays.

Lamb's Restaurant 169 S Main St ☎801/364-7166. Great breakfasts, best eaten at the long shiny counter, and excellent-value set meals throughout the day. Closed Sun.

Market Street Grill 48 W Market St ☎801/322-4668. As close as Salt Lake City comes to a New York City bar and grill, with fresh seafood, especially oysters, plus steaks in all shapes and sizes. $12 lunch specials, full dinners $18–35.

Orbit Café 540 W 200 South ☎801/322-2808. Large, postmodern diner, which serves tasty sandwiches and ethnic specials for lunch, and then fancier late-night meals, with frequent live music. Lunch and dinner weekdays, breakfast and lunch only weekends.

Ruth's Diner 2100 Emigration Canyon Rd ☎801/582-5807. Good-value indoor and patio dining, often accompanied by live music, set in and around old railroad carriages in a narrow canyon just three miles east of town. There's a wide selection of fresh dishes, great salads, and Utah's best breakfasts.

Sage's Café 473 E 300 South ☎801/322-3790. Salt Lake's finest vegetarian restaurant, with a menu that ranges from pizza to raw salads, and great Sunday brunches.

Drinking and nightlife

Salt Lake City doesn't roll up the sidewalks when the sun goes down. Many **drinking** venues are technically private clubs, in which a nominal membership fee entitles the cardholder and up to five guests to two weeks' use of the facilities, but there are also a handful of **brewpubs** for which membership is not required. Good options for an evening out include the *Dead Goat Saloon*, 165 S West Temple Blvd (☎801/328-4628), a raucous, semi-subterranean saloon, with live loud music most nights. The casual, friendly *Squatters Pub*, 147 West Broadway (☎801/363-2739), offers a range of beers available until 1am every day, plus a simple menu. The best place to hear **live music**, surprisingly enough, has to be *The Depot*, in the Union Pacific Station at 400 W South Temple Blvd (☎801/456-2888), though *Zanzibar*, 677 S 200 West (☎801/746-0590), also programs good jazz and blues.

To find out about the broad range of **fringe** art, music, and clubland happenings, pick up free papers such as *City Weekly* (Ⓦwww.slweekly.com) or tune to radio station KRCL 91FM.

Park City

Despite Brigham Young's strictures against prospecting for precious metals – he feared a Gentile "Gold Rush" – the first mining camp at **PARK CITY**, just thirty miles east of downtown Salt Lake City along I-80 through the mountains, was established in the late 1860s. In 1872 George Hearst laid the foundations of the Hearst media empire by paying $27,000 for a claim that became the Ontario Silver Mine, worth $50 million. These days, the **Park City Mountain Resort** (Ⓣ435/649-8111, Ⓦwww.parkcitymountain.com), and the nearby **The Canyons** (Ⓣ435/649-5400, Ⓦwww.thecanyons.com) and (skiers-only) **Deer Valley** (Ⓣ435/649-1000 or 1-800/424-3337, Ⓦwww.deervalley.com) resorts constitute Utah's largest **ski area**, with the season usually running from mid-November to mid-April. Daily lift passes for each resort cost around $75; equipment rental outlets include Park City Sport (Ⓣ1-800/523-3922) and Gart Brothers (Ⓣ1-800/284-4754). In addition, Park City hosts the prestigious **Sundance Film Festival**, held during the second half of January each year (Ⓣ801/328-3456, Ⓦwww.sundance.org).

There's an ever-growing sprawl of new condos, factory outlets, and other developments, while an overhaul for the 2002 Winter Olympics restored **Main Street** with only token gestures mimicking the mountain mining community it used to be. Its shops and restaurants strive instead to emulate the chic resorts of Colorado.

Practicalities

Park City's **visitor center**, 528 Main St (May & Oct daily 11am–5pm; rest of year Mon–Fri 10am–7pm, Sat & Sun noon–6pm; Ⓣ435/649-6100 or 1-800/453-1360, Ⓦwww.parkcityinfo.com), doubles as an enjoyable museum of town history, and stands above the town's original jailhouse. Lewis Bros Stages (Ⓣ435/901-2724 or 1-877/491-8911, Ⓦwww.lewisstages.com) runs scheduled **shuttles** from downtown Salt Lake City ($30) and the airport (up to $60).

Accommodation rates double in the ski season; the visitor center can provide full listings of resorts and other lodgings. The down-to-earth *Chateau Apres*, 1299 Norfolk Ave (Ⓣ435/649-9372 or 1-800/357-3556, Ⓦwww.chateauapres. com; ❶/❹), is a cozy lodge motel with some $30 dorm beds. *Wahso*, 577 Main St (Ⓣ435/615-0300), is an extremely fancy pan-Asian **restaurant** with a sky-high reputation, while *Windy Ridge*, 1250 Iron Horse Drive (Ⓣ435/647-2906), serves good, cheap deli snacks and sandwiches. The *Wasatch Brew Pub*, 250 Main St (Ⓣ435/649-0900), is open until midnight daily and serves good food as well as microbrewed beer.

Nevada

NEVADA is without doubt the most desolate state in the US, consisting largely of endless tracts of bleak, empty desert. Its flat sagebrush plains are cut intermittently by angular mountain ranges and lack rainfall or fertile soil. Apart from the huge acreages given over to mining and grazing, much of Nevada is under the control of the **military**, which uses it to test aircraft and weapons systems. While dozens of intriguing small communities are scattered around the state, many more are decrepit roadside ghost towns, often little more than a gas-station-cum-general-store, flanked by a saloon and perhaps a brothel (Nevada is the only US state not to have outlawed **prostitution**, though it is illegal in Las Vegas.)

Though millions of people pass through on their way to and from California, there's only one real reason why anyone ever *visits* Nevada, and that is to **gamble**: as soon as you cross the state border, you're attacked by a 24-hour onslaught of neon signs and gimmicky architecture, each advertising the best odds and biggest jackpots, nowhere more than in the surreal oasis of **Las Vegas**. Even the smaller and more down-to-earth settlements of **Reno** and state capital **Carson City** revolve around the casino trade. At least the casinos' energetic pursuit of gamblers keeps rooms and especially food inexpensive, so the towns make good places to break a long journey – and, with Nevada's relaxed marriage and divorce laws, make or break a relationship.

Getting around Nevada

Traveling the state's vast empty spaces is nearly impossible without a car. Las Vegas is no longer served by Amtrak, but Reno still welcomes daily trains between San Francisco and Salt Lake City. Both Las Vegas and Reno have airports, and bus service exists between the two cities – though they're well over 400 miles apart.

Las Vegas

Shimmering from the desert haze of Nevada like a latter-day El Dorado, **LAS VEGAS** is the most dynamic, spectacular city on earth. At the start of the twentieth century, it didn't even exist; now it's home to over one million people, and boasts fourteen of the world's twenty largest hotels, whose flamboyant, no-expense-spared **casinos** lure in thirty-seven million tourists each year.

Las Vegas has been stockpiling superlatives since the 1950s, but never rests on its laurels for a moment. First-time visitors tend to expect the city to be a repository of kitsch, but the casino owners are far too canny to be sentimental about the old days. Yes, there are a few Elvis impersonators around, but what characterizes the city far more is its endless quest for **novelty**. Long before they lose their sparkle, yesterday's showpieces are blasted into rubble, to make way for ever more extravagant replacements. A few years ago, when the fashion was for fantasy, Arthurian castles and Egyptian pyramids mushroomed along the legendary Strip; now Vegas demands nothing less than entire cities, and boasts pocket versions of New York, Paris, Monte Carlo, and Venice.

While the city has certainly cleaned up its act since the early days of Mob domination, there's little truth in the notion that it's become a **family** destination. Neither is Vegas as consistently **cheap** as it used to be. It's still possible to find good, inexpensive rooms, and the all-you-care-to-eat buffets offer unbeatable value, but the casino owners have finally discovered that high-rollers happy to lose hundreds of dollars per night don't mind paying premium prices to eat at top-quality restaurants, while the latest developments are charging room rates of more like $300 than $30 per night.

Although Las Vegas is an unmissable destination, it's one that palls for most visitors after a couple of (hectic) days. If you've come solely to gamble, there's not

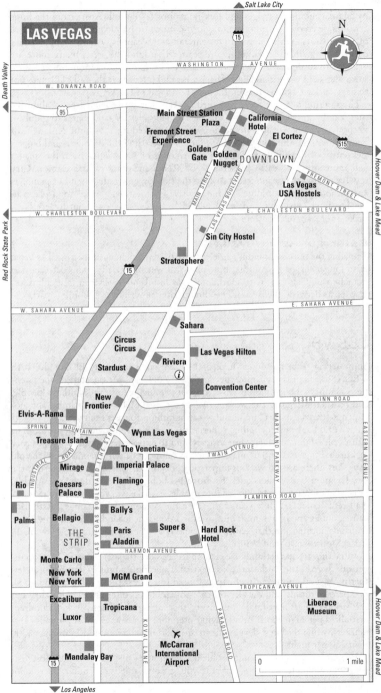

LAS VEGAS

N

▲ Salt Lake City

WASHINGTON AVENUE

◄ Death Valley

W. BONANZA ROAD

◄ Red Rock State Park

Hoover Dam & Lake Mead ►

95

Main Street Station
Plaza
California
Hotel
Fremont Street
Experience
El Cortez
Golden
Gate
Golden
Nugget
DOWNTOWN
FREMONT STREET
Las Vegas
USA Hostels
515

MAIN STREET

LAS VEGAS BOULEVARD

W. CHARLESTON BOULEVARD
E. CHARLESTON BOULEVARD

Sin City Hostel

Stratosphere

15

W. SAHARA AVENUE
E. SAHARA AVENUE

Sahara

Circus
Circus
Las Vegas Hilton

Stardust
Riviera
(i)

Convention Center

DESERT INN ROAD

New
Frontier

MARYLAND PARKWAY

EASTERN AVENUE

Elvis-A-Rama

SPRING MOUNTAIN ROAD

Wynn Las Vegas

Treasure Island

THE STRIP

The Venetian
TWAIN AVENUE

Mirage
Imperial Palace

Rio
Caesars
Palace
Flamingo
FLAMINGO ROAD

LAS VEGAS BOULEVARD

Palms
Bellagio
Bally's

THE
STRIP
Paris
Super 8
Hard Rock
Hotel

Monte Carlo
Aladdin
HARMON AVENUE

New York
New York
MGM Grand

TROPICANA AVENUE

Excalibur
Tropicana
Liberace
Museum

Luxor

KOVAL LANE

PARADISE ROAD

Hoover Dam & Lake Mead ►

✈
McCarran
International
Airport

0   1 mile

15

Mandalay Bay

▼ Los Angeles

much to say beyond the fact that all the casinos are free, and open 24 hours per day, with acres of floor space packed with ways to lose money: million-dollar slots, video poker, blackjack, craps, roulette wheels, and much, much more.

A history of Las Vegas

The name Las Vegas – Spanish for "the meadows" – was originally applied to a group of natural springs that from 1829 onward served as a way-station for travelers on the Old Spanish Trail. In 1900, the valley had a population of just thirty people. Things changed in 1905, with the completion of the now-defunct rail link between Salt Lake City and Los Angeles.

Though Nevada was the first state to outlaw gambling, in 1909, it was made legal once more in 1931, and the workers who built the nearby **Hoover Dam** flocked to Vegas to bet away their pay packets. Providing abundant cheap electricity and water, the dam amounted to a massive federal subsidy for the infant city. Hotel-casinos such as the daring 65-room *El Rancho* began to appear in the early 1940s, and mobster Bugsy Siegel raised $7 million to open the *Flamingo* on the Strip in 1946.

By the 1950s, Las Vegas was booming. The military had arrived – mushroom clouds from **A-bomb tests** in the deserts were visible from the city, and visitors would drive out with picnics to get a better view – and so too had big guns like **Frank Sinatra**, who debuted at the *Desert Inn* in 1951, and **Liberace**, who received $50,000 to open the *Riviera* in 1955. As the stars gravitated toward the Vegas honeypot, nightclubs across America went out of business, and the city became the nation's undisputed live-entertainment capital.

The beginning of the end for Mob rule in Vegas came in 1966, after reclusive airline tycoon **Howard Hughes** sold TWA for $500 million and moved into the *Desert Inn*. When the owners tired of his non-gambling ways, he simply bought the hotel, and his clean-cut image encouraged other entrepreneurs to follow suit. **Elvis** arrived a little later; the young rock 'n' roller had bombed at the *New Frontier* in 1956, but started a triumphant five-year stint as a karate-kicking lounge lizard at the *International* (now the *Las Vegas Hilton*) in 1969.

Endless federal swoops and stings drove the Mob out of sight by the 1980s, in time for Vegas to reinvent itself on a surge of junk-bond megadollars. The success of Steve Wynn's *Mirage* in enticing a new generation of visitors, from 1989 onward, spawned a host of imitators. A spate of casino building saw *Excalibur* and the *MGM Grand* followed first by *Luxor* and *New York–New York* and then, as the millennium approached, by the opulent quartet of *Bellagio*, *Mandalay Bay*, the *Venetian*, and *Paris*. The 21st century, however, started with shockwaves. Unsuccessful investments elsewhere forced Steve Wynn to sell *Bellagio* and the *Mirage* to the MGM group; the new *Aladdin* swiftly went bankrupt; and the tragedy of September 11, 2001, hit the Las Vegas economy hard.

And yet, once again, Las Vegas has bounced back, with the *Venetian* now going from strength to strength as the flagship for all that the city does best, and Wynn himself opening his biggest casino yet, *Wynn Las Vegas*, on the site of the old *Desert Inn*.

Arrival, information, and getting around

Las Vegas's busy **McCarran International Airport** is a mile east of the southern end of the Strip, and four miles from downtown (☎702/261-5211). Some hotels run free shuttle buses for guests, while Bell Trans (☎702/739-7990, ⓦ www.bell-trans.com) runs **minibuses** to the Strip ($5) and downtown ($6). From the airport, a **taxi** to the Strip costs from $15 for the southern end up to $25 for casinos further north, though fares can vary enormously depending on the time taken.

Amtrak **trains** no longer serve Las Vegas, but Greyhound's long-distance **buses** use a terminal at 200 S Main St downtown.

If you plan to see more of Vegas than the Strip and even there, it's too hot in summer to walk more than a couple of the long blocks in the daytime – a **car** is invaluable. **Public transport** does exist, however. The **Las Vegas Monorail** runs along the eastern side of the Strip from the *MGM Grand* to the *Sahara* (daily 6am–2am; single trip $3, 1-day pass $10, 10-ride pass $20; ⊤702/699-8299, Ⓦwww.lvmonorail.com), but doesn't go as far as either the airport or downtown. Separate, free monorail systems also link *Mandalay Bay* with *Excalibur* via *Luxor*, and the *Mirage* with *TI*. In addition, the oak-veneered streetcars of the **Las Vegas Strip Trolley** (⊤702/382-1404) ply the Strip between *Mandalay Bay* and the *Stratosphere*, for a flat fare of $1.65. CAT **buses** (⊤702/228-7433, Ⓦwww.catride.com) serve the whole city; #301 and #302 connect the Strip to downtown ($2).

Although there is a **visitor center** at the vast Convention Center, 3150 Paradise Rd (daily 8am–5pm; ⊤702/892-0711 or 877/VISIT-LV, Ⓦwww.vegasfreedom.com), at half a mile east of the Strip it's too far from the Strip to reach on foot. Better sources of information include the **website** Ⓦwww.lasvegas24hours.com, and the daily *Las Vegas Review-Journal*, which always incorporates a four-page guide to the city.

Getting married in Las Vegas

Second only to making your fortune as a reason to visit Las Vegas is the prospect of **getting married**. Over a hundred thousand weddings are performed here each year, many so informal that bride and groom just wind down the window of their car during the ceremony, and a Vegas wedding has become a byword for tongue-in-cheek chic.

You don't have to be a local resident or take a blood test to get wed here. Assuming you're both at least eighteen years old and carrying picture ID, simply turn up at the Clark County Marriage License Bureau, downtown at 200 S Third St (daily 8am–midnight; ⊤702/455-4415, Ⓦwww.accessclarkcounty.com/clerk/Marriage_Information.htm), and buy a marriage license for $55 cash. You can then walk over to the Clark County Court House at 309 S Third St (daily 8am–10pm), and be married by the Commissioner for Civil Marriages.

Wedding chapels claim to charge as little as $55 for basic ceremonies, but at that sort of rate even the minister is an "extra" costing an additional $45. Reckon on paying at least $150 for the bare minimum, which is liable to be as romantic a process as checking in at a hotel, and to take about as long. The full deluxe service ranges up to whatever you can afford. Novelty options include pledging your eternal loyalty on the deck of the *USS Enterprise* at the *Hilton* (⊤702/697-8750); floating on a gondola in the *Venetian*'s Grand Canal (⊤702/414-4253); or beside your helicopter at the bottom of the Grand Canyon (Papillon; ⊤702/736-7243).

Graceland Wedding Chapel 619 S Las Vegas Blvd ⊤702/474-6655 or 1-800/824-5732, Ⓦwww.gracelandchapel.com. Home of the King – an Elvis impersonator will act as best man, give the bride away, or serenade you, but unfortunately he can't perform the service.

Little Church of the West 4617 Las Vegas Blvd S ⊤702/739-7971 or 1-800/821-2452, Ⓦwww.littlechurchlv.com. This fifty-year-old chapel has moved progressively down the Strip to its current site south of *Mandalay Bay*. Among the more peaceful and quiet places to exchange your Vegas vows – if that's really what you want.

Little White Chapel 1301 S Las Vegas Blvd ⊤702/382-5943 or 1-800/545-8111, Ⓦwww.alittlewhitechapel.com. Where Bruce Willis and Demi Moore married each other, Michael Jordan and Joan Collins married other people, and Britney Spears married Jason Alexander in January 2004. Open all day every day, with ceremonies in the roofed-over driveway (or "Tunnel of Love") for those in a major hurry.

Accommodation

Although Las Vegas has well over 135,000 motel and hotel rooms, it's best to book **accommodation** ahead if you're on a tight budget, or arriving on Friday or Saturday; upwards of two hundred thousand people descend upon the city every weekend. Las Vegas hotels no longer offer incredibly cheap deals at the drop of a hat. It is true that serious gamblers can get their accommodation free, but to count as "serious" you'd have to commit yourself to gambling several thousand dollars.

Even if you stay in the same room for several days, you'll be charged a different rate for each day, depending on the day of the week, and what's going on in town. The only sure-fire way to get a cut-price room is to **visit during the week** rather than on the weekend. Rates rise enormously on Friday or Saturday, by perhaps $30 to $50 extra in a lower-end property, $100 in the big-name casinos. On top of that, many hotels won't accept Saturday arrivals. The **Las Vegas Convention & Visitors Authority** offers an availability and reservations service at ☎ 1-877/847-4858.

Aladdin 3667 Las Vegas Blvd S ☎ 702/785-5555 or 1-877/333-9474, ⊛ www.aladdincasino.com. The financially troubled *Aladdin* may well have been rebranded as *Planet Hollywood* by the time you visit, but hopefully it will remain much more user-friendly than most of its giant neighbors. Each of its 2600 spacious rooms is within easy reach of an elevator, with separate bath and shower, while the dining and shopping are first class. Sun–Thurs ❹, Fri & Sat ❻

Bellagio 3600 Las Vegas Blvd S ☎ 702/693-7111 or 1-888/987-6667, ⊛ www.bellagio.com. Extremely luxurious rooms, with plush European furnishings and marble bathrooms, an amazing pool complex, and some of the best restaurants in town. Sun–Thurs ❻, Fri & Sat ❾

Caesars Palace 3570 Las Vegas Blvd S ☎ 702/731-7222 or 1-800/634-6661, ⊛ www. caesars.com. Right in the heart of the Strip, the epitome of 1960s luxury continues to offer the last word in pseudo-Roman splendor, with top-class restaurants and shops. Sun–Thurs ❺, Fri & Sat ❽

California Hotel 12 Ogden Ave at First St ☎ 702/385-1222 or 1-800/634-6255, ⊛ www. thecal.com. Almost all the guests in this mid-range downtown casino are Hawaiian, and Hawaiian food and drink dominate the bars and restaurants. The actual rooms are plain but adequate. Sun–Thurs ❷, Fri & Sat ❸

Circus Circus 2880 Las Vegas Blvd S ☎ 702/734-0410 or 1-800/444-2472, ⊛ www.circuscircus. com. Venerable Strip hotel popular with budget tour groups. Kids love the theme park and (almost) nonstop circus acts, while adults love the low room rates. ❸

Las Vegas International Hostel 1322 E Fremont St ☎ 702/385-1150 or 1-800/550-8958, ⊛ www. usahostels.com. Former motel, in a slightly forbidding neighborhood ten blocks east of downtown.

It's much the better of the city's two independent hostels, with dorm beds from $13 and private double rooms from $38. Rates include free breakfast; cheap dinners are also available. There's also a heated swimming pool. The friendly staff arrange city and national-park tours, as well as a weekly clubbing night. ❶/❷

🏃 **Luxor Las Vegas** 3900 Las Vegas Blvd S ☎ 702/262-4102 or 1-888/777-0188, ⊛ www.luxor.com. Vast, smoked-glass pyramid, in which all two thousand rooms face outwards, with tremendous views – and they're much larger than usual. Unlike the extra two thousand rooms in the newer tower next door, however, most have showers, not baths. Sun–Thurs ❸, Fri & Sat ❺

Main Street Station 200 N Main St at Ogden ☎ 702/387-1896 or 1-800/465-0711, ⊛ www. mainstreetcasino.com. Downtown's best-value option, with four hundred large guest rooms plus a brewpub and good restaurants. Ask for a room on the south side, rather than right next to the freeway. Mon–Thurs & Sun ❸, Fri & Sat ❹

MGM Grand 3799 Las Vegas Blvd S ☎ 702/891-1111 or 1-800/929-1111, ⊛ www.mgmgrand.com. Waiting for any kind of service, especially check-in, at the largest hotel in the US – 5005 rooms and counting – can be horrendous, but you get a great standard of accommodation for the price. Sun–Thurs ❹, Fri & Sat ❻

🏃 **New York–New York Hotel & Casino** 3790 Las Vegas Blvd S ☎ 702/740-6050 or 1-800/693-6763, ⊛ www.nynyhotelcasino.com. Rooms at the most exuberantly fun Strip casino are very nice, if a bit small, and filled with Art Deco furnishings and flourishes. Sun–Thurs ❹, Fri & Sat ❻

The Palms 4321 W Flamingo Rd ☎ 702/942-7777 or 1-866/942-7777, ⊛ www.palms.com. Although it ranks among the hottest newer casinos in town, thanks to some very fancy nightclubs and restaurants, the *Palms* is really just a presentable but rather dull locals casino. While the rooms are very comfortable, you may not feel it's worth paying premium rates for the inconvenient location a mile west of the Strip. Mon–Thurs & Sun ④, Fri & Sat ⑥

Paris–Las Vegas 3655 Las Vegas Blvd S ☎702/946-7000 or 1-877/796-2096, ⓦwww. parislasvegas.com. If not the absolute pinnacle of luxury, rooms and services at the flamboyant French-themed *Paris* are still pretty good, and for location, views, and ambience it more than holds its own. Sun–Thurs ⑤, Fri & Sat ⑦

The Venetian 3355 Las Vegas Blvd S ☎702/414-1000 or 1-888/283-6423, ⓦwww.venetian.com. Even the standard rooms at this upscale Strip behemoth are split-level suites, with antique-style canopied beds atop raised platforms, plus spacious living rooms. Sun–Thurs ⑦, Fri & Sat ⑨

Wynn Las Vegas 3131 Las Vegas Blvd S ☎702/770-7000 or 1-888/320-7123, ⓦwww. wynnlasvegas.com. Steve Wynn has once again rewritten the Strip's definition of luxury, but the very stylish rooms, most of which offer great views of the "Lake of Dreams," come of course at a substantial price. Sun–Thurs ⑦, Fri & Sat ⑨

The City

Though the Las Vegas sprawl measures fifteen miles wide by fifteen miles long, most tourists stick to the six-mile stretch of **Las Vegas Boulevard** that includes both the **downtown** area, slightly southeast of the intersection of I-15 and US-95, and the **Strip**, home to the major casinos. In between lie two seedy miles of gas stations, fast-food drive-ins, and wedding chapels, while the rest of town is largely residential.

The Strip

For its razor-edge finesse in harnessing sheer, magnificent excess to the deadly serious business of making money, there's no place like the **Las Vegas Strip**. It's hard to imagine that Las Vegas was once an ordinary city, and Las Vegas Boulevard a dusty thoroughfare scattered with the usual edge-of-town motels. After six decades of capitalism run riot, with every new casino-hotel setting out to surpass anything its neighbors ever dreamed of, the Strip seems to be locked into a hyperactive craving for thrills and glamour, forever discarding its latest toy in its frenzied pursuit of the next jackpot.

Each casino is a self-contained fantasyland of high camp and genuine excitement. Huge moving walkways sweep you in from the sidewalk, almost against your will; once inside, it can be almost impossible to find your way out. The action keeps going day and night, and in this sealed and windowless environment you rapidly lose track of time. Even if you do manage to get back onto the streets during the day, the scorching heat is liable to drive you straight back in; night is the best time to venture out, when the neon's blazing at its brightest.

Mandalay Bay

The Strip's procession kicks off at its southern end with the glowing gilded tower of **Mandalay Bay**, which boasts a vaguely Burmese theme. Financed through the profits from its neighbors, *Luxor* and *Excalibur*, *Mandalay Bay* is more upmarket than either, and its excellent restaurants, as well as the *House of Blues* music venue, keep it lively at night. During the day, all it has to offer the casual sightseer is the **Shark Reef** aquarium, right at the back of the property (daily 10am–11pm; $16), a mock-up of a steamy, half-submerged temple complex, inhabited by crocodiles, jellyfish, and, of course, sharks. It's expensive considering how short a time it takes to see it, plus all the so-called "coral" in the tanks is actually a multicolored mix 'n' match plastic kit.

Luxor

A block north of *Mandalay Bay* stands the 36-story pyramid of **Luxor**. From the palm-fringed avenue of sphinxes guarding the entrance, to the reconstruction of

△ The Bellagio, on the Strip

Tutankhamun's tomb inside, the whole building plays endless variations upon the theme of ancient Egypt, and ranks as a real must-see. In Las Vegas's closest approximation to Disneyland, three separate simulator rides and 3D movies combine to relate a confusing saga of derring-do that's overpriced at $25. Meanwhile, the most powerful artificial light-beam ever created shines up from the pyramid's apex.

Excalibur and the MGM Grand

Luxor's architect, Veldon Simpson, had previously designed the less sophisticated **Excalibur**, immediately north. A mock-up of a medieval castle, complete with drawbridge, crenellated towers, and a basement stuffed with fairground-style sideshows for the kids, it's usually packed out with low-budget tour groups. Its brief reign as the world's largest hotel, from 1990 to 1993, ended when the five-thousand-room **MGM Grand** – another Simpson creation – opened across the street. There, the main attraction, the **Lion Habitat**, is a walk-through wooded zoo near the front entrance, where real lions lounge around a ruined temple beneath a naturally lit dome. Admission is free (daily 11am–11pm), and for $20 you can have your photo taken with a cute little lion cub (daily except Tues 11am–5pm).

New York–New York

Excalibur and the *MGM Grand* are not the only giants facing off across the intersection of Las Vegas Boulevard and Tropicana Avenue, said to be the busiest traffic junction in the US. The northwest corner, diagonally opposite the veteran *Tropicana*, is occupied by an exuberantly meticulous recreation of the Big Apple, **New York–New York**. This miniature Manhattan boasts a skyline featuring twelve separate skyscrapers and is fronted, naturally, by the Statue of Liberty. Unusually, the interior is every bit as carefully realized, with a lovely rendition of Central Park at dusk (not perhaps somewhere you'd choose to be in real life). In one respect, it even surpasses New York itself: for $12.50 you can swoop around the whole thing at 65mph on the hair-raising Manhattan Express **roller coaster**.

Aladdin

North of the *MGM Grand*, the $1.4-billion **Aladdin** opened in 2000 as Las Vegas's first megacasino of the new millennium, but it really represented the last gasp of the Strip's 1990s construction boom. The resort was tipped into bankruptcy by the 2001 terrorist attacks of September. The Middle Eastern theme didn't exactly help, and the *Aladdin* is expected to be revamped and renamed *Planet Hollywood* in the very near future. Its gigantic **Desert Passage** shopping mall, and 7000-seat auditorium, will survive the transformation intact.

Paris

Paris was the 1999 handiwork of the same designers as *New York–New York*. With a half-size Eiffel Tower straddling the Arc de Triomphe and the Opera, it all feels a little compressed, but once again the attention to detail is a joy. There's also a fine assortment of top-notch French restaurants. Elevators soar through the roof of the casino and up to the summit of the Eiffel Tower, for stunning views of the city, at their best after dark (daily 10am–midnight; $9).

Bellagio

The Eiffel Tower was cheekily positioned to enjoy a perfect prospect of **Bellagio**, opposite. In 1998, Steve Wynn unveiled the *Bellagio* as his attempt to build the best hotel in world history. *Bellagio* is undeniably a breathtaking achievement, striving to be somehow more authentic than the original town on Lake Como. The trouble is that *Bellagio* is not in Italy; it's in Las Vegas, stuffed full of slot machines (inlaid with jewel-like precision into marble counters, perhaps, but still slot machines). The main hotel block, a stately curve of blue and cream pastels, stands aloof from the Strip behind an eight-acre artificial lake in which hundreds of submerged fountains erupt every half-hour in Busby-Berkeley water-ballets, choreographed with booming music and colored lights.

Otherwise, *Bellagio*'s proudest boasts are the **Via Bellagio**, a covered mall of impossibly glamorous designer boutiques, and its opulent **Conservatory**, where a network of flowerbeds beneath a Belle Epoque canopy of copper-framed glass is replanted every few weeks with ornate seasonal displays.

Caesars Palace

Across Flamingo Road from *Bellagio* – this is the intersection where rapper Tupac Shakur was gunned down in 1996 – the long-established **Caesars Palace** still encapsulates Las Vegas at its best. Here, the walkway delivers you past grand marble staircases that lead nowhere, and full-size replicas of Michelangelo's *David*, into a vast labyrinth of slots and green baize, peopled by strutting half-naked Roman centurions and Cleopatra-cropped waitresses. Above the stores and restaurants of the extraordinary **Forum**, the blue-domed ceiling dims and glows as it endlessly cycles from dawn to dusk and back again, while the animatronic statues that top its ornate fountains come to life at regular intervals.

The Mirage and TI

Nighttime crowds jostle for space on the sidewalk outside the glittering **Mirage**, beyond *Caesars*, to watch the somewhat half-hearted volcano that erupts every fifteen minutes, spewing water and fire into the lagoon below. Although veteran magicians Siegfried and Roy were finally driven into retirement by Roy's near-fatal accident in 2003, their trademark white tigers can still be seen in the *Mirage*'s spacious **Secret Garden & Dolphin Habitat** (daily 10am–7pm; $15, under 13s $10).

Next door, a pirate galleon and a British frigate, crewed by actors, continue to do noisy battle outside **TI**, the former *Treasure Island*, though ludicrously enough the sailors these days are no longer gnarled buccaneers but the scantily-clad **Sirens of TI** (every 90min after dark; free). *Treasure Island* used to be pirate-themed throughout, but when MGM took over the *Mirage* empire in 2000, they hastily abandoned all thoughts of appealing to children. All *Treasure Island*'s lovingly crafted fripperies have therefore been stripped away, from its huge video arcade and bizarre $400,000 bone chandeliers, to the skull motifs that adorned everything from its main sign to the doorhandles.

The Venetian

Across the Strip from *TI*, the facade of the **Venetian** includes loving facsimiles of six major Venice buildings, as well as the Rialto Bridge and the Bridge of Sighs. The main emphasis in the casino itself is on the **Grand Canal Shoppes**, reached via a stairwell topped by vivid frescoes copied from yet more Venice originals. The ludicrous recreation of the **Grand Canal** at the top, complete with gondolas and singing gondoliers ($12.50 a ride), is quintessential Las Vegas, and as such utterly irresistible – it's *upstairs*, for God's sake.

In a thematic non sequitur, the *Venetian* hired Dutch architect Rem Koolhaas to design the on-site **Guggenheim Hermitage** (daily 9.30am–8.30pm; $20, under 13s $14.50) in ultramodern style. The museum aims to provide much-needed funds for St Petersburg's legendary State Hermitage Museum in return for displaying its finest treasures on a six-monthly changing rotation. Exhibitions so far have concentrated on Impressionism and Cubism, with Monet and Picasso well represented.

The *Venetian* also holds an outpost of **Madame Tussaud's** renowned waxwork museum (daily 10am–10pm, some seasonal variation; $23, under 13s $13), which styles itself "Interactive Wax" because visitors can sing karaoke for Simon Cowell or sink a putt with Tiger Woods. The whole experience is ridiculously expensive, its token animatronic showpieces not a patch on the free shows at *Caesars*.

Elvis-A-Rama

At the corner of *TI,* take Spring Mountain one block west of the Strip to reach the Fashion Show Mall at 3401 Industrial Road. Behind the mall, you can admire (if not step on) the King's very own blue suede shoes at **Elvis-A-Rama** (daily 10am–6pm; $10). As well as boasting a fine array of Elvis memorabilia, the museum puts on hourly impersonator shows.

Wynn Las Vegas

Next door to the *Venetian* stands the project into which Steve Wynn sank all the fortune he accrued by building and selling the *Mirage* and *Bellagio*. **Wynn Las Vegas**, which opened in 2005 on the site of the vanished *Desert Inn*, has lived up to its creator's promise that it would be designed to be seen from the inside out. From the Strip, it's largely obscured by an artificial tree-covered mountain; once you find your way inside, you discover that the mountain makes a backdrop for the bizarre, enormous **Lake of Dreams**, an "environmental theater" in which ethereal sculpted figures emerge from a large expanse of water, in front of a massive waterfall that continually changes color, as indeed do the trees and the entire mountain.

Circus Circus

The family-oriented **Circus Circus**, nearly a mile north of *Wynn Las Vegas*, uses live circus acts to pull in the punters – a trapeze artist here, a fire-eater there – and also has an indoor theme park, the **Adventuredome** (Mon–Thurs 10am–6pm, Fri & Sat 10am–midnight, Sun 10am–8pm), where you pay separately for each roller coaster or river-ride, or can buy an all-day pass at $22 for anyone over 4ft, $14 for those under.

The Star Trek Experience

Half a mile east of *Circus Circus* at 3000 Paradise Rd, the **Las Vegas Hilton** is home to the **Star Trek Experience** (daily 11am–11pm; $35, under-13s $32), which is roughly equivalent to a high-echelon ride in an LA or Orlando theme park; it's pretty good, but absurdly expensive. Visits start from the Space Quest Casino, a sort of *Enterprise* with slots. The ramp beyond the ticket booths doubles as a queuing area – you can wait as long as two hours on summer weekends – and a "museum," which recounts an episode-by-episode chronology of every *Star Trek* series. It all culminates in two separate twenty-minute shows: *Klingon Encounter* and *Borg Invasion 4-D*, both of which involve you being caught up in alien plots and sent on stomach-churning motion-simulator rides through deep space.

The Stratosphere

Sahara Avenue traditionally marked the northern limit of the Strip, but the 1996 opening of the **Stratosphere**, a few blocks north, tried to change that. At 1149ft, the *Stratosphere* is the tallest building west of the Mississippi, and the outdoor deck and indoor viewing chamber in the sphere near the summit offer amazing panoramas across the city ($9). Three utterly demented thrill rides can take you even closer to heaven; the world's highest roller coaster ($4) swirls around the outside of the sphere, X-Scream ($8) dangles passengers over the edge in a precarious gondola, and the ludicrous Big Shot ($8) shunts you to the very top of an additional 160ft spire, from which you free-fall back down again.

Downtown and the Liberace Museum

As the Strip has evolved from strength to strength, **downtown** Las Vegas, the city's original core, has by comparison been neglected. Actually it has never really been a "downtown" in the conventional sense, having never developed a significant infrastructure of stores and other businesses apart from its few compact blocks of lower-key casinos. Long known as "Glitter Gulch," it has however repeatedly attempted to revive itself. The principal sign of that is the **Fremont Street Experience**, in which five entire blocks of the central Fremont Street were roofed over with an open-air mesh. This "Celestial Vault" is studded with over twelve million

LED nodules to create a movie screen, choreographed by computer in dazzling nightly displays (hourly, 8pm–midnight; free).

Almost all Las Vegas's handful of off-Strip museums are eminently missable, with one unarguable exception: the **Liberace Museum**, two miles east of the Strip at 1775 E Tropicana Ave (Mon–Sat 10am–5pm, Sun noon–4pm; ☏702/798-5595, ⓦwww.liberace.org; $12). Popularly remembered more for his pompadour and love of rhinestones than his torpid toe-tapper songs, Liberace, who died in 1987, started out as a classically trained pianist playing the rough bars of Milwaukee during the 1940s. A decade later, he was being mobbed by screaming adolescents and ruthlessly hounded by the scandal-hungry press. All this is recalled by a yellowing collection of cuttings and family photos, along with an electric candelabra, bejeweled quail eggs with inlaid pianos, rhinestone-covered fur coats, glittering cars, and more.

Eating

As recently as the early 1990s, the **restaurant** scene in Las Vegas was governed by the notion that visitors were not prepared to pay for gourmet food, and the only quality restaurants were upscale Italian places well away from the Strip. Now, however, the situation has reversed, as the major casinos compete to attract culinary superstars from all over the country to open Vegas outlets. Many tourists now come to the city in order to eat at the best restaurants in the United States, without having to reserve a table months in advance or pay sky-high prices. The choice on the Strip in particular is overwhelming, and you'll almost certainly find a good restaurant in your own hotel. The places reviewed here form only a tiny proportion of the total and tend toward the higher-end restaurants that are worth making a special effort to reach.

Buffets

Almost every casino features an all-you-can-eat **buffet**. At its best, the traditional buffet experience is like being granted unrestricted access to the food court in an upmarket mall: you'll get good fast food, but not great cooking. The best such buffets tend to be in casinos away from both the Strip and downtown that depend on locals as well as tourists. By contrast, those at the largest Strip casinos, like *Excalibur* and the *MGM Grand,* are often poor. A new development, however, has been for high-end casinos like *Bellagio* and *Paris* to raise buffet prices to a level that makes it possible to provide true gourmet feasts.

The Buffet *Bellagio*, 3600 Las Vegas Blvd S ☏702/791-7111. Far and away Las Vegas's best buffet. With other buffets, you may rave about what good value they are; with this one, you'll rave about what good food it is. Breakfast is $14; lunch is $18, and can include sushi, sashimi, and dim sum; and dinner, with choices like lobster claws, fresh oysters, and venison, is $26, or $34 on Fri & Sat.

Carnival World Buffet *Rio*, 3700 W Flamingo Rd ☏702/252-7777. The *Rio* uses its buffet to lure bargain-hunters west from the Strip; its prices are not what they were, at $13 for breakfast, $15 for lunch, and $23 for dinner, but the value is excellent. The variety is immense, with Thai, Chinese, Mexican, and Japanese stations, as well as the usual pasta and barbecue.

Fantasy Market Buffet *The Palms*, 4321 W Flamingo Rd ☏702/942-7777. Easy to find and afford, the *Palms'* buffet is a local favorite. Food and decor alike are bright and appealing, with a broad spectrum that takes in salads, a little sushi, Mexican and Italian specialties, teriyaki chicken, barbecue beef, and a lot of lovely cakes and pies. Breakfast is $6, lunch $7, and dinner $12, rising to $16 on Fri.

Garden Court Buffet *Main Street Station*, 200 N Main St ☏702/387-1896. Downtown's best-value buffet, ranging from fried chicken and corn at the "South to Southwest" station, to tortillas at "Ole," and pork chow mein and oyster tofu at "Pacific Rim." Breakfast is $6, lunch $8, and dinner varies $11–16.

Le Village Buffet *Paris*, 3655 Las Vegas Blvd S ☏702/967-7000. Superb French cuisine, with great seafood, succulent roast chicken, and super-fresh vegetables. The setting is a little cramped, squeezed into a very Disney-esque French village, but the food is *magnifique*. Breakfast is $13, lunch $18, and dinner $25.

Todai Seafood Buffet Desert Passage, *Aladdin*, 3663 Las Vegas Blvd S ☏702/892-

Restaurants

America *New York–New York*, 3790 Las Vegas Blvd S ☏702/740-6451. Cavernous 24-hour diner, with a vast 3D "map" of the United States curling from the ceiling, and a staggeringly eclectic menu. At any hour of the day or night, there really is something for everyone, and it's all surprisingly good.

The Coffee Shop *Binion's Horseshoe*, 128 E Fremont St ☏702/382-1600. The Las Vegas coffee shop of your dreams, in the basement of a veteran downtown casino. Between 10pm and 5am, a steak dinner costs just $5. Breakfast is better value than most buffets: the $4.99 "Benny Binion's Natural," served 2am–2pm, consists of two eggs, bacon, sausage, or ham, toast, tea or coffee, and magnificent home fries. Daily 24 hours.

Bouchon Venezia Tower, *The Venetian*, 3355 Las Vegas Blvd S ☏702/414-6200. Despite its sky-high reputation and exclusive setting, Thomas Keller's spacious recreation of a classic French bistro is both friendly and affordable, and sitting outside on the huge piazza is a real joy. A delicious French onion soup costs $8.50 and a roast chicken flavored with onions and garlic costs $22.50. There's also plenty of seafood. Breakfast is a Francophile's dream of croissants, pastries, yogurt and coffee. Open daily for all meals.

Commander's Palace Desert Passage, 3667 Las Vegas Blvd S ☏702/892-8272. The first-ever outpost of New Orleans' finest (and most expensive) restaurant abuts the Strip at the front of the Desert Passage mall. The decor is formal but redolent of Louisiana atmosphere, and the food is sumptuous. Lunch and dinner daily.

Il Fornaio *New York–New York*, 3790 Las Vegas Blvd S ☏702/650-6500. The nicest place to enjoy the atmosphere of the casino, this rural-Italian restaurant is a real joy. Choose from pizzas for around $12, or full meals like mixed antipasto ($9.50), followed by seafood linguini ($19) or rotisserie chicken ($16). The delicious olive breads, pastries, and espresso coffees are also sold in a separate deli nearby. Open daily for all meals.

0021. Not to be confused with the *Aladdin*'s own (adequate but not exceptional) buffet, *Todai* specializes in magnificent all-you-can-eat Japanese spreads. It's seafood heaven, with unlimited sushi and sashimi plus hot entrées, noodles, and barbecued and teriyaki meats. Lunch Mon–Fri $15, Sat & Sun $17; dinner Sun–Thurs $26, Fri & Sat $28.

Mon Ami Gabi *Paris*, 3655 Las Vegas Blvd S ☏702/944-4224. The first and the finest major casino restaurant to offer open-air seating right on the Strip has the feel of a proper French pavement bistro. At lunch, try the gloriously authentic onion soup ($7), the mussels ($11), or the thin-cut *steak frites* ($21). Dinner features more expensive steak cuts and fish entrées. Lunch and dinner daily.

Mr Lucky's 24/7 *Hard Rock Hotel*, 4455 Paradise Rd ☏702/693-5000. Stylish 24-hour coffee shop, with an open kitchen, faux-fur-clad booths, and a subdued tan-and-cream paint job, where the food is well above average.

Paymon's Mediterranean Cafe and Market 4147 S Maryland Pkwy at Flamingo ☏702/731-6030. This highly recommended Middle Eastern restaurant, with attractive Cretan murals, is simple but also Vegas's best vegetarian option. Salads and pita sandwiches cost $7–9, and spinach pie $10, while dips such as hummus or the eggplant-based *baba ganosh* are $5. A mountainous best-of-every-thing combination plate is just $11. Closed Sun.

Vialé Roman Plaza, *Caesars Palace*, 3500 Las Vegas Blvd S ☏702/731-7110. Inexpensive sidewalk Italian trattoria, outdoors on the Strip, that's almost too good to be true. Lunch is an absolute treat, with a burger or warm panini sandwich costing under $10, and a Caesar salad for $7, or $10 with chicken. The dinner menu offers many of the same salads, plus pasta as both appetizer ($7–9) and entree ($12–17), and more substantial entrees like grilled quail with mascarpone stuffing ($19). Lunch and dinner daily.

Zefferino Grand Canal Shoppes, *The Venetian*, 3355 Las Vegas Blvd S ☏702/414-3500. Very romantic, and yet utterly playful Italian restaurant, with its ornate balconies overlooking the Grand Canal. Dinner entrees can be pricey, with basic ravioli at $26 and fish soup at $45, but the $20 three-course set lunch, served daily except Sun, is exceptional value. Lunch and dinner daily.

Bars and clubs

All the casinos have plenty of bars, but if you want a drink, there's no need to look for one; instead, a tray-toting waitress will come and find you. The old-fashioned **Las Vegas lounge** has returned in force, whether knowingly retro-styled for twenty-something rockers, glammed up as an "ultra-lounge," or lovingly recreated for older visitors looking to recapture the quieter but still decadent flavor of the Rat-Pack era. In addition, Las Vegas has finally come of age as an international **clubbing** capital. The success of nightclubs at hipper casinos like the *Hard Rock* and *Mandalay Bay* has prompted all their major rivals to follow suit, often with spectacular results.

Gaudi Bar *Sunset Station*, 1301 W Sunset Rd, Henderson ☎702/547-7777. Las Vegas's most weird and wonderful casino lounge; a billowing mosaic-encrusted toadstool of a tribute to Spanish architect Gaudi, complete with faux-sky underbelly and best appreciated with the aid of a $4 specialty martini. Daily 24 hrs.

Ghostbar *The Palms*, 4321 W Flamingo Rd ☎702/940-7777. Self-proclaimed "ultra-lounge," whose lack of a dance floor, and low music volume, stops it being categorized as a nightclub. Thirty-something hipsters wait to pay the cover charge, then venture out on its cantilevered open-air deck, which has a terrifying Plexiglass floor. Daily 8pm–dawn. Cover Sun–Thurs $10, Fri & Sat $20.

Gipsy 4605 Paradise Rd ☎702/731-1919. High-profile gay dance club, where apart from the free cruise nights on Wednesdays, there's normally some form of live entertainment to justify the $5 post-midnight cover charge, with go-go boys performing Friday, and beer busts most nights. The elaborate lost-city decor attracts young ingenues and local celebs. Daily 10pm–6am.

House of Blues *Mandalay Bay*, 3950 Las Vegas Blvd S ☎702/632-7600, ⓦwww.hob.com. The Strip's premier live-music venue, the voodoo-tinged, folk-art-decorated *House of Blues* has a definite, but not exclusive, emphasis toward blues, R&B, and the like. Typical prices range from around $30 up to $85 for stars like Aretha Franklin.

Nine Fine Irishmen *New York–New York*, 3790 Las Vegas Blvd S ☎702/740-6463. The affinity between New York and all things Irish finds expression in this two-story wood-paneled pub, shipped over from Ireland and featuring live Irish musicians, singers, and dancers nightly.

Ra *Luxor*, 3900 Las Vegas Blvd S ☎702/262-4400. Despite the splendidly camp Egyptian motifs, *Ra* feels like a real city nightclub, booking big-name DJs to cater to a ferociously hip and very glamorous crowd. Cage dancers watch over a changing schedule of special nights. Wed–Sat 10pm–5am. Cover $10 women, $20 men.

Rain *The Palms*, 4321 W Flamingo Rd ☎702/940-7246. Vast, glitzy, no-expense-spared water-themed 1200-capacity club, featuring spectacular fountains of water and fire. When it's warm enough, the action extends outside into the pool area. Thurs 11pm–5am, $10, Fri & Sat 10pm–5am, $20.

rumjungle *Mandalay Bay*, 3950 Las Vegas Blvd S ☎702/632-7408. You have to run a gauntlet of go-go dancers and volcanic gas jets just to get into this bar-restaurant-nightclub. Inside, the leopardskin-clad staff serve well-priced cocktails, plus a vast menu of rums. It's too loud to do anything more than watch, or join, the dance floor action. Closed Sun.

Entertainment

There was a time when Las Vegas represented the pinnacle of any show-business career. In the early 1960s, when Frank Sinatra's Rat Pack were shooting the original *Ocean's 11* during the day then singing the night away at the *Sands*, the city could claim to be the capital of the international entertainment industry. Then the world moved on. In the last few years, however, Las Vegas has started to come back into its own. One by one, the cheesy, feathers-and-tassels revues have closed down, to be replaced by surprisingly stimulating, postmodern shows by the likes of the now-ubiquitous **Cirque du Soleil** and the **Blue Man Group**. A new generation of big-name stars are taking up the kind of long-term residencies we all thought had vanished with Elvis. **Celine Dion** and **Elton John** at *Caesars'* huge Colosseum are the most conspicuous, but more are expected to follow.

The Amazing Johnathan *The Sahara*, 2535 Las Vegas Blvd S ℡702/737-2111, ⓦwww.amazingj.com. Far from the unbridled craziness his advertising might lead you to expect, Johnathan is a lovable magician whose emphasis on comedy means he barely completes a trick all evening. That's probably for the best, as carefully honed patter and hilarious skits like "Bad Karate Theater" make this one of Las Vegas's funniest shows. Daily except Thurs 10pm. $50 & $60.

Blue Man Group *The Venetian*, 3265 Las Vegas Blvd S ℡1-866/641-7469. Enter a strange and unfamiliar world, in which three bald, blue performance artists sell out a 1750-seat theater every night of the week. Don't expect stars, or a plot, or even words; instead, you get synchronized eating of breakfast cereal and live endoscopies on audience members, plus deafening, exhilarating drumming from the Men themselves, and some stunning special effects. It's not for everyone, but breathtaking novelty is at least part of what Las Vegas is all about. Sun–Fri 7pm, Sat 7pm & 10pm. $79–90.

Celine Dion in A New Day *Caesars Palace*, 3570 Las Vegas Blvd S ℡702/731-7865. Celine Dion serves up Las Vegas entertainment on an epic scale in *Caesars*' vast Colosseum. Unless you're a big fan, however – in which case you'll love the amazing sound – what's been dubbed the "Cirque de Celine" may well leave you cold. Celine herself is all but dwarfed on the gigantic stage, while the abundant trimmings seem at odds with the essentially lightweight songs. Seasonal, Wed–Sun 8.30pm, $87.50–225.

Folies Bergere *Tropicana*, 3801 Las Vegas Blvd S ℡702/739-2411. A fixture since 1959, the *Folies Bergere* is the longest-running show in the US. The basic formula remains the same: a mildly "naughty" Parisian revue designed to blow the minds of stout, bearded farmers from Iowa. Showgirls with fixed grins and feathered headdresses – and topless during certain performances – highkick and waltz through big production numbers, with a break while quick-fire Mexican juggler Wally Eastwood plays the piano with his balls. Mon, Wed, Thurs & Sat 7.30pm & 10pm (topless), Tues & Fri 8.30pm (topless); all shows except 7.30pm over 16s only. $45–55.

Kà *MGM Grand*, 3799 Las Vegas Blvd S ℡702/891-7777, ⓦwww.ka.com. With a budget of $165 million, and nightly cast of 75 performers and 158 technicians, Las Vegas' fourth Cirque du Soleil production, Kà, is the most expensive theatrical production ever staged anywhere. Though more plot-driven than other Cirque shows, telling a complex saga about two Asian twins separated by kidnappers, at heart it's a succession of truly breathtaking vignettes. The maneuverability of the stage allows for some staggering aerial battles, and there's an astonishing "Wheel of Death" routine. Add in some extraordinary puppetry and sumptuous costumes, plus the artful use of fire and fog, and Kà is certain to expand your horizons. Fri–Tues 7pm & 10:30pm. $99, $125, $150.

Lance Burton *Monte Carlo*, 3770 Las Vegas Blvd S ℡702/730-7160. The best family show in Las Vegas, featuring master magician Lance Burton. Most of it consists of traditional but very impressive stunts with playing cards, handkerchiefs, and doves, but large-scale illusions include the disappearance of an entire airplane and a narrow escape from hanging. Tues & Sat 7pm & 10pm, Wed–Fri 7pm. $66 & $73.

Legends in Concert *Imperial Palace*, 3535 Las Vegas Blvd S ℡702/794-3261. Enjoyable celebrity-tribute show, with a changing roster of impersonators posing as stars from Tina Turner to Rod Stewart. Daily except Sun 7.30pm & 10.30pm. $40–60, including one drink; ages 12 and under $25–45.

🏃 **Mystère** *TI*, 3300 Las Vegas Blvd S ℡1-800/392-1999. Fabulous Cirque du Soleil showcase, with tumblers, acrobats, trapeze artists, pole climbers, clowns, and strongmen, but no animals apart from fantastic costumed apparitions. Wed–Sat 7.30pm & 10.30pm, Sun 4.30pm & 7.30pm. $95.

🏃 **O** *Bellagio*, 3600 Las Vegas Blvd S ℡702/693-7722. From the synchronized swimmers onward, the Cirque du Soleil display their magnificent skills to maximum advantage. Any part of the stage at any time may be submerged in water of varying depths – one moment a performer can walk across a particular spot, the next someone may dive headfirst into it from the high wire. Wed–Sun 7.30pm & 10.30pm. $99–150.

V – the Ultimate Variety Show *V Theatre*, *The Aladdin*, 3667 Las Vegas Blvd S ℡702/932-1818. Old-fashioned but enjoyable revue show that gives assorted singers, comedians, jugglers, and the like a few minutes each to prove their worth. If the hilarious Russ Merlin is on the bill, be sure not to miss it. Daily 7.30pm & 9pm, $69–69.

Lake Mead and the Hoover Dam

The vast reservoir thirty miles southeast of the city, **LAKE MEAD**, was created by the construction of the Hoover Dam. As with the similarly incongruous Lake

Powell (see p.1003), it makes a bizarre spectacle, the blue waters a vivid counterpoint to the surrounding desert, but it gets excruciatingly crowded all year round.

Though the Lake Mead National Recreation Area straddles the border between Nevada and Arizona, the best views come from the Nevada side. Even if you don't need details on how to sail, scuba-dive, water-ski, or fish from the marinas along the five-hundred-mile shoreline, call in at the Alan Bible **visitor center** (daily 8.30am–4.30pm; ☎702/293-8990, ⓦwww.nps.gov/lame), four miles northeast of Boulder City on US-93, to enjoy a sweeping prospect of the whole thing.

Eight miles on, beyond the rocky ridges of the Black Mountains, US-93 reaches the **Hoover Dam** itself. Designed to block the Colorado River and provide low-cost electricity for the cities of the Southwest, it's among the tallest dams ever built (760ft high), and used enough concrete to build a two-lane highway from the West Coast to New York. It was completed in 1935, as the first step of the Bureau of Reclamation program that culminated with the Glen Canyon Dam (see p.1003). For security reasons, the dam no longer offers extensive behind-the-scenes tours, but you can still ride an elevator to the turbine room at the bottom. Regular half-hour guided tours leave from the **Hoover Dam Visitor Center** on the Nevada side of the river (daily April–Sept 8.30am–5.45pm, Oct–March 9.15am–4.15pm; $10, plus $5 parking; ☎702/293-1824).

Crossing Nevada

The bulk of Nevada is made up of dry, flat plains sliced by knife-edge volcanic mountain ranges. Called the **Great Basin** because its rivers and streams have no outlet to the ocean, the land has a certain eerie, even hypnotic, beauty. Here you'll find the indefinable, very American sense of the endless frontier.

The main route across Nevada, **I-80**, shoots from Salt Lake City to Reno, skirting dozens of bizarrely named small towns – Winnemucca, Elko, Battle Mountain – packed with casinos, bars, brothels, motels, and little else. The other main route, **US-50**, has a reputation as the loneliest highway in America, with the least traffic and roadside life. Older and slower than I-80, it follows much the same route as did the Pony Express in the 1860s, but many of the towns have faded away, and some have been entirely abandoned.

Great Basin National Park

Just across the border from Utah, **Great Basin National Park** was created in 1986 by the amalgamation of the Lehman Caves National Monument and the Wheeler Peak Scenic Area. It's a distillation of the range of scenery the Nevada desert offers, from angular peaks to high mountain meadows cut by fast-flowing streams. The **Lehman Caves** are some of the most extensive and fascinating limestone caves in the country, not as big as Carlsbad Caverns, but if anything more densely packed with intriguing formations. Guided tours leave regularly throughout the day, costing $4 for 30min, $8 for 1hr, or $10 for 90min, from the **visitor center** near the mouth of the caves (daily: summer 8am–5pm; winter 8am–4.30pm; ☎775/234-7331, ⓦwww.nps.gov/grba), five miles west of the hamlet of **Baker**.

From the Lehman Caves, a twelve-mile road climbs the east flank of the bald and usually snowcapped **Wheeler Peak**, and trails lead past alpine lakes and through a grove of gnarled, ancient bristlecone pines to the 13,063ft summit. Few people ever come here, but in winter the mountains and meadows make for excellent off-track cross-country skiing. The nearest real town, **ELY**, an hour's drive away, has two worthwhile museums – the entertaining **Nevada Northern Railway Museum** (daily except Mon 11am–1pm; $5; ☏1-866/407-8326, ⓦnevadanorthern railway.net), which offers $20 rides on a restored steam train, and the **County Museum** (daily 9am–4pm; free) – as well as a dozen **motels** (like *Motel 6*, 770 Avenue O; ☏775/289-6671; ❷) and a handful of casinos and restaurants.

Elko

One of the few Nevada towns worth aiming for, if you're here at the right time of year, is **ELKO**, a straggling highway town along I-80, a hundred miles from the Utah border. The self-proclaimed last real cowtown in the West is the center of one of the largest open-range cattle-ranching regions in the US, and the fitting home of the annual **Cowboy Poetry Gathering**, held here every January. People get together in a sort of celebration of folk culture, telling stories around campfires, singing about the lonesome life on the range, and keeping alive the dying traditions and tales of the Wild West.

During the 72-hour party of the **National Basque Festival**, each Fourth of July weekend, hulking men throw huge logs at each other amid a whole lot of carousing and downing of platefuls of Basque food. The food is available year-round in restaurants like the *Star Hotel*, two blocks south of the main drag at 246 Silver St (☏775/738-9925). Greyhound and Amtrak both stop in Elko, and there are dozens of budget motels, such as the *Centre Motel*, 475 Third St (☏775/738-7226; ❷). Elko's **visitor center** is at 700 Moren Way (Mon–Fri 9am–5pm; ☏775/738-4091 or 1-800/248-ELKO, ⓦwww.elkocva.com).

Reno and around

If you don't make it to Las Vegas, you can get a feel for the nonstop, neon-lit gambler's lifestyle by stopping in **RENO**, on I-80, very near the California border. "The biggest little city in the world," as it likes to call itself, is a somewhat downmarket version of Vegas, with miles of gleaming slot machines and poker tables, along with tacky wedding chapels and quickie divorce courts. While the town itself may not be much to look at, its setting – at the foot of the snowcapped **Sierra Nevada**, with the Truckee River winding through the center – is superb.

There are three things to do in Reno: gamble, get married, and get divorced. The **casinos** are concentrated in the downtown area, along Virginia Street on either side of the railroad tracks. To get **married**, the requirements are the same as in Las Vegas (see p.1024), though here you obtain your **marriage license** at the **Washoe County Court**, Virginia and Court streets (daily 8am–midnight; $55; ☏775/328-3260). Wedding chapels all around the city will help you tie the knot, including Heart of Reno Wedding Chapel, 243 S Sierra St (☏775/786-6882).

Practicalities

Reno's **Cannon International Airport** is a couple of miles southeast of downtown, a twenty-minute ride on local bus #24. Greyhound **buses** use the terminal at 155 Stevenson St; daily Amtrak **trains** call at 135 E Commercial Row downtown, six hours out of San Francisco en route for Salt Lake City.

The downtown **visitor center**, in the National Bowling Stadium at 300 N Center St (daily 8am–6pm; ☏1-800/FOR-RENO, ⓦwww.renolaketahoe.com), should be able to help you find an inexpensive **place to stay**, though rates tend to double at weekends. All the big casinos offer accommodation – the pick of them are the *Atlantis*, 3800 S Virginia St (☎ 775/825-4700 or 1-800/723-6500, ⓦ www. atlantiscasino.com; ❹); *Silver Legacy*, 407 N Virginia St (☎ 775/325-7401 or 1-800/687-8733, ⓦ www.silverlegacyreno.com; ❸); and *Circus Circus*, 500 N Sierra St (☎ 775/329-0711 or 1-877/213-7709, ⓦ www.circusreno.com; ❷ . Reno's best **buffet** is at the *Eldorado*, 345 N Virginia St (☎ 775/786-5700 or 1-800/648-5966, ⓦ www.eldoradoreno.com; ❸).

Carson City

US-395 heads south from Reno along the jagged spires of the **High Sierra**, en route to **Death Valley**. Just thirty miles south of Reno, **CARSON CITY**, state capital of Nevada, is small by comparison but has a number of elegant buildings, some excellent historical museums, and a handful of world-weary casinos.

Carson City was named after frontier explorer Kit Carson in 1858, and is still redolent with Wild West history. A good introduction to the region is the **Nevada State Museum** at 600 N Carson St (daily 8.30am–4.30pm; $4). Housed in the former Carson Mint, it covers the geology and natural history of the Great Basin, up to the heyday of the 1860s, when the silver mines of the nearby Comstock Lode were at their peak. From its reconstructed **Ghost Town**, a tunnel allows entry down into a full-scale model of an **underground mine**.

Greyhound **buses** between Reno and Los Angeles stop once a day in each direction, at 111 E Telegraph Ave. *Bliss Mansion* is a luxurious **B&B** in a restored Victorian house, downtown at 608 Elizabeth St (☎ 775/887-8988 or 1-800/887-3501, ⓦ www.blissmansion.com; ❼), while *Hardman House* at 917 N Carson St (☎ 775/882-7744; ❸) is an inexpensive **motel**. The **visitor center**, on the south side of town at 1900 S Carson St (Mon–Fri 8am–5pm, Sat & Sun 10am–3pm; ☎ 775/687-7410, ⓦ www.carson-city.org), can help with practical details and provide maps for self-guided architectural walking and driving **tours** of the town.

Virginia City

Much of the wealth on which Carson City – and indeed San Francisco – was built came from the silver mines of the **Comstock Lode**, a solid seam of pure silver discovered underneath Mount Hamilton, fourteen miles northeast of Carson City off US-50, in 1859. Raucous **VIRGINIA CITY** grew up on the steep slopes above the mines, and a young writer named Samuel Clemens made his way here from the east with his older brother, the acting Secretary to the Governor of the Nevada Territory, to see what all the fuss was about. His descriptions of the wild life of the mining camp were published years later under his pseudonym, **Mark Twain**. Collected in *Roughing It*, they form a hilarious eyewitness account of the hard-drinking existence of the frontier miners. There's not much to Virginia City nowadays, since all the old storefronts have been taken over by hot-dog vendors and tacky souvenir stands, but the surrounding landscape of arid mountains still feels remote and undisturbed.

13

California

AL - ALABAMA	IN - INDIANA	MN - MINNESOTA	RI - RHODE ISLAND
AR - ARKANSAS	LA - LOUISIANA	MS - MISSISSIPPI	SC - SOUTH CAROLINA
CT - CONNECTICUT	MA - MASSACHUSETTS	NC - NORTH CAROLINA	VA - VIRGINIA
DE - DELAWARE	MD - MARYLAND	NH - NEW HAMPSHIRE	VT - VERMONT
FL - FLORIDA	ME - MAINE	NJ - NEW JERSEY	WI - WISCONSIN
IL - ILLINOIS	MI - MICHIGAN	PA - PENNSYLVANIA	WV - WEST VIRGINIA

CHAPTER 13

Highlights

✳ **San Diego Zoo** About as humane and "natural" as a zoo can get, with a vast collection of rare species. See p.1038

✳ **Disney Hall** LA's foremost example of modern sculpture—which also happens to be a terrific symphony hall. See p.1052

✳ **Mono Lake** A strange and remote sight that's well worth the trip – prime bird-watching territory amid blue waters and gnarled tufa columns. See p.1085

✳ **Joshua Tree National Park** The eerily twisted "arms" of Joshua trees beckon visitors to explore this long-abandoned mining country. See p.1079

✳ **Highway 1** A thrilling, circuitous drive along the US's West Coast, with pounding Pacific surf and dramatic cliffside vistas. See p.1101

✳ **Yosemite National Park** Giant sequoias, towering waterfalls, the sheer face of Half Dome – pack the camera. See p.1091

✳ **Alcatraz** Eerie, legendary one-time maximum-security prison stuck out on "the Rock" in San Francisco Bay. See p.1121

✳ **Golden Gate Park** San Francisco's famous green patch offers cultural delights and still conjures up images of its hippie heyday. See p.1127

△ Venice Beach, CA

California

P ublicized and idealized all over the world, **CALIFORNIA** has a formidable reputation as a terrestrial paradise of sun, sand, and surf, with high mountain ranges, fast-paced glitzy cities, primeval old-growth forests, and vast stretches of deserts. All this, however, lies under the constant threat of the Big One – a massive **earthquake** of unimaginable destruction – along with the floods, fires, and other assorted disasters. Its politics have also undergone a seismic shift. Although formerly the power base for such right-wing stalwarts as Ronald Reagan and Richard Nixon, California has also been the source of some of the country's most progressive **political movements**. The fierce protests of the Sixties may have died down, but California remains the heart of liberal America, at the forefront of environmental awareness, gay pride, and social experimentation, and a firm bulwark of the Democratic Party. **Economically**, too, the region is crucial, whether in the film and music industries, the financial markets, or the all-consuming sector of real estate.

California is much too large to be fully explored in a single trip – so decide what kind of vacation you're looking for. **Los Angeles** is far and away the biggest and most stimulating city: a maddening collection of freeways, beaches, suburbs, elite enclaves, and extreme lifestyles. To the south, the more conservative metropolis of **San Diego** has broad, welcoming beaches and easy access to Mexico, while further inland, the **deserts**, most notably **Death Valley**, comprise a barren and inhospitable landscape of volcanic craters and salt pans that in summer becomes the hottest place on Earth.

Most people follow the shoreline north up the **central coast**: a gorgeous run that takes in vibrant small towns such as **Santa Barbara** and **Santa Cruz**. California's second city, **San Francisco**, is about as different from LA as it's possible to get: a European-styled jewel whose wooden Victorian houses and steep hills make it one of the world's most distinctive and appealing cities. It is also well placed for the national parks to the east, such as **Yosemite**, where waterfalls cascade into a sheer glacial valley, and **Sequoia/Kings Canyon** with its gigantic trees, as well as the ghost towns of the **Gold Country**. North of San Francisco the countryside becomes wilder, wetter, and greener, passing vineyards, stunning lakes, spectacular **Mt Shasta** and almost deserted volcanic tablelands en route to Oregon.

The **climate** in **southern California** features seemingly endless days of sunshine and warm, dry nights, with occasional bouts of torrential flooding in the winter. All along the **coast** mornings can be hazily overcast, especially in May and June; in the Bay Area around San Francisco it can be chilly all year, and fog rolls in to spoil many a sunny day. Much more so than in the south, winter in **northern California** can bring rain for weeks on end, causing massive mudslides that wipe out roads and hillside homes. Most hiking trails in the **mountains** are blocked between October and June by the snow that keeps California's ski slopes among the busiest in the nation.

Some history

Around half a million people were living in tribal villages along the West Coast when the Spaniard **Juan Cabrillo** first sighted San Diego harbor in 1542, naming it **California** after an imaginary island (inhabited by Amazons) from a Spanish novel. **Sir Francis Drake** landed near Point Reyes, north of San Francisco, in 1579, where the "white bancks and cliffes" reminded him of Dover. In 1602 **Sebastián Vizcáino** bestowed most of the place-names that still survive; his exaggerated description of **Monterey** as a perfect harbor led later colonizers to make it the region's military and administrative center. The Spanish occupation began in earnest in 1769, combining military rule with missionary zeal. Father **Junípero Serra** first established a small mission and *presidio* (fort) at San Diego, before arriving in June 1770 at Monterey. By 1804 a chain of 21 missions, each a long day's

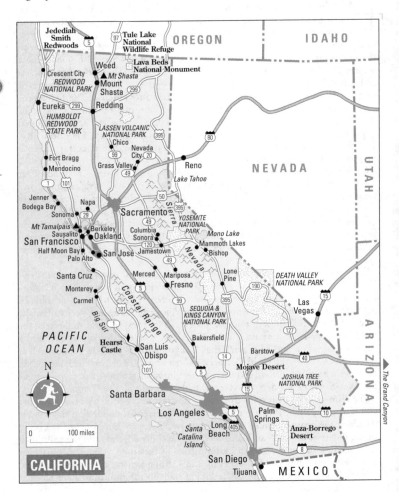

The Grand Canyon ▶

walk from the next along the dirt path of *El Camino Real* (The Royal Road), ran from San Diego to San Francisco. Native Americans were either forcibly converted into Catholicism or killed; though not all gave up without a fight, disease ensured that they were soon wiped out.

When Mexico gained its independence in 1821, in theory it also acquired control of California. However, **Americans** were already starting to arrive, despite the immense difficulty of getting to California – three months by sea or four months overland in a covered wagon. Though the non-native population was a mere ten thousand in 1846, the growing belief that it was the **Manifest Destiny** of the United States to cover the continent from coast to coast, evident in the imperialist policies of President James K. Polk, soon led to the **Mexican–American War**. Virtually all the fighting took place in Texas; Monterey was captured by the US Navy without a shot fired, and by January 1847 the Americans controlled the entire West Coast.

A mere nine days before the signing of the treaty that ended the war, flakes of **gold** were discovered in the Sierra Nevada. Prospectors flooded in from all parts of the world in a madcap migration that led to California joining the US as the **31st state** in 1850. It took just fifteen years to pick the land clean of visible gold, but industrialists like Charles Crocker, Leland Stanford, and Collis Huntington achieved jaw-dropping fortunes. The **transcontinental railroad** was completed in 1869, linking the gold fields to the rest of the US. Built mostly by Chinese laborers, the railway was an engineering feat and a social and cultural turning point. The crossing from New York now took just five days, and a railroad rate war brought fares down to as little as $1 for a one-way ticket, which attracted hordes of newcomers from the Great Plains to Southern California and helped make Los Angeles the state's biggest city.

Thanks to this migration, along with periodic real-estate booms and the rise of the **film industry**, California became the nation's fastest-growing state. Heavy industry followed during **World War II**, in the form of shipyards and airplane factories, and many workers – both white and black – and military personnel stayed on afterwards.

As home to the **beats** in the Fifties and the **hippies** in the Sixties, California was at the cutting edge of cultural change. But when the Vietnam-era protests ended with the abolition of the draft, much of the state's creative ferment did, too – giving rise to the indulgent, cocaine-fueled "Me Generation" of the 1970s. The economic counterpart of this shift also developed when **Proposition 13**, in 1978, augured a national trend to dramatically cut taxes at the cost of government solvency. The 1980s saw further right-wing gains, with a string of laissez-faire Republican governors, the associated decline of public financing for health care and education, and a prison-building boom and "tough on crime" attitude, epitomized by police chiefs like LA's Daryl Gates who used military tanks and SWAT teams. These policies had a predictable outcome in the Nineties, which crash-landed in economic scandal, a depressed real-estate market, rising unemployment, gang violence, and race riots in LA – compounded by **earthquakes**, **drought**, and **flooding**.

After a carnivalesque recall election in 2003 that cut short the term of charisma-challenged **Gray Davis**, action-movie star **Arnold Schwarzenegger** became the Republican governor of the largely Democratic state. California continues to attract countless **new migrants** from the rest of the US and the world. With much of the influx coming from Latin America, Spanish is now the lingua franca in many communities, and **Hispanics** increasingly provide much of the economic growth and cultural vitality of this dynamic, ever-changing place.

To explore California to the fullest, you'll need a **car**. A city such as Los Angeles couldn't exist without the automobile, and in any case driving down the coastal freeways in a sleek convertible is too fun and iconic to resist.

Amtrak **trains** running north-south include the *Pacific Surfliner* that connects **San Diego** and **LA** (and up to San Luis Obispo), with a stop at Fullerton for buses to Disneyland. The daily *Coast Starlight* runs up the coast from LA, stopping at **Oakland** and **Emeryville**, the nearest stations to San Francisco, and continues on via Sacramento to Seattle. The *San Joaquin* from Oakland runs along the Central Valley, connecting with LA by bus. Greyhound **buses** link all the main cities.

For quick hops between the major cities, you can't beat **flying**, though the airline industry has forced cutbacks in many services, and rising gas prices mean hiked costs. If your plans are flexible enough, you can take advantage of off-peak deals.

If you plan to do any **long-distance cycling**, traveling from north to south can make all the difference – the wind blows this direction in the summer, and the ocean side of the road offers the best views. Be careful if you cycle along the coast on Hwy-1: despite the stunning views, the highway has heavy traffic, tight curves, and is prone to fog.

⑬

San Diego

Relatively free from smog and byzantine freeways, **SAN DIEGO**, sits on a gracefully curving bay and represents the conservative side of southern California. The second most-populous city in California may be affluent and libertarian, but it's also easygoing and far from smug. Although it was the site of the first mission in California, the city only really took off with the arrival of the Santa Fe Railroad in the 1880s, and in terms of trade and significance it has long been in the shadow of Los Angeles. However, during World War II the US Navy made San Diego its Pacific Command Center, and the military continues to dominate the local economy, alongside tourism. It's also known for having some of the worst municipal corruption in the country, though travelers will hardly notice this darker side while enjoying the long white beaches, sunny weather, and bronzed bodies – giving rise to the city's nickname, "Sandy Ego."

Arrival, information, and getting around

Both **trains** and **buses** stop in the heart of downtown San Diego: Greyhound at Broadway and First Avenue is more central than Amtrak's Santa Fe Depot, at the west end of Broadway. **Lindbergh Field Airport** is only two miles out, on bus #992 from downtown (daily 5am–midnight; $2.25).

The **International Visitor Information Center** is downtown at 1040 W Broadway (June–Aug daily 9am–5pm, Sept–May Thurs–Tues 9am–4pm; ☎619/236-1212, ⓦwww.sandiego.org). The main downtown post office is at 815 E St, between 8th and 9th avenues (Mon–Fri 8.30am–5pm; ☎619/232-8612; zip code 92101).

Getting around without a car is comparatively easy. Several major companies operate **buses** in the area (ⓦ www.sdcommute.com), with most one-way fares $1–2.50, though long-distance, express and rural routes can reach $4. The main operators are San Diego Transit, or SDTC (ⓣ 619/238-0100), and North County Transit District (ⓣ 760/966-6500). The **Transit Store**, at 1st and Broadway (Mon–Sat 9am–5pm; ⓣ 619/234-1060), has detailed timetables and sells a **Day Tripper Transit Pass** for one- to four-day visits ($5, $9, $12, and $15, respectively). The passes apply also to the tram-like **San Diego Trolley**, which runs throughout the area (one-way tickets $1–3) and covers the sixteen miles from the Santa Fe Depot to the Mexican border-crossing at San Ysidro. It's a 45-minute journey ($5 round-trip; every 15min from 5am to midnight), and the last trolley back leaves at 1am (or Sat 2am). **Bicycle** rental shops include Bicycle Barn, 746 Emerald St, Pacific Beach (ⓣ 858/581-3665), and Cheap Rentals, 3685 Mission Blvd, Mission Beach (ⓣ 858/488-9070, ⓦ www.cheap-rentals.com).

Accommodation

Accommodation is plentiful throughout San Diego. The best-placed, though mall-like, **campground** is *Campland on the Bay*, 2211 Pacific Beach Drive (ⓣ 1-800/4BAY-FUN, ⓦ www.campland.com), linked to downtown by bus #30, where a basic site starts at $39, with more elaborate sites running $56–200. For a more serene camping option, there's **San Elijo Beach State Park**, Rte-21 south of Cardiff-by-the-Sea (ⓣ 1-800/444-7275; $9–25).

Hotels, motels, and B&Bs

Bahia Resort 998 West Mission Bay Drive, Mission Bay ⓣ 1-800/576-4229, ⓦ www.bahiahotel.com. Prime beachside accommodation with expansive ocean views, watersports rentals, pool, and Jacuzzi. There are snug but pleasant rooms in a palm-garden setting and pricier bayside suites. ❼

Balboa Park Inn 3402 Park Blvd, Hillcrest ⓣ 619/298-0823, ⓦ www.balboaparkinn.com. Elegant, gay-oriented B&B, within walking distance of Balboa Park and museums. Offers 26 romantic one- and two-bedroom themed suites (with Parisian, Impressionist, and Tarzan motifs, to name a few) with coffeemakers and mini-fridges. ❹

Beach Haven Inn 4740 Mission Blvd, Pacific Beach ⓣ 858/272-3812 or 1-800/831-6323, ⓦ www.beachhaveninn.com. Nice rooms around a pool and spa; continental breakfast included. With a/c, kitchenettes, and cable TV, it's one of the better values at the beach. ❹

Bristol 1055 1st Ave, downtown ⓣ 619/232-6141, ⓦ www.thebristolsandiego.com. Boutique hotel with stylish modern decor and tasteful amenities, plus in-room CD players and Internet access. ❼

Crystal Pier Hotel and Cottages 4500 Ocean Blvd, Pacific Beach ⓣ 858/483-6983 or 1-800/748-5894, ⓦ www.crystalpier.com. Beautiful, deluxe cottages built in the 1920s, right on the Pacific Beach pier. All units are suites with private deck, and most have kitchenettes. ❽

El Cordova 1351 Orange Ave, Coronado ⓣ 619/435-4131 or 1-800/229-2032, ⓦ www. elcordovahotel.com. The best deal in Coronado, these Spanish Colonial buildings from 1902 are set among lovely gardens. There's a pool, and some rooms have kitchenettes. A huge price spread covers basic units without a/c (❹) and elegant suites (❾).

Heritage Park B&B 2470 Heritage Park Row, Old Town ⓣ 619/299-6832 or 1-800/995-2470, ⓦ www.heritageparkinn.com. Restored Queen Anne mansion in Heritage Park, chock-full of Victorian trappings. Breakfast and afternoon tea are included. Rooms and suites are in the usual lace-and-chintz style. One small unit (❺) undercuts the rest of the rooms. ❻

Horton Grand 311 Island Ave at 3rd Ave, downtown ⓣ 619/544-1886 or 1-800/542-1886, ⓦ www. hortongrand.com. Classy, modernized amalgam of two century-old hotels, with fireplaces in most of the renovated, antique-accented rooms, plus an on-site restaurant and piano bar. The staff dresses in Victorian-era costumes. ❼

Hotel del Coronado 1500 Orange Ave, Coronado ⓣ 619/522-8000 or 1-800/468-3533, ⓦ www.hoteldel.com. This spectacular Victorian confection put Coronado on the map and is still the area's major tourist sight (see p.1036). The striking rooms and suites, expansive bay views, and old-fashioned charm from 1888 give the place much appeal. Modern accommodations in separate buildings. ⑧–⑨

La Pensione 606 W Date St at India St ☎619/236-8000, ⓦwww.lapensionehotel.com. Great-value small hotel within walking distance of the city center and with on-site laundry. The rooms are small but tastefully decorated and equipped with microwaves, fridges, and cable TV.

Manchester Grand Hyatt One Market Place, at Harbor Drive ☎619/232-1234, ⓦwww.manchester grand.hyatt.com. A pair of gleaming white slabs of luxury make up the most prominent hotel along the waterfront. Top-notch amenities include pool, spas, health club, several restaurants and lounges, and rooms with expansive views of the bay. ⑨

Park Manor Suites 525 Spruce St, near Balboa Park ☎619/291-0999 or 1-800/874-2649, ⓦwww.parkmanorsuites.com. Renovated complex that's nearly one hundred years old. Tasteful suites feature kitchens and large sitting areas. Continental breakfast included. ⑤

US Grant Hotel 326 Broadway, downtown ☎619/232-3121 or 1-800/237-5029, ⓦwww.usgrant.net. Downtown's poshest address since 1910, newly renovated with grand Neoclassical design, chandeliers, marble floors, and cozy, but comfortable guestrooms. ⑧

Hostels

Banana Bungalow 707 Reed Ave, Pacific Beach ☎858/273-3060 or 1-800/5-HOSTEL, ⓦwww.bananabungalow.com/sub/bbsd.html. Friendly if scruffy place with access to the beach, along with the free breakfasts, keg nights, barbecues, bonfires, among other things – drawing a party-all-night, sleep-all-day crowd. Dorm beds $18–25, private rooms $55-95. Take bus #34. ①–④

HI-San Diego Downtown 521 Market St at 5th Ave, downtown ☎619/525-1531 or 1-800/909-4776, ⓦwww.sandiegohostels.org. Handy for the Gaslamp District, with free breakfast and high-speed internet access. HI members $19, others $24, and private doubles $47–55. No curfew. ①–③

HI-San Diego Pt Loma/Elliott 3790 Udall St, Ocean Beach ☎619/223-4778 or 1-800/909-4776, ⓦwww.sandiegohostels.org. A couple of miles back from the beach and minus the relentless party atmosphere prevailing in other hostels, offering free breakfast, patio, and common room with TV. Well-run and friendly, with dorms for $20–22 and private rooms $42–54. Take bus #35. ①–③

Ocean Beach International Backpackers Hostel 4961 Newport Ave, Ocean Beach ☎619/223-7873 or 1-800/339-7263, ⓦmembers.aol.com/OBIhostel/hostel. Lively spot a block from the beach, offering barbecues, bike and surfboard rentals, and nightly movies. Space in a four-bed dorm $17–22, with sheets, showers, and continental breakfast. ①

USA Hostels – San Diego 726 5th Ave, downtown ☎619/232-3100 or 1-800/438-8622, ⓦwww.usa-hostels.com/sandiego. Converted 1890s building with a good location on the edge of the Gaslamp District. Rooms accommodate 6 to 8 beds, and cost $24 with sheets and continental breakfast. Doubles $61. Organizes weekly pub crawl and tours to Tijuana, SeaWorld, and the Zoo. ①–③

The City

With its mix of laid-back libertarians and rock-ribbed conservatives, San Diego embodies a work-hard, play-hard ethic, although it leans more toward the latter. Featuring an easily navigable downtown, scenic bay, 42 miles of beaches, and plentiful parks and museums, the city is hard not to like from the moment you arrive.

Downtown San Diego

The vibrant core of **downtown** San Diego is the most convenient place to start exploring, if not the best place to hang out for more than a few hours. Since the late 1970s, several blocks of 1920s architecture have been stylishly renovated, with the sleek modern buildings symbolizing the city's growing economic importance on the Pacific Rim. Downtown is safe by day, but can be unwelcoming at night when the financial zone shuts down – you're better off heading to the restaurants and clubs of the well-lit Gaslamp District.

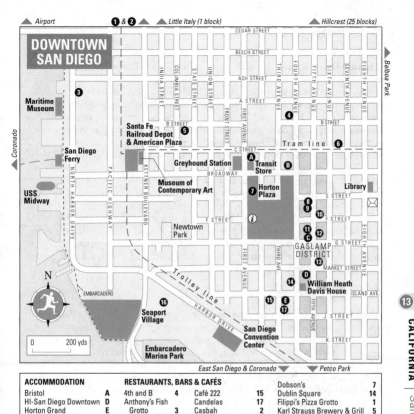

ACCOMMODATION

Bristol	A
HI-San Diego Downtown	D
Horton Grand	E
US Grant Hotel	B
USA Hostels – San Diego	C

RESTAURANTS, BARS & CAFÉS

4th and B	4	Café 222	15
Anthony's Fish		Candelas	17
Grotto	3	Casbah	2
Bella Luna	12	Croce's Restaurant	
Bitter End	11	and Jazz Bar	10
Buffalo Joe's	13	de' Medici	8

Dobson's	7
Dublin Square	14
Filippi's Pizza Grotto	1
Karl Strauss Brewery & Grill	5
Manchester Grand Hyatt	16
On Broadway	6
Onyx Room	9

The tall Moorish archways of the **Santa Fe Railroad Depot**, at the western end of Broadway, built in 1915 for the Panama-California Exposition, still evoke a sense of grandeur. Nearby, the downtown branch of the **Museum of Contemporary Art**, or MCA San Diego, 1001 Kettner Blvd (Thurs–Tues 11am–5pm; free; Ⓦwww.mcasd.org), is a fine first-stop for anyone interested in contemporary art with a California twist. Although its permanent collection focuses on American minimalism, Pop Art, and the indigenous art of Mexico, its temporary shows are the real appeal, often involving irreverent imagery drawn from the intersection of pop-culture surrealism and socioeconomic concerns. Further west, **Broadway** slices through the middle of downtown, at its most hectic between 4th and 5th avenues. Many visitors linger around the fountains on the square outside **Horton Plaza**, between 1st and 4th avenues south of Broadway (Mon–Fri 10am–9pm, Sat 10am–8pm, Sun 11am–7pm; Ⓦwww.westfield.com/hortonplaza), a giant mall of some 140 stores and San Diego's de facto city center. For better or worse, the complex's whimsical, colorful postmodern style, loaded with quasi-Art Deco and southwestern motifs, is inevitably a colossal tourist draw. Its lack of a roof flaunts the region's sunny climate.

Gaslamp District

South of Broadway, a few blocks from Horton Plaza, lies the sixteen-block **Gaslamp District**, once the seedy heart of frontier San Diego but now filled with smart streets lined with cafés, antique stores, art galleries, and, of course, "gas lamps" – powered by electricity. A tad artificial it may be, but its late nineteenth-century buildings are intriguing to explore, especially on the two-hour **walking tour** (Sat 11am; $10; ☎619/233-4692, ⓦwww.gaslampquarter.org/tours) that begins from the small cobbled square at 4th and Island avenues. The square is within the grounds of the **William Heath Davis House**, 410 Island Ave (Tues–Sat 10am–6pm, Sun 9am–3pm; $5), whose owner founded modern San Diego and built his saltbox-styled home here in 1850. Each room of the house commemorates a different period with its decor and copious photographs, and should be fascinating to anyone with an interest in Southern California history.

The district is the focus of San Diego nightlife, especially on the weekend. A flow of visitors has been ensured by the construction of **Petco Park**, 7th Ave at Harbor Drive (ⓦsandiego.padres.mlb.com), which draws plenty of Padres baseball fans but has limited parking options. If you've come to play spectator, make an early trip on the Blue Line trolley (which passes alongside) – mass transit around game time resembles a rail-bound journey into deepest tourist hell.

The Bayfront

Along San Diego's curving, scenic **bayfront**, the pathway of the **Embarcadero** runs a mile or so along the bay, curling around to the western end of downtown. The whole length is used by strollers, joggers, and kite-flyers, but some tourists get no farther than **Seaport Village**, a predictable array of trinket shops and diners. Permanently docked here since 2004, the **USS Midway**, 910 N Harbor Drive (daily 10am–5pm, last admission 4pm; $15; ⓦwww.midway.org), shows off its formidable collection of naval hardware and weapons to the public. For those with a taste for nautical combat from World War II to the first Gulf War (the life cycle of the ship), the experience is a memorable one, enhanced by the presence of flight simulators and seven old-time planes parked at the site. Seven, more vintage ships can be visited further north at the **Maritime Museum**, 1492 Harbor Drive (daily 9am–8pm; $12; ⓦwww.sdmaritime.com), highlighted by the 1863 *Star of India*, the world's oldest iron sailing ship still afloat, and the *Californian*, a modern replica of an 1847 cutter, which served as a federal lawboat patrolling the Pacific during the heady Gold Rush days. Keep in mind that since most of these craft are sea-worthy, some may be cruising when you come to visit; call ahead to make sure your favorite boat is on view.

Coronado

Across San Diego Bay from downtown, the isthmus of **Coronado** is a well-scrubbed resort community with a major naval station occupying its western end. It's reached by the majestically modern **Coronado Bay Bridge**, a curving 11,000-foot span that's one of the area's signature images. The town of Coronado grew up around the **Hotel del Coronado** (see "Accommodation," p.1033), a Victorian whirl of turrets and towers erected as a health resort in 1888. The "Del" is where Edward VIII (then Prince of Wales) first met Coronado housewife Wallis Warfield Simpson in 1920, and where *Some Like It Hot* was filmed in 1958, with the Del posing as a Miami Beach hotel. The grandiose place welcomes non-guests to look around. The **Coronado Museum of History and Art**, 1100 Orange Ave (Mon–Fri 9am–5pm, Sat 10am-5pm, Sun 11am–4pm; $4; ⓦwww.coronado

history.org) chronicles the town's early pioneers and first naval aviators, as well as its history of yachting and architecture. The simplest and most scenic way to get to Coronado is on the **San Diego Bay ferry** ($3 each way; ℡619/234-4111), which leaves Broadway Pier daily on the hour between 9am and 9pm (Fri & Sat 10pm). Tickets are available at San Diego Harbor Excursion, 1050 N Harbor Drive (℡619/234-4111, ⓦww.sdhe.com).

Balboa Park and San Diego Zoo

Northeast of downtown, sumptuous **Balboa Park** contains one of the largest groups of **museums** in the US, as well as charming landscaping, traffic-free promenades, and stately Spanish Colonial-style buildings. The park is large but easy to get around **on foot** – if you get tired, there's always the free tram. The **Balboa Park Passport**, a week-long pass that allows one-time admission to all thirteen of the park's museums and its Japanese garden (plus the San Diego Zoo, for an extra $25), is available for $30 from the **visitor information center** (daily 9.30am–4.30pm; ℡619/239-0512, ⓦwww.balboapark.org), inside the on-site House of Hospitality. Near the center, the **Spreckels Organ Pavilion** (concerts June–Aug Sun 2pm, Mon 7.30pm; ⓦwww.serve.com/sosorgan), is worth a look as the home of one of the world's largest organs, with no less than 4500 pipes.

Most of the major museums flank El Prado, the pedestrian-oriented road that bisects the park. Minor works by Rembrandt and El Greco and a stirring collection of Russian icons make the stifling formality of the **Timkin Museum of Art** (Tues–Sat 10am–4.30pm, Sun 1.30–4.30pm; closed Sept; free; ⓦwww.timkenmuseum.org) worth enduring. The **San Diego Museum of Art** (Tues–Sun 10am–6pm, Thurs closes 9pm; $10; ⓦwww.sdmart.org) is the main venue for any big traveling shows – collections from Egypt, China, and the Vatican (to name a few) usually charge a $5–10 premium beyond museum admission. In the permanent collection, there's a solid stock of European paintings from the Renaissance to the nineteenth century, highlighted by Hals and Rembrandt, matched by curious modern works by California artists. Straddling El Prado, the **Museum of Man** (daily 10am–4.30pm; $6; ⓦwww.museumofman.org) veers from the banal to the engaging to the bizarre, including demonstrations of Mexican loom-weaving, replicas of huge Mayan stones, interesting Native American artifacts, and various Egyptian relics.

Close to the Park Boulevard end of El Prado, the **Reuben H. Fleet Science Center** (Mon–Thurs 9.30am–5pm, Fri 9.30am–9pm, Sat 9.30am–8pm, Sun 9.30am–6pm; Science Center $6.75, Science Center and theater or simulator $11.75, all three $15; ⓦwww.rhfleet.org) presents an assortment of child-oriented exhibits, focusing on the snazzier aspects of contemporary science, as well as the expected IMAX theater and virtual-reality simulator. Across Plaza de Balboa, the **Natural History Museum** (daily 10am–5pm; $11; ⓦwww.sdnhm.org) has a great collection of fossils, hands-on displays of minerals, and entertaining exhibits on dinosaurs and crocodiles. South of El Prado, the **Casa de Balboa** houses four museums, three of which are worth a look: the **Museum of Photographic Arts** (daily 10am–5pm, Thurs closes 9pm; $6; ⓦwww.mopa.org) offers a fine permanent collection that includes the work of Matthew Brady, Alfred Stieglitz, Paul Strand, and other big names; the **San Diego Historical Society Museum** (Tues–Sun 10am–5pm; $5; ⓦwww.sandiegohistory.org) charts the booms that have elevated San Diego from scrubland into metropolis within 150 years; and the **Model Railroad Museum** (Tues–Fri 11am–4pm, Sat & Sun 11am–5pm; $5; ⓦwww.sdmodelrailroadm.com) displays tiny, elaborate replicas of cityscapes, deserts, and mountains, as well as the industrious little trains that chug through them.

At the southern end of Pan American Plaza, the **Aerospace Museum** (daily 10am–4.30pm, summer closes 5.30pm; $10; Ⓦ www.aerospacemuseum.org) recounts the history of aviation, loaded with close to seventy planes including the *Spitfire*, *Hellcat*, and the mysterious spy plane *Blackbird*. Next door at the **Automotive Museum** (daily 10am–5.30pm; $7; Ⓦ www.sdautomuseum.org) car enthusiasts linger over motorcycles and classic cars of all kinds, such as a 1948 Tucker Torpedo – one of only fifty left.

Immediately north of the main museums, the enormous **San Diego Zoo** (daily mid-June to early Sept 7am–10pm; early Sept to mid-June 9am–4pm; Ⓦ www.sandiegozoo.org) is one of the world's most renowned, with more than four thousand animals from eight hundred different species, among them very rare Chinese pheasants, Mhorr gazelles, and a freakish two-headed corn snake. It's an enormous place, and you can easily spend a full day here, soaking in the major sections devoted to the likes of chimps and gorillas, sun and polar bears, lizards and lions, and habitats such as the rain forest. Take a bus tour early on to get a general idea of the layout, or survey the scene on the vertiginous Skyfari overhead tramway. Basic admission, including the children's zoo, is $32 (children 3–11 $19.75). A Two-Park Ticket ($54.45, children $33.55) includes a bus tour, ride on the Skyfari, and admission to the **Wild Animal Park**, near Escondido (daily 9am–4pm, summer closes 8pm; $28.50 adults, $17.50 kids), a two-thousand-acre preserve for big cats, rhinos, giraffes, and the like, conveniently roaming about outside your car's windows.

On the border of Balboa Park, **Hillcrest** is a lively and artsy area at the center of the city's **gay community** – about as close as San Diego gets to having a bohemian air. Come here for the interesting cafés and restaurants around University and 5th streets, or simply to stroll around the fine gathering of Victorian homes.

Old Town San Diego and Presidio Hill

In 1769, Spanish settlers chose **Presidio Hill** as the site of the first of California's missions. They soon began to build homes at the foot of the hill, which was dominated in turn by Mexican officials and then by early arrivals from the eastern US. **Old Town San Diego**, reachable from downtown via the Trolley (Blue Line; $2.25), is now a state historical park and the site of several original adobe dwellings – and the inevitable souvenir shops. Most of the stores and restaurants stay open from 10am until at least 10pm. Highlights include the **Casa de Estudillo** on Mason Street, built by the commander of the **presidio**, José Mariá de Estudillo in 1827, one of the poshest of the original adobes. Next door, the **Casa de Bandini** was the home of the politician and writer Juan Bandini and acted as the social center of San Diego during the mid-nineteenth century. Details on the many structures here are available from the **visitor center**, inside the Robinson-Rose House, near Taylor and Congress streets (daily 10am–5pm; Ⓦ www.oldtownsandiego.org).

The Spanish-style building now atop Presidio Hill is only a rough approximation of the original mission – moved in 1774 – but its **Junipero Serra Museum**, 10818 San Diego Mission Rd (Fri–Sun 10am–4.30pm; $5), offers an intriguing examination of Junípero Serra, the padre who led the Spanish colonization and Catholic conversion of California. The **Mission San Diego de Alcalá** itself was relocated six miles north to 10818 San Diego Mission Rd (daily 8am–4pm; $3; Ⓦ www.missionsandiego.com), to be near a water source and fertile soils – and to be safer from attack. The present building is a working parish church, with a small **museum**; among the craft objects and artifacts from the mission is the crucifix held by Serra at his death in 1834. Despite controversy over his legacy and allegations of mission-led violence against native peoples, Serra was beatified in 1998 in a Vatican ceremony.

Ocean Beach and Point Loma

Ruled by the Hell's Angels in the 1960s, **OCEAN BEACH**, six miles northwest of downtown via bus #35 or #923, is a fun and relaxed beach town whose quaint, old-time streets and shops have preserved some of their ramshackle appeal and funky character. The two big hangouts include **Newport Street**, where backpackers slack around at snack bars, surf and skate rental shops, and some of the best secondhand music stores around; and **Voltaire Street**, which true to its name has a good range of independent-minded local businesses. There is often good surf, and the beach itself can be quite fun – especially on weekends, when the local party scene gets cranking. Where Voltaire Street meets the waves, you can visit Ocean Beach's one major attraction, **Dog Beach**, the only sand-strip in the area where pooches are allowed to frolic without leashes. South from the pier rise the dramatic **Sunset Cliffs**, a prime spot for twilight vistas.

South of Ocean Beach, at the southern end of the hilly green peninsula of **Point Loma**, the **Cabrillo National Monument** (daily 9am–5.15pm; 7-day pass $5 per car, pedestrians and cyclists $3; ⓦwww.nps.gov/cabr) marks the spot where Juan Cabrillo and crew became the first Europeans to land in California, albeit briefly, in 1542. The startling views from this high spot, across San Diego Bay to downtown and down the coast to Mexico, easily repay a trip here. A platform atop the western cliffs of the park makes it easy to view the November-to-March **whale migration**, when scores of gray whales pass by en route to their breeding grounds off Baja California, Mexico. The nearby visitor center (same as park hours) contains information on the history and wildlife of the point, and lies near the **Old Point Loma Lighthouse** (daily 9am–5pm; free), which offers tours that lead past replica Victorian furnishings and equipment from the 1880s.

SeaWorld, Mission Beach, and Pacific Beach

North of Ocean Beach, **Mission Bay** is the site of San Diego's most popular tourist attraction: **SeaWorld** (daily June–Aug 9am–10pm, rest of the year 10am–dusk; $54, children $44, parking $7; ⓦwww.seaworld.com), reachable by bus #9 from downtown. It's undeniably kid-friendly, with rides, attractions, and shows, but make sure young ones are prepared for a full day out to make the park's steep entry prices worthwhile. Amazingly enough, the *Skytower* and *Skyride* attractions charge an extra $5 – so don't assume $54 is all you're going to spend, especially after costs for the pricey junk food are figured in.

The biggest-name public beaches in San Diego are **Mission Beach**, the peninsula that separates Mission Bay from the ocean, and its northern extension, **Pacific Beach**. If you aren't up for bronzing on the sands, you can always nurse a beer at one of the many beachfront bars, or you could rollerblade or bike down **Ocean Front Walk**, the concrete boardwalk running the length of both beaches, and observe the toasty sands overrun with scantily clad babes and surfboard-clutching dudes. A mile north of Pacific Beach's Crystal Pier, **Tourmaline Surfing Park**, La Jolla Blvd at Tourmaline St, is reserved exclusively for the sport, as well as windsurfing – but no swimmers are allowed. If you don't have a board, a good alternative is a few miles north, **Windansea Beach**, a favorite surfing hot spot that's also fine for swimming and hiking alongside the oceanside rocks and reefs.

Near the southern end of Ocean Front Walk at 3146 Mission Blvd once-derelict **Belmont Park** (June–Aug Sun–Thurs 11am–11pm, Sat & Sun 11am–midnight; rides $2–5; ⓦwww.belmontpark.com) has been renovated with eleven official rides, though the two main attractions are both from 1925: the **Giant Dipper** rollercoaster, one of the few of its era still around, and the **Vertical Plunge**, once the largest saltwater plunge in the world, and the setting for famous Hollywood swimmers Johnny Weissmuller and Esther Williams.

La Jolla

A more pretentious air prevails in **La Jolla** (pronounced "La Hoya"), an elegant beach community just to the north. Stroll its immaculate, gallery-filled streets, fuel up on California cuisine at one of the many sidewalk cafés, or visit the La Jolla site of the **Museum of Contemporary Art**, 700 Prospect St (Fri–Tues 11am–5pm, Thurs 11am–7pm; $6, students $2; Ⓦ www.mcasd.org), which has a huge, regularly changing stock of paintings and sculptures from 1955 onwards, highlighted by California pop and minimalism. On the seaward side of the museum lies the small and tasteful **Ellen Scripps Browning Park**, named for the philanthropist whose Irving Gill-designed home now houses the museum. Where the park meets the coast is the popular **La Jolla Cove**, much of it an ecological reserve whose clear waters make it perfect for snorkeling (if you can find a parking space).

Just up the road, architecture fans won't want to miss a chance to tour one of the premier sites for high modernism in the US, the **Salk Institute for Biological Studies**, 10010 N Torrey Pines Rd (Mon–Fri 8.30am–5pm; tours Mon, Wed & Fri noon; reserve at Ⓣ858/453-4100 ext 1200, Ⓦ www.salk.edu), not only a respected institution for molecular biology and physics, but also a considerably influential design by architect Louis I. Kahn. This collection of rigid geometric concrete blocks and walls features stark vistas that look out over the Pacific Ocean, possessing a strange, austere serenity. Further north, the **Stephen Birch Aquarium and Museum**, 2300 Expedition Way (daily 9am–5pm; $11, Ⓦ www.aquarium.ucsd.edu), provides entertaining up-close views of captive marine life, informative displays on the earth's ecology, and exhibits detailing the marine exploration work carried out by the Institute. The highlights include the Hall of Fishes, a huge kelp forest home to countless sea creatures, and the Shark Reef, displaying a nice range of the fearsome creatures, including a few pint-sized versions. Altogether, the museum is a much more edifying experience than anything at SeaWorld, and a lot cheaper, too.

Eating

Wherever you are in San Diego, you'll have few problems finding some place good to **eat** at reasonable prices. Everything from crusty coffee shops to stylish ethnic restaurants is in copious supply here, with seafood at its best around Mission Beach and the Gaslamp District, and the latter also home to the greatest concentration of restaurants, aimed at both tourists and locals.

Anthony's Fish Grotto 1360 Harbor Drive, Downtown Ⓣ619/232-5103. Fish-and-chips and other affordable seafood dishes are the draw at this longstanding bayside favorite. Lunch or dinner; one of several area locations.

Bella Luna 748 5th Ave, downtown Ⓣ619/239-3222. A romantic, moon-themed bistro with an artsy feel, serving up wonderful, mid-priced dishes from different regions of Italy, with hefty servings of pasta and succulent calamari.

Berta's 3928 Twiggs St, Old Town Ⓣ619/295-2343. One of the best-kept secrets in town, offering low-priced, authentic cooking from all over Latin America, with a range of hot and spicy concoctions to make you pound the table for more.

Café 222 222 Island Ave, downtown Ⓣ619/236-9902. Hip café serving some of the city's best breakfasts and lunches, with excellent pancakes and waffles and inventive twists on traditional sandwiches and burgers (including vegetarian), at reasonable prices.

Candelas 416 3rd Ave, downtown Ⓣ619/702-4455. Gaslamp District restaurant offering swank, pricey Mexican fare with inventive combinations of seafood and meat dishes – the California cuisine influence is apparent in items like sea bass with grape sauce and wild mushrooms.

Chez Loma 1132 Loma Ave, Coronado ☎619/435-0661. Intensely aromatic and delicious upscale French cuisine, offering the likes of roasted duck in peppercorn and burnt-orange sauce, and a nice cassoulet with black mussels and salmon sausage.

Chilango's Mexican Grill 142 University Ave, Hillcrest ☎619/294-8646. Regional Mexican food for under $10 is served in this tiny storefront locale, which is packed to the rafters in the evenings. Especially tasty shrimp, served with garlic sauce or in mango and vanilla, among other choices.

Crest Café 425 Robinson Ave, Hillcrest ☎619/295-2510. Don't let the dumpy exterior fool you – this place offers solid, tasty American fare on the cheap. The salads, burgers, and pancakes will make your stomach happy, along with more curious items like jalapeno fettucine.

Croce's Restaurant and Jazz Bar 802 5th Ave, Gaslamp District ☎619/233-4355. Pricey but excellent range of pasta, desserts, and salads; the Sunday jazz brunch is a popular event.

de' Medici 815 5th Ave, downtown ☎619/702-7228. Upscale Italian fare that draws plenty of suits for its scrumptious menu, including some tasty gnocchi, beef filets, and cioppino.

Dobson's 956 Broadway Circle, downtown ☎619/231-6771. An upscale restaurant whose cuisine leans toward Continental, with puff pastries adding some zing to the fare, which includes everything from veal sweetbreads to rock shrimp risotto.

Filippi's Pizza Grotto 1747 India St at Date St, downtown ☎619/232-5094. Great pizzas and a handful of scrumptious pasta dishes served in a small room at the back of an Italian grocery.

Ichiban 1449 University Ave, Hillcrest ☎619/299-7203. Fine Japanese cuisine, featuring good rolls, bentos, soups, and sushi, in an unpretentious and popular setting. The combo platters are extremely

well-priced. Also in Pacific Beach at 1441 Garnet Ave (☎858/270-5755).

Karinya 825 Garnet Ave, Pacific Beach ☎858/270-5050. Hot and spicy soups, firecracker shrimp and coconut curry to set your mouth ablaze, with a good range of Thai staples such as noodle dishes and rolls. A solid, affordable bet.

Kono's 704 Garnet Ave, Pacific Beach ☎858/483-1669. Crowded, touristy place for breakfast or lunch on the boardwalk, with hefty and inexpensive portions of eggs, sandwiches, hamburgers, and other American favorites.

Living Room Coffeehouse 1010 Prospect St, La Jolla ☎858/459-1187. One in a chain of four local coffeeshops, with great sandwiches, soups, quiches, and pastries in a cozy setting.

Mission Café and Coffeehouse 3795 Mission Blvd, Mission Beach ☎858/488-9060. A wide range of eclectic choices, from French toast and tamales with eggs to tortillas with spicy seasonings to "roll-ups" stuffed with meat and pasta.

Old Town Mexican Café 2489 San Diego Ave ☎619/297-4330. Expect to queue up at this lively and informal Mexican diner before dining on Mexican ribs and steak Azteca; only at breakfast are you unlikely to have to wait for a table.

Point Loma Seafoods 2805 Emerson St, Ocean Beach ☎619/223-1109. Fast, inexpensive counter serving up San Diego's freshest fish in a basket, along with mean crabcake and squid sandwiches that make the locals cheer. The justly popular joint is packed on weekends.

Sportsmen's Seafood 1617 Quivira Rd, Mission Beach ☎619/224-3551. For the serious fish-lover, the combo diner/market offers cheap and delicious fare – shrimp cocktails, squid steak, tuna burgers, fish and chips, crab or lobster platters, and fish tacos.

Taste of Thai 527 University Ave, Hillcrest ☎619/291-7525. Terrific Thai staples – spicy noodles, marinated shrimp, pad Thai – for reasonable prices; expect a wait on weekends.

Nightlife

Although San Diego's money is lavished on **classical music**, **opera**, and **theater** (half-priced tickets and information at the **Arts Tix** booth at 28 Horton Plaza, Tues–Thurs 11am–6pm, Fri & Sat 10am–6pm, Sun 10am–5pm; ☎619/497-5000), the crowds flock to beachside **discos** and boozy Gaslamp District **music venues**. For full listings, pick up the free *San Diego Reader* (⊛www.sdreader.com), the Thursday edition of the *San Diego Union-Tribune* (⊛www.signonsandiego.com), or the youth-oriented *San Diego CityBeat* (⊛www.sdcitybeat.com).

Bars, coffeeshops, and clubs

Bitter End 770 5th Ave, Gaslamp District ☎619/338-9300. Two-story venue complete with frenetic dancefloor, martini bar, and private lounge, for the sophisticated poseur who doesn't mind paying $10 for an apple-tini.

Café Crema 1001 Garnet Ave, Pacific Beach ☎858/273-3558. Wake yourself up before going to the bars, or sober up afterwards, with one of their large coffees. Sidewalk seating, late hours, Internet access, and eclectic entertainment from oddball poets to avant-garde tunes.

Claire de Lune 2906 University Ave, Hillcrest ☎619/688-9845. The prototypical coffeehouse, with steaming java, teas, and sandwiches, comfy seating and entertainment that runs from smooth jazz to spoken-word to avant-garde.

Dublin Square 554 4th Ave, Gaslamp District ☎619/239-5818. Get your fill of chicken pot pie and lamb-shank stew as you quaff Irish beer and spirits at this Emerald Isle pub. Even the seafood comes in a broth made from Guinness, and the chocolate cake contains whiskey.

Karl Strauss Brewery & Grill 1157 Columbia St, downtown ☎619/234-2739. Discerning beer hunt-ers enjoy ales and lagers brewed on the premises – consider the sampler tray – while the menu offers a solid array of hefty favorites like ribs and sausages. Five other locations.

Live Wire 2103 El Cajon Blvd, just east of Hill-crest ☎619/291-7450. With a wide selection of imported beers, pinball, pool, and quasi-bohemian decor, this is a fine choice for boozing.

On Broadway 615 Broadway, downtown ☎619/231-0111. The apotheosis of posing in San Diego, a velvet-rope scene that attracts the local celebrity elite (such as they are) and sends you into booty-shaking overdrive as you groove to world-league DJs and thunderous house beats.

Onyx Room 852 5th Ave, Gaslamp District ☎619/235-6699. Groovy underground bar with lush decor, where you can knock back a few cock-tails, then hit the back room for live acid-jazz and dance tunes. The swanky lounge upstairs, *Thin*, has pricier drinks and bigger attitudes.

Thrusters Lounge 4633 Mission Blvd, Pacific Beach ☎858/483-6334. Sleek bar and club where the dance beats come hard and heavy, typically leaning toward hip-hop and 80s favorites.

Live-music venues

4th and B 345 B St, downtown ☎619/231-4343. Hard-thumping live rock and dance club with two rooms and a hormone-fueled crowd of bump 'n' grinders. A funky place to shake your ass.

Blind Melons 710 Garnet Ave, Pacific Beach ☎858/483-7844. College-oriented spot with live rock, blues, and reggae bands nightly, plus the occasional DJ.

Brick by Brick 1130 Buenos Ave, Mission Bay ☎619/675-5483. Cool lounge that's one of the better indie spots around town, attracting up-and-coming alternative, blues, and hard-rock acts.

Buffalo Joe's 600 5th Ave, Gaslamp District ☎619/236-1616. Very popular, almost unavoidable nightspot loaded with tourists and some locals, with a broad selection of live tunes, from aggres-sive rockers to snappy funk and blues to tribal dance-beats.

Casbah 2501 Kettner Blvd, downtown ☎619/232-4355. Grungy joint that hosts a solid, varying roster of blues, funk, reggae, rock, and indie bands.

Humphrey's by the Bay 2241 Shelter Island Drive, Point Loma ☎619/523-1010. Live soul, pop, and R&B from mid-level acts and old timers, make this restaurant a solid choice for mainstream music, as well as seafood.

SOMA 3350 Sports Arena Blvd, west of Old Town ☎619/226-7662. Favorite all-ages spot for thrash-ing to punk acts or head-banging to rockers, set in a former moviehouse complex with two stages. No booze, but the frenetic atmosphere is more than enough to get you high.

Winston's 1921 Bacon St, Ocean Beach ☎619/222-6822. A former bowling alley, this local club has rock bands most nights, with occasional reggae and 1960s-style acts as well.

Out from San Diego: the Anza-Borrego Desert

Most of eastern San Diego County, which otherwise consists largely of sleepy suburban towns, is taken up by the 937-square-mile **Anza–Borrego Desert** ($5 per vehicle; Ⓦwww.anzaborrego.statepark.org), much of it comprising the largest desert state park in the US. Some of it can be covered by car, although four-wheel-drive vehicles are necessary for the more obscure – and most interesting – routes. The best **time to come** is winter, when daytime temperatures stay around 85°F. In the fiercely hot summer, it's best left to the lizards, but when the desert blooms, between March and May, scarlet ocotillo, orange poppies, white lilies, purple verbena, and other wildflowers paint a memorable, and fragrant, picture. To find out more information, stop by the **park visitor center**, near park headquarters at 200 Palm Canyon Drive (daily 9am–5pm, weekends only in summer; Ⓣ760/767-4205).

Approaching from the west, Hwy-78 descends to Scissors Crossing, the junction with Hwy-S2, which follows the **Butterfield Stage Route**, which began service in 1857 as the first regular line of communication between the East and the newly settled West. Further on, the old adobe rest stop of **Vallecito** (pronounced "vie-ay-SEE-toe") **Stage Station** (Sept–May only 9am–sunset; $2, camping $12) gives a good indication of the privations of early desert travel. To the south, **Agua Caliente Regional Park** (Sept–May daily 9.30am–5pm; $5, camping $14–18) features a few naturally fed pools, while around Imperial Valley in the least-visited portion of Anza–Borrego, there's a vivid and spectacular clash as gray rock rises from the edges of the red desert floor.

The only substantial settlement in the desert is **BORREGO SPRINGS**, at the northern end of Hwy-S3 along Hwy-S22, which is a good base for the area's canyon walks, some with free but waterless **campgrounds** (campsites $7–19). Camping is also available at the *Borrego Palm Canyon* campground ($13–19), near the Anza–Borrego park visitor center. From here, a 1.5-mile trail takes you to a small oasis with palms and a waterfall. **Hotels** in town are fairly pricey; the most affordable are the *Starland Resort*, 2771 Borrego Springs Rd (Ⓣ760/767-5501; ❸), and *Hacienda del Sol*, 610 Palm Drive (Ⓣ760/767-5442; ❹), and both are clean but basic. Decent **restaurants** include *Carlee's Place* (Ⓣ760/767-3262), for its service-able burgers and pizza; and the *Krazy Koyote*, 2220 Hoberg Rd (Ⓣ760/767-7788), for upscale steak and seafood inside an appealing retro-chic 1950s motel, *The Palms* (same phone; ❹–❻, depending on season).

Los Angeles

The rambling metropolis of **LOS ANGELES** sprawls across the thousand square miles of a great desert basin, knit together by an intricate network of freeways between the Pacific Ocean and the snowcapped mountains. Its colorful melange of shopping malls, palm trees, and swimming pools is both surreal and familiar, thanks to the potent celluloid self-image it has spread all over the world.

LA is a young city. Although founded by the Spanish in the eighteenth century, only after the completion of the transcontinental railroad, starting in the 1870s, did it really begin to grow. By the mid-twentieth century, the enduring symbol of the city had become the family-sized suburban house, with requisite swimming pool and two-car garage. Although the movie industry, beginning locally in the 1910s, attracted its share of new arrivals, the biggest boom came after World

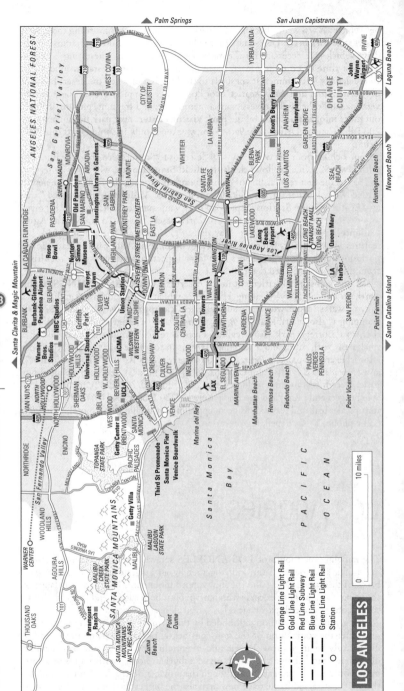

LOS ANGELES

Palm Springs ▲

San Juan Capistrano ▲

▲ Santa Clarita & Magic Mountain

▶ Laguna Beach

▶ Newport Beach

▶ Huntington Beach

▶ Santa Catalina Island

ANGELES NATIONAL FOREST

San Gabriel Valley

San Gabriel River

San Gabriel Mountains

San Fernando Valley

SANTA MONICA MOUNTAINS

SANTA MONICA MOUNTAINS NAT'L REC. AREA

MALIBU CREEK STATE PARK

TOPANGA STATE PARK

MALIBU LAGOON STATE PARK

ORANGE COUNTY

Los Angeles River

Santa Monica Bay

PACIFIC OCEAN

WARNER CENTER

THOUSAND OAKS

AGOURA HILLS

WOODLAND HILLS

NORTHRIDGE

ENCINO

VAN NUYS

NORTH HOLLYWOOD

SHERMAN OAKS

BURBANK

GLENDALE

PASADENA

LA CANADA FLINTRIDGE

SIERRA MADRE

MONROVIA

ARCADIA

WEST COVINA

CITY OF INDUSTRY

MONTEREY PARK

EL MONTE

SAN GABRIEL

SAN MARINO

HIGHLAND PARK

EAST LA

WHITTIER

LA HABRA

SANTA FE SPRINGS

NORWALK

YORBA LINDA

ANAHEIM

BUENA PARK

GARDEN GROVE

LA MIRADA

LOS ALAMITOS

LAKEWOOD

SEAL BEACH

LONG BEACH

IRVINE

WILLINGTON

COMPTON

GARDENA

TORRANCE

HAWTHORNE

INGLEWOOD

CULVER CITY

WESTWOOD

BRENTWOOD

BEL AIR

BEVERLY HILLS

W. HOLLYWOOD

HOLLYWOOD

SILVER LAKE

DOWNTOWN

VERNON

SOUTH CENTRAL LA

CRENSHAW

WATTS

MANHATTAN BEACH

HERMOSA BEACH

REDONDO BEACH

PALOS VERDES PENINSULA

SAN PEDRO

LA Harbor

REDONDO BEACH

EL SEGUNDO

VENICE

Marina del Rey

MALIBU

Point Dume

Zuma Beach

Point Vicente

Point Fermin

Paramount Ranch

Getty Villa

Getty Center

Santa Monica Pier
Venice Boardwalk
Third St Promenade
Santa Monica

UCLA

LAX

Forest Lawn
Union Station
Rose Bowl
Norton Simon Museum
Old Pasadena
Huntington Library & Gardens

Burbank-Glendale-Pasadena Airport
Warner Bros. Studios
NBC Studios
Universal Studios
Griffith Park

LACMA
Wilshire & Western

Exposition Park

Watts Towers

Knott's Berry Farm
Disneyland

Long Beach Airport
Long Beach Transit Mall
Queen Mary

John Wayne Airport

Orange Line Light Rail
Gold Line Light Rail
Red Line Subway
Blue Line Light Rail
Green Line Light Rail
Station

N

0   10 miles

War II with the mushrooming of the aerospace industry. Since then, the city's been driven by finance, media, and real estate.

The first-time visitor may find Los Angeles thrilling and threatening in equal proportions; it's a place that picks you up and sweeps you along whether you like it or not. While it has its fine-art museums, unexpected swaths of parkland, and a few old-fashioned urban plazas, what people really come here for is to experience the fantasy worlds of **Disneyland** and **Hollywood**, as well as the gilded opulence of **Beverly Hills** and **Malibu**.

Arrival, information, and city transportation

All European and many domestic **flights** use LA International Airport – known as **LAX** – sixteen miles southwest of downtown along Santa Monica Bay. **Shuttle buses** "B" and "C" serve their respective parking lots round the clock, and near lot C you can connect with local buses. Minibuses such as SuperShuttle (☎1-800/BLUE-VAN, ⓦ www.supershuttle.com) run all over town, delivering you to your door. Fares depend on your destination but are generally around $25–40 (plus tip), with a journey time of between 30 and 60 minutes. **Taxis** charge at least $35 to West LA or Hollywood, $90 to Disneyland, and a flat $38 to downtown; a $2.50 surcharge applies for all trips starting from LAX.

If you're arriving from elsewhere in the US, or from Mexico, you might just land at one of the **other airports** in the LA area – at Burbank, Long Beach, Ontario, or Orange County's John Wayne Airport in Costa Mesa. **MTA buses** (☎1-800/COMMUTE, outside LA ☎1-800/2-LARIDE, ⓦ www.mta.net) serve them all – phone on arrival and tell them where you are and want to go.

The main **Greyhound** bus terminal, at 1716 E Seventh St (24hr; ☎213/629-8401), is in a seedy section of downtown, but access is restricted to ticket-holders, so it's safe enough inside. To find other local bus stations and stops, check out ⓦ www.greyhound.com. If arriving in LA by **train** you'll be greeted with the Mission Revival architecture of Union Station, 800 N Alameda St (☎213/624-0171), on the north side of downtown, from which you can easily access the city's MTA bus lines.

Information

LA has a number of **visitor centers**. The downtown one is at 685 S Figueroa St (Mon–Fri 9am–5pm; ☎213/689-8822, ⓦ www.lacvb.com); others, all open normal weekday working hours, are in the Hollywood & Highland mall, 6801 Hollywood Blvd (☎323/467-6412); Santa Monica, 1920 Main St (☎310/393-7593, ⓦ www.santamonica.com); near Disneyland, 800 W Katella Ave (☎714/239-1340, ⓦ www.anaheimoc.org); Beverly Hills, 239 S Beverly Drive (☎310/248-1000, ⓦ www.beverlyhillscvb.com); Pasadena, 171 S Los Robles Ave (☎626/795-9311, ⓦ www.pasadenacal.com); and Long Beach, 1 World Trade Center, suite 300 (☎1-800/452-7829, ⓦ www.visitlongbeach.com).

City transportation

The sheer scale of LA – its detractors call it "nineteen suburbs in search of a city" – means that it really is difficult to get around without a car, unless you're confining your visit to more centralized spots like Santa Monica, Pasadena, or downtown LA. Even though the traffic is often bumper-to-bumper, the freeways are the only way to cover long distances quickly. Otherwise, try to relax on the fastest alternative, **express buses**.

Public transportation

LA's **Metrorail** train system comprises five limited lines, distinguished by color: the **Red Line** stretches from Union Station through Hollywood to North Hollywood in the San Fernando Valley; North Hollywood to the western Valley is served by the **Orange Line**; the **Green Line** goes from Hawthorne to Norwalk along the Century Freeway (but stops short of LAX); the **Blue Line** connects downtown through Watts to downtown Long Beach; and the **Gold Line** links downtown to the San Gabriel Valley through Old Pasadena. Tickets cost $1.25 one way, or 75¢ at night 9pm–5am, and trains run every five to fifteen minutes (more infrequently at night). By contrast, **Metrolink** commuter trains ($4.50–12 one way; ☎1-800/371-LINK, ⓦwww.metrolinktrains.com) operate primarily inter-suburban routes on weekdays, though they can be useful if you find yourself in far-flung cities at the fringes of the metropolis.

Car-less Angelenos are still most well served, however, by **buses**, most of which are run by the LA County Metropolitan Transit Authority (MTA or "Metro"; ☎213/626-4455 or 1-800/COMMUTE, ⓦwww.mta.net). Information can also be obtained in person at the East Portal of downtown's Union Station, 800 N Alameda St (Mon–Fri 6am–6.30pm), and 5301 Wilshire Blvd, Mid-Wilshire (Mon–Fri 9am–5pm). Buses on the major streets between downtown and the coast run roughly every fifteen minutes between 5am and 2am; other routes, and the **all-night services** along the major streets, are less frequent. At night, be careful not to get stranded alone downtown waiting for a connection.

The standard **one-way fare** is $1.25; **transfers** cost 25¢ more, but must be made within an hour; **express buses**, and any others using the freeway, are $1.75 up to $3.25. If you're staying a while, you can save some money with a **daily**, **weekly** or **monthly pass**, which cost $3, $14 and $52, respectively. There are also the mini **DASH** buses (☎808-2273 for area codes 213, 310, 323, and 818, ⓦwww.ladottransit.com), with a flat fare of 25¢, and broad coverage throughout downtown and limited routes elsewhere in the city. You'll be hard pressed to find an available **taxi** cruising the streets, so call ahead; among the more reliable companies are the Independent Cab Co. (☎1-800/521-8294),

Yellow Cab (☎ 1-800/200-1085), and United Independent Taxi (☎ 1-800/411-0303). Fares include a base charge of $2; add $2 per mile, and tack on another $2.50 if you're getting picked up from LAX.

Cycling

Cycling in LA may sound perverse, but in some areas it can be one of the better ways of getting around. There are beachside bike paths between Santa Monica and Redondo Beach, and from Long Beach to Newport Beach, and many equally enjoyable inland routes, notably around Griffith Park and Pasadena. Contact AAA, 2601 S Figueroa St (Mon–Fri 9am–5pm; ☎ 213/741-3686), or the LA Department of Transportation, known as CalTrans, 100 S Main St (Mon–Fri 8am–5pm; ☎ 213/897-3656, ⓦ www.dot.ca.gov), for maps and information. The best place to **rent a bike** for the beaches is around the Venice Boardwalk, where numerous outlets include Spokes 'n' Stuff, 4175 Admiralty Way (☎ 310/306-3332) and 1700 Ocean Front Walk (☎ 310/395-4748); in summer, bike rental stands line the beach. Prices range from $10 a day for a clunker to $20 a day or more for a mountain bike. Many beachside stores also rent roller skates and rollerblades.

Accommodation

There's a wide range of **places to stay** in LA. Downtown has both upscale and budget hotels, Hollywood has a wide range of cheap motels, and the Westside and Malibu are mid- to upper-range territory. If you're not driving, choose your base carefully to avoid lengthy cross-town journeys between these areas, or divide your stay between them. The best **campgrounds** in the LA area are along the Orange County coast, such as *Bolsa Chica* in Huntington Beach and the state parks at San Clemente and Crystal Cove (all ☎ 1-800/444-7275), and in the mountains and beaches around Malibu, notably Malibu Creek State Park (☎ 1-800/706-8809) and Leo Carrillo State Beach (☎ 1-818/706-1310). Campsites run $17–25.

Hotels, motels, and B&Bs

Hotels and **motels** are listed by neighborhood. If you're arriving on a late flight, or leaving on an early one, note that hotels near LAX are blandly similar and generally cost around $50–75 a night, but do offer complimentary shuttle service to and from the terminals. Prices increase at many tourist-oriented establishments during peak travel periods, typically over the summer and on weekends, especially those near major attractions like Disneyland and Universal Studios. However, weekday rates at business-oriented hotels, especially during conventions, can be just as expensive, or even more so, than weekend prices.

Downtown and around

Cecil 640 S Main St ☎ 213/624-4545. Grand old 1920s hotel that's been refurbished as a clean, low-budget property; rooms are basic, but have more style than you'd expect, and there's also Internet access. It's in a dicey area, so be cautious after dark. ❸

Hilton Checkers 535 S Grand ☎ 213/624-0000 or 1-800/HILTONS, ⓦ www.hiltoncheckers.com. One of the great LA hotels, with sleek modern appointments in historic 1920s architecture, and

nicely furnished rooms, rooftop pool, and spa. Terrific downtown views, too. ❽ weekdays, ❼ weekends.

Millennium Biltmore 506 S Grand Ave ☎ 213/624-1011 or 1-800/222-8888, ⓦ www.thebiltmore.com. Neoclassical 1923 architecture meets modern luxury, including a health club modeled on a Roman bathhouse. Elegant rooms, and a view overlooking the city. ❼

Miyako Inn 328 E 1st St ☎ 213/617-2000, ⓦ www.miyakoinn.com. Despite the grim concrete exterior, this is a pleasant hotel featuring clean rooms with fridges, spa, and karaoke bar. ❺

Ritz Milner 813 S Flower St ☎213/627-6981, Ⓦwww.milner-hotels.com. Somewhat bare-bones rooms at this restored old building south of Bunker Hill, but still cheap and clean and in a prime location. Larger suites also available. ❹

The Standard 550 S Flower St ☎213/892-8080, Ⓦwww.standardhotel.com. The downtown branch of LA's uber-trendy chain features sleek, modern furnishings and quirky decor, but is best known for its rooftop bar. Although billed as a "business hotel," the party scene is pretty much constant. The cheapest rooms are small and basic. ❹–❾

🏃 **Westin Bonaventure** 404 S Figueroa St ☎213/624-1000 or 1-800/228-3000, Ⓦwww.star woodhotels.com. Modernist luxury hotel with five glass towers that resemble cocktail shakers, a six-story atrium with a "lake," and elegantly remodeled rooms. A breathtaking exterior elevator ride ascends to a rotating cocktail lounge. Suites are upwards of $2000. ❻–❾

Wilshire Grand 930 Wilshire Blvd ☎213/688-7777 or 1-800/695-8284, Ⓦwww.wilshiregrand.com. Large Bunker Hill hotel with health club and pool. Mainly geared toward business travelers, with clean and comfy rooms; pricey during the week ($199), but weekends bring the cost down ($129). ❺–❼

Hollywood

Chateau Marmont 8221 Sunset Blvd ☎323/656-1010, Ⓦwww.chateaumarmont.com. Exclusive Norman Revival hotel resembling a dark fortress that's hosted all manner of celebrities. Largely suites and bungalows, up to $3000. Cheapest rooms are $335. ❾

Grafton 8462 Sunset Blvd ☎323/654-6470, Ⓦwww.graftononsunset.com. Nice boutique hotel with attractive furnishings, in-room stereos and VCRs, plus a pool, fitness center, and complimentary shuttle to nearby malls and businesses. An extra $40 will get you a king bed. ❻–❼

Hollywood Metropolitan 5825 Sunset Blvd ☎323/962-5800 or 1-800/962-5800, Ⓦwww.metropolitanhotel.com. Sleek high-rise in central Hollywood, with flashy exterior elevator, good views, and spacious rooms. Good value for the area, a bit south of major attractions. ❹

Hollywood Roosevelt 7000 Hollywood Blvd ☎323/466-7000, Ⓦwww.hollywoodroosevelt.com. The first hotel built for the movie greats in 1927, now remodeled with a boutique flair. The rooms are still on the smallish side, but the Corinthian-columned lobby reeks of Hollywood atmosphere and the hotel features a hot tub, gym, swimming pool,

and plenty of Tinseltown kitsch. ❽

Orchid Suites 1753 Orchid Ave ☎323/874-9678 or 1-800/537-3052, Ⓦwww.orchidsuites.com. Roomy, if spartan, suites with cable TV, kitchenettes, and heated pool. Very close to the most popular parts of Hollywood – adjacent to the massive Hollywood & Highland mall. ❹

Renaissance Hollywood 1755 N Highland Blvd ☎323/856-1200, Ⓦwww.renaissancehollywood.com. The hotel centerpiece of the Hollywood & Highland mall complex, with arty flair in the overall design, upscale rooms and suites, and a prime location in the heart of tourist central. ❾

West LA and Beverly Hills

🏃 **Bel Air** 701 Stone Canyon Rd ☎310/472-1211 or 1-800/648-1097, Ⓦwww.hotelbelair.com. The nicest hotel in LA bar none – and the only business in Bel Air – in a lushly overgrown canyon above Beverly Hills. If you can't afford the rooms, which can reach $1000 a night, go for a beautiful brunch by Swan Lake. ❾

Beverly Hills Hotel 9641 Sunset Blvd ☎310/276-2251, Ⓦwww.beverlyhillshotel.com. The classic Hollywood resort, with a bold pink-and-green color scheme and Mission-style design, surrounded by its own exotic gardens. Rooms feature marbled bathrooms, VCRs, and hot tubs, and the famed Polo Lounge restaurant is also on-site. ❾

Claremont 1044 Tiverton Ave ☎310/208-5957. An amazingly good deal for the area, this cheerful and inexpensive little hotel sits very close to UCLA and Westwood Village. Rooms are fairly basic, but the main difficulty is the lack of parking. ❸

Culver Hotel 9400 Culver Blvd ☎310/838-7963, Ⓦwww.culverhotel.com. A lovely, restored historic landmark featuring red-and-black decor, old-fashioned iron railings in the lobby, and cozy rooms with good views of Culver City, just south of West LA. ❺

Elan Hotel Modern 8435 Beverly Blvd ☎323/658-6663, Ⓦwww.elanhotel.com. Semi-upscale boutique hotel, located in a busy shopping zone just north of the Beverly Center mall. Rooms are nicely appointed, and there's also a fitness center and spa. ❻

Hotel del Flores 409 N Crescent Drive, Beverly Hills ☎310/274-5115, Ⓦwww.hoteldelflores.com. Three blocks from Rodeo Drive, one of the better deals around. Modest, pleasant and very good value for the area, with simple, quaint rooms. Shared baths bring the cost down to $65. ❸–❹

Le Montrose 900 Hammond St ☎310/855-1115, Ⓦwww.lemontrose.com. Elegant West Hollywood hotel with Art Nouveau stylings, featuring rooftop tennis courts, pool, and Jacuzzi. Most rooms are suites with full amenities. ❽

Orbit Hotel 7950 Melrose Ave, West Hollywood ☎323/655-1510 or 1-877/ORBIT-US, ⊛www.orbit hotel.com. Retro-1960s hotel and hostel with sleek Day-Glo furnishings and ultra-hip modern decor, offering complimentary breakfast, movie screening room, patio, café, private baths in all rooms, shuttle tours, and $20-per-day car rental. Dorms $20, hotel rooms $75. ❶–❸

Santa Monica, Venice, and Malibu

Bayside 2001 Ocean Ave at Bay St, Santa Monica ☎310/396-6000, ⊛www.baysidehotel.com. Just a block from the beach and Main Street. The rooms are fairly bland, but some have fridges, Internet access, and kitchenettes. Generally comfortable, with ocean views from the more expensive rooms. ❺
Cadillac 8 Dudley Ave, Venice ☎310/399-8876, ⊛www.thecadillachotel.com. Restored Art Deco hotel right on the Venice Boardwalk. Bright, airy atmosphere with gym, sauna, and pleasant rooms with Internet access. ❹
Casa Malibu Inn 22752 Pacific Coast HWY ☎310/456-2219. Located opposite Carbon Beach and featuring superb rooms with great modern design. Face a courtyard garden ($109) or the beach ($229); some rooms have fireplaces and balconies. ❺–❽
Channel Road Inn 219 W Channel Rd, Pacific Palisades ☎310/459-1920, ⊛www.channelroad inn.com. Romantic getaway nestled in lower Santa Monica Canyon, with ocean views, hot tub, and free bike rental. Fourteen rooms priced according to view, size, and amenities. ❽
Fairmont Miramar 101 Wilshire Blvd, Santa Monica ☎310/576-7777, ⊛www.fairmont.com. Upscale even for this area, this swanky hotel offers nicely appointed suites and bungalows near the pool, and health club, salon, spa, fitness center, and fine views over the Pacific. ❾
Inn at Venice Beach 327 Washington Blvd, Venice ☎310/821-2557 or 1-800/828-0688, ⊛www. innatvenicebeach.com. Conveniently located near Venice Beach and the canals, with simple, tasteful rooms featuring balconies and fridges. ❺
Malibu Country Inn 6506 Westward Beach Rd ☎310/457-9622, ⊛www.malibucountryinn.com. A B&B in an old-fashioned 1943 structure, with nicely renovated rooms, hot tubs, and fridges. Each unit has a different style and views of either the ocean, gardens, or Santa Monica Mountains. Weekday rates drop by about $40. ❼
Shangri-La 1301 Ocean Ave, Santa Monica ☎310/394-2791, ⊛www.shangrila-hotel.com. Wonderfully restored Art Deco treasure overlooking Palisades Park and the Santa Monica beach, with clean and sleek, if basic, rooms. ❼

The South Bay and LA Harbor

Beach House at Hermosa 1300 Strand, Hermosa Beach ☎310/374-3001, ⊛www.Beach-House. com. The height of luxury in the South Bay, offering two-room suites with fireplaces, wet bars, balconies, hot tubs, stereos, and refrigerators, with many rooms overlooking the sea. ❾
Hotel Hermosa 2515 Pacific Coast HWY, Hermosa Beach ☎310/318-6000, ⊛www.hotelhermosa. com. In a busy part of town, between Hermosa and Manhattan beaches, a sumptuous hotel with decent rooms starting at moderate prices. It's just a short walk to the beach. ❺
Vagabond Inn 150 Alamitos, Long Beach ☎562/435-7621, ⊛www.vagabondinn.com. One of the cheapest, most reliable of the chain lodging options in the area, with a pool, located just a few blocks west of the main downtown action. ❸
Westin Long Beach 333 E Ocean Blvd, Long Beach ☎562/436-3000, ⊛www.westin.com. A solid bet for bayside luxury at affordable prices, right by the convention center, with a spa, fitness center, and pool. ❽

Around Disneyland

Desert Palms 631 W Katella Ave ☎1-800/635-5423, ⊛www.desertpalmshotel.com. Good rooms and suites (for $30 more) with fridges, microwaves, high-speed Internet access, VCRs, and continental breakfast. Conventions in town make prices jump. ❹–❺
Disneyland Hotel 1150 W Cerritos Ave, Anaheim ☎714/956-6400, ⊛disneyland.disney.go.com. Cookie-cutter rooms without much charm but still, an irresistible choice for many. The Disneyland monorail does stop outside (theme park admission is separate). Ultra-basic rooms begin at $205, simple one-bedroom suites at $460. ❽–❾
Park Place Inn 1544 S Harbor Blvd ☎714/776-4800, ⊛www.parkplaceinnandminisuites.com. Best Western chain hotel across from Disneyland, with the customary clean rooms with fridges and microwaves, plus pool, sauna, Jacuzzi, and continental breakfast. ❹
Pavilions 1176 W Katella Ave ☎714/776-0140, ⊛www.pavilionshotel.com. Convenient chain hotel offering basic rooms (some with fridges), and a pool, spa, sauna, and shuttle to Disneyland. ❹

The San Gabriel and San Fernando valleys

Artists Inn 1038 Magnolia St, South Pasadena ☎1-800/799-5668, ⊛www.artistsinns.com. Themed B&B with ten rooms and suites honoring famous painters and styles. Best is the Italian Suite,

CALIFORNIA | Los Angeles: Accommodation

1049

with an antique tub and sun porch. Two blocks from Gold Line Metro. ⑤

Graciela Burbank 322 N Pass Ave ⓣ818/842-8887, ⓦwww.thegraciela.com. Modern boutique accommodations to enliven the drab Valley scene. King rooms ($270) have fridges, DVD and CD players, and Internet access. Also with pool, gym, sauna, and rooftop sundeck with Jacuzzi. ⑦–⑨

Ritz-Carlton Huntington 1401 S Knoll Ave, Pasadena ⓣ626/568-3900, ⓦwww.ritzcarlton.

com. Landmark hotel, c.1900, luxuriously designed and discreetly tucked away in residential Pasadena. Suites start at $649, with more basic rooms for less than half the price. ⑨

Safari Inn 1911 W Olive St, Burbank ⓣ818/845-8586, ⓦwww.safariburbank.com. A classic mid-century motel, renovated but still loaded with pop-architecture touches. Perks include a pool, fitness room, Burbank airport shuttle, and in-room fridges, plus continental breakfast. ⑤

Hostels

Hostels dot the city, though some limit stays to a few nights. Many hostels also offer cut-rate single and double rooms. You can expect little more from your stay than a clean, safe bed, somewhere to lock your valuables, and a typically colorful crowd of visitors – sometimes making for quite the party scene. Some hostels also offer tours of theme parks, shopping malls, and stars' homes, while others organize social activities such as volleyball and pizza parties.

Banana Bungalow 2775 Cahuenga Blvd W, in Cahuenga Pass ⓣ323/851-1129 or 1-800/446-7835, ⓦwww.bananabungalow.com. Popular hostel near Universal City and US-101, with free airport shuttles, tours to Venice Beach and Magic Mountain, and a relaxed atmosphere. Outdoor pool and free parking. Dorms $22–25, private doubles $75–95. ①–④

HI-Anaheim/Fullerton 1700 N Harbor Blvd, Fullerton ⓣ714/738-3721, ⓦwww.hihostels.com. Convenient and comfortable, five miles north of Disneyland on the site of a former dairy farm. The excellent facilities include a grass volleyball court, golf driving range, and picnic area. There are only twenty dorm beds, so reservations are a must. ①

HI-LA/Santa Monica 1436 2nd St, Santa Monica ⓣ310/393-9913, ⓦwww.hilosangeles.org. A few blocks from the beach and pier, this was LA's Town Hall from 1887 to 1889, now renovated with Internet access, nice inner courtyard and a skylight – and 260 beds. Smoking and drinking prohibited. Reservations essential in summer. Open 24hr. ①

HI-LA/South Bay 3601 S Gaffey St #613 ⓣ310/831-8109, ⓦwww.hihostels.com. Sixty beds in old US Army barracks, with a panoramic view of the Pacific Ocean. Ideal for seeing San Pedro, Palos Verdes, and the whole LA Harbor area. Dorms $23, private rooms $50. ①–②

Hollywood International 6820 Hollywood Blvd, Hollywood ⓣ323/463-0797 or 1-800/750-6561, ⓦwww.hollywoodhostels.com. Offers free tea and coffee, game room, gymnasium, patio garden, kitchen, and laundry. Also offers tours of Hollywood, theme parks, Las Vegas, and Tijuana. Shared rooms start at $17, private rooms $40. ①–②

Huntington Beach Hostel 421 8th St, Huntington Beach ⓣ714/536-3315, ⓦwww.huntington-beachhostel.com. Four blocks from the beach and mostly double rooms. Easy access to Disneyland and Knott's Berry Farm, plus free surfing lessons. Sleeping bags allowed. Dorms $22, private rooms $50. ①–②

Orange Drive Manor 1764 N Orange Drive, Hollywood ⓣ323/850-0350, ⓦwww.orangedrivehostel.com. Centrally located hostel (right behind the Chinese Theatre), offering tours to film studios, theme parks, and homes of the stars. Dorms $22–28, private rooms $48–64. ①–③

Venice Beach Cotel 25 Windward Ave, Venice ⓣ310/399-7649, ⓦwww.venicebeachcotel.com. In a historic beachside building, this colonnaded hostel (or "cotel") has dorm rooms for $18, and private rooms for $44. Trips to major theme parks, homes of the stars, and Getty Center. ①–②

The City

If LA has a heart, it's **downtown**, in the center of the basin, which offers a taste of almost everything you'll find elsewhere in the city, from upscale art along Bunker Hill to commercial zones like the Garment District, compressed into an area of small, easily walkable blocks. West from downtown, **Hollywood** has streets imbued with movie myths and legends – even if the genuine glamor is long gone. Adjoining **West LA** is home to the city's newest money, shown off in Beverly Hills and along the Sunset Strip. **Santa Monica** and **Venice** further to the west are the quintessential oceanfront LA of palm trees, white sands, and laid-back living, while the coastline itself stretches another twenty miles northwest to glamorous **Malibu**, home to the film industry elite.

Suburban **Orange County**, to the southeast, holds little of interest apart from **Disneyland**, a few museums, and a handful of libertine beach towns. On the far side of the northern hills lie the **San Gabriel and San Fernando valleys**, or simply "the Valley," seen by mainstream Los Angeles as nothing more than endless tract homes and strip malls, but in reality a bit more interesting.

Downtown LA

Downtown LA embraces the city's every social, economic, and ethnic group, and the whole area can easily be seen in a day on foot. LA's original settlement at **The**

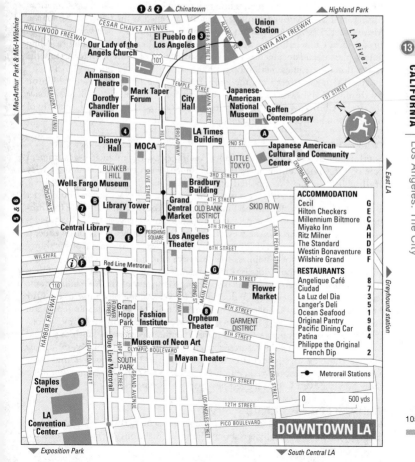

ACCOMMODATION

Cecil	G
Hilton Checkers	E
Millennium Biltmore	C
Miyako Inn	A
Ritz Milner	H
The Standard	D
Westin Bonaventure	B
Wilshire Grand	F

RESTAURANTS

Angelique Café	8
Ciudad	7
La Luz del Dia	3
Langer's Deli	5
Ocean Seafood	1
Original Pantry	9
Pacific Dining Car	6
Patina	4
Philippe the Original French Dip	2

Metrorail Stations

0   500 yds

DOWNTOWN LA

Plaza is the obvious first stop, before crossing into the municipal plazas of the **Civic Center** and the corporate zone of **Bunker Hill**, and continuing through the free-spirited chaos along **Broadway**.

The Plaza

Within the **El Pueblo de Los Angeles Historic Park**, 845 N Alameda St (daily 9am–5pm; free; ⓣ213/628-2381, ⓦwww.ci.la.ca.us/ELP), the square known as **the Plaza** was roughly the site of the city's original 1781 townsite, and a few evocative early buildings remain in situ. The plaza church **La Placita**, 535 N Main St (daily 8am–8pm; ⓦwww.laplacita.org), the city's oldest, is a small adobe structure with a gabled roof. From 1861 to 1923 the building was remodeled or reconstructed four times, but it still evokes a sense of the local heritage. **Mass** (occasionally with Mariachi bands) takes place three or four times daily. **Olvera Street**, which runs north from the plaza, contrived in part as a pseudo-Mexican village market, offers a cheery collection of food and craft stalls and the historic **Avila Adobe** (daily 9am–5pm; free), technically the city's oldest building, though it's been completely rebuilt in the last thirty years. Other worthwhile sights include the **Sepulveda House** (Mon–Sat 10am–3pm; free), an 1887 Eastlake Victorian structure that has rooms highlighting different periods in Mexican-American history, and the **Garnier Building**, recently reopened as the **Chinese American Museum**, 425 N Los Angeles St (Tues–Sun 10am–3pm; $3; ⓦwww.camla.org). Inside, local Chinese history, society, and culture is detailed, including revealing letters, photos, and documents, as well as a smattering of contemporary art and the re-creation of a Chinese herb shop c.1900.

Across Alameda Street from the Plaza, the magnificent Mission Revival **Union Station** is chiefly used as a Metrorail and Amtrak terminal, although it was once the site of **Chinatown**, which now sits a few blocks to the north and is mainly of interest for a host of fine restaurants.

Civic Center

South from the Plaza, across the Santa Ana Freeway, the municipal-government core of the **Civic Center** offers three of the city's most notable buildings. **City Hall**, 200 N Spring St, appeared on TV as *Dragnet*'s imposing symbol of civic virtue and as the Daily Planet office in the original *Superman* show. You can get a good look at the inside of the building on free **tours**, which include its 28th-story 360-degree observation deck (daily 10am–1pm; reserve at ⓣ213/485-4423, ⓦwww.lacityhall.org). To the west, **Disney Hall**, 1st Street at Grand Avenue, is Frank Gehry's grand spectacle of modern architecture, a 2300-seat acoustic showpiece with a curvaceous, stainless-steel exterior and an interior with rich, warm acoustics and a mammoth, intricate pipe organ. It also may be one of the best places to hear music in the country, which you can do courtesy of the LA Philharmonic (ⓦwdch.laphil.com; see p.1073) during the season. A long block north, the **Our Lady of the Angels** Catholic church (Mon–Fri 6.30am–6pm, Sat 9am–6pm, Sun 7am–6pm; tours Mon–Fri 1pm; free; ⓦwww.olacathedral.org) resembles a concrete fortress on the outside – but features exquisite decor inside, such as a grand marble altar and ultra-thin alabaster screens for diffusing light. Finally, though its massive complex isn't particularly distinguished, the **Los Angeles Times**, near Spring and 1st streets (by reservation at ⓣ213/237-5757), offers free tours that show how the West Coast's biggest newspaper is put together.

Bunker Hill and Little Tokyo

Until a century ago the area south of the Civic Center, **Bunker Hill**, was LA's most elegant neighborhood, its elaborate Victorian mansions and houses connected by funicular railroad to the growing business district down below. But after a half-century of decay, a wrecking-ball approach to 1960s urban renewal transformed it into the imperious **Financial District**, sprouting colossal new towers. Amid the fancy offices and luxury condos of the California Plaza at 250 S Grand Avenue, the **Museum of Contemporary Art** (MOCA; Mon & Fri 11am–5pm, Thurs 11am–8pm, Sat & Sun 11am–6pm; $8, free Thurs 5–8pm; Ⓦ www.moca.org) was designed by showman architect Arata Isozaki as a vivid array of reddish geometric blocks. In addition to work by Franz Kline, Mark Rothko, Robert Rauschenberg, and Claes Oldenburg, and some eye-opening temporary exhibits, it features an impressive selection of **Southern California artists**, ranging from Lari Pittman's spooky, sexualized silhouettes to Robert Williams's feverishly violent and satiric comic-book-styled paintings. A ticket also entitles you to same-day entry into **The Geffen Contemporary** (same hours as above), further east at 152 N Central Ave, a former police garage now used for MOCA's edgier temporary shows. Across from the Geffen, **Little Tokyo** is an appealing collection of historic sites, restaurants, and galleries, highlighted by the comprehensive **Japanese American National Museum**, 369 E 1st St (Tues–Sun 11am–5pm, Thurs closes at 8pm; $8; Ⓦ www. janm.org), housed in a former Buddhist temple constructed in 1925. The museum offers everything from origami to traditional furniture and folk craftwork to the story of the internment of Japanese-Americans during World War II.

Back atop Bunker Hill, catercorner to MOCA, the superficial but amusing **Wells Fargo Museum**, 333 S Grand Ave (Mon–Fri 9am–5pm; free; Ⓦ www.wellsfar gohistory.com), displays old mining equipment, antiques, photographs, a two-pound chunk of gold, a re-created assay office from the nineteenth century, and a simulated stagecoach journey from St Louis to San Francisco. A few blocks southwest rise the sparkling glass tubes of the **Westin Bonaventure Hotel**, 404 S Figueroa St (see "Accommodation," p.1048), whose lobby is an Escher-style labyrinth of spiraling ramps and balconies, worth negotiating for a ride in the glass elevators that run up and down the outside of the building, giving splendid views over much of the downtown and beyond. Finally, a short distance away, the **Richard J. Riordan Central Library**, 630 W 5th St (Mon–Thurs 10am–8pm, Fri & Sat 10am–6pm, Sun 1–5pm; tours Mon–Fri 12.30pm, Sat 11am & 2pm, Sun 2pm; Ⓦ www.lapl.org/central), is named for LA's billionaire mayor of the 1990s, but it dates back to 1926, the last work of pioneering architect Bertram Goodhue, and its striking, angular lines set the tone for many LA buildings, most obviously City Hall.

Broadway and the Old Bank District

Although it's hard to picture now, **Broadway** was once LA's most fashionable shopping and entertainment district. Today it's largely taken over by the hustle and bustle of Hispanic clothing and trinket stores, all to a soundtrack of blaring salsa music. You can sample a vivid taste of the area at the broadly ethnic **Grand Central Market**, between 3rd and 4th streets (daily 9am–6pm; Ⓦ www. grandcentralsquare.com), where you'll find everything from pickled pigs' feet to sheeps' brains. Right alongside, the whimsical terracotta facade of the 1918 **Million Dollar Theater** mixes buffalo heads with bald eagles, and was seen in the film *Blade Runner*, as was the neighboring 1893 **Bradbury Building**, no. 304 (Mon–Sat 9am–5pm; free), highlighted by a magnificent sunlit atrium surrounded by stylish wrought-iron balconies and open-cage elevators. While the moviehouse has since closed, the extravagant arches and marble columns of the **Los Angeles Theater**, 615 S Broadway, and the **Orpheum**'s neo–French Renaissance grand staircases and chandeliers, at no. 630, are still on view during the annual "Last Remaining Seats" film festival in June (details at Ⓦ www.laconservancy.org).

If you venture a few blocks west of Broadway, you'll come to the most recent focus of LA's urban-revival efforts, the **Old Bank District**, as developers now have named it, based around Spring Street from 7th to 3rd streets. Although there are no official sights, these stately, hundred-year-old Beaux Arts buildings are now being converted into upscale housing, fancy shops, chic eateries, and the like.

South Park and the Garment District

A few blocks south of Broadway's main sights is **South Park**, named by developers apparently lacking irony or access to cable TV. The highlight is the **Museum of Neon Art**, 501 W Olympic Blvd (Wed–Sat 11am–5pm, Sun noon–5pm; $5; Ⓦ www.neonmona.org), recognizable by the visage of Mona Lisa smiling through blue-and-yellow neon squiggles. The museum's small exhibition space showcases contemporary neon designs and a range of strange kinetic art, plus some great old neon theater signs. Just north across Grand Hope Park, the **Fashion Institute of Design and Merchandising**, 919 S Grand Ave (Mon–Sat 10am–4pm; free; Ⓦ www.fashionmuseum.org), features items drawn from its collection of ten thousand pieces of costume and apparel – French gowns, Russian jewels, quirky shoes, and so on. The main draw is the *Art of Motion Picture Costume Design* show that runs from February to April, displaying colorful outfits that may include anything from Liz Taylor's Cleopatra garb to Austin Powers's retro-60s gear.

Apart from these museums, the other major attraction in the area is the welter of commercial activity in the **Garment District**, bounded by Los Angeles and San Pedro streets and 7th and 9th avenues, where you can pick up decent fabric for as little as $2 per yard.

Around downtown

The LA sprawl begins as soon as you leave downtown. Freeways and boulevards cut through diverse environs, with large distances separating the points of interest. As such, it makes little sense to see them consecutively.

Wilshire Boulevard

Heading west from downtown, Wilshire Boulevard was once a grand commercial corridor, but has fallen on harder times in recent decades. There are a few isolated points of interest before you reach West LA, however, notably the seminal **Bullocks Wilshire** department store, 3050 Wilshire Blvd. This is nothing less than the epitome of 1920s Art Deco on the West Coast, crowned with a colossal copper tower and original "Zigzag" design, now beautifully restored as the law library of adjacent **Southwestern University**. You can reserve space for one of the school's periodic "Tea and Tour" events (Ⓣ 213/738-6814, Ⓔ events@swlaw.edu, Ⓦ www.swlaw.edu/library), though more regular monthly tours are planned for the future. Also in the neighborhood and worth a look is the **First Congregational Church**, 540 S Commonwealth Ave, a 1930s English Gothic-styled cathedral known for its huge and glorious set of pipe organs (free recitals Thurs 12.10pm) and, appropriately, the annual Bach Festival in October ($7–30; information at Ⓣ 213/385-1345, Ⓦ www.fccla.org).

Just south of Wilshire as you continue west, along Olympic Boulevard between Vermont and Western avenues, **Koreatown** is five times larger than the more touristy areas of Chinatown and Little Tokyo, and is home to the largest concentration of Koreans outside Korea. Beyond good authentic restaurants, there's not much for visitors to see here.

Exposition Park

South of downtown, across Exposition Boulevard from the fortress-like USC campus, **Exposition Park** is one of the most appreciated parks in LA. The **California Science Center**, off Figueroa Street at 700 State Drive (daily 10am–5pm; free; ⓦ www.californiasciencecenter.org), contains enough enjoyable working models and thousands of gadgets to keep kids absorbed. Just outside, an **IMAX Theater** ($8, children $4.75) attracts youthful patrons of nature documentaries, while closer to Exposition Boulevard, the Center's **Air and Space Gallery** (Mon–Fri 10am–1pm, Sat & Sun 11am–4pm; free) is marked by a sleek jet stuck to its facade and offers a series of satellites, telescopes, airplanes, and rockets. To the south, the **California African American Museum**, 600 State Drive (Wed–Sat 10am–4pm; free; ⓦ www.caamuseum.org), has stimulating exhibits on the history and culture of America's black communities.

The **Natural History Museum of Los Angeles County**, 900 Exposition Blvd (Mon–Fri 9.30am–5pm, Sat & Sun 10am–5pm; $9; ⓦ www.nhm.org), with its echoey domes and travertine columns, has a tremendous stock of dinosaur skeletons that includes the skull of a Tyrannosaurus rex, and the frame of a Diatryma – a huge flightless bird. Other fascinating displays include Mayan pyramid murals and the reconstructed contents of a Mexican tomb. The last major sights in the park are the **LA Coliseum**, familiar as the site of the 1932 and 1984 Olympics and for its towering headless statues, and the **Rose Garden** (daily 10am–5pm; free), whose 16,000 bushes are at their most fragrant in April and May.

⓭

A brief history of Hollywood

Once the home of the country's largest Presbyterian church, Hollywood started life as a **temperance colony** in 1887, intended to provide a sober, God-fearing alternative to raunchy downtown LA, eight miles away by rough country road. The film industry, of course, was drawn here from the East Coast not by puritanical morality, but by the predictable sunshine, low taxes, cheap labor, and diverse shooting locations – and as a way of dodging Thomas Edison's restrictive motion-picture patents. Nearby **Silver Lake** was the first (temporary) site of the movie business, but the first permanent studio opened in Hollywood in 1911, and within three years the place was packed with filmmakers such as **Cecil B. DeMille**, who shared his barn-converted office space with a horse and other budding magnates like Samuel Goldwyn, Adolph Zukor, and Jesse Lasky. The space is now home to the **Hollywood Heritage Museum**, 2100 N Highland Ave (Sat & Sun 11am–4pm; $5; ⓦ www.hollywoodheritage.org), exhibiting antiques and treasures from the silent era.

The industry expanded fast, and eager new arrivals soon swamped the original small-scaled community. Once movie-making had proved itself to be a financially secure business, film production became a conglomerated, mechanical, and specialized system. Small companies either went bust or were incorporated into the big studios, which had by the 1930s almost all relocated to more distant digs in Culver City, Burbank, and West LA – of the big names, only Paramount remained.

The **demise of the studio system** came in the 1950s, through government anti-trust actions, the postwar revival of the international film industry, and, of course, television. A few lean decades followed. In the 1970s and 1980s, though, directors like Steven Spielberg and George Lucas re-engineered American movies around the concept of the **blockbuster** – high-priced, special-effects-laden epics that would appeal to as a wide range of audiences as possible. Thanks to this trend, and the worldwide financial consolidation of media enterprises, Hollywood continues to be a symbol for the enduring success of American movies – slick, entertaining fare with gorgeous actors, predictable plots, and happy endings – and a mechanized dream factory of international proportions.

The Watts Towers

Several miles south of downtown, **South Central LA** hardly ranks on the tourist circuit, and is well worth avoiding, with the notable exception of the stunning, Gaudíesque **Watts Towers**, 1765 E 107th St. Created by Italian immigrant Simon Rodia from 1921 to 1954, these striking pieces of folk art were constructed from iron, stainless steel, old bedframes, and cement, and decorated with fragments of bottles and around 70,000 crushed seashells. Although routinely threatened with demolition, the towers have survived the decades and open for tours on sunny days (Fri & Sat 11am–2.30pm, Sun 12.30–3pm; free; ⓦwww.trywatts.com). Call the adjacent Watts Towers Arts Center, 1727 E 107th St (ⓣ323/860-9964 or 213/847-4646), for more details. A good time to come is during the Day of the Drum/Simon RodiaWatts Towers Jazz Festival, which takes place in late September at an adjoining amphitheater.

Hollywood

If a single place-name encapsulates the LA dream of glamor, money, and overnight success, it's **Hollywood**. Millions of tourists arrive on pilgrimages, yet the big film companies moved out long ago and you're more likely to spot a porno theater than a movie star. Despite the spate of new malls and hotels and renovated movie palaces, the district can't match the mythical status it holds in the minds of its many star-struck visitors.

Central Hollywood

The lore, magic, and mystery of **Central Hollywood** create a pervasive sense of nostalgia that recent urban-renewal projects and redevelopment plans have tried to capitalize on. The biggest symbol of this newfound investment is the **Hollywood & Highland** mall (ⓦwww.hollywoodandhighland.com) at the eponymous intersection. However, despite hosting a major hotel, boutiques, and chic restaurants, adding grand silent-film-set architecture, and relocating the Oscars to the **Kodak Theater** on-site, this towering beacon of commerce is still no better than your average suburban shopping mall.

In the shadow of the iconic "record stack" of the **Capitol Records Tower**, the obvious place to begin exploring Hollywood Boulevard is the junction of **Hollywood and Vine** – the legendary location where budding stars could be "spotted" by big-shot directors and whisked off to fame and fortune. Nowadays, few aspiring stars loiter in this gritty environment, but many visitors do come to trace the **Walk of Fame**, which officially begins here with a series of gold-inset stars that honor famous and forgotten names of radio, TV, and film. Further west, at 6608 Hollywood Blvd, the purple and pink **Frederick's of Hollywood** has been (under-) dressing Hollywood's sex goddesses since 1947, as well as mortal bodies via mail order. Inside, the **Celebrity Lingerie Hall of Fame** (Mon–Fri 10am–9pm, Sat 10am–6pm, Sun noon–6pm; free) displays some of the company's most famous corsets, bras, and panties, donated by glitterati from Lana Turner to Cher. If you're sufficiently fired up by this, wander down to the **Erotic Museum**, 6741 Hollywood Blvd (Sun–Thurs 11am–8pm, Fri–Sat 11am–11pm; $13; ⓦwww.theeroticmuseum.com), an intellectual attempt to probe the mysteries of libido, as well as Hollywood's latest attempt to contextualize (and profit from) the sleaze that's available for free on the streets outside.

Nearby, the **Egyptian Theater**, at no. 6712, was built in a modest attempt to re-create the Temple of Thebes, and the very first Hollywood premiere (*Robin Hood*) took place here in 1922. Now restored in glorious fashion, movie-lovers should make a special trip here to view an art, foreign, and indie film, or at least the

HOLLYWOOD

ACCOMMODATION
Banana Bungalow   A
Hollywood International   F
Hollywood Metropolitan   G
Hollywood Roosevelt   E
Orange Drive Manor   D
Orchid Suites   C
Renaissance Hollywood   B

**RESTAURANTS, BARS &
CLUBS**
Arena   14
Avalon   3
Baked Potato   1
Bar Sinister   8
Beauty Bar   9
Boardner's   7
Bourgeois Pig   2
Dragonfly   15
El Floridita   16
Formosa Café   12
Knitting Factory   5
Lava Lounge   10
Musso and Frank Grill   4
Roscoe's Chicken
and Waffles   11
The Ruby   6
Tempest   13

Griffith Park

John Anson Ford
Theater

HOLLYWOOD
HILLS

Hollywood Bowl
Museum

Hollywood Bowl

Runyon
Canyon
Park

Wattles Park

Hollywood Heritage
Museum

WHITLEY
HEIGHTS

Capitol
Records
Tower

Pantages Theater

Janes
House

Frederick's of
Hollywood

Erotic Museum

Hollywood &
Highland
Mall

Egyptian
Theater

Stages
Theater
Center

Kodak Theatre

Hollywood
Entertainment
Museum

Chinese
Theatre

Movie star
Sculpture

El
Capitan
Theater

Hollywood History
Museum

Hollywood
Palladium

Cinerama
Dome

GOWER
GULCH

N

500 yds

Downtown

& Los Feliz

Hollywood

Forever Cemetery & Paramount Studios

Mid-Wilshire

Melrose Avenue

Sunset Strip & West Hollywood

documentary chronicling the rise of Hollywood (hour-long shows Sat & Sun 2pm & 3.30pm; $7; ⓦwww.americancinematheque.com). Also worth a look are the famous handprints and footprints in the concrete forecourt of the **Chinese Theatre**, west across Highland Avenue at 6925 Hollywood Blvd. For many decades, this has been *the* spot for movie premieres, an odd version of a classical Chinese temple, replete with quasi-Chinese motifs and upturned dragon tails.

Just west, the **Hollywood Entertainment Museum**, 7021 Hollywood Blvd (Thurs–Tues 11am–6pm; $12; ⓦwww.hollywoodmuseum.com), houses a collection of movie- and TV-related knickknacks highlighted by the full set of the TV show *Cheers* and the bridge of the *Enterprise* from *Star Trek*. Also chiefly of interest for fans of pop-culture ephemera, the **Hollywood History Museum**, just southeast at 1660 N Highland Ave (Thurs–Sun 10am–5pm; $15; ⓦwww.thehollywoodmuseum.com), has four levels of exhibits on the fashion, sets, make-up, special effects, and art design of mainstream American movies.

Further south, near Santa Monica Boulevard and Gower Street, **Hollywood Forever Cemetery** (daily dawn–dusk; free; ⓦwww.hollywoodforever.com) is the district's most famous graveyard, and features all manner of buried stars such as Rudolph Valentino and Douglas Fairbanks Sr, as well as more unexpected grave markers, such as Johnny Ramone playing one last guitar riff. South of the cemetery, **Paramount Studios**, 5555 Melrose Ave (2hr tour, Mon–Fri 10am & 2pm; $35; by reservation at ☎323/956-1777, ⓦwww.paramount.com/studio), is famous for its grand **gate**, though the original studio entrance – which Gloria Swanson rode through in *Sunset Boulevard* – is now inaccessible. The tour isn't quite up to the standard of other studio tours, but if you want to poke around empty soundstages and a mildly interesting backlot, it may be worth it.

Griffith Park

The greenery and mountain slopes that make up vast **Griffith Park** northeast of Hollywood (daily 6am–10pm, mountain roads close at dusk) offer lush fern and azalea gardens, a bird sanctuary, and many miles of fine trails – though the **LA Zoo**, 5333 Zoo Drive (daily 10am–5pm; $10; ⓦwww.lazoo.org), pales in comparison to its San Diego counterpart (see p.1038). The landmark **Griffith Observatory**, 2800 E Observatory Rd (closed for renovation until late 2006), has been used as a backdrop in innumerable Hollywood films, most famously *Rebel Without a Cause*, and the surrounding acres are marked by paths that lead into desolate but unspoiled terrain with great views over the LA basin and out to sea (provided the smog isn't too thick). One way to explore is on a rented **bike** from Spokes 'n' Stuff, near the park ranger station, at 4400 Crystal Springs Rd (weekends during daylight hours; $6–10 per hour; ☎323/662-6573). Definitely meriting a stop is the **Museum of the American West**, near the junction of the Ventura and Golden State freeways at 4700 Western Heritage Way (Tues–Sun 10am–5pm, Thurs closes 8pm; $7.50; ⓦwww.museumoftheamericanwest.org), whose comprehensive collection of artifacts includes sections on native peoples, European exploration, nineteenth-century pioneers, the Wild West, Asian immigrants and, of course, Hollywood's versions of all of the above.

The Hollywood Hills

Around the canyons and slopes of the **Hollywood Hills**, which run from Hollywood itself into Benedict Canyon above Beverly Hills, mansions are so commonplace that only the half-dozen fully blown castles really stand out. Guided tours (see p.1046) can point out which is which, but for the most part you can't get close to them anyway, and none is open to the public. For a more up-close look at landmark architecture, take in a concert at the **Hollywood Bowl**, 2301

N Highland Ave (☎323/850-2000, ⓦwww.hollywoodbowl.org), the massive concrete bandshell whose summer music offerings are rarely highbrow, but it's as good a spot as any to hear the roar of the *1812 Overture*.

Throughout Hollywood, you can see the **Hollywood Sign**, erected as a property advertisement in 1923 (when it spelled "Hollywoodland," until 1949) and illuminated with four thousand light bulbs. Nowadays, infrared cameras and radar-activated zoom lenses have been installed to catch graffiti writers. Curious tourists who can't resist a close look are liable for a steep fine.

West LA

LA's Westside begins immediately beyond Hollywood in **West LA**, roughly bordered by the foothills of the Hollywood Hills to the north and the Santa Monica Freeway (I-10) to the south. West LA is the place where the city's nouveau riche flaunt their fortunes most conspicuously, from the trendy confines of West Hollywood and shadowy wealth of Bel Air to the high-priced shopping strips of Beverly Hills.

The Museum Mile

On the commercial axis of Wilshire Boulevard, the **Miracle Mile**, between La Brea and Fairfax avenues, was the premier property development of the 1930s. The area's department stores have since moved out, but recent development has created a "**Museum Mile**" in their place, also known as **Museum Row**. The first is sited at the **La Brea Tar Pits**, where for thousands of years, animals who tried to drink from the thin layer of water covering this rank pool of tar became stuck fast and preserved for posterity. It's now surrounded by life-sized replicas of such victims as mastodons and saber-toothed tigers, some of them reconstructed next door at the impressive **George C. Page Museum**, 5801 Wilshire Blvd (Mon–Fri 9.30am–5pm, weekends opens at 10am; $7; ⓦwww.tarpits.org). Across the street, the **Craft and Folk Art Museum** (Tues, Wed & Fri 11am–5pm, Thurs 11am–7pm, Sat & Sun noon–6pm; $5; ⓦwww.cafam.org) is best for fans of international folk art – Middle Eastern textiles, Ukrainian easter eggs, and so on – displayed in mildly interesting temporary exhibits.

On the west side of the La Brea Tar Pits, the enormous **LA County Museum of Art (LACMA)**, 5905 Wilshire Blvd (Thurs–Tues noon–8pm, Fri closes 9pm; $9, students $5; ⓦwww.lacma.org), comprises a set of drab blocks (now being remodeled into a more coherent Renzo Piano design), but its collections are among the best in the world. The **Fearing Collection** of funereal masks and sculpted guardian figures from pre-Columbian Mexico is highly impressive, but where the museum really excels is in its specializations: **German Expressionist** prints and drawings, scrolls and ceramics in the **Pavilion for Japanese Art**, and entire rooms devoted to Auguste Rodin, 17th-century Dutch masters, rare jewelry and porcelain, and Hollywood fashion designers. LACMA continues on to the western end of the Museum Mile to Fairfax Avenue, where blockbuster shows and children's art are the highlights of **LACMA West** (same hours and ticket), occupying a former department store building that has been compared to an oversized perfume bottle. Since various museum buildings will be closed until late 2007, if there's a collection you really want to see, call first to make sure it's on view.

Across from LACMA West, the **Petersen Automotive Museum**, 6060 Wilshire Blvd (Tues–Sun 10am–6pm; $10; ⓦwww.petersen.org), pays homage to motorized vehicles of all kinds on three floors, with rotating exhibits such as the Golden Age of customizing, Hollywood prop cars, and "million-dollar" vehicles.

West Hollywood

North along Fairfax Avenue from the Museum Mile, **West Hollywood** is home to Los Angeles's prominent – and affluent – gay community, as well as elderly pensioners and Russian immigrants. **Melrose Avenue**, LA's trendiest shopping street and one of the unmistakable symbols of Southern California, runs parallel to the less eventful main drag of **Santa Monica Boulevard**, where neon and Art Deco abound among a fluorescent rash of designer and secondhand boutiques, exotic antique shops, and avant-garde galleries. **La Brea Avenue** runs perpendicular to the east side of the Melrose district, offering more space, fewer tourists, and chic clothiers, upscale restaurants, and even trendier galleries.

North of West Hollywood, on either side of La Cienega Boulevard, is the two-mile-odd mix of restaurants hotels, billboards, and nightclubs on Sunset Boulevard known as the **Sunset Strip**, one of LA's best areas for nightlife. The scene hit its stride in the 1960s around the landmark *Whisky-a-Go-Go* club, no. 8901, which featured seminal psychedelic rock bands such as The Doors, Love, and Buffalo Springfield. In the 1970s the *Sunset Hyatt* hotel, no. 8401, became the infamous "Riot House" where Led Zeppelin raced motorcycles in the hallways and drugged-out rock stars committed unspeakable acts of debauchery. The hotel's pretty dull and corporate these days, but the music venues are well worth a visit, whether you want to rock, headbang, or just dance.

Beverly Hills and around

Beverly Hills is one of the world's wealthiest residential areas, patrolled by more cops per capita than anywhere else in the US. Glorified by the elite shops of **Rodeo Drive**, squeaky-clean streets, and ostentatious displays of wealth, the city is undoubtedly the height of LA pretension. Still, there are a number of decent and unassuming spots for visitors interested in things other than commodities. The **Museum of Television and Radio** (Wed–Sun noon–5pm; $10 donation; ⓦwww.mtr.org) is one such place, vividly chronicling eighty years of our media-saturated age, while the **Beverly Hills Trolley** (July & Aug & Nov & Dec Tues–Sat 11am–4pm; $5) offers tourists a forty-minute glimpse of the city's highlights, departing hourly from the corner of Dayton Way and Rodeo Drive.

In the northern hills and canyons, a number of well-concealed gardens and parks offer a respite from the shopping frenzy below. The wooded **Virginia Robinson Gardens**, 1008 Elden Way (tours Tues–Fri 10am & 1pm; $10; by appointment only at ⓣ310/276-5367), spreads across six acres, with more than a thousand varieties of flora, including some impressive Australian King Palm trees. To the east, the grounds of the biggest house in Beverly Hills, **Greystone Mansion**, 905 Loma Vista Drive, are now maintained as a public **park** by the city (daily 10am–5pm; free). The fifty-thousand-square-foot manor was once the property of oil titan Edward Doheny, but is rarely open to the public. However, you can admire the mansion's limestone facade and intricately designed chimneys, then stroll through the sixteen-acre park, with its koi-filled ponds and expansive views of the LA sprawl.

Just outside Beverly Hills, **Century City** is a charmless expanse of concrete and steel that was once the studio lot for 20th Century Fox, which now stands off-limits at 10201 Pico Blvd. A bit further east, the **Museum of Tolerance**, 9786 W Pico Blvd (April–Oct Mon–Thurs 11am–6.30pm, Fri 11am–5pm, Sun 11am–7.30pm; Nov–March Fri closes 3pm; $10; ⓦwww.museumoftolerance. com), looks at international hate and intolerance in general, tracing the rise of Nazism to a harrowing conclusion in a replica gas chamber.

Westwood

West of Beverly Hills and north of Wilshire Boulevard, **Westwood** is the home of the **University of California at Los Angeles (UCLA)**, and is known to many as "Westwood Village." Once LA's prime movie-going district, Westwood has lost some of its cinematic eminence due to a lack of parking, but remains the most densely packed movie-theater district in town, and its 1931 **Westwood Village Theater**, 961 Broxton Ave, is still used for Hollywood premieres or "sneak previews" to gauge audience reactions.

The university itself has a number of good gardens and museums worth exploring. The highlights include the **Fowler Museum of Cultural History**, Bruin Walk at Westwood Plaza (Wed–Sun noon–5pm, Thurs closes 8pm; free; Ⓦ www. fowler.ucla.edu), offering an intriguing selection of native masks from around the world, more than ten thousand textile pieces, and an extensive collection of African and Polynesian art. The **Franklin Murphy Sculpture Garden**, in the northeast corner of campus, is LA's best outdoor display of modern sculpture, featuring pieces by Henry Moore, Barbara Hepworth, Henri Matisse, Jacques Lipchitz, and Isamu Noguchi. The **Hannah Carter Japanese Garden**, 10619 Bellagio Rd (Tues, Wed & Fri 10am–3pm; free; by appointment only at Ⓣ 310/794-0320 or Ⓦ www.japanesegarden.ucla.edu), is an idyllic spot featuring magnolias and Japanese maples, and traditional structures and river rocks brought directly from Japan. Finally, art lovers shouldn't miss a trip to the **UCLA Hammer Museum**, 10899 Wilshire Blvd (Tues–Sat 11am–7pm, Thurs 11am–9pm, Sun 11am–5pm; $5, kids free, Thurs free to all; Ⓦ www.hammer.ucla.edu), where the minor Rembrandts and Rubenses may be less than stunning, but there are some impressive early-American works from Gilbert Stuart, Thomas Eakins, and John Singer Sargent, as well as a range of insightful, sometimes risk-taking, modern and avant-garde temporary exhibits.

The Getty Center

Towering over the surrounding area, the **Getty Center**, near the Sepulveda Pass north of Wilshire Blvd (Tues–Sun 10am–6pm, weekends closes 9pm; free, parking

△ The Getty Center

$7; ⓦwww.getty.edu), is Richard Meier's towering modernist temple to high art, clad in acres of travertine, its various buildings devoted to art exhibition, conservation, and acquisition, as well as other philanthropic tasks. Its surrounding gardens are arranged with rigid geometric precision. You can get here by MTA bus #561, which stops on Sepulveda Boulevard, near the lower parking lot.

Obliged by law to spend part of its multi-billion-dollar endowment every year, the Getty can outbid anyone to get what it wants, which is usually anything except contemporary art – a real deficiency in the museum's collections. Still, the quality of the **exhibits** is extraordinary, especially in the rooms devoted to decorative arts, where you can see a formidable array of ornate French furniture from the reign of Louis XIV, with clocks, chandeliers, tapestries, and gilt-edged commodes filling several overwhelmingly opulent chambers. The painting collection features all the major names from the thirteenth century on, including Van Gogh's *Irises* and several Rembrandt portraits. Elsewhere in the museum, photography is well represented by Man Ray, Moholy-Nagy and other notables, and there's also a rich assortment of classical, Renaissance, and Baroque sculpture – highlighted by Bernini's *Boy with a Dragon*, depicting a plump, possibly angelic toddler bending back the jaw of a dragon with surprising ease.

Venice, Santa Monica, and Malibu

Set along an unbroken twenty-mile stretch of white-sand beaches, the cozy, sometime quirky communities that line **Santa Monica Bay** feature some of the best vistas LA has to offer, with none of the smog or searing heat that can make the rest of the metropolis unpleasant. The entire area is well served by public transportation, near enough to the airport, and a wide choice of accommodation makes it a good base for seeing the rest of the city.

Venice

Venice was laid out in 1905 by developer Abbot Kinney as a romantic replica of the northern Italian city, complete with a twenty-mile network of canals. Over the decades it then became an amusement-park zone, grungy oil-drilling site, funky zone for hippies, drugs, and crime, and finally – the current version – a swank, arty district drawing a mix of hipsters, yuppies, and real-estate speculators. The town's main artery, **Windward Avenue**, runs from the sands into what was the Grand Circle of the canal system. An original Neoclassical **arcade**, around the intersection with Pacific Avenue, is alive with health-food shops, secondhand record stores, and roller-skate rental stands. Nearby, the few remaining **canals** display renovated white bridges and pedestrian-friendly footpaths (best accessed northbound on Dell Avenue from Washington Boulevard), along with a bevy of eye-popping housing designs.

Nowhere else does LA parade itself quite so openly as along the wide pathway of **Venice Boardwalk**, packed year-round at weekends and every day in summer with jugglers, fire-eaters, roller-skating guitar players, and people-watchers. South of Windward is **Muscle Beach**, a legendary outdoor weightlifting center where serious-looking dudes pump serious iron, and budding basketballers hold court on the concrete. Around the pier, outlets such as Spokes 'n' Stuff (☎310/395-4748), rent out **bikes** and **rollerblades**. If you've time, other sights worth a peek are Jonathan Borofsky's grotesque and looming sculpture **Ballerina Clown**, at Main Street and Rose Avenue; the chic restaurants and boutiques lining **Abbot Kinney Boulevard**; and, south of the Boardwalk, the latest in sleek modern architecture along **Ocean Front Walk**.

Santa Monica

Immediately north of Venice, **Santa Monica** is the oldest and biggest of LA's resorts, perched on palm-tree-shaded bluffs above the blue Pacific. Once a wild beachfront playground, it's now a self-consciously healthy and very liberal community with a large expatriate British and Irish contingent.

Santa Monica reaches nearly three miles inland, but most spots of interest are within a few blocks of the beach, notably **Palisades Park**, the pleasant, cypress-tree-lined strip along the top of the bluffs which makes for striking views of the surf below. Two blocks east of Ocean Avenue, the **Third Street Promenade**, a pedestrianized stretch with street vendors, buskers, and itinerant evangelists, is the closest LA comes to having a dynamic urban energy, and is by far the best place to come for alfresco dining, beer-drinking, and people-watching.

The real focus of Santa Monica is down below, on the **beach**, which is better for sunbathing than swimming, and on the refurbished **Santa Monica pier**, boasting a well-restored 1922 wooden **carousel** (mid-March to Sept Mon–Thurs 11am–5pm, Fri–Sun 11am–7pm; Oct to mid-March Thurs–Mon only; 50¢ per ride; ☎310/394.8042) that was featured in the 1973 movie *The Sting*. Although the familiar thrill rides of **Pacific Park** (summer daily 11am–11pm, Sat & Sun closes 12.30am; $17, kids $9; ⊛www.pacpark.com) may catch your eye, save your money for the **Santa Monica Pier Aquarium** (summer Mon–Fri 2–6pm, Sat & Sun 12.30–6.30pm; $5; ⊛www.healthebay.org/smpa), below the pier at 1600 Ocean Front Walk, where you can get your fingers wet touching sea anemones and starfish.

Another popular spot in town is the half-mile-long assortment of chic restaurants, boutiques, bookstores, and drinking joints along **Main Street**. Beyond consuming, there's little else to do but visit the **California Heritage Museum**, no. 2612 (Wed–Sun 11am–4pm; $5; ⊛www.californiaheritagemuseum.org), which hosts temporary displays on regional topics like old-time amusement parks, and has permanent exhibits on pottery, furniture, and decorative arts.

Finally, fans of the arts are advised to poke around inland Santa Monica for a trip to **Bergamot Station**, 2525 Michigan Ave, which houses many small art galleries (most open Tues–Fri 10am–6pm; free), as well as the **Santa Monica Museum of Art**, in Building G-1 (Tues–Sat 11am–6pm, $3; ⊛www.smmoa.org), a good space to see some of the most engaging work of the local scene. For some serious art from antiquity, head five miles north along the beautiful, curving **Pacific Coast Highway (PCH)**, to the opulent **Getty Villa**, 17985 PCH (Thurs–Mon 10am–5pm; free; by reservation only at ☎310/440-7300, ⊛www.getty.edu), which re-opened in 2006 after a long renovation and showcases an astounding collection of Greek and Roman antiquities – vases, statues, bowls, and so on – in a replica Roman villa poised high above the sea on a dramatic perch between Santa Monica and Malibu.

Malibu and the Santa Monica Mountains

Twenty miles north of Santa Monica at the top of the bay, **Malibu** is synonymous with luxurious celebrity isolation, but it's not all that impressive on arrival, with ramshackle surf shops and fast-food stands scattered along PCH around the graceful **Malibu Pier**. **Surfrider Beach** here was the surfing capital of the world in the 1950s and early 1960s, and is still a big attraction (the surf is best in late summer; check the surfing report at ⊛www.surfrider.org). Just beyond is **Malibu Lagoon State Park** (daily 8am–dusk), a nature reserve and bird refuge, and nearby is the **Adamson House**, 23200 PCH (grounds 8am–sunset, house Wed–Sat 11am–3pm; $3; ⊛www.adamsonhouse.org), a stunning, historic Spanish Colonial-style home featuring opulent decor and colorful tilework.

Most Malibu homes are tucked away in the narrow canyons on the fringes of town. There's very little to see, despite tourists' futile attempts to peek into the exclusive **Malibu Colony** Hollywood retreat, located along an unmarked stretch near PCH. You'd do better to explore the huge **Santa Monica Mountains National Recreation Area** (ⓦwww.lamountains.org), north of town, which is wilderness in many places, and you can still spot a variety of deer, coyotes, and even the odd mountain lion. If you'd like to find out more about this marvelous protected area, the Santa Monica Mountains **visitor center**, in neighboring Thousand Oaks, 401 W Hillcrest Drive (daily 9am–5pm; ⓣ805/370-2301, ⓦwww.nps.gov/samo), has maps and information. Other good spots here include the 4000-acre **Malibu Creek State Park**, on Las Virgenes Road near Mulholland Drive, where 20th Century Fox filmed many Tarzan pictures, as well as the TV show *M*A*S*H*. The park includes a large lake, waterfalls, and nearly fifteen miles of hiking trails. Further west, the **Paramount Ranch**, 2813 Cornell Rd, is another studio backlot with a phony rail crossing and cemetery, and Western movie set used in countless productions.

Five miles along the coast from Malibu Pier, **Zuma Beach** is the largest and most crowded of the Los Angeles County beaches. Adjacent **Point Dume State Beach**, below the imposing promontory of Point Dume, is a lot more relaxed, and the rocks at its southern tip, **Pirate's Cove**, are a good place to view seals and migrating gray whales in winter. At the northwestern edge of LA County, **Leo Carrillo** ("ca-REE-oh") **State Beach Park**, 35000 PCH, sits at the end of MTA bus route #434. The mile-long sandy beach is divided by Sequit Point, a bluff with underwater caves and a tunnel you can pass through at low tide, and is also one of LA's best campgrounds (see p.1047).

The South Bay and LA Harbor

South from LA along PCH is an eight-mile coastal strip of quiet and unpretentious South Bay beach towns: **Manhattan Beach**, **Hermosa Beach**, and **Redondo Beach**. Each has a beckoning strip of white sand – much more open to the public than those around Malibu – and Manhattan and Hermosa are especially well equipped for surfing and beach sports. They're also well connected by the regular bus lines to downtown LA. To the south are **Long Beach** – site of the LA Harbor – and **Catalina Island**.

Long Beach

Although downtown **Long Beach** offers a pleasant stretch of restored architecture and antique stores around **Pine Avenue** (linked by the Blue Line light rail to downtown LA; see p.1046), the main reason most tourists come is to see the **Queen Mary** (daily 10am–6pm; $23 self-guided tours; ⓦwww.queenmary.com). The Cunard flagship from the 1930s until the 1960s, the boat is now a luxury hotel, and the guided tours ($3–9 extra) present a sentimentalized version of its days of elegance and refinement. Across the bay along Shoreline Drive, the **Aquarium of the Pacific** (daily 9am–6pm; $20, children $12; ⓦwww.aquariumofpacific.org) is a terrific exploration of aquatic flora and fauna from geographic and climatic zones around the world, while further west, the **Long Beach Museum of Art**, 2300 E Ocean Blvd (Tues–Sun 11am–5pm; $7; ⓦwww.lbma.org), is the home of regional LA artworks and tasteful displays of early-20th-century modernist furniture and sculpture.

Catalina Island

The enticing island of **Catalina**, twenty miles offshore from Long Beach, is mostly preserved wilderness, but does have substantial charm and offers a nice break from the metropolis. Indeed, with cars largely forbidden, the two thousand islanders walk, ride bikes, or drive golf carts. **Ferry** trips run several times daily from Long Beach, and cost $52–61 roundtrip (look for discounts for Internet booking). Operators include Catalina Explorer (T 1-877/432-6276, W www.catalinaferry.com), Catalina Express (T 1-800/315-3967, W www.catalinaexpress.com), and, from Newport Beach, Catalina Flyer (T 949/673-5245, W www.catalina-flyer.com).

The island's one town, **AVALON**, can be fully explored on foot in an hour, with maps issued by the Chamber of Commerce at the foot of the ferry pier (T 310/510-1520, W www.visitcatalina.org). Begin at the sumptuous Art Deco **Avalon Casino**, 1 Casino Way, a 1920s structure that still shows movies featuring mermaid murals, gold-leaf ceiling motifs, an Art Deco ballroom, and a small **museum** (daily 10am–4pm, Jan–March closed Thurs; $4) displaying Native American artifacts from Catalina's past. Several miles southwest of Avalon, the **Wrigley Memorial and Botanical Garden**, 1400 Avalon Canyon Rd (daily 8am–5pm; $5), displays all manner of endemic flora and fauna on forty acres. **Santa Catalina Island Company** (T 1-800/446-0266, W www.scico.com), offers tours of the Casino or downtown area (each $15), bus trips through the outback ($32–98), and harbor cruises and glass-bottom-boat rides ($20-35), while **Catalina Adventure Tours** provides cheaper versions of the same ($13–36; T 310/510-2888, W www.catalinaadventuretours.com).

The most interesting **hotel** is the *Zane Grey Pueblo*, 199 Chimes Tower Rd (T 310/510-0966, W www.zanegreypueblohotel.com; ⑥), which has sixteen rooms overlooking the bay or mountains, with an enticing off-season (Oct–May) weekday rate of $59. If you really have a bundle to spend, the *Inn on Mt Ada*, 398 Wrigley Rd (T 310/510-2030, W www.innonmtada.com; ⑨), is the final word in Catalina luxury. The only true budget option is **camping**: *Hermit Gulch* is the closest site to Avalon and the busiest. Four other sites – *Blackjack*, *Little Harbor*, *Parsons Landing*, and *Two Harbors* – in Catalina's interior (all $12 per person, kids $6; bookable at T 310/510-8368, W www.scico.com/camping) are much more distant, but also roomier.

Orange County

Throughout the US, **Orange County** is synonymous with anodyne, white suburbia – most famously as the site of fun and squeaky-clean **Disneyland** – but in recent years it's begun to change, with many new Hispanic arrivals and much more cultural (and culinary) diversity. Still, most tourists come for the theme parks and for the easy-going, upscale beach towns of the **Orange County Coast**.

Disneyland

The pop-culture colossus of **Disneyland**, in Anaheim at 1313 Harbor Blvd (summer daily 8am–midnight; rest of year Mon–Fri 10am–6pm, Sat 9am–midnight, Sun 9am–10pm; $59, kids $49, parking $10; W www.disneyland.com), is one of America's most iconic sights, as well as one of its most expensive – most of the park's hotels are ridiculously overpriced (see p.1049) and there's little quality cuisine in the area. The park is 45 minutes by **car** from downtown LA on the Santa Ana Freeway. Arrive early, as traffic and ride lines quickly become nightmarish, especially in the summer.

Among Disneyland's best **rides** are three in **Adventureland**: the Indiana Jones Adventure, an interactive archeological dig and 1930s-style newsreel show leading up to a giddy journey along 2500ft of skull-encrusted corridors; the Pirates of the Caribbean, a boat trip through underground caverns full of singing rogues; and the Haunted Mansion, a riotous "doom buggy" tour in the company of the house spooks. By contrast, **Frontierland** has mainly lower-end Wild West–themed carnival attractions, **Fantasyland** low-tech fairy-tale rides, "highlighted" by the treacly It's a Small World; and **Toontown**, a cartoonish zone aimed at the kindergarten set. It's more worthwhile to zip right through to **Tomorrowland**, Disney's vision of the future, where the Space Mountain roller coaster plunges through the pitch-blackness of outer space, the Star Tours ride simulates a journey into the world of George Lucas, and Innoventions offers a fun opportunity to look at, and play with, the latest special effects.

The latest adjunct to Disneyland is the **California Adventure**, technically a separate park, and a lot less fun. Aside from its slightly more exciting roller coasters and better food, the Adventure is really just another "land" to visit on your Disney trek, albeit a much bigger and more expensive one: you'll have to shell out another $20 for a one-day pass that covers both this and the main park.

Knott's Berry Farm

More down-to-earth than Disneyland, **Knott's Berry Farm**, four miles northwest, off the Santa Ana Freeway at 8039 Beach Blvd (summer Sun–Thurs 9am–11pm, Fri & Sat 9am–midnight; rest of year Mon–Fri 10am–6pm, Sat 10am–10pm, Sun 10am–7pm; $40, kids $15; Ⓦwww.knotts.com), still has roller coasters far more exciting than anything at its rival. Although there are ostensibly six themed lands here, you should spend most or all of your time in just half of them: **Fiesta Village**, home to the Jaguar, a high-flying coaster that spins you around the park concourse; **Ghost Town**, with fun wooden coasters and log flumes; and the **Boardwalk**, which is all about heart-thumping thrill rides. Knott's also has its own adjacent water park, **Soak City USA** (June–Sept only, hours vary but generally daily 10am–5pm or 6pm; $27, $15 for children or adult entry after 3pm), offering twenty-one drenching rides of various heights and speeds.

Orange County Coast

Stretching from the edge of the LA Harbor to the border of San Diego County 35 miles south, the **Orange County Coast** is chic suburbia with a shoreline: swanky houses line the sands, and the ambiance is easygoing, libertarian, and affluent. As the names of the main towns suggest – **Huntington Beach**, **Newport Beach**, and **Laguna Beach** – most of the good reasons to come here involve sea and sand, though a handful of museums and festivals can also make for an interesting trip. Check out the **International Surfing Museum**, 411 Olive Ave, Huntington Beach (Oct–May Thurs–Mon noon–5pm; June–Sept open daily; $3; Ⓦwww.surfingmuseum.org), loaded with famous legends of the waves, and Laguna Beach's **Pageant of the Masters** (July–Aug daily shows begin at 8.30pm; $20–75; ☎1-800/487-3378, Ⓦwww.foapom.com), a strangely compelling spectacle in which participants dress up as characters from famous paintings. To the far south, **San Juan Capistrano** merits a stop as the site of the best-kept of all the Californian **missions**, Ortega Highway and Camino Capistrano (daily 8.30am–5pm; $6; Ⓦwww.missionsjc.com).

The San Gabriel and San Fernando valleys

The northern limit of LA is defined by two long stretches – the **San Gabriel and San Fernando valleys** – lying over the hills from the central basin, starting close to one another a few miles north of downtown, spanning outwardly in opposite directions – east to the deserts, west to the Central Coast – and featuring a few worthwhile points of interest.

The San Gabriel Valley

Ten miles northeast of downtown LA, the **San Gabriel Valley**'s main appeal is the genteel community of **Pasadena**, best known for its **Rose Parade** in January and **Rose Bowl** stadium west of town. Also distinctive is the historic shopping precinct of **Old Pasadena** along Colorado Boulevard, now fashionable for its restaurants and boutiques (and accessible on the Gold Line light rail).

Pasadena's other best offerings are the splendid collection of the **Norton Simon Museum**, 411 W Colorado Blvd (Wed–Mon noon–6pm, Fri closes 9pm; $8, students free; Ⓦ www.nortonsimon.org), one of LA's greatest art institutions, with a prime selection of Old Masters like Rubens and Rembrandt and modern works by Klee and Picasso, and the **Gamble House**, 4 Westmoreland Place (hour-long tours Thurs–Sun noon–3pm; $10; Ⓦ gamblehouse.usc.edu), a famed Craftsman mansion with Arts and Crafts decor and Japanese-inspired design elements. Maps and booklets on Pasadena, available at the visitors bureau (see p.1045), detail worthwhile self-guided tours of the city's excellent architecture, historical sites, and museums.

South of Pasadena, in dull, upper-crust **San Marino**, the **Huntington Museum and Library**, off Huntington Drive at 1151 Oxford Rd (Tues–Fri noon–4.30pm, Sat & Sun 10.30am–4.30pm; $15; Ⓦ www.huntington.org), contains many historic documents and rare books, such as a Gutenberg Bible and the Ellesmere Chaucer – the latter an illuminated manuscript of *The Canterbury Tales* dating from around 1410. Paintings include Gainsborough's *Blue Boy* and Reynolds's *Mrs Siddons as the Tragic Muse*, and the whole complex is set off by acres of beautiful themed **gardens**.

The San Fernando Valley and Magic Mountain

The **San Fernando Valley**, spreading west, is a vast sprawl of tract homes, minimalls, and fast-food diners, but merits a trip to see **Forest Lawn Cemetery**, in Glendale at 1712 S Glendale Ave (daily 9am–5pm; free; Ⓦ www.forestlawn.org), a fascinating, often kitschy, display of death, Hollywood style. Those buried here include Errol Flynn, Walt Disney, Clara Bow, Nat King Cole, Chico Marx, Clark Gable, and Jean Harlow, among many other notables.

North of the San Fernando Valley, the three-hundred-acre theme park of **Magic Mountain**, Magic Mountain Parkway at I-5 (summer daily 10am–10pm; rest of year Sat & Sun only 10am–8pm; $60, kids $30, $8 parking; Ⓦ www.sixflags.com), holds the region's wildest roller coasters, with a new fright-ride unleashed nearly every summer.

Burbank and the studios

Miles from Hollywood proper, the nitty-gritty business of actually making films goes on over the hills in otherwise boring **BURBANK**. The studio tours include a peek inside **NBC**, 3000 W Alameda Blvd (box office open Mon–Fri 9am–4pm; $7; reserve at ⓣ 818/840-3537), and a fun trek into **Warner Bros Studios**, 3400 Warner Blvd (Mon–Fri 8.30am–4.30pm; $42; Ⓦ www.wbstudiotour.com), but Disney's fortress-like compound, at 500 S Buena Vista St, is strictly off-limits.

The largest of the backlots belongs to **Universal Studios**, whose lengthy tours (daily: summer 9am–8pm or 9pm; rest of year 10am–6pm; $59; Ⓦ www.universalstudioshollywood.com) include high-tech rides and "evening spectaculars" based on current movies. The shows are without exception cheesy, but for fans of explosions and pratfalls, they're an absolute must.

⑬

CALIFORNIA | Los Angeles: The City

Eating

LA **eating** covers every extreme: whatever you want to eat and however much you want to spend, you're spoiled for choice. Try to take at least a few meals in the higher-end restaurants, many of which serve superb food in consciously cultivated surroundings. At the cheaper end of the scale, the options are almost endless, and include terrific burger stands where you can scarf down mountains of fries, and free food available for the price of a drink at **happy hours**.

Downtown and around

Angelique Café 840 S Spring St ☎ 213/623-8698. A marvelous and affordable Continental eatery in the middle of the Garment District, where you can dine on well-crafted pastries for breakfast or savory sandwiches, rich casseroles, and fine salads for lunch.

Ciudad 445 S Figueroa St ☎ 213/486-5171. Roast chicken and quinoa fritters are some of the highlights at this colorful, if pricey, Mexican-influenced spot, where the live Latin music competes with the delicious food for your attention.

Dong Il Jang 3455 W 8th St ☎ 213/383-5757. Cozy little Korean restaurant where the meat is cooked at your table and the food is consistently good, especially the grilled chicken and beef.

La Luz del Dia 107 Paseo de la Plaza ☎ 213/628-7495. Authentic Mexican eatery on Olvera Street, worth seeking out for the fiery burritos, enchiladas, and stews, all served in sizeable portions.

Langer's Deli 704 S Alvarado ☎ 213/483-8050. One of LA's finest delis, with an excellent selection of take-out meats and baked goods. Offers twenty ways of eating what is LA's best pastrami sandwich. Open daylight hours only; curbside pick-up available in a grim area.

Ocean Seafood 750 N Hill ☎ 213/687-3088. Cavernous and often crowded Chinese restaurant serving low-priced, excellent food – try the abalone, crab, shrimp, or duck.

Original Pantry 877 S Figueroa St ☎ 213/972-9279. Former mayor Richard Riordan owns this classic old diner, which serves huge pork chops and American breakfasts 24hrs a day.

Pacific Dining Car 1310 W 6th St ☎ 213/483-6000. Starched linen and very expensive steaks in a former railroad carriage styled after an English supper club. Open until 2am.

Patina 141 S Grand Ave ☎ 213/972-3331. One of LA's signature eateries, a fancy, ultra-swank spot in Disney Hall. Here you can devour pheasant in apple-champagne sauce, pork loin medallions, and other rotating items on the menu if you're prepared to drop a wad of cash.

Philippe the Original French Dip 1001 N Alameda St ☎ 213/628-3781. Renowned sawdust café with long communal tables, a decor unchanged since 1908, and juicy, artery-clogging French dips – first invented here – loaded with turkey, pork, beef, or lamb.

Hollywood

Casa Carnitas 4067 Beverly Blvd ☎ 323/667-9953. On the southeast edge of Hollywood, tasty, cheap Mexican food from the Yucatan, with dishes inspired by Cuban and Caribbean cooking. Lots of seafood, too.

Fred 62 1854 N Vermont Ave ☎ 323/667-0062. Classic 24hr retro-diner offering stylish twists on staples like salads, burgers, and fries, and a tempting array of pancakes and omelets.

Mario's Peruvian Seafood 5786 Melrose Ave ☎ 323/466-4181. Good and authentic Peruvian fare: supremely tender squid, rich and flavorful mussels, with a hint of soy sauce in some dishes. Inexpensive, too.

Mexico City 2121 Hillhurst Ave ☎ 323/661-7227. Spinach enchiladas and other Californian versions of Mexican standards, including a mean *pollo verde* chicken dish, with prices that are easy to stomach.

Palermo 1858 N Vermont Ave ☎ 323/663-1178. Chi-chi Northern Italian cuisine be damned – this joint is as old as Hollywood itself, and with as many devoted fans, who flock here for the rich pizzas, cheesy decor and gallons of affordable red wine.

Pink's Hot Dogs 709 N La Brea Ave ☎ 323/931-4223. The quintessence of chili dogs, featuring items like a cheese-chili-hot dog combo wrapped up in a gooey tortilla package. Open until 2am, or 3am weekends.

Roscoe's Chicken and Waffles 1514 N Gower St ☎ 323/466-7453. An unlikely spot for Hollywood's elite, this LA dining institution attracts all sorts for its fried chicken, greens, goopy gravy, and thick waffles.

Shibucho 3114 Beverly Blvd ☎ 323/387-8498. Seriously tasty, affordable sushi bar where the squid and eel are quite fine, along with the famed *toro*, an expensive but delicious tuna delicacy.

vermont 1714 N Vermont Ave ☎ 323/661-6163. Pretentious lower-case letters aside, this is one of the best upper-end Cal-cuisine spots around, with primo roasted chicken, crab cakes, and ravioli.

West LA

Apple Pan 10801 W Pico Blvd ☎310/475-3585. Grab a spot at the counter and enjoy freshly baked apple pie and greasy hamburgers at an old-time joint that opened just after World War II.

Ca' Brea 346 S La Brea Ave ☎323/938-2863. One of LA's best choices for upscale California and Italian cuisine, and especially good for *osso buco* and risotto.

Campanile 624 S La Brea Ave ☎323/938-1447. Pricey but tremendous Northern Italian dishes – the likes of rosemary-infused lamb and butternut squash ravioli. If you can't afford a dinner, just try the dessert or pick up some of the city's best bread at *La Brea Bakery* next door.

Canter's Deli 419 N Fairfax Ave ☎323/651-2030. Waitresses in pink uniforms and running shoes serve kosher soup and sandwiches in a kitsch, white-vinyl setting, with its own bizarre cabaret.

Cobras and Matadors 7615 Beverly Blvd ☎323/932-6178. A fine, mid-priced tapas spot where you can sample Castilian delights, like spiced pork loin and game hen, in an intimate setting.

Gumbo Pot 6333 W 3rd St, in the Farmers Market ☎323/933-0358. Delicious and dirt-cheap Cajun cooking in a bustling setting; try the *gumbo yaya* of chicken, shrimp, and sausage or the fruit-and-potato salad.

Jar 8225 Beverly Blvd ☎323/655-6566. An upper-end steakhouse featuring all the usual red-meat fare – prime rib, T-bone, even a pot roast – with an inspired Cal-cuisine flair, throwing in different spices and exotic flavors.

Jerry's Famous Deli 8701 Beverly Blvd, Beverly Hills ☎310/289-1811. The most engaging of the many *Jerry's* locations in LA, featuring a sizable deli menu and open 24hrs. Occasionally, celebrities stop in to nosh.

L'Orangerie 903 N La Cienega Blvd ☎310/652-9770. The closest Francophiles can get to Escoffier in LA, though the stylish French food has more than a dash of California cuisine as well. Bring wads of cash and a fancy suit, or be prepared to leave quietly.

Michelia 8738 3rd St ☎310/276-8288. Nouveau, somewhat pricey Southeast Asian eatery with Cal-cuisine versions of traditional spicy salads and fish dishes.

Mishima 8474 W 3rd St ☎323/782-0181. Chic, popular eatery serving bowls of delicious udon and soba noodles at low prices.

Nate 'n' Al's 414 N Beverly Drive ☎310/274-0101. The best-known deli in Beverly Hills, popular with movie people and one of the few reasonable places for dining in the vicinity. Get there early (opens 7am) to grab a booth.

Santa Monica, Venice, and Malibu

Benito's Taco Shop 11614 Santa Monica Blvd ☎310/442-9924. Tacos with beef, pork, or fish, for just a few bucks. Most combos are under $5, making this a good spot to gulp and go.

Border Grill 1445 4th St, Santa Monica ☎310/451-1655. Good place to sup on delicious shrimp, pork, plantains, and other nuevo Latin American-flavored fixings, with excellent desserts, too. Prices are on the expensive side, but the ambiance is always swinging.

Chaya Venice 110 Navy St ☎310/396-1179. Coolly elegant culinary crossroads serving Japanese and Mediterranean foods to a smart clientele.

Chinois on Main 2709 Main St, Santa Monica ☎310/392-9025. One of LA's most renowned, and most expensive, restaurants, run by chef Wolfgang Puck, and serving *nouvelle* Chinese dishes.

Hal's 1349 Abbot Kinney Blvd, Venice ☎310/396-3105. Offers a nice range of well-done, somewhat expensive American standards, including marinated steaks and salmon dishes.

Marix Tex-Mex Playa 118 Entrada Drive, Pacific Palisades ☎310/459-8596. Flavorful fajitas and big margaritas in this rowdy beachfront cantina. Another free-spirited branch at 1108 N Flores St, West Hollywood ☎323/656-8800.

Michael's 1147 3rd St, Santa Monica ☎310/451-0843. Longstanding favorite for California preparations of steak, pasta, and fowl, served here amid modern art. Reservations are essential, prices steep.

Neptune's Net 42505 PCH, Malibu ☎310/457-3095. It's worth a trip to the far reaches of LA County's northwestern border to gorge on clams, shrimp, oysters and lobsters at basic picnic tables for low-end prices.

Valentino 3115 Pico Blvd, Santa Monica ☎310/829-4313. Some call it the finest Italian restaurant in the US – traditional Northern Italian dishes, with an infusion of California cuisine dash and experiment. Expect to max out your credit card.

South Bay and LA Harbor

Bluewater Grill 665 N Harbor Dr, Redondo Beach ☎310/318-3474. Solid seafood spot featuring a slew of mid-priced fresh fish – salmon and catfish to crabs and oysters.

El Pollo Inka 1100 PCH, Hermosa Beach ☎310/372-1433. Cheap Peruvian-style chicken, catfish, and hot and spicy soups to make your mouth water.

Hof's Hut 6257 E 2nd St, Long Beach ☎562/598-

4070. One bite of the *Huf*'s juicy Hofburger and you know you've found the real deal. Four other South Bay locations, and four in Orange County.

New Orleans 140 Pier Ave, Hermosa Beach ☎310/372-8970. Authentic deep-South Cajun cuisine: jambalaya, gumbo, po' boy sandwiches, and fried oysters, all of them plenty tasty and cheap.

Rock 'n Fish 120 Manhattan Beach Blvd, Manhattan Beach ☎310/379-9900. Whether you're in the mood for halibut, sea bass, blackened shrimp, or just a good old prime rib, this cozy surf 'n' turf eatery is a good, affordable spot to indulge. Just make sure to reserve ahead.

Orange County

Angelo's 511 S State College Blvd, Anaheim ☎714/533-1401. Straight out of TV's *Happy Days*, a drive-in complete with roller-skating car-hops and juicy burgers. Open until 2am on weekends.

Claes Seafood in the Hotel Laguna, 425 S Coast Hwy, Laguna Beach ☎949/376-9283. Sample pricey and delicious ahi tuna and halibut, plus Cal-cuisine spins on the same fare, with fine views of the Pacific.

Favori 3502 W First St, Santa Ana ☎714/531-6838. Worth the long drive out for what may be LA's best Vietnamese food, including delicious garlic shrimp, curried chicken with lemon grass, and

savory noodles, all for decent prices.

Ruby's 1 Balboa Pier, Newport Beach ☎949/675-RUBY. A solid spot for burgers and fries – the only eatery on this popular pier and one of the few cheap spots in this upscale burg.

The San Gabriel and San Fernando valleys

Art's Deli 12224 Ventura Blvd, Studio City ☎818/762-1221. Long-time film-industry favorite with a good range of hefty sandwiches and soups.

Dr Hogly-Wogly's Tyler Texas Bar-B-Q 8136 Sepulveda Blvd, Van Nuys ☎818/780-6701. Line up for the chicken, sausages, ribs, and beans – some of the best in LA.

Portos Bakery 315 N Brand Blvd, Glendale ☎818/956-5996. Popular and cheap café serving flaky Cuban pastries, scrumptious sandwiches, cheesecakes soaked in rum, croissants, tarts and tortes, and cappuccino.

Sea Star 740 E Valley Blvd, Alhambra ☎626/282-1883. The one reason to come to this San Gabriel Valley town, for affordable dim sum at its best: pork, *baos*, potstickers and dumplings.

Wolfe Burger 46 N Lake St, Pasadena ☎ 626/792-7292. A great place for chili, tamales, burgers, and *huevos rancheros*, not to mention south- *and* north-of-the-border burritos.

Nightlife and entertainment

Exploring the jungle of LA **nightlife** can be great fun. Even the quietest venue offers a chance to eavesdrop on a bit of vapid dialogue; the most raucous ones will take your breath away. In all the bars, clubs, and discos, you'll need to be 21 and will be asked for ID. The best sources of **listings** are *LA Weekly* and the "Calendar" section in Friday's *LA Times*.

Bars and coffeehouses

LA's **bars** provide a wide range of choices, from the funky dives of Hollywood to the chic enclaves of West LA and Santa Monica. As elsewhere along the West Coast, **coffeehouses** are established all over the city as popular meeting places.

Barney's Beanery 8447 Santa Monica Blvd, West Hollywood ☎310/654-2287. Well-worn poolroom/bar, with 200 beers and a rock'n'roll-hedonist history. Also serves all-American food.

Beauty Bar 1638 N Cahuenga Blvd, Hollywood ☎323/464-7676. Drinking spot devoted to nails, hair, and cosmetics, with a welter of 1950s-style salon gadgets and a similarly themed cocktail list – the Prell, Blue Rinse, Platinum Blonde, etc.

Boardner's 1652 N Cherokee Ave, Hollywood

☎323/462-9621. A likeably unkempt neighborhood bar with a mix of salty old-timers and hip newbies.

Bourgeois Pig 5931 Franklin Ave, Hollywood ☎323/962-6366. Hip environment and overpriced cappuccinos – you really pay for the groovy atmosphere of mirrors, chandeliers, and loveseats – but the tasty java and colorful clientele make it worth your while.

El Carmen 8138 W 3rd St ☎323/852-1552.

Groovy faux dive-bar with a south-of-the-border theme pushed to the extreme, with black-velvet pictures of Mexican wrestlers, steer horns, stuffed snakes, and much tongue-in-cheek grunge, as well as signature margaritas.

Formosa Café 7156 Santa Monica Blvd ☏ 323/850-9050. Started during Prohibition, this tiny bar is said to be alive with the ghosts of Bogie and Marilyn. Indulge in the potent spirits (not the insipid food) and soak in a true Hollywood institution.

Insomnia 7286 Beverly Blvd, West LA ☏ 323/931-4943. A chic spot for chugging cappuccinos while sitting in comfortable sofas and admiring the vivid amateur art on the walls.

Lava Lounge 1533 N La Brea, Hollywood ☏ 323/876-6612. Wallow in the cheesy retro decor and slurp down a glowing cocktail to the sounds of pounding rockabilly and freewheeling surf music.

Library Alehouse 2911 Main St, Santa Monica ☏ 310/314-4855. Presenting the choicest brews from West Coast microbreweries and beyond, this is a good spot to select from a nice range of well-known and obscure labels.

Molly Malone's Irish Pub 575 S Fairfax Ave ☏ 323/935-1577. One of LA's drinking staples: an authentic Irish bar, with a crowd of regulars who

look like they've been there for ages, plus nightly music, shamrock decor, and the requisite pints of thick Guinness.

Musso and Frank Grill 6667 Hollywood Blvd ☏ 323/467-7788. Simply put, if you haven't had a drink in this landmark 1919 bar, you haven't been to Hollywood. You can also have a pricey bite to eat.

Nova Express 426 N Fairfax Ave, south of West Hollywood ☏ 323/658-7533. One of the grooviest coffee joints around, designed with retro-futuristic sci-fi decor, with weird colors and lighting, and dance music most nights. Open until 4am.

Novel Café 212 Pier Ave, Santa Monica ☏ 310/396-8566. Stacks of used books and high-backed wooden chairs set the tone; good coffees, teas, and pastries, with funky old sofas on the mezzanine to curl up in.

Tiki-Ti 4427 W Sunset Blvd, Hollywood ☏ 323/669-9381. Tiny grass-skirted cocktail bar straight out of *Hawaii Five-0*, packed with kitschy pseudo-Polynesian decor, on the edge of Hollywood.

Ye Olde Kings Head 116 Santa Monica Blvd, Santa Monica ☏ 310/451-1402. Prime LA spot for quaffing British ales and munching on steak-and-kidney pie.

Clubs and discos

LA's **clubs** are among the wildest in the country, ranging from posy hangouts to industrial noise cellars. The trendier side of the club scene is, as always, elusive, with some venues changing names and clientele every six months (those below are among the more established). Check the *LA Weekly* before setting out.

Avalon 1735 N Vine St, Hollywood ☏ 323/462-3000. Weekend dance club spinning old-school faves, along with a dash of rock and retro, with the occasional big-name DJ dropping in.

Bar Sinister 1652 N Cherokee, Hollywood ☏ 323/769-7070. A collection of sprightly dance beats most nights of the week, then memorably spooky goth music and anemic-looking vampire types on Sat. Connected to *Boardner's* bar (see p.1070).

Dragonfly 6510 Santa Monica Blvd, Hollywood ☏ 323/466-6111. Unusual decor, two large dance rooms, and house and disco club nights that are continually buzzing on Thurs–Sun nights; live music at other times.

The Echo 1822 Sunset Blvd ☏ 213/413-8200. East Hollywood scene with scrappy dance DJs spinning a range of old- and new-school favorites nightly, and rock and retro DJs on Sun.

Mor 2941 Main St, Santa Monica ☏ 310/455-6720. Techno, trance, house, and soul, mixed up for groovy club nights most evenings in this hip lounge setting, plus new wave and retro-pop.

The Ruby 7070 Hollywood Blvd ☏ 323/467-7070. A wide range of feverish dance nights take turns Thurs–Sun, covering everything from gothic and grinding industrial to perky house and garage.

The Space 2020 Wilshire Blvd, Santa Monica ☏ 310/829-1933. Ground zero for weekend retro vibes, with backward-looking DJs massaging everything from 1980s electro, pop and New Wave to spacey 1970s disco and funk to more current breakbeats.

Tempest 7323 Santa Monica Blvd ☏ 323/850-5115. After 10pm on weekends, the eclectic grooves start to spin here, from retro-funk and disco to the latest hip-hop to 1960s *Austin Powers*-style sing-a-longs.

Gay and lesbian bars and clubs

7969 7969 Santa Monica Blvd, West Hollywood ☎ 323/654-0280. A landmark for its frenetic assortment of gay-themed (but straight-friendly) shows, from go-go girls to male strippers to drag queens. Always one of LA's most colorful spots for dancing and grinding.

Arena 6655 Santa Monica Blvd, Hollywood ☎ 323/462-0714. Work up a sweat to funk, hip-hop and house on a massive dance floor inside a former ice factory. The fervent crowd is diverse, but leans toward a mix of Hispanics and gays. Plays host to many different club nights.

The Factory 652 N La Peer Drive ☎ 310/659-4551. DJs spin house music most nights of the week at what is one of West Hollywood's more popular clubs.

Jewel's Catch One 4067 W Pico Blvd, Mid-Wilshire ☎ 323/734-8849. Sweaty barn catering to a mixed crowd of gays and straights and covering two wild dance floors. A longtime LA favorite, located in the middle of nowhere.

Rage 8911 Santa Monica Blvd, West Hollywood ☎ 310/652-7055. Very flashy gay men's club playing the latest house hits. Also with drag comedy.

Ultra Suede 661 N Robertson Blvd, West Hollywood ☎ 310/659-4551. Featuring various theme nights where a mixed gay and straight crowd gyrates to new wave, rock, house, and retro-pop music.

Live music

LA has an overwhelming choice of venues for **live music**: ever since the 1960s, the local **rock** scene has been excellent, with up-and-comers getting their first break in clubs on the Sunset Strip; **jazz** is played in a few authentic downbeat dives; and **salsa** is immensely popular, and not just among LA's Hispanics. Cover charges can vary widely, depending on the prominence of the headliner and the night of the week, so call ahead.

Babe and Ricky's Inn 4339 Leimert Blvd, South Central LA ☎ 323/295-9112. One of LA's top spots for blues, attracting plenty of quality, nationally known acts.

Baked Potato 3787 Cahuenga Blvd West, North Hollywood ☎ 818/980-1615. A small, near-legendary contemporary jazz spot, where many reputations have been forged. Expect to be surprised.

Doug Weston's Troubadour 9081 Santa Monica Blvd, West Hollywood ☎ 310/276-6168. An old 1960s mainstay that's been through a lot of incarnations. Used to be known for folk and country rock, then metal, now for alternative and acoustic line-ups.

El Floridita 1253 N Vine St, Hollywood ☎ 323/871-8612. Decent Mexican and Cuban food plus a fine line-up of Cuban and salsa artists, who play on weekends and jam on other nights.

El Rey Theater 5515 Wilshire Blvd, Mid-Wilshire ☎ 323/936-4790. Although not as famous as its Sunset Strip counterparts, this rock and alternative venue is possibly the best spot to see explosive new bands and still-engaging oldsters. Also offers a variety of dance club nights.

Gabah 4658 Melrose Ave, Mid-Wilshire ☎ 323/664-8913. Eclectic spot serving up a mix of reggae, funk, dub and rock – even flamenco. The dicey neighborhood leaves much to be desired, though.

Harvelle's 1432 4th St, Santa Monica ☎ 310/395-1676. Near the Promenade, a stellar blues joint for more than six decades, offering a range of performers nightly.

Jazz Bakery 3233 Helms Ave, Culver City ☎ 310/271-9039. More performance space than club, where the best local musicians play alongside big-name visitors in a former bakery building.

Knitting Factory 7021 Hollywood Blvd, Hollywood ☎ 323/463-0204. West Coast branch of landmark New York club (see p.123), with a wide range of interpretation, much of it avant-garde.

Largo 432 N Fairfax Ave, Mid-Wilshire ☎ 323/852-1073. Intimate cabaret venue with interesting jazz, rock, and pop acts.

McCabe's 3101 Pico Blvd, Santa Monica ☎ 310/828-4497. The back room of LA's premier acoustic guitar shop; long the scene of excellent and unusual folk and country shows.

The Roxy 9009 Sunset Blvd, West Hollywood ☎ 310/276-2222. The showcase of the rock industry's new signings, intimate and with a great sound system.

Rusty's Surf Ranch 256 Santa Monica Pier ☎ 310/393-7437. Offers not only surf music but live folk and country as well, along with karaoke. A popular spot for tourists, near the end of the pier.

Spaceland 1717 Silver Lake Blvd, Hollywood ☎ 213/833-2843. Excellent spot to catch up-and-coming local and national rockers and other acts, including punk and alternative musicians.

Viper Room 8852 Sunset Blvd, West Hollywood ☎ 310/358-1881 Great live rockers and a headline-grabbing past have helped boost this club's hip aura.

Whisky-a-Go-Go 8901 Sunset Blvd, West Hollywood ☎ 310/652-4202. For many years LA's most famous rock 'n' roll club, nowadays featuring mainly hard rock.

Classical music, opera, and dance

LA has an increasing number of outlets for **classical music**. The Los Angeles Philharmonic (☎ 213/850-2000, ⓦ www.laphil.org), the city's big name, performs regularly during the year; the Los Angeles Chamber Orchestra (☎ 213/622-7001, ⓦ www.laco.org) performs at assorted venues; and the Da Camera Society (☎ 213/477-2929, ⓦ www.dacamera.org) offers chamber works in stunning settings, from grand churches to legendary modernist homes.

As for **opera**, LA Opera (☎ 213/972-8001, ⓦ www.losangelesopera.com) stages productions between September and June, at downtown's Music Center, while Orange County's Opera Pacific in Costa Mesa (☎ 1-800/34-OPERA, ⓦ www. operapacific.org) is a similar, classics-oriented alternative. The city's most exciting company is Long Beach Opera (☎ 562/439-2580, ⓦ www.longbeachopera.org), which puts on challenging but well-regarded performances of modern and lesser-known operas. **Dance** in Los Angeles has its annual big event with UCLA's Dance Kaleidoscope (☎ 323/343-5120, ⓦ www.performingarts.ucla.edu), held over two weeks in July.

Disney Hall 1st St at Grand Ave, downtown ☎ 213/850-2000, ⓦ wdch.laphil.com. Home of the LA Philharmonic, a striking Frank Gehry design (see p.1052) hosting many kinds of arts groups.
Dorothy Chandler Pavilion in the Music Center, 135 N Grand Ave, downtown ☎ 213/972-7211, ⓦ www.musiccenter.org. Warhorse of the arts world, used by LA Opera and other top names.
Greek Theatre 2700 N Vermont Ave, Griffith Park ☎ 323/665-1927, ⓦ www.greektheatrela.com. A broad range of mainstream music acts at this outdoor, summer-only venue.
Hollywood Bowl 2301 N Highland Ave, Hollywood ☎ 323/850-2000, ⓦ www.hollywoodbowl.org. The LA Philharmonic gives open-air summer concerts (July–Sept Tues–Sat evenings) at this huge bandshell (see p.1058), leaning toward familiar pops offerings.
John Anson Ford Theater 2850 Cahuenga Blvd, Hollywood ☎ 323/461-3673, ⓦ wwww.fordamphi theatre.org. As well as UCLA's summer "Dance

Kaleidoscope," this open-air venue also has eclectic productions by local groups.
Orange County Performing Arts Center 600 Town Center Drive, Costa Mesa ☎ 714/556-ARTS, ⓦ www.pacificsymphony.org. Home of the Pacific Symphony Orchestra and Opera Pacific, as well as touring big names in pop and jazz.
Pasadena Dance Theater 1985 Locust Ave, Pasadena ☎ 626/683-3459, ⓦ www.pasadena dance.org. Prominent San Gabriel Valley dance venue, hosting many diverse groups during the year.
Shrine Auditorium 665 W Jefferson Blvd ☎ 213/749-5123, box office at 655 S Hill St. A striking white Islamic-domed complex hosting shows by choral gospel groups and touring pop acts.
UCLA Center for the Performing Arts ☎ 310/825-4401, ⓦ www.performingarts.ucla.edu. Coordinates a wide range of touring companies, and also runs the experimentally inclined "Art of Dance" series between Sept and June.

Comedy

The **comedy** scene in LA has long been a national proving ground for aspiring jokesters, and it's also a good place to catch live performances by established names as well as up-and-comers. The better-known places are open nightly, but are often solidly booked on weekends. Cover is usually $10–25.

Comedy & Magic Club 1018 Hermosa Ave, Hermosa Beach ☎ 310/372-1193. Strange couplings of magic acts and comedians, highlighted by Jay

Leno occasionally testing material here.
Comedy Store 8433 W Sunset Blvd, West Hollywood ☎ 323/650-6268. LA's premier comedy

showcase and popular enough to be spread over three rooms – which means there's usually space, even at weekends.

Groundlings Theater 7307 Melrose Ave, Hollywood ☎323/934-4747. Only the gifted survive at this pioneering improvisation venue, where Pee Wee Herman got his start.

Improv Olympic West 6366 Santa Monica Blvd, Hollywood ☎323/962-7560. A spot for those who like their improv drawn out and elaborate, with comedy routines more like short theater pieces than wacky one-liners.

The Improvisation 8162 Melrose Ave, West Hollywood ☎323/651-2583. Prime destination for comedy-lovers and known for hosting some of the best acts in the area. Part of a national chain.

Laugh Factory 8001 Sunset Blvd, West Hollywood ☎323/656-1336. Nightly stand-ups of varying standards and reputations, with the occasional big name. Features a variable open-mike night.

Theater

Not surprisingly, LA has a very active **theater** scene, with countless venues large and small spread all over town; ticket services like LA Stage Alliance (☎213/614-0556, ⓦwww.theatrela.org) provide full-price and half-price tickets and take reservations. The *LA Weekly* and the *LA Times* Friday "Calendar" section both have full listings and reviews.

Ahmanson Theatre/Mark Taper Forum at the Music Center, 135 N Grand Ave, downtown ☎213/972-0700, ⓦwww.taperahmanson.com. Institutional, mainstream theater, with agreeable classics and, less frequently, new plays.

Alex Theater 216 N Brand Blvd, Glendale ☎818/243-ALEX, ⓦwww.alextheatre.org. A gloriously restored movie palace – with a great neon spike and quasi-Egyptian forecourt – hosting a fine range of musical theater, dance, comedy, and film.

The Complex 6476 Santa Monica Blvd, Hollywood ☎323/465-0383. An association of five small theaters and studios putting on innovative works you might not see anywhere else.

Odyssey Theatre Ensemble 2055 S Sepulveda Blvd, West LA ☎310/477-2055, ⓦwww.odyssey theatre.com. Well-respected Westside theater company with a modernist bent, offering a range of quality productions on three stages for decent prices.

Pantages Theater 6233 Hollywood Blvd ☎323/468-1770. An exquisite Art Deco theater, in the heart of historic Hollywood, hosting major touring Broadway productions.

Stages Theatre Center 1540 N McCadden Place, Hollywood ☎323/465-1010, ⓦwww.stages theatrecenter.com. With three stages offering twenty to one hundred seats, this is an excellent place to catch a wide range of comedies and dramas.

Theatre West 3333 Cahuenga Blvd W, Hollywood ☎323/851-7977, ⓦwww.theatrewest.org. A fine spot to see inventive, sometimes odd, productions with a troupe of solid up-and-comers.

Pro sports in LA

Baseball: the **LA Dodgers** (☎323/2241-HIT, ⓦwww.dodgers.com) play at Dodger Stadium near downtown, seats $8–30 or more; the renamed **LA Angels** of Anaheim (☎1-888/796-4256, ⓦwww.angelsbaseball.com) at Anaheim Stadium in Orange County, seats $7–35.

Basketball: the **Lakers** (tickets $25–250; ☎213/480-3232, ⓦwww.lakers.com), Clippers ($12–220; ☎213/742-7430, ⓦwww.clippers.com), and women's **Sparks** ($5–50; ☎1-877/44-SPARKS, ⓦwww.wnba.com/sparks) all play at the Staples Center, south of downtown.

Football: the 102,000-seat **Rose Bowl** (☎626/577-3100, ⓦwww.rosebowlstadium. com) is the site of Pasadena's New Years Day college football game, but LA hasn't had a pro franchise in more than a decade.

Hockey: the **Kings** are based at Staples Center ($25–120; ☎1-888/KINGS-LA, ⓦwww.lakings.com), and Orange County's **Anaheim Ducks** play at Arrowhead Pond ($20–175; ☎714/704-2500, ⓦwww.anaheimducks.com).

Soccer: the **Galaxy** ($20–55; ☎1-877/3-GALAXY, ⓦwww.lagalaxy.com) plays at the Home Depot Center in the South Bay city of Carson.

Film

Many films are often released in LA months (or years) before they play anywhere else. You can catch **mainstream releases** in any mall-based multiplex, but if you're after golden-age-of-film **atmosphere**, head for one of the historic movie palaces or evocative second-run houses listed below – or check out the Last Remaining Seats festival in June (ⓦ www.laconservancy.org).

Aero 1328 Montana Ave, Santa Monica ☎ 310/395-4990, ⓦ www.aerotheatre.com. Thanks to a nice restoration, you can watch classic and art-house movies in this fine old venue from 1940.

Bing at the LA County Art Museum, 5905 Wilshire Blvd, Mid-Wilshire ☎ 323/857-6010. Offers afternoon screenings of Warner Brothers classics for just $3, as well as full-priced evening programs of classic, independent, foreign, art-house, and revival cinema.

Chinese 6925 Hollywood Blvd, Hollywood ☎ 323/464-8111. Landmark cinema showing mainstream fare with a large main screen, six-track stereo sound, and wild chinoiserie interior.

Egyptian 6712 Hollywood Blvd, Hollywood ☎ 323/466-FILM. Renovated showcase for classic and foreign films, in the middle of historic Hollywood (see p.1056).

El Capitan 6834 Hollywood Blvd, Hollywood ☎ 323/467-7674. Legendary Hollywood venue restored to full glory and renovated a second time.

Expect to see plenty of animated and live-action Disney fare.

Nuart 11272 Santa Monica Blvd, West LA ☎ 310/478-6379. Rarely seen classics, foreign films, documentaries, and sometimes Oscar contenders in Dec.

Silent Movie 611 N Fairfax Ave, West LA ☎ 323/655-2510. Fine showings of silent Chaplin, Laurel and Hardy, Ramon Navarro thrillers, and so on. Every show is accompanied by an organist.

Village 961 Broxton Ave, Westwood ☎ 310/208-5576. One of the best places to watch a movie in LA, equipped with a giant screen, fine seats, and modern sound system, and a frequent spot for Hollywood premieres.

Warner Grand 478 W 6th St, San Pedro ☎ 310/548-7672, ⓦ www.warnergrand.org. Well worth a trip to the LA harbor to see the glory of this 1931 Art Deco masterpiece. Having been restored twice, the theater is now a repertory cinema and performing arts hall.

Shopping

Not surprisingly for a city identified with mass consumerism, you can buy virtually anything in LA. The big department stores and exclusive **Rodeo Drive** are the first options for many tourists, along with the city's massive **malls**: **CityWalk** at Universal Studios (☎ 818/508-9600) is a bland but popular choice, while West Hollywood's **Beverly Center**, at Beverly and La Cienega boulevards (☎ 310/854-0070), has designer stores and cinemas. The **Century City Mall**, 10250 Santa Monica Blvd (☎ 310/553-5300), West LA's **Grove**, 6301 W 3rd St (☎ 323/571-8830), and **Hollywood & Highland**, at that Hollywood intersection (☎ 323/960-2331), are the other prominent names. Many chic boutiques line **Melrose Avenue** between La Brea and Fairfax avenues.

Books

Acres of Books 240 Long Beach Blvd, Long Beach ☎ 562/437-6980. LA's largest, and most disorganized, secondhand collection. You may not be able to find the exact title you're looking for, but chances are you'll stumble across something good.

Book Soup 8818 Sunset Blvd, West Hollywood ☎ 323/659-3110. Right on the Sunset Strip and packed to the gills with an eclectic selection, this shop is as good for celebrity sightings as it is for browsing.

Dutton's 11975 San Vicente Blvd, Brentwood ☎ 310/476-6263. One of LA's best general bookstores, and very popular with locals. A second branch in Beverly Hills, at 447 N Canon Drive (☎ 310/281-0997).

Hennessey and Ingalls 214 Wilshire Blvd, Santa Monica ☎ 310/458-9074. An impressive range of coffee-table art and architecture books makes this among the best of its kind in LA. While there are many cut-rate remainders, the books you'll likely want are priced at premium.

Larry Edmunds Book Shop 6644 Hollywood Blvd, Hollywood ☎323/463-3273. Stacks of books on every aspect of film and theater, plus movie stills and posters.

Samuel French Theatre & Film Bookshop 7623 Sunset Blvd, Hollywood ☎323/876-0570. Famed for its drama and performing-arts selections, the best in town, with a prime selection of cinema books and media-oriented volumes as well.

Taschen 354 N Beverly Drive, Beverly Hills ☎310/274-4300. Fun, weird, and edifying titles that focus on everything from Renaissance art to kitsch Americana to fetish photography.

Vroman's 695 E Colorado Blvd, Pasadena ☎626/449-5320. One of the San Gabriel Valley's largest retailers for new books, and a good place to browse.

Music

Amoeba Music 6400 W Sunset Blvd, Hollywood ☎323/245-6400. Popular record store whose vast selection of titles supposedly numbers around half a million – on CD, tape, and vinyl. Also presents occasional in-store live music.

Backside Records 139 N San Fernando Rd, Burbank ☎818/559-7573. With a bent toward the vinyl-minded, this two-level, DJ-oriented store stocks both LPs and CDs with a broad range of electronica, plus some jazz, rap, and soul.

Counterpoint 5911 Franklin Ave, Hollywood ☎323/957-7965. Provides a terrific smorgasbord of used vinyl, CDs, movies on cassette and DVD, books, and even antique 78 records. Also connected to its own underground art gallery.

Record Surplus 11609 W Pico Blvd, West LA ☎310/478-4217. The best spot for used music in LA (or anywhere for that matter), loaded with ancient LPs, out-of-print CDs, new releases, and all manner of assorted junk you have to see to believe.

Vinyl Fetish 1614 N Cahuenga Blvd, Hollywood ☎323/957-2290. Loaded with punk, alternative, and indie sounds – plus plenty of vinyl for budding DJs – this is also a good place to discover what's new on the ever-changing LA music scene.

The Deserts

California's **deserts** occupy a quarter of the state. Largely untouched but for the three million acres used for military bases, this hot and forbidding wilderness exerts a powerful fascination for venturesome travelers. The two distinct regions are the **Low Desert** in the south, the most easily reached from LA, containing the opulent oasis of **Palm Springs** and the primeval expanse of **Joshua Tree National Park**; and the **Mojave** or **High Desert**, dominated by **Death Valley** and stretching along Hwy-395 to the sparsely populated **Owens Valley**, infamous as the place from which LA stole its water.

It is impossible to do justice to this area without a car. Palm Springs can be reached on public transit from LA, but only the periphery of Joshua Tree is accessible, and it's a long hot walk to anywhere worth seeing. You can get as far as dreary Barstow on Greyhound and Amtrak, but no transportation traverses Death Valley, leaving only the Owens Valley with daily Greyhound service between LA and Reno.

The Low Desert

Most visitors to the **Low Desert** head straight for its capital, that bastion of libertarian politics and sun-scorched refuge of the Hollywood elite, **Palm Springs**.

It's the first major town east from LA on I-10, at the center of the **Coachella Valley**, an agricultural empire that grows dates and citrus fruits in vast quantities and the toasty location of one of the country's best outdoor music festivals (Ⓦ www. coachella.com). An hour's drive east of Palm Springs is the eerily sublime landscape of **Joshua Tree National Park**.

Palm Springs

Amid lush farmland replete with golf courses, condos, and millionaires, **PALM SPRINGS** embodies a strange mix of Spanish Colonial and mid-twentieth-century modernism. Massive Mount San Jacinto looms over its low-slung buildings, casting a welcome shadow over the town in the late-afternoon heat. Ever since Hollywood stars first came here in the 1930s, laying claim to ranch estates and holing up in elite hotels, the clean dry air and sunshine have made Palm Springs irresistible to the masses. In recent years, the city has also become a major **gay** resort.

Arrival, information, and getting around

Palm Springs is 120 miles east of LA. Arriving by car, you drive into town on N Palm Canyon Drive, passing the **visitor center** at no. 2901 (daily 9am–5pm, Sun closes 4pm; Ⓣ 1-800/347-7746, Ⓦ www.palm-springs.org), a classic piece of pop architecture with an upswept roof and boomerang design. Greyhound **buses** (6 daily from LA; 3–4hr) pull in at 311 N Indian Canyon Drive, while Amtrak **trains** from LA (3 weekly) stop just south of I-10 at N Indian Avenue, about ten minutes from downtown. The local operator SunBus (6am–8pm; tickets $1, day passes $1.50; Ⓣ 760/347-8628, Ⓦ www.sunline.org) circulates in all the local resort towns. One enjoyable option outside the blistering summer months is to rent a **bike** from Bighorn Bicycles, 302 N Palm Canyon Drive (Ⓣ 760/325-3367), who charge $25–35 for a half- to a full-day, depending on the model.

Companies such as Celebrity Tours, 4751 E Palm Canyon Drive (Ⓣ 760/770-2700, Ⓦ www.celebrity-tours.com), offer **tours** past celebrity homes and enclaves from $25 for a basic, 90-minute trip to $40 for more involved, 3–4 hour treks. (You can also do it yourself, with a map of the stars' homes ($7) from the visitor center.) Guided tours of Palm Springs' stash of notable **modernist architecture**, among them designs by R.M. Schindler, Albert Frye and Richard Neutra, are organized by PS Modern Tours (2hr 30min; $55; Ⓣ 760/318-6118, Ⓔ psmodern tours@aol.com).

Accommodation

Luxury **hotels** predominate in Palm Springs, but prices drop by as much as seventy percent as temperatures soar in the summer. The north end of town, along Hwy-111, holds many of the lower-priced places, including countless motels, virtually all of which have pools and air-conditioning. The prices below are **spring** and **autumn rates**; expect to pay about $20–50 more or less for winter and summer, respectively.

Ballantines 1420 N Indian Canyon Drive Ⓣ 760/320-1178, Ⓦ www.ballantineshotels. com. Remodeled motel with modern luxuries and sporting vintage 1950s kitsch in its themed rooms (bachelor pads, Hollywood glamor, etc). ❻
Casa Cody 175 S Cahuilla Rd Ⓣ 760/320-9346 or 1-800/231-2639, Ⓦ www.casacody.com. Built in the 1920s, this historic, but updated,

Southwestern-style B&B offers attractive rooms and a shady garden. A bit more comfortable than higher-priced retro-motels. ❹
Ingleside Inn 200 W Ramon Rd Ⓣ 760/325-0046 or 1-800/772-6655, Ⓦ www.inglesideinn.com. Historic downtown option, where the guest list has included Dalí, Garbo, and Brando. For double the price of a standard unit, you can get a room with

antiques, fireplace, whirlpool tub, or patio. ❹–❻
Orbit Inn 562 W Arenas Rd ☎760/323-3585
Ⓦwww.orbitin.com. About the best that can be
expected when recasting a 1957 motel into a suave,
yuppie-friendly hotel. Drink cutely named cocktails
by the pool and lounge in stylish rooms filled with
arch-modern decor. ❼
Palm Court Inn 1983 N Palm Canyon Drive
☎760/416-2333, Ⓦwww.palmcourt-inn.com.
Nice motel with two pools, a Jacuzzi, and gym,
plus free continental breakfast and comfortable
rooms. ❸

Villa Royale 1620 S Indian Trail ☎760/327-2314,
Ⓦwww.villaroyale.com. Elegant inn with nicely
furnished rooms and suites, as well as in-room
Jacuzzis and a good restaurant. ❼

The Willows 412 W Tahquitz Canyon
☎760/320-0771, Ⓦwww.thewillowspalm
springs.com. The very reason celebrities were first
attracted to Palm Springs in the 1930s: a stunning
hangout for the Hollywood elite that provides great
views and opulent rooms. ❾

Downtown Palm Springs

Downtown Palm Springs stretches for half a mile along **Palm Canyon Drive**, a
wide, bright, and modern strip of chain stores that has engulfed the town's quaint
Spanish Colonial-style buildings. Shops run the gamut from upscale boutiques
and middlebrow art galleries to tacky T-shirt emporia and bookstores devoted
exclusively to dead celebrities.

The luxuriously housed **Palm Springs Desert Museum**, 101 Museum Drive
(Tues, Wed & Fri–Sun 10am–5pm, Thurs noon–8pm; summer Fri–Sun only,
10am–5pm; $12.50, children $5; Ⓦwww.psmuseum.org), is strong on Native
American and Southwestern art, as well as grand American landscaping painting
from the nineteenth century. Some interesting natural-science exhibits focus on
the animal and plant life of the desert, demonstrating that it's not all sandstorms
and rattlesnakes. There is a modern art gallery and some lovely sculpture courts on
the grounds, and the museum hosts performances of music, theater, comedy, and
dance in the 450-seat **Annenberg Theater** (tickets ☎760/325-4490).

There's an anarchic piece of landscape gardening at **Moorten Botanical Gardens**, 1701 S Palm Canyon Drive (Mon, Tues, Thurs–Sat 9am–4.30pm, Sun
10am–4pm; $3; Ⓦwww.palmsprings.com/moorten), an odd cornucopia of desert
plants and cacti, in settings designed to simulate their natural environments,
but lumped together in no particular order. Finally, near the airport, the **Palm
Springs Air Museum**, 745 N Gene Autry Trail (daily 10am–5pm; $10; Ⓦwww.
palmspringsairmuseum.org), has an impressive collection of World War II fighters
and bombers, including Spitfires, Tomcats, and a B-17 Flying Fortress.

Around Palm Springs

Most visitors to Palm Springs never leave the poolside, but desert enthusiasts still
visit to hike and ride in the **Indian Canyons** (daily 8am–5pm, summer schedule
varies; $8; Ⓦwww.indian-canyons.com), three miles southeast of downtown
along S Palm Canyon Drive, where centuries ago, ancestors of the Cahuilla developed extensive agricultural communities. The canyons are about fifteen miles
long, and can be toured by car, although it's worth walking at least a few miles;
the easiest trails lead past the waterfalls, rocky gorges, and copious palm trees of
Palm Canyon (3 miles) and **Andreas Canyon** (1 mile). Some areas are set aside
for **trailblazing** in jeeps and four-wheel-drive vehicles: you can rent one from
Off-Road Rentals, four miles north of town at 59511 Hwy-111 (Sept–June only;
$35 per hour; ☎760/325-0376, Ⓦwww.offroadrentals.com), or take a guided jeep
adventure around the Santa Rosa Mountains with Desert Adventures, 67555 E
Palm Canyon Drive, Cathedral City (2–4hr; $75–125; ☎760/324-JEEP, Ⓦwww.
red-jeep.com).

If the desert heat becomes too much to bear, large cable cars grind and sway
over eight thousand feet up the **Palm Springs Aerial Tramway**, Tramway Road,

just off Hwy-111 north of Palm Springs (daily 10am–9pm, weekends opens 8am; $21.50, children $14.50; ⓦ www.pstramway.com), heading to the striking 10,815-foot summit of Mount San Jacinto, where you can hike, camp, and dine amid spectacular views. In the opposite direction from Palm Springs, a few miles east of town, **PALM DESERT** is, like the sun-baked towns further east, riddled with golf courses and elite resorts. Its other claim to fame is the mile-long **El Paseo**, a boutique-rich strip that some claim as the "Rodeo Drive of the Desert," though it's doubtful that fabled Beverly Hills route ever hosted anything quite so kitschy as an annual golf-cart parade (ⓦ www.golfcartparade.com). Beyond retirees on the green, Palm Desert is also home to the **Living Desert**, a combination garden and zoo at 47900 Portola Ave, Palm Desert (daily: summer 8.30am–1pm; rest of year 9am–5pm; $12, summer $8.75; ⓦ www.livingdesert.org), which is rich with cactus and palm gardens, and throws in an incongruous section devoted to African desert animals, such as giraffes, zebras, cheetahs, and warthogs.

Eating and drinking

Although most of the better **restaurants** in Palm Springs are ultra-expensive, more reasonable options can be found with a little effort; alternatively, head to gay-friendly **Cathedral City** ("Cat City"), five miles east along Hwy-111. All listings are in Palm Springs unless otherwise stated.

Daily Grill 73061 El Paseo, Palm Desert ⓣ 760/779-9911. Busy but stylish diner, with affordable prices for large helpings of steak, fish, and chicken pot pie. Part of a national chain.

El Gallito 68820 Grove St, Cathedral City ⓣ 760/328-7794. Just east of downtown Palm Springs, a busy Mexican cantina that has the best food for miles and often a long wait – get there around 6pm to avoid the masses.

El Mirasol 140 E Palm Canyon Drive ⓣ 760/323-0721. Fine, affordable Mexican dining that offers a mix of familiar, affordable staples and more authentic fare from Zacatecas and other regions.

Las Casuelas 368 N Palm Canyon Drive ⓣ 760/325-3213. Local Mexican favorite that's been around since 1958, and remains popular for its hefty portions and laid-back atmosphere. The best bet in a local chain.

 Le Vallauris 385 W Tahquitz Canyon Way, next to the Desert Museum ⓣ 760/325-

5059. Excellent contemporary California-Mediterranean cuisine in a gorgeous setting, with sky-high prices and the occasional B-list celebrity dropping in. Reservations only.

Native Foods 1775 E Palm Canyon Drive ⓣ 760/416-0070. One of the town's better choices for cheap vegetarian cuisine – with veggie pizzas, burgers, and tacos – located in a shopping mall. Also in Palm Desert at 73-890 El Paseo (ⓣ 760/836-9396).

Shame on the Moon 69950 Frank Sinatra Drive, Rancho Mirage ⓣ 760/324-5515. Upscale California cuisine and excellent service are the draw here, attracting a loyal gay clientele. Located five miles east of downtown Palm Springs.

Thai Smile 651 N Palm Canyon Drive ⓣ 760/320-5503. Uninspiring decor but great, authentic Thai curry and noodle dishes, all at very reasonable prices.

Joshua Tree National Park

Where the low Colorado Desert meets the high Mojave northeast of Palm Springs, **JOSHUA TREE NATIONAL PARK** (ⓦ www.nps.gov/jotr) protects 1250 square miles of grotesquely gnarled plants, which aren't trees at all, but a type of **yucca**, an agave. Joshua trees, named by Mormons in the 1850s who saw in their craggy branches the arms of Joshua pointing to the promised land, can rise up to forty feet tall, but have to contend with extreme aridity and rocky soil. All around lie great heaps of boulders, pushed up by the Pinto Mountain fault, their edges rounded and smoothed by flash floods and harsh winds.

This unearthly landscape is ethereal at sunrise or sunset, when the desert floor is bathed in red light; at noon it can be a threatening furnace, with temperatures sometimes topping 125°F in summer, and rising even higher in the Low Desert section of the park below 3000ft. Still, the park attracts campers, day-trippers, and rock-climbers for its unspoiled beauty, gold-mine ruins, ancient petroglyphs, and incredible rock formations. As with any desert, never venture anywhere without a map and always use four-wheel-drive on unmarked roads. When hiking, stick to the trails: Joshua Tree is full of abandoned gold mines, so watch for loose gravel, never trust the safety of ladders or timber, and bear in mind that the rangers rarely check mines for casualties. Even on the simpler trails, allow around an hour per mile.

One of the easiest hikes (3 miles long, foot-travel only) starts one-and-a-half miles from Canyon Road, six miles from the visitor center at Twentynine Palms,

△ Joshua Tree National Park

at **Fortynine Palms Oasis**. West of the oasis, quartz boulders tower around the *Indian Cove* campground; a trail from the eastern branch of the campground road heads to **Rattlesnake Canyon**, where, after rainfall, the streams and waterfalls break an otherwise eerie silence among the monoliths.

Moving south into the main body of the park, the **Wonderland of Rocks** features rounded granite boulders that draw rock-climbers from around the world. Well-signposted nature trails lead one mile to **Hidden Valley**, where cattle-rustlers used to hide out, and to the rain-fed **Barker Dam**, one mile to the east. The latter is Joshua Tree's crucial water supply, built by cattlemen around the turn of the twentieth century. One negotiable trail climbs four miles past abandoned mines, where some buildings and equipment are still intact, to **Lost Horse Mine**, 450ft up – which once produced around $20,000 in gold a week, and now consists of antiquated foundations and equipment.

You can find a brilliant desert panorama of badlands and mountains at the 5185-foot **Keys View** nearby, from where Geology Tour Road leads down to the east through the best of Joshua Tree's **rock formations** and, further on, to the **Cholla Cactus Garden**.

Practicalities

Less than an hour's drive northeast from Palm Springs, Joshua Tree National Park (always open; $15 per vehicle for 7 days, $5 per cyclist or hiker) is best approached along Hwy-62, which branches off I-10. You can enter the park via the **west entrance**, on Park Blvd in the town of Joshua Tree (daily 8am–5pm; ☏760/366-1855), or the **north entrance** at Twentynine Palms, where you'll also find the **Oasis Visitor Center**, 74485 National Park Drive (daily 8am–5pm; ☏760/367-5500). Alternatively, if you're coming from the south, there's another entry at the **Cottonwood Visitor Center** (daily 9am–3pm; ☏760/367-5500), seven miles north of I-10.

The park has nine established **campgrounds**, all in the northwest except for one at Cottonwood. Only two have water – *Black Rock Canyon* and *Cottonwood* (both $10) – and except for *Indian Cove* ($10), all the others are $5. You can reserve sites at *Black Rock*, *Sheep Pass* and *Indian Cove* by contacting the park reservation center (☏1-800/365-CAMP, ⓦreservations.nps.gov). The rest are operated on a first-come, first-served basis. Come prepared – gathering firewood is not allowed, and you should stock up on water. There are good **motels** and decent restaurants in **TWENTYNINE PALMS**, a small desert town two minutes' drive from the park. The cheapest decent **place to stay** is the *El Rancho Dolores*, 73352 Inn Ave (☏760/367-3528, ⓦwww.virtual29.com/elrancho; ❷), although more pleasant is the historic *Twentynine Palms Inn*, nearby at no. 73950 (☏760/367-3505, ⓦwww.29palmsinn.com; ❺), with its nice wooden cabins and adobe bungalows, and fine **restaurant** where the bread is homemade and the vegetables are fresh from an onsite garden. Otherwise, you can try the tasty, authentic Mexican fare at *Ramona's*, at no. 72115 (☏760/367-1929). Morongo Basin Transit Authority **buses** (☏760/367-7433 or 1-800/794-6282, ⓦwww.mbtabus.com) run between Palm Springs and Twentynine Palms (1 hr 15min; $10 one way, $15 roundtrip), but not into the park itself.

The High Desert

The stretches of the **Mojave Desert** that most people see from the road are predictably desolate. Consequently few visitors are inspired to explore further, but this **High Desert** – sited above 2000ft – offers some of the most dramatic scenery in Southern California, rolling with lush grasses, startling volcanic formations, large stands of Joshua trees, and even, in spots, piñon pines.

Death Valley National Park

DEATH VALLEY is the hottest place on earth. It's also almost entirely devoid of shade, much less water – carry plenty for both car and body. Its sculpted rock layers form deeply shadowed, eroded crevices at the foot of silhouetted hills, their exotic minerals turning ancient mudflats into rainbows of sunlit iridescence. The valley was named by a party of white settlers who stumbled through in 1849, looking for a short cut to the Gold Rush towns; they survived despite running out of food and water. Throughout the summer, the **temperature** in Death Valley averages 112°F, and the ground can reach near boiling point. Better to come during the spring, when wildflowers are in bloom and it's generally mild and dry.

The central north–south valley contains two main outposts, **Stovepipe Wells** and **Furnace Creek**, where the **visitor center** (daily 8am–5pm; seven-day park pass $20 per vehicle, $10 per pedestrian or cyclist; ☎760/786-3200, ⓦwww.nps.gov/deva) is located.

Many of the most unusual sights are located south of Furnace Creek. A good first stop, seven miles along Hwy-178/Badwater Road, is the **Artist's Palette**, an eroded hillside covered in an intensely colored mosaic of red, gold, black, and green. A few miles further south, a dirt road heading west leads to **Devil's Golf Course**, a field of salt pinnacles and hummocks protruding a couple of feet from the desert floor. Another four miles on, **Badwater** is an unpalatable but nonpoisonous 30-foot-wide pool of water, loaded with chloride and sulphates. From the pool, a pair of four-mile hikes crossing the hot valley floor drop two feet down to the lowest point in the western hemisphere, 282ft below sea level.

The badlands around **Zabriskie Point**, overlooking Badwater and the Artist's Palette off Hwy-190, four miles south of Furnace Creek, were the inspiration for Antonioni's eponymous 1970 movie. More visually appealing is **Dante's View**, twenty-one miles south on 190 and ten miles along a very steep access road; its best vista of the wide, parched desert floor is during the early morning, when the pink-and-gold Panamint Mountains are highlighted by the rising sun. Near Stovepipe Wells, some thirty miles northwest of Furnace Creek, spread fifteen rippled and contoured square miles of ever-changing **sand dunes**.

Hordes of overheated tourists wait patiently to wander through the surreal luxury of **Scotty's Castle** (50min tours daily 9.30am–4pm; $11; reservations ☎760/786-2392), forty miles north of Stovepipe Wells. Built in the 1920s as the $2-million desert retreat of Chicago insurance broker Albert Johnson, it was named after "Death Valley" Scotty, a cowboy and prospector who managed the construction and claimed the house was his own and financed by a hidden gold mine. Tours of the opulently furnished house take in the decorative wooden ceilings, indoor waterfalls, and a remote-controlled player piano. The house remains as it was when Johnson died in 1948. Scotty himself lived here until 1954, and is buried just behind the house.

Eight miles west gapes the half-mile-wide **Ubehebe Crater**, the rust-tinged result of a massive volcanic explosion some three thousand years ago; half a mile south sits its thousand-year-old younger brother, **Little Hebe**. Beyond the craters the road continues south for another twenty dusty miles to **Racetrack Valley**, a two-and-a-half-mile mudflat across which giant boulders seem slowly to be racing, leaving faint trails in their wake.

Practicalities

If you plan to **stay**, you must reserve ahead. Furnace Creek Resort (☎760/786-2345 or 1-800/236-7916, ⊛www.furnacecreekresort.com) operates two hotels on natural oases – the gorgeous 1920s adobe *Furnace Creek Inn* (❾), and the ordinary *Furnace Creek Ranch* (❻), which has two **restaurants** and a nice bar. More reasonable is *Stovepipe Wells Village* (☎760/786-2387, ⊛www.stovepipewells.com; ❺) on Hwy-190 about thirty miles northwest of Furnace Creek, offering its own mineral-water pool and restaurant. **Camping** in one of the many park-service campgrounds costs $12–14, depending on facilities and location, or is free if you don't mind being up in the Panamint Range, far from the valley's sights: the only campground that takes reservations is *Furnace Creek* ($12–18; ☎1-800/365-CAMP), just north of town.

The High Sierra and the Owens Valley

The towering **eastern** peaks of the **HIGH SIERRA** drop abruptly to the empty landscape of the **OWENS VALLEY**, sixty miles west of Death Valley. Almost the entire range is wilderness: well-maintained roads lead to trailheads at over ten thousand feet, providing access to the stark terrain of spires, glaciers, and clear mountain lakes. US-395 is the lifeline of the area connecting several small towns, all with plenty of budget motels. As there is virtually **no public transporation** in this area (except for CREST; see p.1085), you'll really need a **car** to get around.

Mount Whitney and Lone Pine

Rising out of the northern Mojave Desert, the mountainous backbone of the Sierra Nevada announces itself with a bang two hundred miles north of Los Angeles at 14,497-foot **Mount Whitney**, the highest point in the lower 48 states. A silver-gray ridge of pinnacles forms a nearly sheer wall of granite, dominating the small roadside town of **LONE PINE** eleven thousand feet below. **Motels** here include the *Dow Villa Motel/Historic Dow Hotel* at 310 S Main St (☎760/876-5521 or 1-800/824-9317, ⊛www.dowvillamotel.com; ❹), where John Wayne always stayed when filming in the area, and the *Best Western Frontier Motel*, 1008 S Main St (☎760/876-5571 or 1-800/780-7234; ❹). Those headed north might want to push on sixteen miles to Independence, where the slightly run-down but atmospheric *Winnedumah Hotel*, 211 N Edwards St (☎760/878-2040, ⊛www.winnedumah.com; B&B ❹). You can **camp** at *Tuttle Creek* campground ($5; no water) on Horseshoe Meadow Road some four miles west of Lone Pine beyond the Alabama Hills (see below). The *Pizza Factory*, 301 S Main St (☎760/876-4707), and the diner-style *Mt Whitney Restaurant*, 227 S Main St (☎760/876-5751), are decent places to **eat**. The **Eastern Sierra Interagency Visitor Center**, a mile south of town on US-395 at the junction of Hwy-136 (daily 8am–5pm; ☎760/876-6222), is a great source of information about the Owens Valley.

Many early Westerns, and the epic *Gunga Din*, were filmed in the **Alabama Hills** to the west, a rugged expanse of bizarrely eroded sedimentary rock. Some of the oddest formations are linked by the **Picture Rocks Circle**, a paved road that loops around from Whitney Portal Road, passing rocks shaped like bullfrogs, walruses, and baboons.

Two thousand eager souls make the strenuous 22-mile roundtrip **hike** (12–16hr; 6100ft ascent) to the summit of Mount Whitney each summer (generally snow free June–Oct), some doing it in a day, others camping along the way. Permits are awarded by lottery: applications (⊛www.fs.fed.us/r5/inyo) are only accepted in February. Any permits left after the lottery are available from the Wilderness Permit Office, Inyo National Forest, 351 Pacu Lane, Suite 200, Bishop, CA 93514 (℡760/873-2400). All hikers pay a $15 fee.

One-day ascents start at dawn from either the *Whitney Portal* **campground** (late May to mid-Oct; ℡1-877/444-6777; $16), or the one-night-only first-come, first-served *Whitney Trailhead* site ($8) at the end of twisting Whitney Portal Road, reachable via shuttle bus with Lonesome Polecat (℡760/876-8232). The trail cuts up to boulder-strewn Trail Crest Pass, the southern end of the 211-mile John Muir Trail to Yosemite, then climbs along the top of vertical cliffs to the rounded summit.

Big Pine and the White Mountains

Nearly fifty miles north, hikes lead from the end of Glacier Lodge Road, ten miles west of nondescript **BIG PINE**, up to the **Palisades Glacier**, the southernmost glacier in the northern hemisphere. Along the opposite wall of the five-mile-wide Owens Valley, the ancient, bald, and dry **White Mountains** are home to the gnarled **bristlecone pines**, the oldest living things on earth, some first sprouting over four thousand years ago. Battered and beaten by the harsh environment into contorted but beautiful shapes, even when dead the wood can withstand the wind-driven ice and sand for another thousand years.

The most accessible trees are in **Schulman Grove**, 24 miles east of Big Pine, (late May–Oct; $3 per person, or $5 per vehicle; recorded info on ℡760/873-2500), where two trails radiate out from the visitor center. The mile-long **Discovery Trail**, which passes some photogenic examples; while a longer loop passes but intentionally fails to identify the oldest tree, the 4700-year-old Methuselah.

In the White Mountains there's the free, waterless *Grandview* **campground**, or you can **stay** back in Big Pine at the *Big Pine Motel*, 370 S Main St (℡760/938-2282; ❹).

Bishop

BISHOP, to a Californian, means outdoor pursuits. The largest town (population 3500) in the Owens Valley, it's an excellent base for cross-country skiing, fly-fishing, and especially rock-climbing. **Motels**, such as the *El Rancho*, 274 W Lagoon St (℡760/872-9251 or 1-888/872-9251; ❸), the *Thunderbird*, 190 W Pine St (℡760/873-4215; ❸), and bargain restaurants can be found within a block of US-395. The **visitor center** at 690 N Main St (Mon–Fri 9am–4.30pm, Sat & Sun 10am–4pm; ℡760/873-8405, ⓦwww.bishopvisitor.com) can provide details of the many **adventure travel specialists** based in town. For **hiking** and **camping** information, the White Mountain Ranger Station, 798 N Main St (May–Oct daily; rest of year Mon–Fri; call for hours; ℡760/873-2500), will be of more use.

Mammoth Lakes

Forty miles north along US-395 from Bishop, then three miles west on Hwy-203, the resort town of **MAMMOTH LAKES** offers the state's premier ski slopes outside the Lake Tahoe basin, and in summer hosts on- and off-road bike races. The setting is stunning, but the town is pricey and prone to testosterone overload. To ski **Mammoth Mountain** (℡1-800/MAMMOTH, ⓦwww.mammothmountain.com), which looms up behind the resort, pick up **lift tickets** ($78 a day) from the Main Lodge on Minaret Road, where you can also rent **equipment** ($32 for basic skis, boots, and poles), and book three-hour **lessons** ($67). In summer, fifty miles of snow-free slopes transform themselves into the 3500-acre **Mammoth Moun-**

tain Bike Park (one-day pass with unlimited rides on the bike shuttle and gondola $35; add $40 for bike rental).

One appealing summer-only destination is the **Devil's Postpile National Monument**, seven miles southwest of Mammoth Mountain ($7, includes shuttle bus; ⓦwww.nps.gov/depo). A collection of slender, blue-gray basaltic columns, some as tall as sixty feet, the Postpile was formed as lava from a volcanic eruption cooled and fractured into multi-sided forms. From here, a two-mile hike along the San Joaquin River leads to the 101-foot **Rainbow Falls**, which refract the midday sun perfectly.

Practicalities

Year-round Carson Ridgecrest Eastern Sierra Transit (CREST) **buses** (ⓣ760/872-1901 or ⓣ1-800/922-1930) stop in the *McDonald's* parking lot on Hwy-203. During the ski season, get around on the five-line Mammoth Shuttle (ⓣ760/934-3030). For information, go to the combined US Forest Service **ranger station** and Mammoth Lakes **visitor center**, on the main highway half a mile east of the town center (daily 8am–5pm; ⓣ760/924-5500, ⓦwww.visitmammoth.com).

Mammoth's plentiful **accommodation** is cheapest in summer (and is what we've quoted here); expect one price range higher during the ski season. For reasonably priced B&B close to downtown visit the rambling *Cinnamon Bear Inn*, 113 Center St (ⓣ1-800/845-2873, ⓦwww.cinnamonbearinn.com; ❺). The *Swiss Chalet Lodge*, 3776 Viewpoint Rd (ⓣ1-800/937-9477, ⓦwww.mammoth-swisschalet.com; ❹) offers motel accommodation with mountain views; while the hostel-style *Davison St. Guesthouse*, 19 Davison St (ⓣ760/924-2188; ⓦwww.mammoth-guest.com; dorms $25, rooms ❸), offers comfortable rooms, four-bed dorms and a kitchen. Central **camping** is at the fairly busy *New Shady Rest* ($15) just as you enter Mammoth from US-395. There are also campgrounds ($15) close to Devil's Postpile National Monument, and free waterless sites in the Inyo National Forest off US-395 around eleven miles north.

Mammoth has the widest selection of **restaurants** in the Owens Valley. The *Looney Bean*, Mammoth Mall, is the most vibrant café; *Schat's Bakery* 3305 Main St, serves sumptuous baked goods; and *The Stove*, 644 Old Mammoth Road, dishes up country cooking in gargantuan portions. *Whiskey Creek*, at Main and Minaret (ⓣ760/934-2555), is a lively **bar** and restaurant, with its own good microbrews; and for something fancy try *The Lakefront Restaurant*, at Tamarack Lodge (ⓣ760/934-2442), which offers superb lake views and good French-Californian cuisine – for a price.

Mono Lake, Lee Vining, and Bodie Ghost Town

The blue expanse of **Mono Lake** sits in the midst of a volcanic desert tableland at the north end of the valley. It looks like a science-fiction landscape, with two large islands, one light-colored, the other black, surrounded by salty, alkaline water. Strange sandcastle-like formations of **tufa** (calcium deposited from springs) were exposed after the City of Los Angeles extended an aqueduct into the Mono Basin through an eleven-mile tunnel. From 1941 until the 1990s the **water level** gradually dropped by over forty feet creating the biggest environmental controversy in California. Mono Lake is the primary nesting ground for the state's **California gull** population – twenty percent of the world total – and a prime stopover point for hundreds of thousands of grebes and phalaropes. Though the California Supreme Court ruled in 1983 that Mono Lake must be saved, it wasn't until 1991 that emergency action was taken.

△ Mono Lake

For more details about Mono Lake and the fight for its survival, stop by the **Mono Lake Committee Information Center**, in the small town of **LEE VINING** on US-395 (daily: July & Aug 9am–10pm; rest of year 9am–5pm; ℡760/647-6595, ⓦwww.leevining.com), or a mile north at the excellent **Mono Basin Scenic Area Visitor Center** (May–Oct daily 9am–5.30pm; ℡760/647-3044). **Motels** along US-395 include *El Mono Motel* (℡760/647-6310; ❸) and *Murphey's* (℡1-800/334-6316, ⓦwww.murpheysyosemite.com; ❹). Excellent budget **food** is served at the 🍴 *Whoa Nellie Deli*, in the Mobil gas station at the junction of US-395 and Hwy-120 just south of town. For fine dining, head five miles north to the *Mono Inn* (℡760/647-6581, ⓦwww.monoinn.com; closed Tues & Nov–April) owned by Ansel Adams's granddaughter and with lovely lake views.

Northeast of Lee Vining, in a remote, high desert valley, stands a well-preserved and evocative relic of the gold-mining 1870s. **Bodie State Park** (open all year but often inaccessible by car in winter; $3 per person; ⓦwww.parks.ca.gov) is perhaps the best **ghost town** in the US, with many of its structures still intact but not gussied up for tourists. With thirty saloons and dance halls and a population of ten thousand, it was once the raunchiest and most lawless mining camp in the west; over 150 wooden buildings survive in a state of arrested decay around the intact town center, littered with old bottles, bits of machinery, and old stagecoaches. The ruins of the mines themselves, in the hills east of town, are off limits to visitors except on the frequent tours.

The San Joaquin Valley

The vast **interior** of California is split down the middle by the **Sierra Nevada** (Spanish for "snowy range"), or High Sierra, a sawtooth range of snow-capped peaks that stands high above the semi-desert of the Owens Valley. The wide **San Joaquin Valley** in the west was made super-fertile by irrigation projects during the 1940s, and is now almost totally agricultural. Even if the nightlife begins and ends with the local ice-cream parlor, after the big cities of the coast the downshift can be quite refreshing. However, the real reason to come here is to reach the **national parks** of **Sequoia** and **Kings Canyon** – whose huge trees form the centerpiece of a rich natural landscape – and **Yosemite**, where waterfalls cascade down towering walls of silvery granite. Few roads penetrate the hundred miles of wilderness to the east, but the entire region is crisscrossed by hiking trails leading up into the pristine alpine backcountry.

The arrow-straight I-5 barrels straight up from LA to San Francisco. Six daily **trains** and frequent Greyhound **buses** run through the valley, calling at the towns along Hwy-99, in particular Merced, which has bus connections to Yosemite but otherwise doesn't merit a look-in.

Bakersfield

The first town you come to across the rocky peaks north of Los Angeles is the flat and featureless oil town of **BAKERSFIELD**. This is the unlikely home of one of the liveliest **country music** scenes in the nation, stemming from the arrival during the Depression of Midwestern farmers, with their hillbilly instruments and camp-fire songs. In the mid-1960s, the gutsy honky-tonk style of Bakersfield artists such as Merle Haggard and Buck Owens challenged the slick commercial output of Nashville, but hopes of luring the major country-music record labels to "Nashville West" foundered with the emergence of rivals like Austin, Texas.

Nevertheless, the numerous honky-tonks of Bakersfield are still jumping every Friday and Saturday night. Stetson hats and rhinestone shirts are the sartorial order of the day, and audiences span generations. Most venues are hotel lounges or restaurant backrooms; don't miss the country bar *Trouts*, 805 N Chester Ave (☎661/399-6700), for a down-to-earth honky-tonk experience. Closer to town, you might also try the *Buck Owens Crystal Palace*, 2800 Buck Owens Blvd (☎661/328-7560, ⓦwww.buckowens.com; closed Mon), where for under $10 you get a live show, dancing and access to a museum of Buck Owens memorabilia. Buck died in 2006, but his band, The Buckaroos, continue to play on Friday and Saturday nights.

Practicalities

From LA, the Amtrak Thruway bus goes to Bakersfield, where you can catch the train through the valley toward San Francisco and northern California. Several Greyhound **bus** routes require changes here too, calling at 1820 18th St. The handiest **visitor center** is at 1725 Eye St (Mon 9am–5pm; Tues–Fri 8am–5pm; ☎661/327-4421; ⓦwww.visitkern.com), and there's good information on the county website. Bargain overnight stays include the *EZ-8*, 2604 Buck Owen Blvd (☎661/322-1901; ❷), and the adjacent *La Quinta*, 3232 Riverside Drive (☎661/325-7400 or 1-800/642-4271; ❹), both pool-equipped and a short stagger from *Buck Owens Crystal Palace* (see opposite). For **food**, Zingo's at 3201 Buck Owen Blvd (☎661/321-0627) is a 24-hour truckstop where frilly-aproned waitresses deliver plates of diner staples; *24th Street Café*, 1415 24th St (☎661/323-8801), does top-rate breakfasts; *Joseph's*, hidden back off the road at 3013 F St (☎661/322-7710), serves huge calzone and other Italian dishes; and the 🌂 *Noriega Hotel*, 525 Sumner St (☎661/322-8419; closed Mon), offers excellent all-you-can-eat Basque meals at long communal tables.

Sequoia and Kings Canyon

The southernmost of the Sierra Nevada national parks, preserving ancient forests of giant sequoia trees, are Sequoia and Kings Canyon. As you might expect, **Sequoia National Park** contains the thickest concentration – and the biggest specimens – of sequoias to be found anywhere, tending (literally) to overshadow

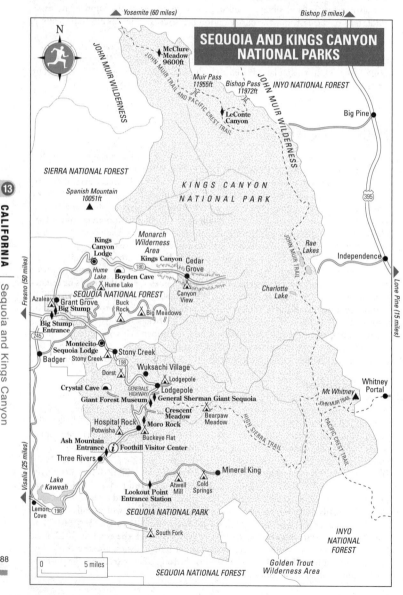

Yosemite (60 miles)

Bishop (5 miles)

SEQUOIA AND KINGS CANYON NATIONAL PARKS

N

JOHN MUIR WILDERNESS

McClure Meadow 9600ft

JOHN MUIR TRAIL AND PACIFIC CREST TRAIL

Muir Pass 11955ft

Bishop Pass 11972ft

JOHN MUIR WILDERNESS

INYO NATIONAL FOREST

LeConte Canyon

Big Pine

SIERRA NATIONAL FOREST

Spanish Mountain 10051ft

KINGS CANYON NATIONAL PARK

395

Monarch Wilderness Area

Kings Canyon Lodge

Kings Canyon

Cedar Grove

Rae Lakes

Independence

Hume Lake

Hume Lake

Boyden Cave

JOHN MUIR TRAIL

Azalea

Grant Grove

Big Stump

SEQUOIA NATIONAL FOREST

Buck Rock

Canyon View

Charlotte Lake

Big Stump Entrance

245

Big Meadows

Montecito Sequoia Lodge

Badger

Stony Creek

198

Stony Creek

Dorst

Wuksachi Village

Crystal Cave

GENERALS HIGHWAY

Lodgepole

Giant Forest Museum

General Sherman Giant Sequoia

Mt Whitney

Whitney Portal

Crescent Meadow

JOHN MUIR TRAIL

Hospital Rock

Potwisha

Moro Rock

Bearpaw Meadow

HIGH SIERRA TRAIL

PACIFIC CREST TRAIL

Ash Mountain Entrance

Buckeye Flat

Foothill Visitor Center

Three Rivers

Lake Kaweah

Atwell Mill

Cold Springs

Mineral King

Lookout Point Entrance Station

Lemon Cove

198

SEQUOIA NATIONAL PARK

South Fork

INYO NATIONAL FOREST

SEQUOIA NATIONAL FOREST

Golden Trout Wilderness Area

0   5 miles

Fresno (50 miles)

Lone Pine (15 miles)

Visalia (25 miles)

its assortment of meadows, peaks, canyons, and caves. **Kings Canyon National Park** has few big trees but compensates with a gaping canyon gored out of the rock by the Kings River as it cascades down from the High Sierra. The few established sights of both parks are near the main roads, leaving the vast majority of the landscape untrammeled and unspoiled, but well within reach for willing hikers.

Arrival and information

No **public transportation** of any kind serves the parks, but they're easily reached by **car**: the closest large town is **Visalia**, just under fifty miles away on Hwy-198, or a slightly longer, but faster, drive uses Hwy-180 from Fresno: note that there is **no gas** available in the parks. The **entrance fee** ($20 per car, $10 per pedestrian or cyclist: valid seven days) entitles you to a detailed map of the paired parks, and a copy of *The Guide*, a free seasonal newspaper which details accommodation, guided hikes, and other activities. The two parks are separate but jointly run; for **information** call ☏559/565-3341 or visit ⓦwww.nps.gov/seki.

Accommodation and eating

The least expensive **rooms** are in the motels near the park entrances: *Sierra Inn Motel* (☏559/338-0678, ⓕ338-0789; ❸), fourteen miles west of the southern entrance on Hwy-180 and, near the southern entrance on Hwy-198, *Gateway Lodge* (☏559/561-4133, ⓦwww.gateway-sequoia.com; ❺). Inside the parks, all facilities are managed by Kings Canyon Park Services (KCPS; ☏559/335-5500 or 1-866/522-6966, ⓦwww.sequoia-kingscanyon.com; ❸–❼) who operate cabins and hotel units at Stony Creek, Grant Grove, and Cedar Grove; and Delaware North Companies Parks and Resorts (DNCPR; ☏559/565-3341 or 1-888/252-5757, ⓦwww.visitsequoia.com; ❼) who run the upmarket *Wuksachi Lodge* in Sequoia. Space is at a premium during the high season (May to mid-Oct), but you can usually pick up cancellations on the day. In winter you can still camp, but the cheapest roofed accommodation is in cabins at Grant Grove for $120.

Campgrounds are dotted all over both parks, most charging $18 a pitch. In **Sequoia**, the busiest campground is *Lodgepole*, which you can reserve up to five months in advance through the National Park Reservation System (☏1-800/444-6777, ⓦwww.recreation.gov). In **Kings Canyon**, the bulk of the sites are around Grant Grove, with another at Cedar Grove – all cost $18. For **backcountry** camping, pick up a free permit from a visitor center or ranger station. And remember this is **bear country**: in established campgrounds use the bearproof food boxes, in the backcountry rent bear canisters from the stores in Cedar Grove, Grant Grove, and Lodgepole.

There are pricey **food** markets and cafeterias in the various villages, and a couple of restaurants, notably bargain buffets at the *Montecito-Sequoia Lodge* in the national forest between the two parks. Three Rivers, on the southern approach to Sequoia, has the best range of places to eat nearby.

Sequoia National Park

While trees are seldom scarce in **SEQUOIA NATIONAL PARK** – patches where the giant sequoias can't grow are thickly swathed with pine and fir – the scenery is quite varied. Paths lead through forests and meadows; longer treks rise above the tree line to the barren peaks of the High Sierra. Soon after entering the park from the south, Hwy-198 becomes the **Generals Highway** and climbs swiftly into the dense woods of the aptly labeled **Giant Forest**, where displays in the modern **Giant Forest Museum** explain the lifecycle of the sequoias and what's being done to protect the remaining groves. From here you can explore along Crescent Meadow Road where a loop road leads to the granite monolith of **Moro Rock** (a three-mile marked trail leads from Giant Forest), which streaks wildly upward from the green hillside. Views from its remarkably level top can stretch 150 miles. A hewn staircase makes it easy to climb the rock in fifteen minutes, although the altitude can be a strain.

Continuing east, Crescent Meadow Road leads to **Crescent Meadow** which, like other grassy fields in the area, is more accurately a marsh, too wet for the sequoias that form an impressive boundary around. A perimeter trail leads to **Tharp's Log**, a cabin hollowed out of a fallen sequoia by Hale Tharp who, while searching for a summer grazing ground for his sheep, was led here by Native Americans in 1856. He was not only the first white man to see the giant sequoias but the first to live in one. Just north of Giant Forest, back on the Generals Highway, is the biggest sequoia of them all, the 2200-year-old, 275-foot **General Sherman Tree**. While it's certainly a thrill to see what is held to be the largest living thing on the planet, its extraordinary dimensions are hard to grasp alongside the almost equally monstrous sequoias all around.

Whatever your plans, you should stop at **Lodgepole Village**, three miles north of the Sherman Tree, for the geological displays and film shows at the **visitor center** (June to Aug daily 7am–6pm; May & Sept daily 7am–5pm). You can explore the glacial canyon on the **Tokopah Valley Trail** (2hr), which leads to the base of Tokopah Falls, beneath the 1600ft **Watchtower** cliff. The top of the Watchtower is accessible by the fatiguing but straightforward six-mile **Lakes Trail**.

Kings Canyon National Park

Kings Canyon National Park is wilder and less visited than Sequoia, with a maze-like collection of canyons and a sprinkling of isolated lakes – the perfect environment for careful self-guided exploration. To reach the canyon proper, you have to pass through the hamlet of **Grant Grove**, where there's a useful **visitor center** (daily: mid-May to Aug 8am–6pm; rest of year 9am–4.30pm) and the 2.5-mile **Big Stump Trail** shows off the remains of the logging that took place in the 1880s. Several massive trees from these parts were sliced up and sent to the Atlantic seaboard to convince cynical easterners that such enormous trees really existed. A mile west of Grant Grove, a large stand of sequoias contains the **General Grant** and **Robert E. Lee** trees, which rival the General Sherman in size.

Kings Canyon Highway (Hwy-180; May–Oct only) descends from Grant Grove into the steep-sided Kings Canyon, cut by the furious gushings of various forks of the Kings River. Whether or not this is the deepest canyon in the US, as some would have it, its wall sections of granite and gleaming blue marble, and the yellow pockmarks of blooming yucca plants (May and early June, in particular), are magnificent. A word of warning: don't be tempted by the clear waters of the river; people have been swept away even when paddling close to the bank in a seemingly placid section.

Once into the national park proper, the canyon sheds its V-shape and gains a floor. **Cedar Grove Village** here is named for its proliferation of incense cedars. There's a **ranger station** across the river (June–Aug daily 9am–5pm; May & Sept hours reduced). Apart from the scenery, you should look out for the **flowers** – leopard lilies, shooting stars, violets, lupins, and others – and **birdlife**, too. The longer hikes beside the creeks are up to eight miles long and fairly strenuous. An easy alternative is to wander around the green **Zumwalt Meadow**, four miles from Cedar Grove Village and a short walk from the road, which spreads beneath the forbidding gray walls of Grand Sentinel and North Dome.

Just a mile further on, Kings Canyon Road comes to an end at **Copper Creek**. Thirty years ago vehicles were prohibited from penetrating further, and instead the multitude of canyons and peaks that constitute the Kings River Sierra are networked by **hiking paths**, almost all best enjoyed armed with a tent, provisions, and a wilderness permit from the trailhead ranger station.

The Sierra National Forest

The entire gaping tract of land between Kings Canyon and Yosemite is taken up by the less-visited **Sierra National Forest**. If you want to hike and camp in complete solitude, this is the place to do it. Buck Rock and Big Meadows campgrounds, not far from either Kings Canyon or Sequoia national parks, are free, waterless sites. Don't try lone exploration without thorough planning – public transportation is nonexistent here, and roads and trails are often closed due to bad weather. The best-placed source for free backcountry permits, and camping and wilderness information is the **Pineridge Ranger Station** (daily 8am–4.30pm; ☎559/855-5360), on Hwy-168 at Prather, five miles west of the forest entrance.

Of the forest's two main regions, the **Pineridge district**, forty miles east from Fresno using Hwy-168, is the best to explore. The popular Shaver Lake and Huntington Lake, rich in campgrounds (reserve in summer on ☎1-877/444-6777), soon give way to the isolated alpine landscapes beyond the 9200-foot Kaiser Pass. The sheer challenge posed by the rugged, unspoiled terrain of the adjoining **John Muir Wilderness** can make the national parks look like holiday camps. You can bathe outdoors at the nearby **Mono Hot Springs**, or for the full hot springs experience, head for the *Mono Hot Springs Resort* here (mid-May to Oct; ☎559/325-1710, ⓦ www.monohotsprings.com; ❸–❺), which has indoor mineral baths along with self-catering cabins. The road narrows and twists on to Edison Lake and the *Vermillion Valley Resort* (☎559/259-4000, ⓦ www.edisonlake.com; ❸–❹), from where you can catch a small ferry across the lake to the trailheads.

Yosemite National Park

More gushing adjectives have been thrown at **YOSEMITE NATIONAL PARK** than at any other part of California. However excessive the hyperbole may seem, the instant you turn the corner that reveals **Yosemite Valley**, you realize it's actually an understatement – this is one of the world's most dramatic geological spectacles. Just seven miles long and never more than one mile across, it is walled by near-vertical three-thousand-foot cliffs, streaked by tumbling waterfalls and topped by domes and pinnacles that form a jagged silhouette against the sky. At ground level, grassy meadows are framed by oak, cedar, and fir trees; deer, coyotes, and even black bears are often seen. Tourists are even commoner, but the park is big enough to absorb the crowds: you can visit at any time of year, even in winter when the waterfalls ice up and the trails are blocked by snow, and excepting summer, the valley itself is rarely overcrowded.

Yosemite Valley was made by glaciers gouging through the canyon of the Merced River: the ice scraped away the softer granite but only scarred the harder sections, which became the existing cliffs. The lake that formed when the glaciers melted eventually silted up to create the present valley floor. Native Americans lived here in comparative peace until the mid-nineteenth century, when the threatening approach of Gold Rush settlers led them to launch raiding parties. In 1851 Major James Savage's

Mariposa Battalion trailed the Native Americans into the foothills and beyond, becoming the first whites to set foot in Yosemite Valley, and the native community were soon forced out to make way for farmers, foresters, and tourists. Thanks in great part to the campaigning work of naturalist **John Muir**, in 1864 Yosemite Valley and Mariposa Grove were set aside as protected wilderness, setting the template for the world's first national park, Yellowstone, formed eight years later. A Scottish immi-

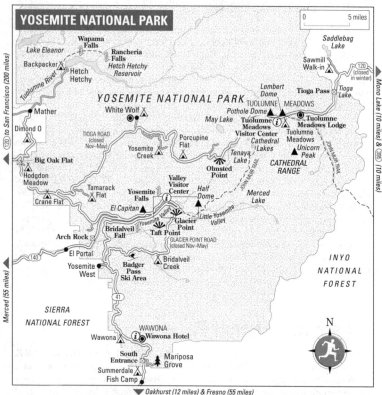

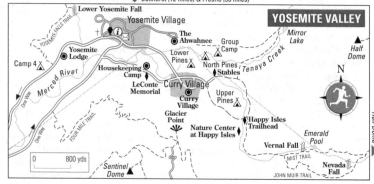

grant who traveled the entire area on foot, Muir spearheaded the conservation movement that led to the founding of the Sierra Club, with the express aim of preserving Yosemite. In 1913, the construction of a dam in the Hetch Hetchy Valley just north, to provide water for San Francisco, was a setback; but the publicity actually aided the formation of the present National Park Service in 1916, which promised – and has since provided – greater protection. **Park entry** costs $20 per vehicle, $10 per pedestrian or cyclist, and is valid for seven days.

Getting there

Getting to Yosemite by car is straightforward, though the only road in from the east, Hwy-120 from Lee Vining, is closed from early November to around the beginning of June. **Gas** is pricey in the park and unavailable in Yosemite Valley. **Public transportation** into the park centers on the Amtrak-accessible Central Valley town of Merced, from where YARTS **buses** (T209/388-9589 or 1-877/989-2787, Wwww.yarts.com) make the two-hour run to Yosemite Valley four or five times a day, charging $13 each way. All services call at Merced Transpo, 710 W 16th St, for Greyhound connections, and at the Amtrak station, 324 W 24th St at K Street, where two of the services connect with trains from San Francisco. YARTS also runs a once-daily summer-only service over the Tioga Pass road from Mammoth Lakes and Lee Vining ($20 roundtrip).

There's also the Yosemite Bug Bus (Wwww.yosemitebugbus.com), which picks up from San Francisco hostels and hotels (Mon, Wed, Fri) for two-day-two-night tours to Yosemite with nights at the Yosemite Bug (see below) in a dorm ($140 total) or private room ($165 total). Bus fares are inclusive of park entry.

If you need somewhere to stay overnight before heading to Yosemite, consider the *HI-Merced Home Hostel* (T209/725-0407; members $15, others $18), where the staff pick you up from the train or bus and drop you off at the appropriate station the following morning. If you'd rather be closer to the park, try the lively ⚑ *Yosemite Bug*, 6979 Hwy-140 (T209/966-6666 or 966-6667, Wwww. YosemiteBug.com; rooms ❷–❹, bunks HI $15, nonmembers $18), at **Midpines**, on the YARTS bus route, where there's a wide range of accommodation and an excellent bar and café.

For recorded **information** on the park, roads, and weather, call T209/372-0200. The park also has a website: Wwww.nps.gov/yose.

Yosemite Valley

The three roads from the Central Valley end up at **Yosemite Valley**, roughly in the center of the park's 1200 square miles, and home to its most dramatic scenery. This is the busiest part of Yosemite, with **Yosemite Village** holding the main shops and the useful **visitor center** (daily: June–Sept 8am–6pm or later; Oct to May 9am–5pm; T209/372-0299).

There's little in the village of any great interest; the reason to come here is to explore the major cliffs that dominate Yosemite Valley. The 3600-foot **El Capitan** is one of the world's biggest pieces of exposed granite, so large that rock-climbers on its face are virtually invisible to the naked eye. The truncated face of **Half Dome** is the sheerest cliff in North America, just seven percent off the vertical.

You can hike to rounded summit of Half Dome by initially following the popular **Mist Trail to Vernal Fall** (3 miles roundtrip; 2–3hr; 1100ft ascent), which winds up so close to the sensual waterfall that during the spring snowmelt period (mid-April to mid-June) hikers are drenched by the spray, but rewarded by vivid rainbows. Vernal Fall never completely dries up, but like all those in the valley, it is best seen in spring; by August, falls can be reduced to a trickle, and others disappear altogether. Continuing on the Mist Trail past Vernal Fall, it's a strenuous ascent, the final section aided by a steel staircase hooked on to Half Dome's curving back (late May to mid-Oct only); if you plan a one-day assault, you'll need to start at the crack of dawn.

An early start is also recommended for the trail to **Upper Yosemite Fall** (7 miles roundtrip; 4–7hr; 2700ft ascent) leads up along a steep switchback path from behind the *Camp 4* campground, near *Yosemite Lodge*. This almost continuous ascent strains the leg muscles, but you get fine views over the valley on the way up, and after about two miles, a chance to appreciate the power (and volume) of the water as it crashes almost 1500ft in a single cascade. A mile and a half further on the same trail, you reach the top of the fall, more spectacular views, and riverside spots for a much deserved picnic.

The most spectacular views of Yosemite Valley are from **Glacier Point**, the top of a 3200ft almost-sheer cliff, 32 miles by road from the valley. It's possible to get there on foot using the vertiginous **Four-Mile Trail** (4.8 miles one way; 3–4hr; 3200ft ascent) though the lazy prefer to take the bus up (details below) and the trail down. The valley floor lies directly beneath the viewing point, and there are tremendous views across to Half Dome and the distant snowcapped summits of the High Sierra.

Practicalities

Prices within Yosemite are uniformly higher than outside the park, but not unaffordable. Of the **hotels** in the valley, try *Yosemite Lodge* (⑤) or *Curry Village*, a mile from Yosemite Village, which has similarly priced rooms, plus fixed tent cabins (④) and cabins (④–⑤); it also offers showers for nonguests ($2). For hotel information and reservations, call ℡559/253-5635 or visit Ⓦwww.yosemitepark.com.

Camping in the valley is only permitted in campgrounds, such as *Camp 4 Walk-in* ($5 per person), just west of *Yosemite Lodge*, which is popular with rock-climbers and has a bohemian reputation; it lacks showers and can only be reserved on the day at the kiosk on-site. Other valley campgrounds cost $20 per site, and you can reserve up to five months ahead in summer (℡1-800/444-6777; Ⓦwww.recreation.gov): reserve as far in advance as you can, though there are occasionally cancellations.

Food in Yosemite is expensive for what you get, though there is reasonable choice. Yosemite Village has a small supermarket and snack bars, the best of which is *Degnan's Deli*, where massive sandwiches cost around $7. The *Food Court* at *Yosemite Lodge* offers filling and inexpensive meals, and the *Pavilion Buffet* at *Curry Village* has an all-you-care-to-eat feast for $13. There's also a great deck at *Curry Village* where you can order pizza and margaritas. The baronial-style *Ahwahnee Dining Room* (℡209/372-1489) has the best (and most expensive) food in Yosemite and a great $34 Sunday brunch; a jacket is required for dinner.

Once in Yosemite Valley, **getting around** is easy, but cars spoil everybody's fun. If you drive in for the day, park at *Yosemite Village* and ride the frequent, free **shuttle buses** that loop around the valley in summer (daily 7am–10pm), calling at all points of interest. A number of bicycle paths cross the valley floor but **bike rental** is limited to outlets at *Yosemite Lodge* and *Curry Village* ($25 a day). There are also **guided tours** (℡209/372-1240), hikes, and horseback trips. Pick up a copy of *Yosemite Today* or browse Ⓦwww.yosemitepark.com for details.

Outside the valley

Mariposa Grove, close to the park's southern entrance, is the biggest and best of Yosemite's groves of **giant sequoia** trees. To get to the towering growths, walk the 2.5-mile loop trail from the parking lot at the end of the road, which is also served by a free bus from the park entrance. The most renowned of the grouping, well marked along the route, is the **Grizzly Giant**, thought to be over 2700 years old.

On the eastern edge of the park, **Tuolumne Meadows** (June–Oct only) has an atmosphere quite different from the valley; here, at 8600 feet, you almost seem to be level with the tops of the surrounding snow-covered mountains. The air always has a crisp bite and early summer reveals a plethora of colorful wildflowers. It's a better starting point than the valley for backcountry hiking into the High Sierra, with eight hundred miles of trails, both long and short, crisscrossing their way along the Sierra Nevada ridges. To spend a night in the backcountry, you must get a **wilderness permit**. You can obtain one up to 24hr in advance (free) at the nearest visitor center, but places are limited so it is best to reserve up to 24 weeks in advance ($5) from the Wilderness Center, Box 545, Yosemite, CA 95389 (T 209/372-0740, W www.nps.gov/yose/wilderness). There are tent cabins at *Tuolumne Meadows Lodge* (T 559/253-5635, W www.yosemitepark.com; ❹) and camping at the *Tuolumne Meadows* campground for $20 per site if you have a vehicle, $5 per person if you're hiking and have a wilderness permit.

The Central Coast

Between the busy sprawl of LA and San Francisco, the four hundred miles of the **Central Coast** come as a welcome respite, home to just a few modest cities and lined by clean sandy beaches. The topography is at its most dramatic along **Big Sur**, one of the most rugged and beautiful stretches of coastline in the world, where the brooding Santa Lucia Mountains rise steeply out of the thundering Pacific surf. To the south, **Santa Barbara** is a wealthy resort full of old and new money, while **Santa Cruz** in the north is a coastal town redolent of the Sixties. In between, languorous **San Luis Obispo** makes a good base for visiting **Hearst Castle**, the hilltop palace of publishing magnate William Randolph Hearst, and the inspiration for the Xanadu pleasure palace in the film *Citizen Kane*.

Almost all of the towns grew up around the original Spanish Catholic **missions**, each a long day's walk from the next, and once enclosed within thick walls to prevent native attacks. Still featuring attractive nineteenth-century architecture, **Monterey**, a hundred miles south of San Francisco, was California's capital under Spain and Mexico, and briefly the state capital in 1850.

Amtrak's *Coast Starlight* and *Pacific Surfliner* **trains** run along the coast up to San Luis Obispo, with the former continuing on to the Bay Area and up to Seattle. Greyhound **buses** stop at most coastal towns, especially along the main highway, US-101.

Santa Barbara

Beautifully sited on gently sloping hills above the Pacific, **SANTA BARBARA**'s low-slung Spanish Revival buildings feature red-tiled roofs and white stucco walls, while its golden beaches are wide and clean, lined by palm trees along a curving bay. The mission-era feel of Santa Barbara is no accident. After a devastating earthquake in 1925, the entire town was rebuilt in the image of an apocryphal Spanish Colonial village, with arcades linking shops, cafés, and restaurants – even the central **El Paseo Nuevo mall** is built in the style.

State Street, the main drag, is home to an appealing assortment of diners, book-shops, coffeehouses, and nightclubs. The few remaining genuine mission struc-tures are preserved as **El Presidio de Santa Barbara** (daily 10.30am–4.30pm; $3; Ⓦwww.sbthp.org/presidio.htm), at the center of which are the barracks of the old fortress **El Cuartel**, standing two blocks east of State Street at 123 Canon Perdido. The second-oldest building in California, it now houses historical exhibits and a scale model of the small Spanish colony. Nearby, the **Santa Barbara Historical Museum**, 136 E De la Guerra St (Tues–Sat 10am–5pm, Sun noon–5pm; donation; Ⓦwww.santabarbaramuseum.com), is built around an 1817 adobe, presenting aspects of the city's past from Ice Age geology to artifacts, from native settlements to modern photo studies. Three blocks north of El Presidio, the still-functional **County Courthouse**, 1100 Anacapa St (Mon–Fri 8.30am–4.30pm, Sat & Sun 10am–4.30pm; free), is a Spanish Revival gem, an idiosyncratic 1929 variation on the Mission theme with striking murals, tilework, and fountain. Take a break in the sunken gardens, explore the quirky staircases, or climb the seventy-foot-high "**El Mirador**" clock tower for a nice view out over the town. Afterwards, drop by the nearby **Santa Barbara Museum of Art**, 1130 State St (Tues–Sun 11am–5pm; $9; Ⓦwww.sbmuseart.org), a fine, if small, museum with classical Greek and Egyptian statuary, a decent array of American paintings, a smattering of French Impressionists, and an Asian collection of some note.

State Street leads half a mile down from the town center to **Stearns Wharf**, the oldest wooden pier in the state, built in 1872. Restoration efforts have now made it home to shopping stalls, food vendors, and the **Sea Center** (daily 10am-5pm; $7), which showcases whale bones and tot-friendly tide pools.

In the hills above the town is the engaging **Museum of Natural History**, 2559 Puesta del Sol Rd (daily 10am–5pm; $8; Ⓦwww.sbnature.org), which has informative displays on the plants and animals of Southern California – and the museum entrance itself is constructed out of the skeleton of a blue whale. Nearby, **Mission Santa Barbara** (daily 9am–5pm; donation; Ⓦwww.sbmission.org) is the so-called "Queen of the Missions," dating from 1820. Its colorful twin-towered facade – facing out over a perfectly manicured garden toward the sea – combines Romanesque and Spanish Mission styles, giving it a formidable character lacking in some of the prettier missions in the chain. If you continue on into the hills from the mission, you come to the splendid **Santa Barbara Botanic Garden**, 1212 Mission Canyon Rd (daily 9am-6pm, summer closes 5pm; $7; Ⓦwww.sbbg.org), whose 65 acres are laced with pleasant hiking trails amid cacti, manzanita, trees, and wildflowers - a relaxing respite through hillside meadows and glades.

Arrival, information, and accommodation

Greyhound **buses** stop every few hours downtown at 34 W Carrillo St; Amtrak **trains** arrive at the old Southern Pacific station at 209 State St, right by US-101. A few blocks away is the **visitor center**, at 1 Garden St, (Mon–Sat 9am–5pm, Sun 10am–5pm; Ⓣ805/965-3021, Ⓦwww.santabarbara.com). You can walk to most places, although a frequent **shuttle bus** (25¢) loops around Santa Barbara during the day, with regional buses ($1.25; Ⓣ805/683-3702, Ⓦwww.sbmtd.gov) cover-ing the outlying areas into the evening.

While there are no **campgrounds** in Santa Barbara proper, there are several spots along the coast to the north, including El Capitan and Refugio state beaches (both at Ⓣ805/968-1033 or 1-800/444-7275; $20–25), and to the south, Carpinteria State Beach (☏ 805/684-2811 or 1-800/444-7275; $20-35); all are accessible through ⓦ www.reserveamerica.com.

Cheshire Cat 36 W Valerio St ☏ 805/569-1610, ⓦ www.cheshirecat.com. B&B that features a hot tub, bikes for guests' use, and Alice in Wonderland theme. Complimentary wine on arrival and breakfast under a palm tree, and loaded with precious Victorian décor. **⑦**
Harbor View Inn 28 W Cabrillo Blvd ☏ 805/963-0780 or 1-800/755-0222, ⓦ www.harbor viewinnsb.com. Appealing luxury hotel offering restaurant, bar, pool and Jacuzzis, and elegant rooms (and ten even better suites) with patios or balconies. **⑨**
Hotel Santa Barbara 533 State St ☏ 805/957-9300 or 1-888/259-7700, ⓦ www.hotelsantabarbara.com. Solid, tasteful choice that provides comfortable, well-decorated rooms, web access, complimentary breakfast, and a prime downtown location. **⑦**
Montecito Inn 1295 Coast Village Rd ☏ 1-800/843-2017, ⓦ www.montecitoinn.com. Spanish

Revival inn with a wide range of rooms and rates, from quaint, basic units to elaborate suites, plus pool, sauna, and Jacuzzi. **⑧**
Sandpiper Lodge 3525 State St ☏ 805/687-5326, ⓦ www.sandpiperlodge.com. Comfortable motel lodging in uptown part of the city, with basic and clean rooms, pool, spa, and complimentary breakfast. Suites cost $30 more than rooms. **④**
Santa Barbara Tourist Hostel 134 Chapala St ☏ 805/963-0154, ⓦ www.sbhostel.com. Dorm beds here are cheap and comfortable ($21), with private rooms also available ($55-85), some with private bath (extra $5-15). Also provides free breakfast and Internet access. **①–④**
State Street 121 State St ☏ 805/966-6586. Near the wharf and beach in a colorful old Mission-style building, though subject to some noise from the nearby railway and only offers communal bathrooms. Cheap rates include breakfast. **④**

Eating, drinking, and nightlife

Although Santa Barbara has plenty of places for munching on comfort food and swilling beer, the unquestioned center for local and tourist activity is **State Street**, which is lined with a number of good **restaurants**, **bars**, and **clubs**.

Chad's 625 Chapala St ☏ 805/568-1876. Stylish nouveau American cuisine – with the Montana pork chops and caramelized halibut as some of the highlights – in the intimate atmosphere of a historic Victorian home.
Edomasa 2710 De la Vina ☏ 805/687-0210. Fine sushi joint with a solid menu and nice presentation – the salmon and marina rolls are top-notch. Open until midnight, or 1am weekends.
El Paseo 10 El Paseo ☏ 805/962-6050. Worthwhile Mexican restaurant serving the familiar staples, but within a historic home with a colorful courtyard and fountain.
Galanga Thai 507 State St ☏ 805/963-6799. Lacking in atmosphere, but still a good spot to drop in for well-prepared and tasty dishes of coconut soup, eggplant curry, and pad Thai.
Natural Café 508 State St ☏ 805/962-9494. Scrumptious, cheap veggie meals – with pasta, sandwiches, salads, falafel, and desserts – in a

prime spot for people-watching.
Santa Barbara Brewing Company 501 State St ☏ 805/730-1040. Serviceable American fare – burgers, seafood, and sandwiches – with solid microbrewed beers and live music on weekends.
sOhO 1221 State St ☏ 805/962-7776. Favorite local place to catch a jazz show and dine on steak, pasta, and seafood. You'll also find rock, acoustic, and world-beat artists and bands here.
Waterfront Grill 113 Harbor Way ☏ 805/564-1200. Specializing in seafood and views. Downstairs is casual fine dining; head upstairs to the *Endless Summer Bar and Café* (☏ 805/564-4666) for cheap and delicious fare of burgers, mussels, oysters, and fish and chips.
Zelo 630 State St ☏ 805/966-5792. Fashionable bar and restaurant that evolves into a dance club as the night wears on, offering dance, Latin, hip-hop, and other eclectic music during the week.

⑬

CALIFORNIA | San Luis Obispo

San Luis Obispo

SAN LUIS OBISPO, 160 miles north of Santa Barbara and halfway between LA and San Francisco, is a few miles inland, but makes the best base for exploring the coast. Still mainly an agricultural center, it holds an attractive lot of nineteenth-century architecture, especially around Buchon Street, as well as good restaurants, pubs, and – outside summer weekends – plenty of accommodation.

The compact core of San Luis is easily walkable, centered on the late- eighteenth-century **Mission San Luis Obispo de Tolosa**, 751 Palm St (daily 9–4pm, summer closes 5pm; donation; Ⓦ www.missionsanluisobispo.org), which was the prototype for the now-ubiquitous red-tile roof church, developed to replace the original, flammable thatch in response to Native American arson attacks. Between the mission and the visitor center, **Mission Plaza**'s terraces step down along San Luis creek, along which footpaths meander. Bridges cross the creek every hundred feet, and the south bank has shops and outdoor restaurants. **Higuera Street**, a block south of Mission Plaza, is the main drag, and springs to life on Thursday afternoons and evenings for the **Farmers' Market**, when the street is closed to cars and filled with vegetable stalls, barbecues, and street musicians. The highlight of the area, though, is the historic **Fremont Theater**, 1035 Monterey St, an Art Deco marvel that becomes a riot of splashy neon at night and still plays movies. A few blocks southeast of the theater, the **Dallidet Adobe and Gardens**, 1185 Pacific St (gardens Thurs 2.30–5.30pm, house tours summer Sun 1–4pm; donation; Ⓣ 805/543-6762), is a handsome 1860s residence and one of the area's oldest buildings, with a pleasant garden sitting in the shadow of a pair of huge redwood trees.

Arrival, information, and accommodation

The Greyhound **bus** depot is at 150 South St, half a mile from the center of town, while Amtrak **trains** stop at the end of Santa Rosa Street, half a mile south of the business district. The **Chamber of Commerce**, 1039 Chorro St (Ⓣ 805/781-2777, Ⓦ www.slochamber.org), provides brochures for self-guided walking tours of town. The local transit company, San Luis Obispo Regional Rideshare (Ⓣ 805/541-2277, Ⓦ www.rideshare.org), has information on transit options in the region, including shuttles and taxis; area **bus** rides cost $1–2.75.

Rates for **accommodation** are generally low, though if you want a nice view of the ocean, you're better off taking a short drive south to **Pismo Beach**, a beach town that makes a pleasant stopover.

Apple Farm 2015 Monterey St Ⓣ 805/544-2040, Ⓦ www.applefarm.com. Charming Victorian inn with canopy beds, complimentary breakfast, and attractive surroundings. The basic units are cheap ($79-99), but more elegant suites may be worth the splurge ($279). ❹–❾
Edgewater 280 Wadsworth Ave, Pismo Beach Ⓣ 805/773-4811, Ⓦ www.edgewater-inn.com. Right on the beach, offering hot tubs, a heated pool, and kitchenettes in some rooms. ❺
Garden Street Inn B&B 1212 Garden St Ⓣ 805/545-9802, Ⓦ www.gardenstreetinn.com. Restored 1880s structure with quaint, pleasant rooms, complimentary wine on arrival, and solid, home-cooked breakfasts. ❼
Hostel Obispo 1617 Santa Rosa St Ⓣ 805/544-4678, Ⓦ www.hostelobispo.com. At $20 a night, this hostel is the best value around, offering convenient central location, cheap bike rentals, and complimentary breakfasts. Private rooms $55–60. ❶–❸
San Luis Inn 404 Santa Rosa St Ⓣ 805/544-0881, Ⓦ www.sanluisinn.com. Clean rooms, complimentary breakfast, and a heated pool. A good, cheap deal. ❸

Eating and drinking

Higuera Street is the prime place to **eat**, with a nice range of unassuming restaurants and **bars**. Other good dining choices can also be found throughout town, along with a few microbreweries.

Buona Tavola 1037 Monterey St ☎805/545-8000. Serviceable bistro featuring a good selection of Northern Italian food and wine.

Mondeo 893 Higuera St ☎805/544-2956. A popular Asian-styled fast-food joint with inventive wraps and bowls, some of the better ones served with swordfish and shrimp.

Oasis 675 Higuera St ☎805/543-1155. Delicious Middle Eastern cuisine – the set lunches are especially good value.

Splash Café 1491 Monterey St ☎805/544-7567. A bit touristy, but this wide-ranging, seafood joint does feature a mean clam chowder. Also in Pismo Beach, 197 Pomeroy Ave, ☎805/773-4653.

Taj Palace 795 E Foothill Blvd ☎805/543-0722. The city's top choice for Indian cuisine, though a bit pricier than other ethnic diners. The $6 buffet lunch is a bargain.

Hearst Castle

Forty-five miles northwest of San Luis Obispo, the hilltop **Hearst Castle** is one of the most extravagant estates in the world. The former holiday home where publisher **William Randolph Hearst** held court for such guests as Winston Churchill, Charlie Chaplin, George Bernard Shaw, and Charles Lindbergh brings in more than a million visitors a year. Its interior is a garish hodgepodge of walls, floors, and ceilings ripped from European churches and castles and mixed with Gothic fireplaces and Moorish tiles, while nearly every room bursts with Greek vases and medieval tapestries.

Work on Hearst's nearly four-hundred-square-mile ranch began in 1919, managed by architect Julia Morgan, but the castle was never truly completed: rooms were torn out as soon as they were finished to accommodate yet more booty. The main facade, a twin-towered copy of a Mudejar cathedral, stands atop steps curving up from the world's most photographed swimming pool, which is filled with spring water and lined by a Greek colonnade and marble statues – the height of aesthetic glory, or irredeemably vulgar, depending on your taste.

The real Citizen Kane

Often portrayed as a power-hungry monster – most memorably by Orson Welles in his thinly veiled *Citizen Kane* – **William Randolph Hearst** was born in 1863 as the only son of a multimillionaire mining engineer, and learned the newspaper trade in New York under Joseph Pulitzer, the inventor of "**Yellow Journalism**," of which Hearst became the greatest practitioner. When he published his own *Morning Journal*, Hearst fanned the flames of American imperialism to ignite the Spanish–American War of 1898. As he told his correspondents in Cuba: "You provide the pictures, and I'll provide the war." Hearst eventually controlled an empire that during the 1930s sold twenty-five percent of the nation's newspapers – and sixty percent of those sold in California.

Hearst was a lifelong Democrat who served two terms in the House of Representatives but failed to be elected mayor of New York, let alone president. Besides his many newspapers, Hearst owned eleven radio stations and two movie studios, which he used to make his longtime mistress, Marion Davies, a star. Both were aboard Hearst's yacht when in 1924 the famed silent-movie producer Thomas Ince – a party guest – died amid suspicious circumstances. Hearst was never prosecuted, but the charge of murder, combined with the more familiar ones of jingoism and corporate monopoly, only helped reinforce the man's dark legend. When the Depression hit, he was forced to sell off most of his holdings, but he continued to exert power and influence – including an attempt to suppress Welles's film and burn the original negative – until his death in 1951, aged 88.

△ Hearst Castle

The most dramatic time to visit is in the morning, when coastal fog often enshrouds the slopes below the castle, making it resemble *Citizen Kane*'s eerily evocative Xanadu, which was modeled on the estate. Five different, two-hour guided **tours** – which are essential, as are reservations – leave from the visitor center just off Hwy-1 (summer daily 8am–4pm; rest of year 8.20am–3.20pm; ☏1-800/444-4445, ⓦwww.hearst-castle.org). New visitors are directed to the

Experience Tour ($24), a basic overview of the castle, while the Garden Tour ($24) offers a peek at the castle's blooms, as well as the guest house and wine cellar. From April to October, docents in period dress take visitors on an Evening Tour of the castle ($30), speaking of Hearst in the present tense.

The Big Sur Coast

Starting just north of Hearst Castle, the ninety wild and undeveloped miles of rocky cliffs along the **Big Sur Coast** form a sublime landscape where redwood groves line river canyons and the Santa Lucia Mountains rise out of the blue-green Pacific. Running through this striking terrain is the serpentine, exhilarating route of **Hwy-1**, carved out of bedrock cliffs 500ft above the ocean, though **public transit** is limited to the Monterey-Salinas Transit (MST) bus (ⓣ 831/899-2555, Ⓦ www.mst.org), which runs south from Monterey to Nepenthe four times daily during the summer (Rte-22; $4 each way). The roads and campgrounds get packed on sunny weekends, and hardly anyone braves the turbulent winters, when violent storms can erode cliffsides. The southern coastline of Big Sur is comparatively gentle, with sandy beaches hiding below crumbling ochre cliffs. To find out more, contact the regional **Chamber of Commerce** (ⓣ 831/667-2100, Ⓦ www. bigsurcalifornia.org).

Roughly midway along the Big Sur Coast, **ESALEN** is named for the long-gone native tribes who once enjoyed its natural **hot spring**, situated on a clifftop high above the raging Pacific. Since the 1960s, when people came to Big Sur to get high and get back to nature, Esalen has been at the forefront of the New Age movement, and the spring is now owned and operated by the Esalen Institute (by reservation only at ⓣ 831/667-3005, Ⓦ www.esalen.org), which aims to train neophytes for the "Olympics of the mind, body, and spirit," although most yuppies simply come for the yoga and massage treatments.

Three miles north on Hwy-1, **Julia Pfeiffer Burns State Park** (daily dawn–dusk; ⓣ 831/667-2315) offers some of the best day-hikes in the Big Sur area, including a short walk along the cliffs to an overlook of McWay Falls, which crash onto a beach below. A less-traveled path leads down from Hwy-1 two miles north of the waterfall through a 200-foot-long tunnel to the remains of a small wharf at **Partington Cove**, one of the few places in Big Sur where you can get to the sea. As with other Big Sur parks, Pfeiffer Burns provides camping sites for $20–25 per night (reserve at ⓣ 831/667-2315, Ⓦ www.reserveamerica.com), while private operations like nearby *Ventana Campground* (ⓣ 831/667-2712; $30–35) offer campsites with bath houses equipped with hot water and electricity. Seven miles north of Pfeiffer Burns, lovely old 🕭 *Deetjen's Big Sur Inn* (ⓣ 831/667-2377; Ⓦ www.deetjens.com; ❹–❼) has log cabins with rooms hand-crafted from thick redwood planks and in-room fireplaces, plus fine breakfasts and dinners on site.

Further north at **NEPENTHE**, the rooftop *Nepenthe* restaurant, just off Hwy-1 (ⓣ 831/667-2345), offers pricey steaks and seafood, though you can find similarly striking views at *Café Kevah* (ⓣ 831/667-2344), which serves organic breakfasts and lunches on its terrace. Across the highway, the **Henry Miller Library** (Wed–Mon 11am–6pm; donation; Ⓦ www.henrymiller.org), displays and sells books by the author, who lived elsewhere in the area intermittently until the 1960s. Two miles north along Hwy-1, unmarked Sycamore Canyon Road leads a mile west to Big Sur's best strip of coast, **Pfeiffer Beach** (daily dawn–dusk; $5 per car; ⓣ 831/667-2315), a white sandy stretch dominated by a large rock whose color varies from brown to red to orange in the changing light.

Big Sur River Valley

Immediately north of the Pfeiffer Beach turnoff, Hwy-1 drops into the valley of the Big Sur River, where many of the accommodation and restaurants are dotted sporadically along six miles of highway. The **ranger station** here (daily 8am–6pm, winter closes 4.30pm; ℡831/667-2315) issues the camping permits required for the Ventana Wilderness in the mountains above, and can provide information on staying at other parks in the area. One of these, sheltered **Pfeiffer Big Sur State Park**, features deep, clear swimming holes that form in the steepwalled river gorge during late spring and summer, and a hiking trail that leads half a mile up a canyon shaded by redwoods to the sixty-foot **Pfeiffer Falls**. The **campgrounds** here charge $20–25 and are often full on summer weekends (℡831/667-2315 or 1-800/444-7275, Ⓦwww.reserveamerica.com).

Just north of Pfeiffer Big Sur, the cluster of shops, lodgings, and restaurants known as **The Village** is the most feasible base for seeing the area. **Accommodation** fills up in summer, but if you can afford it, it's worth spending a night in one of the rustic riverside rooms at the *Big Sur River Inn Resort* (℡831/667-2700 or 1-800/548-3610, Ⓦwww.bigsurriverinn.com; ❺), which has an upscale **restaurant** with decent seafood and American cuisine, which you can enjoy in a garden setting or on a terrace. There are also spacious cabins in the *Big Sur Lodge* (℡831/667-3100 or 1-800/424-4787, Ⓦwww.bigsurlodge.com; ❹, or ❼ summer), where the plush rooms have porches and large showers, but no phones or TVs. Alternatively try the basic cabins at *Big Sur Campgrounds and Cabins*, a mile north of Pfeiffer Big Sur State Park (℡831/667-2322; Ⓦwww.bigsurcamp.com; ❸–❺).

The Monterey Peninsula

At the northern edge of the Big Sur coast, a hundred miles south of San Francisco, are the rocky headlands of the **Monterey Peninsula**, where gnarled cypress trees mark the collision between the cliffs and the sea. The lively harbor town of **Monterey** was the capital of California under the Spanish and briefly under the Mexicans and Americans, and retains many old adobes and historic structures alongside the usual tourist traps. **Carmel**, on the other hand, three miles to the south, is a self-consciously quaint village of million-dollar holiday homes and art galleries, famous for once having Clint Eastwood as its mayor.

Arrival, information, and getting around

Inconveniently, Greyhound **buses** and Amtrak trains avoid the peninsula entirely, so to get there you'll have to first arrive at the sprawling agricultural town of **Salinas** inland, then take a further 55-minute trip on the hourly local bus #20 or 21 into Monterey (see p.1104). Pick up information on Monterey at the **visitor center**, 401 Camino El Estero at Franklin St (℡831/649-1770, Ⓦwww.montereyinfo.org), or the **Chamber of Commerce**, 380 Alvarado St (℡831/648-5360, Ⓦwww.mpcc.com); or on the entire peninsula from the **Monterey County Visitor Center**, 150 Olivier St (℡831/657-6400), which can also help with hotel reservations.

Getting around the area is surprisingly easy on Monterey Salinas Transit buses (℡831/899-2555, Ⓦwww.mst.org). The base charge is $2, though this can double or triple the further you go (eg to Nepenthe or Salinas). There's also a free shuttle bus, the WAVE, from downtown to the Aquarium on Cannery Row.

Another option is to **rent a bike**: try Adventures by the Sea, 201 Alvarado Mall

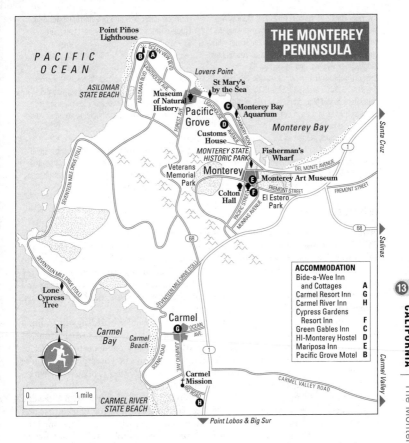

ACCOMMODATION

Bide-a-Wee Inn and Cottages	A
Carmel Resort Inn	G
Carmel River Inn	H
Cypress Gardens Resort Inn	F
Green Gables Inn	C
HI-Monterey Hostel	D
Mariposa Inn	E
Pacific Grove Motel	B

and five other locations ($6 per hour, $24 per day; ⓦ www.adventuresbythesea. com), or Bay Bikes, 585 Cannery Row or 99 Pacific St ($10 per 2hr, $22 per day; ⓦ www.montereybaybikes.com).

Accommodation

Hotels and **B&Bs** can get pricey, but cheap **motels** are clustered along Fremont Street and Munras Avenue, two miles north of the center. The nearest **camping** is in Veterans Memorial Park ($3 per pedestrian, $15 per vehicle; ⓣ 831/646-3865), site of Steinbeck's fictional *Tortilla Flat*, in the hills above town.

Bide-a-Wee Inn and Cottages 221 Asilomar Ave, Pacific Grove ⓣ 831/372-2330, ⓦ www. bideaweeinn.com. Excellent value for the area, with spruced-up rooms, some with kitchenettes and microwaves. Short walk to the ocean. Prices double at weekends. ❸–❻
Carmel Resort Inn Carpenter St and 2nd Ave, Carmel ⓣ 831/624-3113 or 1-800-454-3700, ⓦ www.carmelresortinn.com. One of the better

deals in Carmel: cottage rooms with fireplaces, microwaves, and refrigerators, plus continental breakfast. Prices double at weekends. ❹–❻
Carmel River Inn Hwy-1 at Carmel River Bridge, Carmel ⓣ 831/624-1575 or 1-800/966-6490, ⓦ www.carmelriverinn.com. Pleasant rooms come with patios or private decks, and some with kitchenettes and fireplaces, plus a heated pool and riverside location. ❺

Cypress Gardens Resort Inn 1150 Munras Ave, Monterey ☎831/373-2761, ⓦwww.cypressgardensinn.com. A good, centrally located motel with a pool and Jacuzzi. Recently snazzed-up rooms have fridges, microwaves, and balconies. ❺

Green Gables Inn 104 5th St, Pacific Grove ☎831/375-2095 or 1-800/722-1774, ⓦwww.foursisters.com. Plush doubles in one of the prettiest homes in a town of fine houses, on the waterfront a few blocks from the Aquarium. Two other Four Sisters properties also available on the peninsula, for similar cost. ❻

HI-Monterey Hostel 778 Hawthorne St, Monterey ☎831/649-0375, ⓦwww.montereyhostel.org. Downtown near Cannery Row, a standard hostel with dorms for $23 and private rooms for $54. Three-night maximum stay and 11pm curfew. ❶–❸

🏃 Mariposa Inn 1386 Munras Ave, Monterey ☎831/649-1414, ⓦwww.mariposamonterey.com. The best deal in town. Cozy rooms with fireplaces, plus a hot tub and continental breakfast. Also offers two-story townhouses for larger groups. Rates can double on summer weekends. ❸–❻

Pacific Grove Motel Lighthouse Ave at Grove Acre, Pacific Grove ☎831/372-3218. Nice, small motel in a marvelous setting, 100 yards from the sea. Amenities include a heated pool, hot tub, and in-room refrigerators. ❹

Monterey

Named by the Spanish merchant and explorer Sebastian Vizcaíno in 1602, **MONTEREY** was not colonized until 1770, when it was founded as the military and administrative center of a territory that extended east to the Rockies and north to Canada. By the time the US took over in the mid-nineteenth century, Monterey had become a backwater, though in 1849 it was the site of the negotiating and writing of the state constitution, and soon became the first capital of California, before being superseded by Sacramento (see p.1146).

The compact center features some of the best vernacular **buildings** of California's Spanish and Mexican past, most sitting within a few blocks of the tourist-choked waterfront. A loosely organized **Path of History** connects the 37 sites of the **Monterey State Historic Park**, though most can't be entered unless you're part of a free 45-minute guided **walking tour** (☎831/649-7118, ⓦwww.parks.ca.gov/) that leaves from the Pacific House (see p.1105).

The best place to get a feel for life in old Monterey is the **Larkin House**, Pacific and Jefferson streets (45min tour; Wed & Sat 2pm; free), home of the first and only American consul to Mexican California, Thomas Larkin, who developed the now-common Monterey style of architecture, mixing adobe walls, balconies of Greek Revival Southern plantations, and a dollop of ornament. The house, the first two-story adobe in California, is filled with antiques and memorabilia, and is surrounded by gorgeous gardens. Larkin also helped organize the would-be state's **constitutional convention**, which took place just around the corner at **Colton Hall** (daily 10am–4pm; free; ⓦwww.monterey.org/museum), furnished as it was during the event, with quill pens on the tables and an early map of the West Coast on view – used by delegates to form the boundaries of the 31st state. For a break from history, drop by the **Monterey Art Museum**, across the street at 559 Pacific St (Wed–Sat 11am–5pm, Sun 1–4pm; $5; www.montereyart.org), which along with good regional artworks has some excellent rose gardens.

The **Stevenson House**, three blocks east at 530 Houston St (45min tours; Mon & Fri 2pm, Sat 10.30am; free), is filled with memorabilia belonging to Robert Louis Stevenson, who passed through in 1879 and foresaw that Monterey's easy-going lifestyle was no match for the "Yankee craft" of the "millionaire vulgarians of the Big Bonanza." Six blocks north, tacky **Fisherman's Wharf** is a tourist trap loaded with disused wharves and canneries, some of them converted into boutiques and diners. At the foot of the wharf, the **Customs House** (Thurs–Mon 10am–4pm; free) is the oldest governmental building on the West Coast, with portions built by Spain in 1814, Mexico in 1827, and the US in 1846. Now restored, the site displays ancient crates of seized coffee and liquor in a small museum. Two blocks south, the **Pacific House** on Custom House Plaza (Fri–Mon & Wed 10am–3pm; free) has been a courthouse, boarding house and dance hall since its construction in 1847, and is now has agreeable displays on Monterey history and a decent collection of native artifacts.

Heading north from the wharf, a **bike path** runs two miles to Pacific Grove along **Cannery Row** – named after John Steinbeck's literary portrait of the rough-and-ready workers of its seafood plants. During World War II some 200,000 tons of sardines were processed here each year, but with overfishing the stocks were exhausted by 1945. The abandoned canneries reopened in the 1970s as malls and restaurants, and now teem with tourists instead of fish. Along the route, the engaging **Monterey Bay Aquarium**, 886 Cannery Row (daily 10am–6pm, summer opens 9.30am; $22, kids $13; Ⓦ www.montereybayaquarium.org), has one of the world's largest, most spectacular displays of sealife in the world. Reserve tickets well in advance and allow a day to see everything, including the huge Kelp Forest tank, a touch pool (where you can pet bat rays), the two-story sea otter exhibit, and the dark and evocative rooms with glowing, multicolored jellyfish dipping and swirling before your eyes.

Pacific Grove

Just north of Monterey, counterclockwise on the peninsula, **PACIFIC GROVE** – or "Butterfly Town USA," as it likes to call itself – began as a campground and Methodist retreat in 1875, where Christian revivalists prohibited booze, bare skin, and reading the Sunday newspapers, and which still holds ornate wooden **cottages** from those long-forgotten days, along 16th and 17th streets. One other reminder of that pious period is the deep-red wooden Gothic church **St Mary's by the Sea**, Central Ave at 12th St (Mon & Wed-Fri 9am-4pm; Ⓦ www.stmarysbythesea.org), with a simple interior of polished redwood beams and an authentic signed Tiffany stained-glass window, nearest the altar on the left.

Ocean View Boulevard circles the coast around the town, passing the headland of **Lovers Point** – originally called Lovers of Jesus Point – where preachers used to hold sunrise services. Surrounded in early summer by the red-and-purple blooming ice plant, it's one of the peninsula's best **beaches**. Every year, from November through early March, hundreds of thousands of golden Monarch **butterflies** come here to escape the winter chill, forming orange and black blankets on the **Butterfly Trees**, on Ridge Road, a quarter of a mile inland on Lighthouse Avenue. At the end of the avenue, near the tip of Monterey Peninsula, stands the 150-year-old **Point Piños** lighthouse (Thurs–Sun 1–4pm; $2), the oldest continuously operating lighthouse on the California coast, though basically a quaint farmhouse with a revolving light poking out of its roof. To find out more about the stunning topography and biology of the area, head to the **Pacific Grove Museum of Natural History**, downtown at Forest St and Central Ave (Tues–Sat 10am–5pm; free; Ⓦ www.pgmuseum.org), where you can learn all about the native birds and butterflies, among other wildlife.

If you have time, consider taking the **Seventeen Mile Drive** (daily dawn–dusk; $9 per car), a privately owned, scenic toll road that loops along the coast south to Carmel and provides beautiful vistas of rugged headlands and the glistening shoreline. One particular highlight along the way is the **Lone Cypress Tree**, whose solitary silhouette has been the subject of many a postcard in these parts.

Carmel

Set on gently rising bluffs above a sculpted rocky shore, **CARMEL** is well known for its highly inflated real-estate prices, neat rows of quaint shops and miniature homes along Ocean Avenue, and a largely untouched coastline. Unfortunately, the town also has a thick air of pretension, peppered with tacky middlebrow galleries and mock-Tudor tearooms, and lacking any authentic sense of small-town culture. Don't expect to see street addresses, mail delivery, or franchise businesses in town either: they're all officially banned. Despite the cramped atmosphere, **Carmel Mission Basilica**, 3080 Rio Rd (Mon–Sat 9.30–5.30pm, Sun 10.30am–5pm; $5; ⓦ www.carmelmission.org), provides a rare point of genuine interest as the second of the California Spanish missions, built in 1771. Three small museums in the mission compound trace its history with antiques and memorabilia, while the darker side of the dainty building becomes apparent via the graves of more than three thousand local Native Americans in the adjacent **cemetery**.

The town's best feature, however, is the nearby coastline. **Carmel River State Beach**, west of town, is a tranquil cove of blue water bordered by soft white sand and cypress-covered cliffs, though the tides are deceptively strong and dangerous, so be careful if you chance a swim. **Point Lobos State Reserve**, two miles south of the Carmel Mission on Hwy-1 (daily summer 9am–7pm, winter 9am–5pm; $8 per vehicle; ⓣ831/624-4909), claims, perhaps correctly, to be "the greatest meeting of land and water in the world." Spread over two square miles, the park has more than 250 bird and animal species along its hiking trails, and the sea here is one of the richest underwater habitats in California. Gray whales are often seen offshore - from as little as a hundred yards away - migrating south in January and returning with young calves in April and early May.

Eating

There are many excellent places to **eat** on the peninsula. However, if you're on a tight budget, the best cheap eats are on the north side of Monterey, along Fremont Street and just south of Cannery Row on and around Lighthouse Avenue.

Bookworks 667 Lighthouse Ave, Pacific Grove ⓣ831/372-2242. A book dealer and decent café where you can pick up information about the area while snacking on pastries and drinking coffee.

Fishwife 1996 Sunset Drive at Asilomar Blvd, Pacific Grove ⓣT831/375-7107. Longstanding local favorite, serving great seafood dishes at reasonable prices (around $15 a plate); try the lip-smacking Prawns Belize sautéed in red peppers and lime juice.

India's Clay Oven 150 Del Monte Ave, 2nd floor, Monterey ⓣ831/373-2529. Unexpectedly good Indian food, featuring cheap ($9) buffets for lunch, plus enticing, eight-course combo dinners ($19) with a good range of tandoori, curry, and seafood choices.

La Boheme Dolores and 7th sts, Carmel ⓣ831/624-7500. Cozy French-inspired bistro offering fixed-price, multi-course dinners for $31 per person. Charming, if chintzy.

Old Monterey Café 489 Alvarado St, Monterey ⓣ831/646-1021. Hearty more-than-you-can-eat breakfasts with solid pancakes and omelets, plus tasty sandwiches. Breakfast and lunch only.

Paolina's San Carlos St between Ocean and 7th sts, Carmel ⓣ831/624-5599. Fresh homemade pasta in a casual courtyard setting, at half the price of other Carmel restaurants.

Papa Chano's 462 Alvarado St, Monterey ⓣ831/646-9587. Affordable Mexican fare with juicy, authentic south-of-the-border specialties, highlighted by a mean chorizo.

Robata Grill & Sake Bar 3658 The Barnyard, Carmel ⓣ831/624-2643. One of the few good local choices for sushi and tempura, though it can be pricey.

Sardine Factory 701 Wave St, Monterey ⓣ831/373-3775. Despite the dreadful name, this is where prime California seafood is served in French château splendor, with entrees starting at $25, or fixed-price meals for $30.

Schooner's Grille & Brewery in the *Monterey Plaza Hotel*, 400 Cannery Row, Monterey ⓣ831/372-2628. Colorful California bistro in a historic hotel with views over the bay, offering a good range of steak, seafood, pasta, and microbrews.

Drinking and nightlife

Since Pacific Grove and Carmel offer few decent **nightlife** options, all listings below are for Monterey, though it's hardly regarded as an entertainment hub. Still, mid-September's **Monterey Jazz Festival** (☎1-800/307-3378, ⓦwww.monterey jazzfestival.org) is the oldest of its kind in the world. Check out the widely available *Monterey County Weekly* for current **listings**.

Brittania Arms 444 Alvarado St ☎831/656-9543. British pub with a range of meals – shepherd's pie to sandwiches and burgers – along with karaoke on Wed and Sun and all-you-care-to-eat fish and chips on Sunday.

Crown and Anchor 150 W Franklin St ☎831/649-6496. All your English favorites, from fish and chips to bangers 'n' mash, at this unpretentious local pub, best known for its wide array of brews.

Lallapalooza 474 Alvarado St ☎831/645-9036. Swank martini bar for relaxed social-climbing, with well-mixed, trendy drinks with names like "Grateful Dead" and "Three Mile Island."

Club Octane 321 Alvarado St, ste D ☎831/646-9244. See-and-be-seen downtown nightclub with three throbbing floors playing pop, retro, and hip-hop, plus male and female burlesque spectacles.

Planet Gemini 625 Cannery Row ☎831/373-1449. Upbeat club offering comedy and music (rock, rap, and dance) on weekends with salsa beats on Sun nights.

Santa Cruz

In many ways the quintessential California beach town, **SANTA CRUZ**, 75 miles south of San Francisco, sits at the foot of thickly wooded mountains beside a clean sandy beach. In the 1960s, Ken Kesey's band of Merry Pranksters turned the local youth on to LSD long before it defined a generation, and the area is still among the most liberal in California. It's also surprisingly untouristy: no hotels spoil the miles of coastline, most of the land is agricultural, and roadside stands are more likely to sell apples or sprouts than postcards and trinkets. Still, the recent boom in property prices – endemic to all of coastal California – has driven some of the old-timers out, though the more famous (notably Neil Young) can still be spotted loping around town.

The **Santa Cruz Boardwalk**, 400 Beach St (June–Aug open daily, rest of year Sat & Sun only; hours vary, often 11am–7pm; $1.95–3.60 per ride, unlimited rides $26.95; ⓦwww.beachboardwalk.com), is one of the last surviving beach-front amusement parks on the West Coast. Although it can get packed on weekends, most of the time it's a laid-back fair, where barefoot hippies mix with farmers and tourists. The highlight is the 1924 **Giant Dipper**, a wild wooden roller coaster that often doubles in the movies as a ride in Coney Island, New York.

The **beach** next to the boardwalk is popular, but can get rowdy and dirty. For more peace and quiet, follow the coast out of town to one of the smaller beaches such as Capitola or New Brighton. From **West Cliff Drive**, you'll see some of the biggest waves in California, not least at **Steamer Lane**, beyond the Municipal Pier. **Cowell Beach**, just north of the Municipal Pier, is the best place to give surfing a try; Club Ed (☎831/459-9283, ⓦwww.club-ed.com), in the parking lot, rents boards ($7-15 per hour, $20-45 per day) and assists with lessons. The ghosts of surfers past are animated at the **Surfing Museum**, in the old Abbott Memorial lighthouse on the point (Thurs–Mon noon–4pm; $1; ⓦwww.santacruzsurfing-museum.org), where the boards on display range from early 12-foot redwood planks to modern high-tech multifinned cutters. A clifftop cycle path runs two miles out from here to **Natural Bridges State Beach** (daily 8am–dusk; $6 per car; ⓦwww.santacruzstateparks.org), where waves once cut holes through the cliffs and formed delicate stone arches – though only one remains.

In the hills above Santa Cruz, the local branch of the **University of California** (reachable on Metro bus #1) famously has as its mascot the **banana slug**, and is renowned as a progressive bastion. One of its few highlights for visitors is the **Arboretum** (daily 9am–5pm; free; Ⓦwww2.ucsc.edu/arboretum), world famous for its experimental techniques of cultivation and stocked with plants from around the world.

Arrival, information, and accommodation

Greyhound **buses** stop five times a day at 425 Front St, in the center of town, and Santa Cruz has an excellent public transit system known as the **Metro** (tickets $1.50; day pass $4.50; ☎831/425-8600, Ⓦwww.scmtd.com). Electric Sierra Cycles, 302 Pacific Ave (☎831/425-1593), rents **bikes** for $25-35 per day. The **visitor center** is at 1211 Ocean St (Mon–Sat 9am–5pm, Sun 10am–4pm; ☎831/425-1234 or 1-800/833-3494, Ⓦwww.santacruz.org).

Santa Cruz has plenty of places to **stay**, though rates can be much higher on weekends. Of the many **campgrounds** in the area, the best is at *New Brighton State Beach* (☎831/464-6330 or 1-800/444-7275, Ⓦwww.reserveamerica.com; $25–35), three miles south at 1500 Park Ave, near the town of Capitola.

Capitola Venetian 1500 Wharf Rd, Capitola ☎831/476-6471, Ⓦwww.capitolavenetian.com. Aging beach hotel with one- to three-bed rooms, some with stoves, fridges, fireplaces, and ocean views. Rates vary wildly, from $59 on a winter weekday to $259 on a summer weekend. ❸–❾
Carousel Motel 110 Riverside Ave, Santa Cruz ☎831/425-7090. Clean and centrally located units, all with microwaves and balconies, near the boardwalk. Rates are cheap, but double in the summer. ❸–❻
Cliff Crest B&B Inn 407 Cliff St, Santa Cruz ☎831/427-2609, Ⓦwww.cliffcrestinn.com. An

1887 refurbished Queen Anne with five elegant guest rooms, set in lovely gardens at the top of Beach Hill, with breakfast served in a conservatory. Prices can increase by $20-50 in summer. ❼
HI-Santa Cruz 321 Main St, Santa Cruz ☎831/423-8304, Ⓦwww.hi-santacruz.org. Well-situated hostel set in 1870s cottages, offering dorm beds from $21. Often booked up in advance. ❶
Pleasure Point Inn 2-3665 E Cliff Drive, Santa Cruz ☎408/291-0299, Ⓦwww.pleasurepointinn. com. Stylishly modern B&B boasting clifftop views, a roof sundeck, and hot tub; rooms have stereos and Jacuzzis. Rates go up $25 on weekends. ❽

Eating, drinking, and nightlife

The main drag of **Pacific Avenue** is peppered with many relaxed **restaurants** and **bars**, while the town itself has the Central Coast's rowdiest **nightlife**, ranging from coffeehouses to nightclubs where the music varies from surf-punk and reggae to Sixties-styled rock. Consult the free *Good Times* magazine for listings.

The Catalyst 1011 Pacific Ave ☎831/423-1336. Happening club with nightly entertainment and one of the best bets for catching mid-level touring artists and up-and-coming locals.
Clouds Downtown 110 Church St ☎831/429-2000. A mix of affordable seafood and California cuisine, with hearty but enjoyable items like pretzel chicken and tilapia-and-scallop ceviche.
The Crepe Place 1134 Soquel Ave ☎831/429-6994. Serves up mid-priced crepes with a tasty assortment of both savory and sweet fillings, as well as a few surprises, like jambalaya crepes.
Kuumbwa Jazz Center 320 Cedar St ☎831/427-2227. Friendly and intimate spot showcasing both traditional and modern jazz. Mon draws the big names. Cover anywhere from $1–15.

Rio Theatre 1205 Soquel Ave ☎831/423-8209, Ⓦwww.riotheatre.com. Historic theater that presents a mix of cult films, oddball performances, and eclectic music concerts.
Saturn Café 145 Laurel St ☎831/429-8505. A good place to enjoy the (self-consciously) eccentric flair of Santa Cruz, this vegetarian diner serves tasty items like burgers and nachos. Open until 3am, or 4am weekends.
Tacqueria Vallarta 1101 Pacific Ave #A ☎831/471-2655. Authentic, gut-busting Mexican fare with a self-serve salsa bar. Mighty good, and pretty cheap. Two other local branches.
Zoccoli's Deli 1534 Pacific Ave ☎831/423-1711. Italian deli with rich and hearty staples, including a delicious minestrone soup.

△ Pigeon Point Lighthouse

The coast north to San Francisco

Twenty-five miles north along the coast from Santa Cruz, the beginning of the San Francisco Peninsula is marked by **Pigeon Point Lighthouse**, 210 Pigeon Point Rd, an 1872 structure that took its name from the clipper ship *Carrier Pigeon*, which broke up on the rocks off the point, one of many shipwrecks that led to the construction of the lighthouse in the late nineteenth century. The lighthouse is now closed, but you can still spend the night in the old **keeper's quarters** (ⓣ650/879-0633, ⓦwww.norcalhostels.org; ❶–❸) and soak your bones in a hot tub ($7 per 30min), cantilevered out over the rocks. Dorm beds cost $21 each and there are also four private doubles for $46–59.

Just before Pigeon Point, beautiful **Big Basin Redwoods State Park** ($6 parking; ⓣ831/338-8860) offers 25 square miles of wilderness with 300-foot-tall redwoods and a compelling ten-mile **trail** leading from the fog-shrouded hills to the sparkling ocean. Closer down toward the shore, giant blubbery northern elephant seals can be found mating every December and January in the **Año Nuevo State Reserve**, off New Year's Creek Rd (daily 8am–dusk; $6 parking; ⓣ650/879-0227), a winter ritual in which the males of the species – fifteen-foot-long, three-ton brutes – collide on the rocks and sand dunes to fight for a mate. It's a bizarre spectacle, and one you shouldn't miss.

San Francisco

SAN FRANCISCO proper occupies just 48 hilly square miles at the tip of a slender peninsula, almost perfectly centered along the California coast. Arguably the most beautiful, certainly the most liberal city in the US, it remains true to itself: a funky, individualistic, surprisingly small city whose people pride themselves on being the cultured counterparts to their cousins in LA – the last bastion of civilization on the lunatic fringe of America. It's a compact and approachable place, where downtown streets rise on impossible gradients to reveal stunning views of the city, the bay, and beyond, and blanket fogs roll in unexpectedly to envelop the city in mist. This is not the California of monotonous blue skies and slothful warmth – the temperatures rarely exceed 70°F, and even during summer can drop much lower.

The original inhabitants of this area, the **Ohlone Indians**, were all but wiped out within a few years of the establishment in 1776 of the **Mission Dolores**, the sixth in the chain of Spanish Catholic missions that ran the length of California. Two years after the Americans replaced the Mexicans in 1846, the discovery of gold in the Sierra foothills precipitated the rip-roaring **Gold Rush**. Within a year fifty thousand pioneers had traveled west, and east from China, turning San Francisco from a muddy village and wasteland of sand dunes into a thriving supply center and transit town. By the time the **transcontinental railroad** was completed in 1869, San Francisco was a lawless, rowdy boomtown of bordellos and drinking dens, something the moneyed elite – who hit it big on the much more dependable silver Comstock Load – worked hard to mend, constructing wide boulevards, parks, a cable car system, and elaborate Victorian redwood mansions.

In the midst of the city's golden age, however, a massive **earthquake**, followed by three days of fire, wiped out most of the town in 1906. Rebuilding began immediately, resulting in a city more magnificent than before; in the decades that followed, writers like Dashiell Hammett and Jack London lived and worked here. Many of the city's landmarks, including Coit Tower and both the Golden Gate and Bay bridges, were built in the 1920s and 1930s. By World War II San Francisco had been eclipsed by Los Angeles as the main West Coast city, but it achieved a new cultural eminence with the emergence of the Beats in the 1950s and the hippies in the 1960s, when the fusion of music, protest, rebellion, and of course, drugs that characterized 1967's "Summer of Love" took over the Haight-Ashbury district.

It's estimated that over half of San Francisco's population originates from somewhere else. It is a city in a constant state of evolution, fast gentrifying itself into one of the most high-end towns on earth – thanks, in part, to the disposable incomes pumped into its coffers from its sizeable singles and gay contingents. Gay capital of the world, San Francisco has also been the scene of the dot.com revolution's meteoric rise, fall and steadier recovery. The resultant wealth has pushed housing prices sky high. Despite the city's economic ebbs and flows, your impression of the city will be that of a proudly distinct place.

Arrival and information

All international and most domestic flights arrive at **San Francisco International Airport** (SFO), inconveniently located about fifteen miles south of the city. Regular BART (Bay Area Rapid Transit; ☎415/817-1717, ⓦwww.bart.gov; $5.15) trains get you downtown in thirty minutes. San Mateo County Transit (SamTrans) **buses** (☎1-800/660-4287, ⓦwww.samtrans.org) leave every half-hour from the lower level of the airport; the #KX express ($4) takes around thirty minutes to reach the Transbay Terminal in downtown, while the slower #292 ($1.50) stops everywhere and takes nearly an hour. The SFO Airporter (☎1-877/877-8819) and other **minibuses** depart every five to ten minutes from the lower level of the circular road and take passengers to any city-center destination for $15 a head. **Taxis** from the airport cost $30–40 (plus tip) for any downtown location, more for the East Bay and Marin County – only worth considering if there are more than one of you. If you're planning to drive, the usual **car rental** agencies operate free shuttle buses to their depots, leaving every fifteen minutes from the upper level.

Several domestic airlines (Jet Blue and Southwest are two) and United fly into **Oakland International Airport** (OAK; see p.1137), across the bay. This is actually closer to downtown San Francisco than SFO, and is efficiently connected with the city by the $2 (exact change only) AirBART shuttle bus, which drops you at the Coliseum BART station. From there, hop onto a Daly City BART train and you'll be in downtown San Francisco in around fifteen minutes ($3.35).

By bus and train

All of San Francisco's **Greyhound** services use the **Transbay Terminal** at 425 Mission St, south of Market Street, near the Embarcadero BART station (☎ 1-800/231-2222, ⓦ www.greyhound.com). **Green Tortoise** (☎ 1-800/867-8647, ⓦ www.greentortoise.com) buses pull in behind the Transbay Terminal at First and Natoma streets. **Amtrak** trains stop across the bay in **Richmond** (the most efficient BART transfer point) and continue to **Oakland**, from where free shuttle buses run across the Bay Bridge to the Transbay Terminal, or you can also take BART. Although Emeryville, the stop before Oakland, is technically closer to San Francisco, don't get off there as public transportation to the city is very patchy.

Information

The **San Francisco Visitor Information Center**, on the lower level of Hallidie Plaza at the end of the cable car line at 900 Market St (Mon–Fri 9am–5pm, Sat & Sun 9am–3pm, Nov–April closed Sun; ☎ 415/391-2000, ⓦ www.onlyinsanfrancisco.com), has free maps of the city and the Bay Area, and can help with lodging and travel plans. Its free *San Francisco Book* provides detailed, if a little selective, information about accommodation, entertainment, exhibitions, and stores. The good value **City Pass** (ⓦ www.citypass.com; $49), which allows entry into various attractions, free MUNI rides, and other discounts for seven days, is available here.

San Francisco's two main **post offices**, with telephone and general delivery facilities, are at Sutter Street Station, 150 Sutter St at Montgomery Street, in the Financial District (Mon–Fri 8.30am–5pm), and Rincon Finance Station, 180 Steuart St at Mission Street, SoMa (Mon–Fri 7am–6pm, Sat 9am–2pm).

City transportation

San Francisco is the rare American city where you don't need a car to see everything. In fact, given the chronic shortage of parking downtown, horrible traffic, and zealous meter maids, going carless makes sense. The public transportation system, **MUNI**, though much maligned by locals for its unpredictable schedule, covers every neighborhood inexpensively. Marked bike routes direct riders to all major points of interest. Walking the compact metropolis is the best bet, with each turn revealing surprises like stunning homes and bustling marketplaces. Wear comfortable shoes for the killer hills, some of them angled at a steep 30 degrees.

Useful bus routes

#5 From the Transbay Terminal, west alongside Haight-Ashbury and Golden Gate Park to the ocean.

#7 From the Ferry Terminal (Market St) to the end of Haight Street and to Golden Gate Park.

#15 From 3rd Street (SoMa) to Pier 39, Fisherman's Wharf, via the Financial District and North Beach.

#20 (Golden Gate Transit) From corner of Mission and 1st streets to the Golden Gate Bridge ($1.75).

#22 From the Marina up Pacific Heights and north on Fillmore.

#28 and **#29** From the Marina through the Presidio, north through Golden Gate Park, the Richmond, and the Sunset.

#30 From the Caltrain depot on 3rd Street, north to Ghirardelli Square, via Chinatown and North Beach, and out to Chestnut Street in the Marina district.

#38 From Geary Street via Civic Center, west to the ocean along Geary Boulevard through Japantown and the Richmond, ending at Cliff House.

MUNI train lines

MUNI F-Market line Restored vintage trolleys from other cities run downtown from the Transbay Terminal and Fisherman's Wharf, up Market Street, and into the heart of the Castro.

MUNI J-Church line From downtown to the edge of the Castro and on to the Mission and Noe Valley.

MUNI K-Ingleside line From downtown through the Castro to Balboa Park.

MUNI L-Taraval line From downtown west through the Sunset to the zoo and Ocean Beach.

MUNI M-Ocean View From downtown west by the Stonestown Galleria shopping center and San Francisco State University.

MUNI N-Judah line From downtown west through the Inner Sunset and to Ocean Beach, via the outer Haight.

From the MUNI N-Judah line or #5 and #38 bus routes, you can connect to bus #44, which goes by the De Young Museum, Japanese Tea Garden, California Academy of Sciences, and Steinhart Aquarium in Golden Gate Park. A MUNI transfer will get you discounts at these places.

MUNI

The city's public transportation is run by the **San Francisco Municipal Railway**, or MUNI (☎415/673-6864, ⓦwww.sfmuni.com). A comprehensive network of buses, trolleybuses, and cable cars runs up and over the city's hills, while the underground trains become streetcars when they emerge from downtown to split off and serve the suburbs. On buses and trains the flat **fare** is $1.50 (exact change only); with each ticket you buy, ask for a **free transfer** – good for another two rides on a train or bus, and a fifty-percent reduction on cable cars if used within ninety minutes. Cable cars cost a steep $5 one way (no transfers).

If you're staying a few days, the MUNI **Passport** is available in one-day, three-day, and seven-day denominations ($11, $18, $24) and is valid for unlimited travel on MUNI and also the Bay Area Rapid Transit (BART) system (see p.438) within the city limits. A **Fast Pass** costs $45 for a full calendar month. MUNI trains run **throughout the night** on a limited service, except those on the M-Ocean View line,

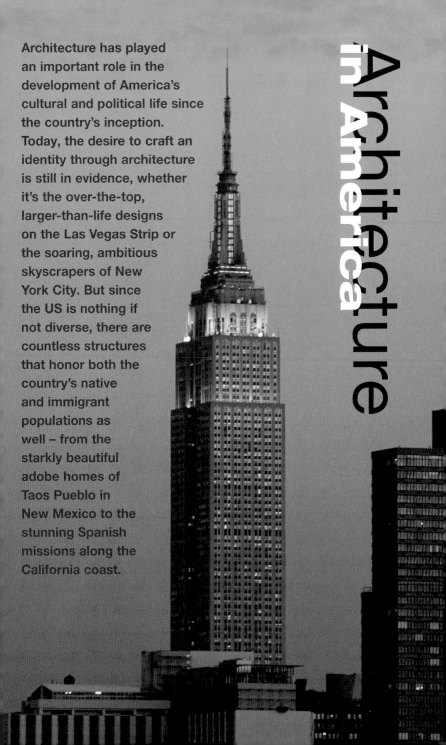

Architecture has played an important role in the development of America's cultural and political life since the country's inception. Today, the desire to craft an identity through architecture is still in evidence, whether it's the over-the-top, larger-than-life designs on the Las Vegas Strip or the soaring, ambitious skyscrapers of New York City. But since the US is nothing if not diverse, there are countless structures that honor both the country's native and immigrant populations as well – from the starkly beautiful adobe homes of Taos Pueblo in New Mexico to the stunning Spanish missions along the California coast.

Architecture in America

Early American style

Savannah, GA

It was no coincidence that the stately, imperial forms of **Greek and Roman architecture** were applied to the buildings of the young republic, given that the founding fathers sought to emulate the classical world's prestige, along with its ideals. Today you can get a good idea of the founders' vision for the country by visiting the National Mall in Washington DC. Though the capital city took 150 years to be fully realized, its imperial design – with grand diagonal boulevards and looming Neoclassical structures, none more recognizable than the Pantheon-inspired US Capitol building – was prescient. On a much humbler scale, architect (and third US president) **Thomas Jefferson**'s detailed plans for the University of Virginia, in Charlottesville, and his nearby estate, Monticello, established a more personal interpretation of classical architecture, re-imagined to fit the rolling green hills and valleys of the country.

Far removed from the budding capital, however, the early American landscape was lined with frontier log cabins (like the simple one Abraham Lincoln was born in; a replica stands at his Kentucky birthplace), wooden forts, and clapboard farmhouses, while Spanish settlers established their own Mission and Colonial styles in isolated southwestern outposts. Soon all these distinct building styles would be incorporated within one, growing country.

European influences

The nineteenth century saw the US awash in imported designs. The stately Georgian manors of the northeast gave the impression of British gentry, though their occupants might have been rum-runners and real-estate speculators; the neo-Gothic cathedrals suggested an old Anglican or Catholic order, but were just as likely to be homegrown Baptist or, later, Mormon; and revivals of Egyptian temples, Swiss chalets, and Tudor mansions were conspicuous sights on a Midwest prairie or New England lakefront.

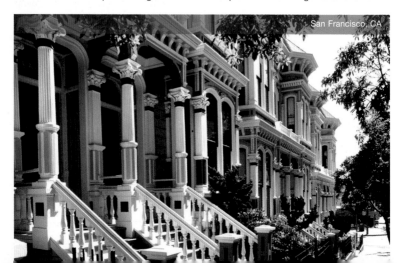

San Francisco, CA

The greatest influence of all, however, was the colorful **Victorian** style, which defined the cityscape of places from San Francisco to Boston to numerous mining towns in the Rocky Mountains (visit places like Crested Butte and Leadville, in Colorado, for a particularly good look). By 1900, though, even these designs weren't monumental enough for the growing ambitions of the US, and only ancient Rome, yet again, seemed to suffice as an equal: over the next couple of decades, stunning banks and libraries were modeled as temples, robber-baron mansions replicated emperors' palaces, and train stations, like the old Penn Station, evoked the Baths of Caracalla.

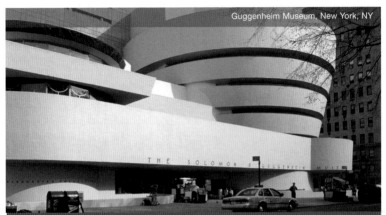

Guggenheim Museum, New York, NY

America's architect: Frank Lloyd Wright

Considered by many to be the greatest American architect, Frank Lloyd Wright (1867–1959) enjoyed a career that spanned more than seven decades, beginning when America was just getting its architectural sea legs in the late-Victorian era and ending in the mid-twentieth century. Wright's influence was huge: with his use of linear, horizontal volumes, he underlined the importance of the native landscape; his inventive engineering and clever use of materials like glass brick, Pyrex tubes, and pre-cast concrete "knit-blocks," helped give rise to architecture as sculpture; and through his pre-designed model "Usonian" homes, he hoped to devise affordable but creative middle-class housing. Some of Wright's greatest masterpieces include the following:

• Fallingwater (see p.184). Innovative environmental architecture built around an enchanting site of forested beauty and cascading water in Mill Run, Pennsylvania.

• Johnson Wax Building. A streamlined office complex in Racine, Wisconsin, with a sleek tower and concrete "lily pads" holding up the roof.

• The Robie House (see p.365). The single most important signpost for the coming suburban ranch home, as well as a lovely piece of design. It sits on the University of Chicago campus, in Hyde Park, Illinois.

• Taliesin (see p.384). Wright's marvelous Wisconsin home and studio lends its name to his Scottsdale, Arizona, architecture and design school.

• Guggenheim Museum (see p.105). This Manhattan art gallery is an abstract design in the form of a circular beehive with a famous sloping interior ramp.

One of the most memorable ways to experience Wright's genius is to visit Oak Park, Illinois (p.363), which offers the most concentrated collection of his early-modern gems, including the stunning Unity Temple and his own house and studio.

Field trips

The Painted Ladies, CA Although many of San Francisco's Victorian homes were destroyed in the 1906 fire and earthquake, what remains – in areas from Haight-Ashbury to Pacific Heights to Alamo Square – is a resplendent reminder of the good old days of the Italianate, Queen Anne, and Eastlake styles.

Anasazi Country, in the Southwest The USA's indigenous peoples were also some of its most inventive architects, none more so than the Anasazi, or Ancient Pueblo, peoples, whose cliff dwellings, kivas, and Great Houses are easily accessible in the Four Corners region of the Southwest. Chaco Canyon, Mesa Verde, and Canyon de Chelly are among the most spectacular ruins, and the striking pueblos at Acoma and Taos are fascinating as well.

South Beach, FL In Miami's fabulous Art Deco District, oceanfront buildings are alive with zigzag lines, neon-rimmed curves, and dynamic letters – all bathed in a warm, moderne glow.

The Serra Missions, CA Although his role as spiritual colonizer of native tribes is still unsettling, Father Junipero Serra and his Catholic missionaries did leave behind a chain of 21 striking, late-eighteenth-century Spanish missions along the coast of California, from San Francisco to San Diego.

Boston, MA The cauldron of the American Revolution has many key sights that span four centuries, but its most eye-catching attractions are the gilded-dome-topped Massachusetts State House, one of Charles Bulfinch's many local designs, and H.H. Richardson's rusticated-stone Romanesque Trinity Church.

Bodie, CA The best place to see the ruins of frontier America. Located in California's Sierra Nevada range, it's nothing less than the nation's best ghost town, its eerie, windswept townscape preserving some 150 homes and businesses in arrested decay.

Charleston, SC and Savannah, GA These small towns offer an ideal place to see both the comfort and gentility of the Old South as well as its darker aspects – from fetching town squares and grand plantations, to grim slave quarters and auction blocks.

Las Vegas, NV Sin City has long been an icon of pop architecture: in the 1960s for its hypnotic neon and glitzy signs, and today for its ersatz castles, pyramids, tropical islands, and pint-sized versions of Paris, Venice, and New York.

Art Deco architecture, South Beach, FL

The Venetian, Las Vegas, NV

Native invention

The 1920s and 30s represented a peak for American architectural creativity – best exemplified by the **Art Deco** towers of the Empire State and Chrysler buildings in New York, descendants of earlier work done in Chicago by Louis Sullivan, who is credited with inventing the skyscraper. Elsewhere in the country, Frank Lloyd Wright was in the middle of a long, exceptional career (see box on previous page) and Europeans like Mies van der Rohe did some of their best work here. Although architectural trends can change like haute couture – modern glass-and-steel boxes giving way to tongue-in-cheek Postmodernism, and so on – the greatest builders have created styles and structures that are here to last. The concrete austerity of Louis Kahn (more famous internationally than at home perhaps; the Salk Institute in La Jolla, CA, is his most acclaimed building) and the sharp white angles of Richard Meier, designer of Los Angeles's Getty Center, are just a couple of the homegrown creations that have had a distinct and lingering impact on the wide American landscape.

which stop around 1am. **Buses** run all night, but services are greatly reduced after midnight. For **more information**, pick up the handy MUNI map from the Visitor Information Center or bookstores. **Bikes** are allowed on MUNI buses equipped with bicycle racks (on the front of the bus) and on BART, except during peak hours.

Other transportation services

Along Market Street in downtown, MUNI shares the station concourses with BART (see p.1138), which runs to the East Bay – including downtown Oakland and Berkeley – and the outer suburbs. The **Caltrain** commuter railway (depot at 4th and King streets, in the SoMa, district; ☎1-800/660-4287, ⓦwww.cal-train.com) links San Francisco along the peninsula south to San Jose. **Golden Gate Ferry** boats (☎415/923-2000, ⓦwww.goldengate.org) leave from the Ferry Building at the Embarcadero, crossing the bay past Alcatraz to Sausalito and Larkspur in Marin County. **Blue & Gold Fleet** (☎415/705-5555, ⓦwww.blueandgoldfleet.com) runs to Sausalito and Tiburon from Pier 41 at Fisherman's Wharf, with some services from the Ferry Building. The **Alameda–Oakland ferry** (☎510/522-3300, ⓦwww.transitinfo.org/AlaOakFerry) operates between Oakland's Jack London Square, the Ferry Building, Fisherman's Wharf (Pier 39), and Pac Bell Park ($5 one way) and, in summer, to Angel Island ($12 roundtrip; daily late May–Oct).

Taxis ply the streets, and you can flag one down (especially downtown), but finding one can be a pain. If you're phoning ahead, try Veterans (☎415/552-1300) or Yellow Cab (☎415/626-2345). Fares within the city are roughly $1.70 for the first mile and $1.80 per mile thereafter, plus a customary fifteen-percent tip.

If you fancy **cycling**, the handiest option is Blazing Saddles (☎415/202-8888, ⓦwww.blazingsaddles.com), which has several locations – two of the most convenient are at 1095 Columbus Ave at Francisco Street, in North Beach, and Pier 41 at Fisherman's Wharf. Rates for a standard bike are $7 per hour, $28 per day (tandem $11 per hour and $48 per day). Another option is Bay City Bikes, 2661 Taylor St at Beach Street, at Fisherman's Wharf, with rates beginning at $27 per day (☎415/346-2453, ⓦwww.baycitybike.com).

Organized tours

One way to orient yourself is with an **organized tour**. Gray Line Tours (from $44; ☎415/434-8687 or 1-888/428-6937, ⓦwww.graylinesanfrancisco.com) trundle round the city in four fairly tedious hours and offer various combo tours. Considerably more thrilling are the one-hour **bay cruises** operated by the Blue & Gold Fleet ($18 before noon, $21 after; ☎415/773-1128, ⓦwww.blueandgoldfleet.com) from piers 39 and 41 – though be warned that everything may be shrouded in fog. If you're feeling flush, the expensive **aerial tours** of the city and Bay Area in light aircraft or helicopters are unbeatable – try San Francisco Helicopter Tours (☎1-800/400-2404, ⓦwww.sfhelicoptertours.com), which offers spectacular flights starting at $130 per passenger.

The best of the **walking tours** include City Guides, sponsored daily by the San Francisco Public Library (free; ☎415/557-4266, ⓦwww.sfcityguides.org); Cruisin' the Castro ($35; ☎415/255-1821, ⓦwww.webcastro.com/castrotour), an absorbing and witty tour of the gay community; the Victorian Home Walk, which swings past the pick of the city's posh old homes ($20; ☎415/252-9485, ⓦwww.victorianwalk.com); and the Barbary Coast Trail, marked by bronze medallions set in the sidewalk, which highlights the oldest parts of the city (audio tours $14; guided tours $20; ☎415/454-2355, ⓦwww.sfhistory.org). Three Babes and a Bus

CALIFORNIA | San Francisco: City transportation

($39, which includes all cover charges; ☏1-800/414-0158, ⓦwww.threebabes. com) takes a luxury coachload of people looking for a good time to different nightclubs around the city – and is less cringe-inducing than it might sound. There are also special mural tours of the Mission by Precita Eyes that take in the district's distinctive street art (see p.1125 for details).

Accommodation

Annual visitors far outnumber San Francisco's 800,000 people, and the city isn't short on lodging, but to get the pick, be sure to reserve well in advance, especially in summer and fall. Expect to pay at least $100 per room in any decent hotel or motel in season; if you want to snag one of the smart bargains or hostel beds we've listed below, make sure to reserve in advance in high season. You'll also normally find significantly better rates for rooms that share baths.

For plentiful **B&Bs**, consult the list below or contact a specialist agency such as California Bed & Breakfast Inns (☏1-800/284-4667, ⓦwww.cabbi.com) or Bed and Breakfast San Francisco (Mon–Fri 9.30am–5pm; ☏1-800/452-8249, ⓦwww. bbsf.com). British visitors can reserve rooms through **Colby International** (ⓦwww.colbyintl.com), while once you're in the city, San Francisco Reservations (☏1-800/677-1500, ⓦwww.hotelres.com) will find you a room starting from around $75 a double off season. If all else fails and you've got a car, **motels** are legion along the highways and bigger roads throughout the Bay Area, at a standard rate of $45–60 a night. In all cases, bear in mind that all quoted room rates are subject to a **fourteen–percent room tax**.

Hotels, motels, and B&Bs

Adagio Hotel 550 Geary St at Jones, Union Square ☏415/775-5000, ⓦwww.jdvhospitality.com. The decor at this hotel echoes its ornate Spanish Revival facade with deep reds and ochres. Rooms are large and, even better, there's free Internet access and printing on-site. ❼

Archbishop's Mansion 1000 Fulton St at Steiner, Fillmore ☏ 415/563-7872 or 1-800/543-5820, ⓦwww.thearchbishopsmansion.com. The last word in camp elegance, this B&B is crammed with $1 million worth of antiques, including the very chandelier that featured in the ballroom of *Gone With the Wind*. ❻

Bohème 444 Columbus Ave at Vallejo, North Beach ☏ 415/433-9111, ⓦwww.hotelboheme.com. Smack in the middle of Beat heartland, this small, 15-room hotel has tiny but dramatic rooms, with canopied beds. Columbus Ave can be noisy, so ask for a room at the back. ❻

The Carl 198 Carl St at Stanyan, Haight-Ashbury ☏ 415/661-5679 or 1-888/661-5679, ⓦcarlhotel. citysearch.com. A bargain for its Golden Gate Park location. The small but florally pretty rooms come with microwaves and fridges; the cheaper ones have shared baths. ❸

Clift 495 Geary St at Taylor, Theater District ☏415/775-4700 or 1-800/658-5492, ⓦwww

.morganshotelgroup.com. The rooms are vaguely oriental with quirky touches like the Louis XIV–style chairs with mirrors on the seat and back, and sleigh beds – pity the bathrooms are so small. ❾

Cow Hollow Motor Inn 2190 Lombard St at Steiner, Cow Hollow ☏415/921-5800, ⓦwww. cowhollowmotorinn.com. Pleasant Swiss-chalet style exterior and large modern rooms in an airy location. Plenty of parking. ❹

Del Sol 3100 Webster St at Lombard, Cow Hollow ☏415/921-5520 or 1-877/433-5765, ⓦwww. jdvhospitality.com. Funky updated motor lodge with a tropical theme, plus a swimming pool: the best place for budget cool in the city. ❺

🏃 **Golden Gate Hotel** 775 Bush St at Mason, Theater District ☏415/392-3702 or 1-800/835-1118, ⓦwww.goldengatehotel.com. Friendly European-style B&B with cozy, warmly-furnished rooms, some with shared baths. Beautiful original iron elevator. Great value. ❹

Hotel Astoria 510 Bush St at Grant, Chinatown ☏415/434-8889 or 1-800/666-6696, ⓦwww. hotelastoria-sf.com. The decor here is friskier than that of many other budget hotels, with TV and full in-room amenities; continental breakfast is included and there's discounted parking nearby ($20/24hr). ❸

Hotel Diva 440 Geary St at Mason, Union Square

415/885-0200 or 1-800/553-1900, ⓦ www. hoteldiva.com. Trendy modern art hotel with spacious rooms and sleek metal and leather furniture. Touts itself as the sexiest downtown hotel. ❺

Monaco 501 Geary St at Taylor, Union Square ☎415/292-0100 or 1-800/214-4220, ⓦ www. monaco-sf.com. Quirky boutique hotel in a historic Beaux Arts building. Canopied beds and goldfish in each room; the Grace Slick suite features her art for wealthy Airplane fans. ❽

The Mosser 54 Fourth St at Market, SoMa ☎415/986-4400 or 1-800/227-3804, ⓦ www. themosser.com. A recent funky conversion fusing Victorian touches like ornamental molding with mod leather sofas. The chocolate and olive rooms may be tiny, but each is artfully crammed with amenities including multi-disc CD players. ❺

Ocean Park Motel 2690 46th Ave at Wawona, Ocean Beach ☎415/566-7020, ⓦ oceanparkmotel. citysearch.com. A fair way from downtown (25min by MUNI), this is nonetheless a great Art Deco motel that's convenient for the beach and the zoo, and has an on-site kids' play area. ❹

The Phoenix 601 Eddy St at Larkin, Tenderloin ☎415/776-1380 or 1-800/248-9466, ⓦ www. thephoenixhotel.com. This raucous retro motel is a favorite with up-and-coming bands when they're in town; there's a small pool, and the rooms are eclectically decorated in tropical colors and have changing local artwork. ❺

Queen Anne 1590 Sutter St at Octavia, Fillmore ☎415/441-2828 or 1-800/227-3970, ⓦ www. queenanne.com. Gloriously excessive restored Victorian with some bargain rates. Each room is stuffed with gold-accented Rococo furniture and bunches of silk flowers: the parlor (where afternoon sherry is served) is over-filled with museum-quality period furniture. ❹

The Red Victorian Bed, Breakfast and Art 1665 Haight St at Cole, Haight-Ashbury ☎415/864-1978, ⓦ www.redvic.com. Homey B&B, decorated with the owner's ethnic arts and exuding her desire for world peace. Rooms vary from simple to opulent: the best feature is the shared bathrooms, including a goldfish-filled toilet cistern. ❹

San Remo Hotel 2237 Mason St at Chestnut, North Beach ☎415/776-8688 or 1-800/352-7366, ⓦ www.sanremohotel.com. Quirky option close to Fisherman's Wharf. Rooms in this warren-like converted house are cozy and chintzy: all share spotless bathrooms and a few have sinks. ❸

Sir Francis Drake 450 Powell St at Sutter, Union Square ☎415/392-7755 or 1-800/227-5480, ⓦ www.sirfrancisdrake.com. The lobby is a riot of marble grandeur and red or purple furnishings – the rooms are calmer, with a gentle apple-green

color scheme and full facilities. ❻

Stanyan Park Hotel 750 Stanyan St at Waller, Haight-Ashbury ☎415/751-1000, ⓦ www.stanyan-park.com. Overlooking Golden Gate Park, this small hotel has 35 sumptuous rooms busily decorated in country florals, heavy drapes, and junior four-poster beds. ❻

Surf Motel 2265 Lombard St at Pierce, Cow Hollow ☎415/922-1950, ⓦ www.surfmotorinn. com. This old-school motel has two tiers of bright, simple rooms that are sparklingly clean. Unbeatable prices. ❸

Hostels

Elements Hostel 2524 Mission St at 21st ☎415/647-4100 or 1-866/327-8407. One of the few places to stay in this area. Most dorms have only four beds and there are some doubles. Good amenities and no curfew. From $25. ❷

The Globe Hostel 10 Hallam Place, SoMa ☎415/431-0540, ⓦ www.hostelz.com. Lively South of Market hostel with a young clientele and 33 rooms, split between dorms and private rooms. There's free coffee and, best of all, no curfew. Dorm beds from $20.

Green Tortoise 494 Broadway at Montgomery, North Beach ☎415/834-1000 or 1-800/867-8647, ⓦ www.greentortoise.com. This laid-back hostel is the best place to stay if money's tight: there's room for 130 people in dorm beds and double rooms (with shared bath). Both options include free Internet access, use of the small on-site sauna, and complimentary breakfast. No curfew. Dorm beds from $20.

HI-San Francisco City Center 685 Ellis St at Larkin, Tenderloin ☎415/474-5721, ⓦ www. norcalhostels.org. Recent conversion from the old *Atherton Hotel*, this is a spiffy new hostel; its 272 beds are divided into four-person dorms, each with en-suite bath. There's no curfew and overall, it's friendly, funky, and oozes California cool. Dorms $23 members, $26 others; private rooms from $66 members. ❶–❸

HI-San Francisco Fisherman's Wharf Building 240, Fort Mason ☎415/771-7277, ⓦ www.hiayh. org. On the waterfront between the wharf and the Golden Gate Bridge, this is a choice option for an outdoorsy traveler, a standard hostel housed in a historic former Civil War barracks. Although public transportation connects the hostel with the main sights, it's a little out of the way on the federal complex at Fort Mason. Beds from $23.

HI-San Francisco Union Square 312 Mason St at Geary, Union Square ☎415/788-5604, ⓦ www. hiayh.org. Despite having almost 300 beds, this downtown hostel still fills up quickly in peak season: four-person dorms are spotless, sharing bathroom facilities between eight people. The private rooms are pricier and sleep two people. Dorms from $23.

Pacific Tradewinds Guesthouse 680 Sacramento St at Kearny, Chinatown ☏ 415/433-7970 or May–Oct only ☏ 1-800/486-7975, ⓦ www.san-francisco-hostel.com. The best budget accommodation in the center of town, this small hostel offers free, high-speed Internet access, a clean kitchen, plus a large, communal dining table that's convivial too. Dorm beds $24. ❶

Gay and lesbian accommodation

24 Henry 24 Henry St at Sanchez, Castro ☏ 415/864-5686 or 1-800/900-5686, ⓦ www.24henry.com. This small blue and white home tucked away on a leafy residential street north of Market is predominantly a gay male guesthouse with 5 simple rooms, one with private bath. Online specials. ❹

Inn on Castro 321 Castro St at Market, Castro

☏ 415/861-0321, ⓦ www.innoncastro.com. This luxurious B&B is spread across two nearby houses: it has eight rooms and three apartments available, all of which are brightly decorated in individual styles and have private baths and phones. ❺

Noe's Nest 3973 23rd St at Noe, Noe Valley ☏ 415/821-0751, ⓦ www.noesnest.com. Seven-room B&B (six with private bath) on a quiet street in Noe Valley. Lavish breakfasts are served each morning, and there's a hot tub too. ❺

The Parker House 520 Church St at 18th, Castro ☏ 415/621-3222 or 1-888/520-7275, ⓦ www.parkerguesthouse.com. This converted Edwardian mansion is set in beautiful gardens and has a friendly vibe, thanks to its ample, large common areas: there's a sunny breakfast room and on-site sauna. ❺

The Renoir 45 McAllister St, at Seventh, Civic Center ☏ 415/626-5200 or 1-800/576-3388, ⓦ www.renoirhotel.com. This wedge-shaped building is a historic landmark with 135 rooms that have recently been unexcitingly refurbished with floral touches. Especially popular during Gay Pride for its Market Street views along the parade route. ❺

The City

San Francisco is a city of hills and distinct neighborhoods. As a general rule, elevation means wealth – the higher up you are, the better off you are. Commercial square-footage is surprisingly small and mostly confined to the downtown area, and the rest of the city is made up of primarily residential neighborhoods with street-level shopping districts, easily explored on foot. Armed with a good map and strong legs, you could plough through much of the city in a day, but the best way to get to know San Francisco is to dawdle.

Union Square

The city's heart can be found around **Union Square**, located north of Market Street and bordered by Powell and Stockton streets, which was recently spruced up with the addition of shady trees and benches. Cable cars clank past shoppers and theater-goers who gravitate to the district's many upscale hotels, department stores, and boutiques. The statue in the center commemorates Admiral Dewey's success in the Spanish–American War, though the square takes its name from its role as gathering place for stumping speechmakers during the US Civil War. The square witnessed the attempted assassination of President Gerald Ford outside the **St Francis Hotel** (now *Westin*) in 1975, and was also the location of Francis Ford Coppola's film *The Conversation*, where Gene Hackman spied on strolling lovers. Many of **Dashiell Hammett**'s detective stories, such as *The Maltese Falcon*, are set partly in the *St Francis*; in fact, during the 1920s, he worked there as a Pinkerton detective.

On Geary Street, on the south side of the square, the **Theater District** is a pint-sized Broadway of restaurants, tourist hotels, and serious and "adult" theaters. On the eastern side of the square, **Maiden Lane** is a chic urban walkway that before

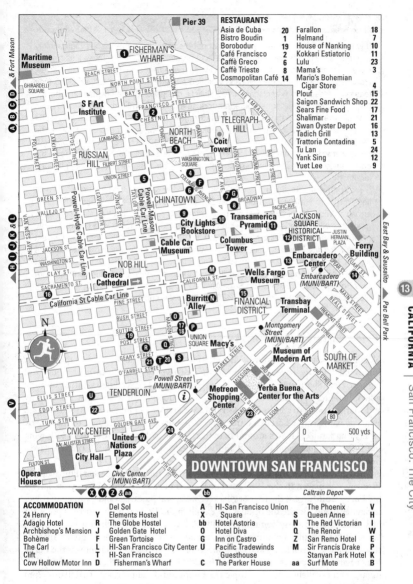

RESTAURANTS

Asia de Cuba	20	Farallon	18
Bistro Boudin	1	Helmand	7
Borobodur	19	House of Nanking	10
Café Francisco	2	Kokkari Estiatorio	11
Caffè Greco	6	Lulu	23
Caffè Trieste	8	Mama's	3
Cosmopolitan Café	14	Mario's Bohemian Cigar Store	4
		Plouf	15
		Saigon Sandwich Shop	22
		Sears Fine Food	17
		Shalimar	21
		Swan Oyster Depot	16
		Tadich Grill	13
		Trattoria Contadina	5
		Tu Lan	24
		Yank Sing	12
		Yuet Lee	9

DOWNTOWN SAN FRANCISCO

0   500 yds

ACCOMMODATION

24 Henry	Y	Del Sol	A	HI-San Francisco Union		The Phoenix	V
Adagio Hotel	R	Elements Hostel	X	Square	S	Queen Anne	H
Archbishop's Mansion	J	The Globe Hostel	bb	Hotel Astoria	N	The Red Victorian	I
Bohème	F	Golden Gate Hotel	O	Hotel Diva	Q	The Renoir	W
The Carl	L	Green Tortoise	G	Inn on Castro	Z	San Remo Hotel	E
Clift	T	HI-San Francisco City Center	U	Pacific Tradewinds		Sir Francis Drake	P
Cow Hollow Motor Inn	D	HI-San Francisco Fisherman's Wharf	C	Guesthouse		Stanyan Park Hotel	K
				The Parker House	aa	Surf Mote	B

the 1906 earthquake and fire was one of the city's roughest areas, where homicides averaged around ten a month. Nowadays, aside from some prohibitively expensive boutiques, its main feature is San Francisco's only **Frank Lloyd Wright building**, an intriguing circular space at no. 140 that was a prototype for the Guggenheim Museum in New York. Now occupied by the Xanadu Tribal Art Gallery, feel free to wander inside, but just don't expect a warm welcome from the tourist-weary staff.

It was the invention of the **cable car** that put the high in San Francisco's high society as it made life on the hills both possible and practical. Since 1873, these little trolleys have been an integral part of life in the city, supposedly thanks to Scots-born Andrew Hallidie's concern for horses. Having watched a team struggle and fall, breaking their legs on a steep San Franciscan street, Hallidie designed a pulley system around the thick wire rope his father had patented for use in the California mines (the Gold Rush was slowing, and so the Hallidies needed a new market for their product). Despite locals' initial doubts, a transportation revolution followed. At their peak, just before the 1906 earthquake, over six hundred cable cars traveled 110 miles of track throughout the city at a maximum 9.5mph; over the years, usage dwindled and, in 1964, nostalgic citizens voted to preserve the last seventeen miles (now just ten) as a moving historic landmark.

Today there are three lines. Two of them, the Powell & Mason and the Powell & Hyde lines run from Hallidie Plaza off Union Square at Powell and Market streets to Fisherman's Wharf. The Powell & Hyde is the steepest, reaching a hair-raising 21-degree grade between Lombard and Chestnut streets. The oldest route, the California line, climbs Nob Hill along California Street from the Embarcadero, rattling past the fanciest hotels in the city. The cars fasten onto a moving two-inch cable, which runs beneath the streets, gripping on the ascent then releasing at the top and gliding down the other side. You can see the huge motors that still power these cables in the **Cable Car Museum and Powerhouse**, 1201 Mason St at Washington Street (daily: April–Sept 10am–6pm; Oct–March 10am–5pm; free; ☎415/474-1887, ⊛www.cablecarmuseum.org).

The Financial District

North of the city's main artery, Market Street, the glass-and-steel skyscrapers of the **Financial District** have sprung up in the last twenty years to form the only real highrise area. Sharp-suited workers clog the streets and coffee kiosks during business hours, but after 6pm, the area pretty much shuts down. Stop at the corner of Kearny and Market streets to admire **Lotta's Fountain**, one of San Francisco's most treasured artifacts, named after Lotta Crabtree, one of the first children brought to the city by pioneering families. It was around here that people gathered to hear news following the 1906 earthquake and fire, and also where famed soprano Luisa Tetrazzini gave a free concert on Christmas Eve, 1910.

Once cut off from the rest of San Francisco by the double-decker Embarcadero Freeway – damaged in the 1989 earthquake and finally torn down two years later – the **Ferry Building**, at the foot of Market Street, was modeled on the cathedral tower in Seville, Spain. Before the bridges were built in the 1930s it was the arrival point for fifty thousand cross-bay commuters daily. A few ferries still dock here (see p.1113), but after years of playing home to colorless offices, it has finally undergone a massive renovation that's seen shops and cafés line its halls. The first new tenant was the **Ferry Plaza Farmers Market**, which moved indoors from its old site in front of the building – it's an excellent place to sample the sumptuous local produce (Tues 10am–2pm & Sat 8am–2pm; ☎415/353-5650, ⊛www.ferryplazafarmersmarket.com).

Since the freeway was pulled down, the area around it, known as **The Embarcadero**, has experienced a dramatic renaissance – from an area of charmless office blocks into a swanky waterfront district with some of the city's finest restaurants and hotels making the most of the bay views.

From the vast and unimaginative **Embarcadero Center** shopping mall and the square concrete tubing of the fountains in **Justin Herman Plaza** at the foot of Market Street, it's a few blocks down to **Montgomery Street**, where the grand pillared entrances and banking halls of the post-1906 earthquake buildings era jostle for attention with a mixed bag of modern towers. The best known is undoubtedly the **Bank of America** monolith, 555 California St, at Kearney, where the state's largest financial institution has its headquarters; this enormous building was initially unpopular when finished in 1971, though affection has grown over the years for the broad-shouldered hulk. The **Wells Fargo History Museum**, 420 Montgomery St (Mon–Fri 9am–5pm; free; ☎ 415/396-2619, ⓦ www.wellsfargo.com), traces the far-from-slick origins of San Francisco's big money, right from the days of the Gold Rush, with mining equipment, gold nuggets, photographs, and a genuine retired stagecoach.

Jackson Square and the Barbary Coast

A century or so ago, the eastern flank of the Financial District formed part of the **Barbary Coast**. This area of landfill appeared thanks to the hundreds of ships that lay abandoned by sailors heading for the Gold Rush; enterprising San Franciscans used the dry ships as hotels, bars, and stores. At the time, the district was a rough-and-tumble place that gave San Francisco an unsavory reputation as **Baghdad by the Bay**, packed as it was with saloons and brothels where hapless young males were given Mickey Finns and forcibly taken aboard merchant ships and pressed into involuntary servitude. William Randolph Hearst's *Examiner* newspaper lobbied frantically to shut down the quarter, resulting in a 1917 California law prohibiting prostitution. Remains of the cradle of San Francisco can be seen in the **Jackson Square Historic District**, not an actual square but an area bordered by Washington, Columbus, Sansome, and Pacific streets; these were the only buildings downtown to escape the catastrophic 1906 fire unharmed, and Jackson Street in particular provides a hint of what early San Francisco looked like. A detour down the redbrick-lined Hotaling Place, with its hitching posts and antique lamps, is similarly revealing.

The landmark **Transamerica Pyramid**, at the foot of diagonal Columbus Avenue and Washington Street, is San Francisco's tallest building. The 48-story structure, capped by a colossal 212-foot hollow spire, arose in 1972 amid a city-planning furor that earned it the name of "Pereira's Prick," after its LA-based architect William Pereira, and since then it's been indisputably the signature of San Francisco's skyline. Though it survived the 1989 earthquake undamaged, for security reasons there's no longer access to the 27th-floor viewing deck. The block on which the Transamerica Pyramid stands is a historic one: Rudyard Kipling, Robert Louis Stevenson, Mark Twain, and William Randolph Hearst all rented office space in the building that originally stood on this site, and regularly hung around the notorious *Bank Exchange* bar within. Legend has it that Dr Sun Yat-sen – whose statue is in Chinatown, three blocks away – wrote the Chinese constitution and orchestrated the successful overthrow of the Manchu Dynasty from his second-floor office here. Next door is the pleasant **Transamerica Redwood Park** with fountains perfect for an outdoor lunch. Heading west on Jackson or Pacific streets from the area leads you back to Columbus and the green-copper siding of the **Columbus Tower**, 906 Kearny St, the de facto beginning of North Beach. Director and San Francisco native Francis Ford Coppola owns the building, and his *Niebaum-Coppola Café* on the ground floor serves sandwiches, pasta, and wine from his Napa Valley winery.

Chinatown

Chinatown's 24 square blocks smack in the middle of San Francisco make up the second-largest Chinese community outside Asia (after New York City). It has its roots in the migration of Chinese laborers to the city after the completion of the transcontinental railroad, and the arrival of Chinese sailors keen to benefit from the Gold Rush. The city didn't extend much of a welcome: they were met by a tide of vicious racial attacks and the 1882 Chinese Exclusion Act, the only law in American history aimed at a single racial group that prevented Chinese immigration and naturalization. Nowadays, the Chinese population has been joined by Vietnamese, Koreans, Thais, and Laotians: by day the area seethes with activity, while by night it's a blaze of neon. Overcrowding is compounded by a brisk tourist trade – sadly, however, Chinatown boasts some of the tackiest stores and facades in the city, making it more akin to shopping in a bad part of Hong Kong than in Beijing. Indeed, Chinese tourists are often disappointed in the neighborhood's disorder – for a truer sense of everyday Chinese life in San Francisco, you're better off heading to the Richmond district in the city's northwestern corner.

Gold-ornamented portals and brightly painted balconies sit above the souvenir shops and restaurants of narrow **Grant Avenue**, the tourist thoroughfare; pass under the entrance arch at Bush Street and you'll be met by an assault of plastic Buddhas, cloisonné "health balls," noisemakers, and chirping mechanical crickets in every doorway. **Old St Mary's Cathedral**, 660 California St at Grant Street, was one of the few San Francisco buildings to survive the 1906 earthquake and fire, and there's a good photo display of the damage to the city in the entranceway.

Parallel to Grant Avenue, **Stockton Street** is crammed with exotic fish and produce markets, bakeries, and herbalists, and is the local main drag. Inside the **Ellison Herb Shop**, 805 Stockton St at Sacramento Street, Chinatown's best-stocked herbal pharmacy, you'll find clerks filling orders the ancient Chinese way – using hand-held scales and abacuses – from cabinets filled with dried bark, roots, sharks' fins, cicadas, ginseng, and other staples. Here, between Grant and Stockton, jumbled alleys hold the most worthwhile stops. The best of these is **Waverly Place,** a two-block corridor of brightly painted balconies that was lined with brothels before the 1906 catastrophe and is now home to three opulent but skillfully hidden **temples:** Norras at no. 109, Jen Sen on the second floor of no. 146, and Tien Hou on the fourth floor of no. 125. The latter is the most impressive, with its ornate interior splashed with gold and vermilion. All three temples are still in use and open to visitors (daily 10am–5pm). Although the temples don't charge admission, it's respectful to leave a donation and not use cameras or camcorders inside.

Some of the hundred-plus **restaurants** in Chinatown (see p.1129) are historical landmarks in themselves. *Sam Wo*, 813 Washington St at Grant Avenue, is a cheap and churlish ex-haunt of the Beats, where Gary Snyder taught Jack Kerouac to eat with chopsticks and had them both thrown out with his loud and passionate interpretation of Zen poetry.

North Beach

Resting in the hollow between Russian and Telegraph hills, and bisected by throbbing Columbus Avenue, **North Beach** has always been a gateway for immigrants, especially the Italians who flocked here during the Gold Rush. It became the center of an alternative scene in 1953, after the opening of the **City Lights Bookstore,** 261 Columbus Ave at Broadway (☎415/362-8193, ⓦ www.citylights.com); the first paperback bookstore in the US stands amid the flashing neon and sleazy clubs at this intersection, open until midnight seven days a week, and still owned by poet and novelist Lawrence Ferlinghetti. The **Beat Generation** briefly made the store (and the city) the literary capital of America, achieving overnight notoriety when charges of obscenity were leveled at Allen Ginsberg's poem *Howl* in 1957, which he first performed in a gallery in Cow Hollow. It was the hedonistic antics of the Beats as much as their literary merits that struck a chord, and North Beach came to symbolize a wild and subversive lifestyle. The roadtrips and riotous partying, the drug-taking, and the embrace of Eastern religions were emulated nationwide, while tourists poured into North Beach for "Beatnik Tours." Then, when the Beat movement imploded, the younger hipsters – whom Kerouac & Co. had derided as juniors, or "hippies," for their dovish views – gathered in Haight-Ashbury, thus beginning the psychedelic Sixties (see p.1126).

Next to the bookstore, **Vesuvio's**, an old North Beach bar where the likes of Dylan Thomas and Kerouac would get loaded, remains a haven for the lesser-knowns to pontificate on the state of the arts. At the crossroads of Columbus and Broadway, poetry meets porn in a raucous assembly of strip joints, coffeehouses, and drag clubs. The most famous of these is the *Condor Club*, 300 Columbus Ave (now reincarnated as the *Condor Sports Bar*), where Carol "44 inches" Doda slipped out of her top one night and kickstarted the concept of topless waitresses in 1964. The landmark site still preserves photos and clippings from the original club's heyday.

As you continue north on Columbus Avenue, you enter the heart of the old **Italian neighborhood**, an enclave of narrow streets and leafy enclosures. Explorations lead to small landmarks like the **Café Trieste**, (see p.1129), where the jukebox blasts out opera classics to a heavy-duty art crowd sipping cappuccinos and browsing slim volumes; legend has it that Francis Ford Coppola wrote the screenplay for *The Godfather* here. Dawdle in the grassy plaza known as **Washington Square Park** that plays host to dozens of local Chinese each morning practising *t'ai chi*, then head up the very steep steps on Filbert Street to reach Telegraph Hill and the **Coit Tower**, which affords grand views of the city and beyond (daily 10am–6pm; $4.50; ☏415/362-0808).

Alcatraz

Before the rocky islet of **Alcatraz** became America's most dreaded **high-security prison**, in 1934, it had already served as a fortress and military jail. Surrounded by the freezing, impassable water of San Francisco Bay, it made an ideal place to hold the nation's most wanted criminals – men such as Al Capone and Machine Gun Kelly. The conditions were inhumane: inmates were kept in solitary confinement, in cells no larger than nine by five feet, most without light. They were not allowed to eat together, read newspapers, play cards, or even talk; relatives could visit for only two hours each month. Escape really was impossible. Nine men managed to get off the rock but none gained his freedom – the only two to make it to land (who had used a jacket stuffed with inflated surgical rings as a raft) were soon apprehended.

Due to its massive running costs, the prison finally closed in 1963. The island remained abandoned until 1969, when a group of Native Americans staged an occupation as part of a peaceful attempt to claim the island for their people, citing treaties that designated all federal land not in use as automatically reverting to their ownership. Using all the bureaucratic trickery it could muster, the government finally ousted them in 1971, claiming the operative lighthouse qualified it as active.

At least 750,000 tourists each year take the excellent hour-long, self-guided audio **tours** of the abandoned prison, which include some sharp anecdotal commentary as well as campy re-enactments of prison life featuring improvised voices of the likes of Capone and Kelly. Note that the island's name is a corruption of the Spanish for pelicans (*alcatraces*), although the only reason the current islet is known as Alcatraz is thanks to a muddle-headed English mapmaker and captain. He confused the names of several outcrops in the bay in 1826 – what we know as Yerba Buena Island was in fact the original Alcatraz.

Boats to Alcatraz leave from Pier 33 ($18.75 including audio tour; 9.30am, then every 30min 10.15am–2.15pm; last tour winter 4.10pm, summer 5.10pm); allow around two hours for a visit. Advance reservations are essential – in peak season, it's impossible to snag a ticket for same-day travel and ideally you should allow two weeks (☏415/981-7625, ⊛www.alcatrazcruises.com).

CALIFORNIA | San Francisco: The City

To the west of Columbus, **Russian Hill** was named for six unknown Russian sailors who died here on an expedition in the early 1800s. In the summer, there's always a long line of cars waiting to drive down the tight curves of **Lombard Street**. Surrounded by palatial dwellings and herbaceous borders, Lombard is an especially thrilling drive at night, when the tourists leave and the city lights twinkle below. Even if you're without a car, the journey up here is worth it for a visit to the **San Francisco Art Institute**, 800 Chestnut St (daily 8am–9pm; free; T 415/771-7020, W www.sanfranciscoart.edu), where the Diego Rivera Gallery has an outstanding mural created by the painter in 1931. Walking south from the Institute for four blocks on Jones Street, you'll find **Macondray Lane**, a pedestrian-only "street" thought to be one of the inspirations for Armistead Maupin's rollicking saga, *Tales of the City* (see p.1322).

Fisherman's Wharf

San Francisco rarely tries to pass off pure, unabashed commercialism as a worthy tourist attraction, but with **Fisherman's Wharf** and the nearby waterfront district, it makes an exception. It's the one place in town guaranteed to produce shudders of embarrassment from most locals.

An inventive use of statistics allows the area to proclaim itself the most-visited tourist attraction in the entire country; in fact, this crowded and hideous ensemble of waterfront kitsch and fast-food stands makes a sad and rather misleading introduction to the city. It may be hard to believe, but this was once a genuine fishing port; the few fishing vessels that can still afford the exorbitant mooring charges are usually finished by early morning and get out before the tourists arrive. The shops and bars here are among the most overpriced in the city, and crowd-weary families do little to add to the ambiance.

If you do brave it, the best diversion is the **Aquarium of the Bay** at Pier 39 (Mon–Thurs 10am–7pm, Fri–Sun 10am–8pm; $13.95; T 415/623-5000, W www.aquariumofthebay.com), which has a transparent tunnel so you can walk among gliding sharks and rays and a hands-on exhibition where you can stroke them. One-hour **bay cruises** depart several times a day from piers 39 and 41 (see p.1113). If you head west to the museums of **Fort Mason** and on to the expanse of green parkland along the **Marina district**, you'll get an excellent view of the Golden Gate Bridge.

Nob Hill

The posh hotels and Masonic institutions of **Nob Hill** exemplify San Francisco's old wealth, which arrived in the late 1800s with the robber-baron industrialists who moved here to build the Central Pacific Railroad. These financiers – who gave Nob Hill its name, after either "nabob," a Moghul prince, or "snob" – all built opulent mansions on the hill, only to see every one of them burn down in the fire caused by the earthquake of 1906. Aside from astounding views over the city and beyond, there are very few real sights to reward the stiff climb (or cable car ride) up the hill.

Begun soon after the fire, lumbering **Grace Cathedral**, perched on top of the hill, is one of the biggest hunks of sham-Gothic architecture in the US. It took more than sixty years to finish and it suffers from a hodgepodge of styles as a result: the ugly reinforced concrete from the 1960s is particularly off-putting. For no reason other than the fact they were available, the entrance is adorned with faithful replicas of the fifteenth-century Ghiberti doors of the Florence Baptistry; the one place worth detouring inside here is the AIDS Interfaith Chapel, adorned with Keith Haring's vibrant cast bronze altar. A block east, be sure to go inside the

Fairmont Hotel, 950 Mason St at Sacramento, to get a sense of the opulence that once ruled the hill: take its elevators up for a great view of the city. Across from the *Fairmont*, the brownstone of the **Pacific Union Club** was the only original Nob Hill structure left standing after the fire.

The Tenderloin, Civic Center, and SoMa

While parts of San Francisco can almost seem to be an urban utopia, the adjoining districts of **the Tenderloin** and **Civic Center** are a gritty reminder that not everybody has it so easy. **SoMa**, the urban district *So*uth of *Ma*rket Street, meanwhile, was transformed by the dot-com boom – from an industrial wasteland to a hive of loft offices and granite-walled eateries, centered on the lovely Yerba Buena Gardens; of course, the Internet crash ended much of its economic upswing, though the area's slowly reviving again.

The majestic federal and municipal buildings of **Civic Center**, squashed between the Tenderloin and SoMa, can't help but look strangely out of sync, both with their immediate neighbors and with San Francisco as a whole. Their grand Beaux Arts style is at odds with the quirky wooden architecture of the rest of the city: little wonder, as they're the sole remnant of a grand architectural plan to transform the city's downtown into a boulevard-dotted, Parisian-inspired place after the buildings there were levelled in the 1906 earthquake. It was at the huge, green-domed **City Hall**, on the northern edge of the dismal **United Nations Plaza**, that Mayor George Moscone and gay Supervisor Harvey Milk were assassinated in 1978 (see p.1125). The recently restored gold plate dome is an impressive relic of Gold Rush-era largesse. If you want to take one of the free, fascinating tours round its interior, sign up at the Docent Tour kiosk on the Van Ness Avenue side of the building (tours Mon–Fri 10am, noon & 2pm, Sat & Sun 12.30pm; ℡415/554-4799, ⓦwww.ci.sf.ca.us/cityhall).

Formerly one of San Francisco's least desirable neighborhoods, SoMa enjoyed a rebirth during the 1990s that converted many of its warehouses to offices for the fledgling Internet industry, but the district has taken a tumble since the dot-crom crash and most of those office spaces now stand empty. The area's anchor attraction, though, is the **SF Museum of Modern Art**, 151 3rd St at Mission (Fri–Tues 11am–5.45pm, Thurs 11am–8.45pm; summer opens at 10am; $12.50, free first Tues; ℡415/357-4000, ⓦwww.sfmoma.org), which opened here in January 1995. Major works include paintings by Jackson Pollock, Frida Kahlo, and Diego Rivera, though the temporary exhibitions are the museum's strongest suit. The building, designed by Swiss architect Mario Botta, is flooded with natural light from a striking cylindrical skylight while the upper galleries are connected by a vertigo-inducing metal catwalk.

Opposite the museum is the other totem of civic pride, the **Yerba Buena Center for the Arts**, 701 Mission St at 3rd **St** (Tues, Wed, Sat & Sun 11am–6pm, Thurs & Fri 11am–8pm; $6, free first Tues of month; ℡415/978-2787, ⓦwww.yerbabuenaarts.org). This spectacular $44-million project features performance and gallery spaces used by both national and international touring exhibitions. Frankly, however, the big draw here is the stunning five and a half acres of gardens in which it sits. The 50-foot Sierra granite waterfall memorial to Martin Luther King Jr is especially moving, inscribed with excerpts from his speeches, Next to the gardens stands the **SONY Metreon** mall (℡415/369-6000, ⓦwww.metreon.com), an enormous 3D advertisement for the electronics giant that is only worth stopping by for its cinema, the most convenient multiscreen to downtown.

An interesting new addition is the **Museum of African Diaspora**, around the corner at 685 Mission St (Mon, Wed & Thurs–Sat 10am–6pm, Sun noon–5pm; $10; ℡415/358-7200, ⓦwww.moadsf.org). Several floors of light, airy space celebrate humanity through four themes – origins, movement, adaptation, and transformation – with subtle modern art, photography, and video displays. A few blocks southwest at 875 Howard St, some of the best exhibits from the **California Academy of Sciences** and **Steinhart Aquarium** (daily 10am–5pm; $10; ☏ 415/321-8000, ⓦ www.calacademy.org), including a dinosaur display, coral reef tank, and penguin feeding, are temporarily housed here pending their return to the usual locations in Golden Gate Park (see p.1127).

Sights in this massive area thin out considerably as you head south into a warehouse-lined former wasteland – though at night, this is the nexus of San Francisco's club culture. There are dozens of dance clubs here (see p.1134) as well as the legendary **Folsom Street**, once synonymous with S&M. Though Folsom has calmed down from its chaps-and-whips heyday in the 1970s, it's still home to bars which cater to the city's leather community and can be quite a scene, especially on weekends.

In the far southern reaches of SoMa stands **AT&T Park**, overlooking the waters at 3rd and King streets. Home to baseball's San Francisco Giants, the stadium is a remarkable addition to the city's waterfront. The faux old-brick building offers superb views of the bay beyond the outfield fences, some of the finest food to ever grace a ballpark, as well as the chance to see the odd home run splash into the bay. If the team's not playing while you're in town, check out the park on one of the twice-hourly tours (non-game days only, 10.30am & 12.30pm; $10; ☏ 415/972-2000, ⓦ www.sfgiants.com).

The Mission

Vibrant, hip, and ethnically mixed, **the Mission** is easily San Francisco's most interesting neighborhood. A mile or so south of downtown, nestled in a basin, it's also the warmest and the summer fogs that dog the rest of the city leave this area alone. The traditional first stop for immigrants, the Mission was initially predominantly Scandinavian, then Irish before becoming a sizeable Latin American settlement. Though hipster Anglos have in recent years swarmed to its old buildings and cheap rents, it's still a joyously Hispanic place and one of the unmissable sights of the city.

The area takes its name from the old **Mission Dolores**, 3321 16th St at Dolores (daily 9am–4pm; $1 suggested donation; ☏ 415/621-8203, ⓦ missiondolores.city search.com), the oldest building to survive the 1906 earthquake and fire. Founded in 1776, it was the sixth in a series of missions built along the Pacific coast as Spain staked its claim to California; the graves of the Native Americans it tried to "civilize" can be seen in the cemetery next door, along with those of white pioneers. Go early in the morning to avoid the tour buses.

The Hispanic heart of the Mission lies east of Mission Street between 16th and 24th streets. Here you'll absorb the district's original Latin flavor among the Nicaraguan, Salvadoran, Costa Rican, and Mexican stores and restaurants, as well as markets selling tropical fruits and *panaderias* baking traditional pastries. Meanwhile, to catch the Anglo pulse of the area, head along to the same stretch along Valencia Street, one block west: the profusion of independent bookstores and thrift stores around here makes for heavenly browsing, and the vicinity of 22nd Street has become a new gourmet-dining scene. It's worth stopping by to take a snap of the huge yellow **Levi Strauss & Co. factory**, 250 Valencia St at 14th Street, constructed after the original factories were destroyed in 1906.

What really sets the Mission apart from the city's other neighborhoods are its **murals** – there are over two hundred in all, though many are more heartfelt than skilled or beautiful. The densest concentration is along **Balmy Alley**, between

△ Mission Dolores

Folsom and Harrison off 24th Street, which is especially known for its politically charged paintings depicting the agonies of many Central American countries. For a more detailed recap of the murals' history and meaning, join one of the **tours** run by the mural organization, Precita Eyes, 2981 24th St at Harrison (tours Sat & Sun 1.30pm; $12; ☎415/285-2287, ⓦwww.precitaeyes.org).

The Castro

Progressive and celebratory, but also increasingly comfortable and wealthy, **the Castro** is the city's gay capital, providing a barometer for the state of the grown-up and sobered gay scene. Some people insist that this is still the wildest place in town, while others reckon it's a shadow of its former self; all agree that things are not the same as a decade or so ago, when a walk down the Castro would have had you gawping at the revelry. Most of the same bars and hangouts still stand, but these days they're host to an altogether different and more conservative breed. Cute shops and restaurants lend a young professional feel to the place. A visit to the district is a must if you're to get any idea of just what San Francisco is all about, though in terms of visible street life, the few blocks around Castro and Market streets contain about all there is to see – the liveliest time to stroll around is on Sunday afternoons, when the streetside cafés are packed with well-groomed Castro residents.

Harvey Milk Plaza, by the Castro MUNI station, is dedicated to the assassinated gay supervisor, who owned a camera store in the Castro. The man who shot Milk and Mayor George Moscone, Dan White, was a disgruntled ex-colleague who resigned in protest at their liberal policies; at the trial, his plea of temporary insanity caused by harmful additives in his fast food – the so-called "Twinkie defense" – won him a sentence of five years' imprisonment for manslaughter and the derision of the local gay community. Reactions were angry enough to spark the violent "White Night" riots, as protesters marched into City Hall, burning police cars as they went. As for White, he was released from prison in 1985 and, unable to find a job, committed suicide soon afterwards.

Before heading down Castro Street into the heart of the neighborhood, take a short walk to the former location of the **Names Project** at 2363A Market St, which sponsored the creation of **"The Quilt"** – a gargantuan blanket in which each panel measures six feet by three feet (the size of a grave site) and bears the name of a person lost to AIDS. Made by lovers, friends, and families, the panels are stitched together and regularly tour the country and the world; it has been spread on the Mall in Washington, DC, several times to dramatize the epidemic. The 54-ton Quilt and Names Project Foundation moved to a permanent home in Atlanta in 2001.

The junction of **Castro and 18th Street**, known as the "gayest four corners of the earth," marks the Castro's center, cluttered with bookstores, clothing stores, cafés, and bars. The side streets offer a slightly more exclusive fare of exotic delicatessens, fine wines, and fancy florists amid manicured and leafy residential roads.

Haight-Ashbury

The fame of **Haight-Ashbury**, two miles west of downtown San Francisco, far outstrips its size and its appeal. No more than eight blocks in length, centered on the junction of Haight and Ashbury streets, "The Haight" was a run-down Victorian neighborhood until it was transformed into the hub of counterculture cool during the 1960s. Since then the area has become gentrified, but it retains a collection of radical bookstores, laid-back cafés, record stores, and secondhand clothing emporia, not to mention a ragged collection of hangers-on.

All there is to do in the Haight today is to stroll around the **shops**, and pick your way past the dozens of beggars. Meanwhile down at the eastern end of Haight Street, around Fillmore Street, is the area known as the **Lower Haight**.

For decades a primarily African-American neighborhood, it has been transformed over the past decade or so by youthful immigrants from Britain and elsewhere into a stomping ground for the city's rave culture.

Golden Gate Park

In a city with an abundance of green space, **Golden Gate Park** stands out as not just the largest, but also the most beautiful, and safest, of its parks. Spreading three miles or so west from the Haight as far as the Pacific, it was constructed on what was then an area of wild sand dunes buffeted by the spray from the ocean. Despite the throngs of joggers, polo players, roller-skaters, cyclists, and strollers, it never seems to get overcrowded and you can always find a spot to be alone.

Of the park's several museums, the best is the completely rebuilt **M.H. de Young Museum** (Tues–Sun 9.30am–5.15pm; $10; ☎415/863-3330, Ⓦwww.thinker.org). Don't be put off by the ugly square black-box exterior because the gems inside, which augment the extensive American art from colonial times up to the present day with superb Native American, Latin American, African and Oceanic pieces, are well worth devoting a couple of hours to. Opposite the museum, the California Academy of Sciences and Steinhart Aquarium buildings are now being renovated but some of their exhibits are on display in the SoMa district (see p.1123). Slightly to the west, the **Japanese Tea Garden** (daily Mar–Oct 8.30am–6pm, Nov–Feb 9am–5pm; $3.50; ☎415/752-1171) is dominated by a massive bronze Buddha, while carp-filled ponds and bonsai and cherry trees lend a tranquil feel, as long as you can ignore the busloads of tourists that pour in regularly throughout the day. The best way to enjoy the garden is to get there around 9am and have a $3 breakfast of tea and fortune cookies in the tea house.

The Golden Gate Bridge and beyond

The orange towers of the **Golden Gate Bridge**, perhaps the best-loved symbol of San Francisco, are visible from almost every high point in the city. The bridge, which spans 4200ft, had taken only 52 months to design and build when it was opened in 1937: note that the ruddy color was originally intended as a temporary undercoat before the gray topcoat was applied, but locals liked it so much, the bridge has stayed orange ever since. Driving on it is a real thrill, while the half-hour walk across allows you to take in its enormous size and absorb the views of the Marin headlands, as well as the city itself. The view is especially beautiful at sunset, when the glow of the waning day paints the white city a delicate pink.

The **Fort Point National Historic Site** beneath the bridge gives a good sense of the place as the westernmost outpost of the nation. This brick fortress, built in the 1850s, has a dramatic site, reachable via Marine Drive in the Presidio, where the surf pounds away beneath the great span of the bridge high above – a view made famous by Kim Novak's suicide attempt in Alfred Hitchcock's *Vertigo*. The other attraction in the shadow of the bridge is the beaches at the tip of the peninsula, though dangerous riptides and excruciatingly cold water make it impossible to swim with any confidence. The **Presidio** itself is another fine expanse of green in which you can escape from the city noise.

Make sure to head inland and west to **Lincoln Park**, at 34th Avenue and Clement Street, which offers striking views of the Marin headlands and is home to the stately **California Palace of the Legion of Honor** (Tues–Sun 9.30am–5pm; $8, free every Tues, surcharge for special exhibitions; ☏415/863-3330, ⓦwww.thinker. org), one of the best museums in the city. Its isolated, windswept location, high on a bluff overlooking the ocean, is unsurpassably romantic, and deters the hordes that swarm the MoMA and the museums in Golden Gate Park. The bronze cast of Rodin's *The Thinker* on a pedestal in the center of the front courtyard offers a foretaste of the museum's expansive holdings by the French sculptor. Sadly, the magnificent museum is somewhat let down by its lackluster collection of Old Masters – many of the artworks, including those by Giambologna, Cellini, and Cranach, are "attributed to" or "the workshop of," rather than bona fide masterpieces. The Impressionist and Post-Impressionist galleries are stronger, though, and contain works by Courbet, Manet, and Monet among others – look for the lively oil sketches by Degas and Seurat's characteristically trippy view of the Eiffel Tower.

Eating

With well over three thousand restaurants crammed onto the small peninsula, and scores of bars and cafés open all day, **eating** in San Francisco is never difficult, and while the hype around the city is relentless, it's in its restaurants where that hype is unquestionably deserved. Be warned: San Francisco closes early, and you'll be struggling to find places that will serve you after 10 or 11pm. **Mexican** food is big in the Mission, **Italian** places abound in North Beach, and, of course, Chinatown naturally has plenty of **Chinese** restaurants, while the **Japan Center** – the heart of Japantown, located at Post Street, a mile west of Union Square – boasts a few fine Japanese places. In health-conscious San Francisco you'll find **vegetarian** entrees on every menu and quite a few entirely vegetarian restaurants. With the vineyards of Napa and Sonoma Valley on the city's doorstep, quality **wines** have a high profile in most San Francisco restaurants. State law prohibits **smoking** in all restaurants, cafés, and bars, as evidenced by the crowds of people puffing on the pavements.

Downtown and Chinatown

Asia de Cuba *Clift Hotel*, 495 Geary St at Taylor, Theater District ☎ 415/923-2300. Cuban food served family-style in huge portions in an extremely trendy setting. It's a delicious experience, enhanced by the opium-den-like ambiance.

Borobodur 700 Post St at Jones, Theater District ☎ 415/775-1512. Small but excellent Indonesian place, serving rich curries. Try the *Rijsttafel*, a selection of small dishes with rice.

Cosmopolitan Café 121 Spear St Unit B-8, in the Rincon Center, Financial District ☎ 415/543-4001. In an otherwise deserted area, this modern American bistro is an appealing choice for dinner. The standard modern American food (entrees around $20) is spruced up with great condiments like sweet, chunky house-made ketchup, not to mention friendly, efficient service.

Farallon 450 Post St at Powell, Union Square ☎ 415/956-6969. Sumptuously styled as an undersea grotto, serving highly creative seafood dishes in small portions. Definitely worth a splurge if you're into elegant dining experiences.

House of Nanking 919 Kearny at Jackson, Chinatown ☎ 415/421-1429. One of the most popular Chinese restaurants, despite the lack of decor and elbow room. You can wait ages for a table, but the inexpensive food doesn't disappoint.

Kokkari Estiatorio 200 Jackson St at Front, Financial District ☎ 415/981-0983. By far, the best Greek restaurant in town, offering staples such as lamb and eggplant that are served both separately or combined as moussaka.

Plouf 40 Belden Lane at Bush, Chinatown ☎ 415/986-6491. Convivial South-of-France seafood bistro, with sidewalk seating in good weather. The garlicky mussels – the house specialty – are the best in the city. Very reasonable prices.

Sears Fine Food 439 Powell St at Post, Union Square ☎ 415/986-1160. A classic breakfast joint with a hearty old-fashioned ambiance: try the plate of eighteen tiny Swedish pancakes, or for groups of six or more, the Ranch Breakfast of pancakes, eggs, bacon, and the works.

Tadich Grill 240 California St at Battery, Financial District ☎ 415/391-1849. Half diner, half gentleman's club, staffed by white-jacketed waiters and serving hearty steaks and salads.

Yank Sing 427 Battery St at Clay, Financial District ☎ 415/781-1111. A cavernous spot that regularly tops locals' lists for the best dim sum in the city. Despite being routinely packed during lunch hours, the waitstaff can almost always find a spot for you in the seemingly endless warren of dining rooms.

North Beach, the Embarcadero, Fisherman's Wharf, and the Marina

Baker Street Bistro 2953 Baker St at Lombard, Cow Hollow ☎ 415/931-1475. Cramped but charming café with a few outdoor tables. The slightly older, neighborhood crowd enjoys simple food served by French staff. Wines are well priced and the $14.50 *prix fixe* dinner is a bargain.

Bistro Boudin 160 Jefferson St at Taylor, Fisherman's Wharf ☎ 415/351-5561. Quality Gallo-American cuisine with great views across the Bay from the dining room above the famous *Boudin Bakery*. Fairly pricey, so look out for coupons in the City Pass (see p.1111).

Bistro Yoffi 2231 Chestnut St at Pierce, Marina ☎ 415/885-5133. Eclectic modern American cuisine served in an attractive bistro that's refreshingly quirky given its location, packed with potted ferns and mismatched chairs. There's a great garden out back.

Café Francisco 2161 Powell St at North Point, Fisherman's Wharf ☎ 415/397-2602. Cheap neighborhood café only blocks from the wharf. Great for a lazy breakfast while reading the newspapers or a quiet lunchtime sandwich.

Caffè Trieste 601 Vallejo St at Grant, North Beach ☎ 415/392-6739. Small, crowded, and authentic Italian coffeehouse – features free music: folk and classical on Sat afternoons and mostly jazz on Thurs evenings.

Greens Fort Mason Center, Building A, Marina ☎ 415/771-6222. The queen of San Francisco's vegetarian restaurants, using the best organic produce, with a gorgeous view of the bay. Book ahead.

Helmand 430 Broadway at Kearny, North Beach ☎ 415/362-0641. The decor here is simple and unassuming – unlike the food, which is unforgettable. The menu features tangy and spicy Afghani staples like *kaddo borwani* (caramelized pumpkin).

Mama's 1701 Stockton St at Washington Square, North Beach ☎ 415/362-6421. Cheery, bright yellow tablecloths and sunny staff give this homey diner a lift: try the crab Benedict or one of the gooey, cake-like French toast specials. Expect lines at the weekend, whatever the time.

Trattoria Contadina 1800 Mason St at Union, North Beach ☎ 415/982-5728. This tiny, family-owned trattoria still caters primarily to the local Italian community, serving outstanding renditions of traditional dishes, like rigatoni with eggplant and smoked mozzarella.

Civic Center, Tenderloin, SoMa, and The Mission

Asia SF 201 9th St at Howard, SoMa ☎415/255-2742. More of an experience than a restaurant, this only-in-San Francisco spot features "gender illusionist" staff who put on a campy nightly revue. Though the show's the real draw, the sushi and cocktails are good.

Betty's Café 167 11th St at Howard, SoMa ☎415/431-2525. Known for its hearty breakfast specials under $3, including choice of meat, eggs, hash browns, and toast. No frills, but who'd expect them at prices like these.

El Perol 2590 Mission St at 22nd ☎415/550-8582. Wonderful cheap Peruvian place serving traditional soups and more substantial Andean fare.

Fringale 570 4th St at Brannan, SoMa ☎415/543-0573. Delightful, low-key charmer on a quiet SoMa block offering service that's as exceptional as the food, which is predominantly French, but with Basque touches like serrano ham.

Lulu 816 Folsom St at 4th, SoMa ☎415/495-5775. Famed Californian restaurant with a rustic, rather cramped dining room serving family-style, Italian-inspired dishes. The wine list is spectacular.

Luna Park 694 Valencia St at 18th, Mission ☎415/553-8584. Groovy local favorite, decked out like a lush bordello with deep red walls and ornamental chandeliers. Most of the entrees, like a tuna salad niçoise or moules frites, hover around $15.

Saigon Sandwich Shop 560 Larkin St at Ellis, Tenderloin ☎415/474-5698. Hole-in-the-wall store selling superb, made-to-order Vietnamese sandwiches for around $2 each: choose from barbecued chicken or pork, and meatballs.

Shalimar 532 Jones St at Geary, Tenderloin ☎415/928-0333. A happy find in the downtrodden Tenderloin, this divey spot serves delicious, cheap Pakistani food, all of it made to order before your eyes.

Swan Oyster Depot 1517 Polk at California, Polk Gulch ☎415/673-1101. No frills – and officially, no full meals – at this cheap seafood counter. Grab a stool and hang onto it (it gets crowded and competitive in here) and suck down some cheap shellfish and seafood.

Ti Couz 3108 16th St at Valencia, Mission ☎415/252-7373. This friendly but hip crêperie was one of the pioneers of the newly groovy Mission scene on Valencia Street. It still holds its place as one of the best cheaper restaurants around, serving buckwheat savory pancakes for $6 or so.

Truly Mediterranean 3109 16th St at Valencia, Mission ☎415/252-7482. Fast threatening to overtake the beloved burrito as the locals' favorite portable dinner item, this hole-in-the-wall's version of the falafel comes wrapped in thin, crispy bread.

Tu Lan 8 6th St at Market, SoMa ☎415/626-0927. A legend ever since Julia Child first sampled the Vietnamese cooking in this cramped, dingy space on one of the seediest blocks in town. The food's consistently fresh, flavorful, and cheap.

The Castro, Haight-Ashbury, and Japantown

Café Flore 2298 Noe St at Market, Castro ☎415/621-8579. Wedged into the triangle at the corner of Market and Noe streets, this café has a sunny, plant-filled courtyard that's a great place to grab a coffee and a gooey cake; be aware that it can be very cruisey, especially during the early evening.

Chow 215 Church St at Market, Castro ☎415/552-2469. Unfussy comfort food, like pasta and wood-fired pizza, some with an Asian twist. Spaghetti and meatballs is great value for $6 and most dishes cost no more than $10.

Late-night eating

For that midnight snack or early-morning binge, check out the following **24-hour** dependables:

Bagdad Café 2295 Market St at 16th St, Castro ☎415/621-4434. The best-price 24-hour option in the neighborhood.

Caffè Greco 423 Columbus Ave at Vallejo, North Beach ☎415/397-6261. The best place to come for a dark, pungent, pick-me-up espresso – you can also graze on pastries.

El Farolito 2779 Mission St at 24th, Mission ☎415/824-7877. Twenty-four-hour taqueria.

Mario's Bohemian Cigar Store 566 Columbus Ave at Union, North Beach ☎415/362-0536. The cigars are long gone, but it's definitely still a boho hangout – they're likely here for the huge, doorstopping panini.

Yuet Lee 1300 Stockton St at Broadway, Chinatown ☎415/982-6020. Terrific Chinese seafood – try the braised catfish; until 3am daily except Tues.

EOS 901 Cole St at Carl, Cole Valley ☎ 415/566-3063. The best place to sip a glass of wine and enjoy Euro-Asian inspired cuisine. The restaurant is very pricey, so stick to the wine bar next door for a similar experience at a lower price.

Frjtz 579 Hayes St at Laguna, Hayes Valley ☎ 415/864-7654. Trendy little *friterie*, serving cones of crunchy Belgian-style fries with dips like tabasco-chive ketchup and spicy yogurt peanut.

Home 2100 Market St at Church, Castro ☎ 415/503-0333. The menu at this mixed-gay diner is designed to offer the things that a chef cooks at home for his friends – primarily comfort food like *moules frites* (around $10–12 per entree). There's an enjoyable patio bar with DJs on the weekend.

Maki Japan Center, 1825 Post St at Webster, Japantown ☎ 415/921-5125. One of the many tasty, tiny places in the Japan Center, this restaurant specializes in *wappan meshi*, a wood steamer filled with vegetables, meat, and rice.

Rosamunde Sausage Grille 545 Haight St at Fillmore, Lower Haight ☎ 415/437-6851. Small storefront grill with a few stools at the bar, serving just-grilled sausages on a sesame roll. Choose from a cherry-laced chicken sausage to the light flavors of a shrimp, scallop, and snapper sausage.

Stelline 330 Gough St at Hayes, Hayes Valley ☎ 415/626-4292. Red-checkered tablecloths, a handwritten and photocopied menu, plus affable, chatty staff make this a cheap, relaxed place to grab home-style Italian food.

Suppenküche 601 Hayes St at Laguna, Hayes Valley ☎ 415/252-9289. Satisfying and delicious German cooking near Civic Center in a loud, lively bar/restaurant decked out like a traditional Bavarian pub. Don't miss the potato pancakes appetizer – it's enough alone for a light supper.

🏃 **Taqueria El Balazo** 1654 Haight St at Belvedere, Haight-Ashbury ☎ 415/864-2140.

Jazzily coloured Mexican canteen serving some of the best inexpensive food in the area. The deluxe burritos are tremendous.

Thep Phanom 400 Waller St at Fillmore, Lower Haight ☎ 415/431-2526. Delicate decor and beautifully prepared Thai dishes in the Lower Haight. Main course around $9–12 and expect to wait for a table.

The Sunset and the Richmond

Chapeau! 1408 Clement St at 15th, Richmond ☎ 415/750-9787. Delicious French food served in a small space crowded with locals enjoying a relaxed provincial atmosphere.

Fountain Court 354 Clement St at 5th Ave, Richmond ☎ 415/668-1100. Unusual Chinese restaurant serving authentic Shanghai food – less familiar than Cantonese staples, perhaps, but just as delicious. Try the Shanghai dumplings or lion's-head soup.

Pizzetta 211 23rd Ave at California, Richmond ☎ 415/379-9880. Inventive and unusual pizzas are featured on a different menu each week, offering whatever's fresh and seasonal as a topping.

PJ's Oyster Bed 737 Irving St at 9th, Sunset ☎ 415/566-7775. This rowdy, unpretentious restaurant offers spicy, tangy Cajun dishes like blackened catfish and alligator eggs. Watch out for the free Jello vodka shots the owner periodically passes around.

Wing Lee Bakery 503 Clement St at 6th Ave, Richmond ☎ 415/668-9481. No-nonsense Chinese dim sum store, one of several on this strip. There's little English spoken, so it's something of a lucky dip snack, but the fillings are more authentic than what you'll find downtown.

🔲 **13**

Nightlife and entertainment

Compared to many US cities, where you need money and attitude in equal measure, San Francisco's **nightlife** scene demands little of either. It is not unusual for restaurants to provide live music, and you can often eat and be entertained for no extra cost. This is no 24-hour city, however, and the approach to socializing is often surprisingly low-key, with little of the pandering to fads and fashions that goes on elsewhere. The club scene is far from the cutting edge of hip, and is inexpensive compared to those in other cities. A decent night out might run you $30–40, including cover charge and a few drinks. As with restaurants, smoking is illegal in bars and clubs, though locals routinely flout the law at the risk of incurring a ticket.

The Sunday *Chronicle*'s "Pink Pages" supplement, along with the free weekly *Bay Guardian* and the *SF Weekly*, are the best sources of **listings**. Ticketmaster

(☎415/421-8497, 🌐www.ticketmaster.com) is the major **ticket** agency, with outlets in Rite Aid stores. Tickets.com (☎415/776-1999, 🌐www.tickets.com) is also worth a try.

Bars

San Francisco, while famous for its restaurants, has a huge number of **drinking establishments**, ranging from comfortably scruffy jukebox joints to chic watering holes.

Bambuddha *The Phoenix Hotel*, 601 Eddy St at Larkin, Tenderloin ☎415/885-5088. Sleek, South Pacific-inspired cocktail lounge with terrific DJs and strong drinks.

Blondie's Bar & No Grill 540 Valencia St at 16th, Mission ☎415/864-2419. Always packed, this fun bar with a good-sized patio serves huge cocktails and often hosts live music. As a bonus, the newly opened *Wetspot* back room is also smoker-friendly.

Edinburgh Castle 950 Geary St at Polk, Tenderloin ☎415/885-4074. Just your average Scottish bar run by Koreans; it's filled with heraldic Highland memorabilia and offers a mean version of fish and chips.

Gordon Biersch Brewery 2 Harrison St at Embarcadero, SoMa ☎415/243-8246. Bayfront microbrewery in a converted coffee warehouse, with a great selection of beers that pulls in a downtown twenty-something crowd.

Kezar 770 Stanyan St at Waller ☎415/386-9292. Large Brit-run pub opposite the park. No great range of beers but the most reliable place to see soccer on TV, even the early games.

Li Po's Bar 916 Grant Ave at Jackson, Chinatown ☎415/982-0072. Named after the Chinese poet, *Li Po's* is a little grotty, although that's part of its charm: it's one of the few places to drink in Chinatown.

Mad Dog in the Fog 530 Haight St at Fillmore, Lower Haight ☎415/626-7279. Aptly named by the two lads from Birmingham, England who own the joint, this is one of the Lower Haight's most loyally patronized bars, with darts, English beer, and soccer on TV.

Persian Aub Zam Zam 1663 Haight St at Clayton, Haight-Ashbury ☎415/861-2545. A Casbah-style cocktail lounge featuring a retro jazz jukebox; the famed and ornery owner may be dead, but his regulars clubbed together and bought the bar to preserve its vibe. Try a signature gin martini.

Red Room *Commodore International Hotel*, 827 Sutter St at Jones, Theater District ☎415/346-7666. This trendy, sexy bar is – as its name implies – completely red: walls, furniture, glasses, and even many of the drinks.

The Redwood Room *Clift Hotel*, 495 Geary St at Taylor, Theater District ☎415/775-4700. This clubby, landmark bar was recently given a hip makeover, with lightboxes on the wall displaying paintings that phase and fade between portraits. It's great fun – just don't choke on the drinks prices.

Tonga Room *Fairmont Hotel*, 950 Mason St at California, Nob Hill ☎415/772-5278. This basement bar is styled like a Polynesian village, complete with a pond and simulated rainstorms, and a grass-skirted band playing terrible jazz and pop covers from a floating raft. The cocktails are outrageously overpriced, but a $7 happy hour buffet makes up for it. Cover $3 after 8pm.

Tunnel Top 601 Bush St at Stockton, Union Square ☎415/986-8900 This funky, industrial bar is hidden behind a seedy storefront on top of the Stockton Street tunnel. One of the few tobacco-friendly places downtown.

Gay and lesbian bars

San Francisco's **gay and lesbian bars** are many and varied, ranging from cozy cocktail lounges to no-holds-barred leather-and-chain hangouts. The scene may no longer be quite as wild as its reputation would have you believe, but at its best it can still be hard to beat.

Badlands 4131 18th St at Castro, Castro ☎415/626-9320, 🌐www.sfbadlands.com. Recently renovated, this video bar attracts a pretty, thirty-something crowd and is usually packed at weekends.

Cat Club 1190 Folsom St at 8th, SoMa ☎415/431-3332. This dark, loud club is one of the city's lesbian

hotspots, mixing dancing and live performances. It's livelier the later you arrive. Cover $5–10.

Cherry Bar 917 Folsom St at 5th, SoMa ☎415/974-1585. Newer lesbian bar with a rock vibe and regular live music. On Sun there is a strip club with butch and trans erotic dancers.

The Eagle Tavern 398 12th St at Harrison, SoMa ⊤415/626-0880. A good old-fashioned leather bar, particularly popular on Sun when it holds a late-afternoon "beer bust" for charity.

Esta Noche 3079 16th St at Valencia, Mission ⊤415/861-5757. This gay Latin drag bar hosts nightly shows that are great fun and attract a young, racially mixed clientele.

Lexington Club 3464 19th St at Lexington, Mission ⊤ 415/863-2052. The only place in the city where the girls outnumber the boys (men must be accompanied by a woman to enter), this bustling lesbian bar attracts all sorts with its no-nonsense decor, friendly atmosphere, and excellent jukebox.

Midnight Sun 4067 18th St at Castro, Castro ⊤415/861-4186, ⓦwww.midnightsunsf.com. Long, narrow video bar, always busy with well-dressed white boys checking out the movies shown on the monitors, as well as each other.

Pilsner Inn 225 Church St at Market, Castro ⊤415/621-7058. The best neighborhood gay bar in the Castro, filled with a diverse, slightly older crowd playing pool and darts. There's a large, smoker-friendly patio out back.

Powerhouse 1347 Folsom St at Doré Alley, SoMa ⊤415/861-1790. One of the prime pick-up joints in the city, this very cruisey old-school leather bar has plenty of convenient dark corners. Leather/uniform dress code enforced.

The Stud 399 Folsom St at 9th, SoMa ⊤415/252-7883. Legendary gay club that's still as popular as ever, attracting a diverse, energetic, and uninhib-ited crowd. Now hosts Planet Big SF for large men on Sun. Cover $5–8.

Live music: rock, jazz, and folk

San Francisco's **music scene** reflects the character of the city: laid-back, eclectic, and not a little nostalgic. The options for live music are wide and the scene is definitely on the up and up, with the city regularly spawning good young bands. In recent years the city has helped launch acid jazz (beat-heavy jazz that's become *de rigueur* dinner-party music across the country), a classic swing revival, and the East Bay pop-punk sound. Check the *San Francisco Bay Guardian* and *SF Weekly* free weeklies, and the *San Francisco Chronicle*, for listings.

Biscuits and Blues 401 Mason St at Geary, Union Square ⊤415/292-2583, ⓦwww.biscuitsandblues.com. Lively blues supper club with inexpensive Southern cuisine and hot blues acts nightly. Reservations recommended for dinner shows. Cover $5–15.

Boom Boom Room 1601 Fillmore St at Geary, Japantown ⊤415/673-8000, ⓦwww.boomboomblues.com. Once owned by the late blues legend John Lee Hooker, this small, intimate bar delivers straight-ahead jazz or classic blues acts nightly. Cover $5–12.

Bottom of the Hill 1233 17th St at Missouri, Potrero Hill ⊤415/621-4455, ⓦwww.bottomofthehill.com. Hangout for rock and country music, live seven nights a week, drawing a late-twenty- to thirty-something crowd. There's an outdoor all-you-care-to-eat barbecue on the patio Sun. Cover $5–10.

Bruno's 2389 Mission St at 20th, Mission ⊤415/648-7701, ⓦwww.brunoslive.com. Like something from a Scorsese movie, this retro-1960s restaurant has an intimate live venue attached where there's usually jazz or nu-school R&B. Cover $5–8 (no cover for diners).

Café du Nord 2170 Market St at Sanchez, Castro ⊤415/861-5016, ⓦwww.cafedunord.com. Primarily a jazz club, this popular bar is also a great place to enjoy live swing, Latin, and world music over good food, or just have a beer and shoot some pool. Cover $3–8.

Elbo Room 647 Valencia St at 17th, Mission ⊤415/552-7788, ⓦwww.elbo.com. The birthplace of acid jazz, often home to world music performers. Cover $5–12.

The Fillmore Auditorium 1805 Geary St at Fillmore, Japantown ⊤ 415/346-6000, ⓦwww.thefillmore.com. A local landmark, *The Fillmore* was at the heart of the 1960s counter-culture, masterminded by the legendary Bill Graham. It reopened in 1994 after several years' hiatus and is home now to rock and alt-rock touring acts. Ticket prices vary.

The Great American Music Hall 859 O'Farrell St at Polk, Tenderloin ⊤415/885-0750, ⓦwww.musichallsf.com. Historic former bordello and saloon that has been converted into a popular venue for rock, blues, and world music acts. Cover $10–20.

The Independent 628 Divisadero St at Hayes, Alamo Square ⊤415/771-1421, ⓦwww.theindependentsf.com. As the name suggests, this mid-sized club specializes in showcasing local and international indie outfits. Cover $5–15.

The Make Out Room 3225 22nd St at Mission, Mission ⊤415/647-2888, ⓦwww.makeoutroom.com. Cozy and laid-back bar featuring worthy but obscure acts and the odd famous maverick like Jonathan Richman. Cover $6–12.

Tongue & Groove 2513 Van Ness Ave at Union, Cow Hollow ☎ 415/928-0404, ⊕ www.tongueand groovesf.com. Local bands ranging from rock and funk to Seventies retro and alternative – one of the most inventive and reliable options in the city. Cover $8–10.

Clubbing

Still trading on a reputation for hedonism earned decades ago, San Francisco's **nightclubs** in fact trail light years behind those of other large American cities. That said, the compensations are manifold – it is rare to encounter high cover charges, ridiculously priced drinks, feverish posing, or long lines, though a few of the cavernous dance clubs in SoMa do have lines on weekends. The greatest concentration of clubs is in **SoMa** and, recently, the **Mission**. You must bring your ID to get in to all clubs; most require you to be at least twenty-one. Unlike most other cities, where the action never gets going until after midnight, many San Francisco clubs have to close at 2am during the week, so you can usually be sure of finding things well under way by 11.30pm.

1015 Folsom 1015 Folsom St at 6th, SoMa ☎ 415/431-1200, ⊕ www.1015.com. Multi-level superclub, popular across-the-board for late-night dancing: the music's largely house and garage, and expect marquee names like Sasha and Digweed on the main floor. $15–20.

DNA Lounge 375 11th St at Harrison, SoMa ☎ 415/626-1409, ⊕ www.dnalounge.com. Changes its music style nightly, but draws the same young hipsters, a mixed gay-straight crowd. $15–20.

The EndUp 401 6th St at Harrison, SoMa ☎ 415/357-0827, ⊕ www.theendup.com. Open all night (though you can only drink until 2am), and attracting hardcore gay and straight clubbers for after-hours dancing on its cramped dance floor. If you want a break from the beats, there's an outdoor patio with plenty of seating.

Hush Hush 496 14th St at Guerrero, Mission ☎ 415/241-9944, ⊕ www.hushhushlounge.com. A great place to hang out or dance, this hidden bar has no sign outside; inside, there's a slightly older crowd, playing pool or dancing to housey disco and classic 1970s funk, Wed to Sat.

Pink 2925 16th St at Capp, Mission ☎ 415/431-8889 This tiny, fun club is one of the city's best places to dance to acid jazz and deep house with a friendly crowd of all sexual orientations. $2–10.

Skylark 3089 16th St at Valencia, Mission ☎ 415/621-9294, ⊕ www.skylarkbar.com. Popular for its intimacy, low lights, strong drinks and varied DJs, this spot makes for an inexpensive night out. No cover.

Sno-Drift 1830 3rd St at 16th, China Basin ☎ 415/431-4766. Alpine ski lodge-themed club where almost everything is igloo-white, including an enormous padded vinyl bar. Music varies, but is mainly house. $15.

Space 550 550 Barneveld Ave at Oakdale, Hunter's Point ☎ 415/289-2001, ⊕ www.space550.com. This enormous warehouse club is known for its trancey, industrial dance programming. Although it's a long way out, in an iffy part of town, serious clubbers think it's worth the trek. $5–15.

Classical music, opera, and dance

Though the San Francisco arts scene has a reputation for provincialism, this is the only city on the West Coast to boast its own professional **symphony**, **ballet**, and **opera** companies. These companies rely entirely on private contributions for their survival and low-priced tickets are rare, if not non-existent. Last-minute standing-room tickets are an option for those on a budget. Look out in summer for the free concerts in Stern Grove (at 19th Avenue and Sloat Boulevard), where the symphony, opera, and ballet give open-air performances for ten successive Sundays (starting in June).

The **San Francisco Opera Association** (tickets and info ☎ 415/864-3330, ⊕ www.sfopera.com) has been performing in the opulent War Memorial Opera House, 301 Van Ness Ave at Grove, in the Civic Center since the building opened in 1932, pulling in big names like Placido Domingo and Kiri Te Kanawa on a regular basis. Its main season runs from the end of September for thirteen weeks, and its opening night is one of the principal social events on the West Coast. Also housed here is the **San Francisco Ballet** (℡415/864-3330, Ⓦ www.sfballet.org), whose regular season starts in February, while performances of *The Nutcracker* occur during the Christmas season.

Next door, the **Louise M. Davies Symphony Hall**, at 201 Van Ness Ave at Hayes (℡415/864-6000, Ⓦ www.sfsymphony.org), is the permanent home of the San Francisco Symphony, hosting a year-round season of classical music and sometimes performances by other, often offbeat musical and touring groups.

Theater

The majority of the **theaters** in downtown's Theater District are not especially innovative, but tickets are reasonably inexpensive – rarely exceeding $25 a seat – and there's usually good availability. For last-minute bargains try the **Tix Bay Area** booth inside the Union Square garage, between Stockton and Powell streets (Tues–Thurs 11am–6pm, Fri & Sat 11am–7pm; recorded info ℡415/433-7827). It's also an outlet for Ticketmaster.

American Conservatory Theater (ACT) Geary Theater, 415 Geary St at Taylor, Theater District ℡415/742-2228, Ⓦ www.act-sfbay.org. San Francisco's flagship theater company, the Tony Award-winning ACT puts on eight major plays each season.

Beach Blanket Babylon *Club Fugazi*, 678 Green St at Powell, North Beach ℡415/421-4222. This legendary musical revue, filled with celebrity impersonations and towering hats, has been running since 1974. Highly recommended, but remember to reserve in advance. Tickets from $25.

Golden Gate Theater 1 Taylor St at Golden Gate Ave and Market, Tenderloin ℡415/551-2000, Ⓦ www.bestofbroadway-sf.com. San Francisco's most elegant theater (in its least elegant neighborhood), with marble flooring, Rococo ceilings, and gilt trimmings. It's a pity the program – generally a mainstream diet of touring musicals – doesn't live up to the decor.

Lorraine Hansberry Theatre 620 Sutter St at Mason, Theater District ℡415/474-8800, Ⓦ www.lorrainehansberrytheatre.com. The mainstay of African-American theater in San Francisco. Traditional theater as well as contemporary political pieces and jazz/blues musical revues.

Magic Theatre Fort Mason Center, Building D, Fort Mason ℡415/441-8822, Ⓦ www.magictheatre.org. Specializes in contemporary American playwrights and emerging new talent; Sam Shepard traditionally premieres his work here.

New Conservatory Theater Center 25 Van Ness Ave at Market, Civic Center ℡415/861-8972, Ⓦ www.nctcsf.org. This mid-sized theater is known for its performances of musicals in concert, youth shows, and pantomime.

Theater Artaud 450 Florida St at Mariposa, Mission ℡415/621-7797, Ⓦ www.artaud.org. Modern theater in a converted warehouse offering dance and theater performances, many less obscure than the theater's arty name might imply.

Shelton Theater 533 Sutter St at Powell, Union Square ℡415/433-1226, Ⓦ www.sheltontheater.com. Small stage featuring mostly highbrow drama, with an even smaller space hosting comedy sketches and the like.

Theater Rhinoceros 2926 16th St at S Van Ness, Mission ℡415/861-5079, Ⓦ www.therhino.org. San Francisco's leading gay theater space, performing everything from light, humorous productions to those that confront gay issues.

Shopping

While boasting the large-scale facilities and international names you'd expect in a major city, San Francisco's **shopping scene** is low-key and unpretentious. If you want to run the gauntlet of designer labels, or just watch the style brigade consume, **Union Square** is the place to be. The heart of the city's shopping territory, it has a good selection of big-name and chic stores worth a few hours if you're into serious dollar-dropping.

Books

Abandoned Planet Bookstore 518 Valencia at 16th, Mission ☎ 415/861-4695. Encouraging its customers to "Break the TV habit!" this eccentric and utterly San Francisco bookstore crams its shelves with left-wing and anarchist volumes.

Borders Books and Music 400 Post St at Powell, Union Square ☎ 415/399-1633. Gargantuan chain bookstore with some 160,000 books to choose from, as well as CDs, videos, and software on four floors. Another massive branch is at 200 King St, opposite AT&T Park.

City Lights Bookstore 261 Columbus Ave at Broadway, North Beach ☎ 415/362-8193. America's first paperback bookstore, and still San Francisco's best. The range of titles includes house publications.

A Different Light 489 Castro St at 18th, Castro ☎ 415/431-0891. Well-stocked and diverse gay bookstore.

Forever After Books 1475 Haight St at Ashbury, Haight-Ashbury ☎ 415/431-8299. The windows of this store are blocked by the piles of accumulated paperbacks – it's worth rifling your way through the mountains given the cheap prices.

Get Lost 1825 Market St at Valencia, Hayes Valley/Mission ☎ 415/437-0529. Tiny travel bookstore, crammed with unusual titles alongside the standard guidebooks.

The Great Overland Bookstore Company 2848 Webster St at Union, Cow Hollow ☎ 415/351-1538. Cluttered with piles of books, this is a first-rate, old-fashioned store with mint-condition first editions as well as cheap paperbacks.

Green Apple 506 Clement St at 6th Ave, Richmond ☎ 415/387-2272. In the heart of the Richmond district, this relaxed and welcoming store features new and used books (rare out-of-print volumes as well as standards), plus a well-priced selection of CDs and vinyl recordings.

Modern Times 888 Valencia St at 20th, Mission ☎ 415/282-9246. Progressive community bookstore with a good selection of Latin American literature and publications on women's issues and contemporary cultural studies.

Music

Amoeba Records 1855 Haight St at Stanyan, Haight-Ashbury ☎ 415/831-1200. A massive, independent record and CD store with one of the largest and best used collections you'll ever find (over one million new and used). They also host frequent live in-store performances.

Sports in San Francisco and the Bay Area

San Francisco's dedication to its **professional sports** teams can verge on the obsessive. Tickets for the big events can sell out, but it's usually possible to show up on the day, and it needn't cost all that much: an outfield seat to watch baseball from the "bleachers" goes for around $8, while promotional specials like Wednesday Dollar Days, run by the Oakland team, can reduce prices of seats and hotdogs to only a couple of bucks. Advance tickets for all Bay Area sports events are available through Ticketmaster's charge-by-phone ticket service (☎ 415/421-8497, ⓦ www.ticketmaster .com), or through the teams' headquarters.

Baseball: The **Oakland A's** play at the usually sunny Coliseum (ⓦ www.oakland-athletics.com), which has a BART stop in front. The **San Francisco Giants** play at AT&T Park, where home runs sometimes land in the bay (☎ 415/972-2000, ⓦ www. sfgiants.com). There are five hundred bleacher-seat tickets made available two-and-a-half hours before game time and long lines form early and often. Walk up to the ticket booths at 24 Willie Mays Plaza, near Third and King streets, to get them.

Football: The **San Francisco 49ers**, five-time Super Bowl champions, also play at 3Com Park, where you may have to pay as much as $100 per seat (☎ 415/656-4900, ⓦ www.sf49ers.com), and the **Oakland Raiders**, blue-collar heroes and runners-up in the 2003 Superbowl, bash heads at the Oakland Coliseum (ⓦ www.raiders.com).

Basketball: The reliably awful **Golden State Warriors** play at the newly renovated Oakland Arena (☎ 510/986-2200, ⓦ www.nba.com/warriors).

Ice hockey: The **San Jose Sharks** (☎ 408/287-7070, ⓦ www.sj-sharks.com) play at their own arena in San Jose.

Soccer: The **San Jose Earthquakes** (☎ 408/985-4625, ⓦ www.sjearthquakes.com), MLS champs in 2001, draw large crowds at San Jose State's Spartan Stadium.

Aquarius Records 1055 Valencia St at 21st, Mission ☎415/647-2272. Small neighborhood store with friendly, knowledgeable staff and a good range of indie rock, jazz, and things experimental and obscure.

BPM 654 Fillmore St at Fell, Lower Haight ☎415/487-8680. One of the top DJ record stores in the city, with the latest UK imports from top-name British DJs and masses of flyers for upcoming events.

CD & Record Rack 3987 18th St at Castro, Castro ☎415/552-4990. Castro emporium with a superb selection of dance music, including a few 1970s twelve-inch singles.

Groove Merchant Records 687 Haight St at Pierce, Lower Haight ☎415/252-5766. Come here for secondhand soul, funk, and jazz: the owner is passionate and knowledgeable, so don't be afraid to ask questions.

Jack's Record Cellar 254 Scott St at Haight, Lower Haight ☎415/431-3047. The city's best source for American roots music – R&B, jazz, country, and Rock 'n' Roll – especially on LP. Closed Sun–Tues.

Mikado 1737 Post St, Japantown ☎415/922-9450. Enormous Japanese record store sprawled across three units of the Japan Center, with an exhaustive selection of Asian music.

Mission Music Center 2653 Mission St at 22nd, Mission ☎415/648-1788. Music from all over the continent, but especially South America.

Virgin Megastore 2 Stockton St at Market, Union Square ☎415/397-4525. Three floors packed with books, videos, and music, plus a café overlooking Market Street.

The Bay Area

Of the six million people who make their home in the vicinity of San Francisco, only a lucky one in eight lives in the city itself. Everyone else is spread around the **Bay Area**, a sharply contrasting patchwork of very rich and very poor towns dotted down the peninsula or across one of the three impressive bridges that span the chilly waters of the exquisite natural harbor. In the **East Bay** are industrial Oakland and intellectual Berkeley, while south of the city, the **Peninsula** holds the gloating wealth of Silicon Valley, which gained its nickname from the multibillion-dollar technology industry. To the north across the Golden Gate Bridge is the woody, leafy landscape and rugged coastline of **Marin County**, an elitest pleasure zone of conspicuous luxury and abundant natural beauty.

The East Bay

The largest and the second-most-traveled bridge in the US, the **Bay Bridge** connects downtown San Francisco to the East Bay, part graceful suspension bridge and part heavy-duty steel truss. Currently being replaced along half its span, the Bay Bridge works a lot harder for a lot less respect than the more famous Golden Gate: a hundred million vehicles cross it each year. The heart of the East Bay is **Oakland**, a resolutely blue-collar city that spreads north to the progressive university town of **Berkeley**; the two communities all but merge into one city, and the hills above them are topped by a twenty-mile string of forested **regional parks**.

Arrival, information, and getting around

Flights direct to the East Bay touch down at **Oakland Airport**, just outside town (☎510/577-4015 or 1-800/992-7433 for automated flight info, ⊛www.oakland-airport.com). The AirBART shuttle van (every 15min; $2; ☎510/577-4294) runs to the Coliseum BART station from where you can hop on BART (see p.1138) to Berkeley, Oakland, or San Francisco. There are numerous door-to-door **shuttle buses** from the airport, such as Bridge Airporter Express (☎510/481-1050 or 1-800/300-1661) – expect to pay around $18 to downtown Oakland, $30–40 to San Francisco. Note that the **Greyhound** station is in a dodgy part of northern Oakland on San Pablo Avenue at 21st Street. **Amtrak** terminates at 2nd Street near Jack London Square in West Oakland, where you can catch a free shuttle bus to downtown San Francisco (a smoother alternative is to get off at Richmond and change onto the nearby BART trains).

There are two main **visitor centers**: Oakland CVB is at 463 11th St (Mon–Fri 8.30am–5pm; ☎510/839-9000, ⓦwww.oaklandcvb.com), while Berkeley's office is at 2015 Center St (Mon–Fri 9am–1pm & 2–5pm; ☎510/549-7040, ⓦwww.visitberkeley.com).

The underground **BART** system links the East Bay with San Francisco (Mon–Fri 4am–midnight, Sat 6am–midnight, Sun 8am–midnight; $1.40–7.65; ☎510/465-BART, ⓦwww.bart.gov). **AC Transit** (☎510/891-4777, ⓦwww.actransit.org) buses cover the entire East Bay area, with a more limited service running to Oakland and Berkeley from the Transbay Terminal in San Francisco; they're the only option for crossing the Bay when BART shuts down for the night.

East Bay accommodation

The East Bay's **motels** and **hotels**, which cost from $55 a night, are barely better value for money than their San Francisco counterparts.

Bancroft Hotel 2680 Bancroft Way, Berkeley ☎510/549-1000 or 1-800/549-1002, ⓦwww.bancrofthotel.com. Small hotel – just 22 rooms – with good location and service. Breakfast included. ❻

The Claremont Resort & Spa 41 Tunnel Rd, Berkeley ☎510/843-3000 or 1-800/551-7266, ⓦwww.claremontresort.com. The lap of luxury among Berkeley hotels in a 1915 building. Even the basic rooms are a treat, but you'll pay for the privilege. Spa sessions start around $100/hour for facials or massages. ❾

Downtown Berkeley YMCA 2001 Allston Way at Milvia St, Berkeley ☎510/848-9622, ⓦwww.baymca.org. Berkeley's best bargain accommodation, just one block from the Berkeley BART stop. Rates, starting at around $39 for a single, $50 for a double, include use of gym and pool. ❷

Hotel Shattuck Plaza 2086 Allston Way, Berkeley ☎510/845-7300, ⓦwww.hotelshattuckplaza.com.

Comfortable, central rooms in a well-restored older hotel. ❹

Jack London Inn 444 Embarcadero West, Oakland ☎510/444-2032, ⓦwww.jacklondoninn.com. Kitschy 1950s-style motor lodge next to Jack London Square. ❺

Maya Motel 4715 Telegraph Ave, North Oakland ☎510/654-5850. Basic motel but neat enough and better than most in this area, which is within walking distance of trendy Rockridge. ❷

Nash Hotel 2045 University Ave, Berkeley ☎510/841-1163, ⓦwww.nashhotel.com. No frills rooms with threadbare carpets in Chinese-run hotel. Cheap and central. ❸

Waterfront Plaza Hotel 10 Washington St, Oakland ☎510/836-3800 or 1-800/729-3638, ⓦwww.waterfrontplaza.com. Plush, modern hotel moored on the best stretch of the Oakland waterfront. ❼

Oakland

OAKLAND, the workhorse of the Bay Area, is one of the largest ports on the West Coast. It has also been the breeding ground of revolutionary **political movements**. In the Sixties, the city's fifty-percent black population found a voice through the militant Black Panthers, and in the Seventies the Symbionese Liberation Army, kidnappers of heiress Patty Hearst, obtained a ransom of free food for the city's poor. It's not all hard graft, though: the climate is often sunny and mild when San Francisco is cold and dreary, and there's great hiking in the redwood- and eucalyptus-covered hills above the city.

There's not much to see within the city. The major concession to the tourist trade is the waterfront Jack London Square, an aseptic cluster of national chains that have nothing to do with the writer. At the far eastern end of the promenade, however, you will find **Heinhold's First and Last Chance Saloon**, a slanting tiny bar built in 1883 from the hull of a whaling ship. Jack London really did drink here, and the collection of yellowed portraits of him on the wall are the only genuine thing about the writer you'll find on the square. A half-mile north up Broadway from the waterfront, Oakland's restored downtown is anchored by chain stores and the gargantuan open-air **City Center** complex of offices and fast-food outlets. Beside it, at Broadway and 14th Street, the massive space of **Frank Ogawa Plaza** is a pleasant place to eat lunch outdoors, while further east on 10th and Oak streets, the **Oakland Museum of California** (Wed–Sat 10am–5pm, Sun noon–5pm; $8, free every second Sunday of month; ⊤510/238-2200, ⓦwww.museumca.org) has a good exhibit of California history, including the Beat Generation.

Writer **Gertrude Stein** was born in Oakland at around the same time as the macho and adventurous London, but she's barely commemorated anywhere. Perhaps it's because it was Stein who wrote "what was the use of me having come from Oakland…*there is no there there*" – a quote that has haunted the city ever since. Oakland residents argue that there is indeed a *there* there, notably in the small, trendy community of **Rockridge** and the lively neighborhoods around Piedmont and Grand avenues, the latter near pleasant **Lake Merrit**.

Joaquin Miller Park, the most easily accessible of Oakland's hilltop parks, stands above East Oakland (take AC Transit bus #64 from downtown). It was once home to the "Poet of the Sierras," Joaquin Miller, who made his name playing the eccentric frontier American in the salons of 1870s London. His poems weren't exactly acclaimed (his greatest poetic achievement was rhyming "teeth" with "Goethe"), but his prose account of the time he spent with the Modoc Indians near Mount Shasta (see p.1161) remains invaluable. His house, a small white cabin called **The Abbey**, still survives here, as do the thousands of trees he planted.

Berkeley

BERKELEY (named for the English philosopher-theologian George Berkeley) is dominated by the **University of California**, one of America's most famous – and infamous – universities. Its grand buildings and thirty thousand students give off an energy that spills south down raucous **Telegraph Avenue**, where aging hippies peddle rainbow bracelets in front of vegetarian restaurants, music stores, and pizza joints. The very name of Berkeley conjures up images of dissent and it remains a solidly left-wing oasis. **Sproul Plaza**, in front of the school's entranceway, Sather Gate, is where the Free Speech Movement began, and, as some historians would argue, the experience known as the Sixties. Among the sites of the almost-daily pitched battles of the Sixties and early Seventies, part of the broad campus revolt against the Vietnam War, is the now-quiet **People's Park**. Today the campus prides itself on its high academic rankings and Nobel-laureate-laden faculty. Stroll the campus's tree-shaded pathways or join the free student-led **tours** that leave from the visitor services office, 101 University Hall (Mon–Sat 10am, Sun 1pm; ⊤ 510/642-5215, ⓦwww.berkeley.edu/visitor).

Telegraph Avenue holds most of the student hangouts, and several excellent bookstores. Older students congregate in **Northside**, popping down from their woodsy hillside homes to partake of goodies from "Gourmet Ghetto" – the restaurants, delis, and bakeries on Shattuck Avenue like the renowned *Chez Panisse* (see p.1140). North of here, on the hills, **Tilden Regional Park** has good trails and a fine rose garden. Along the bay itself, at the **Berkeley Marina**, you can rent windsurfing boards and sailboats, or just watch the sun set behind the Golden Gate.

Eating

As befits the birthplace of California cuisine, the East Bay offers a choice of good **restaurants**. Berkeley is both an upmarket diner's paradise and a student town where you can eat cheaply and well, especially on and around Telegraph Avenue.

Bay Wolf 3853 Piedmont Ave, North Oakland
℡510/655-6004. Chic restaurant whose menu is
influenced by the cuisine of Tuscany, Provence, and
the Basque country. Entrees like double mustard-
tarragon chicken cost mostly over $20.

Café Intermezzo 2442 Telegraph Ave near Haste,
Berkeley ℡510/849-4592. Huge sandwiches on
homemade bread, even bigger salads, and great
coffee.

Cha-Am 1543 Shattuck Ave, North Berkeley
℡510/848-9664. Climb the stairs to this unlikely,
always crowded small restaurant for deliciously
spicy Thai food at bargain prices.

Cheeseboard Pizza 1512 Shattuck Ave, North
Berkeley ℡510/549-3055. Incredibly good gourmet pizza at $2.50 a slice. Irregular hours, but usu-
ally open for lunch and dinner Tues–Sun.

Chez Panisse 1517 Shattuck Ave, North
Berkeley ℡510/548-5525. First and still the
best of the California cuisine restaurants, overseen
by legendary chef Alice Waters. Dinner is served at
two sittings, 6pm and 8.30pm; the *prix fixe* menu
costs $50–75 depending on the day of the week.
The Café upstairs is comparatively inexpensive.
Reservations recommended for the Café, essential
for the main restaurant.

Fenton's Creamery 4226 Piedmont Ave, North
Oakland ℡510/658-7000. The ultimate old-style
ice-cream parlor. Sandwiches, fries, and other
snacks are available to offset the sundae buzz. Open
until 11pm on weeknights, midnight at weekends.

Homemade Café 2454 Sacramento St, Berkeley
℡510/845-1940. Nontraditional California-style
Jewish and Mexican breakfasts and lunches – at
shared tables when it's crowded.

Juan's Place 941 Carleton St, West Berkeley
℡510/845-6904. The original Berkeley Mexican
restaurant, with great food (tons of it) and an interesting mix of people.

La Mediterranee 2936 College Ave, Berkeley
℡510/540-7773. Great Middle Eastern food in a
relaxed atmosphere.

La Note 2377 Shattuck Ave, Berkeley ℡510/843-
1535. The appropriately sunny, light cuisine of
Provence isn't the only flavor you'll find in this
petite dining room: students and teachers from the
jazz school next door routinely stop in for casual
jam sessions.

Le Cheval 1007 Clay St, Oakland
℡510/763-8595. Downtown Vietnamese
place serving exquisitely spiced food at reasonable
prices in comfortable surroundings.

Tropix Backyard Café 3814 Piedmont Ave, North
Oakland ℡510/653-2444. Large portions of fruity
Caribbean delicacies at reasonable prices, with
authentic jerk sauce and thirst-quenching mango
juice. Outside seating on the patio.

Vik's Chaat Corner 726 Allston Way, West Berkeley ℡510/644-4412. Fantastic lunchtime spot,
where you can feast cheaply on authentic South
Indian dishes such as *masala dosa* in a huge, no-
nonsense self-service canteen.

Cafés and bars

The many bohemian **cafés** in Berkeley are full from dawn to near midnight with
earnest characters wearing their intellects on their sleeves; if you're not after a caffeine fix, you can generally get a glass of beer or wine. For serious drinking you're
better off in one of the many **bars**, particularly in rough-hewn Oakland. Grittier
versions of what you'd find in San Francisco, they're mostly blue-collar, convivial,
and almost always less expensive.

The Alley 3325 Grand Ave, Oakland ℡510/444-
8505. Ramshackle old-timers' piano bar where
locals come specifically to sing. Music starts at
9pm. Closed Mon.

Ben 'n' Nick's 5612 College Ave, Rockridge
℡510/933-0327. Lively bar with good taped rock
music and tasty pub food.

Caffè Mediterraneum 2475 Telegraph Ave,
Berkeley ℡510/841-5634. Berkeley's oldest café,
straight out of the Beat Generation archives: beards
and berets optional, books de rigueur.

Coffee Mill 3363 Grand Ave, Oakland ℡ 510/465-
4224. This café doubles as an art gallery and often
hosts poetry readings, too.

Heinhold's First and Last Chance Saloon 56
Jack London Square, Oakland ℡510/839-6761.

Authentic waterfront bar that's hardly changed
since around 1900, when Jack London drank here.
They've never even bothered to fix the slanted floor
that was caused by the 1906 earthquake.

Jupiter 2181 Shattuck Ave, Berkeley ℡510/843-
8277. Many, many beers to select from at this local
favorite, which offers live jazz on weekends and an
outdoor beer garden.

Pacific Coast Brewing Co 906 Washington St,
Oakland ℡510/836-2739. The only real microbrewery downtown, where you can also get decent
grub to wash down with your ale.

Pyramid Brewery 901 Gilman St, Berkeley
℡510/528-9880. Great microbrewed beers in a
popular pub, with industrial-chic decor and outdoor
movie screenings on summer weekends.

Triple Rock Brewery 1920 Shattuck Ave, Berkeley ⓣ510/843-2739. Lively student bar with fine burgers and beers – be sure to check out which two revolving cask-conditioned ales are on.

The White Horse Inn 6551 Telegraph Ave at 66th St, North Oakland ⓣ510/652-3820. Oakland's oldest gay bar – a small, friendly place with mixed dancing for men and women nightly.

Live music and entertainment

Nightlife is where the East Bay really comes into its own. Though traditional **clubs** are virtually nonexistent, there are plenty of **live music venues**, from smoky jazz cafés to sweaty R&B dives. Live dance music thrives here; there's also plenty of holdovers still jangling along in poppy, punky guitar bands that echo Green Day and Nirvana.

The range of **films** screened here is top-notch. Berkeley's **Pacific Film Archives** at 2575 Bancroft Ave ($8; ⓣ510/642-5249 for tickets, ⓦwww.bampfa.berkeley. edu), one of the finest film libraries in California, puts on contemporary international films, plus old favorites. The free *East Bay Express* has the most comprehensive listings of what's on.

Ashkenaz 1317 San Pablo Ave, Berkeley ⓣ510/525-5054, ⓦwww.ashkenaz.com. World music and dance café hosting acts from modern Afro-beat to the best of the Balkans. Kids and under-21s welcome. Cover $5–10.
Blake's on Telegraph 2367 Telegraph Ave, Berkeley ⓣ510/848-0886, ⓦwww.blakesontelegraph. com. Funky student club featuring a variety of live acts from blues and soul through rock to punk and rap. $10–20
Freight and Salvage 1111 Addison St, West Berkeley ⓣ510/548-1761, ⓦwww.thefreight.org. Singer-songwriters perform in a coffeehouse setting. Cover $5–20.
Gilman Street Project 924 Gilman St, West Berkeley ⓣ510/525-9926, ⓦwww.924gilman.org. On the outer edge of the hardcore punk, indie, and experimental scene, this institution helped launch

Green Day and Sleater-Kinney. No alcohol, all ages. Weekends only; cover $5–10.
Starry Plough 3101 Shattuck Ave, Berkeley ⓣ510/841-2082, ⓦwww.starryploughpub.com. Lively Irish bar that features bargain-price live rock and country many nights of the week.
Stork Club 2330 Telegraph Ave, Oakland ⓣ510/444-6174, ⓦwww.storkcluboakland.com. Presently a favorite with DJs and indie bands, this historic club features a jukebox that specializes in country tunes. Closed Mon; cover $5.
Yoshi's World Class Jazz House 510 Embarcadero W, Oakland ⓣ510/238-9200, ⓦwww.yoshis. com. The centerpiece of Oakland's revived Jack London Square, this combination jazz club and sushi bar routinely attracts the biggest names in jazz. Cover $5–40.

The Peninsula

The city of San Francisco sits at the tip of a five-mile-wide neck of land commonly referred to as the **Peninsula**. Home of old money and new technology, the Peninsula stretches for fifty miles through relentless suburbia south from San Francisco along the Bay, winding up in the futuristic roadside landscape of the "Silicon Valley" near **San Jose**.

There was a time when the region was largely agricultural, but the computer boom – spurred by Stanford University in **Palo Alto** – has replaced the orange groves and fig trees of yesteryear with office complexes and parking lots. Most of the land along the **coast** – separated from the bayfront sprawl by a ridge of redwood-covered peaks – remains rural; it also contains some of the best **beaches** in the Bay Area.

Palo Alto

Palo Alto, home of preppy, conservative **Stanford University** (ⓣ650/723-2300, ⓦwww.stanford.edu), has become somewhat of a social center for Silicon Valley's nouveau riche and wealthy students, as evidenced by the trendy cafés and chic new restaurants along its main drag, **University Avenue**. The town doesn't offer a lot in terms of sights other than Spanish Colonial homes, but it's a great place for a lazy stroll and a gourmet meal. Wash down a California-style Greek dish from *Evvia*, 420 Emerson St (T650/326-0983), or Left Bank Parisian cuisine from *La Cheminée*, 530 Bryant St (T650/328-2722), with a microbrewed beer from the *Gordon Biersch Brewery*, 640 Emerson St (T650/323-7723), or a latte from *Caffè Verona*, 236 Hamilton Ave (T650/326-9942). Cheaper but still delicious ethnic fare can be enjoyed at the Thai *Krung Siam* (T650/322-5900) and Indian *Marigold* (T650/327-3455) restaurants, located at nos. 423 and 448 University Ave, respectively. Surprisingly affordable **rooms** are available at the *Cardinal Hotel*, 235 Hamilton Ave, in the heart of downtown (T650/323-5101, Wwww.cardinal hotel.com; shared bath ❸, private bath ❹).

San Jose

Burt Bacharach could easily find **SAN JOSE** today by heading south from San Francisco and following the heat and smog that collects below the Bay. Although one of the fastest-growing cities in California, it is not strong on identity – though in area and population it's close to twice the size of San Francisco. Sitting at the southern end of the peninsula, San Jose has in the past 25 years emerged as the civic heart of Silicon Valley, surrounded by miles of faceless high-tech industrial parks where the next generations of computers are designed and built. Ironically, it's also acknowledged as the first city in California, though the only sign of this is the unremarkable eighteenth-century **Mission Santa Clara de Asis**, on the pleasant campus of the Jesuit-run Santa Clara University.

The area's most famous landmark is the **Winchester Mystery House**, 525 S Winchester Blvd, just off I-280 near Hwy-17 (mid-Oct to April daily 9am–5pm; May to early June & Sept to mid-Oct Sun–Thurs 9am–5pm, Fri & Sat 9am–7pm; mid-June to Aug daily 9am–7pm; tours $18.95–26.95; T408/247-2000, Wwww. winchestermysteryhouse.com). Sarah Winchester, heiress to the Winchester rifle fortune, was convinced upon her husband's death in 1884 that he had been taken by the spirits of men killed with Winchester rifles, and believed that unless a room was built for each of the spirits, the same fate would befall her. The sound of hammers never ceased as work on the mansion went on 24 hours a day for the next thirty years – stairs lead nowhere, windows open on to solid brick. Today it's a relentlessly hyped commercial cash cow, but is still worth a detour. The **Rosicrucian Museum**, 1342 Naglee Ave (Mon–Fri 10am–5pm, Sat & Sun 11am–6pm; $9; T408/947-3636, Wwww.rosicrucian.org), houses a brilliant collection of Assyrian and Babylonian artifacts, while the revamped **Tech Museum of Innovation** (Tues–Sun 10am–5pm; $8; T408/294-8224, Wwww.thetech.org), downtown at 201 S Market St, contains hands-on displays of high-tech engineering as well as an IMAX theater (one show included in admission; extra show $4).

San Jose's **visitor center** is next to the huge Convention Center at 408 Almaden Blvd (Mon–Fri 8am–5pm; T408/295-9600 or 1-800/726-5673, Wwww .sanjose.org), though it is geared more to business people than travelers. Downtown **accommodation** is grossly overpriced, so it's best to try further out. Options include the *Valley Inn*, 2155 The Alameda (T408/241-8500, Wwww .valleyinnsanjose.com; ❸), and the *Howard Johnson Express*, 1215 S 1st St (T408/280-5300 or 1-800/509-7666, Wwww.hojo.com; ❸). Good old-fashioned American **food** is dished up at *Original Joe's*, 301 S First St (T408/292-7030). Grab a stool at the counter or settle into one of the comfy booths at this San Jose institution, where $10 goes a long way (open 11am–1am). For fresh coffee and pastries, head to *Café Matisse*, 371 S 1st St (T408/298-7788).

The coast

The **coastline** of the Peninsula south from San Francisco is a world away from the valley of the inland: mostly undeveloped, with a few small towns, and countless beaches that run 75 miles down to the mellow cities of Santa Cruz and Capitola. Just south of San Francisco, Hwy-1 hugs the precipitous cliffs of Devil's Slide, passing the decent mini-resort of **Pacifica** en route to the clothing-optional sands of **Gray Whale Cove State Beach** (daily 8am–sunset; ☏650/728-5336, Ⓦwww.parks.ca.gov). Despite the name, it's not an especially great place to look for migrating gray whales, but there is a stairway from the bus stop down to a fine strand of sand. Two miles further on Hwy-1, the red-roofed buildings of the 1875 **Point Montara Lighthouse**, set among the windswept Monterey pine trees at the top of a steep cliff, have been converted into a **youth hostel** (☏650/728-7177, Ⓦwww.norcalhostels.org; dorm $19–21; ❸). Just beyond the hostel, down California Street, the **Fitzgerald Marine Reserve** (☏650/728-3584; free) has three miles of diverse oceanic habitat, peaceful trails, and, at low tide, the best tidal pools. But continue a tiny bit further for the historic **Moss Beach Distillery** (☏650/728-5595), a great place to grab a snack and a beer on its windswept patio – they provide enormous blankets to help brave the fog.

A few miles further south on Hwy-1 is **Princeton-by-the-Sea**, where the waterfront *Barbara's Fish Trap* (☏650/728-7049) is a fine spot for good-value seafood, followed by the excellent strand of **Miramar**, the unlikely location of the *Douglass Beach House* (☏650/726-4143, Ⓦwww.bachddsoc.org), an informal jazz pub that attracts some big names. The next town, constantly expanding **Half Moon Bay,** offers camping behind its eponymous state beach (☏650/726-8820; $20), as well as fancier accommodation such as the *Old Thyme Inn*, 779 Main St (☏650/726-1616 or 1-800/720-4277, Ⓦwww.oldthymeinn.com; ❺), and a few eating options – try *Chateau des Fleurs,* 523 Church St (☏650/712-8837), a small French place. Gas up here; fuel stations are rare for the next fifty miles to Santa Cruz.

Marin County

Across the Golden Gate from San Francisco, **Marin County** is an unabashed introduction to Californian self-indulgence: a pleasure zone of conspicuous luxury and abundant natural beauty, with sunshine or fog, sandy beaches, high mountains, and thick redwood forests. Though in the past the region served as logging headquarters, the county is now one of the wealthiest in the US, attracting young professionals to its swanky waterside towns.

The modern **ferries** that travel across the bay from San Francisco can make a great start to a day out. Boats to the chic bayside settlement of **Sausalito** leave from the Ferry Building on the Embarcadero, run by Golden Gate Ferry (Mon–Fri 7.40am–7.55pm, frequency varies; reduced timetable at weekends; $6.75 each way; ☏415/455-2000, Ⓦwww.goldengate.org) or Pier 41 at Fisherman's Wharf, run by Blue & Gold Fleet ferries (6–7 trips daily; $8.50 each way; ☏415/705-8200, Ⓦwww.blueandgoldfleet.com). **Biking** over here means a beautiful ride over the Golden Gate Bridge (unless there's fog) and allows you to explore the headlands freely. Golden Gate Ferries accommodate up to 25 bikes, first-come, first-served.

Across the Golden Gate: the Marin Headlands

The largely undeveloped **Marin Headlands**, across the Golden Gate Bridge from San Francisco, afford some of the most impressive views of the bridge and the city behind. The coastline is much more rugged than it is on the San Francisco side, and it makes a great place for an isolated clifftop scramble among the concrete remains of old forts and gun emplacements. Heading west on Bunker Hill Road takes you up to the brink of the headlands before the road snakes down to Fort Barry and wide, sandy **Rodeo Beach**, from which numerous hiking trails branch out. Check in at the Marin Headlands Visitor Center (daily 9.30am–4.30pm; ℡415/331-1540) above Rodeo Lagoon for free maps. The largest of the fort's old buildings has been converted into the spacious but homey *HI-Marin Headlands* **hostel** (℡415/331-2777 or 1-800/979-4776 ext 168, ⓦwww.norcalhostels.org; dorm $20; ❸), an excellent base for more extended explorations of the inland ridges and valleys.

Sausalito

Attractive, smug little **SAUSALITO**, along the Bay below US-101, was once a gritty community of fishermen and sea traders, full of bars and bordellos. Now exclusive restaurants and pricey boutiques line its picturesque waterfront promenade, and expensive, quirky houses climb the overgrown cliffs above Bridgeway Avenue, the main road and bus route through town. Ferries from San Francisco arrive next to the Sausalito Yacht Club in the town center. If you have sailing experience, split the daily rental fee of a four- to ten-person sailboat at Cass's Marina, 1702 Bridgeway Ave (rates from $124/half-day; ℡415/332-6789, ⓦwww.cassmarina.com).

Aside from walking, shopping, and sucking in the sea air, Sausalito has a one-of-a-kind exhibit in the **Bay Model Visitor Center**, 2100 Bridgeway (Tues–Sat 9am–4pm; donation; ℡415/332-3870, ⓦwww.baymodel.org), where elevated walkways in a huge building lead you around a scale model of the entire bay, surrounding deltas, and its aquatic inhabitants, offering insight on the enormity and diversity of this area.

If you decide **to stay**, *Casa Madrona* at 801 Bridgeway Ave (℡415/332-0502 or 1-800/288-0502, ⓦwww.casamadrona.com; ❼) is a deluxe **hotel** that climbs up the hill opposite the bay and also houses *Mikayla*, a delectable seafood **restaurant** (℡415/331-5888). For less expensive food, head for *Tommy's Wok*, 3001 Bridgeway Ave (℡415/332-1683), a largely organic Chinese restaurant, or try terrific, low-cost curries at *Sartaj India Cafe*, 43 Caledonia St (℡415/332-7103). The *Bar With No Name*, 757 Bridgeway Ave (℡415/332-1392), is an ex-haunt of the Beats hosting frequent live jazz.

Mount Tamalpais and Muir Woods

Mount Tamalpais dominates the skyline of the Marin peninsula, looming over the cool canyons of the rest of the county and dividing it into two distinct parts: the wild western slopes above the Pacific Coast and the increasingly suburban communities along the calmer bay frontage. The Panoramic Highway branches off from Hwy-1 along the crest above Mill Valley, taking ten miles to reach the center of **Mount Tamalpais State Park** (℡415/388-2070, ⓦwww.mtia.net), which has some thirty miles of hiking trails and many campgrounds. While most of the redwood trees that once covered its slopes have long since been chopped down to build San Francisco's Victorian houses, one towering grove remains, protected as the **Muir Woods National Monument** (daily 8am–sunset; $3; ℡415/388-2595, ⓦwww.nps.gov/muwo). It's a tranquil and majestic spot, with sunlight filtering three hundred feet down from the treetops to the laurel- and fern-covered canyon below. Being so close to San Francisco, Muir Woods is a popular target, and the paved trails nearest the car park are often packed with coach-tour hordes; more secluded hiking paths include the Matt Davis Trail, leading south to Stinson Beach and north to Mount Tamalpais.

Mill Valley

From the east peak of Mount Tamalpais, a quick two-mile downhill hike follows the Temelpa Trail through velvety shrubs of chaparral to the town of **MILL VALLEY**, the oldest and most enticing of the inland towns of Marin County. For many years the town has made a healthy living out of tourism and October's annual **Mill Valley Film Festival**, a world-class event that draws Bay Area stars and up-and-coming directors alike.

The restored town centers on the redwood-shaded square of the *Depot Bookstore and Café* (☎415/383-2665), a popular bookstore, café, and meeting place at 87 Throckmorton Ave. The **Chamber of Commerce** is next door at 85 Throckmorton Ave (Mon–Fri 10am–noon and 1–4pm; ☎415/388-9700, ⓦwww.millvalley.org). Far and away the best place to **stay** is the *Mill Valley Inn*, 165 Throckmorton Ave (☎415/389-6608 or 1-800/595-2100, ⓦwww.millvalleyinn.com; ➐), a gorgeous European-style inn with elegant rooms and two private cottages. *Piazza D'Angelo*, at 22 Miller Ave (☎415/388-2000), has delicious pizzas and pastas, while the *Sunnyside Café*, 31 Sunnyside Ave (☎415/388-5260), claims "the customers are rarely right" but serves large, affordable breakfasts and lunches nonetheless. *Sweetwater*, at 153 Throckmorton Ave (☎415/388-2820, ⓦwww.sweetwatersaloon.com), is a comfortable saloon that doubles as Marin's prime **live music** venue, with gigs ranging from jazz and blues all-stars to Jefferson Airplane survivors.

Point Reyes National Seashore

The westernmost tip of Marin County comes at the end of the **Point Reyes National Seashore**, a near-island of wilderness bordered on three sides by over fifty miles of isolated coastline – pine forests and sunny meadows hemmed in by rocky cliffs and sandy, windswept beaches. This wing-shaped landmass is a rogue piece of the earth's crust that has been drifting steadily northward along the San Andreas Fault, having started out some six million years ago as a suburb of Los Angeles. When the great earthquake of 1906 shattered San Francisco, the land here, at the epicenter, shifted over sixteen feet in an instant, though damage was confined to a few skewed cattle fences.

The **Bear Valley visitor center** (Mon–Fri 9am–5pm, Sat & Sun 8am–5pm; ☎415/464-5100, ⓦwww.nps.gov/pore), two miles southwest of Point Reyes Station in Olema, has engaging displays on local geology and natural history, plus details of hiking trails. Just to the north, Limantour Road heads six miles west to the *HI-Point Reyes* **hostel** (closed 10am–4.30pm; ☎415/663-8811, ⓦwww.norcalhostels.org; ➊) in an old ranch house. Nearby **Limantour Beach** is good (and cold) for swimming.

Eight miles west of the hamlet of Inverness, a small road leads down to **Drake's Beach**, the presumed landing spot of Sir Francis Drake in 1579. Appropriately, the coastline resembles the southern coast of England – cold, wet, and windy, with chalk-white cliffs rising above the wide sandy beach. The road continues southwest another four miles to the very tip of Point Reyes, where a precarious-looking **lighthouse** (Thurs–Sun 10am–4.30pm, tours first and third Sat of each month; free; ☎415/669-1534) stands firm against the crashing surf. The bluffs here are excellent for watching sea lions and, from mid-March to April and late December to early February, migrating gray whales.

The Gold Country

More than 150 years before techies from all over the world rushed to California in search of Silicon gold, rough-and-ready forty-niners invaded the **GOLD COUNTRY** of the Sierra Nevada, about 150 miles east of San Francisco, in search of the real thing. The area ranges from the foothills near Yosemite to the deep gorge of the Yuba River two hundred miles north, with **Sacramento** as its largest city. Many of the mining camps that sprang up around the Gold Country vanished as quickly as they appeared, but about half still survive. Some are bustling resorts, standing on the banks of whitewater rivers in the midst of thick pine forests; others are just eerie ghost towns, all but abandoned on the grassy rolling hills. Most of the mountainous forests along the Sierra crest are preserved as near-pristine wilderness, with excellent hiking, camping, and backpacking. There's also great skiing in winter, around the mountainous rim of **Lake Tahoe** on the border between California and Nevada, aglow under the bright lights of the nightclubs and casinos that line its southeastern shore.

⑬ Sacramento

California's state capital, **SACRAMENTO**, in the flatlands of the Central Valley, was founded in 1839 by the Swiss John Sutter. He worked hard for ten years to build a busy trading center and cattle ranch, only to be thwarted by the discovery of gold at a nearby sawmill in 1848. His workers quit their jobs to go prospecting, and thousands more flocked to the goldfields of the Central Mother Lode, without any respect for Sutter's claims to the land. Sacramento became the main supply point for the miners, and remained important as the western headquarters of the transcontinental railroad. Flashy office towers and hotel complexes have now sprung from its rather suburban streetscape, enlivening the flat grid of leafy, tree-lined blocks.

There's not a great deal to see, though the wharves, warehouses, saloons, and stores of the historic core along the **riverfront** have been restored and converted into the touristy shops and restaurants of **Old Sacramento**. On the northern edge of the old town, the **California State Railroad Museum** (daily 10am–5pm; $8; ☎916/445-6645, ⓦwww.csrmf.org) brings together a range of lavishly restored 1860s locomotives, with "cow-catcher" front grilles and bulbous smokestacks.

A mile or so east of downtown, the dome of the **state capitol** stands proudly in a spacious green park two blocks south of K Street Mall. Recently restored to its original elegance, the luxurious building brims over with finely crafted details. Although you're free to walk around, you'll see a lot more on one of the free hourly **tours** (daily 9am–5pm). Further east at 27th and L streets, **Sutter's Fort State Historic Park** (daily 10am–5pm; $3; ☎916/445-4422) is a re-creation of Sacramento's original settlement. An adobe house displays relics from the Gold Rush, and on summer weekends costumed volunteers act out scenes from the 1850s.

Practicalities

Most tourists arrive in Sacramento by car, taking a logical break from driving on Rte-80. **Trains** come in at 4th and I streets, near Old Sacramento, while Greyhound **buses** arrive at 7th and L streets. The **airport** is twelve miles northwest of the city: SuperShuttle Sacramento vans ($13; ☎1-800/258-3826, ⓦwww.supershuttle.com) take you directly to your downtown destination.

Sacramento's most accessible **visitor information center** is at 1102 2nd St (daily 10am–5pm; ℡916/442-7644, ⓦ www.discovergold.org). Besides the central *HI-Sacramento Hostel*, 900 H St (℡916/443-1691, ⓦ www.norcalhostels.org; dorm $20–23, ❷), there are plenty of **places to stay** within walking distance of the city center – the best value being the *Econo Lodge*, 711 16th St (℡916/443-6631 or 1-800/553-2666, ⓦ www.econolodge.com; ❷), while a fancier option is *Amber House B&B* (℡916/444-8085 or 1-800/755-6526, ⓦ www.amberhouse.com; ❺). Further away, the *Vizcaya Mansion*, 2019 21st St (℡916/455-5243 or 1-800/456-2019, ⓦ www. sterlinghotels.com; ❻), offers historic luxury in a quiet residential area. *Paesano's*, at 1806 Capitol Ave (℡916/447-8646), is a deservedly popular pizza **restaurant**; *Tapa the World*, at 2115 J St (℡916/442-4353), serves delicious *tapas* until midnight, often accompanied by live flamenco guitar; and *Centro Cocina Mexicana*, 454 28th St near J Street (℡916/442-2552), offers innovative Californian-Mexican fusion cuisine. For alternative **live music** try *Old Ironsides*, 1901 10th St (℡916/443-9751). Pick up the free weekly *Sacramento News & Review* for more entertainment details.

The Mines

In the romantically rugged landscape of the Gold Country, overshadowed by the 10,000ft granite peaks of the Sierra Nevada, fast-flowing rivers cascade through steeply walled canyons. During the fall, the flaming reds and golds of poplars and sugar maples stand out against an evergreen background of pine and fir. The camps of the **southern mines** were the liveliest and most uproarious of all the Gold Rush settlements, and inspired most of the popular images of the era: Wild West towns full of gambling halls, saloons, and gunfights in the streets. Freebooting prospectors in these "placer" mines sometimes panned for nuggets of gold in the streams and rivers; further **north**, the diggings were far richer and more successful, but the gold was (and still is) buried deep underground, and had to be pounded out of hardrock ore.

Sonora, Columbia, Jamestown, and Mariposa

The center of the southern mining district is **SONORA**, set on steep ravines roughly a hundred miles east of San Francisco. This friendly and animated logging town boasts Victorian houses and false-fronted buildings on its main Washington Street. The Tuolumne County Visitors Bureau, 542 West Stockton Rd off Hwy-49 (Apr–Sep Mon–Fri 9am–7pm, Sat 10am–6pm, Sun 10am–5pm; Oct–Mar Mon–Fri 9am–6pm, Sat 10am–6pm; ℡209/533-4420 or 1-800/446-1333, ⓦ www.thegreatunfenced.com), is the best source of information.

Sonora's onetime arch-rival, **COLUMBIA**, three miles north on Parrots Ferry Road, is now a ghost town (and a state historic park), with a carefully restored Main Street that gives an excellent – if slightly contrived – idea of what Gold Rush life might have been like. In 1854 it was California's second largest city, and it missed becoming the state capital by two votes – just as well, since by 1870 the gold had run out and the town was abandoned.

The **Railtown 1897 State Historic Park** (daily Apr–Oct 9.30am–4.30pm, Nov–Mar 10am–3pm; free, tours $2; ℡209/984-3953, ⓦ www.railtown1897. org), on the corner of 5th and Reservoir streets along the way to Sonora, in **JAMESTOWN**, holds an impressive collection of old steam trains including the one used in *High Noon* and offers rides some weekends. Further south, after a breathtaking drive over the Don Pedro Lake and Merced River, is **MARIPOSA**, gateway to Yosemite and one of the last Gold Rush towns on Hwy-49. Its **California State Mining and Mineral Museum**, a mile or so south of the historic downtown (May–Sept daily 10am–6pm; Oct–April Wed–Mon 10am–4pm; $2; T 209/742-7625), has a working 1860s stamp mill model and hundreds of mineral samples.

Practicalities

In downtown Columbia, the best **place to stay** is right on the historic Main Street in the balconied *City Hotel* (T 209/532-1479 or 1-800/532-1479, W www. cityhotel.com; ❺); in Sonora, *Sterling Gardens* is a comfortable B&B with four guestrooms among ten acres at 18047 Lime Kiln Rd (T 209/533-9300, W www. sterlinggardens.com; ❺), while the well-placed *Gunn House Hotel* (T 209/532-3421, W www.gunnhousehotel.com; ❸) is right in town at 286 S Washington St; motels on Hwy-49 between Sonora and Jamestown include the good-value *Miner's Motel* (T 209/532-7850 or 1-800/451-4176; ❸). Jamestown's Main Street is lined by old Gold Rush hotels such as the fantastic *Jamestown Hotel* (T 209/984-3902 or 1-800/205-4901, W www.jamestownhotel.com; ❹), which boasts an impressive restaurant while being close to other good options, including *Morelia Mexican* (T 209/984-1432), across the street. Sonora has a wide variety of **places to eat** along Washington Street: *Alfredo's* at no. 123 (T 209/532-8332) is a local favorite for Mexican food, and *The Old Stan*, at no. 177 (T 209/536-9598), has *tapas* and Mediterranean dishes.

Grass Valley, Nevada City, and Downieville

The compact communities of **GRASS VALLEY** and **NEVADA CITY**, four miles apart in the Sierra Nevada Mountains, were the most prosperous and substantial of the gold-mining towns. Since the 1960s, artists and craftspeople have settled in the elaborate Victorian homes of the surrounding hills and gorges. In Grass Valley, the **North Star Mining Museum** (May–Oct daily 10am–5pm; donation; T 530/273-4255) at the south end of Mill Street is housed in what used to be the power station for the North Star Mine. Its giant water-driven **Pelton wheel**, fitted with a hundred or so iron buckets, once powered the drills and hoists of the mine. Dioramas show the day-to-day working life of the miners, three-quarters of whom had emigrated here from the depressed tin mines of Cornwall (bringing the Cornish pasty with them).

The last mine in California to shut down was its richest, the **Empire Mine** (May–Aug 9am–6pm; Sept–April 10am–5pm; $3; T 530/273-8522, W www. empiremine.org), now preserved as a state park in the pine forests a mile southeast of Grass Valley off Rte-49. It closed in 1956, after more than six million ounces of gold had been recovered, when the cost of getting the gold out of the ground exceeded $35 an ounce, which was the government-controlled price at the time. Machinery sold off when the mine closed has been replaced from other disused workings and now augments the excellent and very informative **museum** at the entrance.

The excellent Grass Valley **visitor center** at 248 Mill St (Mon–Fri 9am–5pm, Sat 10am–3pm; T 530/273-4667 or 1-800/655-4667, W www.grassvalleychamber. com) is housed in a replica of the original home of Lola Montez, an Irish entertainer and former mistress of Ludwig of Bavaria, who retired here after touring

America with her provocative "Spider Dance" and kept a grizzly bear in her front yard.

Towns don't get much quainter than **Nevada City**. Amid all its shops and restaurants, the lacy-balconied and bell-towered **Old Firehouse** at 214 Main St houses a small **museum** of social history of the region (May–Oct daily 11am–4pm; Nov–April Fri–Sun noon–3pm; donation).

Both towns are very compact and connected every thirty minutes by the Gold Country Stage **minibus** (Mon–Fri 8am–5pm, Sat 9.15am–5.30pm; $1, $2 for a day pass; ☏530/477-0103). These also go to Auburn for connections to the five daily Amtrak Thruway **buses** from Sacramento and Truckee.

North on Rte-49, an hour's drive from Nevada City, you'll head into the most rugged and beautiful part of the Gold Country, where waterfalls tumble over black rocks bordered by pines and maples. **DOWNIEVILLE** is in the midst of an idyllic setting and particularly popular with mountain bikers; it abuts an extensive trail system with moderate to extreme bike trails. Oddly, as the only mining camp to have ever hanged a woman, the town has restored a gallows to commemorate that grisly passage of its history.

Accommodation

Accommodation in the revamped old Gold Rush **hotels** doesn't come cheap, but if you can afford to splash out on a B&B, Nevada City has some excellent options.

Holbrooke Hotel 212 W Main St, Grass Valley ☏530/273-1353 or 1-800/933-7077, ⓦwww.holbrooke.com. Historic hotel, once visited by Mark Twain, and right in the center of town. Breakfast included. **④**

Holiday Lodge 1221 E Main St, Grass Valley ☏530/273-4406 or 1-800/742-7125. Comfortable, basic accommodation with perks such as a swimming pool, free breakfast, and free local calls. **③**

National Hotel 211 Broad St, Nevada City ☏530/265-4551, ⓦwww.thenationalhotel.

com. Oozing faded glory, this historic landmark is the oldest continuously operating hotel in the West and still provides decent rooms

Outside Inn 575 E Broad St, Nevada City ☏530/265-2233, ⓦwww.outsideinn.com. Quiet, 1940s motel with swimming pool, and only a 10min walk from the center of town. **③**

Swan-Levine House 328 S Church St, Grass Valley ☏530/272-1873, ⓦwww.swanlevinehouse.com. Attractively decorated, sunny rooms in an old Victorian hospital run by two artists. **④–⑤**

Eating and drinking

Both Grass Valley and Nevada City have good places to **eat**, as well as many **bars** and **saloons**, where you'll often be treated to free live music.

Café Mekka 237 Commercial St, Nevada City ☏530/478-1517. Relaxed coffeeshop, popular with arty locals.

Cirino's 309 Broad St, Nevada City ☏530/265-2246. Casual Italian place serving filling deli sandwiches and a range of tasty entrees.

Marshall's Pasties 203 Mill St, Grass Valley ☏530/272-2844. Stunning array of freshly filled Cornish-style pasties. Takeout only.

Sopa Thai 312 Commercial St, Nevada City ☏530/470-0101. Beautifully decorated place that dishes up authentic Siamese fare and has become a local favorite.

Swiss House 535 Mill St, Grass Valley ☏530/273-8272. The central European decor seems out of place here but the hearty food such as schnitzel and apple strudel will fill you up.

Lake Tahoe

One of the highest, deepest, cleanest, and coldest lakes in the world, **Lake Tahoe** is perched high above the Gold Country in an alpine bowl of forested granite peaks. Longer than the English Channel is wide, and more than a thousand feet deep, it's so cold that perfectly preserved cowboys who drowned over a century ago have been recovered from its depths. The lake borders Nevada as well and lures weekenders with sunny beaches in the summer, snow-covered slopes in the winter, and bustling casinos year-round.

Arrival, information, and getting around

The nearest you can get to Lake Tahoe on Greyhound or Amtrak from San Francisco and Sacramento is Truckee, fifteen miles north (see p.1153). From there, local TART **buses** (☏530/581-3922 or 1-800/736-6365, ⊛www.laketahoetransit.com) run to Tahoe City and around but, frustratingly, there are only onward services to South Lake Tahoe in the summer months. Transport around the south shore is provided by BlueGo buses and trolleys (☏530/541-7149, ⊛www.bluego.org). There are shuttles from both ends of the lake to Reno airport: North Lake Tahoe Express (☏530/541-4892, ⊛www.laketahoetransit.com) and South Tahoe Express (☏1-866/898-2463, ⊛www.southtahoeexpress.com); prices vary according to the number of passengers. You can rent **bicycles** from numerous outlets, including the Mountain Sports Center (☏530/542-6584, ⊛www.camprichardson.com) in South Lake Tahoe's *Camp Richardson Resort*, and from Olympic Bike Shop (☏530/581-2500) in Tahoe City.

There are four official **visitor centers** around the lake: in California at 3066 US-50, South Lake Tahoe (Mon–Sat 9am–5pm; ☏530/544-5050 or 1-800/288-2463, ⊛www.tahoeinfo.com), and 300 North Lake Blvd, Tahoe City (daily 9am–5pm; ☏530/581-6900, ⊛www.tahoefun.org); and in Nevada at 969 Tahoe Blvd, Incline Village (Mon–Fri 8am–5pm, Sat & Sun 10am–4pm; ☏775/832-1606, ⊛www.gotahoe.com), and at 168 Hwy-50 in Stateline (☏775/588-4591, ⊛www.tahoechamber.org).

Accommodation

There are dozens of bargain **motels** along the Southshore, though weekday rates from $50 can easily more than double on weekends and in summer. In Tahoe City, there are fewer budget choices. If you're stuck, any of the visitor centers will try to help.

Doug's Mellow Mountain Retreat 3787 Forest Ave, South Lake Tahoe ☏530/544-8065, ⊛www.hostelz.com. Basic hostel-style accommodation in essentially Doug's home, with cooking facilities and cheap bike rental. $25 per person. ❶

Inn at Heavenly 1261 Ski Run Blvd ☏530/544-4244 or 1-800/692-2246, ⊛www.innatheavenly.com. Friendly inn with cozy wood-paneled rooms and some huge cabins. Continental breakfast and use of spa included in rates. ❺

River Ranch Hwy-89 and Alpine Meadows Rd, Tahoe City ☏530/583-4264 or 1-800/535-9900, ⊛www.riverranchlodge.com. Historic lodge on the Truckee River with a casual atmosphere and one of the lake's best restaurants. ❹

Royal Valhalla 4104 Lakeshore Blvd, South Lake Tahoe ☏530/544-2233 or 1-800/999-4104, ⊛www.tahoeroyalvalhalla.com. Not exactly regal but one of the better motels, with balconies overlooking the lake and kitchenettes. ❹

Stardust Lodge 4061 Lake Tahoe Blvd, South Lake Tahoe ☏530/544-5211 or 1-800/262-5077, ⊛www.stardust-tahoe.com. Simple suites and guestrooms with kitchenettes, and an easy walk to the casinos and the lake. ❹

Tahoe City Inn 790 North Lake Blvd, Tahoe City ☏530/581-3333 or 1-800/800-8246, ⊛www.tahoecityinn.com. The basic, centrally located rooms can cost as little as $50 midweek in the low season. ❸

South Lake Tahoe and around

In **South Lake Tahoe**, the lakeside's largest community, ranks of restaurants, modest motels, and pine-bound cottages stand cheek by jowl with the high-rise gambling dens of **Stateline**, just across the border in Nevada. If you happen to lose your money at the tables and slot machines, you can always explore the beautiful hiking trails, parks, and beaches in the surrounding area.

The **Heavenly Gondola**, in the heart of town, rises to an elevation of 9136ft (summer daily 10am–5pm; $24, kids $15; see box p.1152). From there, enjoy breathtaking views from East Peak Lake, East Peak Lookout, or Sky Meadows. Hikes are graded from easy to strenuous. Closer to the water, the prettiest part of the lake is along the southwest shore, at **Emerald Bay State Park**, ten miles from South Lake Tahoe, which has a number of good shoreline **campgrounds**. A mile from the parking lot, **Vikingsholm** is a reproduction of a Viking castle, built as a summer home in 1929 and open for hourly tours (summer daily 10am–4pm; $6). In **Sugar Pine Point State Park**, two miles north, the huge **Ehrman Mansion** (daily 11am–4pm; $6) is decorated in Thirties-era furnishings; the extensive lakefront grounds were used as a location in *The Godfather II*.

The rest of the 75-mile **drive** is lovely enough, though certainly not the "most beautiful drive in America," as one locally produced brochure touts. Another way to see the lake is to take a paddlewheel **boat cruise** on the *MS Dixie II* or *Tahoe Queen*, from Zephyr Cove (timetable varies; $33–61, kids $9–31; ☎775/589-4906, ⓦwww.zephyrcove.com), reached on a free shuttle from South Lake Tahoe. You can sign up for other boat tours through one of the casinos.

Tahoe City

Tahoe City, the hub on the lake's northwestern shore manages to retain a more relaxed small-town attitude than South Lake Tahoe. Hwy-89 meets Hwy-28 at Lake Tahoe's only outlet, the **Truckee River**. At the mouth of the river, the **Gatekeeper's Museum** (May to mid-June Wed–Sun 11am–5pm; mid-June to mid-Oct daily 11am–5pm; $2), contains a well-presented hodgepodge of artifacts from the nineteenth century, and a good collection of native basketware. **Rafting** down the Truckee is a common activity in summer, with raft rental companies clustered at the junction of highways 28 and 89.

A couple of miles south along Hwy-89, 500 yards past the Kaspian picnic grounds, hike ten minutes up the unmarked trail to the top of **Eagle Rock** for amazing panoramic views of the royal-blue lake. Several miles further along the highway is **Chamber's Beach**, which in summer is as popular for sunning and swimming as it is for socializing.

Squaw Valley, the site of the 1960 Winter Olympics, is situated five miles west of Tahoe City off of Hwy-89, although the original facilities (except the flame and the Olympic rings) are now swamped by the rampant development that has made this California's largest ski resort (see box, p.1152).

Eating and drinking

Fast food and casino all-you-care-to-eat buffets are standard in Southshore, while Tahoe City has a better range of moderately priced **restaurants** and a couple of good **bars**, all within a few minutes of each other.

CALIFORNIA | Lake Tahoe

Bridgetender Bar & Grill 30 West Lake Blvd, Tahoe City ☎530/583-3342. Friendly rustic bar with good music, a fine range of beers and huge portions of ribs, burgers, etc.

Lakehouse Pizza 120 Grove St, Tahoe City ☎530/583-2222. Tahoe's best place for pizza is also a popular spot for cocktails on the lake at sundown.

Pierce Street Annex in the back of the Safeway complex, Tahoe City ☎530/583-5800. The place for drinking and dancing on the Northshore, but with sometimes-cheesy music. Popular with the younger Tahoe City crowd.

Red Hut Waffle Shop 2749 Lake Tahoe Blvd, South Lake Tahoe ☎530/541-9024. Ever-popular coffee shop, justifiably crowded on early winter mornings with carbo-loading skiers.

River Ranch Hwy-89 and Alpine Meadows Rd, Tahoe City ☎530/583-4264 or 1-800/535-9900. Historic lodge on the Truckee River serving good New American cuisine in a relaxed atmosphere.

Sprouts 3123 Lake Tahoe Blvd near Alameda Ave, South Lake Tahoe ☎530/541-6969. Almost, but not completely, vegetarian, with good organic sandwiches, burritos, and smoothies.

Lake Tahoe skiing

Lake Tahoe has some of the best **downhill skiing** in North America, and its larger resorts rival their Rocky Mountain counterparts. Although skiing is not cheap – the largest ski areas charge at least $50 for a single day – many resorts offer decent-value rental/lift ticket/lesson packages or multiday discounts. **Snowboarding** has caught on in a big way, and the same resorts that once scoffed at the sport have now installed massive snow parks with radical half-pipes and jumps. **Cross-country skiing** is also popular. Most resorts **rent** skis for about $30 and snowboards for $35 or more.

Downhill skiing

Heavenly reachable by shuttle from Southshore, two miles from the casinos, or via the gondola on Hwy-50, next to the state line (☎775/586-7000 or 1-800/243-2836, ⊛www.skiheavenly.com). Prime location and sheer scale (85 runs and 29 lifts) make this one of the lake's most frequented resorts, and it also offers the highest vertical skiing served by a lift. Lift tickets are $65.

Homewood five miles south of Tahoe City on Hwy-89 (☎530/525-2992 or 1-877/525-7669, ⊛www.skihomewood.com). Smaller and more relaxed than its massive resort neighbors, Homewood boasts some surprisingly good skiing with unbeatable views of the lake and reasonable prices. Lift tickets go for $45, and drop as low as $27 midweek.

Kirkwood Ski Resort 35 miles south of South Lake Tahoe on Hwy-88 (☎209/258-6000, ⊛www.kirkwood.com). A bit out of the way if you're in Tahoe but worth the trip as a destination in itself for its recreational possibilities, including excellent hiking and biking trails. Lift tickets are $60.

Squaw Valley USA Squaw Valley Rd, halfway between Truckee and Tahoe City (☎530/583-6955 or 1-888/766-9321, ⊛www.squaw.com). Thirty-three lifts service over four thousand acres of unbeatable terrain at the site of the 1960 Winter Olympics. Non-skiers can take the cable lift ($19) and use the ice-skating/swimming pool complex for the day. Lift tickets are $62.

Cross-country skiing

Royal Gorge in Soda Springs, ten miles west of Truckee (☎530/426-3871 or 1-800/666-3871, ⊛www.royalgorge.com). The largest and best of Tahoe's cross-country resorts has 204 miles of groomed trails. Trail fee $28, rental fee $19.50, and lessons (group $25, private $40).

Spooner Lake in Nevada at the intersection of Hwy-50 and Hwy-28 (☎775/749-5349, ⊛www.spoonerlake.com). The closest cross-country resort to South Lake Tahoe has lake views and 63 miles of groomed trails. Trail fee $20, rental fee $18.50, and lessons $42.50, including pass and rental.

Sunnyside 1850 West Lake Blvd, near Tahoe City ☎530/583-7200. One of the most popular places to have cocktails at sunset on the deck overlooking the lake.

Tahoe House Bakery Hwy-89, half a mile south of Hwy-28, Tahoe City ☎530/583-1377. Family-style bakery and deli, popular with locals.

Taj Mahal 3838 Lake Tahoe Blvd, in the *Quality Inn*, South Lake Tahoe ☎530/541-6495. Basic Indian fare with a daily eleven-dish lunch buffet.

Tep's Villa Roma 3450 Hwy-50, South Lake Tahoe ☎530/541-8227. Longstanding Southshore institution that serves large portions of hearty Italian food.

Truckee and Donner Lake

Fifteen miles north of Tahoe City, the pleasant town of **TRUCKEE** is not only a jumping off point for Lake Tahoe, but a developing tourist destination in its own right. It is well placed for outdoor excursions and it retains a fair amount of nine-teenth-century wooden architecture along its main drag, Donner Pass Road, still referred to as Commercial Row by locals. This strip holds a good choice of **eating** and **drinking** joints, such as *Dragonfly* (☎530/587-0557), a Pacific Rim and Asian fusion restaurant at no. 10118, and *OB's* (☎530/587-4164), a relaxed pub with decent food at no. 10046. Around the corner at 10007 Bridge St, the *Truckee Hotel* (☎530/587-4444 or 1-800/659-6921, ⓦwww.thetruckeehotel.com; ❸) is a central and inexpensive **place to stay**. The Chamber of Commerce, 10065 Donner Pass Rd (Mon–Fri 8.30am–6pm, Sat & Sun 9am–6pm; ☎530/587-2757, ⓦwww.truckee.com) is very helpful and friendly.

Several miles west of Truckee, **DONNER LAKE**, surrounded by alpine cliffs of silver-gray granite, was the site of a gruesome tragedy in 1846, when the **Donner Party**, heading for the Gold Rush, found their route blocked by early snowfall. They stopped and built crude shelters, hoping that the snow would melt; it didn't. Fifteen of their number braved the mountains in search of help from Sutter's Fort in Sacramento; only two men and five women made it, surviving by eating the bodies of the men who died. A rescue party set off immediately, only to find more of the same: thirty or so half-crazed survivors, living off the meat of their fellow travelers. The horrific tale is recounted in the small **Emigrant Trail Museum** (daily summer 9am–5pm, winter 9am–4pm; donation), just off Donner Pass Road in Donner State Park (parking $6 and camping May–Sep; $25; ☎1-800-444-7275, ⓦwww.reserveamerica.com).

Northern California

The massive and eerily silent volcanic lands of **northern California** have more in common with Oregon and Washington than with the rest of the state. Its small settlements live by farming and an ever-decreasing number by logging and fishing, though locals have been joined in recent years by New Agers, ex-hippies, and a growing contingent of tourists. Once you're past the atypically lush valleys of the **Wine Country**, the coast stretches for four hundred miles of rugged bluffs and forests. Aside from the beautiful deserted beaches that stripe the coast, trees are the big attraction, thousands of years old and hundreds of feet high, dominating a landscape swathed in swirling mists. The **Redwood National Park** teems with campers and hikers in summer, but out of season it can be idyllic. The remote wildernesses of the interior can be enchanting, especially around the **Shasta Cascade** and **Lassen Volcanic National Park**.

Public transportation is, not surprisingly, scarce, though Greyhound buses run from San Francisco and Sacramento up and down I-5 into Oregon and US-101 as far as Arcata.

The Wine Country

The warm and sunny hills of **Napa** and **Sonoma valleys**, an hour north of San Francisco, are by reputation at the center of the American wine industry. In truth, less than five percent of California's wine comes from the region, but what it does produce is America's best. In summer, cars jam Hwy-29 through its heart, as visitors embark on a day's hectic tasting.

The Napa Valley

Thirty miles of gently landscaped hillsides, the **Napa Valley** looks more like southern France than a near-neighbor of the Pacific Ocean. The one anomaly is the town of **Napa** itself, a sprawling, ungainly city of 60,000 best avoided in favor of the wineries and small towns north on Hwy-29. Nine miles north is **YOUNTVILLE**, anchored by **Vintage 1870**, 6525 Washington St (daily 10.30am–5.30pm), a shopping and wine complex in a converted winery that's home to Napa Valley Aloft (ⓣ1-800/944-4408, ⓦwww.nvaloft.com), which specializes in sunrise hot-air balloon tours.

Of the large wineries at the valley's southern end, **Robert Mondavi**, at 7801 St Helena Hwy in Oakville (daily 10am–5pm; $10; ⓣ1-888/766-6328, ⓦwww.mondavi.com) offers the most informative and least sales-driven tours and tastings.

Up the valley past the pretty village of **ST HELENA**, **Beringer Vineyards**, at 2000 Main St (daily 10am–5pm; $5; ⓣ707/963-7115, ⓦwww.beringer.com), is modeled on a German Gothic mansion and has graced the cover of many a wine magazine. Spacious lawns and a grand tasting room heavy with dark wood make for quite a regal experience.

Homey **CALISTOGA**, at the very northern tip of the valley, is well known for its mud baths, whirlpools, and mineral water, though its wineries are just as appealing. South of town, **Clos Pegase**, 1060 Dunaweal Lane (daily 10.30am–5pm; $5; ⓣ707/942-4981, ⓦwww.clospegase.com), is a flamboyant, high-profile winery that draws a link between fine wine and fine art, with an excellent sculpture garden; there are tours at 11am and 2pm. The **Chateau Montelena**, 1429 Tubbs Lane (daily 9.30am–4pm; $10; ⓣ707/942-5105, ⓦwww.montelena.com), just north of town, is one of the valley's oldest and smallest wineries, with an impressive medieval facade and a reputation for first-class chardonnays. A mile further up the road, the **Old Faithful Geyser** (daily 9am–6pm; $8; ⓣ707/942-6463) spurts boiling water sixty feet into the air at forty-minute intervals. The water source was discovered during oil drilling here in the 1920s, when search equipment struck a force estimated to be up to a thousand pounds per square foot. In time, landowners turned it into a high-yield tourist attraction, using the same name as the famous spouter in Yellowstone National Park.

△ A Napa Valley vineyard

Practicalities

From San Francisco there are daily Gray Line **bus tours** ($70; ☎415/558-9400 or 1-888/428-6937, ⓦwww.grayline.com) to the Wine Country; otherwise you will need a car. The main **Visitors Bureau** (daily 9am–5pm; ☎707/226-7459, ⓦwww.napavalley.com) is at 1310 Napa Town Center, off First Street in Napa itself, but most towns have their own information outlet.

In **St Helena**, *Hotel St Helena*, 1309 Main St (☎707/963-4388; ❻), provides cozy rooms right in the center of town, while the nearby *Ambrose Bierce House* (☎707/963-3003, ⓦwww.ambrosebiercehouse.com; ❻), is a luxury B&B at 1515 Main St. St Helena's **restaurants** range from the inexpensive Mexican of *Armadillo's*, 1304 Main St (☎707/963-8082), to the haute cuisine and four-hundred-plus wine list at the gigantic *Culinary Institute of America Restaurant*, 2555 Main St (☎707/967-1010).

In **Calistoga**, *Dr Wilkinson's Hot Springs*, 1507 Lincoln Ave (☎707/942-4102, ⓦwww.drwilkinson.com; ❺), is a legendary health spa and hotel, while less expensive lodgings (and spa facilities) lining the main drag, Lincoln Avenue, include the quiet, modern *Comfort Inn* at no. 1865 (☎707/942-9400, ⓦwww.comfortinn.com; ❹). Downtown's most enticing hotel can be found at 1457 Lincoln Ave in the historic *Mount View Hotel and Spa* (☎707/942-6877 or 1-800/816-6877, ⓦwww.mountviewhotel.com; ❼ double, ❾ cottage with patio and Jacuzzi). Creative cuisine, featuring unheard-of combinations such as *chile rellenos* with walnut pomegranate sauce, makes **dining** at the *Wappo Bar & Bistro*, 1226 Washington St (☎707/942-4712), a delicious adventure. The ⚑ *Calistoga Inn*, 1250 Lincoln Ave (☎707/942-4101), serves great seafood appetizers, including wheat-ale steamed clams and mussels, plus a wide range of wines, microbrewed beers, and excellent desserts. *Brannan's Grill*, 1374 Lincoln Ave (☎707/942-2233), serves fresh oysters, salmon, and roasted Sonoma chicken in an airy wood-interior bistro.

Sonoma Valley

On looks alone, the crescent-shaped **Sonoma Valley** beats Napa hands down. This altogether more rustic valley curves between oak-covered mountain ranges from the

Spanish Colonial town of **SONOMA** to Glen Ellen, a few miles north along Hwy-12. It's far smaller than Napa, and many of its wineries are informal, family-run businesses, where a charge for tasting is still frowned upon and visitors are few.

The restored **Mission San Francisco Solano de Sonoma** (daily 10am–5pm; $2), just east of the spacious plaza in Sonoma, was the last and northernmost of the California missions, and the only one established in northern California by the nervous Mexican rulers, who were fearful of expansionist Russian fur-traders. The plaza was also the sight of the Bear Flag Revolt, the 1846 action that propelled California into independence from Mexico, and then statehood. Many of Sonoma's wineries are concentrated a mile east, within walking distance, and include the grand old **Buena Vista Winery**, 18000 Old Winery Rd (free tasting daily 10am–5pm; $5; historical tours daily 2pm; ☎1-800/678-8504, ⓦwww.buenavistawinery.com), which has champagne cellars, tunnels of oak caskets, and a high-ceilinged tasting room. A ten-minute drive further north, in charming Glen Ellen, is the **Benziger Family Winery**, 1883 London Ranch Rd (daily 10am–5pm; $5–10; ☎1-888/490-2739, ⓦwww.benziger.com). A self-guided tour explains how wine grapes are cultivated and flavored, and four times daily a tram tour ($5) takes you around the vineyard along the side of Mount Sonoma. A half-mile up London Ranch Road, **Jack London State Park** (daily 9.30am–5pm, until 7pm in summer; $5 per car) sits on the 140 acres of ranchland owned by the famed author of *The Call of the Wild*. Here you'll find the author's final resting place, along with a decent museum that houses a collection of souvenirs that he picked up while traveling the globe.

Practicalities

Public transportation to the valley is available through Golden Gate Transit's bus services from San Francisco to Petaluma and Santa Rosa (☎707/541-2000, ⓦwww.goldengate.org). For useful **info**, head for the Visitors Bureau (daily 9am–5pm; ☎707/996-1090, ⓦwww.sonomavalley.com), in a cute building right on Sonoma's plaza. **Accommodation** is pricey, though the *Sonoma Hotel*, 110 W Spain St (☎707/996-2996, ⓦwww.sonomahotel.com; ⑥), has French country-style doubles and a great bar, and the *Swiss Hotel*, 18 W Spain St (☎707/938-2884, ⓦwww.swisshotelsonoma.com; ⑥), is in a landmark building on the plaza with four-poster beds in each room. Good shopping and cafés abound on and around the square; *The Girl and the Fig*, 110 W Spain St (☎707/938-3634), is a highly-rated French **restaurant**, while hidden away on 315 Second St E, the *Vella Cheese Company* (Mon–Sat 9am–6pm; ☎1-800/848-0505) attracts cheese aficionados from far and wide with hand-made Monterey Jack, sharp cheddar, and asiago.

The northern coast

The fog-bound towns and windswept, craggy beaches of the **northern coast** that stretches to the Oregon border is better suited for hiking and camping than sunbathing, with cool temperatures year-round and a huge network of national, state, and regional parks preserving magnificent **redwood** trees. Throw on your hiking boots and get out onto the trails that sweep past lolling seals, migrating whales, and some of the oldest, tallest trees on earth.

The Sonoma Coast and Russian River Valley

Despite the weekend influx from San Francisco, the villages of the **Sonoma Coast** and **Russian River Valley** seem all but asleep for most of the year. Tucked along the slow, snaking Hwy-1, towns include **BODEGA BAY**, where Hitchcock filmed *The Birds*. From here, a great thirteen-mile hike leads along the rugged cliffs to busy **Goat Rock Beach**, where the Russian River joins the ocean. A prime seal- and whale-watching spot, the beach is less than a mile from equally pleasing **JENNER**, which is a good place for clam chowder and ocean-staring.

About ten miles inland on Hwy-116, toward the warm and pastoral Russian River Valley, **GUERNEVILLE** is a well-established gay resort. It offers plenty of **places to stay** – though many are expensive. The *New Dynamic Inn*, 14030 Mill St (☎707/869-1563, ⓦ www.newdynamicinn.com; ❹), is one of the more modest places, while the **campground** at *Johnson's Resort* on 1st Street also has cabins (☎707/869-2022, ⓦ www .johnsonsbeach.com; ❷). The popular *Russian River Resort ("Triple R")*, 16390 4th St (☎707/869-0691 or 1-800/417-3767, ⓦ www.russianriverresort.com; ❹), serves alcohol and food, and has comedy and karaoke nights, while *Main St Station*, 16280 Main St (☎707/869-0501), is a great pizzeria with nightly live jazz. The **Armstrong Redwoods State Reserve** ($6 per car), two miles north, contains 750 very dense acres of enormous redwoods interspersed by trails – one of the best ways to see it is on horseback. Guided expeditions run by the Armstrong Woods Pack Station (☎707/887-2939, ⓦ www.redwoodhorses.com) vary in length from half a day (from $70) to overnight rides (from $300) with tented accommodation.

MONTE RIO, four miles back down the river toward the coast, is a lovely old resort town, at the entrance to the 2500-acre **Bohemian Grove**, where the richest and most powerful men in the country traditionally gather in privacy each July for two weeks of (supposedly male-only) high jinks.

The Mendocino coast

The coast of **Mendocino County**, 150 miles north of San Francisco, is a dramatic extension of the Sonoma coastline – the headlands a bit sharper, the surf a bit rougher, but otherwise more of the same. **MENDOCINO** itself looks like a transplanted New England fishing village: weathered and charming, with plenty of art galleries and boutiques. Just south of town, hiking and cycling trails weave through the unusual **Van Damme State Park**, on Hwy-1 ($6 per car; ☎707/937-5804), where the ancient trees of the Pygmy Forest are stunted to waist height because of poor drainage and soil chemicals. Two-hour sea cave tours through the park are available through Lost Coast Kayaking (three times daily; $50; ☎707/937-2434, ⓦ www.lostcoastkayaking.com).

The best of the affordable **accommodations** in the center of town is the *Sea Gull Inn*, 44960 Albion St (☎707/937-5204 or 1-888/937-5204, ⓦ www. seagullbb.com; ❻), though the antique-filled *The Mendocino Hotel and Garden Suites*, 45080 Main St (☎707/937-0511 or 1-800/548-0513, ⓦ www .mendocinohotel.com; ❹), offers some more luxurious suites. The town's oldest **bar** is *Dick's Place* on Main Street, the closest thing you'll find to a local hangout. Of Mendocino's **restaurants**, the most famous is *Café Beaujolais*, 961 Ukiah St (☎707/937-5614), which specializes in organic California cuisine. ⚑ *955 Ukiah Street* (closed Tues; ☎707/937-1955) serves some of the best food in town: entrees are considered a steal for $15–25 a plate. For slightly cheaper fare with a great view, try the *Bay View Café*, 45040 Main St (☎707/937-4197), which serves tasty standards from salads to fish and chips daily.

The Humboldt coast

Humboldt is by far the most beautiful of the coastal counties: almost entirely forestland, overwhelmingly peaceful in places, in others plain eerie. The impassable cliffs of **Kings Range** prevent even the sinuous Hwy-1 from reaching the "Lost Coast" of its southern reaches. To get there you have to detour inland via US-101

Bigfoot Country

Willow Creek, forty miles east of Arcata, is the self-proclaimed gateway to "**Bigfoot Country**." Reports of giant 350- to 800-pound humanoids wandering the forests of northwestern California have circulated since the late nineteenth century, fueled by long-established Indian legends, but weren't taken seriously until 1958, when a road maintenance crew found giant footprints. Thanks to their photos, the Bigfoot story went worldwide. However, in 2002, the bereaved family of Ray L. Wallace claimed he made the 1958 footprints, a hoax they had promised to keep secret until after his death. But the number and variety of prints (over forty, since 1958) still points to a Bigfoot mystery, and the small **visitor center** in Willow Creek has details of Bigfoot's alleged activities. Information on the adjacent **Hoopa Valley Indian Reservation** can be found here and at the **Hoopa Museum** in Hoopa, north of Willow Creek on Highway 96. The site of several violent confrontations between Native Americans and whites over fishing territory, the reservation was finally declared a sovereign territory in 1988, and is currently working on restoration of the Trinity River and its depleted fish stocks.

through the deepest redwood territory as far as **GARBERVILLE**, a one-street town with a few good bars that is the center of the "Emerald Triangle," which produces the majority of California's largest cash crop, marijuana. Every August, the town hosts the enormous **Reggae on the River** festival (information on ℡707/923-4583, Ⓦwww.reggaeontheriver.com).

Redwood country begins in earnest a few miles north, at the **Humboldt Redwoods State Park** (℡707/946-2409, Ⓦwww.humboldtredwoods.org), California's largest redwood park. The serpentine **Avenue of the Giants** weaves for 33 miles through trees that block all but a few strands of sunlight, but you can exit at numerous points to get back on US-101. This is the habitat of *Sequoia sempervirens*, the coastal redwood, with ancestors dating back to the days of the dinosaurs, and some are over 350ft tall. Three campgrounds fill up quickly in summertime (℡1-800/444-7275, Ⓦwww.reserveamerica; $20).

Tiny **SAMOA**, a few minutes by car over the bay from sprawling Eureka, holds the last remaining cookhouse in the West. Lumbermen came to the 🍴 *Samoa Cookhouse* (℡707/442-1659) to eat gargantuan meals after a day of felling redwoods; the oilskin tablecloths and burly workers have gone, but the lumber-camp style remains, with long tables and colossal portions of red meat.

ARCATA, seven miles north of Eureka, a small college town with an earthy, mellow pace, has a grassy central plaza surrounded by good restaurants, and some excellent white-sand, windswept beaches to the north. The *Fairwinds Motel*, 1674 G St (℡707/822-4824 or 1-866/352-5518, Ⓦwww.fairwindsmotelarcata.com; ❸), is probably the best deal in town. More upscale, the *Hotel Arcata*, 708 Ninth St (℡707/826-0217 or 1-800/344-1221, Ⓦwww.hotelarcata.com; ❹), is central and offers standard rooms and nicer suites. *Humboldt Brewery*, 856 10th St, no longer makes its own ale but stocks a good range and has low-priced food.

Redwood National Park

Thirty miles north of Arcata, the small town of **ORICK** marks the southern limit, and busiest section, of the **Redwood National Park**. **Tall Trees Grove** here is home to one of the world's tallest trees — a mighty 367-footer. Many visitors hike to it on the 8.5-mile trail from Bald Hill Road near Orick, but make sure to visit the **Kuchel information center** (daily 9am–5pm; ℡707/464-6101), from which you can obtain the needed free permit to drive along the access road to the trailhead.

Of the three state parks within the Redwood National Park area, **Prairie Creek** is the most varied and popular, and while bear and elk roam in plain sight, rangers lead **tours** through the wild and damp profusion. Highlights include the meadows of **Elk Prairie** in front of the **ranger station** (daily: summer 9am–6pm; rest of year 9am–5pm; ☎707/464-6101), where herds of Roosevelt Elk – massive beasts weighing up to twelve hundred pounds – wander freely.

Spectacular coastal views can be had from trails in the Klamath area, especially the **Klamath Overlook**, two miles up Requa Road and about three-quarters of a mile above the sea. You can jump over, lumber under, or glide through all the naturally contorted and sculpted **Trees of Mystery** (daily: summer 8am–7pm; winter 9am–5pm; $13.50, kids $6.50), except the impressive **Cathedral Tree**, where nine trees have grown from one root structure to form a spooky circle. Further north in a stupendous coastal setting just off US-101, the ☀ *HI-Redwood National Park* **hostel** (☎707/482-8265, ⓦwww.norcalhostels.org; ❷) has dorm beds from $20 and two private rooms.

The park headquarters are in otherwise missable **Crescent City** at 1111 Second St (summer daily 9am–5pm, winter Mon–Sat 9am–5pm; ☎707/464-6101, ⓦwww.nps.gov/redw), but you can pick up information all over the park. There are **campgrounds** everywhere; three that have showers and water are *Prairie Creek* on US-101, *Mill Creek*, five miles south of Crescent City, and *Jedediah Smith*, eight miles north of Crescent City on the Smith River. If you do come in summer, make reservations through ReserveAmerica (☎1-800/444-7275, ⓦwww.reserveamerica.com), and if things get really desperate, head up US-101 to the numerous **motels** around Crescent City.

The northern interior

The remote **northern interior** of California, cut off from the coast by the **Shasta Cascade** range and dominated by forests, lakes, and mountains, is largely uninhabited. Interstate 5 leads through the heart of this near-wilderness, forging straight through the unspectacular farmland of **Sacramento Valley** to **Redding** – the region's only buses follow this route. Redding makes a good base for the **Whiskeytown-Shasta-Trinity area** and the more demanding **Lassen National Volcanic Park**. Mountaineers and the spiritually-minded flock to **Mount Shasta**, which is close enough to the volcanic **Lava Beds** at the very northeastern tip of the state for them to be a long but feasible day's car trip.

Chico

Charming little **CHICO**, about midway between Sacramento and Redding, some twenty miles east of I-5, is a good stopoff if you don't want to cover the whole valley from top to bottom in one day, or if you're here to visit Lassen Volcanic National Park (see p.1160) and need somewhere to stay. Home to **Chico State University**, the laid-back town is loved by mountain bikers for its many trails. Cheap rooms downtown can be found at the *Vagabond Inn*, 630 Main St (☎530/895-1323 or 1-800/522-1555, ⓦwww.vagabondinn-chico-hotel.com; ❸), and there are several good restaurants, notably the 24-hour *Jack's Family Restaurant*, 540 Main St (☎530/343-8383), a great down-home diner.

Redding and Shasta

A sprawling expanse of chain stores with a shopping mall at its heart and a poured-concrete convention center at its gate, **REDDING** appears to be an anomaly amidst the natural splendor of the northern interior. The region's largest city, with over 70,000 people, it has acted as a northern nexus since the late nineteenth century, when the Central Pacific Railroad came through. Today it remains a crossroads, bulging with cookie-cutter motels and fast food outlets, but the superb **Turtle Bay Exploration Park**, 800 Auditorium Drive (March–Oct daily 9am–5pm, Nov–Feb Tues–Sun 9am–5pm; $12; ☎530/243-8850, ⬤www.turtlebay.org), full of fascinating interactive exhibits, and stunning Sundial Bridge, designed by Spanish architect Santiago Calatreva, have greatly enhanced the town's image. If you have a car and need **to stay**, try the *Best Western Hilltop Inn*, 2300 Hilltop Drive (☎530/221-6100 or 1-800/336-4880, ⬤www.bestwestern.com; ❹); the *Deluxe Inn*, 1135 Market St (☎530/243-5141; ❷), is quite at odds with its name but close to the Greyhound station.

SHASTA, four miles west of Redding and not to be confused with Mount Shasta, is somewhat a ghost town. The row of half-ruined brick buildings here represent a once booming gold-mining town, literally at the end of the road from San Francisco and on the very edge of the wilderness. The **Courthouse** has been turned into a museum (Wed–Sun 10am–5pm; $2), full of historical California artwork and mining paraphernalia, while the gallows and prison cells are a grim reminder of the daily executions that went on here.

From Shasta, precipitous Hwy-299 climbs into the **Whiskeytown-Shasta-Trinity National Recreation Area**, which has artificial beaches, forests, and camping facilities at three lakes – Trinity, Whiskeytown, and Shasta. During summer it's completely congested with windsurfers, motorboats, jet skiers, and recreational vehicles block the narrow routes that serve the lakes. An extensive system of tunnels, dams, and aqueducts directs the plentiful waters of the Sacramento River in to California's Central Valley to irrigate cash crops. The lakes are pretty enough, but residents complain they're not a patch on the wild waters that used to flow from the mountains before the Central Valley Project came along in the 1960s.

Lassen Volcanic National Park

About fifty miles over gently-sloping plains east from Red Bluff on Hwy-36, or forty miles east from Redding on Hwy-44, the 106,000 acres that make up the pine forests, crystal-green lakes, and boiling thermal pools of the **LASSEN VOL-CANIC NATIONAL PARK** are one of the most unearthly parts of northern California's forbidding climate, which receives up to fifty feet of snowfall each year, keeping the area pretty much uninhabited outside the brief summer season. **Mount Lassen** itself last erupted in 1915, when the peak blew an enormous mushroom cloud some seven miles skyward, tearing the summit into chunks that landed as far away as Reno; scientists predict that it is the likeliest of all the West Coast volcanoes to blow again.

The thirty-mile tour of the park along Hwy-89 from **Manzanita Lake** in the north should take no more than a few hours. There is a $10 access fee per vehicle to the park, valid for seven days. The Mount Lassen explosion denuded the devastated area, ripping out every tree and patch of grass. Slowly the earth is recovering a green blanket, but the most vivid impression is one of complete destruction. Marking the halfway point, **Summit Lake** is a busy camping area set around a beautiful icy lake, close to which are the park's most manageable hiking trails. From a parking area to the south (8000ft up), the steep, five-mile ascent to Lassen Peak begins. Experienced hikers can do it in four hours, but wilderness seekers will have a better time pushing east to the steep trails of the **Juniper Lake** area.

Continuing south along Hwy-89, Lassen's indisputable show-stealers are **Bumpass Hell** and **Emerald Lake**, the former (named for a man who lost a leg trying to cross it) a steaming valley of active pools and vents that bubble away at a low rumble all around. The trails are sturdy and easy to manage, but you should never venture off them. The crusts over the thermal features are often brittle, and breaking through could plunge you into very hot water. Before leaving the park at **Mineral**, make an effort to stop at **Sulphur Works**, an acrid cauldron of steam vents. A magnificent but grueling trail leads for a mile around the site to the avalanche-prone summit at **Diamond Peak**, which affords great views over the entire park and forestland beyond.

The Park Service has its **headquarters** in Mineral (summer daily 8am–4.30pm, winter Mon–Fri 8am–4.30pm; ℡530/595-4444, ⓦwww.nps.gov/lavo), where you can get free maps and information (there's a box outside when it's closed, and they'll leave your backcountry permits here if you arrive late), including the *Lassen Park Guide*. Another **visitor center** (summer daily 9am–5pm; ℡530/595-4444 ext 5180) is at Manzanita Lake, just inside the northern entrance, and includes the Loomis Museum, which documents the park's eruption cycle.

Mount Shasta City and Mount Shasta

Roughly sixty miles north of Redding, a scenic road branches off I-5 to the tiny town that describes itself as "the best kept secret in California": **MOUNT SHASTA CITY**, hard under the enormous bulk of the 14,162-foot **Mount Shasta**. Still considered active despite not having erupted for two hundred years, this lone peak dominates the landscape for a hundred miles around, and its "energies" attract New Agers by the score. If you want to climb to the summit (10hr; crampons and ice axe needed most of the year), or simply to explore the flanks of the mountain along the many trails, you must obtain a free permit from the **ranger district office**, 204 W Alma St (April–Oct Mon–Sat 8am–4.30pm; rest of year Mon–Fri 8am–4.30pm; ℡530/926-4511), or you can self-issue one at the main trailheads.

The nearest Greyhound stop is at Weed, nine miles north, whence local STAGE **buses** (℡530/842-8295 or 1-800/247-8243) connect to Mt Shasta City. The **Chamber of Commerce** is at 300 Pine St (daily: summer 9am–5.30pm, winter 10am–4pm; ℡530/926-3696 or 1-800/926-4865, ⓦwww.mtshastachamber. com). There's friendly **accommodation** at the excellent *Alpenrose Cottage Guest House*, 204 E Hinkley St (℡530/926-6724, ⓦwww.snowcrest.net/alpenrose; ❹), and more standard rooms at the *Best Western Tree House Motor Inn*, 111 Morgan Way (℡1-800/545-7164 or 530/926-3101, ⓦwww.bestwestern.com; ❹). Nicer still, the ⚞ *McCloud Hotel Bed & Breakfast*, 408 Main St, McCloud (℡530/964-2822 or 1-800/964-2823, ⓦwww.mchotel.com; ❺), has some rooms with Jacuzzis. *Lake Siskiyou Campground* (℡530/926-2618; $20) is four miles west of town and the most picturesque in the area.

Some of the town's best **meals** can be had at *Trinity Café*, 622 N Mount Shasta Blvd (℡530/926-3372), which serves quality California cuisine, and *Vivify* (℡530/926-1345), an upmarket Japanese restaurant at 531 Chestnut St. For good bar food and a chance to meet the locals, head for *Billy Goats*, 107 Chestnut St (℡530/926-0209).

Lava Beds National Monument

Lava Beds National Monument ($10 per vehicle for seven days), in the far north of the state, is one of the most remote and beautiful of California's parks, and also one of its most interesting. The history of these volcanic caves and huge black lava flows is as violent as the natural forces that created them. Before the Gold Rush the area was home to the **Modoc** Indians, but repeated and bloody confrontations with miners led the government to order them into a reservation shared with the Klamath, their traditional enemy. After only a few months the Modocs drifted back to the isolation of the lava beds, and in 1872 the army was sent in. Fifty-five Modoc warriors, under the leadership of "Captain Jack," held back an army ten times the size of theirs for five months from a natural fortress of passageways now known as **Captain Jack's Stronghold**, at the park's northern tip. You can retrace the conflict through well-detailed, self-guided trails in the park and informative exhibits at the **visitor center** (daily: summer 8am–6pm; rest of year 8am–5pm; ☎530/667-2282, ⓦwww.nps.gov/labe).

The bulk of the lava tube caves are close to the visitor center from where you can take the free ranger tours (daily 2pm). With some nerve and a good light source (free loaner flashlights from the visitor center), you can explore the caves alone. You can camp near the visitor center, but there are no shops nearby, so bring everything you'll need with you. Nearby is the **Modoc Ranger Station** (Mon–Fri 8am–5pm; ☎530/233-5811), which has general information on the Modoc National Forest. North and west of the Lava Beds region, the **Klamath Basin National Wildlife Refuge** hosts millions of birds migrating along the Pacific Flyway. The **visitor center** (Mon–Fri 8am–4.30pm, Sat & Sun 10am–4pm; ☎530/667-2231) is off Hill Road near the northwest entrance for the Lava Beds. Surprisingly, the best way of spotting the wildlife is by driving along designated routes; getting out of the car and walking scares the birds off.

The Pacific Northwest

CANADA

WASHINGTON

MONTANA | NORTH DAKOTA | MN | MI

OREGON

IDAHO

WYOMING | SOUTH DAKOTA | WI | MI

NEVADA | NEBRASKA | IOWA | OHIO

UTAH | COLORADO | KANSAS | MISSOURI | IL | IN | WV | VA

CALIFORNIA | NEW MEXICO | OKLAHOMA | AR | KENTUCKY | NC

ARIZONA | TENNESSEE | AL | SC | GEORGIA

MEXICO | TEXAS | MS | LA

PACIFIC OCEAN

ATLANTIC OCEAN

ALASKA | HAWAII

Gulf of Mexico | FL

NEW YORK | PA | NJ | DE | MD

ME | VT | NH | MA | RI | CT

N

AL - ALABAMA	IN - INDIANA	MN - MINNESOTA	RI - RHODE ISLAND
AR - ARKANSAS	LA - LOUISIANA	MS - MISSISSIPPI	SC - SOUTH CAROLINA
CT - CONNECTICUT	MA - MASSACHUSETTS	NC - NORTH CAROLINA	VA - VIRGINIA
DE - DELAWARE	MD - MARYLAND	NH - NEW HAMPSHIRE	VT - VERMONT
FL - FLORIDA	ME - MAINE	NJ - NEW JERSEY	WI - WISCONSIN
IL - ILLINOIS	MI - MICHIGAN	PA - PENNSYLVANIA	WV - WEST VIRGINIA

CHAPTER 14

Highlights

❋ **Pike Place Market, Seattle, WA** Seattle's lively urban market holds an array of fine restaurants, seafood and produce vendors, and street entertainers. See p.1170

❋ **Port Townsend, WA** A charming Victorian town on the Olympic Peninsula, rich with lovely gingerbread homes and waterside vistas. See p.1185

❋ **Columbia River Gorge, WA and OR** One of the USA's best natural attractions, home to precipitous waterfalls, historic highways, and a huge, U-shaped gorge carved from colossal Ice Age floods. See p.1206

❋ **Mount St Helens, WA** Still a haunting sight nearly three decades after it blew its top, the most renowned volcano in North America. See p.1193

❋ **Sandcastle competition, OR** An annual summertime eruption of seaside sculpture and local color, held in the always-popular burg of Cannon Beach. See p.1211

❋ **Crater Lake, OR** Cradled in what's left of a hollowed-out volcano, this sheer blue lake makes a stunning destination. See p.1215

❋ **Hells Canyon, OR** Deeper than the Grand Canyon, this remote gorge boasts excellent white-water rafting on the Snake River. See p.1219

△ Port Townsend, WA

14

The Pacific Northwest

T he **PACIFIC NORTHWEST** states of **Washington** and **Oregon**, while similar in climate, topography, and liberal politics, are quite different in their attitudes toward growth and expansion. Washington's sprawling development, bustling military bases, and notorious freeway gridlock contrast dramatically with Oregon's low-scaled design and easygoing temperament, thanks in no small measure to its stringent land-use laws and "urban-growth boundaries" around its larger cities.

Cooler and wetter than California to the south, both states are split by the great north–south spine of the **Cascade Mountains**, with their western sides more appealing by far to visitors. Here, regular rainfall and a moist climate create a verdant landscape, thick with woodlands that on Washington's **Olympic Peninsula** have become small rainforests. This fertile land is where the region's population is most heavily concentrated, yet much of it remains remarkably pristine – especially in Oregon. Both **Seattle** and **Portland** lie roughly fifty miles from the Pacific Ocean along the I-5 freeway, running from Canada to California. Seattle, the commercial and cultural capital of the Northwest, is a major port sited along the beautiful, island-strewn **Puget Sound.** Portland offers much historic appeal for its old-time terracotta architecture and ten stately bridges crossing the scenic Willamette River.

Beyond the Cascades, the land to the **east** is far drier and less hospitable, peppered with desert and scrubland, as well as bleak stretches of lava beds and cinder cones. Of the towns, only **Spokane** in Washington is of any appreciable size, though Oregon's booming resort town of **Bend** is a far more appealing destination, as its Cascade-straddling location makes it a useful base for sampling the mountains, desert, and especially the beautiful **Columbia River Gorge** to the north. Of outstanding interest also is the scarred territory between Seattle and Portland around **Mount St Helens**, which erupted with devastating effect in 1980.

Some history

The **first inhabitants** of the Pacific Northwest may have reached the continent 12,000 to 20,000 years ago by crossing a land bridge over what is now the Bering Strait between Siberia and Alaska. White newcomers in the early nineteenth century initially focused on trading and exploring along the coast rather than making permanent settlements.

Around the same time, European sea captains such as James Cook and George Vancouver came in search of the fabled **Northwest Passage**, an ice-free route between the Atlantic and the Pacific. Explorers Meriwether Lewis and William Clark, who reached the Oregon coast near present-day Astoria in 1804, were the first whites to cross the interior of the continent, and within forty years American settlers were streaming in along the **Oregon Trail**. This legendary period of

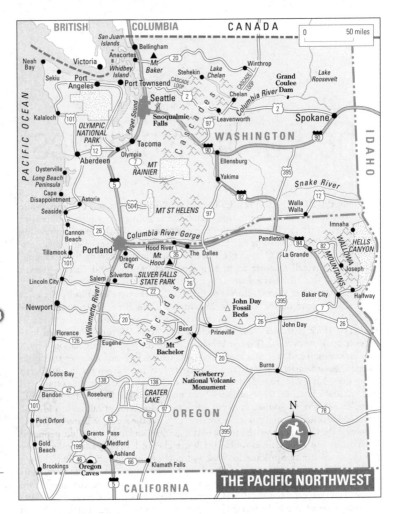

immigration gave de facto control of the region to the United States, and official title followed in 1846 with the signing of a land pact with Britain that established a territorial boundary for the US and Canada at the 49th Parallel. In 1859 Oregon became the second **American state** west of the Great Plains (after California). Thirty more years would pass before Washington entered the Union.

When the railroads reached Portland and Seattle, Oregon and Washington began their economic ascent, aided by timber sales and, in the case of Seattle, the booming trade supplying prospectors on their way to Alaska's Klondike Gold Rush. Later decades would see the rise and fall of the lumber market and the aerospace industry, and, most recently, the **high-tech sector**, which hit a local nadir just after the turn of the millennium. As of 2007, the Pacific Northwest has made a modest economic recovery, though it still regularly posts the nation's highest unemployment rate.

Washington

Although **Seattle** is one of America's most likeable and vibrant cities, perhaps its greatest asset is its proximity to the glorious scenery of **Puget Sound**, the deep-water inlet around which much of the population of Washington lives. Some of the islands here serve as stepping stones to the **Olympic Peninsula** to the west, whose mountains are home to rare elk and lush vegetation that merges into rainforest, and whose rustic beaches have remained pristine for centuries. Dazzling **Olympic National Park** occupies the bulk of the peninsula, and a hike along one of its clearly laid-out trails is a definite highlight of any trip. Wet, often stormy **weather** is almost sure to set the backdrop for many an outdoor pursuit in **western Washington**, though warm temperatures and blue skies reign during the summer.

Not quite as rainy as the mountains to the northeast, the **southern coast** is flatter and more accessible but not as appealing. The nearest real attraction lies a few hours east, where you can marvel at the eye-opening volcanic scenery of **Mount St Helens**.

Dry and desolate, the sprawling prairie-plateau and flood-scoured "channeled scablands" that make up most of **eastern Washington** are a long, slow grind with little of interest, though if a cross-country trek takes you through **Spokane**, the **Grand Coulee Dam** is worth a detour. Otherwise you're only likely to come out here if you're traveling the Cascade loop, a memorable four-hundred-mile round-trip drive through the stunning **Cascade Mountains**.

Getting around Washington

From Seattle, Amtrak runs its *Coast Starlight* **train** once daily south to Portland and LA, while its *Cascades* line runs four times per day south to Eugene, Oregon. Amtrak's twice-daily *Empire Builder* route heads east (to Chicago), just as Greyhound provides **bus** service east across the Cascades to **Spokane** and beyond, with other routes to Wenatchee (for Chelan), Ellensburg, Yakima, and Walla Walla.

Getting to and along the coast is more difficult and requires planning. **Ferries** from Seattle cross to Winslow on **Bainbridge Island**, from where Kitsap Transit services (☎360/373-2877 or 1-800/501-RIDE, ⓦwww.kitsaptransit.org) link with Jefferson Transit (☎360/385-4777 or ☎1-800/371-0497, ⓦwww.jefferson transit.com) for bus access to Port Angeles, Port Townsend, and Olympic National Park. In the Seattle and Puget Sound areas, ferries (mostly run by Washington State Ferries; ☎206/464-6400 or 1-800/84-FERRY, ⓦwww.wsdot.wa.gov/ferries) are a reliable and picturesque way of getting to such places as **Whidbey Island** and the **San Juan Islands**. There are also long-distance services to Canada from Seattle, Anacortes, and Port Angeles, and to Alaska from **Bellingham**; see p.1185.

Seattle

Located on the shore of sparkling Elliott Bay, with attractive Lake Washington behind and the snowy peak of Mount Rainier in the distance, **SEATTLE** has a magnificent setting, with a modern skyline of glass skyscrapers, a friendly charm, and plenty of funky coffeehouses, good restaurants, and engaging clubs.

Seattle's beginnings were inauspiciously muddy. Flooded out of its first location on Alki Point in what is now the suburb of West Seattle, in the 1850s the town shifted to the present location of Pioneer Square, renaming itself after the Native American **Chief Sealth**, who helped reduce violent tensions between whites and local indigenous peoples. As the surrounding forest was gradually felled and the lumber shipped out, Seattle grew slowly until the Klondike Gold Rush of 1897 put it firmly on the national map as a transport and commercial hub. Since the beginning of the twentieth century, the **Boeing** corporation has been crucial to the city's economic strength, booming during World War II and employing one in five of Seattle's workforce by the 1960s. More recent success stories have included **Microsoft** and **Amazon.com**, and the 1990s dot-com boom resulted in an explosion of upscale restaurants, glossy museums, and cultural institutions. This was tempered somewhat by the violent 1999 WTO protests and a February 2001 **earthquake**, as well as a shakeout in the high-tech sector around the same time.

Despite the changes wrought by Seattle's rollercoaster economy as the city grows into an international destination, its more established neighborhoods remain distinctive, and it has a pleasantly down-to-earth ambiance. Unlike the larger cities in California, Seattle's visitors are apt to find many good deals in accommodation, dining, and package sightseeing tours.

Arrival and information

Flights land at **Sea-Tac Airport** (⊤206/433-5388 or 1-800/544-1965, ⓦwww.portseattle.org/seatac), fourteen miles south of downtown Seattle. The Gray Line Airport Express bus (daily 5.30am–11pm every 30min; $10.25, $17 roundtrip ⊤206/626-6088 or 1-800/426-7532, ⓦwww.graylineofseattle.com) drops off at eight major hotels in the downtown area, with connector services to other hotels from 5.30am to 9pm, for $2.50 extra; reserve at least one hour in advance for these connections at ⊤206/255-7159. Shuttle Express has door-to-door service (daily 4am–midnight; ⊤206/622-1424 or 1-800/487-RIDE, ⓦwww.shuttleexpress.com) for $28–30 to downtown. **Taxis** charge $35–40 for the airport-to-downtown route and leave from the taxi stand on the third floor of the parking garage; you can also call ⊤206/246-9999 for pickup once you arrive. The Amtrak station at Third Avenue and Jackson Street (⊤206/382-4125), a dozen blocks south of downtown, and the Greyhound bus terminal, at Eighth Avenue and Stewart Street to the east (⊤206/628-5526), are both an easy bus ride from downtown, or a fifteen-to-twenty-minute walk. Located inside the Washington State Convention and Trade Center, Seventh Ave at Pike St (daily 9am–1pm & 2–5pm; ⊤206/461-5840, ⓦwww.seeseattle.org), the local **visitors bureau** has a "Citywide Concierge Center" that can help with accommodations. The main **post office** is downtown at 301 Union St at Third Avenue (Mon–Fri 7.30am–5.30pm; ⊤206/748-5417 or 1-800/275-8777; zip code 98101).

City transportation

You can get around Seattle for **free** either on foot or by **Metro bus** in the **Downtown Ride Free Area**, bordered by Jackson and Battery streets, 6th Avenue, and the waterfront. Otherwise, adult fares are $1.25, or $1.50–2 during peak hours (Mon–Fri 6–9am & 3–6pm); kids' fares are 50¢, and all tickets are valid for an hour. **Day-passes** ($5) are available from the Citywide Concierge Center (see above) or in King Street Center, 201 S Jackson St (Mon–Fri 8am–5pm; ⊤206/553-3000, ⓦtransit.metrokc.gov). Passes can be used on the elevated monorail (otherwise $3.50 per ride, kids $1.50) between downtown and the Seattle Center, and on the waterfront streetcar (replaced by buses due to construction until 2007; $1.25 off-peak, $1.50 peak). Washington State **ferries** run to Vashon and Bainbridge islands;

tickets from Pier 52, Colman Dock (passengers $4.20–8.50, add $8–10 per vehicle; ☎206/464-6400, ⊛www.wsdot.wa.gov/ferries). Gray Line (☎206/626-5208, ⊛www.graylineofseattle.com) organizes three-hour **bus tours** (3hr; $29) of the city, as well as combination bus-and-**boat tours** (6hr; $54) on an Argosy sightseeing cruise (more tours at ☎206/623-4252, ⊛www.argosycruises.com).

Accommodation

When it comes to **hotels** in Seattle, the best choices are often downtown. Also of good value are the city's **hostels** and **B&Bs**, the latter of which are abundant on Capitol Hill. Specialist **B&B agencies** include A Pacific Reservation Service (☎206/439-7677 or 1-800/684-2932, ⊛www.seattlebedandbreakfast.com) and Seattle Bed and Breakfast Association (☎206/547-1020 or 1-800/348-5630, ⊛www.lodginginseattle.com).

Hotels, motels, and B&Bs

Ace 2423 1st Ave ☎206/448-4721, ⊛www. theacehotel.com. A Seattle favorite with modern, if somewhat austere, rooms and a chic white lobby in the heart of Belltown. Hardwood floors, lofty ceilings, and shared bathrooms for $75; more comfortable suites start at around twice as much. ❹

Alexis 1007 1st Ave, downtown ☎206/624-4844 or 1-800/426-7033, ⊛www.alexishotel.com. Renovated old hotel between Pike Place Market and Pioneer Square. Offers in-room hot tubs, spa, fitness center, and the bright, lurid tentacles of a Dale Chihuly lobby sculpture. Nearly half the rooms are suites that, at their largest, have fireplaces and dining rooms. ❾

Bacon Mansion 959 Broadway E, Capitol Hill ☎206/329-1864 or 1-800/240-1864, ⊛www. baconmansion.com. Eleven elegant rooms and spacious suites in a grand 1909 Tudor Revival structure, just north of Broadway. Well-decorated if a bit small, the least expensive rooms are cheap for Capitol Hill, at $84, although the price is more than double at the high end. Two-night minimum stay on weekends. ❹–❼

Hotel Andra 2000 4th Ave ☎206/448-8600 or 1-877/448-8601, ⊛www.hotelandra.com. An intimate boutique hotel with 120 chic, modern units – more than half of them suites. Onsite gym and restaurant, and high-speed Internet access. An abundance of style for steep rates. ❼–❽

MarQueen 600 Queen Ave N, Seattle Center ☎206/282-7407 or 1-800/445-3076, ⊛www. marqueen.com. Refurbished 1918 building with 56 rooms and suites, period antiques, and amenities like hardwood floors, kitchenettes, microwaves, and fridges, as well as an onsite spa. ❺–❻

Monaco 1101 4th Ave, downtown ☎206/621-1770 or 1-800/715-6513, ⊛www.monaco-seattle. com. Luxurious boutique hotel with bland exterior, but a striking lobby, fitness center, and elegant

suites with CD players and fax machines – some with Jacuzzis as well. ❽

Paramount 724 Pine St, downtown ☎206/292-9500, ⊛www.paramounthotelseattle.com. Luxury chain hotel with impressive European-styled exterior, if somewhat unexciting rooms. Some suites do have hot tubs, though. ❼

Pensione Nichols 1923 1st Ave, Belltown ☎206/441-7125, ⊛www.seattle-bed-breakfast. com. Classy little B&B that's a great deal, with small but clean rooms, shared baths, and simple, tasteful decor in a classic 1904 building. Basic units with shared bath $110; suites with kitchenettes add about $75 per night, but can be shared by four people. ❺

Pioneer Square 77 Yesler Way, Pioneer Square ☎206/340-1234, ⊛www.pioneersquare.com. Restored 1914 brick hotel built by Seattle pioneer Henry Yesler, and one of the few good mid-price establishments with adequate comfort. Saloon on the ground floor. ❻.

Shafer-Baillie Mansion 907 14th Ave E ☎206/322-4654, ⊛shaferbaillie.tripod.com. This mansion's oak-paneled walls and late-Victorian decor echo its 1914 construction. Offers a range of eleven period-furnished B&B rooms, from three cramped "servants' quarters" ($95) to more spacious suites with antique tubs and refrigerators ($140–195). ❹–❼

Sorrento 900 Madison St, First Hill ☎206/622-4400 or 1-800/426-1265, ⊛www.hotelsorrento. com. Modernized, 76-room edifice with a European flair, stylish decor, and posh onsite restaurant, on the east side of I-5 by downtown. The regal exterior surrounds a circular courtyard with palm trees. ❽.

University Inn 4140 Roosevelt Way NE, University District ☎206/632-5055 or 1-800/733-3855, ⊛www.universityinnseattle.com. Business-oriented hotel off University Way. Some rooms have kitchens, all have complimentary breakfast; there's also

THE PACIFIC NORTHWEST | Seattle

an onsite pool and spa. ❹

W Seattle 1112 4th Ave, downtown ☏ 206/264-6000, ⓦ www.whotels.com. Stylish modern tower with a staff of beautiful people and smart, cozy rooms in high style. An even better draw is the ambiance: there's a chic lobby bar with often-packed "cocktail couches" downstairs. ❾

Hostels

Bigfoot Backpackers 126 Broadway Ave E, Capitol Hill ☏ 206/720-2965 or 1-800/600-2965. Reached via an alley near the busiest corner in the area, with 45 beds, including dorms ($18) and a few private rooms ($38 single, $48 double). No curfew and lots of extras: free breakfast, downtown pickup, Internet access, and parking. ❷

Green Tortoise 1525 2nd Ave, between Pike and Pine, downtown ☏ 206/340-1222 or 1-888/424-6783, ⓦ www.greentortoise.net. Old-style hotel digs now functioning as a hostel, with four-to-a-room dorms ($23) and some private doubles ($48).

Free breakfast, Internet access, and pickups at Amtrak, Greyhound, or ferries; they also do summer walking tours. ❷

HI-Seattle 84 Union St, behind Pike Place Market, downtown ☏ 206/622-5443 or 1-888/662-5443, ⓦ www.hiseattle.org. Modern and well-equipped hostel popular with families. Dorm rooms start at $26, though reservations are advisable June–Sept, when the price increases to $35. Private rooms with shared baths cost $55–64, while hotel-type units with private bathrooms and kitchens cost around $100. Free pickup from bus and train stations. ❸–❹

YWCA 1118 5th Ave, downtown ☏ 206/461-4888 ⓦ www.ywcaworks.org. Open to women only, the ambiance here is more functional than colorful, but it's safe and clean, a reasonable choice for visitors on a budget; $46–75 (the higher-priced rooms include a private bath). Twenty-one rooms in all. ❷–❸

The City

Downtown Seattle sits alongside the curve of Elliott Bay just off the I-5 freeway, crowded with plenty of hotels, restaurants, and attractions, but none more popular than **Pike Place Market** and its array of stalls and cafés. Further south, the nineteenth-century center of **Pioneer Square** is lined with bars and clubs, while at the **Seattle Center** in the north, the **Space Needle** presides over museums and carnival rides, as well as the showpiece **Experience Music Project**. Several outlying districts are often livelier than downtown: **Capitol Hill**'s cafés and bars are the heart of the city's hipster and gay scene, and the **University District** is a student area with inexpensive cafés and uptempo nightlife.

Pike Place Market and the Seattle Art Museum

Centrally located at Pike Street and First Avenue, **Pike Place Market** (daily Mon–Sat 9am–6pm, Sun 10am–5pm; ☏ 206/682-7453, ⓦ www.pikeplacemarket.org) began in the early twentieth century and is the oldest continuous working public market in the US. Made up of various buildings stretching over several city blocks, the bustling market makes a real attempt to keep it true to its agrarian roots. Street entertainers play to crowds, the aroma of organic coffee drifts from cafés, and stalls offers piles of lobsters, crabs, salmon, vegetables, fruit, and flowers. Further inside, handmade jewelry, woodcarvings, and silk-screen prints are on sale, while small shops close by stock a massive range of ethnic foods.

Just down the road, the **Seattle Art Museum**, 100 University St and First Ave (Tues–Sun 10am–5pm, Thurs open until 9pm; $7, ticket includes entry to the Seattle Asian Art Museum; free first Thurs of month; ⓦ www.seattleartmuseum.org), features international touring exhibitions and an eclectic array of African, Pacific, and Native American work, with a more limited selection of modern art. Outside the main entrance is the 48ft "**Hammering Man**," a kinetic sculpture by Jonathan Borofsky, which has become the museum's enigmatic emblem. The museum is closed for renovation until spring 2007.

Lake Washington Ship Canal

DOWNTOWN SEATTLE

Seattle Repertory Theater **A**

Intiman Theatre

Marion McCaw Oliver Hall

Key Arena

Center House

Experience Music Project

Children's Museum

SEATTLE CENTER

Monorail Terminal

Space Needle

Pacific Science Center

Olympic Sculpture Park

Victoria BC

Pier 69

Victoria Clipper

Bainbridge Island

Vashon

International District

Capitol Hill

BROAD STREET
MERCER STREET
REPUBLICAN STREET
HARRISON STREET
THOMAS STREET
JOHN STREET

Denny Park
DENNY WAY

Monorail

Roq la Rue

Moore Theater

Westlake Center Mall

Greyhound Bus Depot

Paramount Theatre

Monorail Terminal

PIKE PLACE MARKET HISTORICAL DISTRICT

Waterfront Streetcar

Pike Place Market

Hillclimb

Benaroya Hall

5th Avenue Theatre

New Central Library

Seattle Aquarium

Seattle Art Museum

Bank of America Tower

Elliott Bay

0   200 yards

ACCOMMODATION

Ace	B
Alexis	L
Green Tortoise	F
HI-Seattle	I
Hotel Andra	C
MarQueen	A
Monaco	K
Paramount	D
Pensione Nichols	E
Pioneer Square	M
Sorrento	G
W Seattle	J
YWCA	H

PIONEER SQUARE HISTORICAL DISTRICT

Smith Tower

PIONEER SQUARE
YESLER WAY
S. WASHINGTON STREET
OCCIDENTAL PARK
S. MAIN ST
Klondike National Historical Park
S. JACKSON ST
S. KING ST

Amtrak Station

Seahawks Stadium

Pier 52

Washington State Ferry Terminal

N

RESTAURANTS, BARS & CLUBS

Alibi Room	11	Ivar's Acres of Clams	17
Anthony's Pier 66	7	Kell's Irish Pub	8
Assaggio	4	Noodle Ranch	2
Campagne	9	Panther Room	3
Central Saloon	19	Phnom Penh Noodle House	23
Copacabana	13	Pike Pub & Brewery	15
Crocodile Café	5	Place Pigalle	14
Dahlia Lounge	6	Salumi	20
Dimitriou's Jazz Alley	1	Showbox	10
Doc Maynard's Public House	18	Triple Door	12
Il Terrazzo Carmine	21	Wild Ginger	16
		Zeitgeist Coffee	22

Safeco Field & Museum of Flight & Airport

The Business District

Between Second and Seventh avenues, most of downtown is given over to the steel-and-glass office towers of Seattle's **Business District**. Here, the multi-story **Westlake Center** mall, 400 Pine St (daily 10am–9pm), is only notable for being the southern terminus of the 1.3-mile **monorail** (Mon–Fri 7.30am–11pm, Sat–Sun 9am–11pm; one-way fare $3.50, kids $1.50; ⓦwww.seattlemonorail.com), a holdover from the 1962 Seattle World's Fair that still connects to the Seattle Center and provides the city with one of its prime emblems. Further south, the darkly looming **Bank of America Tower** (nicknamed "the BOAT"), 701 Fifth Ave, has three concave walls that give the structure an oddly curving silhouette. At nearly a thousand feet high, it's the biggest building west of the Mississippi River by number of stories (76). Head to the 73rd-floor **observation deck** (Mon–Fri 8.30am–4.30pm; $5, kids $3) for a predictably good panoramic view.

Just north of the BOAT, the **New Central Library**, 1000 Fourth Ave (Mon–Thurs 10am–8pm, Fri–Sat 10am–6pm, Sun noon–6pm; ⓦwww.spl.org), is a colossal Rem Koolhaas creation that resembles few other libraries in America – and is unmissable for fans of modern architecture. With a facade composed of brilliantly reflective glass panels, unexpected angles, and cantilevered stories looming high above, the library will amaze at street level alone, long before you enter.

The waterfront

Continuing west from Pike Place Market, stairs in the complex lead down to the steep staircase of the **Hillclimb**, in turn conveying foot traffic to the **waterfront** below. Almost opposite the stairway, **Pier 59**, an old wooden jetty that once served tall ships, now houses the underwater viewing dome of the **Seattle Aquarium** (daily June–Aug 9.30am–7pm, rest of year 10am–5pm; $12.50, kids $8.50; ⓣ206/386-4320, ⓦwww.seattleaquarium.org). It has an easily navigable layout, including an outdoor portion near the shoreline, and includes around four hundred species of fish, birds, plants, and marine mammals. On Pier 54 to the south, the most famous of the waterfront's fish-and-chip stands, **Ivar's Acres of Clams** (ⓣ206/624-6852, ⓦwww.ivars.net), is excellent for its streetside **fish bar**, open until 2am, where you can grab a bowl of clam chowder or a helping of cod-and-chips. Along the way, **Colman Dock** at Pier 52 is the terminal for Washington State Ferries (see p.1168).

On the opposite end of the waterfront, at 2901 Western Ave, the 8.5-acre **Olympic Sculpture Park** is a brand-new project by the Seattle Art Museum, highlighted by Richard Serra's five undulating steel panels, known as *Wake*. The free park offers much in the way of hulking, metallic modern sculpture, with pieces by Mark Di Suvero, Tony Smith and Alexander Calder among the other major works.

Pioneer Square

A few blocks inland from the ferry terminal, **Pioneer Square** is Seattle's oldest district, rich with appealing bookshops and galleries amid the old red-brick and wrought-iron buildings. Things get more raucous at night, when rock and jazz boom out from the taverns and many panhandlers take advantage of the foot traffic.

By far the most interesting way to find out about the city's seamy past is on a 90-minute **Underground Tour** from *Doc Maynard's* tavern, 610 First Ave (hours vary by month, usually leaving daily on the hour 11am–4pm, sometimes until 6pm; $11, kids $5; ⓣ206/682-4646, ⓦwww.undergroundtour.com), which details how, after a disastrous 1889 fire, this area was rebuilt with the street level raised by one story, so what used to be storefronts are now underground, linked by subterranean passageways. One long block east, the 1914 white-terracotta **Smith Tower**, 506 Second Ave, was the city's first skyscraper, as well as its longtime-visual icon well before the 1960s arrival of the Space Needle. These days, it's best for the prime views from its 35th-floor **observation deck** (Apr–Oct daily 10am–4pm, rest of year Fri–Sun only; $6; ⓦwww.smithtower.com).

A couple of blocks south at 117 S Main St, **Klondike Gold Rush National Historical Park** (daily 9am–5pm; free; ⓦwww.nps.gov/klse) houses a small museum celebrating the days when Seattle was the gateway to Alaska gold, and prospectors streamed in and traders – and con artists – made their fortunes. Just as interesting, the nearby cobblestoned square of **Occidental Park**, between Main and Washington streets at Occidental, holds four totem poles carved with mythical creatures from Northwest native legends.

Once a month, highbrow culture finds a place at Pioneer Square: the **Gallery Walk** (first Thurs of month 6–8pm; free) showcases nearly forty local art dealers holding simultaneous openings, while **Art in the Park** (3–9pm; free) features a broad range of visual and performance-art pieces in Occidental Park. Both events occur on "**First Thursday**," when the area's ongoing gentrification is most openly on display.

Belltown and the Seattle Center

North of Downtown proper, **Belltown** was the home of the grunge music scene in the 1980s, but has since developed into ground zero for yuppie-friendly condominiums and fancy restaurants. A thin sliver of the good old days is preserved along **Second Avenue**, where diners and clubs like the **Crocodile Café**, 2200 Second Ave (ⓣ206/441-5611, ⓦwww.thecrocodile.com), and funky galleries like **Roq La Rue**, 2312 Second Ave (Wed–Sat 1–6pm, Fri closes 7pm; free; ⓦwww.roqlarue.com), provide a small hint of the neighborhood's lost vitality.

Further north, the **Seattle Center** (ⓦwww.seattlecenter.com) dates from the 1962 Seattle World's Fair and since then the 74-acre complex has become the city's cultural hub, the site of museums, sporting events, concerts, and festivals. The Center is best reached by the **monorail**, which runs from the third floor of Westlake Center (see p.1171) and drops you close to the **Space Needle**, the Space Age-modernist city icon, which is most appealing at night when it's lit up. The panoramic view from the observation deck, where there's a bar, is unmatched (daily 9am–noon; $14, two trips in 24hr $17; ⓦwww.spaceneedle.com).

△ The Space Needle

Southwest of the Needle, the **Pacific Science Center** (Mon–Fri 10am–5pm, Sat & Sun 10am–6pm; $10, kids $7; ☎206/443-2001, ⓦwww.pacsci.org) is full of science-related exhibits for children, and includes a planetarium and IMAX theater. Also good for the kids is the **Children's Museum**, in the Center House complex (Mon–Fri 10am–5pm, Sat & Sun 10am–6pm; $7.50; ⓦwww.thechildrensmuseum. org), which offers plenty of tot-friendly activities and attractions like the **artificial mountain forest**, which lets kids crawl through logs or simulate a rock climb.

The most recent highlight of the Seattle Center, though, is the Frank Gehry-designed **Experience Music Project** (Tues–Thurs 10am–5pm, Sat & Sun 10am–6pm; $20, kids $15; ⓦwww.emplive.com), a giant burst of colored aluminum – into which the monorail passes – that houses an 80,000-piece collection of rock memorabilia divided up into exhibits on different phases of popular music history, as well as rotating exhibits on subjects from Bob Dylan to Brooklyn hip hop. Also on the site, the newer **Science Fiction Museum and Hall of Fame** is supposedly a separate institution, but you'll have to purchase a combined ticket with the EMP ($27, kids $20) to see it. Pop sci-fi fans will delight in the toy spaceships, futuristic sets, and alien attire on display – including sleek costumes from *Blade Runner*, weapons from a simple phaser to a light saber to Jane Fonda's *Barbarella* crossbow, and the iconic captain's chair from *Star Trek*.

Capitol Hill

A fifteen-minute bus ride east of downtown takes you to **Capitol Hill**, the city's alternative center ever since gays, hippies, and assorted radicals moved in during the 1960s and 1970s, and whose **Broadway** axis remains a good choice for eating, buying music, clubbing, and drinking coffee from sidewalk espresso carts. On the northern end of Broadway, between E Roy Street and E Highland Drive, the **Harvard-Belmont Historic District**, along with adjacent Millionaires Row, is rich with huge Neoclassical mansions and sprawling period-revival homes; for a tour, contact the Seattle Architectural Foundation ($10; ☎206/667-9186, ⓦwww .seattlearchitecture.org). East of Broadway from Twelfth to Ninth avenues, the **Pike/Pine Corridor** is filled with all-night coffeehouses, live music venues, and trendy bars. Near its southern end, the **Frye Art Museum**, 704 Terry Ave (Tues–Sat 10am–5pm, Sun noon–5pm, Thurs closes at 8pm; free; ☎206/622-9250, ⓦfryeart.org), is devoted to the figurative painting of American and European artists from the last two centuries, though more daring temporary exhibits have included compelling multimedia, performance, and installation pieces.

The northern end of Capitol Hill is highlighted by **Volunteer Park** 1247 15th Ave (daily 6am–11pm), where you'll find the 1912 **Conservatory**'s hothouses, home to flowers, shrubs, and orchids from jungle, desert, and rainforest habitats (daily 10am–4pm, summer closes 7pm; free), as well as the old **Water Tower** that provides a free, sweeping view of Seattle, albeit through wire mesh. In the same park, the **Seattle Asian Art Museum**, 1400 E Prospect St (Thurs–Sun 10am–5pm, Thurs closes at 9pm; $5; ⓦwww.seattleartmuseum.org), exhibits ceramics, jade, and snuff bottles from Japan, China, Korea, and Southeast Asia.

Ten blocks east, on the other side of Capitol Hill, **Washington Park Arboretum** (daily 7am–dusk; free; ⓦdepts.washington.edu/wpa) is a lush showcase for indigenous vegetation, with many charming footpaths and regional trees, plus the immaculately designed **Japanese Gardens**, where banks of pink flowers sit beside neat little pools with brightly colored carp (March–Nov daily 10am–dusk; $5).

The University District

Across the Lake Washington Ship Canal from Washington Park, the **University District**, or the "U" District, is a busy hodgepodge of coffeehouses, cinemas, and boutiques catering to the University of Washington's 35,000 students. The area centers on University Way, known as **"The Ave,"** and is lined with inexpensive ethnic restaurants and many decent book and record stores.

On campus, the **Henry Art Gallery**, 15th Ave NE and NE 41st St (Tues–Sun 11am–5pm, Thurs closes at 8pm; $10, free for any students with ID; ⓦ www. henryart.org), presents the most imaginative exhibits to be found in any of Seattle's art museums, and houses American and European paintings and photography from the last two centuries. The **Burke Memorial Museum**, 17th Ave NE and NE 45th St (daily 10am–5pm; $8; ⓦ www.washington.edu/burkemuseum), holds the US's largest collection of Native American art and artifacts west of the Mississippi – namely masks, totem poles, and baskets – and presents selections from its huge collection of 2.75 million fossils and Ice Age skeletons, including the remains of a 12,000-year-old sloth.

Along the Lake Washington Ship Canal

As with the "U" District, Seattle's northern neighborhoods are divided from the rest of town by the **Lake Washington Ship Canal**, which connects Lake Union with Elliott Bay to the west and Lake Washington to the east. On the north shore of Lake Union, **Gas Works Park**, 2101 N Northlake Way (daily 6am–11.30pm, parking lot open 6am–9pm; free), is a former gas plant turned postmodern park, where children now play on grassy hills that were once slag heaps and decaying, graffiti-covered machines offer surreal evidence of the site's previous industrial incarnation. Further west, a procession of boats passes through the **Hiram M. Chittenden Locks** (daily 7.30am–9pm; free), and a **fish ladder** is laid out with viewing windows, through which you can see enormous fish leaping up (late summer for salmon, fall and early winter for trout).

Beyond the locks is Salmon Bay, with **Fisherman's Terminal** on its south side, 3919 18th Ave W (daily 7am–4.30pm; ⓦ www.portseattle.org/seaport), crowded with Seattle's fishing fleet and stalls selling freshly caught fish. On the northern side of Salmon Bay, blue-collar **Ballard** appeals for its historic **Ballard Avenue**, between 17th and 22nd avenues NW, home to galleries, bars, and restaurants behind the stately facades of hundred-year-old buildings. The heritage of the Scandinavian fishermen who settled in Ballard in the late nineteenth century is celebrated at the **Nordic Heritage Museum**, 3014 NW 67th St (Tues–Sat 10am–4pm, Sun noon–4pm; $6; ⓦ www.nordicmuseum.org), offering memorabilia and folk art associated with their long journey from the Old World to the West Coast.

Fremont and the Woodland Park Zoo

East of Ballard, **Fremont** is a self-consciously hip area with a spate of used bookshops and artsy cafés, with its hub around Fremont Avenue N from N 34th to N 37th streets. Just off N 34th Street, the **Fremont Sunday Market** (April–Oct 10am–5pm, Nov–March 10am–4pm; free; ⓦ www.fremontmarket. com/fremont) hosts vendors of secondhand jewelry, furniture, clothing, trinkets, and music. Fremont's other main draws are its quirky **public artworks** scattered around the district, most notably the **Fremont Troll** lurking under the Aurora Bridge, 36th St and Aurora Ave, emerging from the gloom with an actual VW Bug in its clutches.

A bit further north, Aurora Avenue leads toward the **Woodland Park Zoo**, N 55th St and Phinney Ave N (daily 9.30am–4pm, summer closes at 6pm; $10.50, kids $7.50; ⓦ www.zoo.org), where more than 250 species reside in a sleek facility with exhibits arranged to reflect different climates and terrains, such as the Northern Trail, Tropical Asia, Tropical Forest, and Temperate Forest.

The Museum of Flight

The biggest of Seattle's museums, the **Museum of Flight**, a twenty-minute bus ride (#174) south of downtown at 9404 E Marginal Way (daily 10am–5pm; $14, kids $7.50; ⓦ www.museumofflight.org), is partly housed in the restored 1909 **"Red Barn"** that was the original Boeing manufacturing plant. It now displays relics from the early days of flight, including the nearly decrepit 1914 *Caproni Ca 20*, the world's first fighter plane. Elsewhere, the **Great Gallery** features more than fifty full-sized airplanes, from ancient prototypes to a replica of John Glenn's 1962 Mercury space capsule, to an SR-71 Blackbird spy plane, which once flew 80,000 feet above the jungles of Vietnam. More icons are on display outside in the museum's expansive **Airpark** (daily 11am–3.30pm, summer closes 4.30pm; free with museum admission), which has a walk-in collection of models that include the 727, 737, and jumbo-jet 747, as well as the supersonic, but now discontinued, Concorde.

Eating

Seattle has many fine choices for **restaurants**, from the funky diners of Capitol Hill and ethnic restaurants of the University District to the delicious seafood of Pike Place Market. Moreover, local **coffeehouses** host an engaging cultural scene, and are inexpensive choices for whiling away the time or surfing the Internet. Corporate giant *Starbucks* started here in the early 1970s (in an extant location in the Pike Place Market), though you're better off sampling a local brew that you can't find in your hometown minimall. Better yet, check out one of the 200-plus **espresso carts** scattered about town, each colorfully styled and uniquely designed.

Restaurants and cafés

The 5 Spot 1502 Queen Anne Ave N, north of Seattle Center ⓣ 206/285-SPOT. Southern-style diner whose "Melting Pot Meals" include Pumpkin Show Pasta in pumpkin-cream sauce, Honey Stung Fried Chicken dipped in buttermilk and honey, and Just So Brisket (with a Coca-Cola and onion marinade).

Anthony's Pier 66 2201 Alaskan Way ⓣ 206/448-6688. Good, expensive seafood – such as shellfish, mahi mahi, and oysters – served in a waterfront restaurant (part of a local chain) with one of the best views of Puget Sound in town.

Assaggio 2010 4th Ave, Belltown ⓣ 206/441-1399. Pleasant, mid-priced Italian restaurant with a friendly ambiance and a menu featuring such items as pan-seared scallops and potato dumplings with gorgonzola, among the expected pizzas, pastas, and veal.

Café Flora 2901 E Madison St, Capitol Hill ⓣ 206/325-9100. One of the city's best vegetarian restaurants, attracting even devout carnivores for its creative, if expensive, soups, salads, and entrees, like Oaxaca tacos or black-eyed pea fritters.

Café Septieme 214 Broadway E, Capitol Hill ⓣ 206/860-8858. A trendy, bustling European-style bistro offering sophisticated but affordable homemade food, with tasty, somewhat unusual breakfasts and lunches like vegetable frittatas and eggplant steaks.

🏃 **Campagne** 1600 Post Alley, downtown ⓣ 206/728-2800. Superb French provincial cooking near the Pike Place Market, with excellent pan-roasted beef entrees and the ever-tasty pommes frites, fried in duck fat. A less expensive branch, Café Campagne, can be found downstairs.

Copacabana 1520 Pike Place, downtown ⓣ 206/622-6359. One of Pike Place's most offbeat eateries, with a concentration on mid-priced Bolivian fare such as stuffed pies (like *huminta*, or corn pie) and seafood soups. The always-popular balcony seating offers a good view of the market hordes.

🏃 **Dahlia Lounge** 1904 4th Ave, Belltown ⓣ 206/682-4142. Upscale restaurant best known for its seafood, featuring delicious main courses like Peking duck and Dungeness crab cakes. If you can't afford to drop a wad on dinner, try the adjoining, excellent Dahlia Bakery.

Il Terrazzo Carmine 411 1st Ave S, Pioneer Square ⓣ 206/467-7797. The height of Italian chic in the city, with splendid risotto, rack of lamb, gnocchi and a fine range of pastas, for steep prices.

Monsoon 615 19th Ave E, Capitol Hill ⓣ 206/325-2111. Upper-end pan-Asian restaurant that's popular for its scrumptious drunken crispy chicken,

Alaska scallops with black-rice risotto, carmelized Idaho catfish, and ginger pork ribs.

Noodle Ranch 2228 2nd Ave, Belltown ⊤206/728-0463. Delicious, pan-Asian cuisine starting at $10 and featuring imaginative noodle-based dishes and other creations, served in a casual atmosphere. The green curry is the chef's specialty and packs quite a punch.

Phnom Penh Noodle House 660 S King St, south of Pioneer Square ⊤206/748-9825. Like the name says, an honest-to-God Cambodian noodle joint that doles out rich helpings of noodles in various sauces, as well as traditional favorites like spicy soups and fishcakes.

Piecora's 1401 E Madison St, Capitol Hill ⊤206/322-9411. The best pizza parlor in a city not known for its pizza, leaning toward the New York style with rich, flavorful, and gooey pies served in a friendly neighborhood environment.

Place Pigalle 81 Pike St, on the staircase behind the Pike Place Market ⊤206/624-1756. Great seafood offerings – mussels, crab, sturgeon – with fine French cuisine make this small spot an excellent choice, despite the high prices. Patio open in warm weather.

Salumi 309 3rd Ave S, Pioneer Square ⊤206/621-8772. Sausages made the old-fashioned way, served on delicious homemade bread, and issued piping hot. Succulent ingredients include the likes of oxtail, prosciutto, lamb, and numerous hog parts.

Wild Ginger 1400 Western Ave, downtown ⊤206/623-4450. Upscale restaurant with fiery dishes from Southeast Asia, India, and China. Try the tuna *manada* – yellowfin tuna fried in spicy Indonesian sauce.

Coffeehouses

Allegro Espresso Bar 4214 University Way ⊤206/633-3030. One of the better spots to taste local brews around the University, with Internet access in an adjoining room, for customers only.

Bauhaus Books & Coffee 301 E Pine St, Capitol Hill ⊤206/625-1600. A hangout for the dressed-in-black crowd with large tables, a used-book section – focusing on art and architecture volumes – and good coffee.

Caffè Ladro 2205 Queen Anne Ave N ⊤206/282-5313. Near the Seattle Center, this neighborhood coffeehouse whose name translates to "coffee thief" has a groovy mix of industrial and organic designs. There's a range of light meals (some veggie options) in addition to hearty coffees.

Online Coffee Company 1720 E Olive Way, Capitol Hill ⊤206/328-3731. Spacious and relaxed Internet café with coffee, beer, wine, and baked goods; the outside patio has a view of Puget Sound.

Verite Coffee 2052 NW Market St ⊤206/709-4497. Fun coffee shop along Ballard's main drag, with excellent coffee and flavorful cupcakes with offbeat toppings like gummy fish and candy flowers.

Vivace Espresso 901 E Denny Way, Capitol Hill ⊤206/860-5869. A large haunt for serious java-drinkers and run by self-proclaimed "espresso roasting and preparation specialists"; their side-walk café at 321 Broadway E is the prime people-watching perch in the area.

Zeitgeist Coffee 171 S Jackson St ⊤206/583-0497. Mostly coffee, a few sandwiches, some pastries, and modern art are found at this pleasant haunt in the heart of Pioneer Square's gallery scene.

Drinking and nightlife

Seattle's **nightlife** revolves around its engaging **live music** venues and **bars**, which pour an excellent selection of microbrewed beers. The tavern scene is most accessible, and touristy, in **Pioneer Square**, where the "joint cover night" plan (weekends $12, weekdays $5) allows you entrance into eight different music venues. Although its grunge heyday is long gone, **Belltown** still hosts well-known bands at the old, atmospheric **Moore Theater**, 1932 Second Ave (⊤206/443-1744, Ⓦwww.themoore.com), among others listed below.

Bars and clubs

Alibi Room 85 Pike St ⊤206/623-3180. Swank martini bar tucked in a dramatic alley behind the Pike Street Market. Excellent food in café-type rooms upstairs, DJs spinning tunes on the dance floor downstairs, and a good selection of film scripts in the library.

Central Saloon 207 1st Ave S, Pioneer Square ⊤206/622-0209. Seattle's oldest saloon

was established in 1892, and is consistently crowded, owing to its location at the tourist district's epicenter. Every night, the live music ranges from alt-rock to punk to metal and eclectic/acoustic.

Comet Tavern 922 E Pike St, Capitol Hill ⊤206/323-9853. The oldest bar on Capitol Hill and a grunge institution – not surprisingly a smoky dive and a bit of a rocker's hangout, with pool tables.

Doc Maynard's Public House 610 1st Ave S, Pioneer Square ℡ 206/682-4649. Pile-driving rock bands entertain tourists in this 1890s saloon. Meeting place for Underground Tours (see p.1172).

Kells Irish Pub 1916 Post Alley, Pike Place Market ℡ 206/728-1916. Fun Irish bar and restaurant in a central location, with patio seating and nightly performances by Irish-oriented folk and rock groups.

Linda's Tavern 707 E Pine St, Capitol Hill ℡ 206/325-1220. Popular with musicians for its jukebox stocked with classics and current indie rock acts. DJs spin two or three nights a week.

Panther Room 2421 1st Ave ℡ 206/441-1677. Swinging Belltown lounge with excellent, quirky drinks like the appropriately potent Latin Fireball and similarly fiery Dragon Mary, and even good happy-hour bar fare (most items $2–6; Mon–Fri 4–6pm) like drunken prawns and marsala mushrooms.

Pike Pub & Brewery 1415 1st Ave, downtown ℡ 206/622-6044. Small craft brewery serving its own beers, as well as numerous bottled brands; has a large wine list and an extensive fish- and pizza-heavy menu to boot.

Pyramid Alehouse 1201 1st Ave S, south of Pioneer Square ℡ 206/682-3377. Excellent regional brewery with a warehouse-like space that serves a dozen Pyramid brands, including some fruit-flavored varieties and an extra-special bitter (ESB).

Music venues

Baltic Room 1207 Pine St E, Capitol Hill ℡ 206/625-4444. Stylish alternative music venue – playing everything from industrial and electronica DJs to rock and jazz bands – comprising three different sections, and selling beer, wine, and cigars.

Crocodile Café 2200 2nd Ave, Belltown ℡ 206/441-5611. A hip alternative joint promoting everything from rock to avant-garde jazz and spoken word. Also a decent diner.

Dimitriou's Jazz Alley 2033 6th Ave, downtown ℡ 206/441-9729. Best big-name jazz spot in town, showcasing international acts, as well as up-and-coming brilliants. Tickets start around $20.

Nuemo's 925 E Pike St, Capitol Hill ℡ 206/709-9467. A hard-thrashing venue that has clawed its way up (almost) to the top of the indie-rock heap. The murals and wall art are splashy and irreverent (themed by a creepy clown), and the bands are of the punk, goth, rock, and alt-anything variety.

Paramount Theatre 911 Pine St, downtown ℡ 206/682-1414. Large 1928 movie palace, seating around three thousand and often hosting well-known rock 'n' roll bands, as well as lectures, classic film programs, comedians, assorted concerts, and more.

Showbox 1426 1st Ave, downtown ℡ 206/628-3151. A good alternative choice for regional rock acts, and quite affordable compared to the bigger-name venues. Grab a drink in the venue's adjacent Green Room bar before the show. Across from Pike Place Market.

Tractor Tavern 5213 Ballard Ave NW, Ballard ℡ 206/789-3599. Solid joint in Ballard with great character, good microbrewed beers, and roots music of all kinds – zydeco, Irish, blues, bluegrass.

Triple Door 216 Union St, Downtown ℡ 206/838-4333. Attractive modern complex that's the apogee of the folk, roots, alt-country, and blues scene in Seattle; the Mainstage has major players and up-and-comers, while the Musicquarium mixes things up with DJs and more experimental fare – it's also free.

Performing arts and festivals

Many of Seattle's **performing arts** venues are based around the Seattle Center; the most prominent of these is **Marion Oliver McCaw Hall**, a sleek, modern facility that hosts the **Seattle Opera** (℡ 206/389-7676, Ⓦ www.seattleopera.org). In the same complex, **Pacific Northwest Ballet** (℡ 206/441-2424, Ⓦ www.pnb.org) puts on around seven programs from September to June and has an active repertoire of seventy works. Away from Seattle Center, **Seattle Symphony Orchestra** performs downtown in the glass-walled **Benaroya Concert Hall**, 3rd and Union streets (℡ 206/215-4747, Ⓦ www.seattlesymphony.org), whose acoustics are heralded as being among the finest in the world for classical performances.

For **theater**, Seattle's longest-established small troupe is the **Seattle Repertory Company** (℡ 206/443-2222, Ⓦ www.seattlerep.org) at the Seattle Center, while next door, the **Intiman Theater** (℡ 206/269-1900, Ⓦ www.intiman.org) performs classics and premieres of innovative new works. A bit to the north at 100 W Roy St, **On the Boards** presents modern performances (℡ 206/217-9888, Ⓦ www.ontheboards.org), while big-name musicals open at the **Fifth Avenue Theatre**, 1308 5th Ave (℡ 206/625-1418, Ⓦ www.5thavenuetheatre.org), or the

Paramount, 911 Pine St (T206/682-1414, Wwww.theparamount.com), both downtown.

Seattle's major **events** include **Bumbershoot**, hosting hundreds of artists on dozens of stages around town on Labor Day weekend (T206/281-7788, Wwww.bumbershoot.org), and the **Northwest Folklife Festival** (T206/684-7300, Wwww.nwfolklife.org), a Memorial Day event at the Seattle Center drawing folk musicians from around the world. In late May and early June, the **Seattle International Film Festival** (T206/464-5830, Wwww.seattlefilm.com) centers on classic moviehouses in Capitol Hill, and from late July to early August, **Seafair** (T206/728-0123 ext 108, Wwww.seafair.com), is a colorful celebration held all over town with airplane spectacles, hydroplane events, and milk-carton boat races.

For **listings**, *Seattle Weekly* and *The Stranger* are free from boxes on the streets and many cafés and stores, and are good for reviews of theater, cinema, and the arts, as is the Friday edition of the *Seattle Post Intelligencer* newspaper.

Day trips to Bainbridge and Vashon islands

For a brief escape from Seattle, the **ferry ride** across Elliott Bay to **Bainbridge Island** provides a relaxing, scenic experience. Washington State Ferries leave from Pier 52 (hourly 5.30am–1.35am; foot passengers $6.50 (collected westbound only in peak season); vehicle and driver $11 non-peak, $14.10 peak season; T206/464-6400 or 1-800/84-FERRY, Wwww.wsdot.wa.gov/ferries) for the 35-minute trip to the island, a green and rural spot occupying less than fifty square miles. The island's only conventional attraction, the **Bloedel Reserve**, 7571 NE Dolphin Drive, off the Agatewood Road exit of Hwy-305 (Wed–Sun 10am–4pm; $10; by reservation only at T206/842-7631, Wwww.bloedelreserve.org), is a natural conservatory containing nearly 150 acres of gardens, ponds, meadows, and wildlife habitats. If you want to pitch a tent on the island, there's **camping** at the far end in Fay Bainbridge State Park ($15–21; T206/842-3931, Wwww.parks.wa.gov). Otherwise, accommodation is limited to **B&Bs**, details of which can be obtained from the **visitor center** in the town of **WINSLOW**, 590 Winslow Way E (T206/842-3700, Wwww.bainbridgechamber.com). Decent choices for eating in Winslow are the Harbour Public House, 231 Parfitt Way SW (T206/842-0969), a renovated 1881 house now used for serving up seafood, salads, burgers, and microbrews, and San Carlos, 279 Madison Ave N (T206/842-1999), which serves nouveau Mexican and Southwestern fare highlighted by mid-priced ribs, chili, garlic prawns, and *chimichangas*.

Other ferries from Seattle and West Seattle make the short trip to easygoing, bicycle-friendly **Vashon Island**. Ferries from downtown Seattle's Pier 50 are passenger-only (Mon–Fri 7.35am–6pm; 35min trip; $8.50), while West Seattle trips are also for vehicles (daily 5.20am–2am; 20min; foot passengers $4.20, vehicle and driver $14.50, $18 peak season). A few pleasant beaches lie along the coast of this island, where the community of **VASHON** is little more than a simple hamlet. The *AYH Ranch Hostel*, 12119 SW Cove Rd (T206/463-2592, Wwww.vashonhostel.com), six miles from the Seattle–Vashon ferry dock at the north end of the island, offers log-cabin dorm beds and tepees for $19, or private rooms for $65. Phone ahead to make a reservation and arrange a free pickup at the jetty. There are also a number of good **B&Bs**, among them *Artist's Studio Loft,* 16592 91st Ave SW (T206/463-2583, Wwww.asl-bnb.com; $110), and the *Swallow's Nest Guest Cottages*, 6030 SW 248th St (T206/463-2646, Wwww.vashonislandcottages.com; $105). Good **places to eat** include *The Hardware Store*, 17601 Vashon Hwy SW (T206/463-1800), a former tool vendor now given over to tasty nouveau American cuisine, and *Rock Island Pizza*, 17322 Vashon Hwy SW (T206/463-6814), which has gourmet pizzas and microbrews.

Puget Sound

The grand waterway of **Puget Sound** hooks far into western Washington, its array of tiny islands and ragged peninsulas the dramatic setting for passing yachts, oceangoing ships, fishing trawlers, and even nuclear submarines. The southern edge of the Sound is increasingly urban, where the formerly industrial **Tacoma** and the small state capital of **Olympia** are slowly becoming known for more than pollution and politicians, respectively, while the waterway itself surrounds countless appealing mountains, forests, and lakes. Popular weekend escapes include rural **Whidbey Island** and the beautiful **San Juan Islands** further north.

Tacoma

Sitting on the Seattle–Portland axis of I-5, **TACOMA** is an old industrial town that's recently experienced a resurgence with a slew of new museums, theaters, and restaurants. Its centerpiece is the massive blue-and-white **Tacoma Dome**, perched just off the freeway, a major concert venue (ⓦ www.tacomadome.org), if something of an eyesore.

Most of Tacoma's attractions sit near each other on the main drag of **Pacific Avenue**, just south of downtown. The most notable of these is unquestionably art celebrity Dale Chihuly's glittering pedestrian overpass, the **Bridge of Glass** (daily dawn–dusk; free), chockablock with crystalline blue spires and glass vases and curiosities on view. It leads to the **Museum of Glass**, 1801 E Dock St (Wed–Sat 10am–5pm, Sun noon–5pm, summer also Mon & Tues 10am–5pm; $10; ⓦ www.museumofglass.org), which resembles a giant metal kiln and presents Chihuly's work and that of other glassblowers, along with a hodgepodge of modern art. On the west side of the bridge is the copper-domed **Union Station** (Mon–Fri 10am–4pm), built in 1911 and now redesigned as a courthouse and display space for some of Chihuly's more extravagant works. On the south side of Union Station, the excellent **Washington State History Museum**, 1911 Pacific Ave (Mon–Sat 10am–5pm, Thurs open until 8pm, Sun noon–5pm; $8; ⓦ www.wshs.org/wshm), has a huge array of exhibits on regional history, with interactive models of covered wagons, coal mines, frontier cabins, and a Depression-era lunch counter, among others. On the north side of the Station is the **Tacoma Art Museum**, 1701 Pacific Ave (Tues–Sat 10am–5pm, Sun noon–5pm; $7.50; ⓦ www.tacomaartmuseum.org), which, like the other museums around here, is most notable for its locally made glassworks.

Further north, the restored historic core of Tacoma is centered around the two-block-long **Antique Row**, Broadway between S 7th and S 9th streets, a popular strip for everything from historic collectibles to modern castoffs, and the **Broadway Center for the Performing Arts**, 901 Broadway (ⓣ 253/591-5894, ⓦ www.broadwaycenter.org), whose two stunning former moviehouses are landmarks with terracotta facades and much historic-revival decor.

If you have time, head four miles north of downtown to picturesque **Point Defiance Park**, at Pearl Street off Ruston Way, which at seven hundred acres is one of the largest urban parks in the USA. Its **Five-Mile-Drive** loop has fine vistas of Puget Sound and many appealing trails branching off from it.

Practicalities

Hotels in Tacoma are less expensive than their counterparts in Seattle. The downtown *Sheraton Tacoma*, 1320 Broadway Plaza (ⓣ 253/572-3200 or 1-800/845-9466, ⓦ www.sheratontacoma.com; ⓞ), has the best chain-hotel rooms in town, though the **B&B** rooms at *The Villa*, about a mile northeast of downtown at 705

N 5th St (☏253/572-1157, ⓦ www.villabb.com; ⑥), are much more appealing, set in a Renaissance Revival mansion surrounded by luxurious gardens. Some of the rooms have private verandas with prime views. Another solid B&B choice is *Geiger Victorian*, 912 North I St (☏253/383-3504, ⓦ www.geigervictorian.com; ⑥), loaded with all the chintz and antiques you'd expect, plus a fireplace, and claw-footed tubs in the rooms. For a bite to **eat**, try the *Southern Kitchen*, 1716 6th Ave (☏253/627-4282), whose delicious gumbo, catfish, hush puppies, candied yams, and fried okra are about as close to Dixie as you're going to get in the Pacific Northwest; and *Spar Tavern*, 2121 N 30th St (☏253/627-8215), a classic brick diner and watering hole serving up burgers, seafood, and microbrews, plus blues on Sunday nights.

Olympia

Picked as Washington's territorial capital in 1853, **OLYMPIA** offers a small but appealing set of attractions that are well worth a look on a stopover between Portland and Seattle. Its compact downtown area is presided over by the **Old Capitol**, Washington St at 7th Ave (Mon–Fri 8am–5pm; free), an 1892 jewel with gothic turrets and arched windows, while nearby along **East Fourth Ave** is one of the prime strips for hearing Northwest rock at its best and cheapest (try Le Voyeur, no. 404, ☏360/943-5710, and The Clipper, no. 402, ☏360/943-6300, for starters). There's also the **Olympia Farmers Market**, 700 N Capitol Way (April–Oct Thurs–Sun 10am–3pm; Nov–Dec Sat & Sun only; ⓦ www.farmers-market.org), with a nice selection of fruits, vegetables, herbs, and handicrafts.

Just south of downtown, the neat lawns of the **Capitol Campus** are the setting for the grand Neoclassical **Legislative Building**, which was completed in 1928 and merits a look for its six gargantuan bronze entry-doors decorated with scenes from state history; a rotunda with a five-ton Tiffany chandelier; and a large circular walnut table in the State Reception Room, whose base was carved from a single tree trunk in the shape of eagles' legs (tours daily on the hour 10am–3pm; self-guided visits daily 10am–4pm; ☏360/753-2580). On the northern side of the campus, the **Capitol Conservatory and Gardens**, 11th Ave at Water St (Mon–Fri 8am–3pm; free), has an eclectic selection of plants from tropical to northern regions, while eight blocks south, the **State Capital Museum**, 211 W 21st Ave (Tues–Fri 10am–4pm, Sat noon–4pm; $2; ⓦ ww.wshs.org/wscm), features local historical artifacts alongside displays of Native American art and Puget Sound natural history.

Practicalities

The **Greyhound** station is at 107 Seventh Ave SE at Capitol Way (☏360/357-5541), just north of the Capitol Campus, and the **Amtrak** station is eight miles southeast, at 6600 Yelm Hwy in the town of Lacey. Intercity Transit runs local **buses** (75¢ ticket, one-day pass $1.50; ☏360/786-1881, ⓦ www.intercitytransit.com), also providing a free DASH shuttle service between downtown, the Farmers Market, and the Capitol Campus. Olympia's **visitor center** (daily 8am–5pm; ☏360/586-3460) is on the Capitol Campus, 14th Avenue and Capitol Way.

Beyond the typical motels, in-town **accommodation** is sparse, highlighted only by the *Swantown Inn*, 1431 11th Ave SE (☏360/753-9123, ⓦ www.swantowninn.com; $99), a striking 1887 Eastlake Victorian, with wireless Internet, savory breakfast, and views of the Capitol; and the *Phoenix Inn*, 415 Capitol Way (☏360/570-0555, ⓦ www.phoenixinnsuites.com; $109), with fridges and microwaves in each room, plus an onsite pool, Jacuzzi, and gym. There's also **camping** at forested Millersylvania State Park, 12245 Tilley Rd ($15–21;

⊕360/753-1519), south of Olympia, two miles east of I-5, exit 99. Of places to **eat**, the *Urban Onion*, 116 Legion Way (⊕360/943-9242), has delicious burgers for vegetarians and carnivores, while a few blocks away, *Spar Café*, 114 Fourth Ave E (⊕360/357-6444), is a 1930s diner with blues and jazz on Saturday nights.

Whidbey Island

With its sheer cliffs and craggy outcrops, rocky beaches and prairie countryside, **WHIDBEY ISLAND** is the second-largest island in the continental US – nearly fifty miles in length from north to south. Although it's possible to reach the island by road – Hwy 20 off I-5 drops into the north end of Whidbey, 85 miles north of Seattle – the **ferry** is usually a better option. The quickest route from Seattle is to head thirty miles north to Mukilteo and catch the ferry to **Clinton** on Whidbey's southern tip (daily 5am–1am; 20min trip; foot passengers $3.85, vehicle and driver $8.35). From Port Townsend on the Olympic Peninsula (see p.1185) another ferry goes to **Keystone**, in the middle of the island (6.30am–8.30pm; 30min; foot passengers $2.50, vehicle and driver $10.90; ⊛www.wsdot.wa.gov /ferries). Whidbey's **bus** system, Island Transit (daily except Sun; ⊕360/321-6688, ⊛www.islandtransit.org), runs eight free routes along the length of the island.

Just a few miles away from where the ferry docks in Clinton, the town of **Langley** offers an Old West main street of wooden storefronts set on a picturesque bluff overlooking the water. First Street is lined with antique stores and galleries such as the Artists Cooperative of Whidbey Island, no. 314 (⊕360/221-7675), and the Hellebore Glass Studio, no. 308 (⊕360/221-2067). Good **places to stay** are *Country Cottage of Langley*, 215 6th St (⊕360/221-8709 or 1-800/718-3860, ⊛www.acountrycottage.com; ⊙), which has five rooms in a restored 1920s farmhouse, all with CD player and fridge; and *The Inn at Langley*, 400 First St (⊕360/221-3033, www.innatlangley.com; ⊙), whose posh rooms have porches and waterfront views. Among the limited **food** options in town, *Langley Village Bakery,* 221 2nd St, #1 (⊕360/221-3525), has great baked goods, pizza, and soups; and *Neil's Clover Patch Cafe*, 2850 SR 525 (⊕360/321-4120), is a buffet spot with gut-busting weekly specials of fish 'n' chips and pork ribs.

The middle part of the island contains **Ebey's Landing National Historic Reserve** (⊛www.nps.gov/ebla), compelling for its turn-of-the-last-century military garrisons **Fort Casey** and **Fort Ebey**, which have since been converted into evocative state parks; Fort Ebey is also a good spot to **camp** ($15–21; ⊕360/678-4636). Nearby, charming little **Coupeville** features preserved Victorian mansions, and its Front Street is where you'll find most of the shops and eateries. Good **accommodation** includes *Captain Whidbey Inn*, 2072 W Captain Whidbey Inn Rd, two miles west of town at Penn Cove (⊕360/678-4097, ⊛www.captain whidbey.com; ⊙), a nautical-themed **hotel** serving superb food; and the *Anchorage Inn*, 807 N Main St (⊕360/678-5581, ⊛www.anchorage-inn.com; ⊙), with seven affordable B&B rooms. For **eating**, try *Knead & Feed,* 4 Front St (⊕360/678-5431), offering homemade bread, pies, and cinnamon rolls, and *Christopher's Front Street Café*, 23 Front St (⊕360/678-5480), which strikes a balance between basic diner food and ritzier dining, with its panini, seafood, pastas, and steaks.

On the northern edge of the island, **Deception Pass State Park** (daily 8am–dusk; ⊕360/675-2417) is not to be missed, sprawling over four thousand acres of rugged land and sea that's great for hiking, fishing, bird-watching, and scuba diving.

The San Juan Islands

North and west of Whidbey Island, midway between Seattle and Vancouver, the beautiful **SAN JUAN ISLANDS** are scattered across the northern reaches of Puget Sound. Every summer brings more visitors than the islands can easily accommodate, especially on the largest ones, San Juan and Orcas, so you'll need to book your stay and transportation in advance.

Arrival and getting around

Washington State Ferries runs a dozen boats per day to the islands from the harbor a few miles west of **Anacortes**, a gritty port 75 miles north of Seattle at the end of Hwy-20. The ferry stops at Lopez, Shaw, Orcas, and San Juan Island (T1-888/808-7977, Wwww.wsdot.wa.gov/ferries), and the slow cruise through the archipelago is a delight. Motorists should get to the port early, as there's often an hour's wait or more to get vehicles onto a summer crossing. Roundtrip **fares** to the islands – $12.80 for foot passengers and $35–50 for a car and driver, depending on the destination and season – are collected only on the westbound journey, and there is no charge for foot passengers on inter-island trips (bringing a bike is an extra $4).

If you want to catch an early ferry from Anacortes, Commercial Avenue is lined with numerous budget **hotels**, the least generic of which is the *Islands Inn*, no. 3401 (T360/293-4644, Wwww.islandsinn.com; $63), offering bayside views and fireplaces, while the *Majestic Hotel*, no. 419 (T360/293-3355; $98), is a nicely renovated option, with old-fashioned decor and a good onsite restaurant and bar.

As an alternative to ferry travel, Kenmore Air (T1-800/543-9595, Wwww .kenmoreair.com) runs **seaplane flights** from Seattle to six stops in the San Juans ($129 one way, $228 roundtrip); booking by Internet can save around $50.

Lopez Island

Pleasant **LOPEZ ISLAND** is a quiet spot whose rolling hills make it an enjoyable place to ride a **bicycle**, which you can rent from Lopez Bicycle Works ($5 per hour, $25 per day; T360/468-2847, Wwww.lopezbicycleworks.com). The main destination is **Shark Reef Park** (T360/378-8420), at the island's southwest tip on Shark Reef Road, where a fifteen-minute walk through dense forest is rewarded by beautiful vistas at the water's edge, where you can spot the occasional sea lion past the tidepools. For **accommodation**, on the edge of little **Lopez Village**, about four miles from the ferry dock, *Lopez Islander*, 2847 Fisherman Bay Rd (T360/468-2233 or 1-800/736-3434, Wwww.lopezislander.com; ❹), is a delightful and spacious resort hotel, not far from the excellent *Bay Café*, 9 Old Post Rd (T360/468-3700). For a change of pace, *Lopez Farm Cottages*, Fisherman Bay Rd south of Military Rd (T1-800/440-3556, Wwww.lopezfarmcottages. com; ❹-❼), offers five comfortable cottages – each with fireplace, porch, and deck – varying from $99–180 according to season.

Orcas Island

Horseshoe-shaped **ORCAS ISLAND** teems with rugged hills and leafy timber that tower over its fetching farm country, craggy beaches, and abundant wildlife. The ferry lands in tiny **Orcas**, mainly interesting for its Victorian *Orcas Hotel* (T360/376-4300, Wwww.orcashotel.com; ❹-❽), whose plushest rooms have Jacuzzis, balconies, and harbor views. You can rent **bicycles** from Dolphin Bay Bicycles, just up from the dock ($30 per day; T360/376-3093, Wwww .rockisland.com/~dolphin), to cycle inland.

Ten miles north, in the drab town of **Eastsound**, the **Chamber of Commerce**, on N Beach Rd past Eastsound Square (T360/376-2273, Wwww.orcasisland. org), provides maps and information. Places to **eat** include *Bilbo's Festivo,* N Beach Road and A Street (T360/376-4728), for its solid Mexican food, and *Portofino Pizzeria*, along A Street (T360/376-2085), for tasty, handcrafted pizzas and calzones.

Nestled at the end of West Beach Road, *Beach Haven Resort* (☎360/376-2288, Ⓦ www.beach-haven.com; ❺) is a great place to **stay**, its beachfront log cabins lining a densely wooded, sunset-facing cove; in summer they are only available by the week.

The island's highlight is **Moran State Park**, off Horseshoe Hwy southeast of Eastsound (Ⓦ www.orcasisle.com/~elc), where more than thirty miles of hiking trails wind through dense forest and open fields to freshwater lakes, to the summit of **Mount Constitution** – the San Juans' highest point – crowned with a rugged stone observation tower. The park's four **campgrounds** ($15–21; ☎1-800/452-5687) fill up early in summer, so book ahead. Further along, lovely *Doe Bay Village & Resort*, Doe Bay Rd, 18 miles east of Eastsound (☎360/376-2291, Ⓦ www. doebay.com), is tucked into a secluded bay and offers everything from hostel beds ($20) to basic campsites ($30) to modern cabins ($75–175). In nearby **Olga**, *Café Olga* (☎360/376-5098) serves tasty **meals** and fruit pies and has an adjoining art gallery.

San Juan Island

SAN JUAN ISLAND is the ferry's last stop before Canada, best known as the home of two harbor towns and, at the southern tip, **American Camp** (dawn–11pm; free; ☎360/378-2902, Ⓦ www.nps.gov/sajh), a national park whose territory once played a role in the infamous "Pig War," an 1859 border conflict between the US and Britain. More appealing is **English Camp**, to the west (same entry as American Camp), where forests overlook pleasant fields and maple trees near the shore, and four buildings from the 1860s and a small formal garden have been restored.

Friday Harbor, the lone incorporated spot in the San Juans, has cafés, shops, and a waterfront that make for pleasant wandering, and its small **Whale Museum**, 62 First St N (daily summer 9am–6pm, rest of year 10am–5pm; $6; Ⓦ www.whale museum.org), offers an interesting look at the sights and sounds of local cetaceans. To see the real thing, head past the coves and bays on the island's west side to **Lime Kiln Point State Park**, 6158 Lighthouse Rd, named after the site's former lime quarry. Orca ("killer") whales come here in summer to feed on migrating salmon, and there's usually at least one sighting a day. San Juan Tours (☎360/378-1323 or 1-800/450-6858, Ⓦ www.sanjuansafaris.com) is one of several companies offering three-hour **whale-watching cruises** (April–Sept only; $59).

From April to September, **San Juan Shuttle** stops at most of the island's principal attractions ($5/one-way, $8/roundtrip, $15/day-pass; ☎360/378-8887 or 1-800/887-8387, Ⓦ www.sanjuantransit.com), and **bikes** ($35/day) can be rented at Island Bicycles, 380 Argyle St (Thurs–Sat only; ☎360/378-4941, Ⓦ www.island bicycles.com). **Maps** are available at the **visitors center**, 91 Front St (Mon–Fri 9am–4.30pm; ☎360/378-8887).

Choices to **stay** include *Friday's*, 35 First St (☎360/378-5848 or 1-800/352-2632, Ⓦ www.friday-harbor.com/lodging; ❹–❺), a cozy inn from 1891, with a range of rooms and suites; *Lakedale Resort* (☎1-800/617-2267, Ⓦ www.lakedale. com; ❼), six miles from the ferry on Roche Harbor Rd (accessible by bus), which has everything from simple campsites ($21) to elegant lodge rooms ($169) and log cabins ($239); and a pleasant, cyclist-only **campground** called *Pedal Inn*, 1300 False Bay Drive (April–Oct only; ☎360/378-3049; $5). The local Bed & Breakfast Association (☎360/378-3030, Ⓦ www.san-juan-island.net) can also hook you up with a room, though it's essential to reserve ahead, especially during late July's popular **San Juan Island Jazz Festival** (☎360/378-5509). Of Friday Harbor's plentiful places to **eat**, *Bella Luna*, 175 First St (☎360/378-4118), is good for Italian fare; *Cannery House*, 174 First St (☎360/378-2500), has fresh seafood,

Eighteen miles south of the Canadian border, **Bellingham** is a pleasant town that's best used as a gateway, either to the winter-sports draw of **Mount Baker**, 56 scenic miles along Hwy-542 (ski season early-Nov to late-May; lift tickets $38 weekends, $32 weekdays; ☏360/734-6771, ⓦ www.mtbaker.us), or west across Puget Sound on the **Alaska Marine Highway,** a three-day ferry ride ($231–352; ☏1-800/382-9229, ⓦ www.akmhs.com) that winds between islands and a fjord-lined coast up to seven Alaska destinations, including Skagway (see p.1235).

If you find yourself in Bellingham for any length of time, the Victorian **Fairhaven** district, three miles south of downtown (I-5 exit 250), is the town's most appealing area, with hip bookstores, cafés, and boutiques – and it's near the ferry terminal, which also hosts Amtrak and Greyhound transit. The best **rooms** are the eight quaint units at the gabled Victorian *North Garden Inn*, 1014 N Garden St (☏ 360/671-7828 or 1-800/922-6414, ⓦ www.northgardeninn.com; ❸), a nice B&B near downtown and just off I-5, with good breakfasts and a great view of the bay; and the *Bellwether*, near Roeder Ave and F Street (☏1-877/411-1200, ⓦ www.hotelbellwether.com; ❻), a large resort hosting spacious rooms and suites with onsite spa, gym, and salon. The best place to **camp** is Larrabee State Park, seven miles south of Bellingham on Hwy-11 ($15–21), though there are other campgrounds on the road to Mount Baker as well.

Downtown has several decent places to **eat**, including *Dirty Dan Harris*, 1211 11th St (☏ 360/676-1011), for solid prime rib and steaks, and *Dos Padres*, 1111 Harris Ave (☏ 360/733-9900), for cheap Mexican staples. Fairhaven's hip coffee shop, *Tony's*, 1101 Harris Ave (☏ 360/733-6319), sometimes hosts live music.

soups, sandwiches, and homemade breads; and *San Juan Donut Shop*, 209 Spring St (☏360/378-5059), serves good, hefty breakfasts from 6.30am.

At the northwest tip of the island is **Roche Harbor**, established in the 1880s around the limestone trade, and highlighted by the gracious white *Hotel de Haro*, 248 Reuben Memorial Drive (☏360/378-2155 or 1-800/451-8910, ⓦ www.rocheharbor.com; ❸–❼), built over the harbor in 1886 and still appealing for its upscale suites, standard rooms, and quaint cottages. At the hotel there are several places to **eat**. The best by far is *McMillen's* (☏360/378-5757), with good, if pricey, steak and seafood entrees and waterside vistas.

The Olympic Peninsula

West of Puget Sound lies the great **Olympic Peninsula**, accessible by US-101, which loops around its coastal perimeter. The **Olympic Mountains** at the peninsula's core are rich with dense vegetation thickening into rainforest. Home to several of these forests and unspoiled Pacific beaches, the peninsula provides habitat for a huge variety of wildlife and seabirds. Luckily, much of the terrain is protected as **Olympic National Park**, a rugged preserve that merits a visit for its excellent hiking, bicycling, climbing and other outdoor activities.

Port Townsend

With its brightly painted mansions, convivial cafés, and easily walkable scale, **PORT TOWNSEND** is a charming, if somewhat isolated, relic from the 1890s that's a great place to spend a day or two before venturing on to the mountains. Perched on the peninsula's northeastern tip across from Keystone on Whidbey Island, Port Townsend's physical split – half on a bluff, half at sea level – reflects nineteenth-century social divisions, when wealthy merchants built their houses uptown, far above the rowdy clamor of the port below.

The downtown area lies at the base of the hill on **Water Street**, which sports an attractive medley of Victorian brick and stone buildings. The area's rich history is detailed in the museum of the **Jefferson County Historical Society**, 210 Polk St (Fri–Mon 11am–4pm; $3; Ⓦ www.jchsmuseum.org), which has an eclectic assortment of items, from a photographer's chair draped with bear and buffalo skins, to unusual late nineteenth- and early twentieth-century two-necked harp guitars. Up on the bluff, and even more eye-catching, is the grand **Jefferson County Courthouse**, Walker and Jefferson streets (Mon–Fri 9am–5pm; Ⓦ www.co.jefferson. wa.us), a towering red Romanesque Revival edifice with a clock tower that looks like a medieval version of Big Ben.

Though bustling year-round, the town is busiest during its **summer festivals** – principally American Fiddle Tunes in early July, Jazz Port Townsend in late July, and the Wooden Boat Festival in September (ⓣ 360/385-4742, Ⓦ www. woodenboat.org). Some of these take place at the state park at **Fort Worden** (ⓣ 360/344-4400, Ⓦ www.fortworden.org), the remains of a military garrison two miles north of town. It offers a wide range of accommodation from dorm beds ($18) to campsites ($22) and former officers' houses (❺–❽), as well as several museums, a science center, and a lighthouse – not to mention dozens of good hiking trails at the edge of Puget Sound.

Practicalities

Although Port Townsend is easily accessed by road, you can also get there by **ferry** from Keystone (see p.1182). Get maps and information at the helpful **visitor center**, 2437 E Sims Way (Mon–Fri 9am–5pm; ⓣ 360/385-2722 or 1-888/365-6978, Ⓦ www.ptguide.com), twelve blocks south of the ferry terminal on Hwy-20.

There's a good choice of places to stay, and the most central is the ⚹ *Palace Hotel*, 1004 Water St (ⓣ 360/385-0773, Ⓦ www.palacehotelpt.com; ❸–❺), a Victorian charmer with an elegant lobby and antique decor, claw-footed tubs, and excellent views of the sound. Rooms range from ultra-cheap units with shared bath to affordable two-room suites. The town's specialty, though, is its B&Bs, the best of which occupy grand Victorian mansions uptown, such as the *Ann Starrett Mansion,* 744 Clay St (ⓣ 360/385-3205 or 1-800/321-0644, Ⓦ www.starrettmansion. com; ❻), an 1889 Queen Anne gem with elegant ceiling frescoes, a splendid spiral staircase, and antique furnishings; and the delightful *Manresa Castle*, Seventh and Sheridan streets (ⓣ 360/385-5750 or 1-800/732-1281, Ⓦ www.manresacastle. com), a quasi-French castle from 1892 that has thirty rooms ranging from affordable cozy single units to swanky suites in the tower (❹–❼).

Port Townsend has many fine places to eat, among them *Fountain Café*, 920 Washington St (ⓣ 360/385-1364), with seafood and pasta specialties like oyster stew and wild mushroom risotto, and the *Silverwater Café*, 237 Taylor St (ⓣ 360/385-6448), with fresh seafood such as Northwest floribunda and ahi tuna. Also excellent is ⚹ *Sweet Laurette Patisserie*, 1029 Lawrence St (ⓣ 360/385-4886), the best French-style bakery in town, featuring elaborate (and expensive) cakes that resemble artworks, and cheaper scones, pies, and pastries.

Port Angeles

PORT ANGELES is the peninsula's main town and the most popular point of entry into Olympic National Park, a few miles to the south. Its working-class harbor is backed by striking mountains, but there are few reasons to linger, except as a stopover to more compelling destinations.

Although it's preferable to stay inside the park, Port Angeles has a number of inexpensive chain **motels** near its uninspiring one-way main drags, First Street and Front Street. The most serviceable is *Best Western Olympic Lodge*, 140 Del Guzzi Drive (☎360/452-2993, ⓦwww.portangeleshotelmotel.com; ❺), but for more upscale accommodation elsewhere in town, try *Domaine Madeleine*, 146 Wild-flower Lane (☎360/457-4174, ⓦwww.domainemadeleine.com; ❼), an elegant B&B with art-themed rooms and a lovely five-acre garden.

For **food**, head for the tiny *First Street Haven*, 107 E First St and Laurel (☎360/457-0352), for its seafood, sandwiches, and pasta; the upscale *Bella Italia*, 118 E First St (☎360/457-5442), has solid seafood and Italian cuisine; and *Thai Peppers*, 222 N Lincoln St (☎360/452-4995), is surprisingly good for Thai fare.

Port Angeles has the peninsula's best **transportation** links. Olympic Bus Lines (☎360/417-0700, ⓦwww.olympicbuslines.com) offers daily trips to Seattle ($39) and Sea-Tac Airport ($49), while Clallam Transit buses (75¢–$2; ☎360/452-4511 or 1-800/858-3747, ⓦwww.clallamtransit.com) go west from Port Angeles around the peninsula and east to Sequim – from there connecting with Jefferson Transit ($1.25; ☎360/371-0497, ⓦwww.jeffersontransit.com) buses to Port Townsend. Black Ball Transport runs **ferries** to Victoria in Canada (May–Dec; $11 passengers, $42.50 vehicle and driver; ☎360/457-4491, ⓦwww.cohoferry.com), while Victoria Express (May–Sept; $12.50; ☎360/452-8088 or 1-800/633-1589, ⓦwww.victoriaexpress.com) operates a faster passenger-only service. Port Angeles' **visitor center**, 121 E Railroad St, beside the ferry terminal (☎360/452-2363, ⓦwww.portangeles.org), has information on the entire peninsula and can put you in touch with river-rafting and sea-kayaking operators.

Neah Bay and Cape Flattery

Whereas US-101 takes a turn inland from Port Angeles to skirt Olympic National Park, Hwy-112 clambers along the coast for seventy miles to **NEAH BAY**, the tiny fishing village that is home to the **Makah** tribe, seagoing Native Americans whose reservation is the site of the **Ozette Dig**. It's among the most significant archeological finds in North America, where erosion in 1970 uncovered thousands of artifacts: harpoons, intricately-carved seal clubs, watertight boxes made without metal, bowls, toys – all from an era before trade with Europeans. The site was reburied in 1981, but the finds are displayed at the **Makah Cultural and Research Center**, Hwy-112 at Bayview Ave (daily summer 10am–5pm, rest of year Wed–Sun only; $5; ⓦwww.makah.com), displaying marine dioramas, dugout cedar canoes, fishing gear, and a life-sized replica of a fifteenth-century Makah longhouse.

At the northern corner of the reservation is **CAPE FLATTERY**, the continental US's northwesternmost point, a remote headland accessible on an unpaved road from Neah Bay. A half-mile hike from the road through the rainforest leads to the cape that once "flattered" Captain Cook with the hope of finding a harbor. Below the cape, the waves have worn caves into the sheer rock of the cliff face, while opposite, on **Tatoosh Island**, the Coast Guard runs a remote lighthouse (closed to the public).

You can get to Neah Bay on Clallam Transit (see above), though there are few good options for **accommodation**. Given the area's drab motels, to find anything special you'll have to head seventeen miles east to **Sekiu**, a sports fishing town, to reach *Van Riper's Resort*, 280 Front St (☎360/963-2334, ⓦwww.vanripersresort.com; ❸–❻), which has a range of motel rooms and campsites, and more elaborate lodge units and waterfront suites, along with beach access and boat rentals.

Olympic National Park

Stunning **Olympic National Park** covers much of the peninsula's mountainous interior and a detached 57-mile strip of the Pacific coast. Created in 1938 by Franklin D. Roosevelt, partly to ensure the survival of the rare Roosevelt elk, it now has the largest remaining herd in the US. More than two hundred miles of wild rivers wind through the park, while the river valleys contain sizeable tracts of **temperate rainforest**.

The main **visitor center**, in Port Angeles at 600 E Park Ave (Mon–Fri 10am–4pm, summer also Sat & Sun 9am–4pm; ☎360/565-3100, ⓦwww.nps.gov/olym), has useful brochures and trail maps, while the **Wilderness Information Center**, 3002 Mount Angeles Rd (May & June daily 8am–4.30pm; July & Aug Sun–Thurs 7.30am–6pm, Fri & Sat 7.30am–7pm), supplies information on trail conditions in the area; smaller visitor centers are located at Hurricane Ridge and Hoh Rainforest. The **entrance fee** is $5 for individuals or $15 per car; both fees are good for seven days of park access. The **weather** is consistently erratic and often rainy – there's even a fair amount of snow as late as June. If you are staying inside the park, at any of the sixteen excellent **campgrounds** ($10–16), you'll need your own vehicle. Try *Heart o' the Hills*, six miles south of Port Angeles, along Hurricane Ridge Road, or further west, *Elwah* and *Altaire* – though these are closed in winter along with several others.

Hurricane Ridge and Lake Crescent

The main visitor center marks the start of a winding, precipitous road that climbs seventeen miles to daunting **Hurricane Ridge**, where the jagged peaks and sparkling glaciers of the Olympic Mountains spread majestically before you. A **day lodge** on the ridge (May–Oct daily 10am–4pm) has tourist facilities and information. From here, **Hurricane Hill Trail** (3-mile roundtrip) is a moderate hike, climbing through wildflower meadows to the peak where, on a clear day, Cape Flattery, the Juan de Fuca Strait, Vancouver Island, and the Cascade Mountains are all in view.

Ten miles west of Port Angeles, glacially carved **Lake Crescent** is popular for trout fishing and hiking on shoreline trails. Good places to stay are *Lake Crescent Lodge* (May–Oct; ☎360/928-3211, ⓦwww.lakecrescentlodge.com; ❸–❽), well placed among dense forest on the lake's south shore, offering simple rooms to elegant cottages; and *Sol Duc Hot Springs Resort* (March–Oct; ☎1-866/4SOLDUC, ⓦvisitsolduc.com; ❺), set deep in the park twelve miles off US-101, providing free guest access to **Sol Duc Hot Springs** (otherwise $11) – three pools with mineral-rich waters bubbling up at 100 to 108F°.

Hoh Rainforest

The **Hoh Rainforest** sits nineteen miles along Upper Hoh River Road, which branches off from US-101 twelve miles south of the town of Forks. From the **visitor center** (Fri–Sun 10am–4pm, summer daily closes 6pm; ☎360/374-6925), there are two short **trails** to explore: the Hall of Mosses Trail, and the slightly longer Spruce Trail, following along the glacier-fed Hoh River. More energetic hikers can try the 36-mile Hoh River Trail up to the base of 8000ft Mount Olympus. Climbing the ice-covered peak is a major undertaking, so you may want to **camp** along the route ($12 per night). Cougars, black bears, eagles, beavers, and other wildlife are very much present, and in winter Roosevelt elk from higher elevations gather here.

South to Kalaloch and the ocean beaches

Beyond the Hoh turnoff, US-101 dips down to the wild **beaches** of the Pacific coast, where black rocks jut out of the sea, and the strong undertow, floating tree trunks, and dramatic tides make the churning waters striking to watch, if rather unsafe for swimming. The hiking can be magnificent, though, and a series of short, appealing trails head down to and along the seashore – **Ruby Beach**, named for its red-and-black-pebbled sand, is the unmistakable highlight. Near the end of the park's coastal stretch, **Kalaloch** has a few **campgrounds** ($14–18; reserve at ☎1-800/365-CAMP), and the impressive *Kalaloch Lodge* (☎360/962-2271, ⓦwww.visitkalaloch.com), has basic lodge rooms (❺–❻) and more upscale cabins (❺–❼), as well as a good onsite restaurant. The **ranger station** here also provides information and suggestions for hiking trips (☎360/962-2283).

The rainforests and Lake Quinault
South of Kalaloch, US-101 turns inland before reaching the 25-mile dirt road that branches northeast to isolated **Queets River Rainforest**, worthwhile for its rustic trails, and for the luxuriant flora and fauna, highlighted by the **world's tallest Douglas fir** – 220ft tall and 45ft around.

△ Hiking the Maple Glade Trail in the Quinault Rainforest

The most accessible of the rainforests is the **Quinault Rainforest**, around the shores of glacier-carved **Lake Quinault**, just off US-101. One of the best hiking trails is the half-mile **Maple Glade Trail** on the north shore, leading through rainforest vegetation. Longer and more difficult trails, such as the dark, four-mile **Quinault Loop Trail**, through looming stands of old-growth trees, take hikers up the forested river valley and into the Olympic Mountains.

The best of Lake Quinault's three **hotels** is the charming 1926 *Quinault Lodge* (☎360/288-2900 or 1-800/562-6672, ⓦwww.visitlakequinault.com; ⓞ), on the shores of Lake Quinault, offering rooms with fireplaces or lakeside views, and a pool and sauna. There are also four lakeside **campgrounds** ($10–15), information for which is available at the **ranger station**, 353 S Shore Rd (Mon–Fri 8am–4.30pm, summer also Sat & Sun 9am–4pm; ☎360/288-2525, ⓦwww. fs.fed.us/r6/olympic).

The southwest coast

Heading south on US-101 from Lake Quinault, leaving the national park, it's about forty hilly miles to industrial **Aberdeen**, from where there's a choice of routes: US-12/Hwy-8 lead east towards Olympia (see p.1181), while Hwy-101 pushes south over the hills, threading along the shore of muddy Willapa Bay and the **southwest coast** of Washington. Here, the **Long Beach Peninsula** is something of a low-rent resort area, offering the usual chain motels and souvenir shops. It's worth a trip to the northern tip, however, to visit **OYSTERVILLE**, a forested collection of rusting old buildings and home to **Oysterville Sea Farms** (☎360/665-6585, ⓦwww.oysterville.net), recognizable by its piles of discarded shells and renowned for its fresh smoked oysters ($6.50 per package). Also good for the palate is the **Pacific Coast Cranberry Museum**, 2907 Pioneer Rd in the town of Long Beach (☎360/642-5553, ⓦwww.cranberrymuseum.com), where you can wander through a cranberry bog and purchase berry-flavored treats.

Down at the far southwestern tip of Washington, near the mouth of the Columbia River, the last points of interest are within scenic **Cape Disappointment State Park** (daily summer 6.30am–10pm, rest of year closes 4pm; ⓦwww. parks.wa.gov). The evocative 1856 **North Head Lighthouse** (summer daily 11am–3pm; $1) still stands watch, and the **Lewis and Clark Interpretive Center** (daily 10am–5pm; $3) can tell you all about the historical hazards of navigating the Columbia River. Fortunately, you'll be spared any such difficulty as you travel south on Hwy-101 over the 1966 span of the **Astoria Bridge**, crossing the state boundary into Oregon (see p.1197).

The Cascade Mountains

The **Cascade Mountains** offer mile upon mile of dense forested wilderness, stretching from Canada to Oregon, traversed by a tangle of beautiful trails – which, for all but a few summer months, you'll need snowshoes to hike. The most popular access point is **Mount Rainier**, set in its own national park ninety miles southeast of Seattle, while the haunting scenery around volcanic **Mount St Helens** compels visitors from near and far. Further north, Hwy-20, the high mountain road that crosses the Cascades, is by far the most spectacular route to eastern Washington, traversing the snow-capped wonder of **North Cascades National Park**.

The North Cascades and the Cascade Loop

When Hwy-20 opened up the rugged **North Cascades** in 1972, the towns of the eastern foothills created the **Cascade Loop** (T509/662-3888, W www .cascadeloop.com), a 400-mile roundtrip that channeled tourist traffic along highways 20, 153, 97, and 2. The full trip is only feasible during the summer, since at other times snow closes the mountain passes; unless you have at least three days to explore the territory in full, you're better off taking a few selected treks through the gorgeous environs, making brief stops along the way. You can find out more details about some of the best hikes at **North Cascades National Park Information Center**, 2105 Hwy-20 near Sedro Woolley, located just east of where Hwy-20 begins its journey inland at Burlington (daily 8am–4.30pm; T360/856-5700, W www.nps.gov/noca). The center also offers information about the area's geology, climate, and wildlife.

Winthrop

From the information center, the highway threads through high mountain passes to tiny **WINTHROP**, an old mining town decked out in a Wild West get-up, and the original setting for Owen Wister's *The Virginian*. While the effect is more than a bit cheesy, the false-fronted "saloons" and "dance halls" do make for some good snapshots. If you'd like to **stay**, the best choice is the *Hotel Rio Vista*, 285 Riverside Ave (T509/996-3535 or 1-800/398-0911, W www.hotelriovista.com; ④), which offers nice suites with hot tubs, kitchenettes, and DVD players.

As for **eating** and **drinking** options, *Winthrop Brewing Co*, 155 Riverside Ave (T509/996-3183), dispenses solid microbrews, and the *Duck Brand Cantina*, 248 Riverside Ave (T509/996-2192, W www.methownet.com/duck), serves up cheap and tasty Mexican fare and has six simple, Western-themed rooms in its onsite B&B (③). The nearby **visitor center**, 202 Riverside Ave (T509/996-2125, W www.winthropwashington.com), offers information and backcountry permits.

Chelan and Stehekin

The fetching resort of **CHELAN**, sixty miles south of Winthrop, nestles at the foot of **Lake Chelan**, whose spectacularly deep waters fill a glacially-carved trough nestled in the mountains. Of several good **lodging** options, *Campbell's Resort*, 104 W Woodin Ave (T509/682-2561 or 1-800/553-8225, W www.campbellsresort. com; ④–⑧), varies by season), is the most appealing for its range of lakeside rooms and suites, some of which come with fireplaces, kitchenettes, and balconies, though cheaper digs are available at the *Apple Inn Motel*, 1002 E Woodin Ave (T509/682-4044; $40–65). For **eating**, *Deepwater Brewing & Public House*, 225 Hwy-150 (T509/682-2720), has burgers, salads, and steaks, as well as its own microbrews. The **ranger station** at 428 W Woodin Ave (daily 7.45am–4.30pm; T509/682-2576) can ply you with hiking maps when you're ready to hit the trails.

The Lake Chelan Boat Company, 1418 W Woodin Ave (T509/682-2224 info, T509/682-4584 reservations, W www.ladyofthelake.com), runs a passenger ferry service to the head of Lake Chelan. Leaving from the jetty a mile west of town on Woodin Avenue, the *Lady of the Lake II* takes four hours to cruise the 55 miles of the nation's deepest gorge (May–Oct; $22.50 one-way, $38 roundtrip); the year-round *Lady Express* (May–Oct $34.50 one-way, $57 roundtrip; Nov–April $38 roundtrip) reaches Lake Chelan's mountainous western tip in half the time; and the high-speed *Lady Cat* takes you on a thrilling 75min jaunt (July–Sept; $63 one-way, $102 roundtrip). All cruises feature 60- to 90-minute layovers at **STEHEKIN**, a tiny, isolated village otherwise accessible only by a Chelan Airways

seaplane ($89 one-way, $149 roundtrip; ℡509/682-5555, ⓦwww.chelanair-
ways.com), which is also available for airborne **tours** of the region ($99–229). At
Stehekin there are **campsites** and trailheads leading to some of the best hiking and
backpacking in the North Cascades. Bikes and canoes are available from the *North
Cascades Stehekin Lodge* (℡509/682-4494, ⓦwww.stehekin.com; ❹–❺), where
the lakeside rooms are a bit pricier than standard units. For camping and hiking
information (and, for some of the trails, a free wilderness permit), visit the **Golden
West Visitor Center** near the Stehekin jetty (April–Oct daily 8.30am–5pm;
℡360/856-5700, ext. 340).

Leavenworth to Snoqualmie Falls

Several miles south of Chelan, the Cascade Loop turns west along US-2 at the
apple-producing town of **Wenatchee**, then heads for pocket-sized **LEAVEN-
WORTH**, a Bavarian theme town where even the fast-food outlets are decked out
in high gables and half-timbered woodwork. It's best as a base for taking in the outdoor activities in the spectacular mountain surroundings. The **ranger station**, just
off US-2 at 600 Sherbourne St (daily 7.45am–4.30pm; ℡509/782-1413), provides
trail guides and hiking information, and **bikes**, **canoes**, and **kayaks** can be rented
from Leavenworth Mountain Sports, 940 Hwy-2 at Icicle Rd (℡509/548-7864).
The nearby **visitor center**, 894 Hwy-2 (℡509/548-5807, ⓦwww.leavenworth.
org), has copious listings of places to **stay** and **eat**. The cozy rooms and suites
of the *Hotel Pension Anna*, 926 Commercial St (℡1-800/509-ANNA, ⓦwww.
pensionanna.com; ❹), are decked out in cheerful Teutonic kitsch, but the rooms
at the stylish *Enzian Motor Inn*, 590 Hwy-2 (℡509/548-5269 or 1-800/223-8511,
ⓦwww.enzianinn.com; ❺), are more tasteful, if blander too. The *Andreas Keller*,
829 Front St (℡509/548-6000), doles out hefty helpings of gut-busting German
cuisine, as does *King Ludwig's*, 921 Front St (℡509/548-6625), which also features
lively Bavarian dancing, hearty pork schnitzel, and beer-bearing barmaids – bring
your Tyrolean hat.

West of Leavenworth, US-2 crosses the mountains over Stevens Pass, but the
principal east–west highway, I-90, lies further south, connecting Seattle with the
Yakima Valley. Near I-90 is the striking, 270ft **Snoqualmie Falls** (℡425/831-
5784, ⓦwww.snoqualmiefalls.com), and behind it the luxurious ⚓ *Salish Lodge*,
6501 Railroad Ave SE (℡425/888-2556 or 1-800/2-SALISH, ⓦwww.salishlodge.
com; ❾), still best known as a location in the David Lynch TV series *Twin Peaks*.

Mount Rainier National Park

Set in its own national park, glacier-clad **MOUNT RAINIER** is the highest
(14,410ft) and most accessible peak in the Cascades, and a major Washington landmark. Not until midsummer does the snow melt enough for roads to open, and
then the deer and mountain goats appear, dazzling wildflowers paint the alpine
meadows, and the mountain makes for some perfect hiking.

More than three hundred miles of **trails** criss-cross Mount Rainier National
Park, ranging from short, simple interpretive walks – such as the 1.2-mile Nisqually Vista Trail loop – to the five-mile Skyline Trail up to Glacier Overlook,
to the 93-mile Wonderland Trail that encircles Mount Rainier itself. If you only
have a day to explore the park, visit the south and east sides from the Nisqually
entrance to **Paradise**, with a side trip to **Sunrise** – a stunning eighty-mile drive
winding through river valleys and lowland forests with glaciated peaks and stunning vistas.

Climbing Mount Rainier itself is hazardous and should only be undertaken by
experienced climbers. The long-established guide service, Rainier Mountaineering,

in Paradise (℡ 1-800/238-5756, ⓦ www.rmiguides.com), offers a one-day training course followed by a two-day guided climb to the summit for $795.

The Paradise **visitor center** (May to mid-Oct daily 10am–6pm; mid-Oct to April Sat & Sun 10am–5pm; ℡ 360/569-2211 ext 2328) has films and exhibits on natural history and a circular observation room for viewing the mountain.

Practicalities

The park is located some seventy miles southeast of Tacoma by way of Hwy-7 and a transfer onto minor route 706. **Admission** is $15 per vehicle, $5 per person, for a one-week pass. The park has four **entrances**: **Nisqually** in the southwest corner, **Stephen's Canyon** in the southeast, **White River** in the northeast, and **Carbon River** in the northwest. Only the Nisqually entrance is open year-round (for cross-country skiing; the others open June–Sept) and the only one serviced by public **transportation** – a ten-hour day-trip with Gray Line from Seattle (May–Sept; $59; ℡ 360/624-5077 or 1-800/426-7505, ⓦ www.graylineseattle.com). For map and trail conditions, stop by the **visitor centers** at Longmire, Ohanapecosh, Paradise, Sunrise and White River (details at ⓦ www.nps.gov/mora).

For **accommodation**, the classic rustic lodge of the *National Park Inn* (℡ 360/569-2275, ⓦ rainier.guestservices.com; $100, plus $34 for private bath), is nestled in a forest at Longmire, open year-round with 25 guestrooms and a restaurant. Make reservations well in advance. Outside the park, in the town of Ashford, *Whittaker's Bunkhouse*, 30205 SR 706 E (℡ **360/569-2439,** ⓦ www.whittakersbunkhouse.com), is an old loggers' bunkhouse with dorm beds ($30) and double rooms with private baths (❸–❹); and *Mounthaven*, 38210 SR 706 E (℡ 360/569-2594 or 1-800/456-9380, ⓦ www.mounthaven.com; ❻), has ten cabins, some with fireplaces, kitchenettes, fridges, wood stoves, and porches. The park's six **campgrounds** require reservations ($8–15; ℡ 1-800/365-CAMP, ⓦ reservations.nps.gov), which you can obtain up to 24 hours in advance from any hiking center in the park. For overnight **backpacking**, pick up a required wilderness permit, free from Longmire, White River, or Paradise ranger stations ($20 if by reservation; ℡ 360/569-2211).

Mount St Helens

The looming volcanic mound of **MOUNT ST HELENS** erupted on May 18, 1980, leaving a scorched area of near-total destruction: its blast wave flattened 230 square miles of surrounding forests, heavy clouds of ash settled as far away as Portland, and a massive mudflow sent an avalanche of debris down the river valleys. Since then, the forests and animal species have begun their recovery, though the scarred landscape still testifies to the awesome force of nature. All this has led to Mount St Helens justifiably becoming a major tourist attraction.

Located in Gifford Pinchot National Forest, the area around the mountain has three entry routes. Most visitors arrive along Hwy-504, off I-5 roughly halfway between Olympia and Portland, which snakes through dark green forests until bald, spiky trees give way to thousands of lifeless gray trees lying in combed-down rows. At the end is the **Johnson Ridge Observatory** (May–Oct daily 10am–6pm; ℡ 360/274-2140, ⓦ www.fs.fed.us/gpnf/mshnvm), which offers breathtaking views of the still-steaming lava dome, a film of the mountain's eruption, and testimony by blast survivors. On bright summer days, **views** of the mountain can be both picturesque and ominous. The only real disadvantage with the Hwy-504 approach to Mount St Helens is its popularity – expect long caravans of SUVs and RVs on any fair-weather day, and huge numbers of tourists at the observatory.

One alternative is to take Hwy-503 from Portland (via I-5) to **Cougar**, on the mountain's southern side – a surprisingly moist and verdant terrain, dotted with ravines and lava caves, as well as ashen lahars (volcanic mudflows) – from where the summer-only forest roads USFS-90, -25, and -99 wind along its flanks to **Windy Ridge** on the northeast side of the mountain. This is the best place to view the volcanic apocalypse up close: entire slopes denuded of foliage, colossal tree husks scattered like twigs, and huge dead zones where anything alive was vaporized. Windy Ridge can also be accessed from the north from **Randle** along USFS-25 and -99, which provides access to what remains of Spirit Lake and passes through lava flows with numerous viewpoints en route.

Practicalities

Although **climbing** Mount St Helens has been forbidden since the mountain began its rumblings again, you can still get the one-day **Monument Pass** ($3 single visit, $6 multiple visits) that allows entry to the Coldwater Ridge and Mount St Helens visitor centers, and the Johnston Ridge Observatory; the **Northwest Forest Pass** ($5) is good for other sites, and is available through putting money in drop boxes at site parking lots. En route to Windy Ridge from Hwy-503 is **Mount St Helens Volcanic Monument Headquarters** (daily 8am–5pm; ☎360/449-7800) in Amboy, which has maps and information. Just off I-5 near Castle Rock is the **Mount St Helens Visitor Center** (daily 9am–5pm; ☎360/274-0962), complete with informative exhibits, while **Coldwater Ridge Visitor Center**, 3029 Spirit Lake Hwy (daily 10am–6pm, winter Thurs–Mon 10am–5pm; ☎360/274-2114), focuses on the ways plants and animals have successfully recolonized the blast zones.

Though there aren't any campgrounds within the national monument, there are **private campgrounds** in the vicinity of Cougar (June–Aug only; ☎503/813-6666 for reservations): the Cougar campsite, located on Yale Reservoir just north of the village (60 sites; $15); Beaver Bay, about a mile north on 503 (78 sites; $15); and Cresap Bay, two miles south of 503 (73 sites; $15). Inside the park, **wilderness camping** is allowed below 4800 feet, and at Climbers Bivouac – the only permit required is the Northwest Forest Pass ($5; see above). Alternately, **Seaquest State Park** (daily summer entry 8am–8pm, rest of year 8am–5pm; campsites $15–27; ☎1-800/452-5687), abuts Silver Lake about five miles east of I-5 on Hwy-504.

Eastern Washington

The dry expanse of **eastern Washington** has little in common with its green, western counterpart: olive-colored sagebrush covers many acres, and massive red rocks loom over the prairies, while huge bare patches of basalt and torn-away groundcover (from centuries of Ice Age floods) give the area the unattractive geological moniker of the "**channeled scablands**." To the south lies the lower Yakima Valley, with miles of orchards and farms, which make it one of the largest producers of apples in the world. Of eastern Washington's major towns, only **Spokane** has any degree of cultural life, but some are decent bases for outdoor activities such as fishing, hiking, and skiing.

Ellensburg and Yakima

East of the mountains along I-90, 130 miles from Seattle, **ELLENSBURG** is the first notable stop. The dusty little burg of fetching nineteenth-century red-brick architecture is mainly known for its **Ellensburg Rodeo** (tickets start at $12; ☎509/962-7831 or 1-800/637-2444, ⓦwww.ellensburgrodeo.com), held over Labor Day weekend, with Stetson-clad cowhands roping steers, riding bulls, and braving bucking broncos.

Greyhound stops at 1512 Hwy-97. The **visitor center**, 609 N Main St (Mon–Fri 8am–5pm; ☎509/925-3138, ⓦwww.ellensburg-chamber.com), provides maps and **hotel** options; one safe choice is the basic *Ellensburg Inn*, 1700 Canyon Rd (☎509/925-9801; ⓦwww.ellensburginn.com; ❹). The Art Deco *Valley Café*, 103 W Third Ave (☎509/925-3050), is a good place to **dine** on eclectic American fare.

To the south on I-82, the agricultural hub of **YAKIMA** has few attractions, but is an excellent base to visit the tasting rooms of the excellent vintners scattered throughout the Yakima Valley (information at ☎1-800/258-7270, ⓦwww.wineyakimavalley.com). Wine-tour maps, as well as lodging and dining information, can be found at the **visitor center**, 10 N Eighth St (Mon–Fri 8.30am–5pm; ☎1-800/221-0751, ⓦwww.visityakima.com). Greyhound stops nearby at 602 E Yakima Ave. Standard-issue **motels** and **diners** abound along N First Street; worth noting are *Gasparetti's*, no. 1013 (☎509/248-0628), and *Santiago's*, 111 E Yakima Ave (☎509/453-1644), providing agreeable Italian and Mexican fare, respectively. There's **camping** across the Yakima River on Hwy-24 at **Sportsman State Park** ($15–21; ☎509/575-2774 or 1-800/562-0990).

Walla Walla

About 120 miles southeast of Yakima along I-82 and US-12, **WALLA WALLA** is an uneventful college and agricultural town best known for its sweet onions – eaten raw like apples. This was the place where the missionary **Marcus Whitman** arrived from the East Coast in 1836, only to be martyred eleven years later when a band of natives murdered him, his wife, and eleven others. The event generated such terror about native uprisings that the government declared the region a US territory and sent in the army to protect the settlers – and deal harshly with native tribes.

The site where the **Whitman Mission** was burned down (daily 8am–4.30pm, summer until 6pm; $3; ☎509/522-6360, ⓦwww.nps.gov/whmi), seven miles west of town off US-12, has basic marks on the ground to illustrate its layout; a **visitor center** shows a film on Whitman and exhibits the weapon thought to have killed him. Of more pseudo-historical value, the **Fort Walla Walla Museum**, 755 Myra Rd (April–Oct daily 10am–5pm; ⓦwww.fortwallawallamuseum.org; $7), is a curious mock-up of a pioneer village, with sixteen shacks loaded with antiques and Old West dioramas.

Walla Walla's **visitor center** is at 29 E Sumach St (Mon–Fri 8.30am–5pm, Sat & Sun 9am–3pm; ☎1-877/WW-VISIT, ⓦwww.wwchamber.com). The *Best Western Walla Walla Suites*, 7 E Oak St (☎509/525-4700; ❹), provides good basic **accommodation**, as do the other familiar chains in town. The decent **eateries** are mostly downtown; *Merchants Delicatessan*, 21 E Main St (☎509/525-0900), is a nice breakfast spot for espresso and pastries, as well as lunchtime deli fare.

Spokane

A few miles past the Idaho border on I-90, **SPOKANE** ("spo-CAN"), eastern Washington's only real city of any size, has some grandiose late nineteenth-century buildings – built on the spoils of nearby Idaho silver mines – though its heyday is long gone. Still, its pleasant parks and striking architecture can nicely fill a half-day. The town's hub, hundred-acre **Riverfront Park**, was the site of the 1974 World's Fair and sprawls over two islands in the middle of the Spokane River, which tumbles down the rocky shelves of **Spokane Falls**. The **attractions** (day-passes $15; June–Aug Sun–Thurs 11am–8pm, Fri & Sat 11am–10pm; ⓦwww.spokaneriverfrontpark.com) include an ice-skating rink, the charming hand-carved **Looff Carousel** ($2), and the **Spokane Falls Skyride** ($6), which rises above the falls to take in a commanding view of the area.

Most of the relics of Spokane's early grandeur can be found several blocks southwest on West Riverside Avenue, where Neoclassical facades cluster around Jefferson Street. The city's other architectural highlights include the **Clark Mansion**, 2208 W Second Ave, an 1897 marvel of lovely classical arcades and red-tiled roofs, and the Tudor Revival splendor of the **Campbell House**, 2316 W First Ave. The latter can be toured as a part of the **Northwest Museum of Art and Culture**, at the same site (Tues–Sun 11am–5pm; $7; ⓦ www.northwestmuseum.org). The museum focuses on regional history and artwork, Native American culture, and fine arts from WPA-era paintings to items from nineteenth-century Japan and seventeenth-century Holland.

Practicalities

Amtrak and Greyhound share the **transit center** at 221 W First St, and the **visitor center** is at 201 W Main St (Mon–Fri 9am–5pm; ⓣ 509/747-3230 or 1-800/776-5263, ⓦ www.visitspokane.com). Nice **accommodations** include the 1914 🏛 *Davenport Hotel*, 10 S Post St (ⓣ 1-800/899-1482, ⓦ www.thedavenporthotel. com; ❼), with its wildly ornate lobby and spacious, well-designed suites; and the *West Coast Ridpath*, 515 W Sprague Ave (ⓣ 509/838-2711, ⓦ www.west-coasthotels.com; ❹), a 265-room hotel with good views over the city. There's also **camping** in Riverside State Park ($15–21; ⓣ 509/456-3964), six miles northwest off Hwy-291. For **eating**, *Luna*, 5620 S Perry St (ⓣ 509/448-2383), serves up delicious, pricey Northwest Cuisine and cheaper gourmet pizzas, while *Mizuna*, 214 N Howard St (ⓣ 509/747-2004), has upscale seafood and regional cuisine, as well as a mean muscovy duck.

The Grand Coulee Dam and Lake Roosevelt

Eighty miles west of Spokane, amid parched and dusty land, the vast **Grand Coulee Dam** is the country's largest concrete structure and was one of the cornerstones of FDR's New Deal, providing jobs for workers from all over the country, including **Woody Guthrie**, who also worked on the Bonneville Dam in the Columbia Gorge (see p.1206) and was commissioned to write twenty songs about the project.

The dam's heyday was during World War II, when its waterpower was harnessed to make the aluminum that became essential to the production of war material, and it continues to be one of the world's top generators of **hydroelectricity**. Heroic tales of power production are detailed in the **visitor center**, on Hwy-155 on the west side of the dam (daily 9am–5pm, summer 8.30am–11pm; free; ⓦ www.grandcouleedam.org), which also runs free tours of the dam and one of its massive generating plants (daily every two hours 10am–4pm). On summer nights (June–Sept) the dam is even lit up by a **laser show** that takes place from 8.30pm to 10pm, depending on the month.

The area offers little in the way of notable accommodation or food, but more than thirty **campgrounds** lie around the 150-mile-long, spindly reservoir of **Lake Roosevelt**, which becomes more woody and secluded as you get further north. Some noteworthy spots include *Spring Canyon Campground*, on the lakeshore ($10 May–Sept, rest of year $5; ⓣ 509/633-9188, ⓦ www.nps.gov/laro), and *Steamboat Rock State Park*, twelve miles south of Grand Coulee ($15–21; ⓣ 509/633-1304).

Oregon

For nineteenth-century pioneers on the arduous Oregon Trail, the rich and fertile **Willamette Valley** was the promised land, and an obvious choice for Oregon's first settlements. Today, the valley is still the heart of the state's social, political, and cultural life. **Portland**, the biggest city, has a cozy European feel; **Salem**, the state capital, maintains a small-town air; and **Eugene**, at the southern foot of the valley, is a likable college community.

East of Portland, waterfalls cascade down mossy cliffs along the **Columbia River Gorge**, south of which looms the imposing presence of **Mount Hood**. Central Oregon, and its popular recreation hub of **Bend**, is located on a high chaparral desert, while further south around **Grants Pass**, the major rivers carve steep gorges and make for some excellent whitewater rafting, and the liberal hamlet of **Ashland** offers a splash of culture with its annual Shakespeare Festival.

Several highways link the Willamette Valley to the coast, whose most northerly town, **Astoria**, enjoys a magnificent setting strewn with imposing Victorian homes. South along the **Oregon coast**, wide expanses of sand are broken by jagged black monoliths, pale lighthouses look out from stark headlands, and rough cliffs conceal small, sheltered coves. The coast is every bit as appealing as its California counterpart, and though colder, is also more protected and accessible. Finally, the rugged deserts and lava fields of **Eastern Oregon** are much more remote, and some small towns still celebrate their cowboy roots with annual rodeos.

Wherever you go, try to pronounce the state's name as "OR-uh-gun"; calling it "ORY-gone" will mark you as a tourist, and is sure to invite a quick correction.

Getting around Oregon

From Union Station at 800 NW Sixth Ave and an adjacent bus station, **Portland** is well connected by **train** and **bus** to Seattle in the north and California to the south. Amtrak runs its *Coast Starlight* train once daily north to Seattle or south to LA; the *Cascades* four times daily between Eugene and Seattle; and the *Empire Builder* twice-daily east to Chicago. Bus routes radiate from Portland out to western and eastern Washington, across southern and central Oregon and to the coast. Finally, **cycling** throughout Oregon is a popular endeavor, especially along majestic stretches of coastal Hwy-101. Having your own vehicle can facilitate access to many of the state's more remote spots, particularly if you're planning to sample the great hiking and camping options on hand (see Ⓦ www.oregon.gov/OPRD).

Portland

With few major attractions and an unpretentious bohemian flavor, **PORTLAND** makes for an excellent spot to slow down and relax in the wealth of good diners, microbreweries, clubs, bookstores, and coffeehouses. Though sporting grand Beaux Arts architecture, Portland has a small-city feel thanks to a walkable urban core of short city blocks and attractions that cluster close together.

The city was named after Portland, Maine, following a coin toss between its two East Coast founders in 1845 ("Boston" was the other option). Its location on the **Willamette River**, just 78 miles from the Pacific, made it a perfect lumber and trading port, and it grew quickly, replacing its clapboard houses with ornate facades and Gothic gables. As a reminder of those days, the town's quirky "**Benson Bubblers**" – four-headed drinking fountains that are prime fixtures on downtown streets – are constantly flowing.

By the 1970s, when the lumber industry started to decline, Portland's historic buildings had decayed or were sacrificed to parking lots and expressways. In the last few decades, however, much effort has been made to salvage what was left of the past, replacing concrete with red brick, and introducing folksy statues and murals. More importantly, Portland's groundbreaking "**urban growth boundary**" has done much to limit unrestrained development, and preserve the low-slung scale and old-fashioned charms of many neighborhoods – thus making the city that much more appealing to refugees from California to New York.

Arrival and information

Portland International Airport (PDX) is a twenty-minute drive from downtown, also accessed by MAX "Red Line" **light rail** (3–5 times hourly, 5am–11pm; $1.95), which connects to the airport near Terminal C and takes about forty minutes to reach Pioneer Courthouse Square downtown. A **cab** from the airport into town costs $30. Greyhound, 550 NW 6th Ave, and Amtrak, close by at 800 NW 6th Ave, are within walking distance of the center; if you arrive at night, take a cab – this part of town is dicey after dark.

The **visitor center**, in Pioneer Square at 701 SW 6th Ave (Mon–Fri 8.30am–5.30pm, Sat 10am–4pm; ☎503/275-8355, ⓦwww.pova.org), has plenty of maps and information on both the city and the state. Portland's main **post office** is at 715 NW Hoyt St (☎503/294-2124; zip code 97205). Unlike most US states, Oregon has **no sales tax**, so buying goods here can be cheaper than in neighboring states.

City transportation

Although you can see much of the compact city center on **foot**, or along the city's impressive, extensive network of **cycling** paths and trails (visit ⓦwww.portlandonline.com/transportation for maps and information), Portland also has an excellent public transit network. Its **MAX light rail** system channels riders around central downtown and Old Town, connects to the western and eastern suburbs, and tunnels under Washington Park and the zoo. Tri-Met **buses** are based at the downtown **transit mall** along Fifth Avenue (southbound) and Sixth Avenue (northbound) – though renovation in coming years may shift buses to adjoining streets. The **Tri-Met Ticket Office** in Pioneer Square (Mon–Fri 8.30am–5.30pm, unstaffed Sat 10am–4pm; ☎503/238-7433, ⓦwww.trimet.org) offers free transit maps and sells all-zone day-tickets ($4), regular fares ($1.65–1.95), and other passes.

The colorful **Portland Streetcar** line runs between the south waterfront, Portland State University, the Pearl District, and Northwest Portland, covering many downtown sights on NW and SW 10th and 11th streets. As with buses, fares are free inside Fareless Square – basically the downtown core – otherwise $1.65 (ⓦwww.portlandstreetcar.org). **Taxis** don't stop in the street; get one at a hotel or call Broadway Cab (☎503/227-1234) or Portland Taxi Co. (☎503/256-5400).

Accommodation

Scads of flavorless **motels** line the interstates, but for a few dollars more you're far better staying downtown, where you'll find **hostels**, **B&Bs**, and a good range of **hotels**, the pick of which occupy grand and elegantly restored old buildings.

Hotels, motels, and B&Bs

Benson 309 SW Broadway ☎503/228-2000 or 1-888/523-6766, ⓦwww.bensonhotel.com. The spot for visiting dignitaries and celebs, this classy hotel has a superb walnut-paneled 1912 lobby, swank bedrooms with modern appointments, and a range of rooms, suites, and penthouses. ❼

Days Inn City Center 1414 SW 6th Ave ☎503/221-1611, ⓦwww.daysinn.com. Great central location with clean, well-tended motel rooms. Excellent value for downtown. ❸

Edgefield 2126 SW Halsey St ☎503/669-8610 or 1-800/669-8610, ⓦwww.mcmenamins.com/edge. Fifteen minutes east of the airport in the drab suburb of Troutdale, this unique brewery-resort features restaurants, bars, winery and tasting room, distillery, movie theater, gardens, and golf course. Also with its own hostel, at $30 per dorm bed. The cheapest doubles have shared baths. ❹

Governor 614 SW 11th Ave ☎1-800/554-3456 or 503-224-3400, ⓦwww.govhotel.com. Rich with elegant rooms and suites with fireplaces, spas, sofas, and stylish decor, plus an onsite pool and fitness center. Centrally located a block from MAX and streetcar lines. ❼

Heathman 1001 SW Broadway ☎503/241-4100 or 1-800/551-0011, ⓦwww.heathmanhotel.com. Occupies a finely restored Neoclassical building, with an elegant, teak-paneled interior and much marble and brass. Splendid rooms and suites, excellent restaurant, and popular lobby-lounge where you can swill among the swells. ❼

Heron Haus 2545 NW Westover Rd ☎503/274-1846, ⓦwww.heronhaus.com. Stylish 1904 Tudor B&B, with some large suites featuring fireplaces, spas, and cozy sitting areas. Excellent continental breakfast and close hiking access to Portland's expansive Forest Park. ❻

Hotel DeLuxe 729 SW 15th Ave ☎1-866/895-2094, ⓦwww.hoteldeluxeportland.com. Stylish old favorite now refurbished into a chic luxury item, with smart décor and onsite gym, plus in-room iPods and HDTVs in all the rooms. Well placed along the MAX tracks, just west of downtown. ❻

Inn at Northrup Station 2025 NW Northrup St ☎503/224-0543, ⓦwww.northrupstation.com.

Poised on the streetcar line in Northwest Portland and offering a range of colorful suites with splashy retro designs, some with kitchens, patios, and wet bars. Excellent value for the area. ❺

Jupiter 800 E Burnside ☎503/230-9200, ⓦwww.jupiterhotel.com. If you're too hip for your own good, you will be irresistibly drawn to this converted chain motel that's now flush with arty minimalism, a party atmosphere, and the uber-cool presence of the adjoining Doug Fir Lounge (see p.1205). ❹

Kennedy School 5736 NE 33rd Ave ☎503/249-3983 or 1-888/249-3983, ⓦwww.mcmenamins.com/kennedy. Thirty-five B&B rooms, in a refurbished 1915 schoolhouse with chalkboards and cloakrooms, plus modern appointments. Excellent breakfast, multiple brewpubs, movie theater, outdoor bathing pool, and "detention bar." ❹

Vintage Plaza 422 SW Broadway ☎503/228-1212 or 1-800/263-2305, ⓦwww.vintageplaza.com. An intimate boutique hotel with tasteful rooms and a calm, relaxed atmosphere. Wine is offered in the afternoons in the lobby. One of the city's few dog-friendly hotels. ❽

White Eagle 836 N Russell St ☎503/282-6810, ⓦwww.mcmenamins.com/eagle. Portland's best deal, a refurbished 1905 hotel and hip brewpub in an industrial-bohemian neighborhood. Rooms are clean, simple and cheap, with shared baths. Live music nightly downstairs – so early sleepers beware. ❷

Hostels

HI-Portland Hawthorne 3031 SE Hawthorne Blvd ☎503/236-3380 or 1-866/447-3031, ⓦwww.portlandhostel.com. Nice Victorian house in the Hawthorne District, offering Web access, tours of local sights, bike rental, and occasional live music. $20 dorms, $49 private rooms.

HI-Portland Northwest 1818 NW Ave at Glisan ☎503/241-2783, ⓦwww.2oregonhostels.com. Located in a nineteenth-century home in Northwest Portland, near the popular Mission Theatre & Brewpub and just east of the main action on 21st and 23rd streets. Contains espresso bar and family rooms. $23 dorms, doubles with private bathrooms.

The City

The **Willamette** (pronounced "wuh-LAM-it") **River** bisects Portland into its east and west sides, with **Burnside Street** delineating the north from the south; each street address describes its relation to these dividers – SE, NW, and SW, and NE (there's also N, which is everything east of the river and roughly west of I-5). The **downtown core** lies between the river's west bank and the I-405 freeway, in the city's southwest section; the rest of town is mostly residential.

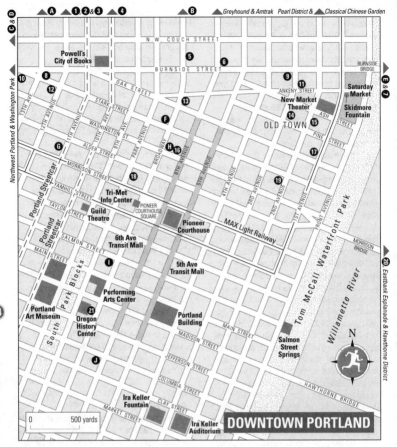

Greyhound & Amtrak   Pearl District &   Classical Chinese Garden

DOWNTOWN PORTLAND

OLD TOWN

Powell's
City of Books

Saturday
Market

Skidmore
Fountain

New Market
Theater

MAX Light Railway

Tri-Met
Info Center

Guild
Theatre

Pioneer
Courthouse

6th Ave
Transit Mall

5th Ave
Transit Mall

Performing
Arts Center

Portland
Art Museum

Oregon
History
Center

Portland
Building

Salmon
Street
Springs

Ira Keller
Fountain

Ira Keller
Auditorium

Portland Streetcar

Portland Streetcar

Tom McCall Waterfront Park

Willamette River

Eastbank Esplanade & Hawthorne District

Northwest Portland & Washington Park

South Park Blocks

N

0   500 yards

N.W. COUCH STREET
BURNSIDE STREET
OAK STREET
STARK STREET
WASHINGTON ST.
ALDER STREET
MORRISON STREET
YAMHILL STREET
TAYLOR STREET
SALMON STREET
MAIN STREET
MADISON STREET
JEFFERSON STREET
COLUMBIA STREET
MARKET STREET
CLAY STREET
ANKENY STREET
ASH STREET
PINE STREET
STARK STREET
MORRISON BRIDGE
HAWTHORNE BRIDGE
BURNSIDE BRIDGE

PIONEER
COURTHOUSE
SQUARE

14

THE PACIFIC NORTHWEST | Portland

ACCOMMODATION

Benson	**F**	
Days Inn		
City Center	**J**	
Governor	**G**	
Heathman	**I**	
Heron Haus	**D**	
Hotel DeLuxe	**C**	
Inn at Northrup Station	**A**	
Jupiter	**E**	
Vintage Plaza	**H**	
White Eagle	**B**	

RESTAURANTS, BARS & CLUBS

Berbati's Pan	**11**	Embers	**5**	McCormick
Brasserie		Higgins	**21**	and Schmick's **17**
Montmartre	**18**	Huber's	**19**	Oba **3**
Crystal		Jake's Famous		Papa Haydn **1**
Ballroom	**10**	Crawfish	**12**	Pazzo **16**
Dante's	**9**	Jimmy Mak's	**4**	Produce Row **20**
Doug Fir	**7**	Kell's	**15**	Ringlers Annex **8**
				Roseland Theater **6**
				Saucebox **13**
				Stumptown Roasters **14**
				Wildwood **2**

Downtown

Named after the adjacent **Pioneer Courthouse**, a squat 1868 structure that still maintains its judicial function, **Pioneer Courthouse Square** is the indisputable center of Portland. Surrounded by **downtown**'s historic terracotta buildings, the square's curving brick terraces are perennially filled with music and people. Close by are some of Portland's leading attractions along SW Broadway and the Park Blocks – where fading plasterwork and ceramic reliefs face concrete and glass. From the square, you can take a two-and-a-half hour **walking tour** of city highlights (Fri–Sun 10am; $15; ⓦ www.portlandwalkingtours.com).

Broadway epitomizes Portland's mix of early grandeur and new wealth, with prestigious hotels sharing space with cultural institutions, such as the grand old

1200

Paramount movie theater, restored as part of the impressive **Portland Center for the Performing Arts**, 1111 SW Broadway (ⓦ www.pcpa.com). One block west, the **Portland Art Museum**, 1219 SW Park Ave (Tues, Wed & Sat 10am–5pm, Thurs & Fri 10am–8pm, Sun noon–5pm; $10; ⓦ www.pam.org), has a wide-ranging collection of Northwest Native American masks, Mexican statues, and ancient Chinese figures, as well as temporary modern American and historic European shows. Nearby, decorated with huge *trompe l'oeil* pioneer murals, the **Oregon History Center**, 1200 SW Park Ave (Mon–Sat 10am–5pm, Sun noon–5pm; $10; ⓦ www.ohs.org), presents imaginative exhibits exploring different facets of the state's history. Between the museum and the history center run the **South Park Blocks**, a twelve-block green belt and favorite Portland hangout, under the shadow of statues of Teddy Roosevelt riding on to victory at San Juan Hill and a dour Abe Lincoln. Twice a week, the park hosts a popular **farmers' market** (May–Oct Wed 10am–2pm, April–Dec Sat 8.30am–2pm; ⓦ www.portlandfarmersmarket. org) that draws fruit and vegetable growers, and other vendors of bread, pastries, candles, and handicrafts.

Several blocks east is a favorite urban oasis, the two-mile-long **Tom McCall Waterfront Park** (created by demolishing the highway in the 1970s), where flocks of Canada geese abound on the grass, and young and old alike dash through the fountains of **Salmon Street Springs**. As a cheap and fun way to get wet, the springs are second only in popularity to the user-friendly **Ira Keller Fountain**, SW 3rd and Clay, a huge concrete water sculpture just west of the riverfront, where you can clamber around and get drenched on huge blocks and pillars.

Old Town and Chinatown

Old Town, the area around and just south of the **Burnside Bridge**, is where Portland was founded in 1843. These days, missions for the homeless coexist with galleries, brewpubs, boutiques, and, especially, clubs – the area is unavoidable if you're in town to dance to DJs or live music. The **Saturday Market** (March–Dec Sat 10am–5pm, Sun 11am–4.30pm; ⓦ www.portlandsaturdaymarket.com) packs the area south of, and under, the Burnside Bridge with arts and crafts stalls, eclectic street musicians, spicy foods, and lively crowds, all right by the MAX tracks (check the website as the market may be moving in 2007). At First and Ankeny stands the **Skidmore Fountain**, a nineteenth-century bronze basin raised by caryatids above a granite pool, designed to provide European elegance for citizens and water for hard-working horses. Across the fountain's plaza, an ornamental colonnade stretches from the side of the **New Market Theater**, an 1899 restored brick treasure.

North of Burnside, the ornamental gate at Fourth Avenue marks **Chinatown**, once the second-largest Chinese community in the US until the 1880s, when racist attacks forced most to leave. There's still enough of a community here to support a range of cheap ethnic restaurants and dive bars, but otherwise the only attraction is the enticing **Classical Chinese Garden**, NW 3rd Ave at Everett (daily: April–Oct 9am–6pm; Nov–March 10am–5pm; $7; ⓦ www.portlandchinesegarden.org), a Suzhou-styled garden with traditional vegetation, ponds, and walkways.

Pearl District and Northwest Portland

Northwest of Chinatown lies the chic **Pearl District**, a gentrified zone thick with lofts, galleries, restaurants, and boutiques, at its swankiest between NW 10th and 12th avenues, and Glisan and Lovejoy streets. On the southern edge of the Pearl is Portland's biggest draw, **Powell's City of Books**, 1005 W Burnside St (daily 9am–11pm; ⓦ www.powells.com). With more than a million new, used, and rare books on four floors, Powell's occupies an entire block, as well as separate branches

around town, and provides free color-coded maps so customers don't get lost.

Further west, what's known in travel brochures as Nob Hill is called **Northwest Portland** by locals. Stretching between Burnside and Pettygrove streets along NW 23rd and 21st avenues, the neighborhood is choked with fine restaurants and boutiques, the assortment of restored Victorian piles adding a San Franciscan tinge.

Forest Park and Washington Park

A few miles west of Northwest Portland, the five-thousand-acre **Forest Park** (Ⓦ www.friendsofforestpark.org) is the country's largest urban green space, interlaced with countless hiking routes, including the thirty-mile **Wildwood Trail**, which can be accessed around NW 31st Avenue and Upshur Street; otherwise, follow NW Thurman until it dead-ends and take **Leif Erickson Drive** (closed to traffic) deep into the hills. South of Forest Park, the elegant houses of the wealthy include **Pittock Mansion**, 3229 NW Pittock Drive (daily noon–4pm, summer 11am–4pm, $6; Ⓦ www.pittockmansion.com), a 1914 Renaissance Revival gem whose most attractive attribute is its stunning – and free – view of the city from the front lawn.

Beyond the mansion, the 130-acre **Washington Park** is home to a number of Portland's top attractions. These include the lovely **International Rose Test Garden** (daily 7am–9pm; free; Ⓦ www.rosegardenstore.org), featuring a wide array of bright summertime blooms; the tranquil **Japanese Garden** (daily: April–Sept 10am–7pm; Oct–March 10am–4pm; $8; Ⓦ www.japanesegarden. com), actually a collection of five traditional gardens with ponds, bridges, foliage, and sand designs; and the **Oregon Zoo** (daily: April–Sept 9am–6pm; Oct–March

9am–4pm; $9.50; ⓦ www.zooregon.org), whose most unusual feature is its Elephant Museum, detailing the biological and cultural history of pachyderms – and decorated with a giant mastodon skeleton. Close by, the **World Forestry Center** (daily 10am–5pm; $7; ⓦ www.worldforestry.org) is largely an ode to the timber industry, but the **Hoyt Arboretum**, 4000 Fairview Blvd (daily 6am–10pm; free; ⓦ www.hoytarboretum.org), merits a leisurely walk for its collection of ten thousand trees and plants from throughout the region and the world.

Most park attractions have easy access to MAX light-rail ($1.65 from downtown), whose station is buried deep underground and accessible only by elevator. Once you get here, you can hop on a summertime **shuttle** (every 15min June–Sept 10am–7pm; $1.65) and access all the park's major sights on a day-pass ticket.

The Eastside

Since the end of the nineteenth century, most of the city's population has lived on the **Eastside**. Perhaps the best reason to venture across the river is to walk or bike the three-mile loop of the **Eastbank Esplanade**, which connects from the Hawthorne to the Steel bridge on floating walkways and cantilevered footpaths, offering striking views of downtown with the roar of nearby I-5 as a soundtrack. Near the loop's south end, the interactive exhibits and high-tech toys of the **Oregon Museum of Science and Industry (OMSI)**, 1945 SE Water Ave (Tues–Sun 9.30am–5.30pm; $9; ⓦ www.omsi.edu), are primarily geared toward children and adults with only a sketchy knowledge of science.

Two miles further east, the **Hawthorne District** is Portland's best alternative culture zone. With Hawthorne Boulevard as its axis between 34th and 45th streets, and dominated by the sparkly, quasi-Moorish 1927 *Bagdad Theater & Pub* at no. 3702 (☎503/236-9234), the area teems with bookstores, hip cafés, dive bars, cheap restaurants, and only a handful of corporate chain stores. Six blocks north, **Belmont Avenue** is a historic corridor thick with boutiques, novelty shops, and ethnic diners, centered around 34th Street, while a mile southwest around 26th Avenue, **Clinton Street** is home to some good restaurants, funky bars, and vintage clothiers.

Finally, intrepid Eastside explorers may wish to venture up to **NE Broadway**, between 12th and 20th streets, good for its ethnic and upscale restaurants; the gallery- and boutique-rich stretch of **NE Alberta Street**, between 20th and 30th avenues, the leading edge of local gentrification, for better or worse; or the antique-buying center of **Sellwood**, several miles south of OMSI along Tacoma Street.

Eating

As in Seattle, Portland's **Northwest Cuisine** is a mix of international cooking and fresh regional produce – emphasizing tasty local favorites like Pacific crabs, clams, and oysters, Hood River Valley fruit and berries, and Eastern Oregon organically raised beef – and the city offers many excellent **dining** options for all palates and pocketbooks. Downtown, the Pearl District and Northwest Portland have swank cocktail bars, sedate bistros, and fun brewpubs, while Hawthorne Boulevard and Belmont Avenue have the best cheap grub and ethnic diners.

Bombay Cricket Club 1925 Hawthorne Blvd ☎503/231-0740. Terrific mid-level restaurant a mile west of the main Hawthorne scene is the town's best Indian food. Dive right into the delicious vindaloos and tandooris.
Brasserie Montmartre 626 SW Park Ave ☎503/224-5552. Popular French bistro with fresh

seafood, tasty pasta, and free live jazz on most evenings.
Clay's Smokehouse Grill 2932 SE Division St ☎503/235-4755. Great barbecue house serving rich and hearty fare like ribs and pork sandwiches, as well as super-sweet, old-fashioned desserts like pineapple upside-down cake.

Genoa 2832 SE Belmont Ave ☎ 503/238-1464. Arguably the region's best, and certainly most expensive, Italian food, on a three- to seven-course rotating seasonal menu ($45–75) that offers a sumptuous taste of northern Italy.

Higgins 1239 SW Broadway ☎ 503/222-9070. Nationally recognized Northwest Cuisine restaurant, where fresh local ingredients and scrumptious desserts are served on a pricy, rotating menu.

Jake's Famous Crawfish 401 SW 12th Ave ☎ 503/226-1419. A landmark for more than a hundred years, with a staggering choice of fresh local seafood like sturgeon and Dungeness crab and spicy crawfish cakes. The "Bag of Chocolate" is a famously delicious, belt-breaking dessert.

Lauro Kitchen 3377 Division St ☎ 503/239-7000 The kind of local favorite that doesn't need any publicity – even the mayor has to wait for a table on weekends. If you don't mind the delay, come for some of the city's best and most affordable Northwest Cuisine.

McCormick and Schmick's 235 SW 1st Ave at Oak St ☎ 503/224-7522. The first location of what's become a national chain of fine seafood restaurants, with fresh nightly specials and a lively oyster bar.

Oba 555 NW 12th Ave ☎ 503/228-6161. Flashy mid-priced eatery that fuses flavors from all over Latin America. It's most inviting during happy hour, when succulent bar-menu entrees (like the artery-clogging *queso fundido*) are $3–5.

Papa Haydn 701 NW 23rd Ave ☎ 503/223-7317. Classic French eatery whose entrees aren't what they used to be, but you can still stop by for a taste of the fifty-odd desserts on offer, including heaping chocolate cakes, Baked Alaska, and others on view under glass.

Pazzo 621 SW Washington St ☎ 503/228-1515. Top-notch Italian and Northwest Cuisine with a solid selection of fresh seafood and inventive pasta, just off the lobby of the Vintage Plaza Hotel (see p.1119).

Pix Patisserie 3402 SE Division ☎ 503/232-4407. Local hot-spot with a colorful range of French desserts made by a Parisian-trained chef known as the "Pixie." Also good for its international beers.

Siam Society 2703 NE Alberta St ☎ 503/922-3675. While there are plenty of excellent, affordable Thai diners around town, this mid-level entry is a welcome newcomer, doling out innovative versions of Southeast Asian fare in a moody modern setting.

Taqueria Nueve 28 NE 28th Ave ☎ 503/236-6195. Supreme new Latin cuisine on a two-block stretch of fine restaurants – this one's best for its seafood, innovative takes on Mexican staples, and rich and tasty desserts.

Wildwood 1221 NW 21st Ave ☎ 503/248-9663. Trendy, upscale restaurant with imaginative food using fresh local ingredients – morel mushrooms, Pacific salmon, Painted Hills beef, and the like.

Nightlife

Portland is a beer-drinker's haven, with more than thirty **microbreweries**, including *Rogue Ales Public House*, 1339 NW Flanders St (☎ 503/222-5910); *Bridgeport Brewing*, 1313 NW Marshall St (☎ 503/233-6540); and *Widmer Gasthaus*, 929 N Russell St (☎ 503/281-3333). McMenamins "concept" brewpubs sell their own locally ales in unique settings, such as former schoolhouses and renovated hotels (ⓦ www.mcmenamins.com). For **music**, Portland maintains a small but vital presence on the national map, with countless alternative bands. The coolest venues are located around east and west Burnside.

Bars, brewpubs, and coffeehouses

The Alibi 4024 N Interstate Ave ☎ 503/287-5335. The pinnacle of Polynesian kitsch, a fun and somewhat divey joint that has cheap, powerful drinks, a spirited atmosphere, and a Thurs–Sun karaoke scene that's among the city's best.

Goose Hollow Inn 1927 SW Jefferson St ☎ 503/228-7010. Great microbrews, the city's top Reuben sandwich, and a convenient location near the MAX tracks, a mile west of downtown. Watch for colorful owner Bud Clark, the city mayor in the 1980s, best known for his slogan "Whoop! Whoop!"

Dot's Café 2521 SE Clinton St ☎ 503/235-0203. Funky late-night spot offering good brews, the classic bacon cheeseburger, cheese fries, and a helluva grilled-cheese sandwich.

Holocene 1001 SE Morrison St ☎ 503/239-7639. Packed with would-be hipsters posing at point-blank range and an essential stop for local DJs, Holocene mixes a range of cocktails and even broader spectrum of nightly electronica.

Huber's 411 SW 3rd Ave ☎ 503/228-5686. Portland's oldest bar is an elegant spot with an arched stained-glass skylight, mahogany paneling, and terrazzo floor. Famous for roast turkey sandwiches and flaming Spanish coffees.

Kell's 112 SW 2nd Ave ☎ 503/227-4057. Long-standing Irish bar, with fine authentic Irish stews and soda bread, and a range of microbrews, imported beers, and of course, Irish (and Scotch) whiskey.

Lucky Labrador 915 SE Hawthorne Blvd ☎ 503/236-3555. Dog-friendly brewpub occupying a large space with an outdoor patio. Fresh ales, great sandwiches, and a mean peanut-curry bento.

Pied Cow 3244 SE Belmont Ave ☎ 503/230-4866. A favorite for its coffee, tea, and dessert. Set in a stately Victorian house, it offers late-night hours, lush garden seating, and the chance to puff fruit-flavored tobacco from a hookah pipe.

Produce Row 204 SE Oak St ☎ 503/232-8355. It's stuck in a gritty location by the railroad tracks in an industrial zone, but it boasts thirty brews on tap and a nice range of live music from country to rock.

Rimsky-Korsakoffee House 707 SE 12th Ave ☎ 503/232-2640. Excellent place to linger for hours over dessert and coffee. Immensely popular with bohemians and slackers.

Ringlers Annex 1223 SW Stark St ☎ 503/525-0520. Great people-watching in the ornate wedge-shaped 1917 Flatiron Building. Companion bar, *Ringlers*, is two blocks away at 1332 W Burnside St (☎ 503/225-0627).

Saucebox 214 SW Broadway ☎ 503/241-3393. Great pan-Asian cuisine, colorful cocktails, and eclectic nightly music that attracts black-clad poseurs and serious hipsters.

Stumptown Roasters 3356 SE Belmont Ave ☎ 503/232-8889. Widely acknowledged as the city's best coffee, made from a blend of seven different types. The best of a local chain of three coffeehouses. Also downtown at 128 SW 3rd Ave (☎ 503/295-6144).

Live music and clubs

Berbati's Pan 10 SW 3rd Ave ☎ 503/248-4579. Overly large space has a nightly selection of eclectic bands – local to international – usually for $8–15 cover.

Crystal Ballroom 1332 W Burnside St ☎ 503/778-5625. This nineteenth-century dance hall, two levels above the *Ringlers* bar, has a "floating" floor on springs. Bands range from hippie to hip-hop, and the best of Portland's indie rock and retro-DJs are show-cased in "Lola's Room" on the floor above the bar.

Dante's 1 SW 3rd Ave ☎ 503/226-6630. Perhaps the city's hippest nightspot. Cabaret acts and live music mix with the club's signature "Sinferno" Sunday strip shows and "Karaoke from Hell" Mondays.

Doug Fir 830 E Burnside ☎ 503/231-WOOD. For a cramped underground space with limited room to groove, this is, surprisingly, one of the city's prime venues for alt-country, dance, and indie rock.

Embers 11 NW Broadway ☎ 503/222-3082. An often-crowded club with drag shows in the gay-oriented front room and high-energy dancing in the straight-leaning room in back.

Goodfoot 2845 SE Stark St ☎ 503/239-9292. Frenetic live-music joint and dance club, always sweaty, smoky, and packed on weekends – but worth it to hear top-notch DJs spinning funk and retro-soul.

Jimmy Mak's 221 NW 10th Ave ☎ 503/295-6542. Newly renovated, this is one of the few choices for nightly jazz in a town not known to swing. Come by to hear local Mel Brown or visiting name acts.

Roseland Theater 8 NW 6th Ave ☎ 503/224-2038. Located in one of the city's dicier corners, but a top spot for rock and alternative acts – often the last affordable venue for fans before the groups start touring stadiums.

Performing arts and film

The **performing arts** scene revolves around the **Portland Center for the Performing Arts**, 1111 SW Broadway (☎ 503/248-4335, ⓦ www.pcpa.com), comprising the **Arlene Schnitzer Concert Hall** and **New Theater Building**. The "Schnitz" is a sumptuously restored 1928 vaudeville and movie house that presents musical extravaganzas, dance, and theater, hosting performances by the **Oregon Symphony** (☎ 503/228-1353, ⓦ www.orsymphony.org) and **Oregon Ballet Theater** (☎ 503/222-5538, ⓦ www.obt.org), among others. Several blocks away at SW 3rd Ave, between Market and Clay, the **Ira Keller Auditorium** is home to traveling musicals and the **Portland Opera** (☎ 503/241-1802, ⓦ www. portlandopera.org).

If you're interested in catching a **film**, local favorites include Cinema 21, 616 NW 21st Ave (☎ 503/223-4515, ⓦ www.cinema21.com), for foreign and independent movies; the Guild, 829 SW 9th Ave (☎ 503/221-1156), for classics and retrospectives; and the historic Hollywood Theatre, 4122 NE Sandy Blvd (☎ 503/281-4215, ⓦ www.hollywoodtheatre.org), for all of the above.

During the summer, **free concerts** are held at Pioneer Courthouse Square, Waterfront Park, the zoo, and the International Rose Test Garden. The free *Willamette Week* (Ⓦwww.wweek.com) carries **listings** of what's on and where, as does the free *Portland Mercury* (Ⓦwww.portlandmercury.com), and the Friday edition of the main local newspaper, *The Oregonian* (Ⓦwww.oregonian.com). *Just Out* is the chief gay/lesbian publication (Ⓦwww.justout.com).

Around Portland: the Columbia River Gorge and Mount Hood

East of Portland along the I-84 interstate, the **Columbia River Gorge** is a striking geological setting with gusty winds, craggy rocks, and incredible views. Scoured into a wide U-shape by huge Ice Age–era floods, the gorge is a nationally protected scenic area (Ⓦwww.fs.fed.us/r6/columbia), where waterfalls tumble down sheer cliffs, and fir and maple trees turn fabulous shades of gold and red in the fall. Much more rugged in the nineteenth century before the arrival of modern dams, this was the ominous final leg of the Oregon Trail, where many pioneers met a dark end negotiating perilous rapids on flimsy wooden rafts.

The most dramatic part of the gorge, around the town of **Hood River**, is just north of the snowy peak of Mount Hood, where a romantic, mist-shrouded river landscape in the spring gives way to colorful windsurfers in the summer bounding over the whitecapped waves. The ideal way to explore the area is by driving along the narrow, winding **Historic Columbia River Highway** (accessible at exits 22 or 35 off I-84), which boasts several excellent vantage points, particularly at **Crown Point**, where the 1915 **Vista House** – a marvelous structure perched high above the gorge about ten miles east of Troutdale – has just been restored to its original rustic grandeur (May–Oct daily 9am–6pm; free; Ⓦwww.vistahouse.com). Further east, some highway sections are closed to automotive traffic, but open to hikers and cyclists.

Back on I-84 below, the most spectacular of the waterfalls en route is **Multnomah Falls** (daily 8am–9pm; free), whose waters plunge 530ft down a rock face, collect in a pool, and then drop another seventy feet. Be warned: this is the state's second most popular attraction (after a casino) and the crowds can get quite thick on the trails and viewing bridges. Further east, **Bonneville Dam** (daily 9am–5pm; free; ⓣ541/374-8820) is a huge New Deal project that generates regional electricity and offers a chamber where you can see salmon making their way upstream.

Mount Hood

To the south along Highway 35, **Mount Hood** is a dormant volcano rising over eleven thousand feet, the tallest peak in the Oregon Cascades. The **Mount Hood Loop** – a combination of highways 35 and 26 – takes in both the mountain and the gorge. One of the joys of the area is to explore the mountain via trails radiating out from its slopes; contact the Mount Hood Information Center (see below) for information. The highest point on the loop at some 4000ft, **Barlow Pass** is named after Sam Barlow, a wagon-train leader who blazed the first "road" around the mountain, which became the unpleasant alternative to the even more dangerous Columbia River route on the Oregon Trail. You can still see deep gashes on some of the trees where ropes were fastened to check the wagons' descent.

Near the intersection of highways 35 and 26, a turn-off leads to the rough-hewn stone of ⚔ *Timberline Lodge* (ⓣ503/231-5400 or 1-800/547-1406, Ⓦwww.timberlinelodge.com; ➐), a colossal New Deal structure that is part of the year-round *Timberline* **ski resort** (ⓣ503/622-0717; lift tickets $43), and the exterior setting for Stanley Kubrick's *The Shining* (though without that film's hedge maze). Two other downhill ski areas – Mount Hood Meadows (Ⓦwww.skihood.com; $45) and Mount Hood SkiBowl (Ⓦwww.skibowl.com; $39) – offer nighttime **skiing** from November to April (around $20). There are also many miles of cross-country skiing trails throughout the **Mount Hood National Forest**. For more information on mountain activities and cheaper area lodging, contact the Mount Hood Information Center (Ⓣ503/622-4822 or 1-888/622-4822, Ⓦwww.mthood. info).

Hood River

Adjacent to the Columbia River, north of Mount Hood, charming little **HOOD RIVER** is a hub for river windsurfing and mountain biking, with outfitters' shops lining the hillside streets and a riverfront **Port Marina Park** to take it all in. One of the most exquisite **places to stay** in the entire region is the *Columbia Gorge Hotel*, just off I-84 at the far west end of town, at 3000 Westcliff Drive (Ⓣ1-800/345-1921, Ⓦwww.columbiagorgehotel.com; Ⓞ), where hacienda-style buildings perch on a clifftop right above the gorge, and the hotel's exquisite gardens even have their own waterfalls. More central, and less expensive, options include *Hood River Hotel*, 102 Oak Ave (Ⓣ541/386-1900 or 1-800/386-1859, Ⓦwww.hoodriverhotel.com; Ⓞ), built in 1913 and featuring tasteful rooms and more elaborate suites; and *Inn at the Gorge*, 1113 Eugene St (Ⓣ541/386-4429, Ⓦwww.innatthegorge.com; Ⓞ), a stately 1908 Colonial Revival home that's been transformed into a tasteful, elegant B&B with minimal Victorian kitsch. For **eating** and **drinking**, *Full Sail Brewing*, 506 Columbia St (Ⓣ541/386-2247), is a fine local microbrewery; the *6th Street Bistro*, 509 Cascade Ave (Ⓣ541/386-5737), has some solid burgers and American fare; and *Mike's Ice Cream*, 504 Oak St (Ⓣ541/386-6260), is known for its marionberry milkshakes. The **visitor center**, in Port Marina Park (Ⓣ1-800/366-3530, Ⓦwww.hoodriver.org), provides information on all the regional attractions, including the engaging summertime **fruit loop** (Ⓦwww.hoodriverfruitloop.com), a driving concourse that connects to growers of cheap and delicious apples, pears, cherries, and peaches.

The Willamette Valley

South of Portland, the **WILLAMETTE VALLEY** has a diverse agricultural scene, but is best known for its grapes. The scenic route through wine country, Hwy-99 W, accesses dozens of acclaimed **wineries**, most of which pour superb pinot noirs, cabernets, and rieslings. Pick up a wine-country tour map from any local visitor center (or Ⓦwww.oregonwine.org), and expect the odd traffic bottleneck in little burgs like **Dundee**, which is roughly in the center of the vineyard zone. A few miles south in Dayton, the renowned *Joel Palmer House*, 600 Ferry St (Ⓣ503/864-2995, Ⓦwww.joelpalmerhouse.com), draws Portland urbanites for its delicious, if expensive, Northwest cuisine. The Valley also has some of the best examples of **covered bridges**, with thirty-four in the state spanning creeks from Albany to Cottage Grove (see Ⓦcoveredbridges.stateoforegon.com).

From Portland, I-5 courses through the Willamette Valley on its way to California, but bypasses historic **Oregon City**, the first state capital, at the end of the Oregon Trail. Today, the only reasons to stop are the **John McLoughlin House**, 713 Center St (Wed–Sat 10am–4pm, Sun 1–4pm; $4; Ⓦwww.mcloughlinhouse. org), the 1846 dwelling of a trail pioneer that's loaded with artifacts and details on local history; and the **End of The Oregon Trail Interpretive Center**, 1726 Washington St (March–Oct: Mon–Sat 9.30am–5pm, Sun 10.30am–5pm; Nov–

Feb: Wed–Sat 11am–4pm, Sun noon–4pm; $9; Ⓦwww.endoftheoregontrail. org), housed in a trio of giant, imitation covered-wagon buildings, which hold a series of dioramas, replica antiques, and documentary films – and a staff in full period costume.

Salem

The main reason to visit **SALEM** is to see the modern, white Vermont-marble **State Capitol**, 900 Court St NE (Mon–Fri 7.30am–5.30pm; free; tours at Ⓣ503/986-1388), whose cupola is topped by a large gold-leaf pioneer, axe in hand, eyes to the West. Also worth a look is **Mission Mill Village**, 1313 Mill St SE (Mon–Sat 10am–5pm; $7; Ⓦwww.missionmill.org), a collection of well-preserved pioneer buildings and a gloomy, nineteenth-century woolen mill.

Greyhound is located at 450 Church St NE, and Amtrak at 500 13th St SE. The **visitor center** (Ⓣ503/581-4325) is in Mission Mill Village. Decent **motels** include *Phoenix Inn Suites*, 4370 Commercial St SE (Ⓣ1-800/445-4498, Ⓦwww.phoenixinn.com; ❹), while the *Creekside Garden Inn*, 333 Wyatt Court NE (Ⓣ503/391-0837, Ⓦwww.salembandb.com; ❹), is a stately **B&B** close to downtown. If you're **camping**, head for the huge waterfalls and lush forests of **Silver Falls State Park** (Ⓣ503/873-8681; $16–21), 26 miles east of Salem, the state's most popular park – so reserve many weeks (or months) in advance. For **food**, you're best off downtown, where *Court Street Dairy Lunch*, 347 Court St NE (Ⓣ503/363-6433), is a classic 1960s diner with primo burgers, and *Jonathan's Oyster Bar*, 445 State St (Ⓣ503/362-7219), serves fresh seafood, Cajun and Southwestern cuisine.

Eugene

Student and hippie central, **EUGENE** is a liberal enclave where Ken Kesey and some of his Merry Pranksters came to live after retreating from California. Although short on sights, it's an energetic cultural center, to which the **University of Oregon** in the city's southeast corner lends a youthful bohemian feel, especially along 13th Avenue just west of campus. For different pursuits, the glassy, modern **Hult Center**, Sixth Ave and Willamette St (Ⓣ541/682-5746, Ⓦwww. hultcenter.org), is home to the local opera, symphony, ballet, and renowned Oregon Bach Festival (Ⓦwww.oregonbachfestival.com) in early July. The other major attraction is the **Saturday Market**, Eighth Ave and Oak St (April–Dec 10am–5pm; Ⓦwww.eugenesaturdaymarket.org), something of a neo-hippie carnival with live folk music, plenty of handicrafts, and street performers. Finally, Eugene is also a prime spot for **sports**, and trails abound in the city center, along the river banks, and up imposing **Spencer's Butte**, a huge basalt monolith south of town.

Ten miles west of Eugene on US-126, little **Veneta** hosts the **Oregon Country Fair** (tickets $14; Ⓣ541/343-4298, Ⓦwww.oregoncountryfair.org) in July, a hippie-flavored festival of music, art, food, and dancing. Traffic can be heavy, and even if you have a car it's easier to go by bus – the LTD (see below) operates special services.

Practicalities

Greyhound stops at 987 Pearl St, and Amtrak at Fourth Ave and Willamette St. Eugene has a terrific bus system, the LTD ($1.25; Ⓣ541/687-5555, Ⓦwww. ltd.org), offering day-passes for $2.50, and 50¢ rides on the "Breeze" shuttle linking downtown and the university. The **visitor center** is at 115 W 8th Ave (Mon–Fri 8.30am–5pm, Sat 10am–4pm; Ⓣ541/484-5307, Ⓦwww.visitlane county.org).

The best **places to stay** include the *Campbell House*, 252 Pearl St (☎541/343-1119 or 1-800/264-2519, ⓦwww.campbellhouse.com; ⑤), an elegant 1892 Victorian mansion with eighteen rooms; and *Franklin Inn*, 1857 Franklin Blvd (☎541/342-4804, ⓦwww.eugenefranklininn.com; ❸), which has affordable motel rooms near the university. The *Eugene International Hostel*, 2352 Willamette St (☎541/349-0589; $20), offers twenty clean and comfortable dorm beds.

Of Eugene's better places to **eat**, *Café Zenon*, 898 Pearl St (☎541/343-3005), has an eclectic menu rich with international fare; *Chanterelle*, 207 E 5th Ave (☎541/484-4065), is an intimate French bistro; the *Oregon Electric Station*, 27 E 5th Ave (☎541/485-4444), serves top-notch prime rib and seafood in renovated railway cars; and the amazingly delicious truffles of ❧*Euphoria Chocolate*, 6 W 17th Ave (☎541/343-9223, ⓦwww.euphoriachocolate.com), are reason alone to visit Eugene.

Live **music** is also big in town. *Jo Federigo's*, 259 E 5th Ave (☎541/343-8488, ⓦwww.jofeds.com), has nightly jazz and serves solid Italian cuisine, while funky *WOW Hall*, 291 W 8th Ave (☎541/687-2746, ⓦwww.wowhall.org), showcases up-and-coming rockers. For a taste of the music scene near the university, stroll along **13th Avenue** and hear the indie rock and punk wafting out from the bars and clubs.

South to California

South of Eugene along I-5, unenticing **Grants Pass** depends on the vigorous Rogue River for its living. Half a day of **whitewater rafting** costs around $50, a full day $70 – the **visitor center**, just off I-5 at 1995 NW Vine St (☎541/476-5510, ⓦwww.visitgrantspass.org), provides brochures from more than a dozen licensed river guides. Beyond Grants Pass, I-5 dips southeast through **Ashland**, taking a mountainous inland route to California, while US-199 heads southwest to the California (and southern Oregon) coast, passing near the **Oregon Caves**.

Oregon Caves National Monument

Thirty miles southwest of Grants Pass along US-199, at the dull burg of **Cave Junction**, Hwy-46 veers east twenty miles to the **Oregon Caves National Monument** (tours daily April–Nov: hours vary, often 9am–5pm; 75min; $8.50; ☎541/592-2100, ⓦwww.nps.gov/orca). Tucked in a wooded canyon at the end of a narrow, twisting road and kept at a constant temperature of 41°F, it's actually one enormous cave, with smaller branching passages, where the dripping marble walls are covered with elaborate stalactites, stalagmites, and flowstone.

Close to the cave entrance is the appealing *Oregon Caves Chateau*, 2000 Caves Hwy (May-Oct; ☎541/592-3400; ❹), an elegant 1930s lodge with grand public rooms; reservations are advised. Since there's little but drab lodging in Cave Junction, try one of the **campgrounds** along Hwy-46, with *Grayback* and *Cave Creek* being the closest to the monument ($10; ☎541/592-2166 for reservations).

Ashland and the Shakespeare Festival

The progressive hamlet of **ASHLAND**, forty miles southeast of Grants Pass, is a real anomaly among the agricultural towns that blanket the state. Since 1945, the **Oregon Shakespeare Festival** has been held here between February and October, packing audiences into the half-timbered **Elizabethan Theatre**, and cycling through the Bard's complete oeuvre every few years. The town's Rogue River Valley setting is magnificent, with good skiing in the winter and rafting in summer. There's also some excellent fringe theater – not to mention pleasant cafés, galleries, and boutiques, especially around the **Historic Railroad District** (ⓦ www.ashlandrrdistrict.com) a few blocks north of the festival.

The **Angus Bowmer Theatre**, adjacent to the Elizabethan Theatre, stages both Shakespearean and more recent works, while the austere **New Theatre** has a mostly modern repertoire. The three theaters share the same box office, 15 S Pioneer St (ⓣ 541/482-4331, ⓦ www.osfashland.org), and tickets average around $35 (with standing room at the Elizabethan Theatre for $10), and summer prices are $10–15 more expensive. For a dose of musical comedy to relieve the drama, try the **Oregon Cabaret Theater**, in a renovated pink church at First and Hargadine ($21–27; ⓣ 541/488-2902, ⓦ www.oregoncabaret.com).

The **visitor center** is at 110 E Main St (Mon–Fri 9am–5pm; ⓣ 541/482-3486, ⓦ www.ashlandchamber.com). Greyhound **buses** drop passengers on the edge of town near the I-5 freeway exit. Ashland has more than sixty **B&Bs**, most of which are in charming Victorian homes; the Ashland B&B Network (ⓣ 1-800/944-0329, ⓦ www.abbnet.com) has information on most of them. The best **hotel** is the grand and centrally located *Ashland Springs*, 212 E Main St (ⓣ 1-888/795-4545, ⓦ www.ashlandspringshotel.com; ⑥), with its charming two-story lobby, day spa, afternoon tea, and nicely appointed rooms. Another good option is the *Winchester Inn*, 35 S 2nd St (ⓣ 541/488-1113, ⓦ www.winchesterinn.com; ⑥), with nineteen en-suite rooms and attractive gardens. The top budget option is the friendly, clean, and well-placed *Ashland Hostel*, 150 N Main St (ⓣ 541/482-9217, ⓦ www.the ashlandhostel.com; $25 dorm beds, $55 private rooms).

The main choices for **eating** are found along **Main Street**, near the entrance to Lithia Park. The choices vary widely, from the eclectic entrees of the upscale French *Chateaulin*, 50 E Main St (ⓣ 503/482-2264), to the cheap but tasty pasta, burgers, salads, and seafood of *Greenleaf*, 49 N Main St (ⓣ 541/482-2808). If you come in the summer, head twenty miles northwest to the preserved Old West hamlet of **Jacksonville** for the annual **Britt Festival** (June–Aug; tickets $20–46; ⓣ 1-800/882-7488; ⓦ www.brittfest.org), to hear the top names in jazz, pop, and country music.

The Oregon Coast

The **Oregon coast** is as beautiful as any stretch of coastline in America, a moody and secluded four-hundred miles of stunning terrain, almost all of it public land. State parks and campgrounds abound, and extensive and often isolated beaches are free for hiking, beachcombing, shell-fishing, and whale-watching. Although the shoreline hasn't escaped commercialism, and it has its occasional eyesores of development, the Oregon coast remains the least exploited in the entire US.

A number of coastal state parks offer novel accommodation in the form of seaside **cabins** and **yurts** – Mongolian-style domed circular tents with wooden floors, electricity, and lockable doors, as well as bunk beds and a futon (yurts $27–30 per night, cabins $35–38; ⓣ 1-800/452-5687, ⓦ www.oregonstateparks.org). Alternatively, you can **camp** for $15–20 at various sites on the coast.

For the most scenic transportation along the waves, **cycling** is always a good option, whether within the state parks, along US-101 (following the coastline to the California border), or on the many smaller "scenic loop" roads. Pick up the *Coast Bike Route Map* from any major visitor center.

Astoria

Set near the mouth of the Columbia River, the port of **ASTORIA** was founded in 1811 as a base for exporting furs to Asia by the millionaire John Jacob Astor.

A small replica of the **old fort** stands at 15th and Exchange streets, but nowadays many of Astoria's canneries and port facilities have vanished, as the city tries to reinvent itself for tourists interested in nautical history and working-class color.

From the east, the main road into Astoria, **Marine Drive**, runs parallel to the waterfront, about eight miles from the Pacific Ocean. Exhibits from Astoria's seafaring past are on display at the **Columbia River Maritime Museum**, 1792 Marine Drive (daily 9.30am–5pm; $8; Ⓦwww.crmm.org), which also features impressive displays of scrimshaw, native artifacts, and reconstructed ships.

From Marine Drive, numbered streets climb up towards fancy Victorian mansions, many now renovated B&Bs. Painted emblems on the street direct you to the top of Coxcomb Hill, where the **Astoria Column** is decorated with a winding mural depicting pioneer history, and offers stunning views for anyone willing to climb its 164 cramped spiral stairs. Back in town, further west, the **Flavel House**, 441 8th St (daily 10am–5pm, summer 11am–4pm; $5), is one of the grandest of the city's mansions, the grand, 1886 Queen Anne home of sea captain George Flavel, featuring main rooms set up as dioramas featuring period furniture and decor.

A few miles southwest of town is **Fort Clatsop** (daily 9am–5pm; $5; Ⓦwww. nps.gov/lewi), a reconstruction of the winter quarters Lewis and Clark built here in 1805. The site mysteriously burned in 2005, but a new version aims to replicate the pioneer living conditions with greater historical accuracy, based on the latest evidence. Further west, also off US-101, **Fort Stevens State Park** (☎503/861-1671) offers good trails and camping and miles of beaches. The fort was developed as a Union post in the Civil War, and was shelled during World War II by a passing Japanese submarine, which makes it the only military installation on the mainland US to have been fired on by a foreign government since 1812.

Practicalities

Bus or train access to this part of the coast is limited, but Amtrak operates a once-daily bus service that drops off at the **visitor center** at 111 W Marine Drive (summer daily 8am–6pm; winter Mon–Fri 9am–5pm; ☎503/325-6311, Ⓦwww.old oregon.com), near the base of the US-101 bridge over the Columbia, which leads into southwest Washington. To make a leisurely trip along the waterfront, hop aboard the **Astoria Trolley** (summer Mon–Thurs 3–9pm, Fri–Sun noon–9pm; rest of year Fri–Sun 1–4pm; $2), historic rail cars that ply a tourist-oriented route. You can **camp** at Fort Stevens State Park ($18–22; ☎1-541/861-1671), but the town's most distinctive offerings are its **B&Bs**, many of them in Victorian mansions. Among the best are *Franklin St Station*, 1140 Franklin St (☎503/325-4314 or 1-800/448-1098, Ⓦwww. franklin-st-station-bb.com; ❹), having six rooms with balconies overlooking town, and the *Rosebriar*, 636 14th St (☎503/325-7427 or 1-800/487-0224, Ⓦwww.rosebri-ar.net; ❹), a renovated, modernized 1902 convent with great river views. For fancier digs, the *Hotel Elliott*, 357 12th St (☎1-877/EST-1924, Ⓦwww.hotelelliott.com; ❺). is a historic 1924 charmer with upscale amenities in its rooms and suites, some with fireplaces and Jacuzzis; rates increase by $60 and up during the summer.

Good places to **eat** include *Columbian Café*, 1114 Marine Drive (☎503/325-2233), which has gourmet seafood and vegetarian meals, and offers tasty pizzas and weekend musical jams in its attached *Voodoo Room*; the *Cannery Cafe*, 1 6th St (☎503/325-8642), a solid breakfast and lunch spot with good pierside views; and the *Home Spirit Baking Company*, 1585 Exchange St (☎503/325-6846), which serves homemade sourdough bread and ice cream in a lovely Victorian home.

Cannon Beach

Seventeen miles south of Astoria, **Seaside** is a rather seedy resort of carnival rides, the one spot on the Oregon coast nature-lovers avoid, but another nine miles south, the more upmarket and pleasant **CANNON BEACH** manages to retain its small-town air despite decades of relentless commercialism. The place is at its liveliest during the mid-June **Sandcastle Competition**, a one-day event that starts when the tide permits, drawing artistic sand-crafters and hapless muck-shovelers from around the region. You're apt to see anything from sand dinosaurs and sphinxes to mermaids and monkeys, with Jesus and Elvis also putting in frequent appearances. Cannon Beach's best natural draw is its 240ft **Haystack Rock**, a black monolith crowned with nesting seagulls – accessible at low tide, though definitely not climbable. To escape the town's crush of tourists, head four miles north to **Ecola State Park**, where dense conifer forests decorate the basaltic cliffs of Tillamook Head, or south to **Oswald West State Park**, named after the pioneering governor who helped preserve most of the state's beaches, where there's a beautiful beach, rocky headland, and coastal rainforest. The park's tent-only campground (Mar–Oct; ☎541/368-3575; $10–14) is popular with surfers and provides wheelbarrows to transport your gear to the site.

The **visitor center** is at 207 N Spruce St (☎503/436-2623, ⓦwww.cannon-beach.org). In town, **accommodation** is tight, especially in the summer. *Cannon Beach Hotel*, 1116 S Hemlock St (☎503/436-1392, ⓦwww.cannonbeachhotel.com; ❹), is a cozy boutique hotel, while the *Waves Motel*, 188 W Second St (☎503/436-2205 or 1-800/822-2468, ⓦwww.thewavesmotel.com; ❺), has studios and suites on the seafront. For **food**, the *Bistro*, 263 N Hemlock St (☎503/436-2661), doles out a fine range of fresh seafood, and *Bill's Tavern & Brewhouse*, 188 N Hemlock St (☎503/436-2202), is the town's busiest **bar**, offering bar food along with their own handcrafted brews.

Tillamook to Newport

Forty-four miles south of Cannon Beach, **TILLAMOOK** provides two good reasons for a stopover: the first is the **Tillamook Cheese Factory** (daily 8am–6pm, summer closes at 8pm; free; ⓦwww.tillamookcheese.com), just north of town on US-101, where on a self-guided tour you can watch cheese evolve from milky liquid in large vats to yellow and orange bricks on conveyor belts. The other milk product you can leave with is an oversized ice-cream cone, scooped from the factory's counter. Tastier cheese can be had a mile south at the **Blue Heron** (daily 9am–6pm, summer 8am–8pm; free; ⓦwww.blueheronoregon.com), where you can sample the pepper brie or taste Oregon wine before heading out back to have a close encounter with a goat or rooster in a quasi-petting zoo.

Forty miles further south, there's no avoiding **Lincoln City**, the ugliest town on the Oregon coast, sprawling along the highway for seven congested, dreadful miles, but hold out for another thirty miles and you'll reach **NEWPORT**, both an active port and something of a resort. While the **Historic Bayfront** along Bay Boulevard is the obvious first stop for many – with its souvenir shops, seafood diners, and sea lions wallowing on the wharves – the town's real highlight is uncrowded **Nye Beach**, a quiet oceanside gem further west. Here, there are few official sights other than a deserted, modern **Vietnam War Memorial** (24hr; free), but the beach makes for an excellent stroll, and the seaside development is far more restrained than elsewhere in town. To the south, across the bridge at 2820 SE Ferry Slip Rd, the impressive **Oregon Coast Aquarium** (daily summer 9am–6pm; rest of year 10am–5pm; $12; ⓦwww.aquarium.org) is home to sea otters, seals, and tufted puffins, as well as Passages of the Deep, a shark-oriented underwater tunnel. Just north of town, Newport's other top attraction is **Yaquina Head** (daily 9am–5pm; $5), an officially decreed "Outstanding Scenic Area" with a marine biology center, cape lighthouse, manmade tidepools, and seals and sea lions playing on the shoreline rocks.

Practicalities

The Greyhound station is at 956 SW 10th St, and the **chamber of commerce** is at 555 SW Coast Hwy (℡541/265-8801, ⊛www.newportchamber.org). The most prominent place to **stay** is the *Sylvia Beach Hotel*, on Nye Beach at 267 NW Cliff St (℡541/265-5428, ⊛www.sylviabeachhotel.com; ➍), whose twenty rooms each bear the name of a famous writer, from Melville to Dickinson. Newport also has a handful of fine **B&Bs** (details at ⊛www.moriah.com/npbba), with charming amenities set in historic houses and estates.

There's a cluster of first-rate **cafés** and **restaurants** on Bay Boulevard at the bayfront. *Mo's Original* (℡541/265-2979) and *Mo's Annex* (℡541/265-7512), both in the 600 block, are two decent local-chain seafood diners that are always thick with tourists. ⚑ *Rogue Ales Public House*, no. 748 (℡541/265-3188), is the liveliest spot for food and beer, and also offers one- and two-bedroom "Bed and Beer" hotel units (➍–➎, plus two complimentary bottles) so you don't have to risk driving away drunk. On Nye Beach, *April's*, 749 NW 3rd St (℡541/265-6855), offers fine Continental cuisine – the town's best restaurant by far.

Bandon

At the mouth of the Coquille River along US-101, easygoing **BANDON** was once one of the Oregon Coast's great hidden jewels, its deserted beaches and quaint, small-town appeal adding to its seaside charm. However, in recent years a successful golf resort has changed the atmosphere, and the usual souvenir shops, chain stores, and motels have all taken root.

Bandon's main attraction is still its rugged **beach**, strewn with unusual rock formations and magnificent in stormy weather. In calmer conditions, clam-diggers head off to the river's mudflats, crabbers gather at the town dock, and the whole scene makes for a nice stroll. The **visitor center** is at 300 SE 2nd St (℡541/347-9616, ⊛www.bandon.com), and there's oceanfront **accommodation** just south of town at the *Sunset Motel*, 1865 Beach Loop Drive (℡541/347-2453 or 1-800/842-2407, ⊛www.sunsetmotel.com; ➍–➎), which offers rooms, condos, and seafront cabins. In town, the place to stay is the harbor-front *Sea Star Guest House*, 370 1st St (℡541/347-9632, ⊛www.seastarbandon.com; ➌–➏), offering rooms, suites, and a penthouse, plus a harbor and sunset view from a deck. You can **camp** just north of town at **Bullards Beach State Park** (℡541/347-2209), where the disused Coquille River Lighthouse casts a romantic silhouette over miles of windswept sands. Try the good **seafood** at *Bandon Boatworks*, 275 Lincoln Ave SW (℡541/347-2111), or pick up a tasty block of cheese at the *Bandon Cheese Factory*, 680 SE 2nd St (℡541/347-2456), or a tangy treat at *Cranberry Sweets*, 1st St at Chicago SE (℡541/347-9475).

Gold Beach and Siskiyou National Forest

Towns are fewer and farther apart going south on US-101 from Bandon, with the coastline at its prettiest beyond **Port Orford**, where forested mountains sweep smoothly down to the sea. These mountains mark the western limit of the **SISKIYOU NATIONAL FOREST**, a vast slab of remote wilderness best explored by boat along the turbulent Rogue River from workaday **GOLD BEACH**. Here, the **visitor center**, on the main road at 29279 S Ellensburg (℡541/247-0923, ⊛www.goldbeachchamber.com), has details of rafting and powerboat excursions plus details for the town's basic motels and hotels. Finally, at the state's far southwestern corner, **Brookings** has a warmer climate, and is best used as a base for exploring northern California's **Redwood National Park** (see p.1158). Contact the local **visitor center** (℡541/469-3181, ⊛www.brookingsor.com) for more details.

Central Oregon

East of the Cascades, Oregon grows warmer, drier, and wilder; green valleys give way to the high desert with sagebrush, juniper trees, craggy hills, and stark rock formations broken up by the occasional tract of pine forest. **Central Oregon's** volcanic landscape features cracked lava beds, towering cone-like hills, and deep craters such as beautiful **Crater Lake** in the south.

Bend and around

BEND is the most useful base for visiting central Oregon, giving access both to mountain grandeur and eerie volcanic landscapes, and packed with restaurants, microbreweries, and outdoor-gear shops. Greyhound is at 20545 Builders St, the **visitor center** is at 917 NW Harriman (℡541/382-8048, ⓦwww.visitbend. com), and the **Central Oregon Welcome Center**, 661 SW Powerhouse Drive (℡1-800/800-8334, ⓦwww.covisitors.com), has brochures and accommodation listings. Beyond recreation, the area's main attraction is the **High Desert Museum**, 59800 US-97 (daily 9am–5pm; $12; ⓦwww.highdesertmuseum.org), a fascinating collection of artifacts from Native American and pioneer history, along with displays of regional flora, and a reconstructed pioneer homestead and sawmill. There are panoramic views over Bend from **Pilot Butte**, the remains of a small volcano a mile east of downtown off US-20; you can drive or walk to the top.

The compact town center is the best place to find **accommodation**, especially in several smart **B&Bs** in stately, early twentieth-century residences, such as the *Lara House*, 640 NW Congress St (℡541/388-4064, ⓦwww.larahouse.com; ⑤), and *Sather House*, 7 NW Tumalo Ave (℡541/388-1065, ⓦwww.satherhouse. com; ④). Alternatively, the *St Francis Hotel*, 700 NW Bond St (℡541/330-8560, ⓦwww.mcmenamins.com; ⑤), is a charmingly renovated, former Catholic school from 1936 that offers rooms with the latest luxuries and the chance to stay in a nunnery, friary and parish house (⑥–⑨). You can also camp in **Tumalo State Park** (℡541/388-6055), a wooded dell by the Deschutes River five miles northwest along US-20. You can rent a **yurt** or a large canvas-covered **tepee** ($27–35).

For **eating** and **drinking**, *Pine Tavern*, 967 NW Brooks St (℡541/382-5581), and *Bend Brewing*, 1019 NW Brooks St (℡541/383-1599), both serve microbrewed ales and stouts and sturdy American cuisine, while the *Deschutes Brewery and Public House*, 1044 NW Bond St (℡541/385-8606), brews and serves some of the Northwest's most prominent beers. *West Side Café & Bakery*, 1005 NW Galveston Ave (℡541/382-3426), has filling breakfasts and delicious baked goods.

Mount Bachelor and the Cascades Lake Highway

The Northwest's largest ski resort, **Mount Bachelor**, 22 miles southwest of Bend (mid-Nov to late-May; ℡541/382-2442 or 1-800/829-2442, ⓦwww. mtbachelor.com; lift tickets $49), caters to downhill and cross-country skiers, and snowboarders alike. It's also the first stop on the **Cascade Lakes Highway**, a hundred-mile mountain loop road giving access to trailheads into the **Three Sisters** – a trio of spiky peaks visible throughout central Oregon – or, further south, the **Diamond Peak** wilderness area and a sprinkling of campgrounds (see ⓦwww. oregonstateparks.org for information). Get details from **Deschutes National Forest Ranger Station**, just outside of Bend at 1645 NE Hwy-20 (℡541/388-2715, ⓦwww.fs.fed.us/r6/centraloregon), or in Bend at 1001 SW Emkay Drive (℡541/383-5300).

Newberry National Volcanic Monument

The so-called **Lava Lands** cover a huge area of central Oregon, but especially in the Bend area at **Newberry National Volcanic Monument** (dawn–dusk; five-day parking passes $5). Dating back seven thousand years to the eruption of Mount Newberry, the monument is actually a huge, gently sloping crater laced with hiking paths, nature trails, campgrounds, and prime fishing spots. Some of the highlights (most free with monument admission) include the chilly, mile-long **Lava River Cave** (summer daily 9am–5pm; $3 for a lamp), an eerie subterranean passage made from a hollow lava tube that remains a steady 42 degrees; the **Lava Cast Forest**, circular, basalt casts of tree trunks burnt by lava before they could fall; and the surreal landscape of the **Big Obsidian Flow**, huge hills of volcanic black glass that native tribes throughout the area once used to make arrowheads. The **Lava Lands visitor center** (May–Oct Wed–Sun 9am–5pm, summer daily; ☎541/593-2421), eleven miles south of Bend on US-97, is an excellent source of maps and information on hiking trails, and provides access to the monument's other major sight, **Lava Butte**, a massive 500ft cinder cone, whose narrow rim you can reach by car and traverse in a short walk.

Crater Lake National Park

Just over a hundred miles south of Bend, the blown-out shell of Mount Mazama holds the resoundingly beautiful **CRATER LAKE** (seven-day access fee $10; ⓦwww.nps.gov/crla), the deepest lake in the Western Hemisphere, formed after an explosion 42 times greater than that of Mount St Helens (see p.1193). The biggest island on the lake, **Wizard Island**, is actually the tip of a still-rising cinder cone. In its snowy isolation, the lake, at a depth of nearly two thousand feet, is awe-inspiring; in summer, wildflowers bloom along its high rim. The most popular hike is up 8054ft **Garfield Peak**, which offers a tremendous vista and is particularly striking in winter. More intrepid hikers can explore the marginally better views offered by the park's tallest outcrop, **Mount Scott**, at almost nine thousand feet.

You'll need a **car** to get to the park, though only the southern roads (US-62 from Medford or US-97 from Klamath Falls) are open year-round. The northern access road (via Hwy-138) is closed from mid-October to June, as is the spectacular, 33-mile "Rim Drive" around the crater's edge. Regular **boats** cruise the lake (July–Sept daily 10am–4pm; 1hr 45min; $22), reached via the sheer, mile-long **Cleetwood Cove trail**, which provides the only access to the lake. The trail is on the north edge, but visitor facilities are clustered on the south edge, at tiny **Rim Village**, where the **visitor center** (June–Sept 9.30am–5pm) is a few steps from *Crater Lake Lodge* (late-May to mid-Oct; ☎541/830-8700, ⓦwww.craterlakelodges.com; $169), a grand old lodge built in 1915; ask for a room overlooking the lake (the lodge perches on the rim of the caldera, nine hundred feet above the water's surface). Operated by the same company, *Mazama Village Cabins* (June–Oct; same phone; $111) is seven miles from the crater, but has an adjoining **campground** ($18) in a quiet wooded setting. There are also two campgrounds, the large *Mazama* ($10) and the much smaller *Lost Creek* ($14.75), both inside the park boundary. The **park headquarters** is at the Steel Visitors Center, a few miles south of the rim on the main access road (May–Oct 9am–5pm; rest of year 10am–4pm; ☎541/594-3100), where you can inquire about the full range of activities on offer, including taking a **scuba dive** (June–Sept; free permits) into the depths of the deep blue lake.

⑭ Klamath Falls

Sixty miles southeast of Crater Lake, the burg of **KLAMATH FALLS** isn't particularly pretty, but it does boast the **Favell Museum**, 125 W Main St (Mon–Sat 9.30am–5.30pm; $6; ⓦwww.favellmuseum.org), which hosts a fine collection of native artifacts and a large assortment of Wild West paintings and sculptures.

Klamath Falls sits in the middle of **Klamath Basin**, whose lakes and marshes once formed a vast wetland stretching far beyond the California border. Much of it has been drained, but six sections are now protected as **national wildlife refuges**, with upwards of a million birds during spring and fall migrations. The **visitor center**, 507 Main St (ⓣ541/882-1501, ⓦklamathcounty.net), has maps and information.

Eastern Oregon

Eastern Oregon, former Wild West country, can be surprisingly beautiful with its bare, sun-scorched landscape of ochre and beige. The unexpected colors of the **John Day Fossil Beds**, the remote, snowcapped **Wallowa Mountains**, and the deep slash of **Hells Canyon** are all very dramatic landscapes, and not to be missed if you have the time to explore them. Eastbound on Hwy-126/26 from Redmond, you'll emerge from a brief passage through the **Ochoco National Forest** – also worth a look for its wooded slopes, craggy canyons, and rocky pillars.

John Day Fossil Beds and around

Many eastern Oregon features are named, oddly enough, after John Jacob Astor's fur-trapping employee **John Day**, best known for being attacked and stripped naked by natives and enduring fits of dementia. As writer Ralph Friedman remarks, places in the state bearing his name are "probably the only ones in

Oregon honoring a man acknowledged to have been violently insane." The most significant of his namesakes are the **John Day Fossil Beds**, preserved in a layer of volcanic ash while the Cascades formed, just after the extinction of the dinosaurs 65 million years ago. There are three fossil sites, with the most interesting being the **Painted Hills** unit, nine miles northwest of Mitchell, just off US-26. Striped in shades of beige, rust, and brown, the surfaces of these evocative, sandcastle-like hills are quilted with rivulets worn by draining water. Thirty miles east is the **Sheep Rock** unit, on Hwy-19, two miles from its junction with US-26. Here, the **Condon Paleontology Center** (Mon–Fri 9am–5pm; free; ☎541/987-2333, ⓦ www.nps.gov/joda) provides a good introduction to the local geology and the world of fossils. (The last site, the **Clarno** unit, is 20 miles west of the town of Fossil, but doesn't have a visitor center.) A mile north of the Condon Center is the **Blue Basin**, a natural amphitheater where a mile-long trail leads past various fossil replicas, like that of a saber-toothed cat and a tortoise that hurtled to its death millions of years ago.

Beyond the fossil beds, the largest town along US-26 between Baker City and Prineville is little **John Day**, home of the fascinating **Kam Wah Chung & Co. Museum**, just off US-26 (May–Sept daily 9am–5pm; free). This was once the residence, opium den, and general store of famed Chinese herbalist **Ing Hay**, whose apothecary wares – five hundred herbs, dried lizard, bear claw, and rattlesnakes – have been preserved and are still on display, providing an authentic, unexpected glimpse into Oregon's pioneer history. Six miles west of John Day, there's **camping** at **Clyde Holliday State Park** (Mar–Nov; $13–17; ☎503/932-4453), which also offers a pair of tepees ($28) and hiker and biker campsites for only $4.

Baker City

In the forested hills east of John Day, US-26 turns southeast for the long run down to Idaho. More enjoyable is the far shorter drive on Hwy-7 through the southern reaches of the **Wallowa-Whitman National Forest** to the Gold Rush boomtown of **BAKER CITY**. The **Oregon Trail Interpretive Center**, five well-signposted miles east of town at Flagstaff Hill (daily: April–Oct 9am–6pm; Nov–Mar 9am–4pm; $5; ⓦ oregontrail.blm.gov), has audiovisual displays and four miles of trails revealing wagon ruts and other points of interest from that historic route (see box overleaf). Back in town, the **Oregon Trail Regional Museum**, 2480 Grove St (April–Oct daily 9am–5pm; $3.50), showcases artifacts from pioneer days, but is most notable for its fine collection of rocks, petrified wood, and fluorescent geodes.

Baker City's Main Street, with its handsome early-twentieth-century, red-brick buildings, has the best **accommodations**, including the *Baer House*, 2333 Main St (☎541/523-1055, ⓦ www.baerhouse.com; ❹), a fetching 1882 Victorian B&B with rooms awash in period antiques, and the opulent *Geiser Grand*, 1996 Main St (☎541/523-1889, ⓦ www.geisergrand.com; ❹), a classic 1889 hotel decked out with a stained-glass ceiling and mahogany fixtures. The surrounding Wallowa-Whitman National Forest has many **campgrounds**; get details from the **visitor center**, 490 Campbell St, beside exit 304 on I-84 (☎541/523-3356, ⓦ www. visitbaker.com). Among the limited choices for **eating**, try *Barley Brown's Brewpub*, 2190 Main St (☎541/523-4266), for its dependable pub fare. Greyhound **buses** connect to Portland from the bus station at 515 Campbell St.

Pendleton

The large, flat **Grande Ronde Valley**, north of Baker City on I-84, is based around the dusty town of **La Grande**, but for local color and history you're better off pushing northwest on I-84, following the route of the Oregon Trail, to

Between the 1840s and 1870s, more than a quarter-million Americans journeyed by wagon train from the Midwest on **the Oregon Trail** in search of a new start. Ever since Lewis and Clark completed their successful survey of the Oregon Country in 1806, the idea of "manifest destiny" had both politicians and prospective settlers keen to see their country expand from coast to coast, regardless of who or what might be in the way. The first migrants were further inspired by the missionaries who went west to try to Christianize Native Americans in the 1830s, and who sent back glowing reports of the region's temperate climate, fertile soil, dense forests, fish-rich rivers, and absence of malaria.

In spring 1843 more than a thousand would-be migrants gathered at Independence and Westport on the banks of the Missouri, preparing for the "**Great Migration**." The pioneers were a remarkably homogenous bunch, nearly all experienced farmers, using ox-pulled wagons with flimsy canvas roofs to transport supplies and often walking alongside their vehicles, instead of riding and adding extra weight to them – as Hollywood would have it.

Traversing almost two thousand miles of the West, the migrants forced their wagons across pristine rivers, forests, and mountains, pausing at the occasional army fort or missionary station to recuperate. After three months on the trail, they arrived at what is now the town of The Dalles. From there the group faced an uneasy choice before reaching the lush Willamette Valley just beyond: build rafts and risk the treacherous currents and whirlpools of the Columbia River or take the equally perilous Barlow Road around Mount Hood (see p.1206), notorious for its swiftly changing weather and steep hillsides.

Over the next thirty years, fifty thousand more settlers arrived in the Willamette Valley, with others moving into Washington and California. Along with helping Oregon to become a state in 1859, the migration spawned a cottage industry of specialist suppliers and wagon-builders. Inevitably, except for some isolated wagon-wheel ruts here and there, there are few surviving signs of the migrants, but they are commemorated by several museums, the best of which is near Baker City (see p.1217).

PENDLETON. The town is best known as the home of the popular, week-long **Pendleton Round-Up** in September ($11–15 per rodeo event; ℡541/276-2553 or 1-800/45-RODEO, ⓦwww.pendletonroundup.com), combining traditional rodeo with extravagant pageantry; the **Round-Up Hall of Fame**, 1205 SW Court Ave (June–Sept Mon–Sat 10am–5pm; free), is stuffed with related memorabilia. The famed **Pendleton Woolen Mills**, 1307 SE Court Place (tours Mon–Fri; free; information at ℡541/276-6911, ⓦwww.pendleton-usa.com), will mainly appeal to textile fans, although you can always pick up a sweater there, while the fascinating **Pendleton Underground**, 37 SW Emigrant Ave (Mar–Oct Mon–Sat 9.30am–3pm, rest of year varies; 90min; $10; ⓦwww.pendletonunderground tours.org), lets you tour the town's many subterranean passageways, used during Prohibition for saloons, card rooms, and brothels.

The **chamber of commerce** is at 501 S Main St (Mon–Fri 9am–5pm; ℡541/276-7411, ⓦwww.pendletonchamber.com), and the Greyhound station is at 801 SE Court Ave. For **accommodation** try the Victorian rooms of the *Parker House B&B*, 311 N Main St (℡541/276-8581, ⓦwww.parkerhousebnb.com; ❹), or the functional *Oxford Suites*, 2400 SW Court Place (℡1-877/545-7848, ⓦwww.oxfordsuites.com; ❹). Most **restaurants** dole out hefty portions of all-American fare like burgers and fries, although *Raphael's*, 233 SE 4th Ave (℡541/276-8500), offers a touch of upscale Northwest cuisine, from crab legs and salmon to barbecued elk chops.

The Wallowa Mountains

The **Wallowa Mountains**, reached by leaving I-84 at La Grande and heading east on Hwy-82, are one of Eastern Oregon's loveliest and least-known areas. At the northern tip of the glacially carved **Wallowa Lake**, tiny **JOSEPH** is a perfect spot to spend the night. There are quite a few **B&Bs** of varying quality, the best of which is the *Bronze Antler*, 309 S Main St (☎541/432-0230, ⓦ www.bronzeantler. com; ❹–❺, by season), with rustic, Arts and Crafts design and antique European furniture. Also on Main Street are many antique stores and the small **Wallowa County Museum**, 110 S Main St (summer daily 10am–5pm; donation), where the story of the Nez Percé tribe is presented along with a collection of pioneer artifacts.

A mile south of Joseph, **Wallowa Lake** is inhabited by the Native American legend of the great horned Wallowa Lake Monster, also known as "Wally." At its far end, the state park has **camping** ($17–21; ⓦ www.wallowalake.net), and the **Wallowa Lake Tramway**, 59919 Wallowa Lake Hwy (daily: June–Aug 10am–5pm; May & Sept 10am–4pm; $20 roundtrip; ⓦ www.wallowalaketramway.com), whisks visitors to the top of 4000ft **Mount Howard**, where short trails lead to magnificent overlooks. Much of the mountain scenery makes up the **Eagle Cap Wilderness** ($5 day-passes; ⓦ www.fs.fed.us/r6/w-w), whose lakes, streams, and peaks are accessible only via hiking trails, and the backcountry camping is strikingly remote. Contact the **Wallowa Mountains Visitor Center**, 88401 Hwy-82 (☎541/426-5546, ⓦ www.wallowacounty.org), for details on the Eagle Cap, as well as Hells Canyon.

Hells Canyon

East of Joseph, marking the Idaho border, the **Snake River** has cut the deepest chasm on the continent – **Hells Canyon**, a 130-mile gorge that's a thousand feet deeper than the Grand Canyon. With the **Seven Devils** mountains rising above it and the river glimmering in its depths, the canyon is still best known as the site of the ill-fated (but non-fatal) 1974 motorcycle jump by daredevil Evel Knievel.

The area is preserved as **Hells Canyon National Recreation Area** (day-pass $5; ⓦ www.fs.fed.us/hellscanyon), where deer, otters, mink, and elk live, along with rattlesnakes, black bears, and mountain lions. Motor vehicles are banned in much of the canyon, so you can only explore by foot or horseback. The forest roads that skirt the area are rough and slippery, and many are closed by snow much of the year. If you intend to use them, check with the **rangers** in Enterprise, 88401 Hwy-82 (☎541/426-5546), or Baker City, 1550 Dewey Ave (☎541/523-6391), before you go.

From Joseph, Little Sheep Creek Highway leads to **Imnaha**, where a narrow and vertiginous graveled Forest Service road leads to the ultimate view from **Hat Point**, site of a campground and lookout tower. The easier approach is at the south end of the canyon, along Hwy-86 east from Baker City. On the way, tiny **Halfway** makes a good stop, with **accommodation** at the three cabins and five rooms available at the rustic farmhouse of the *Clear Creek Farm B&B*, 48212 Clear Creek Rd (☎541/742-2238, ⓦ www.clearcreekfarm.biz; ❸).

The other approach heading into the canyon, from Halfway on Hwy-86, meets the Snake River at Oxbow Dam, where a rough Forest Service road leads to **Hells Canyon Dam**, the launching-point for exhilarating jet-boat and rafting trips through the canyon. *Hells Canyon Adventures* (reserve at ☎541/785-3352 or 1-800/422-3568; ⓦ www.hellscanyonadventures.com) and other companies run sightseeing **tours** in summer (2–3hr; $35–45 per person). Skimming over the rapids, the boats also operate a "drop-off" service, taking you to hiking trails along the canyon and picking you up the same day or later in the week ($35 per person).

15

Alaska

AL - ALABAMA	IN - INDIANA	MN - MINNESOTA	RI - RHODE ISLAND
AR - ARKANSAS	LA - LOUISIANA	MS - MISSISSIPPI	SC - SOUTH CAROLINA
CT - CONNECTICUT	MA - MASSACHUSETTS	NC - NORTH CAROLINA	VA - VIRGINIA
DE - DELAWARE	MD - MARYLAND	NH - NEW HAMPSHIRE	VT - VERMONT
FL - FLORIDA	ME - MAINE	NJ - NEW JERSEY	WI - WISCONSIN
IL - ILLINOIS	MI - MICHIGAN	PA - PENNSYLVANIA	WV - WEST VIRGINIA

CHAPTER 15

Highlights

* **Sitka** Russian influence
blended with Native
heritage and fabulous
coastal scenery, making
this one of Alaska's most
diverting towns.
See p.1230

* **The Chilkoot Trail**
Follow in the (frozen)
footsteps of the Klondike
prospectors on this
demanding 33-mile trail
near Skagway.
See p.1237

* **Talkeetna** Every Alaska
visitor's favorite small
town is the base for
superb flightseeing trips
around Mount McKinley.
See p.1251

* **Denali National Park**
Alaska's finest park offers
superb mountain scenery
and incomparable
wildlife-spotting around
the highest peak in North
America. See p.1252

* **Aurora borealis** The
spectacular after-dark
displays of the Northern
Lights are at their best
around Fairbanks from
mid-September to mid-
March. See p.1258

* **Dalton Highway** This
lonely and grueling 500-
mile road leads north
from Fairbanks to the
Arctic Ocean.
See p.1258

△ Denali National Park

Alaska

No other region in North America fires the imagination like **ALASKA** – a derivation of *Alayeska*, an Athabascan word meaning "great land of the west." Few who see this land of gargantuan ice fields, sweeping tundra, glacially excavated valleys, lush rainforests, deep fjords, and occasionally smoking volcanoes leave unimpressed. **Wildlife** may be under threat elsewhere, but here it is abundant, with Kodiak bears standing twelve feet tall, moose stopping traffic in downtown Anchorage, wolves prowling national parks, bald eagles circling over the trees, and rivers solid with fifty-plus-pound salmon.

Alaska's sheer size is hard to comprehend. If superimposed onto the Lower 48 states, it would stretch from the Atlantic to the Pacific, while its coastline is longer than the rest of the US combined. All but three of the nation's twenty highest peaks are found within its boundaries, and one glacier alone is twice the size of Wales. In addition, not only does it contain America's **northernmost** and **westernmost** points, because the Aleutian Islands stretch across the 180th meridian, it contains the **easternmost** point as well.

Perhaps surprisingly then, a mere 665,000 people live in Alaska, of whom only one-fifth were born in the state: as a rule of thumb, the more winters you have endured, the more Alaskan you are. Often referred to as the **"Last Frontier,"** Alaska in many ways mirrors the American West of the nineteenth century: an endless, undeveloped space in which to stake one's claim and set up a life without interference – or at least that's how Alaskans would like it to be. Throughout the last hundred years or so, tens of thousands have been lured by the promise of wealth, first by gold and then by fishing, logging, and, most recently, oil. However, Alaska's 100,000 **Native peoples** have been greatly marginalized, though Native corporations set up as a result of pre-oil boom land deals have increasing economic clout.

Traveling around Alaska still demands a spirit of adventure, and to make the most of the state you need to have an enthusiasm for striking out on your own and roughing it a bit. Binoculars are an absolute must, as is bug spray; the **mosquito** is referred to as the "Alaska state bird" and it takes industrial-strength repellent to keep it away. On top of that, there's the **climate** – though Alaska is far from the great big icebox people imagine it to be. While winter temperatures of -40°F are commonplace in Fairbanks, the most touristed areas – the southeast and the Kenai Peninsula – enjoy a maritime climate (45–65°F in summer) similar to that of the Pacific Northwest, meaning much more rain (in some towns 180-plus inches per year) than snow. Remarkably, the summer temperature in the Interior often reaches 80°F.

Alaska is far more expensive than most other states: apart from two dozen hostels and myriad campgrounds, there's little budget accommodation, and **eating** and **drinking** will set you back at least twenty percent more than in the Lower 48 (perhaps fifty percent in more remote regions). Still, experiencing Alaska on a **low budget** is possible, though it requires planning and off-peak travel. From June to August room prices are crazy; May and September, when tariffs are relaxed and the weather only slightly chillier, are just as good times to go, and in April or October you'll have the place to yourself, albeit with a smaller range of places to stay and eat. Ground **transportation**, despite the long distances, is reasonable, with backpacker shuttles ferrying budget travelers between major centers. **Winter**, when hotels drop their prices by as much as half, is becoming an increasingly popular time to visit, particularly for the dazzling **aurora borealis** (see box, p.1258).

Some history

It is thought that Alaska has been inhabited for longer than anywhere else in the Americas; it was here that humans first reached the "New World" from eastern Russia, most likely around fourteen thousand years ago. These first settlers can be classified into four groups. The **Aleut**, in the inhospitable Aleutian Islands, built underground homes and hunted sea mammals such as walrus for food and clothing, while the nomadic **Athabascan** herded caribou in the Interior. The warrior **Tlingit** lived in the warmer coastal regions of the southeast, where food was plentiful, while the **Eskimos** (or, more correctly, the Yup'ik and Iñupiat), who inhabited the northwestern coast, lived off fish and larger marine life. Descendants of all these groups can be found in Alaska today, and a few live in much the same way as their ancestors.

In 1741, Danish explorer **Vitus Bering**, working for the Tsar of Russia, became the first Caucasian to set foot on Alaskan soil and found huge numbers of fur seals and **sea otters**, whose treasured pelts were made into hats. Russians, and later British and Spaniards, joined in the ensuing slaughter, both of the otters and the Aleut, who were enslaved and forced to hunt on behalf of the fur traders. By the end of the century, the Russians had established their Alaskan capital at present-day **Sitka**, pushed down the coast as far as Northern California and, in the process, decimated the sea otter colonies.

During the 1860s, limited returns and domestic economic problems forced Russia to sell its lands to America. On October 18, 1867, Secretary of State William Seward purchased what was disparagingly known as "**Seward's Folly**" or "Seward's Icebox" for $7.2 million – less than 2¢ per acre. Alaska soon turned out to be a literal **gold mine** with major discoveries at Juneau (1880), Nome (1898), and Fairbanks (1902). With logging companies and commercial fishing operations soon descending upon Alaska, the government began to take a more active interest in its affairs, and in 1959 Alaska became the **49th state**.

Fortune-seekers headed to Alaska again in the mid-1970s to build the **trans-Alaska pipeline** from Prudhoe Bay to the ice-free port of Valdez. Today, Alaska still derives the majority of its wealth from oil and gas and, consequently, is prone to extreme boom-and-bust cycles. Once-lucrative fishing and lumber industries are fast giving way to tourism as a source of income, and the ethical question of how best to use Alaska lands in the future has led to bitter controversy. Nowhere is this more apparent than in the case of the **Arctic National Wildlife Refuge**, a vast tract of tundra in Alaska's northeast that has some degree of protection, but is constantly under threat from the oil industry and Alaska's Republican governor, senators, and congressman.

Getting to Alaska

Alaska is a long way from the rest of the United States, and however you get there it is going to be **expensive**. Once you accept that, however, there is no question as to the most **enjoyable** method – the memorable ferry trip on the Alaska Marine Highway.

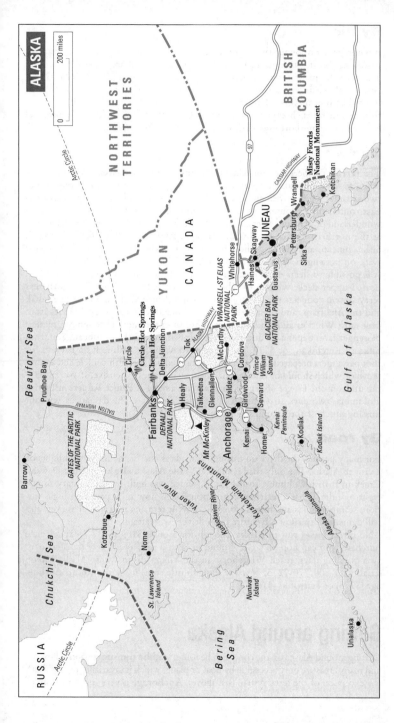

By air

Anchorage is no longer the major air crossroads it was, but it's still easy to **fly** to Alaska. Most, but not all, flights from the Lower 48 are routed via Seattle. The most frequent service is operated by Alaska Airlines (℡1-800/252-7522, ⓦwww.alaskaair.com), whose moneysaving package enables you to stop at towns like Juneau, Sitka, Cordova, and Fairbanks at little extra cost. Roundtrips from Seattle to Anchorage cost around $400 if bought two weeks in advance, and $600 or more on short notice, though there can be Web specials.

By sea

The **ferries** of the state-run **Alaska Marine Highway System** (℡1-800/642-0066, ⓦwww.ferryalaska.com) reaching many places that cars can't, operates in two separate regions with an occasional "Cross-Gulf" link. The popular **southeast** route runs a thousand miles from Bellingham, north of Seattle, through a wonderland of pristine waters, narrow fjords, and untouched forests to Skagway, at the northern end of the **Inside Passage**, stopping at Ketchikan, Wrangell, Sitka, Juneau, and Haines. The whole trip takes three days and costs $342 for walk-on passengers, $448 for a small car, $55 for bicycles, and $85 for kayaks. It is possible to sleep – and even to pitch a tent – on the "solarium," a covered, heated upper deck, while a two-berth cabin costs from $271. The **southwest** ferry system connects the Kenai Peninsula and Prince William Sound to Kodiak and the Aleutians, and the two systems are linked by "Cross-Gulf" ferries from Juneau to Whittier and Kodiak twice a month in summer. Throughout, section passenger fares depend on distance traveled: $44 from Sitka to Juneau; $80 from Sitka to Ketchikan; or $214 from Juneau to Whittier. While it's a bargain for foot passengers prepared to rough it, an extended voyage with vehicle and a cabin (both of which should be reserved in advance) becomes expensive. If you're driving up from the Lower 48, consider boarding a ferry at Prince Rupert in British Columbia, two days' drive north of Seattle. This saves one day at sea without missing much of the natural spectacle.

By road

For many people, the drive up through Canada is one of the major highlights of a visit to Alaska. The only road is the 1500-mile **Alaska Highway** from Dawson Creek in British Columbia to Fairbanks, which was built by the military in just eight months. It has a fearsome reputation, but is now fully paved with gas stations, campgrounds and hotels along the way. It remains as beautiful as ever, and still demands a spirit of adventure from drivers who attempt it.

No direct **buses** run to Alaska, though for around $169 ($107 7-day advance purchase) you can hop on a Greyhound in Seattle and, after a few transfers over two grueling days, reach Whitehorse in the Yukon, from where Alaska/Yukon Trails (℡1-800/770-7275, ⓦwww.alaskashuttle.com) make the run to Anchorage ($175) or Fairbanks ($162).

Getting around Alaska

Getting around Alaska on the cheap can be tough; **public transportation** is limited, and many areas are only accessible by boat or plane, which is invariably pricey. With the exception of the ferry system (see above), **Anchorage** is very much the hub of

Alaska, with several **bus** companies running to major destinations: Seward with Seward Bus Line (℡907/224-3608, ⓦ www.sewardbuslines.com; $45); Homer with Homer Stage Line (℡907/235-2252, ⓦ www.homerstageline.com; $60); Talkeetna with Talkeetna Shuttle Service (℡907/733-17258, ⓦ www.denalicentral.com) and Denali ($65) and Fairbanks ($90) with Alaska/Yukon Trails (℡1-800/770-7275, ⓦ www.alaskashuttle.com). The expensive **Alaska Railroad** runs nearly five hundred miles from Seward north through Anchorage to Fairbanks, with a spur to Whittier for cruise liners and ferries to Valdez and Juneau. One-way summer **fares** from Anchorage are: Denali $129, Fairbanks $185, Whittier $55 and Seward $62.

Driving around Alaska in summer requires no special skills, though minor routes are often gravel, requiring caution. Wildlife, especially moose, can be a danger any time, even on city streets. In spring and fall you should be prepared for snow, and it is wise to carry a **survival kit**, particularly in winter, as traffic can be sparse even on major routes. Road conditions can change rapidly – call ℡511 or 1-866/282-7577 or see ⓦ511.alaska.gov.

Travel by **plane** is not always more expensive than other methods, especially if you can map out your itinerary in advance with the state's largest operator, Alaska Airlines (see opposite), which flies to most major communities and uses partners such as ERA Aviation (℡1-800/866-8394, ⓦ www.flyera.com) and PenAir (℡1-800/448-4226, ⓦ www.penair.com) to get to smaller towns. **Chartering a plane** might sound extravagant but can be inexpensive for groups of four or more, and may be the crowning glory of an Alaska vacation. To arrange this, contact any 'bush plane' operator (every town has at least one). ERA Aviation and PenAir are good starting points, though they may refer you to another company.

Southeast Alaska

Southeast Alaska is archetypal Alaska: an awesome four-hundred-mile-long tableau of fjords, mountains, glaciers, a thousand islands, and thick conifer forests lining the **Inside Passage**. The area's first settlers were the **Tlingit** (*thling-get*), and it was not until the end of the eighteenth century that Russian expansionists burst into the region. Today, southeast Alaska's small communities resound with tales of endurance, folly, and cruelty.

The state's southernmost town, **Ketchikan**, rich in Native heritage, makes a pretty introduction, while **Sitka** retains a Russian influence. Further north are swanky **Juneau**, the capital; **Haines**, with its mix of old-timers and arty newcomers; and

15

ALASKA | Southeast Alaska

Skagway, thoroughly redolent of the old gold-mining days. You could spend months exploring here, but most are content to focus on the the towns of Sitka and Skagway, and **Glacier Bay National Park**, an expensive side-trip from Juneau that penetrates one of Alaska's most stunning regions.

With no roads connecting towns, by far the best way to travel is by **ferry**, though at some stage make sure you take a **floatplane** ride. For a true outdoor adventure, you can rent a **cabin** in the huge Tongass National Forest – which encompasses most of southeast Alaska – for around $35 per night; details from the visitor centers in Juneau (see p.1232) and Ketchikan (see below), or through the NRRS reservation service (Ⓦ www.reserveusa.com).

Ketchikan and around

KETCHIKAN, almost seven hundred miles north of Seattle, is Alaska's "first city." It is the first port of call for many cruise ships and its historic downtown, wedged between water and forested mountains, becomes saturated in summer with elderly tourists. Beyond the souvenir shopping, it can be a delight, built into steep hills and partly propped on wooden pilings, dotted with boardwalks, wooden staircases, and totem poles.

By 1886, white settlers had opened the first of dozens of canneries in what was soon to be the "salmon capital of the world." Forests of cedar, hemlock, and spruce, which had provided timber for Tlingit homes and totems, also fed the town's sawmills. The timber and fishing industries have since declined, and Ketchikan has increasingly looked to tourism as its savior, with the nearby **Misty Fiords National Monument** as the prime draw.

The state's fourth largest city is a strong contender for the nation's wettest; annual precipitation averages 165 inches, but Ketchikan's perennial drizzle and sporadic showers won't spoil your visit.

Arrival and information

Ferries dock two miles north of downtown on Tongass Highway; city **buses** stop here every thirty minutes until 8.30pm. Alaska Airlines serves the **airport**, which is on an island and is linked to town by half-hourly ferries ($5 roundtrip). The **visitor center** stands downtown at 131 Front St (daily 8am–5pm; ☎ 1-800/770-3300, Ⓦ www.visit-ketchikan.com), and for information about the surrounding Tongass forests visit the **Southeast Alaska Discovery Center**, 50 Main St (daily 8am–5pm; ☎ 907/228-6220, Ⓦ www.fs.fed.us/r10/tongass), a striking cedar-framed building which houses absorbing displays ($5) of the region's natural habitats and native culture.

Accommodation

Hotels in Ketchikan vary widely, and the closest **campgrounds** to town ($10) are in the attractive Ward Lake Recreation Area, five miles northwest of the ferry terminal.

Alderhouse 420 Alder Street ☎ 907/247-2537, Ⓦ www.alderhousebnb.com. Very welcoming B&B an easy walk from the AMHS ferry dock and close to buses running between downtown and Totem Bight. Attention to detail makes everything, especially the breakfast, a treat. Open June–Sept; 2 night minimum. ❺

Eagle View Hostel 2305 5th Ave ☎ 907/225-5461, Ⓦ www.eagleviewhostel. com. Suburban house shared with the owner, offering great views of the Narrows. Single-sex dorm beds (as well as one double room) cost $28 including bed linen, towel, and use of the kitchen, barbecue, and sauna. No lockout or curfew. Follow Jefferson off Tongass Highway then turn right onto 5th. Open April–Oct and by reservation.

Ketchikan Youth Hostel in the United Methodist Church, 400 Main St ☎ 907/225-3319, Ⓔ ktnyh@

eagle.ptialaska.net. Very basic youth hostel with beds for $15, June–Aug only.

🏃 **The New York Hotel** 207 Stedman St ☎1-866/225-0246, ⓦwww.thenewyorkhotel.com. Tastefully refurbished hotel by the small boat harbor with cozy, tastefully decorated rooms and a good café. ❺

The town

The bulk of Ketchikan's historic buildings lie on **Creek Street**, a rickety-looking boardwalk along Ketchikan Creek. This was a red-light district until 1954; now all the former houses of ill-repute are given over to gift shops and galleries. **Dolly's House**, 24 Creek St, once the home and workplace of Dolly Arthur, the town's most famous madam, is now a small museum stuffed with saucy memorabilia (generally daily 8am–5pm; $5).

Most of the totem poles you see around town are authentic replicas, but the **Totem Heritage Center**, 601 Deermount St (daily 8am–5pm; $5), exhibits the largest collection of original totem poles in the US: 33 mostly nineteenth-century examples recovered from abandoned Native villages. The Tlingit-run **Saxman Totem Park**, two miles south of town, displays the world's largest standing collection of poles and an authentic tribal house. For $3 you get to see the poles and exterior of the buildings, but you'll need to join the **Saxman Native Village Tour** (May–Sept daily; 1hr; $35; ⓦwww.capefoxtours.com, ⓔinfo@capefoxtours.com; no phone) to see sculptors at work and a dance performance inside the clan house.

Fourteen of the best replica totem poles and a rebuilt tribal house stand in **Totem Bight State Park**, breathtakingly set on a forested strip of coast overlooking the Narrows, ten miles north of town on the Tongass Highway. On the way back, take some time out to do the easy but enjoyable boardwalk trail up to **Perseverance Lake**, starting on Ward Lake Road, four miles north of town.

Eating and drinking

Inexpensive **food** in Ketchikan tends to be rather good, a rare combination in Alaska. The town is also renowned for its hard **drinking**.

Chico's 435 Dock St ☎907/225-2833. Bargain authentic Mexican food and pizza with dinners starting at $10, or just grab a $6.50 burrito to eat in or take out.

Diaz Café 335 Stedman St ☎907/225-2257. Great inexpensive diner food with some tasty Filipino dishes. Closed Mon.

First City Saloon 830 Water Street. Straightforward boozing bar occasionally featuring bands and shows. Probably the mostly likely place to indulge in a little dancing.

🏃 **That One Place** 207 Stedman St ☎907/225-0246. Nonsmoking restaurant and bar with a daytime menu loaded with excellent soups, burgers, wraps, and salads (mostly $9–12), plus some sumptuous desserts. Also open evenings when there's an excellent tapas menu, with most plates $5–7. Closed Sun.

Misty Fiords National Monument

Twenty-two miles east of Ketchikan on the mainland, the awe-inspiring **MISTY FIORDS NATIONAL MONUMENT** consists of 2.3 million acres of deep fjords flanked by sheer 3000ft glacially scoured walls topped by dense rainforest. As befits its name, the monument is at its most atmospheric when swathed in low-lying mists. The best access is with Alaska Cruises (☎1-800/225-1905, ⓦwww.mistyfjord.net) who offer a six-hour cruise ($130) and an excellent four-hour cruise/fly combo ($260, occasional evening specials $200). Fourteen rustic cabins (mostly $35) are rented out by the Forest Service (☎1-877/444-6777). Access is either by floatplane with Taquan Air (☎1-800/770-8800, ⓦwww.taquanair.com), or kayak with Southeast Sea Kayaks (☎1-800/287-1607, ⓦwww.kayakketchikan.com).

Sitka

Perched on the seaward edge of the Inside Passage, **SITKA** ranks as one of Alaska's prettiest and most historic towns. The Russians established a fort here in 1799; three years later, Tlingit warriors massacred the imperialist troops, but were themselves cannoned into submission in 1804. Under Russian occupation the town became the capital of Russian America and witnessed transfer of ownership to the US in 1867. Sitka today earns its keep mostly from fishing and tourism – you'll find more nesting dolls here than in the rest of the US put together – but the town also has a wealth of great outdoor opportunities and a fine reputation for its festivals, especially the chamber-oriented **Summer Music Festival** each June.

Arrival and information

Traditional **ferries** and a new fast catamaran jointly visit Sitka around five times per week, mooring seven miles northwest of town. Sitka Tours **shuttles** (⊤ 907/747-8443; $8 roundtrip) run downtown and offer two-hour town tours ($12). Flights arrive a half-hour walk from downtown. **Mountain bikes** can be rented from Yellow Jersey Cycles, 329 Harbor Drive (⊤ 907/747-6317; $25 a day). You can rent **kayaks** from Sitka Sound Ocean Adventures (⊤ 907/747-6375, ⊛ www.ssoceanadventures .com; $30 a half-day, double $40), who also organize day-long guided trips on the Sound ($132). The **visitor center** is in the Centennial Building, 330 Harbor Drive (daily 8am–5pm; ⊤ 907/747-3220, ⊛ www.sitka.org).

Accommodation

Sitka has a good range of **accommodation**: the historic ⅌ *Sitka Hotel*, 118 Lincoln St (⊤ 907/747-3288, ⊛ www.sitkahotel.com; ❸–❹), offers a touch of old-fashioned style and good-value rooms that come with and without bathrooms; the centrally located *Finn Alley Inn B&B*, 711 Lincoln St (⊤ 907/747-3655, ⊛ www. ptialaska.net/~seakdist/finn; ❺), has one large half-basement apartment with a private entrance, full kitchen, and a continental breakfast; and the new Sitka Youth Hostel, 109 Jeff Davis St ⊤ 907/747-8661), is expected to open in June 2007, with bunk beds around $20. **Campers** should head less than a mile north of the ferry dock to the gorgeous *Starrigavan* Campground, on Halibut Point Rd

△ Sitka Sound

(☏1-877/444-6777; $12), or seven miles east of Sitka to the free but basic *Sawmill Creek Campground*, on Blue Lake Rd, at the start of the Beaver Lake Trail.

The Town

The best place to get a grasp of Sitka's Russian past is from diminutive **Castle Hill**, where Alaska was officially transferred to the US on October 18, 1867; a plaque marks the spot. A two-minute stroll to the heart of downtown leads to **St Michael's Cathedral**, a fine piece of Russian church architecture, completed in 1848 and rebuilt after a disastrous fire in 1966. It displays priceless original icons (Mon–Fri 9am–4pm; $2). Nearby is the large, mustard-colored 1842 **Russian Bishop's House** (daily 9am–5pm; $4). Guided tours take in the restored chapel, schoolroom, and bishop's living quarters. Four blocks further along at 104 College Drive, the **Sheldon Jackson Museum** (daily 9am–5pm; $4) houses a compact but extensive display of Native artifacts accumulated by missionary and educationalist Sheldon Jackson.

At the end of Lincoln Street, **Sitka National Historic Park** stands on the site of a decisive battle between the Tlingit and the Russians. Nothing remains of the fort except a grassy clearing, but the evocative air is enhanced by several vividly painted **totem poles** alongside the footpaths, all replicas of nineteenth-century classic designs. A **visitor center** (summer daily 8am–5pm; $4) features good interpretative displays on what is commonly called the "Battle of Sitka," as well as hosting Native craft workshops.

Sitka's **trail system** ranges from shoreside strolls to harder climbs up Gavan Hill and steep Mount Verstovia: for more information visit the **Forest Service office**, 204 Siganaka Way (☏907/747-6671).

Eating and drinking

Sitka's **restaurants** aren't exactly going to set gourmet tongues wagging, though there are several decent places to dine out. You can duck through Old Harbor Books to access ᴽ*Backdoor,* 104 Barracks St ☏907/747-8856, a daytime café with great coffee, plus tasty sandwiches, pastries, and light lunches, while the simple, cafeteria-style *Sheldon Jackson College Dining Room* has all-you-care-to-eat breakfast (6.30–8am; $5.50), lunch (11.30am–1pm; $8.25), and dinner (5–6pm; $11). Follow the road opposite the entrance to the Sheldon Jackson Museum to reach it. For more upscale dining, try ᴽ*Ludvig's Bistro*, 256 Katlian St (☏907/966-3663), offering expensive but excellent Spanish-, Portuguese-, Italian-, and Moroccan-influenced dishes. Closed Sun. If you're looking for evening drinks, *Pioneer Bar*, 212 Katlian St (☏907/747-3456), is a down-to-earth boozing spot lined with hundreds of black-and-white photographs of fishing boats.

Juneau and around

The sophisticated and vibrant city of **JUNEAU** is the only state capital in the nation not accessible by road. It is exceptionally picturesque, hard against the **Gastineau Channel**, with steep, narrow roads clawing up into the rainforested hills behind. Gold features heavily in its history. In 1880, Joe Juneau made **Alaska's first gold strike** in the rainforest along the banks of the Gastineau Channel. Until the last mine was shut down in 1944, this was the world's largest producer of low-grade ore – all the flat land in Juneau, stretching from downtown to the airport, is landfill from mine tailings. Today, state government provides much of the employment, and tourism plays its part with the drive-to **Mendenhall Glacier** and the watery charms of **Tracy Arm fjord** as temptation.

Arrival, information, and getting around

The **ferry terminal** is fourteen miles northwest of downtown at Auke Bay; ferries often arrive at unearthly hours, so getting into town can be a problem. Apart from taking a $40 taxi ride, the only transport is the city's Capital Transit **bus service** (Mon–Sat hourly 7am–10.30pm, Sun 9am–5pm; ☎907/789-6901; $1.50), which stops a mile and a half south outside DeHarts grocery. Buses also pick up from close to the airport, nine miles north of downtown, which sees daily Alaska Airlines flights.

The main **visitor center**, Centennial Hall, 101 Egan Drive (Mon–Fri 8.30am–5pm, Sat & Sun 9am–5pm; ☎1-888/581-2201, ⓦwww.traveljuneau.com), contains an unstaffed desk devoted to brochures about the Tongass National Forest, including material on Glacier Bay, Tracy Arm fjord, and the trails and cabins in Juneau's wooded surroundings. Popular **hikes** from Juneau include the undemanding Perseverance Trail and, over the bridge on Douglas Island, the Treadwell Mine Historic Trail. *Driftwood Lodge* (☎907/586-2280), rents out **mountain bikes** for $25 a day.

Accommodation

Juneau has the widest range of accommodation in Southeast Alaska, as well as some fine camping.

Alaskan Hotel and Bar 167 S Franklin St ☎1-800/327-9374, ⓦwww.thealaskanhotel.com. Pleasant old hotel with a salacious past and a fine bar in the heart of downtown. Twelve doubles with shared or private bath. ③–④

Gold Street Inn 303 Gold St, downtown ☎907/586-9863, ⓦwww.goldstreetinn.com. Quiet and attractive B&B with self-catering facilities, self-serve breakfast, satellite TV and free WiFi. Suite ⑥, rooms ④

Juneau Hostel 614 Harris St ☎907/586-9559, ⓦwww.juneauhostel.org. Clean, comfortable, and relaxed hostel, in an old home near downtown, with dorm beds ($10) and a family room, but an inconvenient daytime lock-out

(9am–5pm) and an 11pm curfew.

Mendenhall Lake Campground Montana Creek Rd, 13 miles from downtown. A gorgeous Forest Service campground within sight of the Mendenhall Glacier and with space for RVs ($26) and some lovely lakeside walk-in tent sites ($10).

Silverbow Inn 120 2nd St, downtown ☎1-800/586-4146, ⓦwww.silverbowinn.com. Attractive, small hotel with smallish but nicely furnished and tastefully decorated rooms, each with TV, phone and WiFi, and with a good continental breakfast included. ⑥

Thane Road Tent Camping Mile 1 Thane Rd. Primitive site 15min walk south of downtown. $5.

The Town

Many original buildings stand in the **South Franklin Street Historic District** – Juneau managed to avoid the fires that destroyed many other gold towns in Alaska. The onion-domed **St Nicholas Russian Orthodox Church**, on Fifth and Gold (Mon 9am–6pm, Tues & Thurs 9am–5pm, Fri 10am–noon & 3-5pm, Sat 11am–3pm, Sun 1–5pm; $2 donation), contains icons and religious treasures, while the well-presented **Alaska State Museum**, 395 Whittier St (daily 8.30am–5.30pm; $5), covers Native culture, Russian heritage, and the first gold strikes. Its pride and joy is the logbook in which Bering reported his first sighting of Alaska. The smaller **City Museum**, at Main and Fourth streets (Mon–Fri 9am–5pm, Sat & Sun 10am–5pm; $4), displays relics from the mining era. The best views of town are from the top of the **Mount Roberts Tramway** (summer daily 9am–9pm; $24), which careers from the cruise-ship dock 1800 feet up Mount Roberts, where there's a nature center and some easy trails.

Eating and drinking

Downtown has a reasonable selection of places to **eat and drink**, but most fill up very quickly when cruise ships are in town.

Alaskan Hotel Bar 167 S Franklin St. Great old bar, with live music most nights, especially toward the weekend.

The Hanger on the Wharf Merchants Wharf ☎ 907/586-5018. Former float-plane hanger with tremendous waterfront views. There are over twenty beers on tap, plus pool tables and live music on weekends. Also serves wraps and burgers at lunch and the likes of jambalaya and halibut tacos ($10–12) at dinner.

🏃 **Paradise Café** 245 Marine Way. Stylish little café and bakery with excellent soups, salads, phyllo rolls, and wraps, all made from scratch and eaten at tables in an adjacent room. A little pricey but worth it. Open for breakfast and lunch to 3pm.

Rainbow Foods 224 4th St ☎ 907/586-6476. Wholefood and organic grocery serving a limited selection of light lunches (Mon–Fri), plus a salad bar. Try the homemade cookies and espresso.

Silverbow Bakery 120 2nd St ☎ 907/586-4146. Relaxed eat-in bakery and coffee bar with bagels and superb pastries bolstering a menu of homemade breads used in hot and cold deli sandwiches ($6–11).

Uncle Sam's Cafeteria 2nd floor, 709 W 9th St ☎ 907/586-3430. Low-cost dining with a view, inside the Federal Building. Open for breakfast ($5; 7–10.30am) and lunches including daily specials ($7; noon–4pm) such as taco salad and chicken fried steak.

Mendenhall Glacier and Tracy Arm Fjord

Thirteen miles from downtown, the one-and-a-half-mile-wide **Mendenhall Glacier** is the state's most accessible. The **visitor center** (daily 8am–7.30pm; $3) is built on a point occupied by the glacier as recently as 1940. Hiking **trails** include the West Glacier Trail, on which, with extreme caution and without official approval, you can explore the ice caves. Capital Transit **buses** leave for Mendenhall hourly from downtown; get off at Glacier Spur Road for the visitor center, or Montana Creek Road for the West Glacier trail. MGT (☎ 907/789-5460) charges $6 each way from town as part of their Glacier Express tour. Temsco (☎ 1-877/789-9501, ⓦ www.temscoair.com; $199) offers one-hour **helicopter trips** with 25 minutes on the glacier itself.

One of the best day-trips out of Juneau is up the narrow, twisting **Tracy Arm fjord**, with waterfall-fringed cliffs and common sightings of whales and seals. Take one of the day-long **cruises** with Adventure Bound Alaska (☎ 1-800/228-3875, ⓦ ww.adventureboundalaska.com; $120).

Glacier Bay National Park

Alaska's finest array of tidewater glaciers feed into **GLACIER BAY**, sixty miles northwest of Juneau. Sixteen glaciers surround this tranquil 65-mile-long wilderness where the flora ranges from mature spruce forests to delicate plant life. Brown and black bears, moose, mountain goats, sea otters, humpback whales, porpoise, seals, and a colorful array of birds have made the area their home. It is an expensive place to visit requiring a flight from Juneau to Gustavus ($90–130 roundtrip) with either Alaska Airlines or LAB (☎ 907/789-9160, ⓦ www.labflying.com). Glacier access is by **day-cruise** (8hr; $170) from nearby Bartlett Cove, and you'll also need at least one night's **accommodation**. At Bartlett Cove you can camp for free or stay at *Glacier Bay Lodge* (☎ 1-888/229 8687, ⓦ www.visitglacierbay.com; ❼), with tasteful rooms, a good restaurant, and cruise bookings. Further accommodation can be found in Gustavus in the form of 🏃 *Bear's Nest B&B* (☎ 907/679-2440, ⓦ www.gustavus/bearsnest; ❹), a completely self-contained and fully furnished cabin with a double bed upstairs and a single futon down, plus a more basic A-frame. Eat next door to the *Bear's Nest Café*.

Haines

The small community of **HAINES** sits on a peninsula between the Chilkat and the Chilkoot inlets at the northern end of the longest and deepest fjord in the US,

Lynn Canal. The town tends to be overshadowed by its brasher neighbor, Skagway, but it remains a real Alaska experience nonetheless. The community itself is an interesting mix of locals and urban escapees from the Lower 48.

The Tlingit fished and traded here for years before 1881, when the first missionaries arrived. Today, the town survives on fishing and tourism, and though cruise ships tend to press on to Skagway, it remains a popular spot, hosting in mid-August the cookouts, crafts, and log-rolling of the **Southeast Alaska Fair**. The fairgrounds also hold **Dalton City**, a free pioneer theme park notable only in that its buildings came from the movie sets of Jack London's *White Fang*, which was filmed in the Haines area in 1989.

Arrival and information

Haines's AMHS **ferry** terminal is five miles north of town, with a daily service to and from Juneau and Skagway. Local **taxis** meet all ferry arrivals; downtown should cost $10, but ask before you board. Chilkat Cruises & Tours (☎907/766-2100 or 1-888/766-2103, ⓦwww.chilkatcruises.com) runs a convenient passenger-only fast ferry ($25 one-way, $45 roundtrip) between Haines and Skagway from a dock near Fort Seward. The **visitor center**, 122 Second St (Mon–Fri 8am–7pm, Sat & Sun 9am–6pm; ☎1-800/458-3579, ⓦwww.haines.ak.us), has all kinds of maps and information.

Accommodation

As well as the usual mid-range **accommodation**, Haines has half a dozen handy **campgrounds**.

Bear Creek Cabins and Hostel Small Tract Rd ☎907/766-2259, ⓦbearcreekcabinsalaska.com. Good hostel over a mile south of Fort Seward with coin-op laundry and no lock-out or curfew. Campers ($14 for two) can use hostel facilities. Dorms $18, cabins ❷

Port Chilkoot Camper Park Mud Bay Rd beside Fort Seward ☎1-800/542-6363, ⓦwww.hotelhalsingland.com. Central campsite with pay-showers and a laundromat on site. Full hookup $25, dry RV $16, tents $10.

Portage Cove State Recreation Site Beach Rd, half a mile southeast of Fort Seward. A small site for backpackers and cyclists only. It's right by the beach and has great views and potable water. No overnight parking. $5.

Summer Inn B&B 117 2nd Ave ☎907/766-2970, ⓦwww.summerinnbnb.com. Immaculately kept downtown B&B with shared-bath rooms, some with sea views and all including a good cooked breakfast. It has a very homey feel with clawfoot baths, quilts, and fresh flowers. ❻

The Town

In the center of town, the **Sheldon Museum & Cultural Center**, 11 Main St (Mon–Fri 10am–5pm, Sat & Sun 1–4pm; ⓦwww.sheldonmuseum.org; $3), does a great job of showing how Haines fits into its Chilkat environment and the wider Tlingit world, and exhibits fine examples of woodwork, clothing, and the distinctive yellow and black Chilkat blanket in wolf, raven, and killer whale designs.

Half a mile away, grassy **Fort William H. Seward** was established in 1903 to contain general Gold Rush lawlessness, and territorial disputes with Canada. It is now the site of **Alaska Indian Arts** (Mon–Fri 9am–5pm; free), with a gallery for locally produced sculpture, photos, and carving, and a back room where you can watch and chat to carvers as they work on huge totem poles.

Nearby, the stuffed birds of the **American Bald Eagle Foundation**, 113 Haines Hwy at Second Avenue (daily 10am–6pm; $3), make a poor substitute for seeing the world's largest gathering of **bald eagles**, which flock to the banks of the Chilkat River each fall. By November over three thousand of these once-endangered rare birds – as many as two dozen to a tree – are gathered along a five-mile sand bar at the **Chilkat Bald Eagle Preserve**, nine miles north of town on the Haines Highway.

Two great, wild **state parks** – Chilkoot Lake and Chilkat – are just a half-hour cycle ride to the north and south of town respectively. Chilkat in particular has some good trails and vistas, while well-tramped treks lead from town to the summits of Mount Riley and the much more difficult Mount Ripinsky. Haines is also a popular starting point for **rafting trips**: Chilkat Guides on Beach Road (☎907/766-2491, ⓦwww.raftalaska.com) is one of many operators to offer four-hour **float trips** ($79) down the Chilkat River, ideal for viewing eagles and other wildlife.

Eating and drinking

Haines's most exciting **bars** and **restaurants** can be found in the Fort Seward area. In the evening visitors converge on the friendly bar at the *Hotel Hälsingland*, while some locals stick to the more raucous joints downtown.

Bamboo Room 11 2nd St near Main ☎907/766-2800. Standard diner popular for its well-prepared meals (especially the locally caught halibut and chip dinner), and fresh-baked pies.

Chilkat Restaurant and Bakery 5th Ave & Dalton St ☎907/766-3653. A great spot for some of their baked goods with an espresso coffee, or more substantial fare. They do everything from tasty breakfasts, salads and halibut sandwiches to regular Thai lunches for $10, all beautifully cooked.

Mountain Market & Café 151 3rd Ave at Haines Hwy ☎907/766-3340. Combined natural-food grocery and espresso bar that's one of the best places in town for a $6 bagel breakfast, a $7 tortilla wrap, or just a muffin with your mocha.

Skagway and around

SKAGWAY, the northernmost ferry stop on the southeast route, sprang up overnight in 1897 as a trading post serving **Klondike Gold Rush** pioneers about to set off on the five-hundred-mile ordeal. Having grown from one cabin to a town of twenty thousand in three months, Skagway, rife with disease and desperado violence, was reported to be "hell on earth." It boasted over seventy bars and hundreds of prostitutes, and was controlled by organized criminals, including **Jefferson "Soapy" Smith**, notorious for cheating hapless prospectors out of their gold.

By 1899, the Gold Rush was over, but the completion in 1900 of the White Pass and Yukon Route railway from Skagway to Whitehorse, the Yukon capital, ensured Skagway's survival. Today, the town's eight hundred residents have gone to great lengths to maintain (or recreate) the original appearance of their home, much of which lies in the **Klondike Gold Rush National Historic Park**, and in summer as many as five cruise ships a day call in to appreciate the effort.

Arrival, information, and getting around

AMHS ferries and an independent operator (see p.1234) arrive daily from Haines and Juneau at the foot of the main thoroughfare, Broadway, and just a block from the **train station** from where WP&YR trains (see p.1236) head inland. Yukon Alaska Tourist Tours (reservations essential ☎1-866/626-7383, ⓦwww.yatt.ca), run a bus from Skagway to Whitehorse ($40) and a train-bus combo ($95).

Skagway is very compact, and most of the sights can easily be seen on foot. The Klondike Gold Rush National Historic Park **visitor center**, Broadway at 2nd Avenue (daily 8am–6pm; ☎907/983-2223, ⓦwww.nps.gov/klgo), holds talks, leads walking tours, and has historical displays and an impressive movie about the Gold Rush, as well as maps and information on the Chilkoot Trail. Skagway's **visitor center** (daily 8am–6pm; ☎1-888/762-1898, ⓦwww.skagway.org) is on Broadway between Second and Third avenues in the Arctic Brotherhood Hall building.

Accommodation

In such a touristy little town, **accommodation** prices run slightly high, and rooms are often reserved far in advance.

At the White House 475 8th Ave at Main St ☎ 907/983-9000, ⓦ www.atthewhitehouse. com. High-standard B&B in one of Skagway's original homes; restored and modernized rooms with super-comfy beds, cable TV, and ceiling fans. A continental breakfast buffet is served and there's always tea, coffee, and home-baked cookies on hand. ❺

Chilkoot Trail Outpost Dyea ☎ 907/983-3799, ⓦ www.chilkoottrailoutpost.com. Comfortable modern log cabins in the woods at this welcoming B&B located almost 9 miles from Skagway and a quarter mile from the start of the Chilkoot Trail. Cabins sleep up to four and come with bedding, TV, microwave, fridge, and coffeemaker. Cheaper "Hikers' Cabins" come with bunks and bedding but lack microwave and fridge. Free bikes, WiFi, and breakfast are included for all guests. Large cabins ❻, hikers ❺

Cindy's Place Mile 0.2 Dyea Rd ☎ 1-800/831-8095, ⓦ www.alaska.net/~croland. Three cabins in the woods two miles from downtown Skagway, one budget, two more luxurious log-built affairs with private bathrooms (one with a wood-burning stove), phone, and cooking equipment. All guests have free use of the hot tub and there are thoughtful touches like a dozen varieties of tea and coffee in the cabins, plus homemade jams and jellies for breakfast. Deluxe ❺, budget ❷

Skagway Home Hostel 3rd Ave and Main St ☎ 907/983-2131, ⓦ www.skagwayhostel.com. In-with-the-family hostel in a century-old building with bunks in single-sex dorms ($20), mixed dorms ($20) and one private room (❷). There's a communal feel, ample supplies for cooking (honesty box), and an 11pm curfew. ❷

Skagway Mountain View RV Park Broadway at 12th Ave ☎ 1-888/778-7700, ⓦ www.alaskarv .com. Large RV-dominated spot with all the expected facilities, water and electricity hookup ($30), dry sites ($20), and a few wooded tent sites ($17) that are in high demand.

The Town

Strolling up Broadway you can't miss the eye-catching facade of the 1899 **Arctic Brotherhood Hall**, decorated with almost nine thousand pieces of driftwood and housing the Skagway Visitor Center. Many of the other buildings hereabouts form part of the **Klondike Gold Rush National Historic Park**, notably the former **Mascot Saloon** on Broadway (daily 8am–6pm; free), and **Moore House**, Fifth Avenue at Spring Street (daily 10am–5pm; free), a museum **devoted to** Skagway's original resident that features stories and photos of the Gold Rush. There's further detail in the recently refurbished **City of Skagway Museum** (Mon–Fri 9am–5pm, Sat 10am–5pm, Sun 10am–4pm; $2), which contains Soapy's Derringer pistol and good Tlingit artifacts.

If you've had enough of Soapy and his cronies, you may feel like **hiking**. The useful *Skagway Trail Map*, available from the visitor center, details other walks in the area, including those in the Dewey Lakes system, which pass pretty subalpine lakes and tumbling waterfalls, and the more difficult scramble up AB Mountain. Sockeye Cycles, Fifth Avenue and Broadway (☎ 907/983-2851, ⓦ www. cyclealaska.com), rents out well-maintained **mountain bikes** for $20 a half-day, and the neighboring Mountain Shop (☎ 907/983-2544) rents and sells backpacking supplies.

A lazier way to take in the scenery is on the **White Pass and Yukon Route** railway (early May to late Sept; 2–3 departures daily; ☎ 1-800/343-7373, ⓦ wpyr.com), which follows the gushing Skagway River upstream past waterfalls and ice-packed gorges and over a 1000ft-high wooden trestle bridge, stopping at the White Pass summit ($95 roundtrip) before occasionally continuing to Lake Bennett, British Columbia ($150; steam-hauled $180). There's no shortage of riders, so get there early and grab a seat on the left-hand side going up. The company also offers a through bus service to Whitehorse.

Eating and drinking

Most of Skagway's **bars** and **restaurants** line the touristy part of Broadway.

The Haven State St at 9th Ave ☎907/983-3553. Relaxed coffee shop with sofas and stacks of magazines, serving good espresso, egg or granola breakfasts, mouthwatering panini and fresh salads – Santa Fe, Greek, Caesar – all available with added chicken ($7–9).

Red Onion Saloon Broadway at 2nd Ave ☎907/983-2222. An 1898 bar and former bordello with heaps of character, draft beers, and excellent pizza.

Sabrosa Broadway at 6th Ave ☎907/983-2469. Daytime café and bakery tucked in behind the gift shops that's great for breakfast (from $5) and lunches of burritos ($8), vegetarian chili (cup $4, bowl $6), and tarragon, pecan, and chicken salad ($9). Shaded outdoor seating for those hot days.

Stowaway Café 205 Congress Way ☎907/983-3463. Stop by in the evening for the likes of lemongrass halibut ($22), back baby ribs ($22), and peach bread pudding ($6), all served in a congenial atmosphere with views of the small boat harbor. Open nightly 4pm–10pm.

The Chilkoot Trail

Alaska's most famous trail, the 33-mile **CHILKOOT TRAIL**, is a hike through one huge wilderness museum following the footsteps of the original Klondike prospectors. Starting in **Dyea**, nine miles from Skagway, and ending in **Bennett** in Canada, the trail climbs through rainforest to tundra often strewn with haunting reminders of the past, including ancient boilers that once drove aerial tramways, and several collapsed huts.

The three- to five-day hike can be strenuous, especially the final ascent up from Sheep Camp (1000ft) to Chilkoot Pass (3550ft). You must be **self-sufficient** for food, fuel, and shelter, and be prepared for foul weather. Campgrounds line the trail, as well as emergency shelters with stoves and firewood. There are also ranger stations at Dyea, Sheep Camp, and Lindeman City. Dyea is accessible by road, and the White Pass and Yukon Railway runs a service for hikers returning to Skagway (Sun & Mon only; $80).

The main hiking season runs from July to early September, when there is a quota system administered by Parks Canada (🅦www.pc.gc.ca/chilkoot). Whether you

△ Hiking the Chilkoot Trail

15

ALASKA | Southeast Alaska

have a reservation or not, you must first visit the Skagway **Trail Center**, Broadway at 1st Avenue (early June to early Sept daily 8.30am–4.30pm), where rangers make sure you understand the challenges and dangers, and can advise on weather conditions and current bus and train schedules for the trip back to Skagway. While here, you must also pay out a rather extravagant Can$55 for a permit.

Anchorage

Wedged between the two arms of Cook Inlet and the imposing Chugach Mountains, **ANCHORAGE** is home to over forty percent of Alaska's population and is the state's transport hub. A sprawling city on the edge of one of the world's great wildernesses, it often gets bad press from those who live elsewhere in the state and deride it as "just half an hour from Alaska." However, it has its attractions and, with its beautiful setting, can make a pleasant one- or two-day stopover.

Anchorage was born in 1915 as a tent city for Alaska Railroad construction workers. During the 1930s, hopefuls fleeing the Depression poured in from the Lower 48, and World War II – and construction of the Alaska Highway – further boosted the city. The opening of the airport established Anchorage – midway between New York and Tokyo – as the "Crossroads of the World", and statehood in 1959 and the 1970s oil boom brought in yet more optimistic adventurers.

Arrival and information

Anchorage International Airport, five miles southwest of town, is served by bus #7, part of the citywide **People Mover** system (Mon–Fri 6am–11pm, Sat 8am–8pm, Sun 9.30am–6.30pm; $1.75 flat fare or $4 day-pass from the driver). Alaska Shuttle Service (☎907/388-8888) charges $10 to take you downtown ($5 each for three or more passengers), and taxis cost around $20. The **train station** is downtown at 411 W 1st Ave (☎1-800/544-0552, ⓦwww.alaskarailroad.com), and the major sights are easily reached on foot.

The **Log Cabin Visitor Center**, downtown at 4th and F (daily: May & Sept 8am–6pm; June–Aug 7.30am–7pm; Oct–April 9am–4pm; ☎907/274-3531, ⓦwww.anchorage.net), has all the brochures you could need and details of an easy self-guided downtown walking tour. Across the street, the **Alaska Public Lands Information Center** (June–Aug daily 9am–5pm; rest of year Mon–Fri 10am–5pm; ☎907/271-2737, ⓦwww.nps.gov/aplic) has an excellent natural history display plus maps and more brochures. It'll help plan trips into the Interior, and make reservations both for accommodation and the shuttle bus in Denali National Park – vital in summer.

Accommodation

Inexpensive **accommodation** in Anchorage can be hard to find, especially in summer when many places are fully booked. **Campers** should head for the central *Ship Creek Landings RV Park*, 150 N Ingra (☎907/227-0877, ⓦwww.alaskarv. com; $14), or the more woodsy *Centennial Campground* (☎907/343-6986; $15), five miles north on the Glenn Highway.

Anchorage Guesthouse 2001 Hillcrest Drive ☎907/274-0408, ⓦwww.akhouse.com. Upscale backpacker-style hostel, just over a mile from downtown and handy for the Coastal Trail (rent a bike for $2.50 per hour). Other perks include sheets, towels, breakfast, use of kitchen, free gear storage, free local calls, and Internet access. Dorm beds cost $30 and there are private doubles and kings. ❸

Anchorage International Hostel 700 H St ☎907/276-3635, ⓦwww.anchorageinternationalhostel

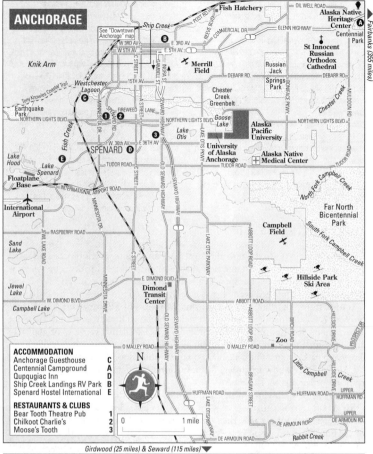

ANCHORAGE

Fish Hatchery
Ship Creek
OIL WELL ROAD
POST RD.
REEVE BLVD.
COMMERCIAL DR.
GLENN HIGHWAY
Alaska Native Heritage Center **A**
Centennial Park
B
W 3RD AV
W 5TH AV
E 3RD AV
E 5TH AV
St Innocent Russian Orthodox Cathedral
Fairbanks (355 miles)

Knik Arm

Merrill Field
15TH AV
DEBARR RD.
Russian Jack Springs Park
DEBARR RD.
Chester Creek Greenbelt
MULDOON RD.

Westchester Lagoon **C**
Tony Knowles Coastal Trail
NORTHERN LIGHTS BLVD.
Goose Lake
Lake Otis
Alaska Pacific University
Chester Creek
NORTHERN LIGHTS BLVD.

Earthquake Park
NORTHERN LIGHTS BLVD.
1 2
FIREWEED LANE
SPENARD **D**
W 36TH AV
E 36TH AV
3
University of Alaska Anchorage
Alaska Native + Medical Center

Fish Creek
MINNESOTA DR.
Lake Hood
Lake Spenard **E**
Floatplane Base
INTERNATIONAL AIRPORT ROAD
TUDOR ROAD
TUDOR ROAD
North Fork Campbell Creek

International Airport

Sand Lake
JEWEL LAKE ROAD
RASPBERRY ROAD
C STREET
LAKE OTIS PARKWAY
ABBOTT LOOP ROAD
Campbell Field
South Fork Campbell Creek
Far North Bicentennial Park

Jewel Lake
E. DIMOND BLVD.
Dimond Transit Center
SEWARD HIGHWAY
OLD SEWARD HIGHWAY
ABBOTT ROAD
Hillside Park Ski Area
BIRCH RD.
HILLSIDE DRIVE

Campbell Lake
W. DIMOND BLVD.
MINNESOTA DRIVE
O MALLEY ROAD
O MALLEY ROAD
Zoo
Little Campbell Creek
PROSPECT

ACCOMMODATION
Anchorage Guesthouse **C**
Centennial Campground **A**
Qupquigiaq Inn **D**
Ship Creek Landings RV Park **B**
Spenard Hostel International **E**

RESTAURANTS & CLUBS
Bear Tooth Theatre Pub **1**
Chilkoot Charlie's **2**
Moose's Tooth **3**

HUFFMAN ROAD
BRAGAW STREET
HUFFMAN ROAD
HILLSIDE DRIVE
UPPER
HUFFMAN RD.

N

0   1 mile

DE ARMOUN ROAD
LAKE OTIS PKWY.
DE ARMOUN ROAD
UPPER
DE ARMOUR ROAD
Rabbit Creek

Girdwood (25 miles) & Seward (115 miles) ▼

15

ALASKA | Anchorage

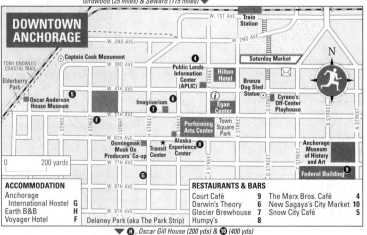

DOWNTOWN ANCHORAGE

W. 1ST AVE
Train Station
W. 2ND AVE

TONY KNOWLES COASTAL TRAIL
Captain Cook Monument
W. 3RD AVE
Public Lands Information Center (APLIC)
4
Hilton Hotel
Saturday Market

N

Elderberry Park
W. 4TH AVE
Imaginarium
6
Bronze Dog Sled Statue
Cyrano's Off-Center Playhouse

Oscar Anderson House Museum **5**
7
Egan Center (i)

F
W. 5TH AVE
Performing Arts Center
Town Square Park

K STREET
L STREET
W. 6TH AVE
Oomingmak Musk Ox Producers' Co-op
Alaska Transit Center
Alaska Experience Center
8
Anchorage Museum of History and Art

W. 7TH AVE
G
Federal Building
9

0   200 yards
W. 8TH AVE

ACCOMMODATION
Anchorage International Hostel **G**
Earth B&B **H**
Voyager Hotel **F**

W. 9TH AVE
Delaney Park (aka The Park Strip)

RESTAURANTS & BARS
Court Café **9**
Darwin's Theory **6**
Glacier Brewhouse **7**
Humpy's **8**
The Marx Bros. Café **4**
New Sagaya's City Market **10**
Snow City Café **5**

▼ **H**, Oscar Gill House (200 yds) & **10** (400 yds)

.org. Functional and very central hostel with luggage storage, Internet access, and laundry along with a daytime lock-out and evening curfew. Dorm beds $20; reserve well ahead in summer.
Earth B&B 1001 W 12th Ave ☎907/279-9907, ⓦwww.earthbb.com. Enthusiastically and liberally run, this is home away from home for Denali-bound climbers. It's simple but very accommodating, with a barbecue out back. Bus #6, #36, or #60 from downtown. ❸
Oscar Gill House 1344 W 10th Ave ☎907/279-1344, ⓦwww.oscargill.com. Lovely B&B in a 1913 house, comprehensively restored while maintaining character and understated elegance. Two rooms share a bath while the largest has its own jacuzzi, all tastefully done and managed by very welcoming hosts. Private bath ❺, shared ❹

Qupqugiac Inn 640 W 36th Ave, midtown ☎907/563-5633, ⓦwww.qupq.com. Great budget hotel with clean, simple rooms with phone and satellite TV, and a communal lounge with kitchen and free Internet. Bus #9 from downtown passes a block away on Arctic Blvd. Rooms with bath ❹, without ❸
Spenard Hostel International 2845 W 42nd Place ☎907/248-5036, ⓦwww.alaskahostel. org. Friendly suburban hostel with nearby mall just a mile and a half from the airport (bus #6). $10 bike rental, no curfew or lock-out, and dorm beds for $21.
Voyager Hotel 501 K St at 5th Ave ☎1-800/247-9070, ⓦwww.voyagerhotel.com. The best of the mid- to upper-range hotels featuring spacious rooms (with kitchenette) and most of the facilities of a business hotel at much lower cost. Reserve well in advance in summer. ❼

The City

Travelers eager to rush off into the "real" Alaska tend to overlook cosmopolitan Anchorage – a blend of old and new, urban blight and rural parks – but there is plenty to see, and it's worth spending some time experiencing it. The city is laid out on a grid; numbered avenues run east–west, lettered streets north–south.

Your first stop should be the **Anchorage Museum of History and Art**, 121 W Seventh Ave (summer daily 9am–6pm and to 9pm on Thurs; rest of year Tues–Sat 10am–6pm, Sun noon–5pm; $8), providing an excellent overview of the state and its history through intricate dioramas, alongside beautiful examples of carved ivory and basketware. The art gallery on the ground floor is notable for the works by Alaska's best-known painter, Sydney Laurence, including a monumental oil painting of Mount McKinley.

The rest of the downtown sights are more modest: the **Imaginarium**, 737 W Fifth Ave (Mon–Sat 10am–6pm, Sun noon–5pm; $5.50) has hands-on displays telling you all about glaciers, the Northern Lights, polar bears, and the private life of the dopey-looking moose; the period-furnished 1915 **Oscar Anderson House Museum**, 420 M St (June to mid-Sept Mon–Fri noon–5pm; $3), illustrates early Anchorage life; and the **Alaska Experience Theater**, Sixth Avenue and G Street (summer daily 9am–9pm; $10), presents forty minutes of Alaska's best scenery, shot from choppers and beamed onto a 180° wraparound screen; the admission price includes a film of the devastating 1964 Good Friday **earthquake** that leveled much of downtown – North America's strongest-ever quake at Magnitude 9.2.

Seven miles east on the edge of town lies the **Alaska Native Heritage Center**, off the Glenn Highway at Muldoon Road (summer daily 9am–6pm; $21). Although pricey, it gives an excellent introduction to the state's five main ethnic groups, each represented by a typical house where Native guides interpret their culture. Throughout the day, cultural groups perform in the main auditorium, where there is also an instructive introductory film. A free shuttle runs to the Center from the Anchorage Museum and Ship Creek Center, while People Mover #4 takes almost an hour to get here from downtown.

On long summer days it is better to stay outside, perhaps strolling (or biking) along the **Tony Knowles Coastal Trail**, which offers restorative views of Turnagain Arm, or exploring the mountains and lakes of the 495,000-acre **Chugach State Park**, just fifteen minutes' drive east from Anchorage. Challenging trails traversing the park include an often treacherous scramble up 4500ft Flattop Mountain, giving spectacular views of the city and Cook Inlet.

Eating, drinking, and nightlife

Nowhere in Alaska will you find a more diverse range of places to eat than in Anchorage. That's not to say you'd make a special journey here for the culinary wonders, but after a few weeks in the wilds, the city can seem like heaven. For groceries, make for Carr's supermarket at the junction of Northern Lights Boulevard and Minnesota Drive (bus #3, #4, or #36), which has a strong deli section.

Good **bars** abound downtown, and the atmosphere varies as much as the clientele. Also visit the lively (and somewhat edgy) neighborhood of **Spenard** – on Spenard Road between Northern Lights Boulevard and International Airport Road – which can be fun as long as you're careful. Women travelers may not find the "bohemian" side of macho Anchorage quite as endearing as some locals do, with some innocent-looking bars turning out to be strip joints. Shows, plays, opera, and concerts take place at the **Center for Performing Arts** (☎907/263-2787).

Bear Tooth Theatre Pub 1230 W 27th Ave ☎907/276-4200, ⒲www.beartooththeatre.net. Top-notch combined restaurant, bar, and cinema where, for $3 on top of your meal price, you can also watch an arthouse movie. The menu has a wide range – halibut chowder ($4), Caesar salads ($6), burritos and tacos ($5–8), and gourmet pizzas ($15 for a 16-inch), and the microbrews are excellent.

Chilkoot Charlie's 2435 Spenard Rd ☎907/272-1010, ⒲www.koots.com. Sawdust-strewn barn that packs them in nightly for pricey drinks, pool, foosball, two floors of DJ-led dance, and live music from 9.30pm.

Court Café 222 W 7th at C St ☎907/277-6736. Breakfast and lunch cafeteria that's about the best budget value downtown, certainly a cut above the fast-food joints and more filling. Steaming clam chowder or an entrée will cost around $5.

Darwin's Theory 426 G St at 4th Ave ☎907/277-5322. Straightforward local bar good for moderately priced boozing and neighborly encounters with colorful local characters.

Glacier Brewhouse 737 W 5th St ☎907/274-2739 ⒲www.glacierbrewhouse.com. Hugely popular restaurant, bar, and microbrewery serving wonderful food and drink. At least half a dozen toothsome house-brewed beers accompany alderwood-baked gourmet pizza ($11), spit-grilled three-peppercorn prime rib ($25), or steamed Alaska King crab legs ($37).

Humpy's 610 W 6th Ave ☎907/276-2337, ⒲www.humpys.com. Popular watering hole with live music and a strong college-bar feel. The likes

of charbroiled salmon, burgers, soups, and salads (mostly about $10) slip down with local microbrews plus English and Belgian bottled beers, and over thirty single malts.

The Marx Bros. Café 627 W 3rd Ave ☎907/278-2133, ⒲www.marxcafe.com. The best all-round fine dining downtown served up in a historic house with views of the water. Start on the likes of Kachemak Bay oysters with pepper vodka and ginger sorbet ($13) or Neapolitan seafood mousse ($15), followed by baked halibut rolled in a macadamia-nut crust and curry sauce and chutney ($30). Dinner only.

Moose's Tooth 3300 Old Seward Hwy at 33rd Ave ☎907/258-2537, ⒲www.moosestooth.net. A perennial favorite, always alive with folks tucking into some of the town's best gourmet pizza or sipping great microbrews.

New Sagaya's City Market 900 W 13th Ave at I St ☎907/274-6173. Trendy and expensive grocery store, deli, and café with a great selection ranging from organic vegetables and great cheeses to pizza, wraps, Thai dishes, and good coffee. The nearest groceries to downtown.

Snow City Café 1034 W 4th Ave ☎907/272-2489. The best place downtown for breakfast– eggs Benedict or Florentine for $9.50, yogurt, fruit & granola for $5 – or relaxing over a pot of Earl Grey and a slice of cake. Lunchtime options include soups, salads, pesto chicken pasta ($9), and tofu stir-fry ($9). Closed for dinner except for soup and sandwiches on Wednesday when there's an Irish music session.

15

ALASKA | Anchorage

Kenai Peninsula and Kodiak Island

South of Anchorage, the Seward Highway hugs the shore of **Turnagain Arm** past **Girdwood** and the ski resort of **Alyeska**. Just beyond, a side road cuts to the ever-popular **Portage Glacier**, and continues through a tunnel to **Whittier**, little more than a ferry dock for accessing Prince William Sound (see p.1247). Beyond Portage, the Seward Highway enters the **Kenai Peninsula**, "Anchorage's playground," which at over nine thousand square miles is larger than some states. The peninsula offers an endless diversity of activities and scenery, mostly concentrated around major communities such as **Seward**, the base for cruises into the inspirational **Kenai Fjords National Park**, and artsy **Homer**, where the waters and shorelines of the glorious **Kachemak Bay State Park** are the main destination. Most Alaskans come to the Kenai Peninsula to **fish**: the Kenai, Russian, and Kasilof rivers host "combat fishing," with thousands of anglers standing elbow to elbow using strength and know-how to pull in thirty-pound-plus king salmon. **Campgrounds** along the rivers fill up fast, especially in July and August.

A hundred miles beyond Homer in the Gulf of Alaska, the "Emerald Isle" of **Kodiak Island** offers some of Alaska's most uncommon and pleasing landscapes, and is home to the **Kodiak bear**, an overgrown subspecies of the grizzly.

Girdwood and Portage Glacier

Outdoorsy **GIRDWOOD**, 37 miles south of Anchorage, lies two miles inland in the shade of the **Alyeska Resort**, Alaska's largest winter sports complex and the lowest-elevation ski resort in the world, starting just 270 feet above sea level. Downhill runs and an extensive night-skiing operation run from November to mid-April (tows $52 a day), and in summer you can ride the Alyeska Tramway ($16) up to stunning views and some good hiking territory. Girdwood Ski and Cyclery, Mile 1.5 Alyeska Highway (T 907/783-2453; closed Mon & Tues), rents city **bikes** ($25 a day) to explore the town and coastal cycle path.

The resort's *Alyeska Prince Hotel* (T 907/754-1111 or 1-800/880-3880, W www. alyeskaresort.com; ●) is a grand ski lodge with half a dozen good restaurants and service to match. Alternatively, try *The Carriage House B&B*, Mile 0.2 Crow Creek Road (T 1-888/961-9464, W www.thecarriagehousebandb.com; ●), or *Alyeska Hostel* (T 907/783-2099), with $15 bunks. There's tasty, inexpensive **food** at ⅋ *The Bake Shop* (T 907/783-2831) on Olympic Mountain Loop at the base of the ski tows, and at the unmissable ⅋ *Double Musky Inn* on Crow Creek Road (T 907/783-2822): budget on $40 a head and a meal to remember.

Eleven miles south of Girdwood, a road leads to Whittier, past **Portage Glacier**, a popular day-tour from Anchorage. Frustratingly, you can't see the glacier from the parking lot; instead you must pay Gray Line $29 for a cruise around the lake's corner to the glacier's snout. Two USFS **campgrounds** ($10–13) can be found two or three miles back down the road.

Seward and Kenai Fjords National Park

SEWARD, ringed by glaciers and mountains 127 miles south of Anchorage, sprang to life in 1903 after engineers declared this ice-free port the ideal starting point for railroad tracks to the Interior. Since then it has been a key freight terminal, but tourism – particularly cruises into Kenai Fjords National Park – is now its most conspicuous business.

Seward's main activities are enjoying the scenery and visiting the wonders at the waterfront **SeaLife Center** (daily: summer 8am–7pm; $15), a successful marriage of marine research and visitor education partly funded by the Exxon Valdez oil spill settlement. The center offers the chance to watch ongoing cold-water research in action and marvel at the underwater antics of stellar sea lions, harbor seals, and adorable puffins. After a visit to the center, another good local option is the four-hour hike up nearby **Mount Marathon** for some glorious views. The trail here is also the scene of an annual Fourth of July race, thanks to the antics of two pioneers who, in 1909, bet each other to run up and down the 3022-foot mountain – the current race record is 43 minutes 23 seconds.

Most visitors also drive thirteen miles out to **Exit Glacier** (24hr; free), one of the few in the state you can approach on land. From the **nature centre** at the end of the road (summer daily 9am–8pm; free), a short stroll leads to the still-active glacier, though signs warn you back from the ice wall and its inviting blue clefts. Exit Glacier is part of **KENAI FJORDS NATIONAL PARK**, a magnificent 580,000-acre region of peaks, glaciers, and craggy coastline. Its towering mountains are mantled by the prodigious three-hundred-square-mile Harding Icefield, feeding the three dozen retreating glaciers, which have exposed the dramatic fjords after which the park is named. Eight of these tidewater glaciers "calve" icebergs into the sea with thunderous booms, and the fjords also hold a wealth of **marine wildlife** – sea otters, porpoises, seals, stellar sea lions, plus orca, gray, humpback, and minke whales – as well as the seabird rookeries on the cliffs of the Chiswell Islands. All the Seward-based **cruise** companies do a good job: try Renown Tours (☎1-888/514-8687; $69–129); pay out for the longer day-tours that go right up to the calving tidewater glaciers.

The park's **visitor center**, 1212 Fourth Ave in Seward's small boat harbor (summer daily 8.30am–7pm; ☎907/224-2125), provides maps, film shows, and details on regional hikes.

Practicalities

Trains from Anchorage (a lovely journey) arrive and depart daily (☎1-800/544-0552; $62 one-way, $103 roundtrip). Seward Bus Line (☎907/224-3608) charges $45 for a one-way ride from Anchorage. Seward's two hubs of activity, the small boat harbor and downtown, are joined by the mile-long Fourth Avenue, while the main **visitor center** is inconveniently situated at Mile 2 Seward Hwy (summer daily 8am–6pm; ☎907/224-8051, ⓦwww.sewardak.org). There's a shuttle bus (☎907/224-5569; $9 roundtrip) running from the small boat harbor hourly to Exit Glacier.

For budget **accommodation** downtown, go to the slightly cramped *Moby Dick Hostel*, 432 3rd Ave (mid-April to Sept; ☎907/224-7072, ⓦwww.mobydickhostel. com; ❸), with bunks ($19), limited kitchen facilities, and small private rooms, or try the more upscale *Murphy's Motel*, 911 Fourth Ave (☎907/224-8090 or 1-800/886-8191, ⓦwww.murphysmotel.com; ❺–❼), close to the small boat harbor. Rooms come with microwave, fridge, dataport, and cable TV, though older rooms are small. Alternatively, head out of town to the lovely ☀ *Alaska's Treehouse* (☎907/224-3867, ⓦwww.seward.net/treehouse; room ❹, suite ❺), a very welcoming B&B in a large timber house seven miles out along the Seward Highway (turn into Timber Lane Drive then Forest Rd). There's one room with a private (but separate) bathroom and a suite that sleeps up to five. Everyone gets a full sourdough-pancake breakfast and access to a hot tub out on the deck among the spruce trees. For campers, there's the excellent, centrally located *Waterfront Campground* (mid-April to Sept; ☎907/224-4055; tents $8, RVs $12–25), off Ballaine Boulevard and so close to the shores of Resurrection Bay you can almost fish from inside your tent.

Food in Seward is fairly reasonably priced: for good coffee or light meals, head to ☀ *Resurrect Art*, 320 3rd Ave (☎907/224-7161), a converted church where you can also play board games, while *Yoly's Bistro*, 220 4th Ave (☎907/224-3295) is a great downtown restaurant and bar serving soups, sandwiches, and the likes of lemongrass chicken ($15) and wasabi halibut ($20), with live music on weekends. For fine dining, try 🛪 *Ray's Waterfront* 1316 4th Ave (April–Oct; ☎907/224-5606), which is near the small boat harbor and has great mountain views. Pan-seared Thai scallops ($24), prime rib ($24), and more are all beautifully cooked. If you're looking for a good range of beers, stop at the lively *Yukon Bar*, 201 4th Ave at Washington St (☎907/224-3063), which also offers live music throughout the summer – jam session (Mon), karaoke (Wed), live bands (Thurs–Sat), and usually a set or two from Kenai Peninsula legend Hobo Jim on Sunday.

Homer and around

HOMER, 226 miles south from Anchorage, is the Kenai Peninsula's south-ernmost road-accessible town. It commands a truly magnificent setting, spread beneath gently sloping verdant bluffs with a four-mile finger of land – **The Spit** – slinking out into the dark waters of Kachemak Bay, into which flow crystal-blue glaciers, framed by dense black forest. With abundant activities, a lively nightlife, and a varied, youthful population that supports a thriving arts com-munity, it's so appealing you'll probably want to linger a few days extra.

Russians, drawn by the abundance of coal, were the first whites to reach the area, and by the mid-1800s several American companies had followed suit. In 1896, **Homer Pennock**, a gold-seeker from Michigan, set up the community that still bears his name. Every summer in recent years, young people from the Lower 48 have arrived here in droves to work on the halibut boats, many living in an impromptu tent city on the beach.

Arrival, information, and getting around

Ferries from Seldovia and Kodiak arrive at the end of The Spit. Homer Stage Lines (☎907/235-7009) runs a daily **bus** service between Anchorage and Homer for $60 each way. Most hotels, restaurants, and shops are in town, while almost all of the fishing charter and tour operators can be found along the twee boardwalks of The Spit. There is no public transport between the town and The Spit so hitch, grab a cab or rent a bike from Homer Saw & Cycle, 1532 Ocean Drive (☎907/235-8405; $25 a day). The main **visitor center** is at 201 Sterling Hwy (summer Mon–Fri 9am–7pm, Sat & Sun 10am–6pm; ☎907/235-7740, ⓦhomeralaska.org).

Accommodation

Homer's good-value **hotels** and **B&Bs** are often fully booked in midsummer; the visitor center, though, can help if you arrive without reservations.

🛪 **Driftwood Inn** 135 W Bunnel Ave ☎1-800/478-8019, ⓦwww.thedriftwoodinn. com. Rambling older hotel with an extensive and varied range of rooms, RV parking, and a com-munal TV lounge with video library. Breakfast is not included, though there is free tea and coffee (breakfast is available for a fee). Private bath ❹–❻, shared bath ❹

🛪 **Homer Hostel** 304 W Pioneer Ave ☎907/235-1463, ⓦwww.homerhostel.com. Centrally located hostel in a converted home where you sleep in made-up beds and bunks ($23), in 4- to 6-bed dorms, and relax in a big lounge with a great view of the mountains. There's no curfew or lock-out. Bikes and fishing rods can be rented for $10 and $5 a day, respectively. Rooms ❷

Homer Spit Camping ☎907235-1583. The classic Homer experience, either in tents on the beach or in RVs around the fishing hole. Within a short walk of each site, you'll find drinking water, toilets, and fish-cleaning tables. $8 per tent, $15 per RV.

Old Town B&B 106 W Bunnell Ave ☎907/235-7558. Beautiful, three-room B&B in a 1936 building. The rooms have wooden floors and a restrained decor of antiques, quilted bed covers, and old-fashioned bathroom fittings; two have tremendous

15

sea views (one with private bathroom). Breakfast (included) is at *Panarelli's*, downstairs. ❺

 Seaside Farm Hostel Mile 5 East End Rd ☏ 907/235-7850, ⓦ www.xyz.net/~seaside.

Small farm hostel with slightly cramped bunks ($20) and a lovely range of rooms, plus small cabins dotted around the property. Open May–Sept. Camping $10, rooms & cabins. ❸

The Town and around

Stop first at the new **Alaska Islands & Ocean Visitor Center**, 95 Sterling Hwy (summer daily 9am–6pm; ☏ 907/235-6961, ⓦ www.islandsandocean.org), designed to showcase various facets of the Alaska Maritime National Wildlife Refuge through interactive exhibits, replica seabird cliffs, and sections on the work of biologists in remote locations. Not far away, the **Pratt Museum**, 3779 Bartlett St (daily 10am–6pm; $6), features excellent displays on Kachemak Bay, its people and history along with remote-controlled cameras trained on nesting seabirds and the salmon-feeding bears. Many of Homer's most popular activities, however, revolve around The Spit. To Alaska anglers, Homer is "**Halibut Central**": a full day's fishing excursion with any of the charter companies begins at around $190. If you don't mind joining the crowds, it's cheaper and simpler to visit the **Fishing Hole**, a tiny bight on The Spit, which is stocked with salmon and offers good fishing from mid-May to mid-September.

The prime tourist attraction in the Homer area is **Kachemak Bay State Park**, directly across the bay, with its 250,000 acres of forested mountains, glaciers, pristine fjords, and inlets. Bird species here include puffin, auklets, kittiwakes, and storm petrels, and marine creatures such as seals, sea otters, and whales are also plentiful. The most popular destination is the gorgeous hamlet of **Halibut Cove**, where boardwalks link art galleries and *The Saltry* restaurant: the *Danny J* **ferry** (☏ 907/235-7847) makes two daily trips to Halibut Cove, on the south shore of the bay, via Gull Island rookery, for $48 roundtrip, $25 if you book in for an evening meal.

The area's best trails, most of them manageable in a day, are those in Kachemak Bay State Park, on the south side of Kachemak Bay: pick up the park's hiking-trails leaflet ($2) and other information from the visitor center. The most-traveled route, up to **Grewingk Glacier**, is an easy three-and-a-half-mile trek above the spruce and cottonwood forest to the foot of the glacier, from where you get splendid views of the bay.

Eating and drinking

Not surprisingly, Homer's culinary scene focuses mostly on fresh fish. For **nightlife**, head out to a colorful bar or to the relaxed **Pier One Theater** (June–Aug; ☏ 907/235-7333), next to the fishing hole on the Spit.

Café Cups 162 Pioneer Ave ☏ 907/235-8330. Relaxing yet vibrant café serving some of the best coffee and great sandwiches and salads.

 Fat Olive's 276 Olsen Lane ☏ 907/235-3448. Chic modern restaurant with strong Italian leanings, excellent pizza, a convivial atmosphere, and a good selection of microbrews.

Lands End Resort at the end of The Spit ☏ 907/235-0400 or 1-800/478-0400. Plush and not-too-pricey restaurant offering an absolutely wonderful view of the bay as well as a fairly

standard but tasty Alaska menu. Breakfast is a must.

Salty Dawg The Spit. No self-respecting drinker should pass up a few jars in the *Dawg* with its dark interior, life preservers pinned to the wall, and what is reliably claimed to be the only surveyors' benchmark located in a bar in the US.

 Two Sisters Espresso/Bakery 233 E Bunnell Ave ☏ 907/235-2280. Great little spot for that morning coffee either in the bakery or at tables out on the deck. Good too for pizza, soups, and quiches at moderate prices.

Kodiak

A nine-hour ferry ride connects Homer with **KODIAK ISLAND**, at a hundred miles long and sixty wide, the largest island in the US. In the north it is thick with spruce forests, but the interior is carpeted by wild grasses studded with marshes, lumpy knolls, and reeded lakes. This is prime territory for the renowned **Kodiak bear**, a sub-species of the grizzly, which weighs up to 1500 pounds. Streams chock-full of spawning salmon allow these monsters to thrive in the **Kodiak National Wildlife Refuge**, covering the southwestern two-thirds of the island. Roughly ten bears inhabit each square mile around Red and Fraser lakes, and bear-watching trips are big business.

The warm **Japanese Current** that flows around the island supports a mild maritime climate along with plenty of rain and fog, creating poor flying conditions and the distinct possibility that your stay could be extended by a day or two. If you want to avoid peak-season prices, note that May and June are notoriously wet, but September weather is usually fairly reliable.

All but two thousand of the island's twelve thousand inhabitants live in and around its only major town, the likeable and busy fishing port of **KODIAK** on the northeastern tip. Before Russian explorers established a community here in 1792, Aleut and Alutiiq had fished the area for millennia. After Alaska was transferred to the US, Kodiak survived as a center for trappers, whale-hunters, and salmon-fishers, and in 1939 was just another sleepy Alaskan village when a massive military base was established here and the population rocketed to around fifty thousand. However, most of Kodiak's wealth comes from fishing the rich waters of the Gulf, and the town maintains a fleet of over six hundred fishing vessels. Tourism definitely plays second fiddle and few cruise ships stop here.

Arrival, information, and getting around

AMHS ferries from Homer dock downtown three times a week in summer. Alaska Airlines and ERA Aviation jointly dispatch eight one-hour flights a day from Anchorage at around $250 roundtrip. The local bus ($3) is very infrequent so you may want to catch a cab the five miles into town ($15). The helpful **visitor center** is by the ferry dock at 100 Marine Way (Mon–Fri 8am–5pm, Sat & Sun dependant on ferry arrivals; ☎907/486-4782, ⓦwww.kodiak.org). The **Kodiak National Wildlife Refuge Visitor Center**, 1390 Buskin River Rd, close to the airport, four miles south of town (April–Sept Mon–Fri 8am–7pm, Sat & Sun noon–4pm; ☎907/487-2600, ⓦwww.r7.fws.gov/nwr/kodiak), stocks a wealth of information on bears and the backcountry. It should move to a site beside the main visitor centre in 2008. **Accommodation** is quite expensive and there's no hostel, but at least there are plenty of good **places to eat**.

Accommodation

Most **lodging** in Kodiak is expensive, but the hotels and B&Bs are generally very good. *Kodiak Inn*, 236 Rezanof Drive West (☎1-888/563-4254, ⓦkodiakinn.com; ❻), the town's fanciest hotel, has eighty pleasant and well-equipped rooms, plus a restaurant and bar, while the *Shelikof Lodge*, 211 Thorsheim Ave (☎907/486-4141, ⓦwww.shelikoflodge.com; ❺), has Kodiak's cheapest hotel rooms, offering an on-site bar and restaurant plus a free airport shuttle. *Bev's Bed And Make Your Own Darn Breakfast!*, 1510 Mission Road (☎907/486-0834, ⓦwww.bevsbedandbreakfast .com; ❸), an easy walk from downtown, has queen-bedded rooms (one with private bath), and ingredients are available in the kitchen for you to cook all your meals. Campers can pitch a tent at *Fort Abercrombie State Historical Park*, four miles north of town (ⓦwww.dnr.state.ak.us/parks; $10 per site), and eat meals in the covered picnic area (prepayment required).

The Town and around

In **downtown Kodiak**, your first stop should be the small **Baranov Museum** (summer Mon–Sat 10am–4pm, Sun noon–4pm; $3), in an old Russian house opposite the dock, which holds Aleut, Russian, and American pioneer artifacts, including an impressive collection of whalebones. Nearby, the small but beautifully formed **Alutiiq Museum**, 215 Mission Rd (June–Aug Mon–Fri 9am-5pm, Sat 10am–5pm; $3), centers on the life and culture of the island's native people.

Etched out of lush rainforest, less than four miles north, **Fort Abercrombie State Historical Park** is a great place to do some seabird- and **whale-watching**, camp or take a shoreline hike: a meadow at the north end provides a dazzling blaze of color in summer. Other moderately easy **hiking trails** originating near town go to the top of Pillar Mountain and Termination Point. However, most trails are not maintained and can be confusing; get precise details from the visitor center or the rangers at Fort Abercrombie. The undulating and unpaved **Chiniak Highway** runs for 48 miles to Cape Greville and the *Road's End Restaurant*, sweeping through tightly bunched spruce and passing many abandoned World War II defenses, plus prime vistas of Chiniak Bay.

Eating and drinking

Food in Kodiak is generally good. *Henry's Great Alaskan*, 512 Marine Way (☎907/486-8844), a restaurant and sports bar with microbrewed beer, has a good range of salads, sandwiches, burgers, and dinners (like the halibut with fries) that cost around $14, while *Harborside Coffee and Goods*, 216 Shelikov St (☎907/486-5862), is just the spot for watching the harbor activity over an espresso or light meal. *Old Powerhouse*, 516 E Marine Way (☎907/481-1088; closed Mon), is a predominantly Japanese seafood restaurant with great views over the channel and excellent box-lunch specials for around $8.

Prince William Sound

Prince William Sound, a largely unspoiled wilderness of steep fjords and mountains, glaciers and rainforest, rests calmly at the head of the Gulf of Alaska. Sheltered by the Chugach Mountains in the north and east, and the Kenai Peninsula in the west, and with its sparkling blue waters full of whales, porpoise, sea otters, and seals, the Sound has a relatively low-key tourist industry. The only significant settlements, spectacular **Valdez**, at the end of the trans-Alaska pipeline, and **Cordova**, a fishing community only accessible by sea or air, are the respective bases for visiting the **Columbia** and **Childs glaciers**.

The region's first settlers, the Chugach Eskimos, were edged out by the more aggressive Tlingit, in their turn displaced by Russian trappers in search of sea otter pelts, and then by American gold prospectors and fishers. The whole glorious show was very nearly spoiled forever on Good Friday 1989, when the **Exxon Valdez** spilled eleven million gallons of its cargo of crude oil. Although the long-term effects have yet to be fully determined, the spill fortunately affected just a fifth of the Sound and today no surface pollution is visible.

Valdez

VALDEZ, 304 road miles from Anchorage and the Western Hemisphere's northernmost ice-free port, lies at the head of a fjord reaching twelve miles inland from Prince William Sound. Sometimes hyped as "Little Switzerland" for its stunning backdrop of mountains, glaciers, and waterfalls, and a record annual snowfall of over forty feet, Valdez (pronounced *val-Deez*) offers great hiking, rafting, sea kayaking, wildlife-viewing, and, of course, fishing.

The 1890s **Gold Rush** transformed Valdez from a remote whaling station into a flourishing settlement, when thousands of prospectors came to cross the deadly Valdez and Klutina glaciers on the Valdez Trail to the mines in the Yukon. Only three hundred of the 3500 miners who set out made it to the goldfield – those that did not perish from frostbite and starvation gave up. Valdez came to depend on fish canneries, logging, and occasional military use for its survival, but nature conspired to finish it off on Good Friday 1964: the epicenter of North America's largest **earthquake** was just 45 miles away. The ground turned to quivering jelly, snapping roads, toppling buildings, and killing 33 residents. However, the citizens of Valdez refused to be intimidated, and moved sixty-odd buildings to the more stable present site four miles away.

The town's fortunes rose again during the 1970s, when oil was found beneath Prudhoe Bay, and Valdez became the southern terminus of the 800-mile **trans-Alaska pipeline,** carrying close to a million barrels of oil per day. Although winds and tides kept the oil from the *Exxon Valdez* out of the port of Valdez, ironically the spill triggered an economic boom as the city became the base for the massive **cleanup.** The operation, which lasted into 1991, cost Exxon three billion dollars, and called on eleven thousand workers in over one thousand boats and three hundred planes to scour the beaches. All seems pristine now, though many species have still not fully recovered their former numbers.

Arrival and information

One of the most exciting things about Valdez is getting here; both car and ferry rides are unforgettable. The **Richardson Highway** holds epic scenery: restful alpine meadows, mountain glaciers, the icy summit of **Thompson Pass**, and the waterfall-fringed **Keystone Canyon**. Alaska/Yukon Trails (☎1-800/700-7275, ⓦwww.alaskashuttle.com) run along this route from Fairbanks, Delta Junction, and Glennallen, but only when numbers make the journey viable. **Ferries** from Cordova or Whittier dock at the end of Hazelet Avenue (☎907/835-4436). ERA Aviation (☎1-800/866-8394, ⓦwww.flyera.com) flies three times daily from Anchorage (from $90 plus tax each way) to the **airport** five miles north, from where **taxis** (☎907/835-2500) run downtown for around $10. The **visitor center** (summer Mon–Fri 8am–7pm, Sat 9am–6pm, Sun 10am–5pm; ☎1-800/770-5954, ⓦwww.valdezalaska.org) is at 200 Fairbanks St.

Accommodation

Valdez's **accommodation** gets snapped up pretty quickly and there's no hostel, but a free phone outside the visitor center connects with some of the fifty-plus **B&Bs**. **Campers** can choose between the central but busy *Bear Paw Camper Park* (☎907/835-2530; $20), and the inconvenient *Valdez Glacier Campground* (☎907/835-2282; $10), five miles from town past the airport. The cheapest rooms are at *L&L's B&B*, 533 W Hanagita St (☎907/835-4447, ⓦwww.lnlalaska.com; ❸), with five comfortable shared-bath rooms ten minutes' walk from the center, but with free bikes and a good breakfast. Other good candidates are the renovated *Keystone Hotel*, 401 Egan Drive (☎1-888/835-0665, ⓦwww.keystonehotel.com; ❹), which has comfortable rooms (some with bath) and a light continental breakfast; the motel-style *Downtown B&B Inn*, 113 Galena Drive (☎ 1-800/478-2791, ⓦwww.alaskaone.com/downinn; ❹); and *Valdez Harbor Inn*, 100 N Harbor Drive (☎1-888/222-3440, ⓦwww.valdezharborinn.com; ❻), a recently renovated *Best Western*, with a great waterside location, where rooms have cable TV, DVD player, microwave, fridge, and free WiFi.

The Town and around

The **Valdez Museum**, 217 Egan Drive (summer daily 9am–6pm; $5), carries just enough detail on the Gold Rush, oil terminal, glaciation, and *Exxon Valdez* oil spill. Its **annex**, at 436 S Hazelet Ave (summer daily 9am–6pm; $1.50), covers the 1964 earthquake at length. For security reasons, you can no longer tour the pipeline terminal; instead, take in the **Alaska Pipeline Media Tour and Exhibit** at the Community College, 303 Lowe St (summer daily 9.30am, 11.30am & 1.30pm; $5).

Out at the airport, the **Maxine & Jesse Whitney Museum** (summer daily 9.30am–7pm; $5) has an astounding collection of carved ivory and an assortment of dead beasts, including a couple of moose hides with Alaskan scenes burned into them by an early pioneer. If you fancy something more active, Anadyr Adventures (☎1-800/865-2925, ⊚www.anadyradventures.com) and Pangaea Adventures (☎1-800/660-9637, ⊚www.alaskasummer.com) offer **sea-kayaking** trips to Duck Flats (3–4hr; $55), or a more ambitious coastal paddle to Gold Creek (6–7hr; $75–80). It is worth making the effort to reach distant paddling destinations, (accessed by water taxi), principally Shoup Glacier (8hr; $150) and Columbia Glacier (10hr; $185–199). Both companies also offer **kayak rentals** (single $45 per day, double $65, triple $80), the rates reducing by $5–10 a day after the first or second day of rental. Anadyr Adventures rents **mountain bikes** as well, for $8 an hour.

You should also take a cruise out into Prince William Sound, principally to see the spectacular **Columbia Glacier**, three miles wide at its face and towering three hundred feet above the sea. Unfortunately it is receding rapidly and the fjord is now so choked with ice that you can't get close to the face. Weather permitting, you can see it at long range from the AMHS **ferries** running between Valdez and Whittier, but for a closer look go with Stan Stephens Glacier & Wildlife Cruises (☎1-866/867-1297, ⊚www.stanstephenscruises.com), who pick their way through a floating icefield and point out such sights as Bligh Reef, where the *Exxon Valdez* grounded. Choose between a six-hour cruise at $90 and the nine-hour cruise that also visits the Meares Glacier ($130).

Eating

The **dining** selection in Valdez, while nothing particularly special, should satisfy for the night or two you're here. The *Alaska Halibut House*, 208 Meals Ave (☎907/835-2788) serves budget halibut sandwiches and salmon wedges, but the best all-around dining is at *Alaska's Bistro* (☎907/835-5688, ⊚www.alaskasbistro .com) in the *Valdez Harbor Inn*. Oil-boom survivor *The Pipeline Club*, 136 Egan Drive (☎907/835-4332), is also worth a try for top-quality steak and seafood, as well as for its lively dark bar.

Cordova and the Copper River Delta

Far quieter than Valdez, and only accessible by sea or air, **CORDOVA** is an unpretentious fishing community on the southeastern edge of the Sound. In 1906 Irish engineer **Michael J. Heney** chose Cordova as the port for the copper mined in Kennicott, a hundred miles northeast, and gambled on cutting a path between two active glaciers for his proposed Copper River and Northwestern Railroad – the CR&NW – ridiculed at the time as the "Can't Run & Never Will." Nonetheless, in 1911 Heney spanned the Copper River with the elaborate **"Million Dollar Bridge"** and the railroad was completed. Even so, the mines were exhausted just 27 years later and Cordova shifted its dependency to fishing, in turn dealt a potentially fatal blow by the grounding of the *Exxon Valdez* in 1989. For the next two seasons, the community reeled from the effects of the **oil spill**; since then fortunes have slowly improved.

Today the "Million Dollar Bridge", battered by the 1964 earthquake, cuts a lonely figure at the end of the Copper River Highway, a 48-mile gravel road across the wondrous wetlands of the **Copper River Delta**, a major breeding ground for America's migratory birds backed by the Chugach Mountains. It is a tranquil spot for fishing, bird-watching, or **hiking** along many of the excellent trails, such as the easy Saddlebag Glacier Trail. The road ends just over the bridge beside the incredibly active **Childs Glacier**.

By far the best way to make the trip is in a **rental car** (from around $70 a day, unlimited mileage) from either Chinook Auto Rentals, in the Airport Depot Diner or at the *Northern Nights Inn* (☎1-877/424-527, ⓦwww.chinookautorentals.com) or Cordova Auto Rental, at the airport (☎907/424-5982, ⓦwww.ptialaska. net/~cars). Alternatively, Copper River and Northwest Tours (☎907/424-5356) runs a five-hour tour to the bridge for $45 including lunch (though currently only on Wednesdays).

Cordova itself has few sights; the **small boat harbor** is the core of the town's activity, particularly when the fleet is in, from May until September. The **Cordova Historical Museum**, 620 First St (summer Mon–Sat 10am–6pm, Sun 2–4pm; rest of year Tues–Fri 10am–5pm, Sat 1–5pm; $1 donation), has quirky exhibits on local history, including the evolution of the little **ice worm** that lives in the glaciers and the funky festival that celebrates its existence each mid-February. The new **Ilanka Cultural Center**, by the harbor at 110 Nicholoff Way (☎907/424-7903, ⓔiccilanka@nveyak.org; end May to mid-Sept Tue–Sat 9am–5pm, rest of year Tues–Fri 10am–4pm; donation), has a complete orca skeleton hanging over the entrance, plus local native arts and crafts and a fine bookshop.

Practicalities

There is no road access to Cordova; daily **flights** from Anchorage and Juneau land at the airport twelve miles down the Copper River Highway, to be met by a **bus** ($12). Near-daily **ferries** from Valdez and Whittier dock a mile north of town. For information, contact the **Chamber of Commerce** at 404 First St (Mon–Fri 9am–4pm; ☎907/424-7260, ⓦwww.cordovachamber.com). Cordova has no **hostel** and the only tent **camping** close to town is at the scruffy *City Camper Park* on Whitshed Road, half a mile south of town (☎907/424-6200; $18), so you might want to rent a car and camp out along the Copper River Delta. The cheapest option in town is the basic *Alaskan Hotel*, 600 First St (☎907/424-3299, ⓔhotelak@yahoo.com; ❷), though you may prefer the *Northern Nights Inn*, 501 Third St (☎907/424-5356; ❸–❹), or the cosy modern *Cordova Lighthouse Inn*, Nicholoff Way (☎907/424-7080, ⓦwww.cordovalighthouseinn.com; ❺), over-looking the small boat harbor. For **food**, try the popular *Killer Whale Café*, 507 First St (☎907/424-7733), or the excellent breakfasts and gourmet pizzas at the *Cordova Lighthouse Café* by the harbor. Wash it down afterwards with a drink at the *Alaskan Hotel*'s **bar**.

Interior and northern Alaska

Interior and northern Alaska is the quintessential "great land." For the most part it's a rolling plateau divided by the Alaska and Brooks ranges, crisscrossed by rivers, punctuated by glaciers, and with views of imposing peaks, above all Mount

McKinley, the nation's highest. Even in high summer, when RVs clog the George Parks Highway, people are still hugely outnumbered by game: moose, Dall sheep, grizzly bears, and herds of caribou sweep over seemingly endless swathes of taiga (sparse birch woodland) and tundra.

Heading north from Anchorage the first essential stop is tiny **Talkeetna**, which has great views of Mount McKinley and the opportunity to fly around it. The mountain is at the heart of **Denali National Park**, the jewel of the Interior. If you prefer your wilderness with fewer people and regulations, head east to the untrammeled vastness of **Wrangell-St Elias National Park**. Alternatively, **Fairbanks**, Alaska's second city, is diverting in its own right and serves as the hub of the North, with roads fanning out to **hot springs** and five hundred miles north to the Arctic Ocean at **Prudhoe Bay**.

Weather here can vary enormously from day to day, with even greater seasonal variations: in winter temperatures can drop to -50°F for days at a time, while summer days reach a sweltering 90°F. However, the major problem during the warmer months is huge mosquitoes; don't forget the insect repellent.

Talkeetna

A hundred miles from Anchorage, **TALKEETNA** has a palpable small-town Alaska feel: this eclectic hamlet was the model for Cicely in TV's *Northern Exposure*, but to its credit Talkeetna doesn't use this as tour-bus bait. The town is lent an international flavor by the world's mountaineers, who come here to scale the 20,320ft **Mount McKinley**, usually referred to in Alaska by its Athabascan name of **Denali**, "the Great One." Whatever you choose to call it, North America's highest peak rises from 2000ft lowlands, making it the world's tallest from base to peak (Everest et al rise from high terrain). Though central to Denali National Park, the mountain is best seen from the **overlook** just south of Talkeetna, which reveals the peak's transcendent white glow, in sharp contrast to the warm colors all around.

From mid-April to mid-July, climbers mass in Talkeetna to be flown to the mountain: only half of the 1200 attempting the climb each year succeed, due to extreme weather. Air-taxi companies also run **flightseeing** trips ranging from a spectacular one-hour ($140) flight to the full ninety-minute grand tour ($200) all around the mountain. K2 Aviation (T 1-800/764-2291, W www.flyk2.com), the choice of most climbers, offers the widest range of options, including glacier landings (extra $60) in planes fitted with skis.

Talkeetna's famed **Moose Dropping Festival** falls on the second weekend of July; little brown balls sell fast (with a sanitary coat of varnish) for use in earrings or necklaces. In addition to these highly desirable lumps of Alaskana, the festival features dancing, drinking, a moose-dropping throwing competition and some more drinking.

Practicalities

Talkeetna is at the end of a fourteen-mile spur off the George Parks Highway, which can usually be hitched. Bus services avoid Talkeetna except for Alaska Park Connection (daily from Anchorage; $41; T 1-800/266-8625, W www.alaskacoach.com); Anchorage to Denali **trains** stop half a mile south of the center of Talkeetna once a day. Information is available from the **Talkeetna Ranger Station**, on B Street (summer daily 8am–6pm; T 907/733-2231).

For a town of just three hundred, Talkeetna teems with good **accommodation**, the cheapest being *House of Seven Trees* on Main St (T 907/733-7733 or 243-3456, E patm_ak@hotmail.com), with bunkhouse (①) and private (③) and family rooms

(**❹**), or the less central *Talkeetna Hostel International* on I Street (☎907/733-4678, ⓦwww.talkeetnahostel.com; bunks $27, rooms **❸**). Dating back to 1917, the central *Talkeetna Roadhouse* (☎907/733-1351, ⓦwww.talkeetnaroadhouse.com; **❶–❹**) bolsters its old-style atmosphere with great home-cooking, bunks ($21) and rooms with shared bathrooms. Easily the fanciest hotel is the *Talkeetna Alaskan Lodge* (☎1-888/959-9590, ⓦwww.talkeetnalodge.com; **❽**), on the hill to the south of town. **Campers** can stay at the *Talkeetna River Park* ($12), at the western end of Main Street, but many stroll another hundred yards west and (unofficially) pitch by the river.

Good places to **eat** include the bakery/diner at the *Talkeetna Roadhouse* (see above), and the *West Rib Pub & Grill*, Main Street (☎907/733-3354), which has good burgers and sandwiches. And make sure you stop for a **drink** in the wonderfully ancient *Fairview Inn* on Main Street.

Denali National Park

The six-million-acre **DENALI NATIONAL PARK**, 240 miles north of Anchorage, is home to **Mount McKinley**, which is often shrouded in cloud. The mountain is far from the park's only attraction, however. Shuttle buses offer a glimpse of a vast world of tundra and taiga, glaciers, huge mountains, and abundant wildlife – the Park Service reports that 95 percent of visitors see **bears**, **caribou**, and **Dall sheep**, 82 percent moose, and over one-fifth **wolves**, along with porcupine, snowshoe hare, red foxes, and over 160 bird species. Visiting Alaska without trying to see Denali is unthinkable for most travelers, and therein lies a problem. In high summer, the visitor center and service areas out on the Parks Highway are a stream of RVs, tour buses, and the like. Things pick up in the park itself, and backcountry hiking, undertaken by only a tiny fraction of visitors, remains a wonderfully solitary experience.

In **winter**, Denali is transformed into a ghostly, snow-covered world. Motorized vehicles are banned and transportation, even for park personnel, is by snowshoe, skis, or dogsled as temperatures dive and northern lights glitter over the snows.

△ Rafting in Denali National Park

Getting to the park

Driving to Denali Park takes about five hours from Anchorage or three from Fairbanks; **hitching** is quite easy with twenty hours of summer daylight. **Bus** services from Anchorage are run by Anchorage Denali Shuttle (☎ 301-5436, ⓦ www.anchoragedenalishuttle .com), Alaska Park Connection (☎ 1-800/266-8625, ⓦ www.alaskacoach.com) and Alaska/Yukon Trails (☎ 1-800/770-7275, ⓦ www.alaskashuttle.com), charging $65–76, with the last continuing to Fairbanks ($46). **Trains** (daily in summer) leave at 8.15am from both Anchorage ($129) and Fairbanks ($56), depositing you at 4pm and noon respectively at the train station a mile and a half inside the park entrance. **Park entry** costs $10 per person and is valid for a week.

Sightseeing, hiking, and other activities

The only vehicles allowed on Denali's narrow, unpaved ninety-mile road are a few tour buses and green **shuttle buses**, which you should book well in advance (☎ 1-800/622-7275, ⓦ www.reservedenali.com) or up to two days ahead at the **wilderness access center** (May–Sept daily 7am–8pm; ☎ 907/683-1266), just inside the park entrance. You can pick up a free copy of the *Denali Alpenglow* paper and a wide range of literature here or at the new visitor center, near the train station, or join ranger-led activities including short hikes and the popular, and free, dogsled demonstration held daily at 10am, 2pm, and 4pm.

Shuttle buses run to either the **Toklat River** at Mile 53 ($19), where rangers lead one-hour tundra tours each day at 1.30pm, or to the aptly named **Wonder Lake** at Mile 84 ($33); roundtrips take about eight and ten hours, respectively. The shuttle drivers don't give guided tours, but with forty pairs of watchful eyes on board, you're almost guaranteed to see the big mammals. You can also hop off at any point for a day-hike (no permits required), returning to the road to flag down the next bus back, if it has room. Buses run at least hourly in each season, and there are others used mainly by campers that will pick up stragglers at day's end.

Backcountry camping is the best way to appreciate Denali's scenery and its inhabitants. Don't expect it to be easy though, as there are no formal trails, and with thick spongy tundra and frequent river crossings even hardy hikers find themselves limited to five miles a day. The park is divided into 87 units and only a designated number of hikers are allowed into each section at a time. Free permits are available, one day in advance, from the **Backcountry Information Center** (daily 7am–8pm), facing the Wilderness Access Center, though high demand means you should be prepared to hike in the less popular areas. The BIC will also teach you about avoiding run-ins with bears and issue you with bear-resistant food containers. Special camper buses reserved for those with campground or backcountry permits cost $24.25. If there's room, buses also carry bikes; cyclists can be dropped anywhere, but are obliged to keep to the road. Another option is to join a **narrated tour** (☎ 1-800/622-7275) along the park road: either the five-hour Natural History Tour ($60) or the full-day Tundra Wilderness Tour ($90), which penetrates as far as Mile 53, stopping frequently to observe wildlife.

Just outside the park entrance, several **rafting** companies offer two-hour trips down the Nenana River: all offer a gentle "scenic float" and an eleven-mile "Canyon Run" through Class III and IV rapids – they cost around $65 individually and $90 for a joint run. Denali Outdoor Center (☎ 1-888/303-1925, ⓦ www. denalioutdoorcenter.com) charges a couple of dollars more than some of the others, but offers a quality experience.

Practicalities

With the exception of several exclusive lodges deep in the heart of the park, there are no hotels in Denali, so your choice is between camping, the $130-a-night gaggle of summer-only hotels a mile north of the park entrance, or the cheaper offerings either ten miles further north in the little coal-mining town of **HEALY**, or spots a few miles south along the George Parks Highway. The only cheap option by the park entrance is to camp at *Denali Rainbow Village RV Park* (Mile 238.6, ☎907/683-7777, Ⓦwww.denalirvrvpark.com; from $20) or *Denali Riverside RV Park* (Mile 240.5, ☎1-866/583-2696, Ⓦwww.denaliriversiderv.com; $16), while the only real hostel hereabouts is the excellent *Denali Mountain Morning Hostel and Lodge*, Mile 224.5, thirteen miles south (☎907/683-7503, Ⓦwww.hostelalaska.com; cabins ❸, rooms ❷, bunks ❶), set in wooded seclusion and with a bargain shuttle service ($3 a day) to the park. Accommodation is in spacious dorms ($25) or separate cabins, there's an efficient kitchen, all manner of games, and the hosts will do everything to facilitate your Denali visit. In Healy there's the high-quality *Motel Nord Haven*, Mile 249.5 Parks Hwy (☎1-800/683-4501, Ⓦwww.motelnordhaven.com; ❺), and the lovely *Earth Song Lodge*, Mile 4, Stampede Rd (☎907/683-2863, Ⓦwww.earthsonglodge.com; ❻), with a cluster of cabins with great mountain views and a café on site.

Camping is the best way to experience Denali up close, with most of the park's six campgrounds open from mid-May to mid-September. The best is **Wonder Lake** ($16), with a stunning view of McKinley; failing that, **Igloo Creek** ($9) is good for spotting Dall sheep, while **Riley Creek** ($12–19), near the entrance, is open year-round. All sites are bookable at the main visitor center or via phone or the Web (☎1-800/622-7275, Ⓦwww.reservedenali.com). If you don't do this you may have to wait a day or two to get a spot. The best alternative is *Denali Grizzly Bear Cabins & Campground*, Mile 231.1, seven miles south of Denali (☎1-866/583-2696,Ⓦwww.denaligrizzlybear.com; ❶–❼), set in the trees close to the Nenana River with a wide variety of attractive cabins all around.

Eating is expensive, with only a limited range of grocery stores and a small selection of fairly pricey restaurants close to the park entrance, such as the *Black Bear Coffee House* (☎907/683-1656), serving light meals, and *Lynx Creek Pizza and Pub* (☎907/683-2547), where the menu includes salads and sandwiches as well as pizza and draft microbrews.

Wrangell-St Elias National Park

As Denali becomes more crowded, people are increasingly making the trip to remoter **WRANGELL-ST ELIAS NATIONAL PARK** in the extreme southeast corner of the Interior, where four of the continent's great mountain ranges – the Wrangell, St Elias, Chugach, and Alaska – cramp up against each other. Everything is writ large: glacier after enormous glacier, canyon after dizzying canyon, and nine of the sixteen highest peaks in the US, all laced together by braided rivers and idyllic lakes where mountain goats, Dall sheep, bears, moose, and caribou roam.

The first whites in the area came in search of gold but instead hit upon one of the continent's richest copper deposits. The mines closed in 1938, after 27 frantic years of production, and today **Kennicott**, with over thirty creaking, disused buildings, is a virtual ghost town. You can visit the mill complex on fascinating two-hour **walking tours** run by St Elias Alpine Guides ($25; ☎1-888/933-5427, Ⓦwww.steliasguides. com), who also run a number of hikes, ice-climbing trips, mountain-bike rides, raft trips, and even glacier skiing adventures out into the virtually trailless park.

Practicalities

Half the fun is getting to McCarthy along 58 rugged miles of the **McCarthy Road**, following the trackbed of the abandoned railroad that once linked the Kennicott mill to the port at Cordova. Take it slow and stop often to admire the scenery and abandoned trestle bridges. At the end of the road you cross the Kennicott River on a footbridge and continue half a mile to the village of McCarthy on foot, from where a shuttle bus runs along the rough five-mile dirt road to Kennicott. Hitching along the McCarthy Road can be a hit-or-miss affair; if you haven't got a vehicle you can go with Backcountry Connections (℡ 1-866/582-5292, ⓦ www.alaska-backcountry-tours.com), who charge $119 roundtrip from Glennallen. The park's **visitor center** is just south of Glennallen at Mile 107 on the Richardson Highway (summer daily 8am–6pm; ℡ 907/822-5234, ⓦ www.nps.gov/wrst).

Accommodation around McCarthy and Kennicott isn't cheap, though there are two hostels. *Kennicott River Lodge and Hostel* (℡ 907/554-4441, ⓦ www.kennicottriverlodge .com; ❹), near the road end, has four-bunk cabins ($28 per person) and nice common areas; *Lancaster's Backpacking Hotel*, in McCarthy (℡ 907/554-4402, ⓦ www .mccarthylodge.com; ❺) has simple shared-bath rooms costing $48 for one, $68 for two. The associated *Ma Johnson Hotel* (same details; ❻) is very pleasant and atmospheric, and *McCarthy Lodge* across the road serves good food. In Kennicott there's the upscale *Kennicott Glacier Lodge* (℡ 1-800/582-5128, ⓦ www.kennicottlodge.com; ❼), which also has the town's one restaurant (reserve for dinner).

Fairbanks

FAIRBANKS, 358 miles north of Anchorage, is at the end of the Alaska Highway from Canada and definitely at the end of the road for most tourists. Though somewhat bland, its central location makes a great base for exploring a hinterland of gold mines and hot springs, and a staging point for trips into the surrounding wilderness and for journeys along the **Dalton Highway** to the Arctic Ocean oil community of **Prudhoe Bay**.

Alaska's second most populous town was founded accidentally, in 1901, when a steamship carrying trader E.T. Barnette ran aground in the shallows of the Chena River. Unable to move his supplies any further, he set up shop in the wilderness and catered to the few trappers and prospectors trying their luck in the area. The following year **gold** was found, a tent city sprang up, and Barnette made a mint. In 1908, at the height of the rush, Fairbanks had a population of 18,500, but by 1920 it had dwindled to only 1100. To thwart possible Japanese attacks during World War II, several huge **military bases** were built and the population rebounded, getting a further boost in the mid-1970s when it became the construction center for the **trans-Alaska pipeline**, causing the population to reach an all-time high. The city's economy dropped dramatically with the oil crash, and unemployment hit twenty percent before government spending put the city back on track.

The spectacular **aurora borealis** is a major winter attraction, as is the **Ice Festival** in mid-March, with its ice-sculpting competition and open-sled dog racing on the frozen downtown streets. Summer visitors should try to catch the three-day **World Eskimo-Indian Olympics** in mid-July, when contestants from around the state compete in the standard dance, art, and sports competitions, as well as some unusual ones like ear-pulling, knuckle hop, high kick, and the blanket toss.

Fairbanks suffers remarkable extremes of climate, with winter temperatures dropping to -70°F and summer highs topping 90°F. Proximity to the Arctic Circle means over 21 hours of sunlight in midsummer, when midnight baseball games take place under natural light, and 2am bar evacuees are confronted by bright sunshine.

Arrival, information, and getting around

Alaska Airlines flies frequently from Anchorage to **Fairbanks Airport**, four miles southwest of downtown; the MACS Yellow Line **bus** (Mon–Sat; $1.50) runs downtown, but the long wait between services means you'll probably want to grab a **taxi** (around $12). Alpenglow's Fairbanks Shuttle (T 1-800/770-2267, W www.alaskashuttles.com) will take you around town for $5 ($8 return) or to the airport or rail depot for $7. The airport is also a gateway for flights into the bush; Frontier Flying Service (T 1-800/478-6779, W www.frontierflying.com) operates a reliable service. **Trains** from Anchorage (daily in summer, weekly in winter) stop beside the Johansen Expressway inconveniently far from downtown. It's cheaper to get here by bus with Alaska/Yukon Trails (T 1-800/770-7275, W www.alaskashuttle.com), who drop off at the visitor center and major hostels and hotels. The best way to get around town is by car, but there's a good riverside cycle trail and the five **bus lines**, run by MACS (T 907/459-1011), provide a reasonable service. Among the companies that can whisk you off into the surrounding bush and fly you to the **Arctic Circle**, the widest choice is with the Northern Alaska Tour Company (T 1-800/474-1986, W www.northernalaska.com).

The **visitor center**, at 550 First Ave (summer daily 8am–8pm; rest of year daily 10am–5pm; T 1-800/327-5774, W www.explorefairbanks.com), carries a vast amount of information on lodging and activities. For information on the area's parks, including Denali, stop by the useful **Alaska Public Land Information Center** (APLIC) at 250 N Cushman St (summer daily 9am–6pm; rest of year Tues–Sat 10am–6pm; T 907/456-0527, W www.nps.gov/aplic).

Accommodation

Downtown motels and hotels tend to be either quite pricey or pretty dodgy. **B&B**s are plentiful, with rooms from $75 a night; the visitor center offers free phone calls and all the brochures. Thankfully there are a couple of good hostels, and for campers there's the tranquil and convenient *Tanana Valley Campground*, 1800 College Rd at Aurora Drive (mid-May to mid-Sept; T 907/456-7956; $10), on the MACS bus Red line and with free bikes for guests.

Ah, Rose Marie 302 Cowles St T 907/456-2040, E ahrosemarie@yahoo.com. Small but well-run and justly popular B&B where a hearty breakfast is served on the glassed-in porch. ❸

Billie's Backpackers 2895 Mack Rd T 907/479-2034, W www.alaskahostel.com. Welcoming though somewhat cramped hostel, in a nice area and handily placed on the bus route between downtown and the university. Bikes and Internet access available. Bunks $25, camping $15. ❶

Golden North Motel 4888 Old Airport Way T 1-800/447-1910, W www.goldennorthmotel.com. Friendly and spotlessly clean motel near the airport with cable TV, WiFi, and continental breakfast. Courtesy pickups are available, and the Yellow and Blue buses pass nearby. ❸–❹

GoNorth Base Camp 3500 Davis Rd T 907/479-7272, W www.paratours.net. A kind of outdoors hostel in a forested area with large fixed tents with five beds ($24; bring a sleeping bag). There's also camping ($12). Bikes available for $18 a day.

Midge's Birch Lane B&B 4335 Birch Lane T 907/388-8084, W www.alaskaone.com/midgebb. Relaxed, welcoming, and spacious house in the quiet University district. Rooms with and without private bathrooms. ❸

Minnie Street B&B Inn 345 Minnie St T 1-888/456-1849, W www.minniestreetbandb.com. Top-line B&B with every luxury, including phones with dataports plus WiFi and a spacious deck with a hot tub. Some rooms have a Jacuzzi and there's a full breakfast. Jacuzzi ❼, private bath ❻, shared bath. ❺

The Town

Besides the visitor center, the main point of interest **downtown** is the small **Fairbanks Community Museum**, 410 Cushman St at 5th Avenue (Tue–Sat 10am–6pm; donation appreciated), containing locally donated trapping, mining, and dogsled racing equipment. The museum also acts as the public face of the **Yukon Quest** dogsled race – a grueling thousand-mile marathon between Fairbanks and Whitehorse – selling related books, videos, and T-shirts. A similarly wintry theme is pursued at the **Ice Museum**, 500 2nd Ave at Lacey Street (summer daily 10am–9pm; $8), a year-round taster of the Ice Sculpting competition by way of a slide show and walk-in refrigerators housing some small carvings. A couple of miles west on the banks of the Chena River, **Pioneer Park** celebrates Alaska history in a very touristy, but not unpleasant way; admission is free, though different attractions charge small fees. Five decent little **museums** cover the early pioneering days, you can board the only large wooden sternwheeler left in the US, and a miniature railway encircles the entire park; there's plenty to amuse the kids. College Road heads west past **Creamer's Field**, thick with sandhill cranes and Canada geese, especially in spring and fall, to the University of Alaska Fairbanks's attractive campus. Here the superb new extension to UAF's **Museum of the North** (summer daily 9am–7pm; winter Mon–Fri 9am–5pm, Sat & Sun noon–5pm; $10; ☎907/474-7505, ⓦwww.uaf.edu/museum) allows it to display its eclectic collection of native and contemporary art, as well as natural and human history displays.

Unashamedly touristy but fun and very popular is a four-hour **cruise** down the Chena River on the "Riverboat Discovery" ($47; ☎907/479-6673, ⓦwww.riverboatdiscovery.com), which includes a visit to a mock Native village.

Eating and nightlife

Fairbanks's **eating** options are varied, with good Thai particularly prevalent. They're also well scattered, with downtown and College Road, toward the university, having the greatest concentrations. Nowhere downtown sells groceries: the closest are Safeway and Fred Meyer at the eastern end of College Road. Fairbanks has its decent **nightspots**, though none lie in hard-drinking downtown.

Alaska Coffee Roasting Co. West Valley Plaza, 4001 Geist Rd ☎907/457-5282. Fairbanks's best coffee, roasted daily on the premises served in a cozy café hung with local art. There's a good selection of wraps, cakes, and muffins, too.

Blue Loon Mile 353.5 Parks Hwy ☎907/457-5666, ⓦwww.theblueloon.com. Late-closing hotspot five miles west of Fairbanks that's always good for a convivial drink. Hosts local and touring bands (sometimes a DJ) several nights a week, and screens cult and art-house movies. Closed Mon.

The Diner 244 Illinois St ☎907/451-0613. Reliable diner fare at good prices.

Gambardella's Pasta Bella 706 2nd Ave, downtown ☎907/457-4992, ⓦwww.gambardellas.com. Fairbanks' best Italian and not wildly expensive, with a pleasant outdoor area for those endless summer evenings.

Hot Tamale 112 N Turner Rd ☎907/457-8350. Authentic downtown Mexican decorated in a kind of "cantina kitsch" style and particularly noted for cheap beer and their all-you-care-to-eat $11 buffet lunch and dinner.

Howling Dog Saloon Mile 11 Old Steese Hwy, Fox ☎907/457-8780. Eleven miles north of town,

but perhaps the north's best bar – unassuming, unpretentious, and fun. Live rock and R&B bands perform and it's the ideal place to play volleyball under the midnight sun.

The Marlin 3412 College Rd ☎907/479-4646. Poky wood-paneled cellar bar at the cutting edge of Fairbanks's music scene with live bands – blues, jazz, and rock – most evenings from around 9pm and only a small cover charge, if any.

Pump House Mile 1.3 Chena Pump Rd ☎907/479-8452, ⓦwww.pumphouse.com. A local favorite in a historic pumphouse, stuffed with gold-mining paraphernalia and with a deck to watch life go by on the Chena River. Great for steak, seafood, and burgers, and also pulls in a substantial drinking crowd.

Second Storey Café 3525 College Rd ☎907/474-9574. Pleasant spot above Gulliver's Bookstore, serving wraps, sandwiches, bagels, biscotti, and coffee, all at reasonable prices, Free Internet access as well.

Thai House 412 5th Ave, downtown ☎907/452-6123. A small but ever-popular restaurant serving the usual range of Thai dishes, but all done to perfection and at very modest prices for around $10. Closed Sun.

Around Fairbanks: two hot springs

Chena Hot Springs, the most accessible and developed resort in the area, stands in a clearing sixty miles east of Fairbanks amid a wonderfully bucolic swath of **mus-**

The **aurora borealis**, or "Northern Lights," an ethereal display of light in the upper-most atmosphere, give their brightest and most colorful displays in the sky above Fairbanks. For up to one hundred winter nights, the sky appears to shimmer with dancing curtains of color ranging from luminescent greens to fantastic veils that run the full spectrum. Named after the Roman goddess of dawn, the aurora is caused by an interaction between the earth's magnetic field and the **solar wind**, an invisible stream of charged electrons and protons continually blown out into space by the innate violence of the sun. The earth deflects the solar wind like a rock in a stream, with the energy released at the magnetic poles – much like a neon sign.

The Northern Lights are at their most dazzling from December to March, when nights are longest and the sky darkest, but late September can be good for summer visitors. They are pretty much visible everywhere, but the further north the better, especially around Fairbanks.

keg (grassy swampland) and forest traversed by good hiking trails and teeming with moose. For $10 a day non-guests can use the hot pools and large outdoor "rock pool", which are free for those staying at the fully-equipped resort (☏1-800/478-4681, Ⓦwww.chenahotsprings.com; ❹–❻), where camping costs $20. The resort also rents out canoes and mountain bikes, as well as offering rafting float trips.

The traditional favorite for Fairbanks folk has been the more rustic **Circle Hot Springs**, 130 miles northeast of the city along scenic Steese Highway. Though the resort has been closed since 2001, the caretaker will usually allow access to the pool. Call first (☏907/520-5113) as it is a long drive through pristine scenery beside the Chatanika River to the tiny mining village of **Central**, then eight miles to the resort; there's camping two miles short of the resort.

The Dalton Highway

Built in the 1970s to service the **trans–Alaska pipeline**, the mostly gravel-surfaced **Dalton Highway**, or Haul Road, runs from Fairbanks five hundred miles to the oil facility of Prudhoe Bay on Alaska's north coast, some three hundred miles beyond the Arctic Circle. It is a long, bumpy, and demanding drive, so take spare tires, gas, provisions, and, ideally, a sturdy four-wheel-drive vehicle: most regular rentals aren't permitted up here. Not far from Fairbanks you start to parallel the pipeline, snaking up hills and in and out of the ground. At 188 miles, a sign announces that you've just crossed the **Arctic Circle**. The **Northern Alaska Tour Company** (☏1-800/474-1986, Ⓦwww.northernalaska.com) will drive you up in a minibus and fly you back down to Fairbanks for around $270 (you can save $130 by taking the minibus back, but it's a long day and you miss out on the flight).

Most people are happy to return south at this point, but the highway plugs on through increasingly barren territory, finally dispensing with trees as you climb through the wilderness of the **Brooks Range**, a 9000ft chain mostly held within the **Gates of the Arctic** National Park. From Atigun Pass you descend through two hundred miles of grand glaciated valleys and blasted arctic plains to the end of the road at dead-boring **Deadhorse**. You can't stroll by the ocean or camp here, so your choices are confined to staying in one of the $120-per-night hotels and taking a $39 tour past the adjacent – and off-limits – **Prudhoe Bay** oil facility to the Arctic Ocean where you can dip your toe or go for the full body immersion. By far the best way to do it is with Northern Alaska, who run a three-day fly/drive tour to Prudhoe Bay for $750.

16

Hawaii

AL - ALABAMA	IN - INDIANA	MN - MINNESOTA	RI - RHODE ISLAND
AR - ARKANSAS	LA - LOUISIANA	MS - MISSISSIPPI	SC - SOUTH CAROLINA
CT - CONNECTICUT	MA - MASSACHUSETTS	NC - NORTH CAROLINA	VA - VIRGINIA
DE - DELAWARE	MD - MARYLAND	NH - NEW HAMPSHIRE	VT - VERMONT
FL - FLORIDA	ME - MAINE	NJ - NEW JERSEY	WI - WISCONSIN
IL - ILLINOIS	MI - MICHIGAN	PA - PENNSYLVANIA	WV - WEST VIRGINIA

CHAPTER 16

Highlights

* **Waikiki Beach, Oahu**
Learn to surf, or just sip a cocktail, on the world's most famous beach. See p.1267

* **Pearl Harbor, Oahu**
Relive December 7, 1941 – the "date that will live in infamy" – by visiting the sunken USS *Arizona*. See p.1268

* **Kilauea Eruption, Big Island** The Big Island gets bigger day by day, thanks to the spectacular eruption of its youngest volcano, Kilauea. See p.1275

* **Downhill biking, Maui**
Freewheel forty miles down the slopes of Maui's mighty Haleakala volcano. See p.1277

* **Lahaina, Maui** This early nineteenth century whaling port ranks among the most historic towns in Hawaii. See p.1279

* **Lumahai Beach, Kauai**
This superb beach has been featured in countless movies, but beware the treacherous waters. See p.1285

* **Kalalau Trail, Kauai**
Admire the magnificent Na Pali coastline of Kauai from one of the world's greatest hiking trails. See p.1285

△ Waikiki Beach

16

Hawaii

With their fiery volcanoes, palm-fringed beaches, verdant valleys, glorious rainbows, and awesome cliffs, the islands of **HAWAII** boast some of the most spectacularly beautiful scenery on earth. Two thousand miles from the country it belongs to, the fiftieth state pulls in seven million tourists per year, including honeymooners from all over the world, frequent fliers cashing in their mileage, and almost two million Japanese. This Pacific archipelago can seem at times like a gigantic theme park.

Honolulu, on **Oahu**, is by far the largest city of Hawaii; its resort annex of Waikiki is the main tourist center. The biggest island, **Hawaii** itself, is known as the **Big Island** in a vain attempt to avoid confusion, while **Maui** and **Kauai** also attract mass tourism. All the islands share a similar topography and **climate**. Ocean winds shed their rain on the northeast, **windward** coast, keeping it wet and green; the southwest, **leeward** (or "Kona") coasts can be almost barren, and so make ideal locations for big resorts. While temperatures remain consistent all year at between 70°F and 85°F, rainfall is heaviest from December to March. That is nonetheless the most popular time to visit, enabling mid- to upper-range hotels to add a premium of at least $30 per night to their standard room rates. A visit to Hawaii doesn't have to cost a fortune, however; **budget** facilities do exist. The one major expense you can't avoid, except possibly on Oahu, is car rental – rates are very reasonable, but gas is pricey.

Some history

Each of the Hawaiian islands was forced up like a vast mass of candle drippings by submarine volcanic action, all fueled by the same "hot spot," which has remained stationary as the Pacific plate drifted above. The process continues at Kilauea on the Big Island, where lava explodes into the sea to add new land day by day, while the oldest islands are now mere atolls way to the northwest. Until two thousand years ago, these unknown specks were populated only by the very few plants, birds, and animals that had chanced to be carried here by wind or wave. The first known human inhabitants were the **Polynesians**, who arrived in two principal migrations: one from the Marquesas in the eighth century, and another from Tahiti four or five hundred years later.

No Western ship chanced upon Hawaii until **Captain Cook** arrived at Kauai in 1778. He was amazed to find a civilization sharing a culture – and language – with the peoples of the South Pacific. Although Cook himself was killed in Hawaii in 1779, his visit started an irreversible process of change. In reshaping the islands to suit their needs, Westerners decimated most of the indigenous flora and fauna – as well as the Hawaiians themselves. Cook's men estimated that there were a million islanders; the population today is roughly the same, but only eight thousand **pure-blood Hawaiians** are left.

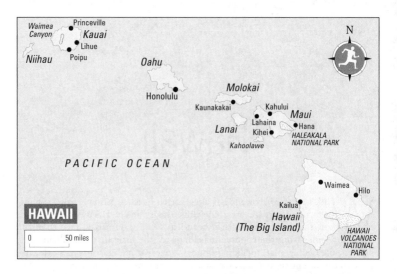

Within a few years of Cook's arrival, **Kamehameha** became the first king to unite all the islands. However, exposure to the world economy swiftly devastated Hawaii's traditional way of life. White advisers and ministers soon dominated the government, and the families of the first missionaries from New England became Hawaii's wealthiest and most powerful class. As the US grew increasingly reliant on Hawaiian-grown **sugar**, Hawaii moved inexorably towards annexation. In 1887 an all-white group of "concerned businessmen" forced King David Kalakaua to surrender power, and subsequently called in the US warship *Boston* and declared a provisional republican government. US President Cleveland (a Democrat) responded that "Hawaii was taken possession of by the United States forces without the consent or wish of the government of the islands . . . (It) was wholly without justification . . . not merely a wrong but a disgrace."

On August 12, 1898, Hawaii was formally **annexed** as a territory of the United States. Its ultimate integration into the American mainstream was hastened by its crucial role in the war against Japan, and the expansion of tourism thereafter. The islands finally became the fiftieth of the United States in 1959, after a plebiscite showed a seventeen-to-one majority in favor. The only group to oppose statehood were the few remaining native Hawaiians.

Modern Hawaii

Roughly sixty percent of the million-plus modern Hawaiians were born here. Around one-third are Caucasian (many of them US military personnel), one-third Japanese, and one-sixth Filipino, with 200,000 claiming at least some Hawaiian ancestry. The traditional reliance on agriculture seems to be in terminal decline, with sugar and pineapple plantations closing one after the other, and the need to import virtually all the basics of life resulting in an extraordinarily high **cost of living**.

Visitors in search of **ancient Hawaii** will find that few vestiges remain. What is presented as "historic" usually postdates the missionary impact. Although the ruins of temples (*heiaus*) to the old gods still stand in some places – notably on the Big Island – the "old towns" are pure nineteenth-century Americana, with false-front stores and raised wooden boardwalks. While authentic **hula** dancing is a powerful art form, you're most likely to encounter it bastardized in a **luau**. Primarily tourist money-spinners, these "traditional feasts" provide an opportunity to sample Hawaiian **foods** such as *kalua* pig, baked underground, and local fish such as *ono*, *ahi*, *mahi mahi*, and *lomi-lomi* (raw salmon). *Poi* – a paste made from mashed taro root – remains a staple of the diet, much as it was when one of Captain Cook's men described it as "a disagreeable mess."

The Hawaiian **language** endures primarily in place names and music. At first glance it looks unpronounceable – especially as it is written using a mere twelve letters (the five vowels, plus *h*, *k*, *l*, *m*, *n*, *p*, and *w*) – but usually, each letter is enunciated individually, and long words often break down into repeated sounds, such as "*meha-meha*" in "Kamehameha."

Getting to and around Hawaii

Honolulu, just under six hours by plane from the US West Coast, is one of the world's busiest centers for air traffic; return fares from **LA**, **San Francisco**, and **Seattle** start at around $350. There are also direct flights from the mainland to Maui, the Big Island, and Kauai. Many flights to the US from **Australia** – such as those on Continental – include free stopovers in Hawaii. **European** travelers should buy all-inclusive tickets from Europe.

The principal **inter-island carriers** are Hawaiian Airlines (T 1-800/882-8811 or 1-800/367-5320, W www.hawaiianair.com) and Aloha Air (T 808/484-1111 or 1-800/367-5250, W www.alohaair.com), together with its subsidiary Island Air (T 808/484-2222 or 1-800/323-3345). They connect all the major islands several times per day, with standard one-way fares of around $85. In 2006, go! (T 1-888/435-9462, W www.iflygo.com) entered the market, offering standard one-way fares of $39 and some as cheap as $19; its survival remains to be seen. A new inter-island **ferry** (W www.hawaiisuperferry.com) promises to start daily sailings between Oahu, Maui and Kauai in July 2007 (from $42 one-way), adding the Big Island in 2009 (from $52 one-way).

All the airports have **car rental** outlets; with the exception of Oahu, however, **bus** services on the islands barely exist.

Oahu

Three-quarters of Hawaii's population live on **OAHU**, which has monopolized the islands' trade and tourism since the first European sailors realized that **Honolulu** offered the safest in-shore anchorage for thousands of miles. Eighty percent of visitors to Hawaii arrive in Honolulu, and most remain for their entire vacation. Oahu effectively confines tourists to the tower-block enclave of **Waikiki**, just east of downtown Honolulu; there are few rooms anywhere else. In much the same way, the **military** are closeted away in relatively inconspicuous camps. On any given day, the numbers of military personnel and tourists on Oahu are roughly the same.

While overcrowding and development mean Oahu can't be recommended over the **Neighbor Islands** (as the other Hawaiian islands are known), it can still give a real flavor of Hawaii. Oahu has some excellent **beaches**, with those on the North Shore a haven for **surfers** and campers, and the **cliffs** of the Windward side are awesome.

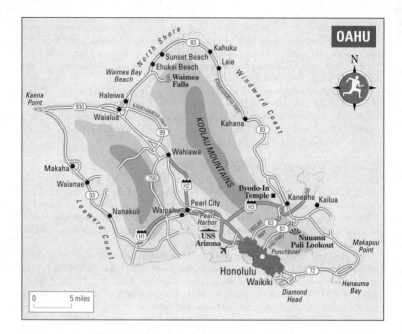

Honolulu

Until the Europeans came, **HONOLULU** was insignificant; soon so many foreign ships were frequenting its waters that it had become Kamehameha's capital, and it remains the economic center of the archipelago. While the city covers a long (if narrow) strip of southern Oahu, **downtown** is a manageable size, and a lot quieter than its glamorous image might suggest. The tourist hotels are concentrated among the skyscrapers of very distinct **Waikiki**, a couple of miles east.

While its setting is beautiful, right on the Pacific and backed by dramatic cliffs and extinct volcanoes, most visitors are here simply to enjoy the sheer **hedonism** of shopping, eating, and generally hanging out in the sun. It's also the center of an exemplary **public transportation** system that facilitates exploration of the whole island.

Arrival, information, and getting around

The runways of Honolulu's **International Airport**, just west of downtown, extend out to sea on a coral reef. **Car rental** outlets abound on the island, but a car is not especially desirable in Honolulu, what with city traffic and hefty parking fees in Waikiki. The nine-mile (not at all scenic) drive to Waikiki takes anything from 25 to 75 minutes; Reliable (one-way $8, roundtrip $15; ☎808/924-9292, ⓦwww.reliableshuttle.com) is one of many **shuttle services** that run to any Waikiki hotel. Regular **buses #19** and **#20** also head to Waikiki, but don't allow large bags, cases, or backpacks. A **taxi** will cost around $25.

Information

The **Hawaii Visitors Bureau** maintains a strong online presence at ⓦwww.gohawaii.com. Free listings magazines and leaflets are everywhere you turn, and all the hotels have information desks. Kiosks around Kalakaua Avenue offer greatly discounted rates for island tours, helicopter rides, dinner cruises, surfing lessons, and so on.

Getting around

A network of over sixty **bus** routes, collectively named TheBus, covers the whole of Oahu. All journeys, however long, cost $2, with free transfers onto any connecting route if you ask as you board (information ☏808/848-5555, ⓦwww.thebus.org). The most popular routes with Waikiki-based tourists are **#2** to downtown, **#8** to Ala Moana Shopping Center, **#20** to Pearl Harbor, **#22** to Hanauma Bay, and the bargain "**Circle Island**" buses (**#52** clockwise and **#55** counterclockwise), which take four hours to loop around the central valley and the east coast, passing the legendary North Shore surf spots.

Among companies running **city and island bus tours**, for anything from $26 up to $75 for a full day, as well as off-island packages, are Polynesian Adventure Tours (☏808/833-3000 or 1-800/622-3011, ⓦwww.polyad.com).

Accommodation

All the accommodation listed below is in or near **Waikiki**; very little is available in central Honolulu. Waikiki accommodation covers a wide range, and the highest rates will bring absolute luxury, but it's possible to find comfortable lodging for much less. An ocean view costs a $50-plus premium; everything is close to the ocean, however.

Aloha Punawai 305 Saratoga Rd ☏808/923-5211 or 1-866/713-9694, ⓦwww.alternative-hawaii.com/alohapunawai/. This 19-room hotel, opposite the post office, offers clean, air-conditioned apartments and studios, all with kitchenettes. ⑤

The Breakers 250 Beach Walk ☏808/923-3181 or 1-800/426-0494, ⓦwww.breakers-hawaii.com. Small, intimate hotel on the western edge of central Waikiki; all rooms have kitchenettes and TV, and there's a bar and grill beside the pool. ⑤

🏃 **Hawaiiana Hotel** 260 Beach Walk ☏808/923-3811 or 1-800/367-5122, ⓦwww.hawaiianahotelatwaikiki.com. Pleasant little family hotel, abounding in tiki images, where the rooms are ranged around two pools; all have kitchenettes, some have balconies. ⑤

New Otani Kaimana Beach Hotel 2863 Kalakaua Ave ☏808/923-1555 or 1-800/421-8795, ⓦwww.kaimana.com. Intimate, Japanese-toned beachfront hotel half a mile east of central Waikiki. ⑥

Outrigger and **Ohana** are linked hotel chains with numerous locations around Waikiki, mostly high-rises (reservations *Outrigger* ☏1-800/688-7444, ⓦwww.outrigger.com; *Ohana* ☏303/369-7777 or 1-800/462-6262, ⓦwww.ohanahotels.com). Choices include the *Ohana Maile Sky Court*, 2058 Kuhio Ave (④), or the more luxurious *Ohana Waiki-*

ki Beachcomber, 2300 Kalakaua Ave (⑦); most of the other *Ohana*s have rooms for around $125, while the *Outrigger*s, such as the *Reef*, 2169 Kalia Rd (⑦), are generally more expensive. ④–⑨

Polynesian Beach Club Hostel 2584 Lemon Rd ☏808/922-1340, ⓦwww.hawaiihostels.com. Clean, efficiently-run hostel, a block from the sea. Some rooms hold four $25 bunk beds, some hold ten at $20, some serve as good-value private doubles, and there are also private suites. Free snorkels and boogie boards are available; there's cheap Internet access; and meals are served in the communal area some nights. ①/③

🏃 **The Royal Hawaiian** 2259 Kalakaua Ave ☏808/923-7311 or 1-800/325-3535, ⓦwww.royal-hawaiian.com. This 1920s "Pink Palace," commanding the beach, is one of Waikiki's best-loved landmarks. The original building looks out across terrace gardens to the sea, but is now flanked by a less atmospheric tower block, which holds the most expensive suites. ⑨

Waikiki Beachside Hostel 2556 Lemon Rd ☏808/923-9566 or 1-866/478-3888, ⓦwww.hokondo.com. Small hotel block near the park in eastern Waikiki that has been converted into a popular, lively private hostel, with dorm beds for $25, plus pricier double rooms, and Internet access. ①/③

The City

Downtown Honolulu is surprisingly small, set back a little from the sea and focused around a spacious plaza on King Street that includes **Iolani Palace** and the **state capitol**. The palace was built for King David Kalakaua in 1882, but, apart from its *koa*-hardwood floors, contains little that is distinctively Hawaiian, or that justifies the high tour price (by reservation, ☏808/522-0832; Tues–Sat 9am–2.15pm; $20). Across the road is a flower-bedecked, gilt statue of Kamehameha the Great.

To reach the nearby ocean, pedestrians have to negotiate fearsome traffic. The **Aloha Tower** on Pier 9 used to be the city's tallest building; the surrounding area is now a mall, fronting onto the docks and better for dining than it is for shopping. The view from the top of the tower is little short of ugly, but is good for getting your bearings (daily 9am–5pm; free). The **Hawaii Maritime Center** just east on Pier 7 (daily 8.30am–5pm; $7.50) documents Hawaii's seafaring past in superb detail, from ancient migrations through to tourism in the twentieth century. A stunning film from 1922 shows the true-life drama of whaling, and there's a wall of gigantic historic surfboards. In the adjacent dock are the fully rigged four-master *Falls of Clyde* and the replica Polynesian canoe *Hokulea*, whose voyages to Tahiti and New Zealand have inspired tremendous interest in traditional methods of navigation.

Honolulu residents take great pride in the stunning fine art on display at the **Academy of Arts**, half a mile east of the capitol at 900 S Beretania St (Tues–Sat 10am–4.30pm, Sun 1–5pm; $7; ☏808/532-8700, ⓦwww.honoluluacademy.org). As well as paintings including Van Gogh's *Wheat Field*, Gauguin's *Two Nudes on a Tahitian Beach*, and one of Monet's *Water Lilies*, the Academy also holds fascinating depictions of Hawaii by visiting artists, including vivid, stylized studies of Maui's Iao Valley and Hana coast by Georgia O'Keeffe, plus magnificent ancient **Chinese** ceramics and bronzes.

Chinatown

Just five minutes' walk down Hotel Street west of downtown Honolulu, the faded green-clapboard storefronts of **Chinatown** seem like another world. Traditionally the city's red-light district, the narrow streets leading down to the Nuuanu Stream are still characterized by pool halls, massage parlors, and heavy-duty bars.

It's well worth delving into a few of Chinatown's inconspicuous alleyways. Some of its old walled courtyards are now malls, but the businesses remain much the same as ever, and you can still find herbalists weighing out dried leaves in front of vast arrays of bottles. Pig snouts and salmon heads are among the food specialties at **Oahu Market**, on N King and Kekaulike streets.

Bishop Museum

The anthropological collection at the **Bishop Museum** at 1525 Bernice St (daily 9am–5pm; $15; ☏808/847-3511, ⓦwww.bishopmuseum.org) – well away from both the ocean and downtown, near the foot of the Likelike Highway – showcases real Polynesian culture. Three floors display ancient carved stone and wooden images of gods, magnificent feather *leis* and cloaks, and a full-sized *hale* (traditional hut) brought here from Kauai, in addition to Japanese samurai armor and even a full-sized sperm whale. There are also excellent exhibitions for kids, and a planetarium. TheBus #2 from Waikiki stops two blocks away on Kapalama Street.

Punchbowl

High above Honolulu, lush lawns growing in the caldera of an extinct volcano are the setting for the **National Memorial Cemetery of the Pacific** (daily:

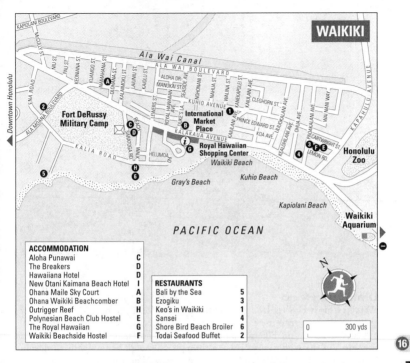

March–Sept 8am–6.30pm; Oct–Feb 8am–5.30pm), which holds casualties from all US Pacific wars, including Vietnam, as well as Hawaiian shuttle astronaut Ellison Onizuka. This spot is said to have held an ancient sacrificial temple, and is on TheBus route #15 from town.

Waikiki

Built on a reclaimed swamp, **Waikiki** is very nearly an island, all but separated from Honolulu between the sea and the Ala Wai canal (which provides the drainage to make its incredible highrise profusion possible). Once home to Kamehameha the Great, the site may be venerable, but these days its *raison d'être* is rampant commercialism. You could, just about, survive here with very little money, but there would be no point – there's nothing to see, and the only thing to do apart from surf and sunbathe is to stroll along the seafront **Kalakaua Avenue** and shop.

The most striking thing about the parallel **Waikiki Beach** is how narrow it is, a thin strip of shipped-in sand. Compared to many other Hawaiian beaches, it's overcrowded and small, but it's still a wonderful place to spend a lazy day, and the fact that it's lined by a pedestrian walkway, with several pleasant gardens en route, makes it a refuge from the frenzy nearby.

Two possible diversions on the eastern fringes of Waikiki are **Honolulu Zoo** (daily 9am–4.30pm; $8; ☎808/971-7171, ⓦwww.honoluluzoo.org), where you can walk through a mock African savannah set against the magnificent backdrop of Diamond Head, and the oceanfront **Waikiki Aquarium** (daily 9am–5pm; $9; ☎808/923-9741, ⓦwww.waquarium.org) which, as well as holding sharks and monkfish seals, has a tank devoted to the many-hued reef fish of Hanauma Bay (see p.1268).

△ Activity along Waikiki Beach

Diamond Head

Waikiki's most famous landmark is the pinnacle of **Diamond Head**, another extinct volcano just to the east. The lawns of the crater interior are oddly bland, but a straightforward hiking trail leads up a mile or so to the summit, and a panorama of the whole coast, passing through a network of tunnels built during World War II. TheBus #22 and #58 stop on the road nearby.

Hanauma Bay

A few miles to the east, the magnificent crescent-shaped **Hanauma Bay**, formed when the wall of a crater collapsed and let in the sea, is renowned as Oahu's best place to **snorkel** (summer daily except Tues 6am–7pm, 2nd and 4th Sat of month 6am–10pm; winter daily except Tues 6am–6pm, 2nd Sat of month 6am–10pm; $5, under-13s free; ☎808/396-4229). Thanks to strict conservation measures, the sea abounds in brightly colored fish. Hourly buses from Waikiki drop passengers at the visitor center, which shows educational videos about the bay's fragile ecology.

Pearl Harbor

Almost the whole of **Pearl Harbor**, the principal base for the US Pacific fleet (just over one hour west of Waikiki on TheBus #20), is off-limits to visitors. However, the surprise Japanese attack of December 7, 1941, which an official US inquiry called "the greatest military and naval disaster in our nation's history," is commemorated by a simple white memorial set above the wreck of the battleship **USS Arizona**, still discernible in the clear blue waters. More than 1100 of its crew lie entombed there.

Free tours of the memorial operate between 8am and 3pm each day, but it can be two or three hours after you pick up your numbered ticket at the **Pearl Harbor visitor center** (daily 7.30am–5pm, last program starts 3pm; ☎808/422-0561) before you're called to board the ferry that takes you there. There's a small museum and bookstore in the visitor center, as well as long-range views of the memorial, which was partly financed by Elvis Presley's 1961 Honolulu concert, his first show after leaving the army. The huge **USS Missouri**, which survived the attack and was used four years later for the ceremony in Tokyo Harbor that ended World War II, is moored alongside the *Arizona*. Guided visits, by bus from alongside the Pearl Harbor visitor center, include the actual surrender site as well as sweeping views of the harbor from the *Missouri*'s bridge (daily 9am–5pm; tours $16–25; ⊤1-877/MIGHTYMO, ⓦwww.ussmissouri.com).

Eating

Honolulu and Waikiki offer an enormous range of **dining** possibilities, and the recommendations below are just a sampling. For fine dining, all the larger Waikiki hotels have good restaurants, and, in Honolulu, **Restaurant Row mall** near the harbor is a good bet. There are excellent fast-food malls in the **Ala Moana Center**, and the much cheaper and more exotic **Maunakea Marketplace** on Maunakea Street in Chinatown, while Waikiki's Kuhio Avenue is lined with snack outlets and fast-food franchises.

Bali by the Sea *Hilton Hawaiian Village*, 2005 Kalia Rd, Waikiki ⊤808/941-2254. Highly refined gourmet restaurant, with irresistible views of the full length of Waikiki and very tasteful (and expensive) Pacific Rim cuisine.

Ezogiku 2546 Lemon Rd, Waikiki ⊤808/923-2013. Plain and very inexpensive Japanese diner, with three branches in Waikiki – the others are at 2420 Koa Ave and 2146 Kalakaua Ave. Ramen soups plus rice and curry dishes, all at around $8, to eat in or take out.

Kakaako Kitchen Ward Center, 1200 Ala Moana Blvd ⊤808/596-7488. Mall diner that dishes up high-quality fast food; pretty much everything, from the hamburger stew to the signature dish chicken linguine, costs $7–10, and there's a menu of daily $8 specials like meat loaf or pot roast.

Keo's in Waikiki 2028 Kuhio Ave, Waikiki ⊤808/951-9355. Hawaii's best Thai restaurant, and though its menu isn't exceptional, everything, from the specialty "Evil Jungle Prince" curries onwards, tastes great, and all entrees cost under $15. Breakfast is both American and Asian; lunch and dinner are entirely Thai.

Sam Choy's Breakfast, Lunch, and Crab 580 N Nimitz Hwy ⊤808/545-7979. Copious quantities of modern Hawaiian cuisine, including the signature raw tuna salad *ahi poke*, plus a microbrewery, located a mile or two west of downtown Honolulu.

🏃 **Sansei** *Waikiki Beach Marriott*, 2552 Kalakaua Ave ⊤808/931-6286. Wonderful, dinner-only Japanese-inspired restaurant, serving superb sushi at around $10 for a specialty roll, and a full Pacific Rim menu with entrees from $20. Late-night dining and free karaoke Fri & Sat.

Shore Bird Beach Broiler *Outrigger Reef on the Beach*, 2169 Kalia Rd, Waikiki ⊤808/922-2887. Open-air oceanfront restaurant serving a $10 breakfast buffet, and dinner with an open salad bar for $15–20, depending on choice of entree. Guests cook their own meat or fish on a communal grill.

🏃 **Todai Seafood Buffet** 1910 Ala Moana Blvd, Waikiki ⊤808/947-1000. Stylish all-you-care-to-eat Japanese buffet in western Waikiki. Lunch costs $16 and dinner $29, but the range and quality of the food, including sushi, shrimp, crab, and lobster, makes it a real bargain.

Yakiniku Canellia 2494 S Beretania St ⊤808/946-7955. Korean buffet restaurant a mile north of Waikiki, where you select slices of marinated beef, chicken, or pork and grill it yourself at the gas-fired burners set into each table. Open daily for lunch ($12) and dinner ($18).

Nightlife

Most of Honolulu's **nightlife** is concentrated in Waikiki, where fun-seeking tourists set the tone. On the whole, the available entertainment is on the bland side. Hawaii tends to be off the circuit for touring musicians, so if you enjoy live music you'll probably have to settle for lesser-known local performers. Look out also for special events at downtown's beautifully restored Hawaii Theatre, 1130 Bethel St (⊤808/528-0506, ⓦwww.hawaiitheatre.com).

🏃 **Chai's Island Bistro** Aloha Tower Marketplace, 101 Ala Moana Blvd ⊤808/585-0011. Sumptuous and very expensive Thai restaurant, where the very finest Hawaiian musicians perform for diners nightly 6.45–8.45pm.

Duke's Canoe Club *Outrigger Waikiki on the Beach*, 2335 Kalakaua Ave ☎808/922-2268. Smooth Hawaiian sounds wash over this oceanfront Waikiki cocktail bar nightly from 4pm to 6pm and 10pm to midnight – including big-name "Concerts on the Beach" Fri–Sun 4–6pm. No cover charge.

Hula's Bar and Lei Stand *Waikiki Grand Hotel*, 134 Kapahulu Ave ☎808/923-0669. Waikiki's most popular gay venue occupies a suite of ocean-view rooms across from the Honolulu Zoo. As well as a state-of-the-art dance floor equipped with giant video screens, there's also a more casual lounge area. Daily 10am–2am.

Ocean Club Restaurant Row, 500 Ala Moana Blvd ☎808/526-9888. Flamboyant, frenetic downtown bar-cum-restaurant that serves inexpensive food in the early evening and turns into a wild dance club as the night wears on. Over-22s only; no T-shirts.

Windward Oahu

The most spectacular moment on a tour of Oahu comes as you cross the Koolau Mountains on the **Pali Highway** (Hwy-61) to see the sheer green cliffs of the windward side of the island, veiled by swirling mists. The highest spot, four miles northeast of Honolulu, is the **Nuuanu Pali Lookout**. Kamehameha the Great finalized his conquest of Oahu here in 1795, forcing hundreds of enemy warriors over the edge of the cliffs.

Oahu's leading paying attraction, with one million annual visitors, is the **Polynesian Cultural Center**, ten miles short of the island's northernmost tip at Laie (Mon–Sat 12.30–9pm; $50–200; ☎1-800/367-7060, ⓦwww.polynesia.com). This haphazard mixture of real and bogus Polynesia – in which the history is firmly on the latter – is owned by the Mormons, and staffed by students from the adjacent Brigham Young University, who perform tired music and dance routines. TheBus #52 takes roughly two hours to get this far.

North Shore Oahu

The **surfing beaches** of northern Oahu are famous the world over, but they're minimally equipped for tourists. **Waimea**, **Sunset**, and **Ehukai** beach parks are

Sea sports and safety

The nation that invented **surfing** – long before the whites came – remains its greatest arena. The sport was popularized early in the twentieth century by Olympic swimmer Duke Kahanamoku, using a 20ft board; these days most are around six feet. As a rule, the best surfing beaches are on the north shore of each island. **Windsurfing**, too, is hugely popular, in similar locations, while smaller **boogie boards** make an exhilarating initiation. **Snorkeling** and **diving** are top-quality, although Hawaii's **coral** has fewer brilliant hues than those seen in warmer equatorial waters.

Bear in mind, however, that **drownings** in Hawaii are all too common. Waves can sweep in from two thousand miles of open ocean onto beaches that are unprotected by any reef. Not all beaches have lifeguards and warning flags, and unattended beaches are not necessarily safe. Watch the sea carefully before going in, and never take your eyes off it thereafter. If you get swept out, don't fight the big waves; wait for the current to die down before trying to swim back to shore.

Sea creatures to avoid include black spiky **sea urchins**, Portuguese man-of-war **jellyfish**, and **coral** in general, which can give painful infected cuts. **Shark attacks** are much rarer than popular imagination suggests; those that do occur are usually due to "misunderstandings," such as surfers idling on their boards looking a bit too much like turtles from below.

all laid-back roadside stretches of sand, where you can usually find a quiet spot to yourself. In summer, the tame waves may leave you wondering what all the fuss is about; see them at full tilt in the winter, and you'll have no doubts.

HALEIWA, the main surfers' hangout, combines alternative shops and cafés with upfront tourist traps. Much of the **food** around is vegetarian; the *Paradise Found Café*, 66-443 Kamehameha Hwy (☎808/637-4640), serves breakfast and lunch, both for about $7, while *Cholo's Homestyle Mexican*, in the North Shore Marketplace across the street (☎808/637-3059), is a busy, plain but very lively Mexican joint.

For **accommodation**, you'll have to head five miles northeast to the *Backpacker's Vacation Inn*, at 59-788 Kamehameha Hwy by Waimea Bay (☎808/638-7838, Ⓦwww.backpackers-hawaii.com; ❶–❾), which has dorm beds for $22–26 a night, as well as some great-value ocean-view private rooms and studios.

The Big Island

Although the **Big Island of Hawaii** could hold all the other islands with room to spare, it has the population of a medium-sized town, with just 150,000 people (half what it was in Captain Cook's day). Visitation is low compared to Oahu or Maui; despite its fair share of restaurants, bars, and facilities, this is basically a rural community, and sleepy old towns all over the island have remained unchanged for a century. The few resorts are built on the barren lava flows of the **Kona** coast to catch maximum sunshine; the beaches are great, but these are otherwise the least beautiful areas on the island.

Thanks to the **Kilauea** volcano, which has destroyed roads and even towns, and spews out pristine beaches of jet-black sand, the Big Island is still growing, its southern shore inching ever further out to sea. **Hawaii Volcanoes National Park**, which includes **Mauna Loa** as well as Kilauea (though not **Mauna Kea**, further to the north and higher than either), is absolutely compelling; you can explore steaming craters and cinder cones, venture into the rainforest, and at times approach within feet of the eruption itself.

As befits the birthplace and base of King Kamehameha, more of the ancient Hawaii survives on the Big Island than anywhere else in the islands. **Puuhonua O Honaunau National Historical Park** preserves a "place of refuge" for defeated warriors and those who ran afoul of society's rules, and there are further temples north along the Kohala coast, while **Waipio Valley**, where Kamehameha spent his youth, remains as lush and green as ever.

Flights to the Big Island arrive at both **Hilo** on the rainy east coast, or near the resort town of **Kailua** (often referred to as Kona) on the west. Public transportation is all but nonexistent.

Windward Hawaii

Almost all the rain that falls on the slopes of Mauna Kea flows down the eastern side of the Big Island. As a result, myriad streams and waterfalls nourish dense jungle-like vegetation, ensuring that the main road north along the coast from Hilo – the only sizeable base for travelers – is alive with flowering trees and orchids.

Hilo

Although it's the Big Island's capital and largest town, just 45,000 people live in **HILO**, which remains endearing and unpressured. Mass tourism has never taken off here, mainly because it rains too much. However, the rain falls mostly at night, and America's wettest city blazes with tropical blooms against a backdrop of rainbows.

With its modest streets and wooden stores, Hilo's **downtown** looks appealingly low-key. Sadly, that's largely because all the buildings that stood on the seaward side of Kamehameha Avenue were destroyed by two tsunami, in 1946 and 1960. The story is told in the **Pacific Tsunami Museum**, on Kamehameha Avenue at Kalakaua Street (Mon–Sat 9am–4pm; $7; ☎808/935-0926, ⓦwww.tsunami. org). A scale model shows how the city looked before the 1946 disaster; contemporary footage and personal letters bring home the full impact of the tragedy.

The focus of the two-part **Lyman Museum** at 276 Haili St (Mon–Sat 9.30am–4.30pm; $7; ☎808/935-5021, ⓦwww.lymanmuseum.org) is the original 1830s **Mission House**, furnished in dark *koa* wood, of Calvinist missionaries David and Sarah Lyman. The museum next door starts with a fascinating display of ancient weapons and then documents Hawaii's various ethnic groups, including the Portuguese brought here in 1878 from the similarly volcanic Azores, whose *braginha* became the ukelele.

A couple of miles up Waianuenue Avenue, at **Rainbow Falls**, just to the right of the road, a spectacular wide waterfall plummets 100ft across the mouth of a huge cavern.

Practicalities

Hilo's **airport** is at **General Lyman Field** (☎808/935-4782), on the eastern outskirts; a taxi into town costs around $8. The **Hawaii Visitors Bureau** is at 250 Keawe St (Mon–Fri 8am–noon & 1–4.30pm; ☎808/961-5797, ⓦwww.bigisland. org). From a terminal on Kamehameha Avenue, Hilo's Hele-On **bus** (☎808/961-8744) operates one daily service to Kailua (Mon–Sat) and down to Hawaii Volcanoes National Park (Mon–Fri).

There are two good **hostels** in town, both with private rooms as well as dorm beds. The attractive ⚓ *Hilo Bay Hostel*, downtown at 101 Waianuenue Ave (☎808/933-2771, ⓦwww.hawaiihostel.net; ❶–❸), offers $18 dorm beds and assorted private rooms. *Arnott's Lodge*, in the woods two miles southeast at 98 Apapane Rd. (☎808/969-7097, ⓦwww.arnottslodge.com; ❶–❸), has tent spots and dorm beds for $10, and you can join organized island tours. Otherwise, the *Dolphin Bay*, 333 Iliahi St (☎808/935-1466 or 1-877/935-1466, ⓦwww.dolphinbayhilo .com; ❹), is a nice, friendly little hotel. *Naung Mai Thai*, 86 Kilauea Ave ☎808/934-7540; closed Sun) is an excellent little Thai café downtown.

North from Hilo

The **Belt Road** (Hwy-19) follows the **Hamakua coast** north of Hilo, clinging to the hillsides and crossing ravines on slender bridges. For a glimpse into the interior, head into the mountains after fifteen miles to the 450ft **Akaka Falls**. A short loop trail through the forest, festooned with wild orchids, offers views of Akaka and other jungle-like tropical waterfalls.

Waipio Valley

Highway 240, which turns north off the Belt Road at **HONOKAA**, comes to an abrupt end after nine miles at the edge of **Waipio Valley**. As the southernmost of six successive sheer-walled valleys, this is the only one accessible by land – and it's as close as Hawaii comes to the classic South Seas image of an isolated and self-sufficient valley, dense with fruit trees and laced by footpaths leading down to the sea.

It's perfectly possible to walk down the steep, mile-long track into Waipio, but most visitors take tours, either in the four-wheel-drive vehicles of the Waipio Valley Shuttle (Mon–Sat 9am, 11am, 1pm & 3pm; ⊤808/775-7121, ⓦwww.waipiovalleytour.com; $45), at the Waipio Valley Art Works in Kukuihaele, a mile from the end of the road, or on horseback (⊤808/775-1007; $85).

The Kona coast

Hawaii's leeward **Kona coast** divides into two distinct areas. To the north of its only sizeable community, **Kailua**, barren lava trails down to the sea from the third highest of the Big Island's volcanoes, Hualalai. Thanks to the relentless sun on its superb beaches, luxury hotels dot the shoreline as incongruous green patches in the wasteland. To the south, the hillsides are more fertile, and although the condos are spreading, you can still get a real feel for the old Hawaii in the land where Captain Cook met his end.

North Kona and the resorts

The best of the spectacular sandy beaches along the Kona coast – safe for summer swimming, though with tempestuous winter surf – lie to the north of Kailua. **Hapuna Beach**, almost forty miles up the coast, is deservedly the most famous, despite being overshadowed by the giant ⚑ *Hapuna Beach Prince Hotel* (⊤808/880-1111 or 1-888/977-4623, ⓦwww.hapunabeachprincehotel; ⓿). For idyllic seclusion, head instead for **Kekaha Kai State Park** (daily except Wed 9am–7pm; free), reached via a bumpy dirt road a couple of miles north of Keahole Airport (see below).

Several extraordinary **resort hotels** lie in the district of South Kohala, thirty miles north of Kailua (see below). Three separate enclaves – Waikoloa, Mauna Kea, and Mauna Lani – have been landscaped out of this inhospitable lava desert, each one a self-contained oasis holding two or three hotels, a beach or two, and nothing else. Although **Waikoloa** is the least exclusive of the three, it's home to the ostentatious, mile-long *Hilton Waikoloa* (⊤808/886-1234 or 1-800/221-2424, ⓦwww.hiltonwaikoloavillage.com; ⓿), where guests travel to and from their rooms by electric boats or monorail.

Kailua (Kona)

Although the Big Island's main resort is officially called **KAILUA**, it's much more commonly referred to as **Kona**. An attractive little town that has played a major part in Hawaiian history, it's more affected by tourism than any other Big Island community, and its seafront row of fast-food restaurants and souvenir shops could be almost anywhere.

Arrival

The largely open-air **Keahole Airport**, situated on a field of black lava nine miles north of Kailua, has the usual car rental places; otherwise Speedishuttle **buses** into town cost around $20 per person (☎808/521-2085, ⓦwww.speedishuttle.com). In Kailua, a regular **shuttle bus** runs the six-mile length of Alii Drive every ninety minutes (Mon–Sat 8.30am–7.30pm; $2; ☎808/775-7121). One daily Hele-On bus (see p.1272) follows Hwy-11 around the north of the island to Hilo, leaving Kailua at 6.45am and returning in the late afternoon.

Accommodation

Alii Drive is lined for about five miles south from Kailua with **hotels and condos**, but none offers much in the way of budget accommodation. The listings below therefore include places a bit further along the coast.

King Kamehameha's Kona Beach Hotel 75-5660 Palani Rd ☎808/329-2911 or 1-800/367-6060, ⓦwww.konabeachhotel.com. Landmark hotel at the northern end of oceanfront Kailua, set around a picturesque little beach. ❼
Kona Seaside Hotel 75-5646 Palani Rd ☎808/329-2455 or 1-800/560-5558, ⓦwww.sand-seaside.com. Six floors of reasonable, air-conditioned rooms, with and without kitchens. ❻

Kona Tiki Hotel 75-5968 Alii Drive ☎808/329-1425, ⓦwww.konatiki.com. This simple three-story motel, beside the ocean a mile south of central Kailua, is very popular with bargain hunters. No phones or TVs, but some rooms have kitchenettes. ❸

The Town

Hulihee Palace (daily 9am–4pm, Sat & Sun 10am–4pm; $6) faces out to sea from the center of Kailua. Built as the governor's residence in 1838, it's not all that imposing from the outside, but within it's notable for massive *koa*-wood furnishings, made to fit the considerable girth of the various members of the Hawaiian royal family who later lived here, such as the redoubtable four-hundred-pound Princess Ruth. The 1836 **Mokuaikaua Church** directly opposite – Hawaii's first church – holds a museum on the early days of Hawaiian Christianity. King Kamehameha's funeral rites were performed in the ancient temple of **Ahuena Heiau**, which juts into the sea at the northern end of the bay.

Some of the world's best fishing, snorkeling, and scuba spots are approached by sea from Kailua. The catamaran *Fair Wind* offers snorkeling cruises to Kealakekua Bay (daily: 9am departure $105, shorter 2pm departure $69; ☎808/322-2788, ⓦwww.fair-wind.com).

Eating and drinking

Competition ensures that the **restaurants** and **bars** of central Kailua – especially those along the seafront – are well priced, though the relentless vacation atmosphere means the place can seem a bit unreal.

Cassandra's Greek Taverna 75-5669 Alii Drive ☎808/334-1066. Greek food might seem incongruous for Hawaii, but the fish specialties taste all the better for the sea view.
Huggo's 76-6828 Kuhakai St ☎808/329-1493. Lunch and dinner served on a large terrace with ocean views. Burgers, salads, and sandwiches, as well as Pacific Rim specialties, plus live evening entertainment.

O's Bistro Crossroads Shopping Center, 75-1027 Henry St ☎808/329-9222. Pan-Asian noodle joint, a mile up from the ocean near the highway, serving great dinners from around $20.
Sibu Café Banyan Court Mall, 75-5695 W Alii Drive ☎808/329-1112. Popular, informal Indonesian restaurant, with atmospheric outdoor seating but no views. Serves $12–15 entrees, including a tasty shrimp *sate*.

Kealakekua Bay

Kealakekua Bay, a dozen miles south of Kailua, was where Captain Cook was killed on February 14, 1779, during his second visit to Hawaii, after a year spent searching for the fabled Northwest Passage. One of ancient Hawaii's major population centers, it's now barely inhabited, and the white **obelisk** on the death site

– legally a small piece of England – is all but inaccessible. You can only get to within a mile of the bay by car, at **Napoopoo Beach**, though you'll get a glimpse of it from the road on the way down. The bay itself is the best place on the Big Island for **snorkeling**, even if there are sharks further out. It's also possible to hike down to the monument, but it's a grueling four-hour roundtrip, for which you need to carry all your water and supplies. The trail starts just before the town of **CAPTAIN COOK**, which is also home to the bargain ⊁ *Manago Hotel* (☏808/323-2642, ⓦ www.managohotel.com; ❶–❸), offering comfortable ocean-view rooms amid flowering Japanese gardens.

This region, South Kona, is the prime source of **Kona coffee**, which sells here for around $26 per pound (including shipping). A mile south of Captain Cook, the ⊁ *Coffee Shack* (daily 7am–4pm; ☏808/328-9555) serves wonderfully fresh coffee and smoothies on a terrace that enjoys staggering views all the way down to Kealakekua Bay.

Puuhonua O Honaunau – "The City of Refuge"

Puuhonua O Honaunau National Historical Park (Mon–Thurs 6am–8pm, Fri–Sun 6am–11pm; $5 per vehicle), four miles on from Kealakekua, is the single most evocative historical site in all of the Hawaiian islands, jutting into the Pacific on a small peninsula of jagged black lava. The grounds include a palace, complete with fishpond and private canoe landing, and three *heiaus* (places of worship), guarded by large carved effigies of gods – reproductions, but still eerie in their original setting. An ancient **"place of refuge"** lies firmly protected behind the mortarless masonry of the sixteenth-century **Great Wall**. Those who broke ancient Hawaii's intricate system of *kapu* (taboo) – perhaps by treading on the shadow of a chief or fishing in the wrong season – could expect summary execution unless they fled to the sanctuary of such a place. As chiefs lived on the surrounding land, transgressors had to swim through the shark-infested seas. If successful, they would be absolved and released overnight.

Hawaii Volcanoes National Park

The Big Island's southernmost volcanoes, **Mauna Loa** and **Kilauea**, jointly constitute **HAWAII VOLCANOES NATIONAL PARK**, thirty miles from Hilo and eighty from Kailua. Possibly the most dramatic of all the US national parks, it includes desert, arctic tundra, and rainforest, besides two active volcanoes.

Evidence is everywhere of the awesome power of the volcanoes to create and destroy; no map can keep up with the latest whims of the lava flow. Whole towns have been engulfed, and what were once prized beachfront properties lie buried hundreds of yards back from the sea.

Kilauea Caldera

The main focus of the park is **Kilauea Caldera**. Close to the rim, on the eleven-mile **Crater Rim Drive**, both the **visitor center** (daily 7.45am–5pm; $10 per vehicle; ☏808/967-7311, ⓦ www.nps.gov/havo) and the fascinating **Jaggar Museum** of geology (daily 8.30am–5pm; free) offer basic orientation. Kilauea is said to be the home of the volcano goddess **Pele**, who has followed the "hot spot" from island to island. In 1824 Queen Kapiolani, a recent convert to Christianity, defied her by descending into the crater, reading aloud from her Bible, eating the *tabu* red *ohelo* berries, and throwing stones into the pit. When Mark Twain came here in 1866, he observed a dazzling lake of liquid fire; since a huge explosion in 1924 it's been shallower and quieter, a black dusty expanse dotted with hissing steam vents. Enthusiastic hikers should set time aside to follow the long trails that explore the caldera floor. Both the **Halemaumau Trail**, a seven-mile roundtrip, and the **Kilauea Iki Trail**, a total of five miles, involve picking your way from cairn to cairn across an eerie landscape of cracked and jagged lava.

Among shorter routes, the mile-long **Devastation Trail** is a boardwalk laid across the scene of a 1959 eruption. Most of what you see is new growth – fresh lava is full of nutrients, and rainwater and seeds soon collect in the recesses – but a few older trees survived partial submersion in ash by growing "aerial roots" some way up their trunks.

Chain of Craters Road

Chain of Craters Road winds down to the sea from Crater Rim Drive, sweeping around a succession of cones and vents in an empty landscape where the occasional dead white tree trunk or flowering shrub pokes up. Fresh sheets of lava constantly ooze down the slopes to cover the road. When a new road is built on top of the flow, more lava covers it. Along the coast, the scale of the damage since 1983 has been too great to repair – over seven miles have been lost – so now the road is a dead end, and getting shorter year by year. One by one the landmarks along its seafront stretch have been destroyed, and before long it may not follow the shoreline at all.

Check current conditions at the **visitor center** when you arrive, and make sure you have enough gas. The end of the road is a fifty-mile roundtrip from the park entrance, and there are no facilities of any kind along the way. For the last few years, depending on where current volcanic activity is concentrated, it has been possible at times to walk across the congealed lava blocking Chain of Craters Road to see molten rock gush from the earth – sometimes directly into the sea. The park's **Volcano Update** (℡808/985-6000, ⓦhvo.wr.usgs.gov) has the latest details; for information on ranger-led tours, call the visitor center.

△ Kilauea Volcano

Practicalities

The national park operates two free **campgrounds** on a first-come, first-served basis, while the famous *Volcano House*, on the very edge of the crater within the park (℡808/967-7321, Ⓦ www.volcanohousehotel.com; cabins ❸, rooms ❹), has spectacular views, and good food in the evening, although the prices for its simple motel-style rooms are rather high. Otherwise, the small and inconspicuous town of **VOLCANO**, just before the park entrance on the Hilo side, provides the best places to **stay** in the vicinity, with B&Bs such as 🍴 *Hale Ohia* (℡808/967-7986, Ⓦ www.haleohia.com; ❹), south of the highway across from the village. *Kilauea Lodge*, on the leafy main street (℡808/967-7366, Ⓦ www.kilauealodge.com; ❻), is a comfortable inn with a very good **restaurant**.

Maui

The island of **MAUI**, the second largest in the Hawaiian chain, is Oahu's principal rival, attracting roughly a third of all visitors to the state. Some would say that things have gone too far, with formerly remote, unspoiled beaches, around **Kaanapali** and **Kihei** for example, now swamped by sprawling resorts. On the other hand, the crowds come to Maui for the good reason that it's still beautiful. This is the best equipped of all the islands for **activity** holidays – whale-watching,

---

Maui activities

From the moment you arrive on Maui, promotional handouts and free newspapers will bombard you with details on the island's wide range of **activities**. Operators in all the tourist areas, especially along Front Street in Lahaina, including Barefoot's Cashback Tours at no. 834 (℡1-888/222-3601, Ⓦ www.tombarefoot.com), offer cut-rate deals.

Snorkeling and diving

Maui's best-known **snorkeling** and **diving** spot is the tiny crescent of **Molokini**, poking above the sea – all that's left of a once-great volcano. There's no beach or landfall, but you do see a lot of fish, including deep-water species. Countless cruises leave early each morning (to avoid the heat) from Maalea Harbor; snorkelers can pay anything from $50 to $110 for a morning trip, and from $35 for a shorter afternoon jaunt. Vessels range from the twenty-passenger *Hokua* (℡808/249-2583, Ⓦ www.alohabluecharters.com) up to the 150-seater *Prince Kuhio* (℡808/242-8777, Ⓦ www.mvprince.com).

Downhill cycle rides

One of Maui's more unusual opportunities is to be taken by van to the top of **Haleakala**, watch the sun rise, and then ride a bicycle 39 miles down to Paia by the sea – without pedaling once. Serious cyclists find the slow pace of the trip frustrating; complete novices or the unfit shouldn't try; in-betweens think it's great. Companies running trips for around $80 (including pickups) include Cruiser Phil's (℡808/893-2332 or 1-877/764-2453, Ⓦ www.cruiserphil.com) and Maui Downhill (℡808/871-2155 or 1-800/535-2453, Ⓦ www.mauidownhill.com).

windsurfing, diving, sailing, snorkeling, and cycling. Temperatures along the coast can be searing, especially at historic **Lahaina**, but it's always possible to escape to somewhere cooler. **Upcountry Maui**, on the slopes of the mighty **Haleakala** volcano, is a delight, well away from the bustle, while the waterfalls and ravines along the tortuous road out west to **Hana** outclass anything on Oahu.

Kahului and Wailuku

Almost half of Maui's 125,000 inhabitants – the workers who keep this fantasy island going – live in the twin towns of **KAHULUI** and **WAILUKU**, to the north of the "neck" connecting its two mountainous sections. The land here can be so flat you fear the waves will wash right over it. Kahului is the main commercial center; Wailuku, if not aesthetically pleasing, is one of the few towns on Maui that feels like a genuine community, and the presence of budget accommodation and restaurants – and the stunning **Iao Needle** nearby – make it a good central base.

Arrival and information

Virtually all visitors to Maui arrive at **Kahului Airport**, which is well placed for all the island's major destinations and has an information booth. Speedishuttle **buses** (T 808/661-6667 or 1-800/977-2605, W www.speedishuttle.com) connect the airport regularly with resorts around the island.

The offices of the **Maui Visitors Bureau** are hard to find, tucked away at 1727 Wili Pa Loop in Wailuku (Mon–Fri 8am–4.30pm; T 808/244-3530 or 1-800/525-6284, W www.visitmaui.com), and it's easier simply to pick up information in major hotels.

Accommodation

Wailuku is nowhere near Maui's main resort areas, and lacks any hotels, but thanks to its two hostels and convenient restaurants, it's the island's most popular destination for budget travelers.

Banana Bungalow 310 N Market St, Wailuku T 808/244-5090 or 1-800/846-7835, W www. mauihostel.com. Friendly, lively hostel that offers $25 dorm beds as well as some bare, basic doubles. Free airport shuttles, a changing schedule of free island tours, and cut-price car rental. ❶–❸

Northshore Hostel 2080 Vineyard St, Wailuku T 808/986-8095 or 1-866/946-7835, W www. northshorehostel.com. Refurbished hostel in central Wailuku, offering $25 dorm beds, plus some private rooms with en-suite facilities. ❶–❸

Exploring Kahului and Wailuku

There's no sightseeing to speak of in either Kahului or Wailuku, though you may become familiar with both while shopping for food and other necessities. **Market Street** in Wailuku also contains several interesting curio and souvenir shops, and commands a view across to Haleakala.

Wailuku's Main Street heads straight into the **West Maui Mountains**, stopping three miles in at **Iao Needle**, a stunning 1200ft pinnacle of green-clad lava that stands, head usually in the clouds, at the intersection of two lush valleys. Kamehameha won control of Maui here in 1790, in a battle determined by a cannonade directed by two European gunners.

Eating

While both Kahului and Wailuku hold a handful of good-value **restaurants**, neither has anything that could be considered fine dining.

AK's Cafe 1237 L Market St, Wailuku ☏808/244-8774. Healthy and very tasty local specialties, with cheap lunches and fish dinners for around $15. Closed Sat & Sun.

Maui Bake Shop & Deli 2092 Vineyard St, Wailuku ☏808/244-7117. Great deli, where you can pick up inexpensive breakfasts and lunches or simply buy superb fresh bread. Closed Sun & Mon.

Maui Coffee Roasters 444 Hana Hwy, Kahului ☏808/877-2877. Relaxed espresso bar serving good breakfasts, lunch specials, and, of course, coffees.

West Maui

Despite largely guaranteed sunshine, you can feel somewhat cut off if you choose to stay on Maui's **west coast**, where the prices are higher than elsewhere, and the long drive is worsened by heavy traffic. The hotels and shopping centers are concentrated in the two main resorts, **Lahaina** and **Kaanapali**, although development has sensibly been restricted to the *makai* (oceanward) side of the Honoapiilani Highway, leaving the inland hills and valleys untouched except by drifting rainbows.

Lahaina

LAHAINA, West Maui's only real town, is one of the prettiest communities in all Hawaii. During the early nineteenth century it served as capital of the entire Kingdom of Hawaii, but it has barely grown since then, and still resembles the peaceful tropical village it used to be. Its main oceanfront street is lined with timber-frame buildings; coconut palms sway to either side of the mighty central banyan tree; surfers swirl into the thin fringe of beach to the south; and the mountains of West Maui dominate the skyline.

16

HAWAII | West Maui

Whale-hunting and whale-watching

The first **whaling ships** arrived in Hawaii in 1820, the same year as the missionaries – and had an equally dramatic impact. With the ports of Japan closed to outsiders, Hawaii swiftly became the center of the industry. Any Pacific port of call must have seemed a godsend to the whalers, who were away from New England for three years at a time, and paid so badly that most were either fugitives from justice or just plain mad. Hawaii was such a paradise that up to fifty percent of each crew would desert, to be replaced by native Hawaiians, born seafarers eager to see the world.

Until the 1840s, Honolulu, which permitted drinking, was the whalers' favorite port. Then potatoes and prostitution lured them to **Lahaina** as well, where the sea was calm enough for ships to dock beside the open road and stock up on provisions at a grassy marketplace beside a central canal.

At the peak of the trade, almost six hundred whaling vessels docked in Honolulu in a single year. Decline came with the Civil War – when many whaling ships were deliberately sunk to blockade Confederate ports – and an 1871 disaster, when 31 vessels lingered in the Arctic too long, became frozen in, and had to be abandoned.

Ironically, the waters off western Maui now rate among the world's best areas for whale-watching and whale research. Between January and March each year, and for up to a month either side of that, **humpback whales** use the ocean channels here as both sanctuary and playground. The whales are often clearly visible from the shore, but specific whale-watching trips can take you much closer (with money-back guarantees if you don't see one). Operators include the nonprofit Pacific Whale Foundation ($20; ☏808/249-8811 or 1-800/942-5311, 🌐www.pacificwhale.org).

△ Lahaina

The view out to sea from Lahaina, towards the island of **Lanai**, is superb. If you have the time, consider taking a ferry there for the day; there's little to see on the island, but the main beach, at Hulopoe Bay, is a delight. Expeditions provides five sailings daily, from Lahaina Harbor ($25 each way; ☎808/661-3756, ⓦwww.go-lanai.com).

Accommodation

If you have the money to spend on resort-style **accommodation**, Lahaina and the coast to the north have some good options, but there's very little available for under $100 per night.

Best Western Pioneer Inn 658 Wharf St ☎808/661-3636 or 1-800/457-5457, ⓦwww.pioneerinnmaui.com. Characterful and very lively old hotel, right in the thick of things. Tastefully furnished rooms come with private bath and air-conditioning. ❻

Old Lahaina House PO Box 10355, Lahaina, HI 96761 ☎808/667-4663 or 1- 800/847-0761, ⓦwww.oldlahaina.com. Good-quality en suite B&B rooms in a friendly private home, complete with pool. ❹

Outrigger Aina Nalu 660 Wainee St ☎808/667-9766 or 1-800/367-5226, ⓦwww.outrigger.com. Very central, low-key but attractively refurbished, mid-range accommodation. ❺

Food and nightlife

Lahaina's harborside malls contain a tremendous selection of **restaurants**, national and local chain outlets, and take-out places, not all of them good by any means, but covering a wider spectrum than the hotels.

David Paul's Lahaina Grill *Lahaina Inn*, 127 Lahainaaluna Rd ☎808/667-5117. Upmarket dinneronly restaurant serving Maui's finest Pacific Rim cooking; it's slightly cramped, but the food is great.

The Feast at Lele 505 Front St ☎808/667-5353. An inspired cross between a *luau* and a gourmet restaurant. Each of the five Polynesian courses consists of at least two dishes – a colossal amount of food, but it's excellent and unusual, and the beachfront setting is superb. The $99 charge, though steep, includes unlimited cocktails and other beverages. Reservations are essential. Daily, April–Sept 6pm, Oct–March 5.30pm.

Sunrise Café 693A Front St at Market St
☎808/661-8558. Small, laid-back, and very
central café, with outdoor seating beside its own

tiny patch of beach. Espressos, smoothies, salads,
sandwiches, and daily specials are all on offer, with
prices starting at around $6.

Kaanapali

KAANAPALI, just a few miles north of Lahaina but reliably cooler, was never a town; fields of sugar cane here were replaced in the 1960s by highrise hotels and condos, each comfortable enough but soulless en masse. Besides several perfect family **beaches** – swimming and snorkeling are best at **Black Rock**, in front of the *Sheraton* – the other main attraction is the **whaling museum** in the Whalers Village mall (daily 9am–10pm; free). Grisly but fascinating exhibits include a cast-iron "try pot," used for reducing whale blubber at sea; such pots gave rise to the stereotyped, but not entirely untrue, image of cannibals cooking missionaries in big black cauldrons.

A free shuttle bus connects Kaanapali with Lahaina, and a trolley operates within the resort. The warnings of the car rental companies concerning the sinuous **Kahekili Highway**, which on the map looks like a good route to continue on around northwest Maui and back to Wailuku, should be taken seriously; it's an exceptionally dangerous drive. However, two of Maui's most famous **surfing** spots, at Mokuleia Bay and Honolua Bay, are a few miles along, before the road gets too hair-raising.

Kihei and Wailea

Maui's other main resort area is south of Kahului, across the isthmus. The long strip of hotels, malls, and condos begins at **KIHEI**, with the road heavily built up on both sides, but thins out beyond the manicured lawns of **WAILEA**, near some superb beaches. **Paluea Beach** is ideal for families, while **Little Beach**, reached by a trail from **Makena (Big) Beach**, is famous for (illegal) nudism.

Few of the **accommodation** options are geared towards budget travelers, though the pretty little *Sunseeker Resort*, 551 S Kihei Rd (☎808/879-1261 or 1-800/532-6284, ⓦwww.mauisunseeker.com; ⓖ), which looks like an old-fashioned motel, has great-value ocean-view rooms, and the *Wailana Inn*, 14 Wailana Place (☎808/874-3131 or 1-800/399-3885, ⓦwww.wailanabeach.com; ⓖ), is a slightly more expensive and comfortable version. For **food**, *Sansei*, at the Kihei Town Center (☎808/879-0004), offers great-value sushi and Pacific Rim concoctions.

Upcountry Maui

Hawaii is not always a land tarnished by civilization. **Central Maui**, in the nineteenth century "a dreary expanse of sand and shifting sandhills, with a dismal growth . . . of thornless thistles," is now a pastoral idyll, thanks to an ingenious system of irrigation channels.

The highway to the top of **Haleakala** climbs higher, at a faster rate, than any road on earth. Starting in rich meadows, it climbs past purple-blossoming jacaranda, firs, and eucalyptus to reach open ranching land, and then ascends in huge curves to the volcanic desert and the crater itself.

Haleakala

Though **HALEAKALA** – "the House of the Sun" – is the world's largest dormant volcano, you may not appreciate its full ten-thousand-foot majesty until you're at the top. Shield volcanoes are not as dramatic as the classic cones, as lava oozes from fissures along broad flanks to create a long, low profile, and the summit is often obscured by clouds. That it hasn't erupted for two hundred years doesn't necessarily mean it won't ever again – in 1979, for example, Haleakala was thought more likely to explode than Mount St Helens (see p.1193).

The higher reaches of the mountain are a **national park**, which never closes (admission $10 per vehicle). Manhattan would fit comfortably into the awe-inspiring **crater**, almost eight miles across, which was for the ancient Hawaiians a site of deep spiritual power. The most popular time to come is for the **sunrise**; the **visitor center** at the top operates from just before dawn until 3pm (☎808/572-4400, ⓦwww.nps.gov/hale). Hiking trails of varying difficulty cross the crater floor, where **camping** is permitted in three remote cabins that are awarded by lottery two months in advance. They require a hike of four to ten miles and a $75 fee per night. In addition, fifteen to twenty-five free tent sites outside the crater are available every day (first-come, first-served).

Makawao and Paia

Coming down from Haleakala, Hwy-365 leads north to two laid-back little country towns populated mainly by old Californian hippies: **MAKAWAO**, five miles up from the ocean, and **PAIA**, Maui's first plantation town, near the great windsurfing beach of **Hookipa**. Neither offers any accommodation, but in the center of Makawao, the friendly Italian restaurant *Casanova's*, 1188 Makawao Ave (☎808/572-0220), puts on live music at night, courtesy of the local community of rock exiles. Fresh fish is the specialty at the oceanfront *Mama's*, a mile east of Paia at 799 Poho Place (☎808/579-8488), while vegetarians will be glad of the top-quality food at *Fresh Mint*, 115 Baldwin Ave, in Paia (☎808/579-9144).

The road to Hana

The rains that fall on Haleakala cascade down Maui's long windward flank, covering it in thick, jungle-like vegetation. Convicts in the 1920s hacked out a road along the coast that has become a major tourist attraction, twisting in and out of gorges, past innumerable waterfalls and over more than fifty tiny one-lane bridges. All year round, and especially in June, the route is ablaze with color from orchids, rainbow eucalyptus, and orange-blossomed African tulip trees. The usual day's excursion is roughly fifty miles (three hours) each way from Paia, to gorgeous **Oheo Gulch**, ten miles beyond Hana, where waterfalls tumble down the hillside to oceanfront meadows.

Hana

The former sugar town of **HANA** itself might seem a disappointment at the end of the road; it's a pleasant enough little community that isn't especially interested in attracting tourists. **Hasegawa's General Store** is a friendly place to pick up supplies, and a **red-sand beach** can be reached by a precarious trail from the end of Uakea Road. Rooms at the deluxe ⚑ *Hotel Hana-Maui* (☎808/248-8211 or 1-800/321-4262, ⓦwww.hotelhanamaui.com; ❾) *start* at around $400; *Joe's Place*

on Uakea Road is a basic but affordable alternative (℡808/248-7033, Ⓦwww. joesrentals.com; ❷). There's also **camping** beside the black-sand beach at lovely Waianapanapa State Park, four miles short of Hana (℡808/984-8109; $5).

Kauai

Although no point on the tiny island of **KAUAI** is as much as a dozen miles from the sea, the variety of its landscapes is quite incredible. This is the oldest of the major islands, and the forces of erosion have had more than six million years to sculpt it into fantastic shapes. The mist-shrouded extinct volcano **Mount Waia-leale** at its heart is the world's wettest spot, draining into a high landlocked swamp, and full of unique plants and animals. Nearby is the chasm of **Waimea Canyon**, while the north shore holds the vertiginous green cliffs of the awe-inspiring **Na Pali** coast, familiar to millions from films such as *Jurassic Park* and *South Pacific*, but the sole preserve of adventurous **hikers**. Kauai is a place to be active, on sea and land; and if you only take one **helicopter** flight in your life, this is the place to do it.

Lihue

Flights to Kauai arrive at the capital, **LIHUE**, which stands slightly inland of little Nawiliwili Harbor at the southeast corner of the island. It's roughly at the mid-point of the one main road that encircles the island (prevented from completing a loop by the Na Pali cliffs), but as a base it's undistinguished. The population is just five thousand, and downtown consists of a few tired plantation-town streets set well back from the sea.

The small **Kauai Museum** at 4428 Rice St (Mon–Fri 9am–4pm, Sat 10am–4pm; $7) traces the island's history from the mythical *menehune* (dwarfs said to have been here before the Polynesians arrived) through Captain Cook's 1778 landfall and on to its sugar-growing heyday. Kauai was the one island not conquered by Kame-hameha the Great; he spent six years amassing a fleet that never sailed, and settled in the end for accepting economic tribute.

Practicalities

Lihue's **airport** is only two miles from downtown ($8 by **taxi**; Wailua or Kapaa cost closer to $20). Along with the usual **car** rental outlets, it also has **helicopters** – Safari Helicopter Tours (℡808/246-0136 or 1-800/326-3356, Ⓦwww.safariair. com) is typical, offering basic tours from $150. The **Hawaii Visitors Bureau** is in town at 4334 Rice St (Mon–Fri 8am–4.30pm; ℡808/245-3971 or 1-800/262-1400, Ⓦwww.kauaidiscovery.com).

There's no great point staying in Lihue rather than along the coast. However, the ⚓ *Garden Island Inn*, near the harbor at 3445 Wilcox Rd (℡808/245-7227 or 1-800/648-0154, Ⓦwww.gardenislandinn.com; ❹), is a lovely refurbished three-story motel, dripping with purple bougainvillea. For a quick meal in the heart of town, call in at *Hamura's Saimin*, 2956 Kress St (℡808/245-3271), a family-run

Japanese food counter which specializes in bowls of *saimin* (noodles) for $4. A mile or two east, the 🜂 *Hanamaulu Restaurant and Tea House* (☎808/245-2511) is a delightful old place, complete with fishponds, that serves both Chinese and Japanese food.

East Kauai

Most Kauaians live between Lihue and the overlapping communities of **WAILUA**, **WAIPOULI**, and **KAPAA**, whose malls, condos, and hotels blend into each other a few miles north of the capital. All the way along there's an exposed thin strip of beach; only Wailua is especially scenic, and you have to go further north for snorkeling.

Accommodation

While most East Shore **hotels** are expensive by any other than Hawaiian standards, there are several possibilities on a more affordable scale.

Hotel Coral Reef 1516 Kuhio Hwy, Kapaa ☎808/822-4481 or 1-800/843-4659, ⓦwww.hotelcoralreef.com. Simple little hotel facing the beach that offers some of Kauai's best rates. ❹

Kauai International Hostel 4532 Lehua St, Kapaa ☎808/823-6142, ⓦwww.kauaihostel.net. Kauai's only hostel, across from Kapaa Beach and open to everyone except Hawaiian residents, with a maxi-

mum one-week stay. $25 dorm beds, and a few private rooms. ❶–❸

Lae Nani 410 Papaloa Rd, Wailua ☎808/822-4938 or book through Outrigger 1-800/688-7444, ⓦwww.outrigger.com. Irresistible complex of luxurious oceanfront apartments and condos, with lovely swimming alongside. ❼

Eating

Kapaa is the only town in East Kauai with anything like a center; you can window-shop for **restaurants** along its street of wooden stores, which are fronted by a beach park.

Caffè Coco 4-1639 Kuhio Hwy, Wailua ☎808/822-7990. Attractively ramshackle café, serving cheap and wholesome, if not entirely vegetarian, breakfasts and lunches for under $10, plus changing dinner specials. Closed Mon.

Coconuts 4-919 Kuhio Hwy, Kapaa ☎808/823-8777. Roomy, attractive (but viewless) Pacific Rim

restaurant, serving flavorful fish and meat entrees for $20 and up. Dinner only.

Korean Bar-B-Q Restaurant 4-3561 Kuhio Hwy, Wailua ☎808/823-6744. Unassuming barbecue diner serving excellent grilled meats and chicken; the best bet for a bargain meal, with large combos for under $10.

North Kauai

Despite the development elsewhere on the island, the astonishing valleys of Kauai's **Na Pali coast** are likely to remain inviolate – though accessible enough by canoe to sustain large Hawaiian populations, their awesome walls shield them from any attempt to build roads.

Long, golden **Secret Beach**, hidden away from the road up from Kapaa, is among Kauai's best-looking beaches, though swimming here is usually unsafe. To get there, drive up Hwy-56 from the south, pass **Kilauea**, and then turn right at Kalihiwai. Take the second right onto a dirt track leading to a parking area, and the beach is a ten-minute walk down through the woods. At the far end, a waterfall of beautiful fresh mountain water cascades down the cliffs, and there are often spinner dolphins just offshore, especially around the picturesque 1913 Kilauea **lighthouse**. The cliffs above are a bird sanctuary.

Hanalei

Major development stops beyond the resort of **Princeville**, mainly because the road then crosses seven successive one-lane bridges. The first is over the Hanalei River, where the valley stretching away inland is a National Wildlife Refuge. Here endangered Hawaiian ducks, coots, and stilts are protected by the preservation of their major habitats – natural wetlands and taro ponds. As a result, this is a rare chance to see a Hawaiian landscape relatively unchanged since ancient times.

The small town of **HANALEI**, set around a magnificent bay, has some low-key apartments for rent, but otherwise little formal accommodation. Of local **restaurants**, the busy *Hanalei Gourmet* in the Hanalei Center mall (☎808/826-2524) makes an ideal stop for breakfast or a sandwich lunch, and also has live music every night.

Gorgeous **Lumahai Beach**, at the western edge of Hanalei Bay, has starred in countless movies, among them *South Pacific*, but is too treacherous for swimming. All the roadside beaches from here on, however, are good for snorkeling. Just two miles from the start of the Na Pali coast (see below), the ⚓ *Hanalei Colony Resort* (☎808/826-6235 or 1-800/628-3004, ⓦ www.hcr.com; ➒) is Kauai's most dramatic waterfront property, within a few feet of the pounding surf; all its units have two bedrooms. The road finally comes to an end at **Kee Beach**, perhaps the loveliest spot of all.

The Na Pali coast

The lush valleys of the **Na Pali coast**, separated by knife-edge ridges of rock thousands of feet high but just a few feet thick, make Kauai one of the world's great hiking destinations. Although many of the best views (other than from a helicopter) are from the trails in Kokee State Park (see p.1286) or boat trips out to sea, the **Kalalau Trail** along the shore is unforgettable. The full eleven miles to Kalalau Valley is arduous and gets progressively more dangerous; in places you have to scramble along a precipitous (and shadeless) wall of crumbly red rock.

However, the first two miles of the trail, to **Hanakapiai Beach**, are probably the most beautiful. They're steep but straightforward, passing through patches of dense vegetation where you clamber over the gnarled root systems of the splay-footed *hala* (pandanus) tree. Creepers and vines hang down, and it's all exposed to the sun. From the beach, a further hour's arduous hike (off the main trail) leads inland to the natural amphitheater of the towering **Hanakapiai Falls**. It takes at least four and a half hours to get to the falls and back from the trailhead at Kee Beach, opposite the ten-mile marker at the end of the road. Hikers and campers doing anything more than a day-hike must obtain **permits**, costing $10 per person per night, from the State Parks Office (3060 Eiwa St, Lihue; ☎808/274-3444). Accidents and drownings are not uncommon, and the staff need a record of who may be missing.

South Kauai

POIPU, Kauai's principal beach resort, lies on the south coast roughly ten miles west of Lihue, where sunshine is more consistent and there's great surfing and snorkeling. Its finest **hotel** is the sumptuous 🏨 *Hyatt Regency*, 1571 Poipu Rd (☎808/742-1234 or 1-800/554-9288, ⓦwww.kauai-hyatt. com; ❾), while *Grantham Resorts* (☎808/742-7220 or 1-800/325-5701, ⓦwww .grantham-resorts.com; ❼–❾) quotes lower prices for local condos than you'll be offered by individual properties. The best restaurants are two upmarket Pacific Rim options: *Casa di Amici*, 2301 Nalo Rd (☎808/742-1555), and 🏨 *Roy's Poipu Bar & Grill* (☎808/742-5000), in the Poipu Shopping Village mall.

West Kauai

Two of the major scenic attractions in all Hawaii – the gorge of **Waimea Canyon** and **Kokee State Park** (with its views of the Na Pali cliffs to one side and the sodden Alakai Swamp to the other) – can only be reached from the **west coast** of Kauai. The coast itself, however, is nondescript. **WAIMEA**, the largest town here, is just one short street at the foot of the poorly marked road up to the canyon. The statue of **Captain Cook**, which commemorates his "discovery" of Hawaii here on January 20, 1778, is an exact replica of one in Cook's home town of Whitby, England. Western Kauai's only **accommodation** option is 🏨 *Waimea Plantation Cottages* (☎808/338-1625 or 1-800/992-4632, ⓦwww.waimea-plantation.com; ❻), set in an attractive coconut grove, and with a good restaurant and brewpub in the main plantation house.

Waimea Canyon and Kokee State Park

It's not unreasonable to call **Waimea Canyon** the "Grand Canyon of the Pacific." At three thousand feet, it may not be quite as deep as its Arizona rival, but the colors – all shades of green against the bare red earth – are absolutely breathtaking. Erosion by torrential rains created this landscape, but the process began when a massive geological fault almost split Kauai in two. The road from Waimea climbs beside the widening gorge, until after eight miles the mile-wide canyon can be seen in all its splendor. Each of the roadside lookouts is definitely worth stopping for.

Explore **Kokee State Park**, higher up, as early in the day as possible; by late morning the valleys may be filled with mist and clouds. Hiking trails lead off from both sides of the highway, and although the ranger station at **KOKEE**, the park headquarters, is often unstaffed, you can pick up trail information from the small but informative **Kokee Natural History Museum** nearby (daily 10am–4pm; $1 donation), where displays center on the area's indigenous wildlife. Kauai is the only island where mongooses have not killed off most native **birds**, and at this height mosquitoes are no threat either, so some of the world's rarest species (such as the *o'o a'a*) survive here and nowhere else.

Kokee Lodge Housekeeping Cabins, next to the park headquarters, are rented by the day (PO Box 819, Waimea, Kauai, HI 96796; ☎808/335-6061; ❷), and there's free **camping**, available with a permit from the parks office in Lihue (see p.1283). For **food**, *Kokee Lodge* has lunch specials for around $8.

Kalalau Lookout and Pihea Trail

A few miles further up, **Kalalau Lookout** stands over the valley where the Kalalau Trail ends – though to attempt a descent would be certain suicide. The **Pihea Trail** follows the course of a lunatic attempt to extend the road beyond its current end. At times it narrows to a few feet, with precipitous drops to either side, and visibility can drop to nothing as the clouds siphon across the ridges. Inland lies the **Alakai Swamp**, where the heaviest rainfall on earth collects in the volcanic rock; the few humans who manage to penetrate the mists are assailed on all sides by the shrills, whistles, and buzzes of a jungle without mammals or snakes. The trail running through the swamp consists of a boardwalk for almost its entire six-mile length, though in places the planks just rest on cloying black mud. Giant ferns dangle above the trail, and orchids gleam from the undergrowth. If you make it all the way to the end, you're rewarded with a stupendous panorama of Hanalei Bay.

Contexts

Contexts

A brief history of the USA

here is much more to the history of North America than the history of the United States alone. In these few pages, however, there's little room to do more than briefly survey the peopling and political development of the disparate regions that now form the USA. Many of the events and issues discussed below are covered in more detail in the relevant chapters, while the books listed on p.1314 onwards are invaluable resources for serious students.

First peoples

The first definitely dated trace of human beings in the Americas stems from just 14,000 years ago, when the true pioneers of North America, nomadic hunter-gatherers from Siberia, reached what's now **Alaska**. Thanks to the last ice age, when sea levels were three hundred feet lower than in the modern Bering Strait, a "**land-bridge**" – actually a vast plain, measuring six hundred miles north to south – connected Eurasia to America.

At that time, Alaska effectively formed part of Asia rather than North America, being separated by impenetrable glacier fields from what is now Canada and points south. Much like an air lock, the region has "opened" in different directions at different times; migrants reaching it from the west, oblivious to the fact that they were leaving Asia, would at first have found their way blocked to the east. Several generations might have passed, and the connection back towards Asia been severed, before an eastward passage appeared. When thawing ice did clear a route into North America, it was not along the Pacific coast but via a corridor that led east of the Rockies and out onto the Great Plains.

This migration was almost certainly spurred not by the urge to explore what must have seemed unpromising territory, but the pursuit of large mammal species, and especially **mammoth**, that had already been harried to extinction throughout almost all of Eurasia. A huge bonanza awaited the hunters when they finally encountered America's own indigenous "**megafauna**," such as mammoths, mastodons, giant ground sloths and enormous long-horned bison, all of which had evolved without fear of, or protection against, human predation.

Within a thousand years, both North and South America were filled with a total of ten million people. Although that sounds like a phenomenal rate of spread, only a small group of original human settlers need have been responsible. To achieve that impact, it would have taken a band of just one hundred individuals to enter the continent, and then advance a mere eight miles per year, with a population growth of 1.1 percent each year. The mass **extinction** of the American megafauna coincided so exactly with the advent of humans that humans must surely have been responsible, eliminating the giant beasts in each locality in one fell swoop, before pressing on in search of the next kill.

Quite apart from its ecological impact, the consequences of the elimination of large land mammals were legion. It precluded future American civilizations from domesticating any of the major animal species that were crucial to Old World economies. Without cattle, horses, sheep, or goats, or significant equivalents, they lacked the resources used elsewhere to supply food and clothing to large settlements, provide draft power to haul ploughs or wheeled vehicles, or increase mobility and the potential for conquest. What's more, most of the human diseases later introduced from the rest of the world evolved in association with domesticated animals; the first Americans developed neither immunity to such diseases, nor any indigenous diseases of their own that might have attacked the invaders.

At least three distinct waves of **migrants** arrived via Alaska, each of whom went on to settle in, and adapt to, a more marginal environment than its predecessors. The second, five thousand years on, were the "**Nadene**" or Athapascans – the ancestors of the Haida of the Northwest, and also the Navajo and Apache of the Southwest – while the third, another two thousand years later, found their niche in the frozen Arctic north and became the **Aleuts** and the **Inuits**.

Within the modern United States, the earliest known settlement site, dating back 12,000 years, has been uncovered at Meadowcroft in southwest Pennsylvania. Five hundred years later, the Southwest was dominated by what archeologists call the **Clovis** culture, whose distinctive arrowheads were first identified at Clovis, New Mexico. Subsequent subgroups ranged from the Algonquin farmers of what's now New England to peoples such as the Chumash and Macah, who lived by catching fish, otters, and even whales along the coasts of the Pacific Northwest.

Nowhere did a civilization emerge that could rival the wealth and sophistication of the great cities of ancient Mexico, such as Teotihuacan or Tenochtitlan. However, the influence of these far-off cultures did filter north; the cultivation of crops such as beans, squash, and maize made the development of large communities possible, and northern religious cults, including those that performed human sacrifice, are thought to owe much to Central American beliefs. The so-called **Moundbuilders** of the **Ohio** and **Mississippi** valleys developed sites such as the Great Serpent Mound in modern Ohio and Poverty Point in Louisiana. The most prominent of these early societies, now known as the **Hopewell** culture, flourished between around 1 and 400 AD. Later on, **Cahokia**, just outside present-day St Louis, became the largest pre-Columbian city in North America, centered on a huge mound topped by some form of temple, and reaching its peak between 1050 and 1250 AD.

In the deserts of the **Southwest**, the **Hohokam** settlement of Snaketown, near what's now Phoenix in Arizona, set about grappling with the same problems of water management that plague the region today. Nearby, the **Ancestral Puebloan** "Basketmakers" developed pottery around 200 AD, and began to gather into the walled villages later known as pueblos, possibly for protection against the threat of Athapascan invaders, such as the Apache, who were arriving from the north. Ancestral Puebloan "cities," such as Pueblo Bonito in New Mexico's Chaco Canyon – a center for the turquoise trade with the mighty Aztec – and the "Cliff Palace" at Mesa Verde in Colorado, are the most impressive monuments to survive from ancient North America. Although the Ancestral Puebloans are no longer identifiable as a group after the twelfth century – they probably dispersed after a devastating drought – many of the settlements created by their immediate descendants have remained in use ever since. Through centuries of migration, war, and changes of government, the desert farmers of the **Hopi Mesas** in Arizona (see p.983), and the pueblos of **Taos** and **Ácoma** in New Mexico, have never been dispossessed of their homes.

Estimates of the total indigenous population held by the Americas before the arrival of the Europeans vary widely. Although serious suggestions for North America range between two and twelve million, an acceptable median figure would be around fifty million people in the Americas as a whole, with five million of those in North America, speaking around four hundred different languages.

European contacts

The greatest seafarers of early medieval Europe, the **Vikings**, established a colony in Greenland around 982 AD. Under the energetic leadership of Eirik the Red, this became a base for voyages along the mysterious coastline to the west. **Leif Eiriksson** – also known as Leif the Lucky – spent the winter of 1001–02 at a site that has been identified with L'Anse aux Meadows in northern Newfoundland. Climatic conditions may well have been much better than they are today, though it remains unclear what were the "grapes" that led him to call it **Vinland**. Subsequent expeditions returned over the next dozen years, and may have ventured as far south as Maine. However, repeated clashes with the people the Vikings knew as **Skraelings** or "wretches" – probably Inuit, also newcomers to the area around this time – led them to abandon plans for permanent settlement.

A further five centuries passed before the crucial moment of contact with the rest of the world came on October 12, 1492, when **Christopher Columbus**, sailing on behalf of the Spanish, reached San Salvador in the Bahamas. A mere four years later the English navigator John Cabot officially "discovered" Newfoundland, and soon British fishermen in particular were setting up makeshift encampments in what became known as **New England**, to spend the winter curing their catch.

Over the next few years various expeditions mapped the eastern seaboard. In 1524, for example, the Italian **Giovanni Verrazano** sailed past Maine, which he characterized as the "Land of Bad People" thanks to the inhospitable and contemptuous behavior of its natives, and reached the mouth of the Hudson River. The great hope initially was to find a sea route in the Northeast that would lead to China – the fabled **Northwest Passage**. To the French **Jacques Cartier**, the St Lawrence Seaway seemed a distinct possibility, and successive expeditions explored and attempted (unsuccessfully) to settle the northern areas of the Great Lakes region from the 1530s onwards. Intrepid trappers and traders began to venture ever further west.

To the south, the Spaniards had started to nose their way up from the Caribbean in 1513, when **Ponce de Leon**'s expedition in search of the Fountain of Youth landed at what is now Palm Beach, and named the region of **Florida**. Spanish attentions for the next few years focused on the lucrative conquest of Mexico, but in 1528 they returned under Panfilo de Narvaez, whose voyage ended in shipwreck somewhere in the Gulf. One of his junior officers, **Cabeza de Vaca**, managed to survive, and together with three shipmates spent the next six years on an extraordinary odyssey across Texas into the Southwest. Sometimes held as slaves, sometimes revered as seers, they finally managed to get back to Mexico in 1534, bringing tales of golden cities deep in the desert, known as the **Seven Cities of Cibola**.

One of Cabeza de Vaca's companions was a black African slave called **Estevanico the Moor**, a giant of a man who had amazed the native peoples they encountered. Rather than return to a life of slavery, he volunteered to map the route for a new expedition; racing alone into the interior, with two colossal greyhounds at his side, he was killed in Zuni Pueblo in 1539. The following year, **Francisco Vázquez de Coronado**'s full party managed to prove to everyone's intense dissatisfaction that the Seven Cities of Cibola did not exist. They reached as far as the Grand Canyon, encountering the Hopi and other pueblo peoples along the way. Hernán Cortés, the conqueror of the Aztec, had meanwhile traced the outline of the peninsula of Baja California, and in 1542 Juan Cabrillo sailed right up the coast of California, failing to spot San Francisco Bay in the usual mists.

Although no treasures were found in North America to match the vast riches plundered from the Aztec and Inca empires, a steady stream of less spectacular discoveries – whether new foodstuffs such as potatoes, or access to the cod fisheries of the northern Atlantic – began to boost economies throughout Europe. It was the Spanish who established the first permanent settlement in the present United States, when they founded **St Augustine** on the coast of Florida in 1565 – permanent, at least, until it was burned to the ground by Sir Francis Drake in 1586. In 1598 the Spanish also succeeded in subjugating the pueblo peoples, and founded the colony of **New Mexico** along the Rio Grande. This was more of a missionary than a military enterprise, and its survival was always precarious due to the vast tracts of empty desert that separated the colony from the rest of Mexico. Nonetheless, the construction of a new capital, **Santa Fe**, began in 1609 (see p.926).

The growth of the colonies

The great rivalry between the English and the Spanish in the late sixteenth century extended right around the world. Freebooting English adventurers-cum-pirates contested Spanish hegemony along both coasts of North America. Sir Francis Drake staked a claim to California in 1579, five years before **Sir Walter Raleigh** claimed **Virginia** in the east, in the name of his Virgin Queen, Elizabeth I. The party of colonists he sent out in 1585 established the short-lived settlement of **Roanoke**, now remembered as the mysterious "Lost Colony" (see p.494).

The Native Americans encountered by the earliest settlers were seldom hostile at the outset. To some extent the European newcomers were obliged to make friends with the locals; most had crossed the Atlantic to find religious freedom or to make their fortunes, and lacked the experience or even the inclination to make a success of the mundane business of subsistence farming. Virginia's first enduring colony, **Jamestown**, was founded by Captain John Smith on May 24, 1607. He bemoaned "though there be Fish in the Sea, and Foules in the ayre, and Beasts in the woods, their bounds are so large, they are so wilde, and we so weake and ignorant, we cannot much trouble them"; not surprisingly, six out of every seven colonists died within a year of their arrival in the New World.

Gradually, however, the settlers learned the techniques necessary to cultivate the strange crops that grew in this unfamiliar terrain. As far as the English government was concerned, the colonies were strictly commercial ventures, intended to produce crops that could not be grown at home, and it was inconceivable to them that the colonists might have goals of their own. After early failures with sugar and rice, Virginia finally found its feet with its first **tobacco** harvest in 1615 (the man responsible, John Rolfe, is now better known as the husband of Pocahontas). A successful tobacco plantation requires two things in abundance: land, which intensified the pressure to dispossess the Indians, and labor. No self-respecting Englishman came to America to work for others; when the first **slave** ship called in at Jamestown in 1619, the captain found an eager market for his cargo of twenty African slaves. By that time there were already a million slaves in South America.

The 102 **Puritans** known to history as the "**Pilgrim Fathers**" were deposited on Cape Cod by the *Mayflower* in late 1620, and soon moved on to set up their own colony at Plymouth (see p.221). Fifty of them died during that winter, and the whole party might well have perished but for their fortuitous encounter with the extraordinary **Squanto**. This Native American had twice been kidnapped and taken to Europe and succeeded in making his way home; during his wanderings he had spent four years working as a merchant in the City of London, and had also lived in Spain. Having recently come home to find his entire tribe exterminated by smallpox, he decided to throw in his lot with the English. With his guidance, they finally managed to reap their first harvest, celebrated with the mighty feast of **Thanksgiving** that is still commemorated today.

Of greater significance to the history of New England was the founding in 1630 of a new colony, further up the coast at Naumkeag (which became Salem), by the Massachusetts Bay Company. Its governor, **John Winthrop**, soon moved to establish a new capital on the Shawmut peninsula – the city of **Boston**, complete with its own university of Harvard. His vision of a Utopian "City on a Hill" did not extend to sharing Paradise with the Indians; he argued that they had not "subdued" the land, and it was therefore a "vacuum" for the Puritans to use as they saw fit. While their faith helped individual colonists to endure the early hardships, the colony as a whole failed to maintain a strong religious identity (the Salem witch trials of 1692 did much to discredit the notion that the New World had any moral superiority to the Old), and breakaway groups soon left to create the rival settlements of Providence and Connecticut.

Between 1620 and 1642, sixty thousand migrants – which amounted to 1.5 percent of the population – left England for America. Those who came in pursuit of economic opportunities tended to join the longer-established colonies, where in effect they diluted the religious zeal of the Puritans. Groups hoping to find spiritual freedom were more inclined to start afresh; thus **Maryland** was created as a haven for Catholics in 1632, and fifty years later **Pennsylvania** was founded by the Quakers.

The English were not alone, however. After Sir Henry Hudson rediscovered Manhattan in 1609, it was "bought" by the **Dutch** in 1624 – though the Indians who took their money were passing nomads with no claim to it either. The Dutch colony of New Amsterdam, founded in 1625, lasted less than forty years before it was captured by the English and renamed **New York**; by that time, there was a strong Dutch presence on the lower reaches of the Hudson River.

From their foothold in the Great Lakes region, meanwhile, the **French** sent the explorers Joliet and Marquette to map the course of the Mississippi in 1673. They turned back once they had established that the river did indeed flow into the Gulf of Mexico, but their trip cleared the way for the foundation of the huge and ill-defined colony of **Louisiana** in 1699. The city of **New Orleans**, at the mouth of the Mississippi, was created in 1718.

While the Spanish remained firmly ensconced in Florida, things were not going so smoothly in the Southwest. In the bloody **Pueblo Revolt** of 1680, the pueblo peoples managed to drive the Spanish out of New Mexico altogether, only to have them return in force a dozen years later. Thereafter, a curious synthesis of traditional and Hispanic religion and culture began to evolve, and, but for hostile raids from the north, the Spanish presence was not seriously challenged.

With the arrival of the foreigners, things were also changing in the unknown hinterland. The frontier in the east was pushing steadily forward, as colonists seized Indian land, with or without the excuse of an "uprising" or "rebellion" to provoke them into bloodshed. The major killer of the indigenous peoples, however, was **smallpox**, which worked its way deep into the interior of the continent long before the Europeans. (Scientists speculate that the Native Americans may have had no equivalent "new" diseases to inflict on the newcomers because of the long period their ancestors had spent crossing the Arctic in subzero temperatures.) As populations were decimated, great migrations took place. In addition, around this time the **horse** arrived on the Great Plains. The original inhabitants of the region were sedentary farmers, who also hunted buffalo by driving them over rocky bluffs. The bow and arrow was discovered around the fifth century, but the acquisition of horses (probably captured from the Spanish, and known at first as "mystery dogs") made possible the emergence of an entirely new, nomadic lifestyle. Groups such as the Cheyenne and the Apache swept their rivals aside to dominate vast territories, and eagerly seized the potential offered by firearms when they were introduced in due course. This created a very dynamic, but fundamentally unstable culture, as they became dependent on trade with Europeans for the necessities of life.

The American Revolution

The American colonies prospered during the **eighteenth century**, with the cities of Boston, New York, and Philadelphia in particular becoming home to a wealthy, well educated, and highly articulate middle class. Frustration began to mount at the inequities of the colonies' relationship with Britain. While they were allowed to trade among themselves, the Americans could otherwise only sell their produce to the British, and all transatlantic commerce had to be undertaken in British ships.

Although full-scale independence was not an explicit goal until late in the century, the main factor that made it possible was the economic impact of the pan-European conflict known as the **Seven Years' War**. Officially, the war in Europe lasted from 1756 to 1763, but fighting among the English, French, and Spanish in North America broke out a little earlier. Beginning in 1755 with the mass expulsion of French settlers from Acadia in Nova Scotia (triggering their epic migration to Louisiana, where as the **Cajuns** they remain to this day), the British went on to conquer all of Canada. In forcing the **surrender of Québec** in 1759, General Wolfe brought the war to a close; the French ceded Louisiana to the Spanish rather than let it fall to the British, while Florida passed into British control for a year before reverting to the Spanish. All the European monarchs were left hamstrung by debts, and it became apparent to the British that colonialism in America was not as profitable a business as in those parts of the world where the native populations could be coerced into working for their overseas masters.

There was one other major player on the scene – the **Iroquois Confederacy**. Evidence of Iroquois culture, characterized by military expansionism and even human sacrifice, has been found in the Great Lakes region dating from around 1000 AD onwards. Forever in competition with the Algonquin and the Huron, the southern Iroquois had by the eighteenth century resolved themselves into a League of Five Nations – the Seneca, Cayuga, Onondaga, Oneida, and Mohawk, all in what's now upstate New York. Wooed by both French and British, the Iroquois for most of the century charted an independent course between the two. During negotiations with the colonists in 1744, an Onondaga chief, unimpressed by the squabbling representatives of Pennsylvania, Virginia, and Maryland, had recommended "by your observing the same methods our wise forefathers have taken, you will acquire fresh strength and power." Benjamin Franklin, who was present, wrote in 1751 that "It would be a very strange thing if . . . ignorant savages should be capable of forming a scheme for such a union . . . that has subsisted ages and appears indissoluble; and yet that a like union should be impracticable for ten or a dozen English colonies."

Shortly after the Seven Years' War, an unsuccessful insurrection by the Ottawa tribe in 1763, led by their chief **Pontiac**, led the cash-strapped British to conclude that, while America needed its own standing army, it was not unreasonable to expect the colonists to pay for it.

In 1765, the British introduced the **Stamp Act**, which required duty on all legal transactions and printed matter in the colonies to be paid to the British Crown. Firm in the belief that there should be "no taxation without representation," delegates from nine of the colonies met in the Stamp Act Congress in October 1765. By that time, however, the British prime minister responsible for the Act had already been dismissed by King George III. Only briefly, in Georgia, were the offending stamps ever distributed, and the Act was repealed in 1766.

However, in 1767, Chancellor Townshend made political capital at home by proclaiming "I dare tax America," as he introduced a program of legislation that included the broadly similar Revenue Act. That led the merchants of Massachusetts, inspired by **Samuel Adams**, to vote to boycott English goods; they were subsequently joined by all the other colonies except New Hampshire. Townshend's Acts were repealed in turn by a new prime minister, Lord North, on March 5, 1770. By chance, on that same day a stone-throwing mob surrounded the Customs House in Boston; shots from the guards killed five people in what became known as the **Boston Massacre**. Even so, most of the colonies resumed trading with Britain, and the crisis was postponed for a few more years.

In May 1773, Lord North's **Tea Act** relieved the debt-ridden East India Company of the need to pay duties on exports to America, while still requiring the Americans to pay duty on tea. Massachusetts called for the colonies to unite in action, and its citizens took the lead on December 16 in the **Boston Tea Party**, when three tea ships were boarded and 342 chests thrown into the sea. As John Adams put it, "to let it be landed would be giving up the principle of taxation by Parliamentary authority."

The infuriated British Parliament thereupon began to pass a body of legislation collectively known as both the "Coercive" and the "Intolerable" Acts, which included closing the port of Boston and disbanding the government of Massachusetts. Thomas Jefferson argued that the acts amounted to "a deliberate and systematical plan of reducing us to slavery." To discuss a response, the first **Continental Congress** was held in Philadelphia on May 5, 1774, and attended by representatives of all the colonies except Georgia.

War finally broke out on April 18, 1775, when General Gage, the newly imposed

C

governor of Massachusetts, dispatched four hundred British soldiers to destroy the arms depot at **Concord**, in order to prevent weapons from falling into rebel hands. Silversmith **Paul Revere** was dispatched by the citizens of Boston on his legendary ride to warn the rebels, and the British were confronted en route at Lexington by 77 American "Minutemen". The resulting skirmish led to the "shot heard 'round the world."

Congress set about forming an army at Boston, and decided for the sake of unity to appoint a Southern commander, **George Washington**. One by one, as the war raged, the colonies set up their own governments and declared themselves to be states, and the politicians set about defining the society they wished to create. The writings of pamphleteer Thomas Paine – especially *Common Sense* – were, together with the Confederacy of the Iroquois, a great influence on the **Declaration of Independence**. Drafted by Thomas Jefferson, this was adopted by the Continental Congress in Philadelphia on July 4, 1776. The anti-slavery clauses originally included by Jefferson – himself a slave-owner – were omitted to spare the feelings of the Southern states, though the section that denounced the King's dealings with "merciless Indian Savages" was left in.

At first, the Revolutionary War went well for the British. General Howe crossed the Atlantic with around twenty thousand men, took New York and New Jersey, and ensconced himself in Philadelphia for the winter of 1777–78. Washington's army was encamped not far away at Valley Forge, freezing cold and all but starving

The Constitution

As signed in 1787 and ratified in 1788, the **Constitution** stipulated the following form of government:

All **legislative** powers were granted to the **Congress of the United States**. The lower of its two distinct houses, the **House of Representatives**, was to be elected every two years, with its members in proportion to the number of each state's "free Persons" plus "three fifths of all other persons" (meaning slaves). The upper house, the **Senate**, would hold two Senators from each state, chosen by state legislatures rather than by direct elections. Each Senator was to serve for six years, with a third of them to be elected every two years.

Executive power was vested in the **President**, who was also Commander in Chief of the Army and Navy. He would be chosen every four years, by as many **"Electors"** from each individual state as it had Senators and Representatives. Each state could decide how to appoint those Electors; almost all chose to have direct popular elections. Nonetheless, the distinction has remained ever since between the number of "popular votes," across the whole country, received by a presidential candidate, and the number of state-by-state "electoral votes," which determines the actual result. Originally, whoever came second in the voting automatically became **Vice President**.

The President could **veto** acts of Congress, but that veto could be overruled by a two-thirds vote in both houses. The House of Representatives could **impeach** the President for treason, bribery, or "other high crimes and misdemeanors," in which instance the Senate could remove him from office with a two-thirds majority.

Judicial power was invested in a **Supreme Court**, and as many "inferior Courts"as Congress should decide.

The Constitution has so far been altered by 27 **Amendments**. Those that have introduced significant governmental changes include **14** and **15**, which extended the vote to black males in 1868 and 1870; **17**, which made senators subject to election by direct popular vote, in 1913; **18**, introducing women's suffrage, in 1920; **22**, restricting the president to two terms, in 1951; **24**, which stopped states using poll taxes to disenfranchise black voters, in 1964; and **26**, which reduced the minimum voting age to 18, in 1971.

to death. It soon became clear, however, that the longer the Americans could avoid losing an all-out battle, the more likely it was that the British would over-extend their lines as they advanced through the vast and unfamiliar continent. Thus, General Burgoyne's expedition, which set out from Canada to march on New England, was so harried by rebel guerrillas that he found himself obliged to surrender at Saratoga in October 1777. As the logistical difficulty of maintaining the British war effort became ever more apparent, other European powers took delight in coming to the aid of the Americans. Benjamin Franklin led a wildly successful delegation to France to request support, and soon the nascent American fleet was being assisted in its bid to cut British naval communications by both the French and the Spanish. The end came when Cornwallis, who had replaced Howe, was instructed to dig in at Yorktown and wait for the Royal Navy to come to his aid, only for the French to seal off Chesapeake Bay and prevent reinforcement. Cornwallis surrendered to Washington on October 17, 1781, just fifteen miles from the site of the first English settlement at Jamestown.

The ensuing **Treaty of Paris** granted the Americans their independence on generous terms – the British completely abandoned their Native American allies, including the Iroquois, to the vengeance of the victors – and Washington entered New York as the British left in November 1783. The Spanish were confirmed in their possession of Florida.

The victorious US Congress met for the first time in 1789, and the tradition of awarding political power to the nation's most successful generals was instigated by the election of George Washington as the first **president**. He was further honored when his name was given to the new capital city of **Washington DC**, deliberately sited between the North and the South.

The nineteenth century

In its first century, the territories and population of the new **United States of America** expanded at a phenomenal rate. The white population of North America in 1800 stood at around five million, and there were another one million African slaves (of whom thirty thousand were in the North). Of that total, 86 percent lived within fifty miles of the Atlantic, but no US city could rival Mexico City, whose population approached 100,000 inhabitants. (Both New York and Philadelphia reached that figure within twenty years, however, and New York had passed a million fifty years later.)

It had suited the British to discourage settlers from venturing west of the Appalachians, where they would be far beyond the reach of British power and therefore inclined to carry on independent existences. For George Washington, however, any agreement to follow such a policy had been a "temporary expedient to quieten the minds of the Indians." Adventurers such as **Daniel Boone** started to cross the mountains into Tennessee and Kentucky during the 1770s. Soon makeshift rafts, made from the planks that would later be assembled to make log cabins, were careering west along the Ohio River (the only westward-flowing river on the continent).

In 1801, the Spanish handed Louisiana back to the French, on the express undertaking that the French would keep it for ever. However, Napoleon swiftly realized that any attempt to hang on to his American possessions would involve spreading his armies too thinly. He chose instead to make the best of things by selling them to the United States for $15 million, in the **Louisiana Purchase** of 1803. The new territories extended far beyond the boundaries of

THE GROWTH OF THE UNITED STATES

present-day Louisiana (see map opposite), and for President Thomas Jefferson it was a matter of urgency to send the explorers **Lewis and Clark** to map them out. With the help of Sacagawea, their female Shoshone guide, they followed the Missouri and Columbia rivers all the way to the Pacific; in their wake, trappers and "mountain men" came to hunt in the wilderness of the Rockies. The **Russians** had already reached the Pacific Northwest by this time and established a network of fortified outposts to trade in the pelts of beaver and otter.

British attempts to blockade the Atlantic, primarily intended as a move against Napoleon, gave the new nation its first chance to flex its military muscles. Although British raiders succeeded in capturing Washington, DC, and burned the White House to the ground, the **War of 1812** most significantly provided the US with a cover for aggression against the Native American allies of the British. Thus **Tecumseh** of the Shawnee was defeated near Detroit, and **Andrew Jackson** moved against the Creek of the southern Mississippi. Jackson's campaign against the Seminole in Florida enabled the US to gain possession of the state from the Spanish; he was rewarded first with the governorship of the new state, and later by his election to the presidency. During his period in office, in the 1830s, Jackson went even further, and set about clearing all states east of the Mississippi of their native populations. The barren region that later became Oklahoma was designated as "Indian Territory," home to the "Five Civilized Tribes." The Creek and the Seminole, and the Choctaw and Chickasaw of Mississippi were eventually joined by the Cherokee of the lower Appalachians there, after four appalling months on the forced march known as the "**Trail of Tears**."

For the citizens of the young republic, it took only a small step from realizing that their country might be capable of spreading across the whole continent to supposing that it had a quasi-religious duty – a "**Manifest Destiny**" – to do so. At its most basic, that doctrine amounted to little more than a belief that might must be right, but the idea that they were fulfilling the will of God inspired countless pioneers to set off across the plains in search of a new life.

Mexico had by now gained its independence from Spain. The Spanish territories of the Southwest had never attracted enough migrants to turn into full-fledged colonies, and the American settlers who arrived in ever-increasing numbers began to dominate their Hispanic counterparts. The Anglos of **Texas** rebelled in 1833, under the leadership of General Sam Houston. Shortly after the legendary setback at the **Alamo** (see p.731), in 1836, they defeated the Mexican army of Santa Anna, and Texas became an independent republic in its own right.

The ensuing **Mexican War** was a bare-faced exercise in American aggression, in which most of the future leading figures of the Civil War received their first experience fighting on the same side. The conflict resulted in the acquisition not only of Texas, but also of Arizona, Utah, Colorado, Nevada, New Mexico, and finally California, in 1848. A token US payment of $15 million to the Mexican government was designed to match the Louisiana Purchase. Controversy over whether slavery would be legal in the new states was rendered academic when it turned out that, on virtually the same day the war ended, gold had been discovered in the Sierra Nevada of California. The resultant **Gold Rush** created California's first significant city, **San Francisco**, and brought a massive influx of free white settlers to a land that was in any case utterly unsuitable for a plantation-based economy.

Proponents of Manifest Destiny seem never to have given much thought to the **Pacific Northwest**, which remained nominally under the control of British Canada. However, once the Oregon Trail started to operate in 1841 (see p.1218), American settlers there swiftly outnumbered the British. In 1846, a surprisingly amicable treaty fixed the border along the 49th parallel, just as it already did across eastern Canada, and left the whole of Vancouver Island to the British.

The Civil War

From the moment of its inception, the unity of the United States had been based on shaky foundations. Great care had gone into devising a **Constitution** that balanced the need for a strong federal government with the aspirations for autonomy of its component states. That was achieved by giving Congress two separate chambers – the **House of Representatives**, in which the number of representatives from each state depended upon its population, and the **Senate**, in which each state, regardless of size, had two members. Thus, although in theory the Constitution remained silent on the issue of **slavery**, it allayed the fears of the less populated Southern states (where although the slaves lacked the vote, each was counted as three-fifths of a person when it came to determining the number of representatives elected per state) that the voters of the North might destroy their economy by forcing them to abandon their "peculiar institution." However, it gradually became apparent that the system only worked so long as there were equal numbers of "Free" and slave-owning states. The only practicable way to keep the balance was to ensure that each time a new state was admitted to the Union, a matching state taking the opposite stance on slavery was also admitted. Thus the admission of every new state became subject to endless intrigue. The 1820 **Missouri Compromise**, under which Missouri joined as a slave-owning state and Maine as a Free one, was straightforward in comparison to the prevarication and chest-beating that surrounded the admission of Texas, while the Mexican War was widely seen in the North as a naked land grab for new slave states.

Abolitionist sentiment in the North was not all that great before the middle of the nineteenth century. At best, after the importation of slaves from Africa ended in 1808, Northerners had vague hopes that slavery was an anachronism that might simply wither away. As it turned out, the profitability of the Southern plantations was dramatically boosted by the development of the cotton gin, and the increased demand for manufactured cotton goods triggered by the **Industrial Revolution**. What ultimately changed the situation was the rapid growth of the nation as a whole, making it ever more difficult to maintain a political balance between North and South.

Matters came to a head in 1854, when the **Kansas–Nebraska Act** sparked guerrilla raids and mini-wars between rival settlers by allowing both prospective states self-determination on the issue. That same year, the **Republican Party** was founded, on the platform of resisting the further expansion of slavery. Escaped former slaves such as Frederick Douglass were by now inspiring Northern audiences to moral outrage, and Harriet Beecher Stowe's *Uncle Tom's Cabin* found unprecedented readership.

In October 1859, **John Brown** – a white-bearded, wild-eyed veteran of some of Kansas's bloodiest infighting – led a dramatic raid on the US Armory at Harpers Ferry, West Virginia, intending to secure arms for a slave insurrection (see p.453). Swiftly captured by forces under the command of Robert E. Lee, he was hanged within a few weeks, proclaiming that "I am now quite certain that the crimes of this guilty land will never be purged away but with blood."

The Republican candidate for the presidency in 1860 was the little-known **Abraham Lincoln** from Kentucky; he won no Southern states, but with the Democrats split into Northern and Southern factions he was elected with 39 percent of the popular vote. Within weeks, on December 20, South Carolina became the first state to secede from the Union; the **Confederacy** was declared on February 4, 1861, when it was joined by Mississippi, Florida, Alabama, Georgia, Louisiana, and Texas. Its first (and only) president was **Jefferson Davis**, also from Kentucky; at their inauguration, his new vice president remarked that their government was "the first in the history of the world based upon the great physical and moral truth that the negro is not equal to the white man." Lincoln was inaugurated in turn in March 1861, proclaiming that "I have no purpose, directly or indirectly, to interfere with the institution of slavery in the States where it exists. I believe I have no lawful right to do so, and I have no inclination to do so." He was completely inflexible, however, on one paramount issue: the survival of the Union.

The **Civil War** began just a few weeks later. The first shots were fired on April 12, when a much-postponed federal attempt to resupply Fort Sumter, in the harbor at Charleston, South Carolina, was greeted by a Confederate bombardment that forced its surrender. Lincoln's immediate call to raise an army against the South was greeted by the further secession of Virginia, Arkansas, Tennessee, and North Carolina. Within a year, both armies had amassed 600,000 men; Robert E. Lee had been offered command of both and opted for the Confederacy, while George McLellan became the first leader of the Union forces. Although the rival capitals of Washington, DC, and Richmond, Virginia, were a mere one hundred miles apart, over the next four years operations of war reached almost everywhere south of Washington and east of the Mississippi.

Tracing the ebb and flow of the military campaigns – from the Confederate victories of the early years, via Grant's successful siege of Vicksburg in 1863 and Sherman's devastating March to the Sea in 1864, to Lee's eventual surrender at Appomattox in April 1865 – it's easy to lose sight of the fact that it was not so much generalship as sheer economic (and man) power that won the war. The war pitted the **Union** of 23 Northern states, holding over 22 million people, against the **Confederacy** of 11 Southern states, with 9 million people. As for potential combatants, the North initially drew upon 3.5 million white males aged between 18 and 45 – and later recruited blacks as well – whereas the South had more like one million. In the end, around 2.1 million men fought for the Union, and 900,000 for the Confederacy. Of the 620,000 soldiers who died during the conflict, a disproportionate 258,000 came from the South – representing one quarter of its white men of military age. Meanwhile, not only was the North able to continue trading with the rest of the world as it maintained its industrial and agricultural output, but it also stifled the Confederacy with a devastating **naval blockade**. The Southern war effort was primarily financed by printing $1.5 billion of paper currency, which with neither reserves nor income to support it was so eroded by inflation that it became worthless.

Even so, the Confederacy came much closer to victory than is usually appreciated. The repeated out-maneuvering of federal forces by General **Robert E. Lee**, and his incursions into Union territory, meant that in each of three successive years, from 1862 to 1864, there was a genuine possibility that Northern morale would collapse, allowing opponents of the war to be elected to power and agree to peace. After all, the Revolutionary War had shown how such a war could be won: for the Union to triumph, it had to invade and occupy the South, and destroy its armies, but for the South to win it only had to survive until the North wearied of the struggle.

The dashing tactics of Confederate generals Lee and Jackson, forever counter-attacking and carrying the fight to the enemy, may have been in the finest romantic traditions of the Old South, but they arguably contributed to the Southern defeat. The grim, relentless total-war campaigning of Grant and Sherman eventually ground the South down. There's a particular irony in the fact that had the Confederacy sued for peace before Lee gave it fresh hope, a negotiated settlement might not have included the abolition of slavery. In the event, as the war went on, with

Southern slaves flocking to the Union flag and black soldiers fighting on the front line, emancipation did indeed become inevitable. Lincoln took the political decision to match his moral conviction by issuing his **Emancipation Proclamation** in 1862, though the **Thirteenth Amendment** outlawing slavery only took effect in 1865.

Lincoln himself was assassinated within a few days of the end of the war, a mark of the deep bitterness that would almost certainly have rendered successful **Reconstruction** impossible even if he had lived. There was a brief period, after black men were granted the vote in 1870, when Southern states elected black political representatives, but without a sustained effort to enable former slaves to acquire land, racial relations in the South swiftly deteriorated. Thanks to white supremacist organizations such as the Ku Klux Klan, nominally clandestine but brazenly public, Southern blacks were soon effectively disenfranchised once more. Anyone working to transform the South came under attack either as a carpetbagger (a Northern opportunist who headed South for personal profit) or a treacherous scalawag (a Southern collaborator).

The aftermath of the Civil War can almost be said to have lasted for a hundred years. While the South condemned itself to a century as a backwater, the rest of the re-United States embarked on a period of expansionism and prosperity.

The Indian Wars

With the completion of the transcontinental railroad in 1867, Manifest Destiny became an undeniable reality. Among the first to head west were the troops of the federal army, with Union and Confederate veterans marching under the same flag to do battle with the remaining Native Americans. Treaty after treaty was signed, only to be broken as it became expedient to do so (usually upon the discovery of gold or precious metals). When the whites overreached themselves, or when driven to desperation, the Indians were capable of fighting back. The defeat of **General George Custer** at Little Bighorn in 1876, by **Sitting Bull** and his Sioux and Cheyenne warriors (see p.894), provoked the full wrath of the government. Within a few years, leaders such as **Crazy Horse** of the Oglala Sioux and **Geronimo** of the Apache had been forced to surrender, and their people were confined to reservations. One final act of resistance came in the form of the visionary, messianic cult of the **Ghost Dance**, whose practitioners hoped that by correct ritual observance they could win back their lost way of life, in a land miraculously free of white intruders. Such aspirations were regarded as hostile, and military harassment of the movement culminated in the massacre at **Wounded Knee** in South Dakota in 1890.

A major tactic in the campaign against the Plains Indians was to starve them into submission, by eliminating the vast herds of bison that were their primary source of food. As General Philip Sheridan put it, "For the sake of a lasting peace . . . kill, skin and sell until the buffalo are exterminated. Then your prairies can be covered by the speckled cow and the festive cowboy." More significant than the activities of the much-mythologized cowboys, however, was the back-breaking toil of the miners up in the mountains, and the homesteading families out on the plains.

Industry and immigration

The late nineteenth century was an era of massive **immigration** to North America from the rest of the world, with influxes from Europe to the East Coast paralleled by those from Asia to the West. As in Colonial times, national groups tended to form enclaves in specific areas – examples range from the Scandinavian farmers of Minnesota and the northern Plains, to the Basque shepherds of Idaho, and the Cornish miners of Colorado. In the Southwest, where individual hard work counted for less than shared communal effort, the **Mormons** of Utah had fled persecution eastward across the United States to become the first white settlers to eke a living from the unforgiving desert.

The fastest growth of all was in the nation's greatest **cities**, especially New York, Chicago, and Boston. Their industrial and commercial strength enabled them to attract and absorb migrants not only from throughout Europe but also from the Old South – particularly ex-slaves, who could now at least vote with their feet.

Now that it stretched "from sea to shining sea," the territorial boundaries of the US had reached almost their current form. In 1867, however, Secretary of State William Seward agreed to buy **Alaska** from the crisis-torn Russian government for $7.2 million. The purchase was at first derided as "Seward's Folly," but it was not long before the familiar Midas touch of the Americans was revealed by the discovery of gold there as well.

The various US presidents of the day, from the victorious General Grant (a man palpably out of his depth) onwards, now seem anonymous figures compared to the industrialists and financiers who manipulated the national economy. These **"robber barons"** included such men as John D. Rockefeller, who controlled seventy percent of the world's oil almost before anyone else had realized it was worth controlling; Andrew Carnegie, who made his fortune introducing the Bessemer process of steel manufacture; and J.P. Morgan, who went for the most basic commodity of all – money. Their success was predicated on the willingness of the government to cooperate in resisting the development of a strong labor movement. A succession of widely publicized strikes – such as those on the railroads in 1877, in the mines of Tennessee in 1891, and in the steel mills of Pittsburgh in 1892 – were forcibly crushed.

The nineteenth century had also seen the development of a distinctive American voice in **literature**, which rendered increasingly superfluous the efforts of passing English visitors – such as Charles Dickens, and the Trollopes, mother and son – to "explain" the United States. From the 1830s onwards, a wide range of writers set out to find new ways to describe their new world, with results as varied as the introspective essays of Henry Thoreau, the morbid visions of Edgar Allan Poe, the all-embracing novels of Herman Melville, and the irrepressible poetry of Walt Whitman, whose endlessly revised *Leaves of Grass* was an exultant hymn to the young republic. Virtually every leading participant in the Civil War wrote at least one highly readable volume of memoirs, while public figures as disparate as Buffalo Bill Cody and the showman P. T. Barnum also produced lively autobiographies. The boundless national self-confidence found its greatest expression in the vigorous vernacular style of **Mark Twain**, whose depictions of frontier life, whether in the journalistic *Roughing It* and *Life on the Mississippi*, or fictionalized in novels like *Huckleberry Finn*, gave the rest of the world perhaps its most abiding impression of the American character.

Many Americans saw the official "closure" of the Western frontier, announced by the Census Bureau in 1890, as tantamount to depriving the country of the Manifest Destiny that was its *raison d'être*, and were prompted to search for new frontiers further afield. Such **imperialist ventures** reached a crescendo in 1898, with the annexation of the Kingdom of **Hawaii** – which even then-President Cleveland condemned as "wholly without justification . . . not merely wrong but a disgrace" – and the double seizure of Cuba and the Philippines in the **Spanish–American War**, which catapulted **Theodore Roosevelt** to the presidency. Though he took the African proverb "speak softly and carry a big stick" as his motto – and was hardly, if truth be told, noted for being soft-spoken – Roosevelt in office did much to heal the divisions within the nation. While new legislation reigned in the worst excesses of the Robber Barons, and of rampant capitalism in general, it alleviated popular discontent without substantially threatening the business community, or empowering the labor movement. A decade into the twentieth century, the United States had advanced to the point that it knew, even if the rest of the world wasn't yet altogether sure, that it was the strongest, wealthiest country on earth.

The twentieth century

It may not have been apparent to everyone at the time, but the first few years of the twentieth century witnessed the emergence of many of the features that came to characterize modern America. In 1903 alone, Wilbur and Orville Wright achieved the first successful powered **flight**, and Henry Ford established his Ford Motor Company. Ford's enthusiastic adoption of the latest technology in mass production – the assembly line – gave Detroit a head start in the new **automobile** industry, which swiftly became the most important business in America. Both **jazz** and **blues** music came to the attention of a national audience for the first time during that same period, while Hollywood acquired its first **movie** studio in 1911, and its first major hit in 1915 with D. W. Griffith's unabashed glorification of the Ku Klux Klan in *Birth of a Nation*.

This was also a time of growing **radicalism**. Both the NAACP (National Association for the Advancement of Colored People) and the socialist International Workers of the World ("the Wobblies") were founded in the early 1900s, while the campaign for women's suffrage also came to the forefront. Writers such as Upton Sinclair, whose *The Jungle* exposed conditions in Chicago's stockyards, and Jack London proselytized to the masses; contemporary improvements in the educational system suggest this may well have been the most literate period in US history.

President Wilson managed to keep the US out of the **Great War** for several years but, when the time came, American intervention was decisive. With the Russian Revolution illustrating the dangers of anarchy, the US also took charge of supervising the peace. However, although Wilson presided over the postwar negotiations that resulted in the Treaty of Versailles in 1919, isolationist sentiment at home kept the US from joining his pet scheme to preserve future world peace, the League of Nations.

Back home, the 18th Amendment to the Constitution, in 1920, forbade the sale and distribution of alcohol, while the 19th finally gave all American women the vote. Quite how **Prohibition** ever became the law of the land is something of a mystery; certainly, in the buzzing metropolises of the Roaring Twenties, it enjoyed little conspicuous support. There was no noticeable elevation in the moral tone of the country, and Chicago in particular became renowned for the street wars between bootlegging gangsters such as Al Capone and his rivals.

The two Republican presidents who followed Wilson did little more than sit back and watch the Roaring Twenties unfold. At least until his premature death, **Warren Harding** enjoyed considerable public affection, but he's now remembered as probably the worst of all US presidents, thanks to the cronyism and corruption of his associates. It's hard to say quite whether **Calvin Coolidge** did anything at all; his laissez-faire attitude extended to working a typical four-hour day, and announcing shortly after his inauguration that "four-fifths of our troubles would disappear if we would sit down and keep still."

The Depression and the New Deal

By the middle of the 1920s, the US was enough of an industrial powerhouse to be responsible for more than half the world's output of manufactured goods. After leading the way into a new era of prosperity, however, it suddenly found itself dragging the rest of the world down into economic collapse. It's hard to say exactly what triggered the **Great Depression**; the consequences were out of all proportion to any one specific cause. Possible factors include American overinvestment in the floundering economy of postwar Europe, combined with high tariffs on imports that effectively precluded European recovery. Conservative commentators at the time chose to interpret the calamitous **Wall Street Crash** of October 1929 as a symptom of impending depression rather than a contributory cause, but the quasi-superstitious faith in the stock market that preceded it showed all the characteristics of such classic speculative booms as Britain's eighteenth-century South Sea Bubble. On "Black Tuesday" alone, enough stocks were sold to produce a total loss of ten thousand million dollars – more than twice the total amount of money in circulation in the US. Within the next three years, industrial production was cut by half, the national income dropped by 38 percent, and, above all, unemployment rose from 1.5 million to 13 million.

National self-confidence, however shaky its foundations, has always played a crucial role in US history, and President Hoover was not the man to restore it. Matters only began to improve in 1932, when the patrician figure of **Franklin Delano Roosevelt** accepted the Democratic nomination for president with the words "I pledge myself to a new deal for America," and went on to win a landslide victory. At the time of his inauguration, early in 1933, the banking system had all but closed down; it took Roosevelt the now-proverbial "Hundred Days" of vigorous legislation to turn around the mood of the country.

Taking advantage of the new medium of radio, he used his "Fireside Chats" to cajole America out of crisis; among his earliest observations was that it was a good time for a beer, and that therefore the experiment of Prohibition was over. The **New Deal** took many forms and worked through many newly created agencies, but was marked throughout by a massive growth in the power of the federal government, which only now seems to be under threat. Among its accomplishments were the National Recovery Administration, which created two million jobs; the Social Security Act, of which Roosevelt declared "no damn politician can ever scrap my social security program"; the Public Works Administration, which built dams and highways the length and breadth of the country; the Tennessee Valley Authority, which by generating electricity under public ownership for the common good was probably the closest the US has ever come to institutionalized socialism; and measures to legitimize the role of the unions and revitalize the "Dust Bowl" farmers out on the plains.

Roosevelt originally saw himself as a populist who could draw support from every sector of society. By 1936, however, business leaders – and the Supreme Court – were making it clear that as far as they were concerned he had done more than enough already to kick-start the economy. From then on, as he secured an unprecedented four consecutive terms as president, he was firmly cast as the champion of the little man.

After the work-creation programs of the New Deal had put America back on its feet, the deadly pressure to achieve victory in **World War II** spurred industrial production and know-how to new heights. Once again the US stayed out of the war at first, until it was finally forced in by the high-stakes gamble of the Japanese, who launched a pre-emptive strike on Hawaii's Pearl Harbor in December 1941. In both the Pacific and in Europe, American manpower and economic muscle eventually carried all before it. Roosevelt died early in 1945, after laying the foundations for the postwar carve-up with Stalin and Churchill at Yalta, and thus was spared the fateful decision, made by his successor Harry Truman, to use the newly developed atomic bomb on Hiroshima and Nagasaki.

The coming of the Cold War

With the war won, Americans were in no mood to revert back to the isolationism of the 1930s. Amid much hopeful rhetoric, Truman enthusiastically participated in the creation of the **United Nations**, and set up the **Marshall Plan** to speed the recovery of Europe – a task in which it was far more successful than any of the corresponding attempts made 25 years earlier. However, as Winston Churchill announced in Missouri in 1946, an "**Iron Curtain**" had descended upon Europe, and Joseph Stalin was transformed from ally to enemy almost overnight.

The ensuing **Cold War** lasted for more than four decades, at times fought in ferocious combat (albeit often by proxy) in scattered corners of the globe, and during the intervals diverting colossal economic resources towards the stockpiling of ever more destructive arsenals. Some of its ugliest moments came in its earliest years; Truman was still in office in 1950 when war broke out in **Korea**. A dispute over the arbitrary division of the Korean peninsula into two separate nations, North and South, soon turned into a stand-off between the US and China (with Russia, in theory at any rate, lurking in the shadows). Two years of bloody stalemate ended with little to show for it, except that Truman had by now been replaced by the genial **Dwight D. Eisenhower**, the latest war hero to turn president.

The Eisenhower years are often seen as an era characterized by bland complacency. Once Senator **Joseph McCarthy**, the "witch-hunting" anti-Communist scourge of the State Department and Hollywood, had finally discredited himself by attacking the army as well, middle-class America seemed to lapse into a wilful suburban stupor. Great social changes were starting to take shape, however. World War II had introduced vast numbers of women and members of ethnic minorities to the rewards of factory work, and it had shown many Americans from less prosperous regions the lifestyle that was attainable in other parts of their own country. The development of a **national highway system**, and a huge increase in automobile ownership, encouraged people to pursue the American Dream wherever they chose. Combined with increasing mechanization on the cotton plantations of the South, this led to another **mass exodus** of blacks from the rural South to the cities of the North, and to a lesser extent the West. The cities of **California** entered a period of rapid growth, with the aeronautical industries of Los Angeles in particular attracting thousands of prospective workers.

It was also during the 1950s that **television** reached every home in the country. Together with the LP record, it created an entertainment industry that seemed designed to promote mass conformity, but which swiftly showed itself capable of addressing the needs of consumers who had previously been barely identified. **Youth culture** burst into public prominence from 1954 onwards, with Elvis Presley's recording of "*That's Alright Mama*" appearing within a few months of Marlon Brando's moody starring role in *On the Waterfront* and James Dean's in *Rebel Without a Cause*.

The civil rights years

Racial segregation of public facilities, which had remained the norm in the South ever since Reconstruction, was in 1954 finally declared illegal by the Supreme Court ruling on *Brown v. Topeka Board of Education*. Just as a century before, however, the Southern states saw the issue more in terms of states' rights than of human rights, and attempting to implement the law, or even to challenge the failure to implement it, required immense courage. The action of Rosa Parks in refusing to give up her seat to a white man on a bus in Montgomery, Alabama, in December 1955 triggered a successful mass boycott (see p.585), and pushed the 27-year-old **Rev Dr Martin Luther King Jr** to the forefront of the civil rights campaign. Further confrontation took place at the Central High School in Little Rock, Arkansas, in 1957 (see p.599), when the reluctant Eisenhower found himself forced to call in federal troops to counter the state's unwillingness to integrate its education system.

The election of **John F. Kennedy** to the presidency in 1960, by the narrowest of margins, marked a sea-change in American politics, even if in retrospect his policies do not seem exactly radical. At 43 the youngest man ever to be elected president, and the first Catholic, he was prepared literally to reach for the moon, urging the US to victory in the Space Race in which it had thus far lagged humiliatingly behind the Soviet Union. The two decades that lay ahead, however, were to be characterized by disillusion, defeat, and despair. If the Eisenhower years had been dull, the 1960s in particular were far too interesting for almost everybody's liking.

Kennedy's sheer glamor made him a popular president during his lifetime, while his assassination suffused his administration with the romantic glow of "Camelot." His one undisputed triumph, however, came with the **Cuban missile crisis** of 1962, when the US military fortunately spotted Russian bases in Cuba before any actual missiles were ready for use, and Kennedy faced down premier Khrushchev to insist they be withdrawn. On the other hand, he'd had rather less success the previous year, in launching the abortive **Bay of Pigs** invasion of Cuba, and he also managed to embroil America deeper in the ongoing war against Communism in Vietnam, by sending more "advisers," including Green Berets, to Saigon.

Although a much-publicized call to the wife of Rev Martin Luther King Jr, during one of King's many sojourns in Southern jails, was a factor in Kennedy's election success, he was rarely keen to identify himself with the **civil rights** movement. The campaign nonetheless made headway, given added momentum by the global television coverage of such horrific confrontations as the onslaught by Birmingham police on peaceful demonstrators in 1963. The movement's defining moment came when Rev King delivered his electrifying "I Have a Dream" speech during the March on Washington later that summer. King was subsequently awarded the Nobel Peace Prize for his unwavering espousal of Gandhian principles of nonviolence. Perhaps an equally powerful factor in middle America's recognition that the time had come to address racial inequalities, however, was the not-so-implicit threat in the rhetoric of **Malcolm X**, who argued that black people had the right to defend themselves against aggression.

After Kennedy's assassination in November 1963, his successor, **Lyndon B. Johnson**, pushed through legislation that enacted most of the civil rights campaigners' key demands. Even then, violent white resistance in the South continued, and only the long, painstaking and dangerous work of registering Southern black voters en masse eventually forced Southern politicians to mend their ways.

Johnson won election by a landslide in 1964, but his vision of a **"Great Society"** soon foundered. Instead, he was brought low by the war in **Vietnam**, where US involvement escalated beyond all reason or apparent control. Broad-based popular opposition to the conflict grew in proportion to the American death toll, and the threat of the draft heightened the mood of youthful rebellion. San Francisco in particular responded to psychedelic prophet Timothy Leary's call to "turn on, tune in, drop out"; 1967's "Summer of Love" saw the lone beatniks of the 1950s transmogrify into an entire generation of hippies.

From the earliest days of the civil rights struggle, Dr King had argued that social justice could only be achieved through economic equality. That message was given a new urgency by riots in the ghettoes of Los Angeles in 1965 and Detroit in 1967, and the emergence of the Black Panthers, an armed defense force in the tradition of the now-dead Malcolm X. King also began to denounce the Vietnam War; meanwhile, after refusing the draft with the words "No Vietcong ever called me nigger," **Muhammad Ali** was stripped of his title as world heavyweight boxing champion.

In 1968, the very social fabric of the US reached the brink of collapse. Shortly after Johnson's plummeting popularity forced the president to withdraw from the year-end elections, Martin Luther King was gunned down in a Memphis motel. Next, JFK's brother **Robert Kennedy**, now redefined as spokesman for the nation's dispossessed, was fatally shot just as he emerged as Democratic front-runner. It didn't take a conspiracy theorist to see that the spate of deaths reflected a malaise in the soul of America.

Richard Nixon to Jimmy Carter

Somehow – perhaps because the brutally suppressed riots at the Chicago Democratic Convention raised the specter of anarchy – the misery of 1968 resulted in the election of Republican **Richard Nixon** as president. Eisenhower's vice president while still in his thirties, Nixon had famously told the press after his failed bid for the governorship of California in 1962 that "you won't have Nixon to kick around any more." Now he was back, and it soon became apparent that he had scores to settle with his countless perceived enemies, above all in the media. Nixon's impeccable conservative credentials enabled him to bring the US to a rapport with China, but the war in Vietnam dragged on, to claim a total of 57,000 American lives. Attempts to win it included the secret and illegal bombing of Cambodia, which raised opposition at home to a new peak, but ultimately it was simpler to abandon the original goals in the name of "peace with honor." The end came either in 1972 – when Henry Kissinger and Le Duc Tho were awarded the Nobel Peace Prize for negotiating a treaty, and Tho at least had the grace to decline the award – or in 1975, when the Americans finally withdrew from Saigon.

During Nixon's first term, many of the disparate individuals politicized by the events and undercurrents of the 1960s coalesced into **activist groupings**. Feminists united to campaign for abortion rights and an Equal Rights Amendment; gay men in New York's *Stonewall* bar fought back after one police raid too many; Native Americans formed the American Indian Movement; and even prisoners attempted to organize themselves, resulting in such bloody debacles as the storming of Attica prison in 1971. Nixon directed various federal agencies to monitor the new radicalism, but his real bugbear was the antiwar protesters. Increasingly ludicrous covert operations against real and potential opponents culminated in a botched attempt to burgle Democratic National Headquarters in the **Watergate** complex in 1972. It took two years of investigation for Nixon's role in the subsequent cover-up to be proved, but in 1974 he **resigned**, one step ahead of impeachment by the Senate, to be succeeded by **Gerald Ford**, his own unelected appointee as vice president.

With the Republicans momentarily discredited, former Georgia governor **Jimmy Carter** was elected president as a clean-handed outsider in the bicentennial year of 1976. His victory showed how far the US had come in a decade, let alone two centuries; a crucial constituency for this new-style Southern Democrat was the recently enfranchised black population of the South. However, Carter's enthusiastic attempts to put his Baptist principles into practice on such issues as global human rights were soon perceived as naive, if not un-American. Misfortune followed misfortune. He had to break the news that the nation was facing an **energy crisis**, following the formation of the OPEC cartel of oil producers. Worse still, the Shah of Iran was overthrown, and staff at the US embassy in Tehran were taken hostage by Islamic revolutionaries. Carter's failed attempts to arrange their release were seized upon by the Republicans as a sign of his weak leadership, and all but destroyed his hopes of winning re-election in 1980. Instead he was replaced by a very different figure, the former Hollywood movie actor **Ronald Reagan**.

The Reagan–Bush years

Reagan was a new kind of president. Unlike his workaholic predecessor, Jimmy Carter, he made a virtue of his hands-off approach to the job, joking that "they say hard work never killed anybody, but I figured why take the risk?" That laissez-faire attitude was especially apparent in his domestic economic policies, under which the rich were left to get as rich as they could. The common perception that Reagan was barely aware of what went on around him allowed his popularity to remain undented by a succession of scandals, including the labyrinthine **Iran-Contra** affair, under which illegal arms sales to Iran were used to fund support for the Contra rebels in Nicaragua. When Reagan was finally confronted with proof that he had been wrong in his insistence that "I did not trade arms for hostages," he produced an extraordinary apology: "My heart and my best intentions still tell me that's true, but the facts and the evidence tell me it is not."

Reagan's most enduring achievement came during his second term, when, with his credentials as a Cold Warrior beyond question, the electorate allowed him greater leeway than a Democrat might have received to negotiate **arms–control** agreements with **Mikhail Gorbachev**, the new leader of what he had previously called the "Evil Empire." On the down side, his successors were left to cope with the explosion in the **national debt** that followed the combination of extensive **tax cuts** alongside the deregulation of the financial markets, the collapse of the savings and loan system, and above all, the enormous increases in defense spending that funded such pet projects as the Strategic Defense Initiative ("**Star Wars**").

In 1988, **George Bush** became the first vice president in 150 years to be immediately elected to the presidency. Despite his unusually broad experience in foreign policy (which included a spell as director of the CIA), Bush did little more than sit back and watch in amazement as the domino theory suddenly went into reverse. One after another, the Communist regimes of eastern Europe collapsed, until finally even the Soviet Union crumbled away. Bush was also president when **Operation Desert Storm** drove the Iraqis out of Kuwait in February 1991, an undertaking that lasted 100 hours and in which virtually no American lives were lost. At the moment of triumph in Kuwait, Bush's soaring popularity seemed certain to guarantee his re-election.

And yet the much-anticipated "**peace dividend**" – the dramatic injection of cash into the economy that voters expected to follow the end of the arms race – never materialized. As one Democrat contender for the 1992 presidential nomination, Paul Tsongas, succinctly put it, "the Cold War is over and Japan won." Between 1980 and 1990, the US had gone from being the world's largest creditor to being the world's largest debtor. The national debt had trebled from $908 billion to $2.9 trillion, and much of the borrowing came from Japan, spared from incurring military expenditures on anything like the same scale. With the 1992 campaign focusing on domestic affairs rather than what was happening overseas, twelve years of Republican government were ended by the election of Arkansas Governor **Bill Clinton**.

Clinton and the end of the century

Clinton's first two years were characterized by his failure to deliver on specific promises – most obviously, to reform the health-care system. That enabled the Republicans to sweep to power in Congress in 1994, and resulted in two years of legislative gridlock. Displaying a better grasp of the popular mood, Clinton managed to assign most of the blame for the government's ineffectiveness to the Republicans and was elected to a second term with surprising ease. However, the "Comeback Kid" found holding on to office more of a challenge when his adulterous affair with White House intern Monica Lewinsky was exposed in 1998. Special Prosecutor Kenneth Starr's exhaustive probing led to the disgrace of **impeachment**, but the Senate ultimately failed to convict, sensing perhaps that the American people did not feel Clinton's indiscretions were serious enough to merit removal.

The new millennium

As Clinton left the presidency, the economy was **booming**, coming to the end of a record ten-year burst of sustained growth that had seen the budget deficit eradicated far ahead of even the most optimistic schedule, and the Dow Jones rise by over 260 percent since the day Clinton came to office. His former vice president, however, **Al Gore**, seemed too ashamed of his boss's character failings to bring himself to campaign on his economic record, and contrived to throw away the 2000 presidential election. Clinton is generally agreed to have won the 1996 election via "**triangulation**," adopting elements of his opponents' agenda to scoop up middle-ground voters; arguably, both Gore and his Republican opponent, **George W. Bush**, followed Clinton's example so well, and so precisely targeted the center of the political spectrum, that the result was inevitable: a **tie**. With the final conclusion depending on a mandatory re-counting of votes in Florida, where various irregularities and mistakes complicated the issue, the impasse was ultimately decided by the conservative **Supreme Court**, and Bush won the presidency. At the time, the charge that he had "stolen" the election was expected to seriously impair his presidency, while the authority of the Supreme Court was also threatened by the perception of its ruling as partisan.

A **recession** was probably due whoever was in the White House, as the bursting of the dot-com bubble drove hundreds of high-tech companies into bankruptcy. However, during his first months in office Bush showed little sign of halting the slide, and also seemed alarmingly indifferent to the concerns of America's friends and neighbors abroad. As well as cutting taxes and federal spending, he alienated environmentalists by rejecting US compliance with the 1997 Kyoto Agreement on global warming.

Then the atrocity of **September 11 2001**, abruptly made matters infinitely worse, inflicting a devastating blow to both the nation's economy and its pride. Over three thousand people were killed in the worst **terrorist attack** in US history, when two hijacked planes were flown into the **World Trade Center** in New York City, and one into the **Pentagon**. (A fourth crashed in Pennsylvania after its passengers and crew attempted to regain control.) The attacks were quickly linked to the al-Qaeda network of Saudi Arabian terrorist **Osama bin Laden**, and within weeks President Bush declared an open-ended "**War on Terror**".

Bush found himself confronting a new, changed world where the costs of maintaining vigilance and military preparedness seem incalculable, and yet the costs of not doing so might prove even higher. Far from balking at the challenge, he set about re-writing the traditional rule-book of diplomacy and international law. In

△ The White House

June 2002, he declared that the US has a right to launch **pre-emptive attacks**: "If we wait for threats to fully materialize, we will have waited too long . . . We must take the battle to the enemy, disrupt his plans, and confront the worst threats before they emerge."

A US-led invasion took control of **Afghanistan** in 2001, and was followed by a similar incursion into **Iraq** in 2003, ostensibly on the grounds that Iraqi dictator **Saddam Hussein** was developing "weapons of mass destruction." Saddam was deposed, apprehended, and in due course executed, but it's now acknowledged that no such weapons existed, and Iraq has both degenerated into a hopeless civil war and become a major recruiting ground for international terrorism. Meanwhile, at the time of writing in early 2007, bin Laden himself has yet to be found.

Despite a wave of financial scandals, spearheaded by the collapse of the mighty energy firm **Enron**, Bush defeated Senator John Kerry of Massachusetts in 2004 to win a second term as president. That election did little to suggest the country had become any less polarized, however, and the Bush administration was widely lambasted for its appalling failure to respond promptly or adequately when **Hurricane Katrina** and consequent floods devastated New Orleans and the Gulf Coast in 2005.

By the mid-term elections of November 2006, the deteriorating situation in Iraq – where the US death toll had topped three thousand and was evoking memories of Vietnam – rather than the legacy of Katrina was the major factor that enabled the Democrats to regain control of both the Senate and the House of Representatives for the first time in twelve years. At press time, Bush still seems determined to escalate rather than end the US presence in Iraq, while Democrat anti-war rhetoric hasn't yet led to a clear withdrawal strategy.

Books

I t would be futile to attempt to provide a comprehensive overview of American literature in the limited space available. The following bibliography is, therefore, an idiosyncratic selection of books intended as a starting point for interested readers. Books tagged with the 🏃 symbol are particularly recommended.

History and society

John Berendt *Midnight in the Garden of Good and Evil*. Voodoo, transvestism, and murder; best-selling true-life tales of life and death in contemporary Savannah (see p.534).

Dee Brown *Bury My Heart at Wounded Knee*. Approaching forty years on from its first publication, this remains the best narrative of the impact of white settlement and expansion on Native Americans across the continent.

Bill Bryson *Made in America*. A compulsively readable history of the American language, packed with bizarre snippets, which does much to illuminate the history of the nation.

🏃 **Mike Davis** *City of Quartz*. City politics, neighborhood gangs, unions, film noir, and religion are drawn together in this award-winning, leftist, hyperbolic history of Los Angeles.

John Demos *The Unredeemed Captive*. This story of the aftermath of a combined French and Indian attack on Deerfield, Massachusetts, in 1704 illuminates frontier life in the eighteenth century.

🏃 **W.E.B. DuBois** *The Souls of Black Folk*. Seminal collection of largely autobiographical essays examining the separation of the races in American society at the start of the twentieth century.

Joseph J. Ellis *Founding Brothers*. Enjoyable and informative essays on the "revolutionary generation" that bring the characters of Washington, Jefferson, et al to life.

Brian Fagan *Ancient North America*. Archeological history of America's native peoples, from the first hunters to cross the Bering Strait up to European contact.

Tim Flannery *The Eternal Frontier*. "Ecological" history of North America that reveals how the continent's physical environment has shaped the destinies of all its inhabitants, from horses to humans.

Shelby Foote *The Civil War: a Narrative*. Epic, three-volume account containing anything you could possibly want to know about the "War Between the States."

John Kenneth Galbraith *The Great Crash 1929*. An elegant and authoritative interpretation of the Wall Street Crash and its implications.

David Halberstam *The Fifties*. A delightfully readable yet satisfyingly comprehensive overview of the Eisenhower years.

Tony Horwitz *Confederates in the Attic: Dispatches from the Unfinished Civil War*. Strange meld of past and present, as journalist Horwitz explores the places in the South where die-hards keep the Civil War very much alive.

Meriwether Lewis and William Clark *The Original Journals of the Lewis and Clark Expedition, 1804–1806*. Eight volumes of meticulous jottings by the Northwest's first inland explorers, scrupulously following President Jefferson's orders to record every detail of flora, fauna, and native inhabitant.

Magnus Magnusson and Herman Pálsson (trans) *The Vinland Sagas*. If you imagine stories that the Vikings reached America to be no more than myths, here's the day-to-day minutiae to convince you otherwise.

James M. McPherson *Battle Cry of Freedom*. Extremely readable history of the Civil War, which integrates and explains the complex social, economic, political, and military factors in one concise volume.

Clyde A. Milner II, Carol A. O'Connor, and Martha A. Sandweiss *The Oxford History of the American West*. Fascinating collection of essays on Western history, covering topics ranging from myths and movies to art and religion.

James Mooney *The Ghost Dance Religion and The Sioux Outbreak of 1890*. An extraordinary Bureau of Ethnology report, first published in 1890 but still available in paperback. Mooney persuaded his Washington superiors to allow him to roam the West in search of first-hand evidence, and even interviewed Wovoka, the Ghost Dance prophet, in person.

Samuel Eliot Morison *The European Discovery of America*. An excellent resource for anyone interested in the early navigators who explored the Americas, divided into two fat volumes – *The Northern Voyages* and *The Southern Voyages* – and written by a former admiral who meticulously retraced many of the routes himself.

Roderick Frazier Nash *Wilderness and the American Mind*. Classic study of the American take on environmental and conservation issues over the past couple of hundred years. Especially good sections on John Muir and his battles to preserve Yosemite.

Stephen Plog *Ancient Peoples of the Southwest*. Much the best single-volume history of the pre-Hispanic Southwest, packed with diagrams and color photographs.

Marc Reisner *Cadillac Desert*. Concise, engaging account of the environmental and political impact on the West of the twentieth-century mania for dam-building and large-scale irrigation projects.

Eric Schlosser *Fast Food Nation*. A century on from *The Jungle*, Eric Schlosser warns America once again that you are what you eat.

Alan Taylor *American Colonies*. Perhaps the best book on any single era of American history – a superb account of every aspect of the peopling of the continent, from remote antiquity until the Declaration of Independence.

Mark Twain *Roughing It*, *Life on the Mississippi*, and many others. Mark Twain was by far the funniest and most vivid chronicler of nineteenth-century America. *Roughing It*, which covers his early wanderings across the continent, all the way to Hawaii, is absolutely compelling.

Geoffrey C. Ward, with Ric and Ken Burns *The Civil War*. Illustrated history of the Civil War, designed to accompany the TV series and using hundreds of the same photographs.

Allen Weinstein and David Rubel *The Story of America*. This glossy volume is so beautifully illustrated you might not expect the text to be first-rate too. In fact, it provides fascinating detail and analysis on the one representative topic it chooses to cover from each of 26 eras.

Richard White *It's Your Misfortune And None of My Own*. Dense, authoritative and all-embracing history of the American West, which debunks the notion of the rugged pioneer by stressing the role of the federal government.

Juan Williams *Eyes on the Prize*. Informative and detailed account of the Civil Rights years from the early 1950s up to 1966, with lots of rare, and some very familiar, photos.

Edmund Wilson *Patriotic Gore*. Fascinating eight-hundred-page survey of the literature of the Civil War, which serves in its own right as an immensely readable narrative of the conflict.

Bob Woodward *Plan Of Attack*, *Bush At War*, and *State Of Denial*. Woodward's role as the ultimate insider journalist dates back to Watergate, of course, but his extraordinary access to the Bush White House makes his ongoing account of the "War On Terror" essential reading.

Biography and oral history

Muhammad Ali *The Greatest*. Powerful and entertaining autobiography of the Louisville boy who grew up to become world heavyweight boxing champion. The most memorable parts deal with his fight against the Vietnam draft and the subsequent stripping away of his world championship title.

Maya Angelou *I Know Why the Caged Bird Sings*. First of a five-volume autobiography that provides an ultimately uplifting account of how a black girl transcended her traumatic childhood in 1930s Arkansas.

Paul Auster (ed) *True Tales of American Life* (UK)/*I Thought My Father Was God* (US). Anthology of true-life stories sent to Auster for a National Public Radio project. Arranged by subject, it's best dipped into at random; among the mawkish and the mundane are just enough quirky, touching, and plain crazy tales to make it worth the while.

Donald A. Barclay, James H. Maguire, and Peter Wild (eds) *Into the Wilderness Dream*. Gripping collection of Western exploration narratives written between 1500 and 1800; thanks to any number of little-known gems, the best of many such anthologies.

Bill Clinton *My Life*. The exhaustive, and exhausting, autobiography of the last twentieth-century president; biased, of course, but the man's sheer energy and commitment are astonishing.

William F. Cody *The Life of Hon. William F. Cody, Known as Buffalo Bill*. Larger-than-life autobiography of one of the great characters of the Wild West. Particularly treasurable for the moment when he refers to himself more formally as "Bison William."

Frederick Douglass, et al *The Classic Slave Narratives*. Compilation of ex-slaves' autobiographies, ranging from Olaudah Equíano's kidnapping in Africa and global wanderings to Frederick Douglass's eloquent denunciation of slavery. Includes Harriet Jacobs' story of her escape from Edenton, North Carolina – see p.490.

Jill Ker Conway (ed) *Written by Herself*. Splendid anthology of women's autobiographies from the mid-1800s to the present, including sections on African-Americans, scientists, artists, and pioneers.

U.S. Grant *Personal Memoirs*. Encouraged by Mark Twain, the Union general and subsequent president wrote his autobiography just before his death, in a (successful) bid to recoup his horrendous debts. At first the book feels oddly downbeat, but the man's down-to-earth modesty grows on you.

Henry Hampton and Steve Fayer *Voices of Freedom*. Hugely impressive oral history of the Civil Rights movement.

Malcolm X, with Alex Haley *The Autobiography of Malcolm X*. Searingly honest and moving account of Malcolm's progress from street hoodlum to political leadership. Written on the hoof over a period of years, it traces the development of Malcolm X's thinking before, during, and after his split from the Nation of Islam. The conclusion, when he talks about his impending assassination, is painful in the extreme.

Edmund Morris *The Rise of Theodore Roosevelt* and *Theodore Rex*. Thoroughly engaging and superbly researched two-volume biography of Theodore Roosevelt, tracing the energetic and controversial president's astonishing trajectory to the White House, and his far-reaching achievements.

Ron Powers *Mark Twain*. Definitive recent biography of America's most compelling literary figure.

Joanna L. Stratton *Pioneer Women*.
Original memoirs of women – mothers, teachers, homesteaders, and circuit riders – who ventured across the Plains from 1854 to 1890. Lively, superbly detailed accounts, with chapters on journeys, homebuilding, daily domestic life, the church, the cowtown, temperance, and suffrage.

Studs Terkel *American Dreams Lost and Found*. Interviews with ordinary American citizens. As illuminating a guide to US life as you could hope for.

🏃 **Frank Waters** *Book of the Hopi*.
Extraordinary insight into the traditions and beliefs of the Hopi, prepared through years of interviews and approved by tribal elders.

Gary Younge *Stranger In A Strange Land* and *No Place Like Home*. Black British journalist Gary Younge is one of the most acute observers of contemporary America; his experiences in the self-proclaimed New South, chronicled in *No Place Like Home*, make fascinating reading.

Entertainment and culture

Kenneth Anger *Hollywood Babylon*.
A vicious yet high-spirited romp through Tinseltown's greatest scandals, amply illustrated with gory and repulsive photographs, and always inclined to bend the facts for the sake of a good story. A shoddily researched second volume covers more recent times.

Joshua Berrett (ed) *The Louis Armstrong Companion: Eight Decades of Commentary*. Broad selection of essays, interviews, letters, reviews, and autobiography, revealing the world's most influential musician in all his complexity. A fine introduction to the subject, featuring lots of previously unpublished material: standouts include Armstrong's own lament about defeatism and negativity in his fellow black men.

Bob Dylan *Chronicles: Volume One*.
Far from the kind of endless stream-of-consciousness he wrote in his younger days, Dylan chose in this long-awaited autobiography to focus in almost microscopic detail on three distinct moments in his life, including Greenwich Village in the early 1960s, and New Orleans in the 1980s. The result is a compelling testament to his place at the epicenter of America's cultural life.

Charlotte Greig *Will You Still Love Me Tomorrow?* Enthusiastic feminist appraisal of (predominantly American) girl groups from the 1950s (the Chan-

tels and the Crystals) through to 1980s rap stars like Salt'n'Pepa. Though inevitably somewhat dated, its many photos and personal recollections still make it a great read.

🏃 **Peter Guralnick** *Lost Highways*, *Feel Like Going Home* and *Sweet Soul Music*. Thoroughly researched personal histories of black popular music, packed with obsessive detail on all the great names. His twin Elvis biographies, *Last Train to Memphis* and *Careless Love*, trace the rise and fall of the iconic star in an unsensational but nonetheless gripping documentary manner, while also performing the rare trick of evaluating him seriously as a musician.

Gerri Hershey *Nowhere to Run: the History of Soul Music*. Definitive run-down on the evolution of soul music from the gospel heyday of the 1940s through the Memphis, Motown, and Philly scenes to the sounds of the early 1980s. Strong on social commentary and political background and studded with anecdotes and interviews.

Michael Ondaatje *Coming through Slaughter*. Extraordinary, dream-like fictionalization of the life of doomed New Orleans cornet player Buddy Bolden, written in a lyrical style that evokes the rhythms and pace of jazz improvisation.

Robert Palmer *Deep Blues*. Readable history of the development and personalities of the Delta Blues.

Geoffrey C. Ward, Ken Burns, et al *Jazz: a History of America's Music*. While the story peters out somewhat after bebop, this highly readable volume (linked to the TV series) boasts hundreds of illustrations and rare photographs, first-hand accounts and lively essays to provide a beautifully drawn picture of America's home-grown music and its icons.

Travel writing

Edward Abbey *The Journey Home*. Hilarious accounts of whitewater rafting and desert hiking trips alternate with essays by the man who inspired the radical environmentalist movement Earth First! All of Abbey's many books, especially *Desert Solitaire*, a journal of time spent as a ranger in Arches National Park, make great traveling companions.

James Agee and Walker Evans *Let Us Now Praise Famous Men*. A deeply personal but also richly evocative journal of travels through the rural lands of the Depression-era Deep South, complemented by Evans's powerful photographs.

Bill Bryson *The Lost Continent*. Using his boyhood home of Des Moines in Iowa as a benchmark, the author travels the length and breadth of America to find the perfect small town. Hilarious, if occasionally a bit smug. *A Walk in the Woods* applies his trademark irony to the Appalachian Trail from Georgia to Maine, but suffers from too much nature and too few quirky characters.

J. Hector St-John de Crèvecoeur *Letters from an American Farmer and Sketches of Eighteenth-Century America*. A remarkable account of the complexities of Revolutionary America, first published in 1782.

Robert Frank *The Americans*. The Swiss photographer's brilliantly evocative portrait of mid-century American life from coast to coast, with striking images contextualized by an introductory essay from Jack Kerouac.

Ian Frazier *Great Plains*. An immaculately researched and well-written travelogue containing a wealth of information on the people of the American prairielands from Native Americans to the soldiers who staff the region's many nuclear installations.

Jack Kerouac *On the Road*. Definitive account of transcontinental Beatnik wanderings, which now reads as a curiously dated period piece. Not as incoherent as you might expect.

James A. MacMahon (ed) *Audubon Society Nature Guides*. Attractively produced, fully illustrated and easy-to-use guides to the flora and fauna of seven different US regional ecosystems, covering the entire country from coast to coast and from grasslands to glaciers.

Virginia and Lee McAlester *A Field Guide to American Houses*. Well-illustrated and engaging guide to America's rich variety of domestic architecture, from pre-Colonial to postmodern.

John McPhee *Encounters with the Arch Druid*. In three interlinked narratives, the late environmental activist and Friends of the Earth founder David Brower confronts developers, miners, and dam-builders, while trying to protect three different American wilderness areas – the Atlantic shoreline, the Grand Canyon, and the Cascades of the Pacific Northwest.

William Least Heat-Moon *Blue Highways*. Account of a mammoth loop tour of the US by back roads, in which the author interviews ordinary people in ordinary places. A good overview of rural America, with lots of interesting details on Native Americans. His next book, *Prairyerth*, opted for the microcosmic approach, taking six hundred loving pages over the story of Chase County, Kansas.

Jonathan Raban *Old Glory*. A somewhat pompous though always interesting account of Raban's journey on a small craft down the Mississippi River from the head-waters in Minnesota to the bayous of Louisiana.

Bernard A. Weisberger (ed) *The WPA Guide to America*. Prepared during the New Deal as part of a make-work program for writers, these guides paint a fairly comprehensive portrait of 1930s and earlier America.

Also available are state-by-state guides, most of them out of print but easily found in US libraries and secondhand bookshops.

Edmund White *States of Desire: Travels in Gay America*. A revealing account of life in gay communities across the country, focusing heavily on San Francisco and New York.

Fiction

General Americana

Raymond Carver *Will You Please Be Quiet Please?* Stories of the American working class, written in a distinctive sparse, almost deadpan style that perhaps owes something to Hemingway and certainly influenced untold numbers of contemporary American writers. The stories served as the basis for Robert Altman's film *Short Cuts*.

Don DeLillo *White Noise*; *Underworld*. The former is his best, a funny and penetrating pop culture exploration, while the latter is one of those typically flawed attempts to pack the twentieth-century American experience into a great big novel. Worthwhile, though.

John Dos Passos *USA*. Hugely ambitious novel (originally a trilogy) that grapples with the US in the early decades of the twentieth century from every possible angle. Gripping

human stories with a strong political and historical point of view.

William Kennedy *Ironweed*. Terse, affecting tale of a couple of down-on-their-luck drunks haunted by ghosts from a checkered past; excellent evocation of 1930s America, specifically working-class Albany, New York.

Herman Melville *Moby-Dick*. Compendious and compelling account of nineteenth-century whaling, packed with details on American life from New England to the Pacific.

E. Annie Proulx *Accordion Crimes*. Proulx's masterly book comes as close to being the fabled "Great American Novel" as anyone could reasonably ask, tracing a fascinating history of immigrants in all parts of North America through the fortunes of a battered old Sicilian accordion.

New York City

Paul Auster *New York Trilogy*. Three Borgesian investigations into the mystery and madness of contemporary New York. Using the conventions of the detective novel, Auster unfolds a disturbed and disturbing picture of the city.

Truman Capote *Breakfast at Tiffany's* and *In Cold Blood*. The first story is about a fictional social climber in New York called Holly Golightly; the

second concerns the true-life stories of two serial killers in the heartland. The subject matter of these two stories could hardly be more different, but the degree of insight drawn from two uniquely American stories is equally high in both accounts.

Michael Chabon *The Amazing Adventures of Kavalier & Clay*. Pulitzer Prize–winning novel charting the rise and fall of comic book-writing cousins in New York City – one a refugee from World War II Prague, the other a closeted Brooklynite.

Jonathan Franzen *The Corrections*. While it never quite lived up to the hype – what could? – this ambitious saga, about a classically dysfunctional American family, manages to capture all that late twentieth-century navel searching in a nutshell. And it's very funny in places, too.

🏃 **Chester Himes** *Cotton Comes to Harlem, Blind Man with a Pistol*, and many others. Action-packed and uproariously violent novels set in New York's Harlem, starring the much-feared detectives Coffin Ed Johnson and Grave Digger Jones.

Grace Paley *Collected Stories*. Shrewd love-hate stories written over a lifetime by the daughter of Russian-Jewish immigrants, who published dead-on accounts of New York life in three installments: her first book of stories came out in the 1950s, her second in the early 1970s and her third in the late 1980s.

🏃 **J.D. Salinger** *The Catcher in the Rye*. Classic novel of adolescence, tracing Holden Caulfield's sardonic journey through the streets of New York.

New England

John Irving *The Cider House Rules*. One of Irving's more successful sprawling novels, weaving themes of love, suffering, and the many facets of the abortion debate against a Maine backdrop.

H.P. Lovecraft *The Best of H.P. Lovecraft: Bloodcurdling Tales of Horror and the Macabre*. Creepy New England stories from the author Stephen King called "the twentieth century's greatest practitioner of the classic horror tale."

Florida and the South

William Faulkner *The Reivers*. The last and most humorous work of this celebrated Southern author. *The Sound and the Fury*, a fascinating study of prejudice, set like most of his books in the fictional Yoknatapawpha County in Mississippi, is a much more difficult read.

Carl Hiaasen *Basket Case*, and many others. Hiaasen is the funniest crime writer on the scene – and a razor-sharp chronicler of Florida's weirder, wilder side. This one sees dead rock stars, a grumpy investigative reporter, and a giant frozen lizard caught up in a fast-moving caper plot.

Zora Neale Hurston *Spunk*. Short stories celebrating black culture and experience from around the country, by a writer from Florida who became one of the bright stars of the Harlem cultural renaissance in the 1920s.

Harper Lee *To Kill a Mockingbird*. Classic tale of racial conflict and soci-ety's view of an outsider, Boo Radley, as seen through the eyes of children.

Cormac McCarthy *Suttree*. McCarthy is better known for his "modern Western" works like *Blood Meridian* and *All the Pretty Horses*, but this beautifully written tale, of a Knoxville, Tennessee, scion opting for a hard-scrabble life among a band of vagrants on the Tennessee River, is his best.

Carson McCullers *The Heart is a Lonely Hunter*. McCullers is unrivaled in her sensitive treatment of misfits, in this case the attitude of a small Southern community to a deaf-mute.

Margaret Mitchell *Gone With the Wind*. Worth a read even if you know the lines of Scarlett and Rhett by heart.

🏃 **Toni Morrison** *Beloved*. Exquisitely written ghost story by the Nobel Prize-winning novelist, which recounts the painful lives of a group of freed slaves after Reconstruction, and the obsession a mother develops after murdering her baby daughter to spare her a life of slavery.

Flannery O'Connor *A Good Man is Hard to Find*. Short stories, featuring strong, obsessed characters, that explore religious tensions and racial conflicts in the Deep South.

Alice Walker *In Love and Trouble*. Moving and powerful stories of black women in the South, from the author of the much-acclaimed *The Color Purple*.

Eudora Welty *The Ponder Heart*. Quirky, humorous evocation of life in a backwater Mississippi town. Her most critically acclaimed work, *The Optimist's Daughter*, explores the tensions between a judge's daughter and her stepmother.

Louisiana

James Lee Burke *Black Cherry Blues*. Perhaps the best in Burke's series featuring Cajun cop Dave Robicheaux. Here Robicheaux sets out to expose alliances between government and organized crime in Louisiana and Montana.

George Washington Cable *The Grandissimes*. Romantic saga of Creole family feuds, written c.1900 but set during the Louisiana Purchase. Superb evocation of steamy Louisiana elite, the Creole lifestyle, and the resistance of New Orleans to its Americanization. Apparently shocking at the time for its sympathetic portrayal of blacks.

🏃 **Kate Chopin** *The Awakening*. Subversive story of a bourgeois married woman whose fight for independence ends in tragedy. The swampy Louisiana of a century ago is portrayed as both a sensual hotbed for her sexual awakening and as her eventual nemesis.

Valerie Martin *Property*. A bleak but wonderfully written tale of the brutalizing effects of slavery, on both mistress and slave, on a Louisiana sugar plantation.

Anne Rice *Feast Of All Saints*. Rice's vampire novels are great fun, but her finest portrait of nineteenth-century New Orleans comes in this sensitive examination of race, sexuality and gender issues in the antebellum period.

🏃 **John Kennedy Toole** *A Confederacy of Dunces*. Anarchic black tragicomedy in which the pompous and repulsive anti-hero Ignatius J. Reilly wreaks havoc through an insalubrious and surreal New Orleans.

🏃 **Robert Penn Warren** *All The King's Men*. This fascinating fictionalized saga of Louisiana's legendary "Kingfish", Huey Long, is also a truly great American novel in its own right.

The Great Lakes and the Great Plains

🏃 **Willa Cather** *My Ántonia*. Stunning book set in Nebraska that provides a great sense of the pioneer hardships on the Plains.

Louise Erdrich *The Beet Queen*. Offbeat tale of passion and obsession among poor white North Dakota folk – particularly women – against the backdrop of an economy and culture changing with the introduction of sugar beet as a crop in the 1940s. Erdrich's other novels play through the tensions between tradition and "progress" in Native American communities.

Garrison Keillor *Lake Wobegon Days*. Wry, witty tales about a mythical Minnesota small town, poking gentle fun at the rural Midwest.

Mari Sandoz *Old Jules*. Written in 1935, this fictionalized biography gives a wonderful insight into the life of the author's pioneer Swiss father on the Nebraskan plains. Sandoz's other major work, *Crazy Horse*, contains great historical overviews but is spoiled somewhat by her insistence on narrating it through Sioux eyes.

Upton Sinclair *The Jungle*. Documenting the horrific unsanitary conditions in Chicago's meat-packing industry, Sinclair's compelling Socialist-tract-cum-novel, first serialized in 1905, ranks among the most influential books in US history.

Richard Wright *Native Son*. The harrowing story of Bigger Thomas, a black chauffeur who accidentally kills his employer's daughter. The story develops his relationship with his lawyer, the closest he has ever come to being on an equal footing with a white.

The Rockies and the Southwest

A.B. Guthrie Jr *Big Sky*. When first published in the Thirties it shattered the image of the mythical West peddled by Hollywood. Realistic historical fiction at its very best, following desperate mountain man and fugitive Boone Caudill, whose idyllic life in Montana was ended by the arrival of white settlers.

Tony Hillerman *The Dark Wind*, and many others. The adventures of Jim Chee of the Navajo Tribal Police on the reservations of northern Arizona, forever dabbling in dark and mysterious forces churned up from the Ancestral Puebloan past.

Barbara Kingsolver *Pigs in Heaven*. A magnificent evocation of tensions and realities in the contemporary Southwest, by a Tucson-based writer who ranks among America's finest prose stylists.

Norman MacLean *A River Runs Through It*. Unputdownable – the best ever novel about fly-fishing, set in beautiful Montana lake country.

California and the West

Raymond Chandler *The Big Sleep* and *Farewell My Lovely*. The original incarnations of archetypal tough guy and iconic private eye Philip Marlowe are far more complex and beautifully written than the related movies would lead you to expect. Pulp fiction at its finest – written by an American raised in London.

David Guterson *Snow Falling on Cedars* and *East Of the Mountains*. Two gripping novels that capture the flavor of the Pacific Northwest; the first is an atmospheric mystery centering on postwar interracial tensions, the second features a dying man looking back on his life.

Jack London *The Call of the Wild and Other Stories*. London's classic tale, of a family pet discovering the ways of the wilderness while forced to pull sleds across Alaska's Gold Rush trails, still makes essential reading before a trip to the far north.

Armistead Maupin *Tales of the City*. Long-running saga comprising sympathetic and entertaining tales of life in San Francisco, that also work surprisingly well as suspenseful stand-alone novels. That many of its key characters are gay meant that over the years the series became a chronicle of the impact of AIDS on the city. Maupin's *Maybe the Moon* is the poignant true-life story of his friend, the short person who played ET in the movie but was never allowed to reveal her true identity.

Thomas Pynchon *The Crying of Lot 49*. Shorter, funnier, and more accessible than *Gravity's Rainbow*, this novel of techno-freaks and potheads in Sixties California reveals, among other things, the sexy side of stamp collecting.

John Steinbeck *The Grapes of Wrath*. The classic account of a migrant family forsaking the Midwest for the Promised Land. Steinbeck's lighthearted but crisply observed novella *Cannery Row* captures daily life on the prewar Monterey waterfront. The epic *East of Eden* updates and resets the Bible in the Salinas Valley and details three generations of familial feuding.

Nathanael West *The Day of the Locust*. West wrote dark novels wholly vested in the American experience; this one, set in LA, is an apocalyptic story of fringe characters at the edge of the film industry.

Film

The list below focuses on key films in certain genres that have helped define the American experience for domestic and foreign audiences alike, cementing cultural stereotypes such as the gangster, cowboy, and blonde chorus girl, as well as national iconography such as expansive prairies, open highways, big-city skyscrapers, and suburban dream homes. Films tagged with the 🎬 symbol are particularly recommended.

Music/musicals

Calamity Jane (David Butler, 1953). The Western gets a rumbustious musical twist with tomboy Doris Day's thigh-slapping gusto in the title role and Howard Keel as the rugged hero who (almost) tames her.

Gimme Shelter (Albert and David Maysles, 1969). Excellent documentary about the ill-fated Rolling Stones concert at Altamont. Its searing look at homegrown American violence and Vietnam-era chaos at the end of the 1960s also includes an on-camera stabbing.

Gold Diggers of 1933 (Mervyn LeRoy/Busby Berkeley, 1933). The most entertaining in a famous trio of 1933 films (including *42nd Street* and *Footlight Parade*), in which genius choreographer Berkeley pioneered stunning overhead-crane shots of flamboyant, mechanized dance numbers featuring lines of glamorous chorines.

Meet Me in St Louis (Vincente Minnelli, 1944). Most famous for its Judy Garland number "The Trolley Song," this charming piece of nostalgia celebrates turn-of-the-century America through the ups and downs of a St Louis family during the 1903 World's Fair.

On the Town (Stanley Donen/Gene Kelly, 1949). An exuberant musical tour of New York City, led by director Kelly and Frank Sinatra, who play sailors on shore leave.

🎬 **Singin' in the Rain** (Stanley Donen/Gene Kelly, 1952). Beloved musical comedy about Hollywood at the dawn of the sound era, featuring memorable tunes like "Make 'Em Laugh" and the title song, along with energetic performances by star Kelly, sidekick Donald O'Connor, and a pixie-ish Debbie Reynolds.

Woodstock (Michael Wadleigh, 1969). *Gimme Shelter*'s upbeat counterpart, documenting the musical pinnacle of the hippie era, showing a half-million flower children peacefully grooving to Jimi Hendrix, The Who, and Sly and the Family Stone while getting stoned, muddy, and wild on an upstate New York farm.

Silent era

Birth of a Nation (D.W. Griffith, 1915). Possibly the most influential film in American history, both for its pioneering film technique (close-ups, cross-cutting, and so on) and appalling racist propaganda, which led to a revival of the KKK and a resurgence in lynchings across the country.

🎬 **The General** (Buster Keaton, 1926). A fine introduction to Keaton's acrobatic brand of slapstick and his inventive cinematic approach, in which the Great Stone Face chases down a stolen locomotive during the Civil War.

The Gold Rush (Charlie Chaplin, 1925). Chaplin's finest film: the Little

Tramp gets trapped in a cabin during an Alaska blizzard in an affecting story that mixes sentiment and high comedy in near-perfect balance.

Greed (Erich von Stroheim, 1923). An audacious scene-by-scene adaptation of Frank Norris's novel *McTeague*, a tragic tale of love and revenge in San Francisco at the end of the nineteenth century. Slashed from ten to two-and-a-half hours by MGM, the film remains a cinematic triumph for its striking compositions, epic drama, and truly bleak ending.

Intolerance (D.W. Griffith, 1916). The greatest debacle of the silent era, a colossal bomb that helped destroy Griffith's career, but still fascinates for its multiple storylines, arch melodrama, and stunning Babylonian set (a replica was built as part of a shopping mall in Hollywood).

Sunrise (F.W. Murnau, 1927). Among the most beautiful Hollywood productions of any era. *Sunrise*'s German émigré director employed striking lighting effects, complex traveling shots, and emotionally compelling performances in a tale of a country boy led astray by a big-city femme fatale.

Westerns

McCabe and Mrs. Miller (Robert Altman, 1971). Entrepreneur Warren Beatty brings prostitution to a Washington State town and tries to reinvent himself as a gunslinger, in what's often referred to as an anti-Western because of its stark, snowy landscapes, soft-focus images, and unromantic outlook.

Once upon a Time in the West (Sergio Leone, 1968). The quintessential spaghetti Western, actually filmed in Spain by an Italian director, steeped in mythic American themes of manifest destiny and rugged individualism.

Red River (Howard Hawks, 1948). Upstart Montgomery Clift battles beef-baron John Wayne on a momentous cattle drive through the Midwest. Prototypical Hawks tale of clashing tough-guy egos and no-nonsense professionals on the range.

The Searchers (John Ford, 1956). Perhaps the most iconic of Ford's many Westerns; a highly influential production with vivid cinematography and epic scale, in which John Wayne relentlessly hunts down the Indian chief who massacred his friends and family.

The Wild Bunch (Sam Peckinpah, 1969). A movie that says as much about the chaotic end of the 1960s as it does about the West, featuring a band of killers who hunt for women and treasure and wind up in a bloodbath unprecedented in film history.

Americana

Breakfast at Tiffany's (Blake Edwards, 1961). Manhattan never looked more chic, and Audrey Hepburn, dressed in Givenchy, gives a quintessentially stylish performance as vulnerable kept-woman Holly Golightly. The theme tune, "Moon River", penned by Henry Mancini, also shines as a perennial classic. Based on a novella by Truman Capote.

Travel store

Small print and

Index

A Rough Guide to Rough Guides

Published in 1982, the first Rough Guide – to Greece – was a student scheme that became a publishing phenomenon. Mark Ellingham, a recent graduate of English from Bristol University, had been traveling in Greece the previous summer and couldn't find the right guidebook. With a small group of friends he wrote his own guide, combining a highly contemporary, journalistic style with a thoroughly practical approach to travelers' needs.

The immediate success of the book spawned a series that rapidly covered dozens of destinations. And, in addition to impecunious backpackers, Rough Guides soon acquired a much broader and older readership that relished the guides' wit and inquisitiveness as much as their enthusiastic, critical approach and value-for-money ethos.

These days, Rough Guides include recommendations from shoestring to luxury and cover more than 200 destinations around the globe, including almost every country in the Americas and Europe, more than half of Africa and most of Asia and Australasia. Our ever-growing team of authors and photographers is spread all over the world, particularly in Europe, the USA, and Australia.

In the early 1990s, Rough Guides branched out of travel, with the publication of Rough Guides to World Music, Classical Music, and the Internet. All three have become benchmark titles in their fields, spearheading the publication of a wide range of books under the Rough Guide name.

Including the travel series, Rough Guides now number more than 350 titles, covering: phrasebooks, waterproofs, music guides from Opera to Heavy Metal, reference works as diverse as Conspiracy Theories and Shakespeare, and popular culture books from iPods to Poker. Rough Guides also produce a series of more than 120 World Music CDs in partnership with World Music Network.

Visit www.roughguides.com to see our latest publications.

Many Rough Guide travel images are available for commercial licensing at www.roughguidespictures.com

Rough Guide credits

Text editor: Amy Hegarty
Layout: Dan May, Diana Jarvis
Cartography: Maxine Repath, Katie Lloyd-Jones, Ed Wright
Picture editor: Sarah Smithies
Production: Katherine Owers
Proofreader: Stewart J. Wild
Cover design: Chloë Roberts
Editorial: London Kate Berens, Claire Saunders, Ruth Blackmore, Polly Thomas, Richard Lim, Alison Murchie, Karoline Densley, Andy Turner, Keith Drew, Edward Aves, Nikki Birrell, Alice Park, Sarah Eno, Lucy White, Jo Kirby, Samantha Cook, James Smart, Natasha Foges, Roisin Cameron, Joe Staines, Duncan Clark, Peter Buckley, Matthew Milton, Tracy Hopkins, Ruth Tidball; **New York** Andrew Rosenberg, Steven Horak, AnneLise Sorensen, Amy Hegarty, April Isaacs, Ella Steim, Anna Owens, Joseph Petta, Sean Mahoney
Design & Pictures: London Scott Stickland, Dan May, Diana Jarvis, Mark Thomas, Jj Luck, Harriet Mills, Chloë Roberts, Nicole Newman; **Delhi** Umesh Aggarwal, Ajay Verma, Jessica Subramanian, Ankur Guha, Pradeep Thapliyal, Sachin Tanwar, Anita Singh, Madhavi Singh

Production: Katherine Owers, Aimee Hampson
Cartography: London Maxine Repath, Ed Wright, Katie Lloyd-Jones; **Delhi** Jai Prakash Mishra, Rajesh Chhibber, Ashutosh Bharti, Rajesh Mishra, Animesh Pathak, Jasbir Sandhu, Karobi Gogoi, Amod Singh, Alakananda Bhattacharya, Athokpam Jotinkumar
Online: New York Jennifer Gold, Kristin Mingrone; **Delhi** Manik Chauhan, Narender Kumar, Rakesh Kumar, Amit Kumar, Amit Verma, Rahul Kumar, Ganesh Sharma, Debojit Borah
Marketing & Publicity: London Liz Statham, Niki Hanmer, Louise Maher, Jess Carter, Vanessa Godden, Anna Paynton, Rachel Sprackett; **New York** Geoff Colquitt, Megan Kennedy, Katy Ball; **Delhi** Reem Khokhar
Special Projects Editor: Philippa Hopkins
Manager India: Punita Singh
Series Editor: Mark Ellingham
Reference Director: Andrew Lockett
Publishing Coordinator: Megan McIntyre
Publishing Director: Martin Dunford
Commercial Manager: Gino Magnotta
Managing Director: John Duhigg

Publishing information

This eighth edition published April 2007 by **Rough Guides Ltd**,
80 Strand, London WC2R 0RL
345 Hudson St, 4th Floor,
New York, NY 10014, USA
14 Local Shopping Centre, Panchsheel Park,
New Delhi 110017, India
Distributed by the Penguin Group
Penguin Books Ltd,
80 Strand, London WC2R 0RL
Penguin Group (USA)
375 Hudson Street, NY 10014, USA
Penguin Group (Australia)
250 Camberwell Road, Camberwell,
Victoria 3124, Australia
Penguin Books Canada Ltd,
10 Alcorn Avenue, Toronto, Ontario,
Canada M4V 1E4
Penguin Group (NZ)
67 Apollo Drive, Mairangi Bay, Auckland 1310,
New Zealand
Cover concept by Peter Dyer.

Typeset in Bembo and Helvetica to an original design by Henry Iles.

Printed in Italy by LegoPrint SpA

© Samantha Cook, Tim Perry, Greg Ward, JD Dickey, Nick Edwards, and Rough Guides 2007

No part of this book may be reproduced in any form without permission from the publisher except for the quotation of brief passages in reviews.

1368pp includes index

A catalogue record for this book is available from the British Library

ISBN: 9-78184-353-786-1

The publishers and authors have done their best to ensure the accuracy and currency of all the information in **The Rough Guide to the USA**, however, they can accept no responsibility for any loss, injury, or inconvenience sustained by any traveler as a result of information or advice contained in the guide.

1 3 5 7 9 8 6 4 2

Help us update

We've gone to a lot of effort to ensure that the eighth edition of **The Rough Guide to the USA** is accurate and up to date. However, things change – places get "discovered", opening hours are notoriously fickle, restaurants and rooms raise prices or lower standards. If you feel we've got it wrong or left something out, we'd like to know, and if you can remember the address, the price, the time, the phone number, so much the better. We'll credit all contributions, and send a copy of the next edition (or any other Rough Guide if you prefer) for the best letters. Everyone who writes to us and isn't already a subscriber will receive a copy of our full-color thrice-yearly newsletter. Please mark letters: "**Rough Guide the USA Update**" and send to: Rough Guides, 80 Strand, London WC2R 0RL, or Rough Guides, 4th Floor, 345 Hudson St, New York, NY 10014. Or send an email to **mail@roughguides.com**
Have your questions answered and tell others about your trip at
www.roughguides.atinfopop.com

SMALL PRINT

Acknowledgments

Sam: At Rough Guides, a very big thank you to Amy Hegarty, a great editor and a pleasure to work with; to new co-authors Jeff and Nick; and above all to dear Greg, for everything. Of the many people who helped in the USA, I am particularly grateful to Jackie Reed and Kelly Earnest in Memphis; Christine deCuir and Meire Ramos in New Orleans; Allie Hardee in Nashville; Jorge Franz and Celia Morales in Houston; Penélope Benedict in San Antonio; and to Kilynn Sommer in Dallas. Thanks also to David Nicholson; Eve Gardiner at First PR; and Susie, Jody, and Kirsty at TTM World.

Greg: Thanks to everyone at Rough Guides for agreeing to delay this new edition while Sam and I got married. Thanks to Sam for every minute, and to Amy for her enthusiasm and precision. On the road, thanks to Chris Nobles in Charleston; Carey Ferrara, Erica Backus, and Teresa Jacobs in Savannah; Elizabeth Walasin Lulla, Robert Prohaska, and Sally Baker in Chicago; Bob Harris in Georgia; Candy Aluli and Nancy Daniels in Hawaii; and Edie Jarolim, Steve Lewis, and Bruce Brossman in the Southwest.

JD would like to thank his family for their support, his editor for her excellent work in managing this project, and other colleagues at Rough Guides, including Steve Horak and Andrew Rosenberg, and all his friends and associates throughout the Northwest, who made useful suggestions, provided illuminating insight, and otherwise made this book worth writing.

Nick would like to thank the many folk at the various CVBs and tourist organizations for their invaluable help: Jill d'Anzeris, NY; Cathy Ellis, Ulster Co, NY; Margaret Marchuk, Lake Placid, NY; Patti Donoghue, Rochester, NY; Nancy Vargo, Buffalo, NY;

Ellen Kornfield, Philadelphia, PA; Terese Balzareit, Harrisburg, PA; Mindy Bianca, Hershey, PA; Tammy Brown, Columbus, OH; DeAnn Hazey, Cleveland, OH; Jeff Blom, Cincinnatti, OH; Kirsten Borgstrom, MI; Carolyn Artman, Detroit, MI; Sally Laukitis, Holland, MI; Nick Miller, Ann Arbor, MI; Marge Bateman, KY; Jennifer Broadwater, Pleasant Hill, KY; Tim Zahner & Kelly Chamberlin, San Francisco, CA; Adele, Berkeley, CA; Sharon Hunt, Lake Tahoe, CA; Suzi Brakken, Plumas Co, CA; Joanne Steele, Siskiyou Co, CA; Richard, Humboldt Co, CA; Sharon Rooney, Mendocino Co, CA; Nina Laramore, Russian River, CA; Jenny Franklin, Truckee, CA; Bob Warren & Karen Whitaker, Shasta Cascades, CA. Many thanks to all the fine places I ate and stayed, too numerous to mention and to the friends who sheltered me at various points: Clint, Anandamayi, & Laramie in Berkeley; Nicki & Eric in Gold Country; and Karen Kaschak in NJ. For spiritual inspiration en route, gratitude goes to the Yogananda retreat near Nevada City and The Beloved Community outside Ashland, OR. Well done to Amy Hegarty at RG in NYC for steering us patiently through the mammoth project. Finally, heartfelt thanks as ever to Maria for teaching all that I could ever want to know about Pittsburgh.

The editor would like to thank Sam, Greg, Jeff, Nick, and all the contributors for their excellent and inspiring work, and for making this book such a pleasure to be a part of. Additional thanks go to Dan May, Diana Jarvis, Maxine Repath, Katie Lloyd-Jones, Ed Wright, Sarah Smithies, Stewart Wild, Christina Knight, Chloë Roberts, Megan McIntyre, Philippa Hopkins, David Paul, Katherine Owers, April Isaacs, Andrew Rosenberg, AnneLise Sorensen, and Steven Horak.

ROUGH GUIDES

SMALL PRINT

Readers' letters

Thanks to all the readers who have taken the time to write in with comments and suggestions (and apologies if we've inadvertently omitted or misspelt anyone's name):

Simon Barnes, Anthea and Roger Bickley, Jonathan Blackstaffe, Jean Bolard, Paul Boys, Tracy Brooks, Wendy S. Brown, Steve Buff, Peter Collister, Natalie Dixon, Peter Floor, Manolo Garcia Angeles, Rona B. Gordon, David Griffiths, Ralph Holmes, Bob Iles, Dave Ingram, Alfred Jacobsen, James and Ann Jordan, Cory Jubitz, Julie Klingenstein, Mike Lewis, Anne Lindsay, Elizabeth Lopez, Andrea & Geoff Major, David Masterton, Geoff May, Alistair McCleery, David Mell, Daniel Mersey, Peter Murphy, David Phillips, Valerie Reynolds, Joe Richardson, Tim Salter, Stuart Saunders, Hermann Schoenecker, Dubnogartos Sexton, Rosalind Stewart, Steve Walzer, Richard and Amy Woodger

Photo credits

All photos © Rough Guides except the following:

Cover
Front picture: Mount Rushmore © Alamy
Back picture: The Bean sculpture © Alamy

Title page
Brooklyn Bridge and Manhattan skyline, dawn © John Lawrence/Getty Images

Full page
California, Big Sur Coastline along Highway 1 © James Randklev/Getty Images

Introduction
Hollywood sign, high above Los Angeles, CA © Neil Setchfield/DK Images
Golden Gate Bridge, San Francisco, CA © Roy Ooms/Masterfile
Washington Monument, Washington DC © Marvin E Newman/Getty Images
John Brown's Fort, Harpers Ferry National Historical Park, WV © Alan Briere /Superstock
Fajada Butte, Chaco Culture National Historical Park, NM © Demetrio Carrasco/DK Images
Avalanche lilies, Glacier National Park, MT © John Warden/Getty Images
Brant Point Lighthouse, Nantucket, MA © Eric Chen/Alamy

Things not to miss
02 Savannah Mission, Savannah, GA © Georgia Department of Tourism
03 Magic Kingdom, Orlando, FL © Katja Kreder/Alamy
05 Kentucky Derby, Churchill Downs, Louisville, KY © Daniel Dempster Photography/Alamy
06 Old Faithful Geyser, Yellowstone National Park, WY © Jim Peaco/National Park Services
07 Mardi Gras, New Orleans, LA © Luis Castaneda Inc/Getty Images
08 Pike Place Market, Seattle, WA © David P. Hall/Masterfile
09 Bighorn sheep on snowy incline, Glacier National Park, MT © Art Wolfe/Getty Images
10 Monticello, Charlottesville, VA © Garry Black/Masterfile
11 Bandelier National Monument, NM © Tony Souter/DK Images
12 North Rim, Grand Canyon National Park, AZ © Les David Manevitz /Superstock
13 Swamp near New Orleans, LA © age fotostock //Superstock
14 Alamo Square, San Francisco, CA © Bill Brooks/Masterfile
15 Path through woodland in autumn © Charles Benes/Getty Images
16 Lower Yosemite Falls in Yosemite National Park, CA © John Heseltine/DK Images
17 Philly cheesesteak © Terry Way

18 Cowboy rodeo, Cheyenne Frontier Days, WY © Holger Leue/Alamy
19 Kilauea Volcano, Hawaii Volcanoes National Park © David Reggie/Pacific Stock/Photolibrary.com
21 Aurora borealis, AK © Kevin Schafer/Alamy
22 Rio Grande River in Santa Elena Canyon, Big Bend National Park, TX © Jeff Foott/Getty Images
23 Mount Rushmore, SD © Garry Black/Masterfile
24 Country Music Hall of Fame, Nashville, TN © Prisma/Superstock
26 The Delano Hotel, South Beach, Miami, FL © Peter Wilson/DK Images
27 Skiing at Alta, UT © Donald C Landwehrle/Getty Images
28 Fenway Park, Boston, MA © James Lemass /Superstock
29 Capitol Hill, Washington DC © Kim Sayer/DK Images
30 Continental Club in Austin, TX © Patrick Byrd/Alamy
31 Looking out across Big Sur, CA © Peter Anderson/DK Images
32 Sears Tower, Chicago, IL © Andrew Leyerle/DK Images
33 Graceland, Memphis, TN © Jon Arnold Images/Alamy
34 Crab Claw in St. Michaels, Maryland © Paul A. Souders/Corbis
36 *Behold* statue at the Martin Luther King Jr Center for Nonviolent Social Change, Atlanta, GA © Robert W. Ginn/Alamy
37 Cactus Saguaro National Park, Tucson, AZ © Jon Arnold Images/Walter Bibikow/Alamy
38 Route 66 signpost © John Crall/Transtock Inc./Alamy

Color section: American food
Chicago hot dog © E. Jane Armstrong /Jupiterimages
Barbecue grill in Texas © SuperStock
Clam chowder © foodfolio/Alamy
Lobster Shack, Pemaquid Point, ME © Walter Bibikow/Jon Arnold Images/Alamy

Color section: Music
Elvis Presley, 1968 © SNAP/Rex Features
Jazz musicians, New Orleans, LA © Cosmo Condina/Getty Images
Rock and Roll Hall of Fame, Cleveland, OH © Richard Cummins/Corbis
Grand Ole Opry, Nashville, TN © Hiroyuki Matsumoto/Getty Images
Jukebox © Robert Karpa/Masterfile
Bob Dylan, Concert for Bangladesh, 1971 © Rex Features

SMALL PRINT

ROUGH
GUIDES

SMALL PRINT

Index

Map entries are in color.

INDEX

INDEX

Rough Guide favorites

Ski resorts

I

INDEX

Rough Guide favorites

Historic sites
The Alamo, San
Antonio, TX   p.731
Fort Sumter, SC   p.517
Ground Zero   p.84
Harpers Ferry, WV p.453
Lexington, MA   p.215
Lincoln Memorial p.410
Little Bighorn Battlefield,
MT   p.894
Mesa Verde, CO   p.870
MLK Jr National Historic
Site, Atlanta, GA p.526
Pearl Harbor, HI p.1268
Roanoke Island,
NC   p.493
St Augustine, FL p.640
The Sixth Floor Museum,
Dallas, TX p.748

INDEX

INDEX

INDEX

1350

Map symbols

maps are listed in the full index using coloured text

------	International border	♟	Museum
--·--·--	State border	🏛	Monument/memorial
---	Chapter boundary	⚞	Ski area
80	Interstate highway	◼	Restaurant
30	US highway	◉	Accommodation
1	State highway	⚠	Campsite
———	Unpaved road	P	Parking
··········	4WD road	★	Bus stop
:::::	Tunnel	⊞	Hospital/medical center
-----	Path/trail	ⓘ	Information center
═══	Railroad	⊠	Post office
— —	Ferry route	⊙	Statue
———	River	⚱	Fountain/gardens
◠	Cave	▃▃▃	Wall
🜲	Mountain range	⌒	Arch
▲	Mountain peak	⊠	Park entrance
🌊	Waterfall	⏟	Church (regional maps)
⚜	Spring	◼	Building
🌿	Marshland/swamp	⊞	Church (town maps)
🌾	Gorge	⬭	Stadium
✕	Battlefield	⊞	Cemetery
♦	Point of interest	▨	Park
✈	Airport	▨	Forest
✗	Airfield	▨	Beach
🌿	Viewpoint/lookout	▨	Indian reservation
⚑	Lighthouse		

MAP SYMBOLS